CONSTITUTIONAL LAW

CASES—COMMENTS—QUESTIONS

Ninth Edition

By

Jesse H. Choper
Earl Warren Professor of Public Law,
University of California, Berkeley

Richard H. Fallon, Jr.
Professor of Law
Harvard University

Yale Kamisar
Clarence Darrow Distinguished University Professor of Law,
University of Michigan,
Visiting Professor of Law,
University of San Diego

Steven H. Shiffrin
Professor of Law,
Cornell University

AMERICAN CASEBOOK SERIES®

WEST
GROUP

A THOMSON COMPANY

ST. PAUL, MINN., 2001

American Casebook Series, and the West Group symbol
are registered trademarks used herein under license.

COPYRIGHT © 1964, 1967, 1970 WEST PUBLISHING CO.

COPYRIGHT © 1975, 1981 LOCKHART, KAMISAR & CHOPER

COPYRIGHT © 1986 LOCKHART, KAMISAR, CHOPER & SHIFFRIN

COPYRIGHT © 1991, 1996 WEST PUBLISHING CO.

COPYRIGHT © 2001 By WEST GROUP
    610 Opperman Drive
    P.O. Box 64526
    St. Paul, MN 55164–0526
    1–800–328–9352

ISBN 0–314–24716–5

Preface

Casebooks are teaching tools, and this is no exception. The hallmark of this book since its original edition is its commitment to the proposition that a student's understanding of constitutional law is greatly enriched by exposure to diverse perspectives drawn from the best of legal scholarship. To that end, we have reproduced many selections from the literature or woven them into notes and questions that follow almost every main case. Overall, the book furnishes the resources to teach a broadly intellectual (as well as doctrinal) Constitutional Law course, but seeks to do so without imposing a comprehensive framework that teachers must either adopt or "teach against."

In the five years since the eighth edition of this book was published, many significant decisions have been handed down and a wealth of scholarly commentary has been generated. Accordingly, this new edition represents a complete revision and a fresh re-evaluation, for purposes of re-editing and re-organizing, of all existing materials. It also constitutes the product of an extensive examination of the recent literature — in an effort to further enrich the notes, comments and questions. We are especially pleased that the task has been accomplished in a book that is even a few pages shorter than its predecessor. In addition to full updating, restructuring has been undertaken where called for by recent developments and (as in the section of Chapter 5 on the origins of substantive due process and the *Lochner* era) to make the materials more effectively teachable. Former Chapter 5 ("State Power to Tax") has been omitted, with an abbreviated presentation of its central doctrinal materials now included in Section 5 of Chapter 4 ("State Power to Regulate"). As a result, long-time users of the book will note that chapters after Chapter 4 have been re-numbered. The most significant substantive revisions appear in Chapter 2 (National Legislative Power) and Chapter 11 (Congressional Enforcement of Civil Rights) to account for the Court's revived interest in judicial protection of states' rights.

The cut-off date for this book is February 20, 2001. Significant cases handed down during the last four months of the 2000-01 Supreme Court Term will appear in a supplement to be published in August 2001. Important developments thereafter will appear in annual supplements.

Case and statute citations, as well as footnotes, of the Court and commentators have been omitted without so specifying; other omissions are indicated by asterisks or by brackets. Numbered footnotes are from the original materials; lettered footnotes are ours. The three editions of Laurence H. Tribe, *American Constitutional Law* are cited simply as "Tribe." The composition of the Court on any date may be obtained by consulting the Table of Justices in Appendix A, originally prepared by Professor John J. Cound, a compilation of basic biographical data on all the individuals who have ever served on the Court.

This edition of the casebook is the first prepared without our senior colleague, William B. Lockhart, who actively participated in all eight editions

iii

before he died in 1996 at the age of 89. We have now arranged the editors' names in alphabetical order rather than by seniority.

Special thanks to Mary Lebert, Florence D. McKnight, Rose Merendino, and Nancy Thompson for exceptionally able secretarial assistance, and to Matt Andelman, Eve Brensike, Justin Deabler, Kathleen Hartnett, Gregory Rapawy, and Ana Reyes for their help as research assistants.

JESSE H. CHOPER
RICHARD H. FALLON, JR.
YALE KAMISAR
STEVEN H. SHIFFRIN

April 2001

A Photograph of the Nine Justices of the U.S. Supreme Court, 1995–2001

From left to right, Justice Sandra Day O'Connor, Justice Anthony M. Kennedy, Justice Antonin Scalia, Chief Justice William H. Rehnquist, Justice David H. Souter, Justice Ruth Bader Ginsburg, Justice Clarence Thomas, Justice Stephen G. Breyer and Justice John Paul Stevens.

This photograph is reprinted with the permission of National Geographic Society/Supreme Court Historical Society

Summary of Contents

*

Table of Contents

Table of Cases

The principal cases are in bold type. Cases cited or discussed
in the text are roman type. References are to pages.

*

Table of Authorities

If extracts have been taken, the page numbers appear in bold; all others are roman.

CONSTITUTIONAL LAW

CASES—COMMENTS—QUESTIONS

Ninth Edition

*

Chapter 1

NATURE AND SCOPE OF JUDICIAL REVIEW

SECTION 1. ORIGINS, EARLY CHALLENGES, AND CONTINUING CONTROVERSY

"Whoever hath an absolute authority to interpret any written or spoken laws, it is he who is truly the lawgiver, to all intents and purposes, and not the person who first spoke or wrote them."

— Bishop Hoadly's Sermon, preached before the King, 1717.

MARBURY v. MADISON

5 U.S. (1 Cranch) 137, 2 L.Ed. 60 (1803).

[Thomas Jefferson, an Anti–Federalist (or Republican), who defeated John Adams, a Federalist, in the presidential election of 1800, was to take office on March 4, 1801. On January 20, 1801, Adams, the defeated incumbent, nominated John Marshall, Adams' Secretary of State, as fourth Chief Justice of the United States. Marshall assumed office on February 4 but continued to serve as Secretary of State until the end of the Adams administration. During February, the Federalist Congress passed (1) the Circuit Court Act, which, inter alia, doubled the number of federal judges and (2) the Organic Act which authorized appointment of 42 justices-of-the-peace in the District of Columbia. Senate confirmation of Adams' "midnight" appointees, virtually all Federalists, was completed on March 3. Their commissions were signed by Adams and sealed by Acting Secretary of State Marshall, but due to time pressures, several for the justices-of-the-peace (including that of William Marbury) remained undelivered when Jefferson assumed the presidency the next day. Jefferson ordered his new Secretary of State, James Madison, to withhold delivery.

[Late in 1801, Marbury and several others sought a writ of mandamus in the Supreme Court to compel Madison to deliver the commissions. The Court ordered Madison "to show cause why a mandamus should not issue" and the case was set for argument in the 1802 Term.

[While the case was pending, the new Republican Congress—incensed at Adams' efforts to entrench a Federalist judiciary and at the "Federalist" Court's

1 — Court did not have jurisdiction over case

order against a Republican cabinet officer—moved to repeal the Circuit Court Act. Federalist congressmen argued that repeal would be unconstitutional as violative of Art. III's assurance of judicial tenure "during good behavior" and of the Constitution's plan for separation of powers assuring the independence of the Judiciary. It "was in this debate that for the first time since the initiation of the new Government under the Constitution there occurred a serious challenge of the power of the Judiciary to pass upon the constitutionality of Acts of Congress. Hitherto, [it had been the Republicans] who had sustained this power as a desirable curb on Congressional aggression and encroachment on the rights of the States, and they had been loud in their complaints at the failure of the Court to hold the Alien and Sedition laws unconstitutional. Now, however, in 1802, in order to counteract the Federalist argument that the Repeal Bill was unconstitutional and would be so held by the Court, [Republicans] advanced the proposition that the Court did not possess the power."[a]

[The Repeal Law passed early in 1802. To forestall its constitutional challenge in the Supreme Court until the political power of the new administration had been strengthened, Congress also eliminated the 1802 Supreme Court Term. Thus, the Court did not meet between December, 1801 and February, 1803.]

[On] 24th February, the following opinion of the court was delivered by CHIEF JUSTICE MARSHALL: * * *

No cause has been shown, and the present motion is for a mandamus. The peculiar delicacy of this case, the novelty of some of its circumstances, and the real difficulty attending the points which occur in it require a complete exposition of the principles on which the opinion to be given by the court is founded. * * *

1st. Has the applicant a right to the commission he demands? * * *

Mr. Marbury, [since] his commission was signed by the President and sealed by the Secretary of State, was appointed; and as the law creating the office gave the officer a right to hold for five years, independent of the executive, the appointment was not revocable, but vested in the officer legal rights, which are protected by the laws of his country.

To withhold his commission, therefore, is an act deemed by the court not warranted by law, but violative of a vested legal right.[b] * * *

2dly. If he has a right, and that right has been violated, do the laws of his country afford him a remedy?

The very essence of civil liberty certainly consists in the right of every individual to claim the protection of the laws, whenever he receives an injury. One of the first duties of government is to afford that protection. * * *

The government of the United States has been emphatically termed a government of laws, and not of men. It will certainly cease to deserve this high appellation, if the laws furnish no remedy for the violation of a vested legal right. * * *

a. 1 Charles Warren, *The Supreme Court in United States History* 215 (1922).

b. Consider William Van Alstyne, *A Critical Guide to Marbury v. Madison,* 1969 Duke L.J. 1, 8: "[T]here is clearly an 'issue' of sorts which preceded any of those touched upon in the opinion. Specifically, it would appear that Marshall should have recused himself in view of his substantial involvement in the background of this controversy. * * * Proof of the status of Marbury's commission not only involved circumstances within the Chief Justice's personal knowledge, it was furnished in the Supreme Court by Marshall's own younger brother who had been with him in his office when, as Secretary of State, he had made out the commissions."

[W]here the heads of departments are the political or confidential agents of the executive, merely to execute the will of the president, or rather to act in cases in which the executive possesses a constitutional or legal discretion, nothing can be more perfectly clear than that their acts are only politically examinable. But where a specific duty is assigned by law, and individual rights depend upon the performance of that duty, it seems equally clear that the individual who considers himself injured, has a right to resort to the laws of his country for a remedy.[c]
* * *

It remains to be inquired whether,

3dly. He is entitled to the remedy for which he applies? This depends on,

1st. The nature of the writ applied for; and,

2dly. The power of this court.

1st. The nature of the writ. * * *

This writ, if awarded, would be directed to an officer of government, and its mandate to him would be, to use the words of Blackstone, "to do a particular thing therein specified, which appertains to his office and duty, and which the court has previously determined, or at least supposes, to be consonant to right and justice." Or, in the words of Lord Mansfield, the applicant, in this case, has a right to execute an office of public concern, and is kept out of possession of that right.

These circumstances certainly concur in this case.

Still, to render the mandamus a proper remedy, the officer to whom it is to be directed, must be one to whom, on legal principles, such writ may be directed; and the person applying for it must be without any other specific and legal remedy.

1st. With respect to the officer to whom it would be directed. The intimate political relation subsisting between the President of the United States and the heads of departments, necessarily renders any legal investigation of the acts of one of those high officers peculiarly irksome, as well as delicate; and excites some hesitation with respect to the propriety of entering into such investigation. Impressions are often received without much reflection or examination, and it is not wonderful that in such a case as this the assertion, by an individual, of his legal claims in a court of justice, to which claims it is the duty of that court to attend, should at first view be considered by some, as an attempt to intrude into the cabinet, and to intermeddle with the prerogatives of the executive.

It is scarcely necessary for the court to disclaim all pretensions to such a jurisdiction. An extravagance, so absurd and excessive, could not have been entertained for a moment. The province of the court is, solely, to decide on the rights of individuals, not to inquire how the executive, or executive officers, perform duties in which they have a discretion. Questions in their nature political, or which are, by the constitution and laws, submitted to the executive, can never be made in this court.

But [what] is there in the exalted station of the officer, which shall bar a citizen from asserting, in a court of justice, his legal rights, or shall forbid a court to listen to the claim, or to issue a mandamus, directing the performance of a

---

c. Consider Norman Redlich, *The Supreme Court—1833 Term,* 40 N.Y.U.L.Rev. 1, 4 (1965): "[T]he Court could have ruled that, since the President had the power to appoint the judges, he also had the power to deliver the commissions which was in a sense the final act of appointment. Viewed as a component of the act of appointment, the delivery of the commissions could have simply been considered as lying within the discretion of the President."

duty, not depending on executive discretion, but on particular acts of congress, and the general principles of law? * * *

This, then, is a plain case for a mandamus, either to deliver the commission, or a copy of it from the record; and it only remains to be inquired,

Whether it can issue from this court.

The act to establish the judicial courts of the United States authorizes the supreme court "to issue writs of mandamus, in cases warranted by the principles and usages of law, to any courts appointed, or persons holding office, under the authority of the United States."[d]

The secretary of state, being a person holding an office under the authority of the United States, is precisely within the letter of the description; and if this court is not authorized to issue a writ of mandamus to such an officer, it must be because the law is unconstitutional, and therefore absolutely incapable of conferring the authority, and assigning the duties which its words purport to confer and assign. * * *

In the distribution of [the judicial power of the United States] it is declared that "the supreme court shall have original jurisdiction in all cases affecting ambassadors, other public ministers and consuls, and those in which a state shall be a party. In all other cases, the supreme court shall have appellate jurisdiction."

It has been insisted, at the bar, that as the original grant of jurisdiction, to the supreme and inferior courts, is general, and the clause, assigning original jurisdiction to the supreme court, contains no negative or restrictive words, the power remains to the legislature, to assign original jurisdiction to that court in other cases than those specified in the article which has been recited; provided those cases belong to the judicial power of the United States.

If it had been intended to leave it in the discretion of the legislature to apportion the judicial power between the supreme and inferior courts according to the will of that body, it would certainly have been useless to have proceeded

---

d. § 13 of the Judiciary Act of 1789 provided: "That the Supreme Court shall have exclusive jurisdiction of all controversies of a civil nature, where a state is a party, except between a state and its citizens; and except also between a state and citizens of other states, or aliens, in which latter case it shall have original but not exclusive jurisdiction. And shall have exclusively all such jurisdiction of suits or proceedings against ambassadors or other public ministers, or their domestics, or domestic servants, as a court of law can have or exercise consistently with the law of nations; and original, but not exclusive jurisdiction of all suits brought by ambassadors or other public ministers, or in which a consul, or vice consul, shall be a party. And the trial of issues of fact in the Supreme Court in all actions at law against citizens of the United States shall be by jury. The Supreme Court shall also have appellate jurisdiction from the circuit courts and courts of the several states, in the cases hereinafter specially provided for; and shall have power to issue writs of prohibition to the district courts, when proceeding as courts of admiralty and maritime jurisdiction, and writs of mandamus, in cases warranted by the principles and usages of law, to any courts appointed, or persons holding office under the authority of the United States."

Consider Van Alstyne, supra, at 15: "Textually, the provision regarding mandamus says nothing expressly as to whether it is part of original or appellate jurisdiction or both, and the clause itself does not speak at all of 'conferring jurisdiction' on the court. The grant of 'power' to issue the writ, however, is juxtaposed with the section of appellate jurisdiction and, in fact, follows the general description of appellate jurisdiction in the same sentence, being separated only by a semicolon. No textual mangling is required to confine it to appellate jurisdiction. Moreover, no mangling is required even if it attaches both to original and to appellate jurisdiction, not as an enlargement of either, but simply as a specification of power which the Court is authorized to use in cases which are *otherwise* appropriately under consideration. Since this case is not otherwise within the specified type of original jurisdiction (e.g., it is not a case in which a state is a party or a case against an ambassador), it should be dismissed."

further than to have defined the judicial power, and the tribunals in which it should be vested. The subsequent part of the section is mere surplusage, is entirely without meaning, if such is to be the construction. If congress remains at liberty to give this court appellate jurisdiction, where the constitution has declared their jurisdiction shall be original; and original jurisdiction where the constitution has declared it shall be appellate; the distribution of jurisdiction, made in the constitution, is form without substance.

Affirmative words are often, in their operation, negative of other objects than those affirmed; and in this case, a negative or exclusive sense must be given to them, or they have no operation at all.

It cannot be presumed that any clause in the constitution is intended to be without effect; and, therefore, such a construction is inadmissible, unless the words require it. * * *

The authority, therefore, given to the Supreme Court, by the Act establishing the judicial courts of the United States, to issue writs of mandamus to public officers, appears not to be warranted by the Constitution; and it becomes necessary to inquire whether a jurisdiction so conferred can be exercised.

The question whether an Act repugnant to the Constitution can become the law of the land, is a question deeply interesting to the United States; but, happily, not of an intricacy proportioned to its interest. It seems only necessary to recognize certain principles, supposed to have been long and well established, to decide it.

That the people have an original right to establish, for their future government, such principles as, in their opinion, shall most conduce to their own happiness, is the basis on which the whole American fabric has been erected. The exercise of this original right is a very great exertion; nor can it nor ought it to be frequently repeated. The principles, therefore, so established, are deemed fundamental. And as the authority from which they proceed is supreme, and can seldom act, they are designed to be permanent.

This original and supreme will organizes the government, and assigns to different departments their respective powers. It may either stop here, or establish certain limits not to be transcended by those departments.

The government of the United States is of the latter description. The powers of the legislature are defined and limited; and that those limits may not be mistaken, or forgotten, the constitution is written. To what purpose are powers limited, and to what purpose is that limitation committed to writing, if these limits may, at any time, be passed by those intended to be restrained? The distinction between a government with limited and unlimited powers is abolished, if those limits do not confine the persons on whom they are imposed, and if acts prohibited and acts allowed, are of equal obligation. It is a proposition too plain to be contested, that the constitution controls any legislative act repugnant to it; or, that the legislature may alter the constitution by an ordinary act.

e. Consider Van Alstyne, supra, at 31: "It can be plausibly argued, however, that the Article III division of judicial power between appellate and original jurisdiction served a useful purpose other than that insisted upon by Marshall. Had Congress *not* adopted the Judiciary Act of 1789 or taken any other action describing Supreme Court jurisdiction, the division itself would have provided a guideline for the Court to follow until Congress was inclined to act." See also id. at 30–33.

By Marshall's interpretation of Art. III, may Congress authorize the Court to exercise appellate jurisdiction in cases involving foreign consuls? See *Bors v. Preston,* 111 U.S. 252, 4 S.Ct. 407, 28 L.Ed. 419 (1884).

Between these alternatives there is no middle ground. The constitution is either a superior paramount law, unchangeable by ordinary means, or it is on a level with ordinary legislative acts, and, like other acts, is alterable when the legislature shall please to alter it.

If the former part of the alternative be true, then a legislative act contrary to the constitution is not law: if the latter part be true, then written constitutions are absurd attempts, on the part of the people, to limit a power in its own nature illimitable.

Certainly all those who have framed written constitutions contemplate them as forming the fundamental and paramount law of the nation, and consequently, the theory of every such government must be, that an act of the legislature, repugnant to the constitution, is void.

This theory is essentially attached to a written constitution, and is, consequently, to be considered, by this court, as one of the fundamental principles of our society. It is not therefore to be lost sight of in the further consideration of this subject.

If an act of the legislature, repugnant to the Constitution, is void, does it, notwithstanding its invalidity, bind the courts, and oblige them to give it effect? Or, in other words, though it be not law, does it constitute a rule as operative as if it was a law? This would be to overthrow in fact what was established in theory; and would seem, at first view, an absurdity too gross to be insisted on. It shall, however, receive a more attentive consideration.

It is emphatically the province and duty of the judicial department to say what the law is. Those who apply the rule to particular cases, must of necessity expound and interpret that rule. If two laws conflict with each other, the courts must decide on the operation of each.

So if a law be in opposition to the constitution; if both the law and the constitution apply to a particular case, so that the court must either decide that case conformably to the law, disregarding the constitution; or conformably to the constitution, disregarding the law; the court must determine which of these conflicting rules governs the case. This is of the very essence of judicial duty.

If, then, the courts are to regard the constitution, and the constitution is superior to any ordinary act of the legislature, the constitution, and not such ordinary act, must govern the case to which they both apply.

Those then who controvert the principle that the constitution is to be considered in court, as a paramount law, are reduced to the necessity of maintaining that courts must close their eyes on the constitution, and see only the law.

This doctrine would subvert the very foundation of all written constitutions. It would declare that an Act which, according to the principles and theory of our government, is entirely void, is yet, in practice, completely obligatory. It would declare that if the legislature shall do what is expressly forbidden, such Act, notwithstanding the express prohibition, is in reality effectual. It would be giving to the legislature a practical and real omnipotence, with the same breath which professes to restrict their powers within narrow limits. It is prescribing limits, and declaring that those limits may be passed at pleasure.

That it thus reduces to nothing what we have deemed the greatest improvement on political institutions, a written constitution, would of itself be sufficient, in America, where written constitutions have been viewed with so much reverence, for rejecting the construction. But the peculiar expressions of the Constitution of the United States furnish additional arguments in favor of its rejection.

The judicial power of the United States is extended to all cases arising under the Constitution.

Could it be the intention of those who gave this power, to say that in using it the Constitution should not be looked into? That a case arising under the Constitution should be decided without examining the instrument under which it arises?

cases which would not be const.

This is too extravagant to be maintained.

In some cases, then, the Constitution must be looked into by the judges. And if they can open it at all, what part of it are they forbidden to read or to obey?

There are many other parts of the Constitution which serve to illustrate this subject.

It is declared that "no tax or duty shall be laid on articles exported from any State." Suppose a duty on the export of cotton, of tobacco, or of flour; and a suit instituted to recover it. Ought judgment to be rendered in such a case? Ought the judges to close their eyes on the Constitution, and only see the law?

The Constitution declares "that no bill of attainder or ex post facto law shall be passed."

If, however, such a bill should be passed, and a person should be prosecuted under it, must the court condemn to death those victims whom the Constitution endeavors to preserve?

✗ LK

"No person," says the Constitution, "shall be convicted of treason unless on the testimony of two witnesses to the same overt act, or on confession in open court."

Here the language of the Constitution is addressed especially to the courts. It prescribes, directly for them, a rule of evidence not to be departed from. If the legislature should change that rule, and declare one witness, or a confession out of court, sufficient for conviction, must the constitutional principle yield to the legislative act?

From these, and many other selections which might be made, it is apparent, that the framers of the constitution contemplated that instrument as a rule for the government of courts, as well as of the legislature.

Why otherwise does it direct the judges to take an oath to support it? This oath certainly applies in an especial manner, to their conduct in their official character. How immoral to impose it on them, if they were to be used as the instruments, and the knowing instruments, for violating what they swear to support!

The oath of office, too, imposed by the legislature, is completely demonstrative of the legislative opinion on this subject. It is in these words: "I do solemnly swear that I will administer justice without respect to persons, and do equal right to the poor and to the rich; and that I will faithfully and impartially discharge all the duties incumbent on me as _____, according to the best of my abilities and understanding agreeably to the constitution and laws of the United States."

- Judges oath

Why does a judge swear to discharge his duties agreeably to the constitution of the United States, if that constitution forms no rule for his government? If it is closed upon him, and cannot be inspected by him?

If such be the real state of things, this is worse than solemn mockery. To prescribe, or to take this oath, becomes equally a crime.

It is also not entirely unworthy of observation, that in declaring what shall be the supreme law of the land, the constitution itself is first mentioned; and not the laws of the United States generally, but those only which shall be made in pursuance of the constitution, have that rank.

Thus, the particular phraseology of the Constitution of the United States confirms and strengthens the principle, supposed to be essential to all written constitutions, that a law repugnant to the constitution is void; and that courts, as well as other departments, are bound by that instrument.

The rule must be discharged.[f]

––––––––

"We are under a Constitution, but the Constitution is what the judges say it is."

—Charles Evans Hughes, Speech, 1907.

Comments and Questions

Further Historical Context

CHARLES WARREN, 1 *The Supreme Court in United States History,* 232, 242–43 (1922): "Contemporary writings make it very clear that the republicans attacked the [*Marbury*] decision, not so much because it sustained the power of the court to determine the validity of congressional legislation, as because it enounced the doctrine that the court might issue mandamus to a cabinet official who was acting by direction of the president. In other words, Jefferson's antagonism to Marshall and the court at that time was due more to his resentment at the alleged invasion of his executive prerogative than to any so-called 'judicial usurpation' of the field of congressional authority. [It] seems plain [that Marshall might] have construed the language of the section of the judiciary act [to escape the necessity] to pass upon its constitutionality. Marshall naturally felt that in view of the recent attacks on judicial power it was important to have the great principle firmly established, and undoubtedly he welcomed the opportunity of fixing the precedent in a case in which his action would necessitate a decision in favor of his political opponents."

––––––––

MORRIS COHEN, *The Faith of a Liberal* 178–80 (1946) (written in 1938): "The section of [the] act of 1789 which Marshall declared unconstitutional had been drawn up by Ellsworth, his predecessor as chief justice, and by others who a short time before had been the very members of the constitutional convention that had drafted its judicial provisions. It was signed by George Washington who had presided over the deliberations of that convention. Fourteen years later, John

f. Six days later, the Circuit Court Act Repeal Law was held to be constitutional. *Stuart v. Laird,* 5 U.S. (1 Cranch) 299, 2 L.Ed. 115 (1803). After *Marbury,* the Court did not hold an act of Congress unconstitutional until *Dred Scott v. Sandford,* 60 U.S. (19 How.) 393, 15 L.Ed. 691 (1857).

Marshall by implication accused his predecessor on the bench, the members of congress such as James Madison, the father of the constitution, and president Washington, of either not understanding the constitution (which some of them had drawn up), or else wilfully disregarding it. [To] a secular historian, it is obvious that John Marshall was motivated by the fear of impeachment if he granted the mandamus or dared to declare the republican judiciary repeal act of 1802 unconstitutional. Having thus refused aid to his fellow federalists ousted from offices created for them by a 'lame duck' congress, he resorted to a line of sophistical dicta to get even with his political enemy, as indeed he did also in the *Aaron Burr* case. In his letter to his colleague Chase, Marshall offered to abandon judicial supremacy in the interpretation of the constitution in return for security against impeachment."[g]

Text of the Constitution

Is the doctrine of "judicial review," which gives the Court power to declare an act of a coordinate branch of the government unconstitutional, compelled because a contrary rule "would subvert the very foundation of all written constitutions"?

WILLIAM VAN ALSTYNE, *A Critical Guide to Marbury v. Madison,* 1969 Duke L.J. 1, 17: "[E]ven in Marshall's time (and to a great extent today), a number of nations maintained written constitutions and yet gave national legislative acts the full force of positive law without providing any constitutional check to guarantee the compatibility of those acts with their constitutions [e.g.,] France, Switzerland, and Belgium (and to some extent Great Britain where magna carta and other written instruments are roughly described as the constitution but where acts of parliament are not reviewable)."[h]

Does the "judges' oath" provision (Art. VI, cl. 3) furnish the necessary textual support for the doctrine of judicial review?

———

JUSTICE GIBSON, dissenting in *Eakin v. Raub,* 12 S. & R. 330 (Pa.1825):[i] "The oath to support the Constitution is not peculiar to the judges, but is taken indiscriminately by every officer of the government, and is designed rather as a test of the political principles of the man, than to bind the officer in the discharge of his duty: otherwise, it were difficult to determine, what operation it is to have in the case of a recorder of deeds, for instance, who, in execution of his office, has nothing to do with the Constitution. But granting it to relate to the official

---

g. In 1804, the House impeached Justice Chase due, inter alia, to what the Republicans believed to be Chase's partisan Federalist activities and statements both on and off the Bench. After a lengthy trial in the Senate, the constitutional majority to convict was not obtained. It was generally assumed that, if the effort had been successful, Marshall and other Federalist judges would suffer the same fate. See generally 1 Warren, supra, ch. 6. For a further account of *Marbury,* see 3 Albert Beveridge, *The Life of John Marshall* 105–156 (1919).

h. Consider Cohen, supra, at 185: "Nor is it necessary to consider in detail the argument that this power is necessary for a federal system. The Swiss constitution is a perfect example of a federal system without the judiciary

having such power. The late Justice Holmes said, 'I do not think the United States would come to an end if we lost our power to declare an Act of Congress void. I do think the Union would be imperiled if we could not make that declaration as to the laws of the several states.'"

For discussion of the modern growth of various forms of judicial review in other countries—Australia, Austria, Canada, Cyprus, Denmark, Germany, India, Italy, Japan, Norway, Sweden, Turkey, Yugoslavia—see Mauro Cappelletti, *Judicial Review in Comparative Perspective,* 58 Calif.L.Rev. 1017 (1970).

i. This opinion is widely regarded as the most effective answer of the era to Marshall's reasoning supporting judicial review.

conduct of the judge, as well as every other officer, and not to his political principles, still, it must be understood in reference to supporting the Constitution, only as far as that may be involved in his official duty; and consequently, if his official duty does not comprehend an inquiry into the authority of the legislature, neither does his oath. * * *

"But do not the judges do a positive act in violation of the Constitution, when they give effect to an unconstitutional law? Not if the law has been passed according to the forms established in the Constitution. The fallacy of the question is, in supposing that the judiciary adopts the acts of the legislature as its own; whereas, the enactment of a law and the interpretation of it are not concurrent acts, and as the judiciary is not required to concur in the enactment, neither is it in the breach of the constitution which may be the consequence of the enactment; the fault is imputable to the legislature, and on it the responsibility exclusively rests."

———

What of Art. III, § 2, cl. 1, extending "the judicial Power" "to *all* cases * * * arising under this Constitution"?

ALEXANDER BICKEL, *The Least Dangerous Branch* 5–6 (1962): "[W]hat the constitution extends to cases arising under it is 'the judicial power.' Whether this power reaches as far as Marshall wanted it to go—namely, to reviewing acts of the legislature—is the question to be decided. What are the nature and extent of the function of the court—the judicial power? Is the court empowered, when it decided a case, to declare that a duly enacted statute violates the constitution, and to invalidate the statute? Article III does not purport to describe the function of the court; it subsumes whatever questions may exist as to that in the phrase 'the judicial power.' It does not purport to tell the court how to decide cases; it only specifies which kinds of case the court shall have jurisdiction to deal with at all. Thus, in giving jurisdiction in cases 'arising under [the] laws' or 'under treaties'' the clause is not read as prescribing the process of decision to be followed. The process varies. In cases 'under [the] laws' courts often leave determination of issues of fact and even issues that may be thought to be 'of law' to administrative agencies. And under both 'the laws [and] treaties,' much of the decision concerning meaning and applicability may be received ready-made from the congress and the president. In some cases of all three descriptions, judicial decision may be withheld altogether[j]—and it is for this reason that it will not do to place reliance on the word 'all' in the phrase 'all cases * * * arising * * *.' To the extent that the constitution speaks to such matters, it does so in the tightly packed phrase 'judicial power.'

"Nevertheless, if it were impossible to conceive a case 'arising under the Constitution' which would not require the Court to pass on the constitutionality of congressional legislation, then the analysis of the text of Article III made above might be found unsatisfactory, for it would render this clause quite senseless. But there are such cases which may call into question the constitutional validity of judicial, administrative, or military actions without attacking legislative or even presidential acts as well, or which call upon the Court, under appropriate statutory authorization, to apply the Constitution to acts of the states."

———

j. See Sec. 2 infra, "Political Questions."

What of the supremacy clause (Art. VI, cl. 2)?

HERBERT WECHSLER, *Toward Neutral Principles of Constitutional Law*, 73 Harv.L.Rev. 1, 3–5 (1959): "Judge Hand [*The Bill of Rights* 28 (1958)] concedes that under this clause 'state courts would at times have to decide whether state laws and constitutions, or even a federal statute, were in conflict with the federal constitution' but he adds that 'the fact that this jurisdiction was confined to such occasions, and that it was thought necessary specifically to provide such a limited jurisdiction, looks rather against than in favor of a general jurisdiction.'

"Are you satisfied, however, to view the supremacy clause in this way, as a grant of jurisdiction to state courts, implying a denial of the power and the duty to all others? This certainly is not its necessary meaning; it may be construed as a mandate to all of officialdom including courts, with a special and emphatic admonition that in binds the judges of the previously independent states. That the latter is the proper reading seems to me persuasive when the other relevant provisions of the Constitution are brought into view.

"Article III, section 1 [represented] one of the major compromises of the Constitutional Convention and relegated the establishment vel non of lower federal courts to the discretion of the Congress. None might have been established, with the consequence that, as in other federalisms, judicial work of first instance would all have been remitted to state courts. Article III, section 2 goes on, however, to delineate the scope of the federal judicial power, providing that it 'shall extend [inter alia] to all Cases, in Law and Equity, arising under this Constitution * * *' and further, that the Supreme Court 'shall have appellate jurisdiction' in such cases 'with such Exceptions, and under such Regulations as the Congress shall make.' Surely this means, as section 25 of the Judiciary Act of 1789 took it to mean, that if a court passes on a constitutional issue, as the supremacy clause provides that it should, its judgment is reviewable, subject to congressional exceptions, by the Supreme Court, in which event that Court must have no less authority and duty to accord priority to constitutional provisions that the court that it review. And such state cases might have encompassed every case in which a constitutional issue could possibly arise, since, as I have said, Congress need not and might not have exerted its authority to establish 'inferior' federal courts.

"If you abide with me thus far, I doubt that you will hesitate upon the final step. Is it a possible construction of the Constitution, measured strictly as Judge Hand admonishes by the test of 'general purpose,' that if Congress opts, as it has opted, to create a set of lower courts, those courts in cases falling within their respective jurisdictions and the Supreme Court when it passes on their judgments are less or differently constrained by the supremacy clause than are the state courts, and the Supreme Court when it reviews their judgments? Yet I cannot escape, what is for me the most astonishing conclusion, that this is the precise result of Judge Hand's reading of the text."

Did Judge Hand concede too much in reading the text of the supremacy clause to empower state courts to decide the constitutionality of *federal* statutes? If so, is Chief Justice Marshall's reference to Art. VI persuasive?[k]

k. Consider Charles Black, *The People and The Court* 23–25 (1960): '[T]he most impressive thing in firming the claims of judicial review is the operation of our history since its beginning. And the most striking thing about this history is that the other departments of government, preeminently Congress, have operated under the assumption (and not through mere oversight, for the assumption has in several epochs been passionately challenged) that

WILLIAM VAN ALSTYNE, supra, at 20–22: "The phrase 'in pursuance thereof' might as easily mean '*in the manner prescribed by this constitution,*' in which case acts of congress might be judicially reviewable as to their procedural integrity, but not as to their substance. An example of this more limited, procedural, judicial review is found in *Field v. Clark* [143 U.S. 649, 12 S.Ct. 495, 36 L.Ed. 294 (1892)]; it is, moreover, far more common in other countries than is substantive constitutional review. * * *

"The phrase might also mean merely that only those statutes adopted by Congress *after* the re-establishment and reconstitution of Congress pursuant to the Constitution itself shall be the supreme law of the land, whereas acts of the earlier Continental Congress, constituted merely under the Articles of Confederation, would not necessarily be supreme and binding upon the several states. Under this view, acts of Congress, like acts of Parliament, *are* the supreme law and not to be second-guessed by any court, state or federal, so long as they postdate ratification of the Constitution.[36]

" * * * *Assuming that an act repugnant to the Constitution is not a law 'in pursuance thereof' and thus must not be given effect as the supreme law of the land, who, according to the Constitution, is to make the determination as to whether any given law is in fact repugnant to the Constitution itself?* [T]he supremacy clause itself cannot be the clear textual basis for a claim by the judiciary that this prerogative to determine repugnancy belongs to it.

"[The phrase] could mean merely that the people should regard the Constitution with deep concern and that *they* should act to prevent Congress from overstepping the Constitution. It might even imply, moreover, a right of civil disobedience or serve as a written reminder to government of the natural right of revolution against tyrannical government which oversteps the terms of the social compact. Such a construction would be consistent with philosophical writings of

judicial review is an authentic part of our system of government. One of the most decisive Congressional expressions of this assumption, of special interest because it was passed by the First Congress, is the 25th Section of the first federal Judiciary Act [which] explicitly recognizes and provides for review of state court decisions by the Supreme Court, and lays it down with certainty that the Supreme Court may, by reversing a state judgment that has upheld a state law as against constitutional attack, hold state laws unconstitutional. But it says more than that. It clearly recognizes, first, that the validity of a 'treaty or statute of [the] United States' may be drawn in question in a state court and that the decision of the state court may be 'against their validity.' It then goes on to say, not only that the Supreme Court may review such a judgment, but that it may be 'reversed or affirmed' in that Court. If the Supreme Court may 'affirm' a state judgment holding a federal law invalid, then the Supreme Court obviously may, in such a case at least, hold a federal law invalid. [But] does it not seem likely that it was also assumed that the federal courts were empowered to pass and would pass, in all cases within their jurisdiction, on the validity of the state laws? Actually, the absurdity of the contrary assumption, in the context of the Judiciary Act of 1789, is

even greater than this bare statement makes it appear. For that Act provided (as the law still provides) that parties from different state could sue and be sued in the federal courts. So the hypothesis that the state courts might, while the federal courts might not, pass on the validity of federal statutes, would necessarily imply that parties who were citizens of the same state could appeal to the federal Constitution in court, while those who were citizens of different states could not. This is sheer lunacy—but to clear the members of the First Congress (as they deserve to be cleared) of this charge of lunacy, we have to assume that they took it for granted that the federal constitutional validity of state and federal laws could be passed on by all courts, state and federal."

36. For a careful elaboration of this point, see 2 William Crosskey, *Politics and the Constitution* 990–1007 (1953).

As distinguished from acts of Congress, treaties were binding upon the several states according to this view merely by having been entered into "under the Authority of the United States," and irrespective of whether they were approved by the Senate as it was proposed to be established pursuant to the new Constitution.

the period, consistent with the Declaration of Independence, and consistent also with the view of some antifederalists of the period."[1]

The Court as "Final" Arbiter

THOMAS JEFFERSON, writing in 1804, 8 *The Writings of Thomas Jefferson* 310 (1897): "The judges, believing the [sedition law] constitutional, had a right to pass a sentence of fine and imprisonment; because that power was placed in their hands by the constitution. But the executive, believing the law to be unconstitutional, was bound to remit the execution of it; because that power has been confided to him by the constitution. The instrument meant that its co-ordinate branches should be checks on each other. But the opinion which gives to the judges the right to decide what laws are constitutional, and what not, not only for themselves in their own sphere of action, but for the legislative and executive also in their spheres, would make the judiciary a despotic branch."

———

ANDREW JACKSON, veto message in 1832 on act to recharter bank of united states (the constitutionality of which had earlier been upheld by the court), 2 Richardson, *Messages and Papers of the Presidents* 576, 581–82 (1900): "It is as much the duty of the house of representatives, of the senate, and of the president to decide upon the constitutionality of any bill or resolution which may be presented to them for passage or approval as it is of the supreme judges when it may be brought before them for judicial decision. The opinion of the judges has no more authority over congress than the opinion of congress has over the judges, and on that point the president is independent of both. The authority of the supreme court must not, therefore, be permitted to control the congress or the executive when acting in their legislative capacities, but to have only such influence as the force of their reasoning may deserve."

———

ABRAHAM LINCOLN, inaugural address in 1861, 2 Richardson, supra, at 5, 9–10: "I do not forget the position assumed by some that constitutional questions are to be decided by the supreme court, nor do I deny that such decisions must be binding in any case upon the parties to a suit as to the object of that suit, while they are also entitled to very high respect and consideration in all parallel cases by all other departments of the government. And while it is obviously possible that such decision may be erroneous in any given case, still the evil effect following it,

1. Much has been written on the matter of "historical original intent" in respect to judicial review—generally examining pre-Convention judicial precedents in England and the colonies, statements of the framers both within and outside the Constitutional Convention (see especially Alexander Hamilton in Nos. 78 and 80 of *The Federalist* (1788)), and debate during the ratification period—arriving at conflicting conclusions. See, e.g., Louis Boudin, *Government by Judiciary* (1932); Edward Corwin, *The Doctrine of Judicial Review* (1914); William Crosskey, *Politics and the Constitution in the History of the United States* (1953); William Nelson, *Changing Conceptions of Judicial Review: The Evolution of Constitutional Theory in the States, 1790–1860*, 120 U.Pa.L.Rev. 1166 (1972); Charles Warren, *Congress, the Constitution, and the Supreme Court* (1925). For brief discussion see Levy, *Judicial Review, History, and Democracy: An Introduction,* in Judicial Review and the Supreme Court 1–12 (1967). For the view that "strict intentionalism" is not a "tenable approach to constitutional decision making," see Paul Brest, *The Misconceived Quest for the Original Understanding,* 60 B.U.L.Rev. 204 (1980).

For review of the broader historical setting, see Bernard Bailyn, *The Ideological Origins of the American Revolution* (1967); Gordon Wood, *The Creation of the American Republic, 1776–1787* (1969).

being limited to that particular case, with the chance that it may be overruled and never become a precedent for other cases, can better be borne than could the evils of a different practice. At the same time, the candid citizen must confess that if the policy of the government upon vital questions affecting the whole people is to be irrevocably fixed by decisions of the supreme court, the instant they are made in ordinary litigation between parties in personal actions the people will have ceased to be their own rulers, having to that extent practically resigned their government into the hands of that eminent tribunal. Nor is there in this view any assault upon the court or the judges. It is a duty from which they may not shrink to decide cases properly brought before them, and it is no fault of theirs if others seek to turn their decisions to political purposes."

Are these views inconsistent with *Marbury?* Does *Marbury* decide anything more than that *"the Court may refuse to give effect to an act of Congress where the act pertains to the judicial power itself"?* Van Alstyne, supra, at 34. Than that the Court claimed the power of judicial review "only in the defensive sense of safeguarding the Court's original jurisdiction from congressional enlargement"? Frank Strong, *Judicial Review: A Tri–Dimensional Concept of Administrative-Constitutional Law,* 69 W.Va.L.Rev. 111, 249 (1967).

If the Court upholds the constitutionality of a federal statute, may the President refuse to enforce it because be believes it to be unconstitutional? May he refuse to enforce it on this ground after Congress has enacted it but before it comes before the Court? May he refuse to enforce it on this ground if Congress overrides his veto? May the President continue to enforce a statute (e.g., by pressing charges for its violation) after the Court has held it unconstitutional? May he refuse to return property that the Court has held was unconstitutionally seized? If Congress forbids the President from taking certain action, may he do so on the ground that Congress' restriction is unconstitutional? Even after the Court has upheld its constitutionality?

LEARNED HAND, *The Bill of Rights* 11–15 (1958): "[L]et us try to imagine what would have been the result if the power [of judicial review] did not exist. There were two alternatives, each prohibitive, I submit. One was that the decision of the first 'department' before which an issue arose should be conclusive whenever it arose later. That doctrine, coupled with its conceded power over the purse, would have made congress substantially omnipotent, for by far the greater number of issues that could arise would depend upon its prior action. * * *

"As Hamilton intimated, every legislator is under constant pressure from groups of constituents whom it does not satisfy to say, 'Although I think what you want is right and that you ought to have it, I cannot bring myself to believe that it is within my constitutional powers.' Such scruples are not convincing to those whose interests are at stake; and the voters at large will not usually care enough about preserving 'the balance of the Constitution' to offset the votes of those whose interests will be disappointed. [But] the second alternative would have been even worse, for under it each 'Department' would have been free to decide constitutional issues as it thought right, regardless of any earlier decision of the others. Thus it would have been the President's privilege, and indeed his duty, to execute only those statutes that seemed to him to be constitutional, regardless even of a decision of the Supreme Court. The courts would have entered such judgments as seemed to them consonant with the Constitution; but neither the

President, nor Congress, would have been bound to enforce them if he or it disagreed, and without their help the judgments would have been waste paper.

"For centuries it has been an accepted canon in interpretation of documents to interpolate into the text such provisions, though not expressed, as are essential to prevent the defeat of the venture at hand; and this applies with especial force to the interpretation of constitutions, which, since they are designed to cover a great multitude of necessarily unforeseen occasions, must be cast in general language, unless they are constantly amended. If so, it was altogether in keeping with established practice for the Supreme Court to assume an authority to keep the states, Congress, and the President within their prescribed powers. Otherwise the government could not proceed as planned; and indeed would almost certainly have foundered, as in fact it almost did over that very issue.

"However, since this power is not a logical deduction from the structure of the Constitution but only a practical condition upon its successful operation, it need not be exercised whenever a court sees, or thinks that it sees, an invasion of the Constitution."

May a Congressman vote against a bill because he believes it to be unconstitutional even though the Court has held to the contrary? May the President veto such a bill on this ground? If the President altogether refuses to "receive Ambassadors and other public Ministers" (see Art. II, § 3), may the Court order him to do so? Or should the "supremacy" of judicial review at least be limited to those decisions that do not "interfere with the procedural machinery of Congress or the federal executive"? Sidney Buchanan, *Judicial Supremacy Reexamined: A Proposed Alternative*, 70 Mich.L.Rev. 1279, 1304 (1972). See Sec. 2 infra—"Political Questions." Is there a distinction between *state* and federal officials in respect to the binding nature of the Court's decisions?

COOPER v. AARON, 358 U.S. 1, 78 S. Ct. 1401, 3 L.Ed.2d 5 (1958) (also discussed at p. 1197), arose several years after the landmark reading in *Brown v. Board of Education* (1954) (set forth at p. 1167 infra) that segregation of public school children on the basis of race violated fourteenth equal protection, a plan approved by the lower federal courts to desegregate Little Rock public schools was blocked by the Governor of Arkansas and other state officials. In the face of a federal court injunction, the Governor backed off, and National Guard soldiers, called out to keep the public schools desegregated, were withdrawn. For a short time, black students were able to attend previously all-white public schools under the protection of federally-commanded troops. However, in early 1958, citing deep tension and concern about violence, the school board sought, and a federal court granted, a long postponement of the desegregation plan. The Court of Appeals reversed, and the Supreme Court affirmed—in an opinion delivered not by any one Justice, as is ordinarily the case, but signed by all nine. Arkansas contended that since it was not a party to the litigation that culminated in the *Brown* ruling, it was not "bound" by that decision. This claim stirred the Supreme court to make a broad and forceful statement about its supremacy in constitutional matters—as Laurence H. Tribe, *American Constitutional Law* 255 (3d ed. 2000) (hereafter Tribe, 3d ed.) described it, "a statement uniquely punctuated by the Justices' individual signatures of the opinion":

"Article VI of the constitution makes the Constitution the 'supreme law of the land.' In 1803, Chief Justice Marshall, speaking for a unanimous Court, referring to the Constitution as 'the fundamental and paramount law of the nation,' declared [in] *Marbury* the basic principle that the federal judiciary is supreme in the exposition of the law of the constitution, and that principle has ever since been respected by this court and the country as a permanent and indispensable feature of our constitutional system. It follows that the interpretation of the Fourteenth Amendment enunciated by this Court in the *Brown* case is the supreme law of the land. [Every] state legislator and executive and judicial officer is solemnly committed by oath taken pursuant to art. VI, cl. 3 'to support this constitution.' No state legislature or executive or judicial officer can war against the Constitution without violating his undertaking to support it. Chief Justice Marshall spoke for a unanimous court in saying that: 'If the legislatures of the several states may, at will, annul the judgments of the courts of the United States, and destroy the rights acquired under those judgments, the constitution itself becomes a solemn mockery * * *.' *United States v. Peters,* 5 Cranch 115. A governor who asserts a power to nullify a federal court order is similarly restrained."[m]

LAURENCE TRIBE, 3d ed., at 255–58, 264–67: *"The meaning of Cooper v. Aaron.* [A] broad reading of *Cooper* would seem to embody two central assumptions. The first is that the Court, in rendering a constitutional decision, announces a general norm of wide applicability. This viewpoint ignores the competing conception that the Court, in making constitutional determinations pursuant to its responsibility under *Marbury*, simply resolves the claims of the parties before it. But an expansive view of the judicial function was clearly warranted in *Brown*; the Court's unanimous opinion was couched in the most general terms and was perceived at the time as applying to all public schools.

"[The] second possible assumption—that the Court's interpretation is *itself* the 'supreme law of the land' and that state officials are directly bound by oath to support that interpretation—is more troubling. This view has been criticized as wrongly equating the Constitution with the Court's interpretation of it—as saying that *Marbury* means that the Constitution is what the Court says it is, no less and no more. So construed, *Cooper* ignores the reality that, at least so long as the manner in which our nation's fundamental document is to be interpreted remains open to question, the 'meaning,' of the Constitution is subject to legitimate dispute, and the Court is not alone in its responsibility to address that meaning. Rather, a variety of actors must make their own constitutional judgments, and possess the power to develop interpretations of the Constitution which do not necessarily conform to the judicially enforced interpretation articulated by the Supreme Court: the president, legislators, state courts and the public at large.

"The *Cooper* opinion as a whole, however, does not require so literal a reading of its invocation of absolute judicial supremacy; conceived with sufficient subtlety, it is readily compatible with American democracy. Plainly, in *Cooper* the Court does say that its *Brown* decision is binding law under the Supremacy Clause. But the Court need not be understood to say anything more than that *Brown* and its progeny, including the case at hand, are binding in the same way that any other judicial decision is binding, so that state officials who interfere with enforcement of a judgment, or act to undermine its goals, are acting unlawfully. On this view,

---

m. For a strong defense of this "judicial supremacy" analysis, see Larry Alexander & Frederick Schauer, *On Extrajudicial* 1997 Con-stitutional Interpretation, *110 Harv.L.Rev. 1359 (1997).*

Brown need not be seen as itself 'part' of the Constitution, but as a constitutional judgment, an exercise of judicial power entitled to respect under the Supremacy Clause not because it *is* the Constitution but because it is an exercise of power *under* the Constitution—just as the [Court's] interpretation of a federal statute, is binding. On this view, to declare that the "federal judiciary is *supreme* in the exposition of the law of the Constitution" is to make a statement more about the role of the federal judiciary than about the content of the Constitution's commands. * * *

"Whether the Court possesses a monopoly on constitutional interpretation. [There] is ample historical support for the power of other branches to construe the Constitution. Thomas Jefferson and Andrew Jackson, among many others, took the view that each branch has the authority to interpret the Constitution for itself and that, in the event of conflict, the views of the Court are no more authoritative than those of the other branches. Indeed, in the Nation's early years, '[i]t was in the legislative and executive branches, not in the courts, that the original understanding of the Constitution was forged.'[62]

[As] Michael Paulsen has observed,[69] just as *Marbury* instructs that an Act of Congress contrary to the Constitution should not be given effect by courts when exercising their power to decide cases, so a judicial decree contrary to the Constitution arguably should not be given effect by the executive when exercising the power to take care that the laws be faithfully executed. Indeed, to do otherwise might be said to violate the President's own oath. What if, for example, Congress enacted a law (over the President's veto) ordering the imprisonment or summary execution of a suspected terrorist by name and a politicized Supreme Court upheld it? Shouldn't the President have the power—even the duty—to refuse to carry out the sentence? Similarly, suppose that in the year 1863 the same Supreme Court that decided *Dred Scott* ruled that the emancipation proclamation was unconstitutional as a taking of property? Would Lincoln have been obligated to return freed blacks to slavery? These examples illustrate the gravity of the separate oath requirement that the Constitution imposes on the President in Article II, § 1, clause 8, and the legitimacy of differing interpretations of the Constitution itself."

JUSTICE BREYER—DISSENTING IN BUSH v. GORE, 121 S.Ct. 525, 550 (2000): To describe this case briefly,[n] the Florida Supreme Court ordered a manual recount of ballots cast in selected, heavily Democratic counties during the 2000 Florida presidential election. This order effectively extended the December 12 deadline set by the Florida Secretary of State.[o] The Florida Supreme Court then ordered a manual recount of all so-called "undervotes" (ballots on which earlier machine counts had failed to record any presidential choice) in all counties,

62. David P. Currie, *The Constitution in Congress: The Federalist Period, 1978–1801,* at 296 (1997) * * *

69. Michael Stokes Paulsen, *The Most Dangerous Branch: Executive Power to Say What the Law Is,* 83 Geo. L.J. 217, 228–61 (1994).

n. The procedural setting of this case is presented more extensively at p. 1356 infra.

o. A majority of the U.S. Supreme Court understood this to be a Florida statutory dead-line for the completion of proceedings bearing on the final certification of the state's electors. But dissenting Justice Breyer, joined by Stevens, Souter and Ginsburg, JJ., maintained that whether there was time to "conduct a recount prior to December 18, when the electors are scheduled to meet," and whether, under Florida law, Florida could take further action, were "matter[s] for Florida courts, not this Court, to decide."

saying only that election officials and lower court judges should follow the legislatively prescribed standard of attempting to discern "the will of the voter." On December 9, the Supreme Court stayed the state supreme court order. Three days later the Supreme Court held (1) that the manual recount of ballots ordered by the state supreme court violated the equal protection clause (see p. ___); and (2) that, in light of the December 12 deadline, remanding the case to the state supreme court for its ordering of a constitutionally proper contest would not be an appropriate remedy.

The per curiam opinion observed that "[n]one are more conscious that are the members of the Court, and none stand more in admiration of the Constitution's design to leave the selection of the President to the people, through their legislatures, and to the political sphere," but added: "When contending parties invoke the process of the courts, however, it becomes our unsought responsibility to resolve the federal and constitutional issues the judicial system has been forced to confront." But dissenting Justice Breyer, joined by Stevens, Souter and Ginsburg, JJ., did not believe that Court had been "forced to confront" any federal and constitutional issues. He maintained that the Court "was wrong to take this case" and "wrong to grant a stay" and "should now vacate that stay and permit the Florida Supreme Court to decide whether the recount should resume." Justice Breyer then continued as follows:

"Despite the reminders that this case involves 'an election for the President of the United States' (Rehnquist, C.J. concurring), no preeminent legal concern, or practical concern related to legal questions, required this Court to hear this case, let alone to issue a stay that stopped Florida's recount process in its tracks. * * * Of course, the selection of the President is of fundamental national importance. But that importance is political, not legal. And this Court should resist the temptation unnecessarily to resolve tangential legal disputes, where doing so threatens to determine the outcome of the election.

"* * * I think it not only legally wrong, but also most unfortunate, for the Court simply to have terminated the Florida recount. Those who caution judicial restraint in resolving political disputes have described the quintessential case for that restraint as a case marked, among other things, by the 'strangeness of the issue,' its 'intractability to principled resolution,' its 'sheer momentousness, [which] tends to unbalance judicial judgement,' and 'the inner vulnerability, the self-doubt of an institution which is electorally irresponsible and has no earth to draw strength from.' Bickel, *The Least Dangerous Branch* 184 (1966). Those characteristics mark this case.

"At the same time, [the] Court is not acting to vindicate a fundamental constitutional principle, such as the need to protect a basic human liberty. No other strong reason to act is present. Congressional statutes tend to obviate the need. And, above all, in this highly politicized matter, the appearance of a split decision runs the risk of undermining the public's confidence in the Court itself. That confidence is a public treasure. It has been built slowly over many years, some of which were marked by a Civil War and the tragedy of segregation. It is a vitally necessary ingredient of any successful effort to protect basic liberty and, indeed, the rule of law itself. We run no risk of returning to the days when a President (responding to this Court's efforts to protect the Cherokee Indians) might have said, 'John Marshall has made this decision; now let him enforce it!' Loth, *Chief Justice John Marshall and The Growth of the American Republic* 365

(1948). But we do risk a self-inflicted wound—a wound that may harm not just the Court, but the Nation.

"I fear that in order to bring this agonizingly long election process to a definitive conclusion, we have not adequately attended to that necessary 'check upon our own exercise of power,' 'our own sense of self-restraint.' *United States v. Butler*, 297 U.S. 1, 79 (1936) (Stone J., dissenting). Justice Brandeis once said of the Court, 'The most important thing we do is not doing.' What it does today, the Court should have left undone. I would repair the damage done as best we now can, by permitting the Florida recount to continue under uniform standards."[p].

Judicial Review and Democracy

ALEXANDER BICKEL, supra, at 16–20: "The root difficulty is that judicial review is a counter-majoritarian force in our system. [W]hen the supreme court declares unconstitutional a legislative act or the action of an elected executive, it thwarts the will of representatives of the actual people of the here and now; it exercises control, not in behalf of the prevailing majority, but against it. That [is] the reason the charge can be made that judicial review is undemocratic.

"Most assuredly, no democracy operates by taking continuous nose counts on the broad range of daily governmental activities. * * * Nevertheless, although democracy does not mean constant reconsideration of decisions once made, it does man that a representative majority has the power to accomplish a reversal. This power is of the essence, and no less so because it is often merely held in reserve.

"It is true, of course, that the process of reflecting the will of a popular majority in the legislature is deflected by various inequalities of representation and by all sorts of institutional habits and characteristics, which perhaps tend most often in favor of inertia.[70] Yet, impurities and imperfections, if such they be, in one part of the system are no argument for total departure from the desired norm in another part. * * *

"No doubt ['interest' or 'pressure groups'] operate forcefully on the electoral process, and no doubt they seek and gain access to and an effective share in the legislative and executive decisional process. Perhaps they constitute also, in some measure, and impurity or imperfection. But no one has claimed that they have been able to capture the governmental process except by combining in some fashion, and thus capturing or constitution (are not the two verbs synonymous?) a majority. They often ten themselves to be majoritarian in composition and to be subject to broader majoritarian influences. And the price of what they sell or buy in the legislature is determined in the biennial or quadrennial electoral market-place. * * * Judicial review works counter to this characteristic.

"It therefore does not follow from the complex nature of a democratic system that, because admirals and generals and the members, say, of the Federal Reserve Board or of this or that administrative agency are not electorally responsible, judges who exercise the power of judicial review need not be responsible either,

---

p. Justice Souter did not join this part of Justice Breyer's dissent.

70. For a forceful position "that there can be no automatic and blanket equation of Congress or the Executive branch with the voice of the people," see Martin Shapiro, *Freedom of Speech*, 17–25 (1966). Consider Samuel Krislov, *The Supreme Court and Political Freedom* 20 (1968): "If one analyzes the actual rules of behavior in the so-called democratic units of government, we find that they also have mixed aspects, the the possibility—sometimes the actuality—of minority control. The power of the Rules Committee, the filibuster, and the Senate are obvious shortcomings; [the] operational consequences of seniority, and the population base of districts likely to maintain continuity in representation are more veiled aspects." See also Donald Kimmers, *Professor Kurland, The Supreme Court, and Political Science*, 15 J.Pub.L. 230 (1966).

and in neither case is there a serious conflict with democratic theory. For admirals and generals and the like are most often responsible to officials who are themselves elected and through whom the line runs directly to a majority. What is more significant, the policies they make are or should be interstitial or technical only and are reversible by legislative majorities * * *—a fact of great consequence. Nor will it do to liken judicial review to the general lawmaking function of judges. In the latter aspect, judges are indeed something like administrative officials, for their decisions are also reversible by any legislative majority—and not infrequently they are reversed.[71] Judicial review, however, is the power to apply and construe the Constitution in matters of the greatest moment, against the wishes of a legislative majority review, however, is the power to apply and construe the constitution in matters of the greatest moment, against the wishes of a legislative majority, which is, in turn, powerless to affect the judicial decision."[q]

————

JESSE CHOPER, *The Supreme Court and the Political Branches: Democratic Theory and Practice,* 122 U.Pa.L.Rev. 810, 830–32 (1974): "In the main, the effect of judicial review in ruling legislation unconstitutional is to nullify the finished product of the lawmaking process. It is the very rare supreme court decision on constitutionality that affirmatively mandates the undertaking of government action. To make the point in another way, when the supreme court finds legislative acts unconstitutional it holds invalid only those enactments that have survived the many hurdles fixed between incipient proposals and standing law.

"The significance of this [is] that most of the antimajoritarian elements that have been found in the American legislative process [are] negative ones. They work to *prevent* the translation of popular wishes into governing rules rather than to *produce* laws that are contrary to majority sentiment. [S]enators representing only fifteen percent of the population may hold sway in the upper house; but their real impact (as is obviously the case with the filibuster as well) is to halt ultimate action rather than facilitate it. For the enactment of law also requires the concurrence of the lower [house]. Furthermore, within each legislative chamber, the ability of the committees and their chairmen and minority members—and frequently of the lobbies and other interest groups as well—to circumvent the majority will of the assembly is most saliently manifested in obstructing the process rather than in making laws. The more formidable task usually is not to stall or defeat a proposal but to organize the requisite support among the dispersed powers so as to form a coalition for its passage. * * *

"Thus, although exceptions exist, '[a] distinguishing feature of our system, perhaps impelled by heritage of sectional division and heterogeneity, is that our governmental structure, institutional habits, and political parties with their internal factional divisions, have combined to produce a system in which major programs and major new directions cannot be undertaken unless supported by a

---

71. Compare William Bishin, *Judicial Review in Democratic Theory*, 50 S.Cal.L.Rev. 1099, 1110 (1977): "Closer examination suggests [that] not all of the decision that such officeholders make can, in fact or theory, be reversed by majoritarian action. [It] must be remembered [that] Congress-especially the Senate-is so structured that representatives of only a minority of the people can prevent the passage of legislation which would overturn prior decisions * * *. Wherever the position of such a minority coincides with the [judges's or administrative officer's] position, therefore, the Constitution gives the principle of reversibility no effect at all."

q. For a different view of the so-called "countermajoritarian difficulty," see Tribe, 3d ed., at 302–10.

fairly broad popular consensus. This normally has been far broader than 51 percent and often bipartisan as well.' [Consequently,] when the Supreme Court, itself without conventional political responsibility, says 'thou shalt not' to acts of Congress, it usually cuts sharply against the grain of majority rule. The relatively few laws that finally overcome the congressional obstacle course generally illustrate the national political branches operating at their majoritarian best while the process of judicial review depicts that element of the Court's work and that exertion of federal authority with the most brittle democratic roots.[59]"

A "Double Standard" of Judicial Review?

For a discussion of the view that the courts should utilize a "double standard" of review, upholding economic legislation so long as it is supported by any rational basis but subjecting laws restricting political processes likely to bring about repeal of undesirable legislation or laws aimed at racial or religious minorities to a more exacting judicial scrutiny, see pp. 298–302 infra.

MARTIN v. HUNTER'S LESSEE

14 U.S. (1 Wheat.) 304, 4 L.Ed. 97 (1816).

[Lord Fairfax, a Virginia citizen, willed his Virginia land known as the Northern Neck of Virginia to his nephew, Martin, a British subject resident in England. In 1789, Virginia, acting pursuant to state laws confiscating lands owned by British subjects, granted land in the Northern Neck to Hunter. The latter brought an action of ejectment against Martin. The Virginia district court ruled for Martin, whose claim was fortified by the anti-confiscation clauses of the treaties of 1783 and 1794 with Great Britain. But the Virginia Court of Appeals reversed, holding that (1) the state's title to the Northern Neck had been perfected before any treaty and (2) in any event, a 1796 Act of Compromise between the Fairfax claimants and the state claimants, formally adopted by the Virginia legislature, had settled the matter against Martin.

[Acting for the purchasers of the Fairfax estate, John Marshall, then a member of the Virginia legislature, had negotiated the compromise. Since he and his brother had organized a syndicate which purchased 160,000 acres of Northern Neck from Martin in 1793, Marshall had a great interest in the case's outcome.

[In *Fairfax's Devisee v. Hunter's Lessee*, 11 U.S. (7 Cranch) 603, 3 L.Ed. 453 (1813), the Supreme Court (Marshall, C.J., not participating) reversed the Virginia Court of Appeals, ruling that Virginia had not perfected title to Northern Neck prior to the grant to Hunter and that therefore the Treaty of 1794 confirmed the title remaining in Martin. Neither Story, J.'s majority opinion nor Johnson, J.'s dissent mentioned the Act of Compromise.

[The cause was remanded to the Virginia Court of Appeals with instructions to enter judgment for appellant, but that court refused to obey the Supreme Court's mandate. All four judges then sitting maintained that in so far as it extended the appellate jurisdiction of the Supreme Court to "this court," § 25 of the Judiciary Act was unconstitutional. Judge Roane—Marshall's arch political enemy—and Judge Fleming (the two judges sitting when the court had decided

---

59. Although no detailed examination of the legislative systems in the states and their political subdivisions has been ventured here, the same conclusion appears to have substantially similar merit in respect to the Court's overturning the laws they produce.

the case against Martin on the merits) contended further that even if the Judiciary Act were valid the case had not properly been before the Supreme Court since the Virginia decision turned not upon a treaty, but "upon another and ordinary ground of jurisdiction—the act of compromise."

[The case again came to the Supreme Court, Marshall again not sitting.[1]]

STORY, J., delivered the opinion of the court. * * *

The third article of the constitution is that which must principally attract our attention. [A]ppellate jurisdiction is given by the constitution to the supreme court, in all cases [within "the judicial power of the United States"] where it has not original jurisdiction; subject, however, to such exceptions and regulations as congress may prescribe. [W]hat is there to restrain its exercise over state tribunals, in the enumerated cases? [If] the judicial power extends to the case, it will be in vain to search in the letter of the constitution for any qualification as to the tribunal where it depends. It [is] plain, that the framers of the constitution did contemplate that cases within the judicial cognisance of the United States, not only might, but would, arise in the state courts, in the exercise of their ordinary jurisdiction [pointing to the supremacy clause]. Suppose, an indictment for a crime, in a state court, and the defendant should allege in his defence, that the crime was created by an ex post facto act of the state, must not the state court [have] a right to pronounce on the validity and sufficiency of the defence? [It] was foreseen, that in the exercise of their ordinary jurisdiction, state courts would incidentally take cognisance of cases arising under the constitution, the laws and treaties of the United States. Yet, to all these cases, the judicial power, by the very terms of the constitution, is to extend. It cannot extend, by original jurisdiction, if that was already rightfully and exclusively attached in the state courts, which (as has been already shown) may occur; it must, therefore, extend by appellate jurisdiction, or not at all. It would seem to follow, that the appellate power of the United States must, in such cases, extend to state tribunals * * *

It has been argued, that such an appellate jurisdiction over state courts is inconsistent with the genius of our governments, and the spirit of the constitution. That the latter was never designed to act upon state sovereignties, but only upon the people, and that if the power exists it will materially impair the sovereignty of the states, and the independence of their courts. [But the Constitution] is crowded with provisions which restrain or annul the sovereignty of the states, in some of the highest branches of their prerogatives. The tenth section of the first article contains a long list of disabilities and prohibitions imposed upon the states. [The] language of the constitution is also imperative upon the states, as to the performance of many duties. It is imperative upon the state legislatures, to make laws prescribing the time, places and manner of holding elections for senators and representatives, and for electors of president and vice-president. And in these, as well as some other cases, congress have a right to revise, amend or supersede the laws which may be passed by state legislatures. When, therefore, the states are stripped of some of the highest attributes of sovereignty, and the same are given to the United States; when the legislatures of the states are, in some respects, under the control of congress, and in every case are, under the constitution, bound by the paramount authority of the United States; it is certainly difficult to support the argument, that the appellate power over the decisions of state courts is contrary to the genius of our institutions. The courts of

1. For further exploration of the historical background, see 4 Albert Beveridge, *The Life of John Marshall* 144–61 (1919); 2 William Crosskey, *Politics and the Constitution* 785–817 (1953); 1 Charles Warren, *The Supreme Court in United States History* 442–53 (1922).

the United States can, without question, revise the proceedings of the executive and legislative authorities of the states, and if they are found to be contrary to the constitution, may declare them to be of no legal validity. Surely, the exercise of the same right over judicial tribunals is not a higher or more dangerous act of sovereign power.

Nor can such a right be deemed to impair the independence of state judges. It is assuming the very ground in controversy, to assert that they possess an absolute independence of the United States. In respect to the powers granted to the United States, they are not independent; they are expressly bound to obedience, by the letter of the constitution * * *.

The argument urged from the possibility of the abuse of the revising power, is equally unsatisfactory. [From] the very nature of things, the absolute right of decision, in the last resort, must rest somewhere—wherever it may be vested, it is susceptible of abuse. [A]dmitting that the judges of the state courts are, and always will be, of as much learning, integrity and wisdom, as those of the courts of the United States (which we very cheerfully admit), it does not aid the argument. It is manifest, that the constitution has proceeded upon a theory of its own, and given or withheld powers according to the judgment of the American people, by whom it was adopted. We can only construe its powers, and cannot inquire into the policy or principles which induced the grant of them. The constitution has presumed (whether rightly or wrongly, we do not inquire), that state attachments, state prejudices, state jealousies, and state interests, might sometimes obstruct, or control, or be supposed to obstruct or control, the regular administration of justice. * * *

This is not all. A motive of another kind, perfectly compatible with the most sincere respect for state tribunals, might induce the grant of appellate power over their decisions. * * * Judges of equal learning and integrity, in different states, might differently interpret the statute, or a treaty of the United States, or even the constitution itself: if there were no revising authority to control these jarring and discordant judgments, and harmonize them into uniformity, the laws, the treaties and the constitution of the United States would be different, in different states, and might, perhaps, never have precisely the same construction, obligation or efficiency, in any two states. The public mischiefs that would attend such a state of things would be truly deplorable * * *.

On the whole, the court are of opinion, that the appellate power of the United States does extend to cases pending in the state courts; and that the 25th section of the judiciary act, which authorizes the exercise of this jurisdiction in the specified cases, by a writ of error, is supported by the letter and spirit of the constitution. [It] is an historical fact, that this exposition of the constitution, extending its appellate power to state courts, was, previous to its adoption, uniformly and publicly avowed by its friends, and admitted by its enemies, as the basis of their respective reasonings, both in and out of the state conventions. It is an historical fact, that at the time when the judiciary act was submitted to the deliberations of the first congress, composed, as it was not only of men of great learning and ability, but of men who acted a principal part in framing, supporting or opposing that constitution, the same exposition was explicitly declared and admitted by the friends and by the opponents of that system. It is an historical fact, that the supreme court of the United States have, from time to time, sustained this appellate jurisdiction, in a great variety of cases, brought from the tribunals of many of the most important states in the Union,[2] and that no state

2. See, e.g., *Clerke v. Harwood*, 3 U.S. (3 Dall.) 342, 1 L.Ed. 628 (1797) (state law in

tribunal has ever breathed a judicial doubt on the subject or declined to obey the mandate of the supreme court, until the present occasion. * * *

[The Court next rejected the contention that the case was not properly before it because the Virginia decision turned on the Act of Compromise.]

We have not thought it incumbent on us to give any opinion upon the question, whether this court have authority to issue a writ of mandamus to the court of appeals, to enforce the former judgments, as we did not think it necessarily involved in the decision of this cause.

It is the opinion of the whole court, that the judgment of the court of appeals of Virginia, rendered on the mandate in this cause, be reversed, and the judgment of the district court [be] affirmed.

JOHNSON, J. It will be observed, in this case, that the court disavows all intention to decide on the right to issue compulsory process to the state courts; thus leaving us, in my opinion, where the constitution and laws place us— supreme over persons and cases, so far as our judicial powers extend, but not asserting any compulsory control over the state tribunals. In this view, I acquiesce in their opinion, but not altogether in the reasoning or opinion of my brother who delivered it. * * *

Notes and Questions

1. *Was the judgment executed?* Charles Warren reports that the Court "decided to avoid the chance of further friction" with the Virginia Court of Appeals "and accordingly, instead of issuing a second mandate to that Court, it issued its process directly to the District Court [in] which the suit had been originally instituted," 1 Warren, supra, at 450.[3] See also Walter Dodd, *Chief Justice Marshall and Virginia 1813–21*, 12 Am.Hist.Rev. 776, 779 (1907), claiming that the United States marshal was eventually ordered to execute the judgment of the Supreme Court. But William Crosskey insists that execution of judgment was neither issued nor required. Under the Virginia practice, he contends, the proceeding under which the case was brought "served much the same purpose in settling points of law in dispute in land-title controversies, as does a modern action for a declaratory judgment," 2 Crosskey, supra, at 786. Moreover, he adds, "upon the peculiar facts of the case, execution of the judgment would have been a completely vain proceeding; for Hunter could at once have brought a successful action to recover possession again, based on the compromise. There was not a word in the Supreme Court's decision that forbade it." Id. at 806 n.[4]

2. COHENS v. VIRGINIA, 19 U.S. (6 Wheat.) 264, 5 L.Ed. 257 (1821)— which sustained the Court's appellate jurisdiction under § 25 of the Judiciary Act to review state criminal proceedings, and is generally viewed as reaffirming and

conflict with treaty). The first Supreme Court decision holding a state law unconstitutional was *Fletcher v. Peck*, 10 U.S. (6 Cranch) 87, 3 L.Ed. 162 (1810) but the case arose in a lower federal court.

3. In respect to its appellate jurisdiction, 28 U.S.C.A. § 2106 presently empowers the Court to "remand the cause and direct the entry of such appropriate judgment, decree or order, or require such further proceedings to be had as may be just under the circumstances."

4. For post-*Martin* instances of state court resistance to Supreme Court orders and vari-

ous efforts to secure compliance see Walter Murphy, *Lower Court Checks on Supreme Court Power*, 53 Am.Pol.Sci.Rev. 1017 (1959); Charles Warren, *Federal and State Court Interference*, 43 Harv.L.Rev. 345 (1930); Jerry Beatty, *State Court Evasion of United States Supreme Court Mandates During the Last Decade of the Warren Court*, 6 Val.L.Rev. 260 (1972); Notes, 67 Harv.L.Rev. 1251 (1954), 56 Yale L.J. 574 (1947). On the theory of "interposition," see Note, 1 Race Rel.L.Rep. 465 (1956).

"supplementing" *Martin,* see 2 Warren, supra, at 10—has stronger historical links with *McCulloch v. Maryland* (set forth, p. 60 infra), see 4 Beveridge, *The Life of John Marshall* 343 (1919).

Appellants were found guilty in a Virginia court of selling lottery tickets in violation of state law. Their defense was that the lottery was organized by the City of Washington, under a congressional statute authorizing the lottery. On appeal to the Supreme Court, they were met with the contentions that the Court had no jurisdiction to review a state criminal case and, in any event, Congress had no power to permit the sale of lottery tickets in a state which prohibited such sale. On the jurisdictional point, Virginia argued that (1) if when the state is a party the Supreme Court has original jurisdiction, this grant excludes appellate jurisdiction; (2) federal courts cannot take original jurisdiction over criminal cases, since that rightfully belongs to the courts of the state whose laws have been violated; (3) consequently, the Supreme Court has no jurisdiction at all. As in *Marbury,* MARSHALL, C.J., used the occasion to express a broad view of the Court's powers, but decided the case on a narrow ground in favor of the Jeffersonians—the federal statute authorizing a lottery had no effect outside the City of Washington.

SECTION 2. POLITICAL QUESTIONS

Does the principle of judicial review comprehend the Court's acting as "final arbiter" on *all* constitutional questions presented by a case properly within its jurisdiction? Or are some constitutional issues inappropriate for judicial resolution and thus "nonjusticiable"?

NIXON v. UNITED STATES

506 U.S. 224, 113 S.Ct. 732, 122 L.Ed.2d 1 (1993).

CHIEF JUSTICE REHNQUIST delivered the opinion of the Court.

Petitioner Walter L. Nixon, Jr., [a] former Chief Judge of the United States District Court for the Southern District of Mississippi, was convicted by a jury of two counts of making false statements before a federal grand jury and sentenced to prison. The grand jury investigation stemmed from reports that Nixon had accepted a gratuity from a Mississippi businessman in exchange for asking a local district attorney to halt the prosecution of the businessman's son. Because Nixon refused to resign from his office as a United States District Judge, he continued to collect his judicial salary while serving out his prison sentence.

On May 10, 1989, the House of Representatives adopted three articles of impeachment for high crimes and misdemeanors. The first two articles charged Nixon with giving false testimony before the grand jury and the third article charged him with bringing disrepute on the Federal Judiciary.

After the House presented the articles to the Senate, the Senate voted to invoke its own Impeachment Rule XI, under which the presiding officer appoints a committee of Senators to "receive evidence and take testimony." The Senate committee held four days of hearings, during which 10 witnesses, including Nixon, testified. Pursuant to Rule XI, the committee presented the full Senate with a complete transcript of the proceeding and a report stating the uncontested facts and summarizing the evidence on the contested facts. Nixon and the House impeachment managers submitted extensive final briefs to the full Senate and delivered arguments from the Senate floor during the three hours set aside for oral argument in front of that body. Nixon himself gave a personal appeal, and several Senators posed questions directly to both parties. The Senate voted by more than the constitutionally required two-thirds majority to convict Nixon on the first two articles. The presiding officer then entered judgment removing Nixon from his office as United States District Judge.

Nixon thereafter commenced the present suit, arguing that Senate Rule XI violates the constitutional grant of authority to the Senate to "try" all impeachments because it prohibits the whole Senate from taking part in the evidentiary hearings. [The] District Court held that his claim was nonjusticiable and the Court of Appeals for the District of Columbia Circuit agreed.

A controversy is nonjusticiable—i.e., involves a political question—where there is "a textually demonstrable constitutional commitment of the issue to a coordinate political department; or a lack of judicially discoverable and manageable standards for resolving it." *Baker v. Carr,* 369 U.S. 186, 217, 82 S.Ct. 691, 7 L.Ed.2d 663 (1962). But [the] lack of judicially manageable standards may strengthen the conclusion that there is a textually demonstrable commitment to a coordinate branch.

In this case, we must examine Art. I, § 3, cl. 6, to determine the scope of authority conferred upon the Senate by the Framers regarding impeachment. It provides: "The Senate shall have the sole Power to try all Impeachments. When sitting for that Purpose, they shall be on Oath or Affirmation. When the President of the United States is tried, the Chief Justice shall preside: And no Person shall be convicted without the Concurrence of two thirds of the Members present." * * *

Petitioner argues that the word "try" in the first sentence imposes by implication an additional requirement on the Senate in that the proceedings must be in the nature of a judicial trial. From there petitioner goes on to argue that this limitation precludes the Senate from delegating to a select committee the task of hearing the testimony of witnesses * * *.

There are several difficulties with this position which lead us ultimately to reject it. The word "try," both in 1787 and later, has considerably broader meanings than those to which petitioner would limit it. [Thus], we cannot say that the Framers used the word "try" as an implied limitation on the method by which the Senate might proceed in trying impeachments. * * *

The conclusion that the use of the word "try" in the first sentence of the Impeachment Trial Clause lacks sufficient precision to afford any judicially manageable standard of review of the Senate's actions is fortified by the existence of the three very specific requirements that the Constitution does impose on the Senate when trying impeachments: the members must be under oath, a two-thirds vote is required to convict, and the Chief Justice presides when the President is tried. These limitations are quite precise, and their nature suggests that the Framers did not intend to impose additional limitations on the form of the Senate proceedings by the use of the word "try" in the first sentence.

Petitioner devotes only two pages in his brief to negating the significance of the word "sole" in the first sentence of Clause 6. [We] think that the word "sole" is of considerable significance. Indeed, the word "sole" appears only one other time in the Constitution—with respect to the House of Representatives' "*sole* Power of Impeachment." Art. I, § 2, cl. 5 (emphasis added). The common sense meaning of the word "sole" is that the Senate alone shall have authority to determine whether an individual should be acquitted or convicted. The dictionary definition bears this out. "Sole" is defined as "having no companion," "solitary," "being the only one," and "functioning ... independently and without assistance or interference." If the courts may review the actions of the Senate in order to determine whether that body "tried" an impeached official, it is difficult to see how the Senate would be "functioning ... independently and without assistance or interference."

Nixon [argues] that even if significance be attributed to the word "sole" in the first sentence of the clause, the authority granted is to the Senate, and this means that "the Senate—not the courts, not a lay jury, not a Senate Committee—shall try impeachments." Brief for Petitioner 42. It would be possible to read the first sentence of the Clause this way, but it is not a natural reading. Petitioner's interpretation would bring into judicial purview not merely the sort of claim made by petitioner, but other similar claims based on the conclusion that the word "Senate" has imposed by implication limitations on procedures which the Senate might adopt. Such limitations would be inconsistent with the construction of the Clause as a whole, which, as we have noted, sets out three express limitations in separate sentences.

The history and contemporary understanding of the impeachment provisions support our reading of the constitutional language. The parties do not offer evidence of a single word in the history of the Constitutional Convention or in contemporary commentary that even alludes to the possibility of judicial review in the context of the impeachment powers. This silence is quite meaningful in light of the several explicit references to the availability of judicial review as a check on the Legislature's power with respect to bills of attainder, ex post facto laws, and statutes. See *The Federalist* No. 78.

The Framers labored over the question of where the impeachment power should lie. Significantly, in at least two considered scenarios the power was placed with the Federal Judiciary. [See] *The Federalist* No. 65. The Supreme Court was not the proper body because the Framers "doubted whether [it] would possess the degree of credit and authority" to carry out its judgment if it conflicted with the accusation brought by the Legislature—the people's representative. In addition, the Framers believed the Court was too small in number: "The awful discretion, which a court of impeachments must necessarily have, to doom to honor or to infamy the most confidential and the most distinguished characters of the community, forbids the commitment of the trust to a small number of persons." Id.

There are two additional reasons why the Judiciary, and the Supreme Court in particular, were not chosen to have any role in impeachments. First, the Framers recognized that most likely there would be two sets of proceedings for individuals who commit impeachable offenses—the impeachment trial and a separate criminal trial. In fact, the Constitution explicitly provides for two separate proceedings. See Art. I, § 3, cl. 7. The Framers deliberately separated the two forums to avoid raising the specter of bias and to ensure independent judgments. [Certainly] judicial review of the Senate's "trial" would introduce the same risk of bias as would participation in the trial itself.

Second, judicial review would be inconsistent with the Framers' insistence that our system be one of checks and balances. In our constitutional system, impeachment was designed to be the *only* check on the Judicial Branch by the Legislature. * * * Judicial involvement in impeachment proceedings, even if only for purposes of judicial review, is counterintuitive because it would eviscerate the "important constitutional check" placed on the Judiciary by the Framers. * * *

Nevertheless, Nixon argues [that] if the Senate is given unreviewable authority to interpret the Impeachment Trial Clause, there is a grave risk that the Senate will usurp judicial power. The Framers anticipated this objection and created two constitutional safeguards to keep the Senate in check. The first safeguard is that the whole of the impeachment power is divided between the two legislative bodies [which] "avoids the inconvenience of making the same persons both accusers and judges; and guards against the danger of persecution from the prevalency of a factious spirit in either of those branches." The second safeguard is the two-thirds supermajority vote requirement. * * *

In addition to the textual commitment argument, we are persuaded that the lack of finality and the difficulty of fashioning relief counsel against justiciability. See *Baker*. We agree with the Court of Appeals that opening the door of judicial review to the procedures used by the Senate in trying impeachments would "expose the political life of the country to months, or perhaps years, of chaos." This lack of finality would manifest itself most dramatically if the President were impeached. The legitimacy of any successor, and hence his effectiveness, would be impaired severely, not merely while the judicial process was running its course, but during any retrial that a differently constituted Senate might conduct if its first judgment of conviction were invalidated. Equally uncertain is the question of what relief a court may give other than simply setting aside the judgment of conviction. Could it order the reinstatement of a convicted federal judge, or order Congress to create an additional judgeship if the seat had been filled in the interim?

Petitioner finally contends that a holding of nonjusticiability cannot be reconciled with our opinion in *Powell v. McCormack,* 395 U.S. 486, 89 S.Ct. 1944, 23 L.Ed.2d 491 (1969). The relevant issue in *Powell* was whether courts could review the House of Representatives' conclusion that Powell was "unqualified" to sit as a Member because he had been accused of misappropriating public funds and abusing the process of the New York courts. We stated that the question of justiciability turned on whether the Constitution committed authority to the House to judge its members' qualifications, and if so, the extent of that commitment. Article I, § 5 provides that "Each House shall be the Judge of the Elections, Returns and Qualifications of its own Members." In turn, Art. I, § 2 specifies three requirements for membership in the House: The candidate must be at least 25 years of age, a citizen of the United States for no less than seven years, and an inhabitant of the State he is chosen to represent. We held that, in light of the three requirements specified in the Constitution, the word "qualifications"—of which the House was to be the Judge—was of a precise, limited nature. [The] claim by the House that its power to "be the Judge of the Elections, Returns and Qualifications of its own Members" was a textual commitment of unreviewable authority was defeated by the existence of this separate provision specifying the only qualifications which might be imposed for House membership. The decision as to whether a member satisfied these qualifications was placed with the House, but the decision as to what these qualifications consisted of was not.

In the case before us, there is no separate provision of the Constitution which could be defeated by allowing the Senate final authority to determine the meaning of the word "try" in the Impeachment Trial Clause. We agree with Nixon that courts possess power to review either legislative or executive action that transgresses identifiable textual limits. [But] we conclude, after exercising that delicate responsibility, that the word "try" in the Impeachment Clause does not provide an identifiable textual limit on the authority which is committed to the Senate.

Affirmed.

Justice Stevens, concurring.

[Respect] for a coordinate Branch of the Government forecloses any assumption that improbable hypotheticals like those mentioned by Justice White and Justice Souter will ever occur. * * *

JUSTICE WHITE, with whom JUSTICE BLACKMUN joins, concurring in the judgment.

[The] Court is of the view that the Constitution forbids us even to consider [petitioner's constitutional] contention. I find no such prohibition and would therefore reach the merits of the claim. I concur in the judgment because the Senate fulfilled its constitutional obligation to "try" petitioner.

I. It should be said at the outset that, as a practical matter, it will likely make little difference whether the Court's or my view controls this case. This is so because the Senate has very wide discretion in specifying impeachment trial procedures and because it is extremely unlikely that the Senate would abuse its discretion and insist on a procedure that could not be deemed a trial by reasonable judges. Even taking a wholly practical approach, I would prefer not to announce an unreviewable discretion in the Senate to ignore completely the constitutional direction to "try" impeachment cases. When asked at oral argument whether that direction would be satisfied if, after a House vote to impeach, the Senate, without any procedure whatsoever, unanimously found the accused guilty of being "a bad guy," counsel for the United States answered that the Government's theory "leads me to answer that question yes." Especially in light of this advice from the Solicitor General, I would not issue an invitation to the Senate to find an excuse, in the name of other pressing business, to be dismissive of its critical role in the impeachment process.

Practicalities aside, however, since the meaning of a constitutional provision is at issue, my disagreement with the Court should be stated.

II. [T]he issue in the political question doctrine is not whether the Constitutional text commits exclusive responsibility for a particular governmental function to one of the political branches. There are numerous instances of this sort of textual commitment, e.g., Art. I, § 8, and it is not thought that disputes implicating these provisions are nonjusticiable. Rather, the issue is whether the Constitution has given one of the political branches final responsibility for interpreting the scope and nature of such a power.

[T]here are few, if any, explicit and unequivocal instances in the Constitution of this sort of textual commitment. [In] drawing the inference that the Constitution has committed final interpretive authority to one of the political branches, courts are sometimes aided by textual evidence that the judiciary was not meant to exercise judicial review—a coordinate inquiry expressed in *Baker's* "lack of judicially discoverable and manageable standards" criterion. See, e.g., *Coleman v. Miller,* 307 U.S. 433, 452–454, 59 S.Ct. 972, 83 L.Ed. 1385 (1939), where the Court refused to determine the life span of a proposed constitutional amendment given Art. V's placement of the amendment process with Congress and the lack of any judicial standard for resolving the question.

A. [That] the word "sole" is found only in the House and Senate Impeachment Clauses demonstrates that its purpose is to emphasize the distinct role of each in the impeachment process. As the majority notes, the Framers, following English practice, were very much concerned to separate the prosecutorial from the adjudicative aspects of impeachment. Giving each House "sole" power with respect to its role in impeachments effected this division of labor. While the majority is thus right to interpret the term "sole" to indicate that the Senate ought to " 'function independently and without assistance or interference,' " it wrongly identifies the judiciary, rather than the House, as the source of potential interference with which the Framers were concerned when they employed the term "sole."

Even if the Impeachment Trial Clause is read without regard to its companion clause, the Court's willingness to abandon its obligation to review the constitutionality of legislative acts merely on the strength of the word "sole" is perplexing. Consider, by comparison, the treatment of Art. I, § 1, which grants "All legislative powers" to the House and Senate. As used in that context "all" is nearly synonymous with "sole"—both connote entire and exclusive authority. Yet the Court has never thought it would unduly interfere with the operation of the Legislative Branch to entertain difficult and important questions as to the extent of the legislative power. * * *

The historical evidence reveals above all else that the Framers were deeply concerned about placing in any branch the "awful discretion, which a court of impeachments must necessarily have." *The Federalist* No. 65. Viewed against this history, the discord between the majority's position and the basic principles of checks and balances underlying the Constitution's separation of powers is clear. In essence, the majority suggests that the Framers conferred upon Congress a potential tool of legislative dominance yet at the same time rendered Congress' exercise of that power one of the very few areas of legislative authority immune from any judicial review. [In] a truly balanced system, impeachments tried by the Senate would serve as a means of controlling the largely unaccountable judiciary, even as judicial review would ensure that the Senate adhered to a minimal set of procedural standards in conducting impeachment trials.

B. [The] majority finds this case different from *Powell* only on the grounds that, whereas the qualifications of Art. I, § 2 are readily susceptible to judicial interpretation, the term "try" does not provide an "identifiable textual limit on the authority which is committed to the Senate."

This argument comes in two variants. The first, which asserts that one simply cannot ascertain the sense of "try" which the Framers employed and hence cannot undertake judicial review, is clearly untenable. To begin with, one would intuitively expect that, in defining the power of a political body to conduct an inquiry into official wrongdoing, the Framers used "try" in its legal sense. * * *

The other variant of the majority position focuses not on which sense of "try" is employed in the Impeachment Trial Clause, but on whether the legal sense of that term creates a judicially manageable standard. The majority concludes that the term provides no "identifiable textual limit." Yet, [the] term "try" is hardly so elusive as the majority would have it. Were the Senate, for example, to adopt the practice of automatically entering a judgment of conviction whenever articles of impeachment were delivered from the House, it is quite clear that the Senate will have failed to "try" impeachments. Indeed in this respect, "try" presents no greater, and perhaps fewer, interpretive difficulties than some other constitutional standards that have been found amenable to familiar techniques of judicial construction, including, for example, "Commerce ... among the several States," Art. I, § 8, cl. 3, and "due process of law." Amdt. 5.[3]

---

3. The majority's in terrorem argument against justiciability—that judicial review of impeachments might cause national disruption and that the courts would be unable to fashion effective relief—merits only brief attention. In the typical instance, court review of impeach- ments would no more render the political system dysfunctional than has this litigation. Moreover, the same capacity for disruption was noted and rejected as a basis for not hearing *Powell*. The relief granted for unconstitutional impeachment trials would presumably be simi-

III. [T]extual and historical evidence reveals that the Impeachment Trial Clause was not meant to bind the hands of the Senate beyond establishing a set of minimal procedures. Without identifying the exact contours of these procedures, it is sufficient to say that the Senate's use of a factfinding committee under Rule XI is entirely compatible with the Constitution's command that the Senate "try all impeachments." * * *

JUSTICE SOUTER, concurring in the judgment.

[As] we cautioned in *Baker,* "the 'political question' label" tends "to obscure the need for case-by-case inquiry." The need for such close examination is nevertheless clear from our precedents, which demonstrate that the functional nature of the political question doctrine requires analysis of "the precise facts and posture of the particular case," and precludes "resolution by any semantic cataloguing."

[Whatever] considerations feature most prominently in a particular case, the political question doctrine is "essentially a function of the separation of powers," ibid., existing to restrain courts "from inappropriate interference in the business of the other branches of [the Federal] Government," and deriving in large part from prudential concerns about the respect we owe the political departments. Not all interference is inappropriate or disrespectful, however, and application of the doctrine ultimately turns, as Learned Hand put it, on "how importunately the occasion demands an answer." Learned Hand, *The Bill of Rights* 15 (1958).

This occasion does not demand an answer. The Impeachment Trial Clause [contemplates] that the Senate may determine, within broad boundaries, such subsidiary issues as the procedures for receipt and consideration of evidence necessary to satisfy its duty to "try" impeachments. Other significant considerations confirm a conclusion that this case presents a nonjusticiable political question: the "unusual need for unquestioning adherence to a political decision already made," as well as "the potentiality of embarrassment from multifarious pronouncements by various departments on one question." * * *

One can, nevertheless, envision different and unusual circumstances that might justify a more searching review of impeachment proceedings. If the Senate were to act in a manner seriously threatening the integrity of its results, convicting, say, upon a coin-toss, or upon a summary determination that an officer of the United States was simply " 'a bad guy,' " judicial interference might well be appropriate. In such circumstances, the Senate's action might be so far beyond the scope of its constitutional authority, and the consequent impact on the Republic so great, as to merit a judicial response despite the prudential concerns that would ordinarily counsel silence. "The political question doctrine, a tool for maintenance of governmental order, will not be so applied as to promote only disorder." *Baker.*

Notes and Questions

1. *Political questions and the judicial function.* Is the Court's decision in *Nixon*—that the constitutional lawfulness of the procedures used in an impeach-

---

lar to the relief granted to other unfairly tried public employee-litigants. Finally, as applied to the special case of the President, the majority's argument merely points out that, were the Senate to convict the President without any kind of a trial, a constitutional crisis might well result. It hardly follows that the Court ought to refrain from upholding the Constitution in all impeachment cases. Nor does it follow that, in cases of Presidential impeachment, the Justices ought to abandon their Constitutional responsibilities because the Senate has precipitated a crisis.

ment trial is a nonjusticiable political question—consistent with *Marbury v. Madison* and its central holding that "[i]t is emphatically the province and duty of the judicial department to say what the law is"? Recall that Marshall, C.J., contemplated that "in cases in which the executive possesses a constitutional or legal discretion," the lawfulness of implementing acts would be "only politically examinable."

(a) Martin H. Redish, *Judicial Review and the "Political Question,"* 79 Nw.U.L.Rev. 1031 (1985), argues that the political question doctrine is irreconcilable with the judicial function as understood since *Marbury* and should therefore be abandoned. Do you agree?

(b) Consider Herbert Wechsler, *Principles, Politics, and Fundamental Law* 11–14 (1961): All the political question "doctrine can defensibly imply is that the courts are called upon to judge whether the Constitution has committed to another agency of government the autonomous determination of the issue raised, a finding that itself requires an interpretation. [T]he only proper judgment that may lead to an abstention from decision is that the Constitution has committed the determination of the issue to another agency of government than the courts. Difficult as it may be to make that judgment wisely, [what] is involved is in itself an act of constitutional interpretation, to be made and judged by standards that should govern the interpretive process generally. [That is totally] different from a broad discretion to abstain or intervene."

(c) Louis Henkin, *Is There a Political Question Doctrine?*, 85 Yale L.J. 597, 622–23 (1976), argues that the political question doctrine is "an unnecessary, deceptive packaging of several established doctrines." According to Henkin, one of these doctrines requires the courts to "accept decisions by the political branches within their constitutional authority," and another recognizes the ability of the courts to "refuse some (or all) remedies for want of equity," but none calls for the Court to turn a blind eye to constitutional violations.

(d) Compare Michael J. Gerhardt, *Rediscovering Nonjusticiability: Judicial Review of Impeachments After Nixon*, 44 Duke L.J. 231, 245–46 (1994): "[A] finding of nonjusticiability [is] different from a court's deciding that a wide realm of governmental behavior is constitutional in that a determination of nonjusticiability forecloses a range of potential litigation and signals once and for all that there is no judicial remedy available for any official misconduct within a certain area."

2. *"Textually demonstrable constitutional commitment."* (a) *Impeachment.* Is the Court persuasive in *Nixon* that the constitutional text gives the Senate exclusive power to determine the requisites of impeachment trials? Does it effectively distinguish *Powell v. McCormack*?[a] Would (should) the Court decline review if an impeached federal judge credibly claimed that the Senate's conviction was by less than a 2/3 vote? If a federal judge sought judicial review of an impeachment and conviction alleging denial of the right to counsel or discrimination based on race or political affiliation? Consider Redish, supra, at 1042–43: "I fail to understand a logic that suggests that an appeal to the due process clause of either the fifth or fourteenth amendments can be precluded by a constitutional provision's vesting of power in one of the political branches of government. If the particular exercise of power violates the due process clause, then the fact that a provision in the body of the Constitution authorizes the practice is wholly

a. On *Powell,* see generally *Symposium,* 17 U.C.L.A.Rev. 1 (1969).

irrelevant. [It] may well be subject to control through protections contained in the constitutional amendments."[b]

Consider also Raoul Berger, *Impeachment: The Constitutional Problems* 117–18, 120 (1973): "Although impeachment was chiefly designed to check Executive abuses and oppressions, there was no thought of delivering either the President or the Judiciary to the unbounded discretion of Congress. This is attested by the Framers' rejection of the unfettered removal by Address [formal request of Congress], by their rejection of 'maladministration' because that was 'so vague' as to [amount to] tenure 'at the pleasure' of the Senate, and by the substitution of 'high crimes and misdemeanors' with knowledge that it had a 'limited' and 'technical meaning.'"

Compare Charles L. Black, Jr., *Impeachment: A Handbook* 61–62 (1974): "If the Supreme Court [were] to order reinstatement of an impeached and convicted president, there would be [a] very grave and quite legitimate doubt whether that decree had any title to being obeyed, or whether it was [as] widely outside judicial jurisdiction as would be a judicial order to Congress to increase the penalty for counterfeiting. To cite the most frightening consequence, our military commanders would have to decide for themselves which president they were bound to obey. [It] would be most unfortunate if the notion got about that the Senate's verdict was somewhat tentative."

(b) *Amending process.* COLEMAN v. MILLER, supra, held that the questions whether a state could ratify a constitutional amendment that it had once rejected and whether a proposed amendment lapses if not ratified within a reasonable time were nonjusticiable political questions. But there was no majority opinion. Concurring, Black, J., joined by Roberts, Frankfurter, and Douglas, JJ., stated that Art. V grants Congress "exclusive power over the amending process" and that Congress "is under no duty to accept the pronouncements upon that exclusive power by this Court." Does the language of Art. V support Black, J.? What if Congress submitted a proposed constitutional amendment to the states and provided that no African–American could participate in the state ratification process? See generally Laurence H. Tribe, *A Constitution We Are Amending: In Defense of a Restrained Judicial Role,* 97 Harv.L.Rev. 433 (1983); Walter Dellinger, *The Legitimacy of Constitutional Change: Rethinking the Amendment Process,* 97 Harv.L.Rev. 386 (1983).

Is it relevant to the question of justiciability that constitutional amendment, like impeachment, is a constitutionally mandated check on judicial power? See Tribe, supra.

If, pursuant to Art. V, "the legislatures of two-thirds of the several states" apply to Congress to "call a convention for proposing amendments" and Congress ignores the application, is an action for a mandatory injunction "nonjusticiable"? See Arthur E. Bonfield, *The Dirksen Amendment and the Article V Convention Process,* 66 Mich.L.Rev. 949, 976–85 (1968). Does it matter that the apparent purpose of this provision is to give states a mechanism to force action by an otherwise resistant Congress?

(c) *Regulating the militia.* In GILLIGAN v. MORGAN, 413 U.S. 1, 93 S.Ct. 2440, 37 L.Ed.2d 407 (1973), students at Kent State University sought various relief against government officials to prevent repetition of events that had

---

b. Compare Rebecca L. Brown, *When Political Questions Affect Individual Rights: The Other Nixon v. United States,* 1993 Sup.Ct.Rev. 125, 143, 153 (arguing that, despite broader formulations, "the Court persists in applying the [political question] doctrine in such a way as, most of the time, to do the least violence to [constitutional] rights").

occurred on that campus in May 1970. The court of appeals instructed the federal district court to evaluate the "pattern of training, weaponry and orders in the Ohio National Guard" so as to determine whether it made "inevitable the use of fatal force in suppressing civilian disorders." The Court, per BURGER, C.J., reversed, relying heavily on Art. I, § 8, cl. 16—which grants to Congress "the responsibility for organizing, arming and disciplining the Militia (now the National Guard), with certain responsibilities being reserved to the respective States"— and on federal legislation enacted pursuant thereto: "[T]he nature of the questions to be resolved on remand are subjects committed expressly to the political branches of government. [It] would be difficult to think of a clearer example of the type of governmental action that was intended by the Constitution to be left to the political branches [or] of an area of governmental activity in which the courts have less competence. The complex, subtle, and professional decisions as to the composition, training, equipping, and control of a military force are essentially professional military judgments, subject *always* to civilian control of the Legislative and Executive Branches [which] are periodically subject to electoral accountability."[c]

Suppose the plaintiffs' lawsuit in *Gilligan* had been adjudged justiciable and the plaintiffs had prevailed on the merits. Would there have been judicially manageable standards to guide the Court in crafting an injunctive remedy? Might *Gilligan* be persuasively rationalized as resting on grounds of equity and the unavailability of appropriate equitable remedies? See Henkin, supra, at 619–22. Cf. *Scheuer v. Rhodes*, 416 U.S. 232, 94 S.Ct. 1683, 40 L.Ed.2d 90 (1974) (holding that *Gilligan* did not bar a damages action by estates of students killed at Kent State).

3. *"Judicially manageable standards."* The plurality opinion in COLEMAN v. MILLER stated: "[T]he question of a reasonable time [for the pendency of a constitutional amendment before the states involves] an appraisal of a great variety of relevant conditions, political, social and economic, which can hardly be said to be within the appropriate range of evidence receivable in a court of justice and as to which it would be an extravagant extension of judicial authority to assert judicial notice. [T]hese conditions are appropriate for the consideration of the political departments of the Government. The questions they involve are essentially political and not justiciable."

Compare Redish, supra, at 1047: "Ultimately, *any* constitutional provision can be supplied with working standards of interpretation. To be sure, those standards often will not clearly flow from either the language or history of the provision, but that fact does not distinguish them from many judicial standards invoked every day."

4. *Prudence.* Consider Maurice Finkelstein, *Judicial Self–Limitation*, 37 Harv.L.Rev. 338, 344 (1924): The term "political question" applies "to all those matters of which the court, at a given time, will be of the opinion that it is impolitic or inexpedient to take jurisdiction. Sometimes this idea of inexpediency will result from the fear of the vastness of the consequences that a decision on the merits might entail." The most famous modern formulation of this view was

---

c. Blackmun, J., joined by Powell, J., concurred: "This case relates to prospective relief in the form of judicial surveillance of highly subjective and technical matters involving military training and command. As such, it presents an '[inappropriate] subject matter for judicial consideration,' for respondents are asking the District Court, in fashioning that prospective relief, 'to enter upon policy determinations for which judicially manageable standards are lacking.' *Baker.* [On] the understanding that this is what the Court's opinion holds, I join that opinion."

Douglas, Brennan, Stewart, and Marshall, JJ., dissented because "this case is now moot."

offered by Alexander M. Bickel, *The Least Dangerous Branch* 125–26, 183–84 (1962). Professor Bickel explicitly took the view that the political question doctrine—though functionally necessary—was "something that cannot exist within the four corners of *Marbury*" and its assumption that the courts have an unyielding duty to apply the law in every case properly before them: "[O]nly by [a] play on words can the broad discretion that the courts have [exercised] be turned into an act of constitutional interpretation governed by the general standards of the interpretive process. The political question doctrine simply resists being domesticated in this fashion. There is [something] different about it, in kind, not in degree; something greatly more flexible, something of prudence, not construction and not principle.

"[Such] is the foundation, in both intellect and instinct, of the political-question doctrine: the Court's sense of lack of capacity, compounded in unequal parts of (a) the strangeness of the issue and its intractability to principled resolution; (b) the sheer momentousness of it, which tends to unbalance judicial judgment; (c) the anxiety, not so much that the judicial judgment will be ignored, as that perhaps it should but will not be; (d) finally ('in a mature democracy'), the inner vulnerability, the self-doubt of an institution which is electorally irresponsible and has no earth to draw strength from."

In his concurring opinion in *Nixon*, Souter, J., described the political question doctrine as "deriving in large part from prudential concerns" and expressly cited to Bickel, supra. Is prudential reasoning appropriate in determining whether a case presents a nonjusticiable political question? Inevitable?

5. *The guarantee clause: republican form of government.* (a) *Initiative process.* In PACIFIC STATES TEL. & T. CO. v. OREGON, 223 U.S. 118, 32 S.Ct. 224, 56 L.Ed. 377 (1912), four years after Oregon amended its constitution to allow the people to enact laws through an initiative process, petitioner challenged a tax enacted by an initiative on the ground that the process violated Art. IV, § 4: "The United States shall guarantee to every State in this Union a Republican Form of Government." In essence, the company argued that the initiative process is democratic, not republican. The Court, per WHITE, J., held that the case presented a political question, quoting from *Luther v. Borden,* 48 U.S. (7 How.) 1, 12 L.Ed 581 (1849), an action arising out of the Dorr Rebellion in Rhode Island, in which the question of whether the defendant's arrest of the plaintiff was a trespass turned on which of two groups was the lawful government of the state: "[Under Art. IV, § 4], it rests with Congress to decide what government is the established one in a State. For, as the United States guarantee to each State a republican government, Congress must necessarily decide what government is established in the State before it can determine whether it is republican or not. And when the senators and representatives of a State are admitted into the councils of the Union, the authority of the government under which they are appointed, as well as its republican character, is recognized by the proper constitutional authority. And its decision is binding on every other department of the government, and could not be questioned in a judicial tribunal. It is true that the contest in this case did not last long enough to bring the matter to this issue; and as no senators or representatives were elected under the authority of the government of which Mr. Dorr was the head, Congress was not called upon to decide the controversy. Yet the right to decide is placed there, and not in the courts."

Turning from *Luther,* the Court noted that the telephone company's argument proceeds "upon the theory that the adoption of the initiative and referendum destroyed all government republican in form in Oregon. This being so, the contention, if held to be sound, would necessarily affect the validity, not only of the particular statute which is before us, but of every other statute passed in Oregon since the adoption of the initiative and referendum. And indeed the propositions go further than this, since in their essence they assert that there is no governmental function, legislative or judicial, in Oregon, because it cannot be assumed, if the proposition be well founded, that there is at one and the same time one and the same government which is republican in form and not of that character.[d] * * *

"Do the provisions of § 4, Art. IV, bring about these strange, far-reaching and injurious results? [D]o they authorize the judiciary to substitute its judgment as to a matter purely political for the judgment of Congress on a subject committed to it and thus overthrow the Constitution upon the ground that thereby the guarantee to the States of a government republican in form may be secured, a conception which after all rests upon the assumption that the States are to be guaranteed a government republican in form by destroying the very existence of a government republican in form in the Nation?

"[The] defendant company does not contend here that it could not have been required to pay a license tax. It does not assert that it was denied an opportunity to be heard as to the amount for which it was taxed, or that there was anything inhering in the tax or involved intrinsically in the law which violated any of its constitutional rights. If such questions had been raised they would have been justiciable, and therefore would have required the calling into operation of judicial power. Instead, however, of doing any of these things, the attack on the statute here made is of a wholly different character. Its essentially political nature is at once made manifest by understanding that the assault which the contention here advanced makes is not on the tax as a tax, but on the State as a State. It is addressed to the framework and political character of the government by which the statute levying the tax was passed. It is the government, the political entity, which (reducing the case to its essence) is called to the bar of this court, not for the purpose of testing judicially some exercise of power assailed, on the ground that its exertion has injuriously affected the rights of an individual because of repugnancy to some constitutional limitation, but to demand of the State that it establish its right to exist as a State, republican in form."

(b) *Malapportionment.* BAKER v. CARR, supra, per Brennan, J., held that a suit challenging Tennessee's legislative apportionment scheme, under which some districts had vastly larger populations than others, presented a justiciable question under the equal protection clause: "Judicial standards under the Equal Protection Clause are well developed. [This] case does, in one sense, involve the allocation of political power within a State, and the appellants might conceivably have added a claim under the Guarantee Clause. [Although such a claim] could not have succeeded it does not follow that appellants may not be heard on the equal protection claim which in fact they tender."

Frankfurter, J., joined by Harlan, J., dissented: "The present case [is], in effect, a Guarantee Clause claim masquerading under a different label. But it cannot make the case more fit for judicial action that appellants invoke the

---

d. Consider Tribe 3d ed., at 369: "[I]f a court found that a particular feature of state government rendered the government unrepublican, why could not the court simply declare that feature invalid?" See also Erwin Chemerinsky, *Cases Under the Guarantee Clause Should Be Justiciable*, 65 U.Colo.L.Rev. 849, 873 (1994).

Fourteenth Amendment rather than Art. IV, § 4, where, in fact, the gist of their complaint is the same. * * *

"Hardly any distribution of political authority that could be assailed as rendering government nonrepublican would fail similarly to operate to the prejudice of some groups, and to the advantage of others, within the body politic. [T]he real battle over the initiative and referendum, or over a delegation of power to local rather than statewide authority, is the battle between forces whose influence is disparate among the various organs of government to whom power may be given. [What] Tennessee illustrates is an old and still widespread method of representation—representation by local geographical division, only in part respective of population—in preference to others, forsooth, more appealing. Appellants contest this choice and seek to make this Court the arbiter of the disagreement. [Certainly], 'equal protection' is no more secure a foundation for judicial judgment of the permissibility of varying forms of representative government than is 'Republican Form.'"

(c) *A softening?* In NEW YORK v. UNITED STATES, p. 36, infra, the Court ruled that a federal statute effectively mandating state legislative action (to deal with nuclear waste within the states' borders) exceeded congressional authority under the commerce clause. Turning to an argument that federal statutory provisions creating incentives for the states to legislate violated the guarantee clause, the Court, per O'CONNOR, J., noted that the Court had ruled on the merits of guarantee clause claims in the late nineteenth and early twentieth centuries, "before the holding of *Luther* was elevated into a general principle of nonjusticiability," but found no need to pronounce on the circumstances under which guarantee clause challenges might be justiciable: "[E]ven indulging the assumption that the Guarantee Clause provides a basis upon which a State or its subdivisions may sue to enjoin the enforcement of a federal statute, petitioners have not made out such a claim in this case," since the challenged provisions did "not pose any realistic threat of altering the form or the method of the functioning of New York's government."

(d) *The meaning of the guarantee clause.* Consider the *substantive* issues that would arise if the Court were to deem guarantee clause issues justiciable. Should the Court hold that the initiative process violates the guarantee clause? Suppose that a city provided all citizens with a technology that made legislative debates on all issues fully available and then allowed citizens to enact legislation on certain issues by popular vote from their own homes. Would legislation through this form be consistent with the structure and history of the Constitution? With its spirit? Consider Chemerinsky, supra, at 868: "Madison was particularly concerned that states might be controlled by stable majority coalitions that would systematically impede minority rights.[78] He saw that an integral part of solving the dangers of democracy is having a republican government where people elect representatives and representatives make laws that must comply with state and federal constitutional provisions. [Recently,] historians such as Bernard Bailyn and Gordon Wood, and law professors such as Cass Sunstein and Frank Michelman have argued that the core of a republican government is citizen participation in important public deliberations.[80] Perspectives from both the republican revival and the founders' debates indicate that the Guarantee Clause is not primarily about guaranteeing a

---

78. *The Federalist* No. 10.

80. See, e.g., Cass R. Sunstein, *Beyond the Republican Revival*, 97 Yale L.J. 1539 (1988); Frank I. Michelman, *Foreword: Traces of Self-* *Government*, 100 Harv.L.Rev. 4 (1986). But see Richard H. Fallon, Jr., *What is Republicanism, and Is It Worth Reviving?*, 102 Harv.L.Rev. 1695 (1989).

particular structure of government in states or even about protecting state governments from federal encroachments. Instead, it is meant to protect the basic individual right of political participation, most notably the right to vote and the right to choose public officeholders."

Is there any sound modern reason why the Court should be unwilling to adjudicate the requirements of a republican form of government? See generally Symposium, *Guaranteeing a Republican Form of Government*, 65 Colo.L.Rev. 709 (1994).[e]

6. *Foreign relations.* (a) BAKER v. CARR, per BRENNAN, J., noted: "[I]t is error to suppose that every case or controversy which touches foreign relations lies beyond judicial cognizance. Our cases in this field seem invariably to show a discriminating analysis of the particular question posed, in terms of the history of its management by the political branches, of its susceptibility to judicial handling in the light of its nature and posture in the specific case, and of the possible consequences of judicial action. For example, [w]hile recognition of foreign governments so strongly defies judicial treatment that without executive recognition a foreign state has been called 'a republic of whose existence we know nothing,' and the judiciary ordinarily follows the executive as to which nation has sovereignty over disputed territory, once sovereignty over an area is politically determined and declared, courts may examine the resulting status and decide independently whether a statute applies to that area. [Also, in respect to dates of duration of hostilities,] analysis reveals isolable reasons for the presence of political questions, underlying this Court's refusal to review the political departments' determination of when or whether a war has ended. Dominant is the need for finality in the political determination, for emergency's nature demands 'A prompt and unhesitating obedience,' *Martin v. Mott,* 12 Wheat. 19, 30, 6 L.Ed. 537 (calling up of militia). [But] deference rests on reason, not habit."

(b) GOLDWATER v. CARTER, 444 U.S. 996, 100 S.Ct. 533, 62 L.Ed.2d 428 (1979), summarily reversed a court of appeals decision that the President had power to terminate a treaty with Taiwan without congressional approval. REHN-QUIST, J., joined by Burger, C.J., and Stewart and Stevens, JJ., believed "that the controversy [is] a nonjusticiable political dispute. [W]hile the Constitution is express as to the manner in which the Senate shall participate in the ratification of a Treaty, it is silent as to that body's participation in the abrogation of a Treaty. In this respect the case is directly analogous to *Coleman.* [In] light of [the] fact that different termination procedures may be appropriate for different treaties, the [case] 'must surely be controlled by political standards.' [T]he justifications for concluding that the question here is political [are] even more compelling than in *Coleman* because it involves foreign relations—specifically a treaty commitment to use military force in the defense of a foreign government if attacked. [W]e are asked to settle a dispute between coequal branches of our government, each of which has resources available to protect and assert its interests, resources not available to private litigants outside the judicial forum."

POWELL, J., concurred because of "prudential considerations": "[A] dispute between Congress and the President is not ready for judicial review unless and until each branch has taken action asserting its constitutional authority. [Since]

---

e. For discussion of whether *state* courts may (or should) enforce the guarantee clause, see Arthur E. Bonfield, *The Guarantee Clause of Article IV, Section 4: A Study in Constitutional Desuetude,* 46 Minn.L.Rev. 513 (1962); Jesse H. Choper, *Observations on the Guaran-* *tee Clause,* 65 U.Cal.L.Rev. 741 (1994); Hans A. Linde, *When Is Initiative Lawmaking Not "Republican Government"?,* 17 Hast.Con.L.Q. 159 (1989); Hans A. Linde, *Who Is Responsible for Republican Government?* 65 U.Colo.L.Rev. 709 (1994).

Congress has taken no official [action], we do not know whether there ever will be an actual confrontation between the Legislative and Executive Branches."

But "reliance upon the political-question doctrine is inconsistent with our precedents. [First,] the text of the Constitution does not unquestionably commit the power to terminate treaties to the President alone. Second, there is no 'lack of judicially discoverable and manageable [standards.]' "

BRENNAN, J., who would have affirmed on the merits, dissented: "[T]he political question doctrine restrains courts from reviewing an exercise of foreign policy judgment by a coordinate political branch [but] the doctrine does not pertain when a court is faced with the *antecedent* question whether a particular branch has been constitutionally designated as the repository of political decision-making power. Cf. *Powell*. The issue of decisionmaking authority must be resolved as a matter of constitutional law, not political discretion; accordingly, it falls within the competence of the courts."[f]

(c) If a soldier seeks a federal declaratory judgment that American participation in a particular armed conflict is "unconstitutional in that it was not initially authorized or subsequently ratified by Congressional declaration," is the question "justiciable"? See the opinions of Marshall and Douglas, JJ., in *Holtzman v. Schlesinger*, 414 U.S. 1304, 1316, 94 S.Ct. 1, 8, 38 L.Ed.2d 18, 28 (1973). Virtually without exception, the federal courts have declined to adjudicate such issues—if not on political question grounds, then on grounds of ripeness or mootness.[g]

Consider Archibald Cox, *The Role of Congress in Constitutional Determinations*, 40 U.Cinc.L.Rev. 199, 204 (1971): "[O]ne might formulate a workable principle for delimiting the President's power to engage in military activities overseas, but the task is far from easy. Should the rule permit the use of troops to protect the lives of United States citizens in a foreign country until they can be safely evacuated? Should it permit sending arms with which another nation may defend itself against foreign aggression? Sending 'technicians' to give battlefield instructions in the use of sophisticated weapons? Sending instructors? Sending support troops to protect the bases where logistic support is delivered but to fight only when themselves attacked? If, through gross miscalculation, measures that the rule permits result in armed combat on a sizeable scale, what then may the Executive do, without a declaration of war, to protect the lives of United States soldiers and the national interest during a process of disengagement? May the adverse effects of declaring war upon international relations be taken into account in determining whether the declaration is essential? These are only a few of the pertinent questions."

Should it make any difference to the justiciability issue if a soldier were court-martialed for refusing to engage in combat and sought federal habeas corpus relief? Consider Michael E. Tigar, *Judicial Power, The "Political Question Doctrine," and Foreign Relations*, 17 UCLA L.Rev. 1135, 1177–78 (1970): "[It is] the duty of the Court to consider the legality of a detention by consideration of all the legal rules which are conceded to be operative under the Constitution, laws and treaties of the United States. This determination does not necessarily involve the

---

f. Blackmun, J., joined by White, J., dissented. They "would set the case for oral argument and give it the plenary consideration it so obviously deserves."

g. See, e.g., *Dellums v. Bush*, 752 F.Supp. 1141 (D.D.C.1990)(dictum)(asserting that the issue of whether Persian Gulf War required congressional authorization was justiciable in principle, but dismissing a challenge for lack of ripeness).

Executive in litigating the validity of its claim to possess lawfully the power it exercises in conducting a war: it says only that [when] the Executive [comes] into court it must be bound by the rules fashioned by the judiciary and the Congress for the protection of litigants' rights." See also John H. Ely, *War and Responsibility: Constitutional Lessons of Vietnam and Its Aftermath* 55–58 (1993).

SECTION 3. CONGRESSIONAL REGULATION OF JUDICIAL POWER

Under the Constitution, Congress possesses undisputed power to regulate the jurisdiction of the federal courts. Article III contemplates that the Supreme Court's appellate jurisdiction shall be subject to "such Exceptions * * * as the Congress shall make." And Congress, if it chose, would not need to create any lower federal courts at all. As a result of a deliberate compromise at the Constitutional Convention between those who favored and those who opposed the establishment of lower federal courts, Article III provides that the judicial power "shall be vested in one supreme Court, and in such inferior Courts as the Congress may from time to time ordain and establish." Beginning with the first Judiciary Act, Congress has *never* invested the lower federal courts with the maximum jurisdiction that the Constitution would allow, and it has always imposed limitations on the appellate jurisdiction of the Supreme Court. For example, it was not until 1914 that the Court was authorized to review state court decisions holding state laws violative of the Constitution.

The Supreme Court's original jurisdiction, which typically comprises at most a handful of cases each year (mainly concerning "controversies between two or more states"), is presently governed by 28 U.S.C.A. § 1251. The most important current provisions respecting the Court's appellate jurisdiction are 28 U.S.C.A. §§ 1254 (federal courts of appeals) and 1257 (state courts).

----

§ 1254. Cases in the courts of appeals may be reviewed by the Supreme Court by the following methods: (1) By writ of certiorari granted upon the petition of any party to any civil or criminal case, before or after rendition of judgment or decree; (2) By certification at any time by a court of appeals of any question of law in any civil or criminal case as to which instructions are desired, and upon such certification the Supreme Court may give binding instructions or require the entire record to be sent up for decision of the entire matter in controversy.

§ 1257. (a) Final judgments or decrees rendered by the highest court of a State in which a decision could be had, may be reviewed by the Supreme Court by writ of certiorari where the validity of a treaty or statute of the United States is drawn in question or where the validity of a statute of any State is drawn in question, on the ground of its being repugnant to the Constitution, treaties, or laws of the United States, or where any title, right, privilege, or immunity is specially set up or claimed under the Constitution or the treaties or statutes of, or any commission held or authority exercised under, the United States. * * *

Sections 1254 and 1257 previously provided for a form of appeal that required the Court to determine some classes of cases on their merits. Congress removed this form of jurisdiction in 1988 to permit the Court to decide for itself which cases most deserved its attention. For discussion of the Court's exercise of discretion, see Sec. 4 infra.

EX PARTE McCARDLE

74 U.S. (7 Wall.) 506, 19 L.Ed. 264 (1869).

[On February 5, 1867, Congress empowered federal courts to grant habeas corpus "in all cases where any person may be restrained of his or her liberty in violation of" federal law. Enacted by a Reconstruction Congress, the 1867 Act was intended primarily to establish federal authority to review detentions by state and local authorities; federal courts already possessed jurisdiction to review federal detentions. Among its incidental provisions, the Act authorized appeals to the Supreme Court in cases in which circuit courts denied applications for the writ of habeas corpus.

[McCardle, the virulently racist editor of the Vicksburg Times, was imprisoned by the military government of Mississippi pursuant to the Reconstruction Acts for publishing "incendiary and libelous" articles tending to incite violence and impede Reconstruction. Alleging "unlawful restraint by military force," he sought habeas corpus, but his petition was denied by the Circuit Court. He thereupon appealed to the Supreme Court under the 1867 Act.

[McCardle's case presented the Supreme Court with the opportunity to rule on the constitutionality of the Military Reconstruction Act, which had placed ten former Confederate states under military jurisdiction. The constitutional arguments were clearly substantial, and the Court, in *Ex parte Milligan*, 71 U.S. (4 Wall.) 2 (1867), had hinted that it might be ready to hold military Reconstruction unconstitutional. Fearing this result, Congress, in 1868, after argument in the *McCardle* case but before the Supreme Court had rendered a decision, passed the following act (over President Johnson's veto):] "That so much of the act approved February 5, 1867 [as] authorized an appeal from the judgment of the Circuit Court to the Supreme Court of the United States, or the exercise of any such jurisdiction by said Supreme Court, on appeals which have been, or may hereafter be taken, [is] hereby repealed."

* * * Argument was now heard upon the effect of the repealing act.

The CHIEF JUSTICE [CHASE] delivered the opinion of the Court.

[T]he appellate jurisdiction of this Court is not derived from acts of Congress. It is, strictly speaking, conferred by the Constitution. But it is conferred "with such exceptions and under such regulations as Congress shall make."

It is unnecessary to consider whether, if Congress had made no exceptions and no regulations, this court might not have exercised general appellate jurisdiction under rules prescribed by itself. For among the earliest acts of the first Congress [was the Judiciary Act of 1789, which] provided for the organization of this court, and prescribed regulations for the exercise of its jurisdiction.

[In] *Durousseau v. United States* [10 U.S. (6 Cranch), 307 (1810)], particularly, the whole matter was carefully examined, and the court held, that [the] judicial act was an exercise of the power given by the Constitution to Congress "of making exceptions to the appellate jurisdiction of the Supreme Court." "They have described affirmatively," said the court, "its jurisdiction, and this affirmative description has been understood to imply a negation of the exercise of such appellate power as is not comprehended within it."

The principle [thus] established, it was an almost necessary consequence that acts of Congress, providing for the exercise of jurisdiction, should come to be spoken of as acts granting jurisdiction and not as acts making exceptions to the constitutional grant of it.

The exception to appellate jurisdiction in the case before us, however, is not an inference from the affirmation of other appellate jurisdiction. It is made in terms. * * *

We are not at liberty to inquire into the motives of the legislature. We can only examine into its power under the Constitution * * *.

What, then, is the effect of the repealing act upon the case before [us?] Jurisdiction is power to declare the law, and when it ceases to exist the only function remaining to the court is that of announcing the fact and dismissing the cause. And this is not less clear upon authority than upon principle. [J]udicial duty is not less fitly performed by declining ungranted jurisdiction than in exercising firmly that which the Constitution and the laws confer.

Counsel seem to have supposed, if effect be given to the repealing act in question, that the whole appellate power of the court, in cases of habeas corpus, is denied. But this is an error. The act of 1868 does not except from that jurisdiction any cases but appeals from Circuit Courts under the act of 1867. It does not affect the jurisdiction which was previously exercised.

The appeal [must] be dismissed for want of jurisdiction.[a]

Notes and Questions

1. *Jurisdiction stripping.* Proposals to restrict federal jurisdiction in response to politically unpopular doctrines and decisions have been common in American history.[b] Since the late 1970s, for example, critics of the Supreme Court's school prayer and abortion decisions have regularly attempted to pass legislation stripping the Supreme Court, the lower federal courts, or both of jurisdiction in school prayer and abortion cases. Although opponents of the Court's decisions would prefer to overturn its rulings by constitutional amendment, amendments are exceedingly difficult to enact. Jurisdiction-stripping bills are thus viewed as substitutes. Their characteristic aim—like that of the legislation involved in *McCardle*—is to achieve, by less onerous means, a de facto change in the substantive law through the procedural device of a limitation on federal jurisdiction.

Does *McCardle* provide square authority for the constitutional permissibility of jurisdiction-stripping legislation?

2. *Diverse issues.* The issues raised by various types of proposed jurisdiction-stripping legislation are diverse. To take a proposal that has surfaced repeatedly for more than three decades, consider the various forms that legislation curbing jurisdiction in cases involving challenges to school prayer might take. In light of the Constitution's language and structure, different issues may be raised by proposed legislation (i) limiting the jurisdiction of the Supreme Court to review

a. For an historical account, see Charles Fairman, *Reconstruction and Reunion, 1864–88, Part One,* c. X (1971).

b. See Max Baucus & Kenneth R. Kay, *The Court Stripping Bills: Their Impact on the Constitution, the Courts, and Congress,* 27 Vill.

L.Rev. 988 (1982); Gerald Gunther, *Congressional Power to Curtail Federal Court Jurisdiction: An Opinionated Guide to the Ongoing Debate,* 36 Stan.L.Rev. 895 (1984); Stuart S. Nagel, *Court-Curbing Periods in American History,* 18 Vand.L.Rev. 925 (1965).

cases that remain subject to the jurisdiction of the lower federal courts, (ii) curbing lower federal court jurisdiction but retaining Supreme Court appellate jurisdiction to review state court judgments, (iii) precluding the exercise of jurisdiction by both the Supreme Court and the lower federal courts but leaving state court jurisdiction intact, and (iv) barring jurisdiction by all courts, state and federal alike.

3. *The appellate jurisdiction of the Supreme Court.* Suppose that Congress were to eliminate the Supreme Court's appellate jurisdiction in cases involving school prayer. Would this be authorized by the language of Article III permitting congressional "exceptions" to the Supreme Court's jurisdiction and by the *McCardle* case?

(a) *The essential functions thesis.* How does Article III's contemplation of "exceptions" to the jurisdiction of the Supreme Court square with the general, structural commitment to an independent federal judiciary and a regime of government under law? In a celebrated and broad-ranging commentary on Congress' power over federal jurisdiction, Professor Henry M. Hart, Jr. suggested that constitutionally permissible exceptions to the Court's jurisdiction "must not be such as will destroy the essential role of the Supreme Court in the constitutional plan." *The Power of Congress to Limit the Jurisdiction of Federal Courts: An Exercise in Dialectic*, 66 Harv.L.Rev. 1362, 1364–65 (1953). Hart acknowledged the indeterminacy of this test, but pointedly queried whether "the difficulties of the test" were not "less [than] the difficulties of reading the Constitution as authorizing its own destruction." See also Leonard G. Ratner, *Congressional Power over the Appellate Jurisdiction of the Supreme Court*, 109 U.Pa.L.Rev. 157, 171–72 (1960). Do you agree? Would elimination of Supreme Court appellate jurisdiction over school prayer cases, for example, deprive the Court of its "essential role [in] the constitutional plan"?

Consider Leonard G. Ratner, *Majoritarian Constraints on Judicial Review: Congressional Control of Supreme Court Jurisdiction*, 27 Vill.L.Rev. 929, 935, 956 (1982): "The supremacy clause of article VI mandates one supreme federal law throughout the land, and article III establishes the Supreme Court as the constitutional instrument for implementing that clause. [As] such, its essential functions under the Constitution are: 1) ultimately to resolve inconsistent or conflicting interpretations of federal law, and particularly of the Constitution, by state and federal courts; 2) to maintain the supremacy of federal law, and particularly the Constitution, when it conflicts with state law or is challenged by state authority."

Note that, prior to 1980, Supreme Court review of federal claims in civil cases was generally subject to a jurisdictional amount limitation; for over a century, federal criminal decisions were appealable only on a certificate of division in the circuit court; and, until the twentieth century, "[r]eview of state court decisions depended on how the state court decided a federal question; thus for a time, when workmen's compensation was held unconstitutional in a state court, there was no possible review in the Supreme Court." Paul A. Freund, *Why We Need the National Court of Appeals*, 59 A.B.A.J. 247, 251 (1973). Does Professor Ratner's version of the "essential functions" argument confuse "the familiar with the necessary, the desirable with the constitutionally mandated"? Gunther, supra at 905.

Compare Martin H. Redish, *Congressional Power to Regulate Supreme Court Appellate Jurisdiction under the Exceptions Clause: An Internal and External Examination*, 27 Vill.L.Rev. 900, 907 (1982): "[I] might well agree, as a policy matter, that Congress should not possess the power to tamper with performance of the Supreme Court's role, [but] I can find no constitutional basis for erecting such a [limitation]." Contrast Lawrence G. Sager, *Constitutional Limitations on Congress' Authority to Regulate the Jurisdiction of the Federal Courts,* 95 Harv. L.Rev. 17, 57 (1981): "The Court must be available to superintend *state compliance* with federal law unless Congress provides effective review elsewhere within the *federal* judiciary" (emphasis added.)[c]

(b) *The pertinence of McCardle.* How great an incursion into the Court's appellate jurisdiction did *McCardle* really permit? In *Ex Parte Yerger,* 75 U.S. (8 Wall.) 85, 19 L.Ed. 332 (1869), also challenging the Reconstruction Acts, the Court upheld its jurisdiction in a habeas corpus proceeding in which the petitioner sought review based on *pre–1867 legislation* that provided for discretionary review by writ of certiorari. Consider Ratner, supra, 109 U.Pa.L.Rev. at 180: "The statute [involved in *McCardle* did] not deprive the Court of jurisdiction to decide McCardle's case; he could still petition the Supreme Court for [an original] writ of habeas corpus. [The] legislation did no more than eliminate one procedure for Supreme Court review of decisions denying habeas corpus while leaving another equally efficacious one available."[d]

The Court followed *Yerger*'s interpretive principle that implied repeals of Supreme Court appellate jurisdiction should be disfavored in FELKER v. TURPIN, 518 U.S. 651, 116 S.Ct. 2333, 135 L.Ed.2d 827 (1996), per REHNQUIST, C.J., holding unanimously that a statute withdrawing its certiorari jurisdiction in certain habeas cases had not affected its authority to review the case before it upon a petition for an original writ of habeas corpus under 28 U.S.C. §§ 2241 and 2254. As in *McCardle,* the availability of an alternative mechanism for the Court to exercise jurisdiction "obviate[d]" any constitutional challenge to the jurisdiction-limiting legislation under Art. III, § 2. In a concurring opinion, Souter, J., joined by Stevens and Breyer, JJ., reserved the question whether the statute might be held unconstitutional as applied to subsequent cases if, in practice, it stopped the Court from reviewing "divergent interpretations" of a federal statute.

(c) *Is motive relevant?* In *McCardle,* the Court observed that it was "not at liberty to inquire into the motives of the legislature." Since *McCardle,* however, the Court has established that legislative motive is relevant to whether government has exercised its power lawfully under, for example, the establishment clause of the first amendment (see e.g., *Wallace v. Jaffree,* Ch. 8, Sec. I, I *infra*) and the equal protection clause (see, e.g., *Washington v. Davis,* Ch. 9, Sec. 2, III *infra*). Suppose that Congress' motive in curbing the Supreme Court's jurisdiction—in school prayer cases, for example—were to invite defiance of the Constitution or of Supreme Court decisions by lower courts or executive officials. Should the legislation be invalidated on this ground?[e] Or, by vesting power to limit

---

c. For the narrower suggestion that Congress may permissibly create exceptions to the Court's appellate jurisdiction only as to questions of fact, not questions of law, see Raoul Berger, *Congress v. The Supreme Court* 285–86 (1969); Henry J. Merry, *Scope of the Supreme Court's Appellate Jurisdiction: Historical Basis,* 47 Minn.L.Rev. 53 (1962).

d. For criticism of *McCardle* on the grounds that the Court (1) dismissed the case "for want of jurisdiction" despite the existence—as evidenced by *Yerger*—of an alternative source of jurisdiction, and (2) treated the

Repealer Act as making an "exception" to the Court's art. III appellate jurisdiction when, in fact, it only repealed a portion of the 1867 Act that had created a special right of appeal not previously authorized by statute, see William W. Van Alstyne, *A Critical Guide to Ex Parte McCardle,* 15 Ariz.L.Rev. 229, 244–54 (1973).

e. See, e.g., John H. Ely, *Legislative and Administrative Motivation in Constitutional Law,* 79 Yale L.J. 1205, 1306–08 (1970). See also Laurence H. Tribe, *Jurisdictional Gerrymandering: Zoning Disfavored Rights Out of*

jurisdiction in Congress, does the Constitution implicitly leave a broad scope for politically motivated decisionmaking?[f]

(d) *Jurisdictional limitations vs. substantive directions.* Suppose that McCardle had been released by the court below and, after the government appealed to the Supreme Court, Congress passed a statute commanding the Supreme Court to resolve all pending habeas corpus appeals in favor of the government. Would such a statute have been constitutional? In UNITED STATES v. KLEIN, 80 U.S. (13 Wall.) 128, 20 L.Ed. 519 (1872), the Court, in a confusing opinion, held unconstitutional a statute directing the federal courts to dismiss for want of jurisdiction any suit in which the plaintiff relied on a presidential pardon to prove loyalty during the Civil War and, thus, entitlement to recover for property seized by the government. An earlier decision had found that a presidential pardon, apparently as a constitutional matter, must be treated as conclusive proof of loyalty. Although Congress could presumably have denied federal jurisdiction over all suits against the United States (under the doctrine of sovereign immunity), it could not use its jurisdiction-stripping power on a selective basis to compel the courts to reach unconstitutional results in particular cases. It could not, in other words, require courts to proceed to the point of receiving evidence that in fact established a legal right to recover and, at that point, to dismiss suits that relied on the President's constitutional pardon power to establish that right. See also Hart, supra, at 1373: "[I]f Congress," rather than withholding jurisdiction altogether, "directs an Article III court to decide a case, I can easily read into Article III a limitation on the power of Congress to tell the court *how* to decide it."[g]

Plaut v. Spendthrift Farm, Inc., 514 U.S. 211, 115 S.Ct. 1447, 131 L.Ed.2d 328 (1995), held that Congress impermissibly intruded on the judicial role under the separation of powers by enacting a statute that required Article III courts to reopen final judgments dismissing suits by one private party against another. Compare *Miller v. French*, 530 U.S. 327, 120 S.Ct. 2246, 147 L.Ed.2d 326 (2000), per O'Connor, J., which sharply distinguished judgments awarding damages from judgments awarding injunctive relief and held that neither *Plaut* nor *Klein* forbade Congress to enact otherwise constitutionally valid legislation "alter[ing] the prospective effect of previously entered injunctions."[h]

4. *Limitation of lower federal court jurisdiction.* It is settled that Congress, which does not need to establish any lower federal courts at all,[i] also has broad, discretionary power to prescribe and limit their jurisdiction. See *Sheldon v. Sill*, 49 U.S. (8 How.) 441, 12 L.Ed. 1147 (1850). It was not until 1875, for example, that Congress gave the lower federal courts general jurisdiction to decide questions "arising under" the Constitution, laws, and treaties of the United States.

---

the Federal Courts, 16 Harv.C.R.C.L.L.Rev. 129, 149–52 (1981).

f. Cf. Paul M. Bator, *Congressional Power over the Jurisdiction of the Federal Courts,* 27 Vill.L.Rev. 1030, 1038–41 (1982); Gunther, supra, at 908–12.

g. The reach of *Klein,* and the principle on which it rests, continues to be much controverted. See, e.g., *Robertson v. Seattle Audubon Soc'y,* 503 U.S. 429, 112 S.Ct. 1407, 118 L.Ed.2d 73 (1992); Lawrence G. Sager, *Klein's First Principle: A Proposed Solution,* 86 Geo. L.J. 2525 (1998); Daniel J. Meltzer, *Congress, Courts, and Constitutional Remedies,* 86 Geo. L.J. 2537 (1998); Gordon G. Young, *Congressional Regulation of Federal Courts' Jurisdiction and Processes: United States v. Klein Revisited,* 1981 Wis.L.Rev. 1189.

h. Souter, J., joined by Ginsburg, J., concurred in part and dissented in part. Breyer, J., joined by Stevens, J., dissented on statutory grounds.

i. But see Theodore Eisenberg, *Congressional Authority to Restrict Lower Federal Court Jurisdiction,* 83 Yale L.J. 498 (1974); cf. Martin H. Redish & Curtis E. Woods, *Congressional Power to Control the Jurisdiction of Lower Federal Courts: A Critical Review and a New Synthesis,* 124 U.Pa.L.Rev. 45 (1975).

Due to jurisdictional amount limitations, among others, the lower federal courts have never enjoyed the full jurisdiction that would be permitted by Article III.

Statutes curbing the jurisdiction of lower federal courts in response to federal decisions on the merits are not unprecedented. Perhaps the most prominent example is the Norris–LaGuardia Act, which greatly restricted federal courts from issuing injunctions in "labor disputes" and from enforcing "yellow-dog" contracts, and expressly framed its prohibitions as restrictions on federal "jurisdiction." Rejecting a constitutional challenge, *Lauf v. E.G. Shinner & Co.,* 303 U.S. 323, 330, 58 S.Ct. 578, 582, 82 L.Ed. 872, 877 (1938), said "[t]here can be no question of the power of Congress thus to define and limit the jurisdiction of the inferior courts of the United States."

Commentators continue to debate whether *Lauf* necessarily contemplated that Congress could purposefully and discriminatorily close the doors of the lower federal courts to cases involving congressionally disfavored *constitutional* rights. For a discussion, see Gordon G. Young, *A Critical Reassessment of the Case Law Bearing on Congress's Power to Restrict the Jurisdiction of the Lower Federal Courts,* 54 Md.L.Rev. 132, 168–82 (1995).

The Norris–LaGuardia Act did not purport to restrict the exercise of state court jurisdiction—a pattern followed by most recent proposals to curb the jurisdiction of the *federal* courts. Even if federal courts were barred from hearing challenges to school prayer, for example, couldn't suit still be brought in state court? And wouldn't state courts, under the Supremacy Clause, be bound to enforce the Constitution? Would they be bound to follow Supreme Court precedent?[j] Could they realistically be expected to do so?

5. *Restraints from constitutional provisions other than Article III.* Congress clearly could not eliminate either Supreme Court or lower federal court jurisdiction in cases brought by African–Americans, Jews, women, or people under five feet tall. Even if hypothetical restrictions of this kind did not violate Article III, they would indisputably violate *other* constitutional provisions, such as the equal protection component of the due process clause. Are proposals to restrict jurisdiction of suits involving challenges to school prayer or restrictions on abortion constitutionally objectionable in the same way? See Tribe, supra, 16 Harv. C.R.C.L.L.Rev at 141–42, 150–52. Or does the argument to that effect "too readily extend[] the analysis of the obvious flaw in laws that distinguish among *litigants* on the basis of race or other forbidden criteria to jurisdictional statutes that differentiate on the basis of *subject matter*"? Gunther, supra, 36 Stan.L.Rev. at 918; see Bator, supra, 27 Vill.L.Rev. at 1034–37.

6. *Curbs of both Supreme Court and lower federal court jurisdiction.* Beginning with Story, J., in *Martin v. Hunter's Lessee,* a line of jurists and scholars has maintained that the Constitution's language and structure require the availability of *some* federal court to rule on claims of federal right. On this view, Congress could eliminate Supreme Court jurisdiction over school prayer cases, for example, but only if it retained jurisdiction in a lower federal court; and it could curb lower federal court jurisdiction in such cases, but only if the Supreme Court retained appellate jurisdiction of suits brought in state court. For prominent theories of this kind, see Sager, supra; Akhil R. Amar, *A Neo–Federalist View of Article III:*

---

j. Compare Evan H. Caminker, *Why Must Inferior Courts Obey Superior Court Precedents,* 46 Stan.L.Rev. 817, 837–38, 868–69 (1994)(arguing that state courts would not be clearly bound to do so in all cases) with Herbert Wechsler, *The Courts and the Constitution,* 65 Colum.L.Rev. 1001, 1006 (1965)(arguing that jurisdictional limitations would entrench Supreme Court precedent).

Separating the Two Tiers of Federal Jurisdiction, 65 B.U.L.Rev. 205 (1985).[k] For criticisms on textual, historical, and precedential grounds, see Daniel J. Meltzer, *The History and Structure of Article III,* 138 U.Pa.L.Rev. 1569 (1990); John Harrison, *The Power of Congress to Limit the Jurisdiction of Federal Courts and the Text of Article III,* 64 U.Chi.L.Rev. 203 (1997).[l]

7. *Prohibitions of jurisdiction by any court.* Suppose that Congress were to deny jurisdiction to *any* court—state or federal—to rule on a claim of constitutional right. Would the prohibition be constitutional? (Note that this is a different question from the constitutionality of proposals to curtail federal jurisdiction, while leaving state courts open to hear federal claims.) The Court has often suggested that the preclusion of all judicial review of constitutional issues would raise a "serious" constitutional question and, accordingly, has frequently construed statutes to permit review at least of constitutional questions. See, e.g., *Webster v. Doe,* 486 U.S. 592, 603, 108 S.Ct. 2047, 2053–54, 100 L.Ed.2d 632, 644–45 (1988); *Bowen v. Michigan Academy of Family Physicians,* 476 U.S. 667, 681 n.12, 106 S.Ct. 2133, 2141–42 n.12, 90 L.Ed.2d 623, 635 n. 12 (1986); *Johnson v. Robison,* 415 U.S. 361, 366–67, 94 S.Ct. 1160, 1165–66, 39 L.Ed.2d 389, 397–98 (1974). See also *Battaglia v. General Motors Corp.,* 169 F.2d 254 (2d Cir.1948).

Can suggestions that due process (or some other constitutional guarantee) requires judicial review of constitutional questions be reconciled with the accepted position that sovereign immunity generally bars unconsented suits against the United States? See Richard H. Fallon, Jr., *Some Confusions About Due Process, Judicial Review, and Constitutional Remedies,* 93 Colum.L.Rev. 309, 329–39, 366–72 (1993).

8. *Congressional power and judicial legitimacy.* According to Charles L. Black, Jr., *The Presidency and Congress,* 32 Wash. & Lee L.Rev. 841, 846 (1975), Congress' power to restrict federal court jurisdiction is "the rock on which rests the legitimacy of the judicial work in a democracy." Do you agree?[m]

9. *Other levers of political control.* Control of federal jurisdiction is by no means the only, and perhaps not even the most important, means by which the political branches may register their disagreement with Supreme Court decision-making or seek to influence its future course.

k. See also Akhil R. Amar, *The Two–Tiered Structure of the Judiciary Act of 1789,* 138 U.Pa.L.Rev. 1499 (1990); Robert Pushaw, *Congressional Power Over Federal Court Jurisdiction: A Defense of the Neo–Federalist Interpretation of Article III,* 1997 BYU L.Rev. 847; Robert N. Clinton, *A Mandatory View of Federal Court Jurisdiction: A Guided Quest for the Original Understanding of Article III,* 132 U.Pa.L.Rev. 741 (1984).

l. Because most proposed legislation curbing federal jurisdiction would leave state courts open, debates about the constitutionality of restrictions on federal jurisdiction are frequently bound up with debates about the "parity" or "disparity" of state and federal courts. For a diversity of perspectives, see, e.g., Michael E. Solimine & James L. Walker, *Respecting State Courts* 37–42 (1999); Paul M. Bator, *The State Courts and Federal Constitutional Litigation,* 22 Wm. & Mary L.Rev. 605 (1981); Erwin Chemerinsky, *Parity Reconsidered: Defining a Role for the Federal Judiciary,* 36 U.C.L.A. L.Rev. 233 (1988); Burt Neuborne, *The Myth of Parity,* 90 Harv.L.Rev. 1105 (1977); Burt Neuborne, *Parity Revisited: The Uses of a Judicial Forum of Excellence,* 44 DePaul L.Rev. 797 (1995); William Rubenstein, *The Myth of Superiority,* 16 Const.Comm. 599 (1999); Michael E. Solimine & James L. Walker, *Constitutional Litigation in Federal and State Courts: An Empirical Analysis of Judicial Parity,* 10 Hast.Con.L.Q. 213 (1983); Michael Wells, *Behind the Parity Debate: The Decline of the Legal Process Tradition in the Law of Federal Courts,* 71 B.U.L.Rev. 609 (1991).

m. Compare Barry Friedman, *A Different Dialogue: The Supreme Court, Congress and Federal Jurisdiction,* 85 Nw.U.L.Rev. 1, 2–3 (1990), arguing that "the contours of federal jurisdiction are resolved as the result of an interactive process between Congress and the Court on the appropriate uses and bounds of the federal judicial power."

(a) Article III leaves it to Congress to determine the number of justices who sit on the Supreme Court. The first Judiciary Act provided for a chief justice and five associate justices. The number of justices briefly grew as high as ten, before settling at the current nine in 1869. When a conservative Court threatened to wreck the New Deal, President Franklin Roosevelt notoriously sought authority to "pack" the Supreme Court by appointing one additional justice for each justice over the age of 70. Although the proposal failed, Roberts, J., nearly contemporaneously altered his voting pattern to create a 5–4 majority upholding key New Deal legislation. Historians continue to debate whether this celebrated "switch in time that saved nine" was in fact motivated by Roosevelt's Court-packing effort.[n] Did Roosevelt's Court-packing plan violate any judicially enforceable constitutional norm? Was it in accord with the Constitution's spirit? Its commitment to an independent judiciary?

(b) Supreme Court justices, like all other Article III judges, must be appointed by the President and confirmed by the Senate. Is it appropriate for the President to seek to appoint only people whose jurisprudential views generally accord with the Administration's political agenda? To apply a "litmus test" concerning potential nominees' views on specific issues (such as abortion rights, for example)? Is it appropriate for the Senate to apply explicitly political criteria in voting on candidates nominated by the President?[o]

SECTION 4. DISCRETIONARY REVIEW

In the words of Vinson, C.J., 69 S.Ct. vi (1949), the Supreme Court is not "primarily concerned with the correction of errors in lower court decisions. In almost all cases within the Court's appellate jurisdiction, the petitioner has already received one appellate review. [If] we took every case in which an interesting legal question is raised, or our *prima facie* impression is that the decision below is erroneous, we could not fulfill the Constitutional and statutory responsibilities placed upon the Court. To remain effective, the Supreme Court must continue to decide only those cases which present questions whose resolution will have immediate importance far beyond the particular facts and parties involved."

UNITED STATES SUPREME COURT RULES

Rule 10. Considerations Governing Review on Writ of Certiorari

1. A review on writ of certiorari is not a matter of right, but of judicial discretion. A petition for a writ of certiorari will be granted only when there are

n. Speculation that Roberts, J., shifted his position for tactical reasons was denied in Felix Frankfurter, *Mr. Justice Roberts*, 104 U.Pa. L.Rev. 311 (1955). Frankfurter's claims are doubted in Michael Ariens, *A Thrice–Told Tale, or Felix the Cat*, 107 Harv.L.Rev. 620 (1994). For a response, see Richard D. Friedman, *A Reaffirmation: The Authenticity of the Roberts Memorandum, or Felix the Non–Forger*, 142 U.Pa.L.Rev. 1985 (1994). For discussion of the historical significance of Roosevelt's attempt at Court-packing, see William E. Leuchtenburg, *The Supreme Court Reborn: The Constitutional Revolution in the Age of Roosevelt* (1995).

o. For historical discussion, see Laurence H. Tribe, *God Save This Honorable Court* (1985); Paul A. Freund, *Appointment of Justices: Some Historical Perspectives*, 101 Harv. L.Rev. 1146 (1988). For a range of views on the role that the Senate ought to play, see, *e.g.*, Stephen L. Carter, *The Confirmation Mess: Cleaning up the Federal Appointments Process* (1994); Tribe, supra; Bruce A. Ackerman, *Transformative Appointments*, 101 Harv.L.Rev. 1164 (1988); David A. Strauss & Cass R. Sunstein, *The Senate, the Constitution, and the Confirmation Process*, 101 Yale L.J. 1491 (1992).

special and important reasons therefor. The following, while neither controlling nor fully measuring the Court's discretion, indicate the character of reasons that will be considered: (a) When a United States court of appeals has rendered a decision in conflict with the decision of another United States court of appeals on the same matter; or has decided a federal question in a way in conflict with a state court of last resort; or has so far departed from the accepted and usual course of judicial proceedings, or sanctioned such a departure by a lower court, as to call for an exercise of this Court's power of supervision. (b) When a state court of last resort has decided a federal question in a way that conflicts with the decision of another state court of last resort or of a United States court of appeals. (c) When a state court or a United States court of appeals has decided an important question of federal law which has not been, but should be, settled by this Court, or has decided a federal question in a way that conflicts with applicable decisions of this Court. * * *

MARYLAND v. BALTIMORE RADIO SHOW, INC.

338 U.S. 912, 70 S.Ct. 252, 94 L.Ed. 562 (1950).

Opinion of JUSTICE FRANKFURTER respecting the denial of the petition for writ of certiorari. * * *

A variety of considerations underlie denials of the writ, and as to the same petition different reasons may lead different Justices to the same result. This is especially true of petitions for review on writ of certiorari to a State court. Narrowly technical reasons may lead to denials. [For detail, see Sec. 5 infra.] A decision may satisfy all these technical requirements and yet may commend itself for review to fewer than four members of the Court. Pertinent considerations of judicial policy here come into play. A case may raise an important question but the record may be cloudy. It may be desirable to have different aspects of an issue further illumined by the lower courts. Wise adjudication has its own time for ripening.

Since there are these conflicting and, to the uninformed, even confusing reasons for denying petitions for certiorari, it has been suggested from time to time that the Court indicate its reasons for denial. Practical considerations preclude. [The] time that would be required is prohibitive, apart from the fact as already indicated that different reasons not infrequently move different members of the Court * * *. It becomes relevant here to note that failure to record a dissent from a denial of a petition for writ of certiorari in nowise implies that only the member of the Court who notes his dissent thought the petition should be granted. * * *

Notes and Questions

1. *The volume of business.* In recent years, roughly 7,000 cases have been filed annually in the Supreme Court. Only a few come within the Court's original jurisdiction or its now-shrunken mandatory appellate jurisdiction; virtually all are petitions for certiorari, which the Court may, but need not, choose to hear. The Court decided only 77 cases with written opinions in the 1999–2000 Term, down from an average of 172 cases each year for the five Terms spanning 1984–88 and an average of 113 for the five Terms spanning 1990–97. See the annual November issue, No. 1, of the Harv.L.Rev. for each Term's statistics.

2. *The screening process.* To assist them in selecting the cases in which to grant certiorari, the justices rely heavily on law clerks to summarize the petitions

and recommend dispositions. As many as eight justices now share "pool memos," which are prepared by law clerks and distributed to all justices participating in the "cert. pool." See H. W. Perry, Jr., *Deciding to Decide: Agenda Setting in the United States Supreme Court* 51–64 (1991); John P. Stevens, *The Life Span of a Judge–Made Rule,* 58 N.Y.U.L.Rev. 1, 13–14 (1983). The justices then meet in conference to decide which cases to accept. The Chief Justice prepares a list of cases potentially worthy of consideration, and any other justice may add a case to the "discuss" list. Cases not put on the list are automatically denied review. At conference, there reportedly is relatively little discussion of which cases to grant and which to deny.

Despite the "cert. pool" and a streamlined process of consideration, the screening process makes heavy demands on the justices' time and energy. From time to time, proposals have surfaced to transfer responsibility for management of the Court's docket to some other tribunal.[a] Among the objections to such proposals is that deciding which cases to review is crucial to the Supreme Court's function of overseeing the coherent development and evolution of a uniform body of federal law.[b]

3. *The "rule of four."* (a) By long tradition, it takes the votes of four justices to put a case on the Court's plenary docket. Does the vote of four justices to hear a case oblige the other five to render a decision on the merits, even if some or all believe that argument and decision would squander the Court's time or otherwise be ill-advised?

(b) When the Court feels on oral argument, upon further study, or due to intervening factors, that the basis upon which certiorari was granted no longer exists, the Court may "dismiss the writ as improvidently granted." See Robert L. Stern, Eugene Gressman, Stephen M. Shapiro, & Kenneth S. Geller, *Supreme Court Practice* 231–32, 258–62 (7th ed. 1993). Suppose, however, that the four justices who voted to grant certiorari continue to want the case to be heard. Is a vote to dismiss at that point inconsistent with the "rule of four"? Compare *Triangle Improvement Council v. Ritchie,* 402 U.S. 497, 91 S.Ct. 1650, 29 L.Ed.2d 61 (1971) (dismissing certiorari as improvidently granted over the dissent of four Justices) with *Burrell v. McCray,* 426 U.S. 471, 96 S.Ct. 2640, 48 L.Ed.2d 788 (1976) (dismissing certiorari with the support of one of the original four). Consider Stevens, J., concurring in *New York v. Uplinger,* 467 U.S. 246, 251, 104 S.Ct. 2332, 2335, 81 L.Ed.2d 201, 206 (1984): "[T]he Rule of Four is [a] device for deciding when a case must be argued, but its force is largely spent once the case has been heard. At that point, a more fully informed majority of the Court must decide whether some countervailing principle outweighs the interest in judicial economy in deciding the case."[c]

(c) Suppose that four justices vote to grant certiorari in a capital case, and the successful petitioner then applies to the Court for a stay of execution, which would ordinarily require the votes of five justices. Are the five justices who would have denied certiorari obliged by the "rule of four" to attempt to protect the

a. The most prominent was advanced by a committee chaired by Professor Paul Freund, Report of the Study Group on the Caseload of the Supreme Court (Federal Judicial Center 1972); see Paul A. Freund, *Why We Need the National Court of Appeals,* 59 A.B.A.J. 247 (1973).

b. See, e.g., Earl Warren, *Let's Not Weaken the Supreme Court,* 60 A.B.A.J. 677 (1974).

c. For consideration of the view "that the Rule of Four must inevitably enlarge the size of the Court's argument docket and cause it to hear a substantial number of cases that a majority of the Court deems unworthy of review," see Stevens, note 2 supra, at 20.

Court's jurisdiction? The Court's practice would suggest not. See, e.g., *Herrera v. Collins*, 502 U.S. 1085, 112 S.Ct. 1074, 117 L.Ed.2d 279 (1992)(denying stay by vote of 5–4); Mark Tushnet, *"The King of France with Forty Thousand Men": Felker v. Turpin and the Supreme Court's Deliberative Process*, 1996 Sup.Ct.Rev. 163, 166–81. For discussion, see Richard L. Revesz & Pamela S. Karlan, *Nonmajority Rules and the Supreme Court*, 136 U.Pa.L.Rev. 1067, 1074–81 (1988).

4. *Criteria for granting the writ.* How satisfactory are the standards for grants of certiorari that are articulated in Rule 10?[d] Although each of the subparagraphs of Rule 10 refers to a "conflict" of authorities as a basis for certiorari, studies indicate that the Court does not invariably grant certiorari in such cases,[e] and commentators are divided both about how to identify "conflicts" and about the importance of resolving conflicts at an early stage before issues have been fully explored in the lower courts.[f]

In recent years, the Court has reversed the judgment below in 60 to 70 percent of the cases in which certiorari is granted[g]—a statistic that seems to confirm the commonsense view that the justices are more likely to vote to hear a case when they believe that it was wrongly decided. See generally Arthur D. Hellman, *Error Correction, Lawmaking, and the Supreme Court's Exercise of Discretionary Review*, 44 U.Pitt.L.Rev. 795 (1983). Nonetheless, other studies indicate that "strategic" voting on whether to grant the writ, including "defensive" votes to deny certiorari based on the fear that a majority of the Court would reverse if review were granted, are the exception rather than the rule. See, e.g., Perry, supra, at 198–207.

5. *Significance of denials of certiorari.* The Court has often asserted that the denial of certiorari carries no precedential significance; the Court does not approve the judgment of the lower court, but merely—for unexplained reasons—allows it to stand. But see *United States v. Kras*, 409 U.S. 434, 93 S.Ct. 631, 34 L.Ed.2d 626 (1973).

Consider Peter Linzer, *The Meaning of Certiorari Denials*, 79 Colum.L.Rev. 1227, 1304–05 (1979): "[A] certiorari denial is often not based on the merits and never should bind anyone. [Yet] it seems time to stop pretending that denial of certiorari means nothing. Many times it gives us a glimpse, imperfect to be sure, into the Justices' preliminary attitudes on a given issue."

6. *Summary reversals.* On relatively rare occasions, the Court will reverse a decision below on the certiorari papers without further briefing or argument; when it does so, the Court usually issues a brief, per curiam opinion explaining its decision. See Hellman, supra, 44 U.Pitt.L.Rev. at 825–36. When, if ever, is it justifiable for the Court to render decision based on so cursory a review?

---

d. For criticisms and reform suggestions, see Samuel Estreicher & John Sexton, *Redefining the Supreme Court's Role: A Theory of Managing the Federal Judicial Process* (1986).

e. See, e.g., Arthur D. Hellman, *By Precedent Unbound: The Nature and Extent of Unresolved Circuit Conflicts*, 56 U.Pitt.L.Rev. 693 (1995); Arthur D. Hellman, *Light on a Darkling Plain: Intercircuit Conflicts in the Perspective of Time and Experience*, 1998 Sup.Ct.Rev. 247.

f. Compare Richard D. Posner, *The Federal Courts: Challenge and Reform* 195 (2d ed.1996)(observing that the Court's diminishing case load indicates that it does not regard unresolved conflicts as a major problem at this time) with Thomas E. Baker & Douglas D. McFarland, *The Need for a New National Court*, 100 Harv.L.Rev. 1400, 1408–09 (1987)(asserting the importance of uniform national law).

g. See Stern et al., supra, § 4.17, at 195 n. 59.

SECTION 5. PREREQUISITES TO FEDERAL JURISDICTION AND JUDICIAL REVIEW: AN INTRODUCTION

Under Article III, federal judicial power extends only to "cases" and "controversies." Thus, federal courts are precluded from giving "advisory opinions" or deciding "moot" cases. Parties asserting constitutional challenges must have "standing." Further, claims must be asserted at a time when they are "ripe" for adjudication: "[a] hypothetical threat is not enough";[a] "[d]etermination of [the] constitutionality of legislation in advance of its immediate adverse effect in the context of a concrete case involves too remote and abstract an inquiry for the proper exercise of the judicial function."[b]

Because all these matters must be resolved before a federal court may consider the merits of a constitutional contention, they could profitably be explored in detail here. But their consideration is often intertwined with and requires understanding of the substantive constitutional provision in issue. Thus, their presentation is deferred to Ch. 12, for study when students will be better equipped to comprehend and evaluate them.

A number of additional requirements must also be satisfied for the Supreme Court to be able to review state court decisions. While these are considered at length in courses on Federal Courts, the most important are briefly described below.

1. *Final judgments or decrees.* The Court will ordinarily review only the final judgment or decree of the highest state court in which review of a decision could be had—typically, though not invariably, the state's supreme court. The "final judgment" rule reflects intertwined policies aimed at avoiding (i) unnecessary constitutional decisions; (ii) inefficient, piecemeal review; and (iii) unnecessary interference with state court processes. In its traditional formulation, the "final judgment" rule barred Supreme Court review until the completion of all lower court proceedings in a case. In recent years, however, the rule has been relaxed somewhat. In the leading case of *Cox Broadcasting Corp. v. Cohn*, 420 U.S. 469, 477, 95 S.Ct. 1029, 1037, 43 L.Ed.2d 328, 339 (1975), the Court acknowledged that there were "at least four categories" of cases in which it had treated and would continue to treat "the decision on the federal issue as [final] without awaiting the completion of the additional proceedings anticipated in the lower state courts."[c] Although important, the exceptions appear not to have

---

a. *United Public Workers v. Mitchell*, Ch. 12, Sec. 3, II infra.

b. *International Longshoremen's and Warehousemen's Union v. Boyd*, 347 U.S. 222, 74 S.Ct. 447, 98 L.Ed. 650 (1954).

c. The Court defined the four categories as follows: (i) those in which, although further state proceedings remain to be completed, the federal issue has been authoritatively decided and is effectively "conclusive" so that the outcome is "preordained"; (ii) cases "in which the federal issue, finally decided by the highest court in the State, will survive and require decision regardless of the outcome of future state-court proceedings"; (iii) "those situations where the federal claim has been finally decided, with further proceedings on the merits in the state courts to come, but in which later review of the federal issue cannot be had"—for example, because a state, having lost on the

appeal of a constitutional issue in a criminal case, would not subsequently be able to appeal if the accused were acquitted at trial; and (iv) "those situations where the federal issue has been finally decided in the state courts with further proceedings pending in which the party seeking review here might prevail on the merits on nonfederal grounds, thus rendering unnecessary review of the federal issue by this Court, and where reversal of the state court on the federal issue would be preclusive of any further litigation on the relevant cause of action rather than merely controlling the nature and character of, or determining the admissibility of evidence in, the state proceedings still to come." Concerning the fourth exception, the Court explained that review would be appropriate only "if a refusal immediately to review the state-court decision might seriously erode federal policy."

swallowed the rule, and review in the Supreme Court is generally not available until a case has come to final judgment in the state system.[d]

2. *Review limited to issues of federal law.* Under *Murdock v. Memphis*, 87 U.S. (20 Wall.) 590, 22 L.Ed. 429 (1875)—a precursor of sorts to the later decision in *Erie Railroad Co. v. Tompkins*, 304 U.S. 64, 58 S.Ct. 817, 82 L.Ed. 1188 (1938)—the Court will generally not review state court decisions of state law issues. Nor, for the most part, will it review determinations of fact. Review, in other words, is generally limited to questions of federal law.

3. *Issues duly raised in state court.* To be litigable in the Supreme Court, a federal issue generally must have been duly raised in state court. This requirement helps to insure that the facts bearing on federal issues will have been adequately explored and the competing arguments ventilated. Sensible exceptions to this requirement exist for cases in which state procedural rules unduly impede the effort to raise a federal issue or the highest state court actually decides a federal question, even if the question was not raised in compliance with state procedural rules.[e]

4. *Adequate and independent state grounds.* Perhaps the most complex limitation on the Court's appellate jurisdiction is the doctrine barring review of decisions that rest on "adequate and independent state grounds." In a nutshell, the rationale of the doctrine is that the Court's "only power over state judgments is to correct them to the extent that they incorrectly adjudge federal rights. [If] the same judgment would be rendered by the state court after we corrected its views of federal laws, our review could amount to nothing more than an advisory opinion." *Herb v. Pitcairn*, 324 U.S. 117, 125–26, 65 S.Ct. 459, 463, 89 L.Ed. 789, 794–95 (1945).

For the most part, a state law ground of decision will be "adequate" to support a judgment if it dictates that a case would come out the same way, regardless of how the Supreme Court might decide a federal issue also presented in the case. Suppose, for example, that a state court were to rule against the plaintiff in a libel case on the alternative grounds that (i) liability was barred by the first amendment to the United States Constitution and (ii) the defendant's allegedly libelous comments were also privileged as a matter of state law. Even if the Supreme Court were to grant review and reverse on the federal constitutional issue, the plaintiff would still not be able to recover on a state law libel claim, due to the state law privilege. The ruling on the state law privilege issue thus would be "adequate" to support the judgment.

The ruling on the state law privilege issue would also be "independent" of the federal first amendment issue, since the rulings on the two issues do not appear to be connected in any way: the state law privilege would apply even if the first amendment should be construed not to preclude liability.

The issue of independence becomes trickier, however, in cases in which it appears that a state court may have decided an issue in a particular way *because of* its arguable misunderstanding of federal law. For example, many states have apparently interpreted provisions of their state constitutions to confer protections identical to those conferred by the parallel provisions of the federal Constitution.

d. For lucid, general discussions of the final judgment rule, see Erwin Chemerinsky, *Federal Jurisdiction* 643–55 (3d ed. 1999); Martin H. Redish, *Federal Jurisdiction: Tensions in the Allocation of Judicial Power* 247–60 (2d ed. 1990).

e. See Daniel J. Meltzer, *State Court Forfeitures of Federal Rights*, 99 Harv.L.Rev. 1128 (1986).

Thus, a state court might hold, for example, that liability for a defamatory publication is barred by the state constitution *because* it is barred by the federal Constitution; in other words, the ruling with respect to state constitutional law might be dictated by the ruling with respect to federal law. In such a case, a state court's determination that speech is not actionable under the state constitution would not be "independent" of its decision of the federal issue. If the Supreme Court were to grant review and reverse on the federal constitutional issue, the state court, on remand, would presumably reverse its ruling on the state constitutional issue, and the outcome of the case could change.

The concept of "independence," which is complicated even in theory, frequently becomes even more complicated in practice, since state courts do not always make clear whether their rulings with respect to state issues are independent of their decisions of federal issues—that is, whether they would decide the state law issue the same way, even if they thought the federal issue should be decided differently. After experimenting with various approaches to cases in which it was unclear whether a state law ground of decision was independent of the federal ground, the Court has now decided to presume, in *ambiguous* cases, that state grounds of decision are *not* independent and thus do not bar Supreme Court review of the federal issues in a case. According to *Michigan v. Long*, 463 U.S. 1032, 1040–41, 103 S.Ct. 3469, 3476, 77 L.Ed.2d 1201, 1214 (1983), "when [a] state court decision fairly appears to rest primarily on federal law, or to be interwoven with the federal law, and when the adequacy and independence of any possible state law ground is not clear from the face of the opinion, we will accept as the most reasonable explanation that the state court decided the case the way it did because it believed that federal law required it to do so."[f]

---

f. For further discussion and critical assessment of the "independent and adequate state ground doctrine," see Chemerinsky, supra, at 661–86.

Chapter 2

NATIONAL LEGISLATIVE POWER

SECTION 1. SOURCES AND NATURE OF NATIONAL LEGISLATIVE POWER

INTRODUCTION

By 1787, the minimal power of the national government under the Articles of Confederation—including its inability to directly raise armies, collect taxes, regulate foreign commerce (in particular to establish tariffs to protect new domestic industries), enforce domestic laws, and require the states to conform to the Peace Treaty with Great Britain[a]—produced what many considered to be a political crisis. Among the major defects in the Articles that led to the Constitutional Convention was the lack of authority to eliminate trade barriers erected by the individual states which treated other states like foreign nations and threatened to result in interstate commercial warfare.[b]

With these concerns in mind, the framers set out to construct a new central government that would have sufficient authority to address national problems, but whose powers would be limited to those designated in the Constitution. The framers recognized the conflict between generalized grants of federal power (which might threaten the liberty of the people) and an overly specific listing of powers (which might leave the new government as ineffective as its predecessor). At one point, the Convention tentatively approved Virginia's proposal that the national legislature should have power "to legislate in all cases for the general interests of the Union, and also in those to which the States are separately incompetent."[c] But the Committee on Detail's final report chose instead to enumerate a series of powers—mainly in Art. I, § 8—and to add at the end the

---

a. *See The Federalist* No. 15 (Alexander Hamilton). The Federalist was a series of essays published in New York newspapers in late 1787 and early 1788 to defend the proposed Constitution against attacks aimed at defeating its ratification in New York. The essays were republished in book form as "The Federalist" in the Spring of 1788. The principal authors, anonymous at the time of publication, were Alexander Hamilton, James Madison, and John Jay.

b. Indeed, it was not until more than 100 years later that the Court held that Congress'

power in Art. I, § 8, cl.3 "to regulate Commerce ... among the several States" (Sec. 2 infra) was not limited to protecting interstate commerce "from acts of interference by state legislation," but also included the regulation of "private contracts between citizens" if they obstruct interstate commerce. *Addyston Pipe & Steel Co. v. United States*, 175 U.S. 211, 227–229, 20 S.Ct. 96, 102–103, 44 L.Ed. 136 (1899).

c. 2 Max Farrand, *Records of the Federal Convention* 26–27 (1911).

power to "make all laws that shall be necessary and proper for carrying into execution the foregoing powers, and all other powers vested, by this Constitution." This change may be interpreted in different ways. It surely might indicate that the Committee intended to reject any generalized grant of power in favor of the more limited enumeration.[d] On the other hand, it has been interpreted to mean that the Committee's report simply confirmed "that the enumeration conformed to the standard previously approved, and that the powers enumerated comprehended those matters as to which the states were separately incompetent and in which national legislation was essential."[e]

Although the necessary and proper clause was adopted by the Convention with little discussion, it was hardly understood uniformly. In 1791, shortly after the Constitution's ratification, before signing a bill chartering a national bank, President Washington sought opinions on its constitutionality. Secretary of the Treasury Alexander Hamilton argued that the necessary and proper clause had to be interpreted broadly, and that the bank legislation was clearly constitutional. To him, laws "necessary" to carry out Congress' powers meant laws "needful, requisite, incidental, useful" to such powers. Limiting Congress' authority to strict necessity would unreasonably curtail the government's ability to act. Although Hamilton acknowledged that there must be limits on the federal legislative power,[f] he took the necessary and proper clause to mean that Congress had implied powers: it was given broad means to achieve its relatively circumscribed ends.

But Secretary of State Thomas Jefferson argued that the bank would be flatly unconstitutional. To him, the necessary and proper clause had to be read strictly: a national bank was in no sense *essential* to carry out the duties of the federal government. If the clause were read so broadly as to make the bank "necessary," then Congress would effectively be authorized to enact any legislation that would be "convenient" in carrying out its goals, thus rendering the Convention's careful enumeration irrelevant.[g]

Hamilton's co-Federalist, James Madison, appeared to believe that the substance of the necessary and proper clause was such an integral part of the Constitution that its explicit presence in the text was unnecessary. He argued that "no axiom is more clearly established in law, or in reason, than that wherever the end is required, the means are authorised; wherever a general power to do a thing is given, every particular power necessary for doing it, is included."[h] And thus, to him, "had the Constitution been silent on this head, there can be no doubt that all the particular powers, requisite as means of executing the general powers, would

---

d. Support for this position comes from the tenth amendment, which ensures that "powers not delegated to the United States ... are reserved to the States respectively, or to the people."

e. Robert L. Stern, *That Commerce Which Concerns More States than One*, 47 Harv. L.Rev. 1335, 1341 (1934) (arguing that the Convention's accepting the replacement in the "absence of objection or comment upon the change" argues for this interpretation). Accord, Donald H. Regan, *How to Think About the Federal Commerce Power and Incidentally Rewrite United States v. Lopez*, 94 Mich.L.Rev. 554, 556 (1995).

f. Hamilton had argued *against* the need for a Bill of Rights on the ground that such

documents normally enumerate rights a monarch's subjects do *not* surrender, whereas the people under the proposed Constitution "surrender nothing, and as they retain every thing, they have no need of particular reservations." *The Federalist* No. 84. Indeed, he had contended that explicitly preventing the federal government from legislating in some areas might give weight to arguments that the power to do so existed in the first place. Id.

g. See John C. Yoo, *McCulloch v. Maryland*, in Constitutional Stupidities, Constitutional Tragedies 241 (1998).

h. *The Federalist* No. 44.

have resulted to the government, by unavoidable implication."[i] Nevertheless, by the time of the bank controversy, Madison had moved to Jefferson's camp, believing that Hamilton's interpretation threatened the delicate balance of federalism. The matter was addressed by the Court in *McCulloch v. Maryland*, the first case in this chapter, involving a second law, again chartering a national bank, passed in 1816 and not vetoed by President Madison.

The early controversy over the contours of America's system of federalism has continued unabated. On the one hand, it is generally agreed that the framers feared that a too powerful federal government might trample the liberties of its citizens. They hoped to check potential tyranny both by limits upon national legislative powers, and also by maintaining viable state governments that would tend to counter efforts by the national government to aggrandize its powers.[j] To this day, the Court adheres to this understanding of a balanced strength between the states and the nation, reiterating that state and federal governments "will act as mutual restraints only if both are credible. In the tension between federal and state power lies the promise of liberty."[k]

As also underlined regularly by the Court, the framers recognized further benefits to the federalist structure: "It assures a decentralized government that will be more sensitive to the diverse needs of a heterogenous society; it increases opportunity for citizen involvement in democratic processes; it allows for more innovation and experimentation in government; and it makes government more responsive by putting the States in competition for a mobile citizenry."[l] For a compact but thorough evaluation of the historic and contemporary values of federalism, see David L. Shapiro, *Federalism: A Dialogue* (1995).

THE NECESSARY AND PROPER CLAUSE

Background of McCulloch v. Maryland. The first Bank of the United States engaged in a private banking business, but also acted as a depository for United States funds wherever it established branches. The preamble of the Act incorporating the Bank stated that its establishment "will be very conducive to the successful conducting of the national finances; will tend to give facility to the obtaining of loans, for the use of the government, in sudden emergencies; and will be productive of considerable advantages to trade and industry in general." The second Bank was incorporated over strenuous political opposition, and made itself extremely unpopular, particularly in the West and South, when it over-expanded credits and later drastically curtailed them, contributing to the failure of many state-incorporated banks. As a result, a number of states sought to exclude the Bank, either by state constitutional prohibitions against operating within the state

---

i. Id. Madison added: "Had the Convention attempted a positive enumeration of the powers necessary and proper for carrying their other powers into effect; the attempt would have involved a complete digest of laws on every subject to which the Constitution relates." Id.

j. See, e.g., The Federalist No. 28 (Alexander Hamilton), No. 51 (James Madison).

k. *Gregory v. Ashcroft*, 501 U.S. 452, 459, 111 S.Ct. 2395, 2400, 115 L.Ed.2d 410 (1991).

l. *Gregory*, supra. For the view that "federalism in America achieves none of the beneficial goals that the Court claims for it," and

that these goals "call for a decentralized regime, not a federal one," see Edward L. Rubin & Malcolm Feeley, *Federalism: Some Notes on a National Neurosis*, 41 UCLA L.Rev. 903 (1994). For the view that the judiciary and academic commentators have largely ignored (1) the widely discussed "justifications for regulating at the central or national level, rather than retaining regulatory authority in the states," and (2) "any serious study" of "the supposed values of federalism" or "any sustained attempt to measure their true worth," see Barry Friedman, *Valuing Federalism*, 82 Minn.L.Rev. 317 (1997).

any bank not chartered by the state, or by imposing heavy discriminatory taxes on such banks. The tax in *McCulloch* was one of the milder taxes.

McCULLOCH v. MARYLAND

17 U.S. (4 Wheat.) 316, 4 L.Ed. 579 (1819).

CHIEF JUSTICE MARSHALL delivered the opinion of the Court.

[Maryland taxed any bank operating in the state without state authority 2% of the face value of all banknotes issued unless it paid in advance a $15,000 tax. The Maryland Court of Appeals upheld a judgment for the statutory penalty against the cashier of the Baltimore branch of the Bank of United States for issuing bank notes without payment of the required tax. The Supreme Court reversed in an opinion handed down only three days after completion of nine days of oral argument.[a]]

The first question [is], has Congress power to incorporate a bank? * * *

This government is acknowledged by all to be one of enumerated powers.[b] [Among] the enumerated powers, we do not find that of establishing a bank or creating a corporation. But there is no phrase in the instrument which, like the Articles of Confederation [Article II: "Each state retains [every] power [not] expressly delegated."] excludes incidental or implied powers; and which requires that everything granted shall be expressly and minutely described. Even the tenth amendment, which was framed for the purpose of quieting the excessive jealousies which had been excited, omits the word "expressly," and declares only that the powers "not delegated to the United States, nor prohibited to the states, are reserved to the states or to the people"; thus leaving the question, whether the particular power which may become the subject of contest has been delegated to the one government, or prohibited to the other, to depend on a fair construction of the whole instrument. The men who drew and adopted this amendment had experienced the embarrassments resulting from the insertion of this word in the Articles of Confederation, and probably omitted it to avoid those embarrassments.

---

a. But see G. Edward White, *The Working Life of the Marshall Court,* 1815–1835, 70 Va. L.Rev. 1, 30–33 (1984), commenting on the frequent short intervals between arguments and decisions during the Marshall period of unlimited oral arguments, unanimous opinions, light appellate calendars, short sojourns in Washington, and heavy circuit-riding duties.

b. The Court rejected Maryland's argument that the Constitution was "the Act of sovereign and independent states," who "delegated" the "powers of the federal government," which must be exercised in subordination to the states: "The convention which framed the Constitution was, indeed, elected by the state legislatures. But the instrument, when it came from their hands, was a mere proposal, without obligation, or pretensions to it. It was reported to the then existing Congress of the United States, with a request that it might 'be submitted to a convention of delegates, chosen in each state, by the people thereof, under the recommendation of its legislature, for their assent and ratification.' This mode of proceeding was adopted; and by the convention, by Congress, and by the state legislatures, the instrument was submitted to the people. They acted upon it, in the only manner in which they can act safely, effectively, and wisely, on such a subject, by assembling in convention [in] their several states * * *.

"From these conventions the Constitution derives its whole authority. The government proceeds directly from the people; is 'ordained and established' in the name of the people. [The] assent of the states, in their sovereign capacity, is implied in calling a convention, and thus submitting that instrument to the people. But the people were at perfect liberty to accept or reject it; and their act was final. [The] Constitution, when thus adopted, was of complete obligation, and bound the state sovereignties. * * *

"The government of the Union, then (whatever may be the influence of this fact on the case), is emphatically and truly a government of the people. In form and in substance it emanates from them, its powers are granted by them, and are to be exercised directly on them, and for their benefit."

A constitution, to contain an accurate detail of all the subdivisions of which its great powers will admit, and of all the means by which they may be carried into execution, would partake of the prolixity of a legal code, and could scarcely be embraced by the human mind. It would probably never be understood by the public. Its nature, therefore, requires, that only its great outlines should be marked, its important objects designated, and the minor ingredients which composed those objects be deduced from the nature of the objects themselves. [In] considering this question, then, we must never forget, that it is *a constitution* we are expounding.

Although, among the enumerated powers of government, we do not find the word "bank," or "incorporation," we find the great powers to lay and collect taxes; to borrow money; to regulate commerce; to declare and conduct a war; and to raise and support armies and navies. The sword and the purse, all the external relations, and no inconsiderable portion of the industry of the nation, are intrusted to its government. It can never be pretended that these vast powers draw after them others of inferior importance, merely because they are inferior. [But] it may, with great reason be contended that a government, intrusted with such ample powers, on the due execution of which the happiness and prosperity of the nation so vitally depends, must also be intrusted with ample means for their execution. The power being given, it is the interest of the nation to facilitate its execution. It can never be their interest, and cannot be presumed to have been their intention, to clog and embarrass its execution by withholding the most appropriate means. Throughout this vast republic * * * revenue is to be collected and expended, armies are to be marched and supported. The exigencies of the nation may require, that the treasure raised in the North should be transported to the South, that raised in the East conveyed to the West, or that this order should be reversed. Is that construction of the Constitution to be preferred which would render these operations difficult, hazardous, and expensive? Can we adopt that construction (unless the words imperiously require it) which would impute to the framers of that instrument, when granting these powers for the public good, the intention of impeding their exercise by withholding a choice of means? * * *

The creation of a corporation, it is said, appertains to sovereignty. This is admitted. But to what portion of sovereignty does it appertain? [In] America, the powers of sovereignty are divided between the government of the Union, and those of the states. They are each sovereign, with respect to the objects committed to it, and neither sovereign with respect to the objects committed to the other. [We] cannot well comprehend the process of reasoning which maintains, that a power appertaining to sovereignty cannot be connected with that vast portion of it which is granted to the general government, so far as it is calculated to subserve the legitimate objects of that government. The power of creating a corporation, though appertaining to sovereignty, is not, like the power of making war, or levying taxes, or of regulating commerce, a great substantive and independent power, which cannot be implied as incidental to other powers, or used as a means of executing them. It is never the end for which other powers are exercised, but a means by which other objects are accomplished. * * *

But the Constitution of the United States has not left the right of Congress to employ the necessary means, for the execution of the powers conferred on the government, to general reasoning. To its enumeration of powers is added that of making "all laws which shall be necessary and proper, for carrying into execution the foregoing powers, and all other powers vested by this Constitution, in the government of the United States, or in any department thereof."

The counsel for the state of Maryland have urged [that] this clause, though in terms a grant of power, is not so in effect; but is really restrictive of the general right, which might otherwise be implied, of selecting means for executing the enumerated powers.

[T]he argument on which most reliance is placed, is drawn from the peculiar language of this clause. Congress is not empowered by it to make all laws, which may have relation to the powers conferred on the government, but such only as may be *"necessary and proper"* for carrying them into execution. The word *"necessary"* is considered as controlling the whole sentence, and as limiting the right to pass laws for the execution of the granted powers, to such as are indispensable, and without which the power would be nugatory. That it excludes the choice of means, and leaves to Congress in each case, that only which is most direct and simple.

Is it true, that this is the sense in which the word "necessary" is always used? [If] reference be had to its use, in the common affairs of the world, or in approved authors, we find that it frequently imports no more than that one thing is convenient, or useful, or essential to another. To employ the means necessary to an end, is generally understood as employing any means calculated to produce the end, and not as being confined to those single means, without which the end would be entirely unattainable. [A] thing may be necessary, very necessary, absolutely or indispensably necessary. To no mind would the same idea be conveyed, by these several phrases. This comment on the word is well illustrated [by] the tenth section of the first article of the Constitution. It is, we think, impossible to compare the sentence which prohibits a state from laying "imposts, or duties on imports or exports, except what may be *absolutely* necessary for executing its inspection laws," with that which authorizes Congress "to make all laws which shall be necessary and proper for carrying into execution" the powers of the general government, without feeling a conviction that the convention understood itself to change materially the meaning of the word "necessary" by prefixing the word "absolutely." This word, then like others, is used in various senses; and in its construction, the subject, the context, the intention of the person using them, are all to be taken into view.

Let this be done in the case under consideration. The subject is the execution of those great powers on which the welfare of a nation essentially depends. It must have been the intention of those who gave these powers, to insure, as far as human prudence could insure, their beneficial execution. [This] provision is made in a constitution intended to endure for ages to come, and, consequently, to be adapted to the various crises of human affairs. To have prescribed the means by which government should, in all future time, execute its powers, would have been to change, entirely, the character of the instrument, and give it the properties of a legal code. It would have been an unwise attempt to provide, by immutable rules, for exigencies which, if foreseen at all must have been seen dimly, and which can be best provided for as they occur. To have declared that the best means shall not be used, but those alone without which the power given would be nugatory, would have been to deprive the legislature of the capacity to avail itself of experience, to exercise its reason, and to accommodate its legislation to circumstances. If we apply this principle of construction to any of the powers of the government, we shall find it so pernicious in its operation that we shall be compelled to discard [it.]

But the argument which most conclusively demonstrates the error of the construction contended for by the counsel for the state of Maryland, is founded on the intention of the convention, as manifested in the whole clause: * * *

1st. The clause is placed among the powers of Congress, not among the limitations on those powers.

2nd. Its terms purport to enlarge, not to diminish the powers vested in the government. It purports to be an additional power, not a restriction on those already granted. [If] no other motive for its insertion can be suggested, a sufficient one is found in the desire to remove all doubts respecting the right to legislate on that vast mass of incidental powers which must be involved in the Constitution, if that instrument be not a splendid bauble.

We admit, as all must admit, that the powers of the government are limited, and that its limits are not to be transcended. But we think the sound construction of the Constitution must allow to the national legislature that discretion, with respect to the means by which the powers it confers are to be carried into execution, which will enable that body to perform the high duties assigned to it, in the manner most beneficial to the people. Let the end be legitimate, let it be within the scope of the Constitution, and all means which are appropriate, which are plainly adapted to that end, which are not prohibited, but consist with the letter and spirit of the Constitution, are constitutional. * * *

If a corporation may be employed indiscriminately with other means to carry into execution the powers of the government, no particular reason can be assigned for excluding the use of a bank, if required for its fiscal operations. [That] it is a convenient, a useful, and essential instrument in the prosecution of its fiscal operations, is not now a subject of controversy. * * *

But were its necessity less apparent, none can deny its being an appropriate measure; and if it is, the degree of its necessity, as has been very justly observed, is to be discussed in another place. [S]hould Congress, under the pretext of executing its powers, pass laws for the accomplishment of objects not entrusted to the government; it would become the painful duty of this tribunal, should a case requiring such a decision come before it, to say that such an act was not the law of the land. But where the law is not prohibited, and is really calculated to effect any of the objects entrusted to the government, to undertake here to inquire into the degree of its necessity, would be to pass the line which circumscribes the judicial department, and to tread on legislative ground. * * *

[The Court invalidated Maryland's tax on the United States Bank, invoking the supremacy clause (Art. VI, cl. 2). This ruling and its progeny are considered in Sec. 5 infra.]

Notes and Questions

1. *McCulloch's reasoning.* (a) Does *McCulloch* leave room for effective judicial review over congressional action not expressly authorized by the Constitution but arguably designed to effectuate one or more of the expressly granted powers? What standard of review does the Court indicate it will apply in deciding such cases? What ought the standard to be? As for a "substantive" limit, is there "a vast difference between those powers reasonably *ancillary* to an enumerated power—in the sense that the powers thus implied are at least useful in effectuating the power expressly enumerated—and the far larger set of powers that merely *relate*, in some loose sense, to the power expressly enumerated"? Tribe 3d. ed., at

801. For a suggested "procedural" limit, consider David E. Engdahl, *Casebooks and Constitutional Competency*, 21 Seattle U.L.Rev. 741, 781–83 (1998): "The principle of enumerated powers precludes any presumption of validity for a federal measure not unmistakably premised on some enumerated power, and to premise anything on the Necessary and Proper Clause requires a sufficient [means-end] link. From the beginning it has been deemed '*the right of the legislature* to exercise *its* best judgment in the selection of measures to carry into execution the constitutional powers of the government,' [*McCulloch*,] and therefore that *judgment by Congress* is the indispensable requisite of this power. [Thus], the Constitution entitles the people to have their electorally answerable *political* organs *actually and openly* inquire, debate, compromise, and resolve whether and how far it is necessary to reach matters otherwise beyond the national government's scope, *in order to* effectuate enumerated federal powers."[c] To what extent would this process help determine whether laws are "really calculated" to accomplish permissible objectives, rather than being a "pretext" to enable Congress to go beyond its delegated powers? *Should* the Court make this determination? (The problem of judicial inquiries into legislative or executive motivation arises in respect to many constitutional issues—e.g., Sec. 2 infra (commerce power); Sec. 3 infra (taxing power); Ch. 4 (state power to regulate commerce); Ch. 7, Sec. 2 (freedom of speech); Ch. 8 (freedom of religion); Ch. 9, Secs. 2, III and 5, I, B (equal protection).)

(b) In particular, keep in mind the issues discussed above as you consider the materials on Congress' power that follow in this chapter.

2. *Contemporary judicial analysis of McCulloch.* (a) In U.S. TERM LIMITS, INC. v. THORNTON, 514 U.S. 779, 115 S.Ct. 1842, 131 L.Ed.2d 881 (1995)—ruling that, like Congress (see *Powell v. McCormack*, p. ___ supra), the states have no power to add to the qualifications for members of Congress in Art. I, § 2, cl. 2 and Art. I, § 3, cl. 3, and thus cannot bar "the name of an otherwise-eligible candidate for Congress from appearing on the general election ballot if that candidate has already served three terms in the House of Representatives or two terms in the Senate"—the Court split sharply over *McCulloch's* meaning. The majority, per STEVENS, J., concluded: (1) "[T]he power to add qualifications is not within the 'original powers' of the States, and thus is not reserved to the States by the Tenth Amendment. [N]o such right existed before the Constitution was ratified. [Similarly, *McCulloch*] rejected the argument that the Constitution's silence on the subject of state power to tax corporations chartered by Congress [Sec.5 infra] implies that the States have 'reserved' power to tax such federal instrumentalities. As Chief Justice Marshall pointed out, an 'original right to tax' such federal entities 'never existed, and the question whether it has been surrendered, cannot arise.' [Since] electing representatives to the National Legislature was a new right, arising from the Constitution [itself,] any state power to set the qualifications for membership in Congress must derive not from the reserved powers of state sovereignty, but rather from the delegated powers of national sovereignty." (2) "[T]he right to choose representatives belongs not to the States, but to the people. [Permitting] individual States to formulate diverse qualifications for their representatives would result in a patchwork of state

---

c. For the view "that legal actors during the founding era understood the words 'necessary' and 'proper' to have distinct meanings in many contexts, [and that the] meaning of 'proper' would require executory laws to be laws that are peculiarly within the jurisdiction or competence of Congress—that is, to be laws that do not tread on the retained rights of individuals or states, or the prerogatives of federal executive or judicial departments," see Gary Lawson & Patricia B. Granger, *The "Proper" Scope of Federal Power: A Jurisdictional Interpretation of the Sweeping Clause*, 43 Duke L.J. 267 (1993).

qualifications, undermining the uniformity and the national character that the Framers envisioned and sought to ensure."

KENNEDY, J., who joined the majority, also concurred: "There can be no doubt, if we are to respect the republican origins of the Nation and preserve its federal character, that there exists a federal right of citizenship, a relationship between the people of the Nation and their National Government, with which the States may not interfere. [*McCulloch* rejected the idea, fn. b supra] that because the States ratified the Constitution, the people can delegate power only through the States or by acting in their capacities as citizens of particular States."

THOMAS, J., joined by Rehnquist, C.J., and O'Connor and Scalia, JJ., dissented: "Our system of government rests on one overriding principle: all power stems from [the] consent of the people of each individual State, not the consent of the undifferentiated people of the Nation as a whole. [In] Madison's words, the popular consent upon which the Constitution's authority rests was 'given by the people, not as individuals composing one entire nation, but as composing the distinct and independent States to which they respectively belong.' *The Federalist* No. 39.[2] [Because] the people of the several States are the only true source of power, [the] Federal Government enjoys no authority beyond what the Constitution confers [and] the States can exercise all powers that the Constitution does not withhold from them. The Federal Government and the States thus face different default rules: where the Constitution is silent about the exercise of a particular power—that is, where the Constitution does not speak either expressly or by necessary implication—the Federal Government lacks that power and the States enjoy it.[d] [The] majority's essential logic is that the state governments could not 'reserve' any powers that they did not control at the time the Constitution was drafted. But it was not the state governments that were doing the reserving. [Given] the fundamental principle that all governmental powers stem from the people of the States, it would simply be incoherent to assert that the people of the States could not reserve any powers that they had not previously controlled."

(b) *McCulloch's* interpretation of the necessary and proper clause has been held to apply to other grants of congressional power, most notably the "enforcement" provisions of the Civil War amendments. (Ch. 11, Sec. 2.) For the view that recent qualifications on the scope of that congressional enforcement power applies as well to the necessary and proper clause, see Engdahl, supra, at 779–80.

SPECIFIED POWERS AS THE ONLY SOURCES OF FEDERAL LEGISLATIVE POWER

1. *Traditional concept.* (a) With one possible exception,[a] the Court has consistently ruled that federal legislation must be based on powers granted to the

2. [Kennedy, J.,] seizes on Marshall's references to "the people," [but] Marshall was merely using that phrase in contra-distinction to "the State governments." Counsel for Maryland had noted that "the constitution was formed and adopted, not by the people of the United States at large, but by the people of the respective States. To suppose that the mere proposition of this fundamental law threw the American people into one aggregate mass, would be to assume what the instrument itself does not profess to establish." Marshall's opinion accepted this premise, even borrowing some of counsel's language. What Marshall rejected was counsel's conclusion that the Con-stitution therefore was merely "a compact between the States." As Marshall explained, the acts of "the people themselves" in the various ratifying conventions should not be confused with "the measures of the State governments." * * *

d. Stevens, J., responded that "the Court has never treated [the] 'default rule' as absolute," pointing to *McCulloch's* rejection of "the argument that the Constitution's silence on state power to tax federal instrumentalities requires that States have the power to do so."

a. For foreign affairs, see Sec. 4 infra.

federal government in the Constitution. KANSAS v. COLORADO, 206 U.S. 46, 27 S.Ct. 655, 51 L.Ed. 956 (1907), ruled that Congress had no legislative power to irrigate non-federal lands: "[I]t is enough to say that no [enumerated power], by any implication, refers to the reclamation of arid lands. The [necessary and proper clause] is not the delegation of a new and independent power, but simply provision for making effective the powers theretofore mentioned. [A]s as our national territory has been enlarged, we have within our borders extensive tracts of arid lands which ought to be reclaimed, and it may well be that no power is adequate for their reclamation other than that of the national government. But, if no such power has been granted, none can be exercised."

(b) Might any of the granted powers reasonably be interpreted as a source of implied power to reclaim arid land? Could Congress authorize federal construction of the Boulder Dam in the Colorado River, and creation of a great reservoir, to be used "first, for river regulation, improvement of navigation, and flood control; second, for irrigation and domestic uses and satisfaction of present perfected [rights]; and third, for power"? If Congress did not provide for improvement of navigation, by what reasoning might the creation of such a dam and reservoir for irrigation, power, and flood control be justified? Cf. *Arizona v. California*, 283 U.S. 423, 51 S.Ct. 522, 75 L.Ed. 1154 (1931); *Ashwander v. TVA*, 297 U.S. 288, 56 S.Ct. 466, 80 L.Ed. 688 (1936); *Oklahoma v. Atkinson Co.*, 313 U.S. 508, 61 S.Ct. 1050, 85 L.Ed. 1487 (1941). Must a *regulatory* power be relied on to sustain federal creation and operation of a dam and reservoir designed for irrigation of privately owned lands? Where else might this power be found without disregarding the necessity to base federal action on some specified power in the Constitution? See *United States v. Gerlach Live Stock Co.*, 339 U.S. 725, 738, 70 S.Ct. 955, 962, 94 L.Ed. 1231 (1950); *Ivanhoe Irr. Dist. v. McCracken*, 357 U.S. 275, 294, 78 S.Ct. 1174, 1185, 2 L.Ed.2d 1313, 1327 (1958).

2. *Sources of legislative power outside Art. I, § 8*. Although Art. I, § 8, contains the principal listing of federal legislative powers, several other constitutional provisions expressly authorize legislative action by Congress, e.g., Art. I, § 4 (alter state regulations for election of Senators and Representatives); Art. III, § 1 (establish a system of "inferior" federal courts and to make "exceptions and regulations" concerning the appellate jurisdiction of the Supreme Court); and Art. IV, § 3 ("make all needful Rules and Regulations respecting the Territory or other Property belonging to the United States.") Amendments 13, 14, 15, 19, 23, 24 and 26 each authorize Congress to enforce the amendment by "appropriate legislation."

May sources of congressional legislative power be found in the powers expressly assigned in the Constitution to the federal courts or the President? Is the necessary and proper clause relevant here? Consider, for example:

(a) *Admiralty and maritime jurisdiction*. Art. III, § 2 extends the federal judicial power "to all Cases of admiralty and maritime Jurisdiction." *Ex parte Garnett*, 141 U.S. 1, 11 S.Ct. 840, 35 L.Ed. 631 (1891), sustaining congressional limitation of liability in admiralty cases,[b] recognized congressional power to legislate substantive rules for admiralty and maritime controversies based on this grant of judicial power, and PANAMA R.R. v. JOHNSON, 264 U.S. 375, 44 S.Ct. 391, 68 L.Ed. 748 (1924), upheld a federal law increasing the rights of injured seamen, reasoning: A "system [of maritime] law existed in colonial times and during the Confederation, and commonly was applied in the adjudication of

b. In 1789, Congress gave the federal courts exclusive jurisdiction of all admiralty and maritime cases. This is still the law. See 28 U.S.C.A. § 1333.

admiralty and maritime cases. [The] framers of the Constitution were familiar with that system and proceeded with it in mind. Their purpose was [to] place the entire subject—its substantive as well as its procedural features—under national control, because of its intimate relation to navigation and to interstate and foreign commerce. [Although] containing no express grant of legislative power over the substantive law, [Art. III, § 2] was regarded from the beginning as implicitly investing such power in the United States. [After] the Constitution went into effect, the substantive law theretofore in force was not regarded as superseded or as being only the law of the several states, but as having become the law of the United States—subject to power in Congress to alter, qualify or supplement it as experience or changing conditions might require. * * *

"In this connection it is well to recall that the Constitution, by section 1 of article 3, declares that the judicial power of the United States shall be vested in one Supreme Court 'and in such inferior courts as the Congress may from time to time ordain and establish,' and, by section 8 of article 1, empowers the Congress to make all laws which shall be necessary and proper for carrying into execution the several powers vested in the government of the United States."

(b) *Diversity jurisdiction.* For auto accident cases in the federal courts on diversity of citizenship, could Congress substitute a federal no-fault statute for state negligence law? Are the admiralty cases distinguishable? ERIE R.R. v. TOMPKINS, 304 U.S. 64, 58 S.Ct. 817, 82 L.Ed. 1188 (1938), per BRANDEIS, J., ruled that in diversity cases federal courts could not disregard the applicable state common law to apply "federal common law": "Congress has no power to declare substantive rules of common law applicable in a state whether they be local in their nature or 'general.' [And] no clause in the Constitution purports to confer such a power upon the federal courts. * * * 'Supervision over either the legislative or the judicial action of the States is in no case permissible except as to matters by the Constitution specifically authorized or delegated to the United States.' "Does this reasoning apply to congressional legislation prescribing the substantive law to be applied to *diversity cases in federal courts*? Cf. Henry Friendly, *In Praise of Erie—and of the New Federal Common Law*, 19 Record of N.Y.C.B.A. 64 (1964).

(c) *Treaties.* May a treaty obligating the United States to adopt laws not otherwise authorized be the source of congressional legislative power? See Sec. 4, I infra.

SECTION 2. THE NATIONAL COMMERCE POWER

I. DEVELOPMENT OF BASIC CONCEPTS

GIBBONS v. OGDEN

22 U.S. (9 Wheat.) 1, 6 L.Ed. 23 (1824).

CHIEF JUSTICE MARSHALL delivered the opinion of the Court.

[A New York statute granted Livingston and Fulton the exclusive right to navigate steamboats in state waters; they assigned to Ogden the right to navigate between New York City and New Jersey. Ogden secured an injunction in the state courts against Gibbons, who was navigating between New York and New Jersey two steamboats licensed under an act of Congress.]

The appellant contends that this decree is erroneous, because the laws which purport to give the exclusive privilege it sustains, are repugnant [to] that clause in the constitution which authorizes Congress to [regulate] "commerce with foreign nations, and among the several states, and with the Indian tribes."

The subject to be regulated is commerce [and to] ascertain the extent of the power, it becomes necessary to settle the meaning of the word. The counsel for the appellee would limit it to traffic, to buying and selling, or the interchange of commodities, and do not admit that it comprehends navigation. This would restrict a general term, applicable to many objects, to one of its significations. Commerce, undoubtedly, is traffic, but it is something more,—it is intercourse. It describes the commercial intercourse between nations, and parts of nations in all its branches, and is regulated by prescribing rules for carrying on that intercourse. [All] America understands, and has uniformly understood the word "commerce" to comprehend navigation. It was so understood, and must have been so understood, when the Constitution was framed. The power over commerce, including navigation, was one of the primary objects for which the people of America adopted their government, and must have been contemplated in forming [it].

To what commerce does this power extend? The Constitution informs us, to commerce "with foreign nations, and among the several states, and with the Indian tribes." It has, we believe, been universally admitted that these words comprehend every species of commercial intercourse between the United States and foreign nations. No sort of trade can be carried on between this country and any other to which this power does not extend. * * *

The subject to which the power is next applied is to commerce "among the several States." The word "among" means intermingled [with.] Commerce among the states cannot stop at the external boundary-line of each state, but may be introduced into the interior. * * *

Comprehensive as the word "among" is, it may very properly be restricted to that commerce which concerns more states than one. [The] enumeration of the particular classes of commerce to which the power was to be extended [presupposes] something not enumerated; and that something, if we regard the language or the subject of the sentence, must be the exclusively internal commerce of a state. The genius and character of the whole government seem to be, that its action is to be applied to all the external concerns of the nation, and to those internal concerns which affect the states generally; but not to those which are completely within a particular state, which do not affect other states, and with which it is not necessary to interfere for the purpose of executing some of the general powers of the government. The completely internal commerce of a state, then, may be considered as reserved for the state itself.

But, in regulating commerce with foreign nations, the power of Congress does not stop at the jurisdictional lines of the several states. It would be a very useless power if it could not pass those lines. The commerce of the United States with foreign nations is that of the whole United States. Every district has a right to participate in it. The deep streams which penetrate our country in every direction pass through the interior of almost every state in the Union, and furnish the means of exercising this right. If Congress has the power to regulate it, that power must be exercised whenever the subject exists. If it exists within the states, if a foreign voyage may commence or terminate at a port within a state, then the power of Congress may be exercised within a state.

This principle is, if possible, still more clear when applied to commerce "among the several states." They either join each other, in which case they are separated by a mathematical line, or they are remote from each other, in which case other states lie between them. What is commerce "among" them; and how is it to be conducted? Can a trading expedition between two adjoining states commence and terminate outside of each? And if the trading intercourse be between two states remote from each other, must it not commence in one, terminate in the other, and probably pass through a third? Commerce among the states must, of necessity, be commerce with the states. [The] power of Congress, then, whatever it may be, must be exercised within the territorial jurisdiction of the several states. * * *

We are now arrived at the inquiry, What is this power? It is the power to regulate; that is, to prescribe the rule by which commerce is to be governed. This power, like all others vested in Congress, is complete in itself, may be exercised to its utmost extent, and acknowledges no limitations other than are prescribed in the Constitution. These are expressed in plain terms, and do not affect the questions which arise in this [case]. If, as has always been understood, the sovereignty of Congress, though limited to specified objects, is plenary as to those objects, the power over commerce with foreign nations, and among the several states, is vested in Congress as absolutely as it would be in a single government, having in its constitution the same restrictions on the exercise of the power as are found in the Constitution of the United States. The wisdom and the discretion of Congress, their identity with the people, and the influence which their constituents possess at elections, are, in this, as in many other instances, as that, for example, of declaring war, the sole restraints on which they have relied, to secure them from its abuse. They are the restraints on which the people must often rely solely, in all representative governments. * * *

[Ch. 4, Sec. 1 considers Marshall, C.J.'s discussion of Gibbons' claim that Congress' power to regulate commerce was exclusive. The Court left that issue unresolved when it ruled that Ogden's claim of a steamboat monopoly under New York's law must yield to the federal law under which Gibbons held a license.]

The boats of the appellant were, we are told, employed in the transportation of passengers, and this is no part of that commerce which Congress may regulate. [But no] clear distinction is perceived between the power to regulate vessels employed in transporting men for hire, and property for hire. The subject is transferred to Congress, and no exception to the grant can be admitted which is not proved by the words or the nature of the thing.* * *a

Notes and Questions

1. *Meaning of "commerce."* (a) The Court's commerce clause concepts were first developed largely in cases challenging state regulatory laws and taxes as regulations of "commerce," which were claimed to be exclusively within the power of Congress. Congress had left most business regulation to the states,[b] and had made little use of its power to regulate commerce until the Interstate Commerce Act in 1887 and the Sherman Act in 1890. Were concepts so developed likely to prove viable when Congress finally enacted substantial business regulations and the true issue became the extent of congressional, not state, power?

a. Johnson, J., concurred on the ground that the power of Congress to regulate commerce was exclusive.

2 Charles Warren, *The Supreme Court in United States History,* 75–76 (1922), pointed out the dramatic effect of *Gibbons* in opening up greater freedom in interstate transporta-

tion: "Marshall's opinion was the emancipation proclamation of American commerce."

b. Ch. 4 concerns the Court's efforts to protect interstate commerce against harmful state regulation and taxation without thwarting state efforts to protect legitimate state interests.

(b) PAUL v. VIRGINIA, 75 U.S. (8 Wall.) 168, 19 L.Ed. 357 (1869), upheld state regulation of interstate insurance business on the ground that "issuing a policy of insurance is not a transaction of commerce" and insurance contracts "are not articles of commerce." Would *Paul* be a persuasive precedent for insurance companies contending that the Sherman Act's bar on restraints of trade in interstate commerce may not apply to an interstate insurance rate-fixing arrangement? See *United States v. South–Eastern Underwriters Ass'n,* 322 U.S. 533, 64 S.Ct. 1162, 88 L.Ed. 1440 (1944) (prosecution upheld under broader approach to Congress' commerce power).

(c) KIDD v. PEARSON, 128 U.S. 1, 9 S.Ct. 6, 32 L.Ed. 346 (1888), upheld Iowa's ban on manufacture of liquor as applied to an Iowa distillery that sold its entire output in other states. It rejected the contention that manufacture for exclusively out-of-state sales was interstate commerce subject only to congressional regulation: "No distinction is more popular to the common mind, or more clearly expressed in economic and political literature, than that between manufacturing and commerce. Manufacturing is transformation—the fashioning of raw materials into a change of form for use. [The] buying and selling and the transportation incident thereto constitute commerce. [If] it be held that the term includes the regulation of all such manufactures as are intended to be the subject of commercial transactions in the future, it is impossible to deny that it would also include all productive industries that contemplate the same thing. The result would be that Congress would be invested, to the exclusion of the States, with the power to regulate, not only manufactures, but also agriculture, horticulture, stock raising, domestic fisheries, mining—in short, every branch of human industry. For is there one of them that does not contemplate, more or less clearly, an interstate or foreign market? [The] power being vested in Congress and denied to the States, it would follow as an inevitable result that the duty would devolve on Congress to regulate all these delicate, multiform and vital interests—interests which in their nature are and must be, local in all details of their successful management."

The Court continued to adhere to the *Pearson* ruling that manufacture and production are not "commerce." See, e.g., *United States v. E.C. Knight Co.,* 156 U.S. 1, 15 S.Ct. 249, 39 L.Ed. 325 (1895) (Sherman Act could not be applied to monopoly of sugar refiners: "commerce succeeds to manufacture, and is not part of it").

2. *Meaning of "among the several states."* (a) THE DANIEL BALL, 77 U.S. (10 Wall.) 557, 19 L.Ed. 999 (1871), sustained a federal safety regulation as applied to a small ship navigating in shallow water on the Grand River exclusively within Michigan: "So far as she was employed in transporting goods destined for other States, or goods brought from without the limits of Michigan and destined to places within that State, she was engaged in commerce between the States. [She] was employed as an instrumentality of that commerce; for whenever a commodity has begun to move as an article of trade from one State to another, commerce in that commodity between the States has commenced. The fact that several different and independent agencies are employed in transporting the commodity, some acting entirely in one State, and some acting through two or more States does in no respect affect the character of the transaction.

"[W]e are unable to draw any clear and distinct line between the authority of Congress to regulate an agency employed in commerce between the States, when that agency extends through two or more States and when it is confined in its action entirely within the limits of a single State. If its authority does not extend to an agency in such commerce, when that agency is confined within the limits of a State, its entire authority over interstate commerce may be defeated."

(b) *"Between the states" or "among the people"*? *The Daniel Ball* referred to commerce "between the states." Could "among" be given a broader meaning than "between"? 1 William W. Crosskey, *Politics and the Constitution in the History of the United States*, c. 3 (1953), contended that the framers intended to give Congress power to regulate all commercial and business activities, irrespective of state lines or interstate movement. Crosskey's view of the 1787 usage and understanding of among and the several states led him to conclude that "commerce among the several states" really meant "commerce among the people of the several states."[c]

3. *Business purpose.* Is a business or "commercial" purpose necessary before Congress can exercise its commerce power to control interstate movement or transportation? See *Caminetti v. United States*, 242 U.S. 470, 37 S.Ct. 192, 61 L.Ed. 442 (1917) (transportation of mistress for non-commercial but immoral purposes). For example, may Congress forbid a fundamentalist Mormon from driving his wives from Utah to Nevada to set up housekeeping? See *Cleveland v. United States*, 329 U.S. 14, 67 S.Ct. 13, 91 L.Ed. 12 (1946). Forbid carrying liquor for one's own use across state lines? See *United States v. Hill*, 248 U.S. 420, 39 S.Ct. 143, 63 L.Ed. 337 (1919). Forbid fleeing from one state to another to avoid state criminal prosecution? See *Hemans v. United States*, 163 F.2d 228 (6th Cir.), cert. denied, 332 U.S. 801 (1947). Forbid a parent from "kidnapping" child from the other parent's custody into another state? See *Gooch v. United States*, 297 U.S. 124, 56 S.Ct. 395, 80 L.Ed. 522 (1936). Under our federal system are there good reasons for making the commerce power applicable to such non-commercial actions?

FOUNDATIONS FOR EXTENDING THE REACH OF CONGRESSIONAL POWER

The more significant problems concerning Congress' commerce power have related to its use to regulate (1) national economic problems by regulating local aspects that may be neither "commerce" nor "among the several states," such as labor relations or wages in a local factory, or crops produced and used on a farm; (2) disfavored local activities, such as gambling, prostitution, distribution of harmful or improperly labeled foods and drugs, and local loan shark enterprises; and (3) other socially undesirable activities, such as discrimination based on race, sex, or age, and activities harmful to the environment.

The next two cases reveal the origins of two different methods of using the commerce clause to deal with such problems. The rest of Sec. 2 deals with the evolution of these two "approaches."

THE LOTTERY CASE (CHAMPION v. AMES)
188 U.S. 321, 23 S.Ct. 321, 47 L.Ed. 492 (1903).

JUSTICE HARLAN delivered the opinion of the Court.

[The Federal Lottery Act, which prohibited interstate carriage of lottery tickets, was applied to shipping a box of lottery tickets from Texas to California.] ⚹ F

---

c. Although Crosskey's views were widely discussed, they appear to have had little influence on constitutional developments.

[handwritten: regulate morality]

These tickets were the subject of traffic; they could have been sold; and the holder was assured that the company would pay to him the amount of the prize drawn. * * * *[handwritten: ×F]*

We are of opinion that lottery tickets are subjects of traffic, and therefore are subjects of commerce, and the regulation of the carriage of such tickets from state to state, at least by independent carriers, is a regulation of commerce among the several states. *[handwritten: ×H]*

* * * Are we prepared to say that a provision which is, in effect, a *prohibition* of the carriage of such articles from state to state is not a fit or appropriate mode for the *regulation* of that particular kind of commerce?[a] If lottery traffic, *carried on through interstate commerce,* is a matter of which Congress may take cognizance and over which its power may be exerted, can it be possible that it must tolerate the traffic, and simply regulate the manner in which it may be carried on? Or may not Congress, for the protection of the people of all the states, and under the power to regulate interstate commerce, devise such means, within the scope of the Constitution, and not prohibited by it, as will drive that traffic out of commerce among the states? * * * *[handwritten: ×L]*

[handwritten in left margin: – Congress is not granted police power.]

If a state, when considering legislation for the suppression of lotteries within its own limits, may properly take into view the evils, that inhere in the raising of money, in that mode, why may not Congress, invested with the power to regulate commerce among the several states, provide that such commerce shall not be polluted by the carrying of lottery tickets from one state to another? In this connection it must not be forgotten that the power of Congress to regulate commerce among the states is plenary, is complete in itself, and is subject to no limitations except such as may be found in the Constitution. [What] clause can be cited which, in any degree, countenances the suggestion that one may, of right, carry or cause to be carried from one state to another that which will harm the public morals? * * * *[handwritten: ×L]*

Congress [does] not assume to interfere with traffic or commerce in lottery tickets carried on exclusively within the limits of any state, but has in view only commerce of that kind <u>among the several</u> states. It has not assumed to interfere with the completely internal affairs of any state, and has only legislated in respect of a matter which concerns the people of the United States. As a state may, for the purpose of guarding the morals of its own people, forbid all sales of lottery tickets within its limits, so Congress, for the purpose of guarding the people of the United States against the "widespread pestilence of lotteries" and to protect the commerce which concerns all the states, <u>may prohibit the carrying of lottery tickets from one state to another.</u> In legislating upon the subject of the traffic in lottery tickets, as carried on through interstate commerce, Congress only supplemented the action of those states—perhaps all of them—which, for the protection of the public morals, prohibit the drawing of lotteries, as well as the sale or circulation of lottery tickets, within their respective limits. It said, in effect, that it would not permit the declared policy of the states, which sought to protect their people against the mischiefs of the lottery business, to be overthrown or disregarded by the agency of interstate commerce. We should hesitate long before adjudging that an evil of such appalling character, carried on through interstate commerce, *[handwritten: ×L]* cannot be met and crushed by the only power competent to that [end.] *[handwritten in right margin: Moral Judgements]* *[handwritten: ×H]*

a. For the view that a law enacted "to effectuate the commerce power [that] purports to regulate, but is really intended as a prohibition" violates the necessary and proper clause, see Randy E. Barnett, *Necessary and Proper,* 44 UCLA L.Rev. 745 (1997).

It is said, however, that if, in order to suppress lotteries carried on through interstate commerce, Congress may exclude lottery tickets from such commerce, that principle leads necessarily to the conclusion that Congress may arbitrarily exclude from commerce among the states any article, commodity, or thing, of whatever kind or nature, or however useful or valuable, which it may choose, no matter with what motive* * *. It will be time enough to consider the constitutionality of such legislation when we must do so. [T]he possible abuse of a power is not an argument against its existence. * * *

CHIEF JUSTICE FULLER, with whom concur JUSTICE BREWER, JUSTICE SHIRAS, and JUSTICE PECKHAM, dissenting.

[D]oubtless an act prohibiting the carriage of lottery matter would be necessary and proper to the execution of a power to suppress lotteries; but that power belongs to the states and not to Congress. To hold that Congress has general police power would be to hold that it may accomplish objects not intrusted to the general government, and to defeat the operation of the 10th Amendment.[b]

But apart from the question of bona fides, this act cannot be brought within the power to regulate commerce among the several states, unless lottery tickets are articles of commerce, and, therefore, when carried across state lines, of interstate commerce; or unless the power to regulate interstate commerce includes the absolute and exclusive power to prohibit the transportation of anything or anybody from one state to [another].

Is the carriage of lottery tickets from one state to another commercial intercourse? The lottery ticket purports to create contractual relations, and to furnish the means of enforcing a contract right. This is true of insurance policies, and both are contingent in their nature. Yet this court has held that the issuing of fire, marine, and life insurance policies, in one state, and sending them to another, to be there delivered to the insured on payment of premium, is not interstate commerce. *Paul v. Virginia.* * * *

If a lottery ticket is not an article of commerce, how can it become so when placed in an envelope or box or other covering, and transported by an express company? [This] would be to say that everything is an article of commerce the moment it is taken to be transported from place to place, and of interstate commerce if from state to state. An invitation to dine, or to take a drive, or a note of introduction, all become articles of commerce under the ruling in this case, by being deposited with an express company for transportation. [The] necessary consequence is to take from the states all jurisdiction over the subject so far as interstate communication is concerned. It is a long step in the direction of wiping out all traces of state lines, and the creation of a centralized [government].[c]

b. Several pages later, the dissent quoted the sentence in *McCulloch* respecting Congress, "under the pretext of executing its powers, pass[ing] laws for the accomplishment of objects not entrusted to the government."

c. Consider Deborah J. Merritt, *The Third Translation of the Commerce Clause: Congressional Power to Regulate Social Problems*, 66 Geo.Wash.L.Rev. 1206, 1209 (1998): "Compared to the constitutional firestorm over Congress's authority to regulate the national economy, a power the Framers clearly intended to confer, barely a candle has flickered over Congress's power to regulate a variety of social issues. Yet it is in the latter cases that the Court has wandered farthest from the apparent meaning of the Commerce Clause and has engaged in the most extreme forms of one type of textualism. The Court has taken the phrase 'Commerce ... among the several States' out of its documentary, historical, and cultural context and has used that phrase to uphold regulation of any activity that has some link to interstate commerce—even if the nexus is purely incidental to the law's purpose."

The power to prohibit the transportation of diseased animals and infected goods over railroads or on steamboats is an entirely different thing, for they would be in themselves injurious to the transaction of interstate commerce, and, moreover, are essentially commercial in their nature. And the exclusion of diseased persons rests on different ground, for nobody would pretend that persons could be kept off the trains because they were going from one state to another to engage in the lottery business. However enticing that business may be, we do not understand these pieces of paper themselves can communicate bad principles by contact.

* * *

Notes and Questions

Commerce clause as source of national police power. (a) In the next 15 years, Congress used its power to exclude from the channels of interstate commerce commodities and activities "which are injurious, not to that commerce or to any of the agencies or facilities thereof, but to the health, morals, safety, and general welfare of the nation." Robert E. Cushman, *The National Police Power Under the Commerce Clause of the Constitution,* 3 Minn.L.Rev. 289 (1919) (analyzing decisions involving obscene materials, traffic in prostitution, misbranded products, and impure, unwholesome or adulterated food or drugs).

(b) In HOKE v. UNITED STATES, 227 U.S. 308, 33 S.Ct. 281, 57 L.Ed. 523 (1913), a unanimous Court explained: "The principle established by the cases is the simple one, when rid of confusing and distracting considerations, that Congress has power over transportation among the several States; that the power is complete in itself, and that Congress, as an incident to it, may adopt not only means necessary but convenient to its exercise, and the means may have the quality of police regulations."

HOUSTON, EAST & WEST TEXAS RY. v. UNITED STATES (SHREVEPORT CASE)
234 U.S. 342, 34 S.Ct. 833, 58 L.Ed. 1341 (1914).

JUSTICE HUGHES delivered the opinion of the Court.

[The Interstate Commerce Commission fixed interstate railroad rates westward from Shreveport, La., to Texas markets and ordered the affected railroads to raise their rates, for intrastate shipments eastward to the same Texas markets, which were prescribed by the Texas Railroad Commission and which discriminated against interstate commerce.[a]

[Where the power of Congress to regulate commerce] exists, it dominates. Interstate trade was not left to be destroyed or impeded by the rivalries of local government. The purpose was to make impossible the recurrence of the evils which had overwhelmed the Confederation, and to provide the necessary basis of national unity by insuring "uniformity of regulation against conflicting and discriminating state legislation." By virtue of the comprehensive terms of the grant, the authority of Congress is at all times adequate to meet the varying exigencies that arise. [Its] authority, extending to these interstate carriers as instruments of interstate commerce, necessarily embraces the right to control

---

a. For example "a rate of 60 cents carried first-class traffic [160 miles] eastward from Dallas, while the same rate [carried] the same class of traffic only 55 miles into Texas from Shreveport. [The] rate on wagons from Dallas to Marshall, Texas, 147.7 miles, was 36.8 cents, and from Shreveport to Marshall, 42 miles, 56 [cents]."

their operations in all matters having such a close and substantial relation to interstate traffic that the control is essential or appropriate to the security of that traffic, to the efficiency of the interstate service, and to the maintenance of conditions under which interstate commerce may be conducted upon fair terms and without molestation or hindrance.

[While *Baltimore & O.R. Co. v. ICC*, 221 U.S. 612, 31 S.Ct. 621, 55 L.Ed. 878 (1911),[b] and *Southern R. Co. v. United States*, 222 U.S. 20, 32 S.Ct. 2, 56 L.Ed. 72 (1911)[c]] relate to measures adopted in the interest of the safety of persons and property, they illustrate the principle that Congress, in the exercise of its paramount power, may prevent the common instrumentalities of interstate and intrastate commercial intercourse from being used in their intrastate operations to the injury of interstate commerce. This is not to say that Congress possesses the authority to regulate the internal commerce of a state, as such, but that it does possess the power to foster and protect interstate commerce, and to take all measures necessary or appropriate to that end, although intrastate transactions of interstate carriers may thereby be controlled.

This principle is applicable here. We find no reason to doubt that Congress is entitled to keep the highways of interstate communication open to interstate traffic upon fair and equal terms. That an unjust discrimination in the rates of a common carrier, by which one person or locality is unduly favored as against another under substantially similar conditions of traffic, constitutes an evil, is undeniable; and where this evil consists in the action of an interstate carrier in unreasonably discriminating against interstate traffic over its line, the authority of Congress to prevent it is equally clear. It is immaterial, so far as the protecting power of Congress is concerned, that the discrimination arises from intrastate rates as compared with interstate rates. The use of the instrument of interstate commerce in a discriminatory manner so as to inflict injury upon that commerce, or some part thereof, furnishes abundant ground for Federal intervention. [In] removing the injurious discriminations against interstate traffic arising from the relation of intrastate to interstate rates, Congress is not bound to reduce the latter below what it may deem to be a proper standard, fair to the carrier and to the public. Otherwise, it could prevent the injury to interstate commerce only by the sacrifice of its judgment as to interstate rates. Congress is entitled to maintain its own standard as to these rates, and to forbid any discriminatory action by interstate carriers which will obstruct the freedom of movement of interstate traffic over their lines in accordance with the terms it establishes. * * *

Justice Lurton and Justice Pitney dissent.

Notes and Questions

1. *Contrasting approaches.* How do the *Shreveport* and *Lottery* methods of regulating local activities differ in terms of the regulatory point of impact, professed objective, and rationale?

2. *Local activities "burdening" interstate commerce.* (a) Does *Shreveport's* rationale apply to rates for *passengers*? WISCONSIN R.R. COM'N v. CHICAGO,

---

b. *Baltimore & O.R.* upheld federal regulation of hours of service of employees working on interstate railroads, even though the effect was to control their hours on intrastate service as well, because of the impracticality of limiting their work to one or the other.

c. *Southern R.* upheld the federal safety appliance act's application to vehicles used by an interstate railroad only in intrastate traffic, as well as those used interstate, in order to assure the safety of interstate traffic moving over the same railroad as the intrastate.

B. & Q. R.R., 257 U.S. 563, 42 S.Ct. 232, 66 L.Ed. 371 (1922), per TAFT, C.J., upheld an ICC order raising Wisconsin-prescribed intrastate railroad passenger fares to equal those in interstate commerce: "Congress as the dominant controller of interstate commerce [may] restrain undue limitation of the earning power of the interstate commerce system doing state work. The affirmative power of Congress in developing interstate commerce agencies is clear [and] it can impose any reasonable conditions on a State's use of interstate carriers for intrastate commerce it deems necessary or desirable." What result in *Shreveport* and *Wisconsin R.R.* if the unduly low, state-prescribed intrastate rates were charged by railroads that operated entirely within Texas and Wisconsin?

(b) STAFFORD v. WALLACE, 258 U.S. 495, 42 S.Ct. 397, 66 L.Ed. 735 (1922), per TAFT, C.J., upheld federal regulation of rates and practices of persons engaged in local buying and selling in stockyards. Relying on an earlier "current of commerce" concept,[a] the Court reasoned that the regulated activities, while "usually lawful and affecting only intrastate commerce," were subject to federal control when Congress "reasonably fear[s] that such [acts] will probably [constitute] a direct and undue burden on [interstate commerce. It] is primarily for Congress to consider and decide the fact of the danger and meet it." McReynolds, J., dissented without opinion.

II. REGULATION OF NATIONAL ECONOMIC PROBLEMS

A. LIMITATIONS ON COMMERCE POWER THROUGH 1936

(child labor)

HAMMER v. DAGENHART

- Cong. Can not regulate manufacture.

247 U.S. 251, 38 S.Ct. 529, 62 L.Ed. 1101 (1918).

JUSTICE DAY delivered the opinion of the Court.

[Ruling that Congress exceeded its commerce power by prohibiting interstate transportation of products from factories that used child labor,] the Court distinguished the *Lottery* line of cases:] In each of these instances the use of interstate transportation was necessary to the accomplishment of harmful results. In other words, although the power over interstate transportation was to regulate, that could only be accomplished by prohibiting the use of the facilities of interstate commerce to effect the evil intended.

This element is wanting in the present case. The thing intended to be accomplished by this statute is the denial of the facilities of interstate commerce to those manufacturers in the states who employ children within the prohibited ages. The act in its effect does not regulate transportation among the states, but aims to standardize the ages at which children may be employed in mining and manufacturing within the states. The goods shipped are of themselves harmless. [When] offered for shipment, and before transportation begins, the labor of their production is over, and the mere fact that they were intended for interstate commerce transportation does not make their production subject to federal control under the commerce power.* * *

Over interstate transportation, or its incidents, the regulatory power of Congress is ample, but the production of articles, intended for interstate commerce, is a matter of local regulation. [If] it were otherwise, all manufacture

a. See *Swift & Co. v. United States,* 196 U.S. 375, 25 S.Ct. 276, 49 L.Ed. 518 (1905) (upholding application of Sherman Act to local sales in stockyards by viewing the sales as part of a "current of commerce" between states).

- Limitation of Federal Power (where does it stop)

intended for interstate shipment would be brought under federal control to the
practical exclusion of the authority of the states, a result certainly not contemplated by the framers of the Constitution when they vested in Congress the authority
to regulate commerce among the States. *Kidd v. Pearson.*

It is further contended that the authority of Congress may be exerted to
control interstate commerce in the shipment of child-made goods because of the
effect of the circulation of such goods in other states where the evil of this class of
labor has been recognized by local legislation, and the right to thus employ child
labor has been more rigorously restrained than in the state of production. In other
words, that the unfair competition, thus engendered, may be controlled by closing
the channels of interstate commerce to manufacturers in those states where the
local laws do not meet what Congress deems to be the more just standard of other
states.

There is no power vested in Congress to require the states to exercise their
police power so as to prevent possible unfair competition. Many causes may
cooperate to give one state, by reason of local laws or conditions, an economic
advantage over others. The commerce clause was not intended to give to Congress
a general authority to equalize such conditions. In some of the states laws have
been passed fixing minimum wages for women, in others the local law regulates
the hours of labor of women in various employments. Business done in such states
may be at an economic disadvantage when compared with states which have no
such regulations; surely, this fact does not give Congress the power to deny
transportation in interstate commerce to those who carry on business where the
hours of labor and the rate of compensation for women have not been fixed by a
standard in use in other states and approved by Congress. [The] grant of power to
Congress over the subject of interstate commerce was to enable it to regulate such
commerce, and not to give it authority to control the states in their exercise of the
police power over local trade and manufacture. [To] sustain this statute [would]
sanction an invasion by the federal power of the control of a matter purely local in
its character, and over which no authority has been delegated to Congress in
conferring the power to regulate commerce among the states. * * *

JUSTICE HOLMES, dissenting.[a]

* * * Regulation means the prohibition of something, and when interstate
commerce is the matter to be regulated I cannot doubt that the regulation may
prohibit any part of such commerce that Congress sees fit to forbid. * * *

The question then is narrowed to whether the exercise of its otherwise
constitutional power by Congress can be pronounced unconstitutional because of
its possible reaction upon the conduct of the States in a matter upon which [they]
are free from direct control. I [should] have thought that the most conspicuous
decisions of this Court had made it clear that the power to regulate commerce and
other constitutional powers could not be cut down or qualified by the fact that it
might interfere with the carrying out of the domestic policy of any [State.]

The Act does not meddle with anything belonging to the States. They may
regulate their internal affairs and their domestic commerce as they like. But when
they seek to send their products across the State line they are no longer within
their rights. If there were no Constitution and no Congress their power to cross
the line would depend upon their neighbors. Under the Constitution such commerce belongs not to the States but to Congress to regulate. It may carry out its
views of public policy whatever indirect effect they may have upon the activities of

a. McKenna, Brandeis, and Clarke, JJ.,
joined this dissent.

the States. Instead of being encountered by a prohibitive tariff at her boundaries the State encounters the public policy of the United States which it is for Congress to express. [The] national welfare as understood by Congress may require a different attitude within its sphere from that of some self-seeking State.
* * *

Notes and Questions

1. *Harmful effects.* Which "harmful results" were more of a threat to the interests the commerce clause was intended to protect—those guarded against by the laws sustained in the *Lottery, Hoke* and similar cases or those guarded against by the law held invalid in *Dagenhart?*

2. *The need for national power.* (a) *Dagenhart* sought to preserve "the authority of the states over matters purely local." Did *Dagenhart's* invalidation of federal control advance or impede the states' ability to make effective their own child labor laws? Without the support of federal laws could New York or Massachusetts protect their textile industries from the competition of child labor mills in North Carolina? Could New York protect its home market by forbidding the sale in New York of the products of child labor? Cf. *Baldwin v. Seelig* (1935), Ch.4, Sec. 2, I (state cannot forbid sale within state of milk bought outside of state at price lower than minimum price established by state for its own milk producers).

(b) Nine months after *Dagenhart,* Congress enacted a law seeking to control child labor through use of the taxing power. See *Child Labor Tax Case,* Sec. 3 infra.

CONSTITUTIONAL STRUGGLE: THE NEW DEAL vs. THE GREAT DEPRESSION

The great depression of the 1930s gave rise to unprecedented unemployment, drastic cutbacks in production, 60% declines in farm and labor income, widespread business and bank failures, devastating home and farm mortgage foreclosures, all reacting on each other in an extraordinary downward spiral. For a classic analysis of the constitutional litigation by a participant in the successful struggle to find bases for national regulatory power, see Robert L. Stern, *The Commerce Clause and the National Economy,* 1933–1946, 59 Harv.L.Rev. 645, 883 (1946): "The problems were economic, and the Commerce Clause was the enumerated power most directly concerned with business and economic, or commercial, matters. ["Although the] ingredients of the economic crises often preceded the movement of goods across state lines and occurred during the course of manufacture and production, they were of national consequence because the products of the national economy were distributed throughout a national market. The channels of interstate commerce were the arteries through which the impact of these forces affected the nation. Because of the nation-wide market, and the constitutional impediment placed by the Commerce Clause itself in the way of regulation by the states, the state governments were unable to cope with economic problems affecting the nation as a whole. The depressed state of business activity obviously affected interstate commerce in the most elementary sense, since it greatly reduced the quantity of products to be transported across state lines.

"Nevertheless there could be no assurance that federal legislation directed at the economic causes of the depression would be constitutional. For that depended on what the Supreme Court thought. And there was ample authority in the Supreme Court opinions looking both ways."

Early in the litigation over New Deal legislation, SCHECHTER POULTRY CORP. v. UNITED STATES, 295 U.S. 495, 55 S.Ct. 837, 79 L.Ed. 1570 (1935), per HUGHES, C.J., struck down a Code, adopted under the National Industrial Recovery Act, to regulate trade practices, wages, hours, and collective bargaining in the New York poultry wholesale slaughtering market where 96% of the poultry came from other states. Schechter bought poultry only on the local market and, after slaughtering, sold it only to local retailers. The opinion ruled that the regulation fell outside the commerce power because the regulated conduct had no "direct" effect upon interstate commerce, but did little to clarify this, possibly because the major basis for invalidity was that the Act unconstitutionally delegated legislative power to the Administrator, see Ch. 3, Sec. 2, I.

One year later, CARTER v. CARTER COAL CO., 298 U.S. 238, 56 S.Ct. 855, 80 L.Ed. 1160 (1936), per SUTHERLAND, J., expanded on *Schechter's* "direct effect" test ruling that the commerce clause did not give Congress power to require Bituminous Coal Code members to observe the hours and wages agreed upon between producers of two-thirds of the bituminous coal volume and one-half of the employed bituminous mine workers: "[T]he effect of the labor provisions of the [act] primarily falls upon production and not upon commerce; [p]roduction is a purely local activity. It follows that none of these essential antecedents of production constitutes a transaction in or forms any part of interstate commerce. [T]he local character of mining, of manufacturing, and of crop growing is a fact, and remains a fact, whatever may be done with the [products].

"That the production of every commodity intended for interstate sale and transportation has some effect upon interstate commerce may [be] freely granted; and we are brought to the final and decisive inquiry, whether here that effect is direct [or] indirect. The distinction is not formal, but substantial in the highest degree, as we pointed out in *Schechter*. 'If the commerce clause were construed [to] reach all enterprises and transactions which could be said to have an indirect effect upon interstate commerce, the federal authority would embrace practically all the activities of the people, and the authority of the state over its domestic concerns would exist only by sufferance of the federal [government].'

"Whether the effect of a given activity or condition is direct or indirect is not always easy to determine. The word 'direct' implies that the activity or condition invoked or blamed shall operate proximately—not mediately, remotely, or collater-ally—to produce the effect. It connotes the absence of an efficient intervening agency or condition. And the extent of the effect bears no logical relation to its character. The distinction between a direct and an indirect effect turns, not upon the magnitude of either the cause or the effect, but entirely upon the manner in which the effect has been brought about. If the production by one man of a single ton of coal intended for interstate sale and shipment, and actually so sold and shipped, affects interstate commerce indirectly, the effect does not become direct by multiplying the tonnage, or increasing the number of men employed, or adding to the expense or complexities of the business, or by all combined. It is quite true that rules of law are sometimes qualified by considerations of degree, as the government argues. But the matter of degree has no bearing upon the question here, since that question is not—What is the *extent* of the local activity or condition, or the *extent* of the effect produced upon interstate commerce? but— What is the *relation* between the activity or condition and the effect?

Kidd v. Pearson
Logic

– Production issue

– beyond Fed power

"Much stress is put upon the evils which come from the struggle between employers and employees over the matter of wages, working conditions, the right of collective bargaining, etc., and the resulting strikes, curtailment, and irregularity of production and effect on prices; and it is insisted that interstate commerce is *greatly* affected thereby. But [the] conclusive answer is that the evils are all local evils over which the federal government has no legislative control. [Such] effect as they may have upon commerce, however extensive it may be, is secondary and indirect. An increase in the greatness of the effect adds to its importance. It does not alter its character.

"[The] only perceptible difference between [*Schechter*] and this is that in the *Schechter Case* the federal power was asserted with respect to commodities which had come to rest after their interstate transportation; while here, the case deals with commodities at rest before interstate commerce has begun. That difference is without significance. The federal regulatory power ceases when interstate commercial intercourse ends; and, correlatively, the power does not attach until interstate commercial intercourse begins."[b]

B. EXPANSION OF COMMERCE POWER AFTER 1936

By the 1936 Presidential election the Court had dealt devastating blows to President Franklin D. Roosevelt's New Deal program for economic recovery. It had invalidated six federal laws designed to advance that program, four of major importance: the National Industrial Recovery Act and the Bituminous Coal Act, both supra, the Agricultural Adjustment Act, *United States v. Butler* (1936) (6–3), Sec. 3, II infra, and the Railway Pension Act, *Railroad Retirement Bd. v. Alton R.R.,* 295 U.S. 330, 55 S.Ct. 758, 79 L.Ed. 1468 (1935) (5–4).[a]

Only one New Deal measure aimed at the economic crisis had been sustained, the Gold Clause legislation. *Norman v. Baltimore & O.R. Co.,* 294 U.S. 240, 55

---

b. For the Court's additional ruling on unconstitutional delegation, see fn. a, p. 157.

Hughes, C.J., concurred in the result, stating only that "Congress may not use this protective authority [over commerce] as a pretext [to] regulate activities and relations within the states which affect interstate commerce only indirectly."

Cardozo, J., joined by Brandeis and Stone, JJ., found the labor provisions not ripe for decision, but would uphold the Code's provisions on fixing intrastate coal prices: "Mining and agriculture and manufacture are not interstate commerce considered by themselves, yet their relation to that commerce may be such that for the protection of the one there is need to regulate the other. *Schechter*. Sometimes it is said that the relation must be 'direct' to bring that power into play. In many circumstances such a description will be sufficiently precise to meet the needs of the occasion. But a great principle of constitutional law is not susceptible of comprehensive statement in an adjective. The underlying thought is merely this, that 'the law is not indifferent to considerations of degree.' It cannot be indifferent to them without an expansion of the commerce clause that would absorb or imperil the re-

served powers of the states. [Holmes, J., made the same point in *Diamond Glue Co. v. U.S. Glue Co.,* 187 U.S. 611, 616, 23 S.Ct. 206, 208, 47 L.Ed. 328 (1903).] At times, as in the case cited, the waves of causation will have radiated so far that their undulatory motion, if discernible at all, will be too faint or obscure, too broken by crosscurrents, to be heeded by the law. In such circumstances the holding is not directed at prices or wages considered in the abstract, but at prices or wages in particular conditions. The relation may be tenuous or the opposite according to the [facts.] Perhaps, if one group of adjectives is to be chosen in preference to another, 'intimate' and 'remote' will be found to be as good as any. At all events, 'direct' and 'indirect,' even if accepted as sufficient, must not be read too narrowly. A survey of the cases shows that the words have been interpreted with suppleness of adaptation and flexibility of meaning. The power is as broad as the need that evokes it."

a. The other two were the Farm Mortgage Act and the Municipal Bankruptcy Act. *Louisville Joint Stock Land Bank v. Radford,* 295 U.S. 555, 55 S.Ct. 854, 79 L.Ed. 1593 (1935) (9–0); *Ashton v. Cameron County Water Imp. Dist.,* 298 U.S. 513, 56 S.Ct. 892, 80 L.Ed. 1309 (1936) (5–4).

S.Ct. 407, 79 L.Ed. 885 (1935) (5–4). More vital Acts of the New Deal legislative program still awaited the Court's scrutiny. These included the National Labor Relations Act, the Social Security Act (both old age pensions and unemployment compensation), and the Public Utility Holding Company Act. In addition, new legislation was needed to replace the minimum labor standards lost in *Schechter* and *Carter Coal* and the control over agricultural surpluses lost in *Butler*.

Viewing his overwhelming victory in the 1936 elections as "an endorsement of his legislative program [despite] the recent Supreme Court opinions which seemingly blocked his path," President Roosevelt "determined not to permit the Court to flout the popular will by what he, as well as Justices Brandeis, Stone and Cardozo, felt to be a reactionary interpretation of the Constitution." Stern, supra at 677. The president sought congressional approval of what became known popularly as the "court packing" plan, which would have authorized appointment of as many as six new justices, one to sit in addition to each justice over seventy years of age. For the story of the battle over the plan, see Joseph Alsop & Turner Catledge, *168 Days* (1938); Robert H. Jackson, *The Struggle for Judicial Supremacy* (1941); 2 Merlo J. Pusey, *Charles Evans Hughes* 759–65 (1951); Alpheus T. Mason, *Harlan Fiske Stone and FDR's Court Plan,* 61 Yale L.J. 791 (1952); William E. Leuchtenburg, *The Origins of Franklin D. Roosevelt's "Court Packing" Plan,* 1966 Sup.Ct.Rev. 347–394. See also fn. n., Ch. 1, Sec. 3.

The first major commerce clause decision after *Carter,* handed down several months before Congress rejected the court-packing plan,[b] NLRB v. JONES & LAUGHLIN STEEL CORP., 301 U.S. 1, 57 S.Ct. 615, 81 L.Ed. 893 (1937), per HUGHES, C.J., upheld application of the National Labor Relations Act to the nation's fourth largest steel producer, with facilities throughout the country, most of whose production was shipped and sold in interstate commerce. The NLRB found that J & L had engaged in unfair labor practices by discharging employees at one of its plants.

— Labor relations effect commerce

"[Respondent's] argument rests upon the proposition that manufacturing in itself is not commerce. [Although] activities may be intrastate in character when separately considered, if they have such a close and substantial relation to interstate commerce that their control is essential or appropriate to protect that commerce from burdens and obstructions, Congress cannot be denied the power to exercise that control. Undoubtedly the scope of this power must be considered in the light of our dual system of government and may not be extended so as to embrace effects upon interstate commerce so indirect and remote that to embrace them, in view of our complex society, would effectually obliterate the distinction between what is national and what is local and create a completely centralized government. The question is necessarily one of degree.   *— goes against Carter Coal*

"[In] *Schechter,* we found that the effect there was so remote as to be beyond the federal power. To find 'immediacy or directness' there was to find it 'almost everywhere,' a result inconsistent with the maintenance of our federal system. In *Carter,* the Court was of the opinion that the provisions of the statute relating to production were invalid upon several grounds,—that there was improper delegation of legislative power, and that the requirements not only went beyond any sustainable measure of protection of interstate commerce but were also inconsistent with due process. These cases are not controlling here.

b. Two weeks earlier, *West Coast Hotel Co. v. Parrish* (1937), Ch. 5, Sec. 3, held that a state minimum wage law did not violate the fourteenth amendment due process clause, overruling several earlier decisions.

"[T]he stoppage of those operations by industrial strife would have a most serious effect upon interstate commerce. In view of respondent's far-flung activities, it is idle to say that the effect would be indirect or remote. It is obvious that it would be immediate and might be catastrophic. We are asked to shut our eyes to the plainest facts of our national life and to deal with the question of direct and indirect effects in an intellectual vacuum. Because there may be but indirect and remote effects upon interstate commerce in connection with a host of local enterprises throughout the country, it does not follow that other industrial activities do not have such a close and intimate relation to interstate commerce as to make the presence of industrial strife a matter of the most urgent national concern."

McReynolds J., joined by Van Devanter, Sutherland and Butler, JJ., dissented: "[At one plant,] ten men out of ten thousand were discharged; in the other cases only a few. The immediate effect in the factory may be to create discontent among all those employed and a strike may follow, which, in turn, may result in reducing production, which ultimately may reduce the volume of goods moving in interstate commerce. By this chain of indirect and progressively remote events we finally reach the evil with which it is said the legislation under consideration undertakes to deal. A more remote and indirect interference with interstate commerce or a more definite invasion of the powers reserved to the states is difficult, if not impossible, to imagine [—] far too indirect to justify congressional regulation. Almost anything—marriage, birth, death—may in some fashion affect commerce."

UNITED STATES v. DARBY
312 U.S. 100, 61 S.Ct. 451, 85 L.Ed. 609 (1941).

Justice Stone delivered the opinion of the Court. * * *

The Fair Labor Standards [Act's] purpose [is] to exclude from interstate commerce goods produced for the commerce and to prevent their production for interstate commerce, under conditions detrimental to the maintenance of the minimum standards of living necessary for health and general well-being; and to prevent the use of interstate commerce as the means of competition in the distribution of goods so produced, and as the means of spreading and perpetuating such substandard labor conditions among the workers of the several [states].

The indictment charges that appellee is engaged, in the state of Georgia, in the business of acquiring raw materials, which he manufactures into finished lumber with the intent when manufactured, to ship it in interstate [commerce].

The prohibition of shipment of the proscribed goods in interstate commerce. Section 15(a)(1) prohibits, and the indictment charges, the shipment in interstate commerce, of goods produced for interstate commerce by employees whose wages and hours of employment do not conform to the requirements of the Act. * * *

While manufacture is not of itself interstate commerce the shipment of manufactured goods interstate is such commerce and the prohibition of such shipment by Congress is indubitably a regulation of the commerce. The power to regulate [commerce] extends not only to those regulations which aid, foster and protect the commerce, but embraces those which prohibit it. It is conceded that the power of Congress to prohibit transportation in interstate commerce includes noxious articles, stolen articles, [and] articles such as intoxicating liquor or convict made goods, traffic in which is forbidden or restricted by the laws of the state of destination.

But it is said that the present prohibition falls within the scope of none of these categories; that while the prohibition is nominally a regulation of the commerce its motive or purpose is regulation of wages and hours of persons engaged in manufacture, the control of which has been reserved to the states and upon which Georgia and some of the states of destination have placed no restriction. [But] Congress, following its own conception of public policy concerning the restrictions which may appropriately be imposed on interstate commerce, is free to exclude from the commerce articles whose use in the states for which they are destined it may conceive to be injurious to the public health, morals or welfare even though the state has not sought to regulate their [use].

The motive and purpose of the present regulation are plainly to make effective the Congressional conception of public policy that interstate commerce should not be made the instrument of competition in the distribution of goods produced under substandard labor conditions, which competition is injurious to the commerce and to the states from and to which the commerce flows. The motive and purpose of a regulation of interstate commerce are matters for the legislative judgment upon the exercise of which the Constitution places no restriction and over, which the courts are given no control [citing cases on Congress' taxing power, Sec. 3, I infra]. Whatever their motive and purpose, regulations of commerce which do not infringe some constitutional prohibition are within the plenary power conferred on Congress by the Commerce Clause. Subject only to that limitation, presently to be considered [fn. a infra], we conclude that the prohibition of the shipment interstate of goods produced under the forbidden substandard labor conditions is within the constitutional authority of Congress.

[T]hese principles of constitutional interpretation have been so long and repeatedly recognized by this Court as applicable to the Commerce Clause, that there would be little occasion for repeating them now were it not for the decision of this Court twenty-two years ago in *Dagenhart*. In that case it was held by a bare majority of the Court over the powerful and now classic dissent of Mr. Justice Holmes setting forth the fundamental issues involved, that Congress was without power to exclude the products of child labor from interstate [commerce.]

Dagenhart has not been followed. The distinction on which the decision was rested that Congressional power to prohibit interstate commerce is limited to articles which in themselves have some harmful or deleterious property—a distinction which was novel when made and unsupported by any provision of the Constitution—has long since been abandoned. The thesis of the opinion that the motive of the prohibition or its effect to control in some measure the use or production within the states of the article thus excluded from the commerce can operate to deprive the regulation of its constitutional authority has long since ceased to have force. [It] should be and now is overruled.

Validity of the wage and hour requirements. Section 15(a)(2) and §§ 6 and 7 require employers to conform to the wage and hour provisions with respect to all employees engaged in the production of goods for interstate commerce. As appellee's employees are not alleged to be "engaged in interstate commerce" the validity of the prohibition turns on the question whether [their employment] in the production of goods for interstate commerce is so related to the commerce and so affects it as to be within the reach of the power of Congress to regulate it.

[The] purpose of the Act was [to] stop the initial step toward transportation, production with the purpose [of] transporting it. [T]he power of Congress to regulate interstate commerce extends to the regulation [of] activities intrastate which have a substantial effect on the commerce or the exercise of the Congressional power over it. In such legislation Congress has sometimes left it to the courts to determine whether the intrastate activities have the prohibited effect on the commerce, as in the Sherman Act. It has sometimes left it to an administrative board or agency to determine whether the activities sought to be regulated or prohibited have such effect, as in the case [of] the National Labor Relations Act. [And] sometimes Congress itself has said that a particular activity affects the commerce, as it did in the present Act, the Safety Appliance Act and the Railway Labor Act. In passing on the validity of legislation of the class last mentioned the only function of courts is to determine whether the particular activity regulated or prohibited is within the reach of the federal power.

Congress, having by the present Act adopted the policy of excluding from interstate commerce all goods produced for the commerce which do not conform to the specified labor standards, it may choose the means reasonably adapted to the attainment of the permitted end, even though they involve control of intrastate activities. Such legislation has often been sustained with respect to powers, other than the commerce power granted to the national government, when the means chosen, although not themselves within the granted power, were nevertheless deemed appropriate aids to the accomplishment of some purpose within an admitted power of the national government. [A] familiar like exercise of power is the regulation of intrastate transactions which are so commingled with or related to interstate commerce that all must be regulated if the interstate commerce is to be effectively controlled. *Shreveport; Wisconsin Railroad Comm.* [Similarly] Congress may require inspection and preventive treatment of all cattle in a disease infected area in order to prevent shipment in interstate commerce of some of the cattle without the treatment. [And] we have recently held that Congress in the exercise of its power to require inspection and grading of tobacco shipped in interstate commerce may compel such inspection and grading of all tobacco sold at local auction rooms from which a substantial part but not all of the tobacco sold is shipped in interstate commerce. *Currin v. Wallace,* 306 U.S. 1, 59 S.Ct. 379, 83 L.Ed. 441 (1939). * * *

We think also that § 15(a)(2), now under consideration, is sustainable independently of § 15(a)(1), which prohibits shipment or transportation of the proscribed goods. As we have said the evils aimed at by the Act are the spread of substandard labor conditions through the use of the facilities of interstate commerce for competition by the goods so produced with those produced under the prescribed or better labor conditions; and the consequent dislocation of the commerce itself caused by the impairment or destruction of local businesses by competition made effective through interstate commerce. The Act is thus directed at the suppression of a method or kind of competition in interstate commerce which it has in effect condemned as "unfair", as the Clayton Act, has condemned other "unfair methods of competition" made effective through interstate commerce. * * *

The means adopted by § 15(a)(2) for the protection of interstate commerce by the suppression of the production of the condemned goods for interstate commerce is so related to the commerce and so affects it as to be within the reach of the commerce power. Congress, to attain its objective in the suppression of nationwide competition in interstate commerce by goods produced under substandard labor conditions, has made no distinction as to the volume or amount of shipments in the commerce or of production for commerce by any particular shipper or producer. * * *

So far as *Carter* is inconsistent with this conclusion, its doctrine is limited in principle by the decisions under the Sherman Act and the National Labor Relations Act, which we have cited and which we follow.

Our conclusion is unaffected by the Tenth Amendment [which] states but a truism that all is retained which has not been surrendered. There is nothing in the history of its adoption to suggest that it was more than declaratory of the relationship between the national and state governments as it had been established by the Constitution before the amendment or that its purpose was other than to allay fears that the new national government might seek to exercise powers not granted, and that the states might not be able to exercise fully their reserved powers.[a]

Reversed.

Notes and Questions

1.   *Unanimity.* The unanimity in *Darby* can be attributed to the departure of the four justices who dissented in *Jones & Laughlin,* Butler, J., by death in 1938, and the other three by retirement: Van Devanter, J., in 1937, Sutherland, J., in 1938 and McReynolds, J., in 1940, just two days before the announcement of *Darby.* Of the five who joined the majority opinion in *Carter Coal,* only Roberts, J., remained, and his views appeared to have undergone much change since 1936.[b]

2.   *Power to exclude from interstate commerce.* (a) *Darby's* revival of *Lottery* and its progeny encouraged widespread use by Congress of its "police" power to exclude from interstate commerce commodities and activities thought harmful to the nation, though the harm itself often occurred only at a local level. (See note 3 after *Gibbons* supra and note 1 after *Lottery* supra.) Additional uses of this power include prohibitions on interstate transportation of stolen vehicles or other stolen goods, and of persons in furtherance of a scheme to defraud; interstate shipment of gambling devices and wagering materials, and of firearms to or by persons indicted or convicted of a serious crime; and interstate travel to incite, encourage or participate in a riot, or in aid of "racketeering enterprises."

(b)   *"Jurisdictional nexus."* What are the limits on Congress' "police" power through this use of the commerce clause? Consider Robert F. Nagel, *The Future of Federalism,* 46 Case W. Res. L.Rev. 643, 648 (1996): "[A]ny conceivable object of regulation will necessarily involve *something* that has traveled in interstate commerce. Everyone knows that schools, police departments, and families all purchase goods that have been a part of commerce. [T]he asserted tie to commerce would potentially allow national regulation of any imaginable activity." May Congress use this "jurisdictional nexus" with interstate commerce to regulate the curricula of schools that buy goods from out of state? To regulate child care providers that deal with parents who make purchases in interstate commerce? To regulate any tortfeasor who wears clothing that was shipped interstate? Of what relevance is the relationship between the movement of goods across state lines and the policy that Congress is seeking to achieve? See Thomas W. Merrill,

a.   The Court also held that the minimum wage and maximum hours provisions did not violate the due process clause of the fifth amendment, citing *West Coast Hotel Co. v. Parrish,* Ch. 5, Sec. 3.

b.   For recent discussion of the shifting positions of the justices, see Michael Ariens, *A Thrice–Told Tale, or Felix the Cat,* 107 Harv.

L.Rev. 620 (1994); Richard D. Friedman, *A Reaffirmation: The Authenticity of the Roberts Memorandum, or Felix the Non–Forger,* 142 U.Pa.L.Rev. 1985 (1994); Richard D. Friedman, *Switching Time and Other Thought Experiments: The Hughes Court and Constitutional Transformation"* 142 U.Pa.L.Rev. 1891 (1994).

Toward a Principled Interpretation of the Commerce Clause, 22 Harv.J.Law & Pub.Pol. 31, 39 (1998) ("we must ask whether the intent of Congress is to regulate commerce insofar as it affects the movement of matter and energy across state lines (a permissible objective) or whether it is to regulate commercial activity without regard to whether there is any effect on interstate movements (an impermissible usurpation of the states' police powers"); Harry Litman & Mark D. Greenberg, *Federal Power and Federalism: A Theory of Commerce–Clause Based Regulation on Traditionally State Crimes*, 47 Case W.Res.L.Rev. 921 (1997) ("an analogy to common law principles of liability is useful," i.e., proximate cause); Thomas R. Powell, *Vagaries and Varieties in Constitutional Interpretation* 63–70 (1956).

(c) *After interstate commerce ends.* May Congress use the commerce clause to pass a law requiring that anyone traveling in interstate commerce for the purpose of getting a divorce must obtain a divorce that meets federal standards? May Congress require compliance with federal divorce standards for anyone who has traveled in interstate commerce in the past or does so in the future? Of what relevance is the amount of time that has passed between the use of interstate commerce and the policy that Congress wishes to implement? What results under the following decisions:

UNITED STATES v. SULLIVAN, 332 U.S. 689, 68 S.Ct. 331, 92 L.Ed. 297 (1948), per BLACK, J. upheld the conviction of a retail druggist under the federal Food, Drug and Cosmetic Act for two pill boxes, in which he had placed 12 tablets, by failing to affix to the required warning label that was printed on the large bottle of pills bought from an in-state wholesaler, who had secured them through interstate commerce: "[The Act] was designed [to] safeguard the consumer by applying the Act to articles from the moment of their introduction into interstate commerce all the way to the moment of their delivery to the ultimate consumer. [We affirm] the constitutional power of Congress under the commerce clause to regulate the branding of articles that have completed an interstate shipment and are being held for future sales in purely local or intrastate commerce."[c]

SCARBOROUGH v. UNITED STATES, 431 U.S. 563, 97 S.Ct. 1963, 52 L.Ed.2d 582 (1977), per MARSHALL, J., interpreted a federal statute as making it a crime for a convicted felon to possess a firearm as long as there existed "the minimal nexus that the firearm have been, at some time, in interstate commerce, [with] little concern for when the nexus with commerce occurred"—even before the accused became a convicted felon. Although the Court did not resolve any constitutional issue, it indicated that "Congress [asserted] its full Commerce Clause power so as to cover all activity substantially affecting interstate commerce."

Of what relevance is it that "at the time of *Lottery*, most if not all of the states had decided that lotteries were immoral and had legislated against them"? Regan, fn. e, Sec. 1, at 576. Consider id.: "[T]here may have been good reason why a federal prohibition on the interstate transportation of lottery tickets was a necessary, or at least a very useful, aid to the states in the enforcement of their own choices about lotteries. Lottery tickets are small, portable, concealable, and in some views dangerous—like guns. Stamping out lotteries may have been something the states were individually incompetent to do, practically speaking. [But] there is all the difference in the world between Congress's legislating against lotteries just because it disapproves of them and Congress's legislating against

---

c. Rutledge, J., concurred. Frankfurter, J., dissented, joined by Reed and Jackson, JJ. All were concerned only with statutory construction.

lotteries to help the states give effect to their own judgments of disapproval. The former is not something we need the national government for."

3. *Power over local activities affecting commerce.* (a) WICKARD v. FILBURN, 317 U.S. 111, 63 S.Ct. 82, 87 L.Ed. 122 (1942), per JACKSON, J., upheld a penalty imposed under the Agricultural Adjustment Act of 1938 on Filburn for raising 239 bushels of wheat in excess of his marketing allotment. Filburn's practice was to plant a small acreage of wheat, to sell some, feed some to livestock, and use some for home-consumed flour and for seed: "[The commerce clause] question would merit little consideration since our decision in [*Darby*], except for the fact that this Act extends federal regulation to production not intended in any part for commerce but wholly for consumption on the farm. [T]he Government argues that the statute regulates neither production nor consumption, but only marketing; and, in the alternative, [is] sustainable as a 'necessary and proper' implementation of the power of Congress over interstate commerce.

"The Government's concern [is] attributable to a few dicta and decisions of this Court which might be understood to lay it down that activities such as 'production,' 'manufacturing,' and 'mining' are strictly 'local' and, except in special circumstances which are not present here, cannot be regulated under the commerce power because their effects upon interstate commerce are, as matter of law, only 'indirect.' [But] questions of the power of Congress are not to be decided by reference to any formula which would give controlling force to nomenclature such as 'production' and 'indirect' and foreclose consideration of the actual effects of the activity in question upon interstate commerce. [Once] an economic measure of the reach of the power granted to Congress in the Commerce Clause is accepted, questions of federal power cannot be decided simply by finding the activity in question to be 'production' nor can consideration of its economic effects be foreclosed by calling them 'indirect.' [E]ven if appellee's activity be local and though it may not be regarded as commerce, it may still, whatever its nature, be reached by Congress if it exerts a substantial economic effect on interstate commerce and this irrespective of whether such effect is what might at some earlier time have been defined as 'direct' or 'indirect.' * * *

"The wheat industry has been a problem industry for some years. Largely as a result of increased foreign production and import restrictions, * * * decline in the export trade has left a large surplus in production which in connection with an abnormally large supply of wheat and other grains in recent years caused congestion in a number of markets; tied up railroad cars; and caused elevators in some instances to turn away grains, and railroads to institute embargoes to prevent further congestion. * * *

"In the absence of regulation the price of wheat in the United States would be much affected by world conditions. During 1941 producers who cooperated with the Agricultural Adjustment program received an average price on the farm of about $1.16 a bushel as compared with the world market price of 40 cents a bushel. [In] 1940 the average percentage of the total wheat production that was sold in each state as measured by value ranged from 29 per cent thereof in Wisconsin to 90 per cent in Washington. [The] effect of consumption of home-grown wheat on interstate commerce is due to the fact that it constitutes the most variable factor in the disappearance of the wheat crop. Consumption on the farm where grown appears to vary in an amount greater than 20 per cent of average production. The total amount of wheat consumed as food varies but relatively little, and use as seed is relatively constant.

"The maintenance by government regulation of a price for wheat undoubtedly can be accomplished as effectively by sustaining or increasing the demand as by limiting the supply. The effect of the statute before us is to restrict the amount which may be produced for market and the extent as well to which one may forestall resort to the market by producing to meet his own needs. That appellee's own contribution to the demand for wheat may be trivial by itself is not enough to remove him from the scope of federal regulation where, as here, his contribution, taken together with that of many others similarly situated, is far from trivial. [*NLRB v. Fainblatt*, 306 U.S. 601, 59 S.Ct. 668, 83 L.Ed. 1014 (1939)[d]; *Darby*].

"It is well established by decisions of this Court that the power to regulate commerce includes the power to regulate the prices at which commodities in that commerce are dealt in and practices affecting such prices. One of the primary purposes of the Act in question was to increase the market price of wheat and to that end to limit the volume thereof that could affect the market. It can hardly be denied that a factor of such volume and variability as home-consumed wheat would have a substantial influence on price and market conditions. This may arise because being in marketable condition such wheat overhangs the market and if induced by rising prices tends to flow into the market and check price increases. But if we assume that it is never marketed, it supplies a need of the man who grew it which would otherwise be reflected by purchases in the open market. Home-grown wheat in this sense competes with wheat in commerce. The stimulation of commerce is a use of the regulatory function quite as definitely as prohibitions or restrictions thereon. This record leaves us in no doubt that Congress may properly have considered that wheat consumed on the farm where grown if wholly outside the scheme of regulation would have a substantial effect in defeating and obstructing its purpose to stimulate trade therein at increased prices."

(b) MARYLAND v. WIRTZ, 392 U.S. 183, 88 S.Ct. 2017, 20 L.Ed.2d 1020 (1968), per HARLAN, J., upheld expanded congressional coverage of the Fair Labor Standards Act (1) from employees "engaged in commerce or in the production of goods for commerce" to *all* employees of any "*enterprise*" so engaged and (2) to include hospitals, nursing homes, and educational institutions—elementary, secondary or higher education—whether private or public.[e] The "enterprise" extension was justified on two grounds: (1) the competitive position of an interstate enterprise is affected by *all* its labor costs, not simply the costs of employees producing goods for commerce; and (2) a labor dispute caused by substandard labor conditions "among any group of employees, whether or not they are personally engaged in commerce or production, may lead to strife disrupting an entire enterprise." Extension of coverage to schools and hospitals was sustained under the commerce power on the ground that these institutions are major users of goods imported from other states, and work stoppages involving their employees would interrupt this flow of goods across state lines.

(c) As indicated in *Wickard* and *Wirtz*, in addition to regulating interstate movement of persons or commodities to achieve police-type objectives, Congress has increasingly resorted to direct regulation of the undesired local activity when

---

d. *Fainblatt* upheld application of the National Labor Relations Act to a New Jersey shop where 60 employees did piece work for a New York company: "[C]ommerce may be affected in the same manner and to the same extent in proportion to its volume, whether it be great or small. [There] are not a few industries in the United States which, though conducted in relatively small units, contribute in the aggregate a vast volume of interstate commerce."

e. For application of the Act to state government activities, see Sec. 5 infra.

it "in any way or degree obstructs, delays or adversely affects [interstate] commerce."[f] In some cases, Congress has simply concluded that the controlled local activity adversely affects interstate commerce.[g] For example, Title VIII of the Organized Crime Control Act of 1970 makes it a federal offense for five or more persons to engage in a "gambling business" illegal under state law. And Title IX of that Act, the now widely used RICO ("Racketeer Influenced and Corrupt Organizations") statute, makes it a federal offense for "any person employed by or associated with any enterprise engaged in, or the activities of which affect, interstate or foreign commerce, [to] participate in the conduct" of its affairs through a "pattern of racketeering activity," defined to embrace two or more of a wide range of acts made criminal by state or federal law.

May these statutes be applied to instances of local gambling or local racketeering not shown to be related to organized crime or to have any discernable impact on interstate commerce? PEREZ v. UNITED STATES, 402 U.S. 146, 91 S.Ct. 1357, 28 L.Ed.2d 686 (1971), per DOUGLAS, J., upheld the federal Consumer Credit Protection Act's ban on "extortionate credit transactions, though purely intrastate, [because they] may in the judgment of Congress affect interstate commerce. [R]eports and hearings [supplied] Congress with the knowledge that the loan shark racket provides organized crime with its second most lucrative source of revenue, exacts millions from the pockets of people, coerces its victims into the commission of crimes against property, and causes the takeover by racketeers of legitimate businesses.

"We have mentioned in detail the economic, financial, and social setting of the problem as revealed to Congress [not] to infer that Congress need make particularized findings in order to legislate [but to] answer the impassioned plea of petitioner that all that is involved in loan sharking is a traditionally local activity. It appears, instead, that loan sharking in its national setting is one way organized interstate crime holds its guns to the heads of the poor and the rich alike and syphons funds from numerous localities to finance its national operations."

The Court rejected the contention that the extortionate activities of Perez were not shown to have any effect on commerce: "Where the *class of activities* is regulated and that *class* is within the reach of federal power, the courts have no power 'to excise, as trivial, individual instances' of the class. *Wirtz*."

STEWART, J., dissented: "[I]t is not enough to say that loan sharking is a national problem, for all crime is a national problem. It is not enough to say that some loan sharking has interstate characteristics, for any crime may have an interstate setting. And the circumstance that loan sharking has an adverse impact on interstate business is not a distinguishing attribute, for interstate business suffers from almost all criminal activity, be it shoplifting or violence in the streets. [The] definition and prosecution of local, intrastate crime are reserved to the States under the Ninth and Tenth Amendments."

4. *"Aggregation" principle (or "cumulative impact" doctrine).* (a) Does *Wickard's* "trivial by itself [but] taken together with that of many others similarly situated" approach give Congress effectively unlimited power? Would this be ameliorated by limiting the commerce power to products and services that have a

---

f. See, e.g., 18 U.S.C.A. § 231 (teaching another to use a firearm or explosive for use in a civil disorder, or interference with fireman or police carrying out duties during civil disorder, where commerce is adversely affected).

g. For a comprehensive summary and discussion of these developments, see Boris I. Bittker, *Regulation of Interstate and Foreign Commerce* chs. 3–5 (1999).

unified national market and thus produce interstate competition? See Regan, supra at 588–90. Consider Grant S. Nelson & Robert J. Pushaw, Jr., *Rethinking the Commerce Clause: Applying First Principles to Uphold Federal Commercial Regulations but Preserve State Control Over Social Issues*, 85 Ia.L.Rev. 1, 111 n. 518 (1999): "This argument is appealing because it limits the *Wickard* 'aggregating' principle to its factual context—a fungible commodity with an interstate market (e.g., wheat) where transactions in one state influence those in another. Aggregation becomes progressively more attenuated as it is extended to more unique goods, to small service providers, and to businesses lacking a multistate organization. Thus, for example, the price charged by an independent, family-run laundry in Los Angeles to press a shirt does not seem to bear any obvious relation to the price of the identical service in Peoria, Illinois. [But] in our integrated national economy almost any commercial activity might reasonably be viewed as affecting interstate commerce. [M]any restaurants and laundries are part of huge franchises, and those that are not compete against these national chains. Hence, it would make little sense to require McDonald's to pay a minimum wage, but not a local burger joint that competes with McDonald's."

(b) *Products "similarly situated."* The law in *Wickard* regulated corn, cotton, rice, peanuts and tobacco, as well as wheat. Could production for home consumption of all these be regulated by "aggregating" them with wheat, even though, unlike wheat, home consumption of none of them had any significant impact on interstate prices? For the view that "that kind of aggregation would justify any federal legislation," see John C. Nagle, *The Commerce Clause Meets the Delhi Sands Flower–Loving Fly*, 97 Mich.L.Rev. 174 (1998) (discussing the Endangered Species Act).

5. *Analogous rationale for war powers.* Invoking the war powers, WOODS v. CLOYD W. MILLER CO., 333 U.S. 138, 68 S.Ct. 421, 92 L.Ed. 596 (1948), per Douglas, J., upheld continuation of federal rent control long after hostilities had ceased, using effect-type reasoning analogous to the foregoing commerce clause opinions: "The legislative history of the present Act makes abundantly clear that there has not yet been eliminated the deficit in housing which in considerable measure was caused by the heavy demobilization of veterans and by the cessation or reduction in residential construction during the period of hostilities due to the allocation of building materials to military projects. Since the war effort contributed heavily to that deficit, Congress has the power even after the cessation of hostilities to act to control the forces that a short supply of the needed article created. If that were not true, the Necessary and Proper Clause would be drastically limited in its application to the several war powers. * * *

"We recognize the force of the argument that the effects of war under modern conditions may be felt in the economy for years and years, and that if the war power can be used in days of peace to treat all the wounds which war inflicts on our society, it may not only swallow up all other powers of Congress but largely obliterate the Ninth and the Tenth Amendments as well. There are no such implications in today's decision. [W]e cannot assume that Congress is not alert to its constitutional responsibilities. And the question whether the war power has been properly employed in cases such as this is open to judicial inquiry."[h]

---

h. For other economic regulations based on the war powers, see *Yakus v. United States,* Ch.3, Sec.2, I.; *Bowles v. Willingham,* 321 U.S. 503, 64 S.Ct. 641, 88 L.Ed. 892 (1944).

III. PROTECTION OF OTHER INTERESTS THROUGH THE COMMERCE CLAUSE

HEART OF ATLANTA MOTEL, INC. v. UNITED STATES

379 U.S. 241, 85 S.Ct. 348, 13 L.Ed.2d 258 (1964).

JUSTICE CLARK delivered the opinion of the Court.

[The Court affirmed an injunction restraining appellant from violating Sec. 201 of the Civil Rights Act of 1964.[a]]

Appellant owns and operates the Heart of Atlanta Motel which has 216 rooms, [readily] accessible to interstate [and] state highways. [Appellant] solicits patronage from outside the State of Georgia through various national advertising [media]; it maintains over 50 billboards and highway signs within the State[;] it accepts convention trade from outside Georgia and approximately 75% of its registered guests are from out of State. Prior to passage of the Act the motel had followed a practice of refusing to rent rooms to Negroes. [The] sole question posed is, therefore, the constitutionality of the Civil Rights Act of 1964 as applied to these facts. * * *

The Senate Commerce Committee made it quite clear that the fundamental object of Title II was to vindicate [pursuant to the equal protection clause of the fourteenth amendment] "the deprivation of personal dignity that surely accompanies denials of equal access to public establishments." At the same time, however, it noted that such an objective has been and could be readily achieved "by congressional action based on the commerce power of the Constitution." Our study of the legislative record [has] brought us to the conclusion that Congress possessed ample power [under the commerce clause], and we have therefore not considered the other grounds relied upon. * * *

While the Act [carried] no congressional findings the [legislative record is] replete with evidence of the burdens that discrimination by race or color places upon interstate commerce. This testimony included the fact that our people have become increasingly mobile with millions of all races traveling from State to State; that Negroes in particular have been the subject of discrimination in transient accommodations, having to travel great distances to secure the same; that often they have been unable to obtain accommodations and have had to call upon friends to put them up overnight; and that these conditions had become so acute as to require the listing of available lodging for Negroes in a special guidebook which was itself "dramatic testimony of the difficulties" Negroes encounter in travel. These exclusionary practices were found to be nationwide, the Under Secretary of Commerce testifying that there is "no question that this discrimination in the North still exists to a large degree" and in the West and Midwest as

---

a. Sec. 201(a) provided: "All persons shall be entitled to the full and equal enjoyment of the goods, services, facilities, [and] accommodations of any place of public accommodation * * * without discrimination or segregation on the ground of race, color, religion, or national origin." Sec. 201(b) defined of several types of establishments as "a place of public accommodation [if] its operations affect commerce [defined to include all interstate and foreign commerce], or if discrimination or segregation by it is supported by State action." Sec. 201(c) provided that "any inn, hotel, motel or other establishment which provides lodging to transient guests" is a place of public accommodation whose "operations * * * affect commerce," except when a live-in owner rents five or less rooms.

Sec. 201(d) defined the banned "discrimination or segregation * * * supported by State action" as that "carried on under color of any law, statute, ordinance or regulation; [or] under color of any custom or usage required or enforced by officials of the State [or] required by action of the State." Section 202 declared the broader right of "all persons to be free [at] *any establishment or place*" from State-required discrimination.

well. This testimony indicated a qualitative as well as quantitative effect on interstate travel by Negroes. The former was the obvious impairment of the Negro traveler's pleasure and convenience that resulted when he continually was uncertain of finding lodging. As for the latter, there was evidence that this uncertainty stemming from racial discrimination had the effect of discouraging travel on the part of a substantial portion of the Negro community. [T]he voluminous testimony presents overwhelming evidence that discrimination by hotels and motels impedes interstate travel.

[The] same interest in protecting interstate commerce which led Congress to deal with segregation in interstate carriers and the white slave traffic has prompted it to extend the exercise of its power to gambling, to criminal enterprises, to deceptive practices in the sale of products, to fraudulent security transactions, to misbranding of drugs, [to] discrimination against shippers, to the protection of small business from injurious price cutting, [and] to racial discrimination by owners and managers of terminal restaurants.

That Congress was legislating against moral wrongs in many of these areas rendered its enactments no less valid. In framing Title II of this Act Congress was also dealing with what it considered a moral problem. But that fact does not detract from the overwhelming evidence of the disruptive effect that racial discrimination has had on commercial intercourse. [G]iven this basis for the exercise of its power, Congress was not restricted by the fact that the particular obstruction to interstate commerce with which it was dealing was also deemed a moral and social wrong.

[T]he power of Congress to promote interstate commerce also includes the power to regulate the local incidents thereof, including local activities in both the States of origin and destination, which might have a substantial and harmful effect upon that commerce. One need only examine the evidence which we have discussed above to see that Congress may—as it has—prohibit racial discrimination by motels serving travelers, however "local" their operations may appear.

* * *

[The concurring opinions of Douglas and Goldberg, JJ., appear after *Katzenbach v. McClung, infra.*]

———————

KATZENBACH v. McCLUNG, 379 U.S. 294, 85 S.Ct. 377, 13 L.Ed.2d 290 (1964), per CLARK, J., upheld application of Sec. 201 to Ollie's Barbecue, a Birmingham restaurant eleven blocks from an interstate highway. It catered to a family and white collar trade with a take-out service for African Americans, whom it had refused to serve since opening in 1927: "There is no claim that interstate travelers frequented the restaurant. The sole question, therefore, narrows down to whether Title II, as applied to a restaurant receiving about $70,000 worth of food which has moved in commerce [out of a total of $150,000], is a valid exercise of the power of Congress.[b] The [legislative] record is replete with testimony of the burdens placed on interstate commerce by racial discrimination in restaurants. A comparison of per capita spending by Negroes in restaurants, theaters, and like

---

b. Sec. 201(b)(2) classified as a public accommodation, "any restaurant [or] other facility principally engaged in selling food for consumption on the premises." Sec. 201(c)(2) stated that the operations of such an establishment "affect commerce [if] it serves or offers to serve interstate travelers or a substantial portion of the food it serves [has] moved in commerce."

establishments indicated less spending, after discounting income differences, in areas where discrimination is widely practiced. This condition, which was especially aggravated in the South, was attributed in the testimony of the Under Secretary of Commerce to racial segregation. This diminutive spending springing from a refusal to serve Negroes and their total loss as customers has, regardless of the absence of direct evidence, a close connection to interstate commerce. The fewer customers a restaurant enjoys the less food it sells and consequently the less it buys. [In] addition, the Attorney General testified that this type of discrimination imposed 'an artificial restriction on the market' and interfered with the flow of merchandise. [In] addition, there were many references to discriminatory situations causing wide unrest and having a depressant effect on general business conditions in the respective communities.

"Moreover there was an impressive array of testimony that discrimination in restaurants had a direct and highly restrictive effect upon interstate travel by Negroes. This resulted, it was said, because discrimination practices prevent Negroes from buying prepared food served on the premises while on a trip, except in isolated and unkempt restaurants and under most unsatisfactory and often unpleasant conditions. This obviously discourages travel and obstructs interstate commerce for one can hardly travel without eating. Likewise, it was said, that discrimination deterred professional, as well as skilled, people from moving into areas where such practices occurred and thereby caused industry to be reluctant to establish there.

"We believe that this testimony afforded ample basis for the conclusion that established restaurants in such areas sold less interstate goods because of the discrimination, that interstate travel was obstructed directly by it, that business in general suffered and that many new businesses refrained from establishing there as a result of it. * * *

"It goes without saying that, viewed in isolation, the volume of food purchased by Ollie's Barbecue from sources supplied from out of state was insignificant when compared with the total foodstuffs moving in commerce. But, as [said] in *Wickard:* 'That appellee's own contribution to the demand for wheat may be trivial by itself is not enough to remove him from the scope of federal regulation where, as here, his contribution, taken together with that of many others similarly situated, is far from trivial.'

"[We] must conclude that while the focus of the legislation was on the individual restaurant's relation to interstate commerce, Congress appropriately considered the importance of that connection with the knowledge that the discrimination was but 'representative of many others throughout the country, the total incidence of which if left unchecked may well become far-reaching in its harm to commerce.'

"[Appellees] object to the omission of a provision for a case-by-case determination—judicial or administrative—that racial discrimination in a particular restaurant affects commerce. [But here, as *in Darby*], Congress has determined for itself that refusals of service to Negroes have imposed burdens both upon the interstate flow of food and upon the movement of products generally. Of course, the mere fact that Congress has said when particular activity shall be deemed to affect commerce does not preclude further examination by this Court. But where we find that the legislators, in light of the facts and testimony before them, have a <u>rational basis</u> for finding a chosen regulatory scheme necessary to the protection of commerce, our investigation is at an end. * * *

4. If statute does pass rational review, purpose for act is irrelevant

"The absence of direct evidence connecting discriminatory restaurant service with the flow of interstate food, a factor on which the appellees place much reliance, is not, given the evidence as to the effect of such practices on other aspects of commerce, a crucial matter.

"The [Act], as here applied, we find to be plainly appropriate in the resolution of what the Congress found to be a national commercial problem of the first magnitude."

DOUGLAS, J., concurred: "Though I join the Court's opinion, I am somewhat reluctant [to] rest solely on the Commerce Clause. My reluctance is not due to any conviction that Congress lacks power to regulate commerce in the interests of human rights. It is rather my belief that the right of people to be free of state action that discriminates against them because of race * * *, 'occupies a more protected position in our constitutional system than does the movement of cattle, fruit, steel and coal across state lines.'

"[Hence] I would prefer to rest on the assertion of legislative power contained in § 5 of the Fourteenth Amendment [which] would have a more settling effect, making unnecessary litigation over whether a particular restaurant or inn is within the commerce definitions of the Act or whether a particular customer is an interstate traveler."[c]

Notes and Questions

1. *The Court's reasoning.* (a) *Congress' "motive."* Do you agree that the fact "that Congress was legislating against moral wrongs" should "render its enactments no less valid"? Does (should) it make any difference that the *Civil Rights Act Cases* were based on the "regulation of local activities that affect commerce" rationale, in contrast to *Lottery*'s and *Darby*'s "plenary power over interstate commerce"?

(b) *Standard of review.* Do you agree that if Congress, "in light of the facts and testimony before [it, has] a rational basis for finding a chosen regulatory scheme necessary to the protection of commerce," then the Court's "investigation is at an end"? Consider Richard A. Epstein, *Constitutional Faith and the Commerce Clause*, 71 Not.D.L.Rev. 167, 188–89 (1996): "The basic design of the Constitution sought to achieve some balance between the powers ceded [to the union] and the powers retained by the states. [This] delicate balance requires that both forms of error have about the same weight, so that the right standard of review under the Commerce Clause [should provide for] a rough parity between the two kinds of error costs."

2. *Employment.* (a) Title VII of the Civil Rights Act of 1964 prohibits discrimination in employment practices based on "race, color, religion, sex, or national origin" when an employer with 25 or more employees is "engaged in an industry affecting commerce," defined as one "in commerce or in which a labor dispute would hinder or obstruct commerce or the free flow of commerce." The Age Discrimination in Employment Act of 1967 also prohibits discrimination in employment because of an individual's age in "industries affecting commerce" as defined above for the Civil Rights Act. On what commerce clause reasoning can such national regulation best be sustained?

c. Goldberg, J., also joined the opinion of the Court but in a separate opinion stated his view that the fourteenth amendment also authorized enactment of the Civil Rights Act, stressing that its "primary purpose" was "vindication of human dignity."

3. *Abatement of trespass convictions.* In a companion case to *Heart of Atlanta* and *McClung*, HAMM v. ROCK HILL, 379 U.S. 306, 85 S.Ct. 384, 13 L.Ed.2d 300 (1964), per CLARK, J., vacated state trespass convictions for peaceful sit-ins at white lunch counters, then pending on appeal in the Supreme Court. Though the convictions had been affirmed in state courts before the Civil Rights Act, the Act had "substituted a right for a crime" under state law, and, "by virtue of the Supremacy Clause," Congress had the power to extend immunity to state prosecutions still pending in the Court. "Even if [it is] true" that allowing the convictions to stand might not affect interstate commerce, Congress "clearly intended to eradicate an unhappy chapter in our history." This justified applying to these state court convictions "the principle of abatement so firmly embedded in our jurisprudence," based on a rule of statutory construction that enactment of a federal statute making former criminal conduct lawful abates federal convictions still under review. Black, Harlan, Stewart and White, JJ., dissented on the ground that Congress did not intend retroactive effect. HARLAN, J., added: "Moreover, the contrary conclusion would confront us with constitutional questions of the gravest import, for the legislative record is barren of any evidence showing that giving effect to *past* state trespass convictions would result in placing any burden on *present* interstate commerce. Such evidence, at the very least, would be a prerequisite to the validity of any purported exercise of the Commerce power in this regard."

4. *Land regulation.* HODEL v. VIRGINIA SURFACE MINING AND REC-LAMATION ASS'N, 452 U.S. 264, 101 S.Ct. 2352, 69 L.Ed.2d 1 (1981), per MARSHALL, J., unanimously upheld the Surface Mining Control and Reclamation Act of 1977: "In light of the evidence available to Congress[a] and the detailed consideration that the legislation received, we cannot say that Congress did not have a rational basis for concluding that surface coal mining has substantial effects on interstate commerce."[b]

REHNQUIST, J., concurred in the judgment, emphasizing that "there *are* constitutional limits on the power of Congress to regulate pursuant to the Commerce Clause. [I]t has long been established that the commerce power does not reach activity which merely 'affects' interstate commerce. There must instead be a showing that regulated activity has a *substantial effect* on that commerce. [Moreover,] simply because Congress may conclude that a particular activity substantially affects interstate commerce does not necessarily make it so. Congress' findings must be supported by a 'rational basis' and are reviewable by the courts."

IV. NEW LIMITATIONS AT THE END OF THE 20th CENTURY

"Violence against woman Act"

UNITED STATES v. MORRISON
529 U.S. 598, 120 S.Ct. 1740, 146 L.Ed.2d 658 (2000).

CHIEF JUSTICE REHNQUIST delivered the opinion of the Court.

[Petitioner Brzonkala, alleging that respondent, a fellow student at Virginia Polytechnic Institute, had assaulted and repeatedly raped her, sued him under 42

---

a. The opinion recited the following findings of Congress: "[M]any surface mining operations result in disturbances of surface areas that burden and adversely affect commerce and the public welfare by destroying or diminishing the utility of land for commercial, industrial, residential, recreational, agricultural, and forestry purposes, by causing erosion and landslides, by contributing to floods, by polluting the water, by destroying fish and wildlife habitats, by impairing natural beauty, by damaging the property of citizens, by creating hazards dangerous to life and property by degrading the quality of life in local communities, and by counteracting governmental programs and efforts to conserve soil, water, and other natural resources."

b. The opinion expressly rejected the claim that "land as such" is not subject to regulation under the commerce clause.

U.S.C. § 13981 (part of the Violence Against Women Act of 1984) which provides a federal civil remedy for the victims of gender-motivated violence. The United States intervened to defend § 13981's constitutionality.]

As we discussed at length in *United States v. Lopez*, 514 U.S. 549, 115 S.Ct. 1624, 131 L.Ed.2d 626 (1995), our interpretation of the Commerce Clause has changed as our Nation has developed. [I]n the years since *Jones & Laughlin*, Congress has had considerably greater latitude in regulating conduct and transactions under the Commerce Clause than our previous case law permitted.

Lopez emphasized, however, [that] Congress' regulatory authority is not without effective bounds. [In] *Jones & Laughlin*, the Court warned that the scope of the interstate commerce power "must be considered in the light of our dual system of government and may not be extended so as to embrace effects upon interstate commerce so indirect and remote that to embrace them, in view of our complex society, would effectually obliterate the distinction between what is national and what is local and create a completely centralized government."

As we observed in *Lopez*, modern Commerce Clause jurisprudence has "identified three broad categories of activity that Congress may regulate under its commerce power." "First, Congress may regulate the use of the channels of interstate commerce" (citing *Heart of Atlanta*; *Darby*). "Second, Congress is empowered to regulate and protect the instrumentalities of interstate commerce, or persons or things in interstate commerce, even though the threat may come only from intrastate activities" (citing *Shreveport*). "Finally, Congress' commerce authority includes the power to regulate those activities having a substantial relation to interstate commerce, i.e., those activities that substantially affect interstate commerce" (citing *Jones & Laughlin*).

Petitioners [seek] to sustain § 13981 as a regulation of activity that substantially affects interstate commerce. Given § 13981's focus on gender-motivated violence wherever it occurs (rather than violence directed at the instrumentalities of interstate commerce, interstate markets, or things or persons in interstate commerce), we agree that this is the proper inquiry.

[In] *Lopez*, we held that the Gun–Free School Zones Act of 1990, 18 U.S.C. § 922(q)(1)(A), which made it a federal crime to knowingly possess a firearm in a school zone, exceeded Congress' authority under the Commerce Clause. Several significant considerations contributed to our decision.

First, we observed that § 922(q) was "a criminal statute that by its terms has nothing to do with 'commerce' or any sort of economic enterprise, however broadly one might define those terms." [A] fair reading of *Lopez* shows that the noneconomic, criminal nature of the conduct at issue was central to our decision in that case. See, e.g., ("Even *Wickard*, which is perhaps the most far reaching example of Commerce Clause authority over intrastate activity, involved economic activity in a way that the possession of a gun in a school zone does not"), ("Admittedly, a determination whether an intrastate activity is commercial or noncommercial may in some cases result in legal uncertainty. But, so long as Congress' authority is limited to those powers enumerated in the Constitution, and so long as those enumerated powers are interpreted as having judicially enforceable outer limits, congressional legislation under the Commerce Clause always will engender 'legal uncertainty'"), ("The possession of a gun in a local school zone is in no sense an economic activity that might, through repetition elsewhere, substantially affect any sort of interstate commerce"); see also id. (Kennedy, J., concurring) (stating that *Lopez* did not alter our "practical conception of commercial regulation" and that Congress may "regulate in the commercial sphere on the assumption that we have a single market and a unified purpose to build a stable national economy"), ("Were the Federal Government to take over the regulation of entire areas of traditional state concern, areas having nothing to do with the regulation of commercial activities, the boundaries between the spheres of federal and state authority would blur"), ("[In] a sense any conduct in this interdependent world of ours has an ultimate commercial origin or consequence, but we have not yet said the commerce power may reach so far"). * * *

The second consideration that we found important in analyzing § 922(q) was that the statute contained "no express jurisdictional element which might limit its reach to a discrete set of firearm possessions that additionally have an explicit connection with or effect on interstate commerce." Such a jurisdictional element may establish that the enactment is in pursuance of Congress' regulation of interstate commerce.[a]

Third, we noted that neither § 922(q) "nor its legislative history contains express congressional findings regarding the effects upon interstate commerce of gun possession in a school zone." While "Congress normally is not required to make formal findings as to the substantial burdens that an activity has on interstate commerce," (citing *McClung, Perez*), the existence of such findings may "enable us to evaluate the legislative judgment that the activity in question substantially affects interstate commerce, even though no such substantial effect [is] visible to the naked eye."

Finally, our decision in *Lopez* rested in part on the fact that the link between gun possession and a substantial effect on interstate commerce was attenuated. The United States argued that the possession of guns may lead to violent crime, and that violent crime "can be expected to affect the functioning of the national economy in two ways. First, the costs of violent crime are substantial, and, through the mechanism of insurance, those costs are spread throughout the population. Second, violent crime reduces the willingness of individuals to travel to areas within the country that are perceived to be unsafe." The Government also argued that the presence of guns at schools poses a threat to the educational process, which in turn threatens to produce a less efficient and productive workforce, which will negatively affect national productivity and thus interstate commerce.

We rejected these "costs of crime" and "national productivity" arguments because they would permit Congress to "regulate not only all violent crime, but all activities that might lead to violent crime, regardless of how tenuously they relate to interstate commerce." We noted that, under this but-for reasoning: "Congress could regulate any activity that it found was related to the economic productivity of individual citizens: family law (including marriage, divorce, and child custody),[b] for example. Under these theories, [it] is difficult to perceive any limitation on

a. After *Lopez*, Congress amended the Gun–Free School Zones Act to add that the prosecution must demonstrate that the gun "has moved in or otherwise affects interstate or foreign commerce."

b. See also Holmes, J., dissenting in *Northern Securities Co. v. United States*, 193 U.S. 197, 24 S.Ct. 436, 48 L.Ed. 679 (1904): "Commerce depends upon population, but Congress could not, on that ground, undertake to regulate marriage and divorce. [Otherwise,] I can see no part of the conduct of life with which on similar principles Congress might not interfere."

federal power, even in areas such as criminal law enforcement or education where States historically have been sovereign.[c] Thus, if we were to accept the Government's arguments, we are hard pressed to posit any activity by an individual that Congress is without power to regulate."

With these principles underlying our Commerce Clause jurisprudence as reference points, the proper resolution of the present cases is clear. Gender-motivated crimes of violence are not, in any sense of the phrase, economic activity. While we need not adopt a categorical rule against aggregating the effects of any noneconomic activity in order to decide these cases, thus far in our Nation's history our cases have upheld Commerce Clause regulation of intrastate activity only where that activity is economic in nature.

Like the Gun–Free School Zones Act at issue in *Lopez*, § 13981 contains no jurisdictional element establishing that the federal cause of action is in pursuance of Congress' power to regulate interstate commerce. Although *Lopez* makes clear that such a jurisdictional element would lend support to the argument that § 13981 is sufficiently tied to interstate commerce, Congress elected to cast § 13981's remedy over a wider, and more purely intrastate, body of violent crime.[5]

In contrast with the lack of congressional findings that we faced in *Lopez*, § 13981 is supported by numerous findings regarding the serious impact that gender-motivated violence has on victims and their families. But [as] we stated in *Lopez*, " 'Simply because Congress may conclude that a particular activity substantially affects interstate commerce does not necessarily make it so.' " (quoting *Hodel* (Rehnquist, J., concurring in judgment)). Rather, " 'whether particular operations affect interstate commerce sufficiently to come under the constitutional power of Congress to regulate them is ultimately a judicial rather than a legislative question, and can be settled finally only by this Court.' " (quoting *Heart of Atlanta* (Black, J., concurring)).

In these cases, Congress [found] that gender-motivated violence affects interstate commerce "by deterring potential victims from traveling interstate, from engaging in employment in interstate business, and from transacting with business, and in places involved in interstate commerce; [by] diminishing national productivity, increasing medical and other costs, and decreasing the supply of and the demand for interstate products." Given these findings and petitioners' arguments, the concern that we expressed in *Lopez* that Congress might use the Commerce Clause to completely obliterate the Constitution's distinction between national and local authority seems well founded. The reasoning that petitioners advance seeks to follow the but-for causal chain from the initial occurrence of violent crime (the suppression of which has always been the prime object of the

---

c. See also Douglas, J., joined by Whittaker, J., dissenting in *United States v. Oregon*, 366 U.S. 643, 81 S.Ct. 1278, 6 L.Ed.2d 575 (1961) (upholding federal escheat to United States of property of veteran who dies in veterans hospital without will or heirs): "[W]hen the Federal Government enters a field as historically local as the administration of decedents' estates, some clear relation of the asserted power to one of the delegated powers should be shown. [Today's] decision does not square with our conception of federalism."

5. Title 42 U.S.C. § 13981 is not the sole provision of the Violence Against Women Act of 1994 to provide a federal remedy for gender-

motivated crime. Section 40221(a) of the Act creates a federal criminal remedy to punish "interstate crimes of abuse including crimes committed against spouses or intimate partners during interstate travel and crimes committed by spouses or intimate partners who cross State lines to continue the abuse." [The] Courts of Appeals have uniformly upheld this criminal sanction as an appropriate exercise of Congress' Commerce Clause authority, reasoning that the provision properly falls within the first of *Lopez's* categories as it regulates the use of channels of interstate commerce—i.e., the use of the interstate transportation routes through which persons and goods move.

States' police power) to every attenuated effect upon interstate commerce. If accepted, petitioners' reasoning would allow Congress to regulate any crime as long as the nationwide, aggregated impact of that crime has substantial effects on employment, production, transit, or consumption. Indeed, if Congress may regulate gender-motivated violence, it would be able to regulate murder or any other type of violence since gender-motivated violence, as a subset of all violent crime, is certain to have lesser economic impacts than the larger class of which it is a part.[7]

[The] regulation and punishment of intrastate violence that is not directed at the instrumentalities, channels, or goods involved in interstate commerce has always been the province of the States. See, e.g., *Cohens v. Virginia,* (Marshall, C. J.) (stating that Congress "has no general right to punish murder committed within any of the States," and that it is "clear [that] congress cannot punish felonies generally").[d] Indeed, we can think of no better example of the police power, which the Founders denied the National Government and reposed in the States, than the suppression of violent crime and vindication of its victims. * * *

[The issue of Congress' power to enact § 13981 under § 5 of the fourteenth amendment is discussed in Ch. 11, Sec. 2.]

JUSTICE THOMAS, concurring.

The majority opinion correctly applies our decision in *Lopez,* and I join it in full. I write separately only to express my view that the very notion of a "substantial effects" test under the Commerce Clause is inconsistent with the original understanding of Congress' powers and with this Court's early Commerce Clause cases. [Thomas, J.'s concurring opinion in *Lopez* contended:

["At the time the original Constitution was ratified, 'commerce' consisted of selling, buying, and bartering, as well as transporting for these purposes [in] contradistinction to productive activities such as manufacturing and agriculture.[e] Alexander Hamilton, for example, repeatedly treated commerce, agriculture, and manufacturing as three separate endeavors. * * *

["The Constitution not only uses the word 'commerce' in a narrower sense than our case law might suggest, it also does not support the proposition that Congress has authority over all activities that 'substantially affect' interstate commerce. [After] all, if Congress may regulate all matters that substantially

---

7. Justice Souter's dissent theory [is] remarkable because it undermines this central principle of our constitutional system. As we have repeatedly noted, the Framers crafted the federal system of government so that the people's rights would be secured by the division of power. [No] doubt the political branches have a role in interpreting and applying the Constitution, but ever since *Marbury* this Court has remained the ultimate expositor of the constitutional text. Contrary to Justice Souter's suggestion, [that] from *Gibbons* on, public opinion has been the only restraint on the congressional exercise of the commerce power is true only insofar as it contends that political accountability is and has been the only limit on Congress' exercise of the commerce power within that power's outer bounds. As the language surrounding that relied upon by Justice Souter makes clear, *Gibbons* did not remove from this Court the authority to define that boundary.

d. For the view that "the Domestic Violence Clause [Art. IV, § 4] plays the role of a Tenth Amendment for crime, [providing] a guarantee to the states that the federal government will not interfere with a state's administration over crime [and creating] a presumption demanding that Congress justify an overlap of federal and state action against crime," see Jay S. Bybee, *Insuring Domestic Tranquility: Lopez, Federalization of Crime, and the Forgotten Role of the Domestic Violence Clause,* 66 Geo.Wash.L.Rev. 1 (1997).

e. For support, see Raoul Berger, *Judicial Manipulation of the Commerce Clause,* 74 Tex. L.Rev. 695 (1996); Richard A. Epstein, *The Proper Scope of the Commerce Power,* 73 Va. L.Rev. 1387 (1987). For the view that "Justice Thomas's list of sources illustrating contemporary usage hardly reflects the range of usages contemporaneous with the framing of the Constitution," see Herbert Hovenkamp, *Judicial Restraint and Constitutional Federalism: The Supreme Court's Lopez and Seminole Tribe Decisions,* 96 Colum.L.Rev. 2213, 2229 (1996).

affect commerce, there is no need for the Constitution to specify that Congress may enact bankruptcy laws, cl. 4, or coin money and fix the standard of weights and measures, cl. 5, or punish counterfeiters of United States coin and securities, cl. 6. Likewise, Congress would not need the separate authority to establish post offices and post roads, cl. 7, or to grant patents and copyrights, cl. 8, or to 'punish Piracies and Felonies committed on the high Seas,' cl. 10. It might not even need the power to raise and support an Army and Navy, cls. 12 and 13, for fewer people would engage in commercial shipping if they thought that a foreign power could expropriate their property with ease. Indeed, if Congress could regulate matters that substantially affect interstate commerce, there would have been no need to specify that Congress can regulate international trade and commerce with the Indians. As the Framers surely understood, these other branches of trade substantially affect interstate commerce. [An] interpretation of cl. 3 that makes the rest of § 8 superfluous simply cannot be correct."]

By continuing to apply this rootless and malleable standard, however circumscribed, the Court has encouraged the Federal Government to persist in its view that the Commerce Clause has virtually no limits. Until this Court replaces its existing Commerce Clause jurisprudence with a standard more consistent with the original understanding, we will continue to see Congress appropriating state police powers under the guise of regulating commerce.

JUSTICE SOUTER, with whom JUSTICE STEVENS, JUSTICE GINSBURG, and JUSTICE BREYER join, dissenting. * * *

One obvious difference from *Lopez* is the mountain of data assembled by Congress, here showing the effects of violence against women on interstate commerce. Passage of the Act in 1994 was preceded by four years of hearings [and] includes reports on gender bias from task forces in 21 [States]. Congress received evidence for the following findings:

"Three out of four American women will be victims of violent crimes sometime during their life."

"[A]s many as 50 percent of homeless women and children are fleeing domestic violence."

"[B]attering 'is the single largest cause of injury to women in the United States.'"

"An estimated 4 million American women are battered each year by their husbands or partners." * * *

"Between 2,000 and 4,000 women die every year from [domestic] abuse."

"[A]rrest rates may be as low as 1 for every 100 domestic assaults."

"[E]stimates suggest that we spend $5 to $10 billion a year on health care, criminal justice, and other social costs of domestic violence."

The evidence as to rape was similarly extensive, supporting these conclusions:

"[The incidence of] rape rose four times as fast as the total national crime rate over the past 10 years."

"According to one study, close to half a million girls now in high school will be raped before they graduate."

"[T]hree-quarters of women never go to the movies alone after dark because of the fear of rape and nearly 50 percent do not use public transit alone after dark for the same reason."

"[Forty-one] percent of judges surveyed believed that juries give sexual assault victims less credibility than other crime victims."

"Less than 1 percent of all [rape] victims have collected damages."

" '[A]n individual who commits rape has only about 4 chances in 100 of being arrested, prosecuted, and found guilty of any offense.' "

"Almost one-quarter of convicted rapists never go to prison and another quarter received sentences in local jails where the average sentence is 11 months."

"[A]lmost 50 percent of rape victims lose their jobs or are forced to quit because of the crime's severity." * * *

Congress thereby explicitly stated the predicate [quoted in the Court's opinion at p. 96 supra] for the exercise of its Commerce Clause power. [T]he sufficiency of the evidence before Congress to provide a rational basis for the finding cannot seriously be questioned. * * *

The Act would have passed muster at any time between *Wickard* in 1942 and *Lopez* in 1995, a period in which the law enjoyed a stable understanding that congressional power under the Commerce Clause, complemented by the authority of the Necessary and Proper Clause, extended to all activity that, when aggregat- ed, has a substantial effect on interstate commerce. [T]his understanding was secure even against the turmoil at the passage of the Civil Rights Act of 1964, in the aftermath of which the Court not only reaffirmed the cumulative effects and rational basis features of the substantial effects test, but declined to limit the commerce power through a formal distinction between legislation focused on "commerce" and statutes addressing "moral and social wrongs," *Heart of Atlanta*.

The fact that the Act does not pass muster before the Court today is therefore proof, to a degree that *Lopez* was not, that the Court's nominal adherence to the substantial effects test is merely that. [I]t is clear that some congressional conclusions about obviously substantial, cumulative effects on commerce are being assigned lesser values than the once-stable doctrine would assign them. These devaluations are accomplished not by any express repudiation of the substantial effects test or its application through the aggregation of individual conduct, but by supplanting rational basis scrutiny with a new criterion of review.

* * * From the fact that Art. I, § 8, cl. 3 grants an authority limited to regulating commerce, [it] does not at all follow that an activity affecting commerce nonetheless falls outside the commerce power, depending on the specific character of the activity, or the authority of a State to regulate it along with Congress. My disagreement with the majority is not, however, confined to logic, for history has shown that categorical exclusions have proven as unworkable in practice as they are unsupportable in theory.

Obviously, it would not be inconsistent with the text of the Commerce Clause itself to declare "noncommercial" primary activity beyond or presumptively beyond the scope of the commerce power. That variant of categorical approach is not, however, the sole textually permissible way of defining the scope of the Commerce Clause, and any such neat limitation would at least be suspect in the light of the [necessary and proper clause]. Accordingly, for significant periods of our history, the Court has defined the commerce power as plenary, unsusceptible to categorical exclusions, and this was the view expressed throughout the latter part of the 20th century in the substantial effects test. These two conceptions of the commerce power, plenary and categorically limited, are in fact old rivals. [T]oday's attempt to distinguish between primary activities affecting commerce in terms of the relatively commercial or noncommercial character of the primary conduct proscribed comes with the pedigree of near-tragedy that I outlined in *Lopez*. In the half century following the modern activation of the commerce power with passage of the Interstate Commerce Act in 1887, this Court from time to time created categorical enclaves beyond congressional reach by declaring such activities as "mining," "production," "manufacturing," and union membership to be outside the definition of "commerce" and by limiting application of the effects test to "direct" rather than "indirect" commercial consequences.

Since adherence to these formalistically contrived confines of commerce power in large measure provoked the judicial crisis of 1937, one might reasonably have doubted that Members of this Court would ever again toy with a return to the days before *Jones & Laughlin,* which brought the earlier and nearly disastrous experiment to an end. And yet today's decision can only be seen as a step toward recapturing the prior mistakes. [Its] enquiry into commercial purpose, first intimated by the *Lopez* concurrence (opinion of Kennedy, J.), is cousin to the intent-based analysis employed in *Hammer*, but rejected for Commerce Clause purposes in *Heart of Atlanta* and *Darby*.

Why is the majority tempted to reject the lesson so painfully learned in 1937? An answer emerges from contrasting *Wickard* with one of the predecessor cases it superseded. It was obvious in *Wickard* that growing wheat for consumption right on the farm was not "commerce" in the common vocabulary.[13] [Just] a few years before *Wickard*, however, it had certainly been no less obvious that "mining" practices could substantially affect commerce, even though *Carter Coal* had held mining regulation beyond the national commerce power. When we try to fathom the difference between the two cases, it is clear that they did not go in different directions because the *Carter Coal* Court could not understand a causal connection that the *Wickard* Court could grasp; the difference, rather, turned on the fact that the Court in *Carter Coal* had a reason for trying to maintain its categorical, formalistic distinction, [it] was still trying to create a laissez-faire world out of the 20th-century economy, and formalistic commercial distinctions were thought to be useful instruments in achieving that object. * * *

The Court finds it relevant that the statute addresses conduct traditionally subject to state prohibition under domestic criminal law, a fact said to have some heightened significance when the violent conduct in question is not itself aimed directly at interstate commerce or its instrumentalities. Again, history seems to be recycling, for the theory of traditional state concern as grounding a limiting principle has [been repudiated in *Garcia v. San Antonio Met. Trans. Auth* (1985) [Sec. 5 infra], which held that the concept of "traditional governmental function" [was] incoherent, there being no explanation that would make sense of the multifarious decisions placing some functions on one side of the line, some on the other. * * *[14]

---

13. [The] *Wickard* Court admitted that Filburn's activity "may not be regarded as commerce" but insisted that "it may still, whatever its nature, be reached by Congress if it exerts a substantial economic effect on interstate commerce." The characterization of home wheat production as "commerce" or not is, however, ultimately beside the point. For if substantial effects on commerce are proper subjects of concern under the Commerce Clause, what difference should it make whether the causes of those effects are themselves commercial? The Court's answer is that it makes a difference to federalism, and the legitimacy of the Court's new judicially derived federalism is the crux of our disagreement.

14. The Constitution of 1787 did, in fact, forbid some exercises of the commerce power. Article I, § 9, cl. 6, barred Congress from giving preference to the ports of one State over those of another. More strikingly, the Framers protected the slave trade from federal interference, see Art. I, § 9, cl. 1. [These] reservations demonstrate the plenary nature of the federal power; the exceptions prove the rule. [T]o suppose that enumerated powers must have limits is sensible; to maintain that there exist judi-

The objection to reviving traditional state spheres of action as a consideration in commerce analysis [is] compounded by a further defect[:] the majority's rejection of the Founders' considered judgment that politics, not judicial review, should mediate between state and national interests as the strength and legislative jurisdiction of the National Government inevitably increased through the expected growth of the national economy. [quoting Madison (in *Federalist* No. 46), James Wilson, and Marshall, C.J., in *Gibbons*]. * * *

The *Garcia* Court's rejection of "judicially created limitations" in favor of the intended reliance on national politics was all the more powerful owing to the Court's explicit recognition that in the centuries since the framing the relative powers of the two sovereign systems have markedly changed. Nationwide economic integration is the norm, the national political power has been augmented by its vast revenues, and the power of the States has been drawn down by the Seventeenth Amendment, eliminating selection of senators by state legislature in favor of direct election. * * *[19]

Amendments that alter the balance of power between the National and State Governments, like the Fourteenth, or that change the way the States are represented within the Federal Government, like the Seventeenth, are not rips in the fabric of the Framers' Constitution, inviting judicial repairs. The Seventeenth Amendment may indeed have lessened the enthusiasm of the Senate to represent the States as discrete sovereignties, but the Amendment did not convert the judiciary into an alternate shield against the commerce power.

The Court [finds] no significance whatever in the state support for the Act based upon the States' acknowledged failure to deal adequately with gender-based violence in state courts, and the belief of their own law enforcement agencies that national action is essential.

The National Association of Attorneys General supported the Act unanimously, and [as] the 1993 Senate Report put it, "The Violence Against Women Act is intended to respond both to the underlying attitude that this violence is somehow less serious than other crime and to the resulting failure of our criminal justice system to address such violence. Its goals are both symbolic and practical." [It] is, then, not the least irony of these cases that the States will be forced to enjoy the new federalism whether they want it or not. * * *

Justice Breyer, with whom Justice Stevens joins, and with whom Justice Souter and Justice Ginsburg join as to Part I–A, dissenting.

No one denies the importance of the Constitution's federalist principles. [The] question is how the judiciary can [best] impose some meaningful limit, but not too great a limit, upon the scope of the legislative authority that the Commerce Clause delegates to Congress.

A. Consider the problems. The "economic/noneconomic" distinction is not easy to apply. Does the local street corner mugger engage in "economic" activity

cially identifiable areas of state regulation immune to the plenary congressional commerce power even though falling within the limits defined by the substantial effects test is to deny our constitutional history.

19. The majority tries to deflect the objection that it blocks an intended political process by explaining that the Framers intended politics to set the federal balance only within the sphere of permissible commerce legislation, whereas we are looking to politics to define

that sphere (in derogation even of *Marbury*). * * * Neither Madison nor Wilson nor Marshall, nor the *Jones & Laughlin, Darby, Wickard*, or *Garcia* Courts, suggested that politics defines the commerce power. Nor do we, even though we recognize that the conditions of the contemporary world result in a vastly greater sphere of influence for politics than the Framers would have envisioned. * * *

or "noneconomic" activity when he mugs for money? Would evidence that desire for economic domination underlies many brutal crimes against women save the present statute?

The line becomes yet harder to draw given the need for exceptions. The Court itself would permit Congress to aggregate, hence regulate, "noneconomic" activity taking place at economic establishments. See *Heart of Atlanta*. And it would permit Congress to regulate where that regulation is "an essential part of a larger regulation of economic activity, in which the regulatory scheme could be undercut unless the intrastate activity were regulated." *Lopez*;[f] cf. Controlled Substances Act (regulating drugs produced for home consumption). Given the former exception, can Congress simply rewrite the present law and limit its application to restaurants, hotels, perhaps universities, and other places of public accommodation? Given the latter exception, can Congress save the present law by including it, or much of it, in a broader "Safe Transport" or "Workplace Safety" act?

More important, why should we give critical constitutional importance to the economic, or noneconomic, nature of an interstate-commerce-affecting cause? If chemical emanations through indirect environmental change cause identical, severe commercial harm outside a State, why should it matter whether local factories or home fireplaces release them? * * *

Most important, the Court's complex rules seem unlikely to help secure the very object that they seek, namely, the protection of "areas of traditional state regulation" from federal intrusion. The Court's rules, even if broadly interpreted, are underinclusive. The local pickpocket is no less a traditional subject of state regulation than is the local gender-motivated assault. Regardless, the Court reaffirms, as it should, Congress' well-established and frequently exercised power to enact laws that satisfy a commerce-related jurisdictional prerequisite—for example, that some item relevant to the federally regulated activity has at some time crossed a state line. *Heart of Atlanta*; see also *Scarborough*.

And in a world where most everyday products or their component parts cross interstate boundaries, Congress will frequently find it possible to redraft a statute using language that ties the regulation to the interstate movement of some relevant object, thereby regulating local criminal activity or, for that matter, family affairs. See, e.g., Child Support Recovery Act of 1992. [How] much would be gained, for example, were Congress to reenact the present law in the form of "An Act Forbidding Violence Against Women Perpetrated at Public Accommodations or by Those Who Have Moved in, or through the Use of Items that Have Moved in, Interstate Commerce"? Complex Commerce Clause rules creating fine distinctions that achieve only random results do little to further the important federalist interests that called them into being. That is why modern (pre-*Lopez*) case law rejected them.

* * * We live in a Nation knit together by two centuries of scientific, technological, commercial, and environmental change. Those changes, taken together, mean that virtually every kind of activity, no matter how local, genuinely can affect commerce, or its conditions, outside the State—at least when considered in the aggregate. And that fact makes it close to impossible for courts to develop meaningful subject-matter categories that would exclude some kinds of local

f. In *Lopez*, Breyer, J., joined by Stevens, Souter and Ginsburg, JJ., dissenting, noted that "although the majority today attempts to categorize *Perez*, *McClung*, and *Wickard*, as involving intrastate 'economic activity,' the Courts that decided each of those cases did *not* focus upon the economic nature of the activity regulated. Rather, they focused upon whether that activity *affected* interstate or foreign commerce."

activities from ordinary Commerce Clause "aggregation" rules without, at the same time, depriving Congress of the power to regulate activities that have a genuine and important effect upon interstate commerce.

Since judges cannot change the [world,] Congress, not the courts, must remain primarily responsible for striking the appropriate state/federal balance. Congress is institutionally motivated to do so. Its Members represent state and local district interests. They consider the views of state and local officials when they legislate, and they have even developed formal procedures to ensure that such consideration takes place. See, e.g., Unfunded Mandates Reform Act of 1995. Moreover, Congress often can better reflect state concerns for autonomy in the details of sophisticated statutory schemes than can the judiciary, which cannot easily gather the relevant facts and which must apply more general legal rules and categories.

B. I would also note [that] attorneys general in the overwhelming majority of States (38) supported congressional legislation, telling Congress that "our experience as Attorneys General strengthens our belief that the problem of violence against women is a national one, requiring federal attention, federal leadership, and federal funds."

Moreover, [Congress] focused the federal law upon documented deficiencies in state legal systems. And it tailored the law to prevent its use in certain areas of traditional state concern, such as divorce, alimony, or child custody. Consequently, the law before us seems to represent an instance, not of state/federal conflict, but of state/federal efforts to cooperate in order to help solve a mutually acknowledged national problem.

[This] Court on occasion has pointed to the importance of procedural limitations in keeping the power of Congress in check. See *Garcia* ("Any substantive [limitations] must be tailored to compensate for possible failings in the national political process rather than to dictate a 'sacred province of state autonomy.'" [Of] course, any judicial insistence that Congress follow particular procedures might itself intrude upon congressional prerogatives and embody difficult definitional problems. But the intrusion, problems, and consequences all would seem less serious than those embodied in the majority's approach.

I continue to agree with Justice Souter that the Court's traditional "rational basis" approach is sufficient. But I recognize that the law in this area is unstable and that time and experience may demonstrate both the unworkability of the majority's rules and the superiority of Congress' own procedural approach—in which case the law may evolve towards a rule that, in certain difficult Commerce Clause cases, takes account of the thoroughness with which Congress has considered the federalism issue.[g] * * *

Notes and Questions

1. *"Substantial effects."* How are, or should these be, defined? Does this criterion help articulate a coherent (principled) limit on the commerce power? Consider Deborah J. Merritt, *Commerce!*, 94 Mich.L.Rev. 674, 679 (1995): "The majority's use of 'substantial effect' is more akin to the notion of proximate cause in tort law [—] that the relationship between the regulated activity and interstate commerce must be strong enough or close enough to justify federal intervention,

---

g. The question of whether the national political process or judicial review is more de- sirable and effective in "safeguarding" federalism is considered further in Sec. 5, IV infra.

just as the concept of proximate cause means that a defendant's negligence must be closely enough related to the plaintiff's injury to justify forcing the defendant to bear the costs of the injury. Both of these judgments are qualitative ones, resting on a host of contextual factors,[a] rather than simple quantitative calculations." See also H. Jefferson Powell, *Enumerated Means and Unlimited Ends,* 94 Mich.L.Rev. 651, 656 (1995): "*Lopez* suggests that it is not enough to make the positive argument that a given statute has a substantial relationship to interstate commerce; it is also necessary to make the essentially negative demonstration that one can with logical consistency prove some other, hypothetical statute unconstitutional. This second, negative requirement—what we might call 'the test of consequences'—serves to confirm that, in upholding the use of the Commerce Clause under review, the Court is not inadvertently 'conclud[ing] that the Constitution's enumeration of powers does not presuppose something not enumerated' [citing *Lopez*] contrary to the principle of enumerated and therefore limited federal power." Compare Bittker, fn. g, Sec. II, B supra at 5–31: "This claim, a species of reductio ad absurdum, depends of course on the threshold premise that the power being examined is vested in Congress *subject to an identifiable outer limit,* which for the Commerce Clause is usually an action that does not affect (or does not substantially affect, in some formulas) interstate commerce. But if changed circumstances have obliterated the presupposed existence in fact of 'activity that does not affect interstate commerce,' at least in the business or economic sphere, then an argument is *not* mistaken merely because it recognizes that there is no longer any economic activity that is beyond the power of Congress to regulate under the Commerce Clause."

2. *The "commercial/economic" criterion.* (a) Should "we give critical constitutional importance to the economic, or noneconomic, nature of an interstate-commerce-affecting cause" (Breyer, J.)? Consider Deborah J. Merritt, *The Third Translation of the Commerce Clause: Congressional Power to Regulate Social Problems,* 66 Geo.Wash.L.Rev. 1206, 1208–09 (1998): "[Art. I, § 8] enumerates more than two dozen specific subjects that Congress may govern. The specificity of each subject, together with the length of the list, suggests that each power is reasonably finite. It is hard to believe that the Framers buried in the middle of this inventory—in the second phrase of the third clause, no less—a cloaked dynamo that one day would generate congressional power over virtually any social problem." Compare Tribe 3d ed., at 825 n. 1: "[E]ven if congressional power to regulate activities that are *neither* interstate *nor* commercial but that, in the aggregate, 'substantially affect' interstate commerce is not contained in the Commerce Clause proper, it is readily located in the doctrine of implied powers, and/or in the Necessary and Proper Clause, *coupled* with the Commerce Clause."

(b) JONES v. UNITED STATES, 529 U.S. 848, 120 S.Ct. 1904, 146 L.Ed.2d 902 (2000), per GINSBURG, J., unanimously held that the federal arson statute (covering buildings "used [in] any activity affecting interstate or foreign commerce") did not apply to an owner-occupied residence not used for commercial purposes, thus avoiding the constitutional question under the commerce clause. THOMAS, J., joined by Scalia, J., went beyond the facts of the case and "express[ed] no view on the question whether the federal arson statute [is] constitutional in its application to all buildings used for commercial activities." Compare Nelson & Pushaw, note 4(a) after *Darby,* at 155: "Arson is a significant and unique concern for insurers, who have been viewed for centuries as 'commercial.' The flaw in this

---

a. "One of those factors is whether the government's argument is so all-encompassing that it sweeps all conduct within congressional control." Deborah J. Merritt, *The Fuzzy Logic of Federalism,* 46 Case W.Res.L.Rev. 685, 692 (1996).

argument is that the statute does not specifically safeguard the insurance industry. Congress could do so, however, by prohibiting arson against 'insured property,' which would include almost all buildings, including personal residences."

(c) *Problems of definition.* Consider Jesse H. Choper & John C. Yoo, *The Scope of the Commerce Clause After Morrison*, 25 Okla.City U.L.Rev. 843, 856–6 (2000): "Given the success that the law and economics movement has encountered in revealing the underlying economic motivations that might underlay many actions, Congress may have little difficulty in persuasively characterizing many activities as economic in nature. [Thus,] while Congress might not be able to enact criminal penalties for all violence, it may still be able to ban any violence that has an economic motive or purpose. Not only would crimes that are fundamentally financial in nature, such as fraud or theft, fall wholly within federal power, but large subsets of other offenses also could come within national jurisdiction. Congress probably cannot, for example, enact a law that prohibits all physical assaults, but it could prohibit all muggings—which are, by definition, physical assaults undertaken to get the victim's money. It probably could not prohibit all breaking-and-entering, [but] could enact a nationwide law that prohibited all robbery. Congress may not be able to prohibit all possession of a certain product, but it could ban any transaction or exchange that involved that product. To push the commercial distinction even further, neither *Lopez* nor *Morrison* prevent Congress from regulating any activity that involved the exchange of a single dollar of U.S. currency or even barter. Congress may well be able to make a federal offense of any crime that involved the use of the federal currency." Compare Nelson & Pushaw, supra at 147–48: "[M]ost criminal behavior does not constitute 'commerce' [which] at its core is a consensual transaction. [For] instance, crimes against the person, such as battery and rape, can hardly be classified as commercial. The addition of a financial purpose does not alter this conclusion. For example, murder is not commerce, even if done to collect under an insurance policy or otherwise to inherit the victim's wealth. The same may be said for armed robbery where, by definition, the impetus is economic. Nor is burglary a commercial transaction, even though most burglars contemplate subsequently selling their loot. Even kidnapping for ransom is not a true commercial transaction. Although there is an 'agreement' to pay money in exchange for the release of the victim, it is made under duress."

(d) *"Instrumentalities of interstate commerce."* May Congress use the commerce clause to regulate the labor relations of a nonprofit organization? See *Polish Nat'l Alliance v. NLRB*, 322 U.S. 643, 64 S.Ct. 1196, 88 L.Ed. 1509 (1944). To make it a crime to obstruct access to abortion clinics? See Note, *Abortion as Commerce: The Impact of United States v. Lopez on the Freedom of Access to Clinic Entrances Act of 1994*, 50 Vand.L.Rev. 239 (1997). To prohibit partial-birth abortions? See David B. Kopel & Glenn H. Reynolds, *Taking Federalism Seriously: Lopez and the Partial–Birth Abortion Ban Act*, 30 Conn.L.Rev. 59 (1997). Are nonprofit organizations and abortion clinics *themselves* "enterprises engaged in interstate commerce" because they purchase materials from other states and have clients and employees that come from other states? Cf. *United States v. Robertson*, 514 U.S. 669, 115 S.Ct. 1732, 131 L.Ed.2d 714 (1995) (gold mine was such an "enterprise" within federal RICO law). If so, do they fall within *Lopez*'s second "broad category of activity that Congress may regulate under its commerce power"?

Consider Choper & Yoo, supra at 863: "While as yet not fully used by Congress, the instrumentalities aspect of the Commerce Clause could sweep a great deal of intrastate, non-economic activity within the ambit of national authority. Mail and wire fraud require only one use of the mails or the phones to trigger federal jurisdiction. Congress could add other common-law crimes in addition to fraud to the mail and wire statutes: conspiracy to commit murder, robbery, assault, and so on. Seemingly, all it would take is one phone call in the course of planning to rob or attack a victim to make something a federal crime. Further, Congress could make it a federal crime to use the interstate highways, or any road connected to a federal road, in the commission of any crime. Congress could make a federal crime out of using the internet or a computer network attached to the internet to commit any crime. As with Congress's power to regulate the channels of interstate commerce, the nationalization of the economy and society gives the legislature's power over the instrumentalities of interstate commerce a sufficiently broad scope to encompass much private, non-economic conduct."

(e) Is it clear that if the Court intends to impose serious restraints on Congress' commerce power, its recent efforts will have to be supplemented by refining its "commercial/economic" criterion and by redefining its "jurisdictional nexus" (see fn. a supra) and "instrumentalities" categories?

(f) *Avoiding the constitutional question.* In addition to *Jones*, note b supra, see SOLID WASTE AGENCY OF NORTHERN COOK COUNTY v. UNITED STATES ARMY CORPS OF ENGINEERS, 531 U.S. 159, 121 S.Ct. 675, 148 L.Ed.2d 576 (2001), per REHNQUIST, C.J., interpreting the Clean Water Act as not covering "nonnavigable, isolated intrastate waters" which were used as a habitat for migratory birds, thus avoiding "significant constitutional and federalism questions." STEVENS, J., joined by Souter, Ginsburg and Breyer, JJ., dissenting, disagreed with "the Court's miserly construction of the statute" and thus "comment[ed] briefly" on Congress' commerce power: First, "unlike the class of activities [in] *Morrison* and *Lopez*, [the] discharge of fill material into the Nation's waters is almost always undertaken for economic reasons." Second, "it is undisputed that literally millions of people regularly participate in birdwatching and hunting [and] those activities generate a host of commercial activities of great value." "Finally, [i]dentifying the Corps' jurisdiction by reference to waters that serve as habitat for birds that migrate over state lines also satisfies this Court's expressed desire for some 'jurisdictional element' that limits federal activity to its proper scope. *Morrison*."

3. *Other proposed approaches.* (a) *"Commerce."* Consider Nelson & Pushaw, supra at 8–12, 113: "[Under] the original meaning of the Commerce Clause by examining its language from an eighteenth-century perspective; its drafting, ratification, and early implementation; and its relationship to other constitutional principles, ['commerce'] covers a wide range of subjects, which fall roughly into two categories. The first includes buying and selling goods; their antecedent production through activities such as manufacturing, farming, and mining; and byproducts of that production, like environmental and safety effects. The second consists of the provision of services for money (e.g., labor, insurance, and banking), which many eighteenth-century commentators deemed 'commercial,' and which form a critical component of our modern economy. [If] a statute meets our 'commerce' requirement, the Court should then determine whether the activity or enterprise at issue has a commercial impact in more than one state. Most commerce does, given America's nationally integrated economy. [Thus,] courts should review Congress's determinations on this score under a 'rational basis' test, which means that virtually all such statutes will be upheld. [Even though] Congress arguably should be permitted to regulate noncommercial activities because many of them have a great impact on interstate commerce, [the] Court

should halt the increasing reliance by Congress on the Commerce Clause to impose a specific cultural or moral viewpoint simply because it disagrees with that taken by certain states. [In] a nutshell, the Framers believed that national uniformity is good in commerce but bad in political, social, cultural, and moral matters.''

(b) *"Separate states' incompetence."* Consider Regan, fn. e, Sec. 1 supra at 555: "[W]hen we are trying to decide whether some federal law or program can be justified under the commerce power, we should [ask]: 'Is there some reason the federal government must be able to do this, some reason why we cannot leave the matter to the states?' Federal power exists where and only where there is special justification for it.'' See also Ann Althouse, *Enforcing Federalism After United States v. Lopez*, 38 Ariz.L.Rev. 793, 818–19 (1996): "Uniformity is frequently a good thing necessary to the solution of the kinds of problems involved in *Wickard*. Individual states cannot impose production caps or price controls without damaging the interests of the citizens in their commercial activities. [In] contrast, the kind of activity involved in *Lopez* was not only susceptible to local regulation, states had traditionally assumed responsibility in this area and were in all likelihood better suited to handle [it.] While violence may be widespread, it does not interlock at the national level like a market. [A] federal law is only passed because a problem has engaged the attention of the national legislature: in that sense all federal law addresses concerns that exist at the national level. But [m]any matters that absorb Congress today do not represent any sort of considered analysis about whether a national *solution* is needed. Indeed, the practice of deferring to the judgment of Congress as to what affects interstate commerce is flawed for this very reason: members of Congress, inclined to pursue their personal political goals, commonly resort to legislative gestures designed to appeal to the passions of the electorate. The expansive federalization of criminal law shows this force in action.''

(c) *Substantive and procedural judicial review.* Consider Stephen Gardbaum, *Rethinking Constitutional Federalism*, 74 Tex.L.Rev. 795, 814, 819, 824 (1996): "[The Court should] prevent Congress from preempting the states or regulating local activities that affect interstate commerce [unless Congress balances] the advantages and disadvantages of its proposed course of action from a federalism perspective [by] deliberating seriously about the need and merits of so doing, [and] having reasonable grounds for its decision.[b] [Under] such an enhanced rational basis test, [even] if there is an extremely tight fit between means and legitimate end, consideration of the interests and capabilities of the states may still render it inappropriate [for Congress to act].'' Compare H. Geoffrey Moulton, Jr., *The Quixotic Search for a Judicially Enforceable Federalism*, 83 Minn.L.Rev. 849, 922–24 (1999): "The critical question is not how do we protect the states from the nation, but how do we allocate particular responsibilities to the level of government best equipped to handle those responsibilities. [As] to choosing between state-and national-level lawmaking, the framers did not claim to have worked out the political science and economics of federalism, and did not contemplate that later courts would do that work for them. As a consequence, the Constitution grants no license to courts to second-guess congressional resolution of questions of institutional choice. Moreover, as a practical matter courts are simply ill-suited for the enormously complex (and contestable) task of determining the optimal allocation of power in a federal system.''

b. See also Vicki C. Jackson, *Federalism and the Uses and Limits of Law: Printz and* *Principle?*, 111 Harv. L. Rev. 2180, 2231–2246 (1998).

(d) *Rethinking the necessary and proper clause.* Consider Bradford R. Clark, *Translating Federalism: A Structural Approach*, 66 Geo.Wash.L.Rev. 1161, 1177 (1998): "Because Congress's commerce power has become so pervasive, the constitutional structure arguably no longer counsels in favor of a broad interpretation of the Necessary and Proper Clause to augment this power. * * * Adhering to a broad interpretation [would] permit Congress to regulate any activity that affects interstate commerce [or] 'practically every activity of social life' [citing Lawrence Lessig, *Translating Federalism: United States v. Lopez*, 1995 Sup.Ct. Rev. 125.]. Thus, even if a plausible interpretation of the clause allowed Congress to regulate *intra*state commerce as a means of regulating *inter*state commerce in 1819, changed circumstances arguably have rendered this reading of the text obsolete today."

SECTION 3. THE NATIONAL TAXING AND SPENDING POWERS

Art. I, § 8, cl. 1, grants Congress power "to lay and collect taxes, duties, imposts and excises, to pay the debts and provide for the common defense and general welfare of the United States." Its terms include both power to tax and to spend.[a] This section is concerned primarily with use of these two related powers to achieve regulatory ends.

The Court has long recognized that Congress may use its taxing power as both a "necessary and proper" way to enforce its regulatory powers, and as a way to raise revenue which may produce "incidental" regulatory effects. The issues raised by the latter use of the taxing power, and analogous use of the spending power, declined in importance as the expanded view of Congress' regulatory powers after 1936 left few occasions for Congress to resort to taxing or spending for regulatory purposes. But the limitations imposed on the commerce power by *Lopez* and *Morrison* (as well as on Congress' ability to enforce the Civil War amendments, see Ch. 11, Sec. 2) have given the national taxing and spending powers a potentially new importance.

I. REGULATION THROUGH TAXING

BAILEY v. DREXEL FURNITURE CO. (CHILD LABOR TAX CASE), 259 U.S. 20, 42 S.Ct. 449, 66 L.Ed. 817 (1922), per TAFT, C.J., held invalid the Child Labor Tax Law which, nine months after *Dagenhart*, imposed a 10% excise tax on the net profits of employers of child labor, defined identically as in the law struck down in *Dagenhart*:

"The law is attacked on the ground that it is a regulation of the employment of child labor in the states—an exclusively state function. [Does] this law impose a tax with only that incidental restraint and regulation which a tax must inevitably involve? Or does it regulate by the use of the so-called tax as a penalty? [If] it were an excise on a commodity or other thing of value, we might not be permitted under previous decisions of this court to infer solely from its heavy burden that the act intends a prohibition instead of a tax. But this [act] provides a heavy

a. For the view that cl.1 does *not* clearly authorize *general* federal "spending" (and is "utterly inadequate to authorize routine *deficit* spending)," and that "a careful parsing of the records of the Constitutional Convention indicates that [the] Article IV Property Clause was specifically designed for the purpose, among several others, of authorizing Congress to spend—even for objects that would not be within any enumerated power," see David E. Engdahl, *The Spending Power*, 44 Duke L.J. 1, 50–51 (1994).

exaction for a departure from a detailed and specified course of conduct in business. [The] amount is not [proportioned] to the extent or frequency of the departures, but is to be paid by the employer in full measure whether he employs 500 children for a year, [or] one for a day. Moreover, if he does not know the child is within the named age limit, he is not to [pay]. Scienters are associated with penalties, not with taxes. The employer's factory is to be subject to inspection at any time not only by the taxing officers of the Treasury, [but] also by the Secretary of Labor and his subordinates, whose normal function is the advancement and protection of the welfare of the workers. In the light of these features of the act, a court must be blind not to see that the so-called tax is imposed to stop the employment of children within the age limits prescribed. Its prohibitory and regulatory effect and purpose are palpable. All others can see and understand this. How can we properly shut our minds to it?

" * * * Grant the validity of this law, and all that Congress would need to do, hereafter, in seeking to control any one of the great number of subjects reserved to [the states] by the Tenth Amendment, would be to enact a detailed measure of complete regulation of the subject and enforce it by a so-called tax upon departures from it. To give such magic to the word 'tax' would be to break down all constitutional limitation of the powers of Congress and completely wipe out the sovereignty of the states.

" * * * Where the sovereign enacting the law has power to impose both tax and penalty, the difference between revenue production and mere regulation may be immaterial, but not so when one sovereign can impose a tax only, and the power of regulation rests in another. Taxes are occasionally imposed in the discretion of the Legislature on proper subjects with the primary motive of obtaining revenue from them and with the incidental motive of discouraging them by making their continuance onerous. They do not lose their character as taxes because of the incidental motive. But there comes a time in the extension of the penalizing features of the so-called tax when it loses its character as such and becomes a mere penalty, with the characteristics of regulation and punishment. Such is the case in the law before us. Although Congress does not invalidate the contract of employment or expressly declare that the employment within the mentioned ages is illegal, it does exhibit its intent practically to achieve the latter result by adopting the criteria of wrongdoing and imposing its principal consequence on those who transgress its standard.

" * * * *Veazie Bank v. Fenno,* 8 Wall. 533, 19 L.Ed. 482, [involved] a law which increased a tax on the circulating notes of persons and state banks from one per centum to 10 per centum. [To the objection that the tax was so excessive as to indicate a purpose to destroy state banks, *Veazie*] answered: 'The first answer to this is that the judicial cannot prescribe to the legislative departments of the government limitations upon the exercise of its acknowledged powers. * * *'

"It will be observed that the sole objection to the [*Veazie* tax] was its excessive character. Nothing else appeared on the face of the act. It was an increase of a tax admittedly legal to a higher rate and that was all. But more than this, what was charged to be the object of the excessive tax was within the congressional authority [to] secure a national [currency.]

"* * * *McCray v. United States,* 195 U.S. 27, 24 S.Ct. 769, 49 L.Ed. 78 (1904), [upheld a federal excise tax of 10 cents per pound on yellow oleomargarine when the tax on white oleo was ¼ cent per pound and when the price of butter was 28 per pound.] This court held that the discretion of Congress [in] selecting its subjects for taxation, might impose the burden where and as it would and that a motive disclosed in its selection to discourage sale or manufacture of an article by a higher tax than on some other did not invalidate the tax. In neither of these cases did the law objected to show on its face as does the law before us the detailed specifications of a regulation of a state concern and business with a heavy exaction to promote the efficacy of such regulation. * * *

" * * * *United States v. Doremus,* 249 U.S. 86, 39 S.Ct. 214, 63 L.Ed. 493 (1919) [upheld the Narcotic Drug Act, which imposed a $1 annual tax on the manufacture, importation and sale of named narcotics. It required all subject to the tax to register with the Commissioner of Internal Revenue and to sell the narcotics only on a written order of the buyer or a physician's prescription. Copies were required to be kept, subject to official inspection, for two years.] The provisions for subjecting the sale and distribution of the drugs to official supervision and inspection were held to have a reasonable relation to the enforcement of the tax and were therefore held valid.[a]

"The court said that the act could not be declared invalid just because another motive than taxation, not shown on the face of the act, might have contributed to its passage. This case does not militate against the conclusion we have reached in respect of the law now before us. The court, there, made manifest its view that the provisions of the so-called taxing act must be naturally and reasonably adapted to the collection of the tax and not solely to the achievement of some other purpose plainly within state power."[b]

Notes and Questions

1. *Legislative motives.* Was *McCray* "blind not to see" that the tax 40 times higher on yellow than on white oleo was imposed to curtail the sale of yellow oleo? Did the *McCray* tax impose a "heavy penalty for departure from a specified course of conduct"—selling only white margarine? Did the *Doremus* detailed record-keeping regulations establish a congressional motive to control the dispensing of narcotics, rather than to produce revenue?[c] Would (should) the amount of revenue produced by the Child Labor Tax Law influence its constitutionality? Does the amount of revenue produced by a tax reveal (indicate) the motive(s) of its enactors?

(b) Might the same concerns over attempts to expand federal legislative power that caused the Court to see a legislative motive behind the power of Congress in *Dagenhart* but not in *Lottery* explain the reliance on such motives in *Child Labor Tax Case* though not in *McCray* or *Doremus*?

2. *Subsequent developments.* While never repudiated, and occasionally cited, the *Child Labor Tax Case* has been applied by the Court to invalidate a federal tax only once since 1922, and that during the *Schechter-Carter* era of restrictive commerce power interpretation. UNITED STATES v. CONSTANTINE, 296 U.S. 287, 56 S.Ct. 223, 80 L.Ed. 233 (1935), per ROBERTS, J., found a "purpose to usurp the police power of the State" in a tax 10 to 40 times heavier on a liquor business

---

a. *Doremus* explained: "The provisions [tend] to keep the traffic aboveboard and subject to inspection by those authorized to collect the revenue. They tend to diminish the opportunity of unauthorized persons to obtain the drugs and sell them clandestinely without paying the tax imposed by the federal law."

b. Clarke, J., dissented without opinion.

c. Nine years after *Doremus, Nigro v. United States,* 276 U.S. 332, 48 S.Ct. 388, 72 L.Ed. 600 (1928), noted that the Narcotic Drug Act rates had been increased to provide substantial revenue, and added: "If there was doubt as to the character of this Act—that it is not as alleged a subterfuge—it has been removed by the change whereby what was a nominal tax before was made a substantial one."

operating "contrary to state law" than on other liquor businesses. Cardozo, J., joined by Brandeis and Stone, JJ., dissented, protesting disregard of the "wise and ancient doctrine that a court will not inquire into the motives of a legislative body or assume them to be wrongful."

Due to the broad expansion of Congress' commerce power after 1936, Congress has had few occasions to use the taxing power for regulatory purposes. Since *Constantine,* no federal tax has been held invalid because of a regulatory motive outside federal power. See *Sonzinsky v. United States,* 300 U.S. 506, 57 S.Ct. 554, 81 L.Ed. 772 (1937), ($200 tax on each transfer of concealable firearms; "inquiry into hidden motive is beyond competence of the courts"); *United States v. Sanchez,* 340 U.S. 42, 71 S.Ct. 108, 95 L.Ed. 47 (1950)(Congress expressed two objectives: raising revenue and making "extremely difficult the acquisition of marihuana"); *United States v. Kahriger,* 345 U.S. 22, 73 S.Ct. 510, 97 L.Ed. 754 (1953) (ten percent tax on all wagers coupled with registration of all wager takers, whose names must be given to state prosecutors, if requested.)[d]

3. *Future potential.* Consider Choper & Yoo, Sec. 2, IV supra, at 859–60: "Even if the Court continues to place restrictions on the Commerce Clause, it is unclear whether it would attempt to impose corresponding limitations upon Congress' ability to enact taxes that went beyond commercial activity. Although much of the income tax code certainly can find justification as the regulation of commercial activity, other provisions that do not might be brought into question on the ground that their purpose and effect is not to raise revenue, but rather to achieve regulatory ends. Moreover, while gift and estates taxes involve the transfer of wealth, large portions do not seem to involve commercial or economic activity of the sort contemplated by *Lopez* and *Morrison.* [Or,] building on the existing tax code, Congress could deny anyone who possessed a handgun near a school zone or who committed gender-motivated violence any deductions or exemptions, or could impose a very high tax on any gifts or inheritances they receive."

II. REGULATION THROUGH SPENDING

UNITED STATES v. BUTLER, 297 U.S. 1, 56 S.Ct. 312, 80 L.Ed. 477 (1936), per ROBERTS, J., held invalid the Agricultural Adjustment Act of 1933. To raise farm prices by reducing supply, the act authorized the government to contract with farmers to reduce their acreage for particular commodities in exchange for benefit payments derived from a tax on processors of that commodity: "The government concedes that the phrase 'to provide for the general welfare' [in cl.1] qualifies the power 'to lay and collect taxes.' The view that the clause grants power to provide for the general welfare, independently of the taxing power, has never been authoritatively accepted. Mr. Justice Story points out that, if it were adopted, ['the] government of the United States [would be], in reality, a government of general and unlimited powers, notwithstanding the subsequent enumeration of specific powers.' The true construction undoubtedly is that the only thing granted is the power to tax for the purpose of providing funds for payment of the nation's debts and making provision for the general [welfare].

---

d. The registration requirement was later held to violate the fifth amendment ban on self-incrimination. *Marchetti v. United States,* 390 U.S. 39, 88 S.Ct. 697, 19 L.Ed.2d 889 (1968).

"Since the foundation of the nation, sharp differences of opinion have persisted as to the true interpretation of the phrase. Madison asserted [that], as the United States is a government of limited and enumerated powers, the grant of power to tax and spend for the general national welfare must be confined to the enumerated legislative fields committed to the Congress. * * * Hamilton, on the other hand, maintained the clause confers a power separate and distinct from those later enumerated, is not restricted in meaning by the grant of them, and Congress consequently has a substantive power to tax and to appropriate, limited only by the requirement that it shall be exercised to provide for the general welfare of the United States. * * * Mr. Justice Story, in his *Commentaries,* espouses the Hamiltonian position. [The] writings of public men and commentators [and] legislative practice [lead] us to conclude that the reading advocated by Mr. Justice Story is the correct one. While, therefore, the power to tax is not unlimited, its confines are set in the clause which confers it, and not in those of section 8 which bestow and define the legislative powers of the Congress. It results that the power of Congress to authorize expenditure of public moneys for public purposes is not limited by the direct grants of legislative power found in the Constitution. * * *

"We are not now required to ascertain the scope of the phrase 'general welfare of the United States' or to determine whether an appropriation in aid of agriculture falls within it. Wholly apart from that question, another principle embedded in our Constitution prohibits the enforcement of the Agricultural Adjustment Act. The act invades the reserved rights of the states. It is a statutory plan to regulate and control agricultural production, a matter beyond the powers delegated to the federal government. * * *

"If the taxing power may not be used as the instrument to enforce a regulation of matters of state concern with respect to which the Congress has no authority to interfere, may it, as in the present case, be employed to raise the money necessary to purchase a compliance which the Congress is powerless to command? The government asserts that whatever might be said against the validity of the plan, if compulsory, it is constitutionally sound because the end is accomplished by voluntary co-operation. [But the] regulation is not in fact voluntary. The farmer, of course, may refuse to comply, but the price of such refusal is the loss of benefits. The amount offered is intended to be sufficient to exert pressure on him to agree to the proposed regulation. The power to confer or withhold unlimited benefits is the power to coerce or destroy. If the cotton grower elects not to accept the benefits, he will receive less for his crops; those who receive payments will be able to undersell him. The result may well be financial ruin. [This] is coercion by economic pressure. * * *

"But if the plan were one for purely voluntary co-operation it would stand no better so far as federal power is concerned. At best, it is a scheme for purchasing with federal funds submission to federal regulation of a subject reserved to the states. [C]ontracts for the reduction of acreage and the control of production are outside the range of [federal power]. Congress cannot invade state jurisdiction to compel individual action; no more can it purchase such action. * * *

"We are not here concerned with a conditional appropriation of money, nor with a provision that if certain conditions are not complied with the appropriation shall no longer be available. [There] is an obvious difference between a statute stating the conditions upon which moneys shall be expended and one effective only upon assumption of a contractual obligation to submit to a regulation which otherwise could not be enforced. Many examples pointing the distinction might be cited. We are referred to appropriations in aid of education, and it is said that no one has doubted the power of Congress to stipulate the sort of education for which money shall be expended. But an appropriation to an educational institution which by its terms is to become available only if the beneficiary enters into a contract to teach doctrines subversive of the Constitution is clearly bad. An affirmance of the authority of Congress so to condition the expenditure of an appropriation would tend to nullify all constitutional limitations upon legislative power."

STONE, J., joined by Brandeis and Cardozo, JJ., dissented: "As the present depressed state of agriculture is nation wide in its extent and effects, there is no basis for saying that the expenditure of public money in aid of farmers is not within the specifically granted power of Congress to levy taxes to 'provide for [the] general welfare.'

"[The] suggestion of coercion finds no support in the record or in any data showing the actual operation of the act. Threat of loss, not hope of gain, is the essence of economic coercion. Members of a long-depressed industry have undoubtedly been tempted to curtail acreage by the hope of resulting better prices and by the proffered opportunity to obtain needed ready money. But there is nothing to indicate that those who accepted benefits were impelled by fear of lower prices if they did not accept, or that at any stage in the operation of the plan a farmer could say whether, apart from the certainty of cash payments at specified times, the advantage would lie with curtailment of production plus compensation, rather than with the same or increased acreage plus the expected rise in prices which actually occurred. [Of] the total number of farms growing cotton, estimated at 1,500,000, 33% in 1934 and 13% in 1935 did not participate. * * *

"The Constitution requires that public funds shall be spent for a defined purpose, the promotion of the general welfare. Their expenditure usually involves payment on terms which will insure use by the selected recipients within the limits of the constitutional purpose. [The] power of Congress to spend is inseparable from persuasion to action over which Congress has no legislative control. Congress may not command that the science of agriculture be taught in state universities. But if it would aid the teaching of that science by grants to state institutions, it is appropriate, if not necessary, that the grant be on the condition [that] it be used for the intended purpose. Similarly it would seem to be compliance with the Constitution, not violation of it, for the government to take and the university to give a contract that the grant would be so [used]. Condition and promise are alike valid since both are in furtherance of the national purpose for which the money is appropriated.

"[The] spending power of Congress is in addition to the legislative power and not subordinate to it. This independent grant of the power of the purse, and its very nature, involving in its exercise the duty to insure expenditure within the granted power, presuppose freedom of selection among divers ends and aims, and the capacity to impose such conditions as will render the choice effective. It is a contradiction in terms to say that there is power to spend for the national welfare, while rejecting any power to impose conditions reasonably adapted to the attainment of the ends which alone would justify the expenditure.

"[If] the expenditure is for a national public purpose, that purpose will not be thwarted because payment is on condition which will advance that purpose. [If] appropriation in aid of a program of curtailment of agricultural production is constitutional, and it is not denied that it is, payment to farmers on condition that they reduce their crop acreage is constitutional. It is not any the less so because the farmer at his own option promises to fulfill the condition.''

Notes and Questions

Butler's reasoning. Did the majority *really* adopt Hamilton's position? Is there a difference of constitutional dimension between educational grants conditioned on the education meeting federal standards beyond the federal power to command and financial grants to farmers conditioned on their reduction of planted acreage?

STEWARD MACHINE CO. v. DAVIS

301 U.S. 548, 57 S.Ct. 883, 81 L.Ed. 1279 (1937).

JUSTICE CARDOZO delivered the opinion of the Court.

[Under Title IX of the Social Security Act, relating to unemployment compensation, the proceeds of a federal payroll tax on employers went into the general federal treasury. But these employers received 90% credit on their federal tax for payments to a state unemployment compensation fund under a state law that met federal requirements.]

The excise is not void as involving the coercion of the states in contravention of the Tenth Amendment. [To] draw the line intelligently between duress and inducement, there is need to remind ourselves of facts as to the problem of unemployment. [During] the years 1929 to 1936, when the country was passing through a cyclical depression, the number of the unemployed mounted to unprecedented heights. [T]he states were unable to give the requisite relief. [It] is too late today for the argument to be heard with tolerance that in a crisis so extreme the use of the moneys of the nation to relieve the unemployed and their dependents is a use for any purpose narrower than the promotion of the general welfare. Cf. *Butler; Helvering v. Davis* [infra], decided herewith.

[The] assailants of the statute say that its dominant end and aim is to drive the state Legislatures under the whip of economic pressure into the enactment of unemployment compensation laws at the bidding of the central government. Supporters of the statute say that its operation is not constraint, but the creation of a larger freedom, the states and the nation joining in a co-operative endeavor to avert a common evil. Before Congress acted, unemployment compensation insurance was still, for the most part, a project and no more. [But] if states had been holding back before the passage of the federal law, inaction was not owing, for the most part, to the lack of sympathetic interest. Many held back through alarm lest in laying such a toll upon their industries, they would place themselves in a position of economic disadvantage as compared with neighbors or competitors. Two consequences ensued. One was that the freedom of a state to contribute its fair share to the solution of a national problem was paralyzed by fear. The other was that in so far as there was failure by the states to contribute relief according to the measure of their capacity, a disproportionate burden, and a mountainous one, was laid upon the resources of the government of the nation.

The Social Security Act is an attempt to find a method by which all these public agencies may work together to a common end. Every dollar of the new taxes will continue in all likelihood to be used and needed by the nation as long as states are unwilling, whether through timidity or for other motives, to do what can be done at home. [On] the other hand, fulfillment of the home duty will be lightened and encouraged by crediting the taxpayer upon his account with the

Treasury of the nation to the extent that his contributions under the laws of the locality have simplified or diminished the problem of relief and the probable demand upon the resources of the fisc. * * *

Who then is coerced through the operation of this statute? Not the taxpayer. He pays in fulfillment of the mandate of the local legislature. Not the state. Even now she does not offer a suggestion that in passing the unemployment law she was affected by duress. For all that appears, she is satisfied with her choice, and would be sorely disappointed if it were now to be annulled. [E]very rebate from a tax when conditioned upon conduct is in some measure a temptation. But to hold that motive or temptation is equivalent to coercion is to plunge the law in endless difficulties. The outcome of such a doctrine is the acceptance of a philosophical determinism by which choice becomes impossible. Till now the law has been guided by a robust common sense which assumes the freedom of the will as a working hypothesis in the solution of its problems. The wisdom of the hypothesis has illustration in this case. [We] cannot say that [Alabama] was acting, not of her unfettered will, but under the strain of a persuasion equivalent to undue influence, when she chose to have relief administered under laws of her own making, by agents of her own selection, instead of under federal laws, administered by federal officers, with all the ensuing evils, at least to many minds, of federal patronage and power. * * *

In ruling as we do, we leave many questions open. We do not say that a tax is valid, when imposed by act of Congress, if it is laid upon the condition that a state may escape its operation through the adoption of a statute unrelated in subject-matter to activities fairly within the scope of national policy and power. No such question is before us. In the tender of this credit Congress does not intrude upon fields foreign to its function. The purpose of its intervention, as we have shown, is to safeguard its own treasury and as an incident to that protection to place the states upon a footing of equal opportunity. [It] is one thing to impose a tax dependent upon the conduct of the taxpayers, or of the state in which they live, where the conduct to be stimulated or discouraged is unrelated to the fiscal need subserved by the tax in its formal operation, or to any other end legitimately national. [It] is quite another thing to say that a tax will be abated upon the doing of an act that will satisfy the fiscal need, the tax and the alternative being approximate equivalents. In such circumstances, if in no others, inducement or persuasion does not go beyond the bounds of power.

[*Butler*] was by a divided court, a minority taking the view that the objections were untenable. None of them is applicable [here].

(a) The proceeds of the tax in controversy are not earmarked for a special group.

(b) The unemployment compensation law which is a condition of the credit has had the approval of the state and could not be a law without it.

(c) The condition is not linked to an irrevocable agreement, for the state at its pleasure may repeal its unemployment [law], terminate the credit, and place itself where it was before the credit was accepted.

(d) The condition is not directed to the attainment of an unlawful end, but to an end, the relief of unemployment, for which nation and state may lawfully cooperate.

[The] statute does not call for a surrender by the states of powers essential to their quasi sovereign existence. [A] credit to taxpayers for payments made to a state under a state unemployment law will be manifestly futile in the absence of some assurance that the law leading to the credit is in truth what it professes to be. [What] is basic and essential may be assured by suitable conditions. The terms embodied in these sections are directed to that end. A wide range of judgment is given to the several states as to the particular type of statute to be spread upon their books. [What] they may not do, if they would earn the credit, is to depart from those standards which in the judgment of Congress are to be ranked as fundamental. * * *a

Notes and Questions

1. *Coercion or inducement?* Which program comes closer to "coercion" or "the strain of persuasion equivalent to undue influence"? Were the farmers in *Butler* or the states in *Steward* more free to resist the federal "inducement" or "coercion" or "temptation"? Consider Jesse H. Choper, *The Supreme Court and Unconstitutional Conditions: Federalism and Individual Rights,* 4 Corn.J.L. & Pub.Pol. 460, 464–65 (1995): "[T]he Court [has] refused to recognize 'coercion,' when it has 'stared the Court in the face.' [T]here is no clearer example [than *Steward*]. The national government took the states' money. The states received nothing in return if they did not comply with the federal government's demands. However, the states did regain 90% of the funds if they established a proper unemployment compensation system." Or do "offers of conditioned benefits expand rather than contract the options of the beneficiary class, and so present beneficiaries with a free choice"? Kathleen M. Sullivan, *Unconstitutional Conditions,* 102 Harv.L.Rev. 1415, 1428 (1989) If Congress offers a state university funds to enhance science education (or build a new athletic stadium), is this "coercive" or does it simply "expand its options"? Consider Tribe 3d ed., at 840–41: "It is not clear what, if any, form of conditional spending could constitute [forbidden] compulsion; the Court has provided little guidance on the question, and it implicates the deeper philosophical question whether—assuming that choice and free will can sometimes be meaningful—there is any form or level of inducement that can truly render someone unable to choose, as well as the question of what choice and compulsion mean when we are talking about *states* rather than persons."

2. *Federal "fiscal needs."* Can the spending in *Butler* (to "purchase" compliance by the farmers with a reduced acreage program in order to provide relief for a depressed national agriculture) be fairly distinguished from the tax and credit device in *Steward* (to induce states to adopt unemployment compensation) on the ground that, in *Steward,* Congress did not "intrude upon fields foreign to its function" in view of the national fiscal responsibility for relief of the unemployed? Can most conditions on federal funding to induce state regulation (or private conduct) that Congress feels are needed to advance the general welfare be justified on the basis of Congress' "fiscal need [to] safeguard its own treasury"?

3. *Definition of "general welfare."* (a) HELVERING v. DAVIS, 301 U.S. 619, 57 S.Ct. 904, 81 L.Ed. 1307 (1937), per CARDOZO, J., upheld the Social Security Act's old age pension program, supported exclusively by federal taxes: "The line must still be drawn between one welfare and another, between the particular and the general. [The] discretion [belongs] to congress, unless the choice is clearly wrong, a display of arbitrary power, not an exercise of judgment. [Nor] is the

---

a. McReynolds and Butler, JJ., dissented in separate opinions. Sutherland, J., joined by Van Devanter, J., agreed that the act did not coerce the states, but contended that the administrative provisions of the act unconstitutionally encroached on state powers (an issue considered in Sec. 5 infra).

concept of the general welfare static. Needs that were narrow or parochial a century ago may be interwoven in our day with the well-being of the nation. * * *

"The problem is plainly national in area and dimensions. Moreover, laws of the separate states cannot deal with it effectively. Congress, at least, had a basis for that belief. States and local governments are often lacking in the resources that are necessary to finance an adequate program of security for the aged. [Apart] from the failure of resources, states and local governments are at times reluctant to increase so heavily the burden of taxation to be borne by their residents for fear of placing themselves in a position of economic disadvantage as compared with neighbors or competitors. [A] system of old age pensions has special dangers of its own, if put in force in one state and rejected in another. The existence of such a system is a bait to the needy and dependent elsewhere, encouraging them to migrate and seek a haven of repose. Only a power that is national can serve the interests of all." Butler and McReynolds, JJ., dissented.

(b) In upholding the power to spend for large scale federal land reclamation projects, *United States v. Gerlach Live Stock Co.*, 339 U.S. 725, 70 S.Ct. 955, 94 L.Ed. 1231 (1950), stated: "Congress has a substantive power to tax and appropriate for the general welfare, limited only by the requirement that it shall be exercised for the common benefit as distinguished from some mere local purpose." Is some nationwide need or some common benefit, widely shared, a requisite for federal spending? Should it be? Would an appropriation for an irrigation project that would only benefit land within a 50 mile radius be valid? An appropriation to prevent the bankruptcy of Detroit?

(c) *Judicial review.* Assuming standing to challenge a federal expenditure,[a] are courts qualified to make independent judgments on "general welfare" spending issues? Could the Court responsibly rule such issues nonjusticiable? By what reasoning might the Court appropriately leave such issues to congressional judgment without abdicating its "duty [to] say what the law is" (*Marbury*) on constitutional issues?

SOUTH DAKOTA v. DOLE

483 U.S. 203, 107 S.Ct. 2793, 97 L.Ed.2d 171 (1987).

CHIEF JUSTICE REHNQUIST delivered the opinion of the Court.

Petitioner South Dakota permits persons 19 years of age or older to purchase beer containing up to 3.2% alcohol. In 1984 Congress enacted 23 U.S.C. § 158 [withholding 5%] of federal highway funds otherwise allocable from States "in which the purchase or public possession [of] any alcoholic beverage by a person who is less than twenty-one years of age is lawful." * * *

The spending power is of course not unlimited, *Pennhurst State School and Hospital v. Halderman*, 451 U.S. 1, 17, and n. 13, 101 S.Ct. 1531, 1540 n. 13, 67 L.Ed.2d 694 (1981), but is instead subject to several general restrictions articulated in our cases. The first of these limitations is derived from the language of the Constitution itself: the exercise of the spending power must be in pursuit of "the general welfare." In considering whether a particular expenditure is intended to serve general public purposes, courts should defer substantially to the judgment of Congress. *Helvering.*[2] Second, we have required that if Congress desires to

---

a. Standing to challenge federal spending is considered in Ch. 12, Sec. 2, II.

2. The level of deference to the congressional decision is such that the Court has more recently questioned whether "general welfare"

condition the States' receipt of federal funds, it "must do so unambiguously, [enabling] the States to exercise their choice knowingly, cognizant of the consequences of their participation." *Pennhurst*. Third, our cases have suggested (without significant elaboration) that conditions on federal grants might be illegitimate if they are unrelated "to the federal interest in particular national projects or programs." *Massachusetts v. United States*, 435 U.S. 444, 461, 98 S.Ct. 1153, 1164, 55 L.Ed.2d 403 (1978) (plurality opinion). Finally, we have noted that other constitutional provisions may provide an independent bar to the conditional grant of federal funds.

South Dakota does not seriously claim that § 158 is inconsistent with any of the first three restrictions mentioned [above.] Indeed, the condition imposed by Congress is directly related to one of the main purposes for which highway funds are expended—safe interstate travel. [A] Presidential commission appointed to study alcohol-related accidents and fatalities on the Nation's highways concluded that the lack of uniformity in the States' drinking ages created "an incentive to drink and drive" because "young persons commut[e] to border States where the drinking age is lower." * * *

The remaining question about the validity of § 158—and the basic point of disagreement between the parties—is whether the Twenty-first Amendment constitutes an "independent constitutional bar." [Petitioner] asserts that "Congress may not use the spending power to regulate that which it is prohibited from regulating directly under the Twenty-first Amendment." But our cases [have] established that the constitutional limitations on Congress when exercising its spending power are less exacting than those on its authority to regulate directly.

We have also held that a perceived Tenth Amendment limitation on congressional regulation of state affairs did not concomitantly limit the range of conditions legitimately placed on federal grants. In *Oklahoma v. Civil Service Comm'n*, 330 U.S. 127, 67 S.Ct. 544, 91 L.Ed. 794 (1947), the Court considered the validity of the Hatch Act insofar as it was applied to political activities of state officials whose employment was financed in whole or in part with federal funds. The State contended that an order under this provision to withhold certain federal funds unless a state official was removed invaded its sovereignty in violation of the Tenth Amendment. Though finding that "the United States is not concerned with, and has no power to regulate, local political activities as such of state officials," the Court nevertheless held that the Federal Government "does have power to fix the terms upon which its money allotments to states shall be disbursed." The Court found no violation of the State's sovereignty because the State could, and did, adopt "the 'simple expedient' of not yielding to what she urges is federal coercion. The offer of benefits to a state by the United States dependent upon cooperation by the state with federal plans, assumedly for the general welfare, is not unusual."

[T]he language in our earlier opinions stands for the unexceptionable proposition that the [spending] power may not be used to induce the States to engage in activities that would themselves be unconstitutional. Thus, for example, a grant of federal funds conditioned on invidiously discriminatory state action or the infliction of cruel and unusual punishment would be an illegitimate exercise of the Congress' broad spending power. But no such claim can be or is made here. Were South Dakota to succumb to the blandishments offered by Congress and raise its

is a judicially enforceable restriction at all. See *Buckley v. Valeo*, 424 U.S. 1, 90–91, 96 S.Ct. 612, 668–669, 46 L.Ed.2d 659 (1976) (per curiam).

drinking age to 21, the State's action in so doing would not violate the constitutional rights of anyone.

Our decisions have recognized that in some circumstances the financial inducement offered by Congress might be so coercive as to pass the point at which "pressure turns into compulsion." *Steward.* Here, however, Congress has directed only that a State desiring to establish a minimum drinking age lower than 21 lose a relatively small percentage of certain federal highway funds. [A] conditional grant of federal money of this sort is [not] unconstitutional simply by reason of its success in achieving the congressional objective.[a] * * *

Here Congress has offered relatively mild encouragement to the States to enact higher minimum drinking ages than they would otherwise choose. But the enactment of such laws remains the prerogative of the States not merely in theory but in fact. Even if Congress might lack the power to impose a national minimum drinking age directly, we conclude that encouragement to state action found in § 158 is a valid use of the spending power. * * *

JUSTICE O'CONNOR, dissenting.

[T]he Court's application of the requirement that the condition imposed be reasonably related to the purpose for which the funds are expended is cursory and unconvincing. * * *

When Congress appropriates money to build a highway, it is entitled to insist that the highway be a safe one. But it is not entitled to insist as a condition of the use of highway funds that the State impose or change regulations in other areas of the State's social and economic life because of an attenuated or tangential relationship to highway use or safety. Indeed, if the rule were otherwise, the Congress could effectively regulate almost any area of a State's social, political, or economic life on the theory that use of the interstate transportation system is somehow enhanced. If, for example, the United States were to condition highway moneys upon moving the state capital, I suppose it might argue that interstate transportation is facilitated by locating local governments in places easily accessible to interstate highways—or, conversely, that highways might become overburdened if they had to carry traffic to and from the state capital. In my mind, such a relationship is hardly more attenuated than the one which the Court finds supports § 158.

There is a clear place at which the Court can draw the line between permissible and impermissible conditions on federal grants. [The] difference turns on whether the requirement specifies in some way how the money should be spent, so that Congress' intent in making the grant will be effectuated. [A] requirement that is not such a specification is not a condition, but a regulation, which is valid only if it falls within one of Congress' delegated regulatory powers. * * *

This approach harks back to *Butler.* [The] error in *Butler* was not the Court's conclusion that the Act was essentially regulatory, but rather its crabbed view of the extent of Congress' regulatory power under the Commerce Clause. The Agricultural Adjustment Act was regulatory but it was regulation that today would likely be considered within Congress' commerce power.

a. *Pennhurst*, per Rehnquist, J., observed that "legislation enacted pursuant to the spending power is much in the nature of a contract: in return for federal funds, the States agree to comply with federally imposed conditions. The legitimacy of Congress' power to legislate under the spending power thus rests on whether the State voluntarily and knowingly accepts the terms of the 'contract.' "

[If] the spending power is to be limited only by Congress' notion of the general welfare, the reality, given the vast financial resources of the Federal Government, is that the Spending Clause gives "power to the Congress to tear down the barriers, to invade the states' jurisdiction, and to become a parliament of the whole people, subject to no restrictions save such as are self-imposed." This, of course, as *Butler* held, was not the Framers' plan and it is not the meaning of the Spending Clause.

Our later cases are consistent with the notion that, under the spending power, the Congress may only condition grants in ways that can fairly be said to be related to the expenditure of federal funds [discussing *Oklahoma v. CSC*. But] a condition that a State will raise its drinking age to 21 [has] nothing to do with how the funds Congress has appropriated are expended. Rather [it] is a regulation determining who shall be able to drink liquor. As such it is not justified by the spending power.

Of the other possible sources of congressional authority for regulating the sale of liquor only the commerce power comes to mind. But in my view, the regulation of the age of the purchasers of liquor, just as the regulation of the price at which liquor may be sold, falls squarely within the scope of those powers reserved to the States by the Twenty-first Amendment.[b] * * *

Notes and Questions

1. *Reach of spending power.* (a) May Congress provide that any person who steals or misappropriates money from any entity that receives federal funds, or who makes corrupt offers to agents of such an entity, is guilty of a federal crime? See George D. Brown, *Stealth Statute—Corruption, The Spending Power, and the Rise of 18 U.S.C. § 666*, 73 Not.D.L.Rev. 247 (1998). May Congress provide that an emergency room doctor, in any hospital that receives federal funds, who withholds emergency room services from persons because of their inability to pay, is guilty of a federal crime? Cf. Emergency Medical Treatment and Active Labor Act, 42 U.S.C. § 1395dd. Do you agree that under *Dole*, "Congress may effectively regulate almost any area of a State's social, political, or economic life" (O'Connor, J.)? Might Congress use the spending power to achieve the results invalidated in *Lopez* and *Morrison*?

(b) Does O'Connor, J.'s approach provide an effective limit on the spending power? Consider Kimberley Sayers–Fay, *Conditional Federal Spending: A Back Door to Enhanced Free Exercise Protection*, 88 Calif.L.Rev. 1281, 1320–21 (2000): "The requirement that conditions 'specify in some way how the money should be spent is exceedingly porous. [After *Dole*, what] if Congress dictated that the funds be expended in order to build 'safe roads' or even 'safe roads where a twenty-one-year-old drinking age obtains'? Would that not be specifying in some way how the money should be spent?" Could Congress allocate funds to pay for many additional state judges, including those needed to adjudicate an effective new civil damages action against perpetrators by victims of gender-motivated violence? Could Congress allocate "Safe School Funds" to those states that make it a crime to possess guns in a school zone?

2. *Other proposed approaches.* (a) Consider Lynn A. Baker, *Conditional Spending After Lopez*, 95 Colum.L.Rev. 1911, 1962–64 (1995): "[T]hose offers of federal funds to the states which, if accepted, would regulate the states in ways that Congress could not directly mandate, will be presumed invalid. This presump-

---

b. Brennan, J., agreed with this point in a brief, separate dissent.

tion will be rebutted upon a determination that the offer of funds constitutes 'reimbursement spending' rather than 'regulatory spending.' 'Reimbursement spending' legislation specifies the *purpose* for which the states are to spend the offered federal funds and simply reimburses the states, in whole or in part, [and "an amount of money no greater than that necessary"] for their expenditures for that purpose."

(b) Consider Choper, note 1 after *Steward*, at 464: "There is a feeling that if the spending power is an independent power, then Congress must be able to engage in conditioned spending. However, that does not logically follow. The Court could hold that Congress has an independent spending power, but does not have authority to condition its spending on conduct it could not directly require using one of its regulatory powers. For example, suppose Congress has no power to require tiny lakes throughout the nation be free of pollution. Nonetheless, if Congress wishes to spend federal money to accomplish this goal, it may accomplish it through the independent use of the spending power."

(c) Consider Albert J. Rosenthal, *Conditional Federal Spending and the Constitution*, 39 Stan.L.Rev. 1103, 1121–23 (1987): "[As] in so many other areas of the law, decisions must be predicated upon some form of balancing of interests. [Where] the validity of coercive conditions on spending has been under consideration, the growing tendency of the Supreme Court has been to weigh them case by case rather than to resolve them by reference to some broad formulation relating to unconstitutional conditions."

SECTION 4. FOREIGN AFFAIRS POWER

The preceding materials on the commerce, taxing, and spending powers should provide adequate background for consideration of issues relating to the many other congressional powers. See, e.g., note 5 after *Darby* (war powers). This section, however, involves a significant, atypical congressional power.

I. TREATIES AS A SOURCE OF LEGISLATIVE POWER

MISSOURI v. HOLLAND, 252 U.S. 416, 40 S.Ct. 382, 64 L.Ed. 641 (1920), per HOLMES, J., upheld the Migratory Bird Treaty Act that regulated the taking of migratory birds in the United States. A treaty with Canada obligated both countries to seek legislation[a] protecting birds that traversed both countries, and were valued for food and as destroyers of insects harmful to vegetation: "[It] is not enough to refer to the Tenth Amendment [because] by Article 2, Section 2, the power to make treaties is delegated expressly, and by Article 6 treaties made under the authority of the United States, along with the Constitution and laws of the United States made in pursuance thereof, are declared the supreme law of the land.[b] If the treaty is valid there can be no dispute about the validity of the statute [as] a necessary and proper means to execute the powers of the Government. * * *

"It is said [that] there are [constitutional limits] to the treaty-making power, and that one such limit is that what an act of Congress could not do unaided, in

a. Thus, the treaty was not, by its terms, "self-executing (see fn. d, p. 186 infra), but rather required congressional implementation.

b. "[A] treaty is placed on the same footing [with] an act of legislation. [When] the two relate to the same subject, the courts will al-ways endeavor to construe them so as to give effect to both, [but] if the two are inconsistent, the one last in date will control the other." *Whitney v. Robertson*, 124 U.S. 190, 8 S.Ct. 456, 31 L.Ed. 386 (1888).

derogation of the powers reserved to the States,[c] a treaty cannot do. [Acts] of Congress are the supreme law of the land only when made in pursuance of the Constitution, while treaties are declared to be so when made under the authority of the United States. It is open to question whether the authority of the United States means more than the formal acts prescribed to make the convention. We do not mean to imply that there are no qualifications to the treaty-making power; but they must be ascertained in a different way. It is obvious that there may be matters of the sharpest exigency for the national well being that an act of Congress could not deal with but that a treaty followed by such an act could, and it is not lightly to be assumed that, in matters requiring national action, 'a power which must belong to and somewhere reside in every civilized government' is not to be found. [W]hen we are dealing with words that also are a constituent act, like the Constitution of the United States, we must realize that they have called into life a being the development of which could not have been foreseen completely by the most gifted of its begetters. It was enough for them to realize or to hope that they had created an organism; it has taken a century and has cost their successors much sweat and blood to prove that they created a nation. The case before us must be considered in the light of our whole experience and not merely in that of what was said a hundred years ago. The treaty in question does not contravene any prohibitory words to be found in the Constitution. The only question is whether it is forbidden by some invisible radiation from the general terms of the Tenth Amendment. We must consider what this country has become in deciding what that amendment has reserved. * * *

"Here a national interest of very nearly the first magnitude is involved. It can be protected only by national action in concert with that of another power. The subject matter is only transitorily within the State and has no permanent habitat therein. But for the treaty and the statute there soon might be no birds for any powers to deal with. We see nothing in the Constitution that compels the Government to sit by while a food supply is cut off and the protectors of our forests and our crops are destroyed. It is not sufficient to rely upon the States. The reliance is vain, and were it otherwise, the question is whether the United States is forbidden to act. We are of opinion that the treaty and statute must be upheld." Van Devanter and Pitney, JJ., dissented without opinion.

Notes and Questions

1. *Scope of treaty power.* (a) Are there judicially manageable limits on the federal government's power to expand its regulatory power through treaties? *De Geofroy v. Riggs*, 133 U.S. 258, 10 S.Ct. 295, 33 L.Ed. 642 (1890), stated that the treaty power "extends to all proper subjects of negotiation between our government and the government of other nations." In 1965, *Restatement (Second) of the Foreign Relations Law of the United States* provided that the treaty power is limited to matters "of international concern," i.e., it "must relate to the external concerns of the nation as distinguished from matters of a purely internal nature." But in 1987, *Restatement (Third)* declared that "contrary to what was once suggested, the Constitution does not require that an international agreement deal

---

c. At the time, "the Commerce Clause had not been read in a sufficiently sweeping fashion to permit birds flying across state lines to be treated as articles in interstate commerce, especially since there was very little evidence that birds were actually transported across state lines, as distinguished from flying across them of their own volition." G. Edward White, *The Transformation of the Constitutional Regime of Foreign Relations*, 85 Va.L.Rev. 1, 65 (1999).

only with 'matters of international concern.' "[a] Consider Curtis A. Bradley, *The Treaty Power and American Federalism*, 97 Mich.L.Rev. 390, 396–97 (1998): "This dichotomy [between internal and external concerns] might have been accurate at one time in American history, when treaties were generally bilateral and regulated matters such as diplomatic immunity, military neutrality, and removal of trade barriers. [During] the latter part of this century, however, there has been a proliferation of treaties [that] take the form of detailed multilateral instruments [designed] to operate as international 'legislation' binding on much of the world. [Many] concern matters that in the past countries would have addressed wholly domestically. This change in treaty-making is most evident in the area of international human rights law, [on] issues such as racial and gender equality, criminal procedure and punishment, and religious freedom [where] conflict is likely to occur at the state level." For the view that the Founders understood "that the treaty power was limited either by subject matter, by the reserved powers of the states, or both" and that, therefore, "the treaty power should be subject to the same federalism limitations that apply to Congress's legislative powers," see id. at 417, 450.[b]

2. *"Prohibitory words."* REID v. COVERT, 354 U.S. 1, 77 S.Ct. 1222, 1 L.Ed.2d 1148 (1957), per BLACK, J. (plurality opinion), reversed murder convictions of U.S. military dependents for denial of jury trials by U.S. military courts in Great Britain, pursuant to jurisdiction under a treaty: "No agreement with a foreign nation can confer power on Congress, or any other branch of Government, which is free from the restraints of the Constitution. [The] reason treaties were not limited [in the Supremacy Clause] to those made in 'pursuance' of the Constitution was so that agreements made by the United States under the Articles of Confederation [would] remain in effect. [*Holland*] carefully noted that the treaty involved was not inconsistent with any specific provision of the Constitution."[c]

II. OTHER BASES FOR LEGISLATIVE POWER OVER FOREIGN AFFAIRS

Is congressional power to legislate on foreign affairs limited to laws implementing treaties and to such sources as are found in Art. I, § 8, the Civil War Amendments, and similar grants of legislative power? Is a broader source of legislative power on foreign affairs needed?

————

PEREZ v. BROWNELL, 356 U.S. 44, 78 S.Ct. 568, 2 L.Ed.2d 603 (1958), per FRANKFURTER, J., upheld a federal statute mandating loss of U.S. citizenship for

a. The Chief Reporter for *Restatement (Third)* had earlier written: "What is of international concern, what affects American foreign relations and is relevant to American foreign policy, what matters the United States wishes to negotiate about, differ from generation to generation, perhaps from year to year, with the ever-changing character of relations between nations." Louis Henkin, *The Constitution, Treaties, and International Human Rights*, 116 U.Pa.L.Rev. 1012, 1025 (1968).

b. For a brief summary of the abortive attack on *Holland* through the proposed

"Bricker Amendment," drawn to limit the "internal law" effect of a treaty to "legislation that would be valid in the absence of a treaty," see Louis Henkin, *Foreign Affairs and the Constitution* 146–47 (1972).

c. Warren, C.J., Douglas and Brennan, JJ., joined in Black, J.'s plurality opinion. Frankfurter and Harlan, JJ., concurred as to capital cases. Clark and Burton, JJ., dissented. Whittaker, J., took no part.

"voting in a political election in a foreign state." The court viewed this effort, to prevent the international tensions risked by a citizen's "participat[ing] in the political or governmental affairs of another country," as based upon Congress' "power to regulate foreign affairs:" "Although there is in the Constitution no specific grant to Congress of power to enact legislation for the effective regulation of foreign affairs, there can be no doubt of the existence of this power in the law-making organ of the nation. See *United States v. Curtiss–Wright Export Corp.* 299 U.S. 304, 318, 57 S.Ct. 216, 81 L.Ed. 255, 261 (1936);[a] *Mackenzie v. Hare,* 239 U.S. 299, 311, 312, 36 S.Ct. 106, 60 L.Ed. 297, 301. The states that joined together to form a single nation and to create, through the constitution, a federal government to conduct the affairs of that nation must be held to have granted that government the powers indispensable to its functioning effectively in the company of sovereign nations. The government must be able not only to deal affirmatively with foreign nations, as it does through the maintenance of diplomatic relations with them and the protection of American citizens sojourning within their territories. It must also be able to reduce to a minimum the frictions that are unavoidable in a world of sovereigns sensitive in matters touching their dignity and interests."[b]

Notes and Questions

Scope of foreign affairs power? Are there manageable standards by which to limit Congress' power over foreign affairs? *Perez* reasoned that "a rational nexus must exist between the content of a specific power in Congress and the action of Congress. [In this case,] withdrawal of citizenship [must] be reasonably related to the end—here, regulation of foreign affairs." For a comprehensive view of Congress' "foreign affairs power" under the *Curtiss-Wright* and *Perez* rationale, coupled with a recognition of the breadth of Congress' power over foreign affairs derived from the specified powers of Congress, see Henkin, fn. b supra, at 69–74.

SECTION 5. APPLYING NATIONAL POWERS TO STATE GOVERNMENTS: INTERGOVERNMENTAL IMMUNITIES

I. ORIGINS OF IMMUNITIES

Intergovernmental immunity as a constitutional limit on state and federal power started with immunity of the federal government from state taxation. McCULLOCH v. MARYLAND, Sec. 1 supra, held invalid Maryland's taxes on the Bank of United States: "[The] great principle [that sustains the bank's] claim to be exempted from the power of the state to tax its operations [is] that the Constitution and the laws made in pursuance thereof are supreme; that they control the Constitution and laws of the respective [states]. From this, [other] propositions are deduced as corollaries[:] 1st. That a power to create implies a power to preserve. 2d. That a power to destroy, if wielded by a different hand, is

---

a. The *Curtiss-Wright* opinion appears in Ch. 3, Sec. 3.

b. In three opinions Warren, C.J., and Black, Douglas and Whittaker, JJ., dissented from the ruling that Congress could impose involuntary expatriation, but did not question

the *Perez* comments on Congress' power to legislate on foreign affairs. Nor did *Afroyim v. Rusk,* 387 U.S. 253, 87 S.Ct. 1660, 18 L.Ed.2d 757 (1967), which overruled the *Perez* expatriation ruling as inconsistent with § 1 of the fourteenth amendment.

hostile to, and incompatible with, these powers to create and to preserve. 3d. That where this repugnancy exists, that authority which is supreme must control * * *.

"That the power of taxing [the bank] by the states may be exercised so as to destroy it, is too obvious to be denied. * * *

"The argument [of] Maryland, is, not that the states may directly resist a law of Congress, but that they may exercise their acknowledged powers upon it, and that the Constitution leaves them this right in the confidence that they will not abuse it. [But this principle is] capable of arresting all the measures of the [government]. If the states may tax one instrument, employed by the government in the execution of its powers, they may tax any and every other instrument. They may tax the mail; they may tax the mint; they may tax patent rights; they may tax the papers of the customhouse; they may tax judicial process; they may tax all the means employed by the government, to an excess which would defeat all the ends of government.

"[If state] supremacy as to taxation be acknowledged; what is to restrain their exercising this control in any shape they may please to give it? Their sovereignty is not confined to taxation. That is not the only mode in which it might be displayed. The question is, in truth, a question of supremacy * * *.

"This opinion does not deprive the states of any resources which they originally possessed. It does not extend to a tax paid by the real property of the bank, in common with the other real property within the state, nor to a tax imposed on the interest which the citizens of Maryland may hold in this institution, in common with other property of the same description throughout the state. But this is [a] tax on the operation of an instrument employed by the government of the Union to carry its powers into execution. Such a tax must be unconstitutional."

Notes and Questions

1. *Birth of state immunity from federal taxes.* Just as *Dobbins v. Commissioners*, 41 U.S. (16 Pet.) 435, 10 L.Ed. 1022 (1842), invoked *McCulloch* to strike down a state tax on the salary of a federal officer, COLLECTOR v. DAY, 78 U.S. (11 Wall.) 113, 20 L.Ed. 122 (1871), invoked *McCulloch* and its reasoning to invalidate a federal income tax on the salary of a state judge as an "instrumentality" of state government. It viewed the independent, "sovereign powers" reserved to the states by the tenth amendment as the foundation for state immunity from federal taxes, analogous to the role of the supremacy clause as the foundation for federal immunity from state taxes: "[If] the means and instrumentalities employed by [the General Government] to carry into operation the powers granted to it are, necessarily, and, for the sake of self-preservation, exempt from taxation by the States, why are not those of the States depending upon their reserved powers, for like reasons, equally exempt from federal taxation? [It] is admitted that there is no express provision in the Constitution that prohibits the General Government from taxing the means and instrumentalities of the States, nor is there any prohibiting the States from taxing the means and instrumentalities of that government. In both cases the exemption rests upon necessary implication, and is upheld by the great law of self-preservation; as any government, whose means employed in conducting its operations, if subject to the control of another and distinct government, can exist only at the mercy of that government. Of what avail are these means if another power may tax them at discretion?"

2. *Expansion and contraction. Dobbins* and *Collector* led to broad expansion of intergovernmental immunities to relieve private taxpayers from state or federal taxes arising from transactions with the other government, even to striking down the application of a state income tax to royalties from a federal patent.[a] But beginning in 1938, this line of cases was abandoned,[b] and the Court has not invoked intergovernmental immunity to protect private taxpayers, even when their tax burden was passed on to the other government,[c] except for discrimination against state employees.[d]

The focus, then, in the following materials is on (1) the remaining immunity from federal taxes for state and local governments, their property and instrumentalities, and vice versa, (2) the criteria for deciding such issues, and (3) the impact of these tax immunity policies upon state immunity from federal regulation.

II. STATE IMMUNITY FROM FEDERAL TAXES

Since 1938, although the Court has invalidated no federal tax on a state, its activities, agencies or property, its opinions have not questioned a state's right to immunity in appropriate situations. Both cases to reach the Court since 1938 upheld the federal tax, but in neither did a majority concur on a statement of the controlling considerations.

NEW YORK v. UNITED STATES, 326 U.S. 572, 66 S.Ct. 310, 90 L.Ed. 326 (1946), upheld application of a federal excise tax to New York's sale of mineral waters bottled and sold by the state to provide funds for a state health resort. FRANKFURTER, J., joined by Rutledge, J., would have accorded state immunity from nondiscriminatory federal taxes only when imposed on "state activities and state-owned property that partake of uniqueness from the point of view of intergovernmental relations. These inherently constitute a class by themselves. Only a state can own a statehouse; only a state can get income by taxing. These could not be included for purposes of federal taxation in any abstract category of taxpayers without taxing the state as a state. But so long as congress generally taps a source of revenue by whomsoever earned and not uniquely capable of being earned only by a state, the Constitution of the United States does not forbid it merely because its incidence falls also on a state."

STONE, C.J. joined by Reed, Murphy and Burton, JJ., would grant a broader state immunity: "It is plain that there may be non-discriminatory taxes which, when laid on a State, would nevertheless impair the sovereign status of the State quite as much as a like tax imposed by a State on property or activities of the

---

a. *Long v. Rockwood,* 277 U.S. 142, 48 S.Ct. 463, 72 L.Ed. 824 (1928).

b. See, e.g., *Helvering v. Gerhardt,* 304 U.S. 405, 58 S.Ct. 969, 82 L.Ed. 1427 (1938) (upheld federal income tax on salaries of state employees); *Alabama v. King & Boozer,* 314 U.S. 1, 62 S.Ct. 43, 86 L.Ed. 3 (1941) (upheld state sales tax on cost-plus federal contractor for material purchased to build army camp). Cf. *United States v. Fresno,* 429 U.S. 452, 97 S.Ct. 699, 50 L.Ed.2d 683 (1977) (upheld equivalent of state property tax on U.S. Forest Service employees for value of U.S.-owned houses provided as mandatory living quarters).

c. See, e.g., *United States v. New Mexico,* 455 U.S. 720, 102 S.Ct. 1373, 71 L.Ed.2d 580 (1982). The latest such decision, *South Car-* olina v. Baker, 485 U.S. 505, 108 S.Ct. 1355, 99 L.Ed.2d 592 (1988) (only O'Connor, J., dissenting), upheld a federal tax on private income from a class of state and municipal bonds, overruling *Pollock v. Farmers' Loan and Trust Co.,* 157 U.S. 429, 15 S.Ct. 673, 39 L.Ed. 759 (1895). *Pollock* had not been challenged earlier, despite the revolutionary change in intergovernmental tax immunity, only because Congress had made no earlier effort to tax income from state bonds.

d. *Davis v. Michigan Dept. of Treasury,* 489 U.S. 803, 109 S.Ct. 1500, 103 L.Ed.2d 891 (1989) (exemption from state income tax of pensions of state, but not federal, retired employes violated "principles of intergovernmental tax immunity").

national government. [This] is not because the tax can be regarded as discriminatory but because a sovereign government is the taxpayer, and the tax, even though non-discriminatory, may be regarded as infringing its sovereignty. [If] a non-discriminatory tax unduly interferes with the performance of the State's functions of government [the] fact that the tax is non-discriminatory does not save it."

DOUGLAS, J., joined by Black, J., dissented: "The fact that local government may enter the domain of private enterprise and operate a project for profit does not put it in the class of private business enterprise for tax purposes. [If] the federal government can place the local governments on its tax collector's list, their capacity to serve the needs of their citizens is at once hampered or curtailed. [Many] state activities are in marginal enterprises where private capital refuses to venture. Add to the cost of these projects a federal tax and the social program may be destroyed before it can be launched."

———

MASSACHUSETTS v. UNITED STATES, 435 U.S. 444, 98 S.Ct. 1153, 55 L.Ed.2d 403 (1978), upheld, as applied to state police planes, a federal registration tax on all civil aircraft, imposed to pay part of the cost of federal air navigational facilities and services. BRENNAN, J., joined by White, Marshall and Stevens, JJ., observed that " 'cogent reasons' were recognized for narrowly limiting the immunity of the States from federal imposts. The first is [that] when the scope of the States' constitutional immunity is enlarged beyond that necessary to protect the continued ability of the States to deliver traditional governmental services, the burden of the immunity is thrown upon the National Government without any corresponding promotion of the constitutionally protected values. The second is that the political process is uniquely adapted to accommodating the competing demands 'for national revenue, on the one hand, and for reasonable scope for the independence of state action, on the other.'

"[In] recognition of these considerations, decisions of the Court [have held] that the National Government may tax revenue-generating activities of the States that are of the same nature as those traditionally engaged in by private persons. See, e.g., *New York v. United States* (1946); *Allen v. Regents,* 304 U.S. 439, 58 S.Ct. 980, 82 L.Ed. 1448 (1938) (tax on admissions to state athletic events approved notwithstanding use of proceeds for essential state functions); *Helvering v. Powers,* 293 U.S. 214, 55 S.Ct. 171, 79 L.Ed. 291 (1934) (tax on operations of railroad by State); *Ohio v. Helvering,* 292 U.S. 360, 54 S.Ct. 725, 78 L.Ed. 1307 (1934) (tax on state liquor operation). It is true that some of the opinions speak of the state activity taxed as 'proprietary' and thus not an immune essential *governmental* activity, [but] *New York v. United States*, the most recent decision, rejected the governmental-proprietary distinction as untenable. * * *

"A nondiscriminatory taxing measure that operates to defray the cost of a federal program by recovering a fair approximation of each beneficiary's share of the cost is surely no more offensive to the constitutional scheme than is either a tax on the income earned by state employees or a tax on a State's sale of bottled water. [There] is no danger that such measures will not be based on benefits conferred or that they will function as regulatory devices unduly burdening essential state activities. It is, of course, the case that a revenue provision that forces a State to pay its own way when performing an essential function will increase the cost of the state activity. But [an] economic burden on traditional state functions without, more is not a sufficient basis for sustaining a claim of immunity."[e]

Notes and Questions

Major issues. What are "traditional state functions"? "Essential state activities"? Can they (always) (almost always) be "of the same nature as those traditionally engaged in by private persons"? When does a federal tax "infringe a state's sovereignty"? "Unduly interfere with the performance of the State's functions of government"? Would Douglas and Black, JJ., immunize state and local governments from *all* federal taxes? To what extent is "the political process uniquely adapted to accommodate the competing demands" of state and federal governments?

These issues are extensively considered in Part IV infra.

III. FEDERAL IMMUNITY FROM STATE TAXES

Federal immunity from state taxes has not undergone the same attrition as state immunity from federal taxes. Indeed, since *McCulloch* "the Court has never questioned the propriety of absolute federal immunity from state taxation," nor has it upheld a single state tax laid "directly upon the United States"[a] without the consent of Congress, despite its elimination of immunity for private taxpayers, starting in 1938.[b] But the Court has restricted such immunity to state taxes imposed "on the United States itself, or an agency or instrumentality so closely connected to the Government that the two cannot realistically be viewed as separate entities, at least insofar as the activity being taxed is concerned."[c]

Is such broad federal immunity justified in view of the much more limited state immunity from federal taxes? What makes the difference? A view that all federal activities are "governmental"? The supremacy clause? Judicial deference due to Congress, as compared to that due a single state legislature whose action has adverse impact on a national interest?

Federal immunity from state regulation. For consideration of analogous federal immunity from state *regulatory* power, and the extent of immunity for individuals acting on behalf of the government, see Tribe 3d ed., at 1223–25.

IV. STATE IMMUNITY FROM FEDERAL REGULATION

MARYLAND v. WIRTZ (1968), Sec. 2, III, B supra, per HARLAN, J., upheld application of the Fair Labor Standards Act to state schools and hospitals, stressing that "Congress has 'interfered with' these state functions only to the extent of providing that when the state employs people in performing such functions it is subject to the same restrictions as a wide range of other employers whose activities affect commerce, including privately operated schools and hospi-

---

e. Stewart and Powell, JJ., saw "no need to discuss the general contours of state immunity from federal taxation," but concurred in the ruling that the registration tax was valid as a "user fee." Rehnquist, J., joined by Burger, C.J., dissented on the user fee issue. Blackmun, J., did not participate.

a. See *United States v. New Mexico,* 455 U.S. 720, 733, 102 S.Ct. 1373, 1382, 71 L.Ed.2d 580, 591 (1982) (government contractors whose tax costs are passed on to the federal government are not to that extent "government instrumentalities" immune from state taxation).

b. See note 3, Part I supra.

c. *United States v. New Mexico,* supra. For more details see Tribe 3d ed., at 1225–37.

tals." In exercising a "delegated power" the federal government "may override countervailing state interests whether these be described as 'governmental' or 'proprietary' in character." The argument that *United States v. California*, 297 U.S. 175, 56 S.Ct. 421, 80 L.Ed. 567 (1936) (unanimously upholding application of the federal Safety Appliance Act to a state-owned railroad, which served San Francisco wharves and industrial plants) was not "controlling" because the "state activity involved there was less central to state sovereignty misses the mark. This Court [will] not carve up the commerce power to protect enterprises indistinguishable in their effect on commerce from private businesses, simply because those enterprises happen to be run by the states for the benefit of their citizens."

Douglas, J., joined by Stewart, J., dissented: "It is one thing to force a State to purchase safety equipment for its railroad and another to force it either to spend several million dollars more on hospitals and schools or substantially reduce services in those areas. [In] this case the State as a sovereign power is being seriously tampered with, potentially crippled."

———

NATIONAL LEAGUE OF CITIES v. USERY, 426 U.S. 833, 96 S.Ct. 2465, 49 L.Ed.2d 245 (1976), per Rehnquist, J., overruled *Wirtz* on this issue: "The Court has never doubted that there are limits upon the power of Congress to override state sovereignty, even when exercising its otherwise plenary powers to tax or to regulate commerce." Federal regulation of the wages, hours, and overtime compensation for those whom states employ "to carry out their governmental functions" would increase costs and "substantially restructure" ways by which "state and local governments [discharge] their dual function of administering the public law and furnishing public services." It is not within Congress' commerce power "to directly displace the States' freedom to structure integral operations in areas of traditional governmental functions."

Though "not untroubled by [possible] implications of the Court's opinion," Blackmun, J., joined it "with the understanding" that it "adopts a balancing approach, and does not outlaw federal power where the federal interest is demonstrably greater and [state compliance] would be essential." Brennan, J., joined by White, Marshall and Stevens, JJ., dissented.

————

During the next seven years, the *National League of Cities* principle was unsuccessfully urged upon the Court five times. The first two decisions were unanimous.[a] In the next two, Blackmun, J., joined the *National League of Cities* dissenters to rule 5 to 4 that the principle was not applicable.[b] The fifth follows:

a. *Hodel v. Virginia Surface Mining* (1981), note 4 after *Heart of Atlanta* (upholding federal regulation of surface mining, displacing state regulation, except when a state adopts the federal regulation, and drawing a "sharp distinction between congressional regulation of private persons and federal regulation 'directed to States as States' "); *United Transp. Union v. Long Island R. R.*, 455 U.S. 678, 102 S.Ct. 1349, 71 L.Ed.2d 547 (1982) (Long Island Railroad ruled not a "traditional government function").

b. *Federal Energy Regulatory Com'n v. Mississippi* (1982), p. 137 infra; *Equal Employment Opportunity Com'n v. Wyoming*, 460 U.S. 226, 103 S.Ct. 1054, 75 L.Ed.2d 18 (1983) (upholding federal ban on mandatory age retirement for state game wardens as not involving a "serious federal intrusion").

Const. recognizes states as sovereign - but this will not be protected by judicial system (courts) but by national political process

130   INTERGOVERNMENTAL IMMUNITIES   Ch. 2

GARCIA v. SAN ANTONIO METROPOLITAN TRANSIT AUTHORITY

- reverses usury

469 U.S. 528, 105 S.Ct. 1005, 83 L.Ed.2d 1016 (1985).

JUSTICE BLACKMUN delivered the opinion of the Court.

[The Court upheld application of the Fair Labor Standards Act to a munici- *∗* pally-owned and operated mass transit system.]

The prerequisites for governmental immunity under *National League of Cities* *∗ P* were summarized by this Court in *Hodel*[:] First, it is said that the federal statute *∗ L* at issue must regulate "the 'States as States.'" Second, the statute must "address matters that are indisputably 'attribute[s] of state sovereignty.'" Third, state compliance with the federal obligation must "directly impair [the States'] ability 'to structure integral operations in areas of traditional governmental functions.'" "Finally, the relation of state and federal interests must not be such that "the nature of the federal [interest] justifies state submission."

The controversy in the present cases has focused on the third *Hodel* requirement. [It] normally might be fair to venture the assumption that case-by-case development would lead to a workable standard for determining whether a particular governmental function should be immune from federal regulation under the Commerce Clause. A further cautionary note is sounded, however, by the Court's experience in the related field of state immunity from federal taxation. * * *

The distinction [between governmental and proprietary functions that] the Court discarded as unworkable in the field of tax immunity has proved no more fruitful in the field of regulatory immunity under the Commerce Clause. Neither do any of the alternative standards that might be employed to distinguish between protected and unprotected governmental functions appear manageable. We rejected the possibility of making immunity turn on a purely historical standard of "tradition" in *Long Island*. [The] most obvious defect of a historical approach to state immunity is that it prevents a court from accommodating changes in the historical functions of States, changes that have resulted in a number of once- *∗ L* private functions like education being assumed by the States and their subdivisions. At the same time, [r]eliance on history as an organizing principle results in linedrawing of the most arbitrary sort; the genesis of state governmental functions stretches over a historical continuum from before the Revolution to the present, and courts would have to decide by fiat precisely how longstanding a pattern of state involvement had to be for federal regulatory authority to be defeated.

A nonhistorical standard for selecting immune governmental functions is likely to be just as unworkable. [I]dentifying "uniquely" governmental functions, for example, has been rejected by the Court in the field of government tort liability in part because the notion of a "uniquely" governmental function is unmanageable. * * *

We believe, however, that there is a more fundamental problem at work here [—] neither the governmental/proprietary distinction nor any other that purports to separate out important governmental functions can be faithful to the role of federalism in a democratic society. The essence of our federal system is that within the realm of authority left open to them under the Constitution, the States *∗ L* must be equally free to engage in any activity that their citizens choose for the common weal, no matter how unorthodox or unnecessary anyone else—including the judiciary—deems state involvement to be. Any rule of state immunity that looks to the "traditional," "integral," or "necessary" nature of governmental functions inevitably invites an unelected federal judiciary to make decisions about

States are well represented in political process (Senators) (electoral college)

which state policies it favors and which ones it dislikes.[a] [If] there are to be limits on the Federal Government's power to interfere with state functions—as undoubtedly there are—we must look elsewhere to find them. We accordingly return to the underlying issue that confronted this Court in *National League of Cities*—the manner in which the Constitution insulates States from the reach of Congress' power under the Commerce Clause.

The central theme of *National League of Cities* was [that] the Constitution precludes "the National Government [from] devour[ing] the essentials of state sovereignty." * * *

We doubt that courts ultimately can identify principled constitutional limitations on the scope of Congress' Commerce Clause powers over the States merely by relying on a priori definitions of state sovereignty. In part, this is because of the elusiveness of objective criteria for "fundamental" elements of state sovereignty, a problem we have witnessed in the search for "traditional governmental functions." There is, however, a more fundamental reason: [the] States unquestionably do "retai[n] a significant measure of sovereign authority." They do so, however, only to the extent that the Constitution has not divested them of their original powers and transferred those powers to the Federal Government. [The] fact that the States remain sovereign as to all powers not vested in Congress or denied them by the Constitution offers no guidance about where the frontier between state and federal power lies. In short, we have no license to employ freestanding conceptions of state sovereignty when measuring congressional authority under the Commerce Clause.

When we look for the States' "residuary and inviolable sovereignty," *The Federalist* No. 39 (J. Madison), in the shape of the constitutional scheme rather than in predetermined notions of sovereign power, a different measure of state sovereignty emerges. Apart from the limitation on federal authority inherent in the delegated nature of Congress' Article I powers, the principal means chosen by the Framers to ensure the role of the States in the federal system lies in the structure of the Federal Government itself. It is no novelty to observe that the composition of the Federal Government was designed in large part to protect the States from overreaching by Congress.[11] [The] States were vested with indirect influence over the House of Representatives and the Presidency by their control of electoral qualifications and their role in presidential elections. They were given

---

a. Consider Jesse H. Choper, *Judicial Review and the National Political Process* 202–03 (1980): "Whatever the judiciary's [special] competence in articulating the values and defining the scope of those constitutional clauses that declare individual rights, when the fundamental issue turns in large measure on the relative competence of different levels of government to deal with societal problems, the Court is no more inherently capable of correct judgment than its companion federal branches. Indeed, the judiciary may well be less capable, given both the highly pragmatic nature of federal-state questions and the forceful representation of the states (which are most directly affected by their resolution) in the national process of political decisionmaking. Thus, for Madison, 'the roles of the two governments would not depend upon legal line-drawing but upon the political process by which they were constituted.'"

11. See, e.g., Jesse H. Choper, *Judicial Review and the National Political Process* 175–184 (1980); Herbert Wechsler, *The Political Safeguards of Federalism: The Role of the States in the Composition and Selection of the National Government,* 54 Colum.L.Rev. 543 (1954); D. Bruce La Pierre, *The Political Safeguards of Federalism, Redux: Intergovernmental Immunity and the States as Agents of the Nation,* 60 Wash.U.L.Q. 779 (1982).

[For the view that "the Wechsler–Choper thesis is wrong, at least in today's political world, insofar as it assumes that national elected officials safely can be made the exclusive enforcers of constitutional federalism guarantees," see Steven G. Calabresi, *"A Government of Limited and Enumerated Powers": In Defense of United States v. Lopez,* 94 Mich.L.Rev. 752 (1995).]

more direct influence in the Senate, where each State received equal representation and each Senator was to be selected by the legislature of his State. The significance attached to the [former] is underscored by the prohibition of any constitutional amendment divesting a State of equal representation without the State's consent. Art. V.

The extent to which the structure of the Federal Government itself was relied on to insulate the interests of the States is evident in the views of the Framers. James Madison explained that the Federal Government "will partake sufficiently of the spirit [of the States], to be disinclined to invade the rights of the individual States, or the prerogatives of their governments." *The Federalist* No. 46.[b] [State] sovereign interests, then, are more properly protected by procedural safeguards inherent in the structure of the federal system than by judicially created limitations on federal power.[c]

The effectiveness of the federal political process in preserving the States' interests is apparent even today in the course of federal legislation. On the one hand, the States have been able to direct a substantial proportion of federal revenues into their own treasuries in the form of general and program-specific grants in aid. [At] the same time [they] have been able to exempt themselves from a wide variety of obligations imposed by Congress under the Commerce Clause. For example, the Federal Power Act, the National Labor Relations Act, the Labor–Management Reporting and Disclosure Act, the Occupational Safety and Health Act, the Employee Retirement Insurance Security Act, and the Sherman Act all contain express or implied exemptions for States and their subdivisions. The fact that some federal statutes such as the FLSA extend general obligations to the States cannot obscure the extent to which the political position of the States in the federal system has served to minimize the burdens that the States bear under the Commerce Clause.[d]

b. For conflicting views on the "original understanding," compare John C. Yoo, *The Judicial Safeguards of Federalism*, 70 So.Cal. L.Rev. 1311, 1313 (1997): "The text, structure and history of the Constitution * * * strongly indicates that the Framers believed judicial review would work in conjunction with the political process to maintain the proper balance between federal and state powers"; with Larry D. Kramer, *Putting the Politics Back into the Political Safeguards of Federalism*, 100 Colum.L.Rev. 215, 233 (2000): "The Founding generation had a widely shared understanding of how Congress would be restrained, an understanding that assigned no meaningful role to courts"; Saikrishna B. Prakash & John C. Yoo, *The Puzzling Persistence of Process–Based Federalism Theories*, 79 Tex.L.Rev.—(June 2001).

c. Consider Jesse H. Choper, *The Scope of National Power Vis–A–Vis the States: The Dispensability of Judicial Review*, 86 Yale L.J. 1552, 1556–57 (1977): "[S]tate representation in the national executive and legislature places the President and Congress in a trustworthy position to view the issues involved in federalism disputes. In contrast, beneficiaries of individual rights, such as members of minority groups, are often not adequately represented in the deliberations of the political branches. A more active judicial role in personal rights

cases is thus necessitated. But when democratic processes may be trusted to produce a fair constitutional judgment, as in cases involving the allocation of power between the states and the national government, it advances the democratic tradition to vest that judgment with popularly responsible institutions."

d. See also Jesse H. Choper, *Federalism and Judicial Review: An Update*, 21 Hast.Con. L.Q. 577, 586–87 (1994): "Since *Garcia*, the record of the states' ability to secure their vital interests against federal encroachments without the aid of judicial review has been consistent with their earlier successes. Perhaps the most dramatic confirmation came within eight months after *Garcia* when Congress amended the Fair Labor Standards Act to substantially reduce its financial impact on state and local governments. The point, of course, is not that Congress *never* overcomes state-voiced protests to proposed national actions that burden local interests. According to a recent study of the processes and outcomes of several congressional endeavors in this area, 'the "political safeguards of federalism" do not operate automatically to protect important state interests. [To] assure that the values of federalism will be considered in Congress, state and local governments must make active efforts to protect their own interests.' But, the study reports, when they do, they often succeed."

[A]gainst this background, we are convinced that the fundamental limitation that the constitutional scheme imposes on the Commerce Clause to protect the "States as States" is one of process rather than one of result. Any substantive restraint on the exercise of Commerce Clause powers must find its justification in the procedural nature of this basic limitation, and it must be tailored to compensate for possible failings in the national political process rather than to dictate a "sacred province of state autonomy." [W]e perceive nothing in the overtime and minimum-wage requirements of the FLSA, as applied to SAMTA, that is destructive of state [sovereignty]. SAMTA faces nothing more than the same minimum-wage and overtime obligations that hundreds of thousands of other employers, public as well as private, have to [meet].[e]

[The] political process ensures that laws that unduly burden the States will not be promulgated. In the factual setting of these cases the internal safeguards of the political process have performed as intended. * * * *National League of Cities* is overruled. * * *

JUSTICE POWELL, with whom THE CHIEF JUSTICE, JUSTICE REHNQUIST, and JUSTICE O'CONNOR join, dissenting.

[T]oday's decision effectively reduces the Tenth Amendment to meaningless rhetoric when Congress acts pursuant to the Commerce Clause. * * *

Much of the Court's opinion is devoted to arguing that it is difficult to define a priori "traditional governmental functions." *National League of Cities* neither engaged in, nor required, such a task [but rather] adopted a familiar type of balancing test for determining whether Commerce Clause enactments transgress constitutional limitations imposed by the federal nature of our system of government. * * *

In reading *National League of Cities* to embrace a balancing approach, Justice Blackmun quite correctly cited the part of the opinion that reaffirmed *Fry v. United States* [which] explicitly weighed the seriousness of the problem addressed by the federal legislation at issue in that case, against the effects of compliance on State sovereignty.[a] Our subsequent decisions also adopted this approach of weighing the respective interests of the States and federal government.[5] * * *

Today's opinion does not explain how the States' role in the electoral process guarantees that particular exercises of the Commerce Clause power will not infringe on residual State sovereignty. Members of Congress are elected from the various States, but once in office they are members of the federal government. Although the States participate in the Electoral College, this is hardly a reason to view the President as a representative of the States' interest against federal

e. The Court noted that when FLSA changes subjected state mass-transit systems to higher costs the federal government simultaneously provided "substantial countervailing financial assistance."

a. *Fry,* 421 U.S. 542, 95 S.Ct. 1792, 44 L.Ed.2d 363 (1975) upheld Congress' commerce power to combat inflation by limiting wage increases for state and local government employees, along with all others, citing *Wirtz:* "It seems inescapable that the effectiveness of federal action would have been drastically impaired if wage increases to this sizeable group of employees (14% of the Nation's work force) were left outside the reach of these emergency federal wage controls." Rehnquist, J., dissent-ed, urging the overruling of *Wirtz.* Douglas, J., would have dismissed the writ as improvidently granted.

5. In undertaking such balancing, we have considered [the] strength of the federal interest in the challenged legislation and the impact of exempting the States from its reach. Central to our inquiry into the federal interest is how closely the challenged action implicates the central concerns of the Commerce Clause, viz., the promotion of a national economy and free trade among the states. [On] the other hand, we have also assessed the injury done to the States if forced to comply with federal Commerce Clause enactments.

encroachment. We noted recently "the hydraulic pressure inherent within each of the separate Branches to exceed the outer limits of its [power]." *INS v. Chadha,* [Ch. 3, Sec. 2, II]. The Court offers no reason to think that this pressure will not operate when Congress seeks to invoke its powers under the Commerce Clause, notwithstanding the electoral role of the States.[9]

[The] States' success at obtaining federal funds for various projects and exemptions from the obligations of some federal statutes [is] not relevant to the question whether the political *processes* are the proper means of enforcing constitutional limitations. The fact that Congress generally does not transgress constitutional limits on its power to reach State activities does not make judicial review any less necessary to rectify the cases in which it does do so. The States' role in our system of government is a matter of constitutional law, not of legislative grace.[b] [Far] from being "unsound in principle," judicial enforcement of the Tenth Amendment is essential to maintaining the federal system so carefully designed by the Framers and adopted in the Constitution. [Indeed,] the Court's view of federalism appears to relegate the States to precisely the trivial role that opponents of the Constitution feared they would occupy.

[handwritten marginal note: A Matter of Constitutional Law — not political grace.]

[Under] the balancing test approved in *National League of Cities* [the] state interest [in this case] is compelling. The financial impact on States and localities of displacing their control over wages, hours, overtime regulations, pensions, and labor relations with their employees could have serious, as well as unanticipated, effects on state and local planning, budgeting, and the levying of taxes. [I]ntracity mass transit system [is] a classic example of the type of service traditionally provided by local government. It [is] indistinguishable in principle from the traditional services of providing and maintaining streets, public lighting, traffic control, water, and sewerage systems. Services of this kind are precisely those "with which citizens are more 'familiarly and minutely conversant.'" The *Federalist*, No. 46. State and local officials [know] that their constituents and the press respond to the adequacy, fair distribution, and cost of these services. It is this kind of state and local control and accountability that the Framers understood would

---

9. * * * Professor Wechsler, whose seminal article in 1954 proposed the view adopted by the Court today, predicated his argument on assumptions that simply do not accord with current reality. Professor Wechsler wrote: "National action [has] always been regarded as exceptional in our polity, an intrusion to be justified by some necessity, the special rather than the ordinary case." Not only is the premise of this view clearly at odds with the proliferation of national legislation over the past 30 years, but "a variety of structural and political changes in this century have combined to make Congress particularly *insensitive* to state and local values." Advisory Comm'n on Intergovernmental Relations [ACIR], *Regulatory Federalism: Policy, Process, Impact and Reform* 50 (1984). The adoption of the Seventeenth Amendment (providing for direct election of senators), the weakening of political parties on the local level, and the rise of national media, among other things, have made Congress increasingly less representative of State and local interests, and more likely to be responsive to the demands of various national constituencies. Id. * * *

[handwritten marginal note: Is Senate really a good representative of the state? — Political parties outside of state funding?]

See also Lewis B. Kaden, *Politics, Money, and State Sovereignty: The Judicial Role,* 79 Colum.L.Rev. 847 (1979). * * *

[For the view that "the development of political parties [has] preserved the states' voice in national councils by linking political fortunes of state and federal officials, [and] has protected federalism" so as to "render the Court's aggressive foray into federalism as unnecessary," see Kramer, fn. b supra. Contra, Prakash & Yoo, fn. b supra.

b. Consider Kennedy, J., joined by O'Connor, J., concurring in *Lopez*, Sec. 2, IV supra: "[T]he federal balance is too essential a part of our constitutional structure and plays too vital a role in securing freedom for us to admit [the Court's] inability to intervene when one or the other level of Government has tipped the scales too far. [T]he substantial element of political judgment in Commerce Clause matters leaves our institutional capacity to intervene more in doubt than when we decide cases, for instance, under the Bill of Rights even though clear and bright lines are often absent in the latter class of disputes. But our cases do not teach that we have no role at all in determining the meaning of the Commerce Clause."

insure the vitality and preservation of the federal system that the Constitution explicitly requires. * * *c

Notes and Questions

1. *"Failings in national political process."* SOUTH CAROLINA v. BAKER, 485 U.S. 505, 108 S.Ct. 1355, 99 L.Ed.2d 592 (1988), per BRENNAN, J., again recognized the possibility of a process-based attack on federal regulation of state government operations, but ruled that the "national political process did not operate in a defective manner" when Congress banned certain types of state bonds by relying on anecdotal, not "concrete" evidence that such bonds were being used to conceal taxable income. For discussion of judicial remedies under a "process-oriented approach to federalism," see Andrzej Rapaczynski, *From Sovereignty to Process: The Jurisprudence of Federalism after Garcia,* 1985 Sup.Ct.Rev. 341.

2. *State "sovereignty."* What is the precise nature of the "state sovereignty" or "state interests" that federalism seeks to safeguard? Is it "the institutional interests of state governments," Deborah J. Merritt, *Three Faces of Federalism: Finding a Formula for the Future,* 47 Vand.L.Rev. 1563, 1568 (1994), or the "viewpoint of the people of the state" Choper, fn. a, at 181–84? (See also fn. b in *McCulloch,* Sec. 1 supra, and note 2 after *McCulloch.*) To what extent does the answer to this question affect the issue in *Garcia?*

3. *Alternative approach.* GREGORY v. ASHCROFT, 501 U.S. 452, 111 S.Ct. 2395, 115 L.Ed.2d 410 (1991), per O'CONNOR, J., advanced many of the considerations in the *Garcia* dissent in refusing to apply the federal Age Discrimination in Employment Act to a state judge required by state law to retire at 70, by importing a "plain statement" rule from eleventh amendment cases: "If Congress intends to alter the 'usual constitutional balance between the States and the Federal Government' it must make its intention to do so unmistakably clear in the language of the statute. *Atascadero State Hospital v. Scanlon,* 473 U.S. 234, 242, 243, 105 S.Ct. 3142, 3147, 3148, 87 L.Ed.2d 171 (1985)." Of the five justices in the *Garcia* majority, the four remaining on the Court dissented from this plain statement reasoning because it "directly contravenes our decision in *Garcia.*" For a critique of the plain statement rule, see Laurence H. Tribe, *Clear Statement Rules, Federalism and Congressional Regulation of States,* 107 Harv.L.Rev. 1941 (1994).

c. O'Connor, J., joined by Rehnquist, C.J., and Powell, J., added a dissent that called for "weighing state autonomy as a factor in the balance when interpreting the means by which Congress can exercise its authority on the State as States."

While joining the Powell and O'Connor dissents, Rehnquist, J., withheld full acceptance of their "balancing" approaches and concluded: "[U]nder any one of these approaches the judgment in this case should be affirmed, and I do not think it incumbent on those of us in dissent to spell out further the fine points of a principle that will, I am confident, in time again command the support of a majority of this Court." O'Connor, J., added her "belief that this Court will in time again assume its constitutional responsibility."

For helpful commentaries on *Garcia* and *National League of Cities,* see Martha A. Field, *Garcia v. San Antonio Metropolitan Transit Authority, The Demise of a Misguided Doctrine,* 99 Harv.L.Rev. 84 (1985); William W. Van Alstyne, *The Second Death of Federalism,* 83 Mich.L.Rev. (1985); Robert F. Nagel, *Federalism as a Fundamental Value: National League of Cities in Perspective,* 1981 Sup.Ct. Rev. 81; Sotirios A. Barber, *National League of Cities v. Usery, New Meaning for the Tenth Amendment?* 1976 Sup.Ct.Rev. 161.

PRINTZ v. UNITED STATES

521 U.S. 898, 117 S.Ct. 2365, 138 L.Ed.2d 914 (1997).

Justice Scalia delivered the opinion of the Court.

[T]he Brady Handgun Violence Prevention Act purports to direct state law enforcement officers to participate, albeit only temporarily, in the administration of a federally enacted regulatory scheme. Regulated firearms dealers are required to forward Brady Forms not to a federal officer or employee, but to the CLEOs ["chief law enforcement officers"], whose obligation to accept those forms is implicit in the duty imposed upon them to make "reasonable efforts" within five days to determine whether the sales reflected in the forms are lawful. While the CLEOs are subjected to no federal requirement that they prevent the sales determined to be unlawful (it is perhaps assumed that their state-law duties will require prevention or apprehension), they are empowered to grant, in effect, waivers of the federally prescribed 5–day waiting period for handgun purchases by notifying the gun dealers that they have no reason to believe the transactions would be illegal.

The petitioners here object to being pressed into federal [service.] Because there is no constitutional text speaking to this precise question, the answer to the CLEOs' challenge must be sought in historical understanding and practice, in the structure of the Constitution, and in the jurisprudence of this Court.

[The Court concluded that the relevant historical practice "tends to negate" Congress' power to impose federal responsibilities on state officers without the States' consent. "[E]nactments of the early Congresses [contain] no evidence of an assumption that the Federal Government may command the States' executive power in the absence of a particularized constitutional authorization," such as the Extradition Clause of Art IV, Sec. 2. The "early laws establish, at most, that the Constitution was originally understood to permit imposition of an obligation on state judges to enforce federal prescriptions, insofar as those prescriptions related to matters appropriate for the judicial power." Finally, there is "an absence of executive-commandeering statutes [in] our later history as well."[a]

* * * We turn next to consideration of the structure of the Constitution, to see if we can discern among its "essential postulate[s]" a principle that controls the present cases.[b] * * * We have set forth the historical record in more detail elsewhere, see *New York v. United States,* [505 U.S. 144, 112 S.Ct. 2408, 120 L.Ed.2d 120 (1992), per O'Connor, J. (discussed below)], and need not repeat it here. It suffices to repeat the conclusion: "The Framers explicitly chose a Constitution that confers upon Congress the power to regulate individuals, not

---

a. The dissents disputed each of these points, as well as the meaning of *The Federalist* Nos. 27 and 44, concluding: "[T]he majority's opinion consists almost entirely of arguments against the substantial evidence weighing in opposition to its view; the Court's ruling is strikingly lacking in affirmative support. Absent even a modicum of textual foundation for its judicially crafted constitutional rule, there should be a presumption that if the Framers had actually intended such a rule, at least one of them would have mentioned it."

b. For the view that *Printz* "embraces [a] formalist approach to interpreting [the] Constitution [and] eschewed a more 'functionalist' approach [in] that it pointedly avoided a sensitive assessment of whether such commandeering undermines any of the diverse values or purposes thought to underlie our various divisions of governmental authority, either at its founding or today," see Evan H. Caminker, *Printz, State Sovereignty, and the Limits of Formalism*, 1997 Sup.Ct.Rev. 199, 201. See also Erwin Chemerinsky, *Formalism and Functionalism in Federalism Analysis*, 19 Ga. St. U.L.Rev. 959 (1997).

States." [This] separation of the two spheres is one of the Constitution's structural protections of liberty. [The] power of the Federal Government would be augmented immeasurably if it were able to impress into its service—and at no cost to itself—the police officers of the 50 States.

[F]ederal control of state officers would [also] have an effect upon [the] separation and equilibration of powers between the three branches of the Federal Government itself. The Constitution does not leave to speculation who is to administer the laws enacted by Congress; the President, it says, "shall take Care that the Laws be faithfully executed," personally and through officers whom he appoints. [The] Brady Act effectively transfers this responsibility to thousands of CLEOs in the 50 States, who are left to implement the program without meaningful Presidential control (if indeed meaningful Presidential control is possible without the power to appoint and remove).[c] [T]he power of the President would be subject to reduction, if Congress could act as effectively without the President as with him, by simply requiring state officers to execute its laws.[12] * * *

Finally, and most conclusively in the present litigation, we turn to the prior jurisprudence of this Court. Federal commandeering of state governments is such a novel phenomenon that this Court's first experience with it did not occur until the 1970's, when [several] opinions of ours have made clear that the Federal Government may not compel the States to implement, by legislation or executive action, federal regulatory programs. [*Hodel*, note 4 after *Katzenbach v. McClung*] concluded that the Surface Mining Control and Reclamation Act of 1977 did not present the problem they raised because it merely made compliance with federal standards a precondition to continued state regulation in an otherwise pre-empted field. In *FERC* [*v. Mississippi*, 456 U.S. 742, 102 S.Ct. 2126, 72 L.Ed.2d 532 (1982),] we construed the most troubling provisions of the Public Utility Regulatory Policies Act of 1978 to contain only the "command" that state agencies "consider" federal standards, and again only as a precondition to continued state regulation of an otherwise pre-empted field.[d] * * *

When we were at last confronted squarely with a federal statute that unambiguously required the States to enact or administer a federal regulatory program, our decision should have come as no surprise. At issue in *New York* were the so-called "take title" provisions of the Low–Level Radioactive Waste Policy Amendments Act of 1985, which required States either to enact legislation providing for the disposal of radioactive waste generated within their borders, or to take title to, and possession of, the waste—effectively requiring the States

---

c. The subject is considered in detail in Ch. 3, Sec. 2, III.

12. There is not, as the dissent believes, "tension" between the proposition that impressing state police officers into federal service will massively augment federal power, and the proposition that it will also sap the power of the Federal Presidency. It is quite possible to have a more powerful Federal Government that is, by reason of the destruction of its Executive unity, a less efficient one. The dissent is correct that control by the unitary Federal Executive is also sacrificed when States voluntarily administer federal programs, but the condition of voluntary state participation significantly reduces the ability of Congress to use this device as a means of reducing the power of the Presidency.

d. *FERC*, per Blackmun, J., emphasized that since "Congress could have preempted the field of utility regulation, at least insofar as private rather than state activity is concerned, [the Act] should not be invalid simply because, out of deference to state authority, Congress adopted a less intrusive scheme and allowed the States to continue regulating in the area on the condition that they *consider* the suggested federal standards. [Thus, the provisions] do not threaten the States' 'separate and independent existence,' and do not impair the ability of the States 'to function effectively in a federal system.' To the contrary, they offer the States a vehicle for remaining active in an area of overriding concern."

either to legislate pursuant to Congress's directions, or to implement an administrative solution. We concluded that Congress could constitutionally require the states to do neither.[e] * * *

The Government contends that *New York* is distinguishable on the following ground: unlike the "take title" provisions invalidated there, the background-check provision of the Brady Act does not require state legislative or executive officials to make policy. [But executive] action that has utterly no policymaking component is rare, particularly at an executive level as high as a jurisdiction's chief law-enforcement officer. Is it really true that there is no policymaking involved in deciding, for example, what "reasonable efforts" shall be expended to conduct a background check? It may well satisfy the Act for a CLEO to direct that (a) no background checks will be conducted that divert personnel time from pending felony investigations, and (b) no background check will be permitted to consume more than one-half hour of an officer's time. [Is] this decision whether to devote maximum "reasonable efforts" or minimum "reasonable efforts" not preeminently a matter of policy?[f] It is quite impossible, in short, to draw the Government's proposed line at "no policymaking," and we would have to fall back upon a line of "not too much policymaking" * * *.

Even assuming, moreover, that the Brady Act leaves no "policymaking" discretion with the States, we fail to see how that improves rather than worsens the intrusion upon state sovereignty. Preservation of the States as independent and autonomous political entities is arguably less undermined by requiring them to make policy in certain fields than [by] "reduc[ing] [them] to puppets of a ventriloquist Congress." * * *

The Government purports to find support for its proffered distinction of *New York* [in] *Testa v. Katt,* 330 U.S. 386, 67 S.Ct. 810, 91 L.Ed. 967 (1947), [which] stands for the proposition that state courts cannot refuse to apply federal law—a conclusion mandated by the terms of the Supremacy Clause. [T]hat says nothing about whether state executive officers must administer federal law. * * *

The Government also maintains that requiring state officers to perform discrete, ministerial tasks specified by Congress does not violate the principle of *New York* because it does not diminish the accountability of state or federal officials.[g] This argument fails even on its own terms. By forcing state governments

---

e. For the view that the original understanding supports this "anti-commandeering" conclusion, see Saikrishna B. Prakash, *Field Office Federalism,* 79 Va.L.Rev. 1957 (1993). For criticism, see H. Jefferson Powell, *The Oldest Question of Constitutional Law,* 79 Va. L.Rev. 633, 681 (1993); Evan H. Caminker, *State Sovereignty and Subordinacy: May Congress Commandeer State Officers to Implement Federal Law?,* 95 Colum.L.Rev. 1001 (1995); Erik M. Jensen & Jonathan L. Entin, *Commandeering, The Tenth Amendment, and the Federal Requisition Power: New York v. United States Revisited,* 15 Const. Comm. 355, 378–81 (1998).

f. Dissenting in *FERC,* O'Connor, J., joined by Burger, C.J. and Rehnquist, J., argued that: "the power to make decisions and set [policy] embraces more than the ultimate authority to enact laws; it also includes the power to decide which proposals are most worthy of consideration, the order in which they should be taken

up, and the precise form in which they should be debated. [The Act] intrudes upon all of these functions. It chooses twelve proposals, forcing their consideration even if the state agency deems other ideas more worthy of immediate attention. [By] taxing the limited resources of these commissions, and decreasing their ability to address local regulatory ills, [the Act] directly impairs the power of state utility commissions to discharge their traditional functions efficiently and effectively."

Query: Does *FERC* survive *Printz* and *New York?*

g. *New York* reasoned that "where the Federal Government compels States to regulate, the accountability of both state and federal officials is diminished. If the citizens of New York, for example, do not consider that making provision for the disposal of radioactive waste is in their best interest, they may elect state officials who share their view. That view can

to absorb the financial burden of implementing a federal regulatory program, Members of Congress can take credit for "solving" problems without having to ask their constituents to pay for the solutions with higher federal taxes. And even when the States are not forced to absorb the costs of implementing a federal program, they are still put in the position of taking the blame for its burdensomeness and for its defects. Under the present law, for example, it will be the CLEO and not some federal official who stands between the gun purchaser and immediate possession of his gun. And it will likely be the CLEO, not some federal official, who will be blamed for any error (even one in the designated federal database) that causes a purchaser to be mistakenly rejected.

[The] Brady Act, the dissent asserts, is different [from] *New York* because the former is addressed to individuals—namely CLEOs—while the latter were directed to the State itself. That is certainly a difference, but it cannot be a constitutionally significant one. While the Brady Act is directed to "individuals," it is directed to them in their official capacities as state officers; it controls their actions, not as private citizens, but as the agents of the State. * * *

Finally, the Government puts forward a cluster of arguments that can be grouped under the heading: "The Brady Act serves very important purposes, is most efficiently administered by CLEOs during the interim period, and places a minimal and only temporary burden upon state officers." * * * Assuming all the mentioned factors were true, they might be relevant if we were evaluating whether the incidental application to the States of a federal law of general applicability excessively interfered with the functioning of state governments. See, e.g., *Fry; National League of Cities*. But where, as here, it is the whole object of the law to direct the functioning of the state executive, and hence to compromise the structural framework of dual sovereignty, such a "balancing" analysis is inappropriate.[17] * * *

JUSTICE O'CONNOR, concurring.

[T]he Court appropriately refrains from deciding [whether] purely ministerial reporting requirements imposed by Congress on state and local authorities pursuant to its Commerce Clause powers are similarly invalid. See, e.g., 42 U.S.C. § 5779(a) (requiring state and local law enforcement agencies to report cases of missing children to the Department of Justice).[a] The provisions invalidated here,

---

always be preempted under the Supremacy Clause if is contrary to the national view, but in such a case it is the Federal Government that makes the decision in full view of the public, and it will be federal officials that suffer the consequences if the decision turns out to be detrimental or unpopular. But where the Federal Government directs the States to regulate, it may be state officials who will bear the brunt of public disapproval, while the federal officials who devised the regulatory program may remain insulated from the electoral ramifications of their decision. [See] D. Bruce La Pierre, *Political Accountability in the National Political Process—The Alternative to Judicial Review of Federalism Issues*, 80 Nw.U.L.Rev. 577, 639–665 (1985)."

17. The dissent observes that "Congress could require private persons, such as hospital executives or school administrators, to provide arms merchants with relevant information about a prospective purchaser's fitness to own

a weapon," and that "the burden on police officers [imposed by the Brady Act] would be permissible if a similar burden were also imposed on private parties with access to relevant data." That is undoubtedly true, but it does not advance the dissent's case. The Brady Act does not merely require CLEOs to report information in their private possession. It requires them to provide information that belongs to the State and is available to them only in their official capacity; and to conduct investigations in their official capacity, by examining databases and records that only state officials have access to. In other words, the suggestion that extension of this statute to private citizens would eliminate the constitutional problem posits the impossible.

a. The Court commented that "federal statutes [which] require only the provision of information to the Federal Government, do not involve the precise issue before us [here]."

however, which directly compel state officials to administer a federal regulatory program, utterly fail to adhere to the design and structure of our constitutional scheme.[b]

JUSTICE STEVENS, with whom JUSTICE SOUTER, JUSTICE GINSBURG, and JUSTICE BREYER join, dissenting. * * *

These cases do not implicate the more difficult questions associated with congressional coercion of state legislatures addressed in *New York*. Nor need we consider the wisdom of relying on local officials rather than federal agents to carry out aspects of a federal program, or even the question whether such officials may be required to perform a federal function on a permanent basis. The question is whether Congress, acting on behalf of the people of the entire Nation, may require local law enforcement officers to perform certain duties during the interim needed for the development of a federal gun control program. * * *

Indeed, since the ultimate issue is one of power, we must consider its implications in times of national emergency. Matters such as the enlistment of air raid wardens, the administration of a military draft, the mass inoculation of children to forestall an epidemic, or perhaps the threat of an international terrorist, may require a national response before federal personnel can be made available to respond. If the Constitution empowers Congress and the President to make an appropriate response, is there anything in the Tenth Amendment, "in historical understanding and practice, in the structure of the Constitution, [or] in the jurisprudence of this Court," that forbids the enlistment of state officers to make that response effective? More narrowly, what basis is there in any of those sources for concluding that it is the Members of this Court, rather than the elected representatives of the people, who should determine whether the Constitution contains the unwritten rule that the Court announces today? * * *

Unlike the First Amendment, which prohibits the enactment of a category of laws that would otherwise be authorized by Article I, the Tenth Amendment [confirms] the principle that the powers of the Federal Government are limited to those affirmatively granted by the Constitution, but it does not purport to limit the scope or the effectiveness of the exercise of powers that are delegated to Congress.[c] Thus, the Amendment provides no support for a rule that immunizes local officials from obligations that might be imposed on ordinary citizens.[2] * * *

---

b. The concurring opinion of Thomas, J., who joined the Court's opinion—and added that if "the Second Amendment is read to confer a *personal* right to 'keep and bear arms,' a colorable argument exists that the Federal Government's regulatory scheme, at least as it pertains to the purely intrastate sale or possession of firearms, runs afoul of that Amendment's protections"—is omitted.

c. *New York*, however, explained that "the Tenth Amendment confirms that the power of the Federal Government is subject to limits that may, in a given instance, reserve power to the States. The Tenth Amendment thus directs us to determine [whether] an incident of state sovereignty is protected by a limitation on an Article I power."

The debate concerning the relationship between the tenth amendment and the "essential postulates" (*Printz* majority) of state sovereignty is helpfully explored in Tribe 3d ed., at 903–12. For the view that the guarantee clause

(Art. IV, § 4) "might plausibly be invoked in support of the proposition that the Constitution recognizes in the National Government a duty, running directly 'to every State in this Union' rather than to individuals, to respect the state's most fundamental structural choices as to how its people are to participate in and shape the processes of their own governance," see id. See also Merritt, note 2 after *Garcia*.

2. Recognizing the force of the argument, the Court suggests that this reasoning is in error because—even if it is responsive to the submission that the Tenth Amendment roots the principle set forth by the majority today—it does not answer the possibility that the Court's holding can be rooted in a "principle of state sovereignty" mentioned nowhere in the constitutional text. As a ground for invalidating important federal legislation, this argument is remarkably weak. The majority's further claim that, while the Brady Act may be

Recent developments demonstrate that the political safeguards protecting Our Federalism are effective. The majority expresses special concern that were its rule not adopted the Federal Government would be able to avail itself of the services of state government officials "at no cost to itself." But this specific problem of federal actions that have the effect of imposing so-called "unfunded mandates" on the States has been identified and meaningfully addressed by Congress in recent legislation.[18] * * *

Perversely, the majority's rule seems more likely to damage than to preserve the safeguards against tyranny provided by the existence of vital state governments. By limiting the ability of the Federal Government to enlist state officials in the implementation of its programs, the Court creates incentives for the National Government to aggrandize itself. In the name of State's rights, the majority would have the Federal Government create vast national bureaucracies to implement its policies.[d]

legislation "necessary" to Congress' execution of its undisputed Commerce Clause authority to regulate firearms sales, it is nevertheless not "proper" because it violates state sovereignty, is wholly circular and provides no traction for its argument. [Our] ruling in *New York* that the Commerce Clause does not provide Congress the authority to require States to enact legislation—a power that affects States far closer to the core of their sovereign authority— does nothing to support the majority's unwarranted extension of that reasoning today.

18. The majority also makes the more general claim that requiring state officials to carry out federal policy causes states to "tak[e] the blame" for failed programs. The Court cites no empirical authority to support the proposition. [This] concern is vastly overstated. Unlike state legislators, local government executive officials routinely take action in response to a variety of sources of authority: local ordinance, state law, and federal law. It doubtless may therefore require some sophistication to discern under which authority an executive official is acting, just as it may not always be immediately obvious what legal source of authority underlies a judicial decision. [But] the majority's rule neither creates nor alters this basic truth. The problem is of little real consequence in any event, because to the extent that a particular action proves politically unpopular, we may be confident that elected officials charged with implementing it will be quite clear to their constituents where the source of the misfortune lies. These cases demonstrate the point. Sheriffs Printz and Mack have made public statements, including their decisions to serve as plaintiffs in these actions, denouncing the Brady Act.

[See also Moulton, note 3(c) after *Morrison*, at 877: "When federal officials persuade the states to regulate, through either financial incentives or preemption threats, then those federal officials 'may remain insulated from the electoral ramifications of their decision' at least to the same extent that they would were they to compel the states to regulate. Indeed,

use of persuasion rather than coercion might make escaping electoral accountability easier for federal officials, since the ultimate decision in fact would be made by the states." See also Mark Tushnet, *Globalization and Federalism in a Post–Printz World*, 36 Tulsa L.J. 11, 28, 37 (2000): "Preemption is an exercise of a power of negative commandeering. If affirmative commandeering is constitutionally impermissible, why is negative commandeering constitutionally unproblematic? [T]ext, history, and structure do not explain why a suitably designed state immunity from preemption should be ruled out."]

d. White, J., joined by Blackmun and Stevens, JJ., dissenting in *New York*, made a similar argument: "The ultimate irony of the decision today is that in its formalistically rigid obeisance to 'federalism,' the Court gives Congress fewer incentives to defer to the wishes of state officials in achieving local solutions to local problems. This legislation was a classic example of Congress acting as arbiter among the States in their attempts to accept responsibility for managing a problem of grave import. The States urged the National Legislature not to impose from Washington a solution to the country's low-level radioactive waste management problems. [By] invalidating the measure designed to ensure compliance for recalcitrant States, such as New York, the Court upsets the delicate compromise achieved among the States."

See also Erwin Chemerinsky, *Federalism Not as Limits, But as Empowerment*, 45 Kan. L.Rev. 1219, 1237 (1997): "Rather than mandate a uniform national approach, Congress left it to each state to decide for itself how best to deal with the contaminated debris. [F]or Congress to impose uniform standards on states would have left states less discretion and power to deal with the problem in an appropriate manner. In other words, the approach that the Court implicitly endorsed would have limited state authority, while the law the Court disapproved empowered states to choose the techniques of clean up that they thought best."

Finally, the majority provides an incomplete explanation of our decision in *Testa* [which] unanimously held that state courts of appropriate jurisdiction must occupy themselves adjudicating claims brought by private litigants under the federal Emergency Price Control Act of 1942, regardless of how otherwise crowded their dockets might be with state-law matters. That is a much greater imposition on state sovereignty than the Court's characterization of the [case].

Even if the Court were correct in its suggestion that it was the reference to judges in the Supremacy Clause, rather than the central message of the entire Clause, that dictated the result in *Testa*, the Court's implied expressio unius argument that the Framers therefore did not intend to permit the enlistment of other state officials is implausible. Throughout our history judges, state as well as federal, have merited as much respect as executive agents. The notion that the Framers would have had no reluctance to "press state judges into federal service" against their will but would have regarded the imposition of a similar—indeed, far lesser—burden on town constables as an intolerable affront to principles of state sovereignty can only be considered perverse. * * *

Justice Breyer, with whom Justice Stevens joins, dissenting.

[T]he United States is not the only nation that seeks to reconcile the practical need for a central authority with the democratic virtues of more local control. At least some other countries, facing the same basic problem, have found that local control is better maintained through application of a principle that is the direct opposite of the principle the majority derives from the silence of our Constitution. The federal systems of Switzerland, Germany, and the European Union, for example, all provide that constituent states, not federal bureaucracies, will themselves implement many of the laws, rules, regulations, or decrees enacted by the central "federal" body. * * *

Of course, we are interpreting our own Constitution, [but] their experience may nonetheless cast an empirical light on the consequences of different solutions to a common legal problem. * * *

[T]he fact that there is not more precedent—that direct federal assignment of duties to state officers is not common—likely reflects, not a widely shared belief that any such assignment is incompatible with basic principles of federalism, but rather a widely shared practice of assigning such duties in other ways. See, e.g., *Dole* (spending power); *New York* (general statutory duty); *FERC* (pre-emption). Thus, there is neither need nor reason to find in the Constitution an absolute principle, the inflexibility of which poses a surprising and technical obstacle to the enactment of a law that Congress believed necessary to solve an important national problem.* * *e

Notes and Questions

1. *Generally applicable laws.* (a) How persuasive is the *Printz* (and *New York*) distinction of *Garcia* on the ground that it involves a "federal law of general applicability"? Consider D. Bruce La Pierre, *The Political Safeguards of Federalism Redux: Intergovernmental Immunity and the States as Agents of the Nation*, 60 Wash.U.L.Rev. 779, 1000–01 (1982): "When a regulation applies both to state

---

e. Souter, J., who reaffirmed his view that *New York* "was rightly decided," filed a separate dissent, noting (1) that "in deciding these cases, which I have found closer than I had anticipated, it is *The Federalist* that finally determines my position," and (2) that "I do not read any of *The Federalist* material as requiring the conclusion that Congress could require administrative support without an obligation to pay fair value for it."

and private activity, the political checks on Congress' power to regulate private activity provide vicarious protection for state interests and make Congress politically accountable. [S]tate interests are protected because they are included in the representation of private interests." For the view that "*New York* and *Printz* do not establish a narrow anti-commandeering rule, but instead prohibit laws that target state and local governments for unique burdens," see Thomas H. Odom & Marc R. Baluda, *The Development of Process–Oriented Federalism: Harmonizing the Supreme Court's Tenth Amendment Jurisprudence from Garcia Through Printz*, 31 Urb.Law. 993 (1999). For the view that *New York* "provides no explanation for why such generally applicable laws burden political accountability less than laws that apply only to governmental entities," see Roderick M. Hills, Jr., *The Political Economy of Cooperative Federalism: Why State Autonomy Makes Sense and "Dual Sovereignty" Doesn't*, 96 Mich.L.Rev. 813, 829 (1998).

(b) *Definitional problems.* Do you agree that Congress "could not impose a minimum wage on the state governor, state legislators, or state judges, because these state workers have no private counterparts"? Ronald D. Rotunda, *The Powers of Congress Under Section 5 of the Fourteenth Amendment After City of Boerne v. Flores*, 32 Ind.L.Rev. 163, 165 (1998). If the minimum wage applied to corporate presidents and boards of directors, might they be "private counterparts"? See further *Reno v. Condon* (last ¶), below.

2. *Purely ministerial reporting.* What result after *Printz* in respect to such requirements? Consider Tribe 3d ed., at 886: "Perhaps requiring state officials to *gather* information would be tantamount to requiring them to play a role in administering a federal program, whereas merely requiring the *reporting* of pre-existing information would not be." Compare Jackson, fn. b after *Morrison*, at 2206: "Given the 'separate sphere' of 'state autonomy' model of sovereignty on which *Printz* is based, the model's logic—that Congress had no power (outside of constitutionally specified exigencies) to compel state or local governments to act—would argue against the constitutionality of many such laws." Contrast Tribe 3d ed., at 893: "Consider, for example, the provision of the Brady Act requiring CLEOs to destroy Brady forms if they find no reason to deem the would-be-purchaser ineligible to receive a handgun—a provision whose constitutionality the Court found it unnecessary to decide. If expressed as a command that local officials exert their sovereign power to destroy certain forms, this requirement would violate the anticommandeering principle; but if expressed as a prohibition against retention of certain forms by anyone, including private citizens, the requirement would seem constitutionally unobjectionable. It is difficult to see, then, why the strict, exceptionless rule of *Printz* is superior to a judicial approach that would permit realistic appraisal of the operation of federal requirements on states and of the extent to which objectionable commandeering has gratuitously taken place."

3. *Scope of "anti-commandeering" principle.* (a) Can Congress make it a crime for state and local officials to *engage* in certain conduct (assuming a substantial effect on interstate commerce), such as engaging in corrupt government practices? See George D. Brown, *Should Federalism Shield Corruption?— Mail Fraud, State Law and Post–Lopez Analysis*, 82 Corn.L.Rev. 225 (1997). Can Congress make it a crime to *fail* to take certain action, such as investigating government corruption? See generally Matthew D. Adler & Seth F. Kreimer, *The New Etiquette of Federalism: New York, Printz, and Yeskey*, 1999 Sup.Ct.Rev. 71.

(b) RENO v. CONDON, 528 U.S. 141, 120 S.Ct. 666, 145 L.Ed.2d 587 (2000), per REHNQUIST, C.J., unanimously sustained Congress' power under the commerce clause to pass the Driver's Privacy Protection Act, which bars state motor vehicle departments from disclosing (or selling) personal information (such as name, address, telephone number, vehicle description, Social Security number, medical information, and photograph) required for a driver's license or car registration: "The motor vehicle information which the States have historically sold is used by insurers, manufacturers, direct marketers, and others engaged in interstate commerce [and] is also used in the stream of interstate commerce by various public and private entities for matters related to interstate motoring. Because drivers' information is, in this context, an article of commerce, its sale or release into the interstate stream of business is sufficient to support congressional regulation. * * *

"We agree [that] the DPPA's provisions will require time and effort on the part of state employees, but reject the State's argument that the DPPA violates the principles laid down in either *New York* or *Printz*. [Such] 'commandeering' [is] an inevitable consequence of regulating a state activity. [That] a State wishing to engage in certain activity must take administrative and sometimes legislative action to comply with federal standards regulating that activity is a commonplace that presents no constitutional defect.

"Like the statute at issue in [*South Carolina v. Baker*, note 1 after *Garcia*, which "prohibited States from issuing unregistered bonds"], the DPPA does not require the States in their sovereign capacity to regulate their own citizens. The DPPA regulates the States as the owners of databases. It does not require the South Carolina Legislature to enact any laws or regulations, and it does not require state officials to assist in the enforcement of federal statutes regulating private individuals. We accordingly conclude that the DPPA is consistent with the constitutional principles enunciated in *New York* and *Printz*."

Nor does the DPPA "regulate the States exclusively. [It] regulates the universe of entities that participate as suppliers to the market for motor vehicle information–the States as initial suppliers of the information in interstate commerce and private resellers or redisclosers of that information in commerce."

Can *Condon* be squared with fn. 17 in *Printz*? Can it be squared with *Printz's* rejection of any "balancing analysis"? See Odom & Baluda, note 1 supra (DPPA invalid under *Printz* analysis). Reconsider note 2 supra.

4. *State "consent."* The *New York* dissenters described the extended negotiations between the states that led to the 1985 Act and viewed New York's participation and its actions under the Act as "approval of the interstate agreement process embodied in the 1980 and 1985 Acts" within the meaning of the interstate compact clause. But the majority reasoned that "the Constitution does not protect the sovereignty of States for the benefit of the States or state governments as abstract political entities, or even for the benefit of the public officials governing the [States]. ['Rather,] federalism secures to citizens the liberties that derive from the diffusion of sovereign power.' [State] officials thus cannot consent to the enlargement of the powers of Congress beyond those enumerated in the Constitution." How does the issue in note 2 after *Garcia* bear on this dispute?

5. *Alternative sources of national power.* (a) *Spending. New York* made clear that there are "a variety of methods, short of outright coercion, by which Congress may urge a State to adopt a legislative program consistent with federal interests. [First,] under Congress' spending power, 'Congress may attach conditions on the receipt of federal funds.' *Dole.*" Is this a less than fully effective method because "with conditional grants, Congress is constrained by its limited

fiscal capacity"? Hills, note 1 (a) supra, at 868. Could Congress easily condition receipt of some portion of *existing* federal law enforcement assistance funds on CLEOs performing background checks? For criticism of the "dim view of states' ability to decline federal money," see id. at 858–71.

(b) *Treaty.* Do the "essential postulates of state sovereignty" impose *New York* and *Printz*-like limits on the treaty power as well as on Art. I powers? Consider Carlos M. Vasquez, *Breard, Printz, and the Treaty Power*, 70 U.Colo. L.Rev. 1317, 1347 (1999): "As a general matter, treaties address the rights and obligations of governments vis-à-vis each other. [Even] when a treaty's ultimate object is the protection or regulation of individuals, it typically accomplishes that goal by placing obligations, whether of an affirmative or negative character, on the states-parties. [Thus,] an anticommandeering rule that bars the imposition of obligations on states that are not also imposed on private individuals would invalidate the typical rather than the odd treaty. The same would be true of a rule barring treaties that affect states 'in their role as governments.' Accordingly, neither rule could plausibly apply to the treaty power." Accord, Martin S. Flaherty, *Are We to be a Nation? Federal Power vs. "States' Rights" in Foreign Affairs*, 70 U.Colo.L.Rev. 1277 (1999). Contra, Tribe 3d ed., at 647–48.

Chapter 3

DISTRIBUTION OF FEDERAL POWERS: SEPARATION OF POWERS

This chapter addresses the distribution of powers *within* the federal government. Its principal concern is the extent to which the Constitution's text and structure, and the separation-of-powers and checks-and-balances concepts embodied therein, define the powers of the branches of government, especially those of the Congress and the Executive. A related issue is the extent to which a power expressly granted to one branch must be exercised with a view to avoiding interference the powers of another branch.

These matters are considered in this chapter's five sections: (1) presidential action affecting "congressional powers"; (2) congressional action affecting "presidential powers"; (3) the foreign affairs and war powers; (4) executive privilege and immunity; and (5) impeachment of the president.

SECTION 1. PRESIDENTIAL ACTION AFFECTING "CONGRESSIONAL" POWERS

YOUNGSTOWN SHEET & TUBE CO. v. SAWYER [THE STEEL SEIZURE CASE]

343 U.S. 579, 72 S.Ct. 863, 96 L.Ed. 1153 (1952).

JUSTICE BLACK delivered the opinion of the Court. * * *

We are asked to decide whether [President Truman] was acting within his constitutional power when he issued an order directing the Secretary of Commerce [Sawyer] to take possession of and operate most of the Nation's steel mills. The mill owners argue that the President's order amounts to lawmaking, a legislative function which the Constitution has expressly confided to the Congress and not to the President. The Government's position is that the order was made on findings of the President and that his action was necessary to avert a national catastrophe which would inevitably result from a stoppage of steel production [during the Korean War].

[When efforts to settle a labor dispute—including reference to the Federal Wage Stabilization Board—failed, the union called a nationwide strike to begin April 9, 1952. Finding that such a strike would jeopardize national defense, a few hours before the strike deadline the President issued Executive Order 10340, directing the Secretary of Commerce to take possession of most of the country's steel mills and keep them operating. The President sent a message to Congress reporting his actions on the next day. On May 3, the Court granted certiorari for direct review of a U.S. District Court order that had enjoined the Secretary's continued possession of the steel mills, and set argument for May 12. On June 2, the Court upheld the injunction, ruling the seizure unconstitutional.]

The President's power, if any, to issue the order must stem either from an act of Congress or from the Constitution itself.

[T]he use of the seizure techniques [to] prevent work stoppage was not only unauthorized by any congressional enactment; prior to this controversy, Congress had refused to adopt that method of settling labor disputes. When the Taft–Hartley Act [Labor Management Relations Act of 1947] was under [consideration], Congress rejected an amendment which would have authorized such governmental seizures in cases of emergency. [Instead], the plan sought to bring about settlements by use of the customary devices of mediation, conciliation, investigation by boards of inquiry, and public reports. In some instances temporary injunctions were authorized to provide cooling-off periods. All this failing, unions were left free to strike after a secret vote by employees * * *.[a]

It is clear that if the President had authority to issue the order he did, it must be found in some provision of the Constitution. [The] contention is that presidential power should be implied from the aggregate of his powers under the Constitution. Particular reliance is placed on provisions in Article II which say that "The executive Power shall be vested in a President"; that "he shall take Care that the Laws be faithfully executed"; and that he "shall be Commander in Chief of the Army and Navy of the United States."

* * * We cannot with faithfulness to our constitutional system hold that the Commander in Chief of the Armed Forces has the ultimate power as such to take possession of private property in order to keep labor disputes from stopping production. This is a job for the Nation's lawmakers, not for its military authorities.

Nor can the seizure order be sustained because of the several constitutional provisions that grant executive power to the President. In the framework of our Constitution, the President's power to see that the laws are faithfully executed refutes the idea that he is to be a lawmaker. The Constitution limits his functions in the lawmaking process to the recommending of laws he thinks wise and the vetoing of laws he thinks bad. And the Constitution is neither silent nor equivocal about who shall make laws which the President is to execute. The first section of the first article says that "All legislative Powers herein granted shall be vested in a Congress of the United States." * * *

The President's order does not direct that a congressional policy be executed in a manner prescribed by Congress—it directs that a presidential policy be executed in a manner prescribed by the President. The preamble of the order itself, like that of many statutes, sets out reasons why the President believes certain policies should be adopted, proclaims these policies as rules of conduct to be followed, and again, like a statute, authorizes a government official to promul-

a. Sections 206–210 of the Act provided that "[w]henever in the opinion of the President [a] threatened or actual strike [will], if permitted to occur or to continue, imperil the national health or safety," on the President's initiative, the strike could be enjoined while a board of inquiry studied the dispute, but that the strike could continue after 80 days if the employees reject the employer's last offer of settlement. The President was then obligated under the Act to report on the emergency to Congress.

gate additional rules and regulations consistent with the policy proclaimed and needed to carry that policy into execution. The power of Congress to adopt such public policies as those proclaimed by the order is beyond question. It can authorize the taking of private property for public use. It can make laws regulating the relationships between employers and employees, prescribing rules designed to settle labor disputes, and fixing wages and working conditions in certain fields of our economy. The Constitution did not subject this lawmaking power of Congress to presidential or military supervision or control.

It is said that other Presidents without congressional authority have taken possession of private business enterprises in order to settle labor disputes. But even if this be true, Congress has not thereby lost its exclusive constitutional authority to make laws necessary and proper to carry out the powers vested by the Constitution "in the Government of the United States."

Affirmed.

JUSTICE FRANKFURTER, concurring in the judgment and opinion of the Court.

Although the considerations relevant to the legal enforcement of the principle of separation of powers seem to me more complicated and flexible than may appear from what Mr. Justice Black has written, I join his opinion because I thoroughly agree with the application of the principle to this case. * * *

[We] must [put] to one side consideration of what powers the President would have had if there had been no legislation whatever bearing on the authority asserted by the seizure, or if the seizure had been only for a short, explicitly temporary period, to be terminated automatically unless Congressional approval were given. These and other questions, like or unlike, are not now here. * * *

[It] cannot be contended that the President would have had power to issue this order had Congress explicitly negated such authority in formal legislation. [And Congress's decision reflected in the Labor Management Relations Act of 1947 should be given the same effect, since] Congress has expressed its will to withhold this power from the President as though it had said so in so many words. [It has] said to the President, "You may not seize. Please report to us and ask for seizure power if you think it is needed in a specific [situation]."

[The] content of the three authorities of government is not to be derived from an abstract analysis. The areas are partly interacting, not wholly disjointed. The Constitution is a framework for government. Therefore the way the framework has consistently operated fairly establishes that it has operated according to its true nature. Deeply embedded traditional ways of conducting government cannot supplant the Constitution or legislation, but they give meaning to the words of a text. [But the] list of executive assertions of the power of seizure in circumstances comparable to the present reduces to three in the six-month period from June to December of 1941. [T]hese three isolated instances do not add up [to] the kind of executive construction of the Constitution [necessary to justify the action here]. Nor do they come to us sanctioned by the long-continued acquiescence of Congress* * *.

JUSTICE DOUGLAS, concurring in the judgment and opinion of the Court.

[The] President might seize and the Congress by subsequent action might ratify the seizure. But until and unless Congress acted, no condemnation would be lawful. The branch of government that has the power to pay compensation for a seizure is the only one able to authorize a seizure or make lawful one that the President has effected. That seems to me to be the necessary result of the condemnation provision in the Fifth Amendment.

JUSTICE JACKSON, concurring in the judgment and opinion of the Court.

The actual art of governing under our Constitution does not and cannot conform to judicial definitions of the power of any of its branches based on isolated clauses or even single Articles torn from context. While the Constitution diffuses power the better to secure liberty, it also contemplates that practice will integrate the dispersed powers into a workable government. It enjoins upon its branches separateness but interdependence, autonomy but reciprocity. Presidential powers are not fixed but fluctuate, depending upon their disjunction or conjunction with those of Congress. We may well begin by a somewhat over-simplified grouping of practical situations in which a President may doubt, or others may challenge, his powers, and by distinguishing roughly the legal consequences of this factor of relativity.

1. When the President acts pursuant to an express or implied authorization of Congress, his authority is at its maximum, for it includes all that he possesses in his own right plus all that Congress can delegate. * * *

2. When the President acts in absence of either a congressional grant or denial of authority, he can only rely upon his own independent powers, but there is a zone of twilight in which he and Congress may have concurrent authority, or in which its distribution is uncertain. Therefore, congressional inertia, indifference or quiescence may sometimes, at least as a practical matter, enable, if not invite, measures on independent presidential responsibility. In this area, any actual test of power is likely to depend on the imperatives of events and contemporary imponderables rather than on abstract theories of law.

3. When the President takes measures incompatible with the expressed or implied will of Congress, his power is at its lowest ebb, for then he can rely only upon his own constitutional powers minus any constitutional powers of Congress over the matter. Courts can sustain exclusive Presidential control in such a case only by disabling the Congress from acting upon the subject. Presidential claim to a power at once so conclusive and preclusive must be scrutinized with caution, for what is at stake is the equilibrium established by our constitutional system.

Into which of these classifications does this executive seizure of the steel industry fit? It is eliminated from the first by admission, for it is conceded that no congressional authorization exists for this seizure. * * *

[It] seems clearly eliminated from [the "second category"] because Congress has not left seizure of private property an open field but has covered it by three statutory policies inconsistent with this seizure [none of which] were invoked. In choosing a different and inconsistent way of his own, the President cannot claim that it is necessitated or invited by failure of Congress to legislate upon the occasions, grounds and methods for seizure of industrial properties.

This leaves the current seizure to be justified only by the severe tests under the third grouping, [where] we can sustain the President only by holding that seizure of such strike-bound industries is within his domain and beyond control by Congress. * * *

[I] cannot accept the view that [Art. II, § 1, cl. 1, vesting "the executive power" in the President] is a grant in bulk of all conceivable executive power but regard it as an allocation to the presidential office of the generic powers thereafter stated.

The [Commander in Chief] appellation is sometimes advanced as support for any presidential action, internal or external, involving use of force, the idea being that it vests power to do anything, anywhere, that can be done with an army or navy. [However, the] Constitution expressly places in Congress power "to raise and *support* Armies" and "to *provide* and *maintain* a Navy." (Emphasis supplied.) This certainly lays upon Congress primary responsibility for supplying the armed forces. Congress alone controls the raising of revenues and their appropriation and may determine in what manner and by what means they shall be spent for military and naval procurement. I suppose no one would doubt that Congress can take over war supply as a Government enterprise. * * *

The third clause in which the Solicitor General finds seizure powers is that "he shall take Care that the Laws be faithfully executed." That authority must be matched against [the due process clause of the fifth amendment]. One [clause] gives a governmental authority that reaches so far as there is law, the other gives a private right that authority shall go no farther. * * *

The Solicitor General lastly grounds support of the seizure upon nebulous, inherent powers never expressly granted but said to have accrued to the office from the customs and claims of preceding administrations. The plea is for a resulting power to deal with a crisis or an emergency according to the necessities of the case, the unarticulated assumption being that necessity knows no law. Loose and irresponsible use of adjectives colors all non-legal and much legal discussion of presidential powers. "Inherent" powers, "implied" powers, "incidental" powers, "plenary" powers, "war" powers and "emergency" powers are used, often interchangeably and without fixed or ascertainable meanings.* * *

In view of the ease, expedition and safety with which Congress can grant and has granted large emergency powers, certainly ample to embrace this crisis, I am quite unimpressed with the argument that we should affirm possession of them without statute. Such power either has no beginning or it has no end. If it exists, it need submit to no legal restraint. I am not alarmed that it would plunge us straightway into dictatorship, but it is at least a step in that wrong direction.

[The] Executive, except for recommendation and veto, has no legislative power. The executive action we have here originates in the individual will of the President and represents an exercise of authority without law. [With] all its defects, delays, and inconveniences, men have discovered no technique for long preserving free government except that the Executive be under the law, and that the law be made by parliamentary deliberations.[b]

CHIEF JUSTICE VINSON, with whom JUSTICE REED and JUSTICE MINTON join, dissenting.

[The dissent emphasized the country's international commitments for economic and military aid to preserve the free world and the congressional action directing the President to strengthen the armed forces. It called attention to the legislation directly related to supporting the Korean War. It quoted affidavits showing the enormous demand for steel in vital defense programs and attesting that a work stoppage would imperil the national defense.]

Accordingly, if the President has any power under the Constitution to meet a critical situation in the absence of express statutory authorization, there is no basis whatever for criticizing the exercise of such power in this case.

---

b. Burton, J., also concurred in Black, J.'s opinion but also wrote a separate concurrence, similar in thrust to those of Frankfurter and Jackson, JJ., stressing that "the President's [order] invaded the jurisdiction of Congress," which "reserved to itself" the remedy of seizure. Clark, J., concurred in the judgment because "Congress had prescribed methods to be followed by the President in meeting the emergency at hand, [but] in the absence of such action by Congress, the President's independent power to act depends upon the gravity of the situation confronting the nation."

[Our] Presidents have on many occasions exhibited the leadership contemplated by the Framers when they made the President Commander in Chief, and imposed upon him the trust to "take Care that the Laws be faithfully executed." With or without explicit statutory authorization, Presidents have [dealt] with national emergencies by acting promptly [to] enforce legislative programs, at least to save those programs until Congress could act. Congress and the courts have responded to such executive initiative with consistent approval. [Historic episodes from George Washington to Franklin D. Roosevelt were summarized in 17 pages. A brief excerpt follows:]

Some six months before Pearl Harbor, a dispute at a single aviation [plant] interrupted a segment of the production of military aircraft. [President] Roosevelt ordered the seizure of the plant "pursuant to the powers vested in [him] by the Constitution and laws of the United States, as President of the United States of America and Commander in Chief of the Army and Navy of the United States." The Attorney General (Jackson) vigorously proclaimed that the President had the moral duty to keep this Nation's defense effort a "going concern." [A]lso prior to Pearl Harbor, the President ordered the seizure of a ship-building company and an aircraft parts plant. Following the declaration of war, [five] additional industrial concerns were seized to avert interruption of needed production. During the same period, the President directed seizure of the Nation's coal mines to remove an obstruction to the effective prosecution of the war.

[This] is but a cursory summary of executive leadership. But it amply demonstrates that Presidents have taken prompt action to enforce the laws and protect the country whether or not Congress happened to provide in advance for the particular method of execution. [T]he fact that Congress and the courts have consistently recognized and given their support to such executive action indicates that such a power of seizure has been accepted throughout our history.

Flexibility as to mode of execution [of the laws] to meet critical situations is a matter of practical necessity. [The] broad executive power granted by Article II [cannot], it is said, be invoked to avert disaster. Instead, the President must confine himself to sending a message to Congress recommending action. Under this messenger-boy concept of the Office, the President cannot even act to preserve legislative programs from destruction so that Congress will have something left to act upon.

[T]here [is no] question of unlimited executive power in this case. The President himself closed the door to any such claim when he sent his Message to Congress stating his purpose to abide by any action of Congress, whether approving or disapproving his seizure action. [There] is no question that the possession was other than temporary in character and subject to congressional direction—either approving, disapproving or regulating the manner in which the mills were to be administered and returned to the owners. [Judicial], legislative and executive precedents throughout our history demonstrate that in this case the President acted in full conformity with his duties under the Constitution.

Notes and Questions

1. *Emergency powers.* Does Black, J.'s opinion for the Court imply that the President has no "emergency" or "implied" powers whatsoever? Is this a workable position? Does a majority of the Court agree?

Should it matter to separation-of-powers analysis that a particular branch of government has exercised the challenged power in the past? Should practical necessities matter? It seems clear, in retrospect, that the government in *Youngstown* much overestimated the practical emergency. In addition, the President had further, statutorily authorized options. Would (and should) the result have been the same if the success of the Korean War effort or the safety of troops in combat were genuinely at risk?

Does the President possess inherent authority, in the absence of congressional authorization, to deploy American troops to repel sudden attacks, to safeguard American property, or to protect or rescue governmental personnel or American citizens abroad? See generally Henry P. Monaghan, *The Protective Power of the Presidency*, 93 Colum.L.Rev. 1 (1993). See also Sec. 3 infra.

2. *Executive "lawmaking."* (a) *Delegation.* As discussed more fully infra, agencies of the executive branch, typically pursuant to authority delegated by Congress, routinely engage in rulemaking, and the President himself has developed and implemented tariff schedules.[a] Is the exercise of delegated rulemaking authority legislative action that is forbidden to executive officials?

(b) *Executive orders.* Presidents have long asserted a power to issue so-called "Executive Orders" relating to the organization of the executive branch, the use of federal property, and the terms on which the federal government will enter contracts. The most prominent include President Lincoln's Emancipation Proclamation and President Truman's racial integration of the armed forces. A much cited example is *United States v. Midwest Oil Co.*, 236 U.S. 459, 35 S.Ct. 309, 59 L.Ed. 673 (1915), upholding presidential authority to protect oil resources on public lands, pending proposed legislation, by suspending statutory entitlements to file oil claims. More recently, Presidents have issued executive orders first forbidding race discrimination by private firms receiving federal contracts, and later mandating "affirmative action" by federal contractors. Does the Constitution permit or authorize such action by the President? See Michael Brody, *Congress, The President, and Federal Equal Employment Policymaking: A Problem in Separation of Powers*, 60 B.U.L.Rev. 239 (1980). Cf. *Minnesota v. Mille Lacs Band of Chippewa Indians*, 526 U.S. 172, 119 S.Ct. 1187, 143 L.Ed.2d 270 (1999) (finding no valid source of authority for an 1850 executive order purporting to require the removal of Chippewa Indians from lands ceded to the United States by an 1837 treaty).

(c) DAMES & MOORE v. REGAN, 453 U.S. 654, 101 S.Ct. 2972, 69 L.Ed.2d 918 (1981), per REHNQUIST, J., unanimously upheld presidential executive orders to implement an executive agreement between Iran and the United States securing the release of American hostages held in Iran from November 1979 until January 1981. The executive agreement called for the termination of "all litigation between the government of each party and the nationals of the other" and for the settlement of pending claims through binding arbitration before a claims tribunal established under the agreement. The executive orders (1) suspended all claims in American courts that were within the jurisdiction of the claims tribunal, (2) nullified all prejudgment attachments against Iran's assets in actions against Iran in American courts, and (3) ordered transfer to Iran of all Iranian assets held in U.S. banks, except for one billion dollars to cover awards against Iran by the claims tribunal.

Dames & Moore's prejudgment attachment of Iranian bank assets, to secure its large claim for services rendered to Iran, was vacated pursuant to the

---

a. See, e.g., *J.W. Hampton, Jr. & Co. v. United States*, 276 U.S. 394, 48 S.Ct. 348, 72 L.Ed. 624 (1928); *Field v. Clark*, 143 U.S. 649, 12 S.Ct. 495, 36 L.Ed. 294 (1892); *The Aurora*, 11 U.S. (7 Cranch) 382, 3 L.Ed. 378 (1813).

Executive Orders. The Court rejected Dames & Moore's challenge: "Because the President's action in nullifying the attachments and ordering the transfer of the assets was taken pursuant to specific congressional authorization [under the International Emergency Economic Powers Act (IEEPA)][b] it is 'supported by the strongest of presumptions and the widest latitude of judicial interpretation, and the burden of persuasion would rest heavily upon any who might attack it.' [*Youngstown*] (Jackson, J., concurring). [We] cannot say that petitioner has sustained that heavy burden. A contrary ruling would mean that the Federal Government as a whole lacked the power exercised by the President, and that we are not prepared to say."

By contrast, "neither the IEEPA nor the Hostage Act constitutes specific authorization of the President's action suspending claims. [But this is] not to say that these statutory provisions are entirely irrelevant to the question of the validity of the President's [action.] Congress cannot anticipate and legislate with regard to every possible action the President may find it necessary to take or every possible situation in which he might act. [T]he enactment of legislation closely related to the question of the President's authority in a particular case which evinces legislative intent to accord the President broad discretion may be considered to 'invite' 'measures on independent presidential responsibility.' *Youngstown* (Jackson, J., concurring). At least this is so where there is no contrary indication of legislative intent and when, as here, there is a history of congressional acquiescence in conduct of the sort engaged in by the [President.]

"Crucial to our decision today is the conclusion that Congress has implicitly approved the practice of claim settlement by executive agreement. This is best demonstrated by Congress' enactment of the International Claims Settlement Act of 1949. The Act had two purposes: (1) to allocate to United States nationals funds received in the course of an executive claims settlement with Yugoslavia, and (2) to provide a procedure whereby funds resulting from future settlements could be distributed. To achieve these ends Congress created the International Claims Commission, now the Foreign Claims Settlement Commission, and gave it jurisdiction to make final and binding decisions with respect to claims by United States nationals against settlement funds. By creating a procedure to implement future settlement agreements, Congress placed its stamp of approval on such agreements. Indeed, the legislative history of the Act observed that the United States was seeking settlements with countries other than Yugoslavia and [stated] that the bill contemplates settlements of a similar nature in the future.

"[As] Justice Frankfurter pointed out in *Youngstown*, 'a systematic, unbroken executive practice, long pursued to the knowledge of the Congress and never before questioned [may] be treated as a gloss on "Executive Power" vested in the President by § 1 of Art. II.' * * *

"Our conclusion is buttressed by the fact that the means chosen by the President to settle the claims of American nationals provided an alternative forum, the Claims Tribunal, which is capable of providing meaningful relief. [Just] as importantly, Congress has not disapproved of the action taken [here.] We are thus clearly not confronted with a situation in which Congress has in some way resisted the exercise of Presidential authority.

"[W]e re-emphasize the narrowness of our decision. We do not decide that the President possesses plenary power to settle claims, even as against foreign

---

b. Section 1702(a)(1)(B) of IEEPA empowered the President to "compel," "nullify," or "prohibit" any "transfer" with respect to, or transactions involving, any property subject to the jurisdiction of the United States in which any foreign country has any interest.

governmental entities. [But] where, as here, the settlement of claims has been determined to be a necessary incident to the resolution of a major foreign policy dispute between our country and another, and where, as here, we can conclude that Congress acquiesced in the President's action, we are not prepared to say that the President lacks the power to settle such claims."[c]

(d) *Congressional "acquiescence."* In neither *Dames & Moore* nor *Youngstown* had Congress either expressly prohibited or authorized the President's challenged action. To what extent should congressional inaction or "silence" amount to "implicit approval"? Consider Tribe 3d ed., at 672–76: "[J]udicial reasoning that allows Congress to legislate by silence is constitutionally dubious: The internal system of checks and balances is thwarted because legislative silences are not subject to presidential veto, and external political accountability is diminished because Congress cannot realistically be held accountable by the electorate for laws it 'enacts' by silence. * * * *Dames & Moore* is not the only twentieth-century case involving foreign affairs in which the Court has strayed from requiring the President to obtain fairly explicit legislative authorization for actions he seeks to take [discussing *Haig v. Agee,* Ch.7, Sec.3]." Whether *Dames & Moore* may be grounded in the President's special authority over foreign affairs is considered in Sec. 3 infra.

3. *The fifth amendment.* How important was (or should it be) that the President in *Youngstown* was claiming a right to act "contra legem"—in violation of the constitutional right against the taking of property for public use without just compensation? Does the Constitution *ever* authorize the President to violate constitutional rights? See Monaghan, supra at 10, asserting this limit on the President's "protective" powers.

4. *Justice Jackson's categories.* As indicated in *Dames & Moore,* the opinion in the *Youngstown* case that has exercised the greatest subsequent influence is that of Jackson, J. Is his analysis consistent with that of Black, J. in whose opinion Jackson, J., purports to join? Are Jackson, J.'s categories analytically helpful?[d]

Within Jackson, J.'s "zone of twilight," where both Congress and the President may reasonably claim independent authority, which should be recognized as paramount? According to Edward S. Corwin, *The Steel Seizure Case: A Judicial Brick Without Straw,* 53 Colum.L.Rev. 53, 66 (1953), the "Court [in *Youngstown*] would unquestionably have assented to the proposition that in all emergency situations the last word lies with Congress when it chooses to speak such last word." Is congressional predominance always appropriate?

5. *Accretion of presidential power.* Consider Charles L. Black, Jr., *The Working Balance of the American Political Departments,* 1 Hast. Con.L.Q. 13, 20 (1974): "On paper, and as a matter of irreducible minimum, the presidency is an office of very little uncontrollable power. [The five powers specifically enumerated

c. The Court did not "think it appropriate at the present time to address petitioner's contention that the suspension of claims, if authorized, would constitute a taking of property in violation of the Fifth Amendment." For consideration of this issue, see Phillip R. Trimble, *Foreign Policy Frustrated—Dames & Moore, Claims Court Jurisdiction and a New Raid on the Treasury,* 84 Colum.L.Rev. 317 (1984).

d. For criticism, see Martin H. Redish & Elizabeth J. Cisar, *"If Angels Were to Govern": The Need for Pragmatic Formalism in Separation of Powers Theory,* 41 Duke L.J. 449, 485–

87 (1991), questioning the suggestion that the President's powers are at a "maximum" when acting pursuant to congressional authorization, since the powers of Congress and the President are substantially distinct, and Congress can neither delegate congressional powers to the President nor nullify presidential power arising from the Constitution. For the suggestion that *more* categories must be recognized, see Abner S. Greene, *Checks and Balances in an Era of Presidential Lawmaking,* 61 U.Chi.L.Rev. 123, 191–92 (1994).

in Art. II that seem most important either (i) do not amount to much, such as the powers to receive ambassadors and to grant pardons, or (ii) are hemmed in by congressional powers, such as the commander-in-chief power, which is limited by Congress' powers to declare war and vote military appropriations, and the power to enforce the law, which depends on the laws that Congress enacts and the enforcement resources that it provides.] Congress, on the other hand, holds virtually all the national power, if only it wants to keep or to resume [it]. But Congress is very poorly structured for initiative and leadership; the presidency is very well structured for these things. The result has been a flow of power from Congress to the presidency. [The] one fundamental error is that of supposing that the modern expansion of presidential power is based on the Constitution by itself, and hence is inaccessible as a matter of law to congressional correction." Should this mean that since the presidency "is now the most powerful office in the nation," our system of checks-and-balances requires "congressional regulation of the executive [to be] presumptively valid"? See Martin S. Flaherty, *The Most Dangerous Branch*, 105 Yale L.J. 1725, 1730, 1737 (1996). Or does the fact that Art. II grants the President an undefined "executive Power," while Art. I only vests Congress with "the legislative Powers herein granted," suggest that the framers intended a more unbounded presidential authority? See Steven G. Calabresi & Saikrishna B. Prakash, *The President's Power to Execute the Law*, 104 Yale L.J. 541 (1994).

6. *Formalism and functionalism.* What does Frankfurter, J. mean when criticizing Black, J.'s opinion as "formalistic"? What is the alternative?

Recent commentators have frequently distinguished between "formal" and "functional" approaches to separation-of-powers issues.[e] Although there is no canonical definition of these terms, formalist approaches, such as Black, J.'s in *Youngstown*, generally assume that the Constitution recognizes three kinds of functions—legislative, executive, and judicial—that must be assigned to the corresponding branch of government. Within this framework, separation-of-powers issues turn largely on classification of functions (as either legislative, executive, or judicial). There can be no inter-branch interference not expressly authorized by the Constitution.

By contrast, functionalism takes as its foundational commitment the different but equally familiar ideal of "checks and balances."[f] According to functionalist approaches, there can be no rigid division of governmental functions into three sharp categories, each the distinctive province of a single branch of government. Functionalists acknowledge that each branch may have certain "core" functions that cannot be curbed or usurped, but beyond the core accept that the constitutionality of challenged actions and institutional arrangements should be measured by reference to such characteristic *functions* of the separation of powers as (i) maintaining a system of checks and balances, (ii) preventing the concentration of excessive power in a single branch, (iii) protecting individual liberty, and (iv)

---

e. For an early and influential development of the distinction, see Peter L. Strauss, *The Place of Agencies in Government: Separation of Powers and the Fourth Branch*, 84 Colum.L.Rev. 573 (1984). For more recent discussion of this and related distinctions that have become prominent in the literature, see Rebecca L. Brown, *Separated Powers and Ordered Liberty*, 139 U.Pa.L.Rev. 1513, 1522–31 (1991); Flaherty, supra.

f. Cf. Garry Wills, *Explaining America: The Federalist* 119 (1981): "Checks and balances do not arise from separation theory, but are at odds with it. Checks and balances have to do with the *invasion* of the separated powers." See generally Lawrence Lessig & Cass R. Sunstein, *The President and the Administration*, 94 Colum. L.Rev. 1 (1994); David A. Strauss, *The Place of Agencies in Government: Separation of Powers and the Fourth Branch*, 84 Colum. L.Rev. 452 (1984).

allowing—subject to check—a cooperative ebb and flow of power among the branches to promote effective government.

Roughly speaking, formalists tend to criticize functionalism as inconsistent with constitutional structure and the framers' intent and as requiring judgments that are too ad hoc and political to be consistent with the rule of law. Functionalists, by contrast, often assert that a formalist methodology is unhistoric and unworkable,[g] since it would require the dismantling of much of the modern administrative state as we know it. Functionalists also claim that formalism is too aridly conceptual to reflect the most basic structural presuppositions of a Constitution designed to be adaptable to unforeseen exigencies.

7. *Impoundment.* May the President withhold expenditures authorized and appropriated by Congress when neither the appropriation act nor other legislation authorizes or forbids impoundment?[h] In 1974, Congress enacted over the President's veto the Congressional Budget and Impoundment Control Act, which gave Congress the last word by requiring that an appropriation be "available for obligation" unless Congress rescinds the appropriation within 45 days after a required notice to Congress that the President "has determined" that the appropriation should be rescinded. 2 U.S.C.A. §§ 681–688. No President has since challenged Congress' assertion of power over impoundment. But note the Line Item Veto Act of 1996, which delegated to the President substantially unrestricted authority to "cancel" certain spending and tax benefit measures after he has signed them into law, held unconstitutional in *Clinton v. New York*, Sec. 2, II infra.

SECTION 2. CONGRESSIONAL ACTION AFFECTING "PRESIDENTIAL" POWERS

I. DELEGATION OF RULEMAKING POWER

YAKUS v. UNITED STATES, 321 U.S. 414, 64 S.Ct. 660, 88 L.Ed. 834 (1944): the 1942 war-time emergency price control act authorized the president-appointed price administrator to issue regulations establishing maximum prices and rents to carry out the act's declared purposes "to stabilize prices and to prevent speculative, unwarranted, and abnormal increases in prices and rents; [and] protect persons with relatively fixed and limited incomes [from] undue impairment of

---

g. Functionalists deny that the framers intended a conceptually rigid division and separation of power among the branches, with no overlap or interbranch checking and balancing. They rely especially on *The Federalist* No. 47 (Madison): "No political truth is certainly of greater intrinsic value [than the maxim requiring the separation of governmental powers]. [But Montesquieu, the theorist whose authority is most often invoked,] did not mean that these departments have no *partial agency* in, or no *control* over, the acts of each other. His meaning, [can] amount to no more than this, that where the *whole* power of the department is exercised by the same hands which possess the *whole* power of another department, the fundamental principles of a free constitution are subverted."

h. Conflicts over presidential impoundment of appropriated funds reached their peak in the Nixon administration. The constitutionality of impoundment has been considered in non-judicial studies and in a few federal court cases, but it has not been addressed by the Supreme Court. See Abner J. Mikva & Michael F. Hertz, *Impoundment of Funds—The Courts, The Congress and The President: A Constitutional Triangle*, 69 Nw.U.L.Rev. 335 (1974); L. Harold Levinson & Jon L. Mills, *Impoundment: A Search for Legal Principles*, 26 U.Fla.L.Rev. 191 (1974); Timothy R. Harner, *Presidential Power to Impound Appropriations for Defense and Foreign Relations*, 5 Harv.J.L. & Pub. Pol. 131 (1982).

their standard of living * * *." When in the administrator's judgment prices "have risen or threaten to rise in a manner inconsistent with the purposes of this act," the administrator was to establish maximum prices and rents that "in his judgment [would] be generally fair and equitable [and] effectuate the purposes of this act." So far as practicable, the administrator was to "give due consideration to the prices prevailing between October 1 and October 15, 1941" and to "make adjustments for such relevant factors as he may determine and deem to be of general applicability." The court, per STONE, C.J., upheld this delegation: "The Act [is] an exercise by Congress of its legislative power. In it Congress has stated the legislative objective, has prescribed the method of achieving that objective— maximum price fixing—, and has laid down standards to guide the administrative determination of both the occasions for the exercise of the price-fixing power, and the particular prices to be established.

"The Act is unlike the National Industrial Recovery Act [in] *Schechter Poultry Corp.*, [Ch. 2, Sec. 2, III, A], which proclaimed in the broadest terms its purpose 'to rehabilitate industry and to conserve natural resources.' It prescribed no method of attaining that end save by the establishment of codes of fair competition, the nature of whose permissible provisions was left undefined. It provided no standards to which those codes were to conform.

"[The] Constitution as a continuously operative charter of government does not demand the impossible or the impracticable. It does not require that Congress find for itself every fact upon which it desires to base legislative action or that it make for itself detailed determinations which it has declared to be prerequisite to the application of the legislative policy to particular facts and circumstances impossible for Congress itself properly to investigate. The essentials of the legislative function are the determination of the legislative policy and its formulation and promulgation as a defined and binding rule of conduct. [These] essentials are preserved when Congress has specified the basic conditions of fact upon whose existence or occurrence, ascertained from relevant data by a designated administrative agency, it directs that its statutory command shall be effective. It is no objection that the determination of facts and the inferences to be drawn from them in the light of the statutory standards and declaration of policy call for the exercise of judgment, and for the formulation of subsidiary administrative policy within the prescribed statutory framework."

Only Roberts, J., dissented on the delegation issue.

Notes and Questions

1. *Nondelegation doctrine.* (a) *Law.* The Court has continued to give voice to a so-called non-delegation doctrine, under which "Congress [cannot] delegate its legislative powers to another branch," *Mistretta v. United States*, Sec. III infra, but has not invalidated legislation under this doctrine since 1935.[a] Although some justices have occasionally sought to enforce this principle,[b] the decisions establish

a. In only two cases, both involving New Deal legislation, has the Court invalidated congressional delegation of legislative power to a federal officer or agency. *Schechter*, supra; *Panama Refining Co. v. Ryan*, 293 U.S. 388, 55 S.Ct. 241, 79 L.Ed. 446 (1935). See also *Carter v. Carter Coal Co.*, Ch. 2, Sec. 2, III, A, invalidating a congressional delegation to a private industry association with a potentially adverse interest to the objects of the regulation. See generally Tribe 3d ed., at 991–93.

b. See, e.g., *American Textile Mfg. Institute, Inc. v. Donovan*, 452 U.S. 490, 101 S.Ct. 2478, 69 L.Ed.2d 185 (1981) (Rehnquist, J., joined by Burger, C.J., dissenting). Cf. the opinions of Breyer and Scalia, JJ., dissenting in *Clinton v. New York*, Sec. II infra.

that delegations will be upheld wherever Congress furnishes an "intelligible principle" that rulemakers are bound to follow, and leave little reason to believe that the requisites stated in *Yakus* are effective limits on the delegation of legislative power. See 1 Kenneth Culp Davis & Richard J. Pierce, Jr., *Administrative Law Treatise* 66–85 (3d ed. 1994); *Mistretta*, Sec. III infra.[c]

The broad scope of Congress' power to delegate in the modern administrative state is further emphasized by CHEVRON U.S.A. INC. v. NATURAL RESOURCES DEFENSE COUNCIL, INC., 467 U.S. 837, 104 S.Ct. 2778, 81 L.Ed.2d 694 (1984), which concerned a federal agency's interpretation of a statutory authorization when "Congress has not directly addressed the precise question at issue." The Court held that "if Congress has explicitly left a gap for the agency to fill," the agency's interpretations of its governing statute are valid "unless they are arbitrary, capricious, or manifestly contrary to the statute"; if the delegation is "implicit rather than explicit," the agency's interpretation is valid if "reasonable." In addition to this judicial "deference" to the agency's interpretations, "an agency to which Congress has delegated policymaking responsibilities may, within the limits of that delegation, properly rely upon the incumbent administration's views of wise policy to inform its judgments. While agencies are not directly accountable to the people, the Chief Executive is, and it is entirely appropriate for this political branch of the Government to make such policy choices—resolving the competing interests which Congress itself either inadvertently did not resolve, or intentionally left to be resolved by the agency charged with the administration of the statute in light of everyday realities."

(b) *Policy.* Should the delegation of rulemaking to an executive agency be rejected as an unconstitutional assignment of legislative power to the executive branch? Consider Cass R. Sunstein, *Is the Clean Air Act Unconstitutional?*, 98 Mich.L.Rev. 303, 336 (1999): "The vesting of lawmaking power in Congress is designed to ensure the combination of deliberation and accountability that comes from saying that government power cannot be brought to bear on individuals unless diverse representatives, from diverse places, have managed to agree on the details. Consider, as an extreme example, the early decision by the German legislature to confer on Adolf Hitler the power to rule by 'decree'; this delegation made possible lawmaking exercises that would otherwise have been extremely cumbersome, and hence removed an important check on arbitrary rule." See generally John H. Ely, *Democracy and Distrust: A Theory of Judicial Review* 131–34 (1980); Martin Redish, *The Constitution as Political Structure* ch. 5 (1995).

---

c. In *American Trucking Assn's v. EPA*, 175 F.3d 1027, modified 195 F.3d 4 (D.C.Cir. 1999), cert. granted, 120 S.Ct. 2193 (2000), holding sections of the Clean Air Act to violate the nondelegation doctrine, the dissent argued: "Section 109 requires EPA to publish air quality standards 'the attainment and maintenance of which in the judgment of the Administrator, based on such criteria and allowing an adequate margin of safety, are requisite to protect the public health.' Compare section 109 to the language of section 303 of the Communications Act of 1934, which gave the FCC authority to regulate broadcast licensing in the 'public interest,' and which the Supreme Court sustained in *National Broadcasting Co. v. United States*, 319 U.S. 190, 225–26, 63 S.Ct. 997, 87 L.Ed. 1344 (1943). The FCC's general authority to issue regulations 'as public convenience, interest, or necessity requires' was sustained in *United States v. Southwestern Cable Co.*, 392 U.S. 157, 178, 88 S.Ct. 1994, 20 L.Ed.2d 1001 (1968). The Supreme Court has sustained equally broad delegations to other agencies, including [the] Federal Power Commission's authority to determine 'just and reasonable' rates, *FPC v. Hope Natural Gas Co.*, 320 U.S. 591, 600, 64 S.Ct. 281, 88 L.Ed. 333 (1944), the War Department's authority to recover 'excessive profits' earned on military contracts, *Lichter v. United States*, 334 U.S. 742, 778–786, 68 S.Ct. 1294, 92 L.Ed. 1694 (1948), and the Attorney General's authority to regulate new drugs that pose an 'imminent hazard to public safety,' *Touby v. United States*, 500 U.S. 160, 165, 111 S.Ct. 1752, 114 L.Ed.2d 219 (1991)."

In contrast, it has been argued that "broad delegation to administrators" *enhances* "accountability." Presidents, who "are heads of administrations," are unlike Congress because they have "no particular constituency [with] special responsibility to deliver benefits." Rather, they are concerned with "the responsiveness of government to the desires of the general electorate." Jerry L. Mashaw, *Greed, Chaos, and Governance* 152 (1997). See also Peter H. Schuck, *Delegation and Democracy*, 20 Cardozo L. Rev. 775, 781–82 (1999): "[T]he agency is often the site in which public participation is most effective. This is not only because [the] policy stakes for individuals and interest groups are most immediate, transparent, and well-defined at the agency level. [It] is also because the agency is where the public can best educate the government about the true nature of the problem that Congress has tried to address." See also Laurence H. Silberman, *Chevron—The Intersection of Law & Policy*, 58 Geo.Wash.L.Rev. 821 (1990).

(c) *Reasons for delegation.* Why does Congress, which might be expected to be jealous of its authority, so frequently delegate rulemaking power to the executive branch? Consider Redish, supra at 35: "One of the key constitutional strategies of the New Deal [was] a dramatic relaxation of the so-called nondelegation doctrine. [This] was dictated by the social goals and political philosophy of the New Deal, which focused on the need for efficiency and expertise in the administration of governmental programs and which therefore called for substantial administrative discretion in substantive policymaking." See also Richard B. Stewart, *The Reformation of American Administrative Law*, 88 Harv.L.Rev. 1667, 1695–96 (1975): "Administration is an exercise in experiment. [C]hanges in the basic parameters of the problem may preclude the development of a detailed policy that can consistently be pursued for any length of time. [In] addition, there appear to be serious institutional constraints on Congress' ability to specify regulatory policy in meaningful detail. Legislative majorities typically represent coalitions of interests that must not only compromise among themselves but also with opponents. Individual politicians often find far more to be lost than gained in taking a readily identifiable stand on a controversial issue. [Furthermore,] detailed legislative specification [of] specialized and complex issues [requires] resources that Congress has, in most instances, been unable or unwilling to muster. [Finally,] one may question whether a legislature is likely in many instances to generate more responsible decisions on questions of policy than agencies." Is the premise that the Constitution requires a rigid separation of functions among the departments of government still valid?[d]

2. *Foreign Affairs.* Did the functional imperative of averting a crippling wartime inflation justify the result in *Yakus*? See also *Loving v. United States,* 517 U.S. 748, 116 S.Ct. 1737, 135 L.Ed.2d 36 (1996), per Kennedy, J., holding unanimously, on the assumption that its death penalty jurisprudence applied to courts-martial, that Congress could delegate to the President responsibility for prescribing aggravating factors warranting capital sentences. Because the assigned duties were "interlinked" with the President's constitutional powers as Commander in Chief, Congress, which had already defined the underlying capital offense, was not required to supply the President with "further guidance" concerning aggravating factors.[e] For further consideration of the foreign affairs

---

d. For an argument that virtually the entire administrative state is unconstitutional and thoughts about what to do about it, see Gary Lawson, *The Rise and Rise of the Administrative State*, 107 Harv.L.Rev. 1231 (1994).

e. Scalia, J., joined by O'Connor, J., concurred in part but declined to join the majority's treating English history as a source of relevant separation-of-powers principles in this case. Thomas, J., concurred in the judgment only.

context, see Sec. 3 infra. Is the judicial branch competent to assess claims of necessity and importance in ruling on congressional delegations in other contexts?

3. *Proposals for revitalization.* (a) "[L]imitations on executive discretion [are] best promoted not by invalidating legislation, but by statutory construction[f] and by clear statement principles[g]—the real place where contemporary American law recognizes a nondelegation doctrine, and where that doctrine now flourishes— and also by judicial invalidation in the extremely rare cases where even aggressive statutory construction is able to identify neither floors nor ceilings." Sunstein, *supra* at 340, 357–58.

(b) "The new delegation doctrine [accepts] Congress's assignment of power and consequent relinquishment of policy control, [but] also ensures that agencies implement their delegated authority in [a manner] necessary for democratic lawmaking [by supplying] a limiting standard, rationally related to the goals of the Act [citing *AT & T Corp. v. Iowa Utilities Bd.*, 525 U.S. 366, 119 S.Ct. 721, 142 L.Ed.2d 835 (1999), a decision yet to be regularly applied]." Lisa S. Bressman, *Schechter Poultry at the Millennium: A Delegation Doctrine for the Administrative State*, 109 Yale L.J. 1399 (2000).

(c) "[T]he inability to retrieve delegated authority accounts for much of the nondelegation principle. [Broad] delegations to the President are thus the most structurally problematic; the President's dual role as recipient of delegated authority and participant in decisions about its retrieval [through the veto] creates the very real potential that lawmaking power is ceded in such a way that Congress's ultimate power to make laws is diminished."[h] Vikram D. Amar, *Indirect Effects of Direct Election: A Structural Examination of the Seventeenth Amendment*, 49 Vand.L.Rev. 1347, 1383–84 (1996).

II. LEGISLATIVE AND LINE ITEM VETOES

INS v. CHADHA

462 U.S. 919, 103 S.Ct. 2764, 77 L.Ed.2d 317 (1983).

CHIEF JUSTICE BURGER delivered the opinion of the Court.

[The Immigration and Nationality Act authorized the Attorney General to suspend deportation of a deportable alien if he met specified conditions and would suffer "extreme hardship" if deported. It required a report to Congress on each suspension. Sec. 244(c)(2) provided that if, within a specified period thereafter, either house of Congress "passes a resolution stating [that] it does not favor the suspension [the] Attorney General shall thereupon deport such alien." The Attorney General suspended the deportation of Chadha. Accepting the House Committee's conclusion that Chadha did not satisfy the hardship requirements, the House of Representatives passed a resolution that the "deportation should not

---

f. "As between an open-ended and less open-ended understanding of agency authority, the less open-ended interpretation should be preferred."

g. "Often courts say that statutes will not be interpreted to allow agencies to engage in certain conduct unless there has been a clear statement of authorization from Congress."

h. Should Congress *ever* be able to delegate governmental power *outside* the federal gov-

ernment? See Harold J. Krent, *Fragmenting the Unitary Executive: Congressional Delegations of Administrative Authority Outside the Federal Government*, 85 Nw.U.L.Rev. 62 (1990); John C. Yoo, *New Sovereignty and the Old Constitution: The Chemical Weapons Convention and the Appointments Clause*, 15 Const. Comment. 87 (1998) (delegation to foreign officials).

be suspended." It was not submitted to the Senate, nor "presented to the President" under Art. I, § 7.]

Although not "hermetically" sealed from one another, the powers delegated to the three Branches are functionally identifiable. When any Branch acts, it is presumptively exercising the power the Constitution has delegated to [it]. Whether actions taken by either House are, in law and fact, an exercise of legislative power depends not on their form but upon "whether they contain matter which is properly to be regarded as legislative in its character and effect."

[In] purporting to exercise power defined in Art. I, § 8, cl. 4, to "establish an uniform Rule of Naturalization," the House took action that had the purpose and effect of altering the legal rights, duties, and relations of persons, including the Attorney General, Executive Branch officials and Chadha, all outside the legislative branch. [The] one-House veto operated in [this case] to overrule the Attorney General and mandate Chadha's deportation; absent the House action, Chadha would remain in the United States. Congress has *acted* and its action has altered Chadha's status.

The legislative character of the one-House veto in [this case] is confirmed by the character of the congressional action it supplants. Neither the House of Representatives nor the Senate contends that, absent the veto provision in § 244(c)(2), either of them, or both of them acting together, could effectively require the Attorney General to deport an alien once the Attorney General, in the exercise of legislatively delegated authority,[16] had determined the alien should remain in the United States. Without the challenged provision in § 244(c)(2), this could have been achieved, if at all, only by legislation requiring deportation. * * *

The nature of the decision implemented by the one-House veto in [this case] further manifests its legislative character. After long experience with the clumsy, time-consuming private bill procedure, Congress made a deliberate choice to delegate to [the] Attorney General, the authority to allow deportable aliens to remain in this country in certain specified circumstances. [Disagreement] with the Attorney General's decision on Chadha's deportation—that is, Congress' decision to deport Chadha—no less than Congress' original choice to delegate to the Attorney General the authority to make that decision, involves determinations of policy that Congress can implement in only one way; bicameral passage followed by presentment to the President. Congress must abide by its delegation of authority until that delegation is legislatively altered or revoked.[19]

---

16. Congress protests that affirming the Court of Appeals in [this case] will sanction "lawmaking by the Attorney General." * * * Executive action under legislatively delegated authority that might resemble "legislative" action in some respects is not subject to the approval of both Houses of Congress and the President for the reason that the Constitution does not so require. That kind of Executive action is always subject to check by the terms of the legislation that authorized it; and if that authority is exceeded it is open to judicial review as well as the power of Congress to modify or revoke the authority entirely. A one-House veto is clearly legislative in both character and effect and is not so checked; the need for the check provided by Art. I, §§ 1, 7, is therefore clear. Congress' authority to delegate portions of its power to administrative agencies provides no support for the argument that Congress can constitutionally control administration of the laws by way of a Congressional veto.

19. This does not mean that Congress is required to capitulate to "the accretion of policy control by forces outside its chambers." [Beyond] the obvious fact that Congress ultimately controls administrative agencies in the legislation that creates them, other means of control, such as durational limits on authorizations and formal reporting requirements, lie well within Congress' constitutional power. See also n.9, supra.

[Fn. 9 stated: "Without the one-House veto, § 244 resembles the 'report and wait' provision approved by the Court in *Sibbach v. Wilson & Co.*, 312 U.S. 1, 61 S.Ct. 422, 85 L.Ed. 479 (1941). [The statute in] *Sibbach* did *not* provide

Finally, we see that when the Framers intended to authorize either House of Congress to act alone and outside of its prescribed bicameral legislative role, they narrowly and precisely defined the procedure for such action. There are [only] four provisions in the Constitution, explicit and unambiguous, by which one House may act alone with the unreviewable force of law, not subject to the President's veto: [the House of Representatives' power to initiate impeachments, and the Senate's powers to try impeachments, to approve presidential appointments, and to ratify treaties.]

The bicameral requirement, the Presentment Clauses, the President's veto, and Congress' power to override a veto were intended to erect enduring checks on each Branch and to protect the people from the improvident exercise of power by mandating certain prescribed steps. To preserve those checks, and maintain the separation of powers, the carefully defined limits on the power of each Branch must not be eroded. [In] purely practical terms, it is obviously easier for action to be taken by one House without submission to the President; but it is crystal clear from the records of the Convention, contemporaneous writings and debates, that the Framers ranked other values higher than efficiency. * * *

The choices we discern as having been made in the Constitutional Convention [were] consciously made by men who had lived under a form of government that permitted arbitrary governmental acts to go unchecked. There is no support in the Constitution or decisions of this Court for the proposition that the cumbersomeness and delays often encountered in complying with explicit constitutional standards may be avoided, either by the Congress or by the President.

JUSTICE POWELL concurring in the judgment.

[In] my view, the case [may] be decided on a narrower ground. When Congress finds that a particular person does not satisfy the statutory criteria for permanent residence in this country it has assumed a judicial function in violation of the principle of separation of powers. [The Framers'] concern that a legislature should not be able unilaterally to impose a substantial deprivation on one person was expressed not only in [the] general allocation of power, but also in more specific provisions, such as the Bill of Attainder Clause, Art. I, § 9, cl. 3 [,both of which] reflect the Framers' concern that trial by a legislature lacks the safeguards necessary to prevent the abuse of power. * * *

JUSTICE WHITE dissenting. * * *

The prominence of the legislative veto mechanism in our contemporary political system and its importance to Congress can hardly be overstated. It has become a central means by which Congress secures the accountability of executive and independent agencies. Without the legislative veto, Congress is faced with a Hobson's choice: either to refrain from delegating the necessary authority, leaving itself with a hopeless task of writing laws with the requisite specificity to cover endless special circumstances across the entire policy landscape, or in the alternative, to abdicate its lawmaking function to the Executive Branch and independent agencies. To choose the former leaves major national problems unresolved; to opt for the latter risks unaccountable policymaking by those not elected to fill that role. Accordingly, over the past five decades, the legislative veto has been placed in nearly 200 statutes. The device is known in every field of governmental concern: reorganization, budgets, foreign affairs, war powers, and regulation of trade,

that Congress could unilaterally veto the Federal Rules. Rather, it gave Congress the opportunity to review the Rules before they became effective and to pass legislation barring their effectiveness if the Rules were found objectionable. This technique was used by Congress when it acted in 1973 to stay, and ultimately to revise, the proposed Rules of Evidence."]

safety, energy, the environment, and the economy. [T]he increasing reliance of Congress upon the legislative veto suggests that the alternatives to which Congress must now turn are not entirely satisfactory.[10]

The history of the legislative veto also makes clear that it has not been a sword with which Congress has struck out to aggrandize itself at the expense of the other branches—the concerns of Madison and Hamilton. Rather, the veto has been a means of defense, a reservation of ultimate authority necessary if Congress is to fulfill its designated role under Art. I as the Nation's lawmaker. While the President has often objected to particular legislative vetoes, generally those left in the hands of congressional Committees, the Executive has more often agreed to legislative review as the price for a broad delegation of authority. * * *

I do not dispute the Court's truismatic exposition of [the prerequisites for lawmaking set forth in Art. I of the Constitution.] [But the] power to exercise a legislative veto is not the power to write new law without bicameral approval or Presidential consideration. The veto must be authorized by statute and may only negative what an Executive department or independent agency has proposed. On its face, the legislative veto no more allows one House of Congress to make law than does the Presidential veto confer such power upon the President. * * *

If Congress may delegate lawmaking power to independent and Executive agencies, it is most difficult to understand Art. I as prohibiting Congress from also reserving a check on legislative power for itself. Absent the veto, the agencies receiving delegations of legislative or quasi-legislative power may issue regulations having the force of law without bicameral approval and without the President's signature. It is thus not apparent why the reservation of a veto over the exercise of that legislative power must be subject to a more exacting test. In both cases, it is enough that the initial statutory authorizations comply with the Art. I requirements. * * *

The central concern of the presentation and bicameralism requirements of Art. I is that when a departure from the legal status quo is undertaken, it is done with the approval of the President and both Houses of Congress—or, in the event of a Presidential veto, a two-thirds majority in both Houses. This interest is fully satisfied by the operation of § 244(c)(2). The President's approval is found in the Attorney General's action in recommending to Congress that the deportation order for a given alien be suspended. The House and the Senate indicate their approval of the Executive's action by not passing a resolution of disapproval within the statutory period. Thus, a change in the legal status quo—the deportability of the alien—is consummated only with the approval of each of the three relevant actors. The disagreement of any one of the three maintains the alien's pre-existing status* * *.[a]

Notes and Questions

1. *Extension to rulemaking by independent regulatory agencies.* Two weeks after *Chadha*, PROCESS GAS CONSUMERS GROUP v. CONSUMER ENERGY

10. While Congress could write certain statutes with greater specificity, it is unlikely that this is a realistic or even desirable substitute for the legislative veto. [Political volatility] and [t]he controversial nature of many issues would prevent Congress from reaching agreement on many major problems if specificity were required in their enactments.

a. For commentaries on *Chadha*, see, e.g., Stephen Breyer, *The Legislative Veto After Chadha*, 72 Geo.L.J. 785 (1984); E. Donald Elliott, *INS v. Chadha: The Administrative Constitution, the Constitution, and the Legislative Veto*, 1983 Sup.Ct.Rev. 125; Peter L. Strauss, *Was There A Baby in the Bathwater? A Comment on the Supreme Court's Legislative Veto Decision*, 1983 Duke L.J. 789 (1983).

COUNCIL OF AMERICA, 463 U.S. 1216, 103 S.Ct. 3556, 77 L.Ed.2d 1402, 1403, 1413 (1983), summarily affirmed court of appeals decisions invalidating a one-house legislative veto of regulatory rulemaking by the Federal Energy Regulatory Commission and a two-house veto of such rulemaking by the Federal Trade Commission. Rehnquist, J., would have noted probable jurisdiction and set the cases for oral argument. Powell, J., took no part. WHITE, J., dissented: "Where the veto is placed as a check upon the actions of the independent regulatory agencies, the Art. I analysis relied upon in *Chadha* has a particularly hollow ring. [These] regulations have the force of law without the President's concurrence; nor can he veto. [To] invalidate the [legislative veto,] which allows Congress to maintain some control over the lawmaking process, merely guarantees that the independent agencies, once created, for all practical purposes are a fourth branch of the Government not subject to the direct control of either Congress or the Executive Branch."

2. *Chadha's broad sweep.* Was it wise for the Court, in invalidating the legislative veto, to paint with so broad a brush?[b]

(a) Should the Court have limited its opinion to the validity of legislative vetoes of individual deportation decisions, like *Chadha,* perhaps recognized as representative of a potentially broader class of decisions on "highly individual matters" involving the application of law to fact?[c]

(b) Does rulemaking raise distinctive issues? What is the answer to White, J.'s argument that the legislative veto would actually promote the Constitution's purpose of requiring the concurrence of both Houses of Congress and of the President for proposed rules of conduct to become law?

(c) In upholding delegation of rulemaking to regulatory agencies, the Court stressed the practical governmental necessity for such delegations. See, e.g., *Yakus.* Should the Court also have considered the practical governmental needs, if any, for legislative vetoes?

3. *Formalism and functionalism.* (a) Since Congress may authorize a regulatory agency to engage in rulemaking without repeating the formalities of bicameral approval and presentment, already satisfied when the law was enacted, why may not the same Act of Congress also authorize one or both houses to review, disapprove, and revoke the resulting rules without repeating those formalities? If the executive branch can make rules with the force of law, why can't Congress exercise quasi-executive authority (analogous to the "quasi-legislative" power recognized in *Yakus*)? Consider Tribe 3d ed., at 146: "The Framers regarded the legislature as the most dangerous branch, and even two centuries later it remains a plausible proposition to many that there is more to fear when Congress—which is the source of all statutorily delegated authority—delegates not to the other branches, but to itself." Compare the *Line Item Veto* case, infra. Is it relevant whether the legislature or executive is the "most dangerous"? If so, which branch is it?

(b) Consider Greene, fn. d, Sec. 1 supra, at 124, 196: "We cannot properly examine the constitutional balance of power between the President and Congress

---

b. For discussion and classification of the various types of legislative veto provisions employed since 1932, when Congress authorized the President to reorganize the executive departments subject to a one-House veto, see Strauss, supra at 790–91.

c. Cf. Rebecca L. Brown, *Separation of Powers and Ordered Liberty*, 139 U.Pa.L.Rev. 1513, 1531 (1991)(arguing that "the Court [should] examine governmental acts in light of the degree to which they tend to detract from [individual] fairness [in] the process of government").

if we assume that Congress legislates and the President executes. Rather, we should begin from a new premise, that of presidential lawmaking. For since the New Deal, Congress has delegated much lawmaking power to the President, without judicial invalidation. The framers of the Constitution were centrally concerned with avoiding the concentration of executive and legislative powers in the same hands. This concern should be ours as well, both because of the harm that concentrated power can bring and the good that can result from diffused power. [I]f we accept sweeping delegations of lawmaking power to the President, then to capture accurately the framers' principles—principles that deserve our continuing adherence—we must also accept some (though not all) congressional efforts at regulating presidential lawmaking. [The legislative veto] might be far from the specific structure that the framers envisioned, but it is far closer to their underlying principles than the present system, which allows the President to make policy while effectively preventing Congress from doing anything about it."

(c) Compare arguments that, measured against the purposes that underlay the framers' design of a system of checks and balances, the legislative veto was *dys*functional. According to Harold H. Bruff & Ernest Gellhorn, *Congressional Control of Administrative Regulation: A Study of Legislative Vetoes*, 90 Harv. L.Rev. 1369, 1417–18 (1977), "[a] primary purpose of the legislative veto [was] to increase the political accountability of administrative rulemaking" by ensuring that agency rulemaking is consistent with the intent of Congress. But "political accountability is likely to be attenuated in practice, [because much] settlement of policy occurred in behind-the-scenes negotiations between the staffs of the committees and the agencies." See also Jonathan R. Macey, *Separated Powers and Positive Political Theory: The Tug of War Over Administrative Agencies*, 80 Geo.L.J. 671, 694–97 (1992): "[T]he subject of a particular legislative veto is extremely narrow. It will commonly be a particular administrative act that has reached the attention of Congress, but rarely will be of such moment that it catches the attention of the popular press or the public. Consequently, the congressional veto inevitably will be the focus of interest group struggle, rather than public-spirited political debate."

4. *Alternatives to legislative veto.* After *Chadha,* what options are available to Congress to ensure that administrative rulemaking, in particular, conforms to statutory policy? See, e.g., *Chadha,* n. 19 and n. 9; Breyer, supra; Elliott H. Levitas & Stanley M. Brand, *Congressional Review of Executive and Agency Actions After Chadha: "The Son of Legislative Veto" Lives On,* 72 Geo.L.J. 801 (1984). Consider Tribe 3d ed., at 149–50: "[C]areful post-*Chadha* case studies of the actual operation of legislative veto provisions indicate [that] the elimination of this short-cut has invigorated the performance by Congress of its traditional role in democratic self-government: bereft of the unilateral power to make binary yea-or-nay decisions such [as in *Chadha*], Members of Congress have instead resorted to raising the public visibility of their policy views, to taking responsibility for the programs that they enact, and to sharpening use of existing mechanisms for ensuring that the regulatory process is responsive to their constituents."

CLINTON v. NEW YORK

524 U.S. 417, 118 S.Ct. 2091, 141 L.Ed.2d 393 (1998).

JUSTICE STEVENS delivered the opinion of the Court.

[The Line Item Veto Act gave the President the power to "cancel in whole" three types of provisions that have been enacted by Congress and signed into law:

"(1) any dollar amount of discretionary budget authority; (2) any item of new direct spending; or (3) any limited tax benefit." The President exercised his "line item veto" to nullify the two provisions involved in this case: a section of the Balanced Budget Act of 1997 that waived the federal government's statutory authority to seek recoupment of as much as $2.6 billion in taxes that New York had levied against Medicare providers, and a section of the Taxpayers Relief Act of 1997, which authorized favorable tax treatment of certain parties selling food processing facilities to farmers' cooperatives.]

It is undisputed that the New York case involves an "item of new direct spending" and that the [other] involves a "limited tax benefit" as those terms are defined in the Act. It is also undisputed that each of those provisions had been signed into law pursuant to Article I, § 7, of the Constitution before it was canceled.

The Act requires the President to adhere to precise procedures whenever he exercises his cancellation authority. [He] must [also] determine, with respect to each cancellation, that it will "(i) reduce the Federal budget deficit; (ii) not impair any essential Government functions; and (iii) not harm the national interest." Moreover, he must transmit a special message to Congress notifying it of each cancellation within five calendar days.

[If] a "disapproval bill" pertaining to a special message is enacted into law, the cancellations set forth in that message become "null and void." The Act sets forth a detailed expedited procedure for the consideration of a "disapproval bill," but no such bill was passed for [the] cancellations involved in these cases. A majority vote of both Houses is sufficient to enact a disapproval bill. The Act does not grant the President the authority to cancel a disapproval bill, but he does, of course, retain his constitutional authority to veto such a bill.

[There] are important differences between the President's "return" of a bill pursuant to Article I, § 7, and the exercise of the President's cancellation authority pursuant to the Line Item Veto Act. The constitutional return takes place before the bill becomes law; the statutory cancellation occurs after the bill becomes law. The constitutional return is of the entire bill; the statutory cancellation is of only a part. Although the Constitution expressly authorizes the President to play a role in the process of enacting statutes, it is silent on the subject of unilateral Presidential action that either repeals or amends parts of duly enacted statutes.

There are powerful reasons for construing constitutional silence on this profoundly important issue as equivalent to an express prohibition. The procedures governing the enactment of statutes set forth [in] Article I were the product of the great debates and compromises that produced the Constitution itself. [Our] first President understood the text of the Presentment Clause as requiring that he either "approve all the parts of a Bill, or reject it in toto." What has emerged in these cases from the President's exercise of his statutory cancellation powers, however, are truncated versions of two bills that passed both Houses of Congress. They are not the product of the "finely wrought" procedure that the Framers designed.

[R]elying primarily on *Field v. Clark* [fn. a, Sec. 1 supra], the Government contends that the cancellations were [not repeals or vetoes in the constitutional sense, but] merely exercises of discretionary authority granted to the President by the Balanced Budget Act and the Taxpayer Relief Act read in light of the previously enacted Line Item Veto Act. [In] *Field*, the Court upheld the constitutionality of the Tariff Act of 1890. That statute contained a "free list" of almost

300 specific articles that were exempted from import duties[, but] directed the President to suspend [the] exemption for sugar, molasses, coffee, tea, and hides "whenever, and so often" as he [determined] that any country producing and exporting those products imposed duties on the agricultural products of the United States that he deemed to be "reciprocally unequal and unreasonable."

[But there are] three critical differences between the power to suspend the exemption from import duties and the power to cancel portions of a duly enacted statute. First, the exercise of the suspension power was contingent upon a condition that did not exist when the Tariff Act was passed: the imposition of "reciprocally unequal and unreasonable" import duties by other countries. In contrast, the exercise of the cancellation power within five days after the enactment of the Balanced Budget and Tax Reform Acts necessarily was based on the same conditions that Congress evaluated when it passed those statutes. Second, under the Tariff Act, when the President determined that the contingency had arisen, he had a duty to suspend; in contrast, [the Line Item Veto Act] did not qualify his discretion to cancel or not to cancel. Finally, whenever the President suspended an exemption under the Tariff Act, he was executing the policy that Congress had embodied in the statute. In contrast, whenever the President cancels an item of new direct spending or a limited tax benefit he is rejecting the policy judgment made by Congress and relying on his own policy judgment.

The Government's reliance upon other tariff and import statutes [that] contain provisions similar to the one challenged in *Field* is unavailing for the same reasons. [In addition, the] cited statutes all relate to foreign trade, and this Court has recognized that in the foreign affairs arena, the President has "a degree of discretion and freedom from statutory restriction which would not be admissible were domestic affairs alone involved." *Curtiss-Wright* [Sec. 3 infra]. Although Congress presumably anticipated that the President might cancel some of the items in the Balanced Budget Act and in the Taxpayer Relief Act, Congress cannot alter the procedures set out in Article I, § 7, without amending the Constitution.[40]

Neither are we persuaded by the Government's contention that the President's authority to cancel new direct spending and tax benefit items is no greater than his traditional authority to decline to spend appropriated funds. [The] critical difference between this statute and all of its predecessors [is] that unlike any of them, this Act gives the President the unilateral power to change the text of duly enacted statutes.

[Because] we conclude that the Act's cancellation provisions violate Article I, § 7, [we] find it unnecessary to consider [whether] the Act [impermissibly delegates lawmaking authority to the President].

JUSTICE KENNEDY, concurring.

[To] say the political branches have a somewhat free hand to reallocate their own authority would seem to require acceptance of two premises: first, that the public good demands it, and second, that liberty is not at risk. The former premise is inadmissible. The Constitution's structure requires a stability which transcends

---

40. The Government argues that the Rules Enabling Act, 28 U.S.C. § 2072(b), permits this Court to "repeal" prior laws without violating Article I, § 7. Section 2072(b) provides that this Court may promulgate rules of procedure for the lower federal courts and that "all laws in conflict with such rules shall be of no further force or effect after such rules have taken effect." In enacting § 2072(b), however, Con-gress expressly provided that laws inconsistent with the procedural rules promulgated by this Court would automatically be repealed upon the enactment of new rules in order to create a uniform system of rules for Article III courts. As in the tariff statutes, Congress itself made the decision to repeal prior rules upon the occurrence of a particular event—here, the promulgation of procedural rules by this Court.

the convenience of the moment. The latter premise, too, is flawed. Liberty is always at stake when one or more of the branches seek to transgress the separation of powers. Separation of powers was designed to implement a fundamental insight: concentration of power in the hands of a single branch is a threat to liberty. [If] a citizen who is taxed has the measure of the tax or the decision to spend determined by the Executive alone, without adequate control by the citizen's Representatives in Congress, liberty is threatened.

JUSTICE BREYER, with whom JUSTICE O'CONNOR and JUSTICE SCALIA join as to Part III, dissenting.* * *

III.   [To] understand why one cannot say, *literally speaking*, that the President has repealed or amended any law, imagine how the provisions of law before us might have been, but were not, written. Imagine that the canceled New York health care tax provision at issue here [said]: "Section One. Taxes [that] were collected by the State of New York from a health care provider before June 1, 1997 and for which a waiver of provisions [requiring payment] have been sought [are] deemed to be permissible health care related taxes *[provided] however that the President may prevent the just-mentioned provision from having legal force or effect if he determines x, y and z.* (Assume x, y and z to be the same determinations required by the Line Item Veto Act)."

Whatever a person might say, or think, about the constitutionality of this imaginary law, [one] could not say that a President who "prevents" the deeming language from "having legal force or effect" has either repealed or amended this particular hypothetical statute. Rather, the President has exercised the power it explicitly delegates to him. He has executed the law, not repealed it.

It could make no significant difference to this linguistic point were the italicized proviso to appear, not as part of what I have called Section One, but, instead, at the bottom of the statute page, say referenced by an asterisk, with a statement that it applies to every spending provision in the act next to which a similar asterisk appears. And that being so, it could make no difference if that proviso appeared, instead, in a different, earlier-enacted law, along with legal language that makes it applicable to every future spending provision picked out according to a specified formula.

But, of course, this last-mentioned possibility is this very case. [Because] one cannot say that the President's exercise of the power the Act grants is, literally speaking, a "repeal" or "amendment," the fact that the Act's procedures differ from the Constitution's exclusive procedures for enacting (or repealing) legislation is beside the point. The Act itself was enacted in accordance with these procedures, and its failure to require the President to satisfy those procedures does not make the Act unconstitutional.

IV.   Because I disagree with the Court's holding of literal violation, I must consider whether the Act nonetheless violates Separation of Powers principles. [O]ne cannot say that the Act "encroaches" upon Congress' power, when Congress retained the power to insert, by simple majority, into any future appropriations bill, into any section of any such bill, or into any phrase of any section, a provision that says the Act will not apply.* * *

Nor can one say the Act's grant of power "aggrandizes" the Presidential office. The grant is limited to the context of the budget. It is limited to the power to spend, or not to spend, particular appropriated items, and the power to permit, or not to permit, specific limited exemptions from generally applicable tax law from taking effect.* * *

The "nondelegation" doctrine [raises] a more serious constitutional obstacle here. [The] Constitution permits only those delegations where Congress "shall lay down by legislative act an intelligible principle to which the person or body authorized to [act] is directed to conform." [The standards in the Act] are broad. But this Court has upheld standards that are equally broad, or broader. See, e.g., *National Broadcasting Co. v. United States*, [fn. c, Sec. 2 supra].

[L]ike statutes delegating power to award broadcast television licenses, [the] Act is aimed at a discrete problem: namely, a particular set of expenditures within the federal budget. [Second], like the award of television licenses, the particular problem involved—determining whether or not a particular amount of money should be spent or whether a particular dispensation from tax law should be granted a few individuals—does not readily lend itself to a significantly more specific standard. [Third], insofar as monetary expenditure (but not "tax expenditure") is at issue, the President acts in an area where [Congress] has frequently delegated the President the authority to spend, or not to spend, particular sums of money.

[The] "limited tax benefit" question [is] more difficult. [But this] Court has upheld tax statutes [involving tariffs] that delegate to the President the power to change taxes under very broad standards. [These] statutory delegations [have often involved] a duty on imports, which is a tax [that] in the last century was as important then as the income tax is now, for it provided most of the Federal Government's revenues.

[I] recognize that the Act before us is novel. [But the] Constitution, in my view, authorizes Congress and the President to try novel methods in this way.

JUSTICE SCALIA, with whom JUSTICE O'CONNOR joins, and with whom JUSTICE BREYER joins as to Part III, concurring in part and dissenting in part. * * *

III.   [Article I, § 7] of the Constitution obviously prevents the President from canceling a law that Congress has not authorized him to cancel. [But] that is not this case. [Article I, § 7] no more categorically prohibits the Executive reduction of congressional dispositions in the course of implementing statutes that authorize such reduction, than it categorically prohibits the Executive augmentation of congressional dispositions in the course of implementing statutes that authorize such augmentation—generally known as substantive rulemaking. * * *[a]

I turn, then, [to] whether Congress's authorizing the President to cancel an item of spending [violates the non-delegation doctrine by giving] him a power that our history and traditions show must reside exclusively in the Legislative Branch. [Insofar] as the degree of political, "law-making" power conferred upon the Executive is concerned, there is not a dime's worth of difference between Congress's authorizing the President to cancel a spending item, and Congress's authorizing money to be spent on a particular item at the President's discretion. And the latter has been done since the Founding of the Nation. From 1789–1791, the First Congress made lump-sum appropriations for the entire Government— "sums not exceeding" specified amounts for broad purposes. From a very early date Congress also made permissive individual appropriations, leaving the decision whether to spend the money to the President's unfettered discretion. * * *[b]

---

a. For detailed description of "numerous statutes authorizing cancellation or modification of statutory provisions of law" and of congressional sanctioning of "regulatory modification of statutes," see Saikrishna B. Prakash, *Deviant Executive Lawmaking*, 67 Geo. Wash.L.Rev. 1, 26–31 (1998).

b. Which of the opinions in *Clinton* was "formalist" or "functionalist"? See Tribe 3d ed., at 748–49.

Notes and Questions

1. *Clinton's reasoning.* "Because the Constitution does not permit the President to veto particular provisions in a bill," does it necessarily follow "that Congress may not convey additional authority"? Prakash, fn. a in *Clinton*, at 40. Consider Elizabeth Garrett, *Accountability and Restraint: The Federal Budget Process and the Line Item Veto Act*, 20 Cardozo L.Rev. 871, 883 (1999): "[In the Line Item Veto Act], Congress seeks to give away power; its instincts for self-preservation should provide some safeguard against decisions resulting in excessive concentrations of governmental power in other branches."

2. *Political accountability.* Consider Tribe 3d ed., at 750: "[T]he Act attempted to hand off to the President the tough decisions about federal spending that Congress was unwilling or unable to make on its own—or that Congress did not want to take the political heat for making. It is hard to imagine a statute much more subversive [of] democratic accountability itself." Do the criteria for the exercise of FCC regulatory authority in *National Broadcasting* ("public interest, convenience, or necessity," fn. c, Part I, supra) assure congressional accountability more so than the criteria for the exercise of presidential cancellation authority in *Clinton*? For the view that the "nondelegation" issue is more difficult than the *Clinton* dissenters acknowledge, see Garrett, supra.

3. *Alternatives to line item veto.* Consider Garrett, supra, at 874, 913: "Congress could adopt a separate enrollment procedure to give the President the same kind of power. Using this process, Congress would disaggregate the provisions usually contained in omnibus spending and revenue bills and pass each provision as a separately enrolled bill. [In] this age of computers, the enrolling clerks have, or could develop, the capacity to follow the directions of separate enrollment." For a more detailed alternative procedure, see Prakash, supra, at 38.

III. APPOINTMENT AND REMOVAL OF OFFICERS

Art. II, Sec. 2, cl.2 states the President's power to "appoint * * * Officers of the United States," but nowhere does the Constitution address the power to remove officers, an issue disputed in the First Congress concerning President Washington's authority to unilaterally remove the Secretary of the new Department of Foreign Affairs. In a sweeping opinion that went well beyond the issues raised, MYERS v. UNITED STATES, 272 U.S. 52, 47 S.Ct. 21, 71 L.Ed. 160 (1926), ruled that the President's executive power included the power to remove executive officers of the United States, even when their appointment was subject to the advice and consent of the Senate.[a] TAFT, C.J., reasoned that, as the President's "selection of administrative officers is essential to the execution of the laws by him, so must be his power of removing those for whom he can not continue to be responsible." This point soon became increasingly important as to the matter of which branch of government would have "control" over the greatly enlarged administrative state.

---

a. *Myers* held unconstitutional a statute establishing a four year term for first class postmasters, subject to removal for cause "by the President [with] the advice and consent of the Senate."

Nine years later, HUMPHREY'S EXECUTOR v. UNITED STATES, 295 U.S. 602, 55 S.Ct. 869, 79 L.Ed. 1611 (1935), per SUTHERLAND, J., held[b] that Congress could limit the grounds for removal of a Commissioner of the Federal Trade Commission: "[*Myers*] cannot be accepted as controlling our decision here. A postmaster is an executive officer restricted to the performance of executive functions. He is charged with no duty at all related to either the legislative or judicial power. [*Myers*] finds support in the theory that such an officer is merely one of the units in the executive department and, hence, inherently subject to the exclusive and illimitable power of removal by the Chief Executive, whose subordinate and aid he is. [The] necessary reach of the decision goes far enough to include all purely executive officers. It goes no [further].

"The authority of Congress, in creating quasi-legislative or quasi-judicial agencies, to require them to act in discharge of their duties independently of executive control, cannot well be doubted; and that authority includes, as an appropriate incident, power to fix the period during which they shall continue in office, and to forbid their removal except for cause in the meantime. For it is quite evident that one who holds his office only during the pleasure of another, cannot be depended upon to maintain an attitude of independence against the latter's will.

"The fundamental necessity of maintaining each of the three general departments of government entirely free from the control or coercive influence, direct or indirect, of either of the others, has often been stressed and is hardly open to serious question.

"[The] power of removal here claimed for the President falls within this principle, since its coercive influence threatens the independence of a commission, which is not only wholly disconnected from the executive department, but [which] was created by Congress [as] an agency of the legislative and judicial departments."

Notes and Questions

1. *A headless fourth branch?* Does the "independence" of the FTC imply that it falls within none of the three branches of government created by the Constitution? Within both the legislative and judicial branches? How may either of these arrangements be justified under the Constitution?[c]

2. *Delegation of judicial power to non-Art. III tribunals.* Where does the Constitution allow Congress to confer judicial powers on bodies other than Art. III courts? Although reliance on non-Art. III tribunals traces to the early years of the republic, the justification for the practice has always been uncertain, and the permissible bounds of adjudication by so-called "legislative courts" and "administrative agencies" have occasioned recurrent litigation in recent years. See generally Erwin Chemerinsky, *Federal Jurisdiction* 207–45 (2d ed.1994); Richard H. Fallon, Jr., *Of Legislative Courts, Administrative Agencies, and Article III*, 101 Harv.L.Rev. 915 (1988). On the relationship between separation-of-powers issues

---

b. McReynolds, J., concurred in the result, noting that his views on the President's removal power were stated in his separate opinion in *Myers*.

c. For a range of views on the status of the so-called "independent" agencies, and whether they should generally be conceptualized as located within the executive branch, see Lawrence Lessig & Cass R. Sunstein, *The President*

and the Administration, 94 Colum.L.Rev. 1, 113–18 (1994); Cass R. Sunstein, *Constitutionalism After the New Deal*, 101 Harv.L.Rev. 421, 452–63, 485–91 (1987); Symposium, *The Independence of Independent Agencies*, 1988 Duke L. J. 215–99; Peter L. Strauss, *The Place of Agencies in Government: Separation of Powers and the Fourth Branch*, 84 Colum.L.Rev. 573 (1984).

involving the judiciary and those involving the executive, see Steven G. Calabresi & Kevin H. Rhodes, *The Structural Constitution: Unitary Executive, Plural Judiciary*, 105 Harv.L.Rev. 1153 (1992).

3. *Executive agencies vs. independent commissions.* Is it clear that Congress *could* have located the FTC within the executive branch? The FTC performs the characteristically executive functions of conducting investigations and initiating prosecutions. Moreover, Congress frequently does delegate both "quasi-legislative" (rulemaking) and "quasi-judicial" functions to executive officials. See, e.g., Strauss, supra at 584 (noting that "regulatory and policymaking responsibilities are scattered among independent and executive-branch agencies in ways that belie explanation in terms of the work agencies do" and that the characterization of agencies as "executive" or "independent" is typically a function of relatively ad hoc political considerations). Is it simply a matter of congressional choice whether an agency with rulemaking and adjudicatory functions should be designated as independent or assigned to the executive branch?

4. *The "unitary" executive? Humphrey's Executor* appears to have been animated largely by the view that the President must have untrammeled authority over officials performing properly "executive" functions in the executive branch. See Strauss, supra at 611. Is the validity of this proposition so clear? Might it be "necessary and proper" for Congress, under Art. I, to establish limits on the removal of at least some executive officials? Is recognizing such a congressional power *less* consistent with the Constitution's structure than the proposition that the Constitution allows the creation of agencies lying wholly outside the constitutionally established departments of government?

Whether the Constitution requires a "unitary executive," i.e., a direct "chain of command" running from the President to all federal officials performing functions not clearly located within the legislative or judicial branch—or whether, on the contrary, Congress has power under the necessary and proper clause to structure the government including the executive branch—is vigorously debated. Among the controverted questions: (i) does the "vesting" clause of Art. II dictate that all executive power necessarily resides *exclusively* in the President;[d] (ii) are the powers specifically vested in the President by Art. II the *only* executive powers that must be assigned to the President (if Congress creates offices or enacts laws that call for the exercise of further executive powers);[e] (iii) do early practice and the framers' intent distinguish between offices and functions that must, and those that need not, be subject to direct presidential control;[f] and (iv) what is the relevance, if any, of later historical practice and functional and policy concerns?[g]

---

d. Compare Calabresi & Rhodes, supra (upholding unitary executive thesis) with A. Michael Froomkin, *The Imperial Presidency's New Vestments*, 88 Nw.U.L.Rev. 1346 (1994)(disputing claims of Calabresi & Rhodes and asserting that the Constitution contemplates broad congressional power to structure the executive branch).

e. Compare Froomkin, supra (so maintaining) with Steven G. Calabresi, *The Vesting Clauses as Power Grants*, 88 Nw.U.L.Rev. 1377 (1994)(disagreeing).

f. Compare Lessig & Sunstein, supra (identifying such a division between "executive"

and "administrative" departments and functions and claiming it to be a "plain myth" that "the framers constitutionalized anything like" a unitary presidency) with Steven G. Calabresi & Saikrishna B. Prakash, *The President's Power To Execute the Laws*, 104 Yale L.J 541 (1994)(attempting to refute claims made by Lessig & Sunstein).

g. See, e.g., Steven G. Calabresi, *Some Normative Arguments for the Unitary Executive*, 48 Ark.L.Rev. 23 (1995); Greene, fn. d, Sec. 1 supra (arguing that current doctrine must allow compensating adjustments to check and balance earlier departures from original intent

BUCKLEY v. VALEO, 424 U.S. 1, 96 S.Ct. 612, 46 L.Ed.2d 659 (1976), per curiam, invalidated the Federal Election Campaign Act's provision for the Federal Election Commission because it assigned the appointment of two commissioners to the President pro tem of the Senate and two to the Speaker of the House of Representatives, leaving two for Presidential appointment: "[A]ny appointee exercising significant authority pursuant to the laws of the United States is an 'Officer of the United States,' and must, therefore, be appointed in the manner prescribed by [the Appointments Clause]. While the second part of the Clause authorizes Congress to vest the appointment of the officers described in that part in 'the Courts of Law, or in the Heads of Departments,' neither the Speaker of the House nor the President pro tempore of the Senate comes within this language.

"[The] position that because Congress has been given explicit and plenary authority to regulate a field of activity, it must therefore have the power to appoint those who are to administer the regulatory statute is both novel and contrary to the language of the Appointments Clause [which] controls the appointment of the members of a typical administrative agency even though its functions, as this Court recognized in *Humphrey's Executor*, may be 'predominantly quasi-judicial and quasi-legislative' rather than executive. The Court in that case carefully emphasized that although the members of such agencies were to be independent of the Executive in their day-to-day operations, the Executive was not excluded from selecting them. * * *

"All aspects of the Act are brought within the Commission's broad administrative powers: rulemaking, advisory opinions, and determinations of eligibility for funds and even for federal elective office itself. These functions [are] of kinds usually performed by independent regulatory agencies or by some department in the Executive Branch under the direction of an Act of Congress. [Yet] each of these functions also represents the performance of a significant governmental duty exercised pursuant to a public law. While the President may not insist that such functions be delegated to an appointee of his removable at will, *Humphrey's Executor,* none of them operates merely in aid of congressional authority to legislate or is sufficiently removed from the administration and enforcement of public law to allow it to be performed by the present Commission."

Notes and Questions

1. *Consistency.* Is the Court's method of analysis in *Buckley* consistent with *Humphrey's Executor?* Is the result?

2. *Reach of the decision.* Can Congress, in creating an independent agency, provide that no more than a certain number of its members shall be members of any one political party? (Congress in fact had done so in a section of the Federal Election Campaign Act that was not challenged in *Buckley.*) How "tightly" may Congress define the criteria for appointment?

---

that unduly aggrandized the executive branch); Martin H. Redish & Elizabeth J. Cisar, *"If Angels Were to Govern": The Need for Pragmatic Formalism in Separation of Powers Theory,* 41 Duke L.J. 449 (1991)(maintaining that "functional" considerations support endorsement of a "formalist" conception of the separa-tion of powers, including presidential power); Strauss, supra (defending a "functional" approach under which a unitary presidency is not required, but the President must retain opportunities to influence policy and policymaking officials).

BOWSHER v. SYNAR, 478 U.S. 714, 106 S.Ct. 3181, 92 L.Ed.2d 583 (1986): The Balanced Budget and Emergency Deficit Act of 1985 set maximum yearly permissible deficits with the goal of reducing the federal deficit to zero in fiscal year 1991. If needed to keep the deficit within the maximum, the Act required across-the-board cuts, half in defense programs and half elsewhere. Sec. 251 set out the procedure: (1) For each year the directors of OMB (Office of Management and Budget) and of CBO (Congressional Budget Office) were each to estimate the deficit and to calculate, program by program, the cuts required to meet the goal; they were to report their estimates and calculations to the Comptroller General. (2) After reviewing the Directors' figures, the Comptroller was to report to the President on the estimates and the required budget reductions. (3) The President was then to issue an order placing in effect the reductions specified by the Comptroller, unless within a specified period congress met the deficit goal in other ways. The Court, per BURGER, C.J., held this procedure unconstitutional: "Congress cannot reserve for itself the power of removal of an officer charged with the execution of the laws except by impeachment. * * * 'Once an officer is appointed, it is only the authority that can remove him, and not the authority that appointed him, that he must fear and, in the performance of his functions, obey.' The structure of the Constitution does not permit Congress to execute the laws; it follows that Congress cannot grant to an officer under its control what it does not possess. [To] permit an officer controlled by Congress to execute the laws would be, in essence, to permit a congressional veto. Congress could simply remove, or threaten to remove, an officer for executing the laws in any fashion found to be unsatisfactory to Congress. [*Chadha.*] With these principles in mind, we turn to consideration of whether the Comptroller General is controlled by Congress.

"[Although] the Comptroller General is nominated by the President from a list of three individuals recommended by the Speaker of the House of Representatives and the President pro tempore of the Senate, and confirmed by the Senate,[a] he is removable only at the initiative of Congress. He may be removed not only by impeachment but also by joint resolution of Congress 'at any [time'].[7] [The] Framers recognized that, in the long term, structural protections against abuse of power were critical to preserving liberty. In constitutional terms, the removal powers over the Comptroller General's office dictate that he will be subservient to Congress.

"[The] dissent is simply in error to suggest that the political realities reveal that the Comptroller General is free from influence by Congress. The Comptroller General heads the General Accounting Office, 'an instrumentality of the United States Government independent of the executive departments,' which was created by Congress [in] 1921. Congress created the office because it believed that it 'needed an officer, responsible to it alone, to check upon the application of public funds in accordance with appropriations.' Harvey C. Mansfield, *The Comptroller General* 65 (1939).

"It is clear that Congress has consistently viewed the Comptroller General as an officer of the Legislative Branch. [Over] the years, the Comptrollers General have also viewed themselves as part of the Legislative Branch. [The] remaining question is whether the Comptroller General has been assigned [executive powers under the Act].

a. The Comptroller General was limited to a single 15–year term.

7. Although the President could veto such a joint resolution, the veto could be overridden by a two-thirds vote of both Houses of Congress. Thus, the Comptroller General could be removed in the face of Presidential opposition. [We] therefore read the removal provision as authorizing removal by Congress alone.

"The primary responsibility of the Comptroller General under the instant Act is the preparation of a 'report.' This report must contain detailed estimates of projected federal revenues and expenditures, [and must] specify the reductions, if any, necessary to reduce the deficit to the target. [Under] § 251, the Comptroller General must exercise judgment concerning facts that affect the application of the Act. He must also interpret the provisions of the Act to determine precisely what budgetary calculations are required. Decisions of that kind are typically made by officers charged with executing a statute.

"The executive nature of the Comptroller General's functions under the Act is revealed in § 252(a)(3) which gives the Comptroller General the ultimate authority to determine the budget cuts to be made. Indeed, the Comptroller General commands the President himself to carry out, without the slightest variation (with exceptions not relevant to the constitutional issues presented), the directive of the Comptroller General as to the budget reductions. * * * 'Congress of course initially determined the content of the Balanced Budget and Emergency Deficit Control Act; and undoubtedly the content of the Act determines the nature of the executive duty.' However, as *Chadha* makes clear, once Congress makes its choice in enacting legislation, its participation ends. Congress can thereafter control the execution of its enactment only indirectly—by passing new legislation."

In deciding the remedy, the Court invalidated the procedure that gave "executive" authority to the Comptroller General, and called for resort to the Act's "fallback" provisions[b] that were to take effect "[i]n the event [any] of the reporting procedures described in section 251 are invalidated."[c]

WHITE, J., dissented: "[The] Court's decision rests on a feature of the legislative scheme that is of minimal practical significance and that presents no substantial threat to the basic scheme of separation of powers. In attaching dispositive significance to what should be regarded as a triviality, the Court neglects what has in the past been recognized as a fundamental principle governing consideration of disputes over separation of powers: 'The actual art of governing under our Constitution does not and cannot conform to judicial definitions of the power of any of its branches based on isolated clauses or even single Articles torn from context. While the Constitution diffuses power the better to secure liberty, it also contemplates that practice will integrate the dispersed powers into a workable government.' *Youngstown* (Jackson, J., concurring). * * *

"Determining the level of spending by the Federal Government is [a] peculiarly legislative function, and one expressly committed to Congress by Art. I, § 9. [Delegating] the execution of this legislation—that is, the power to apply the Act's criteria and make the required calculations—to an officer independent of the President's will does not deprive the President of any power that he would otherwise have or that is essential to the performance of the duties of his office.

b. Under the fallback provision, Congress makes the ultimate budget decision by joint resolution, which is subject to Presidential veto unless overridden by two-thirds votes in both houses of Congress.

c. Stevens, J., joined by Marshall, J., concurred in the judgment but dissented from "labeling the function assigned to the Comptroller General as 'executive powers.'

"I am convinced that the Comptroller General must be characterized as an agent of Congress because of his longstanding statutory responsibilities; that the powers assigned to him under the [Act] require him to make policy that will bind the Nation; and that, when Congress, or a component or an agent of Congress, seeks to make policy that will bind the Nation, it must follow the procedures mandated by Article I of the Constitution—through passage by both Houses and presentment to the President."

Rather, the result of such a delegation, from the standpoint of the President, is no different from the result of more traditional forms of appropriation: under either system, the level of funds available to the Executive Branch to carry out its duties is not within the President's discretionary control.

" * * * Congress may remove the Comptroller only through a joint resolution, which by definition must be passed by both Houses and signed by the President. [In] other words, a removal of the Comptroller under the statute *satisfies the requirements of bicameralism and presentment laid down in Chadha.* * * *

"More importantly, [the] requirement of Presidential approval obviates the possibility that the Comptroller will perceive himself as so completely at the mercy of Congress that he will function as its tool. If the Comptroller's conduct in office is not so unsatisfactory to the President as to convince the latter that removal is required under the statutory standard, Congress will have no independent power to coerce the Comptroller unless it can muster a two-thirds majority in both Houses—a feat of bipartisanship more difficult than that required to impeach and convict. The incremental in terrorem effect of the possibility of congressional removal in the face of a Presidential veto is therefore exceedingly unlikely to have any discernible impact on the extent of congressional influence over the Comptroller.

"[Those] who have studied the office agree that the procedural and substantive limits on the power of Congress and the President to remove the Comptroller make dislodging him against his will practically impossible. [The] majority's contrary conclusion rests on the rigid dogma that, outside of the impeachment process, any 'direct congressional role in the removal of officers charged with the execution of the laws [is] inconsistent with separation of powers.' Reliance on such an unyielding principle to strike down a statute posing no real danger of aggrandizement of congressional power is extremely misguided and insensitive to our constitutional role."[d]

Notes and Questions

1. *The Comptroller's function.* (a) Was the comptroller's function necessarily "executive"? Could Congress have provided for the required calculations to be made by an independent "Balanced Budget Commission" appointed by the President, with Senate confirmation, and removable by the President only for inefficiency, neglect of duty, or malfeasance?

(b) *Bowsher and Clinton.* Is *Bowsher's* holding that the Comptroller's "ultimate authority to determine the budget cuts to be made" is an exercise of *executive* power inconsistent with *Clinton's* conclusion that the President's "cancellation authority pursuant to the Line Item Veto Act" was an exercise of *legislative* power to "effect the repeal of laws"? See H. Jefferson Powell & Jed Rubenfeld, *Laying It on the Line: A Dialogue on Line Item Vetoes and Separation of Powers,* 47 Duke L.J. 1171, 1190–91, 1198 (1998); Garrett, note 1 after *Clinton,* at 886.

2. *Formalism and functionalism.* Did *Bowsher* adopt a "formal" style of separation-of-powers analysis requiring a rigid assignment of "executive," "legis-

d. Blackmun, J., separately dissenting, agreed with White, J., that it was "unrealistic" to claim that the removal power makes the Comptroller General "subservient to Congress." But to the extent removal power was found incompatible with the constitutional separation of powers, he would "cure" it by refusing to allow congressional removal "—if it ever is attempted—and not by striking down the central provisions of the Deficit Control Act."

lative," and "judicial" functions to the corresponding branch of government, with no cross-branch interference. See, e.g., Peter L. Strauss, *Formal and Functional Approaches to Separation-of-Powers Questions—A Foolish Inconsistency?*, 72 Corn. L.Rev. 488 (1987). Did *Bowsher* threaten the underlying premises of *Humphrey's Executor*? The notion, reflected in *Yakus* and a host of other decisions, that Congress can assign rulemaking and adjudicative functions to agencies in the executive branch?

MORRISON v. OLSON

487 U.S. 654, 108 S.Ct. 2597, 101 L.Ed.2d 569 (1988).

CHIEF JUSTICE REHNQUIST delivered the opinion of the Court.

[The Ethics in Government Act of 1978 called for appointment of an "independent counsel" to investigate, and, if appropriate, to prosecute certain high-ranking government officials[a] for violating any federal criminal law.[b] Upon receipt of information that the Attorney General considers "sufficient grounds," the Attorney General conducts a preliminary investigation and then reports to the special division of the Court of Appeals for the District of Columbia Circuit whether there are "reasonable grounds to believe that further investigation or prosecution is warranted." If so, the Attorney General must request the Special Division to appoint, and provide it with sufficient information to enable it to appoint, "an appropriate independent counsel and define that independent counsel's prosecutorial jurisdiction."[c] The act grants the independent counsel the "full power and independent authority" of the Department of Justice to investigate and prosecute. The department must suspend all its investigations and proceedings regarding any matter referred to independent counsel.[d] Pursuant to these procedures, the Special Division appointed Morrison to investigate a charge of perjury before the House Judiciary Committee by Olson, an Assistant Attorney General.]

We now turn to consider whether the Act is invalid under the constitutional principle of separation of powers. [The first issue] is whether the provision of the Act restricting the Attorney General's power to remove the independent counsel to only those instances in which he can show "good cause," taken by itself, impermissibly interferes with the President's exercise of his constitutionally appointed functions. * * *

Unlike both *Bowsher* and *Myers,* this case does not involve an attempt by Congress itself to gain a role in the removal of executive officials other than its established powers of impeachment and conviction. The Act instead puts the removal power squarely in the hands of the Executive Branch. [There] is no

---

a. These include the President, Vice–President, cabinet officers, high ranking officers in the Executive Office of the President and the Justice Department, and the like.

b. Except Class B or C misdemeanors.

c. The Act created the Special Division, consisting of three Circuit Court Judges, appointed by the Chief Justice of the United States for two-year terms. The Court upheld the Special Division's authority to appoint the independent counsel and specify her jurisdiction. It invoked the Appointments Clause reference to courts of law appointing "inferior officers," the congruity of "a court having the power to appoint prosecutorial officers" with a "court's normal functions," and the Act's ban on Special Division judges' participation in other matters relating to the independent counsel.

d. After having been allowed to lapse during the Bush Administration, the statute involved in *Morrison* was substantially re-enacted, with amendments, in the Independent Counsel Reauthorization Act of 1994. Among its more significant changes, the new statute applied to members of Congress. Its most famous use was in the Whitewater/Lewinsky investigation under Kenneth W. Starr, lasting more than six years, costing in excess of $55 million and leading to the impeachment of President Clinton. This new law expired in 1999 and was not reauthorized.

requirement of congressional approval of the Attorney General's removal decision, though the decision is subject to judicial review. * * *

Appellees contend that *Humphrey's Executor* and *Wiener [v. United States,* 357 U.S. 349, 78 S.Ct. 1275, 2 L.Ed.2d 1377 (1958),] are distinguishable from this case because they did not involve officials who performed a "core executive function." They argue [that] when a "purely executive" official is involved, the governing precedent is *Myers,* not *Humphrey's Executor.* And, under *Myers,* the President must have absolute discretion to discharge "purely" executive officials at will.

We undoubtedly did rely on the terms "quasi-legislative" and "quasi-judicial" to distinguish the officials involved in *Humphrey's Executor* and *Wiener* from those in *Myers,* but our present considered view is that the determination of whether the Constitution allows Congress to impose a "good cause"-type restriction on the President's power to remove an official cannot be made to turn on whether or not that official is classified as "purely executive." The analysis contained in our removal cases is designed not to define rigid categories of those officials who may or may not be removed at will by the President, but to ensure that Congress does not interfere with the President's exercise of the "executive power" and his constitutionally appointed duty to "take care that the laws be faithfully executed" under Article II. *Myers* was undoubtedly correct in its holding, and in its broader suggestion that there are some "purely executive" officials who must be removable by the President at will if he is to be able to accomplish his constitutional role.[29] [At] the other end of the spectrum from *Myers,* the characterization of the agencies in *Humphrey's Executor* and *Wiener* as "quasi-legislative" or "quasi-judicial" in large part reflected our judgment that it was not essential to the President's proper execution of his Article II powers that these agencies be headed up by individuals who were removable at will.[30] [But] the real question is whether the removal restrictions are of such a nature that they impede the President's ability to perform his constitutional duty, and the functions of the officials in question must be analyzed in that light.

[There] is no real dispute that the functions performed by the independent counsel are "executive" in the sense that they are law enforcement functions that typically have been undertaken by officials within the Executive Branch.[e] As we noted above, however, the independent counsel is an inferior officer under the Appointments Clause, with limited jurisdiction and tenure and lacking policymaking or significant administrative authority. Although the counsel exercises no

29. The dissent says that the language of Article II vesting the executive power of the United States in the President requires that every officer of the United States exercising any part of that power must serve at the pleasure of the President and be removable by him at will. This rigid demarcation—a demarcation incapable of being altered by law in the slightest degree, and applicable to tens of thousands of holders of offices neither known nor foreseen by the Framers—depends upon an extrapolation from general constitutional language which we think is more than the text will bear. * * *

30. The terms also may be used to describe the circumstances in which Congress might be more inclined to find that a degree of independence from the Executive, such as that afforded by a "good cause" removal standard, is necessary to the proper functioning of the agency or official. It is not difficult to imagine situations in which Congress might desire that an official performing "quasi-judicial" functions, for example, would be free of executive or political control.

e. Compare Tribe 3d ed., at 696–97: "[C]riminal prosecution historically was *not* a core executive function. [In] eighteenth-century England, for example, private individuals could instigate criminal prosecutions, and 'although the Attorney General brought some cases and could defeat a private prosecution by filing a writ of nolle prosequi, the system was essentially private.' In most of the colonies, a dual system of public and private prosecution was the norm."

small amount of discretion and judgment in deciding how to carry out his or her duties under the Act, we simply do not see how the President's need to control the exercise of that discretion is so central to the functioning of the Executive Branch as to require as a matter of constitutional law that the counsel be terminable at will by the President.

[This] is not a case in which the power to remove an executive official has been completely stripped from the President. [Although] we need not decide in this case exactly what is encompassed within the term "good cause" under the Act, the legislative history of the removal provision also makes clear that the Attorney General may remove an independent counsel for "misconduct." Here, as with the provision of the Act conferring the appointment authority of the independent counsel on the special court, the congressional determination to limit the removal power of the Attorney General was essential, in the view of Congress, to establish the necessary independence of the office. We do not think that this limitation as it presently stands sufficiently deprives the President of control over the independent counsel to interfere impermissibly with his constitutional obligation to ensure the faithful execution of the laws.

The final question to be addressed is whether the Act, taken as a whole, violates the principle of separation of powers. [We] observe first that this case does not involve an attempt by Congress to increase its own powers at the expense of the Executive Branch. [W]ith the exception of the power of impeachment—which applies to all officers of the United States—Congress retained for itself no powers of control or supervision over an independent counsel. The Act does empower certain Members of Congress to request the Attorney General to apply for the appointment of an independent counsel, but the Attorney General has no duty to comply with the request, although he must respond within a certain time limit.
* * *

Similarly, we do not think that the Act works any *judicial* usurpation of properly executive functions. [T]he Special Division has no power to appoint an independent counsel sua sponte; it may only do so upon the specific request of the Attorney General, and the courts are specifically prevented from reviewing the Attorney General's decision not to seek appointment. In addition, once the court has appointed a counsel and defined his or her jurisdiction, it has no power to supervise or control the activities of the counsel. [The] Act does give a federal court the power to review the Attorney General's decision to remove an independent counsel, but in our view this is a function that is well within the traditional power of the Judiciary.

Finally, we do not think that the Act "impermissibly undermine[s]" the powers of the Executive Branch. [It] is undeniable that the Act reduces the amount of control or supervision that the Attorney General and, through him, the President exercises over the investigation and prosecution of a certain class of alleged criminal activity. The Attorney General is not allowed to appoint the individual of his choice; he does not determine the counsel's jurisdiction; and his power to remove a counsel is limited. Nonetheless, the Act does give the Attorney General several means of supervising or controlling the prosecutorial powers that may be wielded by an independent counsel. Most importantly, the Attorney General retains the power to remove the counsel for "good cause," [and] the Attorney General's decision not to request appointment if he finds "no reasonable grounds to believe that further investigation is warranted" is committed to his unreviewable discretion. The Act thus gives the Executive a degree of control over the power to initiate an investigation by the independent counsel. In addition, the jurisdiction of the independent counsel is defined with reference to the facts submitted by the Attorney General, and once a counsel is appointed, the Act requires that the counsel abide by Justice Department policy unless it is not "possible" to do so. Notwithstanding the fact that the counsel is to some degree "independent" and free from executive supervision to a greater extent than other federal prosecutors, in our view these features of the Act give the Executive Branch sufficient control over the independent counsel to ensure that the President is able to perform his constitutionally assigned duties.[f]

JUSTICE SCALIA, dissenting.

[It] effects a revolution in our constitutional jurisprudence for the Court, once it has determined that (1) purely executive functions are at issue here, and (2) those functions have been given to a person whose actions are not fully within the supervision and control of the President, nonetheless to proceed further to sit in judgment of whether "the President's need to control the exercise of [the independent counsel's] discretion is *so central* to the functioning of the Executive Branch" as to require complete control (emphasis added), whether the conferral of his powers upon someone else "*sufficiently* deprives the President of control over the independent counsel to interfere impermissibly with [his] constitutional obligation to ensure the faithful execution of the laws" (emphasis added), and whether "the Act give[s] the Executive Branch *sufficient* control over the independent counsel to ensure that the President is able to perform his constitutionally assigned duties" (emphasis added). It is not for us to determine [how] much of the purely executive powers of government must be within the full control of the President. The Constitution prescribes that they *all* are.

[Before] this statute was passed, the President, in taking action disagreeable to the Congress, or an executive officer giving advice to the President or testifying before Congress concerning one of those many matters on which the two branches are from time to time at odds, could be assured that his acts and motives would be adjudged—insofar as the decision whether to conduct a criminal investigation and to prosecute is concerned—in the Executive Branch, that is, in a forum attuned to the interests and the policies of the Presidency. That was one of the natural advantages the Constitution gave to the Presidency, just as it gave Members of Congress (and their staffs) the advantage of not being prosecutable for anything said or done in their legislative capacities. [It] deeply wounds the President, by substantially reducing the President's ability to protect himself and his staff. That is the whole object of the law, of course, and I cannot imagine why the Court believes it does not succeed.

[Worse] than what [the Court] has done, however, is the manner in which it has done it. A government of laws means a government of rules. Today's decision on the basic issue of fragmentation of executive power is ungoverned by rule, and hence ungoverned by law. It extends into the very heart of our most significant constitutional function the "totality of the circumstances" mode of analysis that this Court has in recent years become fond of. Taking all things into account, we conclude that the power taken away from the President here is not really *too* much. The next time executive power is assigned to someone other than the President we may conclude, taking all things into account, that it *is* too much.

f. For the view that "the 'good cause' provision, while surely expected to give the independent counsel *some* insulation from outside executive control, nonetheless might be construed to avoid a serious constitutional question" by "authoriz[ing] the independent counsel's removal for disobeying the President's legal directives, at least on matters of reasonably contestable legal judgment," see John F. Manning, *The Independent Counsel Statute: Reading "Good Cause" in Light of Article II,* 83 Minn.L.Rev. 1285 (1999).

That opinion, like this one, will not be confined by any rule. We will describe, as we have today (though I hope more accurately) the effects of the provision in question, and will authoritatively announce: "The President's need to control the exercise of the [subject officer's] discretion *is* so central to the functioning of the Executive Branch as to require complete control." This is not analysis; it is ad hoc judgment. And it fails to explain why it is not true that—as the text of the Constitution seems to require, as the Founders seemed to expect, and as our past cases have uniformly assumed—all purely executive power must be under the control of the President. * * *[g]

Notes and Questions

1. *Morrison's reasoning.* Consider Tribe 3d ed., at 684: "The Appointments Clause embodies a concern for political accountability in the exercise of executive power. [I]n the particular situation in which an inferior officer is appointed by persons who are themselves not politically accountable—such as the special panel of judges charged with appointing independent counsels—ongoing supervision by a politically accountable official, whether by the President or by someone serving at the President's pleasure, seems particularly important. In such circumstances, where there is little or no political accountability at the front end for the choice of that officer, a 'for cause' limitation on removal that renders political supervision impossible appears troubling from an accountability perspective." Compare Akhil R. Amar, *Intratextualism*, 112 Harv.L.Rev. 747, 803 (1999): "If the President truly disagrees with the Independent Counsel, the President can make the Counsel vanish with one stroke of the presidential pardon pen: no underlying targets of prosecution, no prosecutor. [A] truly skillful chief executive can wield this mighty broadsword as a surgical scalpel by explaining the facts of life to an Independent Counsel (publicly or privately): unless she does *X* and *Y* and refrains from *Z*, the President will be obliged to pardon." Contrast Tribe 3d. ed., at 685 n.42: "When the President is the target of an independent counsel's investigation, however, no supervision is possible [because] the President may not pardon himself. [Arguably,] the pardon power is too blunt a tool to constitute a means of supervision adequate to render an independent counsel an inferior officer; a Chief Executive (or other supervisor) disturbed by an independent counsel's investigatory tactics should not be required to take the extreme step of pardoning the target of investigation in order to rein the independent counsel in."

2. *Alternative plans.* Would the following proposal satisfy the *Morrison* majority *and* Scalia, J.: "[O]nce a preliminary investigation by the Attorney General shows reasonable grounds to believe that further investigation of high executive officials is warranted, just as it was under the recently lapsed Independent Counsel law, [then] *the President* (not a panel of judges) would have the statutory duty to nominate, subject to Senate advice and consent, a three-member panel—the Special Litigation Committee—who would be principal officers within the Executive Branch, serving at the pleasure of the President." Michael S. Paulsen, *A Constitutional Independent Counsel Statute*, 5 Widener L.Symp.J. 111, 113 (2000). How about a congressionally designated "Independent Investigator," who could make a full investigation and recommendation to the Attorney General, but with no authority to initiate a prosecution?

3. *Formalism and functionalism.* Is the only alternative to a "formal" conception of the separation of powers, which requires that all "executive"

g. Kennedy, J., took no part.

functions be vested in officials subject to the direct supervision of the President, a mode of analysis that Scalia, J., castigated in *Morrison* as involving "not analysis" but "ad hoc judgment?"[a] Is a "functional" approach to the separation of powers sufficiently rigorous to satisfy basic requirements of the rule of law?

Is it an answer to Scalia, J.'s objection that many constitutional tests— including those respecting issues of individual rights and federalism—involve multi-factor balancing inquiries? Do structural questions, involving the legitimacy of the basic design of government and the responsibility and accountability of various governmental actors, require clearer, more historically and textually grounded answers?[b] Or should Congress have greater flexibility to structure a workable government?

4. *After Morrison.* (a) MISTRETTA v. UNITED STATES, 488 U.S. 361, 109 S.Ct. 647, 102 L.Ed.2d 714 (1989), per BLACKMUN, J., upheld the Sentence Reform Act of 1984, which created the U.S. Sentencing Commission charged with devising guidelines for federal sentencing that would establish, within the limits of existing law, ranges of determinate sentences for categories of offenses and defendants according to specified factors, "among others." The Commission was established as an independent commission in the Judicial Branch, consisting of seven voting members appointed by the President, of whom three must be federal judges:

"[Jackson, J.'s opinion in *Youngstown*] summarized the pragmatic, flexible view of differentiated governmental power to which we are heir. [As] a general principle, we stated as recently as last Term that 'executive or administrative duties of a nonjudicial nature may not be imposed on [Art. III judges]. *Morrison.* Nonetheless, we have recognized significant exceptions to this general rule [as in] *Sibbach* [fn. 19 in *Chadha*, in which] we upheld a challenge to certain rules promulgated under the Rules Enabling Act of 1934, which conferred upon the Judiciary the power to promulgate federal rules of civil procedure." Thus, the constitutionality of conferring rulemaking authority on federal judges lay within the "twilight area" recognized in Jackson, J.'s opinion in *Youngstown*, and, on the facts, should be upheld. In light of the judiciary's traditional role in sentencing, there was nothing "incongruous" about the judicial role on the Commission and no "vesting within the Judiciary [of] responsibilities that more appropriately belong to another Branch." Whatever "constitutional problems might arise if the powers of the Commission were vested in a court, the Commission is not a court, does not exercise judicial power, and is not controlled by or accountable to members of the Judicial Branch. The Commission [is] an independent agency in every relevant sense." Moreover, "placement of the Sentencing Commission in the Judicial Branch has not increased the Branch's authority. Prior to the passage of the Act, the Judicial Branch, as an aggregate, decided precisely the questions assigned to the Commission: what sentence is appropriate to what criminal conduct under what circumstances." The Court also ruled that this "extrajudicial assignment" did not undermine the integrity or independence of the Judicial Branch, nor "threaten, either in fact or in appearance, [its] impartiality."[c]

a. For critical analysis of the *Morrison* opinion, see Lee S. Liberman, *Morrison v. Olson: A Formalistic Perspective on Why the Court Was Wrong*, 38 Am.U.L.Rev. 313 (1989); Stephen L. Carter, *The Independent Counsel Mess*, 102 Harv.L.Rev. 105 (1988).

b. See Stephen L. Carter, *From Sick Chicken to Synar: The Evolution and Subsequent De–Evolution of the Separation of Powers*, 1987 B.Y.U.L.Rev. 719, 778–800.

c. Only Scalia, J., dissented. He would uphold "delegation of legislative authority" under "congressionally prescribed standards" only "in conjunction with the lawful exercise of executive or judicial power. [The] whole theory of *lawful* congressional 'delegation' is [that] a certain degree of discretion, and thus of lawmaking, *inheres* in most executive or judicial action, and it is up to Congress, by the relative specificity or generality of its statutory com-

(b) METROPOLITAN WASHINGTON AIRPORTS AUTH. v. CITIZENS FOR THE ABATEMENT OF AIRPORT NOISE, INC., 501 U.S. 252, 111 S.Ct. 2298, 115 L.Ed.2d 236 (1991), per STEVENS, J., invalidated a compact between the District of Columbia and Virginia, approved by Congress, leasing Reagan and Dulles airports from the federal government. The compact conditioned the lease on the vesting of veto power over the management of the airports in a Review Board comprised of nine members of Congress, selected from designated congressional committees but serving in their "individual" capacities. If the powers of the Review Board were "executive," congressional involvement in their exercise was impermissible under *Bowsher*. If the functions of the Review Board were instead classified as legislative, the arrangement ran afoul of principles laid down in *Chadha*. "[T]he statutory scheme [provides] a blueprint for extensive expansion of the legislative power beyond its constitutionally defined role. [Congress] could [use] similar expedients to enable its Members or its agents to retain control, outside the ordinary legislative process, of the activities of state grant recipients charged with executing virtually every aspect of national policy."[d]

(c) EDMOND v. UNITED STATES, 520 U.S. 651, 117 S.Ct. 1573, 137 L.Ed.2d 917 (1997), upheld the authority of the Secretary of Transportation to appoint civilian members of the Coast Guard Court of Criminal Appeals, which hears appeals from courts martial. The Court, per SCALIA, J., reasoned that these judges were "inferior" officers, subject to appointment by heads of departments, because they were supervised by the Judge Advocate General, who could remove them without cause, and by the Court of Appeals for the Armed Forces, which has appellate jurisdiction over Coast Guard Court of Criminal Appeals judgments: "Generally speaking, the term 'inferior officer' connotes a relationship with some higher ranking officer or officers below the President: Whether one is an inferior officer depends upon whether he has a superior." Souter, J., concurred in the result.

Is the rationale of *Edmond*, by Scalia, J., consistent with *Morrison*, from which Scalia, J., dissented? Who is the independent counsel's "superior"? See generally Nick Bravin, Note, *Is Morrison v. Olson Still Good Law? The Court's New Appointments Clause Jurisprudence*, 98 Colum.L.Rev. 1103 (1998).

5. *The emerging framework?* Consider Froomkin, fn. d after *Humphrey's*, at 1368–69: "Overall, the Court's decisions fit a pattern in which Congress's power to check the other branches by determining their structure is very great, but Congress is checked by the requirements that it act through persons outside the legislature (which usually means persons in the executive or the judiciary) and that Congress not aggrandize its own powers. Thus, in *Myers, Buckley, Chadha, Bowsher*, and *Metropolitan Airports*, separation of powers was violated by Congress seeking to reserve an executive power for itself. *Humphrey's Executor, Wiener, Morrison*, [and] *Mistretta* all concerned cases in which Congress had lessened the President's power (or increased the judiciary's) without reserving a corresponding power for itself. Indeed, when the issue is an unenumerated presidential power, such as the power to remove executive branch officials, the Supreme Court has, since at least 1838, consistently focused on whether Congress has impermissibly aggrandized itself, not on whether the President's 'nebulous'

mands, to determine—up to a point—how small or how large that degree shall be. [But] the lawmaking function of the Sentencing Commission is completely divorced from any responsibility for execution of the law or adjudication of private rights under the law. [The]

only governmental power the Commission possesses is the power to make law; and it is not the Congress."

d. White, J., joined by Rehnquist, C.J., and Marshall, J., dissented.

executive power is being undermined [citing *Kendall v. United States ex rel. Stokes*, 37 U.S. (12 Pet.) 524, 610, 9 L.Ed. 1181 (1838), which upheld a writ of mandamus directing the performance of a duty by the Postmaster, stating that although the President has a special constitutional position, 'it by no means follows that every officer in every branch of [a] department is under the exclusive direction of the President'.]"[e]

Is this an accurate summary? Does it account for *Clinton v. New York*? (See note 2 after *Clinton*.) Does this framework reflect an analytically sound and practicable approach?

SECTION 3. FOREIGN AFFAIRS AND WAR POWERS

UNITED STATES v. CURTISS–WRIGHT EXPORT CORP.

299 U.S. 304, 57 S.Ct. 216, 81 L.Ed. 255 (1936).

JUSTICE SUTHERLAND delivered the opinion of the Court.

[A joint resolution of Congress authorized the President to prohibit the sale of arms to Bolivia and Paraguay, which were engaged in armed conflict, if the President found that such prohibition would "contribute to the reestablishment of peace between those countries." The President proclaimed an embargo, and Curtiss–Wright was indicted for violating its terms. The lower court found the joint resolution an unconstitutional delegation of legislative power.]

The powers of the federal government in respect of foreign or external affairs and those in respect of domestic or internal affairs [are] different, both in respect of their origin and their nature. The broad statement that the federal government can exercise no powers except those specifically enumerated in the Constitution, and such implied powers as are necessary and proper to carry into effect the enumerated powers, is categorically true only in respect of our internal affairs.

As a result of the separation from Great Britain by the colonies acting as a unit, the powers of external sovereignty passed from the Crown not to the colonies severally, but to the colonies in their collective and corporate capacity as the United States of America. [The] powers to declare and wage war, to conclude peace, to make treaties, to maintain diplomatic relations with other sovereignties, if they had never been mentioned in the Constitution, would have vested in the federal government as necessary concomitants of nationality.

[Another difference is that] participation in the exercise of power [over external affairs] is significantly limited. In this vast external realm, with its important, complicated, delicate and manifold problems, the President alone has the power to speak or listen as a representative of the nation. He *makes* treaties with the advice and consent of the Senate; but he alone negotiates. Into the field of negotiation the Senate cannot intrude; and Congress itself is powerless to invade it. As Marshall said [in] the House of Representatives, "The President is the sole organ of the nation in its external relations, and its sole representative with foreign nations."

It is important [that] we are here dealing not alone with an authority vested in the President by an exertion of legislative power, but with such an authority plus the very delicate, plenary and exclusive power of the President as the sole

---

e. See also Dean Alfange, Jr., *The Supreme Court and the Separation of Powers: A Wel-* come *Return to Normalcy?*, 58 Geo. Wash.L.Rev. 668 (1990).

organ of the federal government in the field of international relations. [If] embarrassment—perhaps serious embarrassment—is to be avoided and success for our aims achieved, congressional legislation [must] often accord to the President a degree of discretion and freedom from statutory restriction which would not be admissible were domestic affairs alone involved. Moreover, he, not Congress, has the better opportunity of knowing the conditions which prevail in foreign countries, and especially is this true in time of war. He has his confidential sources of information. [Secrecy] in respect of information gathered by them may be highly necessary, and the premature disclosure of it productive of harmful results.

[In] the light of the foregoing observations, it is evident that this court should not be in haste to apply a general rule which will have the effect of condemning legislation like that under review as constituting an unlawful delegation of legislative power. * * *

Reversed.[a]

Notes and Questions

1. *Nonenumerated powers.* Is the notion that the federal government possesses unenumerated foreign affairs powers consistent with basic tenets of American constitutionalism?[b] Is the capacity to respond effectively to foreign affairs emergencies a functionally necessary predicate for the maintenance of constitutional democracy?

2. *Presidential power.* (a) Does the constitutional text support the conclusion that the President is "the sole organ of the federal government in the field of international relations"? Compare Joel R. Paul, *The Geopolitical Constitution: Executive Expediency and Executive Agreements*, 86 Calif.L.Rev. 671, 682 (1998): "[M]y reading of the history from the Framers' time to the present reveals a clear, consistent understanding of a more limited role for the President in foreign affairs up until the Cold War." Is it significant that the President can make treaties only with the advice and consent of the Senate and that Congress is vested with authority to regulate foreign commerce, to declare war, and to provide for the funding and regulation of the armed forces? Compare Edwin Corwin, *The President: Office and Powers, 1787–1957*, at 171 (4th ed. 1957): "[T]he Constitution, considered only for its affirmative grants of powers capable of affecting the issue, is an invitation to [Congress and the President] to struggle for the privilege of directing American foreign policy."

(b) Is *Curtiss-Wright* inconsistent with *Youngstown*? See Harold H. Koh, *The National Security Constitution: Sharing Power After the Iran–Contra Affair* 134–43 (1990)(arguing that *Youngstown* and *Curtiss-Wright* reflect different constitutional visions and that, while "the *Youngstown* theory [generally requiring the President to seek congressional concurrence] took hold powerfully" under the

---

a. McReynolds, J., dissented without opinion. Stone, J., did not participate.

b. For a critique of both the historical and constitutional analysis of *Curtiss-Wright*, see Charles A. Lofgren, *"Government From Reflection and Choice": Constitutional Essays on War, Foreign Relations, and Federalism* 167–205 (1986). For support of Sutherland, J.'s view, see Jack N. Rakove, *Original Meanings: Politics and Ideas in the Making of the Consti-* *tution* 163–168 (1996). For a detailed account of the evolution of the view "that there was an essential difference between foreign relations policymaking and domestic policymaking, and that difference reflected the consummate importance of human flexibility and discretion in the delicate realm of international relations," see G. Edward White, *The Transformation of the Constitutional Regime of Foreign Relations*, 85 Va.L.Rev. 1 (1999).

Warren Court, the Burger and Rehnquist Courts—as in *Dames & Moore*—have followed the *Curtiss-Wright* approach of recognizing broad presidential discretion). If there are indeed two approaches, which is the more sound?

3. *Executive agreements.* (a) Executive agreements with foreign nations originally played a minor role as compared to treaties, but since World War II, they have overwhelmed the process.[c] These agreements often have been authorized or approved by congressional action or entered into pursuant to treaties.[d] But from early days Presidents have entered into significant international executive agreements strictly on their own authority.[e] *United States v. Belmont*, 301 U.S. 324, 57 S.Ct. 758, 81 L.Ed. 1134 (1937), *United States v. Pink*, 315 U.S. 203, 62 S.Ct. 552, 86 L.Ed. 796 (1942), and *Dames & Moore* upheld the President's authority to enter into such executive agreements without Senate or congressional approval.[f] Are these decisions consistent with the assertion of Black, J.'s opinion

c. Between 1939–1989, the nation entered into 11,698 non-treaty agreements but only 702 treaties. See Committee on Foreign Relations, United States Senate, *Treaties and Other International Agreements: The Role of the United States Senate*, S. Prt. 103–53, 103d Cong. 1st Sess. 14 (1993). See generally Michael D. Ramsey, *Executive Agreements and the (Non) Treaty Power*, 77 N.C.L.Rev. 133 (1998).

d. See Louis Henkin, *Foreign Affairs and the Constitution* 173–76 (1972). Arthur W. Rovine, *Separation of Powers and International Executive Agreements*, 52 Ind.L.J. 397, 412 (1977), notes a State Department study indicating that 86% of all executive agreements were authorized by prior statute or subsequent joint resolution of Congress.

May a statute or joint resolution, passed by majority vote in both houses of Congress, be a constitutionally adequate substitute for the process of Senatorial advice and consent to treaties, which requires a two-thirds majority (Art. II, § 2, cl. 2)? Compare Bruce Ackerman & David Golove, *Is NAFTA Constitutional?*, 108 Harv.L.Rev. 799 (1995)(arguing that a de facto constitutional amendment has allowed use of congressionally approved executive agreements in circumstances once requiring senatorial consent to a "treaty") with Laurence H. Tribe, *Taking Text and Structure Seriously: Reflections on Free–Form Method in Constitutional Interpretation*, 108 Harv.L.Rev. 1221, 1249–69 (1995)(arguing that, although the President can bind the nation by executive agreement, on matters that do not "seriously affect state or national sovereignty," other international agreements are necessarily "treaties" in the constitutional sense, and are not constitutionally valid without Senate confirmation). According to Tribe, if a matter can be dealt with by executive agreement, congressional approval is unnecessary; if it cannot be dealt with by executive agreement, congressional action (other than treaty ratification) is ineffectual. See also David Golove, *Against Free–Form Formalism*, 73 N.Y.U.L.Rev. 1791 (1998) (responding to Tribe). For the view that "congressional-executive agreements [*must*] be used to approve international agreements that

regulate matters within Congress's Article I powers," and that "treaties [*must*] be used if the nation seeks to make agreements outside of Congress's competence or bind itself in areas where both President and Congress exercise competing, overlapping powers," see John C. Yoo, *Laws as Treaties?: The Constitutionality of Congressional–Executive Agreements*, 99 Mich.L.Rev. ___ (2001).

A similar tension regarding action that may be taken either by (a) the executive and the Senate (treaty), or (b) by Congress and the President (statute) arises in respect to the legitimacy of a *self-executing* treaty. The issue is considered extensively in John C. Yoo, *Globalism and the Constitution: Treaties, Non–Self-Execution, and the Original Understanding*, 99 Colum.L.Rev. 1955 (1999) (since "self-execution invites a conflict between the textual grants of the executive and legislative powers and resolves the clash by allowing the treaty-making authority to trump Congress's Article I powers," the original understanding (as well as the Constitution's text and structure) require that treaties "should not generally be judicially enforceable unless Congress passes implementing legislation"). For the contrary view, see Martin S. Flaherty, *History Right? Historical Scholarship, Original, Understanding, and Treaties as "Supreme Law of the Land,"* 99 Colum.L.Rev. 2095 (1999) ("the Framers crafted a Constitution that made treaties self-executing upon ratification"); Carlos Vasquez, *Laughing at Treaties*, 99 Colum.L.Rev. 2154 (1999).

e. Henkin, supra at 176–180.

f. *Belmont* and *Pink* involved the Soviet Union's assignment to the United States of amounts owed to it by American nationals so that outstanding claims of other American nationals could be paid. The Court ruled that the executive agreement became the "supreme Law of the Land," overriding New York's court-made policy not to recognize government appropriation of property. *Pink* explained: "The powers of the President in the conduct of foreign relations included the power, without

in *Youngstown* that the President is categorically excluded from the exercise of lawmaking authority? Should the President be so excluded?

(b) In 1972, Professor Henkin noted that "[o]ne is compelled to conclude that there are agreements which the President can make on his sole authority and others which he can make only with the consent of the Senate, but neither Justice Sutherland [who wrote *Belmont*] nor any one else has told us which are which."[g] Do *Dames & Moore, Pink,* and *Belmont* provide any guidance to the extent or source of the President's power to enter into such "sole executive agreements?"[h]

CAMPBELL v. CLINTON

203 F.3d 19 (D.C.Cir.2000).

SILBERMAN, CIRCUIT JUDGE.

A number of congressmen [filed] suit claiming that the President violated the War Powers Resolution [WPR] and the War Powers Clause of the Constitution by directing U.S. forces' participation in the recent NATO campaign in Yugoslavia. The district court dismissed for lack of standing. * * *

On March 24, 1999, President Clinton announced the commencement of NATO air and cruise missile attacks on Yugoslav targets. Two days later he submitted to Congress a report, "consistent with the War Powers Resolution," detailing the circumstances necessitating the use of armed forces, the deployment's scope and expected duration, and asserting that he had "taken these actions pursuant to [his] authority [as] Commander in Chief and Chief Executive." On April 28, Congress voted [down] a declaration of war 427 to 2 and an "authorization" of the air strikes 213 to 213, but it also voted against requiring the President to immediately end U.S. participation in the NATO operation and voted to fund that involvement. The conflict between NATO and Yugoslavia continued for 79 days. [The] WPR requires the President to submit a report within 48 hours "in any case in which United States Armed Forces are introduced [into] hostilities or into situations where imminent involvement in hostilities is clearly indicated by the circumstances," and to "terminate any use of United States Armed Forces with respect to which a report was submitted (or required to be submitted), unless the Congress [has] declared war or has enacted a specific authorization" [within] 60 days * * *.[a]

consent of the Senate, to determine the public policy of the United States with respect to the Russian nationalization [decrees]. Power to remove such obstacles to full recognition as [claims settlement] certainly is a modest implied power of the President who is the 'sole organ of the federal government in the field of international relations.' *Curtiss-Wright.* Effectiveness in handling the delicate problems of foreign relations requires no [less]."

g.　Henkin, supra at 179.

h.　For exploration of such issues see Henkin, supra at 177–78; Rovine, supra at 412–415. See also Ackerman & Golove, supra at 856–60; Tribe, supra at 1258–69.

a.　The War Powers Resolution was passed in 1973, in response to the Vietnam War, over presidential veto on the ground, inter alia, that it unconstitutionally constrained the President's war powers. Nearly all commentators agree that the War Powers Resolution has failed to fulfill its intended aims. First, the Resolution does not deal at all with military operations that can be completed in less than 60 days. Second, Presidents have ignored the Resolution in cases—such as President Reagan's dispatch of troops to Lebanon in 1982, President Bush's initial introduction of forces in the Persian Gulf, and President Clinton's sending troops to Haiti in 1994—in which it would seem relevant. See John H. Ely, *War and Responsibility: Constitutional Lessons of Vietnam and Its Aftermath* 49 (1993); Koh, note 2(b) after *Curtiss-Wright*, at 39–40; John C. Yoo, *Kosovo, War Powers, and the Multilateral Future,* 148 U.Pa.L.Rev. 1673, 1677–79 (2000).

For a range of views on legal issues raised by the War Powers Resolution, see Stephen L. Carter, *The Constitutionality of the War Pow-*

[W]e agree with the district court that the congressmen lack standing * * *.

SILBERMAN, CIRCUIT JUDGE, concurring.

[I]n my view, no one is able to bring this challenge because the two claims are not justiciable. We lack "judicially discoverable and manageable standards" for addressing them, and the War Powers Clause claim implicates the political question doctrine. See *Baker v. Carr* [Ch. 1, Sec. 2].

Appellants contend this case is governed by *Mitchell v. Laird*, 488 F.2d 611, 614 (D.C.Cir.1973), where we said that "[t]here would be no insuperable difficulty in a court determining whether" the Vietnam conflict constituted a war in the Constitutional sense. See also *Dellums v. Bush*, 752 F.Supp. 1141, 1146 (D.D.C. 1990) ("[T]he Court has no hesitation in concluding that an offensive entry into Iraq by several hundred thousand United States servicemen [could] be described as a 'war' within the meaning [of] the Constitution."). But a careful reading of both cases reveals that the language upon which appellants rely is only dicta. * * *

Appellants cannot point to any constitutional test for what is war. See, e.g., *Holtzman v. Schlesinger*, 414 U.S. 1316, 94 S.Ct. 8, 38 L.Ed.2d 28 (1973) (Justice Douglas, in chambers, vacating order of Court of Appeals granting stay of district court's injunction against bombing of Cambodia), 414 U.S. at 1321 (Justice Marshall, in chambers, granting stay the same day with the concurrence of the other Justices); *Holtzman v. Schlesinger*, 484 F.2d 1307 (2d Cir.1973) (holding legality of Cambodia bombing nonjusticiable because courts lack expertise to determine import of various military actions). Instead, appellants offer a rough definition of war provided in 1994 by an Assistant Attorney General to four Senators with respect to a planned intervention in Haiti, as well as a number of law review articles each containing its own definition of war. I do not think any of these sources, however, offers a coherent test for judges to apply to the question what constitutes war, a point only accentuated by the variances, for instance, between the numerous law review articles. [Even] if this court knows all there is to know about the Kosovo conflict, we still do not know what standards to apply to those facts.

Judge Tatel points to numerous cases in which a court has determined that our nation was at war, but none of these cases involved the question whether the President had "declared war" in violation of the Constitution. For instance, in *Bas v. Tingy*, 4 U.S. (4 Dall.) 37, 1 L.Ed. 731 (1800), the question whether there was a "war" was only relevant to determining whether France was an "enemy" within the meaning of a prize statute. * * *

Even assuming a court could determine what "war" is, it is important to remember that the Constitution grants Congress the power to declare war, which is not necessarily the same as the power to determine whether U.S. forces will fight in a war. This distinction was drawn in the *Prize Cases*, 67 U.S. (2 Black) 635, 17 L.Ed. 459 (1862). There, petitioners challenged the authority of the President to impose a blockade on the secessionist States, an act of war, where Congress had not declared war against the Confederacy. The Court, while recognizing that the President "has no power to initiate or declare a war," observed that "war may exist without a declaration on either side." In instances where war is declared against the United States by the actions of another country, the President "does not initiate the war, but is bound to accept the challenge without

ers Resolution, 70 Va.L.Rev. 101 (1984); Robert F. Turner, *The War Powers Resolution: Uncon-*   *stitutional, Unnecessary, and Unhelpful*, 17 Loy.L.A.L.Rev. 683 (1984).

waiting for any special legislative authority." Importantly, the Court made clear that it would not dispute the President on measures necessary to repel foreign aggression. * * *

I read the *Prize Cases* to stand for the proposition that the President has independent authority to repel aggressive acts by third parties even without specific congressional authorization, and courts may not review the level of force selected. [If] the President may direct U.S. forces in response to third-party initiated war, then the question any plaintiff who challenges the constitutionality of a war must answer is, who started it? The question of who is responsible for a conflict is, as history reveals, rather difficult to answer, and we lack judicial standards for resolving it. Then there is the problem of actually discovering the necessary information to answer the question, when such information may be unavailable to the U.S. or its allies, or unavailable to courts due to its sensitivity. Perhaps Yugoslavia did pose a threat to a much wider region of Europe and to U.S. civilian and military interests and personnel there.

Judge Tatel does not take into account the *Prize Cases* when he concludes that the President was not exercising his independent authority to respond to foreign aggression because "in fact, the Kosovo issue had been festering for years." As quoted above the President alone "must determine what degree of force the crisis demands." See 67 U.S. at 670. Judge Tatel would substitute our judgment for the President's as to the point at which an intervention for reasons of national security is justified, after which point—when the crisis is no longer acute—the President must obtain a declaration of war. One should bear in mind that Kosovo's tensions antedate the creation of this republic.

In most cases this will also be an issue of the greatest sensitivity for our foreign relations. Here, the President claimed on national television that our country needed to respond to Yugoslav aggression to protect our trading interests in Europe, and to prevent a replay of World War I. A pronouncement by another branch of the U.S. government that U.S. participation in Kosovo was "unjustified" would no doubt cause strains within NATO. * * *[b]

TATEL, CIRCUIT JUDGE, concurring.

* * * I do not agree that courts lack judicially discoverable and manageable standards for "determining the existence of a 'war.'" Whether the military activity in Yugoslavia amounted to "war" within the meaning of the Declare War Clause, is no more standardless than any other question regarding the constitutionality of government action. Precisely what police conduct violates the Fourth Amendment guarantee "against unreasonable searches and seizures"? When does government action amount to "an establishment of religion" prohibited by the First Amendment? [I]n *The Prize Cases,* the Court had to determine whether a state of war, though undeclared, existed "de facto" between the United States and the confederacy, and if so, whether it justified the U.S. naval blockade of confederate ports. [There] was no formal declaration of war, the Court explained, because the Constitution does not permit Congress to "declare war against a State, or any number of States." Yet the Court, guided by the definition of war as "[t]hat state in which a nation prosecutes its right by force," determined that a state of war actually existed. [In] making this determination, the Court looked to the facts of the conflict, to the acts of foreign governments recognizing the war and declaring their neutrality, and to congressional action authorizing the Presi-

b. Randolph, J.'s concurrence in the judg-   omitted.
ment, on grounds of standing and mootness, is

dent's use of force. Given these facts, the Court refused "to affect a technical ignorance of the existence of a war, which all the world acknowledges to be the greatest civil war known in the history of the human race."

[If] in 1799 the Supreme Court could recognize that sporadic battles between American and French vessels amounted to a state of war, and if in 1862 it could examine the record of hostilities and conclude that a state of war existed with the confederacy, then surely we, looking to similar evidence, could determine whether months of daily airstrikes involving 800 U.S. aircraft flying more than 20,000 sorties and causing thousands of enemy casualties amounted to "war" within the meaning of Article I, section 8, clause 11. * * *

The government also claims that this case is nonjusticiable because it "requires a political, not a judicial, judgment." The government has it backwards. Resolving the issue in this case would require us to decide not whether the air campaign was wise—a "policy choice[ ] and value determination [ ] constitutionally committed for resolution to the halls of Congress or the confines of the Executive Branch"—but whether the President possessed legal authority to conduct the military operation. Did the President exceed his constitutional authority as Commander in Chief? Did he intrude on Congress's power to declare war? Did he violate the War Powers Resolution? Presenting purely legal issues, these questions call on us to perform one of the most important functions of Article III courts: determining the proper constitutional allocation of power among the branches of government. Although our answer could well have political implications, "the presence of constitutional issues with significant political overtones does not automatically invoke the political question doctrine. Resolution of litigation challenging the constitutional authority of one of the three branches cannot be evaded by courts because the issues have political implications." This is so even where, as here (and as in the other cases discussed above), the issue relates to foreign policy. See *Baker* ("[I]t is error to suppose that every case or controversy which touches foreign relations lies beyond judicial cognizance"). * * *

The Government's final argument—that entertaining a war powers challenge risks the government speaking with "multifarious voices" on a delicate issue of foreign policy—fails for similar reasons. Because courts are the final arbiters of the constitutionality of the President's actions, "there is no possibility of 'multifarious pronouncements' on this question." Any short-term confusion that judicial action might instill in the mind of an authoritarian enemy, or even an ally, is but a small price to pay for preserving the constitutional separation of powers * * *.c

Notes and Questions

1. *Constitutional sources of power to wage war.* The phrase "war powers" does not appear in the Constitution, but rather "describes a cluster of powers exercised by the President or Congress, together or separately, to combat both domestic insurgency and foreign military enemies." Charles A. Lofgren, *War Powers, in* ENCYC. OF AMER. CONST. 2013 (1986). Art. I, § 8 authorizes Congress to "lay and collect Taxes, [to] provide for the common Defence" (cl. 1); to "declare War (cl. 11);" to "grant Letters of Marque and Reprisal (cl. 11);" to "raise and

c. For the view that *all* separation of powers issues, including the war power, should be nonjusticiable, see Jesse H. Choper, *Judicial Review and the National Political Process* ch. 5 (1980) (arguing that the line between legislative and executive authority is ambiguous and shifting, and that the Court's involvement is unnecessary to police constitutional violations because both branches have enormous incentives and impressive weapons to protect their prerogatives).

support Armies" (cl. 12); to "provide and maintain a Navy" (cl. 13); to "make Rules for the Government and Regulation of the land and naval Forces" (cl. 14); to "provide for calling forth the Militia to execute the Laws of the Union, suppress Insurrections and repel Invasions" (cl. 15); to "provide for organizing, arming, and disciplining, the Militia" (cl. 16); and (in § 9, cl. 2) to suspend the "privilege of the Writ of Habeas Corpus [in] Cases of Rebellion or Invasion." As for the President, Art. II, § 1, cl. 1 grants him the "executive Power," § 2, cl. 1 declares that he "shall be Commander in Chief of the Army and Navy of the United States, and of the Militia of the several States, when called into the actual Service of the United States," and § 3 charges the President to "take Care that the Laws be faithfully executed."

2. *Range of issues and relevance of original understanding.* Especially because relatively few Supreme Court opinions address foreign affairs or war powers, much modern debate involving a host of controversial issues has concerned the original understanding and historical practice.[a]

First, and foremost, who has the power to *"commence* war," the President or Congress? Moreover, may Congress "authorize" a war by mechanisms other than a formal declaration—e.g., what about a joint resolution of Congress, which also requires majority votes of both Houses?

A widely shared view—generally stated, and with various detailed qualifications—is that "Congress exclusively possesses the constitutional power to initiate war, whether declared or undeclared, public or private, perfect or imperfect, de jure or de facto," the only exception being the President's power to repel sudden attacks.[b] These scholars reason that the Founders "fear[ed] that presidents, like kings before them, might be tempted to initiate war for reasons of personal 'ambition' and 'aggrandizement' [Madison]. Vesting the power to declare or commence war in the legislature [would] permit deliberation by a diverse group of people before the nation embarked on a course so full of risks. [Including] the House in the decision to initiate war also ensured that the American people, who would bear the burdens of war, had a voice in that decision through their most immediate federal representatives."[c] A contrary view interprets Congress' power to "declare War" narrowly, merely "trigger[ing] the international laws of war, which would clothe in legitimacy certain actions taken against one's own and enemy citizens"[d]—thus placing in the executive the power to initiate and escalate

a. For recent discussion of the criteria for faithful and persuasive use of historical sources respecting original understanding, see Martin S. Flaherty, *History "Lite" in Modern American Constitutionalism*, 95 Colum.L.Rev. 523 (1995); John C. Yoo, *Clio at War: The Misuse of History in the War Powers Debate*, 70 U. of Colo.L.Rev. 1169 (1999).

b. Francis D. Wormuth & Edwin B. Firmage, *To Chain the Dog of War* 299 (2d ed. 1989). Similarly, see Raoul Berger, *War-Making by the President*, 121 U.Pa.L.Rev. 29 (1972); Arthur Bestor, *Separation of Powers in the Domain of Foreign Affairs: The Intent of the Constitution Historically Examined*, 5 Seton Hall L. Rev. 527, 555–613 (1974); Ely, fn. a in *Campbell* supra, at 3–10, 139–52; Louis Fisher, *Presidential War Power* (1995); Michael J. Glennon, *Constitutional Diplomacy* 80–84 (1990); Louis Henkin, *Constitutionalism, De-*

mocracy, and Foreign Affairs 33 (1990); Louis Henkin, *Foreign Affairs and the Constitution* 80–81 (1972); Koh, note 2(b) after *Curtiss-Wright* supra, at 74–77; Leonard W. Levy, *Original Intent and the Framers' Constitution* 30–53 (1988); Charles A. Lofgren, *War-Making Under the Constitution: The Original Understanding*, 81 Yale L.J. 672 (1972); William M. Treanor, *Fame, The Founding, and the Power to Declare War*, 82 Corn.L.Rev. 695, 772 (1997) (nor did Founders intend to give the President a veto power over a congressional declaration of war).

c. Jane E. Stromseth, *Understanding Constitutional War Powers Today: Why Methodology Matters*, 106 YALE L.J. 845, 852 (1996).

d. John C. Yoo, *The Continuation of Politics by Other Means: The Original Understanding of War Powers*, 84 Calif. L. Rev. 167, 242 (1996) (Congress would use its sole control

hostilities leading to a formal congressional declaration.[e] Advocates of this position contend that "the Founders intended no one procedure for deciding on war or the use of force more generally. The Founders instead gave overlapping war powers to Congress and the President and expected that they would cooperate and struggle in a flexible system of checks and balances."[f]

The *Campbell* decision discusses a second question: What is meant by the word "war" in the phrase "commence *war*"? What about small-scale offensive military operations?[g] Or those that do not clearly involve initiating war or commencing offensive action—such as the U.S. deployment of forces in Somalia to secure humanitarian relief operations, and the U.S. military involvement in Bosnia to implement the Dayton Peace Agreement (in which American forces arrived "not to impose peace, but rather to monitor a negotiated settlement accepted by the parties on the ground."[h]) A somewhat related issue concerns the President's universally acknowledged power to "repel sudden attacks." Did the Founders contemplate imminent as well as actual attacks against the United States? What about attacks against U.S. citizens and vessels beyond the nation's borders? Or attacks that threaten American interests, but against other countries?

Further, to what extent can the Founders basic purposes be effectively "transposed" into the modern world? For example, a highly significant contemporary issue concerns Presidential action taken pursuant to a treaty, such as sending American troops to Iraq by President Bush and to Haiti and Kosovo by President Clinton under auspices of the U.N. Does the fact that the U.S. is a treaty signatory to the U.N. Charter authorize the President to "execute" it in this way without specific approval of Congress? Compare Thomas M. Franck & Faiza Patel, *Agora: The Gulf Crisis in International and Foreign Relations Law, UN Police Action in Lieu of War: "The Old Order Changeth,"* 85 Am.J.Int'l L. 63 (1991) with Michael J. Glennon & Allison R. Hayward, *Collective Security and the Constitution: Can the Commander in Chief Power Be Delegated to the United Nations?*, 82 Geo.L.J. 1573 (1994). If the treaty obligation of the U.S. under international law authorizes the President to do so, may he send American troops to serve under foreign commanders who have not been designated under the Appointments Clause? See generally Yoo, fn. a. in *Campbell*, supra.

Finally, while war powers scholars agree that the historical practices of Presidents and Congress matter for the constitutional division of war powers today, there is considerable disagreement in respect to how those practices should

---

over funding to check the President in foreign affairs). Similarly, see Philip Bobbit, *War Powers: An Essay on John Hart Ely's War and Responsibility: Constitutional Lessons of Vietnam and Its Aftermath*, 92 Mich. L. Rev. 1364, 1370–1388 (1994); Robert Bork, *Erosion of the President's Power in Foreign Affairs*, 68 Wash. U.L.Q. 693, 698 (1990); Henry P. Monaghan, *Presidential War-making*, 50 B.U.L.Rev. 19 (special issue) (Spring, 1970); W. Michael Reisman, *Some Lessons from Iraq: International Law and Democratic Politics*, 16 Yale J.Int'l L. 203, 212 (1991); Eugene V. Rostow, *"Once More unto the Breach": The War Powers Resolution Revisited*, 21 Val. U. L. Rev. 1, 6 (1986).

e. For discussion of the consequences of a formal declaration of war on the Bill of Rights, see Patrick O. Gudridge, *Ely, Black, Grotius & Vattel*, 50 U. Miami L.Rev. 81 (1995).

f. As described in Stromseth, supra at 857–58.

g. Many "exclusively Congress" scholars invoke the Marque and Reprisal Clause as intended "to ensure that lesser forms of hostilities came within congressional power." Jules Lobel, *"Little Wars" and the Constitution*, 50 U.Miami L.Rev. 61, 70 (1995). Indeed, some deny *any* "emergency" war power for the President, arguing, for example, that Lincoln's Civil War blockade (undertaken "in a genuine emergency" when Congress was not in session) lacked "legal or constitutional authority," but was "ventured upon under what appeared to be a popular demand and a public necessity, trusting then, as now, that Congress would readily ratify" it. Fisher, fn. b supra, at 87, 38 (quoting Lincoln).

h. Stromseth, supra at 904.

be characterized. The "exclusively Congress" commentators concede that a number of post Cold War practices—President Truman's sending troops into the Korean War without congressional permission, President Bush's similar conduct in the Gulf War, and President Clinton's military intervention in Kosovo, and in Haiti (in the context of a unanimous Senate Resolution that he had no authorization to do so)—conflict with their position. But they contend that prior history supports them, distinguishing the more than two hundred situations in which the "presidential power" advocates allege unilateral executive uses of force: "Almost seventy of the cases, for instance, involved small, relatively low-risk, and self-contained naval landings to protect or rescue American nationals overseas, which are a far cry from committing U.S. forces to a major and sustained combat operation. At least eight of the cases involved limited military actions against pirates. Many of the cases on the lists, moreover, were in fact authorized by Congress by statute or were taken pursuant to regulations authorized by statute. The lists do not include cases in which presidents refrained from using force because they knew Congress would oppose it or because they were unsuccessful in obtaining congressional authorization. Nor do the lists generally examine whether Congress was presented with a fait accompli that made it practically impossible for it to object or whether Congress protested the action after the fact."[i]

SECTION 4. EXECUTIVE PRIVILEGE AND IMMUNITY

UNITED STATES v. NIXON, 418 U.S. 683, 94 S.Ct. 3090, 41 L.Ed.2d 1039 (1974), grew out of the burglary of Democratic national headquarters in the Watergate hotel, during the 1972 presidential campaign, by employees of the president's re-election committee. After investigations by the press and a Senate select committee revealed involvement by high officials in the Nixon administration, the President authorized the appointment of a special prosecutor,[a] who subpoenaed presidential tapes and documents based on an indictment that named Nixon an unindicted "co-conspirator," and charged seven of his staff and political associates with obstructing justice and other Watergate-related offenses. The Court per BURGER, C.J., rejected the President's claim of executive privilege: "The President's counsel [reads] the Constitution as providing an absolute privilege of confidentiality for all presidential communications. Many decisions of this Court, however, have unequivocally reaffirmed the holding of *Marbury v. Madison* that '[i]t is emphatically the province and duty of the judicial department to say what the law is.' [Notwithstanding] the deference each branch must accord the others, the 'judicial power of the United States' [can] no more be shared with the Executive Branch than the Chief Executive, for example, can share with the Judiciary the veto power.

"[T]he President's counsel urges [the] valid need for protection of communications between high government officials and those who advise and assist them in the performance of their manifold duties; the importance of this confidentiality is too plain to require further discussion. Human experience teaches that those who expect public dissemination of their remarks may well temper candor with a concern for appearances and for their own interests to the detriment of the decisionmaking process. Whatever the nature of the privilege of confidentiality of presidential communications in the exercise of Art. II powers, the privilege can be

---

i. Stromseth, supra at 877.

a. Footnote 8 of the opinion provides details concerning the Special Prosecutor's independence.

said to derive from the supremacy of each branch within its own assigned area of constitutional duties.[b] Certain powers and privileges flow from the nature of enumerated powers; the protection of the confidentiality of presidential communications has similar constitutional underpinnings. * * *

"However, neither the doctrine of separation of powers, nor the need for confidentiality of high level communications, without more, can sustain an absolute, unqualified presidential privilege of immunity from judicial process under all circumstances. [When] the privilege depends solely on the broad, undifferentiated claim of public interest in the confidentiality of such conversations, a confrontation with other values arises. Absent a claim of need to protect military, diplomatic, or sensitive national security secrets, we find it difficult to accept the argument that even the very important interest in confidentiality of presidential communications is significantly diminished by production of such material for in camera inspection with all the protection that a district court will be obliged to provide.

"The impediment that an absolute, unqualified privilege would place in the way of the primary constitutional duty of the Judicial Branch to do justice in criminal prosecutions would plainly conflict with the function of the courts under Art. III. In designing the structure of our Government and dividing and allocating the sovereign power among three coequal branches, the Framers [sought] to provide a comprehensive system, but the separate powers were not intended to operate with absolute independence.

"[A] President and those who assist him must be free to explore alternatives in the process of shaping policies and making decisions and to do so in a way many would be unwilling to express except privately. These are the considerations justifying a presumptive privilege for presidential communications." [But] this presumptive privilege must be considered in light of our historic commitment to the rule of law. [To] ensure that justice is done, it is imperative to the function of courts that compulsory process be available for the production of evidence needed either by the prosecution or by the [defense].

"In this case the President [does] not place his claim of privilege on the ground [of] military or diplomatic secrets [where courts] have traditionally shown the utmost deference to presidential [responsibilities]. No case of the Court [has] extended this high degree of deference to a President's generalized interest in confidentiality. * * *

"The right to the production of all evidence at a criminal trial similarly has constitutional dimensions. The Sixth Amendment explicitly confers upon every defendant in a criminal trial the right 'to be confronted with the witnesses against him' and 'to have compulsory process for obtaining witnesses in his favor.' Moreover, the Fifth Amendment also guarantees that no person shall be deprived of liberty without due process of law. It is the manifest duty of the courts to vindicate those guarantees and to accomplish that it is essential that all relevant and admissible evidence be produced.

"In this case we must weigh the importance of the general privilege of confidentiality of presidential communications in performance of [the President's] responsibilities against the inroads of such a privilege on the fair administration of

b. On the constitutional, political and historical basis for executive privilege, compare Saikrishna B. Prakash, *A Critical Comment on the Constitutionality of Executive Privilege*, 83 Minn.L.Rev. 1143 (1999) (casting doubt "that an executive privilege necessarily emanates from the Constitution itself") and Raoul Berger, *Executive Privilege: A Constitutional Myth* (1974) with Mark J. Rozell, *Executive Privilege: The Dilemma of Secrecy and Democratic Accountability* (1994).

criminal justice.[19] The interest in preserving confidentiality is weighty indeed and entitled to great respect. However, we cannot conclude that advisers will be moved to temper the candor of their remarks by the infrequent occasions of disclosure because of the possibility that such conversations will be called for in the context of a criminal prosecution.

"On the other hand, [the] constitutional need for production of relevant evidence in a criminal proceeding is specific and central to the fair adjudication of a particular criminal case in the administration of justice. Without access to specific facts a criminal prosecution may be totally frustrated. [The] generalized assertion of privilege must yield to the demonstrated, specific need for evidence in a pending criminal trial."[c]

Notes and Questions

1. *Types of privilege.* Consider Tribe 3d ed., at 770–71: "Although it is customary to employ the phrase 'executive privilege,' it is perhaps more accurate to speak of executive *privileges*, for presidential refusals to furnish information may be actuated by any of at least three distinct kinds of considerations. [1.] Presidents of the United States beginning with George Washington have invoked executive privilege on the ground that disclosure of the desired information would subvert crucial military or diplomatic objectives. [The] Supreme Court [relied] upon an executive right to withhold information in *Chicago & Southern Air Lines v. Waterman Steamship Corp.* [333 U.S. 103, 111, 68 S.Ct. 431, 436, 92 L.Ed. 568, 576 (1948)] when [it] proclaimed that '[t]he President has available intelligence services whose reports are not and ought not to be published to the world.' [T]he Court has [also] seen fit to pronounce that the 'privilege against revealing military secrets [is] well established in the law of evidence.' More generally, a President can successfully claim that a measure of secrecy, and thus a qualified executive privilege from required disclosure, is a necessary condition for the successful conduct of foreign affairs.

"[2.] The law of evidence has also long recognized an informer's privilege— that is, 'the Government's privilege to withhold from disclosure the identity of persons who furnish information of violations of law to officers charged with enforcement of that law.' [3.] Finally, a generic privilege for internal deliberations has been said to attach to 'intragovernmental documents reflecting advisory opinions, recommendations and deliberations comprising part of a process by which governmental decisions and policies are formulated.' "

2. *Marbury and judicial resolution of privilege claims.* Does the Court's reliance on *Marbury* for the proposition that it must determine the merits of the President's claim of privilege "convey a misleadingly broad view of judicial competence, exclusivity and supremacy"? See Gerald Gunther, *Judicial Hegemony and Legislative Autonomy: The Nixon Case and the Impeachment Process*, 22 U.C.L.A.Rev. 30, 33–34 (1974). Did *Marbury* prevent the Court from "declar[ing] 'the law' to be that the President is the sole determiner of the need for protecting

---

19. We are not here concerned with the balance between the President's generalized interest in confidentiality and the need for relevant evidence in civil litigation, nor with that between the confidentiality interest and congressional demands for information, nor with the President's interest in preserving state secrets.

c. The Court stressed the obligation of the District Court to examine the tapes and documents in camera and to excise and keep confidential all material not admissible and relevant.

Rehnquist, J., did not participate.

the confidentiality of particular communications, just as 'the law' grants him sole authority over recognition of the legal government of a foreign state''? See Paul A. Freund, *On Presidential Privilege*, 88 Harv.L.Rev. 13, 21–22 (1974). Would (should) the Court proceed in the same way in a case involving a claim that disclosure would damage military or diplomatic efforts? Cf. *Chicago & Southern Air Lines*.

3. *Executive privilege in judicial proceedings*. (a) Does *Nixon* mean that executive privilege must *always* yield when the communications are relevant to criminal cases? Should the constitutionally based executive privilege receive less protection than traditional husband-wife, doctor-patient, lawyer-client privileges that exclude relevant, otherwise admissible evidence? Consider Tribe 3d ed., at 777–78: "Since relevance, admissibility, and necessity must in any event be shown in order to require production of evidence prior to trial, the Court's [statement] that the trial judge should demand a showing that the materials are 'essential to the justice of the [pending criminal] case,' [may] indicate that an even greater showing must be made to overcome the claim of privilege. [*Nixon*] may eventually be construed as dealing only with the scope of presidential privilege when the President appears to have a conflict of interest, hence posing no threat to privileges in a more traditional setting."

Of what relevance are the "constitutional dimensions" of criminal trials— such as the confrontation clause and the due process clause? Consider Akhil R. Amar, *Nixon's Shadow*, 83 Minn. L.Rev. 1405, 1408 (1999): "[In the famous *Aaron Burr Case*, relied on in *Nixon*], a criminal defendant sought to subpoena evidence to prove his innocence. [*Nixon*] turned *Burr* upside down, insisting that due process demanded that all possible evidence of the criminal defendant's guilt *must* be produced, even if both the defendants and the President preferred otherwise. [But due process] says nothing about any government right or duty to prosecute every possible defendant using every possible scrap of evidence." What about "the primary constitutional duty of the Judicial Branch to do justice in criminal prosecutions [under Art III]"? Consider Neil Kinkopf, *Executive Privilege: The Clinton Administration in the Courts*, 8 Wm. & Mary Bill Rts. J. 631, 642 (2000): "Article III does not create a criminal justice system [or] define criminal law. Nothing in Article III required prosecution of the Watergate defendants."

(b) May the lesser protection for the executive privilege in *Nixon* have resulted from the high public interest in making evidence available in a case involving serious criminal charges against high government officials, in which the indictment named the President himself as unindicted co-conspirator? Consider Michael S. Paulsen, *Nixon Now: The Courts and the Presidency After Twenty-five Years*, 83 Minn.L.Rev. 1337, 1381 (1999): "[J]ust as with the attorney-client privilege, [executive privilege should] yield in the face of a sufficient showing of probability that the communication was in furtherance of a crime or fraud, and not for the legitimate purpose of providing or obtaining advice on confidential matters not implicating illegal conduct."

(c) Should the need for relevant evidence in a civil proceeding outweigh the interests underlying the "presumptive executive privilege"? Should the answer depend on whether the government is plaintiff or defendant in the civil case?

4. *After Nixon*. "The post-Watergate period has witnessed a breakdown in the proper exercise of executive privilege. [P]residents either have avoided uttering the words 'executive privilege' and have protected secrecy through other

sources of authority (Ford, Carter, Bush), or they have tried to restore executive privilege and failed (Reagan, Clinton)." Mark J. Rozell, *Restoring Balance to the Debate Over Executive Privilege,* 8 Wm. & Mary Bill Rts. J. 541, 565–66 (2000).

5. *Executive privilege in Congress.* (a) Despite frequent assertion of executive privilege to deny information to Congress, beginning with President Washington's refusal to turn over treaty negotiating records to the House of Representatives, the Court has never adjudicated the issue. Though some commentators have advocated that the Court undertake to resolve such issues,[d] others have counseled restraint. See, e.g. Archibald Cox, *Executive Privilege,* 122 U.Pa.L.Rev. 1383, 1425–32 (1974): "Courts are accustomed to weighing the need for specific pieces of evidence in a judicial proceeding against the public interest in preserving the confidentiality of particular relationships, but they have no experience in weighing the legislative needs of Congress against other public interests. [I] would be content to see the Judicial Branch [leave] questions of executive privilege vis-à-vis Congress to the ebb and flow of political power."

(b) Should any privilege attaching to communications with the President also shield communications among lower executive branch officials? See *In re Sealed Case,* 121 F.3d 729 (D.C.Cir.1997) (yes).

6. *Congressionally-mandated control over a former President's papers.* NIXON v. ADMINISTRATOR OF GENERAL SERVICES, 433 U.S. 425, 97 S.Ct. 2777, 53 L.Ed.2d 867 (1977), per BRENNAN, J., rejected a claim of presidential privilege in upholding the "facial validity" of the Presidential Recordings and Materials Preservation Act. The Act, passed after President Nixon's resignation and pardon by President Ford, required the Administrator to take "possession and control" of Nixon's presidential materials, to screen them and return those that were private and not of "general historical interest," and to promulgate regulations to protect the remaining materials from loss and to govern eventual access to them:

"[A]dequate justifications are shown for this limited intrusion into executive confidentiality comparable to those held to justify the in camera inspection [in *Nixon I.*] Congress acted to establish regular procedures [to] preserve the materials for legitimate historical and governmental purposes. [Other] substantial public interests [were] the desire to restore public confidence in our political processes by preserving the materials as a source for facilitating a full airing of the events leading to appellant's resignation, and Congress' need to understand how those political processes had in fact operated in order to gauge the necessity for remedial legislation. [And], of course, the Congress repeatedly referred to the importance of the materials to the Judiciary in the event that they shed light upon issues in civil or criminal litigation, a social interest that cannot be doubted."[e]

BURGER, C.J., dissented, noting that all prior Presidents were allowed "to provide unilaterally for disposition of [their] workpapers. [No] one has suggested that Congress will find its own 'core' functioning impaired by lack of the impounded papers, as we expressly found the judicial function would be impaired by lack of the material subpoenaed in *Nixon I.*"[f]

---

d. See Norman Dorsen & John H.F. Shattuck, *Executive Privilege, The Congress and the Courts,* 35 Ohio St.L.J. 1, 23, 40 (1974); Berger, fn. b supra, at 340–41.

e. White, Blackmun, Powell, and Stevens, JJ., each concurred separately.

f. Rehnquist, J., dissenting, "fully subscribe[d] to most of what is said respecting the separation of powers" in the Burger dissent.

After his departure from office, President Nixon was sued by Fitzgerald, who claimed that Nixon and various White House aides had caused him to be fired from his federal job (for engaging in "whistle-blowing") and thereby violated his statutory and constitutional rights. NIXON v. FITZGERALD, 457 U.S. 731, 102 S.Ct. 2690, 73 L.Ed.2d 349 (1982), per POWELL, J., affirmed summary dismissal of the action against Nixon: A President is entitled to *absolute immunity* from "damages liability predicated on his official acts."[27] This immunity is "a functionally mandated incident of the President's unique office, rooted in the constitutional tradition of the separation of powers and supported by our [history].

"Because of the singular importance of the President's duties, diversion of his energies by concern with private lawsuits would raise unique risks to the effective functioning of government. As is the case with prosecutors and judges—for whom absolute immunity now is established—a President must concern himself with matters likely to 'arouse the most intense feelings.' Yet [it] is in precisely such cases that there exists the greatest public interest in providing an official 'the maximum ability to deal fearlessly and impartially with' the duties of his office. This concern is compelling where the officeholder must make the most sensitive and far-reaching decisions entrusted to any official under our constitutional system.

"[Frequently] our decisions have held that an official's absolute immunity should extend only to acts in performance of particular functions of his office. [See *Butz v. Economou,* 438 U.S. 478, 98 S.Ct. 2894, 57 L.Ed.2d 895 (1978). But in] view of the special nature of the President's constitutional office and functions, we think it appropriate to recognize absolute Presidential immunity from damages liability for acts within the 'outer perimeter' of his official [responsibility].

"A rule of absolute immunity for the President will not leave the Nation without sufficient protection against misconduct on the part of the chief executive. There remains the constitutional remedy of impeachment. In addition, there are formal and informal checks on Presidential action that do not apply with equal force to other executive officials. The President is subjected to constant scrutiny by the press. Vigilant oversight by Congress also may serve to deter Presidential abuses of office, as well as to make credible the threat of impeachment. Other incentives to avoid misconduct may include a desire to earn re-election, the need to maintain prestige as an element of Presidential influence, and a President's traditional concern for his historical stature."

WHITE, J., joined by Brennan, Marshall and Blackmun, JJ., dissented: "Attaching absolute immunity to the office of the President, rather than to particular activities that the President might perform, places the President above the law. [The] scope of immunity is determined by function, not office. The wholesale claim that the President is entitled to absolute immunity in all of his actions stands on no firmer ground than did the claim that all presidential communications are entitled to an absolute privilege, which was rejected in favor of a functional analysis, by a unanimous Court in *Nixon I.* Therefore, whatever may be true of the necessity of such a broad immunity in certain areas of executive responsibility,[30] the only question that must be answered here is whether the dismissal of

---

27. [Our] holding today need only be that the President is absolutely immune from civil damages liability for his official acts in the absence of explicit affirmative action by Congress. We decide only this constitutional issue, which is necessary to disposition of the case before us.

30. I will not speculate on the presidential functions which may require absolute immunity, but a clear example would be instances in which the President participates in prosecutorial decisions.

employees falls within a constitutionally assigned executive function, the performance of which would be substantially impaired by the possibility of a private action for damages. I believe it does not."[a]

Notes and Questions

1. *Constitutional foundation.* Art. I, § 6, cl. 1, expressly confers a limited immunity on members of Congress by providing that "for any Speech or Debate in either House, they shall not be questioned in any other Place."[b] Should the absence of any comparable immunity in Art. II imply a deliberate denial?

2. *Types of immunity.* (a) Generally, immunity doctrine recognizes two types of immunity from suits for damages: (i) absolute immunity, which establishes that an official cannot be sued even for egregious or intentional constitutional violations, and (ii) "qualified" or "good faith" immunity, which permits an official to be liable only for violations of "clearly established" rights of which a reasonable person would have known. See *Harlow v. Fitzgerald*, infra. Qualified immunity is the norm; absolute immunity is the exception.

(b) Aside from the President, the prevailing doctrine generally establishes that the type of immunity to which an official is entitled depends on the *function* performed when the allegedly unlawful conduct occurred. Within this framework, the judicial, legislative, and prosecutorial functions have been held protected by absolute immunity. But a judge, for example, enjoys only qualified immunity in a suit predicated on the performance of a non-judicial function such as hiring or firing a court employee.[c] Correspondingly, an executive branch employee may claim absolute immunity from suits based on quasi-judicial acts (such as imposing administrative sanctions for violations of a federal regulation).[d]

3. *Immunity and the rule of law.* If it is conceded that many officials can violate constitutional rights without being liable for damages, and that the President should be entitled to at least a qualified immunity from suit, what does the dissent mean by its charge in *Fitzgerald* that the Court has elevated the President "above the law"? How does immunity, for the President and other officials, relate to the famous dictum of *Marbury v. Madison* that for every right the laws of the United States must supply a remedy? See Richard H. Fallon, Jr. & Daniel J. Meltzer, *New Law, Non–Retroactivity, and Constitutional Remedies*, 104 Harv.L.Rev. 1731, 1777–97 (1991)(arguing that individually effective remediation in every case is a constitutional aspiration, not a promise, which must sometimes yield to other values, but that the Constitution minimally requires an adequate structure of remedies—including injunctions and habeas corpus—to keep the government "generally within the bounds of law").

4. *Suits for injunctions.* The immunity doctrines governing suits for damages generally do not apply in suits for injunctions or other specific relief. Under what circumstances could a court enjoin the President? *Mississippi v. Johnson*, 71

---

a. Blackmun, J., joined by Brennan and Marshall, JJ., also dissented.

For commentary, see Stephen L. Carter, *The Political Aspects of Judicial Power: Some Notes on the Presidential Immunity Decision*, 131 U.Pa.L.Rev. 1341 (1983).

b. Decisions have limited the immunity to suits for damages predicated on the performance of expressly *legislative* functions. See, e.g., *Hutchinson v. Proxmire*, 443 U.S. 111, 99

S.Ct. 2675, 61 L.Ed.2d 411 (1979). For critical commentary, see Senator Sam J. Ervin, Jr., *The Gravel and Brewster Cases: An Assault on Congressional Independence*, 59 Va.L.Rev. 175 (1973); Note, 93 Harv.L.Rev. 161 (1979).

c. See *Forrester v. White*, 484 U.S. 219, 108 S.Ct. 538, 98 L.Ed.2d 555 (1988).

d. See *Butz v. Economou*.

U.S. (4 Wall.) 475, 499, 18 L.Ed. 437, 441 (1867), held that it could not enjoin the President from enforcing a law—an act that it classified as "purely executive and political."[e] Compare *Youngstown*, upholding an injunction technically directed at the Secretary of Commerce but in a case in which the Secretary was implementing a presidential order.[f]

5. *Congress and presidential immunity.* Could Congress eliminate the presidential immunity recognized in *Fitzgerald*? See fn. 27 of the Court's opinion. How, if the immunity is constitutionally based, could it be overcome by a mere statute? Is this a case of the kind contemplated by Jackson, J.'s opinion in *Youngstown*, in which presidential power may ebb and flow with congressional action?

6. *President's prior acts.* (a) In CLINTON v. JONES, 520 U.S. 681, 117 S.Ct. 1636, 137 L.Ed.2d 945 (1997), a former Arkansas state employee, filed a federal civil suit against President Clinton, seeking damages for " 'abhorrent' sexual advances that she vehemently rejected," allegedly made while he was governor of Arkansas. The Court, per STEVENS, J., unanimously rejected Clinton's effort to have the suit dismissed without prejudice, and the statute of limitations tolled, until the expiration of his term:

"Petitioner's strongest argument [relies] on separation of powers principles. [He] contends that this particular case—as well as the potential additional litigation that [it] may spawn—may impose an unacceptable burden on the President's time and energy, and thereby impair the effective performance of his office. [But this] predictive judgment finds little support in either history or the relatively narrow compass of the issues raised in this particular case. [In] the more than 200 year history of the Republic, only three sitting Presidents have been subjected to suits for their private actions. [It therefore] seems unlikely that a deluge of such litigation will ever engulf the Presidency. As for the case at hand, if properly managed by the District Court, it appears to us highly unlikely to occupy any substantial amount of petitioner's time.

"[Of] greater significance, petitioner errs by presuming that interactions between the Judicial Branch and the Executive, even quite burdensome interactions, necessarily rise to the level of constitutionally forbidden impairment of the Executive's ability to perform its constitutionally mandated functions. [We] have long held that when the President takes official action, the Court has the authority to determine whether he has acted within the law. [E.g., *Youngstown*.] [If] the Judiciary may severely burden the Executive Branch by reviewing the legality of the President's official conduct, and if it may direct appropriate process to the President himself [e.g., *Nixon*], it must follow that the federal courts have power to determine the legality of his unofficial conduct" [including that occurring before he became President.]

The Court went on to consider whether "a stay of either trial or discovery might be justified [in the discretion of the District Court] by considerations that do not require the recognition of any constitutional immunity. The District Court has broad discretion to stay proceedings as an incident to its power to control its own docket [and] potential burdens on the President [are] appropriate matters for the District Court to evaluate in its management of the case. The high respect that is owed to the Office of the Chief Executive [is] a matter that should inform the conduct of the entire proceeding, including the timing and scope of discovery."

e. See also *Franklin v. Massachusetts*, 505 U.S. 788, 802–03, 112 S.Ct. 2767, 2776–77, 120 L.Ed.2d 636, 651–52 (1992).

f. See also Laura K. Ray, *From Prerogative to Accountability: The Amenability of the President to Suit*, 80 Ky.L.Rev. 739 (1992).

Nonetheless, "the proponent of a stay bears the burden of establishing its need." And so far there was "nothing in the record to enable a judge to assess the potential harm that may ensue from scheduling the trial promptly after discovery is concluded."

BREYER, J., concurred in the judgment only, agreeing "that the Constitution does not automatically grant the President an immunity from civil lawsuits based upon his private conduct." But "once the President sets forth and explains a conflict between judicial proceeding and public duties, [the] Constitution permits a judge to schedule a trial in an ordinary civil damages action [only] within the constraints of a constitutional principle [that] forbids a federal judge in such a case to interfere with the President's discharge of his public duties." Breyer, J., was less "sanguine" than the majority that permitting suits against sitting Presidents would not lead to a proliferation of such actions. He therefore thought that "ordinary case-management principles are unlikely to prove sufficient" and would make clear that the Constitution does "not grant a single judge more than a very limited power to second guess a President's reasonable determination (announced in open court) of his scheduling needs."

(b) *Clinton's reasoning.* Is *Clinton* consistent with *Fitzgerald*? See Akhil R. Amar & Neal K. Katyal, *Executive Privileges and Immunities: the Nixon and Clinton Cases*, 108 Harv.L.Rev. 701 (1994)(arguing that constitutional history and structure more strongly support a suspension of damage actions against the incumbent President than they do the absolute immunity established in *Fitzgerald*). Does *Clinton* apply to a *state* civil damages suit? Or are such suits more vulnerable to constitutional challenge?

Does *Clinton* also cover a federal *criminal* prosecution against the President? At least for "unofficial conduct"? Consider Paulsen, supra at 1372–73: "[T]hat the President may be impeached for commission of criminal offenses does not mean he might not first be tried in the courts for such offenses (as has happened with some federal judges Congress has impeached). And if the President *were* immune from prosecution on this score, that would be in tension with *Clinton* [since] a serious civil wrong could, in the judgment of Congress, constitute an impeachable offense—imagine for example a President who engaged in twelve proven instances of non-criminal quid pro quo sexual harassment with executive branch employees. [If] anything, the judicial system's interest in enforcement of the criminal law would appear to be higher." Compare Tribe 3d ed., at 754–55: "Although the text of the Constitution provides no unambiguous guidance, [b]ecause the Constitution charges one unique official—the President—with the duty to 'take Care that the Laws be faithfully executed,' neither the federal judicial branch nor a state court should be permitted to imprison a sitting President and thereby to threaten the effective execution of the laws."

7. *Presidential aides.* In a companion case to *Nixon v. Fitzgerald*, HARLOW v. FITZGERALD, 457 U.S. 800, 102 S.Ct. 2727, 73 L.Ed.2d 396 (1982), per POWELL, J., rejected a claim that high presidential aides are derivatively entitled to absolute presidential immunity: "For executive officials in general, [our] cases make plain that qualified immunity represents the norm." *Butz* had held that "members of the Cabinet ordinarily enjoy only qualified immunity from suit," and it would be "untenable" to hold that all White House aides enjoy absolute immunity when cabinet members do not," although "aides entrusted with discretionary authority in such sensitive areas as national security or foreign policy"

might require absolute immunity to "protect the unhesitating performance of functions vital to the national interest."[g]

The Court then noted that "qualified immunity" had not always sufficed to permit the early dismissal of frivolous suits, and it concluded that the standard should be reformulated to serve that end: "[B]are allegations of malice"—which, if proved, defeated qualified immunity under the former standard—"should not suffice to subject government officials to either the costs of trial or to the burdens of broad-reaching discovery. We therefore hold that governmental officials performing discretionary functions, generally are shielded from liability for civil damages insofar as their conduct does not violate clearly established statutory or constitutional rights of which a reasonable person would have known." Where the pleadings do not allege a violation of clearly established rights, discovery should not be allowed, and the suit should be dismissed.[h]

BURGER, C.J., dissenting, was "at a loss" to reconcile the Court's decision with the derivative extension of absolute congressional immunity under the Speech and Debate Clause to congressional aides in *Gravel v. United States*, 408 U.S. 606, 92 S.Ct. 2614, 33 L.Ed.2d 583 (1972).

SECTION 5. IMPEACHMENT OF THE PRESIDENT

In 1998, for the second time in our history, the House of Representatives impeached the President who was then tried by the Senate. (In both cases— Andrew Johnson in 1868 and William Clinton in 1999—the Senate voted to acquit.) Because of the Courts' ruling in 1993 (Ch. 1, Sec. 2) that matters respecting congressional impeachments present nonjusticiable political questions, there are no Supreme Court opinions that address any of the important constitutional questions that may arise. The following notes consider some of these:

1. *Definition of impeachable offense.* Art. II, § 4 provides that "all Civil Officers" may be impeached for "Treason, Bribery, or other high Crimes and Misdemeanors."

(a) *Crimes only?* It is generally agreed that an impeachable offense need not be a statutory crime. Consider Frank O. Bowman III & Stephen L. Sepinuck, *"High Crimes & Misdemeanors": Defining the Constitutional Limits on Presidential Impeachment*, 72 So.Calif.L.Rev. 1517, 1526 (1999): "[A] President would certainly be subject to impeachment for refusing to organize the defense of the country against foreign invasion, or refusing to cooperate with military officers charged with command and control of the nuclear arsenal, or firing all cabinet officers and refusing to name replacements. Likewise, it is inconceivable that Congress could not remove a President who drank himself into insensibility by lunchtime on a daily basis." Further, President Johnson was impeached for the noncriminal act of removing the Secretary of War without the Senate consent that was required by statute. President Richard Nixon was impeached for misusing federal agencies to discredit his political opponents and for refusing to comply with congressional demands for information; neither alleged misconduct was criminal. (Nixon resigned before a Senate trial of the charges.) For discussion of

g. But cf. *Mitchell v. Forsyth*, 472 U.S. 511, 105 S.Ct. 2806, 86 L.Ed.2d 411 (1985)(rejecting a claim of absolute immunity by the Attorney General in connection with the approval of a wiretap for purposes of protecting national security).

h. Brennan, J., joined by Marshall and Blackmun, JJ., who joined the Court's opinion, also filed a separate concurrence, as did Rehnquist, J.

"two centuries of practice" involving presidential impeachments, see Cass R. Sunstein, *Impeaching the President*, 147 U.Pa.L.Rev. 279, 294–300 (1998).

(b) *All crimes*? Should *every* criminal offense be impeachable? Consider Jonathan Turley, *Congress As Grand Jury: The Role of the House of Representatives in the Impeachment of an American President*, 67 Geo.Wash.L.Rev. 735, 756, 760 (1999): "Labeling some criminal acts as 'private' [creates] an obvious anomaly in retaining a President under his oath to fully and faithfully enforce federal laws, despite a presumption that he has violated those same laws in office. [C]riminal conduct by a President [should] create a presumption of submission to the Senate." Compare Michael J. Gerhardt, *The Lessons of Impeachment History*, 67 Geo.Wash.L.Rev. 603 (1999): "[The words "other high Crimes and Misdemeanors'] constitute technical terms of art that refer to political crimes [which] the Framers considered [to] consist of 'great' and 'dangerous' offenses committed by certain federal officials. Oftentimes, these offenses were characterized further as serious abuses of official power or serious breaches of the public trust." Accord, Jack Rakove, *Statement on the Background and History of Impeachment*, 67 Geo.Wash.L.Rev. 682, 689 (1999) ("an expansive reading of 'other high Crimes and Misdemeanors' simply cannot be squared with the Framers' desire to insulate the presidency as much as possible from the danger of domination by the legislature"). See also Charles L. Black, Jr., *Impeachment: A Handbook* 27–46 (1974); Michael J. Gerhardt, *The Federal Impeachment Process* 104–05 (1996). Should this exclude "an extremely heinous 'private' crime, such as murder or rape"? See Cass R. Sunstein, *Impeachment and Stability*, 67 Geo.Wash.L.Rev. 699, 709 (1999). Or other "monstrous crimes" such as "child molestation"? See Arthur M. Schlesinger, *Reflections on Impeachment*, 67 Geo.Wash.L.Rev. 693, 695 (1999). How about perjury in a criminal prosecution? In a civil case? Of what significance is it that "the false statement involves conduct that by itself raises serious questions about abuse of office"? Sunstein, note (a) supra, at 308. May a *bribery* occur in a context that does not "raise serious questions about abuse of office"? For the view that perjury is *not* impeachable, see Monroe H. Freedman, *Perjury as a Ground for Impeachment—A Textual and Contextual Analysis*, 28 Hofstra L. Rev. 343 (1999). For the view that it *is*, see Gary L. McDowell, *"High Crimes and Misdemeanors": Recovering the Intentions of the Founders*, 67 Geo.Wash.L.Rev. 626, 646 (1999) ("conclusion seems inescapable" based on "review of the historical record."). See also John O. McGinnis, *Impeachment: The Structural Understanding*, 67 Geo.Wash.L.Rev. 650, 654–55 (1999): "[L]abeling murder 'heinous' and describing perjury or obstruction of justice as 'not heinous' [is] simply a matter of personal judgment. Moreover, it would cause lasting damage to our system of republican government for the House of Representatives to accept a *legal* definition of 'high Crimes and Misdemeanors' [that] tolerates any and all 'private' tax evasion, 'private' perjury, and 'private' obstruction of justice from officials who then would continue to have the power to throw their own citizens into prison for the very same offenses." Accord, Stephen B. Presser, *Would George Washington Have Wanted Bill Clinton Impeached?* 67 Geo.Wash.L.Rev. 666 (1999).

Compare Jonathan Turley, *Reflections on Murder, Misdemeanors, and Madison*, 28 Hofstra L. Rev. 439, 442 (1999): "[T]he most fundamental question of any impeachment is not an abuse of power but the lack of capacity of a President to lead. This is why certain crimes seem to invite impeachment. [It] is not that murder is unique as a crime, but that it is the most obvious example of an act that robs a President of legitimacy to govern." Contrast Tribe 3d ed., at 172–73: Given "the Framers familiarity with [the] long history in English impeachments [of the phrase "high Crimes and Misdemeanors," the discussions] of the Constitutional Convention and the ratification debates therefore strongly reinforce what the Constitution's text suggests—namely, that a civil officer may be impeached only for serious subversions of the government or for grave abuses of power. * * * Impeachment is not a mechanism for addressing generalized concerns of presidential 'legitimacy'; concerns that an executive leader has lost such legitimacy may topple a prime minister in a parliamentary government, but they do not constitute 'high Crimes and Misdemeanors' under our Constitution, where the legislature is merely a coordinate, not a superior, branch of government."

(c) *Differing standards.* Should the definition of an impeachable offense be the same for presidents as for judges? Consider Tribe 3d ed., at 168–69: "There [are] categories of misconduct that one might plausibly argue are *functionally* and *operationally* incompatible with carrying out a *particular* official role. [For] example, it would seem that a person guilty of perjury—on *any* subject, however personal—cannot credibly function for life as a judge, administering oaths to trial witnesses and deciding [who] is telling the truth and who is lying. But it is far from clear that a president who is thought to have committed perjury on income tax returns filed with the IRS, or in the judicial investigation of his sexual conduct, is similarly disabled [to] 'take Care that the Laws be faithfully executed.'

"[I]mpeachable conduct for presidents should therefore be limited to those offenses for which, given the vast power of the presidency, the limited four year term is 'not a sufficient security.' With no analogous safeguard for the conduct of federal judges, the same standard for impeachable offenses [may] well make a judge—whose potential for harming the nation in the future is virtually unlimited due to his life tenure—removable for conduct that would not warrant removal of a president, particularly since Senate removal of a judge entails reversing the Senate's own action in confirming the judge whereas Senate removal of a president entails reversing an action of the entire national electorate." See also Akhil R. Amar, *On Impeaching Presidents*, 28 Hofstra L. Rev. 291, 303–06 (1999).

2. *Roles of House and Senate.* Should the House vote to impeach if it doubts that the Senate will convict? Consider Turley, 67 Geo.Wash.L.Rev. at 780–82: "Academics have stated that such an impeachment would be as improper as a prosecutor indicting with the expectation that he could never secure a conviction. [But if] deterrence is achieved primarily through detection of presidential crimes, [when] credible allegations of impeachable offenses exist, the House performs a vital role in articulating and presenting those allegations for resolution in the Senate. [T]he House should not confuse [its] institutional role with that of the Senate." Should the House exercise something akin to "prosecutor's discretion" in determining whether to impeach? Consider Turley, id. at 787: "To argue in the House for nullification of an incumbent President's crimes is much like arguing for nullification of criminal acts before a grand jury. It would be outrageous for a grand jury to nullify any indictment of an individual for alleged crimes due to his popularity or the unpopularity of his accuser. It is the function of a trial jury to weigh the evidence." If the House votes to impeach, does Art. I, § 3, cl.6 require the Senate to conduct a full trial. Or may it grant a motion to dismiss? See Michael J. Klarman, *Constitutional Fetishism and the Clinton Impeachment Debate*, 85 Va.L.Rev. 631, 635–36 (1999).

3. *Sanctions.* Do Art. II, § 4 and Art.I, § 3, cl.7 require that the President be removed from office if convicted by the Senate? Or may a lesser sanction—such as censure, or a finding of fact—be employed? Does this affect the question of how an impeachable offense should be defined? See generally Akhil R. Amar & Stuart

Taylor, Jr., *On Impeaching Presidents: A Constitutional Conversation*, 28 Hofstra L.Rev. 317 (1999). May both (or either) Houses of Congress censure the President even if he is not impeached or convicted? See Michael J. Gerhardt, *The Historical and Constitutional Significance of the Impeachment and Trial of President Clinton*, 28 Hofstra L.Rev. 349, 377–78 (1999). Whether or not the President is impeached and convicted, may Congress vote to "exact money from the President, whether such an exaction is characterized as the imposition of a fine, the product of a plea bargain or the repayment of costs that Congress believes he has imposed on the government"? Christopher L. Eisgruber & Lawrence G. Sager, *Impeachment and Constitutional Structure*, 5 Widener L. Symp. J. 249, 253 (2000).

Chapter 4

STATE POWER TO REGULATE

INTRODUCTION

As discussed in Ch. 2, the commerce clause is principally a grant of legislative power to Congress. When the Constitution gave Congress the power to regulate commerce, it did not expressly negate state power.[a] From the beginning, however, it has been assumed that the grant of authority to Congress necessarily implies a withdrawal of at least some regulatory power from the states. This chapter explores the impact of national legislative authority on state power to regulate. The focus is on the commerce clause, though similar problems arise under other grants of federal authority.

When Congress enacts valid legislation under the commerce clause, there is no doubt that Congress can preclude, displace, or "preempt" state law. CROSBY v. NATIONAL FOREIGN TRADE COUNCIL, 530 U.S. 363, 363, 120 S.Ct. 2288, 2293–94, 147 L.Ed.2d 352, 361 (2000), summarized the relevant principles as follows: "A fundamental principle of the Constitution is that Congress has the power to preempt state law. Art. VI, cl. 2; *Gibbons v. Ogden* [which appears immediately below]. Even without an express provision for preemption, we have found that state law must yield to a congressional Act in at least two circumstances. When Congress intends federal law to 'occupy the field,' [all] state law in that area is preempted. And even if Congress has not occupied the field, state law is naturally preempted to the extent of any conflict with a federal statute. We will find preemption where it is impossible for a private party to comply with both state and federal law, and where 'under the circumstances of [a] particular case, [the challenged state law] stands as an obstacle to the accomplishment and execution of the full purposes and objectives of Congress.' What is a sufficient obstacle is a matter of judgment, to be informed by examining the federal statute as a whole and identifying its purposes and intended effects."

The preemption of state law by federal legislation is an important topic, but the basic concept of preemption is taken for granted, rather than studied, in the materials that follow.[b] Once the principle is accepted, preemption questions essentially involve the interpretation of federal statutes, not the Constitution, and are better addressed in a course on statutory interpretation.

---

a. Except for the special, express limits on tonnage duties and duties on imports and exports. Art. I, § 10.

b. For a more extensive introduction, see Tribe 3d ed., at 1172–1220.

Accepting that valid federal legislation will displace (or "preempt") any incompatible state law, this chapter considers issues that arise in contexts where Congress' power is unexercised or "dormant"—where Congress has the power to legislate, but has not done so. By the middle of the nineteenth century, the Court had determined that when Congress' power is "dormant," the states retain significant concurrent regulatory powers. But the Court has struggled continuously to define the precise standards (if any) by which to assess the legitimacy of state regulation in the absence of preemptive federal legislation.

The main elements of current doctrine are relatively easy to summarize and can usefully be stated at the outset. Under the most frequently articulated standard, state regulations that purposely or facially discriminate against interstate commerce—such as restrictions on the sale of goods imported from other states—are invalid unless supported by an extraordinary justification. WYOMING v. OKLAHOMA, 502 U.S. 437, 454–55, 112 S.Ct. 789, 800, 117 L.Ed.2d 1, 22 (1992), formulated this aspect of the doctrine as follows: " '[The] "negative" aspect of the Commerce Clause prohibits economic protectionism—that is, regulatory measures designed to benefit in-state economic interests by burdening out-of-state competitors.' When a state statute clearly discriminates against interstate commerce, it will be struck down unless the discrimination is demonstrably justified by a valid factor unrelated to economic protectionism. Indeed, when the state statute amounts to simple economic protectionism, a 'virtually per se rule of invalidity' has applied."

By contrast, when a state regulation only "incidentally" (rather than facially or purposefully) restricts the flow of interstate commerce—for example, by regulating containers in which an item of commerce can be marketed, regardless of where it was produced—the most frequently invoked standard of review was first explicitly stated in PIKE v. BRUCE CHURCH, INC., 397 U.S. 137, 90 S.Ct. 844, 25 L.Ed.2d 174 (1970), considered Sec. 2, II infra: "Where [a state statute] regulates evenhandedly to effectuate a legitimate local public interest, and its effects on interstate commerce are only incidental, it will be upheld unless the burden imposed on such commerce is clearly excessive in relation to the putative local benefits. If a legitimate local purpose is found, then the question [whether the regulation should be invalidated] becomes one of degree. And the extent of the burden that will be tolerated [will] depend on the nature of the local interest involved, and on whether it could be promoted as well with a lesser impact on interstate activities." *—The Balance*

As you study the materials that follow, consider (i) how the current doctrinal structure emerged, (ii) the extent to which the articulated standards actually guide judicial decisions, and (iii) whether prevailing doctrines deserve to endure.

SECTION 1. STATE REGULATION WHEN CONGRESS' POWER IS "DORMANT": HISTORY AND FUNDAMENTAL ISSUES

I. EARLY VIEWS OF THE IMPLICATIONS OF FEDERAL AUTHORITY FOR STATE POWER

In GIBBONS v. OGDEN 22 U.S. (9 Wheat.) 1, 6 L.Ed. 23 (1824), Ch. 2, Sec. 2, MARSHALL, C.J., discussed but did not decide whether the grant of commerce power to Congress impliedly excluded all state regulation of interstate and foreign commerce: "In support of [the argument for concurrent power] it is said, that [the *Issue

states] possessed it as an inseparable attribute of sovereignty, before the formation of the constitution, and still retain it, except so far as they have surrendered
it by that instrument; that this principle results from the nature of the government, and is secured by the tenth amendment; that an affirmative grant of power
is not exclusive, unless in its own nature it be such that the continued exercise of
it by the former possessor is inconsistent with the grant, and that this is not of
that description.

"The appellant [contends], that full power to regulate a particular subject,
implies the whole power, and leaves no residuum; that a grant of the whole is
incompatible with the existence of a right in another to any part of it.

"[The] power of taxation [is] capable of residing in, and being exercised by,
different authorities at the same time. [When], then, each government exercises
the power of taxation, neither is exercising the power of the other. But, when a
State proceeds to regulate commerce with foreign nations, or among the several
States, it is exercising the very power that is granted to Congress, and is doing the
very thing which Congress is authorized to do. There is no analogy, then, between
the power of taxation and the power of regulating commerce.

"[The] inspection laws are said to be regulations of commerce, and are
certainly recognized in the constitution, as being passed in the exercise of a power
remaining with the States. That inspection laws may have a remote and considerable influence on commerce, will not be denied; but that a power to regulate
commerce is the source from which the right to pass them is derived, cannot be
admitted. The object of inspection laws, is to improve the quality of articles
produced by the labor of a [country]. They act upon the subject before it becomes
an article of foreign commerce, or of commerce among the States, and prepare it
for that purpose. They form a portion of that immense mass of legislation, which
embraces every thing within the territory of a State, not surrendered to the
general government: all which can be most advantageously exercised by the States
themselves. Inspection laws, quarantine laws, health laws of every description, as
well as laws for regulating the internal commerce of a State, and those which
respect turnpike roads, ferries, & c., are component parts of this mass.

"No direct general power over these objects is granted to Congress, and,
consequently, they remain subject to State legislation. [It] is obvious that the
government of the Union, in the exercise of its express powers, that, for example,
of regulating commerce with foreign nations and among the States, may use
means that may also be employed by a State, in the exercise of its acknowledged
powers; that, for example, of regulating commerce within the State. [If] a State, in
passing laws on subjects acknowledged to be within its control, and with a view to
those subjects, shall adopt a measure of the same character with one which
Congress may adopt, it does not derive its authority from the particular power
which has been granted, but from some other, which remains with the State, and
may be executed by the same means. All experience shows, that the same
measures, or measures scarcely distinguishable from each other, may flow from
distinct powers; but this does not prove that the powers themselves are [identical].

"It has been contended by the counsel for the appellant, that, as the word to
'regulate' implies in its nature, full power over the thing to be regulated, it
excludes, necessarily, the action of all others that would perform the same
operation on the same thing. That regulation is designed for the entire result,
applying to those parts which remain as they were, as well as to those which are
altered. It produces a uniform whole, which is as much disturbed and deranged by

changing what the regulating power designs to leave untouched, as that on which it has operated.

"There is great force in this argument, and the Court is not satisfied that it has been refuted."

- grant of commerce power to fed, displaces state authority

But: Police power of state might overlap commerce operations

Notes and Questions

1. *Basic questions.* Some powers of Congress are exclusive because the Constitution expressly withholds the power from states,[a] but the commerce clause includes no explicit negative. What inferences, if any, should be drawn from the absence of any express preclusion of state authority? Is it workable for the states to retain a concurrent regulatory authority? Would it be workable for the states *not* to retain a concurrent regulatory authority?

2. *The states' "police" power.* WILLSON v. BLACK–BIRD CREEK MARSH CO., 27 U.S. (2 Pet.) 245, 7 L.Ed. 412 (1829), per MARSHALL, C.J., upheld a Delaware statute authorizing a dam that obstructed a small navigable stream, impeding the passage of a sloop licensed by the federal navigation laws: "The act of assembly by which the plaintiffs were authorized to construct their dam, shows plainly that this is one of those many creeks, passing through a deep level marsh adjoining the Delaware, up which the tide flows for some distance. The value of the property on its banks must be enhanced by excluding the water from the marsh, and the health of the inhabitants probably improved. Measures calculated to produce these objects, provided they do not come into collision with the powers of the general government, are undoubtedly within those which are reserved to the states. But the measure authorized by this act stops a navigable creek, and must be supposed to abridge the rights of those who have been accustomed to use it.

"[If] Congress had passed any act which bore upon the case; any act in execution of the power to regulate commerce, the object of which was to control state legislation over those small navigable creeks into which the tide flows, and which abound throughout the lower country of the middle and southern states; we should feel not much difficulty in saying that a state law coming in conflict with such act would be void. But Congress has passed no such act. The repugnancy of the law of Delaware to the constitution is placed entirely on its repugnancy to the power to regulate commerce with foreign nations and among the several states; a power which has not been so exercised as to affect the question.

"We do not think that the act empowering the [Company] to place a dam across the creek, can, under all the circumstances of the case, be considered as repugnant to the power to regulate commerce in its dormant state, or as being in conflict with any law passed on the subject."

(a) Does "Marshall plainly impl[y] that the Delaware statute falls outside the ban of the 'dormant' commerce clause, because it is not a regulation of commerce, but of 'police' "? Felix Frankfurter, *The Commerce Clause Under Marshall, Taney and Waite* 29 (1937). Consider id. at 27: "Because the 'police power' is a response to the dynamic aspects of the society, it has eluded attempts at definition. But precisely because it is such a response, it is one of the most fertile doctrinal sources for striking an accommodation between local interests and the demands of the commerce clause."

a. E.g., Art. I, § 8 authorizes Congress to "coin money" and Art. 1, § 10 expressly denies such power to states.

(b) Shortly after Marshall, C.J.'s death, *City of New York v. Miln*, 36 U.S. (11 Pet.) 102, 9 L.Ed. 648 (1837), again avoided the exclusive-concurrent power issue by upholding a New York requirement that ships report details on incoming passengers as "not a regulation of commerce, but of police." Story, J., dissenting, contended for exclusive power in Congress, claiming this was Marshall, C.J.'s, view after an earlier argument of the same case. Thompson, J., separately concurring, would have upheld the law under both the Marshall police power theory and the concurrent commerce power theory.

(c) Would a state health law banning entry of unpasteurized milk be any less a regulation of interstate commerce than an act of Congress excluding unpasteurized milk from interstate commerce? Did the term "regulation of police," as used in *Miln*, serve a useful function? Was "[nothing] gained [by] calling [the state's power a] police power?" See *Henderson v. Mayor of the City of New York*, 92 U.S. (2 Otto) 259, 23 L.Ed. 543 (1875).[b]

3. *Exclusive or concurrent?* Although the distinction between the "commerce" and "police" powers introduced a possible basis for accommodating state regulatory authority with congressional power to regulate commerce, the Court remained divided on whether the power to regulate commerce was exclusively in Congress or shared concurrently with the states subject to federal supremacy.[c] Finally, in *Cooley*, infra, in 1851, the Court embraced the basic element of Daniel Webster's argument in *Gibbons* that some "commercial powers [are] exclusive in their nature" and others are not.

COOLEY v. BOARD OF WARDENS

53 U.S. (12 How.) 299, 13 L.Ed. 996 (1851).

JUSTICE CURTIS delivered the opinion of the Court.

[The Court upheld Pennsylvania's 1803 law that required ships using the Philadelphia port to receive a local pilot,[a] considered in the light of a 1789 Act of Congress providing that harbors and ports of the United States shall "continue to be regulated in conformity with the existing laws of the States [or] with such laws as the States [may] hereafter enact."]

If the Constitution excluded the States from making any law regulating commerce, certainly Congress cannot regrant, or in any manner reconvey to the States that power. And yet this act of 1789 gives its sanction only to laws enacted by the [States]. Entertaining these views we are brought [to the] question, whether the grant of the commercial power to Congress, did *per se* deprive the States of all power to regulate [pilots].

[When] it is said that the nature of the power requires that it should be exercised exclusively by Congress, it must be intended to refer to the subjects of that power, and to say they are of such a nature as to require exclusive legislation

---

b. *Henderson* struck down a New York requirement that, for each passenger discharged in New York, carriers pay $1.50 or provide a $300 bond to indemnify the state for relief or support for four years. It ruled that Congress had exclusive authority under the *Cooley* national uniformity test, infra.

c. E.g., the justices wrote six separate opinions in sustaining a requirement of state licenses for the sale of liquor brought from other states. *The License Cases*, 46 U.S. (5 How.)

504, 12 L.Ed. 256 (1847). Eight justices delivered separate opinions in holding invalid state taxes on alien passengers arriving from foreign ports. *The Passenger Cases*, 48 U.S. (7 How.) 283, 12 L.Ed. 702 (1849).

a. Ships not doing so were required to pay half the pilotage fee for "the use of the society for the relief of distressed and decayed pilots" and their families.

by Congress. Now the power to regulate commerce, embraces a vast field, containing not only many, but exceedingly various subjects, quite unlike in their nature; some imperatively demanding a single uniform rule, operating equally on the commerce of the United States in every port; and some, like the subject now in question, as imperatively demanding that diversity, which alone can meet the local necessities of navigation.

Either absolutely to affirm, or deny that the nature of this power requires exclusive legislation by Congress, is to lose sight of the nature of the subjects of this power, and to assert concerning all of them, what is really applicable but to a part. Whatever subjects of this power are in their nature national, or admit only of one uniform system, or plan of regulation, may justly be said to be of such a nature as to require exclusive legislation by Congress. That this cannot be affirmed of laws for the regulation of pilots and pilotage is plain. The act of 1789 contains a clear and authoritative declaration by the first Congress, that the nature of this subject is such, that until Congress should find it necessary to exert its power, it should be left to the legislation of the States; that it is local and not national; that it is likely to be the best provided for, not by one system, or plan of regulations, but by as many as the legislative discretion of the several States should deem applicable to the local peculiarities of the ports within their limits.

[The] practice of the States, and of the national government, has been in conformity with this declaration, from the origin of the national government to this time; and the nature of the subject, when examined, is such as to leave no doubt of the superior fitness and propriety, not to say the absolute necessity, of different systems of regulation, drawn from local knowledge and experience, and conformed to local wants. How then can we say, that by the mere grant of power to regulate commerce, the States are deprived of all the power to legislate on this subject, because from the nature of the power the legislation of Congress must be exclusive. * * *[b]

Notes and Questions

1. *Need for uniform regulation.* (a) Is the need for uniform regulation a manageable standard for deciding which regulations of commerce are exclusively for Congress and which are within concurrent state power?

(b) Is need for uniform regulation a good reason to invalidate state legislation when Congress has not acted and "the only uniformity [the Court can] furnish is uniform lack of regulation?"[c] Should the Court weigh which is preferable—diverse state regulation or no regulation unless Congress acts?[d]

2. *Discrimination against interstate commerce.* An early application of the *Cooley* formula struck down a state statute that required only peddlers of out-of-state merchandise to secure a license and pay a tax. WELTON v. MISSOURI, 91 U.S. (1 Otto) 275, 23 L.Ed. 347 (1876), per FIELD, J.: "[T]ransportation and exchange of commodities is of national importance, and admits and requires uniformity of regulation. The very object of investing this power in the General Government was to insure this uniformity against discriminating State legislation.

---

b. Daniel, J., concurred on other grounds. McLean and Wayne, JJ., dissented.

c. Clarence G. Shenton, *Interstate Commerce During the Silence of Congress*, 23 Dick. L.Rev. 78, 118–19 (1919).

d. Cf. *Wabash, St. Louis and Pac. Ry. Co. v. Illinois,* 118 U.S. 557, 7 S.Ct. 4, 30 L.Ed. 244 (1886), which invalidated state regulation of interstate railroad rates on the need-for-uniformity ground just three months before Congress enacted the Interstate Commerce Act.

[Handwritten margin notes: "Singled out merchandise made outside on state — Unconstitutional. Core purpose of Comm'l. is to assure free channels of distribution. Free Movement no descrimination"]

[If state power to exact such a license tax were admitted,] all the evils of discriminating State legislation, favorable to the interests of one State and injurious to the interests of other states and countries, which existed previous to the adoption of the Constitution, might follow, and the experience of the last fifteen years shows would follow, from the action of some of the States. [It] is sufficient to hold now that the commercial power continues until the commodity has ceased to be the subject of discriminating legislation by reason of its foreign character. That power protects it, even after it has entered the State, from any burdens imposed by reason of its foreign origin."

Might *Welton* more wisely have avoided the sweeping scope of its first quoted sentence and limited its rationale to the need for national "uniformity against discriminating State legislation"?

3. *Weighty state interests.* In determining whether uniformity is needed, does *Cooley* leave room for a judicial determination that important state interests, unrelated to protecting state commercial concerns, outweigh the need for uniformity in interstate trade?[e] Should it? Compare two cases from the 1890s.

(a) LEISY v. HARDIN, 135 U.S. 100, 10 S.Ct. 681, 34 L.Ed. 128 (1890), held that an Iowa prohibition law violated the commerce clause when applied to an in-state sale in the original package[f] of liquor from another state. *Leisy* viewed the need for uniformity rationale as foreclosing state "power to exclude, directly or indirectly," without congressional permission, articles that "Congress recognizes as subjects of interstate commerce." A strong dissent would have given controlling weight to Iowa's social interests.

(b) Four years later, PLUMLEY v. MASSACHUSETTS, 155 U.S. 461, 15 S.Ct. 154, 39 L.Ed. 223 (1894), held that a Massachusetts law forbidding the sale of butter-colored margarine did not violate the commerce clause when applied to in-state sales of colored out-of-state margarine in the original package. The Court gave controlling weight to the state's "police power," including its power to protect its residents from deception in the sale of commodities.

(c) Can *Plumley* and *Leisy* be reconciled? Is it relevant that Congress had expressed early and strong disapproval of *Leisy* in the Wilson Act, which authorized application of state prohibition laws to liquor in the original package?

II. CONGRESSIONAL AUTHORIZATION OF STATE REGULATION

May Congress use its commerce power to authorize state regulation that would otherwise be held by the judiciary to violate the negative implications of the commerce clause?

The year after *Leisy*, WILKERSON v. RAHRER, 140 U.S. 545, 11 S.Ct. 865, 35 L.Ed. 572 (1891), per FULLER, C.J., upheld application of a state prohibition law like that involved in *Leisy* because Congress had authorized it in the Wilson Act. In the Court's view, Congress had concluded "that the common interests did not require entire freedom in the traffic in ardent spirits. [In] so doing Congress has not attempted to delegate the power to regulate commerce, or to exercise any power reserved to the States, or to grant a power not possessed by the [States].

[Handwritten margin note: "Cong May authorize State to regulate commerce"]

---

e. See Noel T. Dowling, *Interstate Commerce and State Power*, 27 Va.L.Rev. 1, 5 (1940).

f. The Court used here the "original package" concept it had developed earlier to decide when imported goods were so "mix[ed] with the common mass of property" in the state as to escape the ban on duties on imports. *Brown v. Maryland*, 25 U.S. (12 Wheat.) 419, 6 L.Ed. 678 (1827).

"[The] power to regulate is solely in the general government, and it is an essential part of that regulation to prescribe the regular means for accomplishing the introduction and incorporation of articles into and with the mass of property in the country or State. No reason is perceived why, if Congress chooses to provide that certain designated subjects of interstate commerce shall be governed by a rule which divests them of that character at an earlier period of time than would otherwise be the case, it is not within its competency to do so.

"[Congress] did not use terms of permission to the State to act, but simply removed an impediment to the enforcement of the state laws in respect to imported packages in their original condition, created by the absence of a specific utterance[a] on its part. It imparted no power to the State not then possessed, but allowed imported property to fall at once upon arrival within the local jurisdiction."

———

Do more fundamental considerations underlie *Rahrer* than whether Congress may redefine the point at which goods from other states become subject to state regulatory power? If the Court concludes that a particular state regulation is invalid because it is unduly harmful to interstate commerce, may Congress override that judgment and authorize such state regulation? By what rationale?

PRUDENTIAL INS. CO. v. BENJAMIN, 328 U.S. 408, 66 S.Ct. 1142, 90 L.Ed. 1342 (1946), per RUTLEDGE, J., reaffirmed *Rahrer* after analyzing the issue anew when it upheld Congress' power to authorize state taxes that discriminate against interstate commerce and thereby insulate such taxes from challenge under the dormant commerce clause:[b] "Prudential chiefly relies [on] the cases which from *Welton* until now have outlawed state taxes found to discriminate against interstate commerce. [Those cases] presented no question of the validity of such a tax where Congress had taken affirmative action consenting to it or purporting to give it validity.

"[In] all the variations of commerce clause theory it has never been the law that what the states may do in the regulation of commerce, Congress being silent, is the full measure of its power. Much less has this boundary been thought to confine what Congress and the states acting together may [accomplish].

"[The] cases most important for the decision in this cause [are] the ones involving situations where the silence of Congress or the dormancy of its power has been taken judicially, [as] forbidding state action, only to have Congress later disclaim the prohibition or undertake to nullify it. Not yet has this Court held such a disclaimer invalid or that state action supported by it could not stand. On the contrary, in each instance it has given effect to the congressional judgment contradicting its own previous one.

a. Earlier opinions had reasoned that when a matter required uniform regulation, the absence of federal regulation reflected Congress' intent that the matter remain unregulated. See *Leisy*. Might other inferences more reasonably be drawn from absence of federal legislation? See Thomas R. Powell, *The Still Small Voice of the Commerce Clause,* Proc. Nat'l Tax Ass'n 337, 338–339 (1938); Henry W. Bikle, *The Silence of Congress,* 41 Harv.L.Rev. 200 (1927).

b. *Prudential* upheld a South Carolina statute that imposed a tax on gross insurance premiums from South Carolina business but exempted South Carolina insurance companies. The Court ruled that Congress had authorized such taxes by the McCarran Act, which made insurance companies subject to state taxes and regulations after *South–Eastern Underwriters,* Ch. 2, Sec. 2, I, had given rise to doubts about state power over interstate insurance business.

"[The McCarran Act] was a determination by Congress that state taxes, which in its silence might be held invalid as discriminatory, do not place on interstate insurance business a burden which it is unable generally to bear or should not bear in the competition with local business. Such taxes were not uncommon among the states, and the statute clearly included South Carolina's tax now in issue.

"That judgment was one of policy and reflected long and clear experience. For, notwithstanding the long incidence of the tax and its payment by Prudential without question prior to the *South–Eastern* decision, the record of Prudential's continuous success in South Carolina over decades refutes any idea that payment of the tax handicapped it in any way tending to exclude it from competition with local business or with domestic insurance companies.

"[This] broad authority [over commerce] Congress may exercise alone [or] in conjunction with coordinated action by the states, in which case limitations imposed for the preservation of their powers become inoperative and only those designed to forbid action altogether by any power or combination of powers in our governmental system remain effective. Here both Congress and South Carolina have acted, and in complete coordination, to sustain the tax. It is therefore reinforced by the exercise of all the power of government residing in our scheme. [Congress and the states] were not forbidden to cooperate or by doing so to achieve legislative consequences, particularly in the great fields of regulating commerce and taxation, which, to some extent at least, neither could accomplish in isolated exertion."

Notes and Questions

1. *Congressionally authorized discrimination.* Might the same structural considerations that have led the Court to invalidate state discrimination when Congress' power is in its "dormant" state also support the conclusion that Congress itself may not use its commerce power in discriminatory ways? See Donald H. Regan, *The Supreme Court and State Protectionism: Making Sense of the Dormant Commerce Clause,* 84 Mich.L.Rev. 1091, 1140, 1205–06 (1986).

Should courts hesitate to construe federal statutes as authorizing discrimination? See *Wyoming v. Oklahoma,* 502 U.S. 437, 458, 112 S.Ct. 789, 802, 117 L.Ed.2d 1, 24–25 (1992)("Congress must manifest its unambiguous intent before a federal statute will be read to permit or to approve" a commerce clause violation).

2. *Other restraints on state discrimination.* Although Congress can waive impediments to state discrimination under the commerce clause, Congress cannot waive individual rights to be free from discrimination under the privileges and immunities clause of Art. IV, see Sec. 4 of this chapter, or the equal protection clause of the fourteenth amendment, see Ch. 9. The leading equal protection case, METROPOLITAN LIFE INS. CO. v. WARD, 470 U.S. 869, 105 S.Ct. 1676, 84 L.Ed.2d 751 (1985), per POWELL, J., struck down a discriminatory state tax on out-of-state insurance companies under the equal protection clause, notwithstanding the statute's immunity from attack on dormant commerce clause grounds under the McCarran Act and *Prudential Ins. Co.* The implications of *Metropolitan Life Ins.* as an equal protection precedent are somewhat uncertain; a leading commentator describes the case as an "aberration." Tribe 2d ed., at 526 n. 34. But whatever discriminations ultimately will survive equal protection challenge, *Metropolitan Life Ins.* establishes that Congress cannot authorize equal protection violations.

III. THE BASIS FOR JUDICIAL ACTION

1. *Basic questions.* Congressional power to overrule judicial decisions invalidating state legislation under the commerce clause has led to difficult questions about the judicial role in this area. Is recognition of this congressional power consistent with *Marbury v. Madison*? Does the Constitution require or even authorize the role that the Court has assumed?

2. *Consistency with Marbury.* For congressional override of the Court's commerce clause decisions to be consistent with *Marbury*, those decisions apparently must either not be "constitutional" decisions at all, or must be "constitutional" decisions of a peculiar kind.

(a) Henry P. Monaghan, *Constitutional Common Law*, 89 Harv.L.Rev. 1, 17 (1975), suggests that "the most satisfactory explanation of the [dormant or negative] commerce clause cases is that the Supreme Court is fashioning federal common law on the authority of the commerce clause. That clause embodies a national, free-trade philosophy" and is the "source of judicial lawmaking authority." But the commerce clause, although it authorizes judicial lawmaking to implement free trade values, does not uniquely require particular rules; and because commerce clause doctrine is judge-made common law, not "*Marbury*-like" constitutional interpretation, "the negative-impact cases are wholly subject to congressional revision."

Although this theory may rationalize congressional overruling of Supreme Court decisions under the commerce clause, does it adequately explain why the commerce clause—a grant of power to *Congress*—should be construed to authorize constitutional common lawmaking by the *courts*?[a]

(b) An alternative theory would portray "dormant commerce clause" doctrine as embodying constitutional "default" rules—rules mandated by considerations of constitutional text, history, and structure, but distinctly subject to override or displacement by express congressional action. See Laurence H. Tribe, *Constitutional Choices* 29–44 (1985). Can the concept of constitutional default rules be reconciled with the judicial role contemplated by *Marbury*? Are there principled grounds for determining which constitutional rules are merely default rules and which are "*Marbury*-like"?

3. *Practical considerations.* Do the political pressures on, and possibly the responsibility of, state legislators to protect and advance local concerns indicate the desirability of review by a body charged to protect truly national interests?[b] Is a judicial role in reviewing state legislation functionally necessary because Congress has "too little time and too few resources to give to give attention to 'low visibility' state programs that have protectionist purposes or effects"?[c] Are judicial

---

a. Cf. Martin H. Redish & Shane V. Nugent, *The Dormant Commerce Clause and the Constitutional Balance of Federalism*, 1987 Duke L.J. 569 (arguing that dormant commerce clause review is a constitutionally illegitimate judicial usurpation).

b. See, e.g., Tribe, 3d. ed. at 1024–29. But see, e.g., Edmund W. Kitch, *Regulation and the American Common Market, in Regulation, Federalism, and Interstate Commerce* 9 (A. Dan Tarlock ed., 1981)(arguing that the costs of judicial oversight exceed the benefits); Patrick C. McGinley, *Trashing the Constitution: Judi-*

cial Activism, the Dormant Commerce Clause, and the Federalism Mantra, 71 Or.L.Rev. 409 (1992)(arguing that dormant commerce clause review reflects a structurally unjustified intrusion on state political autonomy).

c. Dan T. Coenen, *Untangling the Market–Participant Exception to the Dormant Commerce Clause*, 88 Mich.L.Rev. 395, 418 (1989). But see Steven Breker–Cooper, *The Commerce Clause: The Case for Judicial Non–Intervention*, 69 Or.L.Rev. 895 (1990).

decisions more acceptable because they might be viewed as tentative or provisional, subject to congressional revision of future applications?[d]

If the debate is cast in functional terms, a final question must also be asked: are there judicially manageable standards for testing the validity of state legislation under the commerce clause when Congress' powers are "dormant"?

IV. THE QUEST FOR AN ADEQUATE STANDARD

1. *After Cooley.* Although the Court, since *Cooley*, has regularly reviewed state legislation for possible conflict with the negative implications of the commerce clause, uncertainty and controversy have persisted concerning the standard against which legislation should be tested. Through the nineteenth and into the twentieth century, the *Cooley* distinction between subjects that did and did not require national uniformity was consistently applied to invalidate purposefully discriminatory regulations that favored local interests, but other applications were less certain.

After the turn of the century, the Court frequently distinguished between "direct" burdens on commerce, which were impermissible, and "indirect" burdens that could be sustained.[a] But observers complained that these labels were conclusory and, what is more, that it had become "difficult, if not impossible," to tell "whether these expressions merely constituted different methods of stating the *Cooley* doctrine, or whether the Court was applying different tests."[b]

2. *Toward a balancing standard.* (a) In *Di Santo v. Pennsylvania,* 273 U.S. 34, 44, 47 S.Ct. 267, 271, 71 L.Ed. 524, 530 (1927), Stone, J., dissenting, mounted a forceful attack on the direct-indirect "formula." In its place, he suggested a balancing test, under which the validity of a state regulation would depend upon whether "the nature of the regulation, its function, the character of the business involved and the actual effect on the flow of commerce, lead to the conclusion that the regulation concerns interests peculiarly local and does not infringe the national interest in maintaining the freedom of commerce across state lines."[c] Stone, J.'s criticisms were echoed and his suggestion revived and elaborated in an influential article by Professor Noel T. Dowling, *Interstate Commerce and State Power,* 27 Va.L.Rev. 1 (1940).

(b) The Court adopted the balancing approach in *Southern Pacific Co. v. Arizona,* (1945), Sec. 2, V infra, involving a challenge to a state law prohibiting railroad trains of more than 14 passenger or 70 freight cars. In an opinion by now-Chief Justice Stone, the Court framed the judicial inquiry as turning on "the nature and extent of the burden which the state regulation of interstate trains, adopted as a safety measure, imposes on interstate commerce, and whether the relative weights of the state and national interests" justify the prohibition.

Would it be constitutionally permissible and practically desirable for Congress to vest responsibility for reviewing state legislation for compatibility with national interests in an administrative agency or agencies? Cf. Daniel A. Farber, *State Regulation and the Dormant Commerce Clause,* 3 Const.Comm. 395, 407–10 (1986).

d. Cf. Noel T. Dowling, *Interstate Commerce and State Power—Revised Version,* 47 Colum.L.Rev. 547, 558–60 (1947).

a. The Court also "used many other expressions—such as whether the state law was a 'burden,' or a 'substantial' or 'undue' burden, on commerce, [and] whether the regulation was or was not imposed 'on' interstate commerce itself." Robert L. Stern, *The Problems of Yesteryear—Commerce and Due Process,* 4 Vand.L.Rev. 446, 451–52 (1951).

b. Id.

c. Holmes and Brandeis, JJ., joined Stone, J.'s opinion.

3. *Modern formulation of the standard.* The Court articulated the prevailing modern standard, and provided its most quoted formulation, in *Pike v. Bruce Church, Inc.*, quoted in the introduction to this chapter. Under that standard, purposeful and facial discriminations against interstate commerce are virtually per se illegal, whereas "incidental" restrictions trigger judicial balancing.[d]

4. *Continuing controversy and proposed alternatives.* Despite the Court's general agreement on a verbal formula for testing state regulations under the dormant commerce clause, the area continues to be marked by lively methodological debate, especially concerning whether and how the Court should assess regulations that do not facially or purposefully discriminate against interstate commerce, but nonetheless have an incidental effect in restricting it. Scalia and Thomas, JJ., have specifically renounced the balancing approach as unmanageable and unduly legislative. See, e.g., *Bendix Autolite Corp. v. Midwesco Enterprises, Inc.*, Sec. 2, I infra; *Camps Newfound/Owatonna, Inc. v. Harrison*, Sec. 5 infra.[e]

Although there are numerous possible alternatives to an open-ended balancing of state against national interests, two types of approach have attained particular prominence.

(a) *Process-based theories.* A loosely connected family of theories attempts to build on the insight of Stone, J.'s famous footnote four in *United States v. Carolene Products*, Ch. 5, § 3 infra, supra: although courts should generally not reweigh policy judgments made by legislatures, the general presumption that legislatures should be trusted to make such judgments dissolves when affected interests are not fairly represented in a state's political processes.[f] This concern with the fairness of the states' political processes also echoes through much of the caselaw: "Because regulation unduly burdening or discriminating against interstate or foreign commerce or out-of-state enterprise has been thought to result from the inherently limited constituency to which each state or local legislature is accountable, the [Court] has viewed with suspicion any state action which imposes special or distinct burdens on out-of-state interests unrepresented in the state's political process." Tribe 3d ed., at 1052, citing *Southern Pacific*. According to process-based theories, state political judgments should be upheld under the commerce clause, without need for balancing, unless state regulatory legislation disproportionately burdens out-of-staters. In the case of a disproportionate burden on out-of-staters, courts should assess whether the desire to advantage in-state interests by shifting burdens onto or otherwise disadvantaging out-of-state interests was a substantial factor motivating the enactment of a regulation of commerce. If so, the regulation should generally be invalidated. Only (if ever) in cases of disproportionate impact on out-of-staters or out-of-state interests, but no discriminatory intent, should courts engage in an independent judicial balancing of a regulation's costs and benefits.

d. See generally Michael A. Lawrence, *Toward a More Coherent Dormant Commerce Clause: A Proposed Unitary Framework*, 21 Harv.J.L. & Pub.Pol'y 395 (1998) (distilling the Court's commerce clause pronouncements into a "unitary framework").

e. For other attacks on balancing under the commerce clause, see, e.g., Farber, supra; Regan, supra; Earl M. Maltz, *How Much Regulation Is Too Much?—An Examination of Commerce Clause Jurisprudence*, 50 Geo. Wash.L.Rev. 47 (1981).

f. Despite significant differences as to details and applications, important examples of this general approach include Farber, supra; Robert Sedler, *The Negative Commerce Clause As a Restriction on State Regulation and Taxation: An Analysis in Terms of Constitutional Structure*, 31 Wayne L.Rev. 885 (1985); Mark Tushnet, *Rethinking the Dormant Commerce Clause*, 1979 Wis.L.Rev. 125. Cf. Julian N. Eule, *Laying the Dormant Commerce Clause to Rest*, 91 Yale L.J. 425 (1982)(adopting a similar approach, but arguing that the prohibition against discrimination should be rooted in the privileges and immunities clause).

(b) *Anti-protectionist theories.* In an influential article, Professor Donald H. Regan argues that the courts should forego balancing altogether in commerce clause challenges to state restrictions on the sale and movement of goods. *The Supreme Court and State Protectionism: Making Sense of the Dormant Commerce Clause,* 84 Mich.L.Rev. 1091 (1986).[g] Regan denies that state legislatures generally behave in a suspect way when they fail to weigh the interests of outsiders equally with those of insiders (since states are supposed to try to help their citizens). According to him, the Court should largely limit itself to invalidating protective tariffs and analogous barriers to the movement of goods—the historic forms of protectionism with which the framers were concerned and the kind historically likely to provoke retaliation. In Regan's theory, the touchstone is "protectionist" motivation. The states should have political autonomy to enact such regulations as they like (regardless of incidental effects on interstate commerce) as long as they do not impose regulatory barriers that have the *purpose* of advantaging in-state economic interests at the direct expense of out-of-state competitors.

––––––

As you study Sec. 2 infra, consider whether the balancing test articulated in *Pike*: (i) is constitutionally defensible and (ii) actually describes the Court's processes of decision.

SECTION 2. CASES AND DOCTRINE

I. REGULATIONS THAT BURDEN OUT–OF–STATE SUPPLIERS SEEKING IN–STATE MARKETS: BASIC THEMES AND DISTINCTIONS

BALDWIN v. G.A.F. SEELIG, INC.

294 U.S. 511, 55 S.Ct. 497, 79 L.Ed. 1032 (1935).

JUSTICE CARDOZO delivered the opinion of the Court.

[New York regulated minimum milk prices for sales by producers to dealers, and prohibited the sale in New York of milk bought outside the state at lower prices. The Court held the prohibition invalid.]

New York has no power to project its legislation into Vermont by regulating the price to be paid in that state for milk acquired there. [It] is equally without power to prohibit the introduction within her territory of milk of wholesome quality acquired in Vermont, whether at high prices or [low]. Accepting those postulates, New York asserts her power to outlaw milk so introduced by prohibiting its sale thereafter if the price that has been paid for it to the farmers of Vermont is less than would be owing in like circumstances to farmers in New York. The importer in that view may keep his milk or drink it, but sell it he may not.

Such a power, if exerted, will set a barrier to traffic between one state and another as effective as if customs duties, equal to the price differential, had been laid upon the thing transported.

g. See also Catherine Gage O'Grady, *Targeting State Protectionism Instead of Interstate Discrimination Under the Dormant Commerce Clause,* 34 San Diego L.Rev. 571, 574–79 (1997).

[Nice] distinctions [between] direct and indirect burdens [are] irrelevant when the avowed purpose of the obstruction, as well as its necessary tendency, is to suppress or mitigate the consequences of competition between the states. [If] New York, in order to promote the economic welfare of her farmers, may guard them against competition with the cheaper prices of Vermont, the door has been opened to rivalries and reprisals that were meant to be averted by subjecting commerce between the states to the power of the nation.

The argument is pressed upon us, however, that the end to be served by the Milk Control Act is something more than the economic welfare of the farmers. [The] end to be served is the maintenance of a regular and adequate supply of pure and wholesome milk; the supply being put in jeopardy when the farmers of the state are unable to earn a living income. On that assumption we are asked to say that intervention will be upheld as a valid exercise by the state of its internal police power, though there is an incidental obstruction to commerce between one state and another. Let such an exception be admitted, and all that a state will have to do in times of stress and strain is to say that its farmers and merchants and workmen must be protected against competition from without, lest they go upon the poor relief lists or perish altogether. To give entrance to that excuse would be to invite a speedy end of our national solidarity. The Constitution was framed under the dominion of a political philosophy less parochial in range. It was framed upon the theory that the peoples of the several states must sink or swim together, and that in the long run prosperity and salvation are in union and not division.

[T]he evils springing from uncared for cattle must be remedied by measures of repression more direct and certain than the creation of a parity of prices between New York and other states. Appropriate certificates may be exacted from farmers in Vermont and elsewhere (*Mintz v. Baldwin,* 289 U.S. 346, 53 S.Ct. 611, 77 L.Ed. 1245; *Reid v. Colorado,* 187 U.S. 137, 23 S.Ct. 92, 47 L.Ed. 108); milk may be excluded if necessary safeguards have been omitted; but commerce between the states is burdened unduly when one state regulates by indirection the prices to be paid to producers in another, in the faith that augmentation of prices will lift up the level of economic welfare, and that this will stimulate the observance of sanitary requirements in the preparation of the [product.] Whatever relation there may be between earnings and sanitation is too remote and indirect to justify obstructions to the normal flow of commerce in its movement between states.

[The Court applied its ruling both to New York sales in the 40 gallon cans used to import the milk from Vermont and those in retail bottles after transfer from the cans]: The test of the "original package," which came into our law with *Brown v. Maryland*, 25 U.S. (12 Wheat.) 419, 6 L.Ed. 678 (1827), is not inflexible and final for the transactions of interstate commerce. [It] is not an ultimate principle. It is an illustration of a principle. [It] marks a convenient boundary, and one sufficiently precise save in exceptional conditions. What is ultimate is the principle that one state in its dealings with another may not place itself in a position of economic isolation. Formulas and catch-words are subordinate to this over-mastering requirement. Neither the power to tax nor the police power may be used by the state of destination with the aim and effect of establishing an economic barrier against competition with the products of another state or the labor of its residents. Restrictions so contrived are an unreasonable clog upon the mobility of commerce. They set up what is equivalent to a rampart of customs duties designed to neutralize advantages belonging to the place of origin. They are thus hostile in conception as well as burdensome in result. The form of the packages in such circumstances is immaterial, whether they are original or broken. The importer must be free from imposts framed for the very purpose of suppressing competition from without and leading inescapably to the suppression so intended. * * *

Notes and Questions

1. *Continued authority of Baldwin.* Though decided before the emergence of the open balancing process in state commerce regulation cases, *Baldwin* continues to be cited as a basic authority. See, e.g., *Philadelphia v. New Jersey* (1978), Part III infra.

2. *The rationale.* The Court's analysis in *Baldwin* includes at least four strands.

(a) The Court reasons that New York has attempted to "project its legislation into Vermont by regulating the price to be paid in that state for milk acquired there." Is this analysis sound? Would New York be projecting its legislation into Vermont if, to protect the health of its citizens, it forbade the sale in New York of milk produced by cattle (whether in New York, Vermont, or any other state) that had been fed a chemical that New York adjudged dangerous?[a]

(b) The Court suggests that the Constitution embodies a free-trade philosophy, under which "New York, in order to promote the economic welfare of her farmers, may [not] guard them against competition with the cheaper prices of Vermont." Does the Court mean to suggest that New York could take no legislative action, altering the operation of the otherwise free market, aimed distinctly at improving the competitive position of the New York dairy industry for the ultimate benefit of New York citizens?[b] Could New York provide cash subsidies to its dairy industry? For discussion, see pp. 226–31 infra.

(c) The Court analogizes the New York law to an embargo on competing milk from out of state. How close is the analogy? Is it close enough for the New York regulation, if allowed to stand, to open the door "to rivalries and reprisals that were meant to be averted by subjecting commerce between the states to the power of the nation"? Was the New York law more likely to trigger reprisal than a direct subsidy to the dairy industry?

(d) The Court says that commerce is "burdened unduly" by a regulation that ostensibly aims to ensure the observance of sanitary requirements, but does so in a way that is "remote and indirect." Is this another way of saying that the "health" justification for the law was a pretext?

DEAN MILK CO. v. MADISON
340 U.S. 349, 71 S.Ct. 295, 95 L.Ed. 329 (1951).

Justice Clark delivered the opinion of the Court.

[A Madison, Wis., ordinance prohibited sale of milk not processed at approved pasteurization plants within five miles of Madison's central square. Madison officials inspected such plants monthly. Dean Milk, based in Illinois, bought milk

---

a. On extraterritorial legislation, see Sec. 2, IV infra.

b. Cf. Richard B. Collins, *Economic Union as a Constitutional Value*, 63 N.Y.U.L.Rev. 43, 63–64 (1988), arguing that the fundamental national value is national economic union, not economic efficiency, and that some restrictions impeding the latter are not inconsistent with the former.

from Wisconsin and Illinois farms, which it pasteurized at its two Illinois plants 65 and 85 miles from Madison. Chicago public health authorities licensed and inspected these plants under the Chicago ordinance, which required U.S. Public Health Service rating standards. Both ordinances were patterned after the Public Health Service Model Ordinance, though the Court noted that "Madison contends and we assume that in some particulars its ordinance is more rigorous than Chicago's."]

[W]e agree with appellant that the ordinance imposes an undue burden on interstate commerce. [T]his regulation, like the provision invalidated in *Baldwin*, in practical effect excludes from distribution in Madison wholesale milk produced and pasteurized in Illinois. [In] thus erecting an economic barrier protecting a major local industry against competition from without the State, Madison plainly discriminates against interstate commerce.[4] This it cannot do, even in the exercise of its unquestioned power to protect the health and safety of its people, if reasonable nondiscriminatory alternatives, adequate to conserve legitimate local interests, are available. Cf. *Baldwin*. A different view, that the ordinance is valid simply because it professes to be a health measure, would mean that the Commerce Clause of itself imposes no limitations on state action other than those laid down by the Due Process Clause, save for the rare instance where a state artlessly discloses an avowed purpose to discriminate against interstate goods. Our issue then is whether the discrimination inherent in the Madison ordinance can be justified in view of the character of the local interests and the available methods of protecting them.

It appears that reasonable and adequate alternatives are available. If Madison prefers to rely upon its own officials for inspection of distant milk sources, such inspection is readily open to it without hardship for it could charge the actual and reasonable cost of such inspection to the importing producers and processors. Moreover, appellee Health Commissioner of Madison testified that as proponent of the local milk ordinance he had submitted the provisions here in controversy and an alternative proposal based on § 11 of the Model Milk Ordinance recommended by the United States Public Health Service. The model provision imposes no geographical limitation on location of milk sources and processing plants but excludes from the municipality milk not produced and pasteurized conformably to standards as high as those enforced by the receiving city, [subject to verification of ratings through the P.H.S.] The Commissioner testified that Madison consumers "would be safeguarded adequately" under either proposal and that he had expressed no preference.

[To] permit Madison to adopt a regulation not essential for the protection of local health interests and placing a discriminatory burden on interstate commerce would invite a multiplication of preferential trade areas destructive of the very purpose of the Commerce Clause. Under the circumstances here presented, the regulation must yield to the principle that "one state in its dealings with another may not place itself in a position of economic isolation." [*Baldwin*].

JUSTICE BLACK, with whom JUSTICE DOUGLAS, and JUSTICE MINTON concur, dissenting. * * *

Characterization of § 7.21 as a "discriminatory burden" on interstate commerce is merely a statement of the Court's result, which I think incorrect. [B]oth state courts below found that § 7.21 represents a good-faith attempt to safe-guard public health by making adequate sanitation inspection possible. [The] fact that

---

4. It is immaterial that Wisconsin milk from outside the Madison area is subjected to the same proscription as that moving in interstate commerce.

§ 7.21, like all health regulations, imposes some burden on trade, does not mean that it "discriminates" against interstate commerce.

[W]hile the "reasonable alternative" concept has been invoked to protect First Amendment rights, it has not heretofore been considered an appropriate weapon for striking down local health laws. [In] my view, to use this ground now elevates the right to traffic in commerce for profit above the power of the people to guard the purity of their daily diet of [milk].

From what this record shows, and from what it fails to show, I do not think that either of the alternatives suggested by the Court would assure the people of Madison as pure a supply of milk as they receive under their own ordinance. On this record I would uphold the Madison law. At the very least, however, I would not invalidate it without giving the parties a chance to present evidence and get findings on the ultimate issues the Court thinks crucial—namely, the relative merits of the Madison ordinance and the alternatives suggested by the Court today.

Notes and Questions

1. *Effect of intrastate discrimination.* Since the decision was based on "discrimination," why was it "immaterial" that the regulation also excluded *Wisconsin* milk not pasteurized in Madison? Is it an adequate response that discrimination against interstate commerce is constitutionally suspect, even if some intrastate commerce is also discriminated against?[a]

2. *Nature of discrimination.* What did "discrimination" mean, as used in *Dean Milk?* Was the Court concerned with purpose or effect?[b] What, if anything, did the availability of a less restrictive alternative suggest about Madison's *actual* purpose?

———

BREARD v. ALEXANDRIA, 341 U.S. 622, 71 S.Ct. 920, 95 L.Ed. 1233 (1951), per REED, J., upheld, over a commerce clause claim, an ordinance forbidding door-to-door soliciting of orders for the sale of merchandise, as applied to *Breard* and his crew of sales persons seeking subscriptions to out-of-state magazines.[c] The Court viewed the ordinance as protecting an important social interest in residential privacy: "Unwanted knocks on the door by day or night are a nuisance, or worse, to peace and quiet. [As] the exigencies of trade are not ordinarily expected to have a higher rating constitutionally than the tranquillity of the fireside, responsible municipal officers have sought a way to curb the annoyances while preserving complete freedom for desirable visitors to the homes." No less restrictive alternative was available. "The idea of barring classified salesmen from homes by means of notices posted by individual householders was rejected early as less practical than an ordinance regulating solicitors."

a. The Court reaffirmed the holding of *Dean Milk* that limited intrastate discrimination will not excuse otherwise impermissible discrimination against interstate commerce in *Fort Gratiot Sanitary Landfill, Inc. v. Michigan Dept. of Natural Resources,* 504 U.S. 353, 112 S.Ct. 2019, 119 L.Ed.2d 139 (1992), invalidating a Michigan law prohibiting private landfill operators from accepting solid waste originating outside the county in which their facilities operate under the rationale of *Philadelphia v. New Jersey,* Part III.

b. See generally Winkfield F. Twyman, Jr., *Beyond Purpose: Addressing State Discrimination in Interstate Commerce,* 46 S.C.L.Rev. 381 (1995).

c. The Court also denied a freedom of the press claim.

Although acknowledging that "the local retail merchant [has] not been unmindful of the competition furnished by house-to-house selling" and recognizing "the importance to publishers of our many periodicals" of house-to-house solicitation, the Court found it constitutionally adequate that the "usual methods of seeking business are left open by the ordinance." "That such methods do not produce as much business as house-to-house canvassing is, constitutionally, [immaterial.] Taxation that threatens interstate commerce with prohibition or discrimination is bad, but regulation that leaves out-of-state sellers on the same basis as local sellers cannot be invalid for that reason."

The Court was "not willing even to appraise the suggestion, unsupported in the record, that such wide use springs predominantly from the selfish influence of local merchants. When there is a reasonable basis for legislation to protect the social, as distinguished from the economic, welfare of a community, it is not for this Court because of the Commerce Clause to deny the exercise locally of the sovereign power of Louisiana."

VINSON, C.J., joined by Douglas, J., dissented: "I think it plain that a 'blanket prohibition' upon appellant's solicitation discriminates against and unduly burdens interstate commerce in favoring local retail merchants. 'Whether or not it was so intended, those are its necessary effects.' The fact that this ordinance exempts solicitation by the essentially local purveyors of farm products shows that local economic interests are relieved of the burdensome effects of the ordinance."

Notes and Questions

1.   *"Selfish" local influence.* Was it sound for the Court to ignore the possible "selfish influence of local merchants" in securing enactment of the challenged legislation? Consider the suggestion—advanced by "process-based" theories, discussed pp. 217–18 supra—that searching judicial balancing is especially necessary when state legislators and local governing bodies cannot be trusted to represent outsiders' interests or weigh them fairly.

2.   A *different standard for social interests?* Did *Breard* call for heightened judicial deference to legislative judgment in the case of regulations that protect "social, as distinguished from economic," interests?

————

HUNT v. WASHINGTON STATE APPLE ADVERTISING COMM'N, 432 U.S. 333, 97 S.Ct. 2434, 53 L.Ed.2d 383 (1977), ruled unanimously, per BURGER, C.J., that North Carolina violated the commerce clause when it barred from the state closed apple containers bearing any grade marks except those of U.S.D.A. or a "not graded" mark. The regulation was challenged on behalf of Washington apple growers, who routinely packed their apples in containers bearing Washington grades that were viewed in the trade as equivalent or superior to the USDA grades, due to 60 years of state inspection, grading, and advertising of Washington apples.

Though noting "suspect indications" of an "economic protection motive," the Court did not question the "declared purpose of protecting consumers from deception and fraud in the market place," where divergent grading standards from seven states competed with North Carolina apples. But the mere fact that "state legislation furthers matters of legitimate local concern, even in the health and consumer protection areas, does not end the inquiry. [Rather], when such

discriminatory effect on some of I.C., but not protectionist state legislation comes into conflict with the Commerce Clause's overriding requirement of a national 'common market', we are confronted with the task of effecting an accommodation of the competing national and local interests. *Pike.*

"[T]he challenged statute has the practical effect of not only burdening interstate sales of Washington apples, but also discriminating against them. This discrimination takes various forms. [The] statute [raised] the costs of doing business in the North Carolina market for Washington apple growers and dealers, while leaving those of their North Carolina counterparts unaffected.[a] [The] statute [stripped] away from the Washington apple industry the competitive and economic advantages it has earned for itself through its expensive inspection and grading system. [By] prohibiting Washington growers and dealers from marketing apples under their State's grades, the statute has a leveling effect which insidiously operates to the advantage of local apple producers."

The Court further reasoned that the state had not met its "burden [to] justify [the discrimination] in terms of the local benefit flowing from the statute and the unavailability of nondiscriminatory alternatives." By permitting no grades at all the statute "can hardly be thought to eliminate the problems of deception and confusion created by the multiplicity of different state grades." And a nondiscriminatory alternative was available by permitting state grades to be used on the same containers as USDA grades.

BENDIX AUTOLITE CORP. v. MIDWESCO ENTERPRISES, INC., 486 U.S. 888, 108 S.Ct. 2218, 100 L.Ed.2d 896 (1988), per KENNEDY, J., applied *Pike* balancing to invalidate an Ohio statute that tolled the statute of limitations when foreign corporations did not appoint an agent to accept process for the exercise of general judicial jurisdiction: "We find that the burden imposed on interstate commerce by the tolling statute exceeds any local interest that the state might advance. [The] Ohio statutory scheme [forces] a foreign corporation to choose between exposure to the general jurisdiction of Ohio courts or forfeiture of the limitations defense, remaining subject to suit in Ohio in perpetuity. Requiring a foreign corporation to appoint an agent for service in all cases and to defend itself with reference to all transactions, including those in which it did not have the minimum contacts necessary for supporting personal jurisdiction, is a significant [burden]."

"In the particular case before us, the Ohio tolling statute must fall under the Commerce Clause. Ohio cannot justify its statute as a means of protecting its residents from corporations who become liable for acts done within the State but later withdraw from the jurisdiction, for it is conceded by all parties that the Ohio long-arm statute would have permitted service on Midwesco throughout the period of limitations."

SCALIA, J., concurred in the judgment: "I cannot confidently assess whether the Court's evaluation and balancing of interests in this case is right or wrong. [He pointed out uncertainties regarding both the burden on a foreign corporation and the assumed benefits to local interests.]

a. For the North Carolina market, Washington growers had to obliterate Washington grades imprinted on their standard containers, repack all shipments to North Carolina, or pack and store specially marked containers of apples for the estimated North Carolina market.

"Having evaluated the interests on both sides as roughly as this, the Court then proceeds to judge which is more important. This process is ordinarily called 'balancing,' *Pike,* but the scale analogy is not really appropriate, since the interests on both sides are incommensurate. It is more like judging whether a particular line is longer than a particular rock is heavy. All I am really persuaded of by the Court's opinion is that the burdens the Court labels 'significant' are more determinative of its decision than the benefits it labels 'important.' Were it not for the brief implication that there is here a discrimination unjustified by *any* state interest, I suggest an opinion could as persuasively have been written coming out the opposite way. We sometimes make similar 'balancing' judgments in determining how far the needs of the State can intrude upon the liberties of the individual, but that is of the essence of the courts' function as the nonpolitical branch. Weighing the governmental interests of a State against the needs of interstate commerce is, by contrast, a task squarely within the responsibility of Congress, and 'ill suited to the judicial function.' *CTS Corp.,* [Part IV infra] (Scalia, J., concurring in part and concurring in the judgment).

"I would therefore abandon the 'balancing' approach to these negative Commerce Clause cases, first explicitly adopted [in] *Pike,* and leave essentially legislative judgments to the Congress. Issues already decided I would leave untouched, but would adopt for the future an analysis more appropriate to our role and our abilities. [In] my view, a state statute is invalid under the Commerce Clause if, and only if, it accords discriminatory treatment to interstate commerce in a respect not required to achieve a lawful state purpose. When such a validating purpose exists, it is for Congress and not us to determine it is not significant enough to justify the burden on [commerce].

"Because the present statute discriminates against interstate commerce by applying a disadvantageous rule against nonresidents for no valid state purpose that requires such a rule, I concur in the judgment that the Ohio statute violates the Commerce Clause."[a]

Notes and Questions

1. *Balancing and the judicial role.* Is Scalia, J., correct that the balancing called for by *Pike* requires the Court to assess "incommensurate" values? That the balancing function is inherently legislative and not judicial?

Is there a workable alternative? Would it suffice for the Court to limit itself to identifying and invalidating tariff-like restrictions on the interstate movement and sale of goods that are enacted for the "protectionist" purpose of shielding local economic actors from competition with otherwise similarly situated out-of-staters? See Donald H. Regan, *The Supreme Court and State Protectionism: Making Sense of the Dormant Commerce Clause,* 84 Mich.L.Rev. 1091 (1986), discussed p. 218 supra, which so argues.

a. See also *Tyler Pipe Industries, Inc. v. Washington State Dep't of Revenue,* 483 U.S. 232, 265, 107 S.Ct. 2810, 2829, 97 L.Ed.2d 199, 225 (1987)(Scalia, J., concurring in part and dissenting in part). Scalia, J., has since made clear that, despite his "recorded [view] that the Commerce Clause contains no 'negative' component," he will enforce contrary doctrine "[o]n stare decisis grounds [in] two circumstances: (1) against a state law that facially discriminates against interstate commerce, and (2) against a state law that is indistinguishable from a type of law previously held unconstitutional by this Court." *Itel Containers International Corp. v. Huddleston,* 507 U.S. 60, 113 S.Ct. 1095, 1106–07, 122 L.Ed.2d 421, 439 (1993)(Scalia, J., concurring in part and concurring in the judgment). See Richard B. Collins, *Justice Scalia and the Elusive Idea of Discrimination Against Interstate Commerce,* 20 N.Mex.L.Rev. 555 (1990).

2. *Purpose and effect.* Was it plausible to think that the legislation in *Hunt* had any purpose other than economic protectionism? Did the Court "really" balance competing interests in *Hunt* (as it undoubtedly purported to do) or, having found indicia of discriminatory intent, did it in practical effect thrust the burden onto the state to prove otherwise?

Could the rationales and results in other cases be similarly explained as involving the form of balancing, but as having the real purpose of "smoking out" protectionist motivation? See Regan, supra, at 1143–60.

"SUBSIDIES" AND LINKAGES

NEW ENERGY CO. OF IND. v. LIMBACH, 486 U.S. 269, 108 S.Ct. 1803, 100 L.Ed.2d 302 (1988), per SCALIA, J., invalidated an Ohio statute that provided a tax credit to users of a gasoline substitute, ethanol, that was produced in Ohio or in a state that gave a reciprocal tax credit for Ohio-produced ethanol. The Court ruled unanimously that Ohio discriminated in violation of the commerce clause when it denied the tax credit for ethanol produced in Indiana, which granted a direct subsidy to Indiana ethanol producers, but furnished no reciprocal tax credit: "The Ohio provision at issue here explicitly deprives certain products of generally available beneficial tax treatment because they are made in certain other States, and thus on its face appears to violate the cardinal requirement of nondiscrimination.

"[It] has not escaped our notice that the appellant here, which is eligible to receive a cash subsidy under Indiana's program for in-state ethanol producers, is the potential beneficiary of a scheme no less discriminatory than the one that it attacks, and no less effective in conferring a commercial advantage over out-of-state competitors. To believe the Indiana scheme is valid, however, is not to believe that the Ohio scheme must be valid as well. The Commerce Clause does not prohibit all state action designed to give its residents an advantage in the marketplace, but only action of that description *in connection with the State's regulation of interstate commerce.* Direct subsidization of domestic industry does not ordinarily run afoul of that prohibition; discriminatory taxation of out-of-state manufacturers does."

Notes and Questions

1. *Subsidies and regulations.* Does the disparate treatment of "regulation," on the one hand, and "subsidization," on the other, make sense? Both confer economic advantages on local industry and undermine the competitive advantages of out-of-state competitors. And the expense, in both cases, is borne by in-state groups—taxpayers, who pay higher taxes (in the case of a subsidy), or consumers, who pay higher prices (in the case of a price regulation).

2. *Possible distinctions.* Does it matter that subsidies may help, in the long run, to nourish industries that might ultimately produce cheaper or better goods for consumers, including consumers in other states? That a subsidy imposes transparent economic costs on the subsidizing state's taxpayers, and may thus be less likely to result from a stark, discriminatory motivation to help in-staters at the expense of out-of-staters? That subsidies may be less likely to trigger retaliation? That subsidies were not one of the historic evils that the commerce clause was intended to remedy? See generally Regan, supra.

[handwritten margin note: — all sales of milk had uniform tax. But: Tax funds subsidize local milk producers]

WEST LYNN CREAMERY, INC. v. HEALY

512 U.S. 186, 114 S.Ct. 2205, 129 L.Ed.2d 157 (1994).

JUSTICE STEVENS delivered the opinion of the Court.

[Massachusetts taxed all sales of milk by wholesalers to Massachusetts retailers, regardless of whether the milk was produced in or out of state. The proceeds of the tax went to a fund used to make subsidy payments to Massachusetts milk producers.] *[margin: ✶F]*

The paradigmatic example of a law discriminating against interstate commerce is the protective tariff or customs duty, which taxes goods imported from other states, but does not tax similar products produced in state. A tariff is an attractive measure because it simultaneously raises revenue and benefits local producers by burdening their out-of-state competitors. Nevertheless, it violates the principle of the unitary national market by handicapping out-of-state competitors, thus artificially encouraging in-state production even when the same goods could be produced at lower cost in other states.

[Massachusetts' combination of a facially nondiscriminatory tax with a subsidy to in-state farmers] is clearly unconstitutional. Its avowed purpose and its undisputed effect are to enable higher cost Massachusetts dairy farmers to compete with lower cost dairy farmers in other States. [The net result is to make] milk produced out of State more expensive. Although the tax also applies to milk produced in Massachusetts, its effect on Massachusetts producers is entirely (indeed more than) offset by the subsidy provided exclusively to Massachusetts dairy farmers. Like an ordinary tariff, the tax is thus effectively imposed only on out-of-state products. *[margin: ✶H? ... ✶L]*

[Respondent] argues that the payments to Massachusetts dairy farmers from the Dairy Equalization Fund are valid, because subsidies are constitutional exercises of state power, and that the order premium which provides money for the Fund is valid, because it is a nondiscriminatory tax. [But] respondent errs in assuming that the constitutionality of the pricing order follows logically from the constitutionality of its component parts. By conjoining a tax and a subsidy, Massachusetts has created a program more dangerous to interstate commerce than either part alone. Nondiscriminatory measures, like the evenhanded tax at issue here, are generally upheld, in spite of any adverse effects on interstate commerce, in part because "[t]he existence of major in-state interests adversely affected [is] a powerful safeguard against legislative abuse." However, when a nondiscriminatory tax is coupled with a subsidy to one of the groups hurt by the tax, a state's political processes can no longer be relied upon to prevent legislative abuse, because one of the in-state interests which would otherwise lobby against the tax has been mollified by the subsidy. So, in this case, one would ordinarily have expected at least three groups to lobby against the order premium, which, as a tax, raises the price (and hence lowers demand) for milk: dairy farmers, milk dealers, and consumers. But because the tax was coupled with a subsidy, one of the most powerful of these groups, Massachusetts dairy farmers, instead of exerting their influence against the tax, were in fact its primary supporters. *[margin: ✶F ... ✶L]*

[Respondent] also argues that "the operation of the [scheme] disproves any claim of protectionism," because "*only* in-state consumers feel the effect of any retail price increase [and] [t]he dealers themselves [have] a substantial in-state presence." This argument, if accepted, would undermine almost every discriminatory tax case. State taxes are ordinarily paid by in-state businesses and consumers, yet if they discriminate against out-of-state products, they are unconstitutional. [The] cost of a tariff is also borne primarily by local consumers, yet a tariff is the paradigmatic Commerce Clause violation.

SCALIA, J., joined by Thomas, J., concurred in the judgment.

[The] Court notes that, in funding this subsidy, Massachusetts has taxed milk produced in other States, and thus "not only assists local farmers, but burdens interstate commerce." But the same could be said of almost all subsidies funded from general state revenues, which almost invariably include monies from use taxes on out-of-state products. And even where the funding does not come in any part from taxes on out-of-state goods, "merely assist[ing]" in-state businesses unquestionably neutralizes advantages possessed by out-of-state enterprises. Such subsidies, particularly where they are in the form of cash or (what comes to the same thing) tax forgiveness, are often admitted to have as their purpose—*indeed, are nationally advertised as having as their purpose*—making it more profitable to conduct business in-state than elsewhere, i.e., distorting normal market incentives.

[There] are at least four possible devices that would enable a State to produce the economic effect that Massachusetts has produced here: (1) a discriminatory tax upon the industry, imposing a higher liability on out-of-state members than on their in-state competitors; (2) a tax upon the industry that is nondiscriminatory in its assessment, but that has an "exemption" or "credit" for in-state members; (3) a nondiscriminatory tax upon the industry, the revenues from which are placed into a segregated fund, which fund is disbursed as "rebates" or "subsidies" to in-state members of the industry (the situation at issue in this case); and (4) with or without nondiscriminatory taxation of the industry, a subsidy for the in-state members of the industry, funded from the State's general revenues. It is long settled that the first of these methodologies is unconstitutional under the negative Commerce Clause. The second of them, "exemption" from or "credit" against a "neutral" tax, is no different in principle from the first, and has likewise been held invalid. The fourth methodology, application of a state subsidy from general revenues, is so far removed from what we have hitherto held to be unconstitutional, that prohibiting it must be regarded as an extension of our negative-Commerce-Clause jurisprudence and therefore, to me, unacceptable. See *Limbach*.

[The] issue before us in the present case is whether the third of these methodologies must fall. Although the question is close, I conclude it would not be a principled point at which to disembark from the negative-Commerce-Clause train. The only difference between methodology (2) (discriminatory "exemption" from nondiscriminatory tax) and methodology (3) (discriminatory refund of nondiscriminatory tax) is that the money is taken and returned rather than simply left with the favored in-state taxpayer in the first place. The difference between (3) and (4), on the other hand, is the difference between assisting in-state industry through discriminatory taxation, and assisting in-state industry by other means.

I would therefore allow a State to subsidize its domestic industry so long as it does so from nondiscriminatory taxes that go into the State's general revenue fund. Perhaps, as some commentators contend, that line comports with an important economic reality: a State is less likely to maintain a subsidy when its citizens perceive that the money (in the general fund) is available for any number of competing, non-protectionist, purposes. See Dan T. Coenen, *Untangling the Market–Participant Exemption to the Dormant Commerce Clause*, 88 Mich.L.Rev. 395, 479 (1989); Richard B. Collins, *Economic Union as a Constitutional Value*, 63

N.Y.U.L.Rev. 43, 103 (1988); Mark P. Gergen, *The Selfish State and the Market*, 66 Tex.L.Rev. 1097, 1138 (1988). That is not, however, the basis for my position.

REHNQUIST, C.J., joined by Blackmun, J., dissenting: [The] wisdom of a messianic insistence on a grim sink-or-swim policy of laissez-faire economics would be debatable had Congress chosen to enact it; but Congress has done nothing of the kind. It is the Court which has imposed the policy under the dormant Commerce Clause, a policy which bodes ill for the values of federalism which have long animated our constitutional jurisprudence.

Notes and Questions

1. *Themes.* Two themes dominate Stevens, J.'s opinion: (i) "the principle of the unitary national market" and (ii) the notion that discriminatory legislation is suspect because the states' political processes cannot be trusted to balance the interests of in-state against out-of-state interests. How do these themes relate to each other?

2. *Subsidies.* Don't nearly all subsidies, as Scalia, J., suggests, aim to "mak[e] it more profitable to conduct business in-state than elsewhere, i.e., distort[] normal market incentives"? In *West Lynn Creamery*, the Court pointedly noted that it had never directly confronted the constitutionality of subsidies—a disclaimer repeated in the more recent case of *Camps Newfound/Owatonna, Inc. v. Harrison*, Sec. 5 infra. But the Court did recognize in the latter case that "although tax exemptions and subsidies serve similar ends, they differ in important respects, and our cases have recognized these distinctions." See also Walter Hellerstein & Dan T. Coenen, *Commerce Clause Restraints on State Business Development Incentives*, 81 Corn.L.Rev. 789, 791 (1996): "On the one hand, the Court has sustained (or implicitly approved) programs adopted by states—particularly in the form of subsidies—intended to encourage business activities inside their borders. On the other hand, the Court has invalidated [state] programs— particularly in the form of tax incentives—intended to accomplish precisely the same result."

(a) Consider Note, *Functional Analysis, Subsidies, and the Dormant Commerce Clause*, 110 Harv.L.Rev. 1537, 1547–48 (1997): "[S]ubsidies can be a socially beneficial means of encouraging an optimal level of production. When [the production of] a good confers a positive externality on society [for example, by developing a production technique that can subsequently be used by others, or maintaining land in a use that preserves the beauty and integrity of the natural environment, a] firm will not reap all the social benefits of [the] good [that it produces]. By compensating firms for the positive externalities they confer on society, subsidies can function as efficient tools for states to encourage the optimal level of production. Indeed, all states may collectively gain from one state's subsidy if the good confers a positive externality." Consider also Robert M. Stern, *Conflict and Cooperation in International Economic Policy and Law*, 17 U.Pa. J.Int'l Econ.L. 539, 542 (1996): "[When a good confers positive externalities,] a production subsidy would be the best policy [since] it leads firms to increase their [output] while leaving consumers free to consume at undistorted market prices. [A] tariff thus [is less good than] a subsidy."

(b) Apart from issues of economic effects, consider Dan T. Coenen, *Business Subsidies and the Dormant Commerce Clause*, 107 Yale L.J. 965, 1002 (1998): "First, considerations of constitutional history provide a firm 'formal' basis for distinguishing cash grants [which were not one of the historic concerns of the commerce clause] from discriminatory taxation [which was]. Second, a broad state power to subsidize rests on the fairness based notion that state residents should be able to reap where they have sown. Third, the traditional distinction [between permissible subsidies and impermissible tax discrimination] vindicates values of federalism, by granting heightened authority to state governments to direct to the benefit of the state's citizenry those tangible assets that the state itself owns."

(c) Compare Edward A. Zelinsky, *Are Tax 'Benefits' Constitutionally Equivalent to Direct Expenditures?*, 112 Harv.L.Rev. 379, 399, 423–24 (1998): "[T]ax benefits and direct expenditures are economically identical. If that identify has not been recognized in the past, such unawareness should not be celebrated as historical tradition, but rather corrected for the future. [Given] the relative ease with which some tax benefits can be transformed into similar direct spending programs and vice versa, the direct spending/tax border is too porous to be a useful boundary for Commerce Clause purposes."

3. *The political process.* (a) Won't there always be in-state interests—typically including consumers—who are adversely affected by a state regulation that restricts the flow of commerce and thus reduces price competition? If so, why aren't consumers always (or never) adequate surrogates for out-of-staters in the state's legislative debates?

Does the majority's suggestion that commerce clause doctrine should correct "legislative abuse" occurring when "a state's political process can[not] be relied upon" presuppose a theory of interest group politics that distinguishes among the relative capacities of different kinds of groups to affect legislative outcomes? So-called "public choice" theories often postulate that "consumers," as a group, are likely to be diffuse and disorganized; by contrast, the dairy industry, whose members have much more at stake, may be well situated to organize successfully, to mount lobbying campaigns, and to provide or withhold financial or electoral support based on legislators' votes with respect to a single issue.[a] Can courts identify and correct abuses resulting from failures of the political process without making implicit assumptions about the *substantive* outcomes that a properly functioning political process would reach?

(b) Can state political processes be trusted or expected to balance the costs and benefits of subsidies more fairly than those of discriminatory tariffs and taxes? Consider Peter D. Enrich, *Saving the States from Themselves: Commerce Clause Constraints on State Tax Incentives for Business*, 110 Harv.L.Rev. 377, 442–43 (1996): "[Discriminatory tax] incentives, unlike cash subsidies, are typically independent of the annual appropriation process and are authorized as a standing part of the tax code. As a result, they are less politically visible—indeed, their actual costs are often unknown. [This suggests] the need for stricter external constraints on tax incentives than on direct subsidy programs." See also Christopher R. Drahozal, *On Tariffs v. Subsidies in Interstate Trade: A Legal and Economic Analysis*, 74 Wash.U.L.Q. 1127, 1154 (1996).

4. *Linkages.* (a) Consider Dan T. Coenen & Walter Hellerstein, *Suspect Linkage: The Interplay of State Taxing and Spending Measures in the Application of Constitutional Antidiscrimination Rules*, 95 Mich.L.Rev. 2167, 2174–75 (1997): "A fundamental difficulty with the majority's logic [in *West Lynn Creamery*] lies in its [assumption that] what renders [the] local-business-favoring tax break constitutionally odious is its contemporaneous enactment with an otherwise 'neutral' tax that burdens interstate as well as intrastate commerce. [It] is the *fact*

---

a. For an accessible introduction to the relevant concepts and literature, see Daniel A. Farber & Philip P. Frickey, *Law and Public Choice: A Critical Introduction* 12–37 (1991).

of the discrimination—rather than its *timing*—that renders resident-favoring tax relief provisions unconstitutional."

(b) Scalia, J., argued in his concurring opinion that the Massachusetts scheme might have passed constitutional muster if the subsidy had come from general revenues, not a fund specifically created by a tax on the sale of milk. Consider Zelinksy, supra, at 421–22: "[I]t is difficult to see a constitutional difference between the actual Massachusetts program and an entitlement-type alternative placed in the state's general fund budget; in both cases, the program would be permanent, would not be subject to the annual appropriations process, and would have the same rules regarding eligibility and quantitative limits."

5. *The unitary market and laissez faire.* Does *West Lynn Creamery* signal an increasing ascendancy of laissez-faire economic policies in dormant commerce clause doctrine? Should it? Consider Tribe 3d ed., at 1150: "The majority in *West Lynn Creamery* did not purport to apply its prohibitions to all subsidies, and instead indicated that its rule applied only to subsidies coupled with non-discriminatory taxes. [Absent] a clearer definition of coupling, the scope of *West Lynn Creamery* is impossible to ascertain. But that uncertainty is new, and significant. After *West Lynn Creamery*, no state action (other than direct state participation in a market in a purely proprietary capacity)[b] that has the effect of benefiting in-state interests at the expense of out-of-state interests is clearly immune from scrutiny under the dormant Commerce Clause."

II. REGULATION OF OUTGOING TRADE AND OTHER COMMERCE: BURDENS ON OUT–OF–STATE IN-TERESTS SEEKING IN–STATE RESOURCES

H.P. HOOD & SONS, INC. v. DU MOND
336 U.S. 525, 69 S.Ct. 657, 93 L.Ed. 865 (1949).

JUSTICE JACKSON delivered the opinion of the Court.

[Hood operated three licensed milk-receiving depots in New York for milk to be distributed in Boston. New York denied Hood a fourth depot for the same purpose in the same general area under a law requiring that the Commissioner find that "issuance of the license will not tend to a destructive competition in a market already adequately served, [and] is in the public interest." The Commissioner concluded that a fourth depot would (1) divert milk from other distributors' depots, thus tending to reduce their volume and increase their milk-handling costs, and (2) would tend to deprive local markets, like Troy, of a milk supply needed during the short season. The Court held that the law, as applied, violated the commerce clause.]

The present controversy begins where *Eisenberg*[a] left off. [Only] additional restrictions, imposed for the avowed purpose and with the practical effect of curtailing the volume of interstate commerce to aid local economic interests, [are] in question [here].

This distinction between the power of the State to shelter its people from menaces to their health or safety and from fraud, even when those dangers

---

b. See Sec. 3 infra.

a. *Milk Control Bd. v. Eisenberg Farm Products*, 306 U.S. 346, 59 S.Ct. 528, 83 L.Ed. 752 (1939), upheld a Pennsylvania law that required licenses for milk receiving depots, bonds to protect producers, and payment of prescribed prices, as applied to a New York milk distributor operating a receiving depot in Pennsylvania for milk to be shipped to New York.

emanate from interstate commerce, and its lack of power to retard, burden or constrict the flow of such commerce for their economic advantage, is one deeply rooted in both our history and our law. * * *

Baldwin is an explicit, impressive, recent and unanimous condemnation by this Court of economic restraints on interstate commerce for local economic advantage, but it does not stand alone. This Court consistently has rebuffed attempts of states to advance their own commercial interests by curtailing the movement of articles of commerce, either into or out of the state, while generally supporting their right to impose even burdensome regulations in the interest of local health and safety. As most states serve their own interests best by sending their produce to market, the cases in which this Court has been obliged to deal with prohibitions or limitations by states upon exports of articles of commerce are not numerous. However, [in] *West v. Kansas Natural Gas Co.,* 221 U.S. 229, 31 S.Ct. 564, 55 L.Ed. 716 (1911), the Court denied constitutional validity to a statute by which Oklahoma [sought] to restrict the export of natural gas.

[This] principle that our economic unit is the Nation, which alone has the gamut of powers necessary to control of the economy, including the vital power of erecting customs barriers against foreign competition, has as its corollary that the states are not separable economic units. [A] state may not use its admitted powers to protect the health and safety of its people as a basis for suppressing competition.

The material success that has come to inhabitants of the states which make up this federal free trade unit has been the most impressive in the history of commerce, but the established interdependence of the states only emphasizes the necessity of protecting interstate movement of goods against local burdens and repressions. We need only consider the consequences if each of the few states that produce copper, lead, high-grade iron ore, timber, cotton, oil or gas should decree that industries located in that state shall have priority. What fantastic rivalries and dislocations and reprisals would ensue if such practices were begun! Or suppose that the field of discrimination and retaliation be industry. May Michigan provide that automobiles cannot be taken out of that State until local dealers' demands are fully met? Would she not have every argument in the favor of such a statute that can be offered in support of New York's limiting sales of milk for out-of-state shipment to protect the economic interests of her competing dealers and local [consumers]?

Our system, fostered by the Commerce Clause, is that every farmer and every craftsman shall be encouraged to produce by the certainty that he will have free access to every market in the Nation, that no home embargoes will withhold his export, and no foreign state will by customs duties or regulations exclude them. Likewise, every consumer may look to the free competition from every producing area in the Nation to protect him from exploitation by any. Such was the vision of the Founders; such has been the doctrine of this Court which has given it reality. * * *

JUSTICE FRANKFURTER, with whom JUSTICE RUTLEDGE joins, dissenting.

If the Court's opinion has meaning beyond deciding this case in isolation, its effect is to hold that no matter how important to the internal economy of a State may be the prevention of destructive competition, and no matter how unimportant the interstate commerce affected, a State cannot as a means of preventing such competition deny an applicant access to a market within the State if that applicant happens to intend the out-of-state shipment of the product that he buys. I feel constrained to dissent because I cannot agree in treating what is essentially a problem of striking a balance between competing interests as an exercise in absolutes. Nor does it seem to me that such a problem should be disposed of on a record from which we cannot tell what weights to put in which side of the scales.

[In] the determination that an extension of petitioner's license would tend to destructive competition, the fact that petitioner intended the out-of-state shipment of what it bought was, so far as the record tells us, wholly irrelevant; under the circumstances, any other applicant, no matter where he meant to send his milk, would presumably also have been refused a [license].

[The opinion called attention to several questions relevant to a balancing analysis.[b]] We should, I submit, have answers at least to some of these questions before we can say either how seriously interstate commerce is burdened by New York's licensing power or how necessary to New York is that power. [Since] the needed information is neither accessible to judicial notice nor within its proper scope, I believe we should seek further light by remanding the case to the courts of the State. * * *[c]

Notes and Questions

1. *Purpose of the restriction.* Was the restriction in *Hood* "imposed for the avowed purpose and with the practical effect of curtailing the volume of interstate commerce to aid local economic interests"?

2. *Hood and balancing.* Did *Hood* mean that the Court would not use a balancing analysis when the state law protected local economic interests? Might *Hood* be interpreted as an implicit balancing judgment that in such circumstances the state interest was outweighed by the actual or potential harm to commerce?

3. *Local economic interests.* *Hood's* apparent disapproval of "curtailing the volume of interstate commerce to aid local economic interests" should be considered in the light of several earlier cases.

(a) *Eisenberg,* fn. a supra, upheld substantial regulations that raised prices in the producing state and, as a result, burdened interstate commerce in outgoing milk. The opinion recognized that the purpose was to advance the "welfare of the producers and consumers of milk" in the regulating state.

Is permitting a state to regulate the market for this purpose, to the detriment of interstate commerce, consistent with the theory of *Hood* and *Baldwin*? Was it crucial that the regulations in *Eisenberg,* which applied equally to milk not

b. "As matters now stand, however, it is impossible to say whether or not the restriction of competition among dealers in milk does in fact contribute to their economic well-being and, through them, to that of the entire industry. Why, when the State has fixed a minimum price for producers, does it take steps to keep competing dealers from increasing the price by bidding against each other for the existing supply? Is it concerned with protecting consumers from excessive prices? Or is it concerned with seeing that marginal dealers, forced by competition to pay more and charge less, are not driven either to cut corners in the maintenance of their plants or to close them down entirely? Might these consequences follow from operation at less than capacity? What proportion of capacity is necessary to enable the marginal dealer to stay in business? Could

Hood's potential competitors in the Greenwich area maintain efficient and sanitary standards of operation on a lower margin of profit? How would their closing down affect producers? Would the competition of Hood affect dealers other than those in that area? How many of those dealers are also engaged in interstate commerce? How much of a strain would be put on the price structure maintained by the State by a holding that it cannot regulate the competition of dealers buying for an out-of-state market? Is this a situation in which State regulation, by supplementing federal regulation, is of benefit to interstate as well as to intrastate commerce?"

c. Black, J., joined by Murphy, J., also dissented.

shipped out of state, did not *discriminate* against interstate commerce? That they did not attempt to protect the interests of the local dairy industry at the expense of otherwise similarly situated out-of-state dairy producers? That they were unlikely to provoke retaliation or resentment?

(b) PARKER v. BROWN, 317 U.S. 341, 63 S.Ct. 307, 87 L.Ed. 315 (1943), per STONE, C.J., upheld a California statute that, to increase the price of raisins, required producers to give a marketing committee control over the sale of 2/3 of their raisins, 95% of which were shipped in commerce: "Examination of the evidence in this case and of available data of the raisin industry in California, of which we may take judicial notice, leaves no doubt that the evils attending the production and marketing of raisins in that state present a problem local in character and urgently demanding state action for the economic protection of those engaged in one of its important industries. [A spectacular price rise resulted in a large increase in acreage and production, followed by low prices and inability to market the raisins.]

"In comparing the relative weights of the conflicting local and national interests involved it is significant that Congress, by its agricultural legislation, has recognized the distressed condition of much of the agricultural production of the United States, and has authorized marketing procedures, substantially like the California prorate program, for stabilizing the marketing of agricultural products. [Hence] we cannot say that the effect of the state program on interstate commerce is one which conflicts with Congressional policy or is such as to preclude the state from this exercise of its reserved power to regulate domestic agricultural production."

Was it also relevant that the California statute did not discriminate against raisins sold in interstate commerce? That it did not aim to promote the interests of California raisin producers (or consumers) at the expense of similarly situated out-of-staters?

———

PIKE v. BRUCE CHURCH, INC. (1970), quoted in the introduction to this chapter, per STEWART, J., unanimously found that Arizona violated the commerce clause when it required that growers of Arizona's exceptionally high-quality cantaloupes pack them in Arizona in containers bearing the Arizona name and address of the packer: "[Arizona's order] would forbid the company to pack its cantaloupes outside Arizona, not for the purpose of keeping the reputation of its growers unsullied, but to enhance their reputation through the reflected good will of the company's superior produce. The appellant, in other words, is not complaining because the company is putting the good name of Arizona on an inferior or deceptively packaged product, but because it is not putting that name on a product that is superior and well [packaged].

"[T]he State's tenuous interest in having the company's cantaloupes identified as originating in Arizona cannot constitutionally justify the requirement that the company build and operate an unneeded $200,000 packing plant in the State. The nature of that burden is, constitutionally, more significant than its extent. For the Court has viewed with particular suspicion state statutes requiring business operations to be performed in the home State that could more efficiently be performed elsewhere. Even where the State is pursuing a clearly legitimate local interest, this particular burden on commerce has been declared to be virtually per se illegal. *Foster-Fountain Packing Co. v. Haydel*, 278 U.S. 1, 49 S.Ct.

1, 73 L.Ed. 147 (1928);[a] *Toomer v. Witsell,* 334 U.S. 385, 68 S.Ct. 1156, 92 L.Ed. 1460 (1948).

"The appellant argues that the above cases are different because they involved statutes whose express or concealed purpose was to preserve or secure employment for the home State, while here the statute is a regulatory one and there is no hint of such a purpose. But in *Toomer,* the Court indicated that such a burden upon interstate commerce is unconstitutional even in the absence of such a purpose. In *Toomer* the Court held invalid a South Carolina statute requiring that owners of shrimp boats licensed by the State to fish in the maritime belt off South Carolina must unload and pack their catch in that State before 'shipping or transporting it to another State.' What we said there applies to this case as well:

" 'There was also uncontradicted evidence that appellants' costs would be materially increased by the necessity of having their shrimp unloaded and packed in South Carolina ports rather than at their home bases in Georgia where they maintain their own docking, warehousing, refrigeration and packing facilities. In addition, an inevitable concomitant of a statute requiring that work be done in South Carolina, even though that be economically disadvantageous to the fishermen, is to divert to South Carolina employment and business which might otherwise go to Georgia; the necessary tendency of the statute is to impose an artificial rigidity on the economic pattern of the industry.'

"[Here] the State's interest is minimal at best—certainly less substantial than a State's interest in securing employment for its people. If the Commerce Clause forbids a State to require work to be done within its jurisdiction to promote local employment, then surely it cannot permit a State to require a person to go into a local packing business solely for the sake of enhancing the reputation of other producers within its borders."

III. REGULATION TO PROTECT THE ENVIRONMENT AND PRESERVE NATURAL RESOURCES FOR IN-STATE USE

PHILADELPHIA v. NEW JERSEY
437 U.S. 617, 98 S.Ct. 2531, 57 L.Ed.2d 475 (1978).

JUSTICE STEWART delivered the opinion of the Court.

[Operators of New Jersey landfills, and out-of-state cities that had agreements with them for waste disposal, challenged under the commerce clause Ch. 363, N.J.Laws, 1973, which provided: "No person shall bring into this State any solid or liquid waste which originated or was collected outside [the] state." The New Jersey Supreme Court upheld the statute, ruling that it advanced vital health and environmental objectives with no economic discrimination against interstate commerce and that its substantial benefits outweighed its "slight" burden on interstate commerce. The Supreme Court reversed.]

[All] objects of interstate trade merit Commerce Clause protection; none is excluded by definition at the outset. [Just] as Congress has power to regulate the interstate movement of these wastes, States are not free from constitutional scrutiny when they restrict that movement.

---

a. *Foster-Fountain* struck down Louisiana's ban on shipment of shrimp from the state until removal of the hulls and heads, which were useful for fertilizer. The Court found that the purpose was "to bring about the removal of the packing and canning industry from Mississippi to Louisiana."

[The] opinions of the Court through the years have reflected an alertness to the evils of "economic isolation" and protectionism, while at the same time recognizing that incidental burdens on interstate commerce may be unavoidable when a State legislates to safeguard the health and safety of its people. Thus, where simple economic protectionism is effected by state legislation, a virtually per se rule of invalidity has been erected. See, e.g., *Hood; Toomer*. [But] where other legislative objectives are credibly advanced and there is no patent discrimination against interstate trade, the Court has adopted a much more flexible approach, the general contours of which were outlined in [*Pike*]. [The] crucial inquiry, therefore, must be directed to determining whether ch. 363 is basically a protectionist measure, or whether it can fairly be viewed as a law directed to legitimate local concerns, with effects upon interstate commerce that are only incidental.

The purpose of ch. 363 is set out in the [statute]: "The Legislature finds and determines that [the] volume of solid and liquid waste continues to rapidly increase, that the treatment and disposal of these wastes continues to pose an even greater threat to the quality of the environment of New Jersey, that the available and appropriate landfill sites within the State are being diminished, that the environment continues to be threatened by the treatment and disposal of waste which originated or was collected outside the State." [The] state court additionally found that New Jersey's existing landfill sites will be exhausted within a few years; that to go on using these sites or to develop new ones will take a heavy environmental toll, both from pollution and from loss of scarce open lands; that new techniques to divert waste from landfills to other methods of disposal and resource recovery processes are under development, but that these changes will require time; and finally, that "the extension of the lifespan of existing landfills, resulting from the exclusion of out-of-state waste, may be of crucial importance in preventing further virgin wetlands or other undeveloped lands from being devoted to landfill purposes."

[The] evil of protectionism can reside in legislative means as well as legislative ends. Thus, it does not matter whether the ultimate aim of ch. 363 is to reduce the waste disposal costs of New Jersey residents or to save remaining open lands from pollution, for we assume New Jersey has every right to protect its residents' pocketbooks as well as their environment. And it may be assumed as well that New Jersey may pursue those ends by slowing the flow of *all* waste into the State's remaining landfills, even though interstate commerce may incidentally be affected. But whatever New Jersey's ultimate purpose, it may not be accomplished by discriminating against articles of commerce coming from outside the State unless there is some reason, apart from their origin, to treat them differently. Both on its face and in its plain effect, ch. 363 violates this principle of nondiscrimination.

The Court has consistently found parochial legislation of this kind to be constitutionally invalid [citing, e.g., *Baldwin*]. [Also] relevant here are the Court's decisions holding that a State may not accord its own inhabitants a preferred right of access over consumers in other States to natural resources located within its borders. [E.g.,] *West v. Kansas Natural Gas Co.*

[The] New Jersey law at issue in this case falls squarely within the area that the Commerce Clause puts off-limits to state regulation. On its face, it imposes on out-of-state commercial interests the full burden of conserving the State's remaining landfill space. It is true that in our previous cases the scarce natural resource was itself the article of commerce, whereas here the scarce resource and the article of commerce are distinct. But that difference is without consequence. In both instances, the State has overtly moved to slow or freeze the flow of commerce for protectionist reasons. It does not matter that the State has shut the article of commerce inside the State in one case and outside the State in the other. What is crucial is the attempt by one State to isolate itself from a problem common to many by erecting a barrier against the movement of interstate trade.

[It] is true that certain quarantine laws have not been considered forbidden protectionist measures, even though they were directed against out-of-state commerce. But those quarantine laws banned the importation of articles such as diseased livestock that required destruction as soon as possible because their very movement risked contagion and other evils. Those laws thus did not discriminate against interstate commerce as such, but simply prevented traffic in noxious articles, whatever their origin.

The New Jersey statute is not such a quarantine law. There has been no claim here that the very movement of waste into or through New Jersey endangers health, or that waste must be disposed of as soon and as close to its point of generation as possible. The harms caused by waste are said to arise after its disposal in landfill sites, and at that point, as New Jersey concedes, there is no basis to distinguish out-of-state waste from domestic waste. If one is inherently harmful, so is the other. Yet New Jersey has banned the former while leaving its landfill sites open to the latter. The New Jersey law blocks the importation of waste in an obvious effort to saddle those outside the State with the entire burden of slowing the flow of refuse into New Jersey's remaining landfill sites. That legislative effort is clearly impermissible under the Commerce Clause of the Constitution.

Today, cities in Pennsylvania and New York find it expedient or necessary to send their waste into New Jersey for disposal, and New Jersey claims the right to close its borders to such traffic. Tomorrow, cities in New Jersey may find it expedient or necessary to send their waste into Pennsylvania or New York for disposal, and those States might then claim the right to close their borders. The Commerce Clause will protect New Jersey in the future, just as it protects her neighbors now, from efforts by one State to isolate itself in the stream of interstate commerce from a problem shared by all.

JUSTICE REHNQUIST, with whom CHIEF JUSTICE BURGER joins, dissenting.

* * * New Jersey should be free under our past precedents to prohibit the importation of solid waste because of the health and safety problems that such waste poses to its citizens. The fact that New Jersey continues to, and indeed must continue to, dispose of its own solid waste does not mean that New Jersey may not prohibit the importation of even more solid waste into the State.

* * * I do not see why a State may ban the importation of items whose movement risks contagion, but cannot ban the importation of items which, although they may be transported into the State without undue hazard, will then simply pile up in an ever increasing danger to the public's health and safety. The Commerce Clause was not drawn with a view to having the validity of state laws turn on such pointless distinctions.

[T]hat New Jersey has left its landfill sites open for domestic waste does not, of course, mean that solid waste is not innately harmful. Nor does it mean that New Jersey prohibits importation of solid waste for reasons other than the health and safety of its population. New Jersey must out of sheer necessity treat and dispose of its solid waste in some fashion, just as it must treat New Jersey cattle suffering from hoof-and-mouth disease. It does not follow that New Jersey must, under the Commerce Clause, accept solid waste or diseased cattle from outside its borders and thereby exacerbate its problems. * * *

Notes and Questions

1. *Governmental "out-of-state commercial interests."* The only out-of-state litigants in *Philadelphia* were cities claiming the right to continue to "send their waste into New Jersey for disposal"—a governmental function. Was it appropriate to invoke commerce clause concerns to protect such interests? Were they "out-of-state commercial interests"?

2. *"Protectionism" against non-economic problems.* Are the commerce clause considerations underlying the "principle of nondiscrimination" soundly applicable to the conflict between New Jersey's interest in prolonging the life of its limited landfills and other states' interest in using New Jersey's landfills? Is the policy against "protectionism" soundly applicable to a state's efforts to isolate itself from commerce-spread environmental as well as economic problems?[a]

Consider Richard A. Epstein, *Waste and the Dormant Commerce Clause*, 3 Green Bag 29, 35, 37, 39 (1999), which suggests that the Court erred by treating "bads" equivalently with "goods" for purposes of commerce clause analysis: "Waste creates losses; it is far from clear why states should be required to receive them with the same open arms that they receive foreign goods. A new source of goods increases the likelihood that the citizens of any state will receive the benefit of greater competition. [But not so with bads.] Gaining approval for the operation of waste sites is no easy task, given the obvious risks of leakage and pollution. [And states may respond to a judicial requirement that they receive waste from other states on the same terms as intra-state waste by refusing to license waste sites at all, thereby producing] national shortages of waste disposal sites. [The] greater danger lies in using the nondiscrimination principle than in jettisoning it."[b]

Compare Jonathan H. Adler, *Waste and the Dormant Commerce Clause—A Reply*, 3 Green Bag 353, 354–55 (2000): "[E]ncouraging self-sufficiency in waste management makes no more sense than calls for any other sort of economic isolation. [T]here is no more basis for insisting that New Yorkers dispose of all their trash within the state than there is for mandating that they grow all their vegetables in Central Park. [In] addition, the economies of scale in waste management decisively favor larger facilities, which can [operate] at substantially lower costs (and superior environmental performance) than the town dumps of yore, even when long-distance hauling costs are included. Indeed, modern regional 'megafills' can handle waste at less than one-third the cost of older local landfills."

3. *Natural gas cases distinguishable?* Could *Philadelphia* have been soundly distinguished from the natural gas cases there cited, which hold that a state may

a. For critical commentary on Supreme Court decisions applying *Philadelphia* and discussion of the options remaining open to the states to deal with problems involving solid waste disposal, see Stanley E. Cox, *Garbage In, Garbage Out: Court Confusion About the Dormant Commerce Clause*, 50 Okla.L.Rev. 155 (1997); Kirsten Engel, *Reconsidering the National Market in Solid Waste: Trade–Offs in Equity, Efficiency, Environmental Protection,* and State Autonomy, 73 N.C.L.Rev. 1481 (1995).

b. See also Paul E. McGreal, *The Flawed Economics of the Dormant Commerce Clause*, 39 Wm. & Mary L.Rev. 1191 (1998) (offering similar arguments and contending that discriminatory statutes should be deemed to violate the commerce clause only when they harm the national economy).

not require suppliers of natural gas from in-state wells to give priority to in-state domestic and industrial consumers?

4. *Adequate alternatives.* With *Philadelphia* compare MAINE v. TAYLOR, 477 U.S. 131, 106 S.Ct. 2440, 91 L.Ed.2d 110 (1986), per BLACKMUN, J., upholding a Maine law that prohibited importation into Maine of live baitfish that competed with Maine's native baitfish industry. The Court relied on two trial court findings: (1) "Maine 'clearly has a legitimate and substantial purpose in prohibiting the importation of live bait fish' because 'substantive uncertainties' surrounded the effects that baitfish parasites would have on the State's unique population of wild fish, and the [unpredictable] consequences of introducing non-native species." (2) "[L]ess discriminatory means of protecting against these threats were currently unavailable" despite the "abstract possibility" of developing acceptable testing procedures in the future. The Court added:

"[A] State must make reasonable efforts to avoid restraining the free flow of commerce across its borders, but it is not required to develop new and unproven means of protection at an uncertain cost. Appellee, of course, is free to work on his own or in conjunction with other bait dealers to develop scientifically acceptable sampling and inspection procedures for golden shiners; if and when such procedures are developed, Maine no longer may be able to justify its import ban. The State need not join in those efforts, however, and it need not pretend they already have succeeded.

"[The] evidence in this case amply supports the District Court's findings that Maine's ban on the importation of live baitfish serves legitimate local purposes that could not adequately be served by available nondiscriminatory alternatives. This is not a case of arbitrary discrimination against interstate commerce; the record suggests that Maine has legitimate reasons, 'apart from their origin, to treat [out-of-state baitfish] differently,' *Philadelphia*."[c]

———

MINNESOTA v. CLOVER LEAF CREAMERY CO., 449 U.S. 456, 101 S.Ct. 715, 66 L.Ed.2d 659 (1981), per BRENNAN, J., upheld a state law that banned nonreturnable milk containers made of plastic but permitted other nonreturnable milk containers, largely cartons made of pulpwood, though the plastic originated out of state and the pulpwood in state. The legislature had found that use of nonreturnable milk containers "presents a solid waste management problem for the state, promotes energy waste, and depletes natural resources" in violation of a legislative policy to encourage "the reduction of the amount and type of material entering the solid waste stream":

"[Minnesota's statute] does not effect 'simple protectionism,' but 'regulates even-handedly' by prohibiting all milk retailers from selling their products in plastic, nonreturnable milk containers, without regard to whether the milk, the containers, or the sellers are from outside the State. Since the statute does not discriminate between interstate and intrastate commerce, the controlling question is whether the incidental burden imposed on interstate commerce [is] 'clearly excessive in relation to the putative local benefits.' *Pike.* We conclude that it is not. [Within] Minnesota, business will presumably shift from manufacturers of plastic nonreturnable containers to producers of paperboard cartons, refillable bottles, and plastic pouches, but there is no reason to suspect that the gainers will

---

c. Stevens, J., dissented, contending that "uncertainty" and "[a]mbiguity about dangers and alternatives should actually defeat, rather than sustain, the discriminatory measure."

be Minnesota firms, or the losers out-of-state firms. Indeed, two of the three dairies, the sole milk retailer, and the sole milk container producer challenging the statute in this litigation are Minnesota firms.[17]

"Pulpwood producers are the only Minnesota industry likely to benefit significantly from the Act at the expense of out-of-state firms. Respondents point out that plastic resin, the raw material used for making plastic nonreturnable milk jugs, is produced entirely by non-Minnesota firms, while pulpwood, used for making paperboard, is a major Minnesota product. Nevertheless, it is clear that respondents exaggerate the degree of burden on out-of-state interests, both because plastics will continue to be used in the production of plastic pouches, plastic returnable bottles, and paperboard itself, and because out-of-state pulpwood producers will presumably absorb some of the business generated by the Act.

"Even granting that the out-of-state plastics industry is burdened relatively more heavily than the Minnesota pulpwood industry, we find that this burden is not 'clearly excessive' in light of the substantial state interest in promoting conservation of energy and other natural resources and easing solid waste disposal problems, which we have already reviewed in the context of equal protection analysis. We find these local benefits ample to support Minnesota's decision under the Commerce Clause. Moreover, we find that no approach with 'a lesser impact on interstate activities,' *Pike,* is [available].

"In *Exxon [Corp. v. Maryland,* 437 U.S. 117, 98 S.Ct. 2207, 57 L.Ed.2d 91 (1978)], [we] stressed that the Commerce Clause 'protects the interstate market, not particular interstate firms, from prohibitive or burdensome regulations.' A nondiscriminatory regulation serving substantial state purposes is not invalid simply because it causes some business to shift from a predominantly out-of-state industry to a predominantly in-state industry. Only if the burden on interstate commerce clearly outweighs the State's legitimate purposes does such a regulation violate the Commerce Clause."[a]

———

C & A CARBONE, INC. v. CLARKSTOWN, 511 U.S. 383, 114 S.Ct. 1677, 128 L.Ed.2d 399 (1994): Clarkstown, arranged for the construction of a "waste transfer station" to collect waste, separate recyclable from nonrecyclable items, and ship the solid waste to the appropriate disposal facility. The transfer station was built and operated by a private company, but under a contract contemplating that it would be sold to the town for $1 at the end of five years. In order to ensure the transfer station's economic viability, the town adopted a "flow control ordinance" (Local Law No. 9) requiring that all nonrecyclable solid waste generated within the town be processed at the transfer station, which charged a fee in excess of the prevailing private market rate. Ruling on a challenge by a private recycler doing business in Clarkstown, the Court, per KENNEDY, J., held that the ordinance violated the commerce clause:

"[A]s the town itself points out, what makes garbage a profitable business is not its own worth but the fact that its possessor must pay to get rid of it. In other words, the article of commerce is not so much the solid waste itself, but rather the service of processing and disposing of it. With respect to this stream of commerce,

---

17. The existence of major in-state interests adversely affected by the Act is a powerful safeguard against legislative abuse.

a. Powell and Stevens, JJ., dissenting separately, would have referred the commerce clause issue back to the Minnesota Supreme Court. Rehnquist, J., took no part.

the flow control ordinance discriminates, for it allows only the favored operator to process waste that is within the limits of the town. The ordinance is no less discriminatory because in-state or in-town processors are also covered by the prohibition. [*Dean Milk*.]

"[The] flow control ordinance is just one more instance of local processing requirements that we long have held invalid. [It] hoards solid waste, and the demand to get rid of it, for the benefit of the preferred processing facility. The only conceivable distinction from the cases cited above is that the flow control ordinance favors a single local proprietor. But this difference just makes the protectionist effect of the ordinance more acute. In *Dean Milk*, the local processing requirement at least permitted pasteurizers within five miles of the city to compete. An out-of-state pasteurizer who wanted access to that market might have built a pasteurizing facility within the radius. The flow control ordinance at issue here squelches competition in the waste-processing service altogether, leaving no room for investment from outside. * * *

"Clarkstown maintains that special financing is necessary to ensure the long-term survival of the designated facility. If so, the town may subsidize the facility through general taxes or municipal bonds. *Limbach*. But having elected to use the open market to earn revenues for its project, the town may not employ discriminatory regulation to give that project an advantage over rival businesses from out of State."

O'CONNOR, J., concurred in the judgment: "In my view, [the] town's ordinance is unconstitutional not because of facial or effective discrimination against interstate commerce, but rather because it imposes an excessive burden on interstate commerce. [Unlike] the regulations we have previously struck down, Local Law 9 does not give more favorable treatment to local interests as a group as compared to out-of-state or out-of-town economic interests. Rather, the garbage sorting monopoly is achieved at the expense of all competitors, be they local or nonlocal.

"[I] believe this distinction has more doctrinal significance than the majority acknowledges. In considering state health and safety regulations such as Local Law 9, we have consistently recognized that the fact that interests within the regulating jurisdiction are equally affected by the challenged enactment counsels against a finding of discrimination. And for good reason. The existence of substantial in-state interests harmed by a regulation is 'a powerful safeguard' against legislative discrimination. *Clover Leaf Creamery*.

"[Even] a nondiscriminatory regulation may nonetheless impose an excessive burden on interstate trade when considered in relation to the local benefits conferred. '[The] local interest in proper disposal of waste is obviously significant. But this interest could be achieved by simply requiring that all waste disposed of in the town be properly processed *somewhere*.' For example, the town could ensure proper processing by setting specific standards with which all town processors must comply.

"In fact, however, the town's purpose is narrower than merely ensuring proper disposal. Local Law 9 is intended to ensure the financial viability of the transfer facility. I agree with the majority that this purpose can be achieved by other means that would have a less dramatic impact on the flow of goods. For example, the town could finance the project by imposing taxes, by issuing municipal bonds, or even by lowering its price for processing to a level competitive with other waste processing facilities. But by requiring that all waste be processed at the town's facility, the ordinance squelches competition in the waste-processing service altogether, leaving no room for investment from outside,"

SOUTER, J., joined by Rehnquist, C.J., and Blackmun, J., dissented: "[T]he exclusion worked by Clarkstown's Local Law 9 bestows no benefit on a class of local private actors, but instead directly aids the government in satisfying a traditional governmental responsibility. The law does not differentiate between all local and all out-of-town providers of a service, but instead between the one entity responsible for ensuring that the job gets done and all other enterprises, regardless of their location. The ordinance thus falls outside that class of tariff or protectionist measures that the Commerce Clause has traditionally been thought to bar States from enacting against each other.

"[To] the degree Local Law 9 affects the market for trash processing services, it does so only by subjecting Clarkstown residents and businesses to burdens far different from the burdens of local favoritism that dormant Commerce Clause jurisprudence seeks to root out. The town has found a way to finance a public improvement, not by transferring its cost to out-of-state economic interests, but by spreading it among the local generators of trash, an equitable result with tendencies that should not disturb the Commerce Clause and should not be disturbed by us.

"[Clarkstown's] transfer station is essentially a municipal facility, built and operated under a contract with the municipality and soon to revert entirely to municipal ownership. [A] law that favors that single facility over all others is a law that favors the public sector over all private-sector processors, whether local or out of State. Because the favor does not go to local private competitors of out-of-state firms, out-of-state governments will at the least lack a motive to favor their own firms in order to equalize the positions of private competitors.

"[There] is, to be sure, an incidental local economic benefit, for the need to process Clarkstown's trash in Clarkstown will create local jobs. But this local boon is mitigated by another feature of the ordinance, in that it finances whatever benefits it confers on the town from the pockets of the very citizens who passed it into law. On the reasonable assumption that no one can avoid producing some trash, every resident of Clarkstown must bear a portion of the burden Local Law 9 imposes to support the municipal monopoly, an uncharacteristic feature of statutes claimed to violate the Commerce Clause.

"[The] Commerce Clause was not passed to save the citizens of Clarkstown from themselves. It should not be wielded to prevent them from attacking their local garbage problems with an ordinance that does not discriminate between local and out-of-town participants in the private market for trash disposal services and that is not protectionist in its purpose or effect."

Notes and Questions

1. *Monopoly or government function?* How much should turn on the fact that the Clarkstown ordinance had the effect of protecting a single, local enterprise, rather than a class of local businesses? On the fact that the benefitted enterprise was closely connected with the local government and its effort to perform a traditional governmental function?

2. *Bases of disagreement.* Does the majority believe that the commerce clause should be interpreted to "save the citizens of Clarkstown from themselves"? What is the basis of disagreement between the majority and dissenting opinions?

PRESERVING NATURAL RESOURCES FOR IN-STATE USE

HUGHES v. OKLAHOMA, 441 U.S. 322, 99 S.Ct. 1727, 60 L.Ed.2d 250 (1979), per BRENNAN, J., held invalid under the commerce clause an Oklahoma ban on transporting "minnows for sale outside the state which were seined or procured within the waters of this state," as applied to a Texan who transported to Texas a load of minnows taken in Oklahoma waters: "We now conclude that challenges under the Commerce Clause to state regulations of wild animals should be considered according to the same general rule applied to state regulations of other natural resources, and therefore expressly overrule *Geer*.[a] [T]he general rule we adopt in this case makes ample allowance for preserving, in ways not inconsistent with the Commerce Clause, the legitimate state concerns for conservation and protection of wild animals underlying the 19th century legal fiction of state ownership.

"We turn then to the question whether the burden imposed on interstate commerce in wild game by § 4–115(B) is permissible under the general rule articulated in our precedents governing other types of commerce. See, e.g., *Pike*. Under that general rule [we] must inquire (1) whether the challenged statute regulates evenhandedly with only 'incidental' effects on interstate commerce, or discriminates against interstate commerce either on its face or in practical effect; (2) whether the statute serves a legitimate local purpose; and, if so, (3) whether alternative means could promote this local purpose as well without discriminating against interstate commerce. '[When] discrimination against commerce [is] demonstrated, the burden falls on the State to justify it both in terms of the local benefits flowing from the statute and the unavailability of nondiscriminatory alternatives adequate to preserve the local interests at stake.' [*Hunt*].

"[Section 4–115(b)] on its face discriminates against interstate commerce. It forbids the transportation of natural minnows out of the State for purposes of sale, and thus 'overtly blocks the flow of interstate commerce at [the] State's border.' *Philadelphia*. Such facial discrimination by itself may be a fatal defect, regardless of the State's purpose, because 'the evil of protectionism can reside in legislative means as well as legislative ends.' Ibid. At a minimum such facial discrimination invokes the strictest scrutiny of any purported legitimate local purpose and of the absence of nondiscriminatory alternatives.

"[The] State's interest in maintaining the ecological balance in state waters by avoiding the removal of inordinate numbers of minnows may well qualify as a legitimate local purpose. We consider the States' interests in conservation and protection of wild animals as legitimate local purposes. [But] the scope of legitimate state interests in 'conservation' is narrower under this analysis than it was under *Geer*. [The] fiction of state ownership may no longer be used to force those outside the State to bear the full costs of 'conserving' the wild animals within its borders when equally effective nondiscriminatory conservation measures are available.

"Far from choosing the least discriminatory alternative, Oklahoma has chosen to 'conserve' its minnows in the way that most overtly discriminates against interstate commerce. The State places no limits on the numbers of minnows that

---

a. *Geer v. Connecticut*, 161 U.S. 519, 16 S.Ct. 600, 40 L.Ed. 793 (1896), had held that a state ban on exporting wild game from the state was not subject to the commerce clause because of a theory of state ownership of the game, later recognized as a fiction facilitating conservation.

can be taken by licensed minnow dealers; nor [on] how these minnows may be disposed of within the State. Yet it forbids the transportation of any commercially significant number of natural minnows out of the State for sale. Section 4–115(B) is certainly not a 'last ditch' attempt at conservation after nondiscriminatory alternatives have proven unfeasible. It is rather a choice of the most discriminatory means even though nondiscriminatory alternatives would seem likely to fulfill the State's purported legitimate local purpose more effectively.

"[The] overruling of *Geer* does not leave the States powerless to protect and conserve wild animal life within their borders. Today's decision makes clear, however, that States may promote this legitimate purpose only in ways consistent with the basic principle that 'our economic unit is the Nation,' *Hood*, and that when a wild animal 'becomes an article of commerce [its] use cannot be limited to the citizens of one State to the exclusion of citizens of another State.' *Geer* (Field, J., dissenting).''

REHNQUIST, J., joined by Burger, C.J., dissented, concluding that Oklahoma's "substantial interest in conserving and regulating exploitation of its natural minnow population" "outweighed" the "minimal burden" on commerce of requiring all who export minnows from the state, residents as well as nonresidents, to secure them from hatcheries.

———

SPORHASE v. NEBRASKA, 458 U.S. 941, 102 S.Ct. 3456, 73 L.Ed.2d 1254 (1982), per STEVENS, J., held invalid a Nebraska law requiring denial of a permit to withdraw and transport water for use in an adjoining state unless that state "grants reciprocal rights" to withdraw and transport its water for use in Nebraska. Rejecting an earlier precedent,[b] the Court ruled that ground water is an "article of commerce," requiring commerce clause analysis of state laws restricting its transfer to other states: "[Because] Colorado forbids the exportation of its ground water, the reciprocity provision operates as an explicit barrier to commerce between the two States. The State therefore bears the initial burden of demonstrating a close fit between the reciprocity requirement and its asserted local purpose. [The] reciprocity requirement does not survive the 'strictest scrutiny' reserved for facially discriminatory legislation. *Hughes*.''

IV. STATE REGULATION OF TENDER OFFERS

CTS CORP. v. DYNAMICS CORP.

481 U.S. 69, 107 S.Ct. 1637, 95 L.Ed.2d 67 (1987).

JUSTICE POWELL delivered the opinion of the Court.

[An] Indiana takeover law provided that a purchaser who acquired "control shares"[a] in an Indiana corporation would acquire voting rights only to the extent approved by a majority vote of the pre-existing disinterested stockholders.

[The] Indiana Act [has] the same effects on tender offers whether or not the offeror is a domiciliary or resident of Indiana. [Because] nothing in the Indiana

---

b. *Hudson County Water Co. v. McCarter,* 209 U.S. 349, 28 S.Ct. 529, 52 L.Ed. 828 (1908).

a. "Control shares" are reached when the acquired shares would bring the purchaser's voting power to 20, 33 and 1/3, or 50% but for the operation of the Act.

Act imposes a greater burden on out-of-state offerors than it does on similarly situated Indiana offerors, we reject the contention that the Act discriminates against interstate commerce.

[This] Court's recent Commerce Clause cases also have invalidated statutes that adversely may affect interstate commerce by subjecting activities to inconsistent regulations. [The] Indiana Act poses no such problem. So long as each State regulates voting rights only in the corporations it has created, each corporation will be subject to the law of only one State. No principle of corporation law and practice is more firmly established than a State's authority to regulate domestic corporations, including the authority to define the voting rights of [shareholders.]

[The] Court of Appeals [decision] rested on its view of the Act's potential to hinder tender offers. We think the Court of Appeals failed to appreciate the significance for Commerce Clause analysis of the fact that state regulation of corporate governance is regulation of entities whose very existence and attributes are a product of state [law.] By prohibiting certain transactions, and regulating others, such laws necessarily affect certain aspects of interstate [commerce.] Mergers are a typical example. In view of the substantial effect that a merger may have on the shareholders' interests in a corporation, many States require supermajority votes to approve [mergers.] By requiring a greater vote for mergers than is required for other transactions, these laws make it more difficult for corporations to merge. State laws also may provide for 'dissenters' rights' under which minority shareholders who disagree with corporate decisions to take particular actions are entitled to sell their shares to the corporation at fair market value.

[A] State has an interest in promoting stable relationships among parties involved in the corporations it charters, as well as in ensuring that investors in such corporations have an effective voice in corporate affairs. There can be no doubt that the Act reflects these concerns. The primary purpose of the Act is to protect the shareholders of Indiana corporations. It does this by affording shareholders, when a takeover offer is made, an opportunity to decide collectively whether the resulting change in voting control of the corporation, as they perceive it, would be desirable. A change of management may have important effects on the shareholders' interests; it is well within the State's role as overseer of corporate governance to offer this opportunity. The autonomy provided by allowing shareholders collectively to determine whether the takeover is advantageous to their interests may be especially beneficial where a hostile tender offer may coerce shareholders into tendering their shares.

Appellee Dynamics responds to this concern by arguing that the prospect of coercive tender offers is illusory, and that tender offers generally should be favored because they reallocate corporate assets into the hands of management who can use them most effectively.[13] [But] the potentially coercive aspects of tender offers have been recognized by the Securities and Exchange Commission, and by a number of scholarly commentators. The Constitution does not require the States to subscribe to any particular economic theory. We are not inclined "to second-guess the empirical judgments of lawmakers concerning the utility of legislation." In our view, the possibility of coercion in some takeover bids offers

---

13. [No] one doubts that some successful tender offers will provide more effective management or other benefits such as needed diversification. But there is no reason to *assume* that the type of conglomerate corporation that may result from repetitive takeovers necessari-ly will result in more effective management or otherwise be beneficial to shareholders. The divergent views in the literature—and even now being debated in the Congress—reflect the reality that the type and utility of tender offers vary widely. * * *

additional justification for Indiana's decision to promote the autonomy of independent shareholders.

Dynamics argues in any event that the State has "no legitimate interest in protecting the nonresident shareholders." *MITE Corp.*, [note 2 infra]. Dynamics relies heavily on the statement by the *MITE* Court that "[i]nsofar as [the] law burdens out-of-state transactions, there is nothing to be weighed in the balance to sustain the law." But that comment was made in reference to an Illinois law that applied as well to out-of-state corporations as to in-state corporations. We agree that Indiana has no interest in protecting nonresident shareholders *of nonresident corporations*. But this Act applies only to corporations incorporated in Indiana. We reject the contention that Indiana has no interest in providing for the shareholders of its corporations the voting autonomy granted by the Act. Indiana has a substantial interest in preventing the corporate form from becoming a shield for unfair business dealing. Moreover, unlike the Illinois statute invalidated in *MITE,* the Indiana Act applies only to corporations that have a substantial number of shareholders in Indiana. Thus, every application of the Indiana Act will affect a substantial number of Indiana residents, whom Indiana indisputably has an interest in protecting.

Dynamics' argument that the Act is unconstitutional ultimately rests on its contention that the Act will limit the number of successful tender offers. There is little evidence that this will occur. But even if true, this result would not substantially affect our Commerce Clause analysis. We reiterate that this Act does not prohibit any entity—resident or nonresident—from offering to purchase, or from purchasing, shares in Indiana corporations, or from attempting thereby to gain control. It only provides regulatory procedures designed for the better protection of the corporations' shareholders. We have rejected the "notion that the Commerce Clause protects the particular structure or methods of operation in [a] market." The very commodity that is traded in the securities market is one whose characteristics are defined by state law. Similarly, the very commodity that is traded in the "market for corporate control"—the corporation—is one that owes its existence and attributes to state law. Indiana need not define these commodities as other States do; it need only provide that residents and nonresidents have equal access to them. This Indiana has done. * * *[b]

JUSTICE SCALIA, concurring in part and [in] the judgment.

[Whether] the control shares statute "protects shareholders of Indiana corporations," or protects incumbent management seems to me a highly debatable question, but it is extraordinary to think that the constitutionality of the Act should depend on the answer. Nothing in the Constitution says that the protection of entrenched management is any less important a "putative local benefit" than the protection of entrenched shareholders, and I do not know what qualifies us to make that judgment—or the related judgment as to how effective the present statute is in achieving one or the other objective—or the ultimate (and most ineffable) judgment as to whether, given importance-level x, and effectiveness-level y, the worth of the statute is 'outweighed' by impact-on-commerce. * * *

"One commentator has suggested that, at least much of the time, we do not in fact mean what we say when we declare that statutes which neither discriminate against commerce nor present a threat of multiple and inconsistent burdens might nonetheless be unconstitutional under a 'balancing' test. See Regan, [p. 218

b. The Court also ruled that the federal takeover Williams Act did not preempt the Indiana Law.

supra]. If he is not correct, he ought to be. As long as a State's corporation law governs only its own corporations and does not discriminate against out-of-state interests, it should survive this Court's scrutiny under the Commerce Clause, whether it promotes shareholder welfare or industrial stagnation. Beyond that, it is for Congress to prescribe its invalidity."

JUSTICE WHITE, with whom JUSTICE BLACKMUN and JUSTICE STEVENS join, dissenting.

* * * CTS's stock is traded on the New York Stock Exchange, and people from all over the country buy and sell CTS's shares daily. Yet, under Indiana's scheme, any prospective purchaser will be effectively precluded from purchasing CTS's shares if the purchaser crosses one of the Chapter's threshold ownership levels and a majority of CTS's shareholders refuse to give the purchaser voting rights. This Court should not countenance such a restraint on interstate trade.

[A] state law which permits a majority of an Indiana corporation's stockholders to prevent individual investors, including out-of-state stockholders, from selling their stock to an out-of-state tender offeror and thereby frustrate [any] transfer of corporate control, is the archetype of the kind of state law that the Commerce Clause forbids. * * *

Notes and Questions

1. *State interests.* (a) The state's purported interest is protecting shareholders in Indiana corporations, but the challenged statute applies only to corporations that are both chartered in Indiana and located there. "If the legislature was genuinely concerned with protecting *shareholders* [why] would it deny its 'protection' to the shareholders of Indiana corporations just because the principal activities and assets of the firm happen to be in Ohio or New York?" Donald C. Langevoort, *The Supreme Court and the Politics of Corporate Takeovers: A Comment on CTS Corp. v. Dynamics Corp. of America*, 101 Harv.L.Rev. 96, 106–07 (1987). Moreover, if corporate shareholders *want* protection against coercive takeover bids, why do they not provide for such protection by charter amendment?

(b) What if Indiana had attempted to defend the law challenged in *CTS* by citing a state interest in protecting Indiana-based management? What if the state had avowed an interest in protecting entrenched management as a means of preserving Indiana-based jobs? Consider Donald H. Regan, *Siamese Essays: (I) CTS Corp. v. Dynamics Corp. of America and Dormant Commerce Clause Doctrine; (II) Extraterritorial State Legislation*, 85 Mich.L.Rev. 1865, 1872 (1987): "A purpose to protect Indiana workers and suppliers *at the expense of non-Indianans* is impermissible, but a statute which was motivated by a *general* belief that takeovers leading to corporate removals are unacceptably disruptive of established economic relations, and which was limited to Indiana corporations simply because those were the only corporations the Indiana legislature had power to regulate, would be perfectly permissible so far as the dormant commerce clause is concerned."

Compare Lucien A. Bebchuk & Allen Ferrell, *Federalism and Corporate Law: The Race to Protect Managers from Takeovers*, 99 Colum.L.Rev. 1168, 1171 (1999), arguing that state anti-takeover statutes frequently are anti-competitive and inefficient and are designed to protect corporate management: "Because managers play a key role in incorporation decisions, states (especially ones with a large number of already incorporated companies such as Delaware) will give substantial weight to satisfying managers' preferences."

2. *Contrast.* In EDGAR v. MITE CORP., 457 U.S. 624, 102 S.Ct. 2629, 73 L.Ed.2d 269 (1982), Illinois authorized its Secretary of State to adjudicate the substantive fairness of tender offers and to deny the required registration if the Secretary concluded an offer was inequitable or would tend to work a fraud or deceit on the offerees. The statute applied to all corporations 10% of whose shares were owned by Illinois residents, or that had their principal offices in Illinois. The Court, per WHITE, J., ruled that the law violated the commerce clause:

"It is a direct restraint on interstate commerce and [has] an extraterritorial effect" by controlling "conduct beyond the boundary of the state."[a] Applying the *Pike* test, the opinion found harmful effects on interstate commerce by preventing shareholders from selling their shares at a premium, "hindering the reallocation of economic resources to their highest-valued use," and by reducing the incentive "the tender offer mechanism provides incumbent management to perform well." The Court saw "nothing to be weighed in the balance to sustain the law," at least "insofar as the Illinois law burden[ed] out-of-state transactions" of nonresident shareholders.[b]

3. *Extraterritorial reach.* Is it helpful to conceive anti-takeover statutes as impermissibly restricting transactions—i.e., sales of shares—that physically occur out of state? Is corporate law "necessarily extraterritorial in impact" in its regulation of such matters as "the duties of directors, the ease of derivative actions, and the voting rights of shareholders"? See Langevoort, supra at 103.

EXTRATERRITORIAL REGULATION

Perhaps the leading case on impermissibly extraterritorial legislation under the commerce clause is BROWN–FORMAN DISTILLERS CORP. v. NEW YORK STATE LIQUOR AUTH., 476 U.S. 573, 106 S.Ct. 2080, 90 L.Ed.2d 552 (1986), decided one year before *CTS*, which expressly identified extraterritorial regulation as violating the commerce clause. New York had required liquor distillers selling wholesale in the state to file a price schedule monthly, to sell at those prices in New York, and to sell at the lowest prices the distiller charged wholesale in any other state for the same month. The Court, per MARSHALL, J., held that this "lowest-price" provision violated the commerce clause: "[While] a State may seek lower prices for its consumers, it may not insist that producers or consumers in other States surrender whatever competitive advantages they may possess. *Baldwin.* Economic protectionism is not limited to attempts to convey advantages to local merchants; it may include attempts to give local consumers an advantage over consumers in other States.

"[A] 'prospective' statute such as [New York's liquor statute] regulates out-of-state transactions in violation of the Commerce Clause. Once a distiller has posted prices in New York, it is not free to change its price elsewhere in the United States during the relevant month. [While] New York may regulate the sale of liquor within its borders, [it] may not 'project its legislation into [other States] by regulating the price to be paid' for liquor in those States. *Baldwin.*"[a]

---

a. Blackmun, J., did not join in this part of the opinion but joined in the part applying *Pike*.

b. Marshall and Brennan, JJ., dissented, considering the case moot. Rehnquist, J., dissented, considering it nonjusticiable.

a. Blackmun, J., concurred. Stevens, J., joined by White, J. and Rehnquist, C.J. dissented, contending that "in lieu of evidence about the actual impact of the New York statute, the Court speculates that [it] prevents price competition in transactions [in] other States." Brennan, J., did not participate.

Notes and Questions

1. *The meaning of "extraterritorial" regulation.* Suppose that New York forbids the sale within its borders of distilled liquors with more than a specified alcohol content. In order to sell their products in New York, out-of-state manufacturers have no practical choice but to comply; and if it is not economically feasible to undertake separate distillation and bottling for New York and surrounding states, New York's legislation may have the practical effect of determining the alcohol content of liquor marketed in Vermont, too. Does the hypothetical statute have a forbidden extraterritorial effect?

Is the crucial problem in *Brown-Forman* that the effect of the New York statute was to make it unlawful under New York law for liquor wholesalers to sell their products in other states at prices that would be lawful under the law of those states?

2. *Constitutional basis for an extraterritorial limit on state legislative power.* Is the principle that states may not regulate extraterritorially (however the scope of that principle is defined) properly attributable to the commerce clause? Wouldn't some such principle limit state legislative power to deal with matters (in the context of criminal and family law, for example) that have little to do with production of goods or their movement in interstate commerce?

V. REGULATION OF TRANSPORTATION

SOUTHERN PACIFIC CO. v. ARIZONA, 325 U.S. 761, 65 S.Ct. 1515, 89 L.Ed. 1915 (1945), per STONE, C.J., reversed an Arizona Supreme Court decision that upheld an Arizona law limiting the length of trains in Arizona to 70 freight cars: "[E]ver since *Gibbons*, the states have not been deemed to have authority to impede substantially the free flow of commerce from state to state, or to regulate those phases of the national commerce which, because of the need of national uniformity, demand that their regulation, if any, be prescribed by a single authority.[2] [T]he matters for ultimate determination here are the nature and extent of the burden which the state regulation of interstate trains, adopted as a safety measure, imposes on interstate commerce, and whether the relative weights of the state and national interests involved are such as to make inapplicable the rule, generally observed, that the free flow of interstate commerce and its freedom from local restraints in matters requiring uniformity of regulation are interests safeguarded by the commerce clause from state [interference].

"The findings show that the operation [of trains of] more than seventy freight cars is standard practice over the main lines of the railroads of the United States, and that, if the length of trains is to be regulated at all, national uniformity [is] practically indispensable to the operation of an efficient and economical national railway system. [Compliance with the Arizona law increases the costs of operation by $1,000,000 annually for the two railroads in Arizona, and impedes efficient operation by delays in breaking up and remaking long trains.]

"[In] considering the effect of the statute as a safety measure, [the] decisive question is whether in the circumstances the total effect of the law as a safety

2. In applying this rule the Court has often recognized that to the extent that the burden of state regulation falls on interests outside the state, it is unlikely to be alleviated by the operation of those political restraints normally exerted when interests within the state are affected. * * *

measure in reducing accidents and casualties is so slight or problematical as not to outweigh the national interest in keeping interstate commerce free from interferences which seriously impede [it]. [The Court noted that increased crossing accidents from more but shorter trains more than offset the increased risk of accidents from greater 'slack' in longer trains.]

"[The state's] regulation of train lengths, admittedly obstructive to interstate train operation, and having a seriously adverse effect on transportation efficiency and economy, passes beyond what is plainly essential for safety. [E]xamination of all the relevant factors makes it plain that the state interest is outweighed by the interest of the nation in an adequate economical and efficient railway transportation service, which must prevail."[a]

BLACK, J., dissenting, argued that in collecting evidence concerning the efficacy of safety legislation, and in weighing safety against other interests, the trial court "acted, and this Court today is acting, as a 'super-legislature.' [The] balancing of [such] probabilities" as the Court relied on "is not in my judgment a matter for judicial determination, but one which calls for legislative consideration."

KASSEL v. CONSOLIDATED FREIGHTWAYS CORP.

450 U.S. 662, 101 S.Ct. 1309, 67 L.Ed.2d 580 (1981).

JUSTICE POWELL announced the judgment of the Court and delivered an opinion in which JUSTICE WHITE, JUSTICE BLACKMUN, and JUSTICE STEVENS joined.

The question is whether an Iowa statute that prohibits the use of certain large trucks within the State unconstitutionally burdens interstate commerce.

I. Appellee Consolidated Freightways Corporation of Delaware (Consolidated) is one of the largest common carriers in the country. It offers service in 48 States under a certificate of public convenience and necessity issued by the Interstate Commerce Commission. Among other routes, Consolidated carries commodities through Iowa on Interstate 80, the principal east-west route linking New York, Chicago, and the west coast, and on Interstate 35, a major north-south route.

Consolidated mainly uses two kinds of trucks. One consists of a three-axle tractor pulling a 40–foot two-axle trailer. This unit, commonly called a single, or "semi," is 55 feet in length overall. Such trucks have long been used on the Nation's highways. Consolidated also uses a two-axle tractor pulling a single-axle trailer which, in turn, pulls a single-axle dolly and a second single-axle trailer. This combination, known as a double, or twin, is 65 feet long overall. Many trucking companies, including Consolidated, increasingly prefer to use doubles to ship certain kinds of commodities. Doubles have larger capacities, and the trailers can be detached and routed separately if necessary. Consolidated would like to use 65–foot doubles on many of its trips through Iowa.

[Unlike] all other States in the West and Midwest, Iowa generally prohibits the use of 65–foot doubles within its borders. Instead, most truck combinations are restricted to 55 feet in length. Doubles, mobile homes, trucks carrying vehicles such as tractors and other farm equipment, and singles hauling livestock, are permitted to be as long as 60 feet. The statute provided a number of exceptions, discussed infra, but none were available to Consolidated. [T]he District Court found that the "evidence clearly establishes that the twin is as safe as the semi. * * * Twins are more maneuverable, are less sensitive to wind, and create less

---

a. Rutledge, J., concurred only in the result.

splash and spray. However, they are more likely than semis to jackknife or upset. They can be backed only for a short distance. The negative characteristics are not such that they render the twin less safe than semis overall. Semis are more stable but are more likely to 'rear end' another vehicle.''

In light of these findings, the District Court applied the standard we enunciated in *Raymond Motor Transportation, Inc. v. Rice,* 434 U.S. 429, 98 S.Ct. 787, 54 L.Ed.2d 664 (1978), and concluded that the state law impermissibly burdened interstate commerce: "[The] total effect of the law as a safety measure in reducing accidents and casualties is so slight and problematical that it does not outweigh the national interest in keeping interstate commerce free from interferences that seriously impede it.'' The Court of Appeals for the Eighth Circuit affirmed. * * *

II.   [R]egulations that touch upon safety—especially highway safety—are those that "the Court has been most reluctant to invalidate.'' [Indeed], "if safety justifications are not illusory, the Court will not second-guess legislative judgment about their importance in comparison with related burdens on interstate commerce.''

[But] the incantation of a purpose to promote the public health or safety does not insulate a state law from Commerce Clause attack. Regulations designed for that salutary purpose nevertheless may further the purpose so marginally, and interfere with commerce so substantially, as to be invalid under the Commerce Clause. * * *

III.   The State failed to present any persuasive evidence that 65-foot doubles are less safe than 55-foot singles. Moreover, Iowa's law is now out of step with the laws of all other Midwestern and Western States. Iowa thus substantially burdens the interstate flow of goods by truck. [Trucking] companies that wish to continue to use 65-foot doubles must route them around Iowa or detach the trailers of the doubles and ship them through separately. Alternatively, trucking companies must use the smaller 55-foot singles or 60-foot doubles permitted under Iowa law. Each of these options engenders inefficiency and added expense. The record shows that Iowa's law added about $12.6 million each year to the costs of trucking companies. Consolidated alone incurred about $2 million per year in increased costs.

In addition to increasing the costs of the trucking companies (and, indirectly, of the service to consumers), Iowa's law may aggravate, rather than ameliorate, the problem of highway accidents. Fifty-five foot singles carry less freight than 65-foot doubles. Either more small trucks must be used to carry the same quantity of goods through Iowa, or the same number of larger trucks must drive longer distances to bypass Iowa. In either case, as the District Court noted, the restriction requires more highway miles to be driven to transport the same quantity of goods. Other things being equal, accidents are proportional to distance traveled. Thus, if 65-foot doubles are as safe as 55-foot singles, Iowa's law tends to *increase* the number of accidents, and to shift the incidence of them from Iowa to other States.

IV.   [The] Court normally does accord "special deference" to state highway safety regulations. [Less] deference to the legislative judgment is due, however, where the local regulation bears disproportionately on out-of-state residents and businesses. Such a disproportionate burden is apparent here. Iowa's scheme, although generally banning large doubles from the State, nevertheless has several exemptions that secure to Iowans many of the benefits of large trucks while shunting to neighboring States many of the costs associated with their use.

At the time of trial there were two particularly significant exemptions. First, singles hauling livestock or farm vehicles were permitted to be as long as 60 feet. [Second,] cities abutting other States were permitted to enact local ordinances adopting the larger length limitation of the neighboring State. This exemption offered the benefits of longer trucks to individuals and businesses in important border cities without burdening Iowa's highways with interstate through traffic.

The origin of the "border cities exemption" also suggests that Iowa's statute may not have been designed to ban dangerous trucks, but rather to discourage interstate truck traffic. In 1974, the legislature passed a bill that would have permitted 65-foot doubles in the State. Governor Ray vetoed the bill. He said: "I find sympathy with those who are doing business in our state and whose enterprises could gain from increased cargo carrying ability by trucks. However, with this bill, the Legislature has pursued a course that would benefit only a few Iowa-based companies while providing a great advantage for out-of-state trucking firms and competitors at the expense of our Iowa citizens." After the veto, the "border cities exemption" was immediately enacted and signed by the Governor.

[In] the District Court and Court of Appeals, the State explicitly attempted to justify the law by its claimed interest in keeping trucks out of Iowa. The Court of Appeals correctly concluded that a State cannot constitutionally promote its own parochial interests by requiring safe vehicles to detour around [it].

V. Because Iowa has imposed [a] burden [on interstate commerce] without any significant countervailing safety interest, its statute violates the Commerce Clause.

Justice Brennan, with whom Justice Marshall joins, concurring in the judgment.

For me, analysis of Commerce Clause challenges to state regulations must take into account three principles: (1) The courts are not empowered to second-guess the empirical judgments of lawmakers concerning the utility of legislation. (2) The burdens imposed on commerce must be balanced against the local benefits actually sought to be achieved by the State lawmakers, and not against those suggested after the fact by counsel. (3) Protectionist legislation is unconstitutional under the Commerce Clause, even if the burdens and benefits are related to safety rather than economics.

Both the opinion of my Brother Powell and the opinion of my Brother Rehnquist are predicated upon the supposition that the constitutionality of a state regulation is determined by the factual record created by the State's lawyers in trial court. But that supposition cannot be correct, for it would make the constitutionality of state laws and regulations depend on the vagaries of litigation rather than on the judgments made by the State's lawmakers.

[A]lthough Iowa's lawyers in this litigation have defended the truck-length regulation on the basis of the safety advantages of 55-foot singles and 60-foot doubles over 65-foot doubles, Iowa's actual rationale for maintaining the regulation had nothing to do with these purported differences. Rather, Iowa sought to discourage interstate truck traffic on Iowa's highways. Thus, the safety advantages and disadvantages of the types and lengths of trucks involved in this case are irrelevant to the decision.

[Though] my Brother Powell recognizes that the State's actual purpose in maintaining the truck-length regulation was "to limit the use of its highways by deflecting some through traffic," he fails to recognize that this purpose, being *protectionist* in nature, is *impermissible* under the Commerce Clause.

[Iowa] may not shunt off its fair share of the burden of maintaining interstate truck routes, nor may it create increased hazards on the highways of neighboring States in order to decrease the hazards on Iowa highways. Such an attempt has all the hallmarks of the "simple * * * protectionism" this Court has condemned in the economic area. *Philadelphia v. New Jersey.*

JUSTICE REHNQUIST, with whom CHIEF JUSTICE BURGER and JUSTICE STEWART join, dissenting.

A determination that a state law is a rational safety measure does not end the Commerce Clause inquiry. A "sensitive consideration" of the safety purpose in relation to the burden on commerce is required. *Raymond.* When engaging in such a consideration the Court does not directly compare safety benefits to commerce costs and strike down the legislation if the latter can be said in some vague sense to "outweigh" the former. Such an approach would make an empty gesture of the strong presumption of validity accorded state safety measures, particularly those governing highways. It would also arrogate to this Court functions of forming public policy, functions which, in the absence of congressional action, were left by the Framers of the Constitution to state legislatures. [For a court to make such policy judgments would be especially inappropriate] when, as here, the question involves the difficult comparison of financial losses and "the loss of lives and limbs of workers and people using the highways."

The purpose of the "sensitive consideration" referred to above is rather to determine if the asserted safety justification, although rational, is merely a pretext for discrimination against interstate commerce. We will conclude that it is if the safety benefits from the regulation are demonstrably trivial while the burden on commerce is great.

[There] can be no doubt that the challenged statute is a valid highway safety regulation and thus entitled to the strongest presumption of validity against Commerce Clause challenges. As noted, all 50 States regulate the length of trucks which may use their highways. [There] can also be no question that the particular limit chosen by Iowa—60 feet—is rationally related to Iowa's safety objective. Most truck limits are between 55 and 65 feet, and Iowa's choice is thus well within the widely accepted range.

[The] District Court approached the case as if the question were whether Consolidated's 65–foot trucks were as safe as others permitted on Iowa highways, and the Court of Appeals as if its task were to determine if the District Court's factual findings in this regard were "clearly erroneous." The question, however, is whether the Iowa Legislature has acted rationally in regulating vehicle lengths and whether the safety benefits from this regulation are more than slight or problematical.

[The] answering of the relevant question is not appreciably advanced by comparing trucks slightly over the length limit with those at the length limit. It is emphatically not our task to balance any incremental safety benefits from prohibiting 65–foot doubles as opposed to 60–foot doubles against the burden on interstate commerce. Lines drawn for safety purposes will rarely pass muster if the question is whether a slight increment can be permitted without sacrificing safety. [The] particular line chosen by Iowa—60 feet—is relevant only to the question whether the limit is a rational one. Once a court determines that it is, it considers the overall safety benefits *from the regulation* against burdens on interstate commerce, and not any marginal benefits from the scheme the State established as opposed to that the plaintiffs desire.

[The] difficulties with the contrary approach are patent. While it may be clear that there are substantial safety benefits from a 55–foot truck as compared to a 105–foot truck, these benefits may not be discernible in 5–foot jumps. Appellee's approach would permit what could not be accomplished in one lawsuit to be done in 10 separate suits, each challenging an additional five feet.

Notes and Questions

1. *Balancing, protectionism, and highway safety regulations.* (a) Suppose the evidence would have permitted a reasonable person to conclude that the prohibition of double-trailers in Iowa would save, on average, one highway fatality per year in the state of Iowa. By what measure might a court weigh this saving against harm to the national interest in the free flow of interstate commerce?

(b) Suppose the evidence suggested that a ban on double-trailers would prevent one or more traffic fatalities in Iowa each year, but that there would be a corresponding *increase* in traffic fatalities in other states as a result of double-trailers detouring around Iowa. Would legislation aimed at protecting Iowa lives, enacted in full awareness of a likely shift of fatalities out of state, be objectionably discriminatory or protectionist?

(c) Does it matter to the analysis of (b) whether, if all states prohibited double-trailers, there would be a net decrease in traffic fatalities? Should it matter?

2. *Nonillusory highway safety regulations.* After *Kassel*, what appears to be "the law" on whether the Court will balance the anticipated, "nonillusory" benefits of state highway safety regulations against their burden on interstate commerce? What *should* be the law on this matter? What meanings do the different opinions give to "nonillusory?"

3. *The relevance of protectionist purposes.* Is Brennan, J., persuasive that, in the area of safety legislation (at least), the commerce clause prohibits *only* regulations that have a protectionist or discriminatory purpose? Are courts any less competent to balance interests in safety than they are, for example, to weigh those in protecting privacy or the natural environment against a competing interest in the free movement of goods? Compare Regan, note 1 after *Prudential*, at 1183–85, arguing that while there is *not* a general national interest in economic laissez-faire, there *is* a national interest "in the existence of an effective transportation network linking the states," and that balancing may be peculiarly necessary in cases in which state regulations collide with that national interest.

4. *Inconsistency with other states.* BIBB v. NAVAJO FREIGHT LINES, 359 U.S. 520, 79 S.Ct. 962, 3 L.Ed.2d 1003 (1959), per DOUGLAS, J., held invalid an Illinois law that required contour rear fender mudguards on all trucks and trailers on Illinois highways in place of the straight mudflaps that were legal in "at least" 45 states: "[Arkansas requires] that trailers operating in that State be equipped with straight or conventional mud flaps. Vehicles equipped to meet the standards of the Illinois statute would not comply with Arkansas standards, and vice versa. Thus if a trailer is to be operated in both States, mudguards would have to be interchanged, causing a significant delay [of two to four hours] in an operation where prompt movement may be of the [essence].

"This is one of those cases—few in number—where local safety measures that are nondiscriminatory place an unconstitutional burden on interstate commerce. [A] State which insists on a design out of line with the requirements of almost all the other States may sometimes place a great burden of delay and inconvenience on those interstate motor carriers entering or crossing its territory. Such a new safety device—out of line with the requirements of the other States—may be so compelling that the innovating State need not be the one to give-way. But the present showing—balanced against the clear burden on commerce—is far too inconclusive to make this mudguard [law] meet that test.[a] [The] heavy burden which the Illinois mudguard law places on the interstate movement of trucks and trailers seems to us to pass the permissible limits even for safety regulations."[b]

SECTION 3. THE STATE AS A MARKET PARTICIPANT

REEVES, INC. v. STAKE

447 U.S. 429, 100 S.Ct. 2271, 65 L.Ed.2d 244 (1980).

JUSTICE BLACKMUN delivered the opinion of the Court.

[Responding to a 1919 cement shortage, South Dakota built and operated a cement plant, which sold to both in-state and out-of-state buyers. The latter bought 40% of the plant's production in the mid–70's. When booming construction caused a cement shortage in 1978, Reeves, an out-of-state buyer for 20 years, challenged as a commerce clause violation South Dakota's policy of giving preference to South Dakota buyers. The Court upheld the policy, invoking *Hughes v. Alexandria Scrap Corp.*, 426 U.S. 794, 96 S.Ct. 2488, 49 L.Ed.2d 220 (1976). That case had upheld a Maryland subsidy for recycling junk autos that favored local processors by requiring more demanding title documentation from out-of-state processors.]

[*Alexandria Scrap*] did not involve "the kind of action with which the Commerce Clause is concerned." Unlike prior cases voiding state laws inhibiting interstate trade, "Maryland has not sought to prohibit the flow of hulks, or to regulate the conditions under which it may occur. Instead, it has entered into the market itself to bid up their price as a purchaser, in effect, of a potential article of interstate commerce," and has restricted "its trade to its own citizens or businesses within the State."

Having characterized Maryland as a market participant, rather than as a market regulator, the Court found no reason to "believe the Commerce Clause was intended to require independent justification for [the State's] action." The Court couched its holding in unmistakably broad terms. "Nothing in the purposes animating the Commerce Clause prohibits a State, in the absence of congressional action, from participating in the market and exercising the right to favor its own citizens over others."

The basic distinction drawn in *Alexandria Scrap* between States as market participants and States as market regulators makes good sense and sound law. As that case explains, the Commerce Clause responds principally to state taxes and regulatory measures impeding free private trade in the national marketplace. [There] is no indication of a constitutional plan to limit the ability of the States themselves to operate freely in the free market. See Laurence H. Tribe, *American Constitutional Law* 336 (1978)("the commerce clause was directed, as an historical

a. Earlier, the opinion mentioned the District Court's finding that contour mud flaps possessed "no advantages over [straight] mud flaps" and caused heated brake drums that decreased brake effectiveness, and were "susceptible of being hit [when] the trucks backed up and of falling off on the highways."

b. Harlan, J., joined by Stewart, J., concurred.

matter, only at regulatory and taxing actions taken by states in their sovereign capacity"). The precedents comport with this distinction.[9]

Restraint in this area is also counseled by considerations of state sovereignty, the role of each State " 'as guardian and trustee for its people,' " and "the long recognized right of trader or manufacturer, engaged in an entirely private business, freely to exercise his own independent discretion as to parties with whom he will deal." *United States v. Colgate & Co.*, 250 U.S. 300, 307, 39 S.Ct. 465, 63 L.Ed. 992 (1919). Moreover, state proprietary activities may be, and often are, burdened with the same restrictions imposed on private market participants. Evenhandedness suggests that, when acting as proprietors, States should similarly share existing freedoms from federal constraints, including the inherent limits of the Commerce Clause. Finally, as this case illustrates, the competing considerations in cases involving state proprietary action often will be subtle, complex, politically charged, and difficult to assess under traditional Commerce Clause analysis. Given these factors, *Alexandria Scrap* wisely recognizes that, as a rule, the adjustment of interests in this context is a task better suited for Congress than this Court.

South Dakota, as a seller of cement, unquestionably fits the "market participant" label more comfortably than a State acting to subsidize local scrap processors. Thus, the general rule of *Alexandria Scrap* plainly applies here. Petitioner argues, however, that the exemption for marketplace participation necessarily admits of exceptions. While conceding that possibility, we perceive in this case no sufficient reason to depart from the general rule.

[We] find the label "protectionism" of little help in this context. The State's refusal to sell to buyers other than South Dakotans is "protectionist" only in the sense that it limits benefits generated by a state program to those who fund the state treasury and whom the State was created to serve. Petitioner's argument apparently also would characterize as "protectionist" rules restricting to state residents the enjoyment of state educational institutions, energy generated by a state-run plant, police and fire protection, and agricultural improvement and business development programs. Such policies, while perhaps "protectionist" in a loose sense, reflect the essential and patently unobjectionable purpose of state government—to serve the citizens of the State.

[Cement] is not a natural resource, like coal, timber, wild game, or minerals. Cf. *Hughes v. Oklahoma* (minnows); *Philadelphia v. New Jersey* (landfill sites); *Pennsylvania v. West Virginia*, 262 U.S. 553, 43 S.Ct. 658, 67 L.Ed. 1117 (1923)(natural gas). It is the end-product of a complex process whereby a costly physical plant and human labor act on raw materials. South Dakota has not sought to limit access to the State's limestone or other materials used to make cement. Nor has it restricted the ability of private firms or sister States to set up plants within its borders.

JUSTICE POWELL, with whom JUSTICE BRENNAN, JUSTICE WHITE, and JUSTICE STEVENS join, dissenting.

9. *Alexandria Scrap* does not stand alone. In *American Yearbook Co. v. Askew*, 339 F.Supp. 719 (M.D.Fla.1972), a three-judge District Court upheld a Florida statute requiring the State to obtain needed printing services from in-state shops. It reasoned that "state proprietary functions" are exempt from Commerce Clause scrutiny. This Court affirmed summarily. 409 U.S. 904, 93 S.Ct. 230, 34 L.Ed.2d 168 (1972). Numerous courts have rebuffed commerce clause challenges directed at similar preferences that exist in "a substantial majority of the states." Note, 58 Iowa L.Rev. 576, 576 (1973). [The opinion cites state court decisions from eight states.]

[In] procuring goods and services for the operation of government, a State may act without regard to the private marketplace and remove itself from the reach of the Commerce Clause. See *American Yearbook Co.* But when a State itself becomes a participant in the private market for other purposes, the Constitution forbids actions that would impede the flow of interstate commerce. These categories recognize no more than the "constitutional line between the State as Government and the State as trader." *New York v. United States,* [Ch. 2, Sec. 5, II supra].

The Court holds that South Dakota, like a private business, should not be governed by the Commerce Clause when it enters the private market. But precisely because South Dakota is a State, it cannot be presumed to behave like an enterprise "engaged in an entirely private business." A State frequently will respond to market conditions on the basis of political rather than economic concerns. To use the Court's terms, a State may attempt to act as a "market regulator" rather than a "market participant." In that situation, it is a pretense to equate the State with a private economic actor. State action burdening interstate trade is no less state action because it is accomplished by a public agency authorized to participate in the private market.

[Unlike] the market subsidies at issue in *Alexandria Scrap,* the marketing policy of the South Dakota Cement Commission has cut off interstate trade.[3] The State can raise such a bar when it enters the market to supply its own needs. In order to ensure an adequate supply of cement for public uses, the State can withhold from interstate commerce the cement needed for public projects.

The State, however, has no parallel justification for favoring private, in-state customers over out-of-state customers.[4] In response to political concerns that likely would be inconsequential to a private cement producer, South Dakota has shut off its cement sales to customers beyond its borders. That discrimination constitutes a direct barrier to trade "of the type forbidden by the Commerce Clause, and involved in previous cases." *Alexandria Scrap.* The effect on interstate trade is the same as if the state legislature had imposed the policy on private cement producers. The Commerce Clause prohibits this severe restraint on commerce.

Notes and Questions

1. *The rationale.* Does *Reeves* rest, as the dissent suggests, on the "pretense" that a state entering the marketplace should be equated with "a private economic actor"? Or does it rest instead on the view that a state, as a *political* unit, may legitimately take at least some actions with the distinctive aim of benefiting its citizens and its citizens alone? Cf. Dan T. Coenen, *Untangling the Market–Participant Exemption to the Dormant Commerce Clause,* 88 Mich.L.Rev. 395, 479 (1989); Jonathan D. Varat, *State "Citizenship" and Interstate Equality,* 48 U.Chi.L.Rev. 487 (1981).[a]

3. One distinction between a private and a governmental function is whether the activity is supported with general tax funds, as was the case for the reprocessing program in *Alexandria Scrap,* or whether it is financed by the revenues it generates. In this case, South Dakota's cement plant has supported itself for many years. There is thus no need to consider the question whether a state-subsidized business could confine its sales to local residents.

4. The consequences of South Dakota's "residents-first" policy were devastating to petitioner Reeves, Inc., a Wyoming firm. For 20 years, Reeves had purchased about 95% of its cement from the South Dakota plant. When the State imposed its preference for South Dakota residents in 1978, Reeves had to reduce its production by over 75%. As a result, its South Dakota competitors were in a vastly superior position to compete for work in the region.

2. *Discriminatory regulations and permissible preferences.* (a) Consider again the dicta of the unanimous opinion in *Limbach*, Sec. 2, I supra, suggesting that it is permissible under the commerce clause for states to provide subsidies to in-state producers or distributors that are designed to enable them to compete more favorably against out-of-staters. Are the reasons for not applying commerce clause restraints to the state-as-subsidizer applicable to the state-as-trader?

Consider Donald H. Regan, *The Supreme Court and State Protectionism: Making Sense of the Dormant Commerce Clause*, 84 Mich.L.Rev. 1091, 1193–95 (1986): "Many spending programs are [b]eneficial from the point of view of the nation as a whole—agricultural extension services, advertising (to the extent it has information content), certainly welfare programs. But many of these programs would not exist if the state could not channel the primary benefits to locals. Even the construction involved in *White v. Massachusetts Council of Construction Employers* [infra], to the extent it was a public works program, created an unquestioned benefit and probably would not have existed if the local preference aspect had been forbidden. [Moreover, the] very fact that spending programs involve spending and are therefore relatively expensive as a way of securing local benefit makes them less likely to proliferate than measures like tariffs. They are therefore less likely to damage the economy seriously in the aggregate, if they damage it at all."

(b) Should a state university be able to provide preferential admissions and tuition to in-state residents? See *Starns v. Malkerson*, 401 U.S. 985, 91 S.Ct. 1231, 28 L.Ed.2d 527 (1971), summarily aff'g 326 F.Supp. 234 (D.Minn.1970)(upholding one-year residency requirement for lower, instate tuition); *cf. Vlandis v. Kline*, 412 U.S. 441, 93 S.Ct. 2230, 37 L.Ed.2d 63 (1973) (assuming the validity of a preference for residents but invalidating a conclusive presumption that a student who applied from out of state remained a nonresident throughout college).

SOUTH–CENTRAL TIMBER DEVELOPMENT, INC. v. WUNNICKE, 467 U.S. 82, 104 S.Ct. 2237, 81 L.Ed.2d 71 (1984), held that the market participant concept did not free Alaska from commerce clause invalidation of the state's contractual requirement that purchasers of state-owned standing timber must generally saw it into "cants" less than nine inches wide before shipping it out of state. WHITE, J.'s plurality opinion, joined by Brennan, Blackmun, and Stevens, JJ., stressed that the requirement reached beyond the market transaction in which the state participated: "[The] market-participant doctrine permits a state to influence 'a discrete, identifiable class of economic activity in which [it] is a major participant.' Contrary to the state's contention, the doctrine is not carte blanche to impose any conditions that the state has the economic power to dictate, and does not validate any requirement merely because the state imposes it upon someone with whom it is in contractual privity.

"The limit of the market-participant doctrine must be that it allows a State to impose burdens on commerce within the market in which it is a participant, but allows it to go no further. The State may not impose conditions, whether by statute, regulation, or contract, that have a substantial regulatory effect outside of

---

a. For criticism of the market participant doctrine, see Michael J. Polelle, *A Critique of the Market Participation Exception*, 15 Whittier L.Rev. 647 (1994). See also Karl Manheim, *New-Age Federalism and the Market Participant Doctrine*, 22 Ariz.St.L.J. 559 (1990).

that particular market. Unless the 'market' is relatively narrowly defined, the doctrine has the potential of swallowing up the rule that States may not impose substantial burdens on interstate commerce even if they act with the permissible state purpose of fostering local industry.

"[Alaska] contends that it is participating in the processed timber market, although it acknowledges that it participates in no way in the actual processing. South–Central argues, on the other hand, that although the State may be a participant in the timber market, it is using its leverage in that market to exert a regulatory effect in the processing market, in which it is not a participant. We agree with the latter position.

"[We] reject the contention that a State's action as a market regulator may be upheld against Commerce Clause challenge on the ground that the State could achieve the same end as a market participant. We therefore find it unimportant for present purposes that the State could support its processing industry by selling only to Alaska processors, by vertical integration, or by direct subsidy."

Having found the commerce clause applicable, the opinion concluded that Alaska's log processing requirement fell within the *Pike* and *Philadelphia* "rule of virtual per se invalidity" because of its "protectionist nature."[a]

REHNQUIST, J., joined by O'Connor, J., dissented: "Alaska is merely paying the buyer of the timber indirectly, by means of a reduced price, to hire Alaska residents to process the timber. Under existing precedent, the State could accomplish that same result in any number of ways. [T]he State could choose to sell its timber only to those companies that maintain active primary-processing plants in Alaska. *Reeves*. Or the State could directly subsidize the primary-processing industry within the State. *Alexandria Scrap*. The State could even pay to have the logs processed and then enter the market only to sell processed logs. It seems to me unduly formalistic to conclude that the one path chosen by the State as best suited to promote its concerns is the path forbidden it by the Commerce Clause."[b]

Notes and Questions

1. *The distinction of Reeves.* Was the distinction of *Reeves* persuasive? Is a case-by-case, pragmatic analysis necessary or appropriate to determine whether conditions on state contracts favoring in-state interests have more in common with forbidden regulatory discrimination or with permissible preferences by a market participant?

2. *Construction projects.* Suppose that a city raises tax revenues to support a public building project and requires contractors on the project to give an employment preference to city residents. Under the market participant doctrine, the city could prefer local contractors, but does it reach beyond the market in which it is a direct participant in dictating discrimination by its contractors? See *White v. Massachusetts Council of Constr. Employers*, 460 U.S. 204, 103 S.Ct. 1042, 75 L.Ed.2d 1 (1983), (rejecting a commerce clause challenge to a mandate from the Mayor of Boston that had instituted employment preferences for Boston residents on city-funded construction projects).

a. Powell, J., joined by Burger, C.J., would have remanded the foregoing issues for consideration by the court of appeals. But they joined Part II of White, J.'s opinion, which ruled that longstanding federal policy forbidding shipment from Alaska of unprocessed timber from federal lands did not negate the implied inval-idity under the commerce clause of a similar state policy for timber from state lands: for "a state regulation to be removed from the reach of the dormant Commerce Clause, congressional intent must be unmistakably clear."

b. Marshall, J., took no part.

Is *White* persuasively distinguishable from *South-Central Timber*? Should it matter that the state, in *South-Central Timber*, entered the market to sell a natural resource that it had not created, whereas the city in *White* had raised money from taxpayers to create public benefits? Having raised money from its citizens to benefit the political community, did the city in *White* have an especially strong claim to insist that its expenditures redound as broadly as possible to benefit the community and its members? Is this distinction adequate to deal with natural resources (such as the timber in *South-Central Timber*?) that a state may have invested public funds in managing or conserving?

SECTION 4. INTERSTATE PRIVILEGES AND IMMUNITIES CLAUSE

UNITED BUILDING & CONSTRUCTION TRADES COUNCIL v. MAYOR OF CAMDEN

465 U.S. 208, 104 S.Ct. 1020, 79 L.Ed.2d 249 (1984).

JUSTICE REHNQUIST delivered the opinion of the Court.

A municipal ordinance of the city of Camden, New Jersey, requires that at least 40% of the employees of contractors and subcontractors working on city construction projects be Camden residents. Appellant, the United Building and Construction Trades Council of Camden County and Vicinity (Council), challenges that ordinance as a violation of the Privileges and Immunities Clause, Art. IV, § 2, cl. 1, of the United States Constitution.[1] [The City argues] that the Clause only applies to laws passed by a State. [But the] fact that the ordinance [is] municipal [does] not somehow place it outside the scope of the Privileges and Immunities Clause. [What] would be unconstitutional if done directly by the State can no more readily be accomplished by a city deriving its authority from the State. [Nor can we accept] that the Privileges and Immunities Clause does not apply to an ordinance that discriminates solely on the basis of municipal residency. The Clause is phrased in terms of state citizenship and was designed "to place the citizens of each State upon the same footing with citizens of other States, as far as the advantages resulting from citizenship in those States are concerned." [But we] have never read the Clause so literally as to apply it only to distinctions based on state citizenship. [A] person who is not residing in a given State is ipso facto not residing in a city within that State. Thus, whether the exercise of a privilege is conditioned on state residency or on municipal residency he will just as surely be excluded.

[It] is true that New Jersey citizens not residing in Camden will be affected by the ordinance as well as out-of-state citizens. And it is true that the disadvantaged New Jersey residents have no claim under the Privileges and Immunities Clause. *Slaughter-House Cases.* But New Jersey residents at least have a chance to remedy at the polls any discrimination against them. Out-of-state citizens have no similar opportunity. [Application] of the Privileges and Immunities Clause to a particular instance of discrimination against out-of-state residents entails a two-step inquiry. As an initial matter, the Court must decide whether the ordinance burdens one of those privileges and immunities protected by the Clause. *Baldwin v. Montana Fish and Game Comm'n.*, 436 U.S. 371, 98 S.Ct. 1852, 56 L.Ed.2d 354

---

1. "The Citizens of each State shall be enti-   zens in the several States."
tled to all Privileges and Immunities of Citi-

(1978).[a] Not all forms of discrimination against citizens of other States are constitutionally suspect: "Some distinctions between residents and nonresidents merely reflect the fact that this is a Nation composed of individual States, and are permitted; other distinctions are prohibited because they hinder the formation, the purpose, or the development of a single Union of those States. Only with respect to those 'privileges' and 'immunities' bearing upon the vitality of the Nation as a single entity must the State treat all citizens, resident and nonresident, equally." Ibid.

As a threshold matter, then, we must determine whether an out-of-state resident's interest in employment on public works contracts in another State is sufficiently "fundamental" to the promotion of interstate harmony so as to "fall within the purview of the Privileges and Immunities Clause." Id.

Certainly, the pursuit of a common calling is one of the most fundamental of those privileges protected by the Clause. Many, if not most, of our cases expounding the Privileges and Immunities Clause have dealt with this basic and essential activity. See, e.g., *Hicklin v. Orbeck*, 437 U.S. 518, 98 S.Ct. 2482, 57 L.Ed.2d 397 (1978); *Austin v. New Hampshire*, 420 U.S. 656, 95 S.Ct. 1191, 43 L.Ed.2d 530 (1975); *Toomer v. Witsell*, 334 U.S. 385, 68 S.Ct. 1156, 92 L.Ed.2d 1460 (1948). Public employment, however, is qualitatively different from employment in the private sector; it is a subspecies of the broader opportunity to pursue a common calling. We have held that there is no fundamental right to government employment for purposes of the Equal Protection Clause. *Massachusetts Bd. of Retirement v. Murgia*, [Ch. 9, Sec. 4, V]. Cf. *McCarthy v. Philadelphia Civil Service Comm'n*, [Ch. 9, Sec. 5, II] (rejecting equal protection challenge to municipal residency requirement for municipal workers). And in *White*, we held that for purposes of the Commerce Clause everyone employed on a city public works project is, "in a substantial if informal sense, 'working for the city.'"

It can certainly be argued that for purposes of the Privileges and Immunities Clause everyone affected by the Camden ordinance is also "working for the city" and, therefore, has no grounds for complaint when the city favors its own residents. But we decline to transfer mechanically into this context an analysis fashioned to fit the Commerce Clause. Our decision in *White* turned on a distinction between the city acting as a market participant and the city acting as a market regulator. [But] the distinction between market participant and market regulator relied upon in *White* to dispose of the Commerce Clause challenge is not dispositive in this context. The two Clauses have different aims and set different standards for state conduct.

The Commerce Clause acts as an implied restraint upon state regulatory powers. Such powers must give way before the superior authority of Congress to legislate on (or leave unregulated) matters involving interstate commerce. When the State acts solely as a market participant, no conflict between state regulation and federal regulatory authority can arise. *White; Reeves*. The Privileges and Immunities Clause, on the other hand, imposes a direct restraint on state action in the interests of interstate harmony.

In *Hicklin*, we struck down as a violation of the Privileges and Immunities Clause an "Alaska Hire" statute containing a resident-hiring preference for all employment related to the development of the State's oil and gas resources. Alaska argued in that case that "because the oil and gas that are the subject of

a. *Baldwin* upheld Montana's non-resident license fee of $225 for hunting elk, compared with $30 for residents, on the ground that hunting for sport was not a protected "fundamental" right under the Privileges and Immunities Clause.

Alaska Hire are owned by the State, this ownership, of itself, is sufficient justification for the Act's discrimination against nonresidents, and takes the Act totally without the scope of the Privileges and Immunities Clause." We concluded, however, that the State's interest in controlling those things it claims to own is not absolute. "Rather than placing a statute completely beyond the Clause, the State's ownership of the property with which the statute is concerned is a factor— although often the crucial factor—to be considered in evaluating whether the statute's discrimination against noncitizens violates the Clause." Much the same analysis, we think, is appropriate to a city's efforts to bias private employment decisions in favor of its residents on construction projects funded with public moneys. The fact that Camden is expending its own funds or funds its administers in accordance with the terms of a grant is certainly a factor—perhaps the crucial factor—to be considered in evaluating whether the statute's discrimination violates the Privileges and Immunities Clause. But it does not remove the Camden ordinance completely from the purview of the Clause. [Every] inquiry under the Privileges and Immunities Clause "must [be] conducted with due regard for the principle that the States should have considerable leeway in analyzing local evils and in prescribing appropriate cures." This caution is particularly appropriate when a government body is merely setting conditions on the expenditure of funds it controls. The Alaska Hire statute at issue in *Hicklin* swept within its strictures not only contractors and subcontractors dealing directly with the State's oil and gas; it also covered suppliers who provided goods and services to those contractors and subcontractors. We invalidated the Act as "an attempt to force virtually all businesses that benefit in some way from the economic ripple effect of Alaska's decision to develop its oil and gas resources to bias their employment practices in favor of the State's residents." No similar "ripple effect" appears to infect the Camden ordinance. It is limited in scope to employees working directly on city public works projects.

Nonetheless, we find it impossible to evaluate Camden's justification on the record as it now stands. No trial has ever been held in the case. No findings of fact have been made. [We], therefore, [remand for] proceedings not inconsistent with this opinion.

JUSTICE BLACKMUN, dissenting.

[Because] I believe that the [Privileges and Immunities Clause] does not apply to discrimination based on municipal residence, I dissent.

Notes and Questions

1. *Restriction to fundamental rights.* Is the restriction of the privileges and immunities clause to fundamental rights manageable and defensible? In imposing this limitation in *Baldwin,* the Court relied heavily on the opinion of Justice Bushrod Washington in *Corfield v. Coryell,* 6 F.Cas. 546, 552 (No. 3,230)(C.C.E.D.Pa.1825): "The inquiry is, what are the privileges and immunities of citizens in the several states? We feel no hesitation in confining these expressions to those privileges and immunities which are, in their nature, fundamental; which belong, of right, to the citizens of all free governments; and which have, at all times, been enjoyed by the citizens of the several states, [from] the time of their becoming free, independent, and sovereign. What these fundamental principles are, it would perhaps be more tedious than difficult to enumerate. They may, however, be all comprehended under the following general heads: Protection by the government; the enjoyment of life and liberty, with the right to acquire and

possess property of every kind, and to pursue and obtain happiness and safety; subject nevertheless to such restraints as the government may justly prescribe for the general good of the whole."

However, exactly, fundamental rights are to be defined, it seems clear that the "fundamental" rights protected by the privileges and immunities clause are defined differently from the "fundamental" rights entitled to heightened judicial protection under the due process and equal protection clauses, as considered in Ch. 6 and Ch. 9 respectively. See, e.g., Jonathan D. Varat, *State "Citizenship" and Interstate Equality*, 48 U.Chi.L.Rev. 487, 512–16 (1981).

Under the fundamental rights formula, could (should) California, for example, confine to Californians the use of its state-owned parks, campgrounds, and beaches? Cf. Varat, supra, at 509–16.

2. *Applicable test.* In cases where the privileges and immunities clause applies, what test will the Court employ to assess the permissibility of discrimination against out-of-staters?

(a) A much quoted formulation in *Toomer*, which invalidated a discriminatory state tax on non-residents' access to migratory shrimp, said: "Like many other constitutional provisions, the privileges and immunities clause is not an absolute. It does bar discrimination against citizens of other States where there is no substantial reason for the discrimination beyond the mere fact that they are citizens of other States. But it does not preclude disparity of treatment in the many situations where there are perfectly valid independent reasons for it. Thus the inquiry in each case must be concerned with whether such reasons do exist and whether the degree of discrimination bears a close relation to [them. The] purpose [is] to outlaw classifications based on the fact of non-citizenship unless there is something to indicate that non-citizens constitute a peculiar source of the evil at which the statute is aimed."

(b) *Hicklin* framed its rationale as follows: "[No] showing was made on this record that nonresidents were 'a peculiar source of the evil' Alaska Hire was enacted to remedy, namely Alaska's 'uniquely high unemployment.' [Moreover,] even if the State's showing is accepted as sufficient to indicate that nonresidents were 'a peculiar source of evil,' [the] discrimination the Act works against nonresidents does not bear a substantial relationship to the particular 'evil' they are said to present. Alaska Hire simply grants all Alaskans, regardless of their employment status, education, or training, a flat employment preference for all jobs covered by the Act. [If] Alaska is to attempt to ease her unemployment problem by forcing employers within the State to discriminate against nonresidents—again, a policy which may present serious constitutional questions—the means by which she does so must be more closely tailored to aid the unemployed the Act is intended to benefit."

(c) LUNDING v. NEW YORK STATE TAX APPEALS TRIBUNAL, 522 U.S. 287, 118 S.Ct. 766, 139 L.Ed.2d 717 (1998), invalidated a New York statute that effectively denied non-resident taxpayers a state income tax deduction for alimony payments that was available to resident taxpayers. The 6–3 majority, per O'CONNOR, J., found that the state had advanced no justification for the disparate treatment adequate to satisfy the applicable standard, which it stated as follows: "[W]hen confronted with a challenge under the Privileges and Immunities Clause to a law distinguishing between residents and nonresidents, a State may defend its position by demonstrating that '(i) there is a substantial reason for the difference in treatment; and (ii) the discrimination practiced against nonresidents bears a substantial relationship to the State's objective.' " Ginsburg, J., joined by Rehnquist, C.J., and Kennedy, J., dissented.

(d) Are the differences among these formulations potentially significant?

3. *Distinguishing Hicklin?* On the remand, is *United Building* distinguishable from *Hicklin* on the ground that the city of Camden was spending money that it had raised and was therefore entitled to allocate preferentially to city residents—that it was entitled to reap what it had sown—whereas the state of Alaska had not comparably generated the oil involved in *Hicklin* (or, to continue the metaphor, had not sown what it was attempting to reap). Cf. Saul Levmore, *Interstate Exploitation and Judicial Intervention*, 69 Va.L.Rev. 563, 584–86 (1983).[b] Should states be encouraged to "sow" by being permitted to prefer their own citizens in distributing what they have "reaped"? Reconsider at this point the question whether states should be able to subsidize industries by the provision of direct cash subsidies, even though they would be barred by the commerce clause from protecting those same industries by the enactment of discriminatory regulations. See Sec. 2, I supra.

4. *The relation of the commerce and privileges and immunities clauses.* (a) The Court has not abandoned its holding in *Paul v. Virginia*, 75 U.S. (8 Wall.) 168, 19 L.Ed. 357 (1869), that corporations are not "citizens" within the meaning of, and thus are not protected by, the privileges and immunities clause.

(b) Different standards of review apply under the dormant commerce and privileges and immunities clauses, and there may be some additional differences in their coverage.

(c) Is there any persuasive reason why the market participant doctrine should apply to the commerce clause but not the privileges and immunities clause? Is the perceived need for the exception under the commerce clause, but not the privileges and immunities clause, indicative of broader difficulties with dormant commerce clause doctrine more generally? Would it be desirable to "lay the dormant commerce clause to rest" and trust state legislatures to balance state and federal interests, subject to protection of the federal commerce interest by congressional legislation and by judicial review of discriminatory legislation (but not legislation that otherwise burdens commerce) under the privileges and immunities clause?[c]

SECTION 5.   STATE POWER TO TAX

Besides imposing restrictions on state regulatory enactments, the dormant commerce clause constrains state taxation of interstate commerce. In some respects—in particular, in its general prohibition against discrimination—the doctrine applicable to state taxation parallels the doctrine for testing the validity of state regulatory measures.[a] Some dormant commerce clause cases involving tax statutes have, accordingly, appeared already in the preceding materials. But apart

---

b. For an exploration of when state preference laws concerning the expenditure of state funds do and do not yield net economic benefits to the nation as a whole, and a suggestion that courts should weigh this factor in privileges and immunities clause cases, see Werner Z. Hirsch, *An Economic Analysis of the Constitutionality of State Preference Laws*, 14 Int'l Rev.L. & Econ. 299 (1994).

c. For supporting commentary, see Julian N. Eule, *Laying the Dormant Commerce Clause*

to Rest, 91 Yale L.J. 425 (1982); Martin H. Redish & Shane V. Nugent, *The Dormant Commerce Clause and the Constitutional Balance of Federalism*, 1987 Duke L.J. 569; Karl Manheim, *New-Age Federalism and the Market Participant Doctrine*, 22 Ariz.St.L.J. 559, 616–22 (1990).

a. See, e.g., *New Energy Co. of Ind. v. Limbach*, Sec. 2, I supra.

from the parallel condemnation of discrimination, the Court has developed distinctive tests to assess the validity of state taxation (especially of multi-state businesses) under the dormant commerce clause.

This section provides a brief overview of the current doctrinal structure for assessing state taxation of firms engaged in interstate commerce under the dormant commerce clause. The materials aim to do no more than alert the student to basic principles and concerns. Fuller study can be pursued in a course in state and local taxation. In a course in Constitutional Law, among the issues of foremost concern are how and why the Court's stated tests for assessing taxes that are challenged as unduly burdening interstate commerce differ from the stated tests for assessing burdensome regulations.

COMPLETE AUTO TRANSIT, INC. v. BRADY

430 U.S. 274, 97 S.Ct. 1076, 51 L.Ed.2d 326 (1977).

JUSTICE BLACKMUN delivered the opinion of the Court.

[Mississippi imposed "privilege taxes for the privilege of doing business within the state," measured by a percent of gross income. General Motors shipped vehicles by rail from other states to Jackson, Miss., destined for Mississippi dealers. Complete Auto, a contract motor carrier, hauled the cars from Jackson to the dealers. The Court unanimously upheld the application of the tax to Complete Auto's Mississippi gross income.]

Appellant claimed that its transportation was but one part of an interstate movement, and that the taxes assessed were unconstitutional as applied to operations in interstate commerce. [Its] attack is based solely on decisions of this Court holding that a tax on the "privilege" of engaging in an activity in the State may not be applied to an activity that is part of interstate commerce. See, e.g., *Spector Motor Service v. O'Connor,* 340 U.S. 602, 71 S.Ct. 508, 95 L.Ed. 573 (1951); *Freeman v. Hewit,* 329 U.S. 249, 67 S.Ct. 274, 91 L.Ed. 265 (1946). This rule looks only to the fact that the incidence of the tax is the "privilege of doing business"; it deems irrelevant any consideration of the practical effect of the tax. The rule reflects an underlying philosophy that interstate commerce should enjoy a sort of "free trade" immunity from state taxation.

Appellee, in its turn, relies on decisions of this Court stating that "[i]t was not the purpose of the commerce clause to relieve those engaged in interstate commerce from their just share of state tax burden even though it increases the cost of doing the business." *Western Live Stock v. Bureau,* 303 U.S. 250, 58 S.Ct. 546, 82 L.Ed. 823 (1938). These decisions have considered not the formal language of the tax statute, but rather its practical effect, and have sustained a tax against Commerce Clause challenge when the tax is applied to an activity with a substantial nexus with the taxing state, is fairly apportioned, does not discriminate against interstate commerce, and is fairly related to the services provided by the State.

Over the years, the Court has applied this practical analysis in approving many types of tax that avoided running afoul of the prohibition against taxing the "privilege of doing business," but in each instance it has refused to overrule the prohibition. Under the present state of the law, the *Spector* rule [has] no relationship to economic realities. Rather it stands only as a trap for the unwary draftsman.

[Not] only has the philosophy underlying the rule been rejected, but the rule itself has been stripped of any practical significance. If Mississippi had called its tax one on "net income" or on the "going concern value" of appellant's business, the *Spector* rule could not invalidate it. There is no economic consequence that follows necessarily from the use of the particular words, "privilege of doing business," and a focus on that formalism merely obscures the question whether the tax produces a forbidden effect. Simply put, the *Spector* rule does not address the problems with which the Commerce Clause is concerned. Accordingly, we now reject the rule of *Spector* * * *.

Notes and Questions

1. *Break with the past. Complete Auto* marked a sharp break with the "formalist" approach that had "initially gripped and later greatly influenced the Court for about three decades." Jesse H. Choper & Tung Yin, *State Taxation and the Dormant Commerce Clause: The Object–Measure Approach*, 1998 Sup.Ct.Rev. 193, 195.

2. *The modern test.* In assessing the validity of state taxes under the commerce clause, subsequent cases have almost invariably applied the four-part test prescribed in *Complete Auto*, which inquires whether "the tax is applied to an activity with a substantial nexus with the taxing state, is fairly apportioned, does not discriminate against interstate commerce, and is fairly related to the services provided by the State."

———

COMMONWEALTH EDISON CO. v. MONTANA, 453 U.S. 609, 101 S.Ct. 2946, 69 L.Ed.2d 884 (1981), per MARSHALL, J., upheld a Montana severance tax on coal even though 90% of the coal was shipped to other states. The tax produced "almost 20%" of the state revenue, but 50% went to a trust fund to alleviate environmental impact from strip mining and economic problems anticipated upon exhaustion of the coal resources: "Appellants assert that the Montana tax 'discriminate[s]' against interstate commerce because 90% of Montana coal is shipped to other States under contracts that shift the tax burden primarily to non-Montana utility companies and thus to citizens of other States. But the Montana tax is computed at the same rate regardless of the final destination of the coal, and there is no suggestion that the tax is administered in a manner that departs from this even-handed formula. We are not, therefore, confronted here with the type of differential tax treatment that the Court has found in other 'discrimination' cases.

"[Appellants] assume that the Commerce Clause gives residents of one State a right of access at 'reasonable' prices to resources located in another State that is richly endowed with such resources, without regard to whether and on what terms residents of the resource-rich State have access to the resources. We are not convinced that the Commerce Clause, of its own force, gives the residents of one State the right to control in this fashion the terms of resource development and depletion in a sister State. Cf. *Philadelphia v. New Jersey*.

"[The] only remaining foundation for their discrimination theory is a claim that the tax burden borne by the out-of-state consumers of Montana Coal is excessive. This is, of course, merely a variant of appellants' assertion that the Montana tax does not satisfy the 'fairly related' prong of the *Complete Auto* test, and it is to this contention that we now turn.

"[Appellants'] objection is to the *rate* of the Montana tax, and even then, their only complaint is that the *amount* the State receives in taxes far exceeds the *value* of the services provided to the coal mining industry. [To] accept appellants' apparent suggestion that the Commerce Clause prohibits the States from requiring an activity connected to interstate commerce to contribute to the general cost of providing governmental services, as distinct from those costs attributable to the taxed activity, would place such commerce in a privileged position. ['It] was not the purpose of the commerce clause to relieve those engaged in interstate commerce from their just share of state tax [burden.']

"[When,] as here, a general revenue tax does not discriminate against interstate commerce and is apportioned to activities occurring within the State, the State 'is free to pursue its own fiscal policies, [if] the state has exerted its power in relation to opportunities or * * * protection [and] benefits which it has conferred * * *.'

"The relevant inquiry under the fourth prong of the *Complete Auto* test is not, as appellants suggest, the *amount* of the tax or the *value* of the benefits allegedly bestowed as measured by the costs the State incurs on account of the taxpayer's activities. Rather, the test is closely connected to the first prong of the *Complete Auto* test. Under this threshold test, the interstate business must have a substantial nexus with the State before *any* tax may be levied on it. Beyond that threshold requirement, the fourth prong of the *Complete Auto* test imposes the additional limitation that the *measure* of the tax must be reasonably related to the extent of the contact, since it is the activities or presence of the taxpayer in the State that may properly be made to bear a 'just share of state tax burden.'

"[Because the tax] is measured as a percentage of the value of the coal taken, the Montana tax is in 'proper proportion' to appellants' activities within the State and, therefore, to their 'consequent enjoyment of the opportunities and protections which the State has afforded' in connection to those activities. When a tax is assessed in proportion to a taxpayer's activities or presence in a State, the taxpayer is shouldering its fair share of supporting the State's provision of 'police and fire protection, the benefit of a trained work force, and the advantages of a civilized society.'

"[W]hen the measure of a tax is reasonably related to the taxpayer's activities or presence in the State—from which it derives some benefit such as the substantial privilege of mining coal—the taxpayer will realize, in proper proportion to the taxes it pays, '[t]he only benefit to which it is constitutionally entitled[:] that derived from his enjoyment of the privileges of living in an organized society, established and safeguarded by the devotion of taxes to public purposes.' "a

BLACKMUN, J., joined by Powell and Stevens, JJ., dissented: "[The Court concludes] that the relevant inquiry under the fourth prong of the *Complete Auto* test is simply whether the *measure* of the tax is fixed as a percentage of the value of the coal taken. This interpretation emasculates the fourth prong. No trial will ever be necessary on the issue of fair relationship so long as a State is careful to impose a proportional rather than a flat tax rate. * * *

"[The] Clause is violated when, as appellants allege is the case here, the State effectively selects a class of out-of-state taxpayers to shoulder a tax burden grossly in excess of any costs imposed directly or indirectly by such taxpayers on the

a. "With considerable doubt," White, J., joined the Court's opinion, stressing in a short concurrence the power of Congress to protect interstate commerce.

State. [It]is true that a trial in this case would require 'complex factual inquiries' into whether economic conditions are such that Montana is in fact able to export the burden of its severance tax. I do not believe, however, that this threshold inquiry is beyond judicial competence. If the trial court were to determine that the tax is exported, it would then have to determine whether the tax is 'fairly related,' within the meaning of *Complete Auto.* The Court to the contrary, this would not require the trial court 'to second-guess legislative decisions about the amount or disposition of tax revenues.' If the tax is in fact a legitimate general revenue measure identical or roughly comparable to taxes imposed upon similar industries, a court's inquiry is at an end; on the other hand, if the tax singles out this particular interstate activity and charges it with a grossly disproportionate share of the general costs of government, the court must determine whether there is some reasonable basis for the legislative judgment that the tax is necessary to compensate the State for the particular costs imposed by the activity."

Notes and Questions

1. *Discrimination.* (a) "The third prong of the *Complete Auto Transit* test [forbidding discrimination against interstate commerce] has emerged as the dominant one," according to Tribe, 3d ed. at 1107–08: "Among other things, the [Court] has found invalid [those] state taxes that explicitly exempt local activities [such as the tax scheme in *Bacchus Imports, Ltd. v. Dias,* 468 U.S. 263, 104 S.Ct. 3049, 82 L.Ed.2d 200 (1984), which exempted locally produced wines from a Hawaii sales tax. The Court] has also found unconstitutionally discriminatory those state taxes which, though nondiscriminatory on their face, impose economic burdens on interstate enterprises" that are "not in fact imposed on local competitors" (citing cases invalidating fixed fees on solicitation of business, including *Robbins v. Shelby County Taxing Dist.,* 120 U.S. 489, 7 S.Ct. 592, 30 L.Ed. 694 (1887), and *Nippert v. Richmond,* 327 U.S. 416, 66 S.Ct. 586, 90 L.Ed. 760 (1946)).

Is the situation in *Commonwealth Edison Co.* persuasively distinguishable?

(b) CAMPS NEWFOUND/OWATONNA, INC. v. HARRISON, 520 U.S. 564, 117 S.Ct. 1590, 137 L.Ed.2d 852 (1997), held that a Maine statute providing a general property tax exemption for charitable institutions, but withholding the exemption from charitable institutions operated principally for the benefit of non-residents, violates the Commerce Clause. The tax was challenged by the operators of a summer camp for children of the Christian Science faith, about 95% of whose campers are not Maine residents. The Court, per STEVENS, J., viewed the tax as facially discriminatory against interstate commerce. The camp was selling a product that included "in part the natural beauty of Maine itself"; the statute created a financial incentive for the camp and other charitable institutions to prefer state residents over out-of-staters. Reasoning that the statute would be virtually per se illegal as applied to for-profit activities, Stevens, J., saw no reason to make an exception for not-for-profit organizations.

The Court rejected the argument that the "discriminatory tax exemption [at issue] is, in economic reality, no different from a discriminatory subsidy of those charities that cater principally to local needs" and should therefore be upheld. "Assuming, arguendo, that [a] direct subsidy benefitting only those nonprofits serving principally Maine residents would be permissible, our cases do not sanction a tax exemption serving similar ends. [E.g., *Limbach.*]"

SCALIA, J., joined by Rehnquist, C.J., and Thomas and Ginsburg, JJ., dissented. "[T]he provision at issue here is [narrowly] designed [to] compensate or subsidize those organizations that contribute to the public fisc by dispensing public benefits the state might otherwise provide." So understood, the statute did not facially discriminate against interstate commerce; any effect on interstate commerce was "indirect." In any event, the selective exemption was "supported by such traditional and important state interests that it survives scrutiny [even] under the 'virtually per se rule of invalidity.'" Alternatively, the state interests would support recognition of a " 'domestic charity' exception [to] the negative Commerce Clause."[b]

2. *"Fairly related."* Consider Choper & Yin, supra, at 204–05: "The fourth requirement [of *Complete Auto Transit*]—that the tax be fairly related to the services provided by the state—[has become 'insignificant']. The Court has yet to invalidate a tax under it, as 'services' has been defined so broadly—'receipt of police and fire protection, the use of public roads and mass transit, and other advantages of civilized society'—that this condition is virtually meaningless. [Any] taxpayer with a substantial nexus to the taxing state (the first prong) would appear necessarily to benefit from police and fire protection. [The] fourth prong [has] become wholly subordinate to the first." Would a more stringent approach be desirable? Judicially manageable?

CONTAINER CORP. v. FRANCHISE TAX BD., 463 U.S. 159, 103 S.Ct. 2933, 77 L.Ed.2d 545 (1983), per BRENNAN, J., upheld California's unitary "doing business" tax as applied to an Illinois corporation operating in California but also owning all or part of 20 foreign subsidiaries. California calculated the tax by considering the income of the entire integrated business and then using a formula to determine the amount of income attributable to business activity in California. Each subsidiary was relatively autonomous with respect to matters of personnel and day-to-day management, though officers of the parent established standards of professionalism, profitability and ethical practices and dealt with major problems and long term decisions. Neither parent nor subsidiaries depended on each other for a flow of goods used in the business. Only 1% of the subsidiaries' purchases were from the parent.

"Under both the Due Process and the Commerce Clauses [a] State may not, when imposing an income-based tax, 'tax value earned outside its borders.' In the case of a more-or-less integrated business enterprise operating in more than one state, however, arriving at precise territorial allocations of 'value' is often an elusive goal. [For] this reason [the Court has upheld income taxation pursuant to a] unitary business/formula apportionment method. [This method] calculates the local tax base by first determining the scope of the 'unitary business' [and] then apportioning the total income of that 'unitary business' between the taxing

b. Thomas, J., joined by Scalia, J., and in part by Rehnquist, C.J., argued in a separate dissent that the Court should "abandon" its negative Commerce Clause jurisprudence. Rather than continuing with "policy-laden decisionmaking" that is unsupported by the constitutional text, the Court should consider whether there is not a textual prohibition against certain forms of discriminatory taxation in the Import–Export Clause, Art. I, § 10, cl. 2, which provides that "[n]o state shall, without the Consent of Congress, lay any Imposts or Duties on Imports or Exports." Because the Import–Export Clause would not plausibly forbid the property tax at issue, however, Thomas, J., agreed that the constitutional challenge should be rejected. See Brannon P. Denning, *Justice Thomas, The Import–Export Clause, and Camps Newfound/Owatonna v. Harrison,* 70 Colo.L.Rev. 155 (1998), arguing that historical evidence supports Thomas, J.'s, interpretation of the import-export clause as barring discriminatory taxes on imports and exports from other states, but concluding that the import-export clause does not prohibit discriminatory state taxes.

jurisdiction and the rest of the world taking into account objective measures of the corporation's activities within and without the jurisdiction.

"[The] Due Process and Commerce Clauses [do] not allow a State to tax income arising out of interstate activities—even on a proportional basis—unless there is a 'minimum connection' or 'nexus' between the interstate activities and the taxing State.

"[We] address the unitary business issue first. [The] taxpayer always has the 'distinct burden of showing "by clear and cogent evidence" that [the state tax] results in extraterritorial values being taxed.'

"The state Court of Appeals relied on a large number of factors in reaching its judgment that appellant and its foreign subsidiaries constituted a unitary business. These included appellant's assistance to its subsidiaries in obtaining used and new equipment and in filling personnel needs that could not be met locally, the substantial role played by appellant in loaning funds to the subsidiaries and guaranteeing loans provided by others, the 'considerable interplay between appellant and its foreign subsidiaries in the area of corporate expansion,' the 'substantial' technical assistance provided by appellant to the subsidiaries, and the supervisory role played by appellant's officers in providing general guidance to the subsidiaries. [We] need not decide whether any one of these factors would be sufficient as a constitutional matter to prove the existence of a unitary business. Taken in combination, at least, they clearly demonstrate that the state court reached a conclusion 'within the realm of permissible judgment.'

"Having determined that a certain set of activities constitute a 'unitary business,' a state must then apply a formula apportioning the income of that business within and without the state. Such an apportionment formula must, under both the due process and commerce clauses, be fair. See *Hans Rees' Sons v. North Carolina*, 283 U.S. 123, 5 S.Ct. 385, 75 L.Ed. 879 (1931). The first [component] of fairness in an apportionment formula is what might be called internal consistency—that is, the formula must be such that, if applied by every jurisdiction, it would result in no more than all of the unitary business's income being taxed. The second and more difficult requirement is what might be called external consistency—the factor or factors used in the apportionment formula must actually reflect a reasonable sense of how income is generated. The Constitution does not 'invalidat[e] an apportionment formula whenever it *may* result in taxation of some income that did not have its source in the taxing [state].' Nevertheless, we will strike down the application of an apportionment formula if the taxpayer can prove 'by "clear and cogent evidence" that the income attributed to the state is in fact "out of all appropriate proportion to the business transacted in that state," or has "led to a grossly distorted result." '

"California and the other States that have adopted the Uniform [Division of Income for Tax Purposes] Act use a formula—commonly called the 'three-factor' formula—which is based, in equal parts, on the proportion of a unitary business's total payroll, property, and sales which are located in the taxing State. We approved the three-factor formula in *Butler Bros. v. McColgan*, 315 U.S. 501, 62 S.Ct. 701, 86 L.Ed. 991 (1942) [and] it has become [a] benchmark against which other apportionment formulas are judged. * * *

"Appellant challenges the application of California's three-factor formula to its business on two related grounds, both arising as a practical (although not a theoretical) matter out of the international character of the enterprise. First, appellant argues that its foreign subsidiaries are significantly more profitable than it is, and that the three-factor formula, by ignoring that fact and relying instead

on indirect measures of income such as payroll, property, and sales, systematically distorts the true allocation of income between appellant and the subsidiaries. The problem with this argument is obvious: the profit figures relied on by appellant are based on precisely the sort of formal geographical accounting whose basic theoretical weaknesses justify resort to formula apportionment in the first place. [W]henever a unitary business exists, 'separate [geographical] accounting, while it purports to isolate portions of income received in various States, may fail to account for contributions to income resulting from functional integration, centralization of management, and economies of scale. Because these factors of profitability arise from the operation of the business as a whole, it becomes misleading to characterize the income of the business as having a single identifiable "source." '
* * *

"Appellant's second argument [is that the payroll factor in the formula inflated the income attributed to United States operations because of the lower wages and hence lower production costs in the foreign countries.] The problem with all this evidence, however, is that it does not by itself come close to impeaching the basic rationale behind the three-factor formula. Appellant and its foreign subsidiaries have been determined to be a unitary business. It therefore may well be that in addition to the foreign payroll going into the production of any given corrugated container by a foreign subsidiary, there is also California payroll, as well as other California factors, contributing—albeit more indirectly—to the same production. The mere fact that this possibility is not reflected in appellant's accounting does not disturb the underlying premises of the formula apportionment method.

"Both geographical accounting and formula apportionment are imperfect proxies for an ideal which is not only difficult to achieve in practice, but also difficult to describe in theory. Some methods of formula apportionment are particularly problematic because they focus on only a small part of the spectrum of activities by which value is generated. [In] *Hans Rees' Sons,* for example, an apportionment method based entirely on ownership of tangible property resulted in an attribution to North Carolina of between 66 and 85% of the taxpayer's income over the course of a number of years, while a separate accounting analysis purposely skewed to resolve all doubts in favor of the State resulted in an attribution of no more than 21.7%. We struck down the application of the one-factor formula to that particular business, holding that the method, 'albeit fair on its face, operates so as to reach profits which are in no just sense attributable to transactions within its jurisdiction.'[a]

"The three-factor formula used by California has gained wide approval precisely because payroll, property, and sales appear in combination to reflect a very large share of the activities by which value is generated. It is therefore able to avoid the sorts of distortions that were present in *Hans Rees' Sons.*

"Of course, even the three-factor formula is necessarily imperfect. But we have seen no evidence demonstrating that the margin of error (systematic or not) inherent in the three-factor formula is greater than the margin of error (systematic or not) inherent in the sort of separate accounting urged upon us by appellant."

Notes and Questions

1. *Nexus.* (a) *Unrelated business activity.* ASARCO v. IDAHO STATE TAX COMM'N, 458 U.S. 307, 102 S.Ct. 3103, 73 L.Ed.2d 787 (1982), per POWELL, J.,

---

a. Compare *Moorman Mfg. Co. v. Bair,* 437 U.S. 267, 98 S.Ct. 2340, 57 L.Ed.2d 197 (1978) (upholding single factor (sales) apportionment formula).

ruled that ASARCO—engaged in mining, smelting, refining, and selling of non-ferrous metals—could exclude from its apportioned net income, for Idaho's income tax, dividends from partially-owned foreign subsidiaries engaged in similar business abroad over which ASARCO exercised no voting control and for which it made no operational or management decisions: "We cannot accept, consistent with recognized due process standards, a definition of 'unitary business' that would permit nondomiciliary States to apportion and tax dividends '[w]here the business activities of the dividend payor have nothing to do with the activities of the recipient in the taxing State.'

"[In] this case, it is plain that the five dividend-paying subsidiaries 'add to the riches' of ASARCO. But it is also true that they are 'discrete business enterprises' that—in 'any business or economic sense'—have 'nothing to do with the activities' of ASARCO in Idaho. Therefore there is no 'rational relationship between the [ASARCO dividend] income attributed to the State and the intrastate values of the enterprise.' "

(b) *Commerce and due process clauses.* In *ASARCO* as in a number of other cases, the Court did not carefully distinguish the "nexus" inquiries mandated by the commerce and due process clauses. Compare QUILL CORP. v. NORTH DAKOTA, 504 U.S., 298, 112 S.Ct. 1904, 119 L.Ed.2d 91 (1992), which invalidated North Dakota's requirement that out-of-state mail order sellers collect North Dakota's use tax from North Dakota mail order buyers. Although North Dakota had the "minimum contacts" necessary for jurisdiction to tax under the due process clause, the Court, per STEVENS, J., ruled the tax invalid under the commerce clause: "The nexus requirements of the due process and commerce clauses are not identical. [The] 'substantial-nexus' requirement is not, like due process' 'minimum-contacts' requirement, a proxy for notice, but rather a means for limiting state burdens on interstate commerce. [A] corporation may have the 'minimum contacts' with a taxing State as required by the Due Process Clause, and yet lack the 'substantial nexus' with that State as required by the Commerce Clause."[a]

2. *Fair apportionment: internal and external consistency.* According to OKLAHOMA STATE TAX COMM'N v. JEFFERSON LINES, INC., 514 U.S. 175, 115 S.Ct. 1331, 131 L.Ed.2d 261 (1995), the "*internal* consistency" requirement is met "when the imposition of a tax identical to the one in question by every other state would add no burden to interstate commerce that intrastate commerce would not also bear.[b] *[E]xternal* consistency, on the other hand, looks not to the logical consequences of cloning, but to the economic justification for the State's claim upon the value taxed, to discover whether a State's tax reaches beyond that portion of value that is fairly attributable to economic activity within the taxing State." On its facts, the case upheld a state tax on the sale of bus tickets, including interstate bus tickets, that was not apportioned to miles traveled within the state—even though a tax levied by the same state on the gross receipts of an interstate bus company would admittedly have had to apply an apportionment formula. Should this difference in form make a difference as to result? Is it consistent with the anti-formalist aspirations of *Complete Auto*?

a. Scalia, J., joined by Kennedy and Thomas, JJ., concurred in the due process ruling but withheld judgment on the majority's commerce clause reasoning. White, J., accepted the due process ruling but dissented from the commerce clause ruling.

b. For an application, see *American Trucking Ass'ns. v. Scheiner*, 483 U.S. 266, 274, 107 S.Ct. 2829, 97 L.Ed.2d 226 (1987), invalidating a state tax of $36 per vehicle axle per year for the privilege of using the state's highways, on the ground that if all states imposed similar taxes, interstate commerce would be disadvantaged relative to intrastate commerce.

3. *Review of taxes compared with regulations.* (a) Consider Tribe 3d ed., at 1140: "The fair apportionment requirements are [analogous] to the prohibition on extraterritorial regulation discussed in [Sec. 2, IV supra]. By preventing states from effectively imposing their regulations on persons or transactions in other states, the prohibition on extraterritorial regulation prevents states from regulating more than their fair 'share' of national activity."

(b) Compare Choper & Yin, supra, at 199–200: "[T]he theoretical underpinnings of the test announced in *Complete Auto* [can] be seen as securing two precepts that further the Dormant Commerce Clause's core prohibition of discrimination against interstate commerce: avoidance of (a) multiple taxation on interstate commerce and (b) direct commercial advantage of local businesses at the expense of multistate enterprises. This principle—that 'the commerce clause prohibits taxes that bear more heavily on the interstate than the intrastate enterprise merely because the former does business across state lines'—articulated a specially directed, yet expansive conception of nondiscrimination, one that seemingly differs somewhat in both purpose and effect from that concerning judicial review of state *regulation* of interstate commerce. Thus, when a state rule 'regulates evenhandedly to effectuate a legitimate local public interest,' it may still be rejected by the Court if 'the burden imposed on commerce is clearly excessive in relation to the local benefits,' even though neither its purpose nor effect is to treat interstate business any more onerously than local enterprises. This is not the Court's focus, however, when it reviews state taxes. Even though a particular state's system or rates of taxation may impose exceedingly heavy burdens on business enterprises, thus significantly deterring entry of interstate commerce, the decisions show that the Court will not ordinarily invalidate the tax as long as in-state businesses are subject to the same financial disadvantage.

"The bar of discrimination against interstate commerce contributes important clarification of the concept of 'multiple taxation.' The mere fact that a taxpayer is subjected to a number of different taxes does not violate the prohibition against multiple taxation if those taxes are imposed on unrelated activities, such as a sales tax, a property tax, an income tax, and a gasoline tax. On the other hand, if two states both imposed their respective income taxes on all the earnings of a taxpayer who produced income in both states, that taxpayer *would* be subjected to multiple taxation. A business earning $50,000 all in one state would pay income tax to one state on that amount, but a multistate enterprise earning $50,000, half in one state and half in another, would pay income tax on the full amount twice. The obvious effect is discrimination against interstate commerce."[c]

c. For additional commentary on state taxation under the dormant commerce clause, see, e.g., Walter Hellerstein et al., *Commerce Clause Restraints on State Taxation After Jefferson Lines*, 51 Tax L.Rev. 47 (1995); William B. Lockhart, *A Revolution in State Taxation of Commerce*, 85 Minn.L.Rev. 1025 (1981); Ferdinand P. Schoettle, *Commerce Clause Challenges to State Taxes*, 75 Minn.L.Rev. 907 (1991); Daniel A. Shaviro, *An Economic and Political Look at Federalism in Taxation*, 90 Mich.L.Rev. 895 (1992); David F. Shores, *State Taxation of Interstate Commerce: Quill, Allied Signal and a Proposal*, 72 Neb.L.Rev. 682 (1993); Winkfield F. Twyman, Jr., *Beyond Purpose: Addressing State Discrimination in Interstate Commerce*, 46 S.C.L.Rev. 381 (1995).

Chapter 5

SUBSTANTIVE PROTECTION OF ECONOMIC INTERESTS

INTRODUCTION

Most of the remaining chapters are concerned with constitutional limitations on government power, independent of limitations arising out of the distribution of powers within the federal system. Some of the limitations are identical, or nearly so, whether applied to the state or federal governments, but are based on different sources. The major limitations on the federal government are found in the Bill of Rights and in Art. I, § 9, while those on state government are based largely on the thirteenth, fourteenth, and fifteenth amendments and on Art. I, § 10. But the fourteenth amendment has now been held to impose on the states most of the limitations the Bill of Rights imposes on the federal government.

These materials do not deal with all the federal constitutional limitations but only those of major significance and difficulty. State constitutions include additional limitations on state government, some similar to federal limitations though occasionally interpreted differently, and some quite dissimilar in terms and purposes. Study of the federal limitations should provide adequate background for handling many of the state-imposed limitations.

SECTION 1. ORIGINS OF SUBSTANTIVE DUE PROCESS

One important concern of this and later chapters is the extent to which the due process clauses of the fifth and fourteenth amendments may be invoked to impose limits on the *substance* of governmental regulations and other activities, as well as to govern the *procedures* by which government affects "life, liberty and property." That these clauses embody *any* limits on the substance of legislation requires some initial explanation, since their terms refer only to "process."

Professor Edward S. Corwin traced the origin and evolution of due process as a substantive limitation on governmental power in a series of articles, later revised in his *Liberty Against Government* (1948). This book, concerned primarily with judicial evolution of concepts designed to limit government regulation of property and economic interests, provides a valuable background for understanding, as well, some of the underpinnings for the later use of the due process clause and first amendment to limit governmental interference with basic personal liberties.

I. EARLY EXPRESSIONS OF THE NOTION THAT GOVERNMENTAL AUTHORITY HAS IMPLIED LIMITS

The most notable early expression in this country of the view that there are implied or inherent limits on governmental power is CHASE, J.'s opinion in CALDER v. BULL, 3 Dall. (3 U.S.) 386, 1 L.Ed. 648 (1798). Although the Supreme Court rejected the claim of potential heirs that a Connecticut statute amounted to an *ex post facto* law (because the *ex post facto* clause only applied to criminal laws), Chase, J., made plain his willingness in an appropriate case to strike down legislation without regard to explicit constitutional limitations:

"I cannot subscribe to the omnipotence of a State Legislature, or that it is absolute and without control; although its authority should not be expressly restrained by the Constitution, or fundamental law of the State. The people of the United States erected their constitutions, or forms of government, to establish justice, to promote the general welfare, to secure the blessings of liberty, and to protect their persons and property from violence. The purposes for which men enter into society will determine the nature and terms of the social compact; and as they are the foundation of the legislative power, they will decide what are the proper objects of it. The nature and ends of legislative power will limit the exercise of it. This fundamental principle flows from the very nature of our free Republican governments, that no man should be compelled to do what the laws do not require; nor to refrain from acts which the laws permit. There are acts which the Federal, or State, Legislature cannot do, without exceeding their authority. There are certain vital principles in our free Republican governments, which will determine and overrule an apparent and flagrant abuse of legislative power; as to authorize manifest injustice by positive law; to take away that security for personal liberty, or private property, for the protection whereof the government was established. An ACT of the legislature (for I cannot call it a law), contrary to the great first principles of the social compact, cannot be considered a rightful exercise of legislative authority. The obligation of a law in governments established on express compact, and on republican principles, must be determined by the nature of the power on which it is founded. A few instances will suffice to explain what I mean. A law that punished a citizen for an innocent action or, in other words, for an act, which, when done, was in violation of no existing law; a law that destroys, or impairs, the lawful private contracts of citizens; a law that makes a man a Judge in his own cause; or a law that takes property from A and gives it to B: It is against all reason and justice, for a people to intrust a Legislature with SUCH powers; and therefore, it cannot be presumed that they have done it. The genius, the nature, and the spirit, of our State Governments, amount to a prohibition of such acts of legislation; and the general principles of law and reason forbid them. [To] maintain that our Federal, or State Legislature possesses such powers, if they had not been expressly restrained, would, in my opinion, be a political heresy, altogether inadmissible in our free republican governments."[a]

a. For the view that Chase, J.'s opinion is a philosophical, not a constitutional, argument, see John H. Ely, *On Discovering Fundamental Values*, 92 Harv.L.Rev. 5, 26–27 n. 95 (1978).

handwritten margin note: no defined bases judges can use to find natural law

IREDELL, J., disagreed: "[If] a government, composed of Legislative, Executive and Judicial departments, were established, by a constitution which imposed no limits on the legislative power, the consequence would inevitably be, that whatever the legislative power chose to enact, would be lawfully enacted, and the judicial power could never interpose to pronounce it void. It is true, that some speculative jurists have held, that a legislative act against natural justice must, in itself, be void; but I cannot think that, under such a government any Court of Justice would possess a power to declare it so. [I]t has been the policy of all the American states, which have, individually, framed their state constitutions, since the revolution, and of the people of the United States, when they framed the Federal Constitution, to define with precision the objects of the legislative power, and to restrain its exercise within marked and settled boundaries. If any act of Congress, or of the Legislature of a state, violates those constitutional provisions, it is unquestionably void. [If], on the other hand, the Legislature of the Union, or the Legislature of any member of the Union, shall pass a law, within the general scope of their constitutional power, the Court cannot pronounce it to be void, merely because it is, in their judgment, contrary to the principles of natural justice. The ideas of natural justice are regulated by no fixed standard: the ablest and the purest men have differed upon the subject; and all that the Court could properly say, in such an event, would be that the Legislature (possessed of an equal right of opinion) had passed an act which, in the opinion of the judges, was inconsistent with the abstract principles of natural justice."

Notes and Questions

1. Compare Lord Coke in *Dr. Bonham's Case*, 8 Co. 113b, 118a, 77 Eng.Rep. 646, 652 (1610): "And it appears in our books, that in many cases, the common law will controul Acts of Parliament, and sometimes adjudge them to be utterly void: for when an Act of Parliament is against common right and reason, or repugnant, or impossible to be performed, the common law will controul it, and adjudge such Act to be void." For commentary on the influence of the Coke dictum, see Corwin, *Liberty Against Government* 34–40 (1948). For philosophical origins of the Chase viewpoint, see Corwin, *The "Higher Law" Background of American Constitutional Law*, 42 Harv.L.Rev. 149, 365 (1928–1929). For the extent to which similar viewpoints crept into judicial opinions and decisions between the revolution and 1830, see *Liberty Against Government* 58–67: "The truth is that Iredell's tenet that courts were not to appeal to natural rights and the social compact as furnishing a basis for constitutional decisions was disregarded at one time or another by all of the leading judges and advocates of the initial period of our constitutional history, an era which closes about 1830."

2. *Justice Souter calls attention to "two centuries of American constitutional practice in recognizing unenumerated, substantive limits on governmental action."* Concurring in the judgment in *Washington v. Glucksberg*, (1997) (p. 486 infra), which rejected the argument that there is a constitutional right to physician-assisted suicide, SOUTER, J., noted that the physicians who asserted this right "also invoke two centuries of American constitutional practice in recognizing unenumerated substantive limits on governmental action." "Although this practice has neither rested on any single textual basis nor expressed a consistent theory, [the] persistence of substantive due process in our cases points to the legitimacy of the modern justification for such judicial review * * *.

"Before the ratification of the Fourteenth Amendment, substantive constitutional review resting on a theory of unenumerated rights occurred largely in the state courts applying state constitutions that commonly contained either due process clauses like that of the Fifth Amendment (and later the Fourteenth) on the textual antecedents of such clauses, repeating Magna Carta's guarantee of 'the law of the land.' On the basis of such clauses, or of general principles untethered to specific constitutional language, state courts evaluated the constitutionality of a wide range of statutes. [The] middle of the 19th century brought the famous *Wynehamer* case, invalidating a statute purporting to render possession of liquor immediately illegal except when kept for narrow, specified purposes, the state court finding the statute inconsistent with the State's due process clause. WYNE-HAMER v. PEOPLE, 13 N.Y. 378, 486 (1856). The statute was deemed an excessive threat to the 'fundamental rights of the citizen' to property. (opinion of Comstock, J.).

"Even in this early period, however, this Court anticipated the developments that would presage both the Civil War and the ratification of the Fourteenth Amendment, by making it clear on several occasions that it too had no doubt of the judiciary's power to strike down legislation that conflicted with important but unenumerated principles of American government. [In] FLETCHER v. PECK, 6 Cranch 87, 3 L.Ed. 162 (1810), [the Court] struck down an Act of the Georgia Legislature that purported to rescind a sale of public land ab initio and reclaim title for the State, and so deprive subsequent, good-faith purchasers of property conveyed by the original grantees. The Court rested the invalidation on alternative sources of authority: the specific prohibitions against bill of attainder, *ex post facto* laws, laws impairing contracts in Article 1, § 10, of the Constitution; and 'general principles which are common to our free institutions,' by which Chief Justice Marshall meant that a simple deprivation of property by the State could not be an authentically 'legislative' Act.

"*Fletcher* was not, though, the most telling early example of such review. For its most salient instance in the Court before the adoption of the Fourteenth Amendment was, of course, the case that the Amendment would in due course overturn, DRED SCOTT v. SANDFORD, 19 How. 393, 15 L.Ed. 691 (1857). Unlike *Fletcher*, *Dred Scott* was textually based on a Due Process Clause (in the Fifth Amendment, applicable to the National Government), and it was in reliance on that Clauses's protection of property that the Court invalidated the Missouri Compromise. This substantive protection of an owner's property in a slave taken to the territories was traced to the absence of any enumerated power to affect that property granted to the Congress by Article 1 of the Constitution, the implication being that the Government had no legitimate interest that could support the earlier congressional compromise. The ensuing judgment of history needs no recounting here."

II. THE SEARCH FOR A CONSTITUTIONAL BASIS

The philosophical grounds asserted in those early cases for protecting economic interests from legislative power could not long prevail in the face of the growing acceptance of the federal and state constitutions as the only sources of judicially enforceable limitations on legislative power. See Corwin, *Liberty Against Government* 173 (hereinafter Corwin): "The doctrine of vested rights attained its meridian in the early thirties, when it came under attack from two sources. The first [was] the notion that the written constitution, being an expression of popular will, was the supreme law of the State and that judicial review could validly operate only on that basis; the second was the related idea, which is connoted by the term 'police power'—that legislation which was not specifically forbidden by the written constitution must be presumed to have been enacted in the *public interest*. Confronted with these doctrines, the champions of the doctrine of vested rights were compelled to find some clause of the written constitution which could be thrown about the doctrine or else to abandon it."

Before the adoption of the fourteenth amendment in 1868, the federal constitution provided little basis for challenging state regulation of economic interests. In BARRON v. MAYOR AND CITY COUNCIL OF BALTIMORE, 32 U.S. (7 Pet.) 243, 8 L.Ed. 672 (1833), in the course of rejecting appellant's argument that by ruining the use of his wharf the city had violated his fifth amendment guarantee that private property shall not be "taken for public use, without just compensation," the Court, per MARSHALL, C.J., held that the Bill of Rights applied only to the federal government: "[The] great revolution which established the constitution of the United States was not effected without immense opposition. Serious fears were extensively entertained that [the new national powers] might be exercised in a manner dangerous to liberty. In almost every convention by which the constitution was adopted, amendments to guard against the abuse of power were recommended. These amendments demanded security against the apprehended encroachments of the general government. [They] contain no expression indicating an intention to apply them to the state governments. This court cannot so apply them."

Moreover, the Court narrowed the scope of the constitutional provision (Act 1, § 10) prohibiting the states from passing any laws "impairing the obligation of contracts."[b] Indeed, *Charles River Bridge* seemed designed to discourage resort to the federal constitution to escape regulation of economic interests: "It is well settled by the decisions of this court, that a state law may be retrospective in its character, and may divest vested rights; and yet not violate the constitution of the United States, unless it also impairs the obligation of a contract." "Thus it *became more and more evident that the doctrine of vested rights must, to survive, find anchorage in some clause or other of the various State constitutions.*" Corwin 89.

With federal constitutional grounds not available to protect against most encroachments on economic interests, state judges resorted to the "due process" and "law of the land" clauses of state constitutions. These provisions originally referred to proceeding in accordance with the law and accepted legal procedure. Consider Corwin 90–91: "The 'law of the land' clause of the early State constitutions was usually a nearly literal translation of the famous chapter 29 of the Magna Carta of 1225, the Magna Carta of history.[c] [The] phrase 'due process of law' comes from chapter 3 of the statute of 28 Edward III (1355) which [reads]: 'No man of what state or condition he be, shall be put out of his lands or tenements, nor taken, nor imprisoned, nor disinherited, nor put to death, without he be brought to answer by due process of law.'"

The state courts began to evolve out of these clauses a substantive limitation on legislative power, aimed first at special legislation designed to affect the rights of specific individuals, and then applied to general legislation interfering with

---

b. *Proprietors of Charles River Bridge v. Proprietors of Warren Bridge,* 36 U.S. (11 Pet.) 420, 9 L.Ed. 773 (1837) (state grant of right to operate toll bridge did not imply obligation not to authorize competing bridge); *West River Bridge Co. v. Dix,* 47 U.S. (6 How.) 507, 12 L.Ed. 535 (1848) (state grant of exclusive right to operate toll bridge does not bar state from acquiring it by eminent domain); *Stone v. Mississippi,* 101 U.S. (11 Otto) 814, 25 L.Ed. 1079 (1880) (vital public interest permits state to ban lottery business 3 years after it granted 25 year charter).

c. Corwin quoted "its rendition" in the 1780 Massachusetts constitution: "No subject shall be arrested, imprisoned, [or] deprived of his property, [his] life, liberty, or estate, but by the judgment of his peers or the law of the land."

vested rights. See Corwin 89–115, 173–74: "Again the ingenuity of Bench and Bar were equal to the exigency. Most State constitutions contained from the outset a paraphrase of chapter 29 of Magna Carta, which declared that no person should be deprived of his 'estate' 'except by the law of the land or a judgment of his peers'; and following the usage of the Fifth Amendment of the United States Constitution, more and more State constitutions came after 1791 to contain a clause which, paraphrasing a statute of Plantagenet times, declared that 'no person shall be deprived of life, liberty or property without due process of law.' By the outbreak of the Civil War a more or less complete transference of the doctrine of vested rights and most of its Kentian corollaries had been effected in the vast majority of the State jurisdictions. One exception was Kent's distinction between the power of 'regulation,' which he conceded the State, and that of 'destruction,' which he denied it unless it was prepared to compensate disadvantaged owners. The division of judicial opinion on this point was signalized in the middle fifties, when the New York Court of Appeals, in the great *Wynehamer* case, stigmatized a State-wide prohibition statute as an act of destruction, in its application to existing stocks of liquor, which was beyond the power of the State legislature to authorize *even by the procedures of due process of law.* In several other States similar statutes were sustained in the name of the 'police power.'"

III. FOURTEENTH AMENDMENT

Historical background. The history of the Civil War amendments, particularly the fourteenth, insofar as that history relates to the problems considered in this and later chapters, is thoroughly treated elsewhere. See, e.g., Charles Fairman, *Does the Fourteenth Amendment Incorporate the Bill of Rights? The Original Understanding,* 2 Stan.L.Rev. 5 (1949); Alexander M. Bickel, *The Original Understanding and the Segregation Decision,* 69 Harv.L.Rev. 1 (1955); John P. Frank & Robert F. Munro, *The Original Understanding of "Equal Protection of the Laws"* 1972 Wash.U.L.Q. 421 (where other historical studies are cited). Only the barest outline is feasible here.

The thirteenth amendment forbidding involuntary servitude was ratified in 1865, but freeing the slaves did not produce the fruits of freedom, due to the "Black Codes" and other repressive measures. The plight of the blacks and their need at the time was reflected in the Civil Rights Act of 1866, which recognized "all persons born in United States" as United States citizens, and gave to "such citizens, of every race or color, without regard to any previous condition of slavery [the] same right, in every State and Territory in the United States, to make and enforce contracts, to sue, be parties, and give evidence, to inherit, purchase, lease, sell, hold, and convey real and personal property, and to full and equal benefit of all laws and proceedings for the security of person and property, as is enjoyed by white citizens."

Even while that 1866 Civil Rights Act was awaiting enactment, action was under way designed, in part at least, to remove existing doubts as to the power of Congress to enact such legislation. One week after the Senate passed the Civil Rights Act, the Congressional Joint Committee on Reconstruction submitted to both houses of Congress its early version of a fourteenth amendment authorizing Congress to enact laws to protect equal rights. After Congress passed the Civil Rights Act in April over a presidential veto based in part on the view that Congress lacked power to enact the law, the Joint Commission on Reconstruction hammered out a revised proposal that added privileges and immunities, due process, and equal protection provisions as limitations on the states, and authorized Congress to enact legislation to "enforce this article." After further modifications, Congress approved the fourteenth amendment in June, 1866 and sent it to the states for ratification.

———

"A rational reading of [the fourteenth amendment's] Privileges or Immunities Clause ['No State shall make or enforce any law which shall abridge the privileges or immunities of citizens of the United States']" observes Tribe 3d ed., at 1299–1300, "would appear to suggest essentially unqualified federal constitutional protection for at least some personal rights. [There] is no evidence that those who framed [the clause] sought a goal narrower than that suggested by the language they chose. On the contrary, the Privileges or Immunities Clause, it appears from various floor statements by the amendment's drafters and sponsors, was intended essentially to overrule *Barron v. Baltimore* and to secure basic civil rights—most significantly, those enumerated in the federal Bill of Rights—against state as well as federal governments.[a] [But] within a matter of years of the Fourteenth Amendment's adoption, the Supreme Court would squelch the framers' quite unmistakable intentions while twisting the evident import of the text itself and all but remove the Privileges or Immunities Clause from the landscape of American constitutional law."

SLAUGHTER–HOUSE CASES, 16 Wall. (83 U.S.) 36, 21 L.Ed. 394 (1873), per MILLER, J., upheld a Louisiana law granting a monopoly to operate slaughterhouses in the New Orleans area, regarding this an "appropriate, stringent, and effectual" means to "remove from the more densely population of the city, the noxious slaughterhouses and large and offensive collections of animals." Excluded butchers claimed that the law violated their right "to exercise their trade" and invoked the 13th and 14th Amendments: "The challengers claim that the law created an 'involuntary servitude' in violation of the 13th Amendment, and that it violated the 14th Amendment by abridging the 'privileges and immunities' of citizens of the United States, denying them 'of their property without due process of law.' [We are] thus called upon for the first time to [construe these Amendments].

"[The Civil War] being over, those who had succeeded in re-establishing the authority of the Federal government were not content to permit [the] great act of emancipation to rest on the actual results of the contest or the proclamation of the Executive, both of which might have been questioned in after times, and they determined to place this main and most valuable result in the Constitution of the restored Union as one of its fundamental articles. Hence the [13th Amendment]. To withdraw the mind from the contemplation of this grand yet simple declaration of the personal freedom of all the human race within the jurisdiction of this government [and] with a microscopic search endeavor to find in it a reference to servitudes, which may have been attached to property in certain localities, requires an effort, to say the least of it. That a personal servitude was meant is proved by the use of the word 'involuntary,' which can only apply to human beings.

a. Professor Tribe recognizes that Charles Fairman, *Does the Fourteenth Amendment Incorporate the Bill of Rights?*, 2 Stan.L.Rev. 5 (1949), takes a different view of the circumstances surrounding the adoption of the fourteenth amendment, but maintains that although Professor Fairman's "anti-incorporationist interpretation of the Fourteenth Amendment was long accepted as authoritative, more recent scholarship, [cited throughout Tribe's discussion of the subject] has powerfully challenged Fairman's conclusions."

"[The] process of restoring to their proper relations with the Federal government and with the other States those which had sided with the [rebellion] developed the fact that, notwithstanding the formal recognition by those States of the abolition of slavery, the condition of the slave race would, without further protection of the Federal government, be almost as bad as it was before. Among the first acts of legislation adopted by several of the States [were] laws which imposed upon the colored race onerous disabilities and burdens, and curtailed their rights [to] such an extent that their freedom was of little value. [These] circumstances [forced upon those] who had conducted the Federal government in safety through [the war], and who supposed that by [the 13th Amendment] they had secured the result of their labors, the conviction that something more was necessary in the way of constitutional protection to the unfortunate race who had suffered so much. They accordingly [proposed the 14th Amendment]. A few years experience satisfied [those] who had been the authors of the other two amendments that [these] were inadequate for the protection of life, liberty, and property, without which freedom to the slave was no boon. [It] was urged that a race of men distinctively marked as was the negro, living in the midst of another and dominant race, could never be fully secured in their person [and] property without the right of suffrage. Hence [the 15th Amendment].

"[In] the light of this recapitulation of events, almost too recent to be called history, [and] on the most casual examination of the language of these amendments, no one can fail to be impressed with the one pervading purpose found in them all, [and] without which none of them would have been even suggested; we mean the freedom of the slave race [and] the protection of the newly-made freeman and citizen from the oppressions of those who had formerly exercised unlimited dominion over him. It is true that only the 15th amendment, in terms, mentions the negro, [but] it is just as true that each of the other articles was addressed to the grievances of that race, and designed to remedy them as the fifteenth. We do not say that no one else but the negro can share in this protection. [But] what we do say [is] that in any fair and just construction of any section or phrase of these amendments, it is necessary to look to the purpose which [was] the pervading spirit of them all, the evil [they] were designed [to remedy].

"The first section of the [14th Amendment], to which our attention is more specially invited, opens with a definition of citizenship—not only citizenship of the United States, but citizenship of the states. * * * 'All persons born or naturalized in the United States, and subject to the jurisdiction thereof, are citizens of the United States and of the state wherein they reside.' [The section] overturns the *Dred Scott* decision by making *all persons* born within the United States * * * citizens of the United States. [The] next observation is more important in view of the arguments of counsel in the present case. [T]he distinction between citizenship of the United States and citizenship of a State is clearly recognized and established. Not only may a man be a citizen of the United States without being a citizen of a State, but an important element is necessary to convert the former into the latter. He must reside within the state to make him a citizen of it, but it is only necessary that he should be born or naturalized in the United States to be a citizen of the Union. * * *

"We think [the distinction between citizenship of the United states and citizenship of a State] of great weight in this argument, because the next paragraph of this same section, which is the one mainly relied on by plaintiffs in error, speaks only of privileges and immunities of citizens of the United States, and does not speak of those of citizens of the several states. The argument, however, in favor of the plaintiffs, rests wholly on the assumption that the citizenship is the same and the privileges and immunities guaranteed by the clause are the same. The language is, 'No state shall make or enforce any law which shall abridge the privileges or immunities of citizens of the United States.' It is a little remarkable, if this clause was intended as a protection to the citizen of a state against the legislative power of his own state, that the word citizen of the state should be left out when it is so carefully used, and used in contradistinction to citizens of the United States, in the very sentence which precedes it. It is too clear for argument that the change in phraseology was adopted understandingly and with a purpose.

"Of the privileges and immunities of the citizen of the United States, and, of the privileges and immunities of the citizen of the state, and what they respectively are, we will presently consider; but we wish to state here that it is only the former which are placed by this clause under the protection of the federal Constitution, and that the latter, whatever they may be, are not intended to have any additional protection by this paragraph of the amendment.

"[Art. IV, § 2 states:] 'The citizens of each State shall be entitled to all the privileges and immunities of citizens of the several States.'[a] [It] did not create those rights, which it called privileges and immunities of citizens of the States. It threw around them in that clause no security for the citizen of the State in which they claimed or exercised. Nor did it profess to control the power of the State governments over the rights of its own citizens. Its sole purpose was to declare to the several States, that whatever those rights, as you grant or establish them to your own citizens, or as you limit or qualify, [the] same, neither more nor less, shall be the measure of the rights of citizens of other States within your jurisdiction.

"[Up] to the adoption of the recent amendments, no claim or pretense was set up that those rights depended on the Federal government for their existence or protection, beyond the very few express limitations which the Federal Constitution imposed upon the States—such, for instance, as the prohibition against ex post-facto laws, bills of attainder, and laws impairing the obligation of contracts. But with the exception of these and a few other restrictions, the entire domain of the privileges and immunities of citizens of the states [lay] within the constitutional and legislative power of the states, and without that of the Federal government. Was it the purpose of the fourteenth amendment, by the simple declaration that no state should make or enforce any law which shall abridge the privileges and immunities of *citizens of the United States,* to transfer the security and protection of all the civil rights [from] the States to the Federal government? And where it is declared that Congress shall have the power to enforce that article, was it intended to bring within the power of Congress the entire domain of civil rights heretofore belonging exclusively to the States?

a. As pointed out in Tribe 3d ed., at 1306, "Justice Miller's state-citizenship construction of Article IV, § 2 * * * rested entirely upon a *mis*quotation of [that section], inserting the made-up phrase 'privileges and immunities of citizens *of* the several States' in place of the Constitution's *actual* text—'Privileges and Immunities of Citizens *in* the several States.' Whereas the actual language thus spoke of citizens generally and was thought, at least by John Bingham [the Congressman who framed the Privileges or Immunities Clause of the Fourteenth Amendment], to denote citizens of the United States, Justice Miller's paraphrase undoubtedly suggests that the rights protected by the clause are those belonging to citizens of *states as such,* by virtue of *state law.* Although Justice Bradley, writing in dissent, explicitly noted Justice Miller's elementary mistake, the misquotation remained in the published opinion * * *."

"[Such] a construction [would] constitute this court a perpetual censor upon all legislation of the states, on the civil rights of their own citizens, with authority to nullify such as it did not approve as consistent with those rights, as they existed at the time of the adoption of this amendment. [Such a construction] radically changes the whole theory of the relations of the State and Federal governments to each other and of both these governments to the people. [We] are convinced that no such results were intended by the Congress which proposed these amendments, nor by the legislatures of the States which ratified them.

"The argument has not been much pressed in these cases that the defendant's charter deprives the plaintiffs of their property without due process of law, or that it denies to them the equal protection of the law. The first of these paragraphs has been in the Constitution since the adoption of the Fifth Amendment, as a restraint upon the federal power. It is also to be found in some form of expression in the constitutions of nearly all the states, as a restraint upon the power of the States. [U]nder no construction of that provision that we have ever seen, or any that we deem admissible, can the restraint imposed [by] Louisiana upon the exercise of their trade by the butchers of New Orleans be held to be a deprivation of property within the meaning of that provision.

"[In] the light of the history of these amendments, and the pervading purpose of them, which we have already discussed, [it] is not difficult to give a meaning to [the equal protection] clause. [Laws discriminating against 'the newly emancipated negroes'] was the evil to be remedied by this clause, and by it such laws are forbidden. [We] doubt very much whether any action of a state not directed by way of discrimination against the negroes as a class, or on account of their race, will ever be held to come within the purview of this provision. It is so clearly a provision for that race and that emergency, that a strong case would be necessary for its application to any other. Unquestionably [the recent was] added largely to the number of those who believe in the necessity of a strong National government. But, however pervading this sentiment, and however it may have contributed to the adoption of the amendments we have been considering, we do not see in those amendments any purpose to destroy the main features of the general system."

FIELD, J., joined by Chase, J., and Swayne and Bradley, JJ., dissented: "[The] question presented [is] whether the recent [amendments] protect the citizens of the United States against the deprivation of their common rights by State legislation. In my judgment, the fourteenth amendment does afford such [protection]. The amendment does not attempt to confer any new privileges or immunities upon citizens, or to enumerate or define those already existing. It assumes that there are such privileges and immunities which belong of right to citizens as such, and ordains that they shall not be abridged by State legislation. If this inhibition [only] refers, as held by the majority of the court, [to] such privileges and immunities as were before its adoption specially designated in the Constitution or necessarily implied as belonging to citizens of the United States, it was a vain and idle enactment, which accomplished nothing, and most unnecessarily excited Congress and the people on its passage. With privileges and immunities thus designated or implied no State could ever have interfered by its laws, and no new constitutional provision was required to inhibit such interference. The supremacy of the Constitution and the laws of the United States always controlled any State legislation of that character. But if the amendment refers to the natural and inalienable rights which belong to all citizens, the inhibition has a profound significance and consequence. * * *

"The terms, privileges and immunities, are not new in the amendment; they were in the Constitution before the amendment was adopted. They are found in

[Art. IV, § 2.] In *Corfield v. Coryell*, Mr. Justice Washington said he had 'no hesitation in confining these expressions to those privileges and immunities which were, in their nature, fundamental; which belong of right to the citizens of all free governments.' [Field, J., continued with the *Corfield* quotation, p. 262 supra] This appears to me to be a sound construction of the clause in question. Clearly among [these rights] must be placed the right to pursue a lawful employment in a lawful manner, without other restraint than such as equally affects all persons. In the discussions in Congress upon the passage of the Civil Rights Act repeated reference was made to this language of Mr. Justice Washington. It was cited by Senator Trumbull with the observation that it enumerated the very rights belonging to a citizen of the United States set forth in the first section of the act.

"[The] privileges and immunities designated in [Art. IV, § 2] are, then, according to the decision cited, those which of right belong to the citizens of all free governments. [What] the clause in question did for the protection of the citizens of one State against hostile and discriminating legislation of other States, the fourteenth amendment does for the protection of every citizen of the United States against hostile and discriminating legislation against him in favor of others, whether they reside in the same or in different [States].

"This equality of right, with exemption from all disparaging and partial enactments, in the lawful pursuits of life, throughout the whole country, is the distinguishing privilege of citizens of the United States. To them, everywhere, all pursuits, all professions, all avocations are open without other restrictions than such as are imposed equally upon all others of the same age, sex, and condition. The State may prescribe such regulations for every pursuit and calling of life as will promote the public health, secure the good order and advance the general prosperity of society, but when once prescribed, the pursuit or calling must be free to be followed by every citizen who is within the conditions designated, and will conform to the regulations. This is the fundamental idea upon which our institutions rest, and unless adhered to in the legislation of the country our government will be a republic only in name. The fourteenth amendment, in my judgment, makes it essential to the validity of the legislation of every State that this equality of right should be respected."

BRADLEY, J. also dissented: "[C]itizenship is not an empty name. [I]n this country at least, it has connected with it certain incidental rights, privileges, and immunities of the greatest importance. And to say that these rights and immunities attach only to State citizenship, and not citizenship of the United States, appears to me to evince a very narrow and insufficient estimate of constitutional history and the rights of men, not to say the rights of the American people.

"[It] is pertinent to observe that both [Art. IV, § 2], and Justice Washington in his comment on it [in *Corfield*], speak of the privileges and immunities of citizens *in* a State; not of citizens *of* a State. It is the privileges and immunities of citizens, that is, of citizens as such, that are to be accorded to citizens of other States when they are found in any State; or, as Justice Washington says, 'privileges and immunities which are, in their nature, fundamental; which belong, of right, to the citizens of all free governments.

"[In] my judgment, it was the intention of the people of this country in adopting [the 14th] amendment to provide National security against violation by the States of the fundamental rights of the citizen. [A] law which prohibits a large class of citizens from adopting a lawful employment, or from following a lawful employment previously adopted, does deprive them of liberty as well as property, without due process of law. [Such] a law also deprives those citizens of the equal protection of the laws. [It] is futile to argue that none but persons of the African race are intended to be benefitted by this amendment. They may have been the primary cause of the amendment, but its language is general, embracing all citizens, and I think it was purposely so expressed. The mischief to be remedied was not merely slavery and its incidents and consequences; but that spirit of insubordination and disloyalty to the National government which had troubled the country for so many years in some of the States, and that intolerance of free speech and free discussion which often rendered life and property insecure, and led to much unequal legislation.

"[But] great fears are expressed that this construction of the amendment will lead to enactments by Congress interfering with the internal affairs of the States. [In] my judgment no such practical inconveniences would arise. Very little, if any, legislation on the part of Congress would be required to carry the amendment into effect. Like the prohibition against passing a law impairing the obligation of a contract, it would execute itself. [Even] if the business of the National courts should be increased, Congress could easily supply the remedy by increasing their number and efficiency. The great question is: What is the true construction of the amendment? [The] argument from inconvenience ought not to have a very controlling influence in questions of this sort. The National will and National interest are of far greater importance."

Notes and Questions

1. *Objectives of privileges and immunities and citizenship provisions.* An historical study protests that the *Slaughter-House* opinion flies in the face of the congressional purpose for inserting the citizenship sentence. Howard J. Graham, *Our "Declaratory" Fourteenth Amendment,* 7 Stan.L.Rev. 3, 23–26 (1954). "[E]ver since Birney's day, opponents of slavery had regarded all important 'natural' and constitutional rights as being privileges and immunities of *citizens of the United States.* This had been the cardinal premise of antislavery theory from the beginning, and this had been the underlying theory and purpose of Section One from the beginning. The real purpose of adding this citizenship definition was to remove any possible or lingering doubt about the freedman's citizenship."

2. *Resulting scope of privileges and immunities.* Professor McGovney paraphrased the clause as interpreted: "No State shall make or enforce any law which shall abridge any privilege or immunity conferred *by this Constitution, the statutes or treaties of the United States* upon any person who is a citizen of the United States." He then commented, "This narrower construction [renders] it an idle provision, in that it only declares a principle already more amply and more simply expressed in the constitution." Dudley McGovney, *Privileges or Immunities Clause, Fourteenth Amendment,* 4 Iowa Law Bull. (now Iowa L.Rev.) 219, 220, 221 (1918).

3. *The heavy blow Slaughter-House struck the privileges or immunities clause—and the switch to the due process clause.* As pointed out in Tribe 3d ed., at 1316, "[w]ith the Court's announcement of its exceedingly narrow interpretation of the Privileges or Immunities Clause—essentially denying the provision any significant content[a]—responsibility for naturalizing civil rights shifted to the Due

a. As Professor Tribe points out at 1312–14, until 1999, the Clause "had been the basis of a majority opinion of the Supreme Court only once, [in] *Colgate v. Harvey,* 296 U.S. 404, 56 S.Ct. 252, 80 L.Ed. 299 (1935) [invalidating a state tax against residents exclusively upon

Process Clause: 'By strangling the privileges or immunities clause in its crib, *Slaughter-House* forced [litigants] to argue that the original Bill [of Rights] applied against the states either directly of its own force, or via the Fourteenth Amendment's due process clause.'[b] And despite the semantic difficulties that the process-based language of that provision poses for incorporation of the substantive guarantee of the Bill of Rights, the Supreme Court, beginning in the late nineteenth century, has indeed interpreted the Due Process Clause expansively, so that it essentially performs many of the functions for which the Privileges or Immunities Clause was designed."

4. *Creative dicta.* Two closely related factors played important roles in the emergence of substantive due process. (a) Lawyers in speeches, treatises, articles and briefs strongly advanced the laissez faire concept of government, often urging the due process clause as a constitutional limitation on governmental regulation of business. See the study of the influence of lawyers in this respect in Benjamin R. Twiss, *Lawyers and the Constitution* 18–173 (1942). (b) Supreme Court justices in dissenting opinions, and state courts, strongly reflected these views, until majority opinions sustaining state regulation began also to recognize that the due process clause imposes some limits on the regulatory power of government. See Edward S. Corwin, *Liberty Against Government* 129–152 (1948).

* * *

SECTION 2. THE *LOCHNER* ERA

I. THE ROAD TO *LOCHNER*

In *Munn v. Illinois*, 94 U.S. (4 Otto) 113, 24 L.Ed. 77 (1876), although the Court, per Waite, C.J., upheld a state law regulating the rates of grain elevators, pointing out that private property may be regulated when it is "affected with a public interest," the Court made a comment that was to be relied upon years later to justify judicial control of state regulation: "Undoubtedly, in mere private contracts, relating to matters in which the public has no interest, what is reasonable must be ascertained judicially." *Mugler v. Kansas*, 123 U.S. 623, 8 S.Ct. 273, 31 L.Ed. 205 (1887), upheld a state law prohibiting intoxicating beverages, but the Court, per Harlan, J., made clear that not every statute said to be enacted for the promotion of "the public morals, the public health, or the public safety" would be sustained. If a law supposedly enacted pursuant to the police powers of the state "has no real or substantial relation to these objects, or is a palpable invasion of rights secured by the fundamental law, it is the duty of the courts to so adjudge."

ALLGEYER v. LOUISIANA, 165 U.S. 578, 17 S.Ct. 427, 41 L.Ed. 832 (1897), was the first reasoned Supreme Court decision actually to hold that the substance of economic legislation violated fourteenth amendment due process. A unanimous Court, per PECKHAM, J., struck down a Louisiana law prohibiting any act in the

dividends and interest earned outside the state]. However, in *Saenz v. Roe* (p. 1382 infra, a case Tribe calls a "seminal 1999 decision," "a Court majority for the first time protected the right to travel as a privilege or immunity of United States citizenship, treating that right as encompassing the right to enter and leave another state; the right to be treated as a welcome visitor while there [and] the right, upon electing to become a permanent resident of another state, to be treated no less well than residents who have lived there longer."

b. At this point, Tribe is quoting from Akhil R. Amar, *The Bill of Rights and the Fourteenth Amendment*, 101 Yale L.J. 1193, 1259 (1992).

state to effect a contract for marine insurance on state property with a company not licensed to do business in the state. The statute exceeded the police power of the state and deprived the defendants of their fourteenth amendment liberty to contract for insurance. The "liberty" mentioned in that amendment, the Court told us, means not only one's right to be free of physical restraint of his person, but "embrace[s] the right of the citizen to be free in the enjoyment of all his faculties, to be free to use them in all lawful ways; to live and work where he will; [to] pursue any livelihood or avocation; and for that purpose to enter into all contracts which may be proper, necessary, and essential to his carrying out to a successful conclusion the purpose above mentioned."

"Ironically," observes Tribe 3d. ed., at 1311–12, "the *Slaughter-House Cases*' reaffirmation of the [state and federal spheres of power] helped pave the way for the substantive due process doctrine of the post 1890s era. [Miller, J., had] affirmed the duty of the Supreme Court to safeguard the autonomy of the federal and state governments within their respective spheres of power over the same geographical territory. But the Justices of the 1890–1937 era, likewise imbued with Miller's sense of the state and federal spheres and persuaded of the need to protect their sanctity, discerned yet a third sphere—that of the citizen, whose autonomy both required federal protection and could be defended without federal suffocation of the states. [The] Court thus came to perceive a perfect complementarity between the citizens's right to 'life, liberty, and property' and the state's authority to preserve such life, liberty, and property through the exercise of its implied powers within settled common law standards. This complementarity permitted the turn-of-the-century Court to believe that the federal judiciary could protect citizen autonomy without intruding upon the state's sphere—because any state action that *invaded* the liberty or property of its citizens was, by definition, *beyond* the state's sphere."

LOCHNER v. NEW YORK (hand out)

198 U.S. 45, 25 S.Ct. 539, 49 L.Ed. 937 (1905).

JUSTICE PECKHAM delivered the opinion of the Court.

[The Court held invalid a New York statute forbidding employment in a bakery for more than 60 hours a week or 10 hours a day.]

The statute necessarily interferes with the right of contract between the employer and employees. [The] general right to make a contract in relation to his business is part of the liberty of the individual protected by the 14th Amendment. [*Allgeyer*.] The right to purchase or to sell labor is part of the liberty protected by this amendment, unless there are circumstances which exclude the right. [This court has] upheld the exercise of the police powers of the States in many cases, [among them] *Holden v. Hardy*, 169 U.S. 366 (1898), [where it] was held that the kind of employment, mining, smelting, etc., and the character of the employees in such kinds of labor, were such as to make it reasonable and proper for the State to interfere to prevent the employees from being constrained by the rules laid down by the proprietors in regard to labor. [There] is nothing in *Holden v. Hardy* which covers the case now before us.

It must, of course, be conceded that there is a limit to the valid exercise of the police power by the state. [Otherwise] the 14th Amendment would have no efficacy and the legislatures of the states would have unbounded power. [In] every case that comes before this court, therefore, where legislation of this character is concerned, and where the protection of the Federal Constitution is sought, the question necessarily arises: Is this a fair, reasonable, and appropriate exercise of the police power of the state, or is it an unreasonable, unnecessary, and arbitrary interference with the right of the individual to his personal liberty, or to enter into those contracts in relation to labor which may seem to him appropriate or necessary for the support of himself and his family? Of course the liberty of contract relating to labor includes both parties to it. The one has as much right to purchase as the other to sell labor. This is not a question of substituting the judgment of the court for that of the legislature. If the act be within the power of the State it is valid, although the judgment of the court might be totally opposed to the enactment of such a law. But the question would still remain: Is it within the police power of the State? and that question must be answered by the court.

The question whether this act is valid as a labor law, pure and simple, may be dismissed in a few words. There is no reasonable ground for interfering with the liberty of person or the right of free contract, by determining the hours of labor, in the occupation of a baker. There is no contention that bakers as a class are not equal in intelligence and capacity to men in other trades or manual occupations, or that they are not able to assert their rights and care for themselves without the protecting arm of the State. [They] are in no sense wards of the State. Viewed in the light of a purely labor law, with no reference whatever to the question of health, we think that a law like the one before us involves neither the safety, the morals, nor the welfare, of the public, and that the interest of the public is not in the slightest degree affected by such an act. The law must be upheld, if at all, as a law pertaining to the health of the individual engaged in the occupation of a baker. It does not affect any other portion of the public than those who are engaged in that occupation. Clean and wholesome bread does not depend upon whether the baker works but ten hours per day or only sixty hours a week. [There] is, in our judgment, no reasonable foundation for holding this to be necessary or appropriate as a health law to safeguard the public health, or the health of the individuals who are following the trade of a baker. * * *

We think that there can be no fair doubt that the trade of a baker, in and of itself, is not an unhealthy one to that degree which would authorize the legislature to interfere with the right to labor, and with the right of free contract on the part of the individual, either as employer or employee. [Some] occupations are more healthy than others, but we think there are none which might not come under the power of the legislature to supervise and control the hours of working therein, if the mere fact that the occupation is not absolutely and perfectly healthy is to confer that right upon the legislative department of the government. [It] is unfortunately true that labor, even in any department, may possibly carry with it the seeds of unhealthiness. But are we all, on that account, at the mercy of legislative majorities? A printer, a tinsmith, a locksmith, a carpenter, a cabinet maker, a dry goods clerk, a bank's, a lawyer's, or a physician's clerk, or a clerk in almost any kind of business, would all come under the power of the legislature, on this assumption. No trade, no occupation, no mode of earning one's living, could escape this all-pervading power, and the acts of the legislature in limiting the hours of labor in all employments would be valid, although such limitation might seriously cripple the ability of the laborer to support himself and his family.

[It] is also urged [that] it is to the interest of the State that its population should be strong and robust, and therefore any legislation which may be said to tend to make people healthy must be valid as health laws, enacted under the police power. If this be a valid argument and a justification for this kind of legislation, it follows that the protection of the Federal Constitution from undue interference with liberty of person and freedom of contract is visionary, wherever the law is sought to be justified as a valid exercise of the police power. Scarcely any law but might find shelter under such assumptions. [Not] only the hours of employees, but the hours of employers, could be regulated, and doctors, lawyers, scientists, all professional men, as well as athletes and artisans, could be forbidden to fatigue their brains and bodies by prolonged hours of exercise, lest the fighting strength of the state be impaired. We mention these extreme cases because the contention is extreme. We do not believe in the soundness of the views which uphold this law. [The] act is not, within any fair meaning of the term, a health law, but is an illegal interference with the rights of individuals, both employers and employees, to make contracts regarding labor upon such terms as they may think best, or which they may agree upon with the other parties to such contracts. Statutes of the nature of that under review, limiting the hours in which grown and intelligent men may labor to earn their living, are mere meddlesome interferences with the rights of the individual, and they are not saved from condemnation by the claim that they are passed in the exercise of the police power and upon the subject of the health of the individual whose rights are interfered with, unless there be some fair ground, reasonable in and of itself, to say that there is material danger to the public health, or to the health of the employees, if the hours of labor are not curtailed. * * *

This interference on the part of the legislatures of the several states with the ordinary trades and occupations of the people seems to be on the increase. [It] is impossible for us to shut our eyes to the fact that many of the laws of this character, while passed under what is claimed to be the police power for the purpose of protecting the public health or welfare, are, in reality, passed from other motives. We are justified in saying so when, from the character of the law and the subject upon which it legislates, it is apparent that the public health or welfare bears but the most remote relation to the [law].

JUSTICE HARLAN (with whom JUSTICE WHITE and JUSTICE DAY concurred) dissenting:

I take it to be firmly established that what is called the liberty of contract may, within certain limits, be subjected to regulations designed and calculated to promote the general welfare or to guard the public health, the public morals or the public safety. [It] is plain that this statute was enacted in order to protect the physical well-being of those who work in bakery and confectionery establishments. [The] statute must be taken as expressing the belief of the people of New York that, as a general rule, and in the case of the average man, labor in excess of sixty hours during a week in such establishments may endanger the health of those who thus labor. Whether or not this be wise legislation it is not the province of the court to inquire. Under our systems of government the courts are not concerned with the wisdom or policy of legislation. So that in determining the question of power to interfere with liberty or contract, the court may inquire whether the means devised by the State are germane to an end which may be lawfully accomplished and have a real or substantial relation to the protection of health, as involved in the daily work of the persons, male and female, engaged in bakery and confectionery establishments. But when this inquiry is entered upon I find it impossible, in view of common experience, to say that there is here no real or substantial relation between the means employed by the State and the end sought to be accomplished by its legislation. Nor can I say that the statute has no appropriate or direct connection with that protection to health which each State owes to her citizens or that it is not promotive of the health of the employees in question or that the regulation prescribed by the State is utterly unreasonable and extravagant or wholly arbitrary. Still less can I say that the statute is, beyond question, a plain, palpable invasion of rights secured by the fundamental law.

[The opinion quoted from writers on health problems of workers, pointing out that long hours, night hours, and difficult working conditions, such as excessive heat and exposure to flour dust, were injurious to the health of bakers, who "seldom live over their fiftieth year."] We judicially know that the question of the number of hours during which a workman should continuously labor has been, for a long period, and is yet, a subject of serious consideration among civilized peoples, and by those having special knowledge of the laws of health. We also judicially know that the number of hours that should constitute a day's labor in particular occupations involving the physical strength and safety of workmen has been the subject of enactments by Congress and by nearly all of the states. Many, if not most, of those enactments fix eight hours as the proper basis of a day's labor.

I do not stop to consider whether any particular view of this economic question presents the sounder theory. [It] is enough for the determination of this case [that] the question is one about which there is room for debate and for an honest difference of opinion. There are many reasons of a weighty, substantial character, based upon the experience of mankind, in support of the theory that, all things considered, more than ten hours' steady work each day, from week to week, in a bakery or confectionery establishment, may endanger the health and shorten the lives of the workmen, thereby diminishing their physical and mental capacity to serve the State and to provide for those dependent upon them.

If such reasons exist that ought to be the end of this case, for the state is not amenable to the judiciary, in respect of its legislative enactments, unless such enactments are plainly, palpably, beyond all question, inconsistent with the Constitution of the United States. * * *

JUSTICE HOLMES dissenting: * * *

This case is decided upon an economic theory which a large part of the country does not entertain. If it were a question whether I agree with that theory, I should desire to study it further and long before making up my mind. But I do not conceive that to be my duty, because I strongly believe that my agreement or disagreement has nothing to do with the right of a majority to embody their opinions in law. It is settled by various decisions of this court that state constitutions and state laws may regulate life in many ways which we as legislators might think as injudicious, or if you like as tyrannical, as this, and which, equally with this, interfere with the liberty to contract. Sunday laws and usury laws are ancient examples. A more modern one is the prohibition of lotteries. The liberty of the citizen to do as he likes so long as he does not interfere with the liberty of others to do the same, which has been a shibboleth for some well-known writers, is interfered with by school laws, by the Post Office, by every state or municipal institution which takes his money for purposes thought desirable, whether he likes it or not. The 14th Amendment does not enact Mr. Herbert Spencer's *Social Statics*. [A] Constitution is not intended to embody a particular economic theory, whether of paternalism and the organic relation of the citizen to the state or of laissez faire. It is made for people of fundamentally differing views, and the accident of our finding certain opinions natural and familiar, or novel, and even shocking, ought not to conclude our judgment upon the question whether statutes embodying them conflict with the Constitution of the United States.

General propositions do not decide concrete cases. [But] I think that the proposition just stated, if it is accepted, will carry us far toward the end. [I] think that the word "liberty," in the 14th Amendment, is perverted when it is held to prevent the natural outcome of a dominant opinion, unless it can be said that a rational and fair man necessarily would admit that the statute proposed would infringe fundamental principles as they have been understood by the traditions of our people and our law. It does not need research to show that no such sweeping condemnation can be passed upon the statute before us. * * *

Notes and Questions

1. *Holmes and his contemporaries.* In *Lochner*, observes G. Edward White, *Revisiting Substantive Due Process and Holmes's Lochner Dissent*, 63 Brook. L.Rev. 87, 106–07 (1997), "all of the justices save Holmes [simply] applied the constitutional standard for police power cases differently. The majority scrutinized the New York legislation and found that it could not legitimately be directed at the public sphere of political economy because it was not a 'reasonable' exercise of the police power. None of the 'appropriate' rationales for police power legislation [would] have enabled the legislation to be classified as 'general' rather than 'partial.' [Therefore,] the legislation was simply a 'labor law' that imposed unequal benefits and burdens on a class of persons, those engaged in the baking industry, [taking] money from some employers and employees and [giving] it to others. It was a violation of 'free labor' in the deepest sense of the word. It was a violation of the vested rights principle. [Harlan, J.'s] dissent concluded that the New York statute was a legitimate health measure because bakers were more like miners and other persons engaged in dangerous or unhealthful occupations. Legislation limiting the hours of employees in bakeries was thus an appropriate and reasonable method of promoting their health, thereby improving the general welfare. [While] hours legislation in the baking industry did not distribute specific benefits and burdens equally among the entire population, it distributed equally the general benefits and burdens of living and working in an industrializing society."

At the time of *Lochner*, emphasizes Professor White, id. at 89–90, "Holmes's reading of due process cases differed from the general approach of his contemporaries. He did not place much significance on maintaining the boundary between police power and the obligation of legislatures [not to] enact 'class' or 'partial' legislation. [He] believed that nearly any piece of legislation could be shown to rest on some police power. The only limit were arbitrary 'takings' where the property of one citizen was given to another. Because he identified sovereignty so strongly with the legislature in a democracy, Holmes was skeptical about judicial encroachments on that sovereignty; he suspected that judges might overreact to paternalistic legislation because it offended their ideological convictions. He felt that such overreactions precipitated impermissible readings of the Due Process Clauses. Holmes's later admirers came to call what he saw as judicial overreactions 'substantive' interpretations of the Due Process Clause, using the term substantive in a pejorative fashion."

2. *Close scrutiny of means-ends relationship.* "In reviewing state and federal economic regulation during the *Lochner* era," notes Tribe 3d. ed., at 1346–48, "the Supreme Court closely scrutinized both the ends sought and the means employed in challenged legislation. In its analysis of legislative means, the Court

required a 'real and substantial' relationship between a statute and its objectives. * * * *Lochner* itself provides the best example [of] strict and skeptical means analysis. There, the Court rejected New York's claim that its sixty-hour limit on a bakery employee's work week was significantly and directly related to the promotion of employee health. Yet considerable evidence, discussed at length by Justice Harlan in dissent, suggested that limiting the work week as New York had decided to do would enhance the health of bakers. [This] strict scrutiny of means-ends relationships continued to surface in later decisions. Thus, [in *Jay Burns Baking Co. v. Bryan*, 264 U.S. 504, 44 S.Ct. 412, 68 L.Ed. 813 (1924)] the Court invalidated a Nebraska law requiring standardized weights for loaves of bread, finding the statute 'not necessary for the protection of purchasers [against] fraud by short weights,' since that problem 'readily could have been dealt with' without such restrictive regulation. In *Adkins v. Children's Hospital* [1923] [discussed infra], Justice Sutherland asserted for the majority that governmental wage regulation was needed only within limited categories of activity. * * * Stringent analysis of the relationship between a challenged law and its alleged objectives thus formed an important part of the judicial technique rendering much socio-economic legislation vulnerable in the *Lochner* period."

II. THREE DECADES OF CONTROL OVER LEGISLATIVE POLICY

From *Lochner* in 1905 to *Nebbia* in 1934, infra, the Court frequently substituted its judgment for that of Congress and state legislatures on the wisdom of economic regulation said to interfere with contract and property interests.[a] The Court relied mainly upon the due process clauses of the fifth and fourteenth amendments, with occasional resort to the equal protection clause. Between 1899 and 1937, after excluding the civil rights cases, 159 Supreme Court decisions held state statutes unconstitutional under the due process and equal protection clauses and 25 more statutes were struck down under the due process clause coupled with some other provision of the Constitution. Benjamin F. Wright, *The Growth of American Constitutional Law* 154 (1942).

The Court most freely substituted its judgment for that of the legislature in labor legislation, regulation of prices, and limitations on entry into business. It was most tolerant in the regulation of trade and business practices.[b] A few examples will suffice to show the extent to which the Court interfered with legislative policymaking in economic regulation. With regularity Holmes, J., dissented from this use of the due process clause, joined later by Brandeis and Stone, JJ., and Hughes, C.J.

1. *Control over hours of labor.* We have already seen how the Court barred control over the hours of labor, even in an industry where long hours threatened health. *Lochner* (1905). But in 1908 the Court sustained regulation of work hours for women in MULLER v. OREGON, 208 U.S. 412, 28 S.Ct. 324, 52 L.Ed. 551 (1908), basing the decision on special considerations relating to women. The Court, per BREWER, J., thought it plain that "women's physical structure" put her "at a disadvantage in the struggle for subsistence and that since "healthy mothers are essential to vigorous offspring, the physical well-being of woman becomes an object of public interest." The "inherent difference between the two sexes,"

a. See Roscoe Pound, *Liberty of Contract,* 18 Yale L.J. 454 (1909); Ray A. Brown, *Due Process of Law, Police Power, and the Supreme Court,* 40 Harv.L.Rev. 943 (1927).

b. See summary of such cases in *Nebbia v. New York,* infra.

continued the Court, justified "a difference in legislation" upholds that which is designed to compensate for some of the burdens which rest upon her." In 1917 the Court overruled *Lochner* (but not its philosophy) in sustaining a regulation of work hours for men in manufacturing establishments. *Bunting v. Oregon,* 243 U.S. 426, 37 S.Ct. 435, 61 L.Ed. 830. In *Muller,* the majority was influenced by the so-called "Brandeis brief," which furnished the Court with overwhelming documentation justifying regulation of hours of labor for women. Felix Frankfurter, Esq., successfully followed the same technique in *Bunting.* See 208 U.S. at 419–20, and 243 U.S. at 433; Henry W. Bikle, *Judicial Determination of Questions of Fact Affecting the Constitutional Validity of Legislative Action,* 38 Harv.L.Rev. 6, 13 (1924).

2. *Control over anti-union discrimination.* At an early date the Court struck down labor legislation forbidding discrimination by employers for union activity and prohibiting employers from requiring employees to sign "yellow dog" contracts, i.e., agreements not to remain or become union members. ADAIR v. UNITED STATES, 208 U.S. 161, 28 S.Ct. 277, 52 L.Ed. 436 (1908) (5th amendment); COPPAGE v. KANSAS, 236 U.S. 1, 35 S.Ct. 240, 59 L.Ed. 441 (1915) (14th amendment). The opinion in *Adair,* invalidating a federal law banning "yellow-dog" contracts, was written by HARLAN, J., one of the dissenters in *Lochner.* He deemed the "right of a person to sell his labor upon such terms as he considers proper [to be] the same as the right of the purchaser to prescribe the conditions. An employer and his employees "have equality of right, and any legislation that disturbs that equality is an arbitrary interference with the liberty of contract." PITNEY, J.'s majority opinion in *Coppage* has been called "[p]erhaps the clearest and fullest statement of the era's dominant philosophy." Tribe 3d ed., at 1350. The Court told us that the fourteenth amendment protects "the right to make contracts" and an "interference with this liberty so serious as that now under consideration, and so disturbing of equality of right, must be deemed to be arbitrary unless it to be supportable as a reasonable exercise of the police power of the State." The Court was not impressed by the argument that "employees, as a rule, are not financially able to be as independent in making contracts for the sale of their labor as are employers in making contracts of purchase thereof." It is "from the nature of things impossible," responded the Court, "to uphold freedom of contract and the right of private property without at the same time recognizing as legitimate those inequalities of fortune that are the necessary result of the exercise of those rights." And a State could not remove these inequalities directly or indirectly by invoking the police power. HOLMES, J., dissented: "[A] workman not unnaturally may believe that only by belonging to a union can he secure a contract that shall be fair to him. [If] that belief, whether right or wrong, may be held by a reasonable man, it seems to me that it may be enforced by law in order to establish the equality of position between the parties in which liberty of contract begins."

These restrictive decisions were distinguished away in *Texas & N.O.R.R. v. Brotherhood of Ry. & S.S. Clerks,* 281 U.S. 548, 50 S.Ct. 427, 74 L.Ed. 1034 (1930) and *NLRB v. Jones & Laughlin Steel Corp.* (1937). They were finally expressly overruled in *Phelps Dodge Corp. v. NLRB,* 313 U.S. 177, 61 S.Ct. 845, 85 L.Ed. 1271 (1941) and *Lincoln Fed. Labor Union v. Northwestern Iron & Met. Co.* (1949), Sec. 3 infra.

3. *Regulation of wages.* Six years after it had upheld regulation of *hours* of labor in *Bunting,* the Court, per SUTHERLAND, J., ruled that a federal statute prescribing minimum *wages* for women in the District of Columbia violated due process. ADKINS v. CHILDREN'S HOSPITAL, 261 U.S. 525, 43 S.Ct. 394, 67

L.Ed. 785 (1923). The Court emphasized that, although "freedom of contract" is subject to a great variety of restraints, it "is, nevertheless, the general rule and restraint the exception; and the exercise of legislative authority to abridge it can be justified only by the existence of exceptional circumstances." "[This] is not a law dealing with any business charged with a public interest or with public work," continued the Court, nor is it "for the protection of persons under legal disability or for the prevention of fraud. It is simply and exclusively a price-fixing law, confined to adult women, [who] are legally as capable of contracting for themselves as men." The Court noted that the 19th amendment had recently been adopted, thus reducing the civil inferiority of women almost to the "vanishing point." Therefore, "liberty of contract" could not be subjected to greater infringement in the case of women than of men.

HOLMES, J., dissenting, expressed his inability to "understand the principle on which the power to fix a minimum for the wages of women can be denied by those who admit the power to fix a maximum for their hours of work." As he saw it, the bargain is "equally affected whichever half you regulate." As for the recent adoption of the 19th amendment, it "will need more than [that] to convince me that there are no differences between men and women, or that legislation cannot take these differences into account."[c]

4. *Regulation of prices.* The Court also held that regulation of prices for commodities and services violated due process except for a limited class labeled "business affected with a public interest."[d] *Tyson & Bro.-United Theatre Ticket Offices v. Banton,* 273 U.S. 418, 47 S.Ct. 426, 71 L.Ed. 718 (1927) (theatre tickets); *Ribnik v. McBride,* 277 U.S. 350, 48 S.Ct. 545, 72 L.Ed. 913 (1928) (fees of employment agency); *Williams v. Standard Oil Co.,* 278 U.S. 235, 49 S.Ct. 115, 73 L.Ed. 287 (1929) (gasoline prices); cf. *Chas. Wolff Packing Co. v. Court of Industrial Relations,* 262 U.S. 522, 43 S.Ct. 630, 67 L.Ed. 1103 (1923) (compulsory arbitration of wages). *Nebbia v. New York* (1934) severely limited these rulings and they were expressly overruled in *Olsen v. Nebraska ex rel. Western Ref. & Bond Ass'n* (1941), both in Sec. 3 infra.

5. *Limitations on entry into business.* The Court also relied on the "liberty of contract" concept to strike down legislation limiting entry into a business, despite strong demonstrations of need for such limitations. *New State Ice Co. v. Liebmann,* 285 U.S. 262, 52 S.Ct. 371, 76 L.Ed. 747 (1932) (invalid to deny entry into ice business without a finding of "necessity" and that existing facilities are not "sufficient to meet the public needs"); *Liggett Co. v. Baldridge,* 278 U.S. 105, 49 S.Ct. 57, 73 L.Ed. 204 (1928) (invalid to limit new entrants into pharmacy business to pharmacists; *Adams v. Tanner,* 244 U.S. 590, 37 S.Ct. 662, 61 L.Ed. 1336 (1917) (invalid to ban private employment agencies that charge fees paid by employees).

In 1973, *North Dakota State Board v. Snyder's Drug Stores,* Sec. 3 infra, overruled *Liggett.* While no cases precisely like *Adams* or *New State Ice* have arisen, the Court in 1963 asserted in effect that *Adams* had been overruled when it unanimously sustained a state prohibition on engaging in the debt adjusting business. See *Ferguson v. Skrupa,* Sec. 3 infra.

---

c. Not until 1937 were *Adkins* and other cases to the same effect overruled in *West Coast Hotel Co. v. Parrish,* Sec. 3 infra.

d. See Breck P. McAllister, *Lord Hale and Business Affected with a Public Interest,* 43 Harv.L.Rev. 759 (1930); Walton H. Hamilton, *Affectation with Public Interest,* 39 Yale L.J. 1089 (1930); Maurice Finkelstein, *From Munn v. Illinois to Tyson v. Banton: A Study in the Judicial Process,* 27 Colum.L.Rev. 769 (1927).

SECTION 3. THE ABANDONMENT OF *LOCHNER*

NEBBIA v. NEW YORK
291 U.S. 502, 54 S.Ct. 505, 78 L.Ed. 940 (1934).

JUSTICE ROBERTS delivered the opinion of the Court.

[In 1933, after a year's legislative study of the state's dairy industry, New York enacted a law which established a Milk Control Board with power to fix maximum and minimum retail prices. The Board fixed nine cents as the price to be charged by a store. Nebbia, the proprietor of a grocery store, was convicted of selling milk below the minimum price set.]

[Under] our form of government the use of property and the making of contracts are normally matters of private and not of public concern. The general rule is that both shall be free of governmental interference. But neither property rights nor contract rights are absolute; for government cannot exist if the citizen may at will use his property to the detriment of his fellows, or exercise his freedom of contract to work them harm. Equally fundamental with the private right is that of the public to regulate it in the common interest. [T]he guaranty of due process [demands] only that the law shall not be unreasonable, arbitrary, or capricious, and that the means selected shall have a real and substantial relation to the object sought to be attained. [A] regulation valid for one sort of business, or in given circumstances, may be invalid for another sort, or for the same business under other circumstances, because the reasonableness of each regulation depends upon the relevant facts.

[The opinion then summarized many different kinds of business and property regulations and controls previously sustained against due process attacks.]

The legislative investigation of 1932 was persuasive of the fact [that] unrestricted competition aggravated existing evils and the normal law of supply and demand was insufficient to correct maladjustments detrimental to the community. The inquiry disclosed destructive and demoralizing competitive conditions and unfair trade practices which resulted in retail price cutting and reduced the income of the farmer below the cost of production. [The Legislature] believed conditions could be improved by preventing destructive price-cutting by stores which, due to the flood of surplus milk, were able to buy at much lower prices than the larger distributors and to sell without incurring the delivery costs of the latter. [In] the light of the facts the [Milk Control Board's] order appears not to be unreasonable or arbitrary, or without relation to the purpose to prevent ruthless competition from destroying the wholesale price structure on which the farmer depends for his livelihood, and the community for an assured supply of milk. But we are told that because the law essays to control prices it denies due process. Notwithstanding the admitted power to correct existing economic ills by appropriate regulation of business, [the] appellant urges that direct fixation of prices is a type of regulation absolutely forbidden. [The] argument runs that the public control of rates or prices is per se unreasonable and unconstitutional, save as applied to businesses affected with a public interest; that a business so affected is [one] such as is commonly called a public utility; or a business in its nature a monopoly. [But] if, as must be conceded, the industry is subject to regulation in the public interest, what constitutional principle bars the state from correcting existing maladjustments by legislation touching prices? We think there is no such principle. The due process clause makes no mention of sales or of prices any more than it speaks of business or contracts or buildings or other incidents of property. The thought seems nevertheless to have persisted that there is something peculiarly sacrosanct about the price one may charge for what he makes or sells, and that, however able to regulate other elements of manufacture or trade, with incidental effect upon price, the state is incapable of directly controlling the price itself. This view was negatived many years ago. *Munn v. Illinois.*

"[Affected] with a public interest" is the equivalent of "subject to the exercise of the police power" and it is plain that nothing more was intended by the expression. [It] is clear that there is no closed class or category of businesses affected with a public interest, and the function of courts in the application of the Fifth and Fourteenth Amendments is to determine in each case whether circumstances vindicate the challenged regulation as a reasonable exertion of governmental authority or condemn it as arbitrary or discriminatory. The phrase "affected with a public interest" can, in the nature of things, mean no more than that an industry, for adequate reason, is subject to control for the public good. [There] can be no doubt that upon proper occasion and by appropriate measures the state may regulate a business in any of its aspects, including the prices to be charged for the products or commodities it sells.

So far as the requirement of due process is concerned, [a] state is free to adopt whatever economic policy may reasonably be deemed to promote public welfare, and to enforce that policy by legislation adapted to its purpose. The courts are without authority either to declare such policy, or, when it is declared by the legislature, to override it. If the laws passed are seen to have a reasonable relation to a proper legislative purpose, and are neither arbitrary nor discriminatory, the requirements of due process are satisfied. [If] the legislative policy be to curb unrestrained and harmful competition by measures which are not arbitrary or discriminatory it does not lie with the courts to determine that the rule is unwise. With the wisdom of the policy adopted, with the adequacy or practicability of the law enacted to forward it, the courts are both incompetent and unauthorized to deal. * * *

JUSTICE MCREYNOLDS, joined by JUSTICE VAN DEVANTER, JUSTICE SUTHERLAND, and JUSTICE BUTLER, dissenting:

[P]lainly, I think, this Court must have regard to the wisdom of the enactment. At least, we must inquire concerning its purpose and decide whether the means proposed have reasonable relation to something within legislative power— whether the end is legitimate, and the means appropriate. [Here,] we find direct interference with guaranteed rights defended upon the ground that the purpose was to promote the public welfare by increasing milk prices at the farm. [The] court below [has] not attempted to indicate how higher charges at stores to impoverished customers when the output is excessive and sale prices by producers are unrestrained, can possibly increase receipts at the farm. [It] appears to me wholly unreasonable to expect this legislation to accomplish the proposed end— increase of prices at the farm. [Not] only does the statute interfere arbitrarily with the rights of the little grocer to conduct his business according to standards long accepted—complete destruction may follow; but it takes away the liberty of 12,000,000 consumers to buy a necessity of life in an open market. [To] him with less than 9 cents it says: You cannot procure a quart of milk from the grocer although he is anxious to accept what you can pay and the demands of your household are urgent! [Grave] concern for embarrassed farmers is everywhere; but this should neither obscure the rights of others nor obstruct judicial appraisement of measures proposed for relief. The ultimate welfare of the producer, like that of every other class, requires dominance of the Constitution.

Notes and Questions

1. *The Nebbia rationale.* Did *Nebbia* appear to retain any degree of judicial review over legislative policy in state economic regulation? What standards of judgment did *Nebbia* suggest the Court would apply? Do you see any significance in the type of interests the Court found sufficient to justify price controls in *Nebbia?* In the sources relied upon by the Court to establish the factual basis for justifying price regulation?

2. WEST COAST HOTEL CO. v. PARRISH, 300 U.S. 379, 57 S.Ct. 578, 81 L.Ed. 703 (1937), overruled *Adkins v. Children's Hospital* and sustained a state minimum wage law for women. A 5–4 majority, per HUGHES, C.J., devoted substantial space to the reasons for regulation of women's wages: "What can be closer to the public interest than the health of women and their protection from unscrupulous and overreaching employers? [The] Legislature of the state was clearly entitled to consider [the] fact that [women] are in the class receiving the least pay, that their bargaining power is relatively weak, and that they are the ready victims of those who would take advantage of their necessitous circumstances. The Legislature was entitled to adopt measures to reduce the evils of the 'sweating system,' the exploiting of workers at wages so low as to be insufficient to meet the bare cost of living, thus making their very helplessness the occasion of a most injurious competition. [What] these workers lose in wages the taxpayers are called upon to pay. [We] may take judicial notice of the unparalleled demands for relief which arose during the recent period of depression. [The] community is not bound to provide, what is in effect a subsidy for unconscionable employers. [Even] if the wisdom of the policy be regarded as debatable and its effects uncertain, still the Legislature is entitled to its judgment."

As for the contention that the law violated "freedom of contract": "What is this freedom? The Constitution does not speak of freedom of contract. It speaks of liberty [and in] prohibiting that deprivation the Constitution does not recognize an absolute and uncontrollable liberty. [Liberty] under the Constitution [is] necessarily subject to the restraints of due process, and regulation which is reasonable in relation to its subject and is adopted in the interests of the community is due process. [We] think [*Adkins*] was a departure from the true application of the principles governing the regulation by the State of the relation of employer and employed."[a]

3. *What bearing, if any, did President Roosevelt's "Court-packing plan" have on the West Coast Hotel decision? West Coast Hotel* was decided in the midst of the controversy over Roosevelt's "Court-packing plan," leading some to call Roberts, J.'s vote in the case as "the switch in time that saved the Nine" from Roosevelt's plan. But a memorandum left by Roberts, J., makes clear that the conference vote in *West Coast Hotel* took place some weeks before the Court-packing plan was announced. See Felix Frankfurter, *Mr. Justice Roberts*, 104 U.Pa.L.Rev. 311

---

a. Sutherland, J., joined by VanDevanter, McReynolds and Butler, JJ., dissented, emphasizing that "the meaning of the Constitution does not change with the ebb and flow of economic events." As the dissenters saw it, the minimum wage law had no relation to the capacity or earning power of the employee and, to the extent that the law exceeded the fair value of the services rendered, it constituted "a compulsory exaction from the employer for the support of a partially indigent person," thereby unfairly shifting to the employer's shoulders "a burden which, if it belongs to anyone, belongs to society as a whole."

(1955). Compare Michael Ariens, *A Thrice–Told Tale, or Felix the Cat*, 107 Harv.L.Rev. 620 (1994) with Richard D. Friedman, *Switching Time and Other Thought Experiments: The Hughes Court and Constitutional Transformation*, 142 U.Pa.L.Rev. 1891 (1994). (See also the beginning of Ch. 2, Sec. 2, II, B.) It should be recalled, moreover, that Roberts, J., wrote an essentially anti-*Lochner* opinion three years earlier in *Nebbia*.

The Impact on *Lochner* of the Economic Realities of the Depression

Although by the mid–1930s the composition and philosophy of the Supreme Court had changed significantly since *Lochner*, "in large measure," observes Tribe 3d ed., at 1358–59, "it was the economic realities of the Depression that graphically undermined *Lochner*'s premises. No longer could it be argued with great conviction that the invisible hand of economics was functioning simultaneously to protect individual rights and to produce a social optimum. The legal 'freedom' of contract and property came increasingly to be seen as an illusion, subject as it was to impersonal economic forces. [Thus,] the basic justification for judicial intervention under *Lochner*—that the courts were restoring the natural order which had been upset by the legislature—was increasingly perceived as fundamentally flawed. There *was* no "natural" economic order to upset or restore, and legislative decision in any direction could neither be restrained nor justified on any such basis. [The] suffering of the underprivileged, including the misery of underpaid, overburdened, or unemployed workers, came to be seen by many not as an inescapable corollary of personal freedom or an inevitable result of forces beyond human control, but instead as a product of conscious governmental decisions to take *some* steps that might rescue people from conditions of intolerable deprivation."

"The Most Celebrated Footnote in Constitutional Law": Footnote 4 of the *Carolene Products* Case

UNITED STATES v. CAROLENE PRODUCTS CO., 304 U.S. 144, 58 S.Ct. 778, 82 L.Ed. 1234 (1938), upheld the constitutionality of a federal statute that prohibited the shipment in interstate commerce of "filled milk," a product compounded with fat or oil so as to resemble milk or cream. Appellee argued that the legislation violated both the commerce and due process clauses. The government countered that appellee's product was an impure, adulterated substance that posed a danger to the public. Writing for the Court, STONE, J., took the position that economic regulatory legislation, such as the statute at issue, was entitled to a presumption of constitutionality and should be upheld if supported by any rational basis. "Where the existence of a rational basis for legislation whose constitutionality is attacked depends upon facts beyond the sphere of judicial notice," continued Stone, "such facts may properly be made the subject of judicial inquiry, and the constitutionality of a statute predicated upon the existence of a particular state of facts may be challenged by showing to the court that those facts have ceased to exist. [B]y their very nature such inquiries, where the legislative judgment is drawn in question, must be restricted to the issue whether any state of facts either known or which could reasonably be assumed affords support for it." Under this approach, the challenged legislation easily passed constitutional muster.[a] In

---

a. "The plaudits accorded [footnote 4] are matched by the disregard of the case itself." Geoffrey Miller, *The True Story of Carolene Products*, 1987 Sup.Ct.Rev. 397, 398. This is unfortunate, points out Professor Miller, id. at 398–99, "because [the case] is interesting in its own right and because its facts shed light on the meaning of the footnote. The statute upheld in the case was an utterly unprincipled example of special interest legislation. The pur-

the course of writing his opinion, Stone, J., dropped a footnote (fn. 4) that has been called "the most celebrated footnote in constitutional law"[b] and "the great and modern charter for ordering the relations between judges and other agencies of government."[c] That footnote (case citations omitted) reads as follows:

1. "There may be narrower scope for operation of the presumption of constitutionality when legislation appears on its face to be within a specific prohibition of the Constitution, such as those of the first ten amendments, which are deemed equally specific when held to be embraced within the Fourteenth.

2. "It is unnecessary to consider now whether legislation which restricts those political processes which can obviously be expected to bring about repeal of undesirable legislation, is to be subjected to more exacting judicial scrutiny under the general prohibitions of the Fourteenth than are most other types of legislation [referring to cases dealing with restrictions on voting rights and freedom of expression and political association].

3. "Nor need we enquire whether similar considerations enter into the review of statutes directed at particular religions or national or racial minorities[:] whether prejudice against discrete and insular minorities may be a special condition, which tends seriously to curtail the operation of those political processes ordinarily to be relied upon to protect minorities, and which may call for a correspondingly more searching judicial inquiry."[d]

1. *Removing "impurities" in the democratic process.* *Carolene Products* was concerned about the impurity of appellee's product and the need to exclude it from interstate commerce, but, observes, Jack Balkin, *The Footnote*, 83 Nw.U.L.Rev. 275, 283 (1989), "*Carolene Products* is also about another type of purity and impurity, another type of inclusion and exclusion—that which affects the demo-

ported 'public interest' justifications so credulously reported by Justice Stone were patently bogus. [It] is difficult to believe that members of the Court were unaware of the true motivation behind this legislation. That they should nevertheless vote to uphold the statute strongly suggested that all bets were off as far as economic regulation was concerned. Footnote four, in this light, can be seen as indicating that the Court intended to keep its hands off economic regulation, no matter how egregious the discrimination or patent the special interests motivation. Rational basis scrutiny of [this sort] could not be taken seriously if it precluded judicial protection of individual liberties. By separating economic and personal liberties, Justice Stone suggested that the Court might really mean what it said about deference to the legislative will in economic cases."

See also, Neil Komesar, *Taking Institutions Seriously*, 51 U.Chi.L.Rev. 366, 416 (1984): "It does not take much scrutiny to see the dairy lobby at work behind the passage [of] the 'filled milk' act. Indeed, [it] is not too uncharitable [to] suggest that concern for the dairies' pocketbooks rather than for the consumer's health best explains the dairy lobby's efforts."

b. Justice Lewis Powell, *Carolene Products Revisited*, 82 Colum.L.Rev. 1087 (1982).

c. Owen Fiss, *The Forms of Justice*, 93 Harv.L.Rev. 1, 6 (1979).

d. Has the first paragraph of footnote 4 been undervalued in recent years? For an affirmative answer see Peter Linzer, *The Carolene Products Footnote and the Preferred Position of Individual Rights: Louis Lusky and John Hart Ely vs. Harlan Fiske Stone*, 12 Const.Comm. 277 (1995). Observes Professor Linzer at 278: "Early on, [footnote 4] was interpreted to mean that 'personal' rights were to be preferred to economic rights, but in recent years, largely through the efforts of Louis Lusky [who was Stone's law clerk when the famous footnote was written and who wrote the first draft of the footnote] and John Hart Ely, it has been interpreted more narrowly, justifying judicial activism only when the majoritarian democracy does not work: Ely describes it as 'representation-reinforcement,' a process-based notion that the courts should use judicial review aggressively only when the electoral process has broken down or is tampered with or when litigants are deemed not to have a fair chance to achieve change at the ballot box, either because of hostile laws or because of prejudice against them. [In] rereading Stone's contemporaneous opinions and those of his colleagues, however, I have become convinced that the process-based orientation underestimates the substantive content of the footnote, and that the revisionist attack on the 'preferred position' of non-economic rights needs to be refuted."

cratic process. *Carolene Products,* especially in its famous footnote, is concerned with impurities in the democratic process caused by adulteration of the means of political deliberation (the subject of the footnote's second paragraph) or by the exclusion of discrete and insular minorities from full political participation (the footnote's third paragraph). According to the logic of the footnote, certain groups are shut out of the democratic process, relegated to the periphery. They are, to use, Professor Brilmayer's expression, 'insider-outsiders'—persons subject to the power of the political community yet excluded from participation within it.[25] The goal of *Carolene Products* is to restore them to their rightful place within the polity through judicial supervision of the results of the democratic process. The role of the judiciary is to exclude legislation which is the result of impurities in the process, and by this exclusion, include those persons previously excluded, or prevent their future exclusion."

2.   *"Revers[ing] the spin of the countermajoritarian difficulty."* Bruce Ackerman, *Beyond Carolene Products,* 98 Harv.L.Rev. 713, 714–15 (1985), sees the case and footnote 4 as a "brilliant" effort "to turn the Old Court's recent defeat into a judicial victory": *"Carolene* promises relief from the problem of legitimacy raised whenever nine elderly lawyers invalidate the legislative decisions of our elected representatives. The *Carolene* solution is to seize the high ground of democratic theory and establish that the challenged legislation was produced by a profoundly defective process. By demonstrating that the legislative solution itself resulted from an undemocratic procedure, a *Carolene* court hopes to reverse the spin of the countermajoritarian difficulty. For it now may seem that the original legislative decision, not the judicial invalidation, suffers the greater legitimacy deficit."

3.   *Did footnote 4 replace one kind of "judicial activism" with another? Does it cause us to return to another kind of substantive due process?* Consider the remarks of Justice Lewis Powell, fn. b supra, at 1089–91 (1982): "Unlike Holmes, Stone lived to see—and indeed helped to preside over—the passing of the *Lochner* era. [But] Footnote 4, as interpreted by many commentators, represented a radical departure of its own. Far from initiating a jurisprudence of judicial deference to political judgments by the legislature, Footnote 4—on this view—undertook to substitute one activist judicial mission for another. Where once the Court had championed rights of property, now—according to some—it should view its special function as the identification and protection of 'discrete and insular minorities.' Where the Court before had used the substantive due process clause to protect property rights, now it should use the equal protection clause—a generally forgotten provision that Holmes once dismissed as 'the usual last resort of constitutional arguments'—as a sword with which to promote the liberty interests of groups disadvantaged by political decisions.

"The difference—or so runs the argument—is that protection of minority rights occurs in the name of correcting defects of *process,* defects that may have prevented minorities from gaining for themselves a fair bargain in the political arena. The theory is that the Court—in so protecting minority interests—does not risk imposing its own substantive values and distributive preferences on the Constitution and on the people of the United States.

" * * * Stone referred to discrete and insular minorities in a sentence, divided by a colon, in which he had referred earlier to racial, ethnic, and religious groups. Examining the textual evidence only, I think it would be a plausible

25. Lea Brilmayer, *Carolene, Conflicts and the Fate of the "Insider–Outsider,"* 134 U.Pa. L.Rev. 1291, 1294 (1986).

reading that these are the only kinds of groups to which the term 'discrete and insular' was intended to refer. In the normal operation of the political process, the term then would suggest that *some* racial, religious, and ethnic groups are not treated fairly and equally. Courts therefore should apply strict scrutiny to laws 'directed at' these disadvantaged groups.

"This idea has intuitive appeal, and it has been widely accepted. But it too may require some form of limitation in its application. In our uniquely heterogeneous society there are countless groups with some claim to being racial, ethnic, or religious. Over our history many have been minorities, ineffective in politics, and often discriminated against. But these conditions do not remain static. Immigrant groups that once were neglected have become influential participants in the political process. One reasonably may doubt the capacity of courts to distinguish wisely among them or determine which groups—at a given time and place—operate effectively within our politics. One also must inquire how far a court may go in determining when a law, nondiscriminatory on its face, fairly may be considered as 'directed at' a particular group.[e]

"The problem is this: in a democratic society there inevitably are both winners and losers. The fact that one group is disadvantaged by a particular piece of legislation, or action of government, therefore does not prove that the process has failed to function properly. To infer otherwise—that the process has been corrupted by invidious discrimination—a judge must have some *substantive* vision of what results the process should have yielded. Otherwise he has no way to know that the process was unfair.

"Here I must pause to wonder. If I am correct about the implicit link between a substantive judgment and a malfunction of process, then one may inquire whether we have not returned in some cases to a kind of substantive due process. And one also may wonder what Stone—who had fought so vigorously against substantive due process—would have had to say about this."

4. *Is Carolene's conception of the impact of prejudice "underinclusive"?* Should courts protect groups that are "anonymous and diffuse" rather than "discrete and insular"? Is "discreteness and insularity" likely to be a source of important bargaining advantage, not disadvantage, for a group involved in pluralist American politics? Consider Bruce Ackerman, supra, at 731–32, 745: "*Carolene*'s empirical inadequacy stems from its underinclusive conception of the impact of prejudice upon American society. It is easy to identify groups in the population that are not discrete and insular but that are nonetheless the victims of prejudice as that term is commonly understood. Thus, the fact that homosexuals are a relatively anonymous minority has not saved the group from severe prejudice.[f]

e. Does *Carolene* require that "neutral rules" be strictly scrutinized? Would such scrutiny be contrary to its reasoning? See Brilmayer, fn. 25 supra, at 1307–09. Professor Brilmayer concludes at 1334: "*Carolene*'s cruelest hoax is its suggestion that, once the discriminatory rules are invalidated, our political process problems are over. But, as any excluded person surely realizes, after putting the illusion of *Carolene* to one side, discriminatory rules are only a small part of a very large problem. They are only the first hurdle in a long road to political participation and equality. *Carolene*'s approach has led us seriously astray. It suggests that only discriminatory rules have process defects."

f. Earlier in his article, id. at 729, Professor Ackerman notes that he "propose[s] to define a minority as 'discrete' when its members are marked out in ways that make it relatively easy for others to identify them. [In] contrast, other minorities are socially defined in ways that give individual members the chance to avoid easy identification. A homosexual, for example, can keep her sexual preference a very private affair and thereby avoid much of the public opprobrium attached to her minority status. It is for this reason that I shall call homosexuals, and groups like them, 'anonymous' minorities and contrast them with 'discrete' minorities of the kind paradigmatically exemplified by blacks."

Nor is sexism a nonproblem merely because women are a diffuse, if discrete, majority. Prejudice is generated by a bewildering variety of social conditions. Although some *Carolene* minorities are seriously victimized, they are not the only ones stigmatized; nor is it obvious that all *Carolene* minorities are stigmatized more grievously than any other non-*Carolene* group. Why should the concern with 'prejudice' justify *Carolene*'s narrow fixation upon 'discrete and insular' minorities?

"The answer seemed easy in a world in which members of the paradigmatic *Carolene* minority group—blacks—were effectively barred from voting and political participation. [As] we move beyond the pariah model, however, anonymous or diffuse minorities will increasingly emerge as the groups that can raise the most serious complaints of pluralist disempowerment.

"[A]s long as we use *Carolene* rhetoric to express our constitutional concerns with racial equality and religious freedom, we will find ourselves saying things that are increasingly belied by political reality. While constitutional lawyers decry the political powerlessness of discrete and insular groups, representatives of these interests will be wheeling and dealing in the ongoing pluralistic exchange— winning some battles, losing others, but plainly numbering among the organized interests whose electoral power must be treated with respect by their bargaining partners and competitors. * * *

"[I]f we are to remain faithful to *Carolene*'s concern with the fairness of pluralist politics, we must repudiate the bad political science that allows us to ignore those citizens who have the most serious complaints: the anonymous and diffuse victims of poverty and sexual discrimination who find it most difficult to protect their fundamental interests through effective political organization."

The 1940s, 50s and 60s: A Far Cry From *Lochner*

West Coast Hotel was followed quickly by a number of cases upholding New Deal legislation. See, e.g., *NLRB v. Jones & Laughlin Steel Co.,* 301 U.S. 1, 57 S.Ct. 615, 81 L.Ed. 893 (1937) (the States Natural Labor Relations Act); *United States v. Darby*, 312 U.S. 100, 61 S.Ct. 451, 85 L.Ed. 609 (1941) (the Fair Labor Standards Act); *Wickard v. Filburn*, 317 U.S. 111, 63 S.Ct. 82, 87 L.Ed. 122 (1942) (the Agricultural Adjustment Act). A great deal of challenged state economic legislation was also sustained. Some representative cases follow:

OLSEN v. NEBRASKA, 313 U.S. 236, 61 S.Ct. 862, 85 L.Ed. 1305 (1941), upheld a Nebraska statute fixing maximum fees for employment agencies. DOUG-LAS, J.'s, unanimous opinion bluntly rejected the state court's reliance on *Ribnik v. McBride,* 277 U.S. 350, 48 S.Ct. 545, 72 L.Ed. 913 (1928), which had held a similar statute violative of due process: "The drift away from *Ribnik* has been so great that it can no longer be deemed a controlling authority. [But] respondents maintain that the statute here in question is invalid for other reasons. They insist that special circumstances must be shown to support the validity of such drastic legislation as price-fixing, that the executive technical and professional workers which respondents serve have not been shown to be in need of special protection from exploitation, that legislative limitation of maximum fees for employment agencies is certain to react unfavorably upon those members of the community for whom it is most difficult to obtain jobs, that the increasing competition of public employment agencies and of charitable, labor union and employer association employment agencies have curbed excessive fees by private agencies, and [that] there are no conditions which the legislature might reasonably believe would redound to the public injury unless corrected by such legislation.

"We are not concerned, however, with the wisdom, need, or appropriateness of the legislation. Differences of opinion on that score suggest a choice which 'should be left where [it] was left by the Constitution—to the states and to Congress.' *Ribnik,* dissenting opinion. [In] final analysis, the only constitutional prohibitions or restraints which respondents have suggested for the invalidation of this legislation are those notions of public policy embedded in earlier decisions of this Court but which, as Mr. Justice Holmes long ago admonished, should not be read into the Constitution."

In LINCOLN FED. LABOR UNION v. NORTHWESTERN IRON & METAL CO., 335 U.S. 525, 69 S.Ct. 251, 93 L.Ed. 212 (1949), a unanimous Court, per BLACK, J., sustained a state "right-to-work" law that barred a preference for union membership in employment decisions. The Court noted that at least since *Nebbia,* it had "steadily rejected the due process philosophy enunciated in the [*Lochner-Coppage*] line of cases and returned closer to the earlier constitutional principle that states may legislate "against what are found to be injurious practices in their internal commercial and business affairs, so long as they do not run afoul of some specific federal constitutional prohibition [or] some valid federal law."

WILLIAMSON v. LEE OPTICAL OF OKLAHOMA, 348 U.S. 483, 75 S.Ct. 461, 99 L.Ed. 563 (1955), where a unanimous Court, per DOUGLAS, J., upheld an Oklahoma law regulating opticians and optometrists, well demonstrates the great distance the Court had moved away from *Lochner* by the 1950s.

One provision forbid opticians from fitting or duplicating lenses without a prescription from an ophthalmologist or optometrist. "In practical effect, it means that no optician can fit old glasses into new frames or supply a lens, whether it be a new lens or one to duplicate a lost or broken lens, without a prescription." The Court rejected the argument that since an optician, by mechanical devices or ordinary skills, could take a fragment of a broken lens and reduce it to prescriptive terms, the particular means chosen by the legislature were "neither reasonably necessary nor reasonably related to the end sought to be achieved": "The legislature might have concluded that the frequency of occasions when a prescription is necessary was sufficient to justify this regulation of the fitting of eyeglasses. [Or] the legislature may have concluded that eye examinations were so critical [that] every change in frames and every duplication of a lens should be accompanied by a prescription from a medical expert. To be sure, the present law does not require a new examination of the eyes every time the frames are changed or the lenses duplicated. [But] the law need not be in every respect logically consistent with its aims to be constitutional. [The] day is gone when this Court uses the Due Process Clause [to] strike down state laws, regulatory of business and industrial conditions, because they may be unwise, improvident, or out of harmony with a particular school of thought."

As for another provision of the law, which prohibited soliciting the sale of eyeglass frames or any other optical appliances, challenged on the ground that it intruded into a mercantile field "only casually related to the visual care of the public," the Court responded: "[The] legislature might conclude that to regulate [lenses] effectively, it would have to regulate [eyeglass frames]. The advertiser of frames may be using his ads to bring in customers who will buy lenses."

A third provision of the law, one prohibiting retail stores from renting space to optometrists, was also said to violate fourteenth amendment due process. The Court disagreed, viewing the law as "an attempt to free the profession, to as great an extent as possible, from all taints of commercialism. It certainly might be easy for an optometrist with space in a retail store to be merely a front for the retail establishment. [We] cannot say that the regulation has no rational relation [to the objective of raising treatment of the human eye to a strictly professional level] and therefore is beyond constitutional bounds."

In the later case of FERGUSON v. SKRUPA, 372 U.S. 726, 83 S.Ct. 1028, 10 L.Ed.2d 93 (1963), the Court, per BLACK, J., without a dissent, rejected a due process challenge to a state law barring all but lawyers from the business of debt adjusting. And it did so in the strongest terms: "Under the system of government created by our Constitution, it is up to the legislatures, not the courts, to decide on the wisdom and utility of legislation. [The] doctrine that prevailed in *Lochner*, *Coppage*, *Adkins*, and like cases [has] long since been discarded. We have returned to the original constitutional proposition that courts do not substitute their social and economic beliefs for the judgment of legislative bodies, who are elected to pass laws. [Whether] the legislature takes for its textbook Adam Smith, Herbert Spence, Lord Keynes or some other is no concern of ours." Harlan, J., concurred on the ground that "[this] measure bears a rational relation to a constitutionally permissible objective."

SECTION 4. OTHER LIMITS ON ECONOMIC LEGISLATION: THE PROHIBITION AGAINST "TAKING" "PRIVATE PROPERTY" WITHOUT JUST COMPENSATION

INTRODUCTION

As Tribe 2d ed., at 587 observes, "[w]ith the demise of the *Lochner* era, [there] began a search for alternative methods of protecting individuals from majoritarian oppression. [Two] sets of restraints on governmental power both antedated and informed the *Lochner* era and survived that era's eclipse, retaining a measure of vitality even today. One such model, expressed primarily through the ex post facto clauses, the bill of attainder clauses, and the procedural due process requirement, demands *regularity* in the application of governmental power to particular persons. [The other involves] a norm perhaps as basic as that of regularity: the norm of *repose*. We deal here with the idea that government must respect 'vested rights' in property and contract—that certain settled expectations of a focused and crystallized sort should be secure against governmental disruption, at least without appropriate compensation."

The fifth amendment limits the federal government's power of eminent domain: "nor shall private property be taken for a public use without just compensation." This specific provision of the Bill of Rights was one of the first to be deemed binding on the states via fourteenth amendment due process. See *Chicago, B. & Q. R. Co. v. Chicago*, 166 U.S. 226, 17 S.Ct. 581, 41 L.Ed. 979 (1897); *Missouri Pac. Ry. Co. v. Nebraska*, 164 U.S. 403, 17 S.Ct. 130, 41 L.Ed. 489 (1896). This section considers what limits, if any, there are on the purposes for which private property may be taken *even with compensation*, and the circumstances under which a regulation should be regarded a "taking" that requires compensation.

In *Pennsylvania Coal v. Mahon* (1922), the Court, per Holmes, J., told us that "the general rule at least is that while property may be regulated to a certain extent, if regulation goes too far it will be recognized as a taking." Such a rule would strike many as exceedingly hazy and unmanageable. But is the "general rule" (whatever it is) represented by the modern cases any more helpful?

In *Eastern Enterprises v. Apfel* (1998), the most recent case in this section, the Court struck down a federal statute that imposed a monetary assessment on the prior owner of a coal mine that would have been used to fund benefits for now-retired miners who had once worked for the coal mine. There was no opinion of the Court. Speaking for four Justices, O'Connor, J., concluded that as the statute affected Eastern Enterprises, it violated the Takings Clause. Concurring in the judgment, but rejecting the plurality's Takings Clause analysis, Kennedy, J., concluded that the statute "must be invalidated as contrary to essential due process principles" because it went "far outside the bounds of retroactivity permissible under our law." It is noteworthy that (a) the O'Connor plurality seemed to avoid reliance upon the Due Process Clause at least in part out of fear of resurrecting *Lochner*, but (b) Justice Kennedy pointed out that if the plurality had adopted what he called its "novel" concept of a "taking" in order to avoid making a "normative judgment" about the statute it must make the normative judgment anyway. Indeed, maintained Kennedy, the malleability of the Court's takings doctrine "open[s] the door to normative considerations about the wisdom of government decisions." Moreover, dissenting Justice Stevens, joined by Souter, Ginsburg and Breyer, JJ., concluded that whether the statute "is analyzed under the Takings Clause *or* the Due Process Clause" (emphasis added), the company "has not carried its burden of overcoming the presumption of constitutionality accorded to an act of Congress."

I. PURPOSE OF "TAKING"

BERMAN v. PARKER, 348 U.S. 26, 75 S.Ct. 98, 99 L.Ed. 27 (1954): A federal statute authorized an agency to acquire private property for the redevelopment of blighted areas. After the condemnation, the agency could lease or sell portions of the land to private developers who agreed to carry out the redevelopment plan. Appellants owned a well-maintained department store that posed no blight or health problem itself, but was located in a badly blighted area. They argued that their property could not be taken because it was not residential or slum housing. They also maintained that their property was being condemned for a private purpose, not a public one, and therefore could not be taken by the government even upon payment of just compensation. A unanimous Court, per DOUGLAS, J., rejected their contentions: "We deal [with] what traditionally has been known as the police power. [In] such cases the legislature, not the judiciary, is the main guardian of the public needs to be served by social legislation. [This] principle admits of no exception merely because the power of eminent domain is involved. The role of the judiciary in determining whether that power is being exercised for a public purpose is an extremely narrow one.

"Public safety, public health, morality, peace and quiet, law and order—these are some of the more conspicuous examples of the traditional application of the police power to municipal affairs. Yet they merely illustrate the scope of the power and do not delimit it. Miserable and disreputable housing conditions may do more than spread disease and crime and immorality. They may also suffocate the spirit. [They] may [be] a blight on the community which robs it of charm, which is a place from which men turn. * * *

"We do not sit to determine whether a particular housing project is or is not desirable. The concept of the public welfare is broad and inclusive. The values it represents are spiritual as well as physical, aesthetic as well as monetary. It is within the power of the legislature to determine that the community should be beautiful as well as healthy, spacious as well as clean, well-balanced as well as carefully patrolled. [If] those who govern the District of Columbia decide that the Nation's Capital should be beautiful as well as sanitary, there is nothing in the Fifth Amendment that stands in the way.

"[Appellants] maintain that since their building does not imperil health or safety nor contribute to the making of a slum or a blighted area, it cannot be swept into a redevelopment plan. [The] experts concluded that if the community were to be healthy, if it were not to revert again to a blighted or slum area, [the] area must be planned as a whole. It was not enough, they believed, to remove existing buildings that were insanitary or unsightly. [It] was believed that the piecemeal approach, the removal of individual structures that were offensive, would be only a palliative. The entire area needed redesigning so that a balanced, integrated plan could be developed for the region, including not only new homes but also schools, churches, parks, streets, and shopping centers. [Such] diversification in future use is plainly relevant to the maintenance of the desired housing standards and therefore within congressional power."

The Court relied heavily on *Berman* in HAWAII HOUSING AUTHORITY v. MIDKIFF, 467 U.S. 229, 104 S.Ct. 2321, 81 L.Ed.2d 186 (1984), which upheld the use of eminent domain to lessen the concentration of fee simple land ownership, inherited from Hawaii's early feudal land tenure system. The legislature found that the concentration of land ownership in a relatively few hands was, as summarized by the Court, "responsible for skewing the State's residential fee simple market, inflating land prices, and injuring public tranquility and welfare." The resulting legislation authorized the state's housing authority to condemn the land on which "eligible tenants" lived and to sell it to them at a fair market value. A unanimous Court, per O'CONNOR, J., rejected the claim that such taking was not for a public use: "[There] is, of course, a role for courts to play in reviewing a legislature's judgment of what constitutes a public use, even when the eminent domain power is equated with the police power. But the Court in *Berman* made clear that it is 'an extremely narrow' one. [Where] the exercise of the eminent domain power is rationally related to a conceivable public purpose, the Court has never held a compensated taking to be proscribed by the Public Use Clause.

"On this basis, we have no trouble concluding that the Hawaii Act is constitutional. The people of Hawaii have attempted, much as the settlers of the original 13 Colonies did, to reduce the perceived social and economic evils of a land oligopoly traceable to their monarchs. * * * Regulating oligopoly and the evils associated with it is a classic exercise of a State's police powers. We cannot disapprove of Hawaii's exercise of this power.

"[When] the legislature's purpose is legitimate and its means are not irrational, our cases make clear that empirical debates over the wisdom of takings–no less than debates over the wisdom of other kinds of socioeconomic legislation–are not to be carried out in the federal courts. Redistribution of fees simple to correct deficiencies in the market determined by the state legislature to be attributable to land oligopoly is a rational exercise of the eminent domain power. Therefore, the Hawaii statute must pass the scrutiny of the Public Use Clause."

II.   WHEN IS "REGULATION" OF PROPERTY TANTAMOUNT TO A "TAKING"?

PENNSYLVANIA COAL CO. v. MAHON

260 U.S. 393, 43 S.Ct. 158, 67 L.Ed. 322 (1922).

JUSTICE HOLMES delivered the opinion of the Court.

This is a bill in equity brought by the [plaintiffs] to prevent the Pennsylvania Coal company from mining under their property in such way as to remove the supports and cause f subsidence of the surface and of their house. [The] deed conveys the surface, but in express terms reserves the right to remove all the coal under the same, and the grantee takes the premises with [that] risk. [But] the plaintiffs say that whatever may have been the Coal Company's rights, they were taken away by [the] Kohler Act, [a law forbidding] the mining of anthracite coal in such way as to cause the subsidence [of] any structure used as a human habitation, with certain exceptions. [As] applied to this case the statute is admitted to destroy previously existing rights of property and contract. The question is whether the police power can be stretched so far.

Government hardly could go on if to some extent values incident to property could not be diminished without paying for every such change in the general law. As long recognized, some values are enjoyed under an implied limitation and must yield to the police power. But obviously the implied limitation must have its limits, or the contact and due process clauses are gone. One fact for consideration in determining such limits is the extent of the diminution. When it reaches a certain magnitude, in most if not in all cases there must be an exercise of eminent domain and compensation to sustain the act. So the question depends upon the particular facts. The greatest weight is given to the judgment of the legislature, but it always is open to interested parties to contend that the legislature has gone beyond its constitutional power.

[It] is our opinion that the act cannot be sustained as an exercise of the police power, so far as it affects the mining of coal under streets or cities in places where the right to mine such coal has been reserved. [To] make it commercially impracticable to mine certain coal has very nearly the same effect for constitutional purposes as appropriating or destroying it. This we think that we are warranted in assuming that the statute does.

[The] protection of private property in the Fifth amendment presupposes that it is wanted for public use, but provides that it shall not be taken for such use without compensation. [When] this seemingly absolute protection is found to be qualified by the police power, the natural tendency of human nature is to extend the qualification more and more until at last private property disappears. But that cannot be accomplished in this way under the Constitution.

[The] general rule at least is, that while property may be regulated to a certain extent, if regulation goes too far it will be recognized as a taking. [We] are in danger of forgetting that a strong public desire to improve the public condition is not enough to warrant achieving the desire by a shorter cut than the constitutional way of paying for the change. [So] far as private persons or communities have seen fit to take the risk of acquiring only surface rights, we cannot see that the fact that their risk has become a danger warrants the giving to them greater rights than they bought. * * *

JUSTICE BRANDEIS, dissenting.

[If] by mining anthracite coal the owner would necessarily unloose poisonous gasses, I suppose no one would doubt the power of the State to prevent the mining, without buying his coal fields. And why may not the State, likewise, without paying compensation, prohibit one from digging so deep or excavating so near the surface, as to expose the community to like dangers?

It is said that one fact for consideration in determining whether the limits of the police power have been exceeded is the extent of the resulting diminution in value; and that here the restriction destroys existing rights of property and contract. But values are relative. [For] aught that appears the value of the coal kept in place by the restriction may be negligible as compared with the value of the whole property, or even as compared with that part of it which is represented by the coal remaining in place and which may be extracted despite the statute.

[A] prohibition of mining which causes subsidence of [structures] and facilities is obviously enacted for a public purpose. [Yet] it is said that these provisions of the act cannot be sustained as an exercise of the police power where the right to mine such coal has been reserved. The conclusion seems to rest upon the assumption that in order to justify such exercise of the police power there must be "an average reciprocity of advantage" as between the owner of the property restricted and the rest of the community; and that here such reciprocity is absent. [But] where the police power is exercised, not to confer benefits upon property owners, but to protect the public from detriment and danger, there is, in my opinion, no room for considering reciprocity of advantage.

Notes and Questions

1. *The intent of the Framers.* Consider J. Peter Byrne, *Regulatory Takings and "Judicial Supremacy,"* 51 Ala. L. Rev. 949, 955 (2000): "The language of the Takings Clause says nothing about excessive regulatory burdens; indeed, the word 'take' denotes some change in possession or title. Historical research has established beyond reasonable dispute that the Framers intended the Clause only to apply to physical seizures [referring to William M. Treanor, *The Original Understanding of the Takings Clause and the Political Process*, 95 Colum. L. Rev. 782, 791 (1995)]. Courts consistently so interpreted the Clause for more than 100 years, until the Court, in thrall to substantive due process, invented regulatory takings in 1922 in *Pennsylvania Coal.*"

2. Compare *Pennsylvania Coal* with *Miller v. Schoene,* 276 U.S. 272, 48 S.Ct. 246, 72 L.Ed. 568 (1928), upholding a state law authorizing the cutting down of red cedar trees—without any compensation—because they were infected (but not ruined) with a rust disease that might have spread to, and destroyed, a nearby apple orchard. *Miller* is discussed in the next main case set forth in this section, *Penn Central Transp. Co. v. New York City.*

3. Compare *Pennsylvania Coal* with KEYSTONE BITUMINOUS COAL ASS'N v. DEBENEDICTIS, 480 U.S. 470, 107 S.Ct. 1232, 94 L.Ed.2d 472 (1987), upholding a modern-day version of the Kohler Act invalidated in the 1922 case. The 1966 Pennsylvania law prohibited coal mining that caused subsidence damage to preexisting public buildings, dwellings and cemeteries. Regulations issued pursuant to the law required that 50% of the coal beneath such structures be kept in place in order to provide adequate surface support. This time, a 5–4 majority, per STEVENS, J., held that the law did not amount to a "taking," distinguishing *Pennsylvania Coal* on two grounds:

(1) The law "does not merely involve a balancing of the private economic interests of coal companies against the private interests of the surface owners," as did the old Kohler Act, but it represents an effort by the state "to arrest what it perceives to be a significant threat to the public welfare." (2) Unlike the situation in *Pennsylvania Coal*, where the record supported a finding that the Kohler Act had made certain coal mining "commercially impracticable," petitioners "have not even pointed to a single mine that can no longer be mined for profit. [The] total coal in [petitioners'] 13 mines amounts to over 1.46 billion tons. [The challenged law] requires them to leave less than 2% of their coal [albeit 27 million tons] in place. But nowhere near all of the underground coal is extractable even aside from [the law]. [The] 27 million tons of coal do not constitute a separate segment of property for takings law purposes. [When] the coal that must remain beneath the ground is viewed in the context of any reasonable unit of petitioners' coal mining operations, [it] is plain that [they] have not come close to satisfying the burden of proving that they have been denied the economically viable use of that property."

REHNQUIST, C.J., dissented, joined by Powell, O'Connor, and Scalia, JJ., maintaining that both the language and holding of *Pennsylvania Coal* called for the opposite result: "[O]ur cases have never applied that nuisance exception to allow complete extinction of the value of a parcel of property." They thought "[t]here is no question that [the 27 million tons of coal to be left in place] is an identifiable and separate property interest. [From] the relevant perspective—that of the property owners—that interest has been destroyed every bit as much as if the government had proceeded to mine the coal for its own use."

In *Lucas v. South Carolina Coastal Council* (1992), set forth infra, *Pennsylvania Coal* and *Keystone* are compared by both Scalia, J., who wrote the majority opinion (see fn. 7 to his opinion), and by Stevens, J., who dissented.

PENN CENTRAL TRANSP. CO. v. NEW YORK CITY

438 U.S. 104, 98 S.Ct. 2646, 57 L.Ed.2d 631 (1978).

JUSTICE BRENNAN delivered the opinion of the Court.

[Pursuant to New York City's Landmarks Preservation Law, the Preservation Commission designated Grand Central Terminal, owned by Penn Central, as a "landmark." It denied approval for Penn Central to construct a 55 story office building resting on the roof of the Terminal, cantilevered to preserve the existing Terminal facade. The Commission emphasized the harmful effect of the proposed construction on the dramatic view of the Terminal from Park Avenue South.[a] Choosing not to modify its proposal, or to use its right under New York laws to transfer its unused landmark site development rights to one or more of its eight nearby lots, Penn Central unsuccessfully challenged in the New York courts the constitutionality of this application of the Landmarks Law. The Court upheld the Law as applied.]

[The issue is] whether the restrictions [upon] appellants' exploitation of the Terminal site effect a "taking" of appellants' property for a public use within the meaning of the Fifth Amendment, [made] applicable to the States through the Fourteenth.[25]

a. "[To] balance a 55–story office tower above a flamboyant Beaux–Arts facade seems nothing more than an aesthetic joke. Quite simply, the tower would overwhelm the Terminal by its sheer mass. The 'addition' would be four times as high as the existing structure and would reduce the Landmark itself to the status of a curiosity."

25. As is implicit in our opinion, we do not embrace the proposition that a "taking" can

[W]hat constitutes a "taking" [has] proved to be a problem of considerable difficulty. While this Court has recognized that the "Fifth Amendment's guarantee [is] designed to bar Government from forcing some people alone to bear public burdens which, in all fairness and justice, should be borne by the public as a whole," this Court, quite simply, has been unable to develop any "set formula" for determining when "justice and fairness" require that economic injuries caused by public action be compensated by the government, rather than remain disproportionately concentrated on a few persons.

[In] engaging [in] essentially ad hoc, factual inquiries, the Court's decisions have identified several factors that have particular significance. The economic impact of the regulation on the claimant and, particularly, the extent to which the regulation has interfered with distinct investment-backed expectations are, of course, relevant considerations. So, too, is the character of the governmental action. A "taking" may more readily be found when the interference with property can be characterized as a physical invasion by government, see, e.g., *United States v. Causby*, 328 U.S. 256, 66 S.Ct. 1062, 90 L.Ed. 1206 (1946), than when interference arises from some public program adjusting the benefits and burdens of economic life to promote the common good.

[In] instances in which a state tribunal reasonably concluded that "the health, safety, morals, or general welfare" would be promoted by prohibiting particular contemplated uses of land, this Court has upheld land-use regulations that destroyed or adversely affected recognized real property interests [which] have been viewed as permissible governmental action even when prohibiting the most beneficial use of the property. Zoning laws generally do not affect existing uses of real property, but "taking" challenges have also been held to be without merit in a wide variety of situations when the challenged governmental actions prohibited a beneficial use to which individual parcels had previously been devoted and thus caused substantial individualized harm. *Miller v. Schoene*, 276 U.S. 272, 48 S.Ct. 246, 72 L.Ed. 568 (1928), is illustrative. In that case, [an] entomologist, acting pursuant to [a Virginia law], ordered the claimants to cut down a large number of ornamental red cedar trees because they produced cedar rust fatal to apple trees cultivated nearby. [Although the statute] did not provide compensation for the value of the standing trees or for the resulting decrease in market value of the properties as a whole, [a] unanimous Court held that this latter omission did not render the statute invalid. The Court held that the State might properly make "a choice between the preservation of one class of property and that of the other" and since the apple industry was important in the State involved, concluded that the State had not exceeded "its constitutional powers by deciding upon the destruction of one class of property [without compensation] in order to save another which, in the judgment of the legislature, is of greater value to the public."

[*Pennsylvania Coal*] is the leading case for the proposition that a state statute that substantially furthers important public policies may so frustrate distinct investment-backed expectations as to amount to a "taking." [Because] the statute made it commercially impracticable to mine the coal, and thus had nearly the same effect as the complete destruction of rights claimant had reserved from the owners of the surface land, the Court held that the statute was invalid as effecting a "taking" without just compensation. [See] generally Frank I. Michelman, *Property, Utility, and Fairness: Comments on the Ethical Foundations of "Just Compensation" Law*, 80 Harv.L.Rev. 1165, 1229–1234 (1967).

never occur unless government has transferred   physical control over a portion of a parcel.

Finally, government actions that may be characterized as acquisitions of resources to permit or facilitate uniquely public functions have often been held to constitute "takings." *Causby* is illustrative. In holding that direct overflights above the claimant's land, that destroyed the present use of the land as a chicken farm, constituted a "taking," *Causby* emphasized that Government had not "merely destroyed property [but was] using a part of it for the flight of its planes."

[Appellants argue] that the Landmarks Law has deprived them of any gainful use of their "air rights" above the Terminal, [entitling] them to "just compensation" measured by the fair market value of these air rights. [T]he submission that appellants may establish a "taking" simply by showing that they have been denied the ability to exploit a property interest that they heretofore had believed was available for development is quite simply untenable. * * * "Taking" jurisprudence does not divide a single parcel into discrete segments and attempt to determine whether rights in a particular segment have been entirely abrogated. In deciding whether a particular governmental action has effected a taking, this Court focuses rather both on the character of the action and on the nature and extent of the interference with rights in the parcel as a whole—here, the city tax block designated as the "landmark site."

Secondly, appellants [argue that the New York law] effects a "taking" because its operation has significantly diminished the value of the Terminal site. [They claim] that New York City's regulation of individual landmarks is fundamentally different from zoning or from historic district legislation because the controls imposed by New York City's law apply only to individuals who own selected properties. Stated baldly, appellants' position appears to be that the only means of ensuring that selected owners are not singled out to endure financial hardship for no reason is to hold that any restriction imposed on individual landmarks pursuant to the New York City scheme is a "taking" requiring the payment of "just compensation." [C]ontrary to appellants' suggestions, landmark laws are not like discriminatory, or "reverse spot," zoning: that is, a land-use decision which arbitrarily singles out a particular parcel for different, less favorable treatment than the neighboring ones. In contrast to discriminatory zoning, which is the antithesis of land-use control as part of some comprehensive plan, the New York City law embodies a comprehensive plan to preserve structures of historic or aesthetic interest wherever they might be found in the [city].

Next, appellants observe that New York City's law differs from zoning laws and historic-district ordinances in that the Landmarks Law does not impose identical or similar restrictions on all structures located in particular physical communities. It follows, they argue, that New York City's law is inherently incapable of producing the fair and equitable distribution of benefits and burdens of governmental action which is characteristic of zoning laws and historic-district [legislation]. It is, of course, true that the Landmarks Law has a more severe impact on some landowners than on others, but that in itself does not mean that the law effects a "taking." Legislation designed to promote the general welfare commonly burdens some more than others.

[Appellants' claim that they are "solely burdened and unbenefitted"] overlooks the fact that the New York City law applies to vast numbers of structures in the city in addition to the Terminal—all the structures contained in the 31 historic districts and over 400 individual landmarks, many of which are close to the Terminal. Unless we are to reject the judgment of the New York City Council that the preservation of landmarks benefits all New York citizens and all structures, both economically and by improving the quality of life in the city as a whole—which we are unwilling to do—we cannot conclude that the owners of the Terminal have in no sense been benefitted by the Landmarks Law.

[All] we thus far have established is that the [law] is not rendered invalid by its failure to provide "just compensation" whenever a landmark owner is restricted in the exploitation of property [interests], to a greater extent than provided for under applicable zoning laws. We now must consider whether the interference with appellants' property is of such a magnitude that "there must be an exercise of eminent domain and compensation to sustain [it]." *Pennsylvania Coal.* That inquiry may be narrowed to the question of the severity of the impact of the law on appellants' parcel, and its resolution in turn requires a careful assessment of the impact of the regulation on the Terminal site.

[The challenged law] does not interfere in any way with the present uses of the Terminal. Its designation as a landmark not only permits but contemplates that appellants may continue to use the property precisely as it has been used for the past 65 years: as a railroad terminal containing office space and concessions. So the law does not interfere with what must be regarded as Penn Central's primary expectation concerning the use of the parcel. More importantly, on this record, we must regard the [law] as permitting Penn Central not only to profit from the Terminal but also to obtain a "reasonable return" on its investment.

[W]e conclude that the application of New York City's [law] has not effected a "taking" of appellants' property. The restrictions imposed are substantially related to the promotion of the general welfare and not only permit reasonable beneficial use of the landmark site but afford appellants opportunities further to enhance not only the Terminal site proper but also other properties.[a] * * *

Justice Rehnquist, with whom The Chief Justice and Justice Stevens join, dissenting.

[The] question in this case is whether the cost associated with the city of New York's desire to preserve a limited number of "landmarks" within its borders must be borne by all of its taxpayers or whether it can instead be imposed entirely on the owners of the individual properties. [While] neighboring landowners are free to use their land and "air rights" in any way consistent with the broad boundaries of New York zoning, Penn Central, absent the permission of appellees, must forever maintain its property in its present state. The property has been thus subjected to a nonconsensual servitude not borne by any neighboring or similar properties.

Appellees have thus destroyed—in a literal sense, "taken"—substantial property rights of Penn Central. While the term "taken" might have been narrowly interpreted to include only physical seizures of property rights, "the construction of the phrase has not been so narrow. The courts have held that the deprivation of the former owner rather than the accretion of a right or interest to the sovereign constitutes the taking." *United States v. General Motors Corp.,* 323 U.S. 373, 378, 65 S.Ct. 357, 89 L.Ed. 311 (1945). [An] examination of the two exceptions where the destruction of property does *not* constitute a taking demonstrates that a compensable taking has occurred here.

a. We emphasize that our holding today is on the present record which in turn is based on Penn Central's present ability to use the Terminal for its intended purposes and in a gainful fashion. The city conceded at oral argument that if appellants can demonstrate at some point in the future that circumstances have changed such that the Terminal ceases to be, in the city's counsel's words, "economically viable," appellants may obtain relief.

As early as 1887, the Court recognized that the government can prevent a property owner from using his property to injure others without having to compensate the owner for the value of the forbidden use. *Mugler v. Kansas,* 123 U.S. 623, 8 S.Ct. 273, 31 L.Ed. 205 (1887). [Thus], there is no "taking" where a city prohibits the operation of a brickyard within a residential city, or forbids excavation for sand and gravel below the water line. Nor is it relevant, where the government is merely prohibiting a noxious use of property, that the government would seem to be singling out a particular property owner. [Appellees] are not prohibiting a nuisance. [Instead], Penn Central is prevented from further developing its property basically because *too good* a job was done in designing and building [it].

Even where the government prohibits a noninjurious use, the Court has ruled that a taking does not take place if the prohibition applies over a broad cross section of land and thereby "secure[s] an average reciprocity of advantage." *Pennsylvania Coal.* It is for this reason that zoning does not constitute a "taking." While zoning at times reduces *individual* property values, the burden is shared relatively evenly and it is reasonable to conclude that on the whole an individual who is harmed by one aspect of the zoning will be benefitted by another.

Here, however, a multimillion dollar loss has been imposed on appellants; it is uniquely felt and is not offset by any benefits flowing from the preservation of some 400 other "landmarks" in New York City. Appellees have imposed a substantial cost on less than one one-tenth of one percent of the buildings in New York City for the general benefit of all its people. It is exactly this imposition of general costs on a few individuals at which the "taking" protection is [directed.]

[The] benefits that appellees believe will flow from preservation of the Grand Central Terminal will accrue to all the citizens of New York City. There is no reason to believe that appellants will enjoy a substantially greater share of these benefits. If the cost of preserving Grand Central Terminal were spread evenly across the entire population of the city of New York, the burden per person would be in cents per year—a minor cost appellees would surely concede for the benefit accrued. Instead, however, appellees would impose the entire cost of several million dollars per year on Penn Central. But it is precisely this sort of discrimination that the Fifth Amendment prohibits.

[A] taking does not become a noncompensable exercise of police power simply because the government in its grace allows the owner to make some "reasonable" use of his property. "[I]t is the character of the invasion, not the amount of damage resulting from it, so long as the damage is substantial, that determines the question whether it is a taking."

LUCAS v. SOUTH CAROLINA COASTAL COUNCIL

505 U.S. 1003, 112 S.Ct. 2886, 120 L.Ed.2d 798 (1992).

JUSTICE SCALIA delivered the opinion of the Court.

[Lucas bought two lots near a South Carolina beach, at the time zoned for single-family dwellings, intending to build such dwellings on them. But before any construction got underway, the enactment of an anti-erosion law, South Carolina's Beachfront Management Act, prevented Lucas from erecting any permanent habitable structures on his lots. A state trial court found that the new law rendered Lucas's lots "valueless" and ordered compensation of more than one million dollars for this "taking." The state supreme court reversed on the ground that when a law is designed "to prevent serious public harm" no compensation is owed the owner, regardless of the law's impact on the value of his property. The Court granted review to decide whether the state law's "dramatic effect" on the value of Lucas's lots constituted "a taking of private property" and concluded that it did.]

[Holmes, J.,'s opinion in *Pennsylvania Coal*] offered little insight into when, and under what circumstances, a given regulation would be seen as going "too far" for purposes of the Fifth Amendment. [In] 70–odd years [of] "regulatory taking" jurisprudence we [have] described at least two discrete categories of regulatory action as compensable without case-specific inquiry into the public interest advanced in support of the restraint. The first encompasses regulations that compel the property owner to suffer a physical "invasion" of his property. In general (at least with regard to permanent invasions), no matter how minute the intrusion, and no matter how weighty the public purpose behind it, we have required compensation. For example, in *Loretto v. Teleprompter Manhattan CATV Corp.*, 458 U.S. 419, 102 S. Ct. 3164, 73 L. Ed. 2d 868 (1982), we determined that New York's law requiring landlords to allow television cable companies to emplace cable facilities in their apartment buildings constituted a taking, even thought the facilities occupied at most only 1 ½ cubic feet of the landlords' property.[a] [The] second situation in which we have found categorical treatment appropriate is where regulation denies all economically beneficial or productive use of land. [As] we have said on numerous occasions, the Fifth Amendment is violated when the land-use regulation "does not substantially advance legitimate state interests *or denies an owner* economically viable use of his land."[7]

We have never set forth the justification for this rule. Perhaps it is simply, as Justice Brennan suggested, that total deprivation of beneficial use is, from the landowner's point of view, the equivalent of a physical appropriation. [Surely,] at least, in the extraordinary circumstance when *no* productive or economically beneficial use of land is permitted, it is less realistic to indulge our usual

---

a. *Loretto*, per Marshall, J., observed: "When faced with a constitutional challenge to a permanent physical occupation of real property this Court has invariably found a taking." To the extent that the government permanently occupies physical property, it "effectively destroys" the rights to possess, use and dispose of it. "The owner has no right to possess the occupied space himself [or] to exclude the occupier."

Dissenting, Blackmun J., joined by Brennan and White, JJ., protested that "[b]y directing that all 'permanent physical occupations' automatically are compensable, 'without regard to whether the action achieves an important public benefit or has only minimal economic impact on the owner,' the Court does not further equity so much as it encourages litigants to manipulate their factual allegations to gain the benefit of the per se rule."

7. Regrettably, the rhetorical force of our "deprivation of all economically feasible use" rule is greater than its precision, since the rule does not make clear the "property interest" against which the loss of value is to be measured. When, for example, a regulation requires a developer to leave 90% of a rural tract in its natural state, it is unclear whether we

would analyze the situation as one in which the owner has been deprived of all economically beneficial use of the burdened portion of the tract, or as one in which the owner has suffered a mere diminution in value of the tract as a whole. Unsurprisingly, the uncertainty regarding the composition of the denomination in our "deprivation" fraction has produced inconsistent pronouncements by the Court. Compare *Pennsylvania Coal* (law restricting subsurface extraction of coal held to effect a taking) with *Keystone* (nearly identical law held not to effect a taking). [The] answer to this difficult question may lie in how the owner's reasonable expectations have been shaped by the State's law of property—i.e., whether and to what degree the State's law has accorded legal recognition and protection to the particular interest in land with respect to which the takings claimant alleges a diminution in (or elimination of) value. In any event, we avoid this difficulty in the present case, since the "interest in land" that Lucas has pleaded (a fee simple interest) is an estate with a rich tradition of protection at common law, and since the [trial court] found that the [challenged law] left each of Lucas's beachfront lots without economic value.

assumption that the legislature is simply 'adjusting the benefits and burdens of economic life,' *Penn Central,* in a manner that secures an 'average reciprocity of advantage' to everyone concerned, *Pennsylvania Coal.* And the *functional* basis for permitting the government, by regulation, to affect property values without compensation—that "Government hardly could go on if to some extent values incident to property could not be diminished without paying for every such change in the general law," ibid.—does not apply to the relatively rare situations where the government has deprived a landowner of all economically beneficial uses.

On the other side of the balance, affirmatively supporting a compensation requirement, is the fact that regulations that leave the owner of land without economically beneficial or productive options for its use—typically, as here, by requiring land to be left substantially in its natural state—carry with them a heightened risk that private property is being pressed into some form of public service under the guise of mitigating serious public harm. [The] many statutes on the books, both state and federal, that provide for the use of eminent domain to impose servitudes on private scenic lands preventing developmental uses, or to acquire such lands altogether, suggest the practical equivalence in this setting of negative regulation and appropriation. We think, in short, that there are good reasons for our frequently expressed belief that when the owner of real property has been called upon to sacrifice *all* economically beneficial uses in the name of the common good, that is, to leave the property economically idle, he has suffered a taking.[8]

It is correct that many of our prior opinions have suggested that "harmful or noxious uses" of property may be proscribed by government regulation without the requirement of compensation. For a number of reasons, however, we think the [state supreme court] was too quick to conclude that the principle decides the present case. [The] 'harmful or noxious uses' principle was the Court's early attempt to describe in theoretical terms why government may, consistent with the Takings Clause, affect property values by regulation without incurring an obligation to compensate—a reality we nowadays acknowledge explicitly with respect to the full scope of the State's police power. See, e.g., *Penn Central.* "[These] cases are better understood as resting not on any supposed 'noxious' quality of the prohibited uses but rather on the ground that the restrictions were reasonably related to the implementation of a policy—not unlike historic preservation—expected to produce a widespread public benefit and applicable to all similarly situated property." " 'Harmful or noxious use" analysis was, in other words, simply the progenitor of our more contemporary statements that "land-use regulation does not effect a taking if it 'substantially advances legitimate state interests.' " *Nollan v. California Coastal Comm'n,* 483 U.S. 825, 107 S. Ct. 3141, 97 L. Ed. 2d 677 (1987).[b]

The transition from our early focus on control of "noxious" uses to our contemporary understanding of the broad realm within which government may regulate without compensation was an easy one, since the distinction between

---

8. Justice Stevens criticizes the "deprivation of all economically beneficial use" rule as "wholly arbitrary," in that "[the] landowner whose property is diminished in value 95% recovers nothing," while the landowner who suffers a complete elimination of value "recovers the land's full value." This analysis errs in its assumption that the landowner whose deprivation is one step short of complete is not entitled to compensation. Such an owner might

not be able to claim the benefit [and] the extent to which the regulation has interfered with distinct investment-backed expectations" are keenly relevant to takings analysis generally. *Penn Central.* * * *

b. *Nollan,* which held that conditions imposed on a property development permit amounted to an uncompensated "taking," is discussed in note 2 following this case.

"harm-preventing" and "benefit-conferring" regulation is often in the eye of the beholder. It is quite possible, for example, to describe in *either* fashion the ecological, economic, and aesthetic concerns that inspired the South Carolina legislature. [One] could say that imposing a servitude on Lucas's land is necessary in order to prevent his use of it from "harming" South Carolina's ecological resources; or, instead, in order to achieve the "benefits" of an ecological preserve.* * *[12]

When it is understood that "prevention of harmful use" was merely our early formulation of the police power justification necessary to sustain (without compensation) any regulatory diminution in value; and that the distinction between regulation that "prevents harmful use" and that which "confers benefits" is difficult, if not impossible, to discern on an objective, value-free basis; it becomes self-evident that noxious-use logic cannot serve as a touchstone to distinguish regulatory "takings"—which require compensation—from regulatory deprivations that do not require compensation. A fortiori, the legislature's recitation of a noxious-use justification cannot be the basis for departing from our categorical rule that total regulatory takings must be compensated. If it were, departure would virtually always be allowed. * * *

[Where] the State seeks to sustain regulation that deprives land of all economically beneficial use, we think it may resist compensation only if the logically antecedent inquiry into the nature of the owner's estate shows that the proscribed use interests were not part of his title to begin with. This accords, we think, with our "takings" jurisprudence, which has traditionally been guided by the understandings of our citizens regarding the content of, and the State's power over, the "bundle of rights" that they acquire when they obtain title to property. It seems to us that the property owner necessarily expects the uses of his property to be restricted, from time to time, by various measures newly enacted by the State in legitimate exercise of its police powers; "[a]s long recognized, some values are enjoyed under an implied limitation and must yield to the police power." *Pennsylvania Coal.* And in the case of personal property, by reason of the State's traditionally high degree of control over commercial dealings, he ought to be aware of the possibility that new regulation might even render his property economically worthless (at least if the property's only economically productive use is sale or manufacture for sale). See *Andrus v. Allard*, 444 U.S. 51, 100 S. Ct. 318, 62 L. Ed. 2d 210 (1979) (prohibition on sale of eagle feathers).[c] In the case of land,

---

12. In Justice Blackmun's view, even with respect to regulations that deprive an owner of all developmental or economically beneficial land uses, the test for required compensation is whether the legislature has recited a harm-preventing justification for its action. Since such a justification can be formulated in practically every case, this amounts to a test of whether the legislature has a stupid staff. We think the Takings Clause requires courts to do more than insist upon artful harm-preventing characterizations.

c. In *Andrus*, federal regulations issued pursuant to two federal statutes prohibited the sale (but not the possession or transportation) of the parts of certain eagles even though the birds had been lawfully killed before they had come under federal protection. A unanimous Court, per Brennan, J., held that application of the ban to sale of Indian artifacts containing eagle parts taken before the birds were protected did not violate the takings clause:

"[The challenged regulations] do not compel the surrender of the artifacts and there is no physical invasion or restraint upon them. Rather, a significant restriction has been imposed on one means of disposing of the artifacts. But the denial of one traditional property right does not always amount to a taking. At least where an owner possesses a full 'bundle' of property rights, the destruction of one 'strand' of the bundle is not a taking, because the aggregate must be viewed in its entirety. [In] this case it is crucial that appellees return the rights to possess and transport their property, and to donate or devise the protected birds. It is to be sure undeniable that the regulations here prevent the most profitable use of appellees' property. Again, however, that is not dispositive. When we review regulation,

however, [the] notion [that] title is somehow held subject to the "implied limitation" that the State may subsequently eliminate all economically valuable use is inconsistent with the historical compact recorded in the Takings Clause that has become part of our constitutional culture.[15]

Where "permanent physical occupation" of land is concerned, we have refused to allow the government to decree it anew (without compensation), no matter how weighty the asserted "public interests" involved, *Loretto,* though we assuredly *would* permit the government to assert a permanent easement that was a pre-existing limitation upon the landowner's title. We believe similar treatment must be accorded confiscatory regulations, i.e., regulations that prohibit all economically beneficial use of land: Any limitation so severe cannot be newly legislated or decreed (without compensation), but must inhere in the title itself, in the restrictions that background principles of the State's law of property and nuisance already place upon land ownership. A law or decree with such an effect must, in other words, do no more than duplicate the result that could have been achieved in the courts—by adjacent landowners (or other uniquely affected persons) under the State's law of private nuisance, or by the State under its complementary power to abate nuisances that affect the public generally, or otherwise.

On this analysis, the owner of a lake bed, for example, would not be entitled to compensation when he is denied the requisite permit to engage in a landfilling operation that would have the effect of flooding others' land. Nor the corporate owner of a nuclear generating plant, when it is directed to remove all improvements from its land upon discovery that the plant sits astride an earthquake fault. Such regulatory action may well have the effect of eliminating the land's only economically productive use, but it does not proscribe a productive use that was previously permissible under relevant property and nuisance principles. The use of these properties for what are now expressly prohibited purposes was always unlawful, and (subject to other constitutional limitations) it was open to the State at any point to make the implication of those background principles of nuisance and property law explicit. See Michelman, 80 Harv.L.Rev. 1165, 1239–1241 (1967). [When,] however, a regulation that declares 'off-limits' all economically productive or beneficial uses of land goes beyond what the relevant background principles would dictate, compensation must be paid to sustain it.[17]

---

a reduction in the value of property is not necessarily equated with a taking."

15. [Blackmun, J., argues] that our description of the "understanding" of land ownership that informs the Takings Clause is not supported by early American experience. That is largely true, but entirely irrelevant. The practices of the States prior to incorporation of the Takings and Just Compensation Clauses [were] out of accord with any plausible interpretation of those provisions. Justice Blackmun is correct that early constitutional theorists did not believe the Takings Clause embraced regulations of property at all, but even he does not suggest (explicitly, at least) that we renounce the Court's contrary conclusion in *Pennsylvania Coal.* Since the text of the Clause can be read to encompass regulatory as well as physical deprivations [we] decline to do so as well.

17. Of course, the State may elect to rescind its regulation and thereby avoid having

to pay compensation for a permanent deprivation. *First English Evangelical Lutheran Church v. Los Angeles County,* 482 U.S. 304, 107 S. Ct. 2378, 96 L. Ed. 2d 250 (1987). But "where the [regulation has] already worked a taking of all use of property, no subsequent action by the government can relieve it of the duty to provide compensation for the period during which the taking was effective."

[In *First English Evangelical,* a 6–3 majority, per Rehnquist, C.J., held that when a government regulation does amount to a "taking," the mere invalidation of the regulation is a constitutionally inadequate remedy: whether or not the state abandons its intrusion or strikes down the regulation, it must pay compensation for the period of time during which the regulation denied a landowner use of his land.]

The "total taking" inquiry we require today will ordinarily entail (as the application of state nuisance law ordinarily entails) analysis of, among other things, the degree of harm to public lands and resources, or adjacent private property, posed by the claimant's proposed activities, the social value of the claimant's activities and their suitability to the locality in question, and the relative ease with which the alleged harm can be avoided through measures taken by the claimant and the government (or adjacent private landowners) alike. The fact that a particular use has long been engaged in by similarly situated owners ordinarily imports a lack of any common-law prohibition (though changed circumstances or new knowledge may make what was previously permissible no longer so). So also does the fact that other landowners, similarly situated, are permitted to continue the use denied to the claimant.

It seems unlikely that common-law principles would have prevented the erection of any habitable or productive improvements on petitioner's land; they rarely support prohibition of the "essential use" of land. The question, however, is one of state law to be dealt with on remand. We emphasize that to win its case South Carolina must do more than proffer the legislature's declaration that the uses Lucas desires are inconsistent with the public interest. [Instead] as it would be required to do if it sought to restrain Lucas in a common-law action for public nuisance, South Carolina must identify background principles of nuisance and property law that prohibit the uses he now intends in the circumstances in which the property is presently found. Only on this showing can the State fairly claim that, in proscribing all such beneficial uses, the Beachfront Management Act is taking nothing.[d]

JUSTICE BLACKMUN, dissenting.

[The] Court creates its new takings jurisprudence based on the trial court's finding that the property had lost all economic value. This finding is almost certainly erroneous. Petitioner can still enjoy other attributes of ownership, such as the right to exclude others, "one of the most essential sticks in the bundle of rights that are commonly characterized as property." [He] can picnic, swim, camp in a tent, or live on the property in a movable trailer. State courts frequently have recognized that land has economic value where the only residual economic uses are recreation or camping.

[The] Court does not reject the [state supreme court's] decision simply on the basis of its disbelief and distrust of the legislature's findings. It also takes the opportunity to create a new scheme for regulations that eliminate all economic value. From now on, there is a categorical rule finding these regulations to be a taking unless the use they prohibit is a background common-law nuisance or property principle.

[If] one fact about the Court's taking jurisprudence can be stated without contradiction, it is that "the particular circumstances of each case" determine whether a specific restriction will be rendered invalid by the government's failure

---

d. Kennedy, J., concurring in the judgment, observed that the state supreme court had "erred [by] reciting the general purposes for which the state regulations were enacted without a determination that they were in accord with the owner's reasonable expectations and therefore sufficient to support a severe restriction on specific parcels of property. [The] promotion of tourism, for instance, ought not to suffice to deprive specific property of all value without a corresponding duty to compensate. Furthermore, the means as well as the ends of regulations must accord with the owner's reasonable expectations. Here, the State did not act until after the property had been zoned for individual lot development and most other parcels had been improved, throwing the whole burden of the regulation on the remaining lots. This, too, must be measured in the balance."

to pay compensation. *United States v. Central Eureka Mining Co.,* 357 U.S. 155, 168, 78 S.Ct. 1097, 1104, 2 L.Ed.2d 1228 (1958). This is so because although we have articulated certain factors to be considered, including the economic impact on the property owner, the ultimate conclusion "necessarily requires a weighing of private and public interests." When the government regulation prevents the owner from any economically valuable use of his property, the private interest is unquestionably substantial, but we have never before held that no public interest can outweigh it. Instead the Court's prior decisions "uniformly reject the proposition that diminution in property value, standing alone, can establish a 'taking.' " *Penn Central.*

[Even] more perplexing, however, is the Court's reliance on common-law principles of nuisance in its quest for a value-free taking jurisprudence. In determining what is a nuisance at common law, state courts make exactly the decision that the Court finds so troubling when made by the South Carolina General Assembly today: they determine whether the use is harmful. Common-law public and private nuisance law is simply a determination whether a particular use causes harm. [If] judges in the 18th and 19th centuries can distinguish a harm from a benefit, why not judges in the 20th century, and if judges can, why not legislators? There simply is no reason to believe that new interpretations of the hoary common law nuisance doctrine will be particularly "objective" or "value-free." * * *

JUSTICE STEVENS, dissenting.

[As] the Court recognizes, *Pennsylvania Coal* provides no support for its—or, indeed, any—categorical rule. To the contrary, Justice Holmes recognized that such absolute rules ill fit the inquiry into "regulatory takings." [Nor] does the Court's new categorical rule find support in decisions following *Pennsylvania Coal.*

[In] addition to lacking support in past decisions, the Court's new rule is wholly arbitrary. A landowner whose property is diminished in value 95% recovers nothing, while an owner whose property is diminished 100% recovers the land's full value. [Moreover,] because of the elastic nature of property rights, the Court's new rule will also prove unsound in practice. In response to the rule, courts may define "property" broadly and only rarely find regulations to effect total takings. This is the approach the Court itself adopts in its revisionist reading of venerable precedents. * * *[3]

[The] Court's holding today effectively freezes the State's common law, denying the legislature much of its traditional power to revise the law governing the rights and uses of property. Until today, I had thought that we had long abandoned this approach to constitutional law. More than a century ago we recognized that "the great office of statutes is to remedy defects in the common law as they are developed, and to adapt it to the changes of time and circumstances." *Munn v. Illinois* (1877). As Justice Marshall observed about a position similar to that adopted by the Court today: "If accepted, that claim would represent a return to the era of *Lochner,* when common-law rights were also found immune from revision by State or Federal Government. Such an approach would freeze the common law as it has been constructed by the courts, perhaps at its

---

3. Of course, the same could easily be said in this case: Lucas may put his land to "other uses"—fishing or camping, for example–or may sell his land to his neighbors as a buffer. In either event, his land is far from "valueless." This highlights a fundamental weakness in the Court's analysis: its failure to explain why only the impairment of *"economically* beneficial or productive use" (emphasis added) of property is relevant in takings analysis. * * *

19th–century state of development. It would allow no room for change in response to changes in circumstance. The Due Process Clause does not require such a result." *PruneYard Shopping Center v. Robins,* 447 U.S. 74, 93, 100 S.Ct. 2035, 2047, 64 L.Ed.2d 741 (1980) (concurring opinion)."

The Court's categorical approach rule will, I fear, greatly hamper the efforts of local officials and planners who must deal with increasingly planners who must deal with increasingly complex problems in land-use and environmental regulation. As this case—in which the claims of an *individual* property owner exceed $1 million—well demonstrates, these officials face both substantial uncertainty because of the ad hoc nature of takings law and unacceptable penalties if they guess incorrectly about that law.

[It] is well established that a takings case "entails inquiry into [several factors:] the character of the governmental action, its economic impact, and its interference with reasonable investment-backed expectations." *PruneYard.* The Court's analysis today focuses on the last two of these three factors: The categorical rule addresses a regulation's "economic impact," while the nuisance exception recognizes that ownership brings with it only certain "expectations." Neglected by the Court today is the first and, in some ways, the most important factor in takings analysis: the character of the regulatory action.

The Just Compensation clause "was designed to bar Government from forcing some people alone to bear public ,burdens which, in all fairness and justice, should be borne by the public as a whole." [We] have, therefore, in our takings law frequently looked to the *generality* of a regulation of property. For example, in the case of so-called "developmental exactions," we have paid special attention to the risk that particular landowners might "b[e] singled out to bear the burden" of a broader problem not of his own making. *Nollan.* Similarly, in distinguishing between the Kohler Act (at issue in *Pennsylvania Coal*) and the Subsidence Act (at issue in *Keystone*), we found significant that the regulatory function of the latter was substantially broader. Unlike the Kohler Act, which simply transferred back to the surface owners certain rights that they had earlier sold to the coal companies, the Subsidence Act affected all surface owners—including the coal companies—equally. Perhaps the most familiar application of this principle of generality arises in zoning cases. A diminution in value caused by a zoning regulation is far less likely to constitute a taking if it is part of a general and comprehensive land-use plan; conversely, "spot zoning" is far more likely to constitute a taking, see *Penn Central.*

In considering Lucas's claim, the generality of the Beachfront Management Act is significant. The Act does not target particular landowners, but rather regulates the use of the coastline of the entire State. [Moreover,] the Act did not single out owners of undeveloped land. The Act also prohibited owners of developed land from rebuilding if their structures were destroyed. [In] short, the South Carolina Act imposed substantial burdens on owners of developed and undeveloped land alike.[12] This generality indicates that the Act is not an effort to expropriate owners of undeveloped land.

In view of all these factors, even assuming that petitioner's property was rendered valueless, the risk inherent in investments of the sort made by petitioner, the generality of the Act, and the compelling purpose motivating the South

---

12. In this regard, the Act more closely resembles the Subsidence Act in *Keystone* than the Kohler Act in *Pennsylvania Coal.*

Carolina Legislature persuade me that the Act did not effect a taking of petitioner's property.

Notes and Questions

1. *Subsequent history of Lucas.* On remand, the South Carolina Supreme Court ruled, 309 S.C. 424, 424 S.E.2d 484 (1992), that common law principles of nuisance and property could not prohibit the planned construction; hence Lucas was entitled to compensation for the temporary taking of his property. See generally Robert H. Washburn, *Land Use Control, the Individual and Society*, 52 Md. L. Rev. 162 (1993) and a symposium on *Lucas* in 45 Stan. L. Rev. 1369 (1993).

2. *Conditions on property development permits: the need for a "nexus" between permit conditions exacted by the city and the governmental purposes that would justify denial of the permit.* In NOLLAN v. CALIFORNIA COAST COMM'N, 483 U.S. 825, 107 S.Ct. 3141, 97 L.Ed.2d 667 (1987), the Nollans sought a permit to replace their small beachfront cottage with a home nearly five times larger. A state commission granted the permit *only on the condition* that the Nollans allow the public an easement to pass across their beach, located between two public beaches. A 5–4 majority, per Scalia, J., held that imposing this condition constituted an uncompensated "taking": "Had California simply required [the Nollans] to make an easement across their beachfront property available to the public on a permanent [basis] we have no doubt there would have been a taking. [The] question [is] whether requiring [the easement] to be conveyed as a condition for issuing a land use permit alters the outcome.

"[If] the Commission attached to the permit some condition [protecting] the public's ability to see the beach notwithstanding construction of the new house—for example, a height limitation, a width restriction, or a ban on fences—so long as the Commission could have exercised its police power (as we [assume] it could) to forbid construction of the house altogether, imposition of the condition would also be constitutional. [The] evident constitutional propriety disappears, however, if the condition substituted for the prohibition utterly fails to further the end advanced as the justification for the prohibition. When that essential nexus is eliminated, the situation becomes the same as if California forbade shouting fire in a crowded theater, but granted dispensations to those willing to contribute $100 to the state treasury. [Unless] the permit condition serves the same governmental purpose as the development ban, the building restriction is not a valid regulation of land use, but 'an out and out plan of extortion.' "

Dissenting, Brennan, J., joined by Marshall, J., charged that the Court "imposes a standard of precision for the exercise of State's police power that has been discredited for the better part of the century. [It is by] now commonplace that the Court's review of its police power demands only that the State 'could rationally have decided' that the measure adopted might achieve the State's objective. [The] Commission has sought [to] balance private and public interests and to accept tradeoffs: to permit development that reduces access in some ways as long as other means of access are enhanced. In this case, it has determined that the Nollans' burden on access would be offset by a deed restriction that formalizes the public's right to pass along the short. In its informed judgment, such a tradeoff would preserve the net amount of public access to the coastline. The Court's insistence on a precise fit between the forms of burden and condition on each individual parcel along the California coast would penalize the Commission for its flexibility, hampering the ability to fulfill its public trust mandate."

Blackmun and Stevens, JJ., also wrote separate dissents. For commentary on *Nollan*, see Symposium, *The Jurisprudence of Takings*, 88 Colum. L. Rev. 1581 (1988).

3. *The required degree of connection between the permit conditions and the projected impact of the proposed development.* Because the *Nollan* Court did not believe there was any connection between the permit conditions and the projected impact of the proposed development, it did not have to decide what the required relationship had to be. But the Court did reach that question in DOLAN v. TIGARD, 512 U.S. 374, 114 S.Ct. 2309, 129 L.Ed.2d 304 (1994). Dolan sought a permit to double the size of her store in the city's central business district and to pave her gravel parking lot. Dolan's property bordered on Fanno Creek. The city had adopted a draining plan that included recommendations that land adjacent to the creek be used only as "greenways." The city granted a building permit to Dolan on the condition that she dedicate portions of her property for (a) a public greenway along the creek (to minimize flooding that would be exacerbated by the increases in paved surfaces) and (b) a 15–foot strip for a public pedestrian/bicycle path (to relieve traffic congestion). Dolan argued that because one or more of the conditions were insufficiently related to the city's interest in restraining the possible harmful effects of her proposed development, they constituted an uncompensated taking of her property. A 5–4 majority, per REHNQUIST, C.J., agreed:

"[The] conditions imposed were not simply a limitation on the use petitioner might make of her own parcel, but a requirement that she deed portions of the property to the city. In *Nollan* we held that governmental authority to exact such a condition was circumscribed by the Fifth and Fourteenth Amendments. Under the well-settled doctrine of 'unconstitutional conditions,' the government may not require a person to give up a constitutional right—here the right to receive just compensation when property is taken for a public use—in exchange for a discretionary benefit conferred by the government where the benefit sought has little or no relationship to the property.[a]

"[In] evaluating petitioner's claim, we must first determine whether the 'essential nexus' exists between the 'legitimate state interest' and the permit condition exacted by the city. *Nollan*. If we find that a nexus exists, we must then decide the required degree of connection between the exactions and the projected impact of the proposed development. We were not required to reach this question in Nollan, because we concluded that the connection did not meet even the loosest standard. [It seems obvious] that a nexus exists between preventing flooding along Fanno Creek and limiting development within the creek's 100–year floodplain. [The] same may be said for the city's attempt to reduce traffic congestion by providing for alternative means of transportation.

"The second part of our analysis requires us to determine whether the degree of the exactions demanded by the city's permit conditions bear the required relationship to the project impact of petitioner's proposed development. [A majority] of state courts [require] the municipality to show a 'reasonable relationship' between the required dedication and the impact of the proposed development. [We] think [this test] is closer to the federal constitutional norm than [others] previously discussed. [But] we do not adopt it as such, partly because the term 'reasonable relationship' seems confusingly similar to the term 'rational basis' which describes the minimal level of scrutiny under the Equal Protection Clause

---

a. See generally Kathleen M. Sullivan, *Un-* *constitutional Conditions*, 102 Harv. L. Rev.   1415 (1989).

of the Fourteenth Amendment. We think a term such as 'rough proportionality' best encapsulates what we hold to be the requirement of the Fifth Amendment. No precise mathematical calculation is required, but the city must make some sort of individualized determination that the required dedication is related both in nature and extent to the impact of the proposed development.

"[As for Stevens, J.'s dissenting argument that the city's conditional demands are 'a species of business regulation that heretofore warranted a strong presumption of constitutional validity'], simply denominating a governmental measure as a 'business regulation' does not immunize it from constitutional challenge on the ground that it violates a provision of the Bill of Rights. [We] see no reason why the Takings Clause of the Fifth Amendment, as much a part of the Bill of Rights or the First Amendment or Fourth Amendment, should be relegated to the status of a poor relation * * *.

"[It] is axiomatic that increasing the amount of impervious surface will increase the quantity and rate of storm-water flow from petitioner's property. Therefore, keeping the flood plain open and free from development would likely confine the pressures on Fanno Creek created by petitioner's development. [But] the city demanded more—it not only wanted petitioner not to build in the floodplain, but it also wanted petitioner's property along Fanno Creek for its Greenway system. The city has never said why a public greenway, as opposed to a private one, was required in the interest of flood control. [The] difference to petitioner, of course, is the loss of her ability to exclude others. [It] is difficult to see why recreational visitors trampling along petitioner's flood plain easement are sufficiently related to the city's legitimate interest in reducing flooding problems along Fanno Creek, and the city has not attempted to make any individualized determination to support this part of its request.

"[If] petitioner's proposed development had somehow encroached on existing greenway space in the city, it would have been reasonable to require petitioner to provide some alternative greenway space for the public either on her property or elsewhere. [But] that is not the case here. We conclude that the findings upon which the city relies do not show the required reasonable relationship between the flood plain easement and the petitioner's proposed new building.

"With respect to the pedestrian/bicycle pathway, we have no doubt that the city was correct in finding that the larger retail sales facility proposed by the petitioner will increase traffic on the streets of the Central Business District. [But] on the record before us, the city has not met its burden of demonstrating that the additional number of vehicle and bicycle trips generated by the petitioner's development reasonably relate to the city's requirement for a dedication of the pedestrian/bicycle pathway easement. The city simply found that the creation of the pathway 'could offset some of the traffic demand [and] lessen the increase in traffic congestion.' [No] precise mathematical calculation is required, but the city must make some effort to quantify its findings in support of the dedication for the pedestrian/bicycle pathway beyond the conclusory statement that it could offset some of the traffic demand generated.

"[The] city's goals of reducing flooding hazards and traffic congestion, and providing for public greenways, are laudable, but there are outer limits to how this may be done. 'A strong public desire to improve the public condition [will not] warrant achieving the desire by a shorter cut than the constitutional way of paying for the charge.' *Pennsylvania Coal*."

STEVENS, J., joined by Blackmun and Ginsburg, JJ., dissented: "The Court's assurances that its 'rough proportionality' test leaves ample room for cities to pursue the 'commendable task of land use planning' [are] wanting given the result that test compels here. Under the Court's approach, a city must not only 'quantify its findings' and make 'individual determinations' with respect to the nature *and* the extent of the relationship between the conditions and the impact, but also demonstrate 'proportionality.' The correct inquiry should instead concentrate on whether the required nexus is present and venture beyond considerations of a condition's nature or germaneness only if the developer establishes that a concededly germane condition is so grossly disproportionate to the proposed development's adverse effects that it manifests motives other than land use regulation on the part of the city.

"[The] Court has made a serious error by abandoning the traditional presumption of constitutionality and imposing a novel burden of proof on a city implementing an admittedly valid comprehensive land use plan. Even more consequential than its incorrect disposition of the case, however, is the Court's resurrection of a species of substantive due process analysis that it firmly rejected decades ago.

"[In] our changing world one thing is certain: uncertainty will characterize predictions about the impact of new urban developments on the risks of floods, earthquakes, traffic congestion, or environmental harms. When there is doubt concerning the magnitude of those impacts, the public interest in averting them must outweigh the private interest of the commercial entrepreneur. If the government can demonstrate that the conditions it has imposed in a land-use permit are rational, impartial and conducive to fulfilling the aims of a valid land-use plan, a strong presumption of validity should attach to those conditions. The burden of demonstrating that those conditions have unreasonably impaired the economic value of the proposed improvement belongs squarely on the shoulders of the party challenging the state action's constitutionality. That allocation of burdens has served us well in the past. The Court has stumbled badly today by reversing it."[a]

III. WHAT CONSTITUTES "PROPERTY" FOR PURPOSES OF THE TAKINGS CLAUSE?

EASTERN ENTERPRISES v. APFEL, 524 U.S. 498, 118 S.Ct. 2131, 141 L.Ed.2d 451 (1998): As a signatory to various coal wage agreements executed between 1947 and 1964, petitioner Eastern Enterprises (Eastern) made substantial contributions to funds providing health benefits to miners and their dependents. In 1965 Eastern ceased its coal mining operations (transferring these operations to a subsidiary). Thus, Eastern neither participated in negotiations nor agreed to make contributions in connection with benefit plans established under agreements made in the 1970s, agreements suggesting for the first time an industry commitment to the funding of lifetime health benefits for both retirees and their family members.[a]

The decline in coal production, the retirement of a generation of miners, and rapid acceleration in health care caused serious financial problems for the 1950

---

a. Souter, J., also filed a brief, separate dissent, unable to "agree that the application of *Nollan* is a sound one here, since it appears that the Court has placed the burden of producing evidence of relationship on the city, despite the usual rule in cases involving the police power that the government is presumed to have acted constitutionally."

a. Although Eastern's subsidiary continued mining coal until 1987, according to the plural-

ity opinion by O'Connor, J., "Eastern's liability under the Act bears no relationship to [the] ownership of [its subsidiary]; the Act assigns Eastern responsibility for benefits relating to miners that Eastern itself, not [its subsidiary], employed, while [the subsidiary] would be assigned the responsibility for any miners that it had employed."

and 1974 Benefit Plans. As more coal operators abandoned the Benefit Plans, the remaining signatories were forced to absorb the increasing cost of covering retirees left behind by existing employers. Ultimately Congress passed the Coal Industry Retiree Health Benefit Act of 1992 (Coal Act), providing for benefits to retirees by merging the old benefit plans into a new fund (Combined Fund) financed by annual premiums assessed against "signatory coal operators," i.e., coal operators that signed any agreement requiring contributions to the 1950 or 1974 Benefit Plans. When assigned the obligation for Combined Fund premiums respecting some 1,000 retired miners who had worked for it before 1966, Eastern contended that the Coal Act violated both substantive due process and the Takings clause.

Although a 5–4 majority struck down the Coal Act as applied to Eastern, the justices making up the majority disagreed over the basis for the Act's invalidation. Noting that "this Court has expressed concerns about using the Due Process Clause to invalidate economic legislation," a four-Justice plurality—O'CONNOR, J., joined by Rehnquist, C.J., and Scalia and Thomas JJ.—concluded that forcing Eastern "to bear the expense of lifetime health benefits for miners based on [the company's] activities decades before those benefits were promised" violated the Takings Clause.[b] She recognized that prior decisions "make clear that Congress had considerable leeway to fashion economic legislation, including the power to affect contractual commitments between private parties," but maintained that the Court's decisions had left open the possibility that legislation might violate the Takings Clause "if it imposes severe retroactive liability on a limited class of parties that could not have anticipated the liability, and the extent of that liability is substantially disproportionate to the parties' experience. [The] Coal Act's allocation scheme, as applied to Eastern, presents such a case. [T]here is no doubt that the Coal Act has forced a considerable financial burden upon Eastern. The parties estimate that Eastern's cumulative payments under the Act will be on the order of $50 to $100 million. [The] fact that the Federal Government has not specified the assets that Eastern must use to satisfy its obligation does not negate that impact.

"[The Act] substantially interferes with Eastern's reasonable investment-backed expectations. The Act's beneficiary allocation scheme reaches back 30 to 50 years to impose liability against Eastern based on the company's activities between 1946 and 1965. Thus, even though the Act mandates only the payment of future health benefits, it nonetheless 'attaches new legal consequences to [an employment relationship] completed before its enactment.' Retroactivity is generally disfavored in the law in accordance with 'fundamental notions of justice' that have been recognized throughout history. [The] distance into the past that the Act reaches back to impose a liability on Eastern and the magnitude of that liability raise substantial questions of fairness.

"[The] nature of the governmental action in this case is quite unusual. That Congress sought a legislative remedy for what it perceived to be a grave problem in the funding of retired coal miners' health benefits is understandable. [When,]

b. At one point O'Connor, J., noted that the Constitution "expresses concern with retroactive laws through several of its provisions, including the Ex Post Facto and Takings Clauses." Although Thomas, J., joined O'Connor, J.'s opinion in full, he wrote separately to emphasize that the Ex Post Facto Clause even more clearly than the Takings Clause "reflects the principle that retrospective laws are, in-deed, generally unjust.'" Although the Court had long ago considered the Ex Post Facto clause to apply only in the criminal context, Justice Thomas expressed a willingness to reconsider these precedents in order to "determine whether a retroactive civil law that passes muster under our current Taking Clause jurisprudence is nevertheless unconstitutional under the Ex Post Facto Clause."

however, that solution singles out certain employers to bear a burden that is substantial in amount, based on the employers' conduct far in the past, and unrelated to any commitment that the employers made or to any injury they caused, the governmental action implicates fundamental principles of fairness underlying the Takings Clause. Eastern cannot be forced to bear the expense of lifetime health benefits for miners based on its activities decades before these benefits were promised."

When, continued the plurality opinion, a legislative solution to a problem "singles out certain employers to bear a burden that is substantial in amount, based on the employers' conduct far in the past, and unrelated to any commitment that the employers made or to any injury they caused, the governmental action implicates fundamental principles of fairness underlying the Taking Clause."[c]

Concurring in the judgment and dissenting in part, KENNEDY, J., concluded that the Coal Act "must be invalidated as contrary to essential due process principles, without regard to the Takings Clause." It does not apply, he maintained, because the challenged Act "regulates the former mine owner without regard to property. It does not operate upon or alter an identified property interest, and is not applicable to or measured by a property interest. [The] law simply imposes an obligation to perform an act, the payment of benefits. The statute is indifferent as to how the regulated entity elects to comply or the property it uses to do so. To the extent it affects property interests, it does so in a manner similar to many laws; but until today, none were thought to constitute takings. * * *

"[Without] denigrating the importance the regulatory taking concept has assumed in our law, it is fair to say it has proven difficult to explain in theory and to implement in practice. [Until] today, however, one constant limitation has been that in all of the cases where the regulatory taking analysis has been employed, a specific property right or interest has been at stake. [The] plurality's opinion disregards this requirement and, by removing this constant characteristic from takings analysis, would expand an already difficult and uncertain rule to a vast category of cases not deemed, in our law, to implicate the Takings Clause. [The] plurality opinion would [subject] States and municipalities to the potential of new and unforeseen claims in vast amounts. * * * True, the burden imposed by the Coal Act may be just as great if the Government had appropriated one of Eastern's plants, but the mechanism by which the Government injures Eastern is so unlike the act of taking specific property that it is incongruous to call the Coal Act a taking, even as that concept has been expanded by the regulatory principle.

"[If] the plurality is adopting its novel and expansive concept of a taking in order to avoid making normative judgment about the Coal Act, it fails in the attempt; for it must make the normative judgment in all events. [The] imprecision of our regulatory takings doctrine does open the door to normative considerations about the wisdom of government decisions. This sort of analysis is in uneasy tension with our basic understanding of the Takings Clause, which has not been understood to be a substantive or absolute limit on the Government's power to act, [but a provision that] operates as a conditional limitation, permitting the Government to do what it wants so long as it pays the charge."

"Although we have been hesitant to subject economic legislation to due process scrutiny as a general matter, the Court has given careful consideration to

---

c. Because of its determination that the Coal Act's allocation scheme violates the takings clause as applied to Eastern, the plurality saw no need to address Eastern's due process claim.

due process challenges to legislation with retroactive effects. As today's plurality opinion notes, for centuries our law has harbored a singular distrust of retroactive statutes. [The] Court's due process jurisprudence reflects this distrust. [It] is no accident that the primary retroactivity precedents upon which today's plurality opinion relies in its takings analysis were grounded in due process."

Kennedy, J., acknowledged that the Court had upheld the imposition of liability on former employers based on past employment relationships, but "the statutes at issue were remedial, designed to impose an 'actual measurable cost of [the employer's] business' which the employer had been able to avoid in the past. [The] Coal Act, however, does not serve this purpose. Eastern was once in the coal business and employed many of the beneficiaries, but it was not responsible for their expectation of lifetime health benefits or for the perilous financial condition of the [earlier plans] which put the benefits in jeopardy. [This] case is far outside the bounds of retroactivity permissible under our law."

When one accounts for Breyer, J.'s dissenting opinion, Kennedy, J.'s view of the appropriate constitutional provision in the case commands a majority of the Court. Although Breyer, J., joined by Stevens, Souter and Ginsburg, JJ., thought the Coal Act constitutional, "as a preliminary matter" he agreed with Kennedy, J., that "the plurality views this case through the wrong legal lens." The Takings Clause does not apply, maintained Breyer, because "[t]he 'private property' upon which the Clause traditionally has focused is a specific interest in physical or intellectual property." However, the instant case involves not such an interest "but an ordinary liability to pay money, and not to the government, but to third parties." If the Takings Clause "applies when the government simply orders A to pay B," asked Breyer, J., "why does it not apply when the government simply orders A to pay the government, i.e., when it assesses a tax?"[d]

"[The] question involved—the potential unfairness of retroactive liability—finds a natural home in the Due Process Clause. [That clause] can offer protection against legislation that is unfairly retroactive at least as readily as the Takings Clause might, [for] a law that is fundamentally unfair because of its retroactivity is a law which is basically arbitrary. [Insofar] as the plurality avoids reliance upon the Due Process Clause for fear of resurrecting *Lochner* and related doctrines of 'substantive due process,' that fear is misplaced. [To] find that the Due Process Clause protects against this kinds of fundamental unfairness—that it protects against an unfair allocation of public burdens through this kind of specially arbitrary retroactive means—is to read the Clause in light of a basic purpose: the fair application of law. [It] is not to resurrect long-discredited substantive notions of 'freedom of contract.' "

d. Consider Robert Brauneis, *Eastern Enterprises, Phillips, Money, and the Limited Role of the Just Compensation Clause in Protecting Property "in its Larger and Juster Meaning,"* 51 Ala. L. Rev. 937, 944–45 (2000): "The problem with applying the Just Compensation Clause to the practice of taxation [is] a problem of constitutional interpretation. Article 1, § 8 of the Constitution grants Congress [the] power to 'lay and collect Taxes, Duties, Imposts and Excises * * *,' subject only to a few specific limitations. [The] Fifth Amendment, of course, could have added a new limitation, providing that when Congress's otherwise valid exercise of [its] tax power amounted to a taking, it had to pay just compensation. However, there has never been any hint before or after the adoption of the Bill of Rights that anyone understood the Fifth Amendment to add such a limitation. Rather, taxation was thought to be a practice wholly outside the Just Compensation Clause. [Indeed,] it might be argued that the Just Compensation Clause assumes the practice of taxation, for where else, practically speaking, is a government going to get the funds to pay just compensation awards?"

However, Breyer, J., did *not* consider it "fundamentally unfair to require Eastern to make future payments for health care costs of retired miners and their families, on the basis of Eastern's past association with these miners." For one thing the liability imposed upon Eastern "extends only to miners whom Eastern itself employed." Moreover, "the record shows that pre–1965 statements and other conduct led management to understand, and labor legitimately to expect, that health care benefits for retirees and their dependents would continue to be provided." Finally, "Eastern continued to obtain profits from the coal mining industry long after 1965, for it operated a wholly-owned coal-mining subsidiary [until] the late 1980s."[e]

Notes and Questions

1. *The same doctrine as substantive due process?* To what extent does *Eastern Enterprise* support the view, J. Peter Byrnes, *Regulating Takings and "Judicial Supremacy,"* 51 Ala. L. Rev. 949, 954 (2000), that "recent developments in the regulatory takings doctrine share in all the problems associated with substantive due process. Indeed regulatory takings sometimes seems to be the very same doctrine as substantive due process, attached to a different clause only as an alias to avoid the obloquy is which substantive due process is held."

2. *The basic principle.* Did all nine Justices in *Eastern Enterprises* premise their decisions on the same question: whether the Coal Act operated retroactively to hold the company liable "for a problem that the company did not cause, to a degree it could not have expected"? Should this basic principle rise above the complexities of *Eastern Enterprises* and the disputes about the proper doctrinal label for claims of retroactivity? See 112 Harv. L. Rev. 122, 212, 220–22 (2000).

3. *Should the definition of "property" be broadened for takings clause purposes?* Consider James L. Huffman, *Retroactivity, the Rule of Law, and the Constitution*, 51 Ala. L. Rev. 1095, 117–18 (2000): "The objection of Justices Kennedy and Breyer in *Eastern Enterprises* that the Takings Clause is not implicated because no property rights are at issue is not only contradicted by their subsequent analysis of the due process claim, but it is also ill-conceived from the perspective of allowing government to pursue its legitimate ends without sacrificing individual rights. [A] broadened definition of property like that urged by the plurality in *Eastern Enterprises*, will permit governments to rely on the significant power of eminent domain which ensures that the rule of law is not sacrificed to the pursuit of the public good, nor vice versa."

Is interest earned in client funds that is paid to foundations financing legal services for low-income individuals the "private property" of the client for purposes of the Takings Clause? Texas, like 48 other states, has adopted an Interest on Lawyers Trust Account (IOLTA) program. Under these programs an

e. In a separate dissent, Stevens, J., joined by Souter, Ginsburg and Breyer, JJ., concluded that "whether the provision in question is analyzed under the Takings Clause or the Due Process Clause, Eastern has not carried its burden of overcoming the presumption of constitutionality accorded to an act of Congress, by demonstrating that the provision is unsupported by the reasonable expectations of the parties in interest." Stevens emphasized that "there was an implicit understanding on both sides of the bargaining table that the operators would provide the miners with lifetime health benefits. It was this understanding that kept the mines in operations and enabled Eastern to earn handsome profits before it transferred its coal business to a wholly-owned subsidiary."

attorney who receives client funds must place them in a separate, interest-bearing, federally authorized account upon determining that the funds could not reasonably be expected to earn interest for the client or that any interest which might be earned is unlikely to be sufficient to offset the cost of establishing and maintaining the account. IOLTA interest income is paid to foundations that finance legal services for low-income persons. Is the transfer of this interest income to the foundations a "taking" of the clients' property? In PHILLIPS v. WASHINGTON LEGAL FOUNDATION, 524 U.S. 156, S.Ct. 1925, 141 L.Ed.2d 174 (1998), a 5–4 majority, per REHNQUIST, C.J. held that the interest earned on client funds held in IOLTA accounts is the "private property" of the client for Takings Clause purposes, but "express[ed] no view as to whether these funds have been 'taken' by the States" nor "the amount of 'just compensation,' if any, due respondents." Because "the Constitution protects rather than creates property interests," observed the Court, "the existence of a property interest is determined by references to 'existing rules or understanding that stem from an independent source such as state law.'" The firmly embedded and widely held view that "interest follows principal" applies in Texas.

Dissenting, SOUTER, J., joined by Stevens, Ginsburg and Breyer, JJ., maintained that "the Court's limited enquiry has led it to announce an essentially abstract proposition [that] may ultimately turn out to have no significance in resolving the real issue, [which] is whether [the IOLTA] scheme violate the Takings Clause": "The Court recognizes three distinct issues implicated by a takings claim: whether the interest asserted by the plaintiff is property, whether the government has taken that property, and whether the plaintiff has been denied just compensation for the taking. [By addressing] only the first of these questions [the Court has] postponed consideration of the most salient fact relied upon by petitioners in contesting [the] Fifth Amendment claim: that the respondent client would effectively be barred from receiving any net interest on his funds subject to the state IOLTA rule by the combination of an unchallenged federal banking state and regulation [and other rules]. If it should turn out that within the meaning of the Fifth Amendment, the IOLTA scheme had not taken the property recognized today, or if it should turn out that the 'just compensation' for any taking was zero, then there would be no practical consequence for purposes of the Fifth Amendment in recognizing a client's property right in the interest in the first place; any such recognition would be an inconsequential abstraction."

In a separate dissent, BREYER, J., joined by Stevens, Souter and Ginsburg, JJ., criticized the Court's use of the truism that "interest follows principal": "The Question Presented is whether 'interest earned on client trust funds' [which] would 'not earn interest' in the absence of a special 'IOLTA program' amounts to a 'property interest of the client or lawyer' for purposes [of the] Takings Clause. [The] truism [that 'interest follows the principal'] does not help because the Question Presented assumes circumstances that differ dramatically from those in which interest is ordinarily at issue. Ordinarily, principal is capable of generating interest for whoever holds it. Here, by the very terms of the question, we must assume that (because of pre-existing federal law) the client's principal could not generate interest without IOLTA intervention. That is to say, the client could not have had an expectation of receiving interest without intervention. [Thus] the question is whether 'interest,' *earned only as a result of IOLTA rules* and earned upon otherwise *barren* client principal, 'follows principal.'"

Notes and Questions

1. *Putting the cases together*. Consider Brauneis, fn. d supra, at 938: "What are we to learn by putting *Eastern Enterprises* next to *Phillips*? Since there was only one Justice who thought there could be no Just Compensation Clause violation in *Eastern Enterprises* but could be in *Phillips*—Justice Kennedy— maybe the only thing we learn is something about his idiosyncratic preferences. However, the pair of cases can arguably be seen as reinforcing the view that the Just Compensation clause is and should be about government activities that dispossess owners of ordinary objects—in other words, about takings of private property, as we use that term in ordinary language—and not about redefining legal rights or metaphorically taking strands from a bundle of rights."

2. *The use of "physical language" in Phillips*. "The *Phillips* Court," observes Professor Brauneis, supra, at 947, "uses physical language to describe what happens in an ordinary banking transaction: A client or customer deposits money into an account, in much the same way that valuables are placed in a safe deposit box, and that money retains its character as a separate object, "the principal," which is still the property of the banking customer, and when that principal generates interest, that interest is also the property of the banking customer, in the same way that the owner of the cow is also owner of the calf. That description of the banking transaction, as involving an object that is continuously held by a customer and then by the bank, goes a long way towards explaining the *Phillips* Court's conclusion that the interest generated by an [IOLTA] is the private property of the lawyers' clients." Continues Brauneis, id. at 948:

"Should [we] recast *Phillips* as a case about the regulation of the debtor-creditor relationship between lawyers and clients, which does not involve specifically identified property that can be taken? I think it is very difficult to do this, even as an exercise in redescription, and I suggest that the difficulty may be connected to the way that our perception of whether a government action involves 'specific property' or 'general liability' may depend on whether the government action is perceived as singling out particular individuals to bear burdens or whether it is perceived as more general action. In other words, we can describe laws as 'regulating debtor-creditor relations,' with less of a 'property' cast, when they are of a general scheme applicable to debts generally or many different kinds of debts; it is harder to do that when a law singles out one group of people–clients of lawyers–and when the point of the law is to benefit a third party–neither the client, nor the lawyer."

SECTION 5. DECLINE AND REVITALIZATION (?) OF THE CONTRACT CLAUSE

Introduction

Art. 1, § 10, prohibits the state from enacting any "Law impairing the Obligation of Contracts." In *Home Building & Loan Ass'n v. Blaisdell* (1934) (below), Hughes, C.J., recalled the reasons that led to the adoption of this clause: "The widespread distress following the revolutionary period, and the plight of debtors, had called forth in the States an ignoble array of legislative schemes for the defeat of creditors and the invasion of contractual obligations. Legislative interferences had been so numerous and extreme that the confidence essential to prosperous trade had been undermined and the utter destruction of credit was threatened. It was necessary to interpose the restraining power of a central authority in order to secure the foundations even of 'private faith.' "

As pointed out in John E. Nowak & Ronald D. Rotunda, *Constitutional Law* 439 (6th ed. 2000): "Under the leadership of Chief Justice Marshall, [the contract clause] received an expansive reading. During the Marshall years, the Court used the provision to invalidate statutes that retrospectively impaired almost any contractual obligation of private parties. The Court never used the clause to void laws that prospectively modified contractual obligations. Nevertheless, until the late nineteenth century the contract clause was the principal provision the Court used to void legislation that infringed on private property rights."

Then the contract clause lost its importance. For one thing, "the states rarely would enact a statutory grant that [failed] to give [them] the necessary flexibility to pass legislation that [could] modify the previously issued public grant." Moreover, "the Court began to rely on the doctrine of substantive due process to void legislation that would infringe on property or business interests. More often than not, any state legislation that impaired the obligation of contract would not only violate the contract clause but would also violate the Court's notions of economic substantive due process," [a doctrine that] gave the Court more discretion and flexibility than the contract clause in passing on the constitutionality of state legislation. Hence, if the Court had a choice, it would use substantive due process analysis rather than contract clause analysis to void state legislation." Nowak & Rotunda, supra, at 444.

In HOME BUILDING & LOAN ASS'N v. BLAISDELL, 290 U.S. 398, 54 S.Ct. 231, 78 L.Ed. 231, 78 L.Ed. 413 (1934)—decided the same year the *Nebbia* case struck the economic due process doctrine a heavy blow—the Court upheld what might be called a "debtor relief law" despite its retrospective impact. As *Nebbia* and *Blaisdell* indicated, the Court's growing reluctance to invoke the contract clause would parallel its abandonment of substantive due process analysis to strike down economic legislation.

Blaisdell arose as follows: During the Great Depression, Minnesota enacted a Mortgage Moratorium Law—a law that was to remain in effect "only during the continuance of the emergency and in no event beyond May 1, 1935"—which gave the state courts the authority to extend the redemption period after real estate foreclosure sales provided the mortgagor paid a reasonable part of the rental value of the property. Thus mortgagees could not obtain possession of the real estate and convey title in fee as they would have been able to do if a mortgage moratorium law had not been adopted. A 5–4 majority, per HUGHES, C.J., held that the challenged law "does not impair the integrity of the mortgage indebtedness. The obligation for interest remains. [Aside] from the extension of time, the other conditions of redemption are unaltered. [While] the mortgagee-purchaser is debarred from actual possession, he has, so far as rental value is concerned, the equivalent of possession during the extended period. [Not] only is the constitutional provision qualified by the measure of control which the State retains over remedial processes, but the State also continues to possess authority to safeguard the vital interests of its people. [Not] only are existing laws read into contracts in order to fix obligations as between the parties, but the reservation of existing attributes of sovereign power is also read into contracts as a postulate of the legal order. [The Constitution would not] permit the State to adopt as its policy the repudiation of debts or the destruction of contracts or the denial of means to enforce them.[a] But it does not follow that conditions may not arise in which a

---

a. As noted in Nowak & Rotunda, supra, at 444, a very short time after *Blaisdell*, when the Court considered " 'emergency' debtor relief legislation which totally exempted major assets of debtors from creditors' claims or eliminated remedies for claims without protecting the

temporary restraint of enforcement may be consistent with the spirit and purpose of the constitutional provision and thus found to be within the range of the reserved power of the State to protect the vital interests of the community."

In upholding the law, the Court found five factors significant: there was an emergency need "to protect the vital interests of the community"; the law was not designed to favor a special group "but for the protection of a basic interest of society"; the relief was appropriately tailored to the emergency; the conditions imposed were reasonable; and the legislation was "temporary in operation" and "limited to the exigency which called it forth."

As Tribe, 2d ed., at 619, observes, "[the] protective shield of the contract clause lay practically forgotten[b] for three decades until the Court dusted if off and put it to use" in UNITED STATES TRUST CO. v. NEW JERSEY, 431 U.S. 1, 97 S.Ct. 1505, 52 L.Ed.2d 92 (1977). To assure bondholders of the Port Authority of New York and New Jersey that the Authority would not in the future take over mass transit deficit operations beyond its financial reserves in 1962, the two states entered into a covenant limiting the numbers of such operations the Authority would absorb. In 1974, however, in order to permit the Authority to subsidize more mass transportation programs, both states repealed the legislation implementing the covenant. The bondholders sued, claiming that the retroactive repeal of the 1962 covenant, which reduced the financial security of their bonds, violated the contract clause. A 4–3 majority, per BLACKMUN, J., agreed: "[The] Contract Clause is not an absolute bar to subsequent modification of a State's own financial obligations. As with laws impairing the obligations of private contracts, an impairment may be constitutional if it is reasonable and necessary to serve an important public purpose. In applying this standard, however, complete deference to a legislative assessment of reasonableness and necessity is not appropriate because the State's self-interest is at stake. [If] a State could reduce its financial obligations whenever it wanted to spend the money for what it regarded as an important public purpose, the Contract Clause would provide no protection at all.[25]

"[Appellees] contend that [mass transportation, energy conservation, and environmental protection] are so important that any harm to bondholders from repeal of the 1962 covenant is greatly outweighed by the public benefit. We do not accept this invitation to engage in a utilitarian comparison of public benefit and private loss. [A] State cannot refuse to meet its legitimate financial obligations simply because it would prefer to spend the money to promote the public good rather than the private welfare of its creditors. We can only sustain the repeal of

creditors' rights, it found that such legislation violated the contract clause." See *W.B. Worthen Co. v. Thomas*, 292 U.S. 426, 54 S.Ct. 816, 78 L.Ed. 1344 (1934); *W.B. Worthen Co. v. Kavanaugh*, 295 U.S. 56, 55 S.Ct. 555, 79 L.Ed. 1298 (1935).

b. Indeed, as the Court itself noted (fn. 12) in *Allied Structural Steel Co. v. Spannaus* (1978), the next main case in this section, "at least one commentator has suggested that 'the results might be the same if the contract clause were dropped out of the Constitution, and the challenged statutes all judged as reasonable or unreasonable deprivations of property.' Robert L. Hale, *The Supreme Court and the Contract Clause*, 57 Harv.L.Rev. 852, 890–91 (1944)."

25. For similar reasons, a dual standard of review was applied under the Fifth Amendment to federal legislation abrogating contractual gold clauses. "There is a clear distinction between the power of the Congress to control or interdict the contracts of private parties when they interfere with the exercise of its constitutional authority, and the power of the Congress to alter or repudiate the substance of its own engagements when it has borrowed money under the authority which the Constitution confers." *Perry v. United States,* 294 U.S. 330, 55 S.Ct. 432, 79 L.Ed. 912 (1935).

the 1962 covenant if that impairment was both reasonable and necessary to serve the admittedly important purposes claimed by the State.

"[The Court then concluded that the repeal was 'unnecessary' because less drastic alternatives were available and that it was 'unreasonable' because] as early as 1922 [there] were pressures to involve the Port Authority in mass transit. Indeed, the covenant was specifically intended to protect the pledged revenues and reserves against the possibility that such concerns would lead [the] Authority into greater involvement in deficit mass transit."

BRENNAN, J., joined by White and Marshall, JJ., dissented: "Today's [decision] remolds the Contract Clause into a potent instrument for overseeing important policy determinations of the state legislature. At the same time, by creating a constitutional safe haven for property rights embodied in a contract, the decision substantially distorts modern constitutional jurisprudence governing regulation of private economic interests. [Elevation] of the clause to the status of regulator of the municipal bond market at the heavy price of frustration of sound legislative policymaking is as demonstrably unwise as it is unnecessary.

"[Given] that this is the first case in some 40 years in which this Court has seen fit to invalidate purely economic and social legislation on the strength of the Contract Clause, one may only hope that it will prove a rare phenomenon, turning on the Court's particularized appraisal of the facts before it. But there is also is reason for broader concern. [If] today's case signals a return to substantive constitutional review of States' policies, and a new resolve to protect property owners whose interest or circumstances may happen to appeal to Members of the Court, then more than the citizens of New Jersey and New York will be the losers. [In] the final analysis, there is no reason to doubt that appellant's financial welfare is being adequately policed by the political processes and the bond marketplace itself. The role to be played by the Constitution is at most a limited one. For this Court should have learned long ago that the Constitution—be it through the Contract or Due Process Clause can actively intrude into such economic and policy matters only if my Brethren are prepared to bear enormous institutional and social costs."

United States Trust stirred renewed interest in the contract clause, but "the major modern expansion" Tribe, 2d ed., at 620, came a year later:

ALLIED STRUCTURAL STEEL v. SPANNAUS
438 U.S. 234, 98 S.Ct. 2716, 57 L.Ed.2d 727 (1978).

JUSTICE STEWART delivered the opinion of the Court.

[In 1963 Allied Steel adopted a pension plan that vested pension rights only when an employee had worked to age 65, or 15 years to age 60 or 20 years to age 55. Those who quit or were discharged before vesting had no pensions. Allied informed its employees that the plan implied no assurance against dismissal. A 1974 Minnesota Act, the Private Pension Benefits Protection Act, required employers of 100 workers or more (at least one of whom was a Minnesota resident) who had established employee pension plans and who went out of business in Minnesota, to pay full pensions to all its Minnesota employees who had worked 10 years or more, and to pay a "pension funding charge" if their pension funds were insufficient for these employees. As a first step in closing its Minnesota operation, Allied discharged 9 employees who had worked for the company for more than 10 years—but not long enough to have vested pension rights. Under the Act, Allied's "pension funding charge" was $185,000.]

334 PROTECTION OF ECONOMIC INTERESTS Ch. 5

[Although] it was perhaps the strongest single constitutional check on state legislation during our early years as a Nation, the Contract Clause receded into comparative desuetude [with] the development of the large body of jurisprudence under the Due Process Clause. Nonetheless, the Contract Clause remains part of the Constitution. It is not a dead letter. [If] the Contract Clause is to retain any meaning at all, however, it must be understood to impose *some* limits upon the power of a State to abridge existing contractual relationships, even in the exercise of its otherwise legitimate police power. The existence and nature of those limits were clearly indicated in a series of cases in this Court arising from the efforts of the States to deal with the unprecedented emergencies brought on by the severe economic depression of the early 1930's.

[In *Blaisdell*, in] upholding the state mortgage moratorium law, the Court found five factors significant. [The] *Blaisdell* opinion thus clearly implied that if the Minnesota moratorium legislation had not possessed the characteristics attributed to it by the Court, it would have been invalid under the Contract Clause of the Constitution. These implications were given concrete force in [cases] that followed closely in *Blaisdell's* wake. The most recent Contract Clause case in this Court was *United States Trust Co.* * * * Evaluating with particular scrutiny a modification of a contract to which the State itself was a party, the Court in that case held that legislative alteration of the rights and remedies of Port Authority bondholders violated the Contract Clause because the legislation was neither necessary nor reasonable.[15]

In applying [contract clause principles], the first inquiry must be whether the state law has, in fact, operated as a substantial impairment of a contractual relationship. The severity of the impairment measures the height of the hurdle the state legislature must clear. Minimal alteration of contractual obligations may end the inquiry at its first stage. Severe impairment, on the other hand, will push the inquiry to a careful examination of the nature and purpose of the state legislation.

[The] effect of Minnesota's [Act] on this contractual obligation was severe. The company was required in 1974 to have made its contributions throughout the pre–1974 life of its plan as if employees' pension rights had vested after 10 years, instead of vesting in accord with the terms of the plan. Thus a basic term of the pension contract—one on which the company had relied for 10 years—was substantially modified. Not only did the state law thus retroactively modify the compensation that the company had agreed to pay its employees from 1963 to 1974, but it did so by changing the company's obligations in an area where the element of reliance was vital—the funding of a pension [plan]. Thus, the [statute] nullifies express terms of the company's contractual obligations and imposes a completely unexpected liability in potentially disabling amounts. [Yet] there is no showing in the record before us that this severe disruption of contractual expectations was necessary to meet an important general social problem.

[The legislation] clearly has an extremely narrow focus. It applies only to private employers [who] have established voluntary private pension plans, [and] only when such an employer closes his Minnesota office or terminates his pension plan. Thus, this law can hardly be characterized, like the law at issue in [*Blaisdell*], as one enacted to protect a broad societal interest rather than a

---

15. The Court indicated that impairment of a State's own contract would face more stringent examination under the Contract Clause than would laws regulating contractual relationships between private parties, although it was careful to add that "private contracts are not subject to unlimited modification under the police power."

narrow class. Moreover, [this] legislation [was] not enacted to deal with a situation remotely approaching the broad and desperate emergency economic conditions of the early 1930's—conditions of which the Court in *Blaisdell* took judicial notice.

[This] law simply does not possess the attributes of those state laws that in the past have survived challenge under the Contract Clause. [The] law was not even purportedly enacted to deal with a broad, generalized economic or social problem. It did not operate in an area already subject to state regulation at the time the company's contractual obligations were originally undertaken, but invaded an area never before subject to regulation by the State. It did not effect simply a temporary alteration of the contractual relationships of those within its coverage, but worked a severe, permanent, and immediate change in those relationships—irrevocably and retroactively. And its narrow aim was leveled, not at every Minnesota employer, not even at every Minnesota employer who left the State, but only at those who had in the past been sufficiently enlightened as voluntarily to agree to establish pension plans for their employees. * * *

JUSTICE BRENNAN, with whom JUSTICE WHITE and JUSTICE MARSHALL join, dissenting.

[The Minnesota Act] does not abrogate or dilute any obligation due a party to a private contract; rather, like all positive social legislation, the Act imposes new, additional obligations on a particular class of persons. In my view, any constitutional infirmity in the law must therefore derive, not from the Contract Clause, but from the Due Process Clause of the Fourteenth Amendment.

[The Act was] designed to remedy a serious social problem arising from the operation of private pension plans. [B]ecause employers often failed to make contributions to the pension funds large enough adequately to fund their plans, employees often ultimately received only a small amount of those benefits they reasonably anticipated. [Denial] of all pension benefits not because of job related failings but only because the employees are unfortunate enough to be employed at a plant that closes for purely economic reasons is harsh indeed. [The] closing of a plant is a contingency outside the range of normal expectations of both the employer and the employee. [Although] the Court glides over this fact, it should be apparent that the Act will impose only minor economic burdens on employers whose pension plans have been adequately funded.

[It] is nothing less than an abuse of the English language to interpret, as does the Court, the term "impairing" as including laws which create new duties. While such laws may be conceptualized as "enlarging" the obligation of a contract when they add to the burdens that had previously been imposed by a private agreement, such laws cannot be prohibited by the Clause because they do not dilute or nullify a duty a person had previously obligated himself to perform.

[More] fundamentally, the Court's distortion of the meaning of the Contract Clause [threatens] to undermine the jurisprudence of property rights developed over the last 40 years. The Contract Clause, of course, is but one of several clauses in the Constitution that protect existing economic values from governmental interference. The Fifth Amendment's command that "private property [shall not] be taken for public use, without just compensation" is such a clause. A second is the Due Process Clause, which during the heyday of substantive due process, see *Lochner,* largely supplanted the Contract Clause in importance and operated as a potent limitation on Government's ability to interfere with economic expectations. Decisions over the past 50 years have developed a coherent, unified interpretation of all the constitutional provisions that may protect economic expectations and these decisions have recognized a broad latitude in States to effect even severe interference with existing economic values when reasonably necessary to promote the general welfare. At the same time the prohibition of the Contract Clause, consistently with its wording and historic purposes, has been limited in application to state laws that diluted, with utter indifference to the legitimate interests of the beneficiary of a contract duty, the existing contract obligation.

Today's conversion of the Contract Clause into a limitation on the power of States to enact laws that impose duties additional to obligations assumed under private contracts must inevitably produce results difficult to square with any rational conception of a constitutional order. [The] validity of such a law will turn upon whether judges see it as a law that deals with a generalized social problem, whether it is temporary (as few will be) or permanent, whether it operates in an area previously subject to regulation, and, finally, whether its duties apply to a broad class of persons. The necessary consequence of the extreme malleability of these rather vague criteria is to vest judges with broad subjective discretion to protect property interests that happen to appeal to them. * * *a

Notes and Questions

1. *Contract vs. other property rights.* In what respects, if any, is there a significant difference in the Court's review of economic legislation when challenged under the contract clause as compared to due process? Consider particularly (1) the professed standard of review, (2) the degree of deference to the legislature or strictness of judicial scrutiny, (3) the Court's willingness to hypothesize state purposes to justify the legislation. Ought the degree of constitutional protection from legislative interference differ as between preexisting contract interests and preexisting noncontractual property interests? Consider 92 Harv. L.Rev. 57, 86 (1978).

2. *Legislatively-added burdens.* Did *Allied Steel* soundly interpret the contract clause to protect against "impairment" by legislatively-added burdens that increase those stated in the contract? Would it have made a difference in the law's validity if it had added a burden of sounder *funding* of the contractual pension benefits without adding to the *benefits*? Cf. *Connolly v. Pension Benefit Guaranty Corp.*, 475 U.S. 211, 106 S.Ct. 1018, 89 L.Ed.2d 166 (1986) (a taking clause decision).

How Far Has the Court Retreated From *U.S. Trust* and *Allied Steel?*

1. ENERGY RESERVES GROUP v. KANSAS POWER & LIGHT CO., 459 U.S. 400, 103 S.Ct. 697, 74 L.Ed.2d 569 (1983): In 1975 Kansas Power & Light Co. (KPL) agreed to purchase natural gas from Energy Reserves Group (ERG). The contract included provisions for raising the purchase price in the event of changes in the law setting a price higher than the contract price. In 1978, the federal government deregulated natural gas (but allowed the states to regulate the intrastate natural gas market). Kansas promptly imposed price controls on intrastate gas. Because the Kansas law prohibited such recalculation, KPL refused to permit ERG to raise the purchase price under the government escalation clause in their 1975 contract. Without a dissent, the Court, per BLACKMUN, J., held there was no violation of the contract clause:

a. Blackmun, J., did not participate in *Allied Steel*, but Powell and Stevens, JJ., who had not participated in *U.S. Trust*, joined the *Allied Steel* majority, making six Justices voting in the 1970s to revitalize the contract clause.

Because "at the time of the execution of the contracts, ERG did not expect to receive deregulated prices"—indeed, the very existence of the governmental price escalation clause [indicates] that the contracts were structured against the background of regulated prices—ERG's "reasonable expectations have not been impaired by the Kansas Act." To the extent, if any, the Act [does impair] ERG's contractual interests, the Act rests on, and is prompted by, significant and legitimate state interests. Kansas has exercised its police power to protect consumers from the escalation of natural gas prices caused by deregulation." Moreover, it cannot be said that "the means chosen to implement these purposes [are] deficient, particularly in light of the deference to which the Kansas Legislature's judgment is entitled."

Allied Steel was distinguishable, inter alia, on the ground that in that case, unlike the instant one, "[the] State had not acted to meet an important general social problem. The pension statute had a very narrow focus: it was aimed at specific employers. Indeed, it even may have been directed at one particular employer planning to terminate its pension plan when its collective-bargaining agreement expired." Unlike *Allied Steel*, "where a small number of employers were singled out from the larger group," here "there is little or nothing in the record to support [the view] that the Act is special interest legislation."[a]

2. A short time after *Energy Reserves Group*, the Court again rejected a contract clause argument, again distinguishing *U.S. Trust* and *Allied Steel*. At issue in EXXON CORP. v. EAGERTON, 462 U.S. 176, 103 S.Ct. 2296, 76 L.Ed.2d 497 (1983) was an Alabama law increasing the severance tax on oil and gas extracted from Alabama wells, a tax that oil producers were forbidden to pass on, directly or indirectly, to their consumers. Appellant producers were parties to pre-existing contracts that required the purchasers to reimburse them for severance taxes paid. They contended that the pass-through prohibition violated the Contract Clause. A unanimous Court, per MARSHALL, J., disagreed: "[T]he pass-through prohibition did not prescribe a rule limited in effect to contractual obligations or remedies, but instead imposed a generally applicable rule of conduct designed to advance 'a broad societal interest,' *Allied Steel*, protecting consumers from excessive prices. The prohibition applied to all oil and gas producers, regardless of whether they happened to be parties to sale contracts that contained a provision permitting them to pass tax increases through to their purchasers. The effect of the pass-through prohibition on existing contracts that did contain such a provision was incidental to its main effect of shielding consumers from the burden of the tax increase.

"Because the pass-through prohibition imposed a generally applicable rule of conduct, it is sharply distinguishable from the measures struck down in *U.S. Trust* and *Allied Steel*. *U.S. Trust* involved New York and New Jersey statutes whose sole effect was to repeal a covenant that the two States had entered into with the holders of bonds issued by The Port Authority of New York and New Jersey. Similarly, the statute at issue in *Allied Steel* directly 'adjust[ed]' the rights and responsibilities of contracting parties,' [quoting *U.S. Trust*]. The statute [in *Allied Steel*] required a private employer that had contracted with its employees to provide pension benefits to pay additional benefits, beyond those it had agreed to provide. [Since] the statute applied only to employers that had entered into pension agreements, its sole effect was to alter contractual duties. * * *

a. Concurring, Powell, J., joined by Burger, C.J., and Rehnquist, J., thought the Court's conclusion that ERG's reasonable expectations had not been impaired "dispositive" and saw no reason to address other issues.

"Alabama's power to prohibit oil and gas producers from passing the increase in the severance tax on to their purchasers is confirmed by several decisions of this Court rejecting Contract Clause challenges to state rate-setting schemes that displaced any rates previously established by contract. [And] if the Contract Clause does not prevent a State from dictating the price that sellers may charge their customers, plainly it does not prevent a State from requiring that sellers absorb a tax increase themselves rather than pass it through to their customers."

3.   Do *Energy Reserve Group* and *Exxon* make plain that the fears Brennan, J., voiced in his *U.S. Trust* and *Allied Steel* dissents were greatly exaggerated? Do the 1983 cases "distinguish" *U.S. Trust* and *Allied Steel* almost to the vanishing point? See generally Jonathan B. Baker, *Has the Contract Clause Counter-Revolution Halted? Rhetoric, Rights, and Markets in Constitutional Analysis*, 12 Hast. Con.L.Q. 71 (1984); Stewart E. Sterk, *The Continuity of Legislatures: Of Contracts and the Contracts Clause*, 88 Colum.L.Rev. 647 (1988).

Chapter 6

PROTECTION OF INDIVIDUAL RIGHTS: DUE PROCESS, THE BILL OF RIGHTS, AND NONTEXTUAL CONSTITUTIONAL RIGHTS

SECTION 1. NATURE AND SCOPE OF FOURTEENTH AMENDMENT DUE PROCESS; APPLICABILITY OF THE BILL OF RIGHTS TO THE STATES

I. THE "ORDERED LIBERTY—FUNDAMENTAL FAIRNESS," "TOTAL INCORPORATION" AND "SELECTIVE INCORPORATION" THEORIES

Twining v. New Jersey, 211 U.S. 78, 29 S.Ct. 14, 53 L.Ed. 97 (1908); *Palko v. Connecticut,* 302 U.S. 319, 58 S.Ct. 149, 82 L.Ed. 288 (1937); and *Adamson v. California,* 332 U.S. 46, 67 S.Ct. 1672, 91 L.Ed. 1903 (1947), rejected the "total incorporation" view of the history of the fourteenth amendment, the view—which has never commanded a majority—that the fourteenth amendment made all of the provisions of the Bill of Rights fully applicable to the states.[a] But *Twining* recognized that "it is possible that some of the personal rights safeguarded by the first eight Amendments against National action may also be safeguarded against state action, because a denial of them would be a denial of due process" or because "the specific pledge of particular amendments have been found to be implicit in the concept of ordered liberty and thus through the Fourteenth Amendment, become valid as against the states" (*Palko*). And the Court early found among the procedural requirements of fourteenth amendment due process certain rules paralleling provisions of the first eight amendments. For example, *Powell v.*

a. *Palko,* which held that the fourteenth amendment did not encompass at least certain aspects of the double jeopardy prohibition of the fifth amendment, was overruled in *Benton v. Maryland* (1969), discussed below. The *Twining-Adamson* view that the fifth amendment privilege against self-incrimination is not incorporated in the fourteenth was rejected in *Malloy v. Hogan* (1964), discussed below. *Grif-*

fin v. California, 380 U.S. 609, 85 S.Ct. 1229, 14 L.Ed.2d 106 (1965), subsequently applied *Malloy* to overrule the specific holdings of *Twining* and *Adamson,* which had permitted comment on a defendant's failure to take the stand at his criminal trial. These later decisions, however, were still consistent with the rejection of the "total incorporation" interpretation.

339

Alabama, 287 U.S. 45, 53 S.Ct. 55, 77 L.Ed. 158 (1932), held that defendants in a capital case were denied due process when a state refused them the aid of counsel. "The logically critical thing, however," pointed out Harlan, J., years later, "was not that the rights had been found in the Bill of Rights, but that they were deemed * * * fundamental."[b]

Under the "ordered liberty"-"fundamental fairness" test, which procedural safeguards included in the Bill of Rights were applicable to the states and which were not? Consider CARDOZO, J., speaking for the *Palko* Court: "[On reflection and analysis there] emerges the perception of a rationalizing principle which gives to discrete instances a proper order and coherence. The right to trial by jury and the immunity from prosecution except as the result of an indictment [are] not of the very essence of a scheme of ordered liberty. To abolish them is not to violate a 'principle of justice so rooted in the traditions and conscience of our people as to be ranked as fundamental.' [What] is true of jury trials and indictments is true also, as the cases show, of the immunity from compulsory self-incrimination. This too might be lost, and justice still be [done.]"[c]

"We reach a different plane of social and moral values when we pass [to those provisions of the Bill of Rights] brought within the Fourteenth Amendment by a process of absorption. These in their origin were effective against the federal government alone. If the Fourteenth Amendment has absorbed them, the process of absorption has had its course in the belief that neither liberty nor justice would exist if they were sacrificed. This is true, for illustration, of freedom of thought and speech. Of that freedom one may say that it is the matrix, the indispensable condition, of nearly every other form of freedom. * * * Fundamental too in the concept of due process, and so in that of liberty, is the thought that condemnation shall be rendered only after trial. The hearing, moreover, must be a real one, not a sham or pretense [discussing *Powell* which] did not turn upon the fact that the benefit of counsel would have been guaranteed to the defendants by [the] Sixth Amendment if they had been prosecuted in a federal court [but on] the fact that in the particular situation laid before us [the aid of counsel] was essential to the substance of a hearing."

The "total incorporation" position received its strongest support in the *Adamson* dissents. In the principal dissent, BLACK, J., joined by Douglas, J., observed: "I cannot consider the Bill of Rights to be an outworn 18th Century 'strait jacket' as the *Twining* opinion did. Its provisions may be thought outdated

---

b. *Duncan v. Louisiana* (dissent joined by Stewart, J.), discussed below.

c. As pointed out in fn. a supra, the fifth amendment privilege against self-incrimination was subsequently held to be fully applicable to the states via the fourteenth amendment. So was the sixth amendment right to jury trial in criminal cases. *Duncan v. Louisiana* (1968), discussed below.

The above language in *Palko* and language in *Adamson,* infra, and other cases are susceptible of the interpretation that when the Court held that a particular Bill of Rights guarantee was not "incorporated into," or implicit in, fourteenth amendment due process it was *completely* "out." But such a reading of these cases seems unsound. Typically the Court dealt with state procedures transgressing the "outer edges," rather than the basic concept, of a particular Bill of Rights guarantee. It seems

most doubtful that in sustaining such challenged procedures the Court was authorizing the states to abolish completely—or to violate the "hardcore" of—e.g., the protection against double jeopardy, or the privilege against self-incrimination, or the right to trial by jury in criminal cases. Rather the Court probably meant that the state rules did not violate the fourteenth amendment because the Bill of Rights guarantee invoked by defendant did not apply to the states *to the full extent* it applied to the federal government. To hold that a particular provision of the Bill of Rights is not *totally* "incorporated," i.e., not binding on the states *in its entirety,* is not to say it is *completely "out"* of the fourteenth amendment. See generally Louis Henkin, *"Selective Incorporation" in the Fourteenth Amendment,* 73 Yale L.J. 74, 79 & n. 18, 80–81 (1963).

abstractions by some. And it is true that they were designed to meet ancient evils. But they are the same kind of human evils that have emerged from century to century wherever excessive power is sought by the few at the expense of the many. In my judgment the people of no nation can lose their liberty so long as a Bill of Rights like ours survives and its basic purposes are conscientiously interpreted, enforced and respected so as to afford continuous protection against old, as well as new, devices and practices which might thwart those purposes. I fear to see the consequences of the Court's practice of substituting its own concepts of decency and fundamental justice for the language of the Bill of Rights as its point of departure in interpreting and enforcing that Bill of Rights. If the choice must be between the selective process of the *Palko* decision applying some of the Bill of Rights to the States, or the *Twining* rule applying none of them, I would choose the *Palko* selective process. But rather than accept either of these choices, I would follow what I believe was the original purpose of the Fourteenth Amendment—to extend to all the people of the nation the complete protection of the Bill of Rights.

"[T]o pass upon the constitutionality of statutes by looking to the particular standards enumerated in the Bill of Rights and other parts of the Constitution is one thing; to invalidate statutes because of application of 'natural law' deemed to be above and undefined by the Constitution is another. 'In the one instance, courts proceeding within clearly marked constitutional boundaries seek to execute policies written into the Constitution; in the other they roam at will in the limitless area of their own beliefs as to reasonableness and actually select policies, a responsibility which the Constitution entrusts to the legislative representatives of the people.' "[d]

Responding, FRANKFURTER, J.'s concurrence in *Adamson* stressed the "independent potency" of the fourteenth amendment due process clause, maintaining that it "neither comprehends the specific provisions by which the founders deemed it appropriate to restrict the federal government nor is confined to them":[e] "Between the incorporation of the Fourteenth Amendment into the Constitution and the beginning of the present membership of the Court—a period of 70 years—the scope of that Amendment was passed upon by 43 judges. Of all these judges only one, who may respectfully be called an eccentric exception, ever indicated the belief that the Fourteenth Amendment was a shorthand summary of the first eight Amendments theretofore limiting only the Federal Government, and that due process incorporated those eight Amendments as restrictions upon the powers of the States. [To] suggest that it is inconsistent with a truly free society to begin prosecutions without an indictment, to try petty civil cases without the paraphernalia of a common law jury, to take into consideration that one who has full opportunity to make a defense remains silent is, in de Tocqueville's phrase, to confound the familiar with the necessary.

d. Dissenting separately in *Adamson*, Murphy, J., joined by Rutledge, J., "agree[d] that the specific guarantees of the Bill of Rights should be carried over intact into [the fourteenth amendment but was] not prepared to say that the latter is entirely and necessarily limited by the Bill of Rights. Occasions may arise where a proceeding falls so far short of conforming to fundamental standards of procedure as to warrant constitutional condemnation in terms of a lack of due process despite the absence of a specific provision of the Bill of Rights." See also fn. e infra.

e. See also Henry Friendly, *The Bill of Rights as a Code of Criminal Procedure,* 53 Calif.L.Rev. 929, 937 (1965): "[N]o facile formula will enable the Court to escape its assigned task of deciding just what the Constitution protects from state action, as *Estes v. Texas,* 381 U.S. 532, 85 S.Ct. 1628, 14 L.Ed.2d 543 (1965), where no 'specific' could be invoked, showed [for] procedural due process, and *Griswold v. Connecticut* [p. 360 infra] demonstrated for substantive due process."

"[Those] reading the English language with the meaning which it ordinarily conveys, those conversant with the political and legal history of the concept of due process, those sensitive to the relations of the States to the central government as well as the relation of some of the provisions of the Bill of Rights to the process of justice, would hardly recognize the Fourteenth Amendment as a cover for the various explicit provisions of the first eight Amendments. Some of these are enduring reflections of experience with human nature, while some express the restricted views of Eighteenth–Century England regarding the best methods for the ascertainment of facts. The notion that the Fourteenth Amendment was a covert way of imposing upon the States all the rules which it seemed important to Eighteenth Century statesmen to write into the Federal Amendments, was rejected by judges who were themselves witnesses of the process by which the Fourteenth Amendment became part of the Constitution. * * *

"Indeed, the suggestion that the Fourteenth Amendment incorporates the first eight Amendments as such is not unambiguously urged. [There] is suggested merely a selective incorporation of the first eight Amendments into the Fourteenth Amendment. Some are in and some are out, but we are left in the dark as to which are in and which are out. [If] the basis of selection is merely that those provisions of the first eight Amendments are incorporated which commend themselves to individual justices as indispensable to the dignity and happiness of a free man, we are thrown back to a merely subjective test. [In] the history of thought 'natural law' has a much longer and much better founded meaning and justification than such subjective selection of the first eight Amendments for incorporation into the Fourteenth. If all that is meant is that due process contains within itself certain minimal standards which are 'of the very essence of a scheme of ordered liberty,' *Palko,* putting upon this Court the duty of applying these standards from time to time, then we have merely arrived at the insight which our predecessors long ago expressed.

"[A] construction which gives to due process no independent function but turns it into a summary of the specific provisions of the Bill of Rights [would] deprive the States of opportunity for reforms in legal process designed for extending the area of freedom. It would assume that no other abuses would reveal themselves in the course of time than those which had become manifest in 1791. Such a view not only disregards the historic meaning of 'due process.' It leads inevitably to a warped construction of specific provisions of the Bill of Rights to bring within their scope conduct clearly condemned by due process but not easily fitting into the pigeonholes of the specific provisions.

" * * * Judicial review of [the Due Process Clause] of the Fourteenth Amendment inescapably imposes upon this Court an exercise of judgment upon the whole course of the proceedings in order to ascertain whether they offend those canons of decency and fairness which express the notions of justice of English-speaking peoples even toward those charged with the most heinous offenses. These standards of justice are not authoritatively formulated anywhere as though they were prescriptions in a pharmacopoeia. But neither does the application of the Due Process Clause imply that judges are wholly at large. The judicial judgment in applying the Due Process Clause must move within the limits of accepted notions of justice and is not to be based upon the idiosyncracies of a merely personal judgment.''

Notes and Questions

1.   Are Frankfurter and Black, JJ., each more persuasive in demonstrating why the *other's* test is subjective, ill-defined and unilluminating than in explaining why his own is *not*?

2.   *Escape from the "idiosyncrasy of a personal judgment"*. If, as Frankfurter, J., insists, the *Palko-Adamson* test is not based upon "the idiosyncrasies of a merely personal judgment," *whose* moral judgments furnish the answer? And *where* and *how* are they discoverable? The opinions of the progenitors and architects of our institutions? The opinions of the policy-making organs of state governments? Of state courts? The opinions of other countries? Of other countries in the Anglo–Saxon tradition? See Sanford Kadish, *Methodology and Criteria in Due Process Adjudication—A Survey and Criticism,* 66 Yale L.J. 319, 328–333 (1957). What judgments were relied on in *Palko* and *Adamson?* In *Rochin v. California,* Part III infra?

3.   *History.* Historical research has produced ample support—and ample skepticism—for the "incorporation" theory. Is further historical search likely to do more than "further obscure the judicial value-choosing inherent in due process adjudication which can proceed with greater expectation of success if pursued openly and deliberately rather than under disguise"? Is due process more a moral command than a jural or historical concept? Ought it be? See Kadish, supra, at 340–41.

————

Although the Court continued to apply the *"Palko* selective process" approach to the Bill of Rights, DUNCAN v. LOUISIANA, 391 U.S. 145, 88 S.Ct. 1444, 20 L.Ed.2d 491 (1968) (holding the sixth amendment right to jury trial applicable to the states via the fourteenth amendment), no longer employed the Cardozo–Frankfurter terminology (e.g., whether a particular guarantee was "implicit in the concept of ordered liberty" or required by "the 'immutable principles of justice' as conceived by a civilized society") but instead inquired whether the procedural safeguard included in the Bill of Rights was "fundamental to the *American scheme of justice"* (emphasis added) or "fundamental *in the context of the criminal processes maintained by the American states"* (emphasis added). As WHITE, J., noted for the *Duncan* majority (fn. 14), the different phraseology is significant:

"Earlier the Court can be seen as having asked, when inquiring into whether some particular procedural safeguard was required of a State, if a civilized system could be imagined that would not accord the particular protection [quoting from *Palko*]. The recent cases, on the other hand, have proceeded upon the valid assumption that state criminal processes are not imaginary and theoretical schemes but actual systems bearing virtually every characteristic of the common-law system that has been developing contemporaneously in England and this country. The question thus is whether given this kind of system a particular procedure is fundamental—whether, that is, a procedure is necessary to an Anglo–American regime of ordered liberty. It is this sort of inquiry that can justify the conclusions that state courts must exclude evidence seized in violation of the Fourth Amendment, *Mapp v. Ohio* [Part IV infra] [and] that state prosecutors may not comment on a defendant's failure to testify, *Griffin v. California* [fn. a supra]. [Of] each of these determinations that a constitutional provision originally written to bind the Federal Government should bind the States as well it might be said that the limitation in question is not necessarily fundamental to fairness in every criminal system that might be imagined but is fundamental in the context of the criminal processes maintained by the American States.

"When the inquiry is approached in this way the question whether the States can impose criminal punishment without granting a jury trial appears quite different from the way it appeared in the older cases opining that States might abolish jury trial. A criminal process which was fair and equitable but used no juries is easy to imagine. It would make use of alternative guarantees and protections which would serve the purposes that the jury serves in the English and American systems. Yet no American State has undertaken to construct such a system. Instead, every American State, including Louisiana, uses the jury extensively, and imposes very serious punishments only after a trial at which the defendant has a right to a jury's verdict. In every State, including Louisiana, the structure and style of the criminal process—the supporting framework and the subsidiary procedures—are of the sort that naturally complement jury trial, and have developed in connection with and in reliance upon jury trial."[f]

Because the *Duncan* Court believed that "trial by jury in criminal cases is fundamental to the American scheme of justice," it held that it was guaranteed by the fourteenth amendment: "The guarantees of jury trial in the Federal and State Constitutions reflect a profound judgment about the way in which law should be enforced and justice administered. A right to jury trial is granted to criminal defendants in order to prevent oppression by the Government. Those who wrote our constitutions knew from history and experience that it was necessary to protect against unfounded criminal charges brought to eliminate enemies and against judges too responsive to the voice of higher authority. * * * Providing an accused with the right to be tried by a jury of his peers gave him an inestimable safeguard against the corrupt or overzealous prosecutor and against the compliant, biased, or eccentric judge. * * * Fear of unchecked power, so typical of our State and Federal Governments in other respects, found expression in the criminal law in this insistence upon community participation in the determination of guilt or innocence. The deep commitment of the Nation to the right of jury trial in serious criminal cases as a defense against arbitrary law enforcement qualifies for protection under the Due Process Clause of the Fourteenth Amendment, and must therefore be respected by the States."

HARLAN, J., joined by Stewart, J., dissented: "Even if I could agree that the question before us is whether Sixth Amendment jury trial is totally ['incorporated into' the fourteenth amendment] or totally 'out' [see Sec. II infra], I can find in the Court's opinion no real reasons for concluding that it should be 'in'. The basis for distinguishing among clauses in the Bill of Rights cannot be that [only] some are old and much praised, or that only some have played an important role in the development of federal law. These things are true of all. The Court says that some clauses are more 'fundamental' than others, but [uses] this word in a sense that

f. See also Powell, J., concurring in the companion 1972 "jury unanimity" cases of *Johnson v. Louisiana* and *Apodaca v. Oregon*, discussed below: "I agree with Mr. Justice White's analysis in *Duncan* that the departure from earlier decisions was, in large measure, a product of a change in focus in the Court's approach to due process. No longer are questions regarding the constitutionality of particular criminal procedures resolved by focusing alone on the element in question and ascer-taining whether a system of criminal justice might be imagined in which a fair trial could be afforded in the absence of that particular element. Rather, the focus is, as it should be, on the fundamentality of that element viewed in the context of the basic Anglo–American jurisprudential system common to the States. That approach to due process readily accounts both for the conclusion that jury trial *is* fundamental and that unanimity *is not*."

would have astonished Mr. Justice Cardozo and which, in addition, is of no help. The word does not mean 'analytically critical to procedural fairness' for no real analysis of the role of the jury in making procedures fair is even attempted. Instead, the word turns out to mean 'old,' 'much praised,' and 'found in the Bill of Rights.' The definition of 'fundamental' thus turns out to be circular.

"[Jury trial] is of course not without virtues [but its] principal original virtue—[the limitations it] imposes on a tyrannous judiciary—has largely disappeared. [The] jury system [is] a cumbersome process, not only imposing great cost in time and money on both the State and the jurors themselves, but also contributing to delay in the machinery of justice. [That] trial by jury is not the only fair way of adjudicating criminal guilt is well attested by the fact that it is not the prevailing way, either in England or in this country.

"[In] sum, there is a wide range of views on the desirability of trial by jury, and on the ways to make it most effective when it is used; there is also considerable variation from State to State in local conditions such as the size of the criminal caseload, the ease or difficulty of summoning jurors, and other trial conditions bearing on fairness. We have before us, therefore, an almost perfect example of a situation in which [the states should serve as laboratories.] [Instead,] the Court has chosen to impose upon every State one means of trying criminal cases; it is a good means, but it is not the only fair means, and it is not demonstrably better than the alternatives States might devise."

———

Although the Court has remained unwilling to accept the total incorporationists' reading of the fourteenth amendment, in the 1960s it "selectively" "incorporated" or "absorbed" more and more of the specifics of the Bill of Rights into the fourteenth amendment. As White, J., observed in *Duncan*:

"In resolving conflicting claims concerning the meaning of this spacious [fourteenth amendment] language, the Court has looked increasingly to the Bill of Rights for guidance; many of the rights guaranteed by the first eight Amendments to the Constitution have been held to be protected against state action by the Due Process Clause of the Fourteenth Amendment.[g] That clause now protects [the] Fourth Amendment rights to be free from unreasonable searches and seizures and to have excluded from criminal trials any evidence illegally seized; the right guaranteed by the Fifth Amendment to be free of compelled self-incrimination; and the Sixth Amendment rights to counsel, to a speedy and public trial [*Klopfer v. North Carolina*, 386 U.S. 213, 87 S.Ct. 988, 18 L.Ed.2d 1 (1967); *In re Oliver*, 333 U.S. 257, 68 S.Ct. 499, 92 L.Ed. 682 (1948)], to confrontation of opposing witnesses [*Pointer v. Texas*, 380 U.S. 400, 85 S.Ct. 1065, 13 L.Ed.2d 923 (1965)] and to compulsory process for obtaining witnesses [*Washington v. Texas*, 388 U.S. 14, 87 S.Ct. 1920, 18 L.Ed.2d 1019 (1967)]."[h]

g. See also Black, J., joined by Douglas, J., concurring in *Duncan*: "[I] believe as strongly as ever that the Fourteenth Amendment was intended to make the Bill of Rights applicable to the States. I have been willing to support the selective incorporation doctrine, however, as an alternative, although perhaps less historically supportable than complete incorporation [because it] keeps judges from roaming at will in their own notions of what policies outside the Bill of Rights are desirable and what are not. And, most importantly for me, the selective incorporation process has the virtue of having already worked to make most of the Bill of Rights' protections applicable to the States."

h. In the area of criminal procedure, the Court has come very close to incorporating all of the relevant Bill of Rights guarantees. But still on the books, is a lonely exception. *Hurtado v. California*, 110 U.S. 516, 4 S.Ct. 111, 28 L.Ed. 232 (1884), refusing to apply to the

II. SHOULD THE "SELECTED" PROVISION APPLY TO THE STATES "JOT–FOR–JOT"? "BAG AND BAGGAGE"?

In the 1960s, the Court seemed to be "incorporating" not only the basic notion or general concept of the "selected" provision of the Bill of Rights, but applying the provision to the states *to the same extent* it applied to the federal government. Thus, BRENNAN, J., observed for a majority in *Malloy v. Hogan*, 378 U.S. 1, 84 S.Ct. 1489, 12 L.Ed.2d 653 (1964): "We have held that the guarantees of the First Amendment, the prohibition of unreasonable searches and seizures of the Fourth Amendment, and the right to counsel guaranteed by the Sixth Amendment, are all to be enforced against the States under the Fourteenth Amendment *according to the same standards that protect those personal rights against federal encroachment.* [The] Court thus has rejected the notion that the Fourteenth Amendment applies to the States only a 'watered-down, subjective version of the individual guarantees of the Bill of Rights.' " (Emphasis added.) And WHITE, J., put it for a majority in *Duncan:* "Because we believe that trial by jury in criminal cases is fundamental to the American scheme of justice, we hold that the Fourteenth Amendment guarantees a right of jury trial in all criminal cases which—*were they to be tried in a federal court*—would come within the Sixth Amendment's guarantee." (Emphasis added.)[i]

The federal guarantees, protested some justices, were being incorporated into the fourteenth amendment "freighted with their entire accompanying body of federal doctrine" (HARLAN, J., joined by Clark, J., dissenting in *Malloy v. Hogan*); "jot-for-jot and case-for-case" (Harlan, J., joined by Stewart, J., dissenting in *Duncan*); "bag and baggage, however securely or insecurely affixed they may be by law and precedent to federal proceedings" (Fortas, J., concurring in *Duncan*).

Harlan, J., was the most persistent and powerful critic of the *Malloy–Duncan* approach to fourteenth amendment due process. "The consequence," he maintained in his *Malloy* dissent, "is inevitably disregard of all relevant differences which may exist between state and federal criminal law and its enforcement. The ultimate result is compelled uniformity, which is inconsistent with the purpose of our federal system and which is achieved either by encroachment on the State's sovereign powers or by dilution in federal law enforcement of the specific protections found in the Bill of Rights."

Concurring in the result in *Pointer v. Texas,* 380 U.S. 400, 85 S.Ct. 1065, 13 L.Ed.2d 923 (1965) (holding that the Sixth Amendment right of an accused to confront the witnesses against him applies in its entirety to the states via the Fourteenth), HARLAN, J., observed that " 'selective' incorporation or 'absorption' amounts to little more than a diluted form of the full incorporation theory. Whereas it rejects full incorporation because of recognition that not all of the guarantees of the Bill of Rights should be deemed 'fundamental,' it at the same time ignores the possibility that not all phases of any given guaranty are necessarily fundamental."

states the fifth amendment requirement that prosecution be initiated by grand jury indictment. For an overview of the development and application of the selective incorporation doctrine see Jerold Israel, *Selective Incorporation Revisited,* 71 Geo.L.J. 253 (1982).

i. See also Justice Marshall's opinion for the Court in *Benton v. Maryland,* 395 U.S. 784,

89 S.Ct. 2056, 23 L.Ed.2d 707 (1969) (the validity of the state conviction "must be judged not by the watered-down standard enumerated in *Palko,* but *under this Court's interpretations of the Fifth Amendment double jeopardy provision*"). (Emphasis added.)

Dissenting in *Duncan,* HARLAN, J., joined by Stewart, J., protested: "Today's Court still remains unwilling to accept the total incorporationists' view of the history of the Fourteenth Amendment. This, if accepted, would afford a cogent reason for applying the Sixth Amendment to the States. The Court is also, apparently, unwilling to face the task of determining whether denial of trial by jury in the situation before us, or in other situations, is fundamentally unfair. Consequently, the Court has compromised on the ease of the incorporationist position, without its internal logic. It has simply assumed that the question before us is whether the Jury Trial Clause of the Sixth Amendment should be incorporated into the Fourteenth, jot-for-jot and case-for-case, or ignored. Then the Court merely declares that the clause in question is 'in' rather than 'out.'

"The Court has justified neither its starting place nor its conclusion. If the problem is to discover and articulate the rules of fundamental fairness in criminal proceedings, there is no reason to assume that the whole body of rules developed in this Court constituting Sixth Amendment jury trial must be regarded as a unit. The requirement of trial by jury in federal criminal cases has given rise to numerous subsidiary questions respecting the exact scope and content of the right. It surely cannot be that every answer the Court has given, or will give, to such a question is attributable to the Founders; or even that every rule announced carries equal conviction of this Court; still less can it be that every such subprinciple is equally fundamental to ordered liberty."

———

In the 1970s matters were brought to a head by the "right to jury trial" cases: *Baldwin v. New York,* 399 U.S. 66, 90 S.Ct. 1886, 26 L.Ed.2d 437 (1970) (no offense can be deemed "petty," thus dispensing with the fourteenth and sixth amendment rights to jury trial, where more than six months incarceration is authorized); *Williams v. Florida,* 399 U.S. 78, 90 S.Ct. 1893, 26 L.Ed.2d 446 (1970) ("that jury at common law was composed of precisely 12 is an historical accident, unnecessary to effect the purposes of the jury system"; thus 6–person jury in criminal cases does not violate sixth amendment, as applied to the states via fourteenth);[a] and the 1972 *Apodaca* and *Johnson* cases, discussed below, dealing with whether unanimous jury verdicts are required in criminal cases.

Dissenting in *Baldwin* and concurring in *Williams,* HARLAN, J., maintained: "[*Williams*] evinces [a] recognition that the 'incorporationist' view of the Due Process Clause of the Fourteenth Amendment, which underlay *Duncan* and is now carried forward into *Baldwin,* must be tempered to allow the States more elbow room in ordering their own criminal systems. With that much I agree. But to accomplish this by diluting constitutional protections within the federal system itself is something to which I cannot possibly subscribe. Tempering the rigor of *Duncan* should be done forthrightly, by facing up to the fact that at least in this area the 'incorporation' doctrine does not fit well with our federal structure, and by the same token that *Duncan* was wrongly decided.

"[Rather] than bind the States by the hitherto undeviating and unquestioned federal practice of 12–member juries, the Court holds, based on a poll of state practice, that a six-man jury satisfies the guarantee of a trial by jury in a federal criminal system and consequently carries over to the States. This is a constitution-

---

a. But *Ballew v. Georgia,* 435 U.S. 223, 98 S.Ct. 1029, 55 L.Ed.2d 234 (1978), subsequently held that a state trial in a non-petty criminal case to a jury of only five persons did deprive a defendant of the right to trial by jury guaranteed by the sixth and fourteenth amendments.

al renvoi. With all respect, I consider that before today it would have been unthinkable to suggest that the Sixth Amendment's right to a trial by jury is satisfied by a jury of six, or less, as is left open by the Court's opinion in *Williams,* or by less than a unanimous verdict, a question also reserved in today's decision.[b]

"[These decisions] demonstrate that the difference between a 'due process' approach, that considers each particular case on its own bottom to see whether the right alleged is one 'implicit in the concept of ordered liberty,' and 'selective incorporation' is not an abstract one whereby different verbal formulae achieve the same results. The internal logic of the selective incorporation doctrine cannot be respected if the Court is both committed to interpreting faithfully the meaning of the federal Bill of Rights and recognizing the governmental diversity that exists in this country. The 'backlash' in *Williams* exposes the malaise, for there the Court dilutes a federal guarantee in order to reconcile the logic of 'incorporation,' the 'jot-for-jot and case-for-case' application of the federal right to the States, with the reality of federalism. Can one doubt that had Congress tried to undermine the common law right to trial by jury before *Duncan* came on the books the history today recited would have barred such action? Can we expect repeated performances when this Court is called upon to give definition and meaning to other federal guarantees that have been 'incorporated'?

"[I]t is time [for] for this Court to face up to the reality implicit in today's holdings and reconsider the 'incorporation' doctrine before its leveling tendencies further retard development in the field of criminal procedure by stifling flexibility in the States and by discarding the possibility of federal leadership by example."

In *Apodaca v. Oregon,* 406 U.S. 404, 92 S.Ct. 1628, 32 L.Ed.2d 184 (1972) and *Johnson v. Louisiana,* 406 U.S. 356, 92 S.Ct. 1620, 32 L.Ed.2d 152 (1972), upholding the constitutionality of less-than-unanimous jury verdicts in state criminal cases, eight justices adhered to the *Duncan* position that each element of the sixth amendment right to jury trial applies to the states to the same extent it applies to the federal government, but split 4–4 over whether the federal guarantee *did require* jury unanimity in criminal cases. State convictions by less than unanimous votes were sustained only because the ninth member of the Court, newly appointed POWELL, J., read the sixth amendment as requiring jury unanimity, but—taking a Harlan-type approach—concluded that *this feature* of the federal right is not "so fundamental to the essentials of jury trial" as to require unanimity in state criminal cases as a matter of fourteenth amendment due process:[c]

"[I]n holding that the Fourteenth Amendment has incorporated 'jot-for-jot and case-for-case' every element of the Sixth Amendment, the Court derogates principles of federalism that are basic to our system. In the name of uniform application of high standards of due process, the Court has embarked upon a course of constitutional interpretation that deprives the States of freedom to experiment with adjudicatory processes different from the federal model. At the same time, the Court's understandable unwillingness to impose requirements that

b. Cf. Frankfurter, J., for the Court in *Rochin v. California* (1952) (discussed in Part III infra): "Words being symbols do not speak without a gloss. [T]he gloss may be the deposit of history, whereby a term gains technical content. Thus the requirements of the Sixth and Seventh Amendments for trial by jury in the federal courts have a rigid meaning. No changes or chances can alter the content of the verbal symbol of 'jury'—a body of twelve men who must reach a unanimous conclusion if the verdict is to go against the defendant."

c. But *Burch v. Louisiana,* 441 U.S. 130, 99 S.Ct. 1623, 60 L.Ed.2d 96 (1979), subsequently held, without a dissent on this issue, that conviction by a nonunanimous *six-person* jury in a state criminal trial for a nonpetty offense did violate the sixth and fourteenth amendment rights to trial by jury.

it finds unnecessarily rigid (e.g., *Williams*), has culminated in the dilution of federal rights that were, until these decisions, never seriously questioned. The doubly undesirable consequence of this reasoning process, labeled by Mr. Justice Harlan as 'constitutional schizophrenia,' may well be detrimental both to the state and federal criminal justice systems."[d]

BRENNAN, J., joined by Marshall, J., dissented: "Readers of today's opinions may be understandably puzzled why convictions by 11–1 and 10–2 jury votes are affirmed [when] a majority of the Court agrees that the Sixth Amendment requires a unanimous verdict in federal criminal jury trials, and a majority also agrees that the right to jury trial guaranteed by the Sixth Amendment is to be enforced against the States according to the same standards that protect that right against federal encroachment. The reason is that while my Brother Powell agrees that a unanimous verdict is required in federal criminal trials, he does not agree that the Sixth Amendment right to a jury trial is to be applied in the same way to State and Federal Governments. In that circumstance, it is arguable that the affirmance of the convictions [is] not inconsistent with a view that today's decision is a holding that only a unanimous verdict will afford the accused in a state criminal prosecution the jury trial guaranteed him by the Sixth Amendment. In any event, the affirmance must not obscure that the majority of the Court remains of the view that, as in the case of every specific of the Bill of Rights that extends to the States, the Sixth Amendment's jury trial guarantee, however it is to be construed, has identical application against both State and Federal Governments."[e]

III. BODILY EXTRACTIONS: ANOTHER LOOK AT THE "DUE PROCESS" AND "SELECTIVE INCORPORATION" APPROACHES

As noted earlier, Harlan, J., maintained that "the difference between a 'due process' approach [and] 'selective incorporation' is not an abstract one whereby different formulae achieve the same results." But he made this observation in the context of the applicability to the states of the sixth amendment right to trial by jury, which had, or was thought to have, a relatively rigid meaning. Most language in the Bill of Rights, however, is rather vague and general, at least when specific problems arise under a particular phrase. In such cases, does dwelling on the literal language simply *shift the focus of broad judicial inquiry* from "due process" to e.g., "freedom of speech," "establishment of religion," "unreasonable searches and seizures," "excessive bail," "cruel and unusual punishments," and "the assistance of counsel"? See Henry Friendly, *The Bill of Rights as a Code of Criminal Procedure*, 53 Calif.L.Rev. 929, 937 (1965); Jerold Israel, fn. h supra, at 336–38; Kadish, note 2, Part I supra, at 337–39; Herbert Wechsler, *Toward Neutral Principles of Constitutional Law*, 73 Harv.L.Rev. 1, 17–18 (1959). Cf. John

---

d. See also Powell, J., joined by Burger, C.J., and Rehnquist, J., dissenting in *Crist v. Bretz*, 437 U.S. 28, 98 S.Ct. 2156, 57 L.Ed.2d 24 (1978) (holding that federal rule as to when jeopardy "attaches" in jury trials applies to state cases). Consider, too, Burger, C.J.'s separate opinion in *Crist v. Bretz* and Rehnquist, J.'s separate opinion in *Buckley v. Valeo,* p. 1005 infra, maintaining that "not all of the strictures which the First Amendment imposes upon Congress are carried over against the States by the Fourteenth Amendment, [but] only the 'general principle' of free speech."

e. In a separate dissent, Stewart, J., joined by Brennan and Marshall, JJ., protested that "unless *Duncan* is to be overruled," "the only relevant question here is whether the Sixth Amendment's guarantee of trial by jury embraces a guarantee that the verdict of the jury must be unanimous. The answer to that question is clearly 'yes,' as my Brother Powell has cogently demonstrated."

Nowak, *Due Process Methodology in the Postincorporation World*, 70 J.Crim.L. & C. 397, 400–01 (1979) (arguing that decisions based on specific guarantees tend to rely on definitional analysis and fail to explore the interests at stake).

In considering whether the right to counsel "begins" at the time of arrest, preliminary hearing, arraignment, or not until the trial itself, or includes probation and parole revocation hearings or applies to juvenile delinquency proceedings, deportation hearings or civil commitments, or, where the defendant is indigent, includes the right to *assigned* counsel or an assigned psychiatrist at state expense, how helpful is the sixth amendment language entitling an accused to "the assistance of counsel for his defense"? Is the specificity or direction of this language significantly greater than the "due process" clause?

To turn to another cluster of problems—which form the basis for this section—in considering whether, and under what conditions, the police may direct the "pumping" of a person's stomach to uncover incriminating evidence, or the taking of a blood sample from him, without his consent, do the "specific guarantees" in the Bill of Rights against "unreasonable searches and seizures" and against compelling a person to be "a witness against himself" free the Court from the demands of appraising and judging involved in answering these questions by interpreting the "due process" clause?

ROCHIN v. CALIFORNIA, 342 U.S. 165, 72 S.Ct. 205, 96 L.Ed. 183 (1952): Having "some information" that Rochin was selling narcotics, three deputy sheriffs "forced upon the door of [his] room and found him sitting partly dressed on the side of the bed, upon which his wife was lying. On a 'night stand' beside the bed the deputies spied two capsules. When asked 'whose stuff is this?' Rochin seized the capsules and put them in his mouth. A struggle ensued, in the course of which the three officers 'jumped upon him' and [unsuccessfully] attempted to extract the capsules. [Rochin] was handcuffed and taken to a hospital. At the direction of one of the officers a doctor forced an emetic solution through a tube into Rochin's stomach against his will. This 'stomach pumping' produced vomiting. In the vomited matter were found two capsules which proved to contain morphine. [Rochin was convicted of possessing morphine] and sentenced to sixty days' imprisonment. The chief evidence against him was the two capsules."

The Court, per FRANKFURTER, J., concluded that the officers' conduct violated fourteenth amendment due process: "This is conduct that shocks the conscience. Illegally breaking into the privacy of the petitioner, the struggle to open his mouth and remove what was there, the forcible extraction of his stomach's contents—this course of proceeding by agents of government to obtain evidence is bound to offend even hardened sensibilities. They are methods too close to the rack and the screw to permit of constitutional differentiation. * * * Due process of law, as a historic and generative principle, precludes defining, and thereby confining, [civilized] standards of conduct more precisely than to say that convictions cannot be brought about by methods that offend 'a sense of justice.' It would be a stultification of the responsibility which the course of constitutional history has cast upon this Court to hold that in order to convict a man the police cannot extract by force what is in his mind but can extract what is in his stomach. [E]ven though statements contained in them may be independently established as true[,] [c]oerced confessions offend the community's sense of fair play and decency. So here, to sanction the brutal conduct which naturally enough was condemned by the court whose judgment is before us, would be to afford brutality the cloak of law. Nothing would be more calculated to discredit law and thereby to brutalize the temper of a society."

Concurring, BLACK, J., maintained that the fifth amendment's protection against compelled self-incrimination applied to the states and that "a person is compelled to be a witness against himself not only when he is compelled to testify, but also when as here, incriminating evidence is forcibly taken from him by a contrivance of modern science." In his view, "faithful adherence to the specific guarantees in the Bill of Rights insures a more permanent protection of individual liberty than that which can be afforded by the nebulous [fourteenth amendment due process] standards stated by the majority."

DOUGLAS, J., concurring, also criticized the majority's approach. He contended that the privilege against self-incrimination applied to the states as well as the federal government and barred the prosecution's use of capsules seized from a suspect's stomach. "[This] is an unequivocal, definite and workable rule of evidence for state and federal courts. But we cannot in fairness free the state courts from the [restraints of the fifth amendment privilege] and yet excoriate them for flouting the 'decencies of civilized conduct' when they admit the evidence. This is to make the rule turn not on the Constitution but on the idiosyncracies of the judges who sit here."[a]

BREITHAUPT v. ABRAM, 352 U.S. 432, 77 S.Ct. 408, 1 L.Ed.2d 448 (1957), illustrated that under the *Rochin* test state police had considerable leeway even when the body of the accused was "invaded." In *Breithaupt*, the police took a blood sample from an unconscious person who had been involved in a fatal automobile collision. A majority, per CLARK, J., affirmed a manslaughter conviction based on the blood sample (which showed intoxication), stressing that the sample was "taken under the protective eye of a physician" and that "the blood test procedure has become routine in our everyday life." The "interests of society in the scientific determination of intoxication, one of the great causes of the mortal hazards of the road," outweighed "so slight an intrusion" of a person's body.

Dissenting, WARREN, C.J., joined by Black and Douglas, JJ., deemed *Rochin* controlling and argued that police efforts to curb the narcotics traffic, involved in *Rochin*, "is surely a state interest of at least as great magnitude as the interest in highway law enforcement. [Only] personal reaction to the stomach pump and the blood test can distinguish the [two cases]."

a. *Irvine v. California,* 347 U.S. 128, 74 S.Ct. 381, 98 L.Ed. 561 (1954), limited *Rochin* to situations involving coercion, violence or brutality to the person. In *Irvine* the police made repeated illegal entries into petitioner's home, first to install a secret microphone and then to move it to the bedroom, in order to listen to the conversations of the occupants— for over a month. Jackson, J., who announced the judgment of the Court and wrote the principal opinion, recognized that "few police measures have come to our attention that more flagrantly, deliberately, and persistently violated the fundamental principle declared by the Fourth Amendment as a restriction on the Federal Government," but adhered to the holding in *Wolf v. Colorado* (1949) (Part IV infra) that the exclusionary rule in federal search and seizure cases is not binding on the states. (*Wolf* was overruled in *Mapp v. Ohio* (1961) (Part IV infra)). Nor did Jackson, J., deem *Rochin* applicable: "However obnoxious are the facts in the case before us, they do not involve coercion, violence or brutality to the person [as did *Rochin*], but rather a trespass to property, plus eavesdropping."

Because of the "aggravating" and "repulsive" police misconduct in *Irvine*, Frankfurter, J., joined by Burton, J., dissenting, maintained that *Rochin* was controlling, not *Wolf*. (He had written the majority opinions in both cases.) Black, J., joined by Douglas, J., dissented separately, arguing that petitioner had been convicted on the basis of evidence "extorted" from him in violation of the self-incrimination clause, which he considered applicable to the states. Douglas, J., dissenting separately, protested against the use in state prosecutions of evidence seized in violation of the fourth amendment.

DOUGLAS, J., joined by Black, J., dissented, maintaining that "if the decencies of a civilized state are the test, it is repulsive to me for the police to insert needles into an unconscious person in order to get the evidence necessary to convict him, whether they find the person unconscious, give him a pill which puts him to sleep, or use force to subdue him."

Nine years later, even though in the meantime the Court had held in *Mapp v. Ohio,* Part IV infra, that the federal exclusionary rule in search and seizure cases was binding on the states and in *Malloy v. Hogan,* that the fifth amendment's protection against compelled self-incrimination was likewise applicable to the states, the Court upheld the taking by a physician, at police direction, of a blood sample from an injured person, over his objection. SCHMERBER v. CALIFORNIA, 384 U.S. 757, 86 S.Ct. 1826, 16 L.Ed.2d 908 (1966). In affirming the conviction for operating a vehicle while under the influence of intoxicating liquor, a 5–4 majority, per BRENNAN, J., ruled: (1) that the extraction of blood from petitioner under the aforementioned circumstances "did not offend 'that "sense of justice" 'of which we spoke in *Rochin,*" thus reaffirming *Breithaupt;* (2) that the privilege against self-incrimination, now binding on the states, "protects an accused only from being compelled to testify against himself, or otherwise provide the State with evidence of a testimonial or communicative nature and that the withdrawal of blood and use of the analysis in question did not involve compulsion to these ends"; and (3) that the protection against unreasonable search and seizure, now binding on the states, was satisfied because (a) "there was plainly probable cause" to arrest and charge petitioner and to suggest "the required relevance and likely success of a test of petitioner's blood for alcohol"; (b) the officer "might reasonably have believed that he was confronted with an emergency, in which the delay necessary to obtain a warrant, under the circumstances, threatened 'the destruction of evidence' "; and (c) "the test chosen to measure petitioner's blood-alcohol level was [reasonable and] performed in a reasonable manner."

Dissenting, BLACK, J., joined by Douglas, J., expressed amazement at the majority's "conclusion that compelling a person to give his blood to help the State to convict him is not equivalent to compelling him to be a witness against himself." "It is a strange hierarchy of values that allows the State to extract a human being's blood to convict him of a crime because of the blood's content but proscribes compelled production of his lifeless papers."[a]

Notes and Questions

1. In light of *Rochin, Breithaupt* and *Schmerber,* when courts decide constitutional questions by "looking to" the Bill of Rights, to what extent do they proceed, as Black, J., said in *Adamson,* "within clearly marked constitutional boundaries"? To what extent does resort to these "particular standards" enable courts to avoid substituting their "own concepts of decency and fundamental justice" for the language of the Constitution?

2. Did *Mapp* and *Malloy,* decided in the interim between *Breithaupt* and *Schmerber,* affect any justice's vote? Did the applicability of the "particular standards" of the fourth and fifth amendments inhibit Black, Douglas or Bren-

---

a. Warren, C.J., and Douglas, J., dissented in separate opinions, each adhering to his dissenting views in *Breithaupt.* In a third dissent, Fortas, J., maintained that "petitioner's privilege against self-incrimination applies" and, moreover, "under the Due Process Clause, the State, in its role as prosecutor, has no right to extract blood from [anyone] over his protest."

nan, JJ., from employing their own concepts of "decency" and "justice" in *Schmerber?* After *Schmerber,* how much force is there in Black, J.'s view, concurring in *Rochin,* that "faithful adherence to the specific guarantees in the Bill of Rights assures a more permanent protection of individual liberty than that which can be afforded by the nebulous standards stated by the majority"?

3. *The "shocks-the-conscience" test and substantive due process claims.* SAC-RAMENTO v. LEWIS, 523 U.S. 833, 118 S.Ct. 1708, 140 L.Ed.2d 1043 (1998), held, per SOUTER, J., that a police officer did not violate substantive due process by causing death through "reckless indifference" to, or "reckless disregard" for, a person's life in a high-speed automobile chase of a speeding motorcyclist. (The chase resulted in the death of the motorcyclist's passenger when the police car skidded into the passenger after the cycle had tipped over). In such circumstances, concluded the Court, "only a purpose to cause harm unrelated to the legitimate object of arrest will satisfy the element of arbitrary conduct shocking to the conscience, necessary for a due process violation [and for police liability under 42 U.S.C. § 1983]. Since the time of our early explanations of due process," observed the Court, "we have understood the core of the concept to be protection against arbitrary action. [Our] cases dealing with abusive executive action have repeatedly emphasized that only the most egregious official conduct can be said to be 'arbitrary in the constitutional sense.' [Since *Rochin*] we have spoken of the cognizable level of executive abuse of power as that which shocks the conscience. [In] the intervening years we have repeatedly adhered to *Rochin*'s benchmark.' "

The Court emphasized that much turns on the particular context in which the executive misconduct arises. Thus, in a prison custodial situation, when the state has rendered an individual unable to care for himself, and at the same time fails to provide for his basic needs, "the point of the conscience-shocking is reached" when injuries are produced by reckless or grossly negligent executive conduct. On the other hand, "deliberate indifference does not suffice for constitutional liability (albeit under the Eighth Amendment) even in prison circumstances when a prisoner's claim arises not from normal custody but from response to a violent disturbance." Continued the Court:

"Like prison officials facing a riot, the police on an occasion calling for fast action have obligations that tend to tug against each other. [A] police officer deciding whether to give chase must balance on one hand the need to stop a suspect and show that flight from the law is no way to freedom, and, on the other, the high-speed threat to everyone within stopping range, be they suspects, their passengers, other drivers, or bystanders. To recognize a substantive due process violation in these circumstances when only mid-level fault has been shown [i.e., something more than simple negligence, but something less than intentional misconduct] would be to forget that liability for deliberate indifference to inmate welfare rests upon the luxury enjoyed by prison officials of having time to make unhurried judgments, upon the chance for repeated reflection, largely uncomplicated by the pulls of competing obligations. [But] when unforeseen circumstances demand an officer's instant judgment, even precipitate recklessness fails to inch close enough to harmful purpose to spark the shock that implicates 'the large concerns of the governors and the governed.' * * * Regardless whether Smith's behavior offended the reasonableness [of] tort law or the balance struck in law enforcement's own codes of sound practice, it does not shock the conscience."[b]

b. Kennedy, J., joined by O'Connor, J. joined the opinion of the Court, but also wrote separately. They "share[d] Justice Scalia's con-cerns about using the phrase 'shocks the con-science' in a manner suggesting that it is a self-defining test." The phrase, they observed,

4. For other recent illustrations of standards and methodology in due process adjudication, see the "death penalty" cases (although nominally "cruel and unusual punishment" cases), Sec. 4 infra. See also the "right of privacy" cases, Sec. 2 infra.

IV. THE RETROACTIVE EFFECT OF A HOLDING OF UNCONSTITUTIONALITY

In recent years, the Court has considered the retroactive effect of a holding that a law or practice is unconstitutional primarily in the context of criminal procedure decisions.[a] Rejecting what it called the Blackstonian Theory that a new ruling merely sets forth the law as it always existed, *Linkletter v. Walker,* 381 U.S. 618, 85 S.Ct. 1731, 14 L.Ed.2d 601 (1965), took the position that "the Constitution neither prohibits nor requires retrospective effect,"[b] and that a determination of the effect of a judgment of unconstitutionality should turn on "the prior history of the rule in question, its purpose and effect," "whether retrospective operation of the rule will further or retard its operation" and what adverse impact on the administration of justice retroactivity would be likely to have.

The prime purpose of *Mapp v. Ohio,* 367 U.S. 643, 81 S.Ct. 1684, 6 L.Ed.2d 1081 (1961) (imposing the exclusionary rule on the states), emphasized the *Linkletter* Court, was to deter future police misconduct and this purpose would not be advanced by applying the rule to cases which had become "final" (i.e., direct appellate review had been exhausted) prior to the overturning of *Mapp.* The Court recognized that it had given full retroactive effect to some recent law-changing decisions—such as *Gideon v. Wainwright,* 372 U.S. 335, 83 S.Ct. 792, 9 L.Ed.2d 799 (1963) (establishing an absolute right to appointed counsel at least in all serious criminal cases) and the coerced confession cases—but, unlike *Mapp,* the principles in those cases "went to the fairness of the trial—the very integrity of the fact-finding process. [Here] the fairness of the trial is not under attack."

Relying upon the *Linkletter* analysis, STOVALL v. DENNO, 388 U.S. 293, 87 S.Ct. 1967, 18 L.Ed.2d 1199 (1967), set forth a framework for determining whether a new ruling should be given retroactive effect. The "criteria guiding the

"has the unfortunate connotation of a standard laden with subjective assessments. In that respect, it must be viewed with considerable skepticism."

Concurring in the judgment, Scalia, J., joined by Thomas, J., would not have decided the case by applying the "shocks-the-conscience" test but "on the ground that respondents offer no textual or historical support for their alleged due process right."

a. In none of these cases, apparently, did the Court seriously consider applying the new constitutional ruling "purely prospectively," i.e., not even giving the litigant in the very case the benefit of the decision. "Pure prospectivity" raises "difficult problems concerning the nature of a court's functions; persuasive arguments can be made that courts are badly suited for the general determination and proclamation of future rules and, indeed, that for them to do so violates the Constitution's grant to the judiciary only of power over 'cases' and 'controversies.' " 80 Harv.L.Rev. 140 (1966). Another frequently made point, although it may carry less weight in the criminal procedure area, is that "if the Supreme Court begins regularly to announce new rules prospectively only, petitioners, knowing they will be unlikely to benefit personally, will be deterred from pressing for the new rules." Id.

b. "If an unconstitutional statute or practice effectively never existed as a lawful justification for state action [perhaps the dominant view in the era between the Civil War and the Depression], individuals convicted under the statute or in trials which tolerated the practice were convicted unlawfully even if their trials took place before the declaration of unconstitutionality; such a declaration should have a fully retroactive effect, and previously convicted individuals should be able to win their freedom through the writ of habeas corpus. Alternatively, if a judgment of unconstitutionality affects only the case at hand [a view which also had support], the legality of the convictions of individuals previously tried is not affected. In *Linkletter,* the Court rejected both extremes." Tribe 2d ed., at 29–30.

resolution of the question," observed the *Stovall* Court, "implicate (a) the purpose to be served by the new standards, (b) the extent of the reliance by law enforcement authorities on the old standards, [and] (c) the effect on the administration of justice of a retroactive application of the new standards."

Prior to *Linkletter, Mapp* had already been applied to cases still pending on direct appeal, so the only issue considered by *Linkletter* was whether *Mapp* should be applied to a collateral attack upon a conviction. In applying the *Linkletter* standard, however, *Stovall* and subsequent cases did not draw a distinction between final convictions attacked collaterally and those challenged at various stages of direct review.

Moreover, in limiting the retroactive effect of new rulings, cases applying the *Linkletter–Stovall* standard selected different "starting points." Because *Miranda v. Arizona,* 384 U.S. 436, 86 S.Ct. 1602, 16 L.Ed.2d 694 (1966), was viewed as not primarily designed to protect the innocent from wrongful conviction, *Johnson v. New Jersey,* 384 U.S. 719, 86 S.Ct. 1772, 16 L.Ed.2d 882 (1966) held that the new rule in *Miranda* affected only cases in which *the trial began* after the date of that decision. Because the use of improper lineups could be challenged on due process grounds even if the new ruling on lineups were not applied retroactively, *Stovall* declined to give retroactive effect to *United States v. Wade,* 388 U.S. 218, 87 S.Ct. 1926, 18 L.Ed.2d 1149 (1967), the case that established a right to counsel at certain pretrial lineups. But this time the Court selected a different "starting point": the new lineup ruling affected only those pretrial identification procedures *conducted* in the absence of counsel *after the date* of the decisions.[c]

Selection of the date of the challenged *police conduct* as the starting point indicated that *police reliance* on the overturned rule was a major factor in retroactivity disputes. In this respect, DESIST v. UNITED STATES, 394 U.S. 244, 89 S.Ct. 1030, 22 L.Ed.2d 248 (1969) is hardly surprising. *Desist* held that *Katz v. United States,* 389 U.S. 347, 88 S.Ct. 507, 19 L.Ed.2d 576 (1967) (overruling *Olmstead v. United States,* 277 U.S. 438, 48 S.Ct. 564, 72 L.Ed. 944 (1928) and holding that wiretapping and other forms of electronic surveillance are subject to Fourth Amendment restraints) should be given what the Court called "wholly prospective application," i.e., applied only to *police activity* occurring *after* the date of the *Katz* decision.[d]

Desist saw no significant distinction for retroactive purpose between direct review and collateral attack. All of the reasons for making *Katz* prospective only "also undercut any distinction between final convictions and those still pending on direct review. Both the deterrent purpose of the exclusionary rule and the reliance of law enforcement officers focus upon *the time of the search,* not any subsequent point in the prosecution as the relevant date."

HARLAN J., wrote a powerful dissent. Two decades later, this dissent seems a good deal more significant than the opinion of the Court in that case. "[A]ll 'new rules' of constitutional law," maintained Harlan, "must, at a minimum, be applied to all those cases which are still subject to direct review by this Court at the time the 'new' decision is handed down."

c. Although "at first glance the prospectivity rule appears to be an act of judicial self-abnegation," "in reality," observes Francis Allen, *The Judicial Quest for Penal Justice: The Warren Court and the Criminal Cases,* 1975 U.Ill.L.F. 518, 530, such a rule "encourages the making of new law by reducing some of the social costs."

d. The Court recognized that "[o]f course, Katz himself benefitted from the new principle announced [on the date of the *Katz* decision], and [to] that extent the decision has not technically been given wholly prospective application. But [this] is an 'unavoidable consequence of the necessity that constitutional adjudications not stand as mere diction.'"

"[We release a prisoner] only because the Government has offended constitutional principle in the conduct of his case. And when another similarly situated defendant comes before us, we must grant the same relief or give a principled reason for acting differently. We depart from this basic judicial tradition when we simply pick and choose from among similarly situated defendants those who alone will receive the benefit of a 'new' rule of constitutional law.

"[If] a 'new' constitutional doctrine is truly right, we should not reverse lower courts which have accepted it; nor should we affirm those which have rejected the very arguments we have embraced. Anything else would belie the truism that it is the task of this Court, like that of any other, to do justice to each litigant on the merits of his own case. It is only if each of our decisions can be justified in terms of this fundamental premise that they may properly be considered the legitimate products of a court of law, rather than the commands of a super-legislature."

RETHINKING RETROACTIVITY: HARLAN'S VIEWS COME TO THE FORE

Relying heavily on Justice Harlan's reasoning in *Desist,* a 5–4 majority found the distinction between final convictions and those still pending on direct review persuasive for retroactivity purposes and applied it in SHEA v. LOUISIANA, 470 U.S. 51, 105 S.Ct. 1065, 84 L.Ed.2d 38 (1985): When read his *Miranda* rights, Shea asserted his right to counsel. The questioning session was terminated, but the next day, before Shea had communicated with a lawyer, the police again read him his rights. This time he agreed to talk and confessed. The confession was admitted into evidence and Shea was convicted. While his appeal was pending, the Court handed down *Edwards v. Arizona,* 451 U.S. 477, 101 S.Ct. 1880, 68 L.Ed.2d 378 (1981), holding that a custodial suspect's rights are violated when the government uses a confession obtained by police-instigated interrogation—without counsel present—after the suspect has requested a lawyer. The Court, per BLACKMUN, J., held that Shea was entitled to the benefit of *Edwards*: "[It is argued] that drawing a distinction between a case pending on direct review and a case on collateral attack produces inequities and injustices that are not any different from those [we purport] to cure. The argument is that the litigant whose *Edwards* claim will not be considered because it is presented on direct-review will be just as unfairly treated as the direct-review litigant whose claim would be bypassed were *Edwards* not the law. The distinction, however, properly rests on considerations of finality in the judicial process. The one litigant already has taken his case through the primary system. The other has not. For the latter, the curtain of finality has not been drawn. Somewhere, the closing must come.

"[It is also argued] that in every case, *Edwards* alone excepted, reliance on existing law justifies the nonapplication of *Edwards.* [But] there is no difference between the petitioner in *Edwards* and the petitioner in the present case. If the *Edwards* principle is not to be applied retroactively, the only way to dispense equal justice to Edwards and to Shea would be a rule that confined the *Edwards* principle to prospective application unavailable even to Edwards himself."

Dissenting WHITE, J., joined by Burger, C.J., and Rehnquist and O'Connor, JJ., maintained that "the attempt to distinguish between direct and collateral challenges for purposes of retroactivity is misguided": "Under the majority's rule, otherwise identically situated defendants may be subject to different constitutional rules, depending on just how long ago now-unconstitutional conduct occurred and how quickly cases proceed through the criminal justice system. The disparity is no different in kind from that which occurs when the benefit of a new constitutional rule is retroactively afforded to the defendant in whose case it is announced but to no others; the Court's new approach equalizes nothing except the numbers of defendants within the disparately treated classes.

"The majority recognizes that the distinction between direct review and habeas is problematic, but justifies its differential treatment by appealing to the need to draw 'the curtain of finality' on those who were unfortunate enough to have exhausted their last direct appeal at the time *Edwards* was decided. Yet the majority offers no reasons for its conclusion that finality should be the decisive factor. When a conviction is overturned on direct appeal on the basis of an *Edwards* violation, the remedy offered the defendant is a new trial at which any inculpatory statements obtained in violation of *Edwards* will be excluded. It is not clear to me why the majority finds such a burdensome remedy more acceptable when it is imposed on the state on direct review than when it is the result of a collateral attack."

Notes and Questions

1. *Rejection of the "clear break" exception.* Answering a question left open in the *Shea* case, *Griffith v. Kentucky,* 479 U.S. 314, 107 S.Ct. 708, 93 L.Ed.2d 649 (1987), applied *Batson v. Kentucky* (p. 1194 infra) to all convictions not final at the time of the ruling even though *Batson,* which held that a defendant may establish a prima facie case of racial discrimination in the selection of a petit jury on the basis of the prosecution's use of peremptory challenges, was "an explicit and substantial break with prior precedent." "The fact that the new rule may constitute a clear break with the past," observed a 6–3 majority, "has no bearing on the 'actual inequity that results' when only one of many similarly situated defendants receives the benefit of the new rule."

2. *Adoption of the other part of Harlan's approach to retroactivity. What constitutes a "new rule"?* There were two parts to Harlan, J.'s approach to retroactivity. He believed that new rulings should always be applied retroactively to cases on *direct* review (a view adopted in *Shea*), but that generally new rulings should not be applied retroactively to cases on *collateral* review. In TEAGUE v. LANE, 489 U.S. 288, 109 S.Ct. 1060, 103 L.Ed.2d 334 (1989), seven justices adopted this position with respect to retroactivity on collateral attack. However, there was no clear majority as to what the exceptions to this general approach should be.

A four-justice plurality, per O'CONNOR, J. (joined by Rehnquist, C.J., and Scalia and Kennedy, JJ.), identified two exceptions: A new ruling should be applied retroactively to cases on collateral review only (1) if it "places 'certain kinds of primary, private individual conduct beyond the power of the criminal lawmaking authority to proscribe' " or (2) if it mandates "new procedures without which the likelihood of an accurate conviction is seriously diminished." As to what constitutes a "new rule," O'Connor, J., noted for four justices that generally "a case announces a new rule when it breaks new ground or imposes a new obligation" on government or "if the result was not *dictated* by precedent existing at the time the defendant's conviction became final."

3. *Questions about Teague.* Is *Teague's* definition of the claims that will be deemed to rest on new law—and thus be barred from relitigation on habeas unless they fall within a narrow exception—far too expansive? By disabling federal habeas corpus from granting relief whenever reasonable disagreement is possible about the scope or application of an existing rule, does *Teague* "reduce the

incentives for state courts, and state law enforcement officials, to take account of the evolving direction of the law?" Should a "new rule" be defined more narrowly, "to exclude rules and decisions that are clearly foreshadowed, not just those that are 'dictated by precedents' "? See Richard H. Fallon, Jr. & Daniel Meltzer, *New Law, Non–Retroactivity, and Constitutional Remedies,* 104 Harv.L.Rev. 1731, 1816–17 (1991).

SECTION 2. THE RIGHT OF "PRIVACY" (OR "AUTONOMY" OR "PERSONHOOD")

Introductory Note

"Whether as substantive due process or as Privacy, 'fundamentality' needs elaboration, especially with respect to the weight particular rights are to enjoy in the balance against public good. Justices Stone and Cardozo suggested that the freedoms of speech, press and religion required extraordinary judicial protection against invasions even for the public good, because of their place at the foundations of democracy and because of the unreliability of the political process in regard to them. If other rights—those to be described as within the Rights of Privacy—are also to be specially guarded against the democratic political process, similar or other justifications must be found—if there are any. Perhaps unusual respect for autonomy and idiosyncrasy as regards some 'personal' matters is intuitively felt by all of us, including Justices; that such deference is 'self-evident' is not self-evident."

—Louis Henkin, *Privacy and Autonomy,* 74 Colum.L.Rev. 1410, 1428–29 (1974).

As noted in Ira Lupu, *Untangling the Strands of the Fourteenth Amendment,* 77 Mich.L.Rev. 981, 1029–30 (1979), "unlike the all-inclusive theory of the *Lochner* era that held all liberties equally inviolable, and unlike the procedural due process theory that assesses the weight of any protected interest in a refined way for purposes of 'balancing' [Sec. 5 infra], [what might be called] modern substantive due process theory has a distinct all-or-nothing quality to it. Most liberties lacking textual support are of the garden variety—like liberty of contract—and thus their deprivation is constitutional if rationally necessary to the achievement of a public good. [See, e.g., *Williamson v. Lee Optical Co.,* p. 303 supra]. Several select liberties, on the other hand, have attained the status of 'fundamental' or 'preferred,' with the consequence that the Constitution permits a state to abridge them only if it can demonstrate an extraordinary justification." A notable example is *Roe v. Wade,* infra, where the Court held that the "right of privacy" encompassed "a woman's decision whether or not to terminate her pregnancy" and thus certain restrictions on abortion could be justified "only by a 'compelling state interest.' " See also *Shapiro v. Thompson,* p. 1374 infra, which can be viewed as a "right to travel" case, which, in the course of invalidating a one-year durational residence requirement for welfare, rejected the argument that "a mere showing of a rational relationship between the waiting period and [administrative governmental] objectives will suffice [for] in moving from state to state [appellees] were exercising a constitutional right, and any classification which serves to penalize the exercise of that right, unless shown to be necessary to promote a *compelling* governmental interest, is unconstitutional." As Lupu observes, supra, "[b]ecause the review standard for ordinary liberties is so deferential, and the standard for preferred liberties so rigid, outcomes are ordained by the designation of 'preferred' [or 'fundamental'] or not."

Regulations dealing with "fundamental rights" call for "strict scrutiny" review just as government classifications based upon what have come to be known as "suspect" criteria trigger "strict" equal protection review. "[T]here is a case to be made for a significant degree of judicial deference to legislative and administrative choices in some spheres. Yet the idea of strict scrutiny acknowledges that other political choices—those burdening fundamental rights, or suggesting prejudice against racial or other minorities—must be subjected to close analysis in order to preserve substantive values of equality and liberty. Although strict scrutiny in this form ordinarily appears as a standard for judicial review, it may also be understood as admonishing lawmakers and regulators as well to be particularly cautious of their *own* purposes and premises and of the effects of their choices." Tribe 2d ed., at 1451.

Not infrequently, as in *Skinner v. Oklahoma*, 316 U.S. 535, 62 S.Ct. 1110, 86 L.Ed. 1655 (1942),[a] which is an "equal protection" case in form, and which never mentioned any "right of privacy," but to which "the development of the contemporary concept of a constitutionally protected 'right of privacy' in sexual matters can be traced," John Nowak & Ronald Rotunda, *Constitutional Law* 893 (6th ed., 2000) (hereinafter referred to as Nowak & Rotunda), a decision can be viewed as either an "equal protection" or a "fundamental rights" (or "substantive due process") case.

Indeed, observes Lupu, at 983–84, "the tangling [of 'liberty' and 'equality'] is most apparent and most serious when viewed in its relationship to the so-called 'fundamental rights' developments in both equal protection and due process

---

a. *Skinner*, per Douglas, J., held violative of equal protection Oklahoma's Habitual Criminal Sterilization Act, which authorized the sterilization of persons previously convicted and imprisoned two or more times of crimes "amounting to felonies involving moral turpitude" and thereafter convicted of such a felony and sentenced to prison. (Petitioner, previously convicted of "chicken-stealing" and robbery, had again been convicted of robbery.) Expressly exempted were such felonies as embezzlement. Thus one convicted three times of larceny could be subjected to sterilization, but the embezzler could not—although "the nature of the two crimes is intrinsically the same" and they are otherwise punishable in the same manner. The Oklahoma law "runs afoul of the equal protection clause" because—

"We are dealing here with legislation which involves one of the basic civil rights of man. Marriage and procreation are fundamental to the very existence and survival of the race. [In] evil or reckless hands [the power to sterilize] can cause races or types which are criminal to the dominant group to wither and disappear. There is no redemption for the individual whom the law touches. [He] is forever deprived of a basic liberty. We mention these matters [in] emphasis of our view that strict scrutiny of the classification which a State makes in a sterilization law is essential, lest unwittingly, or otherwise, invidious discriminations are made against groups or types of individuals in violation of the constitutional guaranty of just and equal laws."

Stone, C.J., concurring in the result, thought that "the real question [is] not one of equal protection, but whether the wholesale condemnation of a class to such as invasion of personal liberty, without opportunity to any individual to show that his is not the type of case which would justify resort to it, satisfies the demands of due process. [A] law which condemns, without hearing, all the individuals of a class to so harsh a measure as the present because some or even many merit condemnation, is lacking in the first principles of due process."

Skinner distinguished *Buck v. Bell*, 274 U.S. 200, 47 S.Ct. 584, 71 L.Ed.2d 1000 (1927), upholding a sterilization law applicable only to mental defectives in state institutions: "[It] was pointed out [in that case] that 'so far as the operations enable those who otherwise must be kept confined to be returned to the world, and thus open the asylum to others, the equality aimed at will be more nearly reached.' Here there is no such saving feature."

clause interpretation. In the sense used here, fundamental rights include all the claims of individual rights, drawn from sources outside of the first eight amendments, that the Supreme Court has elevated to preferred status (that is, rights which the government may infringe only when it demonstrates extraordinary justification). [Which] new rights properly derive from the liberty strand, and which from the equality strand?[6] Sometimes the Court tells us; other times it does not. Often, members of the Court agree upon the preferred status of an interest but disagree about its textual source.[7] On occasion, members of the Court concede that an interest has no textual source, yet battle still over which strand of the fourteenth amendment protects it from state interference."[8]

———

"[In *Griswold,* Douglas, J.,] skipped through the Bill of Rights like a cheerleader—'Give me a P ... give me an R ... an I ...,' and so on, and found P–R–I–V–A–C–Y as a derivative or penumbral right."

—Robert Dixon, *The "New" Substantive Due Process and the Democratic Ethic: A Prolegomenon,* 1976 B.Y.U.L.Rev. 43, 84.

GRISWOLD v. CONNECTICUT

381 U.S. 479, 85 S.Ct. 1678, 14 L.Ed.2d 510 (1965).

[handwritten: right of married persons from using contraceptives]

JUSTICE DOUGLAS delivered the opinion of the Court.

Appellant Griswold is Executive Director of the Planned Parenthood League of Connecticut. Appellant Buxton [is] Medical Director for the League at its Center in New Haven—a center open [when] appellants were arrested. They gave information, instruction, and medical advice to *married persons* as to the means of preventing conception. [Fees] were usually charged, although some couples were serviced free.

[The constitutionality of two Connecticut statutes is involved.] [One] provides: "Any person who uses any drug, medicinal article or instrument for the purpose of preventing conception shall be fined not less than fifty dollars or imprisoned not less than sixty days nor more than one year or be both fined and imprisoned." [The other] provides: "Any person who assists, abets, counsels, causes, hires or commands another to commit any offense may be prosecuted and punished as if he were the principal offender." The appellants were found guilty as accessories and fined $100 [each].

Coming to the merits,[a] we are met with a wide range of questions that implicate the Due Process Clause * * *. Overtones of some arguments suggest that *Lochner* should be our guide. But we decline that invitation * * *. We do not

[handwritten left margin: Protecting Marriage Relationship]

---

6. Compare *Roe v. Wade* [infra] (due process) with *Eisenstadt v. Baird* [infra] (analogous interests protected by the equal protection clause), and *Loving v. Virginia* [p. 1176 infra] (analogous interests protected by the due process clause) (alternative ground).

7. The reference is to *Griswold v. Connecticut* [infra], in which Bill of Rights' penumbras, the ninth amendment, and "pure" substantive due process compete for attention.

8. In *Shapiro v. Thompson,* the majority held that the equal protection clause protected

the right to travel, while Justice Harlan in dissent believed that the due process clause was the relevant shield. A similar doctrinal dispute split the Court in *Zablocki v. Redhail* [infra], where the majority held that the equal protection clause protected the right to marry. Justice Powell, in a concurring opinion, felt the right found its source in the due process clause.

a. The Court held that appellants had standing to assert the constitutional rights of the married persons they advised.

[handwritten bottom: not a right protected by Constitution -leave it up to Legislative judgement]

sit as a super-legislature to determine the wisdom, need, and propriety of laws that touch economic problems, business affairs, or social conditions. This law, however, operates directly on an intimate relation of husband and wife and their physician's role in one aspect of that relation.

The association of people is not mentioned in the Constitution nor in the Bill of Rights. The right to educate a child in a school of the parents' choice—whether public or private or parochial—is also not mentioned. Nor is the right to study any particular subject or any foreign language. Yet the First Amendment has been construed to include certain of those rights. [See] *Pierce v. Society of Sisters*, 268 U.S. 510 45 S.Ct. 571, 69 L.Ed. 1070 (1925) [and] *Meyer v. Nebraska*, 262 U.S. 390, 43 S.Ct. 625, 67 L.Ed. 1042 (1923).[b] [T]he State may not, consistently with the spirit of the First Amendment, contract the spectrum of available knowledge. The right of freedom of speech and press includes not only the right to utter or to print, but the right to distribute, the right to receive, the right to read and freedom of inquiry, freedom of thought, and freedom to teach—indeed the freedom of the entire university community. Without those peripheral rights the specific rights would be less secure. And so we reaffirm the principle [of] *Pierce* [and] *Meyer*.

In *NAACP v. Alabama* [p. 961 infra], we protected the "freedom to associate and privacy in one's associations," noting that freedom of association was a peripheral First Amendment right. [In] other words, the First Amendment has a penumbra where privacy is protected from governmental intrusion. In like context, we have protected forms of "association" that are not political in the customary sense but pertain to the social, legal, and economic benefit of the members. *NAACP v. Button*, 371 U.S. 415, 83 S.Ct. 328, 9 L.Ed.2d 405 (1963). [W]hile [association] is not expressly included in the First Amendment its existence is necessary in making the express guarantees fully meaningful.

The foregoing cases suggest that specific guarantees in the Bill of Rights have penumbras, formed by emanations from those guarantees that help give them life and substance. Various guarantees create zones of privacy. The right of association contained in the penumbra of the First Amendment is one, as we have seen. The Third Amendment in its prohibition against the quartering of soldiers "in any house" [is] another facet of that privacy. The Fourth Amendment [is another]. The Fifth Amendment in its Self–Incrimination Clause enables the citizen to create a zone of privacy which government may not force him to surrender to his detriment. The Ninth Amendment provides: "The enumeration in the Constitu-

b. Consider Nowak & Rotunda 858: In both *Meyer*, invalidating a state law forbidding all grade schools from teaching subjects in any language other than English, and in *Pierce*, holding a state law requiring students to attend public schools violative of due process, "the majority [per McReynolds, J.] found that the law restricted individual freedom without any relation to a valid public interest. Freedom of choice regarding an individual's personal life was recognized as constitutionally protected. These decisions may only have reflected the attitude of the Court towards government regulation during the apex of 'substantive due process.' While these decisions might today be grounded on the First Amendment, their existence is important to the growth of the right to privacy. If nothing else, they show a historical

recognition of a right to private decision-making regarding family matters as inherent in the concept of liberty."

See also Dennis Hutchinson, *Unanimity and Desegregation: Decisionmaking in the Supreme Court, 1948–58*, 68 Geo.L.J. 1, 49–51 (1979) (Frankfurter, J., long an outspoken critic of the McReynolds opinions in *Meyer* and *Pierce*, warned that the method used in these cases could just as easily produce "another *Lochner*"); Richard Posner, *The Uncertain Protection of Privacy by the Supreme Court*, 1979 Sup.Ct.Rev. 173, 195–96 ("under ostensible modern test of substantive due process," *Meyer* was "incorrectly decided"; its citation in "privacy" cases shows "survival of substantive due process despite frequent disclaimers.")

tion, of certain rights, shall not be construed to deny or disparage others retained by the people." * * *

We have had many controversies over these penumbral rights of "privacy and repose." [*Skinner* and other cases] bear witness that the right of privacy which presses for recognition here is a legitimate one.

The present case, then, concerns a relationship lying within the zone of privacy created by several fundamental constitutional guarantees.[11] And it concerns a law which, in forbidding the *use* of contraceptives rather than regulating their manufacture or sale, seeks to achieve its goals by means having a maximum destructive impact upon that relationship. Such a law cannot stand in light of the familiar principle [that] a "governmental purpose to control or prevent activities constitutionally subject to state regulation may not be achieved by means which sweep unnecessarily broadly and thereby invade the area of protected freedoms." *NAACP v. Alabama*. Would we allow the police to search the sacred precincts of marital bedrooms for telltale signs of the use of contraceptives? The very idea is repulsive to the notions of privacy surrounding the marriage relationship.[12]

We deal with a right of privacy older than the Bill of Rights * * *. Marriage is a coming together for better or for worse, hopefully enduring, and intimate to the degree of being sacred. It is an association that promotes a way of life, not causes; a harmony in living, not political faiths; a bilateral loyalty, not commercial or social projects. Yet it is an association for as noble a purpose as any involved in our prior decisions.

Reversed.

JUSTICE GOLDBERG, whom THE CHIEF JUSTICE and JUSTICE BRENNAN join, concurring.

I [join the Court's opinion]. Although I have not accepted the view that "due process" as used in the Fourteenth Amendment includes all of the first eight Amendments, I do agree that the concept of liberty protects those personal rights that are fundamental, and is not confined to the specific terms of the Bill of Rights. My conclusion [that liberty] embraces the right of marital privacy though that right is not mentioned explicitly in the Constitution is supported both by numerous decisions [and] by the language and history of the Ninth Amendment [which] reveal that the Framers of the Constitution believed that there are additional fundamental rights, protected from governmental infringement. [The] Ninth Amendment [was] proffered to quiet expressed fears that a bill of specifically enumerated rights could not be sufficiently broad to cover all essential rights

---

11. Did the Court omit the free exercise clause of the first amendment? Like religious beliefs, are beliefs in the areas of marriage, procreation and child rearing "often deeply held, involving loyalties fully as powerful as those that bind the citizen to the state"? Will the choice of whom to marry or whether or not to have a child, once taken, "have as strong an impact on the life patterns of the individuals involved [as] any adoption of a religious belief or viewpoint"? See Philip Heymann & Douglas Barzelay, *The Forest and the Trees: Roe v. Wade and Its Critics*, 53 B.U.L.Rev. 765, 773–74 (1973).

12. But consider Posner, fn. b supra, at 194: "Such a search would indeed be an invasion of privacy in a conventional sense. But it would be a justifiable invasion if the statute were not otherwise constitutionally objectionable. This case can be seen by imagining that the statute in question forbade not contraception but murder and that the police had probable cause to believe that the suspected murderer had secreted the weapon to his mattress. Furthermore, even if some methods of enforcing the Connecticut statute [violated the Fourth Amendment], that would mean only that the statute was difficult to enforce. [As] the facts of *Griswold* show, the State could enforce the statute without invading anyone's privacy, simply by prosecuting, as accessories, the employees of birth-control clinics."

and that the specific mention of certain rights would be interpreted as a denial that others were protected.

[While] this Court has had little occasion to interpret the Ninth Amendment,[6] "[i]t cannot be presumed that any clause in the constitution is intended to be without effect." [To] hold that a right so basic and fundamental and so deep-rooted in our society as the right of privacy in marriage may be infringed because that right is not guaranteed in so many words by the first eight amendments to the Constitution is to ignore the Ninth Amendment and to give it no effect whatsoever. [The] Ninth Amendment shows a belief of the Constitution's authors that fundamental rights exist that are not expressly enumerated in the first eight amendments and an intent that the list of rights included there not be deemed exhaustive.

[Surely] the Government, absent a showing of a compelling subordinating state interest, could not decree that all husbands and wives must be sterilized after two children have been born to them. Yet by [the dissenters'] reasoning such an invasion of marital privacy would not be subject to constitutional challenge because, while it might be "silly," no provision of the Constitution specifically prevents the Government from curtailing the marital right to bear children and raise a family. [I]f upon a showing of a slender basis of rationality, a law outlawing voluntary birth control by married persons is valid, then, by the same reasoning, a law requiring compulsory birth control also would seem to be valid. In my view, however, both types of law would unjustifiably intrude upon rights of marital privacy which are constitutionally protected.

In a long series of cases this Court has held that where fundamental personal liberties are involved, they may not be abridged by the States simply on a showing that a regulatory statute has some rational relationship to the effectuation of a proper state purpose. [The] State, at most, argues that there is some rational relation between this statute and what is admittedly a legitimate subject of state concern—the discouraging of extra-marital relations. It says that preventing the use of birth-control devices by married persons helps prevent the indulgence by some in such extra-marital relations. The rationality of this justification is dubious, particularly in light of the admitted widespread availability to all persons [in] Connecticut, unmarried as well as married, of birth-control devices for the prevention of disease, as distinguished from the prevention of conception. But in any event, it is clear that the state interest in safeguarding marital fidelity can be served by a more discriminately tailored statute, which does not, like the present one, sweep unnecessarily broadly, reaching far beyond the evil sought to be dealt with and intruding upon the privacy of all married couples. * * *

JUSTICE HARLAN, concurring in the judgment.

I [cannot] join the Court's opinion [as] it seems to me to evince an approach [that] the Due Process Clause of the Fourteenth Amendment does not touch this Connecticut statute unless the enactment is found to violate some right assured by the letter or penumbra of the Bill of Rights. [W]hat I find implicit in the Court's opinion is that the "incorporation" doctrine may be used to *restrict* the reach of Fourteenth Amendment Due Process. For me this is just as unacceptable constitutional doctrine as is the use of the "incorporation" approach to *impose* upon the States all the requirements of the Bill of Rights. * * *

6. [It] has been referred to as "*The Forgotten Ninth Amendment,*" in a book with that title by Bennett B. Patterson (1955). * * *

[T]he proper constitutional inquiry in this case is whether this Connecticut statute infringes the Due Process Clause of the Fourteenth Amendment because the enactment violates basic values "implicit in the concept of ordered liberty." For reasons stated at length in my dissenting opinion in *Poe v. Ullman* [discussed below], I believe that it does. While the relevant inquiry may be aided by resort to one or more of the provisions of the Bill of Rights, it is not dependent on them or any of their radiations. The Due Process Clause of the Fourteenth Amendment stands, in my opinion, on its own bottom.

[While] I could not more heartily agree that judicial "self restraint" is an indispensable ingredient of sound constitutional adjudication, I do submit that the formula suggested [by the dissenters] for achieving it is more hollow than real. "Specific" provisions of the Constitution, no less than "due process," lend themselves as readily to "personal" interpretations by judges whose constitutional outlook is simply to keep the Constitution in supposed "tune with the times".

[Judicial self-restraint will] be achieved in this area, as in other[s], only by continual insistence upon respect for the teachings of history, solid recognition of the basic values that underlie our society, and wise appreciation of the great roles that the doctrines of federalism and separation of powers have played in establishing and preserving American freedoms. Adherence to these principles will not, of course, obviate all constitutional differences of opinion among judges, nor should it. Their continued recognition will, however, go farther toward keeping most judges from roaming at large in the constitutional field than will the interpolation into the Constitution of an artificial and largely illusory restriction on the content of the Due Process Clause.

[Dissenting in POE v. ULLMAN, 367 U.S. 497, 523, 81 S.Ct. 1752, 6 L.Ed.2d 989 (1961), which failed to reach the merits of the constitutional challenge to the Connecticut anti-birth control statute, Harlan, J., had maintained that the statute, "as construed to apply to these appellants, violates the Fourteenth Amendment" because "a statute making it a criminal offense for *married couples* to use contraceptives is an intolerable and unjustifiable invasion of privacy in the conduct of the most intimate concerns of an individual's personal life." Harlan, J., "would not suggest that adultery, homosexuality, fornication and incest are immune from criminal enquiry, however privately practiced," but "the intimacy of husband and wife is necessarily an essential and accepted feature of the institution of marriage, an institution which the State not only must allow, but which always and every age it has fostered and protected. It is one thing when the State exerts its power either to forbid extra-marital sexuality altogether, or to say who may marry, but it is quite another when, having acknowledged a marriage and the intimacies inherent in it, it undertakes to regulate by means of the criminal law the details of that intimacy."

[Although the state had argued the constitutional permissibility of the moral judgment underlying the challenged statute, Harlan, J., could not find anything that "even remotely suggests a justification for the obnoxiously intrusive means it has chosen to effectuate that policy." He deemed "the utter novelty" of the statute "conclusive." "Although the Federal Government and many States have at one time or another [prohibited or regulated] the distribution of contraceptives, none [has] made the *use* of contraceptives a crime. Indeed, a diligent search has revealed that no nation, including several which quite evidently share Connecticut's moral policy, had seen fit to effectuate that policy by the means presented here."

[Because the constitutional challenges to the Connecticut statute "draw their basis from no explicit language of the Constitution, and have yet to find expression in any decision of this Court," Harlan, J., deemed it "desirable at the outset to state the framework of Constitutional principles in which I think the issue must be judged":

["[Were] due process merely a procedural safeguard it would fail to reach those situations where the deprivation of life, liberty or property was accomplished by legislation which by operating in the future could, given even the fairest possible procedure in application to individuals, nevertheless destroy the enjoyment of all three. [I]t is not the particular enumeration of rights in the first eight Amendments which spells out the reach of Fourteenth Amendment due process, but rather [those concepts embracing] rights 'which [are] *fundamental;* which belong [to] the citizens of all free governments.'

["[T]hrough the course of this Court's decisions [due process] has represented the balance which our Nation, built upon postulates of respect for the liberty of the individual, has struck between that liberty and the demands of organized society. [The] balance of which I speak is the balance struck by this country, having regard to what history teaches are the traditions from which it developed as well as the traditions from which it broke. That tradition is a living thing. A decision of this Court which radically departs from it could not long survive, while a decision which builds on what has survived is likely to be sound. No formula could serve as a substitute, in this area, for judgment and restraint.

["[The] full scope of the liberty guaranteed by the Due Process Clause cannot be found in or limited by the precise terms of the specific guarantees elsewhere provided in the Constitution. This 'liberty' is not a series of isolated points pricked out in terms of [the] freedom of speech, press, and religion; [the] freedom from unreasonable searches and seizures; and so on. It is a rational continuum which, broadly speaking, includes a freedom from all substantial arbitrary impositions and purposeless restraints [and] which also recognizes, what a reasonable and sensitive judgment must, that certain interests require particularly careful scrutiny of the state needs asserted to justify their abridgment. Cf. *Skinner.*"][c]

JUSTICE WHITE, concurring in the judgment.

In my view this Connecticut law as applied to married couples deprives them of "liberty" without [due process] guaranteed by the Fourteenth Amendment against arbitrary or capricious [denials]. Surely the right [to] be free of regulation of the intimacies of the marriage relationship, "come[s] to this Court with a momentum for respect lacking when appeal is made to liberties which derive merely from shifting economic arrangements." *Kovacs v. Cooper*, 336 U.S. 77, 69 S.Ct. 448, 93 L.Ed. 513 (1949) (opinion of Frankfurter, J.).

The Connecticut anti-contraceptive statute deals rather substantially with this relationship. [And] the clear effect of these statutes, as enforced, is to deny disadvantaged citizens of Connecticut, those without either adequate knowledge or resources to obtain private counseling, access to medical assistance and up-to-date information in respect to proper methods of birth control. In my view, a statute with these effects bears a substantial burden of justification when attacked under the Fourteenth Amendment.

An examination of the justification offered, however, cannot be avoided by saying that the Connecticut anti-use statute invades a protected area of privacy and association or that it demeans the marriage relationship. The nature of the

c.   See also the extracts from this dissent in   *Planned Parenthood v. Casey*, infra.

right invaded is pertinent, to be sure, for statutes regulating sensitive areas of liberty do, under the cases of this Court, require "strict scrutiny," *Skinner,* and "must be viewed in the light of less drastic means for achieving the same basic purpose." But such statutes, if reasonably necessary for the effectuation of a legitimate and substantial state interest, and not arbitrary or capricious in application, are not invalid under the Due Process Clause. [There] is no serious contention that Connecticut thinks the use of artificial or external methods of contraception immoral or unwise in itself, or that the anti-use statute is founded upon any policy of promoting population expansion. Rather, the statute is said to serve the State's policy against all forms of promiscuous or illicit sexual relationships, be they premarital or extramarital, concededly a permissible and legitimate legislative goal.

[But] I wholly fail to see how the ban on the use of contraceptives by married couples in any way reinforces the State's ban on illicit sexual relationships. [Perhaps] the theory is that the flat ban on use prevents married people from possessing contraceptives and without the ready availability of such devices for use in the marital relationship, there will be no or less temptation to use them in extramarital ones. This reasoning rests on the premise that married people will comply with the ban in regard to their marital relationship, notwithstanding total nonenforcement in this context and apparent nonenforcibility, but will not comply with criminal statutes prohibiting extramarital affairs and the anti-use statute in respect to illicit sexual relationships, a premise whose validity has not been demonstrated and whose intrinsic validity is not very evident. At most the broad ban is of marginal utility to the declared objective. A statute limiting its prohibition on use to persons engaging in the prohibited relationship would serve the end posited by Connecticut in the same way, and with the same effectiveness, or ineffectiveness, as the broad anti-use statute under attack in this case. I find nothing in this record justifying the sweeping scope of this [statute].

JUSTICE BLACK, with whom JUSTICE STEWART joins, dissenting.

[There are] guarantees in certain specific constitutional provisions which are designed in part to protect privacy at certain times and places with respect to certain activities. [But] I think it belittles [the Fourth] Amendment to talk about it as though it protects nothing but "privacy." [The] average man would very likely not have his feelings soothed any more by having his property seized openly than by having it seized privately and by stealth. [And] a person can be just as much, if not more, irritated, annoyed and injured by an unceremonious public arrest by a policeman as he is by a seizure in the privacy of his office or home.

One of the most effective ways of diluting or expanding a constitutionally guaranteed right is to substitute for the crucial word or words of a constitutional guarantee another word or words, more or less flexible and more or less restricted in meaning. This fact is well illustrated by the use of the term "right of privacy" as a comprehensive substitute for the Fourth Amendment's guarantee against "unreasonable searches and seizures." * * *[1] I like my privacy as well as the next one, but I am nevertheless compelled to admit that government has a right to invade it unless prohibited by some specific constitutional provision.

1. The phrase "right to privacy" appears first to have gained currency from an article written by Messrs. Warren and (later Mr. Justice) Brandeis in 1890 which urged that States should give some form of tort relief to persons whose private affairs were exploited by others. *The Right to Privacy,* 4 Harv.L.Rev. 193. * * *

Observing that "the right of privacy presses for recognition here," today this Court, which I did not understand to have power to sit as a court of common law, now appears to be exalting a phrase which Warren and Brandeis use in discussing grounds for tort relief, to the level of a constitutional [rule].

[This] brings me to the arguments made by [the concurring justices]. I discuss the due process and Ninth Amendment arguments together because on analysis they turn out to be the same thing—merely using different words to claim for this Court and the federal judiciary power to invalidate any legislative act [that] it considers to be arbitrary, capricious, unreasonable, or oppressive, or this Court's belief that a particular state law under scrutiny has no "rational or justifying" purpose, or is offensive to a "sense of fairness and justice." If these formulas based on "natural justice" [are] to prevail, they require judges to determine what is or is not constitutional on the basis of their own appraisal of what laws are unwise or unnecessary. [I] do not believe that we are granted power by the Due Process Clause or any [other] provisions to measure constitutionality by our belief that legislation is arbitrary, capricious or unreasonable, or accomplishes no justifiable purpose, or is offensive to our own notions of "civilized standards of conduct." Such an appraisal of the wisdom of legislation is an attribute of the power to make laws, [a] power which was specifically denied to federal courts by the [Framers].

Of the cases on which my [Brothers] rely so heavily, undoubtedly the reasoning of two of them supports their result here—[*Meyer* and *Pierce*]. *Meyer* [relying on *Lochner*,] held unconstitutional, as an "arbitrary" and unreasonable interference with the right of a teacher to carry on his occupation and of parents to hire him, a state law forbidding the teaching of modern foreign languages to young children in the schools.[7] [*Pierce*, per McReynolds, J.] said that a state law requiring that all children attend public schools interfered unconstitutionally with the property rights of private school corporations because it was an "arbitrary, unreasonable, and unlawful interference" which threatened "destruction of their business and property." Without expressing an opinion as to whether either of those cases reached a correct result in light of our later decisions applying the First Amendment to the States through the Fourteenth, I merely point out that the reasoning stated in *Meyer* and *Pierce* was the same natural law due process philosophy which many later opinions repudiated, and which I cannot accept. * * *

My Brother Goldberg has adopted the recent discovery[12] that the Ninth Amendment as well as the Due Process Clause can be used by this Court as authority to strike down all state legislation which this Court thinks violates "fundamental principles of liberty and justice," or is contrary to the "traditions and collective conscience of our people." [One] would certainly have to look far beyond the language of the Ninth Amendment to find that the Framers vested in this Court any such awesome veto powers over lawmaking. [The Ninth] Amendment was passed [to] limit the Federal Government to the powers granted expressly or by necessary implication. [This] fact is perhaps responsible for the peculiar phenomenon that for a period of a century and a half no serious suggestion was ever made that [that] Amendment, enacted to protect state powers against federal invasion, could be used as a weapon of federal power to prevent state legislatures from passing laws they consider appropriate to govern local affairs. * * *

---

7. In *Meyer*, in the very same sentence quoted in part by my Brethren in which he asserted that the Due Process Clause gave an abstract and inviolable right "to marry, establish a home and bring up children," Justice McReynolds asserted also that the Due Process Clause prevented States from interfering with "the right of the individual to contract."

12. See Patterson, *The Forgotten Ninth Amendment* (1955) [who] urges that the Ninth Amendment be used to protect unspecified "natural and inalienable rights." The Introduction by Roscoe Pound states that "there is a marked revival of natural law ideas throughout the world. Interest in the Ninth Amendment is a symptom of that revival." * * *

I realize that many good and able men have eloquently spoken and written [of] the duty of this Court to keep the Constitution in tune with the times [but I] reject that philosophy. The Constitution makers knew the need for change and provided for it. [The] Due Process Clause with an "arbitrary and capricious" or "shocking to the conscience" formula was liberally used by this Court to strike down economic legislation in the early decades of this century, threatening, many people thought, the tranquility and stability of the Nation. See, e.g., *Lochner*. That formula, based on subjective considerations of "natural justice," is no less dangerous when used to enforce this Court's views about personal rights than those about economic rights. [So] far as I am concerned, Connecticut's law as applied here is not forbidden by any provision of the Federal Constitution as that Constitution was written, and I would therefore affirm.

JUSTICE STEWART, whom JUSTICE BLACK joins, dissenting.

[T]his is an uncommonly silly law. As a practical matter, the law is obviously unenforceable, except in the oblique context of the present case. As a philosophical matter, I believe the use of contraceptives in the relationship of marriage should be left to personal and private [choice]. As a matter of social policy, I think professional counsel about methods of birth control should be available to all, so that each individual's choice can be meaningfully made. But we are not [asked] whether we think this law is unwise, or even asinine. We are asked to hold that it violates the United States Constitution. And that I cannot do.

In the course of its opinion the Court refers to no less than six Amendments [but] does not say which of these Amendments, if any, it thinks is infringed by this Connecticut law. [As] to the First, Third, Fourth, and Fifth Amendments, I can find nothing in any of them to invalidate this Connecticut law, even assuming that all those amendments are fully applicable against the States. [The] Ninth Amendment, like its companion the Tenth [was] simply to make clear that the adoption of the Bill of Rights did not alter the plan that the *Federal* Government was to be a government of express and limited powers, and that all rights and powers not delegated to it were retained by the people and the individual States. Until today no member of this Court has ever suggested that the Ninth Amendment meant anything [else].

What provision of the Constitution, then, does make this state law invalid? The Court says it is the right of privacy "created by several fundamental constitutional guarantees." [I] can find no such general right of privacy in the Bill of Rights, in any other part of the Constitution, or in any case ever before decided by this Court. * * *

Notes and Questions

1. *Is Douglas, J.'s argument logical?* Consider Louis Henkin, *Privacy and Autonomy*, 74 Colum.L.Rev. 1410, 1421–22 (1974): "Although it is not wholly clear, Justice Douglas's argument seems to go something like this: since the Constitution, in various 'specifics' of the Bill of Rights and in their penumbra, protects rights which partake of privacy, it protects other aspects of privacy as well, indeed it recognizes a general, complete right of privacy. And since the right emanates from specific fundamental rights, it too is 'fundamental,' its infringement is suspect and calls for strict scrutiny, and it can be justified only by a high level of public good. A logician, I suppose, might have trouble with that argument. A legal draftsman, indeed, might suggest the opposite: when the Constitution sought to protect private rights it specified them; that it explicitly protects some

elements of privacy, but not others, suggests that it did not mean to protect those not mentioned."

2. *Did Griswold successfully avoid "renewing the romance" with "substantive due process"? Griswold,* observes Lupu, at 994, "provided the severest test for a Court determined to advance chosen values [without] renewing the romance with the dreaded demon of substantive due process. [Douglas, J.,] drew upon the incorporation legacy, rather than a doctrine of 'naked' substantive due process, and tortured the Bill of Rights into yielding a protected zone of privacy that would not tolerate a law banning contraceptive use by married couples. Justice Goldberg's reliance upon the ninth amendment [was] equally disingenuous in its attempt to avoid the jaws of substantive due process. Only Justices White and Harlan were willing to grapple directly with the fearful creature, and concluded that a law invading marital choice about contraception violated the due process clause itself, independent of links with the Bill of Rights. Shocking though that analysis may have been at the time, subsequent developments seem to have confirmed the White–Harlan view, and not the magical mystery tour of the zones of privacy, as the prevailing doctrine of *Griswold* [referring to *Moore v. East Cleveland* (1977), infra]."

3. *Emanations-and-penumbras theory and "economic" vs. "personal" rights.* Do any of the Justices analytically distinguish between "economic" and "personal" rights? Or is the distinction "only self-imposed"? Consider Paul Kauper, *Penumbras, Peripheries, Emanations, Things Fundamental and Things Forgotten: The Griswold Case,* 64 Mich.L.Rev. 235, 253 (1965).

4. *Are the courts authorized to plug glaring gaps in the Constitution?* Consider Richard Posner, *Sex and Reason* 328 (1992). Judge Posner is not interested in "joining the snipe hunt for a convincing legal-doctrinal ground for the *Griswold* decision" and "doubt[s] that one exists." "But," he asks, "should that be the end of the legal analysis?" He continues:

"A constitution that did not invalidate so offensive, oppressive, probably undemocratic, and sectarian a law would stand revealed as containing major gaps. Maybe that is the nature of our, as perhaps any, written Constitution; but yet, perhaps the courts are authorized to plug at least the more glaring gaps. Does anyone really believe, in his heart of hearts, that the Constitution should be interpreted so literally as to authorize every conceivable law that would not violate a specific constitutional clause? This would mean that a state could require everyone to marry, or to have sexual intercourse at least once a month, or that it could take away every couple's second child and place it in a foster home. Of course, no state is likely to do such things; and if it were likely, that would argue such a change of moral outlook in this nation as to make our present institutions a poor guide. Yet we do find it reassuring to think that the courts stand between us and legislative tyranny even if a particular form of tyranny was not foreseen and expressly forbidden by the framers of the Constitution."

5. *The "freedom" of a "talented textualist judge."* Although he recognizes that Justice Douglas's *Griswold* opinion "is widely regarded among law professors as fatally flawed," Mark Tushnet, *Two Notes on the Jurisprudence of Privacy,* 8 Const. Comm. 75, 79 (1991), emphasizes that "Justice Douglas's construct is purely textualist; that is, it pays close attention to the language of the Constitution and to the relations among its specific provisions.[a] * * * Textualism is

a. But cf. Henry Greely, *A Footnote to* "*Penumbra*" *in Griswold v. Connecticut,* 6 Const. Comm. 251, 262–65 (1989).

ordinarily regarded as the most confining technique of constitutional interpretation, the one that places the most severe limits on a judge's ability to enact personal preferences into constitutional law. Justice Douglas's construct shows that this common perception is erroneous. A talented textualist judge has as much freedom as a talented nontextualist, whether the nontextualist is an originalist, an ethicist, or a process theorist. [By] showing that the purportedly most confining technique of constitutional interpretation can be turned to quite unexpected ends, Justice Douglas's opinion in *Griswold* supports the argument that controversies over methods of constitutional interpretation are unlikely to yield fruitful results of any sort."

6. *"Privacy" or "equality"*? "Seen in the context of the Warren Court's general jurisprudence," observes Martin Shapiro, *Fathers and Sons: The Court, the Commentators, and the Search for Values,* in The Burger Court 218, 228 (V. Blasi ed. 1983), "the fact situation in [*Griswold*] was crucial. The living law of Connecticut was that middle-class women received birth control information and purchased birth control supplies, and the Connecticut statute was enforced only to block the operation of birth control clinics that would bring these services to the poor. *Griswold* was an equality not a privacy decision * * *."

7. *Skinner and Griswold taken together.* Consider Tribe 2d ed., at 1340: "Taken together with *Griswold,* which recognized as equally protected the individual's decision *not* to bear a child, the meaning of *Skinner* is that *whether one person's body shall be the source of another's life must be left to that person and that person alone to decide.* That principle seems to collide in the abortion cases [infra] with a command that is no less fundamental: *an innocent life may not be taken except to save the life of another.*"

Griswold invalidated a ban on the *use* of contraceptives by *married* couples. EISENSTADT v. BAIRD, 405 U.S. 438, 92 S.Ct. 1029, 31 L.Ed.2d 349 (1972), overturned a conviction for violating a Massachusetts law making it a felony to *distribute* contraceptive materials, *except* in the case of registered physicians and pharmacists furnishing the materials to *married* persons. Baird had given a woman a package of vaginal foam at the end of his lecture on contraception. He was not charged with distributing to an unmarried person. No proof was offered as to the recipient's marital status. The crime charged was that Baird had no license, and thus no authority, to distribute to anyone. The Court, per BRENNAN, J., concluded that, since the statute is riddled with exceptions making contraceptives freely available and since, if protection of health were the rationale, the statute would be both discriminatory and overbroad, "the goals of deterring premarital sex and regulating the distribution of potentially harmful articles cannot reasonably be regarded as legislative aims." "[V]iewed as a prohibition on contraception per se" the statute "violates the rights of single persons under the Equal Protection Clause." For, "whatever the rights of the individual to access to contraceptives may be, the rights must be the same for the unmarried and the married alike":

"If under *Griswold* the distribution of contraceptives to married persons cannot be prohibited, a ban on distribution to unmarried persons would be equally impermissible. It is true that in *Griswold* the right of privacy in question inhered in the marital relationship. Yet the marital couple is not an independent entity with a mind and heart of its own, but an association of two individuals each with a separate intellectual and emotional make-up. If the right of privacy means anything, it is the right of the *individual,* married or single, to be free from unwarranted governmental intrusion into matters so fundamentally affecting a person as the decision whether to bear or beget a child. On the other hand, if *Griswold* is no bar to a prohibition on the distribution of contraceptives, the State could not, consistently with [equal protection,] outlaw distribution to unmarried but not to married persons. In each case the evil, as perceived by the State, would be identical, and the underinclusion would be invidious."

WHITE, J., joined by Blackmun, J., concurred, emphasizing that "the State did [not] convict Baird for distributing to an unmarried person [but because] Baird had no license and therefore no authority to distribute to anyone." "Given *Griswold,* and absent proof of the possible hazards of using vaginal foam, we could not sustain [Baird's] conviction had it been for selling or giving away foam to a married person. Just as in *Griswold,* where the right of married persons to use contraceptives was 'diluted or adversely affected' by permitting a conviction for giving advice as to its exercise, so here to sanction a medical restriction upon distribution of a contraceptive not proved hazardous to health would impair the exercise of the constitutional right. That Baird could not be convicted for distributing [foam] to a married person disposes of this case. Assuming arguendo that the result would be otherwise had the recipient been unmarried, nothing has been placed in the record to indicate her marital status."[a]

Burger, C.J., dissented, "see[ing] nothing in the Fourteenth Amendment or any other part of the Constitution that even vaguely suggests that these medicinal forms of contraceptives must be available in the open market. [By] relying on *Griswold* in the present context, the Court has passed beyond the penumbras of the specific guarantees into the uncircumscribed area of personal predilections."

Notes and Questions

1. *Does Eisenstadt offer a new rationale for Griswold?* Did *Eisenstadt* decide one of *Griswold's* open issues—the constitutionality of a ban on the use or distribution of contraceptive devices that excluded from its reach the married couple—"by assertion, without a pretext of reasoning"? Harry Wellington, *Common Law Rules and Constitutional Double Standards,* 83 Yale L.J. 221, 296 (1973), so charges: "[W]hether the 'different classes' (married, not married) are [as *Eisenstadt* states] 'wholly unrelated to the objective of the statute,' depends on whether, as *Griswold* insists, the marriage relationship is important to that aspect of liberty that the Court calls privacy. How, then, [could the Court write *Eisenstadt* the way it did] without offering a new rationale for *Griswold*[?]" Cf. Thomas Gerety, *Doing Without Privacy,* 42 Ohio St.L.J. 143–44 (1981).

2. *Griswold "unmasked"?* Consider Richard Posner, *The Uncertain Protection of Privacy by the Supreme Court,* 1979 Sup.Ct.Rev. 173, 198: "*Griswold* had at least attempted to relate the right to use contraceptives to familiar notions of privacy by speculating on the intrusive methods by which a statute banning the use of contraceptives might be enforced. This ground was unavailable in [*Eisenstadt*] because the statute there forbade not the use, but only the distribution, of contraceptives. [*Eisenstadt*] is thus a pure essay in substantive due process. It unmasks *Griswold* as based on the idea of sexual liberty rather than privacy." Cf.

a. Douglas, J., who joined the Court's opinion, also concurred on free speech grounds. Powell and Rehnquist, JJ., did not participate.

Michael Perry, *Abortion, the Public Morals, and the Police Power,* 23 U.C.L.A.L.Rev. 689, 705–06 (1976).

3. *The real objection to the statute at issue in Eisenstadt.* The real objection, observes Richard Posner, *Sex and Reason* 330 (1992), "is not that it cannot deter fornication. It will deter some. Indeed, it will deter a good deal more than a statute, unenforceable as a practical matter, making fornication a misdemeanor— the statute whose constitutionality was not questioned." Continues Posner:

"The real objection to the statute is that there is no good reason to deter premarital sex, a generally harmless source of pleasure and for some people an important stage of marital search. (Yet this is an equal objection to a statute forbidding fornication, and the Court has never questioned the constitutionality of such statutes.) There are good reasons for wanting to deter unwanted pregnancies, but that aim is more likely to be achieved by encouraging than by discouraging the use of contraceptives. [An implication of the Court's opinion] is that notwithstanding the unchallenged misdemeanor fornication law (easily overlooked because totally unenforced), unmarried persons have a constitutional right to engage in sexual intercourse. For if they do not, it is an illegal activity; and how can the Constitution be violated by a state's prohibiting the sale of an input (contraception) into that activity?"

4. *The seed from which Roe grew.* According to Charles Fried, *Order and Law* 77 (1991), when Brennan, J., made the "passing remark" in *Eisenstadt* about the right of the individual to be free from unwarranted governmental intrusion into such matters "as the decision whether to bear or beget a child" he "planted" the "seed [from] which *Roe* grew, so that later [in *Carey* (1977), discussed next], [he] could say that what *Griswold* stood for all along was the proposition that there is a 'constitutional protection of individual autonomy in matters of childbearing.' [When] Justice Brennan, in [*Eisenstadt*], a contraception case, slipped in the irrelevant term 'childbearing,' he was digging a kind of surreptitious doctrinal tunnel to get from *Poe* to *Roe,* a tunnel that a year later would allow Justice Blackmun to get past the critical barrier between contraception and abortion, between what undoubtedly is a matter of privacy and what to some is murder."

5. *From Griswold to Eisenstadt to Carey.* The effect of *Eisenstadt*, notes Tribe, 2d ed., at 1339, was to "single out as decisive in *Griswold* the element of reproductive autonomy, something the Court made clear in 1977, when it extended *Griswold* and *Baird*" in CAREY v. POPULATION SERVICES INTERN., 431 U.S. 678, 97 S.Ct. 2010, 52 L.Ed.2d 675 (1977), to invalidate a New York law which allowed only pharmacists to sell non-medical contraceptive devices to persons over 16 and prohibited the sale of such items to those under 16. (The Court relied in part on the 1973 *Abortion Cases,* infra.) In striking down the restriction on sales to adults, BRENNAN, J., spoke for six justices; in invalidating the ban on sales to those under 16, he spoke for a four-justice plurality.

As for the restriction on distribution to adults, "where a decision as fundamental as that whether to bear or beget a child is involved, regulations imposing a burden on it may be justified only by compelling interests, and must be narrowly drawn to express only those interests"—and the Court found none of the state interests advanced (e.g., protecting health, facilitating enforcement of other laws) to be "compelling."[a] The state argued that *Griswold* dealt only with the *use* of contraceptives, not their manufacture or sale, but read "in light of its progeny, the

---

a. The Court recognized, however, that "other restrictions may well be reasonably related to the objective of quality control," and thus "express[ed] no opinion on, for example, restrictions on the distribution of contraceptives through vending machines."

teaching of *Griswold* is that the Constitution protects individual decisions in matters of childbearing from unjustified intrusion by the State."

As for the ban on sales to those under 16, Brennan, J., joined by Stewart, Marshall, and Blackmun, JJ., applied a test "apparently less rigorous than the 'compelling state interest' test applied to restrictions on the privacy rights of adults"—restrictions inhibiting privacy rights of minors are valid "only if they serve 'any significant state interest [that] is not present in the case of an adult.' *Planned Parenthood v. Danforth,* infra]." The plurality then rejected what it called "the argument [that] minors' sexual activity may be deterred by increasing the hazards attendant on it," pointing out that that argument had already been rejected by the Court in related areas.[b]

Powell, J., concurred in the judgment, observing that by restricting not only the kinds of retail outlets that may distribute contraceptives, "but even prohibit[ing] distribution by mail to adults"—"thus requiring individuals to buy contraceptives over the counter"—the New York provision "heavily burdens constitutionally protected freedom." He saw "no justification for subjecting restrictions on the sexual activity of the young to heightened judicial review"—"a standard that for all practical purposes approaches the 'compelling interest' standard"—but concurred in the invalidation of the "distribution to minors" restriction on narrow grounds.[c]

ORAL ARGUMENTS IN THE ABORTION CASES*

* * *

THE COURT: [I]s it critical to your case that the fetus not be a person under the due process clause? [W]ould you lose your case if the fetus was a person?

SARAH WEDDINGTON [on behalf of appellant Roe]: Then you would have a balancing of interests.

THE COURT: Well you say you have [that] anyway, don't you? * * *

THE COURT: [If] it were established that an unborn fetus is a person, [protected by] the Fourteenth Amendment, you would have almost an impossible case here, would you not?

WEDDINGTON: I would have a very difficult case. * * *

THE COURT: Could Texas constitutionally, in your view, declare [by] statute [that] the fetus is a person, for all constitutional purposes, after the third month of gestation?

---

b. Nor was the restriction on the privacy rights of minors "saved" by another provision authorizing physicians to supply minors with contraceptives. As with limitations on distribution to adults, "less than total restrictions on access to contraceptives that significantly burden the right to decide whether to bear children must also pass constitutional muster. [This provision] delegates the State's authority to disapprove of minors' sexual behavior to physicians, who may exercise it arbitrarily * * *."

c. White and Stevens, JJ., concurred only in the judgment with respect to the restriction on minors. Rehnquist, J., dissented, observing that if those responsible for the Bill of Rights and Civil War Amendments could have lived to know what their efforts had wrought "it is not difficult to imagine their reaction." Burger, C.J., dissented without opinion.

* These extracts are taken from 75 *Landmark Briefs and Arguments of the Supreme Court of the United States: Constitutional Law* 807–33 (Kurland & Casper ed.).

WEDDINGTON: I do not believe that the State legislature can determine the meaning of the Federal Constitution. It is up to this Court to make that determination. * * *

ROBERT FLOWERS [on behalf of appellee]: [I]t is the position of the State of Texas that, upon conception, we have a human being; a person, within the concept of the Constitution of the United States, and that of Texas, also.

THE COURT: Now how should that question be decided? Is it a legal question? A constitutional question? A medical question? A philosophical question? Or, a religious question? Or what is it?

FLOWERS: [W]e feel that it could be best decided by a legislature, in view of the fact that they can bring before it the medical testimony * * *.

THE COURT: So then it's basically a medical question?

FLOWERS: From a constitutional standpoint, no, sir. * * *

THE COURT: Of course, if you're right about [the fetus being a person within the meaning of the Constitution], you can sit down, you've won your case. * * * Except insofar as, maybe, the Texas abortion law presently goes too far in allowing abortions.

FLOWERS: Yes, sir. That's exactly right. * * *

THE COURT: Do you think [you have] lost your case, then, if the fetus or the embryo is not a person? Is that it?

FLOWERS: Yes sir, I would say so. * * *

THE COURT: Well, if you're right that an unborn fetus is a person, then you can't leave it to the legislature to play fast and loose dealing with that person. [I]f you're correct, in your basic submission that an unborn fetus is a person, then abortion laws such as that which New York has are grossly unconstitutional, isn't it?

FLOWERS: That's right, yes.

THE COURT: Allowing the killing of people.

FLOWERS: Yes, sir. * * *

[Rebuttal argument of Weddington]

THE COURT: [I] gather your argument is that a state may not protect the life of the fetus or prevent an abortion [at] any time during pregnancy? Right up until the moment of birth? * * *

WEDDINGTON: [T]here is no indication [that] the Constitution would give any protection prior to birth. That is not before the Court. * * *

THE COURT: Well, I don't know whether it is or isn't. * * *

ROE v. WADE

410 U.S. 113, 93 S.Ct. 705, 35 L.Ed.2d 147 (1973).

JUSTICE BLACKMUN delivered the opinion of the Court.

This Texas federal appeal and its Georgia companion, *Doe v. Bolton,* [infra,] present constitutional challenges to state criminal abortion legislation. The Texas statutes [are] typical of those that have been in effect in many States for approximately a century. The Georgia statutes, in contrast, have a modern cast and are a legislative product that, to an extent at least, obviously reflects the influences of recent attitudinal change, of advancing medical knowledge and techniques, and of new [thinking]. The Texas statutes [make procuring an abortion a crime except] "by medical advice for the purpose of saving the life of the mother."

[Jane] Roe alleged that she was unmarried and pregnant [and] that she was unable to get a "legal" abortion in Texas because her life did not appear to be threatened by the continuation of her pregnancy.[a] [The district court held the Texas abortion statutes unconstitutional, but denied the injunctive relief requested. Roe appealed.]

[R]estrictive criminal abortion laws [like Texas'] in effect in a majority of States [today] derive from statutory changes effected, for the most part, in the latter half of the 19th century. [The Court then reviewed, in some detail, "ancient attitudes," "the Hippocratic Oath" which forbids abortion, "the common law," "the English statutory law," and "the American law." Subsequently, it described the positions of the American Medical Association, the American Public Health Association, and the American Bar Association. Thus,] at common law, at the time of the adoption of our Constitution, and throughout the major portion of the 19th century, [a] woman enjoyed a substantially broader right to terminate a pregnancy than she does in most States today. * * *

Three reasons have been advanced to explain historically the enactment of criminal abortion laws in the 19th century and to justify their [continuance].

It has been argued occasionally that these laws were the product of a Victorian social concern to discourage illicit sexual conduct. Texas, however, does not advance this justification [and] it appears that no court or commentator has taken the argument seriously.

[A] second reason is [that when] most criminal abortion laws were first enacted, the procedure was a hazardous one for the woman. [But] medical data indicat[es] that abortion in early pregnancy, that is, prior to the end of first trimester, although not without its risk, is now relatively safe.

[The] third reason is the State's interest—some phrase it in terms of duty—in protecting prenatal life. Some of the argument for this justification rests on the theory that a new human life is present from the moment of conception. [Only] when the life of the pregnant mother herself is at stake, balanced against the life she carries within her, should the interest of the embryo or fetus not prevail. [In]

---

a. Who was "Jane Roe"? Her real name was Norma McCorvey. Shortly after *Roe* was decided, she revealed who she really was. She explained then that she was an unmarried woman who had become pregnant as a result of a gang rape. She had tried to get an abortion, but had been unable to pay the price ($650) demanded by a doctor she finally found who was willing to perform an abortion. Because she did not want to subject to "public ridicule" a young child she had from a previous marriage, Ms. McCorvey's one condition for going ahead with the legal challenge was that she remain anonymous. See Philip Bobbitt, *Constitutional Fate* 165 (1982); Fred Friendly & Martha Elliott, *The Constitution: That Delicate Balance* 202–04 (1984). But, as noted in Laurence Tribe, *Abortion: The Clash of Abso-* *lutes* 5 (1990), a decade and a half after *Roe* was decided "McCorvey explained, with embarrassment, that she had not been raped after all; she had made up the story to hide the fact that she had gotten 'in trouble' in the more usual way. Many reacted with dismay. How could the heroine of the most important abortion rights case have deceived the advocates of such rights?" Comments Tribe: "Few asked why [McCorvey] had felt a *need* to deceive them. In a different sort of society the life she would have faced as an unwed mother might not have been nearly so lonely. In such a society she might not have made up a story about how she became pregnant. In such a society she might not even have chosen an abortion."

"Bald assertion masquerades as reasoning"
— J. Blackman

assessing the State's interest, recognition may be given to the less rigid claim that as long as at least *potential* life is involved, the State may assert interests beyond the protection of the pregnant woman alone. [It] is with these interests, and the weight to be attached to them, that this case is concerned.

The Constitution does not explicitly mention any right of privacy. [But] the Court has recognized that a right of personal privacy, or a guarantee of certain areas or zones of privacy, does exist under the Constitution. In varying contexts the Court or individual Justices have indeed found at least the roots of that right in the First Amendment, *Stanley v. Georgia* [p. 651 infra]; in the Fourth and Fifth Amendments; in the penumbras of the Bill of Rights, *Griswold;* in the Ninth Amendment, id. (Goldberg, J., concurring); or in the concept of liberty guaranteed by the first section of the Fourteenth Amendment, see *Meyer*. These decisions make it clear that only personal rights that can be deemed "fundamental" or "implicit in the concept of ordered liberty," are included in this guarantee of personal privacy. They also make it clear that the right has some extension to activities relating to marriage, *Loving;* procreation, *Skinner;* contraception, *Eisenstadt;* family relationships, *Prince v. Massachusetts* [discussed at p. 1100 infra]; and child rearing and education, *Pierce*.[b]

This right of privacy, whether it be founded in the Fourteenth Amendment's concept of personal liberty [as] we feel it is, [or] in the [Ninth Amendment], is broad enough to encompass a woman's decision whether or not to terminate her pregnancy. The detriment that the State would impose upon the pregnant woman by denying this choice altogether is apparent. Specific and direct harm medically diagnosable even in early pregnancy may be [involved]. Psychological harm may be imminent. Mental and physical health may be taxed by child care. There is also the distress, for all concerned, associated with the unwanted child, and there is the problem of bringing a child into a family already unable, psychologically and otherwise, to care for it. In other cases, as in this one, the additional difficulties and continuing stigma of unwed motherhood may be involved. All these are factors the woman and her responsible physician necessarily will consider in consultation.

On the basis of elements such as these, appellants and some amici argue that the woman's right is absolute and that she is entitled to terminate her pregnancy at whatever time, in whatever way, and for whatever reason she alone chooses. With this we do not agree. [The] Court's decisions recognizing a right of privacy also acknowledge that some state regulation in areas protected by that right is appropriate. [A] state may properly assert important interests in safeguarding health, in maintaining medical standards, and in protecting potential life. At some point in pregnancy, these respective interests become sufficiently compelling to sustain regulation of the factors that govern the abortion decision.

[Where] certain "fundamental rights" are involved, the Court has held that regulation limiting these rights may be justified only by a "compelling state interest," and that legislative enactments must be narrowly drawn to express only the legitimate state interests at stake.

[Appellee argues] that the fetus is a "person" within the language and meaning of the Fourteenth Amendment. [If so,] appellant's case, of course, collapses, for the fetus' right to life is then guaranteed specifically by the Amendment.

b. Do these parental rights permit parents to forbid public school teachers from imposing corporal punishment on their children? See *Ingraham v. Wright* (1977) (p. 550, fn. e infra).

[The] Constitution does not define "person" in so many words. [The Court then listed each provision in which the word appears.] But in nearly all these instances, the use of the word is such that it has application only postnatally. None indicates, with any assurance, that it has any possible pre-natal application. All this, together with our observation that throughout the major portion of the 19th century prevailing legal abortion practices were far freer [than] today, persuades us that the word "person," as used in the Fourteenth Amendment, does not include the unborn. [Thus,] we pass on to other considerations.

The pregnant woman cannot be isolated in her privacy. She carries an embryo and, later, a fetus. [The] situation therefore is inherently different from marital intimacy, or bedroom possession of obscene material, or marriage, or procreation, or education, with which *Eisenstadt, Griswold, Stanley, Loving, Skinner, Pierce,* and *Meyer* [were] concerned.

[Texas] urges that, apart from the Fourteenth Amendment, life begins at conception and is present throughout pregnancy, and that, therefore, the State has a compelling interest in protecting that life from and after conception. We need not resolve the difficult question of when life begins. When those trained [in] medicine, philosophy, and theology are unable to arrive at any consensus, the judiciary, at this point in the development of man's knowledge, is not in a position to speculate as to the answer.

[W]e do not agree that, by adopting one theory of life, Texas may override the rights of the pregnant woman that are at stake. We repeat, however, that the State does have an important and legitimate interest in preserving and protecting the health of the pregnant woman [and] that it has still *another* important and legitimate interest in protecting the potentiality of human life. These interests are separate and distinct. Each grows in substantiality as the woman approaches term and, at a point during pregnancy, each becomes "compelling."

With respect to [the] interest in the health of the mother, the "compelling" point, in the light of present medical knowledge, is at approximately the end of the first trimester. This is so because of the now established medical fact that until the end of the first trimester mortality in abortion is less than mortality in normal childbirth. It follows that, from and after this point, a State may regulate the abortion procedure to the extent that the regulation reasonably relates to the preservation and protection of maternal health. Examples of permissible state regulation in this area are requirements as to the qualifications of the person who is to perform the abortion; [as] to the facility in which the procedure is to be performed, [and] the like. This means, on the other hand, that, for the period of pregnancy prior to this "compelling" point, the attending physician, in consultation with his patient, is free to determine, without regulation by the State, that in his medical judgment the patient's pregnancy should be terminated. If that decision is reached, the judgment may be effectuated by an abortion free of interference by the State.

With respect to [the] interest in potential life, the "compelling" point is at viability [which "is usually placed at about seven months (28 weeks) but may occur earlier, even at 24 weeks."] This is so because the fetus then presumably has the capability of meaningful life outside the mother's womb.[c] State regulation

c. Earlier in its opinion, the Court described the point "at which the fetus becomes 'viable'" as the point that the fetus is "potentially able to live outside the mother's womb, albeit with artificial aid." *Planned Parenthood v. Danforth*, 428 U.S. 52, 96 S.Ct. 2381, 49 L. Ed.2d 788 (1976), per Blackmun, J., upheld a Missouri abortion statute defining "viability" as "that stage of fetal development when the life of the unborn child may be continued in-

protective of fetal life after viability thus has both logical and biological justifications. If the State is interested in protecting fetal life after viability, it may go as far as to proscribe abortion during that period except when it is necessary to preserve the life or health of the mother.

Measured against these standards, [the Texas statute] sweeps too broadly [and] therefore, cannot survive the constitutional attack made upon it here.

[In] *Doe* [infra], procedural requirements contained in one of the modern abortion statutes are considered. That opinion and this one [are] to be read together.[67]

This holding, we feel, is consistent with the relative weights of the respective interests involved, with the lessons and examples of medical and legal history, with the lenity of the common law, and with the demands of the profound problems of the present day. The decision leaves the State free to place increasing restrictions on abortion as the period of pregnancy lengthens, so long as those restrictions are tailored to the recognized state interests. The decision vindicates the right of the physician to administer medical treatment according to his professional judgment up to the points where important state interests provide compelling justifications for intervention. Up to those points, the abortion decision in all its aspects is inherently, and primarily, a medical decision, and basic responsibility for it must rest with the physician. If an individual practitioner abuses the privilege of exercising proper medical judgment, the usual remedies, judicial and intra-professional, are available. * * *

JUSTICE STEWART, concurring.

In 1963, this Court, in *Ferguson v. Skrupa* [p. 304 supra], purported to sound the death knell for the doctrine of substantive due process, [but] [b]arely two years later, in *Griswold,* the Court held a Connecticut birth control law unconstitutional. [T]he *Griswold* decision can be rationally understood only as a holding that the Connecticut statute substantively invaded the "liberty" that is protected by the Due Process Clause of the Fourteenth Amendment. As so understood, *Griswold* stands as one in a long line of pre-*Skrupa* cases decided under the doctrine of substantive due process, and I now accept it as such.

definitely outside the womb by natural or artificial life-supportive systems." In rejecting contentions that the Missouri statute unduly expanded the *Roe* Court's definition of "viability," failed to contain any reference to a gestational time period, and failed to incorporate and reflect the three stages of pregnancy, the Court observed: "[W]e recognized in *Roe* that viability was a matter of medical judgment, skill, and technical ability, and we preserved the flexibility of the term. [The Missouri statute] does the same. [I]t is not the proper function of the legislature or the courts to place viability, which essentially is a medical concept, at a specific point in the gestation period. The time when viability is achieved may vary with each pregnancy, and the determination of whether a particular fetus is viable is, and must be, a matter for the judgment of the responsible attending physician. [The statutory definition] merely reflects this fact."

Consider, too, *Colautti v. Franklin,* 439 U.S. 379, 99 S.Ct. 675, 58 L.Ed.2d 596 (1979), per

Blackmun, J., [reaffirming] that the determination of "viability" is "a matter for medical judgment" and that viability is reached "when, in the judgment of the attending physician on the particular facts of the case before him, there is a reasonable likelihood of the fetus' sustained survival outside the womb, with or without artificial support. Because this point may differ with each pregnancy, neither the legislature nor the courts may proclaim one of the elements entering into the ascertainment of viability—be it weeks of gestation or fetal weight or any other single factor—as the determinant of when the State has a compelling interest in the life or health of the fetus."

67. Neither in this opinion nor in *Doe* do we discuss the father's rights, if any exist in the constitutional context, in the abortion decision. No paternal right has been asserted in either of the [cases].

[The] Constitution nowhere mentions a specific right of personal choice in matters of marriage and family life, but the "liberty" protected by the Due Process Clause of the Fourteenth Amendment covers more than those freedoms explicitly named in the Bill of Rights. [As] recently as last Term, in *Eisenstadt,* we recognized "the right of the *individual,* married or single, to be free from unwarranted governmental intrusion into matters so fundamentally affecting a person as the decision whether to bear or beget a child." That right necessarily includes the right of a woman to decide whether or not to terminate her pregnancy. [It] is evident that the Texas abortion statute infringes that right directly. [The] question then becomes whether the state interests advanced to justify this abridgment can survive the "particularly careful scrutiny" that the Fourteenth Amendment here requires.

The asserted state interests are protection of the health and safety of the pregnant woman, and protection of the potential future human life within her. These are legitimate objectives, amply sufficient to permit a State to regulate abortions as it does other surgical procedures, and perhaps sufficient to permit a State to regulate abortions more stringently or even to prohibit them in the late stages of pregnancy. But such legislation is not before us, and I think the Court today has thoroughly demonstrated that these state interests cannot constitutionally support the broad abridgment of personal liberty worked by the existing Texas law. * * *

JUSTICE DOUGLAS, concurring [in *Doe* as well as in *Roe*].

While I join the opinion of the Court, I add a few words.

[The] Ninth Amendment obviously does not create federally enforceable rights. [But] a catalogue of [the rights "retained by the people"] includes customary, traditional, and time-honored rights, amenities, privileges, and immunities that come within the sweep of "the Blessings of Liberty" mentioned in the preamble to the Constitution. Many of them in my view come within the meaning of the term "liberty" as used in the Fourteenth Amendment.

First is the autonomous control over the development and expression of one's intellect, interests, tastes, and personality. These are rights protected by the First Amendment and in my view they are absolute * * *.

Second is freedom of choice in the basic decisions of one's life respecting marriage, divorce, procreation, contraception, and the education and upbringing of children. These rights, unlike those protected by the First Amendment, are subject to some control by the police power. [They] are "fundamental" and we have held that in order to support legislative action the statute must be narrowly and precisely drawn and that a "compelling state interest" must be shown in support of the limitation. * * *[4]

[Third] is the freedom to care for one's health and person, freedom from bodily restraint or compulsion, freedom to walk, stroll, or loaf. These rights, though fundamental, are likewise subject to regulation on a showing of "compelling state

---

4. My Brother Stewart, writing in the present cases, says that our decision in *Griswold* reintroduced substantive due process that had been rejected in [*Skrupa*]. There is nothing specific in the Bill of Rights that covers [the marital relation]. Nor is there anything in the Bill of Rights that in terms protects the right of association or the privacy in one's association. [Other] peripheral rights are the right to educate one's children as one chooses, and the right to study the German language. These decisions with all respect, have nothing to do with substantive due process. One may think they are not peripheral rights to other rights that are expressed in the Bill of Rights. But that is not enough to bring into play the protection of substantive due process. * * *

interest." * * * Elaborate argument is hardly necessary to demonstrate that childbirth may deprive a woman of her preferred life style and force upon her a radically different and undesired future.

[Such reasoning] is, however, only the beginning of the problem. [V]oluntary abortion at any time and place regardless of medical standards would impinge on a rightful concern of society. The woman's health is part of that concern; as is the life of the fetus after quickening. These concerns justify the State in treating the procedure as a medical one.

[T]he Georgia statute outlaws virtually all such operations—even in the earliest stages of pregnancy. In light of modern medical evidence [it] cannot be seriously urged that so comprehensive a ban is aimed at protecting the woman's health. Rather, [this ban] can rest only on a public goal of preserving both embryonic and fetal life.

The present statute has struck the balance between the woman and the State's interests wholly in favor of the latter. [We] held in *Griswold* that the States may not preclude spouses from attempting to avoid the joinder of sperm and egg. [I]t is difficult to perceive any overriding public necessity which might attach precisely at the moment of conception.

[The] protection of the fetus when it has acquired life is a legitimate concern of the State. Georgia's law makes no rational, discernible decision on that score. For under the Act the developmental stage of the fetus is irrelevant when pregnancy is the result of rape or when the fetus will very likely be born with a permanent defect or when a continuation of the pregnancy will endanger the life of the mother or permanently injure her health. When life is present is a question we do not try to resolve. While basically a question for medical experts, [it is], of course, caught up in matters of religion and morality. * * *

JUSTICE WHITE, with whom JUSTICE REHNQUIST joins, dissenting [in *Doe* as well as in *Roe*].

At the heart of the controversy in these cases are those recurring pregnancies that pose no danger whatsoever to the life or health of the mother but are nevertheless unwanted for any one or more of a variety of reasons—convenience, family planning, economics, dislike of children, the embarrassment of illegitimacy, etc. The common claim before us is that for any one of such reasons, or for no reason at all, and without asserting or claiming any threat to life or health, any woman is entitled to an abortion at her request if she is able to find a medical advisor willing to [perform it].

The Court for the most part sustains this position [and] simply fashions and announces a new constitutional right [and], with scarcely any reason or authority for its action, invests that right with sufficient substance to override most existing state abortion statutes. The upshot is that the people and the legislatures of the 50 States are constitutionally disentitled to weigh the relative importance of the continued existence and development of the fetus on the one hand against a spectrum of possible impacts on the mother on the other hand. As an exercise of raw judicial power, the Court perhaps has authority [but] in my view its judgment is an improvident and extravagant exercise of the power of judicial review * * *.

JUSTICE REHNQUIST, dissenting. * * *

I have difficulty in concluding [that] the right of "privacy" is involved in this case. [Texas] bars the performance of a medical abortion by a licensed physician on a plaintiff such as Roe. A transaction resulting in an operation such as this is not "private" in the ordinary usage of that word. Nor is the "privacy" which the

Court finds here even a distant relative of the freedom from searches and seizures protected by the Fourth Amendment.

[If] the Court means by the term "privacy" no more than that the claim of a person to be free from unwanted state regulation of consensual transactions may be a form of "liberty" * * * I agree [with] Mr. Justice Stewart [that that "liberty"] embraces more than the rights found in the Bill of Rights. But that liberty is not guaranteed absolutely against deprivation, but only against deprivation without due process of law. The test traditionally applied in the area of social and economic legislation is whether or not a law such as that challenged has a rational relation to a valid state objective. [If] the Texas statute were to prohibit an abortion even where the mother's life is in jeopardy, I have little doubt that such a statute would lack a rational relation to a valid state [objective].[d] But the Court's sweeping invalidation of any restrictions on abortion during the first trimester is impossible to justify under that [standard]. As in *Lochner* and similar cases applying substantive due process standards to economic and social welfare legislation, the adoption of the compelling state interest standard will inevitably require this Court to examine the legislative policies and pass on the wisdom of these policies in the very process of deciding whether a particular state interest put forward may or may not be "compelling." The decision here to break the term of pregnancy into three distinct terms and to outline the permissible restrictions the State may impose in each one, for example, partakes more of judicial legislation than it does of a determination of the intent of the drafters of the Fourteenth Amendment.

The fact that a majority of the States, reflecting after all the majority sentiment in those States, have had restrictions on abortions for at least a century seems to me as strong an indication there is that the asserted right to an abortion is not "so rooted in the traditions and conscience of our people as to be ranked as fundamental." Even today, when society's views on abortion are changing, the very existence of the debate is evidence that the "right" to an abortion is not so universally accepted as the appellants would have us believe.

[By] the time of the adoption of the Fourteenth Amendment in 1868 there were at least 36 laws enacted by state or territorial legislatures limiting abortion. [The] only conclusion possible from this history is that the drafters did not intend to have the Fourteenth Amendment withdraw from the States the power to legislate with respect to this matter. * * *

DOE v. BOLTON, 410 U.S. 179, 93 S.Ct. 739, 35 L.Ed.2d 201 (1973), the companion case to *Roe v. Wade,* sustained, against the contention that it had been rendered unconstitutionally vague by a three-judge district court's interpretation, a Georgia provision that permitted a physician to perform an abortion when "based upon his best clinical judgment that an abortion is necessary." (The district court had struck down the statutorily specified reasons: because continued pregnancy would endanger a pregnant woman's life or injure her health; the fetus would likely be born with a serious defect; or the pregnancy resulted from rape.) "The net result of the district court's decision," observed the Court, "is that the abortion determination, so far as the physician is concerned, is made in the

d. Is it "irrational" or "invalid" for a state to weigh the *possibility* (or even *probability*) that the mother will die without an abortion against the *certainty* that the fetus will not survive with one and then to legislate against abortions in such situations?

exercise of his professional, that is, his 'best clinical,' judgment in the light of all the attendant circumstances. He is not now restricted to the three situations originally specified. Instead, [the] medical judgment may be exercised in light of all factors—physical, emotional, psychological, familial, and the woman's age—relevant to the well-being of the patient. All these factors may relate to health. This allows the attending physician the room he needs to make his best medical judgment. And it is room that operates for the benefit, not the disadvantage, of the pregnant woman.''

However, despite the fact that the Georgia statute was patterned after the American Law Institute's Model Penal Code (1962), which had served as the model for recent legislation in about one-fourth of the states, the Court, per BLACKMUN, J., invalidated substantial portions of the statute. Struck down were requirements (1) that the abortion be performed in a hospital accredited by the Joint Commission on Accreditation of Hospitals (JCAH); (2) that the procedure be approved by a hospital staff abortion committee; and (3) that the performing physician's judgment be confirmed by independent examinations of the patient by two other physicians.

As for (1): There is no restriction of the performance of nonabortion surgery in a hospital not accredited by the JCAH. This requirement is also invalid ''because it fails to exclude the first trimester of pregnancy, see *Roe*. [As] for (2), [we] see no constitutionally justifiable pertinence [for] the advance approval by the abortion committee. We are not cited to any other surgical procedure made subject to committee approval as a matter of state criminal law. The woman's right to receive medical care in accordance with the licensed physician's best judgment and the physician's right to administer it are substantially limited by this statutorily imposed overview.'' As for (3), the two-doctor concurrence, ''the statute's emphasis [is] on the attending physician's 'best clinical judgment that an abortion is necessary.' That should be sufficient. [No] other voluntary medical or surgical procedure for which Georgia requires confirmation by two other physicians has been cited to us.''

COMMENTARY ON THE *ABORTION CASES*: (A) WHETHER AND WHY THE CASES WERE WRONGLY DECIDED; (B) HOW A BETTER OPINION REACHING THE SAME RESULT MIGHT HAVE BEEN WRITTEN; AND (C) WHAT LIGHT THE CASES SHED ON THE NATURE OF THE BURGER COURT'S ACTIVISM

1. *The linkage between the abortion decision and the privacy cases.* Consider Susan Estrich & Kathleen Sullivan, *Abortion Politics: Writing for an Audience of One,* 138 U.Pa.L.Rev. 119, 125–27 (1989): ''The privacy cases rest, on 'the moral fact that a person belongs to himself [or herself] and not others nor to society as a whole.' Extending this principle to the abortion decision follows from the fact that '[f]ew decisions [are] more basic to individual dignity and autonomy' or more appropriate to the 'private sphere of individual liberty' than the uniquely personal, intimate, and self-defining decision whether or not to continue a pregnancy [quoting from Blackmun, J., for the Court, in *Thornburgh*.].

''In two senses, abortion restrictions keep a woman from 'belonging to herself.' First [they] deprive her of bodily self-possession. [P]regnancy increases a woman's uterine size 500–1,000 times, her pulse rate by ten to fifteen beats a minute, and her body weight by 25 pounds or more. [Pregnancy entails] nausea, vomiting, more frequent urination, fatigue, back pain, labored breathing, or water retention. There are also numerous medical risks involved in carrying pregnancy to term. [In] addition, labor and delivery impose extraordinary physical demands, whether over the six to twelve hour or longer course of vaginal delivery, or during the highly invasive surgery involved in a cesarean section, which accounts for one out of four deliveries.

"By compelling pregnancy to term and delivery even where they are unwanted, abortion restrictions thus exert far more profound intrusions into bodily integrity than the stomach pumping the Court invalidated in *Rochin* [p. 350 supra] or the surgical removal of a bullet from a shoulder [invalidated] in *Winston v. Lee* [470 U.S. 753, 105 S.Ct. 1611, 84 L.Ed.2d 662 (1985)]. 'The integrity of an individual's person is a cherished value of our society' [*Winston*] because it is so essential to identity; as former Solicitor General Charles Fried, who argued for the United States in *Webster* [p. 406 infra], recognized in another context: '[to say] that my body can be used is [to say] that I can be used.' "[a]

2. *The precedents relied on by Roe.* Taken together, maintain Philip Heymann & Douglas Barzelay, *The Forest and the Trees: Roe v. Wade and Its Critics,* 53 B.U.L.Rev. 765, 772 (1973), the *Meyer–Pierce–Skinner–Griswold–Eisenstadt* line of cases "clearly delineate a sphere of interests—which the Court now groups and denominates 'privacy'—implicit in the 'liberty' protected by the fourteenth amendment. At the core of this sphere is the right of the individual to make for himself—except where a very good reason exists for placing the decision in society's hands—the fundamental decisions that shape family life: whom to marry; whether and when to have children; and with what values to rear these children." But see Donald Regan, *Rewriting Roe v. Wade,* 77 Mich.L.Rev. 1569, 1639 (1979): "[The *Meyer–Eisenstadt* line of cases which Heymann & Barzelay say] establish a 'realm of private decision as to matters of marriage, procreation and child rearing' [are] a rag-tag lot. Most of them either claim to be or are best understood as being primarily about something other than marriage, procreation and child-rearing." Moreover, continues Regan, supra, at 1641–42: "Whether or not the cases from *Meyer* to *Eisenstadt* establish a right of family-related freedom-of-choice, none of these cases involves a state interest remotely like the interest in protecting 'potential' but *already conceived* human life. Accordingly none of those cases establishes or even suggests that the right of family-related freedom-of-choice is weighty enough to overcome the state's interest in forbidding abortion."

Consider, too, Richard Epstein, *Substantive Due Process by Any Other Name: The Abortion Cases,* 1973 Sup.Ct.Rev. 159, 170–72: "If we must hazard an attempt to find the common thread which runs through [the *Meyer–Eisenstadt* line of cases], it might well be the principle of classic liberalism: the state is entitled to restrict the liberty of any individual within its jurisdiction only where necessary to protect other persons from harm. [But] the general principle will have only an

---

a. For a broader discussion of the bodily integrity approach to the sexual freedom cases, see David B. Cruz, *The "Sexual Freedom Cases"? Contraception, Abortion, Abstinence, and the Constitution,* 35 Harv. C.R.-C.L. Rev. 299, 360–65 (2000), distinguishing between an approach to abortion that relies on a woman's bodily integrity and one that depends on concepts of procreative autonomy: "The bodily integrity view treats the constitutional grava-men of complaints against anticontraception and antiabortion laws as lying primarily in the increased risk from such laws of diseases or of the physical burdens of unwanted pregnancies. The procreative autonomy view, by contrast, attaches constitutional significance to the reduction in control over the circumstances under which persons can choose whether or not to bring new life into the world."

empty exception if 'harm to another' does not cover the death of another person. Let it be accepted that the unborn child is a person (or even is to be treated like one), and it is clear beyond all question that the abortion cases fall not within the general rule that protects the liberty of each person to do as he pleases but within the exception that governs the infliction of harm to others. And the case, moreover, becomes instantly distinguishable from that posed by the state regulation of contraception, because no one claims that there is a person before conception."

3. *Does Roe reflect the same circular reasoning of the earlier substantive due process cases?* Joseph Grano, *Judicial Review and a Written Constitution in a Democratic Society,* 28 Wayne L.Rev. 1, 24 (1981) maintains that it does: The right to terminate a pregnancy can be deemed fundamental only if the fetus is not regarded as a form of life entitled to protection. No a priori moral principle can resolve the question of the fetus' status. By declaring the woman's right 'fundamental,' however, the Court necessarily rejected the legislative judgment that fetal life deserves protection. At this point, some might object that the Court merely concluded that public opinion was too divided to justify such a restraint on the woman's choice, but this conclusion went to the weight of the state's interest. The Court's test required that it first decide whether a fundamental right was implicated, and it could not do this, any more than it could in *Allgeyer* or *Lochner,* or any more than Justice Harlan could in *Poe v. Ullman,* without making its own moral assessment of the activity in question, an assessment not subject to demonstration by analytic reasoning."

4. *"Privacy" or "autonomy"—or "fundamentality"?* Consider Louis Henkin, *Privacy and Autonomy*, 74 Colum.L.Rev. 1410, 1427 (1974): "Most aspects of an individual's life are not 'fundamental,' and in these his liberty is subject to the police power of federal and state governments, with presumptions of statutory validity, and a heavy, generally hopeless, burden on a resisting individual to show that a regulation has no conceivable public purpose, or that there is no rational relation between means and ends. Some, fewer, aspects of individual life are 'fundamental,' constitute a zone of prima facie autonomy (called Privacy), are presumed sacrosanct, and will bow only to a compelling public good clearly established. We are not told the basis—in language, history, or whatever else may be relevant to constitutional interpretation—for concluding that 'liberty' includes some individual autonomy that is 'fundamental' and much that is not. We are not told what is the touchstone for determining 'fundamentality.' We are not told why Privacy satisfies that test (unless Privacy is a tautology for fundamentality). [What] is it that makes my right to use contraceptives a right of Privacy, and fundamental, but my right to contract to work 16 hours a day or to pay more for milk than the law fixes, not a right of Privacy and not fundamental? Is it, as some suspect, that the game is being played backwards: that the private right which intuitively commends itself as valuable in our society in our time, or at least to a majority of our Justices at this time, is called fundamental, and if it cannot fit comfortably into specific constitutional provisions it is included in Privacy?"[b]

5. *Did the Court decide the question without admitting it?* Consider Michael McConnell, *How Not to Promote Serious Deliberation about Abortion,* 58 U.Chi. L.Rev. 1181, 1198 (1991): "Society has no choice but to decide to whom it will extend protection. It is not helpful to call this decision 'private' for there is no

---

b. See also Ira Lupu, *Untangling the Strands of the Fourteenth Amendment*, 77 Mich.L.Rev. 981, 1032–33 (1979); Michael Perry, *Substantive Due Process Revisited*, 71 Nw. U.L.Rev. 417, 440–41 (1976); Richard Posner, *The Uncertain Protection of Privacy in the Supreme Court*, 1979 Sup.Ct.Rev. 173, 199.

more inherently political question than the definition of the political community. When the *Roe* Court stated, '[w]e need not resolve the difficult question of when life begins,' it was deciding the question without admitting it, and thus without having to support its decision with reasons. Worse yet, it was suggesting that the question of human life was irrelevant to the decision. *Any* conscientious determination of when the developing fetus attains a moral-legal status worthy of protection, supported by reasons, would be preferable to that."

6. *Abortion as a Net–Gain.* Consider Richard Posner, *Sex and Reason* 281–283 (1992): "[I]f there were no abortions, and if as a result population grew faster-as almost certainly it would if abortion were effectively repressed-society would reach a condition of perceived overpopulation sooner; the birth rate would fall; and children would not be born who would have been born had abortions been permitted in the earlier period. Those children are saved by allowing abortion. [Abortion] returns a woman to the population that is at risk of becoming pregnant sooner than if she carried the fetus to term, thereby permitting a larger number of completed pregnancies. [Abortion also] enables parents to invest more in their children, thereby increasing the quality of the children at the expense of their quantity, an effect reinforced by the use of abortion to postpone childbearing to a time that may be more opportune for the child as well as for the parents * * *."

7. *Is there no reality in the womb, only theories? Is personhood a biological fact or a legal status?* In one passage, protests John Noonan, *The Root and Branch of Roe v. Wade,* 63 Neb.L.Rev. 668, 672–73 (1984), "[*Roe*] spoke of the unborn before viability as 'a theory of life,' as though there were competing views as to whether life in fact existed before viability. The implication could also be found that there was no reality there in the womb but merely theories about what was there. [To] judge from the weight the Court gave the being in the womb—found to be protectible in any degree only in the last two months of pregnancy—the Court itself must have viewed the unborn as pure potentiality or a mere theory before viability. The Court's opinion appeared to rest on the assumption that the biological reality could be subordinated or ignored by the sovereign speaking through the Court."

But consider Catharine MacKinnon, *Reflections on Sex Equality Under Law,* 100 Yale L.J. 1281, 1315 (1991): "[T]he only point of recognizing fetal personhood, or a separate fetal entity, is to assert the interests of the fetus *against* the pregnant woman. * * * Personhood is a legal and social status, not a biological fact. [In] my opinion and in the experience of many pregnant women, the fetus is a human form of life. It is alive. But the existence of sex inequality in society requires that completed live birth mark the personhood line. If sex equality existed socially—if women were recognized as persons, sexual aggression were truly deviant, and childrearing were shared and consistent with a full life rather than at odds with it—the fetus still might not be considered a person but the question of its political status would be a very different one."[c]

8. *Is the question of when human life begins "nonjusticiable"?* Consider Scalia, J., concurring in *Akron II* (1990) (p. 410, fn. c infra): "I continue to believe [that] the Constitution contains no right to abortion. It is not to be found in the longstanding traditions of our society, nor can it be logically deduced from the text of the Constitution—not, that is, without volunteering a judicial answer to the

c. See also Frances Olsen, *Unravelling Compromise,* 103 Harv.L.Rev. 105, 128 (1989); Rubenfeld, note 8 infra, at 617–20, 627–35 (1991); Mark Tushnet, *Two Notes on the Juris-* *prudence of Privacy,* 8 Const.Comm. 75, 84–85 (1991). But cf. Laurence Tribe, *Abortion: The Clash of Absolutes* 119 (1990).

nonjusticiable question of when human life begins. Leaving this matter to the political process is not only legally correct, it is pragmatically so." Compare Jed Rubenfeld, *On the Legal Status of the Proposition that "Life Begins at Conception,"* 43 Stan.L.Rev. 599, 615–16 (1991): "Justice Scalia has it exactly backward. [G]iven the contraception cases, a right to abortion *cannot be denied* without volunteering a judicial answer to the question of when human life begins. To see why this is [so], suppose an overpopulated state embarked on a campaign of infanticide, supporting its measures with the determination that human life did not begin until age five. Personhood is not and cannot be a 'political question.' It is a question, indeed *the* question, of who holds legal rights. When the rights at stake are *constitutional,* state legislatures plainly are not entitled to the last word. [For] this reason, deference to a state's determination that life begins at conception *is* a judicial answer to Justice Scalia's 'nonjusticiable' question of when life begins. * * * Abortion cannot be flatly prohibited unless the judiciary either (1) abdicates its constitutional responsibility to oversee state determinations of personhood, or (2) concurs that fetuses may be regarded as persons from the moment of conception."

9. *Why must legislation assume that a nonviable fetus is* not *a person?* Consider Richard Posner, *Legal Reasoning from the Bottom Up: The Question of Unenumerated Constitutional Rights,* 59 U.Chi.L.Rev. 433, 444 (1992): "[Professor Ronald Dworkin] is able to make abortion a matter of the varying opinions that Americans hold about the sanctity of life, rather than an issue of life or death,[d] only because he will not allow states to define the fetus as a person and therefore abortion as murder. [Yet] the states are allowed to decide what is property and (in the case of prisoners for example) what is liberty, for purposes of the Due Process Clause; why not what is a person? Can't a state decide that death means brain death rather than a stopped heart? And if it can decide when life ends why can't it decide when life begins? [An] Illinois statute makes abortion murder, and on the civil side wrongful death. The Supremacy Clause prevents its application to abortions privileged by *Roe,* but with that qualification the constitutionality of the statute cannot be doubted. It shows that the states are already in the business of defining human life."

If the Constitution leaves a state free to decide that a fetus is a constitutional person whose rights may be competitive with the rights of a pregnant woman, responds Ronald Dworkin, *Unenumerated Rights: Whether and How Roe Should be Overruled,* 59 U.Chi.L.Rev. 381, 399–402 (1992), "then *Roe* could safely be reversed without the politically impossible implication that states were required to prohibit abortion. The Supreme Court could then say that while some states have chosen to declare fetuses persons within their jurisdiction, other states need not make the same decision." Continues Dworkin:

"There is no doubt that a state can protect the life of a fetus in a variety of ways. A state can make it murder for a third-party intentionally to kill a fetus, as Illinois has done. [Such] laws violate no constitutional rights, because no one has a constitutional right to injure with impunity. [The] suggestion that states are free to declare a fetus a person, and thereby justify outlawing abortion, is a very different matter, however. That suggestion assumes that a state can curtail some persons' constitutional rights by adding new persons to the constitutional population. The constitutional rights of one citizen are of course very much affected by who or what else also has constitutional rights, because the rights of others may compete or conflict with his. So any power to increase the constitutional popula-

d. See the extracts from Dworkin's article
in note 12 infra.

tion by unilateral decision would be, in effect, a power to decrease rights the national Constitution grants to others. * * *

"[Judge Posner] says that states can decide whether 'death means brain death' or 'a stopped heart' and that it follows that they can 'decide when life begins.' [But a state] cannot change constitutional rights by its decisions about when life begins or death happens. It cannot escape its constitutional responsibilities to death-row prisoners by declaring them already dead, or improve its congressional representation by declaring deceased citizens still alive for that purpose. I cannot think of any significant constitutional rights that would be curtailed by treating someone as dead when his brain was dead, however. So none of Posner's examples suggest that he really accepts the position I reject."

10. *When, if ever,* may *a state override a woman's privacy rights by "adopting a theory of life"?* Consider Jed Rubenfeld, note 8 supra, at 628–30, 634–35:

"[T]he right at issue here is the freedom to decide whether and when to bear children. * * * Precisely because it would render abortion completely unavailable, a state determination that life begins at conception would not place an outer limit on this right; it would eviscerate the right at its core. [C]ontraception is no guarantee against pregnancy. Studies indicate that over half of the women who currently obtain abortions do use some form of contraception. [When] abortion is prohibited, no woman is guaranteed the right to decide whether or when to have children, and a large number of women will in fact have childbearing forced upon them against their will.

"[In] light of the state's inability to demonstrate that a fetus is a person, the [*Roe* Court] did 'not agree that, by adopting one theory of life, [a state] may override the rights of pregnant women at stake.' Too strictly construed, this formulation would be incorrect. A state *may* override a woman's privacy rights (indeed may *only* override them) by 'adopting [a] theory of life'—that is, by determining a point at which to recognize the fetus as an independent human being. The Court's essential holding, however, was and remains valid: A state may not completely eviscerate the women's privacy rights by adopting a theory of life that bars abortion altogether.

"[A]ssuming the Court preserves the right to privacy, it can announce as a new constitutional standard that states may deem the fetus a person at any point in pregnancy they choose, *so long as this point affords women a reasonable length of time in which to discover their pregnancy and obtain an abortion.* [This] standard would, however, have obvious disadvantages. It would lack definiteness, invite additional litigation, result in differing state rules, and so forth. On the other hand, the Court would be going no further than it had to go and would be allowing antiabortion states as much leeway in prohibiting abortion as the Constitution could tolerate."[e]

11. *Was the state's justification for interference with individual decision a "moral" one? A "religious" one?* Asks Professor Henkin, note 4 supra, at 1431–32: "Once, [the] promotion and protection of morals was clearly a proper concern of government; does the Right of Privacy imply that it is no longer? While the rights to use contraceptives, to have an abortion, to read obscene materials, were held not offset by hypothesized, particular public goods, were they not all essentially 'morals legislation'? And does it essentially all come down to the Court's saying [in effect] that these are not 'the law's business'? Does the Constitution, then, permit government to be only utilitarian not 'moral'? Or, if

---

e. See also Dworkin, note 9 supra, at 428–32.

that inference is unwarranted, which morals may society promote, by what means? How much attention may it give in legislation to national history, to ancestral or contemporary religion, to the prevailing morality of the time?"

But compare Archibald Cox, *The Role of the Supreme Court* 113–14 (1976): "My criticism of *Roe* is that the Court failed to establish the legitimacy of the decision by not articulating a precept of sufficient abstractness to lift the ruling above the level of a political judgment based upon the evidence currently available from the medical, physical and social sciences. Nor can I articulate such a principle—unless it be that a State cannot interfere with the individual decisions relating to sex, procreation, and family with only a moral or philosophical State justification: a principle which I cannot accept or believe will be accepted by the American people."

"[A]ll normative judgments," observes Tribe 2d ed., at 130, "are rooted in moral premises: surely the judgment that it is wrong to kill a two-week old infant is no less 'moral' in inspiration than the judgment, less frequently made but no less strongly felt by many of those who make it, that it is wrong to kill a two-day old fetus. Archibald Cox seems correct, therefore, when he concludes that *Roe* must be wrong if it rests on the premise that a state can never interfere with individual decisions relating to sex or procreation 'with only moral justification.' But it is clear that *Roe* rests on no such premise."

Is the judgment that it is wrong to kill a two-day old fetus a moral judgment or a *religious* one? How does one distinguish between "moral" and "religious" judgments? Aren't people who hold strong religious beliefs likely to *call them* moral convictions? And to believe sincerely that they *are* moral convictions? If the Court adopted, or allowed a state to adopt, the view that a fetus is in all stages of pregnancy a moral person on a par with an actual person, wouldn't that be the kind of endorsement of nonneutral values which the religion clauses forbid? See David Richards, *Constitutional Privacy, Religious Disestablishment, and the Abortion Decisions,* in *Abortion: Moral and Legal Perspectives* 148, 171–73 (Garfield & Hennessey eds. 1984). See also Thomas Emerson, *The Power of Congress to Change Constitutional Decisions of the Supreme Court: The Human Life Bill,* 77 Nw.U.L.Rev. 129, 131 (1982); Sylvia Law, *Rethinking Sex and the Constitution,* 132 U.Pa.L.Rev. 955, 1026 n. 249 (1984).

12. *What is the most difficult constitutional issue in the abortion controversy?* According to Professor Dworkin, note 9 supra, at 407, it is not some question about the moral personality or rights or interests of a fetus, but "whether states can legitimately claim a detached interest in protecting the intrinsic value, or sanctity, of human life. Does our Constitution allow states to decide [whether] human life is inherently valuable, why it is so, and how that inherent value can be respected?" Continues Dworkin, id. at 411:

"The real question decided in *Roe,* and the heart of the national debate, is the question of conformity [i.e., whether a state can require all its citizens to obey rules and practices that the majority believes best capture and respect the sanctity of life]. I said that government sometimes acts properly when it coerces people in order to protect values the majority endorses: when it collects taxes to support art, or when it requires businessmen to spend money to avoid endangering a species, for example. Why (I asked) can the state not forbid abortion on the same ground: that the majority of its citizens thinks that aborting a fetus, except when the mother's own life is at stake, is an intolerable insult to the inherent value of human life? [The] belief that the value of human life transcends its value for the creature whose life it is—that human life is objectively valuable from the point of view, as it were, of the universe—is plainly a religious belief, even when it is held by people who do not believe in a personal deity" and thus people's beliefs about the inherent value of human life, beliefs deployed in their opinions about abortion (and suicide and euthanasia as well) "should be deemed religious within the meaning of the First Amendment." Do you agree?

13. *The impact of Roe on a pluralistic society.* Consider Guido Calabresi, *Ideals, Beliefs, Attitudes, and the Law* 95–97 (1985): "[When] the Court proclaimed [that] anti-abortion beliefs as to commencement of life, *whether true or not,* are not part of our Constitution [it] said to highly defensive groups composed in significant part of recent immigrants that their highest beliefs [are] not part of *our* law as represented by its most fundamental statement, the Constitution. [This] was catastrophic because it reinforced doubts which the holders of anti-abortion beliefs already had about their full acceptance in American society.

"[Roe] opened wounds one wishes were closed. The decision made it impossible for the opposing views to live with each other, and created a situation in which one side seemed to need to *win* over the other. And, while that may be the side the Court supported, the losers will not quickly forget their exclusion (just as they have not forgotten their treatment as recent immigrants) to the detriment of our pluralistic society."

14. *A defense of Roe even assuming that the fetus is a person.* Agreeing with Professor Ely (see p. 396 infra) that "constitutional argument ought to be based on values that can be inferred from the text of the Constitution, the thinking of the Framers, or the structure of our national government," Donald Regan, note 2 supra, at 1618–42, maintains that such constitutional argument against laws prohibiting abortion may be made, based on three constitutional values: "non-subordination, freedom from physical invasion, and equal protection":[f]

"The non-subordination value that is implicit in the bad-samaritan principle of the common law[g] is at the core of the thirteenth amendment [which] speaks not merely of slavery, but of 'involuntary servitude.' * * * Unwilling pregnancy is not slavery in its fullest sense, [but] it certainly involves the disposition and coercion of the (intensely) personal service of one 'man' for another's benefit. The second value, freedom from physical invasion or imposed physical pain or hardship, is embodied in the eighth amendment and also plainly counts among those fundamental values of our society which are traditionally subsumed under fifth and fourteenth amendment due process. [There] is no other case, I believe, in which the law imposes comparable physical invasion and hardship as an obligation of samaritanism. * * *

"[An anti-abortion statute] picks out certain potential samaritans, namely women who want abortions, and treats them in a way that is at odds with the law's treatment of other potential samaritans. Women who want abortions are

[handwritten margin note: Can state compel you to keep the violinist alive?]

---

f. As Professor Regan acknowledges, his article builds on an argument made in Judith Thomson, *A Defense of Abortion,* 1 Phil. & Pub.Aff. 47 (1971).

g. At the outset of his article, id. at 1569, Professor Regan contends that "abortion should be viewed as presenting a problem in what we might call 'the law of samaritanism,' that is, the law concerning obligations imposed on certain individuals to give aid to others. It is a deeply rooted principle of American law that an individual is ordinarily not required to volunteer aid to another individual who is in danger or in need of assistance. [I]f we require a pregnant woman to carry the fetus to term and deliver it—if we forbid abortion, in other words—we are compelling her to be a Good Samaritan. [I]f we consider the special nature of the burdens imposed on pregnant women by laws forbidding abortion, we must eventually conclude that the equal protection clause forbids imposition of these burdens on pregnant women." Regan refers to "the established principle that one does not have to volunteer aid" as the "bad-samaritan principle," id. at 1572.

required to give aid in circumstances where closely analogous potential samaritans are not. And they are required to give aid of a *kind* and an *extent* that is required of no other potential samaritan.

"[The] inequality of treatment between pregnant women and other potential samaritans touches on the constitutional values of non-subordination and freedom from physical invasion. A woman who is denied an abortion is compelled to serve the fetus and to suffer physical invasion, pain, and hardship. [That it can plausibly] be argued that the Constitution prohibits this imposition outright, [surely] means that any inequality of treatment we can point to becomes harder to justify. * * *

"Other reasons for the Court to give the abortion problem special attention are related to the suspect classification idea. Only women need abortions. [T]he one potential samaritan who is singled out for specially burdensome treatment is a potential samaritan who must, given human physiology, be female. Why is this important?

"First, any inequality that flows from an unchosen and unalterable characteristic is likely to be specially resented. [Since] no one has any choice about whether to be a woman, susceptibility to pregnancy (and to being in the position of wanting an abortion) is a nonchosen characteristic. [Moreover,] the only method of avoiding pregnancy with certainty requires, for many people, extraordinary self-denial [and] does not, to my mind, eliminate the force of the suggestion that pregnancy is often sufficiently 'unchosen' so that laws specially disadvantaging pregnant women limit women's control of their lives, are justifiably resented, and deserve more-than-minimal judicial attention.[h]

"[M]ost legislatures would defend laws against abortion on the ground that they protect human life (or potential life). [But the] inequality between the treatment of pregnant women and the treatment of other potential samaritans who are not required to undertake burdens (often very much smaller burdens) in order to save life is too great. The inequality trenches on two distinct constitutionally protected interests—the interest in non-subordination and the interest in freedom from serious physical invasion. In addition, the inequality disadvantages a class that is defined by a non-chosen characteristic (whether sex or unwanted pregnancy) and that has suffered from a history of discrimination. This is more than any reasonable American legislature would tolerate. * * *

"Perhaps the greatest advantage of my argument is that it makes it possible to avoid the question of whether the fetus is, or may be treated by the state as, a

---

h. Consider Catharine MacKinnon, *Roe v. Wade: A Study in Male Ideology,* in *Abortion: Moral and Legal Perspectives* 45, 46–48 (Garfield & Hennessey eds. 1984): "Feminist investigations suggest [that women do not significantly control sex]. Feminism has found that women feel compelled to preserve the appearance—which, acted upon, becomes the reality—of male direction of sexual expression, as if it is male initiative itself that we want: it is that which turns us on. Men enforce this. It is much of what men want in a woman.

"[Under] these conditions, women often do not use birth control because [it] means acknowledging and planning and taking direction of intercourse, accepting one's sexual availability, and appearing nonspontaneous. [A] good user of contraception is a bad girl. She can be presumed sexually available and, among other consequences, raped with relative impunity. (If you think this isn't true, you should consider rape cases in which the fact that a woman had a diaphragm in is taken as an indication that what happened to her was intercourse, not rape. 'Why did you have your diaphragm in?') * * * I wonder if a woman can be presumed to control access to her sexuality if she feels unable to interrupt intercourse to insert a diaphragm; or worse, cannot even want to, aware that she risks a pregnancy she knows she does not want. [Yet] abortion policy has never been explicitly approached in the context of how women get pregnant; that is, as a consequence of intercourse under conditions of gender inequality; that is, as an issue of forced sex."

person. Justice Blackmun [assumes] that the fetus is *not* a person until the point of viability (at the earliest). Indeed, [he] suggests that if the fetus were a person within the meaning of the fourteenth amendment, the woman's claim to an abortion would be foreclosed by the Constitution itself.

"On the last point, I think Blackmun is mistaken. [The] people who need the assistance of potential samaritans in ordinary samaritan cases are persons under the fourteenth amendment, and yet the general common law bad-samaritan principle is not unconstitutional.

"[M]y argument justifies [the] conclusion that abortion may not be forbidden even in the third trimester when the life or health of the mother is at stake. [Even] the reader who rejects my general conclusions must admit that there is no other case in which we would even consider requiring one individual to sacrifice his life or health to rescue another."[i]

15. *Abortion as self–defense.* Consider Eileen McDonagh's argument in *Breaking the Abortion Deadlock: From Choice to Consent* 6–7 (1996) that a woman's right to an abortion should be understood as "a right to defend herself against the nonconsensual invasion, appropriation, and use of her physical body by an unwelcome fetus." Robin West, *Liberalism and Abortion*, 87 Geo. L.J. 2117, 2118, 2122–23, 2128 (1999) (reviewing McDonagh's book), expanded on this theory:

"[I]f we understand the right to an abortion as a right to defend oneself against nonconsensual, invasive takings of one's body by others, the right is strengthened rather than weakened by the assumption that the fetus is a person. The position of the woman pregnant without her consent [is] basically analogous to the position of the woman or man assaulted by a grown child in need of one of their body parts. If the intercourse was voluntary, she may be partly responsible for having brought the fetus into existence. But likewise, the parent of the grown (or at any rate the born) child is also partly responsible for having brought that child into existence. In either case, the partial responsibility of the parent for the child's existence does not imply the child's right to appropriate the parent's body against the parent's will."

"[In response to the argument that a woman assumed the risk of pregnancy by having sex and therefore consented to the pregnancy, West notes that] we don't consent to the presence of the cancer in our lungs even if we increased the risk of its occurrence by smoking cigarettes. [T]he nonconsensual pregnancy, unlike the nonconsensual assault, threatens not so much to end your life 'from the outside,' so to speak, but to 'take over' your life from the inside. The fear is not that my life will end but that my control over its course will end."

16. *"Privacy" or "sex equality"?* "Nothing the Supreme Court has ever done," observes Sylvia Law, *Rethinking Sex and the Constitution*, 132 U.Pa.L.Rev. 955, 981 (1984), "has been more concretely important for women [than the decision in *Roe*]. Laws restricting abortion have a devastating sex-specific impact." Yet, as Professor Law notes, not only was the abortion decision not grounded on the principle of sex equality, the plaintiffs in *Roe* and *Doe* did not even challenge

i. See also Laurence Tribe, *Abortion: The Clash of Absolutes* 129–35 (1990). But the "Good Samaritan" argument has not escaped criticism. See, e.g., Philip Bobbitt, *Constitutional Fate* 163 (1982); McConnell, note 5 supra, at 1185–86 & n. 8; Rubenfeld, note 7 supra, at 604 n. 35; David Strauss, *Abortion, Toleration, and Moral Uncertainty,* 1992 Sup. Ct.Rev. 1, 10–14.

the abortion restrictions as sex discriminatory. But a growing number of commentators,[j] including Judge (now Justice) Ruth Bader Ginsburg,[k] are maintaining that the best argument for the right to abortion is based on principles of sexual equality, not "due process" or "privacy."

Catharine MacKinnon, note 7 supra, at 1319, puts it powerfully: "Because the social organization of reproduction is a major bulwark of women's social inequality, any constitutional interpretation of a sex equality principle must prohibit laws, state policies, or official practices and acts that deprive women of reproductive control or punish women for their reproductive role or capacity. * * * Women's right to reproductive control is a sex equality right because it is inconsistent with an equality mandate for the state, by law, to collaborate with or mandate social inequality on the basis of sex, as [denials of abortion through criminalization or lack of public funding where needed] do. This is not so much an argument for an extension of the meaning of constitutional sex equality as a recognition that if it does not mean this, it does not mean anything at all.

"Under this sex equality analysis, criminal abortion statutes of the sort invalidated in *Roe* violate equal protection of the laws. They make women criminals for a medical procedure only women need, or make others criminals for performing a procedure on women that only women need, when much of the need for this procedure as well as barriers to access to it have been created by social conditions of sex inequality. Forced motherhood is sex inequality. Because pregnancy can be experienced only by women, and because of the unequal social predicates and consequences pregnancy has for women, any forced pregnancy will always deprive and hurt one sex only as a member of her gender."

But consider Michael McConnell, note 5 supra, at 1187–88: "[A] law does not violate the Equal Protection Clause merely because it burdens one race or sex more heavily than another. Such a law is subject to heightened judicial scrutiny only if the legislature had an intent to discriminate. There exists no substantial evidence that abortion laws, as a matter of historical fact, were motivated by such an intent to discriminate against women. Indeed, the history of abortion laws shows that they were principally a response by the medical profession to improvements in the technology of abortion and to newly-discovered information about embryology. [More] interestingly, the nineteenth century anti-abortion movement was strongly supported by the women's movement." Adds Professor McConnell, id. at 1189–90:

---

j. See Calabresi, note 13 supra, at 99–102; Cass Sunstein, *The Partial Constitution* 272–85 (1993); Tribe, *Abortion* 105; Tribe 2d ed., at 1353–55; Paula Abrams, *The Tradition of Reproduction*, 37 Ariz. L. Rev. 453, 485, 488–89 (1995); Kenneth Karst, *Foreword: Equal Citizenship under the Fourteenth Amendment*, 91 Harv.L.Rev. 1, 57–59 (1977); Seth Kreimer, *Does Pro–Choice Mean Pro–Kevorkian? An Essay on Roe, Casey, and the Right to Die*, 44 Am.U.L.Rev. 803, 849 (1995); Law, supra at 987–1002; Frances Olsen, *Unraveling Compromise*, 103 Harv.L.Rev. 105, 117–26 (1989); Reva Siegel, *Reasoning from the Body: A Historical Perspective on Abortion Regulation and Questions of Equal Protection*, 44 Stan.L.Rev. 261, 350–80 (1992); David Strauss, *Abortion, Toleration, and Moral Uncertainty*, 1992 Sup. Ct.Rev. 1, 18–22.

k. In a lecture delivered shortly before her nomination to the Supreme Court, Judge Ginsburg noted that in *Planned Parenthood v. Casey* (p. 412 infra), which reaffirmed "the essential holding" of *Roe*, the controlling Justices (O'Connor, Kennedy and Souter), speaking for the Court on this point, "added an important strand to the Court's opinions on abortion"— they "acknowledged the intimate connection between a woman's 'ability to control [her] reproductive li[fe]' and her 'ability [to] participate equally in the economic and social life of the Nation.'" Ginsburg, *Speaking in a Judicial Voice*, 67 N.Y.U.L.Rev. 1185, 1199 (1992) (quoting *Casey*, 112 S.Ct. at 2809). See also Ruth Bader Ginsburg, *Some Thoughts on Autonomy and Equality in Relation to Roe v. Wade*, 63 N.C.L.Rev. 375, 382, 386 (1985).

"On Tribe's assumption that 'the fetus [is] a person,'[1] the more natural implication of the Equal Protection Clause is that it stands *against* abortion rights. The Equal Protection Clause is designed to protect members of vulnerable and politically unrepresented minorities from the oppressive measures of the dominant majority. Abortion laws are designed to protect fetuses or unborn children, surely a vulnerable and unrepresented group, from private violence. It is an odd interpretation of the Equal Protection Clause to say that it *prevents* states from extending protection to the vulnerable and unrepresented."

17. *Bridging the Abstinence Gap—A Constitutional Right to Sex?* Consider David B. Cruz, fn. a supra, at 322–23 (2000): "In the vast majority of cases, especially at the time that *Roe* was decided, pregnancy occurs only after peno-vaginal intercourse. If a woman did not wish to bear the burdens of continuing a pregnancy to term and giving birth to a child, or if a couple did not want to risk a pregnancy, she could forgo such intercourse. The availability of this alternative means that most women, at least so far as statutory prohibitions or commands are concerned, could avoid the restrictions imposed by abortion bans, such as the one struck down in Roe, by giving up one kind of sex. Thus, unless one has a specially constitutionally protected interest in engaging in (peno-vaginal) sex, the burden imposed by abortion bans might, in most cases, be seen as a constitutionally permissible restriction of sexual activity."

18. *In Roe did the woman patient take a back seat to the male physician?* In *Roe,* maintains Andrea Asaro, *The Judicial Portrayal of the Physician in Abortion and Sterilization Decisions,* 6 Harv. Women's L.J. 51, 53–55 (1983), "[for] Blackmun, the key issue was quite simply one of medical discretion, in other words: '[F]or the period of pregnancy prior to the "compelling" point, the attending physician, in consultation with his patient, is free to determine [that], in his medical judgment, the patient's pregnancy should be terminated.' Interestingly, the abortion decision is characterized here neither as primarily the woman's nor as fundamentally or initially a moral or personal one. Blackmun's perspective is clinical, and the woman patient has taken a back seat to the male physician-protagonist. [Concluding *Roe,* Blackmun, J., states]: '[The] decision vindicates the right of the physician to administer medical treatment according to his professional judgment up to the points where important state interests provide compelling justifications for intervention. Up to these points, *the abortion decision in all its aspects is inherently, and primarily, a medical decision, and basic responsibility for it must rest with the physician.*' [Emphasis added by Asaro.] Blackmun has neglected even to mention the pregnant woman as party to the abortion decision! The state, the physician, and the court have displaced Ms. Roe altogether."

19. *The "peculiar nature" of the Burger Court's activism.* Unlike the Warren Court, whose justices' doctrinal compromises "took place against a background in which the direction of constitutional development was both clear and, to many, inspiring," observes Vincent Blasi, *The Rootless Activism of the Burger Court,* in *The Burger Court: The Counter–Revolution that Wasn't* 198, 212–13 (V. Blasi ed. 1983), the *Roe* justices "could not plausibly justify their decision as the working out of a theme implicit in several previous decisions, still less as the vindication of values deeply embedded in the nation's constitutional tradition. [T]he peculiar

---

1. At this point, Professor McConnell is referring to a passage in Professor Tribe's book on abortion (p. 135) where Tribe maintains that "even if the fetus [is] regarded as a person," "a powerful case" can be made for the conclusion that laws prohibiting abortion "deny women the equal protection of the laws." As Tribe puts it, the Court might have said that "[e]ven if the fetus *is* a person, our Constitution forbids compelling a woman to carry it for nine months and become a mother."

nature of the Burger Court's activism can be seen from the fact that even so fundamental an issue as abortion was treated by this Court as a conflict of particularized, material interests—a conflict that could be resolved by accommodating those interests in the spirit of compromise. Thus, third trimester abortions can be prohibited but earlier abortions cannot. The state cannot prohibit all abortions outright, but can refuse to fund them [see *Maher v. Roe* and *Harris v. McRae,* infra], even while funding the alternative of childbirth and thereby encouraging pregnant women to forgo the abortion option. The woman's husband cannot veto her choice to have an abortion [*Planned Parenthood v. Danforth,* infra] but a minor's parents can do so under certain limited circumstances. These doctrinal lines are not necessarily incoherent. But each has in fact taken on a highly arbitrary character because in grappling with the issues that followed in *Roe*'s wake, the justices were unable to draw upon any sort of theory, or vision, or even framework for determining the contours of the right they had recognized. Each variation on the abortion issue was treated by the Court as an isolated, practical problem."

20. *The impact of Roe—some surprising aspects.* Although *Roe* increased women's access to safe abortions, "surprisingly," notes Cass Sunstein, *The Partial Constitution* 147 (1993) "it did not dramatically increase the actual number and rate of abortions. [In] fact most states were moving in the direction of liberal abortion laws well before *Roe,* resulting in 600,000 lawful abortions per year. Astonishingly, the rate of increase in *legal* abortions was higher in the three years before that decision than in the three years after. It may well have been the case that states would generally have legalized abortion without *Roe.* Perhaps more fundamentally, the decision probably contributed to the creation of the 'moral majority'; helped defeat the Equal Rights Amendment; prevented the eventual achievement of consensual solutions to the abortion problem; and severely undermined the women's movement, by defining that movement in terms of the single issue of abortion, by spurring and organizing opposition, and by demobilizing potential adherents."

ROE v. WADE AND THE DEBATE IT STIRRED OVER "NONINTERPRETIVIST" OR "NONORIGINALIST" CONSTITUTIONAL DECISIONMAKING[a]

1. Consider Ira Lupu, *Constitutional Theory and the Search for the Workable Premise,* 8 Dayton L.Rev. 579, 583 (1983): "*Roe* clarified, as had no other case

---

a. "Interpretivism" indicates that "judges deciding constitutional issues should confine themselves to enforcing norms that are stated or clearly implicit in the written Constitution"; "noninterpretivism" indicates that "courts should go beyond that set of references and enforce norms that cannot be discovered within the four corners of the document." John Ely, *Democracy and Distrust* 1 (1980). "What distinguishes interpretivism from its opposite is its insistence that the work of the political branches is to be invalidated only in accord with an inference whose starting point, whose underlying premise, is fairly discoverable in the Constitution. That the complete inference will not be found there—because the situation is not likely to have been foreseen—is general common ground." Id. at 1–2.

As might be expected, there is disagreement over the appropriate terminology. In recent years, according to Peter Linzer, *The Carolene Products Footnote and the Preferred Position of Individual Rights,* 12 Const.Comm. 277, 286 (1995), "the term 'originalist' seems to have replaced the awkward 'interpretivist.' " See also Robert Bennett, *Objectivity in Constitutional Law,* 132 U.Pa.L.Rev. 445, 446 & n. 3 (1984), preferring the term "originalists" to describe those who "argue that constitutional language, understood in light of the substantive intentions or values behind its enactment, is the sole proper source for constitutional interpretation," because this term "better captures the static pretense of the approach that seems to me to be its principal flaw." "On the other side of the debate are 'noninterpretivists'

since World War II, the Supreme Court's willingness to reach results which no defensible interpretivist position could support. Although rhetorically tied to the meaning of 'liberty' in the fourteenth amendment due process clause, and loosely aligned with the penumbral analysis developed in *Griswold, Roe* cut fundamental rights adjudication loose from the constitutional text. [Subsequent] scholarly efforts offered a variety of justifications for [this type of] noninterpretive review— natural law underpinnings of the 1787 Constitution, [the] search for enduring or traditional unwritten norms, [and] judicial manifestation of consensus morality."

2. *What happened on the day Roe was decided?* "The subject of abortion," observes Robert Bork, *The Tempting of America* 111–16 (1990), "had been fiercely debated in state legislatures for many years. [Whatever] the proper resolution of the moral debate, [few] imagined that the Constitution resolved it. [The] discovery this late in our history that the question was not one for democratic decision but one of constitutional law was so implausible that it certainly deserved a fifty-one page explanation. Unfortunately, in the entire opinion there is not one line of explanation, not one sentence that qualifies as legal argument. [It] is unlikely that [the Court] ever will [provide the explanation lacking in 1973] because the right to abort, whatever one thinks of it, is not to be found in the Constitution. * * *

"Attempts to overturn *Roe* will continue as long as the Court adheres to it. And, just so long as the decision remains, the Court will be perceived, correctly, as political * * *. *Roe*, as the greatest example and symbol of the judicial usurpation of democratic prerogatives in this century, should be overturned. The Court's integrity requires that."

Compare Laurence Tribe, *Abortion* 99: "Judge Bork says that 'the right to abort, whatever one thinks of it, is not to be found in the Constitution.' In a sense this is obviously right. Indeed, not one of the words 'abortion,' 'pregnancy,' 'reproduction,' 'sex,' 'privacy,' 'bodily integrity,' and 'procreation' appears anywhere in [the] Constitution. But neither do such phrases as 'freedom of thought,' 'rights of parenthood,' 'liberty of association,' 'family self-determination,' and 'freedom of marital choice.' Yet nearly everyone supposes that at least some of these dimensions of personal autonomy and independence are aspects of the 'liberty' which the Fourteenth Amendment says no state may deny to any person 'without due process of law.'

or 'nonoriginalists' who believe it is legitimate for judges to look beyond text and original intention in interpreting constitutional language," but they "are divided on what particular sources should replace or supplement originalist sources and on how to justify their use."

Richard Fallon, *A Constructivist Coherence Theory of Constitutional Interpretation,* 100 Harv.L.Rev. 1189, 1211 (1987), divides "interpretivists" into two camps: "On one side stand 'originalists.' [They] take the rigid view that only the original understanding of the framers' specific intent ought to count. On the other side, 'moderate interpretivists' allow contemporary understandings and the framers' general or abstract intent to enter the constitutional calculus."

Thomas Grey, *Do We Have an Unwritten Constitution?*, 27 Stan.L.Rev. 703 (1975), probably originated the use of the "interpretivist-

noninterpretivist" terminology, but he has since concluded that these labels "distort the debate": "If the current interest in interpretive theory [does] nothing else, at least it shows that the concept of interpretation is broad enough to encompass any plausible mode of constitutional adjudication. We are all interpretivists; the real arguments are not over whether judges should stick to interpreting, but over what they should interpret and what interpretive attitudes they should adopt. Repenting past errors, I will therefore use the less misleading labels 'textualists' and 'supplementers' for, respectively, those who consider the text the sole legitimate source of operative norms in constitutional adjudication, and those who accept supplementary sources of constitutional law [such as 'conventional morality']." Thomas Grey, *The Constitution as Scripture*, 37 Stan.L.Rev. 1 (1984).

3. Consider Joseph Grano, *Judicial Review and a Written Constitution in a Democratic Society,* 28 Wayne L.Rev. 1, 25, 59 (1981): [An objection to criticisms of *Roe*] might be that the Court's poor choice of methodology is not a valid argument against noninterpretivism. The truth, however, is that the Court's methodology is basically all there is. Noninterpretivism is a methodology of *fundamental* rights, [for] no one maintains that the judiciary should require "compelling" reasons for all laws, including those that prohibit swindling or murder. Noninterpretivism's first requirement is that the judiciary separate that which is fundamental from that which is not, and it is this very task that requires the judiciary to take normative and moral positions that cannot be demonstrated.

"[*Roe*] is as wrong as the proposed constitutional amendment to protect the fetus, and for the same reason: it seeks to bind succeeding generations to our generation's thinking, or at least to the thinking of a segment of it. Through the Supreme Court, our generation has dictated to future generations that they can prohibit abortions only by mustering the requisite super-majority to amend the Constitution. [*Roe*] is just one example of judicial noninterpretivism, a methodology that permits the judiciary to decide the difficult moral issues of our time under the rubric of constitutional law. [Every] noninterpretivist decision recognizing one of these claims adds, in effect, a new provision to the written constitution and thereby imposes an additional moral restraint on subsequent generations."

4. *Are the Abortion Cases "bad constitutional law" or "not constitutional law"?* Consider John H. Ely, *The Wages of Crying Wolf: A Comment on Roe v. Wade,* 82 Yale L.J. 920, 935–37, 939, 943, 947–49 (1973): "What is unusual about *Roe* is that the liberty involved is accorded [a] protection more stringent [than] that the present Court accords the freedom of the press explicitly guaranteed by the First Amendment. What is frightening about *Roe* is that this super-protected right is not inferable from the language of the Constitution, the framers' thinking respecting the specific problem in issue, any general value derivable from the provisions they included, or the nation's governmental structure. Nor is it explainable in terms of the unusual political impotence of the group judicially protected vis-á-vis the interest that legislatively prevailed over it.[b]

"[The] problem with *Roe* is not so much that it bungles the question it sets itself, but rather that it sets itself a question the Constitution has not made the Court's business. It *looks* different from *Lochner*—it has the shape if not the

---

b. Professor Ely argues, at 933–35, that Stone, J.'s suggestion in his famous *Carolene Products* footnote that the Court provide extraordinary constitutional protection for " 'discrete and insulate minorities' unable to form effective political alliances" does not apply to *Roe*: "Compared with men, very few women sit in our legislatures, [but] *no* fetuses sit [there]. [Stone's suggestion] was clearly intended and should be reserved for those interests which, as compared with the interests to which they have been subordinated, constitute minorities usually incapable of protecting themselves. Compared with men, women may constitute such a 'minority'; compared with the unborn, they do not."

However, Robert Bennett, *Abortion and Judicial Review,* 75 Nw.U.L.Rev. 978, 995–96 n. 71 (1981), maintains that Professor Ely's challenge of the appropriateness of judicial intervention in *Roe* "is misguided," "because it

assumes that fetuses are political actors—indeed a political minority—whose 'powerlessness' is relevant to assessing the Court's appropriate role in the abortion controversy. Each political system must define, explicitly or implicitly, the universe of relevant political actors. [But] outside the abortion context there are no indications that fetuses are considered relevant political actors. [E]ven within the context of abortion-related issues, the suggestion that fetuses are a part of the larger political community appears, as in Ely's formulation, only incidentally and as part of the abortion discussion. It is, of course, possible for a legislature to take into account interests outside its own political community. [But] with fetuses, as with other interests outside the relevant universe of political actors, the legislative process can only take them into account insofar as relevant political actors subsume those interests into their own."

substance of a judgment that is very much the Court's business, one vindicating an interest the Constitution marks as special—and it is for that reason perhaps more dangerous.

"[*Roe* is] a very bad decision. [It] is bad because it is bad constitutional law, or rather because it is *not* constitutional law and gives almost no sense of an obligation to try to be. [A] neutral and durable principle may be a thing of beauty and joy forever. But if it lacks connection with any value the Constitution marks as special, it is not a constitutional principle and the Court has no business imposing it."[c]

5. *Is it a question of "inventing" a new right, or of the state having to justify an invasion of liberty?* Consider the remarks of Professor Tribe in Choper, Kamisar & Tribe, *The Supreme Court: Trends and Developments 1982–83* (1984) at 215: "[The *Roe* Court] is said to have invented the right to abortion. [But once] one concedes that the word 'liberty' has substantive content in its application against the states through the Fourteenth Amendment—and it must, if any substantive provisions of the Bill of Rights are to be enforced against the states through the Fourteenth Amendment—it becomes not a question of inventing a new right, but of asking what the justification is for a state intrusion into what is indisputably an aspect of someone's personal liberty."[d]

6. *"Enumerated" and "unenumerated" rights.* Although many view the distinction between enumerated and unenumerated rights as presenting the important question whether and when courts have authority to enforce rights not actually enumerated in the Constitution (e.g., the right to travel and the right to privacy, from which the right to an abortion is said to derive), Ronald Dworkin, *Unenumerated Rights,* 59 U.Chi.L.Rev. 381, 387–88 (1992), finds the question "unintelligible":

"The Bill of Rights * * * consists of broad and abstract principles of political morality, which together encompass, in exceptionally abstract form, all the dimensions of political morality that in our political culture can ground an individual constitutional right. The key issue in applying these abstract principles to particular political controversies is not one of reference but of *interpretation,* which is very different. [The distinction between enumerated and unenumerated rights] cannot be sustained. * * * No one thinks that it follows just from the meaning of the words 'freedom of speech' either that people are free to burn flags, or that they are not. No one thinks it follows just from the meaning of the words 'equal protection' that laws excluding women from certain jobs are unconstitutional, or that they are not. [Nor are these arguments] different in how they are interpretive. Each conclusion (if sound) follows, not from some historical hope or belief or intention of a 'framer,' but because the political principle that supports that conclusion best accounts for the general structure and history of constitutional law. [If someone] thinks that the [abortion decision] is wrong, because he abhors, for example, the idea of substantive due process, then he will reject it, but because it is wrong, not because the right it claims would be an unenumerated one."[e]

c. See also Ray Forrester, *Are We Ready for Truth in Judging?,* 63 A.B.A.J. 1212 (1977); Louis Lusky, *By What Right?* 14, 16–17, 20 (1975); Henry Monaghan, *The Constitution Goes to Harvard,* 13 Harv.Civ.Rts.—Civ. Lib.L.Rev. 116, 131 (1978); Richard Posner, *The Uncertain Protection of Privacy in the Supreme Court,* 1979 Sup.Ct.Rev. 173, 199–200.

d. Cf. Walter Dellinger & Gene Sperling, *Abortion and the Supreme Court: The Retreat from Roe v. Wade,* 138 U.Pa.L.Rev. 83, 90–91 (1989).

e. Cf. Thomas Grey, *Do We Have an Unwritten Constitution?,* 27 Stan.L.Rev. 703, 710–14 (1975).

7. *Why noninterpretive review is a "necessary postulate" for constitutional adjudication.* Consider Robert Sedler, *The Legitimacy Debate in Constitutional Adjudication,* 44 Ohio St.L.J. 110, 118–19, 122 (1983): "[The Court] has engaged in noninterpretive review throughout its history, convinced that its actions were legitimate and consistent with the Court's function under our constitutional system. [The] meaning of a constitutional provision develops incrementally, and that provision's line of growth strongly influences its application in particular cases.[167] The framework within which constitutional decision making has operated, then, is a significant constraint on the results that the Court will reach when it is engaged in that decision making.

"[The] argument that noninterpretive review is fully supportive of constitutional governance established by the Constitution proceeds as follows: (1) The overriding principle in the structure of constitutional governance established by the Constitution is the limitation on governmental power. (2) Many of the limitations on governmental power designed to protect individual rights that are contained in the Constitution are broadly phrased and open ended, and these majestic generalities directed toward the protection of individual rights are a part of our constitutional tradition.[f] (3) [These] limitations cannot be fully operable in contemporary society as a limitation on governmental power if their meaning is determined solely or even primarily by referring to values purportedly constitutionalized by the framers at an earlier time. (4) Therefore, given items (1) and (3) above, noninterpretive review is not only legitimate, but is also a necessary postulate for constitutional adjudication under our constitutional system."

ABORTION FUNDING

1. MAHER v. ROE, 432 U.S. 464, 97 S.Ct. 2376, 53 L.Ed.2d 484 (1977) (also discussed at p. 407 infra), per POWELL, J., sustained Connecticut's use of Medicaid funds to reimburse women for the costs of childbirth and "medically necessary" first trimester abortions (defined to include "psychiatric necessity"), but not for the costs of elective or nontherapeutic first trimester abortions.[a]

---

167. [I]t would not have been inconsistent with the line of growth of constitutional protection for reproductive freedom for the Court to have held that the asserted governmental interest in protecting potential human life was constitutionally more important than the woman's interest in reproductive freedom. [But] because the Court had previously held that reproductive freedom is entitled to constitutional protection, the holding in *Roe,* extending that protection to the abortion decision, was fully consistent with the line of growth of constitutional protection for reproductive freedom.

f. "But," maintains Henry Monaghan, *Commentary* (panel discussion), 56 N.Y.U.L.Rev. 525, 526 (1981), "the Constitution doesn't contain generalities. The due process clause and the ninth amendment in my judgment are judge-made and commentator-made generalities. Take the phrase 'due process of law.' If there was ever a phrase that had a fixed, certain meaning when it was introduced in the Constitution and adopted in 1868, it was that phrase. It was the judges who transformed it into a general license to review

the substance of legislation. [Let's] assume that the Constitution contains some generalities like freedom of speech and let's assume that you are going to need a Hercules to interpret such provisions. Even if that Hercules has to rely on some external political theory, which can't be fairly related or thought to underlie the constitutional text, at least the first amendment is a stopping point: it limits the subjects about which judges ought to be concerned. But take the question of abortion. There's nothing in the constitutional text or in its history to 'constitutionalize.' Nor is the theory that would authorize review containable."

a. In a companion case, *Beal v. Doe,* 432 U.S. 438, 97 S.Ct. 2366, 53 L.Ed.2d 464 (1977), per Powell, J., held that the Medicaid Act does not require state funding of nontherapeutic first trimester abortions as a condition of participation in the joint federal-state program.

Poelker v. Doe, 432 U.S. 519, 97 S.Ct. 2391, 53 L.Ed.2d 528 (1977), per curiam, for the reasons set forth in *Maher,* found "no constitutional violation by the city of St. Louis in

On "the central question"—"whether the regulation 'impinges upon a fundamental right explicitly or implicitly protected by the Constitution' "—the Court held that *Roe* did not establish "an unqualified 'constitutional right to an abortion,' " but only a "right protect[ing] the woman from unduly burdensome interference with her freedom to decide whether to terminate her pregnancy. It implies no limitation on the authority of a State to make a value judgment favoring childbirth over abortion, and to implement that judgment by the allocation of public funds. [The] State may have made childbirth a more attractive alternative, thereby influencing the woman's decision, but it has imposed no restriction on access to abortions that was not already there. The indigency that may make it difficult—and in some cases, perhaps, impossible—for some women to have abortions is neither created nor in any way affected by the [regulation.]

"Our conclusion signals no retreat from *Roe* or the cases applying it. There is a basic difference between direct state interference with a protected activity and state encouragement of an alternative activity consonant with legislative policy. * * * We think it abundantly clear that a State is not required to show a compelling interest for its policy choice to favor normal childbirth any more than a State must so justify its election to fund public but not private education."

The Court then sustained the regulation "under the less demanding test of rationality that applies in the absence of a suspect classification or the impingement of a fundamental right." It had little difficulty finding the distinction drawn between childbirth and nontherapeutic abortion " 'rationally related' to a 'constitutionally permissible' purpose." "*Roe* itself explicitly acknowledged the State's strong interest in protecting the potential life of the fetus. [The] State unquestionably has a 'strong and legitimate interest in encouraging normal childbirth' " and subsidizing the substantial and significantly increasing costs incident to childbirth is "a rational means of encouraging childbirth."[13]

BRENNAN, J., joined by Marshall and Blackmun, JJ., dissented, accusing the majority of "a distressing insensitivity to the plight of impoverished pregnant women." The "disparity in funding [clearly] operates to coerce indigent pregnant women to bear children they would not otherwise choose to have, and just as clearly, this coercion can only operate upon the poor, who are uniquely the victims of this form of financial pressure." *Roe* and its progeny held that "an area of privacy invulnerable to the State's intrusion surrounds the decision of a pregnant woman whether or not to carry her pregnancy to term. The Connecticut scheme clearly infringes upon that area of privacy."

In a second dissent, MARSHALL, J., thought it "all too obvious that the governmental actions in these cases, ostensibly taken to 'encourage' women to carry pregnancies to term, are in reality intended to impose a moral viewpoint that no State may constitutionally enforce. [The] impact of the regulations here fall tragically upon those among us least able to help or defend themselves."

electing, as a policy choice, to provide publicly financed hospital services for childbirth without providing corresponding services for nontherapeutic abortions."

13. Much of the rhetoric of the three dissenting opinions would be equally applicable if Connecticut had elected not to fund either abortions or childbirth. Yet none of the dissents goes so far as to argue that the Constitution *requires* such assistance for all indigent pregnant women.

[Compare Gary Simson, *Abortion, Poverty and the Equal Protection of the Laws,* 13 Ga. L.Rev. 505, 508 (1979): "[I]f Connecticut funded neither childbirth nor abortion, poverty would not lead indigent women to prefer childbirth to abortion. Rather, since a safe abortion in the early months of pregnancy is materially cheaper than a safe childbirth, financial considerations probably would militate strongly *in favor of* abortion."]

In a third dissent, BLACKMUN, J., joined by Brennan and Marshall, JJ., charged that "the Court concedes the existence of a constitutional right but denies the realization and enjoyment of that right on the ground that existence and realization are separate and distinct. [Implicit in today's holdings] is the condescension that [the indigent woman] may go elsewhere for her abortion. I find that disingenuous and alarming, almost reminiscent of: 'Let them eat cake.'"

2. *The Hyde Amendment.* Title XIX of the Social Security Act established the Medicaid program to provide federal financial assistance to states choosing to reimburse certain costs of medical treatment for needy persons. Since 1976, various versions of the so-called Hyde Amendment have limited federal funding of abortions under the Medicaid program to those necessary to save the life of the mother and certain other exceptional circumstances.[a] HARRIS v. McRAE, 448 U.S. 297, 100 S.Ct. 2671, 65 L.Ed.2d 784 (1980), per STEWART, J., found no constitutional violation: "The present case does differ factually from *Maher* insofar as that case involved a failure to fund nontherapeutic abortions, whereas the Hyde Amendment withholds funding of certain medically necessary abortions. [But] regardless of [how] the freedom of a woman to choose to terminate her pregnancy for health reasons [is characterized], it simply does not follow that [this freedom] carries with it a constitutional entitlement to the financial resources to avail herself of the full range of protected choices. The reason why was explained in *Maher:* although government may not place obstacles in the path of a woman's exercise of her freedom of choice, it need not remove those not of its own creation. [T]he Hyde Amendment leaves an indigent woman with at least the same range of choice in deciding whether to obtain a medically necessary abortion as she would have had if Congress had chosen to subsidize no health costs at all.

"[Acceptance of appellees' argument] would mark a drastic change in our understanding of the Constitution. It cannot be that because government may not prohibit the use of contraceptives, *Griswold*, or prevent parents from sending their child to a private school, *Pierce,* government, therefore, has an affirmative constitutional obligation to assure that all persons have the financial resources to obtain contraceptives or send their children to private [schools.]"[b]

Four justices dissented—Brennan, Marshall and Blackmun, JJ. (the three *Maher* dissenters), and Stevens, J. who had joined the opinion of the Court in *Maher*. STEVENS, J., maintained that the instant case presented "[a] fundamentally

---

a. The version of the Hyde Amendment applicable for fiscal year 1980 prohibited federal funding of abortions "except where the life of the mother would be endangered if the fetus were carried to term" or except for cases of rape or incest "when such rape or incest has been reported promptly to a law enforcement agency or public health service." But the initial version of the Hyde Amendment, which triggered the instant case, did not include the "rape or incest" exception.

b. The Court then rejected the contention that the Hyde Amendment violates the Establishment Clause because, as the argument ran, "it incorporates into law the doctrines of the Roman Catholic Church": A statute does not run afoul of the Establishment Clause "because it 'happens to coincide or harmonize with the tenets of some or all religions,' *McGowan v. Maryland* [discussed at p. 1058, fn. b infra]"; the Hyde Amendment "is as

much a reflection of 'traditionalist' values toward abortion, as it is an embodiment of the views of any particular religion."

"Again draw[ing] guidance from" *Maher*, the Court also rejected the argument that the Hyde Amendment "violates the equal protection component of the Fifth Amendment": The Hyde Amendment "is not predicated on a constitutionally suspect classification. [Here,] as in *Maher*, the principal impact of [the] Amendment falls on the indigent. But that fact alone does not itself render the funding restriction constitutionally invalid, for this Court has held repeatedly that poverty, standing alone, is not a suspect classification." See generally Ch. 9, Sec. 4, III & IV. Thus, the Hyde Amendment need only satisfy the rational-basis standard of review and it does—"by encouraging childbirth except in the most urgent circumstances, [it] is rationally related to the legitimate governmental objective of protecting potential life."

different question" than the one decided in *Maher*: "This case involves the pool of benefits that Congress created by enacting [Title XIX]. Individuals who satisfy two neutral criteria—financial need and medical need—are entitled to equal access to that pool. The question is whether certain persons who satisfy those criteria may be denied access to benefits solely because they must exercise the constitutional right to have an abortion in order to obtain the medical care they need. Our prior cases plainly dictate [the answer].

"Unlike these plaintiffs, [those] in *Maher* did not satisfy the neutral criterion of medical need; they sought a subsidy for nontherapeutic abortions—medical procedures which by definition they did not need. [This case] involves a special exclusion of women who, by definition, are confronted with a choice between two serious harms: serious health damage to themselves on the one hand and abortion on the other. The competing interests are the interest in maternal health and the interest in protecting potential human life. It is now part of our law that the pregnant woman's decision as to which of these conflicting interests shall prevail is entitled to constitutional protection.

"[If] a woman has a constitutional right to place a higher value on avoiding either serious harm to her own health or perhaps an abnormal childbirth than on protecting potential life, the exercise of that right cannot provide the basis for the denial of a benefit to which she would otherwise be entitled. The Court's sterile equal protection analysis evades this critical though simple point. The Court focuses exclusively on the 'legitimate interest in protecting the potential life of the fetus.' [*Roe*] squarely held that the States may not protect that interest when a conflict with the interest in a pregnant woman's health exists. [The] Court totally fails to explain why this reasoning is not dispositive here.[4] * * *

"Having decided to alleviate some of the hardships of poverty by providing necessary medical care, the Government must use neutral criteria in distributing benefits. [It] may not create exceptions for the sole purpose of furthering a governmental interest that is constitutionally subordinate to the individual interest that the entire program was designed to protect."

The other three dissenters wrote separately, each voicing agreement with Stevens, J.'s analysis. BRENNAN, J., joined by Marshall and Blackmun, JJ., expressed his "continuing disagreement with the Court's mischaracterization of the nature of the fundamental right recognized in *Roe* and its misconception of the manner in which that right is infringed [by] legislation withdrawing all funding for medically necessary abortions": "[W]hat the Court fails to appreciate is that it is not simply the woman's indigency that interferes with her freedom of choice, but the combination of her own poverty and the government's unequal subsidization of abortion and childbirth."[c]

---

4. [In] responding to my analysis of this case, Justice White [in a separate opinion] has described the constitutional right recognized in *Roe* as "the right to choose to undergo an abortion without coercive interference by the Government" or a right "only to be free from unreasonable official interference with private choice." No such language is found in the *Roe* opinion itself. Rather, that case squarely held that State interference is unreasonable if it attaches a greater importance to the interest in potential life than to the interest in protecting the mother's health. One could with equal justification describe the right protected by the First Amendment as the right to make speeches without coercive interference by the Government and then sustain a Government subsidy for all medically needy persons except those who publicly advocate a change of administration.

c. The Court extended *Maher* and *McRae* in *Rust v. Sullivan*, 500 U.S. 173, 111 S.Ct. 1759, 114 L.Ed.2d 233 (1991), upholding federal regulations prohibiting private physicians receiving federal funds for "family planning services" from providing abortion information to a woman client except when a pregnancy

Notes and Questions

(a) *The logic of the abortion funding cases.* "There is," notes Tribe, 2d ed., at 1346, "a certain logic [to the abortion funding cases]: if the abortion choice is constitutionally private, why should the state be prevented from declining to make it a matter for public funding?" "But," continues Tribe, "this logic is far from inexorable":

"The government obviously has the constitutional *authority* to make abortion, like childbirth, available at no charge to the woman, either in a public facility or by public subsidy. The government's *affirmative* choice *not* to do so can fairly be characterized as a decision to enforce alienation of the woman's right to end her pregnancy, whether that alienation—or 'waiver'—was brought about voluntarily (by the woman's failure to save money for an abortion), or involuntarily (by economic circumstances beyond her control). After all, the unavailability of abortion to such a woman follows from her lack of funds only by virtue of the government's quite conscious decision to treat that medical procedure in particular as a purely private commodity available only to those who can pay the market price. The constitutionality of that decision is rendered dubious by the government's simultaneous decision to take *childbirth* procedures for the same poor woman *off* the private market: the result, as Justice Stevens put it, [dissenting in *McRae,*] is a government program that self-consciously 'require[s] the expenditure of millions and millions of dollars in order to thwart the exercise of a constitutional right.' The state's position with respect to reproductive rights—rights it is bound to respect—is therefore neither as neutral nor as passive as a majority of the Court supposed in *Maher* and *McRae.*"[a]

(b) *Preventing constitutional caste.* Where "rights are too important to be reserved for selected privileged groups," observes Kathleen Sullivan, *Unconstitutional Conditions,* 102 Harv.L.Rev. 1413, 1498–99 (1989), "conditions on benefits that affect their exercise can pose a similar danger of hierarchy. * * * Government cannot universally criminalize abortion, nor universally burden it with heavy restrictions, at least in the first trimester. The only difference between such general bans and the selective subsidization of childbirth but not abortion for indigent women is the class affected. Dependency on government defines the class here. But what the government cannot restrict for all, it may not restrict for those over whom it has special leverage because of their dependency—especially where the displacement of private alternatives creates special responsibility. To hold otherwise would sanction a two-tier system of constitutional rights—a system of constitutional caste."

(c) *On looking at the government's purpose.* After pointing out, inter alia, that Congressman Hyde stated that the purpose of his Amendment was "not to fund abortion because it's the killing of an innocently inconvenient pre-born child," Michael Perry, *Why the Supreme Court Was Plainly Wrong in the Hyde Amendment Case,* 32 Stan.L.Rev. 1113, 1126 (1980), concludes that "[i]t strains credulity to the breaking point to suggest that those charged with defending the Hyde Amendment in court could possibly establish that the view that abortion is per se morally objectionable did not play a but-for role in passage of the Amendment."[b]

places her life in peril. (The free speech aspects of this case are discussed at p. 878 infra.)

a. See also Susan Estrich & Kathleen Sullivan, *Abortion Politics: Writing for an Audience of One,* 138 U.Pa.L.Rev. 119, 150 (1989).

b. But consider the remarks of Professor Tribe in Choper, Kamisar & Tribe, *The Su-*

preme Court: Trends and Developments 1979–80 (1981) at 286–87 (ascertaining government purpose is a "treacherous" and "manipulable" inquiry and outside the limited area of suspect classes, "where purpose is critical because we're talking about symbolism and stigma, a strong case can be made for junking the whole issue of purpose."

CONTINUING CONTROVERSY OVER *ROE: AKRON,* *THORNBURGH* AND *WEBSTER*

I. In AKRON v. AKRON CENTER FOR REPRODUCTIVE HEALTH (*Akron I*), 462 U.S. 416, 103 S.Ct. 2481, 76 L.Ed.2d 687 (1983), which struck down various sections of an ordinance regulating abortions,[a] a 6–3 majority, per POWELL, J., declined an invitation to overrule *Roe*. Instead, the Court reaffirmed the central liberty found in *Roe* and its basic trimester decision.

Akron I marked the first time the "undue burden" standard, a test that was to attract much attention later, was suggested. Dissenting Justice O'CONNOR (joined by White and Rehnquist, JJ.), who would have upheld all the challenged regulations, warned that the *Roe* framework is "clearly on a collision course with itself. As the medical risks of various abortion procedures decrease, the point at which the State may regulate for reasons of maternal health is moved further forward to actual childbirth. As medical science becomes better able to provide for the separate existence of the fetus, the point of viability is moved further back toward conception."

The "undue burden" standard, maintained O'Connor, "should be applied to the challenged regulations throughout the entire pregnancy without reference to the particular 'stage' of pregnancy involved." She maintained further that if the particular regulation "does not 'unduly burden' the fundamental right, then our evaluation of that regulation is limited to our determination that the regulation rationally relates to a legitimate state purpose." She continued:

"[The] 'undue burden' required in the abortion cases represents the required threshold inquiry that must be conducted before the Court can require a State to justify its legislative actions under the exacting 'compelling state interest' standard. [In] determining whether the State imposes an 'undue burden,' we must keep in mind that when we are concerned with extremely sensitive issues, such as the one involved here, 'the appropriate forum for their resolution in a democracy is the legislature.'"

In a long footnote, the Court, per POWELL, J., responded that although the dissent "stops short of arguing flatly that *Roe* should be overruled," it "adopts reasoning that, for all practical purposes, would accomplish precisely that result. [The] dissent [maintains that] the State's compelling interests in maternal health and potential life 'are present *throughout* pregnancy.' [The] existence of these compelling interests turn out to be largely unnecessary, however, for the dissent does not think that even one of the numerous abortion regulations at issue imposes a sufficient burden on the 'limited' fundamental right [to] require heightened scrutiny.

"[It] appears that the dissent would uphold virtually any abortion regulation under a rational-basis test. It also appears that even where heightened scrutiny is

---

a. Among the provisions invalidated were a mandatory 24–hour waiting period, which increased the cost of obtaining an abortion by requiring the woman to make two separate trips to the abortion facility; a provision requiring that after the first trimester all abortions be performed in a hospital, thus preventing abortions in outpatient clinics; and an "informed consent" provision that the majority characterized as "designed not to inform the woman's consent but rather to persuade her to withhold it altogether."

deemed appropriate, the dissent would uphold virtually any abortion-inhibiting regulation because of the State's interest in preserving potential human life. [Thus, the dissent argues that] a 24–hour waiting period is justified in part because the abortion decision 'has grave consequences for the fetus.' This analysis is wholly incompatible with the existence of the fundamental right recognized in *Roe*."

II.   In THORNBURGH v. AMERICAN COLLEGE OF OBST. & GYN., 476 U.S. 747, 106 S.Ct. 2169, 90 L.Ed.2d 779 (1986), the United States, in an amicus brief, urged the Court to overrule *Roe*. A 5–4 majority, per BLACKMUN, J., declined. Instead, it invalidated, inter alia, the "reporting requirements" of a Pennsylvania statute and various restrictions on post-viability abortions. Dissenting, WHITE, J., joined by Rehnquist, J., launched a strong attack on the premises of the majority's decision—and the premises of *Roe*: "Fundamental liberties and interests are most clearly present when the Constitution provides specific textual recognition of their existence and importance. Thus, the Court is on relatively firm ground when it deems certain of the liberties set forth in the Bill of Rights to be fundamental and therefore finds them incorporated in the Fourteenth Amendment's guarantee that no State may deprive any person of liberty without due process of law. When the Court ventures further and defines as 'fundamental' liberties that are nowhere mentioned in the Constitution (or that are present only in the so-called 'penumbras' of specifically enumerated rights), it must, of necessity, act with more caution, lest it open itself to the accusation that, in the name of identifying constitutional principles to which the people have consented in framing their Constitution, the Court has done nothing more than impose its own controversial choices of value upon the people.[b]

"[However] one answers the metaphysical or theological question whether the fetus is a 'human being' or the legal question whether it is a 'person' as that term is used in the Constitution, one must at least recognize, first, that the fetus is an entity that bears in its cells all the genetic information that characterizes a member of the species *homo sapiens* and distinguishes an individualized member of that species from all others, and second, that there is no nonarbitrary line separating a fetus from a child or, indeed, an adult human being. Given that the continued existence and development—that is to say, the *life*—of such an entity are so directly at stake in the woman's decision whether or not to terminate her pregnancy, that decision must be recognized as *sui generis*, different in kind from the others that the Court has protected under the rubric of personal or family privacy and autonomy.[2]

"[If] the woman's liberty to choose an abortion is fundamental, then, it is not because any of our precedents (aside from *Roe* itself) command or justify that result; it can only be because protection for this unique choice is itself 'implicit in the concept of ordered liberty' or, perhaps, 'deeply rooted in this Nation's history and tradition.' It seems clear to me that it is neither. The Court's opinion in *Roe* itself convincingly refutes the notion that the abortion liberty is deeply rooted in the history or tradition of our people, as does the continuing and deep division of the people themselves over the question of abortion. As for the notion that choice

b. Compare the language Justice White used later the same term in his opinion of the Court in *Bowers v. Hardwick* (p. 466 infra), upholding a prohibition against consensual sodomy as applied to homosexuals.

2. That the abortion decision, like the decisions in *Griswold, Eisenstadt,* and *Carey,* con-

cerns childbearing (or, more generally, family life) in no sense necessitates a holding that the liberty to choose abortion is "fundamental." That the decision involves the destruction of the fetus renders it different in kind from the decision not to conceive in the first place. * * *

in the matter of abortion is implicit in the concept of ordered liberty, it seems apparent to me that a free, egalitarian, and democratic society does not presuppose any particular rule or set of rules with respect to abortion. * * *

"A second, equally basic error infects the Court's decision in *Roe*. The detailed set of rules governing state restrictions on abortion that the Court first articulated in *Roe* and has since refined and elaborated presupposes not only that the woman's liberty to choose an abortion is fundamental, but also that the state's countervailing interest in protecting fetal life (or, as the Court would have it, 'potential human life') becomes 'compelling' only at the point at which the fetus is viable. As Justice O'Connor pointed out three years ago in her dissent in *Akron I*, the Court's choice of viability as the point at which the State's interest becomes compelling is entirely arbitrary.

" * * * Abortion is a hotly contested moral and political issue. Such issues, in our society, are to be resolved by the will of the people, either as expressed through legislation or through the general principles they have already incorporated into the Constitution they have adopted. *Roe* implies that the people have already resolved the debate by weaving into the Constitution the values and principles that answer the issue. As I have argued, I believe it is clear that the people have never—not in 1787, 1791, 1868, or at any time since—done any such thing. I would return the issue to the people by overruling *Roe*."

STEVENS, J., concurring, responded: "[If] Justice White were correct in regarding the postconception decision of the question whether to bear a child as a relatively unimportant, second-class sort of interest, I might agree with his view that the individual should be required to conform her decision to the will of the majority. But if that decision commands the respect that is traditionally associated with the 'sensitive areas of liberty' protected by the Constitution, as Justice White characterized reproductive decisions in *Griswold*, no individual should be compelled to surrender the freedom to make that decision for herself simply because her 'value preferences' are not shared by the majority. In a sense, the basic question is whether the 'abortion decision' should be made by the individual or by the majority 'in the unrestrained imposition of its own, extraconstitutional value preferences.' But surely Justice White is quite wrong in suggesting that the Court is imposing value preferences on anyone else.

"Justice White is also surely wrong in suggesting that the governmental interest in protecting fetal life is equally compelling during the entire period from the moment of conception until the moment of birth. Again, I recognize that a powerful theological argument can be made for that position, but I believe our jurisdiction is limited to the evaluation of secular state interests. I should think it obvious that the State's interest in the protection of an embryo—even if that interest is defined as 'protecting those who will be citizens'—increases progressively and dramatically as the organism's capacity to feel pain, to experience pleasure, to survive, and to react to its surroundings increases day by day. The development of a fetus—and pregnancy itself—are not static conditions, and the assertion that the government's interest is static simply ignores this reality.

"Nor is it an answer to argue that life itself is not a static condition, and that 'there is no nonarbitrary line separating a fetus from a child, or indeed, an adult human being.' For, unless the religious view that a fetus is a 'person' is adopted—a view Justice White refuses to embrace—there is a fundamental and well-recognized difference between a fetus and a human being; indeed, if there is not such a difference, the permissibility of terminating the life of a fetus could scarcely be left to the will of the state legislatures.[8] * * *

"[In] the final analysis, the holding in *Roe* presumes that it is far better to permit some individuals to make incorrect decisions than to deny all individuals the right to make decisions that have a profound effect upon their destiny. Arguably a very primitive society would have been protected from evil by a rule against eating apples; a majority familiar with Adam's experience might favor such a rule. But the lawmakers who placed a special premium on the protection of individual liberty have recognized that certain values are more important than the will of a transient majority."

III.   In WEBSTER v. REPRODUCTIVE HEALTH SERVICES, 492 U.S. 490, 109 S.Ct. 3040, 106 L.Ed.2d 410 (1989), both the State and the United States urged the Court to overrule *Roe*. Again, the Court declined to do so, but it did significantly modify *Roe*'s trimester approach.

The most hotly disputed section of the challenged Missouri statute required a physician, prior to performing an abortion "on a woman he has reason to believe is carrying an unborn child of twenty or more months gestational age," to ascertain "if the unborn child is viable [by] exercising that degree of care, skill, and proficiency commonly exercised by the ordinarily skillful, careful, and prudent physician engaged in similar practice" and providing further that, in determining viability, "the physician shall perform [such] medical examinations and tests as are necessary to make a finding of the gestational age, weight, and lung maturity of the unborn child." The Court upheld this section but there was no opinion of the Court.

Speaking for a three-Justice plurality (including White and Kennedy, JJ.,) REHNQUIST, C.J., read the section as not requiring the tests to be made under all circumstances—not, for example, "when the physician's reasonable professional judgment indicates that the tests would be irrelevant to determining viability." As so construed, the section was upheld.

As for the doubt cast upon the viability-testing provisions by such cases as *Colautti v. Franklin*, 439 U.S. 379, 99 S.Ct. 675, 58 L.Ed.2d 596 (1979) and *Akron I*, the plurality thought this "is not so much a flaw in the statute as it is a reflection of the fact that the rigid trimester analysis of the course of a pregnancy enunciated in *Roe* has resulted in subsequent [cases] making constitutional law in this area a virtual Procrustean bed. Statutes specifying elements of informed consent to be provided abortion patients, for example, were invalidated if they were thought to 'structure [the] dialogue between the woman and her physician.' * * *

"We have not refrained from reconsideration of a prior construction of the Constitution that has proved 'unsound in principle and unworkable in practice.' * * * We think the *Roe* trimester framework falls into that category.

"In the first place, the rigid *Roe* framework is hardly consistent with the notion of a Constitution cast in general terms, as ours is, and usually speaking in general terms, as ours does. The key elements of the *Roe* framework—trimesters and viability—are not found in the text of the Constitution or in any place else one would expect to find a constitutional principle.

___

8. No member of this Court has ever sug-   meaning of the Fourteenth Amendment.
gested that a fetus is a "person" within the

"[In] the second place, we do not see why the State's interest in protecting potential human life should come into existence only at the point of viability, and that there should therefore be a rigid line allowing state regulation after viability, but prohibiting it before viability. [The plurality then quoted from the dissents of White, J., and O'Connor, J., in *Thornburgh*.]

"[It] is true that the tests in question increase the expense of abortion, and regulate the discretion of the physician in determining the viability of the fetus. Since the tests will undoubtedly show in many cases that the fetus is not viable, the tests will have to be performed for what were in fact second-trimester abortions. But we are satisfied that the requirement of these tests permissibly further the State's interest in protecting societal human life and we therefore believe [the section] to be constitutional."

As for Blackmun, J.'s claim, dissenting, that the plurality's treatment of "the most politically divisive domestic legal issue of our time" is such as to "invite charges of cowardice and illegitimacy to our door," the plurality responded: "[The] goal of constitutional adjudication is surely not to remove inexorably 'politically divisive' issues from the ambit of the legislative process, [but] to hold true the balance between that which the Constitution puts beyond the reach of the democratic process and that which it does not. We think we have done that today."

A majority, per REHNQUIST, C.J., concluded that the law's preamble, which contained "findings" that "[t]he life of each human being begins at conception" and that "unborn children have protectable interests in life, health, and well-being" did not conflict with *Roe*'s statement that "a State may not adopt one theory of when life begins to justify the regulation of abortions." The preamble, noted the Chief Justice, "does not by its terms regulate abortion or any other aspect [of] medical practice"; it can be read simply as expressing a "value judgment favoring childbirth over abortion" (which *Roe* stated is permissible). Thus, there was no need to rule on the preamble's constitutionality.

A majority also sustained provisions prohibiting abortions by state employees and preventing the use of public facilities for abortion, even when a woman paid for the abortion herself: "As in [*Maher*], the State's decision here to use public facilities and staff to encourage childbirth over abortion 'places no governmental obstacle in the path of a woman who chooses to terminate her pregnancy. [It] leaves a pregnant woman with the same choices as if the State had chosen not to operate any hospital at all. The challenged provisions only restrict a woman's ability to obtain an abortion to the extent that she chooses to use a physician affiliated with a public hospital. [*Maher* and *McRae*] support the view that the State need not commit any resources to facilitating abortions, even if it can turn a profit by doing so."

Dissenting, BLACKMUN, J., joined by Brennan and Marshall, JJ., directed his fire at the Rehnquist plurality's consideration of the statute's viability-testing requirement. Contrary to the plurality, he agreed with the Court of Appeals that the "plain language" of the viability-testing provision required that after 20 weeks the specified tests *must* be performed. Therefore, "the statute requires physicians to undertake procedures [that] have no medical justification, impose significant additional health risks on both the pregnant woman and the fetus, and bear no rational relation to the State's interest in protecting fetal life. [Thus,] were it not for the plurality's tortured effort to avoid the plain import of [the provision], it could have struck [it down] as patently irrational irrespective of the *Roe* framework. The plurality eschews this straightforward resolution, in the hope of precipitating a constitutional crisis.

"[Rather] than arguing that the text of the Constitution makes no mention of the right to privacy, the plurality complains that the critical elements of the *Roe* framework—trimesters and viability—do not appear in the Constitution and are, therefore, somehow inconsistent with a Constitution cast in general terms. Were this a true concern, we would have to abandon most of our constitutional jurisprudence. [The] Constitution makes no mention, for example, of the First Amendment's 'actual malice' standard for proving certain libels or of the standard for determining when speech is obscene. * * *

"With respect to the *Roe* framework, [the] trimester framework simply defines and limits that right to privacy in the abortion context to accommodate, not destroy, a State's legitimate interest in protecting the health of pregnant women and in preserving potential human life. Fashioning such accommodations between individual rights and the legitimate interests of government, establishing benchmarks and standards with which to evaluate the competing claims of individuals and government, lies at the very heart of constitutional adjudication. To the extent that the trimester framework is useful in this enterprise, it is not only consistent with constitutional interpretation, but necessary to the wise and just exercise of this Court's paramount authority to define the scope of constitutional rights.

"[The] plurality pretends that *Roe* survives, explaining that the facts of this case differ from those in *Roe:* here, Missouri has chosen to assert its interest in potential life only at the point of viability, whereas, in *Roe,* Texas had asserted that interest from the point of conception, criminalizing all abortions, except where the life of the mother was at stake. This, of course, is a distinction without a difference. [If] the Constitution permits a State to enact any statute that reasonably furthers its interest in potential life, and if that interest arises as of conception, why would the Texas statute fail to pass muster? One suspects that the plurality agrees. It is impossible to read the plurality opinion * * * without recognizing its implicit invitation to every State to enact more and more restrictive abortion laws, and to assert their interest in potential life as of the moment of conception.

"[For] today, at least, the law of abortion stands undisturbed. For today, the women of this Nation still retain the liberty to control their destinies. But the signs are evident and very ominous, and a chill wind blows."[a]

Concurring, O'CONNOR, J., agreed with the Rehnquist plurality that the viability-testing provision did not require a physician to perform examinations and tests when it would be careless and imprudent to do so, but only when useful to make subsidiary findings as to viability. Unlike the plurality, however, Justice O'Connor did not understand the viability testing provision (as so construed) to conflict with any of the Court's past decisions concerning state regulation of abortion. (Thus, there was no need to reexamine the constitutionality of *Roe.*)

---

a. In a separate dissent, Stevens, J., insisted that the viability-testing provision, which was designed to make the abortion more costly, was "manifestly unconstitutional." Because he was unaware of "any secular basis for differentiating between contraceptive procedures that are effective immediately before and those that are effective immediately after fertilization," Stevens thought the preamble invalid under *Griswold* and its progeny. Moreover, "the absence of any secular purpose for the declarations that life begins at conception and that conception occurs at fertilization" made the relevant portion of the preamble invalid under the Establishment Clause of the First Amendment.

Concurring, SCALIA, J., voted to uphold the viability testing requirement, but agreed with dissenting Justice Blackmun (joined by Brennan and Marshall, JJ.) that the portion of the plurality opinion sustaining this provision "effectively would overrule *Roe*." He thought "that should be done," but he would "do it more explicitly." Noting that Justice O'Connor would uphold the provision because "it does not impose an undue burden on a woman's abortion decision," Scalia, J., expressed his unhappiness with that test: "To avoid the question of *Roe* 's validity, with the attendant costs that this will have for the Court and for the principles of self-governance, on the basis of a standard that offers 'no guide but the Court's own discretion' [quoting from a Holmes dissent] merely adds to the irrationality of what we do today."

Notes and Questions

1. *The significance of Webster.* Consider Susan Estrich & Kathleen Sullivan, *Abortion Politics: Writing for an Audience of One*, 138 U.Pa.L.Rev. 119, 120 (1989): "[If] little was decided in *Webster*, a good deal was nonetheless said. The Chief Justice, writing for three members of the Court, made plain that he was ready to jettison [the] trimester approach of *Roe*, presumably finding the state's interest in potential life as compelling in the first month as the last, and leaving it to the state to balance its own interest against the woman's, subject only to some rationality review. The genius of the approach, if you can call it that, is that it effectively overrules *Roe* without ever even suggesting that a woman lacks a privacy or autonomy interest in her own body."

2. *An open invitation to state legislators?* According to Laurence Tribe, *Abortion: The Clash of Absolutes*, 24 (1990), "*Webster* was and remains an open invitation to state legislators to see just how strictly they can regulate abortion without Justice O'Connor finding the burden on the abortion right 'undue.'" At the time Professor Tribe made this observation, O'Connor, J., had never found a restriction on the abortion right "unduly burdensome" and thus constitutionally defective. But shortly thereafter she did—in *Hodgson*, Note 5 infra.

3. *The state's interest in protecting potential human life before viability.* "There is," observe Professors Estrich and Sullivan, note 1, supra, at 146–47, "only one way to protect potential life before a fetus has the potential to survive outside the womb: forbid or discourage abortion. After viability, there are surely other ways abortion regulations can preserve an interest in potential life. * * * Imposing any 'undue burdens,' or indeed any burdens at all, on a woman's right *prior* to viability in the name of preserving life, though, is to say that a woman has a right and then to take it away. By definition, her right is to control her bodily autonomy *even at the expense of potential human life*."

4. *More on the significance of fetal viability.* Consider Jed Rubenfeld, *On the Legal Status of the Proposition that "Life Begins at Conception*," 43 Stan.L.Rev. 599, 622–23, 635 (1991): "The stage in human development currently marked by 'viability' (in its traditional sense) has always carried an implicit significance quite apart from the fetus's chances of survival. Precisely due to the undeveloped state of our medical technology, 'viability' denotes a fairly advanced state in fetal development. Viability occurs not only at the time when the fetus's pulmonary capability begins, but also when its brain begins to take on the cortical structure capable of higher mental functioning. These two important developments provide indicia both of *independent* beingness and of distinctly *human* beingness. [The] reason for *Roe*'s success (such as it was) is that, despite its vocabulary of potential life, the Court in all essential respects made a determination about when the

states could deem the fetus a person. Viability never made sense as the point at which the state interest in potential human life becomes compelling. Its appeal lies in its demarcation of a stage at which the fetus, having become 'capable of meaningful life outside the mother's womb,' may be regarded as a distinct life-in-being with interests of its own—as, in short, a person. Viability, in this sense, is by no means a unique or flawless solution to the problem of locating such a stage in the fetus's development. It is only a *good* solution. Under the circumstances, however, that is an excellent recommendation.''

5. In HODGSON v. MINNESOTA, 497 U.S. 417, 110 S.Ct. 2926, 111 L.Ed.2d 344 (1990), a 5–4 majority (STEVENS, J., joined in principal part by Brennan, Marshall, Blackmun, and O'Connor, JJ.) struck down a state law requiring *both* parents of an unemancipated minor to be notified at least 48 hours before she underwent an abortion.[a] But a different 5–4 majority—O'CONNOR, J., and the four justices who would have sustained the two-parent notification requirement *without* a judicial bypass alternative (Kennedy, J., joined by Rehnquist, C.J., and White and Scalia, JJ.) (the Kennedy group)—upheld the two-parent notification requirement *combined with* a judicial bypass.[b] Thus *Hodgson* produced two distinct majorities and in each instance O'Connor, J., provided the crucial vote. In addition, six justices—Stevens and O'Connor, JJ., and the Kennedy group—upheld a provision that, before proceeding with an abortion, a minor must wait 48 hours after notifying a *single* parent of her intention to obtain an abortion.[c]

In striking down the two-parent notification requirement unaccompanied by a judicial bypass procedure, STEVENS, J., pointed to its many adverse effects, especially on both the minor and the custodial parent when, as is often the case, the parents are divorced or separated. He thought it "clear that the requirement that *both* parents be notified, whether or not both wish to be notified or have assumed responsibility for the upbringing of the child, does not reasonably further any legitimate state interest. [Moreover,] the record reveals that in the thousands of dysfunctional families affected by this statute, the two-parent notice requirement proved positively harmful to the minor and her family, [resulting] in major trauma to the child, and often to a parent as well.''

Applying her "undue burden" test, concurring O'CONNOR, J., concluded that the obstacles imposed by Minnesota's two-parent notice requirement "are not reasonably related to legitimate state interests" and that the requirement "is all the more unreasonable when one considers that only half of the minors [in the state] reside with both biological parents [and a] third live with only one parent.''

a. There were two exceptions: if an immediate abortion was necessary to prevent the minor's death or if she declared she was a victim of parental abuse or neglect (in which event the appropriate authorities had to be notified).

b. The first part of the challenged statute, which required the two-parent notification, provided no alternative means for a pregnant minor to obtain authorization for an abortion. However, the second part of the statute provided that if the first part were ever judicially enjoined the same two-parent notice requirement would be enforced with the addition of a judicial bypass procedure. Under this provision the minor can avoid notifying either parent if she can persuade a judge that she is a "mature" minor or, if immature, that an abortion without notice to her parents would be in her "best interests.''

c. In *Ohio v. Akron Center for Reproductive Health (Akron II)*, 497 U.S. 502, 110 S.Ct. 2972, 111 L.Ed.2d 405 (1990), a companion case to *Hodgson*, the same six justices rejected a facial challenge to a state law prohibiting a physician or other person from performing an abortion on an unemancipated minor absent notice to one of the minor's parents or a court order authorizing the minor to consent.

KENNEDY, J., joined by Rehnquist, C.J., and White and Scalia, JJ., dissented on this issue, reminding his colleagues that the Court "must defer to a reasonable judgment by the state legislature when it determines what is sound public policy" and maintaining "that it was reasonable for the legislature to conclude that in most cases notice to both parents will work to the minor's benefit" (not only where the minor lives in the "ideal family setting," but also where she no longer lives with both parents).

Because O'Connor, J., agreed with the "Kennedy group" that the constitutional objection to the two-parent notification requirement is removed by the judicial bypass—"the interference with the internal operation of the family [simply] does not exist where the minor can avoid notifying one or both parents by use of the bypass procedure"—KENNEDY, J., joined by Rehnquist, C.J., and White and Scalia, JJ., wrote the principal opinion upholding that provision: "The simple fact is that *Bellotti v. Baird* [*Bellotti II*], 443 U.S. 622, 99 S.Ct. 3035, 61 L.Ed.2d 797 (1979), stands for the proposition that a two-parent consent law is constitutional if it provides for a sufficient judicial bypass alternative, and it requires us to sustain the statute before us here."

MARSHALL, J., joined by Brennan and Blackmun, JJ., dissented from the judgment of the Court that the judicial bypass renders the parental notice and 48-hour delay requirements constitutional: "This Court has addressed judicial bypass procedures only in the context of facial challenges. The Court has never considered the actual burdens a particular bypass provision imposes on a woman's right to choose an abortion. Such consideration establishes that, even if judges authorized every abortion sought by petitioning minors,[d] Minnesota's judicial bypass is far too burdensome to remedy an otherwise unconstitutional statute. [It] forces a young woman in an already dire situation to choose between two fundamentally unacceptable alternatives: notifying a possibly dictatorial or even abusive parent and justifying her profoundly personal decision in an intimidating judicial proceeding to a blackrobed stranger. For such a woman, this dilemma is more likely to result in trauma and pain than in an informed and voluntary decision."

In a separate opinion, SCALIA, J., who dissented from the Court's invalidation of the two-parent notification requirement without a bypass but concurred in the Court's other rulings, commented: "One will search in vain the document we are supposed to be construing for text that provides the basis for the argument over these distinctions; and will find in our society's tradition regarding abortion no hint that the distinctions are constitutionally relevant, much less any indication how a constitutional argument about them ought to be resolved. The random and unpredictable results of our consequently unchanneled individual views make it increasingly evident, Term after Term, that the tools for this job are not to be found in the lawyer's—and hence not in the judge's—workbox. I continue to dissent from this enterprise of devising an Abortion Code, and from the illusion that we have authority to do so."

---

d. Of 3,573 judicial bypass petitions filed in Minnesota courts during a period of four and a half years, all but 15 were granted. See also Robert H. Mnookin, *In the Interest of Children*, 262–63 (1985). Professor Mnookin's study of a Massachusetts statute providing a judicial bypass procedure for minors seeking an abortion reveals that it is "a rubber-stamp, administrative procedure." In the first two years after the Massachusetts statute went into effect "none of the 1,300 young women who have gone to court have been successfully refused an abortion."

Notes and Questions

1. In *Hodgson*, did six justices "demote abortion from its fundamental status"? Did they ignore the traditional strict scrutiny applied to fundamental rights and analyze the state restrictions on abortion "under what amounted to a rational basis standard"? See 104 Harv.L.Rev. 253–54 (1990).

2. *Are "the tools for this job" not to be found in the judge's workbox?* Is Justice Scalia right? Consider Jed Rubenfeld, *On the Legal Status of the Proposition that "Life Begins at Conception,"* 43 Stan.L.Rev. 599, 615 (1991): "The 'tools' for this job are not in anyone's workbox. But a judge is not a handyman, and he cannot call in state legislators as professionals whenever he feels out of his depth. Has anyone ever imagined that the tools to determine what counts as 'religion' are ready to the jurist's hand? Yet, when this determination becomes dispositive of first amendment rights, the great difficulty of the question permits the judiciary neither to evade it nor to allow the states to answer it. In determining that life begins at a certain gestational point, a state establishes a compelling interest and thereby delineates the outer limit of a constitutional right. Courts cannot simply defer to state law on this point. They can no more defer here than in the case of a state's enactment of a certain definition of 'clear and present danger' allowing the legislature to prohibit constitutionally protected speech."

THE COURT REAFFIRMS "THE ESSENTIAL HOLDING OF *ROE*"

PLANNED PARENTHOOD OF SOUTHEASTERN PENNSYLVANIA v. CASEY
505 U.S. 833, 112 S.Ct. 2791, 120 L.Ed.2d 674 (1992).

JUSTICE O'CONNOR, JUSTICE KENNEDY, and JUSTICE SOUTER announced the judgment of the Court and delivered the opinion of the Court with respect to Parts I, II, III, V–A, V–C, and VI, an opinion with respect to Part V–E, in which JUSTICE STEVENS joins, and an opinion with respect to Parts IV, V–B, and V–D.

I. Liberty finds no refuge in a jurisprudence of doubt. Yet 19 years after our holding that the Constitution protects a woman's right to terminate her pregnancy in its early stages, *Roe v. Wade*, that definition of liberty is still questioned. Joining the respondents as amicus curiae, the United States, as it has done in five other cases in the last decade, again asks us to overrule *Roe*.

At issue in these cases are five provisions of the Pennsylvania Abortion Control Act of 1982 as amended in 1988 and 1989. [The] Act requires that a woman seeking an abortion give her informed consent prior to the abortion procedure, and specifies that she be provided with certain information at least 24 hours before the abortion is performed. For a minor to obtain an abortion, the Act requires the informed consent of one of her parents, but provides for a judicial bypass option if the minor does not wish to or cannot obtain a parent's consent. Another [provision] of the Act requires that, unless certain exceptions apply, a married woman seeking an abortion must sign a statement indicating that she has notified her husband of her intended abortion. § 3209. The Act exempts compliance with these three requirements in the event of a "medical emergency," which is defined in [§ 3203]. In addition to the above provisions regulating the performance of abortions, the Act imposes certain reporting requirements on facilities that provide abortion services.

Before any of these provisions took effect, the petitioners, who are five abortion clinics and one physician representing himself as well as a class of physicians who provide abortion services, brought this suit seeking declaratory and injunctive relief. [The District Court held all the provisions at issue unconstitutional, but the Court of Appeals sustained all of them except for the husband notification requirement.]

[At] oral argument in this Court, the attorney for the parties challenging the statute took the position that none of the enactments can be upheld without overruling *Roe*. We disagree [but] we acknowledge that our decisions after *Roe* cast doubt upon the meaning and reach of its holding. Further, the Chief Justice admits that he would overrule the central holding of *Roe* and adopt the rational relationship test as the sole criterion of constitutionality. State and federal courts as well as legislatures throughout the Union must have guidance as they seek to address this subject in conformance with the Constitution. Given these premises, we find it imperative to review once more the principles that define the rights of the woman and the legitimate authority of the State respecting the termination of pregnancies by abortion procedures.

After considering the fundamental constitutional questions resolved by *Roe*, principles of institutional integrity, and the rule of *stare decisis*, we are led to conclude this: the essential holding of *Roe* should be retained and once again reaffirmed.

* * * *Roe*'s essential holding, the holding we reaffirm, has three parts. First is a recognition of the right of the woman to choose to have an abortion before viability and to obtain it without undue interference from the State. Before viability, the State's interests are not strong enough to support a prohibition of abortion or the imposition of a substantial obstacle to the woman's effective right to elect the procedure. Second is a confirmation of the State's power to restrict abortions after fetal viability, if the law contains exceptions for pregnancies which endanger a woman's life or health. And third is the principle that the State has legitimate interests from the outset of the pregnancy in protecting the health of the woman and the life of the fetus that may become a child. These principles do not contradict one another; and we adhere to each.

II. Constitutional protection of the woman's decision to terminate her pregnancy derives from the Due Process Clause. [The] controlling word in the case before us is "liberty." Although a literal reading of the Clause might suggest that it governs only the procedures by which a State may deprive persons of liberty, for at least 105 years [the] Clause has been understood to contain a substantive component as well, one "barring certain government actions regardless of the fairness of the procedures used to implement them."

[It] is tempting, as a means of curbing the discretion of federal judges, to suppose that liberty encompasses no more than those rights already guaranteed to the individual against federal interference by the express provisions of the first eight amendments to the Constitution. But of course this Court has never accepted that view.

It is also tempting, for the same reason, to suppose that the Due Process Clause protects only those practices, defined at the most specific level, that were protected against government interference by other rules of law when the Fourteenth Amendment was ratified. See *Michael H. v. Gerald D.*, n. 6 [p. 461 infra] (opinion of Scalia, J.). But such a view would be inconsistent with our law. It is a promise of the Constitution that there is a realm of personal liberty which the government may not enter. We have vindicated this principle before. Marriage is mentioned nowhere in the Bill of Rights and interracial marriage was illegal in most States in the 19th century, but the Court was no doubt correct in finding it to be an aspect of liberty protected against state interference by the substantive component of the Due Process Clause in *Loving v. Virginia* [p. 1176 infra].

Neither the Bill of Rights nor the specific practices of States at the time of the adoption of the Fourteenth Amendment marks the outer limits of the substantive sphere of liberty which the Fourteenth Amendment protects. See U.S. Const., Amend. 9. As the second Justice Harlan recognized: "[T]he full scope of the liberty guaranteed by the Due Process Clause cannot be found in or limited by the precise terms of the specific guarantees elsewhere provided in the Constitution. This 'liberty' is not a series of isolated points pricked out in terms of the taking of property; the freedom of speech, press, and religion; the right to keep and bear arms; the freedom from unreasonable searches and seizures; and so on. It is a rational continuum which, broadly speaking, includes a freedom from all substantial arbitrary impositions and purposeless restraints * * *." *Poe v. Ullman* [p. 364 supra] (Harlan, J., dissenting from dismissal on jurisdictional grounds).

Justice Harlan wrote these words in addressing an issue the full Court did not reach in *Poe,* but the Court adopted his position four Terms later in *Griswold.* [It] is settled now, as it was when the Court heard arguments in *Roe,* that the Constitution places limits on a State's right to interfere with a person's most basic decisions about family and parenthood, as well as bodily integrity.

The inescapable fact is that adjudication of substantive due process claims may call upon the Court in interpreting the Constitution to exercise that same capacity which by tradition courts always have exercised: reasoned judgment. Its boundaries are not susceptible of expression as a simple rule. That does not mean we are free to invalidate state policy choices with which we disagree; yet neither does it permit us to shrink from the duties of our office. * * *

Men and women of good conscience can disagree, and we suppose some always shall disagree, about the profound moral and spiritual implications of terminating a pregnancy, even in its earliest stage. Some of us as individuals find abortion offensive to our most basic principles of morality, but that cannot control our decision. Our obligation is to define the liberty of all, not to mandate our own moral code. The underlying constitutional issue is whether the State can resolve these philosophic questions in such a definitive way that a woman lacks all choice in the matter, except perhaps [where] the pregnancy is itself a danger to her own life or health, or is the result of rape or incest. * * *

Our law affords constitutional protection to personal decisions relating to marriage, procreation, contraception, family relationships, child rearing, and education. [These] matters, involving the most intimate and personal choices a person may make in a lifetime, choices central to personal dignity and autonomy, are central to the liberty protected by the Fourteenth Amendment. At the heart of liberty is the right to define one's own concept of existence, of meaning, of the universe, and of the mystery of human life. Beliefs about these matters could not define the attributes of personhood were they formed under compulsion of the State.

These considerations begin our analysis of the woman's interest in terminating her pregnancy but cannot end it, for this reason: though the abortion decision may originate within the zone of conscience and belief, it is more than a philosophic exercise. Abortion is a unique act. It is an act fraught with consequences for others * * *. Though abortion is conduct, it does not follow that the State is entitled to proscribe it in all instances. That is because the liberty of the woman is at stake in a sense unique to the human condition and so unique to the law. The mother who carries a child to full term is subject to anxieties, to physical constraints, to pain that only she must bear. That these sacrifices have from the beginning of the human race been endured by woman with a pride that ennobles her in the eyes of others and gives to the infant a bond of love cannot alone be grounds for the State to insist she make the sacrifice. Her suffering is too intimate and personal for the State to insist, without more, upon its own vision of the woman's role, however dominant that vision has been in the course of our history and our culture. The destiny of the woman must be shaped to a large extent on her own conception of her spiritual imperatives and her place in society.

[Moreover,] in some critical respects the abortion decision is of the same character as the decision to use contraception, to which [our cases] afford constitutional protection. We have no doubt as to the correctness of those decisions. They support the reasoning in *Roe* relating to the woman's liberty because they involve personal decisions concerning not only the meaning of procreation but also human responsibility and respect for it.

[While] we appreciate the weight of the arguments made on behalf of the State in the case before us, arguments [concluding] that *Roe* should be overruled, the reservations any of us may have in reaffirming the central holding of *Roe* are outweighed by the explication of individual liberty we have given combined with the force of stare decisis. We turn now to that doctrine.

III. The obligation to follow precedent begins with necessity, and a contrary necessity marks its outer limit. [The] very concept of the rule of law underlying our own Constitution requires such continuity over time that a respect for precedent is, by definition, indispensable. At the other extreme, a different necessity would make itself felt if a prior judicial ruling should come to be seen so clearly as error that its enforcement was for that very reason doomed.

[When] this Court reexamines a prior holding, its judgment is customarily informed by a series of prudential and pragmatic considerations designed to test the consistency of overruling a prior decision with the ideal of the rule of law, and to gauge the respective costs of reaffirming and overruling a prior case. Thus, for example, we may ask whether the rule has proved to be intolerable simply in defying practical workability; whether the rule is subject to a kind of reliance that would lend a special hardship to the consequences of overruling and add inequity to the cost of repudiation; whether related principles of law have so far developed as to have left the old rule no more than a remnant of abandoned doctrine; or whether facts have so changed or come to be seen so differently, as to have robbed the old rule of significant application or justification.

So in this case we may inquire whether *Roe*'s central rule has been found unworkable; whether the rule's limitation on state power could be removed without serious inequity to those who have relied upon it or significant damage to the stability of the society governed by the rule in question; whether the law's growth in the intervening years has left *Roe*'s central rule a doctrinal anachronism discounted by society; and whether *Roe*'s premises of fact have so far changed in the ensuing two decades as to render its central holding somehow irrelevant or unjustifiable in dealing with the issue it addressed.

Although *Roe* has engendered opposition, it has in no sense proven "unworkable," representing as it does a simple limitation beyond which a state law is unenforceable.

[One] can readily imagine an argument stressing the dissimilarity of this case to one involving property or contract. Abortion is customarily chosen as an unplanned response to the consequence of unplanned activity or to the failure of conventional birth control, and except on the assumption that no intercourse would have occurred but for *Roe*'s holding, such behavior may appear to justify no reliance claim.

[But to eliminate the issue of reliance] would be simply to refuse to face the fact that for two decades of economic and social developments, people have organized intimate relationships and made choices that define their views of themselves and their places in society, in reliance on the availability of abortion in the event that contraception should fail. The ability of women to participate equally in the economic and social life of the Nation has been facilitated by their ability to control their reproductive lives. [While] the effect of reliance on *Roe* cannot be exactly measured, neither can the certain cost of overruling *Roe* for people who have ordered their thinking and living around that case be dismissed.

No evolution of legal principle has left *Roe*'s doctrinal footings weaker than they were in 1973. No development of constitutional law since the case was decided has implicitly or explicitly left *Roe* behind as a mere survivor of obsolete constitutional thinking.

[*Roe*] stands at an intersection of two lines of decisions, but in whichever doctrinal category one reads the case, the result for present purposes will be the same. The *Roe* Court itself placed its holding in the succession of cases most prominently exemplified by *Griswold*. When it is so seen, *Roe* is clearly in no jeopardy, since subsequent constitutional developments have neither disturbed, nor do they threaten to diminish, the scope of recognized protection accorded to the liberty relating to intimate relationships, the family, and decisions about whether or not to beget or bear a child.

Roe, however, may be seen [as] a rule (whether or not mistaken) of personal autonomy and bodily integrity, with doctrinal affinity to cases recognizing limits on governmental power to mandate medical treatment or to bar its rejection. If so, our cases since *Roe* accord with *Roe*'s view that a State's interest in the protection of life falls short of justifying any plenary override of individual liberty claims. *Cruzan* [p. 480 infra].

Finally, one could classify *Roe* as sui generis. If the case is so viewed, then there clearly has been no erosion of its central determination. [In] *Webster*, although two of the present authors questioned the trimester framework in a way consistent with our judgment today, a majority of the Court either decided to reaffirm or declined to address the constitutional validity of the central holding of *Roe*.

Nor will courts building upon *Roe* be likely to hand down erroneous decisions as a consequence. Even on the assumption that the central holding of *Roe* was in error, that error would go only to the strength of the state interest in fetal protection, not to the recognition afforded by the Constitution to the woman's liberty. The latter aspect of the decision fits comfortably within the framework of the Court's prior decisions including *Skinner*, *Griswold*, *Loving*, and *Eisenstadt*, the holdings of which are "not a series of isolated points," but mark a "rational continuum." *Poe v. Ullman* (Harlan, J., dissenting). * * *

The soundness of this prong of the *Roe* analysis is apparent from a consideration of the alternative. If indeed the woman's interest in deciding whether to bear and beget a child had not been recognized as in *Roe*, the State might as readily restrict a woman's right to choose to carry a pregnancy to term as to terminate it, to further asserted state interests in population control, or eugenics, for example. Yet *Roe* has been sensibly relied upon to counter any such suggestions. * * *

We have seen how time has overtaken some of *Roe*'s factual assumptions: advances in maternal health care allow for abortions safe to the mother later in pregnancy than was true in 1973, and advances in neonatal care have advanced viability to a point somewhat earlier. But these facts go only to the scheme of time limits on the realization of competing interests, and the divergences from the factual premises of 1973 have no bearing on the validity of *Roe*'s central holding, that viability marks the earliest point at which the State's interest in fetal life is constitutionally adequate to justify a legislative ban on nontherapeutic abortions. The soundness or unsoundness of that constitutional judgment in no sense turns on whether viability occurs at approximately 28 weeks, as was usual at the time of *Roe*, at 23 to 24 weeks, as it sometimes does today, or at some moment even slightly earlier in pregnancy, as it may if fetal respiratory capacity can somehow be enhanced in the future. [No] change in *Roe*'s factual underpinning has left its central holding obsolete, and none supports an argument for overruling it.

The sum of the precedential inquiry to this point shows *Roe*'s underpinnings unweakened in any way affecting its central holding. While it has engendered disapproval, it has not been unworkable. An entire generation has come of age free to assume *Roe*'s concept of liberty in defining the capacity of women to act in society, and to make reproductive decisions. [Within] the bounds of normal stare decisis analysis, [the] stronger argument is for affirming *Roe*'s central holding, with whatever degree of personal reluctance any of us may have, not for overruling it.

In a less significant case, *stare decisis* analysis could, and would, stop at the point we have reached. But the sustained and widespread debate *Roe* has provoked calls for some comparison between that case and others of comparable dimension that have responded to national controversies and taken on the impress of the controversies addressed. Only two such decisional lines from the past century present themselves for examination, and in each instance the result reached by the Court accorded with the principles we apply today.

The first example is that line of cases identified with *Lochner v. New York* (1905) [and] *Adkins v. Children's Hospital* (1923). * * * Fourteen years later, *West Coast Hotel Co. v. Parrish* (1937) signaled the demise of *Lochner* by overruling *Adkins*. In the meantime, the Depression had come and, with it, the lesson that seemed unmistakable to most people by 1937, that the interpretation of contractual freedom protected in *Adkins* rested on fundamentally false factual assumptions about the capacity of a relatively unregulated market to satisfy minimal levels of human welfare. [The] facts upon which the earlier case had premised a constitutional resolution of social controversy had proved to be untrue, and history's demonstration of their untruth not only justified but required the new choice of constitutional principle that *West Coast Hotel* announced. Of course, it was true that the Court lost something by its misperception, or its lack of prescience, and the Court-packing crisis only magnified the loss; but the clear demonstration that the facts of economic life were different from those previously assumed warranted the repudiation of the old law.

The second comparison that 20th century history invites is with the cases employing the separate-but-equal rule for applying the Fourteenth Amendment's equal protection guarantee. They began with *Plessy v. Ferguson* [p. 1158 infra], holding that legislatively mandated racial segregation in public transportation works no denial of equal protection. [The] *Plessy* Court considered "the underlying fallacy of the plaintiff's argument to consist in the assumption that the enforced separation of the two races stamps the colored race with a badge of inferiority. If this be so, it is not by reason of anything found in the act, but solely because the colored race chooses to put that construction upon it." [But] this understanding of the facts and the rule it was stated to justify were repudiated in *Brown v. Board of Education* [p. 1167 infra].

The Court in *Brown* [observed] that whatever may have been the understanding in *Plessy*'s time of the power of segregation to stigmatize those who were segregated with a "badge of inferiority," it was clear by 1954 that legally sanctioned segregation had just such an effect, to the point that racially separate public educational facilities were deemed inherently unequal. Society's understanding of the facts upon which a constitutional ruling was sought in 1954 was thus fundamentally different from the basis claimed for the decision in 1896. While we think *Plessy* was wrong the day it was decided, we must also recognize that the *Plessy* Court's explanation for its decision was so clearly at odds with the facts apparent to the Court in 1954 that the decision to reexamine *Plessy* was on this ground alone not only justified but required.

West Coast Hotel and *Brown* each rested on facts, or an understanding of facts, changed from those which furnished the claimed justifications for the earlier constitutional resolutions. [In] constitutional adjudication as elsewhere in life, changed circumstances may impose new obligations, and the thoughtful part of the Nation could accept each decision to overrule a prior case as a response to the Court's constitutional duty.

Because [neither] the factual underpinnings of *Roe*'s central holding nor our understanding of it has changed [the] Court could not pretend to be reexamining the prior law with any justification beyond a present doctrinal disposition to come out differently from the Court of 1973. To overrule prior law for no other reason than that would run counter to the view repeated in our cases, that a decision to overrule should rest on some special reason over and above the belief that a prior case was wrongly decided. * * *

The examination of the conditions justifying the repudiation of *Adkins* by *West Coast Hotel* and *Plessy* by *Brown* is enough to suggest the terrible price that would have been paid if the Court had not overruled as it did. In the present case, however, [the] terrible price would be paid for overruling. Our analysis would not be complete, however, without explaining why overruling *Roe*'s central holding would not only reach an unjustifiable result under principles of stare decisis, but would seriously weaken the Court's capacity to exercise the judicial power and to function as the Supreme Court of a Nation dedicated to the rule of law. [The] Court cannot buy support for its decisions by spending money and, except to a minor degree, it cannot independently coerce obedience to its decrees. The Court's power lies, rather, in its legitimacy, a product of substance and perception that shows itself in the people's acceptance of the Judiciary as fit to determine what the Nation's law means and to declare what it demands.

The underlying substance of this legitimacy is of course the warrant for the Court's decisions in the Constitution and the lesser sources of legal principle on which the Court draws. That substance is expressed in the Court's opinions, and our contemporary understanding is such that a decision without principled justification would be no judicial act at all. But even when justification is furnished by apposite legal principle, something more is required. Because not every conscientious claim of principled justification will be accepted as such, the justification claimed must be beyond dispute. The Court must take care to speak and act in ways that allow people to accept its decisions on the terms the Court claims for them, as grounded truly in principle, not as compromises with social and political pressures having, as such, no bearing on the principled choices that the Court is obliged to make. Thus, the Court's legitimacy depends on making legally principled decisions under circumstances in which their principled character is sufficiently plausible to be accepted by the Nation.

[The] country can accept some correction of error without necessarily questioning the legitimacy of the Court. In two circumstances, however, the Court would almost certainly fail to receive the benefit of the doubt in overruling prior cases. There is, first, [a] limit to the amount of error that can plausibly be imputed to prior courts. If that limit should be exceeded, disturbance of prior rulings would be taken as evidence that justifiable reexamination of principle had given way to drives for particular results in the short term. The legitimacy of the Court would fade with the frequency of its vacillation.

That first circumstance can be described as hypothetical; the second is to the point here and now. Where, in the performance of its judicial duties, the Court decides a case in such a way as to resolve the sort of intensely divisive controversy reflected in *Roe* and those rare, comparable cases, its decision has a dimension that the resolution of the normal case does not carry. It is the dimension present whenever the Court's interpretation of the Constitution calls the contending sides of a national controversy to end their national division by accepting a common mandate rooted in the Constitution.

The Court is not asked to do this very often, having thus addressed the Nation only twice in our lifetime, in the decisions of *Brown* and *Roe*. But when the Court does act in this way, its decision requires an equally rare precedential force to counter the inevitable efforts to overturn it and to thwart its implementation. [To] overrule under fire in the absence of the most compelling reason to reexamine a watershed decision would subvert the Court's legitimacy beyond any serious question.

[The] country's loss of confidence in the judiciary would be underscored by an equally certain and equally reasonable condemnation for another failing in overruling unnecessarily and under pressure. Some cost will be paid by anyone who approves or implements a constitutional decision where it is unpopular, or who refuses to work to undermine the decision or to force its reversal. The price may be criticism or ostracism, or it may be violence. An extra price will be paid by those who themselves disapprove of the decision's results when viewed outside of constitutional terms, but who nevertheless struggle to accept it, because they respect the rule of law. To all those who will be so tested by following, the Court implicitly undertakes to remain steadfast, lest in the end a price be paid for nothing. [N]o Court that broke its faith with the people could sensibly expect credit for principle in the decision by which it did that.

[The] Court's duty in the present case is clear. In 1973, it confronted the already-divisive issue of governmental power to limit personal choice to undergo abortion, for which it provided a new resolution based on the due process guaranteed by the Fourteenth Amendment. Whether or not a new social consensus is developing on that issue, its divisiveness is no less today than in 1973, and pressure to overrule the decision, like pressure to retain it, has grown only more intense. A decision to overrule *Roe*'s essential holding under the existing circumstances would address error, if error there was, at the cost of both profound and unnecessary damage to the Court's legitimacy, and to the Nation's commitment to the rule of law. It is therefore imperative to adhere to the essence of *Roe*'s original decision, and we do so today.

IV. * * * We conclude that the basic decision in *Roe* was based on a constitutional analysis which we cannot now repudiate. The woman's liberty is not so unlimited, however, that from the outset the State cannot show its concern for the life of the unborn, and at a later point in fetal development the State's interest in life has sufficient force so that the right of the woman to terminate the pregnancy can be restricted.

That brings us, of course, to the point where much criticism has been directed at *Roe,* a criticism that always inheres when the Court draws a specific rule from what in the Constitution is but a general standard. [But] [l]iberty must not be extinguished for want of a line that is clear. * * *

We conclude the line should be drawn at viability, so that before that time the woman has a right to choose to terminate her pregnancy. We adhere to this principle for two reasons. First [is] the doctrine of stare decisis. [We] have twice reaffirmed [*Roe*] in the face of great opposition.

[The] second reason is that the concept of viability, as we noted in *Roe,* is the time at which there is a realistic possibility of maintaining and nourishing a life outside the womb, so that the independent existence of the second life can in reason and all fairness be the object of state protection that now overrides the rights of the woman.

[The] woman's right to terminate her pregnancy before viability is the most central principle of *Roe*. It is a rule of law and a component of liberty we cannot renounce.

On the other side of the equation is the interest of the State in the protection of potential life. [The] weight to be given this state interest, not the strength of the woman's interest, was the difficult question faced in *Roe*. We do not need to say whether each of us, had we been Members of the Court when the valuation of the State interest came before it as an original matter, would have concluded, as the *Roe* Court did, that its weight is insufficient to justify a ban on abortions prior to viability even when it is subject to certain exceptions. The matter is not before us in the first instance, and coming as it does after nearly 20 years of litigation in *Roe*'s wake we are satisfied that the immediate question is not the soundness of *Roe*'s resolution of the issue, but the precedential force that must be accorded to its holding. And we have concluded that the essential holding of *Roe* should be reaffirmed.

Yet it must be remembered that *Roe* speaks with clarity in establishing not only the woman's liberty but also the State's "important and legitimate interest in potential life." That portion [of] *Roe* has been given too little acknowledgement and implementation by the Court in its subsequent cases. Those cases decided that any regulation touching upon the abortion decision must survive strict scrutiny, to be sustained only if drawn in narrow terms to further a compelling state interest. Not all of the cases decided under that formulation can be reconciled with the holding in *Roe* itself that the State has legitimate interests in the health of the woman and in protecting the potential life within her. In resolving this tension, we choose to rely upon *Roe,* as against the later cases.

[The] trimester framework no doubt was erected to ensure that the woman's right to choose not become so subordinate to the State's interest in promoting fetal life that her choice exists in theory but not in fact. We do not agree, however, that the trimester approach is necessary to accomplish this objective. [Though] the woman has a right to choose to terminate or continue her pregnancy before viability, it does not at all follow that the State is prohibited from taking steps to ensure that this choice is thoughtful and informed. * * *

We reject the trimester framework, which we do not consider to be part of the essential holding of *Roe*. Measures aimed at ensuring that a woman's choice contemplates the consequences for the fetus do not necessarily interfere with the right recognized in *Roe*, although those measures have been found to be inconsistent with the rigid trimester framework announced in that case. [The] trimester framework suffers from these basic flaws: in its formulation it misconceives the nature of the pregnant woman's interest; and in practice it undervalues the State's interest in potential life, as recognized in *Roe*.

* * * Numerous forms of state regulation might have the incidental effect of increasing the cost or decreasing the availability of medical care, whether for abortion or any other medical procedure. The fact that a law which serves a valid purpose, one not designed to strike at the right itself, has the incidental effect of making it more difficult or more expensive to procure an abortion cannot be enough to invalidate it. Only where state regulation imposes an undue burden on a woman's ability to make this decision does the power of the State reach into the heart of the liberty protected by the Due Process Clause.

[A] finding of an undue burden is a shorthand for the conclusion that a state regulation has the purpose or effect of placing a substantial obstacle in the path of a woman seeking an abortion of a nonviable fetus. A statute with this purpose is invalid because the means chosen by the State to further the interest in potential life must be calculated to inform the woman's free choice, not hinder it. And a statute which, while furthering the interest in potential life or some other valid state interest, has the effect of placing a substantial obstacle in the path of a woman's choice cannot be considered a permissible means of serving its legitimate ends. [In] our considered judgment, an undue burden is an unconstitutional burden. Understood another way, we answer the question, left open in previous opinions discussing the undue burden formulation, whether a law designed to further the State's interest in fetal life which imposes an undue burden on the woman's decision before fetal viability could be constitutional. The answer is no.

Some guiding principles should emerge. What is at stake is the woman's right to make the ultimate decision, not a right to be insulated from all others in doing so. Regulations which do no more than create a structural mechanism by which the State, or the parent or guardian of a minor, may express profound respect for the life of the unborn are permitted, if they are not a substantial obstacle to the woman's exercise of the right to choose. [Unless] it has that effect on her right of choice, a state measure designed to persuade her to choose childbirth over abortion will be upheld if reasonably related to that goal. Regulations designed to foster the health of a woman seeking an abortion are valid if they do not constitute an undue burden.

Even when jurists reason from shared premises, some disagreement is inevitable. [That] is to be expected in the application of any legal standard which must accommodate life's complexity. We do not expect it to be otherwise with respect to the undue burden standard. We give this summary:

(a) To protect the central right recognized by *Roe* while at the same time accommodating the State's profound interest in potential life, we will employ the undue burden analysis as explained in this opinion. An undue burden exists, and therefore a provision of law is invalid, if its purpose or effect is to place a substantial obstacle in the path of a woman seeking an abortion before the fetus attains viability.

(b) We reject the rigid trimester framework of *Roe*. To promote the State's profound interest in potential life, throughout pregnancy the State may take measures to ensure that the woman's choice is informed, and measures designed to advance this interest will not be invalidated as long as their purpose is to persuade the woman to choose childbirth over abortion. These measures must not be an undue burden on the right.

(c) As with any medical procedure, the State may enact regulations to further the health or safety of a woman seeking an abortion. Unnecessary health regulations that have the purpose or effect of presenting a substantial obstacle to a woman seeking an abortion impose an undue burden on the right.

(d) Our adoption of the undue burden analysis does not disturb the central holding of *Roe,* and we reaffirm that holding. [A] State may not prohibit any woman from making the ultimate decision to terminate her pregnancy before viability.

(e) We also reaffirm *Roe*'s holding that "subsequent to viability, the State in promoting its interest in the potentiality of human life may, if it chooses, regulate, and even proscribe, abortion except where it is necessary, in appropriate medical judgment, for the preservation of the life or health of the mother."

These principles control our assessment of the Pennsylvania statute, and we now turn to the issue of the validity of its challenged provisions.

V. * * * A. Because it is central to the operation of various other requirements, we begin with the statute's definition of medical emergency. Under the statute, a medical emergency is "[t]hat condition which, on the basis of the physician's good faith clinical judgment, so complicates the medical condition of a pregnant woman as to necessitate the immediate abortion of her pregnancy to avert her death or for which a delay will create serious risk of substantial and irreversible impairment of a major bodily function."

Petitioners argue that the definition is too narrow, contending that it forecloses the possibility of an immediate abortion despite some significant health risks. [As construed by the Court of Appeals, the statute's definition of medical emergency as] "intended to assure that compliance with [the] abortion regulations would not in any way pose a significant threat to the life or health of a woman" [imposes] no undue burden on a woman's abortion right.

B. [Except] in a medical emergency, the statute requires that at least 24 hours before performing an abortion a physician inform the woman of the nature of the procedure, the health risks of the abortion and of childbirth, and the "probable gestational age of the unborn child." The physician or a qualified nonphysician must inform the woman of the availability of printed materials published by the State describing the fetus and providing information about medical assistance for childbirth, information about child support from the father, and a list of agencies which provide adoption and other services as alternatives to abortion. An abortion may not be performed unless the woman certifies in writing that she has been informed of the availability of these printed materials and has been provided them if she chooses to view them.

[To] the extent *Akron I* and *Thornburgh* find a constitutional violation when the government requires, as it does here, the giving of truthful, nonmisleading information about the nature of the procedure, the attendant health risks and those of childbirth, and the "probable gestational age" of the fetus, those cases go too far, are inconsistent with *Roe*'s acknowledgment of an important interest in potential life, and are overruled. [This] requirement cannot be considered a substantial obstacle to obtaining an abortion, and, it follows, there is no undue burden.

[The] Pennsylvania statute also requires us to reconsider the holding in *Akron I* that the State may not require that a physician, as opposed to a qualified assistant, provide information relevant to a woman's informed consent. Since there is no evidence on this record that requiring a doctor to give the information as provided by the statute would amount in practical terms to a substantial obstacle to a woman seeking an abortion, we conclude that it is not an undue burden. * * *

Our analysis of Pennsylvania's 24–hour waiting period between the provision of the information deemed necessary to informed consent and the performance of an abortion under the undue burden standard requires us to reconsider the premise behind the decision in *Akron I* invalidating a parallel requirement. * * * We consider the [*Akron I*] conclusion to be wrong. The idea that important decisions will be more informed and deliberate if they follow some period of reflection does not strike us as unreasonable, particularly where the statute directs that important information become part of the background of the decision.

[Whether] the mandatory 24–hour waiting period is nonetheless invalid because in practice it is a substantial obstacle to a woman's choice to terminate her pregnancy is a closer question. [The findings of fact indicate that for] those women who have the fewest financial resources, those who must travel long distances, and those who have difficulty explaining their whereabouts to husbands, employers, or others, the 24–hour waiting period will be "particularly burdensome."

These findings are troubling in some respects, but they do not demonstrate that the waiting period constitutes an undue burden. [Under] the undue burden standard a State is permitted to enact persuasive measures which favor childbirth over abortion, even if those measures do not further a health interest. And while the waiting period does limit a physician's discretion, that is not, standing alone, a reason to invalidate it. In light of the construction given the statute's definition of medical emergency by the Court of Appeals, and the District Court's findings, we cannot say that the waiting period imposes a real health risk.

We also disagree with the District Court's conclusion that the "particularly burdensome" effects of the waiting period on some women require its invalidation. A particular burden is not of necessity a substantial obstacle. Whether a burden falls on a particular group is a distinct inquiry from whether it is a substantial obstacle even as to the women in that group. * * *

We are left with the argument that the various aspects of the informed consent requirement are unconstitutional because they place barriers in the way of abortion on demand. Even the broadest reading of *Roe*, however, has not suggested that there is a constitutional right to abortion on demand. Rather, the right protected by *Roe* is a right to decide to terminate a pregnancy free of undue interference by the State. [The] informed consent requirement is not an undue burden on that right.

C. Section 3209 of Pennsylvania's abortion law provides, except in cases of medical emergency, that no physician shall perform an abortion on a married woman without receiving a signed statement from the woman that she has notified her spouse that she is about to undergo an abortion. The woman has the option of providing an alternative signed statement certifying that her husband is not the man who impregnated her; that her husband could not be located; that the pregnancy is the result of spousal sexual assault which she has reported; or that the woman believes that notifying her husband will cause him or someone else to inflict bodily injury upon her. A physician who performs an abortion on a married woman without receiving the appropriate signed statement will have his or her license revoked, and is liable to the husband for damages.

[Among the findings of fact made by the District Court are that '[m]ere notification of pregnancy is frequently a flashpoint for battering and violence within the family [because the] battering husband may deny parentage and use the pregnancy as an excuse for abuse'; a woman's attempt to notify her husband pursuant to § 3209 "could accidentally disclose her whereabouts [in a shelter or safe house] to her husband"; and "[b]ecause of the nature of the battering relationship, battered women are unlikely to avail themselves of the exceptions to § 3209, regardless of whether the section applies to them."]

[Various studies of domestic violence] and the District Court's findings reinforce what common sense would suggest. In well-functioning marriages, spouses discuss important intimate decisions such as whether to bear a child. But there are millions of women in this country who are the victims of regular physical and psychological abuse at the hands of their husbands. Should these women become pregnant, they may have very good reasons for not wishing to inform their husbands of their decision to obtain an abortion. Many may fear devastating forms of psychological abuse from their husbands. [If] anything in this field is certain, it is that victims of spousal sexual assault are extremely reluctant to report the abuse to the government; hence, a great many spousal rape victims will not be exempt from the notification requirement imposed by § 3209.

The spousal notification requirement is thus likely to prevent a significant number of women from obtaining an abortion. It does not merely make abortions a little more difficult or expensive to obtain; for many women, it will impose a substantial obstacle. We must not blind ourselves to the fact that the significant number of women who fear for their safety and the safety of their children are likely to be deterred from procuring an abortion as surely as if the Commonwealth had outlawed abortion in all cases.

[Section] 3209's real target is narrower even than the class of women seeking abortions identified by the State: it is married women seeking abortions who do not wish to notify their husbands of their intentions and who do not qualify for one of the statutory exceptions to the notice requirement. The unfortunate yet persisting conditions we document above will mean that in a large fraction of the cases in which § 3209 is relevant, it will operate as a substantial obstacle to a woman's choice to undergo an abortion. It is an undue burden, and therefore invalid.

This conclusion is in no way inconsistent with our decisions upholding parental notification or consent requirements. Those enactments, and our judgment that they are constitutional, are based on the quite reasonable assumption that minors will benefit from consultation with their parents and that children will often not realize that their parents have their best interests at heart. We cannot adopt a parallel assumption about adult women.

[It] is an inescapable biological fact that state regulation with respect to the child a woman is carrying will have a far greater impact on the mother's liberty than on the father's. The effect of state regulation on a woman's protected liberty is doubly deserving of scrutiny in such a case, as the State has touched not only upon the private sphere of the family but upon the very bodily integrity of the pregnant woman. Cf. *Cruzan*. [The] Constitution protects individuals, men and women alike, from unjustified state interference, even when that interference is enacted into law for the benefit of their spouses.

[In] keeping with our rejection of the common-law understanding of a woman's role within the family, the Court held in *Planned Parenthood v. Danforth*, 428 U.S. 52, 96 S. Ct. 2831, 49 L. Ed. 2d 788 (1976), that the Constitution does not permit a State to require a married woman to obtain her husband's consent before undergoing an abortion. The principles that guided the Court in *Danforth* should be our guides today. For the great many women who are victims of abuse inflicted by their husbands, or whose children are the victims of such abuse, a spousal notice requirement enables the husband to wield an effective veto over his wife's decision.

[The] husband's interest in the life of the child his wife is carrying does not permit the State to empower him with this troubling degree of authority over his wife. The contrary view leads to consequences reminiscent of the common law. A husband has no enforceable right to require a wife to advise him before she exercises her personal choices. * * *

Section 3209 embodies a view of marriage consonant with the common-law status of married women but repugnant to our present understanding of marriage and of the nature of the rights secured by the Constitution. Women do not lose their constitutionally protected liberty when they marry. The Constitution protects all individuals, male or female, married or unmarried, from the abuse of governmental power, even where that power is employed for the supposed benefit of a member of the individual's family. These considerations confirm our conclusion that § 3209 is invalid.

D. [Except] in a medical emergency, an unemancipated young woman under 18 may not obtain an abortion unless she and one of her parents (or guardian) provides informed consent as defined above. If neither a parent nor a guardian provides consent, a court may authorize the performance of an abortion upon a determination that the young woman is mature and capable of giving informed consent and has in fact given her informed consent, or that an abortion would be in her best interests.

We have been over most of this ground before. Our cases establish, and we reaffirm today, that a State may require a minor seeking an abortion to obtain the consent of a parent or guardian, provided that there is an adequate judicial bypass procedure. * * *

E. [As for the provisions imposing certain reporting requirements on facilities that provide abortion services] [in] *Danforth* we held that recordkeeping and reporting provisions "that are reasonably directed to the preservation of maternal health and that properly respect a patient's confidentiality and privacy are permissible." [Under] this standard, all the provisions at issue here except that relating to spousal notice are constitutional. Although they do not relate to the State's interest in informing the woman's choice, they do relate to health. The collection of information with respect to actual patients is a vital element of medical research, and so it cannot be said that the requirements serve no purpose other than to make abortions more difficult. Nor do we find that the requirements impose a substantial obstacle to a woman's choice. At most they might increase the cost of some abortions by a slight amount. * * *

VI.   Our Constitution is a covenant running from the first generation of Americans to us and then to future generations. It is a coherent succession. Each generation must learn anew that the Constitution's written terms embody ideas and aspirations that must survive more ages than one. We accept our responsibility not to retreat from interpreting the full meaning of the covenant in light of all of our precedents. We invoke it once again to define the freedom guaranteed by the Constitution's own promise, the promise of liberty. * * *

JUSTICE STEVENS, concurring in part and dissenting in part.

The portions of the Court's opinion that I have joined are more important than those with which I disagree. I shall therefore first comment on significant areas of agreement, and then explain the limited character of my disagreement.

The Court is unquestionably correct in concluding that the doctrine of stare decisis has controlling significance in a case of this kind, notwithstanding an individual justice's concerns about the merits.[1] [*Roe*] was a natural sequel to the protection of individual liberty established in *Griswold*. *Roe* is an integral part of a correct understanding of both the concept of liberty and the basic equality of men and women.

Stare decisis also provides a sufficient basis for my agreement with the joint opinion's reaffirmation of *Roe*'s post-viability analysis. Specifically, I accept the proposition that "[i]f the State is interested in protecting fetal life after viability, it may go so far as to proscribe abortion during that period, except when it is necessary to preserve the life or health of the mother."

I also accept what is implicit in the Court's analysis, namely, a reaffirmation of *Roe*'s explanation of *why* the State's obligation to protect the life or health of the mother must take precedence over any duty to the unborn. The Court in *Roe* carefully considered, and rejected, the State's argument "that the fetus is a 'person' within the language and meaning of the Fourteenth Amendment." * * * [From] this holding, there was no dissent; indeed, no member of the Court has ever questioned this fundamental proposition. Thus, as a matter of federal constitutional law, a developing organism that is not yet a "person" does not have what is sometimes described as a "right to life."[2]

My disagreement with the joint opinion begins with its understanding of the trimester framework established in *Roe*. Contrary to the suggestion of the joint opinion, it is not a "contradiction" to recognize that the State may have a legitimate interest in potential human life and, at the same time, to conclude that that interest does not justify the regulation of abortion before viability (although other interests, such as maternal health, may). The fact that the State's interest is legitimate does not tell us when, if ever, that interest outweighs the pregnant woman's interest in personal liberty. It is appropriate, therefore, to consider more carefully the nature of the interests at stake. * * *

Identifying the State's interests—which the States rarely articulate with any precision—makes clear that the interest in protecting potential life is not ground-

1.   It is sometimes useful to view the issue of stare decisis from a historical perspective. In the last nineteen years, fifteen Justices have confronted the basic issue presented in *Roe*. Of those, eleven have voted as the majority does today: Chief Justice Burger, Justices Douglas, Brennan, Stewart, Marshall, and Powell, and Justices Blackmun, O'Connor, Kennedy, Souter, and myself. Only four—all of whom happen to be on the Court today—have reached the opposite conclusion.

2.   Professor Dworkin has made this comment on the issue: "The suggestion that states are free to declare a fetus a person * * * assumes that a state can curtail some persons' constitutional rights by adding new persons to the constitutional population." * * *

ed in the Constitution. It is, instead, an indirect interest supported by both humanitarian and pragmatic concerns. Many of our citizens believe that any abortion reflects an unacceptable disrespect for potential human life and that the performance of more than a million abortions each year is intolerable; many find third trimester abortions performed when the fetus is approaching personhood particularly offensive. The State has a legitimate interest in minimizing such offense. * * *

Weighing the State's interest in potential life and the woman's liberty interest, I agree with the joint opinion that the State may " 'expres[s] a preference for normal childbirth,' " that the State may take steps to ensure that a woman's choice "is thoughtful and informed," and that "States are free to enact laws to provide a reasonable framework for a woman to make a decision that has such profound and lasting meaning." Serious questions arise, however, when a State attempts to "persuade the woman to choose childbirth over abortion." Decisional autonomy must limit the State's power to inject into a woman's most personal deliberations its own views of what is best. The State may promote its preferences by funding childbirth, by creating and maintaining alternatives to abortion, and by espousing the virtues of family; but it must respect the individual's freedom to make such judgments.

[Under the principles established in the Court's previous cases, Justice Stevens deemed unconstitutional those sections requiring a woman to be provided with a wide range of materials "clearly designed to persuade her to choose not to undergo the abortion. But he did not find constitutionally objectionable those sections requiring the physician to inform a woman of the nature and risks of the abortion procedure and the medical risks of carrying to term for these "are neutral requirements comparable to those imposed in other medical procedures. These sections indicate no effort by the State to influence the woman's choice in any way."]

The 24–hour waiting period [raises] even more serious concerns. Such a requirement arguably furthers the State's interests in two ways, neither of which is constitutionally permissible.

First, it may be argued that the 24–hour delay is justified by the mere fact that it is likely to reduce the number of abortions, thus furthering the State's interest in potential life. But such an argument would justify any form of coercion that placed an obstacle in the woman's path. * * *

Second, it can more reasonably be argued that the 24–hour delay furthers the State's interest in ensuring that the woman's decision is informed and thoughtful. But there is no evidence that the mandated delay benefits women or that it is necessary to enable the physician to convey any relevant information to the patient. The mandatory delay thus appears to rest on outmoded and unacceptable assumptions about the decisionmaking capacity of women.

[A] correct application of the "undue burden" standard leads to the same conclusion concerning the constitutionality of these requirements. A state-imposed burden on the exercise of a constitutional right is measured both by its effects and by its character: A burden may be "undue" either because the burden is too severe or because it lacks a legitimate, rational justification.

The 24–hour delay requirement fails both parts of this test. [Even] in those cases in which the delay is not especially onerous, it is, in my opinion, "undue" because there is no evidence that such a delay serves a useful and legitimate purpose.

[The] counseling provisions are similarly infirm. [The] statute requires that [information concerning alternatives to abortion, the availability of medical assistance benefits, and the possibility of child-support payments] be given to *all* women seeking abortions, including those for whom such information is clearly useless, such as those who are married, those who have undergone the procedure in the past and are fully aware of the options, and those who are fully convinced that abortion is their only reasonable option. Moreover, [information of probable gestational age] is of little decisional value in most cases, because 90% of all abortions are performed during the first trimester when fetal age has less relevance than when the fetus nears viability. * * * I conclude that [these] requirements do not serve a useful purpose and thus constitute an unnecessary—and therefore undue—burden on the woman's constitutional liberty to decide to terminate her pregnancy.

Accordingly, while I disagree with Parts IV, V–B, and V–D of the joint opinion,[8] I join the remainder of the Court's opinion.

JUSTICE BLACKMUN, concurring in part, concurring in the judgment in part, and dissenting in part.

I join parts I, II, III, V–A, V–C, and VI of the joint opinion * * *.

Three years ago, in *Webster,* four Members of this Court appeared poised to "cas[t] into darkness the hopes and visions of every woman in this country" who had come to believe that the Constitution guaranteed her the right to reproductive choice. (Blackmun, J., dissenting). All that remained between the promise of *Roe* and the darkness of the plurality was a single, flickering flame. Decisions since *Webster* gave little reason to hope that this flame would cast much light. But now, just when so many expected the darkness to fall, the flame has grown bright.

I do not underestimate the significance of today's joint opinion. Yet I remain steadfast in my belief that the right to reproductive choice is entitled to the full protection afforded by this Court before *Webster.* And I fear for the darkness as four Justices anxiously await the single vote necessary to extinguish the light.

Make no mistake, the joint opinion of Justices O'Connor, Kennedy, and Souter is an act of personal courage and constitutional principle. In contrast to previous decisions in which Justices O'Connor and Kennedy postponed reconsideration of *Roe,* the authors of the joint opinion today join Justice Stevens and me in concluding that "the essential holding of *Roe* should be retained and once again reaffirmed." * * *

Today, no less than yesterday, the Constitution and decisions of this Court require that a State's abortion restrictions be subjected to the strictest of judicial scrutiny. Our precedents and the joint opinion's principles require us to subject all non-de-minimis abortion regulations to strict scrutiny. Under this standard, the Pennsylvania statute's provisions requiring content-based counseling, a 24-hour delay, informed parental consent, and reporting of abortion-related information must be invalidated. [R]estrictive abortion laws force women to endure physical invasions far more substantial than those this Court has held to violate the constitutional principle of bodily integrity in other contexts.[3]

---

8. Although I agree that a parental-consent requirement (with the appropriate bypass) is constitutional, I do not join Part V–D of the joint opinion because its approval of Pennsylvania's informed parental-consent requirement is based on the reasons given in Part V–B, with which I disagree.

3. As the joint opinion acknowledges, this Court has recognized the vital liberty interest of persons in refusing unwanted medical treatment. *Cruzan.* Just as the Due Process Clause protects the deeply personal decision of the individual to *refuse* medical treatment, it also

Further, when the State restricts a woman's right to terminate her pregnancy, it deprives a woman of the right to make her own decision about reproduction and family planning—critical life choices that this Court long has deemed central to the right to privacy. The decision to terminate or continue a pregnancy has no less an impact on a woman's life than decisions about contraception or marriage. Because motherhood has a dramatic impact on a woman's educational prospects, employment opportunities, and self-determination, restrictive abortion laws deprive her of basic control over her life.

[A] State's restrictions on a woman's right to terminate her pregnancy also implicate constitutional guarantees of gender equality. [By] restricting the right to terminate pregnancies, the State conscripts women's bodies into its service, forcing women to continue their pregnancies, suffer the pains of childbirth, and in most instances, provide years of maternal care. The State does not compensate women for their services; instead, it assumes that they owe this duty as a matter of course. This assumption—that women can simply be forced to accept the "natural" status and incidents of motherhood—appears to rest upon a conception of women's role that has triggered the protection of the Equal Protection Clause. The joint opinion recognizes that these assumptions about women's place in society "are no longer consistent with our understanding of the family, the individual, or the Constitution."

The Court has held that limitations on the right of privacy are permissible only if they survive "strict" constitutional scrutiny—that is, only if the governmental entity imposing the restriction can demonstrate that the limitation is both necessary and narrowly tailored to serve a compelling governmental interest. *Griswold.* We have applied this principle specifically in the context of abortion regulations. *Roe.*[5]

[In] my view, application of [the] analytical framework [set forth in *Roe*] is no less warranted than when it was approved by seven Members of this Court in *Roe*. [The] factual premises of the trimester framework have not been undermined and the *Roe* framework is far more administrable, and far less manipulable, than the "undue burden" standard adopted by the joint opinion. * * * *Roe*'s requirement of strict scrutiny as implemented through a trimester framework should not be disturbed. No other approach has gained a majority, and no other is more protective of the woman's fundamental right. Lastly, no other approach properly accommodates the woman's constitutional right with the State's legitimate interests. Application of the strict scrutiny standard results in the invalidation of all the challenged provisions. Indeed, as this Court has invalidated virtually identical provisions in prior cases, stare decisis requires that we again strike them down.

This Court has upheld informed and written consent requirements only where the State has demonstrated that they genuinely further important health-related state concerns. * * * Measured against these principles, some aspects of the Pennsylvania informed-consent scheme are unconstitutional. While it is unobjectionable for the Commonwealth to require that the patient be informed of the

must protect the deeply personal decision to *obtain* medical treatment, including a woman's decision to terminate a pregnancy.

5. To say that restrictions on a right are subject to strict scrutiny is not to say that the right is absolute. Regulations can be upheld if they have no significant impact on the woman's exercise of her right and are justified by important state health objectives. See, e.g.,

Danforth (upholding requirements of a woman's written consent and record keeping). But the Court today reaffirms the essential principle of *Roe* that a woman has the right "to choose to have an abortion before viability and to obtain it without undue interference from the State." Under *Roe*, any more than de minimis interference is undue.

nature of the procedure, the health risks of the abortion and of childbirth, and the probable gestational age of the unborn child, I remain unconvinced that there is a vital state need for insisting that the information be provided by a physician rather than a counselor. [Moreover,] *Thornburgh* invalidated biased patient-counseling requirements virtually identical to the one at issue here. * * *

The 24–hour waiting period [is] also clearly unconstitutional. [The] District Court found that the requirement would pose especially significant burdens on women living in rural areas and those women that have difficulty explaining their whereabouts. In *Akron I* this Court invalidated a similarly arbitrary or inflexible waiting period because, as here, it furthered no legitimate state interest.[8] * * *

Finally, [the] statute requires every facility performing abortions to report its activities to the Commonwealth. Pennsylvania [attempts] to justify its required reports on the ground that the public has a right to know how its tax dollars are spent. A regulation designed to inform the public about public expenditures does not further the Commonwealth's interest in protecting maternal health. Accordingly, such a regulation cannot justify a legally significant burden on a woman's right to obtain an abortion.

[If] there is much reason to applaud the advances made by the joint opinion today, there is far more to fear from The Chief Justice's opinion. [His] criticism of *Roe* follows from his stunted conception of individual liberty. While recognizing that the Due Process Clause protects more than simply physical liberty, he then goes on to construe this Court's personal-liberty cases as establishing only a laundry list of particular rights, rather than a principled account of how these particular rights are grounded in a more general right of privacy. This constricted view is reinforced by The Chief Justice's exclusive reliance on tradition as a source of fundamental rights. [P]eople using contraceptives seem the next likely candidate for his list of outcasts.

Even more shocking than The Chief Justice's cramped notion of individual liberty is his complete omission of any discussion of the effects that compelled childbirth and motherhood have on women's lives. The only expression of concern with women's health is purely instrumental—for The Chief Justice, only women's *psychological* health is a concern, and only to the extent that he assumes that every woman who decides to have an abortion does so without serious consideration of the moral implications of their decision. In short, The Chief Justice's view of the State's compelling interest in maternal health has less to do with health than it does with compelling women to be maternal.

Nor does The Chief Justice give any serious consideration to the doctrine of stare decisis. [His] narrow conception of individual liberty and stare decisis leads him to propose the same standard of review proposed by the plurality in *Webster*.

[Under] his standard, States can ban abortion if that ban is rationally related to a legitimate state interest—a standard which the United States calls "deferential, but not toothless." Yet when pressed at oral argument to describe the teeth, the best protection that the Solicitor General could offer to women was that a prohibition, enforced by criminal penalties, *with no exception for the life of the mother*, "could raise very serious questions." * * * [12]

---

8. The Court's decision in *Hodgson v. Minnesota*, validating a 48–hour waiting period for minors seeking an abortion to permit parental involvement does not alter this conclusion. Here the 24–hour delay is imposed on an *adult* woman. Moreover, the statute in *Hodg-* son did not require any delay once the minor obtained the affirmative consent of either a parent or the court.

12. Justice Scalia urges the Court to "get out of this area" and leave questions regarding abortion entirely to the States. Putting aside

[But,] we are reassured, there is always the protection of the democratic process. While there is much to be praised about our democracy, our country since its founding has recognized that there are certain fundamental liberties that are not to be left to the whims of an election. A woman's right to reproductive choice is one of those fundamental liberties. Accordingly, that liberty need not seek refuge at the ballot box.

In one sense, the Court's approach is worlds apart from that of The Chief Justice and Justice Scalia. And yet, in another sense, the distance between the two approaches is short—the distance is but a single vote.

I am 83 years old. I cannot remain on this Court forever, and when I do step down, the confirmation process for my successor well may focus on the issue before us today. That, I regret, may be exactly where the choice between the two worlds will be made.

CHIEF JUSTICE REHNQUIST, with whom JUSTICE WHITE, JUSTICE SCALIA, and JUSTICE THOMAS join, concurring in the judgment in part and dissenting in part.

The joint opinion, following its newly-minted variation on stare decisis, retains the outer shell of *Roe* but beats a wholesale retreat from the substance of that case. We believe that *Roe* was wrongly decided, and that it can and should be overruled consistently with our traditional approach to stare decisis in constitutional cases. We would adopt the approach of the plurality in *Webster* and uphold the challenged provisions of the Pennsylvania statute in their entirety. * * *

Unlike marriage, procreation and contraception, abortion "involves the purposeful termination of potential life." The abortion decision must therefore "be recognized as *sui generis*, different in kind from the others that the Court has protected under the rubric of personal or family privacy and autonomy." *Thornburgh* (White, J., dissenting). One cannot ignore the fact that a woman is not isolated in her pregnancy, and that the decision to abort necessarily involves the destruction of a fetus.

[Nor] do the historical traditions of the American people support the view that the right to terminate one's pregnancy is "fundamental." The common law which we inherited from England made abortion after "quickening" an offense. At the time of the adoption of the Fourteenth Amendment, statutory prohibitions or restrictions on abortion were commonplace; in 1868, at least 28 of the then–37 States and 8 Territories had statutes banning or limiting abortion. By the turn of the century virtually every State had a law prohibiting or restricting abortion on its books. By the middle of the present century, a liberalization trend had set in. But 21 of the restrictive abortion laws in effect in 1868 were still in effect in 1973 when *Roe* was decided, and an overwhelming majority of the States prohibited abortion unless necessary to preserve the life or health of the mother. On this record, it can scarcely be said that any deeply rooted tradition of relatively

the fact that what he advocates is nothing short of an abdication by the Court of its constitutional responsibilities, Justice Scalia is uncharacteristically naive if he thinks that overruling *Roe* and holding that restrictions on a woman's right to an abortion are subject only to rational-basis review will enable the Court henceforth to avoid reviewing abortion-related issues. State efforts to regulate and prohibit abortion in a post-*Roe* world undoubtedly would raise a host of distinct and important constitutional questions meriting review by this Court. For example, does the Eighth Amendment impose any limits on the degree or kind of punishment a State can inflict upon physicians who perform, or women who undergo, abortions? What effect would differences among States in their approaches to abortion have on a woman's right to engage in interstate travel? Does the First Amendment permit States that choose not to criminalize abortion to ban all advertising providing information about where and how to obtain abortions?

unrestricted abortion in our history supported the classification of the right to abortion as "fundamental" under the Due Process Clause of the Fourteenth Amendment.

[The joint opinion] cannot bring itself to say that *Roe* was correct as an original matter, but [instead] contains an elaborate discussion of stare decisis. [This discussion] appears to be almost entirely dicta, because the joint opinion does not apply that principle in dealing with *Roe*. *Roe* decided that a woman had a fundamental right to an abortion. The joint opinion rejects that view. *Roe* decided that abortion regulations were to be subjected to "strict scrutiny" and could be justified only in the light of "compelling state interests." The joint opinion rejects that view. *Roe* analyzed abortion regulation under a rigid trimester framework, a framework which has guided this Court's decisionmaking for 19 years. The joint opinion rejects that framework.

[Having] failed to put forth any evidence to prove any true reliance [on *Roe*], the joint opinion's argument is based solely on generalized assertions about the national psyche, on a belief that the people of this country have grown accustomed to the *Roe* decision over the last 19 years and have "ordered their thinking and living around" it. As an initial matter, one might inquire how the joint opinion can view the "central holding" of *Roe* as so deeply rooted in our constitutional culture, when it so casually uproots and disposes of that same decision's trimester framework. Furthermore, at various points in the past, the same could have been said about this Court's erroneous decisions that the Constitution allowed "separate but equal" treatment of minorities or that "liberty" under the Due Process Clause protected "freedom of contract." [The] simple fact that a generation or more had grown used to these major decisions did not prevent the Court from correcting its errors in those cases, nor should it prevent us from correctly interpreting the Constitution here.

[The joint opinion states] that when the Court "resolve[s] the sort of intensely divisive controversy reflected in *Roe* and those rare, comparable cases," its decision is exempt from reconsideration under established principles of stare decisis in constitutional cases. [Under] this principle, when the Court has ruled on a divisive issue, it is apparently prevented from overruling that decision for the sole reason that it was incorrect, *unless opposition to the original decision has died away*.

The first difficulty with this principle [is that the] question of whether a particular issue is "intensely divisive" enough to qualify for special protection is entirely subjective and dependent on the individual assumptions of the Members of this Court. In addition, because the Court's duty is to ignore public opinion and criticism on issues that come before it, its members are in perhaps the worst position to judge whether a decision divides the Nation deeply enough to justify such uncommon protection.

[The joint opinion] agrees that the Court acted properly in rejecting the doctrine of "separate but equal" in *Brown*. In fact, the opinion lauds *Brown* in comparing it to *Roe*. This is strange, in that under the opinion's "legitimacy" principle the Court would seemingly have been forced to adhere to its erroneous decision in *Plessy* because of its "intensely divisive" character. To us, adherence to *Roe* today under the guise of "legitimacy" would seem to resemble more closely adherence to *Plessy* on the same ground. Fortunately, the Court did not choose that option in *Brown,* and instead frankly repudiated *Plessy*. [The] Court in *Brown* simply recognized, as Justice Harlan had recognized beforehand, that the Fourteenth Amendment does not permit racial segregation. The rule of *Brown* is not tied to popular opinion about the evils of segregation; it is a judgment that the Equal Protection Clause does not permit racial segregation, no matter whether the public might come to believe that it is beneficial. On that ground it stands, and on that ground alone the Court was justified in properly concluding that the *Plessy* Court had erred.

There is also a suggestion in the joint opinion that the propriety of overruling a "divisive" decision depends in part on whether "most people" would now agree that it should be overruled. [How] such agreement would be ascertained, short of a public opinion poll, the joint opinion does not say. [Even] the suggestion is totally at war with the idea of "legitimacy" in whose name it is invoked. The Judicial Branch derives its legitimacy, not from following public opinion, but from deciding by its best lights whether legislative enactments of the popular branches of Government comport with the Constitution. * * *

Roe is not this Court's only decision to generate conflict. Our decisions in some recent capital cases, and in *Bowers v. Hardwick* (1986), have also engendered demonstrations in opposition. The joint opinion's message to such protesters appears to be that they must cease their activities in order to serve their cause, because their protests will only cement in place a decision which by normal standards of stare decisis should be reconsidered. * * *

The end result of the joint opinion's paeans of praise for legitimacy is the enunciation of a brand new standard for evaluating state regulation of a woman's right to abortion—the "undue burden" standard. [While] we disagree with [*Roe*'s "strict scrutiny"] standard, it at least had a recognized basis in constitutional law at the time *Roe* was decided. The same cannot be said for the "undue burden" standard, which is created largely out of whole cloth by the authors of the joint opinion. It is a standard which even today does not command the support of a majority of this Court.

* * * Because the undue burden standard is plucked from nowhere, the question of what is a "substantial obstacle" to abortion will undoubtedly engender a variety of conflicting views. For example, in the very matter before us now, the authors of the joint opinion would uphold Pennsylvania's 24–hour waiting period, concluding that a "particular burden" on some women is not a substantial obstacle. But the authors would at the same time strike down Pennsylvania's spousal notice provision, after finding that in a "large fraction" of cases the provision will be a substantial obstacle. And, while the authors conclude that the informed consent provisions do not constitute an "undue burden," Justice Stevens would hold that they do.

Furthermore, [the] "undue burden" inquiry does not in any way supply the distinction between parental consent and spousal consent which the joint opinion adopts. Despite the efforts of the joint opinion, the undue burden standard presents nothing more workable than the trimester framework which it discards today. Under the guise of the Constitution, this Court will still impart its own preferences on the States in the form of a complex abortion code.

The sum of the joint opinion's labors in the name of stare decisis and "legitimacy" is this: *Roe* stands as a sort of judicial Potemkin Village, which may be pointed out to passers by as a monument to the importance of adhering to precedent. But behind the facade, an entirely new method of analysis, without any roots in constitutional law, is imported to decide the constitutionality of state laws regulating abortion. Neither stare decisis nor "legitimacy" are truly served by such an effort.

We have stated above our belief that the Constitution does not subject state abortion regulations to heightened scrutiny. Accordingly, we think that the correct analysis is that set forth by the plurality opinion in *Webster*. A woman's interest in having an abortion is a form of liberty protected by the Due Process Clause, but States may regulate abortion procedures in ways rationally related to a legitimate state interest.

[The Chief Justice then discussed each of the challenged provisions and concluded that each should be upheld.]

JUSTICE SCALIA, with whom THE CHIEF JUSTICE, JUSTICE WHITE, and JUSTICE THOMAS join, concurring in the judgment in part and dissenting in part.

[The] States may, if they wish, permit abortion-on-demand, but the Constitution does not *require* them to do so. [A] State's choice between two positions on which reasonable people can disagree is constitutional even when (as is often the case) it intrudes upon a "liberty" in the absolute sense. Laws against bigamy, for example—which entire societies of reasonable people disagree with—intrude upon men and women's liberty to marry and live with one another. But bigamy happens not to be a liberty specially "protected" by the Constitution.

That is, quite simply, the issue in this case: not whether the power of a woman to abort her unborn child is a "liberty" in the absolute sense; or even whether it is a liberty of great importance to many women. Of course it is both. The issue is whether it is a liberty protected by the Constitution of the United States. I am sure it is not. I reach that conclusion not because of anything so exalted as my views concerning the "concept of existence, of meaning, of the universe, and of the mystery of human life." Rather, I reach it for the same reason I reach the conclusion that bigamy is not constitutionally protected—because of two simple facts: (1) the Constitution says absolutely nothing about it, and (2) the longstanding traditions of American society have permitted it to be legally proscribed.[1]

The Court destroys the proposition, evidently meant to represent my position, that "liberty" includes "only those practices, defined at the most specific level, that were protected against government interference by other rules of law when the Fourteenth Amendment was ratified" (citing *Michael H. v. Gerald D.*) (opinion of Scalia, J.). That is not, however, what *Michael H.* says; it merely observes that, in defining "liberty," we may not disregard a specific, "relevant tradition protecting, or denying protection to, the asserted right." But the Court does not wish to be fettered by any such limitation on its preferences. The Court's statement that it is "tempting" to acknowledge the authoritativeness of tradition in order to "cur[b] the discretion of federal judges" is of course rhetoric rather than reality; no government official is "tempted" to place restraints upon his own freedom of action, which is why Lord Acton did not say "Power tends to purify."

1. The Court's suggestion that adherence to tradition would require us to uphold laws against interracial marriage is entirely wrong. Any tradition in that case was contradicted *by a text*—an Equal Protection Clause that explicitly establishes racial equality as a constitutional value. [The] enterprise launched in *Roe*, by contrast, sought to *establish*—in the teeth of a clear, contrary tradition—a value found nowhere in the constitutional text.

There is, of course, no comparable tradition barring recognition of a "liberty interest" in carrying one's child to term free from state efforts to kill it. For that reason, it does not follow that the Constitution does not protect childbirth simply because it does not protect abortion. The Court's contention that the only way to protect childbirth is to protect abortion shows the utter bankruptcy of constitutional analysis deprived of tradition as a validating factor. It drives one to say that the only way to protect the right to eat is to acknowledge the constitutional right to starve oneself to death.

The Court's temptation is in the quite opposite and more natural direction—towards systematically eliminating checks upon its own power; and it succumbs.

Beyond that brief summary of the essence of my position, I [must] respond to a few of the more outrageous arguments in today's opinion, which it is beyond human nature to leave unanswered. I shall discuss each of them under a quotation from the Court's opinion to which they pertain.

"The inescapable fact is that adjudication of substantive due process claims may call upon the Court in interpreting the Constitution to exercise that same capacity which by tradition courts always have exercised: reasoned judgment."

[The] whole argument of abortion opponents is that what the Court calls the fetus and what others call the unborn child *is a human life.* Thus, whatever answer *Roe* came up with after conducting its "balancing" is bound to be wrong, unless it is correct that the human fetus is in some critical sense merely potentially human. There is of course no way to determine that as a legal matter; it is in fact a value judgment. Some societies have considered newborn children not yet human, or the incompetent elderly no longer so.

[The] emptiness of the "reasoned judgment" that produced *Roe* is displayed in plain view by the fact that, after more than 19 years of effort by some of the brightest (and most determined) legal minds in the country, after more than 10 cases upholding abortion rights in this Court, and after dozens upon dozens of amicus briefs submitted in this and other cases, the best the Court can do to explain how it is that the word "liberty" *must* be thought to include the right to destroy human fetuses is to rattle off a collection of adjectives that simply decorate a value judgment and conceal a political choice. [But] it is obvious to anyone applying "reasoned judgment" that the same adjectives can be applied to many forms of conduct that this Court (including one of the Justices in today's majority, see *Bowers v. Hardwick*) has held are *not* entitled to constitutional protection—because, like abortion, they are forms of conduct that have long been criminalized in American society. Those adjectives might be applied, for example, to homosexual sodomy, polygamy, adult incest, and suicide * * *.

"Liberty finds no refuge in a jurisprudence of doubt."

One might have feared to encounter this august and sonorous phrase in an opinion defending the real *Roe,* rather than the revised version fabricated today by the authors of the joint opinion. The shortcomings of *Roe* did not include lack of clarity: Virtually all regulation of abortion before the third trimester was invalid. But to come across this phrase in the joint opinion—which calls upon federal district judges to apply an "undue burden" standard as doubtful in application as it is unprincipled in origin—is really more than one should have to bear.

[To] the extent I can discern *any* meaningful content in the "undue burden" standard as applied in the joint opinion, it appears to be that a State may not regulate abortion in such a way as to reduce significantly its incidence. The joint opinion repeatedly emphasizes that an important factor in the "undue burden" analysis is whether the regulation "prevent[s] a significant number of women from obtaining an abortion," whether a "significant number of women [are] likely to be deterred from procuring an abortion," and whether the regulation often "deters" women from seeking abortions. We are not told, however, what forms of "deterrence" are impermissible or what degree of success in deterrence is too much to be tolerated. [As] Justice Blackmun recognizes (with evident hope), the "undue burden" standard may ultimately require the invalidation of each provision upheld today if it can be shown, on a better record, that the State is too effectively "express[ing] a preference for childbirth over abortion." Reason finds no refuge in this jurisprudence of confusion.

*"While we appreciate the weight of the arguments * * * that Roe should be overruled, the reservations any of us may have in reaffirming the central holding of Roe are outweighed by the explication of individual liberty we have given combined with the force of stare decisis."*

The Court's reliance upon stare decisis can best be described as contrived. It insists upon the necessity of adhering not to all of *Roe,* but only to what it calls the "central holding." It seems to me that stare decisis ought to be applied even to the doctrine of stare decisis, and I confess never to have heard of this new, keep-what-you-want-and-throw-away-the-rest version. * * *

I am certainly not in a good position to dispute that the Court *has saved* the "central holding" of *Roe,* since to do that effectively I would have to know what the Court has saved, which in turn would require me to understand (as I do not) what the "undue burden" test means. I must confess, however, that I have always thought, and I think a lot of other people have always thought, that the arbitrary trimester framework, which the Court today discards, was quite as central to *Roe* as the arbitrary viability test, which the Court today retains. * * *

*"Where, in the performance of its judicial duties, the Court decides a case in such a way as to resolve the sort of intensely divisive controversy reflected in Roe * * *, its decision has a dimension that the resolution of the normal case does not carry. It is the dimension present whenever the Court's interpretation of the Constitution calls the contending sides of a national controversy to end their national division by accepting a common mandate rooted in the Constitution."*

[Not] only did *Roe* not, as the Court suggests, *resolve* the deeply divisive issue of abortion; it did more than anything else to nourish it, by elevating it to the national level where it is infinitely more difficult to resolve. National politics were not plagued by abortion protests, national abortion lobbying, or abortion marches on Congress, before *Roe* was decided. Profound disagreement existed among our citizens over the issue—as it does over other issues, such as the death penalty—but that disagreement was being worked out at the state level. As with many other issues, the division of sentiment within each State was not as closely balanced as it was among the population of the Nation as a whole, meaning not only that more people would be satisfied with the results of state-by-state resolution, but also that those results would be more stable. Pre–*Roe,* moreover, political compromise was possible.

Roe's mandate for abortion-on-demand destroyed the compromises of the past, rendered compromise impossible for the future, and required the entire issue to be resolved uniformly, at the national level. At the same time, *Roe* created a vast new class of abortion consumers and abortion proponents by eliminating the moral opprobrium that had attached to the act. ("If the Constitution *guarantees* abortion, how can it be bad?"—not an accurate line of thought, but a natural one.) Many favor all of those developments, and it is not for me to say that they are wrong. But to portray *Roe* as the statesmanlike "settlement" of a divisive issue, a jurisprudential Peace of Westphalia that is worth preserving, is nothing less than Orwellian. *Roe* fanned into life an issue that has inflamed our national politics in general, and has obscured with its smoke the selection of Justices to this Court in particular, ever since. And by keeping us in the abortion-umpiring business, it is the perpetuation of that disruption, rather than of any pax Roeana, that the Court's new majority decrees.

*"[T]o overrule under fire [would] subvert the Court's legitimacy * * *.*

*"To all those who will be * * * tested by following, the Court implicitly undertakes to remain steadfast * * *. The promise of constancy, once given, binds its maker for as long as the power to stand by the decision survives [and] the commitment [is not] obsolete * * *.*

*"[The American people's] belief in themselves as * * * a people [who aspire to live according to the rule of law] is not readily separable from their understanding of the Court invested with the authority to decide their constitutional cases and speak before all others for their constitutional ideals. If the Court's legitimacy should be undermined, then, so would the country be in its very ability to see itself through its constitutional ideals."*

The Imperial Judiciary lives. It is instructive to compare this Nietzschean vision of us unelected, life-tenured judges—leading a Volk who will be "tested by following," and whose very "belief in themselves" is mystically bound up in their "understanding" of a Court that "speak[s] before all others for their constitutional ideals"—with the somewhat more modest role envisioned for these lawyers by the Founders. * * *

I cannot agree with, indeed I am appalled by, the Court's suggestion that the decision whether to stand by an erroneous constitutional decision must be strongly influenced—*against* overruling, no less—by the substantial and continuing public opposition the decision has generated. [In] my history-book, the Court was covered with dishonor and deprived of legitimacy by *Dred Scott,* an erroneous (and widely opposed) opinion that it did not abandon, rather than by *West Coast Hotel,* which produced the famous "switch in time" from the Court's erroneous (and widely opposed) constitutional opposition to the social measures of the New Deal. (Both *Dred Scott* and one line of the cases resisting the New Deal rested upon the concept of "substantive due process" that the Court praises and employs today. Indeed, *Dred Scott* was "very possibly the first application of substantive due process in the Supreme Court, the original precedent for *Lochner* and *Roe.*" David Currie, *The Constitution in the Supreme Court* 271 (1985).)

But whether it would "subvert the Court's legitimacy" or not, the notion that we would decide a case differently from the way we otherwise would have in order to show that we can stand firm against public disapproval is frightening. [Instead] of engaging in the hopeless task of predicting public perception—a job not for lawyers but for political campaign managers—the Justices should do what is *legally* right by asking two questions: (1) Was *Roe* correctly decided? (2) Has *Roe* succeeded in producing a settled body of law? If the answer to both questions is no, *Roe* should undoubtedly be overruled.

[As] long as this Court thought (and the people thought) that we Justices were doing essentially lawyers' work up here—reading text and discerning our society's traditional understanding of that text—the public pretty much left us alone. Texts and traditions are facts to study, not convictions to demonstrate about. But if in reality our process of constitutional adjudication consists primarily of making *value judgments* [then] a free and intelligent people's attitude towards us can be expected to be (*ought* to be) quite different. The people know that their value judgments are quite as good as those taught in any law school—maybe better. * * *

There is a poignant aspect to today's opinion. Its length, and what might be called its epic tone, suggest that its authors believe they are bringing to an end a troublesome era in the history of our Nation and of our Court. "It is the dimension" of authority, they say, to "cal[l] the contending sides of national controversy to end their national division by accepting a common mandate rooted in the Constitution."

[It] is no more realistic for us in this case, than it was for [Taney, C.J.,] in [*Dred Scott*] to think that an issue of the sort they both involved—an issue involving life and death, freedom and subjugation—can be "speedily and finally settled" by the Supreme Court, as President James Buchanan in his inaugural address said the issue of slavery in the territories would be. Quite to the contrary, by foreclosing all democratic outlet for the deep passions this issue arouses, by banishing the issue from the political forum that gives all participants, even the losers, the satisfaction of a fair hearing and an honest fight, by continuing the imposition of a rigid national rule instead of allowing for regional differences, the Court merely prolongs and intensifies the anguish.

We should get out of this area, where we have no right to be, and where we do neither ourselves nor the country any good by remaining.

Notes and Questions

1. *Was continuity and stability given undue prominence?* The authors of the joint opinion in *Casey* "were moved by the need for continuity and stability in constitutional law," observes Charles Fried, *Constitutional Doctrine,* 107 Harv. L.Rev. 1140, 1143 (1994), "yet paradoxically they seemed to give this factor undue prominence relative to their conviction of the rightness of the actual decision— almost as if the decision could not stand on its own and needed an apology." Do you agree?

2. *Removing the Court's ability to hide behind the "mask" of stare decisis.* Michael Stokes Paulsen, *Abrogating Stare Decisis By Statute: May Congress Remove the Precedential Effect of Roe and Casey?*, 109 Yale L.J. 1535, 1541, 1550–51 (2000), argues that Congress should pass a statute abrogating stare decisis in substantive due process abortion cases:

"By virtue of the Necessary and Proper Clause, Congress has enumerated legislative power to pass a statute abrogating stare decisis, as an enactment appropriate to the carrying into execution of the judicial power. The exercise of such legislative power would not intrude on any constitutional province of the judiciary; by the Supreme Court's own admission, stare decisis is merely a rule of policy * * *. Such a statute would merely direct courts to decide such cases in conformity with the Constitution and not to apply precedents to the contrary if they are persuaded that a precedent decision is not a sound interpretation of the Constitution."

"[In the context of the abortion cases, the question is] whether the Justices who relied on stare decisis in *Casey*—Justices who sought to eschew judicial activism, who could not bring themselves to embrace *Roe* as correct, and who (assuming their good faith) resorted to stare decisis as a doctrine of supposed judicial restraint—would strike down an act of Congress that did nothing more than provide that the Court was to decide an important constitutional issue on the merits, using its own best constitutional judgment, without the additional burden imposed by the prudential rule of stare decisis. Were the Justices joining the joint opinion in *Casey* to strike down such an act, it would reveal stare decisis as a mask—a doctrine designed to provide cover for an unpopular or uncomfortable decision on the merits—and reveal at least Justice O'Connor's and Justice Kennedy's explanations for their votes in *Casey* to have been dishonest."

3. *Roe, Lochner, and Brown.* "How," asks Cass Sunstein, *The Partial Constitution* 259–60 (1993), "can one approve of *Roe,* recognizing the abortion right, while disapproving of *Lochner?* The question seems hard to answer if *Lochner* is understood as a case [interpreting] the due process clause to protect a 'fundamental right.' *Roe* used the due process clause in this very way." But "this is a crude and ahistorical approach to the *Lochner* period. [If] we shift our field of vision a little bit, we might as reasonably ask: If you approve of *Brown*'s invalidation of segregation, how can you disapprove of *Roe?* On this view, *Brown* represented a judicial invalidation of a law contributing to second-class citizenship for a group of Americans defined in terms of a morally irrelevant characteristic (race)—and *Roe* represented exactly the same thing (with respect to gender)."

4. *Why should the abortion issue be decided on the level of the individual rather than on the level of the state?* Answers David Strauss, *Abortion, Toleration, and Moral Uncertainty,* 1992 Sup.Ct.Rev. 1, 18–20: "This is the point at which the status of women, properly emphasized by *Casey,* becomes important. Allowing the abortion decision to be made at the political level, instead of the individual level, would create an impermissible risk of subordinating women. [Although] the Court has never made it entirely clear why discrimination against women is unconstitutional, it seems plausible to suppose that at least three aspects of the status of women in society, all relevant to the abortion issue, underlie this principle.

"First, the political process has a persistent tendency generally to undervalue the interests of women. [Second,] women's bodily integrity, in particular, is systematically undervalued. The Court's opinion in *Casey* alluded to this aspect of women's status. [Third,] women are treated as people whose principal responsibility is childbearing and child rearing. They are not seen as full participants in the labor market. [*Casey* did not] make clear the exact connection between the status of women and the abortion issue. The connection, I believe, is this: the tendency to subordinate women in these three ways disqualifies the political process from resolving the moral uncertainty that is central to the abortion debate. There is too great a danger that if the political process decides the abortion issue, that decision will be an act of subordinating women in one or more of these ways."

5. *The worst of all possible worlds?* Consider Sylvia Law, *Abortion Compromise—Inevitable and Impossible,* 1992 U.Ill.L.Rev. 921, 931: "From a pro-choice point of view, one plausible assessment of the *Casey* decision is that is represents the worst of all possible worlds. The joint opinion affirmed a woman's 'fundamental constitutional right' to abortion, but simultaneously allowed the state to adopt measures that effectively curtail *many* women's exercise of the abortion right. This curtailment hits hardest those women who are most vulnerable, i.e., the poor, the unsophisticated, the young, and women who live in rural areas. The abstract recognition of a right to abortion could dampen political enthusiasm in support of reproductive choice.[a]

6. *Spousal notification vs. parental consent.* Consider 106 Harv.L.Rev. 163, 206–08 (1992): "Surface distinctions between pregnant adolescents and pregnant adults notwithstanding, the Court provided no principled basis for striking down the spousal notification clause because of the recognized potential for domestic violence while nonetheless upholding the parental consent requirement. * * *

a. "It is much harder to mobilize pro-choice lobbying, voting and fund-raising efforts, "observes Kathleen Sullivan, *Foreword: The Justices of Rules and Standards,* 106 Harv.L.Rev. 24, 110 (1992), "if *Roe* is nickel-and-dimed away rather than frankly overruled.

* * * Why didn't pro-choice activists celebrate when five Justices reaffirmed 'the essential holding of *Roe*'? Because the Court stole their thunder by adopting a moderate, difference-splitting standard."

Tragically, in its application of the undue burden test, the Court failed to accord pregnant adolescent victims of family violence the same protection it granted similarly victimized pregnant women. [When] inflicted on adolescents, however, domestic violence has even more devastating consequences. * * * Given that '[m]illions of children in the United States are victims of physical, sexual and emotional abuse,' [*Casey*'s] assumption that 'minors will benefit from consultation with their parents and that children will often not realize that their parents have their best interests at heart' must seem a cruel irony to pregnant adolescents trapped in violent homes.''[b]

7. *The spousal notification requirement vs. the 24–hour waiting period.* According to Martha Field, *Abortion Law Today,* 14 J.Legal Med. 3, 13–14 (1993), "the most serious issue *Casey* leaves open" is the scope of the cutback on *Roe:* "*Casey* itself seems utterly inconsistent. The spousal notification requirement is analyzed as posing an undue burden—a substantial obstacle to abortion—while the waiting period is not. [It] was irrelevant that only a small fraction of women seeking abortion would be burdened by the [spousal notification requirement], because '[t]he proper focus of constitutional inquiry is the group for whom the law is a restriction, not the group for whom the law is irrelevant.' But the same conditions obtain with respect to the requirement that a woman wait 24 hours after the 'informed consent' lecture before she can have an abortion. For most or many [the] waiting period may not pose a serious problem, but for rural women who must travel to an urban area to obtain an abortion, the cost of the additional day may be prohibitive. Similarly those who must travel for abortion services and who must be secretive about obtaining an abortion may have much more difficulty explaining their absence if they must be away an extra 24 hours. With a waiting period, these women are as impeded from obtaining an abortion as those who fear husband notification."

8. *The alternative to an undue burden approach.* "[T]he adoption of an expansively applied undue burden standard is hardly a panacea for the protection of fundamental rights," recognizes Alan Brownstein, *How Rights Are Infringed: The Role of Undue Burden Analysis in Constitutional Doctrine,* 45 Hast.L.J. 867, 958 (1994), for the balancing of burdens against the state's interests "is far more conducive to judicial deference to the legislature than are categorical rules of review."[c] The alternative, however, warns Professor Brownstein, "may be even more limited and restrictive": "If the only choice is between protecting the exercise of a right against all burdens under strict scrutiny review or interpreting the interest at stake as something other than a right and providing it no constitutional protection at all, the latter option may be selected in far too many circumstances. It may be implicit in the framework offered by the critics of the

b. The Note goes on to say, id. at 208–09, that the obstacles posed by parental consent are not relieved by a judicial bypass option: "In order to exercise the judicial bypass option, a pregnant minor must navigate the judicial system. The assumption that this process does not present substantial obstacles ignores some basic realities. Teenagers are intimidated by the courts and find them inaccessible. A confused pregnant teen who feels isolated and frightened will be greatly deterred in her abortion choice by the prospect of bypassing her parents and discussing intimate details about her sexual activity with a judge."

c. See also Sullivan, fn. a supra, at 111, noting (shortly after the case was decided) that "*Casey*'s undue burden test will be applied principally by the lower federal courts, and Presidents Reagan and Bush, who ran on anti-abortion platforms, have appointed nearly 70% of the sitting judges. No wonder lawyers for the pro-choice side predict that the undue burden test will be applied in practice to uphold more antiabortion measures than the test will strike down."

'undue burden' standard that rights are rarely recognized, although they receive aggressive protection in those few circumstances when they are found to exist."

ANTI–ABORTION MEASURES POST-*CASEY*: ATTEMPTS TO OUTLAW PARTIAL BIRTH ABORTIONS

STENBERG v. CARHART, 530 U.S. 914 120 S.Ct. 2597, 147 L.Ed.2d 743 (2000): A Nebraska statute prohibited, except where "necessary to save the life of the mother," a medical procedure that abortion opponents call "partial-birth abortion."[a] The statute defined "partial-birth abortion" as "an abortion procedure in which the person performing the abortion partially delivers vaginally a living unborn child before killing the unborn child and completing the delivery." It further defined "partially delivers vaginally a living unborn child before killing [it]" to mean "deliberately and intentionally delivering into the vagina a living unborn child, *or a substantial portion thereof*, for the purpose of performing a procedure [that] will kill [and] does kill the unborn child." (Emphasis added.)

According to defenders of the Nebraska statute, it was meant to ban a specific procedure known in the medical profession as dilation and extraction (D & X). In this procedure, used after 16 weeks of pregnancy, when the fetal skull becomes too large to pass through the cervix, the doctor extracts the fetal body, feet first, up to the head; collapses the skull with a sharp instrument; and then extracts the whole fetus through the cervix. D & X can be distinguished from a more commonly used abortion procedure, dilation and evaluation (D & E), which after the 15th week of pregnancy involves dismemberment of the fetus or the collapse of fetal parts to facilitate evacuation from the uterus. But dismemberment often does not occur until an arm or leg has been pulled into the vagina. Thus the Nebraska statute's definition of "partial-birth abortion" seemed to prohibit D & E as well as the less frequently used D & X.

A 5–4 majority, per BREYER, J., held the statute unconstitutional "for at least two independent reasons": (1) it "lacks any exception 'for the preservation of the health of the mother,'" *Casey* (joint opinion of O'Connor, Kennedy and Souter, JJ.); and (2) it "imposes an undue burden on the woman's ability to chose a D & E abortion, thereby unduly burdening the right to choose abortion itself. *Casey.*"

As for the statute's failure to include an exception for the preservation of the health of the mother: "Justice Thomas [dissenting] says that [our cases] limit [the need for an exception to preserve the health of the mother] to situations where the pregnancy *itself* creates a threat to health. He is wrong. [Our cases,] reaffirmed in *Casey*, recognize that a State cannot subject women's health to significant risks both in that context, *and also* where state regulations force women to use riskier methods of abortion. [Our cases] make clear that a risk to a woman's health is the same whether it happens to arise from regulating a particular method of abortion, or barring abortion entirely. * * *

"Nebraska responds that the law does not require a health exception unless there is a need for such an exception. And here there is no such need, it says. It argues that 'safe alternatives remain available' and 'a ban on partial-birth abortion/D & X would create no risk to the health of women.' [However, there] is

---

a. A violation of the statute was punishable by as much as 20 years' imprisonment. The law also provided for the automatic revocation of a doctor's license to practice medicine in Nebraska.

a District Court finding that D & X significantly obviates health risks in certain circumstances, a highly plausible record-based explanation of why that might be so, a division of opinion among some medical experts over whether D & X is generally safer, and an absence of controlled medical studies that would help answer these medical questions. Given these medically related evidentiary circumstances, we believe the law requires a health exception."

"[Where] a significant body of medical opinion believes a procedure may bring with it greater safety for some patients and explains the medical reasons supporting that view, we cannot say that the presence of a different view by itself proves the contrary. Rather, the uncertainty means a significant likelihood that those who believe that D & X is a safer abortion method in certain circumstances may turn out to be right. If so, then the absence of a health exception will place women at an unnecessary risk of tragic health consequences. If they are wrong, the exception will simply turn out to have been unnecessary."

As for the conclusion that the statute unduly burdens a woman's right to choose abortion: "Nebraska does not deny that the statute imposes an 'undue burden' [upon a woman's right to terminate her pregnancy before viability] if it applies to the more commonly used D & E procedure as well as to D & X. And we agree with the Eighth Circuit that it does so apply. [The] statute forbids 'deliberately and intentionally delivering into the vagina a living unborn child, or a substantial portion thereof, for the purpose of performing a procedure that the person performing such procedure knows will kill the unborn child.' We do not understand how one could distinguish, using this language, between D & E (where a foot or arm is drawn through the cervix) and D & X (where the body up to the head is drawn through the cervix). Evidence before the trial court makes clear that D & E will often involve a physician pulling a 'substantial portion' of a still living fetus, say, an arm or leg, into the vagina prior to the death of the fetus.

"[Even] if the statute's basic aim is to ban D & X, its language makes clear that it also covers a much broader category of procedures. The language does not track the medical differences between D & E and D & X—though it would have been a simple matter, for example, to provide an exception for the performance of D & E and other abortion procedures. Nor does the statute anywhere suggest that its application turns on whether a portion of the fetus' body is drawn into the vagina as part of a process to extract an intact fetus after collapsing the head as opposed to a process that would dismember the fetus. Thus, the dissenters' argument that the law was generally intended to bar D & X can be both correct and irrelevant. The relevant question is *not* whether the legislature wanted to ban D & X; it is whether the law was intended to apply *only* to D & X. The plain language covers both procedures.

"[In] sum, using this law some present prosecutors and future Attorneys General may choose to pursue physicians who use D & E procedures, the most commonly used methods for performing previability second trimester abortions. All those who perform abortion procedures using that method must fear prosecution, conviction, and imprisonment. The result is an undue burden upon the woman's right to make an abortion decision."

O'CONNOR, J., concurring, deemed it "important to note that, unlike Nebraska, some other states have enacted statutes more narrowly tailored to proscribing the D & X procedure alone. [By] restricting their prohibitions to the D & X procedure exclusively, the Kansas Utah, and Montana statutes avoid a principal defect of the Nebraska law." [If] there were adequate alternative methods for a woman safely to obtain an abortion before viability, it is unlikely that prohibiting the D & X procedure alone would 'amount in practical terms to a substantial obstacle to a woman seeking an abortion.' *Casey* (joint opinion). Thus, a ban on partial-birth abortion that only proscribed the D & X method of abortion and that included an exception to preserve the life and health of the mother would be constitutional in my view."[b]

STEVENS, J., joined by Ginsburg, J., concurred: "Although much ink is spilled today describing the gruesome nature of late-term abortion procedures, that rhetoric does not provide me a reason to believe that the procedure Nebraska here claims it seeks to ban is more brutal, more gruesome, or less respectful of 'potential life' than the equally gruesome procedure Nebraska claims it still allows. [The] notion that either of these two equally gruesome procedures performed at this late stage of gestation is more akin to infanticide than the other, or that the State furthers any legitimate interest by banning one but not the other, is simply irrational."

GINSBURG, J., joined by Stevens, J., concurred separately to emphasize that the Nebraska law "does not save any fetus from destruction, for it targets only 'a method of performing abortion.' " As Chief Judge Posner said of a similar law, she observed, "the law prohibits the [abortion] procedure because the State legislators seek to chip away at the private choice shielded by *Roe*, even as modified by *Casey*. [As] stated by Chief Judge Posner, 'if a statute burdens constitutional rights and all that can be said on its behalf is that it is the vehicle that legislators have chosen for expressing their hostility to those rights, the burden is undue.' *Hope Clinic v. Ryan*, 195 F.3d 857, 881 (7th Cir.1999) (dissenting opinion)."

SCALIA, J., dissenting, was "optimistic enough to believe that *Stenberg* will be assigned its rightful place in the history of this Court's jurisprudence beside *Korematsu* and *Dred Scott*. The method of killing a human child—one cannot even accurately say an entirely unborn human child—proscribed by this statute is so horrible that the most clinical description of it evokes a shudder of revulsion. And the Court must know (as most state legislatures banning this procedure have concluded) that demanding a 'health exception'—which requires the abortionist to assure himself that, in his expert medical judgment, this method is, in the case at hand, marginally safer than others (how can one prove the contrary beyond a reasonable doubt?)—[that requires the abortionist to find the method 'marginally safer than others'] is to give live-birth abortion free rein. The notion that the Constitution * * * prohibits the States from simply banning this visibly brutal means of eliminating our half-born posterity is quite simply absurd."

Today's result, continued Scalia, J., is not "merely a regrettable misapplication of *Casey*, [but] *Casey*'s logical and entirely predictable consequence. [In] my dissent in *Casey*, I wrote that the 'undue burden' test made law by the joint opinion created a standard that was 'as doubtful in application as it is unprincipled in origin' * * *. Today's opinion is the proof. [Those] who believe that a 5-to-4 vote on a policy matter by unelected lawyers should not overcome the judgment of 30 state legislatures have a problem, not with the *application of Casey*, but with its *existence*. *Casey* must be overruled.

b. Some proponents of partial-birth abortion bans were not encouraged by O'Connor, J.'s, concurring opinion. They viewed the need for an exception to preserve the health of the mother a "trap" for them. If the exception were too narrow it would be struck down; on the other hand, if it were too broad, e.g., it included factors like a woman's age, psychological or emotional condition, doctors could invoke the exceptions routinely. See William Glaberson, *Foes of Abortion Start New Effort after Court Loss*, N.Y. Times, June 30, 2000, p. 1.

"[If] only for the sake of its own preservation, the Court should return this matter to the people—where the Constitution, by its silence on the subject, left it—and let *them* decide, State by State, whether this practice should be allowed."

KENNEDY, J., joined by Rehnquist, C.J., dissented: "The Court's decision today, in my submission, repudiates [the central premise of *Casey* that the States retain a critical role in legislating on the subject of abortion] by invalidating a statute advancing critical state interests, even though the law denies no woman the right to choose an abortion and places no undue burden upon the right. [The] Court's failure to accord any weight to Nebraska's interest in prohibiting partial-birth abortion is erroneous and undermines its discussion and holding. The Court's approach in this regard is revealed by its description of the abortion methods at issue, which the Court is correct to describe as 'clinically cold or callous.' The majority views the procedures from the perspective of the abortionist, rather than from the perspective of a society shocked when confronted with a new method of ending human life. * * * Repeated references [by the majority] to sources understandable only to a trained physician may obscure matters for persons not trained in medical terminology. Thus it seems necessary at the outset to set forth what may happen during an abortion."

"[As] described by Dr. Carhart, the D & E procedure requires the abortionist to use instruments to grasp a portion (such as a foot or hand) of a developed and living fetus and drag the grasped portion out of the uterus into the vagina. [He] uses the traction created by the opening between the uterus and vagina to dismember the fetus, tearing the grasped portion away from the remainder of the body.

"[The] other procedure implicated today is called 'partial-birth abortion' or the D & X. [In] the D & X, the abortionist initiates the woman's natural delivery process by causing the cervix of the woman to be dilated, sometimes over a sequence of days. The fetus' arms and legs are delivered outside the uterus while the fetus is alive; witnesses to the procedure report seeing the body of the fetus moving outside the woman's body. At this point, the abortion procedure has the appearance of a live birth. [With] only the head of the fetus remaining in utero, the abortionist tears open the skull. According to [a] leading proponent of the procedure, the appropriate instrument to be used at this stage of the abortion is a pair of scissors. Witnesses report observing the portion of the fetus outside the woman react to the skull penetration. The abortionist then inserts a suction tube and vacuums out the developing brain and other matter found within the skull. [Of] the two described procedures, Nebraska seeks only to ban the D & X. In light of the description of the D & X procedure, it should go without saying that Nebraska's ban on partial-birth abortion furthers purposes States are entitled to pursue. * * *

"*Casey* is premised on the States having an important constitutional role in defining their interests in the abortion debate. It is only with this principle in mind that Nebraska's interests can be given proper weight. The State's brief describes its interests as including concern for the life of the unborn and 'for the partially-born,' in preserving the integrity of the medical profession, and in 'erecting a barrier to infanticide.' A review of *Casey* demonstrates the legitimacy of these policies. The Court should say so. * * *

"*Casey* demonstrates that the interests asserted by the State are legitimate and recognized by law. It is argued, however, that a ban on the D & X does not further these interests. This is because, the reasoning continues, the D & E method, which Nebraska claims to be beyond its intent to regulate, can still be used to abort a fetus and is no less dehumanizing than the D & X method. While not adopting the argument in express terms, the Court indicates tacit approval of it by refusing to reject it in a forthright manner. Rendering express what is only implicit in the majority opinion, Justice Stevens and Justice Ginsburg are forthright in declaring that the two procedures are indistinguishable and that Nebraska has acted both irrationally and without a proper purpose in enacting the law. The issue is not whether members of the judiciary can see a difference between the two procedures. It is whether Nebraska can. The Court's refusal to recognize Nebraska's right to declare a moral difference between the procedure is a dispiriting disclosure of the illogic and illegitimacy of the Court's approach to the entire case."

"Nebraska was entitled to find the existence of a consequential moral difference between the procedures. [The] D & X differs from the D & E because in the D & X the fetus is 'killed *outside* of the womb' where the fetus has 'an autonomy which separates it from the right of the woman to choose treatments for her own body.' * * * D & X's stronger resemblance to infanticide means Nebraska could conclude the procedure presents a greater risk of disrespect for life and a consequent greater risk to the profession and society, which depend for their sustenance upon reciprocal recognition of dignity and respect. The Court is without authority to second-guess this conclusion."

THOMAS, J., joined by Rehnquist, C.J., and Scalia, J., dissented: "[Although] in *Casey* the separate opinions of the Chief Justice and Justice Scalia urging the Court to overrule *Roe* did not command a majority, seven Members of that Court, including six Members sitting today, acknowledged that States have a legitimate role in regulating abortion and recognized the States' interest in respecting fetal life at all stages of development. [The] joint opinion [concluded] that prior case law 'went too far' in 'undervaluing the State's interest in potential life' and in 'striking down [some] abortion regulations which in no real sense deprived women of the ultimate decision.' Roe and subsequent cases, according to the joint opinion, had wrongly 'treated all governmental attempts to influence a woman's decision on behalf of the potential life within her as unwarranted,' a treatment that was 'incompatible with the recognition that there is a substantial state interest in potential life throughout pregnancy.' Accordingly, the joint opinion held that so long as state regulation of abortion furthers legitimate interests–that is, interests not designed to strike at the right itself–the regulation is invalid only if it imposes an undue burden on a woman's ability to obtain an abortion, meaning that it places a *substantial obstacle* in the woman's path.

"[The] standard set forth in the *Casey* joint opinion has no historical or doctrinal pedigree. The standard is a product of its authors' own philosophical views about abortion, and it should go without saying that it has no origins in or relationship to the Constitution and is, consequently, as illegitimate as the standard it purported to replace. Even assuming, however, as I will for the remainder of this dissent, that *Casey*'s fabricated undue-burden standard merits adherence (which it does not), today's decision is extraordinary. Today, the Court inexplicably holds that the States cannot constitutionally prohibit a method of abortion that millions find hard to distinguish from infanticide and that the Court hesitates even to describe.

"This holding cannot be reconciled with *Casey*'s undue-burden standard, as that standard was explained to us by the authors of the joint opinion, and the majority hardly pretends otherwise. In striking down this statute—which expresses a profound and legitimate respect for fetal life and which leaves unimpeded several other safe forms of abortion—the majority opinion gives the lie to the promise of *Casey* that regulations that do no more than 'express profound respect for the life of the unborn are permitted, if they are not a substantial obstacle to the woman's exercise of the right to choose' whether or not to have an abortion. Today's decision is so obviously irreconcilable with *Casey*'s explication of what its undue-burden standard requires, let alone the Constitution, that it should be seen for what it is, a reinstitution of the pre-*Webster* abortion-on-demand era in which the mere invocation of 'abortion rights' trumps any contrary societal interest. If this statute is unconstitutional under *Casey*, then *Casey* meant nothing at all, and the Court should candidly admit it.

"[There] is no question that the State of Nebraska has a valid interest—one not designed to strike at the right itself—in prohibiting partial birth abortion. *Casey* itself noted that States may 'express profound respect for the life of the unborn.' States may, without a doubt, express this profound respect by prohibiting a procedure that approaches infanticide, and thereby dehumanizes the fetus and trivializes human life.

"[The] next question, therefore, is whether the Nebraska statute is unconstitutional because it does not contain an exception that would allow use of the procedure whenever 'necessary in appropriate medical judgment, for the preservation of [the] health of the mother.' According to the majority, [unless] a State can conclusively establish that an abortion procedure is no safer than other procedures, the State cannot regulate that procedure without including a health exception. Justice O'Connor agrees. The rule set forth by the majority and Justice O'Connor dramatically expands on our prior abortion cases and threatens to undo any state regulation of abortion procedures.

"[In] *Roe* and *Casey*, the Court stated that the State may 'regulate, and even proscribe, abortion except where it is necessary, in appropriate medical judgment, for the preservation of the life or health of the mother.' *Casey* said that a health exception must be available if '*continuing her pregnancy* would constitute a threat' to the woman (emphasis added). [These] cases addressed only the situation in which a woman must obtain an abortion because of some threat to her health from continued pregnancy. But *Roe* and *Casey* say nothing at all about cases in which a physician considers one prohibited method of abortion to be preferable to permissible methods. [The] majority and Justice O'Connor fail to distinguish between cases in which health concerns require a woman to obtain an abortion and cases in which health concerns cause a woman who desires an abortion (for whatever reason) to prefer one method over another.

"We were reassured repeatedly in *Casey* that not all regulations of abortion are unwarranted and that the States may express profound respect for fetal life. Under *Casey*, the regulation before us today should easily pass constitutional muster. [But] today we are told that 30 States are prohibited from banning one rarely used form of abortion that they believe to border on infanticide. It is clear that the Constitution does not compel this result."

Notes and Questions

1. *Is biased media portrayal responsible for the differential treatment of the D & E and D & X procedures?* Yes, claims Karen E. Walther, Comment, *Partial-Birth Abortion: Should Moral Judgment Prevail Over Medical Judgment?*, 31 Loy. U. Chi. L.J. 693, 722 (2000): "The D & X procedure has been singled out [solely] because the details of the procedure have been publicized." See also Ann MacLean

Massie, *So-Called 'Partial–Birth Abortion' Bans: Bad Medicine? Maybe. Bad Law? Definitely!*, 59 U. Pitt. L. Rev. 301, 379 (1998): "[I]t is the shock value of the physical description of the procedure upon which its opponents often seem to rely in garnering support for their position." Compare the descriptions of the D & E and D & X procedures in the majority and dissenting opinions. Do the procedures sound drastically different to you?

2.   *Hostility toward infanticide coexisting with tolerance for abortion—a utilitarian analysis.* Kennedy, J., talks about the State's interest in "erecting a barrier to infanticide." Can such a barrier coexist with tolerance for abortion? Consider Richard Posner, *Sex and Reason* 285 (1992): "A utilitarian analysis suggests that the later the decision to abort is made, the weaker are the reasons for the law to respect that decision. The benefits to the woman are fewer because she has already borne some of the burdens of the unwanted pregnancy and because the danger and hence the cost of the abortion procedure are higher, while the health and hence the life prospects of the fetus can be better assessed and so the costs of lost life expectancy may be higher too. Thus the medical advances that have made it easier to discover during pregnancy whether the infant will be born with serious deformities or other health problems help explain how hostility to infanticide can coexist with tolerance for abortion: the more feasible abortion is, the more gratuitous infanticide seems."

FAMILY LIVING ARRANGEMENTS, PARENTAL RIGHTS, AND THE "RIGHT TO MARRY"

As illustrated by WHALEN v. ROE, 429 U.S. 589, 97 S.Ct. 869, 51 L.Ed.2d 64 (1977) (sustaining a New York law that doctors disclose the names of persons obtaining certain drugs for storage in a central computer file), those attacking legislation can often cast their challenge in terms of an invasion of a constitutionally protected "zone of privacy." But the Court upheld the legislation as "a reasonable exercise of New York's broad police powers," holding that the program did not require extraordinary justification because it "does not, on its face, pose a sufficiently grievous threat" to either the "privacy" interest "in avoiding disclosure of personal matters"[a] or the "privacy" interest "in independence in making certain kinds of important decisions [e.g., abortion, marriage]." The cases discussed below deal with the latter "privacy" interest.

---

a.   The Court, however, specifically did *not* decide "any question which might be presented by the unwarranted disclosure of accumulated private data—whether intentional or unintentional—or by a system that did not contain [adequate] security provisions."

See also *Paul v. Davis,* per Rehnquist, J., Sec. 5, I infra, holding that police disclosure of a person's shoplifting arrest did not violate his right of privacy: "His claim is based not upon any challenge to the State's ability to restrict his freedom of action in a sphere contended to be 'private,' but instead on a claim that the State may not publicize a record of an official act such as an arrest. None of our substantive privacy decisions hold this or anything like this and we decline to enlarge them in this manner." Brennan, J., joined by Marshall, J., observed that "a host of state and federal courts, relying on both privacy notions and the presumption of innocence, have begun to develop a line of cases holding that there are substantive limits on the power of the Government to disseminate unresolved arrest records outside the law enforcement [system]. I fear that after today's decision, these nascent doctrines will never have the opportunity for full growth and analysis."

1. *Zoning; choice of household companions; "extended family" relationships.* Relying on earlier decisions sustaining local zoning regulations, BELLE TERRE v. BORAAS, 416 U.S. 1, 94 S.Ct. 1536, 39 L.Ed.2d 797 (1974), per DOUGLAS, J., upheld a village ordinance restricting land use to one-family dwellings (defining "family" to mean not more than two unrelated persons living together as a single house-keeping unit, and expressly excluding from the term lodging, boarding, fraternity or multiple-dwelling houses). Appellees, who had leased their houses to six unrelated college students, challenged the ordinance, inter alia, on the ground that it "trenches on the newcomers' rights of privacy." The Court disagreed: "We deal with economic and social legislation where legislatures have historically drawn lines which we respect [if the law] bears 'a rational relationship to a [permissible] state objective.' "[B]oarding houses, fraternity houses, and the like present urban problems. [The] police power is not confined to elimination of filth, stench, and unhealthy places."

MARSHALL, J., dissented: The law burdened "fundamental rights of association and privacy," and thus required extraordinary justification, not a mere showing that the ordinance "bears a rational relationship to the accomplishment of legitimate governmental objectives." He viewed "the right to 'establish a home' " as an "essential part" of fourteenth amendment liberty and maintained that "the choice of household companions"—which "involves deeply personal considerations as to the kind and quality of intimate relationships within the home"—"surely falls within the right to privacy protected by the Constitution." The state's purposes "could be as effectively achieved by means of an ordinance that did not discriminate on the basis of constitutionally protected choices of life style."[b]

Distinguishing *Belle Terre* as involving an ordinance "affect[ing] only *unrelated* individuals," MOORE v. EAST CLEVELAND, 431 U.S. 494, 97 S.Ct. 1932, 52 L.Ed.2d 531 (1977), invalidated a housing ordinance that limited occupancy to single families, but defined "family" so as to forbid appellant from having her two grandsons live with her. (It did not permit living arrangements if, as in this case, the grandchildren were cousins rather than brothers.)[a] POWELL, J., announcing the Court's judgment and joined by Brennan, Marshall, and Blackmun, JJ., struck down the ordinance on substantive due process grounds:

"[O]n its face [the ordinance] selects certain categories of relatives who may live together and declares that others may not. [When] a city undertakes such intrusive regulation of the family [the] usual judicial deference to the legislature is inappropriate. 'This Court has long recognized that freedom of personal choice in matters of marriage and family life is one of the liberties protected by [due process].' [When] the government intrudes on choices concerning family living arrangements, this Court must examine carefully the importance of the governmental interests advanced and the extent to which they are served by the challenged regulation [referring to Harlan, J.'s dissent in *Poe*]." "[T]hus examined, this ordinance cannot survive." Although the city's goals—preventing overcrowding, minimizing congestion and avoiding financial strain on its school system—were "legitimate," the ordinance served them "marginally at best."

"[T]he history of the *Lochner* [era] counsels caution and restraint [but] it does [not] require what the city urges here: cutting off any family rights at the

---

b. Compare Marshall, J.'s views in *Belle Terre* with the Court's discussion of "freedom of intimate association" in *Roberts v. United States Jaycees,* p. 987 infra. See also the Court's discussion of "the freedom to enter into and carry on certain intimate of private relationships" in *Board of Directors of Rotary International v. Rotary Club of Duarte,* p. 990, fn. c infra.

a. The second grandson came to live with his grandmother after the death of his mother.

first convenient, if arbitrary boundary—the boundary of the nuclear family. * * *
Appropriate limits on substantive due process come not from drawing arbitrary
lines but rather from careful 'respect for the teachings of history [and] solid
recognition of the basic values that underlie our society.' *Griswold* (Harlan, J.,
concurring). Our decisions teach that the Constitution protects the sanctity of the
family precisely because the institution of the family is deeply rooted in this
Nation's history and tradition. [Ours] is by no means a tradition limited to respect
for [the] nuclear family. The tradition of uncles, aunts, cousins, and especially
grandparents sharing a household along with parents and children [especially in
times of adversity] has roots equally venerable and equally deserving of constitutional recognition. [In *Pierce,* the Constitution prevented a state from] 'standard-
iz[ing] its children by forcing them to accept instruction from public teachers
only.' By the same token the Constitution prevents East Cleveland from standard-
izing its children—and its adults—by forcing all to live in certain narrowly defined
family patterns."[b]

STEWART, J., joined by Rehnquist, J., dissented, rejecting the argument that
"the importance of the 'extended family' in American society" renders appellant's
"decision to share her residence with her grandsons," like the decisions involved
in bearing and raising children, "an aspect of 'family life' " entitled to substantive
constitutional protection. To equate appellant's interest in sharing her residence
with some of her relatives "with the fundamental decisions to marry and to bear
children," he maintained, "is to extend the limited substantive contours of the
Due Process Clause beyond recognition." He thought the challenged "family"
definition "rationally designed to carry out the legitimate governmental purposes
identified in *Belle Terre.*" A different line "could hardly be drawn that would not
sooner or later become the target of a challenge like the appellant's," such as "the
hard case of an orphaned niece or nephew."

Nor could he understand why "the traditional importance of the extended
family in America" need imply "that the residents of East Cleveland are constitutionally prevented from following what Justice Brennan calls the 'pattern' of
'white suburbia,' even though that choice may reflect 'cultural myopia.' In point
of fact, East Cleveland is a predominantly Negro community, with a Negro City
Manager and City Commission."[c]

b. Brennan, J., joined by Marshall, J., concurred, characterizing the ordinance as "senseless," "arbitrary" and "eccentric" and as reflecting "cultural myopia" and "a distressing
insensitivity toward the economic and emotional needs of a very large part of our society." He
called the "extended family" "virtually a
means of survival" for many poor and black
families. [The] 'nuclear family' is the pattern
so often found in much of white suburbia," but
"the Constitution cannot * * * tolerate the
imposition by government upon the rest of us
of white suburbia's preference in patterns of
family living." But see dissenting Justice Stewart's response, infra.

Stevens, J., concurring, thought this "unprecedented ordinance" unconstitutional even
under the "limited standard of review of zoning decisions": "The city has failed totally to
explain the need for a rule which would allow a
homeowner to have two grandchildren live
with her if they are brothers, but not if they
are cousins. Since the ordinance has not been

shown to have any 'substantial relation to
[East Cleveland's] public health, safety, morals
or general welfare' [and] since it cuts so deeply
into a fundamental right normally associated
with the ownership of residential property—
that of an owner to decide who may reside on
his or her property—it must fall [as] a taking
of property without due process and without
just compensation."

c. "[I]n assessing [appellant's] claim that
the ordinance is 'arbitrary' and 'irrational,' "
Stewart, J., considered a provision permitting
her to request a variance "particularly persuasive evidence to the contrary. [The] variance
procedure, a traditional part of American land-
use law, bends the straight lines of East Cleveland's ordinance, shaping their contours to respond more flexibly to the hard cases that are
the inevitable byproduct of legislative line-
drawing."

Burger, C.J., dissented on the ground that
appellant should have pursued the "plainly

WHITE, J., dissenting, voiced disbelief "that the interest in residing with more than one set of grandchildren is one that calls for any kind of heightened protection under the Due Process Clause. [The] present claim is hardly one of which it could be said that 'neither liberty nor justice would exist if [it] were sacrificed.' *Palko.*"

He maintained that Powell, J.'s approach—construing the Due Process Clause to protect from all but "quite important" state interests any right "that in his estimate is deeply rooted in the country's traditions"—"suggests a far too expansive charter for this Court. [What] the deeply rooted traditions of the country are is arguable; which of them deserve [due process protection] is even more debatable. The suggested view would broaden enormously the horizons of the Clause."[d]

Notes and Questions

(a) *The elusiveness of the search for sources of fundamental rights. Moore v. East Cleveland,* maintains Joseph Grano, *Judicial Review and a Written Constitution in a Democratic Society,* 28 Wayne L.Rev. 1, 25–27 (1981), "demonstrates both how elusive the search for sources of fundamental rights can be and how unsatisfying the Court's attempts at demonstration necessarily are. Justice Powell's plurality opinion concluded that 'the Constitution protects the sanctity of the family precisely because the institution of the family is deeply rooted in the Nation's history and tradition.' Societies do change, however, and cognizant of this, the Court could not have intended to become constitutionally committed to every practice rooted in our history and tradition. In particular, progress toward racial and sexual equality depends upon success in freeing ourselves from the yoke of history and tradition. Moreover, by implication, Justice Powell's opinion suggested that the result would have been different had an unrelated neighbor taken charge of Mrs. Moore's grandson, [but did not explain] why history and tradition would not protect a neighbor's decision to do what Mrs. Moore did. Nor did he explain why, if it would not, history and tradition should be determinative."

(b) *Should Moore have been decided on "naked substantive due process grounds"? Moore's* choice of rationale, comments Ira Lupu, *Untangling the Strands of the Fourteenth Amendment,* 77 Mich.L.Rev. 981, 1017 (1979), "reversed a pattern that had endured for four decades: it was the first decision since the 1937 revolution to invalidate a statute on naked substantive due process grounds when equal protection grounds seemed readily available. [*Griswold* and *Roe*] had not presented such alternatives; in both cases, the complained-of prohibition swept broadly across the state's entire population, and thus offered no classification readily subject to equal protection attack. In *Moore,* by contrast, the 'family' definition in the ordinance seemed perfect for invalidation as an arbitrary [classification]. The plurality opinion stood at least thirty years of conventional wisdom on its head by adopting a substantive due process theory and proclaiming in a one-sentence footnote that the due process holding rendered it unnecessary for the Court to reach the equal protection claims."

If *Moore* had invalidated the ordinance on equal protection grounds, observes Lupu, at 1019, it might have suggested "the permissibility of other, less arbitrary definitions of 'family.' Instead, *Moore* holds that families, defined by blood and

adequate administrative remedy" of seeking a variance, thus finding it "unnecessary to reach the difficult constitutional issue."

d. "[A]n approach grounded in history," replied Justice Powell [fn. 12], "imposes limits on the judiciary that are more meaningful than any based on [White, J.'s] abstract formula taken from *Palko.*"

marriage relations, cannot be carved up unless such limitations are critically necessary to achieve substantial zoning objectives."[a]

(c) *Was the purpose of the ordinance quite straightforward?* How significant is it that "East Cleveland is a predominantly Negro community, with a Negro City Manager and City Commissioner"? Consider Robert Burt, *The Constitution of the Family,* 1979 Sup.Ct.Rev. 329, 389: "The plurality viewed the ordinance as directed against [over-crowding, minimizing traffic and the like, but] did not consider that the purpose of the ordinance was quite straightforward: to exclude from a middle-class, predominantly black community, that saw itself as socially and economically upwardly mobile, other black families most characteristic of lower-class ghetto life. Perhaps the Court did not see this purpose or, if it did, considered this an 'illegitimate goal,' though in other cases the Court had been exceedingly solicitous of white middle-class communities' attempts to preserve a common social identity—'zones,' as the Court had put the matter three years earlier [in *Belle Terre*]—'where family values, youth values, and the blessings of the quiet seclusion and clean air make the area a sanctuary for people.' [Although Brennan, J., had dissented in *Belle Terre*], I find in his characterization of the East Cleveland ordinance as 'senseless' and 'eccentric,' precisely what he alleges in it: 'a depressing insensitivity toward the economic and emotional needs' of the current majority of residents in East Cleveland."

(d) *Was Moore a dispute about the meaning of "family"?* Which way does it cut that the East Cleveland ordinance was "unusual" or even "eccentric"? Was victory for Mrs. Moore "total defeat" for the other city residents, but victory for them "not total defeat for her, except insofar as she wished to remain in their community while transferring its membership to her taste"? Consider Burt, supra, at 391: "[T]he very oddity of the East Cleveland ordinance suggests that Mrs. Moore is not alone in her opposition to it, that the city residents are more the vulnerable, isolated dissenters than she in the broader society, that they more than she deserve special judicial solicitude as a 'discrete and insular minority.' The Court in *Moore* myopically saw the case as a dispute between 'a family' and 'the state' rather than as a dispute among citizens about the meaning of 'family.' "

(e) *The blood relationship of the parties.* The *Moore* plurality emphasized the blood relationship of the parties. Should this factor be regarded as decisive? Consider Tribe 2d ed., at 1420: "If a city or town may require that every home be occupied by a single 'family' consisting entirely of persons related by blood or marriage, it would be difficult to respond to the argument that the same city or town may also decide what a 'family' is: If longtime friends can be excluded by ordinance, why not second cousins? And if second cousins, why not certain grandchildren?" Should governmental interference with *any* "enduring relationships" be invalidated unless compellingly justified? See id. Could a town prohibit unmarried people or homosexuals from living together? Compare Kenneth Karst, *The Freedom of Intimate Association,* 89 Yale L.J. 624, 686–89 (1980) with Bruce Hafen, *The Constitutional Status of Marriage, Kinship, and Sexual Privacy,* 81 Mich.L.Rev. 463, 487, 559 (1983).

---

a. But see Thomas Gerety, *Doing Without Privacy,* 42 Ohio St.L.J. 143, 156–59 (1981) (*Moore* demonstrates need for "privacy" ratio- nale and inadequacy of "pure equal protection theory of individual rights").

2. *Adoption and rights of the natural father.* QUILLOIN v. WALCOTT, 434 U.S. 246, 98 S.Ct. 549, 54 L.Ed.2d 511 (1978): Under Georgia law, if the natural father has not "legitimated" his offspring (appellant had not sought to do so during the 11 years between the child's birth and the adoption petition), only the mother's consent is required for the adoption of the illegitimate child. When the child was 11, the mother consented to his adoption by her husband with whom she and her son were living. Appellant attempted to block the adoption, but did not seek custody or object to the child's continuing to live with his mother and stepfather. On the basis of various findings (e.g., appellant had provided support only on an irregular basis, the child himself expressed a desire to be adopted by his stepfather who was found to be fit to adopt the child), the trial court concluded that the adoption would be in the "best interests of the child."

A unanimous Court, per MARSHALL, J., affirmed: "We have recognized on numerous occasions that the relationship between parent and child is constitutionally protected, e.g. *Wisconsin v. Yoder* [discussed at p. 1044 infra]; *Stanley v. Illinois,* 405 U.S. 645, 92 S.Ct. 1208, 31 L.Ed.2d 551 (1972) [and] [w]e have little doubt that the Due Process Clause would be offended '[i]f a State were to attempt to force the breakup of a natural family, over the objection of the parents and their children, without some showing of unfitness and for the sole reason that to do so was thought to be in the children's best interests.' *Smith v. Organization of Foster Families,* 431 U.S. 816, 862, 97 S.Ct. 2094, 2118, 53 L.Ed.2d 14 (1977) (Stewart, J., concurring). But this is [a case where] the result of the adoption in this case is to give full recognition to a family unit already in existence, a result desired by all concerned, except appellant. [Under these circumstances it suffices that the state found] that the adoption, and denial of legitimation, was in the 'best interests of the child.'"

3. *Non-parental visitation rights vs. rights of parents to make decisions concerning the care, custody, and control of their children.* At issue in TROXEL v. GRANVILLE, 530 U.S. 57, 120 S.Ct. 2054, 147 L.Ed. 2d 49 (2000), was a Washington statute, § 2610.160(3), permitting "[a]ny person" to petition for visitation rights "at any time" and authorizing state superior courts to grant such rights whenever "visitation may serve the best interest of he child." The Troxels petitioned for the right to visit their deceased son's two daughters. Greenville, the girls' mother, did not oppose all visitation, but objected to the amount sought by the girls' grandparents (two weekends of overnight visitation per month and two weeks of visitation each summer). She asked the court to order one day of visitation per month with no overnight stay. The superior court ordered more visitation than Granville desired, and she appealed.

The Washington Supreme Court struck down the statute on its face for two reasons: (1) the Constitution permits a state to interfere with the rights of parents to rear their children only to prevent harm or potential harm to a child and the statute fails that standard "because it recognizes no threshold showing of harm"; (2) by allowing "any person" to petition for forced visitation of a child at "any time," with the only requirement being that the visitation serve "the best interest of the child," the statute sweeps too broadly. The U.S. Supreme Court affirmed, but, as Stevens, J., dissenting, noted, it did not endorse either the holding or the reasoning of the state supreme court. There was no opinion of the Court. The principal opinion was written by O'CONNOR, J., joined by Rehnquist, C.J., and Ginsburg and Breyer, JJ. The plurality found the statute "as applied in this case" unconstitutional:

"The liberty interest at issue in this case—the interests of parents in the care, custody, and control of their children—is perhaps the oldest of the fundamental liberty interests recognized by this Court. [The Court then discussed *Meyer v. Nebraska* (1923); *Pierce v. Society of Sisters* (1925); and *Prince v. Massachusetts* (1944). Next it discussed, e.g., *Stanley v. Illinois* (1972); *Wisconsin v. Yoder* (1972); and *Quilloin*.] In light of this extensive precedent, it cannot now be doubted that the Due Process Clause of the Fourteenth Amendment protects the fundamental right of parents to make decisions concerning the care, custody, and control of their children.

"[The Washington statute], as applied to Granville and her family in this case, unconstitutionally infringes on that fundamental parental right. [The statute] is breathtakingly broad. [Its] language effectively permits any third party seeking visitation to subject any decision by a parent concerning visitation of the parent's children to state-court review. Once [the] matter is placed before a judge, a parent's decision that visitation would not be in the child's best interest is accorded no deference. [The statute] places the best-interest determination solely in the hands of the judge. [Thus,] in practical effect, in the State of Washington, a court can disregard and overturn *any* decision by a fit custodial parent concerning visitation whenever a third party affected by the decision files a visitation petition, based solely on the judge's determination of the child's best interests.

"[The] combination of several factors here compels our conclusion that [the statute], as applied, exceeded the bounds of the Due Process Clause. First, the Troxels did not allege, and no court has found, that Granville was an unfit parent. That aspect of the case is important for there is a presumption that fit parents act in the best interests of their children. [The] problem here is [that the Superior Court] gave no special weight at all to Granville's determination of her daughters' best interests. [Indeed, the] judge's remarks indicate that he [i]n effect * * * placed on Granville, the fit custodial parent, the burden of *disproving* that visitation would be in the best interest of her daughters. [Finally,] we note that there is no allegation that Granville ever sought to cut off visitation entirely. Rather, the present dispute originated when Granville informed the Troxels that she would prefer to restrict their visitation with [the girls] to one short visit per month and special holidays.

"[The circumstances] show that this case involves nothing more than a simple disagreement between the Washington Superior Court and Granville concerning her children's best interest. [The] Due Process Clause does not permit a State to infringe on the fundamental right of parents to make childrearing decisions simply because a state judge believes a 'better' decision could be made. Neither the Washington [statute] generally [nor] the Superior Court in this specific case required anything more. Accordingly, we hold that [the statute], as applied in this case, is unconstitutional."

The plurality also saw no reason to remand the case for further proceedings: "[I]t is apparent that the entry of the visitation order in this case violated the Constitution. We should say so now, without forcing the parties into additional litigation that would further burden Granville's parental right."

SOUTER, J., "concur[red] in the judgment affirming the decision of the Supreme Court of Washington, whose facial invalidation of its own statute is consistent with the Court's prior cases addressing the substantive interests at stake." He saw no error in the state supreme court's second reason for invalidating the statute—"because the state statute authorizes any person at any time to request (and a judge to award) visitation rights, subject only to the State's particular best-interests standard, [it] sweeps too broadly and is unconstitutional on its face.''

THOMAS, J., also concurred in the judgment, "agree[ing] with the plurality that the Court's recognition of a fundamental right of parents to direct the upbringing of their children resolves this case." He "would apply strict scrutiny to infringements of fundamental rights. Here, the State of Washington lacks even a legitimate governmental interest—to say nothing of a compelling one—in second-guessing a fit parent's decision regarding visitation with third parties.''

He "note[d] that neither party has argued that our substantive due process cases were wrongly decided and that the original understanding of the Due Process Clause precludes judicial enforcement of unenumerated rights under that constitutional provision." Thus, he "express[ed] no view on the merits of this matter.''

STEVENS, J., dissenting, maintained that the state supreme court "erred in its federal constitutional analysis because neither the provision granting 'any person' the right to petition the court for visitation nor the absence of a provision requiring a 'threshold [finding] of harm to the child' provides a sufficient basis for holding that the statute is invalid in all its applications." He "believe[d] that a facial challenge should fail whenever a statute has 'a plainly legitimate sweep.' Under the Washington statute, there are plainly any number of cases—indeed, one suspects, the most common to arise—in which the 'person' among 'any' seeking visitation is a once-custodial caregiver, an intimate relation, or even a genetic parent.''

As for "the second key aspect of the Washington Supreme Court's holding—that the Federal Constitution requires a showing of actual or potential 'harm' to the child before a court may order visitation continued over a parent's objections—this "finds no support in the Court's case law":

"A parent's rights with respect to her child [have] never been regarded as absolute, but rather are limited by the existence of an actual, developed relationship with a child, and are tied to the presence or absence of some embodiment of family. [While] this Court has not yet had occasion to elucidate the nature of a child's liberty interests in preserving established familial or family-like bonds, it seems to me extremely likely that, to the extent parents and families have fundamental liberty interests in preserving such intimate relationships, so, too, do children have these interests, and so, too, must their interests be balanced in the equation. At a minimum, our prior cases recognizing that children are, generally speaking, constitutionally protected actors require that this Court reject any suggestion that when it comes to parental rights, children are so much chattel. [The] Due Process Clause of the Fourteenth Amendment leaves room for States to consider the impact on a child of possibly arbitrary parental decisions that neither serve nor are motivated by the best interests of the child.''

SCALIA, J., separately dissenting, thought it "entirely compatible with the commitment to representative democracy set forth in the founding documents to argue, in legislative chambers or in electoral campaigns, that the state has *no power* to interfere with parents' authority over the rearing of their children," but did "not believe that the power which the Constitution confers upon me *as a judge* entitles me to deny legal effect to laws that (in my view) infringe upon what is (in my view) that unenumerated right.'' * * *

"Only three holdings of this Court rest in whole or in part upon a substantive constitutional right of parents to direct the upbringing of their children [citing

Meyer, Pierce, and *Yoder]*—two of them from an era rich in substantive due process holdings that have since been repudiated. The sheer diversity of today's opinion persuades me that the theory of unenumerated parental rights underlying these three cases has small claim to stare decisis protection. A legal principle that can be thought to produce such diverse outcomes in the relatively simple case before us here is not a legal principle that has induced substantial reliance. While I would not now overrule these earlier cases (that has not been urged), neither would I extend the theory upon which they rested to this new context."

KENNEDY, J., wrote a third dissenting opinion. His "principal concern" was that the state court's holding "seems to proceed from the assumption that the parent or parents who resist visitation have always been the child's primary caregivers and that the third parties who seek visitation have no legitimate and established relationship with the child. That idea, in turn, appears influenced by the concept that the conventional nuclear family ought to establish the visitation standard for every domestic relations case. As we all know, this is simply not the structure or prevailing condition in many households. * * *

"Cases are sure to arise—perhaps a substantial number of cases—in which a third party, by acting in a caregiving role over a significant period of time, has developed a relationship with a child which is not necessarily subject to absolute parental veto. * * * Indeed, contemporary practice should give us some pause before rejecting the best interests of the child standard in all third-party visitation cases, as the Washington court has done. The standard has been recognized for many years as a basic tool of domestic relations law in visitation proceedings. [The third-party visitation statutes enacted by all 50 states] include a variety of methods for limiting parents' exposure to third-party visitation petitions and for ensuring parental decisions are given respect. Many States limit the identity of permissible petitioners by restricting visitation petitions to grandparents or by requiring petitioners to show a substantial relationship with a child, or both.

"[In] my view, it would be more appropriate to conclude that the constitutionality of the applications of the best interests standard depends on the more specific factors. In short, a fit parent's rights vis-à-vis a complete stranger is one thing; her right vis-à-vis another parent or a de facto parent may be another."

Did the *Troxel* plurality try to protect parental rights without spelling out the level of protection the Constitution provides? Did the plurality's failure to elaborate on the mechanics of the constitutional standard it announced leave judges, legislators, and individual litigants at sea? See 114 Harv.L.Rev. 179, 229, 234, 238 (2000).

4. *Right to marry.* ZABLOCKI v. REDHAIL, 434 U.S. 374, 98 S.Ct. 673, 54 L.Ed.2d 618 (1978): A Wisconsin law forbade marriage by any resident with minor children not in his custody whom he is under court order to support, unless he proves compliance with the support obligation and that the children "are not then and are not likely thereafter to become public charges." Appellee and the woman he desired to marry were expecting a child, but he was denied a marriage license because he had not satisfied his support obligations to his illegitimate child who had been a public charge since birth. In striking down the marriage prohibition under the "fundamental rights" branch of equal protection doctrine (see Ch. 9, Sec. 4) the Court, per MARSHALL, J., observed:

"Since our past decisions make clear that the right to marry is of fundamental importance, and since the classification at issue here significantly interferes with the exercise of that right, we believe that 'critical examination' of the state's interests advanced in support of the classification is required. [Cases] subsequent to *Griswold* and *Loving v. Virginia* (1967) [p. 1176 infra], invalidating state miscegenation laws] have routinely categorized the decision to marry as among the personal decisions protected by the right of privacy. [It] is not surprising that the decision to marry has been placed on the same level of importance as decisions relating to procreation, childbirth, child rearing, and family relationships [for] it would make little sense to recognize a right of privacy with respect to other matters of family life and not with respect to the decision to enter the relationship that is the foundation of the family in our society. [If] appellee's right to procreate means anything at all, it must imply some right to enter the only relationship in which [the state] allows sexual relations legally to take place.

"By reaffirming the fundamental character of the right to marry, we do not mean to suggest that every state regulation which relates in any way to the incidents of or prerequisites for marriage must be subjected to rigorous scrutiny. [R]easonable regulations that do not significantly interfere with decisions to enter into the marital relationships may legitimately be imposed. See *Califano v. Jobst*, 434 U.S. 47, 98 S.Ct. 95, 54 L.Ed.2d 228 (1977), [discussed fn. 12 infra]." However, because the statute prevents any Wisconsin resident in the affected class from marrying anywhere without a court order, some in the affected class, like appellee, "are absolutely prevented from ever getting married," for "they either lack the financial means to meet their support obligations or cannot prove that their children will not become public charges"; and because "many others [will] be sufficiently burdened by having to [satisfy the statute's requirements] that they will in effect be coerced into foregoing their right to marry," this statute "clearly does interfere directly and substantially with the right to marry.[12]

"When a statutory classification significantly interferes with the exercise of a fundamental right, it cannot be upheld unless it is supported by sufficiently important state interests and is closely tailored to effectuate only those interests. [Assuming that the state interests said to be served by the statute—furnishing an opportunity to counsel the applicant as to the need to fulfill his prior support obligations, and protecting the welfare of the out-of-custody children—] are legitimate and substantial interests, [since] the means selected by the State for achieving these interests unnecessarily impinge on the right to marry, the statute cannot be sustained.

"[As for the argument that the statute provides incentive for the applicant to make support payments to his children], with respect to [those] unable to meet the statutory requirements, the statute merely prevents the applicant from getting married, without delivering any money at all into the hands of the [children]. More importantly, [the] State already has numerous other means for

---

12. The directness and substantiality of the interference with the freedom to marry distinguish the instant case from *Jobst*. In *Jobst* [applying the "rationality" standard of review] we upheld sections of the Social Security Act providing, inter alia, for termination of a dependent child's benefits upon marriage to an individual not entitled to benefits under the Act. As the opinion for the Court expressly noted, the rule terminating benefits upon marriage was not "an attempt to interfere with the individual's freedom to make a decision as important as marriage." The Social Security provisions placed no direct legal obstacle in the path of persons desiring to get married, [and] there was no evidence that the laws significantly discouraged, let alone made "practically impossible," any marriages. Indeed, the provisions had not deterred the individual who challenged the statute from getting married, even though he and his wife were both disabled. * * *

exacting compliance with support obligations, means that are at least as effective as the instant statute's and yet do not impinge upon the right to marry [such as wage assignments, civil contempt proceedings and criminal penalties]."

As for the suggestion that the statute protects the ability of marriage applicants to meet prior support obligations by preventing the applicants from incurring new ones, the statute is "grossly underinclusive" since it in no way limits other new financial commitments and "substantially overinclusive as well," for the new spouse may actually improve the applicant's financial situation. "[P]reventing the marriage may only result in [new] children being born out of wedlock, as in fact occurred in appellee's case. Since the support obligation is the same whether the child is born in or out of wedlock, the net result of preventing the marriage is simply more illegitimate children."[a]

STEWART, J., concurred: "I do not agree [that] there is a 'right to marry' in the constitutional sense. * * * Surely, for example, a State may legitimately say that no one can marry his or her sibling, that no one can marry who is not at least 14 years old, that no one can marry without first passing an examination for venereal disease, or that no one can marry who has a living husband or wife. But, just as surely, in regulating the intimate human relationship of marriage, there is a limit beyond which a State may not constitutionally go.

"[S]ome people simply cannot afford to meet the statute's financial requirements. To deny these people permission to marry penalizes them for failing to do that which they cannot do. Insofar as it applies to indigents, the state law is an irrational means of achieving these objectives of the State. As directed against either the indigent or the delinquent parent, the law is substantially more rational if viewed as a means of assuring the financial viability of future marriages. [But] the State's legitimate concern with the financial soundness of prospective marriages must stop short of telling people they may not marry because they are too poor or because they might persist in their financial irresponsibility. [A] legislative judgment so alien to our traditions and so offensive to our shared notions of fairness offends the Due Process Clause of the Fourteenth Amendment.

"[E]qual protection doctrine has become the Court's chief instrument for invalidating state laws. Yet, in a case like this one, the doctrine is no more than substantive due process by another name. [The] message of the Court's opinion is that Wisconsin may not use its control over marriage to achieve the objectives of the state statute. Such restrictions on basic governmental power are at the heart of substantive due process. The Court is understandably reluctant to rely on substantive due process. But to embrace the essence of that doctrine under the guise of equal protection serves no purpose but obfuscation."

POWELL, J., concurred in the judgment, but wrote separately "because the majority's rationale sweeps too broadly in an area which traditionally has been subject to state regulation": "The Court apparently would subject all state regulation which 'directly and substantially' interferes with the decision to marry in a traditional family setting to 'critical examination' or 'compelling state interest' analysis. Presumably, 'reasonable regulations that do not significantly interfere with decisions to enter into the marital relationship may legitimately be imposed.' The Court does not present, however, any principled means for distinguishing between the two types of regulations. Since state regulation in this area typically takes the form of a prerequisite or barrier to marriage or divorce, the

---

a. Burger, C.J., joined the Court's opinion   and briefly concurred.

degree of 'direct' interference with the decision to marry or to divorce is unlikely to provide either guidance for state legislatures or a basis for judicial oversight.

"[State] regulation has included bans on incest, bigamy, and homosexuality, as well as various preconditions to marriage, such as blood tests. Likewise, a showing of fault on the part of one of the partners traditionally has been a prerequisite to the dissolution of an unsuccessful union. A 'compelling state purpose' inquiry would cast doubt on the network of restrictions that the States have fashioned to govern marriage and divorce.

"State power over domestic relations is not without constitutional limits. The Due Process Clause requires a showing of justification 'when the government intrudes on choices concerning family living arrangements' in a manner which is contrary to deeply rooted traditions, *Moore v. East Cleveland,* [and it also limits] the extent to which the State may monopolize the process of ordering certain human relationships while excluding the truly indigent from that process. *Boddie v. Connecticut* [p. 1390 infra]. Furthermore, under the Equal Protection Clause, the means chosen by the State in this case must bear 'a fair and substantial relation' to the object of the legislation [citing *Reed v. Reed* and his concurring opinion in *Craig v. Boren,* both in Ch. 9, Sec. 3, II.].

"The Wisconsin measure in this case does not pass muster under either due process or equal protection standards. [As for the state's 'collection device' justification, the] vice inheres [in] the failure to make provision for those without the means to comply with child-support obligations. [As for the state interest in preserving 'the ability of marriage applicants to support their prior issue by preventing them from incurring new obligations,' the law is] so grossly underinclusive with respect to this objective, given the many ways that additional financial obligations may be incurred by the applicant quite apart from a contemplated marriage, that the classification 'does not bear a fair and substantial relation to the object of the legislation.' *Craig* (Powell, J., concurring)."

STEVENS, J., concurred: "Under this statute, a person's economic status may determine his eligibility to enter into a lawful marriage. A noncustodial parent whose children are 'public charges' may not marry even if he has met his court-ordered obligations. Thus, within the class of parents who have fulfilled their court-ordered obligations, the rich may marry and the poor may not. This type of statutory discrimination is, I believe, totally unprecedented, as well as inconsistent with our tradition of administering justice equally to the rich and to the [poor.]"[b]

(a) Consider Lupu, supra, at 1072: "[If *Zablocki*] had assessed the Wisconsin statute by analogy to the libertarian principles governing free expression, it would have discovered a significant threat to preferred liberty: the delegation to judges of power to authorize the marriage under the highly discretionary standard 'that such children [are] not likely thereafter to become public charges.' Once the liberty to marry is recognized as fundamental, doctrines requiring clear and imminent danger to legitimate state interests and confining the discretion to make that determination should play as critical a role as they traditionally do in speech cases."

(b) In response to the district court's invalidation of the statute at issue in *Zablocki,* Wisconsin enacted a replacement statute limited to *previously married*

---

b. Rehnquist, J., dissented, "view[ing] this legislative judgment in the light of the traditional presumption of validity, [just as] the traditional standard of review was applied in *Jobst,* despite the claim that the statute there in question burdened [the] right to marry." He concluded that the law, "despite its imperfections, is sufficiently rational to satisfy the demands of the Fourteenth Amendment."

persons who had incurred support obligations and who now intended to marry, establishing a *rebuttable presumption* that the remarriage of a person with support obligations for children not in custody would substantially affect the children's welfare and, finally, providing that the applicant who submits proof that "for reasonable cause" he was unable to meet support obligations may remarry. Under *Zablocki*, would this replacement statute (subsequently repealed) pass constitutional muster? See Note, 1979 Wis.L.Rev. 682.

(c) *The concept of a free society.* Is it consistent with the concept of a free society to let the individual decide whether he or she can meet the burdens of marriage rather than, as in *Zablocki*, to have the state decide whether the burdens of marriage will make it too difficult to manage such problems as satisfying child support payments? See Note, *The Constitution and the Family*, 93 Harv. L. Rev. 1156, 1251–55 (1980).

5. *Civil commitment of children by their parents.* In rejecting the argument that only a formal hearing prior to parents' commitment of their minor children to a mental institution could adequately protect a child's rights, *Parham v. J.R.* (1979), per Burger, C.J. (a case treated more fully in the "procedural due process" section, infra), applied "the traditional presumption that the parents act in the best interests of the child." That some parents may act against the interests of the child some times "is hardly a reason to discard wholesale those pages of human experience that teach that parents generally do act in the child's best interests."

Is *Parham*, like *Planned Parenthood v. Danforth*, ? pp. 377–78 supra, a situation in which the parents cannot be relied on to speak for the child's interests? Consider Note, 93 Harv.L.Rev. 89, 94 (1979): "[*Danforth*] ruled that parents cannot prevent their daughters from having abortions, [reasoning] that the existence of the pregnancy itself fractured the family unit too severely to suggest that parental authority should be upheld to preserve the family structure. This reasoning is clearly applicable to a situation in which parents seek to remove a child from the family." Cf. Burt, supra, at 336; John Garvey, *Children and the Idea of Liberty*, 68 Ky.L.J. 809, 832–33 (1979–80).

MICHAEL H. v. GERALD D.
491 U.S. 110, 109 S.Ct. 2333, 105 L.Ed.2d 91 (1989).

JUSTICE SCALIA announced the judgment of the Court and delivered an opinion in which the CHIEF JUSTICE joins, and in all but footnote 6 of which JUSTICE O'CONNOR and JUSTICE KENNEDY join.

[Claiming to be the father of Victoria, the child of Carole D. and Gerald D., a married couple, Michael H. brought an action in California to establish his paternity and visitation rights. Although Gerald was listed as the father on the birth certificate and has always claimed the child as her father, blood tests showed a 98.07% probability that Michael, with whom the mother had had an adulterous affair, was the father. During the first three years of the child's life, she and her mother resided at times with Michael, who held the child out as his own. During this time, mother and child also resided at times with another man and with Gerald. [Under California law, a child born to a married woman living with her husband, who is neither impotent nor sterile, is presumed to be a child of the marriage, a presumption that may be rebutted only in very limited circumstances. Relying on this presumption, the California courts rejected Michael's claims. The U.S. Supreme Court affirmed.]

Michael contends as a matter of substantive due process that because he has established a parental relationship with Victoria, protection of Gerald's and Carole's marital union is an insufficient state interest to support termination of that relationship. This argument is, of course, predicated on the assertion that Michael has a constitutionally protected liberty interest in his relationship with Victoria. [In] an attempt to limit and guide interpretation of the [Due Process] Clause, we have insisted not merely that the interest denominated as a "liberty" be "fundamental" (a concept that, in isolation, is hard to objectify), but also that it be an interest traditionally protected by our society.[2] As we have put it, the Due Process Clause affords only those protections "so rooted in the traditions and conscience of our people as to be ranked as fundamental." * * *

This insistence that the asserted liberty interest be rooted in history and tradition is evident, as elsewhere, in our cases according constitutional protection to certain parental rights. Michael [reads] *Stanley v. Illinois* 405 U.S. 645, 92 S.Ct. 1208, 31 L.Ed.2d 551 (1972), invalidating an irrebuttable statutory presumption that unwed fathers are unfit parents, and such subsequent cases as *Quilloin*], as establishing that a liberty interest is created by biological fatherhood plus an established parental relationship—factors that exist in the present case as well. [As] we view [these cases], they rest not upon such isolated factors but upon the historic respect—indeed, sanctity would not be too strong a term—traditionally accorded to the relationships that develop within the unitary family.

[Thus,] the legal issue in the present case reduces to whether the relationship between persons in the situation of Michael and Victoria has been treated as a protected family unit under the historic practices of our society, or whether on any other basis it has been accorded special protection. We think it impossible to find that it has. In fact, quite to the contrary, our traditions have protected the marital family (Gerald, Carole, and the child they acknowledge to be theirs) against the sort of claim Michael asserts.[4]

[What] Michael asserts here is a right to have himself declared the natural father *and thereby to obtain parental prerogatives.* What he must establish, therefore, is not that our society has traditionally allowed a natural father in his circumstances to establish paternity, but that it has traditionally accorded such a father parental rights, or at least has not traditionally denied them. [What] counts is whether the States in fact award substantive parental rights to the natural father of a child conceived within and born into an extant marital union that wishes to embrace the child. We are not aware of a single case, old or new, that

---

2. We do not understand what Justice Brennan has in mind by an interest "that society traditionally has thought important [without] protecting it." The protection need not take the form of an explicit constitutional provision or statutory guarantee, but it must at least exclude (all that is necessary to decide the present case) a societal tradition of enacting laws *denying* the interest. Nor do we understand why our practice of limiting the Due Process Clause to traditionally protected interests turns the clause "into a redundancy." Its purpose is to prevent future generations from lightly casting aside important traditional values—not to enable this Court to invent new ones.

4. Justice Brennan insists that in determining whether a liberty interest exists we must look at Michael's relationship with Victoria in isolation, without reference to the circumstance that Victoria's mother was married to someone else when the child was conceived, and that that woman and her husband wish to raise the child as their own. We cannot imagine what compels this strange procedure of looking at the act which is assertedly the subject of a liberty interest in isolation from its effect upon other people—rather like inquiring whether there is a liberty interest in firing a gun where the case at hand happens to involve its discharge into another person's body. The logic of Justice Brennan's position leads to the conclusion that if Michael had begotten Victoria by rape, that fact would in no way affect his possession of a liberty interest in his relationship with her.

has done so. This is not the stuff of which fundamental rights qualifying as liberty interests are made.[6] * * *

JUSTICE O'CONNOR, with whom JUSTICE KENNEDY joins, concurring in part.

I concur in all but footnote 6 of Justice Scalia's opinion. This footnote sketches a mode of historical analysis to be used when identifying liberty interests protected by the Due Process Clause of the Fourteenth Amendment that may be somewhat inconsistent with our past decisions in this area. See *Griswold; Eisenstadt.* On occasion the Court has characterized relevant traditions protecting asserted rights at levels of generality that might not be "the most specific level" available [quoting from fn. 6 of Justice Scalia's opinion]. See *Loving v. Virginia* [p. 1176 infra, invalidating state antimiscegenation laws]; *Turner v. Safley*, 482 U.S. 78, 107 S.Ct. 2254, 96 L.Ed.2d 64 (1987) [where, relying on *Zablocki*, a unanimous Court struck down a prison regulation permitting inmates to marry only when there were "compelling reasons" to do so]. I would not foreclose the unanticipated by the prior imposition of a single mode of historical analysis. *Poe* (Harlan, J., dissenting).[a]

JUSTICE BRENNAN, with whom JUSTICE MARSHALL and JUSTICE BLACKMUN join, dissenting. * * *

Once we recognized that the "liberty" protected by the Due Process Clause of the Fourteenth Amendment encompasses more than freedom from bodily re-

---

6. Justice Brennan criticizes our methodology in using historical traditions specifically relating to the rights of an adulterous natural father, rather than inquiring more generally "whether parenthood is an interest that historically has received our attention and protection." There seems to us no basis for the contention that this methodology is "nove[l]." For example, in *Bowers v. Hardwick* [p. 466 infra], we noted that at the time the Fourteenth Amendment was ratified all but 5 of the 37 States had criminal sodomy laws, that all 50 of the States had such laws prior to 1961, and that 24 States and the District of Columbia continued to have them; and we concluded from that record, regarding that very specific aspect of sexual conduct, that "to claim that a right to engage in such conduct is 'deeply rooted in this Nation's history and tradition' or 'implicit in the concept of ordered liberty' is, at best, facetious." In *Roe* we spent about a fifth of our opinion negating the proposition that there was a longstanding tradition of laws proscribing abortion.

We do not understand why, having rejected our focus upon the societal tradition regarding the natural father's rights vis-à-vis a child whose mother is married to another man, Justice Brennan would choose to focus instead upon "parenthood." Why should the relevant category not be even more general—perhaps "family relationships"; or "personal relationships"; or even "emotional attachments in general"? Though the dissent has no basis for the level of generality it would select, we do: We refer to the most specific level at which a relevant tradition protecting, or denying protection to, the asserted right can be identified. If, for example, there were no societal tradi-

tion, either way, regarding the rights of the natural father of a child adulterously conceived, we would have to consult, and (if possible) reason from, the traditions regarding natural fathers in general. But there is such a more specific tradition, and it unqualifiedly denies protection to such a parent.

[Because] general traditions provide such imprecise guidance, they permit judges to dictate rather than discern the society's views. The need, if arbitrary decision-making is to be avoided, to adopt the most specific tradition as the point of reference—or at least to announce, as Justice Brennan declines to do, some other criterion for selecting among the innumerable relevant traditions that could be consulted—is well enough exemplified by the fact that in the present case Justice Brennan's opinion and Justice O'Connor's opinion, which disapproves this footnote, *both* appeal to tradition, but on the basis of the tradition they select reach opposite results. Although assuredly having the virtue (if it be that) of leaving judges free to decide as they think best when the unanticipated occurs, a rule of law that binds neither by text nor by any particular, identifiable tradition, is no rule of law at all. * * *

a. Stevens, J., who concurred in the judgment, was "willing to assume for the purpose of deciding this case that Michael's relationship with Victoria is strong enough to give him a constitutional right to try to convince a trial judge that Victoria's best interest would be served by granting him visitation rights. I am satisfied, however, that the California statute, as applied in this case, gave him that opportunity."

straint, today's plurality opinion emphasizes, the concept was cut loose from one natural limitation on its meaning. This innovation paved the way, so the plurality hints, for judges to substitute their own preferences for those of elected officials. Dissatisfied with this supposedly unbridled and uncertain state of affairs, the plurality casts about for another limitation on the concept of liberty.

It finds this limitation in "tradition." Apparently oblivious to the fact that this concept can be as malleable and as elusive as "liberty" itself, the plurality pretends that tradition places a discernible border around the Constitution. [Yet,] as Justice White observed in his dissent in *Moore v. East Cleveland:* "What the deeply rooted traditions of the country are is arguable." [Because] reasonable people can disagree about the content of particular traditions, and because they can disagree even about which traditions are relevant to the definition of "liberty," the plurality has not found the objective boundary that it seeks.

Even if we could agree, moreover, on the content and significance of particular traditions, we still would be forced to identify the point at which a tradition becomes firm enough to be relevant to our definition of liberty and the moment at which it becomes too obsolete to be relevant any longer. The plurality supplies no objective means by which we might make these determinations.

[The plurality] does not ask whether parenthood is an interest that historically has received our attention and protection; the answer to that question is too clear for dispute. Instead, the plurality asks whether the specific variety of parenthood under consideration—a natural father's relationship with a child whose mother is married to another man—has enjoyed such protection.

If we had looked to tradition with such specificity in past cases, many a decision would have reached a different result. Surely the use of contraceptives by unmarried couples, *Eisenstadt;* or even by married couples, *Griswold;* [and] even the right to raise one's natural but illegitimate children, *Stanley v. Illinois,* were not "interest[s] traditionally protected by our society" at the time of their consideration by this Court.

[The] plurality's interpretive method is more than novel; it is misguided. It ignores the good reasons for limiting the role of "tradition" in interpreting the Constitution's deliberately capacious language. In the plurality's constitutional universe, we may not take notice of the fact that the original reasons for the conclusive presumption of paternity are out of place in a world in which blood tests can prove virtually beyond a shadow of a doubt who sired a particular child and in which the fact of illegitimacy no longer plays the burdensome and stigmatizing role it once did. [By] describing the decisive question as whether Michael and Victoria's interest is one that has been "traditionally *protected by* our society" (emphasis added), rather than one that society traditionally has thought important (with or without protecting it), and by suggesting that our sole function is to "*discern* the society's views," n. 6 (emphasis added), the plurality acts as if the only purpose of the Due Process Clause is to confirm the importance of interests already protected by a majority of the States. Transforming the protection afforded by the Due Process Clause into a redundancy mocks those who, with care and purpose, wrote the Fourteenth Amendment.

In construing the Fourteenth Amendment to offer shelter only to those interests specifically protected by historical practice, moreover, the plurality ignores the kind of society in which our Constitution exists. We are not an assimilative, homogeneous society, but a facilitative, pluralistic one, in which we must be willing to abide someone else's unfamiliar or even repellant practice because the same tolerant impulse protects our own idiosyncracies. Even if we can agree, therefore, that "family" and "parenthood" are part of the good life, it is absurd to assume that we can agree on the content of those terms and destructive to pretend that we do. In a community such as ours, "liberty" must include the freedom not to conform. The plurality today squashes this freedom by requiring specific approval from history before protecting anything in the name of liberty.

The document that the plurality construes today is unfamiliar to me. It is not the living charter that I have taken to be our Constitution; it is instead a stagnant, archaic, hidebound document steeped in the prejudices and superstitions of a time long past. * * *[b]

DETERMINING THE APPROPRIATE LEVEL OF GENERALITY IN DEFINING RIGHTS; USING TRADITION AS A SUBSTITUTE FOR VALUE CHOICES: CRITICISM OF JUSTICE SCALIA'S APPROACH

1. *Looking to "tradition."* Are legally cognizable "traditions" likely to "mirror majoritan, middle-class conventions"? Are historical traditions susceptible to as much manipulation—or even greater manipulation—than are legal precedents? What if it could be demonstrated unequivocally that public flogging and hand-branding were widely accepted forms of punishment in 1791? How does one know when to *reject* an historical pattern or understanding? See Laurence Tribe & Michael Dorf, *Levels of Generality in the Definition of Rights,* 57 U.Chi.L.Rev. 1057, 1087, 1090 (1990).

2. *What is "tradition"? Does tradition ever speak with one voice?* Consider Jack Balkin, *Tradition, Betrayal, and the Politics of Deconstruction,* 11 Cardozo L.Rev. 1613, 1617 (1990): "If there is a tradition of protecting marital privacy, but not a more specific tradition protecting marital purchase of contraceptives, how do we know whether the latter situation is nevertheless subsumed under the former for purposes of constitutionally protected liberty? Might one not conclude instead that the *real* historical tradition was protection of marital privacy in the home, so that the purchase of contraceptives in the open marketplace could be regulated or even proscribed consistent with the tradition? Would this not be more consistent with the experiences of Margaret Sanger and her followers, who publicly advocated birth control in the early twentieth century, and were met with incredible resistance? Again, if sexual harassment directed toward women in the workplace and respect for marital privacy are both traditions, but only one is worth protecting, how do we tell the difference? If back alley abortions are a tradition in response to the 'traditional' prohibition on abortion in America, does this make abortion (in or out of a back alley) a tradition worth protecting and sustaining? In short, what normative status should be assigned to a set of values given the fact that many people have held these values at one point or another in our nation's history?

"[W]hat is most troubling about Justice Scalia's call for respecting the most specific tradition available is that our most specific historical traditions may often be opposed to our more general commitments to liberty or equality. Curiously, then, different parts of the American tradition may conflict with each other. And indeed, this is one of the untidy facts of historical experience. The fourteenth amendment's abstract commitment to racial equality was accompanied by simulta-

b. White, J., also dissented.

neous acceptance of segregated public schools in the District of Columbia and acquiescence in antimiscegenation laws. The establishment clause and the principle of separation of church and state have coexisted with presidential proclamations of national days of prayer, official congressional chaplains, and national Christmas trees. Traditions do not exist as integrated wholes. They are a motley collection of principles and counterprinciples, standing for one thing when viewed narrowly and standing for another when viewed more generally. Tradition never speaks with one voice, although, to be sure, persons of particular predelictions may hear only one."

3. *In formulating the rights at stake, what information does one "abstract away"?* Consider Tribe & Dorf, note 1 supra, at 1092–93: "Justice Scalia's formulation of the rights at stake [in *Michael H.*] as the rights of "the natural father of a child adulterously conceived" [is] already a considerable abstraction. He has abstracted away lots of information that virtually everybody would agree is irrelevant. But he has also abstracted away some information that many people would see as quite relevant. The natural father in *Michael H.* had a longstanding, albeit adulterous and sporadic, relationship with the mother of his child. He also had fairly extensive, if sporadic, contact with his child. Surely this information is more significant than the plaintiff's race or age. A more specific formulation of the issue than Justice Scalia gives us would be: *what are the rights of the natural father of a child conceived in an adulterous but longstanding relationship, where the father has played a major, if sporadic, role in the child's early development?*

"It is unlikely that any tradition addresses this very question at this precise level of specificity. Thus, we are left with the problem of specifying the *next* most specific tradition. [Do] we abstract away the father's relationship with his child and her mother, as Justice Scalia does? Or do we instead abstract away the fact that the relationship with the mother was an adulterous one, as Justice Brennan does? If we do the latter, then we will find ourselves consulting traditions regarding natural fathers who play major roles in their children's development. This sounds an awful lot like 'traditions regarding natural fathers in general,' which Justice Scalia regarded as less specific than his formulation of the problem. By starting from an even *more* specific description of the case than did Justice Scalia, we have seen that he had no greater justification for abstracting away the father-child relationship than Justice Brennan had for abstracting away the adultery."

4. *The role of "tradition" in due process analysis.* "Cases such as *Michael H.*" notes Frank Easterbrook, *Abstraction and Authority*, 59 U.Chi.L.Rev. 349, 352 (1992), "show the importance of picking a level of generality. [By] choosing narrowly the Court may find no problem in the law. By choosing broadly the Court may find a problem with any law it pleases—invoking 'tradition' to demonstrate that adultery and other things that society has long deprecated are actually *protected* by some traditional freedom,[a] that practices traditionally scorned and punished are no different from practices traditionally praised, such as providing a home for one's grandchild. By reserving the right to choose a level of generality to fit the circumstances, as Justices O'Connor and Kennedy did, the

---

a. Earlier at 351–52, Judge Easterbrook maintains that Brennan, J., dissenting in *Michael H.*, had "proceeded to define the [relevant] tradition as the right of biological parents to raise their children, coupled with 'freedom not to conform'—presumably a fundamental right to commit adultery." "With 'freedom not to conform' as a 'fundamental right,'" adds Easterbrook, "the Court holds the whip hand, for *all* law abridges this freedom, and a judge may deem insufficient the justification asserted by the state for any rule at all."

Court makes a virtue of 'the understandable temptation to vary the relevant tradition's level of abstraction to make it come out right' [quoting John Ely]. Justices O'Connor and Kennedy worried that a rule for selecting a level of generality would change the outcome of some cases. Exactly so, but it is less than clear why that should be troubling.

"Although *Michael H.* vividly demonstrates the importance of the level of abstraction, the Justices' dispute was driven by the need to identify a 'tradition,' which would be used to define a fundamental right. If you assume that the purpose of that enterprise is to increase the number of protected interests, then 'it is crucial to define the liberty at a high enough level to permit unconventional variants to claim protection' [quoting Laurence Tribe]. If you believe that tradition serves to restrict the powers of judges to pursue their vision of a good society, then you will choose a lower level of generality. In either case the selection depends on conclusions about the role of 'tradition' in due process analysis rather than about the function of abstraction in understanding the Constitution itself."

6. *Justice Scalia's footnote 4 approach: incorporating the state's interest into an asserted liberty.* Although footnote 6 to Justice Scalia's plurality opinion in *Michael H.* has generated much comment, worthy of attention, too, is footnote 4—criticizing the Court's practice of first deciding whether a liberty is fundamental and then asking whether a government practice restricting that liberty can be justified. Consider Tribe & Dorf, supra, at 1096–97:

"When we automatically incorporate the factors that provide the state's possible justification for its regulation into the initial definition of a liberty, the fundamental nature of that liberty nearly vanishes. Unless the state's interest is facially absurd, when it is suitably incorporated into an asserted liberty it will render that liberty so specific as to seem insupportable, or at least radically disconnected from precedent. At a minimum, the privacy right protected in *Roe* becomes the implausible 'right' to destroy a living fetus. If one takes footnote 4 to its logical limit in the interpretation of *enumerated* rights, then the free speech right protected in *New York Times Co. v. Sullivan* [p. 613 infra] becomes the dubious 'right' to libel a public official and the right to an exclusionary remedy protected in *Mapp v. Ohio* [p. 354 supra] becomes the counter-intuitive 'right' of a criminal to suppress the truth. To state these cases this way is to decide them in the government's favor. Anyone is free to argue that each of these cases was wrongly decided. But arguments to this effect must explain why the state interest overcomes the liberty interest. Under Justice Scalia's footnote 4 approach, by contrast, the state interest obliterates, without explanation and at the outset, any trace of the individual liberty at stake."

WHAT SHALL WE CALL THIS SEGMENT—THE RIGHT TO ENGAGE IN HOMOSEXUAL SODOMY? ADULT, CONSENSUAL SEXUAL CONDUCT IN THE HOME? THE AUTONOMY OF PRIVATE SEXUAL CHOICES? SEXUAL EXPRESSION AND CONTROL OF ONE'S BODY? UNCONVENTIONAL SEXUAL LIFESTYLES? THE RIGHT TO CONTROL ONE'S INTIMATE ASSOCIATIONS? THE RIGHT TO BE LET ALONE?

BOWERS v. HARDWICK

478 U.S. 186, 106 S.Ct. 2841, 92 L.Ed.2d 140 (1986).

JUSTICE WHITE delivered the opinion of the Court.

In August 1982, respondent, [an adult male,] was charged with violating the Georgia statute criminalizing sodomy[1] by committing that act with another adult male in the bedroom of respondent's home. After a preliminary hearing, the District Attorney decided not to present the matter to the grand jury unless further evidence developed.

Respondent then brought suit in the Federal District Court, challenging the constitutionality of the statute insofar as it criminalized consensual sodomy.[2] He asserted that he was a practicing homosexual, that the Georgia statute [placed] him in imminent danger of arrest, and that the statute [violated the Constitution]. The District Court [dismissed the suit] for failure to state a claim. [The U.S. Court of Appeals for the Eleventh Circuit reversed, holding] that the Georgia statute violated respondent's fundamental rights because his homosexual activity is a private and intimate association that is beyond the reach of state regulation by reason of the Ninth Amendment and the Due Process Clause. [We reverse.]

This case does not require a judgment on whether laws against sodomy between consenting adults in general, or between homosexuals in particular, are wise or desirable. [T]he issue presented is whether the Federal Constitution confers a fundamental right upon homosexuals to engage in sodomy and hence invalidates the laws of the many States that still make such conduct illegal and have done so for a very long time. The case also calls for some judgment about the limits of the Court's role in carrying out its constitutional mandate.

We first register our disagreement with the Court of Appeals [that] the Court's prior cases have construed the Constitution to confer a right of privacy that extends to homosexual sodomy and for all intents and purposes have decided this case. [We] think it evident that none of the rights announced in [such cases as

---

1. Ga.Code Ann. § 16–6–2 (1984) provides, in pertinent part, as follows:

"(a) A person commits the offense of sodomy when he performs or submits to any sexual act involving the sex organs of one person and the mouth or anus of [another].

"(b) A person convicted of the offense of sodomy shall be punished by imprisonment for not less than one nor more than 20 [years]."

2. John and Mary Doe were also plaintiffs in the action. They alleged that they wished to engage in sexual activity proscribed by § 16–6–2 in the privacy of their home, and that they had been "chilled and deterred" from engaging in such activity by both the existence of the

statute and Hardwick's arrest. The District Court held, however, that because they had neither sustained, nor were in immediate danger of sustaining, any direct injury from the enforcement of the statute, they did not have proper standing to maintain the action. The Court of Appeals affirmed [and] the Does do not challenge that holding in this Court.

The only claim properly before the Court, therefore, is Hardwick's challenge to the Georgia statute as applied to consensual homosexual sodomy. We express no opinion on the constitutionality of the Georgia statute as applied to other acts of sodomy.

Skinner, Griswold and *Roe*] bears any resemblance to the claimed constitutional right of homosexuals to engage in acts of sodomy that is asserted in this case. No connection between family, marriage, or procreation on the one hand and homosexual activity on the other has been [demonstrated]. Moreover, any claim that these cases nevertheless stand for the proposition that any kind of private sexual conduct between consenting adults is constitutionally insulated from state proscription is unsupportable. * * * Precedent aside, however, respondent would have us announce [a] fundamental right to engage in homosexual sodomy. This we are quite unwilling to do. * * *

Striving to assure itself and the public that announcing rights not readily identifiable in the Constitution's text involves much more than the imposition of the Justices' own choice of values on the States and the Federal Government, the Court has sought to identify the nature of the rights qualifying for heightened judicial protection. In *Palko* it was said that this category includes those fundamental liberties that are "implicit in the concept of ordered liberty," such that "neither liberty nor justice would exist if [they] were sacrificed." A different description of fundamental liberties appeared in *Moore v. East Cleveland* (opinion of Powell, J.), where they are characterized as those liberties that are "deeply rooted in this Nation's history and tradition."

It is obvious to us that neither of these formulations would extend a fundamental right to homosexuals to engage in acts of consensual sodomy. Proscriptions against that conduct have ancient roots. Sodomy was a criminal offense at common law and was forbidden by the laws of the original thirteen States when they ratified the Bill of Rights. In 1868, when the Fourteenth Amendment was ratified, all but 5 of the 37 States in the Union had criminal sodomy laws. In fact, until 1961, all 50 States outlawed sodomy, and today, 24 States and the District of Columbia continue to provide criminal penalties for sodomy performed in private and between consenting adults. Against this background, to claim that a right to engage in such conduct is "deeply rooted in this Nation's history and tradition" or "implicit in the concept of ordered liberty" is, at best, facetious.

Nor are we inclined to take a more expansive view of our authority to discover new fundamental rights imbedded in the Due Process Clause. The Court is most vulnerable and comes nearest to illegitimacy when it deals with judge-made constitutional law having little or no cognizable roots in the language or design of the Constitution. That this is so was painfully demonstrated by the face-off between the Executive and the Court in the 1930's, which resulted in the repudiation of much of the substantive gloss that the Court had placed on the [due process clause, clauses]. There should be, therefore, great resistance to expand the substantive reach of those Clauses, particularly if it requires redefining the category of rights deemed to be fundamental. Otherwise, the Judiciary necessarily takes to itself further authority to govern the country without express constitutional authority. The claimed right pressed on us today falls far short of overcoming this resistance.

Respondent, however, asserts that the result should be different where the homosexual conduct occurs in the privacy of the home. He relies on *Stanley v. Georgia*, where the Court held that the First Amendment prevents conviction for possessing and reading obscene material in the privacy of [one's home]. *Stanley* did protect conduct that would not have been protected outside the home, and it partially prevented the enforcement of state obscenity laws; but the decision was firmly grounded in the First Amendment. The right pressed upon us here has no similar support in the text of the Constitution, and it does not qualify for recognition under the prevailing principles for construing the Fourteenth Amendment. Its limits are also difficult to discern. Plainly enough, otherwise illegal conduct is not always immunized whenever it occurs in the home. Victimless crimes, such as the possession and use of illegal drugs do not escape the law where they are committed at home. *Stanley* itself recognized that its holding offered no protection for the possession in the home of drugs, firearms, or stolen goods. And if respondent's submission is limited to the voluntary sexual conduct between consenting adults, it would be difficult, except by fiat, to limit the claimed right to homosexual conduct while leaving exposed to prosecution adultery, incest, and other sexual crimes even though they are committed in the home. We are unwilling to start down that road.

Even if the conduct at issue here is not a fundamental right, respondent asserts that there must be a rational basis for the law and that there is none in this case other than the presumed belief of a majority of the electorate in Georgia that homosexual sodomy is immoral and unacceptable. [The] law, however, is constantly based on notions of morality, and if all laws representing essentially moral choices are to be invalidated under the Due Process Clause, the courts will be very busy indeed. Even respondent makes no such claim, but insists that majority sentiments about the morality of homosexuality should be declared inadequate. We do not agree, and are unpersuaded that the sodomy laws of some 25 States should be invalidated on this basis.[8] [Reversed.]

CHIEF JUSTICE BURGER, concurring.

I join the Court's opinion, but I write separately to underscore my view that in constitutional terms there is no such thing as a fundamental right to commit homosexual sodomy. [To] hold that the act of homosexual sodomy is somehow protected as a fundamental right would be to cast aside millennia of moral teaching. * * *

JUSTICE POWELL, concurring.

I join the opinion of the Court. [But the] The Georgia statute at issue in this case authorizes a court to imprison a person for up to 20 years for a single private, consensual act of sodomy. In my view, a prison sentence for such conduct—certainly a sentence of long duration—would create a serious Eighth Amendment issue. [In] this case, however, respondent has not been tried, much less convicted and sentenced.[2] * * *

JUSTICE BLACKMUN, with whom JUSTICE BRENNAN, JUSTICE MARSHALL, and JUSTICE STEVENS join, dissenting.

This case is no more about "a fundamental right to engage in homosexual sodomy," as the Court purports to declare, than *Stanley* was about a fundamental right to watch obscene movies. [Rather,] this case is about "the most comprehen-

---

8. Respondent does not defend the judgment below based on the Ninth Amendment, the Equal Protection Clause or the Eighth Amendment.

2. It was conceded at oral argument that, prior to the complaint against respondent Hardwick, there had been no reported decision involving prosecution for private homosexual sodomy under this Statute for several decades. Moreover, the State has declined to present the criminal charge against Hardwick to a grand jury, and this is a suit for declaratory judgment

brought by respondents challenging the validity of the statute. The history of nonenforcement suggests the moribund character today of laws criminalizing this type of private, consensual conduct. Some 26 states have repealed similar statutes. But the constitutional validity of the Georgia statute was put in issue by respondents, and for the reasons stated by the Court, I cannot say that conduct condemned for hundreds of years has now become a fundamental right.

sive of rights and the right most valued by civilized men," namely, "the right to be let alone." *Olmstead v. United States,* 277 U.S. 438, 478, 48 S.Ct. 564, 572, 72 L.Ed. 944 (1928) (Brandeis, J., dissenting). [T]he fact that the moral judgments expressed by statutes like [this one] may be "natural and familiar [should not] conclude our judgment upon the question whether statutes embodying them conflict with the Constitution of the United States." *Roe,* quoting *Lochner* (Holmes, J., dissenting). [We] must analyze respondent's claim in the light of the values that underlie the constitutional right to privacy. If that right means anything, it means that, before Georgia can prosecute its citizens for making choices about the most intimate aspects of their lives, it must do more than assert that the choice they have made is an " 'abominable crime not fit to be named among Christians.' "

[The] Court's almost obsessive focus on homosexual activity is particularly hard to justify in light of the broad language Georgia has used. Unlike the Court, the Georgia Legislature has not proceeded on the assumption that homosexuals are so different from other citizens that their lives may be controlled in a way that would not be tolerated if it limited the choices of those other citizens. Rather, Georgia has provided that "[a] person commits the offense of sodomy when he performs or submits to any sexual act involving the sex organs of one person and the mouth or anus of another." The sex or status of the persons who engage in the act is irrelevant as a matter of state law. In fact, to the extent I can discern a legislative purpose for Georgia's 1968 enactment, that purpose seems to have been to broaden the coverage of the law to reach heterosexual as well as homosexual activity. I therefore see no basis for the Court's decision to treat this case as an "as applied" challenge to [the law], see n. 2, or for Georgia's attempt, both in its brief and at oral argument, to defend [the law] solely on the grounds that it prohibits homosexual activity. * * *

"Our cases long have recognized that the Constitution embodies a promise that a certain private sphere of individual liberty will be kept largely beyond the reach of government." In construing the right to privacy, the Court has proceeded along two somewhat distinct, albeit complementary, lines. First, it has recognized a privacy interest with reference to certain *decisions* that are properly for the individual to make. E.g., *Roe, Pierce.* Second, it has recognized a privacy interest with reference to certain *places* without regard for the particular activities in which the individuals who occupy them are engaged. The case before us implicates both the decisional and the spatial aspects of the right to privacy. * * *

Only the most willful blindness could obscure the fact that sexual intimacy is "a sensitive, key relationship of human existence, central to family life, community welfare, and the development of human personality." The fact that individuals define themselves in a significant way through their intimate sexual relationships with others suggests, in a Nation as diverse as ours, that there may be many "right" ways of conducting those relationships, and that much of the richness of a relationship will come from the freedom an individual has to *choose* the form and nature of these intensely personal bonds. See Kenneth Karst, *The Freedom of Intimate Association,* 89 Yale L.J. 624, 637 (1980).

In a variety of circumstances we have recognized that a necessary corollary of giving individuals freedom to choose how to conduct their lives is acceptance of the fact that different individuals will make different choices. [The] Court claims that its decision today merely refuses to recognize a fundamental right to engage in homosexual sodomy; what the Court really has refused to recognize is the fundamental interest all individuals have in controlling the nature of their intimate associations with others.

The behavior for which Hardwick faces prosecution occurred in his own home, a place to which the Fourth Amendment attaches special significance. The Court's treatment of this aspect of the case is symptomatic of its overall refusal to consider the broad principles that have informed our treatment of privacy in specific cases. Just as the right to privacy is more than the mere aggregation of a number of entitlements to engage in specific behavior, so too, protecting the physical integrity of the home is more than merely a means of protecting specific activities that often take place there. [The] Court's interpretation of the pivotal case of *Stanley v. Georgia* is entirely unconvincing. [According] to the majority here, *Stanley* relied entirely on the First Amendment, and thus, it is claimed, sheds no light on cases not involving printed materials. But that is not what *Stanley* said. Rather, the *Stanley* Court anchored its holding in the Fourth Amendment's special protection for the individual in his home.

[The] central place that *Stanley* gives Justice Brandeis' dissent in *Olmstead,* a case raising *no* First Amendment claim, shows that *Stanley* rested as much on the Court's understanding of the Fourth Amendment as it did on the First. * * * "The right of the people to be secure in [their] houses," expressly guaranteed by the Fourth Amendment, is perhaps the most "textual" of the various constitutional provisions that inform our understanding of the right to privacy, and thus I cannot agree with the Court's statement that "[t]he right pressed upon us here has [no] support in the text of the Constitution." Indeed, the right of an individual to conduct intimate relationships in the intimacy of his or her own home seems to me to be the heart of the Constitution's protection of privacy.

The Court's failure to comprehend the magnitude of the liberty interests at stake in this case leads it to slight the question whether [petitioner] has justified Georgia's infringement on these interests. I believe that neither of the two general justifications for [that] petitioner has advanced warrants dismissing respondent's challenge for failure to state a claim.

First, petitioner asserts that the acts made criminal by the statute may have serious adverse consequences for "the general public health and welfare," such as spreading communicable diseases or fostering other criminal activity. [Nothing in the record] provides any justification for finding the activity forbidden [to] be physically dangerous, either to the persons engaged in it or to others.[4]

The core of petitioner's defense of [the law], however, is that respondent and others who engage in the [prohibited conduct] interfere with Georgia's exercise of the " 'right of the Nation and of the States to maintain a decent society,' " *Paris*

---

4. Although I do not think it necessary to decide today issues that are not even remotely before us, it does seem to me that a court could find simple, analytically sound distinctions between certain private, consensual sexual conduct, on the one hand, and adultery and incest (the only two vaguely specific "sexual crimes" to which the majority points), on the other. For example, marriage, in addition to its spiritual aspects, is a civil contract that entitles the contracting parties to a variety of governmentally provided benefits. A State might define the contractual commitment necessary to become eligible for these benefits to include a commitment of fidelity and then punish individuals for breaching that contract. Moreover,

a State might conclude that adultery is likely to injure third persons, in particular, spouses and children of persons who engage in extramarital affairs. With respect to incest, a court might well agree with respondent that the nature of familial relationships renders true consent to incestuous activity sufficiently problematical that a blanket prohibition of such activity is warranted. Notably, the Court makes no effort to explain why it has chosen to group private, consensual homosexual activity with adultery and incest rather than with private, consensual heterosexual activity by unmarried persons or, indeed, with oral or anal sex within marriage.

Adult Theatre. Essentially, petitioner argues, and the Court agrees, that the fact that the [prohibited conduct] "for hundreds of years, if not thousands, have been uniformly condemned as immoral" is a sufficient reason to permit a State to ban them today. I cannot agree that either the length of time a majority has held its convictions or the passions with which it defends them can withdraw legislation from this Court's scrutiny. See, e.g., *Roe; Loving; Brown v. Board of Education.*[5] [It] is precisely because the issue raised by this case touches the heart of what makes individuals what they are that we should be especially sensitive to the rights of those whose choices upset the majority.

The assertion that "traditional Judeo–Christian values proscribe" the conduct involved cannot provide an adequate justification for [the law]. That certain, but by no means all, religious groups condemn the behavior at issue gives the State no license to impose their judgments on the entire citizenry. The legitimacy of secular legislation depends instead on whether the State can advance some justification for its law beyond its conformity to religious doctrine. A State can no more punish private behavior because of religious intolerance than it can punish such behavior because of racial animus.

Petitioner and the Court fail to see the difference between laws that protect public sensibilities and those that enforce private morality. Statutes banning public sexual activity are entirely consistent with protecting the individual's liberty interest in decisions concerning sexual relations: the same recognition that those decisions are intensely private which justifies protecting them from governmental interference can justify protecting individuals from unwilling exposure to the sexual activities of others. But the mere fact that intimate behavior may be punished when it takes place in public cannot dictate how States can regulate intimate behavior that occurs in intimate places.

This case involves no real interference with the rights of others, for the mere knowledge that other individuals do not adhere to one's value system cannot be a legally cognizable interest, let alone an interest that can justify invading the houses, hearts, and minds of citizens who choose to live their lives differently. * * * I can only hope that [the] Court soon will reconsider its analysis and conclude that depriving individuals of the right to choose for themselves how to conduct their intimate relationships poses a far greater threat than tolerance of nonconformity could ever do. * * *

JUSTICE STEVENS, with whom JUSTICE BRENNAN and JUSTICE MARSHALL join, dissenting.

Like the statute that is challenged in this case, the rationale of the Court's opinion applies equally to the prohibited conduct regardless of whether the parties who engage in it are married or unmarried, or are of the same or different sexes. Sodomy was condemned as an odious and sinful type of behavior during the formative period of the common law. That condemnation was equally damning for heterosexual and homosexual sodomy. Moreover, it provided no special exemption

---

5. The parallel between *Loving* [which invalidated a Virginia antimiscegenation law] and this case is almost uncanny. There, too, the State relied on a religious justification for its law. [There], too, defenders of the challenged statute relied heavily on the fact that when the Fourteenth Amendment was ratified, most of the States had similar prohibitions. There, too, at the time the case came before the Court, many of the States still had criminal statutes concerning the conduct at issue. [Yet] the Court held, not only that the invidious racism of Virginia's law violated the Equal Protection Clause, but also that the law deprived the Lovings of due process by denying them the "freedom of choice to marry" that had "long been recognized as one of the vital personal rights essential to the orderly pursuit of happiness by free men."

for married couples. The license to cohabit and to produce legitimate offspring simply did not include any permission to engage in sexual conduct that was considered a "crime against nature."

Because the Georgia statute expresses the traditional view that sodomy is an immoral kind of conduct regardless of the identity of the persons who engage in it, I believe that a proper analysis of its constitutionality requires consideration of two questions: First, may a State totally prohibit the described conduct by means of a neutral law applying without exception to all persons subject to its jurisdiction? If not, may the State save the statute by announcing that it will only enforce the law against homosexuals? The two questions merit separate discussion.

Our prior cases make two propositions abundantly clear. First, the fact that the governing majority in a State has traditionally viewed a particular practice as immoral is not a sufficient reason for upholding a law prohibiting the practice; neither history nor tradition could save a law prohibiting miscegenation from constitutional attack.[9] Second, individual decisions by married persons, concerning the intimacies of their physical relationship, even when not intended to produce offspring, are a form of "liberty" protected by [due process]. *Griswold.* Moreover, this protection extends to intimate choices by unmarried as well as married persons. *Carey; Eisenstadt.* * * *

Society has every right to encourage its individual members to follow particular traditions in expressing affection for one another and in gratifying their personal desires. It, of course, may prohibit an individual from imposing his will on another to satisfy his own selfish interests. It also may prevent an individual from interfering with, or violating, a legally sanctioned and protected relationship, such as marriage. And it may explain the relative advantages and disadvantages of different forms of intimate expression. But when individual married couples are isolated from observation by others, the way in which they voluntarily choose to conduct their intimate relations is a matter for them—not the State—to decide.[10] The essential "liberty" that animated the development of the law in cases like *Griswold, Eisenstadt,* and *Carey* surely embraces the right to engage in nonreproductive, sexual conduct that others may consider offensive or immoral.

Paradoxical as it may seem, our prior cases thus establish that a State may not prohibit sodomy within "the sacred precincts of marital bedrooms," *Griswold,* or, indeed, between unmarried heterosexual adults. *Eisenstadt.* [If] the Georgia statute cannot be enforced as it is written—if the conduct it seeks to prohibit is a protected form of liberty for the vast majority of Georgia's citizens—the State must assume the burden of justifying a selective application of its law. Either the persons to whom Georgia seeks to apply its statute do not have the same interest in "liberty" that others have, or there must be a reason why the State may be permitted to apply a generally applicable law to certain persons that it does not apply to others.

The first possibility is plainly unacceptable. Although the meaning of the principle that "all men are created equal" is not always clear, it surely must mean that every free citizen has the same interest in "liberty" that the members of the majority share. From the standpoint of the individual, the homosexual and the heterosexual have the same interest in deciding how he will live his own life, and, more narrowly, how he will conduct himself in his personal and voluntary

---

9. See *Loving.* Interestingly, miscegenation was once treated as a crime similar to sodomy.

10. Indeed, the Georgia Attorney General concedes that Georgia's statute would be un-

constitutional if applied to a married couple. * * * Significantly, Georgia passed the current statute three years after the Court's decision in *Griswold.*

associations with his companions. State intrusion into the private conduct of either is equally burdensome.

The second possibility is similarly unacceptable. A policy of selective application must be supported by a neutral and legitimate interest—something more substantial than a habitual dislike for, or ignorance about, the disfavored group. Neither the State nor the Court has identified any such interest in this case. The Court has posited as a justification for the Georgia statute "the presumed belief of a majority of the electorate in Georgia that homosexual sodomy is immoral and unacceptable." But the Georgia electorate has expressed no such belief—instead, its representatives enacted a law that presumably reflects the belief that *all* *sodomy* is immoral and unacceptable. Unless the Court is prepared to conclude that such a law is constitutional, it may not rely on the work product of the Georgia Legislature to support its holding. For the Georgia statute does not single out homosexuals as a separate class meriting special disfavored treatment. [Moreover, the] record of nonenforcement, in this case and in the last several decades, belies the Attorney General's representations about the importance of the State's selective application of its generally applicable law.

Both the Georgia statute and the Georgia prosecutor thus completely fail to provide the Court with any support for the conclusion that homosexual sodomy, *simpliciter,* is considered unacceptable conduct in that State, and that the burden of justifying a selective application of the generally applicable law has been met.
* * *

CRITICISM OF *BOWERS v. HARDWICK*

1. *"Sever[ing] the roots of the privacy doctrine."* Consider Jed Rubenfeld, *The Right of Privacy,* 102 Harv.L.Rev. 737, 748 (1989): "Justice White stated that the Court's prior cases have recognized three categories of activity protected by the right to privacy: marriage, procreation, and family relationships[, but he] neither sought nor found any unifying principle underlying his three categories. It was as if the Court had said, 'We in the majority barely understand why even these three areas are constitutionally protected; we simply acknowledge them and note that they are not involved here.' The device of compartmentalizing precedent is an old jurisprudential strategy for limiting unruly doctrines. The effect here is that, after *Hardwick,* we know that the right to privacy protects some aspects of marriage, procreation, and child-rearing, but we do not know why. By identifying three disparate applications ungrounded by any unifying principle, the majority effectively severed the roots of the privacy doctrine, leaving only the branches
* * *."

2. *Are Roe and Hardwick irreconcilable?* Consider Frank Easterbrook, *Abstraction and Authority,* 59 U.Chi.L.Rev. 349, 365–66 (1992): "These are irreconcilable decisions—Tribe and Dorf [cited in fn. d infra] think so, I think so, the Justices themselves think so. At least seven of the Justices who voted in *Hardwick* would have treated the abortion and sodomy questions identically: Justices Brennan, Marshall, Blackmun, and Stevens, by protecting both; Justices Burger, White, and Rehnquist (perhaps Justice O'Connor, too), by protecting neither. Only Justice Powell saw a difference—adhering to *Roe* while joining the majority in *Hardwick*—and he is reputed to have changed his mind about *Hardwick* after he left the Court."

Suppose *Hardwick* had been decided in 1973 and the abortion question had come to the Court for the first time in 1986. Would the Court be compelled to decide against the right to abortion in '86? See Easterbrook, supra at 367.

3. *Why didn't the Court dismiss the case as moot?* Consider Richard Posner, *Sex and Reason* 341–42 (1992): "It is unclear whether anyone had been prosecuted in Georgia for a violation of the sodomy law not involving aggravated circumstances for forty years or more. [In] any event, the district attorney's policy was not to prosecute adult consensual violators of the law. [Hardwick] did not try to show that there was a significant probability of his being arrested for sodomy in the future. It was a fluke that the police had seen him commit the crime in the privacy of his own home.

"One might in these circumstances have expected the Court, under its precedents, to dismiss the case as moot,[a] especially given the controversiality of the issue. [The] Court may not have done this because it wanted to cut back on the concept of sexual privacy in a case that some of the justices may have thought an ideal vehicle for doing so—a veritable reductio ad absurdum of the concept. [Had Justice White] noted that besides being about family, marriage and procreation, cases such as *Griswold, Eisenstadt* [and] *Roe* had been about sex, he could not have polished them off so easily. Nor if he had remarked the fact that, on its face anyway, the Georgia statute made sodomy illegal even when heterosexual—even, indeed, when practiced by married persons."[b]

4. *Under the circumstances of the* Hardwick *case, was sexuality "an anatomical irrelevance"?* Criticizing what he calls "Justice White's stunningly harsh and dismissive opinion [in] *Hardwick*," Charles Fried, *Order and Law* 82–84 (1991), observes: "Unless one takes the implausible line that people generally choose their sexual orientation, [to] criminalize any enjoyment of the sexual powers by a whole category of persons is either an imposition of very great cruelty or an exercise in hypocrisy inviting arbitrary and abusive applications of the criminal law. *Poe* and *Griswold* did emphasize the sanctity of marital intimacy, so that a step beyond these cases would have had to be taken to reach the conclusion Justice Blackmun urged in a particularly moving dissent. But it is a short step, and one authorized by reason and tradition: Hardwick was threatened with prosecution for having consensual sex with another man behind a closed bedroom door in his own home. The police found out about it by an uninvited accident. Here the conduct was truly private. It concerned no one else except in the question-begging sense that some may be offended by the very knowledge that such conduct goes unpunished. What is left is an act of private association and communication. The fact that sexuality is implicated seems an anatomical irrelevance."

5. *What was the specific act for which Hardwick has been arrested? Does it matter?* "Overlooked by both opinions," points out Posner, note 3 supra, at 343, "is the fact that at common law sodomy did not include fellatio, the specific act for which Hardwick had been arrested; sodomy at common law was limited to anal intercourse. The extension of the proscription to oral sex came late in the nineteenth century, after the Bill of Rights and the Fourteenth Amendment. White is correct nevertheless that the right to engage in homosexual acts is not deeply rooted in America's history and tradition. [But the] same thing could have been said of the rights recognized in the earlier sexual privacy cases (had, indeed, been said by White himself, in his dissent in *Roe*) * * *."

---

a. See generally pp. 1533–37 infra.

b. "Evidently," observes Judge Posner, id. at 345, "the Georgia legislature that passed the sodomy law was concerned not about homosexuality as such but about 'unnatural' sexual acts by or on whomever committed. Whatever the arguments that might be marshaled in favor of attempts to suppress homosexuality, they are not available as arguments for suppressing 'unnatural' sex acts between men and women—except for the theological arguments, by 1986 made only by orthodox Roman Catholics, and not by many of them, and those are a thin reed to support criminal punishment."

6. *More on Powell's concurring opinion: Was Hardwick really a 4½–4½ decision?* Consider Marc Spindelman, *Reorienting Bowers v. Hardwick*, 79 N.C.L.Rev. 359, 414, 418–19, 425–26 (2001): [The concession that prior to *Hardwick* there had been no reported decision involving prosecution for private homosexual sodomy in Georgia (see fn. 2 to Powell, J.'s opinion)] and the state's choice not to present the criminal charge against Hardwick to a grand jury were strong indications of what 'the law' of sodomy in Georgia (and elsewhere) was at the time *Hardwick* was decided. As Frankfurter expressed the idea [in his plurality opinion in *Poe v. Ullman*]: 'deeply embedded traditional ways of carrying out state policy—*or not carrying it out*—are often tougher and truer law than the dead words of the written act.' (Emphasis added.) Powell captured the gestalt of Frankfurter's *Poe* plurality with his own remark that 'the history of nonenforcement [of Georgia's sodomy ban] suggests the moribund character today of laws criminalizing this type of private consensual conduct'—particularly given that 'some 26 States ha[d] repealed similar statutes.' * * *

"In a letter for posterity to Professor Laurence Tribe [in response to a letter from Tribe],[a] Powell flatly declared, 'The Court should not have granted certiorari in *Hardwick*.' [In light of Powell's qualifications], one might view the decision (as I am inclined to do) as something more akin to 'a vote of four and a half to four and a half,' [with] Powell, on behalf of the Court, reserving judgment on the question that, at first glance, he may have seemed to resolve.

" * * * Powell's opinion can be viewed as an indication that he was awaiting a case in which the state had put its sodomy law into play by breaking the 'tacit agreement' not to punish by prosecuting individuals for private gay sex. In such a case, unlike *Hardwick*, the controversy would have been 'real, [not] hypothetical. [And] in such a case, as I think Powell may have sensed, social disapproval of punishment for gay sex could be used as a constitutional device to trump social disapproval of gay sex itself. With Donald Dripps, I would say that '[i]n such a case, [we] can be confident [Powell] would have voted to reverse a criminal conviction.'[201] [Instead] of interpreting Powell's opinion to have decided the matter once and for all, we can regard it as an effort to split the difference between the Justices who were and those who were not prepared to recognize Hardwick's due process right to engage in consensual, private same-sex sexual activity, an effort that took the form of Powell's staying his hand for another day."[b]

7. *More on the level of generality in defining rights.* Did *Hardwick* define the claim of liberty at the wrong level of generality? Yes, maintains Tribe 2d ed., at 1427–28: "Obviously, the history of homosexuality has been largely a history of opprobrium; indeed, it would not be implausible to find on this basis that homosexuals constitute a discrete and insular minority entitled to heightened protection under the equal protection clause.[c] Yet when the Court uses the history

a. Some years after stepping down from the Court, Justice Powell told a group of law students that he "probably made a mistake" voting with the majority in *Hardwick*. Tribe, who had argued the case for Hardwick in the Supreme Court, then wrote Powell a personal letter praising Powell's "courage and candor" in acknowledging error. See John C. Jeffries, Jr., *Justice Lewis F. Powell, Jr.* 530 (1994).

201. Donald A. Dripps, *Bowers v. Hardwick and the Law of Standing: Noncases Make Bad Law*, 44 Emory L.J. 1417, 1435 (1995).

b. According to Powell's biographer, Jeffries, fn. a supra, at 514, in *Hardwick* Powell sought a middle course, but "did not find the means to translate his moderate impulses into legal doctrine. He failed to craft and publish a clear statement of his own views. In this sense, *Hardwick* was Powell's greatest defeat."

c. Cf. Frank Michelman, *Law's Republic*, 97 Yale L.J. 1493, 1532–33 (1988). Consider, too, Posner, note 3 supra, at 346–48; Sylvia Law, *Homosexuality and the Social Meaning of Gender*, 1988 Wis. L.Rev. 1; David Richards,

of violent disapproval of the behavior that forms part of the very definition of homosexuality as the basis for denying homosexuals' claim to protection, it effectively inverts the equal protection axiom of heightened judicial solicitude for despised groups and their characteristic activities and uses that inverted principle to bootstrap antipathy toward homosexuality into a tautological rationale for continuing to criminalize homosexuality. Therefore, in asking whether an alleged right forms part of a traditional liberty, it is crucial to define the liberty at a high enough level of generality to permit unconventional variants to claim protection along with mainstream versions of protected conduct. The proper question, as the dissent in *Hardwick* recognized, is not whether oral sex as such has long enjoyed a special place in the pantheon of constitutional rights, but whether private, consensual, adult sexual acts partake of traditionally revered liberties of intimate association and individual autonomy."

But consider Robert Bork, *The Tempting of America*, 203–04 (1990): "Tribe [thinks that a] constitutional right to homosexual conduct within the home [is] part of a broader right to sexual intimacies between consenting adults. [The] Court [,he tells us,] must choose the level of generality at which it states 'traditional liberty' at any level that results in a constitutional right for unconventional behavior. This bypasses the question of whether the Constitution contains protection for any sexual conduct or whether that is left to the moral sense of the people. It also fails to come to grips with the central question[:] How can any individual, professor, judge, or moral philosopher tell us convincingly that, regardless of law or our own moral sense, certain forms of unconventional behavior must be allowed? There is no apparent reason why the Court should manipulate the level of generality to protect unconventional sexual behavior any more than liberty should be taken at a high enough level of abstraction to protect kleptomania. Tribe has more sympathy for one than for the other, but that hardly rises to the level of a constitutional principle."[d]

8. *Drawing guidance from the text itself; Hardwick, Roe, and the "right" to use a sperm bank.* "The basic choice," maintain Tribe and Dorf, fn. d below, at 1107 "—and neither the Constitution's text nor its structure nor its history can make it for us—is between emphasizing the 'conservative' functions of both the liberty and equality clauses (as well as others), and emphasizing their potential as generators of critique and change." "We must justify the choice extratextually, but we may and should then implement it in ways that draw as much guidance as possible from the text itself. Justice Harlan exemplified such a program in his [*Poe*] dissent, in which he opted for a moderately conservative orientation toward generalization (one considerably less tradition-conserving than Justice Scalia's, however) and sought unifying structures for specified rights in an intermediate level of generality, drawing heavily upon textual points of reference.

"In the *Hardwick* context, if one is willing to generalize much at all, the Constitution's text—in the First Amendment's protection of peaceful assembly and in the Fourth Amendment's protection of the home—points toward generalizing in the direction of intimate personal association in the privacy of the home rather than generalizing in the direction of, let us say, freedom of choice in matters of procreation. It is for this reason that *Hardwick* seems to us so egregiously wrong; that *Roe* seems a closer and more difficult case; that a supposed 'fundamental right' to use a sperm bank would represent a particularly

Constitutional Legitimacy and Constitutional Privacy, 61 NYU.L.Rev. 800 (1986). See also pp. 1321–28 infra.

d. For a partial response to Judge Bork, see Tribe & Dorf, *Levels of Generality in the Defi-nitions of Rights*, 57 U.Chi.L.Rev. 1057, 1099–1100 (1990).

bold leap; and that a 'right' to enforce a surrogacy contract against a woman who has changed her mind and wishes to keep her gestational child entails a leap across a constitutionally unbridgeable void.''

9. *The Georgia Supreme Court and five other state courts invalidate sodomy laws.* A dozen years after *Hardwick* had upheld Georgia's sodomy law, the Georgia Supreme Court struck down the same law, pointing out that private, consensual, adult sexual activity "is at the heart of the Georgia Constitution's protection of the right to privacy." *Powell v. State*, 270 Ga. 327, 510 S.E.2d 18, 24 (Ga. 1998). In the 1990s five other state courts struck down sodomy laws and three state legislatures repealed their sodomy laws. See Louis Fisher & Neil Devins, *Political Dynamics of Constitutional Law* 223–24 (3d ed. 2001).

10. *Are Romer and Hardwick reconcilable?* Compare *Hardwick* with *Romer v. Evans*, p. 1312 infra, holding that a voter-initiated state constitutional amendment prohibiting state or local governments from acting to protect the status of persons based on their "homosexual, lesbian or bisexual orientation" violates the Equal Protection Clause: "[I]n making a general announcement that gays and lesbians shall not have any particular protections from the law," the amendment inflicts injuries on them "that outrun and belie any legitimate justifications that may be claimed for it"; "it is a classification of persons undertaken for its own sake, something the Equal Protection Clause does not permit." The 6–3 majority did not mention *Hardwick*, but the dissent did. It maintained that the majority had "contradict[ed]" *Hardwick* and "place[d] the prestige of this institution behind the proposition that opposition to homosexuality is as reprehensible as racial or religious bias." Do you share the *Romer* dissenters' view of the Court's holding? Why (not)?

MORE ON PRIVACY AND AUTONOMY

1. *Personal appearance and lifestyles.* KELLEY v. JOHNSON, 425 U.S. 238, 96 S.Ct. 1440, 47 L.Ed.2d 708 (1976), per REHNQUIST, J., held that regulations directed at the style and length of male police officers' hair, sideburns and mustaches, and prohibiting beards and goatees except for medical reasons, violated no " 'liberty' interest protected by the Fourteenth Amendment": "The 'liberty' interest claimed [here] is distinguishable from [those] protected in *Roe, Eisenstadt* [and] *Griswold,* [which] involved a substantial claim of infringement on the individual's freedom of choice with respect to certain basic matters of procreation, marriage, and family life."

Assuming that "the citizenry at large has some sort of 'liberty' interest within the Fourteenth Amendment in matters of personal appearance," this assumption is insufficient to topple the regulation, for respondent has sought constitutional protection "as an employee of the county and, more particularly, as a policeman. [T]he county has chosen a mode of organization which it undoubtedly deems the most efficient in enabling its police to carry out the duties assigned to them under state and local law. Such a choice necessarily gives weight to the overall need for discipline, esprit de corps, and uniformity.

"[The courts are not] in a position to weigh the policy arguments in favor of and against a rule regulating hairstyles as a part of regulations governing a uniformed civilian service. The constitutional issue [is whether the] determination that such regulations should be enacted is so irrational that it may be branded 'arbitrary,' and therefore a deprivation of respondent's 'liberty' interest in freedom to choose his own hairstyle. *Williamson v. Lee Optical Co.* [p. 303 supra]. The overwhelming majority of state and local police of the present day are uniformed. [The view] that similarity in appearance of police officers is desirable may be based on a desire to make police officers readily recognizable to the members of the public, or a desire for the esprit de corps which such similarity is felt to inculcate within the police force itself. Either one is a sufficiently rational justification for" the regulations.[a]

MARSHALL, J., joined by Brennan, J., dissented: "An individual's personal appearance may reflect, sustain, and nourish his personality and may well be used as a means of expressing his attitude and lifestyle. In taking control over a citizen's personal appearance, the Government forces him to sacrifice substantial elements of his integrity and identity as well. To say that the liberty guarantee of the Fourteenth Amendment does not encompass matters of personal appearance would be fundamentally inconsistent with the values of privacy, self-identity, autonomy, and personal integrity that I have always assumed the Constitution was designed to protect [referring, e.g., to *Roe* and *Griswold*].[b]

"[While] fully accepting the aims of 'identifiability' and maintenance of esprit de corps, I find no rational relationship between the challenged regulation and these goals. As for the first justification offered by the Court, I simply do not see how requiring policemen to maintain hair of under a certain length could rationally be argued to contribute to making them identifiable to the public as policemen. [As] for the Court's second justification, the fact that it is the President of the Patrolmen's Benevolent Association, in his official capacity, who has challenged the regulation here would seem to indicate that the regulation would if anything, decrease rather than increase the police force's esprit de corps. [Moreover, while] the regulation prohibits hair below the ears or the collar and limits the length of sideburns, it allows the maintenance of any type of hair style, other than a pony tail. Thus, as long as their hair does not go below their collars, two police officers, with an 'Afro' hair style and the other with a crew cut could both be in full compliance with the regulation * * *[8]."

2. *The substantive due process rights of involuntarily-committed mentally retarded persons.* YOUNGBERG v. ROMEO, 457 U.S. 307, 102 S.Ct. 2452, 73 L.Ed.2d 28 (1982), considered for the first time the substantive due process rights of involuntarily-committed mentally retarded persons. On his mother's petition, Romeo, a profoundly retarded 33–year-old was involuntarily committed to a Pennsylvania state institution (Pennhurst). Subsequently, concerned about injuries Romeo had suffered at Pennhurst, his mother sued institution officials claiming that her son had constitutional rights to (1) safe conditions of confinement, (2) freedom from bodily restraint, and (3) "a constitutional right to minimally adequate habilitation," i.e., minimal training and development of needed skills. (In light of his severe retardation, however, respondent conceded that no amount of training would make his release possible.) The Court, per

---

a. Powell, J., joined the Court's opinion, but underscored that, unlike the dissenters, he found "no negative implications in the opinion with respect to a liberty interest within the Fourteenth Amendment as to matters of personal appearance."

b. See also J. Harvie Wilkinson & G. Edward White, *Constitutional Protection for Personal Lifestyles*, 62 Corn.L.Rev. 562, 605 (1977): "Appearance, like speech, is a chief medium of self-expression that involves important choices about how we wish to project ourselves and be perceived by others. To link appearance with privacy and speech values is not, of course, to require similar constitutional treatment. It does imply, however, that we deal with a substantive constitutional liberty."

8. Because, to my mind, the challenged regulation fails to pass even a minimal degree of scrutiny, there is no need to determine whether, given the nature of the interests involved and the degree to which they are affected, the application of a more heightened scrutiny would be appropriate.

POWELL, J., pointed out that respondent's first two claims "involve liberty interests recognized by prior decisions of this Court, interests that involuntary commitment proceedings do not extinguish," but found respondent's remaining claim "more troubling":

"[If,] as seems the case, respondent seeks only training related to safety and freedom from restraints, this case does not present the difficult question whether a mentally retarded person, involuntarily committed to a state institution, has some general constitutional right to training per se, even when no type or amount of training would lead to freedom. [On the basis of the record], we conclude that respondent's liberty interests require the State to provide minimally adequate or reasonable training to ensure safety and freedom from undue restraint. [W]e need go no further in this case.

"[But the question] is not simply whether a liberty interest has been infringed but whether the extent or nature of the restraint or lack of absolute safety is such as to violate due process. In determining whether a substantive right protected by the Due Process Clause has been violated, it is necessary to balance 'the liberty of the individual' and 'the demands of an organized society.' "

The Court then considered "the proper standard for determining whether a State adequately has protected the rights of the involuntarily-committed mentally retarded." It agreed with the concurring judge below "that 'the Constitution only requires that the courts make certain that professional judgment was in fact exercised. It is not appropriate for the courts to specify which of several professionally acceptable choices should have been made.' Persons who have been involuntarily committed are entitled to more considerate treatment [than] criminals whose conditions of confinement are designed to punish. At the same time, the standard is lower than [a] 'compelling' or 'substantial' necessity [test for justifying restraints] that would place an undue burden on the administration of [state institutions] and also would restrict unnecessarily the exercise of professional judgment as to the needs of residents.

"[In] determining what is 'reasonable'—in this and in any case presenting a claim for training by a state—we emphasize that courts must show deference to the judgment exercised by a qualified professional. [The] decision, if made by a professional, is presumptively valid; liability may be imposed only when the decision by the professional is such a substantial departure from accepted professional judgment, practice or standards as to demonstrate that the person responsible actually did not base the decision on such a judgment.[a] In an action for damages against a professional in his individual capacity, however, the professional will not be liable if he was unable to satisfy his normal professional standards because of budgetary constraints; in such a situation, good-faith immunity would bar liability."[b]

BLACKMUN, J., joined by Brennan and O'Connor, JJ., joined the Court's opinion, but concurred separately to clarify why, because of the uncertainty in the record, "that opinion properly leaves open two difficult and important questions." He believed that whether Pennsylvania could accept respondent for "care and treatment" and then constitutionally refuse to provide him any "treatment," as that term is defined by state law, would, if properly before the Court, present "a serious issue." As for the second difficult question left open—whether respondent had an "independent constitutional claim [to] that 'habilitation' or training

---

a. Does this place "a seemingly insurmountable burden" on plaintiff mental patients? See 96 Harv.L.Rev. 77, 85 (1982).

b. Consider, too, *DeShaney v. Winnebago County*, p. 1463 infra.

necessary to *preserve* those basic self-care skills he possessed when he first entered Pennhurst"—he believed that "it would be consistent with the Court's reasoning today to include within the 'minimally adequate training required by the Constitution' such training as is reasonably necessary to prevent a person's pre-existing self-care skills from *deteriorating* because of his commitment" and he viewed such deterioration "because of the State's unreasonable refusal to provide him training [a] loss of liberty quite distinct from—and as serious as—the loss of safety and freedom from unreasonable restraints."[c]

3. *Freedom of intimate association and expressive association.* See the cases at pp. 987 to 999 infra.

THE "RIGHT TO DIE"

CRUZAN v. DIRECTOR, MISSOURI DEP'T OF HEALTH, 497 U.S. 261, 110 S.Ct. 2841, 111 L.Ed.2d 224 (1990): Since 1983, when, at age 25, she had suffered severe injuries during an automobile accident, Nancy Beth Cruzan had been in a persistent vegetative state, a condition in which a person exhibits motor reflexes, but evinces no indications of significant cognitive function. (At the time some 10,000 persons in the United States were being maintained in that condition.) Medical experts testified that if her life support were not removed Nancy could be kept alive another 30 years. She was able to breathe on her own, but for a number of years she had received all her nutrition and fluids through a gastrostomy tube (a feeding and hydration tube inserted into her stomach). About a month after the accident, when Nancy was unconscious, surgeons implanted the feeding tube with the consent of Nancy's then husband. When it became apparent that Nancy had virtually no chance of regaining her cognitive faculties, Nancy's parents and co-guardians sought to discontinue the tubal feeding. They were rebuffed by officials of the state hospital, where Nancy was a patient. Nancy's parents then obtained a court order directing the removal of the feeding tube.

Before lapsing into her present condition, Nancy had neither executed a living will nor designated anyone to make health-care decisions for her in the event she became incompetent. But when still a vibrant person Nancy had once remarked that she did not want to live "as a vegetable." In another conversation, she had stated that if she couldn't do things for herself "even halfway, let alone not at all," she "wouldn't want to live that way." The trial court concluded that such evidence "suggests that given her present condition [Nancy] would not wish to continue on with her nutrition and hydration." The Missouri Supreme Court reversed (4–3), viewing Nancy's remarks as so remote, general and casual as to be "unreliable for the purposes of establishing her intent." For a guardian to exercise whatever right an incompetent patient may have to be free of life support, ruled the court, the patient must have complied with "the formalities required under Missouri's living will statutes" or there must be "clear and convincing, inherently reliable evidence" of her wishes. Such evidence, concluded the court, was lacking in this case. A 5–4 majority, per Rehnquist, C.J., affirmed: "[The] principle that a competent person has a constitutionally protected liberty interest in refusing unwanted medical treatment may be inferred from our prior decisions. [But] determining that a person has a 'liberty interest' under the Due Process Clause does not end the inquiry;[7] 'whether respondent's constitutional rights have been

---

c. Burger, C.J., concurring, agreed with much of the Court's opinion, but "would hold flatly that respondent has no constitutional right to training, or 'habilitation,' per se."

7. Although many state courts have held that a right to refuse treatment is encom-

violated must be determined by balancing his liberty interests against the relevant state interests.' *Youngberg.*

"[For] purposes of this case, we assume that the United States Constitution would grant a competent person a constitutionally protected right to refuse lifesaving hydration and nutrition. Petitioners [assert] that an incompetent person should possess the same right in this respect as is possessed by a competent person. [The] difficulty with petitioners' claim is that in a sense it begs the question: an incompetent person is not able to make an informed and voluntary choice to exercise a hypothetical right to refuse treatment or any other right. Such a 'right' must be exercised for her, if at all, by some sort of surrogate. Here, Missouri has in effect recognized that under certain circumstances a surrogate may act for the patient, [but] it has established a procedural safeguard to assure that the action of the surrogate conforms as best it may to the wishes expressed by the patient while competent. Missouri requires that evidence of the incompetent's wishes as to the withdrawal of treatment be proved by clear and convincing evidence. The question, then, is whether the United States Constitution forbids the establishment of this procedural requirement by the State. We hold that it does not.

"Whether or not Missouri's clear and convincing evidence requirement comports with [the] Constitution depends in part on what interests the State may properly seek to protect in this situation. Missouri relies on its interest in the protection and preservation of human life, and there can be no gainsaying this interest. As a general matter, the States—indeed, all civilized nations—demonstrate their commitment to life by treating homicide as serious crime. Moreover, the majority of States in this country have laws imposing criminal penalties on one who assists another to commit suicide. We do not think a State is required to remain neutral in the face of an informed and voluntary decision by a physically-able adult to starve to death.

"But in the context presented here, a State has more particular interests at stake. The choice between life and death is a deeply personal decision of obvious and overwhelming finality. We believe Missouri may legitimately seek to safeguard the personal element of this choice through the imposition of heightened evidentiary requirements. It cannot be disputed that the Due Process Clause protects an interest in life as well as an interest in refusing life-sustaining medical treatment. Not all incompetent patients will have loved ones available to serve as surrogate decisionmakers. And even where family members are present, '[t]here will, of course, be some unfortunate situations in which family members will not act to protect a patient.' A State is entitled to guard against potential abuses in such situations. [Finally,] we think a State may properly decline to make judgments about the 'quality' of life that a particular individual may enjoy, and simply assert an unqualified interest in the preservation of human life to be weighed against the constitutionally protected interests of the individual.

"In our view, Missouri has permissibly sought to advance these interests through the adoption of a 'clear and convincing' standard of proof to govern such proceedings. [It] may permissibly place an increased risk of an erroneous decision on those seeking to terminate an incompetent individual's life-sustaining treatment. An erroneous decision not to terminate results in a maintenance of the status quo; the possibility of subsequent developments such as advancements in

passed by a generalized constitutional right of privacy, we have never so held. We believe this issue is more properly analyzed in terms of a Fourteenth Amendment liberty interest. See *Bowers v. Hardwick.*

medical science, the discovery of new evidence regarding the patient's intent, changes in the law, or simply the unexpected death of the patient despite the administration of life-sustaining treatment, at least create the potential that a wrong decision will eventually be corrected or its impact mitigated. An erroneous decision to withdraw life-sustaining treatment, however, is not susceptible of correction.

"[The] Supreme Court of Missouri held that in this case the testimony adduced at trial did not amount to clear and convincing proof of the patient's desire to have hydration and nutrition withdrawn. * * * We cannot say that the [state court] committed constitutional error in reaching the conclusion that it did.

"Petitioners alternatively contend that Missouri must accept the 'substituted judgment' of close family members even in the absence of substantial proof that their views reflect the views of the patient. [But] we do not think the Due Process Clause requires the State to repose judgment on these matters with anyone but the patient herself. Close family members may have a strong feeling—a feeling not at all ignoble or unworthy, but not entirely disinterested, either—that they do not wish to witness the continuation of the life of a loved one which they regard as hopeless, meaningless, and even degrading. But there is no automatic assurance that the view of close family members will necessarily be the same as the patient's would have been had she been confronted with the prospect of her situation while competent."

Concurring, O'Connor J., "agree[d] that a protected liberty interest in refusing unwanted medical treatment may be inferred from our prior decisions and that the refusal of artificially delivered food and water is encompassed within that liberty interest," but wrote separately to clarify why she believed this to be so. "[Because] our notions of liberty are inextricably entwined with our idea of physical freedom and self-determination, the Court has often deemed state incursions into the body repugnant to the interests protected by the Due Process Clause. [The] State's imposition of medical treatment on an unwilling competent adult necessarily involves some form of restraint and intrusion. A seriously ill or dying patient whose wishes are not honored may feel a captive of the machinery required for life-sustaining measures or other medical interventions. Such forced treatment may burden that individual's liberty interests as much as any state coercion. [The] State's artificial provision of nutrition and hydration implicates identical concerns. Artificial feeding cannot readily be distinguished from other forms of medical treatment. [Requiring] a competent adult to endure such procedures against her will burdens the patient's liberty, dignity, and freedom to determine the course of her own treatment. Accordingly, the liberty guaranteed by the Due Process Clause must protect, if it protects anything, an individual's deeply personal decision to reject medical treatment, including the artificial delivery of food and water."

Today's decision, noted O'Connor, J., "does not preclude a future determination that the Constitution requires the States to implement the decisions of a patient's duly appointed surrogate. Nor does it prevent States from developing other approaches for protecting an incompetent individual's liberty interest in refusing medical treatment. [N]o national consensus has yet emerged on the best solution for this difficult and sensitive problem. Today we decide only that one State's practice does not violate the Constitution."

Concurring, Scalia, J., voiced concern that, judging from the tenor of the opinions in *Cruzan*, the Court was poised to confuse the questions raised by the "increasing power of science to keep the body alive" "as successfully as we have confused the enterprise of legislating concerning abortion": "While I agree with the Court's analysis today, and therefore join in its opinion, I would have preferred that we announce, clearly and promptly, that the federal courts have no business in this field; that American law has always accorded the State the power to prevent, by force if necessary, suicide—including suicide by refusing to take appropriate measures necessary to preserve one's life; that the point at which life becomes 'worthless,' and the point at which the means necessary to preserve it become 'extraordinary' or 'inappropriate,' are neither set forth in the Constitution nor known to the nine Justices of this Court any better than they are known to nine people picked at random from the Kansas City telephone directory; and hence, that even when it *is* demonstrated by clear and convincing evidence that a patient no longer wishes certain measures to be taken to preserve her life, it is up to the citizens of Missouri to decide, through their elected representatives, whether that wish will be honored. It is quite impossible (because the Constitution says nothing about the matter) that those citizens will decide upon a line less lawful than the one we would choose; and it is unlikely (because we know no more about 'life-and-death' than they do) that they will decide upon a line less reasonable.

"The text of the Due Process Clause does not protect individuals against deprivations of liberty simpliciter. It protects them against deprivations of liberty 'without due process of law.' [It] is at least true that no 'substantive due process' claim can be maintained unless the claimant demonstrates that the State has deprived him of a right historically and traditionally protected against State interference. *Michael H.* (plurality opinion); *Hardwick.* [That] cannot possibly be established here.

"[The argument] that frustrating Nancy Cruzan's wish to die in the present case requires interference with her bodily integrity [is unpersuasive] because such interference is impermissible only if one begs the question whether her refusal to undergo the treatment on her own is suicide. It has always been lawful not only for the State, but even for private citizens, to interfere with bodily integrity to prevent a felony. That general rule has of course been applied to suicide."

BRENNAN, J., joined by Marshall and Blackmun, JJ., dissented because he "believe[d] that Nancy Cruzan has a fundamental right to be free of unwanted artificial nutrition and hydration, which right is not outweighed by any interests of the State, and because I find that the improperly biased procedural obstacles imposed by the Missouri Supreme Court impermissibly burden that [right]. Nancy Cruzan is entitled to choose to die with dignity. [The] right to be free from medical attention without consent, to determine what shall be done with one's own body, *is* deeply rooted in this Nation's traditions, as the majority acknowledges. [Thus,] freedom from unwanted medical attention is unquestionably among those principles "so rooted in the traditions and conscience of our people as to be ranked as fundamental.'

"[The] only state interest asserted here is a general interest in the preservation of life. But the State has no legitimate general interest in someone's life, completely abstracted from the interest of the person living that life, that could outweigh the person's choice to avoid medical treatment. [Thus,] the State's general interest in life must accede to Nancy Cruzan's particularized and intense interest in self-determination in her choice of medical treatment. There is simply nothing legitimately within the State's purview to be gained by superseding her decision.

"[An] erroneous decision to terminate life-support is irrevocable, says the majority, while an erroneous decision not to terminate 'results in a maintenance of the status quo.'[17] But, from the point of view of the patient, an erroneous decision in either direction is irrevocable. [An] erroneous decision not to terminate [life-support] robs a patient of the very qualities protected by the right to avoid unwanted medical treatment. His own degraded existence is perpetuated; his family's suffering is protracted; the memory he leaves behind becomes more and more distorted."

STEVENS, J., wrote a separate dissent, protesting that the Court "permits the State's abstract, undifferentiated interest in the preservation of life to overwhelm the best interests of Nancy Beth Cruzan, interests which would, according to an undisputed finding, be served by allowing her guardian to exercise her constitutional right to discontinue medical treatment. * * * Choices about death touch the core of liberty. Our duty, and the concomitant freedom, to come to terms with the conditions of our own mortality are undoubtedly 'so rooted in the traditions and conscience of our people as to be ranked as fundamental.' [N]ot much may be said with confidence about death unless it is said from faith, and that alone is reason enough to protect the freedom to conform choices about death to individual conscience. [In] my view, the constitutional answer is clear: the best interests of the individual, especially when buttressed by the interests of all related third parties, must prevail over any general state policy that simply ignores those interests. Indeed, the only apparent *secular* basis for the State's interest in life is the policy's persuasive impact upon people other than Nancy and her family. [Yet, the] State may not pursue its project by infringing constitutionally protected interests for '*symbolic* effect.' [The] Cruzan family's continuing concern provides a concrete reminder that Nancy Cruzan's interests did not disappear with her vitality or her consciousness. However commendable may be the State's interest in human life, it cannot pursue that interest by appropriating Nancy Cruzan's life as a symbol for its own purposes. Lives do not exist in abstraction from persons, and to pretend otherwise is not to honor but to desecrate the State's responsibility for protecting life."

REFLECTIONS ON *CRUZAN* AND THE *"RIGHT TO DIE"*

1. *The death of Nancy Cruzan.* Two months after the Supreme Court's decision, Nancy's parents asked the state probate court for a second hearing. At this new hearing, three of Nancy's former co-workers recalled conversations in which she said she never would want to live "like a vegetable" on medical machines. See N.Y. Times, Nov. 2, 1990, p. A12. Since the State of Missouri withdrew from the case and Nancy's court-appointed guardian sought to disconnect the feeding tube, see N.Y. Times, Dec. 7, 1990, p. A12, all remaining parties agreed that artificial nutrition and hydration should cease. A week later, the probate judge ruled that there was "clear evidence" that the "intent" of Nancy, "if mentally able, would be to terminate her nutrition and hydration" and that there was "no evidence of substance" to the contrary. He then authorized the cessation of nutrition and hydration. See N.Y. Times, Dec. 15, 1990, p. 1. Twelve days later, and nearly eight years after she had lost consciousness and a feeding

---

17. The majority's definition of the "status quo," of course, begs the question. Artificial delivery of nutrition and hydration represents the "status quo" only if the State has chosen to permit doctors and hospitals to keep a pa-tient on life-support systems over the protests of his family or guardian. The "status quo" absent that state interference would be the natural result of his accident or illness (and the family's decision). * * *

tube had first been implanted in her stomach, Nancy Cruzan died. Did the probate court take the "substituted judgment" seriously or did it really apply an objective test? See generally Charles Baron, *On Taking Substantial Judgment Seriously*, Hastings Center Rep., Sept.-Oct., 1990.

2. *Abortion, the "right to die," and the intrinsic value of life.* Did Rehnquist, C.J., and Scalia, J., draw a distinction between the intrinsic value of life and its personal value for the patient? Did they maintain that it is *"intrinsically* a bad thing"* to bring about a person's death even if it is not in the person's own interest to continue living? If so, is this similar to the notion that it is wrong to destroy a fetus *whether or not* a fetus has any interests to protect? See Ronald Dworkin, *Life's Dominion* 12, 198 (1993).[a]

3. *Analogy to suicide.* Consider Note, 104 Harv.L.Rev. 257, 262 (1990): "[T]he common law right to refuse medical treatment has long existed alongside anti-suicide laws. Acting outside the purview of the legal system, doctors have traditionally withheld certain treatments that would delay death on the grounds that the treatment was unnecessarily painful, that it would not improve the patient's condition, or that it was against the patient's wishes. Further, courts have explicitly rejected the notion that terminating treatment constitutes homicide and have held that the right to refuse treatment exists even if the consequence of refusal is death. Thus, even under Justice Scalia's narrow historical test [referring to fn. 6 of the plurality opinion in *Michael H.*], a competent person has a liberty interest in refusing life-sustaining medical treatment. Justice Scalia's zeal for avoiding the entire 'right to die' area led him to evaluate the interest with a history not specifically applicable to the facts of *Cruzan.*"

4. *More on the level of generality in defining rights or liberty interests. How might Chief Justice Rehnquist have been expected to frame the issue in Cruzan?* Rehnquist, C.J., joined Scalia, J.'s plurality in *Michael H.,* including fn. 6. In light of this, would one have expected, or at least not have been surprised, if the Chief Justice had defined the right or liberty interest at issue in *Cruzan* something as follows: "Is the liberty (or right) of an incompetent patient *who is neither dying nor terminally ill,* as those terms are commonly defined, to refuse *lifesaving artificial hydration and nutrition* deeply rooted in the Nation's history and tradition?" Did the Chief Justice assign any particular significance to the fact that the lifesaving measure involved in the *Cruzan* case was artificial feeding? Did he give any weight to the fact that Nancy Cruzan was neither "dying" nor "terminally ill," as those terms are defined by Missouri and many other states?[b] At any point, did he expressly discuss the level of generality at which the liberty interest in *Cruzan* should be defined (and why)?[c]

a. Cf. Tribe, *Abortion* 231. But see Seth Kreimer, *Does Pro–Choice Mean Pro–Kevorkian? An Essay on Roe, Casey, and the Right to Die* (1995); Thomas Mayo, *Constitutionalizing the "Right to Die,"* 49 Md.L.Rev. 103 (1990); Marc Spindelman, *Are the Similarities Between A Woman's Right to Choose an Abortion and the Alleged Right to Assisted Suicide Really Compelling?*, 29 U.Mich.J.L. Ref. 775 (1996).

b. Consider Yale Kamisar, *The "Right to Die": Green Lights and Yellow Lights,* Law Quadrangle Notes, Fall, 1990, pp. 3, 5: "I venture to say that in some future case the Court will make plain what I think is implicit in *Cruzan:* A patient's 'right to die' cannot be denied solely on the ground that she is neither 'dying' nor 'terminally ill'—no more than it can be denied solely for the reason that the life support involved is a feeding tube rather than a respirator."

c. Rehnquist, C.J., might have said, for example, that even under the narrow approach Scalia, J., took in *Michael H.,* "the liberty interest at issue is properly defined at the level of generality of medical treatment, not medical sustenance [because] that is 'the most specific level at which a relevant tradition protecting, or denying protection to, the asserted right can be identified.' Because the technology by which food and water may be routinely provided by means other than oral intake is of relatively recent origin, no societal tradition exists either

5. *Inconsistent views of families: can Cruzan and Akron I be harmonized?* In *Cruzan*, Rehnquist, C.J., noted that close family members might not act to protect a patient, but he joined Kennedy, J.'s lead opinion in *Akron I* (p. 403 supra) (upholding a prohibition against abortions for unemancipated minors absent notice to one of the minor's parents or a court order authorizing the minor to consent), where the majority deemed it fair for a state to assume that "in most instances, the family will strive to give a lonely or even terrified minor advice that is both compassionate and mature." See Martha Minow, *The Role of Families in Medical Decisions*, 1991 Utah L.Rev. 1, 8–11.

IS THERE A CONSTITUTIONAL RIGHT TO PHYSICIAN–ASSISTED SUICIDE?

WASHINGTON v. GLUCKSBERG

521 U.S. 702, 117 S.Ct. 2258, 138 L.Ed.2d 772 (1997).

CHIEF JUSTICE REHNQUIST delivered the opinion of the Court.

The question presented in this case is whether Washington's prohibition against "caus[ing]" or "aid[ing]" a suicide offends the Fourteenth Amendment to the United States Constitution. We hold that it does not.

[Respondents, four physicians who declare they would assist terminally ill, suffering patients in ending their lives if not for Washington's assisted-suicide ban, along with three gravely ill patients, who have since died, and Compassion in Dying, a nonprofit organization that counsels people considering physician-assisted suicide, sought a declaration that Washington's statute is, on its face, unconstitutional. Respondents] asserted "the existence of a liberty interest protected by the Fourteenth Amendment which extends to a personal choice by a mentally competent, terminally ill adult to commit physician-assisted suicide." Relying primarily on *Casey* and *Cruzan*, the District Court agreed and concluded that Washington's assisted suicide ban is unconstitutional because it "places an undue burden on the exercise of [that] constitutionally protected liberty interest."[5]

A panel of the Court of Appeals for the Ninth Circuit reversed, emphasizing that "[i]n the two hundred and five years of our existence no constitutional right to aid in killing oneself has ever been asserted and upheld by a court of final jurisdiction." The Ninth Circuit reheard the case en banc, reversed the panel's decision [8–3]. [Like] the District Court, the Court of Appeals emphasized our *Casey* and *Cruzan* decisions. The court [concluded] that "the Constitution encompasses a due process liberty interest in controlling the time and manner of one's death—that there is, in short, a constitutionally-recognized 'right to die.'" After "[w]eighing and then balancing" this interest against Washington's various interests, the court held that the State's assisted-suicide ban was unconstitutional

permitting or prohibiting individuals to deny themselves medically provided nutrition and hydration." *Developments in the Law—Medical Technology and the Law*, 103 Harv.L.Rev. 1520, 1662 n. 142 (1990).

5. The District Court determined that *Casey's* "undue burden" standard, not the stan-dard from *United States v. Salerno*, 481 U.S. 739, 107 S.Ct. 2095, 95 L.Ed.2d 697 (1987) (requiring a showing that "no set of circumstances exists under which the [law] would be valid"), governed the plaintiffs' facial challenge to the assisted-suicide ban.

"as applied to terminally ill competent adults who wish to hasten their deaths with medication prescribed by their physicians." * * *

We begin, as we do in all due-process cases, by examining our Nation's history, legal traditions, and practices. In almost every State—indeed, in almost every western democracy—it is a crime to assist a suicide. The States' assisted-suicide bans are not innovations. Rather, they are longstanding expressions of the States' commitment to the protection and preservation of all human life. * * * Indeed, opposition to and condemnation of suicide—and, therefore, of assisting suicide—are consistent and enduring themes of our philosophical, legal, and cultural heritages.

More specifically, for over 700 years, the Anglo–American common-law tradition has punished or otherwise disapproved of both suicide and assisting suicide.

[For] the most part, the early American colonies adopted the common-law approach. [Over] time, however, [the] colonies abolished [the] harsh common-law penalties [such as forfeiture of the suicide's property. However,] the movement away from the common law's harsh sanctions did not represent an acceptance of homicide, [but] reflected the growing consensus that it was unfair to punish the suicide's family for his wrongdoing.

[That] suicide remained a grievous, though nonfelonious, wrong is confirmed by the fact that colonial and early state legislatures and courts did not retreat from prohibiting assisting suicide. [And] the prohibitions against assisted suicide never contained exceptions for those who were near death. [In] this century, the [American Law Institute's] Model Penal Code also prohibited "aiding" suicide, prompting many States to enact or revise their assisted-suicide bans. The Code's drafters observed that "the interests in the sanctity of life that are represented by the criminal homicide laws are threatened by one who expresses a willingness to participate in taking the life of another, even though the act may be accomplished with the consent, or at the request, of the suicide victim."

Though deeply rooted, the States' assisted-suicide bans have in recent years been reexamined and, generally, reaffirmed. Because of advances in medicine and technology, Americans today are increasingly likely to die in institutions, from chronic illnesses. Public concern and democratic action are therefore sharply focused on how best to protect dignity and independence at the end of life, with the result that there have been many significant changes in state laws and in the attitudes these laws reflect. Many States, for example, now permit "living wills," surrogate health-care decisionmaking, and the withdrawal or refusal of life-sustaining medical treatment. At the same time, however, voters and legislators continue for the most part to reaffirm their States' prohibitions on assisting suicide.

The Washington statute at issue in this case was enacted in 1975 as part of a revision of that State's criminal code. Four years later, Washington passed its Natural Death Act, which specifically stated that the "withholding or withdrawal of life-sustaining treatment [shall] not, for any purpose, constitute a suicide" and that "[n]othing in this chapter shall be construed to condone, authorize, or approve mercy killing * * *." In 1991, Washington voters rejected a ballot initiative which, had it passed, would have permitted a form of physician-assisted suicide. Washington then added a provision to the Natural Death Act expressly excluding physician-assisted suicide.

California voters rejected an assisted-suicide initiative similar to Washington's in 1993. On the other hand, in 1994, voters in Oregon enacted, also through ballot initiative, that State's "Death With Dignity Act," which legalized physician-assisted suicide for competent, terminally ill adults. Since the Oregon vote, many proposals to legalize assisted-suicide have been and continue to be introduced in the States' legislatures, but none has been enacted. And just last year, Iowa and Rhode Island joined the overwhelming majority of States explicitly prohibiting assisted suicide. Also, on April 30, 1997, President Clinton signed the Federal Assisted Suicide Funding Restriction Act of 1997, which prohibits the use of federal funds in support of physician-assisted suicide.

Thus, the States are currently engaged in serious, thoughtful examinations of physician-assisted suicide and other similar issues. For example, New York State's Task Force on Life and the Law—an ongoing, blue-ribbon commission composed of doctors, ethicists, lawyers, religious leaders, and interested laymen—was convened in 1984 and commissioned with "a broad mandate to recommend public policy on issues raised by medical advances." [After] studying physician-assisted suicide, however, the Task Force unanimously concluded that "[l]egalizing assisted suicide and euthanasia would pose profound risks to many individuals who are ill and vulnerable. [T]he potential dangers of this dramatic change in public policy would outweigh any benefit that might be achieved."

Attitudes toward suicide itself have changed, [but] our laws have consistently condemned, and continue to prohibit, assisting suicide. Despite changes in medical technology and notwithstanding an increased emphasis on the importance of end-of-life decision-making, we have not retreated from this prohibition. Against this backdrop of history, tradition, and practice, we now turn to respondents' constitutional claim.

The Due Process Clause guarantees more than fair process, and the "liberty" it protects includes more than the absence of physical restraint. [The] Clause also provides heightened protection against government interference with certain fundamental rights and liberty interests. [We] have also assumed, and strongly suggested, that the Due Process Clause protects the traditional right to refuse unwanted lifesaving medical treatment. *Cruzan*.

But we "ha[ve] always been reluctant to expand the concept of substantive due process because guideposts for responsible decisionmaking in this unchartered area are scarce and open-ended." By extending constitutional protection to an asserted right or liberty interest, we, to a great extent, place the matter outside the arena of public debate and legislative action. We must therefore "exercise the utmost care whenever we are asked to break new ground in this field," lest the liberty protected by the Due Process Clause be subtly transformed into the policy preferences of the members of this Court.

Our established method of substantive-due-process analysis has two primary features: First, we have regularly observed that the Due Process Clause specially protects those fundamental rights and liberties which are, objectively, "deeply rooted in this Nation's history and tradition." * * * Second, we have required in substantive-due-process cases a "careful description" of the asserted fundamental liberty interest. * * *

Justice Souter, relying on Justice Harlan's dissenting opinion in *Poe v. Ullman,* would largely abandon this restrained methodology, and instead ask "whether [Washington's] statute sets up one of those 'arbitrary impositions' or 'purposeless restraints' at odds with the Due Process Clause of the Fourteenth Amendment."[17] In our view, however, the development of this Court's substan-

17. In Justice Souter's opinion, Justice   Harlan's *Poe* dissent supplies the "modern jus-

tive-due-process jurisprudence, described briefly above, has been a process whereby the outlines of the "liberty" specially protected by the Fourteenth Amendment—never fully clarified, to be sure, and perhaps not capable of being fully clarified—have at least been carefully refined by concrete examples involving fundamental rights found to be deeply rooted in our legal tradition. This approach tends to rein in the subjective elements that are necessarily present in due-process judicial review. In addition, by establishing a threshold requirement—that a challenged state action implicate a fundamental right—before requiring more than a reasonable relation to a legitimate state interest to justify the action, it avoids the need for complex balancing of competing interests in every case.

"[We] have a tradition of carefully formulating the interest at stake in substantive-due-process cases. For example, although *Cruzan* is often described as a "right to die" case, we were, in fact, more precise: we assumed that the Constitution granted competent persons a "constitutionally protected right to refuse lifesaving hydration and nutrition." [The] Washington statute at issue in this case prohibits "aid[ing] another person to attempt suicide" and, thus, the question before us is whether the "liberty" specially protected by the Due Process Clause includes a right to commit suicide which itself includes a right to assistance in doing so.

We now inquire whether this asserted right has any place in our Nation's traditions. [Here,] we are confronted with a consistent and almost universal tradition that has long rejected the asserted right, and continues explicitly to reject it today, even for terminally ill, mentally competent adults. To hold for respondents, we would have to reverse centuries of legal doctrine and practice, and strike down the considered policy choice of almost every State.

[Respondents] contend that in *Cruzan* we "acknowledged that competent, dying persons have the right to direct the removal of life-sustaining medical treatment and thus hasten death" and that "the constitutional principle behind recognizing the patient's liberty to direct the withdrawal of artificial life support applies at least as strongly to the choice to hasten impending death by consuming lethal medication." [The] right assumed in *Cruzan*, however, was not simply deduced from abstract concepts of personal autonomy. Given the common-law rule that forced medication was a battery, and the long legal tradition protecting the decision to refuse unwanted medical treatment, our assumption was entirely consistent with this Nation's history and constitutional traditions. The decision to commit suicide with the assistance of another may be just as personal and profound as the decision to refuse unwanted medical treatment, but it has never enjoyed similar legal protection. Indeed, the two acts are widely and reasonably regarded as quite distinct. In *Cruzan* itself, we recognized that most States outlawed assisted suicide—and even more do today—and we certainly gave no intimation that the right to refuse unwanted medical treatment could be somehow transmuted into a right to assistance in committing suicide.

tification" for substantive-due-process review. But although Justice Harlan's opinion has often been cited in due-process cases, we have never abandoned our fundamental-rights-based analytical method. Just four Terms ago, six of the Justices now sitting joined the Court's opinion in *Reno v. Flores*, 507 U.S. 292, 113 S.Ct. 1439, 123 L.Ed.2d 1 (1993); *Poe* was not even cited. And in *Cruzan*, neither the Court's nor the concurring opinions relied on *Poe*; rather, we concluded that the right to refuse unwanted medical treatment was so rooted in our history, tradition, and practice as to require special protection under the Fourteenth Amendment. True, the Court relied on Justice Harlan's dissent in *Casey*, but, as *Flores* demonstrates, we did not in so doing jettison our established approach. Indeed, to read such a radical move into the Court's opinion in *Casey* would seem to fly in the face of that opinion's emphasis on stare decisis.

Respondents also rely on *Casey*. [The] Court of Appeals, like the District Court, found *Casey* " 'highly instructive' " and " 'almost prescriptive' " for determining " 'what liberty interest may inhere in a terminally ill person's choice to commit suicide' " * * *. Similarly, respondents emphasize the statement in *Casey* that: "At the heart of liberty is the right to define one's own concept of existence, of meaning, of the universe, and of the mystery of human life. Beliefs about these matters could not define the attributes of personhood were they formed under compulsion of the State."

By choosing this language, the Court's opinion in *Casey* described, in a general way and in light of our prior cases, those personal activities and decisions that this Court has identified as so deeply rooted in our history and traditions, or so fundamental to our concept of constitutionally ordered liberty, that they are protected by the Fourteenth Amendment. [That] many of the rights and liberties protected by the Due Process Clause sound in personal autonomy does not warrant the sweeping conclusion that any and all important, intimate, and personal decisions are so protected, and *Casey* did not suggest otherwise.

The history of the law's treatment of assisted suicide in this country has been and continues to be one of the rejection of nearly all efforts to permit it. That being the case, our decisions lead us to conclude that the asserted "right" to assistance in committing suicide is not a fundamental liberty interest protected by the Due Process Clause. The Constitution also requires, however, that Washington's assisted-suicide ban be rationally related to legitimate government interests. This requirement is unquestionably met here. As the court below recognized, Washington's assisted-suicide ban implicates a number of state interests.

First, Washington has an "unqualified interest in the preservation of human life." *Cruzan*. The State's prohibition on assisted suicide, like all homicide laws, both reflects and advances its commitment to this interest.

[The] Court of Appeals also recognized Washington's interest in protecting life, but held that the "weight" of this interest depends on the "medical condition and the wishes of the person whose life is at stake." Washington, however, has rejected this sliding-scale approach and, through its assisted-suicide ban, insists that all persons' lives, from beginning to end, regardless of physical or mental condition, are under the full protection of the law. [As] we have previously affirmed, the States "may properly decline to make judgments about the 'quality' of life that a particular individual may enjoy," *Cruzan*. This remains true, as *Cruzan* makes clear, even for those who are near death.

Relatedly, all admit that suicide is a serious public-health problem, especially among persons in otherwise vulnerable groups. [Those] who attempt suicide— terminally ill or not—often suffer from depression or other mental disorders. [But research indicates] that many people who request physician-assisted suicide withdraw that request if their depression and pain are treated. The New York Task Force, however, expressed its concern that, because depression is difficult to diagnose, physicians and medical professionals often fail to respond adequately to seriously ill patients' needs. Thus, legal physician-assisted suicide could make it more difficult for the State to protect depressed or mentally ill persons, or those who are suffering from untreated pain, from suicidal impulses.

The State also has an interest in protecting the integrity and ethics of the medical profession. [The] American Medical Association, like many other medical and physicians' groups, has concluded that "[p]hysician-assisted suicide is fundamentally incompatible with the physician's role as healer." [And] physician-assisted suicide could, it is argued, undermine the trust that is essential to the doctor-patient relationship by blurring the time-honored line between healing and harming.

[Next,] the State has an interest in protecting vulnerable groups—including the poor, the elderly, and disabled persons—from abuse, neglect, and mistakes. The Court of Appeals dismissed [this] concern, [but we] have recognized [the] real risk of subtle coercion and undue influence in end-of-life situations. *Cruzan*. Similarly, the New York Task Force warned that "[l]egalizing physician-assisted suicide would pose profound risks to many individuals who are ill and vulnerable. [The] risk of harm is greatest for the many individuals in our society whose autonomy and well-being are already compromised by poverty, lack of access to good medical care, advanced age, or membership in a stigmatized social group." [If] physician-assisted suicide were permitted, many might resort to it to spare their families the substantial financial burden of end-of-life health-care costs. The State's interest here goes beyond protecting the vulnerable from coercion; it extends to protecting disabled and terminally ill people from prejudice, negative and inaccurate stereotypes, and "societal indifference."

[Finally,] the State may fear that permitting assisted suicide will start it down the path to voluntary and perhaps even involuntary euthanasia. [The] Court of Appeal's decision, and its expansive reasoning, provide ample support for the State's concerns.[23] [This] concern is further supported by evidence about the practice of euthanasia in the Netherlands. The Dutch government's own [1990 study] suggests that, despite the existence of various reporting procedures, euthanasia in the Netherlands has not been limited to competent, terminally ill adults who are enduring physical suffering, and that regulation of the practice may not have prevented abuses in cases involving vulnerable persons, including severely disabled neonates and elderly persons suffering from dementia. * * * Washington, like most other States, reasonably ensures against this risk by banning, rather than regulating, assisting suicide.

We need not weigh exactingly the relative strengths of these various interests. They are unquestionably important and legitimate, and Washington's ban on assisted suicide is at least reasonably related to their promotion and protection. We therefore hold that [the challenged Washington statute] does not violate the Fourteenth Amendment, either on its face or "as applied to competent, terminally ill adults who wish to hasten their deaths by obtaining medication prescribed by their doctors."[24] * * *

23. Justice Souter concludes that "[t]he case for the slippery slope is fairly made out here, not because recognizing one due process right would leave a court with no principled basis to avoid recognizing another, but because there is a plausible case that the right claimed would not be readily containable by reference to facts about the mind that are matters of difficult judgment, or by gatekeepers who are subject to temptation, noble or not." We agree that the case for a slippery slope has been made out, [but] we also recognize the reasonableness of the widely expressed skepticism about the lack of a principled basis for confining the right. See Brief for United States as Amicus Curiae ("Once a legislature abandons a categorical prohibition against physician-assisted suicide, there is no obvious stopping point) * * *.

24. Justice Stevens states that "the Court does conceive of respondents' claim as a facial challenge—addressing not the application of the statute to a particular set of plaintiffs before it, but the constitutionality of the statute's categorical prohibition...." We emphasize that we today reject the Court of Appeals' specific holding that the statute is unconstitutional "as applied" to a particular class. Justice Stevens agrees with this holding, but would not "foreclose the possibility that an individual plaintiff seeking to hasten her death, or a doctor whose assistance was sought, could prevail in a more particularized challenge." Our opinion does not absolutely foreclose such a claim. However, given our holding that the Due Process Clause of the Fourteenth Amendment does not provide heightened protection to the asserted liberty interest in ending one's life with a physician's assistance, such a claim

Throughout the Nation, Americans are engaged in an earnest and profound debate about the morality, legality, and practicality of physician-assisted suicide. Our holding permits this debate to continue, as it should in a democratic society. * * *

JUSTICE O'CONNOR, concurring.*

[The] Court frames the issue in this case as whether the Due Process Clause of the Constitution protects a "right to commit suicide which itself includes a right to assistance in doing so," and concludes that our Nation's history, legal traditions, and practices do not support the existence of such a right. I join the Court's opinions because I agree that there is no generalized right to "commit suicide." But respondents urge us to address the narrower question whether a mentally competent person who is experiencing great suffering has a constitutionally cognizable interest in controlling the circumstances of his or her imminent death. I see no need to reach that question in the context of the facial challenges to the New York and Washington laws at issue here. [The] parties and *amici* agree that in these States a patient who is suffering from a terminal illness and who is experiencing great pain has no legal barriers to obtaining medication, from qualified physicians, to alleviate that suffering, even to the point of causing unconsciousness and hastening death. In this light, even assuming that we would recognize such an interest, I agree that the State's interests in protecting those who are not truly competent or facing imminent death, or those whose decisions to hasten death would not truly be voluntary, are sufficiently weighty to justify a prohibition against physician-assisted suicide.

Every one of us at some point may be affected by our own or a family member's terminal illness. There is no reason to think the democratic process will not strike the proper balance between the interests of terminally ill, mentally competent individuals who would seek to end their suffering and the State's interests in protecting those who might seek to end life mistakenly or under pressure.

[In] sum, there is no need to address the question whether suffering patients have a constitutionally cognizable interest in obtaining relief from the suffering that they may experience in the last days of their lives. There is no dispute that dying patients in Washington and New York can obtain palliative care, even when doing so would hasten their deaths. The difficulty in defining terminal illness and the risk that a dying patient's request for assistance in ending his or her life might not be truly voluntary justifies the prohibitions on assisted suicide we uphold here.

JUSTICE STEVENS, concurring in the judgments.[a]

[Today,] the Court decides that Washington's statute prohibiting assisted suicide is not invalid "on its face," that is to say, in all or most cases in which it might be applied. That holding, however, does not foreclose the possibility that some applications of the statute might well be invalid. * * *

History and tradition provide ample support for refusing to recognize an open-ended constitutional right to commit suicide. Much more than the State's

would have to be quite different from the ones advanced by respondents here.

* Justice Ginsberg concurs in the Court's judgments substantially for the reasons stated in this opinion. Justice Breyer joins this opinion except insofar as it joins the opinion of the Court.

[O'Connor, J.'s opinion also constitutes her concurring opinion in the companion case of *Vacco v. Quill.*]

a. This opinion also constitutes Stevens, J.'s concurring opinion in *Vacco v. Quill.*

paternalistic interest in protecting the individual from the irrevocable consequences of an ill-advised decision motivated by temporary concerns is at stake.
[The] value to others of a person's life is far too precious to allow the individual to
claim a constitutional entitlement to complete autonomy in making a decision to
end that life. Thus, I fully agree with the Court that the "liberty" protected by the
Due Process Clause does not include a categorical "right to commit suicide which
itself includes a right to assistance in doing so."

But just as our conclusion that capital punishment is not always unconstitutional did not preclude later decisions holding that it is sometimes impermissibly
cruel, so is it equally clear that a decision upholding a general statutory prohibition of assisted suicide does not mean that every possible application of the statute
would be valid.

[The *Cruzan* Court] assumed that the interest in liberty protected by the
Fourteenth Amendment encompassed the right of a terminally ill patient to direct
the withdrawal of life-sustaining treatment. [That] assumption [was] supported by
the common-law tradition protecting the individual's general right to refuse
unwanted medical treatment. [However,] [g]iven the irreversible nature of her
illness and the progressive character of her suffering, Nancy Cruzan's interest in
refusing medical care was incidental to her more basic interest in controlling the
manner and timing of her death. * * * I insist that the source of Nancy Cruzan's
right to refuse treatment was not just a common-law rule. Rather, this right is an
aspect of a far broader and more basic concept of freedom that is even older than
the common law. This freedom embraces, not merely a person's right to refuse a
particular kind of unwanted treatment, but also her interest in dignity, and in
determining the character of the memories that will survive long after her death.

[Thus,] the common-law right to protection from battery, which included the
right to reject medical treatment in most circumstances, did not mark "the outer
limits of the substantive sphere of liberty" that supported the Cruzan family's
decision to hasten Nancy's death. *Casey.* [Whatever] the outer limits of the
concept may be, it definitely includes protection for matters "central to personal
dignity and autonomy." *Casey.*

[The] *Cruzan* case demonstrated that some state intrusions on the right to
decide how death will be encountered are also intolerable. The now-deceased
plaintiffs in this action may in fact have had a liberty interest even stronger than
Nancy Cruzan's because, not only were they terminally ill, they were suffering
constant and severe pain. Avoiding intolerable pain and the indignity of living
one's final days incapacitated and in agony is certainly "[a]t the heart of [the]
liberty [to] define one's own concept of existence, of meaning, of the universe, and
of the mystery of human life."

[Although] there is no absolute right to physician-assisted suicide, *Cruzan*
makes it clear that some individuals who no longer have the option of deciding
whether to live or to die because they are already on the threshold of death have a
constitutionally protected interest that may outweigh the State's interest in
preserving life at all costs. The liberty interest at stake in a case like this differs
from, and is stronger than, both the common-law right to refuse medical treatment and the unbridled interest in deciding whether to live or die. It is an interest
in deciding how, rather than whether, a critical threshold shall be crossed.

The state interests supporting a general rule banning the practice of physician-assisted suicide do not have the same force in all cases. First and foremost of
these interests is the " 'unqualified interest in the preservation of human life,' "
which is equated with " 'the sanctity of life' " * * *. Properly viewed, however,

this interest is not a collective interest that should always outweigh the interests of a person who because of pain, incapacity, or sedation finds her life intolerable, but rather, an aspect of individual freedom.

[Allowing] the individual, rather than the State, to make judgments " 'about the 'quality' of life that a particular individual may enjoy' " does not mean that the lives of terminally-ill, disabled people have less value than the lives of those who are healthy. Rather, it gives proper recognition to the individual's interest in choosing a final chapter that accords with her life story, rather than one that demeans her values and poisons memories of her. See Brief for Bioethicists as Amici Curiae; see also Ronald Dworkin, *Life's Dominion* 213 (1993). * * *

Similarly, the State's legitimate interests in preventing suicide, protecting the vulnerable from coercion and abuse, and preventing euthanasia are less significant in this context. [The] State's legitimate interest in preventing abuse does not apply to an individual who is not victimized by abuse, who is not suffering from depression, and who makes a rational and voluntary decision to seek assistance in dying. * * * Encouraging the development and ensuring the availability of adequate pain treatment is of utmost importance; palliative care, however, cannot alleviate all pain and suffering. [An] individual adequately informed of the care alternatives thus might make a rational choice for assisted suicide. For such an individual, the State's interest in preventing potential abuse and mistake is only minimally implicated.

The final major interest asserted by the State is its interest in preserving the traditional integrity of the medical profession. [But] for some patients, it would be a physician's refusal to dispense medication to ease their suffering and make their death tolerable and dignified that would be inconsistent with the healing role. [Furthermore,] because physicians are already involved in making decisions that hasten the death of terminally ill patients—through termination of life support, withholding of medical treatment, and terminal sedation—there is in fact significant tension between the traditional view of the physician's role and the actual practice in a growing number of cases.

[Unlike] the Court of Appeals, I would not say as a categorical matter that these state interests are invalid as to the entire class of terminally ill, mentally competent patients. I do not, however, foreclose the possibility that an individual plaintiff seeking to hasten her death, or a doctor whose assistance was sought, could prevail in a more particularized challenge. Future cases will determine whether such a challenge may succeed.

JUSTICE SOUTER, concurring in the judgment.

[The] question is whether the statute sets up one of those "arbitrary impositions" or "purposeless restraints" at odds with the Due Process Clause of the Fourteenth Amendment. *Poe v. Ullman* (Harlan, J., dissenting). I conclude that the statute's application to the doctors has not been shown to be unconstitutional, but I write separately to give my reasons for analyzing the substantive due process claims as I do, and for rejecting this one.

[In] their brief to this Court, [the four physicians who brought this challenge to the Washington statute] claim not that they ought to have a right generally to hasten patients' imminent deaths, but only to help patients who have made "personal decisions regarding their own bodies, medical care, and, fundamentally, the future course of their lives," and who have concluded responsibly and with substantial justification that the brief and anguished remainders of their lives have lost virtually all value to them. [In] response, the State argues that the interest asserted by the doctors is beyond constitutional recognition because it has no deep roots in our history and traditions. [Moreover,] the State insists that recognizing the legitimacy of doctors' assistance of their patients as contemplated here would entail a number of adverse consequences that the Washington Legislature was entitled to forestall. The nub of this part of the State's argument is not that such patients are constitutionally undeserving of relief on their own account, but that any attempt to confine a right of physician assistance to the circumstances presented by these doctors is likely to fail.

First, the State argues that the right could not be confined to the terminally ill. [It] asserts that "[t]here is no principled basis on which [the right] can be limited to the prescription of medication for terminally ill patients to administer to themselves" when the right's justifying principle is as broad as " 'merciful termination of suffering' " Second, the State argues that the right could not be confined to the mentally competent, observing that a person's competence cannot always be assessed with certainty, and suggesting further that no principled distinction is possible between a competent patient acting independently and a patient acting through a duly appointed and competent surrogate. Next, according to the State, such a right might entail a right to or at least merge in practice into "other forms of life-ending assistance," such as euthanasia. Finally, the State believes that a right to physician assistance could not easily be distinguished from a right to assistance from others, such as friends, family, and other health-care workers. The State thus argues that recognition of the substantive due process right at issue here would jeopardize the lives of others outside the class defined by the doctors' claim, creating risks of irresponsible suicides and euthanasia, whose dangers are concededly within the State's authority to address.

[The] persistence of substantive due process in our cases points to the legitimacy of the modern justification for such judicial review found in Justice Harlan's dissent in *Poe*,[4] [while] the acknowledged failures of some of these cases point with caution to the difficulty raised by the present claim.

[Justice Harlan's *Poe* dissent] is important for three things that point to our responsibilities today. The first is Justice Harlan's respect for the tradition of substantive due process review itself, and his acknowledgment of the Judiciary's obligation to carry it on. For two centuries American courts, and for much of that time this Court, have thought it necessary to provide some degree of review over the substantive content of legislation under constitutional standards of textual breadth. [This] enduring tradition of American constitutional practice is, in Justice Harlan's view, nothing more than what is required by the judicial authority and obligation to construe constitutional text and review legislation for conformity to that text. * * *

[The *Poe* dissent reminds us] that the business of [substantive due process] review is not the identification of extratextual absolutes but scrutiny of a legislative resolution (perhaps unconscious) of clashing principles, each quite possibly worthy in and of itself, but each to be weighed within the history of our values as a people. It is a comparison of the relative strengths of opposing claims that informs the judicial task, not a deduction from some first premise. Thus informed, judicial review still has no warrant to substitute one reasonable resolution of the contending positions for another, but authority to supplant the balance already

---

4. The status of the Harlan dissent in *Poe v. Ullman* is shown by the Court's adoption of its result in *Griswold* and by the Court's ac-knowledgment of its status and adoption of its reasoning in *Casey*. * * *

struck between the contenders only when it falls outside the realm of the reasonable.

[Justice Harlan's] approach calls for a court to assess the relative "weights" or dignities of the contending interests, and to this extent the judicial method is familiar to the common law. Common law method is subject, however, to two important constraints in the hands of a court engaged in substantive due process review. First, such a court is bound to confine the values that it recognizes to those truly deserving constitutional stature, either to those expressed in constitutional text, or those exemplified by "the traditions from which [the Nation] developed," or revealed by contrast with "the traditions from which it broke." *Poe* (Harlan, J., dissenting).

[The] second constraint, again, simply reflects the fact that constitutional review, not judicial lawmaking, is a court's business here. [It] is only when the legislation's justifying principle, critically valued, is so far from being commensurate with the individual interest as to be arbitrarily or pointlessly applied that the statute must give way. Only if this standard points against the statute can the individual claimant be said to have a constitutional right. * * *[10]

[Harlan, J.,] of course assumed that adjudication under the Due Process Clauses is like any other instance of judgment dependent on common-law method, being more or less persuasive according to the usual canons of critical discourse. [When] identifying and assessing the competing interests of liberty and authority, for example, the breadth of expression that a litigant or a judge selects in stating the competing principles will have much to do with the outcome and may be dispositive. As in any process of rational argumentation, we recognize that when a generally accepted principle is challenged, the broader the attack the less likely it is to succeed. The principle's defenders will, indeed, often try to characterize any challenge as just such a broadside, perhaps by couching the defense as if a broadside attack had occurred. [So] *Dred Scott* treated prohibition of slavery in the Territories as nothing less than a general assault on the concept of property.

Just as results in substantive due process cases are tied to the selections of statements of the competing interests, the acceptability of the results is a function of the good reasons for the selections made. It is here that the value of common-law method becomes apparent, for the usual thinking of the common law is suspicious of the all-or-nothing analysis that tends to produce legal petrification instead of an evolving boundary between the domains of old principles. Common-law method tends to pay respect instead to detail, seeking to understand old principles afresh by new examples and new counterexamples.

[So,] in *Poe,* Justice Harlan viewed it as essential to the plaintiffs' claimed right to use contraceptives that they sought to do so within the privacy of the marital bedroom. This detail in fact served two crucial and complementary functions, and provides a lesson for today. It rescued the individuals' claim from a breadth that would have threatened all state regulation of contraception or intimate relations; extramarital intimacy, no matter how privately practiced, was outside the scope of the right Justice Harlan would have recognized in that case. It was, moreover, this same restriction that allowed the interest to be valued as an aspect of a broader liberty to be free from all unreasonable intrusions into the

---

10. Our cases have used various terms to refer to fundamental liberty interests [and] at times we have also called such an interest a "right" even before balancing it against the government's interest, see, e.g., *Roe; Carey.* * * * Precision in terminology, however, fa-vors reserving the label "right" for instances in which the individual's liberty interest actually trumps the government's countervailing interests; only then does the individual have anything legally enforceable as against the state's attempt at regulation.

privacy of the home and the family life within it, a liberty exemplified in constitutional provisions such as the Third and Fourth Amendments, in prior decisions of the Court involving unreasonable intrusions into the home and family life, and in the then-prevailing status of marriage as the sole lawful locus of intimate relations.[11] The individuals' interest was therefore at its peak in *Poe,* because it was supported by a principle that distinguished of its own force between areas in which government traditionally had regulated (sexual relations outside of marriage) and those in which it had not (private marital intimacies), and thus was broad enough to cover the claim at hand without being so broad as to be shot-through by exceptions.

On the other side of the balance, the State's interest in *Poe* was not fairly characterized simply as preserving sexual morality, or doing so by regulating contraceptive devices. [It] was assumed that the State might legitimately enforce limits on the use of contraceptives through laws regulating divorce and annulment, or even through its tax policy, *ibid.,* but not necessarily be justified in criminalizing the same practice in the marital bedroom, which would entail the consequence of authorizing state enquiry into the intimate relations of a married couple who chose to close their door.

The same insistence on exactitude lies behind questions, in current terminology, about the proper level of generality at which to analyze claims and counterclaims, and the demand for fitness and proper tailoring of a restrictive statute is just another way of testing the legitimacy of the generality at which the government sets up its justification. We may therefore classify Justice Harlan's example of proper analysis in any of these ways: as applying concepts of normal critical reasoning, as pointing to the need to attend to the levels of generality at which countervailing interests are stated, or as examining the concrete application of principles for fitness with their own ostensible justifications. But whatever the categories in which we place the dissent's example, it stands in marked contrast to earlier cases whose reasoning was marked by comparatively less discrimination, and it points to the importance of evaluating the claims of the parties now before us with comparable detail. For here we are faced with an individual claim not to a right on the part of just anyone to help anyone else commit suicide under any circumstances, but to the right of a narrow class to help others also in a narrow class under a set of limited circumstances. And the claimants are met with the State's assertion, among others, that rights of such narrow scope cannot be recognized without jeopardy to individuals whom the State may concededly protect through its regulations.

* * * Constitutional recognition of the right to bodily integrity underlies the assumed right, good against the State, to require physicians to terminate artificial life support, *Cruzan,* [and] the affirmative right to obtain medical intervention to ✳ cause abortion, see *Casey.* It is, indeed, in the abortion cases that the most telling

---

11. Thus, as the *Poe* dissent illustrates, the task of determining whether the concrete right claimed by an individual in a particular case falls within the ambit of a more generalized protected liberty requires explicit analysis when what the individual wants to do could arguably be characterized as belonging to different strands of our legal tradition requiring different degrees of constitutional scrutiny. See also Laurence H. Tribe & Michael C. Dorf, *Levels of Generality in the Definition of Rights,* 57 U.Chi.L.Rev. 1057, 1091 (1990) (abortion might conceivably be assimilated either to the tradition regarding women's reproductive freedom in general, which places a substantial burden of justification on the State, or to the tradition regarding protection of fetuses, as embodied in laws criminalizing feticide by someone other than the mother, which generally requires only rationality on the part of the State). Selecting among such competing characterizations demands reasoned judgment about which broader principle, as exemplified in the concrete privileges and prohibitions embodied in our legal tradition, best fits the particular claim asserted in a particular case.

recognitions of the importance of bodily integrity and the concomitant tradition of medical assistance have occurred. [The] analogies between the abortion cases and this one are several. Even though the State has a legitimate interest in discouraging abortion, the Court recognized a woman's right to a physician's counsel and care. Like the decision to commit suicide, the decision to abort potential life can be made irresponsibly and under the influence of others, and yet the Court has held in the abortion cases that physicians are fit assistants. Without physician assistance in abortion, the woman's right would have too often amounted to nothing more than a right to self-mutilation, and without a physician to assist in the suicide of the dying, the patient's right will often be confined to crude methods of causing death, most shocking and painful to the decedent's survivors.

[The] argument supporting respondents' [position] progresses through three steps of increasing forcefulness. First, it emphasizes the decriminalization of suicide. Reliance on this fact is sanctioned under the standard that looks not only to the tradition retained, but to society's occasional choices to reject traditions of the legal past. See *Poe* (Harlan, J., dissenting). [The] second step in the argument is to emphasize that the State's own act of decriminalization gives a freedom of choice much like the individual's option in recognized instances of bodily autonomy. One of these, abortion, is a legal right to choose in spite of the interest a State may legitimately invoke in discouraging the practice, just as suicide is now subject to choice, despite a state interest in discouraging it. The third step is to emphasize that [respondents] base their claim on the traditional right to medical care and counsel, subject to the limiting conditions of informed, responsible choice when death is imminent, conditions that support a strong analogy to rights of care in other situations in which medical counsel and assistance have been available as a matter of course. There can be no stronger claim to a physician's assistance than at the time when death is imminent, a moral judgment implied by the State's own recognition of the legitimacy of medical procedures necessarily hastening the moment of impending death.

In my judgment, the importance of the individual interest here, as within that class of "certain interests" demanding careful scrutiny of the State's contrary claim, see *Poe,* cannot be gainsaid. Whether that interest might in some circumstances, or at some time, be seen as "fundamental" to the degree entitled to prevail is not, however, a conclusion that I need draw here, for I am satisfied that the State's interests [are] sufficiently serious to defeat the present claim that its law is arbitrary or purposeless.

[Among the interests the State has put forward to justify the Washington law are the] interests in protecting patients from mistakenly and involuntarily deciding to end their lives, and in guarding against both voluntary and involuntary euthanasia. The argument is that a progression would occur, obscuring the line between the ill and the dying, and between the responsible and the unduly influenced, until ultimately doctors and perhaps others would abuse a limited freedom to aid suicides * * *. Respondents propose an answer to all this, the answer of state regulation with teeth. Legislation proposed in several States, for example, would authorize physician-assisted suicide but require two qualified physicians to confirm the patient's diagnosis, prognosis, and competence; and would mandate that the patient make repeated requests witnessed by at least two others over a specified time span; and would impose reporting requirements and criminal penalties for various acts of coercion.

But at least at this moment there are reasons for caution in predicting the effectiveness of the teeth proposed. Respondents' proposals, as it turns out, sound much like the guidelines now in place in the Netherlands, the only place where experience with physician-assisted suicide and euthanasia has yielded empirical evidence about how such regulations might affect actual practice. [There] is, however, a substantial dispute today about what the Dutch experience shows. Some commentators marshall evidence that the Dutch guidelines have in practice failed to protect patients from involuntary euthanasia and have been violated with impunity. This evidence is contested. The day may come when we can say with some assurance which side is right, but for now it is the substantiality of the factual disagreement, and the alternatives for resolving it, that matter. They are, for me, dispositive of the due process claim at this time.

I take it that the basic concept of judicial review with its possible displacement of legislative judgment bars any finding that a legislature has acted arbitrarily when the following conditions are met: there is a serious factual controversy over the feasibility of recognizing the claimed right without at the same time making it impossible for the State to engage in an undoubtedly legitimate exercise of power; facts necessary to resolve the controversy are not readily ascertainable through the judicial process; but they are more readily subject to discovery through legislative factfinding and experimentation. It is assumed in this case, and must be, that a State's interest in protecting those unable to make responsible decisions and those who make no decisions at all entitles the State to bar aid to any but a knowing and responsible person intending suicide, and to prohibit euthanasia. How, and how far, a State should act in that interest are judgments for the State, but the legitimacy of its action to deny a physician the option to aid any but the knowing and responsible is beyond question.

The capacity of the State to protect the others if respondents were to prevail is, however, subject to some genuine question, underscored by the responsible disagreement over the basic facts of the Dutch experience. This factual controversy is not open to a judicial resolution with any substantial degree of assurance at this time. [While] an extensive literature on any subject can raise the hopes for judicial understanding, the literature on this subject is only nascent. Since there is little experience directly bearing on the issue, the most that can be said is that whichever way the Court might rule today, events could overtake its assumptions, as experimentation in some jurisdictions confirmed or discredited the concerns about progression from assisted suicide to euthanasia.

Legislatures, on the other hand, have superior opportunities to obtain the facts necessary for a judgment about the present controversy. [Moreover,] their mechanisms include the power to experiment, moving forward and pulling back as facts emerge within their own jurisdictions. * * * [While] I do not decide for all time that respondents' claim should not be recognized, I acknowledge the legislative institutional competence as the better one to deal with that claim at this time.

JUSTICE GINSBURG, concurring in the judgments.

I concur in the Court's judgments in these cases substantially for the reasons stated by Justice O'Connor in her concurring opinion.

JUSTICE BREYER, concurring in the judgments.

I believe that Justice O'Connor's views, which I share, have greater legal significance than the Court's opinion suggests. I join her separate opinion, except insofar as it joins the majority. And I concur in the judgments. I shall briefly explain how I differ from the Court.

I agree with the Court in *Vacco v. Quill,* [infra] that the articulated state interests justify the distinction drawn between physician assisted suicide and withdrawal of life-support. I also agree [that] the critical question in both of the cases before us is whether "the 'liberty' specially protected by the Due Process Clause includes a right" of the sort that the respondents assert. I do not agree, however, with the Court's formulation of that claimed "liberty" interest. The Court describes it as a "right to commit suicide with another's assistance." But I would not reject the respondents' claim without considering a different formulation, for which our legal tradition may provide greater support. That formulation would use words roughly like a "right to die with dignity." But irrespective of the exact words used, at its core would lie personal control over the manner of death, professional medical assistance, and the avoidance of unnecessary and severe physical suffering—combined.

As Justice Souter points out, Justice Harlan's dissenting opinion in *Poe* offers some support for such a claim. In that opinion, Justice Harlan [recognized] that "*certain interests* require particularly careful scrutiny of the state needs asserted to justify their abridgment." The "certain interests" to which Justice Harlan referred may well be similar (perhaps identical) to the rights, liberties, or interests that the Court today, as in the past, regards as "fundamental."

Justice Harlan concluded that marital privacy was such a "special interest." He found in the Constitution a right of "privacy of the home"—with the home, the bedroom, and "intimate details of the marital relation" at its heart—by examining the protection that the law had earlier provided for related, but not identical, interests described by such words as "privacy," "home," and "family." The respondents here essentially ask us to do the same. They argue that one can find a "right to die with dignity" by examining the protection the law has provided for related, but not identical, interests relating to personal dignity, medical treatment, and freedom from state-inflicted pain.

I do not believe, however, that this Court need or now should decide whether or a not such a right is "fundamental." That is because, in my view, the avoidance of severe physical pain (connected with death) would have to comprise an essential part of any successful claim and because, as Justice O'Connor points out, the laws before us do not *force* a dying person to undergo that kind of pain. Rather, the laws of New York and of Washington do not prohibit doctors from providing patients with drugs sufficient to control pain despite the risk that those drugs themselves will kill. And under these circumstances the laws of New York and Washington would overcome any remaining significant interests and would be justified, regardless.

Medical technology [makes] the administration of pain-relieving drugs sufficient, except for a very few individuals for whom the ineffectiveness of pain control medicines can mean, not pain, but the need for sedation which can end in a coma. We are also told that there are many instances in which patients do not receive the palliative care that, in principle, is available, but that is so for institutional reasons or inadequacies or obstacles, which would seem possible to overcome, and which do *not* include *a prohibitive set of laws.*

This legal circumstance means that the state laws before us do not infringe directly upon the (assumed) central interest (what I have called the core of the interest in dying with dignity) as, by way of contrast, the state anticontraceptive laws at issue in *Poe* did interfere with the central interest there at stake—by bringing the State's police powers to bear upon the marital bedroom.

Were the legal circumstances different—for example, were state law to prevent the provision of palliative care, including the administration of drugs as needed to avoid pain at the end of life—then the law's impact upon serious and otherwise unavoidable physical pain (accompanying death) would be more directly at issue. And as Justice O'Connor suggests, the Court might have to revisit its conclusions in these cases.

————

In a companion case to *Glucksberg*, VACCO v. QUILL, 521 U.S. 793, 117 S.Ct. 2293, 138 L.Ed.2d 834 (1997), the Court without a dissent, rejected the argument that because New York permits competent persons to refuse lifesaving medical treatment, and the refusal of such treatment is "essentially the same thing" as physician-assisted suicide, the state's assisted suicide ban violates the Equal Protection Clause. REHNQUIST, C.J., again wrote for the Court: "[The] Equal Protection Clause [embodies] a general rule that States must treat like cases alike but may treat unlike cases accordingly. If[, as here,] a legislative classification or distinction 'neither burdens a fundamental right nor targets a suspect class, we will uphold [it] so long as it bears a rational relation to some legitimate end.' *Romer v. Evans* [p. 1312 supra]. [On] their faces, neither New York's ban on assisting suicide nor its statutes permitting patients to refuse medical treatment treat anyone differently than anyone else or draw any distinctions between persons. *Everyone,* regardless of physical condition, is entitled, if competent, to refuse unwanted lifesaving medical treatment; *no one* is permitted to assist a suicide.

"[The] Court of Appeals, however, concluded that some terminally ill people— those who are on life-support systems—are treated differently than those who are not, in that the former may 'hasten death' by ending treatment, but the latter may not 'hasten death' through physician-assisted suicide. This conclusion depends on the submission that ending or refusing lifesaving medical treatment 'is nothing more nor less than assisted suicide.' Unlike the Court of Appeals, we think the distinction between assisting suicide and withdrawing life-sustaining treatment, a distinction widely recognized and endorsed in the medical profession and in our legal traditions, is both important and logical; it is certainly rational.

"The distinction comports with fundamental legal principles of causation and intent. First, when a patient refuses life-sustaining medical treatment, he dies from an underlying fatal disease or pathology; but if a patient ingests lethal medication prescribed by a physician, he is killed by that medication. [Furthermore,] a physician who withdraws, or honors a patient's refusal to begin, life-sustaining medical treatment purposefully intends, or may so intend, only to respect his patient's wishes and 'to cease doing useless and futile or degrading things to the patient when [the patient] no longer stands to benefit from them.' The same is true when a doctor provides aggressive palliative care; in some cases, painkilling drugs may hasten a patient's death, but the physician's purpose and intent is, or may be, only to ease his patient's pain. A doctor who assists a suicide, however, 'must, necessarily and indubitably, intend primarily that the patient be made dead.' Similarly, a patient who commits suicide with a doctor's aid necessarily has the specific intent to end his or her own life, while a patient who refuses or discontinues treatment might not. [The] law has long used actors' intent or purpose to distinguish between two acts that may have the same result. [Put] differently, the law distinguishes actions taken 'because of' a given end from actions taken 'in spite of' their unintended but foreseen consequences.

"[Given] these general principles, it is not surprising that many courts, including New York courts, have carefully distinguished refusing life-sustaining treatment from suicide. * * * Similarly, the overwhelming majority of state legislatures have drawn a clear line between assisting suicide and withdrawing or permitting the refusal of unwanted lifesaving medical treatment by prohibiting the former and permitting the latter. * * *

New York is a case in point. [It] has acted several times to protect patients' common-law right to refuse treatment [but] reaffirmed the line between 'killing' and 'letting die.' * * * More recently, the New York State Task Force on Life and the Law studied assisted suicide and euthanasia and, in 1994, unanimously recommended against legalization.

"[This] Court has also recognized, at least implicitly, the distinction between letting a patient die and making that patient die. In *Cruzan* our assumption of a right to refuse treatment was grounded not, as the Court of Appeals supposed, on the proposition that patients have a general and abstract 'right to hasten death,' but on well established, traditional rights to bodily integrity and freedom from unwanted touching. In fact, we observed that 'the majority of States in this country have laws imposing criminal penalties on one who assists another to commit suicide.' *Cruzan* therefore provides no support for the notion that refusing life-sustaining medical treatment is 'nothing more nor less than suicide.'

"For all these reasons, we disagree with respondents' claim that the distinction between refusing lifesaving medical treatment and assisted suicide is 'arbitrary' and 'irrational.'[11] [By] permitting everyone to refuse unwanted medical treatment while prohibiting anyone from assisting a suicide, New York law follows a longstanding and rational distinction.

"New York's reasons for recognizing and acting on this distinction—including prohibiting intentional killing and preserving life; preventing suicide; maintaining physicians' role as their patients' healers; protecting vulnerable people from indifference, prejudice, and psychological and financial pressure to end their lives; and avoiding a possible slide towards euthanasia—are discussed in greater detail in our opinion in *Glucksberg*. These valid and important public interests easily satisfy the constitutional requirement that a legislative classification bear a rational relation to some legitimate end.[13]"

STEVENS, J., concurring in the judgment, "agree[d] that the distinction between permitting death to ensue from an underlying fatal disease and causing it to occur by the administration of medication or other means provides a constitutionally sufficient basis for the State's classification." However, unlike the Court, he was "not persuaded that in all cases there will in fact be a significant difference between the intent of the physicians, the patients or the families in the two situations." He continued:

11. Respondents also argue that the State irrationally distinguishes between physician-assisted suicide and "terminal sedation," a process respondents characterize as "induc[ing] barbiturate coma and then starv[ing] the person to death." Petitioners insist, however, that " '[a]lthough proponents of physician-assisted suicide and euthanasia contend that terminal sedation is covert physician-assisted suicide or euthanasia, the concept of sedating pharmacotherapy is based on informed consent and the principle of double effect.' " Just as a State may prohibit assisting suicide while permitting patients to refuse unwanted lifesaving treatment, it may permit palliative care related to that refusal, which may have the foreseen but unintended "double effect" of hastening the patient's death.

13. Justice Stevens observes that our holding today "does not foreclose the possibility that some applications of the New York statute may impose an intolerable intrusion on the patient's freedom." This is true, but, as we observe in *Glucksberg*, a particular plaintiff hoping to show that New York's assisted-suicide ban was unconstitutional in his particular case would need to present different and considerably stronger arguments than those advanced by respondents here.

"The illusory character of any differences in intent or causation is confirmed by the fact that the American Medical Association unequivocally endorses the practice of terminal sedation—the administration of sufficient dosages of pain-killing medication to terminally ill patients to protect them from excruciating pain even when it is clear that the time of death will be advanced. [Thus,] although the differences the majority notes in causation and intent between terminating life-support and assisting in suicide support the Court's rejection of the respondents' facial challenge, these distinctions may be inapplicable to particular terminally ill patients and their doctors. Our holding today in *Quill* [just] like our holding in [*Glucksberg*,] does not foreclose the possibility that some applications of the New York statute may impose an intolerable intrusion on the patient's freedom."[a]

Notes and Questions

1. *Does Glucksberg mark the end of Roe's constitutional methodology?* Michael McConnell, *The Right to Die and the Jurisprudence of Tradition*, 1997 Utah L. Rev. 665, 666, argues that *Glucksberg* and *Quill* repudiated the notion that federal courts "have authority to resolve contentious questions of social policy on the basis of their own normative judgments": "The Court announced a constitutional jurisprudence of unenumerated rights under the Due Process Clause based not on the normative judgment of courts, but on constitutional text supplemented by the tradition and experience of the nation. *Roe* was not reversed on its facts; the abortion right itself remains secure. But the constitutional methodology under which *Roe* was decided has been repudiated. The era of judicial supremacy epitomized by *Roe* is over."

2. *Preventing pain relief; the "double effect" principle.* Providing medication to terminally ill people knowing that it will have a "double effect"—reduce the patient's pain and hasten death—is widely accepted by the medical profession. Many physicians and bioethicists seem to believe that providing risky pain relief is always justifiable, regardless of how certain or probable the risk of death may be. Recently, however, two law professors have maintained that as a matter of criminal law the physician's motive or desire to relieve pain does not automatically or necessarily justify the administration of pain relief. Norman Cantor & George Thomas, *Pain Relief, Acceleration of Death, and Criminal Law*, 6 Kennedy Inst. of Ethics J. 107 (June, 1996). They argue that if, for example, the situation were such that no analgesic dosage could provide pain relief without also causing prompt death (or if under the circumstances it was almost certain that the required analgesic dosage would cause death) the physician who administered the analgesic would be criminally liable for the resulting death even though death was not intended. According to the authors, as defined by the Model Penal Code these deaths would be "knowing" homicides (acting with awareness that one's conduct is "practically certain" to bring about a particular result). Moreover, according to the authors, if it were *highly likely* that the administration of an analgesic would cause prompt death (for example a 75–90% chance), the physician who used the painkillers that caused the death would also be criminally liable (for having acted "recklessly").

a. Souter, J., who concurred in the judgment, observed that the reasons which led him to conclude that the challenged statute in *Glucksberg* was "not arbitrary under the due process standard also support the distinction between assistance to suicide, which is banned, and practices such as termination of artificial life support and death-hastening pain medication, which are permitted." The concurring opinions of O'Connor, Ginsburg and Breyer, JJ., in *Glucksberg* also constituted their concurrences in *Vacco*.

Suppose, inspired by the Cantor–Thomas article, a state legislature criminalized the use of medication designed to relieve severe pain when it is highly likely (or more probable than not) that administration of such pain relief would cause death. In such an event, how many members of the Supreme Court would be inclined to "revisit" the questions raised by the physician-assisted suicide cases? See Robert A. Burt, *The Supreme Court Speaks—Not Assisted Suicide but a Constitutional Right to Palliative Care*, 337 New Eng. J. Med, 1234 (1997); Lawrence O. Gostin, *Deciding Life and Death in the Courtroom*, 278 JAMA 1523, 1527–28 (1997); Yale Kamisar, *On the Meaning and Impact of the Physician-Assisted Suicide Cases,* 82 Minn. L. Rev. 895, 904–09 (1998).

3. *Judicial "minimalism" and the 1997 physician-assisted suicide cases.* As he explains in his book, *One Case at a Time: Judicial Minimalism on the Supreme Court* (1999), Professor Cass R. Sunstein is a strong proponent of judicial "minimalism," an approach leaving important questions unresolved by saying no more than necessary to justify the outcome of a case. (Judicial "maximalism," on the other hand, is the practice of deciding cases in a way that establishes broad rules for the future.) He maintains (p. 89) that because "it is extremely difficult to produce any verbal formula that is satisfying, consistent with current law, and adequate to resolve the issue of physician-assisted suicide, [the] best and appropriately minimalist route is for the Court simply to assume that the right qualifies as fundamental and to proceed from there to the question of justification." According to Sunstein, although Rehnquist, C.J., rejected this approach, the five justices who wrote concurring opinions did not.[a] "In good minimalist fashion," these five justices "left open the question whether people facing pain and imminent death" may have a constitutional right to physician-assisted suicide and "[t]he Court was right not to decide that question" (p. 76).[b]

Professor Sunstein criticizes Rehnquist, C.J., for writing "the ambitious, emphatically nonminimalist opinion that he and Justice Scalia have been (unsuccessfully) urging on the Court in the abortion cases—an opinion that would limit the right of privacy, and indeed all fundamental rights under the due process clause, to those rights that are 'deeply rooted' in our long-standing traditions and practices" (Preface, p. xii).

But consider Jeffrey Rosen, *The Age of Mixed Results*, (essay review of Sunstein's book), The New Republic, June 28, 1999, pp. 43, 46: "[W]hy is Rehnquist's opinion 'emphatically nonminimalist'? The conventional tools of legal interpretation—text, history, tradition, constitutional structure, and judicial precedent—all fail to support the claim that there is a fundamental right to physician-assisted suicide, even to alleviate great pain when death is imminent. By recognizing the weakness of the argument for a judicially created right to die, and by removing the courts from the debate entirely, Rehnquist's approach would seem to preserve the largest space for democratic deliberation.

a. Professor Sunstein is well aware that five justices signed the Chief Justice's opinion, but he observes that O'Connor, J., who signed the Chief Justice's opinion, "wrote one of her characteristic separate opinions, * * * caution[ing] that the Court had not decided whether a competent person experiencing great suffering had a constitutional right to control the circumstances of an imminent death. That issue remained to be decided on another day." (Preface, p. xii) "What this means is that a majority of five justices on the Court has signaled the possible existence of a right to physician-assisted suicide in compelling circumstances—and thus a five-justice majority has rejected the whole approach in Rehnquist's opinion (for a five-justice majority)." (Id.)

b. Sunstein adds, however, that when and if it is forced to decide that question, the Court should conclude that "the state has sufficient reason to override the individual interest even in such extreme cases" (p. 76).

"Yet Sunstein prefers the far more elusive approach of Justice O'Connor, who stressed that the Court had not decided whether or not a competent person experiencing great suffering might have a constitutional right to control the circumstances of imminent death. * * *

"Sunstein, like O'Connor, says that the Court should assume that the right to physician-assisted suicide is 'presumptively protected' in medically hopeless cases, but should also hold that the state's interests are sufficiently strong to override it. Why is this opaque holding more 'minimalist' than Rehnquist's far less intrusive alternative? Since neither Sunstein nor O'Connor explains the reasons that might persuade the Court to recognize a presumptive right to die under medically hopeless conditions, all this has the feel of a fiat, and it raises the specter that the Court might create other unenumerated rights in the future with similarly thin support in text, history, and precedent. Wasn't it precisely this threat of an untethered court inventing constitutional rights without coherent explanations that the minimalist project was designed to avoid?"

4. *The significance of the informally agreed-upon "right" to assisted suicide, especially in compelling cases.* A number of prominent commentators opposed to the legalization of physician-assisted suicide (e.g., John Arras, Ezekiel Emanuel and Mark Siegler) defend the flat prohibition partly on the ground that it is *not really* a flat ban—that the availability of informal practice and informally agreed-upon "rights," especially in the most compelling cases, *reduces the pressure* to legalize these practices formally. But which way does "the availability of informal practice" cut? See the discussion in Yale Kamisar, *Physician–Assisted Suicide: The Problems Presented by the Compelling, Heartwrenching Case*, 88 J.Crim.L. & Crim. 1121 (1998).

5. *What next?* Should the question of whether and how physician-assisted suicide (PAS) is to be legalized be left to state legislatures? Consider Charles H. Baron, *Pleading for Physician–Assisted Suicide in the Courts*, 19 W. New Eng. L.Rev. 371, 373, 389, 398–99 (1997) (written before the Supreme Court's PAS decisions): "[The] various state supreme courts that have bottomed the right to die on various provisions of their state constitutions and the federal constitutions [have] continually urged the state legislatures to develop comprehensive rules for dealing with the issues that were raised. Indeed, as time has passed, the state supreme courts have emphasized the constitutional aspects less and have used state common law increasingly—in part, presumably, to provide a greater scope of experimentation for state legislatures. The New Jersey Supreme Court, for example, beginning [in 1985], has relied primarily upon the common law principles of informed consent, and only secondarily upon the constitutional right to privacy.

"[The] fears that have kept state legislatures from leading the way in developing the right to die law in the past still seem to haunt the corridors of our legislative assemblies. Oregon has thus far been the only state to legalize [PAS] by legislation, and that law was enacted through a citizen initiative vote—not by the normal legislative process."

6. *After Glucksberg and Quill, how will PAS proponents fare in the state courts? Krischer v. McIver*, 697 So.2d 97 (Fla.1997), indicates that they may meet heavy resistance. About six months *before* the U.S. Supreme Court's decisions in the PAS cases, a Florida trial court held that a terminally ill AIDS patient was entitled, under the Privacy Amendment of the Florida Constitution, to determine the time and manner of his death and that, in order to do so, he had the right to seek and obtain the assistance of his physician in committing suicide. However, a

few weeks *after* the U.S. Supreme Court's PAS decisions, the Florida Supreme Court reversed the trial court (5–1).

Since Florida's Privacy Amendment establishes a right much broader in scope than that of the U.S. Constitution, the Florida Supreme Court could have distinguished *Glucksberg* and *Quill* quite easily. Instead, however, the Court quoted at length from Rehnquist C.J.'s opinion in *Glucksberg* and from the New York Task Force Report on assisted suicide and euthanasia, a report that recommended unanimously that New York's total ban against assisted suicide and euthanasia be maintained. (Rehnquist, C.J., had also relied heavily on the New York report.) After balking at arguments frequently made by PAS proponents, the Florida Supreme Court concluded: "By broadly construing the privacy amendment to include the right to assisted suicide, we would run the risk of arrogating to ourselves those powers to make social policy that as a constitutional matter belong only to the legislature."

7. *The second-degree murder conviction of Dr. Kevorkian.* In March 1999, after having assisted over 100 suicides, and after having been acquitted of assisted suicide in several previous cases, Dr. Jack Kevorkian was convicted of second-degree murder (and sentenced to 10 to 25 years in prison) for administering a lethal injection to Lou Gehrig's disease patient Thomas Youk. *The New York Times* editorialized, March 27, 1999, p. A26: "Most advocates of physician-assisted suicide hold as a first principle that the patient must be the one in full control. The Oregon laws that have legalized assisted suicide, for example, honor that principle. Dr. Kevorkian's mercy killing violates it. Previous juries have let him off the hook for assisting in suicides. But this jury drew the line at direct killing."

Is this the message of the Kevorkian conviction? How significant was it that a videotape of Kevorkian injecting Youk with a lethal dose was shown on CBS's "60 Minutes" in a segment in which Kevorkian dared prosecutors to charge him? How significant was it that the trial judge ruled that the issue of whether Mr. Youk consented to his death was irrelevant and that the jury never heard Youk's wife or mother or brother tell how grateful they were that Kevorkian was available? How significant was it that in all the previous cases Dr. Kevorkian had been represented by Geoffrey Fieger, a prominent trial attorney, but in the Youk case he represented himself?

Many opponents of assisted suicide applauded Kevorkian's conviction and hoped that it signaled a change in public attitude. However, as pointed out in Charles H. Baron, *Assisted Dying*, Trial, July 1999, at 44, recent opinion polls in the United States indicate that this is not so: "[These polls] show a high and increasing level of support for legalization and regulation of physician-assisted suicide. A Field poll taken after [Kevorkian's] conviction shows that support in California has increased in the last two years from 70 percent to 75 percent (from 61 percent to 68 percent among Roman Catholics). An ABC News poll showed that 55 percent of the public disagreed with the jury's verdict [in the trial of Dr. Kevorkian for the death of Mr. Youk], and only 39 percent agreed."[c]

c. *Glucksberg* and *Quill* have generated a considerable amount of commentary. See, e.g., *Symposium: Physician–Assisted Suicide: Facing Death after* Glucksberg *and* Quill, 82 Minn. L. Rev. 885–1101 (1998) (contributions by Howard Brody, Robert Burt, Ezekiel Emanual, Yale Kamisar, Patricia King, Sylvia Law, Kathryn Tucker, Leslie Wolf and Susan Wolf); Lawrence Gostin, note 2 supra; Michael McConnell, note 1 supra; Martha Minow, *Which Question? Which Lie? Reflections on the Physician–Assisted Suicide Case*, 1997 Sup. Ct. Rev. 1; David Orentlicher, *The Supreme Court and Physician–Assisted Suicide—Rejecting Assisted Suicide, but Embracing Euthanasia*, 337 New Eng. J. Med. 1236 (1997); Robert A Sedler, *Abortion, Physician–Assisted Suicide and the Constitution*, 12 Notre Dame J. L., Ethics

SECTION 3. THE RIGHT TO TRAVEL

INTRODUCTION

"The 'right to travel' from state to state has been a favorite of both the Warren and Burger Courts. The Constitution makes no mention of any such right. By now we know that cannot be determinative, but we are entitled to some sort of explanation of why the right is appropriately attributable. In recent years the Court has been almost smug in its refusal to provide one."[a]

—John Hart Ely, *Democracy and Distrust* 177 (1980).

———

Dissenting in *Shapiro v. Thompson* (1969) (discussed at p. 1374 infra), Harlan, J., observed: "Opinions of the Court and of individual Justices have suggested four provisions of the Constitution as possible sources of a right to travel enforceable against the federal or state governments: the Commerce Clause; the Privileges and Immunities Clause of Art. IV, § 2; the Privileges and Immunities Clause of the Fourteenth Amendment; and the Due Process Clause of the Fifth Amendment." (He concluded that "the right to travel interstate is a 'fundamental' right which, for present purposes, should be regarded as having its source in [the fifth amendment due process clause].") Other possible sources for the constitutional right to travel are the equal protection clause, the "penumbra" of the first amendment, the ninth amendment and "the nature of the federal union."[b] One recent constitutional law text discusses the right to travel in its "equal protection" chapter,[c] another treats the subject primarily in a chapter on "rights of privacy and personhood."[d]

———

APTHEKER v. SECRETARY OF STATE, 378 U.S. 500, 84 S.Ct. 1659, 12 L.Ed.2d 992 (1964), concerned an attack by top-ranking leaders of the Communist Party on § 6 of the subversive activities control act of 1950, which denied passports to members of an organization "with knowledge or notice" that it was required to register as "a Communist organization." The Court, per GOLDBERG, J., struck down § 6 as "unconstitutional on its face" because it "too broadly and indiscriminately restricts the right to travel and thereby abridges the liberty guaranteed by the Fifth Amendment." It pointed to the dictum in *Kent v. Dulles,* 357 U.S. 116, 78 S.Ct. 1113, 2 L.Ed.2d 1204 (1958), that "The right to travel is a part of the 'liberty' of which the citizen cannot be deprived without [fifth amendment due process]. Freedom of movement across frontiers in either direction, and inside frontiers as well, was a part of our heritage. Travel abroad, like

---

& Pub. Policy 529 (1998); Sunstein, note 2 supra; Sonia M. Suter, *Ambivalent Unanimity: An Analysis of the Supreme Court's Holding,* in Law at the End of Life 25 (Schneider ed. 2000); Note 111 Harv. L. Rev. 237 (1997).

a. At this point Professor Ely refers to language in *Shapiro v. Thompson* and *United States v. Guest,* both quoted infra. See also Note, 40 U.M.K.C.L.Rev. 66, 77 (1971).

b. See generally Ira Lupu, *Untangling the Strands of the Fourteenth Amendment,* 77 Mich.L.Rev. 981, 993, 1031, 1060–64 (1979); Notes, 22 U.C.L.A.L.Rev. 1129, 1140–45 (1975); 55 Neb.L.Rev. 117–22, 132 (1975) and authorities collected therein.

c. John Nowak & Ronald Rotunda, *Constitutional Law* § 14.38 (6th ed., 2000).

d. Tribe 2d ed., § 15–14.

travel within the country [is] basic in our scheme of values." "Since freedom of association is itself guaranteed in the First Amendment, restrictions imposed upon the right to travel cannot be dismissed by asserting that the right to travel could be fully exercised if the individual would first yield up his membership in a given association."[a]

DOUGLAS, J., joined the Court's opinion, adding that "the right to move freely from State to State is a privilege and immunity of national citizenship." "Absent war, I see no way to keep a citizen from traveling within or without the country [unless] he has been convicted of a crime [or] there is probable cause for issuing a warrant [to arrest him]. Freedom of movement [is] the very essence of our free society, setting us apart."[b]

ZEMEL v. RUSK, 381 U.S. 1, 85 S.Ct. 1271, 14 L.Ed.2d 179 (1965), concerned refusal to issue passports to United States citizens for travel to Cuba "unless specifically endorsed [by] the Secretary of State." Appellant sought a passport "to satisfy my curiosity about the state of affairs in Cuba and to make me a better informed citizen." The Court, per WARREN, C.J., affirmed denial of the request: "The requirements of due process are a function not only of the extent of the governmental restriction imposed, but also of the extent of the necessity for the restriction. [The] United States and other members of the Organization of American States have determined that travel between Cuba and the other countries of the Western Hemisphere is an important element in the spreading of subversion. [in light of this factor and others], the Secretary has justifiably concluded that travel to Cuba by American citizens might involve the Nation in dangerous international incidents, and that the Constitution does not require him to validate passports for such travel.

"The right to travel *within* the United States is of course also constitutionally protected. But that freedom does not mean that areas ravaged by flood, fire or pestilence cannot be quarantined when it can be demonstrated that unlimited travel to the area would directly and materially interfere with the safety and welfare of the area or the Nation as a whole. So it is with international travel. [That the challenged restriction] is supported by the weightiest considerations of national security is perhaps best pointed up by recalling that the Cuban Missile crisis of October 1962 preceded the filing of appellant's complaint by less than two months."

DOUGLAS, J., joined by Goldberg, J., dissented: "[T]here are areas [such as those stricken by pestilence or war] to which Congress can [prohibit] travel. [But] the only so-called danger present here is the Communist regime in Cuba. The world, however, is filled with Communist thought [and] if we are to know them and understand them, we must mingle with [them]."[c]

---

a. *Kent* invalidated State Department regulations denying passports to Communists on the ground they exceeded the congressional grant of authority, thus avoiding the constitutional question.

b. Clark, J., joined by Harlan and White, JJ., dissented, maintaining that the Due Process Clause does not prohibit "reasonable regu-

lation" of the right to travel abroad and that Congress had "a rational basis" for denying passports to members of the Communist Party.

c. Compare *Zemel* with *Regan v. Wald*, 468 U.S. 222, 104 S.Ct. 3026, 82 L.Ed.2d 171 (1984). In 1982, in order to "reduce Cuba's hard currency earnings from travel by U.S.

HAIG v. AGEE, 453 U.S. 280, 101 S.Ct. 2766, 69 L.Ed.2d 640 (1981), arose as follows: Agee, a former CIA employee then residing in West Germany, announced and engaged in a campaign to expose undercover CIA agents stationed abroad and "to drive them out of the countries where they are operating." In carrying out his campaign he traveled in various countries. Because of Agee's activities, his passport was revoked on the basis of a 1966 regulation authorizing passport revocation when the Secretary of state determines that an American citizen's activities abroad "are causing or likely to cause serious damage to the national security or the foreign policy of the United States."[a] A 7–2 majority, per BURGER, C.J., rejected Agee's contention that the revocation violated, inter alia, his "right to travel," stressing the distinction between interstate and international travel:

"Revocation of a passport undeniably curtails travel, but the freedom to travel abroad with a 'letter of introduction' in the form of a passport issued by the sovereign is subordinate to national security and foreign policy considerations; as such, it is subject to reasonable governmental regulation. The Court has made it plain that the *freedom* to travel outside the United States must be distinguished from the *right* to travel within the United States.

"[It] is 'obvious and unarguable' that no governmental interest is more compelling than the security of the Nation. [Not] only has Agee jeopardized the security of the United States, but he has endangered the interests of countries other than the United States—thereby creating serious problems for American foreign relations and foreign policy. Restricting Agee's foreign travel, although perhaps not certain to prevent all of Agee's harmful activities, is the only avenue open to the Government to limit these activities."

BRENNAN, J., joined by Marshall, J., dissenting, devoted most of his opinion to the argument that the regulation under which Agee's passport had been revoked was "invalid as an unlawful exercise of authority by the Secretary [of State] under the Passport Act of 1926." He then cited *Agee* as "a prime example of the adage that 'bad facts make bad law.'"

Notes and Questions

1. *The shift from Kent to Agee.* Consider Daniel Farber, *National Security, The Right to Travel, and the Court,* 1981 Sup.Ct.Rev. 263, 285–87: "[*Agee*] represents a major shift from previous travel cases such as *Kent* [which] laid heavy stress on the importance of the right to travel and took a correspondingly grudging approach to discretionary travel controls. *Agee,* on the other hand, distinguishes the *right* to travel within the United States from the mere *freedom* to travel outside the United States. It takes a correspondingly generous view of executive discretion. For three reasons, the *Kent* approach is preferable * * *.

persons to and from Cuba," a treasury regulation was amended to restrict travel-related economic transactions. Respondents, American citizens who wanted to travel to Cuba, challenged the amendment on both statutory and constitutional grounds. A 5–4 majority, per Rehnquist, J., rejected the constitutional challenge, seeing "no reason to differentiate between the travel restrictions imposed by the President in the present case and the passport restrictions imposed by the Secretary of State in *Zemel.*"

Blackmun, J., joined by Brennan, Marshall and Powell, JJ., dissented, maintaining that the restrictions on travel-related expenditures in Cuba were not authorized by Congress.

a. As a condition for his employment by the CIA, Agee contracted not to make any public statements about Agency matters, either during or after the term of his employment by the Agency, "without specific approval by the Agency." In a separate action brought by the government to enforce Agee's agreement, a federal district court held that "Agee has shown a flagrant disregard for the requirements of the Secrecy Agreement."

"First is the importance of the right to travel itself. [One] important aspect of international travel is its relation to freedom of speech. Without the right to travel, criticism of foreign policy is greatly impeded. [Second,] *Kent's* grudging attitude toward executive discretion is amply supported by history. [The] *Agee* Court seems to have assumed that the discretion to control travel had only been exercised on a principled basis. Too many counterexamples exist to allow reliance on this assumption. The third reason for preferring *Kent* to *Agee* is that *Kent* aligns more closely with congressional intent. Since *Kent*, Congress has strongly supported the principle of freedom of travel. Despite urgent pleas from [President Eisenhower], Congress refused to supply the statutory power held lacking in *Kent*. * * * Twenty years later, Congress abolished the other major elements of the Cold War program of travel control [area restrictions and a penalty for travel without a passport]. In sum, not only the holding but also the underlying policies of *Kent* have received congressional endorsement. This is of critical importance, because both *Kent* and *Agee* proceed from the premise that the President's power flows from Congress. Indeed, even if the President did have some inherent power in the area, that power would be greatly diminished by Congressional disapproval."

2. *A rationale for the right to travel.* Consider Ely, supra, at 178–79: "The right at issue in the modern cases [is] not simply a right to travel to or through a state but rather a right to move there—the right, if you will, to relocate. [To] a large extent America was founded by persons escaping from environments they found oppressive. Mobility was quite free during the colonial period, and '[a]s a result, most colonials who dissented from their own community's conception of right and justice could move without great difficulty to a more congenial community.' And of course the symbolism, and indeed the reality, of 'the frontier' took much of its sustenance from the notion that a person should have the option of pulling up stakes and starting over elsewhere. [I think this tradition] points us in the right direction, one that associates the right to relocate not with the idea that it is some kind of handmaiden of majoritarian democracy but, quite to the contrary, with the notion that one should have an option of escaping an incompatible majority. [A dissenting member of a community] should have the option of exiting and relocating in a community whose values he or she finds more compatible. [I]t's an old idea, dating back at least as far as Rousseau's 'droit d'emigration': it's just that the Court hasn't fixed on it. That is unfortunate, since it provides something the Court hasn't, a rationale for the right to travel it in fact has established."

See also Tribe 2d ed., at 1383–84: "[C]lose surveillance and control of travel in both its senses [as an aspect of expression or education and as a means of changing one's residence and starting life anew] has always been a central technique of the totalitarian state, but centuries of experience should suffice to mark as especially suspect any governmental measure designed to prevent the emigration of those dissatisfied with the existing order, or the immigration of those who might alter the status quo. Just as government should be forbidden to expel the citizen who has become a source of unrest, so it cannot be permitted to imprison the citizen who seeks freedom in another land."

SECTION 4. THE DEATH PENALTY AND RELATED PROBLEMS: CRUEL AND UNUSUAL PUNISHMENT

INTRODUCTION

"The question of capital punishment has been the subject of endless discussion and will probably never be settled so long as men believe in punishment. [The] reasons why it cannot be settled are plain. There is first of all no agreement as to the objects of punishment. Next there is no way to determine the results of punishment. [Moreover,] questions of this sort, or perhaps of any sort, are not settled by reason; they are settled by prejudices and sentiments or by emotion. When they are settled they do not stay settled, for the emotions change as new stimuli are applied to the machine."

—Clarence Darrow, *Crime, Its Cause and Treatment* 166 (1922).

At the time he made it, Darrow's prediction that the question of capital punishment "will probably never be settled" appeared well-founded. That the issue might ever be settled as a matter of constitutional law seemed almost inconceivable. The Court had already specifically sanctioned death by firing squad and by electrocution. Indeed, 25 years after Darrow's remarks, *Louisiana ex rel. Francis v. Resweber,* 329 U.S. 459, 67 S.Ct. 374, 91 L.Ed. 422 (1947), sustained what the dissenters called the horror of "death by installments." (After a first attempt to electrocute petitioner had failed because of mechanical difficulties, the state strapped him in the electric chair a second time and threw the switch again.) And in the 1950s the Court twice upheld the execution of men whose sanity was in doubt, leaving the question to the judgment of a governor and a warden. See Yale Kamisar, *The Reincarnation of the Death Penalty: Is it Possible?* Student Lawyer, May 1973, pp. 22–23.

In *Trop v. Dulles,* 356 U.S. 86, 78 S.Ct. 590, 2 L.Ed.2d 630 (1958), speaking for four justices, (Brennan, J., had found the "expatriation" provision invalid on other grounds), Warren, C.J., deemed deprivation of a native-born American's citizenship because of wartime desertion from the army—leaving him "stateless"—a "fate forbidden by the principle of civilized treatment guaranteed by the Eighth Amendment," but was quick to add: "[W]hatever the arguments may be against the [death penalty, it] has been employed throughout our history, and, in a day when it is still widely accepted, it cannot be said to violate the constitutional concept of cruelty." As late as 1968, a close student of the problem, observed: "[N]ot a single death penalty statute, not a single statutorily imposed mode of execution, not a single attempted execution has ever been held by any court to be 'cruel and unusual punishment' under any state or federal constitution. Nothing less than a mighty counterthrust would appear to be required to alter the direction of these decisions." Hugo Bedau, *The Courts, the Constitution, and Capital Punishment,* 1968 Utah L.Rev. 201.

In the 1960s the NAACP Legal Defense and Educational Fund, Inc. (LDF), led by Professor Anthony Amsterdam, did launch a major constitutional assault on the death penalty. Convinced that "each year the United States went without executions, the more hollow would ring claims that the American people could not do without them" and that "the longer death-row inmates waited, the greater their numbers, the more difficult it would be for the courts to permit the first execution," the LDF developed a "moratorium strategy," creating "a death-row logjam." Michael Meltsner, *Cruel and Unusual: The Supreme Court and Capital Punishment* 107 (1973). Largely as a result of LDF efforts in blocking all executions on every conceivable legal ground, when the Court handed down *Furman,* infra, in 1972, there had not been a single execution in five years. Actually, the number of executions had started to decline as early as the 1940s and had dropped dramatically in the 1960s, several years before the LDF had successfully developed its moratorium strategy. After peaking in the 1930s (152 per year during this decade, and reaching an all-time high of 199 executions in 1935), the annual rate of executions averaged 128 in the 1940s and 72 in the 1950s. There were only 21 executions in 1963, 15 in 1964 and a mere seven in 1965. (In the 1930–50 period, executions had averaged more than ten *a month*). See D. Baldus, G. Woodworth & C. Pulaski, *Equal Justice and the Death Penalty* 9 (1990); Jack Greenberg, *Capital Punishment as a System,* 91 Yale L.J. 908, 924–25 (1982).

I. IS THE DEATH PENALTY ALWAYS—OR EVER—"CRUEL AND UNUSUAL"?

FURMAN v. GEORGIA, 408 U.S. 238, 92 S.Ct. 2726, 33 L.Ed.2d 346 (1972), considered the death sentence in three cases (all involving black defendants), two dealing with a murderer and rapist in Georgia, the third a rapist in Texas.[a] (Each had been sentenced to death after trial by jury. Under the applicable state statutes, the judge or jury had discretion to impose the death penalty.) also at stake, however, were the lives of almost 600 condemned persons who had "piled up" in "death rows" throughout the land in recent years. Striking down the laws of 39 states[b] and various federal statutory provisions, a 5–4 majority, per curiam, held that "the imposition and carrying out" of the death penalty under the current arbitrarily and randomly administered system constitutes "cruel and unusual" punishment in violation of the eighth and fourteenth amendments. Each of the justices wrote a separate concurring or dissenting opinion explaining his reasons for invalidating or upholding the death penalty. (The nine opinions totaled 230 pages in the official reports.) *Furman* has been called "not so much a case as a badly orchestrated opera, with nine characters taking turns to offer their own arias." Robert Weisberg, *Deregulating Death,* 1983 Sup.Ct.Rev. 305, 315.

The pivotal opinions of Stewart and White, JJ., left open the question whether *any* system of capital punishment, as opposed to the presently capriciously administered one, would be unconstitutional. A third member of the majority, Douglas, J., also reserved for another day whether a nondiscriminatorily operated mandatory death penalty would be constitutional.

STEWART, J.: "If we were reviewing death sentences imposed under [laws making death the mandatory punishment for every person convicted of engaging in certain designated criminal conduct] we would be faced with the need to decide

---

a. Since 1930, murder and rape had accounted for nearly 99% of total executions and murder alone for about 87%. But various jurisdictions also permitted capital punishment for other crimes, e.g., kidnapping, treason, espionage, aircraft piracy.

b. Forty states authorized capital punishment for a variety of crimes, but since Rhode Island's only capital statute, murder by a life term prisoner, carried a mandatory death sentence, it was not invalidated by the instant case.

whether capital punishment is unconstitutional for all crimes and under all circumstances. We would need to decide whether a legislature—state or federal— could constitutionally determine that certain criminal conduct is so atrocious that society's interest in deterrence and retribution wholly outweighs any consider- ations of reform or rehabilitation of the perpetrator, and that, despite the inconclusive empirical evidence, only the automatic penalty of death will provide maximum deterrence.

"On that score I would say only that I cannot agree that retribution is a constitutionally impermissible ingredient in the imposition of punishment. The instinct for retribution is part of the nature of man, and channeling that instinct in the administration of criminal justice serves an important purpose in promoting the stability of a society governed by law. When people begin to believe that organized society is unwilling or unable to impose upon criminal offenders the punishment they 'deserve,' then there are sown the seeds of anarchy—of self-help, vigilante justice, and lynch law.

"The constitutionality of capital punishment in the abstract is not, however, before us in these cases. For the Georgia and Texas legislatures have not provided that the death penalty shall be imposed upon all those who are found guilty of forcible rape [or] murder. In a word, neither State has made a legislative determination that forcible rape and murder can be deterred only by imposing the penalty of death upon all who perpetrate those offenses. As [concurring] Justice White so tellingly puts it, the 'legislative will is not frustrated if the penalty is never imposed.'

"Instead, the death sentences now before us are the product of a legal system that brings them, I believe, within the very core of the Eighth Amendment's guarantee against cruel and unusual punishments, a guarantee applicable against the States through the Fourteenth Amendment. In the first place, it is clear that these sentences are 'cruel' in the sense that they excessively go beyond, not in degree but in kind, the punishments that the state legislatures have determined to be necessary. In the second place, it is equally clear that these sentences are 'unusual' in the sense that the penalty of death is infrequently imposed for murder, and that its imposition for rape is extraordinarily rare. But I do not rest my conclusion upon these two propositions alone.

"These death sentences are cruel and unusual in the same way that being struck by lightning is cruel and unusual. For, of all the people convicted of rapes and murders in 1967 and 1968, many just as reprehensible as these, the petition- ers are among a capriciously selected random handful upon whom the sentence of death has in fact been imposed. My concurring Brothers have demonstrated that, if any basis can be discerned for the selection of these few to be sentenced to die, it is the constitutionally impermissible basis of race. But racial discrimination has not been proved, and I put it to one side. I simply conclude that the Eighth and Fourteenth Amendments cannot tolerate the inflicting of a sentence of death under legal systems that permit this unique penalty to be so wantonly and so freakishly imposed."

WHITE, J.: "The imposition and execution of the death penalty are obviously cruel in the dictionary sense. But the penalty has not been considered cruel and unusual punishment in the constitutional sense because it was thought justified by the social ends it was deemed to serve. At the moment that it ceases realistically to further these purposes, however, the emerging question is whether its imposition in such circumstances would violate the Eighth Amendment. It is my view that it would, for its imposition would then be the pointless and needless extinction of life with only marginal contributions to any discernible social or public purposes. A penalty with such negligible returns to the State would be patently excessive and cruel and unusual punishment violative of the Eighth Amendment.

"It is also my judgment that this point has been reached with respect to capital punishment as it is presently administered under the statutes involved in these cases. [A]s the statutes before us are now administered, the penalty is so infrequently imposed that the threat of execution is too attenuated to be of substantial service to criminal justice.

" * * * I must arrive at judgment; and I can do no more than state a conclusion based on 10 years of almost daily exposure to the facts and circumstances of hundreds and hundreds of federal and state criminal cases involving crimes for which death is the authorized penalty. [T]he death penalty is exacted with great infrequency even for the most atrocious crimes [and] there is no meaningful basis for distinguishing the few cases in which it is imposed from the many cases in which it is not.[c] The short of it is that the policy of vesting sentencing authority primarily in juries—a decision largely motivated by the desire to mitigate the harshness of the law and to bring community judgment to bear on the sentence as well as guilt or innocence—has so effectively achieved its aims that capital punishment within the confines of the statutes now before us has for all practical purposes run its course.

"[P]ast and present legislative judgment with respect to the death penalty loses much of its force when viewed in light of the recurring practice of delegating sentencing authority to the jury and the fact that a jury, in its own discretion and without violating its trust or any statutory policy, may refuse to impose the death penalty no matter what the circumstances of the crime. Legislative 'policy' is thus necessarily defined not by what is legislatively authorized but by what juries and judges do in exercising the discretion so regularly conferred upon them. In my judgment what was done in these cases violated the Eighth Amendment."

Douglas, J.: "The words 'cruel and unusual' certainly include penalties that are barbaric. But the words, at least when read in light of the English proscription against selective and irregular use of penalties, suggest that it is 'cruel and unusual' to apply the death penalty—or any other penalty—selectively to minorities whose numbers are few, who are outcasts of society, and who are unpopular, but whom society is willing to see suffer though it would not countenance general application of the same penalty across the board. * * *

"[T]hese discretionary statutes are unconstitutional in their operation. They are pregnant with discrimination and discrimination is an ingredient not compatible with the idea of equal protection of the laws that is implicit in the ban on 'cruel and unusual' punishments."

As Brennan, J., perceived the question, there are four principles "recognized in our cases and inherent in" the eighth amendment prohibition "sufficient to

---

c. But consider Carol Vance, *The Death Penalty after Furman,* 48 Notre Dame Law. 850, 858 (1973): "Actually there is a fairly universal consensus on which cases should receive the harshest penalties. [It] is only in the bizarre murder, the killing for hire or during another serious crime, and a few other isolated instances that the people of this country want to see the death penalty applied. [Any prosecutor] (as well as any judge or defense attorney) can listen to a set of facts and tell you whether it is a death penalty case. [T]here *should* be very few death penalty sentences. Only a very few cases warrant this extreme measure. It takes two essential [ingredients]: (1) overwhelming proof [of] guilt and (2) an extremely aggravated fact situation. What is so surprising is Justice White's and Justice Stewart's conclusion that there is something highly improper in so few people receiving the death penalty."

permit a judicial determination whether a challenged punishment" "does not comport with human dignity" and therefore is "cruel and unusual": (1) "a punishment must not be so severe as to be degrading to the dignity of human beings"; (2) the government "must not arbitrarily inflict a severe punishment"; (3) "a severe punishment must not be unacceptable to contemporary society"; and (4) "a severe punishment must not be excessive," i.e., "unnecessary." Applying the first and "primary" principle, he concluded that capital punishment "involves by its very nature a denial of the executed person's humanity" and, in comparison to all other punishments today, "is uniquely degrading to human dignity." He "would not hesitate to hold, on that ground alone, that death is today a 'cruel and unusual punishment,' *were it not that death is a punishment of longstanding usage and acceptance in this country.*" [Emphasis added.] He then turned to a discussion of the other three principles and, relying heavily upon the fact that today the death sentence is inflicted very rarely and most arbitrarily, concluded that the death penalty is inconsistent with these other principles as well. * * * "The function of these principles is to enable a court to determine whether a punishment comports with human dignity. Death, quite simply, does not."

MARSHALL, J.'s "historical foray" led to the question "whether American society has reached a point where abolition is not dependent on a successful grass roots movement in particular jurisdictions, but is demanded by the Eighth Amendment." He concluded that the death penalty constitutes "cruel and unusual" punishment on two independent grounds: (1) "it is excessive and serves no valid legislative purpose," i.e., it is not a more effective deterrent than life imprisonment; (2) "it is abhorrent to currently existing moral values."

As for the first ground: "Punishment for the sake of retribution" is "not permissible under the Eighth Amendment. [At] times a cry is heard that morality requires vengeance to evidence society's abhorrence of the act. But the Eighth Amendment is our insulation from our baser selves. The cruel and unusual language limits the avenues through which vengeance can be channeled.[d] Were this not so, the language would be empty and a return to the rack and other tortures would be possible in a given case." Nor, "in light of the massive amount of evidence before us, [showing no correlation between the rate of murder or other capital crimes and the presence or absence of the death penalty, can capital punishment] be justified on the basis of its deterrent effect."

As for the second independent ground: Although recent opinion polls indicate that Americans are about equally divided on the question of capital punishment, "whether or not a punishment is cruel or unusual depends, not on whether its mere mention 'shocks the conscience and sense of justice of the people,' but on whether people who were fully informed as to the purposes of the penalty and its liabilities would find the penalty shocking, unjust and unacceptable." He then

---

d. But consider Daniel Polsby, *The Death of Capital Punishment*, 1972 Sup.Ct.Rev. 1, 37, 39–40: "The confusion between the proposition that the death penalty deters and the proposition that it is appropriate is a fairly stable feature of retentionist argument. [I submit] that the declaration that the death penalty is a superior deterrent to serious crime, in spite of evidence to the contrary, amounts to nothing more than the expression of a value preference that, whether the penalty is a superior deterrent or not, it ought to be used. A priori, I can find nothing wrong with this value preference. It may be flinty and stern, but it does not seem to me necessarily barbaric, that someone might believe that certain criminals ought to be put to death, the inhuman brutality of their crimes being so great as to outrun all possibility of forgiveness or amends. But if the argument is to rest upon straight moralistic dogma [why] should it dress itself up in the guise of a utilitarian argument instead? [One] answer may be that retentionists would be ashamed to admit to having such values. If so, surely it is relevant to a judgment whether death is a cruel and unusual punishment." Cf. Charles Black, *Capital Punishment: The Inevitability of Caprice and Mistake* 23–28 (1974).

concluded that *if* the average citizen possessed "knowledge of all the facts presently available" (for example, that death is no more effective a deterrent than life imprisonment; "convicted murderers are rarely executed"; "no attempt is made in the sentencing process to ferret out likely recidivists for execution"; the punishment "is imposed discriminatorily against certain identifiable classes of people"; "innocent people have been executed";) "the average citizen *would,* in my opinion, find [capital punishment] shocking to his conscience and sense of justice. [Emphasis added.]ᵉ For this reason alone capital punishment cannot stand."

There were four separate dissents. BURGER, C.J., warned that "it is essential to our role as a court that we not seize upon the enigmatic character of the [eighth amendment] guarantee as an invitation to enact our personal predilections into law." As for the argument that the death penalty was "excessive" or "unnecessary," he found "no authority suggesting that the Eighth Amendment was intended to purge the law of its retributive elements" nor any basis for prohibiting "all punishments the States are unable to prove necessary to deter crime."

"Real change," maintained the Chief Justice, "could clearly be brought about [by legislatures responding to today's ruling if they] provided mandatory death sentences in such a way as to deny juries the opportunity to bring in a verdict on a lesser charge; under such a system, the death sentence could only be avoided by a verdict of acquittal. If this is the only alternative that the legislatures can safely pursue under today's ruling, I would have preferred that the Court opt for total abolition. * * *

"Quite apart from the limitations of the Eighth Amendment itself, the preference for legislative action is justified by the inability of the courts to participate in the debate at the level where the controversy is focused. The case against capital punishment is not the product of legal dialectic but rests primarily on factual claims, the truth of which cannot be tested by conventional judicial processes."

BLACKMUN, J., dissented, "personally rejoicing" at the Court's result, but unable to accept it "as a matter of history, of law, or of constitutional pronouncement."

POWELL, J.'s, dissent called the Court's ruling "the very sort of judgment that the legislative branch is competent to make and for which the judiciary is ill-equipped." He maintained that "the sweeping judicial action undertaken today reflects a basic lack of faith and confidence in the democratic process."

In a fourth dissent, REHNQUIST, J., concluded that the majority's ruling "significantly lack[ed]" the "humility" and "deference to legislative judgment" with which the task of judging constitutional cases must be approached; indeed, "it is not an act of judgment, but rather an act of will."

Notes and Questions

1. Of *"life"* and *"limb."* Consider Leonard Levy, *Against the Law* 396 (1974): "To argue as a matter of public morality or policy that the state should not take a life as a penalty for crime is an appropriate task for legislation. The

---

e. Is this a valid means of ascertaining whether "popular sentiment" or "the average citizen" abhors capital punishment? Or does Marshall, J.'s approach represent excessive speculation or inappropriate "elitism" about moral judgment? Compare Kamisar, supra, at 48, and Polsby, supra, at 23–24 with Margaret Radin, *The Jurisprudence of Death*, 126 U.Pa. L.Rev. 989, 1040–42 (1978).

responsible [Supreme Court justice] has a different task. In this case the text of the Constitution itself seemed confining, indeed, seemed to erect an insuperable barricade against acceptance of the abolitionist position. The [Eighth Amendment prohibition] appears in the same Bill of Rights that clearly sanctions the death penalty. The Fifth Amendment begins with a guarantee [that] '[n]o person shall be held to answer for a *capital,* or otherwise infamous crime, unless * * *.' The same amendment [also provides]: 'nor shall any person be subject for the same offense to be twice put in jeopardy of *life* or limb' [nor] 'be deprived of *life,* liberty, or property without due process * * *.' In 1868 the Fourteenth Amendment made an identical due-process clause applicable to the [states]. Thus, the Constitution itself in four places recognizes and permits capital punishment, a penalty that was common when the Fifth, Eighth and Fourteenth Amendments were adopted." See also Raoul Berger, *Death Penalties: The Supreme Court's Obstacle Course* 43–50 (1982). But cf. Levy, supra, at 402: "[Brennan, J.,] relegated to one of his footnotes a stunning retort to the dissenters who so heavily stressed the fact that the language of the Fifth Amendment authorized the death penalty. One of its clauses prohibited placing any person in double jeopardy of life 'or limb,' [but] Brennan asserted correctly that no one now contends that the reference to jeopardy of limb 'provides a perpetual constitutional sanction for such corporal punishments as branding and earcropping, which were common punishments when the Bill of Rights was adopted' [fn. 28]. Not one of the four dissenters took note of the point; it was irrefutable."

2. *The "analytic" and "normative" approaches of the Furman majority.* Daniel Polsby has called "the Douglas–Stewart–White approach to the Eighth Amendment 'analytic' to distinguish it from the 'normative' approach of Brennan and Marshall." He observes, Polsby, fn. d supra at 24–25: "[The analytic approach's chief virtue is at the same time its chief vice: it avoids the core normative question whether the 'evolving standards of decency that mark the progress of a maturing society' have now risen high enough to wash the death penalty away. [W]hatever the analytic approach gains in avoiding subjective and impressionistic sallies into the shadow world of language, it also fails to meet Mr. Justice Brennan's implicit objection that the Eighth Amendment—whatever it means—must mean something, and, indeed, must mean something different from the other provisions of the Constitution. The arguments of Justices Douglas, Stewart, and White seem rather intent on avoiding, if possible, that core question. Rather, they prefer to emphasize the use of the Eighth Amendment as a tool for testing whether the penalty of death is evenhandedly applied. Why they should have done this is obscure in view of the fact that existing doctrines of equal protection (which was the emphasis of the Douglas opinion) or due process of law should have furnished more than adequate ground for striking down the death penalty, once the factual premises which these three Justices proffer (relating to the arbitrariness or irrationality of the penalty's use, or in Douglas's case, to its use on despised or dispossessed minorities) are accepted.[f] To view the Eighth Amendment in those terms deprives it of a dimension which is latent in almost all of the previous [decisions]—as an independently potent moral force which is at the disposal of the least dangerous branch of government and which may be used to make the most dangerous branch a little less so."

---

f. But in *Furman* and companion cases certiorari was granted limited to the following question: "Does the imposition and carrying out of the death penalty in [these cases] constitute cruel and unusual punishment in violation of the Eighth and Fourteenth Amendments?"

GREGG v. GEORGIA, 428 U.S. 153, 96 S.Ct. 2909, 49 L.Ed.2d 859 (1976), upheld the constitutionality of Georgia's post-*Furman* capital-sentencing procedures, rejecting the basic contention that "the punishment of death always, regardless of the enormity of the offense or the procedure followed in imposing the sentence, is cruel and unusual punishment in violation of the Constitution." Stewart, Powell and Stevens, JJ., who announced the judgment of the Court and filed an opinion delivered by STEWART, J., concluded that "the concerns expressed in *Furman* that the penalty of death not be imposed in an arbitrary or capricious manner can be met by a carefully drafted statute that ensures that the sentencing authority is given adequate information and guidance. As a general proposition these concerns are best met by a system [such as Georgia's] that provides for a bifurcated proceeding at which the sentencing authority is apprised of the information relevant to the imposition of sentence and provided with standards to guide its use of the information."

Unlike the procedures before the Court in *Furman,* the new Georgia sentencing procedures "focus the jury's attention on the particularized nature of the crime and the particularized characteristics of the individual defendant. While the jury is permitted to consider any aggravating or mitigating circumstances,[a] it must find and identify at least one [of 10 statutory aggravating circumstances[b] beyond a reasonable doubt] before it may impose a penalty of death. In this way the jury's discretion is channeled. No longer can a jury wantonly and freakishly impose the death sentence; it is always circumscribed by the legislative guidelines. In addition, the review function of the Supreme Court of Georgia [which is required to review every death sentence to determine, inter alia, whether it was imposed under the influence of passion or prejudice and whether it is 'excessive or disproportionate to the penalty imposed in similar cases, considering both the crime and the defendant'] affords additional assurance that the concerns that prompted our decision in *Furman* are not present to any significant degree in the Georgia procedure applied here."

At the guilt stage (or guilt trial) of Georgia's bifurcated procedure, the jury found petitioner guilty of two counts of armed robbery and two counts of murder. At the sentencing stage, which took place before the same jury, the judge instructed the jury that it would not be authorized to consider the death penalty unless it first found beyond a reasonable doubt one of these statutorily defined "aggravating circumstances": (1) that murder was committed while the offender was engaged in the commission of "another capital felony," to-wit armed robbery; (2) the offender committed murder "for the purpose of receiving money"; (3) the murder was "outrageously or wantonly vile [in] that it [involved] depravity of the mind." Finding the first two "aggravating circumstances," the jury returned verdicts of death on each count. The Georgia Supreme Court affirmed the

---

a. The plurality pointed out that the jury is not *required* to find any mitigating circumstance in order to make a recommendation of mercy that is binding on the court, "but it must find a *statutory* aggravating circumstance before recommending a sentence of death."

b. Georgia authorized the death penalty for six categories of crime: murder, kidnapping under certain circumstances, rape, treason and aircraft hijacking. The statutory aggravating circumstances for murder include "a prior record of conviction for a capital offense" or "a substantial history of serious assaultive criminal convictions"; commission of the crime

against a police officer or fireman while performing his official duties; commission of the crime while engaged in certain other felonies; or commission of an "outrageously or wantonly vile, horrible or inhuman" murder (§ (b)(7)). *Godfrey v. Georgia,* 446 U.S. 420, 100 S.Ct. 1759, 64 L.Ed.2d 398 (1980), held that the Georgia courts had "adopted such a broad and vague construction" of the § (b)(7) aggravating circumstance as to violate the eighth and fourteenth amendments. But cf. *Walton v. Arizona,* 497 U.S. 639, 110 S.Ct. 3047, 111 L.Ed.2d 511 (1990).

convictions. After reviewing the record and comparing the evidence and sentences in similar cases, the court upheld the death sentences for the murders, but vacated the armed robbery sentences on the ground, inter alia, that the death penalty had rarely been imposed in Georgia for that crime. In rejecting petitioner's claim that his death sentence under the Georgia statute constituted "cruel and unusual" punishment, the plurality observed:

"[A]n assessment of contemporary values concerning the infliction of a challenged sanction is relevant to the application of the Eighth Amendment, [but] our cases also make clear that public perceptions of standards of decency with respect to criminal sanctions are not conclusive. A penalty also must accord with 'the dignity of man,' which is the 'basic concept underlying the Eighth Amendment.' *Trop* (plurality opinion). This means, at least, that the punishment not be 'excessive.' When a form of punishment in the abstract [is challenged], the inquiry into 'excessiveness' has two aspects. First, the punishment must not involve the unnecessary and wanton infliction of pain. Second, the punishment must not be grossly out of proportion to the severity of the crime.

"[I]n assessing a punishment selected by a democratically elected legislature against the constitutional measure, we presume its validity. We may not require the legislature to select the least severe penalty possible so long as the penalty selected is not cruelly inhumane or disproportionate to the crime involved. And a heavy burden rests on those who would attack the judgment of the representatives of the people.

"[Petitioners renew the argument made in *Furman* that 'standards of decency' have evolved to the point where capital punishment no longer can be tolerated, a view accepted only by Justices Brennan and Marshall four years ago], but developments [since] *Furman* have undercut substantially the assumptions upon which [this] argument rested. [It] is now evident that a large proportion of American society continues to regard [capital punishment] as an appropriate and necessary criminal sanction.

"The most marked indication of society's endorsement of the death penalty for murder is the legislative response to *Furman*. The legislatures of at least 35 States have enacted new statutes that provide for the death penalty for at least some crimes that result in the death of another person.[c] And the Congress of the United States, in 1974, enacted a statute providing the death penalty for aircraft piracy that results in death.

"[The] jury also is a significant and reliable objective index of contemporary values because it is so directly involved. [It] may be true that evolving standards have influenced juries in recent decades to be more discriminating in imposing the sentence of death. But the relative infrequency of jury verdicts imposing the death sentence does not indicate rejection of capital punishment per se. Rather, [it] may well reflect the humane feeling that this most irrevocable of sanctions should be reserved for a small number of extreme cases.

c. But consider Franklin Zimring & Gordon Hawkins, *Capital Punishment and the Eighth Amendment: Furman and Gregg in Retrospect*, 18 U.C.Davis L.Rev., 927, 950 (1985): The "legislative extravaganza" of post-*Furman* death penalty statutes "is reminiscent of the 'pouring panic of capital statutes' which was a feature of the history of the criminal law in eighteenth-century England. Whatever the social psychology of that development may have been, the post-*Furman* reaction in America would probably be best characterized as a typical frustration-aggression response. Like parallel incidents in school prayer and pornography, legislative backlash was entirely to be expected by anyone familiar with the history of judicial invalidation in this country."

For a useful summary of the post-*Furman* statutes, see Stephen Gillers, *Deciding Who Dies*, 129 U.Pa.L.Rev. 1, 13, 101–10 (1980).

"[H]owever, the Eighth Amendment demands more than that a challenged punishment be acceptable to contemporary society. The Court also must ask whether is comports with the basic concept of human dignity at the core of the Amendment. *Trop* (plurality opinion).

"[The] death penalty is said to serve two principal social purposes: retribution and deterrence of capital crimes by prospective offenders. In part, capital punishment is an expression of society's moral outrage at particularly offensive conduct. This function [is] essential in an ordered society that asks its citizens to rely on legal processes rather than self-help to vindicate their wrongs. 'The instinct for retribution is part of the nature of man, and channeling that instinct in the administration of criminal justice serves an important purpose in promoting the stability of a society governed by law. * * *'

"[The] value of capital punishment as a deterrent of crime is a complex factual issue the resolution of which properly rests with the legislatures, which can evaluate the results of statistical studies in terms of their own local conditions and with a flexibility of approach that is not available to the courts. Indeed, many of the post-*Furman* statutes reflect just such a responsible effort to define those crimes and those criminals for which capital punishment is most probably an effective deterrent.

"In sum, we cannot say that the judgment of the Georgia legislature that capital punishment may be necessary in some cases is clearly wrong. Considerations of federalism, as well as respect for the ability of a legislature to evaluate, in terms of its particular state the moral consensus concerning the death penalty and its social utility as a sanction, require us to conclude, in the absence of more convincing evidence, that the infliction of death as a punishment for murder is not without justification and thus is not unconstitutionally severe.

"[Petitioner contends] that the changes in the Georgia sentencing procedures are only cosmetic, [focusing] on the opportunities for discretionary action that are inherent in the processing of any murder case under Georgia law. He notes that the state prosecutor has unfettered authority to select those persons whom he wishes to prosecute for a capital offense and to plea bargain with them. Further, at the trial the jury may choose to convict a defendant of a lesser included offense rather than find him guilty of a crime punishable by death, even if the evidence would support a capital verdict. And finally, a defendant who is convicted and sentenced to die may have his sentence commuted by the Governor of the State and the Georgia Board of Pardons and Paroles.[d]

"The existence of these discretionary stages is not determinative of the issues before us. [*Furman*] dealt with the decision to impose the death sentence on a specific individual who had been convicted of a capital offense. Nothing in any of our cases suggests that the decision to afford an individual defendant mercy violates the Constitution. *Furman* held only that, in order to minimize the risk that the death penalty would be imposed on a capriciously selected group of offenders, the decision to impose it had to be guided by standards so that the sentencing authority would focus on the particularized circumstances of the crime and the defendant.[50]"

d. For a forceful statement of the view that the post-*Furman* statutes do not effectively restrict jury discretion by any real standards and that capital sentencing statutes "never will"—"no society is going to kill everybody who meets certain present verbal require-

ments"—see Charles Black, *Capital Punishment: The Inevitability of Caprice and Mistake* 67–68 (1974).

50. The petitioner's argument is nothing more than a veiled contention that *Furman* indirectly outlawed capital punishment by

WHITE, J., joined by Burger, C.J., and Rehnquist, J., concurred in the judgment: "Petitioner's argument that there is an unconstitutional amount of discretion in the system which separates those suspects who receive the death penalty from those who receive life imprisonment, a lesser penalty, or are acquitted or never charged, seems to be in final analysis an indictment of our entire system of justice. Petitioner has argued, in effect, that no matter how effective the death penalty may be as a punishment, government, created and run as it must be by humans, is inevitably incompetent to administer it. This cannot be accepted as a proposition of constitutional law. [I] decline to interfere with the manner in which Georgia has chosen to enforce [the death penalty] on what is simply an assertion of lack of faith in the ability of the system of justice to operate in a fundamentally fair manner."[e]

BRENNAN, J., dissented: "In *Furman*, I read 'evolving standards of decency' as requiring focus upon the essence of the death penalty itself and not primarily or solely upon the procedures under which the determination to inflict the penalty upon a particular person was made. [That] continues to be my view."

MARSHALL, J., also dissented: "The two purposes that sustain the death penalty as nonexcessive in the Court's view are general deterrence and retribution. [The] evidence I reviewed in *Furman* remains convincing, in my view, that 'capital punishment is not necessary as a deterrent to crime in our society.' The justification for the death penalty must be found elsewhere.

"[The plurality's view of the important purpose served by 'channeling' 'the instinct for retribution' in the administration of criminal justice] is wholly inadequate to justify the death penalty. [It] simply defies belief to suggest that the death penalty is necessary to prevent the American people from taking the law into their own hands.

"[The contention] that the expression of moral outrage through the imposition of the death penalty serves to reinforce basic moral values [also] provides no support for the death penalty. It is inconceivable that any individual concerned about conforming his conduct to what society says is 'right' would fail to realize that murder is 'wrong' if the penalty were simply life imprisonment.

"[There] remains for consideration, however, what might be termed the purely retributive justification for the death penalty—that the death penalty is appropriate, not because of its beneficial effect on society, but because the taking of the murderer's life is itself morally good. Some of the language of the plurality's opinion appears positively to embrace this notion of retribution for its own sake as a justification for capital punishment.

"[T]hat society's judgment that the murderer 'deserves' death must be respected not simply because the preservation of order requires it, but because it is appropriate that society make the judgment and carry it out [is a notion]

placing totally unrealistic conditions on its use. In order to repair the alleged defects pointed to by the petitioner, it would be necessary to require that prosecuting authorities charge a capital offense whenever arguably there had been a capital murder and that they refuse to plea bargain with the defendant. If a jury refused to convict even though the evidence supported the charge, its verdict would have to be reversed and a verdict of guilty entered or a new trial ordered, since the discretionary act of jury nullification would not be permitted. Finally, acts of executive clemency would have to be prohibited. Such a system, of course, would be totally alien to our notions of criminal justice.

Moreover, it would be unconstitutional. Such a system in many respects would have the vices of the mandatory death penalty statutes we hold unconstitutional today in *Woodson* and *Stanislaus Roberts* [infra].

e. Blackmun, J., concurred in the judgment, referring solely to his dissent in *Furman*.

fundamentally at odds with the Eighth Amendment. The mere fact that the community demands the murderer's life in return for the evil he has done cannot sustain the death penalty, for as the plurality reminds us, 'the Eighth Amendment demands more than that a challenged punishment be acceptable to contemporary society.' [Under appropriate Eighth Amendment] standards, the taking of life 'because the wrong-doer deserves it' surely must fall, for such a punishment has as its very basis the total denial of the wrong-doer's dignity and worth."

Notes and Questions

1. *The statute upheld in Jurek.* In companion cases to *Gregg,* dividing the same way, the Court upheld the constitutionality of two other state capital-sentencing procedures which, it concluded, essentially resembled the Georgia system. *Proffitt v. Florida,* 428 U.S. 242, 96 S.Ct. 2960, 49 L.Ed.2d 913 (1976); *Jurek v. Texas,* 428 U.S. 262, 96 S.Ct. 2950, 49 L.Ed.2d 929 (1976). For forceful criticism of *Jurek* and for the view that the Texas statute is "much worse than either the Georgia or the Florida statutes, bad as they are," see Charles Black, *Due Process for Death,* 26 Cath.U.L.Rev. 1, 2 (1976).

2. *Gregg, Jurek* and *Proffitt* reached the question reserved in *Furman*—"the constitutionality of capital punishment in the abstract"—and upheld it. But consider Charles Black, *Reflections on Opposing the Penalty of Death,* 10 St. Mary's L.J. 1, 7 (1978): "[T]he *only* question that actually confronts us [is] whether it is right to kill such people as are chosen by our system as it stands. [I]t doesn't really make any difference at all what I think about the abstract rightness of capital punishment. There exists no abstract capital punishment." See also Anthony Amsterdam, *Capital Punishment,* in Bedau, *The Death Penalty in America* 346, 349–51 (3rd ed. 1982).

3. *Public endorsement of the death penalty.* "The critical holding in *Gregg,*" observe Samuel Gross & Robert Mauro, *Death & Discrimination: Racial Dispari-ties in Capital Sentencing* 216 (1990), "was not the endorsement of 'guided discretion' but the decision that the use of the death penalty is consistent with 'contemporary values' and 'public attitude[s]' toward crime, and therefore that it is not constitutionally 'cruel and unusual.' By 1976 the evidence of public endorsement of the death penalty was undeniable." In 1972, when *Furman* was decided, 57% of a national sample favored the death penalty for murder. In 1976, when Gregg was decided, support for the death penalty had increased to 65%. A decade later, the level of support reached about 75% and remained at that high level for many years. See id. at 255 n. 14. (However, between 1996 and 2000— partly because of growing concern that substantial numbers of innocent defen-dants had been, and were being, sentenced to death, public support for the death penalty, although still strong, declined significantly. See p. 535 infra.)

4. *The continuing reluctance to impose the death penalty in all death-eligible cases.* "[O]ne obstacle to eliminating excessive or discriminatory death sentences under the post-*Furman* statutes," note David Baldus, George Woodworth & Charles Pulaski, *Equal Justice and the Death Penalty* 413–14 (1990), "is the continuing reluctance of prosecutors and juries to favor imposition of death sentences in all death-eligible cases. Not only is this reluctance contrary to the Supreme Court's expectations when it decided *Gregg,* but there is no practical remedy for this inaction. No one involved in the criminal-justice process is going to argue that the Eighth Amendment requires the more frequent imposition of death sentences. The fact remains, however, that when only a few of the many defendants convicted of capital murder actually receive death sentences the ability

of the selection process to operate rationally and consistently in each case undergoes substantial strain."

5. *If evidence whether the death penalty is a better deterrent than life imprisonment is "inconclusive," what follows?* Consider Amsterdam, note 2 supra, at 355: "*Because* the [Supreme Court deemed the evidence] inconclusive, [it] held that the Constitution did not forbid judgment either way. But if the evidence is inconclusive, is it *your* judgment that we should conclusively kill people on a factual theory that the evidence does not conclusively sustain?" But see Ernest van den Haag in van den Haag & Conrad, *The Death Penalty: A Debate* 69 (1983).

6. *Whatever the answer when the issue is one of legislative policy, once a state enacts a death penalty statute, is it plain who has the "burden of proof"?* The *Gregg* plurality thought so. It "presumed" the "validity" of the challenged statute, put "a heavy burden [on] those who would attack the judgment of the representatives of the people" and framed the issue in terms of whether the Georgia legislature's judgment was "clearly wrong." But see Margaret Radin, *The Jurisprudence of Death,* 126 U.Pa.L.Rev. 989, 1029–30, 1064 & n. 280 (1978): "The conjunction of the factors of irrevocability, enormity and fundamental right peculiar to the death penalty demands a searching analysis with no initial presumptions in favor of the past. The death penalty should be subject to strict scrutiny for cruelty. [If] we as a society are seriously divided on whether a fundamental interest may be invaded by the government under certain circumstances, it is morally wrong to behave as if there existed a moral consensus that justified invading that interest. [*Roe v. Wade*] recognized that in a conflict between fundamental rights of individuals and the interests of the state, questions of the validity of a moral theory concerning which there exists no consensus should be resolved against the state."

7. *"Mercy."* Consider Black, note 1 supra, at 12: "[T]he question posed is not whether [as the *Gregg* plurality put it] 'the decision to afford an individual defendant mercy violates the Constitution,' [but] whether a 'legal system' which regularly, and in great numbers, runs the death question through a gauntlet of decisions in no way even formally standard-bound, so that, at the end of the process, no one can say why some were selected and others were not selected for death, rises to due process. That is not a trivial question and it cannot [be] answered by calling it, [as Justice White does, concurring in *Gregg*], 'in final analysis an indictment of our entire system of justice.' If it is that, it is an indictment pleading to which would present some difficulty, for it is hard to find informed persons today who think very well of our 'entire system' of criminal justice. But death is unique, and the procedures we must use, having no better, in our entire system of justice—and that is really the kindest thing one can say of that system—may still not be good enough for the death choice. The Court has not really focused on and answered that question—in reason, I mean, and not by fiat." See also Radin, note 6 supra, at 1024.

But consider Ernest van den Haag, *Refuting Reiman and Nathanson,* 14 Philosophy & Public Affairs 165, 173–74 (1985): "Guilt is personal. No murderer becomes less guilty, or less deserving of punishment, because another murderer was punished leniently, or escaped punishment altogether. We should try our best to bring every murderer to justice. But if one got away with murder wherein is that a reason to let anyone else get away? A group of murderers does not become less deserving of punishment because another equally guilty group is not punished, or punished less. We can punish only a very small proportion of all criminals. Unavoidably they are selected accidentally. We should reduce this accidentality as much as possible but we cannot eliminate it."

II.   MANDATORY DEATH SENTENCES; REQUIRING CONSTRAINTS ON THE SENTENCER'S DISCRETION TO IMPOSE THE DEATH PENALTY VS. FORBIDDING RESTRICTIONS ON THE SENTENCER'S DISCRETION TO BE MERCIFUL

1.   Unlike Georgia, Florida and Texas, whose post-*Furman* capital-sentencing procedures were designed to guide and to channel sentencing authority, 10 states responded to *Furman* by replacing discretionary jury sentencing in capital cases with *mandatory death penalties*. These mandatory death statutes were invalidated in WOODSON v. NORTH CAROLINA, 428 U.S. 280, 96 S.Ct. 2978, 49 L.Ed.2d 944 (1976) and ROBERTS (STANISLAUS) v. LOUISIANA, 428 U.S. 325, 96 S.Ct. 3001, 49 L.Ed.2d 974 (1976), both decided the same day as *Gregg*. As occurred in *Gregg,* in both *Woodson* and *Roberts*, STEWART, POWELL and STEVENS, JJ., announced the judgment of the Court. (In each case, for the reasons stated in their *Gregg* dissents, Brennan and Marshall, JJ., concurred in the result.) The history of mandatory death penalty laws in this country, observed the *Woodson* plurality, reveals that the practice "has been rejected as unduly harsh and unworkably rigid." Post–*Furman* enactments were dismissed as merely "attempts [to] retain the death penalty in a form consistent with the Constitution, rather than a renewed social acceptance of mandatory death sentencing."

"A separate deficiency" of the North Carolina statute was its failure to respond adequately to "*Furman's* rejection of unbridled jury discretion in the imposition of capital sentences." In light of the widespread and persistent jury resistance to mandatory death penalties—and the high probability that many juries, despite their oaths, would exercise discretion in deciding which murderers "shall live and which shall die" under these "mandatory" statutes—North Carolina had not remedied "the problem of unguided and unchecked jury discretion" that was "central to the limited holding in *Furman*," but "simply papered over" it. Not only does North Carolina's mandatory death penalty statute provide "no standards to guide the jury in its inevitable exercise" of discretion, but "there is no way under [state law] for the judiciary to check arbitrary and capricious exercise of that power through a review of death sentences. Instead of rationalizing the sentencing process, a mandatory scheme may well exacerbate the problem identified in *Furman* by resting the penalty determination on the particular jury's willingness to act lawlessly."

Another constitutional shortcoming of the statute was "its failure to allow the particularized consideration of relevant aspects of the character and record of each convicted defendant before the imposition upon him of a sentence of death. [D]eath is a punishment different from all other sanctions in kind rather than degree. A process that accords no significance to relevant facets of the character and record of the individual offender or the circumstances of the particular offense excludes from consideration in fixing the ultimate punishment of death the possibility of compassionate or mitigating factors stemming from the diverse frailties of humankind. It treats all persons convicted of a designated offense not as uniquely individual human beings, but as members of a faceless, undifferentiated mass to be subjected to the blind infliction of the penalty of death."[a]

Dissenting, REHNQUIST, J., rejected the view that the 10 post-*Furman* mandatory death statutes represented "a wrong-headed reading [of] *Furman*. While those States may be presumed to have preferred their prior systems reposing sentencing discretion in juries or judges, they indisputably preferred mandatory capital punishment to no capital punishment at all. Their willingness to enact statutes providing that penalty is utterly inconsistent with the notion that they regarded mandatory capital sentencing as beyond 'evolving standards of decency.' "[b]

Dissenting in *Roberts* (which invalidated a Louisiana mandatory death sentence statute the *Woodson* plurality deemed fatally similar to North Carolina's), WHITE, J., joined by Burger, C.J., and Blackmun and Rehnquist, JJ., maintained: "As the plurality now interprets the Eighth Amendment, the Louisiana and North Carolina statutes are infirm because the jury is deprived of all discretion once it finds the defendant guilty. Yet in the next breath it invalidates these statutes because they are said to invite or allow too much discretion: despite their instructions, when they feel that defendants do not deserve to die, juries will so often and systematically disobey their instructions and find the defendant not guilty or guilty of a noncapital offense that the statute fails to satisfy the standards of *Furman*. If it is truly the case that Louisiana juries will exercise *too much* discretion—and I do not agree that it is—then it seems strange indeed that the statute is also invalidated because it purports to give the jury *too little* discretion by making the death penalty mandatory. Furthermore, if there is danger of freakish and too infrequent imposition of capital punishment under a mandatory system such as Louisiana's, there is very little ground for believing that juries will be any more faithful to their instructions under the Georgia and Florida systems where the opportunity is much, much greater for juries to practice their own brand of unbridled discretion."

2. *Gregg and the "mandatory death" cases.* Are *Gregg* and *Woodson* and *Roberts,* handed down the same day, reconcilable? The *Woodson* plurality points out that "instead of rationalizing the sentencing process, a mandatory scheme may well exacerbate the problem identified in *Furman* by resting the penalty determination on the particular jury's willingness to act lawlessly." But are not "these lawless juries, whose lawlessness will taint and bend a mandatory system," the very same juries who are supposed "to follow with patient care the intricacies of the Georgia and Florida statutes [upheld the same day in *Gregg* and *Proffitt*], and the unfathomed mysteries of the Texas statute [upheld the same day in *Jurek*], and base these answers on nothing but sound discretion guided by law"? See Charles Black, *Due Process for Death,* 26 Cath.U.L.Rev. 1, 10 (1976); Charles Black, *The Death Penalty Now,* 51 Tul.L.Rev. 429, 441 (1977). See also Hugo Bedau, *Are Mandatory Capital Statutes Unconstitutional?,* in *The Courts, the Constitution, and Capital Punishment* 106 (1977).

3. LOCKETT v. OHIO, 438 U.S. 586, 98 S.Ct. 2954, 57 L.Ed.2d 973 (1978), struck down a post–*Furman* statute that required the trial judge, once a verdict of

---

a. The *Woodson* Court reserved judgment on the constitutionality of a mandatory death penalty statute "limited to an extremely narrow category of homicide, such as murder by a prisoner serving a life sentence." A decade later, in *Sumner v. Shuman,* 483 U.S. 66, 107 S.Ct. 2716, 97 L.Ed.2d 56 (1987), a 6–3 majority, per Blackmun, J., held that "a departure from the individualized capital-sentencing doctrine is not justified" even in such a case.

b. White, J., joined by Burger, C.J., and Rehnquist, J., also dissented, rejecting the Court's analysis for the reasons stated in his dissent in *Roberts,* infra. Blackmun, J., also dissented in *Woodson* for the reasons stated in his *Furman* dissent. All four *Woodson* dissenters also dissented in *Roberts.*

aggravated murder with specifications had been returned, to impose the death sentence unless he found one of three narrowly defined mitigating circumstances present. A four-justice plurality, BURGER, C.J., joined by Stewart, Powell and Stevens, JJ., concluded that "the sentencer, in all but the rarest kind of capital case, [must] not be precluded from considering *as a mitigating factor,* any aspect of a defendant's character or record and any of the circumstances of the offense that the defendant proffers as a basis for a sentence less than death. [The] nonavailability of corrective or modifying mechanisms with respect to an executed capital sentence underscores the need for individualized consideration as a constitutional requirement in imposing the death sentence." Dissenting Justice REHN-QUIST protested: "By encouraging defendants in capital cases, and presumably sentencing judges and juries, to take into consideration anything under the sun as a 'mitigating circumstance,' it will not guide sentencing discretion but will totally unleash it."

4. EDDINGS v. OKLAHOMA, 455 U.S. 104, 102 S.Ct. 869, 71 L.Ed.2d 1 (1982), underscored the Court's commitment to the principle that *all* mitigating evidence must be considered by the sentencer. The defense offered in mitigation the fact that the defendant, who was 16 at the term of the murder, had a history of beatings by a brutal father and a serious emotional disturbance. Although the state statute permitted consideration of *any* mitigating circumstances, the trial judge refused to consider, as a matter of law, either defendant's emotional disturbance or the circumstances of his unhappy upbringing. The state appellate court found the excluded evidence irrelevant because it did not tend to provide a legal excuse from criminal responsibility. A 5–4 majority, per POWELL, J., vacated the death sentence: "[T]he rule in *Lockett* [reflects] the law's effort to develop a system of capital punishment at once consistent and principled but also humane and sensible to the uniqueness of the individual. [By] holding that the sentencer in capital cases must be permitted to consider any relevant mitigating factor, the rule in *Lockett* recognizes that a consistency produced by ignoring individual differences is a false consistency. [Just] as the State may not by statute preclude the sentencer from considering any mitigating factor, neither may the sentencer refuse to consider, *as a matter of law,* any relevant mitigating evidence. [The] sentencer, and [the state appellate court] on review, may determine the weight to be given relevant mitigating evidence. But they may not give it no weight by excluding such evidence from their consideration."

5. *Exacerbating the disparity in capital defendant's representation.* The sentencer need only consider and, of course, *can* only consider the mitigating evidence that is *introduced.* And the quantity and quality of the mitigating evidence presented turns largely on the skill, dedication, resourcefulness and funding of the capital defendant's attorney. See *Special Project: The Constitutionality of the Death Penalty in New Jersey,* 15 Rutgers L.J. 261, 293–94 (1984). Thus, although the penalty trial affords an able defense lawyer the opportunity to present an enormous amount of material "personalizing" and "humanizing" the capital defendant, "it also exacerbates the disparity in capital defendants' representation at trial, which, in turn, may be expected to exacerbate the death penalty's uneven application." Welsh White, *The Death Penalty in the Eighties* 69 (1987).

IS THE COURT FACED WITH TWO INCOMPATIBLE SETS OF COMMANDS?

Several months before stepping down from the Supreme Court, dissenting from the denial of certiorari in a death penalty case, CALLINS v. COLLINS, 510

U.S. 1141, 114 S.Ct. 1127, 127 L.Ed.2d 435 (1994), BLACKMUN, J., maintained that "the death penalty experiment has failed": "Experience has taught us that the constitutional goal of eliminating arbitrariness and discrimination from the administration of death can never be achieved without compromising an equally essential component of fundamental fairness—individualized sentencing. See *Lockett*. It is tempting, when faced with conflicting constitutional commands, to sacrifice one for the other or to assume that an acceptable balance between them already has been struck. In the context of the death penalty, however, such jurisprudential maneuvers are wholly inappropriate. The death penalty must be imposed 'fairly, and with reasonable consistency, or not at all.' *Eddings*.

"[From] this day forward, I no longer shall tinker with the machinery of death. For more than 20 years I have endeavored—indeed, I have struggled—along with a majority of this Court, to develop procedural and substantive rules that would lend more than the mere appearance of fairness to the death penalty endeavor. Rather than continue to coddle the Court's delusion that the desired level of fairness has been achieved and the need for regulation eviscerated, I feel morally and intellectually obligated simply to concede that the death penalty experiment has failed. It is virtually self-evident to me now that no combination of procedural rules or substantive regulations ever can save the death penalty from its inherent constitutional deficiencies. The basic question—does the system accurately and consistently determine which defendants 'deserve' to die?—cannot be answered in the affirmative. [The] problem is that the inevitability of factual, legal, and moral error gives us a system that we know must wrongly kill some defendants, a system that fails to deliver the fair, consistent, and reliable sentences of death required by the Constitution. * * *

"Experience has shown that the consistency and rationality promised in *Furman* are inversely related to the fairness owed the individual when considering a sentence of death. A step toward consistency is a step away from fairness. * * * I believe the *Woodson–Lockett* line of cases to be fundamentally sound and rooted in American standards of decency that have evolved over time. [Yet,] as several Members of the Court have recognized, there is real 'tension' between the need for fairness to the individual and the consistency promised in *Furman*. [The] power to consider mitigating evidence that would warrant a sentence less than death is meaningless unless the sentencer has the discretion and authority to dispense mercy based on that evidence. Thus, the Constitution, by requiring a heightened degree of fairness to the individual, and also a greater degree of equality and rationality in the administration of death, demands sentencer discretion that is at once generously expanded and severely restricted.

"[The] arbitrariness inherent in the sentencer's discretion to afford mercy is exacerbated by the problem of race. Even under the most sophisticated death penalty statutes, race continues to play a major role in determining who shall live and who shall die. Perhaps it should not be surprising that the biases and prejudices that infect society generally would influence the determination of who is sentenced to death, even within the narrower pool of death-eligible defendants selected according to objective standards. No matter how narrowly the pool of death-eligible defendants is drawn according to objective standards, *Furman's* promise still will go unfulfilled so long as the sentencer is free to exercise unbridled discretion within the smaller group and thereby to discriminate. ' "The power to be lenient [also] is the power to discriminate.' " *McCleskey v. Kemp* [p. 529 infra, quoting Kenneth C. Davis, *Discretionary Justice* 170 (1973).]

"[In] the years since *McCleskey,* I have come to wonder whether there was truth in the majority's suggestion that discrimination and arbitrariness could not be purged from the administration of capital punishment without sacrificing the equally essential component of fairness—individualized sentencing. Viewed in this way, the consistency promised in *Furman* and the fairness to the individual demanded in *Lockett* are not only inversely related, but irreconcilable in the context of capital punishment. Any statute or procedure that could effectively eliminate arbitrariness from the administration of death would also restrict the sentencer's discretion to such an extent that the sentencer would be unable to give full consideration to the unique characteristics of each defendant and the circumstances of the offense. By the same token, any statute or procedure that would provide the sentencer with sufficient discretion to consider fully and act upon the unique circumstances of each defendant would 'thro[w] open the back door to arbitrary and irrational sentencing.' All efforts to strike an appropriate balance between these conflicting constitutional commands are futile because there is a heightened need for both in the administration of death. [In] my view, the proper course when faced with irreconcilable constitutional commands is not to ignore one or the other, nor to pretend that the dilemma does not exist, but to admit the futility of the effort to harmonize them. This means accepting the fact that the death penalty cannot be administered in accord with our Constitution."

Blackmun, J.'s opinion produced a sharp response by SCALIA, J., concurring: "[As] Justice Blackmun [observes], over the years since 1972 this Court has attached to the imposition of the death penalty two quite incompatible sets of commands. [These] commands were invented without benefit of any textual or historical support; they are the products of just such 'intellectual, moral, and personal' perceptions as Justice Blackmun expresses today, some of which (viz., those that have been 'perceived' simultaneously by five members of the Court) have been made part of what is called 'the Court's Eighth Amendment jurisprudence.'

"Though Justice Blackmun joins those of us who have acknowledged the incompatibility of the Court's *Furman* and *Lockett–Eddings* lines of jurisprudence, he unfortunately draws the wrong conclusion from the acknowledgment [quoting Blackmun's statement about 'accepting the fact that the death penalty cannot be administered in accord with our Constitution']. Surely a different conclusion commends itself—to wit, that at least one of these judicially announced irreconcilable commands which cause the Constitution to prohibit what its text explicitly permits must be wrong.[c]

"Convictions in opposition to the death penalty are often passionate and deeply held. That would be no excuse for reading them into a Constitution that does not contain them, even if they represented the convictions of a majority of

c. Concurring in *Walton v. Arizona,* 497 U.S. 639, 110 S.Ct. 3047, 111 L.Ed.2d 511 (1990), Scalia, J., left no doubt as to which irreconcilable command must be rejected: "Our decision in *Furman* was arguably supported by [the text of the Eighth Amendment]. I am therefore willing to adhere to the precedent established by our *Furman* line of cases.

"[The] *Woodson–Lockett* line of cases is another matter. [T]hat bears no relation whatever to the text of the Eighth Amendment. The mandatory imposition of death—without sentencing discretion—for a crime which States have traditionally punished with death cannot possibly violate the Eighth Amendment, because it will not be 'cruel' (neither absolutely nor for the particular crime) and it will not be 'unusual' (neither in the sense of being a type of penalty that is not traditional nor in the sense of being rarely or 'freakishly' imposed). "[My problem] is not that *Woodson* and *Lockett* are wrong, but that [they] are rationally irreconcilable with *Furman.* [Since] I cannot possibly be guided by what seem to me incompatible principles, I must reject the one that is plainly in error."

Americans. Much less is there any excuse for using that course to thrust a minority's views upon the people. [Justice] Blackmun did not select as the vehicle for his announcement that the death penalty is always unconstitutional [one of the other cases currently before us], for example, the case of the 11–year–old girl raped by four men and then killed by stuffing her panties down her throat. How enviable [the] quiet death [of a convicted murderer] by lethal injection compared with that! If the people conclude that such more brutal deaths may be deterred by capital punishment; indeed, if they merely conclude that justice requires such brutal deaths to be avenged by capital punishment; the creation of false, untextual and unhistorical contradictions within 'the Court's Eighth Amendment jurisprudence' should not prevent them."

III. ADMINISTERING THE DEATH PENALTY IN A RACIALLY DISCRIMINATORY MANNER

McCLESKEY v. KEMP

481 U.S. 279, 107 S.Ct. 1756, 95 L.Ed.2d 262 (1987).

JUSTICE POWELL delivered the opinion of the Court.

[Petitioner, a black man, was convicted in a Georgia trial court of armed robbery and the murder of a white police officer in the course of the robbery and sentenced to death. He sought federal habeas corpus relief, contending that the Georgia capital sentencing process was administered in a racially discriminatory manner in violation of the Eighth Amendment and the Equal Protection Clause of the Fourteenth Amendment.[a] In support of his claim, petitioner proffered a statistical study by David Baldus, Charles Pulaski and George Woodworth (the Baldus study).

[This study examined over 2,000 murder cases that occurred in Georgia during the 1970s and concluded that, even after taking account of many nonracial variables, defendants charged with killing white victims were 4.3 times as likely to receive a death sentence as those charged with killing blacks. Moreover, according to this study, black defendants were 1.1 times as likely to receive a death sentence as other defendants. Thus, the study indicates that black defendants, such as petitioner, who kill whites have the greatest likelihood of being sentenced to death.

[The federal district court ruled that the Baldus study "failed to contribute anything of value" to petitioner's claim and denied relief. The U.S. Court of Appeals for the Eleventh Circuit assumed that the Baldus study "showed that systematic and substantial disparities existed in the penalties imposed upon homicide victims in Georgia based on race of the homicide victim, that the disparities existed at a less substantial rate in death sentencing based on race of defendants and that [these factors] were at work in [the county in which petitioner was tried]." Even assuming the validity of the study, however, the Court of Appeals found the statistics "insufficient to demonstrate discriminatory intent or unconstitutional discrimination in the Fourteenth Amendment context [and] insufficient to show irrationality, arbitrariness and capriciousness under any kind of Eighth Amendment analysis." Thus, it affirmed the district court's denial of habeas corpus relief.]

a. For discussion of the portion of Powell, J.'s opinion for the Court rejecting petitioner's equal protection claim, see p. 1195 infra.

[McCleskey argues, inter alia,] that the Baldus study demonstrates that the Georgia capital sentencing system violates the Eighth Amendment.[b] * * *

[O]ur decisions since *Furman* have identified a constitutionally permissible range of discretion in imposing the death penalty. First, there is a required threshold below which the death penalty cannot be imposed. In this context, the State must establish rational criteria that narrow the decisionmaker's judgment as to whether the circumstances of a particular defendant's case meet the threshold. Moreover, a societal consensus that the death penalty is disproportionate to a particular offense prevents a State from imposing the death penalty for that offense. Second, States cannot limit the sentencer's consideration of any relevant circumstance that could cause it to decline to impose the penalty. In this respect, the State cannot channel the sentencer's discretion, but must allow it to consider any relevant information offered by the defendant.

In light of our precedents under the Eighth Amendment, McCleskey cannot argue successfully that his sentence is "disproportionate to the crime in the traditional sense." He does not deny that he committed a murder in the course of a planned robbery, a crime for which this Court has determined that the death penalty constitutionally may be imposed. [He argues, rather,] that the sentence in his case is disproportionate to the sentences in other murder cases.

On the one hand, he cannot base a constitutional claim on an argument that his case differs from other cases in which defendants *did* receive the death penalty. On automatic appeal, the Georgia Supreme Court found that McCleskey's death sentence was not disproportionate to other death sentences imposed in the State. [Moreover,] where the statutory procedures adequately channel the sentencer's discretion, such proportionality review is not constitutionally required.

On the other hand, absent a showing that the Georgia capital punishment system operates in an arbitrary and capricious manner, McCleskey cannot prove a constitutional violation by demonstrating that other defendants who may be similarly situated did *not* receive the death penalty. In *Gregg,* the Court confronted the argument that "the opportunities for discretionary action that are inherent in the processing of any murder case under Georgia law," specifically the opportunities for discretionary leniency, rendered the capital sentences imposed arbitrary and capricious. We rejected this contention. * * *

Because McCleskey's sentence was imposed under Georgia sentencing procedures that focus discretion "on the particularized nature of the crime and the particularized characteristics of the individual defendant," we lawfully may presume that McCleskey's death sentence was not "wantonly and freakishly" imposed and thus that the sentence is not disproportionate within any recognized meaning under the Eighth Amendment.

Although our decision in *Gregg* as to the facial validity of the Georgia capital punishment statute appears to foreclose McCleskey's disproportionality argument, he further contends that the Georgia capital punishment system is arbitrary and capricious in *application,* and therefore his sentence is excessive, because racial

---

b. The Court noted [fn. 7]: "As did the Court of Appeals, we assume the [Baldus] study is valid statistically without reviewing the factual findings of the District Court. Our assumption that the Baldus study is statistically valid does not include the assumption that the study shows that racial considerations actually enter into any sentencing decisions in Georgia. Even a sophisticated multiple regression analysis such as the Baldus study can only demonstrate a *risk* that the factor of race entered into some capital sentencing decisions and a necessarily lesser risk that race entered into any particular sentencing decision."

considerations may influence capital sentencing decisions in Georgia. We now address this claim.

To evaluate McCleskey's challenge, we must examine exactly what the Baldus study may show. Even Professor Baldus does not contend that his statistics *prove* that race enters into any capital sentencing decisions or that race was a factor in McCleskey's particular case. Statistics at most may show only a likelihood that a particular factor entered into some decisions. There is, of course, some risk of racial prejudice influencing a jury's decision in a criminal case. There are similar risks that other kinds of prejudice will influence other criminal trials. The question "is at what point that risk becomes constitutionally unacceptable." McCleskey asks us to accept the likelihood allegedly shown by the Baldus study as the constitutional measure of an unacceptable risk of racial prejudice influencing capital sentencing decisions. This we decline to do.

[At] most, the Baldus study indicates a discrepancy that appears to correlate with race. Apparent disparities in sentencing are an inevitable part of our criminal justice system. The discrepancy indicated by the Baldus study is "a far cry from the major systemic defects identified in *Furman*." [O]ur consistent rule has been that constitutional guarantees are met when "the mode [for determining guilt or punishment] itself has been surrounded with safeguards to make it as fair as possible." Where the discretion that is fundamental to our criminal process is involved, we decline to assume that what is unexplained is invidious. In light of the safeguards designed to minimize racial bias in the process, the fundamental value of jury trial in our criminal justice system, and the benefits that discretion provides to criminal defendants, we hold that the Baldus study does not demonstrate a constitutionally significant risk of racial bias affecting the Georgia capital-sentencing process.[37]

Two additional concerns inform our decision in this case. First, McCleskey's claim, taken to its logical conclusion, throws into serious question the principles that underlie our entire criminal justice system. The Eighth Amendment is not limited in application to capital punishment, but applies to all penalties. Thus, if

---

37. * * * We have held that discretion in a capital punishment system is necessary to satisfy the Constitution. *Woodson*. Yet, the dissent now claims that the "discretion afforded prosecutors and jurors in the Georgia capital sentencing system" violates the Constitution by creating "opportunities for racial considerations to influence criminal proceedings." The dissent contends that in Georgia "[n]o guidelines govern prosecutorial decisions [and] that Georgia provides juries with no list of aggravating and mitigating factors, nor any standard for balancing them against one another." Prosecutorial decisions necessarily involve both judgmental and factual decisions that vary from case to case. Thus, it is difficult to imagine guidelines that would produce the predictability sought by the dissent without sacrificing the discretion essential to a humane and fair system of criminal justice. Indeed, the dissent suggests no such guidelines for prosecutorial discretion.

[The] dissent repeatedly emphasizes the need for "a uniquely high degree of rationality in imposing the death penalty." Again, no suggestion is made as to how greater "rationality" could be achieved under any type of statute that authorizes capital punishment. The *Gregg*-type statute imposes unprecedented safeguards in the special context of capital punishment. These include: (i) a bifurcated sentencing proceeding; (ii) the threshold requirement of one or more aggravating circumstances; and (iii) mandatory state Supreme Court review. All of these are administered pursuant to this Court's decisions interpreting the limits of the Eighth Amendment on the imposition of the death penalty, and all are subject to ultimate review by this Court. These ensure a degree of care in the imposition of the sentence of death that can be described only as unique. Given these safeguards already inherent in the imposition and review of capital sentences, the dissent's call for greater rationality is no less than a claim that a capital-punishment system cannot be administered in accord with the Constitution. As we reiterate, the requirement of heightened rationality in the imposition of capital punishment does not "plac[e] totally unrealistic conditions on its use." *Gregg*.

we accepted McCleskey's claim that racial bias has impermissibly tainted the capital sentencing decision, we could soon be faced with similar claims as to other types of penalty. Moreover, the claim that his sentence rests on the irrelevant factor of race easily could be extended to apply to claims based on unexplained discrepancies that correlate to membership in other minority groups, and even to gender. Similarly, since McCleskey's claim relates to the race of his victim, other claims could apply with equally logical force to statistical disparities that correlate with the race or sex of other actors in the criminal justice system, such as defense attorneys, or judges. Also, there is no logical reason that such a claim need be limited to racial or sexual bias. If arbitrary and capricious punishment is the touchstone under the Eighth Amendment, such a claim could—at least in theory—be based upon any arbitrary variable, such as the defendant's facial characteristics, or the physical attractiveness of the defendant or the victim, that some statistical study indicates may be influential in jury decisionmaking. As these examples illustrate, there is no limiting principle to the type of challenge brought by McCleskey.[45] The Constitution does not require that a State eliminate any demonstrable disparity that correlates with a potentially irrelevant factor in order to operate a criminal justice system that includes capital punishment. * * *

Second, McCleskey's arguments are best presented to the legislative bodies. It is not the responsibility—or indeed even the right—of this Court to determine the appropriate punishment for particular crimes. * * * Despite McCleskey's wide ranging arguments that basically challenge the validity of capital punishment in our multi-racial society, the only question before us is whether in his case, the law of Georgia was properly applied. We agree with the [courts below] that this was carefully and correctly done in this case. * * *

JUSTICE BRENNAN, with whom JUSTICE MARSHALL joins, and with whom JUSTICE BLACKMUN and JUSTICE STEVENS join in all but Part I, dissenting. * * *

II. At some point in this case, Warren McCleskey doubtless asked his lawyer whether a jury was likely to sentence him to die. A candid reply to this question would have been disturbing. First, counsel would have to tell McCleskey that few of the details of the crime or of McCleskey's past criminal conduct were more important than the fact that his victim was white. Furthermore, counsel would feel bound to tell McCleskey that defendants charged with killing white victims in Georgia are 4.3 times as likely to be sentenced to death as defendants charged with killing blacks. [The] story could be told in a variety of ways, but McCleskey could not fail to grasp its essential narrative line: there was a significant chance that race would play a prominent role in determining if he lived or died.

---

45. Justice Stevens, who would not overrule *Gregg,* suggests in his dissent that the infirmities alleged by McCleskey could be remedied by narrowing the class of death-eligible defendants to categories identified by the Baldus study where "prosecutors consistently seek, and juries consistently impose, the death penalty without regard to the race of the victim or the race of the offender." This proposed solution is unconvincing. First, "consistently" is a relative term, and narrowing the category of death-eligible defendants would simply shift the borderline between those defendants who received the death penalty and those who did not. A borderline area would continue to exist and vary in its boundaries. Moreover, because the discrepancy between borderline cases would be difficult to explain, the system would likely remain open to challenge on the basis that the lack of explanation rendered the sentencing decisions unconstitutionally arbitrary.

Second, even assuming that a category with theoretically consistent results could be identified, it is difficult to imagine how Justice Stevens' proposal would or could operate on a case-by-case basis. Whenever a victim is white and the defendant is a member of a different race, what steps would a prosecutor be required to take—in addition to weighing customary prosecutorial considerations—before concluding in the particular case that he lawfully could prosecute? * * *

[The Court] finds no fault in a system in which lawyers must tell their clients that race casts a large shadow on the capital sentencing process. [The] Court's evaluation of the significance of petitioner's evidence is fundamentally at odds with our consistent concern for rationality in capital sentencing, and the considerations that the majority invokes to discount that evidence cannot justify ignoring its force.

III.   It is important to emphasize at the outset that the Court's observation that McCleskey cannot prove the influence of race on any particular sentencing decision is irrelevant in evaluating his Eighth Amendment claim. Since *Furman*, the Court has been concerned with the *risk* of the imposition of an arbitrary sentence, rather than the proven fact of one. * * * This emphasis on risk acknowledges the difficulty of divining the jury's motivation in an individual case. In addition, it reflects the fact that concern for arbitrariness focuses on the rationality of the system as a whole, and that a system that features a significant probability that sentencing decisions are influenced by impermissible considerations cannot be regarded as rational.[1]

[The] statistical evidence in this [case] thus relentlessly documents the risk that McCleskey's sentence was influenced by racial considerations. This evidence shows that there is a better than even chance in Georgia that race will influence the decision to impose the death penalty: a majority of defendants in white-victim crimes would not have been sentenced to die if their victims had been black. [In] determining the guilt of a defendant, a state must prove its case beyond a reasonable doubt. That is, we refuse to convict if the chance of error is simply less likely than not. Surely, we should not be willing to take a person's life if the chance that his death sentence was irrationally imposed is *more* likely than not. In light of the gravity of the interest at stake, petitioner's statistics on their face are a powerful demonstration of the type of risk that our Eighth Amendment jurisprudence has consistently condemned.

Evaluation of McCleskey's evidence cannot rest solely on the numbers themselves. We must also ask whether the conclusion suggested by those numbers is consonant with our understanding of history and human experience. Georgia's legacy of a race-conscious criminal justice system, as well as this Court's own recognition of the persistent danger that racial attitudes may affect criminal proceedings, indicate that McCleskey's claim is not a fanciful product of mere statistical artifice. * * *

IV.   The Court cites four reasons for shrinking from the implications of McCleskey's evidence: the desirability of discretion for actors in the criminal-justice system, the existence of statutory safeguards against abuse of that discretion, the potential consequences for broader challenges to criminal sentencing, and an understanding of the contours of the judicial role. While these concerns

---

1. Once we can identify a pattern of arbitrary sentencing outcomes, we can say that a defendant runs a risk of being sentenced arbitrarily. It is thus immaterial whether the operation of an impermissible influence such as race is intentional. While the Equal Protection Clause forbids racial discrimination, and intent may be critical in a successful claim under that provision, the Eighth Amendment has its own distinct focus: whether punishment comports with social standards of rationality and decency. It may be, as in this case, that on occasion an influence that makes punishment arbitrary is also proscribed under another constitutional provision. That does not mean, however, that the standard for determining an Eighth Amendment violation is superseded by the standard for determining a violation under this other provision. Thus, the fact that McCleskey presents a viable Equal Protection claim does not require that he demonstrate intentional racial discrimination to establish his Eighth Amendment claim.

underscore the need for sober deliberation, they do not justify rejecting evidence as convincing as McCleskey has presented.

[The Court] also declines to find McCleskey's evidence sufficient in view of "the safeguards designed to minimize racial bias in the [capital sentencing] process." [It] is clear that *Gregg* bestowed no permanent approval on the Georgia system. It simply held that the State's statutory safeguards were assumed sufficient to channel discretion without evidence otherwise.

[The] challenge to the Georgia system is not speculative or theoretical; it is empirical. As a result, the Court cannot rely on the statutory safeguards in discounting McCleskey's evidence, for it is the very effectiveness of those safeguards that such evidence calls into question.

[In] fairness, the Court's fear that McCleskey's claim is an invitation to descend a slippery slope also rests on the realization that any humanly imposed system of penalties will exhibit some imperfection. Yet to reject McCleskey's powerful evidence on this basis is to ignore both the qualitatively different character of the death penalty and the particular repugnance of racial discrimination, considerations which may properly be taken into account in determining whether various punishments are "cruel and unusual." Furthermore, it fails to take account of the unprecedented refinement and strength of the Baldus study.

[The] Court also maintains that accepting McCleskey's claim would pose a threat to all sentencing because of the prospect that a correlation might be demonstrated between sentencing outcomes and other personal characteristics. Again, such a view is indifferent to the considerations that enter into a determination of whether punishment is "cruel and unusual." Race is a consideration whose influence is expressly consistently proscribed. We have expressed a moral commitment, as embodied in our fundamental law, that this specific characteristic should not be the basis for allotting burdens and benefits. * * *

[Finally,] the Court justifies its rejection of McCleskey's claim by cautioning against usurpation of the legislatures' role in devising and monitoring criminal punishment. [The] judiciary's role in this society counts for little if the use of governmental power to extinguish life does not elicit close scrutiny. [The Court] fulfills, rather than disrupts, the scheme of separation of powers by closely scrutinizing the imposition of the death penalty, for no decision of a society is more deserving of the "sober second thought." * * *c

---

c. In a separate dissent, Blackmun, J., with whom Marshall and Stevens, JJ., joined and with whom Brennan, J., joined in all but Part IV–B (maintaining that acceptance of petitioner's claim would not eliminate capital punishment in Georgia because "in extremely aggravated murders the risk of discriminatory enforcement of the death penalty is minimized"), concluded that if one assumes that the data presented by petitioner is valid, "as we must in light of the Court of Appeals' assumption, there exists in the Georgia capital-sentencing scheme a risk of racially based discrimination that is so acute that it violates the Eighth Amendment." But the great bulk of Blackmun, J.'s opinion was devoted to a discussion of why he believed the Georgia capital punishment system violates the Equal Protection Clause. See p. 1195 infra.

In a third dissenting opinion, Stevens, J., joined by Blackmun, J., called the majority's evident fear "that the acceptance of McCleskey's claim would sound the death knell for capital punishment in Georgia unfounded": "One of the lessons of the Baldus study is that there exist certain categories of extremely serious crimes for which prosecutors consistently seek, and juries consistently impose, the death penalty without regard to the race of the victim or the race of the offender. If Georgia were to narrow the class of death-eligible defendants to those categories, the danger of arbitrary and discriminatory imposition of the death penalty would be significantly decreased, if not eradicated."

Notes and Questions

1. *The end of doubts?* Consider Robert Burt, *Disorder in the Court: The Death Penalty and the Constitution,* 85 Mich.L.Rev. 1741 (1987): "For twenty years, the Court has struggled to determine the constitutional status of capital punishment. Broadly speaking, there have been three distinct phases in this effort: the first, beginning in 1968, when the Court announced substantial doubts about the constitutional validity of the death penalty; the second, beginning in 1976, when the Court attempted to appease those doubts by rationalizing and routinizing the administration of the penalty; and the third, beginning in 1983 and culminating [in] *McCleskey,* when the Court proclaimed the end of its doubts and correspondingly signaled its intention to turn away from any continuing scrutiny of the enterprise."

2. *The reluctance to "find" racial discrimination.* According to Randall Kennedy, *McCleskey v. Kemp: Race, Capital Punishment and the Supreme Court,* 101 Harv.L.Rev. 1388, 1418 (1988), the *McCleskey* majority manifested a "lack of concern for the feelings of blacks," an attitude that may be related to the Court's "very keen concern for the sensitivities of those—mainly whites—subject to being labeled 'racist.'" Continues Professor Kennedy:

"One of the great achievements of social reform in American history has involved the stigmatization of overt racial prejudice. But this triumph in principle has produced an unforeseen consequence in application: it is precisely the sense that racial discrimination is a terrible evil that inhibits the Justices from 'finding' it in all but the clearest circumstances. Perhaps they assume that conduct so horrible must be plainly observable. Or perhaps their sense of the shamefulness of racism is so intense that they find it difficult to burden an official or agency with the moral opprobrium that the 'racist' label connotes without absolutely positive proof of culpability."

3. *Discretion, arbitrariness and discrimination.* Although the information on discrimination and on arbitrariness was much sketchier in 1972 than in 1988, "to the extent that [comparisons] can be made, they certainly show no marked improvement. The courts' determined assertions that the pre-*Furman* problems have been solved must be seen as statements of faith rather than fact, or perhaps as wishful thinking, since the evidence, if it shows anything, shows remarkable constancy rather than change." Samuel Gross & Robert Mauro, *Death & Discrimination: Racial Disparities in Capital Sentencing* 200 (1989). "Whatever else might be said for the use of death as a punishment," warn Gross and Mauro, "one lesson is clear from experience: this is a power that we cannot exercise fairly and without discrimination."

IV. SUPPORT FOR THE DEATH PENALTY DROPS AS CONCERN ABOUT ERRORS IN THE SYSTEM GROWS

Public support for the death penalty, which had been at about 75% for many years, dropped to about 65% from 1996–2000.[a] Samuel R. Gross & Phoebe C. Ellsworth, *Second Thoughts: Americans' Views on the Death Penalty at the Turn of the Century,* in Capital Punishment and the American Future (Stephen Garvey ed. 2001) (forthcoming), point out:

a. However, in 1999, 75% of Americans took the position that "teens who kill other teens should face the possibility of the death penalty," a view that "probably reflects the continuing demonization of teenage criminals in American popular culture, especially in the wake of the massacre by two students at Co-

By the late 1990s, the crime rate had dropped considerably and the public had noticed. Moreover, capital punishment was no longer a common item on the political agenda and "support for the death penalty had become increasingly reflexive, less thoughtful, and perhaps less passionate." Against that background, stories of innocent people who had almost been executed took root and spread.

Between 1970 and 1997, some 70 defendants had been released from death row, five of them in part through the use of the newly available technology of DNA identification of blood and semen [DPIC]. In November 1998, at a conference on wrongfully convicted capital defendants held at Northwestern University, some thirty persons who had been sentenced to death for murders they did not commit shared the stage in a dramatic demonstration that this was a systematic problem. A year later, the *Chicago Tribune* published a series of articles on the administration of the death penalty in Illinois, reporting that dozens of capital defendants had been represented by attorneys who were later suspended from practice or disbarred. The newspaper articles also disclosed that dozens of murder convictions and death sentences had been based on the highly questionable testimony of jailhouse informants.

Two months later, on January 31, 2000—a short time after the thirteenth innocent inmate had been released from Illinois's death row—Governor George Ryan imposed a moratorium on executions in Illinois, a move approved by two-thirds of Illinois residents. According to the governor, he had taken this action because his confidence in the fairness of the system of capital punishment had been undermined by the findings of the *Chicago Tribune* study.

A study of the death penalty conducted by a team of lawyers and criminologists led by law professor James Liebman and released on June 12, 2000, *A Broken System: Error Rates in Capital Cases, 1973–1995*, revealed that the "overall error rate" for death sentences or the convictions on which they were based for the entire 22–year period, i.e., the proportion of fully reviewed capital judgments overturned at one of three stages (on direct appeal to a higher state court, in a state post-conviction proceeding, or on federal habeas corpus) was an astonishing 68%. The most common error, according to Professor Liebman and his colleagues, was "egregiously incompetent defense lawyering."

Recall Marshall, J.'s argument, concurring in *Furman*, that, despite what the polls show, if the average citizen possessed "knowledge of all the facts presently available" about the administration of the death penalty, he or she would find capital punishment "shocking to his conscience and sense of justice" (p. 516 supra). Comment Gross and Ellsworth:

"Justice Marshall may have been more right than we thought. In the past few years public support for the death penalty has been undercut by growing experience with one of the problems that Marshall addressed, if not the others—the condemnation and possible execution of innocent defendants. The difference in the impact of these issues may reflect the fact that people respond more strongly to concrete cases than to abstract concepts. In the context of the death penalty, this cuts both ways. On one side, advocates of capital punishment use specific stories of terrible murders to generate support for the death penalty in general. On the other, there is a great deal of evidence, from studies and from capital trials alike, that many people who support the death penalty in theory are reluctant to apply it in practice to an individual defendant with a life, a name, and a face. [As Justice Marshall maintained in *Furman*, in] the context of concrete cases, learning

lumbine High School in Colorado." Gross & Ellsworth, infra.

about the operation of capital punishment in practice does sometimes shock people's conscience, and offend their sense of justice. It helps that the issue that did it—capital convictions of innocent defendants—is identified in the public mind with DNA evidence. DNA identification is new, therefore an attractive basis for changing long-held views, and it can provide virtually irrefutable scientific proof of innocence. DNA played no role in 90% of the cases of death row inmates who have been exonerated, but that goes unnoticed."

SECTION 5. PROCEDURAL DUE PROCESS IN NON–CRIMINAL CASES[a]

I. DEPRIVATION OF "LIBERTY" AND "PROPERTY" INTERESTS[b]

"When a litigant is adversely affected entirely as a predictable consequence of procedural grossness and not as a consequence of ulterior design by government (or by its agents) to utilize constitutionally impermissible substantive standards, he is in serious difficulty. The essence of his complaint is to the felt unfairness of procedural grossness itself—that it builds in such a large margin of probable mistake as itself to be intolerable in a humane society. [But] *unlike* his freedom [of expression and religion] (sheltered by the first amendment), and *unlike* his entitlement to privacy (sheltered by the fourth and fifth amendments), [the litigant] cannot anchor a claim to freedom from procedural grossness per se in any clause of the Constitution.

"He cannot rely upon the equal protection clause, for we are here dealing with situations in which all similarly situated persons are uniformly subject to the same degree of procedural grossness * * *. Nor can one say (as doubtless is one's first impulse) that the individual's entitlement to 'due' process is obviously anchored in the very clauses sheltering due process. The difficulty is that such reasoning (ironically akin to the reasoning that created the right-privilege distinction) must imagine a clause *which in fact is not there*. It imagines that the fourteenth amendment (or the same phrase in the fifth amendment) provides something like this: 'No State [shall] deprive any person of life, liberty, property, or of due process of law, without due process of law * * *.' Alternatively, it imagines that the next clause of the fourteenth amendment provides something like this '[Nor shall any State] deny to any person [either] due process of law or the equal protection of the laws.'

"[But as the amendments] read in fact, due process is not itself a protected entitlement. [It] stands in relation to ['life, liberty, [and] property'] not as an equivalent constitutionally established entitlement, but only as a condition to be observed insofar as the state may move to imperil one of the named [interests]. [P]rocedural due process appears never to be anything more than a kind of 'constitutional condition.' It is evidently not a free standing human interest."

—William Van Alstyne, *Cracks in "The New Property": Adjudicative Due Process in the Administrative State*, 62 Corn.L.Rev. 445, 450–52 (1977).[c]

---

a. The creditors' remedies cases are briefly considered in *Flagg Bros. v. Brooks*, p. 1454 infra.

b. See also *DeShaney v. Winnebago County Dep't of Social Servs.*, p. 1463 infra.

c. But Professor Van Alstyne goes on to say at 487, that "it is plausible [to] treat *freedom* *from arbitrary adjudicative procedures* as a substantive element of one's liberty"—"a freedom whose abridgement government must sustain the burden of justifying, even as it must do when it seeks to subordinate other freedoms, such as those of speech and privacy"— "that the protected essences of personal freedom include a freedom from fundamentally

1. According to most commentators, the "procedural due process revolution" began with GOLDBERG v. KELLY, 397 U.S. 254, 90 S.Ct. 1011, 25 L.Ed.2d 287 (1970), holding that due process requires that welfare recipients be afforded an evidentiary hearing *prior* to the termination of benefits. As pointed out in Simon, fn. c supra, at 150, *Goldberg* "did not in fact present the issue of whether welfare benefits were within the 'life, liberty or property' protected by the due process clauses, because [the Social Services Commissioner] conceded that 'the protections of the due process clause apply.'[a] Nevertheless, [the Court] addressed this issue [suggesting] that whether the right to continue receiving a government benefit was within the protection of the due process clause turned upon the importance of the benefit to the individual." Thus, the Court, per BRENNAN, J., observed:

"[Welfare] benefits are a matter of statutory entitlement for persons qualified to receive them.[b] Their termination involves state action that adjudicates important rights. The constitutional challenge cannot be answered by an argument that public assistance benefits are 'a "privilege" and not a "right." ' Relevant constitutional restraints apply as much to the withdrawal of public assistance benefits as to disqualification for unemployment compensation or to denial of a tax exemption or to discharge from public employment. The extent to which procedural due process must be afforded the recipient is influenced by the extent to which he may

unfair modes of governmental action, an immunity (if you will) from procedural arbitrariness." But see Peter Simon, *Liberty and Property in the Supreme Court: A Defense of Roth and Perry,* 71 Calif.L.Rev. 146, 186 (1983). See also Rodney Smolla, *The Reemergency of the Right–Privilege Distinction in Constitutional Law,* 35 Stan.L.Rev. 69, 85–86 (1982); Stephen Williams, *Liberty and Property: The Problem of Government Benefit,* 12 J.Legal Stud. 3, 17–19 (1983).

Compare Van Alstyne, supra, with Ely, *Democracy and Distrust* 19 (1980), maintaining that the phrase "life, liberty or property" used to be, and ought to be, "read as a unit and given an open-ended, functional interpretation," meaning that the government cannot *"seriously hurt* you without due process of law" (emphasis added). But consider Timothy Terrell, *"Property," "Due Process," and the Distinction Between Definition and Theory in Legal Analysis,* 70 Geo.L.J. 861, 899–900 (1982): "[I]f the phrase seriously hurt [has] discoverable substance, then its content necessarily would develop [judicially] in the same manner that the substance of 'life, liberty, or property' has developed. [The] analysis would raise the same sort of questions previously raised about property: what is the definition of 'seriously hurt'? [And] why do we use this phrase rather than one which is more restrictive, such as 'extremely seriously hurt,' or less restrictive, such as 'slightly hurt'? That is, what is the justificatory theory for Ely's substitute phrase?

"This analysis indicates that Ely's objection to the Court's treatment of 'life, liberty, or property' is based on an apparent belief that the Court should not engage in a definitional exercise at all. In effect, he argues that the purpose of the due process clause is to protect citizens from government arbitrariness, and, therefore, that these terms should relate solely to that justification. [Ely] recognizes by his use of the phrase seriously hurt the need for a trigger mechanism that must precede any due process inquiry. Yet if arbitrariness is the evil to avoid, why have any preliminary obstacle to judicial scrutiny, much less the one he has rather casually identified?"

a. "[W]hile there were three dissents in *Goldberg* respecting the *fullness* of the procedure that government would be required to observe before terminating an allegedly ineligible welfare recipient, no one (not even the government itself, as Justice Brennan observed) dissented from the proposition that the due process clause was applicable to the case." Van Alstyne 456.

b. At this point, the Court noted [fn. 8] that "[i]t may be more realistic today to regard welfare entitlements as more like 'property' than a 'gratuity,' " citing Charles Reich, *The New Property,* 73 Yale L.J. 733 (1964), and quoting extensively from Charles Reich, *Individual Rights and Social Welfare: The Emerging Social Issues,* 74 Yale L.J. 1245 (1965). In these articles Professor Reich maintained that public employment, welfare assistance, franchises, licenses and other forms of governmental largess should be given the kind of protection afforded traditional property rights.

be 'condemned to suffer grievous loss,' and depends upon whether the recipient's interest in avoiding the loss outweighs the governmental interest in summary adjudication."

2. As observed in Henry Monaghan, *Of "Liberty" and "Property,"* 62 Corn. L.Rev. 401, 407–08 (1977), BELL v. BURSON, 402 U.S. 535, 91 S.Ct. 1586, 29 L.Ed.2d 90 (1971), "represented the high-water mark of [the] approach [that] whether an interest deserved due process clause process protection involved a simple pragmatic assessment of its 'importance' to the individual." The Court, per BRENNAN, J., invalidated a Georgia statute providing that the vehicle registration and driver's license of an uninsured motorist involved in an accident shall be suspended unless he posts security to cover the damages claimed by agreed parties in accident reports: "[Although a state could bar] the issuance of licenses to all motorists who did not carry liability insurance [or] post security, [o]nce licenses are issued, as in petitioner's case [a clergyman whose ministry requires him to cover three rural communities by car], their continued possession may become *essential* in the pursuit of a livelihood. Suspension of issued licenses thus involves state action that adjudicates *important interests* of the licensees. In such cases the licenses are not to be taken away without that procedural due process required by the Fourteenth Amendment. (Emphasis added.)

"*[Bell]* could have said that the license was sufficient to qualify as 'property,' or that a suspension of an individual's freedom to drive was a restriction on his 'liberty.' The Court said neither; the importance of the interest alone sufficed, and 'importance' was determined as a matter of federal, not state, law."

3. But "*Bell*'s latitudinarian approach to 'liberty' and 'property,' "Monaghan 408, did not prevail. Stressing that before deciding what form of hearing is required by procedural due process the Court must "determine whether due process requirements apply in the first place," i.e., whether one has been deprived of "liberty" or "property"—and in doing so "we must look not to the 'weight' but to the nature of the interest at stake"—BOARD OF REGENTS v. ROTH, 408 U.S. 564, 92 S.Ct. 2701, 33 L.Ed.2d 548 (1972), per STEWART, J., for the first time, rejected a procedural due process claim because it implicated neither "liberty" nor "property." Hired by Wisconsin State University for a fixed term of one year, and given no tenure rights to continued employment, Roth had been informed that he would not be rehired for the next academic year. The Court rejected his contention that the University's failure to give him any reason for its decision or any opportunity to challenge it at any sort of hearing violated procedural due process: "The requirements of procedural due process apply only to the deprivation of interests encompassed within the Fourteenth Amendment's protection of liberty and property. [T]he range of interests protected by procedural due process is not infinite.

"[The] State, in declining to rehire [Roth], did not make any charge against him that might seriously damage his standing and associations in his community [e.g., accuse him of dishonesty or immorality,][a] [nor] impose on him a stigma or

a. "Had it done so," noted the Court, "this would be a different case. For '[w]here a person's good name, reputation, honor, or integrity is at stake because of what the government is doing to him, notice and an opportunity to be heard are essential.' *Wisconsin v. Constantineau,* 400 U.S. 433, 91 S.Ct. 507, 27 L.Ed.2d 515 (1971)." *Constantineau* (Burger, C.J., and Black and Blackmun, JJ., dissenting on proce-dural grounds) invalidated on due process grounds a state law providing that when, by "excessive drinking," one produces certain conditions or exhibits certain traits (e.g., exposing himself or family "to want" or becoming "dangerous to the peace"), designated officials may—without notice or hearing to the person involved—post a notice in all retail liquor stores that sales or gifts of liquor to him

other disability that foreclosed his freedom to take advantage of other employment opportunities. [It did not, for example, bar him] from all other public employment in State universities.[b] [O]n the record before us,[c] all that clearly appears is that [Roth] was not rehired for one year at one University. It stretches the concept too far to suggest that [one] is deprived of 'liberty' when he simply is not rehired in one job but remains as free as before to seek another.

"[As for 'property' interests protected by procedural due process, to] have a property interest in a benefit, [one] must have more than a unilateral expectation of it. He must, instead, have a legitimate claim of entitlement to [it]. Property interests, of course, are not created by the Constitution, [but by, and] defined by existing rules or understandings that stem from an independent source such as state law—rules or understandings that secure certain benefits and that support claims of entitlement to those benefits. [But the terms of Roth's employment] specifically provided that [his] employment was to terminate on June 30. They did not provide for contract renewal absent 'sufficient cause.' Indeed, they made no provision for renewal whatsoever.[d] [Thus, although Roth] surely had an abstract concern in being rehired, [he lacked] a *property* interest sufficient to require the University [to] give him a hearing when [declining] to renew his contract of employment."[e]

4. *"The bitter with the sweet."* ARNETT v. KENNEDY, 416 U.S. 134, 94 S.Ct. 1633, 40 L.Ed.2d 15 (1974): Kennedy, a nonprobationary federal civil service employee in a regional OEO office, was removed by the Regional Director for allegedly publicly accusing the Director of bribery "in reckless disregard" of the facts. The relevant statutes provided, inter alia, that, prior to removal the employee had a right to reply to the charges orally and in writing and to submit affidavits to the official authorized to remove him (the Regional Director).[a] Instead

are forbidden for one year. But cf. *Paul v. Davis* (1976), infra.

b. "Had it done so," noted the Court, "this, again, would be a different case."

c. Roth had also alleged that non-renewal of his contract was based on his exercise of his right to freedom of speech, but this allegation was not before the Court. *Perry v. Sindermann*, 408 U.S. 593, 92 S.Ct. 2694, 33 L.Ed.2d 570 (1972), a companion case, made clear that the lack of a public employee's "right" to reemployment "is immaterial to his free speech claim." For "even though a person has no 'right' to a valuable governmental benefit and even though the government may deny him the benefit for any number of reasons, there are some reasons upon which the government may not act. It may not deny a benefit to a person on a basis that infringes his constitutionally protected interests—especially, his interest in freedom of speech."

d. But *Sindermann*, involving another state college teacher serving on a year-to-year basis whose appointment had not been renewed and who had not received a hearing, per Stewart, J., held that a "lack of a contractual or tenure right to re-employment, taken alone," does not defeat one's claim that nonrenewal of his contract violated procedural due process. Sindermann had ten years service and had alleged, but not been permitted to prove, that the college had a de facto tenure program

and that he had tenure under that program. He must, ruled the Court, be given an opportunity to prove the legitimacy of his claim of entitlement to continued employment absent "sufficient cause" "in light of 'the policies and practices of the institution.'" (Roth, on the other hand, had failed to establish "anything approaching a 'common law' of re-employment.")

e. Dissenting, Marshall, J., maintained that "every citizen who applies for a government job is entitled to it unless the government can establish some reason for denying the employment. This is the 'property' right [that] is protected by the Fourteenth Amendment and that cannot be denied 'without due process of law.' And it is also liberty—liberty to work—which is the 'very essence of the personal freedom and opportunity' secured by the Fourteenth Amendment."

Dissenting, Brennan, J., joined by Douglas, J., agreed with Marshall, J., that Roth had been denied due process when his contract had not been renewed without being informed of the reasons or given a chance to respond. Powell, J., did not participate.

a. The employee may also appeal an adverse decision to a reviewing authority within the agency. Only on appeal is he entitled to an evidentiary trial-type hearing, but if reinstated on appeal he receives full back pay.

of responding to the charges against him in a proceeding to be conducted and decided by the very person he had allegedly slandered, and who had filed the complaint against him, Kennedy instituted a federal suit, asserting that the discharge procedures denied him procedural due process because they failed to provide for a trial-type hearing before an impartial agency official prior to removal. The Court, with no majority opinion, held that the procedures satisfied due process.

The plurality opinion was by REHNQUIST, J., joined by Burger, C.J., and Stewart, J., but (as pointed out by White, J. joined by three other justices, dissenting in *Bishop v. Wood,* infra) the two justices who concurred in *Arnett,* as well as the four who dissented on this issue, rejected the plurality's analysis. As described by Van Alstyne, supra, at 582, according to Rehnquist, J., it was unnecessary to reach step two and "decide whether submitting Mr. Kennedy's fate to the judgment of his accuser was incompatible with [due process] because a close examination of Mr. Kennedy's property interest made it clear that *nothing* was in fact being taken from him to which he had *any* legally recognizable entitlement. In short, he failed at step one." Observed Rehnquist, J.:

"[A]ppellee did have a statutory expectancy that he not be removed other than for 'such cause as will promote the efficiency of the service.' But the very section of the statute [granting him that right] expressly provided also for the procedure by which 'cause' was to be determined, and expressly omitted the procedural guarantees [appellee claims]. [W]here the grant of a substantive right is inextricably intertwined with the limitations on the procedures which are to be employed in determining that right, a litigant in the position of appellee must take the bitter with the sweet."

As for appellee's contention that the charges on which his dismissal was based "in effect accused [him] of dishonesty, and that therefore a hearing was required before he could be deprived of this element of his 'liberty' ": "Since the purpose of [such a hearing] is to provide the person 'an opportunity to clear his name,' a hearing afforded by administrative appeal procedures after the actual dismissal is a sufficient compliance with [due process requirements]."

POWELL, J., joined by Blackmun, J., concurred in the result, but criticized the plurality's approach: "[The Rehnquist analysis] would lead directly to the conclusion that whatever the nature of [one's] statutorily created property interest, deprivation of that interest could be accomplished without notice or a hearing at any time. This view misconceives the origin of the right to procedural due process. That right is conferred not by legislative grace, but by constitutional guarantee. While the legislature may elect not to confer a property interest in federal employment, it may not constitutionally authorize the deprivation of such an interest, once conferred, without appropriate procedural safeguards."[b]

But after "weighing" the government's interest against the affected employee's,[c] Powell concluded that "a prior evidentiary hearing" was not required before removal. "The Government's interest in being able to act expeditiously to remove an unsatisfactory employee is substantial" and, since he would be reinstated and awarded back pay if he prevailed on the merits, Kennedy's "actual injury" would consist only of "a temporary interruption of his income during the interim."

b. This passage was quoted with approval by the Court in *Vitek v. Jones* (1980), *Logan v. Zimmerman Brush Co.* (1982), and *Cleveland Board of Education v. Loudermill* (1985), all discussed infra.

c. For a more extensive articulation of Powell, J.'s "balancing process," see his opinion for the Court in *Mathews v. Eldridge,* Part II infra.

Thus, the challenged statutes and regulations "comport with due process by providing a reasonable accommodation of the competing interests."[d]

Notes and Questions

(a) *Circumventing Goldberg.* "The only difference" between *Arnett* and *Goldberg,* comments David Shapiro, *Mr. Justice Rehnquist: A Preliminary View,* 90 Harv.L.Rev. 293, 324 (1976), "is that [in *Goldberg*] the statutes and regulations governing eligibility were not 'inextricably intertwined' with [those] providing for post-termination but not pre-termination hearings. Thus, under Justice Rehnquist's approach all the legislature would have to do to circumvent [*Goldberg*] would be to place the procedural limitations (which presumably could deny *any* opportunity to be heard at any time) in the same statutory section with the substantive provisions on eligibility. Surely, as six members of the Court seemed to agree, the effect would be to turn what looked like a landmark constitutional decision into the flimsiest of trivia."

(b) *Did Justice Powell miss Rehnquist's point?* Consider Van Alstyne at 464–65: In *Arnett,* Powell, J., "fully recognized the devastating effect of the Rehnquist treatment of the new property, [but] seemed to miss Rehnquist's point in his own reply." Recall that Powell, J., stated that the legislature "may not constitutionally authorize the deprivation of [a property interest in employment], *once conferred,* without appropriate safeguards" (emphasis added). Comments Van Alstyne: "But to speak of '[a property] interest, *once conferred,*' plainly begs the question Justice Rehnquist had raised: What 'interest' *was* 'conferred'? Show us a title or a jot of 'interest' actually 'conferred' by the legislature apart from the interest Kennedy held—the interest exactly bounded, as Rehnquist said, by the procedural provisions of the only source giving it any substance at all."

(c) *Must a government employee always "take the bitter with the sweet"?* "It is clear," comments Van Alstyne at 462, that he "need *not* [if] the bitter is a substantive restriction forbidden to government by the Constitution (which applies, of course, even when the government is operating as an employer), whether the bitter requires one to abstain from insisting upon one's first amendment rights or to relinquish one's rights to due process."

5.   BISHOP v. WOOD, 426 U.S. 341, 96 S.Ct. 2074, 48 L.Ed.2d 684 (1976), per STEVENS, J., held—over the protest of the dissenters that the majority was adopting an analysis rejected by six members of the Court in *Arnett*—that the dismissal of a city policeman implicated neither the "property" or "liberty" interests protected by due process. The City Manager of Marion, North Carolina, terminated petitioner's employment as a policeman without affording him a hearing to determine the sufficiency of the cause for his dismissal. Petitioner brought suit, contending that since he was classified as a "permanent employee"

---

d. White, J., concurring in part and dissenting in part, rejected the Rehnquist plurality's analysis and largely agreed with Powell, J.'s constitutional analysis. (Consider his opinion for the Court in *Vitek v. Jones,* infra). Although he found the pretermination procedures involved in *Arnett* generally adequate, White, J., would affirm the lower court's judgment, ordering reinstatement and backpay, "due to the failure to provide an impartial hearing officer at the pretermination hearing"—a right he maintained that the challenged statute, although silent on the matter, should be construed as requiring in this case.

Dissenting, Marshall, J., joined by Douglas and Brennan, JJ., rejected the plurality's analysis on grounds similar to Powell's, but as Marshall "balanced" the interests involved (stressing the long delay in the processing of adverse personnel actions), Kennedy was entitled to "an evidentiary hearing before an impartial decision-maker prior to dismissal."

he had a constitutional right to a pretermination hearing.[a] During pretrial discovery he was informed that he had been discharged for insubordination, "causing low morale," and "conduct unsuited to an officer."

"[T]he sufficiency of the claim of entitlement," observed the Court, "must be decided by reference to state law. The [state supreme court] has held that an enforceable expectation of continued [state employment] can exist only if the employer, by statute or contract, has actually granted some form of guarantee. [Based] on his understanding of state law, [the federal district court] concluded that petitioner 'held his position at the will and pleasure of the city.' [As the ordinance was thus construed], the City Manager's determination of the adequacy of the grounds for discharge is not subject to judicial review; the employee is merely given certain procedural rights which the District Court found not to have been violated in this case. The District Court's reading of the ordinance is tenable; [and] it was accepted by [the] Fourth Circuit. These reasons are sufficient to foreclose our independent examination of the state law issue. Under [this view], petitioner's discharge did not deprive him of a property interest protected by the Fourteenth Amendment.[b]

"Petitioner's claim that he has been deprived of liberty has two components. He contends that the reasons given for his discharge are so serious as to constitute a stigma that may severely damage his reputation in the community [and] that those reasons were false.[c]

"[In] *Roth,* we recognized that the nonretention of an untenured college teacher might make him somewhat less attractive to other employers, but nevertheless concluded that it would stretch the concept too far 'to suggest that a person is deprived of "liberty" when he simply is not retained in one position but remains as free as before to seek another.' This same conclusion applies to the discharge of a public employee whose position is terminable at the will of the employer when [prior to his instituting a law suit] there is no public disclosure of the reasons for the discharge.

"[Even if the reasons given for petitioner's discharge were false], the reasons stated to him in private had no different impact on his reputation than if they had been true. And the answers to his interrogatories, whether true or false, did not cause the discharge. The truth or falsity of the City Manager's statement determines whether or not his decision to discharge the petitioner was correct or prudent, but neither enhances nor diminishes petitioner's claim that his constitutionally protected interest in liberty has been impaired.[13] A contrary evaluation of

---

a. The relevant provision of the city ordinance provided: "*Dismissal.* A permanent employee whose work is not satisfactory over a period of time shall be notified in what way his work is deficient and what he must do if his work is to be satisfactory. If a permanent employee fails to perform work up to the standard of the classification held, or continues to be negligent, inefficient, or unfit to perform his duties, he may be dismissed by the City Manager. Any discharged employee shall be given written notice of his discharge setting forth the effective date and reasons for his discharge if he shall request such a notice."

b. In *Arnett,* noted Stevens, J., "the Court concluded that because the employee could only be discharged for cause, he had a property interest which was entitled to constitutional

protection. In this case, a holding that as a matter of state law the employee 'held his position at the will and pleasure of the city' necessarily establishes that he had *no* property interest."

c. Since the District Court granted summary judgment against petitioner, noted the Court, "we [must] assume that his discharge was a mistake and based on incorrect information."

13. Indeed, the impact on petitioner's constitutionally protected interest in liberty is no greater even if we assume that the City Manager deliberately lied. Such fact might conceivably provide the basis for a state law claim, the validity of which would be entirely unaffected by our analysis of the federal constitutional question.

his contention would enable every discharged employee to assert a constitutional claim merely by alleging that his former supervisor made a mistake.

"The federal court is not the appropriate forum in which to review the multitude of personnel decisions that are made daily by public agencies.[14] [In] the absence of any claim that the public employer was motivated by a desire to curtail or to penalize the exercise of an employee's constitutionally protected rights, we must presume that official action was regular and, if erroneous, can best be corrected in other ways. [Due Process] is not a guarantee against incorrect or ill-advised personnel decisions."[d]

BRENNAN, J., joined by Marshall, J., dissented: "Petitioner was discharged as a policeman on the grounds of insubordination, 'causing low morale,' and 'conduct unsuited to an officer.' It is difficult to imagine a greater 'badge of infamy' that could be imposed on one following petitioner's calling. [Yet the Court holds] that a State may tell an employee that he is being fired for some nonderogatory reason, and then turn around and inform prospective employers that [he] was in fact discharged for a stigmatizing reason that will effectively preclude future employment.

"The Court purports to limit its holding to situations in which there is 'no public disclosure of the reasons for the discharge,' but in this case the stigmatizing reasons have been disclosed, and there is no reason to believe that respondents will not convey these actual reasons to petitioner's prospective employers. [The stigma was not imposed until after petitioner brought suit, but] the 'claim' does not arise until the State has officially branded petitioner in some way, and the purpose of the due process hearing is to accord him an opportunity to clear his [name].

"[T]he strained reading of the local ordinance, which the Court deems to be 'tenable,' cannot be dispositive of the existence vel non of petitioner's 'property' interest. There is certainly a federal dimension to the definition of 'property' in the Federal Constitution [and] at least before a state law is definitively construed as not securing a 'property' interest, the relevant inquiry is whether it was objectively reasonable for the employee to believe he could rely on continued employment.[4] [At] a minimum, this would require in this case an analysis of the

---

14. [U]nless we were to adopt Justice Brennan's remarkably innovative suggestion that we develop a federal common law of property rights, or his equally far reaching view that almost every discharge implicates a constitutionally protected liberty interest, the ultimate control of state personnel relationships is, and will remain, with the States; they may grant or withhold tenure at their unfettered discretion. In this case, whether we accept or reject the construction of the ordinance adopted by the two lower courts, the power to change or clarify that ordinance will remain in the hands of the City Council of the city of Marion.

[But see Robert Rabin, *Job Security and Due Process: Monitoring Discretion Through a Reasons Requirement,* 44 U.Chi.L.Rev. 60, 72 (1976) "[*Bishop's* reference to] 'Justice Brennan's remarkably innovative suggestion that we develop a federal common law of property' [goes] to the heart of the matter. For if the cases beginning with *Goldberg* were not developing 'a federal common law of property

rights' it is impossible to comprehend the decisions. One would have thought that the dialogue sparked by Justice Rehnquist in *Arnett* made that clear."]

d. Smolla, first fn. c supra, 88–89, points to this "profoundly honest passage" as providing "the best insights into the motivations that underlie the Court's adoption of the entitlement doctrine."

4. By holding that States have "unfettered discretion" in defining "property" for purposes of the Due Process Clause, [the] Court is, as my Brother White argues, effectively adopting the analysis rejected by a majority of the Court in *Arnett*. More basically, the Court's approach is a resurrection of the discredited rights/privileges distinction, for a State may now avoid all due process safeguards attendant upon the loss of even the necessities of life, cf. *Goldberg,* merely by labeling them as not constituting "property."

common practices utilized and the expectations generated by respondents, and the manner in which the local ordinance would reasonably be read by respondents' employees."

WHITE, J., joined by Brennan, Marshall and Blackmun, JJ., also dissented: "The majority's holding that petitioner had no property interest in his job in spite of the unequivocal language in the city ordinance that he may be dismissed only for certain kinds of cause rests [on] the fact that state law provides no *procedures* for assuring that the City Manager dismiss him only for cause.

"[This] is precisely the reasoning which was embraced by only three and expressly rejected by six Members of this Court in [*Kennedy*]. [The] ordinance plainly grants petitioner a right to his job unless there is cause to fire him. Having granted him such a right it is the Federal Constitution,[3] not state law, which determines the process to be applied in connection with any state decision to deprive him of it."[e]

Notes and Questions

(a) Consider Van Alstyne at 468–69: "[According to the Court], Bishop, as a 'permanent employee,' had even less fourteenth amendment property than had Roth, probationary employee at Oshkosh, Wisconsin. Roth had the enforceable assurance of at least the one year of assistant professor status (which he had completed) before encountering the hazard of nonrenewal. Although unknown to him, Bishop as a 'permanent employee' literally had no job *even from day to day*, but was dependent upon the non-happening of an event (receipt of notice of dismissal from the City Manager) as a condition precedent to vest affirmatively in him each day's entitlement to his status."

(b) Does *Roth* leave the courts a role that would allow them to decide for themselves whether interests defined by the state are fourteenth amendment "property"? Compare Monaghan 440 with Simon, first fn. c supra, at 182–83.

(c) *Is there a degree of circularity to the Bishop dissent?* "If the Court were to focus on real expectations and the role a government job actually plays in someone's life," observes Tribe 2d ed., at 698–99, "then it would have to move well beyond the positivist framework it first adopted in *Bishop*. Yet the [*Bishop* dissenters do] not offer a practical alternative. [They] attempt to find a statutory

---

3. The majority intimates in [fn. b] that the views of the three plurality Justices in *Arnett* were rejected because the other six Justices disagreed on the question of how the federal *statute* involved in that case should be construed. This is incorrect. All Justices agreed on the meaning of the statute. [I]t was the constitutional significance of the statute on which the six disagreed with the plurality.

Similarly, here, I do not disagree with the majority or the courts below on the meaning of the state law. If I did, I might be inclined to defer to the judgments of the two lower courts. The state law says that petitioner may be dismissed by the City Manager only for certain kinds of cause and then provides that he will receive notice and an explanation, but no hearing and no review. I agree that as a matter of state law petitioner has no remedy no matter how arbitrarily or erroneously the City Manag-

er has acted. This is what the lower courts say the statute means. I differ with those courts and the majority only with respect to the constitutional significance of an unambiguous state law. A majority of the Justices in *Arnett* stood on the proposition that the Constitution requires procedures *not* required by state law when the state conditions dismissal on "cause."

e. In a third dissent, Blackmun, J., joined by Brennan, J., maintained that the Marion ordinance "contains a 'for cause' standard for dismissal and [thus] creates a proper expectation of privacy of continued employment so long as [the employee] performs his work satisfactorily. At this point, the Federal Constitution steps in and requires that appropriate procedures be followed before the employee may be deprived of his property interest."

entitlement to a job as a policeman. But there is a degree of circularity to their argument that there may have been 'reasonable expectations' in *Bishop* that justified a finding of a property interest: it is questionable whether a person can truly be said to 'justifiably rely' on continued employment where the person's contract or statute expressly indicates either that the employment can be terminated without cause, or that cause is theoretically required but no hearing is to be allowed. This circle can be broken only by an assertion of substantive values or norms in the name of the Constitution—norms as to what an employee, for example, is *entitled* to expect *whatever* the contract or statute may say. Indeed, breaking the circle would require an acceptance of the proposition that due process is not merely a means to the end of implementing the state's own substantive rules and allocations but either a means to some very different and larger purpose, or—as in the intrinsic approach to procedural safeguards—an end in itself."

(d) Since the civil service bureaucracy has great potential for adversely affecting constitutional rights and civil service tenure would help free lower level bureaucrats from political control, should civil service employment be recognized as constitutionally protected? Compare Mark Tushnet, *The Newer Property: Suggestions for the Revival of Substantive Due Process*, 1975 Sup.Ct.Rev. 261, 284 with Van Alstyne at 482–87.

(e) *Public employment, welfare benefits, and the "government as monopolist" theory.* Consider Terrell, first fn. c supra, at 864–65, 902–04, 907–08, "propos[ing] a threshold inquiry for determining whether a particular government entitlement should be considered a protected property interest under the due process clause[,] [the] 'government as monopolist' theory. [W]hen government acts as a 'monopolist' [then] the due process constraint is properly applied to balance the power of government over the individual's life. When the individual is not forced to deal with government, however, but chooses to do so freely and voluntarily, the constitutional protection of due process is misplaced.

"[Based] on this factor of individual choice, cases involving government employment—such as *Roth, Bishop,* and *Arnett*—and potentially other contractual relations would seem to fall generally into the permissible arbitrariness, not the due process, set. Government is rarely a monopolist in these contractual situations, as either the only available employer or the only supplier or purchaser of a particular item. [O]nce an individual voluntarily accepts a job that has less than full due process protections for termination, then the individual has indeed taken 'the bitter with the sweet' and should not be able to base a cause of action on the inadequacy of these protections. [Welfare] benefits cases, like professional licenses cases, should fall in the due process set, just as the Court concluded in *Goldberg.* [The position of welfare recipients] is probably best seen as one of forced association automatically attended by some degree of procedural protection."

6. *Reading "liberty" narrowly.* PAUL v. DAVIS, 424 U.S. 693, 96 S.Ct. 1155, 47 L.Ed.2d 405 (1976), arose as follows: After respondent Davis had been arrested on a shoplifting charge, petitioner police officials circulated a "flyer" to 800 merchants in the Louisville, Ky. area designating him an "active shoplifter." When the shoplifting charge was dismissed, Davis brought a § 1983 action alleging that the police officials' action under color of law had deprived him of his constitutional rights, by inhibiting him from entering business establishments and by impairing his employment opportunities. A 5–3 majority, per REHNQUIST, J., was unimpressed:

"[R]espondent's complaint would appear to state a classical claim for defamation actionable in the courts of virtually every State, [but he] brought his action [not] in the state courts of Kentucky, but in a [federal court]. [He contends that since petitioners are government officials] his action is thereby transmuted into one for deprivation by the State of rights secured under the Fourteenth Amendment. [It] is hard to perceive any logical stopping place to [respondent's] line of reasoning. [His] construction would seem almost necessarily to result in every legally cognizable injury which may have been inflicted by a state official acting under 'color of law' establishing a violation of the Fourteenth Amendment. [But our cases do] not establish the proposition that reputation alone, apart from some more tangible interests such as employment, is either 'liberty' or 'property' by itself sufficient to invoke the procedural protection of the Due Process Clause." Thus, no inquiry had to be made as to whether the police officials had followed adequate procedures before issuing the flyers."

The Court distinguished *Constantineau,* fn. a in *Bell v. Burson,* supra, as dependent on the fact that posting the person's name in liquor stores as a chronic drinker "deprived [him] of a right previously held under state law—the right [to] obtain liquor in common with the rest of the citizenry"—and thus "significantly altered his status as a matter of state law. [I]t was that alteration of legal status which, combined with the injury resulting from the defamation, justified the invocation of procedural safeguards." Interests "comprehended within the meaning of either 'liberty' or 'property' as meant in the Due Process Clause attain this constitutional status by virtue of the fact that they have been initially recognized and protected by state law, and we have repeatedly ruled that the procedural guarantees of the Fourteenth Amendment apply whenever the State seeks to remove or significantly alter that protected status. [But] the interest in reputation alone which respondent seeks to vindicate [is] quite different from the 'liberty' or 'property' recognized in [such decisions as *Bell v. Burson*]. [Although the interest in reputation is protected by the state by virtue of its tort law], any harm or injury to that interest, even where as here inflicted by an officer of the State, does not result in a deprivation of any 'liberty' or 'property' recognized by state or federal law, nor has it worked any change of respondent's status as theretofore recognized under the State's laws."

BRENNAN, J., joined by White and Marshall, JJ., dissented: "The Court today holds that public officials, acting in their official capacities as law enforcers, may on their own initiative and without trial constitutionally condemn innocent individuals as criminals and thereby brand them with one of the most stigmatizing and debilitating labels in our society. "[There] is no attempt by the Court to analyze the question as one of reconciliation of constitutionally protected personal rights and the exigencies of law enforcement. [Rather,] the Court by mere fiat and with no analysis wholly excludes personal interest in reputation from the ambit of 'life, liberty, or property' under the Fifth and Fourteenth Amendments, thus rendering due process concerns *never* applicable to the official stigmatization, however arbitrary, of an individual. The logical and disturbing corollary of this holding is that no due process infirmities would inhere in a statute constituting a commission to conduct *ex parte* trials of individuals, so long as the only official judgment pronounced was limited to the public condemnation and branding of a person as a Communist, a traitor, an 'active murderer,' a homosexual, or any other mark that 'merely' carries social opprobrium. The potential of today's decision is frightening for a free people."

Despite the majority's efforts to distinguish them, cases such as *Roth, Constantineau*[a] and *Goss v. Lopez,*[b] maintained Brennan, J., "are cogent authority that a person's interest in his good name and reputation falls within the broad term 'liberty' and clearly require that the government afford procedural protections before infringing that name and reputation by branding a person as a criminal. [It] is inexplicable how the Court can say that a person's status is 'altered' when the State suspends him from school, revokes his driver's license, fires him from a job, or denies him the right to purchase a drink of alcohol, but is in no way 'altered' when it officially pins upon him the brand of a criminal."[c]

(a) *"An unsettling conception of liberty."* Consider Monaghan at 424–27: "[I]t is an unsettling conception of 'liberty' that protects an individual against state interference with his access to liquor but not with his reputation in the community. * * * Defamation is a serious assault upon an individual's sense of 'self-identity,' and has from ancient times been viewed as 'psychic mayhem.' Accordingly, the Court's conclusion that such an assault implicates no constitutionally protected interest stands wholly at odds with our ethical, political, and constitutional assumption about the worth of each individual."

(b) *A defense of the result, but not the reasoning.* Consider Rodney Smolla, fn. a supra, at 841–47: "The critics of *Paul* have never explained satisfactorily how a section 1983 action is in any substantive law sense an improvement on the law of libel. [A § 1983] action shifts the substantive focus of the lawsuit away from the two issues that have always been at the core of libel actions: the truth or falsity of the defamatory language, and the conduct of the defendant in publishing it. [The] critics of *Paul* have also failed to build a convincing case for construing the fourteenth amendment as mandating an alternate federal forum for what are essentially defamation actions. [Rehnquist, J.,] might have argued, as he would eventually come to argue, that there is no need to treat deprivations of interests in liberty or property as matters of federal concern as long as the state has an adequate system in place to compensate victims of those deprivations.[d] This

a. For the view that "the heart of the complaint" in *Constantineau* was "defamation, not restriction of access to liquor," see Monaghan at 431. See also id. at 423–24; Jerry Mashaw, *Due Process in the Administrative State* 95 (1985); David Shapiro, *Mr. Justice Rehnquist: A Preliminary View,* 90 Harv.L.Rev. 293, 326 (1976); Rodney Smolla, *The Displacement of Federal Due Process Claims by State Tort Remedies,* 1982 U.Ill.L.F. 831, 839–40, 845.

b. *Goss v. Lopez,* 419 U.S. 565, 95 S.Ct. 729, 42 L.Ed.2d 725 (1975) (also discussed in Part II infra), held that students suspended from public high schools for up to ten days were entitled to procedural protections against unfair suspensions. The *Goss* Court, per White, J., pointed out that state law had established a "property interest" in educational benefits, but also recognized "the liberty interest in reputation" implicated by suspensions: "The Due Process Clause also forbids arbitrary deprivations of liberty. 'Where a person's good name, reputation, honor, or integrity is at stake because of what the government is doing to him,' the minimal requirements of the Clause must be satisfied. *Constantineau.* [If] sustained and recorded, [the charges of misconduct] could seriously damage the students' standing with

their fellow pupils and their teachers as well as interfere with later opportunities for higher education and employment. [Neither] the property interest in educational benefits temporarily denied nor the liberty interest in reputation, which is also implicated, is so insubstantial that suspensions may constitutionally be imposed by any procedure the school chooses, no matter how arbitrary."

c. Stevens, J., did not participate, but a year later, dissenting in *Ingraham v. Wright,* discussed in fn. e infra, he suggested that *Paul* "may have been correctly decided on an incorrect rationale."

d. Consider Rehnquist J.'s opinion for the Court in *Parratt v. Taylor,* 451 U.S. 527, 101 S.Ct. 1908, 68 L.Ed.2d 420 (1981). Although the state had a torts claim procedure which provided a remedy for tortious losses at the hands of the state, a state inmate brought a § 1983 action against prison officials, alleging that they had negligently lost certain hobby materials he had ordered by mail, thus depriving him of property without due process of law. The Court thought it plain that the prison officials had acted under color of state law; the lost materials constituted "property"; and that

reasoning would not have denied that reputation was a sufficiently substantial interest to deserve characterization as property or liberty; such a position would merely have held that the interest in reputation was not deprived 'without due process of law' as long as the state courts remain ready, willing and able to provide 'due process' in the form of post-deprivation compensation.

"[In *Constantineau*] the Wisconsin posting statute may very well have pre-empted the normal remedies of the common law by authorizing the very posting procedure used by the police chief against Mrs. Constantineau, in all likelihood immunizing the police chief from the 'common law process' to which the police chiefs in Kentucky were still subject. [The] constitutional fault in Wisconsin's posting statute was thus systemic. It is precisely in cases in which the state enacts a regime that allows the state to visit substantial harm on its citizens without traditional recourse to the courts for compensation that federal constitutional law *should* be activated to override that system and 'superimpose a font of tort law' on the deficient state.

the alleged loss, although negligently caused, amounted to a "deprivation." But standing alone, "these three elements do not establish a violation of the Fourteenth Amendment. Nothing in that Amendment protects against all deprivations of life, liberty, or property by the State. [The Amendment] protects only against deprivations 'without due process of law.'" The Court then addressed the question whether "the tort remedies which Nebraska provides as a means of redress for property deprivations satisfy the requirements of procedural due process" and concluded that they did.

Does *Parratt's* analysis rest on a confusion of *substantive* and *procedural* due process? Consider Richard Fallon, *Some Confusions About Due Process, Judicial Review, and Constitutional Remedies*, 93 Colum.L.Rev. 309, 310–11 (1993): "According to [*Parratt*], the prisoner presented a procedural due process claim, [but] in fact, the inmate's strongest claim sounded in substantive due process: questions of procedure aside, state officials had deprived him of property without adequate justification. Once the substantive element of the inmate's claim is acknowledged, *Parratt* cannot be rationalized as a constitutional case holding that postdeprivation remedies in state court sometimes supply all the procedural due process to which an aggrieved party is entitled. *Parratt* makes most sense if viewed as an abstention decision, which calls upon federal courts to withhold substantive due process rulings in cases in which state tort law adequately protects constitutional values."

According to Fallon at 341–42, *Hudson v. Palmer,* infra, which extended *Parratt* to intentional torts, "reflects a similar confusion of substantive and procedural due process. [In *Hudson,* the] gravamen of the claim, clearly, was that the guard had engaged in substantively arbitrary conduct and thereby deprived the claimant of constitutionally protected property."

In *Hudson v. Palmer*, 468 U.S. 517, 104 S.Ct. 3194, 82 L.Ed.2d 393 (1984), a state inmate brought a § 1983 action against a prison guard, alleging that the latter had engaged in an unreasonable "shakedown" search of the inmate's locker and cell and that, during the search, had intentionally destroyed some of his noncontraband personal property. The Court, per Burger, C.J., deemed the reasoning of *Parratt* applicable to intentional deprivation of property:

"The State can no more anticipate and control in advance the random and unauthorized intentional conduct of its employees than it can anticipate similar negligent conduct. [If] negligent deprivations of property do not violate [due process] because predeprivation process is impracticable, it follows that intentional deprivations do not [either] [provided that] adequate state postdeprivation remedies are available." Because Virginia did furnish such an adequate remedy, "even if [the guard] intentionally destroyed [the inmate's] personal property during the challenged shakedown search, the destruction did not violate the Fourteenth Amendment."

But see Tribe 2d ed., at 727–29: "[T]he magnitude of the [*Hudson*] opinion's apparent leap beyond *Parratt* seems unwarranted. It is one thing to say that no deprivation of life, liberty, or property without due process of law has occurred simply because a state agent negligently injures someone in the course of carrying out his official duties—as the Court was later to hold in *Daniels v. Williams* [474 U.S. 327, 106 S.Ct. 662, 88 L.Ed.2d 662 (1986)] and *Davidson v. Cannon* [474 U.S. 344, 106 S.Ct. 668, 88 L.Ed.2d 677 (1986)]. It is quite another thing to suggest that even an intentional abuse of state authority cannot inflict any constitutional injury unless and until the state has failed to provide redress. * * * Dirty Harry violated the Constitution even if the state made it possible for his victims to sue him. Any contrary intimation in the needlessly broad language of *Hudson* ought to be regarded as dictum, and should be reconsidered when a suitable case presents itself."

"[Rehnquist, J.,] could have finished off Davis' claim by simply pointing out that Davis continued to enjoy precisely the right and status that he always had under Kentucky law: the right to sue the police chiefs in a common law action for damages. [If] Kentucky had taken away from Davis his common law tort cause of action, *then* it would have extinguished 'a right or status previously recognized by state law.' But Kentucky did not.

"[As] much as *Paul*'s language and logic were muddled and misleading, [its] result was sound. The result, however, was not justified by the reason Justice Rehnquist gave—that Kentucky law did not extend its protection to Mr. Davis' reputation—but by precisely the opposite fact: because Kentucky law *did* protect Davis, Kentucky did nothing to violate the due process clause."[e]

7. (a) *In some situations, at least, a litigant need not "take the bitter with the sweet."* A Nebraska law, § 83–180(1), provides that if a designated physician finds that a prisoner "suffers from a mental disease or defect" that cannot be properly treated in prison the Director of Correctional Services may transfer a prisoner to a mental hospital. Jones maintained that a prisoner is entitled to certain procedural protections, including notice, an adversary hearing and provision of counsel, before he is transferred to a state mental hospital for treatment. The Court agreed, VITEK v. JONES, 445 U.S. 480, 100 S.Ct. 1254, 63 L.Ed.2d 552 (1980), per WHITE, J. The involuntary transfer of a state prisoner to a mental hospital implicates a constitutionally protected "liberty interest" and once a state grants prisoners such an interest "due process protections are necessary 'to insure that the state-created right is not arbitrarily abrogated' "—these protections "being a matter of federal law, they are not diminished by the fact that the State may have specified its own procedures that it may deem adequate for determining the preconditions to adverse official action":

"We have repeatedly held that state statutes may create liberty interests that are entitled to the procedural protections of the Due Process Clause of the Fourteenth Amendment. There is no 'constitutional or inherent right' to parole, *Greenholtz v. Nebraska Penal Inmates*, 442 U.S. 1, 7, 99 S.Ct. 2100, 2103, 60 L.Ed.2d 668 (1979),[a] but once a State grants a prisoner the conditional liberty

---

e. Professor Smolla then turns to *Ingraham v. Wright*, 430 U.S. 651, 97 S.Ct. 1401, 51 L.Ed.2d 711 (1977) (also discussed in Part II infra), a case finding that the "paddling" of students as a means of maintaining discipline in the public schools "implicates a constitutionally protected liberty interest," but concluding that the Due Process Clause does not require notice and hearing prior to imposition of corporal punishment as that practice is authorized and limited by the common law— the state's traditional common-law constraints and remedies "are fully adequate to afford due process." Comments Smolla at 847–48:

"As was true in *Paul,* in *Ingraham* state law had in place a remedial scheme that provided redress for the harm that was alleged to form the basis of the due process violation. The Court in *Ingraham* avoided the confusion of *Paul,* however, by steering clear of the notion that the existence of state tort law remedies somehow automatically displaced the due process clause. Instead [*Ingraham*] conceded the logical point that *Paul* had irrationally and

stubbornly seemed to deny, recognizing that at a threshold level, common law protection and constitutional protection could be duplicative. [U]nlike the reputational interest at issue in *Paul,* an interest without independent federal content, the liberty interest in *Ingraham* was undeniably 'constitutional'—the right to be free of physical restraint and punishment, *Ingraham* thus made it clear that state common law remedies could serve as an adequate surrogate for due process safeguards even when 'hard core' constitutional interests in property or liberty were at stake."

a. *Greenholtz* observed, per Burger, C.J., that, absent a statutory entitlement, "there is no constitutional right of a convicted person to be conditionally released before the expiration of a valid sentence. [We] can accept respondents' view that the expectancy of release provided by this statute is entitled to some measure of constitutional protection. However, we emphasize that this statute has unique structure and language and thus whether any other state statute provides a protectible entitlement

properly dependent on the observance of special parole restrictions, due process protections attach to the decision to revoke parole. *Morrissey v. Brewer,* 408 U.S. 471, 92 S.Ct. 2593, 33 L.Ed.2d 484 (1972). The same is true of the revocation of probation. *Gagnon v. Scarpelli,* 411 U.S. 778, 93 S.Ct. 1756, 36 L.Ed.2d 656 (1973). In *Wolff v. McDonnell,* 418 U.S. 539, 94 S.Ct. 2963, 41 L.Ed.2d 935 (1974), we held that a state-created right to good-time credits, which could be forfeited only for serious misbehavior, constituted a liberty interest protected by the Due Process Clause.

"[In] *Meachum v. Fano,* 427 U.S. 215, 96 S.Ct. 2532, 49 L.Ed.2d 451 (1976), and *Montanye v. Haymes,* 427 U.S. 236, 96 S.Ct. 2543, 49 L.Ed.2d 466 (1976), we held that the transfer of a prisoner from one prison to another does not infringe a protected liberty interest. But in those cases transfers were discretionary with the prison authorities, and in neither case did the prisoner possess any right or justifiable expectation that he would not be transferred except for misbehavior or upon the occurrence of other specified events.[b]

"[The] 'objective expectation, firmly fixed in state law and official penal complex practice,' that a prisoner would not be transferred unless he suffered from a mental disease or defect that could not be adequately treated in the prison, gave Jones a liberty interest that entitled him to the benefits of appropriate procedures in connection with determining the conditions that warranted his transfer to a mental hospital. [If] the State grants a prisoner a right or expectation that adverse action will not be taken against him except upon the occurrence of specified behavior, 'the determination of whether such behavior has occurred becomes critical, and the minimum requirements of procedural due process appropriate for the circumstances must be observed.' *Wolff.* These minimum requirements being a matter of federal law, they are not diminished by the fact that the State may have specified its own procedures that it may deem adequate for determining the preconditions to adverse official action. [The state's] reliance on the opinion of a designated physician [for] determining whether the conditions warranting a transfer exist neither removes the prisoner's interest from due process protection nor answers the question of what process is due under the Constitution."

(b) *Recognizing a protected 'liberty interest' independently of state law. Vitek* went on to hold that "independently of § 83–180(1), the transfer of a prisoner

---

must be decided on a case-by-case basis." Consider also Professor Nowak's criticism of *Greenholtz,* p. 566 infra.

Cf. *Connecticut Bd. of Pardons v. Dumschat,* 452 U.S. 458, 101 S.Ct. 2460, 69 L.Ed.2d 158 (1981), per Burger, C.J., rejecting the argument that "the fact that the Connecticut Board of Pardons has granted approximately three-fourths of the applications for commutation of life sentences creates a constitutional 'liberty interest' or 'entitlement' in life-term inmates so as to require that Board to explain its reasons for denial of an application for commutation."

b. *Meachum,* per Rehnquist, J., rejected the contention that "*any* change in the conditions of confinement having a substantial adverse impact on the prisoner involved" invokes due process protections, maintaining instead that the original valid conviction and imprison-

ment decision "sufficiently extinguished the defendant's liberty interest to empower the State to confine him in *any* of its prisons." *Meachum,* observes Tribe 2d ed., at 694, "was wary of subjecting to 'judicial review a wide spectrum of discretionary actions that traditionally have been the business of prison administrations rather than of federal courts.'"

See also *Olim v. Wakinekona,* 461 U.S. 238, 103 S.Ct. 1741, 75 L.Ed.2d 813 (1983), per Blackmun, J., ruling that the transfer of a state prisoner from Hawaii to a maximum security facility in California "does not deprive an inmate of any liberty interest protected by the Due Process Clause in and of itself". Cf. *Hewitt v. Helms,* 459 U.S. 460, 103 S.Ct. 864, 74 L.Ed.2d 675 (1983) (transfer of inmate from general prison population to administrative segregation implicates no liberty interest "independently protected by the Due Process Clause").

from a prison to a mental hospital must be accompanied by appropriate procedural protections": "[F]or the ordinary citizen, [an involuntary] commitment to a mental hospital produces 'a massive curtailment of liberty' [and thus] 'requires due process protection.' [A] convicted felon [as well as an ordinary citizen] is entitled to the benefit of procedures appropriate in the circumstances before he is found to have a mental disease and transferred to a mental hospital. [A] criminal conviction and sentence of imprisonment extinguish an individual's right to freedom from confinement for the term of his sentence, but they do not authorize the State to classify him as mentally ill and to subject him to involuntary psychiatric treatment without affording him additional due process protections."[c]

See also FOUCHA v. LOUISIANA, 504 U.S. 71, 112 S.Ct. 1780, 118 L.Ed.2d 437 (1992), where a 5–4 majority, per White, J., struck down a state statute permitting a person acquitted of a crime by reason of insanity who no longer suffers from a mental illness to be committed indefinitely to a mental institution until he is able to demonstrate that he is not dangerous to himself or to others. Under the Due Process Clause, a state depriving someone of liberty in this way must establish the conditions justifying commitment by "clear and convincing evidence." The Court rejected the state's contention that an insanity acquittee could be confined on the basis of his antisocial personality, a condition that is not a mental disease and that is untreatable:

"First, even if his continued confinement were constitutionally permissible, keeping Foucha against his will in a mental institution is improper absent a determination in civil commitment proceedings of current mental illness and dangerousness. [Due process] requires that the nature of commitment bear some reasonable relation to the purpose for which the individual is committed. [Second,] if Foucha can no longer be held as an insanity acquittee in a mental hospital, he is entitled to constitutionally adequate procedures to establish the grounds for his confinement. [Third,] 'the Due Process Clause contains a substantive component that bars certain arbitrary wrongful government actions regardless of the fairness of the procedures used to implement them.' "

"[A State may] confine a mentally ill person if it shows 'by clear and convincing evidence that the individual is mentally ill and dangerous.' [Here,] the State has not carried that burden; indeed, the State does not claim that Foucha is now mentally ill."

8.   (a) *A state is not free to employ such procedures as it pleases for adjudicating a claim it need not have created.* In LOGAN v. ZIMMERMAN BRUSH CO., 455 U.S. 422, 102 S.Ct. 1148, 71 L.Ed.2d 265 (1982), appellant filed a charge with the Illinois Employment Practices Commission, alleging that his employment had been lawfully terminated because of his physical handicap. This triggered the Commission's statutory obligation to convene a fact-finding conference within 120 days, but, apparently through inadvertence, the conference was scheduled five days *after* expiration of the statutory period. The state court held that the failure to convene a conference within 120 days deprived the Commission of jurisdiction to consider appellant's claim under the Illinois Fair Employment Practices Act

---

c. Cf. *Washington v. Harper,* 494 U.S. 210, 110 S.Ct. 1028, 108 L.Ed.2d 178 (1990) (also discussed in Part II infra). The Court recognized that a state prisoner had a "significant liberty interest," protected by the Due Process Clause, in avoiding the forced administration of antipsychotic drugs. Thus, such treatment could be refused unless certain preconditions were met and procedural safeguards were established to ensure that the prisoners' interests were taken into account. But the Court went on to hold that the state's administrative hearing procedures (an unconsenting prisoner was entitled to a hearing before a committee of medical professionals) satisfied procedural due process; a judicial hearing is not a prerequisite for the involuntary treatment of prison inmates.

(FEPA). The Court, per Blackmun, J., reversed, deeming appellant's FEPA claim "a species of property" protected by fourteenth amendment due process and holding that the state scheme had deprived appellant of his property right.

The Court pointed out that its recent cases had emphasized that "[t]he hallmark of property [is] an individual entitlement grounded in state law, which cannot be removed except 'for cause.' [And] an FEPA claim, which presumably can be surrendered for value, is at least as substantial as the right to an education labeled as property in *Goss v. Lopez.* Certainly, it would require a remarkable reading of a 'broad and majestic term' to conclude that a horse trainer's license is a protected property interest under the Fourteenth Amendment, while a state-created right to redress discrimination is not."

"Because the entitlement arises from statute, the [state supreme court] reasoned, it was the legislature's prerogative to establish the 'procedures to be followed upon a charge.' [This analysis] misunderstands the nature of the Constitution's due process guarantee. [B]ecause 'minimum [procedural] requirements [are] a matter of federal law, they are not diminished by the fact that the State may have specified its own procedures that it may deem adequate for determining the preconditions to adverse official action.' *Vitek.* Indeed, any other conclusion would allow the State to destroy at will virtually any state-created property interest. The Court has considered and rejected such an approach [quoting from that portion of the *Vitek* opinion quoting with approval from Powell, J.'s concurring opinion in *Arnett*]."

"Of course, the State remains free to create substantive defenses or immunities for use in adjudication—or to eliminate its statutorily created causes of action altogether—just as it can amend or terminate its welfare or employment programs [or adjust benefit levels]. [But the 120–day limitation] is a procedural limitation on the claimant's ability to assert his rights, not a substantive element of the FEPA claim."

(b) *Why can't a state "enfeeble" any entitlement it creates?* Consider Frank Easterbrook, *Substance and Due Process,* 1982 Sup.Ct.Rev. 85–86, 109–110, 120: "The process a legislature describes for vindicating the entitlements that it creates is a way of indicating how effective its plan should be. The more process it affords, the more the legislature values the entitlements and thus is willing to sacrifice to avoid mistakes. A court that protects the legislative power to define substantive entitlements ought to give it control of process as well.

"[The] Court's justification for specifying process once the statute has specified substance is that 'any other conclusion would allow the State to destroy at will virtually any state-created property interest.' This would be a good argument if the Court could explain why a state may not destroy the interest it creates, at least prospectively. But the Court has never so argued. Under the Court's decisions legislatures are free to enact precatory statutes, statutes that contain no rules of decision, retroactive statutes, statutes that lack any methods of enforcement, statutes creating absolute immunities, and otherwise to have vacuous 'entitlements.' To use some invented numbers, if states may elect ten percent reliability in enforcement (the amount of adherence to a precatory statute), why can they not elect ninety percent (the amount obtained from rudimentary procedures)? Why, in other words, is the expedient of enfeebling a statutory entitlement by providing 'deficient' procedures out of bounds? The Court's cases contain no answers to this question because they are not consistent. There is no single view that could be respected in the name of stare decisis.

"[Illinois] need not have created any right to be free of discrimination because of handicap or given the right of any particular dimensions. That being so, [Illinois] also should have been allowed to employ such procedure as it pleased for adjudicating (or not adjudicating) Logan's claim.[105]"

(c) *Why wasn't Logan's right to sue the Commission in tort for its negligence in losing his claim sufficient to satisfy due process?* The Zimmerman Brush Company had another argument in support of the Illinois Supreme Court's decision. As described in Smolla, p. 548, fn. a supra, at 860, the Company argued that even if Logan possessed an "entitlement" under Illinois law "no federal due process violation existed, because Logan could sue the Commission for damages under the Illinois Court of Claims Act for having negligently destroyed his 'property'—his [FEPA cause of action]. Logan in effect had an action for 'malpractice' against the Commission, just as he would have had an action against his own attorney if the attorney had negligently caused Logan's claim to lapse. Under the reasoning in *Parratt v. Taylor* [p. 548 fn. d supra], the Company argued, the state had not deprived Logan of property without due process since the state's own tort remedies were adequate to make Logan whole." This argument, responded the Court, "misses *Parratt's* point":

"In *Parratt,* the Court emphasized that it was dealing with 'a tortious loss [of] property as a result of a random and unauthorized act by a state employee [rather than] some established procedure.' Here, in contrast, it is the state system itself that destroys a complainant's property interest, by operation of law, whenever the Commission fails to convene a timely conference—whether the Commission's action is taken through negligence, maliciousness, or otherwise. *Parratt* was not designed to reach such a situation. Unlike the complainant in *Parratt,* Logan is challenging not the Commission's error, but the 'established state procedure' that destroys his entitlement without according him proper procedural safeguards.

"In any event, the Court's decisions suggest that, absent 'the necessity of quick action by the State or the impracticality of providing any predeprivation process,' a post-deprivation hearing here would be constitutionally inadequate. *Parratt.* [That] is particularly true where, as here, the State's only post-termination process comes in the form of an independent tort action.[10] Seeking redress through a tort suit is apt to be a lengthy and speculative process, which in a situation such as this one will never make the complainant entirely whole: the Illinois Court of Claims Act does not provide for reinstatement [and] even a successful suit will not vindicate entirely Logan's right to be free from discriminatory treatment."

(d) *The post-deprivation due process doctrine: reconciling Zimmerman Brush and Parratt.* The relationship between *Zimmerman Brush* and *Parratt,* observes Smolla at 861–62, "parallels the relationship that arguably existed between *Constantineau* and *Paul.* Random and unauthorized harm caused by the state, for

---

105. [As] the Supreme Court of Illinois saw things, the statute (effectively) allowed Logan's claim to be distinguished for no reason at all. Thus the statute gave Logan no property right. *Bishop.* The Court never told us why it was disregarding the state court's construction of the state's statute.

10. In *Ingraham v. Wright* [p. 550 fn. e supra] the Court concluded that state tort remedies provided adequate process for students subjected to corporal punishment in school, [but it] emphasized that the state scheme

"preserved what 'has always been the law of the land,'" [and] that adding additional safeguards would be unduly burdensome. Here neither of those rationales is available. Terminating potentially meritorious claims in a random manner is hardly a practice in line with our common-law traditions. And the State's abandonment of the challenged practice [after the inception of the present litigation] makes it difficult to argue that requiring a determination on the merits will impose undue burdens on the state administrative process.

which the state itself provides a remedy, does not implicate the Constitution. But when the state consciously enacts a system that places its imprimatur on arbitrary conduct, whether it be through a bizarre posting statute or a capricious administrative structure for handling handicap discrimination, federal court intervention under the due process clause is warranted."

9. *"[I]t is settled that the 'bitter with the sweet' approach misconceives the [due process] guarantee."* CLEVELAND BOARD OF EDUCATION v. LOUDERMILL, 470 U.S. 532, 105 S.Ct. 1487, 84 L.Ed.2d 494 (1985): Under Ohio law, respondents Loudermill and Donnelly were "classified civil servants" who could be discharged only for cause. Loudermill, a security guard, was dismissed because of dishonesty in filling out his employment application. He was not afforded an opportunity to respond to the dishonesty charge or to challenge the dismissal.[a] Donnelly was fired as a bus mechanic because he had failed an eye examination. He appealed to the Civil Service Commission, which ordered him reinstated without pay. "The statute plainly supports the conclusion [that] respondents possessed property rights in continued employment," but petitioners [stress] that in addition to specifying the grounds for termination, the statute sets out procedures by which termination may take place [and that these procedures were followed]. [Therefore,] '[t]o require additional procedures would in effect expand the scope of the property interest itself.' " The Court, per WHITE, J., disagreed:

"[Petitioners' argument] has its genesis in the plurality opinion in *Arnett*. [This approach] garnered three votes in *Arnett*, but was specifically rejected by the other six Justices. [I]n light of [*Vitek* and *Zimmerman Brush*], it is settled that the 'bitter with the sweet' approach misconceives the [due process] guarantee. If a clearer holding is needed, we provide it today. The point is straight-forward: the Due Process Clause provides that certain substantive rights—life, liberty, and property—cannot be deprived except pursuant to constitutionally adequate procedures. The categories of substance and procedure are distinct. Were the rule otherwise, the Clause would be reduced to a mere tautology. 'Property' cannot be defined by the procedures provided for its deprivation any more than can life or liberty. The right to due process 'is conferred, not by legislative grace, but by constitutional guarantee. While the legislature may elect not to confer a property interest in [public] employment, it may not constitutionally authorize the deprivation of such an interest, once conferred, without appropriate procedural safeguards.' *Arnett* (Powell, J., [concurring opinion]); see id. (White, J., [concurring in part]). [O]nce it is determined that the Due Process Clause applies, 'the question remains what process is due.' The answer is not to be found in the Ohio statute."[b]

REHNQUIST, J., the sole dissenter on this issue, maintained that the Fourteenth Amendment "does not support the conclusion that Ohio's effort to confer a limited form of tenure upon respondents resulted in the creation of a 'property right' in their employment": "Here, as in *Arnett*, '[t]he employee's statutorily defined right is not a guarantee against removal without cause in the abstract, but such a guarantee as enforced by the procedures which [the Ohio legislature] has designated for the determination of cause' (opinion of Rehnquist, J.). [We] ought

a. On his 1979 job application, Loudermill stated that he had never been convicted of a felony. Eleven months later it was discovered that he had been convicted of grand larceny in 1968. Loudermill maintained that he had thought his larceny conviction was for a misdemeanor rather than a felony.

b. The Court then held that respondents were not entitled to a "full adversarial hearing prior to adverse governmental action. [A]ll the process that is due is provided by a pretermination opportunity to respond, coupled with [a full post-termination hearing] as provided by the Ohio statute." This aspect of *Loudermill* is treated in Part II infra.

to recognize the totality of the State's definition of the property right in question, and not merely seize upon one of several paragraphs in a unitary statute to proclaim that in that paragraph the State has inexorably conferred upon a civil service employee something which it is powerless to qualify in the next paragraph of the statute. [While] it does not impose a federal definition of property, the Court departs from the full breadth of the holding in *Roth* by its selective choice from among the sentences the Ohio legislature chooses to use in establishing and qualifying a right."

10. *A hard look at Loudermill's substance-procedure distinction.* Did the *Loudermill* majority provide a convincing basis for its rejection of Justice Rehnquist's position? Can procedural problems, as the majority seemed to think, be neatly separated from substantive choices? See Tribe 2d ed., at 709–12. If the state is free to define and limit underlying substantive entitlements, why shouldn't it be equally free to define the procedure that goes with each entitlement? If substantive restrictions on entitlements can be adopted which have the effect of limiting procedural rights, why can't the government take the "intermediate course of limiting public benefits and opportunities in an explicitly procedural way"? See id. at 711. "Ultimately," concludes Professor Tribe, at 713, "the clarity of the demarcation the Court declared in *Loudermill* between the rights-conferring function and the process-prescribing function is illusory; the Court must eventually move toward more deference on matters of procedure or less deference on matters of substance. Since the former course would leave the due process clause with little content in the modern state, where so much has come to depend on relationships with government, the latter seems preferable, certainly in relationships created to meet the needs of the individuals involved, and probably also in relationships created to meet the needs of others."

II. WHAT KIND OF HEARING—AND WHEN?

GOLDBERG v. KELLY, 397 U.S. 254, 90 S.Ct. 1011, 25 L.Ed.2d 287 (1970), per Brennan, J. (Burger, C.J., and Black and Stewart, JJ., dissenting), held that due process requires an evidentiary hearing prior to termination of welfare benefits, stressing the "crucial factor [that] termination of aid pending resolution of a controversy over eligibility may deprive an *eligible* recipient of the very means by which to live while he waits. Since he lacks independent resources, his situation becomes immediately desperate. His need to concentrate upon [survival], in turn, adversely affects his ability to seek redress from the welfare bureaucracy." The hearing "need not take the form of a judicial or quasi-judicial trial," but a recipient must have "timely and adequate notice detailing the reasons for a proposed termination, and an effective opportunity to defend by confronting any adverse witnesses and by presenting his own arguments and evidence orally." The Court declined to "say that counsel must be provided" but the recipient must be allowed to retain counsel.

Consider Jerry Mashaw, *Due Process in the Administrative State* 35–36 (1985): "[T]he underprotectionist critic may claim that the due process revolution has stopped short of its essential goals: building legal security and democratic control into the administrative state. Legal security for the welfare claimant, for example, would at a minimum require that the hearing right be oriented to the issues that produce erroneous deprivations and that the recipient class has the necessary resources to make use of hearings to protect its interests. Yet neither condition seems to obtain. A careful study of errors suggests that they occur at least as often through misinterpretation of policy as through mistakes on questions of fact. The *Goldberg* decision limits due process hearings to facts. Moreover, welfare recipients generally lack the human or material resources to make use of the hearings *Goldberg* provided. Except for an occasional flurry of political activism expressed through appeals requests, hearings have been utilized about as infrequently after *Goldberg* as before.

"This sort of criticism may be pressed further to suggest that the hearing technique—the demand for individualized and detailed attention through quasi-judicial process—simply misses the point of the welfare state. The problem has become one of mass, not individual, justice. Legal security for the class of welfare claimants lies, not in hearings, but in good management. Unless due process, therefore, comes to terms with administration, becomes systems—rather than case-oriented, it will be irrelevant.

"The underprotectionist case goes further. *Goldberg*'s hearing rights extend only to the protection of what can be termed 'positive entitlements,' substantive interests already enjoying common law or statutory legal significance. Due process hearings are thus only an addition to the legal security of existing rights. They provide no access to the administrative forums in which rights are being created and no opportunity to avoid the application of general rules on the basis of individual circumstances. *Goldberg*'s hearing rights thus leave untouched the contemporary concern with (1) the remoteness of administrative policy making from immediate participation by affected interests and (2) the unfairness and irrationality that seem to attend bureaucratic implementation of general rules."[b]

MATHEWS v. ELDRIDGE, 424 U.S. 319, 96 S.Ct. 893, 47 L.Ed.2d 18 (1976), per POWELL, J., held that although Social Security disability benefits constitute "a statutorily created 'property' interest protected by the Fifth Amendment," due process does not require a *Goldberg*-type hearing prior to their termination on the ground that "the worker is no longer disabled": "In recent years this Court increasingly has had occasion to consider the extent to which due process requires an evidentiary hearing prior to the deprivation of some type of property interest even if such a hearing is provided thereafter. In only one case, *Goldberg*, has the Court held that a hearing closely approximating a judicial trial is necessary. [for example,] *Bell v. Burson* [held] that due process required only that the prerev-

b. At this point, Professor Mashaw turns to *O'Bannon v. Town Court Nursing Center*, 447 U.S. 773, 100 S.Ct. 2467, 65 L.Ed.2d 506 (1980), per Stevens, J., holding that, because nursing home residents had no government-established entitlement to continued residence at a particular home, they had no right to a hearing before the government decertified the home as provider of services at government expenses under Medicare and Medicaid agreements. Decertification would force the patients to seek care elsewhere and would probably mean that they would be separated from each and might mean that they would have to relocate away from their friends and families. But, responded the Court, Medicaid provisions only give recipients "the right to choose among a range of *qualified* providers, without government interference, [not the right] to enter an unqualified home and demand a hearing to

certify it, nor [the right] to continue to receive benefits for care in a home that has been decertified. [A]lthough the regulations do protect patients by limiting the circumstances under which a *home* may transfer or discharge a Medicaid recipient, they do not purport to limit the Government's right to make a transfer necessary by decertifying a facility. [Whatever rights the patients may have against the nursing home] for failing to maintain its status[,] enforcement by [state and federal agencies] of their valid regulations did not directly affect their legal rights or deprive them of any constitutionally protected interest in life, liberty or property."

Blackmun, J., concurred, but found the Court's analysis "simplistic and unsatisfactory." For extensive criticism of *O'Bannon*, see Mashaw, supra, at 36–41; Tribe, supra, at 766–67; Terrell, supra, at 927–35.

ocation hearing involve a probable-cause determination as to the fault of the licensee, noting that the hearing 'need not take the form of a full adjudication of the question of liability.' [O]ur prior decisions indicate that identification of the specific dictates of due process generally requires consideration of three distinct factors: first, the private interest that will be affected by the official action; second, the risk of an erroneous deprivation of such interest through the procedures used, and the probable value, if any, of additional or substitute procedural safeguards; and finally, the government's interest, including the function involved and the fiscal and administrative burdens that the additional or substitute procedural requirement would entail."[a]

First, in contrast to *Goldberg,* "eligibility for disability benefits [is] not based upon financial need." Rather, such benefits are "wholly unrelated to the worker's income or support from many other sources, such as earnings of other family members, workmen's compensation awards, tort claims awards, savings, [insurance, pensions and public assistance.]" Thus, "there is less reason here than in *Goldberg* to depart from the ordinary principle, established by our decisions, that something less than an evidentiary hearing is sufficient prior to adverse administrative action."

Second, "the potential value of an evidentiary hearing, or even oral presentation to the decisionmaker, is substantially less in this context than in *Goldberg.*" Here, "a medical assessment of the worker's physical or mental condition is required. This is a more sharply focused and easily documented decision than the typical determination of welfare entitlement [where] a wide variety of information may be deemed relevant, and issues of witness credibility and veracity often are critical to the decision-making process." Further, "the information critical [in the disability case] usually is derived from medical sources, [which are likely] to communicate more effectively through written documents than are welfare recipients or the lay witnesses supporting their cause."

Third, as to the "additional cost in terms of money and administrative burden" if pretermination hearings were required, "at some point the benefit of an additional safeguard to the individual affected by the administrative action and to society in terms of increased assurance that the action is just, may be

a. The Court subsequently utilized the factors set forth in *Eldridge* in analyzing *Ingraham v. Wright* (corporal punishment in public schools) and *Parham v. J.R.* (parents' commitment of minor children), both discussed in the notes following this case. The *Eldridge* "balancing approach" was also utilized in, e.g., *Dixon v. Love,* 431 U.S. 105, 97 S.Ct. 1723, 52 L.Ed.2d 172 (1977) (Blackmun, J.) (no prior evidentiary hearing required for driver license revocation pursuant to regulation mandating such revocation if license had been suspended three times within 10 years for conviction of traffic violations); *Memphis Light, Gas & Water Division v. Craft,* 436 U.S. 1, 98 S.Ct. 1554, 56 L.Ed.2d 30 (1978) (Powell, J.) (municipal utility must provide its customers with some administrative procedure for entertaining complaints before cutting off services); *Mackey v. Montrym,* 443 U.S. 1, 99 S.Ct. 2612, 61 L.Ed.2d 321 (1979) (Burger, C.J.) (license of driver lawfully arrested for drunk driving may be suspended for 90 days without prior hearing for refusing to take breath-analysis test so long as immediate post-suspension hearing is available; *Little v. Streater,* 452 U.S. 1, 101 S.Ct. 2202, 68 L.Ed.2d 627 (1981) (Burger, C.J.) (state's refusal to pay cost of blood grouping test for indigent defendant in paternity action, a proceeding with " 'quasi-criminal' overtones," denies him "meaningful opportunity to be heard" and thus violates procedural due process); *Walters v. National Association of Radiation Survivors,* 473 U.S. 305, 105 S.Ct. 3180, 87 L.Ed.2d 220 (1985) (Rehnquist, J.) (federal statute limiting to $10 the fee that may be paid an attorney or agent representing one seeking benefits from Veterans Administration (VA) for service-connected death or disability does not violate procedural due process; since benefits are not granted on basis of need, they are more like social security benefits involved in *Eldridge* than welfare benefits involved in *Goldberg;* elimination of fee limitation "would bid fair to complicate a proceeding which Congress wished to keep as simple as possible").

outweighed by the cost. Significantly, the cost of protecting those whom the preliminary administrative process has identified as likely to be found undeserving may in the end come out of the pockets of the deserving since resources available for any particular program of social welfare are not unlimited."

Finally, "in assessing what process is due in this case, substantial weight must be given to the good-faith judgments of the individuals charged by Congress with the administration of the social welfare system that the procedures they have provided assure fair consideration of the entitlement claims of individuals."[b]

The *Eldridge* approach, observes Jerry Mashaw, *The Supreme Court's Due Process Calculus for Administrative Adjudication in Mathews v. Eldridge*, 44 U.Chi.L.Rev. 28, 39 (1976), "is subjective and impressionistic. [The Court] assumes that disability recipients are less dependent on income support than welfare recipients. This assumption is buttressed only by the notion that welfare is for the needy and disability insurance is for prior taxpayers. [But], any number of circumstances might make a terminated welfare recipient's plight less desperate than that of his disabled SSA counterpart,[42] or vice versa." Mashaw finds several of the *Eldridge* conclusions questionable, especially that it was dealing with an essentially medical determination. Id. at 40. "The *Goldberg* decision's approach to prescribing due process—specification of the attributes of adjudicatory hearings by analogy to judicial trial—makes the Court resemble an administrative engineer with an outdated professional education. It is at once intrusive and ineffectual. Retreating from this stance, [*Eldridge*] relies on the administrator's good faith— an equally troublesome posture in a political system that depends heavily on judicial review for the protection of countermajoritarian values." Id. at 58.

Consider, too, Tribe 2d ed., at 718: "[The *Eldridge*] Court's unwillingness to consider values beyond accuracy of result in the context of a utilitarian balancing test when deciding what process is due, and the Court's grant of a strong presumption of constitutionality to statutory procedural provisions, amount to a serious abdication of traditional notions of judicial responsibility under the due process clauses. Like many other provisions of the Constitution, the due process requirement represented a decision on the part of the Framers to safeguard certain rights and values, those considered fundamental in a free society and yet unusually vulnerable to the risk of denial by the majority. Adequate protection of such 'core' concerns cannot be afforded by 'balancing' the general interests of the majority against those of the individual. [Moreover, there] is no reason to believe that the judiciary would be better suited to that task of utilitarian comparison than the legislature even if it were called for."

"Although the Supreme Court has treated *Mathews v. Eldridge* as furnishing a test for all seasons," the test, points out Richard H. Fallon, Jr., *Some Confusions about Due Process, Judicial Review, and Constitutional Remedies*, 93 Colum.L.Rev. 309, 331 (1993), "was designed for resolving claims of entitlement to

---

b. Brennan, J., joined by Marshall, J., dissented: "[I]n the present case, it is indicated that because disability benefits were terminated there was a foreclosure upon the Eldridge home and the family's furniture was repossessed, forcing Eldridge, his wife and children to sleep in one bed. [It] is also no argument that a worker, who has been placed in the untenable position of having been denied disability benefits, may still seek other forms of public assistance." Stevens, J., took no part.

42. The terminated [welfare] recipient may have access to home or general relief depending upon his residence, whereas the disability claimant in a different state or locality may not. The disability claimant may be totally dependent for his livelihood on the disability payments, whereas the welfare recipient who is terminated may have been receiving a small AFDC payment to supplement inadequate family earnings.

particular types of *administrative,* rather than judicial, procedures. Claims of a right to judicial review raise issues lying beyond the [*Eldridge*] framework."

---

1. *"Educational due process" cases.* (a) GOSS v. LOPEZ, 419 U.S. 565, 95 S.Ct. 729, 42 L.Ed.2d 725 (1975) (also discussed at p. 548 fn. b supra), per White, J., held that "as a general rule," before a student is given a temporary suspension (ten days or less) from public school, due process requires "that the student be given oral or written notice of the charges against him and, if he denies them, an explanation of the evidence the authorities have and an opportunity to present his side of the story": "[T]otal exclusion from the educational process for more than a trivial period, and certainly if the suspension is for 10 days, is a serious event in the life of the suspended child. [T]he State is constrained to recognize a student's legitimate entitlement to a public education as a property interest which is protected by the Due Process Clause and which may not be taken away for misconduct without adherence to the minimum procedures required by that clause. [Due process] also forbids arbitrary deprivations of liberty. [Many] charges could seriously damage the students' standing with their fellow pupils and their teachers as well as interfere with later opportunities for higher education and employment."

Powell, J., joined by Burger, C.J., and Blackmun and Rehnquist, JJ., dissented: "Whether *any* procedural protections are due" turns on the extent to which one will be "condemned to suffer *grievous* loss," [but] the record in this case reflects no educational injury to appellees. Each completed the semester in which the suspension occurred and performed at least as well as he or she had in previous years. [Few] rulings would interfere more extensively in the daily functioning of schools than subjecting routine discipline to the formalities and judicial oversight of due process."[a]

(b) But cf. INGRAHAM v. WRIGHT (1977) (also discussed at p. 550 fn. e supra), per Powell, J., holding that disciplinary corporal punishment in public school "implicates a constitutionally protected liberty interest," but that procedural due process does not require notice and an opportunity to be heard prior to imposition of that punishment as it is authorized and limited by Florida common law: "Were it not for the common-law privilege permitting teachers to inflict reasonable corporal punishment [and] the availability of the traditional remedies for abuse, the case for requiring advance procedural safeguards would be strong indeed. [But the disciplinarian] must exercise prudence and restraint. [And if] the punishment inflicted is later found to have been excessive [the] school authorities inflicting it may be held liable in damages to the child and, if malice is shown, they may be subject to criminal penalties.

a. Compare *Goss* with *Bethel School Dist. v. Fraser* (1986) (also discussed at p. 905 infra). Fraser, a high school senior, was suspended for two days for making a sexually suggestive speech at a school-sponsored assembly. The Court, per Burger, C.J., rejected Fraser's contention that his suspension violated due process because he had no way of knowing that his speech would subject him to disciplinary sanctions: "Given the school's need to be able to impose disciplinary sanctions for a wide range of unanticipated conduct disruptive of the educational process, the school disciplinary rules need not be as detailed as a criminal code which imposes criminal sanctions. Cf. *Arnett.* Two days' suspension from school does not rise to the level of a penal sanction calling for the full panoply of procedural due process protections applicable to a criminal prosecution. Cf. *Goss.* The school disciplinary rule proscribing 'obscene' language and the prespeech admonition of teachers gave adequate warning to Fraser that his lewd speech could subject him to sanctions."

"[Moreover,] because paddlings are usually inflicted in response to conduct directly observed by teachers in their presence, the risk that a child will be paddled without cause is typically insignificant. In the ordinary case, a disciplinary paddling neither threatens seriously to violate any substantive rights nor condemns the child 'to suffer grievous loss of any kind.'

"[T]he low incidence of abuse, and the availability of established judicial remedies in the event of abuse, distinguish this case from *Goss*. [The] subsequent [proceedings] available in this case may be viewed as affording substantially greater protection to the child than the informal conference mandated by *Goss*. [E]ven if the need for advance procedural safeguards were clear, the question would remain whether the incremental benefit could justify the [cost.] 'At some point the benefit of an additional safeguard [may] be outweighed by the cost.' *Eldridge*. We think that point has been reached in this case."

WHITE, J., joined by Brennan, Marshall and Stevens, JJ., dissented: "[The common law] tort action is utterly inadequate to protect against erroneous infliction of punishment for two reasons. First, under Florida law [the] student has no remedy at all for punishment imposed on the basis of mistaken facts, at least as long as the punishment was reasonable from the point of view of the disciplinarian, uninformed by any prior hearing. [Second], [the] lawsuit occurs after the punishment has been finally imposed. The infliction of physical pain is final and irreparable; it cannot be undone in a subsequent proceeding."[b]

(c) *Criticism of Ingraham.* "Government's interests in punishing guilty students first and asking questions about guilt later," maintain Lawrence Alexander & Paul Horton, *Ingraham v. Wright: A Primer for Cruel and Unusual Jurisprudence,* 52 S.Cal.L.Rev. 1305, 1384–85 (1979), "surely pale in significance when compared to the interests of innocent students in avoiding punishment.[282] Usually no emergency is averted by instantaneous corporal punishment.[283] The costs—monetary and otherwise—of providing pre-punishment hearings for the guilty are more than justified by the savings to the innocent. Finally, the burden imposed on the innocent in bringing post-deprivation actions is undoubtedly heavier than the burden imposed on government by a requirement of pre-punishment hearings. [In] none of the cases [upholding] a post-deprivation hearing was there both the strong likelihood of irreparable injury and the absence of a compelling justification for prompt action precluding a prior hearing."

"In other cases in which a post-deprivation hearing has been held adequate," emphasizes Irene Rosenberg, *Ingraham v. Wright: The Supreme Court's Whipping Boy,* 78 Colum.L.Rev. 75, 91–94 (1978), "the interest involved was 'property' rather than 'liberty.' [Where] a liberty interest is invoked, the injured person is considerably less likely to be made whole by a belated award of damages. Particularly is this true in the case of corporal punishment, where the liberty interest is freedom from 'infliction of appreciable physical pain.' * * *

"To [the] very real barriers impairing vindication of the child's rights [by bringing a tort action][c] must be added not only the defense of sovereign immunity

b. Compare *Ingraham* and *Parratt* (p. 548 fn. d supra) with *Zimmerman Brush* (p. 552 supra).

282. [*Ingraham*] is an easy case in this respect, considering that a more reparable student interest (freedom from 10–day suspension) outweighed similar government interests in *Goss*.

283. In that respect, corporal punishment differs from temporary suspensions, without pre-deprivation hearings, which may avert dangers to persons and property.

c. Rosenberg notes, e.g., that it may prove difficult to secure an attorney willing to accept a case of this sort; completion of state court actions may take years, during which time

available to school boards, and the possible defense of good faith mistake available to teachers, but also the inadequacy of money damages as a means of repairing physical and psychological injury deliberately inflicted on a child.

"[*Ingraham*] refused to attempt to distinguish between trivial and severe corporal punishment, while at the same time invoking [the] existence of common law and statutory restraints against *unreasonable* corporal punishment. In effect, the majority was asking the nation's school teachers to make the sorts of decisions about reasonableness that, if erroneous, could lead to tort liability, while at the same time acknowledging its own inability (or unwillingness) to make such judgments."

(d) *In defense of Ingraham.* "Tort law," observes Rodney Smolla, *The Displacement of Federal Due Process Claims by State Tort Remedies,* 1982 U.Ill.L.Rev. 831, 850–51, "has always awarded money for the taking of interests without any objectively discernable value—millions of dollars are awarded for lost reputation, for emotional distress, and for pain and suffering. [A] substantial damage award against a school teacher for excessive corporal punishment is easily conceivable, particularly in communities in which a consensus against such conduct prevails. It is not at all obvious that the threat of such awards is any less a deterrent to misconduct than internal administrative hearings, in which teachers who know the administrative ropes may often be able to prevail in proceedings stacked against students.

"[Professor Rosenberg's point] that the Supreme Court preferred to allow school teachers to make decisions about the reasonableness of discipline that the Court felt unable or unwilling to make is correct, but the Court's reticence is grounds for criticism only if one first assumes that federal court judges are or should be better qualified than school teachers to make such judgments.

"[*Ingraham*] did not totally eliminate federal concern with paddling—a due process violation could still exist if a state were to disable its own courts in their policing of local practices—but it placed federal law in a back-up role. *Ingraham* is in this sense consistent with the Court's general movement in procedural due process cases, toward initial deference to local prerogative in setting procedural norms when the substantive interests at stake are heavily imbued with localized values."

(e) BOARD OF CURATORS v. HOROWITZ, 435 U.S. 78, 98 S.Ct. 948, 55 L.Ed.2d 124 (1978), per REHNQUIST, J., "decline[d] to ignore the historic judgment of educators [and] formalize the academic dismissal process by requiring a hearing." Because of dissatisfaction with her clinical performance and personal hygiene, and after notice from and discussion with the dean of the medical school, a state medical school student was put on probation. After continued dissatisfaction with her work, and pursuant to a faculty-student council recommendation (supported by the dean and the provost), she was dismissed from school in her final year. Assuming but not deciding that there was "a liberty interest" in pursuing a medical career, "respondent has been awarded at least as much due process as the Fourteenth Amendment requires." The Court underscored the distinction between "academic evaluations of a student" and "disciplinary determinations," contrasting the instant case with *Goss*, where "[t]he requirement of a hearing [could] 'provide a meaningful hedge against erroneous action.' The

"the child's memory of the controverted events may dim"; the formality of a jury trial is "considerably less conducive to articulate testimony by the public than an informal pre-

punishment hearing would be"; and that a teacher is more likely to be believed than his or her ex-pupil. See id. at 92–93.

decision to dismiss respondent, by comparison, rested on the academic judgment of school officials," a judgment "by its nature more subjective and evaluative than the typical factual questions presented in the average disciplinary decision."

2. *"Family due process."* (a) Balancing the three factors set forth in *Eldridge,* PARHAM v. J.R., 442 U.S. 584, 99 S.Ct. 2493, 61 L.Ed.2d 101 (1979) (also discussed at p. 558, fn. a supra), per BURGER, C.J., held that a preadmission adversary hearing is not required when parents (or a state agency acting in loco parentis) seek to commit their minor children to a mental institution—so long as the commitment is approved by an "independent medical judgment." The Court "assume[d] that a child has a protectible interest not only in being free of unnecessary bodily restraints but also in not being labeled erroneously" as "mentally ill," but concluded that "our precedents permit the parents to retain a substantial, if not the dominant, role in the decision, absent a finding of neglect or abuse, and that the traditional presumption that the parents act in the best interests of the child should apply. [But the] child's rights and the nature of the commitment decision are such that parents cannot always have absolute and unreviewable discretion [to institutionalize their child]. [They] retain plenary authority [to do so], subject to a physician's independent examination and medical judgment." In the course of a wide-ranging opinion the Court observed:

"That some parents 'may at times be acting against the interests of their children' [is reason] for caution, [but] hardly a reason to discard wholesale those pages of human experience that teach that parents generally do act in the child's best interests. The statist notion that governmental power should supersede parental authority in *all* cases because *some* parents abuse and neglect children is repugnant to American tradition.

"[Appellees] place particular reliance on *Planned Parenthood v. Danforth* [Sec. 2 supra], arguing that its holding indicates how little deference to parents is appropriate when the child is exercising a constitutional right. [But that case] involved an absolute parental veto over the child's ability to obtain an abortion. Parents in Georgia in no sense have an absolute right to commit their children to state mental hospitals; the statute requires [each regional hospital superintendent] to exercise independent judgment as to the child's need for confinement.

"[W]hat process is constitutionally due cannot be divorced from the nature of the ultimate decision that is being made. [Here,] the questions are essentially medical in character. [W]e recently stated in *Addington v. Texas,* 439 U.S. 908, 99 S.Ct. 276, 58 L.Ed.2d 254 (1978),[a] that the determination of 'whether a person is mentally ill turns on the *meaning* of the facts which must be interpreted by expert psychiatrists and psychologists.' [We reject] the notion that the shortcomings of specialists can always be avoided by shifting the decision [to] an untrained judge or administrative hearing officer after a judicial-type hearing. Even after a hearing, the nonspecialist decisionmaker must make a medical-psychiatric decision. Common human experience and scholarly opinions suggest that the supposed protections of an adversary proceeding to determine the appropriateness of

---

a. *Addington* held that one's interest in the outcome of a civil commitment proceeding is so important that due process requires the state to justify confinement by "clear and convincing" evidence, rather than the normal "preponderance of the evidence" standard. See also *Foucha v. Louisiana,* p. 552 supra. Consider Note, 93 Harv.L.Rev. 89, 98 (1979): "It is difficult to reconcile *Parham* with *Addington.* [In] insisting on a strict standard of proof

[*Addington*] assumed that an individual could not be confined without an adversary hearing. In *Parham,* by contrast, the Court allowed minors to be institutionalized with fewer procedural standards than is required for the termination of welfare benefits. The presumption that parents or state agencies will act in a child's best interests is too tenuous a rationale to justify the denial of an adversary hearing."

medical decisions for the commitment and treatment of mental and emotional illness may well be more illusory than real. * * *

" '[P]rocedural due process rules are shaped by the risk of error inherent in the truthfinding process as applied to the generality of cases, not the rare exceptions.' *Eldridge.* In general, we are satisfied that an independent medical decision-making process, [followed] by additional periodic review of a child's condition, will protect children who should not be admitted; we do not believe the risks of error in that process would be significantly reduced by a more formal, judicial-type hearing."

Concurring and dissenting in part, BRENNAN, J., joined by Marshall and Stevens, JJ., agreed that the parent-child relationship "militate[s] in favor of postponement of formal commitment proceedings and against mandatory adversary preconfinement commitment hearings." But "[w]hile the question of the frequency of postadmission review hearings may properly be deferred, the right to at least one post-admission hearing can and should be affirmed now." "This case is governed by the rule of *Danforth.* The right to be free from wrongful incarceration, physical intrusion, and stigmatization has significance for the individual surely as great as the right to an abortion. [Indeed,] *Danforth* involved only a potential dispute between parent and child, whereas here a break in family autonomy has actually resulted in the parents' decision to surrender custody of their child to a state mental institution. [A] child who has been ousted from his family has even greater need for an independent advocate."[b]

(b) *Parental prerogatives and governmental intrusions: Parham and Ingraham compared.* Consider Robert Burt, *The Constitution of the Family,* 1979 Sup.Ct.Rev. 329, 332–33: "The Court spoke in *Parham* as if it were upholding parental prerogatives against governmental intrusions. [But the parents in that case] were not seeking to resist governmental power over their children; they were invoking that power by attempting to confine their children in state psychiatric institutions.

"This paean to parental prerogatives would have had greater relevance if state officials had sought to impose behavioral controls on children against their parent's wishes. The Court did consider a case two years earlier that directly implicated that question. School officials had administered corporal punishment to children. [In *Ingraham,* the] Court majority, composed of the same conservative nucleus as in *Parham* [but here joined by Stewart, J., with White, J., dissenting], ruled that school officials were free to disregard parental objections to this form of behavior control of their children. Justice Powell [said this] for the Court: 'Although the early cases viewed the authority of the teacher as deriving from the parents, [this concept] has been replaced by the view [that] the State itself may impose such corporal punishment as is reasonably necessary for the proper education of the child and for the maintenance of group discipline.' So much for the American tradition—paraded in *Parham* as well as 'the early cases'—that 'governmental power should [not] supersede parental authority.' "

(c) *"The subtleties and nuances of psychiatric diagnoses": Parham and Vitek compared.* The *Parham* Court, observes Jerry Mashaw, *Due Process in the Administrative State* 111 (1985), did not believe that a minor need be given a hearing prior to commitment to a mental institution, "apparently in substantial part because a hearing could provide little additional protection from error. [Yet,] somehow, when in *Vitek* [p. 550 supra] the question was whether a prisoner

b. See also Note, 93 Harv.L.Rev. 89, 94 (1979).

should have a hearing prior to being transferred to a mental hospital, the suggestion that psychiatric judgment was involved elicited the following judicial response: 'The medical nature of the [inquiry] does not justify dispensing with due process requirements. *It is precisely the subtleties and nuances of psychiatric diagnoses that justify the requirement of adversary hearings.' "* [Emphasis added by Mashaw.] See also John Garvey, *Children and the Idea of Liberty*, 68 Ky.L.J. 809, 826–30 (1979–80).

(d) *Parental status termination proceedings.* LASSITER v. DEPARTMENT OF SOCIAL SERVICES, 452 U.S. 18, 101 S.Ct. 2153, 68 L.Ed.2d 640 (1981), per STEWART, J., rejected the view that due process requires the appointment of counsel in every parental status termination proceeding involving indigent parents and left the appointment of counsel in such proceedings to be determined by the state courts on a case-by-case basis: "The pre-eminent generalization that emerges from this Court's precedents on an indigent's right to appointed counsel is that such a right has been recognized to exist only where the litigant may lose his physical liberty if he loses the litigation. * * * Significantly, as a litigant's interest in personal liberty diminishes, so does his right to appointed counsel. [Thus, *Gagnon v. Scarpelli*, 411 U.S. 778, 93 S.Ct. 1756, 36 L.Ed.2d 656 (1973),] declined to hold that indigent probationers have, per se, a right to counsel at revocation hearings, and instead left the decision whether counsel should be appointed to be made on a case-by-case basis."

The Court then held that in the circumstances of this case the trial judge did not deny Ms. Lassiter due process when he failed to appoint counsel for her: "[The] case presented no specially troublesome points of law, either procedural or substantive. While hearsay evidence was no doubt admitted, and while Ms. Lassiter no doubt left incomplete her defense that the Department had not adequately assisted her in rekindling her interest in her son, the weight of the evidence that she had few sparks of such an interest was sufficiently great that the presence of counsel for [her] could not have made a determinative difference."[c]

BLACKMUN, J., joined by Brennan and Marshall, JJ., dissented: "In this case, the State's aim is not simply to influence the parent-child relationship but to *extinguish* it. A termination of parental rights is both total and irrevocable. [It] is hardly surprising that this forced dissolution of the parent-child relationship has been recognized as a punitive sanction by courts, Congress, and commentators.

"[Faced] with a formal accusatory adjudication, with an adversary—the State—that commands great investigative and prosecutorial resources, with standards that involve ill-defined notions of fault and adequate parenting, and with the inevitable tendency of a court to apply subjective values or to defer to the State's 'expertise,' the defendant parent plainly is outstripped if he or she is without the assistance of 'the guiding hand of counsel.' When the parent is indigent, lacking in education, and easily intimidated by figures of authority, the imbalance may well become insuperable. [W]here as here, the threatened loss of liberty is severe and absolute, the State's role is so clearly adversarial and punitive, and the cost involved is relatively slight, there is no sound basis for refusing to recognize the right to counsel as a requisite of due process in a proceeding initiated by the State to terminate parental rights."[d]

c. Burger, C.J., who joined the Court's opinion, also added, in a brief concurrence responding to the dissenters, that the purpose of the parental status termination proceeding "was not 'punitive' " but *"protective* of the child's best interests."

d. The dissent then examined the termination hearing in considerable detail and, "[i]n

STEVENS, J., also dissented: "[The] reasons supporting the conclusion that [due process] entitle the defendant in a criminal case to representation by counsel apply with equal force to a case of this kind. The issue is one of fundamental fairness, not of weighing the pecuniary costs against the societal benefits. Accordingly, even if the costs to the State were not relatively insignificant but rather were just as great as the costs of providing prosecutors, judges, and defense counsel to ensure the fairness of criminal proceedings, I would reach the same result in this category of cases. For the value of protecting our liberty from deprivation by the State without due process of law is priceless."[e]

Compare *Lassiter* with SANTOSKY v. KRAMER, 455 U.S. 745, 102 S.Ct. 1388, 71 L.Ed.2d 599 (1982). Under New York law, the state may terminate, over parental objection, the rights of parents in their natural child upon a finding that the child is "permanently neglected," a finding that need be supported only by a "fair preponderance of the evidence." Because "the private interest affected is commanding; the risk of error from using a preponderance standard is substantial; and the countervailing government interest favoring that standard is comparatively slight," a 5–4 majority, per BLACKMUN, J., held that a "fair preponderance of the evidence" standard in such proceedings violates due process. Thus, before a state may terminate permanently the rights of parents in their natural child, it must support its allegations by at least "clear and convincing evidence. [Unlike] a constitutional requirement of hearings or court-appointed counsel, a stricter standard of proof [than 'preponderance'] would reduce factual error without imposing substantial fiscal burdens upon the State."

Given the flexibility of the due process principle, REHNQUIST, J., joined by Burger, C.J., and White and O'Connor, JJ., dissenting thought it "obvious that a proper due process inquiry cannot be made by focusing upon one narrow provision of the challenged statutory scheme. [Courts] must examine *all* procedural protections offered by the State, and must assess the *cumulative* effect of such safeguards." The dissent then pointed to the "host of procedural protections" the state had "placed around parental rights and interests." In addition to the basic fairness of the statutory scheme, "the standard of proof chosen by New York clearly reflects a constitutionally permissible balance of the interests at stake in this case. [When] the interests of the child and the State in a stable, nurturing homelife are balanced against the interests of the parents in the rearing of their child, it cannot be said that either set of interests is so clearly paramount as to require that the risk of error be allocated to one side or the other."

3. *"Open analysis of the values at stake."* Consider John Nowak, *Due Process Methodology in the Postincorporation World,* 70 J.Crim.L. & C. 397, 403 (1979): "Although one may disagree with the results in [cases such as *Parham,* which employed the *Eldridge* 'balancing test,'] the Court's open analysis of the values at stake [and] its attempt to accommodate the competing values of liberty and efficient administrative procedures certainly is preferable to the masking of such decisions through vaguely worded opinions or formalistic interpretations of constitutional provisions. [By contrast], in *Greenholtz* (1979) [p. 550 fn. a supra], [holding] that inmates of penal institutions were not entitled to due process

---

light of the unpursued avenues of defense, and of the experience petitioner underwent at this hearing," found "virtually incredible" the Court's conclusion that the termination proceeding was fundamentally fair.

e. For the view that the *Lassiter* Court forgot the teaching of *Gideon*—a reviewing

court *cannot* conclude that "the case presented no specially troublesome points of law" on the basis of a record made *without* the assistance of counsel—see Yale Kamisar, *Gideon v. Wainwright A Quarter–Century Later,* 10 Pace L.Rev. 343, 354–55 (1990).

protection in decisionmaking processes related to their possible release on parole, a majority of the Justices totally failed to analyze the basic due process question. [*Greenholtz,* per Burger, C.J., found] no liberty interest meriting protection by the due process clause at issue in these proceedings. The four Justices [Brennan, Marshall, Powell and Stevens] who dissented, at least in part, found that the individual prisoners had a liberty interest at stake [and thus] struggled openly with the problem of determining what, if any, procedural safeguards should be given to [them]. Even if one agreed with the majority's conclusion[,] [it is] easier to accept the separate opinion of Justice Powell, [recognizing] that inmates had an interest worthy of protection by the due process clause [but finding] that the need of efficiently processing inmate files outweighed the interest in freedom preceding the expiration of a properly imposed sentence. [Powell, J.'s] balancing approach is more satisfying than the majority's simple assertion that the possibility of parole is no more than a hope—'a hope which is not protected by due process.' By failing to adopt the Powell approach it was possible to avoid questions of fairness and value identification even in due process decisions."

4. *Separating the "property" or "liberty" issue from that of "what process is due."* While recent cases "fall short of providing the full inventory of procedural safeguards required by *Goldberg,*" observes Robert Rabin, *Job Security and Due Process: Monitoring Administrative Discretion Through A Reasons Requirement,* 44 U.Chi.L.Rev. 60, 74–79 (1976), "they proceed from the same basic assumption about the relationship between property interests and procedural due process: at a minimum, procedural due process contemplates some kind of a hearing—an opportunity to join issue, through the presentation of evidence to a decision maker who is then obliged to reach a reasoned determination on the basis of the submissions. Underlying this conception is the vital interest in promoting an accurate decision, in assuring that facts have been correctly established and properly characterized in conformity with the applicable legal [standard.]

"By equating procedural due process with a value that seems to require a right to some kind of a hearing, the Court has correspondingly been driven to set too high a threshold when arriving at an initial determination of whether a property interest exists. In theory, of course, the inquiry into whether a form of government largess creates a property interest can, as the Court and commentators [and, in a way, the editors of this casebook] suggest, be neatly separated from the question of 'what process is due.' In practice, however, whether an entitlement is established or not is determined with an eye to the minimum procedural requirements that would follow as a consequence of a decision in favor of the recipient's claim. A threshold perception of security of interest focuses both on the existence of a 'property' interest and the procedural safeguards attendant upon its recognition. [The] result, as *Roth* and *Bishop* illustrate, is that when the state equivocates about job security, a court cognizant of the high costs of a hearing requirement in terms of administrative efficiency is likely to be reluctant to recognize a property interest. The court then ends up affording no procedural protection at all, even though the employee in such a case may be on a tenure track or even in a 'permanent' position. * * *

"Fundamental to the concept of procedural due process is the right to a reasoned explanation of government conduct that is contrary to the expectations the government has created by conferring a special status upon an individual. [It] is crucial that this value be seen as distinct from the concern about administrative accuracy—the interest in correcting wrong decisions. Obviously, the two are related[, but] I would insist that the respect for individual autonomy that is at the foundation of procedural due process imposes a distinct obligation upon the government to explain fully its adverse status decision. * * *

"Procedural due process can be viewed as a layered approach aimed at accomplishing a fundamental objective—protection against arbitrary conduct by the state. One could view the [various rights][a] as various layers intended to provide increasingly effective insulation from arbitrariness: each layer adds something to the defensive capacity to ward off an arbitrary effort to destroy a status relationship. In some cases—a job security case involving a first amendment claim, for example—the balance struck between the individual values to be protected and the costs of administration weighs so heavily in favor of the individual claimant that a many-layered approach, some form of 'evidentiary hearing,' seems clearly required. But as we respond to less exigent claims by peeling away the layers of protection—indeed as we strip away any semblance of a 'hearing'—it is essential that we retain the core safeguard against arbitrariness, the right to receive a meaningful explanation of what is being done to the individual."

a. For factors—"roughly in order of priority"—that have been considered to be elements of a fair hearing, see Henry Friendly, *"Some Kind of Hearing,"* 123 U.Pa.L.Rev. 1267, 1279–95 (1975): (1) "an unbiased tribunal" (but recall *Arnett v. Kennedy*); (2) "notice of the proposed action and the grounds asserted for it"; (3) "an opportunity to present reasons why the proposed action should not be taken"; (4), (5) and (6) "the right to call witnesses, to know the evidence against one, and to have decision based only on the evidence presented"; (7) "counsel"; (8) and (9), "the making of a record and a statement of reasons"; (10) "public attendance"; and (11) "judicial review."

Chapter 7

FREEDOM OF EXPRESSION
AND ASSOCIATION

SECTION 1. WHAT SPEECH IS NOT PROTECTED?

The first amendment provides that "Congress shall make no law * * * abridging the freedom of speech, or of the press." Some have stressed that no law means NO LAW. For example, Black, J., dissenting in *Konigsberg v. State Bar,* 366 U.S. 36, 81 S.Ct. 997, 6 L.Ed.2d 105 (1961) argued that the "First Amendment's unequivocal command * * * shows that the men who drafted our Bill of Rights did all the 'balancing' that was to be done in this field."

Laws forbidding speech, however, are commonplace. Laws against perjury, blackmail, and fraud prohibit speech.[a] So does much of the law of contracts. Black, J., himself conceded that speech pursued as an integral part of criminal conduct was beyond first amendment protection. Indeed no one contends that citizens are free to say anything, anywhere, at any time. As Holmes, J., observed, citizens are not free to yell "fire" falsely in a crowded theater.

The spectre of a man crying fire falsely in the theater, however, has plagued first amendment theory. The task is to formulate principles that separate the protected from the unprotected. But speech interacts with too many other values in too many complicated ways to expect that a single formula will prove productive.

Are advocates of illegal action, pornographers selling magazines, or publishers of defamation like that person in the theater or are they engaged in freedom of speech? Do citizens have a right to speak on government property? Which property? Is there a right of access to the print or broadcast media? Can government force private owners to grant access for speakers? Does the first amendment offer protection for the wealthy, powerful corporations, and media conglomerates against government attempts to assure greater equality in the intellectual marketplace? Can government demand information about private political associations or reporters' confidential sources without first amendment limits? Does the first amendment require government to produce information it might otherwise withhold?

a. Nonetheless, for a sophisticated defense of Black, J.'s position, see Charles Black, *Mr.* *Justice Black, the Supreme Court, and the Bill of Rights,* 222 Harper's Mag. 63 (1961).

The Court has approached questions such as these without much attention to the language[b] or history[c] of the first amendment and without a commitment to any general theory.[d] Rather it has sought to develop principles on a case-by-case basis and has produced a complex and conflicting body of constitutional precedent. Many of the basic principles were developed in a line of cases involving the advocacy of illegal action.

I. ADVOCACY OF ILLEGAL ACTION

A. EMERGING PRINCIPLES

SCHENCK v. UNITED STATES, 249 U.S. 47, 39 S.Ct. 247, 63 L.Ed. 470 (1919): Defendants were convicted of a conspiracy to violate the 1917 Espionage Act by conspiring to cause and attempting to cause insubordination in the armed forces of the United States, and obstruction of the recruiting and enlistment service of the United States, when at war with Germany, by printing and circulating to men accepted for military service approximately fifteen thousand copies of the document described in the opinion. In affirming, HOLMES, J., said for a unanimous Court: "The document in question upon its first printed side recited the first section of the Thirteenth Amendment, said that the idea embodied in it was violated by the conscription act and that a conscript is little better than a convict. In impassioned language it intimated that conscription was despotism in its worst form and a monstrous wrong against humanity in the interest of Wall Street's chosen few. It said, 'Do not submit to intimidation,' but in form at least confined itself to peaceful measures such as a petition for the repeal of the act.

b. But compare fn. b. in *Roth v. United States*, Sec. 1, III, A infra. For the contention that comparing the speech clause with other clauses of the Constitution yields insight, see Akhil Reed Amar, *Intratextualism*, 112 Harv. L.Rev. 747, 810–17 (1999).

c. But see, *McIntyre v. Ohio Elections Comm'n*, Sec. 9, I (Thomas, J., concurring) (Scalia, J., dissenting). See, e.g., Michael Perry, *The Constitution, The Courts, and Human Rights*, 63–64 (1982). For a variety of views about the history surrounding the adoption of the first amendment, compare Leonard Levy, *Legacy of Suppression* (1960) with Leonard Levy, *Emergence of a Free Press* (1985); Leonard Levy, *The Legacy Reexamined*, 37 Stan. L.Rev. 767 (1985); Leonard Levy, *On the Origins of the Free Press Clause*, 32 U.C.L.A.L.Rev. 177 (1984) and George Anastaplo, *Book Review*, 39 N.Y.U.L.Rev. 735 (1964); David Anderson, *The Origins of the Press Clause*, 30 U.C.L.A.L.Rev. 455 (1983); Phillip Hamburger, *The Development of the Law of Seditious Libel and the Control of the Press*, 37 Stan.L.Rev. 661 (1985); William Mayton, *Seditious Libel and the Lost Guarantee of a Freedom of Expression*, 84 Colum.L.Rev. 91 (1984); William Mayton, *From a Legacy of Suppression to the 'Metaphor of the Fourth Estate,'* 39 Stan. L.Rev. 139 (1986); Lucas Powe, *The Fourth Estate and the Constitution* 22–50 (1991). David Rabban, *The Ahistorical Historian: Leonard Levy on Freedom of Expression in*

Early American History, 37 Stan.L.Rev. 795 (1985).

For the contention that post-adoption history should play a larger role than philosophy in first amendment analysis, see L.A. Powe, *Situating Schauer,* 72 Notre D. L.Rev. 1519 (1997). For work focusing on post-adoption periods, see Michael Kent Curtis, *Free Speech, "The People's Darling Privilege"* (2000); David Rabban, *Free Speech in its Forgotten Years* (1997). Michael Gibson, *The Supreme Court and Freedom of Expression from 1791 to 1917*, 55 Fordham L.Rev. 263 (1986). See also Zechariah Chafee, *Free Speech in the United States* (1941); Leon Whipple, *The Story of Civil Liberty in the United States* (1927); David Kairys, *Freedom of Speech* in The Politics of Law 160 (Kairys ed. 1982). For an ambitious attempt to marry history, philosophy, and the first amendment, see David Richards, *A Theory of Free Speech,* 34 UCLA L.Rev. 1837 (1987).

d. On the difficulties involved in developing general theory, see Larry Alexander & Paul Horton, *The Impossibility of a Free Speech Principle,* 78 Nw.U.L.Rev. 1319 (1983); Daniel Farber & Phillip Frickey, *Practical Reason and the First Amendment,* 34 UCLA L.Rev. 1615 (1987); Steven Shiffrin, *The First Amendment and Economic Regulation: Away From a General Theory of the First Amendment,* 78 Nw. U.L.Rev. 1212 (1983); Laurence Tribe, *Toward A Metatheory of Free Speech,* 10 Sw.U.L.Rev. 237 (1978).

The other and later printed side of the sheet was headed 'Assert Your Rights.' It stated reasons for alleging that any one violated the Constitution when he refused to recognize 'your right to assert your opposition to the draft,' and went on, 'If you do not assert and support your rights, you are helping to deny or disparage rights which it is the solemn duty of all citizens and residents of the United States to retain.' It described the arguments on the other side as coming from cunning politicians and a mercenary capitalist press, and even silent consent to the conscription law as helping to support an infamous conspiracy. It denied the power to send our citizens away to foreign shores to shoot up the people of other lands, and added that words could not express the condemnation such cold-blooded ruthlessness deserves, & c., & c., winding up, 'You must do your share to maintain, support and uphold the rights of the people of this country.' Of course the document would not have been sent unless it had been intended to have some effect, and we do not see what effect it could be expected to have upon persons subject to the draft except to influence them to obstruct the carrying of it out. The defendants do not deny that the jury might find against them on this point.

"But it is said, suppose that that was the tendency of this circular, it is protected by the First Amendment to the Constitution. [We] admit that in many places and in ordinary times the defendants in saying all that was said in the circular would have been within their constitutional rights. But the character of every act depends upon the circumstances in which it is done. The most stringent protection of free speech would not protect a man in falsely shouting fire in a theatre and causing a panic. [The] question in every case is whether the words used are used in such circumstances and are of such a nature as to create a clear and present danger that they will bring about the substantive evils that Congress has a right to prevent. It is a question of proximity and degree.[a] When a nation is at war many things that might be said in time of peace are such a hindrance to its effort that their utterance will not be endured so long as men fight and that no Court could regard them as protected by any constitutional right. It seems to be admitted that if an actual obstruction of the recruiting service were proved, liability for words that produced that effect might be enforced. The statute of 1917 punishes conspiracies to obstruct as well as actual obstruction. If the act, (speaking, or circulating a paper), its tendency and the intent with which it is done are the same, we perceive no ground for saying that success alone warrants making the act a crime."[b]

---

a. Although Schenck was convicted for violating a conspiracy statute, Holmes appears to have used the occasion to import the law of criminal attempts into the freedom of expression area. "In *Schenck*, 'clear and present danger,' 'a question of proximity and degree' bridged the gap between the defendant's acts of publication and the [prohibited interferences with the war.] This connection was strikingly similar to the Holmesian analysis of the requirement of 'dangerous proximity to success' [quoting from an earlier Holmes opinion] that, in the law of attempts, bridges the gap between the defendant's acts and the completed crime. In either context, innocuous efforts are to be ignored." Yogal Rogat, *Mr. Justice Holmes: Some Modern Views—The Judge as Spectator,* 31 U.Chi.L.Rev. 213, 215 (1964). See also Chaf-

ee, *Free Speech in the United States* 81–82 (1941); Shapiro, *Freedom of Speech* 55–58 (1966). But see Holmes, J., dissenting in *Abrams* infra, and fn. b below.

b. See also *Frohwerk v. United States,* 249 U.S. 204, 39 S.Ct. 249, 63 L.Ed. 561 (1919), where a unanimous Court, per Holmes, J., sustained a conviction for conspiracy to obstruct recruiting in violation of the Espionage Act, by means of a dozen newspaper articles praising the spirit and strength of the German nation, criticizing the decision to send American troops to France, maintaining that the government was giving false and hypocritical reasons for its course of action and implying that "the guilt of those who voted the unnatural sacrifice" is greater than the wrong of those who seek to escape by resistance:

DEBS v. UNITED STATES, 249 U.S. 211, 39 S.Ct. 252, 63 L.Ed. 566 (1919): Defendant was convicted of violating the Espionage Act for obstructing and attempting to obstruct the recruiting service and for causing and attempting to cause insubordination and disloyalty in the armed services. He was given a ten-year prison sentence on each count, to run concurrently. His criminal conduct consisted of giving the anti-war speech described in the opinion at the state convention of the Socialist Party of Ohio, held at a park in Canton, Ohio, on a June 16, 1918 Sunday afternoon before a general audience of 1,200 persons. At the time of the speech, defendant was a national political figure.[a] In affirming, HOLMES, J., observed for a unanimous Court:

"The main theme of the speech was socialism, its growth, and a prophecy of its ultimate success. With that we have nothing to do, but if a part or the manifest intent of the more general utterances was to encourage those present to obstruct the recruiting service and if in passages such encouragement was directly given, the immunity of the general theme may not be enough to protect the speech. [Defendant had come to the park directly from a nearby jail, where he had visited three socialists imprisoned for obstructing the recruiting service. He expressed sympathy and admiration for these persons and others convicted of similar offenses, and then] said that the master class has always declared the war and the subject class has always fought the battles—that the subject class has had nothing to gain and all to lose, including their lives; [and that] 'You have your lives to lose; you certainly ought to have the right to declare war if you consider a war necessary.' [He next said of a woman serving a ten-year sentence for obstructing the recruiting service] that she had said no more than the speaker had said that afternoon; that if she was guilty so was [he].

"There followed personal experiences and illustrations of the growth of socialism, a glorification of minorities, and a prophecy of the success of [socialism], with the interjection that 'you need to know that you are fit for something better than slavery and cannon fodder.' [Defendant's] final exhortation [was] 'Don't worry about the charge of treason to your masters; but be concerned about the treason that involves yourselves.' The defendant addressed the jury himself, and while contending that his speech did not warrant the charges said 'I have been accused of obstructing the war. I admit it. Gentlemen, I abhor war. I would oppose the war if I stood alone.' The statement was not necessary to warrant the jury in finding that one purpose of the speech, whether incidental or not does not matter, was to oppose not only war in general but this war, and that the opposition was so expressed that its natural and intended effect would be to obstruct recruiting. If that was intended and if, in all the circumstances, that would be its probable effect, it would not be protected by reason of its being part of a general program and expressions of a general and conscientious belief.

"[*Schenck* decided] that a person may be convicted of a conspiracy to obstruct recruiting by words of persuasion. [S]o far as the language of the articles goes there is not much to choose between expressions to be found in them and those before us in *Schenck*." Consider Powe, supra, at 71: "The case against Frohwerk was [weaker] than that against Schenck on both contested points; the recipients of the writing and the intensity of the writing. [Even] the government attorney who prevailed in *Frohwerk* [concluded that he was] 'one of the clearest examples of the political prisoner.' "

a. Debs had run for the Presidency on the Socialist ticket for the fourth time in 1912. At the 1920 election, while in prison, Debs ran again and received over 900,000 votes as the Socialist candidate, a significant portion of all votes cast in that election. Consider Harry Kalven, *Ernst Freund and the First Amendment Tradition*, 40 U.Chi.L.Rev. 235, 237 (1973): "To put the case in modern context, it is somewhat as though George McGovern had been sent to prison for his criticism of the [Vietnam] war."

"[Defendant's constitutional objections] based upon the First Amendment [were] disposed of in *Schenck*. [T]he admission in evidence of the record of the conviction [of various persons he mentioned in his speech was proper] to show what he was talking about, to explain the true import of his expression of sympathy and to throw light on the intent of the address. [Properly admitted, too, was an 'Anti-war Proclamation and Program' adopted the previous year, coupled with testimony that shortly before his speech defendant had stated that he approved it]. Its first recommendation was, 'continuous, active, and public opposition to the war, through demonstrations, mass petitions, and all other means within our power.' Evidence that the defendant accepted this view and this declaration of his duties at the time that he made his speech is evidence that if in that speech he used words tending to obstruct the recruiting service he meant that they should have that effect. [T]he jury were most carefully instructed that they could not find the defendant guilty for advocacy of any of his opinions unless the words used had as their natural tendency and reasonably probable effect to obstruct the recruiting service [and] unless the defendant had the specific intent to do so in his mind."

Notes and Questions

1. *The man in the theater.* Consider Harry Kalven, *A Worthy Tradition* 133–34 (1988): "*Schenck*—and perhaps even Holmes himself—are best remembered for the example of the man 'falsely shouting fire' in a crowded theater. Judge Hand said in *Masses* that 'words are not only the keys of persuasion, but the triggers of action.' Justice Holmes makes the same point by means of the 'fire' example, an image which was to catch the fancy of the culture. But the example has long seemed to me trivial and misleading. It is as if the only conceivable controversy over speech policy were with an adversary who asserts that *all* use of words is absolutely immunized under the First Amendment. The 'fire' example then triumphantly impeaches this massive major premise. Beyond that, it adds nothing to our understanding. If the point were that *only* speech which is a comparable 'trigger of action' could be regulated, the example might prove a stirring way of drawing the line at incitement, but it is abundantly clear that Justice Holmes is not comparing Schenck's leaflet to the shouting of 'fire.' Moreover, because the example is so wholly apolitical, it lacks the requisite complexity for dealing with any serious speech problem likely to confront the legal system. The man shouting 'fire' does not offer premises resembling those underlying radical political rhetoric—premises that constitute criticism of government."

2. *Schenck and Debs.* Consider Harry Kalven, *Ernst Freund and the First Amendment Tradition,* 40 U.Chi.L.Rev. 235, 236–38 (1973): "It has been customary to lavish care and attention on the *Schenck* case, [but *Debs*, argued well before *Schenck* was handed down and decided just one week later,] represented the first effort by Justice Holmes to apply what he had worked out about freedom of speech in *Schenck*. The start of the law of the first amendment is not *Schenck;* it is *Schenck* and *Debs* read together. [Debs' speech] fell into the genre of bitter criticism of government and government policy, sometimes called seditious libel; freedom of such criticism from government marks, we have come to understand, 'the central meaning of the First Amendment' [*New York Times v. Sullivan,* Sec. 1, II, B infra]. During the Vietnam War thousands of utterances strictly comparable in bitterness and sharpness of criticism, if not in literacy, were made; it was pretty much taken for granted they were beyond the reach of government.[b] [*Debs*]

b. Compare *Debs* with *Bond v. Floyd,* Sec. 1, I, C infra.

raises serious questions as to what the first amendment, and more especially, what the clear and present danger formula can possibly have meant at the time. [Holmes] does not comment on the fact difference between [*Schenck* and *Debs*]: the defendant in *Schenck* had sent his leaflets directly to men who awaited draft call whereas [*Debs*] was addressing a general audience at a public meeting. Holmes offers no discussion of the sense in which Debss' speech presented a clear and present danger. [In fact, *Debs*] did not move [Holmes] to discuss free speech at all; his brief opinion is occupied with two points about admissibility of [evidence]. It was for Holmes a routine criminal appeal.''

3. *Governmental legitimacy.* Consider Lawrence B. Solum, *Freedom of Communicative Action,* 83 Nw.U.L.Rev. 54, 122–23 (1989): "Government claims a legitimate monopoly on the use of force. Any fundamental challenge to the legitimacy of this monopoly must include implicit justification or explicit advocacy of illegal action, either of nonviolent civil disobedience or of violent revolution. [S]uch fundamental challenges must be allowed if the government claims that the rightfulness of its monopoly on the use of force would be accepted in rational discourse. [I]f a violent revolutionary movement were actually likely to succeed in overthrowing the present government and if we had good reason to believe that the new regime would be worse than the present government, then we would have good reasons to temporarily suspend the right to question fundamental legitimacy in order to avoid this immediate and serious danger. The 'clear and present danger' test operationalizes a qualification of the right to advocate illegal conduct."

4. MASSES PUBLISHING CO. v. PATTEN, 244 Fed. 535 (S.D.N.Y.1917): The Postmaster of New York advised plaintiff that an issue of his monthly revolutionary journal, *The Masses,* would be denied the mails under the Espionage Act since it tended to encourage the enemies of the United States and to hamper the government in its conduct of the war. The Postmaster subsequently specified as objectionable several cartoons entitled, e.g., "Conscription," "Making the World Safe for Capitalism"; several articles admiring the "sacrifice" of conscientious objectors and a poem praising two persons imprisoned for conspiracy to resist the draft. Plaintiff sought a preliminary injunction against the postmaster from excluding its magazine from the mails. LEARNED HAND, D.J., granted relief:

"[The postmaster maintains] that to arouse discontent and disaffection among the people with the prosecution of the war and with the draft tends to promote a mutinous and insubordinate temper among the troops. This [is] true; men who become satisfied that they are engaged in an enterprise dictated by the unconscionable selfishness of the rich, and effectuated by a tyrannous disregard for the will of those who must suffer and die, will be more prone to insubordination than those who have faith in the cause and acquiesce in the means. Yet to interpret the word 'cause' [in the statutory language forbidding one to 'willfully cause' insubordination in the armed forces] so broadly would [necessarily involve] the suppression of all hostile criticism, and of all opinion except what encouraged and supported the existing policies, or which fell within the range of temperate argument. It would contradict the normal assumption of democratic government that the suppression of hostile criticism does not turn upon the justice of its substance or the decency and propriety of its temper. Assuming that the power to repress such opinion may rest in Congress in the throes of a struggle for the very existence of the state, its exercise is so contrary to the use and wont of our people that only the clearest expression of such a power justifies the conclusion that it was intended.

"The defendant's position, therefore, in so far as it involves the suppression of the free utterance of abuse and criticism of the existing law, or of the policies of the war, is not, in my judgment, supported by the language of the statute. Yet there has always been a recognized limit to such expressions, incident indeed to the existence of any compulsive power of the state itself. One may not counsel or advise others to violate the law as it stands. Words are not only the keys of persuasion, but the triggers of action, and those which have no purport but to counsel the violation of law cannot by any latitude of interpretation be a part of that public opinion which is the final source of government in a democratic state. [To] counsel or advise a man to an act is to urge upon him either that it is his interest or his duty to do it. While, of course, this may be accomplished as well by indirection as expressly, since words carry the meaning that they impart, the definition is exhaustive, I think, and I shall use it. [If] one stops short of urging upon others that it is their duty or their interest to resist the law, it seems to me one should not be held to have attempted to cause its violation.[c] If that be not the test, I can see no escape from the conclusion that under this section every political agitation which can be shown to be apt to create a seditious temper is illegal. I am confident that by such language Congress had no such revolutionary purpose in view.

"It seems to me, however, quite plain that none of the language and none of the cartoons in this paper can be thought directly to counsel or advise insubordination or mutiny, without a violation of their meaning quite beyond any tolerable understanding. I come, therefore to the [provision of the Act forbidding] any one from willfully obstructing [recruiting or enlistment]. I am not prepared to assent to the plaintiff's position that this only refers to acts other than words, nor that the act thus defined must be shown to have been successful. One may obstruct without preventing, and the mere obstruction is an injury to the service; for it throws impediments in its way. Here again, however, since the question is of the expression of opinion, I construe the sentence, so far as it restrains public utterance, [as] limited to the direct advocacy of resistance to the recruiting and enlistment service. If so, the inquiry is narrowed to the question whether any of the challenged matter may be said to advocate resistance to the draft, taking the meaning of the words with the utmost latitude which they can bear.

"As to the cartoons it seems to me quite clear that they do not fall within such a test. [T]he most that can be said [is that they] may breed such animosity to the draft as will promote resistance and strengthen the determination of those disposed to be recalcitrant. There is no intimation that, however, hateful the draft may be, one is in duty bound to resist it, certainly none that such resistance is to one's interest. I cannot, therefore, even with the limitations which surround the power of the court, assent to the assertion that any of the cartoons violate the act.

"[As for the text], it is plain enough that the [magazine] has the fullest sympathy for [those who resist the draft or obstruct recruiting], that it admires their courage, and that it presumptively approves their conduct. [Moreover,] these passages, it must be remembered, occur in a magazine which attacks with the utmost violence the draft and the war. That such comments have a tendency to arouse emulation in others is clear enough, but that they counsel others to follow these examples is not so plain. Literally at least they do not, and while, as I have

---

c. Charles Fried, *Perfect Freedom, Perfect Justice,* 78 B.U.L.Rev. 717, 725 (1998): "Hand's test both excludes and includes too much. It denies First Amendment protection to pacifist teaching that it is a person's duty peaceably to disobey certain laws, while granting it—to use Mill's example—to the inflammatory denunciation of food speculation to a hungry mob assembled at a corn dealer's house."

said, the words are to be taken, not literally, but according to their full import, the literal meaning is the starting point for interpretation. One may admire and approve the course of a hero without feeling any duty to follow him. There is not the least implied intimation in these words that others are under a duty to follow. The most that can be said is that, if others do follow, they will get the same admiration and the same approval. Now, there is surely an appreciable distance between esteem and emulation; and unless there is here some advocacy of such emulation, I cannot see how the passages can be said to fall within the [law.] Surely, if the draft had not excepted Quakers, it would be too strong a doctrine to say that any who openly admire their fortitude or even approved their conduct was willfully obstructing the draft.

"When the question is of a statute constituting a crime, it seems to me that there should be more definite evidence of the act. The question before me is quite the same as what would arise upon a motion to dismiss an indictment at the close of the proof: Could any reasonable man say, not that the indirect result of the language might be to arouse a seditious disposition, for that would not be enough, but that the language directly advocated resistance to the draft? I cannot think that upon such language any verdict would stand."[d]

JUSTICE HOLMES—DISSENTING IN
ABRAMS v. UNITED STATES
250 U.S. 616, 624, 40 S.Ct. 17, 20, 63 L.Ed. 1173, 1178 (1919).

[In the summer of 1918, the United States sent a small body of marines to Siberia. Although the defendants maintained a strong socialist opposition to "German militarism," they opposed the "capitalist" invasion of Russia, and characterized it as an attempt to crush the Russian Revolution. Shortly thereafter, they printed two leaflets and distributed several thousand copies in New York City. Many of the copies were thrown from a window where one defendant was employed; others were passed around at radical meetings. Both leaflets supported Russia against the United States; one called upon workers to unite in a general strike. There was no evidence that workers responded to the call.

[The Court upheld the defendants' convictions for conspiring to violate two provisions of the 1918 amendments to the Espionage Act. One count prohibited language intended to "incite, provoke and encourage resistance to the United States"; the other punished those who urged curtailment of war production. As the Court interpreted the statute, an intent to interfere with efforts against a *declared* war was a necessary element of both offenses. Since the United States had not declared war upon Russia, "the main task of the government was to establish an [*intention*] *to interfere with the war with Germany.*" Chafee, supra, at 115. The Court found intent on the principle that "Men must be held to have intended, and to be accountable for, the effects which their acts were likely to produce. Even if their primary purpose and intent was to aid the cause of the

---

d. In reversing, 246 Fed. 24 (1917), the Second Circuit observed: "If the natural and probable effect of what is said is to encourage resistance to a law, and the words are used in an endeavor to persuade to resistance, it is immaterial that the duty to resist is not mentioned, or the interest of the person addressed in resistance is not suggested. That one may willfully obstruct the enlistment service, without advising in direct language against enlistments, and without stating that to refrain from enlistment is a duty or in one's interest, seems to us too plain for controversy."

For diverse views concerning Judge Hand's opinion and its importance, see Gerald Gunther, *Learned Hand* 151–70, 603 (1994); Bernard Schwartz, *Holmes v. Hand,* 1994 S.Ct. Rev. 209; Vincent Blasi, *Learned Hand and the Self–Government Theory of the First Amendment,* 61 U.Col.L.Rev. 1 (1990).

Russian Revolution, the plan of action which they adopted necessarily involved, before it could be realized, defeat of the war program of the United States * * *."

[Holmes, J., dissented in an opinion with which Brandeis, J., concurred:][a]

[I] am aware of course that the word "intent" as vaguely used in ordinary legal discussion means no more than knowledge at the time of the act that the consequences said to be intended will ensue. [But,] when words are used exactly, a deed is not done with intent to produce a consequence unless that consequence is the aim of the deed. It may be obvious, and obvious to the actor, that the consequence will follow, and he may be liable for it even if he regrets it, but he does not do the act with intent to produce it unless the aim to produce it is the proximate motive of the specific act although there may be some deeper motive behind.

It seems to me that this statute must be taken to use its words in a strict and accurate sense. They would be absurd in any other. A patriot might think that we were wasting money on aeroplanes, or making more cannon of a certain kind than we needed, and might advocate curtailment with success, yet even if it turned out that the curtailment hindered and was thought by other minds to have been obviously likely to hinder the United States in the prosecution of the war, no one would hold such conduct a crime. * * *

I never have seen any reason to doubt that the questions of law that alone were before this Court in the cases of *Schenck, Frohwerk* and *Debs* were rightly decided. I do not doubt for a moment that by the same reasoning that would justify punishing persuasion to murder, the United States constitutionally may punish speech that produces or is intended to produce a clear and imminent danger that it will bring about forthwith certain substantive evils that the United States constitutionally may seek to prevent. The power undoubtedly is greater in time of war than in time of peace because war opens dangers that do not exist at other times.

But as against dangers peculiar to war, as against others, the principle of the right to free speech is always the same. It is only the present danger of immediate evil or an intent to bring it about that warrants Congress in setting a limit to the expression of opinion where private rights are not concerned. Congress certainly cannot forbid all effort to change the mind of the country. Now nobody can suppose that the surreptitious publishing of a silly leaflet by an unknown man, without more, would present any immediate danger that its opinions would hinder the success of the government arms or have any appreciable tendency to do so.[b]

---

a. Consider Sheldon Novick, *Honorable Justice, The Life of Oliver Wendell Holmes* 331 (1989): "The majority did very highly disapprove of Holmes's dissent, and White tried to persuade him to be silent. When Holmes clung to what he thought his duty, three of the justices came to call on him in his library, and [his wife] Fanny joined them in trying to dissuade him from publishing his dissent."

b. But cf. John Wigmore, *Abrams v. U.S.: Freedom of Speech and Freedom of Thuggery in War–Time and Peace–Time,* 14 Ill.L.Rev. 539, 549–50 (1920): "[The *Abrams* dissent] is dallying with the facts and the law. None know better than judges that what is lawful for one is lawful for a thousand others. If these five men could, without the law's restraint, urge munition workers to a general strike and armed violences then others could lawfully do so; and a thousand disaffected undesirables, aliens and natives alike, were ready and waiting to do so. Though this circular was 'surreptitious,' the next ones need not be so. If such urgings were lawful, every munitions factory in the country could be stopped by them. The relative amount of harm that one criminal act can effect is no measure of its criminality, and no measure of the danger of its criminality. [At a time] when the fate of the civilized world hung in the balance, how could the Minority Opinion interpret law and conduct in such a way as to let loose men who were doing their hardest to paralyze the supreme war efforts of our country?"

Publishing those opinions for the very purpose of obstructing, however, might indicate a greater danger and at any rate would have the quality of an attempt.[c]
* * *

I do not see how anyone can find the intent required by the statute in any of the defendants' words. The leaflet advocating a general strike is the only one that affords even a foundation for the charge, and [its only object] is to help Russia and stop American intervention there against the popular government—not to impede the United States in the war that it was carrying on. * * *

In this case sentences of twenty years imprisonment have been imposed for the publishing of two leaflets that I believe the defendants had as much right to publish as the Government has to publish the Constitution of the United States now vainly invoked by them. [E]ven if what I think the necessary intent were shown; the most nominal punishment seems to me all that possibly could be inflicted, unless the defendants are to be made to suffer not for what the indictment alleges but for the creed that they avow—[which,] although made the subject of examination at the trial, no one has a right even to consider in dealing with the charges before the Court.

Persecution for the expression of opinions seems to me perfectly logical. If you have no doubt of your premises or your power and want a certain result with all your heart you naturally express your wishes in law and sweep away all opposition. To allow opposition by speech seems to indicate that you think the speech impotent, as when a man says that he has squared the circle, or that you do not care whole-heartedly for the result, or that you doubt either your power or your premises. But when men have realized that time has upset many fighting faiths,[d] they may come to believe even more than they believe the very foundations of their own conduct that the ultimate good desired is better reached by free trade in ideas—that the best test of truth is the power of the thought to get itself accepted in the competition of the market, and that truth is the only ground upon which their wishes safely can be carried out. That at any rate is the theory of our Constitution. It is an experiment, as all life is an experiment. Every year if not every day we have to wager our salvation upon some prophecy based upon imperfect knowledge. While that experiment is part of our system I think that we should be eternally vigilant against attempts to check the expression of opinions that we loathe and believe to be fraught with death, unless they so imminently threaten immediate interference with the lawful and pressing purposes of the law

---

c. Would it, if, under the circumstances, the defendant had no reasonable prospect of success? If his efforts were utterly ineffectual? Is bad intention or purpose, without more, an attempt? Or even everything done in furtherance of that bad intention? Or is unlawful "intention" or "purpose" merely one factor in determining whether defendant's conduct comes dangerously near success or stamps the actor as sufficiently dangerous? Cf. Oliver Wendall Holmes, *The Common Law* 65–66, 68–69 (1881): "Intent to commit a crime is not itself criminal. [Moreover], the law does not punish every act which is done with the intent to bring about a crime. [We] have seen what amounts to an attempt to burn a haystack [lighting a match with intent to start fire to a haystack]; but it was said in the same case, that, if the defendant had gone no further than to buy a box of matches for the purpose, he

would not have been liable. [Relevant considerations are] the nearness of the danger, the greatness of the harm and the degree of apprehension felt." See generally Chafee, supra, at 46–47; Hans Linde, *"Clear and Present Danger" Reexamined,* 22 Stan.L.Rev. 1163, 1168–69, 1183–86 (1970); Martin Shapiro, *Freedom of Speech* 55–58 (1966).

d. "In referring to 'fighting faiths,' Holmes may well have been thinking in part of the abolitionism to which he had been committed in his youth, and which he believed had led to the devastation of the Civil War. In this way, he laid the foundations of modern free speech jurisprudence on the ruins of the natural rights theory which originally supported the First Amendment." Steven J. Heyman, *Righting the Balance: An Inquiry into the Foundations and Limits of Freedom of Expression,* 78 B.U.L.Rev. 1275, 1303 (1998).

that an immediate check is required to save the country. [Only] the emergency that makes it immediately dangerous to leave the correction of evil counsels to time warrants making any exception to the sweeping command, "Congress shall make no law * * * abridging the freedom of speech." Of course I am speaking only of expressions of opinion and exhortations, which were all that were uttered [here].[e]

Notes and Questions

1. *"Marketplace of ideas."* (a) Consider G. Edward White, *Justice Holmes and the Modernization of Free Speech Jurisprudence: The Human Dimension,* 80 Calif.L.Rev. 439 (1992): "For Chafee and those who emphasized the social interest in free speech, the search for truth was part of a process in which public opinion could become more informed and enlightened. For Holmes, 'truth' was the equivalent of majoritarian prejudice at any point in time. He defined it to Laski as 'the prevailing can't help of the majority,' and to Learned Hand as 'the majority vote of that nation that can lick all others.' The optimistic, democratic vision of Chafee and his progressive contemporaries had resonated with Holmes' skeptical resignation about the primacy of majoritarian sentiment. The 'search for truth' metaphor, embodying both of those perspectives, had arrived in American free speech jurisprudence."

(b) Contrast Holmes, J.'s statement of the "marketplace of ideas" argument with John Milton's statement in *Areopagitica:* "And though all the winds of doctrine were let loose to play upon the earth, so Truth be in the field, we do injuriously by licensing and prohibiting to misdoubt her strength. Let her and Falsehood grapple; who ever knew Truth put to the worse, in a free and open encounter?"[f] Holmes, J., claims that the competition of the market is the best test of truth; Milton maintains that truth will emerge in a free and open encounter. How would one verify either hypothesis?

Is the "marketplace of ideas" a "free and open encounter"? Consider Charles Lindblom, *Politics and Markets* 207 (1977): "Early, persuasive, unconscious conditioning—[to] believe in the fundamental politico-economic institutions of one's society is ubiquitous in every society. These institutions come to be taken for granted. Many people grow up to regard them not as institutions to be tested but as standards against which the correctness of new policies and institutions can be tested. When that happens, as is common, processes of critical judgment are short-circuited." Consider also Tribe 2d ed., at 786: "Especially when the wealthy have more access to the most potent media of communication than the poor, how sure can we be that 'free trade in ideas' is likely to generate truth?"

For a specific example, see Steven Shiffrin, *The First Amendment and Economic Regulation: Away From A General Theory of the First Amendment,* 78 Nw.U.L.Rev. 1212, 1281 (1983): "Living in a society in which children and adults

---

e. Consider Vincent Blasi, *Reading Holmes through the Lens of Schauer: The Abrams Dissent,* 72 Notre Dame L. Rev. 1343, 1354–55 (1997): "Nothing [Holmes] says in Abrams by his own injunction, applies to regulations of speech predicated on misstatements of verifiable fact, such as the standard action for defamation. Likewise, disclosures of sensitive information remain outside the ambit of Holmes's argument for free speech, however much such disclosures might contribute to public debate or the checking of government power. The

graphic depictions of pornographers, even the soft-core variety, also appear not to be the type of speech that Holmes insists must be tested in the competition of the market."

f. For commentary explaining Milton's argument, suggesting that Milton's most important contributions to free speech lie elsewhere, see Vincent Blasi, *Milton's Areopagitica and the Modern First Amendment,* 13 Communications Lawyer 1 (1996).

are daily confronted with multiple communications that ask them to purchase products inevitably places emphasis on materialistic values. The authors of the individual messages may not intend that general emphasis, but the whole is greater than the sum of the parts. [Advertisers] spend some sixty billion dollars per year. [Those] who would oppose the materialist message must combat forces that have a massive economic advantage. Any confidence that we will know what is truth by seeing what emerges from such combat is ill placed."

Do the different market failure considerations offered by Lindblom, Tribe, and Shiffrin add up to a rebuttal of the marketplace argument? Consider Melvin Nimmer, *Nimmer on Freedom of Speech* 1–12 (1984): "If acceptance of an idea in the competition of the market is not the 'best test' [what] is the alternative? It can only be acceptance of an idea by some individual or group narrower than that of the public at large. Thus, the alternative to competition in the market must be some form of elitism. It seems hardly necessary to enlarge on the dangers of that path." Is elitism the only alternative to the marketplace perspective? Is elitism always wrong?

(c) Evaluate the following hypothetical commentary: "Liberals have favored government intervention in the economic marketplace but pressed for laissez-faire in the intellectual marketplace. Conservatives have done the reverse. Liberals and conservatives have one thing in common: inconsistent positions."

(d) Does the marketplace argument overvalue truth? Consider Frederick Schauer, *Free Speech: A Philosophical Enquiry* 23 (1982). Government may seek to suppress opinions "because their expression is thought to impair the authority of a lawful and effective government, interfere with the administration of justice (such as publication of a defendant's criminal record in advance of a jury trial), cause offence, invade someone's privacy, or cause a decrease in public order. When these are the motives for suppression, the possibility of losing some truth is relevant but hardly dispositive. [In such circumstances] the argument from truth [is] not wholly to the point." Is Holmes, J., persuasive when he maintains that before we can suppress opinion we must wait until "an immediate check is required to save the country"?

(e) Does the marketplace argument threaten first amendment values? Consider Stanley Ingber, *The Marketplace of Ideas: A Legitimizing Myth*, 1984 Duke L.J. 1, 4–5 "[C]ourts that invoke the marketplace model of the first amendment justify free expression because of the aggregate benefits to society, and not because an individual speaker receives a particular benefit. Courts that focus their concern on the audience rather than the speaker relegate free expression to an instrumental value, a means toward some other goal, rather than a value unto itself. Once free expression is viewed solely as an instrumental value, however, it is easier to allow government regulation of speech if society as a whole 'benefits' from a regulated system of expression."

(f) Does the marketplace argument slight other important free speech values? Consider Robert Wolff, *The Poverty of Liberalism* 18 (1968) "[I]t is not to assist the advance of knowledge that free debate is needed. Rather, it is in order to guarantee that every legitimate interest shall make itself known and felt in the political [process]. Justice, not truth, is the ideal served by liberty of speech." Compare Paul Chevigny, *Philosophy of Language and Free Expression*, 55 N.Y.U.L.Rev. 157 (1980); Mark Leitner, *Liberalism, Separation and Speech*, 1985 Wis.L.Rev. 79, 89–90 & 103–04. The standard discussion of free speech values continues to be Thomas Emerson, *The System of Freedom of Expression* 6–9 (1970).

(g) Would an emphasis on dissent be preferable to an emphasis on the marketplace metaphor? Consider Steven Shiffrin, *The First Amendment, Democracy, and Romance* (1990): "[A] commitment to sponsoring dissent does not require a belief that what emerges in the 'market' is usually right or that the 'market' is the best test of truth. Quite the contrary, the commitment to sponsor dissent assumes that societal pressures to conform are strong and that incentives to keep quiet are often great. If the marketplace metaphor encourages the view that an invisible hand or voluntaristic arrangements have guided us patiently, but slowly, to Burkean harmony, the commitment to sponsoring dissent encourages us to believe that the cozy arrangements of the status quo have settled on something less than the true or the just. If the marketplace metaphor encourages the view that conventions, habits, and traditions have emerged as our best sense of the truth from the rigorous testing ground of the marketplace of ideas, the commitment to sponsoring dissent encourages the view that conventions, habits, and traditions are compromises open to challenge. If the marketplace metaphor counsels us that the market's version of truth is more worthy of trust than any that the government might dictate, a commitment to sponsoring dissent counsels us to be suspicious of both. If the marketplace metaphor encourages a sloppy form of relativism (whatever has emerged in the marketplace is right for now), the commitment to sponsoring dissent emphasizes that truth is not decided in public opinion polls."[g]

2. *Pragmatism and scientific method.* Consider Vincent Blasi, *Reading Holmes through the Lens of Schauer: The Abrams Dissent*, 72 Notre D. L. Rev. 1343, 1344–45 (1997): "Once the eloquence has been savored (and the false modesty noted), the reader wonders whether Holmes can possibly mean what he seems to be saying about 'the best test of truth.' Is he really so cynical, or fatalistic? Is he asserting a Chicago-school level of faith in markets combined with a willingness both to commodify truth and to ignore the various sources of market failure that operate in the flesh-and-blood society he is supposedly discussing? And even if Holmes wishes to embrace such a mundane conception of truth, how then does truth become 'the only ground' of social organization and aspiration? [H]ow does the author of the quip 'the Fourteenth Amendment does not enact Mr. Herbert Spencer's Social Statics' justify the position that the First Amendment enacts an extreme version of epistemological skepticism and/or moral relativism?

"One possible response is to read Holmes as neither a borderline cynic nor a model-building neoclassical economist but rather a pragmatist impressed by how free speech can foster a culture of productive adaptation. In this view, the reference to 'the market'—observe that Holmes never employs the phrase 'marketplace of ideas'—is not meant to evoke anything so elegant and implausible as a fair procedure for determining society's finely calibrated, self-correcting cognitive equilibrium. Rather the claim is simply that the human understanding is eternally fluctuating and incomplete, and constantly in need of inquisitive energy much the way commercial prosperity depends on entrepreneurial energy. In addition, Holmes's allusion to Darwinian forces and his assertion that life is an experiment suggests his embrace of the scientific method, with the implication that the First

g. For a powerful critique of marketplace models, see C. Edwin Baker, *Human Liberty and Freedom of Speech* 6–24, 37–46 (1989). For qualified defenses, see Kent Greenawalt, *Free Speech Justifications*, 89 Colum.L.Rev. 119, 130–41, 153–54 (1989); Frederick Schauer, *Language, Truth, and the First Amendment*, 64 Va.L.Rev. 263 (1978). For the proposition that free speech protects the pursuit of knowledge, an intrinsic good, see John H. Garvey, *What are Freedoms For* ch. 4 (1996). For commentary on metaphors in general and the marketplace metaphor in particular, see Steven Winter, *Transcendental Nonsense, Metaphoric Reasoning, and the Cognitive Stakes for Law*, 137 U.Pa.L.Rev. 1105 (1989).

Amendment represents a commitment by this society to test its truths continually and revise them regularly."[h]

B. STATE SEDITION LAWS

The second main group of cases in the initial development of first amendment doctrine involved state "sedition laws" of two basic types: criminal anarchy laws, typified by the New York statute in *Gitlow*, infra, and criminal syndicalism laws similar to the California statute in *Whitney*, infra. Most states enacted anarchy and syndicalism statutes between 1917 and 1921, in response to World War I and the fear of Bolshevism that developed in its wake, but the first modern sedition law was passed by New York in 1902, soon after the assassination of President McKinley. The law, which prohibited not only actual or attempted assassinations or conspiracies to assassinate, but advocacy of anarchy as well, lay idle for nearly twenty years, until the *Gitlow* prosecution.

GITLOW v. NEW YORK, 268 U.S. 652, 45 S.Ct. 625, 69 L.Ed. 1138 (1925): Defendant was a member of the Left Wing Section of the Socialist Party and a member of its National Council, which adopted a "Left Wing Manifesto," condemning the dominant "moderate Socialism" for its recognition of the necessity of the democratic parliamentary state; advocating the necessity of accomplishing the "Communist Revolution" by a militant and "revolutionary Socialism" based on "the class struggle"; and urging the development of mass political strikes for the destruction of the parliamentary state. Defendant arranged for printing and distributing, through the mails and otherwise, 16,000 copies of the Manifesto in the Left Wing's official organ, The Revolutionary Age. There was no evidence of any effect from the publication and circulation of the Manifesto.

In sustaining a conviction under the New York "criminal anarchy" statutes, prohibiting the "advocacy, advising or teaching the duty, necessity or propriety of overthrowing or overturning organized government by force or violence" and the publication or distribution of such matter, the majority, per SANFORD, J., stated that for present purposes we may and do assume[a] that first amendment freedoms of expression "are among the fundamental personal rights and 'liberties' protected by the due process clause of the Fourteenth Amendment from impairment by the States," but ruled:

"By enacting the present statute the State has determined, through its legislative body, that utterances advocating the overthrow of organized government by force, violence and unlawful means, are so inimical to the general welfare and involve such danger of substantive evil that they may be penalized in the exercise of its police power. That determination must be given great weight. Every

---

h. The literature on Holmes, J.'s first amendment views and their connection to his larger world view is substantial. See, e.g., G. Edward White, *Justice Oliver Wendell Holmes* 412–54 (1993); Yogal Rogat & James O'Fallon, *Mr. Justice Holmes: A Dissenting Opinion— The Speech Cases*, 36 Stan.L.Rev. 1349 (1984); David Rabban, *The Emergence of Modern First Amendment Doctrine*, 50 U.Chi.L.Rev. 1205 (1983); David M. Rabban, *Free Speech in Progressive Social Thought*, 74 Texas L.Rev. 951 (1996). For further analysis of the Holmes– Hand correspondence, see Gerald Gunther, *Learned Hand and the Origins of Modern First Amendment Doctrine: Some Fragments of His-*

tory, 27 Stan.L.Rev. 719 (1975). For illuminating discussion of *Abrams* and the period of which it is a part, see Richard Polenberg, *Fighting Faiths* (1987).

a. Although *Gitlow* is often cited for the proposition that first amendment freedoms apply to restrict state conduct, its language is dictum. Some would say the first case so holding is *Fiske v. Kansas*, 274 U.S. 380, 47 S.Ct. 655, 71 L.Ed. 1108 (1927) (no evidence to support criminal syndicalism conviction) even though no reference to the first amendment appears in the opinion. Perhaps the honor belongs to *Near v. Minnesota* (1931), Sec. 4, I, B infra.

presumption is to be indulged in favor of the validity of the statute. And the case is to be considered 'in the light of the principle that the State is primarily the judge of regulations required in the interest of public safety and welfare'; and that its police 'statutes may only be declared unconstitutional where they are arbitrary or unreasonable attempts to exercise authority vested in the State in the public interest.' That utterances inciting to the overthrow of organized government by unlawful means, present a sufficient danger of substantive evil to bring their punishment within the range of legislative discretion, is clear. Such utterances, by their very nature, involve danger to the public peace and to the security of the State. They threaten breaches of the peace and ultimate revolution. And the immediate danger is none the less real and substantial, because the effect of a given utterance cannot be accurately foreseen. The State cannot reasonably be required to measure the danger from every such utterance in the nice balance of a jeweler's scale. A single revolutionary spark may kindle a fire that, smoldering for a time, may burst into a sweeping and destructive conflagration. It cannot be said that the State is acting arbitrarily or unreasonably when in the exercise of its judgment as to the measures necessary to protect the public peace and safety, it seeks to extinguish the spark without waiting until it has enkindled the flame or blazed into the conflagration. It cannot reasonably be required to defer the adoption of measures for its own peace and safety until the revolutionary utterances lead to actual disturbances of the public peace or imminent and immediate danger of its own destruction; but it may, in the exercise of its judgment, suppress the threatened danger in its incipiency.

"[It] is clear that the question in [this case] is entirely different from that involved in those cases where the statute merely prohibits certain acts involving the danger of substantive evil, without any reference to language itself, and it is sought to apply its provisions to language used by the defendant for the purpose of bringing about the prohibited results. There, if it be contended that the statute cannot be applied to the language used by the defendant because of its protection by the freedom of speech or press, it must necessarily be found, as an original question, without any previous determination by the legislative body, whether the specific language used involved such likelihood of bringing about the substantive evil as to deprive it of the constitutional protection. In such cases it has been held that the general provisions of the statute may be constitutionally applied to the specific utterance of the defendant if its natural tendency and probable effect was to bring about the substantive evil which the legislative body might prevent. *Schenck; Debs.* And the general statement in the *Schenck* case that the 'question in every case is whether the words are used in such circumstances and are of such a nature as to create a clear and present danger that they will bring about the substantive evils,' [was] manifestly intended, as shown by the context, to apply only in cases of this class, and has no application to those like the present, where the legislative body itself has previously determined the danger of substantive evil arising from utterances of a specified character."

HOLMES, J., joined by Brandeis, J., dissented: "The general principle of free speech, it seems to me, must be taken to be included in the Fourteenth Amendment, in view of the scope that has been given to the word 'liberty' as there used, although perhaps it may be accepted with a somewhat larger latitude of interpretation than is allowed to Congress by the sweeping language that governs or ought to govern the laws of the United States. If I am right then I think that the criterion sanctioned by the full Court in *Schenck* applies. [It] is true that in my opinion this criterion was departed from in *Abrams,* but the convictions that I expressed in that case are too deep for it to be possible for me as yet to believe that it [has] settled the law. If what I think the correct test is applied it is manifest that there was no present danger of an attempt to overthrow the government by force on the part of the admittedly small minority who shared the defendant's views. It is said that this manifesto was more than a theory, that it was an incitement. Every idea is an incitement. It offers itself for belief and if believed it is acted on unless some other belief outweighs it or some failure of energy stifles the movement at its birth. The only difference between the expression of an opinion and an incitement in the narrower sense is the speaker's enthusiasm for the result. Eloquence may set fire to reason. But whatever may be thought of the redundant discourse before us it had no chance of starting a present conflagration.[b] If in the long run the beliefs expressed in proletarian dictatorship are destined to be accepted by the dominant forces of the community, the only meaning of free speech is that they should be given their chance and have their way.[c]

"If the publication of this document had been laid as an attempt to induce an uprising against government at once and not at some indefinite time in the future it would have presented a different question. The object would have been one with which the law might deal, subject to the doubt whether there was any danger that the publication could produce any result, or in other words, whether it was not futile and too remote from possible consequences. But the indictment alleges the publication and nothing more."

Notes and Questions

1. The statute in *Schenck* was not aimed directly at expression, but at conduct, i.e., certain actual or attempted interferences with the war effort. Thus, an analysis in terms of proximity between the words and the conduct prohibited (by a concededly valid law) seemed useful. But in *Gitlow* (and in *Dennis*, p. ___ infra) the statute was directed expressly against *advocacy* of a certain doctrine. Once the legislature *designates the point at which words became unlawful,* how helpful is the clear and present danger test? Is the question still how close words come to achieving certain consequences? In *Gitlow*, did Holmes "evade" the difficulty of applying an unmodified *Schenck* test to a different kind of problem? See Yogal Rogat, *Mr. Justice Holmes: Some Modern Views—The Judge as Specta-*

b. Consider Harry Kalven, *A Worthy Tradition* 156 (1988): "This famous passage points up the ironies in tradition building. The basic problem of finding an accommodation between speech too close to action and censorship too close to criticism might, we have argued, have been tolerably solved by settling on 'incitement' as the key term. It is a term which came easily to the mind of Learned Hand. But for Holmes it does not resonate as it did for Hand. It strikes his ear as a loose, expansible term. At an inopportune moment in the history of free speech the great master of the common law turns poet: 'Every idea is an incitement.' There is of course a sense in which this is true and in which it is a 'scholastic subterfuge' to pretend that speech can be arrayed in firm categories. But the defendants' proposed instruction had offered a sense in which it was not true, in which incitement required advocacy of some definite and immediate acts of force. The weakness of the prosecution's case was not that the defendants' radicalism was not dangerous; it was that their manifesto was not concrete enough to be an incitement.

"Justice Holmes's dissent in *Gitlow*, like his *Abrams* peroration, is extraordinary prose to find in a judicial opinion, and I suspect it has contributed beyond measure to the charisma of the First Amendment. But it also carries the disturbing suggestion that the defendants' speech is to be protected precisely because it is harmless and unimportant. It smacks, as will the later protections of Jehovah's Witnesses, of a luxury civil liberty."

c. But see Richard Posner, *Free Speech in an Economic Perspective,* 20 Suff.L.Rev. 1, 7 (1986): "If those beliefs are destined to prevail, free speech is irrelevant. Holmes is not describing a competitive market in ideas but a natural monopoly."

tor, 31 U.Chi.L.Rev. 213, 217 (1964). See also Walter Berns, *Freedom, Virtue and the First Amendment* 63 (Gateway ed. 1965); Hans Linde, *"Clear and Present Danger" Reexamined,* 22 Stan.L.Rev. 1163, 1169–79 (1970).

2. Consider Linde, supra, at 1171: "Since New York's law itself defined the prohibited speech, the [*Gitlow*] Court could choose among three positions. It could (1) accept this legislative judgment of the harmful potential of the proscribed words, subject to conventional judicial review; (2) independently scrutinize the facts to see whether a 'danger,' as stated in *Schenck,* justified suppression of the particular expression; or (3) hold that by legislating directly against the words rather than the effects, the lawmaker had gone beyond the leeway left to trial and proof by the holding in *Schenck* and had made a law forbidden by the first amendment." Which course did the *Gitlow* majority choose? The dissenters? Which position should the Court have chosen?

––––––––

Cases such as *Whitney,* infra, raise questions not only about freedom of speech, but also about the right of assembly. In turn, *Whitney* raises the issue of the existence and scope of a right not mentioned in the first amendment: freedom of association. Freedom of association is explored in Sec. 9 infra. Several of the cases which follow are primarily characterized as speech cases because the assemblies or associations at issue were designed for the purpose of organizing future speech activity.

WHITNEY v. CALIFORNIA

274 U.S. 357, 47 S.Ct. 641, 71 L.Ed. 1095 (1927).

JUSTICE SANFORD delivered the opinion of the Court.

[Charlotte Anita Whitney was convicted of violating the 1919 Criminal Syndicalism Act of California whose pertinent provisions were]:

"Section 1. The term 'criminal syndicalism' as used in this act is hereby defined as any doctrine or precept advocating, teaching or aiding and abetting the commission of crime, sabotage (which word is hereby defined as meaning willful and malicious physical damage or injury to physical property), or unlawful acts of force and violence or unlawful methods of terrorism as a means of accomplishing a change in industrial ownership or control, or effecting any political change.

"Sec. 2. Any person who: * * * 4. Organizes or assists in organizing, or is or knowingly becomes a member of, any organization, society, group or assemblage of persons organized or assembled to advocate, teach or aid and abet criminal syndicalism; * * *

"Is guilty of a felony and punishable by imprisonment."

The first count of the information, on which the conviction was had, charged that on or about November 28, 1919, in Alameda County, the defendant, in violation of the Criminal Syndicalism Act, "did then and there unlawfully, willfully, wrongfully, deliberately and feloniously organize and assist in organizing, and was, is, and knowingly became a member of [a group] organized and assembled to advocate, teach, aid and abet criminal syndicalism." * * *

1. While it is not denied that the evidence warranted the jury in finding that the defendant became a member of and assisted in organizing the Communist Labor Party of California, and that this was organized to advocate, teach, aid or

abet criminal syndicalism as defined by the Act, it is urged that the Act, as here construed and applied, deprived the defendant of her liberty without due process of law. [Defendant's] argument is, in effect, that the character of the state organization could not be forecast when she attended the convention; that she had no purpose of helping to create an instrument of terrorism and violence; that she "took part in formulating and presenting to the convention a resolution which, if adopted, would have committed the new organization to a legitimate policy of political reform by the use of the ballot"; that it was not until after the majority of the convention turned out to be "contrary minded, and other less temperate policies prevailed" that the convention could have taken on the character of criminal syndicalism; and that as this was done over her protest, her mere presence in the convention, however violent the opinions expressed therein, could not thereby become a crime. This contention [is in effect] an effort to review the weight of the evidence for the purpose of showing that the defendant did not join and assist in organizing the Communist Labor Party of California with a knowledge of its unlawful character and purpose. This question, which is foreclosed by the verdict of the jury, [is] one of fact merely which is not open to review in this Court, involving as it does no constitutional question whatever. * * *

[That a state] may punish those who abuse [freedom of speech] by utterances inimical to the public welfare, tending to incite to crime, disturb the public peace, or endanger the foundations of organized government and threaten its overthrow by unlawful means, is not open to question. [*Gitlow*].

The essence of the offense denounced by the Act is the combining with others in an association for the accomplishment of the desired ends through the advocacy and use of criminal and unlawful methods. It partakes of the nature of a criminal conspiracy. That such united and joint action involves even greater danger to the public peace and security than the isolated utterances and acts of individuals is clear. We cannot hold that, as here applied, the Act is an unreasonable or arbitrary exercise of the police power of the State, unwarrantably infringing any right of free speech, assembly or association, or that those persons are protected from punishment by the due process clause who abuse such rights by joining and furthering an organization thus menacing the peace and welfare of the State. * * *

Affirmed.

JUSTICE BRANDEIS (concurring.) * * *

The felony which the statute created is a crime very unlike the old felony of conspiracy or the old misdemeanor of unlawful assembly. The mere act of assisting in forming a society for teaching syndicalism, of becoming a member of it, or assembling with others for that purpose is given the dynamic quality of crime. There is guilt although the society may not contemplate immediate promulgation of the doctrine. Thus the accused is to be punished, not for attempt, incitement or conspiracy, but for a step in preparation, which, if it threatens the public order at all, does so only remotely. The novelty in the prohibition introduced is that the statute aims, not at the practice of criminal syndicalism, nor even directly at the preaching of it, but at association with those who propose to preach it.

Despite arguments to the contrary which had seemed to me persuasive, it is settled that the due process clause of the Fourteenth Amendment applies to matters of substantive law as well as to matters of procedure. Thus all fundamental rights comprised within the term liberty are protected by the federal Constitution from invasion by the states. The right of free speech, the right to teach and the right of assembly are, of course, fundamental rights. These may not be denied or abridged. But, although the rights of free speech and assembly are fundamental, they are not in their nature absolute. Their exercise is subject to restriction, if the particular restriction proposed is required in order to protect the state from destruction or from serious injury, political, economic or moral. That the necessity which is essential to a valid restriction does not exist unless speech would produce, or is intended to produce,[a] a clear and imminent danger of some substantive evil which the state constitutionally may seek to prevent has been settled. See *Schenck.*

[The] Legislature must obviously decide, in the first instance, whether a danger exists which calls for a particular protective measure. But where a statute is valid only in case certain conditions exist, the enactment of the statute cannot alone establish the facts which are essential to its validity. Prohibitory legislation has repeatedly been held invalid, because unnecessary, where the denial of liberty involved was that of engaging in a particular business. The powers of the courts to strike down an offending law are no less when the interests involved are not property rights, but the fundamental personal rights of free speech and assembly.

This Court has not yet fixed the standard by which to determine when a danger shall be deemed clear; how remote the danger may be and yet be deemed present; and what degree of evil shall be deemed sufficiently substantial to justify resort to abridgment of free speech and assembly as the means of protection. To reach sound conclusions on these matters, we must bear in mind why a state is, ordinarily, denied the power to prohibit dissemination of social, economic and political doctrine which a vast majority of its citizens believes to be false and fraught with evil consequence.

Those who won our independence believed that the final end of the state was to make men free to develop their faculties, and that in its government the deliberative forces should prevail over the arbitrary.[b] They valued liberty both as an end and as a means. They believed liberty to be the secret of happiness and courage to be the secret of liberty. They believed that freedom to think as you will and to speak as you think are means indispensable to the discovery and spread of political truth;[c] that without free speech and assembly discussion would be futile; that with them, discussion affords ordinarily adequate protection against the dissemination of noxious doctrine;[d] that the greatest menace to freedom is an

a. Unless speech would produce, *or* is intended to produce? Unless speech *would produce* a clear and imminent danger, although the harm produced was neither advocated nor intended by the speaker? Unless the speaker *intended* to produce a clear and imminent danger, even under extrinsic conditions of actual harmlessness? Compare *Brandenburg v. Ohio,* p. 656 infra. See generally Linde, supra, at 1168–69, 1181, 1185.

b. For commentary on Brandeis, J.'s use of history, see Bradley C. Bobertz, *The Brandeis Gambit: The Making of America's "First Freedom," 1909–1931,* 40 Wm. & Mary L.Rev. 557 (1999).

c. Consider Vincent Blasi, *The First Amendment and the Ideal of Civic Courage,* 29 Wm. & Mary L.Rev. 653, 673–74 (1988): "This is as close as Brandeis gets to the claim that unregulated discussion yields truth. Notice that, in contrast to Holmes, Brandeis never

tells us what is 'the best test of truth.' He never employs the metaphor of the marketplace. He speaks only of 'political truth,' and he uses the phrase 'means indispensable' to link activities described in highly personal terms—'think as you will,' 'speak as you think'—with the collective social goal of 'political truth.' I think his emphasis in this passage is on the attitudes and atmosphere that must prevail if the ideals of self-government and happiness through courage are to be realized. Brandeis is sketching a good society here, but not, I think, an all-conquering dialectic."

d. Consider Blasi, supra, at 674–75: "It is noteworthy that Brandeis never speaks of noxious doctrine being refuted or eliminated or defeated. He talks of societal self-protection and the fitting remedy. He warns us not to underestimate the value of discussion, education, good counsels. To me, his point is that noxious doctrine is most likely to flourish when

inert people; that public discussion is a political duty; and that this should be a fundamental principle of the American government. They recognized the risks to which all human institutions are subject. But they knew that order cannot be secured merely through fear of punishment for its infraction; that it is hazardous to discourage thought, hope and imagination; that fear breeds repression; that repression breeds hate; that hate menaces stable government; that the path of safety lies in the opportunity to discuss freely supposed grievances and proposed remedies; and that the fitting remedy for evil counsels is good ones. Believing in the power of reason as applied through public discussion, they eschewed silence coerced by law—the argument of force in its worst form. Recognizing the occasional tyrannies of governing majorities, they amended the Constitution so that free speech and assembly should be guaranteed.

Fear of serious injury cannot alone justify suppression of free speech and assembly. Men feared witches and burnt women. It is the function of speech to free men from the bondage of irrational fears. To justify suppression of free speech there must be reasonable ground to fear that serious evil will result if free speech is practiced. There must be reasonable ground to believe that the danger apprehended is imminent. There must be reasonable ground to believe that the evil to be prevented is a serious one.[e] Every denunciation of existing law tends in some measure to increase the probability that there will be violation of it. Condonation of a breach enhances the probability. Expressions of approval add to the probability. Propagation of the criminal state of mind by teaching syndicalism increases it. Advocacy of lawbreaking heightens it still further. But even advocacy of violation, however reprehensible morally, is not a justification for denying free speech where the advocacy falls short of incitement and there is nothing to indicate that the advocacy would be immediately acted on. The wide difference between advocacy and incitement, between preparation and attempt, between assembling and conspiracy, must be borne in mind. In order to support a finding of clear and present danger it must be shown either that immediate serious violence was to be expected or was advocated,[f] or that the past conduct furnished reason to believe that such advocacy was then contemplated.

Those who won our independence by revolution were not cowards. They did not fear political change. They did not exalt order at the cost of liberty. To courageous, self-reliant men, with confidence in the power of free and fearless reasoning applied through the processes of popular government, no danger flowing from speech can be deemed clear and present, unless the incidence of the evil apprehended is so imminent that it may befall before there is opportunity for full discussion. If there be time to expose through discussion the falsehood and fallacies, to avert the evil by the processes of education, the remedy to be applied is more speech, not enforced silence.[g] Only an emergency can justify repression. Such must be the rule if authority is to be reconciled with freedom. Such, in my opinion, is the command of the Constitution. It is therefore always open to

its opponents lack the personal qualities of wisdom, creativity, and confidence. And those qualities, he suggests, are best developed by discussion and education, not by lazy and impatient reliance on the coercive authority of the state."

e. Does this suffice, regardless of the intent of the speaker? Regardless of the nature of the words he uses?

f. What if violence is advocated, but the advocacy is utterly ineffectual? What if the

speaker neither desires nor advocates violence, but, under the circumstances the speech nevertheless is "expected" to produce violence?

g. But see Richard Delgado & Jean Stefanic, *Images of the Outsider in American Law and Culture: Can Free Expression Remedy Systematic Social Ills?*, 77 Corn.L.Rev. 1258 (1992); Lawrence Lessig, *The Regulation of Social Meaning*, 62 U.Chi.L.Rev. 943, 1036–39 (1995).

Americans to challenge a law abridging free speech and assembly by showing that there was no emergency justifying it.

Moreover, even imminent danger cannot justify resort to prohibition of these functions essential to effective democracy, unless the evil apprehended is relatively serious. Prohibition of free speech and assembly is a measure so stringent that it would be inappropriate as the means for averting a relatively trivial harm to society. A police measure may be unconstitutional merely because the remedy, although effective as means of protection, is unduly harsh or oppressive. Thus, a state might, in the exercise of its police power, make any trespass upon the land of another a crime, regardless of the results or of the intent or purpose of the trespasser. It might, also, punish an attempt, a conspiracy, or an incitement to commit the trespass. But it is hardly conceivable that this court would hold constitutional a statute which punished as a felony the mere voluntary assembly with a society formed to teach that pedestrians had the moral right to cross uninclosed, unposted, waste lands and to advocate their doing so, even if there was imminent danger that advocacy would lead to a trespass. The fact that speech is likely to result in some violence or in destruction of property is not enough to justify its suppression. There must be the probability of serious injury to the State.[h] Among free men, the deterrents ordinarily to be applied to prevent crime are education and punishment for violations of the law, not abridgement of the rights of free speech and assembly.

* * * Whenever the fundamental rights of free speech and assembly are alleged to have been invaded, it must remain open to a defendant to present the issue whether there actually did exist at the time a clear danger, whether the danger, if any, was imminent, and whether the evil apprehended was one so substantial as to justify the stringent restriction interposed by the Legislature. The legislative declaration, like the fact that the statute was passed and was sustained by the highest court of the State, creates merely a rebuttable presumption that these conditions have been satisfied.

Whether in 1919, when Miss Whitney did the things complained of, there was in California such clear and present danger of serious evil, might have been made the important issue in the case. She might have required that the issue be determined either by the court or the jury. She claimed below that the statute as applied to her violated the federal Constitution; but she did not claim that it was void because there was no clear and present danger of serious evil, nor did she request that the existence of these conditions of a valid measure thus restricting the rights of free speech and assembly be passed upon by the court or a jury. On the other hand, there was evidence on which the court or jury might have found that such danger existed. I am unable to assent to the suggestion in the opinion of the court that assembling with a political party, formed to advocate the desirability of a proletarian revolution by mass action at some date necessarily far in the future, is not a right within the protection of the Fourteenth Amendment. In the present case, however, there was other testimony which tended to establish the existence of a conspiracy, on the part of members of the International Workers of the World, to commit present serious crimes, and likewise to show that such a conspiracy would be furthered by the activity of the society of which Miss Whitney

---

h. But see Robert Bork, *Neutral Principles and Some First Amendment Problems*, 47 Ind. L.J. 1, 34 (1971): "It is difficult to see how a constitutional court could properly draw the distinction proposed. Brandeis offered no analysis to show that advocacy of law violation merited protection by the Court. Worse, the criterion he advanced is the importance, in the judge's eye, of the law whose violation is urged."

was a member. Under these circumstances the judgment of the State court cannot be disturbed. * * *

JUSTICE HOLMES joins in this opinion.

Notes and Questions

1. *"They valued liberty both as an end and as a means."* Should recognition of the value of liberty[i] as an end augment the marketplace perspective or replace it?[j]

2. *Brandeis and Republicanism.* Consider Pnina Lahav, *Holmes and Brandeis: Libertarian and Republican Justifications for Free Speech,* 4 J.L. & Pol. 451, 460–461 (1987): "[I]n his *Whitney* concurrence, Brandeis tells us, that in the American polity, 'the deliberative forces should prevail over the arbitrary,' that 'public discussion is a political duty,' and that 'the occasional tyranny of governing

---

i. For literature contending that the related value of autonomy should play a central role in most (or all) aspects of first amendment law, see C. Edwin Baker, *Human Liberty and Freedom of Speech* 47–51 (1989); David Richards, Toleration and the Constitution 165–77 (1986); Robert Post, *Constitutional Domains* 268–331 (1995); Charles Fried, *The New First Amendment Jurisprudence: A Threat to Liberty,* 59 U.Chi.L.Rev. 225, 233–37 (1992); Robert Post, *Managing Deliberation: The Quandary of Democratic Dialogue,* 103 Ethics 654, 664–66 (1993); Robert Post, *Racist Speech, Democracy, and the First Amendment,* 32 Wm. & Mary L.Rev. 267, 279–85 (1991); Thomas Scanlon, *A Theory of Freedom of Expression,* 1 Phil. & Pub.Aff. 204, 215–22 (1972); David Strauss, *Persuasion, Autonomy, and Freedom of Expression,* 91 Colum.L.Rev. 334, 353–71 (1991); Christina Wells, *Reinvigorating Autonomy,* 32 Harv. C.R.-C.L. L. Rev. 159 (1997). Cf. D.F.B. Tucker, *Law, Liberalism, and Free Speech* (1985)(qualified endorsement of autonomy from a Rawlsian perspective).

For discussion of the value of autonomy and its connection to the problem of advocacy of illegal action, compare Scanlon, supra, with Thomas Scanlon, *Freedom of Expression and Categories of Expression,* 40 U.Pitt.L.Rev. 519 (1979). For commentary on the differences between speaker and listener autonomy, see Cass Sunstein, *Democracy and the Problem of Free Speech* 139–44 (1993); C. Edwin Baker, *Turner Broadcasting: Content–Based Regulation of Persons and Presses,* 1994 Sup.Ct.Rev. 57, 72–80. For the contention that the literature confuses philosophical assumptions of autonomy and empirical claims of autonomy and for doubts about the resolving power of either conception, see Richard Fallon, *Two Senses of Autonomy,* 46 Stan.L.Rev. 875 (1994). For the suggestion that the value of autonomy depends upon open and rich public discussion, see Sunstein, supra. For the contention that the value of autonomy should be subservient to open and rich discussion, see Owen Fiss, *State Activism and State Censorship,* 100 Yale L.J. 2087

(1991). Owen Fiss, *Why the State,* 100 Harv. L.Rev. 781 (1987); Owen Fiss, *Free Speech and Social Structure,* 71 Iowa L.Rev. 1405 (1986); but see Robert Post, *Equality and Autonomy in First Amendment Discourse,* 95 Mich. L.Rev. 1517 (1997).

j. Compare C. Edwin Baker, *Human Liberty and Freedom of Speech* (1989) (liberty theory should replace marketplace theory); C. Edwin Baker, *Scope of the First Amendment Freedom of Speech,* 25 U.C.L.A.L.Rev. 964 (1978)(accord); C. Edwin Baker, *Harm, Liberty, and Free Speech,* 70 So.Cal.L.Rev. 979 (1997)(harm does not justify invasion of liberty); Steven J. Heyman, *Righting the Balance: An Inquiry into the Foundations and Limits of Freedom of Expression,* 78 B.U.L.Rev. 1275 (1998)(endorsing natural rights theory of liberty as basis for free speech); and Martin Redish, *The Value of Free Speech,* 130 U.Pa.L.Rev. 591 (1982) (self-realization should be regarded as the first amendment's exclusive value) and Rodney Smolla, *Free Speech in an Open Society* 5 (1992) ("There is no logical reason, however, why the preferred position of freedom of speech might not be buttressed by multiple rationales. Acceptance of one rationale need not bump another from the list, as if this were First Amendment musical chairs"); Steven Shiffrin, *The First Amendment and Economic Regulation: Away From a General Theory of the First Amendment,* 78 Nw.U.L.Rev. 1212 (1983) (many values including liberty and self-realization underpin the first amendment; single valued orientations are reductionist); Brian C. Murchison, *Speech and the Self–Realization Value,* 33 Harv.C.R.-C.L. L.Rev. 443 (1998)(emphasizing and illuminating the self-realization value while recognizing other values); But see Frederick Schauer, *Must Speech Be Special,* 78 Nw.U.L.Rev. 1284 (1983) (neither liberty nor self-realization should play *any* role in first amendment theory). See also Joshua Cohen, *Freedom of Expression,* 19 Phil. & Pub.Aff. 207 (1993); Joseph Raz, *Free Expression and Personal Identification,* 11 Oxford J.Legal St. 311 (1991).

majorities' should be thwarted. This is radically different from the notion that individuals are free to remain aloof from politics if they so choose (a notion espoused by Holmes), and from the principle of the separation of the state from society. Implied here is the notion of civic virtue—the duty to participate in politics, the importance of deliberation, and the notion that the end of the state is not neutrality but active assistance in providing conditions of freedom which in turn are the 'secret of happiness.' One may even speculate that Brandeis, the progressive leader, believed that the final end of the state was the happiness of mankind.

"These ingredients of the Brandeis position in *Whitney* resonate with republican theory. The theory rests on two central themes: the idea of civic virtue and the idea that the end of politics (or the state) is the common good, which in turn is more than the sum of individual wills. Thus, the state is not separated from society, but rather is committed to the public good, and to a substantive notion of public morality. The members of society are not individuals encased in their autonomous zones, but rather social beings who recognize that they are an integral part of the society. This organic sense of belonging implicitly rejects the notion of combat zones. The republic and its citizens care for the welfare of all. Correctly understood, Brandeis' concurrence in *Whitney* is more than a justification from self-fulfillment or from self-rule. It is a justification from civic virtue."[k]

3. In keeping with the positions of Holmes and Brandeis, is the first amendment best defended as proceeding from a "special kind of argument from character that builds from the claim that a culture that prizes and protects expressive liberty nurtures in its members certain character traits such as inquisitiveness, independence of judgment, distrust of authority, willingness to take initiative, perseverance, and the courage to confront evil"? Vincent Blasi, *Free Speech and Good Character,* 46 UCLA L.Rev. 1567 (1999).

4. Consider Eugene Volokh, *Freedom of Speech, Permissible Tailoring, and Transcending Strict Scrutiny,* 144 U.Pa.L.Rev. 2417, 2446 (1996): "Holmes and Brandeis were not condemning the restrictions simply because the government's goals were not important enough, or arguing that the speech-restrictive means were unnecessary. Rather, they were arguing that the means were impermissible (except where a clear and present danger was present). Even if the speech was likely, through its persuasive powers, to undermine the most compelling of interests, the 'meaning of free speech,' 'the theory of our Constitution,' the judgment of '[t]hose who won our independence' about the 'fundamental principle[s] of the American government,' required that the nation run the risk of the compelling interest being undermined."

5. Ten years after *Whitney, DeJonge v. Oregon,* 299 U.S. 353, 57 S.Ct. 255, 81 L.Ed. 278 (1937) held that mere participation in a meeting called by the Communist party could not be made a crime. The right of peaceable assembly was declared to be "cognate to those of free speech and free press and is equally fundamental."

C. COMMUNISM AND ILLEGAL ADVOCACY

Kent Greenawalt has well described the pattern of decisions for much of the period between *Whitney* and *Dennis* infra: "[T]he clear and present danger

---

k. For further background comparing the views of Brandeis and Holmes, JJ., see Blasi, fn. b supra; Robert Cover, *The Left, The Right and the First Amendment: 1919–28,* 40 Md. L.Rev. 349 (1981).

formula emerged as the applicable standard not only for the kinds of issues with respect to which it originated but also for a wide variety of other First Amendment problems. If the Court was not always very clear about the relevance of that formula to those different problems, its use of the test, and its employment of ancillary doctrines, did evince a growing disposition to protect expression." *Speech and Crime*, 1980 Am.B.Found.Res.J. 645, 706. By 1951, however, anti-communist sentiment was a powerful theme in American politics. The Soviet Union had detonated a nuclear weapon; communists had firm control of the Chinese mainland; the Korean War had reached a stalemate; Alger Hiss had been convicted of perjury in congressional testimony concerning alleged spying activities for the Soviet Union while he was a State Department official; and Senator Joseph McCarthy of Wisconsin had created a national sensation by accusations that many "card carrying Communists" held important State Department jobs. In this context, the top leaders of the American Communist Party asked the Court to reverse their criminal conspiracy convictions.

DENNIS v. UNITED STATES

341 U.S. 494, 71 S.Ct. 857, 95 L.Ed. 1137 (1951).

CHIEF JUSTICE VINSON announced the judgment of the Court and an opinion in which JUSTICE REED, JUSTICE BURTON and JUSTICE MINTON join.

Petitioners were indicted in July, 1948, for violation of the conspiracy provisions of the Smith Act during the period of April, 1945, to July, 1948. * * * A verdict of guilty as to all the petitioners was [affirmed by the Second Circuit]. We granted certiorari, limited to the following two questions: (1) Whether either § 2 or § 3 of the Smith Act, inherently or as construed and applied in the instant case, violates the First Amendment and other provisions of the Bill of Rights; (2) whether either § 2 or § 3 of the Act, inherently or as construed and applied in the instant case, violates the First and Fifth Amendments, because of indefiniteness.

Sections 2 and 3 of the Smith Act provide as follows:

"Sec. 2.

"(a) It shall be unlawful for any person—

"(1) to knowingly or willfully advocate, abet, advise, or teach the duty, necessity, desirability, or propriety of overthrowing or destroying any government in the United States by force or violence, or by the assassination of any officer of any such government; * * *

"Sec. 3. It shall be unlawful for any person to attempt to commit, or to conspire to commit, any of the acts prohibited by the provisions [of] this title."

The indictment charged the petitioners with wilfully and knowingly conspiring (1) to organize as the Communist Party of the United States of America a society, group and assembly of persons who teach and advocate the overthrow and destruction of the Government of the United States by force and violence, and (2) knowingly and wilfully to advocate and teach the duty and necessity of overthrowing and destroying the Government of the United States by force and violence. The indictment further alleged that § 2 of the Smith Act proscribes these acts and that any conspiracy to take such action is a violation of § 3 of the Act.

The trial of the case extended over nine months, six of which were devoted to the taking of evidence, resulting in a record of 16,000 pages. Our limited grant of the writ of certiorari has removed from our consideration any question as to the sufficiency of the evidence to support the jury's determination that petitioners are guilty of the offense charged. Whether on this record petitioners did in fact advocate the overthrow of the Government by force and violence is not before us, and we must base any discussion of this point upon the conclusions stated in the opinion of the Court of Appeals, which treated the issue in great detail [and] held that the record supports the following broad conclusions: [that] the Communist Party is a highly disciplined organization, adept at infiltration into strategic positions, use of aliases, and double-meaning language; that the Party is rigidly controlled; that Communists, unlike other political parties, tolerate no dissension from the policy laid down by the guiding [forces]; that the literature of the Party and the statements and activities of its leaders, petitioners here, advocate, and the general goal of the Party was, during the period in question, to achieve a successful overthrow of the existing order by force and violence. * * *

The obvious purpose of the statute is to protect existing Government, not from change by peaceable, lawful and constitutional means, but from change by violence, revolution and terrorism. That it is within the *power* of the Congress to protect the Government of the United States from armed rebellion is a proposition which requires little discussion. Whatever theoretical merit there may be to the argument that there is a "right" to rebellion against dictatorial governments is without force where the existing structure of the government provides for peaceful and orderly change. We reject any principle of governmental helplessness in the face of preparation for revolution, which principle, carried to its logical conclusion, must lead to anarchy. No one could conceive that it is not within the power of Congress to prohibit acts intended to overthrow the Government by force and violence. The question with which we are concerned here is not whether Congress has such *power*, but whether the *means* which it has employed conflict with the First and Fifth Amendments to the Constitution.

One of the bases for the contention that the means which Congress has employed are invalid takes the form of an attack on the face of the statute on the grounds that by its terms it prohibits academic discussion of the merits of Marxism–Leninism, that it stifles ideas and is contrary to all concepts of a free speech and a free press. [This] is a federal statute which we must interpret as well as judge. Herein lies the fallacy of reliance upon the manner in which this Court has treated judgments of state courts. Where the statute as construed by the state court transgressed the First Amendment, we could not but invalidate the judgments of conviction.

The very language of the Smith Act negates the interpretation which petitioners would have us impose on that Act. It is directed at advocacy, not discussion. Thus, the trial judge properly charged the jury that they could not convict if they found that petitioners did "no more than pursue peaceful studies and discussions or teaching and advocacy in the realm of ideas." * * * Congress did not intend to eradicate the free discussion of political theories, to destroy the traditional rights of Americans to discuss and evaluate ideas without fear of governmental sanction. * * *

But although the statute is not directed at the hypothetical cases which petitioners have conjured, its application in this case has resulted in convictions for the teaching and advocacy of the overthrow of the Government by force and violence, which, even though coupled with the intent to accomplish that overthrow, contains an element of speech. For this reason, we must pay special heed to the demands of the First Amendment marking out the boundaries of speech.

[T]he basis of the First Amendment is the hypothesis that speech can rebut speech, propaganda will answer propaganda, free debate of ideas will result in the wisest governmental policies. [An] analysis of the leading cases in this Court which have involved direct limitations on speech, however, will demonstrate that both the majority of the Court and the dissenters in particular cases have recognized that this is not an unlimited, unqualified right, but that the societal value of speech must, on occasion, be subordinated to other values and considerations. * * *

Although no case subsequent to *Whitney* and *Gitlow* has expressly overruled the majority opinions in those cases, there is little doubt that subsequent opinions have inclined toward the Holmes–Brandeis rationale. * * *

In this case we are squarely presented with the application of the "clear and present danger" test, and must decide what that phrase imports.[a] We first note that many of the cases in which this Court has reversed convictions by use of this or similar tests have been based on the fact that the interest which the State was attempting to protect was itself too insubstantial to warrant restriction of speech. * * * Overthrow of the Government by force and violence is certainly a substantial enough interest for the Government to limit speech. Indeed, this is the ultimate value of any society, for if a society cannot protect its very structure from armed internal attack, it must follow that no subordinate value can be protected. If, then, this interest may be protected, the literal problem which is presented is what has been meant by the use of the phrase "clear and present danger" of the utterances bringing about the evil within the power of Congress to punish.

Obviously, the words cannot mean that before the Government may act, it must wait until the putsch is about to be executed, the plans have been laid and the signal is awaited. If Government is aware that a group aiming at its overthrow is attempting to indoctrinate its members and to commit them to a course whereby they will strike when the leaders feel the circumstances permit, action by the Government is required. The argument that there is no need for Government to concern itself, for Government is strong, it possesses ample powers to put down a rebellion, it may defeat the revolution with ease needs no answer. For that is not the question. Certainly an attempt to overthrow the Government by force, even though doomed from the outset because of inadequate numbers or power of the revolutionists, is a sufficient evil for Congress to prevent. The damage which such attempts create both physically and politically to a nation makes it impossible to measure the validity in terms of the probability of success, or the immediacy of a successful attempt. In the instant case the trial judge charged the jury that they could not convict unless they found that petitioners intended to overthrow the Government "as speedily as circumstances would permit." This does not mean, and could not properly mean, that they would not strike until there was certainty of success. What was meant was that the revolutionists would strike when they thought the time was ripe. We must therefore reject the contention that success or probability of success is the criterion.

The situation with which Justices Holmes and Brandeis were concerned in *Gitlow* was a comparatively isolated event, bearing little relation in their minds to any substantial threat to the safety of the community. [They] were not confronted with any situation comparable to the instant one—the development of an apparatus designed and dedicated to the overthrow of the Government, in the context of world crisis after crisis.

---

a. Consider Harry Kalven, *A Worthy Tradition* 190–91 (1988): "The [Vinson opinion] acknowledges clear and present danger as the constitutional measure of free speech, but in the process, to meet the political exigencies of the case, it officially adjusts the test, giving it the kiss of death."

Chief Judge Learned Hand, writing for the majority below, interpreted the phrase as follows: "In each case [courts] must ask whether the gravity of the 'evil,' discounted by its improbability, justifies such invasion of free speech as is necessary to avoid the danger." We adopt this statement of the rule. As articulated by Chief Judge Hand, it is as succinct and inclusive as any other we might devise at this time. * * *

Likewise, we are in accord with the court below, which affirmed the trial court's finding that the requisite danger existed. The mere fact that from the period 1945 to 1948 petitioners' activities did not result in an attempt to overthrow the Government by force and violence is of course no answer to the fact that there was a group that was ready to make the attempt. The formation by petitioners of such a highly organized conspiracy, with rigidly disciplined members subject to call when the leaders, these petitioners, felt that the time had come for action, coupled with the inflammable nature of world conditions, similar uprisings in other countries, and the touch-and-go nature of our relations with countries with whom petitioners were in the very least ideologically attuned, convince us that their convictions were justified on this score. And this analysis disposes of the contention that a conspiracy to advocate, as distinguished from the advocacy itself, cannot be constitutionally restrained, because it comprises only the preparation. It is the existence of the conspiracy which creates the danger. * * *

Although we have concluded that the finding that there was a sufficient danger to warrant the application of the statute was justified on the merits, there remains the problem of whether the trial judge's treatment of the issue was correct. He charged the jury, in relevant part, as follows:

"In further construction and interpretation of the statute I charge you that it is not the abstract doctrine of overthrowing or destroying organized government by unlawful means which is denounced by this law, but the teaching and advocacy of action for the accomplishment of that purpose, by language reasonably and ordinarily calculated to incite persons to such action. Accordingly, you cannot find the defendants or any of them guilty of the crime charged unless you are satisfied beyond a reasonable doubt that they conspired to organize a society, group and assembly of persons who teach and advocate the overthrow or destruction of the Government of the United States by force and violence and to advocate and teach the duty and necessity of overthrowing or destroying the Government of the United States by force and violence, with the intent that such teaching and advocacy be of a rule or principle of action and by language reasonably and ordinarily calculated to incite persons to such action, all with the intent to cause the overthrow or destruction of the Government of the United States by force and violence as speedily as circumstances would permit. * * *

"If you are satisfied that the evidence establishes beyond a reasonable doubt that the defendants, or any of them, are guilty of a violation of the statute, as I have interpreted it to you, I find as matter of law that there is sufficient danger of a substantive evil that the Congress has a right to prevent to justify the application of the statute under the First Amendment of the Constitution. This is matter of law about which you have no concern. * * * * "

It is thus clear that he reserved the question of the existence of the danger for his own determination, and the question becomes whether the issue is of such a nature that it should have been submitted to the jury.

[When] facts are found that establish the violation of a statute, the protection against conviction afforded by the First Amendment is a matter of law. The doctrine that there must be a clear and present danger of a substantive evil that

Congress has a right to prevent is a judicial rule to be applied as a matter of law by the courts. The guilt is established by proof of facts. Whether the First Amendment protects the activity which constitutes the violation of the statute must depend upon a judicial determination of the scope of the First Amendment applied to the circumstances of the case.

[In] *Schenck* this Court itself examined the record to find whether the requisite danger appeared, and the issue was not submitted to a jury. And in every later case in which the Court has measured the validity of a statute by the "clear and present danger" test, that determination has been by the court, the question of the danger not being submitted to the jury. * * * Petitioners intended to overthrow the Government of the United States as speedily as the circumstances would permit. Their conspiracy to organize the Communist Party and to teach and advocate the overthrow of the Government of the United States by force and violence created a "clear and present danger" of an attempt to overthrow the Government by force and violence. They were properly and constitutionally convicted * * *.

Affirmed.

JUSTICE CLARK took no part in the consideration or decision of this case.

JUSTICE FRANKFURTER, concurring in affirmance of the judgment.

[The] demands of free speech in a democratic society as well as the interest in national security are better served by candid and informed weighing of the competing interests, within the confines of the judicial process, than by announcing dogmas too inflexible for the non-Euclidian problems to be solved.

But how are competing interests to be assessed? Since they are not subject to quantitative ascertainment, the issue necessarily resolves itself into asking, who is to make the adjustment?—who is to balance the relevant factors and ascertain which interest is in the circumstances to prevail? Full responsibility for the choice cannot be given to the courts. Courts are not representative bodies. They are not designed to be a good reflex of a democratic society. Their judgment is best informed, and therefore most dependable, within narrow limits. Their essential quality is detachment, founded on independence. History teaches that the independence of the judiciary is jeopardized when courts become embroiled in the passions of the day and assume primary responsibility in choosing between competing political, economic and social pressures.

Primary responsibility for adjusting the interests which compete in the situation before us of necessity belongs to the Congress. [We] are to set aside the judgment of those whose duty it is to legislate only if there is no reasonable basis for [it]. Free-speech cases are not an exception to the principle that we are not legislators, that direct policy-making is not our province. How best to reconcile competing interests is the business of legislatures, and the balance they strike is a judgment not to be displaced by ours, but to be respected unless outside the pale of fair judgment. [A] survey of the relevant decisions indicates that the results which we have reached are on the whole those that would ensue from careful weighing of conflicting interests. The complex issues presented by regulation of speech in public places by picketing, and by legislation prohibiting advocacy of crime have been resolved by scrutiny of many factors besides the imminence and gravity of the evil threatened. The matter has been well summarized by a reflective student of the Court's work. "The truth is that the clear-and-present-danger test is an oversimplified judgment unless it takes account also of a number of other factors: the relative seriousness of the danger in comparison with the value of the occasion for speech or political activity; the availability of more moderate controls than those which the state has imposed; and perhaps the specific intent with which the speech or activity is launched. No matter how rapidly we utter the phrase 'clear and present danger,' or how closely we hyphenate the words, they are not a substitute for the weighing of values. They tend to convey a delusion of certitude when what is most certain is the complexity of the strands in the web of freedoms which the judge must disentangle." Paul Freund, *On Understanding the Supreme Court* 27–28 [1949]. * * *

To make validity of legislation depend on judicial reading of events still in the womb of time—a forecast, that is, of the outcome of forces at best appreciated only with knowledge of the topmost secrets of nations—is to charge the judiciary with duties beyond its equipment. * * *

Even when moving strictly within the limits of constitutional adjudication, judges are concerned with issues that may be said to involve vital finalities. The too easy transition from disapproval of what is undesirable to condemnation as unconstitutional, has led some of the wisest judges to question the wisdom of our scheme in lodging such authority in courts. But it is relevant to remind that in sustaining the power of Congress in a case like this nothing irrevocable is done. The democratic process at all events is not impaired or restricted. Power and responsibility remain with the people and immediately with their representation. All the Court says is that Congress was not forbidden by the Constitution to pass this enactment and that a prosecution under it may be brought against a conspiracy such as the one before us. * * *

Justice Jackson, concurring.

[E]ither by accident or design, the Communist stratagem outwits the anti-anarchist pattern of statute aimed against "overthrow by force and violence" if qualified by the doctrine that only "clear and present danger" of accomplishing that result will sustain the prosecution.

The "clear and present danger" test was an innovation by Mr. Justice Holmes in the *Schenck* case, reiterated and refined by him and Mr. Justice Brandeis in later cases, all arising before the era of World War II revealed the subtlety and efficacy of modernized revolutionary techniques used by totalitarian parties. In those cases, they were faced with convictions under so-called criminal syndicalism statutes aimed at anarchists but which, loosely construed, had been applied to punish socialism, pacifism, and left-wing ideologies, the charges often resting on farfetched inferences which, if true, would establish only technical or trivial violations. They proposed "clear and present danger" as a test for the sufficiency of evidence in particular cases.

I would save it, unmodified, for application as a "rule of reason" in the kind of case for which it was devised. When the issue is criminality of a hotheaded speech on a street corner, or circulation of a few incendiary pamphlets, or parading by some zealots behind a red flag, or refusal of a handful of school children to salute our flag, it is not beyond the capacity of the judicial process to gather, comprehend, and weigh the necessary materials for decision whether it is a clear and present danger of substantive evil or a harmless letting off of steam. It is not a prophecy, for the danger in such cases has matured by the time of trial or it was never present. The test applies and has meaning where a conviction is sought to be based on a speech or writing which does not directly or explicitly advocate a crime but to which such tendency is sought to be attributed by construction or by implication from external circumstances. The formula in such cases favors freedoms that are vital to our society, and, even if sometimes applied too generously, the consequences cannot be grave. But its recent expansion has extended, in particular to Communists, unprecedented immunities. Unless we are to hold our Government captive in a judge-made verbal trap, we must approach the problem of a well-organized, nation-wide conspiracy, such as I have described, as realistically as our predecessors faced the trivialities that were being prosecuted until they were checked with a rule of reason.

I think reason is lacking for applying that test to this case.

If we must decide that this Act and its application are constitutional only if we are convinced that petitioner's conduct creates a "clear and present danger" of violent overthrow, we must appraise imponderables, including international and national phenomena which baffle the best informed foreign offices and our most experienced politicians. We would have to foresee and predict the effectiveness of Communist propaganda, opportunities for infiltration, whether, and when, a time will come that they consider propitious for action, and whether and how fast our existing government will deteriorate. And we would have to speculate as to whether an approaching Communist coup would not be anticipated by a nationalistic fascist movement. No doctrine can be sound whose application requires us to make a prophecy of that sort in the guise of a legal decision. The judicial process simply is not adequate to a trial of such far-flung issues. The answers given would reflect our own political predilections and nothing more.

The authors of the clear and present danger test never applied it to a case like this, nor would I. If applied as it is proposed here, it means that the Communist plotting is protected during its period of incubation; its preliminary stages of organization and preparation are immune from the law; the Government can move only after imminent action is manifest, when it would, of course, be too late.

The highest degree of constitutional protection is due to the individual acting without conspiracy. But even an individual cannot claim that the Constitution protects him in advocating or teaching overthrow of government by force or violence. I should suppose no one would doubt that Congress has power to make such attempted overthrow a crime. But the contention is that one has the constitutional right to work up a public desire and will to do what it is a crime to attempt. I think direct incitement by speech or writing can be made a crime, and I think there can be a conviction without also proving that the odds favored its success by 99 to 1, or some other extremely high ratio. * * *

What really is under review here is a conviction of conspiracy, after a trial for conspiracy, on an indictment charging conspiracy, brought under a statute outlawing conspiracy. With due respect to my colleagues, they seem to me to discuss anything under the sun except the law of conspiracy. * * *

The Constitution does not make conspiracy a civil right. [Although] I consider criminal conspiracy a dragnet device capable of perversion into an instrument of injustice in the hands of a partisan or complacent judiciary, it has an established place in our system of law, and no reason appears for applying it only to concerted action claimed to disturb interstate commerce and withholding it from those claimed to undermine our whole Government. * * *

I do not suggest that Congress could punish conspiracy to advocate something, the doing of which it may not punish. Advocacy or exposition of the doctrine of communal property ownership, or any political philosophy unassociated with advocacy of its imposition by force or seizure of government by unlawful means could not be reached through conspiracy prosecution. But it is not forbidden to put down force or violence, it is not forbidden to punish its teaching or advocacy, and the end being punishable, there is no doubt of the power to punish conspiracy for the purpose. * * *

JUSTICE BLACK, dissenting. * * *

So long as this Court exercises the power of judicial review of legislation, I cannot agree that the First Amendment permits us to sustain laws suppressing freedom of speech and press on the basis of Congress' or our own notions of mere "reasonableness." Such a doctrine waters down the First Amendment so that it amounts to little more than an admonition to Congress. The Amendment as so construed is not likely to protect any but those "safe" or orthodox views which rarely need its protection. I must also express my objection to the holding because, as Mr. Justice Douglas' dissent shows, it sanctions the determination of a crucial issue of fact by the judge rather than by the jury. * * *

Public opinion being what it now is, few will protest the conviction of these Communist petitioners. There is hope, however, that in calmer times, when present pressures, passions and fears subside, this or some later Court will restore the First Amendment liberties to the high preferred place where they belong in a free society.

JUSTICE DOUGLAS, dissenting.

If this were a case where those who claimed protection under the First Amendment were teaching the techniques of sabotage, the assassination of the President, the filching of documents from public files, the planting of bombs, the art of street warfare, and the like, I would have no doubts. The freedom to speak is not absolute; the teaching of methods of terror and other seditious conduct should be beyond the pale along with obscenity and immorality. This case was argued as if those were the facts. The argument imported much seditious conduct into the record. That is easy and it has popular appeal, for the activities of Communists in plotting and scheming against the free world are common knowledge. But the fact is that no such evidence was introduced at the trial. There is a statute which makes a seditious conspiracy unlawful. Petitioners, however, were not charged with a "conspiracy to overthrow" the Government. They were charged with a conspiracy to form a party and groups and assemblies of people who teach and advocate the overthrow of our Government by force or violence and with a conspiracy to advocate and teach its overthrow by force and violence. It may well be that indoctrination in the techniques of terror to destroy the Government would be indictable under either statute. But the teaching which is condemned here is of a different character.

So far as the present record is concerned, what petitioners did was to organize people to teach and themselves teach the Marxist–Leninist doctrine contained chiefly in four books: *Foundations of Leninism* by Stalin (1924); *The Communist Manifesto* by Marx and Engels (1848); *State and Revolution* by Lenin (1917); *History of the Communist Party of the Soviet Union* (B.) (1939).

Those books are to Soviet Communism what *Mein Kampf* was to Nazism. If they are understood, the ugliness of Communism is revealed, its deceit and cunning are exposed, the nature of its activities becomes apparent, and the chances of its success less likely. That is not, of course, the reason why petitioners chose these books for their classrooms. They are fervent Communists to whom these volumes are gospel. They preached the creed with the hope that some day it would be acted upon.

The opinion of the Court does not outlaw these texts nor condemn them to the fire, as the Communists do literature offensive to their creed. But if the books themselves are not outlawed, if they can lawfully remain on library shelves, by what reasoning does their use in a classroom become a crime? It would not be a crime under the Act to introduce these books to a class, though that would be teaching what the creed of violent overthrow of the Government is. The Act, as construed, requires the element of intent—that those who teach the creed believe in it. The crime then depends not on what is taught but on who the teacher is. That is to make freedom of speech turn not on *what is said,* but on the *intent* with which it is said. Once we start down that road we enter territory dangerous to the liberties of every citizen. * * *

The vice of treating speech as the equivalent of overt acts of a treasonable or seditious character is emphasized by a concurring opinion, which by invoking the law of conspiracy makes speech do service for deeds which are dangerous to society. [N]ever until today has anyone seriously thought that the ancient law of conspiracy could constitutionally be used to turn speech into seditious conduct. Yet that is precisely what is suggested. I repeat that we deal here with speech alone, not with speech *plus* acts of sabotage or unlawful conduct. Not a single seditious act is charged in the indictment. To make a lawful speech unlawful because two men conceive it is to raise the law of conspiracy to appalling proportions. * * *

There comes a time when even speech loses its constitutional immunity. Speech innocuous one year may at another time fan such destructive flames that it must be halted in the interests of the safety of the Republic. That is the meaning of the clear and present danger test. When conditions are so critical that there will be no time to avoid the evil that the speech threatens, it is time to call a halt. Otherwise, free speech which is the strength of the Nation will be the cause of its destruction.

Yet free speech is the rule, not the exception. The restraint to be constitutional must be based on more than fear, on more than passionate opposition against the speech, on more than a revolted dislike for its contents. There must be some immediate injury to society that is likely if speech is allowed. * * *

I had assumed that the question of the clear and present danger, being so critical an issue in the case, would be a matter for submission to the jury. [The] Court, I think, errs when it treats the question as one of law.

Yet, whether the question is one for the Court or the jury, there should be evidence of record on the issue. This record, however, contains no evidence whatsoever showing that the acts charged viz., the teaching of the Soviet theory of revolution with the hope that it will be realized, have created any clear and present danger to the Nation. The Court, however, rules to the contrary. [The majority] might as well say that the speech of petitioners is outlawed because Soviet Russia and her Red Army are a threat to world peace.

The nature of Communism as a force on the world scene would, of course, be relevant to the issue of clear and present danger of petitioners' advocacy within the United States. But the primary consideration is the strength and tactical position of petitioners and their converts in this country. On that there is no evidence in the record. If we are to take judicial notice of the threat of Communists within the nation, it should not be difficult to conclude that *as a political party* they are of little consequence. Communists in this country have never made a respectable or serious showing in any election. I would doubt that there is a village, let alone a city or county or state, which the Communists could carry. Communism in the world scene is no bogeyman; but Communism as a political faction or party in this country plainly is. Communism has been so thoroughly exposed in this country that it has been crippled as a political force. Free speech has destroyed it as an effective political party. It is inconceivable that those who went up and down this country preaching the doctrine of revolution which petitioners espouse would have any success. In days of trouble and confusion, when bread lines were long, when the unemployed walked the streets, when people were starving, the advocates of a short-cut by revolution might have a chance to gain adherents. But today there are no such conditions. The country is not in despair; the people know Soviet Communism; the doctrine of Soviet revolution is exposed in all of its ugliness and the American people want none of it.

[Unless] and until extreme and necessitous circumstances are shown our aim should be to keep speech unfettered and to allow the processes of law to be invoked only when the provocateurs among us move from speech to action. * * *[b]

Notes and Questions

1.   What was the "substantive evil" in the *Dennis* case, the danger of which was sufficiently "clear and present" to warrant the application of the rule as originally formulated by Holmes and Brandeis? A *successful* revolution? An *attempted* revolution, however futile such an attempt might be? A *conspiracy* to plan the overthrow of the government by force and violence? A "conspiracy *to advocate*" such overthrow? See John Gorfinkel & John Mack, *Dennis v. United States and the Clear and Present Danger Rule*, 39 Calif.L.Rev. 475, 496–501 (1951); Nathaniel Nathanson, *The Communist Trial and the Clear-and-Present–Danger Test*, 63 Harv.L.Rev. 1167, 1168, 1173–75 (1950). Suppose it were established in *Dennis* that the odds were 99–1 against the Communists attempting an overthrow of the Government until 1961? 1971? Same result?

2.   *Suppression of "totalitarian movements"*. Consider Carl Auerbach, *The Communist Control Act of 1954*, 23 U.Chi.L.Rev. 173, 188–89 (1956): "[I]n suppressing totalitarian movements a democratic society is not acting to protect the status quo, but the very same interests which freedom of speech itself seeks to secure—the possibility of peaceful progress under freedom. That suppression may sometimes have to be the means of securing and enlarging freedom is a paradox which is not unknown in other areas of the law of modern democratic states. The basic 'postulate,' therefore, which should 'limit and control' the First Amendment is that it is part of the framework for a constitutional democracy and should, therefore, not be used to curb the power of Congress to exclude from the political struggle those groups which, if victorious, would crush democracy and impose totalitarianism. See also Robert Bork, *Neutral Principles and Some First Amendment Problems*, 47 Ind.L.J. 1, 30–33 (1971).[c]

---

b.   Eighteen years later, concurring in *Brandenburg*, Sec. 1, I, D infra, Douglas, J., declared: "I see no place in the regime of the First Amendment for any 'clear and present danger' test whether strict and tight as some would make it or free-wheeling as the Court in *Dennis* rephrased it. When one reads the opinions closely and sees when and how the 'clear and present danger' test has been applied, great misgivings are aroused. First, the threats were often loud but always puny and made serious only by judges so wedded to the status quo that critical analysis made them nervous.

Second, the test was so twisted and perverted in *Dennis* as to make the trial of those teachers of Marxism an all-out political trial which was part and parcel of the cold war that has eroded substantial parts of the First Amendment."

c.   For different perspectives, see John Rawls, *A Theory of Justice* 216–21 (1971); Steven Shiffrin, *Racist Speech Outsider Jurisprudence, and the Meaning of America*, 80 Cornell L.Rev. 43, 88 n. 220, 90 n. 232 (1994); Stephen Smith, *Radically Subversive Speech and the Authority of Law*, 94 Mich.L.Rev. 348 (1995).

3. Does the second amendment guarantee individuals (or groups) the right to bear arms for protection including protection against government tyranny?[d] If the second amendment is so construed, does the second amendment shed light on the first?

4. *Dennis distinguished.* In 1954, Senator McCarthy was censured by the United States Senate for acting contrary to its ethics and impairing its dignity. In 1957, when the convictions of 14 "second string" communist leaders reached the Supreme Court in YATES v. UNITED STATES, 354 U.S. 298, 77 S.Ct. 1064, 1 L.Ed.2d 1356 (1957), McCarthy had died, and so had McCarthyism. Although strong anti-communist sentiment persisted, the political atmosphere in *Yates'* 1957 was profoundly different from that of *Dennis'* 1951. Harlan, J., distinguishing *Dennis*, construed the Smith Act narrowly: "[The] essence of the *Dennis* holding was that indoctrination of a group in preparation for future violent action, as well as exhortation to immediate action, by advocacy found to be directed to 'action for the accomplishment' of forcible overthrow, to violence as 'a rule or principle of action,' and employing 'language of incitement,' is not constitutionally protected when the group is of sufficient size and cohesiveness, is sufficiently oriented towards action, and other circumstances are such as reasonably to justify apprehension that action will occur. This is quite a different thing from the view of the District Court here that mere doctrinal justification of forcible overthrow, if engaged in with the intent to accomplish overthrow, is punishable per se under the Smith Act. [T]he trial court's statement that the proscribed advocacy must include the 'urging,' 'necessity,' and 'duty' of forcible overthrow, and not merely its 'desirability' and 'propriety,' may not be regarded as a sufficient substitute for charging that the Smith Act reaches only advocacy of action for the overthrow of government by force and violence. The essential distinction is that those to whom the advocacy is addressed must be urged to *do* something, now or in the future, rather than merely to *believe* in something." Applying this standard, Harlan J., acquitted 5 defendants and remanded to the lower court for proceedings against the remaining defendants.[e]

d. Is the second amendment an embarrassment to liberals? See Sanford Levinson, *The Embarrassing Second Amendment,* 99 Yale L.J. 637 (1989). For a variety of perspectives on the second amendment, see Symposium, *A Second Amendment Symposium Issue,* 62 Tenn.L.Rev. 443 (1995); Lawrence Cress, *An Armed Community,* 71 J.Am.Hist. 22 (1984); Robert Cottrol & Raymond Diamond, *The Second Amendment: Toward an Afro–Americanist Reconsideration,* 90 Geo.L.Rev. 309 (1991); Andrew Hertz, *Gun Crazy,* 75 B.U.L.Rev. 57 (1995); Donald Kates, *Handgun Prohibition and the Original Meaning of the Second Amendment,* 82 Mich.L.Rev. 204 (1983); David B. Kopel, *The Second Amendment in the Nineteenth Century,* I 1998 B.Y.U.L. Rev. 1359 (1998); William Van Alstyne, *The Second Amendment and the Personal Right to Bear Arms,* 43 Duke L.J. 1236 (1994); Eugene Volokh, Robert Cottrol, Sanford Levinson, L.A. Powe, Jr. & Glenn Harlan Reynolds, *The Second Amendment as A Teaching Tool in Constitutional Law Classes,* 48 J.Legal Ed. 591

(1998); David C. Williams, *The Constitutional Right to "Conservative" Revolution,* 32 Harv. C.R.-C.L.L.Rev. 413 (1997); David C. Williams, *The Militia Movement and the Second Amendment Revolution,* 81 Cornell L.Rev. 879 (1996); David Williams, *Civic Republicanism and the Citizen Militia,* 101 Yale L.J. 551 (1991).

e. Burton, J., concurred. Black, joined by Douglas, JJ., dissenting, would have acquitted all defendants. Clark, J., dissenting, would have affirmed the convictions of all defendants. Brennan and Whittaker, JJ., took no part. On remand, the government requested dismissal of the indictments, explaining that it could not meet *Yates'* evidentiary requirements. For commentary, see Gerald Gunther, *Learned Hand* 603 (1994); Christina E. Wells, *Of Communists and Anti-Abortion Protestors: The Consequences of Falling into the Theoretical Abyss,* 33 Ga. L. Rev. 1 (1998); Kent Greenawalt, *Speech and Crime,* 1980 Am. B.Foun.Res.J. 645, 720 n. 279; Robert Mollan, *Smith Act Prosecutions,* 26 U.Pitt.L. 705 (1965).

5. *The membership clause of the Smith Act.* After *Yates*, the government sought to prosecute communists for being members of an organization advocating the overthrow of the government by force and violence. The Court in *Scales v. United States,* 367 U.S. 203, 81 S.Ct. 1469, 6 L.Ed.2d 782 (1961) and *Noto v. United States,* 367 U.S. 290, 81 S.Ct. 1517, 6 L.Ed.2d 836 (1961) interpreted the membership clause to require that the organization engage in advocacy of the sort described in *Yates* and that the members be active with knowledge of the organization's advocacy and the specific intent to bring about violent overthrow as speedily as circumstances permit.

6. *Spock.* Dr. Spock, Rev. Coffin and others were convicted of conspiring to counsel and abet Selective Service registrants to refuse to have their draft cards in their possession and to disobey other duties imposed by the Selective Service Act of 1967. Spock signed a document entitled "A Call to Resist Illegitimate Authority," which "had 'a double aspect: in part it was a denunciation of governmental policy [in Vietnam] and, in part, it involved a public call to resist the duties imposed by the [Selective Service] Act.'" Several weeks later, Spock attended a demonstration in Washington, D.C., where an unsuccessful attempt was made to present collected draft cards to the Attorney General. *United States v. Spock,* 416 F.2d 165 (1st Cir.1969), per Aldrich, J., ruled that Spock should have been acquitted: "[Spock] was one of the drafters of the Call, but this does not evidence the necessary intent to adhere to its illegal aspects. [H]is speech was limited to condemnation of the war and the draft, and lacked any words or content of counselling. The jury could not find proscribed advocacy from the mere fact [that] he hoped the frequent stating of his views might give young men 'courage to take active steps in draft resistance.' This is a natural consequence of vigorous speech. Similarly, Spock's actions lacked the clear character necessary to imply specific intent under the First Amendment standard. [H]e was at the Washington demonstration, [but took] no part in its planning. [His statements at this demonstration did not extend] beyond the general anti-war, anti-draft remarks he had made before. His attendance is as consistent with a desire to repeat this speech as it is to aid a violation of the law. The dissent would fault us for drawing such distinctions, but it forgets the teaching of [*Bond v. Floyd*[f]] that expressing one's views in broad areas is not foreclosed by knowledge of the consequences, and the important lesson of *Noto, Scales* and *Yates* that one may belong to a group, knowing of its illegal aspects, and still not be found to adhere thereto."

D.   A MODERN "RESTATEMENT"

BRANDENBURG v. OHIO

395 U.S. 444, 89 S.Ct. 1827, 23 L.Ed.2d 430 (1969).

PER CURIAM.[a]

The appellant, a leader of a Ku Klux Klan group, was convicted under [a 1919] Ohio Criminal Syndicalism statute of "advocat[ing] the duty, necessity, or

f. *Bond,* 385 U.S. 116, 87 S.Ct. 339, 17 L.Ed.2d 235 (1966) found ambiguity in expressions of support for those unwilling to respond to the draft that earlier opinions would have characterized as clear advocacy of illegal action. As Thomas Emerson puts it "the distance traversed [from *Schenck* and *Debs* to *Bond*] is quite apparent." *Freedom of Expression in Wartime,* 116 U.Pa.L.Rev. 975, 988 (1968).

a. See Bernard Schwartz, *Holmes Versus Hand: Clear and Present Danger or Advocacy of Unlawful Action?* 1995 S.Ct.Rev. 237:

"*Brandenburg* was assigned to Justice Fortas. The draft opinion that he circulated stated a modified version of the Clear and Present test. [As] it turned out, *Brandenburg* did not come down as a Fortas opinion. Though the Justice had circulated his draft opinion in April 1969 and quickly secured the necessary votes, he followed Justice Harlan's suggestion to delay its announcement. Before then, the events occurred that led to Justice Fortas's forced resignation from the Court. The *Brandenburg* opinion was then redrafted by Justice Brennan,

Imminent (right now)

Likely (to be successful in inciting) *Tough Standard

propriety of crime, sabotage, violence, or unlawful methods of terrorism as a means of accomplishing industrial or political reform" and of "voluntarily assembl[ing] with any society, group or assemblage of persons formed to teach or advocate the doctrines of criminal syndicalism." He was fined $1,000 and sentenced to one to 10 years' imprisonment. * * *

The record shows that a man, identified at trial as the appellant, telephoned an announcer-reporter on the staff of a Cincinnati television station and invited him to come to a Ku Klux Klan "rally" to be held at a farm in Hamilton County. With the cooperation of the organizers, the reporter and a cameraman attended the meeting and filmed the events. Portions of the films were later broadcast on the local station and on a national network.

The prosecution's case rested on the films and on testimony identifying the appellant as the person who communicated with the reporter and who spoke at the rally. The State also introduced into evidence several articles appearing in the film, including a pistol, a rifle, a shotgun, ammunition, a Bible, and a red hood worn by the speaker in the films.

One film showed 12 hooded figures, some of whom carried firearms. They were gathered around a large wooden cross, which they burned. No one was present other than the participants and the newsmen who made the film. Most of the words uttered during the scene were incomprehensible when the film was projected, but scattered phrases could be understood that were derogatory of Negroes and, in one instance, of Jews. Another scene on the same film showed the appellant, in Klan regalia, making a speech. The speech, in full, was as follows:

"This is an organizers' meeting. We have had quite a few members here today which are—we have hundreds, hundreds of members throughout the State of Ohio. I can quote from a newspaper clipping from the Columbus Ohio Dispatch, five weeks ago Sunday morning. The Klan has more members in the State of Ohio than does any other organization. We're not a revengent organization, but if our President, our Congress, our Supreme Court, continues to suppress the white, Caucasian race, it's possible that there might have to be some revengence taken.

"We are marching on Congress July the Fourth, four hundred thousand strong. From there we are dividing into two groups, one group to march on St. Augustine, Florida, the other group to march into Mississippi. Thank you."

The second film showed six hooded figures one of whom, later identified as the appellant, repeated a speech very similar to that recorded on the first film. The reference to the possibility of "revengence" was omitted, and one sentence was added: "Personally, I believe the nigger should be returned to Africa, the Jew returned to Israel." Though some of the figures in the films carried weapons, the speaker did not.

[Whitney] sustained the constitutionality of California's Criminal Syndicalism Act, the text of which is quite similar to that of the laws of Ohio. The Court upheld the statute on the ground that, without more, "advocating" violent means to effect political and economic change involves such danger to the security of the State that the State may outlaw it. But Whitney has been thoroughly discredited

who eliminated all references to the Clear and Present Danger test and substituted the present Brandenburg language: 'where such advocacy is directed to inciting or producing imminent lawless action and is likely to incite or produce such action.' The Brennan redraft was issued as a per curiam opinion."

by later decisions [such as *Dennis* which] have fashioned the principle that the
constitutional guarantees of free speech and free press do not permit a State to
forbid or proscribe advocacy of the use of force or of law violation except where
such advocacy is directed to inciting or producing imminent lawless action[b] and is
likely to incite or produce such action.[2] As we said in *Noto*, "the mere abstract
teaching [of] the moral propriety or even moral necessity for a resort to force and
violence, is not the same as preparing a group for violent action and steeling it to
such action." See also *Bond v. Floyd*. A statute which fails to draw this distinction
impermissibly intrudes upon the freedoms guaranteed by the First and Fourteenth Amendments. It sweeps within its condemnation speech which our Constitution has immunized from governmental control. Cf. *Yates* * * *.

Measured by this test, Ohio's Criminal Syndicalism Act cannot be sustained.
The Act punishes persons who "advocate or teach the duty, necessity, or propriety" of violence "as a means of accomplishing industrial or political reform"; or
who publish or circulate or display any book or paper containing such advocacy; or
who "justify" the commission of violent acts "with intent to exemplify, spread or
advocate the propriety of the doctrines of criminal syndicalism"; or [who] "voluntarily assemble" with a group formed "to teach or advocate the doctrines of
criminal syndicalism." Neither the indictment nor the trial judge's instructions to
the jury in any way refined the statute's bald definition of the crime in terms of
mere advocacy not distinguished from incitement to imminent lawless action.[3]

Accordingly, we are here confronted with a statute which, by its own words
and as applied, purports to punish mere advocacy and to forbid, on pain of
criminal punishment, assembly with others merely to advocate the described type
of action.[4] Such a statute falls within the condemnation of the First and Fourteenth Amendments. The contrary teaching of *Whitney* cannot be supported, and
that decision is therefore overruled.

Reversed.

Justice Black, concurring.

b. Consider Christina Wells, *Reinvigorat-ing Autonomy*, 32 Harv. C.R.-C.L. L. Rev. 159, 179 (1997), "The Court's requirement of immi-nent lawless action is easily justified as based upon concern for autonomy. Speech designed to incite immediate violence or lawless action does not appeal to our thought processes. Rather, it disrespects our rationality and is de-signed to elicit an unthinking, animalistic re-sponse. * * * Speech designed to persuade peo-ple to violate the law is not coercive in the same sense as speech designed to incite immi-nent lawlessness; the former contributes to rather than detracts from our deliberative pro-cesses." Compare David R. Dow & R. Scott Shieldes, *Rethinking the Clear and Present Danger Test*, 73 Indiana L.J. 1217 (1998); David R. Dow, 6 Wm. & Mary Bill of Rts. J. 733 (1998)(clear and present danger test incon-sistent with appropriate notions of moral re-sponsibility).

2. It was on the theory that the Smith Act embodied such a principle and that it had been applied only in conformity with it that this Court sustained the Act's constitutionality. That this was the basis for *Dennis* was empha-sized in *Yates*, in which the Court overturned convictions for advocacy of the forcible over-throw of the Government under the Smith Act, because the trial judge's instructions had al-lowed conviction for mere advocacy, unrelated to its tendency to produce forcible action.

3. The first count of the indictment charged that appellant "did unlawfully by word of mouth advocate the necessity, or pro-priety of crime, violence, or unlawful methods of terrorism as a means of accomplishing politi-cal reform * * *." The second count charged that appellant "did unlawfully voluntarily as-semble with a group or assemblage of persons formed to advocate the doctrines of criminal syndicalism * * *." The trial judge's charge merely followed the language of the indict-ment. * * *

4. Statutes affecting the right of assembly, like those touching on freedom of speech, must observe the established distinctions between mere advocacy and incitement to lawless action * * *.

I agree with the views expressed by Mr. Justice Douglas in his concurring opinion in this case that the "clear and present danger" doctrine should have no place in the interpretation of the First Amendment. I join the Court's opinion, which, as I understand it, simply cites *Dennis*, but does not indicate any agreement on the Court's part with the "clear and present danger" doctrine on which *Dennis* purported to rely.

JUSTICE DOUGLAS, concurring.

While I join the opinion of the Court, I desire to enter a caveat.

[Whether] the war power—the greatest leveler of them all—is adequate to sustain [the "clear and present danger"] doctrine is debatable. The dissents in *Abrams* [and other cases] show how easily "clear and present danger" is manipulated to crush what Brandeis called "the fundamental right of free men to strive for better conditions through new legislation and new institutions" by argument and discourse even in time of war. Though I doubt if the "clear and present danger" test is congenial to the First Amendment in time of a declared war, I am certain it is not reconcilable with the First Amendment in days of peace. * * *

Mr. Justice Holmes, though never formally abandoning the "clear and present danger" test, moved closer to the First Amendment ideal when he said in dissent in *Gitlow* [quoting the passage beginning, "Every idea is an incitement."] We have never been faithful to the philosophy of that dissent.

"[In *Dennis*, we distorted] the 'clear and present danger' test beyond recognition. [I] see no place in the regime of the First Amendment for any 'clear and present danger' test whether strict and tight as some would make it or free-wheeling as the Court in *Dennis* rephrased it.

Notes and Questions

1. What pre-*Brandenburg* decisions, if any, "have fashioned the principle" that advocacy may not be prohibited "except [where] directed to inciting or producing *imminent* lawless action *and * * * likely* to incite or produce such action"? (Emphasis added.) Did *Dennis*, *Yates* and *Scales* take pains to *deny* that the unlawful action advocated need be "imminent" or that the advocacy must be "likely" to produce the forbidden action? See Hans Linde, *"Clear and Present Danger" Reexamined,* 22 Stan.L.Rev. 1163, 1166–67, 1183–86 (1970).

2. Does *Brandenburg* adopt the *Masses* incitement test as a major part of the required showing? Consider Gerald Gunther, *Learned Hand and the Origins of Modern First Amendment Doctrine: Some Fragments of History,*" 27 Stan. L.Rev. 719, 754–55 (1975): "An incitement-nonincitement distinction had only fragmentary and ambiguous antecedents in the pre-*Brandenburg* era; it was *Brandenburg* that really 'established' it; and, it was essentially an establishment of the legacy of Learned Hand. [Under] *Brandenburg*, probability of harm is no longer the central criterion for speech limitations. The inciting language of the speaker—the Hand focus on 'objective' words—is the major consideration. And punishment of the harmless inciter is prevented by the *Schenck*–derived requirement of a likelihood of dangerous consequences." (citing *Brandenburg*'s note 4.) But see Steven Shiffrin, *Defamatory Non–Media Speech and First Amendment Methodology,* 25 U.C.L.A.L.Rev. 915, 947 n. 206 (1978): "Several leading commentators assume that *Brandenburg* adopts an incitement requirement. [The] conclusion is apparently based on this line from *Brandenburg*: 'Neither the indictment nor the trial judge's instructions to the jury in any way refined the statute's bald definition of the crime in terms of mere advocacy, not distinguished from incite-

ment to imminent lawless action' [also citing note 4]. The difficulty with attaching significance to this ambiguous statement is that the term 'incitement' is used in the alternative in the Court's statement of its test. Thus, advocacy of imminent lawless action is protected unless it is directed to inciting *or* producing imminent lawless action and is likely to incite *or* produce imminent lawless action. Thus, even assuming that the use of the word incitement refers to express use of language, as opposed to the nature of results (an interpretation which is strained in light of the Court's wording of the test), incitement is not necessary to divorce the speech from first amendment protection. It is enough that the speech is directed to producing imminent lawless action and is likely to produce such action."

If one wants to argue that *Brandenburg* adopted *Masses*, is there anything to be made of the phrase "directed to" in the *Brandenburg* test? Alternatively, did *Yates* adopt the *Masses* test? If so, does its favorable citation in *Brandenburg* constitute an adoption of the *Masses* test?

3. The *Brandenburg* "inciting or producing imminent lawless action" standard was the basis for reversal of a disorderly conduct conviction in HESS v. INDIANA, 414 U.S. 105, 94 S.Ct. 326, 38 L.Ed.2d 303 (1973) (per curiam). After antiwar demonstrators on the Indiana University campus had blocked a public street, police moved them to the curbs on either side. As an officer passed him, appellant stated loudly, "We'll take the fucking street later [or again]," which led to his disorderly conduct conviction. His statement, observed the Court, "was not addressed to any person or group in particular" and "his tone, although loud, was no louder than that of the other people in the area. [At] best, [the] statement could be taken as counsel for present moderation; at worst, it amounted to nothing more than advocacy of illegal action at some indefinite future time." This was insufficient, under *Brandenburg*, to punish appellant's words, as the State had, on the ground that they had a "tendency to produce violence." It could not be said that appellant "was advocating, in the normal sense, any action" and there was "no evidence" that "his words were intended to produce, and likely to produce, *imminent* disorder."

REHNQUIST, J., joined by Burger, C.J., and Blackmun, J., dissented: "The simple explanation for the result in this case is that the majority has interpreted the evidence differently from the courts below." The dissenters quarreled with the Court's conclusion that appellant's advocacy "was not directed towards inciting imminent action. [T]here are surely possible constructions of the statement which would encompass more or less immediate and continuing action against the police. They should not be rejected out of hand because of an unexplained preference for other acceptable alternatives."[c]

---

c. See also *NAACP v. Claiborne Hardware Co.,* 458 U.S. 886, 102 S.Ct. 3409, 73 L.Ed.2d 1215 (1982). The Court stated that the remarks of Charles Evers "might have been understood" as inviting violence, but stated that when "such appeals do not incite lawless action, they must be regarded as protected speech." If violent action had followed his remarks, a "substantial question" of liability would have been raised. The Court also observed, however, that the defendant might be held criminally liable for the acts of others if the speeches could be taken as evidence that the defendant gave "other specific instructions to carry out violent acts or threats." Compare

Watts v. United States, 394 U.S. 705, 89 S.Ct. 1399, 22 L.Ed.2d 664 (1969) (statute prohibiting knowing and wilful threat of bodily harm upon the President is constitutional on its face) (dictum); *Rankin v. McPherson,* Sec. 9, II infra (clerical employee's private expression of desire that Presidential assassination attempt be successful is insufficient justification for dismissal even in a law enforcement agency). For commentary on threats and the first amendment, see Justice Linde's opinion in *State v. Robertson,* 293 Or. 402, 649 P.2d 569 (1982); C. Edwin Baker, *Human Liberty and Freedom of Speech* 54–69 (1989); Steven G. Gey, *The Nuremberg Files and the First Amendment Value*

4. Does *Yates* survive *Brandenburg*'s emphasis on *imminent* lawless action? Consider Harry Kalven, *A Worthy Tradition* 234 (1988): "It is [possible] that [*Brandenburg*] has preserved the group/individual distinction. Under such an approach the *Yates* incitement-to-future-action standard would apply to group speech and the *Brandenburg* incitement-to-immediate-action standard would apply to the individual speaker." Is light shed on the question by *Communist Party of Indiana v. Whitcomb*, 414 U.S. 441, 94 S.Ct. 656, 38 L.Ed.2d 635 (1974), invalidating an Indiana statute denying a political party or its candidates access to the ballot unless the party files an affidavit that it "does not advocate the overthrow of local, state or national government by force or violence"? The Court, per Brennan J., maintained that the required oath (which had been interpreted to include advocacy of abstract doctrine) violated the principle of *Brandenburg* and stated that the principle applied not only to attempted denials of public employment, bar licensing, and tax exemption, but also to ballot access denials. The flaw with the state's position was that it furnished access to the ballot "not because the Party urges others 'to *do* something now *or in the future* [but] merely to believe in something,' [*Yates*]" (second emphasis added).

What happened to the "imminent lawless action" requirement? Does the *Whitcomb* language clarify *Brandenburg*? Modify it?

5. Does *Brandenburg* apply to the advocacy of trivial crimes? Suppose the advocacy of trespass across a lawn? What result under *Brandenburg*? What result under *Dennis*? Is *Dennis* potentially more speech protective than *Brandenburg*?

6. Does *Brandenburg* apply to solicitation of crime in private or non-ideological contexts? Consider Shiffrin, note 2 supra, at 950: "How different it might be if the factual context were to involve advocacy of murder in a non-socio-political context. One suspects that little rhetoric about the marketplace of ideas or other first amendment values would be employed and that the serious and explicit advocacy of murder in a concrete way would suffice to divorce the speech from first amendment protection even in the absence of a specific showing of likelihood." Would it matter if it were not explicit or not concrete? For trenchant analysis of the issues raised by the shift in context from public to private or in subject matter from ideological to non-ideological, see Kent Greenawalt, *Speech and Crime*, 1980 Am.B.Found.Res.J. 645.

7. Nuremberg Files, an anti-abortion Web site included the names, addresses, photographs, and license plate numbers of those who provided abortions or were prominent pro-choice advocates together with their family members. Paladin Press published *Hit Man: A Technical Manual for Independent Contractors*. James Perry relied on the book's instructions to kill three people. Should the Web site and book be protected under *Brandenburg*?[d]

8. Should the line of cases from *Schenck* to *Brandenburg* fuel cynicism about the binding force of legal doctrine and about the willingness or capacity of the judiciary to protect dissent?[e] To what extent does the focus on Supreme Court cases exaggerate the frailty of legal doctrine?[f]

of Threats, 78 Tex. L.Rev. 541 (2000); Kent Greenawalt, *Criminal Coercion and Freedom of Speech*, 78 Nw.U.L.Rev. 1081 (1984); Note, *United States v. Jake Baker: Revisiting Threats and the First Amendment*, 84 Va. L.Rev. 287 (1998).

d. See generally Rodney A. Smolla, *Deliberate Intent* (1999); Cass R. Sunstein, *One Case at a Time* 191–96 (1999); S. Elizabeth Wilborn Malloy & Ronald J. Krotoszynski, Jr., *Recali-*

brating the Cost of Harm Advocacy, 41 Wm. & Mary L.Rev. 1159 (2000); John Rothchild, *Menacing Speech and the First Amendment*, 8 Tex. J. Women & L. 207 (1999); Note, *Adjusting Absolutism: First Amendment Protection for the Fringe*, 80 B.U.L.Rev. 907 (2000).

e. In fashioning first amendment doctrine, should the overriding objective be at "all times [to] equip the first amendment to do maximum service in those historical periods when intoler-

II. REPUTATION AND PRIVACY

In an important article, Harry Kalven coined the phrase "two level theory." Kalven, *The Metaphysics of the Law of Obscenity,* 1960 Sup.Ct.Rev. 1, 11. As he described it, *Beauharnais,* infra, and other cases employed a first amendment methodology that classified speech at two levels. Some speech—libel, obscenity, "fighting words"—was thought to be so bereft of social utility as to be beneath first amendment protection. At the second level, speech of constitutional value was thought to be protected unless it presented a clear and present danger of a substantive evil.

In considering libel and privacy, we will witness the collapse of "two level theory." The purpose is not a detailed examination of libel and privacy law. Our interests include the initial exclusion of defamation from first amendment protection, the themes and methods contributing to the erosion of that exclusion, and the articulation of basic first amendment values having implications and applications beyond defamation and the right to privacy.

A. GROUP LIBEL

BEAUHARNAIS v. ILLINOIS, 343 U.S. 250, 72 S.Ct. 725, 96 L.Ed. 919 (1952), per FRANKFURTER, J., sustained a statute prohibiting exhibition in any public place of any publication portraying "depravity, criminality, unchastity, or lack of virtue of a class of citizens, of any race, color, creed or religion [which exposes such citizens] to contempt, derision or obloquy or which is productive of breach of the peace or riots." The Court affirmed a conviction for organizing the distribution of a leaflet which petitioned the Mayor and City Council of Chicago "to halt the further encroachment, harassment and invasion of white people, their property, neighborhoods and persons by the Negro"; called for "one million self respecting white people in Chicago to unite"; and warned that if "the need to prevent the white race from becoming mongrelized by the Negro will not unite us, then the [aggressions], rapes, robberies, knives, guns, and marijuana of the Negro, surely will.":

"Today every American jurisdiction [punishes] libels directed at individuals. '[There] are certain well-defined and narrowly limited classes of speech, the prevention and punishment of which have never been thought to raise any constitutional problem. These include the lewd and obscene, the profane, the libelous, and the insulting or "fighting" words—those which by their very utterance inflict injury or tend to incite to an immediate breach of the peace. It has been well observed that such utterances are no essential part of any exposition of ideas, and are of such slight social value as a step to truth that any benefit

---

ance of unorthodox ideas is most prevalent and when governments are most able and most likely to stifle dissent systematically"? Should the first amendment "be targeted for the worst of times"? What impact would such a perspective have on the general development of first amendment doctrine? See Vincent Blasi, *The Pathological Perspective and the First Amendment,* 85 Colum.L.Rev. 449 (1985).

f. For a comprehensive review and critical analysis of the problems and policies raised by advocacy of illegal action, see Greenawalt, note

6 supra. See generally Kent Greenawalt, *Speech, Crime, and the Uses of Language* (1989); Harry Kalven, *A Worthy Tradition* (1987).For comparative perspectives, see Zana v. Turkey, 1997–VII Eur. Ct. H.R. 2533; Ruth Gavison, *Incitement and the Limits of Law* in *Censorship and Silencing* 43 (Post ed. 1998)(discussing Israeli law and the speech surrounding the assassination of Prime Minister Rabin).

that may be derived from them is clearly outweighed by the social interest in order and morality. "Resort to epithets or personal abuse is not in any proper sense communication of information or opinion safeguarded by the Constitution, and its punishment as a criminal act would raise no question under that instrument." *Cantwell v. Connecticut,* [Ch. 8, Sec. 2, I infra].' Such were the views of a unanimous Court in *Chaplinsky v. New Hampshire,* Sec. 1, IV, A infra.[6]

"No one will gainsay that it is libelous falsely to charge another with being a rapist, robber, carrier of knives and guns, and user of marijuana. The [question is whether the fourteenth amendment] prevents a State from punishing such libels—as criminal libel has been defined, limited and constitutionally recognized time out of mind—directed at designated collectivities and flagrantly disseminated. [I]f an utterance directed at an individual may be the object of criminal sanctions, we cannot deny to a State power to punish the same utterance directed at a defined group, unless we can say that this is a wilful and purposeless restriction unrelated to the peace and well-being of the State.

"Illinois did not have to look beyond her own borders to await the tragic experience of the last three decades to conclude that wilful purveyors of falsehood concerning racial and religious groups promote strife and tend powerfully to obstruct the manifold adjustments required for free, orderly life in a metropolitan, polyglot community. From the murder of the abolitionist Lovejoy in 1837 to the Cicero riots of 1951, Illinois has been the scene of exacerbated tension between races, often flaring into violence and destruction. In many of these outbreaks, utterances of the character here in question, so the Illinois legislature could conclude, played a significant [part.]

"In the face of this history and its frequent obligato of extreme racial and religious propaganda, we would deny experience to say that the Illinois legislature was without reason in seeking ways to curb false or malicious defamation of racial and religious groups, made in public places and by means calculated to have a powerful emotional impact on those to whom it was presented.

"[It would] be arrant dogmatism, quite outside the scope of our authority [for] us to deny that the Illinois Legislature may warrantably believe that a man's job and his educational opportunities and the dignity accorded him may depend as much on the reputation of the racial and religious group to which he willynilly belongs, as on his own merits. This being so, we are precluded from saying that speech concededly punishable when immediately directed at individuals cannot be outlawed if directed at groups with whose position and esteem in society the affiliated individual may be inextricably involved. * * *[18]

"As to the defense of truth, Illinois in common with many States requires a showing not only that the utterance state the facts, but also that the publication be made 'with good motives and for justifiable ends'. Both elements are necessary if the defense is to prevail. [The] teaching of a century and a half of criminal libel prosecutions in this country would go by the board if we were to hold that Illinois was not within her rights in making this combined requirement. Assuming that defendant's offer of proof directed to a part of the defense was adequate, it did not satisfy the entire requirement which Illinois could exact."

---

6. In all but five States, the constitutional guarantee of free speech to every person is explicitly qualified by holding him "responsible for the abuse of that right." * * *

18. [If] a statute sought to outlaw libels of political parties, quite different problems not now before us would be raised. For one thing, the whole doctrine of fair comment as indispensable to the democratic political process would come into play. Political parties, like public men, are, as it were, public property.

The Court ruled that the trial court properly declined to require the jury to find a "clear and present danger": "Libelous utterances not being within the area of constitutionally protected speech, it is unnecessary, either for us or for the State courts, to consider the issues behind the phrase 'clear and present danger.' Certainly no one would contend that obscene speech, for example, may be punished only upon a showing of such circumstances. Libel, as we have seen, is in the same class."

BLACK, J., joined by Douglas, J., dissented: "[The Court] acts on the bland assumption that the First Amendment is wholly irrelevant. [Today's] case degrades First Amendment freedoms to the 'rational basis' level. [We] are cautioned that state legislatures must be left free to 'experiment' and to make legislative judgments. [State] experimentation in curbing freedom of expression is startling and frightening doctrine in a country dedicated to self-government by its people.

"[As] 'constitutionally recognized,' [criminal libel] has provided for punishment of false, malicious, scurrilous charges against individuals, not against huge groups. This limited scope of the law of criminal libel is of no small importance. It has confined state punishment of speech and expression to the narrowest of areas involving nothing more than private feuds. Every expansion of the law of criminal libel so as to punish discussion of matters of public concern means a corresponding invasion of the area dedicated to free expression by the First Amendment.

"[If] there be minority groups who hail this holding as their victory, they might consider the possible relevancy of this ancient remark: 'Another such victory and I am undone.' "

REED, J., joined by Douglas, J., dissenting, argued that the statute was unconstitutionally vague: "These words—'virtue,' 'derision,' and 'obloquy'—have neither general nor special meanings well enough known to apprise those within their reach as to limitations on speech. Philosophers and poets, thinkers of high and low degree from every age and race have sought to expound the meaning of virtue. [Are] the tests of the Puritan or the Cavalier to be applied, those of the city or the farm, the Christian or non-Christian, the old or the young?"

DOUGLAS, J., dissented: "Hitler and his Nazis showed how evil a conspiracy could be which was aimed at destroying a race by exposing it to contempt, derision, and obloquy. I would be willing to concede that such conduct directed at a race or group in this country could be made an indictable offense. For such a project would be more than the exercise of free speech. [It] would be free speech plus.

"I would also be willing to concede that even without the element of conspiracy there might be times and occasions when the legislative or executive branch might call a halt to inflammatory talk, such as the shouting of 'fire' in a school or a theatre.

"My view is that if in any case other public interests are to override the plain command of the First Amendment, the peril of speech must be clear and present, leaving no room for argument, raising no doubts as to the necessity of curbing speech in order to prevent disaster."

JACKSON, J., dissenting, argued that the fourteenth amendment does not incorporate the first, as such, but permits the states more latitude than the Congress. He concluded, however, that due process required the trier of fact to evaluate the evidence as to the truth and good faith of the speaker and the clarity and presence of the danger. He was unwilling to assume danger from the tendency of the words and felt that the trial court had precluded the defendant's efforts to show truth and good motives.

Notes and Questions

1. *The right to petition.* Should it make a difference that the leaflet was in the form of a petition to the mayor and city council? Does the right of the people "to petition the Government for a redress of grievances" add anything of substance to Beauharnais' other first amendment arguments? Consider Harry Kalven, *The Negro and the First Amendment* 40 (1965): "If it would make a difference whether the petition was genuine and not just a trick of form, can the Court penetrate the form and appraise the true motivation or must it, as it does with congressional committees accept the official motivation?"[a]

2. *Equality and freedom of speech.* Consider the following hypothetical commentary: "Group libel statutes pose uniquely difficult issues for they involve a clash between two constitutional commitments: the principle of equality and the principle of free speech. They force us to decide what we want to express as a nation: Do we want a powerful symbol of our belief in uninhibited debate or do we want to be the kind of nation that will not tolerate the public calumny of religious, ethnic, and racial groups?"[b] Does the emphasis on equality shortchange the case for prohibiting racist speech? See Robin West, *Progressive Constitutionalism: Reconstructing the Fourteenth Amendment* 147–51 (1994).

3. *Tolerance and freedom of speech.* Should the first amendment be a means of institutionalizing a national commitment to the value of tolerance? By tolerating the intolerable, would we carve out one area of social interaction for extraordinary self-restraint and thereby develop[c] and demonstrate a vital social capacity? See generally Lee Bollinger, *The Tolerant Society: Freedom of Speech and Extremist Speech in America* (1986); Lee Bollinger, *Free Speech and Intellectual Values,* 92 Yale L.J. 438 (1983); Lee Bollinger, *Book Review,* 80 Mich.L.Rev. 617 (1982).

4. *Libel, group libel, and seditious libel.* Consider Kalven, supra, at 15, 16 and 50–51: Seditious libel "is the doctrine that criticism of government officials and policy may be viewed as defamation of government and may be punished as a serious crime. [On] my view, the absence of seditious libel as a crime is the true pragmatic test of freedom of speech. This I would argue is what freedom of speech is about. [The] most revealing aspect of the opinions, and particularly that of Justice Frankfurter, is the absence of any sense of the proximity of the case before them to seditious libel. The case presents almost a perfect instance of that competition among analogies which Edward Levi has emphasized as the essential circumstance of legal reasoning. In the middle we have group libel and Justice Frankfurter's urging its many resemblances to individual libel. [If] the Court's speech theory had been more grounded, as it seems to me it should be, on the relevance of the concept of seditious libel and less on the analogy to the law of

---

a. See *McDonald v. Smith,* 472 U.S. 479, 105 S.Ct. 2787, 86 L.Ed.2d 384 (1985) (denying any special first amendment status for the Petition Clause).

b. See, e.g., *The Price We Pay: The Case Against Racist Speech* (Laura J. Lederer & Richard Delgado eds. 1995); Robin West, *Progressive Constitutionalism: Reconstructing the Fourteenth Amendment* (1994); Mari J. Matsuda et al., *Words that Wound* (Itzin ed. 1993);

Gary Goodpaster, *Equality and Free Speech: The Case Against Substantive Equality,* 82 Ia. L.Rev. 645 (1997); Loren Beth, *Group Libel and Free Speech,* 39 Minn.L.Rev. 167, 180–81 (1955) and sources cited in Sec. 1, V, C.

c. For skepticism about the capacity of courts to achieve any substantial impact in promoting tolerance, see Robert Nagel, *Constitutional Cultures* 27–59 (1989).

attempts found in the slogan 'clear and present danger,' it is difficult to believe that either the debate or the result in *Beauharnais* would have been the same."

B. PUBLIC OFFICIALS AND SEDITIOUS LIBEL

NEW YORK TIMES CO. v. SULLIVAN

376 U.S. 254, 84 S.Ct. 710, 11 L.Ed.2d 686 (1964).

JUSTICE BRENNAN delivered the opinion of the Court.

[Sullivan, the Montgomery, Ala. police commissioner, sued the New York Times and four black Alabama clergymen for alleged libelous statements in a paid, full-page fund-raising advertisement signed by a "Committee to defend Martin Luther King and the struggle for freedom in the South." The advertisement stated that "truckloads of police armed with shotguns and tear-gas ringed Alabama State College Campus" in Montgomery, and that "the Southern violators [have] bombed [Dr. King's] home, assaulted his person [and] arrested him seven times." In several respects the statements were untrue. Several witnesses testified that they understood the statements to refer to Sullivan because he supervised Montgomery police. Sullivan proved he did not participate in the events described. He offered no proof of pecuniary loss.[3] Pursuant to Alabama law, the trial court submitted the libel issue to the jury, giving general and punitive damages instructions. It returned a $500,000 verdict for Sullivan against all of the defendants.] We hold that the rule of law applied by the Alabama courts is constitutionally deficient for failure to provide the safeguards for freedom of speech and of the press that are required by the First and Fourteenth Amendments in a libel action brought by a public official against critics of his official conduct.[4] We further hold that under the proper safeguards the evidence presented in this case is constitutionally insufficient to support the judgment for respondent.

I. [The] publication here [communicated] information, expressed opinion, recited grievances, protested claimed abuses, and sought financial support on behalf of a movement whose existence and objectives are matters of the highest public interest and concern. That the Times was paid for publishing the advertisement is as immaterial in this connection as is the fact that newspapers and books are sold. *Smith v. California* [p. 718 infra]. Any other conclusion would discourage newspapers from carrying "editorial advertisements" of this type, and so might shut off an important outlet for the promulgation of information and ideas by persons who do not themselves have access to publishing facilities.

II. Under Alabama law [once] "libel per se" has been established, the defendant has no defense as to stated facts unless he can persuade the jury that they were true in all their particulars. [His] privilege of "fair comment" for

3. Approximately 394 copies of the edition of the Times containing the advertisement were circulated in Alabama. Of these, about 35 copies were distributed in Montgomery County. The total circulation of the Times for that day was approximately 650,000 copies.

4. [The] Times contends that the assumption of jurisdiction over its corporate person by the Alabama courts overreaches the territorial limits of the Due Process Clause. The latter claim is foreclosed from our review by the ruling of the Alabama courts that the Times entered a general appearance in the action and thus waived its jurisdictional objection. * * *

[Since *New York Times* the Court has upheld expansive personal jurisdiction against media defendants. *Calder v. Jones*, 465 U.S. 783, 104 S.Ct. 1482, 79 L.Ed.2d 804 (1984); *Keeton v. Hustler*, 465 U.S. 770, 104 S.Ct. 1473, 79 L.Ed.2d 790 (1984). *Calder* rejected the suggestion that first amendment concerns enter into jurisdictional analysis. It feared complicating the inquiry and argued that because first amendment concerns are taken into account in limiting the substantive law of defamation, "to reintroduce those concerns at the jurisdictional stage would be a form of double counting."]

expressions of opinion depends on the truth of the facts upon which the comment is based. [Unless] he can discharge the burden of proving truth, general damages are presumed, and may be awarded without proof of pecuniary injury.

[Respondent] relies heavily, as did the Alabama courts, on statements of this Court to the effect that the Constitution does not protect libelous publications. Those statements do not foreclose our inquiry here. None of the cases sustained the use of libel laws to impose sanctions upon expression critical of the official conduct of public officials. [L]ibel can claim no talismanic immunity from constitutional limitations. It must be measured by standards that satisfy the First Amendment.

The First Amendment, said Judge Learned Hand, "presupposes that right conclusions are more likely to be gathered out of a multitude of tongues, than through any kind of authoritative selection. To many this is, and always will be, folly; but we have staked upon it our all." [Thus] we consider this case against the background of a profound national commitment to the principle that debate on public issues should be uninhibited, robust, and wide-open, and that it may well include vehement, caustic, and sometimes unpleasantly sharp attacks on government and public officials. The present advertisement, as an expression of grievance and protest on one of the major public issues of our time, would seem clearly to qualify for the constitutional protection. The question is whether it forfeits that protection by the falsity of some of its factual statements and by its alleged defamation of respondent.

Authoritative interpretations of the First Amendment guarantees have consistently refused to recognize an exception for any test of truth—whether administered by judges, juries, or administrative officials—and especially not one that puts the burden of proving truth on the speaker. [E]rroneous statement is inevitable in free debate, and [it] must be protected if the freedoms of expression are to have the "breathing space" that they "need [to] survive."

[Injury] to official reputation affords no more warrant for repressing speech that would otherwise be free than does factual error. Where judicial officers are involved, this Court has held that concern for the dignity and reputation of the courts does not justify the punishment as criminal contempt of criticism of the judge or his decision. This is true even though the utterance contains "half-truths" and "misinformation." Such repression can be justified, if at all, only by a clear and present danger of the obstruction of justice. If judges are to be treated as "men of fortitude, able to thrive in a hardy climate," surely the same must be true of other government officials, such as elected city commissioners. Criticism of their official conduct does not lose its constitutional protection merely because it is effective criticism and hence diminishes their official reputations.

If neither factual error nor defamatory content suffices to remove the constitutional shield from criticism of official conduct, the combination of the two elements is no less inadequate. This is the lesson to be drawn from the great controversy over the Sedition Act of 1798, 1 Stat. 596, which first crystallized a national awareness of the central meaning of the First Amendment. [Although] the Sedition Act was never tested in this Court, the attack upon its validity has carried the day in the court of history. Fines levied in its prosecution were repaid by Act of Congress on the ground that it was unconstitutional. * * * Jefferson, as President, pardoned those who had been convicted and sentenced under the Act and remitted their fines. [Its] invalidity [has] also been assumed by Justices of this Court. [These] views reflect a broad consensus that the Act, because of the restraint it imposed upon criticism of government and public officials, was inconsistent with the First Amendment. * * *

What a State may not constitutionally bring about by means of a criminal statute is likewise beyond the reach of its civil law of libel. The fear of damage awards under a rule such as that invoked by the Alabama courts here may be markedly more inhibiting than the fear of prosecution under a criminal statute. [The] judgment awarded in this case—without the need for any proof of actual pecuniary loss—was one thousand times greater than the maximum fine provided by the Alabama criminal [libel law], and one hundred times greater than that provided by the Sedition Act. And since there is no double-jeopardy limitation applicable to civil lawsuits, this is not the only judgment that may be awarded against petitioners for the same publication.[18] Whether or not a newspaper can survive a succession of such judgments, the pall of fear and timidity imposed upon those who would give voice to public criticism is an atmosphere in which the First Amendment freedoms cannot [survive].

The state rule of law is not saved by its allowance of the defense of truth. A defense for erroneous statements honestly made is no less essential here than was the requirement of proof of guilty knowledge which, in *Smith v. California,* we held indispensable to a valid conviction of a bookseller for possessing obscene writings for [sale].

A rule compelling the critic of official conduct to guarantee the truth of all his factual assertions—and to do so on pain of libel judgments virtually unlimited in amount—leads to a comparable "self-censorship." Allowance of the defense of truth, with the burden of proving it on the defendant, does not mean that only false speech will be deterred.[19] [Under] such a rule, would-be critics of official conduct may be deterred from voicing their criticism, even though it is believed to be true and even though it is in fact true, because of doubt whether it can be proved in court or fear of the expense of having to do so. They tend to make only statements which "steer far wider of the unlawful zone." The rule thus dampens the vigor and limits the variety of public [debate].

The constitutional guarantees require, we think, a federal rule that prohibits a public official from recovering damages for a defamatory falsehood relating to his official conduct unless he proves that the statement was made with "actual malice"—that is, with knowledge that it was false or with reckless disregard of whether it was false or [not].[a]

18. The Times states that four other libel suits based on the advertisement have been filed against it by [others]; that another $500,000 verdict has been awarded in [one]; and that the damages sought in the other three total $2,000,000.

19. Even a false statement may be deemed to make a valuable contribution to the public debate, since it brings about "the clearer perception and livelier impression of truth, produced by its collision with error." Mill, *On Liberty* 15 (1955).

a. Compare *St. Amant v. Thompson,* 390 U.S. 727, 88 S.Ct. 1323, 20 L.Ed.2d 262 (1968) (publishing while "in fact entertain[ing] serious doubts about the truth of the publication" satisfies standard) with *Garrison v. Louisiana,* 379 U.S. 64, 85 S.Ct. 209, 13 L.Ed.2d 125 (1964) (standard requires "high degree of awareness of probable falsity"). See also *Masson v. New Yorker Magazine, Inc.,* 501 U.S. 496, 111 S.Ct. 2419, 115 L.Ed.2d 447 (1991) ("a deliberate alteration of the words uttered by a plaintiff does not equate with knowledge of falsity [unless] the alteration results in a material change of meaning conveyed by the statement"). For discussion of malice and docudrama, see Rodney Smolla, *Harlot's Ghost and JFK: A Fictional Conversation with Norman Mailer, Oliver Stone, Earl Warren and Hugo Black,* 26 Suffolk U.L.Rev. 587 (1992).

For discussion of the malice doctrine's operation in practice, see Brian C. Murchison, John Soloski, Randall Bezanson, Gilbert Cranberg, & Roselle Wissler, *Sullivan's Paradox: The Emergence of Judicial Standards of Journalism,* 73 N.C.L.Rev. 7 (1994).

Such a privilege for criticism of official conduct is appropriately analogous to the protection accorded a public official when *he* is sued for libel by a private citizen. In *Barr v. Matteo,* 360 U.S. 564, 575, 79 S.Ct. 1335, 1341, 3 L.Ed.2d 1434 (1959), this Court held the utterance of a federal official to be absolutely privileged if made "within the outer perimeter" of his duties. The States accord the same immunity to statements of their highest officers, although some differentiate their lesser officials and qualify the privilege they enjoy. But all hold that all officials are protected unless actual malice can be proved. The reason for the official privilege is said to be that the threat of damage suits would otherwise "inhibit the fearless, vigorous, and effective administration of policies of government" and "dampen the ardor of all but the most resolute, or the most irresponsible, in the unflinching discharge of their duties." *Barr.* Analogous considerations support the privilege for the citizen-critic of government. It is as much his duty to criticize as it is the official's duty to administer. [It] would give public servants an unjustified preference over the public they serve, if critics of official conduct did not have a fair equivalent of the immunity granted to the officials themselves. We conclude that such a privilege is required by the First and Fourteenth Amendments.[23]

III. [W]e consider that the proof presented to show actual malice lacks the convincing clarity[b] which the constitutional standard demands, and hence that it would not constitutionally sustain the judgment for respondent under the proper rule of law. [T]here is evidence that the Times published the advertisement without checking its accuracy against the news stories in the Times' own files. The mere presence of the stories in the files does [not] establish that the Times "knew" the advertisement was false, since the state of mind required for actual malice would have to be brought home to the persons in the Times' organization having responsibility for the publication of the advertisement. With respect to the failure of those persons to make the check, the record shows that they relied upon their knowledge of the good reputation of many [whose] names were listed as sponsors of the advertisement, and upon the letter from A. Philip Randolph, known to them as a responsible individual, certifying that the use of the names was authorized. There was testimony that the persons handling the advertisement saw nothing in it that would render it unacceptable under the Times' policy of rejecting advertisements containing "attacks of a personal character"; their failure to reject it on this ground was not unreasonable. We think the evidence against the Times supports at most a finding of negligence in failing to discover the misstatements, and is constitutionally insufficient to show the recklessness that is required for a finding of actual malice.

---

23. We have no occasion here to determine how far down into the lower ranks of government employees the "public official" designation would extend for purposes of this rule, or otherwise to specify categories of persons who would or would not be included. [Nor] need we here determine the boundaries of the "official conduct" concept. * * *

b. Compare *Bose Corp. v. Consumers Union,* 466 U.S. 485, 104 S.Ct. 1949, 80 L.Ed.2d 502 (1984) (appellate courts "must exercise independent judgment and determine whether the record establishes actual malice with convincing clarity."). Accord *Harte–Hanks Communications, Inc. v. Connaughton,* 491 U.S. 657, 109 S.Ct. 2678, 105 L.Ed.2d 562 (1989). See also *Anderson v. Liberty Lobby, Inc.,* 477 U.S. 242, 106 S.Ct. 2505, 91 L.Ed.2d 202 (1986) (same standard at summary judgment). Should independent appellate judgment be required in all first amendment cases? All constitutional cases? For commentary, see Henry Monaghan, *Constitutional Fact Review,* 85 Colum.L.Rev. 229 (1985); Eugene Volokh & Brett McDonnell, *Freedom of Speech and Independent Judgment Review in Copyright Cases,* 107 Yale L.J. 2431 (1998); Eugene Volokh, *Freedom of Speech and Appellate Review in Workplace Harassment Cases,* 90 Nw. U.L.Rev. 1009 (1996). On the impact of *Bose,* see Susan M. Gilles, *Taking First Amendment Procedure Seriously,* 58 Ohio St.L.J. 1752, 1774–79 (1998).

[T]he evidence was constitutionally defective in another respect:[c] it was incapable of supporting the jury's finding that the allegedly libelous statements were made "of and concerning" respondent. [On this point, the Supreme Court of Alabama] based its ruling on the proposition that: "[The] average person knows that municipal agents, such as police and firemen, and others, are under the control and direction of the city governing body, and more particularly under the direction and control of a single commissioner. In measuring the performance or deficiencies of such groups, praise or criticism is usually attached to the official in complete control of the body."

This proposition has disquieting implications for criticism of governmental conduct. [It would transmute] criticism of government, however impersonal it may seem on its face, into personal criticism, and hence potential libel, of the officials of whom the government is composed. [Raising] as it does the possibility that a good-faith critic of government will be penalized for his criticism, the proposition relied on by the Alabama courts strikes at the very center of the constitutionally protected area of free expression. We hold that such a proposition may not constitutionally be utilized to establish that an otherwise impersonal attack on governmental operations was a libel of an official responsible for those operations. Since it was relied on exclusively here, and there was no other evidence to connect the statements with respondent, the evidence was constitutionally insufficient to support a finding that the statements referred to respondent. * * *[d]

JUSTICE BLACK, with whom JUSTICE DOUGLAS joins (concurring).

* * * "Malice," even as defined by the Court, is an elusive, abstract concept, hard to prove and hard to disprove. The requirement that malice be proved provides at best an evanescent protection for the right critically to discuss public affairs and certainly does not measure up to the sturdy safeguard embodied in the First Amendment. Unlike the Court, therefore, I vote to reverse exclusively on the ground that the Times and the individual defendants had an absolute, unconditional constitutional right to publish in the Times advertisement their criticisms of the Montgomery agencies and [officials].

The half-million-dollar verdict [gives] dramatic proof [that] state libel laws threaten the very existence of an American press virile enough to publish unpopular views on public affairs and bold enough to criticize the conduct of public officials. [B]riefs before us show that in Alabama there are now pending eleven libel suits by local and state officials against the Times seeking $5,600,000, and five such suits against the Columbia Broadcasting System seeking $1,700,000. Moreover, this technique for harassing and punishing a free press—now that it has been shown to be possible—is by no means limited to cases with racial overtones; it can be used in other fields where public feelings may make local as well as out-of-state newspapers easy prey for libel verdict seekers.

In my opinion the Federal Constitution has dealt with this deadly danger to the press in the only way possible without leaving the press open to destruction— by granting the press an absolute immunity for criticism of the way public officials do their public duty.

c. Implicitly, the Court left open the possibility of a new trial with new evidence. For discussion of the Court's internal debate on the question, see Bernard Schwartz, *Super Chief* 531–41 (1983).

d. For a similar ruling that impersonal criticism of a government operation cannot be the basis for defamation "of and concerning" the supervisor of the operation, see *Rosenblatt v. Baer*, 383 U.S. 75, 86 S.Ct. 669, 15 L.Ed.2d 597 (1966): "[T]antamount to a demand for recovery based on libel of government."

[This] Nation, I suspect, can live in peace without libel suits based on public discussions of public affairs and public officials. But I doubt that a country can live in freedom where its people can be made to suffer physically or financially for criticizing their government, its actions, or its officials. * * *e

Professor Kalven observed that the Court in *New York Times* was moving toward "the theory of free speech that Alexander Meiklejohn has been offering us for some fifteen years now." Harry Kalven, *The New York Times Case: A Note On "The Central Meaning of the First Amendment,"* 1964 Sup.Ct.Rev. 191, 221. Indeed Kalven reported Alexander Meiklejohn's view that the case was " 'an occasion for dancing in the streets.' " Id. at 221 n. 125. Consider the following excerpts from Meiklejohn's most significant work and Zechariah Chafee's pointed response.

ALEXANDER MEIKLEJOHN—FREE SPEECH AND ITS RELATION TO SELF–GOVERNMENT

Meiklejohn, *Political Freedom* 9, 27–28, 79–80, 75–77 (1960).
Reprinted with permission of the publisher; copyright
© 1948, 1960 by Harper Collins Publishers.

We Americans think of ourselves as politically free. We believe in self-government. If men are to be governed, we say, then that governing must be done, not by others, but by themselves. So far, therefore, as our own affairs are concerned, we refuse to submit to alien control. That refusal, if need be, we will carry to the point of rebellion, of revolution. And if other men, within the jurisdiction of our laws, are denied their right to political freedom, we will, in the same spirit, rise to their defense. Governments, we insist, derive their just powers from the consent of the governed. If that consent be lacking, governments have no just powers.

[The] principle of the freedom of speech springs from the necessities of the program of self-government. It is not a Law of Nature or of Reason in the abstract. It is a deduction from the basic American agreement that public issues shall be decided by universal suffrage.[a]

e. Goldberg, J., joined by Douglas, J., concurring, also asserted for "the citizen and [the] press an absolute unconditional privilege to criticize official conduct," but maintained that the imposition of liability for "[p]urely private defamation" did not abridge the first amendment because it had "little to do with the political ends of a self-governing society." For background on the *New York Times* case, see Anthony Lewis, *Make No Law* (1991); Rodney Smolla, *Suing The Press* 26–52 (1986). For the Canadian approach, see *Hill v. Church of Scientology of Ontario* [1995], 126 D.L.R. 4th 129.

a. Consider David Cole, *Beyond Unconstitutional Conditions: Charting Spheres of Neutrality in Government–Funded Speech,* 67 N.Y.U.L.Rev. 675, 710 (1992): "If Holmes's 'free trade' metaphor represents the paradigmatic liberal vision of free speech, Meiklejohn's town meeting captures the republican vision of an inclusive public exchange in which ordinary people actively participate as citizens, engaged in an ongoing dialogue about public values and norms. Where the liberal view sees an 'invisible hand' reaching truth through the self-interested behavior of atomistic individuals, the republican vision emphasizes the constitutive role of public dialogue in shaping our collective identity as a community, and the importance of maintaining public institutions for speech to that end." For discussion of the Meiklejohn perspective in the Japanese context, Ronald J. Krotoszynski, Jr., *The Chrysanthemum, the Sword, and the First Amendment,* 1998 Wisc. L.Rev. 905 (1998).

If, then, on any occasion in the United States it is allowable to say that the Constitution is a good document it is equally allowable, in that situation, to say that the Constitution is a bad document. If a public building may be used in which to say, in time of war, that the war is justified, then the same building may be used in which to say that it is not justified. If it be publicly argued that conscription for armed service is moral and necessary, it may likewise be publicly argued that it is immoral and unnecessary. If it may be said that American political institutions are superior to those of England or Russia or Germany, it may, with equal freedom, be said that those of England or Russia or Germany are superior to ours. These conflicting views may be expressed, must be expressed, not because they are valid, but because they are relevant. If they are responsibly entertained by anyone, we, the voters, need to hear them. When a question of policy is "before the house," free men choose to meet it not with their eyes shut, but with their eyes open. To be afraid of ideas, any idea, is to be unfit for self-government. Any such suppression of ideas about the common good, the First Amendment condemns with its absolute disapproval. The freedom of ideas shall not be abridged. * * *

If, however, as our argument has tried to show [T]he principle of the freedom of speech is derived, not from some supposed "Natural Right," but from the necessities of self-government by universal suffrage, there follows at once a very large limitation of the scope of the principle. The guarantee given by the First Amendment is not, then, assured to all speaking. It is assured only to speech which bears, directly or indirectly, upon issues with which voters have to deal— only, therefore, to the consideration of matters of public interest. Private speech, or private interest in speech, on the other hand, has no claim whatever to the protection of the First Amendment. If men are engaged, as we so commonly are, in argument, or inquiry, or advocacy, or incitement which is directed toward our private interests, private privileges, private possessions, we are, of course, entitled to "due process" protection of those activities. But the First Amendment has no concern over such protection. * * *

Here, then, are the charges which I would bring against the "clear and present danger" theory. They are all, it is clear, differing forms of the basic accusation that the compact of self-government has been ignored or repudiated.

First, the theory denies or obscures the fact that free citizens have two distinct sets of civil liberties. As the makers of the laws, they have duties and responsibilities which require an absolute freedom. As the subjects of the laws, they have possessions and rights, to which belongs a relative freedom.

Second, the theory fails to keep clear the distinction between the constitutional status of discussions of public policy and the corresponding status of discussions of private policy.

Third, the theory fails to recognize that, under the Constitution, the freedom of advocacy or incitement to action *by the government* may never be abridged. It is only advocacy or incitement to action by individuals or nonpolitical groups which is open to regulation.

Fourth, the theory regards the freedom of speech as a mere device which is to be abandoned when dangers threaten the public welfare. On the contrary, it is the very presence of those dangers which makes it imperative that, in the midst of our fears, we remember and observe a principle upon whose integrity rests the entire structure of government by consent of the governed.

Fifth, the Supreme Court, by adopting a theory which annuls the First Amendment, has struck a disastrous blow at our national education. It has denied the belief that men can, by processes of free public discussion, govern themselves. * * *

The unabridged freedom of public discussion is the rock on which our government stands. With that foundation beneath us, we shall not flinch in the face of any clear and present—or, even, terrific—danger.

ZECHARIAH CHAFEE, JR.—BOOK REVIEW

62 Harv.L.Rev. 891, 894–901 (1949).
Reprinted with permission of the publisher; copyright
© 1949, by the Harvard Law Review Association.

[M]y main objection to Mr. Meiklejohn's book [is that he] places virtually all his argument against current proposals for suppression on a constitutional position which is extremely dubious. Whereas the supporters of these measures are genuinely worried by the dangers of Communism, he refuses to argue that these dangers are actually small. Instead, his constitutional position obliges him to argue that these dangers are irrelevant. No matter how terrible and immediate the dangers may be, he keeps saying, the First Amendment will not let Congress or anybody else in the Government try to deal with Communists who have not yet committed unlawful [acts.]

Mr. Meiklejohn's basic proposition is that there are two distinct kinds of freedom of speech, protected by quite different clauses of the Constitution. Freedom of speech on matters affecting self-government is protected by the First Amendment and is not open to restrictions by the Government. [By] contrast, private discussion is open to restrictions because it is protected by [fifth amendment due process].

The truth is, I think, that the framers had no very clear idea as to what they meant by "the freedom of speech or of the press," but we can say three things with reasonable assurance. First, these politicians, lawyers, scholars, churchgoers and philosophers, scientists, agriculturalists, and wide readers used the phrase to embrace the whole realm of thought. Second, they intended the First Amendment to give all the protection they desired, and had no idea of supplementing it by the Fifth Amendment. Finally, the freedom which Congress was forbidden to abridge was not, for them, some absolute concept which had never existed on earth. It was the freedom which they believed they already had—what they had wanted before the Revolution and had acquired through independence. In thinking about it, they took for granted the limitations which had been customarily applied in the day-to-day work of colonial courts. Now, they were setting up a new federal government of great potential strength, and (as in the rest of Bill of Rights) they were determined to make sure that it would not take away the freedoms which they then enjoyed in their thirteen sovereign states.

Still, the First Amendment has the power of growing to meet new needs. As Marshall said, it is a *Constitution* which we are interpreting. Although in 1791 the Amendment did not mean what Mr. Meiklejohn says, perhaps it ought to mean that now. But the Supreme Court is unlikely to think so in any foreseeable future. The author condemns the clear and present danger test as "a peculiarly inept and unsuccessful attempt to formulate an exception" to the constitutional protection of public discussion, but he does not realize how unworkable his own views would prove when applied in litigation.

In the first place, although it may be possible to draw a fairly bright line between speech which is completely immune and action which may be punished, some speech on public questions is so hateful that the Court would be very reluctant to protect it from statutory penalties. We are not dealing with a philosopher who can write what he pleases, but with at least five men who are asked to block legislators and prosecutors. The history of the Court Plan in 1937 shows how sure judges have to be of their ground to do that. Take a few examples. A newspaper charges the mayor with taking bribes. Ezra Pound broadcasts from an Italian radio station that our participation in the war is an abominable mistake. A speaker during a very bad food shortage tells a hungry mass of voters that the rationing board is so incompetent and corrupt that the best way to avoid starvation is to demand the immediate death of its members, unless they are ready to resign. Plainly few judges can grant constitutional protection to such speeches.

Even the author begins to hedge. Although his main insistence is on immunity for all speech connected with self-government, as my examples surely are, occasionally he concedes that "repressive action by the government is imperative for the sake of the general welfare," e.g., against libelous assertions, slander, words inciting men to crime, sedition, and treason by words. Here he is diving into very deep water. Once you push punishment beyond action into the realm of language, then you have to say pretty plainly how far back the law should go. You must enable future judges and jurymen to know where to stop. That is just what Holmes did when he drew his line at clear and present danger and the author gives us no substitute test for distinguishing between good public speech and bad public speech. He never faces the problem of Mark Anthony's Oration—discussion which is calculated to produce unlawful acts without ever mentioning them.

At times he hints that the line depends on the falsity of the assertions or the bad motives of the speakers. In the mayor's case, it is no answer to say that false charges are outside the Constitution; the issue is whether a jury shall be permitted to find them false even if they are in fact true. Moreover, in such charges a good deal of truth which might be useful to the voters is frequently mixed with some falsehood, so that the possibility of a damage action often keeps genuine information away from voters. And the low character of speakers and writers does not necessarily prevent them from uttering wholesome truths about politics. Witness the Essays of Francis Bacon. Mr. Meiklejohn has a special dislike for paid "lobbyists for special interests." But if discussing public questions with money in sight is outside the First Amendment, how about speeches by aspirants to a $75,000 job in Washington or editorials in newspapers or books on Free Speech? Dr. Johnson declared that any man who writes except for money is a fool. In short, the trouble with the bad-motive test is that courts and juries would apply it only to the exponents of unpopular views. If what is said happens to be our way, the speaker is as welcome as an ex-revolutionist to the Un–American Committee.

The most serious weakness in Mr. Meiklejohn's argument is that it rests on his supposed boundary between public speech and private speech. That line is extremely blurred. Take the novel *Strange Fruit*, which was lately suppressed in Massachusetts. It did not discuss any question then before the voters, but it dealt thoughtfully with many problems of the relations between whites and Negroes, a matter of great national concern. Was this under the First Amendment or the Fifth? [The] truth is that there are public aspects to practically every subject. [The] author recognizes this when he says that the First Amendment is directed against "mutilation of the thinking process of the community." [This] attitude, however, offers such a wide area for the First Amendment that very little is left for his private speech under the Fifth Amendment. For example, if books and plays are public speech, how can they be penalized for gross obscenity or libels?

On the other hand, if private speech does include scholarship (as the author suggests) and also art and literature, it is shocking to deprive these vital matters of the protection of the inspiring words of the First Amendment. The individual interest in freedom of speech, which Socrates voiced when he said that he would rather die than stop talking, is too precious to be left altogether to the vague words of the due process clause. Valuable as self-government is, it is in itself only a small part of our lives. That a philosopher should subordinate all other activities to it is indeed surprising.

[Even] if Holmes had agreed with Mr. Meiklejohn's view of the First Amendment, his insistence on such absolutism would not have persuaded a single colleague, and scores of men would have gone to prison who have been speaking freely for three decades. After all, a judge who is trying to establish a doctrine which the Supreme Court will promulgate as law cannot write like a solitary philosopher. He has to convince at least four men in a specific group and convince them very soon. The true alternative to Holmes' view of the First Amendment was not at all the perfect immunity for public discussion which Mr. Meiklejohn desires. It was no immunity at all in the face of legislation. Any danger, any tendency in speech to produce bad acts, no matter how remote, would suffice to validate a repressive statute, and the only hope for speakers and writers would lie in being tried by liberal jurymen. * * * Holmes worked out a formula which would invalidate a great deal of suppression, and won for it the solid authority of a unanimous Court. Afterwards, again and again, when his test was misapplied by the majority, Holmes restated his position in ringing words which, with the help of Brandeis and Hughes, eventually inspired the whole Court.

Notes and Questions

1. To what extent does *New York Times* incorporate Meiklejohn's perspective?[b] What is the "central meaning" of the first amendment?

Consider Burt Neuborne, *Toward a Democracy–Centered Reading of the First Amendment,* 93 Nw.U.L.Rev. 1055, 1069 (1999): "It is no coincidence that the textual rhythm of the First Amendment moves from protection of internal

b. For elaboration and modification of Meiklejohn's views, see Alexander Meiklejohn, *The First Amendment Is an Absolute,* 1961 Sup.Ct.Rev. 245. For commentary, see Lee Bollinger, *Free Speech and Intellectual Values,* 92 Yale L.J. 438 (1983); Kalven, supra. For work proceeding from a politically based interpretation of the first amendment, see Akhil Reed Amar, *The Bill of Rights* 20–32 (1998); George Anastaplo, *The Constitutionalist* (1971); Cass Sunstein, *Democracy and the Problem of Free Speech* (1993); Lillian BeVier, *The First Amendment and Political Speech: An Inquiry Into the Substance and Limits of Principle,* 30 Stan.L.Rev. 299 (1978); Edward Bloustein, *The First Amendment and Privacy: The Supreme Court Justice and the Philosopher,* 28 Rutg. L.Rev. 41 (1974); Robert Bork, *Neutral Principles and Some First Amendment Problems,* 47 Ind.L.J. 1 (1971); Owen Fiss, *State Activism*

and State Censorship, 100 Yale L.J. 2087 (1991). Owen Fiss, *Why the State,* 100 Harv. L.Rev. 781 (1987); Owen Fiss, *Free Speech and Social Structure,* 71 Iowa L.Rev. 1405 (1986). See also William Brennan, *The Supreme Court and the Meiklejohn Interpretation of the First Amendment,* 79 Harv.L.Rev. 1 (1965); Daniel Farber, *Free Speech Without Romance,* 105 Harv.L.Rev. 554 (1991) (arriving at a politically centered perspective after applying economic analysis).

For criticism of Sunstein's position, see J.M. Balkin, *Populism and Progressivism as Constitutional Categories,* 104 Yale L.J. (1995); Robert Lipkin, *The Quest for the Common Good: Neutrality and Deliberative Democracy in Sunstein's Conception of American Constitutionalism,* 26 Conn.L.Rev. 1039 (1994); William Marshall, *Free Speech and the "Problem" of Democracy,* 89 Nw.U.L.Rev. 191 (1994).

conscience in the religion clauses, to protection of individual expression in the speech clause, to broad community-wide discussion in the press clause, to concerted action in the assembly (and implied association) clause, and, finally, to formal political activity in the petition clause. Indeed, no rights-bearing document in the Western tradition approximates the precise organizational clarity of the First Amendment as a road map of democracy."

If the first amendment is rooted in a conception of democracy, or even partially rooted in such a conception, does it matter which theory of democracy is entertained? For the suggestion that the particular theory of democracy has implications for a range of first amendment questions, see, C. Edwin Baker, *The Media That Citizens Need,* 147 U.Pa.L.Rev. 317 (1998).

2. *New York Times, definitional balancing, and the two-level theory of the first amendment.* By holding that some libel was within the protection of the first amendment, did the Court dismantle its two-level theory? See Kalven, supra, at 217–218. Or did the Court merely rearrange its conception of what was protected and what was not?

Does *Garrison v. Louisiana,* 379 U.S. 64, 85 S.Ct. 209, 13 L.Ed.2d 125 (1964) shed light on the question? The Court stated: "Calculated falsehood falls into that class of utterances '[of] such slight social value as a step to truth that any benefit that may be derived from them is clearly outweighed by the social interest in order and morality.' *Chaplinsky.*"

Could the judicial process here fairly be called *definitional* classification— defining which categories of libel are to be viewed as "speech" within the first amendment, and which are not? Consider Melville Nimmer, *The Right to Speak from Times to Time: First Amendment Theory Applied to Libel and Misapplied to Privacy,* 56 Calif.L.Rev. 935, 942–43 (1968): "[*New York Times*] points the way to the employment of the balancing process on the definitional rather than the litigation or ad hoc level, [that is,] balancing not for the purpose of determining which litigant deserves to prevail in the particular case, but only for the purpose of defining which forms of speech are to be regarded as 'speech' within the meaning of the first amendment. [By] in effect holding that knowingly and recklessly false speech was not 'speech' within the meaning of the first amendment, the Court must have implicitly (since no explicit explanation was offered) referred to certain competing policy considerations. This is surely a kind of balancing, but it is just as surely not ad hoc balancing."[c]

c. The literature about balancing is voluminous. Compare, e.g., Laurent Frantz, *The First Amendment in the Balance,* 71 Yale L.J. 1424 (1962); Laurent Frantz, *Is the First Amendment Law?—A Reply to Professor Mendelson,* 51 Calif.L.Rev. 729 (1963) with Wallace Mendelson, *On the Meaning of the First Amendment: Absolutes in the Balance,* 50 Calif.L.Rev. 821 (1962); Wallace Mendelson, *The First Amendment and the Judicial Process: A Reply to Mr. Frantz,* 17 Vand.L.Rev. 479 (1984). For recent criticism of balancing, see T. Alexander Aleinikoff, *Constitutional Law in the Age of Balancing,* 96 Yale L.J. 943 (1987); Robert Nagel, *Constitutional Cultures* (1989); Robert Nagel, *Rationalism in Constitutional Law,* 4 Const.Comm. 9 (1987); Robert Nagel, *The Formulaic Constitution,* 84 Mich.L.Rev. 165 (1985). For a philosophical attack on cost benefit analysis, see Laurence Tribe, *Policy Science:* *Analysis or Ideology?,* 2 Phil. & Pub.Aff. 66 (1972); Laurence Tribe, *Technology Assessment and the Fourth Discontinuity: The Limits of Instrumental Rationality,* 46 So.Cal.L.Rev. 617 (1973). For philosophical defenses of balancing, see Pierre Schlag, *An Attack on Categorical Approaches to Freedom of Speech,* 30 U.C.L.A.L.Rev. 671 (1983); Steven Shiffrin, *Liberalism, Radicalism, and Legal Scholarship,* 30 U.C.L.A.L.Rev. 1103 (1983) (both resisting any necessary connection between balancing and instrumentalism or cost-benefit analysis). For more doctrinally focused analysis, compare, e.g., Thomas Emerson, *First Amendment Doctrine and the Burger Court,* 68 Calif.L.Rev. 422 (1980); Laurence Tribe, *Constitutional Calculus: Equal Justice or Economic Efficiency?,* 98 Harv.L.Rev. 592 (1985) with Frederick Schauer, *Categories and the First*

3.   *The scope of New York Times.* Professor Kalven argued that given the Court's conception of freedom of speech, its holding could not be confined: "the invitation to follow a dialectic progression from public official to government policy to public policy to matters in the public domain, like art, seems * * * overwhelming." Kalven, supra, at 221.

(a) *Public officials. New York Times,* fn. 23 left open "how far down into the lower ranks of governmental employees" the rule would extend, and *Rosenblatt v. Baer,* 383 U.S. 75, 86 S.Ct. 669, 15 L.Ed.2d 597 (1966) suggested the rule might apply to the supervisor of a publicly owned ski resort, saying it applies to among other things to those who "appear to the public to [have] substantial responsibility for or control over the conduct of government affairs."[d] Should criticism of the official conduct of *very* high ranking government officials (e.g., the President, the Secretary of State, a general commanding troops in war) be given greater protection than that afforded in *New York Times?*

(b) *Private conduct of public officials and candidates. Garrison,* extended *New York Times* to "anything which might touch on an official's fitness for office," even if the defamation did not concern official conduct in office. Invoking that standard, *Monitor Patriot Co. v. Roy,* 401 U.S. 265, 91 S.Ct. 621, 28 L.Ed.2d 35 (1971) applied *New York Times* to a news column describing a candidate for public office as a "former small-time bootlegger."

(c) *Public figures.* In CURTIS PUB. CO. v. BUTTS and ASSOCIATED PRESS v. WALKER, 388 U.S. 130, 87 S.Ct. 1975, 18 L.Ed.2d 1094 (1967), HARLAN, J., contended that because public figures were not subject to the restraints of the political process, any criticism of them was not akin to seditious libel and was, therefore, a step removed from the central meaning of the first amendment. Nonetheless, he argued that public figure actions should not be left entirely to the vagaries of state defamation law and would have required that public figures show "highly unreasonable conduct constituting an extreme departure from the standards of investigation and reporting ordinarily adhered to by responsible publishers" as a prerequisite to recovery. In response, WARREN, C.J., argued that the inapplicability of the restraints of the political process to public figures underscored the importance for uninhibited debate about their activities since "public opinion may be the only instrument by which society can attempt to influence their conduct." He observed that increasingly "the distinctions between governmental and private sectors are blurred," that public figures, like public officials, "often play an influential role in ordering society," and as a class have a ready access to the mass media "both to influence policy and to counter criticism of their views and activities." He accordingly concluded that the *New York Times* rule should be extended to public figures. Four other justices in *Butts* and *Walker* were willing to go at least as far as Warren, C.J., and subsequent cases have settled on the position that public figures must meet the *New York Times* requirements in order to recover in a defamation action. The critical issues are how to define the concept of public figure and how to apply it in practice. See *Gertz,* infra.

Amendment: A Play in Three Acts, 34 Vand. L.Rev. 265 (1981); Steven Shiffrin, *The First Amendment and Economic Regulation: Away From a General Theory of the First Amendment,* 78 Nw.U.L.Rev. 1212 (1983); William Van Alstyne, *A Graphic Review of the Free Speech Clause,* 70 Calif.L.Rev. 107 (1982).

d. For criticism of *Rosenblatt,* see Note, *The Status/Conduct Continuum: Injecting Rhyme and Reason into Contemporary Public Official Doctrine,* 84 Va.L.Rev 871 (1998).

(d) *Private plaintiffs and public issues.* Without deciding whether any first amendment protection should extend to matters not of general or public interest, a plurality led by BRENNAN, J., joined by Burger, C.J., and Blackmun, J., argued in ROSENBLOOM v. METROMEDIA, INC., 403 U.S. 29, 91 S.Ct. 1811, 29 L.Ed.2d 296 (1971), that the *New York Times* rule should be extended to defamatory statements involving matters of public or general interest "without regard to whether the persons involved are famous or anonymous." Black, J., would have gone further, opining that the first amendment "does not permit the recovery of libel judgments against the news media even when statements are broadcast with knowledge they are false," and Douglas, J., shared Black, J.'s approach (at least with respect to matters of public interest, although he did not participate in *Rosenbloom.*) WHITE, J., felt that the *New York Times* rule should apply to reporting on the official actions of public servants and to reporting on those involved in or affected by their official action. That principle was broad enough to cover Rosenbloom, a distributor of nudist magazines who had been arrested by the Philadelphia police for distributing obscene materials. The defamatory broadcast wrongly assumed his guilt. Dissenting, Harlan, Stewart and Marshall, JJ., counseled an approach similar to that taken in *Gertz,* infra.

After *Rosenbloom* the lower courts rather uniformly followed the approach taken by the plurality. By 1974, however, the composition of the Court had changed and so had the minds of some of the justices.

C.   PRIVATE INDIVIDUALS AND PUBLIC FIGURES

GERTZ v. ROBERT WELCH, INC.

418 U.S. 323, 94 S.Ct. 2997, 41 L.Ed.2d 789 (1974).

JUSTICE POWELL delivered the opinion of the Court.

[Respondent published *American Opinion,* a monthly outlet for the John Birch Society. It published an article falsely stating that Gertz, a lawyer, was the "architect" in a "communist frameup" of a policeman convicted of murdering a youth whose family Gertz represented in resultant civil proceedings, and that Gertz had a "criminal record" and had been an officer in a named "Communist-fronter" organization that advocated violent seizure of our government. In Gertz' libel action there was evidence that *Opinion* 's managing editor did not know the statements were false and had relied on the reputation of the article's author and prior experience with the accuracy of his articles. After a $50,000 verdict for Gertz, the trial court entered judgment n.o.v., concluding that the *New York Times* rule applied to any discussion of a "public issue." The court of appeals affirmed, ruling that the publisher did not have the requisite "awareness of probable falsity." The Court held that *New York Times* did not apply to defamation of private individuals, but remanded for a new trial "because the jury was allowed to impose liability without fault [and] to presume damages without proof of injury."]

II.   The principal issue in this case is whether a newspaper or broadcaster that publishes defamatory falsehoods about an individual who is neither a public official nor a public figure may claim a constitutional privilege against liability for the injury inflicted by those statements. * * *

In his opinion for the plurality in *Rosenbloom,* Mr. Justice Brennan took the *Times* privilege one step further [than *Butts* and *Walker*]. He concluded that its protection should extend to defamatory falsehoods relating to private persons if the statements concerned matters of general or public interest. He abjured the suggested distinction between public officials and public figures on the one hand and private individuals on the other. He focused instead on society's interest in learning about certain issues: "If a matter is a subject of public or general interest, it cannot suddenly become less so merely because a private individual is involved or because in some sense the individual did not choose to become involved." Thus, under the plurality opinion, a private citizen involuntarily associated with a matter of general interest has no recourse for injury to his reputation unless he can satisfy the demanding requirements of the *Times* [test].

III. [Under] the First Amendment there is no such thing as a false idea. However pernicious an opinion may seem, we depend for its correction not on the conscience of the judges and juries but on the competition of other ideas.[a] But there is no constitutional value in false statements of fact. Neither the intentional lie nor the careless error materially advances society's interest in "uninhibited, robust, and wide-open" debate on public issues. * * *

Although the erroneous statement of fact is not worthy of constitutional protection, it is nevertheless inevitable in free debate. [P]unishment of error runs the risk of inducing a cautious and restrictive exercise of the constitutionally guaranteed freedoms of speech and press. [The] First Amendment requires that we protect some falsehood in order to protect speech that matters.

The need to avoid self-censorship by the news media is, however, not the only societal value at issue. [The] legitimate state interest underlying the law of libel is the compensation of individuals for the harm inflicted on them by defamatory falsehoods. We would not lightly require the State to abandon this purpose, for, as Mr. Justice Stewart has reminded us, the individual's right to the protection of his own good name "reflects no more than our basic concept of the essential dignity and worth of every human being—a concept at the root of any decent system of ordered liberty. * * * " *Rosenblatt*.[b]

Some tension necessarily exists between the need for a vigorous and uninhibited press and the legitimate interest in redressing wrongful injury. [In] our continuing effort to define the proper accommodation between these competing concerns, we have been especially anxious to assure to the freedoms of speech and press that "breathing space" essential to their fruitful exercise. To that end this Court has extended a measure of strategic protection to defamatory falsehood.

---

a. For many years the lower courts took this language seriously and deemed opinion to be absolutely protected (see, e.g., *Ollman v. Evans,* 750 F.2d 970 (D.C.Cir.1984)), but *Milkovich v. Lorain Journal Co.,* 497 U.S. 1, 110 S.Ct. 2695, 111 L.Ed.2d 1 (1990), per Rehnquist, C.J., ultimately denied that there is any "wholesale defamation exception for anything that might be labeled 'opinion.' " For the impact of *Milkovich,* see Kathryn Dix Sowle, *A Matter of Opinion,* 3 Wm. & Mary L.Rev. 467 (1994); Note, *Eight Years After Milkovich: Applying A Constitutional Privilege for Opinions Under the Wrong Constitution,* 31 Ind. L.Rev. 1107 (1998). On opinion, see Mark Franklin, *Constitutional Libel Law: The Role of Content,* 34 UCLA L.Rev. 1657 (1987); M. Jeffrey E. Thomas, *A Pragmatic Approach to meaning in Defamation Law,* 34 Wake Forest L.Rev. 333 (1999); Marshall Shapo, *Editorial: Fact/Opin-*

ion = Evidence/Argument, 91 Nw. U.L. Rev. 1108 (1997).

b. Stewart J., continued: "The protection of private personality, like the protection of life itself, is left primarily to the individual States under the Ninth and Tenth Amendments. But this does not mean that the right is entitled to any less recognition by this Court as a basic of our constitutional system." Consider Robert Post, *The Social Foundations of Defamation Law,* 74 Calif.L.Rev. 691, 708 (1986): "[I]t is not immediately clear how reputation, which is social and public, and which resides in the 'common or general estimate of person,' can possibly affect the 'essential dignity' of a person's 'private personality.' The gulf that appears to separate reputation from dignity can be spanned only if defamation law contains an implicit theory of the relationship between the private and public aspects of the self."

The *New York Times* standard defines the level of constitutional protection appropriate to the context of defamation of [public figures and those who hold governmental office]. Plainly many deserving plaintiffs, including some intentionally subjected to injury, will be unable to surmount the barrier of the *New York Times* test. [For] the reasons stated below, we conclude that the state interest in compensating injury to the reputation of private individuals requires that a different rule should obtain with respect to them.

[W]e have no difficulty in distinguishing among defamation plaintiffs. The first remedy of any victim of defamation is self-help—using available opportunities to contradict the lie or correct the error and thereby to minimize its adverse impact on reputation. Public officials and public figures usually enjoy significantly greater access to the channels of effective communication and hence have a more realistic opportunity to counteract false statements than private individuals normally enjoy.[9] Private individuals are therefore more vulnerable to injury, and the state interest in protecting them is correspondingly greater.[c]

More important than the likelihood that private individuals will lack effective opportunities for rebuttal, there is a compelling normative consideration underlying the distinction between public and private defamation plaintiffs. An individual who decides to seek governmental office must accept certain necessary consequences of that involvement in public affairs. He runs the risk of closer public scrutiny than might otherwise be the case. [Those] classed as public figures stand in a similar [position.][d]

Even if the foregoing generalities do not obtain in every instance, the communications media are entitled to act on the assumption that public officials and public figures have voluntarily exposed themselves to increased risk of injury from defamatory falsehoods concerning them. No such assumption is justified with respect to a private individual. He has not accepted public office nor assumed an "influential role in ordering society." *Butts*. He has relinquished no part of his interest in the protection of his own good name, and consequently he has a more compelling call on the courts for redress of injury inflicted by defamatory false-

9. Of course, an opportunity for rebuttal seldom suffices to undo harm of defamatory falsehood. Indeed, the law of defamation is rooted in our experience that the truth rarely catches up with a lie. But the fact that the self-help remedy of rebuttal, standing alone, is inadequate to its task does not mean that it is irrelevant to our inquiry. [Consider Steven Shiffrin, *Defamatory Non–Media Speech and First Amendment Methodology*, 25 U.C.L.A.L.Rev. 915, 952–53 (1978): "[F]ootnote nine, has seemingly left the first amendment in a peculiar spot. *Gertz* holds that the first amendment offers some protection for defamatory utterances presumably so that our Constitution can continue 'to preserve an uninhibited marketplace of ideas in which truth will ultimately prevail. * * * 'And yet the Court recognizes that 'an opportunity for rebuttal seldom suffices to undo [the] harm of defamatory falsehood,' i.e., truth does not emerge in the marketplace of ideas. Is the Court trapped in an obvious contradiction?"]

c. Suppose otherwise private persons have access to and have freely participated in electronic bulletin boards in which they have been defamed? In this context, should they be regarded as public figures? See Note, *The Gertz Doctrine and Internet Behavior*, 84 Va.L.Rev. 477 (1998); Note, *Defining Cyberlibel: A First Amendment Limit for Libel Suits Against Individuals Arising From Computer Bulletin Board Speech*, 46 Case W.Res.L.Rev. 235 (1995).

d. Consider Lee Bollinger, *Images of a Free Press* 25–26 (1994): "Essentially, the Court has said that, since these individuals have freely chosen a public life, what happens to them is their own doing, just as it is for a man who breaks his leg while hiking in the wilderness. Putting aside for the moment the fact that we also have an interest in encouraging people to enter public affairs, it simply is wrong to suppose that the pain inflicted by defamatory statements about public officials and figures is not our responsibility or concern. It should always be open to people to object to the way the world works under the rules we create, and not be dismissed by the claim that they have chosen to continue living in that world and, therefore, can be taken as having assented to it."

hood. Thus, private individuals are not only more vulnerable to injury than public officials and public figures; they are also more deserving of recovery.

For these reasons we conclude that the States should retain substantial latitude in their efforts to enforce a legal remedy for defamatory falsehood injurious to the reputation of a private individual. The extension of the *Times* test proposed by the *Rosenbloom* plurality would abridge this legitimate state interest to a degree that we find unacceptable. And it would occasion the additional difficulty of forcing state and federal judges to decide on an ad hoc basis which publications address issues of "general or public interest" and which do not—to determine, in the words of Mr. Justice Marshall, "what information is relevant to self-government." *Rosenbloom*. We doubt the wisdom of committing this task to the conscience of judges. [The] "public or general interest" test for determining the applicability of the *Times* standard to private defamation actions inadequately serves both of the competing values at stake. On the one hand, a private individual whose reputation is injured by defamatory falsehood that does concern an issue of public or general interest has no recourse unless he can meet the rigorous requirements of *Times*. This is true despite the factors that distinguish the state interest in compensating private individuals from the analogous interest involved in the context of public persons. On the other hand, a publisher or broadcaster of a defamatory error which a court deems unrelated to an issue of public or general interest may be held liable in damages even if it took every reasonable precaution to ensure the accuracy of its assertions. And liability may far exceed compensation for any actual injury to the plaintiff, for the jury may be permitted to presume damages without proof of loss and even to award punitive damages.

We hold that, so long as they do not impose liability without fault, the States may define for themselves the appropriate standard of liability for a publisher or broadcaster of defamatory falsehood injurious to a private individual. This approach provides a more equitable boundary between the competing concerns involved here. It recognizes the strength of the legitimate state interest in compensating private individuals for wrongful injury to reputation, yet shields the press and broadcast media from the rigors of strict liability for defamation. At least this conclusion obtains where, as here, the substance of the defamatory statement "makes substantial danger to reputation apparent." *Butts*. This phrase places in perspective the conclusion we announce today. Our inquiry would involve considerations somewhat different from those discussed above if a State purported to condition civil liability on a factual misstatement whose content did not warn a reasonably prudent editor or broadcaster of its defamatory potential. Cf. *Time, Inc. v. Hill* [Part D infra]. Such a case is not now before us, and we intimate no view as to its proper resolution.

IV. [T]he strong and legitimate state interest in compensating private individuals for injury to reputation [extends] no further than compensation for actual injury. For the reasons stated below, we hold that the States may not permit recovery of presumed or punitive damages, at least when liability is not based on a showing of knowledge of falsity or reckless disregard for the truth.

The common law of defamation is an oddity of tort [law]. Juries may award substantial sums as compensation for supposed damage to reputation without any proof that such harm actually occurred. [This] unnecessarily compounds the potential of any system of liability for defamatory falsehood to inhibit the vigorous exercise of First Amendment freedoms [and] invites juries to punish unpopular opinion rather than to compensate individuals for injury sustained by the publication of a false fact. More to the point, the States have no substantial interest in securing for plaintiffs such as this petitioner gratuitous awards of money damages far in excess of any actual injury.

We would not, of course, invalidate state law simply because we doubt its wisdom, but here we are attempting to reconcile state law with a competing interest grounded in the constitutional command of the First Amendment. It is therefore appropriate to require that state remedies for defamatory falsehood reach no farther than is necessary to protect the legitimate interest involved. It is necessary to restrict defamation plaintiffs who do not prove knowledge of falsity or reckless disregard for the truth to compensation for actual injury. We need not define "actual injury," as trial courts have wide experience in framing appropriate jury instructions in tort action. Suffice it to say that actual injury is not limited to out-of-pocket loss. Indeed, the more customary types of actual harm inflicted by defamatory falsehood include impairment of reputation and standing in the community, personal humiliation, and mental anguish and suffering. Of course, juries must be limited by appropriate instructions, and all awards must be supported by competent evidence concerning the injury, although there need be no evidence which assigns an actual dollar value to the injury.

We also find no justification for allowing awards of punitive damages against publishers and broadcasters held liable under state-defined standards of liability for defamation. In most jurisdictions jury discretion over the amounts awarded is limited only by the gentle rule that they not be excessive. Consequently, juries assess punitive damages in wholly unpredictable amounts bearing no necessary relation to the actual harm caused. And they remain free to use their discretion selectively to punish expressions of unpopular views. [J]ury discretion to award punitive damages unnecessarily exacerbates the danger of media self-censorship; [punitive] damages are wholly irrelevant to the state interest that justifies a negligence standard for private defamation actions. They are not compensation for injury. Instead, they are private fines levied by civil juries to punish reprehensible conduct and to deter its future occurrence. In short, the private defamation plaintiff who establishes liability under a less demanding standard than that stated by *Times* may recover only such damages as are sufficient to compensate him for actual injury.[e]

V. Notwithstanding our refusal to extend the *New York Times* privilege to defamation of private individuals, respondent contends that we should affirm the judgment below on the ground that petitioner is [a] public figure. [That] designation may rest on either of two alternative bases. In some instances an individual may achieve such pervasive fame or notoriety that he becomes a public figure for all purposes and in all contexts. More commonly, an individual voluntarily injects himself or is drawn into a particular public controversy and thereby becomes a public figure for a limited range of issues. In either case such persons assume special prominence in the resolution of public questions.

Petitioner has long been active in community and professional affairs. He has served as an officer of local civic groups and of various professional organizations, and he has published several books and articles on legal subjects. Although petitioner was consequently well known in some circles, he had achieved no general fame or notoriety in the community. None of the prospective jurors called at the trial had ever heard of petitioner prior to this litigation, and respondent

---

e. On remand, Gertz was awarded $100,000 in compensatory damages and $300,000 in punitive damages. In the prior trial, he had been awarded only $50,000 in damages.

offered no proof that this response was atypical of the local population. We would not lightly assume that a citizen's participation in community and professional affairs rendered him a public figure for all purposes. Absent clear evidence of general fame or notoriety in the community, and pervasive involvement in the affairs of society, an individual should not be deemed a public personality for all aspects of his life. It is preferable to reduce the public-figure question to a more meaningful context by looking to the nature and extent of an individual's participation in the particular controversy giving rise to the defamation.

In this context it is plain that petitioner was not a public figure. He played a minimal role at the coroner's inquest, and his participation related solely to his representation of a private client. He took no part in the criminal prosecution of Officer Nuccio. Moreover, he never discussed either the criminal or civil litigation with the press and was never quoted as having done so. He plainly did not thrust himself into the vortex of this public issue, nor did he engage the public's attention in an attempt to influence its outcome. We are persuaded that the trial court did not err in refusing to characterize petitioner as a public figure for the purpose of this litigation.

We therefore conclude that the *New York Times* standard is inapplicable to this case and that the trial court erred in entering judgment for respondent. Because the jury was allowed to impose liability without fault and was permitted to presume damages without proof of injury, a new trial is necessary.[f]

JUSTICE BRENNAN, dissenting.

[While the Court's] arguments are forcefully and eloquently presented, I cannot accept them for the reasons I stated in *Rosenbloom:* "The *New York Times* standard was applied to libel of a public official or public figure to give effect to the Amendment's function to encourage ventilation of public issues, not because the public official has any less interest in protecting his reputation than an individual in private life. [In] the vast majority of libels involving public officials or public figures, the ability to respond through the media will depend on the same complex factor on which the ability of a private individual depends: the unpredictable event of the media's continuing interest in the story. Thus the unproved, and highly improbable, generalization that an as yet [not fully defined] class of 'public figures' involved in matters of public concern will be better able to respond through the media than private individuals also involved in such matters seems too insubstantial a reed on which to rest a constitutional distinction."

[Adoption], by many States, of a reasonable care standard in cases where private individuals are involved in matters of public interest—the probable result of today's decision—[will] lead to self-censorship since publishers will be required carefully to weigh a myriad of uncertain factors before publication. The reasonable care standard is "elusive," *Time, Inc. v. Hill;* it saddles the press with "the

f. Blackmun, J., concurred: "[Although I joined Brennan, J.'s plurality opinion in *Rosenbloom,* from which the Court's opinion in the present case departs, I join] the Court's opinion and its judgment for two reasons:

"1. By removing the spectres of presumed and punitive damages in the absence of *Times* malice, the Court eliminates significant and powerful motives for self-censorship that otherwise are present in the traditional libel action. By so doing, the Court leaves what should prove to be sufficient and adequate breathing space for a vigorous press. What the Court has

done, I believe, will have little, if any, practical effect on the functioning of responsible journalism.

"2. The Court was sadly fractionated in *Rosenbloom.* A result of that kind inevitably leads to uncertainty. I feel that it is of profound importance for the Court to come to rest in the defamation area and to have a clearly defined majority position that eliminates the unsureness engendered by *Rosenbloom's* diversity. If my vote were not needed to create a majority, I would adhere to my prior view. A definitive ruling, however, is paramount."

intolerable burden of guessing how a jury might assess the reasonableness of steps taken by it to verify the accuracy of every reference to a name, picture or portrait." Ibid. Under a reasonable care regime, publishers and broadcasters will have to make pre-publication judgments about juror assessment of such diverse considerations as the size, operating procedures, and financial condition of the news gathering system, as well as the relative costs and benefits of instituting less frequent and more costly reporting at a higher level of accuracy. [And] most hazardous, the flexibility which inheres in the reasonable care standard will create the danger that a jury will convert it into "an instrument for the suppression of those 'vehement, caustic, and sometimes unpleasantly sharp attacks,' [which] must be protected if the guarantees of the First and Fourteenth Amendments are to prevail." *Monitor Patriot Co.*

[A] jury's latitude to impose liability for want of due care poses a far greater threat of suppressing unpopular views than does a possible recovery of presumed or punitive damages. Moreover, the Court's broad-ranging examples of "actual injury" [allow] a jury bent on punishing expression of unpopular views a formidable weapon for doing so. [E]ven a limitation of recovery to "actual injury"— however much it reduces the size or frequency of recoveries—will not provide the necessary elbow room for First Amendment expression. "[The] very possibility of having to engage in litigation, an expensive and protracted process, is threat enough to cause discussion and debate to 'steer far wider of the unlawful zone' thereby keeping protected discussion from public cognizance. * * * "*Rosenbloom.*

[I] reject the argument that my *Rosenbloom* view improperly commits to judges the task of determining what is and what is not an issue of "general or public interest."[3] I noted in *Rosenbloom* that performance of this task would not always be easy. But surely the courts, the ultimate arbiters of all disputes concerning clashes of constitutional values, would only be performing one of their traditional functions in undertaking this duty. [The] public interest is necessarily broad; any residual self-censorship that may result from the uncertain contours of the "general or public interest" concept should be of far less concern to publishers and broadcasters than that occasioned by state laws imposing liability for negligent falsehood. * * * *g*

---

3. The Court, taking a novel step, would not limit application of First Amendment protection to private libels involving issues of general or public interest, but would forbid the States from imposing liability without fault in any case where the substance of the defamatory statement made substantial danger to reputation apparent. As in *Rosenbloom,* I would leave open the question of what constitutional standard, if any, applies when defamatory falsehoods are published or broadcast concerning either a private or public person's activities not within the scope of the general or public interest.

Parenthetically, my Brother White argues that the Court's view and mine will prevent a plaintiff—unable to demonstrate some degree of fault—from vindicating his reputation by securing a judgment that the publication was false. This argument overlooks the possible enactment of statutes, not requiring proof of fault, which provide for an action for retraction or for publication of a court's determination of falsity if the plaintiff is able to demonstrate

that false statements have been published concerning his activities. Although it may be that questions could be raised concerning the constitutionality of such statutes, certainly nothing I have said today (and, as I read the Court's opinion, nothing said there) should be read to imply that a private plaintiff, unable to prove fault, must inevitably be denied the opportunity to secure a judgment upon the truth or falsity of statements published about him.

g. Douglas, J., dissented, objecting to "continued recognition of the possibility of state libel suits for public discussion of public issues" as diluting first amendment protection. He added: "Since this case involves a discussion of public affairs, I need not decide at this point whether the First Amendment prohibits all libel actions. 'An unconditional right to say what one pleases about public affairs is what I consider to be *the minimum guarantee* of the First Amendment.' *New York Times* (Black, J., concurring) (emphasis added). But 'public affairs' includes a great deal more than merely political affairs. Matters of science, economics,

JUSTICE WHITE, dissenting.

[T]he Court, in a few printed pages, has federalized major aspects of libel law by declaring unconstitutional in important respects the prevailing defamation law in all or most of the 50 States. * * *

I. [These] radical changes in the law and severe invasions of the prerogatives of the States [should] at least be shown to be required by the First Amendment or necessitated by our present circumstances. Neither has been [demonstrated.]

The central meaning of *New York Times,* and for me the First Amendment as it relates to libel laws, is that seditious libel—criticism of government and public officials—falls beyond the police power of the State. In a democratic society such as ours, the citizen has the privilege of criticizing his government and its officials. But neither *New York Times* nor its progeny suggest that the First Amendment intended in all circumstances to deprive the private citizen of his historic recourse to redress published falsehoods damaging to reputation or that, contrary to history and precedent, the amendment should now be so interpreted. Simply put, the First Amendment did not confer a "license to defame the citizen." Douglas, *The Right of the People* 38 (1958).

[T]he law has heretofore put the risk of falsehood on the publisher where the victim is a private citizen and no grounds of special privilege are invoked. The Court would now shift this risk to the victim, even though he has done nothing to invite the calumny, is wholly innocent of fault, and is helpless to avoid his injury. I doubt that jurisprudential resistance to liability without fault is sufficient ground for employing the First Amendment to revolutionize the law of libel, and in my view, that body of legal rules poses no realistic threat to the press and its service to the public. The press today is vigorous and robust. To me, it is quite incredible to suggest that threats of libel suits from private citizens are causing the press to refrain from publishing the truth. I know of no hard facts to support that proposition, and the Court furnishes none.

[I]f the Court's principal concern is to protect the communications industry from large libel judgments, it would appear that its new requirements with respect to general and punitive damages would be ample protection. Why it also feels compelled to escalate the threshold standard of liability I cannot fathom, particularly when this will eliminate in many instances the plaintiff's possibility of securing a judicial determination that the damaging publication was indeed false, whether or not he is entitled to recover money damages. [I] find it unacceptable to distribute the risk in this manner and force the wholly innocent victim to bear the injury; for, as between the two, the defamer is the only culpable party. It is he who circulated a falsehood that he was not required to publish. * * *h

V. [I] fail to see how the quality or quantity of public debate will be promoted by further emasculation of state libel laws for the benefit of the news media.[41] If anything, this trend may provoke a new and radical imbalance in the

business, art, literature, etc., are all matters of interest to the general public. Indeed, any matter of sufficient general interest to prompt media coverage may be said to be a public affair. Certainly police killings, 'Communist conspiracies,' and the like qualify."

h. White, J., also argued strongly against the Court's rulings on actual and punitive damages.

41. Cf. Willard Pedrick, *Freedom of the Press and the Law of Libel: The Modern Revised Translation,* 49 Cornell L.Q. 581, 601–02 (1964): "A great many forces in our society operate to determine the extent to which men are free in fact to express their ideas. Whether there is a privilege for good faith defamatory misstatements on matters of public concern or whether there is strict liability for such statements may not greatly affect the course of public discussion. How different has life been

communications process. Cf. Jerome Barron, *Access to the Press—A New First Amendment Right,* 80 Harv.L.Rev. 1641, 1657 (1967). It is not at all inconceivable that virtually unrestrained defamatory remarks about private citizens will discourage them from speaking out and concerning themselves with social problems. This would turn the First Amendment on its head. * * *[i]

Notes and Questions

1. *Gertz and Meiklejohn.* By affording some constitutional protection to all media defamatory speech whether or not it relates to public issues, does the Court squarely reject the Meiklejohn theory of the first amendment? Consider Steven Shiffrin, *Defamatory Non–Media Speech and First Amendment Methodology,* 25 U.C.L.A.L.Rev. 915, 929 (1978): "It may be that the Court has refused to adopt the Meiklejohn 'public issues' test not because it believes that private speech (i.e., speech unrelated to public issues) is as important as public speech but rather because it doubts its ability to distinguish unerringly between the two. [B]y placing all defamatory media speech within the scope of the first amendment, the Court may believe it has protected relatively little non-public speech. On the other hand, [putting aside comments about public officials and public figures], the Court may fear that if *Gertz* were extended to non-media speech, the result would be to protect much speech having nothing to do with public issues, while safeguarding relatively little that does."[j] For consideration of the distinction between public and private speech and of the media non-media distinction, see *Greenmoss,* p. 832 infra. See also *Philadelphia Newspapers, Inc. v. Hepps,* 475 U.S. 767, 106 S.Ct. 1558, 89 L.Ed.2d 783 (1986) (private figure plaintiff has burden of showing falsity at least when issue is of "public concern" and leaving open the question of what standards apply to non-media defendants).[k]

2. *Public figures.* TIME, INC. v. FIRESTONE, 424 U.S. 448, 96 S.Ct. 958, 47 L.Ed.2d 154 (1976), per Rehnquist, J., declared that persons who have not assumed a role of especial prominence in the affairs of society are not public figures unless they have " 'thrust themselves to the forefront of particular public controversies in order to influence the resolution of the issues involved.' " It held that a divorce

in those states which heretofore followed the majority rule imposing strict liability for misstatements of fact defaming public figures from life in the minority states where the good faith privilege held sway?"

i. Burger, C.J., also dissented: "I am frank to say I do not know the parameters of a 'negligence' doctrine as applied to the news media. [I] would prefer to allow this area of law to continue to evolve as it has up to now with respect to private citizens rather then embark on a new doctrinal theory which has no jurisprudential ancestry. [I would remand] for reinstatement of the verdict of the jury and the entry of an appropriate judgment on that verdict."

j. For the claim that speech on private matters deserves as much protection as speech on public matters, see id. at 938–42. For discussion of the different meanings of public and private speech, see Frederick Schauer, *"Private" Speech and the "Private" Forum: Givhan v. Western Line School District,* 1979 Sup.Ct. Rev. 217. For additional commentary on the question of whether *Gertz* should extend to

non-media defendants see, e.g., Albert Hill, *Defamation and Privacy Under the First Amendment,* 76 Colum.L.Rev. 1205 (1976); David Lange, *The Speech and Press Clauses,* 23 U.C.L.A.L.Rev. 77 (1975); Melville Nimmer, *Is Freedom of the Press a Redundancy: What Does It Add to Freedom of Speech?,* 26 Hast. L.J. 639 (1975); William Van Alstyne, Comment: *The Hazards to the Press of Claiming a "Preferred Position,"* 28 Hast.L.J. 761 (1977); Note, *Mediaocracy and Mistrust: Extending New York Times Defamation Protection to Non-media Defendants,* 95 Harv.L.Rev. 1876 (1982).

k. The Communications Decency Act immunizes those who manage electronic bulletin boards and the like from defamation liability for information provided by another. So the *Los Angeles Times* could be liable for defamation published on the letters page of its newspaper, but could not be liable for the same letter if it were published on its web site. Constitutional? See *Zeran v. America Online, Inc.,* 129 F.3d 327 (4th Cir. 1997).

proceeding involving one of America's wealthiest industrial families and containing testimony concerning the extramarital sexual activities of the parties did not involve a "public controversy," "even though the marital difficulties of extremely wealthy individuals may be of interest to some portion of the reading public." Nor was the filing of a divorce suit, or the holding of press conferences ("to satisfy inquiring reporters") thought to be freely publicizing the issues in order to influence their outcome. Recall *Gertz* doubted the wisdom of forcing judges to determine on an ad hoc basis what is and is not of "general or public interest." Is there a basis for distinguishing a public figure test requiring judges to determine on an ad hoc basis what is or is not a "public controversy"?

What does it mean to assume a role of especial prominence in the affairs of society? If Elmer Gertz, a prominent Illinois attorney, does not qualify, does Johnny Carson? Julia Child? Mr. Rogers? If so, is the slide from public officials to television chefs and personalities too precipitous because the latter "have little, if any effect, on questions of politics, public policy, or the organization and determination of societal affairs"? See Frederick Schauer, *Public Figures,* 25 Wm. & Mary L.Rev. 905 (1984): Consider Marie A. Failinger, *Five Modern Notions in Search of an Author: The Ideology of the Intimate Society in Constitutional Speech Law,* 30 U.Tol. L.Rev. 251, 299 (1999): "[T]he Court merely adds fuel to the cultural fire created by [the] 'star' system—people who want to know intimate details that confirm their trust in those selected by the public to be 'stars,' and yet, they have a secret desire to know 'dirt' on those same persons to justify their beliefs that people just like themselves have been randomly enriched with fame, power, and wealth. [T]his politics of resentment, parlay[s] the shame and envy of those who find themselves in a lower-than-deserved status into a rising backlash against those who have unfairly taken 'their' place. Thus, protection of the cult of personality in the Court's speech doctrine only serves to fuel the fires of self-interested, mean-spirited public life." Does a narrow definition of public figures discriminate in favor of orthodox media and discourage attempts "to illuminate previously unexposed aspects of society." Does the negligence concept itself threaten to discriminate "against media or outlets whose philosophies and methods deviate from those of the mainstream"? See generally David Anderson, *Libel and Press Self–Censorship,* 53 Tex.L.Rev. 422, 453, 455 (1975).

3. *Taking reputation too seriously?* Consider Rodney Smolla, *Suing the Press* 257 (1986): "[I]f we take the libel suit too seriously, we are in danger of raising our collective cultural sensitivity to reputation to unhealthy levels. We are in danger of surrendering a wonderful part of our national identity—our strapping, scrambling, free-wheeling individualism, in danger of becoming less American, less robust, wild-eyed, pluralistic and free, and more decorous, image-conscious, and narcissistic. The media is itself partly to blame for this direction, and it would be dangerous to release it totally from the important check and balance that the libel laws provide. But in the United States, the balance that must be struck between reputation and expression should never be tilted too far against expression, for the right to defiantly, robustly, and irreverently speak one's mind just because it is one's mind is quintessentially what it means to be an American."[1]

1. For historical perspective on the social messages communicated by defamation law, see Norman Rosenberg, *Protecting the Best Men* (1986). For valuable material on how the *Gertz* rules work in practice, see Randall P. Bezanson, *The Developing Law of Editorial Judgment,* 78 Neb.L.Rev. 754 (1999); Randall Bezanson, Gilbert Cranberg & John Soloski, *Libel Law and the Press: Myth and Reality* (1987); Henry Kaufman, *Libel 1980–85: Promises and Realities,* 90 Dick.L.Rev. 545 (1985); Marc Franklin, *Suing Media for Libel: A Litigation Study,* 1981 Am.B.Found.Res.J. 795; Marc Franklin, *Winners and Losers and Why:*

D. FALSE LIGHT PRIVACY

TIME, INC. v. HILL, 385 U.S. 374, 87 S.Ct. 534, 17 L.Ed.2d 456 (1967), applied the *New York Times* knowing and reckless falsity standard to a right of privacy action for publishing an erroneous but not defamatory report about private individuals involved in an incident of public interest. In 1952 the Hill family was the subject of national news coverage when held hostage in its home for 19 hours by three escaped convicts who treated the family courteously with no violence. This incident formed part of the basis for a novel, later made into a play, which involved violence against the hostage family. In 1955 *Life* published a picture story that showed the play's cast reenacting scenes from the play in the former Hill home. According to *Life*, the play "inspired by the [Hill] family's experience" "is a heartstopping account of how a family arose to heroism in a crisis." Hill secured a $30,000 judgment for compensatory damages against the publisher under the New York Right to Privacy Statute, which, as interpreted, made truth a complete defense to actions based on "newsworthy people or events" but gave a right of action to one whose name or picture was the subject of an article containing "material and substantial falsification." The court, per BRENNAN, J., reversed, holding that "the constitutional protections for speech and press preclude the application of the New York statute to redress false reports of matters of public interest in the absence of proof that the defendant published the report with knowledge of its falsity or in reckless disregard of the truth," and that the instructions did not adequately advise the jury that a verdict for Hill required a finding of knowing or reckless falsity:

"The guarantees for speech and press are not the preserve of political expression or comment upon public affairs, essential as those are to healthy government. One need only pick up any newspaper or magazine to comprehend the vast range of published matter which exposes persons to public view, both private citizens and public officials. Exposure of the self to others in varying degrees is a concomitant of life in a civilized community. The risk of this exposure is an essential incident of life in a society which places a primary value on freedom of speech and press. [We] have no doubt that the subject of the *Life* article, the opening of a new play linked to an actual incident, is a matter of public interest. 'The line between the informing and the entertaining is too elusive for the protection of [freedom of the press.]' Erroneous statement is no less inevitable in

A Study of Defamation Litigation, 1980 Am. B.Found.Res.J. 455. For commentary suggesting reforms, see Annenberg Washington Program, *Libel Law* (1988). See also Robert Ackerman, *Bringing Coherence to Defamation Law Through Uniform Legislation: The Search for an Elegant Solution*, 72 N.C.L.Rev. 291 (1994); David Anderson, *Is Libel Law Worth Reforming?*, 140 U.Pa.L.Rev. 487 (1991); Randall Bezanson, *The Libel Tort Today*, 45 Wash. & Lee L.Rev. 535 (1988); C. Thomas Dienes, *Libel Reform: An Appraisal*, 23 U.Mich.J.L.Ref. (1989); Richard Epstein, *Was New York Times v. Sullivan Wrong?*, 53 U.Chi.L.Rev. 782 (1986); Bruce Fein, *New York Times v. Sullivan: An Obstacle to Enlightened Public Discourse and Government Responsiveness to the People* (1984); Marc Franklin, *Public Officials and Libel: In Defense of New York Times Co. v. Sullivan*, 5 Cardozo Arts & Ent.L.J. 51 (1986);

Marc Franklin, *Constitutional Libel Law: The Role of Content*, 34 UCLA L.Rev. 1657 (1987); Marc Franklin, *A Declaratory Judgment Alternative to Current Libel Law*, 74 Calif.L.Rev. 809 (1986); Stanley Ingber, *Defamation: A Conflict Between Reason and Decency*, 65 Va. L.Rev. 785 (1979); Pierre Leval, *The No–Money, No–Fault Libel Suit: Keeping Sullivan in Its Proper Place*, 101 Harv.L.Rev. 1287 (1988); Lee Levine, *Book Review*, 56 G.W.U.L.Rev. 246 (1987); Anthony Lewis, *New York Times v. Sullivan Reconsidered: Time to Return to "The Central Meaning of the First Amendment,"* 83 Colum.L.Rev. 603 (1983); John Martin, *The Role of Retraction in Defamation Suits*, 1993 U.Chi. Legal F. 293; Frederick Schauer, *Uncoupling Free Speech*, 92 Colum.L.Rev. 1321 (1992); Rodney Smolla, *Let the Author Beware: The Rejuvenation of the American Law of Libel*, 132 U.Pa.L.Rev. 1 (1983).

such case than in the case of comment upon public affairs, and in both, if innocent or merely negligent, '[it] must be protected if the freedoms of expression are to have the "breathing space" that they "need [to] survive' ". [*New York Times*] We create a grave risk of serious impairment of the indispensable service of a free press in a free society if we saddle the press with the impossible burden of verifying to a certainty the facts associated in news articles with a person's name, picture or portrait, particularly as related to non-defamatory matter. Even negligence would be a most elusive standard, especially when the content of the speech itself affords no warning of prospective harm to another through falsity. A negligence test would place on the press the intolerable burden of guessing how a jury might assess the reasonableness of steps taken by it to verify the accuracy of every reference to a name, picture or [portrait].

"We find applicable here the standard of knowing or reckless falsehood not through blind application of *New York Times,* relating solely to libel actions by public officials, but only upon consideration of the factors which arise in the particular context of the application of the New York statute in cases involving private individuals."

BLACK, J., joined by Douglas, J., concurred in reversal on the grounds stated in the Brennan opinion "in order for the Court to be able at this time to agree on an opinion in this important case based on the prevailing constitutional doctrine expressed in *New York Times,*" but reaffirmed their belief that the "malicious," "reckless disregard of the truth" and "knowing and reckless falsity" exceptions were impermissible "abridgments" of freedom of expression. Douglas, J., also filed a separate concurrence, deeming it "irrelevant to talk of any right of privacy in this context. Here a private person is catapulted into the news by events over which he had no control. He and his activities are then in the public domain as fully as the matters at issue in *New York Times.* Such privacy as a person normally has ceases when his life has ceased to be private."

HARLAN, J., concurring in part and dissenting in part, would have made the test of liability negligence, rather than the *New York Times* "reckless falsity": "It would be unreasonable to assume that Mr. Hill could find a forum for making a successful refutation of the *Life* material or that the public's interest in it would be sufficient for the truth to win out by comparison as it might in that area of discussion central to a free society. Thus the state interest in encouraging careful checking and preparation of published material is far stronger than in *Times.* The dangers of unchallengeable untruth are far too well documented to be summarily dismissed.

"Second, there is a vast difference in the state interest in protecting individuals like Mr. Hill from irresponsibly prepared publicity and the state interest in similar protection for a public official. In *Times* we acknowledged public officials to be a breed from whom hardiness to exposure to charges, innuendos, and criticisms might be demanded and who voluntarily assumed the risk of such things by entry into the public arena. But Mr. Hill came to public attention through an unfortunate circumstance not of his making rather than his voluntary actions and he can in no sense be considered to have 'waived' any protection the State might justifiably afford him from irresponsible publicity. Not being inured to the vicissitudes of journalistic scrutiny such an individual is more easily injured and his means of self-defense are more limited. The public is less likely to view with normal skepticism what is written about him because it is not accustomed to seeing his name in the press and expects only a disinterested report.

"The coincidence of these factors in this situation leads me to the view that a State should be free to hold the press to a duty of making a reasonable investigation of the underlying facts and limiting itself to 'fair comment' on the materials so gathered. Theoretically, of course, such a rule might slightly limit press discussion of matters touching individuals like Mr. Hill. But, from a pragmatic standpoint, until now the press, at least in New York, labored under the more exacting handicap of the existing New York privacy law and has certainly remained robust. Other professional activity of great social value is carried on under a duty of reasonable care and there is no reason to suspect the press would be less hardy than medical practitioners or attorneys."[a]

Notes and Questions

1. Compare ZACCHINI v. SCRIPPS–HOWARD BROADCASTING CO., 433 U.S. 562, 97 S.Ct. 2849, 53 L.Ed.2d 965 (1977): Zacchini performed as a "human cannonball," being shot from a cannon into a net some 200 feet away. Without Zacchini's permission to film or broadcast his act, Scripps–Howard obtained and broadcast the tape of his "shot" on the news. The Ohio Supreme Court held the telecast was protected under *Time, Inc. v. Hill* as a newsworthy event. The Court, per WHITE, J., reversed. *Hill* was distinguishable because Zacchini's claim was based not on privacy or reputation but "in protecting the proprietary interest," an interest "closely analogous to the goals of patent and copyright law." Unlike *Hill,* the issue was not whether Zacchini's act would be available to the public: "[T]he only question is who gets to do the publishing."[b]

2. Does *Hill* survive *Gertz?* Consider the following statement: "In *Hill* and *Gertz* the same class of plaintiffs have to meet different constitutional standards in order to recover. Only the name of the tort has changed. This makes no sense." Is the state interest significantly different in *Gertz* than in *Hill?* Should it matter whether the statement at issue would appear innocuous to a reasonable editor? Offensive? See Diane Zimmerman, *False Light Invasion of Privacy: The Light that Failed,* 64 N.Y.U.L.Rev. 364 (1989).

3. *False news.* Should injury to any particular person be a prerequisite to state regulation of false publications? Consider *Keeton v. Hustler Magazine, Inc.,* 465 U.S. 770, 104 S.Ct. 1473, 79 L.Ed.2d 790 (1984): "False statements of fact harm both the subject of the falsehood *and* the readers of the statement. New Hampshire may rightly employ its libel laws to discourage the deception of its citizens." Could New Hampshire make it a criminal offense to publish false statements with knowledge of their falsity without any requirement of injury to any particular person? See Zimmerman, supra.

E. EMOTIONAL DISTRESS

HUSTLER MAGAZINE v. FALWELL, 485 U.S. 46, 108 S.Ct. 876, 99 L.Ed.2d 41 (1988), per REHNQUIST, C.J., held that public figures and public officials offended

---

a. Fortas, J., joined by Warren, C.J., and Clark, J., dissented, because "the jury instructions, although [not] a textbook model, satisfied [the *New York Times*] standard." For cogent commentary concerning false light privacy, see Gary Schwartz, *Explaining and Justifying a Limited Tort of False Light Invasion of Privacy,* 41 Case West.L.Rev. 886 (1991).

b. Powell, J., joined by Brennan and Marshall, JJ., dissented, observing that there was no showing that the broadcast was a "subterfuge or cover for private or commercial exploitation." Stevens, J., dissented on procedural grounds.

by a mass media parody could not recover for the tort of intentional infliction of emotional distress without a showing of *New York Times* malice. Parodying a series of liquor advertisements in which celebrities speak about their "first time," the editors of *Hustler* chose plaintiff Jerry Falwell (a nationally famous minister, host of a nationally syndicated television show, and founder of the Moral Majority political organization) "as the featured celebrity and drafted an alleged 'interview' with him in which he states that his 'first time' was during a drunken incestuous rendezvous with his mother in an outhouse. The *Hustler* parody portrays [Falwell] and his mother[a] 'as drunk and immoral,' and suggests that [Falwell] is a hypocrite who preaches only when he is drunk. In small print at the bottom of the page, the ad contains the disclaimer, 'ad parody—not to be taken seriously.' The magazine's table of contents also lists the ad as 'Fiction; Ad and Personality Parody.' * * *

"We must decide whether a public figure may recover damages for emotional harm caused by the publication of an ad parody offensive to him, and doubtless gross and repugnant in the eyes of most.[3] [Falwell] would have us find that a State's interest in protecting public figures from emotional distress is sufficient to deny First Amendment protection to speech that is patently offensive and is intended to inflict emotional injury, even when that speech could not reasonably have been interpreted as stating actual facts about the public figure involved. * * *

"Generally speaking the law does not regard the intent to inflict emotional distress as one which should receive much solicitude, and it is quite understandable that most if not all jurisdictions have chosen to make it civilly culpable where the conduct in question is sufficiently 'outrageous.' But in the world of debate about public affairs, many things done with motives that are less than admirable are protected by the First Amendment. '[Debate] on public issues will not be uninhibited if the speaker must run the risk that it will be proved in court that he spoke out of hatred; even if he did speak out of hatred, utterances honestly believed contribute to the free interchange of ideas and the ascertainment of truth.' *Garrison.* Thus while such a bad motive may be deemed controlling for purposes of tort liability in other areas of the law, we think the First Amendment prohibits such a result in the area of public debate about public figures.

"Were we to hold otherwise, there can be little doubt that political cartoonists and satirists would be subjected to damage awards without any showing that their work falsely defamed its subject. * * *

"There is no doubt that the caricature of [Falwell] and his mother published in Hustler is at best a distant cousin of [traditional] political cartoons * * * and a rather poor relation at that. If it were possible by laying down a principled standard to separate the one from the other, public discourse would probably suffer little or no harm. But we doubt that there is any such standard, and we are quite sure that the pejorative description 'outrageous' does not supply one. 'Outrageousness' in the area of political and social discourse has an inherent subjectiveness about it which would allow a jury to impose liability on the basis of the jurors' tastes or views, or perhaps on the basis of their dislike of a particular expression.

a. Falwell's mother was not a plaintiff. What result if she were?

3. Under Virginia law, in an action for intentional infliction of emotional distress a plaintiff must show that the defendant's conduct (1) is intentional or reckless; (2) offends generally accepted standards of decency or morality; (3) is causally connected with the plaintiff's emotional distress; and (4) caused emotional distress that was severe.

"We conclude that public figures and public officials may not recover for the tort of intentional infliction of emotional distress by reason of publications such as the one here at issue without showing in addition that the publication contains a false statement of fact which was made with 'actual malice,' i.e., with knowledge that the statement was false or with reckless disregard as to whether or not it was true."[b]

Notes and Questions

1. Does the rationale sweep beyond the holding? If debate on public issues should be uninhibited and if speakers filled with hatred have a place in that debate, why is the holding confined to suits brought by public officials and public figures? Is the holding likely to follow a "dialectic progression" from public official and public figure to all matters in the public domain? Should it? Is that far enough? Should the holding encompass all media speech? All non-media speech? Consider Rodney Smolla, *Emotional Distress and the First Amendment,* 20 Ariz.St. L.J. 423, 427 (1988): "The intellectual challenge posed by Falwell's suit is not how to construct a convincing rationale for rejecting his claim, but rather how to articulate limits on that rationale that will permit suits for emotional distress inflicted through speech in other contexts to survive." See generally Rodney Smolla, *Jerry Falwell v. Larry Flynt: The First Amendment on Trial* (1988). To what extent should the tort of intentional infliction of emotional distress raise constitutional problems? Compare Franklyn Haiman, *Speech and Law in a Free Society* 148–56 (1981) with Donald Downs, *Skokie Revisited: Hate Group Speech and the First Amendment,* 60 Not.D.Law. 629, 673–85 (1985). See generally Kent Greenawalt, *Speech, Crime, and the Uses of Language* 143–48 (1989) (discussing personal insults).

2. Is the problem with the outrageousness standard less its subjectivity than its enabling "a single community to use the authority of the state to confine speech within its own notions of propriety." Does *Falwell* exhibit a need to respect a "marketplace of communities?" Can we respect that marketplace without "blunt[ing the] rules of civility that define the essence of reason and dignity within community life?" Compare Robert Post, *The Constitutional Concept of Public Discourse,* 103 Harv.L.Rev. 601, 632, 643 (1990) with Joshua Cohen, *Freedom of Expression,* 21 Phil. & Pub. Aff. 207, 227 n. 62 (1993).

3. Is there any distinction to be made between persons and trademarks? The Second Circuit permitted an injunction to issue against exhibition of the film *Debbie Does Dallas* on the ground that it infringed on the trademarked uniform of the Dallas Cowboys Cheerleaders. *Dallas Cowboys Cheerleaders, Inc. v. Pussycat Cinema, Ltd.* 604 F.2d 200 (2d Cir.1979). The movie involves women performing sexual services for a fee so they can go to Dallas to become "Texas Cowgirls." Consistent with *Falwell?* Consider Robert Kravitz, *Trademarks, Speech, and the Gay Olympics Case,* 69 B.U.L.Rev. 131 (1989): "If Rev. Jerry Falwell cannot succeed on a cause of action against an advertising parody suggesting he had a sexual encounter with his mother while drunk in an outhouse, why should an inanimate trademark enjoy greater protection against similar slurs? If Falwell cannot recover, surely Campari, whose trademark was also parodied in the fake ad, should not. [Broadly] interpreted, the holding in *Dallas Cowboys Cheerleaders* suggests that Ford Motor Company might enjoin the distribution of a book or a

b. White, J., concurred, but stated that *New York Times* was irrelevant because of the jury's finding that the parody contained no assertion of fact. Kennedy, J., took no part.

film that portrayed teenagers having sex in the back of a Ford car." See also Robert Denicola, *Trademarks as Speech,* 1982 Wis.L.Rev. 158.

F. DISCLOSURE OF PRIVATE FACTS

FLORIDA STAR v. B.J.F.

491 U.S. 524, 109 S.Ct. 2603, 105 L.Ed.2d 443 (1989).

JUSTICE MARSHALL delivered the opinion of the Court.

Florida Stat. § 794.03 (1987) makes it unlawful to "print, publish, or broadcast [in] any instrument of mass communication" the name of the victim of a sexual offense. Pursuant to this statute, appellant The Florida Star was found civilly liable for publishing the name of a rape victim which it had obtained from a publicly released police report. [B.J.F.] testified that she had suffered emotional distress from the publication of her name. She stated that she had heard about the article from fellow workers and acquaintances; that her mother had received several threatening phone calls from a man who stated that he would rape B.J.F. again; and that these events had forced B.J.F. to change her phone number and residence, to seek police protection, and to obtain mental health counseling. [The jury] awarded B.J.F. $75,000 in compensatory damages and $25,000 in punitive damages. * * *

[We do not] accept appellant's invitation to hold broadly that truthful publication may never be punished consistent with the First Amendment. Our cases have carefully eschewed reaching this ultimate question, mindful that the future may bring scenarios which prudence counsels our not resolving anticipatorily. See, e.g., *Near v. Minnesota,* [Section 4, I, B] (hypothesizing "publication of the sailing dates of transports or the number and location of troops"); see also *Garrison v. Louisiana* (endorsing absolute defense of truth "where discussion of public affairs is concerned," but leaving unsettled the constitutional implications of truthfulness "in the discrete area of purely private libels"). Indeed, in [*Cox Broadcasting v. Cohn,* 420 U.S. 469, 95 S.Ct. 1029, 43 L.Ed.2d 328 (1975)], we pointedly refused to answer even the less sweeping question "whether truthful publications may ever be subjected to civil or criminal liability" for invading "an area of privacy" defined by the State. [We] continue to believe that the sensitivity and significance of the interests presented in clashes between First Amendment and privacy rights counsel relying on limited principles that sweep no more broadly than the appropriate context of the instant case.

In our view, this case is appropriately analyzed with reference to such a limited First Amendment principle. It is the one, in fact, which we articulated in *Smith v. Daily Mail Pub. Co.,* [Section 5, I] in our synthesis of prior cases involving attempts to punish truthful publication: "[I]f a newspaper lawfully obtains truthful information about a matter of public significance then state officials may not constitutionally punish publication of the information, absent a need to further a state interest of the highest order."[a] * * *

Applied to the instant case, the *Daily Mail* principle clearly commands reversal. The first inquiry is whether the newspaper "lawfully obtain[ed] truthful

---

a. Suppose a newspaper publishes the name of a confidential source who it believes has misled it for political reasons and suppose the source sues the newspaper for breach of contract? Should the *Daily Mail* principle ap-ply? See *Cohen v. Cowles Media Co.,* 501 U.S. 663, 111 S.Ct. 2513, 115 L.Ed.2d 586 (1991). Should the *Daily Mail* principle apply in copyright cases?

information about a matter of public significance." It is undisputed that the news article describing the assault on B.J.F. was accurate. In addition, appellant lawfully obtained B.J.F.'s name. Appellee's argument to the contrary is based on the fact that under Florida law, police reports which reveal the identity of the victim of a sexual offense are not among the matters of "public record" which the public, by law, is entitled to inspect. But the fact that state officials are not required to disclose such reports does not make it unlawful for a newspaper to receive them when furnished by the government. Nor does the fact that the Department apparently failed to fulfill its obligation under § 794.03 not to "cause or allow to [be] published" the name of a sexual offense victim make the newspaper's ensuing receipt of this information unlawful. Even assuming the Constitution permitted a State to proscribe *receipt* of information, Florida has not taken this step. It is, clear, furthermore, that the news article concerned "a matter of public significance[.]" That is, the article generally, as opposed to the specific identity contained within it, involved a matter of paramount public import: the commission, and investigation, of a violent crime which had been reported to authorities.

The second inquiry is whether imposing liability on appellant pursuant to § 794.03 serves "a need to further a state interest of the highest order." Appellee argues that a rule punishing publication furthers three closely related interests: the privacy of victims of sexual offenses; the physical safety of such victims, who may be targeted for retaliation if their names become known to their assailants; and the goal of encouraging victims of such crimes to report these offenses without fear of exposure.

At a time in which we are daily reminded of the tragic reality of rape, it is undeniable that these are highly significant interests. [We] accordingly do not rule out the possibility that, in a proper case, imposing civil sanctions for publication of the name of a rape victim might be so overwhelmingly necessary to advance these interests as to satisfy the *Daily Mail* standard. For three independent reasons, however, imposing liability for publication under the circumstances of this case is too precipitous a means of advancing these interests to convince us that there is a "need" within the meaning of the *Daily Mail* formulation for Florida to take this extreme step.

First is the manner in which appellant obtained the identifying information in question. [B.J.F.'s] identity would never have come to light were it not for the erroneous, if inadvertent, inclusion by the Department of her full name in an incident report made available in a press room open to the public. [Where] as here, the government has failed to police itself in disseminating information, it is clear [that] the imposition of damages against the press for its subsequent publication can hardly be said to be a narrowly tailored means of safeguarding anonymity.

That appellant gained access to the information in question through a government news release makes it especially likely that, if liability were to be imposed, self-censorship would result. Reliance on a news release is a paradigmatically "routine newspaper reporting techniqu[e]." The government's issuance of such a release, without qualification, can only convey to recipients that the government considered dissemination lawful, and indeed expected the recipients to disseminate the information further. Had appellant merely reproduced the news release prepared and released by the Department, imposing civil damages would surely violate the First Amendment. The fact that appellant converted the police report into a news story by adding the linguistic connecting tissue necessary to transform the report's facts into full sentences cannot change this result.

A second problem with Florida's imposition of liability for publication is the broad sweep of the negligence per se standard applied under the civil cause of action implied from § 794.03. Unlike claims based on the common law tort of invasion of privacy, civil actions based on § 794.03 require no case-by-case findings that the disclosure of a fact about a person's private life was one that a reasonable person would find highly offensive. On the contrary, under the per se theory of negligence adopted by the courts below, liability follows automatically from publication. This is so regardless of whether the identity of the victim is already known throughout the community; whether the victim has voluntarily called public attention to the offense; or whether the identity of the victim has otherwise become a reasonable subject of public concern—because, perhaps, questions have arisen whether the victim fabricated an assault by a particular person. Nor is there a scienter requirement of any kind under § 794.03, engendering the perverse result that truthful publications challenged pursuant to this cause of action are less protected by the First Amendment than even the least protected defamatory falsehoods: those involving purely private figures, where liability is evaluated under a standard, usually applied by a jury, of ordinary negligence. See *Gertz.* * * *

Third, and finally, the facial underinclusiveness of § 794.03 raises serious doubts about whether Florida is, in fact, serving, with this statute, the significant interests which appellee invokes in support of affirmance. Section 794.03 prohibits the publication of identifying information only if this information appears in an "instrument of mass communication," a term the statute does not define. Section 794.03 does not prohibit the spread by other means of the identities of victims of sexual offenses. An individual who maliciously spreads word of the identity of a rape victim is thus not covered, despite the fact that the communication of such information to persons who live near, or work with, the victim may have consequences equally devastating as the exposure of her name to large numbers of strangers.

When a State attempts the extraordinary measure of punishing truthful publication in the name of privacy, it must demonstrate its commitment to advancing this interest by applying its prohibition evenhandedly, to the small-time disseminator as well as the media giant. Where important First Amendment interests are at stake, the mass scope of disclosure is not an acceptable surrogate for injury. Without more careful and inclusive precautions against alternative forms of dissemination, we cannot conclude that Florida's selective ban on publication by the mass media satisfactorily accomplishes its stated purpose.

Our holding today is limited. We do not hold that truthful publication is automatically constitutionally protected, or that there is no zone of personal privacy within which the State may protect the individual from intrusion by the press, or even that a State may never punish publication of the name of a victim of a sexual offense. We hold only that where a newspaper publishes truthful information which it has lawfully obtained, punishment may lawfully be imposed, if at all, only when narrowly tailored to a state interest of the highest order, and that no such interest is satisfactorily served by imposing liability under § 794.03 to appellant under the facts of this case. * * *

JUSTICE SCALIA, concurring in part and concurring in the judgment.

I think it sufficient to decide this case to rely upon the third ground set forth in the Court's opinion: that a law cannot be regarded as protecting an interest "of the highest order" and thus as justifying a restriction upon truthful speech, when it leaves appreciable damage to that supposedly vital interest unprohibited. In the present case, I would anticipate that the rape victim's discomfort at the dissemination of news of her misfortune among friends and acquaintances would be at least as great as her discomfort at its publication by the media to people to whom she is only a name. Yet the law in question does not prohibit the former in either oral or written form. Nor is it at all clear, as I think it must be to validate this statute, that Florida's general privacy law would prohibit such gossip. Nor, finally, is it credible that the interest meant to be served by the statute is the protection of the victim against a rapist still at large—an interest that arguably would extend only to mass publication. There would be little reason to limit a statute with that objective to rape alone; or to extend it to all rapes, whether or not the felon has been apprehended and confined. In any case, the instructions here did not require the jury to find that the rapist was at large.

This law has every appearance of a prohibition that society is prepared to impose upon the press but not upon itself. Such a prohibition does not protect an interest "of the highest order." For that reason, I agree that the judgment of the court below must be reversed.

JUSTICE WHITE, with whom THE CHIEF JUSTICE and JUSTICE O'CONNOR join, dissenting.

"Short of homicide, [rape] is the 'ultimate violation of self.' " *Coker v. Georgia,* [433 U.S. 584, 97 S.Ct. 2861, 53 L.Ed.2d 982 (1977)] (opinion of White, J.). For B.J.F., however, the violation she suffered at a rapist's knife-point marked only the beginning of her ordeal. [Yet] today, the Court holds that a jury award of $75,000 to compensate B.J.F. for the harm she suffered due to the Star's negligence is at odds with the First Amendment. I do not accept this result.

[T]he three "independent reasons" the Court cites for reversing the judgment for B.J.F. [do not] support its result.

The first of these reasons [is] the fact "appellant gained access to [B.J.F.'s name] through a government news release." [But the] "release" of information provided by the government was not, as the Court says, "without qualification." As the Star's own reporter conceded at trial, the crime incident report that inadvertently included B.J.F.'s name was posted in a room that contained signs making it clear that the names of rape victims were not matters of public record, and were not to be published. The Star's reporter indicated that she understood that she "[was not] allowed to take down that information" (i.e., B.J.F.'s name) and that she "[was] not supposed to take the information from the police department." Thus, by her own admission the posting of the incident report did not convey to the Star's reporter the idea that "the government considered dissemination lawful"; the Court's suggestion to the contrary is inapt. * * *

Unfortunately, as this case illustrates, mistakes happen: even when States take measures to "avoid" disclosure, sometimes rape victim's names are found out. As I see it, it is not too much to ask the press, in instances such as this, to respect simple standards of decency and refrain from publishing a victim's name, address, and/or phone number.

Second, the Court complains [that] a newspaper might be found liable under the Florida courts' negligence per se theory without regard to a newspaper's scienter or degree of fault. The short answer to this complaint is that whatever merit the Court's argument might have, it is wholly inapposite here, where the jury found that appellant acted with "reckless indifference towards the rights of others," a standard far higher than the *Gertz* standard the Court urges as a constitutional minimum today.

But even taking the Court's concerns in the abstract, they miss the mark. [The] Court says that negligence per se permits a plaintiff to hold a defendant liable without a showing that the disclosure was "of a fact about a person's private life [that] a reasonable person would find highly offensive." But the point here is that the legislature—reflecting popular sentiment—has determined that disclosure of the fact that a person was raped is categorically a revelation that reasonable people find offensive. And as for the Court's suggestion that the Florida courts' theory permits liability without regard for whether the victim's identity is already known, or whether she herself has made it known—these are facts that would surely enter into the calculation of damages in such a case. In any event, none of these mitigating factors was present [here].

Third, the Court faults the Florida criminal statute for being underinclusive. [But] our cases which have struck down laws that limit or burden the press due to their underinclusiveness have involved situations where a legislature has singled out one segment of the news media or press for adverse treatment. Here, the Florida law evenhandedly covers all "instrument[s] of mass communication" no matter their form, media, content, nature or purpose. It excludes neighborhood gossips because presumably the Florida Legislature has determined that neighborhood gossips do not pose the danger and intrusion to rape victims that "instrument[s] of mass communication" do. Simply put: Florida wanted to prevent the widespread distribution of rape victim's names, and therefore enacted a statute tailored almost as precisely as possible to achieving that end. * * *

At issue in this case is whether there is any information about people, which—though true—may not be published in the press. [The] Court accepts appellant's invitation to obliterate one of the most note-worthy legal inventions of the 20th–Century: the tort of the publication of private facts. William Prosser, John Wade, & Victor Schwartz, *Torts* 951–952 (8th ed. 1988). Even if the Court's opinion does not say as much today, such obliteration will follow inevitably from the Court's conclusion here. [The] Court's ruling has been foreshadowed. In *Time, Inc. v. Hill,* we observed that—after a brief period early in this century where Brandeis' view was ascendant—the trend in "modern" jurisprudence has been to eclipse an individual's right to maintain private any truthful information that the press wished to publish. More recently, in *Cox Broadcasting,* we acknowledged the possibility that the First Amendment may prevent a State from ever subjecting the publication of truthful but private information to civil liability. Today, we hit the bottom of the slippery slope.

I would find a place to draw the line higher on the hillside: a spot high enough to protect B.J.F.'s desire for privacy and peace-of-mind in the wake of a horrible personal tragedy. There is no public interest in publishing the names, addresses, and phone numbers of persons who are the victims of crime—and no public interest in immunizing the press from liability in the rare cases where a State's efforts to protect a victim's privacy have failed. Consequently, I respectfully dissent.[5]

---

5. The Court does not address the distinct constitutional questions raised by the award of punitive damages in this case. Consequently, I do not do so either. That award is more troublesome than the compensatory award discussed above. Cf. Note, *Punitive Damages and Libel Law,* 98 Harv.L.Rev. 847 (1985).

Notes and Questions

1. *Journalistic practice.* Consider Paul Marcus & Tara McMahon, *Limiting Disclosure of Rape Victims' Identities,* 64 S.Cal.L.Rev. 1019, 1046–47 (1991): "The journalists' code of ethics and the policies of most members of the media currently prohibit publication of a rape victim's name. [T]he New York Times calls the policy 'one of modern journalism's few conspiracies of silence.' And even though a few members of the media, such as [former] NBC News president Michael Gartner, disagree with the policy because, as Gartner says, 'it's not the job of the media to keep secrets,' the majority supports exercising such restraint. Furthermore, it is doubtful many would argue that as a result of working within this established policy of not disclosing rape victims' names, members of the media have become more timid in their endeavor to investigate and report the [news]. Codifying in a rule of law what is already the prevailing practice would not have a chilling effect on the media."

2. *Outing.* Should the first amendment preclude a privacy cause of action against those who publicly disclose that a private person is gay? What if the person is a public official, e.g., a member of a board of education?[b]

3. *Buying habits.* Suppose government prohibits or provides tort relief against merchants who disseminate information about the buying habits of their customers or firms that traffic in similar data. Constitutional?[c]

4. *Voyeurism.* Is the direction of television programming less about encouraging democratic dialogue and more about encouraging a nation of voyeurs, people who watch others, but do not engage with them, people who enjoy prying into the affairs of others? Do voyeuristic desires deserve substantial first amendment protection? See Clay Calvert, *The Voyeurism Value in First Amendment Jurisprudence,* 17 Cardoza Arts & Ent.L.J. 273 (1999). Does the casting of privacy as a private value shortchange the interest in the quality of public discourse?[d]

III. OBSCENITY

A. THE SEARCH FOR A RATIONALE

Roth v. United States, infra, contains the Court's first extended discussion of the constitutionality of obscenity laws. The Court's opinion was framed by briefs that proceeded from sharply different visions of first amendment law. Roth argued that no speech including obscenity could be prohibited without meeting the clear and present danger test, that a danger of lustful thoughts was not the type of evil

b. For diverse perspectives, see Rodney Smolla, *Free Speech in an Open Society,* 137–39 (1992); Susan Becker, *The Immorality of Publicly Outing Private People,* 73 Ore.L.Rev. 159 (1994); Barbara Moretti, *Outing: Justifiable or Unwarranted Invasion of Privacy? The Private Facts Tort As a Remedy for Disclosures of Sexual Orientation,* 11 Cardozo Arts & Ent.L.J. 857 (1993); Comment, *Forced Out of the Closet,* 46 U.Miami L.Rev. 413 (1992); Note, *Outing, Privacy, and the First Amendment,* 102 Yale L.J. 747 (1992); Note, *"Outing" and Freedom of the Press: Sexual Orientation's Challenge to the Supreme Court's Categorical Jurisprudence,* 77 Corn.L.Rev. 103 (1992).

c. See Michael Froomkin, *The Death of Privacy,* 52 Stan. L.Rev. 1049, 1461 (2000) Jessica Litman, *Information Privacy/Information Property,* 52 Stan.L.Rev. 1049, 1283 (2000); Julie E.

Cohen, *Examined Lives: Informational Privacy and the Subject as Object,* 52 Stan. L.Rev. 1049 (2000); Eugene Volokh, *Freedom of Speech and Information Privacy: The Troubling Implications of a Right to Stop People from Speaking about You,* 52 Stan. L. Rev. 1049 (2000).

d. On the relationship between privacy and public discourse, see J.M. Balkin, *How Mass Media Simulate Political Transparency,* 3 Cultural Values 393 (1999); Lee Bollinger, *Images of a Free Press* 34–35 (1991); Lili Levi, *Challenging the Autonomous Press,* 78 Cornell L.Rev. 665, 669–700 (1993); Robert. F. Nagel, *Privacy and Celebrity: An Essay on the Nationalization of Intimacy,* 33 U.Rich.L.Rev. 1121 (2000); Sean M. Scott, *The Hidden First Amendment Values of Privacy,* 71 Wash.L.Rev. 683 (1996); Volokh, supra fn. c.

with which a legislature could be legitimately concerned, and that no danger of anti-social conduct had been shown. On the other hand, the government urged the Court to adopt a balancing test that prominently featured a consideration of the value of the speech involved. The government tendered an illustrative hierarchy of nineteen speech categories with political, religious, economic, and scientific speech at the top; entertainment, music, and humor in the middle; and libel, obscenity, profanity, and commercial pornography at the bottom.

ROTH v. UNITED STATES

ALBERTS v. CALIFORNIA

354 U.S. 476, 77 S.Ct. 1304, 1 L.Ed.2d 1498 (1957).

JUSTICE BRENNAN delivered the opinion of the Court. [Roth and Alberts were convicted of violating the federal and California obscenity laws respectively. The issues raised were whether the statutes, *"on their faces and in a vacuum,* violated the freedom of expression and definiteness requirements of the Constitution."[a]]

The dispositive question is whether obscenity is utterance within the area of protected speech and press.[8] Although this is the first time the question has been squarely presented to this Court [expressions] found in numerous opinions indicate that this Court has always assumed that obscenity is not protected by the freedoms of speech and press.

The guaranties of freedom of expression in effect in 10 of the 14 States which by 1792 had ratified the Constitution, gave no absolute protection for every utterance. Thirteen of the 14 States provided for the prosecution of libel, and all of those States made either blasphemy or profanity, or both, statutory crimes. As early as 1712, Massachusetts made it criminal to publish "any filthy, obscene, or profane song, pamphlet, libel or mock sermon" in imitation or mimicking of religious services. * * *

In light of this history, it is apparent that the unconditional phrasing of the First Amendment was not intended to protect every utterance. This phrasing did not prevent this Court from concluding that libelous utterances are not within the area of constitutionally protected speech. *Beauharnais.* At the time of the adoption of the First Amendment, obscenity law was not as fully developed as libel law, but there is sufficiently contemporaneous evidence to show that obscenity, too, was outside the protection intended for speech and press.[b]

---

a. See William Lockhart & Robert McClure, *Censorship of Obscenity: The Developing Constitutional Standards,* 45 Minn. L.Rev. 5, 13 (1960).

8. No issue is presented in either case concerning the obscenity of the material involved.

b. The Court here cited three state court decisions (1808 to 1821) recognizing as a common law offense the distribution or display of obscene or indecent materials, and four state statutes aimed at similar conduct (1800 to 1842). For the contention that obscenity is not "speech" within the meaning of the first amendment (let alone, not *protected* speech), see Frederick Schauer, *Free Speech: A Philosophical Enquiry* 181–84 (1982) (a sex aid, not speech). See generally Frederick Schauer, *Speech and "Speech"—Obscenity and "Obscen-*

ity": An Exercise in the Interpretation of Constitutional Language, 67 Geo.L.J. 899 (1979). But see Larry Alexander & Paul Horton, *The Impossibility of a Free Speech Principle,* 78 Nw.U.L.Rev. 1319, 1331–34 (1984). Compare Kent Greenawalt, *Criminal Coercion and Freedom of Speech,* 78 Nw.U.L.Rev. 1081 (1984) (discussing the question of whether all ordinary language should be included within the scope of the first amendment, even if much is ultimately unprotected, and contending that some ordinary language should be wholly outside the scope of the first amendment); Kent Greenawalt, *Speech, Crime and the Uses of Language.* But see Franklyn Haiman, *Comments on Kent Greenawalt's Criminal Coercion and Freedom of Speech,* 78 Nw.U.L.Rev. 1125 (1983).

The protection given speech and press was fashioned to assure unfettered interchange of ideas for the bringing about of political and social changes desired by the people. [All] ideas having even the slightest redeeming social importance—unorthodox ideas, controversial ideas, even ideas hateful to the prevailing climate of opinion—have the full protection of the guaranties, unless excludable because they encroach upon the limited area of more important interests. But implicit in the history of the First Amendment is the rejection of obscenity as utterly without redeeming social importance. This rejection for that reason is mirrored in the universal judgment that obscenity should be restrained, reflected in the international agreement of over 50 nations, in the obscenity laws of all of the 48 States, and in the 20 obscenity laws enacted by the Congress from 1842 to 1956. This is the same judgment expressed by this Court in *Chaplinsky* [Sec. I, IV, A infra]: "There are certain well-defined and narrowly limited classes of speech, the prevention and punishment of which have never been thought to raise any Constitutional problem. *These include the lewd and obscene. [It] has been well observed that such utterances are no essential part of any exposition of ideas, and are of such slight social value as a step to truth that any benefit that may be derived from them is clearly outweighed by the social interest in order and morality.*" (Emphasis added [by Court].)

We hold that obscenity is not within the area of constitutionally protected speech or press.

It is strenuously urged that these obscenity statutes offend the constitutional guaranties because they punish incitation to impure sexual *thoughts,* not shown to be related to any overt antisocial conduct which is or may be incited in the persons stimulated to such *thoughts.* [It] is insisted that the constitutional guaranties are violated because convictions may be had without proof either that obscene material will perceptibly create a clear and present danger of antisocial conduct, or will probably induce its recipients to such conduct. But, in light of our holding that obscenity is not protected speech, the complete answer to this argument is in the holding of this Court in *Beauharnais:* "Libelous utterances not being within the area of constitutionally protected speech, it is unnecessary, either for us or for the State courts, to consider the issues behind the phrase 'clear and present danger.' Certainly no one would contend that obscene speech, for example, may be punished only upon a showing of such circumstances. * * * "

However, sex and obscenity are not synonymous. Obscene material is material which deals with sex in a manner appealing to prurient interest.[20] The portrayal of sex, e.g., in art, literature and scientific works, is not itself sufficient reason to deny material the constitutional protection of freedom of speech and press. Sex, a great and mysterious motive force in human life, has indisputably been a subject of absorbing interest to mankind through the ages; it is one of the vital problems of human interest and public [concern].

---

20. I.e., material having a tendency to excite lustful thoughts. *Webster's New International Dictionary* (unabridged, 2d ed., 1949) defines *prurient,* in pertinent part, as follows:

"Itching; longing; uneasy with desire or longing; of persons, having itching, morbid, or lascivious longings; of desire, curiosity, or propensity, lewd * * *."

We perceive no significant difference between the meaning of obscenity developed in the case law and the definition of the A.L.I., *Model Penal Code,* § 207.10(2) (Tent. Draft No. 6, 1957), viz.: "[A] thing is obscene if, considered as a whole, its predominant appeal is to prurient interest, i.e. a shameful or morbid interest in nudity, sex, or excretion, and if it goes substantially beyond customary limits of candor in description or representation of such [matters]." See Comment, id. at 10, and the discussion at page 29 et seq.

The fundamental freedoms of speech and press have contributed greatly to the development and well-being of our free society and are indispensable to its continued growth. [It] is therefore vital that the standards for judging obscenity safeguard the protection of freedom of speech and press for material which does not treat sex in a manner appealing to prurient interest.

The early leading standard of obscenity allowed material to be judged merely by the effect of an isolated excerpt upon particularly susceptible persons. *Regina v. Hicklin,* [1868] L.R. 3 Q.B. 360. Some American courts adopted this standard but later decisions have rejected it and substituted this test: whether to the average person, applying contemporary community standards, the dominant theme of the material taken as a whole appeals to prurient interest. The *Hicklin* test, judging obscenity by the effect of isolated passages upon the most susceptible persons, might well encompass material legitimately treating with sex, and so it must be rejected as unconstitutionally restrictive of the freedoms of speech and press. On the other hand, the substituted standard provides safeguards adequate to withstand the charge of constitutional infirmity. Both trial courts below sufficiently followed the proper standard. Both courts used the proper definition of obscenity.[c]

[It] is argued that the statutes do not provide reasonably ascertainable standards of guilt and therefore violate the constitutional requirements of due process. *Winters v. New York,* 333 U.S. 507, 68 S.Ct. 665, 92 L.Ed. 840 (1948). The federal obscenity statute makes punishable the mailing of material that is "obscene, lewd, lascivious, or filthy [or] other publication of an indecent character." The California statute makes punishable, inter alia, the keeping for sale or advertising material that is "obscene or indecent." The thrust of the argument is that these words are not sufficiently precise because they do not mean the same thing to all people, all the time, everywhere. Many decisions have recognized that these terms of obscenity statutes are not precise. This Court, however, has consistently held that lack of precision is not itself offensive to the requirements of due process. "[T]he Constitution does not require impossible standards"; all that is required is that the language "conveys sufficiently definite warning as to the proscribed conduct when measured by common understanding and [practices.]" * * *

In summary, then, we hold that these statutes, applied according to the proper standard for judging obscenity, do not offend constitutional safeguards against convictions based upon protected material, or fail to give men in acting adequate notice of what is prohibited. * * *[d]

Affirmed.

CHIEF JUSTICE WARREN, concurring in the result.

c. The opinion quoted with apparent approval from the trial court's instruction in *Roth:* "[The] test is not whether it would arouse sexual desires or sexual impure thoughts in those comprising a particular segment of the community, the young, the immature or the highly prudish or would leave another segment, the scientific or highly educated or the so-called worldly-wise and sophisticated indifferent and unmoved. [The] test in each case is the effect of the book, picture or publication considered as a whole, not upon any particular class, but upon all those whom it is likely to reach. In other words, you determine its impact upon the average person in the community. The books, pictures and circulars must be judged as a whole, in their entire context, and you are not to consider detached or separate portions in reaching a conclusion. You judge the circulars, pictures and publications which have been put in evidence by present-day standards of the community. You may ask yourselves does it offend the common conscience of the community by present-day standards."

d. Harlan, J., dissented in *Roth* and concurred in *Alberts.*

[It] is not the book that is on trial; it is a person. The conduct of the defendant is the central issue, not the obscenity of a book or picture. The nature of the materials is, of course, relevant as an attribute of the defendant's conduct. [The] defendants in both these cases were engaged in the business of purveying textual or graphic matter openly advertised to appeal to the erotic interest of their customers. They were plainly engaged in the commercial exploitation of the morbid and shameful craving for materials with prurient effect. * * *

JUSTICE DOUGLAS, with whom JUSTICE BLACK concurs, dissenting.

When we sustain these convictions, we make the legality of a publication turn on the purity of thought which a book or tract instills in the mind of the reader. I do not think we can approve that standard and be faithful to the command of the First Amendment * * *.

I would give the broad sweep of the First Amendment full support. I have the same confidence in the ability of our people to reject noxious literature as I have in their capacity to sort out the true from the false in theology, economics, politics, or any other field.

Notes and Questions

1. *Non-obscene advocacy of "sexual immorality."* Two years after *Roth*, KINGSLEY INT'L. PICTURES CORP. v. REGENTS, 360 U.S. 684, 79 S.Ct. 1362, 3 L.Ed.2d 1512 (1959), per STEWART, J., underlined the distinction between obscenity and non-obscene "portrayal of sex" in art and literature. *Kingsley* held invalid New York's denial of a license to exhibit the film *Lady Chatterley's Lover* pursuant to a statute requiring such denial when a film "portrays acts of sexual immorality [as] desirable, acceptable or proper patterns of behavior":

"The Court of Appeals unanimously and explicitly rejected any notion that the film is obscene [but] found that the picture as a whole 'alluringly portrays adultery as proper behavior.' [What] New York has done, [is] to prevent the exhibition of a motion picture because that picture advocates an idea—that adultery under certain circumstances may be proper behavior. Yet the First Amendment's basic guarantee is of freedom to advocate ideas. The State, quite simply, has thus struck at the very heart of constitutionally protected liberty.

"[T]he guarantee is not confined to the expression of ideas that are conventional or shared by a majority. It protects advocacy of the opinion that adultery may sometimes be proper, no less than advocacy of socialism or the single tax. And in the realm of ideas it protects expression which is eloquent no less than that which is unconvincing. Advocacy of conduct proscribed by law is not, as Mr. Justice Brandeis long ago pointed out, 'a justification for denying free speech where the advocacy falls short of incitement and there is nothing to indicate that the advocacy would be immediately acted on.' *Whitney*."[e]

2. *Ideas and the first amendment.* Consider Harry Kalven, *The Metaphysics of the Law of Obscenity,* 1960 Sup.Ct.Rev. 1, 15–16: "The classic defense of John

e. While joining the opinion, Black and Douglas, JJ., also stated that prior censorship of motion pictures violates the first amendment. See discussion of this issue in Sec. 4, II infra. Harlan, J., joined by Frankfurter and Whittaker, JJ., concurred in the result. While "granting that abstract public discussion [of] adultery, unaccompanied by obscene portrayal or actual incitement [may] not constitutionally be proscribed," they concluded that the New York Court of Appeals had found the film obscene, but on viewing the film they concluded it was not obscene. Clark, J., concurred in the result because the statutory standard was too vague.

Stuart Mill and the modern defense of Alexander Meiklejohn do not help much when the question is why the novel, the poem, the painting, the drama, or the piece of sculpture falls within the protection of the First Amendment. Nor do the famous opinions of Hand, Holmes, and Brandeis. [The] people do not need novels or dramas or paintings or poems because they will be called upon to vote. Art and belles-lettres do not deal in such ideas—at least not good art or belles-lettres—and it makes little sense here to talk [of] whether there is still time for counter-speech.

"[B]eauty has constitutional status too, [and] the life of the imagination is as important to the human adult as the life of the intellect. I do not think that the Court would find it difficult to protect Shakespeare, even though it is hard to enumerate the important ideas in the plays and poems. I am only suggesting that Mr. Justice Brennan might not have found it so easy to dismiss obscenity because it lacked socially useful ideas if he had recognized that as to this point, at least, obscenity is in the same position as all art and literature."[f]

3. *The moral rationale for prohibition.* Consider Harry Clor, *Obscenity and Public Morality* 41–43 (1969): *Roth* "rejected the government's formula for the decision of obscenity cases, a formula which would have involved it in judgments concerning the importance of public morality and the role of government, as well as judgments concerning the effects of obscenity and the relative value of different forms of speech. The Court preferred to decide the case on the narrow and negative grounds that obscenity is without redeeming social importance. [W]hile the idea of redeeming social importance can be valuable as a definition of what should be protected, it cannot serve as a defense of regulation. Justices Harlan and Douglas can be answered only by a course of reasoning which provides some grounds for government activity in the area of morality, showing that the ends are legitimate and important, which provides some justification for the claims of community conscience, and which explores, more thoroughly than does the Court, the character of the 'thoughts' with which the law is here concerned."

The Court does assert that any value of obscenity as a step to truth is "outweighed by the social interest in order and morality." But consider David Richards, *Free Speech and Obscenity Law: Toward A Moral Theory of the First Amendment,* 123 U.Pa.L.Rev. 45, 81 (1974): "[P]ornography can be seen as the unique medium of a vision of sexuality [a] view of sensual delight in the erotic celebration of the body, a concept of easy freedom without consequences, a fantasy of timelessly repetitive indulgence. In opposition to the Victorian view that narrowly defines proper sexual function in a rigid way that is analogous to ideas of excremental regularity and moderation, pornography builds a model of plastic variety and joyful excess in sexuality. In opposition to the sorrowing Catholic dismissal of sexuality as an unfortunate and spiritually superficial concomitant of propagation, pornography affords the alternative idea of the independent status of sexuality as a profound and shattering ecstasy."[g]

f. For the relationship between art and the first amendment, see Marci A. Hamilton, *Art Speech,* 49 Vand.L.Rev. 73 (1996); Sheldon Nahmod, *Artistic Expression and Aesthetic Theory: The Beautiful, The Sublime and The First Amendment,* 1987 Wisc.L.Rev. 221.

g. For the view that pornography can best be defended as a form of anti-social dissent, consider Steven Gey, *The Apologetics of Suppression,* 86 Mich.L.Rev. 1564, 1630 (1988): "Porn exposes a rot in the framework of society, and the great popularity of porn makes the burghers uneasily suspicious that the surface rot may evidence a more deeply rooted degeneration of their moral and political primacy. Thus, the imperative to suppress pornography reveals a much deeper and more insidious insecurity than the moralists will ever acknowledge." Cf. Robin West, *The Feminist–Conservative Anti–Pornography Alliance and the 1986 Attorney General's Commission on Pornography Report,* 1987 Am.B.Found.Res.J. 681, 686–99 (discussing victimizing and liberating aspects of pornography from the perspectives of

Even if these characterizations were somewhat overwrought with respect to Roth's publications (e.g., *Wild Passion* and *Wanton By Night*) what of the view that individuals should be able to decide what they want to read and make moral decisions for themselves? Consider John Stuart Mill's statement of the harm principle in *On Liberty:* "[T]he only purpose for which power can be rightfully exercised over any member of a civilized community, against his will is to prevent harm to others."

Does the liberal view overestimate human rational capacity and underestimate the importance of the state in promoting a virtuous citizenry? See generally Clor, supra. Do liberals fail to appreciate the morally corrosive effects of obscenity? Consider the following observation: "Obscenity emphasizes the base animality of our nature, reduces the spirituality of humanity to mere bodily functions, and debases civilization by transforming the private into the public." Consider Irving Kristol, *Reflections of a Neoconservative* 45, 47 (1983): "Bearbaiting and cockfighting are prohibited only in part out of compassion for the suffering animals; the main reason they were abolished was because it was felt that they debased and brutalized the citizenry who flocked to witness such spectacles. And the question we face with regard to pornography and obscenity is whether [they] can or will brutalize and debase our citizenry. We are, after all, not dealing with one passing incident—one book, or one play, or one movie. We are dealing with a general tendency that is suffusing our entire culture. [W]hen men and women make love, as we say, they prefer to be alone—because it is only when you are alone that you can make love, as distinct from merely copulating in an animal and casual way. And that, too, is why those who are voyeurs, if they are not irredeemably sick, also feel ashamed at what they are witnessing. When sex is a public spectacle, a human relationship has been debased into a mere animal connection."[h]

———

STANLEY v. GEORGIA, 394 U.S. 557, 89 S.Ct. 1243, 22 L.Ed.2d 542 (1969), per MARSHALL, J., reversed a conviction for knowing "possession of obscene matter," based on three reels of obscene films found in Stanley's home when police entered under a search warrant for other purposes: "[*Roth*] and the cases following it discerned [an] 'important interest' in the regulation of commercial distribution of obscene material. That holding cannot foreclose an examination of the constitutional implications of a statute forbidding mere private possession of such material. [The constitutional] right to receive information and ideas, regardless of their social worth [*Winters*] is fundamental to our free society. Moreover, in the context of this case—a prosecution for mere possession of printed or filmed matter in the privacy of a person's own home—that right takes on an added dimension. For also fundamental is the right to be free, except in very limited circumstances, from unwanted governmental intrusions into one's privacy.

" 'The makers of our Constitution undertook to secure conditions favorable to the pursuit of happiness. They recognized the significance of man's spiritual nature, of his feelings and of his intellect. [They] sought to protect Americans in their beliefs, their thoughts, their emotions and their sensations. They conferred,

women while contending that women's experience of pornography, albeit diverse, is different from that of men).

h. See also Clor, supra; Walter Berns, *Pornography vs. Democracy: The Case for Censorship,* 22 Pub.Int. 13 (1971); Robert George, *Making Children Moral: Pornography, Parents, and the Public Interest,* 29 Ariz.St.L.J. 569 (1997). For the relationship between pornography, commerce, and culture, see Ronald Collins & David Skover, *The Pornographic State,* 107 Harv.L.Rev. 1374 (1994).

as against the government, the right to be let alone—the most comprehensive of rights and the right most valued by civilized man.' *Olmstead v. United States,* 277 U.S. 438, 48 S.Ct. 564, 72 L.Ed. 944 (1928) (Brandeis, J., dissenting). * * *

"These are the rights that appellant is asserting in the case before us. He is asserting the right to read or observe what he pleases—the right to satisfy his intellectual and emotional needs in the privacy of his own home. He is asserting the right to be free from state inquiry into the contents of his library. Georgia contends that appellant does not have these rights, that there are certain types of materials that the individual may not read or even possess. [W]e think that mere categorization of these films as 'obscene' is insufficient justification for such a drastic invasion of personal liberties guaranteed by the First and Fourteenth Amendments. Whatever may be the justifications for other statutes regulating obscenity, we do not think they reach into the privacy of one's own home. If the First Amendment means anything, it means that a State has no business telling a man, sitting alone in his own house, what books he may read or what films he may watch. Our whole constitutional heritage rebels at the thought of giving government the power to control men's minds.

"[I]n the face of these traditional notions of individual liberty, Georgia asserts the right to protect the individual's mind from the effects of obscenity. We are not certain that this argument amounts to anything more than the assertion that the State has the right to control the moral content of a person's thoughts.[9] To some, this may be a noble purpose, but it is wholly inconsistent with the philosophy of the First Amendment. [*Kingsley Pictures.*] Nor is it relevant that obscenity in general, or the particular films before the Court, are arguably devoid of any ideological content. The line between the transmission of ideas and mere entertainment is much too elusive for this Court to draw, if indeed such a line can be drawn at all. [*Winters*]. Whatever the power of the state to control public dissemination of ideas inimical to the public morality, it cannot constitutionally premise legislation on the desirability of controlling a person's private thoughts.

"[Georgia] asserts that exposure to obscenity may lead to deviant sexual behavior or crimes of sexual violence. There appears to be little empirical basis for that assertion. But more importantly, if the State is only concerned about literature inducing antisocial conduct, we believe that in the context of private consumption of ideas and information we should adhere to the view that '[a]mong free men, the deterrents ordinarily to be applied to prevent crime are education and punishment for violations of the [law].' *Whitney* (Brandeis, J., concurring). See Emerson, *Toward a General Theory of the First Amendment,* 72 Yale L.J. 877, 938 (1963). Given the present state of knowledge, the State may no more prohibit mere possession of obscenity on the ground that it may lead to antisocial conduct than it may prohibit possession of chemistry books on the ground that they may lead to the manufacture of homemade spirits.

"It is true that in *Roth* this Court rejected the necessity of proving that exposure to obscene material would create a clear and present danger of antisocial conduct or would probably induce its recipients to such conduct. But that case dealt with public distribution of obscene materials and such distribution is subject

---

9. "Communities believe, and act on the belief, that obscenity is immoral, is wrong for the individual, and has no place in a decent society. They believe, too, that adults as well as children are corruptible in morals and character, and that obscenity is a source of corruption that should be eliminated. Obscenity is not suppressed primarily for the protection of others. Much of it is suppressed for the purity of the community and for the salvation and welfare of the 'consumer.' Obscenity, at bottom, is not crime. Obscenity is sin." Louis Henkin, *Morals and the Constitution: The Sin of Obscenity,* 63 Col.L.Rev. 391, 395 (1963).

to different objections. For example, there is always the danger that obscene material might fall into the hands of children, see *Ginsberg*, [fn. d, p. 712 infra], or that it might intrude upon the sensibilities or privacy of the general public. No such dangers are present in this [case.]

"We hold that the First and Fourteenth Amendments prohibit making mere private possession of obscene material a crime. *Roth* and the cases following that decision are not impaired by today's holding. As we have said, the States retain broad power to regulate obscenity; that power simply does not extend to mere possession by the individual in the privacy of his own home."[a]

Notes and Questions

1. *Obscenity and the first amendment.* Is *Stanley* consistent with the constitutional theory of *Roth?* Can the first amendment rationally be viewed as applicable to *private use* but not to *public distribution* of obscenity? Cf. Al Katz, *Privacy and Pornography,* 1969 Sup.Ct.Rev. 203, 210–11. Might the definitional two-level approach reconcile *Stanley* with *Roth?*

2. *Implications of Stanley.* Could *Stanley*'s recognition of a first amendment right to "receive" and use obscene matter in the home fairly be viewed as implying a right to purchase it from commercial suppliers, or to import it for personal use, or to view it in a theater limited to consenting adults?

PARIS ADULT THEATRE I v. SLATON

413 U.S. 49, 93 S.Ct. 2628, 37 L.Ed.2d 446 (1973).

CHIEF JUSTICE BURGER delivered the opinion of the Court.

[The entrance to Paris Adult Theatres I & II was conventional and inoffensive without any pictures. Signs read: "Adult Theatre—You must be 21 and able to prove it. If viewing the nude body offends you, Please Do Not Enter." The District Attorney, nonetheless, had brought an action to enjoin the showing of two films that the Georgia Supreme Court described as "hard core pornography" leaving "little to the imagination." The Georgia Supreme Court assumed that the adult theaters in question barred minors and gave a full warning to the general public of the nature of the films involved, but held that the showing of the films was not constitutionally protected.]

[We] categorically disapprove the theory [that] obscene, pornographic films acquire constitutional immunity from state regulation simply because they are exhibited for consenting adults only. [Although we have] recognized the high importance of the state interest in regulating the exposure of obscene materials to juveniles and unconsenting adults, this Court has never declared these to be the only legitimate state interests permitting regulation of obscene material.

[W]e hold that there are legitimate state interests at stake in stemming the tide of commercialized obscenity, even assuming it is feasible to enforce effective safeguards against exposure to juveniles and to the passerby.[7] [These] include the

---

a. Black, J., concurred separately. Stewart, J., joined by Brennan and White, JJ., concurred in the result on search and seizure grounds.

7. It is conceivable that an "adult" theatre can—if it really insists—prevent the exposure of its obscene wares to juveniles. An "adult"

bookstore, dealing in obscene books, magazines, and pictures, cannot realistically make this claim. The Hill–Link Minority Report of the Commission on Obscenity and Pornography emphasizes evidence (the Abelson National Survey of Youth and Adults) that, although most pornography may be bought by elders,

interest of the public in the quality of life and the total community environment, the tone of commerce in the great city centers, and, possibly, the public safety itself. The Hill–Link Minority Report of the Commission on Obscenity and Pornography indicates that there is at least an arguable correlation between obscene material and crime. Quite apart from sex crimes, however, there remains one problem of large proportions aptly described by Professor Bickel: "It concerns the tone of the society, the mode, or to use terms that have perhaps greater currency, the style and quality of life, now and in the future. A man may be entitled to read an obscene book in his room, or expose himself indecently there. [We] should protect his privacy. But if he demands a right to obtain the books and pictures he wants in the market, and to foregather in public places—discreet, if you will, but accessible to all—with others who share his tastes, *then to grant him his right is to affect the world about the rest of us, and to impinge on other privacies.* Even supposing that each of us can, if he wishes, effectively avert the eye and stop the ear (which, in truth, we cannot), what is commonly read and seen and heard and done intrudes upon us all, want it or not." 22 *The Public Interest* 25, 25–26 (Winter, 1971). (Emphasis supplied.) [T]here is a "right of the Nation and of the States to maintain a decent [society]," *Jacobellis* (Warren, C.J., dissenting).

But, it is argued, there is no scientific data which conclusively demonstrates that exposure to obscene materials adversely affects men and women or their society. It is urged [that], absent such a demonstration, any kind of state regulation is "impermissible." We reject this argument. It is not for us to resolve empirical uncertainties underlying state legislation, save in the exceptional case where that legislation plainly impinges upon rights protected by the Constitution itself. [Although] there is no conclusive proof of a connection between antisocial behavior and obscene material, the legislature of Georgia could quite reasonably determine that such a connection does or might exist. In deciding *Roth,* this Court implicitly accepted that a legislature could legitimately act on such a conclusion to protect *"the social interest in order and morality."*

From the beginning of civilized societies, legislators and judges have acted on various unprovable assumptions. Such assumptions underlie much lawful state regulation of commercial and business affairs. The same is true of the federal securities, antitrust laws and a host of other federal regulations. [Likewise], when legislatures and administrators act to protect the physical environment from pollution and to preserve our resources of forests, streams and parks, they must act on such imponderables as the impact of a new highway near or through an existing park or wilderness area. [The] fact that a congressional directive reflects unprovable assumptions about what is good for the people, including imponderable aesthetic assumptions, is not a sufficient reason to find that statute unconstitutional.

If we accept the unprovable assumption that a complete education requires certain books, and the well nigh universal belief that good books, plays, and art lift the spirit, improve the mind, enrich the human personality and develop character, can we then say that a state legislature may not act on the corollary

"the heavy users and most highly exposed people to pornography are adolescent females (among women) and adolescent and young males (among men)." *The Report of the Commission on Obscenity* 401 (1970). The legitimate interest in preventing exposure of juveniles to obscene materials cannot be fully served by simply barring juveniles from the immediate physical premises of "adult" bookstores, when there is a flourishing "outside business" in these materials.

assumption that commerce in obscene books,[a] or public exhibitions focused on obscene conduct, have a tendency to exert a corrupting and debasing impact leading to antisocial behavior? [The] sum of experience, including that of the past two decades, affords an ample basis for legislatures to conclude that a sensitive, key relationship of human existence, central to family life, community welfare, and the development of human personality, can be debased and distorted by crass commercial exploitation of sex. Nothing in the Constitution prohibits a State from reaching such a conclusion and acting on it legislatively simply because there is no conclusive evidence or empirical data.

[Nothing] in this Court's decisions intimates that there is any "fundamental" privacy right "implicit in the concept of ordered liberty" to watch obscene movies in places of public accommodation. [W]e have declined to equate the privacy of the home relied on in *Stanley* with a "zone" of "privacy" that follows a distributor or a consumer of obscene materials wherever he goes.[b]

[W]e reject the claim that Georgia is here attempting to control the minds or thoughts of those who patronize theatres. Preventing unlimited display or distribution of obscene material, which by definition lacks any serious literary, artistic, political, or scientific value as communication, is distinct from a control of reason and the intellect. Cf. John Finnis, *"Reason and Passion": The Constitutional Dialectic of Free Speech and Obscenity*, 116 U.Pa.L.Rev. 222, 229–230, 241–243 (1967).

[Finally], petitioners argue that conduct which directly involves "consenting adults" only has, for that sole reason, a special claim to constitutional protection. Our Constitution establishes a broad range of conditions on the exercise of power by the States, but for us to say that our Constitution incorporates the proposition that conduct involving consenting adults only is always beyond state regulation,[14] is a step we are unable to take.[15] [The] issue in this context goes beyond whether

---

a. The only case after *Roth* in which the Court upheld a conviction based upon books was in *Mishkin* [Sec. 1, III, B infra] and most, if not all, of those books were illustrated. *Kaplan v. California*, 413 U.S. 115, 93 S.Ct. 2680, 37 L.Ed.2d 492 (1973) held that books without pictures can be legally obscene "in the sense of being unprotected by the First Amendment." It observed that books are "passed hand to hand, and we can take note of the tendency of widely circulated books of this category to reach the impressionable young and have a continuing impact. A State could reasonably regard the 'hard core' conduct described by *Suite 69* as capable of encouraging or causing antisocial behavior, especially in its impact on young people." Is *Kaplan*'s explanation in tension with *Butler v. Michigan* [Sec. 1, III, B infra]? Why should the obscenity standard focus on the average adult if the underlying worry is that books will fall in the hands of children?

b. In a series of cases, the Court limited *Stanley* to its facts. It held that *Stanley* did not protect the mailing of obscene material to consenting adults, *United States v. Reidel*, 402 U.S. 351, 91 S.Ct. 1410, 28 L.Ed.2d 813 (1971) or the transporting or importing of obscene materials for private use, *United States v. Orito*, 413 U.S. 139, 93 S.Ct. 2674, 37 L.Ed.2d 513

(1973) (transporting); *United States v. 12 200–Ft. Reels*, 413 U.S. 123, 93 S.Ct. 2665, 37 L.Ed.2d 500 (1973) (importing). Dissenting in *Reels*, Douglas, J., argued that *Stanley* rights could legally be realized "only if one wrote or designed a tract in his attic and printed or processed it in his basement, so as to be able to read it in his study." Do these decisions take the first amendment out of *Stanley*? Are they justified by the rationale in *Paris Adult Theatre*? For example, does importation for personal use intrude "upon us all"? Affect the total community environment?

For the declaration that *Stanley's* "privacy of the home" principle is "firmly grounded" in the first amendment while resisting the principle's expansion to protect consensual adult homosexual sodomy in the home, see *Bowers v. Hardwick*, Ch. 6, Sec. II supra. But see Blackmun, J., joined by Brennan, Marshall, and Stevens, JJ., dissenting in *Bowers* ("*Stanley* rested as much on the Court's understanding of the Fourth Amendment as it did on the First").

14. Cf. John Stuart Mill, *On Liberty* 13 (1955).

15. The state statute books are replete with constitutionally unchallenged laws against prostitution, suicide, voluntary self-mutilation, brutalizing "bare fist" prize fights,

someone, or even the majority, considers the conduct depicted as "wrong" or "sinful." The States have the power to make a morally neutral judgment that public exhibition of obscene material, or commerce in such material, has a tendency to injure the community as a whole, to endanger the public safety, or to jeopardize, in Mr. Chief Justice Warren's words, the States' "right [to] maintain a decent society." *Jacobellis* (dissenting). * * *

JUSTICE BRENNAN, with whom JUSTICE STEWART and JUSTICE MARSHALL join, dissenting.

[I] am convinced that the approach initiated 15 years ago in *Roth* and culminating in the Court's decision today, cannot bring stability to this area of the law without jeopardizing fundamental First Amendment values, and I have concluded that the time has come to make a significant departure from that [approach.]

[The] decision of the Georgia Supreme Court rested squarely on its conclusion that the State could constitutionally suppress these films even if they were displayed only to persons over the age of 21 who were aware of the nature of their contents and who had consented to viewing them. [I] am convinced of the invalidity of that conclusion [and] would therefore vacate the [judgment]. I have no occasion to consider the extent of State power to regulate the distribution of sexually oriented materials to juveniles or to unconsenting [adults.] [*Stanley*] reflected our emerging view that the state interests in protecting children and in protecting unconsenting adults may stand on a different footing from the other asserted state interests. It may well be, as one commentator has argued, that "exposure to [erotic material] is for some persons an intense emotional experience. A communication of this nature, imposed upon a person contrary to his wishes, has all the characteristics of a physical assault. [And it] constitutes an invasion of his [privacy]." [But] whatever the strength of the state interests in protecting juveniles and unconsenting adults from exposure to sexually oriented materials, those interests cannot be asserted in defense of the holding of the Georgia Supreme Court, [which] assumed for the purposes of its decision that the films in issue were exhibited only to persons over the age of 21 who viewed them willingly and with prior knowledge of the nature of their contents. [The] justification for the suppression must be found, therefore, in some independent interest in regulating the reading and viewing habits of consenting [adults].

In *Stanley* we pointed out that "[t]here appears to be little empirical basis for" the assertion that "exposure to obscene materials may lead to deviant sexual behavior or crimes of sexual violence." In any event, we added that "if the State is only concerned about printed or filmed materials inducing antisocial conduct, we believe that in the context of private consumption of ideas and information we should adhere to the view that '[a]mong free men, the deterrents ordinarily to be applied to prevent crime are education and punishment for violations of the [law].' "

Moreover, in *Stanley* we rejected as "wholly inconsistent with the philosophy of the First Amendment," the notion that there is a legitimate state concern in the "control [of] the moral content of a person's thoughts." [The] traditional description of state police power does embrace the regulation of morals as well as the health, safety, and general welfare of the citizenry. [But] the State's interest

and duels, although these crimes may only directly involve "consenting adults." Statutes making bigamy a crime surely cut into an individual's freedom to associate, but few today seriously claim such statutes violate the First Amendment or any other constitutional provision.

in regulating morality by suppressing obscenity, while often asserted, remains essentially unfocused and ill-defined. And, since the attempt to curtail unprotected speech necessarily spills over into the area of protected speech, the effort to serve this speculative interest through the suppression of obscene material must tread heavily on rights protected by the First Amendment. * * *

In short, while I cannot say that the interests of the State—apart from the question of juveniles and unconsenting adults—are trivial or nonexistent, I am compelled to conclude that these interests cannot justify the substantial damage to constitutional rights and to this Nation's judicial machinery that inevitably results from state efforts to bar the distribution even of unprotected material to consenting adults.[c]

JUSTICE DOUGLAS, dissenting. * * *

"Obscenity" at most is the expression of offensive ideas. There are regimes in the world where ideas "offensive" to the majority (or at least to those who control the majority) are suppressed. There life proceeds at a monotonous pace. Most of us would find that world offensive. One of the most offensive experiences in my life was a visit to a nation where bookstalls were filled only with books on mathematics and books on religion.

I am sure I would find offensive most of the books and movies charged with being obscene. But in a life that has not been short, I have yet to be trapped into seeing or reading something that would offend me. I never read or see the materials coming to the Court under charges of "obscenity," because I have thought the First Amendment made it unconstitutional for me to act as a censor. * * *

B.   A REVISED STANDARD

MILLER v. CALIFORNIA

413 U.S. 15, 93 S.Ct. 2607, 37 L.Ed.2d 419 (1973).

CHIEF JUSTICE BURGER delivered the opinion of the Court. [The Court remanded, "for proceedings not inconsistent" with the opinion's obscenity standard, Miller's conviction under California's obscenity law for mass mailing of unsolicited pictorial advertising brochures depicting men and women in a variety of group sexual activities.]

This is one of a group of "obscenity-pornography" cases being reviewed by the Court in a re-examination of standards enunciated in earlier cases involving what Mr. Justice Harlan called "the intractable obscenity problem." [I]n this context[a] [we] are called on to define the standards which must be used to identify obscene material that a State may [regulate].

[Nine years after *Roth*], in *Memoirs v. Massachusetts*, 383 U.S. 413, 86 S.Ct. 975, 16 L.Ed.2d 1 (1966), the Court veered sharply away from the Roth concept and, with only three Justices in the plurality opinion, articulated a new test of obscenity. The plurality held that under the Roth definition "as elaborated in subsequent cases, three elements must coalesce: it must be established that (a) the

---

c. For the portion of Brennan, J.'s dissent addressing the difficulties of formulating an acceptable constitutional standard, see *Miller v. California,* infra.

a. The "context" was that in *Miller* "sexually explicit materials have been thrust by aggressive sales action upon unwilling recipients." But nothing in *Miller* limited the revised standard to that context, and the companion case, *Paris Adult Theatre,* applied the same standard to dissemination limited to consenting adults.

dominant theme of the material taken as a whole appeals to a prurient interest in sex; (b) the material is patently offensive because it affronts contemporary community standards relating to the description or representation of sexual matters; and (c) the material is utterly without redeeming social value." * * *

While *Roth* presumed "obscenity" to be "utterly without redeeming social importance," *Memoirs* required that to prove obscenity it must be affirmatively established that the material is "*utterly* without redeeming social value."

Thus, even as they repeated the words of *Roth,* the *Memoirs* plurality produced a drastically altered test that called on the prosecution to prove a negative, i.e., that the material was "*utterly* without redeeming social value"—a burden virtually impossible to discharge under our criminal standards of proof. [Apart] from the initial formulation in *Roth,* no majority of the Court has at any given time been able to agree on a standard to determine what constitutes obscene, pornographic material subject to regulation under the States' police power. See, e.g., *Redrup v. New York,* 386 U.S. 767, 87 S.Ct. 1414, 18 L.Ed.2d 515 (1967).[3] This is not remarkable, for in the area of freedom of speech and press the courts must always remain sensitive to any infringement on genuinely serious literary, artistic, political, or scientific expression. * * *

II.   This much has been categorically settled by the Court, that obscene material is unprotected by the First Amendment. [We] acknowledge, however, the inherent dangers of undertaking to regulate any form of expression. State statutes designed to regulate obscene materials must be carefully limited. As a result, we now confine the permissible scope of such regulation to works which depict or describe sexual conduct. That conduct must be specifically defined by the applicable state law, as written or authoritatively construed.[6] A state offense must also be limited to works which, taken as a whole, appeal to the prurient interest in sex, which portray sexual conduct in a patently offensive way, and which, taken as a whole, do not have serious literary, artistic, political, or scientific value.

The basic guidelines for the trier of fact must be: (a) whether "the average person, applying contemporary community standards" would find that the work, taken as a whole, appeals to the prurient interest, (b) whether the work depicts or describes, in a patently offensive way, sexual conduct specifically defined by the applicable state law,[b] and (c) whether the work, taken as a whole, lacks serious literary, artistic, political, or scientific value. We do not adopt as a constitutional standard the "*utterly* without redeeming social value" test of *Memoirs;* that concept has never commanded the adherence of more than three Justices at one time.[7] If a state law that regulates obscene material is thus limited, as written or

---

3. In the absence of a majority view, this Court was compelled to embark on the practice of summarily reversing convictions for the dissemination of materials that at least five members of the Court, applying their separate tests, found to be protected by the First Amendment. *Redrup.* [Beyond] the necessity of circumstances, however, no justification has ever been offered in support of the *Redrup* "policy." The *Redrup* procedure has cast us in the role of an unreviewable board of censorship for the 50 States, subjectively judging each piece of material brought before us.

6. See, e.g., Oregon Laws 1971, c. 743, Art. 29, §§ 255–262, and Hawaii Penal Code, Tit. 37, §§ 1210–1216, 1972 Hawaii Session Laws, pp. 126–129, Act 9, Pt. II, as examples of state

laws directed at depiction of defined physical conduct, as opposed to expression. [We] do not hold, as Mr. Justice Brennan intimates, that all States other than Oregon must now enact new obscenity statutes. Other existing state statutes, as construed heretofore or hereafter, may well be adequate.

b. On the use of guidelines (a) and (b) against sexual minorities, see Comment, *Behind the Curtain of Privacy: How Obscenity Laws Inhibit the Expression of Ideas About Sex and Gender,* 1998 Wis. L. Rev. 625 (1998).

7. "[We] also reject, as a constitutional standard, the ambiguous concept of 'social importance'." [*Hamling v. United States,* 418 U.S. 87, 94 S.Ct. 2887, 41 L.Ed.2d 590 (1974) upheld a conviction in which the jury had been

construed, the First Amendment values applicable to the States [are] adequately protected by the ultimate power of appellate courts to conduct an independent review of constitutional claims when necessary.

We emphasize that it is not our function to propose regulatory schemes for the States. [It] is possible, however, to give a few plain examples of what a state statute could define for regulation under the second part (b) of the standard announced in this opinion, supra:

(a) Patently offensive representations or descriptions of ultimate sexual acts, normal or perverted, actual or simulated.

(b) Patently offensive representations or descriptions of masturbation, excretory functions, and lewd exhibition of the genitals.[c]

Sex and nudity may not be exploited without limit by films or pictures exhibited or sold in places of public accommodation any more than live sex and nudity can be exhibited or sold without limit in such public places.[8] At a minimum, prurient,[d] patently offensive depiction or description of sexual conduct must have serious literary, artistic, political, or scientific value to merit First Amendment protection. For example, medical books for the education of physicians and related personnel necessarily use graphic illustrations and descriptions of human anatomy. In resolving the inevitably sensitive questions of fact and law, we must continue to rely on the jury system, accompanied by the safeguards that judges, rules of evidence, presumption of innocence and other protective features [provide].

Mr. Justice Brennan [has] abandoned his former positions and now maintains that no formulation of this Court, the Congress, or the States can adequately distinguish obscene material unprotected by the First Amendment from protected

instructed to find that the material was "utterly without redeeming social value." Defendant argued that the latter phrase was unconstitutionally vague and cited *Miller*. The Court rejected the vagueness challenge: "[O]ur opinion in *Miller* plainly indicates that we rejected the '[social] value' formulation, not because it was so vague as to deprive criminal defendants of adequate notice, but instead because it represented a departure from [*Roth*], and because in calling on the prosecution to 'prove a negative,' it imposed a '[prosecutorial] burden virtually impossible to discharge' and which was not constitutionally required."]

c. *Jenkins v. Georgia*, 418 U.S. 153, 94 S.Ct. 2750, 41 L.Ed.2d 642 (1974) held the film *Carnal Knowledge* not obscene because it did not " 'depict or describe patently offensive 'hard core' sexual conduct' " as required by *Miller:* "[While there] are scenes in which sexual conduct including 'ultimate sexual acts' is to be understood to be taking place, the camera does not focus on the bodies of the actors at such times. There is no exhibition whatever of the actors' genitals, lewd or otherwise, during these scenes. There are occasional scenes of nudity, but nudity alone is not enough to make material legally obscene under the *Miller* standards." *Ward v. Illinois*, 431 U.S. 767, 97 S.Ct. 2085, 52 L.Ed.2d 738 (1977) held that it was not necessary for the legislature or the courts to provide an "exhaustive list of the sexual conduct [the] description of which may be held

obscene." It is enough that a state adopt *Miller*'s explanatory examples. Stevens, J., joined by Brennan, Stewart and Marshall, JJ., dissented: "[I]f the statute need only describe the 'kinds' of proscribed sexual conduct, it adds no protection to what the Constitution itself creates. [The] specificity requirement as described in *Miller* held out the promise of a principled effort to respond to [the vagueness] argument. By abandoning that effort today, the Court withdraws the cornerstone of the *Miller* [structure]."

8. Although we are not presented here with the problem of regulating lewd public conduct itself, the States have greater power to regulate nonverbal, physical conduct than to suppress depictions or descriptions of the same behavior. * * *

d. *Brockett v. Spokane Arcades, Inc.*, 472 U.S. 491, 105 S.Ct. 2794, 86 L.Ed.2d 394 (1985) held that appeals to prurient interest could not be taken to include appeals to "normal" interests in sex. Only appeals to a "shameful or morbid interest in sex" are prurient. Although the Court was resolute in its position that appeals to "good, old fashioned, healthy" interests in sex were constitutionally protected, it did not further specify how "normal" sex was to be distinguished from the "shameful" or "morbid."

expression, *Paris Adult Theatre I v. Slaton* (Brennan, J., dissenting). Paradoxically, Mr. Justice Brennan indicates that suppression of unprotected obscene material is permissible to avoid exposure to unconsenting adults, as in this case, and to juveniles, although he gives no indication of how the division between protected and nonprotected materials may be drawn with greater precision for these purposes than for regulation of commercial exposure to consenting adults only. Nor does he indicate where in the Constitution he finds the authority to distinguish between a willing "adult" one month past the state law age of majority and a willing "juvenile" one month younger.[e]

Under the holdings announced today, no one will be subject to prosecution for the sale or exposure of obscene materials unless these materials depict or describe patently offensive "hard core" sexual conduct specifically defined by the regulating state law, as written or construed. We are satisfied that these specific prerequisites will provide fair notice to a dealer in such materials that his public and commercial activities may bring prosecution. If the inability to define regulated materials with ultimate, god-like precision altogether removes the power of the States or the Congress to regulate, then "hard core" pornography may be exposed without limit to the juvenile, the passerby, and the consenting adult alike, as indeed, Mr. Justice Douglas contends.

[N]o amount of "fatigue" should lead us to adopt a convenient "institutional" rationale—an absolutist, "anything goes" view of the First Amendment—because it will lighten our burdens. [Nor] should we remedy "tension between state and federal courts" by arbitrarily depriving the States of a power reserved to them under the Constitution, a power which they have enjoyed and exercised continuously from before the adoption of the First Amendment to this day. See *Roth*. "Our duty admits of no 'substitute for facing up to the tough individual problems of constitutional judgment involved in every obscenity case.'" *Jacobellis* (opinion of Brennan, J.).

III. Under a national Constitution, fundamental First Amendment limitations on the powers of the States do not vary from community to community, but this does not mean that there are, or should or can be, fixed, uniform national standards of precisely what appeals to the "prurient interest" or is "patently offensive." These are essentially questions of fact, and our nation is simply too big and too diverse for this Court to reasonably expect that such standards could be articulated for all 50 States in a single formulation, even assuming the prerequi-

---

e. The suggestion that the same book may be obscene in some contexts but not in others has been endorsed in several different contexts. *Butler v. Michigan,* 352 U.S. 380, 77 S.Ct. 524, 1 L.Ed.2d 412 (1957) held that the state could not ban sales to the general public of material unsuitable for children: "The State insists that [by] quarantining the general reading public against books not too rugged for grown men and women in order to shield juvenile innocence, it is exercising its power to promote the general welfare. Surely, this is to burn the house to roast the pig. [The] incidence of this enactment is to reduce the adult population of Michigan to reading only what is fit for children." *Ginsberg v. New York,* 390 U.S. 629, 88 S.Ct. 1274, 20 L.Ed.2d 195 (1968), however, held that the state could bar the distribution to children of books that were suitable for adults, the Court recognizing it

was adopting a "variable" concept of obscenity. See also *Ginzburg v. United States,* 383 U.S. 463, 86 S.Ct. 942, 16 L.Ed.2d 31 (1966) ("pandering" method of marketing supports obscenity conviction even though the materials might not otherwise have been considered obscene); *Mishkin v. New York,* 383 U.S. 502, 86 S.Ct. 958, 16 L.Ed.2d 56 (1966) (material designed for and primarily disseminated to deviant sexual group can meet prurient appeal requirement even if the material lacks appeal to an average member of the general public; appeal is to be tested with reference to the sexual interests of the intended and probable recipient group).

The variable obscenity approach had previously been advocated and elaborated by William Lockhart & Robert McClure, *Censorship of Obscenity: The Developing Constitutional Standards,* 45 Minn.L.Rev. 5, 77 (1960).

site consensus exists. When triers of fact are asked to decide whether "the average person, applying contemporary community standards" would consider certain materials "prurient," it would be unrealistic to require that the answer be based on some abstract formulation. The adversary system, with lay jurors as the usual ultimate fact finders in criminal prosecutions, has historically permitted triers-of-fact to draw on the standards of their community, guided always by limiting instructions on the law. To require a State to structure obscenity proceedings around evidence of a *national* "community standard" would be an exercise in [futility].

We conclude that neither the State's alleged failure to offer evidence of "national standards," nor the trial court's charge that the jury consider state community standards, were constitutional errors. Nothing in the First Amendment requires that a jury must consider hypothetical and unascertainable "national standards" when attempting to determine whether certain materials are obscene as a matter of [fact].

It is neither realistic nor constitutionally sound to read the First Amendment as requiring that the people of Maine or Mississippi accept public depiction of conduct found tolerable in Las Vegas, or New York City. People in different States vary in their tastes and attitudes, and this diversity is not to be strangled by the absolutism of imposed uniformity. As the Court made clear in *Mishkin,* the primary concern with requiring a jury to apply the standard of "the average person, applying contemporary community standards" is to be certain that, so far as material is not aimed at a deviant group, it will be judged by its impact on an average person, rather than a particularly susceptible or sensitive person—or indeed a totally insensitive one.[f] [We] hold the requirement that the jury evaluate the materials with reference to "contemporary standards of the State of California" serves this protective purpose and is constitutionally adequate.[g] * * *

In sum we (a) reaffirm the *Roth* holding that obscene material is not protected by the First Amendment, (b) hold that such material can be regulated by the States, subject to the specific safeguards enunciated above, without a showing that the material is "*utterly* without redeeming social value," and (c) hold that obscenity is to be determined by applying "contemporary community standards," not "national standards." * * *

f.   *Pinkus v. United States,* 436 U.S. 293, 98 S.Ct. 1808, 56 L.Ed.2d 293 (1978) upheld a jury instruction stating "you are to judge these materials by the standard of the hypothetical average person in the community, but in determining this average standard you must include the *sensitive and the insensitive,* in other words, [everyone] in the community." On the other hand, in the absence of evidence that "children were the intended recipients" or that defendant "had reason to know children were likely to receive the materials," it was considered erroneous to instruct the jury that children were part of the relevant community. *Butler.* When the evidence would support such a charge, the Court stated that prurient appeal to deviant sexual groups could be substituted for appeal to the average person; moreover, the jury was entitled to take pandering into account. *Ginzburg.*

g.   *Jenkins,* fn. b supra, stated that a judge may instruct a jury to apply "contemporary community standards" without any further specification. Alternatively, the state may choose "to define the standards in more precise geographic terms, as was done by California in *Miller.*" *Hamling,* fn. 7 supra, interpreted a federal obscenity statute to make the relevant community the one from which the jury was drawn. The judge's instruction to consider the "community standards of the 'nation as a whole' delineated a wider geographical area than would be warranted by [*Miller*]" or the Court's construction of the statute, but the error was regarded as harmless under the circumstances. See also *Sable Communications v. FCC,* Sec. 9, II, infra ("dial-a-porn" company bears burden of complying with congressional obscenity ban despite diverse local community standards). After these decisions, what advice should lawyers give to publishers who distribute in national markets?

JUSTICE DOUGLAS, dissenting. * * *

My contention is that until a civil proceeding has placed a tract beyond the pale, no criminal prosecution should be sustained. For no more vivid illustration of vague and uncertain laws could be designed than those we have fashioned. [If] a specific book [or] motion picture has in a civil proceeding been condemned as obscene and review of that finding has been completed, and thereafter a person publishes [or] displays that particular book or film, then a vague law has been made specific. There would remain the underlying question whether the First Amendment allows an implied exception in the case of obscenity. I do not think it does and my views on the issue have been stated over and again. But at least a criminal prosecution brought at that juncture would not violate the time-honored void-for-vagueness test.[8]

No such protective procedure has been designed by California in this case. Obscenity—which even we cannot define with precision—is a hodge-podge. To send men to jail for violating standards they cannot understand, construe, and apply is a monstrous thing to do in a Nation dedicated to fair trials and due process. * * *

JUSTICE BRENNAN, with whom JUSTICE STEWART and JUSTICE MARSHALL join, dissenting.

In my dissent in *Paris Adult Theatre,* decided this date, I noted that I had no occasion to consider the extent of state power to regulate the distribution of sexually oriented material to juveniles or the offensive exposure of such material to unconsenting adults. [I] need not now decide whether a statute might be drawn to impose, within the requirements of the First Amendment, criminal penalties for the precise conduct at issue here. For it is clear that under my dissent in *Paris Adult Theatre,* the statute under which the prosecution was brought is unconstitutionally overbroad, and therefore invalid on its face. * * *

[In his *Paris Adult Theatre* dissent, Brennan, J., joined by Stewart and Marshall, JJ., argued that the state interests in regulating obscenity were not strong enough to justify the degree of vagueness. He criticized not only the Court's standard in *Miller,* but also a range of alternatives:]

II. [The] essence of our problem [is] that we have been unable to provide "sensitive tools" to separate obscenity from other sexually oriented but constitutionally protected speech, so that efforts to suppress the former do not spill over into the suppression of the latter. [The dissent traced the Court's experience with *Roth* and its progeny.]

III. Our experience with the *Roth* approach has certainly taught us that the outright suppression of obscenity cannot be reconciled with the fundamental principles of the First and Fourteenth Amendments. For we have failed to formulate a standard that sharply distinguishes protected from unprotected speech, and out of necessity, we have resorted to the *Redrup* approach, which resolves cases as between the parties, but offers only the most obscure guidance to legislation, adjudication by other courts, and primary conduct. [T]he vagueness problem would be largely of our own creation if it stemmed primarily from our failure to reach a consensus on any one standard. But after 15 years of experimentation and debate I am reluctantly forced to the conclusion that none of the available formulas, including the one announced today, can reduce the vagueness to a tolerable level while at the same time striking an acceptable balance between

---

8. The Commission on Obscenity and Pornography has advocated such a procedure. [See] *Report of the Commission on Obscenity and Pornography* 70–71 (1970).

the protections of the First and Fourteenth Amendments, on the one hand, and on the other the asserted state interest in regulating the dissemination of certain sexually oriented materials. Any effort to draw a constitutionally acceptable boundary on state power must resort to such indefinite concepts as "prurient interest," "patent offensiveness," "serious literary value," and the like. The meaning of these concepts necessarily varies with the experience, outlook, and even idiosyncracies of the person defining them. Although we have assumed that obscenity does exist and that we "know it when [we] see it," *Jacobellis* (Stewart, J., concurring), we are manifestly unable to describe it in advance except by reference to concepts so elusive that they fail to distinguish clearly between protected and unprotected speech.

[Added to the inherent vagueness of standards] is the further complication that the obscenity of any particular item may depend upon nuances of presentation and the context of its dissemination. See *Ginzburg*. [N]o one definition, no matter how precisely or narrowly drawn, can possibly suffice for all situations, or carve out fully suppressible expression from all media without also creating a substantial risk of encroachment upon the guarantees of the Due Process Clause and the First Amendment.

[The] resulting level of uncertainty is utterly intolerable, not alone because it makes "[b]ookselling [a] hazardous profession," *Ginsberg* (Fortas, J., dissenting), but as well because it invites arbitrary and erratic enforcement of the law. [We] have indicated that "stricter standards of permissible statutory vagueness may be applied to a statute having a potentially inhibiting effect on speech; a man may the less be required to act at his peril here, because the free dissemination of ideas may be the loser." * * *

The problems of fair notice and chilling protected speech are very grave standing alone. But [a] vague statute in this area creates a third [set] of problems. These [concern] the institutional stress that inevitably results where the line separating protected from unprotected speech is excessively vague. [Almost] every obscenity case presents a constitutional question of exceptional difficulty. [As] a result of our failure to define standards with predictable application to any given piece of material, there is no probability of regularity in obscenity decisions by state and lower federal courts. [O]ne cannot say with certainty that material is obscene until at least five members of this Court, applying inevitably obscure standards, have pronounced it [so].

We have managed the burden of deciding scores of obscenity cases by relying on per curiam reversals or denials of certiorari—a practice which conceals the rationale of decision and gives at least the appearance of arbitrary action by this Court. More important, [the] practice effectively censors protected expression by leaving lower court determinations of obscenity intact even though the status of the allegedly obscene material is entirely unsettled until final review here. In addition, the uncertainty of the standards creates a continuing source of tension between state and federal [courts].

The severe problems arising from the lack of fair notice, from the chill on protected expression, and from the stress imposed on the state and federal judicial machinery persuade me that a significant change in direction is urgently required. I turn, therefore, to the alternatives that are now open.

IV. 1. The approach requiring the smallest deviation from our present course would be to draw a new line between protected and unprotected speech, still permitting the States to suppress all material on the unprotected side of the line. In my view, clarity cannot be obtained pursuant to this approach except by drawing a line that resolves all doubts in favor of state power and against the guarantees of the First Amendment. We could hold, for example, that any depiction or description of human sexual organs, irrespective of the manner or purpose of the portrayal, is outside the protection of the First Amendment and therefore open to suppression by the States. That formula would, no doubt, offer much fairer notice [and] give rise to a substantial probability of regularity in most judicial determinations under the standard. But such a standard would be appallingly overbroad, permitting the suppression of a vast range of literary, scientific, and artistic masterpieces. Neither the First Amendment nor any free community could possibly tolerate such a standard.

2. [T]he Court today recognizes that a prohibition against any depiction or description of human sexual organs could not be reconciled with the guarantees of the First Amendment. But the Court [adopts] a restatement of the *Roth-Memoirs* definition of obscenity [that] permits suppression if the government can prove that the materials lack "*serious* literary, artistic, political or scientific value." [In] *Roth* we held that certain expression is obscene, and thus outside the protection of the First Amendment, precisely *because* it lacks even the slightest redeeming social value. [The] Court's approach necessarily assumes that some works will be deemed obscene—even though they clearly have *some* social value—because the State was able to prove that the value, measured by some unspecified standard, was not sufficiently "serious" to warrant constitutional protection. That result [is] nothing less than a rejection of the fundamental First Amendment premises and rationale of the *Roth* opinion and an invitation to widespread suppression of sexually oriented speech. Before today, the protections of the First Amendment have never been thought limited to expressions of *serious* literary or political value. *Gooding v. Wilson; Cohen v. California; Terminiello v. Chicago* [Part V infra].

[T]he Court's approach [can] have no ameliorative impact on the cluster of problems that grow out of the vagueness of our current standards. Indeed, even the Court makes no argument that the reformulation will provide fairer notice to booksellers, theatre owners, and the reading and viewing public. Nor does the Court contend that the approach will provide clearer guidance to law enforcement officials or reduce the chill on protected expression [or] mitigate [the] institutional [problems].

Of course, the Court's restated *Roth* test does limit the definition of obscenity to depictions of physical conduct and explicit sexual acts. And that limitation may seem, at first glance, a welcome and clarifying addition to the *Roth-Memoirs* formula. But just as the agreement in *Roth* on an abstract definition of obscenity gave little hint of the extreme difficulty that was to follow in attempting to apply that definition to specific material, the mere formulation of a "physical conduct" test is no assurance that it can be applied with any greater facility. [The] Court surely demonstrates little sensitivity to our own institutional problems, much less the other vagueness-related difficulties, in establishing a system that requires us to consider whether a description of human genitals is sufficiently "lewd" to deprive it of constitutional protection; whether a sexual act is "ultimate"; whether the conduct depicted in materials before us fits within one of the categories of conduct whose depiction the state or federal governments have attempted to suppress; and a host of equally pointless inquiries. * * *

If the application of the "physical conduct" test to pictorial material is fraught with difficulty, its application to textual material carries the potential for extraordinary abuse. Surely we have passed the point where the mere written description of sexual conduct is deprived of First Amendment protection. Yet the test offers no guidance to us, or anyone else, in determining which written descriptions of sexual conduct are protected, and which are not.

Ultimately, the reformulation must fail because it still leaves in this Court the responsibility of determining in each case whether the materials are protected by the First Amendment. * * *

3. I have also considered the possibility of reducing our own role, and the role of appellate courts generally, in determining whether particular matter is obscene. Thus, [we] might adopt the position that where a lower federal or state court has conscientiously applied the constitutional standard, its finding of obscenity will be no more vulnerable to reversal by this Court than any finding of fact. [E]ven if the Constitution would permit us to refrain from judging for ourselves the alleged obscenity of particular materials, that approach would solve at best only a small part of our problem. For while it would mitigate the institutional stress, [it] would neither offer nor produce any cure for the other vices of vagueness. Far from providing a clearer guide to permissible primary conduct, the approach would inevitably lead to even greater uncertainty and the consequent due process problems of fair notice. And the approach would expose much protected, sexually oriented expression to the vagaries of jury determinations. Plainly, the institutional gain would be more than offset by the unprecedented infringement of First Amendment rights.

4. Finally, I have considered the view, urged so forcefully since 1957 by our Brothers Black and Douglas, that the First Amendment bars the suppression of any sexually oriented expression. That position would effect a sharp reduction, although perhaps not a total elimination, of the uncertainty that surrounds our current approach. Nevertheless, I am convinced that it would achieve that desirable goal only by stripping the States of power to an extent that cannot be justified by the commands of the Constitution, at least so long as there is available an alternative approach that strikes a better balance between the guarantee of free expression and the States' legitimate interests.

* * * I would hold, therefore, that at least in the absence of distribution to juveniles or obtrusive exposure to unconsenting adults, the First and Fourteenth Amendments prohibit the state and federal governments from attempting wholly to suppress sexually oriented materials on the basis of their allegedly "obscene" contents.[h] Nothing in this approach precludes those governments from taking action to serve what may be strong and legitimate interests through regulation of the manner of distribution of sexually oriented material.

VI. * * * I do not pretend to have found a complete and infallible [answer]. Difficult questions must still be faced, notably in the areas of distribution to juveniles and offensive exposure to unconsenting adults. Whatever the extent of state power to regulate in those areas,[29] it should be clear that the view I espouse today would introduce a large measure of clarity to this troubled area, would reduce the institutional pressure on this Court and the rest of the State and Federal judiciary, and would guarantee fuller freedom of expression while leaving room for the protection of legitimate governmental interests. * * *

h. For the portion of Brennan, J.'s dissent addressing the strength and legitimacy of the state interests, see *Paris Adult Theatre,* supra.

29. The Court erroneously states, *Miller,* that the author of this opinion "indicates that suppression of unprotected obscene material is permissible to avoid exposure to unconsenting adults [and] to juveniles * * *." I defer expression of my views as to the scope of state power in these areas until cases squarely presenting these questions are before the Court.

Notes and Questions

1. *Serious value.* Consider Harry Clor, *Obscenity and the First Amendment: Round Three,* 7 Loy.L.A.L.Rev. 207, 210, 218 (1974): "The *Miller* decision abandons the requirement that a censorable work must be *'utterly* without redeeming social value' and substitutes the rule of 'serious value'—literary, artistic, political, or scientific. This is the most important innovation in the law of obscenity introduced by these decisions. [Serious] literature is to be protected regardless of majority opinions about prurience and offensiveness. *This* is the national principle which is not subject to variation from community to community. If it is to perform this function, the rule will have to be elaborated and the meaning of 'serious value' articulated in some measure. This is the most important item on the legal agenda."

(a) *An independent factor?* Under *Miller* would material found to have "serious artistic value" be entitled to first amendment protection regardless of how offensive or prurient? Must each factor in the *Miller* guidelines be independently satisfied, as in *Memoirs? Should* that be so? Would or should that preclude the degree of offensiveness or prurient appeal from affecting the conclusion on the value factor?

(b) *"Serious."* Do you find any guidance for determining when a first amendment value in material depicting sexual conduct is sufficiently "serious" to preclude finding it obscene? Does *Pope v. Illinois,* 481 U.S. 497, 107 S.Ct. 1918, 95 L.Ed.2d 439 (1987) assist?: "The proper inquiry is not whether an ordinary member of any given community would find serious literary, artistic, political, or scientific value[,] but whether a reasonable person would find such value in the material taken as a whole."

(c) *Scope of protected values.* Could the Court consistent with the first amendment exclude serious educational value from those that preclude a finding of obscenity? Serious entertainment value? Could the guidelines be interpreted to include such values? What might explain their omission?

2. *Vagueness and scienter.* Is the *Miller* test intolerably vague? Are there any alternatives that could mitigate the problem? Consider William Lockhart, *Escape from the Chill of Uncertainty: Explicit Sex and the First Amendment,* 9 Ga.L.Rev. 533, 563 (1975): "[E]ither legislative action, or constitutional adjudication, could establish as a defense to a criminal obscenity prosecution that the defendant *reasonably believed* that the material involved was not obscene, that is, was constitutionally protected. [Material] that would support such a court or jury finding is not the kind that requires or justifies quick action by the police and prosecutor. The public interest in preventing distribution of borderline material that can reasonably be believed not obscene is not so pressing as to require immediate criminal sanctions and can adequately be protected by a declaratory judgment or injunction action to establish the obscenity of the material."

Smith v. California, 361 U.S. 147, 80 S.Ct. 215, 4 L.Ed.2d 205 (1959) invalidated an ordinance that dispensed with any requirement that a seller of an obscene book have knowledge of its contents, but did not decide what sort of mental element was needed to prosecute. *Hamling v. United States,* supra, stated that it was constitutionally sufficient to show that a distributor of an advertising collage of pictures of sexual acts "had knowledge of the contents of the materials [and] that he knew the character and nature of the materials." Would it be consistent with *Hamling* to afford constitutional protection to a distributor who reasonably believed the material disseminated was not obscene? See Lockhart, supra, at 568.

3. *The practical impact of Miller.* Consider Edward de Grazia, *Girls Lean Back Everywhere: The Law of Obscenity and the Assault on Genius* 561–62, 571 (1992); Until Powell, J., switched his vote, Brennan, J., and "a Court majority were preparing to reverse [Miller's] obscenity conviction. [T]he Burger revision of the Brennan doctrine was soon revealed to be a sort of paper tiger[, however]; by and large, there in fact occurred no observable retardation of the country's move during the decade that followed toward nearly absolute freedom for sexual expression in literary and artistic modes, including graphic or pictorial pornography; no increase in lower court convictions for obscenity; and no increase in prosecutorial [activity]." See also David Cole, *Playing by Pornography's Rules: The Regulation of Sexual Expression,* 143 U.Pa.L.Rev. 111, 170, 173 (1994): "Because this prohibition is so narrow, it serves in practice not so much to purge the community of explicit sexually arousing speech as to validate everything that remains as nonoffensive, 'normal,' or socially valuable. In this way, obscenity doctrine collectively assures the community that the pornography it consumes at such a high rate is acceptable. [There] are the few who are actually prosecuted; given the remarkable amount and variety of sexual expression that goes without prosecution, to be prosecuted for obscenity these days is akin to being struck by lightning."

C. VAGUENESS AND OVERBREADTH: AN OVERVIEW

In *Paris Adult Theatre,* Brennan, J., dissents on the ground that the obscenity statute is unconstitutionally vague. He envisions the possibility that an obscenity statute might overcome his vagueness objection if it were tailored to combat distribution to unconsenting adults or to children. In *Miller,* the materials were in fact distributed to unconsenting adults. There Brennan, J., does not reach the vagueness question but objects on the ground that the statute is overbroad,—i.e., it is not confined to the protection of unconsenting adults and children, but also prohibits distribution of obscene materials to consenting adults. In Brennan, J.'s view, even if the particular conduct at issue in *Miller* might be constitutionally prohibited by a narrower statute, it cannot be reached under a statute that sweeps so much protected speech within its terms.

The doctrines of "vagueness" and "overbreadth" referred to in Brennan, J.'s dissents are deeply embedded in first amendment jurisprudence. At first glance, the doctrines appear discrete. A statute that prohibits the use of the words "kill" and "President" in the same sentence may not be vague, but it is certainly overbroad even though some sentences using those words may be unprotected. Conversely, a vague statute may not be overbroad; it may not pertain to first amendment freedoms at all, or it may clearly be intended to exclude all protected speech from its prohibition but use vague language to accomplish that purpose.

Ordinarily, however, the problems of "vagueness" and "overbreadth" are closely related. An Airport Commissioners resolution banning all "First Amendment activities" in the Los Angeles International Airport was declared overbroad in *Board of Airport Commissioners v. Jews for Jesus,* 482 U.S. 569, 107 S.Ct. 2568, 96 L.Ed.2d 500 (1987). Literally read the statute would have prevented anyone from talking or reading in the airport. But if the language literally covers a variety of constitutionally protected activities, it *cannot be read literally.* If the statute cannot be read according to its terms, however, problems of vagueness will often emerge. To be sure, statutes may be interpreted in ways that will avoid vagueness or overbreadth difficulties. See, e.g., *Scales v. United States,* Sec. 1, I, D supra. It is established doctrine, for example, that an attack based either upon vagueness or overbreadth will be unsuccessful in federal court if the statute in question is "readily subject to a narrowing construction by the state courts." *Young v. American Mini Theatres, Inc.; Erznoznik v. Jacksonville,* Sec. 3, A infra. Moreover, "[f]or the purpose of determining whether a state statute is too vague and indefinite to constitute valid legislation [the Court takes] 'the statute as though it read precisely as the highest court of the State has interpreted it.'" *Wainwright v. Stone,* 414 U.S. 21, 94 S.Ct. 190, 38 L.Ed.2d 179 (1973). Under this policy, a litigant can be prosecuted successfully for violating a statute that by its terms appears vague or overbroad but is interpreted by the state court in the same prosecution to mean something clearer or narrower than its literal language would dictate. *Cox v. New Hampshire,* Sec. 7, I, A infra. The harshness of this doctrine is mitigated somewhat by the fact that "unexpected" or "unforeseeable" judicial constructions in such contexts violate due process. See *Marks v. United States,* 430 U.S. 188, 97 S.Ct. 990, 51 L.Ed.2d 260 (1977).[a]

Somewhat more complicated is the issue of when general attacks on a statute are permitted. Plainly litigants may argue that statutes are vague as to their own conduct or that their own speech is protected. In other words, litigants are always free to argue that a statute is invalid "as applied" to their own conduct. The dispute concerns when litigants can attack a statute without reference to their own conduct, an attack sometimes called "on its face."

A separate question is: when should such attacks result in partial or total invalidation of a statute? The terminology here has become as confused as the issues. In the past, the Court has frequently referred to facial attacks on statutes in a way that embraces attempts at either partial or total invalidation. In some recent opinions, however, including those quoted below, it uses the term "facial attack" or "on its face" to refer only to arguments seeking total invalidation of a statute.

Terminology aside, one of the recurrent questions has been the extent to which litigants may argue that a statute is unconstitutionally overbroad even though their own conduct would not otherwise be constitutionally protected. This is often characterized as a standing issue. Ordinarily litigants do not have standing to raise the rights of others. See Ch. 12, Sec. 1, II, B. But it has been argued that litigants should have standing to challenge overbroad statutes even if their own conduct would be otherwise unprotected in order to prevent a chilling effect on freedom of speech. Alternatively, it has been argued that no standing problem is genuinely presented because "[u]nder 'conventional' standing principles, a litigant has always had the right to be judged in accordance with a constitutionally valid rule of law." Henry Monaghan, *Overbreadth,* 1981 S.Ct.Rev. 1, 3. On this view, if a statute is unconstitutionally overbroad, it is not a valid rule of law, and any defendant prosecuted under the statute has standing to make that claim.[b] However the issue may be characterized, White, J., contended for many

a. For commentary on overbreadth with special focus on the implications of the doctrine mentioned in this paragraph, see Richard Fallon, *Making Sense of Overbreadth,* 100 Yale L.J. 853 (1991).

b. See also Henry Monaghan, *Third Party Standing,* 84 Colum.L.Rev. 277 (1984). See also Robert Sedler, *The Assertion of Constitutional Jus Tertii: A Substantive Approach,* 70 Calif.L.Rev. 1308, 1327 (1982) ("It may be the

potential chilling effect upon others' expression that makes the statute invalid, but the litigant has his own right not to be subject to the operation of an invalid statute."). For criticism of the Monaghan position, see Richard Fallon, supra note a, at 871–75; Alfred Hill, *The Puzzling Overbreadth Doctrine,* 25 Hofstra L.Rev. 1063 (1997); Lawrence Gene Sager, *Foreword: State Courts and the Strategic Space Between*

years that a litigant whose own conduct is unprotected should not prevail on an overbreadth challenge without a showing that the statute's overbreadth is "real and substantial." After much litigation, White, J., finally prevailed. The "substantial" overbreadth doctrine now burdens all litigants who argue that a statute should be declared overbroad when their own conduct would otherwise be unprotected.[c] *Brockett v. Spokane Arcades, Inc.; New York v. Ferber,* Sec. 1, V, A infra.

Less clear are the circumstances in which a litigant whose conduct *is* protected can go beyond a claim that the statute is unconstitutional "as applied." Again, litigants are always free to argue that their own conduct is protected. Moreover, the Court has stated that "[t]here is no reason to limit challenges to case-by-case 'as applied' challenges when the statute [in] all its applications falls short of constitutional demands."[d] *Secretary of State of Maryland v. Joseph H. Munson Co.,* 467 U.S. 947, 104 S.Ct. 2839, 81 L.Ed.2d 786 (1984). How far beyond this the Court will go is unclear. In *Brockett v. Spokane Arcades, Inc.,* Sec. 1, III, B supra, it referred to the "normal rule that partial, rather than facial invalidation" of statutes is to be preferred and observed that: "[A]n individual whose own speech or expressive conduct may validly be prohibited or sanctioned is permitted to challenge a statute on its face because it also threatens others not before the court—those who desire to engage in legally protected expression but who may refrain from doing so rather than risk prosecution or undertake to have the law declared partially invalid. If the overbreadth is 'substantial,' the law may not be enforced against anyone, including the party before the court, until it is narrowed to reach only unprotected activity, whether by legislative action or by judicial construction or partial invalidation.

"It is otherwise where the parties challenging the statute are those who desire to engage in protected speech that the overbroad statute purports to punish, or who seek to publish both protected and unprotected material. There is then no want of a proper party to challenge the statute, no concern that an attack on the statute will be unduly delayed or protected speech discouraged. The statute may forthwith be declared invalid to the extent that it reaches too far, but otherwise left intact."[e]

Brockett takes the view that it must give standing to the otherwise unprotected to raise an overbreadth challenge, in order to secure the rights of those whose speech should be protected. But it sees no purpose in giving standing to the protected in order to secure rights for those whose speech should not be protected. This position is not without its ironies. In some circumstances, a litigant whose speech is unprotected will be in a better position than one whose speech is

---

the Norms and Rules of Constitutional Law, 63 Tex. L.Rev. 959, 967 & n. 22 (1985).

c. For commentary on the concept of "substantial" overbreadth, see Fallon, supra; Lawrence A. Alexander, *Is There an Overbreadth Doctrine,* 22 San Diego L.Rev. 541, 553–54 (1985); Martin Redish, *The Warren Court, The Burger Court and the First Amendment Overbreadth Doctrine,* 78 Nw.U.L.Rev. 1031, 1056–69 (1983).

d. There is a terminological dispute here. Compare *Los Angeles City Council v. Taxpayers For Vincent,* Sec. 7, II infra (such challenges are not overbreadth challenges) with *Munson,* supra (such challenges are properly called overbreadth challenges).

e. After the Court has declared that the statute is invalid to the extent it reaches too far, the remaining portion of the statute will be examined to determine whether that portion is severable. That is, it could well be the intent of the legislature that the statute stands or falls as a single package. To invalidate a part, then, could be to invalidate the whole. Alternatively, the legislature may have intended to salvage whatever it might. The question of severability is regarded as one of legislative intent, but, at least with respect to federal legislation, courts will presume that severability was intended. See, e.g., *Regan v. Time, Inc.,* 468 U.S. 641, 104 S.Ct. 3262, 82 L.Ed.2d 487 (1984). The question of whether a provision of a state statute is severable is one of state law.

protected, at least if the litigant's goal is completely to stop enforcement of a statute.

Finally, what of the cases when it is uncertain whether the litigant's speech is protected? Should courts consider as applied attacks before proceeding to overbreadth attacks? *Board of Trustees v. Fox,* Sec. 3, II infra, declared it "not the usual judicial practice" and "generally undesirable" to proceed to an overbreadth challenge without first determining whether the statute would be valid as applied.[f] Yet the Court has frequently (see, e.g., Sec. 1, IV, C infra (fighting words cases; *Jews For Jesus*)) declared statutes overbroad without an as applied determination. The Court has yet systematically to detail the considerations relevant to separating the "usual" judicial practice from the unusual.

The issues with respect to vagueness challenges are similar. It remains possible, however, that the Court will resolve them in ways different from the approaches it has fashioned in the law of overbreadth. White, J., argued for a different course. He maintained that vagueness challenges should be confined to "as applied" attacks unless a statute were vague in all of its applications. Accordingly, if a statute clearly proscribed the conduct of a particular defendant, to allow that defendant to challenge a statute for vagueness would in his view have been "to confound vagueness and overbreadth." *Kolender v. Lawson,* 461 U.S. 352, 103 S.Ct. 1855, 75 L.Ed.2d 903 (1983) (White, J., dissenting). In response, the Court stated that a facial attack upon a statute need not depend upon a showing of vagueness in all of a statute's applications: "[W]e permit a facial challenge if a law reaches 'a substantial amount of constitutionally protected conduct,'" *Kolender.* Moreover, the Court has previously allowed litigants to raise the vagueness issue "even though there is no uncertainty about the impact of the ordinances on their own rights." *Young.* But see, e.g., *Broadrick v. Oklahoma,* Sec. 1, V, A infra, in which White, J., writing for the Court suggested that standing to raise the vagueness argument should not be permitted in this situation.

Much less clear are the circumstances in which litigants whose conduct is *not* clearly covered by a statute can go beyond an "as applied" attack.[g] One approach would be to apply the same rule to all litigants, e.g., allowing total invalidation of statutes upon a showing of a "substantial" vagueness. In *Kolender,* the Court made no determination whether the statute involved was vague as to the defendant's own conduct; arguably, the opinion implied that it made no difference. Another approach would analogize to the approach suggested in *Brockett* for overbreadth challenges. Thus, a court might refrain from total invalidation of a statute and confine itself to striking the vague part insofar as the vague part seems to cover protected speech, leaving the balance of the statute intact. *Kolender* itself recites that the Court has "traditionally regarded vagueness and overbreadth as logically related and similar doctrines," but the Court's attitudes toward vagueness remain unclear. The questions of what standards should govern challenges to statutes that go beyond the facts before the Court, who should be able to raise the challenges, and under what circumstances have not been systematically and consistently addressed.[h]

f. The case arose in the federal courts, and the Court might be less likely to remand to a state court for an as applied determination, but the Court did not address that distinction.

g. Conceivably, it could make a difference whether the litigants in this class of those "not clearly covered" have engaged in protected or unprotected conduct.

h. For commentary on vagueness and overbreadth, see, e.g., Melville Nimmer, *Nimmer on Freedom of Speech,* 4–147—4–162 (1984); Larry Alexander, *Is There an Overbreadth Doctrine?,* 22 San Diego L.Rev. 541 (1985); Anthony Amsterdam, *The Void–For–Vagueness Doctrine in the Supreme Court,* 109 U.Pa.L.Rev. 67 (1960); David Bogen, *First Amendment Ancil-*

IV. "FIGHTING WORDS," OFFENSIVE WORDS AND HOSTILE AUDIENCES

A. FIGHTING WORDS

CHAPLINSKY v. NEW HAMPSHIRE, 315 U.S. 568, 62 S.Ct. 766, 86 L.Ed. 1031 (1942): In the course of proselytizing on the streets, appellant, a Jehovah's Witness, denounced organized religion. Despite the city marshal's warning to "go slow" because his listeners were upset with his attacks on religion, appellant continued and a disturbance occurred. At this point, a police officer led appellant toward the police station, without arresting him. While en route, appellant again encountered the city marshal who had previously admonished him. Appellant then said to the marshal (he claimed, but the marshal denied, in response to the marshal's cursing him): "You are a God damned racketeer" and "a damned Fascist and the whole government of Rochester are Fascists or agents of Fascists." He was convicted of violating a state statute forbidding anyone to address "any offensive, derisive or annoying word to any other person who is lawfully in any [public place] [or] call[ing] him by any offensive or derisive name." The Court, per MURPHY, J., upheld the conviction:

"There are certain well-defined and narrowly limited classes of speech, the prevention and punishment of which have never been thought to raise any Constitutional problem.[a] These include the lewd and obscene, the profane, the libelous, and the insulting or 'fighting' words—those which by their very utterance inflict injury (or) tend to incite an immediate breach of the peace. [S]uch utterances are no essential part of any exposition of ideas, and are of such slight social value as a step to truth that any benefit that may be derived from them is clearly outweighed by the social interest in order and morality. * * *

"On the authority of its earlier decisions, the state court declared that the statute's purpose was to preserve the public peace, no words being 'forbidden except such as have a direct tendency to cause acts of violence by the person to whom, individually, the remark is addressed'. It was further said: 'The word "offensive" is not to be defined in terms of what a particular addressee thinks. [The] test is what men of common intelligence would understand would be words likely to cause an average addressee to fight. [The] English language has a number of words and expressions which by general consent are "fighting words"

lary Doctrines, 37 Md.L.Rev. 679, 705–26 (1978); Monaghan, supra; Redish, supra; Note, *The First Amendment Overbreadth Doctrine,* 83 Harv.L.Rev. 844 (1970).

a. See Franklyn Haiman, *How Much of Our Speech is Free?,* The Civ.Lib.Rev., Winter, 1975, pp. 111, 123: "[T]his discrimination between two classes of speech made its first U.S. Supreme Court appearance in *Cantwell v. Connecticut* (1940) [Ch. 8, Sec. 2, I infra]." Jehovah's Witnesses had been convicted of religious solicitation without a permit and of breach of the peace. The Court set aside both convictions. It invalidated the permit system for "religious" solicitation, because it permitted the licensing official to determine what causes were "religious," thus allowing a "censorship of religion." In setting aside the breach of peace conviction, because the offense covered much protected conduct and left "too wide a discretion in its application," the Court, per Roberts, J., noted: "One may, however, be guilty of [breach of the peace] if he commits acts or makes statements likely to provoke violence and disturbance of good order. [I]n practically all [such decisions to this effect], the provocative language [held to constitute] a breach of the peace consisted of profane, indecent or abusive remarks directed to the person of the hearer. *Resort to epithets or personal abuse is not in any proper sense communication of information or opinion safeguarded by the Constitution,* and its punishment as a criminal act [under a narrowly drawn statute] would raise no question under that instrument." (Emphasis added). For commentary, see Robert Post, *Cultural Heterogeneity and Law,* 76 Calif.L.Rev. 297 (1988).

when said without a disarming smile. [Such] words, as ordinary men know, are likely to cause a fight. So are threatening, profane or obscene revilings. Derisive and annoying words can be taken as coming within the purview of the statute as heretofore interpreted only when they have this characteristic of plainly tending to excite the addressee to a breach of the peace. [The] statute, as construed, does no more than prohibit the face-to-face words plainly likely to cause a breach of the peace by the addressee, words whose speaking constitute a breach of the peace by the speaker—including "classical fighting words", words in current use less "classical" but equally likely to cause violence, and other disorderly words, including profanity, obscenity and threats.'

"[A] statute punishing verbal acts, carefully drawn so as not unduly to impair liberty of expression, is not too vague for a criminal law. * * *[8]

"Nor can we say that the application of the statute to the facts disclosed by the record substantially or unreasonably impinges upon the privilege of free speech. Argument is unnecessary to demonstrate that the appellations 'damn racketeer' and 'damn Fascist' are epithets likely to provoke the average person to retaliation, and thereby cause a breach of the peace.

"The refusal of the state court to admit evidence of provocation and evidence bearing on the truth or falsity of the utterances is open to no Constitutional objection. Whether the facts sought to be proved by such evidence constitute a defense to the charge or may be shown in mitigation are questions for the state court to determine. Our function is fulfilled by a determination that the challenged statute, on its face and as applied, does not contravene the Fourteenth Amendment."

Notes and Questions

1. *Fighting words and free speech values.* (a) *Self realization.* Does speech have to step toward truth to be of first amendment value? Consider Martin Redish, *The Value of Free Speech,* 130 U.Pa.L.Rev. 591, 626 (1982): "Why not view Chaplinsky's comments as a personal catharsis, as a means to vent his frustration at a system he deemed—whether rightly or wrongly—to be oppressive? Is it not a mark of individuality to be able to cry out at a society viewed as crushing the individual? Under this analysis, so-called 'fighting words' represent a significant means of self-realization, whether or not they can be considered a means of attaining some elusive 'truth.' "

(b) *Fighting words and truth.* Are fighting words always false? Should truth be a defense? Always?

(c) *Fighting words and self-government.* Was Chaplinsky's statement *something other than* the expression of an idea? Did he wish to inform the marshal of his opinion of him and did he do so "in a way which was not only unquestionably clear, [but] all too clear"? Arnold Loewy, *Punishing Flag Desecrators,* 49 N.C.L.Rev. 48, 82 (1970). How significant is it that Chaplinsky's remarks were not made in the context of a public debate or discussion of political or social issues? Taking into account the events preceding Chaplinsky's remarks, and that the addressee was "an important representative of the Rochester city government,"

---

8. [Even] if the interpretative gloss placed on the statute by the court below be disregarded, the statute had been previously construed as intended to preserve the public peace by punishing conduct, the direct tendency of which was to provoke the person against whom it was directed to acts of violence.

Appellant need not therefore have been a prophet to understand what the statute condemned.

may Chaplinsky's epithets be viewed as "a sharply-expressed form of political protest against indifferent or biased police services in the enforcement of his right to free speech"? Mark Rutzick, *Offensive Language and the Evolution of First Amendment Protection,* 9 Harv.Civ.Rts.—Civ.Lib.L.Rev. 1 (1974). If the speech is directed at a police officer or other official in his representative capacity, is "the real target the government"? See id.

2. *The social interest in order and morality.* What was the social interest in this case? (a) *The likelihood and immediacy of violent retaliation?* Should the Court have considered whether a *law enforcement officer* so reviled would have been provoked to retaliate? Whatever is assumed about the reaction of an average citizen to offensive words, may it be assumed that police are "trained to remain calm in the face of citizen anger such as that expressed by Chaplinsky"? Rutzick, supra, at 10. See also Powell, J., concurring in *Lewis v. New Orleans,* Sec. 1, IV, C infra; Note, 53 B.U.L.Rev. 834, 847 (1973).

(b) *The highly personal nature of the insult, delivered face to face?* Was the marshal "verbally slapped in the face"? May the *Chaplinsky* statute be viewed as "a special type of assault statute"? See Loewy, supra, at 83–84. See also Thomas Emerson, *The System of Freedom of Expression* 337–38 (1970).

B. HOSTILE AUDIENCES

TERMINIELLO v. CHICAGO, 337 U.S. 1, 69 S.Ct. 894, 93 L.Ed. 1131 (1949): Petitioner "vigorously, if not viciously" criticized various political and racial groups and condemned "a surging, howling mob" gathered in protest outside the auditorium in which he spoke. He called his adversaries "slimy scum," "snakes," "bedbugs," and the like. Those inside the hall could hear those on the outside yell, "Fascists, Hitlers!" The crowd outside tried to tear the clothes off those who entered. About 28 windows were broken; stink bombs were thrown. But in charging the jury, the trial court defined "breach of the peace" to include speech which "stirs the public to anger, *invites dispute,* [or] brings about a condition of unrest (emphasis added)." A 5–4 majority, per Douglas, J., struck down the breach of peace ordinance as thus construed: "[A] function of free speech under our system of government is to invite dispute. It may indeed best serve its high purpose when it induces a condition of unrest, creates dissatisfaction with conditions as they are, or even stirs people to anger. [That] is why freedom of speech, though not absolute, *Chaplinsky,* is nevertheless protected against censorship or punishment, unless shown likely to produce a clear and present danger of a serious substantive evil that rises far above public inconvenience, annoyance, or unrest."

FEINER v. NEW YORK, 340 U.S. 315, 71 S.Ct. 303, 95 L.Ed. 295 (1951): Petitioner made a speech on a street corner in a predominantly black residential section of Syracuse, N.Y. A crowd of 75 to 80 persons, black and white, gathered around him, and several pedestrians had to go into the highway in order to pass by. A few minutes after he started, two police officers arrived and observed the rest of the meeting. In the course of his speech, publicizing a meeting of the Young Progressives of America to be held that evening in a local hotel and protesting the revocation of a permit to hold the meeting in a public school auditorium, petitioner referred to the President as a "bum," to the American Legion as "a Nazi Gestapo," and to the Mayor of Syracuse as a "champagne-sipping bum" who "does not speak for the Negro people." He also indicated in an excited manner: "The Negroes don't have equal rights; they should rise up in arms and fight for them."

These statements "stirred up a little excitement." One man indicated that if the police did not get that "S * * * O * * * B* * *" off the stand, he would do so himself. There was not yet a disturbance, but according to police testimony "angry muttering and pushing." In the words of the arresting officer whose testimony was accepted by the trial judge, he "stepped in to prevent it from resulting in a fight." After disregarding two requests to stop speaking, petitioner was arrested and convicted for disorderly conduct. The Court, per VINSON, C.J., affirmed: "The language of *Cantwell* is appropriate here. '[Nobody would] suggest that the principle of freedom of speech sanctions incitement to riot or that religious liberty connotes the privilege to exhort others to physical attack upon those belonging to another sect. When clear and present danger of riot, disorder, interference with traffic upon the public street or other immediate threat to public safety, peace, or order, appears, the power of the State to prevent or punish is obvious.'

"[It] is one thing to say that the police cannot be used as an instrument for the suppression of unpopular views, and another to say that, when as here the speaker passes the bounds of argument or persuasion and undertakes incitement to riot, they are powerless to prevent a breach of the peace. Nor in this case can we condemn the considered judgment of three New York courts approving the means which the police, faced with a crisis, used in the exercise of their power and duty to preserve peace and order."

BLACK, J., dissented: "The Court's opinion apparently rests on this reasoning: The policeman, under the circumstances detailed, could reasonably conclude that serious fighting or even riot was imminent; therefore he could stop petitioner's speech to prevent a breach of peace; accordingly, it was 'disorderly conduct' for petitioner to continue speaking in disobedience of the officer's request. As to the existence of a dangerous situation on the street corner, it seems far-fetched to suggest that the 'facts' show any imminent threat of riot or uncontrollable disorder. It is neither unusual nor unexpected that some people at public street meetings mutter, mill about, push, shove, or disagree, even violently, with the speaker. Indeed, it is rare where controversial topics are discussed that an outdoor crowd does not do some or all of these things. Nor does one isolated threat to assault the speaker forebode disorder. Especially should the danger be discounted where, as here, the person threatening was a man whose wife and two small children accompanied him and who, so far as the record shows, was never close enough to petitioner to carry out the threat.

"Moreover, assuming that the 'facts' did indicate a critical situation, I reject the implication of the Court's opinion that the police had no obligation to protect petitioner's constitutional right to talk. The police of course have power to prevent breaches of the peace. But if, in the name of preserving order, they ever can interfere with a lawful public speaker, they first must make all reasonable efforts to protect him. Here the policemen did not even pretend to try to protect petitioner. According to the officers' testimony, the crowd was restless but there is no showing of any attempt to quiet it; pedestrians were forced to walk into the street, but there was no effort to clear a path on the sidewalk; one person threatened to assault petitioner but the officers did nothing to discourage this when even a word might have sufficed. Their duty was to protect petitioner's right to talk, even to the extent of arresting the man who threatened to interfere. Instead, they shirked that duty and acted only to suppress the right to speak.

"Finally, I cannot agree with the Court's statement that petitioner's disregard of the policeman's unexplained request amounted to such 'deliberate defiance' as would justify an arrest or conviction for disorderly conduct. On the contrary, I think that the policeman's action was a 'deliberate defiance' of ordinary official duty as well as of the constitutional right of free speech. For at least where time allows, courtesy and explanation of commands are basic elements of good official conduct in a democratic society. Here petitioner was 'asked' then 'told' then 'commanded' to stop speaking, but a man making a lawful address is certainly not required to be silent merely because an officer directs it. Petitioner was entitled to know why he should cease doing a lawful act. Not once was he told."

DOUGLAS, J., joined by Minton, J., dissented: "A speaker may not, of course, incite a riot any more than he may incite a breach of the peace by the use of 'fighting words'. But this record shows no such extremes. It shows an unsympathetic audience and the threat of one man to haul the speaker from the stage. It is against that kind of threat that speakers need police protection. If they do not receive it and instead the police throw their weight on the side of those who would break up the meetings, the police become the new censors of speech. Police censorship has all the vices of the censorship from city halls which we have repeatedly struck down."

Notes and Questions

1. What was the subject of disagreement in *Feiner*? (1) The standard for police interruption of a speech when danger of violence exists and the speaker intends to create disorder rather than to communicate ideas? (2) The standard when such danger exists, but the speaker only desires to communicate ideas? (3) Whether the danger of disorder and violence *was* plain and imminent? (4) Whether the speaker *did* intend to create disorder and violence?

May *Feiner* be limited to the proposition that when a speaker "incites to riot"—but only then—police may stop him without bothering to keep his audience in check? Cf. *Sellers v. Johnson,* 163 F.2d 877 (8th Cir.1947), cert. denied, 332 U.S. 851, 68 S.Ct. 356, 92 L.Ed. 421 (1948). See Richard Stewart, *Public Speech and Public Order in Britain and the United States,* 13 Vand.L.Rev. 625, 632–33 (1960).

Should the speech *always* be prohibitable when the speaker intends to create disorder, rather than communicate ideas? Should the speech be prohibitable *only* under these circumstances? Should a speech *ever* be prohibitable because listeners arrive or will arrive, as they would have in *Sellers,* with a preconceived intent to create disturbance? Is the only really difficult problem in this area posed when *neither* the speaker *nor* the audience which gathers intends to create disorder, but the audience becomes *genuinely* aroused, honestly—whether or not justifiably—enraged? Here, should the police protect the speech to the fullest extent possible? If they are firmly told they must before they can arrest the speaker, what is the likelihood that adequate preventive steps will be taken? See Walter Gellhorn, *American Rights* 55–62 (1960); Note, 49 Colum.L.Rev. 1118, 1123–24 (1949).

2. *Edwards v. South Carolina,* 372 U.S. 229, 83 S.Ct. 680, 9 L.Ed.2d 697 (1963) reversed a breach of the peace conviction of civil rights demonstrators who refused to disperse within 15 minutes of a police command. The Court maintained

that the 200 to 300 onlookers did not threaten violence and that the police protection was ample. It described the situation as a "far cry from [*Feiner*]." Clark, J., dissenting, pointed to the racially charged atmosphere ("200 youthful Negro demonstrators were being aroused to a 'fever pitch' before a crowd of some 300 people who undoubtedly were hostile.") and concluded that city officials in good faith believed that disorder and violence were imminent. Did *Edwards* miss a golden opportunity to clarify *Feiner*? What if the crowd had been pushing, shoving and pressing more closely around the demonstrators in *Edwards*? Would the case still be a "far cry" from *Feiner* because the demonstrators had not "passed the bounds of argument or persuasion and undertaken incitement to riot"?

3. In the advocacy of illegal action context, the fear of violence arises from audience cooperation with the speaker. In the hostile audience context, the fear of violence arises from audience conflict with the speaker. How do the elements set out in *Brandenburg* relate to those implied in *Feiner*? How should they relate? Should the standard for "fighting words" cases be different from the "hostile audience" cases?

4. Should police be able to prosecute or silence disruptive audiences? Heckling audiences? In what contexts? See generally *In re Kay,* 1 Cal.3d 930, 83 Cal.Rptr. 686, 464 P.2d 142 (1970).

C. OFFENSIVE WORDS

COHEN v. CALIFORNIA

403 U.S. 15, 91 S.Ct. 1780, 29 L.Ed.2d 284 (1971).

JUSTICE HARLAN delivered the opinion of the Court.

[Defendant was convicted of violating that part of a general California disturbing-the-peace statute which prohibits "maliciously and willfully disturb[ing] the peace or quiet of any neighborhood or person" by "offensive conduct." He had worn a jacket bearing the plainly visible words "Fuck the Draft" in a Los Angeles courthouse corridor, where women and children were present. He testified that he did so as a means of informing the public of the depth of his feelings against the Vietnam War and the draft. He did not engage in, nor threaten, any violence, nor was anyone who saw him violently aroused. Nor was there any evidence that he uttered any sound prior to his arrest. In affirming, the California Court of Appeal construed "offensive conduct" to mean "behavior which has a tendency to provoke *others* to acts of violence or to in turn disturb the peace" and held that the state had proved this element because it was "reasonably foreseeable" that defendant's conduct "might cause others to rise up to commit a violent act against [him] or attempt to forceably remove his jacket."]

In order to lay hands on the precise issue which this case involves, it is useful first to canvass various matters which this record does *not* present.

The conviction quite clearly rests upon the asserted offensiveness of the *words* Cohen used to convey his message to the public. The only "conduct" which the State sought to punish is the fact of communication. Thus, we deal here with a conviction resting solely upon "speech," not upon any separately identifiable conduct which allegedly was intended by Cohen to be perceived by others as expressive of particular views but which, on its face, does not necessarily convey any message and hence arguably could be regulated without effectively repressing Cohen's ability to express himself. Cf. *United States v. O'Brien* [Sec. 2 infra]. Further, the State certainly lacks power to punish Cohen for the underlying content of the message the inscription conveyed. At least so long as there is no showing of an intent to incite disobedience to or disruption of the draft, Cohen could not, consistently with the First and Fourteenth Amendments, be punished for asserting the evident position on the inutility or immorality of the draft his jacket reflected. *Yates.*

Appellant's conviction, then, rests squarely upon his exercise [of] "freedom of speech" [and] can be justified, if at all, only as a valid regulation of the manner in which he exercised that freedom, not as a permissible prohibition on the substantive message it conveys. This does not end the inquiry, of course, for the First and Fourteenth Amendments have never been thought to give absolute protection to every individual to speak whenever or wherever he pleases, or to use any form of address in any circumstances that he chooses. In this vein, too, however, we think it important to note that several issues typically associated with such problems are not presented here.

In the first place, Cohen was tried under a statute applicable throughout the entire State. Any attempt to support this conviction on the ground that the statute seeks to preserve an appropriately decorous atmosphere in the courthouse where Cohen was arrested must fail in the absence of any language in the statute that would have put appellant on notice that certain kinds of otherwise permissible speech or conduct would nevertheless, under California law, not be tolerated in certain places. No fair reading of the phrase "offensive conduct" can be said sufficiently to inform the ordinary person that distinctions between certain locations are thereby created.[3]

In the second place, as it comes to us, this case cannot be said to fall within those relatively few categories of instances where prior decisions have established the power of government to deal more comprehensively with certain forms of individual expression simply upon a showing that such a form was employed. This is not, for example, an obscenity case. Whatever else may be necessary to give rise to the States' broader power to prohibit obscene expression, such expression must be, in some significant way, erotic. *Roth.* It cannot plausibly be maintained that this vulgar allusion to the Selective Service System would conjure up such psychic stimulation in anyone likely to be confronted with Cohen's crudely defaced jacket.

This Court has also held that the States are free to ban the simple use, without a demonstration of additional justifying circumstances, of so-called "fighting words," those personally abusive epithets which, when addressed to the ordinary citizen, are, as a matter of common knowledge, inherently likely to provoke violent reaction. *Chaplinsky.* While the four-letter word displayed by Cohen in relation to the draft is not uncommonly employed in a personally provocative fashion, in this instance it was clearly not "directed to the person of the hearer." No individual actually or likely to be present could reasonably have regarded the words on appellant's jacket as a direct personal insult. Nor do we have here an instance of the exercise of the State's police power to prevent a speaker from intentionally provoking a given group to hostile reaction. Cf. *Feiner; Terminiello.* There is, as noted above, no showing that anyone who saw Cohen was in fact violently aroused or that appellant intended such a result.

---

3. It is illuminating to note what transpired when Cohen entered a courtroom in the building. He removed his jacket and stood with it folded over his arm. Meanwhile, a policeman sent the presiding judge a note suggesting that Cohen be held in contempt of court. The judge declined to do so and Cohen was arrested by the officer only after he emerged from the courtroom.

[T]he mere presumed presence of unwitting listeners or viewers does not serve automatically to justify curtailing all speech capable of giving offense. While this Court has recognized that government may properly act in many situations to prohibit intrusion into the privacy of the home of unwelcome views and ideas which cannot be totally banned from the public dialogue, we have at the same time consistently stressed that "we are often 'captives' outside the sanctuary of the home and subject to objectionable speech."[a] The ability of government, consonant with the Constitution, to shut off discourse solely to protect others from hearing it is, in other words, dependent upon a showing that substantial privacy interests are being invaded in an essentially intolerable manner. Any broader view of this authority would effectively empower a majority to silence dissidents simply as a matter of personal predilections.

[Given] the subtlety and complexity of the factors involved if Cohen's "speech" was otherwise entitled to constitutional protection, we do not think the fact that some unwilling "listeners" in a public building may have been briefly exposed to it can serve to justify this breach of the peace conviction where, as here, there was no evidence that persons powerless to avoid appellant's conduct did in fact object to it, and where [unlike another portion of the same statute barring the use of "vulgar, profane or indecent language within [the] hearing of women or children, in a loud and boisterous manner"], the [challenged statutory provision] evinces no concern [with] the special plight of the captive auditor, but, instead, indiscriminately sweeps within its prohibitions all "offensive conduct" that disturbs "any neighborhood or person."

Against this background, the issue flushed by this case stands out in bold relief. It is whether California can excise, as "offensive conduct," one particular scurrilous epithet from the public discourse, either upon the theory of the court below that its use is inherently likely to cause violent reaction or upon a more general assertion that the States, acting as guardians of public morality, may properly remove this offensive word from the public vocabulary.

The rationale of the California court is plainly untenable. At most it reflects an "undifferentiated fear or apprehension of disturbance [which] is not enough to overcome the right to freedom of expression." *Tinker* [Sec. 7, II infra]. We have been shown no evidence that substantial numbers of citizens are standing ready to strike out physically at whoever may assault their sensibilities with execrations like that uttered by Cohen. There may be some persons about with such lawless and violent proclivities, but that is an insufficient base upon which to erect, consistently with constitutional values, a governmental power to force persons who wish to ventilate their dissident views into avoiding particular forms of expression. The argument amounts to little more than the self-defeating proposition that to avoid physical censorship of one who has not sought to provoke such a response by a hypothetical coterie of the violent and lawless, the States may more appropriately effectuate that censorship themselves.

Admittedly, it is not so obvious that the First and Fourteenth Amendments must be taken to disable the States from punishing public utterance of this unseemly expletive in order to maintain what they regard as a suitable level of discourse within the body politic. We think, however, that examination and reflection will reveal the shortcomings of a contrary viewpoint.

[The] constitutional right of free expression is powerful medicine in a society as diverse and populous as ours. It is designed and intended to remove govern-

---

a. For commentary on the captive audience concept, see J.M. Balkin, *Free Speech and Hos-* *tile Environments*, 99 Colum. L.Rev. 2295, 2306–18 (1999).

mental restraints from the arena of public discussion, putting the decision as to what views shall be voiced largely into the hands of each of us, in the hope that use of such freedom will ultimately produce a more capable citizenry and more perfect polity and in the belief that no other approach would comport with the premise of individual dignity and choice upon which our political system rests.

To many, the immediate consequence of this freedom may often appear to be only verbal tumult, discord, and even offensive utterance. These are, however, within established limits, in truth necessary side effects of the broader enduring values which the process of open debate permits us to achieve. That the air may at times seem filled with verbal cacophony is, in this sense not a sign of weakness but of strength. We cannot lose sight of the fact that, in what otherwise might seem a trifling and annoying instance of individual distasteful abuse of a privilege, these fundamental societal values are truly implicated. * * *

Against this perception of the constitutional policies involved, we discern certain more particularized considerations that peculiarly call for reversal of this conviction. First, the principle contended for by the State seems inherently boundless. How is one to distinguish this from any other offensive word? Surely the State has no right to cleanse public debate to the point where it is grammatically palatable to the most squeamish among us. Yet no readily ascertainable general principle exists for stopping short of that result were we to affirm the judgment below. For, while the particular four-letter word being litigated here is perhaps more distasteful than most others of its genre, it is nevertheless often true that one man's vulgarity is another's lyric. Indeed, we think it is largely because governmental officials cannot make principled distinctions in this area that the Constitution leaves matters of taste and style so largely to the individual.

Additionally, we cannot overlook the fact, because it is well illustrated by the episode involved here, that much linguistic expression serves a dual communicative function: it conveys not only ideas capable of relatively precise, detached explication, but otherwise inexpressible emotions as well. In fact, words are often chosen as much for their emotive as their cognitive force. We cannot sanction the view that the Constitution, while solicitous of the cognitive content of individual speech, has little or no regard for that emotive function which, practically speaking, may often be the more important element of the overall message sought to be communicated. * * *

Finally, and in the same vein, we cannot indulge the facile assumption that one can forbid particular words without also running a substantial risk of suppressing ideas in the process. Indeed, governments might soon seize upon the censorship of particular words as a convenient guise for banning the expression of unpopular views. We have been able [to] discern little social benefit that might result from running the risk of opening the door to such grave results.

It is, in sum, our judgment that, absent a more particularized and compelling reason for its actions, the State may not, consistently with the First and Fourteenth Amendments, make the simple public display here involved of this single four-letter expletive a criminal offense. * * *

[BLACKMUN, J., joined by Burger, C.J., and Black, J., dissented for two reasons: (1) "Cohen's absurd and immature antic [was] mainly conduct and little speech" and the case falls "well within the sphere of Chaplinsky"; (2) although it declined to review the state court of appeals' decision in Cohen, the California Supreme Court subsequently narrowly construed the breach-of-the-peace statute in another case and Cohen should be remanded to the California Court of Appeal in the light of this subsequent construction. White, J., concurred with the dissent on the latter ground.]

Notes and Questions

1.   For criticism of *Cohen*, see Alexander Bickel, *The Morality of Consent* 72 (1975) (Cohen's speech "constitutes an assault" and this sort of speech "may create [an] environment [in which] actions that were not possible before become possible"); Archibald Cox, *The Role of the Supreme Court in American Government* 47–48 (1976) (state has interest in "level at which public discourse is conducted"; state should not have to "allow exhibitionists and [others] trading upon our lower prurient interests to inflict themselves upon the public consciousness and dull its sensibilities"). For a defense (but what not a few would consider a narrow reading) of *Cohen*, see Daniel Farber, *Civilizing Public Discourse: An Essay on Professor Bickel, Justice Harlan, and the Enduring Significance of Cohen v. California*, 1980 Duke L.J. 283. See also John Hart Ely, *Democracy and Distrust* 114 (1980); Tribe, 2d ed., at 787–88, 851–52, 916–17, 953–54. For an overview of Harlan, J.'s approach to the first amendment, see Daniel Farber & John Nowak, *Justice Harlan and the First Amendment*, 2 Const.Comm. 425 (1985).

2.   To what extent, if at all, and in what ways, if any, does *Cohen* restrict the "fighting words" doctrine? Consider Hadley Arkes, *Civility and the Restriction of Speech: Rediscovering the Defamation of Groups*, 1974 Sup.Ct.Rev. 281, 316: *Cohen* turned "the presumptions in *Chaplinsky* around: instead of presuming that profane or defamatory speech was beneath constitutional protection, he presumed that the speech was protected and that the burden of proof lay with those who would restrict it." If "one man's vulgarity is another's lyric," how are discriminations to be made in the "fighting words" area?

3.   Does the "use of elaborate explanations and high sounding principles to resolve" cases like *Cohen* erect "obstacles to an enhanced public appreciation of free speech?" Does systematic judicial protection of "seemingly silly, unsavory, or dangerous activities" ultimately undermine public support for the idea of free speech? See Robert Nagel, *Constitutional Cultures* 47 (1989).

4.   What does *Cohen* decide? Consider William Cohen, *A Look Back at Cohen v. California*, 34 UCLA L.Rev. 1595, 1602–03 (1987): "Unless it is overruled or dishonestly distinguished, [*Cohen*] has settled [that] a criminal statute is unconstitutional if it punishes all public use of profanity without reference to details such as the nature of the location and the audience. The opinion, however, left much to be decided about government controls on the use of profanity based on considerations of time, place, and manner. To what extent can profanity be punished because of the nature of the audience, the nature of the occasion on which it is uttered or displayed, or the manner of its utterance or display."

5.   A series of cases in the early 1970s reversed convictions involving abusive language. GOODING v. WILSON, 405 U.S. 518, 92 S.Ct. 1103, 31 L.Ed.2d 408 (1972), invalidated a Georgia ordinance primarily because it had been previously applied to "utterances where there was no likelihood that the person addressed would make an immediate violent response." LEWIS v. NEW ORLEANS, 415 U.S. 130, 94 S.Ct. 970, 39 L.Ed.2d 214 (1974), ruled that vulgar or offensive speech was protected under the first amendment. Because the statute punished "opprobrious

language," it was deemed by the Court to embrace words that do not " 'by their very utterance inflict injury or tend to invite an immediate breach of the peace.' "

Although *Gooding* seemed to require a danger of immediate violence, *Lewis* recited that infliction of injury was sufficient. Dissenting in both cases, BURGER, C.J., and Blackmun and Rehnquist, JJ., complained that the majority invoked vagueness and overbreadth analysis "indiscriminately without regard to the nature of the speech in question, the possible effect the statute or ordinance has upon such speech, the importance of the speech in relation to the exposition of ideas, or the purported or asserted community interest in preventing that speech." The dissenters focused upon the facts of the cases (e.g., Gooding to a police officer: "White son of a bitch, I'll kill you," "You son of a bitch, I'll choke you to death," and "You son of a bitch, if you ever put your hands on me again, I'll cut you to pieces."). They complained that the majority had relegated the facts to "footnote status, conveniently distant and in less disturbing focus." In *Gooding, Lewis,* and the other cases, POWELL, J., insisted upon the importance of context in decision making. Dissenting in *Rosenfeld v. New Jersey,* 408 U.S. 901, 92 S.Ct. 2479, 33 L.Ed.2d 321 (1972), he suggested that *Chaplinsky* be extended to the "wilful use of scurrilous language calculated to offend the sensibilities of an unwilling audience"; concurring in *Lewis,* he maintained that allowing prosecutions for offensive language directed at police officers invited law enforcement abuse. Finally, he suggested in *Rosenfeld* that whatever the scope of the "fighting words" doctrine, overbreadth analysis was inappropriate in such cases. He doubted that such statutes deter others from exercising first amendment rights.[b]

V. SHOULD NEW CATEGORIES BE CREATED?

Suppose a legislature were to outlaw speech whose dominant theme appeals to a morbid interest in violence, that is patently offensive to contemporary community standards, and that lacks serious literary, artistic, political or scientific value. Constitutional?[a] One approach would be to contend that speech is protected unless it falls into already established categorical exceptions to first amendment protection. Another would be to argue by analogy, e.g., if obscenity is beneath first amendment protection, this speech should (or should not) be beneath such protection. Similarly, one could argue that exceptions to first amendment protection has been fashioned by resort to a balancing methodology and that balancing the relevant interests is the right approach. Alternatively, one could proceed from a particular substantive vision of the first amendment, such as the Meiklejohn view. Which approach has been applied by the Court?[b]

b. For commentary on Powell, J.'s approach, see Gerald Gunther, *In Search of Judicial Quality on a Changing Court: The Case of Justice Powell,* 24 Stan.L.Rev. 1001, 1029–35 (1972).

a. See Kevin W. Sanders, *Media Violence and the Obscenity Exception to the First Amendment,* 3 Wm. & Mary Bill Rts. J. 107 (1994); Lucas Powe & Thomas Krattenmaker, *Televised Violence: First Amendment Principles and Social Science Theory,* 64 Va. L.Rev. 1123 (1978).

b. For commentary on the Court's methodology, see Daniel A. Farber, *The First Amendment* (1998); Martin Redish, *Freedom of Expression: A Critical Analysis* (1984); Steven

Shiffrin, *The First Amendment, Democracy, and Romance* (1990); William Van Alstyne, *Interpretations of the First Amendment* (1984); William Van Alstyne, *A Graphic Review of the Free Speech Clause,* 70 Calif.L.Rev. 107 (1982); T. Alexander Alcinikoff, *Constitutional Law in the Age of Balancing,* 96 Yale L.J. 943 (1987); Randall P. Bezanson, *The Quality of First Amendment Speech,* 20 Hastings Comm/Ent L.J. 275 (1998); Richard Fallon, *A Constructivist Coherence Theory of Constitutional Interpretation,* 100 Harv.L.Rev. 1189, 1228 n.191 (1987); Elena Kagan, *Private Speech, Public Purpose: The Role of Governmental Motive in First Amendment Doctrine,* 63 U. Chi.L.Rev. 413 (1996); Robert Post, *Recuperating First Amendment Doctrine,* 47 Stan.L.Rev.

New York v. Ferber, infra, is interesting because it involves the question of whether to create a new category.

A. HARM TO CHILDREN AND THE OVERBREADTH DOCTRINE

NEW YORK v. FERBER, 458 U.S. 747, 102 S.Ct. 3348, 73 L.Ed.2d 1113 (1982), per WHITE, J., upheld conviction of a seller of films depicting young boys masturbating, under N.Y.Penal Law § 263.15, for "promoting[a] a sexual performance," defined as "any performance [which] includes sexual conduct[b] by a child" under 16. The Court addressed the "single question": " 'To prevent the abuse of children who are made to engage in sexual conduct for commercial purposes, could the New York State Legislature, consistent with the First Amendment, prohibit the dissemination of material which shows children engaged in sexual conduct, regardless of whether such material is obscene?'[c] * * *

"The *Miller* standard, like its predecessors, was an accommodation between the state's interests in protecting the 'sensibilities of unwilling recipients' from exposure to pornographic material and the dangers of censorship inherent in unabashedly content-based laws. Like obscenity statutes, laws directed at the dissemination of child pornography run the risk of suppressing protected expression by allowing the hand of the censor to become unduly heavy. For the following reasons, however, we are persuaded that the States are entitled to greater leeway in the regulation of pornographic depictions of children.

"First. [The] prevention of sexual exploitation and abuse of children constitutes a government objective of surpassing importance. The legislative findings accompanying passage of the New York laws reflect this concern. * * *

"We shall not second-guess this legislative judgment. Respondent has not intimated that we do so. Suffice it to say that virtually all of the States and the United States have passed legislation proscribing the production of or otherwise combating 'child pornography.' The legislative judgment, as well as the judgment found in the relevant literature, is that the use of children as subjects of pornographic materials is harmful to the physiological, emotional, and mental health of the child. That judgment, we think, easily passes muster under the First Amendment.

1249(1995); Frederick Schauer, *The Speech of Law and the Law of Speech,* Ark. L.Rev. 687 (1997); Frederick Schauer, *Mrs. Palsgraf and the First Amendment,* 47 Wash. & Lee L.Rev. 161 (1990); Frederick Schauer, *The Second–Best First Amendment,* 31 Wm. & M.L.Rev. 1 (1989); Frederick Schauer, *Categories and the First Amendment: A Play in Three Acts,* 34 Vand.L.Rev. 265 (1981); Pierre Schlag, *Rules and Standards,* 33 U.C.L.A.L.Rev. 379 (1985); Geoffrey Stone, *Content Regulation and the First Amendment,* 25 Wm. & Mary L.Rev. 189 (1983); Geoffrey Stone, *Content–Neutral Restrictions,* 54 U.Chi.L.Rev. 46 (1987).

a. "Promote" was defined to include all aspects of production, distribution, exhibition and sale.

b. Sec. 263.3 defined "sexual conduct" as "actual or simulated sexual intercourse, deviate sexual intercourse, sexual bestiality, mas-

turbation, sado-masochistic abuse, or lewd exhibition of the genitals."

c. The opinion gave the background for such legislation: "In recent years, the exploitive use of children in the production of pornography has become a serious national problem. The federal government and forty-seven States have sought to combat the problem with statutes specifically directed at the production of child pornography. At least half of such statutes do not require that the materials produced be legally obscene. Thirty-five States and the United States Congress have also passed legislation prohibiting the distribution of such materials; twenty States prohibit the distribution of material depicting children engaged in sexual conduct without requiring that the material be legally obscene. New York is one of the twenty."

"Second. The distribution of photographs and films depicting sexual activity by juveniles is intrinsically related to the sexual abuse of children in at least two ways. First, the materials produced are a permanent record of the children's participation and the harm to the child is exacerbated by their circulation. Second, the distribution network for child pornography must be closed if the production of material which requires the sexual exploitation of children is to be effectively controlled. Indeed, there is no serious contention that the legislature was unjustified in believing that it is difficult, if not impossible, to halt the exploitation of children by pursuing only those who produce the photographs and movies. While the production of pornographic materials is a low-profile, clandestine industry, the need to market the resulting products requires a visible apparatus of distribution. The most expeditious if not the only practical method of law enforcement may be to dry up the market for this material by imposing severe criminal penalties on persons selling, advertising, or otherwise promoting the product. Thirty-five States and Congress have concluded that restraints on the distribution of pornographic materials are required in order to effectively combat the problem, and there is a body of literature and testimony to support these legislative conclusions.

"[The] *Miller* standard, like all general definitions of what may be banned as obscene, does not reflect the State's particular and more compelling interest in prosecuting those who promote the sexual exploitation of children. Thus, the question under the *Miller* test of whether a work, taken as a whole, appeals to the prurient interest of the average person bears no connection to the issue of whether a child has been physically or psychologically harmed in the production of the work. Similarly, a sexual explicit depiction need not be 'patently offensive' in order to have required the sexual exploitation of a child for its production. In addition, a work which, taken on the whole, contains serious literary, artistic, political, or scientific value may nevertheless embody the hardest core of child pornography. 'It is irrelevant to the child [who has been abused] whether or not the material [has] a literary, artistic, political, or social value.' We therefore cannot conclude that the *Miller* standard is a satisfactory solution to the child pornography problem.

"Third. The advertising and selling of child pornography provides an economic motive for and is thus an integral part of the production of such materials, an activity illegal throughout the nation. 'It rarely has been suggested that the constitutional freedom for speech and press extends its immunity to speech or writing used as an integral part of conduct in violation of a valid criminal statute.' * * *

"Fourth. The value of permitting live performances and photographic reproductions of children engaged in lewd sexual conduct is exceedingly modest, if not de minimis. We consider it unlikely that visual depictions of children performing sexual acts or lewdly exhibiting their genitals would often constitute an important and necessary part of a literary performance or scientific or educational work. As the trial court in this case observed, if it were necessary for literary or artistic value, a person over the statutory age who perhaps looked younger could be utilized. * * *

"Fifth. Recognizing and classifying child pornography as a category of material outside the protection of the First Amendment is not incompatible with our earlier decisions. 'The question whether speech is, or is not protected by the First Amendment often depends on the content of the speech.' *Young v. American Mini Theatres, Inc.* [Sec. 3, I infra]. '[I]t is the content of an utterance that determines whether it is a protected epithet or [an] unprotected "fighting comment"'.

Leaving aside the special considerations when public officials are the target, *New York Times Co. v. Sullivan,* a libelous publication is not protected by the Constitution. *Beauharnais.* [It] is not rare that a content-based classification of speech has been accepted because it may be appropriately generalized that within the confines of the given classification, the evil to be restricted so overwhelmingly outweighs the expressive interests, if any, at stake, that no process of case-by-case adjudication is required. When a definable class of material, such as that covered by § 263.15, bears so heavily and pervasively on the welfare of children engaged in its production, we think the balance of competing interests is clearly struck and that it is permissible to consider these materials as without the protection of the First Amendment.

"There are, of course, limits on the category of child pornography which, like obscenity, is unprotected by the First Amendment. As with all legislation in this sensitive area, the conduct to be prohibited must be adequately defined by the applicable state law, as written or authoritatively construed. Here the nature of the harm to be combated requires that the state offense be limited to works that *visually* depict sexual conduct by children below a specified age. The category of 'sexual conduct' proscribed must also be suitably limited and described.

"The test for child pornography is separate from the obscenity standard enunciated in *Miller,* but may be compared to it for purpose of clarity. The *Miller* formulation is adjusted in the following respects: A trier of fact need not find that the material appeals to the prurient interest of the average person; it is not required that sexual conduct portrayed be done so in a patently offensive manner; and the material at issue need not be considered as a whole. We note that the distribution of descriptions or other depictions of sexual conduct, not otherwise obscene, which do not involve live performance or photographic or other visual reproduction of live performances, retains First Amendment protection. As with obscenity laws, criminal responsibility may not be imposed without some element of scienter on the part of the defendant. * * *

"It remains to address the claim that the New York statute is unconstitutionally overbroad because it would forbid the distribution of material with serious literary, scientific, or educational value or material which does not threaten the harms sought to be combated by the State. * * *

"The traditional rule is that a person to whom a statute may constitutionally be applied may not challenge that statute on the ground that it may conceivably be applied unconstitutionally to others in situations not before the Court. *Broadrick v. Oklahoma,* 413 U.S. 601, 93 S.Ct. 2908, 37 L.Ed.2d 830 (1973). In *Broadrick,* we recognized that this rule reflects two cardinal principles of our constitutional order: the personal nature of constitutional rights and prudential limitations on constitutional adjudication.[20] [By] focusing on the factual situation before us, and similar cases necessary for development of a constitutional rule,[21] we face 'flesh-and-blood' legal problems with data 'relevant and adequate to an informed judgment.' This practice also fulfills a valuable institutional purpose: it allows state courts the opportunity to construe a law to avoid constitutional infirmities.

20. In addition to prudential restraints, the traditional rule is grounded in Art. III limits on the jurisdiction of federal courts to actual cases and controversies. * * *

21. Overbreadth challenges are only one type of facial attack. A person whose activity may be constitutionally regulated nevertheless may argue that the statute under which he is convicted or regulated is invalid on its face. See, e.g., *Terminiello.* See generally Henry Monaghan, *Overbreadth,* 1981 S.Ct.Rev. 1, 10–14.

"What has come to be known as the First Amendment overbreadth doctrine is one of the few exceptions to this principle and must be justified by weighty countervailing policies. The doctrine is predicated on the sensitive nature of protected expression: persons whose expression is constitutionally protected may well refrain from exercising their rights for fear of criminal sanctions by a statute susceptible of application to protected expression. * * *

"In *Broadrick,* we explained [that]: '[T]he plain import of our cases is, at the very least, that facial overbreadth adjudication is an exception to our traditional rules of practice and that its function, a limited one at the outset, attenuates as the otherwise unprotected behavior that it forbids the State to sanction moves from "pure speech" toward conduct and that conduct—even if expressive—falls within the scope of otherwise valid criminal laws that reflect legitimate state interests in maintaining comprehensive controls over harmful, constitutionally unprotected conduct. * * * '

"[*Broadrick*] examined a regulation involving restrictions on political campaign activity, an area not considered 'pure speech,' and thus it was unnecessary to consider the proper overbreadth test when a law arguably reaches traditional forms of expression such as books and films. As we intimated in *Broadrick,* the requirement of substantial overbreadth extended 'at the very least' to cases involving conduct plus speech. This case, which poses the question squarely, convinces us that the rationale of *Broadrick* is sound and should be applied in the present context involving the harmful employment of children to make sexually explicit materials for distribution.

"The premise that a law should not be invalidated for overbreadth unless it reaches a substantial number of impermissible applications is hardly novel.[d] On most occasions involving facial invalidation, the Court has stressed the embracing sweep of the statute over protected expression.[26] Indeed, Justice Brennan observed in his dissenting opinion in *Broadrick:* 'We have never held that a statute should be held invalid on its face merely because it is possible to conceive of a single impermissible application, and in that sense a requirement of substantial overbreadth is already implicit in the doctrine.'

"The requirement of substantial overbreadth is directly derived from the purpose and nature of the doctrine. While a sweeping statute, or one incapable of limitation, has the potential to repeatedly chill the exercise of expressive activity by many individuals, the extent of deterrence of protected speech can be expected to decrease with the declining reach of the regulation. This observation appears equally applicable to the publication of books and films as it is to activities, such as picketing or participation in election campaigns, which have previously been categorized as involving conduct plus speech. We see no appreciable difference between the position of a publisher or bookseller in doubt as to the reach of New York's child pornography law and the situation faced by the Oklahoma state employees with respect to the State's restriction on partisan political activity.[e]
* * *

---

d. Scalia, J., dissenting in *Chicago v. Morales,* 527 U.S. 41, 119 S.Ct. 1849, 144 L.Ed.2d 67 (1999), argues that in order to avoid advisory opinions, federal courts should limit themselves to as applied attacks, but that if they insist on considering facial attacks, they should insist that a statute be unconstitutional in all its applications before declaring it unconstitutional. Are either of these positions acceptable?

26. In *Gooding v. Wilson,* the Court's invalidation of a Georgia statute making it a misdemeanor to use " 'opprobrious words or abusive language, tending to cause a breach of the peace' " followed from state judicial decisions indicating that "merely to speak words offensive to some who hear them" could constitute a "breach of the peace." * * *

e. *Brockett v. Spokane Arcades, Inc.,* Sec. 1, III, B supra, stated: "The Court of Appeals

"Applying these principles, we hold that § 263.15 is not substantially over-broad. We consider this the paradigmatic case of a state statute whose legitimate reach dwarfs its arguably impermissible applications. [While] the reach of the statute is directed at the hard core of child pornography, the Court of Appeals was understandably concerned that some protected expression, ranging from medical textbooks to pictorials in the National Geographic would fall prey to the statute. How often, if ever, it may be necessary to employ children to engage in conduct clearly within the reach of § 263.15 in order to produce educational, medical, or artistic works cannot be known with certainty. Yet we seriously doubt, and it has not been suggested, that these arguably impermissible applications of the statute amount to more than a tiny fraction of the materials within the statute's reach."[f]

Notes and Questions

1. Consider Frederick Schauer, *Codifying the First Amendment: New York v. Ferber,* 1982 Sup.Ct.Rev. 285, 295: The new category created in *Ferber* "bears little resemblance to the category of obscenity delineated by *Miller.* The Court in *Ferber* explicitly held that child pornography need not appeal to the prurient interest, need not be patently offensive, and need not be based on a consideration of the material as a whole. This last aspect is most important, because it means that the presence of some serious literary, artistic, political, or scientific matter will not constitutionally redeem material containing depictions of sexual conduct by children. The Court referred to the foregoing factors in terms of having 'adjusted' the *Miller* test, but that is like saying a butterfly is an adjusted camel." What precisely is the new category created in *Ferber*?

erred in holding that the *Broadrick* substantial overbreadth requirement is inapplicable where pure speech rather than conduct is at issue. *Ferber* specifically held to the contrary." For commentary on the overbreadth discussion in *Broadrick* and *Ferber,* see Martin Redish, *The Warren Court, The Burger Court and the First Amendment Overbreadth Doctrine,* 78 Nw. U.L.Rev. 1031, 1056–69 (1983).

f. Brennan, J., joined by Marshall, J., agreed "with much of what is said in the Court's opinion. [This] special and compelling interest (in protecting the well-being of the State's youth), and the particular vulnerability of children, afford the State the leeway to regulate pornographic material, the promotion of which is harmful to children, even though the State does not have such leeway when it seeks only to protect consenting adults from exposure to such materials. * * * I also agree with the Court that the 'tiny fraction' of material of serious artistic, scientific or educational value that could conceivably fall within the reach of the statute is insufficient to justify striking the statute on grounds of over-breadth." But the concurrence stated that application of the statute to such materials as "do have serious artistic, scientific or medical value would violate the First Amendment."

On that issue O'Connor, J., wrote a short concurrence: "Although I join the Court's opin-ion, I write separately to stress that the Court does not hold that New York must except 'material with serious literary, scientific or ed-ucational value' from its statute. The Court merely holds that, even if the First Amend-ment shelters such material, New York's cur-rent statute is not sufficiently overbroad to support respondent's facial attack. The compel-ling interests identified in today's opinion sug-gest that the Constitution might in fact permit New York to ban knowing distribution of works depicting minors engaged in explicit sex-ual conduct, regardless of the social value of the depictions. For example, a 12–year-old child photographed while masturbating surely suffers the same psychological harm whether the community labels the photograph 'edifying' or 'tasteless.' The audience's appreciation of the depiction is simply irrelevant to New York's asserted interest in protecting children from psychological, emotional, and mental harm."

Stevens, J., also concurred in the judgment in a short opinion that noted his conclusion that the films in the case were not entitled to first amendment protection, and his view that overbreadth analysis should be avoided by waiting until the hypothetical case actually arises.

Blackmun, J., concurred in the result with-out opinion.

2. What test or standard of review did the Court use to determine whether the speech should be protected? For general discussion, see Schauer, supra. Did it apply a different test or a standard of review when it formulated its rules in *Gertz*? Are tests or standards of review needed in these contexts? Desirable? Consider Steven Shiffrin, *The First Amendment and Economic Regulation: Away From a General Theory of the First Amendment,* 78 Nw.U.L.Rev. 1212, 1268 (1983): "The complex set of rules produced in *Gertz,* right or wrong, resulted from an appreciation that the protection of truth was important but that the protection of reputation also was important. The Court wisely avoided discussion of levels of scrutiny because any resort to such abstractions would have constitutionalized reductionism." Is "constitutionalized reductionism" desirable because it protects speech and provides guidance to the lower courts?

3. *The absence of children.* SIMON & SCHUSTER, INC. v. MEMBERS OF NEW YORK STATE CRIME VICTIMS BD., 502 U.S. 105, 112 S.Ct. 501, 116 L.Ed.2d 476 (1991), per O'CONNOR, J., struck down a law requiring that income derived from works in which individuals admit to crime involving victims be used to compensate the victims: "[T]he State has a compelling interest in compensating victims from the fruits of the crime, but little if any interest in limiting such compensation to the proceeds of the wrongdoer's speech about the crime."[g]

4. *Overbreadth without a chilling effect?* Massachusetts prohibited adults from posing or exhibiting nude children for purposes of photographs, publications, or pictures, moving or otherwise. Bona fide scientific or medical purposes were excepted as were educational or cultural purposes for a bona fide school, museum, or library. Douglas Oakes was prosecuted for taking 10 color photographs of his 14–year–old stepdaughter in a state of nudity covered by the statute. The Massachusetts Supreme Judicial Court declared the statute overbroad. After certiorari was granted in MASSACHUSETTS v. OAKES, 491 U.S. 576, 109 S.Ct. 2633, 105 L.Ed.2d 493 (1989), Massachusetts added a "lascivious intent" requirement to the statute and eliminated the exemptions. O'CONNOR, J., joined by Rehnquist, C.J., and White and Kennedy, JJ., accordingly refused to entertain the overbreadth challenge and voted to remand the case for determination of the statute's constitutionality as applied: "Because it has been repealed, the former version of [the Massachusetts law] cannot chill protected speech."

SCALIA, J., joined by Blackmun, Brennan, Marshall, and Stevens, JJ., disagreed:[h] "It seems to me strange judicial theory that a conviction initially invalid can be resuscitated by postconviction alteration of the statute under which it was obtained. [Even as a policy matter, the] overbreadth doctrine serves to protect constitutionally legitimate speech not merely *ex post,* that is, after the offending statute is enacted, but also *ex ante,* that is, when the legislature is contemplating what sort of statute to enact. If the promulgation of overbroad laws affecting

g. Kennedy, J., concurring, would have stricken the statute without reference to the compelling state interest test which he condemned as ad hoc balancing. Blackmun, J., also concurred. Thomas, J., did not participate. For extensive criticism of the strict scrutiny test, see Eugene Volokh, *Freedom of Speech, Permissible Tailoring, and Transcending Strict Scrutiny,* 144 U.Pa.L.Rev. 2417, 2446 (1996).

h. Although these five justices agreed that the overbreadth challenge should be entertained, they divided on the merits of the challenge. Scalia, J., joined by Blackmun, J., found no merit in the overbreadth claim (see note 5 infra) and voted to reverse and to remand for determination of the statute's constitutionality as applied. The three remaining justices (see note 5 infra) agreed with the overbreadth challenge and voted to affirm the judgment below. O'Connor, J.'s opinion, therefore, became the plurality opinion, and the Court's judgment was to vacate the judgment below and to remand. In the end, six justices voted against the overbreadth challenge: four because it was moot; two because it did not meet the requirement of substantial overbreadth.

speech was cost free[,] if *no* conviction of constitutionally proscribable conduct would be lost, so long as the offending statute was narrowed before the final appeal—then legislatures would have significantly reduced incentive to stay within constitutional bounds in the first place.[i] [More] fundamentally, however, [it] seems to me that we are only free to pursue policy objectives through the modes of action traditionally followed by the courts and by the law. [I] have heard of a voidable contract, but never of a voidable law. The notion is bizarre."

5. *How substantial is substantial overbreadth?* Five justices addressed the overbreadth question in *Oakes,* but the substantive issue was not resolved. BRENNAN, J., joined by Marshall and Stevens, JJ., objected that the statute would make it criminal for parents "to photograph their infant children or toddlers in the bath or romping naked on the beach." More generally, he argued that the first amendment "blocks the prohibition of nude posing by minors in connection with the production of works of art not depicting lewd behavior. [Many] of the world's great artists—Degas, Renoir, Donatello, to name but a few—have worked from models under 18 years of age, and many acclaimed photographs have included nude or partially clad minors."

SCALIA, J., joined by Blackmun, J., disagreed: "[G]iven the known extent of the kiddie-porn industry[,] I would estimate that the legitimate scope [of the statute] vastly exceeds the illegitimate. [Even] assuming that proscribing artistic depictions of preadolescent genitals and postadolescent breasts is impermissible,[2] the body of material that would be covered is, as far as I am aware, insignificant compared with the lawful scope of the statute. That leaves the family photos. [Assuming] that it is unconstitutional (as opposed to merely foolish) to prohibit such photography, I do not think it so common as to make the statute *substantially* overbroad. [My] perception differs, for example, from Justice Brennan's belief that there is an 'abundance of baby and child photographs taken every day' depicting genitals."[j]

Ohio prohibited possession of material showing a minor in a state of nudity, subject to exceptions.[a] Clyde Osborne was convicted for possessing photographs of a nude male adolescent in a variety of sexually explicit poses.[b] The photographs were secured in his home pursuant to a valid search warrant. The Ohio Supreme

i. For criticism of this point, see Alfred Hill, *The Puzzling First Amendment Overbreadth Doctrine,* 25 Hof.L.Rev. 1063, 1071 (1997).

2. [Most] adults, I expect, would not hire themselves out as nude models, whatever the intention of the photographer or artist, and however unerotic the pose. There is no cause to think children are less sensitive. It is not unreasonable, therefore, for a State to regard parents' using (or permitting the use) of their children as nude models, or other adults' use of consenting minors, as a form of child exploitation.

j. For the argument that the Court should balance a number of factors including the "state's substantive interest in being able to impose sanctions for a particular kind of conduct under a particular legal standard, as opposed to being forced to rely on other, less restrictive substitutes" instead of trying to determine the number of constitutional and unconstitutional applications, see Richard Fallon, *Making Sense of Overbreadth,* 100 Yale L.J. 853, 894 (1991).

a. Ohio excepted material possessed for "bona fide" purposes (e.g., artistic or scientific) or that showed the possessor's child or ward or where the possessor knew that the parents or guardians had consented in writing to the photography and to the manner in which it had been transferred.

b. Two of the photographs focused on the anus of the boy, one with a plastic object apparently inserted; another on his erect penis with an electric object in his hand.

Court narrowed the statute to apply only to depictions of nudity involving a lewd exhibition or a graphic focus on the genitals.

OSBORNE v. OHIO, 495 U.S. 103, 110 S.Ct. 1691, 109 L.Ed.2d 98 (1990), per WHITE, J., upheld the statute as construed: "In *Stanley,* we struck down a Georgia law outlawing the private possession of obscene material. We recognized that the statute impinged upon Stanley's right to receive information in the privacy of his home, and we found Georgia's justifications for its law inadequate.[3]

"*Stanley* should not be read too broadly. We have previously noted that *Stanley* was a narrow holding and, since the decision in that case, the value of permitting child pornography has been characterized as 'exceedingly modest, if not de minimis.' *Ferber.* But assuming, for the sake of argument, that Osborne has a First Amendment interest in viewing and possessing child pornography, we nonetheless find this case distinct from *Stanley* because the interests underlying child pornography prohibitions far exceed the interests justifying the Georgia law at issue in *Stanley.* * * *

"In *Stanley,* Georgia primarily sought to proscribe the private possession of obscenity because it was concerned that obscenity would poison the minds of its viewers. [The] difference here is obvious: the State does not rely on a paternalistic interest in regulating Osborne's mind. Rather, Ohio has [acted] in order to protect the victims of child pornography; it hopes to destroy a market for the exploitative use of children. [*Stanley*] itself emphasized that we did not 'mean to express any opinion on statutes making criminal possession of other types of printed, filmed, or recorded materials. [In] such cases, compelling reasons may exist for overriding the right of the individual to possess those materials.'[5]

"Given the importance of the State's interest in protecting the victims of child pornography, we cannot fault Ohio for attempting to stamp out this vice at all levels in the distribution chain. * * *

"Osborne contends that it was impermissible for the Ohio Supreme Court to apply its [narrowed] construction of the statute when evaluating his overbreadth claim.[c] Our cases, however, have long held that a statute as construed 'may be applied to conduct occurring prior to the construction, provided such application affords fair warning to the defendan[t].'[12] [That] Osborne's photographs of adolescent boys in sexually explicit situations constitute child pornography hardly needs elaboration. Therefore, although [Ohio's statute] as written may have been imprecise at its fringes, someone in Osborne's position would not be surprised to

---

3. We have since indicated that our decision in *Stanley* was "firmly grounded in the First Amendment." *Bowers v. Hardwick,* [Ch. 6, Sec. 2 supra.]

5. [T]he *Stanley* Court cited illicit possession of defense information as an example of the type of offense for which compelling state interests might justify a ban on possession. *Stanley,* however, did not suggest that this crime exhausted the entire category of proscribable offenses.

c. Given the statutory limitations and exceptions (see fn. a supra), the Court expressed doubt that the statute was substantially overbroad even without the Ohio Supreme Court's limiting construction although it conceded that the statute by its terms seemed to criminalize some constitutionally protected conduct.

12. This principle, of course, accords with the rationale underlying overbreadth challenges. We normally do not allow a defendant to challenge a law as it is applied to others. In the First Amendment context, however, we have said that "[b]ecause of the sensitive nature of constitutionally protected expression, we have not required that all those subject to overbroad regulations risk prosecution to test their rights. For free expression—of transcendent value to all society, and not merely to those exercising their rights—might be the loser." But once a statute is authoritatively construed, there is no longer any danger that protected speech will be deterred and therefore no longer any reason to entertain the defendant's challenge to the statute on its face.

learn that his possession of the four photographs at issue in this case constituted a crime. * * *

"Finally, despite Osborne's contention to the contrary, we do not believe that *Massachusetts v. Oakes,* supports his theory of this case.

"[F]ive of the *Oakes* Justices feared that if we allowed a legislature to correct its mistakes without paying for them (beyond the inconvenience of passing a new law), we would decrease the legislature's incentive to draft a narrowly tailored law in the first place. [But] a similar effect will not be likely if a judicial construction of a statute to eliminate overbreadth is allowed to be applied in the case before the Court. This is so primarily because the legislatures cannot be sure that the statute, when examined by a court, will be saved by a narrowing construction rather than invalidated for overbreadth. In the latter event, there could be no convictions under that law even of those whose own conduct is unprotected by the First Amendment. Even if construed to obviate overbreadth, applying the statute to pending cases might be barred by the Due Process Clause. Thus, careless drafting cannot be considered to be cost free based on the power of the courts to eliminate overbreadth by statutory construction. * * *

"To conclude, although we find Osborne's First Amendment arguments unpersuasive, we reverse his conviction and remand for a new trial in order to ensure that Osborne's conviction stemmed from a finding that the State had proved each of the elements of the Ohio statute."[d]

BRENNAN, J., joined by Marshall, J., and Stevens, J., dissented: "As written, the Ohio statute is plainly overbroad.[2] * * *

"Wary of the statute's use of the 'nudity' standard, the Ohio Supreme Court construed § 2907.323(A)(3) to apply only 'where such nudity constitutes a lewd exhibition or involves a graphic focus on the genitals.' The 'lewd exhibition' and 'graphic focus' tests not only fail to cure the overbreadth of the statute, but they also create a new problem of vagueness. * * *

"The Ohio law is distinguishable [from *Ferber*] for several reasons. First, the New York statute did not criminalize materials with a '*graphic focus* 'on the genitals, and, as discussed further below, Ohio's 'graphic focus' test is impermissibly capacious. Even setting aside the 'graphic focus' element, the Ohio Supreme Court's narrowing construction is still overbroad because it focuses on 'lewd

---

d. Defendant's attorney did not ask for a scienter instruction (even though Ohio law generally provides for a scienter requirement in criminal cases) and the Court stated that Osborne could be precluded from raising the question on remand. But Osborne did raise the overbreadth issue and was, therefore, entitled to dispute the application of the statute, as construed, to the photographs in his possession even though Osborne's attorney had not specifically objected to the jury instructions.

BLACKMUN, J., concurring, agreed with the dissent's position that due process entitled the defendant to instructions on "lewd exhibition" and "graphic focus" without regard to whether an objection had been lodged at trial.

2. The Court hints that § 2907.323's exemptions and "proper purposes" provisions might save it from being overbroad. I disagree. The enumerated "proper purposes" (e.g., a "bona fide artistic, medical, scientific, edu-

cational [or] other proper purpose") are simultaneously too vague and too narrow. What is an acceptable "artistic" purpose? Would erotic art along the lines of Robert Mapplethorpe's qualify? What is a valid "scientific" or "educational" purpose? What about sex manuals? What is a permissible "other proper purpose"? What about photos taken for one purpose and recirculated for other, more prurient purposes? The "proper purposes" standard appears to create problems analogous to those this Court has encountered in describing the "redeeming social importance" of obscenity.

At the same time, however, Ohio's list of "proper purposes" is too limited; it excludes such obviously permissible uses as the commercial distribution of fashion photographs or the simple exchange of pictures among family and friends. Thus, a neighbor or grandparent who receives a photograph of an unclothed toddler might be subject to criminal sanctions.

exhibitions of *nudity*' rather than 'lewd exhibitions of *the genitals*' in the context of *sexual conduct,* as in the New York statute at issue in *Ferber*.ᵉ Ohio law defines 'nudity' to include depictions of pubic areas, buttocks, the female breast, and covered male genitals 'in a discernibly turgid state,' *as well as* depictions of the genitals. On its face, then, the Ohio law is much broader than New York's. * * *

"Indeed, the broad definition of nudity in the Ohio statutory scheme means that 'child pornography' could include any photograph depicting a 'lewd exhibition' of even a small portion of a minor's buttocks or any part of the female breast below the nipple. Pictures of topless bathers at a Mediterranean beach, of teenagers in revealing dresses, and even of toddlers romping unclothed, all might be prohibited.[5]

"It might be objected that many of these depictions of nudity do not amount to 'lewd exhibitions.' But in the absence of *any* authoritative definition of that phrase by the Ohio Supreme Court, we cannot predict which ones. * * *

"The Ohio Supreme Court, moreover, did not specify the perspective from which 'lewdness' is to be determined. A 'reasonable' person's view of 'lewdness'? A reasonable pedophile's? An 'average' person applying contemporary local community standards? Statewide standards? Nationwide standards? In sum, the addition of a 'lewd exhibition' standard does not narrow adequately the statute's reach. If anything, it creates a new problem of vagueness, affording the public little notice of the statute's ambit and providing an avenue for 'policemen, prosecutors, and juries to pursue their personal predilections.'[12] Given the important First Amendment interests at issue, the vague, broad sweep of the 'lewd exhibition' language means that it cannot cure [the overbreadth problem].

"The Ohio Supreme Court also added a 'graphic focus' element to the nudity definition. This phrase, a stranger to obscenity regulation, suffers from the same vagueness difficulty as 'lewd exhibition.' Although the Ohio Supreme Court failed to elaborate what a 'graphic focus' might be, the test appears to involve nothing more than a subjective estimation of the centrality or prominence of the genitals in a picture or other representation. Not only is this factor dependent on the perspective and idiosyncrasies of the observer, it also is unconnected to whether the material at issue merits constitutional protection. Simple nudity, no matter how prominent or 'graphic,' is within the bounds of the First Amendment. Michelangelo's 'David' might be said to have a 'graphic focus' on the genitals, for it plainly portrays them in a manner unavoidable to even a casual observer. Similarly, a painting of a partially clad girl could be said to involve a 'graphic focus,' depending on the picture's lighting and emphasis, as could the depictions of nude children on the friezes that adorn our Courtroom. Even a photograph of a child running naked on the beach or playing in the bathtub might run afoul of the law, depending on the focus and camera angle. * * *

"Even if the statute was not overbroad, our decision in *Stanley* forbids the criminalization of appellant's private possession in his home of the materials at

---

e. The Court read the Ohio Court's opinion to refer to the lewd exhibition of the genitals rather than the lewd exhibition of nudity, but maintained that the distinction was not important anyway.

5. [A] well-known commercial advertisement for a suntan lotion shows a dog pulling down the bottom half of a young girl's bikini, revealing a stark contrast between her suntanned back and pale buttocks. That this advertisement might be illegal in Ohio is an absurd yet altogether too conceivable conclusion under the language of the [statute.]

12. The danger of discriminatory enforcement assumes particular importance of the context of the instant case, which involves child pornography with male homosexual overtones. Sadly, evidence indicates that the overwhelming majority of arrests for violations of "lewdness" laws involve male homosexuals.

issue. [Appellant] testified that he had been given the pictures in his home by a friend. There was no evidence that the photographs had been produced commercially or distributed. All were kept in an album that appellant had assembled for his personal use and had possessed privately for several years.

"In these circumstances, the Court's focus on *Ferber* rather than *Stanley* is misplaced. [*Ferber*] did nothing more than place child pornography on the same level of First Amendment protection as *obscene* adult pornography, meaning that its production and distribution could be proscribed. The distinction established in *Stanley* between *what* materials may be regulated and *how* they may be regulated still stands. * * *

"At bottom, the Court today is so disquieted by the possible exploitation of children in the *production* of the pornography that it is willing to tolerate the imposition of criminal penalties for simple *possession*. While I share the majority's concerns, I do not believe that it has struck the proper balance between the First Amendment and the State's interests, especially in light of the other means available to Ohio to protect children from exploitation and the State's failure to demonstrate a causal link between a ban on possession of child pornography and a decrease in its production. * * *

"When speech is eloquent and the ideas expressed lofty, it is easy to find restrictions on them invalid. But were the First Amendment limited to such discourse, our freedom would be sterile indeed. Mr. Osborne's pictures may be distasteful, but the Constitution guarantees both his right to possess them privately and his right to avoid punishment under an overbroad law."

B. HARM TO WOMEN: FEMINISM AND PORNOGRAPHY

Catharine MacKinnon and Andrea Dworkin drafted an anti-pornography ordinance that was considered in a number of jurisdictions.[a]

PROPOSED LOS ANGELES COUNTY ANTI-PORNOGRAPHY CIVIL RIGHTS LAW

Section 1. Statement of Policy

Pornography is sex discrimination. It exists in the County of Los Angeles, posing a substantial threat to the health, safety, welfare and equality of citizens in the community. Existing state and federal laws are inadequate to solve these problems in the County of Los Angeles.

Section 2. Findings

Pornography is a systematic practice of exploitation and subordination based on sex which differentially harms women. The harm of pornography includes dehumanization, sexual exploitation, forced sex, forced prostitution, physical injury, and social and sexual terrorism and inferiority presented as entertainment. The bigotry and contempt pornography promotes, with the acts of aggression it fosters, diminish opportunities for equality of rights in employment, education,

---

a. The ordinance was first considered in Minneapolis. For political, rhetorical, and sociological discussion, see Paul Brest & Ann Vandenberg, *Politics, Feminism, and the Constitution: The Anti–Pornography Movement in Minneapolis*, 39 Stan.L.Rev. 607 (1987). Different versions of the ordinance were passed in Indianapolis, Indiana and Bellingham, Washington (see Margaret Baldwin, *Pornography and the Traffic in Women*, 1 Yale J.L. & Fem. 111 (1989)). Both versions were declared unconstitutional.

property, public accommodations and public services; create public and private harassment, persecution and denigration; promote injury and degradation such as rape, battery, child sexual abuse, and prostitution and inhibit just enforcement of laws against these acts; contribute significantly to restricting women in particular from full exercise of citizenship and participation in public life, including in neighborhoods; damage relations between the sexes; and undermine women's equal exercise of rights to speech and action guaranteed to all citizens under the Constitutions and laws of the United States, the State of California and the County of Los Angeles.

Section 3. Definitions

1. *Pornography* is the graphic sexually explicit subordination of women through pictures and/or words that also includes one or more of the following: (i) women are presented dehumanized as sexual objects, things or commodities; or (ii) women are presented as sexual objects who enjoy pain or humiliation; or (iii) women are presented as sexual objects who experience sexual pleasure in being raped; or (iv) women are presented as sexual objects tied up or cut up or mutilated or bruised or physically hurt; or (v) women are presented in postures of sexual submission, servility, or display; or (vi) women's body parts—including but not limited to vaginas, breasts, or buttocks—are exhibited such that women are reduced to those parts; or (vii) women are presented as whores by nature; or (viii) women are presented as being penetrated by objects or animals; or (ix) women are presented in scenarios of degradation, injury, torture, shown as filthy or inferior, bleeding, bruised or hurt in a context that makes these conditions sexual.

2. The use of men,[b] children, or transsexuals in the place of women in (1) above is also pornography for purposes of this law.

Section 4. Unlawful Practices

1. *Coercion into pornography*: It shall be sex discrimination to coerce, intimidate, or fraudulently induce (hereafter, "coerce") any person, including transsexual, into performing for pornography, which injury may date from any appearance or sale of any product(s) of such performance(s). The maker(s), seller(s), exhibitor(s) and/or distributor(s) of said pornography may be sued, including for an injunction to eliminate the product(s) of the performance(s) from the public view.

Proof of one or more of the following facts or conditions shall not, without more, negate a finding of coercion:

(i) that the person is a woman; or

(ii) that the person is or has been a prostitute; or

(iii) that the person has attained the age of majority; or

(iv) that the person is connected by blood or marriage to anyone involved in or related to the making of the pornography; or

(v) that the person has previously had, or been thought to have had, sexual relations with anyone, including anyone involved in or related to the making of the pornography; or

b. Does this provision wrongly conflate gay pornography with stereotypical heterosexual pornography? See Leslie Green, *Pornographies*, 8 J. of Pol. Phil. 27 (2000). For criticism of the ordinance from a lesbian perspective, see Becki L. Ross, *'It's Merely Designed for Sexual Arousal,'* Feminism & Pornography 264–317 (Cornell ed. 1999).

(vi) that the person has previously posed for sexually explicit pictures with or for anyone, including anyone involved in or related to the making of the pornography at issue; or

(vii) that anyone else, including a spouse or other relative, has given permission on the person's behalf; or

(viii) that the person actually consented to a use of the performance that is changed into pornography; or

(ix) that the person knew that the purpose of the acts or events in question was to make pornography; or

(x) that the person showed no resistance or appeared to cooperate actively in the photographic sessions or in the events that produced the pornography; or

(xi) that the person signed a contract, or made statements affirming a willingness to cooperate in the production of pornography; or

(xii) that no physical force, threats, or weapons were used in the making of the pornography; or

(xiii) that the person was paid or otherwise compensated.

2. *Trafficking in pornography:* It shall be sex discrimination to produce, sell, exhibit, or distribute pornography, including through private clubs.

(i) City, state, and federally funded public libraries or private and public university and college libraries in which pornography is available for study, including on open shelves but excluding special display presentations, shall not be construed to be trafficking in pornography.

(ii) Isolated passages or isolated parts shall not be actionable under this section.

(iii) Any woman has a claim hereunder as a woman acting against the subordination of women. Any man, child, or transsexual who alleges injury by pornography in the way women are injured by it also has a claim.

3. *Forcing pornography on a person:* It shall be sex discrimination to force pornography on a person, including child or transsexual, in any place of employment, education, home, or public place. Only the perpetrator of the force and/or institution responsible for the force may be sued.

4. *Assault or physical attack due to pornography:* It shall be sex discrimination to assault, physically attack or injure any person, including child or transsexual, in a way that is directly caused by specific pornography. The perpetrator of the assault or attack may be sued. The maker(s), distributor(s), seller(s), and/or exhibitor(s) may also be sued, including for an injunction against the specific pornography's further exhibition, distribution or sale.

Section 5. Defenses

1. It shall not be a defense that the defendant in an action under this law did not know or intend that the materials were pornography or sex discrimination.

2. No damages or compensation for losses shall be recoverable under Sec. 4(2) or other than against the perpetrator of the assault or attack in Sec. 4(4) unless the defendant knew or had reason to know that the materials were pornography.

3. In actions under Sec. 4(2) or other than against the perpetrator of the assault or attack in Sec. 4(4), no damages or compensation for losses shall be recoverable against maker(s) for pornography made, against distributor(s) for pornography distributed, against seller(s) for pornography sold, or against exhibitor(s) for pornography exhibited, prior to the effective date of this law.

Section 6. Enforcement

a. Civil Action: Any person, or their estate, aggrieved by violations of this law may enforce its provisions by means of a civil action. No criminal penalties shall attach for any violation of the provisions of this law. Relief for violations of this law, except as expressly restricted or precluded herein, may include compensatory and punitive damages and reasonable attorney's fees, costs and disbursements.

b. Injunction: Any person who violates this law may be enjoined except that:

(i) In actions under Sec. 4(2), and other than against the perpetrator of the assault or attack under Sec. 4(4), no temporary or permanent injunction shall issue prior to a final judicial determination that the challenged activities constitute a violation of this law.

(ii) No temporary or permanent injunction shall extend beyond such material(s) that, having been described with reasonable specificity by the injunction, have been determined to be validly proscribed under this law.

Section 7. Severability

Should any part(s) of this law be found legally invalid, the remaining part(s) remain valid. A judicial declaration that any part(s) of this law cannot be applied validly in a particular manner or to a particular case or category of cases shall not affect the validity of that part(s) as otherwise applied, unless such other application would clearly frustrate the intent of the Board of Supervisors in adopting this law.

Section 8. Limitation of Action

Actions under this law must be filed within one year of the alleged discriminatory acts.

Notes and Questions

1. *The Ferber analogy.* Consider Cass Sunstein, *Neutrality in Constitutional Law (With Special Reference to Pornography, Abortion, and Surrogacy),* 92 Colum.L.Rev. 1, 24 (1992): "A successful action for rape and sexual assault is difficult enough. The difficulty becomes all the greater when the victims are young women coerced into, and abused during, the production of pornography. Often those victims will be reluctant to put themselves through the experience and possible humiliation and expense of initiating a proceeding. Often prosecutors will be reluctant to act on their behalf. Often they will have extremely little credibility even if they are willing to come forward. In this light, the only realistically effective way to eliminate the practice is to eliminate or reduce the financial benefits." If all women in pornographic films were coerced, would the analogy to *Ferber* be airtight? If not, how much coercion is acceptable? What is the relationship between prostitution and pornography? On the latter, see *Feminism & Pornography* (Cornell ed. 1999).[c]

2. *Relationship between obscenity and pornography.* Consider Andrea Dworkin, *Against the Male Flood: Censorship, Pornography, and Equality,* 8 Harv. Women's L.J. 1, 8–9 (1985): "What is at stake in obscenity law is always erection: under what conditions, in what circumstances, how, by whom, by what materials men want it produced in themselves. Men have made this public policy. Why they want to regulate their own erections through law is a question of endless interest and importance to feminists. * * *

"The insult pornography offers, invariably, to sex is accomplished in the active subordination of women: the creation of a sexual dynamic in which the putting-down of women, the suppression of women, and ultimately the brutalization of women, *is* what sex is taken to be. Obscenity in law, and in what it does socially, is erection. Law recognizes the act in this. Pornography, however, is a broader, more comprehensive act, because it crushes a whole class of people through violence and subjugation: and sex is the vehicle that does the crushing. The penis is not the test, as it is in obscenity. Instead, the status of women is the issue. Erection is implicated in the subordinating, but who it reaches and how are the pressing legal and social questions. Pornography, unlike obscenity, is a discrete, identifiable system of sexual exploitation that hurts women as a class by creating inequality and abuse."

Consider Catharine MacKinnon, *Pornography, Civil Rights, and Speech,* 20 Harv.Civ.Rts.—Civ.Lib.L.Rev. 1, 50–52 & 16–17 (1985): "Under the obscenity rubric, much legal and psychological scholarship has centered on a search for the elusive link between pornography defined as obscenity and harm. They have looked high and low—in the mind of the male consumer, in society or in its 'moral fabric,' in correlations between variations in levels of anti-social acts and liberalization of obscenity laws. The only harm they have found has been one they have attributed to 'the social interests in order and morality.' Until recently, no one looked very persistently for harm to women, particularly harm to women through men. The rather obvious fact that the sexes *relate* has been overlooked in the inquiry into the male consumer and his mind. The pornography doesn't just drop out of the sky, go into his head and stop there. Specifically, men rape, batter, prostitute, molest, and sexually harass women. Under conditions of inequality, they also hire, fire, promote, and grade women, decide how much or whether or not we are worth paying and for what, define and approve and disapprove of women in ways that count, that determine our lives.

"In pornography, there it is, in one place, all of the abuses that women had to struggle so long even to begin to articulate, all the *unspeakable* abuse: the rape, the battery, the sexual harassment, the prostitution, and the sexual abuse of children. Only in the pornography it is called something else: sex, sex, sex, sex, and sex, respectively. Pornography sexualizes rape, battery, sexual harassment, prostitution, and child sexual abuse; it thereby celebrates, promotes, authorizes, and legitimizes them. More generally, it eroticizes the dominance and submission that is the dynamic common to them all. It makes hierarchy sexy and calls that 'the truth about sex' or just a mirror of reality." See generally Andrea Dworkin, *Pornography: Men Possessing Women* (1981). Catharine MacKinnon, *Only Words* (1993); Catharine MacKinnon, *Toward a Feminist Theory of the State* 195–214 (1989); Catharine MacKinnon, *Feminism Unmodified* 127–228 (1987).

c. See also Cynthia Chandler, *Feminists as Collaborators and Prostitutes as Autobiographers,* 10 Hastings L.J. 135 (1999).

3. *The trafficking section.* Is the trafficking section constitutional under *Miller?* Consider the following hypothetical commentary: "The Dworkin–Mac-Kinnon proposal focuses on a narrower class of material than *Miller* because it excludes erotic materials that do not involve subordination. That class of material upon which it does focus appeals to prurient interest because it is graphic and sexually explicit. Moreover, the eroticization of dominance in the ways specified in the ordinance is so patently offensive to community standards that it can be said as a matter of law that this class of materials lacks *serious* literary, artistic, political, or scientific value as a matter of law." Do you agree?

Is there a good analogy to *Beauharnais?* To *Ferber?* Did more or less harm exist in *Gertz? Miller? Ferber?* Was there more or less of a threat to first amendment values in *Gertz? Miller? Ferber?* Should this be accepted as a new category? Consider Wendy Kaminer, *Pornography and the First Amendment: Prior Restraints and Private Action,* 239, 245 in *Take Back the Night: Women on Pornography* (Laura Lederer ed. 1980): "The Women's Movement is a civil rights movement, and we should appreciate the importance of individual freedom of choice and the danger of turning popular sentiment into law in areas affecting individual privacy.

"Legislative or judicial control of pornography is simply not possible without breaking down the legal principles and procedures that are essential to our own right to speak and, ultimately, our freedom to control our own lives. We must continue to organize against pornography and the degradation and abuse of women, but we must not ask the government to take up our struggle for us. The power it will assume to do so will be far more dangerous to us all than the 'power' of pornography."[d]

d. Compare Nan Hunter & Sylvia Law, *Brief Amici Curiae of Feminist Anti–Censorship Taskforce* (on appeal in *Hudnut,* below), 21 U.Mich.J.L.Ref. 69, 109 & 129–30 (1987–88). The ordinance conceivably "would require the judiciary to impose its views of correct sexuality on a diverse community. The inevitable result would be to disapprove those images that are least conventional and privilege those that are closest to majoritarian beliefs about proper sexuality. [Moreover] [b]y defining sexually explicit images of women as subordinating and degrading to them, the ordinance reinforces the stereotypical view that 'good' women do not seek and enjoy sex. [Finally], the ordinance perpetuates a stereotype of women as helpless victims, incapable of consent, and in need of protection." See generally Nadine Strossen, *Defending Pornography* (1995).

For collections of feminist perspectives, see Drucilla Cornell, ed., *Feminism and* Pornography (2000); Take *Back the Night,* supra; Varda Burstyn, ed., *Women Against Censorship* (1985); Ann Snitow, Christine Stansell & Sharon Thompson, etc., *Powers of Desire* 419–67 (1983). For a variety of views (including feminist views), see James Weinstein, *Hate Speech, Pornography, and the Radical Attack on Free Speech Doctrine* (1999); Richard Delgado & Jean Stefanic, *Must We Defend Nazis* (1997); Nicholas Wolfson, *Hate Speech, Sex Speech, Free Speech* (1997); Michelle Chernikoff Anderson, *Speaking Freely About Reducing Vi-* olence Against Women, 10 U.Fla. J.L. & Pub. Pol. 173 (1998); Joshua Cohen, *Freedom of Expression,* 21 Phil. & Pub.Aff. 207 (1993); Deborah Rhode, *Justice and Gender,* 263–73 (1989); Mark Tushnet, *Red, White, and Blue* 293–312 (1988); Donald Downs, *The Attorney General's Commission and the New Politics of Pornography,* 1987 Am.B.Found.Res.J. 641; Steven Gey, *The Apologetics of Suppression,* 86 Mich.L.Rev. 1564 (1988); Eric Hoffman, *Feminism, Pornography, and the Law,* 133 U.Pa. L.Rev. 497 (1985); Robert Post, *Cultural Heterogeneity and the Law,* 76 Calif.L.Rev. 297 (1988); David Richards, *Pornography Commissions and the First Amendment,* 39 Me.L.Rev. 275 (1987); Frederick Schauer, *Causation Theory and the Causes of Sexual Violence,* 1987 Am.B.Found.Res.J. 737; Suzanna Sherry, *An Essay Concerning Toleration,* 71 Minn.L.Rev. 963 (1987); Geoffrey Stone, *Anti–Pornography Legislation as Viewpoint–Discrimination,* 9 Harv.J.Pub.Pol'y 461 (1986); Nadine Strossen, *The Convergence of Feminist and Civil Liberties Principles in the Pornography Debate,* 62 N.Y.U.L.Rev. 201 (1987); Cass Sunstein, *Pornography and the First Amendment,* 1986 Duke L.J. 589; Robin West, *The Feminist-Conservative Anti-Pornography Alliance and the 1986 Attorney General's Commission on Pornography Report,* 1987 Am.B.Found.Res.J. 681. For the Canadian approach, see *Regina v. Butler,* [1992] 1 S.C.R. 452. For comparative commentary, see Kent Greenawalt, *Fighting Words* 99–123 (1995).

4. *Pornography and Dissent.* See Rae Langton, *Speech Acts and Unspeakable Acts,* 22 Phil. & Pub.Aff. 293, 311–312 (1993): "What is important here is not whether the speech of pornographers is universally held in high esteem: it is not— hence the common assumption among liberals that in defending pornographers they are defending the underdog. What is important is whether it is authoritative in the domain that counts—the domain of speech about sex—and whether it is authoritative for the hearers that count: people, men, boys, who in addition to wanting 'entertainment,' want to discover the right way to do things, want to know which moves in the sexual game are legitimate. What is important is whether it is authoritative for those hearers who—one way or another—do seem to learn that violence is sexy and coercion legitimate: the fifty percent of boys who 'think it is okay for a man to rape a woman if he is sexually aroused by her,' the fifteen percent of male college undergraduates who say they have raped a woman on a date, the eighty-six percent who say that they enjoy the conquest part of sex, the thirty percent who rank faces of women displaying pain and fear to be more sexually attractive than faces showing pleasure."

5. *Subordination.* Is the absence of subordination an appropriate ideal? Consider Carlin Meyer, *Sex, Sin, and Women's Liberation: Against Porn–Suppression,* 72 Tex.L.Rev. 1097, 1133 n. 156, 1154–55 (1994): "I am not suggesting that sex accompanied by intimacy, respect, and caring is not an appropriate ideal. Rather, I mean to argue that the sort of equality in which no one is ever the aggressor in fantasy or in reality is, at best, a 'utopian vision of sexual relations: sex without power, sex without persuasion, sex without pursuit.' [S]exual discourse needs to be free-wheeling and uncontrolled because of the hotly contested nature of issues concerning sexuality. Such issues as what constitutes pleasure for women and its connection to danger, to power, to men, and to aggression and inequality; of what sex is 'good' and 'bad'; and of whether women can escape inequality and coercion within Western sexual culture are debated and dissected with little agreement across boundaries of class, race, and nationality. Allies on other issues disagree about whether all violence is bad, over what constitutes violence or pleasure, and over the meaning of such terms as 'objectified,' 'degraded,' or 'demeaned.'" See also Susan Keller, *Viewing and Doing: Complicating Pornography's Meaning,* 81 Geo.L.J. 2195, 2231 (1993): "[R]obin West critiques MacKinnon and Dworkin for their failure to acknowledge the 'meaning and the value, to women, of the pleasure we take in our fantasies of eroticized submission.' Some like Jessica Benjamin and Kate Ellis have attempted to explain psychologically why pleasure can be found by women, as well as men, in submission and power. Of the various meanings pornography could have for a variety of audience members, one meaning for women could be pleasure in depictions of power."

6. *The pornography definition.* Is the proposed definition too vague? Is it more or less vague than the terminology employed in *Miller?* Is there a core of clear meaning? How would you clarify its meaning? Is the definition overbroad? What revisions, if any, would you suggest to narrow its scope?

Consider Thomas Emerson, *Pornography and the First Amendment: A Reply to Professor MacKinnon,* 3 Yale L. & Pol. Rev. 130, 131–32 (1985): "The sweep of the Indianapolis Ordinance is breathtaking. It would subject to governmental ban virtually all depictions of rape, verbal or pictorial, and a substantial proportion of other presentations of sexual encounters. More specifically, it would outlaw such works of literature as the *Arabian Nights,* John Cleland's *Fanny Hill,* Henry Miller's *Tropic of Cancer,* William Faulkner's *Sanctuary,* and Norman Mailer's *Ancient Evenings,* to name but a few. The ban would extend from Greek mythology and Shakespeare to the millions of copies of 'romance novels' now being sold in the supermarkets. It would embrace much of the world's art, from ancient carvings to Picasso, well-known films too numerous to mention, and a large amount of commercial advertising.

"The scope of the Indianapolis Ordinance is not accidental. * * * As Professor MacKinnon emphasizes, male domination has deep, pervasive and ancient roots in our society, so it is not surprising that our literature, art, entertainment and commercial practices are permeated by attitudes and behavior that create and reflect the inferior status of women. If the answer to the problem, as Professor MacKinnon describes it, is government suppression of sexual expression that contributes to female subordination, then the net of restraint has to be cast on a nearly limitless scale." Would the ordinance inadvertently cover activist anti-pornographic art that uses violent sexual images to make its point. If not, does the intent of the artist excuse any unintended effects? See Amy Adler, *What's Left?: Hate Speech, Pornography, and the Problem of Artistic Expression,* 84 Calif.L.Rev. 1499 (1996).

7. *The assault provision.* Should the maker of a pornographic work be responsible for assaults prompted by the work? Should the maker of non-pornographic works be responsible for imitative assaults. In *Olivia N. v. NBC,* 126 Cal.App.3d 488, 178 Cal.Rptr. 888 (1981), the victim of a sexual assault allegedly imitating a sexual assault in NBC's "Born Innocent" sued the network. Olivia N. claimed that NBC negligently exposed her to serious risk because it knew or should have known that someone would imitate the act portrayed in the movie. Suppose Olivia N. could show that NBC had been advised that such an assault was likely if the movie were shown? Should a court analogize to cases like *Gertz?* The California court ruled that Olivia N. could not prevail unless she met the *Brandenburg* standard.[e]

The Indianapolis version of the anti-pornography civil rights ordinance was struck down in AMERICAN BOOKSELLERS ASS'N v. HUDNUT, 771 F.2d 323 (7th Cir.1985), affirmed, 475 U.S. 1001, 106 S.Ct. 1172, 89 L.Ed.2d 291 (1986). The Seventh Circuit, per EASTERBROOK, J., ruled that the definition of pornography infected the entire ordinance (including provisions against trafficking, coercion into pornography, forcing pornography on a person, and assault or physical attack due to pornography) because it impermissibly discriminated on the basis of point of view: "Indianapolis enacted an ordinance defining 'pornography' as a practice that discriminates against women. * * *

"The Indianapolis ordinance does not refer to the prurient interest, to offensiveness, or to the standards of the community. It demands attention to particular depictions, not to the work judged as a whole. It is irrelevant under the ordinance whether the work has literary, artistic, political, or scientific value. The City and many amici point to these omissions as virtues. They maintain that pornography influences attitudes, and the statute is a way to alter the socialization of men and women rather than to vindicate community standards of offensiveness. And as one of the principal drafters of the ordinance has asserted, 'if a woman is subjected, why should it matter that the work has other value?'

e. For relevant commentary, see J.M. Balkin, *The Rhetoric of Responsibility,* 76 Va. L.Rev. 197 (1990); Frederick Schauer, *Uncoupling Free Speech,* 92 Colum.L.Rev. 1321 (1992); Frederick Schauer, *Mrs. Palsgraf and the First Amendment,* 47 Wash. & Lee L.Rev. 161 (1990).

Catharine MacKinnon, *Pornography, Civil Rights, and Speech*, 20 Harv.Civ.Rts.—Civ.Lib.L.Rev. 1, 21 (1985).

"Civil rights groups and feminists have entered this case as amici on both sides. Those supporting the ordinance say that it will play an important role in reducing the tendency of men to view women as sexual objects, a tendency that leads to both unacceptable attitudes and discrimination in the workplace and violence away from it. Those opposing the ordinance point out that much radical feminist literature is explicit and depicts women in ways forbidden by the ordinance and that the ordinance would reopen old battles. It is unclear how Indianapolis would treat works from James Joyce's *Ulysses* to Homer's *Iliad;* both depict women as submissive objects for conquest and domination.

"We do not try to balance the arguments for and against an ordinance such as this. The ordinance discriminates on the ground of the content of the speech. Speech treating women in the approved way—in sexual encounters 'premised on equality' (MacKinnon, supra, at 22)—is lawful no matter how sexually explicit. Speech treating women in the disapproved way—as submissive in matters sexual or as enjoying humiliation—is unlawful no matter how significant the literary, artistic, or political qualities of the work taken as a whole. The state may not ordain preferred viewpoints in this way. The Constitution forbids the state to declare one perspective right and silence opponents.[a] [Under] the First Amendment the government must leave to the people the evaluation of ideas. Bald or subtle, an idea is as powerful as the audience allows it to be. A belief may be pernicious—the beliefs of Nazis led to the death of millions, those of the Klan to the repression of millions. A pernicious belief may prevail. Totalitarian governments today rule much of the planet, practicing suppression of billions and spreading dogma that may enslave others. One of the things that separates our society from theirs is our absolute right to propagate opinions that the government finds wrong or even hateful. * * *

"Under the ordinance graphic sexually explicit speech is 'pornography' or not depending on the perspective the author adopts. Speech that 'subordinates' women and also, for example, presents women as enjoying pain, humiliation, or rape, or even simply presents women in 'positions of servility or submission or display' is forbidden, no matter how great the literary or political value of the work taken as a whole. Speech that portrays women in positions of equality is lawful, no matter how graphic the sexual content. This is thought control. It establishes an 'approved' view of women, of how they may react to sexual encounters, of how the sexes may relate to each other. Those who espouse the approved view may use sexual images; those who do not, may not.

"Indianapolis justifies the ordinance on the ground that pornography affects thoughts. Men who see women depicted as subordinate are more likely to treat them so. Pornography is an aspect of dominance.[1] It does not persuade people so

---

a. But consider Alon Harel, *Bigotry, Pornography, and The First Amendment: A Theory of Unprotected Speech*, 65 S.Cal.L.Rev. 1887, 1889 (1992): "Some ideas and values cannot aid in the process of shaping our political obligations. This is not because these 'values' do not, as a matter of fact, influence the output of the political process but because any influence they do exert does not generate legitimate political obligations. Racist and sexist values cannot participate in the shaping of political obligations because the legal obli-

gations they generate do not have morally binding force."

1. "Pornography constructs what a woman is in terms of its view of what men want sexually. * * * Pornography's world of equality is a harmonious and balanced place. Men and women are perfectly complementary and perfectly bipolar. [All] the ways men love to take and violate women, women love to be taken and violated. [What] pornography *does* goes beyond its content: It eroticizes hierarchy,

much as change them. It works by socializing, by establishing the expected and the permissible. In this view pornography is not an idea; pornography is the injury.

"There is much to this perspective. Beliefs are also facts. People often act in accordance with the images and patterns they find around them. People raised in a religion tend to accept the tenets of that religion, often without independent examination. People taught from birth that black people are fit only for slavery rarely rebelled against that creed; beliefs coupled with the self-interest of the masters established a social structure that inflicted great harm while enduring for centuries. Words and images act at the level of the subconscious before they persuade at the level of the conscious. Even the truth has little chance unless a statement fits within the framework of beliefs that may never have been subjected to rational study.

"Therefore we accept the premises of this legislation. Depictions of subordination tend to perpetuate subordination. The subordinate status of women in turn leads to affront and lower pay at work, insult and injury at home, battery and rape on the streets.[2] * * *

"Yet this simply demonstrates the power of pornography as speech. All of these unhappy effects depend on mental intermediation. Pornography affects how people see the world, their fellows, and social relations. If pornography is what pornography does, so is other speech. Hitler's orations affected how some Germans saw Jews. Communism is a world view, not simply a *Manifesto* by Marx and Engels or a set of speeches. Efforts to suppress communist speech in the United States were based on the belief that the public acceptability of such ideas would increase the likelihood of totalitarian government. [Many] people believe that the existence of television, apart from the content of specific programs, leads to intellectual laziness, to a penchant for violence, to many other ills. The Alien and Sedition Acts passed during the administration of John Adams rested on a sincerely held belief that disrespect for the government leads to social collapse and revolution—a belief with support in the history of many nations. Most govern-

---

it sexualizes inequality. It makes dominance and submission sex. Inequality is its central dynamic; the illusion of freedom coming together with the reality of force is central to its working. [P]ornography is neither harmless fantasy nor a corrupt and confused misrepresentation of an otherwise neutral and healthy sexual situation. It institutionalizes the sexuality of male supremacy, fusing the erotization of dominance and submission with the social construction of male and female. * * * Men treat women as who they see women as being. Pornography constructs who that is. Men's power over women means that the way men see women defines who women can be. Pornography [is] a sexual reality." MacKinnon, supra, at 17–18 (emphasis in original). See also Andrea Dworkin, *Pornography: Men Possessing Women* (1981). A national commission in Canada recently adopted a similar rationale for controlling pornography. Special Commission on Pornography and Prostitution, 1 *Pornography and Prostitution in Canada* 49–59 (1985).

2. MacKinnon's article collects empirical work that supports this proposition. The social science studies are very difficult to interpret,

however, and they conflict. Because much of the effect of speech comes through a process of socialization, it is difficult to measure incremental benefits and injuries caused by particular speech. Several psychologists have found, for example, that those who see violent, sexually explicit films tend to have more violent thoughts. But how often does this lead to actual violence? National commissions on obscenity here, in the United Kingdom, and in Canada have found that it is not possible to demonstrate a direct link between obscenity and rape or exhibitionism. The opinions in *Miller* discuss the U.S. commission. See also *Report of the Committee on Obscenity and Film Censorship* 61–95 (Home Office, Her Majesty's Stationery Office, 1979); 1 *Pornography and Prostitution in Canada* 71–73, 95–103. In saying that we accept the finding that pornography as the ordinance defines it leads to unhappy consequences, we mean only that there is evidence to this effect, that this evidence is consistent with much human experience, and that as judges we must accept the legislative resolution of such disputed empirical questions.

ments of the world act on this empirical regularity, suppressing critical speech. In the United States, however, the strength of the support for this belief is irrelevant. Seditious libel is protected speech unless the danger is not only grave but also imminent. See *New York Times*; cf. *Brandenburg*.

"Racial bigotry, anti-semitism, violence on television, reporters' biases—these and many more influence the culture and shape our socialization. None is directly answerable by more speech, unless that speech too finds its place in the popular culture. Yet all is protected as speech, however insidious. Any other answer leaves the government in control of all of the institutions of culture, the great censor and director of which thoughts are good for us.

"Sexual responses often are unthinking responses, and the association of sexual arousal with the subordination of women therefore may have a substantial effect. But almost all cultural stimuli provoke unconscious responses. Religious ceremonies condition their participants. Teachers convey messages by selecting what not to cover; the implicit message about what is off limits or unthinkable may be more powerful than the messages for which they present rational argument. Television scripts contain unarticulated assumptions. People may be conditioned in subtle ways. If the fact that speech plays a role in a process of conditioning were enough to permit governmental regulation, that would be the end of freedom of speech. * * *

"Much of Indianapolis's argument rests on the belief that when speech is 'unanswerable,' and the metaphor that there is a 'marketplace of ideas' does not apply, the First Amendment does not apply either. The metaphor is honored; Milton's *Aeropagitica* and John Stewart Mill's *On Liberty* defend freedom of speech on the ground that the truth will prevail, and many of the most important cases under the First Amendment recite this position. The Framers undoubtedly believed it. As a general matter it is true. But the Constitution does not make the dominance of truth a necessary condition of freedom of speech. To say that it does would be to confuse an outcome of free speech with a necessary condition for the application of the amendment.

"A power to limit speech on the ground that truth has not yet prevailed and is not likely to prevail implies the power to declare truth. At some point the government must be able to say (as Indianapolis has said): 'We know what the truth is, yet a free exchange of speech has not driven out falsity, so that we must now prohibit falsity.' If the government may declare the truth, why wait for the failure of speech? Under the First Amendment, however, there is no such thing as a false idea, *Gertz*, so the government may not restrict speech on the ground that in a free exchange truth is not yet dominant. * * *

"We come, finally, to the argument that pornography is 'low value' speech, that it is enough like obscenity that Indianapolis may prohibit it. Some cases hold that speech far removed from politics and other subjects at the core of the Framers' concerns may be subjected to special regulation. E.g., *FCC v. Pacifica Foundation* Sec. 8, II; *Young v. American Mini Theatres*; *Chaplinsky*. These cases do not sustain statutes that select among viewpoints, however. In *Pacifica* the FCC sought to keep vile language off the air during certain times. The Court held that it may; but the Court would not have sustained a regulation prohibiting scatological descriptions of Republicans but not scatological descriptions of Democrats, or any other form of selection among viewpoints.

"At all events, pornography is not low value speech within the meaning of these cases. Indianapolis seeks to prohibit certain speech because it believes this speech influences social relations and politics on a grand scale, that it controls attitudes at home and in the legislature. This precludes a characterization of the speech as low value. True, pornography and obscenity have sex in common. But Indianapolis left out of its definition any reference to literary, artistic, political, or scientific value. The ordinance applies to graphic sexually explicit subordination in works great and small.[3] The Court sometimes balances the value of speech against the costs of its restriction, but it does this by category of speech and not by the content of particular works. See John Hart Ely, *Flag Desecration: A Case Study in the Roles of Categorization and Balancing in First Amendment Analysis,* 88 Harv.L.Rev. 1482 (1975); Geoffrey Stone, *Restrictions of Speech Because of its Content: The Strange Case of Subject–Matter Restrictions,* 46 U.Chi.L.Rev. 81 (1978). Indianapolis has created an approved point of view and so loses the support of these cases.

"Any rationale we could imagine in support of this ordinance could not be limited to sex discrimination. Free speech has been on balance an ally of those seeking change. Governments that want stasis start by restricting speech. Culture is a powerful force of continuity; Indianapolis paints pornography as a part of the culture of power. Change in any complex system ultimately depends on the ability of outsiders to challenge accepted views and the reigning institutions. Without a strong guarantee of freedom of speech, there is no effective right to challenge what is."[b]

Notes and Questions

1. In response to the last paragraph, supra, Professor Frank Michelman observes: "[I]t is a fair and obvious question why preservation of 'effective right[s] to challenge what is' does not require protection of a 'freedom of speech' more broadly conceived to protect social critics—'outsiders,' in Judge Easterbrook's phrase—against suppression by nongovernmental as well as by governmental power. It is a fair and obvious question why the assertion that '[g]overnments that want stasis start by restricting speech' does not apply equally to the nongovernmental agencies of power in society. It is a fair and obvious question why our society's openness to challenge does not need protection against repressive private as well as public action." *Conceptions of Democracy in American Constitutional Argument: The Case of Pornography Regulation,* 56 Tenn.L.Rev. 291 (1989), citing MacKinnon, *Feminism Unmodified* 155–58 (1987).

2. *Free speech and silence.* Consider Catharine MacKinnon, *Toward a Feminist Theory of the State* 206 (1989): "That pornography chills women's expression

3. Indianapolis briefly argues that *Beauharnais,* which allowed a state to penalize "group libel," supports the ordinance. In *Collin v. Smith,* [Sec. 1, V, C infra], we concluded that cases such as *New York Times v. Sullivan* had so washed away the foundations of *Beauharnais* that it could not be considered authoritative. If we are wrong in this, however, the case still does not support the ordinance. It is not clear that depicting women as subordinate in sexually explicit ways, even combined with a depiction of pleasure in rape, would fit within the definition of a group libel. The well received film *Swept Away* used explicit sex, plus taking pleasure in rape, to make a political statement, not to defame. Work must be an insult or slur for its own sake to come within the ambit of *Beauharnais,* and a work need not be scurrilous at all to be pornography under the ordinance.

b. The balance of the opinion suggested ways that parts of the ordinance might be salvaged, if redrafted. It suggested, for example, that the city might forbid coerced participation in any film or in "any film containing explicit sex." If the latter were adopted, would it make a difference if the section applied to persons coerced into participation in such films without regard to whether they were forced into explicit sex scenes? Swygert, J., concurring, joined part of Easterbrook, J.'s opinion for the court, but objected both to the "questionable and broad assertions regarding how human behavior can be conditioned" and to the "advisory" opinion on how parts of the ordinance might be redrafted.

is difficult to demonstrate empirically because silence is not eloquent. Yet on no more of the same kind of evidence, the argument that suppressing pornography might chill legitimate speech has supported its protection. [T]he law of the First Amendment comprehends that freedom of expression, in the abstract, is a system but fails to comprehend that sexism (and racism), in the concrete, are also systems."[c] But see Charles Fried, *Perfect Freedom, Perfect Justice*, 78 B.U. L.Rev. 717, 737 (1998): "[R]acist or sexist speech, if it has the effect attributed to it, produces it through the mind: Potential speakers are persuaded that they are less worthy individuals and so they are less inclined to contribute their voices in debate; and potential listeners are persuaded that these speakers are not worth attending to. But as the argument must concede that the mechanism of the silencing is through persuasion, it must also concede that the government's countermeasures must be directed at silencing the attempt to persuade: The government stops the message because of what it says and the evil the government fears works through the channels of the mind. I do not see how we can escape the conclusion that the government is stopping the message because it is afraid that people might believe it. But that is precisely what the First Amendment has consistently identified as what government may not do * * *."

3. *"We do not try to balance * * *."* Does the existence of point of view discrimination preclude balancing under existing law? Consider Marjorie Heins, *Viewpoint Discrimination*, 24 Hastings L.Q. 99, 136 (1996) "Judge Easterbrook's point is well-taken, but it reaches beyond the MacKinnon/Dworkin type of ordinance. The First Amendment does not allow the government to dictate 'which thoughts are good for us,' whether it be in the guise of 'feminist' antipornography laws, indecency laws that turn on notions of 'patent offensiveness,' or obscenity laws of the type upheld in *Miller* and *Slaton* because of the lascivious, family-undermining, personality-distorting, and generally immoral thoughts that the Court felt pornography inspires."

4. Does pornography as defined by Indianapolis (or some part of that category) implicate such little first amendment value as to foreclose constitutional protection? How should such value be assessed? Consider Cass Sunstein, *Pornography and the First Amendment*, 1986 Duke Law Journal 603–04: "First, the speech must be far afield from the central concern of the first amendment, which, broadly speaking, is effective popular control of public affairs. Speech that concerns governmental processes is entitled to the highest level of protection; speech that has little or nothing to do with public affairs may be accorded less protection. Second, a distinction is drawn between cognitive and noncognitive aspects of speech. Speech that has purely noncognitive appeal will be entitled to less constitutional protection.[d] Third, the purpose of the speaker is relevant: if the speaker is seeking to communicate a message, he will be treated more favorably than if he is not. Fourth, the various classes of low-value speech reflect judgments that in certain areas, government is unlikely to be acting for constitutionally impermissible reasons or producing constitutionally troublesome harms."

c. To what extent is discourse inherently empowering and silencing in its effects? To what extent is pornography unique? For rich commentary, see the essays collected in *Censorship and Silencing* (Post ed. 1998); Langton, note 4 supra; Jennifer Hornsby, *Disempowered Speech*, 23 Philos. Topics 127 (1997); Daniel Jacobson, *Freedom of Speech Acts?*, 24 Phil. & Pub. Aff. 64 (1995); Wojciech Sadurski,

On Seeing Speech Through An Equality Lens, 16 Oxford J. of Leg. Stud. 713 (1996).

d. For debate about this factor compare Paul Chevigny, *Pornography and Cognition*, 1989 Duke L.J. 420 with Cass Sunstein, *The First Amendment and Cognition*, 1989 Duke L.J. 433. See also Kenneth Karst, *Boundaries and Reasons: Freedom of Expression and the Subordination of Groups*, 1990 U.Ill.L.Rev. 95.

How do Sunstein's factors apply to the Indianapolis ordinance?

To what extent is it desirable to consider the value of speech in forging a balance?[e]

C. RACIST SPEECH REVISITED: THE NAZIS

"What do you want to sell in the marketplace? What idea? The idea of murder?"

Erna Gans, a concentration camp survivor and active leader in the Skokie B'nai B'rith.[a]

COLLIN v. SMITH, 578 F.2d 1197 (7th Cir.), cert. denied, 439 U.S. 916 (1978), per PELL, J., struck down a Village of Skokie "Racial Slur" Ordinance, making it a misdemeanor to disseminate any material (defined to include "public display of markings and clothing of symbolic significance") promoting and inciting racial or religious hatred. The Village would apparently apply this ordinance to the display of swastikas and military uniforms by the NSPA, a "Nazi organization" which planned to peacefully demonstrate for some 20–30 minutes in front of the Skokie Village Hall.

Although there was some evidence that some individuals "might have difficulty restraining their reactions to the Nazi demonstration," the Village "does not rely on a fear of responsive violence to justify the ordinance, and does not even suggest that there will be any physical violence if the march is held. This confession takes the case out of the scope of *Brandenburg* and *Feiner*. [It] also eliminates any argument based on the fighting words doctrine of *Chaplinsky*, [which] applied only to words with a direct tendency to cause violence by the persons to whom, individually, the words were addressed."

The court rejected, inter alia, the argument that the Nazi march, with its display of swastikas and uniforms, "will create a substantive evil that it has a right to prohibit: the infliction of psychic trauma on resident holocaust survivors [some 5,000] and other Jewish residents. [The] problem with engrafting an exception on the First Amendment for such situations is that they are indistinguishable in principle from speech that 'invite[s] dispute [or] induces a condition of unrest [or] even stirs people to anger,' *Terminiello*. Yet these are among the 'high purposes' of the First Amendment. [Where,] as here, a crime is made of a silent march, attended only by symbols and not by extrinsic conduct offensive in itself, we think the words of *Street v. New York* [Sec. 2 infra] are very much on point: '[A]ny shock effect [must] be attributed to the content of the ideas expressed. [P]ublic expression of ideas may not be prohibited merely because the ideas are themselves offensive to some of their hearers.' "

Nor was the court impressed with the argument that the proposed march was "not speech, [but] rather an invasion, intensely menacing no matter how peacefully conducted" (most of Skokie's residents are Jewish): "There *need be* no captive audience, as Village residents may, if they wish, simply avoid the Village Hall for thirty minutes on a Sunday afternoon, which no doubt would be their normal course of conduct on a day when the Village Hall was not open in the regular

e. Compare, e.g., Martin Redish, *The Value of Free Speech*, 130 U.Pa.L.Rev. 591, 596–611 (1982) and Larry Alexander, *Low Value Speech*, 83 Nw.U.L.Rev. 547 (1989) with Cass Sunstein, *Low Value Speech Revisited*, 83 Nw. U.L.Rev. 555 (1989). Reconsider the question after completing Sec. 3.

a. Quoted in Fred Friendly & Martha Elliot, *The Constitution: That Delicate Balance* 83 (1984).

course of business. Absent such intrusion or captivity, there is no justifiable substantial privacy interest to save [the ordinance], when it attempts, by fiat, to declare the entire Village, at all times, a privacy zone that may be sanitized from the offensiveness of Nazi ideology and symbols."[b]

Notes and Questions

1. Is *Beauharnais,* Sec. 1, II, A supra, still "good law"? Should it be?

2. *Abstraction and the first amendment.* Consider Frederick Schauer, *Harry Kalven and the Perils of Particularism,* 56 U.Chi.L.Rev. 397, 408 (1989): "[O]ne sees in the *Skokie* litigation an available distinction between Nazis and others, an equally available distinction between speech designed to persuade and speech designed to assault, and a decision made by the people rather than a decision designed to interfere with the people's wishes. If doctrinal development under the free speech clause were merely an instance of common law decision making, one might expect to see some or all of these factors treated as relevant, and new distinctions developed in order to make relevant those factors, such as the ones just enumerated, that had been suppressed by previous formulations. Yet we know that this is not what happened. The particular events were abstracted in numerous ways. Nazis became political speakers, a suburban community populated by Holocaust survivors became a public forum, and popularly inspired restrictions became governmental censorship. The resolution of the controversy, therefore, stands not as a monument to the ever-more-sensitive development of common law doctrine, but instead as an embodiment of the way in which the First Amendment operates precisely by the entrenchment of categories whose breadth prevents the consideration of some number of relevant factors, and prevents the free speech decision maker from 'thinking small.'"

3. *The Klan and the Communists.* Are the arguments of those who would prohibit racist speech (or pornography), the same as those who would have restricted the speech of the communists (or anarchists). See Steven G. Gey, *The Case Against Postmodern Censorship Theory,* 145 U.Pa. L.Rev. 193 (1996). But consider Steven H. Shiffrin, *Dissent, Injustice, and the Meanings of America* 78, 79 n. 184 (1999): "Racist speakers seek to persuade people that government (and others) should not treat all persons with equal concern and respect. If our legal system has even a prayer of claiming to be legitimate, however, it must start from the premise that all citizens are worthy of equal concern and respect. * * * In this limited context, the best test of truth is the system's foundational premise of equality,[c] not whether racist speech can emerge in the marketplace of ideas. [To] the extent the communists argue against free speech, [they] are in the same

---

b. See also *Skokie v. National Socialist Party,* 69 Ill.2d 605, 14 Ill.Dec. 890, 373 N.E.2d 21 (1978). For commentary relating the Skokie issue to regulation of pornography, and of commercial speech, for the purpose of asking whether there are general principles of freedom of expression and whether freedom of expression should be category-dependent, see Thomas Scanlon, *Freedom of Expression and Categories of Expression,* 40 U.Pitt.L.Rev. 519 (1979). For assessment of the complicated connection between Skokie and equality values especially in light of the rest of first amendment law, see Laurence Tribe, *Constitutional Choices* 219–20 (1985). Compare Donald Downs, *Skokie Revisited: Hate Group Speech and the First Amendment,* 60 Not.D.Law. 629 (1985). More generally, see David Kretzmer, *Freedom of Speech and Racism,* 8 Cardozo L.Rev. 445 (1987).

c. Are there many conceptions of equality in the American system which those who would regulate racist speech need to take account? See Gary Goodpaster, *Equality and Free Speech: The Case Against Substantive Equality,* 82 Iowa L. Rev 645 (1997).

position as the Ku Klux Klan, but the harm of that speech is not in the same league as racist speech."

4. Consider Sionaidh Douglas-Scott, *The Hatefulness of Protected Speech: A Comparison of the American and European Approaches,* 7 Wm. & Mary Bill Rts.J. 305, 343–44 (1999): "There clearly is a radical difference between the German or, more generally, the European and American approach to the regulation of speech. [First], European and, especially, German jurisprudence emphasize particular values-dignity, protection of personal identity, and equality. German judgments stress the potential of racist insults and denials of Nazi atrocities to affect the very core of the identities of members of certain groups, even if those individuals have not been specifically targeted for abuse. [European] case law rejects a conception of individuals as beings who merely should be left to their own devices to make up their own minds about the value of expression in the public domain, to be free to ignore it, or to counter it with more speech. Such an approach isolates human beings by forcing them to take the consequences of painful conduct and ignores the particular susceptibility of certain groups to injury, especially when the offense of the speech seems to be targeted at such groups because of their identity. Under the American model, the individual will be left to his or her less communal and somewhat atomistic existence.

"Second, the European approach is fundamentally more sympathetic to a conception in which the state plays a role in facilitating the realization of freedom, democracy, and equality. Under the European approach, it becomes natural for the state to assume a more affirmative role in actualizing specific constitutional rights. Within the area of freedom of speech this would require the state not only to refrain from violating certain constitutional norms, but also to participate in their realization-an approach which usually is assumed only to be required of socio-economic rights, such as the right to work. Surely it is not enough for societies that claim to be committed to the ideals of social and political equality and respect for individual dignity to remain neutral and passive when threats to these values exist. Sometimes the State must take steps to protect democracy itself, which may involve repressing speech."

For a Canadian perspective, consider Kathleen E. Mahoney, *Hate Speech: Affirmation or Contradiction of Freedom of Expression,* 1996 U.Ill.L.Rev. 789, 796 (1996): "[G]enuine democracies that respect the inherent dignity of the [person], social justice, and equality accept the fundamental principle that legislative protection and government regulation are required to protect the vulnerable. It follows that when free speech doctrine is used by more powerful groups to seriously harm less powerful, vulnerable ones, some government action is required."

5. Should the first amendment bar an action for intentional infliction of emotional distress for face-to-face racial insults?[d] Is it enough that the words in question inflict injury or must the victim show that the words were likely to promote a fight? Suppose a crowd of whites gathers to taunt a young black child on the way to a previously all white school? Suppose short of using violence, they do everything they can to harm the child? Is it the case that "no government that would call itself a decent government would fail to intervene [and] disperse the crowd" and that "the rights of the crowd [cannot] really stand on the same plane" as the child on the way to school? See Hadley Arkes, *Civility and the Restriction of*

---

d. On the relationship between discriminatory speech and the tort of intentional infliction of emotional distress, see Jean Love, *Dis-* *criminatory Speech and the Tort of Intentional Infliction of Emotional Distress,* 47 Wash. & Lee L.Rev. 123 (1990).

Speech: Rediscovering the Defamation of Groups, 1974 Sup.Ct.Rev. 281, 310–11. Should the first amendment bar state criminal or civil actions precisely tailored to punish racial insults? Insults directed against the handicapped? For the case in favor of a tort action against racial insults, see Richard Delgado, *Words That Wound: A Tort Action for Racial Insults, Epithets, and Name–Calling,* 17 Harv. Civ.Rts.—Civ.Lib.L.Rev. 133 (1982). For a spirited exchange, see Marjorie Heins, *Banning Words: A Comment on "Words that Wound,"* 18 Harv.Civ.Rts.—Civ. Lib.L.Rev. 585 (1983) and *Professor Richard Delgado Replies,* Id. at 593.

(6.) Is one person's "racialist's plea" another person's act of intimidation? Are these responses patterned? Consider Mari Matsuda, *Public Response to Racist Speech: Considering the Victim's Story,* 87 Mich.L.Rev. 2320, 2326–27 (1989): "[I] am forced to ask why the world looks so different to me from how it looks to many of the civil libertarians whom I consider my allies. [In] advocating legal restriction of hate speech, I have found my most sympathetic audience in people who identify with target groups, while I have encountered incredulity, skepticism, and even hostility from others.

"This split in reaction is also evident in case studies of hate speech. The typical reaction of target-group members to an incident of racist propaganda is alarm and immediate calls for redress. The typical reaction of non-target-group members is to consider the incidents isolated pranks, the product of sick-but-harmless minds. This is in part a defensive reaction: a refusal to believe that real people, people just like us, are racists. This disassociation leads logically to the claim that there is no institutional or state responsibility to respond to the incident.[e] It is not the kind of real and pervasive threat that requires the state's power to quell."[f]

See also Charles Lawrence, *If He Hollers Let Him Go: Regulating Racist Speech on Campus,* 1990 Duke L.J. 431, 474–75: "If one asks why we always begin by asking whether we can afford to fight racism rather than asking whether we can afford not to, or if one asks why my colleagues who oppose all regulation of racist speech do not feel the burden is theirs (to justify a reading of the first amendment that requires sacrificing rights guaranteed under the equal protection clause), then one sees an example of how unconscious racism operates in the marketplace of ideas. [O]ur unconscious racism causes us (even those of us who are the direct victims of racism) to view the first amendment as the 'regular' amendment—an amendment that works for all people—and the equal protection clause and racial equality as a special interest-amendment important to groups that are less valued."[g]

7. *Effects of regulation.* Consider Steven Shiffrin, *Racist Speech, Outsider Jurisprudence, and the Meaning of America,* 80 Corn.L.Rev. 43, 96–97, 103 (1994): "From the perspective of many millions of Americans, to enact racist speech regulations would be to pass yet another law exhibiting special favoritism for

---

e. For the argument that the best interpretation of *Brown v. Board of Education requires* government to respond, see Lawrence, infra. For response, see Strossen, infra.

f. Are victims in a better position to evaluate the truth? Compare Richard Delgado & Jean Stefanic, *Must We Defend Nazis* 86–87 (1997) with Gey, note 3 supra.

g. For discussion of the extent and character of the harm, see Delgado & Stefanic, fn. f supra, at 4–10; Matsuda, supra; Lawrence, in-

fra; Richard Delgado, *Campus Antiracism Rules Constitutional Narratives in Collision,* 85 Nw.U.L.Rev. 343, 384 (1991) ("The ubiquity and incessancy of harmful racial depiction are [the] source of its virulence. Like water dripping on sandstone, it is a pervasive harm which only the most hardy can resist. Yet the prevailing first amendment paradigm predisposes us to treat racist speech as individual harm, as though we only had to evaluate the effect of a single drop of water.").

people of color. What makes this kind of law so potentially counterproductive is that its transformation of public racists into public martyrs would tap into widespread political traditions and understanding in our culture. In short, the case of the martyr would be appealingly wrapped in the banner of the American flag. Millions of white Americans already resent people of color to some degree. To fuse that resentment with Americans' love for the first amendment is risky business. [America] would still have a FIRST AMENDMENT and a strong first amendment tradition even if it enacted general racist speech regulations. The problem is not the first amendment; the problem is that racism is now and always has been a central part of the meaning of America." Would hate legislation have the "unfortunate effect of focusing on the individual perpetrator rather than on the victims or on social forces that assist and inform the perpetrator"? Would attention "more fruitfully turn to both the lives and the circumstances of the victims as well as the surrounding social traditions and practices that have made and continue to make that group subject to dehumanization"? Martha Minow, *Regulating Hatred*, 47 UCLA L.Rev. 1253, 1274 (2000).

8. Consider Kenneth Karst, *Boundaries and Reasons: Freedom of Expression and the Subordination of Groups*, 1990 U.Ill.L.Rev. 95, 140–41: "Group libel and pornography each respond to a sense of inadequacy, but the two types of hate literature are circulated differently. Where the defamation of racial or religious groups is driven by the felt inadequacies of its distributors, today's pornography is largely driven by the inadequacies of its consumers, with most distributors simply profiting from that demand and seeking to increase it. In neither case will elimination of the literature cause the underlying sense of inadequacy to disappear. Anxious hatemongers, thwarted in purveying their racist leaflets, can find plenty of other ways to express their fear and hate, as the Ku Klux Klan and the Nazis have made clear. And anxious men, thwarted in the consumption of pornography, can find substitute symbols of sexual objectification not just in magazine ads or on television but in every woman they see."

10. Consider Stanford University's definition of harassment by personal vilification: "Speech or other expression constitutes harassment by personal vilification if it a) is intended to insult or stigmatize an individual or a small number of individuals on the basis of their sex, race, color, handicap, religion, sexual orientation, or national and ethnic origin; and b) is addressed directly to the individual or individuals whom it insults or stigmatizes; and c) makes use of insulting or 'fighting words' or non-verbal symbols." Is this appropriate? See Thomas Grey, *Civil Rights v. Civil Liberties*, Soc. Phil. & Pol'y 81 (Spring 1991). Does this go too far? See Nadine Strossen, *Regulating Racist Speech on Campus: A Modest Proposal?* 1990 Duke L.J. 484. Does it not go far enough? See Lawrence, supra at 450 n. 82: "I supported a proposal which would have been broader in scope by prohibiting speech of this nature in all common areas, excepting organized rallies and speeches. It would have been narrower in its protection in that it would not have protected persons who were vilified on the basis of their membership in dominant majority groups." Compare Matsuda, supra at 2357, arguing that speech with a message of racial inferiority, that is directed against a historically oppressed group, and that is persecutorial, hateful, and degrading should be outlawed.[h]

h. For other relevant literature, see, e.g., Sec. 3, IV supra; James Weinstein, *Hate Speech, Pornography, and the Radical Attack on Free Speech Doctrine* (1999); Nicholas Wolfson, *Hate Speech, Sex Speech, Free Speech* (1997); Kent Greenawalt, *Fighting Words* (1995); Mari Matsuda, Charles Lawrence, Richard Delgado, & Kimberle Crenshaw, eds., *Words that Wound* (1993); Laura Lederer &

If racial vilification can be prohibited, can religious vilification in the form of blasphemy be outlawed as well? See Wojciech Sadurski, *Freedom of Speech and Its Limits* 210–17 (1999).

SECTION 2. DISTINGUISHING BETWEEN CONTENT REGULATION AND MANNER REGULATION: UNCONVENTIONAL FORMS OF COMMUNICATION

Special first amendment questions are often said to arise by regulation of the time, place, and manner of speech as opposed to regulation of its content. But the two types of regulation are not mutually exclusive. It is possible to regulate time, place, manner, and content in the same regulation. For example, in *Linmark*, p. 821 infra, the township outlawed signs (but not leaflets) advertising a house for sale (but not other advertisements or other messages) on front lawns (but not other places).

Further, the terms, manner and content are strongly contested concepts. Indeed, an issue recurring in this section is whether the regulations in question are of manner or content. To the extent this section is about manner regulation, it is not exhaustive—much comes later. Most of the cases in this section involve unconventional forms of expression. Speakers claim protection for burning draft cards, wearing armbands, mutilating flags, nude dancing, wearing long hair. Fact patterns such as these fix renewed attention on the question of how "speech" should be defined. It may be a nice question as to whether obscenity is not speech within the first amendment lexicon, whether it is such speech but has been balanced into an unprotected state, or whether it is not *freedom* of speech or *the* freedom of speech.[a] But assassinating a public figure, even to send a message, raises no first amendment problem. Robbing a bank does not raise a free speech issue. What does? How do we decide?

The fact patterns in this section also invite scrutiny of other issues that appear in succeeding sections. Should it make a difference if the state's interest in regulating speech is unrelated to what is being said? Suppose the state's concern arises from the non-communicative impact of the speech act—from its manner. Should that distinction make a constitutional difference, and, if so, how much? These questions become more complicated because in context it is often difficult to determine what the state interest is and sometimes difficult to determine whether there is a meaningful distinction between what is said and how it is said.

Richard Delgado, eds., *The Price We Pay: The Case Against Racist Speech, Hate Propaganda and Pornography* (1995); Samuel Walker, *Hate Speech: The History of an American Controversy* (1994); Symposium, *Campus Hate Speech and the Constitution in the Aftermath of Doe v. University of Michigan,* 37 Wayne L.Rev. 1309 (1991); Symposium, *Free Speech & Religious, Racial & Sexual Harassment,* 32 Wm. & Mary L.Rev. 207 (1991); Symposium, *Frontiers of Legal Thought: The New First Amendment,* 1990 Duke L.J. 375; Symposium, *Hate Speech and the First Amendment: On A Collision Course?,* 37 Vill.L.Rev. 723 (1992); Symposium, *Hate Speech After R.A.V.: More Conflict Be-* *tween Free Speech and Equality,* 18 Wm. Mitchell L.Rev. 889 (1992); See also sources cited in connection with *R.A.V. v. City of St. Paul,* p. 837 infra and sources cited in Steven Shiffrin, *Racist Speech, Outsider Jurisprudence, and the Meaning of America,* 80 Corn. L.Rev. 43, 44 n. 6 (1994). For the Canadian perspective, see *Regina v. Keegstra,* [1990] 3 S.C.R. 697. For relevant commentary, see Greenawalt, supra; Lawrence Douglas, *Policing the Past* in *Censorship and Silencing* 67 (Robert C. Post ed. 1998); Lorraine Weinrib, *Hate Promotion in a Democratic Society,* 36 McGill L.Rev. 1416 (1991).

a. See fn. b in *Roth,* Sec. 1, IV, A supra.

Even when the distinction between the manner of the speech and the content of the speech is clear, further doctrinal complications abound. Sometimes the regulation considered by the Court is described as one regulating the "time, place, or manner" of speech, and the Court employs the "time, place, or manner test" which is itself differently phrased in different cases. On other occasions the regulation is described as having an "incidental" impact on freedom of speech, and the Court turns to a different test. These different tests are sometimes described by the Court as functional equivalents. Should there be different tests? In what circumstances? See generally Susan Williams, *Content Discrimination and the First Amendment,* 139 U.Pa.L.Rev. 201 (1991).

Finally, in this and succeeding sections the question arises of the extent to which freedom of speech should require special sensitivity to the methods and communications needs of the less powerful.

UNITED STATES v. O'BRIEN

391 U.S. 367, 88 S.Ct. 1673, 20 L.Ed.2d 672 (1968).

CHIEF JUSTICE WARREN delivered the opinion of the Court.

On the morning of March 31, 1966, David Paul O'Brien and three companions burned their Selective Service registration certificates on the steps of the South Boston Courthouse. A sizable crowd, including several [FBI agents] witnessed the event. Immediately after the burning, members of the crowd began attacking O'Brien [and he was ushered to safety by an FBI agent.] O'Brien stated to FBI agents that he had burned his registration certificate because of his beliefs, knowing that he was violating federal law.

[For this act, O'Brien was convicted in federal court.] He [told] the jury that he burned the certificate publicly to influence others to adopt his antiwar beliefs, as he put it, "so that other people would reevaluate their positions with Selective Service, with the armed forces, and reevaluate their place in the culture of today, to hopefully consider my position."

The indictment upon which he was tried charged that he "wilfully and knowingly did mutilate, destroy, and change by burning [his] Registration Certificate; in violation of [§ 462(b)(3) of the Universal Military Training and Service Act of 1948], amended by Congress in 1965 (adding the words italicized below), so that at the time O'Brien burned his certificate an offense was committed by any person, "who forges, alters, *knowingly destroys, knowingly mutilates,* or in any manner changes any such certificate * * *." (Italics supplied.)

[On appeal, the] First Circuit held the 1965 Amendment unconstitutional as a law abridging freedom of speech. At the time the Amendment was enacted, a regulation of the Selective Service System required registrants to keep their registration certificates in their "personal possession at all times." Wilful violations of regulations promulgated pursuant to the Universal Military Training and Service Act were made criminal by statute. The Court of Appeals, therefore, was of the opinion that conduct punishable under the 1965 Amendment was already punishable under the nonpossession regulation, and consequently that the Amendment served no valid purpose; further, that in light of the prior regulation, the Amendment must have been "directed at public as distinguished from private destruction." On this basis, the Court concluded that the 1965 Amendment ran afoul of the First Amendment by singling out persons engaged in protests for special treatment. * * *

When a male reaches the age of 18, he is required by the Universal Military Training and Service Act to register with a local draft board. He is assigned a Selective Service number, and within five days he is issued a registration certificate. Subsequently, and based on a questionnaire completed by the registrant, he is assigned a classification denoting his eligibility for induction, and "[a]s soon as practicable" thereafter he is issued a Notice of Classification. * * *

Both the registration and classification certificates bear notices that the registrant must notify his local board in writing of every change in address, physical condition, and occupational, marital, family, dependency, and military status, and of any other fact which might change his classification. Both also contain a notice that the registrant's Selective Service number should appear on all communications to his local board.

[The 1965] Amendment does not distinguish between public and private destruction, and it does not punish only destruction engaged in for the purpose of expressing views.[a] A law prohibiting destruction of Selective Service certificates no more abridges free speech on its face than a motor vehicle law prohibiting the destruction of drivers' licenses, or a tax law prohibiting the destruction of books and records.

O'Brien nonetheless argues [first] that the 1965 Amendment is unconstitutional [as] applied to him because his act of burning his registration certificate was protected "symbolic speech" within the First Amendment. [He claims that] the First Amendment guarantees include all modes of "communication of ideas by conduct," and that his conduct is within this definition because he did it in "demonstration against the war and against the draft."

We cannot accept the view that an apparently limitless variety of conduct can be labeled "speech" whenever the person engaging in the conduct intends thereby to express an idea. However, even on the assumption that the alleged communicative element in O'Brien's conduct is sufficient to bring into play the First Amendment, it does not necessarily follow that the destruction of a registration certificate is constitutionally protected activity. This Court has held that when "speech" and "nonspeech" elements are combined in the same course of conduct, a sufficiently important governmental interest in regulating the nonspeech element can justify incidental limitations on First Amendment freedoms. To characterize the quality of the governmental interest which must appear, the Court has employed a variety of descriptive terms: compelling; substantial; subordinating; paramount; cogent; strong. [W]e think it clear that a government regulation is sufficiently justified if it is within the constitutional power of the government; if it furthers an important or substantial governmental interest; if the governmental interest is unrelated to the suppression of free expression;[b] and if the incidental restriction on alleged First Amendment freedom is no greater than is essential to the furtherance of that interest. We find that the 1965 Amendment meets all of these requirements, and consequently that O'Brien can be constitutionally con-

a. But compare Chief Judge Aldrich below, 376 F.2d at 541: "We would be closing our eyes in the light of the prior law if we did not see on the face of the amendment that it was precisely directed at public as distinguished from private destruction. [In] singling out persons engaging in protest for special treatment the amendment strikes at the very core of what the First Amendment protects."

b. For the contention that the many tests formulated by the Court are best regarded as prophylactic rules designed to assure that the forbidden purpose of suppressing ideas does not underlie government acts, see David Bogen, *Balancing Freedom of Speech*, 38 Md. L.Rev. 387 (1979); David Bogen, *The Supreme Court's Interpretation of the Guarantee of Freedom of Speech*, 35 Md.L.Rev. 555 (1976). See generally David Bogen, *Bulwark of Liberty: The Court and the First Amendment* (1984).

victed for violating it. [Pursuant to its power to classify and conscript manpower for military service], Congress may establish a system of registration for individuals liable for training and service, and may require such individuals within reason to cooperate in the registration system. The issuance of certificates indicating the registration and eligibility classification of individuals is a legitimate and substantial administrative aid in the functioning of this system. And legislation to insure the continuing availability of issued certificates serves a legitimate and substantial purpose in the system's administration.

[O'Brien] essentially adopts the position that [Selective Service] certificates are so many pieces of paper designed to notify registrants of their registration or classification, to be retained or tossed in the wastebasket according to the convenience or taste of the registrant. Once the registrant has received notification, according to this view, there is no reason for him to retain the certificates. [However, the registration and classification certificates serve] purposes in addition to initial notification. Many of these purposes would be defeated by the certificates' destruction or mutilation. Among these are [simplifying verification of the registration and classification of suspected delinquents, evidence of availability for induction in the event of emergency, ease of communication between registrants and local boards, continually reminding registrants of the need to notify local boards of changes in status].

The many functions performed by Selective Service certificates establish beyond doubt that Congress has a legitimate and substantial interest in preventing their wanton and unrestrained destruction and assuring their continuing availability by punishing people who knowingly and wilfully destroy or mutilate them. And we are unpersuaded that the pre-existence of the nonpossession regulations in any way negates this interest.

In the absence of a question as to multiple punishment, it has never been suggested that there is anything improper in Congress providing alternative statutory avenues of prosecution to assure the effective protection of one and the same interest. Here, the pre-existing avenue of prosecution was not even statutory. Regulations may be modified or revoked from time to time by administrative discretion. Certainly, the Congress may change or supplement a regulation.

[The] gravamen of the offense defined by the statute is the deliberate rendering of certificates unavailable for the various purposes which they may serve. Whether registrants keep their certificates in their personal possession at all times, as required by the regulations, is of no particular concern under the 1965 Amendment, as long as they do not mutilate or destroy the certificates so as to render them unavailable. [The 1965 amendment] is concerned with abuses involving *any* issued Selective Service certificates, not only with the registrant's own certificates. The knowing destruction or mutilation of someone else's certificates would therefore violate the statute but not the nonpossession regulations.

We think it apparent that the continuing availability to each registrant of his Selective Service certificates substantially furthers the smooth and proper functioning of the system that Congress has established to raise armies. * * *

It is equally clear that the 1965 Amendment specifically protects this substantial governmental interest. We perceive no alternative means that would more precisely and narrowly assure the continuing availability of issued Selective Service certificates than a law which prohibits their wilful mutilation or destruction. The 1965 Amendment prohibits such conduct and does nothing more. [The] governmental interest and the scope of the 1965 Amendment are limited to preventing a harm to the smooth and efficient functioning of the Selective Service

System. When O'Brien deliberately rendered unavailable his registration certificate, he wilfully frustrated this governmental interest. For this noncommunicative impact of his conduct, and for nothing else, he was convicted.* * *

O'Brien finally argues that the 1965 Amendment is unconstitutional as enacted because what he calls the "purpose" of Congress was "to suppress freedom of speech." We reject this argument because under settled principles the purpose of Congress, as O'Brien uses that term, is not a basis for declaring this legislation unconstitutional.

It is a familiar principle of constitutional law that this Court will not strike down an otherwise constitutional statute on the basis of an alleged illicit legislative motive.[c]

[I]f we were to examine legislative purpose in the instant case, we would be obliged to consider not only [the statements of the three members of Congress who addressed themselves to the amendment, all viewing draft-card burning as a brazen display of unpatriotism] but also the more authoritative reports of the Senate and House Armed Services Committees. [B]oth reports make clear a concern with the "defiant" destruction of so-called "draft cards" and with "open" encouragement to others to destroy their cards, [but they] also indicate that this concern stemmed from an apprehension that unrestrained destruction of cards would disrupt the smooth functioning of the Selective Service System. * * *

Reversed.[d]

JUSTICE HARLAN concurring. * * *

I wish to make explicit my understanding that [the Court's analysis] does not foreclose consideration of First Amendment claims in those rare instances when an "incidental" restriction upon expression, imposed by a regulation which furthers an "important or substantial" governmental interest and satisfies the Court's other criteria, in practice has the effect of entirely preventing a "speaker" from reaching a significant audience with whom he could not otherwise lawfully communicate. This is not such a case, since O'Brien manifestly could have conveyed his message in many ways other than by burning his draft card.

JUSTICE DOUGLAS, dissenting.

[Douglas, J., thought that "the underlying and basic problem in this case" was the constitutionality of a draft "in the absence of a declaration of war" and that the case should be put down for reargument on this question. The following Term, concurring in *Brandenburg,* he criticized *O'Brien* on the merits. After recalling that the Court had rejected O'Brien's first amendment argument on the ground that "legislation to insure the continuing availability of issued certificates serves a legitimate and substantial purpose in the [selective service] system's administration," he commented: "But O'Brien was not prosecuted for not having his draft card available when asked for by a federal agent. He was indicted, tried, and convicted for burning the card. And this Court's affirmance [was not] consistent with the First Amendment." He observed, more generally in *Brandenburg:*

["Action is often a method of expression and within the protection of the First Amendment. Suppose one tears up his own copy of the Constitution in eloquent protest to a decision of this Court. May he be indicted? Suppose one rips his own

---

c. See generally Ch. 9, Sec. 2, III.   **d.** Marshall, J., took no part.

Bible to shreds to celebrate his departure from one 'faith' and his embrace of atheism. May he be indicted? * * *

["The act of praying often involves body posture and movement as well as utterances. It is nonetheless protected by the Free Exercise Clause. Picketing [is] 'free speech plus.' [Therefore], it can be regulated when it comes to the 'plus' or 'action' side of the protest. It can be regulated as to the number of pickets and the place and hours, because traffic and other community problems would otherwise suffer. But none of these considerations are implicated in the symbolic protest of the Vietnam war in the burning of a draft card."]

Notes and Questions

1. *Expression vs. action.* What of the Court's rejection of the idea that conduct is speech "whenever the person engaging in the conduct intends thereby to express an idea." Was it right to question whether O'Brien's conduct was speech? What was it about O'Brien's conduct that made the Court doubt that it was speech? What if O'Brien had burned a copy of the Constitution? Consider Thomas Emerson, *The System of Freedom of Expression* 80 & 84 (1970): "To some extent expression and action are always mingled; most conduct includes elements of both. Even the clearest manifestations of expression involve some action, as in the case of holding a meeting, publishing a newspaper, or merely talking. At the other extreme, a political assassination includes a substantial mixture of expression. The guiding principle must be to determine which element is predominant in the conduct under consideration. Is expression the major element and the action only secondary? Or is the action the essence and the expression incidental? The answer, to a great extent, must be based on a common-sense reaction, made in light of the functions and operations of a system of freedom of expression. * * *

"The burning of a draft card is, of course, conduct that involves both communication and physical acts. Yet it seems quite clear that the predominant element in such conduct is expression (opposition to the draft) rather than action (destruction of a piece of cardboard). The registrant is not concerned with secret or inadvertent burning of his draft card, involving no communication with other persons. The main feature, for him, is the public nature of the burning, through which he expresses to the community his ideas and feelings about the war and the draft."

Compare John Hart Ely, *Flag Desecration: A Case Study in the Roles of Categorization and Balancing in First Amendment Analysis*, 88 Harv.L.Rev. 1482, 1495 (1975): "[B]urning a draft card to express opposition to the draft is an undifferentiated whole, 100% action and 100% expression. It involves no conduct that is not at the same time communication, and no communication that does not result from conduct. Attempts to determine which element 'predominates' will therefore inevitably degenerate into question-begging judgments about whether the activity should be protected. The *O'Brien* Court thus quite wisely dropped the 'speech-conduct' distinction as quickly as it had picked it up."[e]

2. *Nature of the state interest and first amendment methodology.* Melville Nimmer, *The Meaning of Symbolic Speech under the First Amendment*, 21

e. But, as Professor Ely recognizes, the Court picked it up again in *Cohen,* Sec. 1, IV, C supra: "[W]e deal here with a conviction resting solely upon 'speech', cf. *Stromberg,* not upon any separately identifiable conduct which allegedly was intended by Cohen to be perceived by others as expressive of particular views but which, on its face, does not necessarily convey any message and hence arguably could be regulated without effectively repressing Cohen's ability to express himself. Cf. *O'Brien.*"

U.C.L.A.L.Rev. 29 (1973), followed by Ely, note 1 supra, and Tribe, infra, has proposed that the crucial starting point for first amendment methodology is and should be the nature of the state interest.[f] As Ely puts it, at 1497: "The critical question would therefore seem to be whether the harm that the state is seeking to avert is one that grows out of the fact that the defendant is communicating, and more particularly out of the way people can be expected to react to his message, or rather would arise even if the defendant's conduct had no communicative significance whatever."

For one view of the difference that the distinction makes, see Tribe 2d ed., at 791–92: "The Supreme Court has evolved two distinct approaches to the resolution of first amendment claims; the two correspond to the two ways in which government may 'abridge' speech. If a government regulation is aimed at the communicative impact of an act, analysis should proceed along what we will call *track one.* On that track, a regulation is unconstitutional unless government shows that the message being suppressed poses a 'clear and present danger,' constitutes a defamatory falsehood, or otherwise falls on the unprotected side of one of the lines the Court has drawn to distinguish those expressive acts privileged by the first amendment from those open to government regulation with only minimal due process scrutiny. If a government regulation is aimed at the noncommunicative impact of an act, its analysis proceeds on what we will call *track two.* On that track, a regulation is constitutional, even as applied to expressive conduct, so long as it does not unduly constrict the flow of information and ideas. On track two, the 'balance' between the values of freedom of expression and the government's regulatory interests is struck on a case-by-case basis, guided by whatever unifying principles may be articulated."

Professor Nimmer, in distinguishing between anti-speech interests (track one) and non-speech interests (track two), would apply definitional balancing (with a presumption in favor of speech) to the former and the *O'Brien* test to the latter. Dean Ely would protect all regulations on track one except for speech that falls "within a few clearly and narrowly defined categories." John Hart Ely, *Democracy and Distrust* 110 (1980) (emphasis deleted). On track two, Ely insists that balancing is desirable and unavoidable. Ely, note 1 supra, at 1496–1502.

(a) *Normative value of the distinction.* Is balancing unavoidable on either track? How does one decide what the categories should be without balancing? Does the metaphor of balancing wrongly imply that all values are reduced to a single measure and imply non-existent quantitative capacities? Is the distinction between the tracks important enough always to require rules on track one, even if ad hoc procedures are allowable on track two?

Is the distinction between the two tracks at least strong enough to justify a rebuttable presumption that regulation on track one is invalid, but regulation on track two is not? Consider a regulation governing express warranties in commercial advertising. Is much of contract law on track one?[g] Consider "a nationwide ban on *all* posters (intended to conserve paper)." Isn't that on track two? Do these examples suggest that too much emphasis is being placed on a single factor? See

---

f. The distinction is a major organizing principle in Rodney Smolla, *Smolla and Nimmer on Freedom of Speech* (1984).

g. For the suggestion that virtually all laws have information effects and that track two embraces virtually all laws not covered by track one, see Larry Alexander, *Trouble on Track Two: Incidental Regulations of Speech and Free Speech,* 44 Hastings L.J. 921 (1993) (arguing that track two countenances an unconstitutional evaluation of the value of speech).

Daniel Farber, *Content Regulation and the First Amendment: A Revisionist View*, 68 Geo.U.L.Rev. 727, 746–47 (1980).[h]

(b) *Application to O'Brien.* Consider Ely, note 1 supra, at 1498–99: "The interests upon which the government relied were interests, having mainly to do with the preservation of selective service records, that would have been equally threatened had O'Brien's destruction of his draft card totally lacked communicative significance—had he, for example, used it to start a campfire for a solitary cookout or dropped it in his garbage disposal for a lark. (The law prohibited all knowing destructions, public or private)."

Compare Melville Nimmer, note 2 supra, at 41—contending that the *O'Brien* statute was "overnarrow": "[An overnarrow statute] may be said to create a conclusive presumption that in fact the state interest which the statute serves is an anti-rather than a non-speech interest. If the state interest asserted in *O'Brien* were truly the non-speech interest of assuring availability of draft cards, why did Congress choose not to prohibit any knowing conduct which leads to unavailability, rather than limiting the scope of the statute to those instances in which the proscribed conduct carries with it a speech component hostile to governmental policy? The obvious inference to be drawn is that in fact the Congress was completely indifferent to the 'availability' objective, and was concerned only with an interest which the *O'Brien* opinion states is impermissible—an interest in the suppression of free expression."[i]

(c) *Descriptive value of the distinction.* Does the distinction between the two tracks fully explain the Court's approach in *O'Brien* ? Suppose again that an assassin truthfully claims that his or her killing was intended to and did communicate an idea? The assassin's first amendment claim would not prevail, but would it fail because the *O'Brien* test was not met or because no first amendment problem was implicated at all? Is a speech/conduct distinction a necessary prerequisite to the application of the *O'Brien* test?[j]

How different is the *O'Brien* test from the methods used to make decisions on track one? Is the *O'Brien* test as phrased potentially more speech protective than its application in the principal case would suggest? More speech protective than tests sometimes used on track one? Does the application in *O'Brien* offer "little more than the minimal rational-basis test applied in economic due process cases"? See Keith Werhan, *The O'Briening of First Amendment Methodology,* 19 Ariz.St. L.J. 635, 641 (1987): "There is no speech side to the Court's balance. [T]he absence of true balancing within the *O'Brien* methodology can be traced to the origins of the *O'Brien* test. [Having] avoided deciding whether O'Brien's act was protected expression, the Court hardly was in a position to take the next step of incorporating expressive interests into its balance." Id. at 641–42.

3. Does *O'Brien* shortchange the value of dissent? Consider Steven Shiffrin, *The First Amendment, Democracy, and Romance* 5–6, 81 (1990): "If an organizing symbol makes sense in first amendment jurisprudence, it is not the image of a content-neutral government; it is not a town hall meeting or even a robust marketplace of ideas; still less is it liberty, equality, self-realization, respect,

h. See generally Martin Redish, *The Content Distinction in First Amendment Analysis,* 34 Stan.L.Rev. 113 (1981). See notes after *Chicago Police Dept. v. Mosley,* Sec. 6, I, B infra.

i. On the inadequacy of the *O'Brien* methodology to serve as a proxy for problematic motivation, see Lee Bollinger, *The Tolerant Society* 206–12 (1986). On its inadequacy as an organizing principle for first amendment doctrine, see Shiffrin, note 3 infra, ch. 1.

j. For commentary on the difficulties in defining speech, see Larry Alexander & Paul Horton, *The Impossibility of a Free Speech Principle,* 78 Nw.U.L.Rev. 1319 (1984).

dignity, autonomy, or even tolerance. If the first amendment is to have an organizing symbol, let it be an Emersonian[k] symbol, let it be the image of the dissenter. A major purpose of the first amendment [is] to protect the romantics— those who would break out of classical forms: the dissenters, the unorthodox, the outcasts. [That] Emersonian ideal of freedom of speech has deep roots in the nation's culture, but it has been subtly denigrated in recent first amendment theory and seriously abused in practice.

"[N]either the town hall metaphor nor the marketplace of ideas metaphor[, for example,] is quite apt as a symbol for why *O'Brien* is a first amendment horror story. Town hall meetings can function without the burning of draft cards. And it is hard to claim that truth was kept from the marketplace of ideas. *O'Brien* is one of those not infrequent cases where government prosecutions assist the dissemination of the dissenter's message. Yet, *O'Brien* is perhaps the ultimate first amendment insult. O'Brien is jailed because the authorities find his manner of expression unpatriotic, threatening, and offensive. When he complains that his freedom of speech has been abridged, the authorities deny that he has spoken."

4. *Scope of O'Brien*. Should the *O'Brien* test be confined to unconventional forms of communication? Would a distinction of this type be defensible? See Ely, note 1 supra, at 1489: "The distinction is its own objection."[l]

TEXAS v. JOHNSON

491 U.S. 397, 109 S.Ct. 2533, 105 L.Ed.2d 342 (1989).

JUSTICE BRENNAN delivered the opinion of the Court.

[Gregory] Lee Johnson was convicted of desecrating a flag in violation of Texas law.[1]

I. While the Republican National Convention was taking place in Dallas in 1984, respondent Johnson participated in a political demonstration dubbed the "Republican War Chest Tour." [The] demonstration ended in front of Dallas City Hall, where Johnson unfurled the American flag, doused it with kerosene, and set it on fire. While the flag burned, the protestors chanted, "America, the red, white, and blue, we spit on you." [No] one was physically injured or threatened with injury, though several witnesses testified that they had been seriously offended by the flag-burning. * * *

II. Johnson was convicted of flag desecration for burning the flag rather than for uttering insulting words.[2] [We] must first determine whether Johnson's

k. See generally Joel Porte ed. (1983), *Ralph Waldo Emerson: Essays and Lectures.*

l. See also Dean Alfange, *Free Speech and Symbolic Conduct: The Draft–Card Burning Case,* 1968 Sup.Ct.Rev. 1, 23–24; Lawrence Velvel, *Freedom of Speech and the Draft Card Burning Cases,* 16 U.Kan.L.Rev. 149, 153 (1968); Louis Henkin, *On Drawing Lines,* 82 Harv.L.Rev. 63, 79 (1968).

1. Tex.Penal Code Ann. § 42.09 (1989) provides in full: "§ 42.09. Desecration of Venerated Object

"(a) A person commits an offense if he intentionally or knowingly desecrates:

"(1) a public monument;

"(2) a place of worship or burial; or

"(3) a state or national flag.

"(b) For purposes of this section, 'desecrate' means deface, damage, or otherwise physically mistreat in a way that the actor knows will seriously offend one or more persons likely to observe or discover his action.

"(c) An offense under this section is a Class A misdemeanor."

2. Because the prosecutor's closing argument observed that Johnson had led the protestors in chants denouncing the flag while it burned, Johnson suggests that he may have been convicted for uttering critical words rather than for burning the flag. He relies on *Street v. New York,* 394 U.S. 576, 89 S.Ct. 1354, 22 L.Ed.2d 572 (1969), in which we reversed a

*[handwritten margin notes at top: "Even this 'repulsive' act protected by Constitution. *That's what 1st Amend. is all about"]*

burning of the flag constituted expressive conduct, permitting him to invoke the First Amendment in challenging his conviction. If his conduct was expressive, we next decide whether the State's regulation is related to the suppression of free expression. *O'Brien.* If the State's regulation is not related to expression, then the less stringent standard we announced in *O'Brien* for regulations of noncommunicative conduct controls. If it is, then we are outside of *O'Brien*'s test, and we must ask whether this interest justifies Johnson's conviction under a more demanding standard.[3] A third possibility is that the State's asserted interest is simply not implicated on these facts, and in that event the interest drops out of the picture.
* * *

In deciding whether particular conduct possesses sufficient communicative elements to bring the First Amendment into play, we have asked whether "[a]n intent to convey a particularized message was present, and [whether] the likelihood was great that the message would be understood by those who viewed it."[a] [In] *Spence v. Washington,* 418 U.S. 405, 94 S.Ct. 2727, 41 L.Ed.2d 842 (1974), for example, we emphasized that Spence's taping of a peace sign to his flag was "roughly simultaneous with and concededly triggered by the Cambodian incursion and the Kent State tragedy." The State of Washington had conceded, in fact, that Spence's conduct was a form of communication, and we stated that "the State's concession is inevitable on this record."

The State of Texas conceded for purposes of its oral argument in this case that Johnson's conduct was expressive conduct and this concession seems to us as prudent as was Washington's in *Spence.* * * *

III. In order to decide whether *O'Brien*'s test [applies] we must decide whether Texas has asserted an interest in support of Johnson's conviction that is unrelated to the suppression of expression.

A. Texas claims that its interest in preventing breaches of the peace justifies Johnson's conviction for flag desecration.[4] However, no disturbance of the peace

---

conviction obtained under a New York statute that prohibited publicly defying or casting contempt on the flag "either by words or act" because we were persuaded that the defendant may have been convicted for his words alone. Unlike the law we faced in *Street,* however, the Texas flag-desecration statute does not on its face permit conviction for remarks critical of the flag, as Johnson himself admits. Nor was the jury in this case told that it could convict Johnson of flag desecration if it found only that he had uttered words critical of the flag and its referents. * * *

3. [Johnson] has raised a facial challenge to Texas' flag-desecration [statute]. Section 42.09 regulates only physical conduct with respect to the flag, not the written or spoken word, and although one violates the statute only if one "knows" that one's physical treatment of the flag "will seriously offend one or more persons likely to observe or discover his action," this fact does not necessarily mean that the statute applies only to *expressive* conduct protected by the First Amendment. A tired person might, for example, drag a flag through the mud, knowing that this conduct is likely to offend others, and yet have no thought of expressing any idea; neither the language nor the Texas courts' interpretations of the statute precludes

the possibility that such a person would be prosecuted for flag desecration. Because the prosecution of a person who had not engaged in expressive conduct would pose a different case, and because we are capable of disposing of this case on narrower grounds, we address only Johnson's claim that § 42.09 as applied to political expression like his violates the First Amendment.

a. For criticism of this standard, see Robert Post, *Recuperating First Amendment Doctrine,* 47 Stan.L.Rev. 1249 (1995).

4. Relying on our decision in *Boos v. Barry,* Johnson argues [that] the violent reaction to flag burning feared by Texas would be the result of the message conveyed by them, and that this fact connects the State's interest to the suppression of expression. This view has found some favor in the lower courts. Johnson's theory may overread *Boos* insofar as it suggests that a desire to prevent a violent audience reaction is "related to expression" in the same way that a desire to prevent an audience from being offended is "related to expression." Because we find that the State's interest in preventing breaches of the peace is not implicated on these facts, however, we need not venture further into this area.

actually occurred or threatened to occur because of Johnson's burning of the flag. [The] only evidence offered by the State at trial to show the reaction to Johnson's actions was the testimony of several persons who had been seriously offended by the flag-burning.

The State's position, therefore, amounts to a claim that an audience that takes serious offense at particular expression is necessarily likely to disturb the peace and that the expression may be prohibited on this basis. [W]e have not permitted the Government to assume that every expression of a provocative idea will incite a riot, but have instead required careful consideration of the actual circumstances surrounding such expression, asking whether the expression "is directed to inciting or producing imminent lawless action and is likely to incite or produce such action." *Brandenburg*. To accept Texas' arguments that it need only demonstrate "the potential for a breach of the peace," and that every flag-burning necessarily possesses that potential, would be to eviscerate our holding in *Brandenburg*. This we decline to do.

Nor does Johnson's expressive conduct fall within that small class of "fighting words" that are "likely to provoke the average person to retaliation, and thereby cause a breach of the peace." *Chaplinsky*. No reasonable onlooker would have regarded Johnson's generalized expression of dissatisfaction with the policies of the Federal Government as a direct personal insult or an invitation to exchange fisticuffs.

We thus conclude that the State's interest in maintaining order is not implicated on these facts. * * *

B.   The State also asserts an interest in preserving the flag as a symbol of nationhood and national unity. [The] State, apparently, is concerned that such conduct will lead people to believe either that the flag does not stand for nationhood and national unity, but instead reflects other, less positive concepts, or that the concepts reflected in the flag do not in fact exist, that is, we do not enjoy unity as a Nation. These concerns blossom only when a person's treatment of the flag communicates some message, and thus are related "to the suppression of free expression" within the meaning of *O'Brien*. We are thus outside of *O'Brien*'s test altogether.

IV.   It remains to consider whether the State's interest in preserving the flag as a symbol of nationhood and national unity justifies Johnson's conviction. [If Johnson] had burned the flag as a means of disposing of it because it was dirty or torn, he would not have been convicted of flag desecration under this Texas law: federal law designates burning as the preferred means of disposing of a flag "when it is in such condition that it is no longer a fitting emblem for display," 36 U.S.C. § 176(k), and Texas has no quarrel with this means of disposal. The Texas law is thus not aimed at protecting the physical integrity of the flag in all circumstances, but is designed instead to protect it only against impairments that would cause serious offense to others.[6]

Whether Johnson's treatment of the flag violated Texas law thus depended on the likely communicative impact of his expressive conduct. Our decision in *Boos v.*

---

6.   *Cf. Smith v. Goguen*, 415 U.S. 566, 94 S.Ct. 1242, 39 L.Ed.2d 605 (1974) (Blackmun, J., dissenting) (emphasizing that lower court appeared to have construed state statute so as to protect physical integrity of the flag in all circumstances); id. (Rehnquist, J., dissenting) (same). [In *Goguen*, Blackmun, J., argued that

"Goguen's punishment was constitutionally permissible for harming the physical integrity of the flag by wearing it affixed to the seat of his pants" and emphasized that such punishment would not be for "speech—a communicative element."].

Barry, 485 U.S. 312, 108 S.Ct. 1157, 99 L.Ed.2d 333 (1988), tells us that this restriction on Johnson's expression is content-based. In *Boos,* we considered the constitutionality of a law prohibiting "the display of any sign within 50 feet of a foreign embassy if that sign tends to bring that foreign government into 'public odium' or 'public disrepute.' " Rejecting the argument that the law was content-neutral because it was justified by "our international law obligation to shield diplomats from speech that offends their dignity," we held that "[t]he emotive impact of speech on its audience is not a 'secondary effect' " unrelated to the content of the expression itself.

According to the principles announced in *Boos,* Johnson's political expression was restricted because of the content of the message he conveyed. We must therefore subject the State's asserted interest in preserving the special symbolic character of the flag to "the most exacting scrutiny." *Boos.*[8] * * *

If there is a bedrock principle underlying the First Amendment, it is that the Government may not prohibit the expression of an idea simply because society finds the idea itself offensive or disagreeable. [We] have not recognized an exception to this principle even where our flag has been involved. [We] never before have held that the Government may ensure that a symbol be used to express only one view of that symbol or its referents. Indeed, in *Schacht v. United States,* 398 U.S. 58, 90 S.Ct. 1555, 26 L.Ed.2d 44 (1970), we invalidated a federal statute permitting an actor portraying a member of one of our armed forces to " 'wear the uniform of that armed force if the portrayal does not tend to discredit that armed force.' " This proviso, we held, "which leaves Americans free to praise the war in Vietnam but can send persons like Schacht to prison for opposing it, cannot survive in a country which has the First Amendment."

We perceive no basis on which to hold that the principle underlying our decision in *Schacht* does not apply to this case. To conclude that the Government may permit designated symbols to be used to communicate only a limited set of messages would be to enter territory having no discernible or defensible boundaries. Could the Government, on this theory, prohibit the burning of state flags? Of copies of the Presidential seal? Of the Constitution? In evaluating these choices under the First Amendment, how would we decide which symbols were sufficiently special to warrant this unique status? To do so, we would be forced to consult our own political preferences, and impose them on the citizenry, in the very way that the First Amendment forbids us to do.

There is, moreover, no indication—either in the text of the Constitution or in our cases interpreting it—that a separate judicial category exists for the American flag alone. Indeed, we would not be surprised to learn that the persons who framed our Constitution and wrote the Amendment that we now construe were not known for their reverence for the Union Jack. The First Amendment does not guarantee that other concepts virtually sacred to our Nation as a whole—such as the principle that discrimination on the basis of race is odious and destructive—will go unquestioned in the marketplace of ideas. See *Brandenburg.* We decline, therefore, to create for the flag an exception to the joust of principles protected by the First Amendment.

8. Our inquiry is, of course, bounded by the particular facts of this case and by the statute under which Johnson was convicted. There was no evidence that Johnson himself stole the flag he burned, nor did the prosecution or the arguments urged in support of it depend on the theory that the flag was stolen. [Thus] nothing in our opinion should be taken to suggest that one is free to steal a flag so long as one later uses it to communicate an idea. We also emphasize that Johnson was prosecuted *only* for flag desecration—not for trespass, disorderly conduct, or arson.

It is not the State's ends, but its means, to which we object. It cannot be gainsaid that there is a special place reserved for the flag in this Nation, and thus we do not doubt that the Government has a legitimate interest in making efforts to "preserv[e] the national flag as an unalloyed symbol of our country." We reject the suggestion, urged at oral argument by counsel for Johnson, that the Government lacks "any state interest whatsoever" in regulating the manner in which the flag may be displayed. Congress has, for example, enacted precatory regulations describing the proper treatment of the flag, see 36 U.S.C. §§ 173–177, and we cast no doubt on the legitimacy of its interest in making such recommendations. To say that the Government has an interest in encouraging proper treatment of the flag, however, is not to say that it may criminally punish a person for burning a flag as a means of political protest. "National unity as an end which officials may foster by persuasion and example is not in question. The problem is whether under our Constitution compulsion as here employed is a permissible means for its achievement."

[W]e submit that nobody can suppose that this one gesture of an unknown man will change our Nation's attitude towards its flag. See *Abrams* (Holmes, J., dissenting). Indeed, Texas' argument that the burning of an American flag " 'is an act having a high likelihood to cause a breach of the peace,' " and its statute's implicit assumption that physical mistreatment of the flag will lead to "serious offense," tend to confirm that the flag's special role is not in danger; if it were, no one would riot or take offense because a flag had been burned.

We are tempted to say, in fact, that the flag's deservedly cherished place in our community will be strengthened, not weakened, by our holding today. Our decision is a reaffirmation of the principles of freedom and inclusiveness that the flag best reflects, and of the conviction that our toleration of criticism such as Johnson's is a sign and source of our strength. Indeed, one of the proudest images of our flag, the one immortalized in our own national anthem, is of the bombardment it survived at Fort McHenry. It is the Nation's resilience, not its rigidity, that Texas sees reflected in the flag—and it is that resilience that we reassert today.

The way to preserve the flag's special role is not to punish those who feel differently about these matters. It is to persuade them that they are wrong. [We] can imagine no more appropriate response to burning a flag than waving one's own, no better way to counter a flag-burner's message than by saluting the flag that burns, no surer means of preserving the dignity even of the flag that burned than by—as one witness here did—according its remains a respectful burial. * * *

JUSTICE KENNEDY, concurring. * * *

Our colleagues in dissent advance powerful arguments why respondent may be convicted for his expression, reminding us that among those who will be dismayed by our holding will be some who have had the singular honor of carrying the flag in battle. And I agree that the flag holds a lonely place of honor in an age when absolutes are distrusted and simple truths are burdened by unneeded apologetics.

With all respect to those views, I do not believe the Constitution gives us the right to rule as the dissenting members of the Court urge, however painful this judgment is to announce. Though symbols often are what we ourselves make of them, the flag is constant in expressing beliefs Americans share, beliefs in law and peace and that freedom which sustains the human spirit. The case here today forces recognition of the costs to which those beliefs commit us. It is poignant but fundamental that the flag protects those who hold it in contempt.

For all the record shows, this respondent was not a philosopher and perhaps did not even possess the ability to comprehend how repellent his statements must be to the Republic itself. But whether or not he could appreciate the enormity of the offense he gave, the fact remains that his acts were speech, in both the technical and the fundamental meaning of the Constitution. So I agree with the Court that he must go free.

CHIEF JUSTICE REHNQUIST, with whom JUSTICE WHITE and JUSTICE O'CONNOR join, dissenting.

In holding this Texas statute unconstitutional, the Court ignores Justice Holmes' familiar aphorism that "a page of history is worth a volume of logic." *New York Trust Co. v. Eisner,* 256 U.S. 345, 41 S.Ct. 506, 65 L.Ed. 963 (1921). * * *

The American flag [throughout] more than 200 years of our history, has come to be the visible symbol embodying our Nation.[b] It does not represent the views of any particular political party, and it does not represent any particular political philosophy. The flag is not simply another "idea" or "point of view" competing for recognition in the marketplace of ideas. Millions and millions of Americans regard it with an almost mystical reverence regardless of what sort of social, political, or philosophical beliefs they may have. I cannot agree that the First Amendment invalidates the Act of Congress, and the laws of 48 of the 50 States, which make criminal the public burning of the flag.

More than 80 years ago in *Halter v. Nebraska* [205 U.S. 34, 27 S.Ct. 419, 51 L.Ed. 696 (1907)], this Court upheld the constitutionality of a Nebraska statute that forbade the use of representations of the American flag for advertising purposes upon articles of merchandise. The Court there said: "For that flag every true American has not simply an appreciation but a deep affection. * * * Hence, it has often occurred that insults to a flag have been the cause of war, and indignities put upon it, in the presence of those who revere it, have often been resented and sometimes punished on the spot."

Only two Terms ago, in *San Francisco Arts & Athletics, Inc. v. United States Olympic Committee,* [483 U.S. 522, 107 S.Ct. 2971, 97 L.Ed.2d 427 (1987)], the Court held that Congress could grant exclusive use of the word "Olympic" to the United States Olympic Committee. The Court thought that this "restrictio[n] on expressive speech properly [was] characterized as incidental to the primary congressional purpose of encouraging and rewarding the USOC's activities." As the Court stated, "when a word [or symbol] acquires value 'as the result of organization and the expenditure of labor, skill, and money' by an entity, that entity constitutionally may obtain a limited property right in the word [or symbol]."[c] Surely Congress or the States may recognize a similar interest in the flag.[d]

---

b. Rehnquist, C.J., invoked a legacy of prose, poetry, and law in honor of flags in general and the American flag in particular both in peace and in war, quoting from, among others, Ralph Waldo Emerson and John Greenleaf Whittier. Emerson's poem referred to the Union Jack, but he did not always speak warmly of the American flag. After passage of the Fugitive Slave Law Emerson wrote, "We sneak about with the infamy of crime in the streets, & cowardice in ourselves and frankly once for all the Union is sunk, the flag is hateful, and shall be hissed." *Emerson in His Journals* 421 (Joel Porte ed. 1982).

c. For criticism, see James Boyle, *Shamans, Software, and Spleens* 145–48 (1996); Yochai Benkler, *Constitutional Bounds of Database Protection,* 15 Berkeley L.J. 535 (2000), Robert Kravitz, *Trademarks, Speech, and the Gay Olympics Case,* 69 B.U.L.Rev. 131 (1989).

d. In response, Brennan, J., observed that *Halter* was decided "nearly twenty years" before the first amendment was applied to the states and "[m]ore important" that *Halter* in-

[T]he public burning of the American flag by Johnson was no essential part of any exposition of ideas, and at the same time it had a tendency to incite a breach of the peace. Johnson was free to make any verbal denunciation of the flag that he wished; indeed, he was free to burn the flag in private. He could publicly burn other symbols of the Government or effigies of political leaders. He did lead a march through the streets of Dallas, and conducted a rally in front of the Dallas City Hall. He engaged in a "die-in" to protest nuclear weapons. He shouted out various slogans during the march, including: "Reagan, Mondale which will it be? Either one means World War III"; "Ronald Reagan, killer of the hour, Perfect example of U.S. power"; and "red, white and blue, we spit on you, you stand for plunder, you will go under." For none of these acts was he arrested or prosecuted. [As] with "fighting words," so with flag burning, for purposes of the First Amendment: It is "no essential part of any exposition of ideas, and [is] of such slight social value as a step to truth that any benefit that may be derived from [it] is clearly outweighed" by the public interest in avoiding a probable breach of the peace. * * *

The result of the Texas statute is obviously to deny one in Johnson's frame of mind one of many means of "symbolic speech." Far from being a case of "one picture being worth a thousand words," flag burning is the equivalent of an inarticulate grunt or roar that, it seems fair to say, is most likely to be indulged in not to express any particular idea, but to antagonize others. [The] Texas statute [left Johnson] with a full panoply of other symbols and every conceivable form of verbal expression to express his deep disapproval of national policy. Thus, in no way can it be said that Texas is punishing him because his hearers—or any other group of people—were profoundly opposed to the message that he sought to convey. Such opposition is no proper basis for restricting speech or expression under the First Amendment. It was Johnson's use of this particular symbol, and not the idea that he sought to convey by it or by his many other expressions, for which he was punished. * * *

The Court concludes its opinion with a regrettably patronizing civics lecture, presumably addressed to the Members of both Houses of Congress, the members of the 48 state legislatures that enacted prohibitions against flag burning, and the troops fighting under that flag in Vietnam who objected to its being burned: "The way to preserve the flag's special role is not to punish those who feel differently about these matters. It is to persuade them that they are wrong." The Court's role as the final expositor of the Constitution is well established, but its role as a platonic guardian admonishing those responsible to public opinion as if they were truant school children has no similar place in our system of government. * * *

Uncritical extension of constitutional protection to the burning of the flag risks the frustration of the very purpose for which organized governments are instituted. The Court decides that the American flag is just another symbol, about which not only must opinions pro and con be tolerated, but for which the most minimal public respect may not be enjoined. The government may conscript men into the Armed Forces where they must fight and perhaps die for the flag, but the government may not prohibit the public burning of the banner under which they fight. I would uphold the Texas statute as applied in this case.[2]

volved "purely commercial rather than political speech." Similarly, he stated that the authorization "to prohibit certain commercial and promotional uses of the word 'Olympic' [does not] even begin to tell us whether the Government may criminally punish physical conduct towards the flag engaged in as a means of political protest."

2. In holding that the Texas statute as applied to Johnson violates the First Amendment, the Court does not consider Johnson's

JUSTICE STEVENS, dissenting. * * *

Even if flag burning could be considered just another species of symbolic speech under the logical application of the rules that the Court has developed in its interpretation of the First Amendment in other contexts, this case has an intangible dimension that makes those rules inapplicable.

A country's flag is a symbol of more than "nationhood and national unity." [T]he American flag * * * is more than a proud symbol of the courage, the determination, and the gifts of nature that transformed 13 fledgling Colonies into a world power. It is a symbol of freedom, of equal opportunity, of religious tolerance, and of goodwill for other peoples who share our aspirations. The symbol carries its message to dissidents both at home and abroad who may have no interest at all in our national unity or survival.

The value of the flag as a symbol cannot be measured. Even so, I have no doubt that the interest in preserving that value for the future is both significant and legitimate. Conceivably that value will be enhanced by the Court's conclusion that our national commitment to free expression is so strong that even the United States as ultimate guarantor of that freedom is without power to prohibit the desecration of its unique symbol. But I am unpersuaded. The creation of a federal right to post bulletin boards and graffiti on the Washington Monument might enlarge the market for free expression, but at a cost I would not pay. Similarly, in my considered judgment, sanctioning the public desecration of the flag will tarnish its value—both for those who cherish the ideas for which it waves and for those who desire to don the robes of martyrdom by burning it. That tarnish is not justified by the trivial burden on free expression occasioned by requiring that an available, alternative mode of expression—including uttering words critical of the flag be employed.

It is appropriate to emphasize certain propositions that are not implicated by this case. [The] statute does not compel any conduct or any profession of respect for any idea or any symbol. [Nor] does the statute violate "the government's paramount obligation of neutrality in its regulation of protected communication." The content of respondent's message has no relevance whatsoever to the case. The concept of "desecration" does not turn on the substance of the message the actor intends to convey, but rather on whether those who view the act will take serious offense. Accordingly, one intending to convey a message of respect for the flag by burning it in a public square might nonetheless be guilty of desecration if he knows that others—perhaps simply because they misperceive the intended message—will be seriously offended. Indeed, even if the actor knows that all possible witnesses will understand that he intends to send a message of respect, he might still be guilty of desecration if he also knows that this understanding does not lessen the offense taken by some of those witnesses. The case has nothing to do with "disagreeable ideas." It involves disagreeable conduct that, in my opinion, diminishes the value of an important national asset.

[Had respondent] chosen to spray paint—or perhaps convey with a motion picture projector—his message of dissatisfaction on the facade of the Lincoln Memorial, there would be no question about the power of the Government to prohibit his means of expression. The prohibition would be supported by the

claims that the statute is unconstitutionally vague or overbroad. I think those claims are without merit. [By] defining "desecrate" as "deface," "damage" or otherwise "physically mistreat" in a manner that the actor knows will "seriously offend" others, § 42.09 only prohibits flagrant acts of physical abuse and destruction of the flag of the sort at issue here—soaking a flag with lighter fluid and igniting it in public—and not any of the examples of improper flag etiquette cited in Respondent's brief.

legitimate interest in preserving the quality of an important national asset. Though the asset at stake in this case is intangible, given its unique value, the same interest supports a prohibition on the desecration of the American flag.*

The ideas of liberty and equality have been an irresistible force in motivating leaders like Patrick Henry, Susan B. Anthony, and Abraham Lincoln, schoolteachers like Nathan Hale and Booker T. Washington, the Philippine Scouts who fought at Bataan, and the soldiers who scaled the bluff at Omaha Beach. If those ideas are worth fighting for—and our history demonstrates that they are—it cannot be true that the flag that uniquely symbolizes their power is not itself worthy of protection from unnecessary desecration.

Notes and Questions

1. *Patriotism.* Consider George Fletcher, *Loyalty* 141 (1993): "The [question] is whether the Congress has a sufficiently clear interest in promoting national loyalty to interpret the crime of flag burning as a sanction aimed not at the message of protest, but at the act, regardless of its political slant. Whether Congress and the country possess this interest depends, of course, on what one thinks of loyalty and devotion to country as a value. A high regard for patriotism, for sharing a common purpose in cherishing our people and seeking to solve our problems, leads one easily to perceive the expression of our unity as a value important in itself. The flag is at least as important—to go from the sublime to the ridiculous—as protecting draft cards so that the Selective Service System can function efficiently."

2. *Dissent.* Consider Steven Shiffrin, *The First Amendment and the Meaning of America,* in *Identities, Politics, and Rights* 318 (Sarat & Kearnes eds. 1996): "The flag-burning prohibition is uniquely troubling not because it interferes with the metaphorical marketplace of ideas, not because it topples our image of a content neutral government (*that* has fallen many times), and not merely because it suppresses political speech. The flag-burning prohibition is a naked attempt to smother dissent. If we must have a 'central meaning' of the first amendment, we should recognize that the dissenters—those who attack existing customs, habits, traditions and authorities—stand at the center of the first amendment and not at its periphery. Gregory Johnson was attacking a symbol which the vast majority of Americans regard with reverence. But that is *exactly* why he deserved first amendment protection. The first amendment has a special regard for those who swim against the current, for those who would shake us to our foundations, for those who reject prevailing authority. In burning the flag, Gregory Johnson rejected, opposed, even blasphemed the Nation's most important political, social,

---

* The Court suggested that a prohibition against flag desecration is not content-neutral because this form of symbolic speech is only used by persons who are critical of the flag or the ideas it represents. In making this suggestion the Court does not pause to consider the far-reaching consequences of its introduction of disparate impact analysis into our First Amendment jurisprudence. It seems obvious that a prohibition against the desecration of a gravesite is content-neutral even if it denies some protesters the right to make a symbolic statement by extinguishing the flame in Arlington Cemetery where John F. Kennedy is buried while permitting others to salute the flame by bowing their heads. Few would doubt that a protester who extinguishes the flame has desecrated the gravesite, regardless of whether he prefaces that act with a speech explaining that his purpose is to express deep admiration or unmitigated scorn for the late President. Likewise, few would claim that the protester who bows his head has desecrated the gravesite, even if he makes clear that his purpose is to show disrespect. In such a case, as in a flag burning case, the prohibition against desecration has absolutely nothing to do with the content of the message that the symbolic speech is intended to convey.

and cultural icon. Clearly Gregory Johnson's alleged act of burning the flag was a quintessential act of dissent. A dissent centered conception of the first amendment would make it clear that *Johnson* was an easy case—rightly decided."

3. *The meaning of the flag.* Consider Kenneth Karst, *Law's Promise, Law's Expression: Visions of Power in the Politics of Race, Gender, and Religion* 165 (1993): "According to those opinions the flag stands for our nationhood or national unity (Brennan, paraphrasing the state's lawyers); for principles of freedom or inclusiveness (Brennan); for the nation's resiliency (Brennan); for the nation itself (Rehnquist); for something men will die for in war (Rehnquist); for 'America's imagined past and present' (Rehnquist, in Sheldon Nahmod's apt paraphrase); for courage, freedom, equal opportunity, religious tolerance, and 'goodwill for other peoples who share our aspirations' (Stevens); and for shared beliefs in law and peace and 'the freedom that sustains the human spirit' (Kennedy). So, even within the Supreme Court, the flag stands at once for freedom and for obedience to law, for war and for peace, for unity and for tolerance of difference."

4. *The flag's "physical integrity."* Brennan, J., observes that the Texas law is "not aimed at protecting the physical integrity of the flag in all circumstances." What if it were?[e]

In response to *Johnson,* Congress passed the Flag Protection Act of 1989 which attached criminal penalties to the knowing mutilation, defacement, burning, maintaining on the floor or ground, or trampling upon any flag of the United States. UNITED STATES v. EICHMAN, 496 U.S. 310, 110 S.Ct. 2404, 110 L.Ed.2d 287 (1990), per BRENNAN, J., invalidated the statute: "Although the Flag Protection Act contains no explicit content-based limitation on the scope of prohibited conduct, it is nevertheless clear that the Government's asserted *interest* is 'related 'to the suppression of free expression' 'and concerned with the content of such expression. The Government's interest in protecting the 'physical integrity' of a privately owned flag rests upon a perceived need to preserve the flag's status as a symbol of our Nation and certain national ideals. But the mere destruction or disfigurement of a particular physical manifestation of the symbol, without more, does not diminish or otherwise affect the symbol itself in any way. For example, the secret destruction of a flag in one's own basement would not threaten the flag's recognized meaning. Rather, the Government's desire to preserve the flag as a symbol for certain national ideals is implicated 'only when a person's treatment of the flag communicates [a] message' to others that is inconsistent with those ideals."

STEVENS, J., joined by Rehnquist, C.J., White and O'Connor, JJ., dissenting, argued that the government's "legitimate interest in protecting the symbolic value of the American flag" outweighed the free speech interest. In describing the flag's symbolic value he stated that the flag "inspires and motivates the average citizen to make personal sacrifices in order to achieve societal goals of overriding importance; at all times, it serves as a reminder of the paramount importance of pursuing the ideals that characterize our society. * * * [T]he communicative value of a well-placed bomb in the Capital does not entitle it to the protection of the First Amendment. Burning a flag is not, of course, equivalent to burning a

---

e. For commentary concerning the extent to which a focus on physical integrity can be separated from a concern with content, see Kent Greenawalt, *O'er the Land of the Free: Flag Burning as Speech,* 37 UCLA L.Rev. 925 (1990); Frank Michelman, *Saving Old Glory: On Constitutional Iconography,* 42 Stan.L.Rev. 1337 (1990); Geoffrey Stone, *Flag Burning and the Constitution,* 75 Ia.L.Rev. 111 (1989); Mark Tushnet, *The Flag–Burning Episode: An Essay on the Constitution,* 61 U.Col.L.Rev. 39 (1990).

public building. Assuming that the protester is burning his own flag, it causes no physical harm to other persons or to their property. The impact is purely symbolic, and it is apparent that some thoughtful persons believe that impact far from depreciating the value of the symbol, will actually enhance its meaning. I most respectfully disagree."[f]

5. Prior to adopting the Flag Protection Act, the Senate by a vote of 97–3 had passed a resolution expressing "profound disappointment with the [*Johnson*] decision." The House had approved a similar resolution by a vote of 411–5, and President Bush had proposed a constitutional amendment to overrule *Johnson.* Opponents of the amendment argued that a carefully drawn statute might (or would) be upheld by the Court. Suppose you were a member of the House or Senate at that time. Suppose you supported *Johnson* but believed that the statute might be held constitutional, even though you did not think it should be. Suppose you also believed that if a statute were not passed an amendment would.[g]

Consider this exchange during hearings of the House Subcommittee on Civil and Constitutional Rights in *Statutory and Constitutional Responses to the Supreme Court Decision in Texas v. Johnson* (1989): Former Solicitor General Charles Fried: "My good friends and colleagues, Rex Lee and Laurence Tribe, have testified that a statute might be drawn that would pass constitutional muster. [I] hope and urge and pray that we will not act—that no statute be passed and of course that the Constitution not be amended. In short, I believe that *Johnson* is right [in] principle." * * *

Representative Schroeder: "I thought your testimony was eloquent. I think in a purist world, that is where we should go. But [we] are not talking about a purist world. We are talking about a very political world." * * *

Mr. Fried: "There are times when you earn your rather inadequate salary by just doing the right thing, and where you seem to agree with me is that the right thing to do is to do neither one of these. * * * It is called leadership."

Representative Schroeder: "It is called leadership. * * * But I guess what I am saying is if we can't stop a stampede on an amendment without something, isn't it better to try to save the Bill of Rights and the Constitution?"

————

Community for Creative Non–Violence (CCNV) sought to conduct a winter-time demonstration near the White House in Lafayette Park and the Mall to dramatize the plight of the homeless. The National Park Service authorized the erection of two symbolic tent cities for purposes of the demonstration, but denied CCNV's request that demonstrators be permitted to sleep in the tents. National Park Service regulations permit camping (the "use of park land for living accommodation purposes such as sleeping activities") in National Parks only in campgrounds designated for that purpose.

f. But see Arnold Loewy, *The Flag–Burning Case: Freedom of Speech When We Need It Most,* 68 N.C.L.Rev. 165, 174 (1989): "Perhaps the ultimate irony is that *Johnson* has done more to preserve the flag as a symbol of liberty than any prior decision, while the decision's detractors would allow real desecration of the flag by making it a symbol of political oppression." Compare Robin West, *Taking Freedom*

Seriously, 104 Harv.L.Rev. 43, 97–98 (1990) (the militaristic patriotism associated with the flag menaces dissent); see also Greenawalt, fn. e supra.

g. For commentary, compare Michelman, fn. e supra with Steven H. Shiffrin, *Dissent, Injustice, and the Meanings of America* ch. 1 (1990).

CLARK v. COMMUNITY FOR CREATIVE NON–VIOLENCE, 468 U.S. 288, 104 S.Ct. 3065, 82 L.Ed.2d 221 (1984), per WHITE, J., rejected CCNV's claim that the regulations could not be constitutionally applied against its demonstration: "We need not differ with the view of the Court of Appeals that overnight sleeping in connection with the demonstration is expressive conduct protected to some extent by the First Amendment.[5] We assume for present purposes, but do not decide, that such is the case, cf. *O'Brien,* but this assumption only begins the inquiry. Expression, whether oral or written or symbolized by conduct, is subject to reasonable time, place, or manner restrictions. We have often noted that restrictions of this kind are valid provided that they are justified without reference to the content of the regulated speech, that they are narrowly tailored to serve a significant governmental interest, and that they leave open ample alternative channels for communication of the information.

"It is also true that a message may be delivered by conduct that is intended to be communicative and that, in context, would reasonably be understood by the viewer to be communicative. Symbolic expression of this kind may be forbidden or regulated if the conduct itself may constitutionally be regulated, if the regulation is narrowly drawn to further a substantial governmental interest, and if the interest is unrelated to the suppression of free speech. *O'Brien.*

"[That] sleeping, like the symbolic tents themselves, may be expressive and part of the message delivered by the demonstration does not make the ban any less a limitation on the manner of demonstrating, for reasonable time, place, or manner regulations normally have the purpose and direct effect of limiting expression but are nevertheless valid. Neither does the fact that sleeping, arguendo, may be expressive conduct, rather than oral or written expression, render the sleeping prohibition any less a time, place, or manner regulation. To the contrary, the Park Service neither attempts to ban sleeping generally nor to ban it everywhere in the parks. It has established areas for camping and forbids it elsewhere, including Lafayette Park and the Mall. Considered as such, we have very little trouble concluding that the Park Service may prohibit overnight sleeping in the parks involved here.

"The requirement that the regulation be content-neutral is clearly satisfied. The courts below accepted that view, and it is not disputed here that the prohibition on camping, and on sleeping specifically, is content-neutral and is not being applied because of disagreement with the message presented.[a] Neither was the regulation faulted, nor could it be, on the ground that without overnight sleeping the plight of the homeless could not be communicated in other ways. The regulation otherwise left the demonstration intact, with its symbolic city, signs, and the presence of those who were willing to take their turns in a day-and-night vigil. Respondents do not suggest that there was, or is, any barrier to delivering to the media, or to the public by other means, the intended message concerning the plight of the homeless.

---

5. We reject the suggestion of the plurality below, however, that the burden on the demonstrators is limited to "the advancement of a plausible contention" that their conduct is expressive. Although it is common to place the burden upon the Government to justify impingements on First Amendment interests, it is the obligation of the person desiring to engage in assertedly expressive conduct to demonstrate that the First Amendment even applies.

To hold otherwise would be to create a rule that all conduct is presumptively expressive.

a. Marshall, J., dissenting, observed that CCNV had held a demonstration the previous winter in which it set up nine tents and slept in Lafayette Park. The D.C. Circuit held that the regulations did not preclude such a demonstration. According to Marshall, J., "The regulations at issue in this case were passed in direct response" to that holding.

"It is also apparent to us that the regulation narrowly focuses on the Government's substantial interest in maintaining the parks in the heart of our Capital in an attractive and intact condition, readily available to the millions of people who wish to see and enjoy them by their presence. To permit camping—using these areas as living accommodations—would be totally inimical to these purposes, as would be readily understood by those who have frequented the National Parks across the country and observed the unfortunate consequences of the activities of those who refuse to confine their camping to designated areas.

"It is urged by [CCNV] that if the symbolic city of tents was to be permitted and if the demonstrators did not intend to cook, dig, or engage in aspects of camping other than sleeping, the incremental benefit to the parks could not justify the ban on sleeping, which was here an expressive activity said to enhance the message concerning the plight of the poor and homeless. We cannot agree. In the first place, we seriously doubt that the First Amendment requires the Park Service to permit a demonstration in Lafayette Park and the Mall involving a 24–hour vigil and the erection of tents to accommodate 150 people. Furthermore, although we have assumed for present purposes that the sleeping banned in this case would have an expressive element, it is evident that its major value to this demonstration would be facilitative. Without a permit to sleep, it would be difficult to get the poor and homeless to participate or to be present at all.[b]

"Beyond this, however, it is evident from our cases that the validity of this regulation need not be judged solely by reference to the demonstration at hand.[c] Absent the prohibition on sleeping, there would be other groups who would demand permission to deliver an asserted message by camping in Lafayette Park. Some of them would surely have as credible a claim in this regard as does CCNV, and the denial of permits to still others would present difficult problems for the Park Service. With the prohibition, however, as is evident in the case before us, at least some around-the-clock demonstrations lasting for days on end will not materialize, others will be limited in size and duration, and the purposes of the regulation will thus be materially served. Perhaps these purposes would be more effectively and not so clumsily achieved by preventing tents and 24–hour vigils entirely in the core areas. But the Park Service's decision to permit nonsleeping demonstrations does not, in our view, impugn the camping prohibition as a valuable, but perhaps imperfect, protection to the parks. If the Government has a legitimate interest in ensuring that the National Parks are adequately protected, which we think it has, and if the parks would be more exposed to harm without the sleeping prohibition than with it, the ban is safe from invalidation under the First Amendment as a reasonable regulation of the manner in which a demonstration may be carried out.[d] * * *

"[The] foregoing analysis demonstrates that the Park Service regulation is sustainable under the four-factor standard of *O'Brien,* for validating a regulation of expressive conduct, which, in the last analysis is little, if any, different from the

---

b. What if it were the exclusive value? For discussion, see Gary Francione, *Experimentation and the Marketplace Theory of the First Amendment,* 136 U.Pa.L.Rev. 417 (1987).

c. For debate about this point and its implications, compare Frank Easterbrook, *Foreword: The Court and the Economic System,* 98 Harv.L.Rev. 4, 19–21 (1984) with Laurence Tribe, *Constitutional Calculus: Equal Justice or Economic Efficiency?* 98 Harv.L.Rev. 592, 599–603 (1985) and Frank Easterbrook, *Meth-*

od, Result, and Authority: A Reply, 98 Harv.L.Rev. 622, 626 (1985).

d. Alan E. Brownstein, *Alternative Maps for Navigating the First Amendment Maze,* 16 Const. Comm. 101, 117 (1999): "It seems clear that a similar argument could be applied to prohibit leafleting (or all demonstrations for that matter) in Lafayette Park. * * * I do not believe that a ban on leafleting in Lafayette Park would be as cavalierly upheld by the Court as the ban on camping, however."

standard applied to time, place, or manner restrictions.[8] No one contends that aside from its impact on speech a rule against camping or overnight sleeping in public parks is beyond the constitutional power of the Government to enforce. And for the reasons we have discussed above, there is a substantial Government interest in conserving park property, an interest that is plainly served by, and requires for its implementation, measures such as the proscription of sleeping that are designed to limit the wear and tear on park properties. That interest is unrelated to suppression of expression.

"We are unmoved by the Court of Appeals' view that the challenged regulation is unnecessary, and hence invalid, because there are less speech-restrictive alternatives that could have satisfied the Government interest in preserving park lands. [The] Court of Appeals' suggestions that the Park Service minimize the possible injury by reducing the size, duration, or frequency of demonstrations would still curtail the total allowable expression in which demonstrators could engage, whether by sleeping or otherwise, and these suggestions represent no more than a disagreement with the Park Service over how much protection the core parks require or how an acceptable level of preservation is to be attained. We do not believe, however, that either *United States v. O'Brien* or the time, place, or manner decisions assign to the judiciary the authority to replace the Park Service as the manager of the Nation's parks or endow the judiciary with the competence to judge how much protection of park lands is wise and how that level of conservation is to be [attained.]"

BURGER, C.J., joined in the Court's opinion, adding: "[CCNV's] attempt at camping in the park is a form of 'picketing'; it is conduct, not speech. [It] trivializes the First Amendment to seek to use it as a shield in the manner asserted here."

MARSHALL, J., joined by Brennan, J., dissented: "The majority assumes, without deciding, that the respondents' conduct is entitled to constitutional protection. The problem with this assumption is that the Court thereby avoids examining closely the reality of respondents' planned expression. The majority's approach denatures respondents' asserted right and thus makes all too easy identification of a Government interest sufficient to warrant its abridgment.

"[Missing] from the majority's description is any inkling that Lafayette Park and the Mall have served as the sites for some of the most rousing political demonstrations in the Nation's history.[2] [The] primary purpose for making *sleep* an integral part of the demonstration was 'to re-enact the central reality of homelessness' and to impress upon public consciousness, in as dramatic a way as possible, that homelessness is a widespread problem, often ignored, that confronts its victims with life-threatening deprivations. As one of the homeless men seeking

8. Reasonable time, place, or manner restrictions are valid even though they directly limit oral or written expression. It would be odd to insist on a higher standard for limitations aimed at regulable conduct and having only an incidental impact on speech. Thus, if the time, place, or manner restriction on expressive sleeping, if that is what is involved in this case, sufficiently and narrowly serves a substantial enough governmental interest to escape First Amendment condemnation, it is untenable to invalidate it under *O'Brien* on the ground that the governmental interest is insufficient to warrant the intrusion on First Amendment concerns or that there is an inade-

quate nexus between the regulation and the interest sought to be served. We note that only recently, in a case dealing with the regulation of signs, the Court framed the issue under *O'Brien* and then based a crucial part of its analysis on the time, place, or manner cases.

2. At oral argument, the Government informed the Court "that on any given day there will be an average of three or so demonstrations going on" in the Mall–Lafayette Park area. Respondents accurately describe Lafayette Park "as the American analogue to 'Speaker's Corner' in Hyde Park."

to demonstrate explained: 'Sleeping in Lafayette Park or on the Mall, for me, is to show people that conditions are so poor for the homeless and poor in this city that we would actually sleep *outside* in the winter to get the point across.' * * * Here respondents clearly intended to protest the reality of homelessness by sleeping outdoors in the winter in the near vicinity of the magisterial residence of the President of the United States. In addition to accentuating the political character of their protest by their choice of location and mode of communication, respondents also intended to underline the meaning of their protest by giving their demonstration satirical names. Respondents planned to name the demonstration on the Mall 'Congressional Village,' and the demonstration in Lafayette Park, 'Reaganville II.' * * *

"Although sleep in the context of this case is symbolic speech protected by the First Amendment, it is nonetheless subject to reasonable time, place, and manner restrictions. I agree with the standard enunciated by the majority.[6] I conclude, however, that the regulations at issue in this case, as applied to respondents, fail to satisfy this [standard].

"[T]here are no substantial Government interests advanced by the Government's regulations as applied to respondents. All that the Court's decision advances are the prerogatives of a bureaucracy that over the years has shown an implacable hostility toward citizens' exercise of First Amendment [rights].

"The disposition of this case impels me to make two additional observations. First, in this case, as in some others involving time, place, and manner restrictions, the Court has dramatically lowered its scrutiny of governmental regulations once it has determined that such regulations are content-neutral.[e] The result has been the creation of a two-tiered approach to First Amendment cases: while regulations that turn on the content of the expression are subjected to a strict form of judicial review, regulations that are aimed at matters other than expression receive only a minimal level of scrutiny. [The] Court has seemingly overlooked the fact that content-neutral restrictions are also capable of unnecessarily restricting protected expressive activity.[13] [The] Court [has] transformed the ban against content distinctions from a floor that offers all persons at least equal liberty under the First Amendment into a ceiling that restricts persons to the protection of First Amendment equality—but nothing more.[14] The consistent imposition of silence upon all may fulfill the dictates of an evenhanded content-neutrality. But it offends our 'profound national commitment to the principle that debate on public issues should be uninhibited, robust, and wide-open'. *New York Times Co. v. Sullivan.*

6. I also agree with the majority that no substantial difference distinguishes the test applicable to time, place, and manner restrictions and the test articulated in *O'Brien.*

e. In support of Marshall, J.'s contention, see generally William Lee, *Lonely Pamphleteers, Little People, and the Supreme Court,* 54 G.W.U.L.Rev. 757 (1986).

13. See Martin Redish, *The Content Distinction in First Amendment Analysis,* 34 Stan. L.Rev. 113 (1981).

14. Furthermore, [a] content-neutral regulation that restricts an inexpensive mode of communication will fall most heavily upon relatively poor speakers and to points of view that such speakers typically espouse. [See Lee, fn. d supra.] This sort of latent inequality is very much in evidence in this case, for respondents lack the financial means necessary to buy access to more conventional modes of persuasion.

A disquieting feature about the disposition of this case is that it lends credence to the charge that judicial administration of the First Amendment, in conjunction with a social order marked by large disparities of wealth and other sources of power, tends systematically to discriminate against efforts by the relatively disadvantaged to convey their political ideas. * * *

"Second, the disposition of this case reveals a mistaken assumption regarding the motives and behavior of Government officials who create and administer content-neutral regulations. The Court's salutary skepticism of governmental decisionmaking in First Amendment matters suddenly dissipates once it determines that a restriction is not content-based. The Court evidently assumes that the balance struck by officials is deserving of deference so long as it does not appear to be tainted by content discrimination. What the Court fails to recognize is that public officials have strong incentives to overregulate even in the absence of an intent to censor particular views. This incentive stems from the fact that of the two groups whose interests officials must accommodate—on the one hand, the interests of the general public and, on the other, the interests of those who seek to use a particular forum for First Amendment activity—the political power of the former is likely to be far greater than that of the latter.[16]"

Notes and Questions

1. Consider Mark Tushnet, *Character as Argument,* 14 Law and Social Inquiry 539, 549 (1989) (reviewing Harry Kalven, *A Worthy Tradition*): "To capture the attention of a public accustomed to dignified protest, and able to screen it from consciousness, dissidents may have to adopt novel forms of protest, such as sleeping in a national park overnight to draw attention to the disgrace of a national policy that deprives many people of decent shelter. Yet, precisely because their protests take a novel form, they may not be covered by the worthy tradition that Kalven honors. In this sense the dynamics of protest may make the protection of free speech what Kalven tellingly calls a 'luxury civil liberty,' a civil liberty to be enjoyed when nothing of consequence turns on protecting speech and to be abandoned when it really matters."

2. Should the Court have decided whether sleeping in the park in these circumstances was a form of expression entitled to some degree of first amendment protection? Should all forms of expression receive some level of first amendment protection? Is the presence of an "idea" a necessary condition for expression to come within the first amendment's scope? Should nude dancing be excluded from the first amendment's scope because it is not intended to communicate ideas? Should protection for paintings depend upon whether "ideas" are expressed? See *Schad v. Mount Ephraim,* Sec. 3, I infra: "[N]ude dancing is not without its First Amendment protections from official regulation." Should hair styles be afforded first amendment protection? Are hair styles distinguishable from nude dancing on the ground that the latter is a form of expressive entertainment? If so, should video games be afforded first amendment protection? See Note, *The First Amendment Side Effects of Curing Pac–Man Fever,* 84 Colum.L.Rev. 744 (1984). But see Frederick Schauer, *Free Speech and the Demise of the Soapbox* Book Review, 84 Colum.L.Rev. 558, 565 (1984) ("[T]he first amendment importance of the messages from an automatic teller to the bank's central computer completely escapes me, as does the first amendment importance of the mutual exchange of electronic and visual symbols between me and the Pac–Man machine.").[f]

---

16. See David Goldberger, *Judicial Scrutiny in Public Forum Cases: Misplaced Trust in the Judgment of Public Officials,* 32 Buffalo L.Rev. 175, 208 (1983).

f. See Robert Post, *Recuperating First Amendment Doctrine,* 47 Stan.L.Rev. 1249

(1995) (speech in its ordinary language sense has no inherent constitutional value and should be defined to include only those social practices which implicate free speech values). Cf. Stanley Fish, *There's No Such Thing as Free Speech,* 102 (1994) (" 'Free speech' is just

3. The "time, place, or manner" test set out in *Clark* is differently stated in different cases. For example, *U.S. Postal Service v. Council of Greenburgh*, 453 U.S. 114, 101 S.Ct. 2676, 69 L.Ed.2d 517 (1981), speaks of "adequate" as opposed to "ample" alternative channels of communication, and *Renton v. Playtime Theatres, Inc.*, Sec. 3, I infra, transcends the difference by requiring that the restriction not "unreasonably limit" alternative channels of communication. Beyond these differences, a number of cases state that the regulation must serve a significant government interest without stating that it must be "narrowly tailored" to serve a significant government interest. See e.g., *Heffron v. International Soc. For Krishna Consciousness*, Sec. 6, I, A infra. But see *Ward v. Rock Against Racism*, Sec. 6, I, A infra (reaffirming and defining narrowly tailored requirement). Assuming sleeping in the *Clark* context implicates first amendment values, what test should apply?

New York Public Health law authorizes the forced closure of a building for one year if it has been used for the purpose of "lewdness, assignation or prostitution." A civil complaint alleged that prostitution solicitation and sexual activities by patrons were occurring at an adult bookstore within observation of the proprietor. Accordingly, the complaint called for the closure of the building for one year. There was no claim that any books in the store were obscene. The New York Court of Appeals held that the closure remedy violated the first amendment because it was broader than necessary to achieve the restriction against illicit sexual activities. It reasoned that an injunction against the alleged sexual conduct could further the state interest without infringing on first amendment values. ARCARA v. CLOUD BOOKS, INC., 478 U.S. 697, 106 S.Ct. 3172, 92 L.Ed.2d 568 (1986), per Burger, C.J., reversed, holding that the closure remedy did not require any first amendment scrutiny: "This Court has applied First Amendment scrutiny to a statute regulating conduct which has the incidental effect of burdening the expression of a particular political opinion. *O'Brien*. * * *

"We have also applied First Amendment scrutiny to some statutes which, although directed at activity with no expressive component, impose a disproportionate burden upon those engaged in protected First Amendment activities. In *Minneapolis Star & Tribune v. Minnesota Commissioner of Revenue*, 460 U.S. 575, 103 S.Ct. 1365, 75 L.Ed.2d 295 (1983), we struck down a tax imposed on the sale of large quantities of newsprint and ink because the tax had the effect of singling out newspapers to shoulder its burden. [Even] while striking down the tax in *Minneapolis Star*, we emphasized: 'Clearly, the First Amendment does not prohibit all regulation of the press. It is beyond dispute that the States and the Federal Government can subject newspapers to generally applicable economic regulations without creating constitutional problems.'

"The New York Court of Appeals held that the *O'Brien* test for permissible governmental regulation was applicable to this case because the closure order sought by petitioner would also impose an incidental burden upon respondents' bookselling activities. [But] unlike the symbolic draft card burning in *O'Brien*, the sexual activity carried on in this case manifests absolutely no element of protected expression.[a] In *Paris Adult Theatre*, we underscored the fallacy of seeking to use

the name we give to verbal behavior that serves the substantive agendas we wish to advance").

a. In an earlier section of the opinion, Burger, C.J., stated that, "petitioners in *O'Brien* had, as respondents here do not, at least the semblance of expressive activity in

the First Amendment as a cloak for obviously unlawful public sexual conduct by the diaphanous device of attributing protected expressive attributes to that conduct. First Amendment values may not be invoked by merely linking the words 'sex' and 'books.'

"Nor does the distinction drawn by the New York Public Health Law inevitably single out bookstores or others engaged in First Amendment protected activities for the imposition of its burden, as did the tax struck down in *Minneapolis Star*. [If] the city imposed closure penalties for demonstrated Fire Code violations or health hazards from inadequate sewage treatment, the First Amendment would not aid the owner of premises who had knowingly allowed such violations to persist. * * *

"It is true that the closure order in this case would require respondents to move their bookselling business to another location. Yet we have not traditionally subjected every criminal and civil sanction imposed through legal process to 'least restrictive means' scrutiny simply because each particular remedy will have some effect on the First Amendment activities of those subject to sanction.[4]"[b]

O'Connor, J., joined by Stevens, J., concurred: "I agree that the Court of Appeals erred in applying a First Amendment standard of review where, as here, the government is regulating neither speech nor an incidental, non-expressive effect of speech. Any other conclusion would lead to the absurd result that any government action that had some conceivable speech-inhibiting consequences, such as the arrest of a newscaster for a traffic violation, would require analysis under the First Amendment."

Blackmun, JJ., joined by Brennan and Marshall, JJ., dissented: "Until today, this Court has never suggested that a State may suppress speech as much as it likes, without justification, so long as it does so through generally applicable regulations that have 'nothing to do with any expressive conduct.' * * *

"At some point, of course, the impact of state regulation on First Amendment rights become so attenuated that it is easily outweighed by the state interest. But when a State directly and substantially impairs First Amendment activities, such as by shutting down a bookstore, I believe that the State must show, at a minimum, that it has chosen the least restrictive means of pursuing its legitimate objectives. The closure of a bookstore can no more be compared to a traffic arrest of a reporter than the closure of a church could be compared to the traffic arrest of its clergyman.

"A State has a legitimate interest in forbidding sexual acts committed in public, including a bookstore. An obvious method of eliminating such acts is to

their claim that the otherwise unlawful burning of a draft card was to 'carry a message' of the actor's opposition to the draft."

4. [T]here is no suggestion on the record before us that the closure of respondents' bookstore was sought under the public health nuisance statute as a pretext for the suppression of First Amendment protected material. Were respondents able to establish the existence of such a speech suppressive motivation or policy on the part of the District Attorney, they might have a claim of selective prosecution. Respondents in this case made no such assertion before the trial court.

b. On remand, the New York Court of Appeals held that, in the absence of a showing that the state had chosen a course no broader than necessary to accomplish its purpose, any forced closure of the bookstore would unduly impair the bookseller's rights of free expression under the New York State constitution. From New York's perspective, the question is not "who is aimed at but who is hit." *People ex rel. Arcara v. Cloud Books, Inc.*, 68 N.Y.2d 553, 510 N.Y.S.2d 844, 503 N.E.2d 492 (1986). But see *Alexander v. United States*, 509 U.S. 544, 113 S.Ct. 2766, 125 L.Ed.2d 441 (1993)(confiscation and destruction of protected materials for distribution of obscene materials does not violate first amendment).

arrest the patron committing them. But the statute in issue does not provide for that. Instead, it imposes absolute liability on the bookstore simply because the activity occurs on the premises. And the penalty—a mandatory 1–year closure— imposes an unnecessary burden on speech. Of course 'linking the words "sex" and "books" is not enough to extend First Amendment protection to illegal sexual activity, but neither should it suffice to remove First Amendment protection from books situated near the site of such activity. The State's purpose in stopping public lewdness cannot justify such a substantial infringement of First Amendment rights. * * *

"Petitioner has not demonstrated that a less restrictive remedy would be inadequate to abate the nuisance. The Court improperly attempts to shift to the bookseller the responsibility for finding an alternative site. But surely the Court would not uphold a city ordinance banning all public debate on the theory that the residents could move somewhere else.

Notes and Questions

1. Should the state's closing of a bookstore *always* trigger heightened judicial scrutiny? Is the first amendment really "not implicated" in *Arcara?* Should fire code regulations trigger first amendment scrutiny? Consider Comment, *Padlock Orders and Nuisance Laws,* 51 Albany L.Rev. 1007, 1026–27 (1987): "Closure penalties for fire code violations or health hazards from inadequate sewage treatment were offered as examples of generally applicable regulations which could constitutionally be applied to bookstores where the owner 'had knowingly allowed such violations to persist.' Few would argue with this conclusion. These generally applicable regulations would be within the state's constitutional power, would further a substantial governmental interest unrelated to the suppression of free expression, and the incidental restriction on first amendment freedoms, where the owner knowingly allowed the violations to persist, would be no greater than is essential to further the state's interest. Concluding that the *O'Brien* test is satisfied, however, does not support the conclusion that the test does not apply."

2. *Negative theory.* Should the scope of the first amendment be confined to instances in which government may have acted in a biased way? Consider Ronald Cass, *Commercial Speech, Constitutionalism, Collective Choice,* 56 U.Cin.L.Rev. 1317, 1352 (1988): "There is widespread agreement that limitation of official bias is the principal aim of the first amendment, historically and as amplified over the past half-century by the courts." See generally Ronald Cass, *The Perils of Positive Thinking: Constitutional Interpretation and Negative First Amendment Theory,* 34 U.C.L.A. L.Rev. 1405 (1987) (emphasizing official self interest and, to a lesser extent, intolerance as the principal motives of concern).

Professor Schauer has also attempted a justification for freedom of speech not based on any positive aspects of speech, but based on the premise that governments are "less capable of regulating speech than they are of regulating other forms of conduct." He suggests that bias, self-interest, and a general urge to suppress that with which one disagrees are significant reasons for this incapability. Frederick Schauer, *Free Speech: A Philosophical Enquiry* 80–86 (1982). See also Frederick Schauer, *Must Speech Be Special?,* 78 Nw.U.L.Rev. 1284 (1983). As he interprets the first amendment, therefore, its "focus * * * is on the motivations of the government." Frederick Schauer, *Cuban Cigars, Cuban Books, and* *the Problem of Incidental Restrictions on Communications,* 26 Wm. & Mary L.Rev. 779, 780 (1985).[c]

Is negative theory consistent with what the Court has *said* about free speech? With the doctrine it has produced? Consider, e.g., *Arcara. O'Brien.* The defamation line of cases. Compare Frederick Schauer, *Cuban Cigars,* supra with Steven Shiffrin, *The First Amendment, Democracy, and Romance* (1990). Is the content-based/content-neutral distinction founded exclusively on a concern with government motive? See generally Geoffrey Stone, *Content Regulation and the First Amendment,* 25 Wm. & Mary L.Rev. 189 (1983) (arguing that the basis for the distinction is more complicated). Does an emphasis on motive or content unreasonably downplay the notion that the *effect* of government conduct on the quantity or quality of speech is of independent first amendment value? See generally Martin Redish, *The Content Distinction in First Amendment Analysis,* 34 Stan. L.Rev. 113 (1981); Susan Williams, *Content Discrimination and the First Amendment,* 139 U.Pa.L.Rev. 201 (1991).

3. Could *Arcara's* failure to find the first amendment implicated be justified without resort to negative theory or motive theory? Consider Tribe 2d ed., at 978–79 n. 2: "[W]hen *neither* the law, *nor* the act triggering its enforcement has any significant first amendment dimension,[d] the fact that the law *incidentally* operates to restrict first amendment activity, and that some alternative state measure might offer a less restrictive means of pursuing the state's legitimate objectives, should not serve to condemn what the state has done as unconstitutional." Why not?

SECTION 3. IS SOME PROTECTED SPEECH LESS EQUAL THAN OTHER PROTECTED SPEECH?

I. NEAR OBSCENE SPEECH

YOUNG v. AMERICAN MINI THEATRES, INC.

427 U.S. 50, 96 S.Ct. 2440, 49 L.Ed.2d 310 (1976).

JUSTICE STEVENS delivered the opinion of the Court.[*]

[Detroit "Anti–Skid Row" ordinances prohibited "adult motion picture theaters" and "adult book stores" within 1,000 feet of any two other "regulated uses," which included such theaters and book stores, liquor stores, pool halls, pawnshops, and the like. The ordinances defined "adult motion picture theater" as one "presenting material distinguished or characterized by an emphasis on matter depicting, describing or relating to 'Specified Sexual Activities'[a] or 'Speci-

---

c. See also Frederick Schauer, *The Phenomenology of Speech and Harm,* 103 Ethics 635 (1993) (disputing the hypothesis that the harmful consequences of speech are less than those associated with other forms of conduct); Frederick Schauer, *The Sociology of the Hate Speech Debate,* 37 Vill.L.Rev. 805 (1992).

d. For relevant commentary, see Michael C. Dorf, *Incidental Burdens on Fundamental Rights,* 109 Harv. L. Rev. 1175 (1996).

* Part III of this opinion is joined only by The Chief Justice, Mr. Justice White, and Mr. Justice Rehnquist.

a. "Specified Sexual Activities" were defined thus:

"1. Human genitals in a state of sexual stimulation or arousal;

"2. Acts of human masturbation, sexual intercourse or sodomy;

"3. Fondling or other erotic touching of human genitals, pubic region, buttock or female breast."

fied Anatomical Areas' "[b] and "adult book store" in substantially the same terms. The Court upheld the ordinances, reversing a decision in a federal declaratory judgment action by two theater owners wishing regularly to exhibit "adult" motion pictures.]

I. [R]espondents claim that the ordinances are too vague [because] they cannot determine how much of the ["specified"] activity may be permissible before the exhibition is "characterized by an emphasis" on such matter. [We] find it unnecessary to consider the validity of [this argument. Both] theaters propose to offer adult fare on a regular basis. [Therefore], the element of vagueness in these ordinances has not affected these respondents. * * *

Because the ordinances affect communication protected by the First Amendment, respondents argue that they may raise the vagueness issue even though there is no uncertainty about the impact of the ordinances on their own rights. On several occasions we have determined that a defendant whose own speech was unprotected had standing to challenge the constitutionality of a statute which purported to prohibit protected speech, or even speech arguably protected. *Broadrick.* The exception is justified by the overriding importance of maintaining a free and open market for the interchange of ideas. Nevertheless, if the statute's deterrent effect of legitimate expression is not "both real and substantial" and if the statute is "readily subject to a narrowing construction by the state courts" the litigant is not permitted to assert the rights of third parties.

We are not persuaded that the Detroit Zoning Ordinances will have a significant deterrent effect on the exhibition of films protected by the First Amendment. [T]he only vagueness in the ordinances relates to the amount of sexually explicit activity that may be portrayed before the material can be said to be "characterized by an emphasis" on such matter. For most films the question will be readily answerable; to the extent that an area of doubt exists, we see no reason why the statute is not "readily subject to a narrowing construction by the state courts." Since there is surely a less vital interest in the uninhibited exhibition of material that is on the borderline between pornography and artistic expression than in the free dissemination of ideas of social and political significance,[c] and since the limited amount of uncertainty in the statute is easily susceptible of a narrowing construction, we think this is an inappropriate case in which to adjudicate the hypothetical claims of persons not before the Court. * * *

III. [T]he use of streets and parks for the free expression of views on national affairs may not be conditioned upon the sovereign's agreement with what a speaker may intend to say. [If] picketing in the vicinity of a school is to be allowed to express the point of view of labor, that means of expression in that place must be allowed for other points of view as well. As we said in [*Chicago*

---

b. "Specified Anatomical Areas" were defined thus:

"1. Less than completely and opaquely covered: (a) human genitals, pubic region, (b) buttock, and (c) female breast below a point immediately above the top of the areola, and

"2. Human male genitals in a discernibly turgid state, even if completely and opaquely covered."

c. But see Hunter & Law, Sec. 1, V, B supra, at 119–20: "[S]exual speech is political. One core insight of modern feminism is that the person is political. The question of who does the dishes and rocks the cradle affects

both the nature of the home and the composition of the legislature. The dynamics of intimate relations are likewise political, both to the individuals involved and by their multiplied effects to the wider society. To argue [that] sexually explicit speech is less important than other categories of discourse reinforces the conceptual structures that have identified women's concerns with relationships and intimacy as less significant and valuable precisely because those concerns are falsely regarded as having no bearing on the structure of social and political life."

Police Dep't v. Mosley, Sec. 6, I, B infra], "The central problem with Chicago's ordinance is that it describes permissible picketing in terms of its subject matter. [A]bove all else, the First Amendment means that government has no power to restrict expression because of its message, its ideas, its subject matter, or its content. [Any] restriction on expressive activity because of its content would completely undercut the 'profound national commitment to the principle that debate on public issues should be uninhibited, robust, and wide-open.' [*New York Times*]. Selective exclusions from a public forum may not be based on content alone, and may not be justified by reference to content alone."

This statement, and others to the same effect, read literally and without regard for the facts of the case in which it was made, would absolutely preclude any regulation of expressive activity predicated in whole or in part on the content of the communication. But we learned long ago that broad statements of principle, no matter how correct in the context in which they are made, are sometimes qualified by contrary decisions before the absolute limit of the stated principle is reached. When we review this Court's actual adjudications in the First Amendment area, we find this to have been the case with the stated principle that there may be no restriction whatever on expressive activity because of its content. * * *

The question whether speech is, or is not, protected by the First Amendment often depends on the content of the speech. Thus, the line between permissible advocacy and impermissible incitation to crime or violence depends, not merely on the setting in which the speech occurs, but also on exactly what the speaker had to say. Similarly, it is the content of the utterance that determines whether it is a protected epithet or an unprotected "fighting comment." * * *

Even within the area of protected speech, a difference in content may require a different governmental response. [*New York Times*] held that a public official may not recover damages from a critic of his official conduct without proof of "malice" as specially defined in that opinion. Implicit in the opinion is the assumption that if the content of the newspaper article had been different—that is, if its subject matter had not been a public official—a lesser standard of proof would have been adequate. [We] have recently held that the First Amendment affords some protection to commercial speech. [The] measure of [protection] to commercial speech will surely be governed largely by the content of the communication.[32] * * *

More directly in point are opinions dealing with the question whether the First Amendment prohibits the state and federal governments from wholly suppressing sexually oriented materials on the basis of their "obscene character." In *Ginsberg,* the Court upheld a conviction for selling to a minor magazines which were concededly not "obscene" if shown to adults. Indeed, the Members of the Court who would accord the greatest protection to such materials have repeatedly indicated that the State could prohibit the distribution or exhibition of such materials to juveniles and unconsenting adults. Surely the First Amendment does not foreclose such a prohibition; yet it is equally clear that any such prohibition must rest squarely on an appraisal of the content of material otherwise within a constitutionally protected area.

Such a line may be drawn on the basis of content without violating the Government's paramount obligation of neutrality in its regulation of protected

---

32. As Mr. Justice Stewart pointed out in *Virginia Pharmacy* [Sec. 3, II infra], the "differences between commercial price and product advertising [and] ideological communication" permits regulation of the former that the First Amendment would not tolerate with respect to the latter (concurring opinion).

communication. For the regulation of the places where sexually explicit films may be exhibited is unaffected by whatever social, political, or philosophical message the film may be intended to communicate; whether the motion picture ridicules or characterizes one point of view or another, the effect of the ordinances is exactly the same.

Moreover, even though we recognize that the First Amendment will not tolerate the total suppression of erotic materials that have some arguably artistic value, it is manifest that society's interest in protecting this type of expression is of a wholly different, and lesser, magnitude than the interest in untrammeled political debate that inspired Voltaire's immortal comment.[d] Whether political oratory or philosophical discussion moves us to applaud or to despise what is said, every school-child can understand why our duty to defend the right to speak remains the same. But few of us would march our sons and daughters off to war to preserve the citizen's right to see "Specified Sexual Activities" exhibited in the theaters of our choice. Even though the First Amendment protects communication in this area from total suppression, we hold that the State may legitimately use the content of these materials as the basis for placing them in a different classification from other motion pictures.

The remaining question is whether the line drawn by these ordinances is justified by the city's interest in preserving the character of its neighborhoods. [The] record discloses a factual basis for the Common Council's conclusion that this kind of restriction will have the desired effect.[34] It is not our function to appraise the wisdom of its decision to require adult theaters to be separated rather than concentrated in the same areas. In either event, the city's interest in attempting to preserve the quality of urban life is one that must be accorded high respect. Moreover, the city must be allowed a reasonable opportunity to experiment with solutions to admittedly serious problems.

Since what is ultimately at stake is nothing more than a limitation on the place where adult films may be exhibited,[35] even though the determination of whether a particular film fits that characterization turns on the nature of its content, we conclude that the city's interest in the present and future character of its neighborhoods adequately supports its classification of motion pictures. * * *

JUSTICE POWELL, concurring in the judgment and portions of the opinion.

Although I agree with much of what is said in the plurality opinion, [my] approach to the resolution of this case is sufficiently different to prompt me to write separately.[1] I view the case as presenting an example of innovative land-use

---

d. The opinion had earlier quoted Voltaire: "I disapprove of what you say, but I will defend to the death your right to say it."

34. The City Council's determination was that a concentration of "adult" movie theaters causes the area to deteriorate and become a focus of crime, effects which are not attributable to theaters showing other types of films. It is this secondary effect which this zoning ordinance attempts to avoid, not the dissemination of "offensive" speech. In contrast, in *Erznoznik,* the justifications offered by the city rested primarily on the city's interest in protecting its citizens from exposure to unwanted "offensive" speech. * * *

35. The situation would be quite different if the ordinance had the effect of suppressing,

or greatly restricting access to, lawful speech. Here, however, the District Court specifically found that "[t]he Ordinances do not affect the operation of existing establishments but only the location of new ones. There are myriad locations in the City of Detroit which must be over 1000 feet from existing regulated establishments. This burden on First Amendment rights is slight." * * *

1. I do not think we need reach, nor am I inclined to agree with, the holding in Part III (and supporting discussion) that nonobscene, erotic materials may be treated differently under First Amendment principles from other forms of protected expression. I do not consider the conclusions in Part I of the opinion to

regulation, implicating First Amendment concerns only incidentally and to a limited extent. * * *

In this case, there is no indication that the application of the Anti–Skid Row Ordinance to adult theaters has the effect of suppressing production of or, to any significant degree, restricting access to adult movies. Nortown concededly will not be able to exhibit adult movies at its present location, and the ordinance limits the potential location of the proposed Pussy Cat. The constraints of the ordinance with respect to location may indeed create economic loss for some who are engaged in this business. But in this respect they are affected no differently than any other commercial enterprise that suffers economic detriment as a result of land-use regulation. The cases are legion that sustained zoning against claims of serious economic damage.

The inquiry for First Amendment purposes is not concerned with economic impact; rather, it looks only to the effect of this ordinance upon freedom of expression. This prompts essentially two inquiries: (i) does the ordinance impose any content limitation on the creators of adult movies or their ability to make them available to whom they desire, and (ii) does it restrict in any significant way the viewing of these movies by those who desire to see them? On the record in this case, these inquiries must be answered in the negative. At most the impact of the ordinance on these interests is incidental and minimal.[2] Detroit has silenced no message, has invoked no censorship, and has imposed no limitation upon those who wish to view them. The ordinance is addressed only to the places at which this type of expression may be presented, a restriction that does not interfere with content. Nor is there any significant overall curtailment of adult movie presentations, or the opportunity for a message to reach an audience. On the basis of the District Court's finding, it appears that if a sufficient market exists to support them the number of adult movie theaters in Detroit will remain approximately the same, free to purvey the same message. To be sure some prospective patrons may be inconvenienced by this dispersal. But other patrons, depending upon where they live or work, may find it more convenient to view an adult movie when adult theaters are not concentrated in a particular section of the city.

In these circumstances, it is appropriate to analyze the permissibility of Detroit's action under the four-part test of *United States v. O'Brien*. Under that test, a governmental regulation is sufficiently justified, despite its incidental impact upon First Amendment interests, "if it is within the constitutional power of the Government; if it furthers an important government interest; if the government interest is unrelated to the suppression of free expression; and if the incidental restriction [on] First Amendment freedoms is no greater than is essential to the furtherance of that interest." [Powell, J., concluded that the Detroit ordinance satisfied the *O'Brien* test.]

JUSTICE STEWART, with whom JUSTICE BRENNAN, JUSTICE MARSHALL and JUSTICE BLACKMUN join, dissenting.

[This case involves] the constitutional permissibility of selective interference with protected speech whose content is thought to produce distasteful effects. It is elementary that a prime function of the First Amendment is to guard against just such interference. By refusing to invalidate Detroit's ordinance the Court rides roughshod over cardinal principles of First Amendment law, which require that

depend on distinctions between protected speech.

2. The communication involved here is not a kind in which the content or effectiveness of the message depends in some measure upon where or how it is conveyed. * * *

time, place and manner regulations that affect protected expression be content-neutral except in the limited context of a captive or juvenile audience. In place of these principles the Court invokes a concept wholly alien to the First Amendment. Since "few of us would march our sons and daughters off to war to preserve the citizen's right to see 'Specified Sexual Activities' exhibited in the theaters of our choice," the Court implies that these films are not entitled to the full protection of the Constitution. This stands "Voltaire's immortal comment," on its head. For if the guarantees of the First Amendment were reserved for expression that more than a "few of us" would take up arms to defend, then the right of free expression would be defined and circumscribed by current popular opinion. The guarantees of the Bill of Rights were designed to protect against precisely such majoritarian limitations on individual liberty.

The fact that the "offensive" speech here may not address "important" topics—"ideas of social and political significance," in the Court's terminology—does not mean that it is less worthy of constitutional protection. "Wholly neutral futilities [come] under the protection of free speech as fully as do Keats' poems or Donne's sermons." *Winters* (Frankfurter, J., dissenting), accord, *Cohen v. California.* Moreover, in the absence of a judicial determination of obscenity, it is by no means clear that the speech is not "important" even on the Court's terms [*Roth; Kingsley Pictures*].

I can only interpret today's decision as an aberration. The Court is undoubtedly sympathetic, as am I, to the well-intentioned efforts of Detroit to "clean up" its streets and prevent the proliferation of "skid rows." But it is in those instances where protected speech grates most unpleasantly against the sensibilities that judicial vigilance must be at its [height].

The factual parallels between [*Erznoznik* and this case] are striking. There, as here, the ordinance did not forbid altogether the "distasteful" expression but merely required an alteration in the physical setting of the forum. There, as here, the city's principal asserted interest was in minimizing the "undesirable" effects of speech having a particular content. [And] the particular content of the restricted speech at issue in *Erznoznik* precisely parallels the content restricted in [Detroit's] definition of "Specified Anatomical Areas." * * *

The Court must never forget that the consequences of rigorously enforcing the guarantees of the First Amendment are frequently unpleasant. Much speech that seems to be of little or no value will enter the marketplace of ideas, threatening the quality of our social discourse and, more generally, the serenity of our lives. But that is the price to be paid for constitutional freedom. * * *e

Notes and Questions

1. *A hierarchy of protected speech.* Stevens, J., contends that as a matter of law some "protected" speech is less worthy than other protected speech. The dissenters and Powell, J., reject that view. Which approach is more likely to preserve First Amendment values? Would treating all protected speech equally invite a dilution of the force of the First Amendment with respect to the speech that "really" matters? Is the process of allowing judges to pick and choose

e. Blackmun, J., joined by the other three dissenters, also filed a dissent that protested the rejection of the vagueness argument, concluding on this issue: "As to the third reason, that 'adult' material is simply entitled to less protection, it certainly explains the lapse in applying settled vagueness principles, as indeed it explains this whole case. In joining Mr. Justice Stewart I have joined his forthright rejection of the notion that First Amendment protection is diminished for 'erotic materials' that only a 'few of us' see the need to protect."

between types of protected speech too dangerous? Would it be dangerous to protect political speech more than sexually explicit speech? Is sexually explicit speech non-political? If the plaintiff's approach were accepted, would the Court ultimately "rank speech in all its myriad forms, in order of its perceived importance," with new rankings being "created and old ones rejected depending on the Court's view of the worthiness of the speech at issue"? Roger Goldman, *A Doctrine of Worthier Speech,* 21 St. L.U.L.J. 281, 300–01 (1977).

2. *The exhibitor's free expression.* Did Powell, J., assume that the "first amendment rights [involved] in *Young* were primarily vested in creator and audience"? Note, 42 Mo.L.Rev. 461, 468 (1977); Note, 28 Case W.Res.L.Rev. 456, 482 (1978). Does the plurality opinion and its fn. 35 reflect similar lack of concern for exhibitor's interests? How would a record be built to distinguish *Young* from a similar ordinance in another city?

3. *Exclusionary zoning. Schad v. Mt. Ephraim,* 452 U.S. 61, 101 S.Ct. 2176, 68 L.Ed.2d 671 (1981) invalidated a Borough ordinance that permitted adult theaters and bookstores, but excluded live entertainment from its commercial zone. Even as applied to nude dancing, the Court found that the ordinance was not narrowly drawn to serve a sufficiently substantial state interest.[f] The Court observed that there was no evidence to show that the entertainment at issue was available in reasonably nearby areas. What if it were? Suppose the Borough banned adult theaters and bookstores, but could show they were available nearby?

RENTON v. PLAYTIME THEATRES, INC., 475 U.S. 41, 106 S.Ct. 925, 89 L.Ed.2d 29 (1986), per REHNQUIST, J., upheld a zoning ordinance that prohibited adult motion picture theaters from locating within 1,000 feet of any residential zone, church, park, or school. The effect was to exclude such theaters from approximately 94% of the land in the city. Of the remaining 520 acres, a substantial part was occupied by a sewage disposal and treatment plant, a horse racing track and environs, a warehouse and manufacturing facilities, a Mobil Oil tank farm, and a fully-developed shopping center: "[T]he resolution of this case is largely dictated by our decision in *Young.* There, although five Members of the Court did not agree on a single rationale for the decision, we held that the city of Detroit's zoning ordinance, which prohibited locating an adult theater within 1,000 feet of any two other 'regulated uses' or within 500 feet of any residential zone, did not violate the First and Fourteenth amendments. The Renton ordinance, like the one in *Young,* does not ban adult theaters altogether, but merely provides that such theaters may not be located within 1,000 feet of any residential zone, single- or multiple-family dwelling, church, park, or school. The ordinance is therefore properly analyzed as a form of time, place, and manner regulation.

This Court has long held that regulations enacted for the purpose of restraining speech on the basis of its content presumptively violate the First Amendment. See *Chicago Police Dept. v. Mosley,* [Sec. 6, I, B].[a] On the other hand, so-called 'content-neutral' time, place, and manner regulations are acceptable so long as

---

f. But cf. *Newport v. Iacobucci,* 479 U.S. 92, 107 S.Ct. 383, 93 L.Ed.2d 334 (1986) (upholding ordinance prohibiting nude or nearly nude dancing in establishments serving liquor).

a. *Mosley* involved an ordinance that banned picketing near a school building except the "peaceful picketing of any school involved in a labor dispute." The Court stated: "The regulation '[slips] from the neutrality of time, place, and circumstance into a concern about content.' This is never permitted."

they are designed to serve a substantial governmental interest and do not unreasonably limit alternative avenues of communication.[b]

"At first glance, the Renton ordinance, like the ordinance in *Young,* does not appear to fit neatly into either the 'content-based' or the 'content-neutral' category. To be sure, the ordinance treats theaters that specialize in adult films differently from other kinds of theaters. Nevertheless, [the] City Council's *'predominate* concerns' were with the secondary effects of adult theaters, and not with the content of adult films themselves. * * *

"[This] finding as to 'predominate' intent is more than adequate to establish that the city's pursuit of its zoning interests here was unrelated to the suppression of free expression.[c] The ordinance by its terms is designed to prevent crime, protect the city's retail trade, maintain property values,[d] and generally 'protec[t] and preserv[e] the quality of [the city's] neighborhoods, commercial districts, and the quality of urban life,' not to suppress the expression of unpopular views. As Justice Powell observed in *Young,* '[i]f [the city] had been concerned with restricting the message purveyed by adult theaters, it would have tried to close them or restrict their number rather than circumscribe their choice as to location.'

"In short, the [ordinance] does not contravene the fundamental principle that underlies our concern about 'content-based' speech regulations: that 'government may not grant the use of a forum to people whose views it finds acceptable, but deny use to those wishing to express less favored or more controversial views.' *Mosley.*

"It was with this understanding in mind that, in *Young,* a majority of this Court decided that at least with respect to businesses that purvey sexually explicit materials,[e] zoning ordinances designed to combat the undesirable secondary effects of such businesses are to be reviewed under the standards applicable to 'content-neutral' time, place, and manner regulations.[2]

"The appropriate inquiry in this case, then, is whether the Renton ordinance is designed to serve a substantial governmental interest and allows for reasonable alternative avenues of communication."

After concluding that the ordinance was designed to serve substantial government interests, the Court ruled that the Renton ordinance allowed "for reasonable

b. Compare the statement of the time, place, and manner test in *Clark,* Sec. 2 supra. For commentary, see David Day, *The Hybridization of the Content–Neutral Standards for the Free Speech Clause,* 19 Ariz.St.L.J. 195 (1987).

c. The Court interpreted the court of appeals opinion to require the invalidation of the ordinance if a "motivating factor" to restrict the exercise of first amendment rights was present "apparently no matter how small a part this motivating factor may have played in the City Council's decision." This view of the law, the Court continued, "was rejected in *O'Brien:* 'It is a familiar principle of constitutional law that this Court will not strike down an otherwise constitutional statute on the basis of an alleged illicit legislative motive. [What] motivates one legislator to make a speech about a statute is not necessarily what motivates scores of others to enact it, and the

stakes are sufficiently high for us to eschew guesswork.' "

d. For support, see Charles Clarke, *Freedom of Speech and the Problem of the Lawful Harmful Public Reaction,* 20 Akron L.Rev. 187 (1986).

e. The secondary effects justification was deemed to distinguish *Erznoznik v. City of Jacksonville,* 422 U.S. 205, 95 S.Ct. 2268, 45 L.Ed.2d 125 (1975) (invalidating ordinance prohibiting drive-in theaters from showing films containing nudity) and *Schad v. Mount Ephraim,* (invalidating ordinance prohibiting live entertainment, as applied to nude dancing, in commercial zone).

2. See *Young* (plurality opinion) ("[I]t is manifest that society's interest in protecting this type of expression is of a wholly different, and lesser, magnitude than the interest in untrammeled political debate * * *.").

alternative avenues of communication": "[W]e note that the ordinance leaves some 520 acres, or more than five percent of the entire land area of Renton, open to use as adult theater sites. [Respondents] argue, however, that some of the land in question is already occupied by existing businesses, that 'practically none' of the undeveloped land is currently for sale or lease, and that in general there are no 'commercially viable' adult theater sites within the 520 acres left open by the Renton ordinance. The Court of Appeals accepted these arguments. * * *

"We disagree. [That] respondents must fend for themselves in the real estate market, on an equal footing with other prospective purchasers and lessees, does not give rise to a First Amendment violation. And although we have cautioned against the enactment of zoning regulations that have 'the effect of suppressing, or greatly restricting access to, lawful speech,' *Young* (plurality opinion), we have never suggested that the First Amendment compels the Government to ensure that adult theaters, or any other kinds of speech-related businesses for that matter, will be able to obtain sites at bargain prices. [T]he First Amendment requires only that Renton refrain from effectively denying respondents a reasonable opportunity to open and operate an adult theater within the city, and the ordinance before us easily meets this requirement. * * *[4]"f

BRENNAN, J., joined by Marshall, J., dissented: "The fact that adult movie theaters may cause harmful 'secondary' land use effects may arguably give Renton a compelling reason to regulate such establishments; it does not mean, however, that such regulations are content neutral. * * *

"The ordinance discriminates on its face against certain forms of speech based on content. Movie theaters specializing in 'adult motion pictures' may not be located within 1,000 feet of any residential zone, single-or multiple-family dwelling, church, park, or school. Other motion picture theaters, and other forms of 'adult entertainment,' such as bars, massage parlors, and adult bookstores, are not subject to the same restrictions. This selective treatment strongly suggests that Renton was interested not in controlling the 'secondary effects' associated with adult businesses, but in discriminating against adult theaters based on the content of the films they exhibit. [Moreover,] [a]s the Court of Appeals observed, '[b]oth the magistrate and the district court recognized that many of the stated reasons for the ordinance were no more than expressions of dislike for the subject matter.'[3] That some residents may be offended by the *content* of the films shown at adult movie theaters cannot form the basis for state regulation of speech. See *Terminiello.*

4. [We] reject respondents' "vagueness" argument for the same reasons that led us to reject a similar challenge in *Young.* There, the Detroit ordinance applied to theaters "used to present material distinguished or characterized by an emphasis on [sexually explicit matter]." We held that "even if there may be some uncertainty about the effect of the ordinances on other litigants, they are unquestionably applicable to these respondents." We also held that the Detroit ordinance created no "significant deterrent effect" that might justify invocation of the First Amendment "overbreadth" doctrine.

f. Blackmun, J., concurred in the result without opinion.

3. For example, "finding" number 2 states that "[l]ocation of adult entertainment land uses on the main commercial thoroughfares of the City gives an impression of legitimacy to, and causes a loss of sensitivity to the adverse effect of pornography upon children, established family relations, respect for marital relationship and for the sanctity of marriage relations of others, and the concept of nonaggressive, consensual sexual relations."

"Finding" number 6 states that "[l]ocation of adult land uses in close proximity to residential uses, churches, parks, and other public facilities, and schools, will cause a degradation of the community standard of morality. Pornographic material has a degrading effect upon the relationship between spouses."

"Some of the 'findings' [do] relate to supposed 'secondary effects' associated with adult movie theaters[4] [but they were added by the City Council only after this law suit was filed and the Court should not] accept these post-hoc statements at face value. [As] the Court of Appeals concluded, '[t]he record presented by Renton to support its asserted interest in enacting the zoning ordinance is very thin.' [5] * * *[7]

"Even assuming that the ordinance should be treated like a content-neutral time, place, and manner restriction, I would still find it unconstitutional. [T]he ordinance is invalid because it does not provide for reasonable alternative avenues of communication.[g] [R]espondents do not ask Renton to guarantee low-price sites for their businesses, but seek, only a reasonable opportunity to operate adult theaters in the city. By denying them this opportunity, Renton can effectively ban a form of protected speech from its borders. The ordinance 'greatly restrict[s] access to, lawful speech,' *Young*, and is plainly unconstitutional."

Notes and Questions

1. Does *Renton*—see fn. 2—endorse a hierarchy of categories among types of protected speech? Consider Tribe 2d ed., at 939 n. 66: "[I]t is doubtful that *Renton* can fairly be read as endorsing the concept of a hierarchy of intermediate categories, because the case turned on the majority's characterization of the restriction as content-neutral, and the issue of the relative importance of the speech involved, was, strictly speaking, irrelevant." But cf. Philip Prygoski, *Low Value Speech: From Young to Fraser*, 32 St. L.U.L.J. 317, 345 (1987) (despite the content-neutral language, "antipathy toward the kind of expression involved" swayed the case).

2. Was the ordinance fairly characterized as content-neutral? Is the focus on "secondary effects" convincing? Consider Geoffrey Stone, *Content–Neutral Restrictions,* 54 U.Chi.L.Rev. 46, 115–117 (1987): "[T]he Court had never before *Renton* suggested that the absence of a constitutionally disfavored justification is in itself a justification for treating an expressly content-based restriction as if it

4. For example, "finding" number 12 states that "[l]ocation of adult entertainment land uses in proximity to residential uses, churches, parks and other public facilities, and schools, may lead to increased levels of criminal activities, including prostitution, rape, incest and assaults in the vicinity of such adult entertainment land uses."

5. As part of the amendment passed after this lawsuit commenced, the City Council added a statement that it had intended to rely on the Washington Supreme Court's opinion in *Northend Cinema, Inc. v. Seattle,* 90 Wash.2d 709, 585 P.2d 1153 (1978), cert. denied, 441 U.S. 946 (1979), which upheld Seattle's zoning regulations against constitutional attack. Again, despite the suspicious coincidental timing of the amendment, the Court holds that "Renton was entitled to rely [on] the 'detailed findings' summarized in [the] *Northend Cinema* opinion." In *Northend Cinema,* the court noted that "[t]he record is replete with testimony regarding the effects of adult movie theater locations on residential neighborhoods." The opinion however, does not explain the evidence it purports to summarize, and provid-

ed no basis for determining whether Seattle's experience is relevant to Renton's.

7. As one commentator has noted: "[A]nyone with any knowledge of human nature should naturally assume that the decision to adopt almost any content-based restriction might have been affected by an antipathy on the part of at least some legislators to the ideas or information being suppressed. The logical assumption, in other words, is not that there is not improper motivation but, rather, because legislators are only human, that there is a substantial risk that an impermissible consideration has in fact colored the deliberative process." Geoffrey Stone, *Restrictions on Speech Because of its Content: The Peculiar Case of Subject–Matter Restrictions,* 46 U.Chi. L.Rev. 81, 106 (1978).

g. Brennan, J., argued that the ordinance also failed as an acceptable time, place, and manner restriction because it was not narrowly tailored to serve a significant governmental interest.

were content-neutral. To the contrary, with the single exception of *Renton,* the Court in such circumstances has always invoked the stringent standards of content-based review. [For example, *Ferber*] treated as content-based a law prohibiting 'child pornography,' even though the government defended the law not in terms of communicative impact, but on the ground that the law was necessary to protect children who participate in 'sexual performances.' [I]f taken seriously, and extended to other contexts, the Court's transmogrification in *Renton* of an expressly content-based restriction into one that is content-neutral threatens to undermine the very foundation of the content-based/content-neutral distinction. This would in turn erode the coherence and predictability of first amendment doctrine. One can only hope that this aspect of *Renton* is soon forgotten."

But cf. Daniel Farber & Philip Frickey, *The Jurisprudence of Public Choice,* 65 Tex.L.Rev. 873 (1987): "[*Renton*] appears to adopt the view that the government generally may take into account the content of speech when channeling speech, but may only rarely consider content when the purpose is censorship. We believe that in doing so *Renton* merely states explicitly what was implicit in a long line of prior cases."

Are subject matter restrictions as a class less problematic than other forms of content discrimination in that they often do not discriminate on the basis of point of view? Should *Renton's* secondary effects emphasis be limited to subject-matter-based restrictions? See Note, *The Content Distinction in Free Speech Analysis After Renton,* 102 Harv.L.Rev. 1904 (1989). Even if some subject matter restrictions are less problematic, is the Renton ordinance neutral as to point of view? Consider Geoffrey Stone, *Restrictions of Speech Because of its Content: The Peculiar Case of Subject–Matter Restrictions,* 46 U.Chi.L.Rev. 81, 111–12 (1978): "[T]he speech suppressed by restrictions such as those involved in [cases like *Erznoznik* and *Young*] will almost invariably carry an implicit, if not explicit, message in favor of more relaxed sexual mores. Such restrictions, in other words, have a potent viewpoint-differential impact. [I]n our society, the very presence of sexual explicitness in speech seems ideologically significant, without regard to whatever other messages might be intended. To treat such restrictions as viewpoint-neutral seems simply to ignore reality. Finally, [a] large percentage of citizens apparently feel threatened by nonobscene, sexually-explicit speech and believe it to be morally reprehensible. If it were not for the Court's relatively narrow construction of the obscenity concept, much of this speech would undoubtedly be banned outright. Thus, any restriction along these lines will carry an extraordinarily high risk that its enactment was tainted by this fundamentally illegitimate consideration. Such restrictions, although superficially viewpoint-neutral, pose a uniquely compelling case for content-based scrutiny." Are feminist or neo-conservative objections to near obscene speech both "fundamentally illegitimate." Should all content-based scrutiny be the same? Does *Renton* reconstruct the Court's "narrow construction of the obscenity concept"?

Is the concept of viewpoint neutrality itself problematic? Consider Cass Sunstein, *Pornography and the First Amendment,* 1986 Duke L.J. 589, 615: "One does not 'see' a viewpoint-based restriction when the harms invoked in defense of a regulation are obvious and so widely supported by social consensus that they allay any concern about impermissible government motivation. Whether a classification is viewpoint-based thus ultimately turns on the viewpoint of the decisionmaker." See generally Catharine MacKinnon, *Feminism, Marxism, Method, and the State,* 7 Signs 515, 535–36 (1981).

3. *Renton's* "secondary effects" notion was revisited by several justices in BOOS v. BARRY, Sec. 2: A District of Columbia ordinance banned the display of any sign within 500 feet of a foreign embassy that would tend to bring the embassy into "public odium" or "public disrepute." O'CONNOR, J., joined by Stevens and Scalia, JJ., distinguished *Renton:* "Respondents and the United States do not point to the 'secondary effects' of picket signs in front of embassies. They do not point to congestion, to interference with ingress or egress, to visual clutter, or to the need to protect the security of embassies. Rather, they rely on the need to protect the dignity of foreign diplomatic personnel by shielding them from speech that is critical of their governments. This justification focuses *only* on the content of the speech and the direct impact that speech has on its listeners. The emotive impact of speech on its audience is not a 'secondary effect.'[h] Because the display clause regulates speech due to its potential primary impact, we conclude it must be considered content-based."[i]

BRENNAN, J., joined by Marshall, J., agreed with the conclusion that the ordinance was content-based, but objected to O'Connor, J.'s "assumption that the *Renton* analysis applies not only outside the context of businesses purveying sexually explicit materials but even to political speech."[j]

———

Five years after *Renton*, the Court held that an Indiana statute prohibiting the knowing or intentional appearing in a public place in a state of nudity could constitutionally be applied to require that any female dancer at a minimum wear "pasties" and a "G-string" when she dances. *Barnes v. Glen Theatre, Inc.*, 501 U.S. 560, 111 S.Ct. 2456, 115 L.Ed.2d 504 (1991). The Justices upholding the ordinance were divided upon the rationale for doing so. Rehnquist, C.J., joined by O'Connor and Kennedy, JJ., applied the *O'Brien* test, characterized the statute as a "public indecency" statute, and concluded that the interests in order and morality justified the statute. Souter, J., concurring, also applied the *O'Brien* test, but concluded that the statute was justified by the "secondary effects" of prostitution, sexual assaults, and other criminal activity even though this justification had not been articulated by the Indiana legislature or its courts. Scalia, J., argued against the plurality that the interest in morality was not substantial enough to

h. See *Forsyth County v. The Nationalist Movement*, 505 U.S. 123, 112 S.Ct. 2395, 120 L.Ed.2d 101 (1992)("Listener's reaction to speech is not a content-neutral basis for regulation,"—not secondary effects).

i. In an earlier passage O'Connor, J., responded to the argument that the ordinance was not content-based on the theory that the government was not selecting between viewpoints. The argument was instead that "the permissible message on a picket sign is determined solely by the policies of a foreign government. We reject this contention, although we agree the provision is not viewpoint-based. The display clause determines which viewpoint is acceptable in a neutral fashion by looking to the policies of foreign governments. While this prevents the display clause from being directly viewpoint-based, a label with potential First Amendment ramifications of its own, it does not render the statute content-neutral. Rather, we have held that a regulation that 'does not

favor either side of a political controversy' is nonetheless impermissible because the 'First Amendment's hostility to content-based regulation extends [to] prohibition of public discussion of an entire topic.' Here the government has determined that an entire category of speech—signs or displays critical of foreign governments—is not to be permitted."

j. Rehnquist, J., joined by White and Blackmun, JJ., voted to uphold the ordinance on the basis of Bork, J's opinion below in *Finzer v. Barry*, 798 F.2d 1450 (D.C.Cir.1986). Bork, J., stated that the need to adhere to principles of international law might constitute a secondary effect under *Renton* but was not "entirely sure" whether *Renton* alone could dictate that result and did not resolve the issue. Id. at 1469–70 n. 15. For a review of secondary effects doctrine see Philip Prygoski, *The Supreme Court's "Secondary Effects" Analysis in Free Speech Cases*, 6 Cooley L.Rev. 1 (1989).

pass muster under *O'Brien*; nonetheless, he voted to uphold the statute by repudiating the *O'Brien* test. He argued that when a general law is directed at conduct, not specifically against expression, it is subject to no first amendment test even if it is applied against expression. White, joined by Marshall, Blackmun, and Stevens, J., dissenting, argued that the Indiana statute was directed at expression and did not survive close scrutiny.

The fragmented character of the *Barnes* majority created interpretive difficulties for the Pennsylvania Supreme Court in considering an ordinance of Erie, Pennsylvania. Like Indiana, Erie enacted an ordinance making it a offense to knowingly or intentionally appear in public in a "state of nudity." Unlike Indiana, however, the Erie city council made it clear that nude dancing was a special concern. The preamble to the ordinance stated that "Council specifically wishes to adopt the concept of Public Indecency prohibited by the laws of the State of Indiana, which was approved by the U.S. Supreme Court in *Barnes* (for) the purpose of limiting a recent increase in nude live entertainment within the City" which led to prostitution and other crime.

Pap's A.M., operated "Kandyland," featuring nude erotic dancing by women. To comply with the ordinance, as written, these dancers had to wear, at a minimum, "pasties" and a "G-string." Pap's sought declaratory relief and a permanent injunction against the ordinance's enforcement. The Pennsylvania Supreme Court was unable to find a lowest common denominator uniting the *Barnes* majority; so it felt free to reach an independent judgment, and found that the Erie ordinance, although also directed at secondary effects, was primarily directed at expression and did not survive close scrutiny.

ERIE v. PAP'S A.M., 529 U.S. 277, 120 S.Ct. 1382, 146 L.Ed.2d 265 (2000), per O'CONNOR, J., joined by Rehnquist, C.J., Kennedy, and Breyer, JJ., upheld application of the ordinance to prevent nude dancing:[a] "Being 'in a state of nudity' is not an inherently expressive condition. As we explained in *Barnes*, however, nude dancing of the type at issue here is expressive conduct, although we think that it falls only within the outer ambit of the First Amendment's protection. [G]overnment restrictions on public nudity such as the ordinance at issue here should be evaluated under the framework set forth in *O'Brien* for content-neutral restrictions on symbolic speech. * * *

"The ordinance [does] not target nudity that contains an erotic message; rather, it bans all public nudity, regardless of whether that nudity is accompanied by expressive activity. And like the statute in *Barnes*, the Erie ordinance replaces and updates provisions of an 'Indecency and Immorality' ordinance that has been on the books since 1866, predating the prevalence of nude dancing establishments such as Kandyland. * * *

"Although the Pennsylvania Supreme Court acknowledged that one goal of the ordinance was to combat the negative secondary effects associated with nude dancing establishments, the court concluded that the ordinance was nevertheless content based, relying on Justice White's position in dissent in *Barnes* for the proposition that a ban of this type *necessarily* has the purpose of suppressing the erotic message of the dance. [T]he Pennsylvania court adopted the dissent's view in *Barnes* that '[s]ince the State permits the dancers to perform if they wear pasties and G-strings but forbids nude dancing, it is precisely because of the distinctive, expressive content of the nude dancing performances at issue in this

---

a. O'Connor, J., rebuffed a contention that the case was moot. Scalia, J., joined by Thomas, J., would have sustained the mootness claim. Stevens, J., joined by Ginsburg, J., did not address the issue.

case that the State seeks to apply the statutory prohibition.' A majority of the Court rejected that view in *Barnes*, and we do so again here.

"Respondent's argument that the ordinance is 'aimed' at suppressing expression through a ban on nude dancing—an argument that respondent supports by pointing to statements by the city attorney that the public nudity ban was not intended to apply to 'legitimate' theater productions—is really an argument that the city council also had an illicit motive in enacting the ordinance. As we have said before, however, this Court will not strike down an otherwise constitutional statute on the basis of an alleged illicit motive. In light of the Pennsylvania court's determination that one purpose of the ordinance is to combat harmful secondary effects, the ban on public nudity here is no different from the ban on burning draft registration cards in *O'Brien*, where the Government sought to prevent the means of the expression and not the expression of antiwar sentiment itself.

"Justice Stevens argues that the ordinance enacts a complete ban on expression. [But] simply to define what is being banned as the 'message' is to assume the conclusion. We did not analyze the regulation in *O'Brien* as having enacted a total ban on expression. Instead, the Court recognized that the regulation against destroying one's draft card was justified by the Government's interest in preventing the harmful 'secondary effects' of that conduct (disruption to the Selective Service System), even though that regulation may have some incidental effect on the expressive element of the conduct. Because this justification was unrelated to the suppression of O'Brien's antiwar message, the regulation was content neutral. Although there may be cases in which banning the means of expression so interferes with the message that it essentially bans the message, that is not the case here. * * *

"Similarly, even if Erie's public nudity ban has some minimal effect on the erotic message by muting that portion of the expression that occurs when the last stitch is dropped, [a]ny effect on the overall expression is de minimis. And as Justice Stevens eloquently stated for the plurality in *Young*, 'even though we recognize that the First Amendment will not tolerate the total suppression of erotic materials that have some arguably artistic value, it is manifest that society's interest in protecting this type of expression is of a wholly different, and lesser, magnitude than the interest in untrammeled political debate.' [If] States are to be able to regulate secondary effects, then de minimis intrusions on expression such as those at issue here cannot be sufficient to render the ordinance content based.

"This case is, in fact, similar to *O'Brien*, *Community for Creative Non-Violence*, and *Ward*. The justification for the government regulation in each case prevents harmful 'secondary' effects that are unrelated to the suppression of expression. See, e.g., *Ward* v. *Rock Against Racism* (noting that '[t]he principal justification for the sound-amplification guideline is the city's desire to control noise levels at bandshell events, in order to retain the character of [the adjacent] Sheep Meadow and its more sedate activities,' and citing *Renton* for the proposition that '[a] regulation that serves purposes unrelated to the content of expression is deemed neutral, even if it has an incidental effect on some speakers or messages but not others'). While the doctrinal theories behind 'incidental burdens' and 'secondary effects' are, of course, not identical, there is nothing objectionable about a city passing a general ordinance to ban public nudity (even though such a ban may place incidental burdens on some protected speech) and at the same time recognizing that one specific occurrence of public nudity—nude erotic dancing—is particularly problematic because it produces harmful secondary effects.

"[E]rie's efforts to protect public health and safety are clearly within the city's police powers [and] are undeniably important. And in terms of demonstrating that such secondary effects pose a threat, the city need not 'conduct new studies or produce evidence independent of that already generated by other cities' to demonstrate the problem of secondary effects, 'so long as whatever evidence the city relies upon is reasonably believed to be relevant to the problem that the city addresses.' *Renton.* * * * In fact, Erie expressly relied on *Barnes* and its discussion of secondary effects, including its reference to *Renton* and *American Mini Theatres.* * * *

"In any event, Erie also relied on its own findings. The preamble to the ordinance states that 'the Council of the City of Erie *has, at various times over more than a century, expressed its findings* that certain lewd, immoral activities carried on in public places for profit are highly detrimental to the public health, safety and welfare, and lead to the debasement of both women and men, promote violence, public intoxication, prostitution and other serious criminal activity.' The city council members, familiar with commercial downtown Erie, are the individuals who would likely have had first-hand knowledge of what took place at and around nude dancing establishments in Erie, and can make particularized, expert judgments about the resulting harmful secondary effects. * * *

"Justice Souter, however, would require Erie to develop a specific evidentiary record supporting its ordinance * * *. *O'Brien*, of course, required no evidentiary showing at all that the threatened harm was real. But that case is different, Justice Souter contends, because in *O'Brien* 'there could be no doubt' that a regulation prohibiting the destruction of draft cards would alleviate the harmful secondary effects flowing from the destruction of those cards.

"But whether the harm is evident to our 'intuition,' is not the proper inquiry. If it were, we would simply say there is no doubt that a regulation prohibiting public nudity would alleviate the harmful secondary effects associated with nude dancing. * * * Justice Souter attempts to denigrate the city council's conclusion that the threatened harm was real, arguing that we cannot accept Erie's findings because the subject of nude dancing is 'fraught with some emotionalism,' Yet surely the subject of drafting our citizens into the military is 'fraught' with more emotionalism than the subject of regulating nude dancing.

"As to [whether] the regulation furthers the government interest—it is evident that, since crime and other public health and safety problems are caused by the presence of nude dancing establishments like Kandyland, a ban on such nude dancing would further Erie's interest in preventing such secondary effects. To be sure, requiring dancers to wear pasties and G-strings may not greatly reduce these secondary effects, but *O'Brien* requires only that the regulation further the interest in combating such effects. [It may] be true that a pasties and G-string requirement would not be as effective as, for example, a requirement that the dancers be fully clothed, but the city must balance its efforts to address the problem with the requirement that the restriction be no greater than necessary to further the city's interest.

"[The requirement that the restriction be] no greater than is essential to the furtherance of the government interest—is satisfied as well. * * * The requirement that dancers wear pasties and G-strings is a minimal restriction in furtherance of the asserted government interests, and the restriction leaves ample capacity to convey the dancer's erotic message. Justice Souter points out that zoning is an alternative means of addressing this problem. It is far from clear, however, that zoning imposes less of a burden on expression than the minimal requirement implemented here. In any event, since this is a content-neutral restriction, least restrictive means analysis is not required."

SCALIA, J., joined by Thomas., J., concurred: In *Barnes*, I voted to uphold the challenged Indiana statute 'not because it survives some lower level of First Amendment scrutiny, but because, as a general law regulating conduct and not specifically directed at expression, it is not subject to First Amendment scrutiny at all.' Erie's ordinance, too, by its terms prohibits not merely nude dancing, but the act—irrespective of whether it is engaged in for expressive purposes—of going nude in public. The facts that a preamble to the ordinance explains that its purpose, in part, is to 'limi[t] a recent increase in nude live entertainment,' that city councilmembers in supporting the ordinance commented to that effect, and that the ordinance includes in the definition of nudity the exposure of devices simulating that condition, neither make the law any less general in its reach nor demonstrate that what the municipal authorities *really* find objectionable is expression rather than public nakedness. As far as appears (and as seems overwhelmingly likely), the preamble, the councilmembers' comments, and the chosen definition of the prohibited conduct simply reflect the fact that Erie had recently been having a public nudity problem not with streakers, sunbathers or hot-dog vendors, but with lap dancers.

"There is no basis for the contention that the ordinance does not apply to nudity in theatrical productions such as Equus or Hair. Its text contains no such limitation. It was stipulated in the trial court that no effort was made to enforce the ordinance against a production of Equus involving nudity that was being staged in Erie at the time the ordinance became effective. [But], neither in the stipulation, nor elsewhere in the record, does it appear that the city was aware of the nudity—and before this Court counsel for the city attributed nonenforcement not to a general exception for theatrical productions, but to the fact that no one had complained. One instance of nonenforcement—against a play already in production that prosecutorial discretion might reasonably have 'grandfathered'— does not render this ordinance discriminatory on its face. To be sure, in the trial court counsel for the city said that '[t]o the extent that the expressive activity that is contained in [such] productions rises to a higher level of protected expression, they would not be [covered],'—but he rested this assertion upon the provision in the preamble that expressed respect for 'fundamental Constitutional guarantees of free speech and free expression.' [What] he was saying there [was] essentially what he said at oral argument before this Court: that the ordinance would not be enforceable against theatrical productions if the Constitution forbade it. Surely that limitation does not cause the ordinance to be not generally applicable, in the relevant sense of being *targeted* against expressive conduct.

"Moreover, even were I to conclude that the city of Erie had specifically singled out the activity of nude dancing, I still would not find that this regulation violated the First Amendment unless I could be persuaded (as on this record I cannot) that it was the communicative character of nude dancing that prompted the ban. When conduct other than speech itself is regulated, it is my view that the First Amendment is violated only '[w]here the government prohibits conduct precisely because of its communicative attributes.' I do not feel the need, as the Court does, to identify some 'secondary effects' associated with nude dancing that the city could properly seek to eliminate. (I am highly skeptical, to tell the truth, that the addition of pasties and g-strings will at all reduce the tendency of establishments such as Kandyland to attract crime and prostitution, and hence to foster sexually transmitted disease.) The traditional power of government to foster good morals (bonos mores), and the acceptability of the traditional judgment (if

Erie wishes to endorse it) that nude public dancing *itself* is immoral, have not been repealed by the First Amendment.''

SOUTER, J., concurred in part and dissented in part: "I [agree] with the analytical approach that the plurality employs in deciding this case. * * * I do not believe, however, that the current record allows us to say that the city has made a sufficient evidentiary showing to sustain its [regulation].

"[I]ntermediate scrutiny requires a regulating government to make some demonstration of an evidentiary basis for the harm it claims to flow from the expressive activity, and for the alleviation expected from the restriction imposed. That evidentiary basis may be borrowed from the records made by other governments if the experience elsewhere is germane to the measure under consideration and actually relied upon. I will assume, further, that the reliance may be shown by legislative invocation of a judicial opinion that accepted an evidentiary foundation as sufficient for a similar regulation. What is clear is that the evidence of reliance must be a matter of demonstrated fact, not speculative supposition.

"By these standards, the record before us today is deficient in its failure to reveal any evidence on which Erie may have relied, either for the seriousness of the threatened harm or for the efficacy of its chosen remedy. The plurality does the best it can with the materials to hand, but the pickings are slim. [T]he ordinance's preamble assert[s] that over the course of more than a century the city council had expressed 'findings' of detrimental secondary effects flowing from lewd and immoral profitmaking activity in public places. But however accurate the recital may be and however honestly the councilors may have held those conclusions to be true over the years, the recitation does not get beyond conclusions on a subject usually fraught with some emotionalism. [T]he invocation of *Barnes* in one paragraph of the preamble to Erie's ordinance [does not] suffice. The plurality opinion in *Barnes* made no mention of evidentiary showings at all, and though my separate opinion did make a pass at the issue, I did not demand reliance on germane evidentiary demonstrations, whether specific to the statute in question or developed elsewhere. To invoke *Barnes*, therefore, does not indicate that the issue of evidence has been addressed.

"There is one point, however, on which an evidentiary record is not quite so hard to find, but it hurts, not helps, the city. The final *O'Brien* requirement is that the incidental speech restriction be shown to be no greater than essential to achieve the government's legitimate purpose. To deal with this issue, we have to ask what basis there is to think that the city would be unsuccessful in countering any secondary effects by the significantly lesser restriction of zoning to control the location of nude dancing, thus allowing for efficient law enforcement, restricting effects on property values, and limiting exposure of the public. The record shows that for 23 years there has been a zoning ordinance on the books to regulate the location of establishments like Kandyland, but the city has not enforced it. [Even] on the plurality's view of the evidentiary burden, this hurdle to the application of *O'Brien* requires an evidentiary response. * * *

"Careful readers, and not just those on the Erie City Council, will of course realize that my partial dissent rests on a demand for an evidentiary basis that I failed to make when I concurred in *Barnes*. I should have demanded the evidence then, too, and my mistake calls to mind Justice Jackson's foolproof explanation of a lapse of his own, when he quoted Samuel Johnson, 'Ignorance, sir, ignorance.' *McGrath* v. *Kristensen*, 340 U.S. 162, 178, 71 S.Ct. 224, 95 L.Ed. 173 (1950) (concurring opinion). I may not be less ignorant of nude dancing than I was nine years ago, but after many subsequent occasions to think further about the needs of the First Amendment, I have come to believe that a government must toe the mark more carefully than I first insisted."

Stevens, J., joined by Ginsburg, J., dissented: "Far more important than the question whether nude dancing is entitled to the protection of the First Amendment are the dramatic changes in legal doctrine that the Court endorses today. Until now, the 'secondary effects' of commercial enterprises featuring indecent entertainment have justified only the regulation of their location. For the first time, the Court has now held that such effects may justify the total suppression of protected speech. * * *

"As the preamble to Ordinance No. 75–1994 candidly acknowledges, the council of the city of Erie enacted the restriction at issue 'for the purpose of limiting a recent increase in nude live entertainment within the City.' Prior to the enactment of the ordinance, the dancers at Kandyland performed in the nude. As the Court recognizes, after its enactment they can perform precisely the same dances if they wear 'pasties and G-strings.' In both instances, the erotic messages conveyed by the dancers to a willing audience are a form of expression protected by the First Amendment. Despite the similarity between the messages conveyed by the two forms of dance, they are not identical.

"If we accept Chief Judge Posner's evaluation of this art form, see *Miller* v. *South Bend*, 904 F.2d 1081, 1089–1104 (7th Cir. 1990) (en banc), the difference between the two messages is significant. The plurality assumes, however, that the difference in the content of the message resulting from the mandated costume change is '*de minimis.*' Although I suspect that the patrons of Kandyland are more likely to share Chief Judge Posner's view than the plurality's, for present purposes I shall accept the assumption that the difference in the message is small. The crucial point to remember, however, is that whether one views the difference as large or small, nude dancing still receives First Amendment protection, even if that protection lies only in the 'outer ambit' of that Amendment. Erie's ordinance, therefore, burdens a message protected by the First Amendment. If one assumes that the same erotic message is conveyed by nude dancers as by those wearing miniscule costumes, one means of expressing that message is banned;[2] if one assumes that the messages are different, one of those messages is banned. In either event, the ordinance is a total ban.

"The Court relies on the so-called 'secondary effects' test to defend the ordinance. [Never] before have we approved the use of that doctrine to justify a total ban on protected First Amendment expression. On the contrary, we have been quite clear that the doctrine would not support that end. * * *[3] * * *[4]

---

2. Although nude dancing might be described as one protected "means" of conveying an erotic message, it does not follow that a protected message has not been totally banned simply because there are other, similar ways to convey erotic messages. A State's prohibition of a particular book, for example, does not fail to be a total ban simply because other books conveying a similar message are available.

3. The Court contends *Ward* shows that we have used the secondary effects rationale to justify more burdensome restrictions than those approved in *Renton* and *American Mini Theatres*. That argument is unpersuasive for two reasons. First, as in the two cases just mentioned, the regulation in *Ward* was as a time, place, and manner restriction. Second, [*Ward*] is not a secondary effects case.

4. We [held] in *Renton* [that] the city [was] permitted to rely on a detailed study conducted by the city of Seattle that examined the relationship between zoning controls and the secondary effects of adult theaters. (It was permitted to rely as well on "the 'detailed findings' summarized" in an opinion of the Washington Supreme Court to the same effect.) Renton, having identified the same problem in its own city as that experienced in Seattle, quite logically drew on Seattle's experience and adopted a similar solution. But if Erie is relying on the Seattle study as well, its use of that study is most peculiar. After identifying a problem in its own city similar to that in Seattle, Erie has

"The reason we have limited our secondary effects cases to zoning and declined to extend their reasoning to total bans is clear and straightforward: A dispersal that simply limits the places where speech may occur is a minimal imposition whereas a total ban is the most exacting of restrictions. [The] fact that this censorship may have a laudable ulterior purpose cannot mean that censorship is not censorship. For these reasons, the Court's holding rejects the explicit reasoning in *American Mini Theatres* and *Renton* and the express holding in *Schad.* * * *

"The Court * * * compounds that error by dramatically reducing the degree to which the State's interest must be furthered by the restriction imposed on speech, and by ignoring the critical difference between secondary effects caused by speech and the incidental effects on speech that may be caused by a regulation of conduct.

"In what can most delicately be characterized as an enormous understatement, the plurality concedes that 'requiring dancers to wear pasties and G-strings may not greatly reduce these secondary effects.' To believe that the mandatory addition of pasties and a G-string will have *any* kind of noticeable impact on secondary effects requires nothing short of a titanic surrender to the implausible. * * *

"The Court is also mistaken in equating our secondary effects cases with the 'incidental burdens' doctrine applied in cases such as *O'Brien*; and it aggravates the error by invoking the latter line of cases to support its assertion that Erie's ordinance is unrelated to speech. The incidental burdens doctrine applies when 'speech' and 'nonspeech' elements are combined in the same course of conduct,' and the government's interest in regulating the latter justifies incidental burdens on the former. *O'Brien.* Secondary effects, on the other hand, are indirect consequences of protected speech and may justify regulation of the places where that speech may occur. See *American Mini Theatres.* When a State enacts a regulation, it might focus on the secondary effects of speech as its aim, or it might concentrate on nonspeech related concerns, having no thoughts at all with respect to how its regulation will affect speech—and only later, when the regulation is found to burden speech, justify the imposition as an unintended incidental consequence. But those interests are not the same, and the Court cannot ignore their differences and insist that both aims are equally unrelated to speech simply because Erie might have 'recogniz[ed]' that it could possibly have had either aim in mind. One can think of an apple and an orange at the same time; that does not turn them into the same fruit.

"[Erie] has expressly justified its ordinance with reference to secondary effects. [Thus] the Court's argument that 'this case is similar to *O'Brien*,' is quite wrong, as are its citations to *Clark* v. *Community for Creative Non–Violence*, and *Ward*, neither of which involved secondary effects. The Court cannot have its cake and eat it too—either Erie's ordinance was not aimed at speech and the Court may attempt to justify the regulation under the incidental burdens test, or Erie has aimed its law at the secondary effects of speech, and the Court can try to

implemented a solution (pasties and G-strings) bearing no relationship to the efficacious remedy identified by the Seattle study (dispersal through zoning).

But the city of Erie, of course, has not in fact pointed to any study by anyone suggesting that the adverse secondary effects of commercial enterprises featuring erotic dancing depends in the slightest on the precise costume worn by the performers—it merely assumes it to be so. If the city is permitted simply to assume that a slight addition to the dancers' costumes will sufficiently decrease secondary effects, then presumably the city can require more and more clothing as long as any danger of adverse effects remains.

justify the law under that doctrine. But it cannot conflate the two with the expectation that Erie's interests aimed at secondary effects will be rendered unrelated to speech by virtue of this doctrinal polyglot. * * *

"The censorial purpose of Erie's ordinance precludes reliance on the judgment in *Barnes*. [As] its preamble forthrightly admits, the ordinance's 'purpose' is to 'limi[t]' a protected form of speech; its invocation of *Barnes* cannot obliterate that professed aim.

"Erie's ordinance differs from the statute in *Barnes* in another respect. [T]he city permitted a production of Equus to proceed without prosecution, even after the ordinance was in effect, and despite its awareness of the nudity involved in the production. [As] presented to us, the ordinance is deliberately targeted at Kandyland's type of nude dancing (to the exclusion of plays like Equus), in terms of both its applicable scope and the city's enforcement.[14]

"This narrow aim is confirmed by the expressed views of the Erie City Councilmembers who voted for the ordinance. The four city councilmembers who approved the measure (of the six total councilmembers) each stated his or her view that the ordinance was aimed specifically at nude adult entertainment, and not at more mainstream forms of entertainment that include total nudity, nor even at nudity in general. One lawmaker observed: 'We're not talking about nudity. We're not talking about the theater or art * * * * We're talking about what is indecent and immoral* * * * We're not prohibiting nudity, we're prohibiting nudity when it's used in a lewd and immoral fashion.' * * * In my view, we need not strain to find consistency with more general purposes when the most natural reading of the record reflects a near obsessive preoccupation with a single target of the law.[16]"

Notes and Questions

1. Is Scalia, J., correct in arguing that no first amendment test should apply? Suppose a bookstore is closed for one year because the premises were knowingly used for purposes of prostitution. Is his analysis consistent with the language of *O'Brien?* The holding in *Falwell?* Is *Arcara*, Sec. 2 supra, (no first amendment scrutiny; statute directed at prostitution and premises used regardless of other uses) consistent with *Barnes* and *Pap's?*

2. *Is nude dancing speech?* Consider Robert Post, *Recuperating First Amendment Doctrine*, 47 Stan.L.Rev. 1249, 1259 (1995): "[T]he outcome in *Barnes* would have been different if Indiana were to have applied its statute to accepted media for the communication of ideas, as for example by attempting to prohibit nudity in movies or in the theater. Any such prohibition would serve interests

---

14. Justice Scalia [opines] that here, the basis for singling out Kandyland is morality. But since the "morality" of the public nudity in Hair is left untouched by the ordinance, while the "immorality" of the public nudity in Kandyland is singled out, the distinction cannot be that 'nude public dancing *itself* is immoral.' Rather, the only arguable difference between the two is that one's message is more immoral than the other's.

16. The Court dismisses this evidence, declaring that it "will not strike down an otherwise constitutional statute on the basis of an alleged illicit motive." *O'Brien* [said] only that

we would not strike down a law 'on the *assumption* that a wrongful purpose or motive has caused the power to be exerted,' (emphasis added), and that statement was due to our recognition that it is a "hazardous matter" to determine the actual intent of a body as large as Congress "on the basis of what fewer than a handful of Congressmen said about [a law]," [We] need not base our inquiry on an "assumption," nor must we infer the collective intent of a large body based on the statements of a few, for we have in the record the actual statements of all the city councilmembers who voted in favor of the ordinance.

deemed highly problematic by fully elaborated principles of First Amendment jurisprudence. Crucial to the result in *Barnes,* then, is the distinction between what the Court is prepared to accept as a medium for the communication of ideas, and its implicit understanding of nude dancing in nightclubs, which at least three of the majority Justices explicitly characterized as merely 'expressive conduct.' "

3. *Law and morals.* Consider Vincent Blasi, *Six Conservatives in Search of the First Amendment: The Revealing Case of Nude Dancing,* 33 Wm. and Mary L.Rev. 611, 621–22 (1992): "Can a principled conservative approve the enforcement of morals in the context of group vilification? Can a principled liberal argue that topless dancing is protected by the First Amendment but not the shouting of racial epithets? Important differences between the two categories of speech regulation may exist—hate speech ordinarily is not confined to settings in which every member of the audience has made a choice to receive the message, but hate speech also seems more political in character—but the response of many conservatives to the hate speech issue at least suggests that they do not invariably prefer a narrow interpretation of the First Amendment and do not always take a broad view of the state's power to enforce morality."

II. COMMERCIAL SPEECH

VIRGINIA STATE BOARD OF PHARMACY v. VIRGINIA CITIZENS CONSUMER COUNCIL

425 U.S. 748, 96 S.Ct. 1817, 48 L.Ed.2d 346 (1976).

Justice Blackmun delivered the opinion of the Court.

[The Court held invalid a Virginia statute that made advertising the prices of prescription drugs "unprofessional conduct," subjecting pharmacists to license suspension or revocation. Prescription drug prices strikingly varied within the same locality, in Virginia and nationally, sometimes by several hundred percent. Such drugs were dispensed exclusively by licensed pharmacists but 95% were prepared by manufacturers, not compounded by the pharmacists.]

[Appellants] contend that the advertisement of prescription drug prices is outside the protection of the First Amendment because it is "commercial speech." There can be no question that in past decisions the Court has given some indication that commercial speech is unprotected.[a]

Last Term, in *Bigelow v. Virginia,* 421 U.S. 809, 95 S.Ct. 2222, 44 L.Ed.2d 600 (1975), the notion of unprotected "commercial speech" all but passed from the scene. We reversed a conviction for violation of a Virginia statute that made the circulation of any publication to encourage or promote the processing of an abortion in Virginia a misdemeanor. The defendant had published in his newspaper the availability of abortions in New York. The advertisement in question, in addition to announcing that abortions were legal in New York, offered the services of a referral agency in that State. [We] concluded that "the Virginia courts erred in their assumptions that advertising, as such, was entitled to no First Amendment protection," and we observed that the "relationship of speech to the

---

a. Starting with *Valentine v. Chrestensen,* 316 U.S. 52, 62 S.Ct. 920, 86 L.Ed. 1262 (1942), the opinion summarized the decisions and dicta that gave such "indication." Long after *Chrestensen,* strong arguments against a first amendment exception for commercial speech had appeared. See Martin Redish, *The First Amendment in the Market Place,* 39 Geo. Wash.L.Rev. 420 (1971); Note, 50 Ore.L.Rev. 177 (1971); cf. Note, 78 Harv.L.Rev. 1191 (1965).

marketplace of products or of services does not make it valueless in the marketplace of ideas."

Some fragment of hope for the continuing validity of a "commercial speech" exception arguably might have persisted because of the subject matter of the advertisement in *Bigelow*. We noted that in announcing the availability of legal abortions in New York, the advertisement "did more than simply propose a commercial transaction. It contained factual material of clear 'public interest.'" And, of course, the advertisement related to activity with which, at least in some respects, the State could not interfere. See *Roe v. Wade* [p. 409 infra]. Indeed, we observed: "We need not decide in this case the precise extent to which the First Amendment permits regulation of advertising that is related to activities the State may legitimately regulate or even prohibit."

Here, [the] question whether there is a First Amendment exception for "commercial speech" is squarely before us. Our pharmacist does not wish to editorialize on any subject, cultural, philosophical, or political. He does not wish to report any particularly newsworthy fact, or to make generalized observations even about commercial matters. The "idea" he wishes to communicate is simply this: "I will sell you the X prescription drug at the Y price." Our question, then, is whether this communication is wholly outside the protection of the First Amendment.

V. [Speech] does not lose its First Amendment protection because money is spent to project it, as in a paid advertisement of one form or another. *New York Times Co. v. Sullivan*. Speech likewise is protected even though it is carried in a form that is "sold" for profit. *Smith v. California*. [Our] question is whether speech which does "no more than propose a commercial transaction," is so removed from any "exposition of ideas," and from "truth, science, morality, and arts in general, in its diffusion of liberal sentiments on the administration of Government", *Roth,* that it lacks all protection. Our answer is that it is not.

Focusing first on the individual parties to the transaction that is proposed in the commercial advertisement, we may assume that the advertiser's interest is a purely economic one. That hardly disqualifies him for protection under the First Amendment. The interests of the contestants in a labor dispute are primarily economic, but it has long been settled that both the employee and the employer are protected by the First Amendment when they express themselves on the merits of the dispute in order to influence its outcome. * * *[17]

As to the particular consumer's interest in the free flow of commercial information, that interest may be as keen, if not keener by far, than his interest in the day's most urgent political debate.[b] Appellees' case in this respect is a

---

17. The speech of labor disputants, of course, is subject to a number of restrictions. The Court stated in *NLRB v. Gissel Packing Co.,* 395 U.S., at 618, 89 S.Ct., at 1942, 23 L.Ed.2d, at 581 (1969), for example, that an employer's threats of retaliation for the labor actions of his employees are "without the protection of the First Amendment." The constitutionality of restrictions upon speech in the special context of labor disputes is not before us here. We express no views on that complex subject, and advert to cases in the labor field only to note that in some circumstances speech of an entirely private and economic character enjoys the protection of the First Amendment.

[For the contention that labor speech receives less protection than commercial speech, see James Pope, *The Three–Systems Ladder of First Amendment Values: Two Rungs and a Black Hole,* 11 Hast.Con.L.Q. 189 (1984)].

b. "After all. As the National Enquirer likes to observe, 'Inquiring Minds Want to Know.' They 'want to know' about the kind of creme rinse Cindi Lauper uses as much as, perhaps even more than, they want to know whether the CIA may have helped bring down the government in South Vietnam." William Van Alstyne, *Remembering Melville Nimmer: Some Cautionary Notes on Commercial Speech,* 43 UCLA L.Rev. 1635 (1996); Consider Mark

convincing one. Those whom the suppression of prescription drug price information hits the hardest are the poor, the sick, and particularly the aged. A disproportionate amount of their income tends to be spent on prescription drugs; yet they are the least able to learn, by shopping from pharmacist to pharmacist, where their scarce dollars are best spent. When drug prices vary as strikingly as they do, information as to who is charging what becomes more than a convenience. It could mean the alleviation of physical pain or the enjoyment of basic necessities.

Generalizing, society also may have a strong interest in the free flow of commercial information. Even an individual advertisement, though entirely "commercial," may be of general public interest. The facts of decided cases furnish illustrations: advertisements stating that referral services for legal abortions are available, *Bigelow;* that a manufacturer of artificial furs promotes his product as an alternative to the extinction by his competitors of fur-bearing mammals, see *Fur Information & Fashion Council, Inc. v. E.F. Timme & Son,* 364 F.Supp. 16 (S.D.N.Y.1973); and that a domestic producer advertises his product as an alternative to imports that tend to deprive American residents of their jobs, cf. *Chicago Joint Board v. Chicago Tribune Co.,* 435 F.2d 470 (C.A.7 1970), cert. denied, 402 U.S. 973 (1971). Obviously, not all commercial messages contain the same or even a very great public interest element. There are few to which such an element, however, could not be added. Our pharmacist, for example, could cast himself as a commentator on store-to-store disparities in drug prices, giving his own and those of a competitor as proof. We see little point in requiring him to do so, and little difference if he does not.

Moreover, there is another consideration that suggests that no line between publicly "interesting" or "important" commercial advertising and the opposite kind could ever be drawn. Advertising, however tasteless and excessive it sometimes may seem, is nonetheless dissemination of information as to who is producing and selling what product, for what reason, and at what price. So long as we preserve a predominantly free enterprise economy, the allocation of our resources in large measure will be made through numerous private economic decisions. It is a matter of public interest that those decisions, in the aggregate, be intelligent and well informed. To this end, the free flow of commercial information is indispensable. And if it is indispensable to the proper allocation of resources in a free enterprise system, it is also indispensable to the formation of intelligent opinions as to how that system ought to be regulated or altered. Therefore, even if the First Amendment were thought to be primarily an instrument to enlighten public decision making in a democracy, we could not say that the free flow of information does not serve that goal.[c]

Tushnet, *Red, White, and Blue* 290 (1988): "The listener's interest in receiving information, a private interest, thus prevails over a more republican vision of politics, in which political discussion is, at least on the level of public norms, 'keener by far' than private interest."

c. Consider Steven H. Shiffrin, *Dissent, Injustice, and the Meaning of America* 40 (1999): "Suppose that the private allocation of resources is a part of public decision making in a democracy. [Government allocation of resources[, however,] is also part of public decision making in a democracy. That one predominates over the other (for many wealthy corporations, of course, free enterprise is the exception, not the rule) seems quite beside the point. Even if we suppose that commercial advertising is political, protection of 'political speech' in this context seems dramatically less important than in others if all that is at stake is the efficient allocation of resources. Moreover, since government frequently departs from the enterprise with constitutional blessing, perhaps the proper allocation of resources as seen by the market should not be privileged at all. [Why] should allocation of resources be a First Amendment worry?" Compare Robert Post, *The Constitutional Status of Commercial Speech,* 48 UCLA L.Rev. 1 (2000)(commercial

Arrayed against these substantial individual and societal interests are a number of justifications for the advertising ban. These have to do principally with maintaining a high degree of professionalism on the part of licensed pharmacists. [Price] advertising, it is argued, will place in jeopardy the pharmacist's expertise and, with it, the customer's health. It is claimed that the aggressive price competition that will result from unlimited advertising will make it impossible for the pharmacist to supply professional services in the compounding, handling, and dispensing of prescription drugs. Such services are time-consuming and expensive; if competitors who economize by eliminating them are permitted to advertise their resulting lower prices, the more painstaking and conscientious pharmacist will be forced either to follow suit or to go out of business. [It] is further claimed that advertising will lead people to shop for their prescription drugs among the various pharmacists who offer the lowest prices, and the loss of stable pharmacist-customer relationships will make individual [attention] impossible. Finally, it is argued that damage will be done to the professional image of the pharmacist. This image, that of a skilled and specialized craftsman, attracts talent to the profession and reinforces the better habits of those who are in [it].

The strength of these proffered justifications is greatly undermined by the fact that high professional standards, to a substantial extent, are guaranteed by the close regulation to which pharmacists in Virginia are subject. [At] the same time, we cannot discount the Board's justifications entirely. The Court regarded justifications of this type sufficient to sustain the advertising bans challenged on due process and equal protection [grounds].[d]

The challenge now made, however, is based on the First Amendment. This casts the Board's justifications in a different light, for on close inspection it is seen that the State's protectiveness of its citizens rests in large measure on the advantages of their being kept in ignorance. The advertising ban does not directly affect professional standards one way or the other. It affects them only through the reactions it is assumed people will have to the free flow of drug price information. There is no claim that the advertising ban in any way prevents the cutting of corners by the pharmacist who is so inclined. That pharmacist is likely to cut corners in any event. The only effect the advertising ban has on him is to insulate him from price competition and to open the way for him to make a substantial, and perhaps even excessive, profit in addition to providing an inferior service. The more painstaking pharmacist is also protected but, again, it is a protection based in large part on public ignorance.

It appears to be feared that if the pharmacist who wishes to provide low cost, and assertedly low quality, services is permitted to advertise, he will be taken up on his offer by too many unwitting customers. They will choose the low-cost, low-quality service and drive the "professional" pharmacist out of business. [They] will go from one pharmacist to another, following the discount, and destroy the pharmacist-customer relationship. They will lose respect for the profession because it advertises. All this is not in their best interests, and all this can be avoided if they are not permitted to know who is charging what.

[A]n alternative to this highly paternalistic[e] approach [is] to assume that this information is not in itself harmful, that people will perceive their own best

speech provides information necessary for public decision making though it is not as important as "public discourse."

d. The Court referred here to cases upholding bans on advertising prices for eyeglass frames and optometrist and dental services.

e. Consider Frederick Schauer, *The Role of the People in First Amendment Theory*, 74 Cal-

interests if only they are well enough informed, and that the best means to that end is to open the channels of communication rather than to close them. If they are truly open, nothing prevents the "professional" pharmacist from marketing his own assertedly superior product, and contrasting it with that of the low-cost, high-volume prescription drug retailer. But the choice among these alternative approaches is not ours to make or the Virginia General Assembly's. It is precisely this kind of choice, between the dangers of suppressing information, and the dangers of its misuse if it is freely available, that the First Amendment makes for [us].

VI. In concluding that commercial speech, like other varieties, is protected, we of course do not hold that it can never be regulated in any way. Some forms of commercial speech regulation are surely permissible. We mention a few. [There] is no claim, for example, that the prohibition on prescription drug price advertising is a mere time, place, and manner restriction. We have often approved restrictions of that kind provided that they are justified without reference to the content of the regulated speech, that they serve a significant governmental interest, and that in so doing they leave open ample alternative channels for communication of the information. Whatever may be the proper bounds of time, place, and manner restrictions on commercial speech, they are plainly exceeded by this Virginia statute, which singles out speech of a particular content and seeks to prevent its dissemination completely.

Nor is there any claim that prescription drug price advertisements are forbidden because they are false or misleading in any way. Untruthful speech, commercial or otherwise, has never been protected for its own sake. *Gertz*. Obviously much commercial speech is not provably false, or even wholly false, but only deceptive or misleading. We foresee no obstacle to a State's dealing effectively with this problem.[24] The First Amendment, as we construe it today, does not prohibit the State from insuring that the stream of commercial information flows cleanly as well as freely.

Also, there is no claim that the transactions proposed in the forbidden advertisements are themselves illegal in any way. Finally, the special problems of the electronic broadcast media are likewise not in this case.

if.L.Rev. 761, 788 (1986): "We ought to recognize that popular control over nonpolitical speech may in some circumstances be a bad idea and address directly just why this is so. Perhaps it is time to face up to the paternalism of the first amendment, and maybe much of the rest of the Constitution as well." Is the Court's anti-paternalism paternalistic? For the contention that the Virginia price advertising ban was not paternalistic, see Daniel Lowenstein, *"Too Much Puff": Persuasion, Paternalism, and Commercial Speech*, 56 U.Cin.L.Rev. 1205, 1238 (1988).

24. [C]ommon sense differences between speech that does "no more than propose a commercial transaction," *Pittsburgh Press* and other varieties [suggest] that a different degree of protection is necessary to insure that the flow of truthful and legitimate commercial information is unimpaired. The truth of commercial speech, for example, may be more easily verifiable by its disseminator than, let us say, news reporting or political commentary, in that ordinarily the advertiser seeks to disseminate information about a specific product or service that he himself provides and presumably knows more about than anyone else. Also, commercial speech may be more durable than other kinds. Since advertising is the sine qua non of commercial profits, there is little likelihood of its being chilled by proper regulation and foregone entirely.

Attributes such as these, the greater objectivity and hardiness of commercial speech, may make it less necessary to tolerate inaccurate statements for fear of silencing the speaker. They may also make it appropriate to require that a commercial message appear in such a form, or include such additional information, warnings and disclaimers, as are necessary to prevent its being deceptive. They may also make inapplicable the prohibition on prior restraints. Compare *New York Times v. United States* [Sec. 4, III infra] with *Donaldson v. Read Magazine*, 333 U.S. 178, 68 S.Ct. 591, 92 L.Ed. 628 (1948).

What is at issue is whether a State may completely suppress the dissemination of concededly truthful information about entirely lawful activity, fearful of that information's effect upon its disseminators and its recipients. Reserving other questions,[25] we conclude that the answer to this one is in the [negative].

JUSTICE STEWART, concurring.[f]

[I] write separately to explain why I think today's decision does not preclude [governmental regulation of false or deceptive advertising]. The Court has on several occasions addressed the problems posed by false statements of fact in libel cases. [Factual] errors are inevitable in free debate, and the imposition of liability for [such errors] can "dampe[n] the vigor and limi[t] the variety of public debate" by inducing "self-censorship." [In] contrast to the press, which must often attempt to assemble the true facts from sketchy and sometimes conflicting sources under the pressure of publication deadlines, the commercial advertiser generally knows the product or service he seeks to sell and is in a position to verify the accuracy of his factual representations before he disseminates them. The advertiser's access to the truth about his product and its price substantially eliminates any danger that governmental regulation of false or misleading price or product advertising will chill accurate and nondeceptive commercial [expression].

Since the factual claims contained in commercial price or product advertisements relate to tangible goods or services, they may be tested empirically and corrected to reflect the truth without in any manner jeopardizing the free dissemination of thought. Indeed, the elimination of false and deceptive claims serves to promote the one facet of commercial price and product advertising that warrants First Amendment protection—its contribution to the flow of accurate and reliable information relevant to public and private decision making.

JUSTICE REHNQUIST, dissenting.

[Under] the Court's opinion the way will be open not only for dissemination of price information but for active promotion of prescription drugs, liquor, cigarettes and other products the use of which it has previously been thought desirable to discourage. Now, however, such promotion is protected by the First Amendment so long as it is not misleading or does not promote an illegal product or [enterprise].

The Court speaks of the consumer's interest in the free flow of commercial information. [This] should presumptively be the concern of the Virginia Legislature, which sits to balance [this] and other claims in the process of making laws such as the one here under attack. The Court speaks of the importance in a "predominantly free enterprise economy" of intelligent and well-informed decisions as to allocation of resources. While there is again much to be said for the Court's observation as a matter of desirable public policy, there is certainly nothing in the United States Constitution which requires the Virginia Legislature to hew to the teachings of Adam Smith in its legislative decisions regulating the pharmacy profession. E.g., *Nebbia v. New York; Olsen v. Nebraska* [Ch. 5, Sec. 3].

---

25. We stress that we have considered in this case the regulation of commercial advertising by pharmacists. Although we express no opinion as to other professions, the distinctions, historical and functional, between professions, may require consideration of quite different factors. Physicians and lawyers, for example, do not dispense standardized products; they render professional *services* of al-

most infinite variety and nature, with the consequent enhanced possibility for confusion and deception if they were to undertake certain kinds of advertising.

f. Burger, C.J., separately concurring, stressed the reservation in fn. 25 of the opinion with respect to advertising by attorneys and physicians. Stevens, J., took no part.

[There] are undoubted difficulties with an effort to draw a bright line between "commercial speech" on the one hand and "protected speech" on the other, and the Court does better to face up to these difficulties than to attempt to hide them under labels. In this case, however, the Court has unfortunately substituted for the wavering line previously thought to exist between commercial speech and protected speech a no more satisfactory line of its own—that between "truthful" commercial speech, on the one hand, and that which is "false and misleading" on the other. The difficulty with this line is not that it wavers, but on the contrary that it is simply too Procrustean to take into account the congeries of factors which I believe could, quite consistently with the First and Fourteenth Amendments, properly influence a legislative decision with respect to commercial advertising.

[S]uch a line simply makes no allowance whatever for what appears to have been a considered legislative judgment in most States that while prescription drugs are a necessary and vital part of medical care and treatment, there are sufficient dangers attending their widespread use that they simply may not be promoted in the same manner as hair creams, deodorants, and toothpaste. The very real dangers that general advertising for such drugs might create in terms of encouraging, even though not sanctioning, illicit use of them by individuals for whom they have not been prescribed, or by generating patient pressure upon physicians to prescribe them are simply not dealt with in the Court's [opinion].

Notes and Questions

1. As compared to political decision making, is commercial advertising "neither more nor less significant than a host of other market activities that legislatures concededly may regulate"? Is there an "absence of any principled distinction between commercial soliciting and other aspects of economic activity"? Has economic due process been "resurrected, clothed in the ill-fitting garb of the first amendment"? See Thomas Jackson & John Jeffries, *Commercial Speech: Economic Due Process and the First Amendment,* 65 Va.L.Rev. 1, 18 and 30 (1979). Why may government "be paternalistic regarding the purchase of goods but may not be paternalistic regarding information about those goods"? Larry Alexander, *Speech in the Local Marketplace: Implications of Virginia State Board of Pharmacy v. Virginia Citizens Consumer Council, Inc. for Local Regulatory Power,* 14 San Diego L.Rev. 357, 376 (1977).

2. Does the rationale of *Virginia Pharmacy* extend to image or non-informational advertising? Should such advertising be protected? For relevant discussion, see Daniel Lowenstein, *"Too Much Puff": Persuasion, Paternalism, and Commercial Speech,* 56 U.Cin.L.Rev. 1205 (1988); Note, *The "Persuasion Route" of the Law: Advertising and Legal Persuasion,* 100 Colum. L.Rev. 1281 (2000). For the cultural implications of image advertising, see Ronald Collins & David Skover, *Commerce and Communication,* 71 Tex.L.Rev. 697 (1993).[g] But see Sylvia Law, *Addiction, Autonomy, and Advertising,* 77 Iowa L.Rev. 909, 932 (1992): "A broad-sweeping principle denying constitutional protection to noninformational commercial speech reinforces a narrow vision of First Amendment values focusing on political participation and rationality. * * * Film, music, and novels are protected, not because they necessarily provide 'information' or facilitate participation in

g. For the negative implications of advertising (informational or non-informational) for democratic politics and culture, see C. Edwin Baker, *Advertising and a Democratic Press* (1994). See also Ronald Collins, *Dictating Content: How Advertising Pressure Can Corrupt A Free Press* (1992).

formal political processes, but because the First Amendment protects 'not only ideas capable of relatively precise, detached explication, but otherwise inexpressible emotions as well.' "

3. Footnote 24 suggests that *deceptive* commercial speech may be regulated in ways that would be barred if the speech were political. Sound distinction?

(a) *"Commonsense" differences between commercial speech and other speech.* (1) *Verifiability.* Consider Daniel Farber, *Commercial Speech and First Amendment Theory,* 74 Nw.U.L.Rev. 372, 385–86 (1979): "[C]ommercial speech is not necessarily more verifiable than other speech. There may well be uncertainty about some quality of a product, such as the health effect of eggs. On the other hand, political speech is often quite verifiable by the speaker. A political candidate knows the truth about his own past and his present intentions, yet misrepresentations on these subjects are immune from state regulation." (2) *Durability.* Consider Martin Redish, *The Value of Free Speech,* 130 U.Pa.L.Rev. 591, 633 (1982): "[I]t is also incorrect to distinguish commercial from political expression on the ground that the former is somehow hardier because of the inherent profit motive. It could just as easily be said that we need not fear that commercial magazines and newspapers will cease publication for fear of governmental regulation, because they are in business for profit. Of course, the proper response to this contention is that our concern is not *whether* they will publish, but *what* they will publish: fear of regulation might deter them from dealing with controversial subjects." But see Ronald Cass, *Commercial Speech, Constitutionalism, Collective Choice,* 56 U.Cin.L.Rev. 1317, 1368–73 (1988).

(b) *Commercial speech and self-expression.* Is commercial speech distinguishable from political speech because it is unrelated to self-expression? Consider C. Edwin Baker, *Commercial Speech: A Problem in the Theory of Freedom,* 62 Iowa L.Rev. 1, 17 (1976): In commercial speech, the dissemination of the profit motive "breaks the connection between speech and any vision, or attitude, or value of the individual or group engaged in advocacy. Thus the content and form of commercial speech cannot be attributed to individual value allegiances." See generally C. Edwin Baker, *Human Liberty and Freedom of Speech* chs. 3, 9, 10 (1989). For criticism, see, e.g., Pierre Schlag, *An Attack on Categorical Approaches to Freedom of Speech,* 30 UCLA L.Rev. 671, 710–21 (1983); Steven Shiffrin, *The First Amendment and Economic Regulation: Away From A General Theory of the First Amendment,* 78 Nw.U.L.Rev. 1212 (1983). Even if commercial speech is divorced from self expression (or dignity), should it merit substantial protection, nonetheless. See Aleita Estreicher, *Securities Regulation and the First Amendment,* 24 Ga.L.Rev. 223 (1990); Burt Neuborne, *The First Amendment and Government Regulation of Capital Markets,* 55 Brook.L.Rev. 5 (1989).

(c) *Contract approach to commercial speech.* Is commercial advertising distinguishable from other forms of speech because of the state interest in regulating contracts? Consider Farber, supra, at 389: "The unique aspect of commercial speech is that it is a prelude to, and therefore becomes integrated into, a contract, the essence of which is the presence of a promise. Because a promise is an undertaking to ensure that a certain state of affairs takes place, promises obviously have a closer connection with conduct than with self-expression. Second, [in] a fundamentally market economy, the government understandably is given particular deference in its enforcement of contractual expectations. Indeed, the Constitution itself gives special protection to contractual expectations in the contract clause. Finally, [the] technicalities of contract law, with its doctrines of privity, consideration, and the like, should not be blindly translated into first amendment jurisprudence. The basic doctrines of contract law, however, provide a helpful guide in considering commercial speech problems." For discussion, see Larry Alexander & Daniel Farber, *Commercial Speech and First Amendment Theory: A Critical Exchange,* 75 Nw.U.L.Rev. 307 (1980).

(d) *Error costs.* Is commercial speech distinguishable because the risks of error are less? Consider Cass, supra at 1360: "[T]he inquiry can be framed as asking four questions: (1) will officials err less systematically or less often in regulation of commercial speech than in regulation of other speech?; (2) will officials err less systematically or less often in regulation of commerce than in regulation of speech?; (3) will the consequences of errors in regulation of one sort of activity generally be less significant than the consequences of errors in the other?; and (4) will the process costs associated with error correction be lower in respect of one activity than the other?" On the risks of error, see generally Cass, supra; Fred McChesney, *A Positive Regulatory Theory of the First Amendment,* 20 Conn.L.Rev. 335 (1988). See also Ronald Coase, *Advertising and Free Speech,* 6 J.Legal Stud. 1 (1977); Richard Posner, *Free Speech in an Economic Perspective,* 20 Suffolk U.L.Rev. 1 (1986); Thomas Scanlon, *Freedom of Expression and Categories of Expression,* 40 U.Pitt.L.Rev. 519 (1979).

4. *Limits on regulation of deceptive advertising. Bates v. State Bar,* 433 U.S. 350, 97 S.Ct. 2691, 53 L.Ed.2d 810 (1977), struck down an Arizona Supreme Court rule against a lawyer "publicizing himself" through advertising. It rejected the claim that attorney price advertising was inherently misleading, but left open the "peculiar problems" associated with advertising claims regarding the quality of legal services.[h] Could a lawyer truthfully advertise that he or she has (1) tried twice as many personal injury cases as any other lawyer in the country? (2) averaged $10,000 more in recoveries per case than any other lawyer in the county? (3) graduated from Harvard Law School in the upper 10% of the class? (4) received "the best legal education this country offers"? Should an advertisement be protected if it is "sufficiently factual to be subject to verification" even if "implications of quality might be drawn from it"? See William Canby and Ernest Gellhorn, *Physician Advertising: The First Amendment and the Sherman Act,* 1978 Duke L.J. 543, 560–62. Should the Court have deferred to the judgment of the State Bar of Arizona? If not, should it defer to the SEC when it regulates the advertising of securities? The FTC when it regulates automobile advertising? The Virginia Board of Pharmacy when it regulates quality advertising by pharmacists? For deferential treatment of a state ban on the use of tradenames by optometrists, see *Friedman v. Rogers,* 440 U.S. 1, 99 S.Ct. 887, 59 L.Ed.2d 100 (1979).

5. *Paternalism and Democracy.* Is it a part of democratic theory that "individual citizens can be trusted to make legally valid life-affecting choices on the basis of an open marketplace of ideas of information and opinion ." Martin H. Redish, *Tobacco Advertising and the First Amendment,* 81 Ia. L.Rev. 589, 604–05 (1996). Consider Steven H. Shiffrin, *Dissent, Injustice, and the Meanings of*

---

h. *Zauderer v. Office of Disciplinary Counsel,* Sec. 9, I infra, held that a state may not discipline attorneys who solicit legal business through newspaper advertisements containing "truthful and nondeceptive information and advice regarding the legal rights of potential clients" or for the advertising use of "accurate and nondeceptive" illustrations. Zauderer had placed illustrated ads in 36 Ohio newspapers publicizing his availability to represent women who had suffered injuries from use of a contra-ceptive device known as the Dalkon Shield Intrauterine Device. In the ad Zauderer stated that he had represented other women in Dalkon Shield litigation. The Court observed that accurate statements of fact cannot be proscribed "merely because it is possible that some readers will infer that he has some expertise in those areas." But it continued to "leave open the possibility that States may prevent attorneys from making non-verifiable claims regarding the quality of their services. *Bates.*"

America 143–44 n. 41 (1999): "This argument would seem to prove too much. If democratic theory assumes citizens can be trusted to make such choices in an open marketplace, one would imagine government would be foreclosed not only from fixing prices to discourage consumption, but also from regulating false and misleading advertising. In addition, it would be unclear why government should be permitted to make products illegal for paternalistic reasons—-if citizens can truly be trusted. Assuming it were consistent with this version of democratic theory for government to ban products, it would be unclear why its paternalism could not extend to product advertising of legal products. It would not do, for example, to claim that products not made illegal have been certified as safe. To outlaw cigarettes, for example, might create black markets and enormous attendant enforcement problems. The failure to outlaw cigarettes need not suggest that government thinks of them as any less a public health problem than numerous other drugs that are currently outlawed. Whether individual citizens can be 'trusted,' seems to bear no relationship to the legal status of the product. In addition, one could argue that the notion of democracy makes no claims about the quality of *individual* decision making, but makes some relative claims about the quality of *public* decision making."

6. *Truth and commercial advertising.* Should Mercedes Benz be able to truthfully advertise that Elton John drives its car without getting John's permission?[i] Should the state be able to prevent homeowners from posting "for sale" signs in order to prevent panic selling in order to maintain an integrated neighborhood? See *Linmark Associates v. Willingboro*, 431 U.S. 85, 97 S.Ct. 1614, 52 L.Ed.2d 155 (1977). May a state regulate the content of contraceptive advertising in order to minimize its offensive character? Cf. *Carey v. Population Services Int'l.*, Ch. 6, Sec. 2 (total ban on contraceptive advertising unconstitutional).[j]

———

OHRALIK v. OHIO STATE BAR ASS'N, 436 U.S. 447, 98 S.Ct. 1912, 56 L.Ed.2d 444 (1978) upheld the indefinite suspension of an attorney for violating the anti-solicitation provisions of the Ohio Code of Professional Responsibility. Those provisions generally do not allow lawyers to recommend themselves to anyone who has not sought "their advice regarding employment of a lawyer." Albert Ohralik had approached two young accident victims to solicit employment—Carol McClintock in a hospital room where she lay in traction and Wanda Lou Holbert on the day she came home from the hospital. He employed a concealed tape recorder with Holbert, apparently to insure he would have evidence of her assent to his representation. The next day, when Holbert's mother informed Ohralik that she and her daughter did not want to have appellant represent them, he insisted that the daughter had entered into a binding agreement. McClintock also discharged Ohralik, and Ohralik sued her for breach of contract. The Court ruled, per POWELL, J., that a state may forbid in-person solicitation of clients by lawyers for pecuniary gain:

i. See Alice Haemmerli, *Whose Who? The Case for a Kantian Right of Publicity*, 49 Duke L.J. 383 (1999); Wesley Liebeler, *A Property Rights Approach to Judicial Decision Making*, 4 Cato J. 783, 802–03 (1985); Shiffrin, supra note 3, at 1257–58 n. 275; Peter Felcher & Edward Rubin, *Privacy, Publicity, and the Portrayal of Real People by the Media*, 88 Yale L.J.

1577 (1979); James Treece, *Commercial Exploitation of Names, Likenesses, and Personal Histories*, 51 Tex.L.Rev. 637 (1973).

j. Does protection for commercial speech threaten the tort for interference with contract? See David A. Anderson, *Torts, Speech, and Contracts*, 75 Texas L.Rev. 1499 (1977).

"Expression concerning purely commercial transactions has come within the ambit of the Amendment's protection only recently. In rejecting the notion that such speech is wholly outside the protection of the First Amendment, *Virginia Pharmacy,* we were careful not to hold that it is wholly undifferentiable from other forms of speech.

"We have not discarded the common sense distinction between speech proposing a commercial transaction, which occurs in an area traditionally subject to government regulation, and other varieties of speech. To require a parity of constitutional protection for commercial and noncommercial speech alike could invite dilution, simply by a leveling process, of the force of the Amendment's guarantee with respect to the latter kind of speech. Rather than subject the First Amendment to such a devitalization, we instead have afforded commercial speech a limited measure of protection, commensurate with its subordinate position in the scale of First Amendment values, while allowing modes of regulation that might be impermissible in the realm of noncommercial expression.

"Moreover, 'it has never been deemed an abridgment of freedom of speech or press to make a course of conduct illegal merely because the conduct was in part initiated, evidenced, or carried out by means of language, either spoken, written, or printed.' *Giboney v. Empire Storage & Ice Co.,* 336 U.S. 490, 502, 69 S.Ct. 684, 691, 93 L.Ed. 834 (1949). Numerous examples could be cited of communications that are regulated without offending the First Amendment, such as the exchange of information about securities, *SEC v. Texas Gulf Sulphur Co.,* 401 F.2d 833 (C.A.2 1968), cert. denied, 394 U.S. 976, 89 S.Ct. 1454, 22 L.Ed.2d 756 (1969), corporate proxy statements, *Mills v. Electric Auto–Lite Co.,* 396 U.S. 375, 90 S.Ct. 616, 24 L.Ed.2d 593 (1970), the exchange of price and production information among competitors, *American Column & Lumber Co. v. United States,* 257 U.S. 377, 42 S.Ct. 114, 66 L.Ed. 284 (1921), and employers' threats of retaliation for the labor activities of employees, *NLRB v. Gissel Packing Co.,* 395 U.S. 575, 618, 89 S.Ct. 1918, 1942, 23 L.Ed.2d 547 (1969). Each of these examples illustrates that the State does not lose its power to regulate commercial activity deemed harmful to the public whenever speech is a component of that activity. Neither *Virginia Pharmacy* nor *Bates* purported to cast doubt on the permissibility of these kinds of commercial regulation.

"In-person solicitation by a lawyer of remunerative employment is a business transaction in which speech is an essential but subordinate component. While this does not remove the speech from the protection of the First Amendment, as was held in *Bates* and *Virginia Pharmacy,* it lowers the level of appropriate judicial scrutiny. [A] lawyer's procurement of remunerative employment is a subject only marginally affected with First Amendment concerns. It falls within the State's proper sphere of economic and professional regulation. While entitled to some constitutional protection, appellant's conduct is subject to regulation in furtherance of important state [interests].

" "The interest of the States in regulating lawyers is especially great since lawyers are essential to the primary function of administering justice and have historically been officers of the courts' [and] act 'as trusted agents of their clients and as assistants to the court in search of a just solution to disputes.'

"[The] substantive evils of solicitation have been stated over the years in sweeping terms: stirring up litigation, assertion of fraudulent claims, debasing the legal profession, and potential harm to the solicited client in the form of overreaching, overcharging, underrepresentation, and misrepresentation." In providing information about the availability and terms of proposed legal services "in-person solicitation serves much the same function as the advertisement at issue in *Bates*. But there are significant differences as well. Unlike a public advertisement, which simply provides information and leaves the recipient free to act upon it or not, in-person solicitation may exert pressure and often demands an immediate response, without providing an opportunity for comparison or reflection. The aim and effect of in-person solicitation may be to provide a one-sided presentation and to encourage speedy and perhaps uninformed decision making; there is no opportunity for intervention or counter-education by agencies of the Bar, supervisory authorities, or persons close to the solicited individual. The admonition that 'the fitting remedy for evil counsels is good ones' is of little value when the circumstances provide no opportunity for any remedy at all. In-person solicitation is as likely as not to discourage persons needing counsel from engaging in a critical comparison of the 'availability, nature, and prices' of legal services; it actually may disserve the individual and societal interest, identified in *Bates,* in facilitating 'informed and reliable decision making.'

"[Appellant's argument that none of the evils of solicitation was found in his case] misconceives the nature of the State's interest. The rules prohibiting solicitation are prophylactic measures whose objective is the prevention of harm before it occurs.[a] The rules were applied in this case to discipline a lawyer for soliciting employment for pecuniary gain under circumstances likely to result in the adverse consequences the State seeks to avert. In such a situation, which is inherently conducive to overreaching and other forms of misconduct, the State has a strong interest in adopting and enforcing rules of conduct designed to protect the public from harmful solicitation by lawyers whom it has [licensed].

"The efficacy of the State's effort to prevent such harm to prospective clients would be substantially diminished if, having proved a solicitation in circumstances like those of this case, the State were required in addition to prove actual injury. Unlike the advertising in *Bates,* in-person solicitation is not visible or otherwise open to public scrutiny. Often there is no witness other than the lawyer and the lay person whom he has solicited, rendering it difficult or impossible to obtain reliable proof of what actually took place. This would be especially true if the lay person were so distressed at the time of the solicitation that he or she could not recall specific details at a later date. If appellant's view were sustained, in-person solicitation would be virtually immune to effective oversight and regulation by the State or by the legal profession, in contravention of the State's strong interest in regulating members of the Bar in an effective, objective, and self-enforcing manner. It therefore is not unreasonable, or violative of the Constitution, for a State to respond with what in effect is a prophylactic rule."[b]

Notes and Questions

1. *Companion case.* IN RE PRIMUS, 436 U.S. 412, 98 S.Ct. 1893, 56 L.Ed.2d 417 (1978), per POWELL, J., held that a state could not constitutionally discipline an ACLU "cooperating lawyer" who, after advising a gathering of allegedly illegally sterilized women of their rights, initiated further contact with one of the women by writing her a letter informing her of the ACLU's willingness to provide free legal representation for women in her situation and of the organization's desire to file a lawsuit on her behalf. "South Carolina's action in punishing appellant for

---

a. But see Fred McChesney, *Commercial Speech in the Professions,* 134 U.Pa.L.Rev. 45 (1985) (anti-solicitation provisions may be motivated by anti-competitive considerations).

b. Marshall and Rehnquist, JJ., each separately concurred in the judgment. Brennan, J., did not participate.

soliciting a prospective litigant by mail, on behalf of ACLU, must withstand the 'exacting scrutiny applicable to limitations on core First Amendment rights.' [Where] political expression or association is at issue, this Court has not tolerated the degree of imprecision that often characterizes government regulation of the conduct of commercial affairs. The approach we adopt today in *Ohralik* that the State may proscribe in-person solicitation for pecuniary gain under circumstances likely to result in adverse consequences, cannot be applied to appellant's activity on behalf of the ACLU. Although a showing of potential danger may suffice in the former context, appellant may not be disciplined unless her activity in fact involved the type of misconduct at which South Carolina's broad prohibition is said to be directed. The record does not support appellee's contention that undue influence, overreaching, misrepresentation, or invasion of privacy actually occurred in this case."

2. *Related cases. Edenfield v. Fane,* 507 U.S. 761, 113 S.Ct. 1792, 123 L.Ed.2d 543 (1993) held that direct personal solicitation of prospective business clients by Certified Public Accountants is protected under the first amendment,[c] but *Florida Bar v. Went For It, Inc.,* 515 U.S. 618, 115 S.Ct. 2371, 132 L.Ed.2d 541 (1995) held that targeted direct-mail solicitations by personal injury attorneys to victims and their relatives for thirty days following an accident were not protected under the first amendment.

3. *A hierarchy of protected speech.* Consider Steven Shiffrin, note 3 supra, at 1218–21 (1983): In *Virginia Pharmacy,* "the Court never admitted that commercial speech was less valuable than political speech. The 'commonsense differences' had nothing to do with value. [Although] Justice Blackmun labored to defend the asserted equal relationship between commercial speech and political speech for the *Virginia Pharmacy* majority, Justice Powell in *Ohralik* was content to lead the Court to an opposite position without explanation. In so doing, Justice Powell steered the Court to accept a hierarchy of protected speech for the first time, despite his own stated opposition [in *Young*] to creating any such hierarchy." Does the concern that the protection of non-commercial speech would be subject to dilution if it were placed on a par with commercial speech presuppose an unexplained difference between the two types of speech? See id. at 1221 n. 59. For discussion of the dilution argument, see William Marshall, *The Dilution of the First Amendment and the Equality of Ideas,* 38 Case W.Res.L.Rev. 566 (1988).

4. *Muddying the hierarchy.* Cincinnati permitted 1,500–2,000 news racks throughout the city for publications not classified as commercial speech, but refused to allow an additional 62 news racks that contained two publications classified as commercial speech. CINCINNATI v. DISCOVERY NETWORK, 507 U.S. 410, 113 S.Ct. 1505, 123 L.Ed.2d 99 (1993), per STEVENS, J., held that this discrimination violated the first amendment: "The major premise supporting the city's argument is the proposition that commercial speech has only a low value. Based on that premise, the city contends that the fact that assertedly more valuable publications are allowed to use news racks does not undermine its judgment that its esthetic and safety interests are stronger than the interest in allowing commercial speakers to have similar access to the reading public. [In] our

---

c. Blackmun, J., concurred; O'Connor, J., dissented. Compare Ibanez v. Florida Dep't of Business and Professional Regulation, 512 U.S. 136, 114 S.Ct. 2084, 129 L.Ed.2d 118 (1994) (attorney's references in advertising, business cards and stationery to her credentials as a CPA and a Certified Financial Planner are not deceptive or misleading and are protected commercial speech); Accord, Peel v. Attorney Registration and Disciplinary Comm'n, 496 U.S. 91, 110 S.Ct. 2281, 110 L.Ed.2d 83 (1990) (reference on letterhead to prestigious certification is protected speech).

view, the city's argument attaches more importance to the distinction between commercial and non-commercial speech than our cases warrant and seriously underestimates the value of commercial speech.[20]''d

5. *The reach of Discovery Network.* (a) In MARTIN v. STRUTHERS, 319 U.S. 141, 63 S.Ct. 862, 87 L.Ed. 1313 (1943), a city forbade knocking on the door or ringing the doorbell of a resident in order to deliver handbills (in an industrial community where many worked night shifts and slept during the day). In striking down the ordinance, the Court, per BLACK, J., pointed out that the city's objectives could be achieved by means of a law making it an offense for any person to ring the doorbell of a householder who has "appropriately indicated that he is unwilling to be disturbed. This or any similar regulation leaves the decision as to whether distributors of literature may lawfully call at a home where it belongs— with the homeowner himself." By contrast, *Breard v. Alexandria,* 341 U.S. 622, 71 S.Ct. 920, 95 L.Ed. 1233 (1951) upheld an ordinance forbidding the practice of going door to door to solicit orders for the sale of goods. The commercial element was said to distinguish *Martin. Does Breard* survive *Virginia Pharmacy?* Does (should) *Discovery Network* settle the issue? What if, as in *Breard,* the solicitor is selling subscriptions for magazines?

(b) Compare *Schneider,* Sec. 6, I, A infra (prohibition against leaflet distribution on streets unconstitutional) with *Valentine,* Sec. 3, II supra (prohibition against distribution of commercial leaflets upheld). Does (should) the *holding* of *Valentine* survive *Virginia Pharmacy?* Does *Discovery Network* settle the issue?[e]

(c) *Linmark* held it unconstitutional for a locality to prohibit "For Sale" signs on residential property. Similarly, the Court has held it unconstitutional to prohibit property owners from displaying political signs at their residences. *Ladue v. Gilleo,* 512 U.S. 43, 114 S.Ct. 2038, 129 L.Ed.2d 36 (1994). After *Linmark, Ladue,* and *Discovery Network,* would it be unconstitutional to prohibit signs on residential property that advertise goods and services sold elsewhere?

---

20. Metromedia, Inc. v. San Diego, 453 U.S. 490, 101 S.Ct. 2882, 69 L.Ed.2d 800 (1981), upon which the city heavily relies, is not to the contrary. In that case, a plurality of the Court found as a permissible restriction on commercial speech a city ordinance that, for the most part, banned outdoor "offsite" advertising billboards, but permitted "onsite" advertising signs identifying the owner of the premises and the goods sold or manufactured on the site. Unlike this case, which involves discrimination between commercial and noncommercial speech, the "offsite-onsite" distinction involved disparate treatment of two types of commercial speech. Only the onsite signs served both the commercial and public interest in guiding potential visitors to their intended destinations; moreover, the plurality concluded that a "city may believe that offsite advertising, with its periodically changing content, presents a more acute problem than does onsite advertising." Neither of these bases has any application to the disparate treatment of news racks in this case.

The Chief Justice is correct that seven Justices in the Metromedia case were of the view that San Diego could completely ban offsite commercial billboards for reasons unrelated to the content of those billboards. Those seven Justices did not say, however, that San Diego could distinguish between commercial and noncommercial offsite billboards that cause the same esthetic and safety concerns. That question was not presented in Metromedia, for the regulation at issue in that case did not draw a distinction between commercial and noncommercial offsite billboards; with a few exceptions, it essentially banned all offsite billboards.

d. Rehnquist, C.J., joined by White & Thomas, JJ., dissented.

e. For relevant commentary on the normative issues, see C. Edwin Baker, *Commercial Speech: A Problem in the Theory of Freedom,* 62 Iowa L.Rev. 1 (1976); Martin Redish, *The First Amendment in the Marketplace: Commercial Speech and the Values of Free Expression,* 39 Geo.Wash.L.Rev. 429 (1971); Martin Redish, *The Value of Free Speech,* 130 U.Pa.L.Rev. 591 (1982); Steven Shiffrin, *The First Amendment and Economic Regulation: Away From a General Theory of the First Amendment,* 78 Nw. U.L.Rev. 1212, 1220, 1276–82 (1983).

In CENTRAL HUDSON GAS & ELEC. CORP. v. PUBLIC SERV. COMM'N, 447 U.S. 557, 100 S.Ct. 2343, 65 L.Ed.2d 341 (1980), the Court, per POWELL, J., characterized the prior commercial speech cases as embracing a special test: "In commercial speech cases, then, a four-part analysis has developed. At the outset, we must determine whether the expression is protected by the First Amendment. For commercial speech to come within that provision, it at least must concern lawful activity and not be misleading. Next, we ask whether the asserted governmental interest is substantial. If both inquiries yield positive answers, we must determine whether the regulation directly advances the governmental interest asserted, and whether it is not more extensive than is necessary to serve that interest." Sixteen years later, the members of the Court raised issues about the strength of the test and the circumstances in which it should apply.

44 LIQUORMART, INC. v. RHODE ISLAND

517 U.S. 484, 116 S.Ct. 1495, 134 L.Ed.2d 711 (1996).

JUSTICE STEVENS announced the judgment of the Court and delivered the opinion of the Court with respect to Parts I, II, VII,[a] and VIII,[b] an opinion with respect to Parts III and V, in which JUSTICE KENNEDY, JUSTICE SOUTER, and JUSTICE GINSBURG join, an opinion with respect to Part VI, in which JUSTICE KENNEDY, JUSTICE THOMAS, and JUSTICE GINSBURG join, and an opinion with respect to Part IV, in which JUSTICE KENNEDY and JUSTICE GINSBURG join. * * *

I.   In 1956, the Rhode Island Legislature enacted two separate prohibitions against advertising the retail price of alcoholic beverages. The first applies to vendors licensed in Rhode Island as well as to out-of-state manufacturers, wholesalers, and shippers. It prohibits them from "advertising in any manner whatsoever" the price of any alcoholic beverage offered for sale in the State; the only exception is for price tags or signs displayed with the merchandise within licensed premises and not visible from the street. The second statute applies to the Rhode Island news media. It contains a categorical prohibition against the publication or broadcast of any advertisements—even those referring to sales in other States—that "make reference to the price of any alcoholic beverages." * * *

III.   Advertising has been a part of our culture throughout our history. Even in colonial days, the public relied on "commercial speech" for vital information about the market. Early newspapers displayed advertisements for goods and services on their front pages, and town criers called out prices in public squares. Indeed, commercial messages played such a central role in public life prior to the Founding that Benjamin Franklin authored his early defense of a free press in support of his decision to print, of all things, an advertisement for voyages to Barbados.

In accord with the role that commercial messages have long played, the law has developed to ensure that advertising provides consumers with accurate information about the availability of goods and services. In the early years, the common law, and later, statutes, served the consumers' interest in the receipt of accurate information in the commercial market by prohibiting fraudulent and misleading advertising. It was not until the 1970's, however, that this Court held

---

a. Scalia, Kennedy, Souter, Thomas, and Ginsburg, JJ., joined parts I, II, and VII of the Stevens, J., opinion. Section VII concluded that the twenty-first amendment does not qualify the first. The same conclusion was reached in

O'Connor, J.'s concurring opinion joined by Rehnquist, C.J., Souter and Breyer, JJ.

b. Scalia, Kennedy, Souter, and Ginsburg, JJ., joined part VIII of the Stevens, J.'s opinion.

that the First Amendment protected the dissemination of truthful and nonmis-leading commercial messages about lawful products and services. See generally Alex Kozinski & Stuart Banner, *The Anti–History and Pre–History of Commercial Speech*, 71 Texas L.Rev. 747 (1993). * * *

[O]ur early cases uniformly struck down several broadly based bans on truthful, nonmisleading commercial speech, each of which served ends unrelated to consumer protection.[8] Indeed, one of those cases [*Linmark*] expressly likened the rationale that *Virginia Pharmacy* employed to the one that Justice Brandeis adopted in his concurrence in *Whitney v. California*[:] "the remedy to be applied is more speech, not enforced silence. Only an emergency can justify repression." * * *

At the same time, our early cases recognized that the State may regulate some types of commercial advertising more freely than other forms of protected speech. * * *

In *Central Hudson*, we took stock of our developing commercial speech jurisprudence. In that case, we considered a regulation "completely" banning all promotional advertising by electric utilities. Our decision acknowledged the special features of commercial speech but identified the serious First Amendment con-cerns that attend blanket advertising prohibitions that do not protect consumers from commercial harms.[c]

Five Members of the Court recognized that the state interest in the conserva-tion of energy was substantial, and that there was "an immediate connection between advertising and demand for electricity." Nevertheless, they concluded that the regulation was invalid because the Commission had failed to make a showing that a more limited speech regulation would not have adequately served the State's interest.

In reaching its conclusion, the majority explained that although the special nature of commercial speech may require less than strict review of its regulation, special concerns arise from "regulations that entirely suppress commercial speech in order to pursue a nonspeech-related policy." Id. n. 9. In those circumstances, "a ban on speech could screen from public view the underlying governmental policy." As a result, the Court concluded that "special care" should attend the review of such blanket bans, and it pointedly remarked that "in recent years this Court has not approved a blanket ban on commercial speech unless the speech itself was flawed in some way, either because it was deceptive or related to unlawful activity."[10]

---

8. See *Bates* (ban on lawyer advertising); *Carey* (ban on contraceptive advertising); *Linmark* (ban on "For Sale" signs); *Virginia Bd. of Pharmacy* (ban on prescription drug prices); *Bigelow* (ban on abortion advertising). Al-though *Linmark* involved a prohibition against a particular means of advertising the sale of one's home, we treated the restriction as if it were a complete ban because it did not leave open "satisfactory" alternative channels of communication.

c. *Central Hudson* referred to commercial speech as "expression related solely to the eco-nomic interests of the speaker and its audi-ence." Was the speech in *Central Hudson* sole-ly in the economic interests of the speaker and

its audience? Is the *Central Hudson* locution broader or narrower than the category of pro-moting a commercial transaction? Reconsider this question in connection with the *Green-moss* case, Sec. 3, III infra.

10. The Justices concurring in the judg-ment adopted a somewhat broader view. They expressed "doubt whether suppression of infor-mation concerning the availability and price of a legally offered product is ever a permissible way for the State to 'dampen' the demand for or use of the product." Indeed, Justice Black-mun believed that even "though 'commercial' speech is involved, such a regulation strikes at the heart of the First Amendment."

IV. [W]hen a State entirely prohibits the dissemination of truthful, nonmisleading commercial messages for reasons unrelated to the preservation of a fair bargaining process, there is far less reason to depart from the rigorous review that the First Amendment generally demands. * * *

The special dangers that attend complete bans on truthful, nonmisleading commercial speech cannot be explained away by appeals to the "commonsense distinctions" that exist between commercial and noncommercial speech. Regulations that suppress the truth are no less troubling because they target objectively verifiable information, nor are they less effective because they aim at durable messages. As a result, neither the "greater objectivity" nor the "greater hardiness" of truthful, nonmisleading commercial speech justifies reviewing its complete suppression with added deference. * * *

Precisely because bans against truthful, nonmisleading commercial speech rarely seek to protect consumers from either deception or overreaching, they usually rest solely on the offensive assumption that the public will respond "irrationally" to the truth. The First Amendment directs us to be especially skeptical of regulations that seek to keep people in the dark for what the government perceives to be their own good.[d]

V. [Although] the record suggests that the price advertising ban may have some impact on the purchasing patterns of temperate drinkers of modest means, the State has presented no evidence to suggest that its speech prohibition will significantly reduce market-wide consumption. Indeed, the District Court's considered and uncontradicted finding on this point is directly to the contrary. Moreover, the evidence suggests that the abusive drinker will probably not be deterred by a marginal price increase, and that the true alcoholic may simply reduce his purchases of other necessities. * * *

As is evident, any conclusion that elimination of the ban would significantly increase alcohol consumption would require us to engage in the sort of "speculation or conjecture" that is an unacceptable means of demonstrating that a restriction on commercial speech directly advances the State's asserted interest. Such speculation certainly does not suffice when the State takes aim at accurate commercial information for paternalistic ends.

The State also cannot satisfy the requirement that its restriction on speech be no more extensive than necessary. It is perfectly obvious that alternative forms of regulation that would not involve any restriction on speech would be more likely to achieve the State's goal of promoting temperance. As the State's own expert conceded, higher prices can be maintained either by direct regulation or by increased taxation. Per capita purchases could be limited as is the case with prescription drugs. Even educational campaigns focused on the problems of excessive, or even moderate, drinking might prove to be more effective.

As a result, even under the less than strict standard that generally applies in commercial speech cases, the State has failed to establish a "reasonable fit" between its abridgment of speech and its temperance goal. *Board of Trustees v. Fox*, 492 U.S. 469, 109 S.Ct. 3028, 106 L.Ed.2d 388 (1989);[e] see also *Rubin v.*

---

d. See William Van Alstyne, *Quo Vadis, Posadas?*, 25 N.Ky.L.Rev. 505 (1998).

e. *Fox*, per Scalia, J., joined by Rehnquist, C.J., White, Stevens, O'Connor, and Kennedy, JJ., in the course of considering a provision that operated to bar commercial organizations from making sales demonstrations in students'

dormitory rooms, held that the *Central Hudson* test did not require government to foreclose the possibility of all less restrictive alternatives. The university sought to promote an educational rather than a commercial atmosphere and to prevent commercial exploitation. Scalia, J., characterized these interests as sub-

Coors Brewing Co., 514 U.S. 476, 115 S.Ct. 1585, 131 L.Ed.2d 532 (1995)(explaining that defects in a federal ban on alcohol advertising are "further highlighted by the availability of alternatives that would prove less intrusive to the First Amendment's protections for commercial speech").[f] It necessarily follows that the price advertising ban cannot survive the more stringent constitutional review that *Central Hudson* itself concluded was appropriate for the complete suppression of truthful, nonmisleading commercial speech.

VI. The State responds by arguing that it merely exercised appropriate "legislative judgment" in determining that a price advertising ban would best promote temperance. Relying on the *Central Hudson* analysis set forth in *Posadas de Puerto Rico Associates v. Tourism Co. of P. R.*, 478 U.S. 328, 106 S.Ct. 2968, 92 L.Ed.2d 266 (1986), and *United States v. Edge Broadcasting Co.*, 509 U.S. 418, 113 S.Ct. 2696, 125 L.Ed.2d 345 (1993), Rhode Island first argues that, because expert opinions as to the effectiveness of the price advertising ban "go both ways," the Court of Appeals correctly concluded that the ban constituted a "reasonable choice" by the legislature. The State next contends that precedent requires us to give particular deference to that legislative choice because the State could, if it chose, ban the sale of alcoholic beverages outright. See *Posadas*. Finally, the State argues that deference is appropriate because alcoholic beverages are so-called "vice" products. We consider each of these contentions in turn.

The State's first argument fails to justify the speech prohibition at issue. Our commercial speech cases recognize some room for the exercise of legislative judgment. See *Metromedia*. However, Rhode Island errs in concluding that *Edge* and *Posadas* establish the degree of deference that its decision to impose a price advertising ban warrants.

In *Edge*, we upheld a federal statute that permitted only those broadcasters located in States that had legalized lotteries to air lottery advertising. The statute was designed to regulate advertising about an activity that had been deemed illegal in the jurisdiction in which the broadcaster was located. Here, by contrast, the commercial speech ban targets information about entirely lawful behavior.[g]

Posadas is more directly relevant. There, a five-Member majority held that, under the *Central Hudson* test, it was "up to the legislature" to choose to reduce gambling by suppressing in-state casino advertising rather than engaging in

---

stantial, but stated that it was enough if the fit between means and ends were "reasonable." It did not need to be "perfect." Like time, place, and manner regulations, however, the relationship between means and ends had to be "narrowly tailored to achieve the desired objective." Under that standard, as interpreted, government may not " 'burden substantially more speech than is necessary to further the government's legitimate interest,' " but need not foreclose "all conceivable alternatives." Scalia, J., argued that to have a more demanding test in commercial speech than that used for time, place, and manner regulations would be inappropriate because time, place, and manner regulations can apply to political speech.

f. *Rubin* held that a federal provision prohibiting the display of alcoholic content on beer labels violated the first amendment. The Court argued among other things that the overall federal scheme was irrational in that it prohibited alcoholic beverage advertising from men-

tioning alcoholic content in many circumstances and required disclosures of alcoholic content in the labeling of wines in some circumstances.

g. *Edge* upheld federal legislation prohibiting the broadcast of lottery advertising if the broadcaster were located in a state that does not permit lotteries even in circumstances where 92% of the broadcaster's audience resided in a state that permitted lotteries and where the advertisement was for the lottery in the state where it was legal.

Greater New Orleans Broadcasting v. United States, 527 U.S. 173, 119 S.Ct. 1923, 144 L.Ed.2d 161 (1999), held that the congressional ban on the broadcasting of lottery information could not constitutionally be applied to advertisements of casino gambling when the broadcaster was located in a state where such gambling was legal. In addition, as in *Rubin*, fn. f, the Court objected to the lack of rationale for many of the exceptions to the legislation.

educational speech. Rhode Island argues that this logic demonstrates the constitutionality of its own decision to ban price advertising in lieu of raising taxes or employing some other less speech-restrictive means of promoting temperance.

The reasoning in *Posadas* does support the State's argument, but, on reflection, we are now persuaded that *Posadas* erroneously performed the First Amendment analysis. The casino advertising ban was designed to keep truthful, nonmisleading speech from members of the public for fear that they would be more likely to gamble if they received it. * * *

Because the 5–to–4 decision in *Posadas* marked such a sharp break from our prior precedent, and because it concerned a constitutional question about which this Court is the final arbiter, we decline to give force to its highly deferential approach.

Instead, in keeping with our prior holdings, we conclude that a state legislature does not have the broad discretion to suppress truthful, nonmisleading information for paternalistic purposes that the *Posadas* majority was willing to tolerate. * * *

We also cannot accept the State's second contention, which is premised entirely on the "greater-includes-the-lesser" reasoning endorsed toward the end of the majority's opinion in *Posadas*. [The] majority concluded that it would "surely be a strange constitutional doctrine which would concede to the legislature the authority to totally ban a product or activity, but deny to the legislature the authority to forbid the stimulation of demand for the product or activity through advertising on behalf of those who would profit from such increased demand." * * *

Although we do not dispute the proposition that greater powers include lesser ones, we fail to see how that syllogism requires the conclusion that the State's power to regulate commercial activity is "greater" than its power to ban truthful, nonmisleading commercial speech. Contrary to the assumption made in *Posadas*, we think it quite clear that banning speech may sometimes prove far more intrusive than banning conduct. As a venerable proverb teaches, it may prove more injurious to prevent people from teaching others how to fish than to prevent fish from being sold.[19] Similarly, a local ordinance banning bicycle lessons may curtail freedom far more than one that prohibits bicycle riding within city limits. In short, we reject the assumption that words are necessarily less vital to freedom than actions, or that logic somehow proves that the power to prohibit an activity is necessarily "greater" than the power to suppress speech about it.

As a matter of First Amendment doctrine, the *Posadas* syllogism is even less defensible. The text of the First Amendment makes clear that the Constitution presumes that attempts to regulate speech are more dangerous than attempts to regulate conduct.

[J]ust as it is perfectly clear that Rhode Island could not ban all obscene liquor ads except those that advocated temperance, we think it equally clear that its power to ban the sale of liquor entirely does not include a power to censor all advertisements that contain accurate and nonmisleading information about the price of the product. As the entire Court apparently now agrees, the statements in the *Posadas* opinion on which Rhode Island relies are no longer persuasive.

---

19. "Give a man a fish, and you feed him for a day. Teach a man to fish, and you feed him for a lifetime." *The International Thesau-* *rus of Quotations* 646 (compiled by R. Tripp 1970).

Finally, we find unpersuasive the State's contention that, under *Posadas* and *Edge*, the price advertising ban should be upheld because it targets commercial speech that pertains to a "vice" activity.

[T]he scope of any "vice" exception to the protection afforded by the First Amendment would be difficult, if not impossible, to define. Almost any product that poses some threat to public health or public morals might reasonably be characterized by a state legislature as relating to "vice activity". Such characterization, however, is anomalous when applied to products such as alcoholic beverages, lottery tickets, or playing cards, that may be lawfully purchased on the open market.[h] The recognition of such an exception would also have the unfortunate consequence of either allowing state legislatures to justify censorship by the simple expedient of placing the "vice" label on selected lawful activities, or requiring the federal courts to establish a federal common law of vice. * * *

VIII.   Because Rhode Island has failed to carry its heavy burden of justifying its complete ban on price advertising, we conclude that R.I. Gen. Laws §§ 3–8–7 and 3–8–8.1, as well as Regulation 32 of the Rhode Island Liquor Control Administration, abridge speech in violation of the First Amendment as made applicable to the States by the Due Process Clause of the Fourteenth Amendment. * * *

JUSTICE SCALIA, concurring in part and concurring in the judgment.

I share Justice Thomas's discomfort with the *Central Hudson* test, which seems to me to have nothing more than policy intuition to support it. I also share Justice Stevens' aversion towards paternalistic governmental policies that prevent men and women from hearing facts that might not be good for them. On the other hand, it would also be paternalism for us to prevent the people of the States from enacting laws that we consider paternalistic, unless we have good reason to believe that the Constitution itself forbids them. I will take my guidance as to what the Constitution forbids, with regard to a text as indeterminate as the First Amendment's preservation of "the freedom of speech," and where the core offense of suppressing particular political ideas is not at issue, from the long accepted practices of the American people.

The briefs and arguments of the parties in the present case provide no illumination on that point; understandably so, since both sides accepted *Central Hudson*. The amicus brief on behalf of the American Advertising Federation et al. did examine various expressions of view at the time the First Amendment was adopted; they are consistent with First Amendment protection for commercial speech, but certainly not dispositive. I consider more relevant the state legislative practices prevalent at the time the First Amendment was adopted, since almost all of the States had free-speech constitutional guarantees of their own, whose meaning was not likely to have been different from the federal constitutional provision derived from them. Perhaps more relevant still are the state legislative practices at the time the Fourteenth Amendment was adopted, since it is most improbable that that adoption was meant to overturn any existing national consensus regarding free speech. Indeed, it is rare that any nationwide practice would develop contrary to a proper understanding of the First Amendment itself—

---

h. For material relevant to the prohibition of tobacco advertising, see Steven H. Shiffrin, *Dissent, Injustice, and the Meanings of America* ch. 2 (1999); Kathleen M. Sullivan, *Cheap Spirits, Cigarettes, and Free Speech: The Implications of 44 Liquormart*, 1996 Sup.Ct. Rev. 123 (1996); Martin H. Redish, *Tobacco Advertising and the First Amendment*, 81 Ia. L.Rev. 589 (1996); Sylvia Law, *Addiction, Autonomy, and Advertising*, 77 Iowa L.Rev. 909, 932 (1992); Daniel Lowenstein, *"Too Much Puff": Persuasion, Paternalism, and Commercial Speech*, 56 U.Cin.L.Rev. 1205, 1238 (1988).

for which reason I think also relevant any national consensus that had formed regarding state regulation of advertising after the Fourteenth Amendment, and before this Court's entry into the field. The parties and their amici provide no evidence on these points.

Since I do not believe we have before us the wherewithal to declare *Central Hudson* wrong—or at least the wherewithal to say what ought to replace it—I must resolve this case in accord with our existing jurisprudence, which [would] prohibit the challenged regulation. [A]ccordingly [I] join Parts I, II, VII, and VIII of Justice Stevens' opinion.

JUSTICE THOMAS, concurring in Parts I, II, VI, and VII, and concurring in the judgment.

In cases such as this, in which the government's asserted interest is to keep legal users of a product or service ignorant in order to manipulate their choices in the marketplace, the balancing test adopted in *Central Hudson* should not be applied, in my view. Rather, such an "interest" is per se illegitimate and can no more justify regulation of "commercial" speech than it can justify regulation of "noncommercial" speech. * * *

Although the Court took a sudden turn away from *Virginia Pharmacy Bd.* in *Central Hudson*, it has never explained why manipulating the choices of consumers by keeping them ignorant is more legitimate when the ignorance is maintained through suppression of "commercial" speech than when the same ignorance is maintained through suppression of "noncommercial" speech. * * *

JUSTICE O'CONNOR, with whom THE CHIEF JUSTICE, JUSTICE SOUTER, and JUSTICE BREYER join, concurring in the judgment. * * *

I agree with the Court that Rhode Island's price-advertising ban is invalid. I would resolve this case more narrowly, however, by applying our established *Central Hudson* test to determine whether this commercial-speech regulation survives First Amendment scrutiny. * * *

The fit between Rhode Island's method and [its goal of reducing consumption] is not reasonable. If the target is simply higher prices generally to discourage consumption, the regulation imposes too great, and unnecessary, a prohibition on speech in order to achieve it. The State has other methods at its disposal—methods that would more directly accomplish this stated goal without intruding on sellers' ability to provide truthful, nonmisleading information to customers. [A] tax, for example, is not normally very difficult to administer and would have a far more certain and direct effect on prices, without any restriction on speech. The principal opinion suggests further alternatives, such as limiting per capita purchases or conducting an educational campaign about the dangers of alcohol consumption. The ready availability of such alternatives—at least some of which would far more effectively achieve Rhode Island's only professed goal, at comparatively small additional administrative cost—demonstrates that the fit between ends and means is not narrowly tailored. Too, this regulation prevents sellers of alcohol from communicating price information anywhere but at the point of purchase. No channels exist at all to permit them to publicize the price of their products.

Respondents point for support to *Posadas*. The closer look that we have required since *Posadas* comports better with the purpose of the analysis set out in *Central Hudson*, by requiring the State to show that the speech restriction directly advances its interest and is narrowly tailored. Under such a closer look, Rhode Island's price-advertising ban clearly fails to pass muster.

Because Rhode Island's regulation fails even the less stringent standard set out in *Central Hudson*, nothing here requires adoption of a new analysis for the evaluation of commercial speech regulation. [Because] we need go no further, I would not here undertake the question whether the test we have employed since *Central Hudson* should be displaced. * * *

Notes and Questions

1. Consider Kathleen M. Sullivan, *Cheap Spirits, Cigarettes, and Free Speech: The Implications of 44 Liquormart,* 1996 Sup.Ct. Rev. 123, 160 (1996): "A plurality [is] willing to move commercial speech somewhat closer to the core of the First Amendment applying strict scrutiny to paternalistic interventions between speaker and listener for the listener's own good. It remains to be seen whether this group of Justices would extend that approach to all content-based commercial speech regulations, whether a fifth or more will join them, and whether such a move would prompt any change in the Court's currently exceptional treatment of false and misleading commercial speech." Should the category "commercial speech" be abandoned altogether?

2. Consider Akhil Reed Amar, *Intratextualism,* 112 Harv. L.Rev. 747, 810 (1999): "The Justices are beginning to detach the First Amendment from democracy and graft it onto property, moving from free speech to free markets."

III. PRIVATE SPEECH

Before studying *Dun & Bradstreet*, below, review *Gertz*, Sec. 1, II, C supra.

Dun & Bradstreet, Inc., a credit reporting agency, falsely and negligently reported to five of its subscribers that Greenmoss Builders, Inc. had filed a petition for bankruptcy and also negligently misrepresented Greenmoss' assets and liabilities. In the ensuing defamation action, Greenmoss recovered $50,000 in compensatory damages and $300,000 in punitive damages. Dun & Bradstreet argued that, under *Gertz*, its first amendment rights had been violated because presumed and punitive damages had been imposed without instructions requiring a showing of *New York Times* malice. Greenmoss argued that the *Gertz* protections did not extend to non-media defendants and, in any event, did not extend to commercial speech. DUN & BRADSTREET, INC. v. GREENMOSS BUILDERS, INC., 472 U.S. 749, 105 S.Ct. 2939, 86 L.Ed.2d 593 (1985), rejected Dun & Bradstreet's contention, but there was no opinion of the Court. The common theme of the five justices siding with Greenmoss was that the first amendment places less value on "private" speech than upon "public" speech.

POWELL, J., joined by Rehnquist and O'Connor, JJ., noted that the Vermont Supreme Court below had held "as a matter of federal constitutional law" that "the media protections outlined in *Gertz* are inapplicable to nonmedia defamation actions." In affirming, Powell, J., stated that his reasons were "different from those relied upon by the Vermont Supreme Court": "Like every other case in which this Court has found constitutional limits to state defamation laws, *Gertz* involved expression on a matter of undoubted public concern. * * *

"We have never considered whether the *Gertz* balance obtains when the defamatory statements involve no issue of public concern. To make this determination, we must employ the approach approved in *Gertz* and balance the State's interest in compensating private individuals for injury to their reputation against the First Amendment interest in protecting this type of expression. This state interest is identical to the one weighed in *Gertz*. * * *

"The First Amendment interest, on the other hand, is less important than the one weighed in *Gertz*. We have long recognized that not all speech is of equal First Amendment importance.[5] It is speech on 'matters of public concern' that is 'at the heart of the First Amendment's protection.' [In] contrast, speech on matters of purely private concern is of less First Amendment concern. As a number of state courts, including the court below, have recognized, the role of the Constitution in regulating state libel law is far more limited when the concerns that activated *New York Times* and *Gertz* are absent.[6] In such a case, '[t]here is no threat to the free and robust debate of public issues; there is no potential interference with a meaningful dialogue of ideas concerning self-government; and there is no threat of liability causing a reaction of self-censorship by the press. The facts of the present case are wholly without the First Amendment concerns with which the Supreme Court of the United States has been struggling.' *Harley-Davidson Motorsports, Inc. v. Markley*, 279 Or. 361, 366, 568 P.2d 1359, 1363 (1977).

"While such speech is not totally unprotected by the First Amendment, see *Connick v. Myers* [Sec. 9, II infra], its protections are less stringent. [In] light of the reduced constitutional value of speech involving no matters of public concern, we hold that the state interest adequately supports awards of presumed and punitive damages—even absent a showing of 'actual malice.'[7]

"The only remaining issue is whether petitioner's credit report involved a matter of public concern. In a related context, we have held that '[w]hether [speech] addresses a matter of public concern must be determined by [the expression's] content, form, and context [as] revealed by the whole record.'

---

5. This Court on many occasions has recognized that certain kinds of speech are less central to the interests of the First Amendment than others. Obscene speech and "fighting words" long have been accorded no protection. *Roth; Chaplinsky*. In the area of protected speech, the most prominent example of reduced protection for certain kinds of speech concerns commercial speech. Such speech, we have noted, occupies a "subordinate position in the scale of First Amendment values." *Ohralik*. * * *

Other areas of the law provide further examples. In *Ohralik* we noted that there are "[n]umerous examples [of] communications that are regulated without offending the First Amendment, such as the exchange of information about securities, * * * corporate proxy statements, [the] exchange of price and production information among competitors, [and] employers' threats of retaliation for the labor activities of employees." Yet similar regulation of political speech is subject to the most rigorous scrutiny. Likewise, while the power of the State to license lawyers, psychiatrists, and public school teachers—all of whom speak for a living—is unquestioned, this Court has held that a law requiring licensing of union organizers is unconstitutional under the First Amendment. *Thomas v. Collins*, [Sec. 4, I, A infra]; see also *Rosenbloom v. Metromedia* (opinion of Brennan, J.) ("the determinant whether the

First Amendment applies to state libel actions is whether the utterance involved concerns an issue of public or general concern").

6. As one commentator has remarked with respect to "the case of a commercial supplier of credit information that defames a person applying for credit"—the case before us today— "If the first amendment requirements outlined in *Gertz* apply, there is something clearly wrong with the first amendment or with *Gertz*." Steven Shiffrin, *The First Amendment and Economic Regulation: Away From a General Theory of the First Amendment*, 78 Nw. L.Rev. 1212, 1268 (1983).

7. The dissent, purporting to apply the same balancing test that we do today, concludes that even speech on purely private matters is entitled to the protections of *Gertz*. * * *

The dissent's "balance" [would] lead to the protection of all libels—no matter how attenuated their constitutional interest. If the dissent were the law, a woman of impeccable character who was branded a "whore" by a jealous neighbor would have no effective recourse unless she could prove "actual malice" by clear and convincing evidence. This is not malice in the ordinary sense, but in the more demanding sense of *New York Times*. The dissent would, in effect, constitutionalize the entire common law of libel.

Connick. These factors indicate that petitioner's credit report concerns no public issue.[8] It was speech solely in the individual interest of the speaker and its specific business audience. Cf. *Central Hudson*. This particular interest warrants no special protection when—as in this case—the speech is wholly false and clearly damaging to the victim's business reputation. Moreover, since the credit report was made available to only five subscribers, who, under the terms of the subscription agreement, could not disseminate it further, it cannot be said that the report involves any 'strong interest in the free flow of commercial information.' *Virginia Pharmacy*. There is simply no credible argument that this type of credit reporting requires special protection to ensure that 'debate on public issues [will] be uninhibited, robust, and wide-open.' *New York Times*.

"In addition, the speech here, like advertising, is hardy and unlikely to be deterred by incidental state regulation. See *Virginia Pharmacy*. It is solely motivated by the desire for profit, which, we have noted, is a force less likely to be deterred than others. Arguably, the reporting here was also more objectively verifiable than speech deserving of greater protection. In any case, the market provides a powerful incentive to a credit reporting agency to be accurate, since false credit reporting is of no use to creditors. Thus, any incremental 'chilling' effect of libel suits would be of decreased significance.

"We conclude that permitting recovery of presumed and punitive damages in defamation cases absent a showing of 'actual malice' does not violate the First Amendment when the defamatory statements do not involve matters of public concern."

Although expressing the view that *Gertz* should be overruled and that the *New York Times* malice definition should be reconsidered, BURGER, C.J., concurring, stated that: "The single question before the Court today is whether *Gertz* applies to this case. The plurality opinion holds that *Gertz* does not apply because, unlike the challenged expression in *Gertz,* the alleged defamatory expression in this case does not relate to a matter of public concern. I agree that *Gertz* is limited to circumstances in which the alleged defamatory expression concerns a matter of general public importance, and that the expression in question here relates to a matter of essentially private concern. I therefore agree with the plurality opinion to the extent that it holds that *Gertz* is inapplicable in this case for the two reasons indicated. No more is needed to dispose of the present case."

WHITE, J., who had dissented in *Gertz*, was prepared to overrule that case or to limit it, but he disagreed with Powell, J.'s, suggestion that the plurality's resolution of the case was faithful to *Gertz*:

"It is interesting that Justice Powell declines to follow the *Gertz* approach in this case. I had thought that the decision in *Gertz* was intended to reach cases that involve any false statements of fact injurious to reputation, whether the statement is made privately or publicly and whether or not it implicates a matter of public importance. Justice Powell, however, distinguishes *Gertz* as a case that involved a matter of public concern, an element absent here. Wisely, in my view, Justice Powell does not rest his application of a different rule here on a distinction drawn

---

8. The dissent suggests that our holding today leaves all credit reporting subject to reduced First Amendment protection. This is incorrect. The protection to be accorded a particular credit report depends on whether the report's "content, form, and context" indicate that it concerns a public matter. We also do not hold, as the dissent suggests we do, that the report is subject to reduced constitutional protection because it constitutes economic or commercial speech. We discuss such speech, along with advertising, only to show how many of the same concerns that argue in favor of reduced constitutional protection in those areas apply here as well.

between media and non-media defendants. On that issue, I agree with Justice Brennan that the First Amendment gives no more protection to the press in defamation suits than it does to others exercising their freedom of speech. None of our cases affords such a distinction; to the contrary, the Court has rejected it at every turn. It should be rejected again, particularly in this context, since it makes no sense to give the most protection to those publishers who reach the most readers and therefore pollute the channels of communication with the most misinformation and do the most damage to private reputation. If *Gertz* is to be distinguished from this case, on the ground that it applies only where the allegedly false publication deals with a matter of general or public importance, then where the false publication does not deal with such a matter, the common-law rules would apply whether the defendant is a member of the media or other public disseminator or a non-media individual publishing privately. Although Justice Powell speaks only of the inapplicability of the *Gertz* rule with respect to presumed and punitive damages, it must be that the *Gertz* requirement of some kind of fault on the part of the defendant is also inapplicable in cases such as this. * * *

"The question before us is whether *Gertz* is to be applied in this case. For either of two reasons, I believe that it should not. First, I am unreconciled to the *Gertz* holding and believe that it should be overruled. Second, as Justice Powell indicates, the defamatory publication in this case does not deal with a matter of public importance."

BRENNAN, J., joined by Marshall, Blackmun and Stevens, JJ., dissented: "This case involves a difficult question of the proper application of *Gertz* to credit reporting—a type of speech at some remove from that which first gave rise to explicit First Amendment restrictions on state defamation law—and has produced a diversity of considered opinions, none of which speaks for the Court. Justice Powell's plurality opinion affirming the judgment below would not apply the *Gertz* limitations on presumed and punitive damages [because] the speech involved a subject of purely private concern and was circulated to an extremely limited audience. * * * Justice White also would affirm; he would not apply *Gertz* to this case on the ground that the subject matter of the publication does not deal with a matter of general or public importance. The Chief Justice apparently agrees with Justice White. The four who join this opinion would reverse the judgment of the Vermont Supreme Court. We believe that, although protection of the type of expression at issue is admittedly not the 'central meaning of the First Amendment,' *Gertz* makes clear that the First Amendment nonetheless requires restraints on presumed and punitive damage awards for this expression. * * *

"[Respondent urged that *Gertz* be restricted] to cases in which the defendant is a 'media' entity. Such a distinction is irreconcilable with the fundamental First Amendment principle that '[t]he inherent worth [of] speech in terms of its capacity for informing the public does not depend upon the identity of its source, whether corporation, association, union, or individual.' *First National Bank v. Bellotti* [Sec. 10 infra]. First Amendment difficulties lurk in the definitional questions such an approach would generate. And the distinction would likely be born an anachronism.[7] Perhaps most importantly, the argument that *Gertz* should be limited to the media misapprehends our cases. We protect the press to ensure the vitality of First Amendment guarantees. This solicitude implies no endorse-

---

7. Owing to transformations in the technological and economic structure of the communications industry, there has been an increasing convergence of what might be labeled "media" and "nonmedia."

ment of the principle that speakers other than the press deserve lesser First Amendment protection. * * *

"The free speech guarantee gives each citizen an equal right to self-expression and to participation in self-government. [Accordingly,] at least six Members of this Court (the four who join this opinion and Justice White and The Chief Justice) agree today that, in the context of defamation law, the rights of the institutional media are no greater and no less than those enjoyed by other individuals or organizations engaged in the same activities.[10] * * *

"Purporting to 'employ the approach approved in *Gertz,*' Justice Powell balances the state interest in protecting private reputation against the First Amendment interest in protecting expression on matters not of public concern.[11]

"The five Members of the Court voting to affirm the damage award in this case have provided almost no guidance as to what constitutes a protected 'matter of public concern.' Justice White offers nothing at all, but his opinion does indicate that the distinction turns on solely the subject matter of the expression and not on the extent or conditions of dissemination of that expression. Justice Powell adumbrates a rationale that would appear to focus primarily on subject matter.[12] The opinion relies on the fact that the speech at issue was 'solely in the individual interest of the speaker and its *business* audience.' Analogizing explicitly to advertising, the opinion also states that credit reporting is 'hardy' and 'solely motivated by the desire for profit.' These two strains of analysis suggest that Justice Powell is excluding the subject matter of credit reports from 'matters of public concern' because the speech is predominantly in the realm of matters of economic concern."

Brennan, J., pointed to precedents (particularly labor cases) protecting speech on economic matters and argued that, "the breadth of this protection evinces recognition that freedom of expression is not only essential to check tyranny and foster self-government but also intrinsic to individual liberty and dignity and instrumental in society's search for truth."

Moreover, he emphasized the importance of credit reporting: "The credit reporting of Dun & Bradstreet falls within any reasonable definition of 'public concern' consistent with our precedents. Justice Powell's reliance on the fact that Dun & Bradstreet publishes credit reports 'for profit' is wholly unwarranted.

---

10. Justice Powell's opinion does not expressly reject the media/nonmedia distinction, but does expressly decline to apply that distinction to resolve this case.

11. One searches *Gertz* in vain for a single word to support the proposition that limits on presumed and punitive damages obtained only when speech involved matters of public concern. *Gertz* could not have been grounded in such a premise. Distrust of placing in the courts the power to decide what speech was of public concern was precisely the rationale *Gertz* offered for rejecting the *Rosenbloom* plurality approach. * * *

12. Justice Powell also appears to rely in part on the fact that communication was limited and confidential. Given that his analysis also relies on the subject matter of the credit report, it is difficult to decipher exactly what role the nature and extent of dissemination plays in Justice Powell's analysis. But because

the subject matter of the expression at issue is properly understood as a matter of public concern, it may well be that this element of confidentiality is crucial to the outcome as far as Justice Powell's opinion is concerned. In other words, it may be that Justice Powell thinks this particular expression could not contribute to public welfare because the public generally does not receive it. This factor does not suffice to save the analysis. See n. 18 infra.

[In fn. 18, Brennan, J., indicated that, "Dun & Bradstreet doubtless provides thousands of credit reports to thousands of subscribers who receive the information pursuant to the same strictures imposed on the recipients in this case. As a systemic matter, therefore, today's decision diminishes the free flow of information because Dun & Bradstreet will generally be made more reticent in providing information to all its subscribers."]

Time and again we have made clear that speech loses none of its constitutional protection 'even though it is carried in a form that is "sold" for profit.' *Virginia Pharmacy*. More importantly, an announcement of the bankruptcy of a local company is information of potentially great concern to residents of the community where the company is [located]. And knowledge about solvency and the effect and prevalence of bankruptcy certainly would inform citizen opinions about questions of economic regulation. It is difficult to suggest that a bankruptcy is not a subject matter of public concern when federal law requires invocation of judicial mechanisms to effectuate it and makes the fact of the bankruptcy a matter of public record. * * *

"Even if the subject matter of credit reporting were properly considered—in the terms of Justice White and Justice Powell—as purely a matter of private discourse, this speech would fall well within the range of valuable expression for which the First Amendment demands protection. Much expression that does not directly involve public issues receives significant protection. Our cases do permit some diminution in the degree of protection afforded one category of speech about economic or commercial matters. 'Commercial speech'—defined as advertisements that 'do no more than propose a commercial transaction'—may be more closely regulated than other types of speech. [Credit] reporting is not 'commercial speech' as this Court has defined the term.

"[In] *every* case in which we have permitted more extensive state regulation on the basis of a commercial speech rationale—the speech being regulated was pure advertising—an offer to buy or sell goods and services or encouraging such buying and selling. Credit reports are not commercial advertisements for a good or service or a proposal to buy or sell such a product. We have been extremely chary about extending the 'commercial speech' doctrine beyond this narrowly circumscribed category of advertising because often vitally important speech will be uttered to advance economic interests and because the profit motive making such speech hardy dissipates rapidly when the speech is not advertising."[a]

Finally, Brennan, J., argued that even if credit reports were characterized as commercial speech, "unrestrained" presumed and punitive damages would violate the commercial speech requirement that "the regulatory means chosen be narrowly tailored so as to avoid any unnecessary chilling of protected expression. [Accordingly,] Greenmoss Builders should be permitted to recover for any actual damage it can show resulted from Dun & Bradstreet's negligently false credit report, but should be required to show actual malice to receive presumed or punitive damages."

Notes and Questions

1. Which of the following are "private" according to the opinions of Powell, J., Burger, C.J., and White, J.? (a) a report in the *Wall Street Journal* that Greenmoss has gone bankrupt; (b) a confidential report by Dun & Bradstreet to a bank that a famous politician has poor credit. Would it be different if the subject of the report were an actor? (c) a statement in the campus newspaper or by one student to another that a law professor is an alcoholic. Would it make a difference if the law professor was being considered for a Supreme Court appointment?

a. Brennan, J., cited *Consolidated Edison*, Sec. 10 infra, which invalidated a regulation that prohibited a utility company from inserting its views on "controversial issues of public policy" into its monthly electrical bill mailings. The mailing that prompted the regulation advocated nuclear power.

Consider the relationship between the public/private focus of the *Greenmoss* decision and the "public controversy" aspect of the public figure definition. If the speech does not relate to a "public" controversy, can it be "public" within the terms of *Greenmoss*? See Rodney Smolla, *Law of Defamation* 3–15 (1986). Reconsider *Time, Inc. v. Firestone*, Sec. 1, II, C supra.[b]

Finally, does it matter why the D & B subscribers received the information about Greenmoss? Suppose, for investment or insurance purposes, the subscribers had asked for reports on all aspects of the construction industry in Vermont? Compare *Lowe v. SEC*, Sec. 4, III infra.

2. What standard should apply to employers who make negative statements about former employees? Should employers be liable to a subsequently injured person if they fail to disclose an individual's sexual or violent misconduct? Should they be required to disclose such conduct? If they are required to disclose such conduct, is a "good faith" standard appropriate? See Susan Oliver, *Opening the Channels of Communication Among Employers*, 33 Val.U.L.Rev. 687 (1999); J. Hoult Verkerke, *Legal Regulation of Employment Reference Practices*, 65 U.Chi. L.Rev. 111 (1998).

3. What standard should be applied to publicly disseminated defamatory comments made about apples or eggs?[c]

4. Should the focus of the decision have been commercial speech instead of private speech? Would an expansion of the commercial speech definition have been preferable to the promotion of ad hoc decisionmaking about the nature of "private" speech? Consider Shiffrin, *The First Amendment and Economic Regulation: Away From A General Theory of the First Amendment*, 78 Nw.U.L.Rev. 1212, 1269 n. 327 (1983): "[D]rawing lines based on underlying first amendment values is a far cry from sending out the judiciary on a general ad hoc expedition to separate matters of general public interest from matters that are not. A commitment to segregate certain commercial speech from *Gertz* protection is not a commitment to general ad hoc determinations."

5. According to Powell, J., in fn. 5, are the *Ohralik* examples, i.e., exchange of information about securities, corporate proxy statements and the like, examples of protected speech subject to regulation? In what sense, are those examples of communication protected? What is the significance of Powell, J.'s suggestion that they are something other than commercial speech?[d] Where do those examples fit into Brennan, J.'s view of the first amendment? For general discussion, see Shiffrin, note 2 supra; Nicholas Wolfson, *The First Amendment and the SEC*, 20

---

b. For discussion of the different meanings of public and private speech, see Schauer, *"Private" Speech and the "Private" Forum: Givhan v. Western Line School District*, 1979 Sup.Ct. Rev. 217. Compare Michael Perry, *Freedom of Expression: An Essay on Theory and Doctrine*, 78 Nw.U.L.Rev. 1137 (1983) (denying any meaningful distinction between personal and political decisions). See generally Symposium, *The Public/Private Distinction*, 130 U.Pa. L.Rev. 1289 (1982); Risa Lieberwitz, *Freedom of Speech in Public Sector Employment: The Deconstitutionalization of the Public Sector Workplace*, 19 U.C.Davis L.Rev. 597 (1986); Toni Massaro, *Significant Silences: Freedom of Speech in the Public Sector Workplace*, 61 S.Cal.L.Rev. 1, 68–76 (1987). Comment, *A Conflict in the Public Interest*, 31 Santa Clara

L.Rev. 997 (1991). For commentary on the question of whether Gertz should extend to non-media defendants see e.g. sources cited in note 1 after *Gertz*, Sec. 1, II, C supra.

c. Ronald K.L. Collins, *Free Speech, Food Libel, & The First Amendment * * * in Ohio*, 26 Ohio N.U. L.Rev. 1 (2000); Howard M. Wasserman, *Two Degrees of Speech Protection: Free Speech Through the Prism of Agricultural Disparagement Laws*, 8 Wm. & Mary Bill Rts. J. 323 (2000).

d. Consider *Board of Trustees v. Fox*, Sec. 3, II supra (dictum stating that attorneys or tutors dispensing advice for a fee is not commercial speech and strongly suggesting that regulations prohibiting such speech in college dormitories may be unconstitutional).

Conn.L.Rev. 265 (1988). See also Comment, *A Political Speech Exception to the Regulation of Proxy Solicitations,* 86 Colum.L.Rev. 1453 (1986).

IV. CONCEIVING AND RECONCEIVING THE STRUCTURE OF FIRST AMENDMENT DOCTRINE: HATE SPEECH REVISITED—AGAIN

R.A.V. v. ST. PAUL

505 U.S. 377, 112 S.Ct. 2538, 120 L.Ed.2d 305 (1992).

JUSTICE SCALIA delivered the opinion of the Court.

In the predawn hours of June 21, 1990, petitioner and several other teenagers allegedly assembled a crudely-made cross by taping together broken chair legs. They then allegedly burned the cross inside the fenced yard of a black family that lived across the street from the house where petitioner was staying. Although this conduct could have been punished under any of a number of laws, one of the two provisions under which respondent city of St. Paul chose to charge petitioner (then a juvenile) was the St. Paul Bias–Motivated Crime Ordinance, which provides: "Whoever places on public or private property a symbol, object, appellation, characterization or graffiti, including, but not limited to, a burning cross or Nazi swastika, which one knows or has reasonable grounds to know arouses anger, alarm or resentment in others on the basis of race, color, creed, religion or gender commits disorderly conduct and shall be guilty of a misdemeanor." * * *

I. [W]e accept the Minnesota Supreme Court's authoritative statement that the ordinance reaches only those expressions that constitute "fighting words" within the meaning of Chaplinsky. [W]e nonetheless conclude that the ordinance is facially unconstitutional in that it prohibits otherwise permitted speech solely on the basis of the subjects the speech addresses.

[From] 1791 to the present, our society, like other free but civilized societies, has permitted restrictions upon the content of speech in a few limited areas, which are "of such slight social value as a step to truth that any benefit that may be derived from them is clearly outweighed by the social interest in order and morality." *Chaplinsky.* * * *

We have sometimes said that these categories of expression are "not within the area of constitutionally protected speech," *Roth; Beauharnais; Chaplinsky;* or that the "protection of the First Amendment does not extend" to them, *Bose Corp. v. Consumers Union of United States, Inc.* [Sec. 1, II, B supra]; *Sable Communications of Cal., Inc. v. FCC* [Sec. 8, II supra]. Such statements must be taken in context, however, and are no more literally true than is the occasionally repeated shorthand characterizing obscenity "as not being speech at all," Cass Sunstein, *Pornography and the First Amendment,* 1986 Duke L.J. 589, 615, n. 146. What they mean is that these areas of speech can, consistently with the First Amendment, be regulated *because of their constitutionally proscribable content* (obscenity, defamation, etc.)—not that they are categories of speech entirely invisible to the Constitution, so that they may be made the vehicles for content discrimination unrelated to their distinctively proscribable content. Thus, the government may proscribe libel; but it may not make the further content discrimination of proscribing *only* libel critical of the government. * * *

Our cases surely do not establish the proposition that the First Amendment imposes no obstacle whatsoever to regulation of particular instances of such proscribable expression, so that the government "may regulate [them] freely,"

(White, J., concurring in judgment). That would mean that a city council could enact an ordinance prohibiting only those legally obscene works that contain criticism of the city government or, indeed, that do not include endorsement of the city government. Such a simplistic, all-or-nothing-at-all approach to First Amendment protection is at odds with common sense and with our jurisprudence as well.[1] It is not true that "fighting words" have at most a "de minimis" expressive content or that their content is *in all respects* "worthless and undeserving of constitutional protection"; sometimes they are quite expressive indeed. We have not said that they constitute "*no* part of the expression of ideas," but only that they constitute "no *essential* part of any exposition of ideas." *Chaplinsky.*

The proposition that a particular instance of speech can be proscribable on the basis of one feature (e.g., obscenity) but not on the basis of another (e.g., opposition to the city government) is commonplace, and has found application in many contexts. We have long held, for example, that nonverbal expressive activity can be banned because of the action it entails, but not because of the ideas it expresses—so that burning a flag in violation of an ordinance against outdoor fires could be punishable, whereas burning a flag in violation of an ordinance against dishonoring the flag is not. See *Johnson.* See also *Barnes* (Scalia, J., concurring in judgment) (Souter, J., concurring in judgment); *O'Brien.* Similarly, we have upheld reasonable "time, place, or manner" restrictions, but only if they are "justified without reference to the content of the regulated speech." *Ward;* see also *Clark* (noting that the *O'Brien* test differs little from the standard applied to time, place, or manner restrictions). And just as the power to proscribe particular speech on the basis of a noncontent element (e.g., noise) does not entail the power to proscribe the same speech on the basis of a content element; so also, the power to proscribe it on the basis of *one* content element (e.g., obscenity) does not entail the power to proscribe it on the basis of *other* content elements.

In other words, the exclusion of "fighting words" from the scope of the First Amendment simply means that, for purposes of that Amendment, the unprotected features of the words are, despite their verbal character, essentially a "non-speech" element of communication. Fighting words are thus analogous to a noisy sound truck: Each [is,] a "mode of speech,"; both can be used to convey an idea; but neither has, in and of itself, a claim upon the First Amendment. As with the sound truck, however, so also with fighting words: The government may not regulate use based on hostility—or favoritism—towards the underlying message expressed.

The concurrences describe us as setting forth a new First Amendment principle that prohibition of constitutionally proscribable speech cannot be "underinclusiv[e]" (White, J., concurring in judgment)—a First Amendment "absolutism" whereby "within a particular 'proscribable' category of expression, [a] government must either proscribe *all* speech or no speech at all" (Stevens, J., concurring in judgment). That easy target is of the concurrences' own invention. In our view, the First Amendment imposes not an "underinclusiveness" limitation but a "content discrimination" limitation upon a State's prohibition of proscriba-

---

1. Justice White concedes that a city council cannot prohibit only those legally obscene works that contain criticism of the city government, but asserts that to be the consequence, not of the First Amendment, but of the Equal Protection Clause. Such content-based discrimination would not, he asserts, "be rationally related to a legitimate government interest." But of course the only *reason* that government interest is not a "legitimate" one is that it violates the First Amendment. This Court itself has occasionally fused the First Amendment into the Equal Protection Clause in this fashion, but at least with the acknowledgment (which Justice White cannot afford to make) that the First Amendment underlies its analysis. * * *

ble speech. There is no problem whatever, for example, with a State's prohibiting obscenity (and other forms of proscribable expression) only in certain media or markets, for although that prohibition would be "underinclusive," it would not discriminate on the basis of content. See, e.g., *Sable Communications* (upholding 47 U.S.C. § 223(b)(1) (1988), which prohibits obscene *telephone* communications).

Even the prohibition against content discrimination that we assert the First Amendment requires is not absolute. It applies differently in the context of proscribable speech than in the area of fully protected speech. The rationale of the general prohibition, after all, is that content discrimination "rais[es] the specter that the Government may effectively drive certain ideas or viewpoints from the marketplace," *Simon & Schuster,* [Sec. 1, V infra]. But content discrimination among various instances of a class of proscribable speech often does not pose this threat.

When the basis for the content discrimination consists entirely of the very reason the entire class of speech at issue is proscribable, no significant danger of idea or viewpoint discrimination exists. Such a reason, having been adjudged neutral enough to support exclusion of the entire class of speech from First Amendment protection, is also neutral enough to form the basis of distinction within the class. To illustrate: A State might choose to prohibit only that obscenity which is the most patently offensive *in its prurience*—i.e., that which involves the most lascivious displays of sexual activity. But it may not prohibit, for example, only that obscenity which includes offensive *political* messages. And the Federal Government can criminalize only those threats of violence that are directed against the President, see 18 U.S.C. § 871—since the reasons why threats of violence are outside the First Amendment (protecting individuals from the fear of violence, from the disruption that fear engenders, and from the possibility that the threatened violence will occur) have special force when applied to the person of the President. See *Watts* [Sec. 1, I, D supra] (upholding the facial validity of § 871 because of the "overwhelmin[g] interest in protecting the safety of [the] Chief Executive and in allowing him to perform his duties without interference from threats of physical violence"). But the Federal Government may not criminalize only those threats against the President that mention his policy on aid to inner cities. And to take a final example (one mentioned by Justice Stevens), a State may choose to regulate price advertising in one industry but not in others, because the risk of fraud (one of the characteristics of commercial speech that justifies depriving it of full First Amendment protection) is in its view greater there. Cf. *Morales v. Trans World Airlines, Inc.,* 504 U.S. 374, 112 S.Ct. 2031, 119 L.Ed.2d 157 (1992) (state regulation of airline advertising); *Ohralik* (state regulation of lawyer advertising). But a State may not prohibit only that commercial advertising that depicts men in a demeaning fashion.

Another valid basis for according differential treatment to even a content-defined subclass of proscribable speech is that the subclass happens to be associated with particular "secondary effects" of the speech, so that the regulation is "*justified* without reference to the content of [the] speech," *Renton.* A State could, for example, permit all obscene live performances except those involving minors. Moreover, since words can in some circumstances violate laws directed not against speech but against conduct (a law against treason, for example, is violated by telling the enemy the nation's defense secrets), a particular content-based subcategory of a proscribable class of speech can be swept up incidentally within the reach of a statute directed at conduct rather than speech. Thus, for example, sexually derogatory "fighting words," among other words, may produce a violation of Title VII's general prohibition against sexual discrimination in employment practices. Where the government does not target conduct on the basis of its expressive content, acts are not shielded from regulation merely because they express a discriminatory idea or philosophy.

These bases for distinction refute the proposition that the selectivity of the restriction is "even arguably 'conditioned upon the sovereign's agreement with what a speaker may intend to say.'" There may be other such bases as well. Indeed, to validate such selectivity (where totally proscribable speech is at issue) it may not even be necessary to identify any particular "neutral" basis, so long as the nature of the content discrimination is such that there is no realistic possibility that official suppression of ideas is afoot. (We cannot think of any First Amendment interest that would stand in the way of a State's prohibiting only those obscene motion pictures with blue-eyed actresses.) Save for that limitation, the regulation of "fighting words," like the regulation of noisy speech, may address some offensive instances and leave other, equally offensive, instances alone. See *Posadas*.[2]

II. [Although] the phrase in the ordinance, "arouses anger, alarm or resentment in others," has been limited by the Minnesota Supreme Court's construction to reach only those symbols or displays that amount to "fighting words," the remaining, unmodified terms make clear that the ordinance applies only to "fighting words" that insult, or provoke violence, "on the basis of race, color, creed, religion or gender." Displays containing abusive invective, no matter how vicious or severe, are permissible unless they are addressed to one of the specified disfavored topics. Those who wish to use "fighting words" in connection with other ideas—to express hostility, for example, on the basis of political affiliation, union membership, or homosexuality—are not covered. The First Amendment does not permit St. Paul to impose special prohibitions on those speakers who express views on disfavored subjects.

In its practical operation, moreover, the ordinance goes even beyond mere content discrimination, to actual viewpoint discrimination.[a] Displays containing some words—odious racial epithets, for example—would be prohibited to proponents of all views. But "fighting words" that do not themselves invoke race, color, creed, religion, or gender—aspersions upon a person's mother, for example— would seemingly be usable ad libitum in the placards of those arguing *in favor* of racial, color, etc. tolerance and equality, but could not be used by that speaker's opponents. One could hold up a sign saying, for example, that all "anti-Catholic bigots" are misbegotten; but not that all "papists" are, for that would insult and provoke violence "on the basis of religion." St. Paul has no such authority to license one side of a debate to fight freestyle, while requiring the other to follow Marquis of Queensbury Rules.

What we have here, it must be emphasized, is not a prohibition of fighting words that are directed at certain persons or groups (which would be *facially* valid if it met the requirements of the Equal Protection Clause); but rather, a prohibi-

2. Justice Stevens cites a string of opinions as supporting his assertion that "selective regulation of speech based on content" is not presumptively invalid. [A]ll that their contents establish is what we readily concede: that presumptive invalidity does not mean invariable invalidity, leaving room for such exceptions as reasonable and viewpoint-neutral content-based discrimination in nonpublic forums, or with respect to certain speech by government employees.

a. Consider Alan E. Brownstein, *Alternative Maps for Navigating the First Amendment Maze*, 16 Const. Comm. 101, 105 (1999): "Even an ostensibly innocuous subject matter regulation that prohibits speech about dogs, for example, may directly restrict at least one of the viewpoints that might be expressed in a debate about what constitutes the best household pet."

tion of fighting words that contain (as the Minnesota Supreme Court repeatedly emphasized) messages of "bias-motivated" hatred and in particular, as applied to this case, messages "based on virulent notions of racial supremacy." One must wholeheartedly agree with the Minnesota Supreme Court that "[i]t is the responsibility, even the obligation, of diverse communities to confront such notions in whatever form they appear," but the manner of that confrontation cannot consist of selective limitations upon speech. St. Paul's brief asserts that a general "fighting words" law would not meet the city's needs because only a content-specific measure can communicate to minority groups that the "group hatred" aspect of such speech "is not condoned by the majority." The point of the First Amendment is that majority preferences must be expressed in some fashion other than silencing speech on the basis of its content. * * *

[T]he reason why fighting words are categorically excluded from the protection of the First Amendment is not that their content communicates any particular idea, but that their content embodies a particularly intolerable (and socially unnecessary) *mode* of expressing *whatever* idea the speaker wishes to convey. St. Paul has not singled out an especially offensive mode of expression—it has not, for example, selected for prohibition only those fighting words that communicate ideas in a threatening (as opposed to a merely obnoxious) manner. Rather, it has proscribed fighting words of whatever manner that communicate messages of racial, gender, or religious intolerance. Selectivity of this sort creates the possibility that the city is seeking to handicap the expression of particular ideas.[b]

* * * St. Paul argues that the ordinance [is] aimed only at the "secondary effects" of the speech, see *Renton*. According to St. Paul, the ordinance is intended, "not to impact on [sic] the right of free expression of the accused," but rather to "protect against the victimization of a person or persons who are particularly vulnerable because of their membership in a group that historically has been discriminated against." Even assuming that an ordinance that completely proscribes, rather than merely regulates, a specified category of speech can ever be considered to be directed only to the secondary effects of such speech, it is clear that the St. Paul ordinance is not directed to secondary effects within the meaning of *Renton*. As we said in *Boos* "[l]isteners' reactions to speech are not the type of 'secondary effects' we referred to in *Renton*." * * *[7]

---

b. Consider Steven Shiffrin, *Racist Speech, Outsider Jurisprudence, and the Meaning of America,* 80 Corn.L.Rev. 43, 59, 57 (1994): "If the argument is that a particular subject matter implicates the very risks the category was designed to cover, but in a more severe way, what difference does it make that the category of speech involved is not the most offensive *mode* of speech? The question is whether it causes the most serious form of injury. Since when is the mere possibility of idea discrimination in regulating less than fully protected speech of such enormous constitutional import? [Scalia, J.'s] description of the case law breathes new life into the expression about ostriches hiding their heads in the sand. When the government outlaws threats against the President, advertisements for casino gambling or alcoholic beverages, or the burning of draft cards, or when it engages in a campaign of zoning adult theaters out of neighborhoods, no one but a person wearing a black robe with a strong will to believe or befuddle could possibly suppose that 'there is no realistic possibility that official suppression of ideas is afoot.' Point-of-view discrimination permeates these categories. If point-of-view discrimination were as major an evil as the Court often supposes, one would think that a demanding test would have been applied in some of these cases. But many of the justices presumably share the governmental view that advertisements for casino gambling or alcoholic beverages, the burning of draft cards, and the kind of films shown in adult theaters are not worth much. They either do not look for point-of-view discrimination or devise tests that command them not to look. Perhaps they cannot see the ways in which they themselves discriminate."

7. St. Paul has not argued in this case that the ordinance merely regulates that subclass of fighting words which is most likely to provoke a violent response. But even if one assumes (as appears unlikely) that the categories selected may be so described, that would not justify

Finally, St. Paul [asserts] that the ordinance helps to ensure the basic human rights of members of groups that have historically been subjected to discrimination, including the right of such group members to live in peace where they wish. We do not doubt that these interests are compelling, and that the ordinance can be said to promote them. But the "danger of censorship" presented by a facially content-based statute requires that that weapon be employed only where it is *necessary* to serve the asserted [compelling] interest". The existence of adequate content-neutral alternatives thus "undercut[s] significantly" any defense of such a statute, casting considerable doubt on the government's protestations that "the asserted justification is in fact an accurate description of the purpose and effect of the law." [An] ordinance not limited to the favored topics, for example, would have precisely the same beneficial effect. In fact the only interest distinctively served by the content limitation is that of displaying the city council's special hostility towards the particular biases thus singled out. That is precisely what the First Amendment forbids. The politicians of St. Paul are entitled to express that hostility—but not through the means of imposing unique limitations upon speakers who (however benightedly) disagree. * * *

Let there be no mistake about our belief that burning a cross in someone's front yard is reprehensible. But St. Paul has sufficient means at its disposal to prevent such behavior without adding the First Amendment to the fire. * * *

JUSTICE WHITE, with whom JUSTICE BLACKMUN and JUSTICE O'CONNOR join, and with whom JUSTICE STEVENS joins except as to Part I(A), concurring in the judgment. * * *

I.A. [T]he majority holds that the First Amendment protects those narrow categories of expression long held to be undeserving of First Amendment protection—at least to the extent that lawmakers may not regulate some fighting words more strictly than others because of their content. [Should] the government want to criminalize certain fighting words, the Court now requires it to criminalize all fighting words.

To borrow a phrase, "Such a simplistic, all-or-nothing-at-all approach to First Amendment protection is at odds with common sense and with our jurisprudence as well." It is inconsistent to hold that the government may proscribe an entire category of speech because the content of that speech is evil, but that the government may not treat a subset of that category differently without violating the First Amendment; the content of the subset is by definition worthless and undeserving of constitutional protection.

The majority's observation that fighting words are "quite expressive indeed," is no answer. Fighting words are not a means of exchanging views, rallying supporters, or registering a protest; they are directed against individuals to provoke violence or to inflict injury. Therefore, a ban on all fighting words or on a subset of the fighting words category would restrict only the social evil of hate speech, without creating the danger of driving viewpoints from the marketplace.

Therefore, the Court's insistence on inventing its brand of First Amendment underinclusiveness puzzles me.[3] [T]he Court's new "underbreadth" creation [in-

selective regulation under a "secondary effects" theory. The only reason why such expressive conduct would be especially correlated with violence is that it conveys a particularly odious message; because the "chain of causation" thus *necessarily* "run[s] through the persuasive effect of the expressive component" of

the conduct, it is clear that the St. Paul ordinance regulates on the basis of the "primary" effect of the speech—i.e., its persuasive (or repellent) force.

3. The assortment of exceptions the Court attaches to its rule belies the majority's claim that its new theory is truly concerned with

vites] the continuation of expressive conduct that in this case is evil and worthless in First Amendment terms until the city of St. Paul cures the underbreadth by adding to its ordinance a catch-all phrase such as "and all other fighting words that may constitutionally be subject to this ordinance."

Any contribution of this holding to First Amendment jurisprudence is surely a negative one, since it necessarily signals that expressions of violence, such as the message of intimidation and racial hatred conveyed by burning a cross on someone's lawn, are of sufficient value to outweigh the social interest in order and morality that has traditionally placed such fighting words outside the First Amendment.[4] Indeed, by characterizing fighting words as a form of "debate" the majority legitimates hate speech as a form of public discussion. * * *

B. [Although] the First Amendment does not apply to categories of unprotected speech, such as fighting words, the Equal Protection Clause requires that the regulation of unprotected speech be rationally related to a legitimate government interest. A defamation statute that drew distinctions on the basis of political affiliation or "an ordinance prohibiting only those legally obscene works that contain criticism of the city government" would unquestionably fail rational basis review.[9]

Turning to the St. Paul ordinance and assuming arguendo, as the majority does, that the ordinance is not constitutionally overbroad (but see Part II, infra), there is no question that it would pass equal protection review. The ordinance [reflects] the City's judgment that harms based on race, color, creed, religion, or gender are more pressing public concerns than the harms caused by other fighting words. In light of our Nation's long and painful experience with discrimination, this determination is plainly reasonable. Indeed, as the majority concedes, the interest is compelling.

C. The Court has patched up its argument with an apparently nonexhaustive list of ad hoc exceptions, in what can be viewed either as an attempt to confine the effects of its decision to the facts of this case, or as an effort to anticipate some of the questions that will arise from its radical revision of First Amendment law. * * *

To save the statute [making it illegal to threaten the life of the President], the majority has engrafted the following exception onto its newly announced First Amendment rule: Content-based distinctions may be drawn within an unprotected category of speech if the basis for the distinctions is "the very reason the entire class of speech at issue is proscribable." * * *

The exception swallows the majority's rule. Certainly, it should apply to the St. Paul ordinance, since "the reasons why [fighting words] are outside the First

---

content discrimination. See Part I(C), infra (discussing the exceptions).

4. This does not suggest, of course, that cross burning is always unprotected. Burning a cross at a political rally would almost certainly be protected expression. Cf. *Brandenburg.* But in such a context, the cross burning could not be characterized as a "direct personal insult or an invitation to exchange fisticuffs," *Texas v. Johnson,* to which the fighting words doctrine, see Part II, infra, applies.

9. The majority is mistaken in stating that a ban on obscene works critical of government

would fail equal protection review only because the ban would violate the First Amendment. While decisions such as *Mosley* recognize that First Amendment principles may be relevant to an equal protection claim challenging distinctions that impact on protected expression, there is no basis for linking First and Fourteenth Amendment analysis in a case involving unprotected expression. Certainly, one need not resort to First Amendment principles to conclude that the sort of improbable legislation the majority hypothesizes is based on senseless distinctions.

Amendment [have] special force when applied to [groups that have historically been subjected to discrimination]."

To avoid the result of its own analysis, the Court suggests that fighting words are simply a mode of communication, rather than a content-based category, and that the St. Paul ordinance has not singled out a particularly objectionable mode of communication. Again, the majority confuses the issue. A prohibition on fighting words is not a time, place, or manner restriction; it is a ban on a class of speech that conveys an overriding message of personal injury and imminent violence, a message that is at its ugliest when directed against groups that have long been the targets of discrimination. Accordingly, the ordinance falls within the first exception to the majority's theory.

As its second exception, the Court posits that certain content-based regulations will survive under the new regime if the regulated subclass "happens to be associated with particular 'secondary effects' of the speech" which the majority treats as encompassing instances in which "words [can] violate laws directed not against speech but against conduct.".[11] Again, there is a simple explanation for the Court's eagerness to craft an exception to its new First Amendment rule: Under the general rule the Court applies in this case, Title VII hostile work environment claims would suddenly be unconstitutional.

Title VII * * * regulations covering hostile workplace claims forbid "sexual harassment," which includes "[u]nwelcome sexual advances, requests for sexual favors, and other verbal or physical conduct of a sexual nature" which creates "an intimidating, hostile, or offensive working environment." The regulation does not prohibit workplace harassment generally; it focuses on what the majority would characterize as the "disfavored topi[c]" of sexual harassment. In this way, Title VII is similar to the St. Paul ordinance that the majority condemns because it "impose[s] special prohibitions on those speakers who express views on disfavored subjects." * * *

Hence, the majority's second exception, which the Court indicates would insulate a Title VII hostile work environment claim from an underinclusiveness challenge because "sexually derogatory 'fighting words' [may] produce a violation of Title VII's general prohibition against sexual discrimination in employment practices." But application of this exception to a hostile work environment claim does not hold up under close examination.

First, the hostile work environment regulation is not keyed to the presence or absence of an economic quid pro quo, but to the impact of the speech on the victimized worker. Consequently, the regulation would no more fall within a secondary effects exception than does the St. Paul ordinance. Second, the majority's focus on the statute's general prohibition on discrimination glosses over the language of the specific regulation governing hostile working environment, which reaches beyond any "incidental" effect on speech. If the relationship between the broader statute and specific regulation is sufficient to bring the Title VII regulation within *O'Brien*, then all St. Paul need do to bring its ordinance within this exception is to add some prefatory language concerning discrimination generally.

As the third exception to the Court's theory for deciding this case, the majority concocts a catchall exclusion to protect against unforeseen problems. [It] would apply in cases in which "there is no realistic possibility that official

---

11. The consequences of the majority's conflation of the rarely-used secondary effects standard and the *O'Brien* test for conduct incorporating "speech" and "nonspeech" elements, see generally *O'Brien,* present another question that I fear will haunt us and the lower courts in the aftermath of the majority's opinion.

suppression of ideas is afoot." As I have demonstrated, this case does not concern the official suppression of ideas. The majority discards this notion out-of-hand. * * *

II.   * * * I would decide the case on overbreadth grounds. * * *

In construing the St. Paul ordinance, [I understand the Minnesota Supreme Court] to have ruled that St. Paul may constitutionally prohibit expression that "by its very utterance" causes "anger, alarm or resentment."

Our fighting words cases have made clear, however, that [t]he mere fact that expressive activity causes hurt feelings, offense, or resentment does not render the expression unprotected. See *Eichman; Texas v. Johnson; Falwell.* * * *[13] The ordinance is therefore fatally overbroad and invalid on its face.

JUSTICE BLACKMUN, concurring in the judgment.

[B]y deciding that a State cannot regulate speech that causes great harm unless it also regulates speech that does not (setting law and logic on their heads), the Court seems to abandon the categorical approach, and inevitably to relax the level of scrutiny applicable to content-based laws. [The] simple reality is that the Court will never provide child pornography or cigarette advertising the level of protection customarily granted political speech. If we are forbidden from categorizing, as the Court has done here, we shall reduce protection across the board. * * *

[There] is the possibility that this case will not significantly alter First Amendment jurisprudence, but, instead, will be regarded as an aberration—a case where the Court manipulated doctrine to strike down an ordinance whose premise it opposed, namely, that racial threats and verbal assaults are of greater harm than other fighting words. I fear that the Court has been distracted from its proper mission by the temptation to decide the issue over "politically correct speech" and "cultural diversity," neither of which is presented here. If this is the meaning of today's opinion, it is perhaps even more regrettable.

I see no First Amendment values that are compromised by a law that prohibits hoodlums from driving minorities out of their homes by burning crosses on their lawns, but I see great harm in preventing the people of Saint Paul from specifically punishing the race-based fighting words that so prejudice their community. * * *

JUSTICE STEVENS, with whom JUSTICE WHITE and JUSTICE BLACKMUN join as to Part I, concurring in the judgment. * * *

I.   [Our] First Amendment decisions have created a rough hierarchy in the constitutional protection of speech. Core political speech occupies the highest, most protected position; commercial speech and nonobscene, sexually explicit speech are regarded as a sort of second-class expression; obscenity and fighting words receive the least protection of all. Assuming that the Court is correct that this last class of speech is not wholly "unprotected," it certainly does not follow that fighting words and obscenity receive the *same* sort of protection afforded core political speech. Yet in ruling that proscribable speech cannot be regulated based on subject matter, the Court does just that. Perversely, this gives fighting words

---

13. Although the First Amendment protects offensive speech, it does not require us to be subjected to such expression at all times, in all settings. We have held that such expression may be proscribed when it intrudes upon a "captive audience." And expression may be limited when it merges into conduct. *O'Brien.* However, because of the manner in which the Minnesota Supreme Court construed the St. Paul ordinance, those issues are not before us in this case.

greater protection than is afforded commercial speech. If Congress can prohibit false advertising directed at airline passengers without also prohibiting false advertising directed at bus passengers and if a city can prohibit political advertisements in its buses while allowing other advertisements, it is ironic to hold that a city cannot regulate fighting words based on "race, color, creed, religion or gender" while leaving unregulated fighting words based on "union membership or homosexuality." * * * Perhaps because the Court recognizes these perversities, it quickly offers some ad hoc limitations on its newly extended prohibition on content-based regulations.[c]

[T]he Court recognizes that a State may regulate advertising in one industry but not another because "the risk of fraud (one of the characteristics that justifies depriving [commercial speech] of full First Amendment protection)" in the regulated industry is "greater" than in other industries. "[O]ne of the characteristics that justifies" the constitutional status of fighting words is that such words "by their very utterance inflict injury or tend to incite an immediate breach of the peace." *Chaplinsky.* Certainly a legislature that may determine that the risk of fraud is greater in the legal trade than in the medical trade may determine that the risk of injury or breach of peace created by race-based threats is greater than that created by other threats.

Similarly, it is impossible to reconcile the Court's analysis of the St. Paul ordinance with its recognition that "a prohibition of fighting words that are directed at certain persons or groups [would] be facially valid." A selective proscription of unprotected expression designed to protect "certain persons or groups" (for example, a law proscribing threats directed at the elderly) would be constitutional if it were based on a legitimate determination that the harm created by the regulated expression differs from that created by the unregulated expression (that is, if the elderly are more severely injured by threats than are the nonelderly). Such selective protection is no different from a law prohibiting minors (and only minors) from obtaining obscene publications. St. Paul has determined—reasonably in my judgment—that fighting-word injuries "based on race, color, creed, religion or gender" are qualitatively different and more severe than fighting-word injuries based on other characteristics. Whether the selective proscription of proscribable speech is defined by the protected target ("certain persons or groups") or the basis of the harm (injuries "based on race, color, creed, religion or gender") makes no constitutional difference: what matters is whether the legislature's selection is based on a legitimate, neutral, and reasonable distinction. * * *

III.   [Unlike] the Court, I do not believe that all content-based regulations are equally infirm and presumptively invalid; unlike Justice White, I do not believe that fighting words are wholly unprotected by the First Amendment. To

---

c.   In an earlier passage and footnote of his opinion, Stevens, J., argued: "[W]hile the Court rejects the 'all-or-nothing-at-all' nature of the categorical approach, it promptly embraces an absolutism of its own: within a particular 'proscribable' category of expression, the Court holds, a government must either proscribe all speech or no speech at all. The Court disputes this characterization because it has crafted two exceptions, one for 'certain media or markets' and the other for content discrimination based upon 'the very reason that the entire class of speech at issue is proscribable.' These exceptions are, at best, ill- defined. The Court does not tell us whether, with respect to the former, fighting words such as cross-burning could be proscribed only in certain neighborhoods where the threat of violence is particularly severe, or whether, with respect to the second category, fighting words that create a particular risk of harm (such as a race riot) would be proscribable. The hypothetical and illusory category of these two exceptions persuades me that either my description of the Court's analysis is accurate or that the Court does not in fact mean much of what it says in its opinion."

the contrary, I believe our decisions establish a more complex and subtle analysis, one that considers the content and context of the regulated speech, and the nature and scope of the restriction on speech. * * * Whatever the allure of absolute doctrines, it is just too simple to declare expression "protected" or "unprotected" or to proclaim a regulation "content-based" or "content-neutral."

In applying this analysis to the St. Paul ordinance, I assume arguendo—as the Court does—that the ordinance regulates *only* fighting words and therefore is *not* overbroad. Looking to the content and character of the regulated activity, two things are clear. First, by hypothesis the ordinance bars only low-value speech, namely, fighting words. * * * Second, the ordinance regulates "expressive conduct [rather] than [the] written or spoken word."

Looking to the context of the regulated activity, it is again significant that the statute (by hypothesis) regulates *only* fighting words. Whether words are fighting words is determined in part by their context. Fighting words are not words that merely cause offense; fighting words must be directed at individuals so as to "by their very utterance inflict injury." By hypothesis, then, the St. Paul ordinance restricts speech in confrontational and potentially violent situations. The case at hand is illustrative. The cross-burning in this case—directed as it was to a single African–American family trapped in their home—was nothing more than a crude form of physical intimidation. That this cross-burning sends a message of racial hostility does not automatically endow it with complete constitutional protection.

Significantly, the St. Paul ordinance regulates speech not on the basis of its subject matter or the viewpoint expressed, but rather on the basis of the *harm* the speech causes. * * * Contrary to the Court's suggestion, the ordinance regulates only a subcategory of expression that causes *injuries based on* "race, color, creed, religion or gender," not a subcategory that involves *discussions* that concern those characteristics.[9] * * *

Finally, it is noteworthy that the St. Paul ordinance is, as construed by the Court today, quite narrow. The St. Paul ordinance does not ban all "hate speech," nor does it ban, say, all cross-burnings or all swastika displays. Rather it only bans a subcategory of the already narrow category of fighting words. Such a limited ordinance leaves open and protected a vast range of expression on the subjects of racial, religious, and gender equality. As construed by the Court today, the ordinance certainly does not " 'raise the specter that the Government may effectively drive certain ideas or viewpoints from the marketplace.' " Petitioner is free to burn a cross to announce a rally or to express his views about racial supremacy, he may do so on private property or public land, at day or at night, so long as the burning is not so threatening and so directed at an individual as to "by

---

9. The Court contends that this distinction is "wordplay," reasoning that "[w]hat makes [the harms caused by race-based threats] distinct from [the harms] produced by other fighting words [is] the fact that [the former are] caused by a *distinctive idea*." In this way, the Court concludes that regulating speech based on the injury it causes is no different from regulating speech based on its subject matter. This analysis fundamentally miscomprehends the role of "race, color, creed, religion [and] gender" in contemporary American society. One need look no further than the recent so-cial unrest in the Nation's cities to see that race-based threats may cause more harm to society and to individuals than other threats. Just as the statute prohibiting threats against the President is justifiable because of the place of the President in our social and political order, so a statute prohibiting race-based threats is justifiable because of the place of race in our social and political order. * * * [S]uch a place and is so incendiary an issue, until the Nation matures beyond that condition, laws such as St. Paul's ordinance will remain reasonable and justifiable.

its very [execution] inflict injury." Such a limited proscription scarcely offends the First Amendment. * * *[d]

Notes and Questions

1. At the capital sentencing phase of a murder case, the prosecution sought to introduce evidence that the defendant was a member of the Aryan Brotherhood which was stipulated to be a "white racist gang." DAWSON v. DELAWARE, 503 U.S. 159, 112 S.Ct. 1093, 117 L.Ed.2d 309 (1992), per REHNQUIST, C.J., held that its admission violated the first amendment: "Even if the Delaware group to which Dawson allegedly belongs is racist, those beliefs, so far as we can determine, had no relevance to the sentencing proceeding in this case. For example, the Aryan Brotherhood evidence was not tied in any way to the murder of Dawson's [white] victim. [Moreover], we conclude that Dawson's First Amendment rights were violated by the admission of the Aryan Brotherhood evidence in this case, because the evidence proved nothing more than Dawson's abstract beliefs. [Delaware] might have avoided this problem if it had presented evidence showing more than mere abstract beliefs on Dawson's part, but on the present record one is left with the feeling that the Aryan Brotherhood evidence was employed simply because the jury would find these beliefs morally reprehensible."

THOMAS, J., dissented: "Dawson introduced mitigating character evidence that he had acted kindly toward his family. The stipulation tended to undercut this showing by suggesting that Dawson's kindness did not extend to members of other racial groups. Although we do not sit in judgment of the morality of particular creeds, we cannot bend traditional concepts of relevance to exempt the antisocial."

WISCONSIN v. MITCHELL, 508 U.S. 476, 113 S.Ct. 2194, 124 L.Ed.2d 436 (1993), per REHNQUIST, C.J., found no first amendment violation when Wisconsin permitted a sentence for aggravated battery to be enhanced on the ground that the white victim had been selected because of his race. The Court observed that, unlike *R.A.V.*, the Wisconsin statute was aimed at conduct, not speech, that a chilling effect on speech was unlikely, that the focus on motive was no different than that employed in anti-discrimination statutes, and that bias-inspired conduct is more likely "to provoke retaliatory crimes, inflict distinct emotional harms on their victims, and incite community unrest." Consistent with *R.A.V.*?[e] After *Mitchell*, could the state "enact a general regulation against the use of fighting words, and then have a sentence enhancement based on racial motivation." See Daniel A. Farber, *The First Amendment* 115 (1998): "There seems to be a

---

d. For background on *R.A.V.*, see Edward Cleary, *Beyond the Burning Cross* (1994). For additional commentary, see Symposium, *Hate Speech After R.A.V.: More Conflict Between Free Speech and Equality,* 18 Wm. Mitchell L.Rev. 889 (1992); Akhil Amar, *The Case of the Missing Amendments,* 106 Harv.L.Rev. 124 (1992); Joshua Cohen, *Freedom of Expression,* 19 Phil. & Pub.Aff. 207 (1993); Elena Kagan, *The Changing Faces of First Amendment Neutrality,* 1992 Sup.Ct.Rev. 29; Elena Kagan, *Regulation of Hate Speech and Pornography After R.A.V.,* 60 U.Chi.L.Rev. 873 (1993); Charles Lawrence, *Crossburning and the Sound of Silence,* 37 Vill.L.Rev. 787 (1992); Shiffrin, supra.

e. See Frederick Lawrence, *Punishing Hate: Bias Crimes Under American Law* (1999); James B. Jacobs & Kimberly Potter, *Hate Crimes, Criminal Law and Identity Politics* (1998); Alon Herel & Gideon Parchomovsky, *On Hate and Equality,* 109 Yale L.J 507 (1999); Alan E. Brownstein, *Rules of Engagement for Cultural Wars,* 29 U.C. Davis L.Rev. 553 (1996); Susan Gellman, *Sticks and Stones Can Put You in Jail, But Can Words Increase Your Sentence?,* 39 U.C.L.A.L.Rev. 333 (1991); See generally Laurence Tribe, *The Mystery of Motive, Private and Public: Some Notes Inspired by the Problems of Hate Crime and Animal Sacrifice,* 1993 Sup.Ct.Rev. 1.

reasonable argument for distinguishing R.A.V. even when the enhancement is applied to a speech-based regulation."[f]

2. Consider Shiffrin, fn. b supra, at 65: "Justice Scalia [maintains] that the rationale of the prohibition against content discrimination is the 'specter that the government may effectively drive certain ideas or viewpoints from the marketplace.' That concern, however, is difficult to take seriously in the context of *R.A.V.* St. Paul prohibited only a small class of 'fighting words,' words which make a slight contribution to truth—just a particular socially unacceptable *mode* of presentation in Justice Scalia's view. It is hard to see how that raises the 'specter that the Government may effectively drive certain ideas or viewpoints from the marketplace.' Even more telling is Justice Scalia's 'content-neutral' alternative to the St. Paul ordinance: a 'pure' fighting words statute, which, he maintains, could serve the valid government interests in protecting basic human rights of members of groups historically subject to discrimination. But this content-neutral alternative would drive the very same ideas and viewpoints (along with others) from the marketplace." Is there a better rationale?

3. Consider Elena Kagan, *Private Speech, Public Purpose: The Role of Governmental Motive in First Amendment Doctrine*, 63 U.Chi.L.Rev. 413 (1996): "[H]alf hidden beneath a swirl of doctrinal formulations, the crux of the dispute between the majority and the concurring opinions concerned the proper understanding of St. Paul's motive in enacting its hate-speech law. The majority understood this motive as purely censorial—a simple desire to blot out ideas of which the government or a majority of its citizens disapproved. The concurring Justices saw something different: an effort by the government, divorced from mere hostility toward ideas, to counter a severe and objectively ascertainable harm caused by (one form of) an idea's expression."

4. In distinguishing Title VII law, Scalia, J., states that if government does not target discriminatory conduct on the basis of its expressive content, government may regulate, apparently without first amendment scrutiny, even if the conduct expresses a discriminatory idea or philosophy. Is this consistent with *O'Brien*? The opinions in *Barnes* other than Scalia, J.'s? Suppose St. Paul outlawed all conduct that tended to create a racially or sexually hostile environment. Consider Richard Fallon, *Sexual Harassment, Content Neutrality, and the First Amendment Dog That Didn't Bark*, 1994 Sup.Ct.Rev. 1, 16: "A statute of this kind, which would restrict the press, political orators, and private citizens engaged in conversation in their homes, would surely offend the First Amendment. Certainly Justice Scalia [does] not believe otherwise." Could St. Paul outlaw racial harassment under Scalia, J.'s rationale and apply it to the facts of *R.A.V.* without first amendment scrutiny?

Are many applications of sexual harassment law problematic under the first amendment?[g]

---

f. California's anti-paparazzi legislation provides stiffer penalties for trespass if the purpose is to photograph or videotape someone without their permission. Constitutional?

g. For a variety of views, see Kent Greenawalt, *Fighting Words* 77–96 (1995); J.M. Balkin, *Free Speech and Hostile Environments*, 99 Colum. L.Rev. 2295 (1999); Kingsley Browne, *Title VII as Censorship: Hostile–Environment Harassment and the First Amendment*, 52 Ohio St.L.J. 481 (1991); Cynthia L. Estlund, *Free-*

dom of Expression in the Workplace and the Problem of Discriminatory Harassment, 75 Texas L.Rev. 687 (1997); Cynthia L. Estlund, *The Architecture of the First Amendment and the Case of Workplace Harassment*, 72 Notre Dame L.Rev. 1361 (1997); Fallon, supra; Jules B. Gerard, *The First Amendment in a Hostile Environment: A Primer on Free Speech and Sexual Harassment*, 68 Notre D.L.Rev. 579 (1995); Linda S. Greene, *Sexual Harassment Law and the First Amendment*, 71 Chi.-Kent

[margin note, top: 1st Amendment was response to]

SECTION 4. PRIOR RESTRAINTS

[left margin notes: restraining speech before it's Published... • Can be unconstitutional even if the form of speech could be lawfully Punished. - Problem w/ means of restriction, not what is being stopped.]

Prior restraint is a technical term in first amendment law. A criminal statute prohibiting all advocacy of violent action would *restrain* speech and would have been enacted *prior* to any restrained communication. The statute would be overbroad, but it would not be a prior restraint. A prior restraint refers only to closely related, distinctive methods of regulating expression that are said to have in common their own peculiar set of evils and problems, in addition to those that accompany most any governmental interference with free expression. "The issue is not whether the government may impose a particular restriction of substance in an area of public expression, such as forbidding obscenity in newspapers, but whether it may do so by a particular method, such as advance screening of newspaper copy. In other words, restrictions which could be validly imposed when enforced by subsequent punishment are, nevertheless, forbidden if attempted by prior restraint." Thomas Emerson, *The Doctrine of Prior Restraint,* 20 Law and Contemp.Prob. 648 (1955).

The classic prior restraints were the English licensing laws which required a license in advance to print any material or to import or to sell any book.[a] One of the questions raised in this chapter concerns the types of government conduct beyond the classic licensing laws that should be characterized as prior restraints. Another concerns the question of when government licensing of speech, press, or assembly should be countenanced. Perhaps, most important, the Section explores the circumstances in which otherwise protected speech may be restrained on an ad hoc basis.

[margin note: Prior to 1925: only Fed, or state constitutions]

I. FOUNDATION CASES

*[margin note: * Jehovas witnesses challenged licence requirement - must get licence to hand out Pamflets.]*

A. LICENSING

[left margin notes: 1st Amend: Congress → not States (14th Amend) • due process - Speech = Press - Cong. Shall make "No Law"]

LOVELL v. GRIFFIN, 303 U.S. 444, 58 S.Ct. 666, 82 L.Ed. 949 (1938), per HUGHES, C.J., invalidated an ordinance prohibiting the distribution of handbooks, advertising or literature within the city of Griffin, Georgia without obtaining written permission of the City Manager: "[T]he ordinance is invalid on its face. Whatever the motive which induced its adoption, its character is such that it strikes at the very foundation of the freedom of the press by subjecting it to license and censorship. The struggle for the freedom of the press was primarily directed against the power of the licensor. It was against that power that John Milton directed his assault by his 'Appeal for the Liberty of Unlicensed Printing.' And the liberty of the press became initially a right to publish '*without* a license what formerly could be published only *with* one.' While this freedom from previous restraint upon publication cannot be regarded as exhausting the guaranty of liberty, the prevention of that restraint was a leading purpose in the

L.Rev. 729 (1995); Susanne Sangree, *Title VII Prohibitions Against Hostile Environment Sexual Harassment and the First Amendment: No Collision in Sight,* 47 Rutgers L.Rev. 461 (1995); Marcy Strauss, *Sexist Speech in the Workplace,* 25 Harv.C.R.–C.L.L.Rev. 1 (1990); Nadine Strossen, *Regulating Workplace Sexual Harassment and Upholding the First Amendment—Avoiding a Collision,* 37 Vill. L.Rev. 757 (1992); Eugene Volokh, *Freedom of Speech and Workplace Harassment,* 39 U.C.L.A.L.Rev. 1791 (1992); Eugene Volokh, *How Harassment*

Law Restricts Free Speech, 47 Rutgers L.Rev. 563 (1995); Eugene Volokh, *What Speech Does "Hostile Work Environment" Harassment Law Restrict?,* 85 Geo. L.J. 627, 647 (1997). See also *Davis v. Monroe County Board of Educ.,* 526 U.S. 629, 119 S.Ct. 1661, 143 L.Ed.2d. 839 (1999) (Kennedy, J., dissenting).

a. For a persuasive chronicling of the abuses in a modern licensing system, see generally Lucas Powe, *American Broadcasting and the First Amendment* (1987).

*[bottom margin notes: * Facially invalid - the Fects of ordinance make it invalid: Prior restraint vs. invalid as applied - have to read into effect of ordinance]*

Problem w/ Prior restraint: Its Breadth, built in bias

adoption of the constitutional provision. Legislation of the type of the ordinance in question would restore the system of license and censorship in its baldest form.

"The liberty of the press is not confined to newspapers and periodicals. It necessarily embraces pamphlets and leaflets. These indeed have been historic weapons in the defense of liberty, as the pamphlets of Thomas Paine and others in our own history abundantly attest. The press in its historic connotation comprehends every sort of publication which affords a vehicle of information and opinion. * * *

"The ordinance cannot be saved because it relates to distribution and not to publication. 'Liberty of circulating is as essential to that freedom as liberty of publishing; indeed, without the circulation, the publication would be of little value.' *Ex parte Jackson,* 96 U.S. (6 Otto) 727, 733, 24 L.Ed. 877 (1877).

"[As] the ordinance is void on its face, it was not necessary for appellant to seek a permit under it. She was entitled to contest its validity in answer to the charge against her."[a]

Notes and Questions

1. *First amendment procedure.* Notice that Lovell would get the benefit of the prior restraint doctrine even if the material she distributed was obscene or otherwise unprotected. In that respect, the prior restraint doctrine is similar to the doctrines of overbreadth and vagueness. For particular concerns that underlie the prior restraint doctrine, consider Thomas Emerson, *The System of Freedom of Expression* 506 (1970): "A system of prior restraint is in many ways more inhibiting than a system of subsequent punishment: It is likely to bring under government scrutiny a far wider range of expression; it shuts off communication before it takes place; suppression by a stroke of the pen is more likely to be applied than suppression through a criminal process; the procedures do not require attention to the safeguards of the criminal process; the system allows less opportunity for public appraisal and criticism; the dynamics of the system drive toward excesses, as the history of all censorship shows."[b]

2. *Scope and character of the doctrine.* What is the vice of the licensing scheme in *Lovell*? Is the concern that like vague statutes it affords undue discretion and potential for abuse? Is the real concern the uncontrolled power of the licensor to deny licenses? Suppose licenses were automatically issued to anyone who applied?

To what extent should the prior restraint doctrine apply to non-press activities? To a licensing ordinance that otherwise forbids soliciting membership in organizations that exact fees of their members? See *Staub v. Baxley,* 355 U.S. 313, 78 S.Ct. 277, 2 L.Ed.2d 302 (1958) (yes). To a licensing ordinance that otherwise prohibits attempts to secure contributions for charitable or religious causes? See *Cantwell v. Connecticut,* 310 U.S. 296, 60 S.Ct. 900, 84 L.Ed. 1213 (1940) (yes).

Should the prior restraint doctrine apply to all aspects of newspaper circulation? See *Lakewood v. Plain Dealer Publishing Co.,* 486 U.S. 750, 108 S.Ct. 2138,

---

a. Cardozo, J., took no part.

b. But see Richard Posner, *Free Speech in an Economic Perspective,* 20 Suff.L.Rev. 1, 13 (1986): "The conventional arguments for why censorship is worse than criminal punishment are little better than plausible (though I think there is at least one good argument)" [observing that speech ordinarily does not produce sufficient damage to justify sifting through massive materials].

100 L.Ed.2d 771 (1988) (invalidating ordinance granting Mayor power to grant or deny annual permits to place newsracks on public property).[c]

Suppose, in the above cases, that the authority of the licensor were confined by narrow, objective, and definite standards or that licenses were automatically issued to anyone who applied. *Hynes v. Mayor,* 425 U.S. 610, 96 S.Ct. 1755, 48 L.Ed.2d 243 (1976), per Burger, C.J., stated in dictum that a municipality could regulate house to house soliciting by requiring advance notice to the police department in order to protect its citizens from crime and undue annoyance: "A narrowly drawn ordinance, that does not vest in municipal officials the undefined power to determine what messages residents will hear, may serve these important interests without running afoul of the First Amendment." But cf. *Thomas v. Collins,* 323 U.S. 516, 65 S.Ct. 315, 89 L.Ed. 430 (1945) (registration requirement for paid union organizers invalid prior restraint); *Talley v. California,* 362 U.S. 60, 80 S.Ct. 536, 4 L.Ed.2d 559 (1960) (ban on anonymous handbills "void on its face," noting that the "obnoxious press licensing law of England, which was also enforced on the Colonies was due in part to the knowledge that exposure of the names of printers, writers and distributors would lessen the circulation of literature critical of the government").

B. INJUNCTIONS

NEAR v. MINNESOTA

283 U.S. 697, 51 S.Ct. 625, 75 L.Ed. 1357 (1931).

CHIEF JUSTICE HUGHES delivered the opinion of the Court.

[The *Saturday Press* published articles charging that through graft and incompetence named public officials failed to expose and punish gangsters responsible for gambling, bootlegging, and racketeering in Minneapolis. It demanded a special grand jury and special prosecutor to deal with the situation and to investigate an alleged attempt to assassinate one of its publishers. Under a statute that authorized abatement of a "malicious, scandalous and defamatory newspaper" the state secured, and its supreme court affirmed, a court order that "abated" the Press and perpetually enjoined the defendants from publishing or circulating "any publication whatsoever which is a malicious, scandalous or defamatory newspaper." The order did not restrain the defendants from operating a newspaper "in harmony with the general welfare."]

The object of the statute is not punishment, in the ordinary sense, but suppression of the offending newspaper. [In] the case of public officers, it is the reiteration of charges of official misconduct, and the fact that the newspaper [is] principally devoted to that purpose, that exposes it to suppression. [T]he operation and effect of the statute [is] that public authorities may bring the owner or publisher of a newspaper or periodical before a judge upon a charge of conducting a business of publishing scandalous and defamatory matter—in particular that the matter consists of charges against public officers of official dereliction—and, unless the owner or publisher is able and disposed to bring competent evidence to satisfy the judge that the charges are true and are published with good motives and for justifiable ends, his newspaper or periodical is suppressed and further publication is made punishable as a contempt. This is of the essence of censorship.

---

c. White, J., joined by Stevens and O'Connor, JJ., dissenting, contended that *Lovell* should apply only if the newspaper had a constitutional right to place newsracks on public sidewalks. Otherwise, the newspaper should be required to show that a denial was based on improper reasons.

The question is whether a statute authorizing such proceedings [is] consistent with the conception of the liberty of the press as historically conceived and guaranteed. [I]t has been generally, if not universally, considered that it is the chief purpose of the guaranty to prevent previous restraints upon publication. The struggle in England, directed against the legislative power of the licenser, resulted in renunciation of the censorship of the press. The liberty deemed to be established was thus described by Blackstone: "The liberty of the press is indeed essential to the nature of a free state; but this consists in laying no *previous* restraints upon publications, and not in freedom from censure for criminal matter when published. Every freeman has an undoubted right to lay what sentiments he pleases before the public; to forbid this, is to destroy the freedom of the press; but if he publishes what is improper, mischievous or illegal, he must take the consequence of his own temerity." [The] criticism upon Blackstone's statement has not been because immunity from previous restraint upon publication has not been regarded as deserving of special emphasis, but chiefly because that immunity cannot be deemed to exhaust the conception of the liberty guaranteed by State and Federal Constitutions.

[T]he protection even as to previous restraint is not absolutely unlimited. But the limitation has been recognized only in exceptional cases. [N]o one would question but that a government might prevent actual obstruction to its recruiting service or the publication of the sailing dates of transports or the number and location of troops. On similar grounds, the primary requirements of decency may be enforced against obscene publications. The security of the community life may be protected against incitements to acts of violence and the overthrow by force of orderly [government].[a] * * *

The fact that for approximately one hundred and fifty years there has been almost an entire absence of attempts to impose previous restraints upon publications relating to the malfeasance of public officers is significant of the deep-seated conviction that such restraints would violate constitutional right. Public officers, whose character and conduct remain open to debate and free discussion in the press, find their remedies for false accusations in actions under libel laws providing for redress and punishment, and not in proceedings to restrain the publication of newspapers and periodicals. [The] fact that the liberty of the press may be abused by miscreant purveyors of scandal does not make any the less necessary the immunity of the press from previous restraint in dealing with official misconduct. Subsequent punishment for such abuses as may exist is the appropriate remedy, consistent with constitutional [privilege].

The statute in question cannot be justified by reason of the fact that the publisher is permitted to show, before injunction issues, that the matter published is true and is published with good motives and for justifiable ends. If such a statute, authorizing suppression and injunction on such a basis, is constitutionally valid, it would be equally permissible for the Legislature to provide that at any time the publisher of any newspaper could be brought before a court, or even an administrative officer (as the constitutional protection may not be regarded as resting on mere procedural details), and required to produce proof of the truth of his publication, or of what he intended to publish and of his motives, or stand

a. For critical commentary on the concessions in *Near*, see Hans Linde, *Courts and Censorship*, 66 Minn.L.Rev. 171 (1981); Jeffery Smith, *Prior Restraint: Original Intentions and Modern Interpretations*, 28 Wm. & M.Rev. 439, 462 (1987). For criticism of the overuse of preliminary injunctions in a variety of intellectual property contexts, see Mark A. Lemley & Eugene Volokh, *Freedom of Speech and Injunctions in Intellectual Property Cases*, 48 Duke L.J. 147 (1998).

enjoined. If this can be done, the Legislature may provide machinery for determining in the complete exercise of its discretion what are justifiable ends and restrain publication accordingly. And it would be but a step to a complete system of censorship.

[For] these reasons we hold the statute, so far as it authorized the proceedings in this action, [to] be an infringement of the liberty of the press guaranteed by the Fourteenth Amendment. * * *

JUSTICE BUTLER (dissenting).

[T]he *previous restraints* referred to by [Blackstone] subjected the press to the arbitrary will of an administrative officer. [The] Minnesota statute does not operate as a *previous* restraint on publication within the proper meaning of that phrase. It does not authorize administrative control in advance such as was formerly exercised by the licensers and censors, but prescribes a remedy to be enforced by a suit in equity. In this case [t]he business and publications unquestionably constitute an abuse of the right of free press. [A]s stated by the state Supreme Court [they] threaten morals, peace, and good order. [The] restraint authorized is only in respect of continuing to do what has been duly adjudged to constitute a nuisance. [It] is fanciful to suggest similarity between the granting or enforcement of the decree authorized by this statute to prevent *further* publication of malicious, scandalous, and defamatory articles and the *previous restraint* upon the press by licensers as referred to by Blackstone and described in the history of the times to which he alludes. * * *

It is well known, as found by the state supreme court, that existing libel laws are inadequate effectively to suppress evils resulting from the kind of business and publications that are shown in this case. The doctrine [of this decision] exposes the peace and good order of every community and the business and private affairs of every individual to the constant and protracted false and malicious assaults of any insolvent publisher who may have purpose and sufficient capacity to contrive and put into effect a scheme or program for oppression, blackmail or extortion. * * *

JUSTICE VAN DEVANTER, JUSTICE McREYNOLDS, and JUSTICE SUTHERLAND concur in this opinion.[b]

Notes and Questions

1. *Near and seditious libel: a misuse of prior restraint? Near* was decided three decades before *New York Times v. Sullivan.* Should the Court have looked to the substance of the regulation rather than its form? Consider John Jeffries, *Rethinking Prior Restraint,* 92 Yale L.J. 409, 416–17 (1983): "In truth, *Near* involved nothing more or less than a repackaged version of the law of seditious libel, and this the majority rightly refused to countenance. Hence, there was pressure, so typical of this doctrine, to cram the law into the disfavored category of prior restraint, even though it in fact functioned very differently from a scheme of official licensing. Here there was no license and no censor, no ex parte determination of what was prohibited, and no suppression of publication based on speculation about what somebody might say. Here the decision to suppress was made by a judge (not a bureaucrat), after adversarial (not ex parte) proceedings, to determine the legal character of what had been (and not what might be) publish-

b. For background, see Fred Friendly, *Minnesota Rag* (1981); Paul Murphy, *Near v.* *Minnesota in the Context of Historical Developments,* 66 Minn.L.Rev. 95, 133–60 (1981).

ed. The only aspect of prior restraint was the incidental fact that the defendants were commanded not to repeat that which they were proved to have done.

"[I]f *Near* reached the right result, does it really matter that it gave the wrong reason? The answer [is that] *Near* has become a prominent feature of the First Amendment landscape—a landmark, as the case is so often called, from which we chart our course to future decisions. [T]he Court has yet to explain (at least in terms that I understand) what it is about an injunction that justifies this independent rule of constitutional disfavor."

Should a court be able to enjoin the continued distribution of material it has finally adjudicated to be unprotected defamation under existing law? Suppose it enjoins the publication of any material that does not comply with the mandates of *New York Times* and *Gertz*?

2. *The collateral bar rule.* Does the collateral bar rule shed light on the relationship between prior restraints and injunctions? That rule insists "that a court order must be obeyed until it is set aside, and that persons subject to the order who disobey it may not defend against the ensuing charge of criminal contempt on the ground that the order was erroneous or even unconstitutional." Stephen Barnett, *The Puzzle of Prior Restraint*, 29 Stan.L.Rev. 539, 552 (1977). WALKER v. BIRMINGHAM, 388 U.S. 307, 87 S.Ct. 1824, 18 L.Ed.2d 1210 (1967) upheld the rule against a first amendment challenge in affirming the contempt conviction of defendants for violating an ex parte injunction issued by an Alabama court enjoining them from engaging in street parades without a municipal permit issued pursuant to the city's parade ordinance. The Court, per STEWART, J., (Warren, C.J., Brennan, Douglas, and Fortas, JJ., dissenting) held that because the petitioners neither moved to dissolve the injunction nor sought to comply with the city's parade ordinance, their claim that the injunction and ordinance were unconstitutional[c] did not need to be considered: "This Court cannot hold that the petitioners were constitutionally free to ignore all the procedures of the law and carry their battle to the streets. [R]espect for judicial process is a small price to pay for the civilizing hand of law, which alone can give abiding meaning to constitutional freedom." Although *Walker* suggested that its holding might be different if the court issuing the injunction lacked jurisdiction or if the injunction were "transparently invalid or had only a frivolous pretense to validity," it held that Alabama's invocation of the collateral bar rule was not itself unconstitutional.

Cf. *Poulos v. New Hampshire,* 345 U.S. 395, 73 S.Ct. 760, 97 L.Ed. 1105 (1953) (claim of arbitrary refusal to issue license for open air meeting need not be entertained when a licensing statute is considered to be valid on its face in circumstance where speaker fails to seek direct judicial relief and proceeds without a license).[d] Does *Poulos* pose considerable danger to first amendment interests because the low visibility of the administrative decision permits easy abridgement of free expression? See Henry Monaghan, *First Amendment "Due Process,"* 83 Harv.L.Rev. 518, 543 (1970). Do *Lovell, Walker,* and *Poulos* fit easily together? Consider Vincent Blasi, *Prior Restraints on Demonstrations*, 68 Mich. L.Rev. 1482, 1555 (1970): "A refuses to apply for a permit; he undertakes a march that could have been prohibited in the first place; he is prosecuted for parading

c. Indeed, the ordinance in question was declared unconstitutional two years later. *Shuttlesworth v. Birmingham*, 394 U.S. 147, 89 S.Ct. 935, 22 L.Ed.2d 162 (1969) (ordinance conferring unbridled discretion to prohibit any

parade or demonstration is unconstitutional prior restraint).

d. For consideration of when licensing statutes for assemblies are valid, see *Cox v. New Hampshire,* Sec. 6, I, A infra.

without a permit under a statute that is defective for overbreadth. B applies for a permit; he is rudely rebuffed by a city official in clear violation of the state permit statute (which is not invalid on its face); he marches anyway in a manner that would be protected by the first amendment, he is prosecuted for parading without a permit. C applies for a permit; he is rudely rebuffed; he notifies city officials that he will march anyway; the officials obtain an injunction against the march; the injunction is overbroad and is also based on a state statute that is overbroad; C marches in a manner ordinarily within his constitutional rights; he is prosecuted for contempt. Under the law as it now stands, A wins, but B and C lose!"

3. *Time, place, and manner regulations.* Should injunctions that impose time, place, or manner regulations in response to proven wrongdoing be subjected to more stringent examination than that ordinarily applied to general regulations imposed by legislative or executive action? See *Madsen v. Women's Health Center,* 512 U.S. 753, 114 S.Ct. 2516, 129 L.Ed.2d 593 (1994).

4. *The commentators, injunctions, and prior restraint.* Should the link between prior restraint doctrine and injunctions depend upon the collateral bar rule? Does the analogy between licensing systems and injunctions hold only in that event? See Owen Fiss, *The Civil Rights Injunction* 30, 69–74 (1978); Barnett, note 2 supra, at 553–54. Should the prior restraint doctrine be wholly inapplicable to injunctions so long as "expedited appellate review allows an immediate opportunity to test the validity of an injunction against speech and only so long as that opportunity is genuinely effective to allow timely publication should the injunction ultimately be adjudged invalid"? Jeffries, note 1 supra, at 433.[e] Indeed should the whole concept of prior restraint be abandoned? Consider id. at 433–34: "In the context of administrative preclearance, talking of prior restraint is unhelpful, though not inapt. A more informative frame of reference would be overbreadth, the doctrine that explicitly identifies why preclearance is specially objectionable. In the context of injunctions, however, the traditional doctrine of prior restraint is not merely unhelpful, but positively misleading. It focuses on a constitutionally inconsequential consideration of form and diverts attention away from the critical substantive issues of First Amendment coverage. The result is a two-pronged danger. On the one hand, vindication of First Amendment freedoms in the name of prior restraint may exaggerate the legitimate reach of official competence to suppress by subsequent punishment. On the other hand, insistence on special disfavor for prior restraints outside the realm of substantive protection under the First Amendment may deny to the government an appropriate choice of means to vindicate legitimate interests. In my view, neither risk is justified by any compelling reason to continue prior restraint as a doctrinally independent category of contemporary First Amendment analysis."[f]

For a nuanced argument that the prior restraint doctrine should apply to injunctions even in those jurisdictions that reject the applicability of the collateral bar rule to first amendment arguments, see Vincent Blasi, *Toward a Theory of Prior Restraint: The Central Linkage,* 66 Minn.L.Rev. 11 (1981). Except in

---

e. For the argument that regulation by injunction is generally more speech protective than regulation via subsequent punishment, see William Mayton, *Toward A Theory of First Amendment Process: Injunctions of Speech, Subsequent Punishment, and the Costs of the Prior Restraint Doctrine,* 67 Corn.L.Rev. 245 (1982). For the contention that this should count in favor of subsequent punishment in many contexts, see Martin Redish, *The Proper*

Role of the Prior Restraint Doctrine in First Amendment Theory, 70 Va.L.Rev. 53, 92–93 (1984).

f. See also Marin Scordato, *Distinction Without a Difference,* 68 N.C.L.Rev. 1 (1989) (generally agreeing with Jeffries but arguing that a small part of prior restraint doctrine should be salvaged).

particular contexts, Professor Blasi does not claim that the chilling effect of injunctions on speech is more severe than those associated with criminal laws and civil liability rules. He does argue that unlike criminal laws and civil liability rules, regulation of speech by licensing and injunctions requires abstract and unduly speculative adjudication, stimulates overuse by regulatory agents, can to some extent distort the way in which audiences perceive the message at issue, and unreasonably implies that the activity of disseminating controversial communications is "a threat to, rather than an integral feature of, the social order." Id. at 85. He argues that many of these factors are aggravated if the collateral bar rule applies and that other undesirable features are added. For example, speakers are forced to reveal planned details about their communication. He concludes that the "concept of prior restraint is coherent at the core." Id. at 93.[g]

II. PRIOR RESTRAINTS, OBSCENITY, AND COMMERCIAL SPEECH

KINGSLEY BOOKS, INC. v. BROWN, 354 U.S. 436, 77 S.Ct. 1325, 1 L.Ed.2d 1469 (1957), per FRANKFURTER, J., upheld a state court decree, issued pursuant to a New York statute, enjoining the publisher from further distribution of 14 booklets the state court found obscene. On appeal to the Supreme Court the publisher challenged only the prior restraint, not the obscenity finding: "The phrase 'prior restraint' is not a self-wielding sword. Nor can it serve as a talismatic test. The duty of closer analysis and critical judgment in applying the thought behind the phrase has thus been authoritatively put by one who brings weighty learning to his support of constitutionally protected liberties: 'What is needed,' writes Professor Paul A. Freund, 'is a pragmatic assessment of its operation in the particular circumstances. The generalization that prior restraint is particularly obnoxious in civil liberties cases must yield to more particularistic analysis.' *The Supreme Court and Civil Liberties*, 4 Vand.L.Rev. 533, 539.

"Wherein does § 22–a differ in its effective operation from the type of statute upheld in *Alberts,* [p. 697 supra]. One would be bold to assert that the in terrorem effect of [criminal] statutes less restrains booksellers in the period before the law strikes than does § 22–a. Instead of requiring the bookseller to dread that the offer for sale of a book may, without prior warning, subject him to a criminal prosecution with the hazard of imprisonment, the civil procedure assures him that such consequences cannot follow unless he ignores a court order specifically directed to him for a prompt and carefully circumscribed determination of the issue of obscenity. Until then, he may keep the book for sale and sell it on his own judgment rather than steer 'nervously among the treacherous shoals.'[a]

"Criminal enforcement and the proceeding under § 22–a interfere with a book's solicitation of the public precisely at the same stage. In each situation the law moves after publication; the book need not in either case have yet passed into the hands of the public. [H]ere as a matter of fact copies of the booklets whose distribution was enjoined had been on sale for several weeks when process was served. In each case the bookseller is put on notice by the complaint that sale of the publication charged with obscenity in the period before trial may subject him

g. See also Daniel A. Farber, *The First Amendment* 48–49 (1998). For detailed criticism of Blasi's position, all in defense of a different core, see Redish, fn. e supra, at 59–75.

a. In fact, § 22–a did not require a civil adjudication before criminal prosecution, as in-

timated by the opinion. The feasibility of such a requirement is considered in William Lockhart, *Escape from the Chill of Uncertainty,* 9 Ga.L.Rev. 533, 569–86 (1975).

to penal consequences. In the one case he may suffer fine and imprisonment for violation of the criminal statute, in the other, for disobedience of the temporary injunction. The bookseller may of course stand his ground and confidently believe that in any judicial proceeding the book could not be condemned as obscene, but both modes of procedure provide an effective deterrent against distribution prior to adjudication of the book's content—the threat of subsequent penalization.[2]"

The Court pointed out that in both criminal misdemeanor prosecutions and injunction proceedings a jury could be called as a matter of discretion, but that defendant did not request a jury trial and did not attack the statute for its failure to require a jury.

"Nor are the consequences of a judicial condemnation for obscenity under § 22–a more restrictive of freedom of expression than the result of conviction for a misdemeanor. In *Alberts,* the defendant was fined $500, sentenced to sixty days in prison, and put on probation for two years on condition that he not violate the obscenity statute. Not only was he completely separated from society for two months but he was also seriously restrained from trafficking in all obscene publications for a considerable time. Appellants, on the other hand, were enjoined from displaying for sale or distributing only the particular booklets theretofore published and adjudged to be obscene. Thus, the restraint upon appellants as merchants in obscenity was narrower than that imposed on *Alberts.*

"Section 22–a's provision for the seizure and destruction of the instruments of ascertained wrongdoing expresses resort to a legal remedy sanctioned by the long history of Anglo–American law. See Oliver Holmes, *The Common Law,* 24–26.

"[It] only remains to say that the difference between *Near* and this case is glaring in fact. The two cases are no less glaringly different when judged by the appropriate criteria of constitutional law. Minnesota empowered its courts to enjoin the dissemination of future issues of a publication because its past issues had been found offensive. In the language of Mr. Chief Justice Hughes, 'This is of the essence of censorship.' As such, it was enough to condemn the statute wholly apart from the fact that the proceeding in *Near* involved not obscenity but matters deemed to be derogatory to a public officer. Unlike *Near,* § 22–a is concerned solely with obscenity and, as authoritatively construed, it studiously withholds restraint upon matters not already published and not yet found to be offensive."[b]

TIMES FILM CORP. v. CHICAGO

365 U.S. 43, 81 S.Ct. 391, 5 L.Ed.2d 403 (1961).

JUSTICE CLARK delivered the opinion of the Court.

Petitioner challenges on constitutional grounds the validity on its face of that portion of § 155–4[1] of the Municipal Code of the City of Chicago which requires

2. This comparison of remedies takes note of the fact that we do not have before us a case where, although the issue of obscenity is ultimately decided in favor of the bookseller, the State nevertheless attempts to punish him for disobedience of the interim injunction. For all we know, New York may impliedly condition the temporary injunction so as not to subject the bookseller to a charge of contempt if he prevails on the issue of obscenity.

b. Warren, C.J., dissented, objecting that the New York law "places the book on trial" without any consideration of its "manner of use." Black and Douglas, JJ., dissented, objecting to a state-wide decree depriving the publisher of separate trials in different communities, and to substituting "punishment by contempt for punishment by jury trial." Brennan, J., dissenting, contended that a jury trial is required to apply properly the *Roth* standard for obscenity.

1. The portion of the section here under attack is as follows: "Such permit shall be granted only after the motion picture film for

submission of all motion pictures for examination prior to their public exhibition. Petitioner is a New York corporation owning the exclusive right to publicly exhibit in Chicago the film known as "Don Juan." It applied for a permit, as Chicago's ordinance required, and tendered the license fee but refused to submit the film for examination. The appropriate city official refused to issue the permit and his order was made final on appeal to the Mayor. The sole ground for denial was petitioner's refusal to submit the film for examination as required. Petitioner then brought this suit seeking injunctive relief ordering the issuance of the permit without submission of the [film]. Its sole ground is that the provision of the ordinance requiring submission of the film constitutes, on its face, a prior restraint.[2] [Admittedly,] the challenged section of the ordinance imposes a previous restraint, and the broad justiciable issue is therefore present as to whether the ambit of constitutional protection includes complete and absolute freedom to exhibit, at least once, any and every kind of motion picture. It is that question alone which we decide.

[T]here is not a word in the record as to the nature and content of "Don Juan." We are left entirely in the dark in this regard, as were the city officials and the other reviewing courts. Petitioner claims that the nature of the film is irrelevant, and that even if this film contains the basest type of pornography, or incitement to riot, or forceful overthrow of orderly government, it may nonetheless be shown without prior submission for examination. The challenge here is to the censor's basic authority; it does not go to any statutory standards employed by the censor or procedural requirements as to the submission of the film. * * *

Petitioner would have us hold that the public exhibition of motion pictures must be allowed under any circumstances. The State's sole remedy, it says, is the invocation of criminal process under the Illinois pornography statute and then only after a transgression. But this position [is] founded upon the claim of absolute privilege against prior restraint under the First Amendment—a claim without sanction in our cases. To illustrate its fallacy, we need only point to one of the "exceptional cases" which Chief Justice Hughes enumerated in *Near*, namely, "the primary requirements of decency [that] may be enforced against obscene publications." Moreover, we later held specifically "that obscenity is not within the area of constitutionally protected speech or press." *Roth*. Chicago emphasizes here its duty to protect its people against the dangers of obscenity in the public exhibition of motion pictures. [It] is not for this Court to limit the State in its selection of the remedy it deems most effective to cope with such a problem, absent, of course, a showing of unreasonable strictures on individual liberty resulting from its application in particular circumstances. * * *

As to what may be decided when a concrete case involving a specific standard provided by this ordinance is presented, we intimate no opinion. [At] this time we

---

which said permit is requested has been produced at the office of the commissioner of police for examination or [censorship]."

2. That portion of § 155-4 of the Code providing standards is as follows: "If a picture or series of pictures, for the showing or exhibition of which an application for a permit is made, is immoral or obscene, or portrays, depravity, criminality, or lack of virtue of a class of citizens of any race, color, creed, or religion and exposes them to contempt, derision, or obloquy, or tends to produce a breach of the peace or riots, or purports to represent any

hanging, lynching, or burning of a human being, it shall be the duty of the commissioner of police to refuse such permit; otherwise it shall be his duty to grant such permit.

"In case the commissioner of police shall refuse to grant a permit as hereinbefore provided, the applicant for the same may appeal to the mayor. Such appeal shall be presented in the same manner as the original application to the commissioner of police. The action of the mayor on any application for a permit shall be final." * * *

say no more than this—that we are dealing only with motion pictures and, even as to them, only in the context of the broadside attack presented on this record.

Affirmed.

CHIEF JUSTICE WARREN, with whom JUSTICE BLACK, JUSTICE DOUGLAS and JUSTICE BRENNAN join, dissenting. * * *

I hesitate to disagree with the Court's formulation of the issue before us, but, with all deference, I must insist that the question presented in this case is *not* whether a motion picture exhibitor has a constitutionally protected, "complete and absolute freedom to exhibit, at least once, any and every kind of motion picture." [The] question here presented is whether the City of Chicago—or, for that matter, any city, any State or the Federal Government—may require all motion picture exhibitors to submit all films to a police chief, mayor or other administrative official, for licensing and censorship prior to public exhibition within the jurisdiction. * * *

The booklets enjoined from distribution in *Kingsley* were concededly obscene. There is no indication that this is true of the moving picture here. This was treated as a particularly crucial distinction. Thus, the Court has suggested that, in times of national emergency, the Government might impose a prior restraint upon "the publication of the sailing dates of transports or the number and location of troops." *Near.* But, surely this is not to suggest that the Government might require that all newspapers be submitted to a censor in order to assist it in preventing such information from reaching print. Yet in this case the Court gives its blessing to the censorship of all motion pictures in order to prevent the exhibition of those it feels to be constitutionally unprotected.

[E]ven if the impact of the motion picture is greater than that of some other media, that fact constitutes no basis for the argument that motion pictures should be subject to greater suppression. This is the traditional argument made in the censor's behalf; this is the argument advanced against newspapers at the time of the invention of the printing press. The argument was ultimately rejected in England, and has consistently been held to be contrary to our Constitution.[a] No compelling reason has been predicated for accepting the contention now. * * *[b]

Notes and Questions

1. Should the producers of *Bambi* be forced to submit their film to show it in a particular city? Should they be forced to pay a license fee? Suppose hundreds of cities adopted the Chicago system? If films must be submitted before exhibition, can a city constitutionally require that books be submitted before distribution? What are the "peculiar problems" associated with films?

2. *Procedural safeguards.* FREEDMAN v. MARYLAND, 380 U.S. 51, 85 S.Ct. 734, 13 L.Ed.2d 649 (1965), per BRENNAN, J., set out procedural safeguards designed to reduce the dangers associated with prior restraints of films. It required that the procedure must "assure a prompt final judicial decision, to minimize the deterrent effect of an interim and possibly erroneous denial of a license," that the censor must promptly institute the proceedings, that the burden

a. For the contention that the argument has in fact received a warm reception in the twentieth century, see Donald Lively, *Fear and the Media: A First Amendment Horror Show,* 69 Minn.L.Rev. 1071 (1985).

b. Douglas, J., joined by Warren, C.J., and Black, J., dissenting, elaborated on the evils connected with systems of censorship.

of proof to show that the speech in question is unprotected must rest on the censor, and that the proceedings be adversarial. The *Freedman* standards have been applied in other contexts. *Blount v. Rizzi,* 400 U.S. 410, 91 S.Ct. 423, 27 L.Ed.2d 498 (1971) (postal stop orders of obscene materials); *United States v. Thirty–Seven Photographs,* 402 U.S. 363, 91 S.Ct. 1400, 28 L.Ed.2d 822 (1971) (customs seizure of obscene materials); *Southeastern Promotions Ltd. v. Conrad,* 420 U.S. 546, 95 S.Ct. 1239, 43 L.Ed.2d 448 (1975) (denial of permit to use municipal theater for the musical, Hair); *Carroll v. President and Commissioners,* 393 U.S. 175, 89 S.Ct. 347, 21 L.Ed.2d 325 (1968) (10 day restraining order against particular rallies or meetings invalid because *ex parte*). But cf. *FW/PBS v. Dallas,* 493 U.S. 215, 110 S.Ct. 596, 107 L.Ed.2d 603 (1990) (suggesting that partial application of *Freedman* standards (dispensing with burden of going to court and burden of proof, but retaining assurance of timely decision making by licensor and prompt judicial review) to ordinance licensing sexually oriented businesses ostensibly without regard to content of films or books would be appropriate). Should the collateral bar rule apply to *Carroll?* Do the *Freedman* standards make the *Times Film* decision palatable?[c] For thorough discussion of the procedural issues, see Henry Monaghan, *First Amendment "Due Process,"* 83 Harv.L.Rev. 518 (1970).

3. *Informal prior restraints.* BANTAM BOOKS, INC. v. SULLIVAN, 372 U.S. 58, 83 S.Ct. 631, 9 L.Ed.2d 584 (1963), per Brennan, J., (Harlan, J. dissenting) held unconstitutional the activities of a government commission that would identify "objectionable" books (some admittedly not obscene), notify the distributor in writing, inform the distributor of the Commission's duty to recommend obscenity prosecutions to the Attorney General and that the Commission's list of objectionable books was distributed to local police departments. The Commission thanked distributors in advance for their "cooperation," and a police officer usually visited the distributor to learn what action had been taken. In characterizing these practices as a system of prior administrative restraints, rather than mere legal advice, the Court observed that it did not mean to foreclose private consultation between law enforcement officers and distributors so long as such consultations were "genuinely undertaken with the purpose of aiding the distributor to comply" with the laws and avoid prosecution. What if the Commission circulated its list to distributors, police and prosecutors without mentioning prosecution? What if the prosecutor circulates a list of sixty books he or she regards as obscene and subject to prosecution?

4. *Comparing obscenity and commercial speech.* To combat deception, could commercial advertising be constitutionally subjected to a *Times Film* regime? Would such a scheme be permissible for advertising via some media, but not others? Reconsider fn. 24 in *Virginia Pharmacy,* p. 809 supra. Should the prohibition on prior restraints be inapplicable to injunctions against commercial advertising? Should *Freedman* standards be required? Should injunctions be permitted against a newspaper that carries unprotected advertising in addition to the advertiser? PITTSBURGH PRESS CO. v. PITTSBURGH COMM'N ON HUMAN RELATIONS, 413 U.S. 376, 93 S.Ct. 2553, 37 L.Ed.2d 669 (1973), per Powell, J., upheld an order forbidding Pittsburgh Press to carry sex-designated "help wanted" ads, except for exempt jobs: "As described by Blackstone, the protection against prior restraint at common law barred only a system of administrative censorship. [While] the Court boldly stepped beyond this narrow doctrine

---

c. For the contention that *Freedman* procedures fail to address the main concern of the prior restraint doctrine, see Martin Redish, *The Proper Role of the Prior Restraint Doctrine in First Amendment Theory,* 70 Va.L.Rev. 53, 75–89 (1984).

in *Near* [it] has never held that all injunctions are impermissible. See *Lorain Journal Co. v. United States,* 342 U.S. 143, 72 S.Ct. 181, 96 L.Ed. 162 (1951).[d] The special vice of a prior restraint is that communication will be suppressed, either directly or by inducing excessive caution in the speaker, before an adequate determination that it is unprotected by the First Amendment.

"The present order does not endanger arguably protected speech. Because the order is based on a continuing course of repetitive conduct, this is not a case in which the Court is asked to speculate as to the effect of publication. Moreover, the order is clear and sweeps no more broadly than necessary. And because no interim relief was granted, the order will not have gone into effect until it was finally determined that the actions of Pittsburgh Press were unprotected."

STEWART, J., joined by Douglas, J., dissented: Putting to one side "the question of governmental power to prevent publication of information that would clearly imperil the military defense of our Nation," "no government agency can tell a newspaper in advance what it can print and what it cannot."[e]

III. LICENSING "PROFESSIONALS": A DICHOTOMY BETWEEN SPEECH AND PRESS?

LOWE v. SEC, 472 U.S. 181, 105 S.Ct. 2557, 86 L.Ed.2d 130 (1985): The Investment Advisors Act of 1940 provides for injunctions and criminal penalties against anyone using the mails in conjunction with the advisory business who is not registered with the SEC or otherwise exempt from registration. The SEC sought an injunction against Lowe and his affiliated businesses primarily alleging that Lowe's registration with the SEC had been properly revoked because of various fraudulent activities,[a] and that by publishing investment newsletters, Lowe was using the mails as an investment advisor. The SEC did not claim that any information in the newsletters had been false or materially misleading or that Lowe had yet profited from the advice tendered. The SEC did contend that Lowe's prior criminal conduct showed his "total lack of fitness" to remain in an occupation with "numerous opportunities for dishonesty and self-dealing." Lowe denied that his newsletters were covered by the act and argued that, in any event, they were protected against registration and restraint under the first amendment.

The Court, per STEVENS, J., denied that Lowe's publication of financial newsletters made him an investment advisor under the act. The Court's interpretation was strongly influenced by first amendment considerations. The doctrine against prior restraints and the notion that freedom of the press includes everything from distributing leaflets to mass circulation of magazines was said to support a "broad reading" of the exclusion "that encompasses any newspaper, business publication, or financial publication provided that two conditions are met. The publication must be 'bona fide,' and it must be 'of regular and general circulation.' Neither of these conditions is defined, but the two qualifications precisely differentiate 'hit and run tipsters' and 'touts' from genuine publishers. Presumably a 'bona fide' publication would be genuine in the sense that it would

---

d. *Lorain* upheld a Sherman Act injunction restraining a newspaper from seeking to monopolize commerce by refusing to carry advertising from merchants who advertised through a competing radio station.

e. Blackmun, J., dissented "for substantially the reasons stated by" Stewart, J. Burger, C.J., dissenting, argued that the majority had mischaracterized the character and interim effect of the Commission's order.

a. For example, during the period that he was giving personal investment advice, Lowe had been convicted of misappropriating funds of a client, tampering with evidence to cover up fraud of a client, and stealing from a bank.

contain disinterested commentary and analysis as opposed to promotional material disseminated by a 'tout.' Moreover, publications with a 'general and regular' circulation would not include 'people who send out bulletins from time to time on the advisability of buying and selling stocks' or 'hit and run tipsters.' Because the content of petitioners' newsletters was completely disinterested, and because they were offered[b] to the general public on a regular schedule, they are described by the plain language of the [exclusion].

"The dangers of fraud, deception, or overreaching that motivated the enactment of the statute are present in personalized communications but are not replicated in publications that are advertised and sold in an open market.[57] To the extent that the chart service contains factual information about past transactions and market trends, and the newsletters contain commentary on general market conditions, there can be no doubt about the protected character of the communications,[58] a matter that concerned Congress when the exclusion was drafted. The content of the publications and the audience to which they are directed in this case reveal the specific limits of the exclusion. As long as the communications between petitioners and their subscribers remain entirely impersonal and do not develop into the kind of fiduciary, person-to-person relationships that were discussed at length in the legislative history of the Act and that are characteristic of investment adviser-client relationships, we believe the publications are, at least presumptively, within the exclusion."[c]

WHITE, J., joined by Burger, C.J., and Rehnquist, J., concurring, argued that the Court's statutory interpretation was "improvident" and "based on a thinly disguised conviction" that the Act was unconstitutional as applied to prohibit publication by unregistered advisors. "[While] purporting not to decide the question, the Court bases its statutory holding in large measure on the assumption that Congress already knew the answer to it when the statute was enacted. The Court thus attributes to the 76th Congress a clairvoyance the Solicitor General and the Second Circuit apparently lack—that is, the ability to predict our constitutional holdings 45 years in advance of our declining to reach them." Finding it necessary to reach the constitutional question, White, J., argued that an injunction against Lowe's publications would violate the first amendment: "The power of government to regulate the professions is not lost whenever the practice of a profession entails speech. The underlying principle was expressed by the Court in *Giboney v. Empire Storage & Ice Co.*, 336 U.S. 490, 69 S.Ct. 684, 93 L.Ed. 834 (1949): 'it has never been deemed an abridgment of freedom of speech or press to make a course of conduct illegal merely because the conduct was in part initiated, evidenced, or carried out by means of language, either spoken, written, or printed.'

b. Lowe's newsletters in fact did not appear according to schedule. White, J., concurring, remarked: "As is evident from the Court's conclusion that petitioner's publications meet the regularity requirement, the Court's construction of the requirement adopts the view of our major law reviews on the issue of regular publication: good intentions are enough."

57. Cf. *Ohralik*. It is significant that the Commission has not established that petitioners have had authority over the funds of subscribers; that petitioners have been delegated decisionmaking authority to handle subscribers' portfolios or accounts; or that there have been individualized, investment-related interactions between petitioners and subscribers.

58. Moreover, because we have squarely held that the expression of opinion about a commercial product such as a loudspeaker is protected by the First Amendment, *Bose Corp.*, Sec. 1, II, B supra, it is difficult to see why the expression of an opinion about a marketable security should not also be protected.

c. Powell, J., took no part.

"Perhaps the most obvious example of a 'speaking profession' that is subject to governmental licensing is the legal profession. Although a lawyer's work is almost entirely devoted to the sort of communicative acts that, viewed in isolation, fall within the First Amendment's protection, we have never doubted that '[a] State can require high standards of qualification, such as good moral character or proficiency in its law, before it admits an applicant to the [bar].' [To] protect investors, the Government insists, it may require that investment advisers, like lawyers, evince the qualities of truth-speaking, honor, discretion, and fiduciary responsibility.

"But the principle that the government may restrict entry into professions and vocations through licensing schemes has never been extended to encompass the licensing of speech per se or of the press. At some point, a measure is no longer a regulation of a profession but a regulation of speech or of the press; beyond that point, the statute must survive the level of scrutiny demanded by the First Amendment." [It] is for us, then, to find some principle by which to answer the question whether the Investment Advisers Act as applied to petitioner operates as a regulation of speech or of professional conduct.

"This is a problem Justice Jackson wrestled with in his concurring opinion in *Thomas v. Collins*. His words are instructive: '[A] rough distinction always exists, I think, which is more shortly illustrated than explained. A state may forbid one without its license to practice law as a vocation, but I think it could not stop an unlicensed person from making a speech about the rights of man or the rights of labor, or any other kind of right, including recommending that his hearers organize to support his views. Likewise, the state may prohibit the pursuit of medicine as an occupation without its license, but I do not think it could make it a crime publicly or privately to speak urging persons to follow or reject any school of medical thought. So the state to an extent not necessary now to determine may regulate one who makes a business or a livelihood of soliciting funds or memberships for unions. But I do not think it can prohibit one, even if he is a salaried labor leader, from making an address to a public meeting of workmen, telling them their rights as he sees them and urging them to unite in general or to join a specific union.'

"Justice Jackson concluded that the distinguishing factor was whether the speech in any particular case was 'associat[ed] [with] some other factor which the state may regulate so as to bring the whole within its official control.' If 'in a particular case the association or characterization is a proven and valid one,' he concluded, the regulation may stand.

"These ideas help to locate the point where regulation of a profession leaves off and prohibitions on speech begin. One who takes the affairs of a client personally in hand and purports to exercise judgment on behalf of the client in the light of the client's individual needs and circumstances is properly viewed as engaging in the practice of a profession. Just as offer and acceptance are communications incidental to the regulable transaction called a contract, the professional's speech is incidental to the conduct of the profession. [Where] the personal nexus between professional and client does not exist, and a speaker does not purport to be exercising judgment on behalf of any particular individual with whose circumstances he is directly acquainted, government regulation ceases to function as legitimate regulation of professional practice with only incidental impact on speech; it becomes regulation of speaking or publishing as such, subject to the First Amendment's [command].

"[E]ven where mere 'commercial speech' is concerned, the First Amendment permits restraints on speech only when they are narrowly tailored to advance a legitimate governmental interest. The interest here is certainly legitimate: the Government wants to prevent investors from falling into the hands of scoundrels and swindlers. The means chosen, however, is extreme. [Our] commercial speech cases have consistently rejected the proposition that such drastic prohibitions on speech may be justified by a mere possibility that the prohibited speech will be fraudulent. See *Zauderer; Bates.* * * *

"I emphasize the narrowness of the constitutional basis on which I would decide this case. [I] would by no means foreclose the application of, for example, the Act's antifraud or reporting provisions to investment advisers (registered or unregistered) who offer their advice through publications. Nor do I intend to suggest that it is unconstitutional to invoke the Act's provisions for injunctive relief and criminal penalties against unregistered persons who, for compensation, offer personal investment advice to individual clients. I would hold only that the Act may not constitutionally be applied to prevent persons who are unregistered (including persons whose registration has been denied or revoked) from offering impersonal investment advice through publications such as the newsletters published by petitioner."

Notes and Questions

1. Is White, J.'s speech/profession dichotomy persuasive? Should the existence of a "profession" justify prior restraints?

2. Does White, J., suggest an element of special privilege for the press? Consider Steven Shiffrin, *The First Amendment and Economic Regulation: Away From a General Theory of the First Amendment,* 78 Nw.U.L.Rev. 1212, 1276 (1983): "The doctrine of prior restraint may have been designed to put the press on an equal footing. People could speak or write without a license and that ought not to change merely because they used a printing press. Yet we now license a good deal of speech (for example, of lawyers), and those licenses are clearly prior restraints. So we have turned the law upside down. To speak you sometimes need a license; to use the press you almost never do. A doctrine designed to create equality for the press has evolved into one that gives it a special place."

3. If lawyers, psychiatrists, and investment advisors can be licensed, what about fortune tellers? Union organizers? Journalists?

4. Does *Lowe* threaten the "foundations of SEC financial disclosure regulation [and cast] a pall on the validity of government regulation of the professions." See generally Nicholas Wolfson, *The First Amendment and the SEC,* 20 Conn. L.Rev. 265 (1988) (arguing that much securities and professional regulation violates the first amendment). See also Alcta Estreicher, *Securities Regulation and the First Amendment,* 24 Ga.L.Rev. 223 (1990) (arguing against restrictions of securities' advertising). For general commentary, see Symposium, *The First Amendment and Federal Securities Regulation,* 20 Conn.L.Rev. 261 (1988).

———

RILEY v. NATIONAL FEDERATION OF THE BLIND, 487 U.S. 781, 108 S.Ct. 2667, 101 L.Ed.2d 669 (1988), per BRENNAN, J., invalidated a scheme for licensing professional fundraisers who were soliciting on behalf of charitable organizations: "[North Carolina's] provision requires professional fundraisers to await a determination regarding their license application before engaging in solicitation, while volunteer fundraisers, or those employed by the charity, may solicit immediately upon submitting an application. [It] is well settled that a speaker's rights are not lost merely because compensation is received; a speaker is no less a speaker because he or she is paid to speak. [Generally,] speakers need not obtain a license to speak. However, that rule is not absolute. For example, states may impose valid time, place, or manner restrictions. North Carolina seeks to come within the exception by alleging a heightened interest in regulating those who solicit money. Even assuming that the State's interest does justify requiring fundraisers to obtain a license before soliciting, such a regulation must provide that the licensor 'will, within a specified brief period, either issue a license or go to court.' *Freedman.* [The] statute on its face does not purport to require when a determination must be made, nor is there an administrative regulation or interpretation doing so."

REHNQUIST, C.J., joined by O'Connor, J., dissented: "It simply is not true that [fundraisers] are prevented from engaging in any protected speech on their own behalf by the State's licensing requirements; the requirements only restrict their ability to engage in the profession of 'solicitation' without a license. We do not view bar admission requirements as invalid because they restrict a prospective lawyer's 'right' to be hired as an advocate by a client. So in this case we should not subject to strict scrutiny the State's attempt to license a business—professional fundraising—some of whose members might reasonably be thought to pose a risk of fraudulent activity."[d]

IV.   PRIOR RESTRAINTS AND NATIONAL SECURITY

NEW YORK TIMES CO. v. UNITED STATES
[THE PENTAGON PAPERS CASE]

403 U.S. 713, 91 S.Ct. 2140, 29 L.Ed.2d 822 (1971).

PER CURIAM.

We granted certiorari in these cases in which the United States seeks to enjoin the *New York Times* and the *Washington Post* from publishing the contents of a classified study entitled "History of U.S. Decision–Making Process on Viet Nam Policy."[a]

"Any system of prior restraints of expression comes to this Court bearing a heavy presumption against its constitutional validity." *Bantam Books;* see also *Near.* The Government "thus carries a heavy burden of showing justification for the enforcement of such a restraint." [The district court in the *Times* case and both lower federal courts] in the *Post* case held that the Government had not met that burden. We agree. [T]he stays entered [by this Court five days previously] are vacated. * * *

JUSTICE BLACK, with whom JUSTICE DOUGLAS joins, concurring.

I adhere to the view that the Government's case against the *Post* should have been dismissed and that the injunction against the *Times* should have been

----

d. Stevens, J., also dissented from the Court's treatment of the licensing issue. For other aspects of the case.

a. On June 12–14, 1971 the *New York Times* and on June 18 the *Washington Post* published portions of this "top secret" Penta-

gon study. Government actions seeking temporary restraining orders and injunctions progressed through two district courts and two courts of appeals between June 15–23. After a June 26 argument, ten Supreme Court opinions were issued on June 30, 1971.

vacated without oral argument when the cases were first presented to this Court. I believe that every moment's continuance of the injunctions against these newspapers amounts to a flagrant, indefensible, and continuing violation of the First Amendment. Furthermore, after oral arguments, I agree [with] the reasons stated by my Brothers Douglas and Brennan. In my view it is unfortunate that some of my Brethren are apparently willing to hold that the publication of news may sometimes be enjoined. Such a holding would make a shambles of the First Amendment.

[F]or the first time in the 182 years since the founding of the Republic, the federal courts are asked to hold that the First Amendment does not mean what it says, but rather means that the Government can halt the publication of current news of vital importance to the people of this country. * * *

The Government does not even attempt to rely on any act of Congress. Instead it makes the bold and dangerously far-reaching contention that the courts should take it upon themselves to "make" a law abridging freedom of the press in the name of equity, presidential power and national security, even when the representatives of the people in Congress have adhered to the command of the First Amendment and refused to make such a law. To find that the President has "inherent power" to halt the publication of news by resort to the courts would wipe out the First Amendment and destroy the fundamental liberty and security of the very people the Government hopes to make "secure." [The] word "security" is a broad, vague generality whose contours should not be invoked to abrogate the fundamental law embodied in the First Amendment. * * *

JUSTICE DOUGLAS, with whom JUSTICE BLACK joins, concurring.

While I join the opinion of the Court I believe it necessary to express my views more fully.

[The First Amendment leaves] no room for governmental[b] restraint on the press. There is, moreover, no statute barring the publication by the press of the material which the *Times* and *Post* seek to use. [These] disclosures may have a serious impact. But that is no basis for sanctioning a previous restraint on the press * * *.

The dominant purpose of the First Amendment was to prohibit the widespread practice of governmental suppression of embarrassing information. [A] debate of large proportions goes on in the Nation over our posture in Vietnam. That debate antedated the disclosure of the contents of the present documents. The latter are highly relevant to the debate in progress.

Secrecy in government is fundamentally anti-democratic, perpetuating bureaucratic errors. Open debate and discussion of public issues are vital to our national health. [The] stays in these cases that have been in effect for more than a week constitute a flouting of the principles of the First Amendment as interpreted in *Near*.

JUSTICE BRENNAN, concurring.

I write separately [to] emphasize what should be apparent: that our judgment in the present cases may not be taken to indicate the propriety, in the future, of issuing temporary stays and restraining orders to block the publication of material sought to be suppressed by the Government. So far as I can determine, never

b. But see Mark Denbeaux, *The First Word* (1986).
of the First Amendment, 80 Nw.U.L.Rev. 1156

before has the United States sought to enjoin a newspaper from publishing information in its possession. * * *

The entire thrust of the Government's claim throughout these cases has been that publication of the material sought to be enjoined "could," or "might," or "may" prejudice the national interest in various ways. But the First Amendment tolerates absolutely no prior judicial restraints of the press predicated upon surmise or conjecture that untoward consequences may result.* Our cases, it is true, have indicated that there is a single, extremely narrow class of cases in which the First Amendment's ban on prior judicial restraint may be overridden. Our cases have thus far indicated that such cases may arise only when the Nation "is at war," [*Schenck*]. Even if the present world situation were assumed to be tantamount to a time of war, or if the power of presently available armaments would justify even in peacetime the suppression of information that would set in motion a nuclear holocaust, in neither of these actions has the Government presented or even alleged that publication of items from or based upon the material at issue would cause the happening of an event of that nature. [Thus,] only governmental allegation and proof that publication must inevitably, directly and immediately cause the occurrence of an event kindred to imperiling the safety of a transport already at sea can support even the issuance of an interim restraining order. In no event may mere conclusions be sufficient: for if the Executive Branch seeks judicial aid in preventing publication, it must inevitably submit the basis upon which that aid is sought to scrutiny by the judiciary. And therefore, every restraint issued in this case, whatever its form, has violated the First Amendment—and not less so because that restraint was justified as necessary to afford the courts an opportunity to examine the claim more thoroughly. Unless and until the Government has clearly made out its case, the First Amendment commands that no injunction may issue.

Justice Stewart, with whom Justice White joins, concurring.

[I]n the cases before us we are asked neither to construe specific regulations nor to apply specific laws. [We] are asked, quite simply, to prevent the publication by two newspapers of material that the Executive Branch insists should not, in the national interest, be published. I am convinced that the Executive is correct with respect to some of the documents involved. But I cannot say that disclosure of any of them will surely result in direct, immediate, and irreparable damage to our Nation or its people. That being so, there can under the First Amendment be but one judicial resolution of the issues before us. I join the judgments * * *.

Justice White, with whom Justice Stewart joins, concurring.

I concur in today's judgments, but only because of the concededly extraordinary protection against prior restraints enjoyed by the press under our constitutional system. I do not say that in no circumstances would the First Amendment permit an injunction against publishing information about government plans or operations. Nor, after examining the materials the Government characterizes as the most sensitive and destructive, can I deny that revelation of these documents will do substantial damage to public interests. Indeed, I am confident that their disclosure will have that result. But I nevertheless agree that the United States has not satisfied the very heavy burden which it must meet to warrant an

---

* *Freedman* and similar cases regarding temporary restraints of allegedly obscene materials are not in point. For those cases rest upon the proposition that "obscenity is not protected by the freedoms of speech and press." *Roth.* Here there is no question but that the material sought to be suppressed is within the protection of the First Amendment; the only question is whether, notwithstanding that fact, its publication may be enjoined for a time because of the presence of an overwhelming national interest. * * *

injunction against publication in these cases, at least in the absence of express and appropriately limited congressional authorization for prior restraints in circumstances such as these.

The Government's position is simply stated: The responsibility of the Executive for the conduct of the foreign affairs and for the security of the Nation is so basic that the President is entitled to an injunction against publication of a newspaper story whenever he can convince a court that the information to be revealed threatens "grave and irreparable" injury to the public interest; and the injunction should issue whether or not the material to be published is classified, whether or not publication would be lawful under relevant criminal statutes enacted by Congress and regardless of the circumstances by which the newspaper came into possession of the information.

At least in the absence of legislation by Congress, based on its own investigations and findings, I am quite unable to agree that the inherent powers of the Executive and the courts reach so far as to authorize remedies having such sweeping potential for inhibiting publications by the press. [To] sustain the Government in these cases would start the courts down a long and hazardous road that I am not willing to travel at least without congressional guidance and direction.

* * * Prior restraints require an unusually heavy justification under the First Amendment; but failure by the Government to justify prior restraints does not measure its constitutional entitlement to a conviction for criminal publication. That the Government mistakenly chose to proceed by injunction does not mean that it could not successfully proceed in another way.

* * * Congress has addressed itself to the problems of protecting the security of the country and the national defense from unauthorized disclosure of potentially damaging information. It has not, however, authorized the injunctive remedy against threatened publication It has apparently been satisfied to rely on criminal sanctions and their deterrent effect on the responsible as well as the irresponsible press. * * *

JUSTICE HARLAN, with whom THE CHIEF JUSTICE and JUSTICE BLACKMUN join, dissenting. * * *

With all respect, I consider that the Court has been almost irresponsibly feverish in dealing with these cases. Both [the] Second Circuit and [the] District of Columbia Circuit rendered judgment on June 23. [This] Court's order setting a hearing before us on June 26 at 11 a.m., a course which I joined only to avoid the possibility of even more peremptory action by the Court, was issued less than 24 hours before. The record in the *Post* case was filed with the Clerk shortly before 1 p.m. on June 25; the record in the *Times* case did not arrive until 7 or 8 o'clock that same night. The briefs of the parties were received less than two hours before argument on June 26.

This frenzied train of events took place in the name of the presumption against prior restraints created by the First Amendment. Due regard for the extraordinarily important and difficult questions involved in these litigations should have led the Court to shun such a precipitate timetable. In order to decide the merits of these cases properly, some or all of the following questions should have been faced: * * *

2. Whether the First Amendment permits the federal courts to enjoin publication of stories which would present a serious threat to national security. See *Near* (dictum). * * *

4. Whether the unauthorized disclosure of any of these particular documents would seriously impair the national security.

5. What weight should be given to the opinion of high officers in the Executive Branch of the Government with respect to [question 4]. * * *

7. Whether the threatened harm to the national security or the Government's possessory interest in the documents justifies the issuance of an injunction against publication in light of—

a. The strong First Amendment policy against prior restraints on publication; b. The doctrine against enjoining conduct in violation of criminal statutes; and c. The extent to which the materials at issue have apparently already been otherwise disseminated.

These are difficult questions of fact, of law, and of judgment; the potential consequences of erroneous decision are enormous. The time which has been available to us, to the lower courts, and to the parties has been wholly inadequate for giving these cases the kind of consideration they deserve. It is a reflection on the stability of the judicial process that these great issues—as important as any that have arisen during my time on the Court—should have been decided under the pressures engendered by the torrent of publicity that has attended these litigations from their inception.

Forced as I am to reach the merits of these cases, I dissent from the opinion and judgments of the Court. Within the severe limitations imposed by the time constraints under which I have been required to operate, I can only state my reasons in telescoped form, even though in different circumstances I would have felt constrained to deal with the cases in the fuller sweep indicated above.

[It] is plain to me that the scope of the judicial function in passing upon the activities of the Executive Branch of the Government in the field of foreign affairs is very narrowly restricted. This view is, I think, dictated by the concept of separation of powers upon which our constitutional system [rests.] I agree that, in performance of its duty to protect the values of the First Amendment against political pressures, the judiciary must review the initial Executive determination to the point of satisfying itself that the subject matter of the dispute does lie within the proper compass of the President's foreign relations power. Constitutional considerations forbid "a complete abandonment of judicial control." Moreover, the judiciary may properly insist that the determination that disclosure of the subject matter would irreparably impair the national security be made by the head of the Executive Department concerned—here the Secretary of State or the Secretary of Defense—after actual personal consideration by that officer.[c] This safeguard is required in the analogous area of executive claims of privilege for secrets of state.

But in my judgment the judiciary may not properly go beyond these two inquiries and redetermine for itself the probable impact of disclosure on the national security. "[T]he very nature of executive decisions as to foreign policy is

c. Consider Stanley Godofsky & Howard Rogatnick, *Prior Restraints: The Pentagon Papers Case Revisited*, 18 Cum.L.Rev. 527, 536–37 (1988): "Ironically, Justice Harlan's view of the Constitution might, ultimately, have presented more problems for the Government than those of most of the other Justices. Realistically, how often can the Secretary of State or Secretary of Defense devote 'actual personal consideration' to the question of whether material about to be published should be suppressed? And of what does 'actual personal consideration' consist? Must the Secretary himself read the documents? Is it sufficient 'consideration' by a Cabinet officer to act on the advice of his subordinates? If so, is not the 'actual personal consideration' test substantially meaningless? Could a Cabinet officer be required to testify as to the basis for his decision in order to test his 'bona fides'?"

political, not judicial. Such decisions are wholly confided by our Constitution to the political departments of the government, Executive and Legislative. They are delicate, complex, and involve large elements of prophecy. They are and should be undertaken only by those directly responsible to the people whose welfare they advance or imperil. They are decisions of a kind for which the judiciary has neither aptitude, facilities nor responsibility and which has long been held to belong in the domain of political power not subject to judicial intrusion or inquiry." *Chicago & S. Air Lines v. Waterman S.S. Corp.* (Jackson, J.), 333 U.S. 103, 68 S.Ct. 431, 92 L.Ed. 568 (1948).

Even if there is some room for the judiciary to override the executive determination, it is plain that the scope of review must be exceedingly narrow. I can see no indication in the opinions of either the District Court or the Court of Appeals in the *Post* litigation that the conclusions of the Executive were given even the deference owing to an administrative agency, much less that owing to a co-equal branch of the Government operating within the field of its constitutional prerogative. * * *

Pending further hearings in each case conducted under the appropriate ground rules, I would continue the restraints on publication. I cannot believe that the doctrine prohibiting prior restraints reaches to the point of preventing courts from maintaining the status quo long enough to act responsibly in matters of such national importance as those involved here.

Justice Blackmun, dissenting.

[The First Amendment] is only one part of an entire Constitution. Article II of the great document vests in the Executive Branch primary power over the conduct of foreign affairs and places in that branch the responsibility for the Nation's safety. Each provision of the Constitution is important, and I cannot subscribe to a doctrine of unlimited absolutism for the First Amendment at the cost of downgrading other provisions. First Amendment absolutism has never commanded a majority of this Court. What is needed here is a weighing, upon properly developed standards, of the broad right of the press to print and of the very narrow right of the Government to prevent. Such standards are not yet developed. The parties here are in disagreement as to what those standards should be. But even the newspapers concede that there are situations where restraint is in order and is constitutional. Mr. Justice Holmes gave us a suggestion when he said in *Schenck*, "It is a question of proximity and degree. When a nation is at war many things that might be said in time of peace are such a hindrance to its effort that their utterance will not be endured so long as men fight and that no Court could regard them as protected by any constitutional right."

I therefore would remand these cases to be developed expeditiously, of course, but on a schedule permitting the orderly presentation of evidence from both sides [and] with the preparation of briefs, oral argument and court opinions of a quality better than has been seen to this point. [T]hese cases and the issues involved and the courts, including this one, deserve better than has been produced thus far. * * *d

---

d. Marshall, J., concurring, did not deal with first amendment issues but only with separation of powers—the government's attempt to secure through the Court injunctive relief that Congress had refused to authorize.

Burger, C.J., dissenting, complained that because of "unseemly haste," "we do not know

the facts of this case. [W]e literally do not know what we are acting on." He expressed no views on the merits, apart from his joinder in Harlan, J.'s opinion, and a statement that he would have continued the temporary restraints in effect while returning the cases to the lower

Notes and Questions

1. *What did the case decide?* Do you agree that "the case [did] not make any law at all, good or bad"? That on the question "whether injunctions against the press are permissible, it is clear that [the case] can supply no precedent?" See Peter Junger, *Down Memory Lane: The Case of the Pentagon Papers*, 23 Case W.Res.L.Rev. 3, 4–5 (1971). Or do you find in several concurring opinions a discernible standard that must be satisfied before a majority of the Court would permit an injunction against the press on national security grounds? Cf. 85 Harv.L.Rev. 199, 205–06 (1971). Do you find guidance as to the outcome if Congress were to authorize an injunction in narrow terms to protect national security? Cf. id. at 204–05. Might it fairly be said that this is a separation of powers decision, like the *Steel Seizure* case, as well as a first amendment decision? See Junger, supra, at 19.

2. *"De facto" prior restraint.* One difficulty with viewing the prior restraint doctrine as "simply creat[ing] a 'presumption' against the validity of the restraint" (Emerson's characterization of the current approach) rather than as "a prohibition on all restraints subject to certain categorical exceptions," observes Thomas Emerson, *First Amendment Doctrine and the Burger Court*, 68 Calif.L.Rev. 422, 457–58 (1980), is that "the requirement of ad hoc scrutiny of prior restraints is itself likely to result in a 'de facto' prior restraint." Pointing to Brennan, J.'s comment in *Pentagon Papers* that "every restraint issued in this case [has] violated the First Amendment—and not less so because that restraint was justified as necessary to afford the courts an opportunity to examine the claim more thoroughly," Emerson notes that "[t]his is exactly what happened when the government sought to enjoin *The Progressive* magazine from publishing an article on the manufacture of the hydrogen bomb. The Supreme Court refused to order an expedited appeal from the [federal district court] injunction against publication [and, although the case was ultimately dismissed by the Seventh Circuit,] *The Progressive* remained under effective prior restraint for nearly seven months."

Compare *Near* and *Pentagon Papers* with UNITED STATES v. PROGRESSIVE, INC., 467 F.Supp. 990 (W.D.Wis.) (preliminary injunction issued Mar. 28, 1979), request for writ of mandamus den. sub nom. *Morland v. Sprecher*, 443 U.S. 709 (1979), case dismissed, 610 F.2d 819 (7th Cir.1979).[e] *The Progressive* planned to publish an article. "The H–Bomb Secret—How We Got It, Why We're Telling It," maintaining that the article would contribute to informed opinion about nuclear weapons and demonstrate the inadequacies of a system of secrecy and classification. Although the government conceded that at least some of the information contained in the article was "in the public domain" or had been "declassified," it argued that "national security" permitted it to censor information originating in the public domain "if when drawn together, synthesized and collated, such information acquires the character of presenting immediate, direct and irreparable harm to the interests of the United States." The Secretary of State stated that publication would increase thermonuclear proliferation and that this would "irreparably impair the national security of the United States." The Secretary of Defense maintained that dissemination of the Morland article would lead to a substantial increase in the risk of thermonuclear proliferation and to use

courts for more thorough exploration of the facts and issues.

e. The government's action against *The Progressive* was abandoned after information similar to that it sought to enjoin was published elsewhere.

or threats that would "adversely affect the national security of the United States."

Although recognizing that this constituted "the first instance of prior restraint against a publication in this fashion in the [nation's history]," the district court enjoined defendants, pending final resolution of the litigation, from publishing or otherwise disclosing any information designated by the government as "restricted data" within the meaning of The Atomic Energy Act of 1954: "What is involved here is information dealing with the most destructive weapon in the history of mankind, information of sufficient destructive potential to nullify the right to free speech and to endanger the right to life itself. [Faced] with a stark choice between upholding the right to continued life and the right to freedom of the press, most jurists would have no difficulty in opting for the chance to continue to breathe and function as they work to achieve perfect freedom of expression.

"[A] mistake in ruling against *The Progressive* will seriously infringe cherished First Amendment rights. [A] mistake in ruling against the United States could pave the way for thermonuclear annihilation for us all. In that event, our right to life is extinguished and the right to publish becomes moot.

"[W]ar by foot soldiers has been replaced in large part by machines and bombs. No longer need there be any advance warning or any preparation time before a nuclear war could be commenced. [In light of these factors] publication of the technical information on the hydrogen bomb contained in the article is analogous to publication of troop movements or locations in time of war and falls within the extremely narrow exception to the rule against prior restraint [recognized in *Near*].f

"The government has met its burden under § 2274 of The Atomic Energy Act [which authorizes injunctive relief against one who would communicate or disclose restricted data 'with reason to believe such data will be utilized to injure the United States or to secure an advantage to any foreign nation.'] [I]t has also met the test enunciated by two Justices in *Pentagon Papers*, namely grave, direct, immediate and irreparable harm to the United States."

The court distinguished *Pentagon Papers*: "[T]he study involved [there] contained historical data relating to events some three to twenty years previously. Secondly, the Supreme Court agreed with the lower court that no cogent reasons were advanced by the government as to why the article affected national security except that publication might cause some embarrassment to the United States. A final and most vital difference between these two cases is the fact that a specific statute is involved here [§ 2274 of The Atomic Energy Act]."

3. *CIA secrecy agreement.* The Central Intelligence Agency requires employees to sign a "secrecy agreement" as a condition of employment, an agreement committing the employee not to reveal classified information nor to publish any information obtained during the course of employment without prior approval of the Agency. In SNEPP v. UNITED STATES, 444 U.S. 507, 100 S.Ct. 763, 62 L.Ed.2d 704 (1980), Snepp had published a book called *Decent Interval* about certain CIA activities in South Vietnam based on his experiences as an agency

---

f. One of the reasons the court gave for finding that the objected-to technical portions of the article fell within the *Near* exception was that it was "unconvinced that suppression of [these portions] would in any plausible fashion impede the defendants in their laudable crusade to stimulate public knowledge of nuclear armament and bring about enlightened debate on national policy questions." Should this have been a factor in the decision to issue the preliminary injunction?

employee without seeking prepublication review. At least for purposes of the litigation, the government conceded that Snepp's book divulged no confidential information. The Court, per curiam (Stevens, J., joined by Brennan and Marshall, JJ., dissenting) held that Snepp's failure to submit the book was a breach of trust and the government was entitled to a constructive trust on the proceeds of the book: "[E]ven in the absence of an express agreement, the CIA could have acted to protect substantial government interests by imposing reasonable restrictions on employee activities that in other contexts might be protected by the First Amendment. The Government has a compelling interest in protecting both the secrecy of information important to our national security and the appearance of confidentiality so essential to the effective operation of our foreign intelligence service."[g] When employees or past employees do submit publications for clearance, should *Freedman* standards apply? Can former CIA employees be required to submit all public speeches relating to their former employment for clearance? Are extemporaneous remarks permitted? To what extent can secrecy agreements be required of public employees outside the national security area?[h]

SECTION 5. JUSTICE AND NEWSGATHERING

This section explores three problems connected with the fair administration of justice or with newsgathering or with both. The first problem involves pre-trial publicity. The government seeks to deter or punish speech by the press that it fears will threaten the fair administration of justice, but speech of that character falls into no recognized category of unprotected speech. Thus, the courts must consider whether absolute protection is called for, or, alternatively, whether new categories or ad hoc determinations are appropriate, and whether prior restraints are permissible. Alternatively, if the press cannot be prevented from speaking about trials, can prosecutors, defense attorneys, litigants and potential witnesses be prevented from speaking to the press?

In the second problem the government seeks to fairly administer the justice system by forcing reporters to reveal their confidential sources. The press maintains that any such authorized compulsion would have a chilling effect on its ability to gather the news.

In the final problem, government seeks not to punish speech, but to administer justice in private. It refuses to let the public or press witness its handling of prisoners, or its conduct of trial or pre-trial proceedings. The question is whether the first amendment can serve as a sword allowing the press or citizen-critics to gather information. Assuming it can, what are its limits within the justice system? Does any right of access reach beyond the justice system? Does the first amend-

---

g. Compare *Haig v. Agee*, 453 U.S. 280, 101 S.Ct. 2766, 69 L.Ed.2d 640 (1981), stating that "repeated disclosures of intelligence operations and names of intelligence personnel" for the "purpose of obstructing intelligence operations and the recruiting of intelligence personnel" are "clearly not protected by the Constitution." What if the publisher of the information merely has "reason to believe that such activities would impair or impede the foreign intelligence activities of the United States"? See 50 U.S.C. § 421.

h. For discussion of *Snepp*, see Mary Cheh, *Judicial Supervision of Executive Secrecy*, 69 Corn.L.Rev. 690 (1984); Frank Easterbrook,

Insider Trading, Secret Agents, Evidentiary Privileges, and the Production of Information, 1981 Sup.Ct.Rev. 309, 339–53; Stanley Godofsky & Howard Rogatnick, *Prior Restraints: The Pentagon Papers Case Revisited*, fn. c supra, at 543–54 (1988); Judith Koffler & Bennett Gershman, *The New Seditious Libel*, 69 Corn. L.Rev. 816 (1984); Jonathan Medow, *The First Amendment and the Secrecy State: Snepp v. United States*, 130 U.Pa.L.Rev. 775 (1982). For a thorough exploration of the occasions in which secrecy has been preferred over public knowledge, see Benjamin DuVal, *The Occasions of Secrecy*, 47 U.Pitt.L.Rev. 579 (1986).

ment require that the press be granted access not afforded the public? Does the first amendment permit differential access? If so, what are the limits on how government defines the press?

I. PUBLICITY ABOUT TRIALS

In a number of cases, defendants have asserted that their rights to a fair trial have been abridged by newspaper publicity. SHEPPARD v. MAXWELL, 384 U.S. 333, 86 S.Ct. 1507, 16 L.Ed.2d 600 (1966), is probably the most notorious "trial by newspaper" case. The Court, per CLARK, J., (Black, J. dissenting) agreed with the "finding" of the Ohio Supreme Court that the atmosphere of defendant's murder trial was that of a " 'Roman holiday' for the news media." The courtroom was jammed with reporters. And in the corridors outside the courtroom, "a host of photographers and television personnel" photographed witnesses, counsel and jurors as they entered and left the courtroom. Throughout the trial, there was a deluge of publicity, much of which contained information never presented at trial, yet the jurors were not sequestered until the trial was over and they had begun their deliberations.

The Court placed the primary blame on the trial judge. He could "easily" have prevented "the carnival atmosphere of the trial" since "the courtroom and courthouse premises" were subject to his control. For example, he should have provided privacy for the jury, insulated witnesses from the media, instead of allowing them to be interviewed at will, and "made some effort to control the release of leads, information, and gossip to the press by police officers, witnesses, and the counsel for both sides." No one "coming under the jurisdiction of the court should be permitted to frustrate its function."

The Court recognized that "there is nothing that proscribes the press from reporting events that transpire in the courtroom. But where there is a reasonable likelihood that prejudicial news prior to trial will prevent a fair trial, the judge should continue the case until the threat abates, or transfer it to another county not so permeated with publicity. In addition, sequestration of the jury was something the judge should have raised sua sponte with counsel. If publicity during the proceedings threatens the fairness of the trial, a new trial should be ordered. But we must remember that reversals are but palliatives; the cure lies in those remedial measures that will prevent the prejudice at its inception."

The Court, however, reiterated its extreme reluctance "to place any direct limitations on the freedom traditionally exercised by the news media for '[w]hat transpires in the courtroom is public property.' " The press "does not simply publish information about trials but guards against the miscarriage of justice by subjecting the police, prosecutors, and judicial processes to extensive public scrutiny and criticism."

In anticipation of the trial of Simants for a mass murder which had attracted widespread news coverage, the county court prohibited everyone in attendance from, inter alia, releasing or authorizing for publication "any testimony given or evidence adduced." Simants' preliminary hearing (open to the public) was held the same day, subject to the restrictive order. Simants was bound over for trial. Respondent Nebraska state trial judge then entered an order which, as modified by the state supreme court, restrained the press and broadcasting media from reporting any confessions or incriminating statements made by Simants to law enforcement officers or third parties, except members of the press, and from reporting other facts "strongly implicative" of the defendant. The order expired when the jury was impaneled.

NEBRASKA PRESS ASS'N v. STUART, 427 U.S. 539, 96 S.Ct. 2791, 49 L.Ed.2d 683 (1976), per BURGER, C.J., struck down the state court order: "To the extent that the order prohibited the reporting of evidence adduced at the open preliminary hearing, it plainly violated settled principles: 'There is nothing that proscribes the press from reporting events that transpire in the courtroom.' *Sheppard.*"[a] To the extent that the order prohibited publication "based on information gained from other sources, [the] heavy burden imposed as a condition to securing a prior restraint was not met." The portion of the order regarding "implicative" information was also "too vague and too broad" to survive scrutiny of restraints on first amendment rights.

"[P]retrial publicity—even pervasive, adverse publicity—does not inevitably lead to an unfair trial. The capacity of the jury eventually impaneled to decide the case fairly is influenced by the tone and extent of the publicity, which is in part, and often in large part, shaped by what attorneys, police and other officials do to precipitate news coverage. [T]he measures a judge takes or fails to take to mitigate the effects of pretrial publicity—the measures described in *Sheppard*— may well determine whether the defendant receives a trial consistent [with] due process.

"[The] Court has interpreted [first amendment] guarantees to afford special protection against orders that prohibit the publication or broadcast of particular information or commentary—orders that impose [a] 'prior' restraint on speech. None of our decided cases on prior restraint involved restrictive orders entered to protect a defendant's right to a fair and impartial jury, but [they] have a common thread relevant to this case. * * *

"The thread running through [*Near* and *Pentagon Papers*], is that prior restraints on speech and publication are the most serious and the least tolerable infringement on First Amendment rights. A criminal penalty or a judgment in a defamation case is subject to the whole panoply of protections afforded by deferring the impact of the judgment until all avenues of appellate review have been exhausted. [But] a prior restraint [has] an immediate and irreversible sanction. If it can be said that a threat of criminal or civil sanctions after publication 'chills' speech, prior restraint 'freezes' it at least for the time.

"[I]f the authors of [the first and sixth amendments], fully aware of the potential conflicts between them, were unwilling or unable to resolve the issue by assigning to one priority over the other, it is not for us to rewrite the Constitution by undertaking what they declined. [Yet] it is nonetheless clear that the barriers to prior restraint remain high unless we are to abandon what the Court has said for nearly a quarter of our national existence and implied throughout all of [it.]

"We turn now to the record in this case to determine whether, as Learned Hand put it, 'the gravity of the 'evil,' discounted by its improbability, justifies such invasion of free speech as is necessary to avoid the danger,' *Dennis* [2d Cir.], aff'd. To do so, we must examine the evidence before the trial judge when the order was entered to determine (a) the nature and extent of pretrial news coverage; (b) whether other measures would be likely to mitigate the effects of

---

a. The Court added, however, that the county court "could not know that closure of the preliminary hearing was an alternative open to it until the Nebraska Supreme Court so construed state law."

unrestrained pretrial publicity; (c) how effectively a restraining order would operate to prevent the threatened danger. The precise terms of the restraining order are also important. We must then consider whether the record supports the entry of a prior restraint on publication, one of the most extraordinary remedies known to our jurisprudence."

As to (a), although the trial judge was justified in concluding there would be extensive pretrial publicity concerning this case, he "found only 'a clear and present danger that pretrial publicity *could* impinge upon the defendant's right to a fair trial.' [Emphasis added by the Court]. His conclusion as to the impact of such publicity on prospective jurors was of necessity speculative, dealing as he was with factors unknown and unknowable."

As to (b), "there is no finding that alternative means [e.g., change of venue, postponement of trial to allow public attention to subside, searching questions of prospective jurors] would not have protected Simants' rights, and the Nebraska Supreme Court did no more than imply that such measures might not be adequate. Moreover, the record is lacking in evidence to support such a finding."

As to (c), in view of such practical problems as the limited territorial jurisdiction of the trial court issuing the order, the difficulties of predicting what information "will in fact undermine the impartiality of jurors," the problem of drafting an order that will "effectively keep prejudicial information from prospective jurors," and that the events "took place in a community of only 850 people"—throughout which, "it is reasonable to assume," rumors that "could well be more damaging than reasonably accurate news accounts" would "travel swiftly by word of mouth"—"it is far from clear that prior restraint on publication would have protected Simants' rights."

"[It] is significant that when this Court has reversed a state conviction because of prejudicial publicity, it has carefully noted that some course of action short of prior restraint would have made a critical difference. However difficult it may be, we need not rule out the possibility of showing the kind of threat to fair trial rights that would possess the requisite degree of certainty to justify restraint. [We] reaffirm that the guarantees of freedom of expression are not an absolute prohibition under all circumstances, but the barriers to prior restraint remain high and the presumption against its use continues intact. We hold that, with respect to the order entered in this case [the] heavy burden imposed as a condition to securing a prior restraint was not [met]."

BRENNAN, J., joined by Stewart and Marshall, JJ., concurring, would hold that "resort to prior restraints on the freedom of the press is a constitutionally impermissible method for enforcing [the right to a fair trial by a jury]; judges have at their disposal a broad spectrum of devices for ensuring that fundamental fairness is accorded the accused without necessitating so drastic an incursion on the equally fundamental and salutary constitutional mandate that discussion of public affairs in a free society cannot depend on the preliminary grace of judicial censors": " * * * Settled case law concerning the impropriety and constitutional invalidity of prior restraints on the press compels the conclusion that there can be no prohibition on the publication by the press of any information pertaining to pending judicial proceedings or the operation of the criminal justice system, no matter how shabby the means by which the information is obtained.[15] This does

---

15. Of course, even if the press cannot be enjoined from reporting certain information, that does not necessarily immunize it from civil liability for libel or invasion of privacy or from criminal liability for transgressions of

not imply, however, any subordination of Sixth Amendment rights, for an accused's right to a fair trial may be adequately assured through methods that do not infringe First Amendment values.

"[The narrow national security exception mentioned in *Near* and *Pentagon Papers*] does not mean [that] prior restraints can be justified on an ad hoc balancing approach that concludes that the 'presumption' must be overcome in light of some perceived 'justification.' Rather, this language refers to the fact that, as a matter of procedural safeguards and burden of proof, prior restraints even within a recognized exception to the rule against prior restraints will be extremely difficult to justify; but as an initial matter, the purpose for which a prior restraint is sought to be imposed 'must fit within one of the narrowly defined exceptions to the prohibition against prior restraints.' Indeed, two Justices in [*Pentagon Papers*] apparently controverted the existence of even a limited 'military security' exception to the rule against prior restraints on the publication of otherwise protected material. (Black, J., concurring); (Douglas, J., concurring). And a majority of the other Justices who expressed their views on the merits made it clear that they would take cognizance only of a 'single, extremely narrow class of cases in which the First Amendment's ban on prior judicial restraint may be overridden.' (Brennan, J., concurring). * * *

"The only exception that has thus far been recognized even in dictum to the blanket prohibition against prior restraints against publication of material which would otherwise be constitutionally shielded was the 'military security' situation addressed in [*Pentagon Papers*]. But unlike the virtually certain, direct, and immediate harm required for such a restraint [the] harm to a fair trial that might otherwise eventuate from publications which are suppressed pursuant to orders such as that under review must inherently remain speculative."

Although they joined the Court's opinion, White and Powell, JJ., also filed brief concurrences. WHITE, J., expressed "grave doubts" that these types of restrictive orders "would ever be justifiable." POWELL, J., "emphasize[d] the unique burden" resting upon one who "undertakes to show the necessity for prior restraint on pretrial publicity." In his judgment, a prior restraint "requires a showing that (i) there is a clear threat to the fairness of trial, (ii) such a threat is posed by the actual publicity to be restrained, and (iii) no less restrictive alternatives are available. Notwithstanding such a showing, a restraint may not issue unless it also is shown that previous publicity or publicity from unrestrained sources will not render the restraint inefficacious. [A]ny restraint must comply with the standards of specificity always required in the First Amendment context."

STEVENS, J., concurred in the judgment. He agreed with Brennan, J., that the "judiciary is capable of protecting the defendant's right to a fair trial without enjoining the press from publishing information in the public domain, and that it may not do so." But he reserved judgment, until further argument, on "[w]hether the same absolute protection would apply no matter how shabby or illegal the means by which the information is obtained, no matter how serious an intrusion on privacy might be involved, no matter how demonstrably false the information might be, no matter how prejudicial it might be to the interests of innocent persons, and no matter how perverse the motivation for publishing it." He indicated that "if ever required to face the issue squarely" he "may well accept [Brennan, J.'s] ultimate conclusion."[b]

---

general criminal laws during the course of obtaining that information.

b. For background on *Nebraska Press,* see Fred Friendly & Martha Elliot, *The Constitu-*

Notes and Questions

1. *Why the prior restraint reliance?* Does "the reasoning used by all of the justices premised solely on the traditional aversion to prior restraints, insufficiently" protect the press? Robert Sack, *Principle and Nebraska Press Association v. Stuart,* 29 Stan.L.Rev. 411, 411 (1977). Would the *Nebraska Press* order have been "equally objectionable" if "framed as a statutory sanction punishing publication after it had occurred"?[c]

2. *Why the Dennis citation?* Consider Benno Schmidt, *Nebraska Press Association: An Expansion of Freedom and Contraction of Theory,* 29 Stan.L.Rev. 431, 459–60 (1977): Burger, C.J.'s reliance on *Dennis* "is remarkable, almost unbelievable, because that test is both an exceedingly odd means of determining the validity of a prior restraint and a controversial and recently neglected technique of first amendment adjudication. [If] the [*Dennis*] test is the right one for prior restraints, what tests should govern a subsequent punishment case resting on legislation?" See also Barnett, note c supra, at 542–44. Burger, C.J.'s citation to *Dennis* should be read in conjunction with dictum in his majority opinion in *Landmark Communications, Inc. v. Virginia,* note 6 infra. There he questioned reliance upon the clear and present danger standard but observed: "Properly applied, the test requires a court to make its own inquiry into the imminence and magnitude of the danger said to flow from the particular utterance and then to balance the character of the evil, as well as its likelihood, against the need for free and unfettered expression. The possibility that other measures will serve the State's interests should also be weighed."

3. *Future press restraints.* Was *Nebraska Press* a strong case for restraint? Is it "difficult to believe that any other case will provide an exception to the rule against prior restraints in fair trial/free press cases"? James Goodale, *The Press Ungagged: The Practical Effect on Gag Order Litigation of Nebraska Press,* 29 Stan.L.Rev. 497, 504 (1977). If so, does the dispute between the justices over the right standard make a difference? Does the collateral bar rule shed light on that question? See id. at 511–12; Barnett, note c supra, at 553–58. Should the collateral bar rule apply in this situation?

4. *Application to non-press defendants.* Should *Nebraska Press* standards apply to court orders preventing prosecutors, witnesses, potential witnesses, jurors,[d] defendants, or defense attorneys from talking to the press about the case? Should different standards apply to each category—e.g., do defense attorneys deserve as much protection as the press? See *Gentile v. State Bar,* 501 U.S. 1030, 111 S.Ct. 2720, 115 L.Ed.2d 888 (1991) (less stringent standard ("substantial likelihood of material prejudice") applies to defense attorneys not clear and present danger).[e]

tion: That Delicate Balance 148–58 (1984).

c. Id. at 415. See also Stephen Barnett, *The Puzzle of Prior Restraint,* 29 Stan.L.Rev. 539, 542–44, 560 (1977). But see Note, *Punishing the Press: Using contempt of Court to Secure the Right to a Free Trial,* 76 B.U.L. Rev. 537 (1996).

d. Marcy Strauss, *Juror Journalism,* 12 Yale L. & Pol'y Rev. 389 (1994); Comment, *Checkbook Journalism, Free Speech, and Fair Trials,* 143 U.Pa.L.Rev. 1739 (1995).

e. For relevant commentary, see Erwin Chemerinsky, *Silence is Not Golden,* 47 Emory L.Rev. 859 (1998); David A. Strauss, *Why It's Not Free Speech versus Fair Trial,* 1998 U.Chi.Legal F. 109; Lloyd Weinreb, *Speaking Out Outside the Courtroom,* 47 Emory L.J. 889 (1998); Monroe Freedman & Janet Starwood, *Prior Restraints on Freedom of Expression by Defendants and Defense Attorneys: Ratio Decidendi v. Obiter Dictum,* 29 Stan.L.Rev. 607 (1977); Comment, *First Amendment Protection*

5. *Obstructing justice.* A series of cases have held that the first amendment greatly restricts contempt sanctions against persons whose comments on pending cases were alleged to have created a danger of obstruction of the judicial process. "Such repression can be justified, if at all, only by a clear and present danger of the obstruction of justice." *New York Times.* In *Bridges v. California,* 314 U.S. 252, 62 S.Ct. 190, 86 L.Ed. 192 (1941), union leader Bridges had caused publication or acquiesced in publication of a telegram threatening a strike if an "outrageous" California state decision involving Bridges' dock workers were enforced. The Court reversed Bridges' contempt citation. Consider Tribe 1st ed., at 624: "If Bridges' threat to cripple the economy of the entire West Coast did not present danger enough, the lesson of the case must be that almost nothing said outside the courtroom is punishable as contempt."[f]

Would it make a difference if a petit jury were impaneled? Suppose Bridges published an open letter to petit jurors? What if copies were sent by Bridges to each juror? Cf. *Wood v. Georgia,* 370 U.S. 375, 82 S.Ct. 1364, 8 L.Ed.2d 569 (1962) (open letter to press and grand jury—contempt citation reversed). But cf. *Cox v. Louisiana,* 379 U.S. 559, 85 S.Ct. 476, 13 L.Ed.2d 487 (1965) (statute forbidding parades near courthouse with intent to interfere with administration of justice upheld): ("[W]e deal not with the contempt power [but] a statute narrowly drawn to punish" not a pure form of speech but expression mixed with conduct "that infringes a substantial state interest in protecting the judicial process.").

6. *Confidentiality and privacy.* A series of cases has rebuffed state efforts to protect confidentiality or privacy by prohibiting publication. *Cox Broadcasting Corp. v. Cohn,* Sec. 1, II, F supra (state could not impose liability for public dissemination of the name of rape victim derived from public court documents); *Oklahoma Pub. Co. v. District Court,* 430 U.S. 308, 97 S.Ct. 1045, 51 L.Ed.2d 355 (1977) (pretrial order enjoining press from publishing name or picture of 11–year-old boy accused of murder invalid when reporters had been lawfully present at a prior public hearing and had photographed him en route from the courthouse); *Landmark Communications, Inc. v. Virginia,* 435 U.S. 829, 98 S.Ct. 1535, 56 L.Ed.2d 1 (1978) (statute making it a crime to publish information about particular confidential proceedings invalid as applied to non-participant in the proceedings, at least when the information had been lawfully acquired); *Smith v. Daily Mail Pub. Co.,* 443 U.S. 97, 99 S.Ct. 2667, 61 L.Ed.2d 399 (1979) (statute making it a crime for newspapers (but not broadcasters) to publish the name of any youth charged as a juvenile offender invalid as applied to information lawfully acquired from private sources). But cf. *Seattle Times Co. v. Rhinehart,* 467 U.S. 20, 104 S.Ct. 2199, 81 L.Ed.2d 17 (1984) (order enjoining newspaper from disseminating information acquired as a litigant in pretrial discovery valid so long as order is entered on a showing of good cause and does not restrict the dissemination of the information if gained from other sources).

of Criminal Defense Attorneys' Extrajudicial [Statements], 8 Whittier L.Rev. 1021 (1987).

f. Compare Carol Rieger, *Lawyers' Criticism of Judges: Is Freedom of Speech A Figure of Speech?,* 2 Const.Comm. 69 (1985).

II. NEWSGATHERING

A. PROTECTION OF CONFIDENTIAL SOURCES

BRANZBURG v. HAYES

408 U.S. 665, 92 S.Ct. 2646, 33 L.Ed.2d 626 (1972).

JUSTICE WHITE delivered the opinion of the Court.

[Branzburg, a Kentucky reporter, wrote articles describing his observations of local hashish-making and other drug violations. He refused to testify before a grand jury regarding his information. The state courts rejected his claim of a first amendment privilege.

[Pappas, a Massachusetts TV newsman-photographer, was allowed to enter and remain inside a Black Panther headquarters on condition he disclose nothing. When an anticipated police raid did not occur, he wrote no story. Summoned before a local grand jury, he refused to answer any questions about what had occurred inside the Panther headquarters or to identify those he had observed. The state courts denied his claim of a first amendment privilege.

[Caldwell, a N.Y. Times reporter covering the Black Panthers, was summoned to appear before a federal grand jury investigating Panther activities. A federal court issued a protective order providing that although he had to divulge information given him "for publication," he could withhold "confidential" information "developed or maintained by him as a professional journalist." Maintaining that absent a specific need for his testimony he should be excused from attending the grand jury altogether, Caldwell disregarded the order and was held in contempt. The Ninth Circuit reversed, holding that absent "compelling reasons" Caldwell could refuse even to attend the grand jury, because of the potential impact of such an appearance on the flow of news to the public.]

[Petitioners' first amendment claims] may be simply put: that to gather news it is often necessary to agree either not to identify [sources] or to publish only part of the facts revealed, or both; that if the reporter is nevertheless forced to reveal these confidences to a grand jury, the source so identified and other confidential sources of other reporters will be measurably deterred from furnishing publishable information, all to the detriment of the free flow of information protected by the First Amendment. Although petitioners do not claim an absolute privilege [they] assert that the reporter should not be forced either to appear or to testify before a grand jury or at trial until and unless sufficient grounds are shown for believing that the reporter possesses information relevant to a crime the grand jury is investigating, that the information the reporter has is unavailable from other sources, and that the need for the information is sufficiently compelling to override the claimed invasion of First Amendment interests occasioned by the disclosure. [The] heart of the claim is that the burden on news gathering resulting from compelling reporters to disclose confidential information outweighs any public interest in obtaining the information.

[We agree] that news gathering [qualifies] for First Amendment protection; without some protection for seeking out the news, freedom of the press could be eviscerated. But this case involves no intrusions upon speech [and no] command that the press publish what it prefers to withhold. [N]o penalty, civil or criminal, related to the content of published material is at issue here. The use of confidential sources by the press is not forbidden or restricted; reporters remain free to seek news from any source by means within the law. No attempt is made to require the press to publish its sources of information or indiscriminately to disclose them on request.

The sole issue before us is the obligation of reporters to respond to grand jury subpoenas as other citizens do and to answer questions relevant to an investigation into the commission of crime.

[T]he First Amendment does not guarantee the press a constitutional right of special access to information not available to the public generally. [Although] news gathering may be hampered, the press is regularly excluded from grand jury proceedings, our own conferences, the meetings of other official bodies gathered in executive session, and the meetings of private organizations. Newsmen have no constitutional right of access to the scenes of crime or disaster when the general public is excluded, and they may be prohibited from attending or publishing information about trials if such restrictions are necessary to assure a defendant a fair trial before an impartial tribunal. [It] is thus not surprising that the great weight of authority is that newsmen are not exempt from the normal duty of appearing before a grand jury and answering questions relevant to a criminal investigation.

[Because] its task is to inquire into the existence of possible criminal conduct and to return only well-founded indictments, [the grand jury's] investigative powers are necessarily broad. [T]he long standing principle that "the public has a right to every man's evidence," except for those persons protected by a constitutional, common law, or statutory privilege, is particularly applicable to grand jury proceedings.

A [minority] of States have provided newsmen a statutory privilege of varying breadth, [but] none has been provided by federal statute. [We decline to create one] by interpreting the First Amendment to grant newsmen a testimonial privilege that other citizens do not enjoy. [On] the records now before us, we perceive no basis for holding that the public interest in law enforcement and in ensuring effective grand jury proceedings is insufficient to override the consequential, but uncertain, burden on news gathering which is said to result from insisting that reporters, like other citizens, respond to relevant questions put to them in the course of a valid grand jury investigation or criminal trial.

This conclusion [does not] threaten the vast bulk of confidential relationships between reporters and their sources. Grand juries address themselves to the issues of whether crimes have been committed and who committed them. Only where news sources themselves are implicated in crime or possess information relevant to the grand jury's task need they or the reporter be concerned about grand jury subpoenas. Nothing before us indicates that a large number or percentage of *all* confidential news sources fall into either category and would in any way be deterred by [our holding]. * * *[33]

Accepting the fact, however, that an undetermined number of informants not themselves implicated in crime will nevertheless, for whatever reason, refuse to talk to newsmen if they fear identification by a reporter in an official investiga-

---

33. In his *Press Subpoenas: An Empirical and Legal Analysis* 6–12 (1971), Prof. Blasi found that slightly more than half of the 975 reporters questioned said that they relied on regular confidential sources for at least 10% of their stories. Of this group of reporters, only 8% were able to say with some certainty that their professional functioning had been adversely affected by the threat of subpoena; another 11% were not certain whether or not they had been adversely affected. [See also Vincent Blasi, *The Newsman's Privilege: An Empirical Study*, 70 Mich.L.Rev. 229 (1971).]

tion, we cannot accept the argument that the public interest in possible future news about crime from undisclosed, unverified sources must take precedence over the public interest in pursuing and prosecuting those crimes reported to the press by informants and in thus deterring the commission of such crimes in the future. * * *

[The] privilege claimed here is conditional, not absolute; given the suggested preliminary showings and compelling need, the reporter would be required to testify. [If] newsmen's confidential sources are as sensitive as they are claimed to be, the prospect of being unmasked whenever a judge determines the situation justifies it is hardly a satisfactory solution to the problem. For them, it would appear that only an absolute privilege would suffice.

We are unwilling to embark the judiciary on a long and difficult journey to such an uncertain destination. The administration of a constitutional newsman's privilege would present practical and conceptual difficulties of a high order. Sooner or later, it would be necessary to define those categories of newsmen who qualified for the privilege, a questionable procedure in light of the traditional doctrine that liberty of the press is the right of the lonely pamphleteer who uses carbon paper or a mimeograph just as much as of the large metropolitan publisher who utilizes the latest photocomposition methods. [The] informative function asserted by representatives of the organized press in the present cases is also performed by lecturers, political pollsters, novelists, academic researchers, and dramatists. Almost any author may quite accurately assert that he is contributing to the flow of information to the public, that he relies on confidential sources of information, and that these sources will be silenced if he is forced to make disclosures before a grand jury.

In each instance where a reporter is subpoenaed to testify, the courts would also be embroiled in preliminary factual and legal determinations with respect to whether the proper predicate had been laid for the reporters' appearance. [I]n the end, by considering whether enforcement of a particular law served a "compelling" governmental interest, the courts would be inextricably involved in distinguishing between the value of enforcing different criminal laws. By requiring testimony from a reporter in investigations involving some crimes but not in others, they would be making a value judgment which a legislature had declined to [make.]

At the federal level, Congress has freedom to determine whether a statutory newsman's privilege is necessary and desirable and to fashion standards and rules as narrow or broad as deemed necessary [and], equally important, to re-fashion those rules as experience from time to time may dictate. There is also merit in leaving state legislatures free, within First Amendment limits, to fashion their own standards in light of the conditions and problems with respect to the relations between law enforcement officials and press in their own [areas]. * * *

[G]rand jury investigations if instituted or conducted other than in good faith, would pose wholly different issues for resolution under the First Amendment. Official harassment of the press undertaken not for purposes of law enforcement but to disrupt a reporter's relationship with his news sources would have no justification. Grand juries are subject to judicial control and subpoenas to motions to quash. We do not expect courts will forget that grand juries must operate within the limits of the First Amendment as well as the Fifth.

We turn, therefore, to the disposition of the cases before us. [*Caldwell*] must be reversed. If there is no First Amendment privilege to refuse to answer the relevant and material questions asked during a good-faith grand jury investigation, then it is a fortiori true that there is no privilege to refuse to appear before such a grand jury until the Government demonstrates some "compelling need" for a newsman's testimony. [*Branzburg*] must be affirmed. [P]etitioner refused to answer questions that directly related to criminal conduct which he had observed and written about. [If] what petitioner wrote was true, he had direct information to provide the grand jury concerning the commission of serious crimes. [In *Pappas,* we] affirm [and] hold that petitioner must appear before the grand jury to answer the questions put to him, subject, of course, to the supervision of the presiding judge as to "the propriety, purposes, and scope of the grand jury inquiry and the pertinence of the probable testimony."

JUSTICE POWELL, concurring in the opinion of the Court.

I add this brief statement to emphasize what seems to me to be the limited nature of the Court's holding. The Court does not hold that newsmen, subpoenaed to testify before a grand jury, are without constitutional rights with respect to the gathering of news or in safeguarding their sources. [As] indicated in the concluding portion of the opinion, the Court states that no harassment of newsmen will be tolerated. If a newsman believes that the grand jury investigation is not being conducted in good faith he is not without remedy. Indeed, if the newsman is called upon to give information bearing only a remote and tenuous relationship to the subject of the investigation, or if he has some other reason to believe that his testimony implicates confidential source relationships without a legitimate need of law enforcement, he will have access to the Court on a motion to quash and an appropriate protective order may be entered. The asserted claim to privilege should be judged on its facts by the striking of a proper balance between freedom of the press and the obligation of all citizens to give relevant testimony with respect to criminal conduct. The balance of these vital constitutional and societal interests on a case-by-case basis accords with the tried and traditional way of adjudicating such questions.*

In short, the courts will be available to newsmen under circumstances where legitimate First Amendment interests require protection.

JUSTICE DOUGLAS, dissenting.

[T]here is no "compelling need" that can be shown [by the Government] which qualifies the reporter's immunity from appearing or testifying before a grand jury, unless the reporter himself is implicated in a crime. His immunity in my view is therefore quite complete, for absent his involvement in a crime, the First Amendment protects him against an appearance before a grand jury and if he is involved in a crime, the Fifth Amendment stands as a barrier. Since in my view there is no area of inquiry not protected by a privilege, the reporter need not appear for the futile purpose of invoking one to each [question.]

---

* It is to be remembered that Caldwell asserts a constitutional privilege not even to appear before the grand jury unless a court decides that the government has made a showing that meets the three preconditions specified in [Stewart, J.'s dissent]. To be sure, this would require a "balancing" of interests by the Court, but under circumstances and constraints significantly different from the balancing that will be appropriate under the Court's decision. The newsman witness, like all other witnesses, will have to appear; he will not be in a position to litigate at the threshold the State's very authority to subpoena him. Moreover, absent the constitutional preconditions that [the dissent] would impose as heavy burdens of proof to be carried by the State, the court—when called upon to protect a newsman from improper or prejudicial questioning—would be free to balance the competing interests on their merits in the particular case. The new constitutional rule endorsed by [the dissent] would, as a practical matter, defeat such a fair balancing and the essential societal interest in the detection and prosecution of crime would be heavily subordinated.

Two principles which follow from [Alexander Meiklejohn's] understanding of the First Amendment are at stake here. One is that the people, the ultimate governors, must have absolute freedom of and therefore privacy of their individual opinions and beliefs regardless of how suspect or strange they may appear to others. Ancillary to that principle is the conclusion that an individual must also have absolute privacy over whatever information he may generate in the course of testing his opinions and beliefs. In this regard, Caldwell's status as a reporter is less relevant than is his status as a student who affirmatively pursued empirical research to enlarge his own intellectual viewpoint. The second principle is that effective self-government cannot succeed unless the people are immersed in a steady, robust, unimpeded, and uncensored flow of opinion and reporting which are continuously subjected to critique, rebuttal, and re-examination. In this respect, Caldwell's status as a newsgatherer and an integral part of that process becomes critical. * * *

Sooner or later any test which provides less than blanket protection to beliefs and associations will be twisted and relaxed so as to provide virtually no protection at [all]. Perceptions of the worth of state objectives will change with the composition of the Court and with the intensity of the politics of the [times.]

JUSTICE STEWART, with whom JUSTICE BRENNAN and JUSTICE MARSHALL join, dissenting.

The Court's crabbed view of the First Amendment reflects a disturbing insensitivity to the critical role of an independent press in our society. [While] Mr. Justice Powell's enigmatic concurring opinion gives some hope of a more flexible view in the future, the Court in these cases holds that a newsman has no First Amendment right to protect his sources when called before a grand jury. The Court thus invites state and federal authorities to undermine the historic independence of the press by attempting to annex the journalistic profession as an investigative arm of government. Not only will this decision impair performance of the press' constitutionally protected functions, but it will, I am convinced, in the long run, harm rather than help the administration of justice.

[As] private and public aggregations of power burgeon in size and the pressures for conformity necessarily mount, there is obviously a continuing need for an independent press to disseminate a robust variety of information and opinion through reportage, investigation and criticism, if we are to preserve our constitutional tradition of maximizing freedom of choice by encouraging diversity of expression. * * *

A corollary of the right to publish must be the right to gather news. [This right] implies, in turn, a right to a confidential relationship between a reporter and his source. This proposition follows as a matter of simple logic once three factual predicates are recognized: (1) newsmen require informants to gather news; (2) confidentiality—the promise or understanding that names or certain aspects of communications will be kept off-the-record—is essential to the creation and maintenance of a news-gathering relationship with informants; and (3) the existence of an unbridled subpoena power—the absence of a constitutional right protecting, in *any* way, a confidential relationship from compulsory process—will either deter sources from divulging information or deter reporters from gathering and publishing information. * * *

After today's decision, the potential informant can never be sure that his identity or off-the-record communications will not subsequently be revealed through the compelled testimony of a newsman. A public spirited person inside government, who is not implicated in any crime, will now be fearful of revealing corruption or other governmental wrong-doing, because he will now know he can subsequently be identified by use of compulsory process. The potential source must, therefore, choose between risking exposure by giving information or avoiding the risk by remaining silent.

The reporter must speculate about whether contact with a controversial source or publication of controversial material will lead to a subpoena. In the event of a subpoena, under today's decision, the newsman will know that he must choose between being punished for contempt if he refuses to testify, or violating his profession's ethics[10] and impairing his resourcefulness as a reporter if he discloses confidential information. * * *

The impairment of the flow of news cannot, of course, be proven with scientific precision, as the Court seems to demand. [But] we have never before demanded that First Amendment rights rest on elaborate empirical studies demonstrating beyond any conceivable doubt that deterrent effects exist; we have never before required proof of the exact number of people potentially affected by governmental action, who would actually be dissuaded from engaging in First Amendment activity. * * *

We cannot await an unequivocal—and therefore unattainable—imprimatur from empirical studies. We can and must accept the evidence developed in the record, and elsewhere, that overwhelmingly supports the premise that deterrence will occur with regularity in important types of newsgathering relationships. Thus, we cannot escape the conclusion that when neither the reporter nor his source can rely on the shield of confidentiality against unrestrained use of the grand jury's subpoena power, valuable information will not be published and the public dialogue will inevitably be impoverished.

[W]hen a reporter is asked to appear before a grand jury and reveal confidences, I would hold that the government must (1) show that there is probable cause to believe that the newsman has information which is clearly relevant to a specific probable violation of law; (2) demonstrate that the information sought cannot be obtained by alternative means less destructive of First Amendment rights; and (3) demonstrate a compelling and overriding interest in the information. * * *

Both the "probable cause" and "alternative means" requirements [would] serve the vital function of mediating between the public interest in the administration of justice and the constitutional protection of the full flow of information. These requirements would avoid a direct conflict between these competing concerns, and they would generally provide adequate protection for newsmen. No doubt the courts would be required to make some delicate judgments in working out this accommodation. But that, after all, is the function of courts of law. Better such judgments, however difficult, than the simplistic and stultifying absolutism adopted by the Court in denying any force to the First Amendment in these cases.[36] * * *

[In Stewart, J.'s view, the Ninth Circuit correctly ruled that in the circumstances of the case, Caldwell need not divulge confidential information and, moreover, that in this case Caldwell had established that "his very appearance

---

10. The American Newspaper Guild has adopted the following rule as part of the newsman's code of ethics: "Newspaper men shall refuse to reveal confidences or disclose sources of confidential information in court or before other judicial or investigative bodies."

36. The disclaimers in Mr. Justice Powell's concurring opinion leave room for the hope that in some future case the Court may take a less absolute position in this area.

[before] the grand jury would jeopardize his relationship with his sources, leading to a severance of the news gathering relationship and impairment of the flow of news to the public." But because "only in very rare circumstances would a confidential relationship between a reporter and his source be so sensitive [as to preclude] his mere appearance before the grand jury," Stewart, J., would confine "*this* aspect of the *Caldwell* judgment [to] its own facts." Thus, he would affirm in *Caldwell* and remand the other cases for further proceedings not inconsistent with his views.]

Notes and Questions

1. *The role of the press.* Consider Vincent Blasi, *The Checking Value in First Amendment Theory,* 1977 Am.B.Found.Res.J. 521, 593: The White, J., opinion "characterized the press as a private-interest group rather than an institution with a central function to perform in the constitutional system of checks and balances [and] labeled the source relationships that the reporters sought to maintain 'a private system of informers operated by the press to report on criminal conduct' [cautioning] that this system would be 'unaccountable to the public' were a reporter's privilege to be recognized." In contrast to White, J.'s perspective, consider the remarks of Stewart, J., in a much-discussed address, *"Or of the Press,"* 26 Hast.L.J. 631, 634 (1975): "In setting up the three branches of the Federal Government, the Founders deliberately created an internally competitive[a] system. [The] primary purpose[b] of [the Free Press Clause] was a similar one: to create a fourth institution outside the Government as an additional check on the three official branches."[c] Proceeding from variations of this fourth estate view of the press, most commentators endorse a reporter's privilege. See, e.g., C. Edwin Baker, *Press Rights and Government Power to Structure the Press,* 34 U.Miami L.Rev. 819, 858 (1980) (absolute protection). But see Randall Bezanson, *The New Free Press Guarantee,* 63 Va.L.Rev. 731, 759–62 (1977) (press clause prevents special governmental assistance for press). Claims for an independent press-clause, however, need not interpret the press clause along fourth estate lines, see Rodney Smolla, *Smolla and Nimmer on Freedom of Speech* 2–104—2–129 (1984).[d]

a. For commentary on how the "cozy connections" between press and government demonstrate that the relationship is often more cooperative than adversarial, see Aviam Soifer, *Freedom of the Press in the United States* in Press Law in Modern Democracies 79, 108–110 (Lahav, ed., 1985).

b. For spirited debate about the historical evidence, compare David Anderson, *The Origins of the Press Clause,* 30 U.C.L.A.L.Rev. 455 (1983) with Leonard Levy, *On the Origins of the Free Press Clause,* 32 U.C.L.A. L.Rev. 177 (1984). See generally Leonard Levy, *Emergence of a Free Press* (1985).

c. For Brennan, J.'s views, see *Address,* 32 Rutg.L.Rev. 173 (1979).

d. For criticism of the notion of an independent press clause, see David Lange, *The Speech and Press Clauses,* 23 UCLA L.Rev. 77 (1975); Anthony Lewis, *A Preferred Position for Journalism?,* 7 Hof.L.Rev. 595 (1979); William Van Alstyne, *The First Amendment and the Free Press: A Comment on Some New Trends and Some Old Theories,* 9 Hof.L.Rev. 1 (1980); William Van Alstyne, *The Hazards to the Press of Claiming a "Preferred Position",* 28 Hast.L.J. 761 (1977). But see Floyd Abrams, *The Press is Different: Reflections on Justice Stewart and the Autonomous Press,* 7 Hof. L.Rev. 563 (1979). For an effort to transcend the issues involved, see generally Robert Sack, *Reflections on the Wrong Question: Special Constitutional Privilege for the Institutional Press,* 7 Hof.L.Rev. 629 (1979). Finally, for commentary on the "tension between journalism as the political, sometimes partisan fourth estate and journalism as a profession" purporting to operate as a "neutral and objective medium," see Pnina Lahav, *An Outline for a General Theory of Press Law in Democracy* in Press Law in Modern Democracies 339, 352–54 (Lahav ed. 1985). See also Lee Bollinger, *The Press and the Public Interest: An Essay on the Relationship Between Social Behavior and the Language of First Amendment Theory,* 82 Mich.L.Rev. 1447, 1457 (1984) (commenting generally on the pitfalls connected with justifying a free press by arguing that it serves the public interest: "More than most groups (com-

2. *Evaluating Powell, J.'s concurrence.* Did five justices— or only four—hold that grand juries may pursue their goals by any means short of bad faith? May one conclude that the information sought bears "only a remote and tenuous relationship to the subject of investigation" on grounds falling short of demonstrating "bad faith"? Does Powell, J.'s suggested test—the privilege claim "should be judged on its facts by [balancing the] vital constitutional and societal interests on a case-by-case basis"—resemble Stewart, J.'s dissenting approach more than White, J.'s? Extrajudicially, Stewart, J., has referred to *Branzburg* as a case which rejected claims for a journalist's privilege "by a vote of 5–4, or, considering Mr. Justice Powell's concurring opinion, perhaps by a vote of 4½–4½." Potter Stewart, *"Or of the Press,"* 26 Hast.L.J. 631, 635 (1975). The majority of courts applying *Branzburg* have concluded that Powell, J.'s opinion read together with the dissents affords the basis for a qualified privilege. Among the issues litigated are whether the privilege should be confined to journalists (or extended e.g. to academics) and the related question of how to define journalists and whether the privilege belongs to the source, the reporter, or both. For an exhaustive survey, see James Goodale, Joseph Moodhe & Rodney Ott, *Reporter's Privilege Cases,* 421 PLI/PAT 63 (1995).

The Court's most recent expression unanimously refuses, at least in the absence of bad faith, to extend a qualified first amendment privilege to "confidential" tenure files and, in dictum, confines *Branzburg* to the recognition that the "'bad faith' exercise of grand jury powers might raise First Amendment concerns." *University of Pennsylvania v. EEOC,* 493 U.S. 182, 110 S.Ct. 577, 107 L.Ed.2d 571 (1990) (gender discrimination claim). For commentary, see Byrne, *Academic Freedom: A "Special Concern of the First Amendment,"* 99 Yale L.J. 251 (1989).

3. *Other contexts.* Does *Branzburg's* emphasis on the grand jury's special role in the American criminal justice system warrant different treatment of the journalist's privilege when a prosecutor seeks disclosure? See Donna Murasky, *The Journalist's Privilege: Branzburg and Its Aftermath,* 52 Tex.L.Rev. 829, 885 (1974). Are the interests of civil litigants in compelling disclosure of a journalist's confidences significantly weaker than those of criminal litigants? Should there be an absolute journalist's privilege in civil discovery proceedings? See id. at 898–903. What if the journalist is a party to the litigation? Should journalists have greater protection for non-confidential information than other potential witnesses? See *Gonzales v. National Broadcasting Co.,* 155 F.3d 618 (2d Cir.1998).

4. *Reverse Branzburg.* Suppose a reporter reveals a confidential source who sues for redress. Any first amendment protection? See *Cohen v. Cowles Media Co.,* 501 U.S. 663, 669, 111 S.Ct. 2513, 115 L.Ed.2d 586 (1991).[e]

5. *State "shield laws" and a criminal defendant's right to compulsory process.* As of 1984, 26 states had enacted "shield" laws.[f] Some protect only

pare lawyers, for example) the press is in conflict over its relationship to the world on which it regularly reports.").

e. For commentary on *Cohen,* see Jerome A. Barron, *Cohen v. Cowles Media and Its Significance for First Amendment Law and Journalism,* 3 Wm. & Mary Bill Rts. J. 419 (1994); Eric B. Easton, *Two Wrongs Mock a Right: Overcoming the Cohen Maledicta that Bar First Amendment Protection for Newsgathering,* 58 Ohio St. L.J. 1135 (1997); Lili Levi, *Dangerous Liasons: Seduction and Betrayal in*

Confidential Press–Source Relations, 43 Rutgers L.Rev. 609 (1991).

f. Consider Gerald F. Uelmen, *Leaks, Gags and Shields: Taking Responsibility,* 37 Santa Clara L.Rev. 943, 945 (1997): "Current 'shield laws' encourage the leaking of information by protecting the leaker from any consequences for his breach of confidentiality, and place no responsibility on reporters for lack of restraint in promising confidentiality to their sources. Somehow the irony has escaped us, that we encourage irresponsible breaches of confiden-

journalists' sources; some (including New Jersey) protect undisclosed information obtained in the course of a journalist's professional activities as well as sources.

In re Farber, 78 N.J. 259, 394 A.2d 330 (1978), cert. denied, 439 U.S. 997, 99 S.Ct. 598, 58 L.Ed.2d 670 (1978): *New York Times* investigative reporter Myron Farber wrote a series of articles claiming that an unidentified "Doctor X" had caused the death of several patients by poisoning. This led to the indictment and eventual prosecution of Dr. Jascalevich for murder. (He was ultimately acquitted.) In response to the defendant's request, the trial court demanded the disclosure of Farber's sources and the production of his interview notes and other information for his in camera inspection. Relying on the first amendment and the state shield law, Farber refused to comply with the subpoenas. After White, J., and then Marshall, J., had denied stays, each deeming it unlikely that four justices would grant certiorari at this stage of the case, Farber was jailed for civil contempt and the *Times* heavily fined.

The state supreme court (5–2) upheld civil and criminal convictions of the *Times* and Farber. Under the circumstances, it ruled, the first amendment did not protect Farber against disclosure. Nor did the New Jersey shield law, for Farber's statutory rights had to yield to Dr. Jascalevich's sixth amendment right "to have compulsory process for obtaining witnesses in his favor."[g]

ZURCHER v. STANFORD DAILY, 436 U.S. 547, 98 S.Ct. 1970, 56 L.Ed.2d 525 (1978), again declined to afford the press special protection—dividing very much as in *Branzburg*.[a] A student newspaper that had published articles and photographs of a clash between demonstrators and police brought this federal action, claiming that a search of its offices for film and pictures showing events at the scene of the police-demonstrators clash (the newspaper was not involved in the unlawful acts) had violated its first and fourth amendment rights. A 5–3 majority, per WHITE, J., held that the fourth amendment does not prevent the government from issuing a search warrant (based on reasonable cause to believe that the "things" to be searched for are located on the property) simply because the owner or possessor of the place to be searched is not reasonably suspected of criminal involvement. The Court also rejected the argument that "whatever may be true of third-party searches generally, where the third party is a newspaper, there are additional [first amendment factors justifying] a nearly per se rule forbidding the search warrant and permitting only the subpoena duces tecum. The general submission is that searches of newspaper offices for evidence of crime reasonably believed to be on the premises will seriously threaten the ability of the press to gather, analyze, and disseminate news.

tiality by guaranteeing to violaters that we will protect the confidentiality of their breach! Those who have no respect for confidentiality that protects others are rewarded by our guarantee of absolute confidentiality for their treachery."

g. For analysis of the case, see Note, 32 Rutg.L.Rev. 545 (1979). The case is also discussed at length by *New York Times* columnist Anthony Lewis, *A Preferred Position for Journalism?,* 7 Hof.L.Rev. 595, 610–18 (1979).

a. In both cases, White, J., joined by Burger, C.J., Blackmun, Powell and Rehnquist, JJ.,

delivered the opinion of the Court and in both cases the "fifth vote"—Powell, J.,—also wrote a separate opinion which seemed to meet the concerns of the dissent part way. In both cases Stewart, J., dissented, maintaining that the Court's holding would seriously impair "newsgathering." Stevens, J., who had replaced Douglas, J., also dissented in Zurcher, as had Douglas in *Branzburg*. Brennan, J., who had joined Stewart, J.'s dissent in *Branzburg,* did not participate in *Zurcher.*

"[Although] [a]ware of the long struggle between Crown and press and desiring to curb unjustified official intrusions, [the Framers] did not forbid warrants where the press was involved, did not require special showing that subpoenas would be impractical, and did not insist that the owner of the place to be searched, if connected with the press, must be shown to be implicated in the offense being investigated. Further, the prior cases do no more than insist that the courts apply the warrant requirements with particular exactitude when First Amendment interests would be endangered by the search. [N]o more than this is required where the warrant requested is for the seizure of criminal evidence reasonably believed to be on the premises occupied by a newspaper. Properly administered, the preconditions for a warrant—probable cause, specificity [as to] place [and] things to be seized and overall reasonableness—should afford [the press] sufficient protection * * *.

"[R]espondents and amici have pointed to only a very few instances [since] 1971 involving [newspaper office searches]. This reality hardly suggests abuse, and if abuse occurs, there will be time enough to deal with it. Furthermore, the press [is] not easily intimidated—nor should it be."

POWELL, J., concurring, rejected Stewart, J.'s dissenting view that the press is entitled to "a special procedure, not available to others," when the government requires evidence in its possession, but added: "This is not to say [that a warrant] sufficient to support the search of an apartment or an automobile would be reasonable in supporting the search of a newspaper office. [While] there is no justification for the establishment of a separate Fourth Amendment procedure for the press, a magistrate asked to issue a warrant for the search of press offices can and should take cognizance of the independent values protected by the First Amendment—such as those highlighted by [Stewart, J., dissenting]—when he weighs such factors."[b]

STEWART, joined by Marshall, J., dissented: "A search warrant allows police officers to ransack the files of a newspaper, reading each and every document until they have found the one named in the warrant, while a subpoena would permit the newspaper itself to produce only the specific documents requested. A search, unlike a subpoena, will therefore lead to the needless exposure of confidential information completely unrelated to the purpose of the investigation. The knowledge that police officers can make an unannounced raid on a newsroom is thus bound to have a deterrent effect on the availability of confidential news sources. [The result] will be a diminishing flow of potentially important information to the public.

"[Here, unlike *Branzburg,* the newspaper does] not claim that any of the evidence sought was privileged[, but] only that a subpoena would have served equally well to produce that evidence. Thus, we are not concerned with the principle, central to *Branzburg,* that ' "the public [has] a right to everyman's evidence," ' but only with whether any significant social interest would be impaired if the police were generally required to obtain evidence from the press by means of a subpoena rather than a search. * * *

"Perhaps as a matter of abstract policy a newspaper office should receive no more protection from unannounced police searches than, say, the office of a doctor or the office of a bank. But we are here to uphold a Constitution. And our

---

b. Powell, J., noted that his *Branzburg* concurrence may "properly be read as supporting the view expressed in the text above, and in the Court's [*Zurcher*] opinion," that under the warrant requirement "the magistrate should consider the values of a free press as well as the societal interest in enforcing the criminal laws."

Constitution does not explicitly protect the practice of medicine or the business of banking from all abridgement by government. It does explicitly protect the freedom of the press.'"[c]

Notes and Questions

The distinctions between search and subpoena are underscored in Tribe 2d ed., at 973 (2d ed. 1988): "When a subpoena is served on a newspaper, it has the opportunity to assert constitutional and statutory rights [such as 'shield laws,' enacted in many states, protecting reporters from divulging information given them in confidence] to keep certain materials confidential. Such protection is circumvented when officials can proceed *ex parte,* by search warrant. And the risk of abuse may be greatest exactly when the press plays its most vital and creative role in our political system, the role of watchdog on official corruption and abuse. Officials who find themselves the targets [of] media investigations may well be tempted to conduct searches to find out precisely what various journalists have discovered, and to retaliate against reporters who have unearthed and reported official wrongdoing."

B. ACCESS TO TRIALS AND OTHER GOVERNMENTALLY CONTROLLED INFORMATION AND INSTITUTIONS

By 1978, no Supreme Court holding contradicted Burger, C.J.'s contention for the plurality in *Houchins v. KQED,* 438 U.S. 1, 98 S.Ct. 2588, 57 L.Ed.2d 553 (1978) that, "neither the First Amendment nor the Fourteenth Amendment mandates a right of access to government information or sources of information within the government's control." Or as Stewart, J., put it in an often-quoted statement, "The Constitution itself is neither a Freedom of Information Act nor an Official Secrets Act." *"Or of the Press,"* 26 Hast.L.J. 631, 636 (1975). *Richmond Newspapers, infra,* constitutes the Court's first break with its past denials of first amendment rights to information within governmental control.

RICHMOND NEWSPAPERS, INC. v. VIRGINIA
448 U.S. 555, 100 S.Ct. 2814, 65 L.Ed.2d 973 (1980).

[At the commencement of his fourth trial on a murder charge (his first conviction having been reversed and two subsequent retrials having ended in mistrials), defendant moved, without objection by the prosecutor or two reporters present, that the trial be closed to the public-defense counsel stating that he did not "want any information being shuffled back and forth when we have a recess as [to] who testified to what." The trial judge granted the motion, stating that "the statute gives me that power specifically." He presumably referred to Virginia Code § 19.2–266, providing that in all criminal trials "the court may, in its discretion, exclude [any] persons whose presence would impair the conduct of a fair trial, provided that the [defendant's right] to a public trial shall not be violated." Later the same day the trial court granted appellants' request for a hearing on a motion to vacate the closure order. At the closed hearing, appellants observed that prior to the entry of its closure order the court had failed to make any evidentiary findings or to consider any other, less drastic measures to ensure a fair trial. Defendant stated that he "didn't want information to leak out," be

---

c. Stevens, J., dissented on the general fourth amendment issue.

published by the media, perhaps inaccurately, and then be seen by the jurors. Noting inter alia that "having people in the Courtroom is distracting to the jury" and that if "the rights of the defendant are infringed in any way [and if his closure motion] doesn't completely override all rights of everyone else, then I'm inclined to go along with" the defendant, the court denied the motion to vacate the closure order. Defendant was subsequently found not guilty.]

CHIEF JUSTICE BURGER announced the judgment of the Court and delivered an opinion in which JUSTICE WHITE and JUSTICE STEVENS joined.

[T]he precise issue presented here has not previously been before this Court for decision. [Gannett Co. v. DePasquale, 443 U.S. 368, 99 S.Ct. 2898, 61 L.Ed.2d 608 (1979)] was not required to decide whether a right of access to *trials*, as distinguished from hearings on *pre*trial motions, was constitutionally guaranteed. The Court held that the Sixth Amendment's guarantee to the accused of a public trial gave neither the public nor the press an enforceable right of access to a *pre*trial suppression hearing. One concurring opinion specifically emphasized that "a hearing on a motion before trial to suppress evidence is not a *trial*." (Burger, C.J., concurring). Moreover, the Court did not decide whether the First and Fourteenth Amendments guarantee a right of the public to attend trials; nor did the dissenting opinion reach this issue. [H]ere for the first time the Court is asked to decide whether a criminal trial itself may be closed to the public upon the unopposed request of a defendant, without any demonstration that closure is required to protect the defendant's superior right to a fair trial, or that some other overriding consideration requires closure.

[T]he historical evidence demonstrates conclusively that at the time when our organic laws were adopted, criminal trials both here and in England had long been presumptively open[, thus giving] assurance that the proceedings were conducted fairly to all concerned, [and] discourag[ing] perjury, the misconduct of participants, and decisions based on secret bias or partiality. [Moreover, the] early history of open trials in part reflects the widespread acknowledgment [that] public trials had significant therapeutic value. [When] a shocking crime occurs, a community reaction of outrage and public protest often follows. Thereafter the open processes of justice serve an important prophylactic purpose, providing an outlet for community concern, hostility, and emotion.

[The] crucial prophylactic aspects of the administration of justice cannot function in the dark; no community catharsis can occur if justice is "done in a corner [or] in any covert manner." [To] work effectively, it is important that society's criminal process "satisfy the appearance of justice," and the appearance of justice can best be provided by allowing people to observe it.

[From] this unbroken, uncontradicted history, supported by reasons as valid today as in centuries past, we are bound to conclude that a presumption of openness inheres in the very nature of a criminal trial under our system of criminal justice. [Nevertheless,] the State presses its contention that neither the Constitution nor the Bill of Rights contains any provision which by its terms guarantees to the public the right to attend criminal trials. Standing alone, this is correct, but there remains the question whether, absent an explicit provision, the Constitution affords protection against exclusion of the public from criminal trials.

[The] expressly guaranteed [first amendment] freedoms share a common core purpose of assuring freedom of communication on matters relating to the functioning of government. Plainly it would be difficult to single out any aspect of government of higher concern and importance to the people than the manner in which criminal trials are conducted * * *.

The Bill of Rights was enacted against the backdrop of the long history of trials being presumptively open. [In] guaranteeing freedoms such as those of speech and press, the First Amendment can be read as protecting the right of everyone to attend trials so as to give meaning to those explicit guarantees. * * * Free speech carries with it some freedom to listen. "In a variety of contexts this Court has referred to a First Amendment right to 'receive information and ideas.'" *Kleindienst v. Mandel,* 408 U.S. 753, 762, 92 S.Ct. 2576, 2581, 33 L.Ed.2d 683 (1972).ᵃ What this means in the context of trials is that the First Amendment guarantees of speech and press, standing alone, prohibit government from summarily closing courtroom doors which had long been open to the public at the time that amendment was adopted.

[It] is not crucial whether we describe this right to attend criminal trials to hear, see, and communicate observations concerning them as a "right of access," cf. *Gannett* (Powell, J., concurring); *Saxbe v. Washington Post Co.,* 417 U.S. 843, 94 S.Ct. 2811, 41 L.Ed.2d 514 (1974); *Pell v. Procunier,* 417 U.S. 817, 94 S.Ct. 2800, 41 L.Ed.2d 495 (1974),[11] or a "right to gather information," for we have recognized that "without some protection for seeking out the news, freedom of the press could be eviscerated." *Branzburg v. Hayes.* The explicit, guaranteed rights to speak and to publish concerning what takes place at a trial would lose much meaning if access to observe the trial could, as it was here, be foreclosed arbitrarily.

The right of access to places traditionally open to the public, as criminal trials have long been, may be seen as assured by the amalgam of the First Amendment guarantees of speech and press; and their affinity to the right of assembly is not without relevance. From the outset, the right of assembly was regarded not only as an independent right but also as a catalyst to augment the free exercise of the other First Amendment rights with which it was deliberately linked by the draftsmen. * * * Subject to the traditional time, place, and manner restrictions, streets, sidewalks, and parks are places traditionally open, where First Amendment rights may be exercised [see generally Sec. 6 infra]; a trial courtroom also is a public place where the people generally—and representatives of the media—have a right to be present, and where their presence historically has been thought to enhance the integrity and quality of what takes place.

* * * Notwithstanding the appropriate caution against reading into the Constitution rights not explicitly defined, the Court has acknowledged that certain unarticulated rights are implicit in enumerated guarantees [referring, inter alia, to the rights of association and of privacy and the right to travel. See generally Ch. 6, Secs. 2 & 3]. [T]hese important but unarticulated rights [have] been found to share constitutional protection in common with explicit guarantees. The concerns expressed by Madison and others have thus been [resolved].ᵇ

---

a. *Mandel* held that the Executive had plenary power to exclude a Belgium journalist from the country, at least so long as it operated on the basis of a facially legitimate and bona fide reason for exclusion. Although the Court decided ultimately not to balance the government's particular justification against the first amendment interest, it recognized that those who sought personal communication with the excluded alien did have a first amendment interest at stake. The Court apparently assumed that the excluded speaker had no rights at stake, and none were asserted on his behalf.

11. *Procunier* and *Saxbe* are distinguishable in the sense that they were concerned with penal institutions which, by definition, are not "open" or public places. * * * See also *Greer v. Spock* (military bases) [Sec. 6, II infra].

b. The Chief Justice noted "the perceived need" of the Constitution's draftsmen "for some sort of constitutional 'saving clause' [which] would serve to foreclose application to the Bill of Rights of the maxim that the affirmation of particular rights implies a negation of those not expressly defined. Madison's ef-

We hold that the right to attend criminal trials[17] is implicit in the guarantees of the First Amendment; without the freedom to attend such trials, which people have exercised for centuries, important aspects of freedom of speech and "of the press could be eviscerated." *Branzburg.*

[In the present case,] the trial court made no findings to support closure; no inquiry was made as to whether alternative solutions would have met the need to ensure fairness; there was no recognition of any right under the Constitution for the public or press to attend the trial. In contrast to the pretrial proceeding dealt with in *Gannett,* there exist in the context of the trial itself various tested alternatives to satisfy the constitutional demands of fairness. [For example, there was nothing] to indicate that sequestration of the jurors would not have guarded against their being subjected to any improper information.[c] * * * Absent an overriding interest articulated in findings, the trial of a criminal case must be open to the public. * * *

Reversed.[d]

JUSTICE BRENNAN, with whom JUSTICE MARSHALL joins, concurring in the judgment.

[*Gannett*] held that the Sixth Amendment right to a public trial was personal to the accused, conferring no right of access to pretrial proceedings that is separately enforceable by the public or the press. [This case] raises the question whether the First Amendment, of its own force and as applied to the States through the Fourteenth Amendment, secures the public an independent right of access to trial proceedings. Because I believe that [it does secure] such a public right of access, I agree [that], without more, agreement of the trial judge and the parties cannot constitutionally close a trial to the public.[1]

While freedom of expression is made inviolate by the First Amendment, and with only rare and stringent exceptions, may not be suppressed, the First Amendment has not been viewed by the Court in all settings as providing an equally categorical assurance of the correlative freedom of access to information.[2] Yet the Court has not ruled out a public access component to the First Amendment in every circumstance. Read with care and in context, our decisions must therefore be understood as holding only that any privilege of access to governmental information is subject to a degree of restraint dictated by the nature of the

forts, culminating in the Ninth Amendment, served to allay the fears of those who were concerned that expressing certain guarantees could be read as excluding others."

17. Whether the public has a right to attend [civil trials is] not raised by this case, but we note that historically both civil and criminal trials have been presumptively open.

c. Once the jurors are selected, when, if ever, will their sequestration *not* be a satisfactory alternative to closure?

d. Powell, J., took no part. In *Gannett,* he took the position that a first amendment right of access applied to courtroom proceedings, albeit subject to overriding when justice so demanded or when confidentiality was necessary.

l. Of course, the Sixth Amendment remains the source of the *accused's* own right to insist upon public judicial proceedings. *Gannett.*

That the Sixth Amendment explicitly establishes a public trial right does not impliedly foreclose the derivation of such a right from other provisions of the Constitution. The Constitution was not framed as a work of carpentry, in which all joints must fit snugly without overlapping. * * *

2. A conceptually separate, yet related, question is whether the media should enjoy greater access rights than the general public. But no such contention is at stake here. Since the media's right of access is at least equal to that of the general public, this case is resolved by a decision that the state statute unconstitutionally restricts public access to trials. As a practical matter, however, the institutional press is the likely, and fitting, chief beneficiary of a right of access because it serves as the "agent" of interested citizens, and funnels information about trials to a large number of individuals.

information and countervailing interests in security or confidentiality. [Cases such as *Houchins, Saxbe* and *Pell*] neither comprehensively nor absolutely deny that public access to information may at times be implied by the First Amendment and the principles which animate it.

The Court's approach in right of access cases simply reflects the special nature of a claim of First Amendment right to gather information. Customarily, First Amendment guarantees are interposed to protect communication between speaker and listener. When so employed against prior restraints, free speech protections are almost insurmountable. See generally Brennan, *Address,* 32 Rutg. L.Rev. 173, 176 (1979). But the First Amendment embodies more than a commitment to free expression and communicative interchange for their own sakes; it has a *structural* role to play in securing and fostering our republican system of self-government. Implicit in this structural role is not only "the principle that debate on public issues should be uninhibited, robust, and wide-open," but the antecedent assumption that valuable public debate—as well as other civic behavior—must be informed. The structural model links the First Amendment to that process of communication necessary for a democracy to survive, and thus entails solicitude not only for communication itself, but for the indispensable conditions of meaningful communication.

[A]n assertion of the prerogative to gather information must [be] assayed by considering the information sought and the opposing interests invaded. This judicial task is as much a matter of sensitivity to practical necessities as it is of abstract reasoning. But at least two helpful principles may be sketched. First, the case for a right of access has special force when drawn from an enduring and vital tradition of public entree to particular proceedings or information. Such a tradition commands respect in part because the Constitution carries the gloss of history. More importantly, a tradition of accessibility implies the favorable judgment of experience. Second, the value of access must be measured in specifics. Analysis is not advanced by rhetorical statements that all information bears upon public issues; what is crucial in individual cases is whether access to a particular government process is important in terms of that very process.

[This Court has] persistently defended the public character of the trial process. *In re Oliver,* 333 U.S. 257, 68 S.Ct. 499, 92 L.Ed. 682 (1948), established that [fourteenth amendment due process] forbids closed criminal trials [and] acknowledged that open trials are indispensable to First Amendment political and religious freedoms.

By the same token, a special solicitude for the public character of judicial proceedings is evident in the Court's rulings upholding the right to report about the administration of justice. While these decisions are impelled by the classic protections afforded by the First Amendment to pure communication, they are also bottomed upon a keen appreciation of the structural interest served in opening the judicial system to public inspection. So, in upholding a privilege for reporting truthful information about judicial misconduct proceedings, *Landmark* emphasized that public scrutiny of the operation of a judicial disciplinary body implicates a major purpose of the First Amendment—"discussion of governmental affairs." Again, *Nebraska Press* noted that the traditional guarantee against prior restraint "should have particular force as applied to reporting of criminal proceedings." And *Cox Broadcasting* instructed that "[w]ith respect to judicial proceedings in particular, the function of the press serves to guarantee the fairness of trials and to bring to bear the beneficial effects of public scrutiny upon the administration of justice."

[Open] trials play a fundamental role in furthering the efforts of our judicial system to assure the criminal defendant a fair and accurate adjudication of guilt or innocence. But, as a feature of our governing system of justice, the trial process serves other, broadly political, interests, and public access advances these objectives as well. To that extent, trial access possesses specific structural significance.

[For] a civilization founded upon principles of ordered liberty to survive and flourish, its members must share the conviction that they are governed equitably. That necessity * * * mandates a system of justice that demonstrates the fairness of the law to our citizens. One major function of the trial is to make that demonstration.

Secrecy is profoundly inimical to this demonstrative [purpose]. Public access is essential, therefore, if trial adjudication is to achieve the objective of maintaining public confidence in the administration of justice. But the trial [also] plays a pivotal role in the entire judicial process, and, by extension, in our form of government. Under our system, judges are not mere umpires, but, in their own sphere, lawmakers—a coordinate branch of *government*. [Thus], so far as the trial is the mechanism for judicial factfinding, as well as the initial forum for legal decisionmaking, it is a genuine governmental proceeding.

[More] importantly, public access to trials acts as an important check, akin in purpose to the other checks and balances that infuse our system of government. "The knowledge that every criminal trial is subject to contemporaneous review in the forum of public opinion is an effective restraint on possible abuse of judicial power," *Oliver*—an abuse that, in many cases, would have ramifications beyond the impact upon the parties before the court. * * *

Popular attendance at trials, in sum, substantially furthers the particular public purposes of that critical judicial proceeding. In that sense, public access is an indispensable element of the trial process itself. Trial access, therefore, assumes structural importance in our "government of laws."

As previously noted, resolution of First Amendment public access claims in individual cases must be strongly influenced by the weight of historical practice and by an assessment of the specific structural value of public access in the circumstances. With regard to the case at hand, our ingrained tradition of public trials and the importance of public access to the broader purposes of the trial process, tip the balance strongly toward the rule that trials be open.[23] What countervailing interests might be sufficiently compelling to reverse this presumption of openness need not concern us now,[24] for the statute at stake here authorizes trial closures at the unfettered discretion of the judge and parties.[25] [Thus it] violates the First and Fourteenth Amendments * * *.

JUSTICE STEWART, concurring in the judgment.

23. The presumption of public trials is, of course, not at all incompatible with reasonable restrictions imposed upon courtroom behavior in the interests of decorum. Thus, when engaging in interchanges at the bench, the trial judge is not required to allow public or press intrusion upon the huddle. Nor does this opinion intimate that judges are restricted in their ability to conduct conferences in chambers, inasmuch as such conferences are distinct from trial proceedings.

24. For example, national security concerns about confidentiality may sometimes warrant closures during sensitive portions of trial proceedings, such as testimony about state secrets.

25. Significantly, closing a trial lacks even the justification for barring the door to pretrial hearings: the necessity of preventing dissemination of suppressible prejudicial evidence to the public before the jury pool has become, in a practical sense, finite and subject to sequestration.

Whatever the ultimate answer [may] be with respect to pretrial suppression hearings in criminal cases, the First and Fourteenth Amendments clearly give the press and the public a right of access to trials themselves, civil as well as criminal. * * *

In conspicuous contrast to a military base, *Greer*; a jail, *Adderley v. Florida,* 385 U.S. 39, 87 S.Ct. 242, 17 L.Ed.2d 149 (1966); or a prison, *Pell,* a trial courtroom is a public place. Even more than city streets, sidewalks, and parks as areas of traditional First Amendment activity, a trial courtroom is a place where representatives of the press and of the public are not only free to be, but where their presence serves to assure the integrity of what goes on.

But this does not mean that the First Amendment right of members of the public and representatives of the press to attend civil and criminal trials is absolute. Just as a legislature may impose reasonable time, place and manner restrictions upon the exercise of First Amendment freedoms, so may a trial judge impose reasonable limitations upon the unrestricted occupation of a courtroom by representatives of the press and members of the public. Moreover, [there] may be occasions when not all who wish to attend a trial may do so.[3] And while there exist many alternative ways to satisfy the constitutional demands of a fair trial, those demands may also sometimes justify limitations upon the unrestricted presence of spectators in the courtroom.[5]

Since in the present case the trial judge appears to have given no recognition to the right [of] the press and [the] public to be present at [the] murder trial over which he was presiding, the judgment under review must be [reversed.]

Justice White, concurring.

This case would have been unnecessary had *Gannett* construed the Sixth Amendment to forbid excluding the public from criminal proceedings except in narrowly defined circumstances. But the Court there rejected the submission of four of us to this effect, thus requiring that the First Amendment issue involved here be addressed. On this issue, I concur in the opinion of the Chief Justice.

Justice Blackmun, concurring in the judgment.

My opinion and vote in partial dissent [in] *Gannett* compels my vote to reverse the judgment. [It] is gratifying [to] see the Court now looking to and relying upon legal history in determining the fundamental public character of the criminal trial. * * *

The Court's ultimate ruling in *Gannett,* with such clarification as is provided by the opinions in this case today, apparently is now to the effect that there is no *Sixth* Amendment right on the part of the public—or the press—to an open hearing on a motion to suppress. I, of course, continue to believe that *Gannett* was in error, both in its interpretation of the Sixth Amendment generally, and in its application to the suppression hearing, for I remain convinced that the right to a public trial is to be found where the Constitution explicitly placed it—in the Sixth Amendment.

---

3. In such situations, representatives of the press must be assured access, *Houchins* (concurring opinion).

5. This is not to say that only constitutional considerations can justify such restrictions. The preservation of trade secrets, for example, might justify the exclusion of the public from at least some segments of a civil trial. And the sensibilities of a youthful prosecution witness, for example, might justify similar exclusion in a criminal trial for rape, so long as the defendant's Sixth Amendment right to a public trial were not impaired.

[But] with the Sixth Amendment set to one side in this case, I am driven to conclude, as a secondary position, that the First Amendment must provide some measure of protection for public access to the trial. The opinion in partial dissent in *Gannett* explained that the public has an intense need and a deserved right to know about the administration of justice in general; about the prosecution of local crimes in particular; about the conduct of the judge, the prosecutor, defense counsel, police officers, other public servants, and all the actors in the judicial arena; and about the trial itself. It is clear and obvious to me, on the approach the Court has chosen to take, that, by closing this criminal trial, the trial judge abridged these First Amendment interests of the public. * * *

JUSTICE STEVENS, concurring.

This is a watershed case. Until today the Court has accorded virtually absolute protection to the dissemination of information or ideas, but never before has it squarely held that the acquisition of newsworthy matter is entitled to any constitutional protection whatsoever. An additional word of emphasis is therefore appropriate.

Twice before, the Court has implied that any governmental restriction on access to information, no matter how severe and no matter how unjustified, would be constitutionally acceptable so long as it did not single out the press for special disabilities not applicable to the public at large. In a dissent joined by [Brennan and Marshall, JJ.] in *Saxbe,* Justice Powell unequivocally rejected [that conclusion.] And in *Houchins,* I explained at length why [Brennan, Powell, JJ.] and I were convinced that "[a]n official prison policy of concealing * * * knowledge from the public by arbitrarily cutting off the flow of information at its source abridges [first amendment freedoms]." Since [Marshall and Blackmun, JJ.] were unable to participate in that case, a majority of the Court neither accepted nor rejected that conclusion or the contrary conclusion expressed in the prevailing opinions. Today, however, for the first time, the Court unequivocally holds that an arbitrary interference with access to important information is an abridgment of the freedoms of speech and of the press protected by the First Amendment.

It is somewhat ironic that the Court should find more reason to recognize a right of access today than it did in *Houchins.* For *Houchins* involved the plight of a segment of society least able to protect itself, an attack on a longstanding policy of concealment, and an absence of any legitimate justification for abridging public access to information about how government operates. In this case we are protecting the interests of the most powerful voices in the community, we are concerned with an almost unique exception to an established tradition of openness in the conduct of criminal trials, and it is likely that the closure order was motivated by the judge's desire to protect the individual defendant from the burden of a fourth criminal trial.[2]

In any event, for the reasons stated [in] my *Houchins* opinion, as well as those stated by the Chief Justice today, I agree that the First Amendment protects the public and the press from abridgment of their rights of access to information about the operation of their government, including the Judicial Branch; given the total absence of any record justification for the closure order entered in this case, that order violated the First Amendment * * *.

---

2. Neither that likely motivation nor facts showing the risk that a fifth trial would have been necessary without closure of the fourth are disclosed in this record, however. The absence of any articulated reason for the closure order is a sufficient basis for distinguishing this case from *Gannett.* The decision today is in no way inconsistent with the perfectly unambiguous holding in *Gannett* that the rights guaranteed by the Sixth Amendment are rights that may be asserted by the accused rather than members of the general public. * * *

JUSTICE REHNQUIST, dissenting.

[I] do not believe that [anything in the Constitution] require[s] that a State's reasons for denying public access to a trial, where both [the prosecution and defense] have consented to [a court-approved closure order], are subject to any additional constitutional review at our hands.

[The] issue here is not whether the "right" to freedom of the press * * * overrides the defendant's "right" to a fair trial, [but] whether any provision in the Constitution may fairly be read to prohibit what the [trial court] did in this case. Being unable to find any such prohibition in the First, Sixth, Ninth, or any other Amendments [or] in the Constitution itself, I dissent.

Notes and Questions

1. *Beyond the justice system.* May (should) "public access to information about how government operates" (to use Stevens, J.'s phrase) be denied, as the Chief Justice suggests, simply on the ground that the place at issue has not been *traditionally* open to the public (recall how the Chief Justice distinguishes penal institutions from criminal trials) or should the government also have to advance, as Stevens, J., suggests, "legitimate justification" for "abridging" public access? Compare the controversy over whether "the right to a public forum" should turn on whether the place at issue has *historically* been dedicated to the exercise of first amendment rights or on whether the manner of expression is *basically incompatible* with the normal activity of the place at a particular time. See generally the materials on the Public Forum: New Forums, Sec. 6, II infra. See also Note, *The First Amendment Right to Gather State–Held Information,* 89 Yale L.J. 923, 933–39 (1979). Consider, too, Vincent Blasi, *The Checking Value in First Amendment Theory,* 1977 Am.B.Found.Res.J. 521, 609–10: "[U]nder the checking value, the interest of the press (and ultimately the public) in learning certain information relevant to the abuse of official power would sometimes take precedence over perfectly legitimate and substantial government interests such as efficiency and confidentiality. Thus, the First Amendment may require that journalists have access as a general matter to some records, such as certain financial documents, which anyone investigating common abuses of the public trust would routinely want to inspect, even though the granting of such access would undoubtedly entail some costs and risks. Also, the balance might be tilted even more in the direction of access if a journalist could demonstrate that there are reasonable grounds to believe that certain records contain evidence of misconduct by public officials."

But cf. Yale Kamisar, *Right of Access to Information Generated or Controlled by the Government: Richmond Newspapers Examined and Gannett Revisited* in Jesse Choper, Yale Kamisar & Lawrence Tribe, The Supreme Court: Trends and Developments, 1979–80 145, 166 (1981): "[T]hese law review commentaries go quite far. But *someday* the views they advance may be the law of the land. In the meantime, however, many more battles will have to be fought. *Someday* we may look back on *Richmond Newspapers* as the '*Powell v. Alabama*' of the right of access to government-controlled information—but it was a long, hard road from *Powell* to *Gideon.*"[e]

e. For endorsements of generous access, see Franklyn Haiman, *Speech and Law in a Free Society* 108–14, 368–97 (1981); Mark Yudof, *When Government Speaks* 246–55 (1983); Thomas Emerson, *Legal Foundations of the Right to Know,* 1976 Wash.U.L.Q. 1, 14–17; Anthony Lewis, *A Public Right to Know about Public Institutions: The First Amendment as*

2. *Within the justice system.* How far does (should) *Richmond Newspapers* extend within the justice system? To criminal pre-trial proceedings?[f] How is a trial defined? Should it extend to conferences in chambers or at the bench? To grand jury hearings? To civil trials? To depositions? To records of any or all of the above? Should it apply outside judicial proceedings? Should wardens be permitted to completely preclude access by the public and press to prisons? To executions? What if the prisoner wants to close the execution? For wide-ranging discussion of these and related questions, see Choper, Kamisar, and Tribe, note 1 supra, at 145–206 (Professor Tribe was winning counsel in *Richmond Newspapers*). See also G. Michael Fenner & James Koley, *Access to Judicial Proceedings: To Richmond Newspapers and Beyond,* 16 Harv.Civ.Rts—Civ.Lib.L.Rev. 415 (1981).

3. *Closing trials.* After *Richmond Newspapers,* what showing should suffice to justify closure of a criminal trial? See *Globe Newspaper Co. v. Superior Court,* 457 U.S. 596, 102 S.Ct. 2613, 73 L.Ed.2d 248 (1982) (routine exclusion of press and public during testimony of minor victim of sex offense unconstitutional); *Press-Enterprise Co. v. Superior Court,* 464 U.S. 501, 104 S.Ct. 819, 78 L.Ed.2d 629 (1984) (extending *Richmond Newspapers* to voir dire examination of jurors). To overcome either the first amendment or the sixth amendment right to a public trial, the Court has required that the party seeking to close the proceedings "must advance an overriding interest that is likely to be prejudiced, the closure must be no broader than necessary to protect that interest, the trial court must consider reasonable alternatives to closing the proceeding, and it must make findings adequate to support the closure." *Waller v. Georgia,* 467 U.S. 39, 104 S.Ct. 2210, 81 L.Ed.2d 31 (1984).

4. *Special access rights for the press.* Is a press section in public trials required when the seating capacity would be exhausted by the public? Is a press section permitted? What limits attach to government determinations of who shall get press passes? See, e.g., *Sherrill v. Knight,* 569 F.2d 124 (D.C.Cir.1977) (denial of White House press pass infringes upon first amendment guarantees in the absence of adequate process); *Borreca v. Fasi,* 369 F.Supp. 906 (D.Haw.1974) (preliminary injunction against denial of access of a reporter to Mayor's press conferences justified when basis for exclusion is allegedly "inaccurate" and "irresponsible" reporting); *Los Angeles Free Press, Inc. v. Los Angeles,* 9 Cal. App.3d 448, 88 Cal.Rptr. 605 (1970) (exclusion of weekly newspaper from scenes of disaster and police press conferences upheld when newspaper did not report police and fire events "with some regularity"). Cf. *Los Angeles Police Department v. United Reporting Publishing Corp.,* 528 U.S. 32, 120 S.Ct. 483, 145 L.Ed.2d 451 (1999)(law mandating release of arrest records for a scholarly, journalistic, political, or governmental purpose, but not to sell a product or service, may not be challenged on its face; remanded for as applied attack).

When access is required, may the press be prevented from taking notes? Is the right to bring tape recorders into public trials protected under *Richmond Newspapers?* What about "unobtrusive" television cameras? Consider Charles Ares, *Chandler v. Florida: Television, Criminal Trials, and Due Process,* 1981 Sup.Ct. Rev. 157, 174: "Television in the courtroom expands public access to public

---

Sword, 1980 Sup.Ct.Rev. 1. But see Lillian Bevier, *An Informed Public, an Informing Press: The Search for a Constitutional Principle,* 68 Calif.L.Rev. 482 (1980).

f. See *Press–Enterprise Co. v. Superior Court,* 478 U.S. 1, 106 S.Ct. 2735, 92 L.Ed.2d 1 (1986) ("California preliminary hearings are

sufficiently like a trial" to implicate *Richmond Newspapers'* "qualified First Amendment right of access"), in addition, see *El Vocero de Puerto Rico v. Puerto Rico,* 508 U.S. 147, 113 S.Ct. 2004, 124 L.Ed.2d 60 (1993) (reaching same conclusion as to Puerto Rican preliminary hearings).

institutions both qualitatively, because of its immediacy, and quantitatively, because of its reach. It is reported that a majority of Americans acquire their news primarily from television rather than from newspapers. To exclude the most important source of information about the working of courts without some compelling reason cannot be squared with the First Amendment." Cf. *Chandler v. Florida,* 449 U.S. 560, 101 S.Ct. 802, 66 L.Ed.2d 740 (1981) (subject to certain safeguards a state may *permit* electronic media and still photography coverage of public criminal proceedings over the objection of the accused).

Does *Chandler's* holding demean the interest in fair trials? Consider Erwin Griswold, *The Standards of the Legal Profession: Canon 35 Should Not Be Surrendered,* 48 A.B.A.J. 615, 617 (1962): "The presence of cameras and television [has] an inhibiting effect on some people, and an exhilarating effect on others. In either event, there would be distortion, and an inevitable interference with the administration of justice. With all the improved techniques in the world, the introduction of radio and television to the courtroom will surely and naturally convert it into a stage for those who can act, and into a place of additional burden for those who cannot."[g] Do these objections apply with the same force to appellate proceedings?[h] Consider Yale Kamisar, *Chandler v. Florida: What Can Be Said for a "Right of Access" to Televise Judicial Proceedings?* in Choper, Kamisar, & Tribe, note 1 supra, 1980–81, at 149, 168 (1982): "At the present time, no federal court allows TV coverage. *The place to begin* may well be the place that is likely to be the last holdout—the United States Supreme Court."

SECTION 6. GOVERNMENT PROPERTY AND THE PUBLIC FORUM[a]

The case law treating the question of when persons can speak on public property has come to be known as public forum doctrine. But "[t]he public forum saga began, and very nearly ended," Geoffrey Stone, *Fora Americana: Speech in Public Places,* 1974 Sup.Ct.Rev. 233, 236, with an effort by Holmes, J., then on the Supreme Judicial Court of Massachusetts, "to solve a difficult first amendment problem by simplistic resort to a common-law concept," Vincent Blasi, *Prior Restraints on Demonstrations,* 68 Mich.L.Rev. 1482, 1484 (1970). For holding religious meetings on the Boston Common, a preacher was convicted under an ordinance prohibiting "any public address" upon publicly-owned property without a permit from the mayor. In upholding the permit ordinance Holmes, J., observed: "For the legislature absolutely or conditionally to forbid public speaking in a highway or public park is no more an infringement of rights of a member of the public than for the owner of a private house to forbid it in the house." *Massachusetts v. Davis,* 162 Mass. 510, 511, 39 N.E. 113, 113 (1895). On appeal, a unanimous Supreme Court adopted the Holmes position, 167 U.S. 43, 17 S.Ct. 731, 42 L.Ed. 71 (1897): "[T]he right to absolutely exclude all right to use [public property], necessarily includes the authority to determine under what circumstances such use may be availed of, as the greater power contains the lesser."

---

g. Compare Peter L. Arenella, *Televising High Profile Trials: Are We Better Off Pulling the Plug,* 37 Santa Clara L. Rev. 879 (1997)(suggesting that most high profile trials should not be televised). But see Kelli L. Sager & Karen N. Frederikson, *Televising the Judicial Branch: In Furtherance of the Public's First Amendment Rights,* 69 S. Cal. L.Rev. 1519 (1996).

h. See Ares, supra, at 189–90.

a. For treatment of the related question whether, and if so under what circumstances, there is a first amendment right of access to privately-owned facilities, such as shopping centers, see *Marsh v. Alabama,* Ch. 11, Sec. II infra; *Hudgens v. NLRB,* Ch. 11, Sec. II infra; *PruneYard Shopping Center v. Robins,* Sec. 9, I infra.

This view survived until *Hague v. CIO,* 307 U.S. 496, 59 S.Ct. 954, 83 L.Ed. 1423 (1939), which rejected Jersey City's claim that its ordinance requiring a permit for an open air meeting was justified by the "plenary power" rationale of *Davis.* In rejecting the implications of the *Davis* dictum, Roberts, J., in a plurality opinion, uttered a famous "counter dictum," which has played a central role in the evolution of public forum theory: "Wherever the title of streets and parks may rest, they have immemorially been held in trust for the use of the public and, time out of mind, have been used for purposes of assembly, communicating thoughts between citizens, and discussing public questions. Such use of the streets and public places has, from ancient times, been a part of the privileges, immunities, rights, and liberties of citizens. [This privilege of a citizen] is not absolute, but relative, and must be exercised in subordination to the general comfort and convenience, and in consonance with peace and good order; but it must not, in the guise of regulation, be abridged or denied." Eight months later, the *Hague* dictum was given impressive content by Roberts, J., for the Court, in *Schneider* infra.

I. FOUNDATION CASES

A. MANDATORY ACCESS

SCHNEIDER v. IRVINGTON, 308 U.S. 147, 60 S.Ct. 146, 84 L.Ed. 155 (1939), per ROBERTS, J., invalidated several ordinances prohibiting leafleting on public streets or other public places: "Municipal authorities, as trustees for the public, have the duty to keep their communities' streets open and available for movement of people and property, the primary purpose to which the streets are dedicated. So long as legislation to this end does not abridge the constitutional liberty of one rightfully upon the street to impart information through speech or the distribution of literature, it may lawfully regulate the conduct of those using the streets. For example, a person could not exercise this liberty by taking his stand in the middle of a crowded street, contrary to traffic regulations, and maintain his position to the stoppage of all traffic; a group of distributors could not insist upon a constitutional right to form a cordon across the street and to allow no pedestrian to pass who did not accept a tendered leaflet; nor does the guarantee of freedom of speech or of the press deprive a municipality of power to enact regulations against throwing literature broadcast in the streets. Prohibition of such conduct would not abridge the constitutional liberty since such activity bears no necessary relationship to the freedom to speak, write, print or distribute information or opinion. * * *

"In *Lovell* [Sec. 4, I, A supra] this court held void an ordinance which forbade the distribution by hand or otherwise of literature of any kind without written permission from the city manager. [Similarly] in *Hague v. C.I.O.*, an ordinance was held void on its face because it provided for previous administrative censorship of the exercise of the right of speech and assembly in appropriate public places." The [ordinances] under review do not purport to license distribution but all of them absolutely prohibit it in the streets and, one of them, in other public places as well.

"The motive of the legislation under attack in Numbers 13, 18 and 29 is held by the courts below to be the prevention of littering of the streets and, although the alleged offenders were not charged with themselves scattering paper in the streets, their convictions were sustained upon the theory that distribution by them encouraged or resulted in such littering. We are of opinion that the purpose to keep the streets clean and of good appearance is insufficient to justify an ordinance which prohibits a person rightfully on a public street from handing literature to one willing to receive it. Any burden imposed upon the city authorities in cleaning and caring for the streets as an indirect consequence of such distribution results from the constitutional protection of the freedom of speech and press. This constitutional protection does not deprive a city of all power to prevent street littering. There are obvious methods of preventing littering. Amongst these is the punishment of those who actually throw papers on the streets.

"It is suggested that [the] ordinances are valid because their operation is limited to streets and alleys and leaves persons free to distribute printed matter in other public places. But, as we have said, the streets are natural and proper places for the dissemination of information and opinion; and one is not to have the exercise of his liberty of expression in appropriate places abridged on the plea that it may be exercised in some other place."

MCREYNOLDS, J., "is of opinion that the judgment in each case should be affirmed."

Notes and Questions

1. *Leaflets and the streets as public forum.* Consider Harry Kalven, *The Concept of the Public Forum: Cox v. Louisiana*, 1965 S.Ct.Rev. 1, 18 & 21: "Leaflet distribution in public places in a city is a method of communication that carries as an inextricable and expected consequence substantial littering of the streets, which the city has an obligation to keep clean. It is also a method of communication of some annoyance to a majority of people so addressed; that its impact on its audience is very high is doubtful. Yet the constitutional balance in *Schneider* was struck emphatically in favor of keeping the public forum open for this mode of communication. "[The] operative theory of the Court, at least for the leaflet situation, is that, although it is a method of communication that interferes with the public use of the streets, the right to the streets as a public forum is such that leaflet distribution cannot be prohibited and can be regulated only for weighty reasons."

2. *Litter prevention as a substantial interest.* Does the interest in distributing leaflets always outweigh the interest in preventing littering? Suppose helicopters regularly dropped tons of leaflets on the town of Irvington?

3. *Beyond leaflets.* COX v. NEW HAMPSHIRE, 312 U.S. 569, 61 S.Ct. 762, 85 L.Ed. 1049 (1941), per HUGHES, C.J., upheld convictions of sixty-eight Jehovah's Witnesses for parading without a permit. They had marched in four or five groups (with perhaps twenty others) along the sidewalk in single file carrying signs and handing out leaflets: "[T]he state court considered and defined the duty of the licensing authority and the rights of the appellants to a license for their parade, with regard only to consideration of time, place and manner so as to conserve the public convenience." The licensing procedure was said to "afford opportunity for proper policing" and " 'to prevent confusion by overlapping parades, [to] secure convenient use of the streets by other travelers, and to minimize the risk of disorder.' " A municipality "undoubtedly" has "authority to control the use of its public streets for parades or processions." But see C. Edwin Baker, *Unreasoned Reasonableness: Mandatory Parade Permits and Time, Place, and Manner Regulations*, 78 Nw.U.L.Rev. 937, 992 (1984): Approximately 26,000 people walked on the same sidewalks during the same hour the defendants in *Cox* "marched." "This single difference in what [the defendants] did—'marching in formation,' which

they did for expressive purposes and which presumably is an 'assembly' that the first amendment protects—turned out to have crucial significance. This sole difference, engaging in first amendment protected conduct, made them guilty of a criminal offense. [Surely] something is wrong with this result."

4. *Charging for use of public forum. Cox* said there was nothing "contrary to the Constitution" in the exaction of a fee " 'incident to the administration of the [licensing] Act and to the maintenance of public order in the matter licensed.' " But see *Forsyth County v. The Nationalist Movement,* 505 U.S. 123, 112 S.Ct. 2395, 120 L.Ed.2d 101 (1992)(speech cannot be financially burdened for expenses associated with hostile audience in a licensing context).

5. *Reasonable time, place, and manner regulations.* As *Cox* reveals, a right of access to a public forum does not guarantee immunity from reasonable time, place, and manner regulations. In HEFFRON v. INTERNATIONAL SOC. FOR KRISHNA CONSCIOUSNESS, 452 U.S. 640, 101 S.Ct. 2559, 69 L.Ed.2d 298 (1981), for example, the Court, per WHITE, J., upheld a state fair rule prohibiting the distribution of printed material or the solicitation of funds except from a duly licensed booth on the fairgrounds. The Court noted that consideration of a forum's special attributes is relevant to the determination of reasonableness, and the test of reasonableness is whether the restrictions "are justified without reference to the content of the regulated speech, that they serve a significant governmental interest, and that in doing so they leave open ample alternative channels for communication of the information"[a]

WARD v. ROCK AGAINST RACISM, 491 U.S. 781, 109 S.Ct. 2746, 105 L.Ed.2d 661 (1989), per KENNEDY, J., observes that "[E]ven in a public forum the government may impose reasonable restrictions on the time, place, or manner of protected speech, provided the restrictions 'are justified without reference to the content of the regulated speech, that they are narrowly tailored to serve a significant governmental interest, and that they leave open ample alternative channels for communication of the information.' " The case reasserts that the *O'Brien* test is little different from the time, place, and manner test, and then states: "[A] regulation of the time, place, or manner of protected speech must be narrowly tailored to serve the government's legitimate content-neutral interests but [it] need not be the least-restrictive or least-intrusive means of doing so. Rather, the requirement of narrow tailoring is satisfied 'so long as [the] regulation promotes a substantial government interest that would be achieved less effectively absent the regulation.' To be sure, this standard does not mean that a time, place, or manner regulation may burden substantially more speech than is necessary to further the government's legitimate interests. Government may not regulate expression in such a manner that a substantial portion of the burden on speech does not serve to advance its goals."[7]"

MARSHALL, J., dissenting, joined by Brennan and Stevens, JJ., complains of the Court's "serious distortion of the narrowly tailoring requirement" and states that the Court's rejection of the less restrictive alternative test relies on "language in a few opinions [taken] out of context." Should the time, place, and manner test be

---

a. Brennan, J., joined by Marshall and Stevens, JJ., dissented in part as did Blackmun, J., in a separate opinion. Their dispute was not with the Court's test, but its application.

7. A ban on handbilling, of course, would suppress a great quantity of speech that does not cause the evils that it seeks to eliminate, whether they be fraud, crime, litter, traffic congestion, or noise. For that reason, a complete ban on handbilling would be substantially broader than necessary to achieve the interests justifying it.

different from the *O'Brien* test? Is there any difference between those tests and the approach employed in *Schneider*?

B.   EQUAL ACCESS

CHICAGO POLICE DEPT. v. MOSLEY, 408 U.S. 92, 92 S.Ct. 2286, 33 L.Ed.2d 212 (1972), invalidated an ordinance banning all picketing within 150 feet of a school building while the school is in session and one half-hour before and afterwards, except "the peaceful picketing of any school involved in a labor dispute." The suit was brought by a federal postal employee who, for seven months prior to enactment of the ordinance, had frequently picketed a high school in Chicago. "During school hours and usually by himself, Mosley would walk the public sidewalk adjoining the school, carrying a sign that read: 'Jones High School practices black discrimination. Jones High School has a black quota.' His lonely crusade was always peaceful, orderly, and [quiet]." The Court, per MARSHALL, J., viewed the ordinance as drawing "an impermissible distinction between labor picketing and other peaceful picketing": "The central problem with Chicago's ordinance is that it describes permissible picketing in terms of its subject matter. Peaceful picketing on the subject of a school's labor-management dispute is permitted, but all other peaceful picketing is prohibited. The operative distinction is the message on a picket sign. But, above all else, the First Amendment means that government has no power to restrict expression because of its message, its ideas, its subject matter, or its content.

"[U]nder the Equal Protection Clause, not to mention the First Amendment itself,[a] government may not grant the use of a forum to people whose views it finds acceptable, but deny use to those wishing to express less favored or more controversial views. And it may not select which issues are worth discussing or debating in public facilities. There is an 'equality of status in the field of ideas,' and government must afford all points of view an equal opportunity to be heard. Once a forum is opened up to assembly or speaking by some groups, government may not prohibit others from assembling or speaking on the basis of what they intend to say. Selective exclusions from a public forum may not be based on content alone, and may not be justified by reference to content alone.

"[Not] all picketing must always be allowed. We have continually recognized that reasonable 'time, place and manner' regulations of picketing may be necessary to further significant governmental interests. Similarly, under an equal protection analysis, there may be sufficient regulatory interests justifying selective exclusions or distinctions among picketers. [But] [b]ecause picketing plainly involves expressive conduct within the protection of the First Amendment, discriminations among picketers must be tailored to serve a substantial governmental interest. In this case, the ordinance itself describes impermissible picketing not in terms of time, place and manner, but in terms of subject matter. The regulation 'thus slip[s] from the neutrality of time, place and circumstance into a concern about content.' This is never permitted.[b] * * *

a. *Consolidated Edison Co. v. Service Comm'n,* Sec. 10 infra, abandoned equal protection and cited *Mosley* as a first amendment case: "The First Amendment's hostility to content-based regulation extends not only to restrictions on particular viewpoints, but also to prohibition of public discussion of an entire topic." But see, e.g., *Minnesota State Board v. Knight,* 465 U.S. 271, 104 S.Ct. 1058, 79

L.Ed.2d 299 (1984) (stating that *Mosley* is an equal protection case).

b. Consider Daniel A. Farber, *The First Amendment* 23 (1998): "[T]he Court never really explained the basis for its rule. On the face of things, it is not clear that distinctions based on subject matter should always be considered particularly troublesome. For instance, there

"Although preventing school disruption is a city's legitimate concern, Chicago itself has determined that peaceful labor picketing during school hours is not an undue interference with school. Therefore, under the Equal Protection clause, Chicago may not maintain that other picketing disrupts the school unless that picketing is clearly more disruptive than the picketing Chicago already permits. If peaceful labor picketing is permitted, there is no justification for prohibiting all nonlabor picketing, both peaceful and nonpeaceful. 'Peaceful' labor picketing, however the term 'peaceful' is defined, is obviously no less disruptive than 'peaceful' nonlabor picketing. But Chicago's ordinance permits the former and prohibits the latter.

"[We also] reject the city's argument that, although it permits peaceful labor picketing, it may prohibit all nonlabor picketing because, as a class, nonlabor picketing is more prone to produce violence than labor picketing. Predictions about imminent disruption from picketing involve judgments appropriately made on an individualized basis, not by means of broad classifications, especially those based on subject matter. Freedom of expression, and its intersection with the guarantee of equal protection, would rest on a soft foundation indeed if government could distinguish among picketers on such a wholesale and categorical basis. '[I]n our system, undifferentiated fear or apprehension of disturbance is not enough to overcome the right to freedom of expression.' *Tinker.* Some labor picketing is peaceful, some disorderly; the same is true for picketing on other themes. No labor picketing could be more peaceful or less prone to violence than Mosley's solitary vigil. In seeking to restrict nonlabor picketing which is clearly more disruptive than peaceful labor picketing, Chicago may not prohibit all nonlabor picketing at the school forum."[c]

Notes and Questions

1. Consider Kenneth Karst, *Equality as a Central Principle in the First Amendment*, 43 U.Chi.L.Rev. 20, 28 (1975): "*Mosley* is a landmark first amendment decision. It makes two principal points: (1) the essence of the first amendment is its denial to government of the power to determine which messages shall be heard and which suppressed * * *. (2) Any 'time, place and manner' restriction that selectively excludes speakers from a public forum must survive careful judicial scrutiny to ensure that the exclusion is the minimum necessary to further a significant government interest. Taken together, these statements declare a principle of major importance. The Court has explicitly adopted the principle of equal liberty of expression. [The] principle requires courts to start from the assumption that all speakers and all points of view are entitled to a hearing, and permits deviation from this basic assumption only upon a showing of substantial necessity."[d]

2. What if the *Mosley* ordinance had not excepted labor picketing, but had banned *all* picketing within 150 feet of a school during school hours? Consider Karst 37–38: "The burden of this restriction would fall most heavily on those who

seems to be nothing suspicious about the decisions of the drafters of the National Labor Relations Act and the Taft–Hartley Act to regulate labor picketing but not antiwar picketing."

c. Burger, C.J., joined the Court's opinion, but also concurred. Blackmun and Rehnquist, JJ., concurred in the result.

d. For commentary on the relationship between equality and freedom of speech borrowing and adapting the theory of Jurgen Habermas, see Lawrence B. Solum, *Freedom of Communicative Action*, 83 Nw.U.L.Rev. 54 (1989).

have something to communicate to the school [population]. Student picketers presenting a grievance against a principal, or striking custodians with a message growing out of a labor dispute, would be affected more seriously by this ostensibly content-neutral ordinance than would, say the proponents of a candidate for Governor [who could just as effectively carry their message elsewhere]. This differential impact amounts to de facto content discrimination, presumptively invalid under the first amendment equality principle. "[The city faces] an apparent dilemma. [If it] bars all picketing within a certain area, it will effectively discriminate against those groups that can communicate to their audience only by picketing within that area. But if the city adjusts its ordinance to this differential impact, as by providing a student-picketing or labor-picketing exemption, [it runs] afoul of *Mosley* itself. The city can avoid the dilemma by amending the ordinance to ban not all picketing but only noisy picketing."[e]

3.   Does equality fully explain the special concern with content regulation? Consider Geoffrey Stone, *Content Regulation and the First Amendment*, 25 Wm. & Mary L.Rev. 189, 207 (1983): "The problem, quite simply, is that restrictions on expression are rife with 'inequalities,' many of which have nothing whatever to do with content. The ordinance at issue in *Mosley*, for example, restricted picketing near schools, but left unrestricted picketing near hospitals, libraries, courthouses, and private homes. The ordinance at issue in *Erznoznik* restricted drive-in theaters that are visible from a public street, but did not restrict billboards. [Whatever] the effect of these content-neutral inequalities on first amendment analysis, they are not scrutinized in the same way as content-based inequalities. Not all inequalities, in other words, are equal. And although the concern with equality may support the content-based/content-neutral distinction, it does not in itself have much explanatory power."

Is the concern with content discrimination explainable because of concerns about communicative impact, distortion of public debate, or government motivation? See generally Stone, supra. See also sources cited in notes 1 & 2 after *O'Brien*, Sec. 2 supra and Ronald Cass, *First Amendment Access to Government Facilities*, 65 Va.L.Rev. 1287, 1323–25 (1979); Paul Stephan, *The First Amendment and Content Discrimination*, 68 Va.L.Rev. 203 (1982); Geoffrey Stone, *Restrictions of Speech Because of its Content: The Peculiar Case of Subject–Matter Restrictions*, 46 U.Chi.L.Rev. 81 (1978).

4.   An Illinois statute prohibited picketing residences or dwellings—except when the dwelling is "used as a place of business," or is "a place of employment involved in a labor dispute or the place of holding a meeting [on] premises commonly used to discuss subjects of general public interest," or when a "person is picketing his own [dwelling]. Can a conviction for picketing the Mayor of Chicago's home be upheld? Is *Mosley* distinguishable? See *Carey v. Brown*, 447 U.S. 455, 100 S.Ct. 2286, 65 L.Ed.2d 263 (1980).

II.   NEW FORUMS

Are first amendment rights on government property confined to streets and parks? "[W]hat about other publicly owned property, ranging from the grounds surrounding a public building, to the inside of a welfare office, publicly run bus, or library, to a legislative gallery?" Stone, *Fora Americana*, supra, at 245.

---

e. As Professor Karst notes, such an ordinance was upheld in *Grayned v. Rockford*, 408   U.S. 104, 92 S.Ct. 2294, 33 L.Ed.2d 222 (1972), the companion case to *Mosley*.

INTERNATIONAL SOCIETY FOR KRISHNA CONSCIOUSNESS, INC. v. LEE

505 U.S. 672, 112 S.Ct. 2701, 120 L.Ed.2d 541 (1992).

CHIEF JUSTICE REHNQUIST delivered the opinion of the Court.

* * * Petitioner International Society for Krishna Consciousness, Inc. (ISK-CON) is a not-for-profit religious corporation whose members perform a ritual known as sankirtan. The ritual consists of " 'going into public places, disseminating religious literature and soliciting funds to support the religion.' " The primary purpose of this ritual is raising funds for the movement.

Respondent [was] the police superintendent of the Port Authority of New York and New Jersey and was charged with enforcing the regulation at issue. The Port Authority owns and operates three major airports in the greater New York City area [which] collectively form one of the world's busiest metropolitan airport complexes. By decade's end they are expected to serve at least 110 million passengers annually. * * *

The Port Authority has adopted a regulation forbidding within the terminals the repetitive solicitation of money or distribution of literature [but] permits solicitation and distribution on the sidewalks outside the terminal buildings. The regulation effectively prohibits petitioner from performing sankirtan in the terminals. * * *

It is uncontested that the solicitation at issue in this case is a form of speech protected under the First Amendment.[c] But it is also well settled that the government need not permit all forms of speech on property that it owns and controls.

United States Postal Service v. Council of Greenburgh Civic Assns., 453 U.S. 114, 129, 101 S.Ct. 2676, 2685, 69 L.Ed.2d 517 (1981);[a] *Greer v. Spock*, 424 U.S. 828, 96 S.Ct. 1211, 47 L.Ed.2d 505 (1976).[b] Where the government is acting as a proprietor, managing its internal operations, rather than acting as lawmaker with the power to regulate or license, its action will not be subjected to the heightened review to which its actions as a lawmaker may be subject. Thus, we have upheld a ban on political advertisements in city-operated transit vehicles, *Lehman v. City of Shaker Heights*, 418 U.S. 298, 94 S.Ct. 2714, 41 L.Ed.2d 770 (1974), even though the city permitted other types of advertising on those vehicles. Similarly, we have permitted a school district to limit access to an internal mail system used to communicate with teachers employed by the district. *Perry Education Assn. v. Perry Local Educators' Ass'n*, 460 U.S. 37, 103 S.Ct. 948, 74 L.Ed.2d 794 (1983).[c]

---

c. We deal here only with ISKCON's petition raising the permissibility of solicitation. Respondent's cross-petition concerning the leafletting ban is disposed of in the companion case, *Lee v. International Society for Krishna Consciousness, Inc.*, infra.

a. *Greenburgh* held that the post office could prevent individuals from placing unstamped material in residential mail boxes.

b. *Greer* held that the military could bar a presidential candidate from speaking on a military base even though members of the public were free to visit the base, the President had spoken on the base, and other speakers (e.g.,

entertainers and anti-drug speakers) had spoken by invitation on the base.

c. *Perry* held it permissible to deny access to the mailboxes for a competing union despite permitting access for the duly elected union and access for various community groups such as the cub scouts, the YMCA, and other civic and church organizations. *Mosley* and *Carey* were distinguished: "[The] key to those decisions [was] the presence of a public forum." Compare *Lamb's Chapel v. Center Moriches Union Free School Dist.*, 508 U.S. 384, 113 S.Ct. 2141, 124 L.Ed.2d 352 (1993) (school could not exclude religious groups from access

These cases reflect, either implicitly or explicitly, a "forum-based" approach for assessing restrictions that the government seeks to place on the use of its property. *Cornelius v. NAACP Legal Defense and Educational Fund, Inc.,* 473 U.S. 788, 800, 105 S.Ct. 3439, 3448, 87 L.Ed.2d 567 (1985).[d] Under this approach, regulation of speech on government property that has traditionally been available for public expression is subject to the highest scrutiny. Such regulations survive only if they are narrowly drawn to achieve a compelling state interest. *Perry.* The second category of public property is the designated public forum, whether of a limited or unlimited character—property that the state has opened for expressive activity by part or all of the public. Id.[e] Regulation of such property is subject to the same limitations as that governing a traditional public forum. Finally, there is all remaining public property. Limitations on expressive activity conducted on this last category of property must survive only a much more limited review. The challenged regulation need only be reasonable, as long as the regulation is not an effort to suppress the speaker's activity due to disagreement with the speaker's view.

[Our] precedents foreclose the conclusion that airport terminals are public fora. Reflecting the general growth of the air travel industry, airport terminals have only recently achieved their contemporary size and character. [Moreover,] even within the rather short history of air transport, it is only "[i]n recent years [that] it has become a common practice for various religious and non-profit organizations to use commercial airports as a forum for the distribution of literature, the solicitation of funds, the proselytizing of new members, and other similar activities." 45 Fed.Reg. 35314 (1980). Thus, the tradition of airport activity does not demonstrate that airports have historically been made available for speech activity. Nor can we say that these particular terminals, or airport terminals generally, have been intentionally opened by their operators to such activity; the frequent and continuing litigation evidencing the operators' objections belies any such claim. * * *

Petitioner attempts to circumvent the history and practice governing airport activity by pointing our attention to the variety of speech activity that it claims

to school property for after school meetings so long as it held the property generally open for meetings by social, civic, and recreation groups).

d. *Cornelius* upheld an executive order that included organizations providing direct health and welfare services to individuals or their families in a charity drive in the federal workplace while excluding legal defense and political advocacy organizations.

A 4–3 majority, per O'Connor, J., determined that "government does not create a public forum by inaction or by permitting limited discourse, but only by intentionally opening a non-traditional forum for public discourse." Observing that the Court will look to the policy and practice of the government, the nature of the property and its compatibility with expressive activity in discerning intent, O'Connor, J., insisted that "we will not find that a public forum has been created in the face of clear evidence of a contrary intent, nor will we infer that the Government intended to create a public forum when the nature of the property is inconsistent with expressive activity."

Blackmun, J., dissented: "If the Government does not create a limited public forum unless it intends to provide an 'open forum' for expressive activity, and if the exclusion of some speakers is evidence that the Government did not intend to create such a forum, no speaker challenging denial of access will ever be able to prove that the forum is a limited public forum. The very fact that the Government denied access to the speaker indicates that the Government did not intend to provide an open forum for expressive activity, and [that] fact alone would demonstrate that the forum is not a limited public forum."

e. In interpreting this approach, *Perry* also stated in footnote 7 that: "a public forum may be created for a limited purpose such as use by certain groups, e.g., *Widmar v. Vincent* [p. ___ infra] (student groups), or for the discussion of certain subjects, e.g., *Madison Joint School District v. Wisconsin Pub. Employ. Relat. Comm'n,* 429 U.S. 167, 97 S.Ct. 421, 50 L.Ed.2d 376 (1976) (school board business).

historically occurred at various "transportation nodes" such as rail stations, bus stations, wharves, and Ellis Island. Even if we were inclined to accept petitioner's historical account[,] we think that such evidence is of little import for two reasons. First, much of the evidence is irrelevant to *public* fora analysis, because sites such as bus and rail terminals traditionally have had *private* ownership. The development of privately owned parks that ban speech activity would not change the public fora status of publicly held parks. But the reverse is also true. The practices of privately held transportation centers do not bear on the government's regulatory authority over a publicly owned airport.

Second, the relevant unit for our inquiry is an airport, not "transportation nodes" generally. When new methods of transportation develop, new methods for accommodating that transportation are also likely to be needed. And with each new step, it therefore will be a new inquiry whether the transportation necessities are compatible with various kinds of expressive activity. [The] "security magnet," for example, is an airport commonplace that lacks a counterpart in bus terminals and train stations. And public access to air terminals is also not infrequently restricted—just last year the Federal Aviation Administration required airports for a 4–month period to limit access to areas normally publicly accessible. To blithely equate airports with other transportation centers, therefore, would be a mistake. [T]he record demonstrates that Port Authority management considers the purpose of the terminals to be the facilitation of passenger air travel, not the promotion of expression. Even if we look beyond the intent of the Port Authority to the manner in which the terminals have been operated, the terminals have never been dedicated (except under the threat of court order) to expression in the form sought to be exercised [here]. Thus, we think that neither by tradition nor purpose can the terminals be described as satisfying the standards we have previously set out for identifying a public forum.

The restrictions here challenged, therefore, need only satisfy a requirement of reasonableness. * * *

We have on many prior occasions noted the disruptive effect that solicitation may have on business. "Solicitation requires action by those who would respond: The individual solicited must decide whether or not to contribute (which itself might involve reading the solicitor's literature or hearing his pitch), and then, having decided to do so, reach for a wallet, search it for money, write a check, or produce a credit card." *United States v. Kokinda*, 497 U.S. 720, 110 S.Ct. 3123, 111 L.Ed.2d 571 (1990). Passengers who wish to avoid the solicitor may have to alter their path, slowing both themselves and those around them. The result is that the normal flow of traffic is impeded. This is especially so in an airport, where "air travelers, who are often weighted down by cumbersome baggage [may] be hurrying to catch a plane or to arrange ground transportation." Delays may be particularly costly in this setting, as a flight missed by only a few minutes can result in hours worth of subsequent inconvenience.

In addition, face to face solicitation presents risks of duress that are an appropriate target of regulation. The skillful, and unprincipled, solicitor can target the most vulnerable, including those accompanying children or those suffering physical impairment and who cannot easily avoid the solicitation. The unsavory solicitor can also commit fraud through concealment of his affiliation or through deliberate efforts to shortchange those who agree to purchase. Compounding this problem is the fact that, in an airport, the targets of such activity frequently are on tight schedules. This in turn makes such visitors unlikely to stop and formally complain to airport authorities. As a result, the airport faces considerable difficulty in achieving its legitimate interest in monitoring solicitation activity to assure that travelers are not interfered with unduly.

[T]he sidewalk areas outside the terminals [are] frequented by an overwhelming percentage of airport users. [W]e think it would be odd to conclude that the Port Authority's terminal regulation is unreasonable despite the Port Authority having otherwise assured access to an area universally traveled. * * *

Moreover, "[if] petitioner is given access, so too must other groups. "Obviously, there would be a much larger threat to the State's interest in crowd control if all other religious, nonreligious, and noncommercial organizations could likewise move freely." As a result, we conclude that the solicitation ban is reasonable. * * *

JUSTICE O'CONNOR, concurring in 91–155 [on the solicitation issue] and concurring in the judgment in 91–339 [on the distribution of literature issue]. * * *

I concur in the Court's opinion in No. 91–155 and agree that publicly owned airports are not public fora.

[This], however, does not mean that the government can restrict speech in whatever way it likes. * * *

"The reasonableness of the Government's restriction [on speech in a nonpublic forum] must be assessed in light of the purpose of the forum and all the surrounding circumstances." *Cornelius.* " '[C]onsideration of a forum's special attributes is relevant to the constitutionality of a regulation since the significance of the governmental interest must be assessed in light of the characteristic nature and function of the particular forum involved.' " *Kokinda.* In this case, the "special attributes" and "surrounding circumstances" of the airports operated by the Port Authority are determinative. Not only has the Port Authority chosen *not* to limit access to the airports under its control, it has created a huge complex open to travelers and nontravelers alike. The airports house restaurants, cafeterias, snack bars, coffee shops, cocktail lounges, post offices, banks, telegraph offices, clothing shops, drug stores, food stores, nurseries, barber shops, currency exchanges, art exhibits, commercial advertising displays, bookstores, newsstands, dental offices and private clubs. The International Arrivals Building at JFK Airport even has two branches of Bloomingdale's.

We have said that a restriction on speech in a nonpublic forum is "reasonable" when it is "consistent with the [government's] legitimate interest in 'preserv[ing] the property [for] the use to which it is lawfully dedicated.' " *Perry.* [The] reasonableness inquiry, therefore, is not whether the restrictions on speech are "consistent [with] preserving the property" for air travel, but whether they are reasonably related to maintaining the multipurpose environment that the Port Authority has deliberately created.

Applying that standard, I agree with the Court in No. 91–155 that the ban on solicitation is reasonable. * * *

In my view, however, the regulation banning leafletting [cannot] be upheld as reasonable on this record. I therefore concur in the judgment in No. 91–339 striking down that prohibition. [W]e have expressly noted that leafletting does not entail the same kinds of problems presented by face-to-face solicitation. Specifically, "[o]ne need not ponder the contents of a leaflet or pamphlet in order mechanically to take it out of someone's [hand]. 'The distribution of literature does not require that the recipient stop in order to receive the message the speaker wishes to convey; instead the recipient is free to read the message at a later time.' " With the possible exception of avoiding litter, it is difficult to point to any problems intrinsic to the act of leafletting that would make it naturally incompatible with a large, multipurpose forum such as those at issue here. * * *

Of course, it is still open for the Port Authority to promulgate regulations of the time, place, and manner of leafletting which are "content-neutral, narrowly tailored to serve a significant government interest, and leave open ample alternative channels of communication." For example, during the many years that this litigation has been in progress, the Port Authority has not banned sankirtan completely from JFK International Airport, but has restricted it to a relatively uncongested part of the airport terminals, the same part that houses the airport chapel. In my view, that regulation meets the standards we have applied * * *.

JUSTICE KENNEDY, with whom JUSTICE BLACKMUN, JUSTICE STEVENS, and JUSTICE SOUTER join as to Part I, concurring in the judgment.

I. [The Court] leaves the government with almost unlimited authority to restrict speech on its property by doing nothing more than articulating a non-speech-related purpose for the area, and it leaves almost no scope for the development of new public forums absent the rare approval of the government. The Court's error [in] analysis is a classification of the property that turns on the government's own definition or decision, unconstrained by an independent duty to respect the speech its citizens can voice there. The Court acknowledges as much, by reintroducing today into our First Amendment law a strict doctrinal line between the proprietary and regulatory functions of government which I thought had been abandoned long ago. *Schneider; Grayned v. Rockford,* 408 U.S. 104, 92 S.Ct. 2294, 33 L.Ed.2d 222 (1972).[f]

[Public] places are of necessity the locus for discussion of public issues, as well as protest against arbitrary government action. At the heart of our jurisprudence lies the principle that in a free nation citizens must have the right to gather and speak with other persons in public places. The recognition that certain government-owned property is a public forum provides open notice to citizens that their freedoms may be exercised there without fear of a censorial government, adding tangible reinforcement to the idea that we are a free people. * * *

The Court's analysis rests on an inaccurate view of history. The notion that traditional public forums are property which have public discourse as their principal purpose is a most doubtful fiction. The types of property that we have recognized as the quintessential public forums are streets, parks, and sidewalks. It would seem apparent that the principal purpose of streets and sidewalks, like airports, is to facilitate transportation, not public discourse. [Similarly,] the purpose for the creation of public parks may be as much for beauty and open space as for discourse. Thus under the Court's analysis, even the quintessential public forums would appear to lack the necessary elements of what the Court defines as a public forum. * * *

One of the places left in our mobile society that is suitable for discourse is a metropolitan airport [because] in these days an airport is one of the few government-owned spaces where many persons have extensive contact with other members of the public. Given that private spaces of similar character are not subject to the dictates of the First Amendment, it is critical that we preserve these areas for protected speech. [If] the objective, physical characteristics of the property at issue and the actual public access and uses which have been permitted by the govern-

---

f. *Grayned* stated that: "The crucial question is whether the manner of expression is basically incompatible with the normal activity of a particular place at a particular time." Applying that test, the Court held constitutional an ordinance forbidding the making of noise which disturbs or tends to disturb the peace or good order of a school session.

ment indicate that expressive activity would be appropriate and compatible with those uses, the property is a public forum. [The] possibility of some theoretical inconsistency between expressive activities and the property's uses should not bar a finding of a public forum, if those inconsistencies can be avoided through simple and permitted regulations.

The second category of the Court's jurisprudence, the so-called designated forum, provides little, if any, additional protection for speech. [I] do not quarrel with the fact that speech must often be restricted on property of this kind to retain the purpose for which it has been designated. And I recognize that when property has been designated for a particular expressive use, the government may choose to eliminate that designation. But this increases the need to protect speech in other places, where discourse may occur free of such restrictions. In some sense the government always retains authority to close a public forum, by selling the property, changing its physical character, or changing its principal use. Otherwise the State would be prohibited from closing a park, or eliminating a street or sidewalk, which no one has understood the public forum doctrine to require. The difference is that when property is a protected public forum the State may not by fiat assert broad control over speech or expressive activities; it must alter the objective physical character or uses of the property, and bear the attendant costs, to change the property's forum status.

Under this analysis, it is evident that the public spaces of the Port Authority's airports are public forums. First, the District Court made detailed findings [that] show that the public spaces in the airports are broad, public thoroughfares full of people and lined with stores and other commercial activities. An airport corridor is of course not a street, but that is not the proper inquiry. The question is one of physical similarities, sufficient to suggest that the airport corridor should be a public forum for the same reasons that streets and sidewalks have been treated as public forums by the people who use them.

Second, the airport areas involved here are open to the public without restriction. Plaintiffs do not seek access to the secured areas of the airports, nor do I suggest that these areas would be public forums. And while most people who come to the Port Authority's airports do so for a reason related to air travel, [this] does not distinguish an airport from streets or sidewalks, which most people use for travel. * * *

Third, and perhaps most important, it is apparent from the record, and from the recent history of airports, that when adequate time, place, and manner regulations are in place, expressive activity is quite compatible with the uses of major airports. The Port Authority [argues] that the problem of congestion in its airports' corridors makes expressive activity inconsistent with the airports' primary purpose, which is to facilitate air travel. The First Amendment is often inconvenient. But that is besides the point. Inconvenience does not absolve the government of its obligation to tolerate speech. * * *

[A] grant of plenary power allows the government to tilt the dialogue heard by the public, to exclude many, more marginal voices. [We] have long recognized that the right to distribute flyers and literature lies at the heart of the liberties guaranteed by the Speech and Press Clauses of the First Amendment. The Port Authority's rule, which prohibits almost all such activity, is among the most restrictive possible of those liberties. The regulation is in fact so broad and restrictive of speech, Justice O'Connor finds it void even under the standards applicable to government regulations in nonpublic forums. I have no difficulty deciding the regulation cannot survive the far more stringent rules applicable to regulations in public forums. The regulation is not drawn in narrow terms and it does not leave open ample alternative channels for communication. * * *

II.　It is my view, however, that the Port Authority's ban on the "solicitation and receipt of funds" [may] be upheld as either a reasonable time, place, and manner restriction, or as a regulation directed at the nonspeech element of expressive conduct. The two standards have considerable overlap in a case like this one. * * *

I am in full agreement with the statement of the Court that solicitation is a form of protected speech. If the Port Authority's solicitation regulation prohibited all speech which requested the contribution of funds, I would conclude that it was a direct, content-based restriction of speech in clear violation of the First Amendment. The Authority's regulation does not prohibit all solicitation, however; it prohibits the "solicitation and receipt of funds." [It] reaches only personal solicitations for immediate payment of money. [The] regulation does not cover, for example, the distribution of preaddressed envelopes along with a plea to contribute money to the distributor or his organization. As I understand the restriction it is directed only at the physical exchange of money, which is an element of conduct interwoven with otherwise expressive solicitation.

[T]he government interest in regulating the sales of literature[, however,] is not as powerful as in the case of solicitation. The danger of a fraud arising from such sales is much more limited than from pure solicitation, because in the case of a sale the nature of the exchange tends to be clearer to both parties. Also, the Port Authority's sale regulation is not as narrowly drawn as the solicitation rule, since it does not specify the receipt of money as a critical element of a violation. And perhaps most important, the flat ban on sales of literature leaves open fewer alternative channels of communication than the Port Authority's more limited prohibition on the solicitation and receipt of funds. Given the practicalities and ad hoc nature of much expressive activity in the public forum, sales of literature must be completed in one transaction to be workable. Attempting to collect money at another time or place is a far less plausible option in the context of a sale than when soliciting donations, because the literature sought to be sold will under normal circumstances be distributed within the forum. * * *

Against all of this must be balanced the great need, recognized by our precedents, to give the sale of literature full First Amendment protection. We have long recognized that to prohibit distribution of literature for the mere reason that it is sold would leave organizations seeking to spread their message without funds to operate. "It should be remembered that the pamphlets of Thomas Paine were not distributed free of charge." *Murdock v. Pennsylvania,* 319 U.S. 105, 63 S.Ct. 870, 87 L.Ed. 1292 (1943). The effect of a rule of law distinguishing between sales and distribution would be to close the marketplace of ideas to less affluent organizations and speakers, leaving speech as the preserve of those who are able to fund themselves. One of the primary purposes of the public forum is to provide persons who lack access to more sophisticated media the opportunity to speak. [And] while the same arguments might be made regarding solicitation of funds, the answer is that the Port Authority has not prohibited all solicitation, but only a narrow class of conduct associated with a particular manner of solicitation. * * * *g

g.　For commentary on Kennedy, J.'s perspective, see Steven G. Gey, *Reopening the Public Forum–From Sidewalks to Cyberspace,* 58 Ohio St. L.J. 1535 (1998); Comment, *"Objective" Approaches to the Public Forum Doctrine,* 90 Nw. U.L.Rev. 1185 (1996).

JUSTICE SOUTER, with whom JUSTICE BLACKMUN and JUSTICE STEVENS join, concurring in the judgment in No. 91–339 [on the distribution of literature issue] and dissenting in No. 91–155 [on the solicitation issue].

[R]espondent comes closest to justifying the [total ban on solicitation of money for immediate payment] as one furthering the government's interest in preventing coercion and fraud.[1] [While] a solicitor can be insistent, a pedestrian on the street or airport concourse can simply walk [away]. Since there is here no evidence of any type of coercive conduct, over and above the merely importunate character of the open and public solicitation, that might justify a ban, the regulation cannot be sustained to avoid coercion.

As for fraud, our cases do not provide government with plenary authority to ban solicitation just because it could be [fraudulent.] The evidence of fraudulent conduct here is virtually nonexistent. It consists of one affidavit describing eight complaints, none of them substantiated, "involving some form of fraud, deception, or larceny" over an entire 11–year period between 1975 and 1986, during which the regulation at issue here was, by agreement, not enforced. [B]y the Port Authority's own calculation, there has not been a single claim of fraud or misrepresentation since 1981. * * *

Even assuming a governmental interest adequate to justify some regulation, the present ban would fall when subjected to the requirement of narrow tailoring. Thus, in *Schaumburg v. Citizens for a Better Environment,* 444 U.S. 620, 100 S.Ct. 826, 63 L.Ed.2d 73 (1980), we said: "The Village's legitimate interest in preventing fraud can be better served by measures less intrusive than a direct prohibition on solicitation. Fraudulent misrepresentations can be prohibited and the penal laws used to punish such conduct directly."

[Finally,] I do not think the Port Authority's solicitation ban leaves open the "ample" channels of communication required of a valid content-neutral time, place and manner restriction. A distribution of preaddressed envelopes is unlikely to be much of an alternative. The practical reality of the regulation, which this Court can never ignore, is that it shuts off a uniquely powerful avenue of communication for organizations like the International Society for Krishna Consciousness, and may, in effect, completely prohibit unpopular and poorly funded groups from receiving funds in response to protected solicitation. * * *

LEE v. INTERNATIONAL SOCIETY FOR
KRISHNA CONSCIOUSNESS, INC.
505 U.S. 830, 112 S.Ct. 2709, 120 L.Ed.2d 669 (1992).

PER CURIAM.

For the reasons expressed in the opinions of Justice O'Connor, Justice Kennedy, and Justice Souter in *ISKCON v. Lee,* the judgment of the Court of

---

1. Respondent also attempts to justify its regulation on the alternative basis of "interference with air travelers," referring in particular to problems of "annoyance," and "congestion." The First Amendment inevitably requires people to put up with annoyance and uninvited persuasion. Indeed, in such cases we need to scrutinize restrictions on speech with special care. In their degree of congestion, most of the public spaces of these airports are probably more comparable to public streets than to the fairground as we described it in *Heffron.* Consequently, the congestion argument, which was held there to justify a regulation confining solicitation to a fixed location, should have less force here. Be that as it may, the conclusion of a majority of the Court today that the Constitution forbids the ban on the sale [Ed. Does the majority of the Court conclude that the Constitution forbids the ban on the *sale* of literature?] as well as the distribution, of leaflets puts to rest respondent's argument that congestion justifies a total ban on solicitation. While there may, of course, be congested locations where solicitation could severely compromise the efficient flow of pedestrians, the proper response would be to tailor the restrictions to those choke points.

Appeals holding that the ban on distribution of literature in the Port Authority airport terminals is invalid under the First Amendment is affirmed.

CHIEF JUSTICE REHNQUIST, with whom JUSTICE WHITE, JUSTICE SCALIA and JUSTICE THOMAS join, dissenting.

Leafletting [must] be evaluated against a backdrop of the substantial congestion problem facing the Port Authority and with an eye to the cumulative impact that will result if all groups are permitted terminal access. Viewed in this light, I conclude that the distribution ban, no less than the solicitation ban, is reasonable.

[The] weary, harried, or hurried traveler may have no less desire and need to avoid the delays generated by having literature foisted upon him than he does to avoid delays from a financial solicitation. And while a busy passenger perhaps may succeed in fending off a leafletter with minimal disruption to himself by agreeing simply to take the proffered material, this does not completely ameliorate the dangers of congestion flowing from such leafletting. Others may choose not simply to accept the material but also to stop and engage the leafletter in debate, obstructing those who follow. Moreover, those who accept material may often simply drop it on the floor once out of the leafletter's range, creating an eyesore, a safety hazard, and additional cleanup work for airport staff. See *Los Angeles City Council v. Taxpayers for Vincent,* 466 U.S. 789, 104 S.Ct. 2118, 80 L.Ed.2d 772 (1984) (aesthetic interests may provide basis for restricting speech).

[Under] the regime that is today sustained, the Port Authority is obliged to permit leafletting. But monitoring leafletting activity in order to ensure that it is *only* leafletting that occurs, and not also soliciting, may prove little less burdensome than the monitoring that would be required if solicitation were permitted. At a minimum, therefore, I think it remains open whether at some future date the Port Authority may be able to reimpose a complete ban, having developed evidence that enforcement of a differential ban is overly burdensome. * * *

Notes and Questions

1. *The first amendment and geography.* Consider Daniel Farber & John Nowak, *The Misleading Nature of Public Forum Analysis: Content and Context in First Amendment Adjudication,* 70 Va.L.Rev., 1219, 1234–35 (1984): "Classification of public places as various types of forums has only confused judicial opinions by diverting attention from the real first amendment issues involved in the cases. Like the fourth amendment, the first amendment protects people, not places. Constitutional protection should depend not on labeling the speaker's physical location but on the first amendment values and governmental interests involved in the case. Of course, governmental interests are often tied to the nature of the place. [To] this extent, the public forum doctrine is a useful heuristic [device]. But when the heuristic device becomes the exclusive method of analysis, only confusion and mistakes can result." Compare Robert Post, *Between Governance and Management: The History and Theory of the Public Forum,* 34 U.C.L.A.L.Rev. 1713, 1777 (1987): "*Grayned's* 'incompatibility' test takes into account only the specific harm incident to a plaintiff's proposed speech; it does not recognize the generic damage to managerial authority flowing from the very process of independent judicial review of institutional decisionmaking. [The Court's] present focus 'on the character of the property at issue' is a theoretical dead end, because there is no satisfactory theory connecting the classification of government property with

the exercise of first amendment rights. But there is great potential for a rich and principled jurisprudence if the Court were to focus instead on the relationship between judicial review and the functioning of institutional authority."

2. Would the Arlington National Cemetery be open to solicitation and the distribution of literature under Kennedy, J.'s approach? Consider Comment, *"Objective" Approaches to the Public Forum Doctrine,* 90 Nw. U.L.Rev. 1185, 1240 (1996): "The only differences between the Cemetery and the typical park might be concrete tombstones instead of bird baths and the increased likelihood of solemn expressions on the faces of Cemetery visitors."

3. *Footnote 7 forums.* What is the relationship between the Court's second category of property in *Perry* and its fn. 7 (see fn. e. supra)? Is the discretion to create forums limited? Is it necessary to show that restrictions on such forums are necessary to achieve a compelling state interest? If a restriction (to certain speakers or subjects) is challenged, can the restrictions be used to show that that the property is not a public forum of the second category? Is this inadmissible circularity? See Laurence Tribe, *Equality as a First Amendment Theme: The "Government-as-Private Actor" Exception* in Jesse Choper, Yale Kamisar & Lawrence Tribe, The Supreme Court: Trends and Developments 1982–1983, at 221, 226 (1984); Post, supra at 1752–56. In any event, does fn. 7 create a fourth category of property without setting guiding stands? Are the *Perry* mailboxes fn. 7 forums?

LEHMAN v. SHAKER HEIGHTS, 418 U.S. 298, 94 S.Ct. 2714, 41 L.Ed.2d 770 (1974), held that a public transit system could sell commercial advertising space for cards on its vehicles while refusing to sell space for "political" or "public issue" advertising. BLACKMUN, J., joined by Burger, C.J., White and Rehnquist, J.J., ruled the bus cards not be a public forum and found the city's decision reasonable because it minimized "chances of abuse, the appearance of favoritism, and the risk of imposing upon a captive audience." DOUGLAS, J., concurring, maintained that political messages and commercial messages were both offensive and intrusive to captive audiences, noted that the commercial advertising policy was not before the Court, and voted to deny a right to spread a political message to a captive audience. BRENNAN, J., joined by Stewart, Marshall, and Powell, JJ., dissenting, observed that the "city's solicitous regard for 'captive riders' [has] a hollow ring in the present case where [it] has opened its rapid transit system as a forum for communication."

Is *Lehman* a fn. 7 forum?

4. *The relationship between the public forum tests and other tests.* In *Vincent,* a political candidate had placed signs on publicly owned utility poles, and the Court assessed the constitutionality of an ordinance that prohibited the placing of signs on public property. What test applies? A public forum test? A time, place, and manner test? The *O'Brien* test?[h]

---

h. For additional commentary on public forum issues, see Curtis Berger, *Pruneyard Revisited: Political Activity on Private Lands,* 66 N.Y.U.L.Rev. 650 (1991); G. Sidney Buchanan, *The Case of the Vanishing Public Forum,* 1991 U.Ill.L.Rev. 949 (1991); David Day, *The End of the Public Forum Doctrine,* 78 Iowa L.Rev. 143 (1992); Steven G. Gey, *Reopening the Public Forum—From Public Sidewalks to Cyberspace,* 58 Ohio St.L.J. 1535 (1998); David Goldstone, *The Public Forum Doctrine in the Age of the Information Superhighway (Where Are the* *Public Forums on the Information Superhighway?),* 46 Hastings L.J. 335 (1995); Ronald Krotoszynski, Jr., *Celebrating Selma: The Importance of Context in Public Forum Analysis,* 104 Yale L.J. 1411 (1995); Edward Naughton, *Is Cyberspace A Public Forum? Computer Bulletin Boards, Free Speech, and State Action,* 81 Geo.L.J. 409 (1992); Note, 46 Okla.L.Rev. 155 (1993). For commentary on speaker-based restrictions, see Geoffrey Stone, *Content Regula-*

5. In order to prevent voter intimidation and election fraud, Tennessee prohibits the soliciting of votes and the display or distribution of campaign materials within 100 feet of the entrance to a polling place. Is the campaign-free zone, a public forum? Is the permitting of charitable or religious speech (including solicitation) or commercial speech while banning election speech (but not exit polling) impermissible content discrimination?

BURSON v. FREEMAN, 504 U.S. 191, 112 S.Ct. 1846, 119 L.Ed.2d 5 (1992) upheld the statute. BLACKMUN, J., joined by Rehnquist, C.J., and White and Kennedy, J.J., argued that the 100 foot zone was a public forum, that the regulation was based on the content of the speech, that the state was required to show that its statute was necessary to achieve a compelling state interest and narrowly drawn to achieve that end, and determined that this was the "rare case" in which strict scrutiny against content regulation could be satisfied: "There is [ample evidence] that political candidates have used campaign workers to commit voter intimidation or electoral fraud. In contrast, there is simply no evidence that political candidates have used other forms of solicitation or exit polling to commit such electoral abuses. [The] First Amendment does not require states to regulate for problems that do not exist. * * *

"Here, the State, as recognized administrator of elections, has asserted that the exercise of free speech rights conflicts with another fundamental right, the right to cast a ballot in an election free from the taint of intimidation and fraud. A long history, a substantial consensus, and simple common sense shows that some restricted zone around polling places is necessary to protect that fundamental right. Given the conflict between those two rights, we hold that requiring solicitors to stand 100 feet[i] from the entrances to polling places does not constitute an unconstitutional compromise."[j]

SCALIA, J., agreed with Blackmun, J., that the regulation was justified, but maintained that the area around a polling place is not a public forum: "If the category of 'traditional public forum' is to be a tool of analysis rather than a conclusory label, it must remain faithful to its name and derive its content from *tradition*. Because restrictions on speech around polling places are as venerable a part of the American tradition as the secret ballot, [Tennessee's statute] does not restrict speech in a traditional public forum. [I] believe that the [statute] though content-based, is constitutional because it is a reasonable, viewpoint-neutral regulation of a non-public forum."

STEVENS, J., joined by O'Connor and Souter, JJ., did not address the question of whether the area around a polling place was a public forum, but agreed with Blackmun, J., that the regulation could not be upheld without showing that it was necessary to serve a compelling state interest by means narrowly tailored to that end. He contended that the existence of the secret ballot was a sufficient safeguard against intimidation[k] and that the fear of fraud from last minute

tion and the First Amendment, 25 Wm. & Mary L.Rev. 189, 244–51 (1983).

i. Blackmun, J., argued that the question of whether the state should be required to set a smaller zone, perhaps 25 feet, would put the state to an unreasonable burden of proof, and that the difference between such zones was not of constitutional moment.

j. Kennedy, J., concurring, reaffirmed the views he had put forward in *Simon and Schuster*, but noted that the first amendment must

appropriately give way in some cases where other constitutional rights are at stake. Thomas, J., took no part.

k. Stevens, J., argued that the record showed no evidence of intimidation or abuse, nor did it offer a basis for denying election advocacy, while permitting other forms of political advocacy, e.g., environmental advocacy. He maintained that the plurality had shifted the strict scrutiny standard from the state to the candidate who wished to speak.

campaigning could not be reconciled with *Mills v. Alabama,* 384 U.S. 214, 86 S.Ct. 1434, 16 L.Ed.2d 484 (1966)(prohibition on election day editorials unconstitutional). In addition, Stevens, J., argued that the prohibition disproportionately affects candidates with "fewer resources, candidates from lesser visibility offices, and 'grassroots' candidates" who specially profit from "last-minute campaigning near the polling place. [The] hubbub of campaign workers outside a polling place may be a nuisance, but it is also the sound of a vibrant democracy."

III. PRIVACY AND THE PUBLIC FORUM

A Colorado statute regulates speech-related conduct within 100 feet of the entrance to any health care facility, making it unlawful within the regulated areas for any person to "knowingly approach" within eight feet of another person, without that person's consent, "for the purpose of passing a leaflet or handbill to, displaying a sign to, or engaging in oral protest, education, or counseling with such other person * * *." HILL v. COLORADO, 530 U.S. 703, 120 S.Ct. 2480, 147 L.Ed.2d 597 (2000), per STEVENS, J., upheld the statute: "Although the statute [prohibits] speakers from approaching unwilling listeners, it does not require a standing speaker to move away from anyone passing by. Nor does it place any restriction on the content of any message that anyone may wish to communicate to anyone else, either inside or outside the regulated areas. It does, however, make it more difficult to give unwanted advice, particularly in the form of a handbill or leaflet, to persons entering or leaving medical facilities.

"[As] a preface to their legal challenge, petitioners emphasize three propositions. First, they accurately explain that the areas protected by the statute encompass all the public ways within 100 feet of every entrance to every health care facility everywhere in the State of Colorado. There is no disagreement on this point, even though the legislative history makes it clear that its enactment was primarily motivated by activities in the vicinity of abortion clinics. Second, they correctly state that their leafletting, sign displays, and oral communications are protected by the First Amendment. The fact that the messages conveyed by those communications may be offensive to their recipients does not deprive them of constitutional protection. Third, the public sidewalks, streets, and ways affected by the statute are 'quintessential' public forums for free speech. Finally, although there is debate about the magnitude of the statutory impediment to their ability to communicate effectively with persons in the regulated zones, that ability, particularly the ability to distribute leaflets, is unquestionably lessened by this statute.

"On the other hand, it is a traditional exercise of the States' 'police powers to protect the health and safety of their citizens.' That interest may justify a special focus on unimpeded access to health care facilities and the avoidance of potential trauma to patients associated with confrontational protests. See *Madsen* Sec. 5, I, B supra. Moreover, as with every exercise of a State's police powers, rules that provide specific guidance to enforcement authorities serve the interest in even-handed application of the law. Whether or not those interests justify the particular regulation at issue, they are unquestionably legitimate.

"It is also important when conducting this interest analysis to recognize the significant difference between state restrictions on a speaker's right to address a willing audience and those that protect listeners from unwanted communication. This statute deals only with the latter. * * *

"[The] right to avoid unwelcome speech has special force in the privacy of the home, *Rowan v. Post Office Dept.,* 397 U.S. 728, 90 S.Ct. 1484, 25 L.Ed.2d 736 (1970), and its immediate surroundings, *Frisby v. Schultz,* 487 U.S. 474, 108 S.Ct. 2495, 101 L.Ed.2d 420 (1988)[a] but can also be protected in confrontational settings. * * *

"The dissenters argue that we depart from precedent by recognizing a 'right to avoid unpopular speech in a public forum,' We, of course, are not addressing whether there is such a 'right.' Rather, we are merely noting that our cases have repeatedly recognized the interests of unwilling listeners in situations where 'the degree of captivity makes it impractical for the unwilling viewer or auditor to avoid exposure. * * * [25]

"Theoretically, of course, cases may arise in which it is necessary to review the content of the statements made by a person approaching within eight feet of an unwilling listener to determine whether the approach is covered by the statute. But that review need be no more extensive than a determination of whether a general prohibition of 'picketing' or 'demonstrating' applies to innocuous speech. The regulation of such expressive activities, by definition, does not cover social, random, or other everyday communications. See *Webster's Third New International Dictionary* 600, 1710 (1993) (defining 'demonstrate' as 'to make a public display of sentiment for or against a person or cause' and 'picket' as an effort 'to persuade or otherwise influence'). Nevertheless, we have never suggested that the kind of cursory examination that might be required to exclude casual conversation from the coverage of a regulation of picketing would be problematic. * * *

"The Colorado statute's regulation [places] no restrictions on—and clearly does not prohibit—either a particular viewpoint or any subject matter that may be discussed by a speaker. Rather, it simply establishes a minor place restriction on an extremely broad category of communications with unwilling listeners. Instead of drawing distinctions based on the subject that the approaching speaker may wish to address, the statute applies equally to used car salesmen, animal rights activists, fundraisers, environmentalists, and missionaries.

"Here, the statute's restriction seeks to protect those who enter a health care facility from the harassment, the nuisance, the persistent importuning, the following, the dogging, and the implied threat of physical touching that can accompany an unwelcome approach within eight feet of a patient by a person wishing to argue vociferously face-to-face and perhaps thrust an undesired hand-

a. Anti-abortion demonstrators picketed on a number of occasions outside a doctor's home. In response, the Town Board passed an ordinance that was interpreted to prohibit picketing taking place solely in front of a residence and directed at a residence. *Frisby*, per O'Connor, J., upheld the ordinance: "The state's interest in protecting the well-being, tranquility, and privacy of the home is certainly of the highest order in a free and civilized society." Brennan, joined by Marshall, dissenting, would have permitted the town to regulate the number of residential picketers, the hours, and the noise level of the pickets. Stevens, J., dissenting, would have limited the ban to conduct that "unreasonably interferes with the privacy of the home and does not serve a reasonable communicate purpose." He worried that a sign such as "GET WELL CHARLIE—OUR TEAM

NEEDS YOU," would fall within the sweep of the ordinance.

25. Furthermore, whether there is a 'right' to avoid unwelcome expression is not before us in this case. The purpose of the Colorado statute is not to protect a potential listener from hearing a particular message. It is to protect those who seek medical treatment from the potential physical and emotional harm suffered when an unwelcome individual delivers a message (whatever its content) by physically approaching an individual at close range, i.e., within eight feet. In offering protection from that harm, while maintaining free access to health clinics, the State pursues interests constitutionally distinct from the freedom from unpopular speech to which Justice Kennedy refers.

bill upon her. The statutory phrases, 'oral protest, education, or counseling,' distinguish speech activities likely to have those consequences from speech activities (such as Justice Scalia's 'happy speech' that are most unlikely to have those consequences. The statute does not distinguish among speech instances that are similarly likely to raise the legitimate concerns to which it responds. Hence, the statute cannot be struck down for failure to maintain 'content neutrality,' or for 'underbreadth.'

"Also flawed is Justice Kennedy's theory that a statute restricting speech becomes unconstitutionally content based because of its application 'to the specific locations where that discourse occurs.' A statute prohibiting solicitation in airports that was motivated by the aggressive approaches of Hari–Krishnas does not become content based solely because its application is confined to airports—'the specific location where that discourse occurs.' A statute making it a misdemeanor to sit at a lunch counter for an hour without ordering any food would also not be 'content based' even if it were enacted by a racist legislature that hated civil rights protesters (although it might raise separate questions about the State's legitimate interest at issue).

"Similarly, the contention that a statute is 'viewpoint based' simply because its enactment was motivated by the conduct of the partisans on one side of a debate is without support. The antipicketing ordinance upheld in *Frisby*, a decision in which both of today's dissenters joined, was obviously enacted in response to the activities of antiabortion protesters * * *. We nonetheless summarily concluded that the statute was content neutral."

Stevens, J., maintained that the statute was a reasonable place regulation: "The 8–foot separation between the speaker and the audience should not have any adverse impact on the readers' ability to read signs displayed by demonstrators. In fact, the separation might actually aid the pedestrians' ability to see the signs by preventing others from surrounding them and impeding their view. Furthermore, the statute places no limitations on the number, size, text, or images of the placards. And, as with all of the restrictions, the 8–foot zone does not affect demonstrators with signs who remain in place.

"With respect to oral statements, the distance certainly can make it more difficult for a speaker to be heard, particularly if the level of background noise is high and other speakers are competing for the pedestrian's attention. Notably, the statute places no limitation on the number of speakers or the noise level, including the use of amplification equipment, although we have upheld such restrictions in past [cases]. Finally, here there is a 'knowing' requirement that protects speakers 'who thought they were keeping pace with the targeted individual' at the proscribed distance from inadvertently violating the statute.

"It is also not clear that the statute's restrictions will necessarily impede, rather than assist, the speakers' efforts to communicate their messages. The statute might encourage the most aggressive and vociferous protesters to moderate their confrontational and harassing conduct, and thereby make it easier for thoughtful and law-abiding sidewalk counselors like petitioners to make themselves heard. But whether or not the 8–foot interval is the best possible accommodation of the competing interests at stake, we must accord a measure of deference to the judgment of the Colorado Legislature. * * *

"The burden on the ability to distribute handbills is more serious because it seems possible that an 8–foot interval could hinder the ability of a leafletter to deliver handbills to some unwilling recipients. The statute does not, however, prevent a leafletter from simply standing near the path of oncoming pedestrians and proffering his or her material, which the pedestrians can easily accept.

"Justice Kennedy [argues] that the statute leaves petitioners without adequate means of communication. This is a considerable overstatement. The statute seeks to protect those who wish to enter health care facilities, many of whom may be under special physical or emotional stress, from close physical approaches by demonstrators. In doing so, [it] will sometimes inhibit a demonstrator whose approach in fact would have proved harmless. But the statute's prophylactic aspect is justified by the great difficulty of protecting, say, a pregnant woman from physical harassment with legal rules that focus exclusively on the individual impact of each instance of behavior, demanding in each case an accurate characterization (as harassing or not harassing) of each individual movement within the 8–foot boundary. Such individualized characterization of each individual movement is often difficult to make accurately. [A] bright-line prophylactic rule may be the best way to provide protection, and, at the same time, by offering clear guidance and avoiding subjectivity, to protect speech itself. * * *

"[There] are two parts to petitioners' 'overbreadth' argument. On the one hand, they argue that the statute is too broad because it protects too many people in too many places, rather than just the patients at the facilities where confrontational speech had occurred. Similarly, it burdens all speakers, rather than just persons with a history of bad conduct. On the other hand, petitioners also contend that the statute is overbroad because it 'bans virtually the universe of protected expression, including displays of signs, distribution of literature, and mere verbal statements.'

"[The] fact that the coverage of a statute is broader than the specific concern that led to its enactment is of no constitutional significance. What is important is that all persons entering or leaving health care facilities share the interests served by the statute. It is precisely because the Colorado Legislature made a general policy choice that the statute is assessed under the constitutional standard set forth in *Ward*, rather than a more strict standard. In this case, it is not disputed that the regulation affects protected speech activity, the question is thus whether it is a 'reasonable restrictio[n] on the time, place, or manner of protected speech.' * * *

"The second part of the argument is based on a misreading of the statute [which] does not 'ban' any messages, and likewise it does not 'ban' any signs, literature, or oral statements. It merely regulates the places where communications may occur. [Petitioners] have not persuaded us that the impact of the statute on the conduct of other speakers will differ from its impact on their own sidewalk counseling. Like petitioners' own activities, the conduct of other protesters and counselors at all health care facilities are encompassed within the statute's 'legitimate sweep.' Therefore, the statute is not overly broad.

"Petitioners also claim that [the statute] is unconstitutionally vague. * * * [This] concern is ameliorated by the fact that [it] contains a scienter requirement. The statute only applies to a person who 'knowingly' approaches within eight feet of another, without that person's consent, for the purpose of engaging in oral protest, education, or counseling. The likelihood that anyone would not understand any of those common words seems quite remote."

SOUTER, J., joined by O'Connor, Ginsburg, and Breyer, JJ., concurred: "[c]ontent-based discriminations are subject to strict scrutiny because they place the weight of government behind the disparagement or suppression of some messages, whether or not with the effect of approving or promoting others. [This concern] is not, however, raised in the same way when a law addresses not the content of speech but the circumstances of its delivery. The right to express unpopular views does not necessarily immunize a speaker from liability for resorting to otherwise impermissible behavior meant to shock members of the speaker's audience, see *O'Brien* (burning draft card), or to guarantee their attention, see *Kovacs v. Cooper*, 336 U.S. 77, 69 S.Ct. 448, 93 L.Ed. 513 (1949) (sound trucks); *Frisby* (residential picketing); *Heffron*, Sec. 6, I, B (soliciting). Unless regulation limited to the details of a speaker's delivery results in removing a subject or viewpoint from effective discourse (or otherwise fails to advance a significant public interest in a way narrowly fitted to that objective), a reasonable restriction intended to affect only the time, place, or manner of speaking is perfectly valid. * * *

"It is important to recognize that the validity of punishing some expressive conduct, and the permissibility of a time, place, or manner restriction, does not depend on showing that the particular behavior or mode of delivery has no association with a particular subject or opinion. Draft card burners disapprove of the draft, see *O'Brien*, and abortion protesters believe abortion is morally wrong, *Madsen*.[b] There is always a correlation with subject and viewpoint when the law regulates conduct that has become the signature of one side of a controversy. But that does not mean that every regulation of such distinctive behavior is content based as First Amendment doctrine employs that term. The correct rule, rather, is captured in the formulation that a restriction is content based only if it is imposed because of the content of the speech. * * *

"No one disputes the substantiality of the government's interest in protecting people already tense or distressed in anticipation of medical attention (whether an abortion or some other procedure) from the unwanted intrusion of close personal importunity by strangers. The issues dividing the Court, then, go to the content neutrality of the regulation, its fit with the interest to be served by it, and the availability of other means of expressing the desired message (however offensive it may be even without physically close communication).

"Each of these issues is addressed principally by the fact that [does] not declare any view as unfit for expression within the 100–foot zone or beyond it. What it forbids, and all it forbids, is approaching another person closer than eight feet (absent permission) to deliver the message. * * *

"This is not to say that enforcement of the approach restriction will have no effect on speech; of course it will make some difference. The effect of speech is a product of ideas and circumstances, and time, place, and manner are circumstances. The question is simply whether the ostensible reason for regulating the circumstances is really something about the ideas. Here, the evidence indicates that the ostensible reason is the true reason."

b. *Madsen*, per Rehnquist, C.J., struck down an injunction creating a 300–foot buffer zone around the homes of those who worked in abortion clinics: "The 300–foot zone around the residence is much larger than the zone approved in *Frisby*. [The] 300–foot zone would ban '[g]eneral marching through residential neighborhoods, or even walking a route in front of an entire block of houses.' The record before us does not contain sufficient justification for this broad a ban on picketing; it appears that a limitation on the time, duration of picketing, and number of pickets outside a smaller zone could have accomplished the desired result." In separate opinions Stevens, J., Souter, J., and Scalia, J., joined by Kennedy and Thomas, JJ., joined in the judgment of the Court on this issue. For commentary, see Christina Wells, *Of Communists and Anti-Abortion Protestors: The Consequences of Falling into the Theoretical Abyss*, 33 Ga. L. Rev. 1 (1998); Alan E. Brownstein, *Rules of Engagement for Cultural Wars: Regulating Conduct, Unprotected Speech, and Protected Expression in Anti–Abortion Protests–Section II*, 29 U.C.Davis L.Rev. 1163 (1996).

SCALIA, J., joined by Thomas, J., dissented: "What is before us [is] a speech regulation directed against the opponents of abortion, and it therefore enjoys the benefit of the 'ad hoc nullification machine' that the Court has set in motion to push aside whatever doctrines of constitutional law stand in the way of that highly favored practice. [T]he regulation as it applies to oral communications is obviously and undeniably content-based. A speaker wishing to approach another for the purpose of communicating any message except one of protest, education, or counseling may do so without first securing the other's consent. Whether a speaker must obtain permission before approaching within eight feet—and whether he will be sent to prison for failing to do so—depends entirely on *what he intends to say* when he gets there. I have no doubt that this regulation would be deemed content-based *in an instant* if the case before us involved antiwar protesters, or union members seeking to 'educate' the public about the reasons for their strike. * * *

"The Court asserts that this statute is not content-based for purposes of our First Amendment analysis because it neither (1) discriminates among viewpoints nor (2) places restrictions on 'any subject matter that may be discussed by a speaker.' But we have never held that the universe of content-based regulations is limited to those two categories, and such a holding would be absurd. Imagine, for instance, special place-and-manner restrictions on all speech except that which 'conveys a sense of contentment or happiness.' This 'happy speech' limitation would not be 'viewpoint-based'—citizens would be able to express their joy in equal measure at either the rise or fall of the NASDAQ, at either the success or the failure of the Republican Party—and would not discriminate on the basis of subject matter, since gratification could be expressed about anything at all. Or consider a law restricting the writing or recitation of poetry—neither viewpoint-based nor limited to any particular subject matter. Surely this Court would consider such regulations to be 'content-based' and deserving of the most exacting scrutiny.

"[The] Court's confident assurance that the statute poses no special threat to First Amendment freedoms because it applies alike to 'used car salesmen, animal rights activists, fundraisers, environmentalists, and missionaries,' is a wonderful replication (except for its lack of sarcasm) of Anatole France's observation that '[t]he law, in its majestic equality, forbids the rich as well as the poor to sleep under bridges * * *.' [We] know what the Colorado legislators, by their careful selection of content ('protest, education, and counseling'), were taking aim at, for they set it forth in the statute itself: the 'right to protest or counsel against certain medical procedures' on the sidewalks and streets surrounding health care facilities.

"The Court is unpersuasive in its attempt to equate the present restriction with content-neutral regulation of demonstrations and picketing—as one may immediately suspect from the opinion's wildly expansive definitions of demonstrations as 'public display[s] of sentiment for or against a person or cause,' and of picketing as an effort 'to persuade or otherwise influence.' (On these terms, Nathan Hale was a demonstrator and Patrick Henry a picket.) When the government regulates 'picketing,' or 'demonstrating,' it restricts a particular manner of expression that is, as the author of today's opinion has several times explained, 'a mixture of conduct and communication.' [Today], of course, Justice Stevens gives us an opinion restricting not only handbilling but even one-on-one conversation of a particular content. * * *

"The Court makes too much of the statement in *Ward* that '[t]he principal inquiry in determining content neutrality ... is whether the government has adopted a regulation of speech because of disagreement with the message it conveys.' That is indeed 'the *principal* inquiry'—but it is not the *only* inquiry. Even a law that has as its purpose something unrelated to the suppression of particular content cannot irrationally single out that content for its prohibition. An ordinance directed at the suppression of noise (and therefore 'justified without reference to the content of regulated speech') cannot be applied only to sound trucks delivering messages of 'protest.' Our very first use of the 'justified by reference to content' language made clear that it is a prohibition *in addition to*, rather than in place of, the prohibition of facially content-based restrictions. 'Selective exclusions from a public forum' we said, 'may not be based on content alone, and may not be justified by reference to content alone.' *Mosley.*[2]"

Scalia, J., argued that the statute could not pass muster even if it were content neutral: "Just three Terms ago, in upholding an injunction against antiabortion activities, the Court refused to rely on any supposed 'right of the people approaching and entering the facilities to be left alone.' *Schenck v. Pro–Choice Network,* 519 U.S. 357, 117 S.Ct. 855, 137 L.Ed.2d 1 (1997)[c] Finding itself in something of a jam (the State here has passed a regulation that is obviously not narrowly tailored to advance any other interest) the Court today neatly repackages the repudiated 'right' as an 'interest' the State may decide to protect and then places it onto the scales opposite the right to free speech in a traditional public forum.

"[T]he Court's attempt to disguise the 'right to be let alone' as a 'governmental interest in protecting the right to be let alone' is unavailing for the simple reason that this is not an interest that may be legitimately weighed against the speakers' First Amendment rights (which the Court demotes to the status of First Amendment 'interests') We have consistently held that 'the Constitution does not permit the government to decide which types of otherwise protected speech are sufficiently offensive to require protection *for the unwilling listener or viewer.*' *Erznoznik.* * * * [We] have upheld limitations on a speaker's exercise of his right to speak on the public streets *when that speech intrudes into the privacy of the home. Frisby.* [As] the universally understood state of First Amendment law is described in a leading treatise: 'Outside the home, the burden is generally on the observer or listener to avert his eyes or plug his ears against the verbal assaults,

2. The Court's contention that the statute is content-neutral because it is not a 'regulation of speech' but a 'regulation of the places where some speech may occur,' is simply baffling. First, because the proposition that a restriction upon the places where speech may occur is not a restriction upon speech is both absurd and contradicted by innumerable cases. And second, because the fact that a restriction is framed as a 'regulation of the places where some speech may occur' has nothing whatever to do with whether the restriction is content-neutral—which is why *Boos* held to be content-based the ban on displaying, within 500 feet of foreign embassies, banners designed to 'bring into public odium any foreign government.'

c. *Schenck*, per Rehnquist, C.J., maintained that an injunction ordering abortion protesters to cease and desist from "counseling" women entering abortion clinics, who indicate they do not wish to be counseled, could not be sustained in order to protect privacy: "As [a] general matter, we have indicated that in public debate our own citizens must tolerate insulting, and often outrageous, speech in order to provide adequate breathing space to the freedoms protected by the First Amendment." This portion of the injunction was sustained on other grounds. Demonstrators had previously engaged in physical intimidation against women and their escorts. The lower court ordered demonstrators to stay 15 feet away from doorways, driveways, and driveway entrances except for two sidewalk counselors in order to accommodate free speech rights. The Court observed that the counselors, if ordered to desist, and other demonstrators could present their messages outside the 15–foot buffer zone and that their consignment to that area was a result of their own previous intimidation.

lurid advertisements, tawdry books and magazines, and other 'offensive' intrusions which increasingly attend urban life.' L. Tribe, *American Constitutional Law* § 12–19, p. 948 (2d ed. 1988).

"The burdens this law imposes upon the right to speak are substantial, despite an attempt to minimize them that is not even embarrassed to make the suggestion that they might actually 'assist * * * the speakers' efforts to communicate their messages.' [The] Court displays a willful ignorance of the type and nature of communication affected by the statute's restrictions. It seriously asserts, for example, that the 8–foot zone allows a speaker to communicate at a 'normal conversational distance.' I have certainly held conversations at a distance of eight feet seated in the quiet of my chambers, but I have never walked along the public sidewalk—and have not seen others do so—'conversing' at an 8–foot remove. The suggestion is absurd. So is the suggestion that the opponents of abortion can take comfort in the fact that the statute 'places no limitation on the number of speakers or the noise level, including the use of amplification equipment.' That is good enough, I suppose, for 'protesting'; but the Court must know that most of the 'counseling' and 'educating' likely to take place outside a health care facility cannot be done at a distance and at a high-decibel level. The availability of a powerful amplification system will be of little help to the woman who hopes to forge, in the last moments before another of her sex is to have an abortion, a bond of concern and intimacy that might enable her to persuade the woman to change her mind and heart. The counselor may wish to walk alongside and to say, sympathetically and as softly as the circumstances allow, something like: 'My dear, I know what you are going through. I've been through it myself. You're not alone and you do not have to do this. There are other alternatives. Will you let me help you? May I show you a picture of what your child looks like at this stage of her human development?' The Court would have us believe that this can be done effectively—yea, perhaps even *more* effectively—by shouting through a bullhorn at a distance of eight feet.

"The Court seems prepared, if only for a moment, to take seriously the magnitude of the burden the statute imposes on simple handbilling and leafletting. That concern is fleeting, however, since it is promptly assuaged by the realization that a leafletter may, without violating the statute, stand 'near the path' of oncoming pedestrians and make his 'proffe[r] * * * which the pedestrians can easily accept.' It does not take a veteran labor organizer to recognize—although surely any would, see Brief for American Federation of Labor and Congress of Industrial Organization as Amicus Curiae—that leafletting will be rendered utterly ineffectual by a requirement that the leafletter obtain from each subject permission to approach, or else man a stationary post (one that does not obstruct access to the facility, lest he violate subsection (2) of statute) and wait for passersby voluntarily to approach an outstretched hand. That simply is not how it is done, and the Court knows it—or should. A leafletter, whether he is working on behalf of Operation Rescue, Local 109, or Bubba's Bar–B–Que, stakes out the best piece of real estate he can, and then walks a few steps toward individuals passing in his vicinity, extending his arm and making it *as easy as possible* for the passerby, whose natural inclination is generally not to seek out such distributions, to simply accept the offering. Few pedestrians are likely to give their 'consent' to the approach of a handbiller (indeed, by the time he requested it they would likely have passed by), and even fewer are likely to walk over in order to pick up a leaflet."

Scalia, J., also questioned the breadth of the statute: " 'The fact,' the Court says, 'that the coverage of a statute is broader than the specific concern that led to its enactment is of no constitutional significance.' That is true enough ordinarily, but it is not true with respect to restraints upon speech, which is what the doctrine of overbreadth is all about. [Again], the Court says that the overbreadth doctrine is not applicable because this law simply 'does not 'ban' any signs, literature, or oral statements,' but 'merely regulates the places where communications may occur.' I know of no precedent for the proposition that time, place, and manner restrictions are not subject to the doctrine of overbreadth. Our decision in *United States v. Grace*, 461 U.S. 171, 103 S.Ct. 1702, 75 L.Ed.2d 736 (1983), demonstrates the contrary: Restriction of speech on the sidewalks around the Supreme Court was invalidated because it went further than the needs of security justified. Surely New York City cannot require a parade permit and a security bond for any individual who carries a sign on the sidewalks of Fifth Avenue. * * *

"[T]he Court acknowledged—indeed, boasted—that the statute it approves 'takes a prophylactic approach,' and adopts '[a] bright-line prophylactic rule.'[5] I scarcely know how to respond to such an unabashed repudiation of our First Amendment doctrine. Prophylaxis is the antithesis of narrow tailoring.

"[T]he public forum involved here—the public spaces outside of health care facilities—has become, by necessity and by virtue of this Court's decisions, a forum of last resort for those who oppose abortion. As a general matter, the most effective place, if not the only place, where that persuasion can occur, is outside the entrances to abortion facilities. By upholding these restrictions on speech in this place the Court ratifies the State's attempt to make even that task an impossible one.

"Those whose concern is for the physical safety and security of clinic patients, workers, and doctors should take no comfort from today's decision. Individuals or groups intent on bullying or frightening women out of an abortion, or doctors out of performing that procedure, will not be deterred by Colorado's statute; bullhorns and screaming from eight feet away will serve their purposes well. But those who would accomplish their moral and religious objectives by peaceful and civil means, by trying to persuade individual women of the rightness of their cause, will be deterred; and that is not a good thing in a democracy."

KENNEDY, J., dissented: "For the first time, the Court approves a law which bars a private citizen from passing a message, in a peaceful manner and on a profound moral issue, to a fellow citizen on a public sidewalk. If from this time forward the Court repeats its grave errors of analysis, we shall have no longer the proud tradition of free and open discourse in a public forum. * * *

"[The] prohibitions against 'picketing' and/or 'leafleting' upheld in *Frisby*, *Grace*, and *Mosley*, the Court says are no different from the restrictions on 'protest, education, or counseling' imposed by the Colorado statute. [But no] examination of the content of a speaker's message is required to determine whether an individual is picketing, or distributing a leaflet, or impeding free access to a building. Under the Colorado enactment, however, [w]hen a citizen approaches another on the sidewalk in a disfavored-speech zone, an officer of the State must listen to what the speaker says. If, in the officer's judgment, the

---

5. Of course the Court greatly understates the scope of the prophylaxis, saying that 'the statute's prophylactic aspect is justified by the great difficulty of protecting, say, a pregnant woman from physical harassment with legal rules that focus exclusively on the individual impact of each instance of behavior.' But the statute prevents the 'physically harassing' act of (shudder!) approaching within closer than eight feet not only when it is directed against pregnant women, but also (just to be safe) when it is directed against 300–pound, male, and unpregnant truck drivers—surely a distinction that is not 'difficult to make accurately.'

speaker's words stray too far toward 'protest, education, or counseling'—the boundaries of which are far from clear—the officer may decide the speech has moved from the permissible to the criminal. The First Amendment does not give the government such power.

"The statute is content based for an additional reason: [We] would close our eyes to reality were we to deny that 'oral protest, education, or counseling' outside the entrances to medical facilities concern a narrow range of topics—indeed, one topic in particular. [If], just a few decades ago, a State with a history of enforcing racial discrimination had enacted a statute like this one, regulating 'oral protest, education, or counseling' within 100 feet of the entrance to any lunch counter, our predecessors would not have hesitated to hold it was content based or viewpoint based. [To] say that one citizen can approach another to ask the time or the weather forecast or the directions to Main Street but not to initiate discussion on one of the most basic moral and political issues in all of contemporary discourse, a question touching profound ideas in philosophy and theology, is an astonishing view of the First Amendment. * * *

"In a further glaring departure from precedent we learn today that citizens have a right to avoid unpopular speech in a public forum. [*Rowan*] did not hold, contrary to statements in today's opinion that the First Amendment permits the government to restrict private speech in a public forum. Indeed, the Court in Rowan recognized what everyone, before today, understood to be true: '[W]e are often 'captives' outside the sanctuary of the home and subject to objectionable speech and other sound.' "[A]nd *Lehman v. Shaker Heights* [did] not, contrary to the majority's assertions, suggest that government is free to enact categorical measures restricting traditional, peaceful communications among citizens in a public forum. Instead, the Court admonished that citizens usually bear the burden of disregarding unwelcome messages.

Kennedy, J., argued that the terms "protest, "counseling," "education," and "consent" were undefined and unduly vague. "The statute's vagueness [becomes] as well one source of its overbreadth. The only sure way to avoid violating the law is to refrain from picketing, leafleting, or oral advocacy altogether. Scienter cannot save so vague a statute as this."

Kennedy, J., also argued that the State and the Court attempt to sidestep the enactment's obvious content-based restriction by praising the statute's breadth, by telling us all topics of conversation, not just discourse on abortion, are banned within the statutory proscription. [Our] precedents do not permit content censoring to be cured by taking even more protected speech within a statute's reach. [If] it indeed proscribes 'oral protest, education, or counseling' on all subjects across the board, it by definition becomes 'substantially broader than necessary to achieve the government's interest.' [*Ward*].

"The whimsical, arbitrary nature of the statute's operation is further demonstration of a restriction upon more speech than necessary. The happenstance of a dental office being located in a building brings the restricted-speech zone into play. If the same building also houses an organization dedicated, say, to environmental issues, a protest against the group's policies would be barred. Yet if, on the next block there were a public interest enterprise in a building with no health care facility, the speech would be unrestricted. The statute is a classic example of a proscription not narrowly tailored and resulting in restrictions of far more speech than necessary to achieve the legislature's object. * * *

"The majority insists the statute aims to protect distraught women who are embarrassed, vexed, or harassed as they attempt to enter abortion clinics. If these are punishable acts, they should be prohibited in those terms. In the course of praising Colorado's approach, the majority does not pause to tell us why, in its view, substantially less restrictive means cannot be employed to ensure citizens access to health care facilities or to prevent physical contact between citizens. * * *

"The means of expression at stake here are of controlling importance. Citizens desiring to impart messages to women considering abortions likely do not have resources to use the mainstream media for their message, much less resources to locate women contemplating the option of abortion. [Nowhere] is the speech more important than at the time and place where the act is about to occur. As the named plaintiff, Leila Jeanne Hill, explained, 'In my many years of sidewalk counseling I have seen a number of [these] women change their minds about aborting their unborn children as a result of my sidewalk counseling, and God's grace.' * * *

"The Court now strikes at the heart of the reasoned, careful balance I had believed was the basis for the joint opinion in *Casey*. The vital principle of the opinion was that in defined instances the woman's decision whether to abort her child was in its essence a moral one, a choice the State could not dictate. Foreclosed from using the machinery of government to ban abortions in early term, those who oppose it are remitted to debate the issue in its moral dimensions. In a cruel way, the Court today turns its back on that balance."

SECTION 7. GOVERNMENT SUPPORT OF SPEECH

Public forum doctrine recognizes that government is obligated to permit some of its property to be used for communicative purposes without content discrimination, but public forum doctrine also allows other government property to be restricted to some speakers or for talk about selected subjects. In short, in some circumstances government can provide resources for some speech while denying support for other speech. Indeed, government is a significant actor in the marketplace of ideas. Sometimes the government speaks as government; sometimes it subsidizes speech without purporting to claim that the resulting message is its own. It supports speech in many ways: official government messages; statements of public officials at publicly subsidized press conferences; artistic, scientific, or political subsidies, even the classroom communications of public school teachers.

If content distinctions are suspect when government acts as censor, they are the norm when government speaks or otherwise subsidizes speech. Government makes editorial judgments; it decides that some content is appropriate for the occasion and other content is not. The public museum curator makes content decisions in selecting exhibits; the librarian in selecting books; the public board in selecting recipients for research grants; the public official in composing press releases.

The line between support for speech and censorship of speech is not always bright, however. In any event, the Constitution limits the choices government may make in supporting speech. For example, government support of religious speech is limited under the establishment clause. See Ch. 8. This section explores the extent to which the speech clause or constitutional conceptions of equality should limit government discretion in supporting speech.

I. SUBSIDIES OF SPEECH

RUST v. SULLIVAN

500 U.S. 173, 111 S.Ct. 1759, 114 L.Ed.2d 233 (1991).

CHIEF JUSTICE REHNQUIST delivered the opinion of the Court.

These cases concern a facial challenge to Department of Health and Human Services (HHS) regulations which limit the ability of Title X fund recipients to engage in abortion-related activities. * * *

A. In 1970, Congress enacted Title X of the Public Health Service Act (Act), 84 Stat. 1506, as amended, 42 U.S.C. §§ 300–300a–41, which provides federal funding for family-planning services. The Act authorizes the Secretary to "make grants to and enter into contracts with public or nonprofit private entities to assist in the establishment and operation of voluntary family planning projects which shall offer a broad range of acceptable and effective family planning methods and services." 42 U.S.C. § 300(a). Grants and contracts under Title X must "be made in accordance with such regulations as the Secretary may promulgate." 42 U.S.C. § 300a–4. Section 1008 of the Act, however, provides that "[n]one of the funds appropriated under this subchapter shall be used in programs where abortion is a method of family planning." 42 U.S.C. § 300a–6. * * *

In 1988, the Secretary promulgated new regulations designed to provide " 'clear and operational guidance' to grantees about how to preserve the distinction between Title X programs and abortion as a method of family planning." 53 Fed.Reg. 2923–2924 (1988). * * *

The regulations attach three principal conditions on the grant of federal funds for Title X projects. First, the regulations specify that a "Title X project may not provide counseling concerning the use of abortion as a method of family planning or provide referral for abortion as a method of family planning." 42 CFR § 59.8(a)(1) (1989). Because Title X is limited to preconceptional services, the program does not furnish services related to childbirth. Only in the context of a referral out of the Title X program is a pregnant woman given transitional information. § 59.8(a)(2). Title X projects must refer every pregnant client "for appropriate prenatal and/or social services by furnishing a list of available providers that promote the welfare of the mother and the unborn child." Id. The list may not be used indirectly to encourage or promote abortion, "such as by weighing the list of referrals in favor of health care providers which perform abortions, by including on the list of referral providers health care providers whose principal business is the provision of abortions, by excluding available providers who do not provide abortions, or by 'steering' clients to providers who offer abortion as a method of family planning." § 59.8(a)(3). The Title X project is expressly prohibited from referring a pregnant woman to an abortion provider, even upon specific request. One permissible response to such an inquiry is that "the project does not consider abortion an appropriate method of family planning and therefore does not counsel or refer for abortion." § 59.8(b)(5).

Second, the regulations broadly prohibit a Title X project from engaging in activities that "encourage, promote or advocate abortion as a method of family planning." § 59.10(a). Forbidden activities include lobbying for legislation that would increase the availability of abortion as a method of family planning, developing or disseminating materials advocating abortion as a method of family planning, providing speakers to promote abortion as a method of family planning, using legal action to make abortion available in any way as a method of family planning, and paying dues to any group that advocates abortion as a method of family planning as a substantial part of its activities. Id.

Third, the regulations require that Title X projects be organized so that they are "physically and financially separate" from prohibited abortion activities. § 59.9. To be deemed physically and financially separate, "a Title X project must have an objective integrity and independence from prohibited activities. Mere bookkeeping separation of Title X funds from other monies is not sufficient." Id. The regulations provide a list of nonexclusive factors for the Secretary to consider in conducting a case-by-case determination of objective integrity and independence, such as the existence of separate accounting records and separate personnel, and the degree of physical separation of the project from facilities for prohibited activities. Id.

[Petitioners] are Title X grantees and doctors who supervise Title X funds suing on behalf of themselves and their patients. Respondent is the Secretary of the Department of Health and Human Services. [Petitioners] contend that the regulations violate the First Amendment by impermissibly discriminating based on viewpoint because they prohibit "all discussion about abortion as a lawful option—including counseling, referral, and the provision of neutral and accurate information about ending a pregnancy—while compelling the clinic or counselor to provide information that promotes continuing a pregnancy to term." They assert that the regulations violate the "free speech rights of private health care organizations that receive Title X funds, of their staff, and of their patients" by impermissibly imposing "viewpoint-discriminatory conditions on government subsidies" and thus "penaliz[e] speech funded with non-Title X monies." Because "Title X continues to fund speech ancillary to pregnancy testing in a manner that is not even-handed with respect to views and information about abortion, it invidiously discriminates on the basis of viewpoint." Relying on *Regan v. Taxation with Representation of Washington*, 461 U.S. 540, 103 S.Ct. 1997, 76 L.Ed.2d 129 (1983)[a] and *Arkansas Writers' Project, Inc. v. Ragland*, 481 U.S. 221, 107 S.Ct. 1722, 95 L.Ed.2d 209 (1987),[b] petitioners also assert that while the Government may place certain conditions on the receipt of federal subsidies, it may not "discriminate invidiously in its subsidies in such a way as to 'ai[m] at the suppression of dangerous ideas.'" *Regan*.

There is no question but that the statutory prohibition contained in § 1008 is constitutional. [The] Government can, without violating the Constitution, selectively fund a program to encourage certain activities it believes to be in the public interest, without at the same time funding an alternate program which seeks to deal with the problem in another way.[c] In so doing, the Government has not

a. *Regan* upheld tax code provisions that permitted contributions to veteran's organizations to be deductible even if they engaged in substantial lobbying while denying deductions for contributions to other religious, charitable, scientific, or educational organizations if they engaged in substantial lobbying.

b. *Arkansas Writers' Project* held it unconstitutional to impose a sales tax on general interest magazines while exempting newspapers, religious, professional, trade, and sports journals. Discriminatory taxation against the press or segments of it has generally been invalidated. *Minneapolis Star & Tribune v. Minnesota Comm. of Rev.*, 460 U.S. 575, 103 S.Ct. 1365, 75 L.Ed.2d 295 (1983) (some press treated more favorably and press treated differently from other enterprises); *Grosjean v. American Press Co.*, 297 U.S. 233, 56 S.Ct. 444, 80 L.Ed. 660 (1936) (same). But see *Leathers v. Medlock*, 499 U.S. 439, 111 S.Ct. 1438, 113 L.Ed.2d 494 (1991) (upholding general sales tax extension to cable that was not applicable to the print media on the grounds that it did not suppress ideas and that the tax did not target a small group of speakers).

c. The Court cited *Maher v. Roe*, 432 U.S. 464, 97 S.Ct. 2376, 53 L.Ed.2d 484 (1977) (constitutional for government to subsidize childbirth without subsidizing abortions) and

discriminated on the basis of viewpoint; it has merely chosen to fund one activity to the exclusion of the other. "[A] legislature's decision not to subsidize the exercise of a fundamental right does not infringe the right." *Regan.* * * *

The challenged regulations implement the statutory prohibition by prohibiting counseling, referral, and the provision of information regarding abortion as a method of family planning. They are designed to ensure that the limits of the federal program are observed. The Title X program is designed not for prenatal care, but to encourage family planning. A doctor who wished to offer prenatal care to a project patient who became pregnant could properly be prohibited from doing so because such service is outside the scope of the federally funded program. The regulations prohibiting abortion counseling and referral are of the same ilk; "no funds appropriated for the project may be used in programs where abortion is a method of family planning," and a doctor employed by the project may be prohibited in the course of his project duties from counseling abortion or referring for abortion. This is not a case of the Government "suppressing a dangerous idea," but of a prohibition on a project grantee or its employees from engaging in activities outside of its scope.

To hold that the Government unconstitutionally discriminates on the basis of viewpoint when it chooses to fund a program dedicated to advance certain permissible goals, because the program in advancing those goals necessarily discourages alternate goals, would render numerous government programs constitutionally suspect. When Congress established a National Endowment for Democracy to encourage other countries to adopt democratic principles, 22 U.S.C. § 4411(b), it was not constitutionally required to fund a program to encourage competing lines of political philosophy such as Communism and Fascism. Petitioners' assertions ultimately boil down to the position that if the government chooses to subsidize one protected right, it must subsidize analogous counterpart rights. But the Court has soundly rejected that proposition. Within far broader limits than petitioners are willing to concede, when the government appropriates public funds to establish a program it is entitled to define the limits of that program.

We believe that petitioners' reliance upon our decision in *Arkansas Writers' Project* is misplaced. That case involved a state sales tax which discriminated between magazines on the basis of their content. Relying on this fact, and on the fact that the tax "targets a small group within the press," contrary to our decision in *Minneapolis Star,* the Court held the tax invalid. But we have here not the case of a general law singling out a disfavored group on the basis of speech content, but a case of the Government refusing to fund activities, including speech, which are specifically excluded from the scope of the project funded.

Petitioners rely heavily on their claim that the regulations would not, in the circumstance of a medical emergency, permit a Title X project to refer a woman whose pregnancy places her life in imminent peril to a provider of abortions or abortion-related services. This case, of course, involves only a facial challenge to the regulations, and we do not have before us any application by the Secretary to a specific fact situation. On their face, we do not read the regulations to bar abortion referral or counseling in such circumstances. * * *

Petitioners also contend that the restrictions on the subsidization of abortion-related speech contained in the regulations are impermissible because they condition the receipt of a benefit, in this case Title X funding, on the relinquishment of a constitutional right, the right to engage in abortion advocacy and counseling.

Harris v. McRae, 448 U.S. 297, 100 S.Ct. 2671, 65 L.Ed.2d 784 (1980) (accord).

[H]ere the government is not denying a benefit to anyone, but is instead simply insisting that public funds be spent for the purposes for which they were authorized. The Secretary's regulations do not force the Title X grantee to give up abortion-related speech; they merely require that the grantee keep such activities separate and distinct from Title X activities. Title X expressly distinguishes between a Title X *grantee* and a Title X *project*. The grantee, which normally is a health care organization, may receive funds from a variety of sources for a variety of purposes. The grantee receives Title X funds, however, for the specific and limited purpose of establishing and operating a Title X project. 42 U.S.C. § 300(a). The regulations govern the scope of the Title X *project's* activities, and leave the grantee unfettered in its other activities. The Title X *grantee* can continue to perform abortions, provide abortion-related services, and engage in abortion advocacy; it simply is required to conduct those activities through programs that are separate and independent from the project that receives Title X funds.

In contrast, our "unconstitutional conditions" cases involve situations in which the government has placed a condition on the *recipient* of the subsidy rather than on a particular program or service, thus effectively prohibiting the recipient from engaging in the protected conduct outside the scope of the federally funded program. [By] requiring that the Title X grantee engage in abortion-related activity separately from activity receiving federal funding, Congress has, consistent with our teachings in *League of Women Voters*, [Sec. 8, II infra], and *Regan*, not denied it the right to engage in abortion-related activities. Congress has merely refused to fund such activities out of the public fisc, and the Secretary has simply required a certain degree of separation from the Title X project in order to ensure the integrity of the federally funded program.

The same principles apply to petitioners' claim that the regulations abridge the free speech rights of the grantee's staff. Individuals who are voluntarily employed for a Title X project must perform their duties in accordance with the regulation's restrictions on abortion counseling and referral. The employees remain free, however, to pursue abortion-related activities when they are not acting under the auspices of the Title X project. The regulations, which govern solely the scope of the Title X project's activities, do not in any way restrict the activities of those persons acting as private individuals. The employees' freedom of expression is limited during the time that they actually work for the project; but this limitation is a consequence of their decision to accept employment in a project, the scope of which is permissibly restricted by the funding authority.

This is not to suggest that funding by the Government, even when coupled with the freedom of the fund recipients to speak outside the scope of the Government-funded project, is invariably sufficient to justify government control over the content of expression. For example, this Court has recognized that the existence of a Government "subsidy," in the form of Government-owned property, does not justify the restriction of speech in areas that have "been traditionally open to the public for expressive activity," or have been "expressly dedicated to speech activity." Similarly, we have recognized that the university is a traditional sphere of free expression so fundamental to the functioning of our society that the Government's ability to control speech within that sphere by means of conditions attached to the expenditure of Government funds is restricted by the vagueness and overbreadth doctrines of the First Amendment, *Keyishian v. Board of Regents*. It could be argued by analogy that traditional relationships such as that between doctor and patient should enjoy protection under the First Amendment from government regulation, even when subsidized by the Government. We need not resolve that question here, however, because the Title X program regulations do not significantly impinge upon the doctor-patient relationship. Nothing in them requires a doctor to represent as his own any opinion that he does not in fact hold. Nor is the doctor-patient relationship established by the Title X program sufficiently all-encompassing so as to justify an expectation on the part of the patient of comprehensive medical advice. The program does not provide post-conception medical care, and therefore a doctor's silence with regard to abortion cannot reasonably be thought to mislead a client into thinking that the doctor does not consider abortion an appropriate option for her. The doctor is always free to make clear that advice regarding abortion is simply beyond the scope of the program. In these circumstances, the general rule that the Government may choose not to subsidize speech applies with full force. * * *

Justice Blackmun, with whom Justice Marshall joins, with whom Justice Stevens joins as to Parts II[d] and III,[e] and with whom Justice O'Connor joins as to Part I,[f] dissenting. * * *

II.   A.   Until today, the Court never has upheld viewpoint-based suppression of speech simply because that suppression was a condition upon the acceptance of public funds. Whatever may be the Government's power to condition the receipt of its largess upon the relinquishment of constitutional rights, it surely does not extend to a condition that suppresses the recipient's cherished freedom of speech based solely upon the content or viewpoint of that speech. * * *

It cannot seriously be disputed that the counseling and referral provisions at issue in the present cases constitute content-based regulation of speech. Title X grantees may provide counseling and referral regarding any of a wide range of family planning and other topics, save abortion.

The Regulations are also clearly viewpoint-based. While suppressing speech favorable to abortion with one hand, the Secretary compels anti-abortion speech with the other. For example, the Department of Health and Human Services' own description of the Regulations makes plain that "Title X projects are *required* to facilitate access to prenatal care and social services, including adoption services, that might be needed by the pregnant client to promote her well-being and that of her child, while making it abundantly clear that the project is not permitted to promote abortion by facilitating access to abortion through the referral process." 53 Fed.Reg. 2927 (1988) (emphasis added).

Moreover, the Regulations command that a project refer for prenatal care each woman diagnosed as pregnant, irrespective of the woman's expressed desire to continue or terminate her pregnancy. 42 CFR § 59.8(a)(2) (1990). If a client asks directly about abortion, a Title X physician or counselor is required to say, in essence, that the project does not consider abortion to be an appropriate method of family planning. § 59.8(b)(4). Both requirements are antithetical to the First Amendment. See *Wooley v. Maynard*.

The Regulations pertaining to "advocacy" are even more explicitly viewpoint-based. These provide: "A Title X project may not *encourage, promote or advocate* abortion as a method of family planning." § 59.10 (emphasis added). They explain: "This requirement prohibits actions to *assist* women to obtain abortions or *increase* the availability or accessibility of abortion for family planning purposes." § 59.10(a) (emphasis added). The Regulations do not, however, proscribe

---

d. Part II discussed freedom of speech and portions of it are set out below.

e. Part III argued that the regulations violated the fifth amendment due process clause.

f. Part I contended that the regulations were not authorized by the statute. O'Connor, and Stevens, JJ., each filed separate dissents advancing the same contention.

or even regulate anti-abortion advocacy. These are clearly restrictions aimed at the suppression of "dangerous ideas."

Remarkably, the majority concludes that "the Government has not discriminated on the basis of viewpoint; it has merely chosen to fund one activity to the exclusion of another." But the majority's claim that the Regulations merely limit a Title X project's speech to preventive or preconceptional services rings hollow in light of the broad range of nonpreventive services that the Regulations authorize Title X projects to provide.[2] By refusing to fund those family-planning projects that advocate abortion *because* they advocate abortion, the Government plainly has targeted a particular viewpoint. The majority's reliance on the fact that the Regulations pertain solely to funding decisions simply begs the question. Clearly, there are some bases upon which government may not rest its decision to fund or not to fund. For example, the Members of the majority surely would agree that government may not base its decision to support an activity upon considerations of race. As demonstrated above, our cases make clear that ideological viewpoint is a similarly repugnant ground upon which to base funding decisions.

The majority's reliance upon *Regan* in this connection is [misplaced]. That case stands for the proposition that government has no obligation to subsidize a private party's efforts to petition the legislature regarding its views. Thus, if the challenged Regulations were confined to non-ideological limitations upon the use of Title X funds for lobbying activities, there would exist no violation of the First Amendment. The advocacy Regulations at issue here, however, are not limited to lobbying but extend to all speech having the effect of encouraging, promoting, or advocating abortion as a method of family planning. § 59.10(a). Thus, in addition to their impermissible focus upon the viewpoint of regulated speech, the provisions intrude upon a wide range of communicative conduct, including the very words spoken to a woman by her physician. By manipulating the content of the doctor/patient dialogue, the Regulations upheld today force each of the petitioners "to be an instrument for fostering public adherence to an ideological point of view [he or she] finds unacceptable." *Wooley v. Maynard.* This type of intrusive, ideologically based regulation of speech goes far beyond the narrow lobbying limitations approved in *Regan,* and cannot be justified simply because it is a condition upon the receipt of a governmental benefit.[3]

B. The Court concludes that the challenged Regulations do not violate the First Amendment rights of Title X staff members because any limitation of the

---

2. In addition to requiring referral for prenatal care and adoption services, the Regulations permit general health services such as physical examinations, screening for breast cancer, treatment of gynecological problems, and treatment for sexually transmitted diseases. 53 Fed.Reg. 2927 (1988). None of the latter are strictly preventive, preconceptional services.

3. The majority attempts to obscure the breadth of its decision through its curious contention that "the Title X program regulations do not significantly impinge upon the doctor-patient relationship." That the doctor-patient relationship is substantially burdened by a rule prohibiting the dissemination by the physician of pertinent medical information is beyond serious dispute. This burden is undiminished by the fact that the relationship at issue here is not an "all-encompassing" one. A woman seek-

ing the services of a Title X clinic has every reason to expect, as do we all, that her physician will not withhold relevant information regarding the very purpose of her visit. To suggest otherwise is to engage in uninformed fantasy. Further, to hold that the doctor-patient relationship is somehow incomplete where a patient lacks the resources to seek comprehensive healthcare from a single provider is to ignore the situation of a vast number of Americans. As Justice Marshall has noted in a different context: "It is perfectly proper for judges to disagree about what the Constitution requires. But it is disgraceful for an interpretation of the Constitution to be premised upon unfounded assumptions about how people live." *United States v. Kras,* 409 U.S. 434, 93 S.Ct. 631, 34 L.Ed.2d 626 (1973) (dissenting opinion).

employees' freedom of expression is simply a consequence of their decision to accept employment at a federally funded project. Ante, at 22. But it has never been sufficient to justify an otherwise unconstitutional condition upon public employment that the employee may escape the condition by relinquishing his or her job.

The majority attempts to circumvent this principle by emphasizing that Title X physicians and counselors "remain free * * * to pursue abortion-related activities when they are not acting under the auspices of the Title X project." "The regulations," the majority explains, "do not in any way restrict the activities of those persons acting as private individuals." Under the majority's reasoning, the First Amendment could be read to tolerate *any* governmental restriction upon an employee's speech so long as that restriction is limited to the funded workplace. This is a dangerous proposition, and one the Court has rightly rejected in the past.

In *Abood,* it was no answer to the petitioners' claim of compelled speech as a condition upon public employment that their speech outside the workplace remained unregulated by the State.[g] Nor was the public employee's First Amendment claim in *Rankin v. McPherson,* 483 U.S. 378, 107 S.Ct. 2891, 97 L.Ed.2d 315 (1987), derogated because the communication that her employer sought to punish occurred during business hours.[h] At the least, such conditions require courts to balance the speaker's interest in the message against those of government in preventing its dissemination.

In the cases at bar, the speaker's interest in the communication is both clear and vital. In addressing the family-planning needs of their clients, the physicians and counselors who staff Title X projects seek to provide them with the full range of information and options regarding their health and reproductive freedom. Indeed, the legitimate expectations of the patient and the ethical responsibilities of the medical profession demand no less. "The patient's right of self-decision can be effectively exercised only if the patient possesses enough information to enable an intelligent choice. * * * The physician has an ethical obligation to help the patient make choices from among the therapeutic alternatives consistent with good medical practice." Current Opinions, the Council on Ethical and Judicial Affairs of the American Medical Association ¶ 8.08 (1989). * * *

The Government's articulated interest in distorting the doctor/patient dialogue—ensuring that federal funds are not spent for a purpose outside the scope of the program—falls far short of that necessary to justify the suppression of truthful information and professional medical opinion regarding constitutionally protected conduct.[4] Moreover, the offending Regulation is not narrowly tailored to serve this interest. For example, the governmental interest at stake could be served by imposing rigorous bookkeeping standards to ensure financial separation or adopting content-neutral rules for the balanced dissemination of family-planning and health information. By failing to balance or even to consider the free speech interests claimed by Title X physicians against the Government's asserted interest in suppressing the speech, the Court falters in its duty to implement the protection that the First Amendment clearly provides for this important message.

---

g. *Abood v. Detroit Board of Education,* Sec. 9, II infra (compelled funding of ideological activities of union violates freedom of speech).

h. *Rankin* (expressed hope that assassination attempt of president be successful is pro-tected speech when uttered in private to fellow employee during working hours).

4. It is to be noted that the Secretary has made no claim that the Regulations at issue reflect any concern for the health or welfare of Title X clients.

C. Finally, it is of no small significance that the speech the Secretary would suppress is truthful information regarding constitutionally protected conduct of vital importance to the listener. One can imagine no legitimate governmental interest that might be served by suppressing such information. * * *

Notes and Questions

1. *Free speech?* Is the problem in *Rust* one of free speech or of the right to secure an abortion? Consider Abner S. Greene, *Government of the Good,* 53 Vand. L.Rev. 1, 5 (2000): "Should it be improper as a matter of political theory, or unconstitutional, for government to condition the funding of health clinics on their advocating condom use by teens?"

2. *Political Speech.* Are there first amendment limits on the extent to which government can subsidize political speech. Suppose government itself enters the political fray. Should a city government be able to buy media time to speak on behalf of candidates? To influence the outcome of initiative campaigns?[i]

3. *Managerial domains.* Consider Robert C. Post, *Subsidized Speech,* 106 Yale L.J. 151, 164 (1996): "Public discourse must be distinguished from ['managerial'] domains * * * Within managerial domains, the state organizes its resources so as to achieve specified ends. The constitutional value of managerial domains is that of instrumental rationality, a value that conceptualizes persons as means to an end rather than as autonomous agents. * * * Within managerial domains, therefore, ends may be imposed upon persons.

"Managerial domains are necessary so that a democratic state can actually achieve objectives that have been democratically agreed upon. [Thus] the state can regulate speech within public educational institutions so as to achieve the purposes of education; it can regulate speech within the judicial system so as to attain the ends of justice; it can regulate speech within the military so as to preserve the national defense; it can regulate the speech of government employees so as to promote 'the efficiency of the public services [the government] performs through its employees'; and so forth.

"As a result of this instrumental orientation, viewpoint discrimination occurs frequently within managerial domains. To give but a few obvious examples: the president may fire cabinet officials who publicly challenge rather than support Administration policies; the military may discipline officers who publicly attack rather than uphold the principle of civilian control over the armed forces; public defenders who prosecute instead of defend their clients may be sanctioned; prison guards who encourage instead of condemn drug use may be chastised. Viewpoint discrimination occurs within managerial domains whenever the attainment of legitimate managerial objectives requires it.

i. For relevant commentary, see Mark Yudof, *When Government Speaks: Politics, Law, and Government Expression in America* (1983); David Cole, *Beyond Unconstitutional Conditions: Charting Spheres of Neutrality in Government–Funded Speech,* 67 N.Y.U.L.Rev. 675 (1992). Richard Delgado, *The Language of the Arms Race,* 64 B.U.L.Rev. 961 (1984); Thomas Emerson, *The Affirmative Side of the First Amendment,* 15 Ga.L.Rev. 795 (1981); Robert Kamenshine, *The First Amendment's Implied Political Establishment Clause,* 67 Calif.L.Rev. 1104 (1979); Steven Shiffrin, *Government Speech,* 27 UCLA L.Rev. 565 (1980); Martin H. Redish & Daryl I. Kessler, *Government Subsidies and Free Expression,* 80 Minn.L.Rev. 543 (1996); Frederick Schauer, *Book Review,* 35 Stan.L.Rev. 373 (1983); Mark Yudof, *When Governments Speak: Toward A Theory of Government Expression and the First Amendment,* 57 Tex.L.Rev. 863 (1979); Edward Ziegler, *Government Speech and the Constitution: The Limits of Official Partisanship,* 21 B.C.L.Rev. 578 (1980); Note, *The Constitutionality of Municipal Advocacy in Statewide Referendum Campaigns,* 93 Harv.L.Rev. 535 (1980).

"[Clearly], First Amendment doctrine within managerial domains differs fundamentally from First Amendment doctrine within public discourse."[j]

Is the *Rust* situation an appropriate instance to invoke the managerial domain perspective? Or does it matter that the speakers whose speech is limited are not bureaucrats, but professionals who "must always qualify their loyalty and commitment to the vertical hierarchy of an organization by their horizontal commitment to general professional norms and standards." See id. at 172.

4. *Private speakers.* Consider Steven G. Gey, *Reopening the Public Forum–From Sidewalks to Cyberspace,* 58 Ohio St. L. J. 1535, 1601 (1998): "[C]ertainly the government may express its point of view on any matter of public policy. Indeed, creating public policy, informing the public about the policy's content, and defending the policy against political opponents is the central purpose of a democratic government. But extending the capacity of the government to control speech beyond the narrow confines of the government itself—that is, beyond the agencies of government, individuals who are elected members of the government, or employees of the government speaking on the government's behalf—is neither necessary to the process of governing nor consistent with the democratic premise that no government can use its general policymaking authority to suppress or overwhelm its opposition and thereby perpetuate its control of the government indefinitely.

"It is crucial to remember that references to speech by 'the government' are really references to the speech of whatever political faction happened to capture control of the government at the last election. One of the primary purposes of the First Amendment is to ensure that the political faction that won the last election does not abuse the legitimate power it obtains from that victory to manipulate the results of the next election. Therefore, it is necessary to impose strict limits on any victorious faction's ability to 'speak' on behalf of the government."

5. *Deception.* Consider Dorothy E. Roberts, *Rust v. Sullivan and the Control of Knowledge,* 61 Geo.Wash.L.Rev. 587, 594–95 (1993): "[P]regnancy may accelerate the progression of certain serious medical conditions, such as heart disease, hypertension, diabetes, sickle cell anemia, cancer and AIDS. For example, a woman with diabetic retinopathy who becomes pregnant may go blind. The regulations prohibited doctors from advising women suffering from these conditions that abortion may reduce the long-term risks to their health. Moreover, the recommendation of prenatal care may give the false impression that pregnancy does not jeopardize these women's health."

6. *Domination.* Note, *Unconstitutional Conditions as "Nonsubsidies": When is Deference Inappropriate?* 80 Geo.L.J. 131, 135 (1991): "*Rust* was wrongly decided because the government's domination of the entire family planning dialogue for many of those who seek such information has made private alternatives unavailable. Poor women have a right to this information because the Constitution respects the interests of those who want to receive a particular message, not just the interests of those who speak. In the limited context of the

---

j. For similar first amendment perspectives, see C. Edwin Baker, *Campaign Expenditures and Free Speech,* 33 Harv. C.R.-C.L.Rev. 1 (1998)(referring to bounded contexts); Daniel Halberstam, *Commercial Speech, Professional Speech, and the Constitutional Status of Social Institutions,* 147 U.Pa.L.Rev. 771 (1991)(referring to bounded speech institutions). For sympathetic criticism, see Mark Tushnet, *The Pos-* *sibilities of Comparative Constitutional Law,* 108 Yale L.J. 1225 (1999). On the other hand, are their circumstances in which the problem of government supported speech should be regarded as outside the managerial domain and inside the realm of distributive justice where individuals are not treated as a means to an end? See Stephen J. Heyman, *State-Supported Speech,* 1999 Wisc. L.Rev. 1119, 1139–40.

exchange between the family planning counselor and the poor pregnant woman who wants information concerning a range of options, government has gone far toward creating a monopoly. By contrast, a broad portion of government's speech-related subsidies, such as those for the Kennedy Center, do not involve 'crowding out' of private alternatives and thus do not raise analogous First Amendment concerns."

7. *Rust distinguished.* The University of Virginia subsidized the printing costs of a wide variety of student organizations, but refused to fund religious activities (those that "primarily promote or manifest a particular belief in or about a deity or an ultimate reality"). ROSENBERGER v. UNIVERSITY OF VIRGINIA, 515 U.S. 819, 115 S.Ct. 2510, 132 L.Ed.2d 700 (1995), per KENNEDY, J., also set forth Ch. 8, Sec. I infra held that the refusal to fund religious speech violated the free speech clause: "[In *Rust*] the government did not create a program to encourage private speech but instead used private speakers to transmit specific information pertaining to its own program. We recognized that when the government appropriates public funds to promote a particular policy of its own it is entitled to say what it wishes.

"It does not follow [that] viewpoint-based restrictions are proper when the University does not itself speak or subsidize transmittal of a message it favors but instead expends funds to encourage a diversity of views from private speakers."[k]

SOUTER, J., joined by Stevens, Ginsburg and Breyer, JJ., dissented: "If the Guidelines were written or applied so as to limit only such Christian advocacy and no other evangelical efforts that might compete with it, the discrimination would be based on viewpoint. But that is not what the regulation authorizes; it applies to Muslim and Jewish and Buddhist advocacy as well as to Christian. And since it limits funding to activities promoting or manifesting a particular belief not only 'in' but 'about' a deity or ultimate reality, it applies to agnostics and atheists as well as it does to deists and theists. The Guidelines [thus] do not skew debate by funding one position but not its competitors. [T]hey simply deny funding for hortatory speech that 'primarily promotes or manifests' any view on the merits of religion; they deny funding for the entire subject matter of religious apologetics."[l]

In 1989 the National Endowment for the Arts ("NEA") supported two artists whose work sparked controversy: Robert Mapplethorpe's exhibit, *The Perfect Moment*, included homoerotic photographs; Andres Serrano's photograph, *Piss Christ*, showed a crucifix immersed in urine. In reaction, Congress reduced appropriations in 1990 by the amount that had been granted to the two recipients and took a number of steps leading up to the passage of Title 20 U.S.C. § 954(d) which provided that, "No payment shall be made under this section except upon application therefor which is submitted to the National Endowment for the Arts in accordance with regulations issued and procedures established by the Chairperson. In establishing such regulations and procedures, the Chairperson shall ensure that (1) artistic excellence and artistic merit are the criteria by which applications are judged, taking into consideration general standards of decency and respect for the diverse beliefs and values of the American public; and (2) applications are consistent with the purposes of this section. Such regulations and procedures shall

k. O'Connor, J., and Thomas, J., filed concurring opinions.

l. For commentary on whether the Virginia practice constitutes viewpoint discrimination, see Kent Greenawalt, *Viewpoints From Olympus*, 96 Colum. L.Rev. 697 (1996).

clearly indicate that obscenity is without artistic merit, is not protected speech, and shall not be funded."

The National Council on the Arts which advises the NEA Chairperson resolved to implement the provision by ensuring that the panels conducting initial reviews of grant applications represent geographic, ethnic, and aesthetic diversity, and the Chairperson agreed. Several artists, whose grant applications had been approved before the passage of § 954(d), but reconsidered and denied afterwards, brought suit, challenging § 954(d)(1) on its face. The district court and the court of appeals declared § 954(d)(1) unconstitutional.

NATIONAL ENDOWMENT FOR THE ARTS v. FINLEY, 524 U.S. 569, 118 S.Ct. 2168, 141 L.Ed.2d 500 (1998), per O'CONNOR, J., upheld § 954(d)(1) maintaining that it did not impermissibly discriminate on the basis of point of view and was not unconstitutionally vague: "Respondents argue that the provision is a paradigmatic example of viewpoint discrimination because it rejects any artistic speech that either fails to respect mainstream values or offends standards of decency. The premise of respondents' claim is that § 954(d)(1) constrains the agency's ability to fund certain categories of artistic expression. The NEA, however, reads the provision as merely hortatory, and contends that it stops well short of an absolute restriction. Section 954(d)(1) adds 'considerations' to the grant-making process; it does not preclude awards to projects that might be deemed 'indecent' or 'disrespectful,' nor place conditions on grants, or even specify that those factors must be given any particular weight in reviewing an application. Indeed, the agency asserts that it has adequately implemented § 954(d)(1) merely by ensuring the representation of various backgrounds and points of view on the advisory panels that analyze grant applications. We do not decide whether the NEA's view—that the formulation of diverse advisory panels is sufficient to comply with Congress' command—is in fact a reasonable reading of the statute. It is clear, however, that the text of § 954(d)(1) imposes no categorical requirement. The advisory language stands in sharp contrast to congressional efforts to prohibit the funding of certain classes of speech. When Congress has in fact intended to affirmatively constrain the NEA's grant-making authority, it has done so in no uncertain terms. See § 954(d)(2) ('[O]bscenity is without artistic merit, is not protected speech, and shall not be funded').

"Furthermore, like the plain language of § 954(d), the political context surrounding the adoption of the 'decency and respect' clause is inconsistent with respondents' assertion that the provision compels the NEA to deny funding on the basis of viewpoint discriminatory criteria. The legislation was a bipartisan proposal introduced as a counterweight to amendments aimed at eliminating the NEA's funding or substantially constraining its grant-making authority. [B]efore the vote on § 954(d)(1), one of its sponsors stated: 'If we have done one important thing in this amendment, it is this. We have maintained the integrity of freedom of expression in the United States.'

"That § 954(d)(1) admonishes the NEA merely to take 'decency and respect' into consideration, and that the legislation was aimed at reforming procedures rather than precluding speech, undercut respondents' argument that the provision inevitably will be utilized as a tool for invidious viewpoint discrimination.

"Respondents' claim that the provision is facially unconstitutional may be reduced to the argument that the criteria in § 954(d)(1) are sufficiently subjective that the agency could utilize them to engage in viewpoint discrimination. Given the varied interpretations of the criteria and the vague exhortation to 'take them into consideration,' it seems unlikely that this provision will introduce any greater element of selectivity than the determination of 'artistic excellence' itself. * * *

"Any content-based considerations that may be taken into account in the grant-making process are a consequence of the nature of arts funding. The NEA has limited resources and it must deny the majority of the grant applications that it receives, including many that propose 'artistically excellent' projects. The agency may decide to fund particular projects for a wide variety of reasons, 'such as the technical proficiency of the artist, the creativity of the work, the anticipated public interest in or appreciation of the work, the work's contemporary relevance, its educational value, its suitability for or appeal to special audiences (such as children or the disabled), its service to a rural or isolated community, or even simply that the work could increase public knowledge of an art form.'

"Respondent's reliance on our decision in *Rosenberger*, is therefore misplaced. In *Rosenberger*, a public university declined to authorize disbursements from its Student Activities Fund to finance the printing of a Christian student newspaper. We held that by subsidizing the Student Activities Fund, the University had created a limited public forum, from which it impermissibly excluded all publications with religious editorial viewpoints. Although the scarcity of NEA funding does not distinguish this case from *Rosenberger*, the competitive process according to which the grants are allocated does. In the context of arts funding, in contrast to many other subsidies, the Government does not indiscriminately 'encourage a diversity of views from private speakers.' The NEA's mandate is to make aesthetic judgments, and the inherently content-based 'excellence' threshold for NEA support sets it apart from the subsidy at issue in *Rosenberger*—which was available to all student organizations that were 'related to the educational purpose of the University'—and from comparably objective decisions on allocating public benefits, such as access to a school auditorium or a municipal theater, see *Lamb's Chapel v. Center Moriches Union Free School Dist.*, 508 U.S. 384, 386, 113 S.Ct. 2141, 124 L.Ed.2d 352 (1993); *Southeastern Promotions, Ltd. v. Conrad*, 420 U.S. 546, 555, 95 S.Ct. 1239, 43 L.Ed.2d 448 (1975), or the second class mailing privileges available to 'all newspapers and other periodical publications,' see *Hannegan v. Esquire, Inc.*, 327 U.S. 146, 148, n. 1, 66 S.Ct. 456, 90 L.Ed. 586 (1946).

"Respondents do not allege discrimination in any particular funding decision. [Thus,] we have no occasion here to address an as-applied challenge in a situation where the denial of a grant may be shown to be the product of invidious viewpoint discrimination. If the NEA were to leverage its power to award subsidies on the basis of subjective criteria into a penalty on disfavored viewpoints, then we would confront a different case. We have stated that, even in the provision of subsidies, the Government may not 'ai[m] at the suppression of dangerous ideas, 'and if a subsidy were 'manipulated' to have a 'coercive effect,' then relief could be appropriate. [Unless] and until § 954(d)(1) is applied in a manner that raises concern about the suppression of disfavored viewpoints, however, we uphold the constitutionality of the provision.

"Finally, although the First Amendment certainly has application in the subsidy context, we note that the Government may allocate competitive funding according to criteria that would be impermissible were direct regulation of speech or a criminal penalty at stake. So long as legislation does not infringe on other constitutionally protected rights, Congress has wide latitude to set spending priorities. See *Regan v. Taxation with Representation*. In the 1990 Amendments that incorporated § 954(d)(1), Congress modified the declaration of purpose in the

NEA's enabling act to provide that arts funding should 'contribute to public support and confidence in the use of taxpayer funds,' and that '[p]ublic funds [must] ultimately serve public purposes the Congress defines.' § 951(5). And as we held in *Rust*, Congress may 'selectively fund a program to encourage certain activities it believes to be in the public interest, without at the same time funding an alternative program which seeks to deal with the problem in another way.' In doing so, 'the Government has not discriminated on the basis of viewpoint; it has merely chosen to fund one activity to the exclusion of the other.'[a]

"The lower courts also erred in invalidating § 954(d)(1) as unconstitutionally vague. [The] terms of the provision are undeniably opaque, and if they appeared in a criminal statute or regulatory scheme, they could raise substantial vagueness concerns. It is unlikely, however, that speakers will be compelled to steer too far clear of any 'forbidden area' in the context of grants of this nature. But when the Government is acting as patron rather than as sovereign, the consequences of imprecision are not constitutionally severe.

"In the context of selective subsidies, it is not always feasible for Congress to legislate with clarity. Indeed, if this statute is unconstitutionally vague, then so too are all government programs awarding scholarships and grants on the basis of subjective criteria such as 'excellence.' To accept respondents' vagueness argument would be to call into question the constitutionality of these valuable government programs and countless others like them.

"Section 954(d)(1) merely adds some imprecise considerations to an already subjective selection process. It does not, on its face, impermissibly infringe on First or Fifth Amendment rights."

SCALIA, J., joined by Thomas, J., concurred in the judgment: " 'The operation was a success, but the patient died.' What such a procedure is to medicine, the Court's opinion in this case is to law. It sustains the constitutionality of 20 U.S.C. § 954(d)(1) by gutting it. The most avid congressional opponents of the provision could not have asked for more. I write separately because, unlike the Court, I think that § 954(d)(1) must be evaluated as written, rather than as distorted by the agency it was meant to control. By its terms, it establishes content-and-viewpoint-based criteria upon which grant applications are to be evaluated. And that is perfectly constitutional.

"[The statute means what it says. Under the statute, the] application reviewers must take into account 'general standards of decency' and 'respect for the diverse beliefs and values of the American public' when evaluating artistic excellence and merit. One can regard this as either suggesting that decency and respect are elements of what Congress regards as artistic excellence and merit, or as suggesting that decency and respect are factors to be taken into account in addition to artistic excellence and merit. But either way, it is entirely, 100% clear that decency and respect are to be taken into account in evaluating applications.

"This is so apparent that I am at a loss to understand what the Court has in mind (other than the gutting of the statute) when it speculates that the statute is merely 'advisory.' General standards of decency and respect for Americans' beliefs and values *must* (for the statute says that the Chairperson 'shall ensure' this result) be taken into account [in] evaluating all applications. This does not mean that those factors must always be dispositive, but it *does* mean that they must

---

a. Ginsburg, J., joined O'Connor, J.'s opinion with the exception of the paragraph accompanying this footnote.

always be considered. The method of compliance proposed by the National Endowment for the Arts (NEA)—selecting diverse review panels of artists and nonartists that reflect a wide range of geographic and cultural perspectives—is so obviously inadequate that it insults the intelligence. A diverse panel membership increases the odds that, *if and when* the panel takes the factors into account, it will reach an accurate assessment of what they demand. But it in no way increases the odds that the panel *will* take the factors into consideration—much less *ensures* that the panel will do so, which is the Chairperson's duty under the statute. Moreover, the NEA's fanciful reading of § 954(d)(1) would make it wholly superfluous. Section 959(c) already requires the Chairperson to 'issue regulations and establish procedures [to] ensure that all panels are composed, to the extent practicable, of individuals [reflecting] diverse artistic and cultural points of view.'

"I agree with the Court that § 954(d)(1) 'imposes no categorical requirement' in the sense that it does not require the denial of all applications that violate general standards of decency or exhibit disrespect for the diverse beliefs and values of Americans. Compare § 954(d)(2) ('[O]bscenity [shall] not be funded'). But the factors need not be conclusive to be discriminatory. To the extent a particular applicant exhibits disrespect for the diverse beliefs and values of the American public or fails to comport with general standards of decency, the likelihood that he will receive a grant diminishes. In other words, the presence of the 'tak[e] into consideration' clause 'cannot be regarded as mere surplusage; it means something.' And the 'something' is that the decision maker, all else being equal, will favor applications that display decency and respect, and disfavor applications that do not.

"This unquestionably constitutes viewpoint discrimination.[1] That conclusion is not altered by the fact that the statute does not 'compe[l]' the denial of funding any more than a provision imposing a five-point handicap on all black applicants for civil service jobs is saved from being race discrimination by the fact that it does not compel the rejection of black applicants. If viewpoint discrimination in this context is unconstitutional (a point I shall address anon), the law is invalid unless there are some situations in which the decency and respect factors *do not constitute viewpoint discrimination*. And there is none. [T]he conclusion of viewpoint discrimination is not affected by the fact that what constitutes 'decency' or 'the diverse beliefs and values of the American people' is difficult to pin down—any more than a civil-service preference in favor of those who display 'Republican-party values' would be rendered nondiscriminatory by the fact that there is plenty of room for argument as to what Republican-party values might be.

"The 'political context surrounding the adoption of the "decency and respect" clause,' [does] not change its meaning or affect its constitutionality. All that is proved by the various statements [from] the floor debates is (1) that the provision was not meant categorically to exclude any particular viewpoint (which I have conceded, and which is plain from the text), and (2) that the language was not meant to do anything that is unconstitutional. That in no way propels the Court's leap to the countertextual conclusion that the provision was merely 'aimed at reforming procedures,' and cannot be 'utilized as a tool for invidious viewpoint discrimination.' It is evident in the legislative history that § 954(d)(1) was prompted by, and directed at, the public funding of such offensive productions as Serrano's 'Piss Christ,' the portrayal of a crucifix immersed in urine, and

---

1. [O]ne might argue that the decency and respect factors constitute content discrimination rather than viewpoint discrimination, which would render them easier to uphold. Since I believe this statute must be upheld in either event, I pass over this conundrum and assume the worst.

Mapplethorpe's show of lurid homoerotic photographs. Thus, even if one strays beyond the plain text it is perfectly clear that the statute was meant to disfavor—that is, to discriminate against—such productions. Not to ban their funding absolutely, to be sure (though as I shall discuss, that also would not have been unconstitutional); but to make their funding more difficult.

"More fundamentally, of course, all this legislative history has no valid claim upon our attention at all. It is a virtual certainty that very few of the Members of Congress who voted for this language both (1) knew of, and (2) agreed with, the various statements that the Court has culled from [the] floor debate (probably conducted on an almost empty floor). And it is wholly irrelevant that the statute was a 'bipartisan proposal introduced as a counterweight' to an alternative proposal that would directly restrict funding on the basis of viewpoint. We do not judge statutes as if we are surveying the scene of an accident; each one is reviewed, not on the basis of how much worse it could have been, but on the basis of what it says. It matters not whether this enactment was the product of the most partisan alignment in history or whether, upon its passage, the Members all linked arms and sang, 'The more we get together, the happier we'll be.' It is 'not consonant with our scheme of government for a court to inquire into the motives of legislators.' The law at issue in this case is to be found in the text of § 954(d)(1), which passed both Houses and was signed by the President. And that law unquestionably disfavors—discriminates against—indecency and disrespect for the diverse beliefs and values of the American people. * * *

"With the enactment of § 954(d)(1), Congress did not *abridge* the speech of those who disdain the beliefs and values of the American public, nor did it *abridge* indecent speech. Those who wish to create indecent and disrespectful art are as unconstrained now as they were before the enactment of this statute. Avant-garde artistes such as respondents remain entirely free to epater les bourgeois; they are merely deprived of the additional satisfaction of having the bourgeoisie taxed to pay for it. * * *

"As we noted in *Rust*, when Congress chose to establish the National Endowment for Democracy it was not constitutionally required to fund programs encouraging competing philosophies of government—an example of funding discrimination that cuts much closer than this one to the core of political speech which is the primary concern of the First Amendment. It takes a particularly high degree of chutzpah for the NEA to contradict this proposition, since the agency itself discriminates—and is required by law to discriminate—in favor of artistic (as opposed to scientific, or political, or theological) expression. Not all the common folk, or even all great minds, for that matter, think that is a good idea. In 1800, when John Marshall told John Adams that a recent immigration of Frenchmen would include talented artists, 'Adams denounced all Frenchmen, but most especially 'schoolmasters, painters, poets, & C.' He warned Marshall that the fine arts were like germs that infected healthy constitutions.' J. Ellis, *After the Revolution: Profiles of Early American Culture* 36 (1979). Surely the NEA itself is nothing less than an institutionalized discrimination against that point of view. Nonetheless it is constitutional, as is the congressional determination to favor decency and respect for beliefs and values over the opposite.[3]

3. I suppose it would be unconstitutional for the government to give money to an organization devoted to the promotion of candidates nominated by the Republican party—but it would be just as unconstitutional for the government itself to promote candidates nominated by the Republican party, and I do not think that that unconstitutionality has anything to do with the First Amendment.

"The nub of the difference between me and the Court is that I regard the distinction between 'abridging' speech and funding it as a fundamental divide, on this side of which the First Amendment is inapplicable. The Court, by contrast, seems to believe that the First Amendment, despite its words, has some ineffable effect upon funding, imposing constraints of an indeterminate nature which it announces (without troubling to enunciate any particular test) are not violated by the statute here—or, more accurately, are not violated by the quite different, emasculated statute that it imagines."

SOUTER, J., dissented: "The decency and respect proviso mandates viewpoint-based decisions in the disbursement of government subsidies, and the Government has wholly failed to explain why the statute should be afforded an exemption from the fundamental rule of the First Amendment that viewpoint discrimination in the exercise of public authority over expressive activity is unconstitutional.[2]

"[An argument] for avoiding unconstitutionality that the Court appears to regard with some favor is the Government's argument that the NEA may comply with § 954(d) merely by populating the advisory panels that analyze grant applications with members of diverse backgrounds. Would that it were so easy; this asserted implementation of the law fails even to 'reflec[t] a plausible construction of the plain language of the statute.' Rust.

"The Government notes that § 954(d) actually provides that '[i]n establishing [regulations] and procedures, the Chairperson [of the NEA] shall ensure that (1) artistic excellence and artistic merit are the criteria by which applications are judged, taking into consideration general standards of decency and respect for the diverse beliefs and values of the American public.' According to the Government, this language requires decency and respect to be considered not in judging applications, but in making regulations. If, then, the Chairperson takes decency and respect into consideration through regulations ensuring diverse panels, the statute is satisfied. But it would take a great act of will to find any plausibility in this reading. The reference to considering decency and respect occurs in the subparagraph speaking to the 'criteria by which applications are judged,' not in the preamble directing the Chairperson to adopt regulations; it is in judging applications that decency and respect are most obviously to be considered. * * *

"[Another] try at avoiding constitutional problems is the Court's disclaimer of any constitutional issue here because '[s]ection 954(d)(1) adds "considerations' to the grant-making process; it does not preclude awards to projects that might be deemed "indecent" or "disrespectful," nor place conditions on grants, or even specify that those factors must be given any particular weight in reviewing an application.' * * *

"That is not a fair reading. Just as the statute cannot be read as anything but viewpoint based, or as requiring nothing more than diverse review panels, it cannot be read as tolerating awards to spread indecency or disrespect, so long as the review panel, the National Counsel on the Arts, and the Chairperson have given some thought to the offending qualities and decided to underwrite them anyway. That, after all, is presumably just what prompted the congressional outrage in the first place, and there was nothing naive about the Representative

2. [Congress] has no obligation to support artistic enterprises that many people detest. The First Amendment speaks up only when Congress decides to participate in the Nation's artistic life by legal regulation, as it does through a subsidy scheme like the NEA. If Congress does choose to spend public funds in this manner, it may not discriminate by viewpoint in deciding who gets the money.

who said he voted for the bill because it does 'not tolerate wasting Federal funds for sexually explicit photographs [or] sacrilegious works.'

"But even if I found the Court's view of 'consideration' plausible, that would make no difference at all on the question of constitutionality. What if the statute required a panel to apply criteria 'taking into consideration the centrality of Christianity to the American cultural experience,' or 'taking into consideration whether the artist is a communist,' or 'taking into consideration the political message conveyed by the art,' or even 'taking into consideration the superiority of the white race'? Would the Court hold these considerations facially constitutional, merely because the statute had no requirement to give them any particular, much less controlling, weight? I assume not.

"A second basic strand in the Court's treatment of today's question and the heart of Justice Scalia's in effect assumes that whether or not the statute mandates viewpoint discrimination, there is no constitutional issue here because government art subsidies fall within a zone of activity free from First Amendment restraints. The Government calls attention to the roles of government-as-speaker [in] which the government is of course entitled to engage in viewpoint discrimination: if the Food and Drug Administration launches an advertising campaign on the subject of smoking, it may condemn the habit without also having to show a cowboy taking a puff on the opposite page; and if the Secretary of Defense wishes to buy a portrait to decorate the Pentagon, he is free to prefer George Washington over George the Third.

"The Government freely admits, however, that it neither speaks through the expression subsidized by the NEA,[6] nor buys anything for itself with its NEA grants. On the contrary, believing that '[t]he arts [reflect] the high place accorded by the American people to the nation's rich cultural heritage,' § 951(6), and that '[i]t is vital to a democracy [to] provide financial assistance to its artists and the organizations that support their work,' § 951(10), the Government acts as a patron, financially underwriting the production of art by private artists and impresarios for independent consumption. Accordingly, the Government would have us liberate government-as-patron from First Amendment strictures not by placing it squarely within the categories of government-as-buyer or government-as-speaker, but by recognizing a new category by analogy to those accepted ones. The analogy is, however, a very poor fit, and this patronage falls embarrassingly on the wrong side of the line between government-as-buyer or-speaker and government-as-regulator-of-private-speech.

"[*Rosenberger*] controls here. The NEA, like the student activities fund in *Rosenberger*, is a subsidy scheme created to encourage expression of a diversity of views from private speakers. Congress brought the NEA into being to help all Americans 'achieve a better understanding of the past, a better analysis of the present, and a better view of the future.' § 951(3). The NEA's purpose is to 'support new ideas' and 'to help create and sustain [a] climate encouraging freedom of thought, imagination, and inquiry.' §§ 951(10), (7). Given this congressional choice to sustain freedom of expression, *Rosenberger* teaches that the First Amendment forbids decisions based on viewpoint popularity. So long as Congress chooses to subsidize expressive endeavors at large, it has no business requiring the NEA to turn down funding applications of artists and exhibitors who devote their 'freedom of thought, imagination, and inquiry' to defying our tastes, our beliefs, or

---

6. Here, the 'communicative element inherent in the very act of funding itself,' *Rosenberger* (Souter, J., dissenting), is an endorsement of the importance of the arts collectively, not an endorsement of the individual message espoused in a given work of art.

our values. It may not use the NEA's purse to 'suppres[s] dangerous ideas.' *Regan v. Taxation with Representation.*

"The Court says otherwise, claiming to distinguish *Rosenberger* on the ground that the student activities funds in that case were generally available to most applicants, whereas NEA funds are disbursed selectively and competitively to a choice few. But the Court in *Rosenberger* anticipated and specifically rejected just this distinction when it held in no uncertain terms that '[t]he government cannot justify viewpoint discrimination among private speakers on the economic fact of scarcity.'[8] Scarce money demands choices, of course, but choices 'on some acceptable [viewpoint] neutral principle,' like artistic excellence and artistic merit;[9] 'nothing in our decision[s] indicate[s] that scarcity would give the State the right to exercise viewpoint discrimination that is otherwise impermissible.'[10]."

Notes and Questions

1.   Consider Randall P. Bezanson, *The Government Speech Forum: Forbes and Finley and Government Speech Selection Judgments,* 83 Iowa L.Rev. 953, 969 (1998): "How can we know when government acts only to subsidize the expression of others with no communicative design of its own, as in *Rosenberger,* and when government's subsidy of others' speech is simply an efficient means of communicating the government's own expressive design? Are the answers to these questions important, as the Court's majority and Justice Souter in dissent believed, or are they irrelevant, as Justices Scalia and Thomas believed? These are the central questions posed by the *Finley* case."

2.   Consider David Cole, *Symposium: Art, Distribution & the State: Perspectives in the National Endowment for the Arts,* 17 Cardoza Arts & Ent.L.J. 705, 721 (1999): "[If] as Justice Scalia says, when the government funds rather than directly regulates speech, the First Amendment is simply irrelevant, then the public debate would be greatly impoverished * * * . The print press is subsidized by mailing privileges. The broadcast media is subsidized by free access to the air waves. Public broadcasting is also subsidized by tax payer dollars. Political organizations are subsidized by free access to public property for demonstrations. Non-profit organizations and advocacy groups are subsidized through tax exemptions. Public universities are subsidized through the public payroll. Private universities are subsidized through tax subsidies, grants, and financial aid for students. That is where the public debate takes place—in the press, in the

---

8.   The Court's attempt to avoid *Rosenberger* by describing NEA funding in terms of competition, not scarcity, will not work. Competition implies scarcity, without which there is no exclusive prize to compete for; the Court's 'competition' is merely a surrogate for 'scarcity.'

9.   While criteria of 'artistic excellence and artistic merit' may raise intractable issues about the identification of artistic worth, and could no doubt be used covertly to filter out unwanted ideas, there is nothing inherently viewpoint discriminatory about such merit-based criteria. [Decency] and respect, on the other hand, are inherently and facially viewpoint based, and serve no legitimate and permissible end. The Court's assertion that the mere fact that grants must be awarded according to artistic merit precludes 'absolute neu-

trality' on the part of the NEA is therefore misdirected. It is not to the point that the government necessarily makes choices among competing applications, or even that its judgments about artistic quality may be branded as subjective to some greater or lesser degree; the question here is whether the government may apply patently viewpoint-based criteria in making those choices.

10.   [Leaving] aside the proper application of forum analysis to the NEA and its projects, I cannot agree that the holding of *Rosenberger* turned on characterizing its metaphorical forum as public in some degree. Like this case, *Rosenberger* involved viewpoint discrimination, and we have made it clear that such discrimination is impermissible in all forums, even non-public [ones].

universities, and in political organizations. Every one of those organizations is ultimately speaking with government funds. If the government could impose whatever restrictions it wants on who gets funding to speak, we would have a much less free public debate."

3. If government consistently with the first amendment can impose a point of view on bureaucrats or on doctors when they are subsidized with government funds (*Rust*), is it nonetheless barred from telling academics the point of view they can advance in the classroom? If so, should artists on panels be considered more like bureaucrats and doctors or more like academics. How does one decide which actors favor some speech over other speech? See Frederick Schauer, *The Ontology of Censorship*, in Censorship and Silencing 147 (Post ed. 1998). Is there a problem with giving special protection for some institutions or professionals and not others? See generally Frederick Schauer, *Principles, Institutions, and the First Amendment,* 112 Harv. L.Rev. 84 (1998).[b]

4. Suppose the Endowment refuses to fund a work of considerable artistic merit on the ground that it is racist. Constitutional? If so, could one consistently argue that the Endowment could not constitutionally refuse to fund art on the ground that it is indecent? Consider also Steven J. Heyman, *State-Supported Speech,* 1999 Wisc. L.Rev. 1119, 1139–40: "Suppose [a] state legislature becomes concerned about violence in popular culture and the impact it may have on young people. Instead of attempting to regulate violent entertainment, the legislature decides to create a program to support art and culture, with the proviso that no funds should be awarded to works that glorify violence. There can be little doubt that this would constitute viewpoint discrimination. Yet it seems highly implausible to suggest that if the government chooses to support non-violent art, it must support violent art as well. Instead, the proviso should be upheld on the same ground that Souter offers in defending criteria of artistic merit—that it serves a 'perfectly legitimate' governmental goal."[c]

II. GOVERNMENT AS EDUCATOR AND EDITOR

Oregon's Compulsory Education Act of 1922 required all students to attend public schools through the eighth grade.[a] Two operators of private schools, the Society of the Sisters of the Holy Names of Jesus and Mary and the Hill Military Academy secured an injunction against the act's enforcement. PIERCE v. SOCIETY OF SISTERS, 268 U.S. 510, 45 S.Ct. 571, 69 L.Ed. 1070 (1925), per McReynolds, J., held that the law violated the substantive due process rights of the parents and the schools: "The manifest purpose is to compel general attendance at public schools by normal children, between 8 and 16, who have not completed the eighth grade. [No] question is raised concerning the power of the state reasonably to regulate all schools, to inspect, supervise and examine them, their teachers and pupils; to require that all children of proper age attend some school, that teachers

---

b. Are the issues involved in supporting some speech over other speech different in the sciences than the arts? See David Wasserman, *Public Funding for Science and Art*, in Censorship and Silencing 169 (Post ed. 1998).

c. For additional commentary, see Steven H. Shiffrin, *Dissent, Injustice, and the Meanings of America* ch.1 (1999); Owen J. Fiss, *State Activism and State Censorship,* 100 Yale L.J. 2087, 2101 (1991); Amy Sabrin, *Thinking About Content: Can It Play An Appropriate*

Role in Government Funding of the Arts? 102 Yale L.J. 1209 (1993).

a. The statute provided exemptions for children with disabilities, or who had completed the eighth grade, or who lived considerable distances from a public school, or who held a special permit from the county superintendent. The Court did not believe these exemptions were especially important.

shall be of good moral character and patriotic disposition, that certain studies plainly essential to good citizenship must be taught, and that nothing be taught which is manifestly inimical to the public welfare.

"The inevitable practical result of enforcing the act under consideration would be destruction of appellees' primary schools, and perhaps all other private primary schools for normal children within the state of Oregon. Appellees are engaged in a kind of undertaking not inherently harmful, but long regarded as useful and meritorious. Certainly there is nothing in the present records to indicate that they have failed to discharge their obligations to patrons, students, or the state. And there are no peculiar circumstances or present emergencies which demand extraordinary measures relative to primary education.

"Under the doctrine of *Meyer v. Nebraska*, 262 U.S. 390, 43 S.Ct. 625, 67 L.Ed. 1042, (1923), we think it entirely plain that the Act of 1922 unreasonably interferes with the liberty of parents and guardians to direct the upbringing and education of children under their control. [The] fundamental theory of liberty upon which all governments in this Union repose excludes any general power of the state to standardize its children by forcing them to accept instruction from public teachers only. The child is not the mere creature of the state; those who nurture him and direct his destiny have the right, coupled with the high duty, to recognize and prepare him for additional obligations.

"Appellees are corporations, and therefore, it is said, they cannot claim for themselves the liberty which the Fourteenth Amendment guarantees. [But] they have business and property for which they claim protection. These are threatened with destruction through the unwarranted compulsion which appellants are exercising over present and prospective patrons of their schools. * * * Generally, it is entirely true, as urged by counsel, that no person in any business has such an interest in possible customers as to enable him to restrain exercise of proper power of the state upon the ground that he will be deprived of patronage. But the injunctions here sought are not against the exercise of any proper power. Appellees asked protection against arbitrary, unreasonable, and unlawful interference with their patrons and the consequent destruction of their business and property. Their interest is clear and immediate * * * ."

Notes and Questions

1.   Apart from due process, did the Oregon law violate the free speech rights of the affected parents? The schools? The children?

2.   Can a law like that in *Pierce* be defended on the ground that private schools siphon off the wealthy and the academically talented from the public schools while undermining a strong base of political support for generous financing of the schools?[b] On the ground that democratic education depends on schools that are integrated in terms of race, class, and religion?

3.   If parents have a right to send their children to private schools, do they also have a right to have their children excused from instruction they find objectionable? If so, what limits, if any, accompany that right?[c] Do captive

---

b. Is the empirical assumption correct, see Amy Gutmann, *Democratic Education* 117 (1987).

c. See generally Nomi M. Stolzenberg, *"He Drew a Circle that Shut Me Out": Assimila-* *tion, Indoctrination, and the Paradox of a Liberal Education*, 106 Harv. L. Rev. 581 (1993). On parents' free speech rights, see generally, Stephen G. Gilles, *On Educating Children: A Parentalist Manifesto*, 63 U.Chi.L.Rev. (1996).

audiences of government speech have a first amendment right not to be propagandized? Do children educated in public schools particularly have such a right? See Stephen Gottlieb, *In The Name of Patriotism: The Constitutionality of "Bending" History in Public Secondary Schools,* 62 N.Y.U.L.Rev. 497 (1987). If ad hoc methods of separating education from propaganda are unreliable, are any institutional structures or processes required? Should this be a constitutional right without a remedy?[d]

4. Is public education itself objectionable? Consider John Stuart Mill, *On Liberty* 98 (D. Spitz ed. 1975): "A general State education is a mere contrivance for moulding people to be exactly like one another. An education established and controlled by the State should only exist, if it exist at all, as one of many competing experiments carried on for the purpose of example and stimulus, to keep the others up to a certain standard of excellence."

5. Consider Mark G. Yudof, *When Government Speaks: Politics, Law, and Government Expression in America* 229–230 (1983): "*Pierce* may be construed (whatever the original motivations of the justices) as telling governments that they are free to establish their own public schools and to make education compulsory for certain age groups, but not free to eliminate competing, private-sector educational institutions that may serve to create heterogeneity and to counter the state's dominance over the education of the young. * * * *Pierce* represents a reasonable, if imperfect, accommodation of conflicting pressures. The state may promulgate its messages in the public school, while parents are free to choose private schools with different orientations. The state must tolerate private education, but need not fund it. The state may make some demands of private schools to satisfy compulsory schooling laws, but those demands may not be so excessive as to turn private schools into public schools managed and funded by the public sector. The integrity of the communications and socialization processes in private schools and families remains intact, while the state's interest in producing informed, educated, and productive citizens is not sacrificed."

But consider Abner S. Greene, *Why Vouchers are Constitutional and Why They are Not,* 13 Notre Dame J. of L.Ethics & Pub. Policy 397, 407 (1999): "[T]he *Pierce* assumption-although, in one view, assuring multiple repositories of power by counteracting the state's school monopoly—in fact assures that children will get their basic education not from multiple sources, but rather from their parents or their parent's agents alone. [Overruling] *Pierce* would free up funds used for private schooling and would direct parental energies at improving the private schools. Different public schools would, of course, focus on different values, and parents would still therefore have significant input into the curriculum of their local public schools. But we would remove some children from the monopoly of their parents and substitute a plural system of education."

6. A Nebraska law that outlawed the teaching of languages other than English[e] in any school to students who had yet to pass the eighth grade. The Nebraska Supreme Court upheld the conviction of an instructor who taught reading in the German language in a private elementary school during recess. The Nebraska Supreme Court thought the law had a defensible purpose: "The Legislature had seen the baneful effects of permitting foreigners, who had taken

---

d. Consider also captive audiences of prisoners, soldiers, or workers in public institutions. Do "informed consent" provisions concerning abortion raise first amendment captive audience issues? Cf. *Public Utilities Comm'n v.*

Pollak, 343 U.S. 451, 72 S.Ct. 813, 96 L.Ed. 1068 (1952)(city transit company's playing of radio programs does not violate Constitution).

e. The teaching of Latin, Greek, and Hebrew was permitted.

residence in this country, to rear and educate their children in the language of their native land. The result of that condition was found to be inimical to our own safety. To allow the children of foreigners, who had emigrated here, to be taught from early childhood the language of the country of their parents was to rear them with that language as their mother tongue. It was to educate them so that they must always think in that language, and, as a consequence, naturally inculcate in them the ideas and sentiments foreign to the best interests of this country. The statute, therefore, was intended not only to require that the education of all children be conducted in the English language, but that, until they had grown into that language and until it had become a part of them, they should not in the schools be taught any other language. [The] hours which a child is able to devote to study in the confinement of school are limited. It must have ample time for exercise or play. Its daily capacity for learning is comparatively small."

MEYER v. NEBRASKA, supra, per McREYNOLDS, J., held that the statute violated due process: "While this court has not attempted to define with exactness the liberty [guaranteed under the fourteenth amendment], the term has received much consideration and some of the included things have been definitely stated. Without doubt, it denotes not merely freedom from bodily restraint but also the right of the individual to contract, to engage in any of the common occupations of life, to acquire useful knowledge, to marry, establish a home and bring up children, to worship God according to the dictates of his own conscience, and generally to enjoy those privileges long recognized at common law as essential to the orderly pursuit of happiness by free men. [Corresponding] to the right of control, it is the natural duty of the parent to give his children education suitable to their station in life; and nearly all the states, including Nebraska, enforce this obligation by compulsory laws. Practically, education of the young is only possible in schools conducted by especially qualified persons who devote themselves thereto. The calling always has been regarded as useful and honorable, essential, indeed, to the public welfare. Mere knowledge of the German language cannot reasonably be regarded as harmful. Heretofore it has been commonly looked upon as helpful and desirable. Plaintiff in error taught this language in school as part of his occupation. His right thus to teach and the right of parents to engage him so to instruct their children, we think, are within the liberty of the amendment. * * *

"It is said the purpose of the legislation was to promote civic development by inhibiting training and education of the immature in foreign tongues and ideals before they could learn English and acquire American ideals, and 'that the English language should be and become the mother tongue of all children reared in this state.' It is also affirmed that the foreign born population is very large, that certain communities commonly use foreign words, follow foreign leaders, move in a foreign atmosphere, and that the children are thereby hindered from becoming citizens of the most useful type and the public safety is imperiled. * * *

"For the welfare of his Ideal Commonwealth, Plato suggested a law which should provide: 'That the wives of our guardians are to be common, and their children are to be common, and no parent is to know his own child, nor any child his parent. [The] proper officers will take the offspring of the good parents to the pen or fold, and there they will deposit them with certain nurses who dwell in a separate quarter; but the offspring of the inferior, or of the better when they chance to be deformed, will be put away in some mysterious, unknown place, as they should be.' In order to submerge the individual and develop ideal citizens, Sparta assembled the males at seven into barracks and intrusted their subsequent education and training to official guardians. Although such measures have been deliberately approved by men of great genius their ideas touching the relation between individual and state were wholly different from those upon which our institutions rest; and it hardly will be affirmed that any Legislature could impose such restrictions upon the people of a state without doing violence to both letter and spirit of the Constitution.

"The desire of the Legislature to foster a homogeneous people with American ideals prepared readily to understand current discussions of civic matters is easy to appreciate. Unfortunate experiences during the late war and aversion toward every character of truculent adversaries were certainly enough to quicken that aspiration. But the means adopted, we think, exceed the limitations upon the power of the state and conflict with rights assured to plaintiff in error.[f] The interference is plain enough and no adequate reason therefor in time of peace and domestic tranquility has been shown.

"As the statute undertakes to interfere only with teaching which involves a modern language, leaving complete freedom as to other matters, there seems no adequate foundation for the suggestion that the purpose was to protect the child's health by limiting his mental activities. It is well known that proficiency in a foreign language seldom comes to one not instructed at an early age, and experience shows that this is not injurious to the health, morals or understanding of the ordinary child."[g]

TINKER v. DES MOINES SCHOOL DISTRICT

393 U.S. 503, 89 S.Ct. 733, 21 L.Ed.2d 731 (1969).

JUSTICE FORTAS delivered the opinion of the Court.

[Petitioners, two high school students and one junior high student, wore black armbands to school to publicize their objections to the Vietnam conflict and their advocacy of a truce. They refused to remove the armbands when asked to do so. In accordance with a ban on armbands which the city's school principals had adopted two days before in anticipation of such a protest, petitioners were sent home and suspended from school until they would return without the armbands. They sought a federal injunction restraining school officials from disciplining them, but the lower federal courts upheld the constitutionality of the school authorities' action on the ground that it was reasonable in order to prevent a disturbance which might result from the wearing of the armbands.]

[T]he wearing of armbands in the circumstances of this case was entirely divorced from actually or potentially disruptive conduct by those participating in it. It was closely akin to "pure speech" which, we have repeatedly held, is entitled to comprehensive protection under the First Amendment. * * *

f. Are statutes mandating English as the only language of government constitutional? See Drucilla Cornell & William W. Bratton, *Deadweight Costs and Intrinsic Wrongs of Nativism*, 84 Corn.L.Rev. 595 (1999).

g. Holmes and Sutherland, JJ., dissented, arguing, that the Court should defer to the state's interest. In addition, to studying *Pierce* and *Meyer* in connection with due process, the student may wish to reconsider them in the course of studying freedom of religion. In that connection, consider the argument that the law in *Pierce* was substantially motivated by anti-Catholic sentiment, that the law in *Meyer* was substantially motivated by anti-German sentiment and that the purpose of teaching German in *Meyer* was to help children participate in Lutheran services which were taught in German. For rich discussion of the other purposes present in *Pierce* and *Meyer*, see Barbara B. Woodhouse, *"Who Owns the Child?": Meyer and Pierce and the Child as Property*, 33 Wm. & Mary L. Rev. 995 (1992). See generally William J. Ross, *Nativism, Education, and the Constitution, 1917–1927* (1994).

First Amendment rights, applied in light of the special characteristics of the school environment, are available to teachers and students. It can hardly be argued that either students or teachers shed their constitutional rights to freedom of speech or expression at the schoolhouse gate. This has been the unmistakable holding of this Court for almost 50 years. In *Meyer*, this Court [held that fourteenth amendment due process] prevents States from forbidding the teaching of a foreign language to young students. Statutes to this effect, the Court held, unconstitutionally interfere with the liberty of teacher, student, and parent. * * *

The problem presented by the present case does not relate to regulation of the length of skirts or the type of clothing, to hair style or deportment. [It] does not concern aggressive, disruptive action or even group demonstrations. Our problem involves direct, primary First Amendment rights akin to "pure speech."

The school officials banned and sought to punish petitioners for a silent, passive, expression of opinion, unaccompanied by any disorder or disturbance on the part of petitioners. There is here no evidence whatever of petitioners' interference, actual or nascent, with the school's work or of collision with the rights of other students to be secure and to be let alone. Accordingly, this case does not concern speech or action that intrudes upon the work of the school or the rights of other students.

Only a few of the 18,000 students in the school system wore the black armbands. Only five students were suspended for wearing them. There is no indication that the work of the school or any class was disrupted. Outside the classrooms, a few students made hostile remarks to the children wearing armbands, but there were no threats or acts of violence on school premises.

[I]n our system, undifferentiated fear or apprehension of disturbance [the District Court's basis for sustaining the school authorities' action] is not enough to overcome the right to freedom of expression. Any departure from absolute regimentation may cause trouble. Any variation from the majority's opinion may inspire fear. Any words spoken, in class, in the lunchroom or on the campus, that deviates from the views of another person, may start an argument or cause a disturbance. But our Constitution says we must take this risk [and] our history says that it is this sort of hazardous freedom—this kind of openness—that is the basis of our national strength and of the independence and vigor of Americans who grow up and live in this relatively permissive, often disputatious society.

In order for the State in the person of school officials to justify prohibition of a particular expression of opinion, it must be able to show that its action was caused by something more than a mere desire to avoid the discomfort and unpleasantness that always accompany an unpopular viewpoint. Certainly where there is no finding and no showing that the exercise of the forbidden right would "materially and substantially interfere with the requirements of appropriate discipline in the operation of the school," the prohibition cannot be sustained.

In the present case, the District Court made no such finding, and our independent examination of the record fails to yield evidence that the school authorities had reason to anticipate that the wearing of the armbands would substantially interfere with the work of the school or impinge upon the rights of other students. Even an official memorandum prepared after the suspension that listed the reasons for the ban on wearing the armbands made no reference to the anticipation of such disruption.[3]

---

3. The only suggestions of fear of disorder in the report are these: "A former student of one of our high schools was killed in Viet Nam. Some of his friends are still in school and it

On the contrary, the action of the school authorities appears to have been based upon an urgent wish to avoid the controversy which might result from the expression, even by the silent symbol of armbands, of opposition to this Nation's part in the conflagration in Vietnam. * * *

It is also relevant that the school authorities did not purport to prohibit the wearing of all symbols of political or controversial significance. The record shows that students in some of the schools wore buttons relating to national political campaigns, and some even wore the Iron Cross, traditionally a symbol of Nazism. The order prohibiting the wearing of armbands did not extend to these. Instead, a particular symbol—black armbands worn to exhibit opposition to this Nation's involvement in Vietnam—was singled out for prohibition. Clearly, the prohibition of expression of one particular opinion, at least without evidence that it is necessary to avoid material and substantial interference with school work or discipline, is not constitutionally permissible.

In our system, state-operated schools may not be enclaves of totalitarianism. School officials do not possess absolute authority over their students. Students in school as well as out of school are "persons" under our Constitution. They are possessed of fundamental rights which the State must respect, just as they themselves must respect their obligations to the State. In our system, students may not be regarded as closed-circuit recipients of only that which the State chooses to communicate. They may not be confined to the expression of those sentiments that are officially approved. In the absence of a specific showing of constitutionally valid reasons to regulate their speech, students are entitled to freedom of expression of their views.

[The principle of prior cases underscoring the importance of diversity and exchange of ideas in the schools,] is not confined to the supervised and ordained discussion which takes place in the classroom. The principal use to which the schools are dedicated is to accommodate students during prescribed hours for the purpose of certain types of activities. Among those activities is personal intercommunication among the students. This is not only an inevitable part of the process of attending school. It is also an important part of the educational process.

A student's rights therefore, do not embrace merely the classroom hours. When he is in the cafeteria, or on the playing field, or on the campus during the authorized hours, he may express his opinions, even on controversial subjects like the conflict in Vietnam, if he does so "[without] materially and substantially interfering [with] appropriate discipline in the operation of the school" and without colliding with the rights of others. *Burnside*. But conduct by the student, in class or out of it, which for any reason—whether it stems from time, place, or type of behavior—materially disrupts classwork or involves substantial disorder or invasion of the rights of others is, of course, not immunized by the [first amendment].

We properly read [the first amendment] to permit reasonable regulation of speech-connected activities in carefully restricted circumstances. But we do not

was felt that if any kind of a demonstration existed, it might evolve into something which would be difficult to control.

"Students at one of the high schools were heard to say they would wear arm bands of other colors if the black bands prevailed."

Moreover, the testimony of school authorities at trial indicates that it was not fear of disruption that motivated the regulation pro-

hibiting the armbands; the regulation was directed against "the principle of the demonstration" itself. School authorities simply felt that "the schools are no place for demonstrations," and if the students "didn't like the way our elected officials were handling things, it should be handled with the ballot box and not in the halls of our public schools."

confine the permissible exercise of First Amendment rights to a telephone booth or the four corners of a pamphlet, or to supervised and ordained discussion in a school classroom.[a] * * *

Reversed and remanded.

JUSTICE STEWART, concurring.[b]

Although I agree with much of what is said in the Court's opinion, and with its judgment in this case, I cannot share the Court's uncritical assumption that, school discipline aside, the First Amendment rights of children are co-extensive with those of adults. Indeed, I had thought the Court decided otherwise just last Term in *Ginsberg v. New York* [Sec. 1, III, B supra.] I continue to hold the view I expressed in that case: "[A] State may permissibly determine that, at least in some precisely delineated areas, a child—like someone in a captive audience—is not possessed of that full capacity for individual choice which is the presupposition of First Amendment guarantees." (concurring opinion). * * *

JUSTICE BLACK, dissenting. * * *

Assuming that the Court is correct in holding that the conduct of wearing armbands for the purpose of conveying political ideas is protected by the First Amendment [the] crucial remaining questions are whether students and teachers may use the schools at their whim as a platform for the exercise of free speech—"symbolic" or "pure"—and whether the Courts will allocate to themselves the function of deciding how the pupils' school day will be spent. * * *

While the record does not show that any of these armband students shouted, used profane language, or were violent in any manner, detailed testimony by some of them shows their armbands caused comments, warnings by other students, the poking of fun at them, and a warning by an older football player that other, nonprotesting students had better let them alone. There is also evidence that the professor of mathematics had his lesson period practically "wrecked" chiefly by disputes with Beth Tinker, who wore her armband for her "demonstration." Even a casual reading of the record shows that this armband did divert students' minds from their regular lessons, and that talk, comments, etc., made John Tinker "self-conscious" in attending school with his armband. While the absence of obscene or boisterous and loud disorder perhaps justifies the Court's statement that the few armband students did not actually "disrupt" the classwork, I think the record overwhelmingly shows that the armbands did exactly what the elected school officials and principals foresaw it would, that is, took the students' minds off their classwork and diverted them to thoughts about the highly emotional subject of the Vietnam war.

[E]ven if the record were silent as to protests against the Vietnam war distracting students from their assigned class work, members of this Court, like all other citizens, know, without being told, that the disputes over the wisdom of the Vietnam war have disrupted and divided this country as few other issues ever have. Of course students, like other people, cannot concentrate on lesser issues when black armbands are being ostentatiously displayed in their presence to call attention to the wounded and dead of the war, some of the wounded and the dead

a. See also Akhil Reed Amar, *A Tale of Three Wars: Tinker in Constitutional Context*, 48 Drake L.Rev. 507 (2000); Erwin Chemerinsky, *Students Do Leave Their First Amendment Rights at the Schoolhouse Door: What's Left of Tinker?*, 48 Drake L.Rev. 527 (2000); Nadine Strossen, *Keeping the Constitution Inside the Schoolhouse Gate*, 48 Drake L.Rev. 445 (2000); Mark Yudof, *When Governments Speak: Toward a Theory of Government Expression and the First Amendment*, 57 Tex.L.Rev. 863, 884–85 (1979).

b. White, J., also briefly concurred.

being their friends and neighbors. It was, of course, to distract the attention of other students that some students insisted up to the very point of their own suspension from school that they were determined to sit in school with their symbolic armbands. * * *

JUSTICE HARLAN, dissenting.

I certainly agree that state public school authorities in the discharge of their responsibilities are not wholly exempt from the requirements of the Fourteenth Amendment respecting the freedoms of expression and association. At the same time I am reluctant to believe that there is any disagreement between the majority and myself on the proposition that school officials should be accorded the widest authority in maintaining discipline and good order in their institutions. To translate that proposition into a workable constitutional rule, I would, in cases like this, cast upon those complaining the burden of showing that a particular school measure was motivated by other than legitimate school concerns—for example, a desire to prohibit the expression of an unpopular point of view, while permitting expression of the dominant opinion.

Finding nothing in this record which impugns the good faith of respondents in promulgating the arm band regulation, I would affirm the judgment below.

Notes and Questions

1. Should the government's interest in education trump the school child's interest in speaking in the classroom? Are the two interests compatible in this case? May students be prohibited from voicing their opinions of the Vietnam War in the middle of a math class? If so, why can't they be prevented from expressing their views on the same issue in the same class by means of "symbolic speech"? Cf. Sheldon Nahmod, *Beyond Tinker: The High School as an Educational Public Forum,* 5 Harv.Civ.Rts. & Civ.Lib.L.Rev. 278 (1970).

2. Could school authorities adopt a regulation forbidding *teachers* to wear black armbands in the classroom? Or prohibiting teachers from wearing *all* symbols of political or controversial significance in the classroom or anywhere on school property? Are students a "captive" group? Do the views of a teacher occupying a position of authority carry much more influence with a student than would those of students inter sese? Consider *James v. Board of Educ.,* 461 F.2d 566 (2d Cir.1972), holding that school officials violated a high school teacher's constitutional rights by discharging him because he had worn a black armband in class in symbolic protest of the Vietnam War. But the court stressed that "the armband did not disrupt classroom activities [nor] have any influence on any students and did not engender protest from any student, teacher or parent." What if it had? By implication, did the court confirm the potency of the "heckler's veto"? See Note, 39 Brook.L.Rev. 918 (1973). Same result if appellant had been a 3rd grade teacher rather than an 11th grade teacher? See Steven Shiffrin, *Government Speech,* 27 U.C.L.A.L.Rev. 565, 647–53 (1980).

3. Consider Chemerinsky, fn. a supra, at 529: "[I]n the three decades since *Tinker,* the courts have made it clear that students leave most of their constitutional rights at the schoolhouse gate. The judiciary's unquestioning acceptance of the need for deference to school authority leaves relatively little room for protecting student's constitutional rights. The decisions over the past thirty years are far closer to Justice Black's dissent in *Tinker* than they are to Justice Fortas's majority opinion."

HAZELWOOD SCHOOL DISTRICT V. KUHLMEIER

484 U.S. 260, 108 S.Ct. 562, 98 L.Ed.2d 592 (1988).

JUSTICE WHITE delivered the opinion of the Court. * * *

Petitioners are the Hazelwood School District in St. Louis County, Missouri; various school officials; Robert Eugene Reynolds, the principal of Hazelwood East High School, and Howard Emerson, a teacher in the school district. Respondents are three former Hazelwood East students who were staff members of Spectrum, the school newspaper. * * *

The practice at Hazelwood East during the spring 1983 semester was for the journalism teacher to submit page proofs of each Spectrum issue to Principal Reynolds for his review prior to publication. On May 10, Emerson delivered the proofs of the May 13 edition to Reynolds, who objected to two of the articles scheduled to appear in that edition. One of the stories described three Hazelwood East students' experiences with pregnancy; the other discussed the impact of divorce on students at the school.

Reynolds was concerned that, although the pregnancy story used false names "to keep the identity of these girls a secret," the pregnant students still might be identifiable from the text. He also believed that the article's references to sexual activity and birth control were inappropriate for some of the younger students at the school. In addition, Reynolds was concerned that a student identified by name in the divorce story had complained [about] her father * * *. Reynolds believed that the student's parents should have been given an opportunity to respond to these remarks or to consent to their publication. He was unaware that Emerson had deleted the student's name from the final version of the article.

Reynolds believed that there was no time to make the necessary changes in the stories before the scheduled press run and that the newspaper would not appear before the end of the school year if printing were delayed to any significant extent. He concluded that his only options under the circumstances were to publish a four-page newspaper instead of the planned six-page newspaper, eliminating the two pages on which the offending stories appeared, or to publish no newspaper at all. Accordingly, he directed Emerson to withhold from publication the two pages containing the stories on pregnancy and divorce.[1] He informed his superiors of the decision, and they concurred. * * *

[T]he First Amendment rights of students in the public schools "are not automatically coextensive with the rights of adults in other settings," *Bethel School District No. 403 v. Fraser,* 478 U.S. 675, 106 S.Ct. 3159, 92 L.Ed.2d 549 (1986), and must be "applied in light of the special characteristics of the school environment." *Tinker.* A school need not tolerate student speech that is inconsistent with its "basic educational mission," *Fraser,* even though the government could not censor similar speech outside the school. Accordingly, we held in *Fraser* that a student could be disciplined for having delivered a speech that was "sexually explicit" but not legally obscene at an official school [assembly]. We thus recognized that "[t]he determination of what manner of speech in the classroom or in school assembly is inappropriate properly rests with the school board," rather than with the federal courts. * * *

---

1. The two pages deleted from the newspaper also contained articles on teenage marriage, runaways, and juvenile delinquents, as well as a general article on teenage pregnancy. Reynolds testified that he had no objection to these articles and that they were deleted only because they appeared on the same pages as the two objectionable articles.

We deal first with the question whether Spectrum may appropriately be characterized as a forum for public expression. [T]he evidence relied upon by the Court of Appeals fails to demonstrate the "clear intent to create a public forum," *Cornelius,* that existed in cases in which we found public forums to have been created. School [officials] "reserve[d] the forum for its intended purpos[e]," *Perry,* as a supervised learning experience for journalism students. Accordingly, school officials were entitled to regulate the contents of Spectrum in any reasonable manner. * * *

The question whether the First Amendment requires a school to tolerate particular student speech—the question that we addressed in *Tinker*—is different from the question whether the First Amendment requires a school affirmatively to promote particular student speech. The former question addresses educators' ability to silence a student's personal expression that happens to occur on the school premises. The latter question concerns educators' authority over school-sponsored publications, theatrical productions, and other expressive activities that students, parents, and members of the public might reasonably perceive to bear the imprimatur of the school. These activities may fairly be characterized as part of the school curriculum, whether or not they occur in a traditional classroom setting, so long as they are supervised by faculty members and designed to impart particular knowledge or skills to student participants and audiences.

[A] school may in its capacity as publisher of a school newspaper or producer of a school play "disassociate itself," *Fraser,* not only from speech that would "substantially interfere with [its] work [or] impinge upon the rights of other students," *Tinker,* but also from speech that is, for example, ungrammatical, poorly written, inadequately researched, biased or prejudiced, vulgar or profane, or unsuitable for immature audiences.[4] A school must be able to set high standards for the student speech that is disseminated under its auspices— standards that may be higher than those demanded by some newspaper publishers or theatrical producers in the "real" world—and may refuse to disseminate student speech that does not meet those standards. [Otherwise,] the schools would be unduly constrained from fulfilling their role as "a principal instrument in awakening the child to cultural values, in preparing him for later professional training, and in helping him to adjust normally to his environment." *Brown v. Board of Education.*

Accordingly, we conclude that the standard articulated in *Tinker* for determining when a school may punish student expression need not also be the standard for determining when a school may refuse to lend its name and resources to the dissemination of student expression. Instead, we hold that educators do not offend the First Amendment by exercising editorial control over the style and content of student speech in school-sponsored expressive activities so long as their actions are reasonably related to legitimate pedagogical concerns.[7] * * * *a

---

4. [The] decision in *Fraser* rested on the "vulgar," "lewd," and "plainly offensive" character of a speech delivered at an official school assembly rather than on any propensity of the speech to "materially disrupt[ ] class- work or involve[ ] substantial disorder or inva- sion of the rights of others." Indeed, the *Fraser* Court cited as "especially relevant" a portion of Justice Black's dissenting opinion in *Tinker* "disclaim[ing] any purpose [to] hold that the Federal Constitution compels the teachers, parents and elected school officials to surren-

der control of the American public school sys- tem to public school students." Of course, Jus- tice Black's observations are equally relevant to the instant case.

7. A number of lower federal courts have similarly recognized that educators' decisions with regard to the content of school sponsored newspapers, dramatic productions, and other expressive activities are entitled to substantial deference. We need not now decide whether the same degree of deference is appropriate

JUSTICE BRENNAN, with whom JUSTICE MARSHALL and JUSTICE BLACKMUN join, dissenting.

[Under] *Tinker*, school officials may censor only such student speech as would "materially disrup[t]" a legitimate curricular function. Manifestly, student speech is more likely to disrupt a curricular function when it arises in the context of a curricular activity—one that "is designed to teach" something—than when it arises in the context of a noncurricular activity. Thus, under *Tinker,* the school may constitutionally punish the budding political orator if he disrupts calculus class but not if he holds his tongue for the cafeteria. That is not because some more stringent standard applies in the curricular context. (After all, this Court applied the same standard whether the Tinkers wore their armbands to the "classroom" or the "cafeteria.") It is because student speech in the noncurricular context is less likely to disrupt materially any legitimate pedagogical purpose.

I fully agree with the Court that the First Amendment should afford an educator the prerogative not to sponsor the publication of a newspaper article that is "ungrammatical, poorly written, inadequately researched, biased or prejudiced," or that falls short of the "high standards [for] student speech that is disseminated under [the school's] auspices." But we need not abandon *Tinker* to reach that conclusion; we need only apply it. The enumerated criteria reflect the skills that the curricular newspaper "is designed to teach." The educator may, under *Tinker,* constitutionally "censor" poor grammar, writing, or research because to reward such expression would "materially disrup[t]" the newspaper's curricular purpose. * * *

The Court relies on bits of testimony to portray the principal's conduct as a pedagogical lesson to Journalism II students who "had not sufficiently mastered those portions of [the] curriculum that pertained to the treatment of controversial issues and personal attacks, the need to protect the privacy of individuals [and] 'the legal, moral, and ethical restrictions imposed upon journalists * * *.'"

But the principal never consulted the students before censoring their work. [T]hey learned of the deletions when the paper was released. [Further,] he explained the deletions only in the broadest of generalities. In one meeting called at the behest of seven protesting Spectrum staff members (presumably a fraction of the full class), he characterized the articles as "'too sensitive' for 'our immature audience of readers,'" and in a later meeting he deemed them simply "inappropriate, personal, sensitive and unsuitable for the newspaper." The Court's supposition that the principal intended (or the protesters understood) those generalities as a lesson on the nuances of journalistic responsibility is utterly incredible. If he did, a fact that neither the District Court nor the Court of Appeals found, the lesson was lost on all but the psychic Spectrum staffer.

The Court's second excuse for deviating from precedent is the school's interest in shielding an impressionable high school audience from material whose substance is "unsuitable for immature audiences." [*Tinker*] teaches us that the state educator's undeniable, and undeniably vital, mandate to inculcate moral and political values is not a general warrant to act as "thought police" stifling

with respect to school-sponsored expressive activities at the college and university level.

a. White, J., concluded that Principal Reynolds acted reasonably in requiring deletion of the pages from the newspaper. In addition to concerns about privacy and failure to contact persons discussed in the stories, it was "not unreasonable for the principal to have concluded that [frank talk about sexual histories, albeit not graphic, with comments about use or nonuse of birth control] was inappropriate in a school-sponsored publication distributed to 14–year-old freshmen and presumably taken home to be read by students' even younger brothers and sisters."

discussion of all but state-approved topics and advocacy of all but the official position. [The] mere fact of school sponsorship does not, as the Court suggests, license such thought control in the high school, whether through school suppression of disfavored viewpoints or through official assessment of topic sensitivity. [Moreover, the] State's prerogative to dissolve the student newspaper entirely (or to limit its subject matter) no more entitles it to dictate which viewpoints students may express on its pages, than the State's prerogative to close down the schoolhouse entitles it to prohibit the nondisruptive expression of antiwar sentiment within its gates.

Official censorship of student speech on the ground that it addresses "potentially sensitive topics" is, for related reasons, equally impermissible. I would not begrudge an educator the authority to limit the substantive scope of a school-sponsored publication to a certain, objectively definable topic, such as literary criticism, school sports, or an overview of the school year. Unlike those determinate limitations, "potential topic sensitivity" is a vaporous nonstandard [that] invites manipulation to achieve ends that cannot permissibly be achieved through blatant viewpoint discrimination and chills student speech to which school officials might not object. * * *[b]

Notes and Questions

1.   Consider Bruce Hafen, *Hazelwood School District and the Role of First Amendment Institutions,* 1988 Duke L.J. 685, 701, 704–05: "[T]he question whether authoritarian or anti-authoritarian approaches will best develop the minds and expressive powers of children is more a matter of educational philosophy and practice than of constitutional law. For that reason alone, first amendment theories applied by courts largely on the basis of anti-authoritarian assumptions are at best a clumsy and limited means of ensuring optimal educational development, whether the goal is an understanding of democratic values or a mastery of basic intellectual skills. Thus, one of *Hazelwood's* major contributions is its reaffirmation of schools' institutional role—and their accountability to the public for fulfilling it responsibly—in nurturing the underlying values of the first amendment. * * *

"The first amendment must [protect] not only individual writers, but newspapers; not only religious persons, but churches; not only individual students and teachers, but schools. These 'intellectual and moral associations' form a crucial part of the constitutional structure, for they help teach the peculiar and sometimes paradoxical blend of liberty and duty that sustains both individual freedom and the entire culture from one generation to the next."

2.   Consider Martha Minow & Elizabeth Spellman, *Passion For Justice,* 10 Cardozo L.Rev. 37, 68–69 (1988): "The majority does not acknowledge the power it is exercising in the act of deferring to the 'reasonable' judgments of the [principal:] the power to signal to school officials all around the country, that it is all right to err on the side of eliminating student speech, it is all right to indulge your paternalistic attitudes toward the students; you do not need to guard against your own discomfort with what students want to discuss, for the 'rights' really lie within your own judgment about what they need. [The] dissent is acutely sensitive to the impact of censorship on students, but less attentive to the impact of judicial review on the school officials. Although equal attention to competing sides may

b. Brennan, J. further argued that the material deleted was not conceivably tortious and that less restrictive alternatives, such as more precise deletions, were readily available.

make a decision more difficult, refraining from seeing the power of competing arguments itself may lead to tragic blindness.''

3.   Does *Kuhlmeier* apply to high school teacher's educational judgments? Is a school board's action against classroom speech sufficient if it is reasonably related to legitimate pedagogical concerns or do considerations of academic freedom require a more demanding standard? See *Boring v. Buncombe County Board of Education*, 136 F.3d 364 (4th Cir.1998)(drama teacher selects play involving a dysfunctional divorced single parent family including a lesbian daughter and an unmarried pregnant daughter); *Ward v. Hickey*, 996 F.2d 448 (1st Cir. 1993)(teacher discusses abortion of Down's Syndrome fetus in ninth grade biology class). Should *Kuhlmeier* have any application at the college level?[c]

BOARD OF EDUC. v. PICO, 457 U.S. 853, 102 S.Ct. 2799, 73 L.Ed.2d 435 (1982): On ascertaining that its school libraries contained eleven books that they described as "objectionable" and "improper fare for school students,"[a] the Board informally directed, over the objection of the school superintendent, that the books be delivered to the Board's offices so that Board members could read them. The Board characterized the listed books as "anti-American, anti-Christian, anti-Semitic, and just plain filthy" and concluded that it had a "duty" and a "moral obligation" "to protect the children in our school from this moral danger." Although an appointed parent-teacher "Book Review Committee" recommended that only two books be removed and a third be available to students only with parental approval, the Board decided that nine books should be removed and that another should be made available subject to parental approval. Respondent students contended that the Board's actions violated their first amendment rights. The district court granted summary judgment for the Board, stating that the Board had "restricted access only to certain books which [it] believed to be, in essence, vulgar." A 2–1 majority of the Second Circuit reversed. One member of the majority concluded that at least at the summary judgment stage, the Board had not offered sufficient justification for its action. A second member of the majority "viewed the case as turning on the contested factual issue of whether [the Board's] removal decision was motivated by a justifiable desire to remove books containing vulgarities and sexual explicitness, or rather by an impermissible

---

c. See Gail Sorenson & Andrew S. LaManque, *The Application of Hazelwood v. Kuhlmeier in College Litigation*, 22 J. of College & Univ. Law 971 (1996). For a range of views on academic freedom, consider Ronald Dworkin, *Freedom's Law* ch. 11 (1996); Amy Gutmann, Democratic Education (rev. ed. 1999); William G. Buss, *Academic Freedom and Freedom of Speech: Communicating the Curriculum*, 2 J. of Gender, Race & Justice 213 (1999); J. Peter Byrne, *Academic Freedom: A "Special Concern of the First Amendment,"* 99 Yale L.J. 251 (1989); Merle H. Weiner, *Dirty Words in the Classroom: Teaching the Limits of the First Amendment*, 66 Tenn.L.Rev. 597 (1999); William W. Van Alstyne, *Academic Freedom and the First Amendment in the Supreme Court of the United States: An Unhurried Historical Review*, 53 Law & Contemp. Probs. 79 (1990).

a. As the plurality opinion noted: "The nine [listed] books in the High School library

were: *Slaughter House Five*, by Kurt Vonnegut, Jr.; *The Naked Ape*, by Desmond Morris; *Down These Mean Streets*, by Piri Thomas; *Best Short Stories of Negro Writers*, edited by Langston Hughes; *Go Ask Alice*, of anonymous authorship; *Laughing Boy*, by Oliver LaFarge; *Black Boy*, by Richard Wright; *A Hero Ain't Nothin' But A Sandwich*, by Alice Childress; and *Soul On Ice*, by Eldridge Cleaver. The [listed] book in the Junior High School library was *A Reader for Writers*, edited by Jerome Archer. Still another listed book, *The Fixer*, by Bernard Malamud, was found to be included in the curriculum of a twelfth grade literature course."

  The Board subsequently decided that only *Laughing Boy* should be returned to the library without restriction, and that *Black Boy* should be made available subject to parental approval.

desire to suppress ideas." Affirming, BRENNAN, J., announced the judgment of the court in an opinion joined by Marshall and Stevens, JJ., and in part by Blackmun, J.: "Respondents do not seek [to] impose limitations upon their school Board's discretion to prescribe the curricula of the Island Trees schools. On the contrary, the only books at issue in this case are *library* books, books that by their nature are optional rather than required reading. [Furthermore,] even as to library books, the action before us does not involve the *acquisition* of books. [Rather,] the only action challenged in this case is the *removal* from school libraries of books originally placed there by the school authorities, or without objection from them.

[W]e do not deny that local school boards have a substantial legitimate role to play in the determination of school library content. [But] that discretion may not be exercised in a narrowly partisan or political manner. If a Democratic school board, motivated by party affiliation, ordered the removal of all books written by or in favor of Republicans, few would doubt that the order violated the constitutional rights of the students denied access to those books. The same conclusion would surely apply if an all-white school board, motivated by racial animus, decided to remove all books authored by blacks or advocating racial equality and integration. Our Constitution does not permit the official suppression of *ideas.* [If] petitioners *intended* by their removal decision to deny respondents access to ideas with which petitioners disagreed, and if this intent was the decisive factor in petitioners' decision,[22] then petitioners have exercised their discretion in violation of the Constitution. [On] the other hand, respondents implicitly concede that an unconstitutional motivation would *not* be demonstrated if it were shown that petitioners had decided to remove the books at issue because those books were pervasively vulgar. And again, respondents concede that if it were demonstrated that the removal decision was based solely upon the 'educational suitability' of the books in question, then their removal would be 'perfectly permissible.' "[This] would be a very different case if the record demonstrated that petitioners had employed established, regular, and facially unbiased procedures for the review of controversial materials. But [respondents'] allegations and some of the evidentiary materials presented below do not rule out the possibility that petitioners' removal procedures were highly irregular and ad hoc—the antithesis of those procedures that might tend to allay suspicions regarding petitioners' motivations.

"Construing these claims, affidavit statements, and other evidentiary materials in a manner favorable to respondents, we cannot conclude that petitioners were 'entitled to a judgment as a matter of law.' The evidence plainly does not foreclose the possibility that petitioners' decision to remove the books rested decisively upon disagreement with constitutionally protected ideas in those books, or upon a desire on petitioners' part to impose upon the students of the Island Trees High School and Junior High School a political orthodoxy to which petitioners and their constituents adhered."[b]

BLACKMUN, J., concurred, "I do not believe, as the plurality suggests, that the right at issue here is somehow associated with the peculiar nature of the school library; if schools may be used to inculcate ideas, surely libraries may play a role in that process. [S]chool officials may seek to instill certain values 'by persuasion and example,' or by choice of emphasis. That sort of positive educational action, however, is the converse of an intentional attempt to shield students from certain ideas that officials find politically distasteful.

22. By "decisive factor" we mean a "substantial factor" in the absence of which the opposite decision would have been reached.

b. For criticism of Brennan, J.'s opinion, see William Lee, *The Supreme Court and the Right to Receive Expression,* 1987 Sup.Ct.Rev. 303, 323–27.

WHITE, J., who concurred in the judgment, noted that "[t]he unresolved factual issue [is] the reason or reasons underlying the school board's removal of the books" and he was "not inclined to disagree with the Court of Appeals on such a fact-bound issue. [The] Court seems compelled to go further and issue a dissertation on the extent to which the First Amendment limits the discretion of the school board to remove books from the school library. I see no necessity for doing so at this point."

BURGER, C.J., joined by Powell, Rehnquist, and O'Connor, JJ., dissented: "[The] plurality concludes that under the Constitution school boards cannot choose to retain or dispense with books if their discretion is exercised in a 'narrowly partisan or political manner.' The plurality concedes that permissible factors are whether the books are 'pervasively vulgar' or educationally unsuitable. 'Educational suitability,' however, is a standardless phrase. * * * Ultimately the federal courts will be the judge of whether the motivation for book removal was 'valid' or 'reasonable.' Undoubtedly the validity of many book removals will ultimately turn on a judge's evaluation of the books. Discretion must be used, and the appropriate body to exercise that discretion is the local elected school board, not judges."

POWELL, J., also dissented: "In different contexts and in different times, the destruction of written materials has been the symbol of despotism and intolerance. But the removal of nine vulgar or racist books from a high school library by a concerned local school board does not raise this specter."[c]

REHNQUIST, J., joined by Burger, C.J., and Powell, J., dissented: "The nine books removed undoubtedly did contain 'ideas,' but in the light of the excerpts from them found in the dissenting opinion [in the court below], it is apparent that eight of them contained demonstrable amounts of vulgarity and profanity and the ninth contained nothing that could be considered partisan or political. [R]espondents admitted as much. Petitioners did not, for the reasons stated hereafter, run afoul of the First and Fourteenth Amendments by removing these particular books from the library in the manner in which they did. I would save for another day—feeling quite confident that that day will not arrive—the extreme examples posed in Justice Brennan's opinion.

[Had] petitioners been the members of a town council, I suppose all would agree that, absent a good deal more than is present in this record, they could not have prohibited the sale of these books by private booksellers within the municipality. But we have also recognized that the government may act in other capacities than as sovereign, and when it does the First Amendment may speak with a different voice. [By] the same token, expressive conduct which may not be prohibited by the State as sovereign may be proscribed by the State as property owner [quoting from *Adderley*.

When it acts as an educator, at least at the elementary and secondary school level, the government is engaged in inculcating social values and knowledge in relatively impressionable young people. Obviously there are innumerable decisions to be made as to what courses should be taught, what books should be purchased, or what teachers should be employed. In every one of these areas the members of a school board will act on the basis of their own personal or moral values, will attempt to mirror those of the community, or will abdicate the making of such decisions to so-called 'experts.' [In] the very course of administering the many-

c. Powell, J., appended a summary of excerpts from the books at issue collected in the opinion of Judge Mansfield dissenting below.

faceted operations of a school district, the mere decision to purchase some books will necessarily preclude the possibility of purchasing others. The decision to teach a particular subject may preclude the possibility of teaching another subject. A decision to replace a teacher because of ineffectiveness may by implication be seen as a disparagement of the subject matter taught. In each of these instances, however, the book or the exposure to the subject matter may be acquired elsewhere. The managers of the school district are not proscribing it as to the citizenry in general, but are simply determining that it will not be included in the curriculum or school library. In short, actions by the government as educator do not raise the same First Amendment concerns as actions by the government as sovereign. * * *

"Education consists of the selective presentation and explanation of ideas. The effective acquisition of knowledge depends upon an orderly exposure to relevant information. Nowhere is this more true than in elementary and secondary schools, where, unlike the broad-ranging inquiry available to university students, the courses taught are those thought most relevant to the young students' individual development. [Determining] what information *not* to present to the students is often as important as identifying relevant material. This winnowing process necessarily leaves much information to be discovered by students at another time or in another place, and is fundamentally inconsistent with any constitutionally required eclecticism in public education.

"[Unlike] university or public libraries, elementary and secondary school libraries are not designed for free-wheeling inquiry; they are tailored, as the public school curriculum is tailored, to the teaching of basic skills and [ideas.]"

In a brief separate dissent, O'CONNOR, J., observed: "If the school board can set the curriculum, select teachers, and determine initially what books to purchase for the school library, it surely can decide which books to discontinue or remove from the school library so long as it does not also interfere with the right of students to read the material and to discuss it. As Justice Rehnquist persuasively argues, the plurality's analysis overlooks the fact that in this case the government is acting in its special role as educator."

Notes and Questions

1. Consider Mark Yudof, *Tinker Tailored: Good Faith, Civility, and Student Expression*, 69 St. John's L.Rev. 365, 371 (1965): "[Justice Brennan's] application of a right to know in the context of public schooling is not coherent. [The] problem with Justice Brennan's rationale is that it indicates that there are good and bad reasons to remove books from the library. In either instance, however, the right to know has been violated because the book has been removed. [In] one scenario [a] book is excised from the library for poor grammar, and in another, [because] it is ideologically repugnant. [Regardless] of the reason for its removal, the same book is gone."

2. Consider Mark Yudof, *Library Book Selection and Public Schools: The Quest for the Archimedean Point*, 59 Ind.L.J. 527, 530 (1984): The critical questions in *Pico* are "who will control socialization of the young, what are the values to which they will be socialized, and how will cultural grounding and critical reflection be accommodated." On the latter point, see Mendelson, *The Habermas–Gadamer Debate*, New German Critique 18 (1979). See also Roberto Unger, *Knowledge and Politics* (1975).[d]

d. For a range of views on the scope and   propriety of government promotion of particu-

3.   Should librarians have a first amendment right to select and retain books against the objections of a school board? Against a city council in a non-school context?[e] Should elementary school teachers have a first amendment right to resist interference with their teaching by "politically" motivated administrators or school boards? At secondary levels? See William Canby, *The First Amendment and the State as Editor: Implications for Public Broadcasting,* 52 Tex.L.Rev. 1123 (1974). What of an approach that allows (requires?) administrators to set policies and procedures but prohibits ad hoc intervention?

4.   Every justice recognizes that some content discrimination is permitted in selecting books and making curricular decisions. The line between a public forum and a facility subject to the government's editorial discretion, however, may be hard to draw. In SOUTHEASTERN PROMOTIONS, LTD. v. CONRAD, 420 U.S. 546, 95 S.Ct. 1239, 43 L.Ed.2d 448 (1975), reacting to reports that the musical *Hair* included nudity and was obscene, a publicly-appointed board denied *Hair's* producers a permit to use a theater dedicated for "cultural advancement and for clean, healthful, entertainment which will make for the upbuilding of a better citizenship." The Court, per BLACKMUN, J., held that the theater was a public forum "designed for and dedicated to expressive activities" and that the board's procedures amounted to a prior restraint in violation of *Freedman* requirements, p. 861 supra. One of the dissenters, REHNQUIST, J., asked: "May a municipal theater devote an entire season to Shakespeare, or is it required to book any potential producer on a first come, first served basis? [T]he Court's opinion [seems] to give no constitutionally permissible role in the way of selection to the municipal authorities." For commentary, see Kenneth Karst, *Public Enterprise and the Public Forum: A Comment on Southeastern Promotions, Ltd. v. Conrad,* 37 Ohio St.L.J. 247 (1976); Steven Shiffrin, fn. i after *Regan,* supra, at 581–88; Comment, *Access to State–Owned Communications Media—The Public Forum Doctrine,* 26 U.C.L.A.L.Rev. 1410, 1440–44 (1979).

5.   Blackmun, J., states in fn. 2 that the crucial point is the state's decision to "single out an idea for disapproval and then deny access to it." Suppose the government does not deny access to speech but officially denounces it?[f]

---

lar values, see sources collected in fn. i after *Rust* supra. See also Ronald Dworkin, *A Matter of Principle* 181–204, 221–33 (1985); David Moshman, *Children, Education, and the First Amendment* (1989); Joseph Tussman, *Government and the Mind* (1977); Susan Bitensky, *A Contemporary Proposal for Reconciling the Free Speech Clause With Curricular Values Inculcation in the Public Schools,* 70 Notre Dame L.Rev. 769 (1995); David Diamond, *The First Amendment and Public Schools: The Case Against Judicial Intervention,* 59 Tex. L.Rev. 477 (1981); John Garvey, *Children and the First Amendment,* 57 Tex.L.Rev. 321 (1979); Abner S. Greene, *Government of the Good,* 53 Vand. L.Rev. 1 (2000); Stephen Goldstein, *The Asserted Constitutional Right of Public School Teachers to Determine What They Teach,* 124 U.Pa.L.Rev. 1293 (1976); Stephen Gottlieb, *In The Name of Patriotism: The Constitutionality of "Bending" History in Public Secondary Schools,* 62 N.Y.U.L.Rev. 497 (1987); Sanford Levinson, *The Tutelary State*

in *Censorship and Silencing* 169 (Robert C. Post ed. 1998). Sheldon Nahmod, *Controversy in the Classroom: The High School Teacher and Freedom of Expression,* 39 Geo. Wash.L.Rev. 1032 (1971); Suzanna Sherry, *Responsible Republicanism: Educating for Citizenship,* 62 U.Chi.L.Rev. 131 (1995); Tyll van Geel, *The Search for Constitutional Limits on Governmental Authority to Inculcate Youth,* 62 Tex.L.Rev. 197 (1983).

e.   See Robert O'Neil, *Libraries, Librarians and First Amendment Freedoms,* 4 Hum.Rts. 295 (1975); Robert O'Neil, *Libraries, Liberties and the First Amendment,* 42 U.Cin.L.Rev. 209 (1973). But see Abner S. Greene, fn. d supra.

f.   Consider Professor Lawrence's suggestion that segregation's "*only* purpose is to label or define blacks as inferior." Charles Lawrence, " *'One More River to Cross'—Recognizing the Real Injury in Brown,*" in Shades of Brown 49, 50 (Bell ed. 1980). See also Charles Lawrence, *If He Hollers Let Him Go: Regulat-*

LAMONT v. POSTMASTER GENERAL, 381 U.S. 301, 85 S.Ct. 1493, 14 L.Ed.2d 398 (1965), per DOUGLAS, J., invalidated a federal statute permitting delivery of "communist political propaganda" only if the addressee specifically requested in writing that it be delivered: "We rest on the narrow ground that the addressee in order to receive his mail must request in writing that it be delivered. [The] addressee carries an affirmative obligation which we do not think the government may impose on him. This requirement is almost certain to have a deterrent effect, especially as respects those who have sensitive positions. [Public] officials, like school teachers who have no tenure, might think they would invite disaster if they read what the Federal Government says contains the seeds of treason. Apart from them, any addressee is likely to feel some inhibition in sending for literature which federal officials have condemned as 'communist political propaganda.' "

MEESE v. KEENE, 481 U.S. 465, 107 S.Ct. 1862, 95 L.Ed.2d 415 (1987), per STEVENS, J., held that the government could label a film as "political propaganda" without violating the first amendment: "The Foreign Agents Registration Act [uses] the term 'political propaganda,[g] [to] identify those expressive materials that must comply with the Act's registration, filing, and disclosure requirements." The government had identified three Canadian films as "political propaganda." Keene maintained that he should be free to exhibit the three films without being considered an exhibitor of governmentally designated "propaganda." Without otherwise reaching the Act's requirements, the Court rejected Keene's claim: "The statute itself neither prohibits nor censors the dissemination of advocacy materials by agents of foreign principals.[h] [To] the contrary, Congress simply required the disseminators of such material to make additional disclosures that would better enable the public to evaluate the import of the propaganda. The

ing Racist Speech on Campus, 1990 Duke L.J. 431. When should governmental denunciation of persons or groups be considered a violation of the first amendment?

g. The Act defines political propaganda to include: "any oral, visual, graphic, written, pictorial, or other communication or expression by any person (1) which is reasonably adapted to, or which the person disseminating the same believes will, or which he intends to, prevail upon, indoctrinate, convert, induce, or in any other way influence a recipient or any section of the public within the United States with reference to the political or public interests, policies, or relations of a government or a foreign country or a foreign political party or with reference to the foreign policies of the United States or promote in the United States racial, religious, or social dissensions, or (2) which advocates, advises, instigates, or promotes any racial, social, political, or religious disorder, civil riot, or other conflict involving the use of force or violence in any other American republic or the overthrow of any government or political subdivision of any other American republic by any means involving the use of force or violence."

Stevens, J., commented, "As defined in the Act, the term political propaganda includes

misleading advocacy. [But] it also includes advocacy materials that are completely accurate and merit the closest attention and the highest respect. Standard reference works include both broad, neutral definitions of the word 'propaganda' that are consistent with the way the word is defined in this statute, and also the narrower, pejorative definition."

h. The Court distinguished *Lamont* stating that the physical detention of mail, not its mere designation as "communist political propaganda" was the offending element of the statutory scheme. By contrast, the Court argued that the Foreign Agents Registration Act posed no obstacle to Keene's access to the materials. In response, Blackmun, J., dissenting, observed that the "communist political propaganda [detained in *Lamont*] and delivered only upon the addressee's request was defined by reference to the same 'neutral' definition of 'political propaganda' in the Act that is at issue here. Yet the Court examined the effects of the statutory requirements and had no trouble concluding that the need to request delivery of mail classified as 'communist political propaganda' was almost certain to have a deterrent effect upon debate."

statute does not prohibit appellee from advising his audience that the films have not been officially censured in any way. Disseminators of propaganda may go beyond the disclosures required by statute and add any further information they think germane to the public's viewing of the materials. By compelling some disclosure of information and permitting more, the Act's approach recognizes that the best remedy for misleading or inaccurate speech contained within materials subject to the Act is fair, truthful, and accurate speech. * * * ironically, it is the injunction entered by the District Court that withholds information from the public. The suppressed information is the fact that the films fall within the category of materials that Congress has judged to be 'political propaganda'. A similar paternalistic strategy of protecting the public from information was followed by the Virginia Assembly, which enacted a ban on the advertising of prescription drug prices by pharmacists. See *Virginia Pharmacy*."[i]

BLACKMUN, J., joined by Brennan and Marshall, JJ., dissented: "[T]here is a significant difference between the 'paternalistic strategy of protecting the public from information,' by way of a *ban* on information and a prohibition of the government disparagement at issue in this case. [Under] the District Court's ruling, opponents of the viewpoint expressed by the [film] remained completely free to point out [its] foreign [source]. The difference was that dialogue on the value of the films and the viewpoints they express could occur in an atmosphere free of the constraint imposed by government condemnation. It is the Government's classification of those films as 'political propaganda' that is paternalistic. For that government action does more than simply provide additional information. It places the power of the Federal Government, with its authority, presumed neutrality, and assumed access to all the facts, behind an appellation *designed* to reduce the effectiveness of the speech in the eyes of the public."

SECTION 8. THE ELECTRONIC MEDIA

The mass media are not invariably the most effective means of communication. For example, the right to place messages on utility poles concerning a lost dog may be more important than access to a radio or a television station. In some circumstances, picketing outside a school or placing leaflets in teachers' mailboxes may be the most effective communications medium. Nonetheless, the law regulating access to the mass media is of vital societal importance. This section considers first, cases in which government seeks to force newspapers and broadcasters to grant access and cases in which the first amendment is claimed to demand access. Second, this section considers cases involving content regulation of the electronic media, particularly those where government seeks to regulate "indecency" in broadcasting, cable, and on the internet.

---

i. Scalia, J., took no part. In *Block v. Meese*, 793 F.2d 1303 (D.C.Cir.1986), however, then Circuit Judge Scalia ruled on the issue. "[E]ven if classification as 'propaganda' constituted an expression of official government disapproval of the ideas in question, neither precedent nor reason would justify us in finding such an expression *in itself* unlawful. [W]e know of no case in which the first amendment has been held to be implicated by governmental action consisting of no more than governmental criticism of the speech's content. [A] rule excluding official praise or criticism of ideas would lead to the strange conclusion that it is permissible for the government to prohibit racial discrimination, but not to criticize racial bias; to criminalize polygamy, but not to praise the monogamous family; to make war on Hitler's Germany, but not to denounce Nazism. [The] line of permissibility [falls] not between criticism of ideas in general and criticism of the ideas contained in specific books or expressed by specific persons; but between the disparagement of ideas general or specific and the suppression of ideas through the exercise or threat of state power. If the latter is rigorously prescribed, see *Bantam Books*, the former can hold no terror."

I. ACCESS TO THE MASS MEDIA

MIAMI HERALD PUB. CO. v. TORNILLO, 418 U.S. 241, 94 S.Ct. 2831, 41 L.Ed.2d 730 (1974), per BURGER, C.J., unanimously struck down a Florida "right of reply" statute, which required any newspaper that "assails" the personal character or official record of a candidate in any election to print, on demand, free of cost, any reply the candidate may make to the charges, in as conspicuous a place and the same kind of type, provided the reply takes up no more space than the charges. The opinion carefully explained the aim of the statute to "ensure that a wide variety of views reach the public" even though "chains of newspapers, national newspapers, national wire and news services, and one-newspaper towns, are the dominant features of a press that has become noncompetitive and enormously powerful and influential in its capacity to manipulate popular opinion and change the course of events," placing "in a few hands the power to inform the American people and shape public opinion."[a] Nonetheless, the Court concluded that to require the printing of a reply violated the first amendment: "Compelling editors or publishers to publish that which ' "reason" tells them should not be published' is what is at issue in this case. The Florida statute operates as a command in the same sense as a statute or regulation forbidding appellant from publishing specified matter. [The] Florida statute exacts a penalty on the basis of the content of a newspaper. The first phase of the penalty resulting from the compelled printing of a reply is exacted in terms of the cost in printing and composing time and materials and in taking up space that could be devoted to other material the newspaper may have preferred to print. It is correct, as appellee contends, that a newspaper is not subject to the finite technological limitations of time that confront a broadcaster but it is not correct to say that, as an economic reality, a newspaper can proceed to infinite expansion of its column space to accommodate the replies that a government agency determines or a statute commands the readers should have available.

"Faced with the penalties that would accrue to any newspaper that published news or commentary arguably within the reach of the right of access statute, editors might well conclude that the safe course is to avoid controversy and that, under the operation of the Florida statute, political and electoral coverage would be blunted or reduced. Government enforced right of access inescapably 'dampens the vigor and limits the variety of public debate,' *New York Times.*

"Even if a newspaper would face no additional costs to comply with a compulsory access law and would not be forced to forego publication of news or opinion by the inclusion of a reply, the Florida statute fails to clear the barriers of the First Amendment because of its intrusion into the function of editors. A newspaper is more than a passive receptacle or conduit for news, comment, and advertising. The choice of material to go into a newspaper, and the decisions made as to limitations on the size of the paper, and content, and treatment of public issues and public officials—whether fair or unfair—constitutes the exercise of editorial control and judgment. It has yet to be demonstrated how governmental regulation of this crucial process can be exercised consistent with First Amend-

a. The opinion developed these views at greater length, citing "generally" Jerome Barron, *Access to the Press—A New First Amendment Right,* 80 Harv.L.Rev. 1641 (1967); David Lange, *The Role of the Access Doctrine in the Regulation of the Mass Media: A Critical Review and Assessment,* 52 N.C.L.Rev. 1, 8–9 (1973). For historical background and a spirited criticism of the statute, see Lucas Powe, *Tornillo,* 1987 Sup.Ct.Rev. 345.

ment guarantees of a free press as they have evolved to this time."[b]

The Federal Communications Commission for many years imposed on radio and television broadcasters the "fairness doctrine"—requiring that stations (1) devote a reasonable percentage of broadcast time to discussion of public issues and (2) assure fair coverage for each side.[a] At issue in RED LION BROADCASTING CO. v. FCC, 395 U.S. 367, 89 S.Ct. 1794, 23 L.Ed.2d 371 (1969), were the application of the fairness doctrine to a particular broadcast[b] and two specific access regulations promulgated under the doctrine: (1) the "political editorial" rule, requiring that when a broadcaster, in an editorial, "endorses or opposes" a political candidate, it must notify the candidate opposed, or the rivals of the candidate supported, and afford them a "reasonable opportunity" to respond; (2) the "personal attack" rule, requiring that "when, during the presentation of views on a controversial issue of public importance, an attack is made on the honesty, character [or] integrity [of] an identified person or group," the person or group attacked must be given notice, a transcript of the attack, and an opportunity to respond.[c] "[I]n view of [the] scarcity of broadcast frequencies, the Government's role in allocating those frequencies, and the legitimate claims of those unable without government assistance to gain access to those frequencies for expression of their views," a 7–0 majority, per WHITE, J., upheld both access regulations:[d]

"[The broadcasters] contention is that the First Amendment protects their desire to use their allotted frequencies continuously to broadcast whatever they choose, and to exclude whomever they choose from ever using that frequency. No man may be prevented from saying or publishing what he thinks, or from refusing

---

b. Brennan, J., joined by Rehnquist, J., joined the Court's opinion in a short statement to express the understanding that it "implies no view upon the constitutionality of 'retraction' statutes affording plaintiffs able to prove defamatory falsehoods a statutory action to require publication of a retraction."

White, J., concurred. After agreeing that "prior compulsion by government in matters going to the very nerve center of a newspaper—the decision as to what copy will or will not be included in any given edition—collides with the First Amendment," he returned to his attack on *Gertz*, decided the same day: "Reaffirming the rule that the press cannot be forced to print an answer to a personal attack made by it [throws] into stark relief the consequences of the new balance forged by the Court in the companion case also announced today. *Gertz* goes far toward eviscerating the effectiveness of the ordinary libel action, which has long been the only potent response available to the private citizen libeled by the press. [To] me it is a near absurdity to so deprecate individual dignity, as the Court does in *Gertz*, and to leave the people at the complete mercy of the press, at least in this stage of our history when the press, as the majority in this case so well documents, is steadily becoming more powerful and much less likely to be deterred by threats of libel suits."

a. For helpful background on the origins, justification and administration of the fairness doctrine, see Roscoe Barrow, *The Fairness Doctrine: A Double Standard for Electronic and Print Media*, 26 Hast.L.J. 659 (1975); Benno Schmidt, *Freedom of the Press vs. Public Access* 157–98 (1976).

b. *Red Lion* grew out of a series of radio broadcasts by fundamentalist preacher Billy James Hargis, who had attacked Fred J. Cook, author of an article attacking Hargis and "hate clubs of the air." When Cook heard about the broadcast, he demanded that the station give him an opportunity to reply. Cook refused to pay for his "reply time" and the FCC ordered the station to give Cook the opportunity to reply whether or not he would pay for it. The Supreme Court upheld the order of free reply time. See Schmidt, fn. a supra, at 161–63.

c. Excepted were "personal attacks [by] legally qualified candidates [on] other such candidates" and "bona fide newscasts, bona fide news interviews, and on-the-spot coverage of a bona fide news event."

d. Surprisingly, none of the justices joining White, J.'s opinion felt the need to make additional remarks, but Douglas, J., who did not participate in *Red Lion*, expressed his disagreement with it in the *CBS* case, infra.

[Handwritten margin notes:] Still dealing w/ Access. FCC requires broadcast License. B/C there is a finite amount of airwaves

* Permits 1st Amend restrictions against broadcasters

1. Political editorial rule - when a broadcaster endorses or opposes a candidate, must afford candidate reasonable opp. to respond.
2. Personal Attack rule: when broadcaster attacks honesty/Integrity, or character of identified person or group it must afford reasonable opp. to respond.
(clearly content based)

in his speech or other utterances to give equal weight to the views of his opponents. This right, they say, applies equally to broadcasters.

"Although broadcasting is clearly a medium affected by a First Amendment interest, differences in the characteristics of new media justify differences in the First Amendment standards applied to [them]. Just as the Government may limit the use of sound-amplifying equipment potentially so noisy that it drowns out civilized private speech, so may the Government limit the use of broadcast equipment. The right of free speech of a broadcaster, the user of a sound truck, or any other individual does not embrace a right to snuff out the free speech of [others].

"Where there are substantially more individuals who want to broadcast than there are frequencies to allocate, it is idle to posit an unabridgeable First Amendment right to broadcast comparable to the right of every individual to speak, write, or publish. [It] would be strange if the First Amendment, aimed at protecting and furthering communications, prevented the Government from making radio communication possible by requiring licenses to broadcast and by limiting the number of licenses so as not to overcrowd the spectrum. * * *

"By the same token, as far as the First Amendment is concerned those who are licensed stand no better than those to whom licenses are refused. A license permits broadcasting, but the licensee has no constitutional right [to] monopolize a radio frequency to the exclusion of his fellow citizens. There is nothing in the First Amendment which prevents the Government from requiring a licensee to share his frequency with others and to conduct himself as a proxy or fiduciary with obligations to present those views and voices which are representative of his community and which would otherwise, by necessity, be barred from the airwaves.

"[The] people as a whole retain their interest in free speech by radio and their collective right to have the medium function consistently with the ends and purposes of the First Amendment. It is the right of the viewers and listeners, not the right of the broadcasters, which is paramount. [It] is the purpose of the First Amendment to preserve an uninhibited marketplace of ideas in which truth will ultimately prevail, rather than to countenance monopolization of that market, whether it be by the Government itself or a private licensee. [It] is the right of the public to receive suitable access to social, political, esthetic, moral, and other ideas and experiences which is crucial [here.]

"In terms of constitutional principle, and as enforced sharing of a scarce resource, the personal attack and political editorial rules are indistinguishable from the equal-time provision of § 315 [of the Communications Act], a specific enactment of Congress requiring [that stations allot equal time to qualified candidates for public office] and to which the fairness doctrine and these constituent regulations are important complements. [Nor] can we say that it is inconsistent with the First Amendment goal of producing an informed public capable of conducting its own affairs to require a broadcaster to permit answers to personal attacks occurring in the course of discussing controversial issues, or to require that the political opponents of those endorsed by the station be given a chance to communicate with the public. Otherwise, station owners and a few networks would have unfettered power to make time available only to the highest bidders, to communicate only their own views on public issues, people and candidates, and to permit on the air only those with whom they agreed. There is no sanctuary in the First Amendment for unlimited private censorship operating in a medium not open to all.

"[It is contended] that if political editorials or personal attacks will trigger an obligation in broadcasters to afford the opportunity for expression to speakers who need not pay for time and whose views are unpalatable to the licensees, then broadcasters will be irresistibly forced to self-censorship and their coverage of controversial public issues will be eliminated or at least rendered wholly ineffective. Such a result would indeed be a serious matter, [but] that possibility is at best speculative. [If these doctrines turn out to have this effect], there will be time enough to reconsider the constitutional implications. The fairness doctrine in the past has had no such overall effect. That this will occur now seems unlikely, however, since if present licensees should suddenly prove timorous, the Commission is not powerless to insist that they give adequate and fair attention to public issues. It does not violate the First Amendment to treat licensees given the privilege of using scarce radio frequencies as proxies for the entire community, obligated to give suitable time and attention to matters of great public concern. To condition the granting or renewal of licenses on a willingness to present representative community views on controversial issues is consistent with the ends and purposes of those constitutional provisions forbidding the abridgment of freedom of speech and freedom of the press."[e]

Notes and Questions

1. *Tension between Miami Herald and Red Lion.* Consider Lee Bollinger, *Freedom of the Press and Public Access: Toward a Theory of Partial Regulation of the Mass Media,* 75 Mich.L.Rev. 1, 4–6, 10–12 (1976): "What seems so remarkable about the unanimous *Miami Herald* opinion is the complete absence of any reference to the Court's unanimous decision five years earlier in *Red Lion*[, upholding] the so-called personal attack rule, [which] is almost identical in substance to the Florida statute declared unconstitutional in *Miami Herald.* That omission, however, is no more surprising than the absence of any discussion in *Red Lion* of the cases in which the Court expressed great concern about the risks attending government regulation of the print media.

"[The] scarcity rationale [articulated in *Red Lion* does not] explain why what appears to be a similar phenomenon of natural monopolization within the newspaper industry does not constitute an equally appropriate occasion for access regulation. A difference in the cause of concentration—the exhaustion of a physical element necessary for communication in broadcasting as contrasted with the economic constraints on the number of possible competitors in the print media—would seem far less relevant from a first amendment standpoint than the fact of concentration itself. [Instead] of exploring the relevance for the print media of the new principle developed in broadcasting, the Court merely reiterated the opposing, more traditional, principle that the government cannot tell editors what

---

e. The Court noted that it "need not deal with the argument that even if there is no longer a technological scarcity of frequencies limiting the number of broadcasters, there nevertheless is an economic scarcity in the sense that the Commission could or does limit entry to the broadcasting market on economic grounds and license no more stations than the market will support. Hence, it is said, the fairness doctrine or its equivalent is essential to satisfy the claims of those excluded and of the public generally. A related argument, which we also put side, is that quite apart from scarcity of frequencies, technological or economic, Congress does not abridge freedom of speech or press by legislation directly or indirectly multiplying the voices and views presented to the public through time sharing, fairness doctrines, or other devices which limit or dissipate the power of those who sit astride the channels of communication with the general public." For background and discussion of *Red Lion,* see Fred Friendly, *The Good Guys, The Bad Guys and the First Amendment* (1975).

to publish. It thus created a paradox, leaving the new principle unscathed while preserving tradition."

2. *The absence of balancing in Miami Herald.* Did *Miami Herald* present a confrontation between the rights of speech and press? "Nowhere does [*Miami Herald*] explicitly acknowledge [such a confrontation], but implicit recognition of the speech interest," observes Melville Nimmer, *Is Freedom of the Press a Redundancy? What Does it Add to Freedom of Speech?*, 26 Hast.L.J. 639, 645, 657 (1975), "may be found in the Court's reference to the access advocates' argument that, given the present semimonopolistic posture of the press, speech can be effective and therefore free only if enhanced by devices such as a right of reply statute. The Court in accepting the press clause argument in effect necessarily found it to be superior to any competing speech clause claims. [But] the issue cannot be resolved merely by noting, as did [*Miami Herald*], that a right of reply statute 'constitutes the [state] exercise of editorial control and judgment.' This is but one half of the equation. [*Miami Herald*] ignored the strong conflicting claims of 'speech.' Perhaps on balance the press should still prevail, but those who doubt the efficacy of such a result are hardly persuaded by an approach that apparently fails to recognize that any balancing of speech and press rights is required."[f]

3. *Scope of Miami Herald.* Consider Schmidt, fn. a supra, at 233–35: "From the perspective of First Amendment law generally, *Miami Herald* would be a stark and unexplained deviation if one were to read the decision as creating absolute prohibitions on access obligations.[g] [The] fact the Court offers no discussion as to why First Amendment rules respecting access should be absolute, while all other rules emanating from that Amendment are relative, suggests that the principle of *Miami Herald* probably is destined for uncharted qualifications and exceptions." But see Lucas Powe, *Tornillo*, 1987 Sup.Ct.Rev. 345, 391, 390: "Quite frankly I do not believe that a twenty page Supreme Court opinion meeting all the standards of craft (all considerations are ventilated fully and the opinion be of publishable quality for a good legal journal) can as effectively protect the right of press autonomy as the blunt rejection in *Miami Herald.* Chief Justice Burger's failure to engage, so annoying to Schmidt and other commentators, is in fact a great strength of the opinion."

Would a statute requiring nondiscriminatory access to the classified ads section of a newspaper pass muster under *Miami Herald?* A requirement that legal notices be published?

4. *Absolute editorial autonomy—some of the time.* Is it ironic that *Gertz* was decided the same day as *Miami Herald?* Which poses a greater threat to editorial autonomy—a negligence standard in defamation cases or the guaranteed access contemplated by the Florida statute? Whose autonomy is important—the editors or the owners? May government protect editors from ad hoc intervention by corporate owners? See generally C. Edwin Baker, *Human Liberty and Freedom of Speech* 225–71 (1989).

f. Does *Miami Herald* demonstrate, as Professor Nimmer believes, at 644–46, that free speech and press can be distinct, even conflicting interests? Anthony Lewis, *A Preferred Position for Journalism?*, 7 Hof.L.Rev. 595, 603 (1979), thinks not: "[T]he vice of the [Florida right of reply] law lay in the compulsion to publish; and I think the result would be no different if the case involved a compulsion to speak. If a state statute required any candidate who spoke falsely about another to make a corrective speech, would it survive challenge under the first amendment?"

g. "Even in the area of 'the central freedom of the First Amendment,' which is criticism of the governmental acts of public officials," recalls Professor Schmidt, fn. a supra, at 232, "there is no absolute protection for expression."

5. *The threat to editorial autonomy in Red Lion.* Consider Schmidt, fn. c supra, at 166: *Red Lion* "left broadcaster autonomy almost entirely at the mercy of the FCC." See also William Van Alstyne, *The Möbius Strip of the First Amendment: Perspectives on Red Lion,* 29 S.C.L.Rev. 539, 571 (1978): "Indeed, if one continues to be troubled by *Red Lion,* I think it is not because one takes lightly the difficulty of forum allocation in a society of scarce resources. Rather, it is because one believes that the technique of the fairness doctrine in particular may represent a very trivial egalitarian gain and a major first amendment loss; that a twist has been given to the equal protection idea by a device the principal effect of which is merely to level down the most vivid and versatile forum we have, to flatten it out and to render it a mere commercial mirror of each community. What may have been lost is a willingness to risk the partisanship of licensees as catalysts and as active advocates with a freedom to exhort, a freedom that dares to exclaim 'Fuck the draft,' and not be made to yield by government at once to add, 'but on the other hand there is also the view, held by many.'"

6. *The best of both worlds.* "[T]he critical difference between what the Court was asked to do in *Red Lion* and what it was asked to do in *Miami Herald,*" maintains Professor Bollinger note 1 supra, at 27, 32–33, 36–37, "involved choosing between a partial regulatory system and a universal one. Viewed from that perspective, the Court reached the correct result in both cases": "[T]here are good first amendment reasons for being both receptive to and wary of access regulation. This dual nature of access legislation suggests the need to limit carefully the intrusiveness of the regulation in order safely to enjoy its remedial benefits. Thus, a proper judicial response is one that will permit the legislature to provide the public with access *somewhere* within the mass media, but not throughout the press. The Court should not, and need not, be forced into an all-or-nothing position on this matter; there is nothing in the first amendment that forbids having the best of both worlds."[h]

For a powerful critique of the regulated world, see Lucas Powe, *American Broadcasting and the First Amendment* (1987). For a powerful critique of the unregulated world, see C. Edwin Baker, *The First Amendment in Modern Garb,* 58 Ohio St.L.J. 311 (1997).

———

"Like many equal protection issues," observes Karst, Sec. 6, I, B supra, at 45, "the media-access problem should be approached from two separate constitutional directions. First, what does the Constitution *compel* government to do in the way of equalizing? Second, what does the Constitution *permit* government to do in equalizing by statute?" *Red Lion* and *Miami Herald* presented the second question; the first is raised by COLUMBIA BROADCASTING SYSTEM, INC. v. DEMOCRATIC NAT'L COMMITTEE, 412 U.S. 94, 93 S.Ct. 2080, 36 L.Ed.2d 772 (1973) (*CBS*): The FCC rejected the claims of Business Executives' Move for Vietnam Peace (BEM) and the Democratic National Committee (DNC) that "responsible" individuals and groups are entitled to purchase advertising time to comment on public issues, even though the broadcaster has complied with the fairness doctrine. The District of Columbia Circuit held that "a flat ban on paid public issue announcements" violates the first amendment "at least when other

---

h. Does the existence of the threat of regulation or the Court's rhetoric about the press have a substantial impact on press decisions? Compare Lee C. Bollinger, *Images of a Free*

Press (1991) with Lili Levi, *Challenging the Autonomous Press,* 78 Cornell L.Rev. 665 (1993).

sorts of paid announcements are accepted,'' and remanded to the FCC to develop "reasonable procedures and regulations determining which and how many 'editorial advertisements' will be put on the air.'' The Supreme Court, per BURGER, C.J., reversed, holding that neither the "public interest" standard of the Communications Act (which draws heavily from the first amendment) nor the first amendment itself—assuming that refusal to accept such advertising constituted "governmental action" for first amendment purposes[a]—requires broadcasters to accept paid editorial announcements. As pointed out in Vincent Blasi, *The Checking Value in First Amendment Theory*, 1977 Am.B.Found.Res.J. 521, 613–14 although the Chief Justice "built to some extent" on *Red Lion*, his opinion "evinced a most important change of emphasis. For whereas White, J., based his argument in *Red Lion* on the premise that broadcasters are mere 'proxies' or 'fiduciaries' for the general public, the Chief Justice's opinion [in *CBS*] invoked a concept of 'journalistic independence' or 'journalistic discretion,' the essence of which is that broadcasters do indeed have special First Amendment interests which have to be considered in the constitutional calculus.''

Observed the Chief Justice: "[From various provisions of the Communications Act of 1934] it seems clear that Congress intended to permit private broadcasting to develop with the widest journalistic freedom consistent with its public obligations. Only when the interests of the public are found to outweigh the private journalistic interests of the broadcasters will government power be asserted within the framework of the Act. License renewal proceedings, in which the listening public can be heard, are a principal means of such regulation.

"[W]ith the advent of radio a half century ago, Congress was faced with a fundamental choice between total Government ownership and control of the new medium—the choice of most other countries—or some other alternative. Long before the impact and potential of the medium was realized, Congress opted for a system of private broadcasters licensed and regulated by Government. The legislative history suggests that this choice was influenced not only by traditional attitudes toward private enterprise, but by a desire to maintain for licensees, so far as consistent with necessary regulation, a traditional journalistic [role.]

"The regulatory scheme evolved slowly, but very early the licensee's role developed in terms of a 'public trustee' charged with the duty of fairly and impartially informing the public audience. In this structure the Commission acts in essence as an 'overseer,' but the initial and primary responsibility for fairness, balance, and objectivity rests with the licensee. This role of the Government as an overseer and ultimate arbiter and guardian of the public interest and the role of the licensee as a journalistic 'free agent' call for a delicate balancing of competing interests. The maintenance of this balance for more than 40 years has called on both the regulators and the licensees to walk a 'tightrope' to preserve the First Amendment values written into the Radio Act and its successor, the Communications Act.

"The tensions inherent in such a regulatory structure emerge more clearly when we compare a private newspaper with a broadcast licensee. The power of a privately owned newspaper to advance its own political, social, and economic views

---

a. Burger, C.J., joined by Stewart and Rehnquist, JJ., concluded that a broadcast licensee's refusal to accept an advertisement was not "governmental action" for first amendment purposes. Although White, Blackmun and Powell, JJ., concurred in parts of the Chief Justice's opinion, they did not decide this question for, *assuming* governmental action, they found that the challenged ban did not violate the first amendment. Douglas, J., who concurred in the result, assumed *no* governmental action. Dissenting, Brennan, J., joined by Marshall, J., found that the challenged ban did constitute "governmental action."

[handwritten margin notes: "Constitution does not mandate broadcasters to give access. But: regulation has been made OK. So: must be enforced." / "Balance" / "broadcaster rights (journalist) vs. Public rights (medium)"]

is bounded by only two factors: first, the acceptance of a sufficient number of readers—and hence advertisers—to assure financial success; and, second, the journalistic integrity of its editors and publishers. A broadcast licensee has a large measure of journalistic freedom but not as large as that exercised by a newspaper. A licensee must balance what it might prefer to do as a private entrepreneur with what it is required to do as a 'public trustee.' To perform its statutory duties, the Commission must oversee without censoring. This suggests something of the difficulty and delicacy of administering the Communications Act—a function calling for flexibility and the capacity to adjust and readjust the regulatory mechanism to meet changing problems and needs.

"The licensee policy challenged in this case is intimately related to the journalistic role of a licensee for which it has been given initial and primary responsibility by Congress. The licensee's policy against accepting editorial advertising cannot be examined as an abstract proposition, but must be viewed in the context of its journalistic role. It does not help to press on us the idea that editorial ads are 'like' commercial ads, for the licensee's policy against editorial spot ads is expressly based on a journalistic judgment that 10- to 60-second spot announcements are ill-suited to intelligible and intelligent treatment of public issues; the broadcaster has chosen to provide a balanced treatment of controversial questions in a more comprehensive form. Obviously, the licensee's evaluation is based on its own journalistic judgment of priorities and newsworthiness.

"Moreover, the Commission has not fostered the licensee policy challenged here; it has simply declined to command particular action because it fell within the area of journalistic discretion. [The] Commission's reasoning, consistent with nearly 40 years of precedent, is that so long as a licensee meets its 'public trustee' obligation to provide balanced coverage of issues and events, it has broad discretion to decide how that obligation will be met. We do not reach the question whether the First Amendment or the Act can be read to preclude the Commission from determining that in some situations the public interest requires licensees to re-examine their policies with respect to editorial advertisements.[b] The Commission has not yet made such a determination; it has, for the present at least, found the policy to be within the sphere of journalistic discretion which Congress has left with the licensee.

"[I]t must constantly be kept in mind that the interest of the public is our foremost concern. With broadcasting, where the available means of communication are limited in both space and time, [Meiklejohn's admonition] that '[w]hat is essential is not that everyone shall speak, but that everything worth saying shall be said' is peculiarly appropriate.

"[Congress] has time and again rejected various legislative attempts that would have mandated a variety of forms of individual access. [It] has chosen to leave such questions with the Commission, to which it has given the flexibility to experiment with new ideas as changing conditions require. In this case, the

b. *Columbia Broadcasting System, Inc. v. FCC*, 453 U.S. 367, 101 S.Ct. 2813, 69 L.Ed.2d 706 (1981) upheld FCC administration of a statutory provision guaranteeing "reasonable" access to the airwaves for federal election candidates. The Court, per Burger, C.J., observed that "the Court has never approved a *general* right of access to the media. *Miami Herald; CBS v. DNC*. Nor do we do so today." But it found that the limited right of access "properly balances the First Amendment rights of federal candidates, the public, and broadcasters." White, J., joined by Rehnquist and Stevens, JJ., dissented on statutory grounds. For criticism, see Daniel Polsby, *Candidate Access to the Air: The Uncertain Future of Broadcaster Discretion*, 1981 Sup.Ct.Rev. 223.

Commission has decided that on balance the undesirable effects of the right of access urged by respondents would outweigh the asserted [benefits.]

"The Commission was justified in concluding that the public interest in providing access to the marketplace of 'ideas and experiences' would scarcely be served by a system so heavily weighted in favor of the financially affluent, or those with access to wealth. Even under a first-come-first-served system [the] views of the affluent could well prevail over those of others, since they would have it within their power to purchase time more frequently. Moreover, there is the substantial danger [that] the time allotted for editorial advertising could be monopolized by those of one political persuasion.

"These problems would not necessarily be solved by applying the Fairness Doctrine, including the *Cullman* doctrine [requiring broadcasters to provide free time for the presentation of opposing views if a paid sponsor is unavailable], to editorial advertising. If broadcasters were required to provide time, free when necessary, for the discussion of the various shades of opinion on the issue discussed in the advertisement, the affluent could still determine in large part the issues to be discussed. Thus, the very premise of the Court of Appeals' holding—that a right of access is necessary to allow individuals and groups the opportunity for self-initiated speech—would have little meaning to those who could not afford to purchase time in the first instance.

"If the Fairness Doctrine were applied to editorial advertising, there is also the substantial danger that the effective operation of that doctrine would be jeopardized. To minimize financial hardship and to comply fully with its public responsibilities a broadcaster might well be forced to make regular programming time available to those holding a view different from that expressed in an editorial advertisement. [The] result would be a further erosion of the journalistic discretion of broadcasters in the coverage of public issues, and a transfer of control over the treatment of public issues from the licensees who are accountable for broadcast performance to private individuals who are not. The public interest would no longer be 'paramount' but rather subordinate to private whim especially since, under the Court of Appeals' decision, a broadcaster would be largely precluded from rejecting editorial advertisements that dealt with matters trivial or insignificant or already fairly covered by the broadcaster. If the Fairness Doctrine and the *Cullman* doctrine were suspended to alleviate these problems, as respondents suggest might be appropriate, the question arises whether we would have abandoned more than we have gained. Under such a regime the congressional objective of balanced coverage of public issues would be seriously threatened.

"Nor can we accept the Court of Appeals' view that every potential speaker is 'the best judge' of what the listening public ought to hear or indeed the best judge of the merits of his or her views. All journalistic tradition and experience is to the contrary. For better or worse, editing is what editors are for; and editing is selection and choice of material. That editors—newspaper or broadcast—can and do abuse this power is beyond doubt, but that is not reason to deny the discretion Congress provided. Calculated risks of abuse are taken in order to preserve higher values. The presence of these risks is nothing new; the authors of the Bill of Rights accepted the reality that these risks were evils for which there was no acceptable remedy other than a spirit of moderation and a sense of responsibility—and civility—on the part of those who exercise the guaranteed freedoms of expression.

"It was reasonable for Congress to conclude that the public interest in being informed requires periodic accountability on the part of those who are entrusted with the use of broadcast frequencies, scarce as they are. In the delicate balancing historically followed in the regulation of broadcasting Congress and the Commission could appropriately conclude that the allocation of journalistic priorities should be concentrated in the licensee rather than diffused among many. This policy gives the public some assurance that the broadcaster will be answerable if he fails to meet their legitimate needs. No such accountability attaches to the private individual, whose only qualifications for using the broadcast facility may be abundant funds and a point of view. To agree that debate on public issues should be 'robust, and wide-open' does not mean that we should exchange 'public trustee' broadcasting, with all its limitations, for a system of self-appointed editorial commentators.

"[T]he risk of an enlargement of Government control over the content of broadcast discussion of public issues [is] inherent in the Court of Appeals' remand requiring regulations and procedures to sort out requests to be heard—a process involving the very editing that licensees now perform as to regular programming. [Under] a constitutionally commanded and government supervised right-of-access system urged by respondents and mandated by the Court of Appeals, the Commission would be required to oversee far more of the day-to-day operations of broadcasters' conduct, deciding such questions as whether a particular individual or group has had sufficient opportunity to present its viewpoint and whether a particular viewpoint has already been sufficiently aired. Regimenting broadcasters is too radical a therapy for the ailment respondents complain of. * * *

"The Commission is also entitled to take into account the reality that in a very real sense listeners and viewers constitute a 'captive audience.' [It] is no answer to say that because we tolerate pervasive commercial advertisement [we] can also live with its political counterparts.

"The rationale for the Court of Appeals' decision imposing a constitutional right of access on the broadcast media was that the licensee impermissibly discriminates by accepting commercial advertisements while refusing editorial advertisements. The court relied on [lower court cases] holding that state-supported school newspapers and public transit companies were forbidden by the First Amendment from excluding controversial editorial advertisements in favor of commercial advertisements.[c] The court also attempted to analogize this case to some of our decisions holding that States may not constitutionally ban certain protected speech while at the same time permitting other speech in public areas [citing e.g., *Grayned* and *Mosley,* Sec. 6 supra].

"These decisions provide little guidance, however, in resolving the question whether the First Amendment required the Commission to mandate a private right of access to the broadcast media. In none of those cases did the forum sought for expression have an affirmative and independent statutory obligation to provide full and fair coverage of public issues, such as Congress has imposed on all broadcast licensees. In short, there is no 'discrimination' against controversial speech present in this case. The question here is not whether there is to be discussion of controversial issues of public importance on the broadcast media, but rather who shall determine what issues are to be discussed by whom, and when."

DOUGLAS, J., concurred in the result, but "for quite different reasons." Because the Court did not decide whether a broadcast licensee is "a federal agency within the context of this case," he assumed that it was not. He "fail[ed] to see," then "how constitutionally we can treat TV and the radio differently than we treat

c. But see *Lehman v. Shaker Heights,* Sec. 6, II supra.

newspapers": "I did not participate in [*Red Lion* and] would not support it. The Fairness Doctrine has no place in our First Amendment regime. It puts the head of the camel inside the tent and enables administration after administration to toy with TV or radio in order to serve its sordid or its benevolent ends. [The uniqueness of radio and TV] is due to engineering and technical problems. But the press in a realistic sense is likewise not available to all. [T]he daily newspapers now established are unique in the sense that it would be virtually impossible for a competitor to enter the field due to the financial exigencies of this era. The result is that in practical terms the newspapers and magazines, like the TV and radio, are available only to a select few. [That] may argue for a redefinition of the responsibilities of the press in First Amendment terms. But I do not think it gives us carte blanche to design systems of supervision and control nor empower [the government to] make 'some' laws 'abridging' freedom of the press. * * *

"Licenses are, of course, restricted in time and while, in my view, Congress has the power to make each license limited to a fixed term and nonreviewable, there is no power to deny renewals for editorial or ideological reasons [for] the First Amendment gives no preference to one school of thought over the others.

"The Court in today's decision by endorsing the Fairness Doctrine sanctions a federal saddle on broadcast licensees that is agreeable to the traditions of nations that never have known freedom of press and that is tolerable in countries that do not have a written constitution containing prohibitions as absolute as those in the First Amendment."[d]

BRENNAN, J., joined by Marshall, J., dissented, viewing "the *absolute* ban on the sale of air time for the discussion of controversial issues" as "governmental action"[e] violating the first amendment: "As a practical matter, the Court's reliance on the Fairness Doctrine as an 'adequate' alternative to editorial advertising seriously overestimates the ability—or willingness—of broadcasters to expose the public to the 'widest possible dissemination of information from diverse and antagonistic sources.' [Indeed,] in light of the strong interest of broadcasters in maximizing their audience, and therefore their profits, it seems almost naive to expect the majority of broadcasters to produce the variety and controversiality of material necessary to reflect a full spectrum of viewpoints. Stated simply, angry customers are not good customers and, in the commercial world of mass communications, it is simply 'bad business' to espouse—or even to allow others to espouse—the heterodox or the controversial. As a result, even under the Fairness Doctrine, broadcasters generally tend to permit only established—or at least moderated—views to enter the broadcast world's 'marketplace of ideas.'[24]

"Moreover, the Court's reliance on the Fairness Doctrine as the *sole* means of informing the public seriously misconceives and underestimates the public's interest in receiving ideas and information directly from the advocates of those ideas without the interposition of journalistic middlemen. Under the Fairness Doctrine, broadcasters decide what issues are 'important,' how 'fully' to cover them, and what format, time and style of coverage are 'appropriate.' The retention of such *absolute* control in the hands of a few government licensees is inimical to the First Amendment, for vigorous, free debate can be attained only when members of the public have at least *some* opportunity to take the initiative and editorial control into their own hands.

d. Noting that his views "closely approach those expressed by Mr. Justice Douglas," Stewart, J., also concurred.

e. See fn. a supra and Ch. 10, Sec. 2 infra.
24. [Citing many secondary sources to support this statement.]

"[S]tanding alone, [the Fairness Doctrine] simply cannot eliminate the need for a further, complementary airing of controversial views through the limited availability of editorial advertising. Indeed, the availability of at least *some* opportunity for editorial advertising is imperative if we are ever to attain the 'free and general discussion of public matters [that] seems absolutely essential to prepare the people for an intelligent exercise of their rights as citizens.'

"Moreover, a proper balancing of the competing First Amendment interests at stake in this controversy must consider, not only the interests of broadcasters and of the listening and viewing public, but also the independent First Amendment interest of groups and individuals in effective self-expression. [I]n a time of apparently growing anonymity of the individual in our society, it is imperative that we take special care to preserve the vital First Amendment interest in assuring 'self-fulfillment [of expression] for each individual.' For our citizens may now find greater than ever the need to express their own views directly to the public, rather than through a governmentally appointed surrogate, if they are to feel that they can achieve at least some measure of control over their own destinies.

"[F]reedom of speech does not exist in the abstract. [It] can flourish only if it is allowed to operate in an effective forum—whether it be a public park, a schoolroom, a town meeting hall, a soapbox, or a radio and television frequency. For in the absence of an effective means of communication, the right to speak would ring hollow indeed. And, in recognition of these principles, we have consistently held that the First Amendment embodies not only the abstract right to be free from censorship, but also the right of an individual to utilize an appropriate and effective medium for the expression of his views.

"[W]ith the assistance of the Federal Government, the broadcast industry has become what is potentially the most efficient and effective 'marketplace of ideas' ever devised. [Thus], although 'full and free discussion' of ideas may have been a reality in the heyday of political pamphleteering, modern technological developments in the field of communications have made the soapbox orator and the leafleteer virtually obsolete. And, in light of the current dominance of the electronic media as the most effective means of reaching the public, any policy that *absolutely* denies citizens access to the airwaves necessarily renders even the concept of 'full and free discussion' practically meaningless.

"[T]he challenged ban can be upheld only if it is determined that such editorial advertising would unjustifiably impair the broadcaster's assertedly overriding interest in exercising *absolute* control over 'his' frequency. Such an analysis, however, hardly reflects the delicate balancing of interests that this sensitive question demands. Indeed, this 'absolutist' approach wholly disregards the competing First Amendment rights of all 'nonbroadcaster' citizens, ignores the teachings of our recent decision in *Red Lion*, and is not supported by the historical purposes underlying broadcast regulation in this Nation. [T]here is simply no overriding First Amendment interest of broadcasters that can justify the *absolute* exclusion of virtually all of our citizens from the most effective 'marketplace of ideas' ever devised.

"[T]his case deals *only* with the allocation of *advertising* time—airtime that broadcasters regularly relinquish to others without the retention of significant editorial control. Thus, we are concerned here not with the speech of broadcasters themselves but, rather, with their 'right' to decide which *other* individuals will be given an opportunity to speak in a forum that has already been opened to the public.

"Viewed in this context, the *absolute* ban on editorial advertising seems particularly offensive because, although broadcasters refuse to sell any airtime whatever to groups or individuals wishing to speak out on controversial issues of public importance, they make such airtime readily available to those 'commercial' advertisers who seek to peddle their goods and services to the public. [Yet an] individual seeking to discuss war, peace, pollution, or the suffering of the poor is denied this right to speak. Instead, he is compelled to rely on the beneficence of a corporate 'trustee' appointed by the Government to argue his case for him.

"It has been long recognized, however, that although access to public forums may be subjected to reasonable 'time, place, and manner' regulations, '[s]elective exclusions from a public forum, may not be based on *content* alone.' *Mosley* (emphasis added). Here, of course, the differential treatment accorded 'commercial' and 'controversial' speech clearly violates that principle. Moreover, and not without some irony, the favored treatment given 'commercial' speech under the existing scheme clearly reverses traditional First Amendment priorities. For it has generally been understood that 'commercial' speech enjoys *less* First Amendment protection than speech directed at the discussion of controversial issues of public importance."

Notes and Questions

1. *Confronting scarcity.* Consider Tribe 2d ed., at 1005: "*CBS* took a step away from *Red Lion* by its treatment of broadcasters as part of the 'press' with an important editorial function to perform rather than as analogous to the postal or telephone systems, but *CBS* was firmly in the *Red Lion* tradition when it refused to consider the possibility that either the technologically scarce radio and television channels, or the finite time available on such channels, might be allocated much as economically scarce newspaper opportunities are allocated: by a combination of market mechanisms and chance rather than by government design coupled with broadcaster autonomy."

Suppose the government sold the airwaves to the highest bidder and allowed subsequent exchange according to property and contract law. Consider Note, *Reconciling Red Lion and Tornillo: A Consistent Theory of Media Regulation,* 28 Stan.L.Rev. 563, 583 (1976): "This regulatory strategy would remove the government from direct determination of the particular individuals who are allowed to broadcast, leaving this decision to market forces, and would avoid the need for specific behavioral commands and sanctions now necessary to secure compliance by broadcasters with the various obligations imposed by the public interest standard. [Under] strict scrutiny, then, the existence of this clearly identifiable less restrictive alternative indicates that the Communications Act is unconstitutional."

But see Van Alstyne, at 563: "Congress may indeed be free to 'sell off' the airwaves, and it may be wholly feasible to allocate most currently established broadcast signals by competitive bidding that, when done, may well produce private licensees operating truly without subsidy. But only a singularly insensitive observer would believe that this choice is not implicitly also a highly speech-restrictive choice by Congress. It is fully as speech-restrictive as though, in the case of land, government were to withdraw from *all* ownership and all subsidized maintenance of all land, including parks, auditoriums, and streets and to remain in the field exclusively as a policeman to enforce the proprietary decisions of all private landowners."[f]

Should it be constitutional for the government to exercise "ownership" over the entire broadcast spectrum?[g]

2. *The "fairness" doctrine criticized.* The Court's assumption that the fairness doctrine works tolerably well has been roasted by the commentators. See, e.g., Ford Rowan, *Broadcast Fairness: Doctrine, Practice, Prospects* (1984); Steven Simmons, *The Fairness Doctrine and the Media* (1978); Johnson & Dystel, *A Day in the Life: The Federal Communications Commission,* 82 Yale L.J. 1575 (1973). Consider Thomas Krattenmaker & Lucas Powe, *The Fairness Doctrine Today: A Constitutional Curiosity and an Impossible Dream,* 1985 Duke L.J. 151, 175: "If the doctrine is to be taken seriously then suspected violations lurk everywhere and the FCC should undertake continuous oversight of the industry. If the FCC will not—or cannot—do that, then the doctrine must be toothless except for the randomly-selected few who are surprised to feel its bite after the fact." For a vigorous defense of the fairness doctrine, see Charles Ferris & James Kirkland, *Fairness—The Broadcaster's Hippocratic Oath,* 34 Cath.U.L.Rev. 605 (1985).

3. *The fairness doctrine repealed.* The FCC concluded a 15 month administrative proceeding with an official denunciation of the fairness doctrine, pointing in particular to the marked increase in the information services marketplace since *Red Lion* and the effects of the doctrine in application. FCC, *[General] Fairness Doctrine Obligations of Broadcast Licensees,* 102 F.C.C.2d 143 (1985). *Syracuse Peace Council,* 2 FCC Rcd 5043 (1987) held that "under the constitutional standard established by *Red Lion* and its progeny, the fairness doctrine contravenes the First Amendment and its enforcement is no longer in the public interest."[h]

4. *The worst of both worlds.* Evaluate the following hypothetical commentary: "*CBS v. DNC* allows government to grant virtually exclusive control over American's most valuable communication medium to corporations who regard it as their mission to 'deliver' audiences to advertisers. The system gives us the worst of both worlds: the world of profit-seeking—without a free market; the world of regulation—without planning." For discussion of alternatives, see Ronald Cass, *Revolution in the Wasteland* (1981); Bruce Owen, *Economics and Freedom of Expression: Media Structure and the First Amendment* (1975); Charles Firestone & Phillip Jacklin, *Deregulation and the Pursuit of Fairness* in Telecommunications Policy and the Citizen 107 (Timothy Haight ed. 1979); Ralph Nader & Claire

f. For detailed, but traditional, criticism of the scarcity argument, see Matthew Spitzer, *Controlling the Content of Print and Broadcast,* 58 S.Cal.L.Rev. 1349 (1985). But see *Metro Broadcasting v. FCC,* 497 U.S. 547, 110 S.Ct. 2997, 111 L.Ed.2d 445 (1990)(reaffirming the government's power to regulate the "limited number" of broadcast licensees in the context of upholding minority ownership policies designed to effectuate more diverse programming and to safeguard the "rights of the viewing and listening audiences"). For criticism of the scarcity argument in light of new technology, see Lawrence Lessig, *Code* 182–85 (1999).

g. See Glen O. Robinson, *The Electronic First Amendment: An Essay for the New Age,* 47 Duke L.J. 899, 911–13 (1998); Matthew Spitzer, *The Constitutionality of Licensing Broadcasters,* 64 N.Y.U.L.Rev. 990 (1989); Ste-

ven Shiffrin, *Government Speech,* 27 UCLA L.Rev. 565, 587 n. 122, 644–45 (1980).

h. *Syracuse Peace Council v. FCC,* 867 F.2d 654 (D.C.Cir.1989) affirmed the FCC's determination that the fairness doctrine no longer serves the public interest without reaching constitutional issues. On June 20, 1987 President had vetoed congressional legislation designed to preserve the fairness doctrine on the ground that the legislation was unconstitutional. *Radio-Television News Directors Assoc. v. FCC,* 229 F.3d 269 (D.C.Cir.2000) ordered the FCC to vacate the personal attack rules with the understanding that the rules might be reinstituted if the Commission conducted a new rule-making proceeding to determine whether the public interest, consistent with the first amendment, required them.

Riley, *Oh Say Can You See: A Broadcast Network for the Audience,* 5 J.L. & Pol. 1 (1988). Bruce Owen, *Structural Approaches to the Problem of Television Network Economic Dominance,* 1979 Duke L.J. 191.

5. Do access proposals miss the central problem? Is television at the heart of an "amusement-centered culture" that substitutes images and sound bites for serious public discourse while encouraging a privatized nonengaged citizenry? Consider Ronald Collins and David Skover, *The First Amendment in an Age of Paratroopers,* 68 Tex.L.Rev. 1087, 1088–89 (1990): "With entertainment as the paradigm for most public discourse, traditional first amendment values—which stress civic restraint and serious dialogue—are overshadowed. Given these core values and the anticensorial direction of first amendment theory, is there anything that could (or should) be done to thwart, rather than to feed, an amusement-centered culture?

"In attempting to answer this question, we confront a paradox: by saving itself, the first amendment destroys itself. On the one hand, to preserve its anticensorial ideals, the first amendment must protect both the old and new media cultures. Accordingly, it must constrain most governmental controls over expression, including those over the commercial use of electronic media. On the other hand, if the first amendment's protections do not differentiate between the old and new media cultures, the modern obsession with self-amusement will trivialize public discourse and undermine the traditional aim of the first amendment."[i]

6. Consider Henry Geller, *The Transformation of Television News: Articles and Comments: Fairness and the Public Trustee Concept: Time to Move On,* 47 Fed.Com.L.J. 79, 83–84 (1994): "It makes no sense to try to impose effective, behavioral regulation [when] conventional television faces such fierce and increasing competition, and viewership is declining rather than growing. It would be much sounder to truly deregulate broadcasting by eliminating the public trustee requirement and in its place substituting a reasonable spectrum fee imposed on existing stations (and an auction for all new frequency assignments), with the sums so obtained dedicated to public telecommunications. [For] the first time, we would have a structure that works to accomplish explicit policy goals. The commercial system would continue to do what it already does—deliver a great variety of entertainment and news-type programs. The noncommercial system would have the funds to accomplish its goals—to supply needed public service such as educational programming for children, cultural fare, minority presentations, and in-depth informational programs."

7. *Cable television.* Can government require cable operators to grant an access channel for the public, for the government, and for educational institutions? Which is the better analogy: *Red Lion* or *Miami Herald?* Need government lease space or otherwise afford access to utility poles under its control (and grant rights of way) to all competing cable companies? Is the appropriate analogy to *Schneider? Perry? Vincent? Red Lion? Miami Herald?*

LOS ANGELES v. PREFERRED COMMUNICATIONS, INC., 476 U.S. 488, 106 S.Ct. 2034, 90 L.Ed.2d 480 (1986), per REHNQUIST, J., upheld the refusal to dismiss a complaint brought by a cable company demanding access to a city's utility poles and asserting a right to be free of government-mandated channels: "Cable television partakes of some of the aspects of speech and the communica-

---

i. For discussion of the Collins–Skover paradox by Max Lerner, David M. O'Brien, Martin Redish, Edward Rubin, Herbert Schiller, and   Mark Tushnet, see Colloquy: *The First Amendment and the Paratroopers Paradox,* 68 Texas L.Rev. 1087 (1990).

tion of ideas as do the traditional enterprises of newspapers and [book publishers]. Respondent's proposed activities would seem to implicate First Amendment interests as do the activities of wireless broadcasters, which were found to fall within the ambit of the First Amendment in [*Red Lion*]. Of course, ['Even] protected speech is not equally permissible in all places and at all times.' *Cornelius*. Moreover, where speech and conduct are joined in a single course of action, the First Amendment values must be balanced against competing societal interests. See, e.g., *Vincent; O'Brien*." The Court postponed fuller discussion of any cable rights until a factual record had been developed.[j]

———

The Cable Television and Consumer Protection and Competition Act of 1992 required cable television systems to devote a portion of their channels to local broadcasters including commercial stations and public broadcast stations.[a] Congress was concerned about the monopolistic character of cable operations in most localities and the economic incentives for cable operators to favor their own programming. It also pointed to the importance of maintaining local broadcasting. TURNER BROADCASTING SYSTEM, INC. v. FCC, 512 U.S. 622, 114 S.Ct. 2445, 129 L.Ed.2d 497 (1994), per KENNEDY, J., joined by Rehnquist, C.J., and Blackmun and Souter, JJ., upheld the requirement so long as the Government could demonstrate on remand that in the absence of legislation, a large number of broadcast stations would not be carried or would be adversely repositioned, that such stations would be at serious risk of financial difficulty, that the cable operators' programming selections (as opposed to using unused channel capacity) would not be excessively affected, and that no less restrictive alternative means existed. The plurality, joined by Stevens, J., argued that the antitrust interests of government were content neutral, but concluded that "some measure of heightened First Amendment scrutiny" was appropriate because the act was not a generally applicable law but directed at cable operators: "The scope and operation of the challenged provisions make clear [that] Congress designed the must-carry provisions not to promote speech of a particular content, but to prevent cable operators from exploiting their economic power to the detriment of broadcasters, and thereby to ensure that all Americans, especially those unable to subscribe to cable, have access to free television programming—whatever its content."[b]

O'CONNOR, J., joined by Scalia, Ginsburg, and Thomas, JJ., concurring and dissenting in part, would have held the requirements unconstitutional without a remand. They argued that strict scrutiny was appropriate because the preference

j. For cogent discussion, see Daniel Brenner, *Cable Television and the Freedom of Expression*, 1988 Duke L.J. 329. See also Powe, supra, at 216–47; David Saylor, *Municipal Ripoff: The Unconstitutionality of Cable Television Franchise Fees and Access Support Payments*, 35 Cath.U.L.Rev. 671 (1986); Ithiel de Sola Pool, *Technologies of Freedom* 151–88 (1983); Monroe Price, *Taming Red Lion: The First Amendment and Structural Approaches to Media Regulation*, 31 Fed.Comm.L.J. 215 (1979); Comment, *Access to Cable Television: A Critique of the Affirmative Duty Theory of the First Amendment*, 70 Calif.L.Rev. 1393 (1982). For discussion of other technologies, see Special Issue, *Videotex*, 36 Fed.Comm.L.J. 119 (1984). Monroe Price, *Free Expression and Di-*

gital Dreams: The Open and Closed Terrain of Speech, 22 Critical Inquiry 64 (1995).

a. It also required that they be placed in the same numerical position as when broadcast over the air.

b. Blackmun, J., concurring, emphasized the importance of deferring to Congress during the new proceedings. Stevens, J., concurring, reluctantly joined the order to remand; he would have preferred to affirm the must-carry legislation without further proceedings. Ginsburg, J., concurred in parts of the Court's opinion (including the section arguing for intermediate first amendment scrutiny regarding the antitrust interest), filed a separate concurring opinion, and joined O'Connor, J's opinion.

for broadcasters over cable programmers on many channels was based on content (referring to findings about local public affairs programming and public television).[c] Although the interest in public affairs programming was said to be weighty, O'Connor, J., observed that public affairs cable-programming could be displaced: "In the rare circumstances where the government may draw content-based distinctions to serve its goals, the restrictions must serve the goals a good deal more precisely than this." O'Connor, J., also argued that the requirements should fail content neutral scrutiny as well because the act disadvantaged cable operators with no anti-competitive motives and favored broadcasters who could financially survive even if dropped from a cable system.[d]

Remanded

Notes and Questions

1. Has the United States "consistently and properly engaged in content-motivated structuring of the communications realm" in ways that have usually "benefited the nation." See C. Edwin Baker, *Turner Broadcasting: Content–Based Regulation of Persons and Presses,* 1994 Sup.Ct.Rev. 57, 94. Does the dissent's emphasis on content discrimination shortchange the government's interest in assuring a robust communications system? Would such an emphasis lead to the conclusion that commercial broadcasters deserved no preference but public broadcasters did? Consider Donald Hawthorne & Monroe Price, *Rewiring the First Amendment: Meaning, Content and Public Broadcasting,* 12 Cardozo Arts & Ent.L.J. 499, 504 (1994): "If the absence of a meaningful content basis for preferring commercial broadcasters should impair their entitlement to 'must-carry' treatment, precisely the converse is true for noncommercial broadcasters. These entities have been mandated to carry on government's historic responsibility to educate the citizenry and more recent undertaking to subsidize the arts."[e]

2. After remand, TURNER BROADCASTING SYSTEM, INC. v. FCC, 520 U.S. 180, 117 S.Ct. 1174, 137 L.Ed.2d 369 (1997), per KENNEDY, J., joined by Rehnquist, C.J., Stevens, and Souter, JJ., upheld the must-carry provisions. Applying the *O'Brien* test, he emphasized the importance of deferring to Congress so long as it had "drawn reasonable inferences based upon substantial evidence." He found that the legislation was narrowly tailored to preserve the benefits of local broadcast television, to promote widespread dissemination of information from a multiplicity of sources, and to promote fair competition.

BREYER, J., concurring, joined Kennedy, J.'s opinion except for his discussion and conclusion regarding the fair competition rationale.[f]

O'CONNOR, J., joined by Scalia, Thomas, and Ginsburg, JJ., dissenting, argued again that strict scrutiny should apply, agreed that deference was owed to Congress "in its predictive judgments and its evaluation of complex economic questions," but maintained that even under intermediate scrutiny, the Court had an independent duty to examine with care the Congressional interests, the

c. Kennedy, J., argued that such findings showed "nothing more than the recognition that the services provided by broadcast television have some intrinsic value and, thus, are worth preserving against the threats posed by cable."

d. Thomas, J., did not join this section of the opinion.

e. For additional commentary, see Cass R. Sunstein, *One Case at a Time* 172–82 (1999); Glen O. Robinson, *The Electronic First Amend-*

ment: *An Essay for the New Age,* 47 Duke L.J. 899, 933–39 (1998); Jerome Barron, *Reading Turner through a Tornillo Lens,* 13 Comm. Lawyer (1995); Monroe Price & Donald Hawthorne, *Saving Public Television,* Hast.Comm./Ent.L.J. 65 (1994); Cass Sunstein, *The First Amendment in Cyberspace,* 104 Yale L.J. 1757 (1995).

f. Stevens, J., also filed a concurring opinion.

findings, and the fit between the goals and consequences. She criticized the Court for being too deferential even on the assumption that the legislation was content neutral. On her analysis, the record did not support either the conclusion that cable posed a significant threat to local broadcast markets or that the act was narrowly tailored to deal with anti-competitive conduct.[g]

ARKANSAS EDUCATIONAL TELEVISION COMM'N v. FORBES, 523 U.S. 666, 118 S.Ct. 1633, 140 L.Ed.2d 875 (1998), per KENNEDY, J., concluded that a candidate debate sponsored by a state-owned public television broadcaster was a nonpublic forum subject to constitutional restraints, but that the broadcaster's decision to exclude a candidate was reasonable: "A state-owned public television broadcaster [Arkansas Educational Television Commission 'AETC'] sponsored a candidate debate from which it excluded an independent congressional candidate [Ralph Forbes] with little popular support. The issue before us is whether, by reason of its state ownership, the station had a constitutional obligation to allow every candidate access to the debate. We conclude that, unlike most other public television programs, the candidate debate was subject to constitutional constraints applicable to nonpublic fora under our forum precedents. Even so, the broadcaster's decision to exclude the candidate was a reasonable, viewpoint-neutral exercise of journalistic discretion. * * *

"Although public broadcasting as a general matter does not lend itself to scrutiny under the forum doctrine, candidate debates present the narrow exception to the rule. For two reasons, a candidate debate like the one at issue here is different from other programming. First, unlike AETC's other broadcasts, the debate was by design a forum for political speech by the candidates. Consistent with the long tradition of candidate debates, the implicit representation of the broadcaster was that the views expressed were those of the candidates, not its own. The very purpose of the debate was to allow the candidates to express their views with minimal intrusion by the broadcaster. In this respect the debate differed even from a political talk show, whose host can express partisan views and then limit the discussion to those ideas.

"Second, in our tradition, candidate debates are of exceptional significance in the electoral process. [Deliberation] on the positions and qualifications of candidates is integral to our system of government, and electoral speech may have its most profound and widespread impact when it is disseminated through televised debates. * * *

"Under our precedents, the AETC debate was not a designated public forum. [T]he government creates a designated public forum when it makes its property generally available to a certain class of speakers, as the university made its facilities generally available to student groups in *Widmar*. On the other hand, the government does not create a designated public forum when it does no more than reserve eligibility for access to the forum to a particular class of speakers, whose members must then, as individuals, 'obtain permission,' to use it. For instance, the Federal Government did not create a designated public forum in Cornelius when it reserved eligibility for participation in the CFC drive to charitable

---

g. Would *Turner* justify the application of "must carry" rules to segments of the Internet such as Netscape. See Andrew Chin, *Making the World Wide Web Safe for Democracy: A Medium-Specific First Amendment Analysis,* 19 Hastings Comm/Ent L.J. 309 (1997).

agencies, and then made individual, non-ministerial judgments as to which of the eligible agencies would participate.

"The [distinction] between general and selective access furthers First Amendment interests. By recognizing the distinction, we encourage the government to open its property to some expressive activity in cases where, if faced with an all-or-nothing choice, it might not open the property at all.[a] That this distinction turns on governmental intent does not render it unprotective of speech. Rather, it reflects the reality that, with the exception of traditional public fora, the government retains the choice of whether to designate its property as a forum for specified classes of speakers.

"Here, the debate did not have an open-microphone format. [AETC] did not make its debate generally available to candidates for Arkansas' Third Congressional District seat. Instead, just as the Federal Government in *Cornelius* reserved eligibility for participation in the CFC program to certain classes of voluntary agencies, AETC reserved eligibility for participation in the debate to candidates for the Third Congressional District seat (as opposed to some other seat). At that point, just as the Government in *Cornelius* made agency-by-agency determinations as to which of the eligible agencies would participate in the CFC, AETC made candidate-by-candidate determinations as to which of the eligible candidates would participate in the debate. 'Such selective access, unsupported by evidence of a purposeful designation for public use, does not create a public forum.' Thus the debate was a nonpublic forum.

"The debate's status as a nonpublic forum, however, did not give AETC unfettered power to exclude any candidate it wished. [To] be consistent with the First Amendment, the exclusion of a speaker from a nonpublic forum must not be based on the speaker's viewpoint and must otherwise be reasonable in light of the purpose of the property. *Cornelius*. * * *

"There is no substance to Forbes' suggestion that he was excluded because his views were unpopular or out of the mainstream. [Nor] did AETC exclude Forbes in an attempted manipulation of the political process. The evidence provided powerful support for the jury's express finding that AETC's exclusion of Forbes was not the result of 'political pressure from anyone inside or outside [AETC].' There is no serious argument that AETC did not act in good faith in this case. AETC excluded Forbes because the voters lacked interest in his candidacy, not because AETC itself did. The broadcaster's decision to exclude Forbes was a reasonable, viewpoint-neutral exercise of journalistic discretion consistent with the First Amendment."

a. In a later section, the Court stated: "In each of the 1988, 1992, and 1996 Presidential elections, for example, no fewer than 22 candidates appeared on the ballot in at least one State. In the 1996 congressional elections, it was common for 6 to 11 candidates to qualify for the ballot for a particular seat. In the 1993 New Jersey gubernatorial election, to illustrate further, sample ballot mailings included the written statements of 19 candidates. On logistical grounds alone, a public television editor might, with reason, decide that the inclusion of all ballot-qualified candidates would 'actually undermine the educational value and quality of debates.'

"Were it faced with the prospect of cacophony, on the one hand, and First Amendment liability, on the other, a public television broadcaster might choose not to air candidates' views at all.

"These concerns are more than speculative. As a direct result of the Court of Appeals' decision in this case, the Nebraska Educational Television Network canceled a scheduled debate between candidates in Nebraska's 1996 United States Senate race. A First Amendment jurisprudence yielding these results does not promote speech but represses it."

STEVENS, J., joined by Souter and Ginsburg, JJ., dissented: "The official action that led to the exclusion of respondent Forbes from a debate with the two major-party candidates for election to one of Arkansas' four seats in Congress does not adhere to well-settled constitutional principles. The ad hoc decision of the staff of [AETC] raises precisely the concerns addressed by 'the many decisions of this Court over the last 30 years, holding that a law subjecting the exercise of First Amendment freedoms to the prior restraint of a license, without narrow, objective, and definite standards to guide the licensing authority, is unconstitutional.' *Shuttlesworth v. Birmingham.*

"Given the fact that the Republican winner in the Third Congressional District race in 1992 received only 50.22% of the vote and the Democrat received 47.20%, it would have been necessary for Forbes, who had made a strong showing in recent Republican primaries, to divert only a handful of votes from the Republican candidate to cause his defeat. Thus, even though the AETC staff may have correctly concluded that Forbes was 'not a serious candidate,' their decision to exclude him from the debate may have determined the outcome of the election in the Third District.

"If a comparable decision were made today by a privately owned network, it would be subject to scrutiny under the Federal Election Campaign Act unless the network used 'pre-established objective criteria to determine which candidates may participate in [the] debate.' 11 CFR § 110.13(c) (1997). No such criteria governed AETC's refusal to permit Forbes to participate in the debate. Indeed, whether that refusal was based on a judgment about 'newsworthiness'—as AETC has argued in this Court—or a judgment about 'political viability'—as it argued in the Court of Appeals—the facts in the record presumably would have provided an adequate basis either for a decision to include Forbes in the Third District debate or a decision to exclude him * * *.

"The apparent flexibility of AETC's purported standard suggests the extent to which the staff had nearly limitless discretion to exclude Forbes from the debate based on ad hoc justifications. Thus, the Court of Appeals correctly concluded that the staff's appraisal of 'political viability' was 'so subjective, so arguable, so susceptible of variation in individual opinion, as to provide no secure basis for the exercise of governmental power consistent with the First Amendment.' * * *

"The reasons that support the need for narrow, objective, and definite standards to guide licensing decisions apply directly to the wholly subjective access decisions made by the staff of AETC.[18] The importance of avoiding arbitrary or viewpoint-based exclusions from political debates militates strongly in favor of requiring the controlling state agency to use (and adhere to) pre-established, objective criteria to determine who among qualified candidates may participate. A constitutional duty to use objective standards—i.e., 'neutral principles'—for determining whether and when to adjust a debate format would impose only a modest requirement that would fall far short of a duty to grant every multiple-party request. Such standards would also have the benefit of providing the public with

---

18. Ironically, it is the standardless character of the decision to exclude Forbes that provides the basis for the Court's conclusion that the debates were a nonpublic forum rather than a limited public forum. [T]he Court explains that "[a] designated public forum is not created when the government allows selective access for individual speakers rather than general access for a class of speakers." If, as AETC claims, it did invite either the entire class of "viable" candidates, or the entire class of "newsworthy" candidates, under the Court's reasoning, it created a designated public forum.

some assurance that state-owned broadcasters cannot select debate participants on arbitrary grounds."

Notes and Questions

1. Consider Frederick Schauer, *Principles, Institutions, and the First Amendment*, 112 Harv. L. Rev. 84 (1998): "Beyond designated public forums, [it] is hard to see the point of forum analysis in government enterprise cases. In the typical case, the complaint is not about access, but about discriminatory treatment. And at the heart of this issue is the seemingly banal but quite important point that content-based discriminatory treatment is appropriate in some contexts, but not in others. Yet once we recognize this idea, the point of combining the determination of which contexts permit content discrimination and which do not with public forum analysis is elusive. If access is mandatory, then the focus on content discrimination is redundant. But if access is not mandatory, then the existence (or not) of a public forum is superfluous. What is not superfluous is the question whether this is one of the government enterprises which may control for content or viewpoint, and as to this question public forum doctrine offers no assistance. [That] forum analysis plays no role at all in *Finley*, and that the conclusory distinction between a nonpublic forum and a not-forum does all of the work in *Forbes*, serves only to underscore the point."

2. *No point of view discrimination?* Consider Frederick Schauer & Richard H. Pildes, *Electoral Exceptionalism and the First Amendment*, 77 Texas L.Rev. 1803, 1804 n. 5: "[A] standard of electoral viability serves to entrench accepted views against the challenge of non-accepted views. [The] role of challenges is not to displace the two-party system, as that is unlikely for many reasons, but precisely to shift the terms of electoral debate." Does that amount to point of view discrimination? See generally Jamin B. Raskin, *The Debate Gerrymander*, 77 Texas L.Rev. 1943 (1999). If not, should the exclusion of Forbes have been invalidated anyway on the ground that the exclusion skews public debate? Should the state's purpose matter? See Owen Fiss, *The Censorship of Television*, 93 Nw.U.L.Rev. 1215, 1233 (1999).

3. *Congressional action.* Suppose Congress required state owned broadcast stations to admit all official candidates to televised debates. Constitutional?

II. THE ELECTRONIC MEDIA AND CONTENT REGULATION

FCC v. PACIFICA FOUNDATION

438 U.S. 726, 98 S.Ct. 3026, 57 L.Ed.2d 1073 (1978).

Justice Stevens delivered the opinion of the Court (Parts I, II, III, and IV–C) and an opinion in which Chief Justice Burger and Justice Rehnquist joined (Parts IV–A and IV–B).

[In an early afternoon weekday broadcast which was devoted that day to contemporary attitudes toward the use of language, respondent's New York radio station aired a 12–minute selection called "Filthy Words," from a comedy album by a satiric humorist, George Carlin. The monologue, which had evoked frequent laughter from a live theater audience, began by referring to Carlin's thought about the seven words you can't say on the public airwaves, "the ones you definitely wouldn't say ever." He then listed the words ("shit," "piss," "fuck," "motherfucker," "cocksucker," "cunt," and "tits"), "the ones that will curve your spine, grow hair on your hands and (laughter) maybe, even bring us, God help us, peace without honor (laughter) um, and a bourbon (laughter)," and repeated them over and over in a variety of colloquialisms. Immediately prior to the monologue, listeners were advised that it included sensitive language which some might regard as offensive. Those who might be offended were advised to change the station and return in fifteen minutes.

[The FCC received a complaint from a man stating that while driving in his car with his young son he had heard the broadcast of the Carlin monologue. The FCC issued an order to be "associated with the station's license file, and in the event that subsequent complaints are received, the Commission will then decide whether it should utilize any of the available sanctions it has been granted by Congress."][a]

The Commission characterized the language used in the Carlin monologue as "patently offensive," though not necessarily obscene, and expressed the opinion that it should be regulated by principles analogous to those found in the law of nuisance where the "law generally speaks to *channeling* behavior more than actually prohibiting [it]."[5]

Applying these considerations to the language used in the monologue as broadcast by respondent, the Commission concluded that certain words depicted sexual and excretory activities in a patently offensive manner, noted that they "were broadcast at a time when children were undoubtedly in the audience (i.e., in the early afternoon)," and that the prerecorded language, with these offensive words "repeated over and over," was "deliberately broadcast." In summary, the Commission stated: "We therefore hold that the language as broadcast was indecent [under 18 U.S.C. 1464]."

IV. Pacifica [argues] that the Commission's construction of the statutory language broadly encompasses so much constitutionally protected speech that reversal is required even if Pacifica's broadcast of the "Filthy Words" monologue is not itself protected by the First Amendment. * * *

A. The first argument fails because our review is limited to the question whether the Commission has the authority to proscribe this particular broadcast. As the Commission itself emphasized, its order was "issued in a specific factual context." That approach is appropriate for courts as well as the Commission when regulation of indecency is at stake, for indecency is largely a function of context—it cannot be adequately judged in the abstract. * * *

It is true that the Commission's order may lead some broadcasters to censor themselves. At most, however, the Commission's definition of indecency will deter only the broadcasting of patently offensive references to excretory and sexual organs and activities.[18] While some of these references may be protected, they surely lie at the periphery of First Amendment concern. * * * Invalidating any rule on the basis of its hypothetical application to situations not before the Court is "strong medicine" to be applied "sparingly and only as a last resort." *Broadrick*

---

a. The FCC's action is placed in the context of other similar actions in Lucas Powe, *American Broadcasting and the First Amendment* 162–90 (1987).

5. Thus, the Commission suggested, if an offensive broadcast had literary, artistic, political or scientific value, and were preceded by warnings, it might not be indecent in the late evening, but would be so during the day, when children are in the audience.

18. A requirement that indecent language be avoided will have its primary effect on the form, rather than the content, of serious communication. There are few, if any, thoughts that cannot be expressed by the use of less offensive language.

[Sec. I, 5 supra]. We decline to administer that medicine to preserve the vigor of patently offensive sexual and excretory speech.

B. [The] words of the Carlin monologue are unquestionably "speech" within the meaning of the First Amendment. [The] question in this case is whether a broadcast of patently offensive words dealing with sex and excretion may be regulated because of its content.[20] Obscene materials have been denied the protection of the First Amendment because their content is so offensive to contemporary moral standards. *Roth.* But the fact that society may find speech offensive is not a sufficient reason for suppressing it. Indeed, if it is the speaker's opinion that gives offense, that consequence is a reason for according it constitutional protection. For it is a central tenet of the First Amendment that the government must remain neutral in the marketplace of ideas. If there were any reason to believe that the Commission's characterization of the Carlin monologue as offensive could be traced to its political content—or even to the fact that it satirized contemporary attitudes about four letter words[22]—First Amendment protection might be required. But that is simply not this case. These words offend for the same reasons that obscenity offends. Their place in the hierarchy of First Amendment values was aptly sketched by Justice Murphy when he said, "such utterances are no essential part of any exposition of ideas, and are of such slight social value as a step to truth that any benefit that may be derived from them is clearly outweighed by the social interest in order and morality." *Chaplinsky.*

Although these words ordinarily lack literary, political, or scientific value, they are not entirely outside the protection of the First Amendment. Some uses of even the most offensive words are unquestionably protected. Indeed, we may assume, arguendo, that this monologue would be protected in other contexts. [It] is a characteristic of speech such as this that both its capacity to offend and its "social value," to use Justice Murphy's term, vary with the circumstances. Words that are commonplace in one setting are shocking in another. To paraphrase Justice Harlan, one occasion's lyric is another's vulgarity. Cf. *Cohen v. California.*[25]

In this case it is undisputed that the content of Pacifica's broadcast was "vulgar," "offensive," and "shocking." Because content of that character is not entitled to absolute constitutional protection under all circumstances, we must

---

20. Although neither Justice Powell nor Justice Brennan directly confronts this question, both have answered it affirmatively, the latter explicitly, at fn. 3, infra, and the former implicitly by concurring in a judgment that could not otherwise stand.

22. The monologue does present a point of view; it attempts to show that the words it uses are "harmless" and that our attitudes toward them are "essentially silly." The Commission objects, not to this point of view, but to the way in which it is expressed. The belief that these words are harmless does not necessarily confer a First Amendment privilege to use them while proselytizing just as the conviction that obscenity is harmless does not license one to communicate that conviction by the indiscriminate distribution of an obscene leaflet.

25. The importance of context is illustrated by the *Cohen* case. [So] far as the evidence

showed no one in the courthouse was offended by [Cohen's jacket.]

In holding that criminal sanctions could not be imposed on Cohen for his political statement in a public place, the Court rejected the argument that his speech would offend unwilling viewers; it noted that "there was no evidence that persons powerless to avoid [his] conduct did in fact object to it." In contrast, in this case the Commission was responding to a listener's strenuous complaint, and Pacifica does not question its determination that this afternoon broadcast was likely to offend listeners. It should be noted that the Commission imposed a far more moderate penalty on Pacifica than the state court imposed on Cohen. Even the strongest civil penalty at the Commission's command does not include criminal prosecution.

consider its context in order to determine whether the Commission's action was constitutionally permissible.

C.   We have long recognized that each medium of expression presents special First Amendment problems. And of all forms of communication, it is broadcasting that has received the most limited First Amendment [protection.]

The reasons for these distinctions are complex, but two have relevance to the present case. First, the broadcast media have established a uniquely pervasive presence in the lives of all Americans. Patently offensive, indecent material presented over the airwaves confronts the citizen, not only in public, but also in the privacy of the home, where the individual's right to be let alone plainly outweighs the First Amendment rights of an intruder. *Rowan v. Post Office Dept.,* 397 U.S. 728, 90 S.Ct. 1484, 25 L.Ed.2d 736. Because the broadcast audience is constantly tuning in and out, prior warnings cannot completely protect the listener or viewer from unexpected program content. To say that one may avoid further offense by turning off the radio when he hears indecent language is like saying that the remedy for an assault is to run away after the first blow.[27] * * *

Second, broadcasting is uniquely accessible to children, even those too young to read. Although Cohen's written message might have been incomprehensible to a first grader, Pacifica's broadcast could have enlarged a child's vocabulary in an instant. Other forms of offensive expression may be withheld from the young without restricting the expression at its source. Bookstores and motion picture theaters, for example, may be prohibited from making indecent material available to children. We held in *Ginsberg* [Sec. 1, III, B supra] that the government's interest in the "well being of its youth" and in supporting "parents' claim to authority in their own household" justified the regulation of otherwise protected expression.[28] * * *

It is appropriate, in conclusion, to emphasize the narrowness of our holding. This case does not involve a two-way radio conversation between a cab driver and a dispatcher, or a telecast of an Elizabethan comedy. We have not decided that an occasional expletive in either setting would justify any sanction or, indeed, that this broadcast would justify a criminal prosecution. The Commission's decision rested entirely on a nuisance rationale under which context is all-important.

[R]eversed.

JUSTICE POWELL, with whom JUSTICE BLACKMUN joins, concurring.

[T]he language employed is, to most people, vulgar and offensive. It was chosen specifically for this quality, and it was repeated over and over as a sort of verbal shock treatment. [In] essence, the Commission sought to "channel" the monologue to hours when the fewest unsupervised children would be exposed to it. In my view, this consideration provides strong support for the Commission's holding.

---

27. Outside the home, the balance between the offensive speaker and the unwilling audience may sometimes tip in favor of the speaker, requiring the offended listener to turn away. See *Erznoznik.* * * *

28. The Commission's action does not by any means reduce adults to hearing only what is fit for children. Cf. *Butler v. Michigan* [Sec. 1, III, B supra]. Adults who feel the need may purchase tapes and records or go to theatres and nightclubs to hear these words. In fact, the Commission has not unequivocally closed even

broadcasting to speech of this sort; whether broadcast audiences in the late evening contain so few children that playing this monologue would be permissible is an issue neither the Commission nor this Court has decided. [Would the rationale based on supporting parental authority rule out banning Carlin's monologue in the early evening? See Baker, *The Evening Hours During Pacifica Standard Time,* 3 Vill. Sports & Ent. L.J. 45 (1996)].

[The] Commission properly held that the speech from which society may attempt to shield its children is not limited to that which appeals to the youthful prurient interest. The language involved in this case is as potentially degrading and harmful to children as representations of many erotic acts.

In most instances, the dissemination of this kind of speech to children may be limited without also limiting willing adults' access to it. Sellers of printed and recorded matter and exhibitors of motion pictures and live performances may be required to shut their doors to children, but such a requirement has no effect on adults' access. See *Ginsberg*. The difficulty is that [d]uring most of the broadcast hours, both adults and unsupervised children are likely to be in the broadcast audience, and the broadcaster cannot reach willing adults without also reaching children. This, as the Court emphasizes, is one of the distinctions between the broadcast and other media to which we often have adverted as justifying a different treatment of the broadcast media for First Amendment purposes. In my view, the Commission was entitled to give substantial weight to this difference in reaching its decision in this case.

[Another difference] is that broadcasting—unlike most other forms of communication—comes directly into the home, the one place where people ordinarily have the right not to be assaulted by uninvited and offensive sights and sounds. *Erznoznik; Cohen; Rowan.* * * * "That we are often 'captives' outside the sanctuary of the home and subject to objectionable speech and other sound does not mean we must be captives everywhere." *Rowan.* The Commission also was entitled to give this factor appropriate weight in the circumstances of the instant case. This is not to say, however, that the Commission has an unrestricted license to decide what speech, protected in other media, may be banned from the airwaves in order to protect unwilling adults from momentary exposure to it in their homes.[2] * * *

[M]y views are generally in accord with what is said in Part IV(C) of opinion. I therefore join that portion of his opinion. I do not join Part IV(B), however, because I do not subscribe to the theory that the Justices of this Court are free generally to decide on the basis of its content which speech protected by the First Amendment is most "valuable" and hence deserving of the most protection, and which is less "valuable" and hence deserving of less protection.[3] In my view, the result in this case does not turn on whether Carlin's monologue, viewed as a whole, or the words that comprise it, have more or less "value" than a candidate's campaign speech. This is a judgment for each person to make, not one for the judges to impose upon him.[4]

2. It is true that the radio listener quickly may tune out speech that is offensive to him. In addition, broadcasters may preface potentially offensive programs with warnings. But such warnings do not help the unsuspecting listener who tunes in at the middle of a program. In this respect, too, broadcasting appears to differ from books and records, which may carry warnings on their faces, and from motion pictures and live performances, which may carry warnings on their marquees.

3. The Court has, however, created a limited exception to this rule in order to bring commercial speech within the protection of the First Amendment. See *Ohralik* [Sec. 3, II supra].

4. For much the same reason, I also do not join Part IV(A). I had not thought that the application vel non of overbreadth analysis should depend on the Court's judgment as to the value of the protected speech that might be deterred. Except in the context of commercial speech, see *Bates* [Sec. 3, II supra], it has not in the past. See, e.g., *Lewis v. New Orleans; Gooding.*

As Justice Stevens points out, however, the Commission's order was limited to the facts of this case; "it did not purport to engage in formal rulemaking or in the promulgation of any regulations." In addition, since the Commission may be expected to proceed cautiously, as it has in the past, I do not foresee an undue "chilling" effect on broadcasters' exercise of

The result turns instead on the unique characteristics of the broadcast media, combined with society's right to protect its children from speech generally agreed to be inappropriate for their years, and with the interest of unwilling adults in not being assaulted by such offensive speech in their homes. Moreover, I doubt whether today's decision will prevent any adult who wishes to receive Carlin's message in Carlin's own words from doing so, and from making for himself a value judgment as to the merit of the message and words. These are the grounds upon which I join the judgment of the Court as to Part IV.

JUSTICE BRENNAN, with whom JUSTICE MARSHALL joins, dissenting.

[T]he Court refuses to embrace the notion, completely antithetical to basic First Amendment values, that the degree of protection the First Amendment affords protected speech varies with the social value ascribed to that speech by five Members of this Court. See opinion of Justice Powell. Moreover, [all] Members of the Court agree that [the monologue] does not fall within one of the categories of speech, such as "fighting words," or obscenity, that is totally without First Amendment protection. [Yet] a majority of the Court[1] nevertheless finds that, on the facts of this case, the FCC is not constitutionally barred from imposing sanctions on Pacifica for its airing of the Carlin monologue. * * *

[A]n individual's actions in switching on and listening to communications transmitted over the public airways and directed to the public at-large do not implicate fundamental privacy interests, even when engaged in within the home. Instead, because the radio is undeniably a public medium, these actions are more properly viewed as a decision to take part, if only as a listener, in an ongoing public discourse. Although an individual's decision to allow public radio communications into his home undoubtedly does not abrogate all of his privacy interests, the residual privacy interests he retains vis-à-vis the communication he voluntarily admits into his home are surely no greater than those of the people present in the corridor of the Los Angeles courthouse in [Cohen].

Even if an individual who voluntarily opens his home to radio communications retains privacy interests of sufficient moment to justify a ban on protected speech if those interests are "invaded in an essentially intolerable manner," Cohen, the very fact that those interests are threatened only by a radio broadcast precludes any intolerable invasion of privacy; for unlike other intrusive modes of communication, such as sound trucks, "[t]he radio can be turned off"—and with a minimum of effort. [Whatever] the minimal discomfort suffered by a listener who inadvertently tunes into a program he finds offensive during the brief interval before he can simply extend his arm and switch stations or flick the "off" button, it is surely worth the candle to preserve the broadcaster's right to send, and the right of those interested to receive, a message entitled to full First Amendment protection. * * *

The Court's balance, of necessity, fails to accord proper weight to the interests of listeners who wish to hear broadcasts the FCC deems offensive. It permits majoritarian tastes completely to preclude a protected message from entering the homes of a receptive, unoffended minority. No decision of this Court supports such a result. Where the individuals comprising the offended majority may freely choose to reject the material being offered, we have never found their privacy interests of such moment to warrant the suppression of speech on privacy

their rights. I agree, therefore, that respondent's overbreadth challenge is meritless.

1. Where I refer without differentiation to the actions of "the Court," my reference is to this majority, which consists of my Brothers Powell and Stevens and those Members of the Court joining their separate opinions.

grounds. [In] *Rowan,* the Court upheld a statute, permitting householders to require that mail advertisers stop sending them lewd or offensive materials and remove their names from mailing lists. Unlike the situation here, householders who wished to receive the sender's communications were not prevented from doing so. Equally important, the determination of offensiveness vel non under the statute involved in *Rowan* was completely within the hands of the individual householder; no governmental evaluation of the worth of the mail's content stood between the mailer and the householder. In contrast, the visage of the censor is all too discernable here. * * *

*[handwritten margin note: * Permitted to each person to decide what they would recieve, choice made by individual]*

Because the Carlin monologue is obviously not an erotic appeal to the prurient interests of children, the Court, for the first time, allows the government to prevent minors from gaining access to materials that are not obscene, and are therefore protected, as to them.[2] It thus ignores our recent admonition that "[s]peech that is neither obscene as to youths nor subject to some other legitimate proscription cannot be suppressed solely to protect the young from ideas or images that a legislative body thinks unsuitable for them." *Erznoznik.*[3] The Court's refusal to follow its own pronouncements is especially lamentable since it has the anomalous subsidiary effect, at least in the radio context at issue here, of making completely unavailable to adults material which may not constitutionally be kept even from children. * * * *Yoder* and *Pierce,* hold that parents, *not* the government, have the right to make certain decisions regarding the upbringing of their children. As surprising as it may be to individual Members of this Court, some parents may actually find Mr. Carlin's unabashed attitude towards the seven "dirty words" healthy, and deem it desirable to expose their children to the manner in which Mr. Carlin defuses the taboo surrounding the words. Such parents may constitute a minority of the American public, but the absence of great numbers willing to exercise the right to raise their children in this fashion does not alter the right's nature or its existence. Only the Court's regrettable decision does that.

As demonstrated above, neither of the factors relied on by both [Powell and Stevens, JJ.]—the intrusive nature of radio and the presence of children in the listening audience—can, when taken on its own terms, support the FCC's disapproval of the Carlin monologue. [A] neither of the opinions comprising the Court serve to clarify the extent to which the FCC may assert the privacy and children-in-the-audience rationales as justification for expunging from the airways protected communications the Commission finds offensive. Taken to their logical extreme, these rationales would support the cleansing of public radio of any "four-letter words" whatsoever, regardless of their context. The rationales could justify the banning from radio of a myriad of literary works, novels, poems, and plays by the likes of Shakespeare, Joyce, Hemingway, Ben Jonson, Henry Fielding, Robert

2. Even if the monologue appealed to the prurient interest of minors, it would not be obscene as to them unless, as to them, "the work, taken as a whole, lacks serious literary, artistic, political, or scientific value." *Miller.*

3. It may be that a narrowly drawn regulation prohibiting the use of offensive language on broadcasts directed specifically at younger children constitutes one of the "other legitimate proscription[s]" alluded to in *Erznoznik.* This is so both because of the difficulties inherent in adapting the *Miller* formulation to communications received by young children, and because such children are "not possessed of

that full capacity for individual choice which is the presupposition of the First Amendment guarantees." *Ginsberg.* (Stewart, J., concurring). I doubt, as my Brother Stevens suggests, that such a limited regulation amounts to a regulation of speech based on its content, since, by hypothesis, the only persons at whom the regulated communication is directed are incapable of evaluating its content. To the extent that such a regulation is viewed as a regulation based on content, it marks the outermost limits to which content regulation is permissible.

Burns, and Chaucer; they could support the suppression of a good deal of political speech, such as the Nixon tapes; and they could even provide the basis for imposing sanctions for the broadcast of certain portions of the Bible.

In order to dispel the spectre of the possibility of so unpalatable a degree of censorship, and to defuse Pacifica's overbreadth challenge, the FCC insists that it desires only the authority to reprimand a broadcaster on facts analogous to those present in this case. [Powell and Stevens, JJ.] take the FCC at its word, and consequently do no more than permit the Commission to censor the afternoon broadcast of the "sort of verbal shock treatment" involved [here]. I would place the responsibility and the right to weed worthless and offensive communications from the public airways where it belongs and where, until today, it resided: in a public free to choose those communications worthy of its attention from a marketplace unsullied by the censor's hand. * * *

My Brother Stevens [finds] solace in his conviction that "[t]here are few, if any, thoughts that cannot be expressed by the use of less offensive language." The idea that the content of a message and its potential impact on any who might receive it can be divorced from the words that are the vehicle for its expression is transparently fallacious. A given word may have a unique capacity to capsule an idea, evoke an emotion, or conjure up an image. Indeed, for those of us who place an appropriately high value on our cherished First Amendment rights, the word "censor" is such a word. Justice Harlan, speaking for the Court, recognized the truism that a speaker's choice of words cannot surgically be separated from the ideas he desires to express when he warned that "we cannot indulge the facile assumption that one can forbid particular words without also running a substantial risk of suppressing ideas in the process."

[Stevens, J.] also finds relevant to his First Amendment analysis the fact that "[a]dults who feel the need may purchase tapes and records or go to theatres and nightclubs to hear [the tabooed] words." [Powell, J.,] agrees. [The] opinions of my Brethren display both a sad insensitivity to the fact that these alternatives involve the expenditure of money, time, and effort that many of those wishing to hear Mr. Carlin's message may not be able to afford, and a naive innocence of the reality that in many cases, the medium may well be the message.

The Court apparently believes that the FCC's actions here can be analogized to the zoning ordinances upheld in *American Mini Theatres*. For two reasons, it is wrong. First, the zoning ordinances found to pass constitutional muster [had] valid goals other than the channeling of protected speech. No such goals are present here. Second, [the] ordinances did not restrict the access of distributors or exhibitors to the market or impair the viewing public's access to the regulated material. Again, this is not the situation here.

[T]here runs throughout the opinions of my Brothers Powell and Stevens [a] depressing inability to appreciate that in our land of cultural pluralism, there are many who think, act, and talk differently from the Members of this Court, and who do not share their fragile sensibilities. It is only an acute ethnocentric myopia that enables the Court [to blink at] persons who do not share the Court's view as to which words or expressions are acceptable and who, for a variety of reasons, including a conscious desire to flout majoritarian conventions, express themselves using words that may be regarded as offensive by those from different socio-economic backgrounds.[8] In this context, the Court's decision may be seen for

8. Under the approach taken by my Brother Powell, the availability of broadcasts *about* groups whose members comprise such audiences might also be affected. Both news broad-

what, in the broader perspective, it really is: another of the dominant culture's inevitable efforts to force those groups who do not share its mores to conform to its way of thinking, acting, and speaking. * * *[b]

Notes and Questions

1. Consider Steven H. Shiffrin, *The First Amendment, Democracy, and Romance* 80 (1990): "Most people with any first amendment bones in their bodies are troubled by [*Pacifica*]. But the nub of the first amendment insult has little to do with self-government or with the marketplace of ideas. The concern does not flow from a worry that voters will be deprived of valuable information. Concern that the truth about vulgar language might not emerge in the marketplace of ideas may be well placed, but is not a sufficient concern to explain the widespread outrage against the decision. Again, the decision is an affront to a notion of content neutrality, but there are many of those. The *Pacifica* case produces heat precisely because Carlin's speech is considered by many to be precisely what the first amendment is *supposed* to protect. Carlin is attacking conventions; assaulting the prescribed orthodoxy; mocking the stuffed shirts; Carlin *is* the prototypical dissenter.

"It matters not at all whether the target of his invective is society at large or a public official. The outrage is that the stuffed shirts are in a position to silence Carlin, or at least in a position to keep him from 'offending' the mass audience."

2. *Implications for broadcasting.* Consider Thomas Krattenmaker & Lucas Powe, *Televised Violence: First Amendment Principles and Social Science Theory,* 64 Va.L.Rev. 1123, 1228 (1978): *Pacifica* "marks the first time any theory other than scarcity has received the official imprimatur of the Court. [S]carcity could not have authorized the result in *Pacifica* because regardless of whether one thinks the incredible abundance of radio stations in the United States (and especially in New York City) is insufficient, scarcity supports adding voices not banning them." What is the significance of the Court's comment that "the broadcast media have established a uniquely pervasive presence in the lives of all Americans"? Consider Daniel Brenner, *Censoring the Airwaves: The Supreme Court's Pacifica Decision* in Free But Regulated: Conflicting Traditions in Media Law 175, 177 & 79 (1982): "[N]ewspapers, drive-in movies, direct mail advertisements and imprinted T-shirts are media that have also 'established a uniquely pervasive presence' in our lives, in and out of [home]. Offhand comments about broadcasting enjoying 'the most limited' First Amendment protection—What of comic books? Playing cards? Chinese cookie fortunes?—are not simply harmless baffle; they constitute Delphic pronouncements made at a watershed period in the development of electronic media." See also Powe, supra fn. a, at 210–11.

Is the Court suggesting that the broadcast media are uniquely powerful? If so, should that factor cut for or against government regulation?[c] Does *Pacifica*

casts about activities involving these groups and public affairs broadcasts about their concerns are apt to contain interviews, statements, or remarks by group leaders and members which may contain offensive language to an extent my Brother Powell finds unacceptable.

b. Stewart, J., joined by Brennan, White, and Marshall, JJ., dissenting maintained that the Commission lacked statutory authority to

issue its order and did not reach the constitutional question.

c. See Powe, supra, at 211–15; Lucas Powe, *"Or of the [Broadcast] Press,"* 55 Tex.L.Rev. 39, 58–62 (1976). On the various justifications for broadcast regulation, see J.M. Balkin, *Media Filters, the V–Chip, and the Foundations of Broadcast Regulation,* 45 Duke L.J. 1131 (1996).

support regulation of sex and violence on television, of "offensive" commercials, of advertising directed toward children? See generally Matthew Spitzer, *Seven Dirty Words and Six Other Stories* (1986) (criticizing *Pacifica*'s distinctions between print and broadcast).

3.   FCC v. LEAGUE OF WOMEN VOTERS, 468 U.S. 364, 104 S.Ct. 3106, 82 L.Ed.2d 278 (1984), per BRENNAN, J., invalidated a federal law prohibiting editorializing on public broadcast stations: "As our cases attest, [broadcast restrictions] have been upheld only when we were satisfied that the restriction is narrowly tailored to further a substantial governmental interest, such as ensuring adequate and balanced coverage of public issues.[13]"

4.   *Public/Private.* David Cole, *Playing by Pornography's Rules: The Regulation of Sexual Expression,* 143 U.Pa.L.Rev. 111, 140 (1994); "The Court's sexual expression decisions can be organized along a similar public/private axis. The Court's zoning decisions allow communities to demand that when sexually explicit speech appears in public, it must be relegated to dark and distant parts of town. The Court's affirmance of the FCC's 'indecency' regulation permits the zoning of sexual speech to less 'public' times of day. And while private possession of obscenity cannot be regulated, the state is free to regulate obscenity in a public place even if it is enjoyed only by consenting adults, and even where it is only being transported through public channels for private home use. What is immune from regulation in private becomes suppressible in public, even if the very same speakers, listeners, and speech are involved."

5.   *Anti-abortion advertising.* Is graphic anti-abortion advertising indecent? Should it be channeled to the late evening hours? From the perspective of Stevens, J.? Powell, J.? See Lili Levi, *The FCC, Indecency, and Anti–Abortion Political Advertising,* 3 Vill.Spts. & Ent.L.J. 85 (1996).

6.   *Telephonic "indecency" compared.* SABLE COMMUNICATIONS v. FCC, 492 U.S. 115, 109 S.Ct. 2829, 106 L.Ed.2d 93 (1989), per WHITE, J., invalidated a congressional ban on "indecent" interstate commercial telephone messages, i.e., "dial-a-porn."[d] The Court thought *Pacifica* was "readily distinguishable from this case, most obviously because it did not involve a total ban on broadcasting indecent material. [Second,] there is no 'captive audience' problem here; callers will generally not be unwilling listeners. [Third,] the congressional record contains no legislative findings that would justify us in concluding that there is no

---

13. [*Pacifica*] is consistent with the approach taken in our other broadcast cases. There, the Court focused on certain physical characteristics of broadcasting—specifically, that the medium's uniquely pervasive presence renders impossible any prior warning for those listeners who may be offended by indecent language, and, second, that the case with which children may gain access to the medium, especially during daytime hours, creates a substantial risk that they may be exposed to such offensive expression without parental supervision. The governmental interest in reduction of those risks through Commission regulation of the timing and character of such "indecent broadcasting" was thought sufficiently substantial to outweigh the broadcaster's First Amendment interest in controlling the presentation of its programming. In this case, by

contrast, we are faced not with indecent expression, but rather with expression that is at the core of First Amendment protections, and no claim is made by the Government that the expression of editorial opinion by noncommercial stations will create a substantial "nuisance" of the kind addressed in *Pacifica*.

d. The Court upheld a ban on "obscene" interstate commercial telephonic messages. Scalia, J., concurring, noted: "[W]hile we hold the Constitution prevents Congress from banning indecent speech in this fashion, we do not hold that the Constitution requires public utilities to carry it." Brennan, J., joined by Marshall and Stevens, JJ., concurred on the indecency issue and dissented on the obscenity issue.

constitutionally acceptable less restrictive means, short of a total ban, to achieve the Government's interest in protecting minors.''

———

Cable operators are required under federal law to reserve channels for commercial lease ("leased access channels") and are routinely required by their franchise agreements with municipalities to reserve channels for public, educational, and governmental access ("public access channels" or "pegs"). For some years federal law prevented cable operators from employing any editorial control over the content of leased access or public access channels. The Cable Television Consumer Protection and Competition of 1992, however, permitted cable operators to prohibit the broadcast of material that the cable operator "reasonably believes describes or depicts sexual or excretory activities or organs in a patently offensive manner" on leased access channels (47 U.S.C.§ 10(a)) and public access channels (47 U.S.C.§ 10(c)). In addition, if the cable operator did not prohibit such material from being broadcast on leased access channels, the Act required the cable operator to provide a separate channel for the material, to scramble or otherwise block its presentation, and to permit its viewing only upon written request (47 U.S.C.§ 10(b))(the "block and segregate requirements"). After the adoption of § 10(b), Congress passed block and segregate requirements for channels primarily dedicated to sexual programming and required cable operators to honor a subscriber's request to block any undesired programs.

DENVER AREA EDUCATIONAL TELECOMMUNICATIONS CONSORTIUM, INC. v. FCC, 518 U.S. 727, 116 S.Ct. 2374, 135 L.Ed.2d 888 (1996) upheld the constitutionality of § 10(a), but invalidated §§ 10 (b) and (c). Breyer, J., joined by Stevens, O'Connor, Kennedy, and Souter, JJ., held that the segregate and block requirements (§ 10(b)) were invalid: "We agree with the Government that protection of children is a 'compelling interest.' But we do not agree that the 'segregate and block' requirements properly accommodate the speech restrictions they impose and the legitimate objective they seek to attain. Nor need we here determine whether, or the extent to which, *Pacifica* does, or does not, impose some lesser standard of review where indecent speech is at issue, compare (opinion of Stevens, J.)(indecent materials enjoy lesser First Amendment protection), with (Powell, J., concurring in part and concurring in judgment)(refusing to accept a lesser standard for nonobscene, indecent material). That is because once one examines this governmental restriction, it becomes apparent that, not only is it not a 'least restrictive alternative,' and is not 'narrowly tailored' to meet its legitimate objective, it also seems considerably 'more extensive than necessary.' That is to say, it fails to satisfy this Court's formulations of the First Amendment's 'strictest,' as well as its somewhat less 'strict,' requirements. * * *

"The record does not explain why, under the new Act, blocking alone—without written access-requests—adequately protects children from exposure to regular sex-dedicated channels, but cannot adequately protect those children from programming on similarly sex-dedicated channels that are leased. It does not explain why a simple subscriber blocking request system, perhaps a phone-call based system, would adequately protect children from 'patently offensive' material broadcast on ordinary non-sex-dedicated channels (i.e., almost all channels) but a far more restrictive segregate/block/written-access system is needed to protect children from similar broadcasts on what (in the absence of the segregation requirement) would be non-sex-dedicated channels that are leased. Nor is there any indication Congress thought the new ordinary channel protections less than adequate."

In a portion of his opinion joined by Stevens, O'Connor, and Souter, JJ., Breyer, J., concluded that § 10(a) was valid, but, in a portion of his opinion joined by Stevens and Souter, JJ., he concluded that § 10(c) was invalid. As to § 10(a), Breyer, J., observed: "Justices Kennedy and Thomas would have us decide this case simply by transferring and applying literally categorical standards this Court has developed in other contexts. For Justice Kennedy, leased access channels are like a common carrier, cablecast is a protected medium, strict scrutiny applies, § 10(a) fails this test, and, therefore, § 10(a) is invalid. For Justice Thomas, the case is simple because the cable operator who owns the system over which access channels are broadcast, like a bookstore owner with respect to what it displays on the shelves, has a predominant First Amendment interest. Both categorical approaches suffer from the same flaws: they import law developed in very different contexts into a new and changing environment, and they lack the flexibility necessary to allow government to respond to very serious practical problems without sacrificing the free exchange of ideas the First Amendment is designed to protect. * * *

"Over the years, this Court has restated and refined [basic] First Amendment principles, adopting them more particularly to the balance of competing interests and the special circumstances of each field of application. [This] tradition teaches that the First Amendment embodies an overarching commitment to protect speech from Government regulation through close judicial scrutiny, thereby enforcing the Constitution's constraints, but without imposing judicial formulae so rigid that they become a straightjacket that disables Government from responding to serious problems. This Court, in different contexts, has consistently held that the Government may directly regulate speech to address extraordinary problems, where its regulations are appropriately tailored to resolve those problems without imposing an unnecessarily great restriction on speech. Justices Kennedy and Thomas would have us further declare which, among the many applications of the general approach that this Court has developed over the years, we are applying here. But no definitive choice among competing analogies (broadcast, common carrier, bookstore) allows us to declare a rigid single standard, good for now and for all future media and purposes. That is not to say that we reject all the more specific formulations of the standard—they appropriately cover the vast majority of cases involving Government regulation of speech. Rather, aware as we are of the changes taking place in the law, the technology, and the industrial structure, related to telecommunications, we believe it unwise and unnecessary definitively to pick one analogy or one specific set of words now.

"[W]e can decide this case more narrowly, by closely scrutinizing § 10(a) to assure that it properly addresses an extremely important problem, without imposing, in light of the relevant interests, an unnecessarily great restriction on speech. The importance of the interest at stake here—protecting children from exposure to patently offensive depictions of sex; the accommodation of the interests of programmers in maintaining access channels and of cable operators in editing the contents of their channels; the similarity of the problem and its solution to those at issue in *Pacifica*, and the flexibility inherent in an approach that permits private cable operators to make editorial decisions, lead us to conclude that § 10(a) is a sufficiently tailored response to an extraordinarily important problem. * * *

"[W]e part company with Justice Kennedy on two issues. First, Justice Kennedy's focus on categorical analysis forces him to disregard the cable system operators' interests. We, on the other hand, recognize that in the context of cable broadcast that involves an access requirement (here, its partial removal), and unlike in most cases where we have explicitly required 'narrow tailoring,' the expressive interests of cable operators do play a legitimate role. Cf. *Turner*. While we cannot agree with Justice Thomas that everything turns on the rights of the cable owner, we also cannot agree with Justice Kennedy that we must ignore the expressive interests of cable operators altogether. Second, Justice Kennedy's application of a very strict 'narrow tailoring' test depends upon an analogy with a category ('the public forum cases'), which has been distilled over time from the similarities of many cases. Rather than seeking an analogy to a category of cases, however, we have looked to the cases themselves. And, [we find] that *Pacifica* provides the closest analogy. * * *

"The Court's distinction in *Turner*, [between] cable and broadcast television, relied on the inapplicability of the spectrum scarcity problem to cable. While that distinction was relevant in *Turner* to the justification for structural regulations at issue there (the 'must carry' rules), it has little to do with a case that involves the effects of television viewing on children. Those effects are the result of how parents and children view television programming, and how pervasive and intrusive that programming is. In that respect, cable and broadcast television differ little, if at all.

"[I]f one wishes to view the permissive provisions before us through a 'public forum' lens, one should view those provisions as limiting the otherwise totally open nature of the forum that leased access channels provide for communication of other than patently offensive sexual material—taking account of the fact that the limitation was imposed in light of experience gained from maintaining a totally open 'forum.' One must still ask whether the First Amendment forbids the limitation. But unless a label alone were to make a critical First Amendment difference (and we think here it does not), the features of this case that we have already discussed—the government's interest in protecting children, the 'permissive' aspect of the statute, and the nature of the medium—sufficiently justify the 'limitation' on the availability of this forum."

Breyer, J., argued that the balance was different in § 10(c): "[C]able operators have traditionally agreed to reserve channel capacity for public, governmental, and educational channels as part of the consideration they give municipalities that award them cable franchises. [Thus] these are channels over which cable operators have not historically exercised editorial control. Unlike § 10(a) therefore, s 10(c) does not restore to cable operators editorial rights that they once had, and the countervailing First Amendment interest is nonexistent, or at least much diminished.

"[A] second difference is the institutional background that has developed as a result of the historical difference. When a 'leased channel' is made available by the operator to a private lessee, the lessee has total control of programming during the leased time slot. Public access channels, on the other hand, are normally subject to complex supervisory systems of various sorts, often with both public and private elements. [G]iven present supervisory mechanisms, the need for this particular provision, aimed directly at public access channels, is not obvious."

Stevens, J., concurring, agreed with Breyer, J., that it was unwise to characterize leased channels as public fora: "When the Federal Government opens cable channels that would otherwise be left entirely in private hands, it deserves more deference than a rigid application of the public forum doctrine would allow. At this early stage in the regulation of this developing industry, Congress should not be put to an all or nothing-at-all choice in deciding whether to open certain cable channels to programmers who would otherwise lack the resources to participate in the marketplace of ideas."

With respect to § 10(c), Stevens, J., stated: "What is of critical importance to me, however, is that if left to their own devices, those authorities may choose to carry some programming that the Federal Government has decided to restrict. As I read § 10(c), the federal statute would disable local governments from making that choice. It would inject federally authorized private censors into forums from which they might otherwise be excluded, and it would therefore limit local forums that might otherwise be open to all constitutionally protected speech."[3]

SOUTER, J., concurred: "All of the relevant characteristics of cable are presently in a state of technological and regulatory flux. Recent and far-reaching legislation not only affects the technical feasibility of parental control over children's access to undesirable material but portends fundamental changes in the competitive structure of the industry and, therefore, the ability of individual entities to act as bottlenecks to the free flow of information. As cable and telephone companies begin their competition for control over the single wire that will carry both their services, we can hardly settle rules for review of regulation on the assumption that cable will remain a separable and useful category of First Amendment scrutiny. And as broadcast, cable, and the cyber-technology of the Internet and the World Wide Web approach the day of using a common receiver, we can hardly assume that standards for judging the regulation of one of them will not have immense, but now unknown and unknowable, effects on the others. * * *

"The upshot of appreciating the fluidity of the subject that Congress must regulate is simply to accept the fact that not every nuance of our old standards will necessarily do for the new technology, and that a proper choice among existing doctrinal categories is not obvious. Rather than definitively settling the issue now, Justice Breyer wisely reasons by direct analogy rather than by rule, concluding that the speech and the restriction at issue in this case may usefully be measured against the ones at issue in *Pacifica*. If that means it will take some time before reaching a final method of review for cases like this one, there may be consolation in recalling that 16 years passed, from *Roth* to *Miller*, before the modern obscenity rule jelled; that it took over 40 years, from *Hague v. CIO* to *Perry*, for the public forum category to settle out; and that a round half-century passed before the clear and present danger of *Schenck* evolved into the modern incitement rule of *Brandenburg*.

"I cannot guess how much time will go by until the technologies of communication before us today have matured and their relationships become known. But until a category of indecency can be defined both with reference to the new technology and with a prospect of durability, the job of the courts will be just what Justice Breyer does today: recognizing established First Amendment interests through a close analysis that constrains the Congress, without wholly incapacitating it in all matters of the significance apparent here, maintaining the high value

---

3. Although in 1984 Congress essentially barred cable operators from exercising editorial control over PEG channels, see 47 U.S.C. § 531(e), Section 10(c) does not merely restore the status quo ante. Section 10(c) authorizes private operators to exercise editorial discre-

tion over "indecent" programming even if the franchising authority objects. Under the pre-1984 practice, local franchising authorities were free to exclude operators from exercising any such control on PEG channels.

of open communication, measuring the costs of regulation by exact attention to fact, and compiling a pedigree of experience with the changing subject. These are familiar judicial responsibilities in times when we know too little to risk the finality of precision, and attention to them will probably take us through the communications revolution. Maybe the judicial obligation to shoulder these responsibilities can itself be captured by a much older rule, familiar to every doctor of medicine: 'First, do no harm.' ''

O'CONNOR, J., concurring in part and dissenting in part, agreed with Breyer, J.'s assessment that § 10(a) was valid and § 10(b) invalid. She argued, however, that Breyer, J.'s distinctions regarding § 10(c) were insufficiently weighty: "The interest in protecting children remains the same, whether on a leased access channel or a public access channel, and allowing the cable operator the option of prohibiting the transmission of indecent speech seems a constitutionally permissible means of addressing that interest. Nor is the fact that public access programming may be subject to supervisory systems in addition to the cable operator sufficient in my mind to render § 10(c) so ill-tailored to its goal as to be unconstitutional."

KENNEDY, J., joined by Ginsburg, J., concurring in part and dissenting in part, agreed that § 10(b) and (c) were invalid, but faulted the plurality opinion for its upholding of § 10(a): "The plurality opinion, insofar as it upholds § 10(a) [is] adrift. The opinion treats concepts such as public forum, broadcaster, and common carrier as mere labels rather than as categories with settled legal significance; it applies no standard, and by this omission loses sight of existing First Amendment doctrine. When confronted with a threat to free speech in the context of an emerging technology, we ought to have the discipline to analyze the case by reference to existing elaborations of constant First Amendment principles. This is the essence of the case-by-case approach to ensuring protection of speech under the First Amendment, even in novel settings. * * *

"The plurality begins its flight from standards with a number of assertions nobody disputes. I agree, of course, that it would be unwise 'to declare a rigid single standard, good for now and for all future media and purposes.' I do think it necessary, however, to decide what standard applies to discrimination against indecent programming on cable access channels in the present state of the industry. We owe at least that much to public and leased access programmers whose speech is put at risk nationwide by these laws. * * *

"The plurality claims its resistance to standards is in keeping with our case law, where we have shown a willingness to be flexible in confronting novel First Amendment problems. [W]e have developed specialized or more or less stringent standards when certain contexts demanded them; we did not avoid the use of standards altogether. Indeed, the creation of standards and adherence to them, even when it means affording protection to speech unpopular or distasteful, is the central achievement of our First Amendment jurisprudence. Standards are the means by which we state in advance how to test a law's validity, rather than letting the height of the bar be determined by the apparent exigencies of the day. They also provide notice and fair warning to those who must predict how the courts will respond to attempts to suppress their speech. Yet formulations like strict scrutiny, used in a number of constitutional settings to ensure that the inequities of the moment are subordinated to commitments made for the long run mean little if they can be watered down whenever they seem too strong. They mean still less if they can be ignored altogether when considering a case not on all fours with what we have seen before.

"The plurality seems distracted by the many changes in technology and competition in the cable industry. The laws challenged here, however, do not retool the structure of the cable industry or (with the exception of § 10(b)) involve intricate technologies. The straightforward issue here is whether the Government can deprive certain speakers, on the basis of the content of their speech, of protections afforded all others. There is no reason to discard our existing First Amendment jurisprudence in answering this question.

"While it protests against standards, the plurality does seem to favor one formulation of the question in this case: namely, whether the Act 'properly addresses an extremely important problem, without imposing, in light of the relevant interests, an unnecessarily great restriction on speech.' [This] description of the question accomplishes little, save to clutter our First Amendment case law by adding an untested rule with an uncertain relationship to the others we use to evaluate laws restricting speech. * * *

"Justice Souter recommends to the Court the precept 'First, do no harm.' The question, though, is whether the harm is in sustaining the law or striking it down. If the plurality is concerned about technology's direction, it ought to begin by allowing speech, not suppressing it. We have before us an urgent claim for relief against content-based discrimination, not a dry run.

"The constitutionality under *Turner Broadcasting* of requiring a cable operator to set aside leased access channels is not before us. For purposes of this case, we should treat the cable operator's rights in these channels as extinguished, and address the issue these petitioners present: namely, whether the Government can discriminate on the basis of content in affording protection to certain programmers. I cannot agree with Justice Thomas that the cable operator's rights inform this analysis.

"Laws requiring cable operators to provide leased access are the practical equivalent of making them common carriers, analogous in this respect to telephone companies: They are obliged to provide a conduit for the speech of others. [Laws] removing common-carriage protection from a single form of speech based on its content should be reviewed under the same standard as content-based restrictions on speech in a public forum. Making a cable operator a common carrier does not create a public forum in the sense of taking property from private control and dedicating it to public use; rather, regulations of a common carrier dictate the manner in which private control is exercised. A common-carriage mandate, nonetheless, serves the same function as a public forum. It ensures open, nondiscriminatory access to the means of communication.

"*Pacifica* did not purport, however, to apply a special standard for indecent broadcasting. Emphasizing the narrowness of its holding, the Court in *Pacifica* conducted a context-specific analysis of the FCC's restriction on indecent programming during daytime hours. It relied on the general rule that 'broadcasting * * * has received the most limited First Amendment protection.' We already have rejected the application of this lower broadcast standard of review to infringements on the liberties of cable operators, even though they control an important communications medium. *Turner.* * * *

"[Indecency] often is inseparable from the ideas and viewpoints conveyed, or separable only with loss of truth or expressive power. Under our traditional First Amendment jurisprudence, factors perhaps justifying some restriction on indecent cable programming may all be taken into account without derogating this category of protected speech as marginal.

"Congress does have, however, a compelling interest in protecting children from indecent speech. So long as society gives proper respect to parental choices, it may, under an appropriate standard, intervene to spare children exposure to material not suitable for minors. This interest is substantial enough to justify some regulation of indecent speech even under, I will assume, the [strict scrutiny standard].

"Sections 10(a) and (c) nonetheless are not narrowly tailored to protect children from indecent programs on access channels. First, to the extent some operators may allow indecent programming, children in localities those operators serve will be left unprotected. Partial service of a compelling interest is not narrow tailoring. Put another way, the interest in protecting children from indecency only at the caprice of the cable operator is not compelling. Perhaps Congress drafted the law this way to avoid the clear constitutional difficulties of banning indecent speech from access channels, but the First Amendment does not permit this sort of ill fit between a law restricting speech and the interest it is said to serve.

"Second, to the extent cable operators prohibit indecent programming on access channels, not only children but adults will be deprived of it."

THOMAS, J., joined by Rehnquist, C.J., and Scalia, J., concurring in part and dissenting in part, argued that §§ 10(a),(b), and (c) validly protected the constitutional rights of cable operators: "It is one thing to compel an operator to carry leased and public access speech, in apparent violation of *Tornillo*, but it is another thing altogether to say that the First Amendment forbids Congress to give back part of the operators' editorial discretion, which all recognize as fundamentally protected, in favor of a broader access right. It is no answer to say that leased and public access are content neutral and that §§ 10(a) and (c) are not, for that does not change the fundamental fact, which petitioners never address, that it is the operators' journalistic freedom that is infringed, whether the challenged restrictions be content neutral or content based.

"Because the access provisions are part of a scheme that restricts the free speech rights of cable operators, and expands the speaking opportunities of access programmers, who have no underlying constitutional right to speak through the cable medium, I do not believe that access programmers can challenge the scheme, or a particular part of it, as an abridgment of their 'freedom of speech.' Outside the public forum doctrine, government intervention that grants access programmers an opportunity to speak that they would not otherwise enjoy—and which does not directly limit programmers' underlying speech rights—cannot be an abridgement of the same programmers' First Amendment rights, even if the new speaking opportunity is content-based.

"The permissive nature of §§ 10(a) and (c) is important in this regard. If Congress had forbidden cable operators to carry indecent programming on leased and public access channels, that law would have burdened the programmer's right, recognized in *Turner* to compete for space on an operator's system. The Court would undoubtedly strictly scrutinize such a law. * * *

"Petitioners argue that public access channels are public fora in which they have First Amendment rights to speak and that § 10(c) is invalid because it imposes content-based burdens on those rights. * * *

"Cable systems are not public property. Cable systems are privately owned and privately managed, and petitioners point to no case in which we have held that government may designate private property as a public forum.

"Pursuant to federal and state law, franchising authorities require cable operators to create public access channels, but nothing in the record suggests that local franchising authorities take any formal easement or other property interest in those channels that would permit the government to designate that property as a public forum.

"Public access channels are not public fora, and, therefore, petitioners' attempt to redistribute cable speech rights in their favor must fail. For this reason, and the other reasons articulated earlier, I would sustain both § 10(a) and § 10(c).

"Unlike §§ 10(a) and (c), § 10(b) clearly implicates petitioners' free speech rights. Though § 10(b) by no means bans indecent speech, it clearly places content-based restrictions on the transmission of private speech by requiring cable operators to block and segregate indecent programming that the operator has agreed to carry. Consequently, § 10(b) must be subjected to strict scrutiny and can be upheld only if it furthers a compelling governmental interest by the least restrictive means available.

"The Court strikes down § 10(b) by pointing to alternatives, such as reverse-blocking [that] it says are less restrictive than segregation and blocking. Though these methods attempt to place in parents' hands the ability to permit their children to watch as little, or as much, indecent programming as the parents think proper, they do not effectively support parents' authority to direct the moral upbringing of their children. The FCC recognized that leased-access programming comes 'from a wide variety of independent sources, with no single editor controlling [its] selection and presentation.' Thus, indecent programming on leased access channels is 'especially likely to be shown randomly or intermittently between non-indecent programs.' Rather than being able to simply block out certain channels at certain times, a subscriber [must] carefully monitor all leased-access programming. [The Court's alternative is] largely ineffective."

Notes and Questions

1. Consider Yochai Benkler, *Free as the Air to Common Use: First Amendment Constraints on Enclosure of the Public Domain*, 74 N.Y.U. L. Rev. 354 (1999): "Beneath the veneer of an indecency case, *Denver Area* was a case about access rights. [A] majority of the justices acknowledged that access rights to the cable medium served the First Amendment by permitting many and diverse sources to reach viewers over this concentrated medium. These justices treated decisions by cable operators not to carry programming as 'censorial,' and acknowledged that the availability of access to the medium was a question of constitutional moment. Only the partial dissent by Justice Thomas thought that government intervention by requiring access rights was the relevant constitutional concern." Compare Jerome A. Barron, *The Electronic Media and the Flight From First Amendment Doctrine: Justice Breyer's New Balancing Approach*, 31 U. Mich. J.L. Ref. 817, 868, 870 (1998): "Justice Breyer's [balancing] approach [provided] specific consideration to the access for expression dimension of the cable regulations under review in *Denver Area*. Access rights must be weighed against the free speech rights of the cable operator. For Justice Thomas, no First Amendment rights conflicted in *Denver Area* because the only rights asserted that merit First Amendment status were those of the cable operator. [Thomas, J.,] noted that the rationale behind the plurality was not 'intuitively obvious' as to why programmers and viewers have any First Amendment rights. In reality, however, it is not intuitively obvious that cable operators enjoy the whole panoply of First Amend-

ment rights either. [T]o say that mandatory public access and leased access channels violate *Tornillo* would be an extravagant statement. If the rights of the communications entity's owners were intended to trump all other claims to First Amendment protection for all media, *Tornillo* would have been the ideal occasion to make that statement. The *Tornillo* Court instead directed itself to the print media alone and did not so much as cite *Red Lion*, the most obvious contrary electronic media precedent then extant."

2. Consider Jonathan Weinberg, *Cable TV, Indecency and the Court*, 21 Colum.-VLA J.L. & Arts 95, 128 (1997): '[*Pacifica*'s] reasoning and jurisprudential approach are back. This is disturbing. The history of First Amendment decision making in this century suggests that rules are more effective than ad hoc analysis in protecting speech from the fears and repression of the moment. Justice Breyer, in the *Denver Area* plurality opinion, attributed his contextual approach to 'the changes taking place in the law, the technology, and the industrial structure,' which, he said, made any attempt to enunciate abstract doctrine premature. The deeper message of the plurality opinion, though, is that no matter how technology evolves, *Pacifica*'s contextual approach—not the law of rules—will continue to guide content-based regulation of media that feel like television."

3. § 505 of the Telecommunications Act of 1996 requires that cable television operators who provide channels "primarily dedicated to sexually-oriented programming" either "fully scramble or otherwise fully block" the channels so that non-subscribers to the programming would not be able to hear or see it. The art of scrambling has not been perfected, however. "Signal bleed" occurs on many channels, allowing some of the visual and audio aspects of the programming to be heard or seen. In the case of signal bleed, the act requires that the programming be blocked except during hours when children are unlikely to be viewing. The F.C.C.'s regulations provide that those hours are between 10 p.m. and 6 a.m ("the safe harbor provision"). § 504 of the same act required operators to block other programming upon a subscriber's request. A cable television programmer challenged § 505.

———

UNITED STATES v. PLAYBOY ENTERTAINMENT GROUP, 529 U.S. 803, 120 S.Ct. 1878, 146 L.Ed.2d 865 (2000), per KENNEDY, J., declared the restriction to be content-based with a serious impact on protected speech and held that it did not survive strict scrutiny. Kennedy, J., doubted that signal bleed was sufficiently substantial to imperil children and argued that the government had not demonstrated that a requirement to block upon request with notice of the option provided to the subscriber could not be an effective, but less restrictive alternative: "When the statute became operative, most cable operators had 'no practical choice but to curtail [the targeted] programming during the [regulated] sixteen hours or risk the penalties imposed [i]f any audio or video signal bleed occur[red] during [those] times.' The majority of operators—[in one survey, 69%]—complied with § 505 by time channeling the targeted programmers. Since '30 to 50% of all adult programming is viewed by households prior to 10 p.m.,' the result was a significant restriction of communication, with a corresponding reduction in Playboy's revenues. * * *

"Our zoning cases [a]re irrelevant to the question here. We have made clear that the lesser scrutiny afforded regulations targeting the secondary effects of crime or declining property values has no application to content-based regulations

Strict Scrutiny (handwritten note)

targeting the primary effects of protected speech. The statute now before us burdens speech because of its content; it must receive strict scrutiny.

"[A] key difference between cable television and the broadcasting media [is] the point on which this case turns: Cable systems have the capacity to block unwanted channels on a household-by-household basis. The option to block reduces the likelihood, so concerning to the Court in *Pacifica*, that traditional First Amendment scrutiny would deprive the Government of all authority to address this sort of problem. The corollary, of course, is that targeted blocking enables the Government to support parental authority without affecting the First Amendment interests of speakers and willing listeners—listeners for whom, if the speech is unpopular or indecent, the privacy of their own homes may be the optimal place of receipt. Simply put, targeted blocking is less restrictive than banning, and the Government cannot ban speech if targeted blocking is a feasible and effective means of furthering its compelling interests. [When] a plausible, less restrictive alternative is offered to a content-based speech restriction, it is the Government's obligation to prove that the alternative will be ineffective to achieve its goals. The Government has not met that burden here."

STEVENS, J., concurred: "Because Justice Scalia has advanced an argument that the parties have not addressed, a brief response is in order. Relying on *Ginzburg v. United States*, Justice Scalia would treat programs whose content is, he assumes, protected by the First Amendment as though they were obscene because of the way they are advertised. The [*Ginzburg*] theory of obscenity is a legal fiction premised upon a logical bait-and-switch; advertising a bareheaded dancer as 'topless' might be deceptive, but it would not make her performance obscene."[a]

SCALIA, J., dissenting, thought that obscenity law was relevant even if none of the programming was obscene: "We have recognized that commercial entities which engage in 'the sordid business of pandering' by 'deliberately emphasiz[ing] the sexually provocative aspects of [their nonobscene products], in order to catch the salaciously disposed,' engage in constitutionally unprotected behavior. *Ginzburg* . We are more permissive of government regulation in these circumstances because it is clear from the context in which exchanges between such businesses and their customers occur that neither the merchant nor the buyer is interested in the work's literary, artistic, political, or scientific value.

"Section 505 regulates just this sort of business. [It] is conceivable, I suppose, that a channel which is primarily dedicated to sex might not hold itself forth as primarily dedicated to sex—in which case its productions which contain 'serious literary, artistic, political, or scientific value' (if any) would be as entitled to First Amendment protection as the statuary rooms of the National Gallery. But in the competitive world of cable programming, the possibility that a channel devoted to sex would not advertise itself as such is sufficiently remote, and the number of such channels sufficiently small (if not indeed nonexistent), as not to render the provision substantially overbroad."[2]

---

a. Thomas, J., concurring, indicated that the case would be different if the government had proceeded against aspects of the programming that were obscene.

2. Justice Stevens misapprehends in several respects the nature of the test I would apply. First, he mistakenly believes that the nature of the advertising controls the obscenity analysis, regardless of the nature of the material being advertised. I entirely agree with him that 'advertising a bareheaded dancer as "topless"' might be deceptive, but it would not make her performance obscene.' I believe, however, that if the material is 'patently offensive' and it is being advertised as such, we have little reason to think it is being proffered for its socially redeeming value. * * *

Breyer, J., joined by Rehnquist, C.J., and O'Connor, and Scalia, JJ., dissenting, argued that the section was justified by the compelling interest in protecting children. He maintained that the suggested alternative of having subscribers ask for blocking if they wished was impractical: "As the majority observes, during the 14 months the Government was enjoined from enforcing § 505, 'fewer than 0.5% of cable subscribers requested full blocking' under § 504. The majority describes this public reaction as 'a collective yawn,' adding that the Government failed to prove that the 'yawn' reflected anything other than the lack of a serious signal bleed problem or a lack of notice which better information about § 504 might cure. The record excludes the first possibility—at least in respect to exposure, as discussed above. And I doubt that the public, though it may well consider the viewing habits of adults a matter of personal choice, would 'yawn' when the exposure in question concerns young children, the absence of parental consent, and the sexually explicit material here at issue.

"Neither is the record neutral in respect to the curative power of better notice. [An] opt-out right works only when parents (1) become aware of their [rights], (2) discover that their children are watching sexually-explicit signal 'bleed,' (3) reach their cable operator and ask that it block the sending of its signal to their home, (4) await installation of an individual blocking device, and, perhaps (5) (where the block fails or the channel number changes) make a new request. Better notice of [blocking rights] does little to help parents discover their children's viewing habits (step two). And it does nothing at all in respect to steps three through five. Yet the record contains considerable evidence that those problems matter, i.e., evidence of endlessly delayed phone call responses, faulty installations, blocking failures, and other mishaps, leaving those steps as significant [obstacles]."

Two provisions of the Communications Decency Act ("CDA") seek to protect minors from material on the Internet. 47 U.S.C. § 223(a) prohibits the knowing transmission of indecent messages to any recipient under 18 years of age. 47 U.S.C. § 223(d) prohibits the knowing sending or displaying of patently offensive messages in a manner that is available to a person under 18 years of age. Patently offensive is defined as any "image or other communication that in context, depicts or describes, in terms patently offensive as measured by contemporary community standards, sexual or excretory activities or organs * * * ."

RENO v. AMERICAN CIVIL LIBERTIES UNION, 521 U.S. 844, 117 S.Ct. 2329, 138 L.Ed.2d 874 (1997), per Stevens, J., after providing a lengthy description of the Internet focusing on e-mail, automatic mailing list services, newsgroups, chatrooms, and the WORLD Wide Web held that both provisions were too vague and overbroad to withstand first amendment scrutiny.[a] "In four important respects, the statute upheld in *Ginsberg* was narrower than the CDA. First, we noted in *Ginsberg* that 'the prohibition against sales to minors does not bar parents who so desire from purchasing the magazines for their children.' Under the CDA, by contrast, neither the parents' consent—nor even their participation—in the communication would avoid the application of the statute.[32] Second, the

---

a. The CDA also prohibited obscenity on the Internet. That portion of the statute was not challenged, and the Court noted that it had not struck it down.

32. Given the likelihood that many E-mail transmissions from an adult to a minor are conversations between family members, it is therefore incorrect for the dissent to suggest

New York statute applied only to commercial transactions, whereas the CDA contains no such limitation. Third, the New York statute cabined its definition of material that is harmful to minors with the requirement that it be 'utterly without redeeming social importance for minors.' The CDA fails to provide us with any definition of the term 'indecent' as used in § 223(a)(1) and, importantly, omits any requirement that the 'patently offensive' material covered by § 223(d) lack serious literary, artistic, political, or scientific value. Fourth, the New York statute defined a minor as a person under the age of 17, whereas the CDA, in applying to all those under 18 years, includes an additional year of those nearest majority. [Those] factors are not present in cyberspace. Neither before nor after the enactment of the CDA have the vast democratic fora of the Internet been subject to the type of government supervision and regulation that has attended the broadcast industry. Moreover, the Internet is not as 'invasive' as radio or television. The District Court specifically found that '[c]ommunications over the Internet do not 'invade' an individual's home or appear on one's computer screen unbidden. * * * 'It also found that '[a]lmost all sexually explicit images are preceded by warnings as to the content,' and cited testimony that "odds are slim" that a user would come across a sexually explicit sight by accident.' * * *

"Finally, unlike the conditions that prevailed when Congress first authorized regulation of the broadcast spectrum, the Internet can hardly be considered a 'scarce' expressive commodity. It provides relatively unlimited, low-cost capacity for communication of all kinds. [As] the District Court found, 'the content on the Internet is as diverse as human thought.' * * *

"Regardless of whether the CDA is so vague that it violates the Fifth Amendment, the many ambiguities concerning the scope of its coverage render it problematic for purposes of the First Amendment. For instance, each of the two parts of the CDA uses a different linguistic form. The first uses the word 'indecent,' 47 U.S.C.A. § 223(a), while the second speaks of material that 'in context, depicts or describes, in terms patently offensive as measured by contemporary community standards, sexual or excretory activities or organs,' § 223(d). Given the absence of a definition of either term,[35] this difference in language will provoke uncertainty among speakers about how the two standards relate to each other and just what they mean.[37] Could a speaker confidently assume that a serious discussion about birth control practices, homosexuality, the First Amendment issues raised by the Appendix to our *Pacifica* opinion, or the consequences of prison rape would not violate the CDA? This uncertainty undermines the likelihood that the CDA has been carefully tailored to the congressional goal of protecting minors from potentially harmful materials.

"The vagueness of the CDA is a matter of special concern for two reasons. First, the CDA is a content-based regulation of speech [with] penalties including up to two years in prison for each act of violation. The severity of criminal sanctions may well cause speakers to remain silent rather than communicate even arguably unlawful words, ideas, and images. As a practical matter, this increased

that the provisions of the CDA, even in this narrow area, "are no different from the law we sustained in *Ginsberg*."

35. "Indecent" does not benefit from any textual embellishment at all. "Patently offensive" is qualified only to the extent that it involves "sexual or excretory activities or organs" taken "in context" and "measured by contemporary community standards."

37. The statute does not indicate whether the "patently offensive" and "indecent" determinations should be made with respect to minors or the population as a whole. The Government asserts that the appropriate standard is "what is suitable material for minors." But the Conferees expressly rejected amendments that would have imposed such a "harmful to minors" standard.

deterrent effect, coupled with the 'risk of discriminatory enforcement' of vague regulations, poses greater First Amendment concerns than those implicated by the civil regulation reviewed in *Denver Area Ed. Telecommunications Consortium*. * * *

"Because the CDA's 'patently offensive' standard (and, we assume arguendo, its synonymous 'indecent' standard) is one part of the three-prong *Miller* test, the Government reasons, it cannot be unconstitutionally vague. [The] Government's assertion is incorrect as a matter of fact. The second prong of the *Miller* test—the purportedly analogous standard—contains a critical requirement that is omitted from the CDA: that the proscribed material be 'specifically defined by the applicable state law.' [Moreover,] the *Miller* definition is limited to 'sexual conduct,' whereas the CDA extends also to include (1) 'excretory activities' as well as (2) 'organs' of both a sexual and excretory nature.

"The Government's reasoning is also flawed. [Each] of *Miller's* additional two prongs—(1) that, taken as a whole, the material appeal to the 'prurient' interest, and (2) that it 'lac[k] serious literary, artistic, political, or scientific value'—critically limits the uncertain sweep of the obscenity definition. The second requirement is particularly important because, unlike the 'patently offensive' and 'prurient interest' criteria, it is not judged by contemporary community standards. This 'societal value' requirement, absent in the CDA, allows appellate courts to impose some limitations and regularity on the definition by setting, as a matter of law, a national floor for socially redeeming value. The Government's contention that courts will be able to give such legal limitations to the CDA's standards is belied by *Miller's* own rationale for having juries determine whether material is 'patently offensive' according to community standards: that such questions are essentially ones of fact. * * *

"It is true that we have repeatedly recognized the governmental interest in protecting children from harmful materials. But that interest does not justify an unnecessarily broad suppression of speech addressed to adults. [In] arguing that the CDA does not so diminish adult communication, the Government relies on the incorrect factual premise that prohibiting a transmission whenever it is known that one of its recipients is a minor would not interfere with adult-to-adult communication. The findings of the District Court make clear that this premise is untenable. Given the size of the potential audience for most messages, in the absence of a viable age verification process, the sender must be charged with knowing that one or more minors will likely view it. Knowledge that, for instance, one or more members of a 100–person chat group will be [a] minor—and therefore that it would be a crime to send the group an indecent message—would surely burden communication among adults.

"The District Court found that at the time of trial existing technology did not include any effective method for a sender to prevent minors from obtaining access to its communications on the Internet without also denying access to adults. The Court found no effective way to determine the age of a user who is accessing material through e-mail, mail exploders, newsgroups, or chat rooms. As a practical matter, the Court also found that it would be prohibitively expensive for noncommercial—as well as some commercial—speakers who have Web sites to verify that their users are adults. These limitations must inevitably curtail a significant amount of adult communication on the Internet. By contrast, the District Court found that '[d]espite its limitations, currently available user-based software suggests that a reasonably effective method by which parents can prevent their children from accessing sexually explicit and other material which parents may believe is inappropriate for their children will soon be widely available.'

"The breadth of the CDA's coverage is wholly unprecedented. Unlike the regulations upheld in *Ginsberg* and *Pacifica,* the scope of the CDA is not limited to commercial speech or commercial entities. [The] general, undefined terms 'indecent' and 'patently offensive' cover large amounts of nonpornographic material with serious educational or other value. Moreover, the 'community standards' criterion as applied to the Internet means that any communication available to a nation-wide audience will be judged by the standards of the community most likely to be offended by the message. The regulated subject matter includes any of the seven 'dirty words' used in the *Pacifica* monologue, the use of which the Government's expert acknowledged could constitute a felony. It may also extend to discussions about prison rape or safe sexual practices, artistic images that include nude subjects, and arguably the card catalogue of the Carnegie Library.

"For the purposes of our decision, we need neither accept nor reject the Government's submission that the First Amendment does not forbid a blanket prohibition on all 'indecent' and 'patently offensive' messages communicated to a 17–year old—no matter how much value the message may contain and regardless of parental approval. It is at least clear that the strength of the Government's interest in protecting minors is not equally strong throughout the coverage of this broad statute. Under the CDA, a parent allowing her 17–year–old to use the family computer to obtain information on the Internet that she, in her parental judgment, deems appropriate could face a lengthy prison term. Similarly, a parent who sent his 17–year–old college freshman information on birth control via e-mail could be incarcerated even though neither he, his child, nor anyone in their home community, found the material 'indecent' or 'patently offensive,' if the college town's community thought otherwise.

"The breadth of this content-based restriction of speech imposes an especially heavy burden on the Government to explain why a less restrictive provision would not be as effective as the CDA. It has not done so. The arguments in this Court have referred to possible alternatives such as requiring that indecent material be 'tagged' in a way that facilitates parental control of material coming into their homes, making exceptions for messages with artistic or educational value, providing some tolerance for parental choice, and regulating some portions of the Internet—such as commercial web sites—differently than others, such as chat rooms. Particularly in the light of the absence of any detailed findings by the Congress, or even hearings addressing the special problems of the CDA, we are persuaded that the CDA is not narrowly tailored if that requirement has any meaning at all."

O'CONNOR, J., joined by Rehnquist, C.J., concurred in part and dissented in part: "Given the present state of cyberspace, I agree with the Court that the 'display' provision cannot pass muster. Until gateway technology is available throughout cyberspace, and it is not in 1997, a speaker cannot be reasonably assured that the speech he displays will reach only adults because it is impossible to confine speech to an 'adult zone.' Thus, the only way for a speaker to avoid liability under the CDA is to refrain completely from using indecent speech.

"[T]he 'indecency transmission' provision makes it a crime to transmit knowingly an indecent message to a person the sender knows is under 18 years of age. The 'specific person' provision proscribes the same conduct, although it does not as explicitly require the sender to know that the intended recipient of his indecent message is a minor. Appellant urges the Court to construe the provision to impose such a knowledge requirement, and I would do so.

"So construed, both provisions are constitutional as applied to a conversation involving only an adult and one or more minors—e.g., when an adult speaker sends an e-mail knowing the addressee is a minor, or when an adult and minor converse by themselves or with other minors in a chat room. In this context, these provisions are no different from the law we sustained in *Ginsberg*. Restricting what the adult may say to the minors in no way restricts the adult's ability to communicate with other adults. * * *

"The analogy to *Ginsberg* breaks down, however, when more than one adult is a party to the conversation. If a minor enters a chat room otherwise occupied by adults, the CDA effectively requires the adults in the room to stop using indecent speech. [The] CDA is therefore akin to a law that makes it a crime for a bookstore owner to sell pornographic magazines to anyone once a minor enters his store. Even assuming such a law might be constitutional in the physical world as a reasonable alternative to excluding minors completely from the store, the absence of any means of excluding minors from chat rooms in cyberspace restricts the rights of adults to engage in indecent speech in those rooms. [The] Court neither 'accept[s] nor reject[s]' the argument that the CDA is facially overbroad because it substantially interferes with the First Amendment rights of minors. I would reject it. [In] my view, the universe of speech constitutionally protected as to minors but banned by the CDA—i.e., the universe of material that is 'patently offensive,' but which nonetheless has some redeeming value for minors or does not appeal to their prurient interest—is a very small one. Appellees cite no examples of speech falling within this universe and do not attempt to explain why that universe is substantial 'in relation to the statute's plainly legitimate sweep.' [There] is also no evidence in the record to support the contention that 'many [e]-mail transmissions from an adult to a minor are conversations between family members,' and no support for the legal proposition that such speech is absolutely immune from regulation. Accordingly, in my view, the CDA does not burden a substantial amount of minors' constitutionally protected speech."[b]

Notes and Questions

1. Consider Marjorie Heins, *Indecency: The Ongoing American Debate Over Sex, Children, Free Speech, and Dirty Words* (1997): "It remains to be see whether *Reno* will prove an idiosycratically broad response to a broadly drafted law, or whether its recognition of the positive value of some speech about some speech, even for minors, will mark the beginning of a long-overdue process of actually examining the presumption that sexual explicitness or crude language is intrinsically harmful to the young."[c]

2. Was it a mistake for the Court to suggest that a heavy burden on protected speech might be salvaged if a compelling governmental interest test could be satisfied? To what extent does first amendment doctrine permit substantial burdens on otherwise protected speech? See Eugene Volokh, *Freedom of Speech, Shielding Children, and Transcending Balancing*, 1997 Sup.Ct.Rev. 141.

b. Stevens, J., argued that Congress had not provided guidance as to where lines should be drawn if the statute were otherwise to be struck down. Lacking guidance, he declined to find that the statute was readily subject to a narrowing construction.

c. See generally Catherine J. Ross, *Anything Goes: Examining the State's Interest in Protecting Children From Controversial Speech*, 53 Vand. L.Rev. 427 (2000).

3.   Are the application of obscenity laws to the internet problematic since the manager of a website can not discern the jurisdiction from which a person is seeking to gain access. Does this force sexually oriented speech to comply with the most conservative jurisdiction and substantially burden protected speech?[d]

4.   Suppose a public library installs filter software on its computers designed to block websites with material that could be harmful to children. If a patron wishes to gain access to an excluded site, the librarian would decide if the material was age appropriate. Constitutional?

5.   Suppose the government outlawed filter software. Would this be constitutional as "a market-structuring device designed content-neutrally to make unrated fare more competitive and available to a wider variety of households, akin to the cable must-carry regulations upheld in *Turner.*" Kathleen M. Sullivan, *First Amendment Intermediaries in the Age of Cyberspace*, 45 UCLA L.Rev. 1653, 1678 (1998).

6.   The Child Online Protection Act prohibits any person with commercial purposes from knowingly causing material that is obscene for children to be placed on the World Wide Web. It is a defense under the act that the defendant has required proof of age by credit card or adult verification screens, or any reasonable measure that is feasible under available technology. Constitutional? Would blocking software installed by parents be a less restrictive alternative? See *American Civil Liberties Union v. Reno*, 31 F.Supp.2d 473 (1999).[e] Would the best solution be to require that net browsers provide a preference that, if elected, would signal to web sites that the recipient is a child?[f] How serious is it that children might evade this by using a computer at a friend's house?[g]

SECTION 9. THE RIGHT NOT TO SPEAK, THE RIGHT TO ASSOCIATE, AND THE RIGHT NOT TO ASSOCIATE

NAACP v. Alabama ex rel. Patterson, 357 U.S. 449, 78 S.Ct. 1163, 2 L.Ed.2d 1488 (1958), per Harlan, J., held that the first amendment barred Alabama from compelling production of NAACP membership lists. The opinion used the phrase freedom of association repeatedly, "elevat[ing] freedom of association to an independent right, possessing an equal status with the other rights specifically enumerated in the first amendment." Thomas Emerson, *Freedom of Association and Freedom of Expression*, 74 Yale L.J. 1, 2 (1964).

From the materials on advocacy of illegal action (Sec. 1, I supra) onward, it has been evident that individuals have rights to join with others for expressive purposes. This section explores other aspects of the freedom to associate and its corollary, the freedom not to associate. First, we explore cases which the Court bases on a right not to speak, but might better be understood as establishing a right not to be associated with particular ideas. Second, we explore aspects of free association in the employment context—in particular the claims of employees not

---

d.   I. Trotter Hardy, *The Proper Legal Regime for "Cyberspace,"* 55 U.Pitt.L.Rev. 993, 1012–13 (1994).

e.   See Nadine Strossen, *Children's Rights v. Adult Free Speech: Can They Be Reconciled?*, 29 Conn. L.Rev. 873, 876 (1997).

f.   Lawrence Lessig & Paul Resnick, *Zoning Speech on the Internet: A Legal and Technical Model*, 98 Mich. L.Rev 395 (1999).

g.   Eugene Volokh, *Freedom of Speech in Cyberspace From the Listener's Perspective: Private Speech Restrictions, Libel State Action, Harassment, and Sex*, 1996 U.Chi. Legal F. 377, 434 (1996).

to be associated with a political party, or a union or its policies. Those claims are to some extent derived from the cases establishing a right not to be associated with particular ideas. Third, instead of persons resisting forced membership in a group, we confront groups resisting members. Finally, the section explores conflicts between association in political parties and election regulations.

I. THE RIGHT NOT TO BE ASSOCIATED WITH PARTICULAR IDEAS

> *"If there is any fixed star in our constitutional constellation, it is that no official, high or petty, can prescribe what shall be orthodox in politics, nationalism, religion, or other matter of opinion or force citizens to confess by word or act their faith therein."*

West Virginia State Bd. of Educ. v. Barnette, infra (Jackson, J.) (upholding right of public school students to refuse to salute flag).

New Hampshire required that noncommercial vehicles bear license plates embossed with the state motto, "Live Free or Die." "Refus[ing] to be coerced by the State into advertising a slogan which I find morally, ethically, religiously and politically abhorrent," appellee, a Jehovah's Witness, covered up the motto on his license plate, a misdemeanor under state law. After being convicted several times of violating the misdemeanor statute, appellee sought federal injunctive and declaratory relief. WOOLEY v. MAYNARD, 430 U.S. 705, 97 S.Ct. 1428, 51 L.Ed.2d 752 (1977), per BURGER, C.J., held that requiring appellee to display the motto on his license plates violated his first amendment right to "refrain from speaking": "[T]he freedom of thought protected by the First Amendment [includes] both the right to speak freely and the right to refrain from speaking at all. See *Barnette.* The right to speak and the right to refrain from speaking are complementary components of the broader concept of 'individual freedom of mind.' This is illustrated [by] *Miami Herald* [infra], where we held unconstitutional a Florida statute placing an affirmative duty upon newspapers to publish the replies of political candidates whom they had criticized.

" * * * Compelling the affirmative act of a flag salute [the situation in *Barnette*] involved a more serious infringement upon personal liberties than the passive act of carrying the state motto on a license plate, but the difference is essentially one of degree.[a] Here, as in *Barnette,* we are faced with a state measure which forces an individual as part of his daily life—indeed constantly while his automobile is in public view—to be an instrument for fostering public adherence to an ideological point of view he finds unacceptable. In doing so, the State 'invades the sphere of intellect and spirit which it is the purpose of the First Amendment [to] reserve from all official control.' *Barnette.*

"New Hampshire's statute in effect requires that appellees use their private property as a 'mobile billboard' for the State's ideological message—or suffer a penalty, as Maynard already has. [The] fact that most individuals agree with the thrust of [the] motto is not the test; most Americans also find the flag salute

---

a. If a teacher leads a class in the pledge of allegiance, is psychological coercion involved even in the absence of a legal requirement? Is psychological coercion sufficient to trigger a free speech violation. See Abner Greene, *The Pledge of Allegiance Problem,* 44 Ford.L.Rev. 451 (1995).

acceptable. The First Amendment protects the right of individuals to hold a point of view different from the majority and to refuse to foster, in the way New Hampshire commands, an idea they find morally objectionable."

The Court next considered whether "the State's countervailing interest" was "sufficiently compelling" to justify appellees to display the motto on their license plates. The two interests claimed by the state were (1) facilitating the identification of state license plates from those of similar colors of other states and (2) promoting "appreciation of history, state pride, [and] individualism." As to (1), the record revealed that these state license plates were readily distinguishable from others without reference to the state motto and, in any event, the state's purpose could be achieved by "less drastic means," i.e., by alternative methods less restrictive of first amendment freedoms. As to (2), where the State's interest is to communicate an "official view" as to history and state pride or to disseminate any other "ideology," "such interest cannot outweigh an individual's First Amendment right to avoid becoming the courier for such message."

REHNQUIST, J., joined by Blackmun, J., dissented, not only agreeing with what he called "the Court's implicit recognition that there is no protected 'symbolic speech' in this case," but maintaining that "that conclusion goes far to undermine the Court's ultimate holding that there is an element of protected expression here. The State has not forced appellees to 'say' anything; and it has not forced them to communicate ideas with nonverbal actions reasonably likened to 'speech,' such as wearing a lapel button promoting a political candidate or waving a flag as a symbolic gesture.[b] The State has simply required that *all* noncommercial automobiles bear license tags with the state motto. [Appellees] have not been forced to affirm or reject that motto; they are simply required by the State [to] carry a state auto license tag for identification and registration purposes. [The] issue, unconfronted by the Court, is whether appellees, in displaying, as they are required to do, state license tags, the format of which is known to all as having been prescribed by the State, would be considered to be advocating political or ideological views.

"[H]aving recognized the rather obvious differences between [*Barnette* and this case], the Court does not explain why the same result should obtain. The Court suggests that the test is whether the individual is forced 'to be an instrument for fostering public adherence to an ideological point of view he finds unacceptable,' [but] these are merely conclusory words. [For] example, were New Hampshire to erect a multitude of billboards, each proclaiming 'Live Free or Die,' and tax all citizens for the cost of erection and maintenance, clearly the message would be 'fostered' by the individual citizen-taxpayers and just as clearly those individuals would be 'instruments' in that communication. Certainly, however, that case would not fall within the ambit of *Barnette*. In that case, as in this case, there is no *affirmation* of belief. For First Amendment principles to be implicated, the State must place the citizen in the position of either appearing to, or actually, 'asserting as true' the message. This was the focus of *Barnette,* and clearly distinguishes this case from that one."[c]

---

b. Should compelled speech cases be characterized as personhood or autonomy cases rather than free speech cases? See Abner Greene, supra note a. Does *compelled* expression have to be understood by others to be "speech" or does it suffice that the Maynards *subjectively believed* that they were being forced to make an expression? See note 1 following this case.

c. White, J., joined by Blackmun and Rehnquist, JJ., dissented on procedural grounds.

Notes and Questions

1. Consider Laurence Tribe, *The Curvature of Constitutional Space: What Lawyers Can Learn From Modern Physics,* 103 Harv.L.Rev. 1, 22 (1989): "[T]he very existence of the challenged New Hampshire Law in a sense *protected* free speech rights. For it was well known that people had no choice about whether the state motto was to appear on their license plates. [Ironically], by requiring the state to give people the option whether or not to have its motto displayed on their license plates, the *Wooley* Court forced people into a symbolic expression. [An] adequate constitutional analysis cannot ignore the impact on social meaning of the Court's own action."

2. *Use of private property as a forum for the speech of others.* (a) Appellees sought to enjoin a shopping center from denying them access to the center's central courtyard in order to solicit signatures from passersby for petitions opposing a U.N. resolution. The California Supreme Court held they were entitled to conduct their activity at the center, construing the state constitution to protect "speech and petitioning, reasonably exercised, in shopping centers, even [when] privately owned." PRUNEYARD SHOPPING CENTER v. ROBINS, 447 U.S. 74, 100 S.Ct. 2035, 64 L.Ed.2d 741 (1980) per REHNQUIST, J., affirmed: "[In *Wooley,*] the government itself prescribed the message, required it to be displayed openly on appellee's personal property that was used 'as part of his daily life,' and refused to permit him [to] cover up the motto even though the Court found that the display of the motto served no important state interest. Here, by contrast, [the center] is not limited to the personal use of appellants, [but is] a business establishment that is open to the public to come and go as they please. The views expressed by members of the public in passing out pamphlets or seeking signatures for a petition thus will not likely be identified with those of the owner. Second, no specific message is dictated by the State to be displayed on appellants' property. There consequently is no danger of government discrimination for or against a particular message. Finally, [it appears] appellants can expressly disavow any connection with the message by simply posting signs in the area where the speakers or handbillers stand."

Unlike *Barnette,* appellants "are not [being] compelled to affirm their belief in any governmentally prescribed position or view, and they are free to publicly dissociate themselves from the views of the speakers or handbillers. [*Miami Herald*] rests on the principle that the State cannot tell a newspaper what it must print. [There was also a danger that the statute requiring a newspaper to publish a political candidate's reply to previously published criticism would deter] editors from publishing controversial political [statements]. Thus, the statute was found to be an 'intrusion into the function of editors.' These concerns obviously are not present here."[d]

POWELL, J., joined by White, J., concurring in the judgment, maintained that "state action that transforms privately owned property into a forum for the expression of the public's views could raise serious First Amendment questions": "I do not believe that the result in *Wooley* would have changed had [the state] directed its citizens to place the slogan 'Live Free or Die' in their shop windows

---

d. Could *PruneYard* be extended to parts of the Internet? To America Online? To Netscape? Are parts of the Internet already public fora. For various views, see Laurence H. Tribe, *The Constitution in Cyberspace,* The Humanist, Sept.–Oct. 1991, at 15; Edward V. Di Lello, *Functional Equivalency and Its Application to Freedom of Speech on Computer Bulletin* Boards, 26 Colum. J.L. & Soc. Probs. 199 (1993); Note, *Sidewalks in Cyberspace: Making Space for Public Forums in the Electronic Environment,* 12 Harv. J.L. & Tech. 149 (1998); Note, *Is Cyberspace a Public Forum? Computer Bulletin Boards, Free Speech, and State Action,* 81 Geo.L.J. 409 (1992).

rather than on their automobiles. [*Wooley*] protects a person who refuses to allow use of his property as a market place for the ideas of others. [One] who has merely invited the public onto his property for commercial purposes cannot fairly be said to have relinquished his right 'to decline to be an instrument for fostering public adherence to an ideological point of view he finds unacceptable.' *Wooley.*

"[E]ven when [as here] no particular message is mandated by the State, First Amendment interests are affected by state action that forces a property owner to admit third-party speakers. [A] right of access [may be] no less intrusive than speech compelled by the State itself. [A] law requiring that a newspaper permit others to use its columns imposes an unacceptable burden upon the newspaper's First Amendment right to select material for publication. *Miami Herald.*

"[If] a state law mandated public access to the bulletin board of a freestanding store [or] small shopping center [or allowed soliciting or pamphleteering in the entrance area of a store,] customers might well conclude that the messages reflect the view of the proprietor. [He] either could permit his customers to receive a mistaken impression [or] disavow the messages. Should he take the first course, he effectively has been compelled to affirm someone else's belief. Should he choose the second, he has been forced to speak when he would prefer to remain silent. In short, he has lost control over his freedom to speak or not to speak on certain issues. The mere fact that he is free to dissociate himself from the views expressed on his property cannot restore his 'right to refrain from speaking at all.' *Wooley.*

"A property owner may also be faced with speakers who wish to use his premises as a platform for views that he finds morally repugnant[, for example, a] minority-owned business confronted with leafleters from the American Nazi Party or the Ku Klux Klan, [or] a church-operated enterprise asked to host demonstrations in favor of abortion. [The] pressure to respond is particularly apparent [in the above cases, but] an owner who strongly objects to some of the causes to which the state-imposed right of access would extend may oppose ideological activities 'of *any* sort' that are not related to the purposes for which he has invited the public onto his property. See *Abood.* To require the owner to specify the particular ideas he finds objectionable enough to compel a response would force him to relinquish his 'freedom to maintain his own beliefs without public disclosure.' *Abood.* * * *

"[On this record] I cannot say that customers of this vast center [occupying several city blocks and containing more than 65 shops] would be likely to assume that appellees' limited speech activity expressed the views of [the center]. [Moreover, appellants] have not alleged that they object to [appellees' views, nor asserted] that some groups who reasonably might be expected to speak at [the center] will express views that are so objectionable as to require a response even when listeners will not mistake their source. [Thus,] I join the judgment of the Court, [but] I do not interpret our decision today as a blanket approval for state efforts to transform privately owned commercial property into public forums."[e]

Pacific Gas & Electric Co. v. Public Utilities Comm'n, 475 U.S. 1, 106 S.Ct. 903, 89 L.Ed.2d 1 (1986), per Powell, J., joined by Burger, C.J., and Brennan and O'Connor, JJ., (together with Marshall, J., concurring), struck down a commission requirement that a private utility company include in its billing envelope materi-

e. For commentary, see Curtis Berger, *Pruneyard Revisited: Political Activity on Private Lands,* 66 N.Y.U.L.Rev. 633 (1991); Sanford Levinson, *Freedom of Speech and the* *Right of Access to Private Property Under State Constitutional Law* in Developments in State Constitutional Law 51 (McGraw ed. 1985).

als supplied by a public interest group that were critical of some of the company's positions.[f] Was the result required by *Miami Herald*? Consistent with *PruneYard?*

3. *Paraders' rights.* The City of Boston authorized the South Boston Allied War Veterans Council to conduct the St. Patrick's Day–Evacuation parade (commemorating the evacuation of British troops from the city in 1776). The Veterans Council refused to let the Irish–American Gay, Lesbian and Bisexual Group of Boston march in the parade, but the Massachusetts courts ruled that the Council's refusal violated a public accommodations law in that the parade was an "open recreational event." HURLEY v. IRISH–AMERICAN GAY, LESBIAN AND BISEXUAL GROUP OF BOSTON, 515 U.S. 557, 115 S.Ct. 2338, 132 L.Ed.2d 487 (1995), per SOUTER, J., held that "[t]his use of the State's power violates the fundamental rule of protection under the First Amendment, that a speaker has the autonomy to choose the content of his own message. * * *

"[The Council's] claim to the benefit of this principle of autonomy to control one's own speech is as sound as the South Boston parade is expressive. Rather like a composer, the Council selects the expressive units of the parade from potential participants, and though the score may not produce a particularized message, each contingent's expression in the Council's eyes comports with what merits celebration on that day. Even if this view gives the Council credit for a more considered judgment than it actively made, the Council clearly decided to exclude a message it did not like from the communication it chose to make, and that is enough to invoke its right as a private speaker to shape its expression by speaking on one subject while remaining silent on another. * * *

"Unlike the programming offered on various channels by a cable network, the parade does not consist of individual, unrelated segments that happen to be transmitted together for individual selection by members of the audience. Although each parade unit generally identifies itself, each is understood to contribute something to a common theme, and accordingly there is no customary practice whereby private sponsors disavow any 'identity of viewpoint' between themselves and the selected participants. Practice follows practicability here, for such disclaimers would be quite curious in a moving parade. [*PruneYard* found] that the proprietors were running 'a business establishment that is open to the public to come and go as they please,' that the solicitations would 'not likely be identified with those of the owner,' and that the proprietors could 'expressly disavow any connection with the message by simply posting signs in the area where the speakers or handbillers stand.' "[g]

4. *Economic pressure to engage in political activity.* NAACP v. CLAIBORNE HARDWARE CO., 458 U.S. 886, 102 S.Ct. 3409, 73 L.Ed.2d 1215 (1982): The NAACP had organized a consumer boycott whose principal objective was, according to the lower court, "to force the white merchants [to] bring pressure upon [the government] to grant defendants' demands or, in the alternative, to suffer economic ruin." Mississippi characterized the boycott as a tortious and malicious interference with the plaintiffs' businesses. The Court, per STEVENS, J., held for the NAACP: Although labor boycotts organized for economic ends had long been subject to prohibition, "speech to protest racial discrimination" was "essential political speech lying at the core of the First Amendment" and was therefore distinguishable. Is the boycott protected association? Are there association rights

---

f. Burger, C.J., filed a concurring opinion; Rehnquist, J., joined by White and Stevens, JJ., dissented; Stevens, J., filed a separate dissent; Blackmun, J., took no part.

g. For incisive pre-*Hurley* commentary, see Larry W. Yackle, *Parading Ourselves: Freedom of Speech at the Feast of St. Patrick,* 73 B.U.L.Rev. 791 (1993).

on the other side? Does the state have a legitimate interest in protecting merchants from being forced to support political change they would otherwise oppose? Cf. *NLRB v. Retail Store Employees Union,* 447 U.S. 607, 100 S.Ct. 2372, 65 L.Ed.2d 377 (1980) (ban on labor picketing encouraging consumer boycott of neutral employer upheld). Are the white merchants neutral?[h] For commentary, compare Michael Harper, *The Consumer's Emerging Right to Boycott: NAACP v. Claiborne Hardware and Its Implications for American Labor Law,* 93 Yale L.J. 409 (1984) with Maimon Schwarzschild & Larry Alexander, *Consumer Boycotts and Freedom of Association: Comment on a Recently Proposed Theory,* 22 San Diego L.Rev. 555 (1985).

5. *Orthodoxy and commercial advertising.* ZAUDERER v. OFFICE OF DIS-CIPLINARY COUNSEL, 471 U.S. 626, 105 S.Ct. 2265, 85 L.Ed.2d 652 (1985), per WHITE, J., upheld an Ohio requirement that an attorney advertising availability on a contingency basis must disclose in the ad whether the clients would have to pay costs if their lawsuits should prove unsuccessful: "[T]he interests at stake in this case are not of the same order as those discussed in *Wooley, Miami Herald,* and *Barnette.* Ohio has not attempted to 'prescribe what shall be orthodox in politics, nationalism, religion, or other matters of opinion or force citizens to confess by word or act their faith therein.' The State has attempted only to prescribe what shall be orthodox in commercial advertising [regarding] purely factual and un-controversial[i] information about the terms under which his services will be available. Because the extension of First Amendment protection to commercial speech is justified principally by the value to consumers of the information such speech provides, *Virginia Pharmacy,* appellant's constitutionally protected interest in *not* providing any particular factual information in his advertising is minimal. [We] recognize that unjustified or unduly burdensome disclosure requirements might offend the First Amendment by chilling protected commercial speech. But we hold that an advertiser's rights are adequately protected as long as disclosure requirements are reasonably related to the State's interest in preventing decep-tion of consumers."

The Court stated that the first amendment interests "implicated by disclosure requirements are substantially weaker than those at stake when speech is [actu-ally suppressed." Accordingly it rejected any requirement that the advertisement in question be shown to be deceptive absent the disclosure or that the state meet a "least restrictive means" analysis.

BRENNAN, J., joined by Marshall, J., dissenting on this issue, conceded that the distinction between disclosure and suppression "supports some differences in analysis," but thought the Court had exaggerated the importance of the distinc-

h. Stevens, J., also argued in *Claiborne* that the boycott was protected as a right to petition the government. Are the white mer-chants the government?

i. What if the requested disclosures are controverted? Do cigarette companies have first amendment grounds to resist forced dis-closures?

Do doctors have a first amendment right to resist state mandated disclosures to patients regarding abortion? Consider joint opinion of O'Connor, Kennedy, and Souter, JJ., in *Planned Parenthood v. Casey,* 505 U.S. 833, 112 S.Ct. 2791, 120 L.Ed.2d 674 (1992): "[This] is, for constitutional purposes, no dif-ferent from a requirement that a doctor give

certain specific information about any medical procedure. [To] be sure, the physician's First Amendment rights not to speak are implicated, see *Wooley,* but only as part of the practice of medicine, subject to reasonable licensing and regulation by the State."

Can professional fundraisers be required to disclose their professional status before solicit-ing funds? The percent of charitable contribu-tions that have been turned over to charity in the past 12 months? See *Riley v. National Federation of the Blind,* Sec. 4, III supra (the former can be required, not the latter). On compelled commercial speech, see generally Note, *Can the Budweiser Frogs Be Forced to Sing A New Tune?,* 84 Va. L.Rev. 1195 (1998).

tion: "[A]n affirmative publication requirement 'operates as a command in the same sense as a statute or regulation forbidding [someone] to publish specified matter,' and that [a] compulsion to publish that which 'reason tells [one] should not be published' therefore raises substantial first amendment concerns. *Miami Herald*." Accordingly, he would have required a demonstration that the advertising was inherently likely to deceive or record evidence that the advertising was in fact deceptive, or a showing that another substantial interest was directly [advanced]. Applying this standard, Brennan, J., agreed with the Court that a state may require an advertising attorney to include a costs disclaimer, but concluded that the state had provided Zauderer with inadequate notice of what he was required to include in the advertisement.

6. *A right not to speak? Wooley* and succeeding cases establish a right not to be associated with ideas to which one is ideologically opposed. Yet individuals are forced to speak in a wide variety of situations. Does it violate the first amendment to compel witnesses to speak in court or legislative proceedings? Should such compulsion have limits? Consider *Barenblatt v. United States,* 360 U.S. 109, 79 S.Ct. 1081, 3 L.Ed.2d 1115 (1959)(witness can be compelled before Congress to testify about his political connections with the Communist Party if he does not invoke the fifth amendment). Other cases are more sympathetic to those who choose to remain silent.

(a) *Anonymous political speech.* McINTYRE v. OHIO ELECTIONS COMM'N, 514 U.S. 334, 115 S.Ct. 1511, 131 L.Ed.2d 426 (1995), per STEVENS, J., held that Ohio's prohibition against the distribution of anonymous campaign literature was unconstitutional: "Under our Constitution, anonymous pamphleteering is not a pernicious, fraudulent practice, but an honorable tradition of advocacy and of dissent. * * * The State may and does punish fraud directly. But it cannot seek to punish fraud indirectly by indiscriminately outlawing a category of speech, based on its content, with no necessary relationship to the danger sought to be prevented."[j]

THOMAS, J., concurred, but argued that instead of asking whether " 'an honorable tradition' of free speech has existed throughout American history. [We] should seek the original understanding when we interpret the Speech and Press clauses, just as we do when we read the Religion Clauses of the First Amendment." According to Thomas, J., the original understanding approach also protected anonymous speech.

SCALIA, joined by Rehnquist, C.J., dissenting, asserted that it was the "Court's (and society's) traditional view that the Constitution bears its original meaning and is unchanging." Applying that approach, he concluded that anonymous political speech is not protected under the first amendment.

(b) *Compelled election disclosures.* BROWN v. SOCIALIST WORKERS, 459 U.S. 87, 103 S.Ct. 416, 74 L.Ed.2d 250 (1982), per MARSHALL, J., held that an Ohio statute requiring every political party to report the names and addresses of campaign contributors and recipients of campaign disbursements could not be

j. Ginsburg, J., concurred. *Buckley v. American Constitutional Law Foundation,* 525 U.S. 182, 119 S.Ct. 636, 142 L.Ed.2d 599 (1999), per Ginsburg, J., held unconstitutional a Colorado statute requiring that circulators of initiatives wear identification badges bearing their names and that sponsors of the initiative report the names and addresses of all paid circulators. By contrast, the Court was satisfied that the requirement of the filing of an affidavit containing the name and address of the circulator of petitions was consistent with the first amendment. For broad-ranging commentary on the relationship between privacy and disclosure, see Kreimer, *Sunlight, Secrets, and Scarlet Letter: The Tension Between Privacy and Disclosure in Constitutional Law,* 140 U.Pa.L.Rev. 1, 70 (1991).

applied to the Socialist Workers Party. Citing *Buckley v. Valeo*, Sec. 10 infra, the Court held that the " 'evidence offered [by a minor party] need show only a reasonable probability that the compelled disclosure [of] names will subject them to threats, harassment, or reprisals from either Government officials or private parties.' " Consider Geoffrey Stone & William Marshall, *Brown v. Socialist Workers: Inequality As A Command of the First Amendment*, 1983 Sup.Ct.Rev. 583, 592: "[I]n *Brown* the Court expressly exempted particular political parties from an otherwise content-neutral regulation for reasons directly related to the content of their expression. [The] constitutionally compelled exemption substitutes a content-based law for one that is content neutral. It stands the presumption in favor of 'content neutrality' on its head." Is the decision, nonetheless, consistent with first amendment values? See Stone & Marshall, supra.

II. FREEDOM OF ASSOCIATION AND EMPLOYMENT

ELROD v. BURNS, 427 U.S. 347, 96 S.Ct. 2673, 49 L.Ed.2d 547 (1976), (Stevens, J., not participating) declared unconstitutional the dismissal of non-policymaking and nonconfidential state and local government employees solely on the ground that they were not affiliated with or sponsored by a particular political party. (The newly elected Democratic Sheriff of Cook County, Illinois, had sought to replace noncivil-service employees in his office, all Republicans, with members of his own party. The employees who brought suit were process servers and a juvenile court bailiff). BRENNAN, J., announced the judgment and an opinion joined by White and Marshall, JJ.: "The cost of the practice of patronage is the restraint it places on freedoms of belief and association. [The] free functioning of the electoral process also suffers. Conditioning political employment on partisan support prevents support of competing public interests. [As] government employment, state or federal, becomes more pervasive, the greater the dependence on it becomes, and therefore the greater becomes the power to starve political [opposition]. Patronage thus tips the electoral process in favor of the incumbent party.

"[P]olitical belief and association constitute the core of those activities protected by the First Amendment." [The] Court recognized in *United Public Workers v. Mitchell*, 330 U.S. 75, 100, 67 S.Ct. 556, 569, 91 L.Ed. 754 (1947), that 'Congress may not "enact a regulation providing that no Republican, Jew or Negro shall be appointed to federal office." ' This principle was reaffirmed in *Wieman v. Updegraff*, 344 U.S. 183, 73 S.Ct. 215, 97 L.Ed. 216 (1952), which held that a State could not require its employees to establish their loyalty by extracting an oath denying past affiliation with Communists. And in *Cafeteria & Restaurant Workers v. McElroy*, 367 U.S. 886, 898, 81 S.Ct. 1743, 1750, 6 L.Ed.2d 1230 (1961), the Court recognized again that the government could not deny employment because of previous membership in a particular party.[11]

"Particularly pertinent to the constitutionality of the practice of patronage dismissals are *Keyishian v. Board of Regents*, 385 U.S. 589, 87 S.Ct. 675, 17 L.Ed.2d 629 (1967), and *Perry v. Sindermann*, 408 U.S. 593, 92 S.Ct. 2694, 33 L.Ed.2d 570 (1972). In *Keyishian*, the Court invalidated New York statutes

---

11. Protection of First Amendment interests has not been limited to invalidation of conditions on government employment requiring allegiance to a particular political party. This Court's decisions have prohibited conditions on public benefits, in the form of jobs or otherwise, which dampen the exercise generally of First Amendment rights, however slight

the inducement to the individual to forsake those rights.

[T]he First Amendment prohibits limiting the grant of a tax exemption to only those who affirm their loyalty to the State granting the exemption. *Speiser v. Randall*, 357 U.S. 513, 78 S.Ct. 1332, 2 L.Ed.2d 1460 (1958).

barring employment merely on the basis of membership in 'subversive' organizations. *Keyishian* squarely held that political association alone could not, consistently with the First Amendment, constitute an adequate ground for denying public employment.[12] In *Perry,* the Court broadly rejected the validity of limitations on First Amendment rights as a condition to the receipt of a governmental benefit, stating that the government 'may not deny a benefit to a person on a basis that infringes his constitutionally protected interests—especially, his interest in freedom of speech. For if the government could deny a benefit to a person because of his constitutionally protected speech or associations, his exercise of those freedoms would in effect be penalized and inhibited. This would allow the government to "produce a result which [it] could not command directly." *Speiser.* Such interference with constitutional rights is impermissible.' * * *[13]"

If the practice is to survive constitutional challenge, "it must further some vital government end by a means that is least restrictive of freedom of belief and association in achieving that end, and the benefit gained must outweigh the loss of constitutionally protected rights." The plurality then considered and rejected three interests offered in justification of patronage—(1) "the need to insure effective government"; (2) "the need for political loyalty of employees" to assure implementation of the new administration's policies; and (3) "the preservation of the democratic process" and the continued vitality of "party politics":

As to (1), the argument fails, inter alia, "because it is doubtful that the mere difference of political persuasion motivates poor performance; nor do we think it legitimately may be used for imputing such behavior. [At] all events, less drastic means for insuring [this interest] are available"—discharge for good cause, "such as insubordination or poor job performance, when those bases exist."

"[Moreover] the lack of any justification for patronage dismissals as a means of furthering government effectiveness and efficiency distinguishes this case from *U.S. Civil Service Comm'n v. Letter Carriers,* 413 U.S. 548, 93 S.Ct. 2880, 37 L.Ed.2d 796 (1973), and *Mitchell.* In both of those cases, legislative restraints on political management and campaigning by public employees were upheld despite their encroachment on First Amendment rights because, inter alia, they did serve in a necessary manner to foster and protect efficient and effective government. Interestingly, the activities that were restrained by the legislation involved in those cases are characteristic of patronage practices. As the Court observed in *Mitchell,* 'The conviction that an actively partisan governmental personnel threatens good administration has deepened since [1882]. Congress recognizes danger to

---

12. Thereafter, *United States v. Robel,* 389 U.S. 258, 88 S.Ct. 419, 19 L.Ed.2d 508 (1967), similarly held that mere membership in the Communist Party could not bar a person from employment in private defense establishments important to national security.

13. The increasingly pervasive nature of public employment provides officials with substantial power through conditioning jobs on partisan support, particularly in this time of high unemployment. Since the government however, may not seek to achieve an unlawful end either directly or indirectly, the inducement afforded by placing conditions on a benefit need not be particularly great in order to find that rights have been violated. Rights are infringed both where the government fines a person a penny for being a Republican and

where it withholds the grant of a penny for the same reason.

Petitioners contend that even though the government may not provide that public employees may retain their jobs only if they become affiliated with or provide support for the in-party, respondents here have waived any objection to such requirements. The difficulty with this argument is that it completely swallows the rule. Since the qualification may not be constitutionally imposed absent an appropriate justification, to accept the waiver argument is to say that the government may do what it may not do. A finding of waiver in this case, therefore, would be contrary to our view that a partisan job qualification abridges the First Amendment.

the service in that political rather than official effort may earn advancement and to the public in that governmental favor may be channeled through political connections.' "

As for the second interest, the need for political loyalty and implementation of new policies "may be adequately met" by limiting patronage dismissals to "policy-making positions." As for the third interest—one "premised on the centrality of partisan politics in the democratic process"—"we are not persuaded [that] the interdiction of patronage dismissals [will cause] the demise of party politics." Political parties existed prior to active patronage and "they have survived substantial reduction in their patronage power through the establishment of the merit system.

"Patronage dismissals thus are not the least restrictive alternative to achieving the contributions they may make to the democratic process. The process functions as well without the practice, perhaps even better, for patronage dismissals clearly also retard that practice. [U]nlike the gain to representative government provided by the Hatch Act in *Letter Carriers* and *Mitchell,* the gain to representative government provided by [the practice], if any, would be insufficient to justify its sacrifice of First Amendment rights.

"To be sure, *Letter Carriers* and *Mitchell* upheld Hatch Act restraints sacrificing political campaigning and management, activities themselves protected by the First Amendment. But in those cases it was the Court's judgment that congressional subordination of those activities was permissible to safeguard the core interests of individual belief and association. Subordination of some First Amendment activity was permissible to protect other such activity. Today, we hold that subordination of other First Amendment activity, that is, patronage dismissals, not only is permissible, but also is mandated by the First Amendment. And since patronage dismissals fall within the category of political campaigning and management, this conclusion irresistibly flows from *Mitchell* and *Letter Carriers.* For if the First Amendment did not place individual belief and association above political campaigning and management, at least in the setting of public employment, the restraints on those latter activities could not have been judged permissible in *Mitchell* and *Letter Carriers.*"

STEWART, J., joined by Blackmun, J., concurred: "This case does not require us to consider the broad contours of the so-called patronage system, with all its variations and permutations. In particular, it does not require us to consider the constitutional validity of a system that confines the hiring of some governmental employees to those of a particular political party, and I would intimate no views whatever on that question.

"The single substantive question involved in this case is whether a nonpolicymaking, nonconfidential government employee can be discharged or threatened with discharge from a job that he is satisfactorily performing upon the sole ground of his political beliefs. I agree with the plurality that he cannot. See *Perry v. Sindermann.*"

POWELL, J., joined by Burger, C.J., and Rehnquist, J., dissented: "[Here, we have] complaining employees who apparently accepted patronage jobs knowingly and willingly, while fully familiar with the 'tenure' practices long prevailing in the Sheriff's Office. Such employees have *benefitted* from their political beliefs and activities; they have not been penalized for them. In these circumstances, I am inclined to [the view that they] may not be heard to challenge [the patronage system] when it comes their turn to be replaced."

Beyond waiver, he complained that the Court "unnecessarily constitutionalizes another element of American life—an element not without its faults but one which generations have accepted on balance as having merit." Powell, J., stressed the importance of political parties and their dependency upon patronage. "History and long prevailing practice across the country support the view that patronage hiring practices make a sufficiently substantial contribution to the practical functioning of our democratic system to support their relatively modest intrusion on First Amendment interests. * * *

"It is difficult to disagree with the view, as an abstract proposition, that government employment ordinarily should not be conditioned upon one's political beliefs or activities. But we deal here with a highly practical and rather fundamental element of our political system, not the theoretical abstraction of a political science seminar. [T]he plurality seriously underestimates the strength of the government interest—especially at the local level—in allowing some patronage hiring practices, and it exaggerates the perceived burden on First Amendment rights. * * *

"It is naive to think that [local political activity supporting parties is] motivated [by] some academic interest in 'democracy' or other public service impulse. For the most part, the hope of some reward generates a major portion of [such activity]. It is difficult to overestimate the contributions to our system by the major political parties, fortunately limited in number compared to the fractionalization that has made the continued existence of democratic government doubtful in some other countries. * * *

"It is against decades of experience to the contrary, then, that the plurality opinion concludes that patronage hiring practices interfere with the 'free functioning of the electoral process.' This *ad hoc* judicial judgment runs counter to the judgments of the representatives of the people in state and local governments, representatives who have chosen, in most instances, to retain some patronage practices in combination with a merit-oriented civil service. One would think that elected representatives of the people are better equipped than we to weigh the need for some continuation of patronage practices in light of the interests above identified,[9] and particularly in view of local conditions. *Letter Carriers; Mitchell.*"[a]

Notes and Questions

1. BRANTI v. FINKEL, 445 U.S. 507, 100 S.Ct. 1287, 63 L.Ed.2d 574 (1980), per STEVENS, J., applied *Elrod* to "protect an assistant public defender who is satisfactorily performing his job from discharge solely because of his political beliefs."[b] The Court rejected the argument that even if party sponsorship is an

9. The plurality might be taken to concede some promotion of the democratic process by patronage hiring practices but to conclude that in net effect such practices will reduce political debate impermissibly by affecting some employees or potential employees and thereby depriving society of the 'unfettered judgment of each citizen on matters of political concern.' In the past the Court has upheld congressional actions designed to increase the overall level of political discourse but affecting adversely the First Amendment interests of some individuals. In *Letter Carriers* we indicated specifically that the First Amendment freedoms of federal employees could be limited in an effort to further the functioning of the democratic process.

I do not believe that local legislative judgments as to what will further the democratic process in light of local conditions should receive less weight than these congressional judgments. Surely that should be the case until we have a record, if one could be created, showing the fears of the plurality to be justified.

a. Burger, C.J., dissented, contending that the decision "represents a significant intrusion into the area of legislative and policy concerns."

b. The Court noted that in *Elrod*, as in the instant case, "the only practice at issue was the *dismissal* of public employees for partisan reasons" and thus there was "no occasion to

unconstitutional condition for retaining low-level public employees it is a permissible requirement for an assistant public defender: "[P]arty affiliation is not necessarily relevant to every policymaking or confidential position. The coach of a state university's football team formulates policy, but no one could seriously claim that Republicans make better coaches than Democrats, or vice versa, no matter which party is in control of the state government. On the other hand, it is equally clear that the governor of a state may appropriately believe that the official duties of various assistants who help him write speeches, explain his views to the press, or communicate with the legislature cannot be performed effectively unless those persons share his political beliefs and party commitments. In sum, the ultimate inquiry is not whether the label 'policymaker' or 'confidential' fits a particular position; rather, the question is whether the hiring authority can demonstrate that party affiliation is an appropriate requirement for the effective performance of the public office involved." The Court concluded that neither the policymaking of an assistant public defender nor the access of client's confidential information had any bearing on partisan political considerations.

2. RUTAN v. REPUBLICAN PARTY OF ILLINOIS, 497 U.S. 62, 110 S.Ct. 2729, 111 L.Ed.2d 52 (1990), per BRENNAN, J., extended *Elrod* and *Branti* not only to promotion, transfer, and recall decisions, but also to hiring decisions: "It is unnecessary here to consider whether not being hired is less burdensome than being discharged because the government is not pressed to do *either* on the basis of political affiliation."[c]

STEVENS, J., concurred: "[T]he entire rationale for patronage hiring [rests] on the assumption that the patronage employee filling the government position must be paid a premium to reward him for his partisan services. [This assumes] that governmental power and public resources—in this case employment opportunities—may appropriately be used to subsidize partisan activities[4] even when the political affiliation of the employee or the job applicant is entirely unrelated to his or her public service. The premise on which this position rests would justify the

address petitioner's argument that there is a compelling governmental interest in maintaining a political sponsorship system for *filling vacancies* in the public defender's office." (Emphasis added.) Should *Elrod* and *Branti* be extended to independent contractors? See *O'Hare Truck Service v. City of Northlake*, 518 U.S. 712, 116 S.Ct. 2353, 135 L.Ed.2d 874 (1996).

c. The opinion excepted employment decisions where party affiliation or support was an "appropriate requirement for the position involved." Illinois, according to the complaint, however, was operating a wholesale patronage system out of the governor's office that functioned broadly to limit state hiring to those supported by the Republican Party.

4. [Scalia, J.'s opinion] is devoid of reference to meaningful evidence that patronage practices have played a significant role in the preservation of the two-party system. In each of the examples that he cites—"the Boss Tweeds, the Tammany Halls, the Pendergast Machines, the Byrd Machines and the Daley Machines," patronage practices were used solely to protect the power of an entrenched majority. See Douglas Laycock, *Notes on the Role of Judicial Review, the Expansion of Federal Power, and the Structure of Constitutional Rights*, 99 Yale L.J. 1711, 1722 (1990) (describing the "hopelessness of contesting elections" in Chicago's "one-party system" when "half a dozen employees of the city and of city contractors were paid with public funds to work [a precinct] for the other side"); Richard Johnson, *Successful Reform Litigation: The Shakman Patronage Case*, 64 Chi.–Kent L.Rev. 479, 481 (1988) (the "massive Democratic patronage employment system" maintained a "noncompetitive political system" in Cook County in the 1960's).

Without repeating the Court's studied rejection of the policy arguments for patronage practices in *Elrod*, I note only that many commentators agree more with Justice Scalia's admissions of the systemic costs of patronage practices—the "financial corruption, such as salary kickbacks and partisan political activity on government-paid time," the reduced efficiency of government, and the undeniable constraint upon the expression of views by employees than with his belief that patronage is necessary to political stability and integration of powerless groups. * * *

use of public funds to compensate party members for their campaign work, or conversely, a legislative enactment denying public employment to nonmembers of the majority party."

SCALIA, J., joined by Rehnquist, C.J., and Kennedy, J., and in part by O'Connor, J.,[d] dissenting, argued that *Elrod* and *Branti* were wrongly decided and opposed their extension: "As the merit principle [for government employment] has been extended and its effects increasingly felt; as the Boss Tweeds, the Tammany Halls, the Pendergast Machines, the Byrd Machines and the Daley Machines have faded into history; we find that political leaders at all levels increasingly complain of the helplessness of elected government, unprotected by 'party discipline,' before the demands of small and cohesive interest-groups.

"The choice between patronage and the merit principle—or, to be more realistic about it, the choice between the desirable mix of merit and patronage principles in widely varying federal, state, and local political contexts—is not so clear that I would be prepared, as an original matter, to chisel a single, inflexible prescription into the Constitution. * * *

"The provisions of the Bill of Rights were designed to restrain transient majorities from impairing long-recognized personal liberties. They did not create by implication novel individual rights overturning accepted political norms. Thus, when a practice not expressly prohibited by the text of the Bill of Rights bears the endorsement of a long tradition of open, wide-spread, and unchallenged use that dates back to the beginning of the Republic, we have no proper basis for striking it down.[1] Such a venerable and accepted tradition is not to be laid on the examining table and scrutinized for its conformity to some abstract principle of First–Amendment adjudication devised by this Court. To the contrary, such traditions are themselves the stuff out of which the Court's principles are to be formed. They are, in these uncertain areas, the very points of reference by which the legitimacy or illegitimacy of *other* practices are to be figured out. When it appears that the latest 'rule,' or 'three-part test,' or 'balancing test' devised by the Court has placed us on a collision course with such a landmark practice, it is the former that must be recalculated by us, and not the latter that must be abandoned by our citizens. I know of no other way to formulate a constitutional jurisprudence that reflects, as it should, the principles adhered to, over time, by the American people, rather than those favored by the personal (and necessarily shifting) philosophical dispositions of a majority of this Court.

"I will not describe at length the claim of patronage to landmark status as one of our accepted political traditions. Justice Powell discussed it in his dissenting opinions in *Elrod* and *Branti*. Suffice it to say that patronage was, without any thought that it could be unconstitutional, a basis for government employment

---

d. O'Connor, J., did not join the sections of Scalia, J's opinion quoted infra, but did join sections arguing that *Elrod* and *Branti* were wrongly decided.

1. The customary invocation of *Brown v. Board of Education* as demonstrating the dangerous consequences of this principle, (Stevens, J., concurring), is unsupportable. I argue for the role of tradition in giving content only to *ambiguous* constitutional text; no tradition can supersede the Constitution. In my view the Fourteenth Amendment's requirement of "equal protection of the laws," combined with the Thirteenth Amendment's abolition of the institution of black slavery, leaves no room for doubt that laws treating people differently because of their race are invalid. Moreover, even if one does not regard the Fourteenth Amendment as crystal clear on this point, a tradition of *unchallenged* validity did not exist with respect to the practice in *Brown*. To the contrary, in the 19th century the principle of "separate-but-equal" had been vigorously opposed on constitutional grounds, litigated up to this Court, and upheld only over the dissent of one of our historically most respected Justices. See *Plessy v. Ferguson* (Harlan, J., dissenting).

from the earliest days of the Republic until *Elrod*—and has continued unabated since *Elrod,* to the extent still permitted by that unfortunate decision.* * * [2]"e

3. Might Communists be treated differently from Republican or Democrats for some confidential employment? Consider White, J., dissenting in *Robel* (cited in Brennan, J.'s *Elrod* opinion fn. 12): "[D]enying the opportunity to be employed in some defense plants is a much smaller deterrent to the exercise of associational rights than [a] criminal penalty attached solely to membership, and the Government's interest in keeping potential spies and saboteurs from defense plants is much greater than its interest [in] committing all Party members to prison." Compare Jerold Israel, *Elfbrandt v. Russell: The Demise of the Oath?,* 1966 Sup.Ct.Rev. 193, 201–07 and Robert O'Neil, *Unconstitutional Conditions,* 54 Calif.L.Rev. 443 (1966) with William Van Alstyne, *The Constitutional Rights of Employees,* 16 UCLA L.Rev. 751 (1969).

COLE v. RICHARDSON, 405 U.S. 676, 92 S.Ct. 1332, 31 L.Ed.2d 593 (1972), per BURGER, C.J. (Over the dissents of Douglas, J., and Marshall, J., joined by Brennan, J.), upheld the dismissal of Richardson's employment at a state hospital for refusing to sign a loyalty oath calling in part for an affirmation that "i will oppose the overthrow of the government [by] force, violence, or by any illegal or unconstitutional method": "Since there is no constitutionally protected right to overthrow a government by force, violence, or illegal or unconstitutional means, no constitutional right is infringed by an oath to abide by the constitutional system in the future."[f] Should the first amendment permit requiring public employees to oppose that which they have a right to advocate? Is *Cole* consistent with the cases cited in *Elrod*'s plurality opinion? With *Robel*? With *Wooley*?

4. The *Elrod* plurality argues that its conclusion flows irresistibly from *Mitchell* and *Letter Carriers*? Were these cases rightly decided? Is a ban on active participation in political campaigns by government employees necessary (as the Court thought in *Letter Carriers*) to avoid the impression that the government practices "political justice" or to prevent the government work force from becom-

---

2. Justice Stevens seeks to counteract this tradition by relying upon the supposed "unequivocal repudiation" of the right-privilege distinction. That will not do. If the right-privilege distinction was once used to explain the practice, and if that distinction is to be repudiated, then one must simply devise some other theory to explain it. The order of precedence is that a constitutional theory must be wrong if its application contradicts a clear constitutional tradition; not that a clear constitutional tradition must be wrong if it does not conform to the current constitutional theory. On Justice Stevens' view of the matter, this Court examines a historical practice, endows it with an intellectual foundation, and later, by simply undermining that foundation, relegates the constitutional tradition to the dustbin of history. That is not how constitutional adjudication works. I am not sure, in any event, that the right-privilege distinction has been as unequivocally rejected as Justice Stevens supposes. It has certainly been recognized that the fact that the government need not confer a certain benefit does not mean that it can attach any conditions whatever to the conferral of that benefit. But it remains true that certain conditions can be attached to benefits that cannot be imposed

as prescriptions upon the public at large. If Justice Stevens chooses to call this something other than a right-privilege distinction, that is fine and good—but it is in any case what explains the nonpatronage restrictions upon federal employees that the Court continues to approve, and there is no reason why it cannot support patronage restrictions as well.

e. In addition to the arguments referred to in footnotes 1 and 2 of Scalia, J.'s opinion, Stevens, J., maintained in response: "The tradition that is relevant in this case is the American commitment to examine and reexamine past and present practices against the basic principles embodied in the Constitution. the inspirational command by our President in 1961 is entirely consistent with that tradition: 'Ask not what your country can do for you— ask what you can do for your country.' This case involves a contrary command: 'Ask not what job applicants can do for the State—ask what they can do for our party.' Whatever traditional support may remain for a command of that ilk, it is plainly an illegitimate excuse for the practices rejected by the Court today."

f. Powell and Rehnquist, JJ., took no part.

ing a "peaceful, invincible, and perhaps corrupt political machine"? Would prohibitions against coercion (such as those commanded by *Elrod*) be sufficient? If not, is the concern about coercion relevant only to participation on behalf of incumbents? See Vincent Blasi, *The Checking Value in First Amendment Theory*, 1977 Am.B.Found.Res.J. 521, 634–35. Is it of major import that the restrictions are "not aimed at particular parties, groups or points of [view]"? *Letter Carriers*. Does an emphasis on this factor, denigrate the liberty and associational interests of government employees? See Martin Redish, *The Content Distinction in First Amendment Analysis*, 34 Stan.L.Rev. 113 (1981). See also Note, *"Un–Hatching" Federal Employee Political Endorsements*, 134 U.Pa.L.Rev. 1497 (1986) (criticizing Hatch Act policies).

5. *Beyond loyalty and partisanship.* A provision of the Ethics in Government Act prohibited receipt of honoraria for speeches or writings by federal employees. *United States v. National Treasury Employees Union*, 513 U.S. 454, 115 S.Ct. 1003, 130 L.Ed.2d 964 (1995), per Stevens, J., invalidated that provision as applied to lower level executive branch employees, the only parties before the Court. O'Connor, J., concurring and dissenting, would have upheld the provision as applied to *work related* speeches and writings, by lower level executive branch employees (the majority thought this would rewrite the statute).[g]

When District Attorney Connick proposed to transfer Assistant D.A. Myers to a different section, she strongly opposed it. Myers prepared and distributed to the other assistants a questionnaire concerning office transfer policy, office morale, the need for a grievance committee and two questions Connick particularly objected to—the level of confidence in various supervisors and whether employees felt pressured to work in political campaigns. Connick terminated Myers for refusal to accept the transfer and for distributing the questionnaire. CONNICK v. MYERS, 461 U.S. 138, 103 S.Ct. 1684, 75 L.Ed.2d 708 (1983), per WHITE, J., held that her discharge "did not offend the first amendment:"

"For most of this century, the unchallenged dogma was that a public employee had no right to object to conditions placed upon the terms of employment—including those which restricted the exercise of constitutional rights. The classic formulation of this position was Justice Holmes', who, when sitting on the Supreme Judicial Court of Massachusetts, observed: 'A policeman may have a constitutional right to talk politics, but he has no constitutional right to be a policeman.' *McAuliffe v. Mayor*, 155 Mass. 216, 220, 29 N.E. 517, 517 (1892). For many years, Holmes' epigram expressed this Court's law. *Adler v. Bd. of Educ.*, 342 U.S. 485, 72 S.Ct. 380, 96 L.Ed. 517 (1952); *Garner v. Bd. of Pub. Works*, 341 U.S. 716, 71 S.Ct. 909, 95 L.Ed. 1317 (1951)."

The Court proceeded, however, to recount a series of cases[a] repudiating Holmes' epigram. Those cases stood for the idea that it was wholly impermissible to deny freedom of expression "by the denial of or placing of conditions upon a benefit or a privilege." As the Court characterized the public employee cases, they were all rooted in the rights of public employees to participate in public affairs.[b] In particular, the Court focused upon *Pickering v. Bd. of Educ.*, 391 U.S. 563, 88

---

g. Rehnquist, C.J., joined by Scalia and Thomas, JJ., dissented.

a. Most of the cases involved the right of public employees to associate.

b. But see *Letter Carriers*, p. 972 supra.

S.Ct. 1731, 20 L.Ed.2d 811 (1968): "The repeated emphasis in *Pickering* on the right of a public employee 'as a citizen, in commenting upon matters of public concern,' [reflects] both the historical evolvement of the rights of public employees, and the common sense realization that government offices could not function if every employment decision became a constitutional matter.[5] * * *

"*Pickering* [held] impermissible under the First Amendment the dismissal of a high school teacher for openly criticizing the Board of Education on its allocation of school funds between athletics and education and its methods of informing taxpayers about the need for additional revenue. Pickering's subject was a matter of legitimate public concern upon which free and open debate is vital to informed decision-making by the electorate. [I]n *Givhan v. Western Line Cons. School Dist.*, 439 U.S. 410, 99 S.Ct. 693, 58 L.Ed.2d 619 (1979), we held that First Amendment protection applies when a public employee arranges to communicate privately with his employer rather than to express his views publicly. Although the subject-matter of Mrs. Givhan's statements were not the issue before the Court, it is clear that her statements concerning the school district's allegedly racially discriminatory policies involved a matter of public concern.

"*Pickering*, its antecedents and progeny, lead us to conclude that [w]hen employee expression cannot be fairly considered as relating to any matter of political, social, or other concern to the community, government officials should enjoy wide latitude in managing their offices, without intrusive oversight by the judiciary in the name of the First Amendment.[c] [We] do not suggest, however, [that] speech on private matters falls into one of the narrow and well-defined classes of expression which carries so little social value, such as obscenity, that the state can prohibit and punish such expression by all persons in its jurisdiction. See *Chaplinsky; Roth; Ferber.* For example, an employee's false criticism of his employer on grounds not of public concern may be cause for his discharge but would be entitled to the same protection in a libel action accorded an identical statement made by a man on the street. We hold only that when a public employee speaks not as a citizen upon matters of public concern, but instead as an employee upon matters only of personal interest, absent the most unusual circumstances, a federal court is not the appropriate forum in which to review the wisdom of a personnel decision taken by a public agency allegedly in reaction to the employee's behavior. Our responsibility is to ensure that citizens are not deprived of fundamental rights by virtue of working for the government; this does not require a grant of immunity for employee grievances not afforded by the First Amendment to those who do not work for the state.

"Whether an employee's speech addresses a matter of public concern must be determined by the content, form, and context of a given statement, as revealed by the whole record. [We] view the questions pertaining to the confidence and trust that Myers' coworkers possess in various supervisors, the level of office morale, and the need for a grievance committee as mere extensions of Myers' dispute over

---

5. The question of whether expression is of a kind that is of legitimate concern to the public is also the standard in determining whether a common-law action for invasion of privacy is present. See *Restatement (Second) of Torts,* § 652D. See also *Cox Broadcasting Co. v. Cohn* (action for invasion of privacy cannot be maintained when the subject-matter of the publicity is matter of public record); *Time, Inc. v. Hill.* [Should *Pickering* be extended to independent contractors? See *Board of County*

Commissioners v. Umbehr, 518 U.S. 668, 116 S.Ct. 2342, 135 L.Ed.2d 843 (1996)].

c. If there is dispute about what an employee said, does the first amendment require the trier of fact to determine that the statement was made or is it enough that the employer reasonably thought the statement was made? See *Waters v. Churchill*, 511 U.S. 661, 114 S.Ct. 1878, 128 L.Ed.2d 686 (1994) (enough that employer reasonably thought statement was made).

her transfer to another section of the criminal court. [T]he questionnaire, if released to the public, would convey no information at all other than the fact that a single employee is upset with the status quo. [T]he focus of Myers' questions is not to evaluate the performance of the office but rather [to] reflect one employee's dissatisfaction with a transfer and an attempt to turn that displeasure into a cause celèbre.[8] * * *

"One question in Myers' questionnaire, however, [whether] assistant district attorneys 'ever feel pressured to work in political campaigns on behalf of office supported candidates,' [is] a matter of interest to the community upon which it is essential that public employees be able to speak out freely without fear of retaliatory dismissal.

"Because one of the questions in Myers' survey touched upon a matter of public concern, and contributed to her discharge we must determine whether Connick was justified in discharging Myers. [The] District Court viewed the issue of whether Myers' speech was upon a matter of 'public concern' as a threshold inquiry, after which it became the government's burden to 'clearly demonstrate' that the speech involved 'substantially interfered' with official responsibilities. Yet *Pickering* unmistakably states [that] the state's burden in justifying a particular discharge varies depending upon the nature of the employee's expression. Although such particularized balancing is difficult, the courts must reach the most appropriate possible balance of the competing interests. * * *

"We agree with the District Court that there is no demonstration here that the questionnaire impeded Myers' ability to perform her responsibilities. The District Court was also correct to recognize that 'it is important to the efficient and successful operation of the District Attorney's office for Assistants to maintain close working relationships with their superiors.' Connick's judgment, and apparently also that of his first assistant [who] characterized Myers' actions as causing a 'mini-insurrection', was that Myers' questionnaire was an act of insubordination which interfered with working relationships. When close working relationships are essential to fulfilling public responsibilities, a wide degree of deference to the employer's judgment is appropriate. Furthermore, we do not see the necessity for an employer to allow events to unfold to the extent that the disruption of the office and the destruction of working relationships is manifest before taking action. We caution that a stronger showing may be necessary if the employee's speech more substantially involved matters of public [concern].

"Myers' questionnaire touched upon matters of public concern in only a most limited sense; her survey, in our view, is most accurately characterized as an employee grievance concerning internal office policy. The limited First Amendment interest involved here does not require that Connick tolerate action which he reasonably believed would disrupt the office, undermine his authority, and destroy close working relationships."

BRENNAN, J., joined by Marshall, Blackmun and Stevens, JJ., dissented: "[S]peech about 'the manner in which government is operated or should be

---

8. This is not a case like *Givhan*, where an employee speaks out as a citizen on a matter of general concern, not tied to a personal employment dispute, but arranges to do so privately. Mrs. Givhan's right to protest racial discrimination—a matter inherently of public concern—is not forfeited by her choice of a private forum. Here, however, a questionnaire not otherwise of public concern does not attain that status because its subject matter could, in different circumstances, have been the topic of a communication to the public that might be of general interest. The dissent's analysis of whether discussions of office morale and discipline could be matters of public concern is beside the point—it does not answer whether *this* questionnaire is such speech.

operated' is an essential part of the communications necessary for self-governance the protection of which was a central purpose of the First Amendment. Because the questionnaire addressed such matters and its distribution did not adversely affect the operations of the District Attorney's Office or interfere with Myers' working relationship with her fellow employees, I dissent. * * *

"The balancing test articulated in *Pickering* comes into play only when a public employee's speech implicates the government's interests as an employer. When public employees engage in expression unrelated to their employment while away from the work place, their First Amendment rights are, of course, no different from those of the general public. Thus, whether a public employee's speech addresses a matter of public concern is relevant to the constitutional inquiry only when the statements at issue—by virtue of their content or the context in which they were made—may have an adverse impact on the government's ability to perform its duties efficiently.

"The Court's decision today is flawed in three respects. First, the Court distorts the balancing analysis required under *Pickering* by suggesting that one factor, the context in which a statement is made, is to be weighed *twice*—first in determining whether an employee's speech addresses a matter of public concern and then in deciding whether the statement adversely affected the government's interest as an employer. Second, in concluding that the effect of respondent's personnel policies on employee morale and the work performance of the District Attorney's Office is not a matter of public concern, the Court impermissibly narrows the class of subjects on which public employees may speak out without fear of retaliatory dismissal. Third, the Court misapplies the *Pickering* balancing test in holding that Myers could constitutionally be dismissed for circulating a questionnaire addressed to at least one subject that *was* 'a matter of interest to the community,' in the absence of evidence that her conduct disrupted the efficient functioning of the District Attorney's Office.

"[The] proper means to ensure that the courts are not swamped with routine employee grievances mischaracterized as First Amendment cases is not to restrict artificially the concept of 'public concern,' but to require that adequate weight be given to the public's important interests in the efficient performance of governmental functions and in preserving employee discipline and harmony sufficient to achieve that end.

"[The Court's] extreme deference to the employer's judgment is not appropriate when public employees voice critical views concerning the operations of the agency for which they work. Although an employer's determination that an employee's statements have undermined essential working relationships must be carefully weighed in the *Pickering* balance, we must bear in mind that 'the threat of dismissal from public employment is [a] potent means of inhibiting speech.' [As] a result, the public will be deprived of valuable information with which to evaluate the performance of elected officials."

Notes and Questions

1. *Holmes' epigram.* Does the Court reject Holmes' epigram with one hand and embrace it with the other? Does it to some extent hold that because there is no right to hold a job, its retention is a revocable privilege? Consider Laurence Tribe, *Constitutional Choices* 208 (1985): "*Connick* resurrects the right-privilege doctrine for 'private' speech by government employees. By hinging protection on the distinction between public and private speech, the Court has embarked on a

difficult definitional course. The stated test, which includes the 'content, form, and context' of the expression, provides little guidance. As Justice Brennan pointed out in dissent, the Court significantly narrowed the concept of a public issue in holding that criticism of governmental officials is not necessarily of public concern, but provided no clear alternative formulation. The mere fact that expression constitutes an employee grievance surely cannot be decisive, since the Court found that pressure upon employees to work on political campaigns was of public concern. Nor can the absence of partisan political concerns be determinative, since an employee grievance criticizing hiring and personnel management policies is of public concern if based upon a claim of racial discrimination. What is clear is that, at least until the precise reach of *Connick* is determined, public employees, who often possess unique information, will be discouraged from adding their voices to the debate on government performance."[d]

2. Consider the tension between *Letter Carriers* and *Pickering* or *Connick*. Consider also the relationship between *Pickering, Connick,* and *Elrod*. Suppose a deputy sheriff is discharged for meeting with a political opponent of the incumbent sheriff. Does *Elrod* apply or *Pickering–Connick*?[e] What is the difference? For discussion, see Note, *Politics and the Non–Civil Service Public Employee: A Categorical Approach to First Amendment Protection,* 85 Colum.L.Rev. 558 (1985).

3. Does *Connick* provide less protection for the public employee than is afforded to the school child in *Tinker,* supra? Does the public/private distinction distinguish *Tinker?* If *Tinker's* black arm band symbolized criticism of the school principal, would the outcome have been different?

4. After hearing of an assassination attempt on the life of the President, a clerical employee in a county constable's office remarked to a friend in the office, "If they go after him again, I hope they get him." Free speech? See *Rankin v. McPherson,* 483 U.S. 378, 107 S.Ct. 2891, 97 L.Ed.2d 315 (1987). For discussion, see Steven Shiffrin, *The First Amendment, Democracy, and Romance* (1990); Toni Massaro, *Significant Silences: Freedom of Speech in the Public Sector Workplace,* 61 S.Cal.L.Rev. 1, 68–76 (1987).[f]

———

A 1981 amendment to the Food Stamp Act provides that no family shall become eligible to participate in the program during the time that any member of the household is on strike nor shall receive any increase in food stamp allotments by virtue of decreased income of the striking member. LYNG v. UAW, 485 U.S. 360, 108 S.Ct. 1184, 99 L.Ed.2d 380 (1988), per WHITE, J., stated that associational

---

d. Much of the literature relevant to the "right-privilege" distinction is cited in Ch. 5, Sec. 5.

e. Should the standards for public teachers, professors, professionals, and non-professional employees be controlled by *Connick?* Should academic freedom apply to "intramural" speech in ways that permit freer speech than that available to other public employees? See Matthew Finkin, *Intramural Speech, Academic Freedom, and the First Amendment,* 66 Texas L.Rev. 1323 (1988); Mark Yudof, *Intramural Musings on Academic Freedom,* 66 Texas L.Rev. 1351 (1988); Paul Brest, *Protecting Academic Freedom Through the First Amendment,* 66 Texas L.Rev. 1359 (1988).

f. For discussion of *Connick,* see e.g., Shiffrin, supra, Massaro, supra, Risa Lieberwitz, *Freedom of Speech in Public Sector Employment: The Deconstitutionalization of the Public Sector Workplace,* 19 U.C.Davis L.Rev. 597 (1986); Robert Post, *Between Governance and Management,* 34 UCLA L.Rev. 1713, 1813–16 (1987); Comment, *The Public Employee's Right of Free Speech,* 55 U.Cin.L.Rev. 449 (1986). For relevant pre-*Connick* commentary, see Frederick Schauer, *"Private" Speech and the "Private" Forum: Givhan v. Western Line School District,* 1979 Sup.Ct.Rev. 217.

rights included the "combination of workers together in order better to assert their lawful rights" but found no interference with such association: "[The statute] does not 'order' appellees not to associate together for the purpose of conducting a strike, or for any other purpose, and it does not 'prevent' them from associating together or burden their ability to do so in any significant manner. [I]t seems 'exceedingly unlikely' that this statute will prevent individuals from continuing to associate together in unions to promote their lawful objectives.[a] [A] 'legislature's decision not to subsidize the exercise of a fundamental right does not infringe the right.' *Regan.*"[b]

MARSHALL, J., joined by Brennan and Blackmun, JJ., dissenting, saw no need to reach the first amendment issue (although he was "unconvinced" by the Court's treatment of the issue) because, he argued, the statute failed to meet even the most deferential scrutiny. In light of a variety of statutory benefits easing management's burden in labor disputes, he concluded: "Altering the backdrop of governmental support in this one-sided and devastating way amounts to a penalty on strikers, not neutrality."[c]

In ABOOD v. DETROIT BD. OF EDUC., 431 U.S. 209, 97 S.Ct. 1782, 52 L.Ed.2d 261 (1977), a Michigan statute permitted an "agency shop" arrangement, whereby all local governmental employees represented by a union, even though not themselves union members, must, as a condition of employment, pay to the union "service charges" equal in amount to union dues. Alleging that they were unwilling to pay union dues, that (1) they opposed public sector collective bargaining and that (2) the union was engaged in non-collective bargaining political-ideological activities which they disapproved, public school teachers challenged the validity of the agency-shop clause in a collective bargaining agreement between the Board of Education and the union. The Court, per STEWART, J., rejected plaintiffs' first contention, but sustained the second—the union's expenditure of a part of such "service charges" "to contribute to political candidates and to express political views unrelated to its duties as exclusive bargaining representative" violates the first amendment rights of non-union employees who oppose such causes.

"To compel employees financially to support their collective-bargaining representative has an impact upon their First Amendment interests. An employee may very well have ideological objections to a wide variety of activities undertaken by the union in its role as exclusive representative. His moral or religious views about the desirability of abortion may not square with the union's policy in negotiating a medical benefits plan. One individual might disagree with a union policy of negotiating limits on the right to strike, believing that to be the road to serfdom for the working class, while another might have economic or political objections to unionism itself. An employee might object to the union's wage policy because it violates guidelines designed to limit inflation, or might object to the union's seeking a clause in the collective-bargaining agreement proscribing racial

a. Should a penalty for the exercise of a right be unconstitutional even if it does not inhibit the exercise of that right?

b. How does one distinguish the mere failure to subsidize from a penalty? Is participation in a strike protected association? For commentary discussing and ranging beyond

Lyng, see Kathleen Sullivan, *Unconstitutional Conditions,* 102 Harv.L.Rev. 1413, 1428–56, 1474 (1989).

c. The government had argued that the statute was justified by the interest of governmental neutrality in private labor disputes.

discrimination. The examples could be multiplied. To be required to help finance the union as a collective-bargaining agent might well be thought, therefore, to interfere in some way with an employee's freedom to associate for the advancement of ideas, or to refrain from doing so, as he sees fit. But the judgment clearly made in [*Railway Employees' Dep't v. Hanson,* 351 U.S. 225, 76 S.Ct. 714, 100 L.Ed. 1112 (1956), upholding against first amendment challenge a union-shop clause, authorized by the Railway Labor Act (RLA), requiring financial support of the union by every member of the bargaining unit, and *International Ass'n of Machinists v. Street,* 367 U.S. 740, 81 S.Ct. 1784, 6 L.Ed.2d 1141 (1961), avoiding serious constitutional issues by construing RLA to prohibit the use of compulsory union dues for political purposes] is that such interference as exists is constitutionally justified by the legislative assessment of the important contribution of the union shop to the system of labor relations established by the Congress. '[As long as the union leadership acts] to promote the cause which justified bringing the group together, the individual cannot withdraw his financial support merely because he disagrees with the group's strategy.' *Street* (Douglas, J., concurring).

"[The] desirability of labor peace is no less important in the public sector, nor is the risk of 'free riders' any smaller. [Thus], insofar as the service charge is used to finance expenditures by the union for the purposes of collective bargaining, contract administration, and grievance adjustment, [*Hanson* and *Street*] appear to require validation of the agency-shop agreement before us."

In agreeing with plaintiffs' contention that they fall within the protection of *Elrod* and other cases guaranteeing the freedom to associate for the purpose of advancing ideas and forbidding the government to require one to relinquish first amendment rights as a condition of public employment "because they have been prohibited not from actively associating, but rather from refusing to associate," and in ruling that plaintiffs could constitutionally prevent the union's spending a part of their required service fees for political and ideological purposes unrelated to collective bargaining, the Court pointed out: "The fact that [plaintiffs] are compelled to make, rather than prohibited from making, contributions for political purposes works no less an infringement of their constitutional rights. For at the heart of the First Amendment is the notion that an individual should be free to believe as he will, and that in a free society one's beliefs should be shaped by his mind and his conscience rather than coerced by the State. See [*Elrod.*]

"These principles prohibit a State from compelling an individual [to] associate with a political party, *Elrod,* as a condition of employment. They are no less applicable to the case at bar, and they thus prohibit the [union] from requiring any [plaintiff] to contribute to the support of an ideological cause he may oppose as a condition of holding a job as a public school teacher.

"We do not hold that a union cannot constitutionally spend funds for the expression of political views, on behalf of political candidates, or towards the advancement of other ideological causes not germane to its duties as collective bargaining representative. Rather, the Constitution requires only that expenditures be financed from [charges] paid by employees who do not object to advancing those ideas and who are not coerced into doing so against their will by the threat of loss of government employment."

The Court remanded to devise an appropriate "way of preventing subsidization of ideological activity by employees who object thereto without restricting the union's ability to require every employee to contribute to the cost of collective-bargaining activities."[a]

POWELL, J., joined by Burger, C.J., and Blackmun, J., agreed that a state cannot constitutionally compel public employees to contribute to union political activities which they oppose and thus joined the Court's judgment remanding the case for further proceedings, but balked at the Court's apparent ruling "that public employees can be compelled by the State to pay full union dues to a union with which they disagree, subject only to a possible rebate or deduction if they are willing to step forward, declare their opposition to the union, and initiate a proceeding to establish that some portion of their dues has been spent on 'ideological activities unrelated to collective bargaining.' Such a sweeping limitation of First Amendment rights by the Court is not only unnecessary on this record; it [is] unsupported by either precedent or reason. * * *

"The Court's extensive reliance on *Hanson* and *Street* requires it to rule that there is no constitutional distinction between what the Government can require of its own employees and what it can permit private employees to do. To me the distinction is fundamental. Under the First Amendment the Government may authorize private parties to enter into voluntary agreements whose terms it could not adopt as its own.

"[The] collective-bargaining agreement to which a public agency is a party is not merely analogous to legislation; it has all of the attributes of legislation for the subjects [e.g., residency requirements for state employees] with which it deals. [The] State in this case has not merely authorized union-shop agreements between willing parties; it has negotiated and adopted such an agreement itself. [It] has undertaken to compel employees to pay full dues [to] a union as a condition of employment. Accordingly, the [Board of Education's] collective-bargaining agreement, like any other enactment of state law, is fully subject to the constraints that the Constitution imposes on coercive governmental regulation.

"[I] would make it more explicit [than has the majority] that compelling a government employee to give financial support to a union in the public sector regardless of the use to which the union puts the contribution—impinges seriously upon interests in free speech and association protected by the First Amendment.

"[*Buckley* held that] limitations on political contributions 'impinge on protected associational freedoms.' [That] *Buckley* dealt with a contribution limitation requirement does not alter its importance for this case. An individual can no more be required to affiliate with a candidate by making a contribution than he can be prohibited from such affiliation. The only question after *Buckley* is whether a union in the public sector is sufficiently distinguishable from a political candidate or committee to remove the withholding of financial contributions from First Amendment protection. In my view no principled distinction exists.

"The ultimate objective of a union in the public sector, like that of a political party, is to influence public decisionmaking in accordance with the views and perceived interests of the membership. [In this sense], the public sector union is indistinguishable from the traditional political party in this country.

"[It] is possible that paramount governmental interests may be found—at least with respect to certain narrowly defined subjects of bargaining—that would support this restriction on First Amendment rights. But 'the burden is on the government to show the existence of such an interest.' *Elrod*. Because this appeal reaches this Court on a motion to dismiss, the record is barren of any demonstra-

---

a. For procedural aspects of the implementation, see *Chicago Teachers Union v. Hudson,*   475 U.S. 292, 106 S.Ct. 1066, 89 L.Ed.2d 232 (1986).

tion by the State that excluding minority views from the processes by which governmental policy is made is necessary to serve overriding governmental objectives. * * *

"Before today it had been well established that when state law intrudes upon protected speech, the State itself must shoulder the burden of proving that its action is justified by overriding state interests. See *Elrod; Speiser v. Randall.* The Court, for the first time in a First Amendment case, simply reverses this principle. Under today's decision, a nonunion employee who would vindicate his First Amendment rights apparently must initiate a proceeding to prove that the union has allocated some portion of its budget to 'ideological activities unrelated to collective bargaining.' I would adhere to established First Amendment principles and require the State to come forward and demonstrate, as to each union expenditure for which it would exact support from minority employees, that the compelled contribution is necessary to serve overriding governmental objectives."[b]

REHNQUIST, J., concurring, noted that had he joined the *Elrod* plurality, he "would find it virtually impossible to join the Court's opinion in this case." He did not "read the Court's opinion as leaving intact the 'unfettered judgment of each citizen on matters of political concern' [*Elrod*] when it holds that Michigan [may] require an objecting member of a public employees' union to contribute to the funds necessary for the union to carry out its bargaining activities. Nor does the Court's opinion leave such a member free 'to believe as he will and to act and associate according to his beliefs' [*Elrod*]." He was "unable to see a constitutional distinction between a governmentally imposed requirement that a public employee be a Democrat or Republican or else lose his job, and a similar requirement that a public employee contribute to the collective-bargaining expenses of a labor union."[c]

Notes and Questions

1. How should the *Abood* rules apply to forced employee payments for union conventions, union newsletters, union social activities or union organizing? See *Lehnert v. Ferris Faculty Ass'n,* 500 U.S. 507, 111 S.Ct. 1950, 114 L.Ed.2d 572 (1991); *Ellis v. Brotherhood of Railway, Airline & Steamship Clerks,* 466 U.S. 435, 104 S.Ct. 1883, 80 L.Ed.2d 428 (1984). See also *Communications Workers v. Beck,* 487 U.S. 735, 108 S.Ct. 2641, 101 L.Ed.2d 634 (1988) (forced expenditures for purposes other than collective bargaining including non-germane-non-ideological activities violates National Labor Relations Act). For exploration of the issues raised by *Abood,* see Norman Cantor, *Forced Payments to Service Institutions and Constitutional Interests in Ideological Non–Association,* 36 Rut.L.Rev. 3 (1984).

2. Does *Abood* exaggerate the first amendment interests? See generally, Gaebler, *First Amendment Protection Against Government Compelled Expression*

---

b. Reading *Elrod* and *Abood* together, Powell, J., maintains that public employees may be forced to support a political party, but not the union which represents them in collective bargaining. For revealing commentary, see Paul Kahn, *The Court, the Community and the Judicial Balance: The Jurisprudence of Justice Powell,* 97 Yale L.J. 1, 45–47 (1987).

c. Stevens, J., also filed a brief concurrence: "The Court's opinion does not foreclose the argument that the Union should not be permitted to exact a service fee from nonmembers without first establishing a procedure which will avoid the risk that their funds will be used, even temporarily, to finance ideological activities unrelated to collective bargaining." For light on the application of *Abood* to a mandatory university student activity fee, see *Board of Regents v. Southworth,* 529 U.S. 217, 120 S.Ct. 1346, 146 L.Ed.2d 193 (2000)(no refund appropriate so long as allocation of funding is viewpoint neutral; interest in stimulating diverse ideas on campus outweighs the interests of objecting students).

and Association, 23 B.C.L.R. 995 (1982). If Michigan subsidized unions directly, would dissenting taxpayers have a first amendment claim? Suppose Michigan taxed those most likely to benefit from union activity, i.e., the employees? Are compelled contributions different from government taxation? See Steven Shiffrin, *Government Speech,* 27 UCLA L.Rev. 565, 594 (1980). Suppose the union contract provided for a direct payment from the employer and that union dues were not required of employees? Would this arrangement affect the rules set out in *Abood* ?

3.   Although *Abood* limits the sources of funding for union speech, it does not question union rights of free speech and association. Such rights include not only the endorsement of political candidates and causes, but also associational rights to pursue legal claims. Even as against state bar regulations, for example, unions are free to recommend attorneys to their members and to hire or engage in contracts with attorneys to represent individual union members. See *United Transportation Union v. State Bar,* 401 U.S. 576, 91 S.Ct. 1076, 28 L.Ed.2d 339 (1971): "[C]ollective activity undertaken to obtain meaningful access to the courts is a fundamental right within the protection of the First Amendment. [T]hat right would be a hollow promise if courts could deny associations of workers or others the means of enabling their members to meet the costs of legal representation."

4.   California requires all attorneys to join and pay dues to the State Bar, a regulated state agency authorized not only to examine prospective attorneys and to recommend bar admission or discipline, but also to use compulsory dues for a broad range of lobbying and amicus curiae activities. KELLER v. STATE BAR OF CALIFORNIA, 496 U.S. 1, 110 S.Ct. 2228, 110 L.Ed.2d 1 (1990), per REHNQUIST, C.J., unanimously held that compulsory bar dues could only be used if "reasonably incurred for the purpose of regulating the legal profession or improving the quality of the legal service available to the people of the State." Recognizing that difficult line-drawing questions could arise, the Court observed that the case presented clear ends of a spectrum: "Compulsory dues may not be expended to endorse or advance a gun control or nuclear weapons freeze initiative; at the other end of the spectrum petitioners have no valid constitutional objection to their compulsory dues being spent for activities connected with disciplining members of the bar or proposing ethical codes for the profession.

"[The] State Bar of California is a good deal different from most other entities that would be regarded in common parlance as 'governmental agencies.' Its principal funding comes not from appropriations made to it by the legislature, but from dues levied on its members by the Board of Governors. [It] undoubtedly performs important and valuable services for the State by way of governance of the profession, but those services are essentially advisory in nature. The State Bar does not admit anyone to the practice of law, it does not finally disbar or suspend anyone, nor does it ultimately establish ethical codes of conduct. All of those functions are reserved by California law to the State Supreme Court. * * *

"The State Bar of California was created, not to participate in the general government of the State, but to provide specialized professional advice to those with the ultimate responsibility of governing the legal profession. Its members and officers are such not because they are citizens or voters, but because they are lawyers. We think that these differences between the State Bar, on the one hand, and traditional government agencies and officials, on the other hand, render unavailing respondent's argument that it is not subject to the same constitutional rule with respect to the use of compulsory dues as are labor unions representing public and private employees."

5.   The Agricultural Marketing Agreement Act of 1937 enables committees of producers appointed by the Secretary of Agriculture to issue certain marketing orders without violating the antitrust laws provided that two thirds of the producers who market at least two thirds of the volume of a product approve. The purpose of such orders is to establish and maintain orderly marketing conditions and fair prices for agricultural commodities. Such orders, which are restricted to the smallest practicable production area, range from price fixing, joint research projects, standardized packaging, and joint advertising. Expenses of administering an order are paid from funds collected pursuant to the marketing order. Some producers of California nectarines, plums, and peaches brought a proceeding challenging marketing orders requiring them to pay for generic advertising. They invoked a first amendment right not to be compelled to subsidize the speech of others. GLICKMAN v. WILEMAN BROTHERS & ELLIOTT, INC., 521 U.S. 457, 117 S.Ct. 2130, 138 L.Ed.2d 585 (1997), per STEVENS, J., held that the compelled funding of generic advertising did not violate the first amendment: "The legal question that we address is whether being compelled to fund this advertising raises a First Amendment issue for us to resolve, or rather is simply a question of economic policy for Congress and the Executive to resolve.

"Three characteristics of the regulatory scheme at issue distinguish it from laws that we have found to abridge the freedom of speech protected by the First Amendment. First, the marketing orders impose no restraint on the freedom of any producer to communicate any message to any audience. Second, they do not compel any person to engage in any actual or symbolic speech. Third, they do not compel the producers to endorse or to finance any political or ideological views. Indeed, since all of the respondents are engaged in the business of marketing California nectarines, plums, and peaches, it is fair to presume that they agree with the central message of the speech that is generated by the generic program.[d] Thus, none of our First Amendment jurisprudence provides any support for the suggestion that the promotional regulations should be scrutinized under a different standard than that applicable to the other anticompetitive features of the marketing orders. * * *

"None of the advertising in this record promotes any particular message other than encouraging consumers to buy California tree fruit. Neither the fact that respondents may prefer to foster that message independently in order to promote and distinguish their own products, nor the fact that they think more or less money should be spent fostering it, makes this case comparable to those in which an objection rested on political or ideological disagreement with the content of the message. The mere fact that objectors believe their money is not being well spent 'does not mean [that] they have a First Amendment complaint.' "

THOMAS, J., joined by Scalia, J., dissenting observed: "What we are now left with, if we are to take the majority opinion at face value, is one of two disturbing consequences: Either (1) paying for advertising is not speech at all, while such activities as draft card burning, flag burning, armband wearing, public sleeping, and nude dancing are, or (2) compelling payment for third party communication does not implicate speech, and thus the Government would be free to force payment for a whole variety of expressive conduct that it could not restrict. In either case, surely we have lost our way."[e]

---

d.   The producers objected to the content of some of the advertisements. Stevens, J., stated that these concerns might call into question portions of the program, but had no bearing on its entirety. He also stated that these concerns were more properly addressed to the Secretary.

e.   Souter, J., joined by Rehnquist, C.J., and Scalia and Thomas, JJ., also dissented.

III. INTIMATE ASSOCIATION AND EXPRESSIVE ASSOCIATION

ROBERTS v. UNITED STATES JAYCEES, 468 U.S. 609, 104 S.Ct. 3244, 82 L.Ed.2d 462 (1984): Appellee U.S. Jaycees, a nonprofit national membership corporation whose objective is to pursue educational and charitable purposes that promote the growth and development of young men's civic organizations, limits regular membership to young men between the ages of 18 and 35. Associate membership is available to women and older men. An associate member may not vote or hold local or national office. Two local chapters in Minnesota violated appellee's bylaws by admitting women as regular members. When they learned that revocation of their charters was to be considered, members of both chapters filed discrimination charges with the Minnesota Department of Human Rights, alleging that the exclusion of women from full membership violated the Minnesota Human Rights Act (Act), which makes it an "unfair discriminatory practice" to deny anyone "the full and equal enjoyment of goods, services, facilities, privileges, advantages, and accommodations of a place of accommodation" because, inter alia, of sex.

Before a hearing on the state charge took place, appellee brought federal suit, alleging that requiring it to accept women as regular members would violate the male members' constitutional "freedom of association." A state hearing officer decided against appellee and the federal district court certified to the Minnesota Supreme Court the question whether appellee is "a place of public accommodation" within the meaning of the Act. With the record of the administrative hearing before it, the state Supreme Court answered that question in the affirmative. The U.S. Court of Appeals held that application of the Act to appellee's membership policies would violate its freedom of association.[a]

In rejecting appellee's claims,[b] the Court, per BRENNAN, J., pointed out that the Constitution protects " 'freedom of association' in two distinct senses," what might be called "freedom of intimate association" and "freedom of expressive association": "In one line of decisions, the Court has concluded that choices to enter into and maintain certain intimate human relationships must be secured against undue intrusion by the State because of the role of such relationships in safeguarding the individual freedom that is central to our constitutional scheme. In this respect, freedom of association receives protection as a fundamental element of personal liberty. In another set of decisions, the Court has recognized a right to associate for the purpose of engaging in those activities protected by the First Amendment—speech, assembly, petition for the redress of grievances, [and] religion. The Constitution guarantees freedom of association of this kind as an indispensable means of preserving other individual liberties."

The freedom of intimate association was deemed important because, "certain kinds of personal bonds have played a critical role in the culture and traditions of the Nation by cultivating and transmitting shared ideals and beliefs; they thereby

a. When the state supreme court held that appellee was "a place of public accommodation" within the meaning of the Act, it suggested that, unlike appellee, the Kiwanis Club might be sufficiently "private" to be outside the scope of the Act. Appellee then amended its complaint to allege that the state court's interpretation of the Act rendered it unconstitution-

ally vague. The Eighth Circuit so held, but the Supreme Court reversed.

b. There was no dissent. Rehnquist, J., concurred in the judgment. O'Connor, J., joined part of the Court's opinion and concurred in the judgment. See infra. Burger, C.J., and Blackmun, J., took no part.

foster diversity and act as critical buffers between the individual and the power of the State. Moreover, the constitutional shelter afforded such relationships reflects the realization that individuals draw much of their emotional enrichment from close ties with others. Protecting these relationships from unwarranted state interference therefore safeguards the ability independently to define one's identity that is central to any concept of liberty.

"The personal affiliations that exemplify these considerations [are] distinguished by such attributes as relative smallness, a high degree of selectivity in decisions to begin and maintain the affiliation, and seclusion from others in critical aspects of the relationship. [A]n association lacking these qualities—such as a large business enterprise—seems remote from the concerns giving rise to this constitutional protection. * * *

"Between these poles, of course, lies a broad range of human relationships that may make greater or lesser claims to constitutional protection from particular incursions by the State. [We] need not mark the potentially significant points on this terrain with any precision. We note only that factors that may be relevant include size, purpose, policies, selectivity, congeniality, and other characteristics that in a particular case may be pertinent. In this case, however, several features of the Jaycees clearly place the organization outside of the category of relationships worthy of this kind of constitutional protection.

"[T]he local chapters of the Jaycees are large and basically unselective groups. [Apart] from age and sex, neither the national organization nor the local chapters employs any criteria for judging applicants for membership, and new members are routinely recruited and admitted with no inquiry into their backgrounds. In fact, a local officer testified that he could recall no instance in which an applicant had been denied membership on any basis other than age or sex. [Furthermore], numerous non-members of both genders regularly participate in a substantial portion of activities central to the decision of many members to associate with one another, including many of the organization's various community programs, awards ceremonies, and recruitment meetings.

"[We] turn therefore to consider the extent to which application of the Minnesota statute to compel the Jaycees to accept women infringes the group's freedom of expressive association. * * *

"Government actions that may unconstitutionally infringe upon [freedom of expressive association] can take a number of forms. Among other things, government may seek to impose penalties or withhold benefits from individuals because of their membership in a disfavored group; it may attempt to require disclosure of the fact of membership in a group seeking anonymity; and it may try to interfere with the internal organization or affairs of the group. [There] can be no clearer example of an intrusion into the internal structure or affairs of an association than a regulation that forces the group to accept members it does not desire. Such a regulation may impair the ability of the original members to express only those views that brought them together. Freedom of association therefore plainly presupposes a freedom not to associate. See *Abood*.

"The right to associate for expressive purposes is not, however, absolute. Infringements on that right may be justified by regulations adopted to serve compelling state interests, unrelated to the suppression of ideas, that cannot be achieved through means significantly less restrictive of associational freedoms.

"[I]n upholding Title II of the Civil Rights Act of 1964, which forbids race discrimination in public accommodations, we emphasized that its 'fundamental object [was] to vindicate "the deprivation of personal dignity that surely accompanies denials of equal access to public establishments." ' *Heart of Atlanta Motel,* [Ch. 2, Sec. 2, III]. That stigmatizing injury, and the denial of equal opportunities that accompanies it, is surely felt as strongly by persons suffering discrimination on the basis of their sex as by those treated differently because of their race.

"Nor is the state interest in assuring equal access limited to the provision of purely tangible goods and services. A State enjoys broad authority to create rights of public access on behalf of its citizens. *PruneYard.* Like many States and municipalities, Minnesota has adopted a functional definition of public accommodations that reaches various forms of public, quasi-commercial conduct. This expansive definition reflects a recognition of the changing nature of the American economy and of the importance, both to the individual and to society, of removing the barriers to economic advancement and political and social integration that have historically plagued certain disadvantaged groups, including women. * * *

"In applying the Act to the Jaycees, the State has advanced those interests through the least restrictive means of achieving its ends. Indeed, the Jaycees have failed to demonstrate that the Act imposes any serious burdens on the male members' freedom of expressive association. See *Hishon v. King & Spalding,* 467 U.S. 69, 104 S.Ct. 2229, 81 L.Ed.2d 59 (1984) (law firm 'has not shown how its ability to fulfill [protected] function[s] would be inhibited by a requirement that it consider [a woman lawyer] for partnership on her merits'). To be sure, a 'not insubstantial part' of the Jaycees' activities constitutes protected expression on political, economic, cultural, and social affairs. [There] is, however, no basis in the record for concluding that admission of women as full voting members will impede the organization's ability to engage in these protected activities or to disseminate its preferred views. The Act requires no change in the Jaycees' creed of promoting the interests of young men, and it imposes no restrictions on the organization's ability to exclude individuals with ideologies or philosophies different from those of its existing members. Moreover, the Jaycees already invite women to share the group's views and philosophy and to participate in much of [its] activities. Accordingly, any claim that admission of women as full voting members will impair a symbolic message conveyed by the very fact that women are not permitted to vote is attenuated at best.

"[In] claiming that women might have a different attitude about such issues as the federal budget, school prayer, voting rights, and foreign relations, or that the organization's public positions would have a different effect if the group were not 'a purely young men's association,' the Jaycees rely solely on unsupported generalizations about the relative interests and perspectives of men and women. Although such generalizations may or may not have a statistical basis in fact with respect to particular positions adopted by the Jaycees, we have repeatedly condemned legal decisionmaking that relies uncritically on such assumptions. In the absence of a showing far more substantial than that attempted by the Jaycees, we decline to indulge in the sexual stereotyping [of appellees].

"In any event, even if enforcement of the Act causes some incidental abridgement of the Jaycees' protected speech, that effect is no greater than is necessary to accomplish the State's legitimate purposes. [A]cts of invidious discrimination in the distribution of publicly available goods, services, and other advantages cause unique evils that government has a compelling interest to prevent—wholly apart from the point of view such conduct may transmit. Accordingly, like violence or other types of potentially expressive activities that produce special harms distinct from their communicative impact, such practices are entitled to no constitutional protection."[c]

O'CONNOR, J., concurring, joined the Court's opinion except for its analysis of freedom of expressive association: "[T]hat the Court has adopted a test that unadvisedly casts doubt on the power of States to pursue the profoundly important goal of ensuring nondiscriminatory access to commercial opportunities" yet "accords insufficient protection to expressive associations and places inappropriate burdens on groups claiming the protection of the First Amendment":

"[The] Court declares that the Jaycees' right of association depends on the organization's making a 'substantial' showing that the admission of unwelcome members 'will change the message communicated by the group's speech. [S]uch a requirement, especially in the context of the balancing-of-interests test articulated by the Court, raises the possibility that certain commercial associations, by engaging occasionally in certain kinds of expressive activities, might improperly gain protection for discrimination. The Court's focus raises other problems as well. [W]ould the Court's analysis of this case be different if, for example, the Jaycees membership had a steady history of opposing public issues thought (by the Court) to be favored by women? It might seem easy to conclude, in the latter case, that the admission of women to the Jaycees' ranks would affect the content of the organization's message, but I do not believe that should change the outcome of this case. Whether an association is or is not constitutionally protected in the selection of its membership should not depend on what the association says or why its members say it.

"The Court's readiness to inquire into the connection between membership and message reveals a more fundamental flaw in its analysis. The Court pursues this inquiry as part of its mechanical application of a 'compelling interest' test, [and] entirely neglects to establish at the threshold that the Jaycees is an association whose activities or purposes should engage the strong protections that the First Amendment extends to expressive associations.

"On the one hand, an association engaged exclusively in protected expression enjoys First Amendment protection of both the content of its message and the choice of its members. * * * Protection of the association's right to define its membership derives from the recognition that the formation of an expressive association is the creation of a voice, and the selection of members is the definition of that voice. [A] ban on specific group voices on public affairs violates the most basic guarantee of the First Amendment—that citizens, not the government, control the content of public discussion.

"On the other hand, there is only minimal constitutional protection of the freedom of *commercial* association. There are, of course, some constitutional protections of commercial speech—speech intended and used to promote a commercial transaction with the speaker. But the State is free to impose any rational regulation on the commercial transaction itself. The Constitution does not guaran-

---

c. For cases following or extending *Roberts,* see *Board of Directors of Rotary International v. Rotary Club of Duarte,* 481 U.S. 537, 107 S.Ct. 1940, 95 L.Ed.2d 474 (1987); *New York State Club Ass'n v. New York,* 487 U.S. 1, 108 S.Ct. 2225, 101 L.Ed.2d 1 (1988) (upholding city ordinance against facial challenge that prohibits discrimination based on race, creed, or sex by institutions (except benevolent orders or religious corporations) with more than 400 members that provide regular meal service and receive payment from nonmembers for the furtherance of trade or business); *Dallas v. Stanglin,* 490 U.S. 19, 109 S.Ct. 1591, 104 L.Ed.2d 18 (1989) (upholding ordinance restricting admission to certain dance halls to persons between the ages of 14 and 18).

tee a right to choose employees, customers, suppliers, or those with whom one engages in simple commercial transactions, without restraint from the State.

"[A]n association should be characterized as commercial, and therefore subject to rationally related state regulation of its membership and other associational activities, when, and only when, the association's activities are not predominantly of the type protected by the First Amendment. It is only when the association is predominantly engaged in protected expression that state regulation of its membership will necessarily affect, change, dilute, or silence one collective voice that would otherwise be heard. An association must choose its market. Once it enters the marketplace of commerce in any substantial degree it loses the complete control over its membership that it would otherwise enjoy if it confined its affairs to the marketplace of ideas.

"[N]otwithstanding its protected expressive activities, [appellee] is, first and foremost, an organization that, at both the national and local levels, promotes and practices the art of solicitation and management. The organization claims that the training it offers its members gives them an advantage in business, and business firms do indeed sometimes pay the dues of individual memberships for their employees. Jaycees members hone their solicitation and management skills, under the direction and supervision of the organization, primarily through their active recruitment of new members. [The] 'not insubstantial' volume of protected Jaycees activity found by the Court of Appeals is simply not enough to preclude state regulation of the Jaycees' commercial activities. The State of Minnesota has a legitimate interest in ensuring nondiscriminatory access to the commercial opportunity presented by membership in the Jaycees."

Notes and Questions

1. *Freedom of intimate association.* The reference to the freedom of intimate association is the first in the Court's history, but the notion that the concept should serve as an organizing principle is found in Kenneth Karst, *Freedom of Intimate Association,* 89 Yale L.J. 624 (1980). To what extent should freedom of intimate association itself be regarded as a first amendment right? Compare Karst with C. Edwin Baker, *Scope of the First Amendment Freedom of Speech,* 25 UCLA L.Rev. 964 (1978) and Reena Raggi, *An Independent Right to Freedom of Association,* 12 Harv.Civ.Rts.-Civ.Lib.L.Rev. 1 (1977).

2. Is Brennan, J.'s conception of association's value too narrowly conceived? Consider George Kateb, *The Value of Association* in *Freedom of Association* 35, 49(Amy Gutmann ed. 1998): "The intrinsic value of association cannot be exclusively confined to close, intimate, or personal relationships, any more than pleasure or experience or adventure is found only in such relationships. If intrinsic value is present wherever a significant contribution to identity is present, then many relationships that are not close or intimate or deeply personal may have intrinsic value. Distant or formal or mediated or even abstract relationships contribute to the process of self-discovery and self-expression; so may chance or casual encounters or dealings with strangers; they can all help to shape or reshape an identity. It is an unattractive romanticism to believe that a self discloses or enhances itself only amid loving immediacy. * * *

"Different people will, of course, vary in the proportions of intimate and unintimate relationships they want; and many choices are made without reference to a concern to achieve or maintain or reform identity. [They] may think that by serving as a national or state officer of the Jaycees, or by being a member of a local chapter that excludes women as full members, they are engaged in a relationship of association that means a great deal to them. They may prefer to imagine that they are reduced in their identities by being told their choices are illegal, rather than constitutionally protected. We may—I do—think that it is unadult, bigoted, silly, to think as they do, and to wish to remain constitutionally free to choose to do what they want in this particular instance. I do not believe, however, that the Court should have interfered with the internal organization of an association on the grounds (partly) that such an association consisted of relationships that lacked intrinsic value * * *."[d] Does the concept of intimate association have "important implications for other private associations with discriminatory membership policies." Douglas Linder, *Freedom of Association After Roberts v. United States Jaycees,* 82 Mich.L.Rev. 1878, 1885 (1984). What are (should be) the implications for golf and country clubs, fraternal societies, athletic clubs and downtown or city clubs? Consider Comment, *Discrimination in Private Social Clubs: Freedom of Association and Right to Privacy,* 1970 Duke L.J. 1181, 1222: "Whether this society is capable of free evolution to social equality seems irrelevant in light of the influence of the social club in perpetuating general racial and religious economic and social inferiority and in light of the urgent need for reversal of racial polarization. Many private social clubs have become so affected with the public interest that some regulation of their membership practices is not only a proper but also a necessary exercise of legislative power."[e] Would such sentiments allow equality to run roughshod over other values? Consider Nancy L. Rosenblum, *Compelled Association* in *Freedom of Association* 75, 98, 101 (Amy Gutmann ed. 1998): "Regardless of an association's purpose or members' intentions, selective groups will be seen as advancing some claim to preference, privilege, or desert, and they will provoke accusations that they violate the public ethos of democratic equality. As *Roberts* demonstrates, egalitarian opposition to restrictive secular associations is endemic in the United States. [In] liberal democracy, romantic aloofness is as insufferable as exclusive groups; it too is perceived as aristocratic self-distancing, and generally despised. Nonetheless, romantic individualism points up the dark underside of gregariousness: dependence, craving for the good opinion of others, hypocrisy, and the desire of those excluded to join together and inflict the same on others. These are not just incidental accompaniments of voluntary association; they are among its sources."

James Dale's position as an assistant scoutmaster of a New Jersey troop of the Boy Scouts of America was revoked when the Boy Scouts learned that he, an Eagle Scout, was gay, the co-President of the Rutgers University Lesbian/Gay Alliance, who had been publicly quoted on the importance in his own life on the need for gay role models. Dale sued, and the New Jersey Supreme Court ultimately held that New Jersey's anti-discrimination public accommodation law required that the Scouts readmit him.

BOY SCOUTS OF AMERICA v. DALE, 530 U.S. 640, 120 S.Ct. 2446, 147 L.Ed.2d 554 (2000), per Rehnquist, C.J., held that the New Jersey accommodations law violated the expressive association rights of the Boy Scouts: "To determine

d. On the value of association, see generally Nancy L. Rosenblum, *Membership and Morals* (1998).

e. See generally Michael Burns, *The Exclusion of Women From Influential Men's Clubs:*

The Inner Sanctum and the Myth of Full Equality, 18 Harv.Civ.Rts.-Civ.Lib.L.Rev. 321 (1983).

whether a group is protected by the First Amendment's expressive associational right, we must determine whether the group engages in 'expressive association.' The First Amendment's protection of expressive association is not reserved for advocacy groups. But to come within its ambit, a group must engage in some form of expression, whether it be public or private.

"Because this is a First Amendment case where the ultimate conclusions of law are virtually inseparable from findings of fact, we are obligated to independently review the factual record to ensure that the state court's judgment does not unlawfully intrude on free expression. The record reveals the following. The Boy Scouts is a private, nonprofit organization. According to its mission statement: 'It is the mission of the Boy Scouts of America to serve others by helping to instill values in young people and, in other ways, to prepare them to make ethical choices over their lifetime in achieving their full potential. 'The values we strive to instill are based on those found in the Scout Oath and Law"

Rehnquist, C.J., cited a portion of the Scout Oath requiring Scouts to be "morally straight" and a portion of Scout law requiring Scouts to be "Clean": "Thus, the general mission of the Boy Scouts is clear: '[T]o instill values in young people.' The Boy Scouts seeks to instill these values by having its adult leaders spend time with the youth members, instructing and engaging them in activities like camping, archery, and fishing. During the time spent with the youth members, the scoutmasters and assistant scoutmasters inculcate them with the Boy Scouts' values—both expressly and by example. It seems indisputable that an association that seeks to transmit such a system of values engages in expressive activity. * * *

"Obviously, the Scout Oath and Law do not expressly mention sexuality or sexual orientation. And the terms 'morally straight' and 'clean' are by no means self-defining. Different people would attribute to those terms very different meanings. For example, some people may believe that engaging in homosexual conduct is not at odds with being 'morally straight' and 'clean.' And others may believe that engaging in homosexual conduct is contrary to being 'morally straight' and 'clean.' The Boy Scouts says it falls within the latter category.

"The Boy Scouts asserts that it 'teach[es] that homosexual conduct is not morally straight,' Brief for Petitioners 39, and that it does 'not want to promote homosexual conduct as a legitimate form of behavior,' Reply Brief for Petitioners 5. We accept the Boy Scouts' assertion. We need not inquire further to determine the nature of the Boy Scouts' expression with respect to homosexuality. But because the record before us contains written evidence of the Boy Scouts' viewpoint, we look to it as instructive, if only on the question of the sincerity of the professed beliefs."

Rehnquist, C.J., recounted a 1978 position statement to the Boy Scouts' Executive Committee, signed by the President of the Boy Scouts and the Chief Scout Executive, expressing the 'official position' that openly declared homosexuals could not be Scout leaders, a 1991 public position statement (issued after Dale's membership revocation, but before the litigation) asserting that homosexual conduct was inconsistent with being morally straight and clean, a 1993 public position statement maintaining that homosexual role models did not reflect the expectations that scouting families have had for the organization, and the Scouts' participation in litigation throughout the 80's and the 90's defending its position in litigation: "We cannot doubt that the Boy Scouts sincerely holds this view. We must then determine whether Dale's presence as an assistant scoutmaster would significantly burden the Boy Scouts' desire to not 'promote homosexual conduct as a legitimate form of behavior.' As we give deference to an association's assertions regarding the nature of its expression, we must also give deference to an association's view of what would impair its expression. [That] is not to say that an expressive association can erect a shield against antidiscrimination laws simply by asserting that mere acceptance of a member from a particular group would impair its message. But here Dale, by his own admission, is one of a group of gay Scouts who have 'become leaders in their community and are open and honest about their sexual orientation.'' Dale was the copresident of a gay and lesbian organization at college and remains a gay rights activist. Dale's presence in the Boy Scouts would, at the very least, force the organization to send a message, both to the youth members and the world, that the Boy Scouts accepts homosexual conduct as a legitimate form of behavior. * * *

"*Hurley* is illustrative on this point. There we considered whether the application of Massachusetts' public accommodations law to require the organizers of a private St. Patrick's Day parade to include among the marchers an Irish—American gay, lesbian, and bisexual group, GLIB, violated the parade organizers' First Amendment rights. We noted that the parade organizers did not wish to exclude the GLIB members because of their sexual orientations, but because they wanted to march behind a GLIB banner. We observed: '[A] contingent marching behind the organization's banner would at least bear witness to the fact that some Irish are gay, lesbian, or bisexual, and the presence of the organized marchers would suggest their view that people of their sexual orientations have as much claim to unqualified social acceptance as heterosexuals. * * * The parade's organizers may not believe these facts about Irish sexuality to be so, or they may object to unqualified social acceptance of gays and lesbians or have some other reason for wishing to keep GLIB's message out of the parade. But whatever the reason, it boils down to the choice of a speaker not to propound a particular point of view, and that choice is presumed to lie beyond the government's power to control.'

"Here, we have found that the Boy Scouts believes that homosexual conduct is inconsistent with the values it seeks to instill in its youth members; it will not 'promote homosexual conduct as a legitimate form of behavior.' Reply Brief for Petitioners 5. As the presence of GLIB in Boston's St. Patrick's Day parade would have interfered with the parade organizers' choice not to propound a particular point of view, the presence of Dale as an assistant scoutmaster would just as surely interfere with the Boy Scout's choice not to propound a point of view contrary to its beliefs.

"[A]ssociations do not have to associate for the 'purpose' of disseminating a certain message in order to be entitled to the protections of the First Amendment. An association must merely engage in expressive activity that could be impaired in order to be entitled to protection. For example, the purpose of the St. Patrick's Day parade in Hurley was not to espouse any views about sexual orientation, but we held that the parade organizers had a right to exclude certain participants nonetheless.

"[E]ven if the Boy Scouts discourages Scout leaders from disseminating views on sexual issues—a fact that the Boy Scouts disputes with contrary evidence—the First Amendment protects the Boy Scouts' method of expression. If the Boy Scouts wishes Scout leaders to avoid questions of sexuality and teach only by example, this fact does not negate the sincerity of its belief discussed above. * * *

"Dale makes much of the claim that the Boy Scouts does not revoke the membership of heterosexual Scout leaders that openly disagree with the Boy

Scouts' policy on sexual orientation. But if this is true, it is irrelevant. The presence of an avowed homosexual and gay rights activist in an assistant scoutmaster's uniform sends a distinctly different message from the presence of a heterosexual assistant scoutmaster who is on record as disagreeing with Boy Scouts policy. The Boy Scouts has a First Amendment right to choose to send one message but not the other. The fact that the organization does not trumpet its views from the housetops, or that it tolerates dissent within its ranks, does not mean that its views receive no First Amendment protection. * * *

"We recognized in cases such as *Roberts* and *Duarte* that States have a compelling interest in eliminating discrimination against women in public accommodations. But in each of these cases we went on to conclude that the enforcement of these statutes would not materially interfere with the ideas that the organization sought to express. * * *

"Dale contends that we should apply the intermediate standard of review enunciated in *O'Brien* to evaluate the competing interests. [But] New Jersey's public accommodations law directly and immediately affects associational rights, in this case associational rights that enjoy First Amendment protection. Thus, *O'Brien* is inapplicable.

"In *Hurley*, we applied traditional First Amendment analysis to hold that the application of the Massachusetts public accommodations law to a parade violated the First Amendment rights of the parade organizers. Although we did not explicitly deem the parade in Hurley an expressive association, the analysis we applied there is similar to the analysis we apply here. We have already concluded that a state requirement that the Boy Scouts retain Dale as an assistant scoutmaster would significantly burden the organization's right to oppose or disfavor homosexual conduct. The state interests embodied in New Jersey's public accommodations law do not justify such a severe intrusion on the Boy Scouts' rights to freedom of expressive association. That being the case, we hold that the First Amendment prohibits the State from imposing such a requirement through the application of its public accommodations law."

STEVENS, J., joined by Souter, Ginsburg, and Breyer, JJ., dissenting, argued that nothing in the Scout Oath or Scout Law spoke of sexual orientation even in the definitions of morally straight and clean. Moreover, he observed that Scoutmasters are instructed not to instruct Scouts in any formalized manner regarding sex because it is not "Scouting's proper area" and they are advised to steer questions about sexual matters to spiritual leaders, family, or doctors, if possible, otherwise "you may just have to do the best you can. Stevens, J., observed that the 1978 statement (made before Dale entered scouting) was never distributed to the public and itself stated that termination of an individual because of homosexuality should ensue unless a law to the contrary existed. In that case the Scouts should obey the law. Stevens, J., added that statements issued in 1991 and a similar statement in 1992 about the relationship between homosexuality and morality and cleanliness was abandoned by the 1993 statement focusing on family expectations and could not ground an adequate claim of expressive association: "[E]ven during the brief period in 1991 and 1992, when BSA tried to connect its exclusion of homosexuals to its definition of terms found in the Oath and Law, there is no evidence that Scouts were actually taught anything about homosexuality's alleged inconsistency with those principles. Beyond the single sentence in these policy statements, there is no indication of any shared goal of teaching that homosexuality is incompatible with being 'morally straight' and 'clean.' Neither BSA's mission statement nor its official membership policy was altered; no Boy

Scout or Scoutmaster Handbook was amended to reflect the policy statement; no lessons were imparted to Scouts; no change was made to BSA's policy on limiting discussion of sexual matters; and no effort was made to restrict acceptable religious affiliations to those that condemn homosexuality. In short, there is no evidence that this view was part of any collective effort to foster beliefs about homosexuality.

"[BSA] never took any clear and unequivocal position on homosexuality. Though the 1991 and 1992 policies state one interpretation of 'morally straight' and 'clean,' the group's published definitions appearing in the Boy Scout and Scoutmaster Handbooks take quite another view. And BSA's broad religious tolerance combined with its declaration that sexual matters are not its 'proper area' render its views on the issue equivocal at best and incoherent at worst. We have never held, however, that a group can throw together any mixture of contradictory positions and then invoke the right to associate to defend any one of those views. At a minimum, a group seeking to prevail over an antidiscrimination law must adhere to a clear and unequivocal view.

"[A]t most the 1991 and 1992 statements declare only that BSA believed 'homosexual conduct is inconsistent with the requirement in the Scout Oath that a Scout be morally straight and in the Scout Law that a Scout be clean in word and deed.' But New Jersey's law prohibits discrimination on the basis of sexual *orientation*. And when Dale was expelled from the Boy Scouts, BSA said it did so because of his sexual orientation, not because of his sexual conduct.

"It is clear, then, that nothing in these policy statements supports BSA's claim. The only policy written before the revocation of Dale's membership was an equivocal, undisclosed statement that evidences no connection between the group's discriminatory intentions and its expressive interests. The later policies demonstrate a brief—though ultimately abandoned—attempt to tie BSA's exclusion to its expression, but other than a single sentence, BSA fails to show that it ever taught Scouts that homosexuality is not 'morally straight' or 'clean,' or that such a view was part of the group's collective efforts to foster a belief. Furthermore, BSA's policy statements fail to establish any clear, consistent, and unequivocal position on homosexuality. Nor did BSA have any reason to think Dale's sexual conduct, as opposed to his orientation, was contrary to the group's values. * * *

"It speaks volumes about the credibility of BSA's claim to a shared goal that homosexuality is incompatible with Scouting that since at least 1984 it had been aware of this issue—indeed, concerned enough to twice file amicus briefs before this Court—yet it did nothing in the intervening six years (or even in the years after Dale's expulsion) to explain clearly and openly why the presence of homosexuals would affect its expressive activities, or to make the view of 'morally straight' and 'clean' taken in its 1991 and 1992 policies a part of the values actually instilled in Scouts through the Handbook, lessons, or otherwise.

"Several principles are made perfectly clear by *Jaycees* and *Rotary Club*. First, to prevail on a claim of expressive association in the face of a State's antidiscrimination law, it is not enough simply to engage in *some kind* of expressive activity. Both the Jaycees and the Rotary Club engaged in expressive activity protected by the First Amendment, yet that fact was not dispositive. Second, it is not enough to adopt an openly avowed exclusionary membership policy. Both the Jaycees and the Rotary Club did that as well. Third, it is not sufficient merely to articulate *some* connection between the group's expressive activities and its exclusionary policy. The Rotary Club, for example, justified its male-only membership policy by pointing to the 'aspect of fellowship ... that is enjoyed by the [exclusively] male membership' and by claiming that only with an exclusively male membership could it 'operate effectively' in foreign countries.

"Rather, in *Jaycees*, we asked whether Minnesota's Human Rights Law requiring the admission of women 'impose[d] any *serious burdens*' on the group's 'collective effort on behalf of [its] *shared goals*.' Notwithstanding the group's obvious publicly stated exclusionary policy, we did not view the inclusion of women as a 'serious burden' on the Jaycees' ability to engage in the protected speech of its choice. Similarly, in *Rotary Club*, we asked whether California's law would 'affect in any *significant* way the existing members' ability' to engage in their protected speech, or whether the law would require the clubs 'to abandon their basic goals.' * * *

"The evidence before this Court makes it exceptionally clear that BSA has, at most, simply adopted an exclusionary membership policy and has no shared goal of disapproving of homosexuality. BSA's mission statement and federal charter say nothing on the matter; its official membership policy is silent; its Scout Oath and Law—and accompanying definitions—are devoid of any view on the topic; its guidance for Scouts and Scoutmasters on sexuality declare that such matters are 'not construed to be Scouting's proper area,' but are the province of a Scout's parents and pastor; and BSA's posture respecting religion tolerates a wide variety of views on the issue of homosexuality. Moreover, there is simply no evidence that BSA otherwise teaches anything in this area, or that it instructs Scouts on matters involving homosexuality in ways not conveyed in the Boy Scout or Scoutmaster Handbooks. In short, Boy Scouts of America is simply silent on homosexuality. There is no shared goal or collective effort to foster a belief about homosexuality at all—let alone one that is significantly burdened by admitting homosexuals. * * *

"The majority pretermits this entire analysis. It finds that BSA in fact 'teach[es] that homosexual conduct is not morally straight.' 'This conclusion, remarkably, rests entirely on statements in BSA's briefs. Moreover, the majority insists that we must 'give deference to an association's assertions regarding the nature of its expression' and 'we must also give deference to an association's view of what would impair its expression.' So long as the record 'contains written evidence' to support a group's bare assertion, '[w]e need not inquire further.' Once the organization 'asserts' that it engages in particular expression, '[w]e cannot doubt' the truth of that assertion.

"This is an astounding view of the law. I am unaware of any previous instance in which our analysis of the scope of a constitutional right was determined by looking at what a litigant asserts in his or her brief and inquiring no further. It is even more astonishing in the First Amendment area, because, as the majority itself acknowledges, 'we are obligated to independently review the factual record.' It is an odd form of independent review that consists of deferring entirely to whatever a litigant claims. But the majority insists that our inquiry must be 'limited' because 'it is not the role of the courts to reject a group's expressed values because they disagree with those values or find them internally inconsistent.'

"But nothing in our cases calls for this Court to do any such thing. An organization can adopt the message of its choice, and it is not this Court's place to disagree with it. But we must inquire whether the group is, in fact, expressing a message (whatever it may be) and whether that message (if one is expressed) is significantly affected by a State's antidiscrimination law. More critically, that inquiry requires our *independent* analysis, rather than deference to a group's litigating posture. Reflection on the subject dictates that such an inquiry is required. * * *

"If this Court were to defer to whatever position an organization is prepared to assert in its briefs, there would be no way to mark the proper boundary between genuine exercises of the right to associate, on the one hand, and sham claims that are simply attempts to insulate nonexpressive private discrimination, on the other hand. Shielding a litigant's claim from judicial scrutiny would, in turn, render civil rights legislation a nullity, and turn this important constitutional right into a farce. Accordingly, the Court's prescription of total deference will not do. * * *

"In its briefs, BSA implies, even if it does not directly argue, that Dale would use his Scoutmaster position as a 'bully pulpit' to convey immoral messages to his troop, and therefore his inclusion in the group would compel BSA to include a message it does not want to impart. Even though the majority does not endorse that argument, I think it is important to explain why it lacks merit, before considering the argument the majority does accept. BSA has not contended, nor does the record support, that Dale had ever advocated a view on homosexuality to his troop before his membership was revoked. Accordingly, BSA's revocation could only have been based on an assumption that he would do so in the future. * * *

"But there is no basis for BSA to presume that a homosexual will be unable to comply with BSA's policy not to discuss sexual matters any more than it would presume that politically or religiously active members could not resist the urge to proselytize or politicize during troop meetings. As BSA itself puts it, its rights are 'not implicated unless a prospective leader presents himself as a role model inconsistent with Boy Scouting's understanding of the Scout Oath and Law.'

"The majority, though, does not rest its conclusion on the claim that Dale will use his position as a bully pulpit. Rather, it contends that Dale's mere presence among the Boy Scouts will itself force the group to convey a message about homosexuality—even if Dale has no intention of doing so. The majority holds that '[t]he presence of an avowed homosexual and gay rights activist in an assistant scoutmaster's uniform sends a distinc[t] message,' and, accordingly, BSA is entitled to exclude that message. In particular, 'Dale's presence in the Boy Scouts would, at the very least, force the organization to send a message, both to the youth members and the world, that the Boy Scouts accepts homosexual conduct as a legitimate form of behavior.'

"[Though]*Hurley* has a superficial similarity to the present case, a close inspection reveals a wide gulf between that case and the one before us today.

"First, it was critical to our analysis that GLIB was actually conveying a message by participating in the parade—otherwise, the parade organizers could hardly claim that they were being forced to include any unwanted message at all. Our conclusion that GLIB was conveying a message was inextricably tied to the fact that GLIB wanted to march in a parade, as well as the manner in which it intended to march. [Indeed,] we expressly distinguished between the members of GLIB, who marched as a unit to express their views about their own sexual orientation, on the one hand, and homosexuals who might participate as individuals in the parade without intending to express anything about their sexuality by doing so.

"Second, we found it relevant that GLIB's message 'would likely be perceived' as the parade organizers' own speech. That was so because '[p]arades and demonstrations [are] not understood to be so neutrally presented or selectively viewed' as, say, a broadcast by a cable operator, who is usually considered to be 'merely 'a conduit' for the speech' produced by others. Rather, parade organizers are usually understood to make the 'customary determination about a unit admitted to the parade.'

"Dale's inclusion in the Boy Scouts is nothing like the case in *Hurley*. His participation sends no cognizable message to the Scouts or to the world. Unlike GLIB, Dale did not carry a banner or a sign; he did not distribute any fact sheet; and he expressed no intent to send any message. If there is any kind of message being sent, then, it is by the mere act of joining the Boy Scouts. Such an act does not constitute an instance of symbolic speech under the First Amendment.

"It is true, of course, that some acts are so imbued with symbolic meaning that they qualify as 'speech' under the First Amendment. At the same time, however, '[w]e cannot accept the view that an apparently limitless variety of conduct can be labeled 'speech' whenever the person engaging in the conduct intends thereby to express an idea.' *O'Brien*. [Indeed], if merely joining a group did constitute symbolic speech; and such speech were attributable to the group being joined; and that group has the right to exclude that speech (and hence, the right to exclude that person from joining), then the right of free speech effectively becomes a limitless right to exclude for every organization, whether or not it engages in any expressive activities. That cannot be, and never has been, the law.

"The only apparent explanation for the majority's holding, then, is that homosexuals are simply so different from the rest of society that their presence alone—unlike any other individual's—should be singled out for special First Amendment treatment. Under the majority's reasoning, an openly gay male is irreversibly affixed with the label 'homosexual.' That label, even though unseen, communicates a message that permits his exclusion wherever he goes. His openness is the sole and sufficient justification for his ostracism. Though unintended, reliance on such a justification is tantamount to a constitutionally prescribed symbol of inferiority. As counsel for the Boy Scouts remarked, Dale 'put a banner around his neck when he [got] himself into the newspaper [He] created a reputation. [He] can't take that banner off. He put it on himself and, indeed, he has continued to put it on himself.'

"Another difference between this case and *Hurley* lies in the fact that *Hurley* involved the parade organizers' claim to determine the content of the message they wish to give at a particular time and place. The standards governing such a claim are simply different from the standards that govern BSA's claim of a right of expressive association. Generally, a private person or a private organization has a right to refuse to broadcast a message with which it disagrees, and a right to refuse to contradict or garble its own specific statement at any given place or time by including the messages of others. An expressive association claim, however, normally involves the avowal and advocacy of a consistent position on some issue over time. This is why a different kind of scrutiny must be given to an expressive association claim, lest the right of expressive association simply turn into a right to discriminate whenever some group can think of an expressive object that would seem to be inconsistent with the admission of some person as a member or at odds with the appointment of a person to a leadership position in the group."[a]

a. Souter, J., joined by Ginsburg, J., and Breyer, J., also dissented.

IV. POLITICAL ASSOCIATION AND POLITICAL PARTIES

Minnesota's "antifusion" laws prohibit political candidates from appearing on the ballot as candidates for more than one party. Twin Cities Area New Party ("New Party") named a candidate for state representative, Andy Dawkins, who also was a candidate of the Minnesota–Democratic–Farmer–Labor Party ("DFL"). Dawkins signed an affidavit for the New Party, but local election officials refused to accept it since his affidavit of candidacy for DFL had already been filed.[a] TIMMONS v. TWIN CITIES AREA NEW PARTY, 520 U.S. 351, 117 S.Ct. 1364, 137 L.Ed.2d 589 (1997), per REHNQUIST, C.J., upheld the antifusion laws: "The First Amendment protects the right of citizens to associate and to form political parties for the advancement of common political goals and ideas. * * * [On] the other hand, it is also clear that States may, and inevitably must, enact reasonable regulations of parties, elections, and ballots to reduce election- and campaign-related disorder. [When] deciding whether a state election law violates First and Fourteenth Amendment associational rights, we weigh the ' "character and magnitude" ' of the burden the State's rule imposes on those rights against the interests the State contends justify that burden, and consider the extent to which the State's concerns make the burden necessary. Regulations imposing severe burdens on plaintiffs' rights must be narrowly tailored and advance a compelling state interest. Lesser burdens, however, trigger less exacting review, and a State's ' "important regulatory interests" ' will usually be enough to justify ' "reasonable, nondiscriminatory restrictions." ' No bright line separates permissible election-related regulation from unconstitutional infringements on First Amendment freedoms.

"The New Party [has] the right to select the New Party's 'standard bearer.' It does not follow, though, that a party is absolutely entitled to have its nominee appear on the ballot as that party's candidate. A particular candidate might be ineligible for office, unwilling to serve, or, as here, another party's candidate. That a particular individual may not appear on the ballot as a particular party's candidate does not severely burden that party's association rights.

"The New Party relies on *Eu v. San Francisco County Democratic Central Comm.,* 489 U.S. 214, 109 S.Ct. 1013, 103 L.Ed.2d 271 (1989)[b] and *Tashjian v. Republican Party of Conn.,* 479 U.S. 208, 107 S.Ct. 544, 93 L.Ed.2d 514 (1986). In *Eu,* we struck down California election provisions that prohibited political parties from endorsing candidates in party primaries and regulated parties' internal affairs and structure. And in *Tashjian,* we held that Connecticut's closed-primary statute, which required voters in a party primary to be registered party members, interfered with a party's associational rights by limiting 'the group of registered voters whom the Party may invite to participate in the basic function of selecting the Party's candidates.'[c] But while *Tashjian* and *Eu* involved regulation of political parties' internal affairs and core associational activities,[d] Minnesota's fusion ban does not. The ban, which applies to major and minor parties alike, simply precludes one party's candidate from appearing on the ballot, as that

---

a. The DFL did not object.

b. For commentary, see Daniel Lowenstein, *Associational Rights of Major Political Parties: A Skeptical Inquiry,* 71 Tex. L.Rev. 1741 (1993).

c. *California Democratic Party v. Jones,* 530 U.S. 567, 120 S.Ct. 2402, 147 L.Ed.2d 502 (2000) invalidated California's "blanket primary" which required parties to permit citizens to vote in the primary of any party for any office regardless of their party membership.

d. But see *Morse v. Republican Party of Va.,* 517 U.S. 186, 116 S.Ct. 1186, 134 L.Ed.2d 347 (1996)(requiring for preclearance by Attorney General fee requirement to become a delegate to a state nomination convention under the Voting Rights Act does not violate freedom of association rights).

party's candidate, if already nominated by another party. Respondent is free to try to convince Representative Dawkins to be the New Party's, not the DFL's, candidate. * * *

"It is true that Minnesota's fusion ban prevents the New Party from using the ballot to communicate to the public that it supports a particular candidate who is already another party's candidate. In addition, the ban shuts off one possible avenue a party might use to send a message to its preferred *candidate* because, with fusion, a candidate who wins an election on the basis of two parties' votes will likely know more—if the parties' votes are counted separately—about the particular wishes and ideals of his constituency. [But] ballots serve primarily to elect candidates, not as fora for political expression. [We] conclude that the burdens Minnesota imposes on the Party's First and Fourteenth Amendment associational rights—though not trivial—are not severe. "[Therefore,] the State's asserted regulatory interests need only be 'sufficiently weighty to justify the limitation' imposed on the Party's rights. Nor do we require elaborate, empirical verification of the weightiness of the State's asserted justifications. * * *

"Minnesota argues here that its fusion ban is justified by its interests in avoiding voter confusion, promoting candidate competition (by reserving limited ballot space for opposing candidates), preventing electoral distortions and ballot manipulations, and discouraging party splintering and 'unrestrained factionalism.' * * * Petitioners contend that a candidate or party could easily exploit fusion as a way of associating his or its name with popular slogans and catch phrases. For example, members of a major party could decide that a powerful way of 'sending a message' via the ballot would be for various factions of that party to nominate the major party's candidate as the candidate for the newly-formed 'No New Taxes,' 'Conserve Our Environment,' and 'Stop Crime Now' parties. In response, an opposing major party would likely instruct its factions to nominate that party's candidate as the 'Fiscal Responsibility,' 'Healthy Planet,' and 'Safe Streets' parties' candidate.

[The] New Party responds to this concern, ironically enough, by insisting that the State could avoid such manipulation by adopting more demanding ballot-access standards rather than prohibiting multiple-party nomination. However, [because] the burdens the fusion ban imposes on the Party's associational rights are not severe, the State need not narrowly tailor the means it chooses to promote ballot integrity. The Constitution does not require that Minnesota compromise the policy choices embodied in its ballot-access requirements to accommodate the New Party's fusion strategy.

"Relatedly, petitioners urge that permitting fusion would undercut Minnesota's ballot-access regime. [That] is, voters who might not sign a minor party's nominating petition based on the party's own views and candidates might do so if they viewed the minor party as just another way of nominating the same person nominated by one of the major parties. * * * [The] State surely has a valid interest in making sure that minor and third parties who are granted access to the ballot are bona fide and actually supported, on their own merits, by those who have provided the statutorily required petition or ballot support.

"States also have a strong interest in the stability of their political systems. This interest does not permit a State to completely insulate the two-party system from minor parties' or independent candidates' competition and influence, nor is it a paternalistic license for States to protect political parties from the consequences of their own internal disagreements. That said, the States' interest permits them to enact reasonable election regulations that may, in practice, favor the traditional two-party system, and that temper the destabilizing effects of party-splintering and excessive factionalism. [And] while an interest in securing the perceived benefits of a stable two-party system will not justify unreasonably exclusionary restrictions, States need not remove all of the many hurdles third parties face in the American political arena today.

"In *Storer v. Brown,* 415 U.S. 724, 94 S.Ct. 1274, 39 L.Ed.2d 714 (1974), we upheld a California statute that denied ballot positions to independent candidates who had voted in the immediately preceding primary elections or had a registered party affiliation at any time during the year before the same primary elections.[11] [We] noted that the provision did not discriminate against independent candidates. We concluded [that] California apparently believes with the Founding Fathers that splintered parties and unrestrained factionalism may do significant damage to the fabric of government. It appears obvious to us that the one-year disaffiliation provision furthers the State's interest in the stability of its political system.'[12]

"Our decision in *Burdick v. Takushi,* 504 U.S. 428, 112 S.Ct. 2059, 119 L.Ed.2d 245 (1992) is also relevant. There, we upheld Hawaii's ban on write-in voting [we] rejected the petitioner's argument that the ban 'deprive[d] him of the opportunity to cast a meaningful ballot,' emphasizing that the function of elections is to elect candidates and that 'we have repeatedly upheld reasonable, politically neutral regulations that have the effect of channeling expressive activit[ies] at the polls.'

"[Under] the California disaffiliation statute at issue in *Storer, any* person affiliated with a party at any time during the year leading up to the primary election was absolutely precluded from appearing on the ballot as an independent or as the candidate of another party. Minnesota's fusion ban is not nearly so restrictive * * * California's disaffiliation rule limited the field of candidates by thousands; Minnesota's precludes only a handful who freely choose to be so limited. It is also worth noting that while California's disaffiliation statute absolutely banned many candidacies, Minnesota's fusion ban only prohibits a candidate from being named twice.

"[T]he Constitution does not require Minnesota, and the approximately 40 other States that do not permit fusion, to allow it."[e]

STEVENS, J., joined in part by Ginsburg and Souter, JJ., dissented: "The members of a recognized political party unquestionably have a constitutional right to select their nominees for public office and to communicate the identity of their

---

11. A similar provision applied to party candidates, and imposed a "flat disqualification upon any candidate seeking to run in a party primary if he has been 'registered as affiliated with a political party other than that political party the nomination of which he seeks within 12 months immediately prior to the filing of the declaration.' " Another provision stated that "no person may file nomination papers for a party nomination and an independent nomination for the same office...."

12. The dissent insists that New York's experience with fusion politics undermines Minnesota's contention that its fusion ban promotes political stability. California's experiment with cross-filing, on the other hand, provides some justification for Minnesota's concerns. In 1946, for example, Earl Warren was the nominee of both major parties, and was therefore able to run unopposed in California's general election. It appears to be widely accepted that California's cross-filing system stifled electoral competition and undermined the role of distinctive political parties.

e. For relevant commentary, see James Gray Pope, *Fusion, Timmons v. Twin Cities Area New Party, and the Future of Third Parties in the United States,* 50 Rutgers. L.Rev. 473 (1998); Note, *Fusion Candidacies, Disaggregation, and Freedom of Association,* 109 Harv. L.Rev. 1302 (1996); Note, *Fusion and the Associational Rights of Minor Political Parties,* 95 Colum. L.Rev. 683 (1995).

nominees to the voting public. Both the right to choose and the right to advise voters of that choice are entitled to the highest respect.

"The Minnesota statutes place a significant burden on both of those rights. [The] fact that the Party may nominate its second choice surely does not diminish the significance of a restriction that denies it the right to have the name of its first choice appear on the ballot. Nor does the point that it may use some of its limited resources to publicize the fact that its first choice is the nominee of some other party provide an adequate substitute for the message that is conveyed to every person who actually votes when a party's nominees appear on the ballot.[1] [T]he right to be on the election ballot is precisely what separates a political party from any other interest group.

"The majority rejects as unimportant the limits that the fusion ban may impose on the Party's ability to express its political views. [But] the long-recognized right to choose a ' "standard bearer who best represents the party's ideologies and preferences," ' *Eu,* is inescapably an expressive right. 'To the extent that party labels provide a shorthand designation of the views of party candidates on matters of public concern, the identification of candidates with particular parties plays a role in the process by which voters inform themselves for the exercise of the franchise.' *Tashjian.*

"[E]ven accepting the majority's view that the burdens imposed by the law are not weighty, the State's asserted interests must at least bear some plausible relationship to the burdens it places on political parties. * * *

"While the State describes some imaginative theoretical sources of voter confusion that could result from fusion candidacies, in my judgment the argument that the burden on First Amendment interests is justified by this concern is meritless and severely underestimates the intelligence of the typical voter. We have noted more than once that ' "[a] State's claim that it is enhancing the ability of its citizenry to make wise decisions by restricting the flow of information to them must be viewed with some skepticism." ' *Eu*; *Tashjian.*

"The State's concern about ballot manipulation, readily accepted by the majority, is similarly farfetched. The possibility that members of the major parties will begin to create dozens of minor parties with detailed, issue-oriented titles for the sole purpose of nominating candidates under those titles is entirely hypothetical. The majority dismisses out-of-hand the Party's argument that the risk of this type of ballot manipulation and crowding is more easily averted by maintaining reasonably stringent requirements for the creation of minor parties. '[The] State has the undoubted right to require candidates to make a preliminary showing of substantial support in order to qualify for a place on the ballot, because it is both wasteful and confusing to encumber the ballot with the names of frivolous candidates.' But once the State has established a standard for achieving party status, forbidding an acknowledged party from putting on the ballot its chosen candidate clearly frustrates core associational rights.

---

1. [A] fusion ban [also] burdens the right of a minor party to broaden its base of support because of the political reality that the dominance of the major parties frequently makes a vote for a minor party or independent candidate a "wasted" vote. When minor parties can nominate a candidate also nominated by a major party, they are able to present their members with an opportunity to cast a vote for a candidate who will actually be elected. Although this aspect of a party's effort to broaden support is distinct from the ability to nominate the candidate who best represents the party's views, it is important to note that the party's right to broaden the base of its support is burdened in both ways by the fusion ban.

"[The interest in preserving the two-party system is not] sufficient to justify the fusion ban.[f] In most States, perhaps in all, there are two and only two major political parties. It is not surprising, therefore, that most States have enacted election laws that impose burdens on the development and growth of third parties. The law at issue in this case is undeniably such a law. The fact that the law was both intended to disadvantage minor parties and has had that effect is a matter that should weigh against, rather than in favor of, its constitutionality.

"Our jurisprudence in this area reflects a certain tension: on the one hand, we have been clear that political stability is an important state interest and that incidental burdens on the formation of minor parties are reasonable to protect that interest, see *Storer;* on the other, we have struck down state elections laws specifically because they give 'the two old, established parties a decided advantage over any new parties struggling for existence,' *Williams v. Rhodes,* 393 U.S. 23, 89 S.Ct. 5, 21 L.Ed.2d 24 (1968).[7] * * *[g]

"Nothing in the Constitution prohibits the States from maintaining single-member districts with winner-take-all voting arrangements. And these elements of an election system do make it significantly more difficult for third parties to thrive. But these laws are different in two respects from the fusion bans at issue here. First, the method by which they hamper third-party development is not one that impinges on the associational rights of those third parties; minor parties remain free to nominate candidates of their choice, and to rally support for those candidates. The small parties' relatively limited likelihood of ultimate success on election day does not deprive them of the right to try. Second, the establishment of single-member districts correlates directly with the States' interests in political stability. Systems of proportional representation, for example, may tend toward factionalism and fragile coalitions that diminish legislative effectiveness. In the context of fusion candidacies, the risks to political stability are extremely attenuated.[8] Of course, the reason minor parties so ardently support fusion politics is because it allows the parties to build up a greater base of support, as potential minor party members realize that a vote for the smaller party candidate is not necessarily a 'wasted' vote. Eventually, a minor party might gather sufficient strength that—were its members so inclined—it could successfully run a candidate not endorsed by any major party, and legislative coalition-building will be made more difficult by the presence of third party legislators. But the risks to political stability in that scenario are speculative at best. * * *

f. Stevens, J., maintained that the majority should not have considered the interest in maintaining the two-party system because it was not argued in the briefs and was rejected by the state at oral arguments. Ginsburg and Souter, JJ., did not join the section of Stevens, J.'s opinion about the two-party system.

7. In *Anderson v. Celebrezze,* 460 U.S. 780, 103 S.Ct. 1564, 75 L.Ed.2d 547 (1983) the State argued that its interest in political stability justified the early filing deadline for presidential candidates at issue in the case. We recognized that the 'asserted interest in political stability amounts to a desire to protect existing political parties from competition,' and rejected that interest.

g. *Williams* dealt with ballot access requirements making it virtually impossible for new political parties, even ones with hundreds

of thousands of members, to gain access to the ballot. In Presidential elections, for example, Ohio had required new parties to submit petitions totaling 15% of the number of ballots cast in the prior gubernatorial election. (Most states require less than 1% of the ballots cast). The result was to confine the ballot to the two major parties. The Court struck down the statute on equal protection grounds: "There is, of course, no reason why two parties should retain a permanent monopoly on the right to have people vote for or against them."

8. Even in a system that allows fusion, a candidate for election must assemble majority support, so the State's concern cannot logically be about risks to political stability in the particular election in which the fusion candidate is running.

"The strength of the two-party system—and of each of its major components—is the product of the power of the ideas, the traditions, the candidates, and the voters that constitute the parties. It demeans the strength of the two-party system to assume that the major parties need to rely on laws that discriminate against independent voters and minor parties in order to preserve their positions of power.[12] Indeed, it is a central theme of our jurisprudence that the entire electorate, which necessarily includes the members of the major parties, will benefit from robust competition in ideas and governmental [policies]."

SOUTER, J., dissenting, was willing to "judge the challenged statutes only on the interests the State has raised in their defense and would hold them unconstitutional. [Surely] the majority is right that States 'have a strong interest in the stability of their political systems,' that is, in preserving a political system capable of governing effectively. If it could be shown that the disappearance of the two-party system would undermine that interest, and that permitting fusion candidacies poses a substantial threat to the two-party scheme, there might well be a sufficient predicate for recognizing the constitutionality of the state action presented by this case. Right now, however, no State has attempted even to make this argument, and I would therefore leave its consideration for another day."

SECTION 10. WEALTH AND THE POLITICAL PROCESS: CONCERNS FOR EQUALITY

The idea of equality has loomed large throughout this chapter. Some feel it should be a central concern of the first amendment. See Laurence Tribe, *Constitutional Choices* 188–220 (1985); Kenneth Karst, *Equality as a Central Principle in the First Amendment*, 43 U.Chi.L.Rev. 20 (1975). Equality has been championed by those who seek access to government property and to media facilities. It has been invoked in support of content regulation and against it. This section considers government efforts to prevent the domination of the political process by wealthy individuals and business corporations. In the end, it would be appropriate to reconsider the arguments for and against a marketplace conception of the first amendment, to ask whether the Court's interpretations overall (e.g., taking the public forum materials, the media materials, and the election materials together) have adequately considered the interest in equality, and to inquire generally about the relationship between liberty and equality in the constitutional scheme.

BUCKLEY v. VALEO

424 U.S. 1, 96 S.Ct. 612, 46 L.Ed.2d 659 (1976).

PER CURIAM.

[In this portion of a lengthy opinion dealing with the validity of the Federal Election Campaign Act of 1971, as amended in 1974, the Court considers those parts of the Act limiting *contributions* to a candidate for federal office (all sustained), and those parts limiting *expenditures* in support of such candidacy (all held invalid).]

A. *General Principles.* The Act's contribution and expenditure limitations operate in an area of the most fundamental First Amendment activities. Discus-

---

12. The experience in New York with fusion politics provides considerable evidence that neither political stability nor the ultimate strength of the two major parties is truly risked by the existence of successful minor parties.

sion of public issues and debate on the qualifications of candidates are integral to the operation of the system of government established by our Constitution.

[Appellees] contend that what the Act regulates is conduct, and that its effect on speech and association is incidental at most. Appellants respond that contributions and expenditures are at the very core of political speech, and that the Act's limitations thus constitute restraints on First Amendment liberty that are both gross and [direct.]

We cannot share the view [that] the present Act's contribution and expenditure limitations are comparable to the restrictions on conduct upheld in *O'Brien* [p. 762 supra]. The expenditure of money simply cannot be equated with such conduct as destruction of a draft card. Some forms of communication made possible by the giving and spending of money involve speech alone, some involve conduct primarily, and some involve a combination of the two. Yet this Court has never suggested that the dependence of a communication on the expenditure of money operates itself to introduce a non-speech element or to reduce the exacting scrutiny required by the First Amendment. * * *

Even if the categorization of the expenditure of money as conduct were accepted, the limitations challenged here would not meet the *O'Brien* test because the governmental interests advanced in support of the Act involve "suppressing communication." The interests served by the Act include restricting the voices of people and interest groups who have money to spend and reducing the overall scope of federal election campaigns. [Unlike] *O'Brien*, where [the] interest in the preservation of draft cards was wholly unrelated to their use as a means of communication, it is beyond dispute that the interest in regulating the alleged "conduct" of giving or spending money "arises in some measure because the communication allegedly integral to the conduct is itself thought to be harmful."

Nor can the Act's contribution and expenditure limitations be sustained, as some of the parties suggest, by reference to the constitutional principles reflected in such decisions as *Cox v. Louisiana, Adderley,* and *Kovacs,* [Secs. 6, II and III, Ch. 6, Sec. 2 supra]. [The] critical difference between this case and those time, place and manner cases is that the present Act's contribution and expenditure limitations impose direct quantity restrictions on political communication and association by persons, groups, candidates and political parties in addition to any reasonable time, place, and manner regulations otherwise imposed.

A restriction on the amount of money a person or group can spend on political communication during a campaign necessarily reduces the quantity of expression by restricting the number of issues discussed, the depth of their exploration, and the size of the audience reached. This is because virtually every means of communicating ideas in today's mass society requires the expenditure of [money].

The expenditure limitations contained in the Act represent substantial rather than merely theoretical restraints on the quantity and diversity of political speech. The $1,000 ceiling on spending "relative to a clearly identified candidate," 18 U.S.C. § 608(e)(1), would appear to exclude all citizens and groups except candidates, political parties and the institutional press from any significant use of the most effective modes of communication.[20] * * *

---

20. The record indicates that, as of January 1, 1975, one full-page advertisement in a daily edition of a certain metropolitan newspaper costs $6,971.04—almost seven times the annu- al limit on expenditures "relative to" a particular candidate imposed on the vast majority of individual citizens and associations by § 608(e)(1).

By contrast with a limitation upon expenditures for political expression, a limitation [on] the amount of money a person may give to a candidate or campaign organization [involves] little direct restraint on his political communication, for it permits the symbolic expression of support evidenced by a contribution but does not in any way infringe the contributor's freedom to discuss candidates and issues. While contributions may result in political expression if spent by a candidate or an association to present views to the voters, the transformation of contributions into political debate involves speech by someone other than the contributor.

[There] is no indication [that] the contribution limitations imposed by the Act would have any dramatic adverse effect on the funding of campaigns and political associations.[23] The overall effect of the Act's contribution ceilings is merely to require candidates and political committees to raise funds from a greater number of persons and to compel people who would otherwise contribute amounts greater than the statutory limits to expend such funds on direct political expression, rather than to reduce the total amount of money potentially available to promote political expression. * * *

In sum, although the Act's contribution and expenditure limitations both implicate fundamental First Amendment interests, its expenditure ceilings impose significantly more severe restrictions on protected freedoms of political expression and association than do its limitations on financial contributions.

B. *Contribution Limitations.* [Section] 608(b) provides, with certain limited exceptions, that "no person shall make contributions to any candidate with respect to any election for Federal office which, in the aggregate, exceeds $1,000."[a] * * *

Appellants contend that the $1,000 contribution ceiling unjustifiably burdens First Amendment freedoms, employs overbroad dollar limits, and discriminates against candidates opposing incumbent officeholders and against minor-party candidates in violation of the Fifth Amendment.

[In] view of the fundamental nature of the right to associate, governmental "action which may have the effect of curtailing the freedom to associate is subject to the closest scrutiny." Yet, it is clear that "[n]either the right to associate nor the right to participate in political activities is absolute." *Letter Carriers* [p. 972 supra]. Even a " 'significant interference' with protected rights of political association" may be sustained if the State demonstrates a sufficiently important interest and employs means closely drawn to avoid unnecessary abridgment of associational freedoms. * * *

It is unnecessary to look beyond the Act's primary purpose—to limit the actuality and appearance of corruption resulting from large individual financial contributions—in order to find a constitutionally sufficient justification for the $1,000 contribution limitation. [The] increasing importance of the communications media and sophisticated mass mailing and polling operations to effective

---

23. Statistical findings agreed to by the parties reveal that approximately 5.1% of the $73,483,613 raised by the 1161 candidates for Congress in 1974 was obtained in amounts in excess of $1,000. In 1974, two major-party senatorial candidates, Ramsey Clark and Senator Charles Mathias, Jr., operated large-scale campaigns on contributions raised under a voluntarily imposed $100 contribution limitation.

a. As defined, "person" includes "an individual, partnership, committee, association, corporation or any other organization or group." The limitation applies to: (1) anything of value, such as gifts, loans, advances, and promises to give, (2) contributions made direct to the candidate or to an intermediary, or a committee authorized by the candidate, (3) the aggregate amounts contributed to the candidate for each election, treating primaries, runoff elections and general elections separately and all Presidential primaries within a single calendar year as one election.

campaigning make the raising of large sums of money an ever more essential ingredient of an effective candidacy. To the extent that large contributions are given to secure political quid pro quos from current and potential office holders, the integrity of our system of representative democracy is undermined. Although the scope of such pernicious practices can never be reliably ascertained, the deeply disturbing examples surfacing after the 1972 election demonstrate that the problem is not an illusory one.

Of almost equal concern as the danger of actual quid pro quo arrangements is the impact of the appearance of corruption stemming from public awareness of the opportunities for abuse inherent in a regime of large individual financial contributions. In *Letter Carriers,* the Court found that the danger to "fair and effective government" posed by partisan political conduct on the part of federal employees charged with administering the law was a sufficiently important concern to justify broad restrictions on the employees' right of partisan political association. Here, as there, Congress could legitimately conclude that the avoidance of the appearance of improper influence "is also critical [if] confidence in the system of representative Government is not to be eroded to a disastrous extent."[29]

Appellants contend that the contribution limitations must be invalidated because bribery laws and narrowly-drawn disclosure requirements constitute a less restrictive means of dealing with "proven and suspected quid pro quo arrangements." But laws [against] bribes deal with only the most blatant and specific attempts of those with money to influence governmental action. [And] Congress was surely entitled to conclude that disclosure was only a partial measure, and that contribution ceilings were a necessary legislative concomitant to deal with the reality or appearance of corruption inherent in a system permitting unlimited financial contributions, even when the identities of the contributors and the amounts of their contributions are fully disclosed.

The Act's $1,000 contribution limitation focuses precisely on the problem of large campaign contributions—the narrow aspect of political association where the actuality and potential for corruption have been identified—while leaving persons free to engage in independent political expression, to associate actively through volunteering their services. [The] Act's contribution limitations [do] not undermine to any material degree the potential for robust and effective discussion of candidates and campaign [issues].

We find that, under the rigorous standard of review established by our prior decisions, the weighty interests served by restricting the size of financial contributions to political candidates are sufficient to justify the limited effect upon First Amendment freedoms caused by the $1,000 contribution ceiling.[b]

---

29. Although the Court in *Letter Carriers* found that this interest was constitutionally sufficient to justify legislation prohibiting federal employees from engaging in certain partisan political activities, it was careful to emphasize that the limitations did not restrict an employee's right to express his views on political issues and candidates.

b. The Court rejected the challenges that the $1,000 limit was overbroad because (1) most large contributors do not seek improper influence over a candidate, and (2) much more than $1,000 would still not be enough to influence improperly a candidate or office holder. With respect to (1), "Congress was justified in concluding that the interest in safeguarding

against the appearance of impropriety requires that the opportunity for abuse inherent in the process of raising large monetary contributions be eliminated." With respect to (2), "As the Court of Appeals observed, '[a] court has no scalpel to probe, whether, say, a $2,000 ceiling might not serve as well as $1,000.' Such distinctions in degree become significant only when they can be said to amount to differences in kind."

The Court also rejected as without support in the record the claims that the contribution limitations worked invidious discrimination between incumbents and challengers to whom the same limitations applied.

C. *Expenditure Limitations.* [1.] Section 608(e)(1) provides that "[n]o person may make any expenditure [relative] to a clearly identified candidate during a calendar year which, when added to all other expenditures made by such person during the year advocating the election or defeat of such candidate, exceeds $1,000." [Its] plain effect [is] to prohibit all individuals, who are neither candidates nor owners of institutional press facilities, and all groups, except political parties and campaign organizations, from voicing their views "relative to a clearly identified candidate" through means that entail aggregate expenditures of more than $1,000 during a calendar year. The provision, for example, would make it a federal criminal offense for a person or association to place a single one-quarter page advertisement "relative to a clearly identified candidate" in a major metropolitan newspaper.

[Although] "expenditure," "clearly identified," and "candidate" are defined in the Act, there is no definition clarifying what expenditures are "relative to" a candidate. [But the "when" clause in § 608(e)(1)] clearly permits, if indeed it does not require, the phrase "relative to" a candidate to be read to mean "advocating the election or defeat of" a candidate.

But while such a construction of § 608(e)(1) refocuses the vagueness question, [it hardly] eliminates the problem of unconstitutional vagueness altogether. For the distinction between discussion of issues and candidates and advocacy of election or defeat of candidates may often dissolve in practical application. Candidates, especially incumbents, are intimately tied to public issues involving legislative proposals and governmental actions. Not only do candidates campaign on the basis of their positions on various public issues, but campaigns themselves generate issues of public interest.

[Constitutionally deficient uncertainty which "compels the speaker to hedge and trim"] can be avoided only by reading § 608(e)(1) as limited to communications that include explicit words of advocacy of election or defeat of a candidate, much as the definition of "clearly identified" in § 608(e)(2) requires that an explicit and unambiguous reference to the candidate appear as part of the communication. This is the reading of the provision suggested by the nongovernmental appellees in arguing that "[f]unds spent to propagate one's views on issues without expressly calling for a candidate's election or defeat are thus not covered." We agree that in order to preserve the provision against invalidation on vagueness grounds, § 608(e)(1) must be construed to apply only to expenditures for communications that in express terms advocate the election or defeat of a clearly identified candidate for federal office.[c]

We turn then to the basic First Amendment question—whether § 608(e)(1), even as thus narrowly and explicitly construed, impermissibly burdens the constitutional right of free expression. * * *

We find that the governmental interest in preventing corruption and the appearance of corruption is inadequate to justify § 608(e)(1)'s ceiling on indepen-

---

The Court then upheld (1) exclusion from the $1,000 limit of the value of unpaid volunteer services and of certain expenses paid by the volunteer up to a maximum of $500; (2) the higher limit of $5,000 for contributions to a candidate by established, registered political committees with at least 50 contributing supporters and fielding at least five candidates for federal office; and (3) the $25,000 limit on total contributions to all candidates by one person in one calendar year.

c. On the issues raised by this interpretation, see Richard Briffault, *Issue Advocacy: Redrawing the Elections/Politics Line,* 77 Texas L.Rev. 1751 (1999); Allison R. Hayward, *When Does an Advertisement about Issues Become an "Issues" Ad,* 49 Cath. U.L.Rev. 63 (1999); Glenn J. Moramarco, *Beyond "Magic Words": Using Self–Disclosure to Regulate Electioneering,* 49 Cath. U.L.Rev. 107 (1999).

dent expenditures. First, assuming arguendo that large independent expenditures pose the same dangers of actual or apparent quid pro quo arrangements as do large contributions, § 608(e)(1) does not provide an answer that sufficiently relates to the elimination of those dangers. Unlike the contribution limitations' total ban on the giving of large amounts of money to candidates, § 608(e)(1) prevents only some large expenditures. So long as persons and groups eschew expenditures that in express terms advocate the election or defeat of a clearly identified candidate, they are free to spend as much as they want to promote the candidate and his views. The exacting interpretation of the statutory language necessary to avoid unconstitutional vagueness thus undermines the limitation's effectiveness as a loophole-closing provision by facilitating circumvention by those seeking to exert improper influence upon a candidate or office-holder. It would naively underestimate the ingenuity and resourcefulness of persons and groups desiring to buy influence to believe that they would have much difficulty devising expenditures that skirted the restriction on express advocacy of election or defeat but nevertheless benefitted the candidate's campaign. * * *

Second, [the] independent advocacy restricted by the provision does not presently appear to pose dangers of real or apparent corruption comparable to those identified with large campaign contributions. The parties defending § 608(e)(1) contend that it is necessary to prevent would-be contributors from avoiding the contribution limitations by the simple expedient of paying directly for media advertisements or for other portions of the candidate's campaign activities. [Section] 608(b)'s contribution ceilings rather than § 608(e)(1)'s independent expenditure limitation prevent attempts to circumvent the Act through prearranged or coordinated expenditures amounting to disguised contributions.[53] By contrast, § 608(e)(1) limits expenditures for express advocacy of candidates made totally independently of the candidate and his campaign. [The] absence of prearrangement and coordination of an expenditure with the candidate or his agent not only undermines the value of the expenditure to the candidate, but also alleviates the danger that expenditures will be given as a quid pro quo for improper commitments from the candidate. Rather than preventing circumvention of the contribution limitations, § 608(e)(1) severely restricts all independent advocacy despite its substantially diminished potential for abuse.

While the independent expenditure ceiling thus fails to serve any substantial governmental interest in stemming the reality or appearance of corruption in the electoral process, it heavily burdens core First Amendment expression. [Advocacy] of the election or defeat of candidates for federal office is no less entitled to protection under the First Amendment than the discussion of political policy generally or advocacy of the passage or defeat of legislation.

It is argued, however, that the ancillary governmental interest in equalizing the relative ability of individuals and groups to influence the outcome of elections serves to justify the limitation on express advocacy of the election or defeat of

---

53. Section 608(e)(1) does not apply to expenditures "on behalf of a candidate within the meaning of" § 608(2)(B). That section provides that expenditures "authorized or requested by the candidate, an authorized committee of the candidate, or an agent of the candidate" are to be treated as expenditures of the candidate and contributions by the person or group making the expenditure. [In] view of [the] legislative history and the purposes of the Act, we find that the "authorized or requested" standard of the Act operates to treat all expenditures placed in cooperation with or with the consent of a candidate, his agents, or an authorized committee of the candidate as contributions subject to the limitations set forth in § 608(b). [Eds. Subsequent cases have held that group expenditures on behalf of a candidate that are not coordinated with the candidate may not constitutionally be restricted. FEC v. National Conservative Political Action Comm., 470 U.S. 480, 105 S.Ct. 1459, 84 L.Ed.2d 455 (1985)].

candidates imposed by § 608(e)(1)'s expenditure ceiling. But the concept that government may restrict the speech of some elements of our society in order to enhance the relative voice of others[d] is wholly foreign to the First Amendment, which was designed "to secure 'the widest possible dissemination of information from diverse and antagonistic sources,'" and "'to assure unfettered interchange of ideas for the bringing about of political and social changes desired by the people.'" *New York Times Co. v. Sullivan.* The First Amendment's protection against governmental abridgement of free expression cannot properly be made to depend on a person's financial ability to engage in public discussion.[55]

* * * *Mills v. Alabama,* 384 U.S. 214, 86 S.Ct. 1434, 16 L.Ed.2d 484 (1966), held that legislative restrictions on advocacy of the election or defeat of political candidates are wholly at odds with the guarantees of the First Amendment. [Yet] the prohibition on election day editorials invalidated in *Mills* is clearly a lesser intrusion on constitutional freedom than a $1,000 limitation on the amount of money any person or association can spend *during an entire election year* in advocating the election or defeat of a candidate for public office.

For the reasons stated, we conclude that § 608(e)(1)'s independent expenditure limitation is unconstitutional under the First Amendment. * * *[e]

2. [The] Act also sets limits on expenditures by a candidate "from his personal funds, or the personal funds of his immediate family, in connection with his campaigns during any calendar year." § 608(a)(1).[f]

The ceiling on personal expenditures by candidates on their own behalf [imposes] a substantial restraint on the ability of persons to engage in protected First Amendment expression. The candidate, no less than any other person, has a First Amendment right to engage in the discussion of public issues and vigorously and tirelessly to advocate his own election and the election of other candidates. Indeed, it is of particular importance that candidates have the unfettered opportunity to make their views known so that the electorate may intelligently evaluate the candidates' personal qualities and their positions on vital public issues before choosing among them on election day. [Section] 608(a)'s ceiling on personal expenditures by a candidate in furtherance of his own candidacy thus clearly and directly interferes with constitutionally protected freedoms.

The primary governmental interest served by the Act—the prevention of actual and apparent corruption of the political process—does not support the limitation on the candidate's expenditure of his own personal funds. [Indeed], the

---

d. For sustained defense of this aspect of *Buckley,* see Martin H. Redish & Kirk J. Kaludis, *The Right of Expressive Access in First Amendment Theory: Redistributive Values and the Democratic Dilemma,* 93 Nw.U.L.Rev. 1083 (1999). On the other hand, the lower court characterized the issue somewhat differently: Can "the wealthy few [claim] a constitutional guarantee to a stronger political voice than the unwealthy many because they are able to give and spend more money, and because the amounts they give and spend cannot be limited"? 519 F.2d 821, 841 (D.C.Cir.1975).

55. Neither the voting rights cases [Ch. 10, Sec. 4, I, A] nor the Court's decision upholding the FCC's fairness doctrine [p. 938 supra] lends support to appellees' position that the First Amendment permits Congress to abridge the rights of some persons to engage in politi-

cal expression in order to enhance the relative voice of other segments of our [society].

e. The Court invalidated restrictions on the amount of personal funds candidates could spend on their own behalf and on the amount of overall campaign expenditures by federal candidates. The anti-corruption rationale did not apply in the former instance and was already served by the act's contribution and disclosure provisions. On the other hand, the Court also stated that, "[A]cceptance of federal funding entails voluntary acceptance of an expenditure ceiling."

f. $50,000 for Presidential or Vice Presidential candidates; $35,000 for Senate candidates; $25,000 for most candidates for the House of Representatives.

use of personal funds reduces the candidate's dependence on outside contributions and thereby counteracts the coercive pressures and attendant risks of abuse to which the Act's contribution limitations are directed.

The ancillary interest in equalizing the relative financial resources of candidates competing for elective office, therefore, provides the sole relevant rationale for Section 608(a)'s expenditure ceiling. That interest is clearly not sufficient to justify the provision's infringement of fundamental First Amendment rights. First, the limitation may fail to promote financial equality among candidates. [Indeed], a candidate's personal wealth may impede his [fundraising efforts]. Second, and more fundamentally, the First Amendment simply cannot tolerate § 608(a)'s restriction upon the freedom of a candidate to speak without legislative limit on behalf of his own candidacy. We therefore hold that § 608(a)'s restrictions on a candidate's personal expenditures is unconstitutional.

3. [Section] 608(c) of the Act places limitations on overall campaign expenditures by candidates [seeking] election to federal office. [For Presidential candidates the ceiling is $10,000,000 in seeking nomination and $20,000,000 in the general election campaign; for House of Representatives candidates it is $70,000 for each campaign—primary and general; for candidates for Senator the ceiling depends on the size of the voting age population.]

No governmental interest that has been suggested is sufficient to justify [these restrictions] on the quantity of political expression. [The] interest in alleviating the corrupting influence of large contributions is served by the Act's contribution limitations and disclosure provisions rather than by § 608(c)'s campaign expenditure ceilings. [There] is no indication that the substantial criminal penalties for violating the contribution ceilings combined with the political repercussion of such violations will be insufficient to police the contribution provisions. Extensive reporting, auditing, and disclosure requirements applicable to both contributions and expenditures by political campaigns are designed to facilitate the detection of illegal contributions. * * *

The interest in equalizing the financial resources of candidates competing for federal office is no more convincing a justification for restricting the scope of federal election campaigns. Given the limitation on the size of outside contributions, the financial resources available to a candidate's campaign, like the number of volunteers recruited, will normally vary with the size and intensity of the candidate's support. There is nothing invidious, improper, or unhealthy in permitting such funds to be spent to carry the candidate's message to the electorate. Moreover, the equalization of permissible campaign expenditures might serve not to equalize the opportunities of all candidates but to handicap a candidate who lacked substantial name recognition or exposure of his views before the start of the campaign.

The campaign expenditure ceilings appear to be designed primarily to serve the governmental interests in reducing the allegedly skyrocketing costs of political campaigns. [But the] First Amendment denies government the power to determine that spending to promote one's political views is wasteful, excessive, or unwise. In the free society ordained by our Constitution it is not the government but the people individually as citizens and candidates and collectively as associations and political committees who must retain control over the quantity and range of debate on public issues in a political campaign.[65]

65. [Congress] may engage in public financing of election campaigns and may condition acceptance of public funds on an agreement by the candidate to abide by specified expenditure

For these reasons we hold that § 608(c) is constitutionally invalid. * * *

CHIEF JUSTICE BURGER, concurring in part and dissenting in part.

[I] agree fully with that part of the Court's opinion that holds unconstitutional the limitations the Act puts on campaign expenditures. [Yet] when it approves similarly stringent limitations on contributions, the Court ignores the reasons it finds so persuasive in the context of expenditures. For me contributions and expenditures are two sides of the same First Amendment coin.

[Limiting] contributions, as a practical matter, will limit expenditures and will put an effective ceiling on the amount of political activity and debate that the Government will permit to take place.[5]

The Court attempts to separate the two communicative aspects of political contributions—the "moral" support that the gift itself conveys, which the Court suggests is the same whether the gift is of $10 or $10,000,[6] and the fact that money translates into communication. The Court dismisses the effect of the limitations on the second aspect of contributions: "[T]he transformation of contributions into political debate involves speech by someone other than the contributor." On this premise—that contribution limitations restrict only the speech of "someone other than the contributor"—rests the Court's justification for treating contributions differently from expenditures. The premise is demonstrably flawed; the contribution limitations will, in specific instances, limit exactly the same political activity that the expenditure ceilings limit, and at least one of the "expenditure" limitations the Court finds objectionable operates precisely like the "contribution" limitations.[8]

The Court's attempt to distinguish the communication inherent in political *contributions* from the speech aspects of political *expenditures* simply will not wash. We do little but engage in word games unless we recognize that people—candidates and contributors—spend money on political activity because they wish to communicate ideas, and their constitutional interest in doing so is precisely the same whether they or someone else utter the words.

[T]he restrictions are hardly incidental in their effect upon particular campaigns. Judges are ill-equipped to gauge the precise impact of legislation, but a law that impinges upon First Amendment rights requires us to make the attempt. It is

limitations. Just as a candidate may voluntarily limit the size of the contributions he chooses to accept he may decide to forgo private fundraising and accept public funding. [On the merits and demerits of public financing, compare Richard Briffault, *Public Funding and Democratic Elections,* 148 U.Pa.L.Rev. 563 (1999) with Bradley A. Smith, *Some Problems with Taxpayer-funded Political Campaigns,* id. at 591].

5. The Court notes that 94.9% of the funds raised by congressional candidates in 1974 came in contributions of less than $1,000, n. 27, and suggests that the effect of the contribution limitations will be minimal. This logic ignores the disproportionate influence large contributions may have when they are made early in a campaign; "seed money" can be essential, and the inability to obtain it may effectively end some candidacies before they begin. Appellants have excerpted from the rec-

ord data on nine campaigns to which large, initial contributions were critical. Campaigns such as these will be much harder, and perhaps impossible, to mount under the Act.

6. Whatever the effect of the limitation, it is clearly arbitrary—Congress has imposed the same ceiling on contributions to a New York or California senatorial campaign that it has put on House races in Alaska or Wyoming. Both the strength of support conveyed by the gift of $1,000 *and* the gift's potential for corruptly influencing the recipient will vary enormously from place to place. * * *

8. The Court treats the Act's provisions limiting a candidate's spending from his *personal resources* as *expenditure* limits, as indeed the Act characterizes them, and holds them unconstitutional. As Mr. Justice Marshall points out, infra, by the Court's logic these provisions could as easily be treated as limits on *contributions,* since they limit what the candidate can give to his own campaign.

not simply speculation to think that the limitations on contributions will foreclose some candidacies.[9] The limitations will also alter the nature of some electoral contests drastically.[10]

[In] striking down the limitations on campaign expenditures, the Court relies in part on its conclusion that other means—namely, disclosure and contribution ceilings—will adequately serve the statute's aim. It is not clear why the same analysis is not also appropriate in weighing the need for contribution ceilings in addition to disclosure requirements. Congress may well be entitled to conclude that disclosure was a "partial measure," but I had not thought until today that Congress could enact its conclusions in the First Amendment area into laws immune from the most searching review by this Court. * * *[g]

Justice White, concurring in part and dissenting in part. * * *

I [agree] with the Court's judgment upholding the limitations on contributions. I dissent [from] the Court's view that the expenditure limitations [violate] the First Amendment. [This] case depends on whether the nonspeech interests of the Federal Government in regulating the use of money in political campaigns are sufficiently urgent to justify the incidental effects that the limitations visit upon the First Amendment interests of candidates and their supporters.

[The Court] accepts the congressional judgment that the evils of unlimited contributions are sufficiently threatening to warrant restriction regardless of the impact of the limits on the contributor's opportunity for effective speech and in turn on the total volume of the candidate's political communications by reason of his inability to accept large sums from those willing to give.

The congressional judgment, which I would also accept, was that other steps must be taken to counter the corrosive effects of money in federal election campaigns. One of these steps is § 608(e), which [limits] what a contributor may independently spend in support or denigration of one running for federal office. Congress was plainly of the view that these expenditures also have corruptive potential; but the Court strikes down the provision, strangely enough claiming more insight as to what may improperly influence candidates than is possessed by the majority of Congress that passed this Bill and the President who signed it. Those supporting the Bill undeniably included many seasoned professionals who have been deeply involved in elective processes and who have viewed them at close range over many years.

It would make little sense to me, and apparently made none to Congress, to limit the amounts an individual may give to a candidate or spend with his approval but fail to limit the amounts that could be spent on his behalf. Yet the Court permits the former while striking down the latter limitation. [I] would take the word of those who know—that limiting independent expenditures is essential to prevent transparent and widespread evasion of the contribution limits. * * *

---

9. Candidates who must raise large initial contributions in order to appeal for more funds to a broader audience will be handicapped. See n. 5, supra. It is not enough to say that the contribution ceilings "merely require candidates [to] raise funds from a greater number of persons," where the limitations will effectively prevent candidates without substantial personal resources from doing just that.

10. Under the Court's holding, candidates with personal fortunes will be free to contribute to their own campaigns as much as they like, since the Court chooses to view the Act's provisions in this regard as unconstitutional "expenditure" limitations rather than "contribution" limitations. See n. 8, supra.

g. Blackmun, J., also dissented separately from that part of the Court's opinion upholding the Act's restrictions on campaign contributions, unpersuaded that "a principled constitutional distinction" could be made between the contribution and expenditure limitations involved.

The Court also rejects Congress' judgment manifested in § 608(c) that the federal interest in limiting total campaign expenditures by individual candidates justifies the incidental effect on their opportunity for effective political speech. I disagree both with the Court's assessment of the impact on speech and with its narrow view of the values the limitations will serve.

[M]oney is not always equivalent to or used for speech, even in the context of political campaigns. [There are] many expensive campaign activities that are not themselves communicative or remotely related to speech. Furthermore, campaigns differ among themselves. Some seem to spend much less money than others and yet communicate as much or more than those supported by enormous bureaucracies with unlimited financing. The record before us no more supports the conclusion that the communicative efforts of congressional and Presidential candidates will be crippled by the expenditure limitations than it supports the contrary. The judgment of Congress was that reasonably effective campaigns could be conducted within the limits established by the Act and that the communicative efforts of these campaigns would not seriously suffer. In this posture of the case, there is no sound basis for invalidating the expenditure limitations, so long as the purposes they serve are legitimate and sufficiently substantial, which in my view they are.

[E]xpenditure ceilings reinforce the contribution limits and help eradicate the hazard of corruption. [Without] limits on total expenditures, campaign costs will inevitably and endlessly escalate. Pressure to raise funds will constantly build and with it the temptation to resort in "emergencies" to those sources of large sums, who, history shows, are sufficiently confident of not being caught to risk flouting contribution [limits.]

The ceiling on candidate expenditures represents the considered judgment of Congress that elections are to be decided among candidates none of whom has overpowering advantage by reason of a huge campaign war chest. At least so long as the ceiling placed upon the candidates is not plainly too low, elections are not to turn on the difference in the amounts of money that candidates have to spend. This seems an acceptable purpose and the means chosen a common sense way to achieve [it.]

I also disagree with the Court's judgment that § 608(a), which limits the amount of money that a candidate or his family may spend on his campaign, violates the Constitution. Although it is true that this provision does not promote any interest in preventing the corruption of candidates, the provision does, nevertheless, serve salutary purposes related to the integrity of federal campaigns. By limiting the importance of personal wealth, § 608(a) helps to assure that only individuals with a modicum of support from others will be viable candidates. This in turn would tend to discourage any notion that the outcome of elections is primarily a function of money. Similarly, § 608(a) tends to equalize access to the political arena, encouraging the less wealthy, unable to bankroll their own campaigns, to run for political office.[h]

h. Marshall, J., dissented from that part of the Court's opinion invalidating the limitation on the amount a candidate or his family may spend on his campaign. He considered "the interest in promoting the reality and appearance of equal access to the political arena" sufficient to justify the limitation: "[T]he wealthy candidate's immediate access to a substantial personal fortune may give him an initial advantage that his less wealthy opponent can never overcome. [With the option of large contributions removed by § 608(b)], the less wealthy candidate is without the means to match the large initial expenditures of money of which the wealthy candidate is capable. In short, the limitations on contributions put a premium on a candidate's personal wealth. [Section 608(a) then] emerges not simply as a device to reduce the natural advantage of the wealthy candidate, but as a provision providing some symmetry to a regulatory scheme that

Notes and Questions

1. *Equality and Democracy.* Is it "foreign" to the first amendment to curb the spending of the wealthy in an effort to preserve the integrity of the elections process? Would it have been "foreign" to first amendment doctrine to engage in some type of balancing? Does the Court's expenditure ruling denigrate the interests in equality and democracy?[i] Even if the concept of political equity is a "legitimizing myth," is *Buckley* flawed because it underestimates the necessity of promoting political leadership that is autonomous and independent of pluralistic forces? Is government autonomy necessary for minimally adequate regulation of the economy? See Jeffrey Blum, *The Divisible First Amendment: A Critical Functionalist Approach to Freedom of Speech and Electoral Campaign Spending,* 58 N.Y.U.L.Rev. 1273, 1369–78 (1983). Alternatively, would it be better to solve the wealth problem by redistribution (and control of corporate power), while holding fast to a strong liberty principle?[j]

2. To what extent are campaign finance laws likely to advance equality values?[k] Aren't they most likely to benefit incumbents? See Richard Epstein, *Modern Republicanism—Or the Flight From Substance,* 97 Yale L.J. 1633, 1643–45 (1988); Jon Macey, *The Missing Element in the Republican Revival,* 97 Yale L.J. 1673, 1680–81 (1988). Do incumbents possess ordinarily insuperable advantages apart from the campaign finance system? Would campaign finance legislation free incumbents from the need to rely on interest group funding and improve the quality of representation? Vincent Blasi, *Free Speech and the Widening Gyre of Fund–Raising,* 94 Columbia L.Rev. 1281 (1994). Is increased legislative autonomy desirable?[l]

3. *Varying scrutiny.* (a) Did *Buckley* apply less exacting scrutiny to impairment of associational freedoms by contribution limits than to impairment of free expression by expenditure limits? Cf. 90 Harv.L.Rev. 178–79 (1976). "Granted that freedom of association is merely ancillary to speech, a means of amplifying and effectuating communication but logically secondary to speech," is this also "true of expenditures of money in aid of speech"? See Daniel Polsby, *Buckley v.*

---

otherwise enhances the natural advantage of the wealthy."

For background on the *Buckley* case, see Fred Friendly & Martha Elliot, *The Constitution: That Delicate Balance* 91–107 (1984).

i. See, e.g., Laurence Tribe, *Constitutional Choices* 193–94 (1985); Owen Fiss, *Money and Politics,* 97 Colum. L.Rev. 2470 (1997; Burt Neuborne, *Toward a Democracy–Centered Reading of the First Amendment,* 93 Nw. U.L.Rev. 1055 (1999); Marlene Nicholson, *Buckley v. Valeo: The Constitutionality of the Federal Election Campaign Act Amendments of 1974,* 1977 Wis.L.Rev. 323, 336; J. Skelly Wright, *Money and the Pollution of Politics: Is the First Amendment an Obstacle to Political Equality?,* 82 Colum.L.Rev. 609 (1982).

j. See C. Edwin Baker, *Realizing Self–Realization: Corporate Political Expenditures and Redish's The Value of Free Speech,* 130 U.Pa. L.Rev. 646, 652 (1982); C. Edwin Baker, *Scope of the First Amendment Freedom of Speech,* 25 U.C.L.A.L.Rev. 964, 983–90 (1978).

k. Consider Paul Brest, *Further Beyond the Republican Revival,* 97 Yale L.J. 1623, 1627 (1988): " 'Those who are better off participate more, and by participating more they exercise more influence on government officials.' Unequal resources produce unequal influence in determining which issues get on the political [agenda]. Campaign finance regulations barely begin to remedy the systematic ways in which inequalities of wealth distort the political process." But see Edward B. Foley, *Equal–Dollars–Per Voter: A Constitutional Principle of Campaign Finance,* 94 Colum.L.Rev. 1204 (1994); Jamin Raskin & John Bonifaz, *Equal Protection and the Wealth Primary,* 11 Yale L. & Pol'y Rev. 273 (1993). For a variety of views, see *Symposium on Campaign Finance Reform,* 94 Colum.L.Rev. 1125 (1994).

l. Compare Cass Sunstein, *Beyond the Republican Revival,* 97 Yale L.J. 1539 (1988) with Michael Fitts, *Look Before You Leap,* 97 Yale L.J. 1651 (1988); Michael Fitts, *The Vices of Virtue,* 136 U.Pa.L.Rev. 1567 (1988).

Valeo: The Special Nature of Political Speech, 1976 Sup.Ct.Rev. 1, 22. Can a lesser scrutiny be justified for contributions? Or were the differing results based on the Court's perceiving a greater threat to first amendment interests in expenditure limits and less risk of corruption and undue influence in unlimited independent expenditures? Cf. Nicholson, note 1 supra, at 340–45. For a defense of strict scrutiny across the board, see Lillian BeVier, *Money and Politics: A Perspective on the First Amendment and Campaign Finance Reform,* 73 Calif.L.Rev. 1045 (1985). For the argument that strict scrutiny is inappropriate in institutionally bounded contexts and that elections are such contexts, see C. Edwin Baker, *Campaign Expenditures and Free Speech,* 33 Harv. C.R.-C.L.Rev. 1 (1998).[m]

(b) *The O'Brien analogy.* May the Court's rejection of the less-exacting *O'Brien* standard on the ground that the expenditure of money did not introduce a non-speech element fairly be criticized for asking the wrong question: whether *"pure speech* can be regulated where there is some incidental effect on *money,"* rather than whether "the use of *money* can be regulated, by analogy to such conduct as draft-card burning, where there is an undoubted incidental effect on *speech"*? See J. Skelly Wright, *Politics and the Constitution: Is Money Speech?,* 85 Yale L.J. 1001, 1007 (1976). But compare J.M. Balkin, *Some Realism About Pluralism: Legal Realist Approaches to the First Amendment,* 1990 Duke L.J. 375, 414: "I suspect that the slogan 'money is not speech' is attractive because it appeals to a certain humanistic vision—that there is something quite different between the situation of a lone individual expressing her views and the purchase of hired mouths using hired expressions created by hired minds to saturate the airwaves with ideological drivel. Yet in one sense, this humanistic vision really turns upon a set of unstated egalitarian assumptions about economic and social power. Certainly we would have no objection to a person with a speech impediment hiring someone to do her talking for her; that is because we think that, under these circumstances, it is fair for such a person to boost her communicative powers. Modern political campaigns seem a far cry from this example because of the massive amounts of economic power expended to get the message across. I think we should isolate the egalitarian assumptions implicit in the 'money is not speech' position and put them to their best use—the justification of campaign finance reforms on the ground that gross inequalities of economic power destroy the integrity of the political process. [G]overnment is responsible for inequalities in access to the means of communication because it has created the system of property rights that makes such inequalities possible. Therefore, it is not only wrong but also incoherent for opponents of campaign finance reform to contend that the government should not regulate access to the political process. Government already regulates access to the political process—the first amendment simply demands that it do so fairly."

4. *Expenditure limitations and political parties.* COLORADO REPUBLICAN FED. CAMPAIGN COMMITTEE v. FEDERAL ELECTION COMM'N, 518 U.S. 604, 116 S.Ct. 2309, 135 L.Ed.2d 795 (1996) ruled that the Federal Election

---

m. For similar views, see Richard Briffault, *Issue Advocacy: Redrawing the Elections/Politics Line,* 77 Texas L.Rev. 1751 (1999); Frederick Schauer & Richard H. Pildes, *Electoral Exceptionalism and the First Amendment,* 77 Texas L. Rev. 1803 (1999); and Burt Neuborne, *The Supreme Court and Free Speech: Love and A Question,* 42 St. Louis U.L.J. 789, 800 (1998): "If we can conceive of an election campaign as a great deliberative assembly of the people, why shouldn't we allow ourselves to establish a content-neutral, meta-Roberts' Rules of Order to help assure that our elections are preceded by debate calculated to permit our democratic institutions to perform at an acceptable level, an electoral debate where political discourse is not completely dominated by the wealthy?" But see Kathleen M. Sullivan, *Against Campaign Finance Reform,* 1998 Utah L.Rev. 311, 318–20 (1998); Robert Post, *Commentary: Regulating Election Speech Under the First Amendment,* 77 Texas L.Rev 1837 (1999).

Campaign Act's limitation on independent expenditures by political parties was unconstitutional. BREYER, J., joined by O'Connor and Souter, JJ., announced the judgment of the Court, but did not reach the question whether the limitation of expenditures coordinated with the candidate were similarly unconstitutional.

KENNEDY, J., joined by Scalia, J., concurring in part and dissenting in part, argued that the limitation on coordinated expenditures between political parties and their candidates was also unconstitutional: "We have a constitutional tradition of political parties and their candidates engaging in joint first amendment activity. [Congress] may have authority, consistent with the first amendment, to restrict undifferentiated political party contributions [as discussed in] *Buckley*, but that type of regulation is not at issue here." Kennedy, J., dissented from the judgment's failure to reach the question of coordinated expenditures.[n]

STEVENS, J., joined by Ginsburg, J., dissenting, maintained that independent expenditures by parties were contributions and that federal limits were justified by the need to level "the electoral playing field," and to avoid corruption or its appearance.

5.   Under existing law, individuals, groups (with the exception of profit-organizations or unions) or political parties can spend unlimited sums in support of or against a federal candidate so long as there expenditures are not coordinated with the candidate, and profit-organizations or unions may do the same so long as they do not explicitly urge the candidate's election or defeat. Such advertising often takes the form of attack ads. In addition, parties may engage in voter registration and get out the vote campaigns that assist candidates. Unlimited contributions to parties and advocacy organizations may be made for some of these purposes and arguably for all of them. Commentators widely agree that loopholes such as these drastically undercut the effectiveness of the act. They disagree whether it is constitutional, wise or even possible effectively to close the loopholes.[o] If it is not possible to close the loopholes, or so long as they remain, should the contributions limitations be stricken on the ground that they are ineffective and/or that campaigns are better run by parties and candidates?

NIXON v. SHRINK MISSOURI GOVERNMENT PAC, 528 U.S. 377, 120 S.Ct. 897, 145 L.Ed.2d 886 (2000), per SOUTER, J., upheld a Missouri scheme for restricting campaign contributions despite the fact that the limits were lower in real dollar value than those upheld in *Buckley*: "Precision about the relative rigor of the standard to review contribution limits was not a pretense of the *Buckley* per curiam opinion. [While] we did not then say in so many words that different standards might govern expenditure and contribution limits affecting associational rights, [i]t has [been] plain ever since *Buckley* that contribution limits would more readily clear the hurdles before them. [While] the record does not show that the

---

n. Thomas, J., joined by Rehnquist, C.J., and Scalia, J., would also have reached the question, arguing that *Buckley*'s anti-corruption rationale did not apply to associations between political parties and candidates. Thomas, J., on his own, additionally argued that the distinction between contributions and expenditures was generally unsatisfactory and that both should receive first amendment protection.

o. For a sampling, see Stephen Ansolabehere & James M. Snyder, Jr., *Money and Institutional Power*, 77 Texas L.Rev. 1673 (1999); Richard Briffault, *Issue Advocacy: Redrawing the Elections/Politics Line*, 77 Texas L.Rev. 1751(1999); Samuel Issacharoff & Pamela S. Karlan, *The Hydraulics of Campaign Finance Reform*, 77 Texas L.Rev. 1705 (1999); Todd Lochner & Bruce E. Cain, *Equity and Efficacy in the Enforcement of Campaign Finance Laws*, 77 Texas L. Rev. 1891 (1999); Daniel H. Lowenstein, *Election Law Miscellany*, 77 Texas L.Rev. 2001 (1999); Daniel R. Ortiz, Commentary: Water, Water Everywhere, 77 Texas L.Rev. 1837 (1999); Kathleen Sullivan, *Against Campaign Finance Reform*, 1998 Utah L.Rev. 311, 318–20 (1998).

Missouri Legislature relied on the evidence and findings accepted in *Buckley*, the evidence introduced into the record by respondents or cited by the lower courts in this action is enough to show that the substantiation of the congressional concerns reflected in *Buckley* has its counterpart supporting the Missouri law.

"Each dissenter would overrule *Buckley* and thinks we should do the same. The answer is that we are supposed to decide this case. [The plaintiffs] did not request that *Buckley* be overruled; the furthest reach of their arguments about the law was that subsequent decisions already on the books had enhanced the State's burden of justification beyond what *Buckley* required, a proposition we [reject] as mistaken."

STEVENS, J., who joined the Court's opinion, concurred: "Money is property; it is not speech. [Because] I did not participate in the Court's decision in *Buckley*, I did not have the opportunity to suggest then that [property] and liberty concerns adequately explain the Court's decision to invalidate the expenditure limitations in the 1974 Act. * * *

"The right to use one's own money to hire gladiators, or to fund 'speech by proxy,' certainly merits significant constitutional protection. These property rights, however, are not entitled to the same protection as the right to say what one pleases."

BREYER, J., joined by Ginsburg, J., who joined the Court's opinion, concurred: "The dissenters accuse the Court of weakening the First Amendment. [But] this is a case where constitutionally protected interests lie on both sides of the legal equation. For that reason there is no place for a strong presumption against constitutionality, of the sort often thought to accompany the words 'strict scrutiny.'

"On the one hand, a decision to contribute money to a campaign is a matter of First Amendment concern—not because money is speech (it is not); but because it enables speech. Through contributions the contributor associates himself with the candidate's cause, helps the candidate communicate a political message with which the contributor agrees, and helps the candidate win by attracting the votes of similarly minded voters. *Buckley*. Both political association and political communication are at stake.

"On the other hand, restrictions upon the amount any one individual can contribute to a particular candidate seek to protect the integrity of the electoral process—the means through which a free society democratically translates political speech into concrete governmental action. Moreover, by limiting the size of the largest contributions, such restrictions aim to democratize the influence that money itself may bring to bear upon the electoral process. In doing so, they seek to build public confidence in that process and broaden the base of a candidate's meaningful financial support, encouraging the public participation and open discussion that the First Amendment itself presupposes. * * *

I would uphold the statute essentially for the reasons stated by the Court. [But] what if [*Buckley*] denies the political branches sufficient leeway to enact comprehensive solutions to the problems posed by campaign finance. If so, like Justice Kennedy, I believe the Constitution would require us to reconsider *Buckley*. With that understanding I join the Court's opinion."

KENNEDY, J., dissented: "The plain fact is that the compromise the Court invented in *Buckley* set the stage for a new kind of speech to enter the political system. It is covert speech. The Court has forced a substantial amount of political speech underground, as contributors and candidates devise ever more elaborate methods of avoiding contribution limits, limits which take no account of rising campaign costs. The preferred method has been to conceal the real purpose of the speech. Soft money may be contributed to political parties in unlimited amounts, and is used often to fund so-called issue advocacy, advertisements that promote or attack a candidate's positions without specifically urging his or her election or defeat. Richard Briffault, *Issue Advocacy: Redrawing the Elections/Politics Line*, 77 Tex. L.Rev. 1751, 1752–1753 (1999). Issue advocacy, like soft money, is unrestricted, while straightforward speech in the form of financial contributions paid to a candidate, speech subject to full disclosure and prompt evaluation by the public, is not. Thus has the Court's decision given us covert speech. This mocks the First Amendment. I would overrule *Buckley* and then free Congress or state legislatures to attempt some new reform, if, based upon their own considered view of the First Amendment, it is possible to do so. [The] First Amendment ought to be allowed to take its own course without further obstruction from the artificial system we have imposed. It suffices here to say that the law in question does not come even close to passing any serious scrutiny."

THOMAS, J., joined by Scalia, J., dissented: "For nearly half a century, this Court has extended First Amendment protection to a multitude of forms of 'speech,' such as making false defamatory statements, filing lawsuits, dancing nude, exhibiting drive-in movies with nudity, burning flags, and wearing military uniforms. Not surprisingly, the Courts of Appeals have followed our lead and concluded that the First Amendment protects, for example, begging, shouting obscenities, erecting tables on a sidewalk, and refusing to wear a necktie. In light of the many cases of this sort, today's decision is a most curious anomaly. Whatever the proper status of such activities under the First Amendment, I am confident that they are less integral to the functioning of our Republic than campaign contributions. Yet the majority today, rather than going out of its way to protect political speech, goes out of its way to avoid protecting it. * * *

"Because the Court [fails] to strictly scrutinize the inhibition of political speech and competition, I respectfully dissent."

———————

FIRST NAT'L. BANK v. BELLOTTI, 435 U.S. 765, 98 S.Ct. 1407, 55 L.Ed.2d 707 (1978), per POWELL, J., held invalid under the first and fourteenth amendments a Massachusetts criminal statute prohibiting banks or business corporations from making contributions or expenditures to influence the vote in certain initiative campaigns: "The speech proposed by appellants is at the heart of the first amendment's protection. [If] the speakers here were not corporations, no one would suggest that the state could silence their proposed speech. It is the type of speech indispensable to decision making in a democracy, and this is no less true because the speech comes from a corporation rather than an individual. The inherent worth of the speech in terms of its capacity for informing the public does not depend upon the identity of its source, whether corporation, association, union or individual.

"[Nonetheless,] preserving the integrity of the electoral process, preventing corruption, and 'sustain[ing] the active, alert responsibility of the individual citizen in a democracy for the wise conduct of government' are interests of the highest importance. *Buckley*. Preservation of the individual citizen's confidence in government is equally important.

"[Appellee's arguments] that these interests are endangered by corporate participation in discussion of a referendum [issue] hinge upon the assumption that such participation would exert an undue influence on the outcome of a referendum vote, and—in the end—destroy the confidence of the people in the democratic process and the integrity of government. According to appellee, corporations are wealthy and powerful and their views may drown out other points of view. If appellee's arguments were supported by record or legislative findings that corporate advocacy threatened imminently to undermine democratic processes, thereby denigrating rather than serving First Amendment interests,[a] these arguments would merit our consideration.[b] Cf. *Red Lion*. But there has been no showing that the relative voice of corporations has been overwhelming or even significant in influencing referenda in Massachusetts, or that there has been any threat to the confidence of the citizenry in government.

"[Referenda] are held on issues, not candidates for public office. The risk of corruption perceived in cases involving candidate elections simply is not present in a popular vote on a public issue. To be sure, corporate advertising may influence the outcome of the vote; this would be its purpose. But the fact that advocacy may persuade the electorate is hardly a reason to suppress [it]. [T]he people in our democracy are entrusted with the responsibility for judging and evaluating the relative merits of conflicting arguments. They may consider, in making their judgment, the source and credibility of the advocate. But if there be any danger that the people cannot evaluate the information and arguments advanced by appellants, it is a danger contemplated by the Framers of the First Amendment."[c]

WHITE, J., joined by Brennan and Marshall, JJ., dissented, arguing among other things, a proposition that was taken up by the Court in *Austin*, infra: "The statute was designed to protect first amendment rights by 'preventing institutions which have been permitted to amass wealth as a result of special advantages extended by the State for certain economic purposes from using that wealth to acquire an unfair advantage in the political process.'"

Notes and Questions

1. *Protecting the privileged.* Consider Mark Tushnet, *An Essay on Rights,* 62 Tex.L.Rev. 1363, 1387 (1984): "The first amendment has replaced the due process clause as the primary guarantor of the privileged. [Even] in its heyday the due process clause stood in the way only of specific legislation designed to reduce the benefits of privilege. Today, in contrast, the first amendment stands as a general obstruction to all progressive legislative efforts. To protect their positions of privilege, the wealthy can make prudent investments either in political action or, more conventionally, in factories or stocks. But since the demise of substantive due process, their investments in factories and stocks can be regulated by legislatures. Under *Buckley* and *Bellotti*, however, their investments in politics— or politicians—cannot be regulated significantly. Needless to say, careful invest-

---

a. Legislatures wishing to support such findings need not look far. See, e.g., Daniel Lowenstein, *Campaign Spending and Ballot Propositions: Recent Experience, Public Choice Theory and the First Amendment,* 29 UCLA L.Rev. 505 (1982); John Schockley, *Direct Democracy, Campaign Finance, and the Courts: Can Corruption, Undue Influence, and Declining Voter Confidence Be Found?,* 39 U.Miami L.Rev. 377 (1985).

b. "[I]f *Tornillo* and *Buckley* slammed the door on excessive power arguments, [*Bellotti*] opened a window. [The] Court did not pause, however, to explain why factors found in *Buckley* and *Tornillo* to be foreign to the first amendment would have 'merited consideration' in *Bellotti*." Steven Shiffrin, *Government Speech,* 27 U.C.L.A. L.Rev. 565, 598–99 (1980).

c. Burger, C.J., concurred; Rehnquist, J., dissented.

ment in politics may prevent effective regulation of traditional investments." See also Mark Tushnet, *Corporations and Free Speech* in The Politics of Law 253 (David Kairys ed. 1982).[d] Compare Sanford Levinson, *Book Review,* 83 Mich. L.Rev. 939, 945 (1985): "Overtly, justifying restriction of campaign spending by reference to the idea of fair access to the public forum may seem content neutral. However, it is worth considering to what extent we in fact support such restrictions because of tacit assumptions about the contents of the views held by the rich, who would obviously feel most of the burden of the restrictions. If both political views and the propensity to spend money on politics were distributed randomly among the entire populace, it is hard to see why anyone would be very excited about the whole issue of campaign finance."

Does Levinson's observation shortchange participatory values? Consider Cass Sunstein, *Beyond the Republican Revival,* 97 Yale L.J. 1539, 1577 (1988): "[R]epublican understandings would point toward large reforms of the electoral process in an effort to improve political deliberation and to promote political equality and citizenship." Is it reasonable to take the views of the rich into account? See Burt Neuborne, *Is Money Different?,* 77 Texas L.Rev. 1609, 1612–13 (1999).

2. *Protecting listeners.* Is *Bellotti* justifiable because of listeners' rights? See Martin Redish, *Self-Realization, Democracy, and Freedom of Expression: A Reply to Professor Baker,* 130 U.Pa.L.Rev. 678–79 (1982). But see Note, *Statutory Limitations on Corporate Spending in Ballot Measure Campaigns: The Case for Constitutionality,* 36 Hast.L.J. 433 (1985) (legal and market limitations on corporate speech inherently negate its value for listeners). Reconsider the arguments for and against the marketplace of ideas argument, Sec. 1, I supra.

3. *Post-Bellotti initiative cases.* The city of Berkeley placed a $250 limitation on contributions to committees formed to support or oppose ballot measures submitted to popular vote. Constitutional? See *Citizens Against Rent Control v. Berkeley,* 454 U.S. 290, 102 S.Ct. 434, 70 L.Ed.2d 492 (1981)(invalidating statute).[e]

Colorado made it a felony to pay persons to circulate initiative or referendum petitions. The purposes of the provision were to assure that a ballot measure had a sufficiently broad base of popular support to warrant its placement on the ballot and to eliminate an incentive to produce fraudulent signatures. Constitutional?

d. For suggestions that the first amendment may be generally harmful from a progressive perspective, see J.M. Balkin, *Some Realism About Pluralism: Legal Realist Approaches to the First Amendment,* 1990 Duke L.J. 375; Mary E. Becker, *The Politics of Women's Wrongs and the Bill of "Rights": A Bicentennial Perspective,* 59 U.Chi.L.Rev. 453, 486–94 (1992); Mary E. Becker, *Conservative Free Speech and the Uneasy Case for Judicial Review,* 64 U.Colo. L.Rev. 975 (1993); Richard Delgado, *Comments About Mary Becker,* 64 U.Colo.L.Rev. 1051 (1993); Morton Horwitz, *Rights,* 23 Harv. CR–CL L.Rev. 393, 397–98, 402–03 (1988); Frederick Schauer, *The Political Incidence of the Free Speech Principle,* 64 U.Colo.L.Rev. 935 (1993); Mark Tushnet, *An Essay on Rights,* 62 Tex.L.Rev. 1363, 1386–92 (1984). For contrary considerations, see David Rabban, *Free Speech in its Forgotten Years* 388–93 (1997); Steven H. Shiffrin, *Dissent, Injustice and the Meanings of America* ch. 5 (1999); Burt Neuborne, *Blues for the Left*

Hand, 62 U.Chi.L.Rev. 423 (1995); Kathleen Sullivan, *Discrimination, Distribution and Free Speech,* 37 Ariz.L.Rev. 439 (1995); Kathleen Sullivan, *Free Speech and Unfree Markets,* 42 U.C.L.A.L.Rev. 949 (1995); Kathleen Sullivan, *Resurrecting Free Speech,* 63 Ford. L.Rev. 971 (1995); Kathleen Sullivan, *Free Speech Wars,* 48 S.M.U.L.Rev. 203 (1994). See also Mark Graber, *Old Wine in New Bottles,* 48 Vand.L.Rev. 349 (1995). For discussion on a broad range of issues concerning the relationship between speech values and property values in Burger Court decisions, see Norman Dorsen & Gara, *Free Speech, Property, and the Burger Court: Old Values, New Balances,* 1982 Sup.Ct.Rev. 195.

e. For commentary, see Laurence Tribe, Constitutional Choices 195–97 (1985); Lowenstein, fn. a supra, at 584–602; Marlene Nicholson, *The Constitutionality of Contribution Limitations in Ballot Measure Elections,* 9 Ecol. L.Q. 683 (1981).

See *Meyer v. Grant,* 486 U.S. 414, 108 S.Ct. 1886, 100 L.Ed.2d 425 (1988) (invalidating statute).[f]

———

Michigan law prohibits corporations, profit or nonprofit, from making contributions to candidates or independent expenditures on behalf of or opposed to candidates. The law entitles such corporations, however, to solicit contributions for allowable expenditures from a segregated fund. The Michigan State Chamber of Commerce, a nonprofit corporation with more than 8,000 members (three quarters of whom are profit corporations), sought to place a newspaper advertisement in support of a Congressional candidate and argued that Michigan's prohibition of such corporate ads was unconstitutional. AUSTIN v. MICHIGAN STATE CHAMBER OF COMMERCE, 494 U.S. 652, 110 S.Ct. 1391, 108 L.Ed.2d 652 (1990), per MARSHALL, J., upheld the scheme as applied to these facts: "[T]he political advantage of corporations is unfair because '[t]he resources in the treasury of a business corporation [are] not an indication of popular support for the corporation's political ideas. They reflect instead the economically motivated decisions of investors and customers. The availability of these resources may make a corporation a formidable political presence, even though the power of the corporation may be no reflection of the power of its ideas.' *FEC v. Massachusetts Citizens for Life, Inc.,* 479 U.S. 238, 107 S.Ct. 616, 93 L.Ed.2d 539 (1986) [MCFL].

"The Chamber argues that this concern about corporate domination of the political process is insufficient to justify restrictions on independent expenditures. Although this Court has distinguished these expenditures from direct contributions in the context of federal laws regulating individual donors, it has also recognized that a legislature might demonstrate a danger of real or apparent corruption posed by such expenditures when made by corporations to influence candidate elections, *Bellotti,* n. 26. Regardless of whether this danger of 'financial quid pro quo' corruption may be sufficient to justify a restriction on independent expenditures, Michigan's regulation aims at a different type of corruption in the political arena: the corrosive and distorting effects of immense aggregations of wealth that are accumulated with the help of the corporate form and that have little or no correlation to the public's support for the corporation's political ideas. The Act does not attempt 'to equalize the relative influence of speakers on elections'; rather, it ensures that expenditures reflect actual public support for the political ideas espoused by corporations. We emphasize that the mere fact that corporations may accumulate large amounts of wealth is not the justification for [the statute]; rather, the unique state-conferred corporate structure that facilitates the amassing of large treasuries warrants the limit on independent expenditures. [We] therefore hold that the State has articulated a sufficiently compelling rationale to support its restriction on independent expenditures by corporations.

"We next turn to the question whether the Act is sufficiently narrowly tailored to achieve its goal. We find that the Act is precisely targeted to eliminate the distortion caused by corporate spending while also allowing corporations to express their political views. [T]he Act does not impose an *absolute* ban on all forms of corporate political spending but permits corporations to make indepen-

f. For criticism, see Daniel Lowenstein & Robert Stern, *The First Amendment and Paid Initiative Petition Circulators: A Dissenting View and a Proposal,* 17 Hast. Con.L.Q. 175 (1989). But see *Buckley v. American Constitu-* *tional Law Found.,* 525 U.S. 182, 119 S.Ct. 636, 142 L.Ed.2d 599 (1999) (extending *Meyer* to a requirement that paid circulators be registered voters).

dent political expenditures through separate segregated funds. Because persons contributing to such funds understand that their money will be used solely for political purposes, the speech generated accurately reflects contributors' support for the corporation's political views.

"[Although] some closely held corporations, just as some publicly held ones, may not have accumulated significant amounts of wealth, they receive from the State the special benefits conferred by the corporate structure and present the potential for distorting the political process. This potential for distortion justifies § 54(1)'s general applicability to all corporations. The section therefore is not substantially overbroad.

"The Chamber contends that [the Act] cannot be applied to a nonprofit ideological corporation like a chamber of commerce. [The Chamber relied on *MCFL,* per Brennan, J., which held that 2 U.S.C. § 441b, prohibiting corporations from using their treasury funds for the purpose of influencing any election for public office, was unconstitutional as applied to the expenditures of a nonprofit, nonstock corporation. Specifically, MCFL an anti-abortion organization had printed and distributed some 100,000 'newsletters' advocating the election of a number of candidates. Rehnquist, C.J., joined by White, Blackmun, and Stevens, JJ., dissenting, argued that organizations opting for a corporate form could be barred from using treasury funds for election purposes.][a] In *MCFL,* we held that the nonprofit organization there had 'features more akin to voluntary political associations than business firms, and therefore should not have to bear burdens on independent spending solely because of [its] incorporated status.' In reaching that conclusion, we enumerated three characteristics of the corporation that were 'essential' to our holding. * * *

"The first characteristic of MCFL that distinguished it from ordinary business corporations was that the organization 'was formed for the express purpose of promoting political ideas, and cannot engage in business activities.' [MCFL's] narrow political focus thus 'ensure[d] that [its] political resources reflect[ed] political support.'

"In contrast, the Chamber's bylaws set forth more varied purposes, several of which are not inherently political. For instance, the Chamber compiles and disseminates information relating to social, civic, and economic conditions, trains and educates its members, and promotes ethical business practices. Unlike MCFL's, the Chamber's educational activities are not expressly tied to political goals; many of its seminars, conventions, and publications are politically neutral and focus on business and economic issues. The Chamber's President and Chief Executive Officer stated that one of the corporation's main purposes is to provide 'service to [its] membership that includes everything from group insurance to educational seminars, [and] litigation activities on behalf of the business community.' * * *

"We described the second feature of MCFL as the absence of 'shareholders or other persons affiliated so as to have a claim on its assets or earnings. This ensures that persons connected with the organization will have no economic disincentive for disassociating with it if they disagree with its political activity.' Although the Chamber also lacks shareholders, many of its members may be similarly reluctant to withdraw as members even if they disagree with the

---

a. For commentary on *MCFL,* see Louis Seidman, *Reflections on Context and the Con-* *stitution,* 73 Minn.L.Rev. 73, 80–84 (1988).

Chamber's political expression, because they wish to benefit from the Chamber's nonpolitical [programs].[2]

"The final characteristic upon which we relied in *MCFL* was [that] the organization [was] not established by, and had a policy of not accepting contributions from, business corporations. Thus it could not 'serv[e] as [a] condui[t] for the type of direct spending that creates a threat to the political marketplace.' In striking contrast, more than three-quarters of the Chamber's members are business corporations, whose political contributions and expenditures can constitutionally be regulated by the [State].[3] Because the Chamber accepts money from for-profit corporations, it could, absent application of § 54(1), serve as a conduit for corporate political spending. * * *

"The Chamber also attacks § 54(1) as underinclusive because it does not regulate the independent expenditures of unincorporated labor unions.[4] Whereas unincorporated unions, and indeed individuals, may be able to amass large treasuries, they do so without the significant state-conferred advantages of the corporate structure; corporations are 'by far the most prominent example of entities that enjoy legal advantages enhancing their ability to accumulate wealth.' The desire to counterbalance those advantages unique to the corporate form is the State's compelling interest in this case * * *.

"[We now] address the Chamber's contention that the provision infringes its rights under the Fourteenth Amendment. The Chamber argues [that] the State should also restrict the independent expenditures of [corporations] engaged in the media business.[5] [But] media corporations differ significantly from other corporations in that their resources are devoted to the collection of information and its dissemination to the public. We have consistently recognized the unique role that the press plays in 'informing and educating the public, offering criticism, and providing a forum for discussion and debate.' *Bellotti.* See also *Mills v. Alabama* ('[T]he press serves and was designed to serve as a powerful antidote to any abuses of power by governmental officials and as a constitutionally chosen means for keeping officials elected by the people responsible to all the people whom they were selected to serve'). [The] media exception ensures that the Act does not hinder or prevent the institutional press from reporting on and publishing editorials about newsworthy events. Cf. 15 U.S.C. §§ 1801–1804 (enacting a limited exemption from the antitrust laws for newspapers in part because of the recognition of the special role of the press). [Although] the press' unique societal role may not entitle the press to greater protection under the Constitution, it does provide a compelling reason for the State to exempt media corporations from the

---

2. A requirement that the Chamber disclose the nature and extent of its political activities would not eliminate the possible distortion of the political process inherent in independent expenditures from general corporate funds. Given the significant incentive for members to continue their financial support for the Chamber in spite of their disagreement with its political agenda, disclosure will not ensure that the funds in the Chamber's treasury correspond to members' support for its ideas.

3. A nonprofit corporation's segregated fund, on the other hand, apparently cannot receive contributions from corporations. * * *

4. The Federal Election Campaign Act restricts the independent expenditures of labor organizations as well as those of corporations. 2 U.S.C. § 441b(a).

5. The Federal Election Campaign Act contains a similar exemption that excludes from the definition of expenditure "any news story, commentary, or editorial distributed through the facilities of any broadcasting station, newspaper, magazine, or other periodical publication, unless such facilities are owned or controlled by any political party, political committee, or candidate." 2 U.S.C. § 431(9)(B)(I). [For discussion, see Richard L. Hasen, *Campaign Finance Laws and the Rupert Murdoch Problem,* 77 Texas L.Rev. 1627 (1999); L.A. Powe, Jr., *Boiling Blood,* 77 Texas L.Rev. 1667 (1999)]

scope of political expenditure limitations. We therefore hold that the Act does not violate the Equal Protection Clause."

BRENNAN, J., joined the Court's opinion, but referring to himself as "one of the 'Orwellian' 'censors' derided by the dissents and as the author of [*MCFL*]," also concurred to express his views: "The requirement that corporate independent expenditures be financed through a segregated fund or political action committee [may] be unconstitutional as applied to some corporations because they do not present the dangers at which expenditure limitations are aimed. Indeed, we determined that [*MCFL*] fell into this category.[3] [4]

"The Michigan law is concededly 'underinclusive' insofar as it does not ban other types of political expenditures to which a dissenting Chamber member or corporate shareholder might object. [A] corporation remains free, for example, to use general treasury funds to support an initiative proposal in a state referendum. See *Bellotti.*

"I do not find this underinclusiveness fatal, for several reasons.[8] First, as the dissents recognize, discussions on candidate elections lie 'at the heart of political debate.' But just as speech interests are at their zenith in this area, so too are the interests of unwilling Chamber members and corporate shareholders forced to subsidize that speech. The State's decision to focus on this especially sensitive context is a justifiable one. Second, in light of our decisions in *Bellotti, Consolidated Edison Co. v. Public Service Comm'n,* and related cases, a State cannot prohibit corporations from making many other types of political expenditures. [T]o the extent that the Michigan statute is 'underinclusive' only because it does not regulate corporate expenditures in referenda or other corporate expression (besides merely commercial speech), this reflects the requirements of our decisions rather than the lack of an important state interest on the part of Michigan in regulating expenditures in *candidate* elections. In this sense, the Michigan law is not 'underinclusive' at all. Finally, the provision in Michigan corporate law authorizing shareholder actions against corporate waste might serve as a remedy for other types of political expenditures that have no legitimate connection to the corporation's business."

STEVENS, J., joined the Court's opinion and concurred: "[T]he distinction between individual expenditures and individual contributions that the Court

---

3. [Whether] an organization presents the threat at which the campaign finance laws are aimed has to do with the particular characteristics of the organization at issue and not with the content of its speech. Of course, if a correlation between the two factors could be shown to exist, a group would be free to mount a First Amendment challenge on that basis. * * *

4. According to Justice Kennedy's dissent, the majority holds that "it is now a felony in Michigan for the Sierra Club, or the American Civil Liberties Union" to make independent expenditures. This characterization [overlooks] the central lesson of *MCFL* that the First Amendment may require exemptions, on an as-applied basis, from expenditure restrictions. * * *

8. [In] the context of labor unions, [r]ather than assuming that an employee accepts as "the deal," that the union will use his dues for any purpose that will advance the interests of the bargaining unit, including political contri-

butions and expenditures, we have determined that "the authority to impose dues and fees [is] restricted at least to the 'extent of denying the unions the right, over the employee's objection, to use his money to support political causes which he opposes,' even though Congress was well aware that *unions had historically expended funds in the support of political candidates and issues." Ellis v. Railway Clerks* [supra].

Given the extensive state regulation of corporations, shareholder expectations are always a function of *state law.* It is circular to say, as does Justice Scalia, that *if* a State did not protect shareholders, they would have no expectation of being protected, and therefore that the State has no legitimate interest in protecting them. [I] believe it entirely proper for a State to decide to promote the ability of investors to purchase stock in corporations without fear that their money will be used to support candidates with whom they do not agree.

identified in *Buckley,* should have little, if any, weight in reviewing corporate participation in candidate elections. In that context, I believe the danger of either the fact, or the appearance, of quid pro quo relationships provides an adequate justification for state regulation of both expenditures and contributions. Moreover, as we recognized in *Bellotti,* there is a vast difference between lobbying and debating public issues on the one hand, and political campaigns for election to public office on the other."

SCALIA, J., dissented: " 'Attention all citizens. To assure the fairness of elections by preventing disproportionate expression of the views of any single powerful group, your Government has decided that the following associations of persons shall be prohibited from speaking or writing in support of any candidate: _____'. In permitting Michigan to make private corporations the first object of this Orwellian announcement, the Court today endorses the principle that too much speech is an evil that the democratic majority can proscribe. I dissent because that principle is contrary to our case law and incompatible with the absolutely central truth of the First Amendment: that government cannot be trusted to assure, through censorship, the 'fairness' of political debate.

"The Court's opinion says that political speech of corporations can be regulated because '[s]tate law grants [them] special advantages' and because this 'unique state-conferred corporate structure * * * facilitates the amassing of large treasuries.' This analysis seeks to create one good argument by combining two bad ones. Those individuals who form that type of voluntary association known as a corporation are, to be sure, given special advantages—notably, the immunization of their personal fortunes from liability for the actions of the association—that the State is under no obligation to confer. But so are other associations and private individuals given all sorts of special advantages that the State need not confer, ranging from tax breaks to contract awards to public employment to outright cash subsidies. It is rudimentary that the State cannot exact as the price of those special advantages the forfeiture of First Amendment rights. The categorical suspension of the right of any person, or of any association of persons, to speak out on political matters must be justified by a compelling state need. Which is why the Court puts forward its second bad argument, the fact [t]hat corporations 'amas[s] large treasuries [is] also not sufficient justification for the suppression of political speech, unless one thinks it would be lawful to prohibit men and women whose net worth is above a certain figure from endorsing political candidates. Neither of these two flawed arguments is improved by combining them.

"In *FCC v. League of Women Voters of California,* [supra], striking down a congressionally imposed ban upon editorializing by noncommercial broadcasting stations that receive federal funds, the *only* respect in which we considered the receipt of that 'special advantage' relevant was in determining whether the speech limitation could be justified under Congress' spending power, as a means of assuring that the subsidy was devoted only to the purposes Congress intended, which did not include political editorializing. We held it could not be justified on that basis, since 'a noncommercial educational station that receives only 1% of its overall income from [federal] grants is barred absolutely from all editorializing. [The] station has no way of limiting the use of its federal funds to all noneditorializing activities, and, more importantly, it is barred from using even wholly private funds to finance its editorial activity.' Of course the same is true here, even assuming that tax exemptions and other benefits accorded to incorporated associations constitute an exercise of the spending power. It is not just that portion of the corporation's assets attributable to the gratuitously conferred 'special advantages' that is prohibited from being used for political endorsements, but *all* of the corporation's [assets.] Commercial corporations may not have a public persona as sympathetic as that of public broadcasters, but they are no less entitled to this Court's concern.[b]

"As for the second part of the Court's argumentation, [c]ertain uses of 'massive wealth' in the electoral process—whether or not the wealth is the result of 'special advantages' conferred by the State—pose a substantial risk of corruption which constitutes a compelling need for the regulation of speech. Such a risk plainly exists when the wealth is given directly to the political candidate, to be used under his direction and control. [But the] contention that prohibiting overt advocacy for or against a political candidate satisfies a 'compelling need' to avoid 'corruption' is easily dismissed. As we said in *Buckley*, '[i]t would naively underestimate the ingenuity and resourcefulness of persons and groups desiring to buy influence to believe that they would have much difficulty devising expenditures that skirted the restriction on express advocacy of election or defeat but nevertheless benefitted the candidate's campaign.' Independent advocacy, moreover, unlike contributions, 'may well provide little assistance to the candidate's campaign and indeed may prove counterproductive,' thus reducing the danger that it will be exchanged 'as a quid pro quo for improper commitments from the candidate.' The latter point seems even more plainly true with respect to corporate advocates than it is with respect to individuals. I expect I could count on the fingers of one hand the candidates who would generally welcome, much less negotiate for, a formal endorsement by AT & T or General Motors. The advocacy of such entities that have 'amassed great wealth' will be effective only to the extent that it brings to the people's attention *ideas* which—despite the invariably self-interested and probably uncongenial source—strike them as true.

"The Court does not try to defend the proposition that independent advocacy poses a substantial risk of political 'corruption,' as English-speakers understand that term. Rather, [its] opinion ultimately rests upon that proposition whose violation constitutes the New Corruption: expenditures must 'reflect actual public support for the political ideas espoused.' This illiberal free-speech principle of 'one man, one minute' was proposed and soundly rejected in *Buckley*. [And the Court's limitation of this principle to corporations] is of course entirely irrational. Why is it perfectly all right if advocacy by an individual billionaire is out of proportion with 'actual public support' for his positions? * * *

"Justice Brennan's concurrence would have us believe that the prohibition [is] a paternalistic measure to protect the corporate shareholder of America. [But] the Michigan [statute] permits corporations to take as many ideological and political positions as they please, so long as they are not 'in assistance of, or in opposition to, the nomination or election of a candidate.' That is indeed the Court's sole basis for distinguishing *Bellotti*, which invalidated restriction of a corporation's general political speech. The Michigan law appears to be designed, in other words, neither to protect shareholders, nor even (impermissibly) to 'balance' general political debate, but to protect political candidates. * * *

"But even if the object of the prohibition could plausibly be portrayed as the protection of shareholders (which the Court's opinion, at least, does not even assert), that would not suffice as a 'compelling need' to support this blatant restriction upon core political speech. A person becomes a member of that form of

---

b. Scalia, J., also argued that *Buckley* had decided the question of independent corporate political expenditures. He observed that *Buckley* had included corporate plaintiffs. Those plaintiffs apparently were the New York Civil Liberties Union, Inc. and Human Events, Inc. Can *Buckley* be distinguished?

association known as a for-profit corporation in order to pursue economic objectives. [In] joining such an association, the shareholder knows that management may take any action that is ultimately in accord with what the majority (or a specified supermajority) of the shareholders wishes, so long as that action is designed to make a profit. That is the deal. The corporate actions to which the shareholder exposes himself, therefore, include many things that he may find politically or ideologically uncongenial: investment in South Africa, operation of an abortion clinic, publication of a pornographic magazine, or even publication of a newspaper that adopts absurd political views and makes catastrophic political endorsements. His only protections against such assaults upon his ideological commitments are (1) his ability to persuade a majority (or the requisite minority) of his fellow shareholders that the action should not be taken, and ultimately (2) his ability to sell his stock. (The latter course, by the way, does not ordinarily involve the severe psychic trauma or economic disaster that Justice Brennan's opinion suggests.) It seems to me entirely fanciful, in other words, to suggest that the Michigan statute makes any significant contribution towards insulating the exclusively profit-motivated shareholder from the rude world of politics and ideology.

"But even if that were not fanciful, it would be fanciful to think, as Justice Brennan's opinion assumes, that there is any difference between for-profit and not-for-profit corporations insofar as the need for protection of the individual member's ideological psyche is concerned. Would it be any more upsetting to a shareholder of General Motors that it endorsed the election of Henry Wallace (to stay comfortably in the past) than it would be to a member of the American Civil Liberties Union that it endorsed the election of George Wallace?

"Finally, a few words are in order concerning the Court's approval of the Michigan law's exception for 'media corporations.' [I]f one believes in the Court's rationale of 'compelling state need' to prevent amassed corporate wealth from skewing the political debate, surely that 'unique role' of the press does not give Michigan justification for *excluding* media corporations from coverage, but provides especially strong reason to *include* them. Amassed corporate wealth that regularly sits astride the ordinary channels of information is much more likely to produce the New Corruption (too much of one point of view) than amassed corporate wealth that is generally busy making money elsewhere. Such media corporations not only have vastly greater power to perpetrate the evil of overinforming, they also have vastly greater opportunity. General Motors, after all, will risk a stockholder suit if it makes a political endorsement that is not plausibly tied to its ability to make money for its shareholders. But media corporations make money *by* making political commentary, including endorsements. * * *

"Members of the institutional press, despite the Court's approval of their illogical exemption from the Michigan law, will find little reason for comfort in today's decision. The theory of New Corruption it espouses is a dagger at their throat. The Court today holds merely that media corporations *may* be excluded from the Michigan law, not that they *must* be."[c]

c. Kennedy, J., joined by O'Connor and Scalia, JJ., also dissented. For valuable commentary relevant to the issues raised in *Austin,* see C. Edwin Baker, *Turner Broadcasting: Content–Based Regulation of Persons and Presses,* 1994 Sup.Ct.Rev. 57; Victor Brudney, *Association, Advocacy, and the First Amendment,* 4 Wm. & Mary Bill of Rts.J. 3 (1995); Julian Eule, *Promoting Speaker Diversity: Austin and Metro Broadcasting,* 1990 Sup.Ct.Rev. 105; Jill Fisch, *Frankenstein's Monster Hits the Campaign Trail: An Approach to Regulation of Corporate Political Expenditures,* 32 Wm. & Mary L.Rev. 587 (1991); Daniel Lowenstein, *A Patternless Mosaic,* 21 Capital U.L.Rev. 381 (1992); Andrew Stark, *Strange Bedfellows:*

Notes and Questions

1. *Distinguishing wealthy individuals.* Does *Austin* adequately distinguish spending by business corporations from that of wealthy individuals? Can the two be distinguished because (a) corporations in spending shareholders' money do not represent the overall interests of particular shareholders, but only their economic interests in the corporation; (b) the managers of corporations may lobby for structures that benefit managers at the expense of shareholders; and (c) the damage to equality interests is more pervasive? To what extent is spending by unions subject to these concerns? To a greater or lesser degree? See generally Samuel Issacharoff & Daniel R. Ortiz, *Governing Through Intermediaries,* 85 Va.L.Rev. 1627 (1999).

2. *Distinguishing media corporations.* BURGER, C.J., concurring in *Bellotti,* addressed the difficulty of distinguishing media corporations from business corporations: "A disquieting aspect of Massachusetts' position is that it may carry the risk of impinging on the First Amendment rights of those who employ the corporate form—as most do—to carry on the business of mass communications, particularly the large media conglomerates. This is so because of the difficulty, and perhaps impossibility, of distinguishing, either as a matter of fact or constitutional law, media corporations from corporations such as appellants.

"Making traditional use of the corporate form, some media enterprises have amassed vast wealth and power and conduct many activities, some directly related—and some not—to their publishing and broadcasting activities. Today, a corporation might own the dominant newspaper in one or more large metropolitan centers, television and radio stations in those same centers and others, a newspaper chain, news magazines with nationwide circulation, national or worldwide wire news services, and substantial interests in book publishing and distribution enterprises. Corporate ownership may extend, vertically, to pulp mills and pulp timberlands to insure an adequate, continuing supply of newsprint and to trucking and steamship lines for the purpose of transporting the newsprint to the presses. Such activities would be logical economic auxiliaries to a publishing conglomerate. Ownership also may extend beyond to business activities unrelated to the task of publishing newspapers and magazines or broadcasting radio and television programs. Obviously, such far-reaching ownership would not be possible without the state-provided corporate form and its 'special rules relating to such matters as limited liability, perpetual life, and the accumulation, distribution, and taxation of assets.'

"In terms of 'unfair advantage in the political process' and 'corporate domination of the electoral process,' it could be argued that such media conglomerates as I describe pose a much more realistic threat to valid interests than do appellants and similar entities not regularly concerned with shaping popular opinion on public issues."

Consider Marlene Nicholson, *The Constitutionality of the Federal Restrictions on Corporate and Union Campaign Contributions and Expenditures,* 65 Corn. L.Rev. 945, 959 (1980): "A solution may be to focus on the distinction between media activities and other activities. A diversified corporation, partially involved in the media, would be entitled to full first amendment protection for its media-

Two Paradoxes in Constitutional Discourse   ty, 14 Cardozo L.Rev. 1347 (1993).
Over Corporate and Individual Political Activi-

related operations. Under this approach, a newspaper would not lose its first amendment rights because it purchased a pulp mill, but it could not extend these rights to its pulp mill operations. An oil company that purchased a newspaper would not gain first amendment rights for its oil operations, but it would be able to assert these first amendment rights in the operation of its newspaper. The problem is not, to paraphrase Chief Justice Burger, the impracticability of making a distinction, but rather the difficulty of finding a theory that will justify a distinction."

Can self-expression serve as a distinguishing factor? See id. at 959–60. Is there more freedom "to choose and create the content of the delivered speech in the communications industry than in other industries"? Does the communication industry "display less allegiance to the profit motive than other industries"? Does it matter that the communications industry's product is speech? Can a fourth estate theory distinguish the press? On that premise, is there no reason to expand the definition of the press to include business corporations?[d]

3. *Distinguishing non-profit advocacy corporations.* 2 U.S.C.A. § 441(b) prohibits corporations or unions from making contributions or expenditures in connection with federal elections, but allows corporations and unions to establish and pay the expenses of segregated funds to be used for political purposes during federal elections. It prohibits corporations from soliciting contributions from persons other than its "stockholders and their families and its executive or administrative personnel and their families." In lieu of shareholders, corporations without capital stock are permitted to solicit contributions for such a fund from their "members." FEC v. NATIONAL RIGHT TO WORK COMM., 459 U.S. 197, 103 S.Ct. 552, 74 L.Ed.2d 364 (1982), per Rehnquist, J., characterized these provisions as sufficiently tailored to prevent corruption or its appearance and to protect corporate contributors as to negate any judgment that restriction on associational interests was "undue." The National Right to Work Committee is an advocacy group organized as a nonprofit corporation without capital stock. It conceded that it was required to set up a segregated fund under § 441(b) but argued that it was entitled to solicit contributions from anyone that had previously responded to any of its prior mass mailings. The Court unanimously held that this conception of membership would render the statutory corporation "meaningless." Without requiring any evidentiary showing, the Court stated that the interest in avoiding corruption or its appearance justified "treating unions, corporations, and similar organizations differently from individuals."

FEC v. NATIONAL CONSERVATIVE POLITICAL ACTION COMM., 470 U.S. 480, 105 S.Ct. 1459, 84 L.Ed.2d 455 (1985), per Rehnquist, J., characterized *National Right to Work Comm.* as proceeding from the premise that "in return for the special advantages that the State confers on the corporate form, individuals acting jointly through corporations forgo some of the rights they have as individuals." But he suggested that the question of whether a corporation could constitutionally be restricted in making independent expenditures to influence elections for public office was still open. Should advocacy groups organized in corporate form be treated like business corporations? White and Marshall, JJ., dissented.

4. *Protecting shareholders.* After *Bellotti*, could government "authorize management to make some kinds of corporate speech, such as commercial speech, but

---

d. See generally C. Edwin Baker, *Human Liberty and Freedom of Speech*, Chs. 10, 11 (1989); C. Edwin Baker, *Commercial Speech: A Problem in the Theory of Freedom*, 62 Iowa

L.Rev. 1, 25–40 (1976); C. Edwin Baker, *Press Rights and Government Power to Structure the Press*, 34 U.Miami L.Rev. 819, 822–36 (1980).

not others, such as political or noncommercial speech, without the approval or express consent of stockholders?" See generally Victor Brudney, *Business Corporations and Stockholders' Rights Under the First Amendment,* 91 Yale L.J. 235 (1981).

5. After *Austin* and *Bellotti,* could a state prevent non-voters including corporations and out of state citizens from make contributions to candidate or to initiatives within its state? See Note, *"Foreign" Campaign Contributions and the First Amendment,* 110 Harv. L.Rev. 1886 (1997)(discussing permanent resident aliens and American subsidiaries of foreign corporations).

Chapter 8

FREEDOM OF RELIGION

This chapter concerns the "religion clauses" of the first amendment, commonly known as the "establishment clause" (forbidding laws "respecting an establishment of religion") and the "free exercise clause" (forbidding laws "prohibiting the free exercise thereof"). It is difficult to explore either clause in isolation from the other. The extent to which the clauses interact may be illustrated by the matter of public financial aid to parochial schools, the subject of Sec. 1, II. On the one hand, does such aid violate the establishment clause? On the other hand, does a state's failure to provide such aid violate the free exercise clause? Another example of the potential conflict between the clauses—also considered in the materials below—is whether, on the one hand, a state's exemption of church buildings from property taxes contravenes the establishment clause or whether, on the other hand, a state's taxing these buildings contravenes the free exercise clause.

Despite this interrelationship of the two clauses, Sec. 1 deals almost exclusively with the establishment clause. Sec. 2, I then considers conventional problems under the free exercise clause. Sec. 2, II examines the complex issues of defining "religion" for purposes of the first amendment and determining the bona fides of an asserted "religious" belief—both matters usually presumed in the cases decided by the Supreme Court and the former never specifically addressed by a majority of the justices. Issues under each clause having been explored in some detail, Sec. 3 presents the subject of preference among religions that has both establishment and free exercise ramifications, and, finally, Sec. 4 discusses problems presented by government action that attempts to accommodate the seemingly opposing demands of the two religion clauses.[a]

SECTION 1. ESTABLISHMENT CLAUSE

I. INTRODUCTION

It is generally agreed that the establishment clause seeks to assure the separation of church and state in a nation characterized by religious pluralism. Prior to 1947, only two decisions concerning the establishment clause produced any significant consideration by the Court. *Bradfield v. Roberts,* 175 U.S. 291, 20

a. For discussion of the various "articulated justifications for the special constitutional place of religion" by the Justices, see Michael E. Smith, *The Special Place of Religion in the Constitution,* 1983 Sup.Ct.Rev. 83.

S.Ct. 121, 44 L.Ed. 168 (1899) upheld federal appropriations to a hospital in the District of Columbia, operated by the Catholic Church, for ward construction and care of indigent patients. *Quick Bear v. Leupp*, 210 U.S. 50, 28 S.Ct. 690, 52 L.Ed. 954 (1908) upheld federal disbursement of funds, held in trust for the Sioux Indians, to Catholic schools designated by the Sioux for payment of tuition costs.

In the Court's first modern decision, *Everson v. Board of Educ.* (1947), Part II infra, Rutledge, J., observed that "no provision of the Constitution is more closely tied to or given content by its generating history than the religious clause of the First Amendment." Black, J., writing for the majority, recounted that the religion clauses "reflected in the minds of early Americans a vivid mental picture of conditions and practices which they fervently wished to stamp out in order to preserve liberty for themselves and for their posterity." Black, J., detailed the history of religious persecution in Europe "before and contemporaneous with the colonization of America" and the "repetition of many of the old world practices" in the colonies. For example, in Massachusetts, Quakers, Baptists, and other religious minorities suffered harshly and were taxed for the established Congregational Church. In 1776, the Maryland "Declaration of Rights" stated that "only persons professing the Christian religion" were entitled to religious freedom, and not until 1826 were Jews permitted to hold public office. The South Carolina Constitution of 1778 stated that "the Christian Protestant religion shall be deemed [the] established religion of this state." Black, J., explained that "abhorrence" of these practices "reached its dramatic climax in Virginia in 1785–86" when "Madison wrote his great Memorial and Remonstrance" against renewal of "Virginia's tax levy for support of the established church" and the Virginia Assembly "enacted the famous 'Virginia Bill for Religious Liberty' originally written by Thomas Jefferson. [T]he provisions of the First Amendment, in the drafting and adoption of which Madison and Jefferson played such leading roles, had the same objective and were intended to provide the same protection against governmental intrusion on religious liberty as the Virginia statute."

Still, the specific historical record suggests that rather than disclosing a coherent "intent of the Framers," those who influenced the framing of the First Amendment were animated by several distinct and sometimes conflicting goals. Thus, Jefferson believed that the integrity of government could be preserved only by erecting "a wall of separation" between church and state. A sharp division of authority was essential, in his view, to insulate the democratic process from ecclesiastical depradations and excursions. Madison shared this view, but also perceived church-state separation as benefiting religious institutions.[a] Even more strongly, Roger Williams, one of the earliest colonial proponents of religious freedom, posited an evangelical theory of separation, believing it vital to protect the sanctity of the church's "garden" from the "wilderness" of the state. Finally, there is evidence that one purpose of the establishment clause was to protect the existing state-established churches from the newly ordained national government.[b]

a. For the view that "the Constitution was written on the assumption [that] government is a threat to human liberty [and] not the other way around [i.e.,] the First Amendment constrains Congress, not churches," see Douglas Laycock, *Continuity and Change in the Threat to Religious Liberty: The Reformation Era and the Late Twentieth Century*, 80 Minn. L.Rev. 1047 (1996).

b. For the view that "the religion clauses amounted to a decision by the national govern-

ment not to address substantive questions concerning the proper relationship between religion and government," but rather "did no more and no less than confirm the constitutional allocation of jurisdiction over religion to the states," see Steven D. Smith, *Foreordained Failure: The Quest for a Constitutional Principle of Religious Freedom* (1995). Compare Kurt T. Lash, *The Second Adoption of the Establishment Clause: The Rise of the Nonestablishment Principle*, 27 Ariz.St.L.J. 1085 (1995) this un-

(Indeed, although disestablishment was then well under way, the epoch of state-sponsored churches did not close until 1833 when Massachusetts separated church and state.)

The varied ideologies that prompted the founders do, however, disclose a dominant theme: according constitutional status to the integrity of individual conscience. Moreover, as revealed in Virginia's Bill for Religious Liberty, one practice seen by many as anathema to religious freedom was forcing the people to support religion through compulsory taxation, although there was a division of opinion as to whether non-preferential aid to religion violated liberty of conscience.[c]

A final matter involving the history of the establishment clause concerns *Everson*'s unanimous ruling that it was "made applicable to the states" by the fourteenth amendment.[d]

derstanding had changed by the time of the fourteenth amendment).

c. The view that it did not do so was endorsed by Rehnquist, J., in *Wallace v. Jaffree*, Part III, and in *Rosenberger v. University of Virginia*, Part II infra, Thomas, J., found "much to commend" this position.

d. *Application of the establishment clause to the states.* Is nonestablishment as "implicit in the concept of ordered liberty" as the freedoms of speech, press, religious exercise, and assembly? See *Palko v. Connecticut*, Ch. 6, Sec. 1, I. Is it "fundamental to the American scheme"? See *Duncan v. Louisiana*, Ch. 6, Sec. 1, I.

Brennan, J., stated: "It has been suggested [that] absorption of the First Amendment's ban against congressional legislation 'respecting an establishment of religion' is conceptually impossible because the Framers meant the Establishment Clause also to foreclose any attempt by Congress to disestablish the existing official state churches. [But] the last of the formal state establishments was dissolved more than three decades before the Fourteenth Amendment was ratified, and thus the problem of protecting official state churches from federal encroachments could hardly have been any concern of those who framed the post-Civil War Amendments. [T]he Fourteenth Amendment created a panoply of new federal rights for the protection of citizens of the various States. And among those rights was freedom from such state governmental involvement in the affairs of religion as the Establishment Clause had originally foreclosed on the part of Congress.

"It has also been suggested that the 'liberty' guaranteed by the Fourteenth Amendment logically cannot absorb the Establishment Clause because that clause is not one of the provisions of the Bill of Rights which in terms protects a 'freedom' of the individual. The fallacy in this contention, I think, is that it underestimates the role of the Establishment Clause as a co-guarantor, with the Free Exercise Clause, of religious liberty. * * *

"Finally, it has been contended that absorption of the Establishment Clause is precluded by the absence of any intention on the part of the Framers of the Fourteenth Amendment to circumscribe the residual powers of the States to aid religious activities and institutions in ways which fell short of formal establishments. That argument relies in part upon the express terms of the abortive Blaine Amendment—proposed several years after the adoption of the Fourteenth Amendment—which would have added to the First Amendment a provision that '[n]o state shall make any law respecting an establishment of religion.' Such a restriction would have been superfluous, it is said, if the Fourteenth Amendment had already made the Establishment Clause binding upon the States.

"The argument proves too much, for the Fourteenth Amendment's protection of the free exercise of religion can hardly be questioned; yet the Blaine Amendment would also have added an explicit protection against state laws abridging that liberty." *School Dist. v. Schempp*, Part III infra (concurring opinion).

Consider Mark D. Howe, *The Constitutional Question,* in Religion and the Free Society 49, 55 (1958): "The Court did not seem to be aware [that] some legislative enactments respecting an establishment of religion affect most remotely, if at all, the personal rights of religious liberty. [If the Court] reexamined its own interpretations of history [it might allow] the states to take such action in aid of religion as does not appreciably affect the religious or other constitutional rights of individuals."

Compare Jesse H. Choper, *The Establishment Clause and Aid to Parochial Schools,* 56 Calif.L.Rev. 260, 274–75 (1968): "[Howe] assumes that while the fourteenth amendment prevents infringements of liberty which 'significantly affect' the individual, the first amendment forbids abridgements which do not do so. [A] central design of the establishment clause was that it [prevent] government generally from coercing religious belief and specifically from compulsorily taxing individuals for strict-

II. AID TO RELIGION

EVERSON v. BOARD OF EDUC., 330 U.S. 1, 67 S.Ct. 504, 91 L.Ed. 711 (1947), involved one of the major areas of controversy under the establishment clause: public financial assistance to church-related institutions (mainly parochial schools). A New Jersey township reimbursed parents for the cost of sending their children "on regular buses operated by the public transportation system," to and from schools, including nonprofit private and parochial schools. The Court, per BLACK, J., rejected a municipal taxpayer's contention that payment for Catholic parochial school students violated the establishment clause:

"The 'establishment of religion' clause of the First Amendment means at least this: Neither a state nor the Federal Government can set up a church. Neither can pass laws which aid one religion, aid all religions, or prefer one religion over another. Neither can force nor influence a person to go to or to remain away from church against his will or force him to profess a belief or disbelief in any religion. No person can be punished for entertaining or professing religious beliefs or disbeliefs, for church attendance or non-attendance. No tax in any amount, large or small can be levied to support any religious activities or institutions, whatever they may be called, or whatever form they may adopt to teach or practice religion. Neither a state nor the Federal Government can, openly or secretly, participate in the affairs of any religious organizations or groups and vice versa. In the words of Jefferson, the clause against establishment of religion by law was intended to erect 'a wall of separation between Church and State.'

"We must [not invalidate the New Jersey statute] if it is within the state's constitutional power even though it approaches the verge of that power. New Jersey [cannot] contribute tax-raised funds to the support of an institution which teaches the tenets and faith of any church. On the other hand, other language of the amendment commands that New Jersey cannot hamper its citizens in the free exercise of their own religion. Consequently, it cannot exclude individual Catholics, Lutherans, Mohammedans, Baptists, Jews, Methodists, Non-believers, Presbyterians, or the members of any other faith, *because of their faith, or lack of it,* from receiving the benefits of public welfare legislation. While we do not mean to intimate that a state could not provide transportation only to children attending public schools, we must be careful, in protecting the citizens of New Jersey against state-established churches, to be sure that we do not inadvertently prohibit New Jersey from extending its general State law benefits to all its citizens without regard to their religious belief."

Noting that "the New Jersey legislature has decided that a public purpose will be served" by having children "ride in public buses to and from schools rather than run the risk of traffic and other hazards incident to walking or 'hitchhiking,' " the Court conceded "that children are helped to get to church schools. There is even a possibility that some of the children might not be sent to the church schools if the parents were compelled to pay their children's bus fares out of their own pockets when transportation to a public school would have been paid for by the State. [But] state-paid policemen, detailed to protect children going to and from church schools from the very real hazards of traffic, would serve much

---

ly religious purposes. If nonsecular federal action involves either of these consequences, [it] has seemingly violated the fourteenth amendment by 'significantly' affecting personal liberty. However, if federal action involves neither consequence, then [the] establishment clause itself—as a matter of constitutional construction—has probably not been breached." See also Note, *Toward a Uniform Valuation of the Religion Guarantees*, 80 Yale L.J. 77 (1970).

the same [purpose]. Similarly, parents might be reluctant to permit their children to attend schools which the state had cut off from such general government services as ordinary police and fire protection, connections for sewage disposal, public highways and sidewalks. Of course, cutting off church schools from these services, so separate and so indisputably marked off from the religious function, would make it far more difficult for the schools to operate. But such is obviously not the purpose of the First Amendment. That Amendment requires the state to be a neutral in its relations with groups of religious believers and non-believers; it does not require the state to be their adversary. * * *

"This Court had said that parents may, in the discharge of their duty under state compulsory education laws, send their children to a religious rather than a public school if the school meets the secular educational requirements which the state has power to impose. See *Pierce v. Society of Sisters,* [Ch. 7, Sec. 7, II]. It appears that these parochial schools meet New Jersey's requirements. The State contributes no money to the schools. [Its] legislation, as applied, does no more than provide a general program to help parents get their children, regardless of their religion, safely and expeditiously to and from accredited schools.

"The First Amendment has erected a wall between church and state. That wall must be kept high and impregnable. We could not approve the slightest breach. New Jersey has not breached it here."

RUTLEDGE, J., joined by Frankfurter, Jackson and Burton, JJ., filed the principal dissent, arguing that the statute aided children "in a substantial way to get the very thing which they are sent to the particular school to secure, namely, religious training and teaching. * * * Commingling the religious with the secular teaching does not divest the whole of its religious permeation and emphasis or make them of minor part, if proportion were material. Indeed, on any other view, the constitutional prohibition always could be brought to naught by adding a modicum of the secular. [Transportation] cost is as much a part of the total expense, except at times in amount, as the cost of textbooks, of school lunches, of athletic equipment, of writing and other [materials]. Payment of transportation is [no] less essential to education, whether religious or secular, than payment for tuitions, for teachers' salaries, for buildings, equipment and necessary materials. [No] rational line can be drawn between payment for such larger, but not more necessary, items and payment for transportation. [Now], as in Madison's time, not the amount but the principle of assessment is wrong.

" * * * Public money devoted to payment of religious costs, educational or other, brings the quest for more. It brings too the struggle of sect against sect for the larger share or for any. Here one by numbers alone will benefit most, there another. That is precisely the history of societies which have had an established religion and dissident groups. It is the very thing Jefferson and Madison experienced and sought to guard against, whether in its blunt or in its more screened forms. The end of such strife cannot be other than to destroy the cherished liberty. The dominating group will achieve the dominant benefit; or all will embroil the state in their dissensions. * * *

"Nor is the case comparable to one of furnishing fire or police protection, or access to public highways. These things are matters of common right, part of the general need for safety. Certainly the fire department must not stand idly by while the church burns."

The Court did not again confront the subject of aid to parochial schools for more than two decades.[a] During the intervening years, however, the Court continued to develop its establishment clause rationale in cases involving other issues, emphasizing the "purpose and primary effect" of the challenged government action (see Part III infra).

WALZ v. TAX COMM'N, 397 U.S. 664, 90 S.Ct. 1409, 25 L.Ed.2d 697 (1970), per BURGER, C.J., upheld state tax exemption for "real or personal property used exclusively for religious, educational or charitable purposes": "The legislative purpose of a property tax exemption is neither the advancement nor the inhibition of religion; it is neither sponsorship nor hostility. New York, in common with the other states, has determined that certain entities that exist in a harmonious relationship to the community at large, and that foster its 'moral or mental improvement,' should not be inhibited in their activities by property taxation or the hazard of loss of those properties for nonpayment of taxes. It [has] granted exemption to all houses of religious worship within a broad class of property owned by nonprofit, quasi-public corporations which include hospitals, libraries, playgrounds, scientific, professional, historical and patriotic groups. * * *

"We find it unnecessary to justify the tax exemption on the social welfare services or 'good works' that some churches perform for parishioners and others— family counselling, aid to the elderly and the infirm, and to children. [To] give emphasis to so variable an aspect of the work of religious bodies would introduce an element of governmental evaluation and standards as to the worth of particular social welfare programs, thus producing a kind of continuing day-to-day relationship which the policy of neutrality seeks to minimize. * * * We must also be sure that the end result—the effect—is not an excessive government entanglement with religion. The test is inescapably one of degree. * * * Elimination of exemption would tend to expand the involvement of government by giving rise to tax valuation of church property, tax liens, tax foreclosures, and the direct confrontations and conflicts that follow in the train of those legal processes.

"Granting tax exemptions to churches necessarily operates to afford an indirect economic benefit and also gives rise to some, but yet a lesser, involvement than taxing them. * * * Obviously a direct money subsidy would be a relationship pregnant with involvement and, as with most governmental grant programs, could encompass sustained and detailed administrative relationships for enforcement of statutory or administrative standards, but that is not this case. * * *

"It is obviously correct that no one acquires a vested or protected right in violation of the Constitution by long use * * *. Yet an unbroken practice of according the exemption to churches [is] not something to be lightly cast aside."

BRENNAN, J., concurred: "Tax exemptions and general subsidies [both] provide economic assistance, [but a] subsidy involves the direct transfer of public monies to the subsidized enterprise and uses resources exacted from taxpayers as a whole. An exemption, on the other hand, involves no such transfer.[b] It assists the exempted enterprise only passively." Harlan, J., also concurred.

---

a. See *Board of Educ. v. Allen*, 392 U.S. 236, 88 S.Ct. 1923, 20 L.Ed.2d 1060 (1968), upholding a program for lending state approved secular textbooks to all schoolchildren, including those attending church-related schools.

b. What of the fact that exemption for churches augments the tax bills of others? For the view that there is a constitutional distinction between tax exemptions ("a standing arrangement open to a wide array of organizations") and annual appropriations, see Edward A. Zelinsky, *Are Tax "Benefits" Constitutionally Equivalent to Direct Expenditures*, 112 Harv. L.Rev. 379 (1998).

DOUGLAS, J., dissented: "If history be our guide, then tax exemption of church property in this country is indeed highly suspect, as it arose in the early days when the church was an agency of the state. [The] financial support rendered here is to the church, the place of worship. A tax exemption is a subsidy."

Notes and Questions

1. *Size of government.* Consider William W. Van Alstyne, *Constitutional Separation of Church and State: The Quest for a Coherent Position,* 57 Am. Pol.Sci.Rev. 865, 881 (1963): "To finance expanding government services, [taxes] may gradually divert an increasing fraction of total personal income, necessarily leaving proportionately less money in the private sector to each person to spend according to his individual choice, in support of religion or other undertakings. To the extent that the tax revenues thus collected may not be spent by government to support religious enterprises, but must be used exclusively for secular purposes, the net effect, arguably, is to reduce the relative supply of funds available to religion." Does this warrant tax exemption for "religion"? Does it "warrant the judicial junking of the establishment clause"? Id. Is it "equally arguable that government fiscal activity, far from reducing disposable personal income, actually increases it"? Id. See also Alan Schwarz, *The Nonestablishment Principle: A Reply to Professor Giannella,* 81 Harv.L.Rev. 1465, 1469–70 (1968).

2. *"Neutrality" and "endorsement."* TEXAS MONTHLY, INC. v. BULL-OCK, 489 U.S. 1, 109 S.Ct. 890, 103 L.Ed.2d 1 (1989), held violative of the establishment clause a Texas sales tax exemption for books and "periodicals that are published or distributed by a religious faith and that consist wholly of writings promulgating the teaching of the faith." BRENNAN, J., joined by Marshall and Stevens, JJ., referred to several important themes in the Court's developing establishment clause rationale:[c] "[*Walz*] emphasized that the benefits derived by religious organizations flowed to a large number of nonreligious groups as [well]. However, when government directs a subsidy exclusively to religious organizations [that] either burdens nonbeneficiaries markedly or cannot reasonably be seen as removing a significant state-imposed deterrent to the free exercise of religion, as Texas has done, it 'provide[s] unjustifiable awards of assistance to religious organizations' and cannot but 'conve[y] a message of endorsement' to slighted members of the community. This is particularly true where, as here, the subsidy is targeted at writings that *promulgate* the teachings of religious faiths. It is difficult to view Texas' narrow exemption as anything but state sponsorship of religious belief [which] lacks a secular objective."

BLACKMUN, J., joined by O'Connor, J., concurred: "[A] tax exemption *limited* to the sale of religious literature * * * offends our most basic understanding of what the establishment clause is all about." White, J., concurred on freedom of press grounds. Scalia, J., joined by Rehnquist, C.J., and Kennedy, J., dissented from Brennan, J.'s distinction of *Walz.*

———

In 1971, LEMON v. KURTZMAN, 403 U.S. 602, 91 S.Ct. 2105, 29 L.Ed.2d 745, per BURGER C.J., which invalidated state salary supplements to teachers of secular subjects in nonpublic schools, articulated a three-part test for judging

---

c. In addition to "neutrality" and "endorsement," a third theme—"coercion"—is discussed more fully in Part IV infra.

establishment clause issues. This test is most frequently invoked by the lower courts and—as the materials that follow indicate—formally (if not operatively) has yet to be overruled: "First, the statute must have a secular legislative purpose; second, its principal or primary effect must be one that neither advances nor inhibits religion,[d] finally, the statute must not foster "an excessive government entanglement with religion." During the next fifteen years, the Court, using the *Lemon* test, invalidated a large number of aid programs for elementary and secondary schools, even though it found that virtually all had a "secular" purpose.[e] The *Lemon* Court began with a critical premise: the mission of church related elementary and secondary schools is to teach religion, and all subjects either are, or carry the potential of being, permeated with religion. Thus, states would have to engage in a "comprehensive, discriminating, and continuing state surveillance" to prevent misuse of tax funds for religious purposes, which would be impermissibly entangling, and "pregnant with dangers of excessive government direction of church schools and hence of churches."[f] Furthermore, state assistance risked another sort of entanglement: "divisive political potential" along religious lines.[g]

d. Compare Douglas Laycock, *Towards a General Theory of the Religion Clauses: The Case of Church Labor Relations and the Right to Church Autonomy*, 81 Colum.L.Rev. 1373, 1381, 1384 (1981): "The 'inhibits' language is at odds with the constitutional text and with the Court's own statements of the origins and purposes of [the] clause. Government support for religion is an element of every establishment claim, just as a burden or restriction on religion is an element of every free exercise claim. Regulation that burdens religion, enacted because of the government's general interest in regulation, is simply not establishment."

e. "This reflects, at least in part, our reluctance to attribute unconstitutional motives to the states, particularly when a plausible secular purpose for the state's program may be discerned from the face of the statute." *Mueller v. Allen*, cited infra. *Mueller* added: "A state's decision to defray the cost of educational expenses incurred by parents—regardless of the type of schools their children attend—evidences a purpose that is both secular and understandable. An educated populace is essential to the political and economic health of any community, and a state's efforts to assist parents in meeting the rising cost of educational expenses plainly serves this secular purpose of ensuring that the state's citizenry is well-educated. Similarly, [states] could conclude that there is a strong public interest in assuring the continued financial health of private schools, both sectarian and non-sectarian. By educating a substantial number of students such schools relieve public schools of a correspondingly great burden—to the benefit of all taxpayers. In addition, private schools may serve as a benchmark for public schools."

f. White, J., dissenting in *Lemon*, accused the Court of "creat[ing] an insoluble paradox for the State and the parochial schools. The State cannot finance secular instruction if it permits religion to be taught in the same class-room; but if it exacts a promise that religion not be so taught—a promise the school and its teachers are quite willing and on this record able to give—and enforces it, it is then entangled in the 'no entanglement' aspect of the Court's Establishment Clause jurisprudence."

g. *Lemon* reasoned: "In a community where such a large number of pupils are served by church-related schools, it can be assumed that state assistance will entail considerable political activity [by partisans and opponents]. Candidates will be forced to declare and voters to choose. It would be unrealistic to ignore the fact that many people confronted with issues of this kind will find their votes aligned with their faith.

"Ordinarily political debate and division, however vigorous or even partisan, are normal and healthy manifestations of our democratic system of government, but political division along religious lines was one of the principal evils against which the First Amendment was intended to protect. Paul A. Freund, *Public Aid to Parochial Schools*, 82 Harv.L.Rev. 1680, 1692 (1969)."

Compare Alan Schwarz, *No Imposition of Religion: The Establishment Clause Value*, 77 Yale L.J. 692, 711 (1968): "If avoidance of strife were an independent [establishment clause] value, no legislation could be adopted on any subject which aroused strong and divided [religious] feelings." See Jesse H. Choper, *The Establishment Clause and Aid to Parochial Schools*, 56 Calif.L.Rev. 260, 273 (1968): "Nor would a denial of aid to parochial schools largely diminish the extent of religious political activity. In fact, it 'might lead to greater political ruptures caused by the alienation of segments of the religious community.' Those who send their children to parochial schools might intensify opposition to increased governmental aid to public education." Contrast William D.

The case that follows reviews the important subsequent decisions and, although there is no opinion for the Court, brings the matter up to date.

MITCHELL v. HELMS

530 U.S. 793, 120 S.Ct. 2530, 147 L.Ed.2d 660 (2000).

JUSTICE THOMAS announced the judgment of the Court and delivered an opinion, in which THE CHIEF JUSTICE, JUSTICE SCALIA, and JUSTICE KENNEDY join. * * *

Chapter 2 of the Education Consolidation and Improvement Act of 1981, has its origins in the Elementary and Secondary Education Act of 1965 (ESEA), and is a close cousin of the provision of the ESEA that we recently considered in *Agostini v. Felton*, 521 U.S. 203, 117 S.Ct. 1997, 138 L.Ed.2d 391 (1997). [Chapter 2 lends educational materials (mainly for libraries and computers)—which may not "supplant funds from non-Federal sources"—to elementary and secondary schools, both public and private. The "services, materials, and equipment" for participating private schools (which were required to be nonprofit) must be "secular, neutral and nonideological."] It appears that, in an average year, about 30% of Chapter 2 funds spent in Jefferson Parish [La.] are allocated for private schools. [Since 1986, 46 private schools participated.] Of these 46, 34 were Roman Catholic; 7 were otherwise religiously affiliated; and 5 were not religiously affiliated.

Respondents filed suit in December 1985, alleging, among other things, that Chapter 2, as applied in Jefferson Parish, violated the Establishment Clause. The case's tortuous history over the next 15 years indicates well the degree to which our Establishment Clause jurisprudence has shifted in recent times.[a] [In] 1990, after extended discovery, Chief Judge Heebe of the District Court for the Eastern District of Louisiana granted summary judgment in favor of respondents [because] under the second part of our three-part test in *Lemon,* the program had the primary effect of advancing religion. Chapter 2 had such effect, in his view, because the materials and equipment loaned to the Catholic schools were direct aid to those schools and because the Catholic schools [were] "pervasively sectarian." Chief Judge Heebe relied primarily on *Meek v. Pittenger*, 421 U.S. 349, 95 S.Ct. 1753, 44 L.Ed.2d 217 (1975), and *Wolman v. Walter*, 433 U.S. 229, 97 S.Ct. 2593, 53 L.Ed.2d 714 (1977), in which we held unconstitutional programs that provided many of the same sorts of materials and equipment as does Chapter 2.

Valente & William A. Stanmeyer, *Public Aid to Parochial Schools—A Reply to Professor Freund,* 59 Geo.L.J. 59, 70 n. 46 (1970): "[O]ne's assessment of the accuracy of the views of Professors Freund, Schwartz, and Choper as to likely political repercussions is itself a political judgment and not judicial, and [the] weighing of political reactions is a function of legislatures and not of courts." For the view that the historical evidence shows "that it is misguided to interpret the first amendment as prohibiting legislative consideration of an issue affecting religion on the ground that the very act of consideration will spawn impermissible religious division," see Peter M. Schotten, *The Establishment Clause and Excessive Gov-ernmental–Religious Entanglement*, 15 Wake For.L.Rev. 207, 225 (1979).

a. As early as *Lemon* in 1971, the Court observed that, on the issue of financial assistance to sectarian schools, "we can only dimly perceive the lines of demarcation in this extraordinarily sensitive area of constitutional law." *Committee for Pub. Educ. v. Regan*, 444 U.S. 646, 100 S.Ct. 840, 63 L.Ed.2d 94 (1980)—holding that states may reimburse parochial schools for the cost of routine recordkeeping and administering state-prepared tests—observed that the "decisions have tended to avoid categorical imperatives and absolutist approaches at either end of the range of possible outcomes. This course sacrifices clarity and predictability for flexibility."

[Six] years later, Chief Judge Heebe having retired, Judge Livaudais [upheld] Chapter 2, pointing [to] our 1993 decision in *Zobrest v. Catalina Foothills School Dist.*, 509 U.S. 1, 113 S.Ct. 2462, 125 L.Ed.2d 1, in which we held that a State could, as part of a federal program for the disabled, provide a sign-language interpreter to a deaf student at a Catholic high school. Judge Livaudais [also] invoked *Rosenberger v. Rector and Visitors of Univ. of Va.*, 515 U.S. 819, 115 S.Ct. 2510, 132 L.Ed.2d 700 (1995), in [which], we held that the Establishment Clause does not require a public university to exclude a student-run religious publication from assistance available to numerous other student-run publications.[b] [While respondents'] appeal was pending, we decided *Agostini*, in which we approved a program [that] provided public employees to teach remedial classes at private schools, including religious schools. In so holding, we overruled *Aguilar v. Felton*, 473 U.S. 402, 105 S.Ct. 3232, 87 L.Ed.2d 290 (1985), and partially overruled *School Dist. of Grand Rapids v. Ball*, 473 U.S. 373, 105 S.Ct. 3248, 87 L.Ed.2d 267 (1985), both of which had involved such a program. [*Agostini*] acknowledged that our cases discussing excessive entanglement had applied many of the same considerations as had our cases discussing primary effect, and we therefore recast *Lemon's* entanglement inquiry as simply one criterion relevant to determining a statute's effect. We also acknowledged that our cases had pared somewhat the factors that could justify a finding of excessive entanglement. * * *

In this case, our inquiry under *Agostini's* purpose and effect test is a narrow one. Because respondents do not challenge the District Court's holding that Chapter 2 has a secular purpose, [we] will consider only Chapter 2's effect. Further, in determining that effect, we will consider only the first two *Agostini* criteria, since [respondents agree] that Chapter 2 does not create an excessive entanglement. Considering Chapter 2 in light of our more recent case law, we conclude that it neither results in religious indoctrination by the government nor defines its recipients by reference to religion. [For] the same reason, Chapter 2 also "cannot reasonably be viewed as an endorsement of religion," *Agostini*. [We] therefore hold that Chapter 2 is not a "law respecting an establishment of religion." In so holding, we acknowledge [that] *Meek* and *Wolman* are anomalies [and] therefore conclude that they are no longer good law.

As we indicated in *Agostini*, [the] question whether governmental aid to religious schools results in governmental indoctrination is ultimately a question whether any religious indoctrination that occurs in those schools could reasonably be attributed to governmental action. We have also indicated that the answer to the question of indoctrination will resolve the question whether a program of educational aid 'subsidizes' religion, as our religion cases use that term.

In distinguishing between indoctrination that is attributable to the State and indoctrination that is not, we have consistently turned to the principle of neutrality. [If] the religious, irreligious, and areligious are all alike eligible for governmental aid, no one would conclude that any indoctrination that any particular recipient conducts has been done at the behest of the government. [To] put the point differently, if the government, seeking to further some legitimate secular purpose, offers aid on the same terms, without regard to religion, to all who adequately further that purpose, then it is fair to say that any aid going to a religious recipient only has the effect of furthering that secular purpose. The

---

b. The student publication "offered a Christian perspective on both personal and community issues." Souter, J., joined by Stevens, Ginsburg and Breyer, JJ., dissenting, described the magazine as "straightforward exhortation to enter into a relationship with God as revealed in Jesus Christ, and to satisfy a series of moral obligations derived from the teachings of Jesus Christ."

government, in crafting such an aid program, has had to conclude that a given level of aid is necessary to further that purpose among secular recipients and has provided no more than that same level to religious recipients.

As a way of assuring neutrality, we have repeatedly considered whether any governmental aid that goes to a religious institution does so "only as a result of the genuinely independent and private choices of individuals." [For] if numerous private choices, rather than the single choice of a government, determine the distribution of aid pursuant to neutral eligibility criteria, then a government cannot, or at least cannot easily, grant special favors that might lead to a religious establishment. Private choice also helps guarantee neutrality by mitigating the preference for pre-existing recipients that is arguably inherent in any governmental aid program, and that could lead to a program inadvertently favoring one religion or favoring religious private schools in general over nonreligious ones. * * *

The principles of neutrality and private choice, and their relationship to each other, were prominent not only in *Agostini*, but also in *Zobrest, Witters* [*v. Washington Dept. of Servs. for Blind*, 474 U.S. 481, 488–489, 106 S.Ct. 748, 88 L.Ed.2d 846 (1986)], and *Mueller* [*v. Allen*, 463 U.S. 388, 397, 103 S.Ct. 3062, 77 L.Ed.2d 721 (1983)]. The heart of our reasoning in *Zobrest*, [was that] neutrality and private choices together eliminated any possible attribution to the government even when the interpreter translated classes on Catholic doctrine.

Witters and *Mueller* employed similar reasoning. In *Witters*, we held that the Establishment Clause did not bar a State from including within a neutral program providing tuition payments for vocational rehabilitation a blind person studying at a Christian college to become a pastor, missionary, or youth director.[6]c

The [state income] tax deduction for educational expenses [incurred at any nonprofit elementary or secondary school] that we upheld in *Mueller* was, in these respects, the same as the tuition grant in *Witters*. We upheld it chiefly because it "neutrally provides state assistance to a broad spectrum of citizens," and because "numerous, private choices of individual parents of school-age children," determined which schools would benefit from the deductions. * * *

Agostini's [second] criterion requires a court to consider whether an aid program "define[s] its recipients by reference to religion" [—i.e.] whether the criteria for allocating the aid "creat[e] a financial incentive to undertake religious indoctrination." [*Agostini* made] clear the close relationship between this rule, incentives, and private choice. For to say that a program does not create an incentive to choose religious schools is to say that the private choice is truly "independent." When such an incentive does exist, there is a greater risk that one could attribute to the government any indoctrination by the religious schools.

We hasten to add, what should be obvious from the rule itself, that simply because an aid program offers private schools, and thus religious schools, a benefit that they did not previously receive does not mean that the program, by reducing the cost of securing a religious education, creates, under *Agostini's* second

---

6. The majority opinion also noted that only a small portion of the overall aid under the State's program would go to religious education, [but more] recently, in *Agostini*, we held that the proportion of aid benefiting students at religious schools pursuant to a neutral program involving private choices was irrelevant to the constitutional inquiry.

c. On remand, the state court held that the aid in this case would violate the Washington constitution's provision that "no public money [shall] be appropriated for [any] religious instruction." *Witters v. State Commission for the Blind*, 112 Wash.2d 363, 771 P.2d 1119, cert. denied, 493 U.S. 850 (1989).

criterion, an "incentive" for parents to choose such an education for their children. For *any* aid will have some such effect.

Respondents [argue] first, and chiefly, that "direct, nonincidental" aid to the primary educational mission of religious schools is always impermissible.[7]

Although some of our earlier cases [did] emphasize the distinction between direct and indirect aid, the purpose of this distinction was merely to prevent "subsidization" of religion. [O]ur more recent cases address this purpose not through the direct/indirect distinction but rather through the principle of private choice. [If] aid to schools, even "direct aid," is neutrally available and, before reaching or benefiting any religious school, first passes through the hands (literally or figuratively) of numerous private citizens who are free to direct the aid elsewhere, the government has not provided any "support of religion." [It] was undeniable in *Witters* that the aid (tuition) would ultimately go to the Inland Empire School of the Bible and would support religious education. We viewed this arrangement, however, as no different from a government issuing a paycheck to one of its employees knowing that the employee would direct the funds to a religious institution. Both arrangements would be valid * * *. Whether one chooses to label this program "direct" or "indirect" is a rather arbitrary choice, one that does not further the constitutional analysis.

Of course, we have seen "special Establishment Clause dangers," *Rosenberger*, when money is given to religious schools or entities directly[d] rather than, as in *Witters* and *Mueller*, indirectly.[8] But direct payments of money are not at issue in this case, and we refuse to allow a "special" case to create a rule for all cases.

---

7. Respondents also contend that Chapter 2 aid supplants, rather than supplements, the core educational function of parochial schools and therefore has the effect of furthering religion. Our case law does provide some indication that this distinction may be relevant to determining whether aid results in governmental indoctrination, but we have never delineated the distinction's contours or held that it is constitutionally required. Nor, [do] we need to resolve the distinction's constitutional status today, [for] Chapter 2 itself requires that aid may only be supplemental. * * *

d. The *Rosenberger* majority, which consisted of the *Mitchell* plurality and O'Connor, J., noted that its decision "cannot be read as addressing an expenditure from a general tax fund." Rather, the money came from a "special student activities fund from which any group of students with [recognized] status can draw for purposes consistent with the University's educational mission." As in *Lamb's Chapel*, fn. 9 infra, "a public university may maintain its own computer facility and give student groups access to that facility, including the use of the printers, on a religion neutral, say first-come-first-served, basis." This is no different than "a school paying a third-party contractor to operate the facility on its behalf. The latter occurs here." Since the University made payments for publication costs directly to the printing companies, "we do not confront a case where, even under a neutral program that includes nonsectarian recipients, the government is making direct money payments to an institu-

tion or group that is engaged in religious activity." Moreover, "the student publication is not a religious institution, at least in the usual sense of that term as used in our case law."

In a separate concurrence, O'Connor, J., noted that "unlike monies dispensed from state or federal treasuries, the Student Activities Fund is collected from students who themselves administer the fund." Thus, there is a "possibility that the student fee is susceptible to a Free Speech Clause challenge by an objecting student that she should not be compelled to pay for speech with which she disagrees. See, e.g., *Keller; Abood* [Ch. 7, Sec. 9, II]. The existence of such an opt-out possibility not available to citizens generally, provides a potential basis for distinguishing proceeds of the student fees in this case from proceeds of the general assessments in support of religion that lie at the core of the prohibition against religious funding, and from government funds generally."

The dissenters distinguished cases like *Lamb's Chapel* as based "on the recognition that all speakers are entitled to use the street corner (even though the State paves the roads and provides police protection to everyone on the street) and on the analogy between the public street corner and open classroom space. [T]he cases cannot be lifted to a higher plane of generalization without admitting that new economic benefits are being extended directly to religion in clear violation of the principle barring direct aid."

8. The reason for such concern is not that the form per se is bad, but that such a form

Respondents also contend that the Establishment Clause requires that aid to religious schools not be impermissibly religious in nature or be divertible to religious use. We agree with the first part of this argument but not the second. Respondents' "no divertibility" rule is inconsistent with our more recent case law and is unworkable. So long as the governmental aid is not itself "unsuitable for use in the public schools because of religious content," and eligibility for aid is determined in a constitutionally permissible manner, any use of that aid to indoctrinate cannot be attributed to the government and is thus not of constitutional concern [discussing *Zobrest, Witters* and *Mueller*]. [J]ust as a government interpreter does not herself inculcate a religious message—even when she is conveying one—so also a government computer or overhead projector does not itself inculcate a religious message, even when it is conveying one.[9] * * *

A concern for divertibility, as opposed to improper content, is misplaced not only because it fails to explain why the sort of aid that we have allowed is permissible, but also because it is boundless—enveloping all aid, no matter how trivial—and thus has only the most attenuated (if any) link to any realistic concern for preventing an "establishment of religion." Presumably, for example, government-provided lecterns, chalk, crayons, pens, paper, and paintbrushes would have to be excluded from religious schools under respondents' proposed rule. But we fail to see how indoctrination by means of (i.e., diversion of) such aid could be attributed to the government. In fact, the risk of improper attribution is less when the aid lacks content, for there is no risk (as there is with books), of the government inadvertently providing improper content. See *Allen* (Douglas, J., dissenting). Finally, any aid, with or without content, is "divertible" in the sense that it allows schools to "divert" resources. Yet we have "not accepted the recurrent argument that all aid is forbidden because aid to one aspect of an institution frees it to spend its other resources on religious ends."

It is perhaps conceivable that courts could take upon themselves the task of distinguishing among the myriad kinds of possible aid based on the ease of diverting each kind. But it escapes us how a court might coherently draw any such line. * * *

---

creates special risks that governmental aid will have the effect of advancing religion (or, even more, a purpose of doing so). An indirect form of payment reduces these risks. It is arguable, however, at least after *Witters*, that the principles of neutrality and private choice would be adequate to address those special risks, for it is hard to see the basis for deciding *Witters* differently simply if the State had sent the tuition check directly to whichever school Witters chose to attend. Similarly, we doubt it would be unconstitutional if, to modify *Witters*'s hypothetical, a government employer directly sent a portion of an employee's paycheck to a religious institution designated by that employee pursuant to a neutral charitable program. [Finally,] at least some of our prior cases striking down direct payments involved serious concerns about whether the payments were truly neutral. See, e.g., *Committee for Pub. Educ. v. Nyquist*, 413 U.S. 756, 93 S.Ct. 2955, 37 L.Ed.2d 948 (1973) [involving a state partial tuition tax credit to parents who sent their children to nonpublic schools. For parents too poor to be liable for income taxes and therefore unable to benefit from a tax credit, the state gave an outright grant of up to fifty percent of tuition].

9. The dissent would find an establishment of religion if a government-provided projector were used in a religious school to show a privately purchased religious film, even though a public school that possessed the same kind of projector would likely be constitutionally barred from refusing to allow a student bible club to use that projector in a classroom to show the very same film, where the classrooms and projectors were generally available to student groups. See *Lamb's Chapel v. Center Moriches Union Free School Dist.*, 508 U.S. 384, 113 S.Ct. 2141, 124 L.Ed.2d 352 (1993), [holding that a school district did not violate the establishment clause in permitting a church's after-hours use of school facilities to show a religiously oriented film series on family values when the school district also permitted presentation of views on the subject by nonreligious groups].

The dissent serves up a smorgasbord of 11 factors that, depending on the facts of each case "in all its particularity," could be relevant to the constitutionality of a school-aid program. [The] dissent resurrects the concern for political divisiveness that once occupied the Court but that post-*Aguilar* cases have rightly disregarded. As Justice O'Connor explained in dissent in *Aguilar*: "It is curious indeed to base our interpretation of the Constitution on speculation as to the likelihood of a phenomenon which the parties may create merely by prosecuting a lawsuit." * * *

One of the dissent's factors deserves special mention: whether a school that receives aid (or whose students receive aid) is pervasively sectarian. The dissent is correct that there was a period when this factor mattered, particularly if the pervasively sectarian school was a primary or secondary school. But that period [is] thankfully long past [discussing *Witters*, *Zobrest* and *Agostini*. The] religious nature of a recipient should not matter to the constitutional analysis, so long as the recipient adequately furthers the government's secular purpose. If a program offers permissible aid to the religious (including the pervasively sectarian), the areligious, and the irreligious, it is a mystery which view of religion the government has established, and thus a mystery what the constitutional violation would be. The pervasively sectarian recipient has not received any special favor, and it is most bizarre that the Court would, as the dissent seemingly does, reserve special hostility for those who take their religion seriously * * *.

[T]he inquiry into the recipient's religious views required by a focus on whether a school is pervasively sectarian is not only unnecessary but also offensive.[e] It is well established, in numerous other contexts, that courts should refrain from trolling through a person's or institution's religious beliefs. [In] addition, and related, the application of the "pervasively sectarian" factor collides with our decisions that have prohibited governments from discriminating in the distribution of public benefits based upon religious status or sincerity. See *Rosenberger*; *Lamb's Chapel*.[19]

Finally, hostility to aid to pervasively sectarian schools has a shameful pedigree * * *. Opposition to aid to "sectarian" schools acquired prominence in the 1870's with Congress's consideration (and near passage) of the Blaine Amendment, which would have amended the Constitution to bar any aid to sectarian institutions. Consideration of the amendment arose at a time of pervasive hostility to the Catholic Church and to Catholics in general, and it was an open secret that "sectarian" was code for "Catholic." Notwithstanding its history, of course, "sectarian" could, on its face, describe the school of any religious sect, but the Court eliminated this possibility of confusion when [it] coined the term "pervasively sectarian"—a term which, at that time, could be applied almost exclusively to Catholic parochial schools and which even today's dissent exemplifies chiefly by reference to such schools. [This] doctrine, born of bigotry, should be buried now. * * *

[W]e agree with the dissent that there is evidence of actual diversion [in this case] and that, were the safeguards anything other than anemic, there would

---

e. For the view that "the possibilities for misunderstandings, spiritual insensitivity, and outright sectarian bigotry wrought by the 'pervasively sectarian' test is breathtaking," see Carl H. Esbeck, *Myths, Miscues, and Misconceptions: No–Aid Separatism and the Establishment Clause,* 13 Not.D.J.L. Eth. & Pub.Pol. 285 (1999).

19. Indeed, [to] require exclusion of religious schools from such a program would raise serious questions under the Free Exercise Clause. See, e.g., *Church of Lukumi Babalu Aye, Inc. v. Hialeah,* [Sec. 2, I infra]; *Everson.*

almost certainly be more such evidence. In any event, for reasons we discussed supra, the evidence of actual diversion and the weakness of the safeguards against actual diversion are not relevant to the constitutional inquiry * * *.

Respondents do, however, point to some religious books that [were] improperly allowed to be loaned to several religious schools, and they contend that the monitoring programs [are] insufficient to prevent such errors. The evidence, however, establishes just the opposite, for the improper lending of library books occurred—and was discovered and remedied—before this litigation began almost 15 years [ago]. We are unwilling to elevate scattered de minimis statutory violations, discovered and remedied by the relevant authorities themselves prior to any litigation, to such a level as to convert an otherwise unobjectionable parish-wide program into a law that has the effect of advancing religion. * * *

Justice O'Connor, with whom Justice Breyer joins, concurring in the judgment.

* * * I believe that *Agostini* likewise controls the constitutional inquiry respecting Title II. [To] the extent our decisions in *Meek* and *Wolman* are inconsistent with the Court's judgment today, I agree that those decisions should be overruled. * * *

I write separately because, in my view, the plurality announces a rule of unprecedented breadth for the evaluation of Establishment Clause challenges to government school-aid programs. Reduced to its essentials, the plurality's rule states that government aid to religious schools does not have the effect of advancing religion so long as the aid is offered on a neutral basis and the aid is secular in content. [First,] the plurality's treatment of neutrality comes close to assigning that factor singular importance in the future adjudication of Establishment Clause challenges to government school-aid programs. Second, the plurality's approval of actual diversion of government aid to religious indoctrination is in tension with our precedents and, in any event, unnecessary to decide the instant case.

[W]e have never held that a government-aid program passes constitutional muster solely because of the neutral criteria it employs as a basis for distributing aid. For example, in *Agostini*, neutrality was only one of several factors we considered * * * (noting lack of evidence of inculcation of religion by Title I instructors, legal requirement that Title I services be supplemental to regular curricula, and that no Title I funds reached religious schools' coffers). Indeed, given that the aid in *Agostini* had secular content and was distributed on the basis of wholly neutral criteria, our consideration of additional factors demonstrates that the plurality's rule does not accurately describe our recent Establishment Clause jurisprudence. See also *Zobrest*, (noting that no government funds reached religious school's coffers, aid did not relieve school of expense it otherwise would have assumed, and aid was not distributed to school but to the child).

[At] least two of the decisions at the heart of today's case demonstrate that we have long been concerned that secular government aid not be diverted to the advancement of religion. [See] *Agostini*, ("[N]o evidence has ever shown that any New York City Title I instructor teaching on parochial school premises attempted to inculcate religion in students"); *Allen* ("Nothing in this record supports the proposition that all textbooks, whether they deal with mathematics, physics, foreign languages, history, or literature, are used by the parochial schools to teach religion"). * * *

The plurality bases its holding that actual diversion is permissible on *Witters* and *Zobrest*. Those decisions, however, rested [on] the understanding that the aid was provided directly to the individual student who, in turn, made the choice of where to put that aid to [use.] This characteristic of both programs made them less like a direct subsidy, which would be impermissible under the Establishment Clause, and more akin to the government issuing a paycheck to an employee who, in turn, donates a portion of that check to a religious institution. [Like] Justice Souter, I do not believe that we should treat a per-capita-aid program the same as the true private-choice programs considered in *Witters* and *Zobrest*. First, when the government provides aid directly to the student beneficiary, that student can attend a religious school and yet retain control over whether the secular government aid will be applied toward the religious education. The fact that aid flows to the religious school and is used for the advancement of religion is therefore *wholly* dependent on the student's private decision.

Second, [i]n terms of public perception, a government program of direct aid to religious schools based on the number of students attending each school differs meaningfully from the government distributing aid directly to individual students who, in turn, decide to use the aid at the same religious schools. In the former example, if the religious school uses the aid to inculcate religion in its students, it is reasonable to say that the government has communicated a message of endorsement. Because the religious indoctrination is supported by government assistance, the reasonable observer would naturally perceive the aid program as *government* support for the advancement of religion. That the amount of aid received by the school is based on the school's enrollment does not separate the government from the endorsement of the religious message. The aid formula does not—and could not—indicate to a reasonable observer that the inculcation of religion is endorsed only by the individuals attending the religious school, who each affirmatively choose to direct the secular government aid to the school and its religious mission. No such choices have been made. In contrast, when government aid supports a school's religious mission only because of independent decisions made by numerous individuals to guide their secular aid to that [school,] endorsement of the religious message is reasonably attributed to the individuals who select the path of the aid.[a]

[If,] as the plurality contends, a per-capita-aid program is identical in relevant constitutional respects to a true private-choice program, then there is no reason that, under the plurality's reasoning, the government should be precluded from providing direct money payments to religious organizations (including churches) based on the number of persons belonging to each organization. And, because actual diversion is permissible under the plurality's holding, the participating religious organizations (including churches) could use that aid to support religious indoctrination. * * *

Our school-aid cases often pose difficult questions at the intersection of the [principle of government neutrality and the prohibition of state funding of religious activities] and therefore defy simple categorization under either rule. As I explained in *Rosenberger*, "[r]esolution instead depends on the hard task of judging—sifting through the details and determining whether the challenged program offends the Establishment Clause. Such judgment requires courts to draw lines, sometimes quite fine, based on the particular facts of each case."

---

a. The "endorsement" theme—highly influential in the present Court's reasoning—is considered in further detail in Part IV infra.

[Under *Agostini*], we need ask only whether the [Jefferson Parish] program results in governmental indoctrination or defines its recipients by reference to religion. * * *

Respondents [claim] that the presumption that religious schools will use instructional materials and equipment [as in *Meek* and *Wolman*] to inculcate religion is sound because such materials and equipment, unlike textbooks [as in *Allen*] are reasonably divertible to religious uses. For example, no matter what secular criteria the government employs in selecting a film projector to lend to a religious school, school officials can always divert that projector to religious instruction. [But *Wolman*] never justified the inconsistent treatment it accorded the lending of textbooks and the lending of instructional materials and equipment based on the items' reasonable divertibility. * * *

In any event, [the] divertibility rationale urged by respondents and Justice Souter, [does] not provide a logical distinction between the lending of textbooks and the lending of instructional materials and equipment. An educator can use virtually any instructional tool, whether it has ascertainable content or not, to teach a religious message. [For] example, even a publicly financed lunch would apparently be unconstitutional under a divertibility rationale because religious-school officials conceivably could use the lunch to lead the students in a blessing over the bread. * * *

Because divertibility fails to explain the distinction our cases have drawn between textbooks and instructional materials and equipment,[b] there remains the question of which of the two irreconcilable strands of our Establishment Clause jurisprudence we should now follow. Between the two, I would adhere to the rule that we have applied in the context of textbook lending programs: To establish a First Amendment violation, plaintiffs must prove that the aid in question actually is, or has been, used for religious purposes. [In] *Agostini*, we repeatedly emphasized [that] plaintiffs raising an Establishment Clause challenge must present evidence that the government aid in question has resulted in religious indoctrination. * * *

Respondents note that in *Agostini* we did not overrule that portion of *Grand Rapids* holding the Community Education program unconstitutional. Under that program, the government paid religious-school teachers to operate as part-time public teachers at their religious schools by teaching secular classes at the conclusion of the regular school day. Relying on both the majority opinion and my separate opinion in *Grand Rapids*, respondents therefore contend that we must presume that religious-school teachers will inculcate religion in their students. If that is so, they argue, we must also presume that religious-school teachers will be unable to follow secular restrictions on the use of instructional materials and equipment lent to their schools by the government.

I disagree, however, that the latter proposition follows from the former. [When] a religious school receives textbooks or instructional materials and equipment lent with secular restrictions, the school's teachers need not refrain from teaching religion altogether. Rather, the instructors need only ensure that any such religious teaching is done without the instructional aids provided by the

---

b. O'Connor, J.'s opinion stated further: "[T]he most important reason for according special treatment to direct money grants is that this form of aid falls precariously close to the original object of the Establishment Clause's prohibition. Statements concerning the constitutionally suspect status of direct cash aid, accordingly, provide no justification for applying an absolute rule against divertibility when the aid consists instead of instructional materials and equipment."

government. We have always been willing to assume that religious-school instructors can abide by such restrictions when the aid consists of textbooks. [The] same assumption should extend to instructional materials and equipment.

For the same reason, my position in *Grand Rapids* is distinguishable. [In] that context, I was willing to presume that the religious-school teacher who works throughout the day to advance the school's religious mission would also do so, at least to some extent, during the supplemental classes provided at the end of the day. Because the government financed the entirety of such classes, any religious indoctrination taking place therein would be directly attributable to the government. In the instant case, because the Chapter 2 aid concerns only teaching tools that must remain supplementary, the aid comprises only a portion of the teacher's educational efforts during any single class.* * *

The plurality and Justice Souter [proceed] from the premise that, so long as actual diversion presents a constitutional problem, the government must have a failsafe mechanism capable of detecting any instance of diversion. We rejected that very assumption, however, in *Agostini*. There, we explained that because we had "abandoned the assumption that properly instructed public employees will fail to discharge their duties faithfully, we must also discard the assumption that pervasive monitoring of Title I teachers is required." Because I believe that the Court should abandon the presumption adopted in *Meek* and *Wolman* respecting the use of instructional materials and equipment by religious-school teachers, I see no constitutional need for pervasive monitoring under the Chapter 2 program. * * *

Justice Souter contends that *any* evidence of actual diversion requires the Court to declare the Chapter 2 program unconstitutional as applied in Jefferson Parish [but] I know of no case in which we have declared an entire aid program unconstitutional on Establishment Clause grounds solely because of violations on the miniscule scale of those at issue here. * * *

JUSTICE SOUTER, with whom JUSTICE STEVENS and JUSTICE GINSBURG join, dissenting.

The First Amendment's Establishment Clause [bars] the use of public funds for religious aid. * * *

In all the years of its effort, the Court has isolated no single test of constitutional sufficiency, and the question in every case addresses the substantive principle of no aid: what reasons are there to characterize this benefit as aid to the sectarian school in discharging its religious mission? Particular factual circumstances control, and the answer is a matter of judgment.

[The] Court's decisions demonstrate its repeated attempts to isolate considerations relevant in classifying particular benefits as between those that do not discernibly support or threaten support of a school's religious mission, and those that cross or threaten to cross the line into support for religion.[a]

The most deceptively familiar of those considerations is "neutrality" * * *.

There is, of course, good reason for considering the generality of aid and the evenhandedness of its distribution in making close calls between benefits that in

---

a. See Marshall, J., joined by Brennan, Blackmun and Stevens, JJ., dissenting in *Mueller*: "While 'services such as police and fire protection, sewage disposal, highways, and sidewalks,' may be provided to parochial schools in common with other institutions, because this type of assistance is clearly 'marked off from the religious function' of those schools, unrestricted financial assistance, such as grants for the maintenance and construction of parochial schools, may not be provided."

purpose or effect support a school's religious mission and those that do not. [O]n the face of it aid distributed generally and without a religious criterion is less likely to be meant to aid religion than a benefit going only to religious institutions or people. [And,] evenhandedness is a way of asking whether a benefit can reasonably be seen to aid religion in fact; we do not regard the postal system as aiding religion, even though parochial schools get mail. Given the legitimacy of considering evenhandedness, then, there is no reason to avoid the term "neutrality" to refer to it. But one crucial point must be borne in mind. [I]f we looked no further than evenhandedness, and failed to ask what activities the aid might support, or in fact did support, religious schools could be blessed with government funding as massive as expenditures made for the benefit of their public school counterparts, and religious missions would thrive on public money. This is why the consideration of less than universal neutrality has never been recognized as dispositive and has always been teamed with attention to other facts bearing on the substantive prohibition of support for a school's religious objective.

At least three main lines of enquiry addressed particularly to school aid have emerged to complement evenhandedness neutrality. First, we have noted that two types of aid recipients heighten Establishment Clause concern: pervasively religious schools[6] and primary and secondary religious schools.[b] Second, we have identified two important characteristics of the method of distributing aid: directness or indirectness of distribution and distribution by genuinely independent choice. Third, we have found relevance in at least five characteristics of the aid itself: its religious content; its cash form; its divertibility or actual diversion to religious support;[13] its supplantation of traditional items of religious school expense; and its substantiality. * * *

The plurality, however, would reject that lesson. The majority misapplies it. * * *

First, the plurality treats an external observer's attribution of religious support to the government as the sole impermissible effect of a government aid scheme. While perceived state endorsement of religion is undoubtedly a relevant concern under the Establishment Clause, it is certainly not the only [one.] State aid not attributed to the government would still violate a taxpayer's liberty of conscience, threaten to corrupt religion, and generate disputes over aid.* * *[19]

Second, the plurality apparently assumes as a fact that equal amounts of aid to religious and nonreligious schools will have exclusively secular and equal

6. In fact, religious education in Roman Catholic schools is defined as part of required religious practice; aiding it is thus akin to aiding a church service. See 1983 *Code of Canon Law*, Canon 798 (directing parents to entrust children to Roman Catholic schools or otherwise provide for Roman Catholic education) * * *.

b. Aid to higher education is considered in note 1(a) infra.

13. I reject the plurality's argument that divertibility is a boundless principle. Our long experience of evaluating this consideration demonstrates its practical limits. Moreover, the Establishment Clause charges us with making such enquiries, regardless of their difficulty. Finally, the First Amendment's rule permitting only aid with fixed secular content seems no more difficult to apply than the plurality's

rule prohibiting only aid with fixed religious content.

19. Adopting the plurality's rule would permit practically any government aid to religion so long as it could be supplied on terms ostensibly comparable to the terms under which aid was provided to nonreligious recipients. As a principle of constitutional sufficiency, the manipulability of this rule is breathtaking. A legislature would merely need to state a secular objective in order to legalize massive aid to all religions, one religion, or even one sect, to which its largess could be directed through the easy exercise of crafting facially neutral terms under which to offer aid favoring that religious group. Short of formally replacing the Establishment Clause, a more dependable key to the public fisc or a cleaner break with prior law would be difficult to imagine.

effects, on both external perception and on incentives to attend different schools. But there is no reason to believe that this will be the case; the effects of same-terms aid may not be confined to the secular sphere at all.* * *

Third, the plurality assumes that per capita distribution rules safeguard the same principles as independent, private choices. But [n]ot the least of the significant differences [is] the right and genuine opportunity of the recipient to choose not to give the aid. To hold otherwise would be to license the government to donate funds to churches based on the number of their members, on the patent fiction of independent private choice. * * *

The plurality's conception of evenhandedness does not, however, control [this case]. The facts most obviously relevant to the Chapter 2 scheme in Jefferson Parish are those showing divertibility and actual diversion in the circumstance of pervasively sectarian religious schools [and] the lack of effective safeguards. [First,] the record shows actual diversion in the library book program. [D]iscovery revealed that under Chapter 2, nonpublic schools requested and the government purchased at least 191 religious books with taxpayer funds by December 1985. Books such as *A Child's Book of Prayers* and *The Illustrated Life of Jesus* were discovered among others that had been ordered under the program.

The evidence persuasively suggests that other aid was actually diverted as well. The principal of one religious school testified, for example, that computers lent with Chapter 2 funds were joined in a network with other non-Chapter 2 computers in some schools, and [that] the Chapter 2 computer took over the support of the computing system whenever there was a breakdown of the master computer purchased with the religious school's own funds. [Moreover,] film projectors and videotape machines purchased with public funds were [seemingly] used in religious indoctrination over a period of at least seven years. [The] Court has no choice but to hold that the program as applied violated the Establishment Clause.[28]

The plurality would break with the law. [Its] choice to employ imputations of bigotry and irreligion as terms in the Court's debate makes one point clear: that in rejecting the principle of no aid to a school's religious mission the plurality is attacking the most fundamental assumption underlying the Establishment Clause * * *.

Notes and Questions

1. *Direct payments to religious institutions.* (a) *Higher education.* TILTON v. RICHARDSON, 403 U.S. 672, 91 S.Ct. 2091, 29 L.Ed.2d 790 (1971) and ROEMER v. BOARD OF PUB. WORKS, 426 U.S. 736, 96 S.Ct. 2337, 49 L.Ed.2d 179 (1976), upheld direct government grants to church-related colleges and universities as part of general programs for construction of buildings and other activities not involving sectarian activities. *Roemer* noted "what is crucial to a nonentangling aid program: the ability of the State to identify and subsidize separate secular functions carried out at the school, without on-the-site inspections being necessary to prevent diversion of the funds to sectarian purposes." *Tilton* added: "There are generally significant differences between the religious aspects of church-related institutions of higher learning and parochial elementary and secondary schools. The 'affirmative, if not dominant, policy' of the instruction in pre-college church-

---

28. Since the divertibility and diversion require a finding of unconstitutionality, I will not explore other grounds, beyond noting the like- lihood that unconstitutional supplantation occurred as well. * * *

schools is 'to assure future adherents to a particular faith by having control of their total education at an early age.' There is substance to the contention that college students are less impressionable and less susceptible to religious indoctrination. [Further], by their very nature, college and postgraduate courses tend to limit the opportunities for sectarian influence by virtue of their own internal disciplines. Many church-related colleges and universities are characterized by a high degree of academic freedom and seek to evoke free and critical responses from their students."

Brennan, J., dissented in *Tilton:* "[A] sectarian university is the equivalent in the realm of higher education of the Catholic elementary [schools]; it is an educational institution in which the propagation and advancement of a particular religion is a primary function of the institution. [It] is not that religion 'permeates' the secular education that is provided. Rather, it is that the secular education is provided within the environment of religion; the institution is dedicated to two goals, secular education *and* religious instruction. When aid flows directly to the institution, both functions benefit."

(b) *Social welfare programs.* BOWEN v. KENDRICK, 487 U.S. 589, 108 S.Ct. 2562, 101 L.Ed.2d 520 (1988), per Rehnquist, C.J., held that the Adolescent Family Life Act (AFLA)—which grants funds to a variety of public and private agencies (including religious organizations) to provide counseling for prevention of adolescent sexual relations and care for pregnant adolescents and adolescent parents—did not, on its face, violate the establishment clause. "As in *Tilton* and *Roemer*, we do not think the possibility that AFLA grants may go to religious institutions that can be considered 'pervasively sectarian' is sufficient to conclude that no grants whatsoever can be given under the statute to religious organizations."[a] It was to be determined on remand "whether in particular cases AFLA aid has been used to fund 'specifically religious activit(ies) in an otherwise substantially secular setting,' [for example], whether [grantees] use materials that have an explicitly religious content or are designed to inculcate the views of a particular religious faith."[b]

(c) *Burden of proof.* After *Mitchell*, is a *majority* now willing to apply the approach of the above decisions to elementary and secondary schools? If "plaintiffs must prove that the aid in question [is] used for religious purposes" ("O'Connor, J.), is a majority now willing *at least* to uphold previously invalidated programs on a showing that religion no more "permeates the secular education" in primary and secondary parochial schools than it does in church-related colleges?

(d) *"Endorsement."* Consider Tribe 2d ed., at 1221: "Another reason that religious colleges are treated differently from parochial schools is the *public's* view of the aid programs. Aid for secular programs in all colleges, including those with church affiliation, is generally perceived as assistance to non-religious activities. But the moment aid is sent to a parochial school as such, it is widely seen as aid to religion. The number of dollars released for religious purposes may be identical; the symbolism is not."

2. *Vouchers.* After *Mitchell*, would an "education voucher" plan pass muster if the vouchers were given to *all* parents for use in *any* school?

---

a. Prior to *Mitchell*, in *Columbia Union College v. Clarke*, 527 U.S. 1013, 119 S.Ct. 2357, 144 L.Ed.2d 252 (1999), Thomas J., dissented from the Court's denial of certiorari from a decision excluding a "pervasively sec-

tarian" Seventh-day Adventist college from a state aid program.

b. The 5–4 majority included O'Connor, Scalia and Kennedy, JJ.

(a) *"Endorsement."* Consider Kathleen M. Sullivan, *Parades, Public Squares and Voucher Payments: Problems of Government Neutrality*, 28 Conn.L.Rev. 243, 255–58 (1996): "Public education [is] a form of government speech in which government is exercising a massive degree of content control. [The] Establishment Clause operates as a unique gag order on government speech and symbolism. Government itself may espouse any viewpoint a democratic majority wishes *except* a religious viewpoint. Thus, if [a] state extended its voucher system to religious schools, the Court still would, and should, strike it down." Compare Abner S. Greene, *Why Vouchers are Unconstitutional, and Why They're Not*, 13 Not. D.J.L.Eth. & Pub.Pol. 397, 400 (1999): "The generality of voucher programs, combined with the fact that each family, and not the government, decides how to use the voucher money, belies Sullivan's argument. [The] reasonable observer would not attribute to the government the message of any school benefited by voucher money. Rather, such an observer would assume that the government is funding all schools, and thus is supporting the message of none." Contrast Eugene Volokh, *Equal Treatment Is Not Establishment*, id. at 341, 368–70: "Under the endorsement test, the government may not express endorsement *or disapproval* of religion [citing, inter alia, *Wallace v. Jaffree*, Sec. III infra]. [I]f giving special benefits to religion [is] endorsement, then discriminating against religion [is] disapproval."

(b) *"Neutrality."* Do vouchers for religious schools violate "neutrality" because of the government support of "religious values"? Consider Volokh, supra, at 346: "The religious schools do teach a religious value system—just as secular schools teach a secular value system. There's [no] reason why the government is obligated to discriminate against one or the other system, and thus against the parents who choose to teach their children one or the other system. Just as we wouldn't tolerate discrimination against atheistic schools, or discrimination against secular schools, so we shouldn't assume that the Constitution requires discrimination against religious schools."

(c) *"Private choice."* Would a voucher be "no different from a government issuing a paycheck to one of its employees knowing that the employee would direct the funds to a religious institution" (Thomas, J.)? Consider Ira C. Lupu, *The Increasingly Anachronistic Case Against School Vouchers*, id. at 375, 379–80: "When the state pays its employees a wage, they can spend the money for any lawful purpose, including for the advancement of religion. In such circumstances, the state cannot be held responsible for any religious benefit arising from the unfettered spending choices of its employees. By contrast, when the state constrains the benefit in certain ways—for example, a state income tax deduction for all charitable contributions—the probability and forseeability of a boost to religion are markedly increased. Contemporary voucher programs tend to constrain yet further, limiting parents to the mix of participating schools, in which sectarian institutions will be heavily represented, at least in the short run." If a voucher program is the same as a charitable tax deduction, what follows?

(d) *"Religious purpose."* If at least *some* voucher funds might be used to support "religious indoctrination," would the program fail O'Connor, J.'s burden of proof standard in note 1(c) supra. If so, what of *Witters* (and the GI Bill)?

3. *"Neutrality" and political divisiveness.* To what extent does a "broad class" of beneficiary groups affect this criterion? Consider Note, *The Constitutionality of Tax Relief for Parents of Children Attending Public and Nonpublic Schools*, 67 Minn.L.Rev. 793, 820–21 (1983): "Legislation that primarily aids sectarian education disrupts political equality and promotes rivalry among reli-

gious sects by favoring those groups that emphasize private primary and secondary education. [In] contrast, aid which broadly benefits secular as well as sectarian groups is less likely to generate interfaith rivalries or imbalances of power. Even if only some sects receive aid directly, members of other faiths will probably benefit as members of the broader legislative class. Because particular religious groups will not be perceived as the primary beneficiaries of state aid, competition among sects for government funds will also be reduced." Compare Laura Underkuffler–Freund, *The Separation of the Religious and the Secular,* 36 Wm. & M.L.Rev. 837, 975 (1995): "The concerns of reformers—that governmental financial support of religious institutions would promote their involvement in government, their meddling with laws, their grasping for money, and their attempts to protect governmentally-bestowed privileges and emoluments—are presented no less by the public funding of all religious institutions than by the funding of few. Rather, the answer becomes [one] of degree: while incidental public support for sectarian institutions (on a basis equal to public institutions and to each other) probably presents little danger of institutional alliance of church and state, extensive funding may pose significant danger."

4. *Other approaches.* Commentators have proposed various "tests" to measure the validity of public aid to church-related schools. In evaluating those that follow, what results would they produce in the decided cases?

(a) Jesse H. Choper, *The Establishment Clause and Aid to Parochial Schools,* 56 Calif.L.Rev. 260, 265–66 (1968): "[G]overnmental financial aid may be extended directly or indirectly to support parochial schools [so] long as such aid does not exceed the value of the secular educational service rendered by the school."[c] Would such aid have "a secular legislative purpose and a primary effect that neither advances nor inhibits religion"? Compare Harold D. Hammett, *The Homogenized Wall,* 53 A.B.A.J. 929, 932–33 (1967): "If the net effect of the financial aid is to increase proportionally the influence of both the church and the state, so that their influence relative to each other remains at the same original ratio, the 'primary' effect on religion has been neutral." Contrast Stephen D. Sugarman, *New Perspectives on "Aid" to Private School Users,* in Nonpublic School Aid 64, 66 (West ed. 1976): "Even if the [effect] principle were limited to cases in which there was (or the legislature knew there would be) a *large* beneficial impact on religion, it would intolerably inhibit secular government action. For example, perhaps building roads and running public transportation on Sunday may be shown to have large beneficial impacts on religion. [For] me the concerns underlying the Establishment clause could be satisfied with an affirmative answer to this hypothetical question: Would the legislature have acted as it did were there no interdependency with religion involved? If so, then I think it would be fair to say that there is no subsidy of religion, that the religious benefits are constitutionally permitted side effects."[d]

(b) Ira C. Lupu, *To Control Faction and Protect Liberty: A General Theory of the Religion Clauses,* 7 J.Contemp.Leg.Issues 357, 373 (1996): "The worry expressed so widely [about] coercive taxation to support religious teaching is a holdover relic from the Virginia story of coercive assessments earmarked for the support of Christian ministers and teachers. Such an exaction, taking from all to

c. For further analysis, see Michael W. McConnell & Richard Posner, *An Economic Approach to Issues of Religious Freedom,* 56 U.Chi.L.Rev. 1 (1989); Note, *The Supreme Court, Effect Inquiry, and Aid to Parochial Education,* 37 Stan.L.Rev. 219 (1984).

d. Problems under the free exercise clause raised by the exclusion of parochial schools from public aid programs are considered in note 2, p. 1110 infra.

support a few on religious grounds and for religious ends, of course violates the Establishment Clause. [When] the state, however, makes funds available in a religion-neutral way for secular ends ["such as educational attainment, health care, or social services"], those objections quickly become attenuated. Such programs should survive, unless the challenger can persuasively demonstrate that the program (despite facially neutral criteria) is in essence a cover for sectarian discrimination."

III. RELIGION AND PUBLIC SCHOOLS

WALLACE v. JAFFREE

472 U.S. 38, 105 S.Ct. 2479, 86 L.Ed.2d 29 (1985).

JUSTICE STEVENS delivered the opinion of the Court.

[In 1978, Alabama enacted § 16–1–20 authorizing a one-minute period of silence in all public schools "for meditation"; in 1981, it enacted § 16–1–20.1 authorizing a period of silence "for meditation or voluntary prayer." Appellees, parents of second graders,] have not questioned the holding that § 16–1–20 is valid. Thus, the narrow question for decision [concerns § 16–1–20.1].

[T]he Court has unambiguously concluded that the individual freedom of conscience protected by the First Amendment embraces the right to select any religious faith or none at all. This conclusion derives [from] the conviction that religious beliefs worthy of respect are the product of free and voluntary choice by the faithful, and from recognition of the fact that the political interest in forestalling intolerance extends beyond intolerance among Christian sects—or even intolerance among "religions"—to encompass intolerance of the disbeliever and the uncertain. * * *

[Under *Lemon*,] even though a statute that is motivated in part by a religious purpose may satisfy the first criterion, the First Amendment requires that a statute must be invalidated if it is entirely motivated by a purpose to advance religion.

In applying the purpose test, it is appropriate to ask "whether government's actual purpose is to endorse or disapprove of religion."[42] In this case, the answer to that question is dispositive. * * *

The sponsor of the bill that became § 16–1–20.1, Senator Donald Holmes, inserted into the legislative record—apparently without dissent—a statement indicating that the legislation was an "effort to return voluntary prayer" to the public schools. Later Senator Holmes confirmed this purpose before the District Court. In response to the question whether he had any purpose for the legislation other than returning voluntary prayer to public schools, he stated: "No, I did not have no other purpose in mind."[44] The State did not present evidence of *any* secular purpose. * * *

42. *Lynch v. Donnelly,* [Part IV infra] (O'Connor, J., concurring) ("The purpose prong of the *Lemon* test asks whether government's actual purpose is to endorse or disapprove of religion. The effect prong asks whether, irrespective of government's actual purpose, the practice under review in fact conveys a message of endorsement or disapproval. An affirmative answer to either question should render the challenged practice invalid").

44. [The] evidence presented to the District Court elaborated on the express admission of the Governor of Alabama (then Fob James) that the enactment of § 16–1–20.1 was intended to "clarify [the State's] intent to have prayer as part of the daily classroom activity," and that the "expressed legislative purpose in enacting Section 16–1–20.1 (1981) was to 'return voluntary prayer to public schools.'"

The legislative intent to return prayer to the public schools is, of course, quite different from merely protecting every student's right to engage in voluntary prayer during an appropriate moment of silence during the schoolday. The 1978 statute already protected that right, containing nothing that prevented any student from engaging in voluntary prayer during a silent minute of meditation. [The] legislature enacted § 16–1–20.1, despite the existence of § 16–1–20 for the sole purpose of expressing the State's endorsement of prayer activities for one minute at the beginning of each schoolday. The addition of "or voluntary prayer" indicates that the State intended to characterize prayer as a favored practice. Such an endorsement is not consistent with the established principle that the government must pursue a course of complete neutrality toward religion.

The importance of that principle does not permit us to treat this as an inconsequential case involving nothing more than a few words of symbolic speech on behalf of the political majority.[51] For whenever the State itself speaks on a religious subject, one of the questions that we must ask is "whether the government intends to convey a message of endorsement or disapproval of religion." * * *

JUSTICE O'CONNOR concurring in the judgment.

* * * Although a distinct jurisprudence has enveloped each of [the Religion] Clauses, their common purpose is to secure religious liberty. On these principles the Court has been and remains unanimous. [O]ur goal should be "to frame a principle for constitutional adjudication that is not only grounded in the history and language of the first amendment, but one that is also capable of consistent application to the relevant problems." Jesse H. Choper, *Religion in the Public Schools: A Proposed Constitutional Standard,* 47 Minn.L.Rev. 329, 332–333 (1963). Last Term, I proposed a refinement of the *Lemon* test with this goal in mind. *Lynch v. Donnelly* (concurring opinion).

The *Lynch* concurrence suggested that the religious liberty protected by the Establishment Clause is infringed when the government makes adherence to religion relevant to a person's standing in the political community. Direct government action endorsing religion or a particular religious practice is invalid under this approach because it "sends a message to nonadherents that they are outsiders, not full members of the political community, and an accompanying message to adherents that they are insiders, favored members of the political community." [In] this country, church and state must necessarily operate within the same community. Because of this coexistence, it is inevitable that the secular interests of government and the religious interests of various sects and their adherents will frequently intersect, conflict, and combine. A statute that ostensibly promotes a secular interest often has an incidental or even a primary effect of helping or hindering a sectarian belief. Chaos would ensue if every such statute were invalid

---

51. As this Court stated in *Engel v. Vitale,* [infra]: "The Establishment Clause, unlike the Free Exercise Clause, does not depend upon any showing of direct governmental compulsion and is violated by the enactment of laws which establish an official religion whether those laws operate directly to coerce nonobserving individuals or not." Moreover, this Court has noted that "[w]hen the power, prestige and financial support of government is placed behind a particular religious belief, the indirect coercive pressure upon religious minorities to conform to the prevailing officially approved religion is plain." Id. This comment has special force in the public-school context where attendance is mandatory. Justice Frankfurter acknowledged this reality in *McCollum v. Board of Education,* [note 1(a) infra] (concurring opinion): "That a child is offered an alternative may reduce the constraint; it does not eliminate the operation of influence by the school in matters sacred to conscience and outside the school's domain. The law of imitation operates, and non-conformity is not an outstanding characteristic of children." * * *

under the Establishment Clause. For example, the State could not criminalize murder for fear that it would thereby promote the Biblical command against killing.[b] The task for the Court is to sort out those statutes and government practices whose purpose and effect go against the grain of religious liberty protected by the First Amendment.

The endorsement test does not preclude government from acknowledging religion or from taking religion into account in making law and policy. It does preclude government from conveying or attempting to convey a message that religion or a particular religious belief is favored or preferred. Such an endorsement infringes the religious liberty of the nonadherent * * *.

Twenty-five states permit or require public school teachers to have students observe [a] moment of silence at the beginning of the schoolday during which students may meditate, pray, or reflect on the activities of the day. * * * Relying on this Court's decisions disapproving vocal prayer and Bible reading in the public schools, see *School Dist. v. Schempp,* 374 U.S. 203, 83 S.Ct. 1560, 10 L.Ed.2d 844 (1963); *Engel v. Vitale,* 370 U.S. 421, 82 S.Ct. 1261, 8 L.Ed.2d 601 (1962), the courts that have struck down the moment of silence statutes generally conclude that their purpose and effect are to encourage prayer in public schools.

The *Engel* and *Schempp* decisions are not dispositive. [In] *Engel,* a New York statute required teachers to lead their classes in a vocal prayer.[c] The Court concluded that "it is no part of the business of government to compose official prayers for any group of the American people to recite as part of a religious program carried on by the government." In *Schempp,* the Court addressed Pennsylvania and Maryland statutes that authorized morning Bible readings in public schools.[d] The Court reviewed the purpose and effect of the statutes, concluded that they required religious exercises, and therefore found them to violate the Establishment Clause. Under all of these statutes, a student who did not share the religious beliefs expressed in the course of the exercise was left with the choice of participating, thereby compromising the nonadherent's beliefs, or withdrawing, thereby calling attention to his or her nonconformity. The decisions

---

b. On this analysis, *McGowan v. Maryland,* 366 U.S. 420, 81 S.Ct. 1101, 6 L.Ed.2d 393 (1961), per Warren, C.J., held that the "present purpose and effect" of Maryland's Sunday Closing Laws were not religious and did not violate the establishment clause. Although "the original laws which dealt with Sunday labor were motivated by religious forces," the Court showed that secular emphases in language and interpretation have come about, that recent "legislation was supported by labor groups and trade associations," and that "secular justifications have been advanced for making Sunday a day of rest, a day when people may recover from the labors of the week just passed and may physically and mentally prepare for the week's work to come. [It] would seem unrealistic for enforcement purposes and perhaps detrimental to the general welfare to require a State to choose a common day of rest other than that which most persons would select of their own accord."

Douglas, J., dissented: "No matter how much is written, no matter what is said," Sunday is a Christian holiday. "There is an 'establishment' of religion in the constitutional sense if any practice of any religious group has the sanction of law behind it."

c. The prayer, composed by the N.Y. Board of Regents, provided: "Almighty God, we acknowledge our dependence upon Thee, and we beg Thy blessings upon us, our parents, our teachers and our country."

d. The reading of the Bible, without comment, was followed by recitation of the Lord's Prayer. In Pennsylvania, various students read passages they selected from any version of the Bible. Plaintiff father testified that "specific religious doctrines purveyed by a literal reading of the Bible" were contrary to the family's Unitarian religious beliefs; one expert testified that "portions of the New Testament were offensive to Jewish tradition" and, if "read without explanation, they could [be] psychologically harmful to the child and had caused a divisive force within the social media of the school"; a defense expert testified "that the Bible [was] non-sectarian within the Christian faiths."

acknowledged the coercion implicit under the statutory schemes, see *Engel*,[e] but they expressly turned only on the fact that the government was sponsoring a manifestly religious exercise.[f]

A state-sponsored moment of silence in the public schools is different from state-sponsored vocal prayer or Bible reading. First, a moment of silence [unlike] prayer or Bible reading, need not be associated with a religious exercise. Second, [d]uring a moment of silence, a student who objects to prayer is left to his or her own thoughts, and is not compelled to listen to the prayers or thoughts of others. [It] is difficult to discern a serious threat to religious liberty from a room of silent, thoughtful schoolchildren.

By mandating a moment of silence, a State does not necessarily endorse any activity that might occur during the period. Even if a statute specifies that a student may choose to pray silently during a quiet moment, the State has not thereby encouraged prayer over other specified alternatives. Nonetheless, it is also possible that a moment of silence statute, either as drafted or as actually implemented, could effectively favor the child who prays over the child who does not. For example, the message of endorsement would seem inescapable if the teacher exhorts children to use the designated time to pray. Similarly, the fact of the statute or its legislative history may clearly establish that it seeks to encourage or promote voluntary prayer over other alternatives, rather than merely provide a quiet moment that may be dedicated to prayer by those so inclined. The crucial question is whether the State has conveyed or attempted to convey the message that children should use the moment of silence for prayer.[2] This question cannot be answered in the abstract, but instead requires courts to examine the history, language, and administration of a particular statute to determine whether it operates as an endorsement of religion.

[T]he inquiry into the purpose of the legislature in enacting a moment of silence law should be deferential and limited. In determining whether the government intends a moment of silence statute to convey a message of endorsement or disapproval of religion, a court has no license to psychoanalyze the legislators. If a legislature expresses a plausible secular purpose for a moment of silence statute in either the text or the legislative history, or if the statute disclaims an intent to encourage prayer over alternatives during a moment of silence, then courts should generally defer to that stated intent. It is particularly troublesome to denigrate an expressed secular purpose due to postenactment testimony by particular legislators or by interested persons who witnessed the drafting of the statute.[g] Even if the text and official history of a statute express no secular purpose, the statute

---

e. See fn. 51 in the Court's opinion, supra.

f. *Engel* distinguished "the fact that school children and others are officially encouraged to express love for our country by reciting historical documents such as the Declaration of Independence which contain references to the Deity or by singing officially espoused anthems which include the composer's professions of faith in a Supreme Being, or with the fact that there are many manifestations in our public life of belief in God. Such patriotic or ceremonial occasions bear no true resemblance to the unquestioned religious exercise that the State of New York has sponsored in this instance."

2. Appellants argue that *Zorach v. Clauson*, [note 1(b) infra], suggests there is no constitutional infirmity in a State's encouraging a child to pray during a moment of silence. [There]

the Court stated that "[w]hen the state encourages religious instruction—[by] *adjusting the schedule of public events to sectarian needs,* it follows the best of our traditions." When the State provides a moment of silence during which prayer may occur at the election of the student, it can be said to be adjusting the schedule of public events to sectarian needs. But when the State also encourages the student to pray during a moment of silence, it converts an otherwise inoffensive moment of silence into an effort by the majority to use the machinery of the State to encourage the minority to participate in a religious exercise.

g. For further discussion of this point, see Burger, C.J.'s opinion infra.

should be held to have an improper purpose only if it is beyond purview that endorsement of religion or a religious belief "was and is the law's reason for existence." *Epperson v. Arkansas*, [note 3(b) infra]. Since there is arguably a secular pedagogical value to a moment of silence in public schools, courts should find an improper purpose behind such a statute only if the statute on its face, in its official legislative history, or in its interpretation by a responsible administrative agency suggests it has the primary purpose of endorsing prayer.

[It] is of course possible that a legislature will enunciate a sham secular purpose for a statute. I have little doubt that our courts are capable of distinguishing a sham secular purpose from a sincere one, or that the *Lemon* inquiry into the effect of an enactment would help decide those close cases where the validity of an expressed secular purpose is in doubt. [T]he *Lynch* concurrence suggested that the effect of a moment of silence law is not entirely a question of [fact]. The relevant issue is whether an objective observer, acquainted with the text, legislative history, and implementation of the statute, would perceive it as a state endorsement of prayer in public schools. A moment of silence law that is clearly drafted and implemented so as to permit prayer, meditation, and reflection within the prescribed period, without endorsing one alternative over the others, should pass this test.

The analysis above suggests that moment of silence laws in many States should pass Establishment Clause scrutiny because they do not favor the child who chooses to pray during a moment of silence over the child who chooses to meditate or reflect. § 16–1–20.1 does not stand on the same footing. However deferentially one examines its text and legislative history, however objectively one views the message attempted to be conveyed to the public, the conclusion is unavoidable that the purpose of the statute is to endorse prayer in public [schools.][5] * * *[h]

CHIEF JUSTICE BURGER dissenting.

* * * Today's decision recalls the observations of Justice Goldberg: "[U]ntutored devotion to the concept of neutrality can lead to invocation or approval of results which partake not simply of that noninterference and noninvolvement with the religious which the Constitution commands, but of a brooding and pervasive dedication to the secular and a passive, or even active, hostility to the religious. Such results are not only not compelled by the Constitution, but, it seems to me, are prohibited by it." *Schempp* (concurring opinion). * * *

Curiously, the opinions do not mention that *all* of the sponsor's statements relied upon—including the statement "inserted" into the Senate Journal—were made *after* the legislature had passed the statute; [there] is not a shred of evidence that the legislature as a whole shared the sponsor's motive or that a majority in either house was even aware of the sponsor's view of the bill when it was [passed.]

Even if an individual legislator's after-the-fact statements could rationally be considered relevant, all of the opinions fail to mention that the sponsor also

---

5. The Chief Justice suggests that one consequence of the Court's emphasis on the difference between § 16–1–20.1 and its predecessor statute might be to render the Pledge of Allegiance unconstitutional because Congress amended it in 1954 to add the words "under God". I disagree. In my view, the words "under God" in the Pledge serve as an acknowledgement of religion with "the legitimate secu-

lar purposes of solemnizing public occasions, [and] expressing confidence in the future." *Lynch* (concurring opinion).

h. Powell, J., who was the fifth justice to join the Court's opinion, also separately concurred, agreeing "fully with Justice O'Connor's assertion that some moment-of-silence statutes may be constitutional, a suggestion set forth in the Court's opinion as well."

testified that one of his purposes in drafting and sponsoring the moment-of-silence bill was to clear up a widespread misunderstanding that a schoolchild is legally *prohibited* from engaging in silent, individual prayer once he steps inside a public school building. That testimony is at least as important as the statements the Court relies upon, and surely that testimony manifests a permissible purpose. * * *

The several preceding opinions conclude that the principal difference between § 16–1–20.1 and its predecessor statute proves that the sole purpose behind the inclusion of the phrase "or voluntary prayer" in § 16–1–20.1 was to endorse and promote prayer. This reasoning is simply a subtle way of focusing exclusively on the religious component of the statute rather than examining the statute as a whole. Such logic—if it can be called that—would lead the Court to hold, for example, that a state may enact a statute that provides reimbursement for bus transportation to the parents of all schoolchildren, but may not *add* parents of parochial school students to an existing program providing reimbursement for parents of public school students. Congress amended the statutory Pledge of Allegiance 31 years ago to add the words "under God." Do the several opinions in support of the judgment today render the Pledge unconstitutional? [3]

* * * Without pressuring those who do not wish to pray, the statute simply creates an opportunity to think, to plan, or to pray if one wishes—as Congress does by providing chaplains and chapels. [If] the government may not accommodate religious needs when it does so in a wholly neutral and noncoercive manner, the "benevolent neutrality" that we have long considered the correct constitutional standard will quickly translate into the "callous indifference" that the Court has consistently held the Establishment Clause does not require. * * *

JUSTICE REHNQUIST, dissenting.

[There] is simply no historical foundation for the proposition that the Framers intended to build the "wall of separation" that was constitutionalized in *Everson.* [And the "purpose and effect" tests] are in no way based on either the language or intent of the drafters. [If] the purpose prong is intended to void those aids to sectarian institutions accompanied by a stated legislative purpose to aid religion, the prong will condemn nothing so long as the legislature utters a secular purpose and says nothing about aiding religion. * * *

However, if the purpose prong is aimed to void all statutes enacted with the intent to aid sectarian institutions, whether stated or not, then most statutes providing any aid, such as textbooks or bus rides for sectarian school children, will fail because one of the purposes behind every statute, whether stated or not, is to aid the target of its largesse. * * *

If a constitutional theory has no basis in the history of the amendment it seeks to interpret, is difficult to apply and yields unprincipled results, I see little use in it. [It] would come as much of a shock to those who drafted the Bill of Rights as it will to a large number of thoughtful Americans today to learn that the

---

3. The House Report on the legislation amending the Pledge states that the purpose of the amendment was to affirm the principle that "our people and our Government [are dependent] upon the moral directions of the Creator." If this is simply "acknowledgement," not "endorsement," of religion, the distinction is far too infinitesimal for me to grasp.

[Compare Jefferson B. Fordham, *The Implications of the Supreme Court Decisions Dealing* *with Religious Practices in the Public Schools,* 6 J. of Chur. & St. 44, 56 (1964): "In view of the patriotic element here, one may suggest that the likelihood of indirect compulsion is much greater than in the simple prayer case. Here the individual dissenter is made to stand out as one unwilling to engage in a patriotic act and recital."]

Constitution, as construed by the majority, prohibits the Alabama Legislature from "endorsing" prayer. George Washington himself, at the request of the very Congress which passed the Bill of Rights, proclaimed a day of "public thanksgiving and prayer, to be observed by acknowledging with grateful hearts the many and signal favors of Almighty God." History must judge whether it was the Father of his Country in 1789, or a majority of the Court today, which has strayed from the meaning of the Establishment Clause. * * *

Notes and Questions

1. *Released time.* (a) McCOLLUM v. BOARD OF EDUC., 333 U.S. 203, 68 S.Ct. 461, 92 L.Ed. 649 (1948), per BLACK, J., held that a public school released time program violated the establishment clause. Privately employed religious teachers held weekly classes, on public school premises, in their respective religions, for students whose parents signed request cards, while non-attending students pursued secular studies in other parts of the building: "Here not only are the state's tax-supported public school buildings used for the dissemination of religious doctrines. The State also affords sectarian groups an invaluable aid in that it helps to provide pupils for their religious classes through use of the state's compulsory public school machinery."[a]

(b) ZORACH v. CLAUSON, 343 U.S. 306, 72 S.Ct. 679, 96 L.Ed. 954 (1952), per DOUGLAS, J., upheld a released time program in which the religious classes were held in church buildings: "[This] program involves neither religious instruction in public school classrooms nor the expenditure of public funds. All costs, including the application blanks, are paid by the religious organizations. The case is therefore unlike *McCollum*.

"[The] nullification of this law would have wide and profound effects. A Catholic student applies to his teacher for permission to leave the school during hours on a Holy Day of Obligation to attend a mass. A Jewish student asks his teacher for permission to be excused for Yom Kippur. A Protestant wants the afternoon off for a family baptismal ceremony. In each case the teacher requires parental consent in writing. In each case the teacher, in order to make sure the student is not a truant, goes further and requires a report from the priest, the rabbi, or the minister. The teacher in other words cooperates in a religious program to the extent of making it possible for her students to participate in it. Whether she does it occasionally for a few students, regularly for one, or pursuant to a systematized program designed to further the religious needs of all the students does not alter the character of the act.

"We are a religious people whose institutions presuppose a Supreme Being. We guarantee the freedom to worship as one chooses. [When] the state encourages religious instruction or cooperates with religious authorities by adjusting the schedule of public events to sectarian needs, [it] respects the religious nature of our people and accommodates the public service to their spiritual needs. To hold that it may not would [be] preferring those who believe in no religion over those who do believe. [The] problem, like many problems in constitutional law, is one of degree."

JACKSON, J., dissented: "If public education were taking so much of the pupils' time as to [encroach] upon their religious opportunity, simply shortening everyone's school day would facilitate voluntary and optional attendance at Church classes. But that suggestion is rejected upon the ground that if they are made free

---

a. Frankfurter and Jackson, JJ., each filed   concurrences. Reed, J., dissented.

many students will not go to the Church. [Here] schooling is more or less suspended during the 'released time' so the nonreligious attendants will not forge ahead of the churchgoing absentees. But it serves as a temporary jail for a pupil who will not go to Church. It takes more subtlety of mind than I possess to deny that this is governmental constraint in support of religion."[b]

(c) *Cost.* Brennan, J., has distinguished the cases "not [because] of the difference in public expenditures involved. True, the *McCollum* program involved the regular use of school facilities, classrooms, heat and light and time from the regular school day—even though the actual incremental cost may have been negligible. [But the] deeper difference was that the *McCollum* program placed the religious instructor in the public school classroom in precisely the position of authority held by the regular teachers of secular subjects, while the *Zorach* program did not. [This] brought government and religion into that proximity which the Establishment Clause forbids." *Schempp* (concurring opinion).

(d) *Coercion. Zorach* found "no evidence [that] the system involves the use of coercion to get public school students into religious classrooms. [If] it were established that any one or more teachers were using their office to persuade or force students to take the religious instruction, a wholly different case would be presented."[7] Would the *Zorach* plan be inherently coercive, and therefore unconstitutional, if it were shown that most children found religious instruction more appealing than remaining in the public schools? Even if the alternative for those remaining was secular instruction with academic credit? If so, would it be permissible to excuse children from classes to enable them to attend special religious services of their faith? Would the first amendment forbid attendance at parochial schools, as an alternative to public schools, on the ground that this was simply one hundred per cent released time?

Under this analysis, would a program of "dismissed time" as described by Jackson, J., in *Zorach* (all children released early permitting those who so wish to attend religious schools) be unconstitutional? Would "dismissed time" be nonetheless invalid if it could be shown that the *purpose* for the early school closing was to facilitate religious education? Or is this merely an accommodation "adjusting the schedule of public events to sectarian needs"?

What of the argument that the *Zorach* program is inherently coercive, and therefore unconstitutional, because, as Frankfurter, J., contended in *McCollum,* "the law of imitation operates" placing "an obvious pressure upon children to attend" religious classes? Under this analysis, what result in the case of excusing students to attend a religious service? In the case of parochial schools? In the case of "dismissed time"? Do you agree with Jackson, J.'s assertion in *McCollum* that "it may be doubted whether the Constitution [protects] one from the embarrassment that always attends nonconformity, whether in religion, politics, behavior or dress"?

(e) *Use of public property.* Is the use of public school classrooms for religious education during nonschool hours distinguishable from *McCollum?* Consider Tribe 2d ed., at 1175: "Religious instructors will no longer stand in 'the position of

---

b. Black and Frankfurter, JJ., also filed separate dissents.

For a description of the interaction of the justices in fashioning the *Everson, McCollum* and *Zorach* opinions, see Note, *The "Released Time" Cases Revisited: A Study of Group Decisionmaking by the Supreme Court,* 83 Yale L.J. 1202 (1974).

7. [The] only allegation in the complaint that bears on the issue is that the operation of the program "has resulted and inevitably results in the exercise of pressure and coercion upon parents and children to secure attendance by the children for religious instruction." But this charge does not even implicate the school authorities. * * *

authority held by the regular teachers,' because the activities lie outside the mandatory school day. Although coercion is conceivable, it is not inherent, as it probably is with official school prayer; students who do not want to take part in the religious activities may take part in other activities or leave the campus. [Thus,] the state neither lends power to religion, nor borrows legitimacy from religion. Permitting a religious group to use school facilities during non-school hours, accordingly, conveys no message of endorsement."

2. *School prayer and the relevance of coercion.* (a) Should *Engel* and *Schempp* (and *McCollum*) have been explicitly based on "the coercion implicit under the statutory schemes"? Consider Stewart, J., dissenting in *Schempp:* "[T]he duty laid upon government in connection with religious exercises in the public schools is that of refraining from so structuring the school environment as to put any kind of pressure on a child to participate in those exercises; it is not that of providing an atmosphere in which children are kept scrupulously insulated from any awareness that some of their fellows may want to open the school day with prayer, or of the fact that there exist in our pluralistic society differences of religious belief. [A] law which provided for religious exercises during the school day and which contained no excusal provision would obviously be unconstitutionally coercive upon those who did not wish to participate. And even under a law containing an excusal provision, if the exercises were held during the school day, and no equally desirable alternative were provided by the school authorities, the likelihood that children might be under at least some psychological compulsion to participate would be great. [Here,] the record shows no more than a subjective prophecy by a parent of what he thought would happen if a request were made to be excused from participation in the exercises under the amended statute. * * * I think we must not assume that school boards so lack the qualities of inventiveness and good will as to make impossible the achievement of that goal."

What evidence of coercion does Stewart, J. require? That the objectors first ask to be excused from participation and then show that social pressures were brought to bear on them? Would this force an objector to surrender his rights in order to vindicate them? Or would Stewart, J., accept the testimony of social scientists that the program was coercive? Could this be judicially noticed? Or would he require a showing that these particular objectors were coerced? Were likely to be coerced? If so, is this a desirable test?

(b) *Establishment vs. free exercise.* If the decisions *should* turn on the element of coercion, would it have been preferable to base them on "the narrower ground of freedom of religion or of conscience, explaining why the considerations advanced in support of the prayer were outweighed by the rights of the objectors, and why under the circumstances the feature of voluntary participation did not sufficiently protect the interests of objectors"? Paul Kauper, *Prayer, Public Schools and the Supreme Court,* 61 Mich.L.Rev. 1031, 1065–66 (1963). Would this analysis permit prayer in an elementary school where every child was willing to participate? In *any* high school? Consider Louis Pollak, *Public Prayers in Public Schools,* 77 Harv.L.Rev. 62, 70 (1963): "[T]o have pitched the decision [on the free exercise clause] would presumably have meant that the prayer programs were constitutionally unobjectionable unless and until challenged, and, therefore, that school boards would have been under no discernible legal obligation, as assuredly they now are, to suspend ongoing prayer programs on their own initiative. [Indeed,] the hypothetical schoolchild plaintiff, whose free exercise rights would thus be enforced, would have to be a child with the gumption not only to disassociate himself from the prayer program but to prefer litigation to the relatively expeditious exit procedure contemplated by the excusal proviso."

3. *Secular purpose.* Several decisions, in addition to *Jaffree,* have invalidated public school practices because their "purpose" has been found to be "religious":

(a) STONE v. GRAHAM, 449 U.S. 39, 101 S.Ct. 192, 66 L.Ed.2d 199 (1980), per curiam, held that a Kentucky statute—requiring "the posting of a copy of the Ten Commandments, purchased with private contributions, on the wall of each public classroom in the State," with the notation at the bottom that "The secular application of the Ten Commandments is clearly seen in its adoption as the fundamental legal code of Western Civilization and the Common Law of the United States"—had "no secular legislative purpose": "The Ten Commandments is undeniably a sacred text in the Jewish and Christian faiths, and no legislative recitation of a supposed secular purpose can blind us to that [fact]. Posting of religious texts on the wall serves [no] educational function. If the posted copies of the Ten Commandments are to have any effect at all, it will be to induce the school children to read, meditate upon, perhaps to venerate and obey, the Commandments. However desirable this might be as a matter of private devotion, it is not a permissible state objective under the Establishment Clause."

REHNQUIST, J., dissented: "The Court's summary rejection of a secular purpose articulated by the legislature and confirmed by the state court is without precedent in Establishment Clause jurisprudence. [This] Court has recognized that 'religion has been closely identified with our history and government,' *Schempp,* and that 'the history of man is inseparable from the history of religion,' *Engel.* Kentucky has decided to make students aware of this fact by demonstrating the secular impact of the Ten Commandments."[a]

(b) EPPERSON v. ARKANSAS, 393 U.S. 97, 89 S.Ct. 266, 21 L.Ed.2d 228 (1968), per FORTAS, J., held that an "anti-evolution" statute, forbidding teachers in public schools "to teach the theory or doctrine that mankind ascended or descended from a lower order of animals," violated both religion clauses: "Arkansas' law selects from the body of knowledge a particular segment which it proscribes for the sole reason that it is deemed to conflict with a particular religious doctrine." Citing newspaper advertisements and letters supporting adoption of the statute in 1928, the Court found it "clear that fundamentalist sectarian conviction was and is the law's reason for existence. [The] law cannot be defended as an act of religious neutrality. Arkansas did not seek to excise from the curricula of its schools and universities all discussion of the origin of man."

BLACK, J., concurring on the ground of "vagueness," found the first amendment questions "troublesome": "Since there is no indication that the literal Biblical doctrine of the origin of man is included in the curriculum of Arkansas schools, does not the removal of the subject of evolution leave the State in a neutral position. [It] is plain that a state law prohibiting all teaching of human development or biology is constitutionally quite different from a law that compels a teacher to teach as true only one theory of a given doctrine. It would be difficult to make a First Amendment case out of a state law eliminating the subject of higher mathematics, or astronomy, or biology from its curriculum. [T]here is no reason I can imagine why a State is without power to withdraw from its curriculum any subject deemed too emotional and controversial for its public schools."[b]

---

a. Stewart, J., also dissented. Burger, C.J., and Blackmun, J., dissented from not giving the case plenary consideration.

b. Harlan, J., concurred in the Court's "establishment of religion" rationale. Stewart, J., concurred on the ground of vagueness.

(c) EDWARDS v. AGUILLARD, 482 U.S. 578, 107 S.Ct. 2573, 96 L.Ed.2d 510 (1987), per BRENNAN, J., held that a Louisiana statute, which forebade "the teaching of the theory of evolution in public schools unless accompanied by instruction in 'creation science,'" had "no clear secular purpose": "True, the Act's stated purpose is to protect academic freedom. [While] the Court is normally deferential to a State's articulation of a secular purpose, it is required that the statement of such purpose be sincere and not a sham. See *Jaffree; Stone; Schempp.* [It] is clear from the legislative history [that] requiring schools to teach creation science with evolution does not advance academic freedom. The Act does not grant teachers a flexibility that they did not already possess to supplement the present science curriculum with the presentation of theories, besides evolution, about the origin of life. [While] requiring that curriculum guides be developed for creation science, the Act says nothing of comparable guides for evolution. [The] Act forbids school boards to discriminate against anyone who 'chooses to be a creation-scientist' or to teach 'creationism,' but fails to protect those who choose to teach evolution or any other non-creation science theory, or who refuse to teach creation science.

"If the Louisiana legislature's purpose was solely to maximize the comprehensiveness and effectiveness of science instruction, it would have encouraged the teaching of all scientific theories about the origins of humankind. But [the] legislative history documents that the Act's primary purpose was to change the science curriculum of public schools in order to provide persuasive advantage to a particular religious doctrine that rejects the factual basis of evolution in its entirety [and that] embodies the religious belief that a supernatural creator was responsible for the creation of humankind. * * *

"[T]eaching a variety of scientific theories about the origins of humankind to school children might be validly done with the clear secular intent of enhancing the effectiveness of science instruction. But because the primary purpose of the Creationism Act is to endorse a particular religious doctrine, the Act furthers religion in violation of the Establishment Clause."[a]

SCALIA, J., joined by Rehnquist, C.J., dissented: "Even if I agreed with the questionable premise that legislation can be invalidated under the Establishment Clause on the basis of its motivation alone, without regard to its effects, I would still find no justification for today's decision. [The] Legislature explicitly set forth its secular purpose ('protecting academic freedom') [which] meant: *students'* freedom from *indoctrination.* The legislature wanted to ensure that students would be free to decide for themselves how life began, based upon a fair and balanced presentation of the scientific evidence. [The] legislature did not care *whether* the topic of origins was taught; it simply wished to ensure that *when* the topic was taught, [it] be 'taught as a theory, rather than as proven scientific fact' and that scientific evidence inconsistent with the theory of evolution (viz., 'creation science') be taught as well. [The law] treats the teaching of creation the same way. It does *not* mandate instruction in creation science; *forbids* teachers to present creation science 'as proven scientific fact'; and *bans* the teaching of creation science unless the theory [is] 'discredit[ed] at every turn' with the teaching of evolution. It surpasses understanding how the Court can see in this a purpose 'to restructure the science curriculum to conform with a particular religious viewpoint,' 'to provide a persuasive advantage to a particular religious

---

a. Powell, J., joined by O'Connor, J., joined the Court's opinion but wrote separately "to emphasize that nothing in the Court's opinion diminishes the traditionally broad discretion accorded state and local school officials in the selection of the public school curriculum." White, J., concurred only in the judgment.

doctrine,' 'to promote the theory of creation science which embodies a particular religious tenet,' and 'to endorse a particular religious doctrine.'

"[The] Louisiana legislators had been told repeatedly that creation scientists were scorned by most educators and scientists, who themselves had an almost religious faith in evolution. It is hardly surprising, then, that in seeking to achieve a balanced, 'nonindoctrinating' curriculum, the legislators protected from discrimination only those teachers whom they thought were *suffering* from discrimination. [In] light of the unavailability of works on creation science suitable for classroom use (a fact appellees concede) and the existence of ample materials on evolution, it was entirely reasonable for the Legislature to conclude that science teachers attempting to implement the Act would need a curriculum guide on creation science, but not on evolution. * * *

"It is undoubtedly true that what prompted the Legislature to direct its attention to the misrepresentation of evolution in the schools (rather than the inaccurate presentation of other topics) was its awareness of the tension between evolution and the religious beliefs of many children. But [a] valid secular purpose is not rendered impermissible simply because its pursuit is prompted by concern for religious sensitivities.[b] [I] am astonished by the Court's unprecedented readiness to [disbelieve] the secular purpose set forth in the Act [and to conclude] that it is a sham. [I] can only attribute [this] to an intellectual predisposition [and] an instinctive reaction that any governmentally imposed requirements bearing upon the teaching of evolution must be a manifestation of Christian fundamentalist repression. In this case, however, it seems to me the Court's position is the repressive one. [Perhaps] what the Louisiana Legislature has done is unconstitutional because there *is* no [scientific] evidence, and the scheme they have established will amount to no more than a presentation of the Book of Genesis. But we cannot say that on the evidence before us in this summary judgment context, which includes ample uncontradicted testimony that 'creation science' is a body of scientific knowledge rather than revealed belief.[c] *Infinitely less* can we say (or should we say) that the scientific evidence for evolution is so conclusive that no one could be gullible enough to believe that there is any real scientific evidence to the contrary, so that the legislation's stated purpose must be a lie. Yet that illiberal judgment, that *Scopes*-in-reverse, is ultimately the basis on which the Court's facile rejection of the Louisiana Legislature's purpose must rest. * * *

"I [think the *Lemon* 'purpose' test] is 'a constitutional theory [that] has no basis in the history of the amendment it seeks to interpret, is difficult to apply and yields unprincipled results.' *Jaffree* (Rehnquist, J., dissenting).

"[D]iscerning the subjective motivation of those enacting the statute [is] almost always an impossible task. The number of possible motivations [is] not binary, or indeed even finite. In the present case, for example, a particular legislator need not have voted for the Act either because he wanted to foster

---

b. See also Scalia, J., joined by Rehnquist, C.J., and Thomas, J., dissenting from denial of certiorari in *Tangipahoa Parish Board of Educ. v. Freiler*, 530 U.S. 1251, 120 S.Ct. 2706, 147 L.Ed.2d 974 (2000), which invalidated, as "not sufficiently neutral," a policy that when "the scientific theory of evolution" is taught, a statement of "disclaimer from endorsement of such theory" shall be made "to inform students of the scientific concept and not intended to influence or dissuade the Biblical version of Creation," and urging students "to exercise

critical thinking and gather all information possible and closely examine each alternative."

c. "The only evidence in the record [defining] 'creation science' is found in five affidavits filed by appellants. In those affidavits, two scientists, a philosopher, a theologian, and an educator, all of whom claim extensive knowledge of creation science, swear that it is essentially a collection of scientific data supporting the theory that the physical universe and life within it appeared suddenly and have not changed substantially since appearing."

religion or because he wanted to improve education. He may have thought the bill would provide jobs for his district, or may have wanted to make amends with a faction of his party he had alienated on another vote, or he may have been a close friend of the bill's sponsor, or he may have been repaying a favor he owed the Majority Leader, or he may have hoped the Governor would appreciate his vote and make a fundraising appearance for him, or he may have been pressured to vote for a bill he disliked by a wealthy contributor or by a flood of constituent mail, or he may have been seeking favorable publicity, or he may have been reluctant to hurt the feelings of a loyal staff member who worked on the bill, or he may have been settling an old score with a legislator who opposed the bill, or he may have been mad at his wife who opposed the bill, or he may have been intoxicated and utterly *un*motivated when the vote was called, or he may have accidentally voted 'yes' instead of 'no,' or, of course, he may have had (and very likely did have) a combination of some of the above and many other motivations. To look for *the sole purpose* of even a single legislator is probably to look for something that does not exist."

(d) Is it meaningful to distinguish between *secular* vs. *religious* purposes? Consider Phillip E. Johnson, *Concepts and Compromise in First Amendment Religious Doctrine,* 72 Calif.L.Rev. 817, 827 (1984): "Governments usually act out of secular motives, even when they are directly aiding a particular religious sect. An atheistic ruler might well create an established church because he thinks it a useful way of raising money, or of ensuring that the clergy do not preach seditious doctrines. In democratic societies, elected officials have an excellent secular reason to accommodate (or at least to avoid offending) groups and individuals who are religious, as well as groups and individuals who are not. They wish to be re-elected, and they do not want important groups to feel that the community does not honor their values."

(e) If the "purpose" of government action is found to be "religious," *should* that alone be enough to invalidate it under the establishment clause? If so, what result in *Zorach?* For a public school "dismissed time" program implemented to facilitate religious education?[d] Consider Tribe 2d ed., at 1211: "The secular purpose requirement [might] be used to strike down laws whose effects are utterly secular. A legislature might, for example, vote to increase welfare benefits because individual legislators feel religiously compelled to do so. So too, when a legislature passes a neutral moment-of-silence statute, many legislators may hope that students will use the time for prayer. However improper these purposes may be, it is hard to see a meaningful establishment clause problem so long as the statute's effects are completely secular. A visible religious purpose may independently convey a message of endorsement or exclusion, but such a message, standing alone, should rarely if ever suffice to transform a secular action into an establishment clause violation. A religious message may be conveyed by the legislative debates concerning a bill, but the same result is possible from debates that lead to no legislation; it can hardly be said that the debates themselves establish a religion."

See also Jesse H. Choper, *The Religion Clauses of the First Amendment: Reconciling the Conflict,* 41 U.Pitt.L.Rev. 673, 686–87 (1980): "[I]t is only when religious purpose is coupled with threatened impairment of religious freedom that government action should be held to violate the Establishment Clause. [Conceding] that the [*Epperson*] statute had a solely religious purpose, [there] was no

---

d. For use of this test to invalidate the "religiously motivated" Utah firing squad, see Martin R. Gardner, *Illicit Legislative Motiva-* *tion as a Sufficient Condition for Unconstitutionality Under the Establishment Clause,* 1979 Wash.U.L.Q. 435.

evidence that religious beliefs were either coerced, compromised or influenced. That is, it was not shown, nor do I believe that it could be persuasively argued, that the anti-evolution law either (1) induced children of fundamentalist religions to accept the biblical theory of creation, or (2) conditioned other children for conversion to fundamentalism. [Thus, it] should have survived the Establishment Clause challenge." Similarly, "I would find that the creation science law had a religious purpose [to] placate those religious fundamentalists whose beliefs rejected the Darwinian theory of evolution. But [so] long as the theory of creation science is taught in an objective rather than a proselytizing fashion, it does not seem to me to pose a danger to religious liberty [and] should not be held to violate the Establishment Clause." Jesse H. Choper, *Church, State and the Supreme Court: Current Controversy,* 29 Ariz.L.Rev. 551, 557 (1987).

4. *Purpose, primary effect, and "neutrality."* BOARD OF EDUC. v. MERGENS, 496 U.S. 226, 110 S.Ct. 2356, 110 L.Ed.2d 191 (1990), interpreted the Equal Access Act, passed by Congress in 1984, to apply to public secondary schools that (a) receive federal financial assistance, and (b) give official recognition to noncurriculum related student groups (e.g., chess club and scuba diving club in contrast to Latin club and math club) in such ways as allowing them to meet on school premises during noninstructional time. The Act prohibited these schools from denying equal access to, or otherwise discriminating against, student groups "on the basis of the religious, political, philosophical, or other content of the speech at [their] meetings." O'CONNOR, J., joined by Rehnquist, C.J., and White and Blackmun, JJ., held that the establishment clause did not forbid Westside High School from including within its thirty recognized student groups a Christian club "to read and discuss the Bible, to have fellowship and to pray together": "In *Widmar v. Vincent,* 454 U.S. 263, 102 S.Ct. 269, 70 L.Ed.2d 440 (1981), we applied the three-part *Lemon* test to hold that an 'equal access' policy, at the university level, does not violate the Establishment Clause. We concluded that 'an open-forum policy, including nondiscrimination against religious speech, would have a secular purpose,' and would in fact *avoid* entanglement with religion. See id. ("'[T]he University would risk greater 'entanglement' by attempting to enforce its exclusion of 'religious worship' and 'religious speech'"). We also found that although incidental benefits accrued to religious groups who used university facilities, this result did not amount to an establishment of religion. First, we stated that a university's forum does not 'confer any imprimatur of state approval on religious sects or practices.' Indeed, the message is one of neutrality rather than endorsement; if a State refused to let religious groups use facilities open to others, then it would demonstrate not neutrality but hostility toward religion. Second, we noted that '[t]he [University's] provision of benefits to [a] broad spectrum of groups'—both nonreligious and religious speakers—was 'an important index of secular effect.'

"We think the logic of *Widmar* applies [here.] Congress' avowed purpose—to prevent discrimination against religious and other types of speech—is undeniably secular. Even if some legislators were motivated by a conviction that religious speech in particular was valuable and worthy of protection, that alone would not invalidate the Act, because what is relevant is the legislative *purpose* of the statute, not the possibly religious *motives* of the legislators who enacted the law. Because the Act on its face grants equal access to both secular and religious speech, we think it clear that the Act's purpose was not to 'endorse or disapprove of religion,' *Jaffree* (O'Connor, J., concurring).

"Petitioners' principal contention is that the Act has the primary effect of advancing religion. Specifically, petitioners urge that, because the student religious meetings are held under school aegis, and because the state's compulsory attendance laws bring the students together (and thereby provide a ready-made audience for student evangelists), an objective observer in the position of a secondary school student will perceive official school support for such religious meetings.

"We disagree. First, [there] is a crucial difference between *government* speech endorsing religion, which the Establishment Clause forbids, and *private* speech endorsing religion, which the Free Speech and Free Exercise Clauses protect. We think that secondary school students are mature enough and are likely to understand that a school does not endorse or support student speech that it merely permits on a nondiscriminatory basis. * . * *

"Second, we note that the Act expressly limits participation by school officials at meetings of student religious groups, and that any such meetings must be held during 'noninstructional time.' The Act therefore avoids the problems of 'the students' emulation of teachers as role models' and 'mandatory attendance requirements,' *Aguillard;* see also *McCollum.* To be sure, the possibility of *student* peer pressure remains, but there is little if any risk of official state endorsement or coercion where no formal classroom activities are involved and no school officials actively participate. * * *

"Third, the broad spectrum of officially recognized student clubs at Westside, and the fact that Westside students are free to initiate and organize additional student clubs counteract any possible message of official endorsement of or preference for religion or a particular religious belief."

KENNEDY, J., joined by Scalia, J., concurred, emphasizing his disagreement with the plurality's "endorsement test" developed further in *Allegheny County v. ACLU,* Part IV infra: "I should think it inevitable that a public high school 'endorses' a religious club, in a common-sense use of the term, if the club happens to be one of many activities that the school permits students to choose in order to further the development of their intellect and character in an extracurricular setting. But no constitutional violation occurs if the school's action is based upon a recognition of the fact that membership in a religious club is one of many permissible ways for a student to further his or her own personal enrichment. The inquiry with respect to coercion must be whether the government imposes pressure upon a student to participate in a religious activity. This inquiry, of course, must be undertaken with sensitivity to the special circumstances that exist in a secondary school where the line between voluntary and coerced participation may be difficult to draw. No such coercion, however, has been shown to exist as a necessary result of this statute, either on its face [or] on the facts of this case."

MARSHALL, J., joined by Brennan, J., concurred "to emphasize the steps Westside must take to avoid appearing to endorse the Christian Club's goals."

STEVENS, J., dissented: "Under the Court's interpretation of the Act, Congress has imposed a difficult choice on public high schools receiving federal financial assistance. If such a school continues to allow students to participate in such familiar and innocuous activities as a school chess or scuba diving club, it must also allow religious groups to make use of school facilities. [This] comes perilously close to an outright command to allow organized prayer [on] school premises."[a]

a. May elementary or secondary schools permit their facilities to be used for instruction by religious groups if they also permit instruction by outside teachers of art, music, crafts, dance, etc. (cf. *McCollum*)? May they post the Ten Commandments if they also post the symbols of other civic or charitable groups (cf. *Stone*)? See Douglas Laycock, *Equal Access and*

5. *Military chaplains.* In rejecting the argument that Bible reading and prayer exercises in public schools furthered "the majority's right to free exercise of religion," *Schempp* did "not pass upon a situation such as military service, where the Government regulates the temporal and geographic environment of individuals to a point that, unless it permits voluntary religious services to be conducted with the use of government facilities, military personnel would be unable to engage in the practice of their faiths." Might it be that, while free exercise considerations may justify government provision for opportunity to worship, the establishment clause nonetheless bars a government subsidized ministry? "Could the governmental interest be satisfied merely by allowing free time for the serviceman to seek non-military worship or by merely giving the religious orders the right to come into the military environment, at their own expense, to provide the opportunity for worship?" M. Albert Figinski, *Military Chaplains—A Constitutionally Permissible Accommodation Between Church and State,* 24 Md. L.Rev. 377, 409 (1964). Or might it be "that the Government need not necessarily provide chapels and chaplains to those of its armed personnel who are *not* cut off from civilian church facilities"? Klaus J. Herrmann, *Some Considerations on the Constitutionality of the United States Military Chaplaincy,* 14 Am.U.L.Rev. 24, 34 (1964). For fuller consideration of the "conflict" between the religion clauses, see Sec. 4 infra.

6. *Public school secularism. Schempp* emphasized that "it might well be said that one's education is not complete without a study of comparative religion or the history of religion and its relationship to the advancement of civilization. It certainly may be said that the Bible is worthy of study for its literary and historic qualities. Nothing we have said here indicates that such study of the Bible or of religion, when presented objectively as part of a secular program of education, may not be [effected]." May public schools inculcate "fundamental civic and democratic" values? Consider William H. Clune, *The Constitution and Vouchers for Religious Schools: The Demise of Separatism and the Rise of Non-discrimination as Measures of State Neutrality,* Working Paper No. 31 of the Earl Warren Legal Institute, Law School, University of California–Berkeley (1999): "The idea of brainwashing in religious schools only makes sense if it is contrasted with a supposed condition of free choice in secular public education. [But principles] of secularism and secular humanism, that the child should be able to choose among ultimate values on the basis of individual rational choice (as that faculty gradually matures) now seems just as much a value position and a value choice by parents and society as the opposite view that certain values have absolute priority and should be strongly socialized into the child's value system. Indeed the idea that individuals should choose values according to 'rational' criteria operates conceptually as the ultimate value position of secular humanism, just as the idea that individuals should choose values on the basis of religious criteria operates as the ultimate value in religious education." If government requires that public employees be of "good moral character," is this a "religious test" for public office? Contrast Stewart, J., dissenting in *Schempp:* "[A] compulsory state educational system so structures a child's life that if religious exercises are held to be an impermissible activity in schools, [this] is seen, not as the realization of state neutrality, but rather as the establishment of a religion of secularism, or at the least, as government support of the beliefs of those who think that religious exercises should be conducted only in private."

Moments of Silence: The Equal Status of Religious Speech by Private Speakers, 81 Nw. U.L.Rev. 1, 33–35 (1986).

IV. OFFICIAL ACKNOWLEDGMENT OF RELIGION

ALLEGHENY COUNTY v. ACLU

492 U.S. 573, 109 S.Ct. 3086, 106 L.Ed.2d 472 (1989).

JUSTICE BLACKMUN announced the judgment of the Court and delivered the opinion of the Court with respect to Parts III–A, IV, and V, an opinion with respect to Parts I and II, in which JUSTICE O'CONNOR and JUSTICE STEVENS join, an opinion with respect to Part III–B, in which JUSTICE STEVENS joins, and an opinion with respect to Part VI.

This litigation concerns the constitutionality of two recurring holiday displays located on public property in downtown Pittsburgh. The first is a crèche placed on the Grand Staircase of the Allegheny County Courthouse. The second is a Chanukah menorah placed just outside the City–County Building, next to a Christmas tree and a sign saluting liberty. The Court of Appeals for the Third Circuit ruled that each display violates the Establishment Clause [because] each has the impermissible effect of endorsing religion. We agree that the crèche display has that unconstitutional effect but reverse the Court of Appeals' judgment regarding the menorah display.

I.A. [The] crèche [is] a visual representation of the scene in the manger in Bethlehem shortly after the birth of Jesus, as described in the Gospels of Luke and Matthew. The crèche includes [an] angel bearing a banner that proclaims "Gloria in Excelsis Deo!"

[III.A.] Although "the myriad, subtle ways in which Establishment Clause values can be eroded," are not susceptible to a single verbal formulation, this Court has attempted to encapsulate the essential precepts of the Establishment Clause. Thus, in *Everson,* the Court gave this often-repeated summary [stating the second ¶ on p. 1036]. In *Lemon,* the Court sought to refine these principles by focusing on three "tests." [In] recent years, we have paid particularly close attention to whether the challenged governmental practice either has the purpose or effect of "endorsing" religion * * *.

Of course, the word "endorsement" is not self-defining. Rather, it derives its meaning from other words that this Court has found useful over the years in interpreting the Establishment Clause. [Whether] the key word is "endorsement," "favoritism," or "promotion," the essential principle remains the same. The Establishment Clause, at the very least, prohibits government from appearing to take a position on questions of religious belief or from "making adherence to a religion relevant in any way to a person's standing in the political community." *Lynch v. Donnelly,* 465 U.S. 668, 687, 104 S.Ct. 1355, 1386, 79 L.Ed.2d 604 (1984) (O'Connor, J., concurring).

B. [In *Lynch,*] we considered whether the city of Pawtucket, R.I., had violated the Establishment Clause by including a crèche in its annual Christmas display, located in a private park within the downtown shopping district.[a] By a 5–4 decision in that difficult case, the Court [held] that the inclusion of the crèche did not have the impermissible effect of advancing or promoting religion. [First,] the opinion states that the inclusion of the crèche in the display was "no more an

---

a. "[Ten years ago], when [the] crèche was acquired, it cost the City $1365; it now is valued at $200. The erection and dismantling of the crèche costs the City about $20 per year; nominal expenses are incurred in lighting the crèche. No money has been expended on its maintenance for the past 10 years."

advancement or endorsement of religion" than other "endorsements" this Court has approved in the past—but the opinion offers no discernible measure for distinguishing between permissible and impermissible endorsements. Second, the opinion observes that any benefit the government's display of the crèche gave to religion was no more than "indirect, remote, and incidental"—without saying how or why.

Although Justice O'Connor joined the majority opinion in *Lynch,* she wrote a concurrence [that] provides a sound analytical framework for evaluating governmental use of religious symbols.

First and foremost, the concurrence [recognizes] any endorsement of religion as "invalid," because it "sends a message to nonadherents that they are outsiders, not full members of the political community, and an accompanying message to adherents that they are insiders, favored members of the political community."

Second, the concurrence articulates a method for determining whether the government's use of an object with religious meaning has the effect of endorsing religion[:] the question is "what viewers may fairly understand to be the purpose of the display." That inquiry, of necessity, turns upon the context in which the contested object appears: "a typical museum setting, though not neutralizing the religious content of a religious painting, negates any message of endorsement of that content." * * *

The concurrence applied this mode of analysis to the Pawtucket crèche, seen in the context of that city's holiday celebration as a whole. In addition to the crèche the city's display contained: a Santa Claus House with a live Santa distributing candy, reindeer pulling Santa's sleigh; a live 40–foot Christmas tree strung with lights; statues of carolers in old-fashioned dress; candy-striped poles; a "talking" wishing well; a large banner proclaiming "SEASONS GREETINGS"; a miniature "village" with several houses and a church, and various "cut-out" figures, including those of a clown, a dancing elephant, a robot, and a teddy bear. The concurrence concluded that both because the crèche is "a traditional symbol" of Christmas, a holiday with strong secular elements, and because the crèche was "displayed along with purely secular symbols," the crèche's setting "changes what viewers may fairly understand to be the purpose of the display" and "negates any message of endorsement" of "the Christian beliefs represented by the crèche."

The four *Lynch* dissenters agreed with the concurrence that the controlling question was "whether Pawtucket ha[d] run afoul of the Establishment Clause by endorsing religion through its display of the crèche." The dissenters also agreed with the [relevance of] context [but] concluded that the other elements of the Pawtucket display did not negate the endorsement of Christian faith caused by the presence of the crèche. * * *

Thus, despite divergence at the bottom line, the five Justices in concurrence and dissent in *Lynch* agreed upon the relevant constitutional principles [which] are sound, and have been adopted by the Court in subsequent cases. [*Grand Rapids.*]

IV.   We turn first to the county's crèche display. [U]nlike *Lynch,* nothing in the context of the display detracts from the crèche's religious message. [Furthermore,] the crèche sits on the Grand Staircase, the "main" and "most beautiful part" of the building that is the seat of county government. No viewer could reasonably think that it occupies this location without the support and approval of the government [which] has chosen to celebrate Christmas in a way that has the effect of endorsing a patently Christian message: Glory to God for the birth of Jesus Christ. * * *

V. Justice Kennedy and the three Justices who join him would find the display of the crèche consistent with the Establishment Clause. [The] reasons for deciding otherwise are so far-reaching in their implications that they require a response in some depth:

A. In *Marsh v. Chambers*, 463 U.S. 783, 103 S.Ct. 3330, 77 L.Ed.2d 1019 (1983) [upholding the practice of legislative prayer], the Court relied specifically on the fact that Congress authorized legislative prayer at the same time that it produced the Bill of Rights.[b] Justice Kennedy, however, argues that *Marsh* legitimates all "practices with no greater potential for an establishment of religion" than those "accepted traditions dating back to the Founding." Otherwise, the Justice asserts, such practices as our national motto ("In God We Trust") and our Pledge of Allegiance (with the phrase "under God," added in 1954) are in danger of invalidity.

Our previous opinions have considered in dicta the motto and the pledge, characterizing them as consistent with the proposition that government may not communicate an endorsement of religious belief. We need not return to the subject of "ceremonial deism,"[c] because there is an obvious distinction between crèche displays and references to God in the motto and the pledge. However history may affect the constitutionality of nonsectarian references to religion by the government,[52] history cannot legitimate practices that demonstrate the government's allegiance to a particular sect or creed. [The] history of this Nation, it is perhaps sad to say, contains numerous examples of official acts that endorsed Christianity specifically [but] this heritage of official discrimination against non-Christians has no place in the jurisprudence of the Establishment Clause. * * *

b. *Marsh* also pointed, inter alia, to the practice in the colonies (including Virginia after adopting its Declaration of Rights which has been "considered the precursor of both the Free Exercise and Establishment Clauses"), to the opening invocations in federal courts (including the Supreme Court), and in the Continental Congress and First Congress: "[T]he practice of opening sessions with prayer has continued without interruption ever since that early session of Congress. It has also been followed consistently in most of the states." Brennan, Marshall and Stevens, JJ., dissented.

Of what relevance is it that, subsequently, "Madison acknowledged that he had been quite mistaken in approving—as a member of the House, in 1789—bills for the payment of congressional chaplains"? William W. Van Alstyne, *Trends in the Supreme Court: Mr. Jefferson's Crumbling Wall*, 1984 Duke L.J. 770, 776.

c. Brennan, J., joined by Marshall, Blackmun and Stevens, JJ., dissenting in *Lynch* "suggest[ed] that such practices as the designation of 'In God We Trust' as our national motto, or the references to God contained in the Pledge of Allegiance can best be understood [as] a form of 'ceremonial deism,' protected from Establishment Clause scrutiny chiefly because they have lost through rote repetition any significant religious content."

For the view that "secularizing religious practices conveniently preserves the inclusion of symbols and practices that many Americans understand as fundamental to American identity, [but] it also threatens the purity and integrity of both government and religion. In addition, such strained legal justification jeopardizes the historically neutral relationship between religion and the state," see Alexandra D. Furth, *Secular Idolatry and Sacred Traditions: A Critique of the Supreme Court's Secularization Analysis.* 146 U.Pa.L.Rev. 579 (1998). See also Steven B. Epstein, *Rethinking the Constitutionality of Ceremonial Deism*, 96 Colum.L.Rev. 2083 (1996) (extensive review concluding that most forms "violate a core purpose of the Establishment Clause").

52. It is worth noting that just because *Marsh* sustained the validity of legislative prayer, it does not necessarily follow that practices like proclaiming a National Day of Prayer are constitutional. Legislative prayer does not urge citizens to engage in religious practices, and on that basis could well be distinguishable from an exhortation from government to the people that they engage in religious conduct. But, as this practice is not before us, we express no judgment about its constitutionality.

C. Although Justice Kennedy repeatedly accuses the Court of harboring a "latent hostility" or "callous indifference" toward religion, nothing could be further from the truth. [The] government does not discriminate against any citizen on the basis of the citizen's religious faith if the government is secular in its functions and operations. On the contrary, the Constitution mandates that the government remain secular, rather than affiliating itself with religious beliefs or institutions, precisely in order to avoid discriminating among citizens on the basis of their religious faiths.

A secular state, it must be remembered, is not the same as an atheistic or antireligious state. A secular state establishes neither atheism nor religion as its official creed. * * *[59]

VI. The display of the Chanukah menorah in front of the City–County Building may well present a closer [issue. The] relevant question for Establishment Clause purposes is whether the combined display of the tree, the sign, and the menorah has the effect of endorsing both Christian and Jewish faiths, or rather simply recognizes that both Christmas and Chanukah are part of the same winter-holiday season, which has attained a secular status in our society. Of the two interpretations of this particular display, the latter seems far more plausible and is also in line with *Lynch*.[64]

The Christmas tree, unlike the menorah, is not itself a religious symbol. [The] widely accepted view of the Christmas tree as the preeminent secular symbol of the Christmas holiday season serves to emphasize the secular component of the message communicated by other elements of an accompanying holiday display, including the Chanukah menorah.[66]

The tree, moreover, is clearly the predominant element in the city's display. The 45–foot tree occupies the central position [in] the City–County Building; the 18–foot menorah is positioned to one side. Given this configuration, it is much more sensible to interpret the meaning of the menorah in light of the tree, rather than vice versa. * * *

Although the city has used a symbol with religious meaning as its representation of Chanukah, this is not a case in which the city has reasonable alternatives that are less religious in nature. [Where] the government's secular message can be conveyed by two symbols, only one of which carries religious meaning, an observer

59. In his attempt to legitimate the display of the crèche on the Grand Staircase, Justice Kennedy repeatedly characterizes it as an "accommodation" of religion. But an accommodation of religion, in order to be permitted under the Establishment Clause, must lift "an identifiable burden *on the exercise of religion*." *Corporation of Presiding Bishop v. Amos*, [Sec. 4 infra]. Prohibiting the display of a crèche at this location [does] not impose a burden on the practice of Christianity (except to the extent some Christian sect seeks to be an officially approved religion), and therefore permitting the display is not an "accommodation" of religion in the conventional sense.

["Accommodation" of religion and the relationship between the establishment and free exercise clauses is considered in detail in Sec. 3 infra.]

64. [The] conclusion that Pittsburgh's combined Christmas–Chanukah display cannot be interpreted as endorsing Judaism alone does not mean, however, that it is implausible, as a general matter, for a city like Pittsburgh to endorse a minority faith. The display of a menorah alone might well have that effect.

66. Although the Christmas tree represents the secular celebration of Christmas, its very association with Christmas (a holiday with religious dimensions) makes it conceivable that the tree might be seen as representing Christian religion when displayed next to an object associated with Jewish religion. For this reason, I agree with Justice Brennan and Justice Stevens that one must ask whether the tree and the menorah together endorse the *religious* beliefs of Christians and Jews. For the reasons stated in the text, however, I conclude the city's overall display does not have this impermissible effect.

reasonably might infer from the fact that the government has chosen to use the religious symbol that the government means to promote religious faith. See *Schempp* (Brennan, J., concurring) (Establishment Clause forbids use of religious means to serve secular ends when secular means suffice). But where, as here, no such choice has been made, this inference of endorsement is not present.[68]

The Mayor's sign further diminishes the possibility that the tree and the menorah will be interpreted as a dual endorsement of Christianity and Judaism. The sign states that during the holiday season the city salutes liberty. Moreover, the sign draws upon the theme of light, common to both Chanukah and Christmas as winter festivals, and links that theme with this Nation's legacy of freedom, which allows an American to celebrate the holiday season in whatever way he wishes, religiously or otherwise. [While] an adjudication of the display's effect must take into account the perspective of one who is neither Christian nor Jewish, as well as of those who adhere to either of these religions, the constitutionality of its effect must also be judged according to the standard of a "reasonable observer." When measured against this standard, the menorah need not be excluded from this particular display.

The conclusion [here] does not foreclose the possibility that the display of the menorah might violate either the "purpose" or "entanglement" prong of the *Lemon* analysis. These issues [may] be considered [on] remand. * * *

JUSTICE KENNEDY, with whom THE CHIEF JUSTICE, JUSTICE WHITE, and JUSTICE SCALIA join, concurring in the judgment in part and dissenting in part. * * *

I. In keeping with the usual fashion of recent years, the majority applies the *Lemon* [test]. Persuasive criticism of *Lemon* has emerged. See *Aguillard* (Scalia, J., dissenting); *Aguilar v. Felton* (O'Connor, J., dissenting); *Jaffree* (Rehnquist, J., dissenting); *Roemer* (White, J., concurring in judgment). Our cases often question its utility in providing concrete answers to Establishment Clause questions, calling it but a "helpful signpos[t]" or "guidelin[e]", to assist our deliberations rather than a comprehensive test. *Mueller;* See *Lynch* ("we have repeatedly emphasized our unwillingness to be confined to any single test or criterion in this sensitive area").[d] Substantial revision of our Establishment Clause doctrine may be in order;[e] but it is unnecessary to undertake that task today, for even the *Lemon*

---

68. In *Lynch,* in contrast, there was no need for Pawtucket to include a crèche in order to convey a secular message about Christmas. (Blackmun, J., dissenting). [In] displaying the menorah next to the tree, the city has demonstrated no preference for the *religious* celebration of the holiday season. This conclusion, however, would be untenable had the city substituted a crèche for its Christmas tree or if the city had failed to substitute for the menorah an alternative, more secular, representation of Chanukah.

d. In *Marsh,* Brennan, J., joined by Marshall, J. dissenting, noted that "the Court makes no pretense of subjecting Nebraska's practice of legislative prayer to any of the formal 'tests' that have traditionally structured our inquiry under the Establishment Clause": "I have no doubt that, if any group of law students were asked to apply the principles of *Lemon* to the question of legislative prayer, they would nearly unanimously find the practice to be unconstitutional. [W]e are faced here

with the regularized practice of conducting official prayers, on behalf of the entire legislature, as part of the order of business constituting the formal opening of every single session of the legislative term."

e. Four year later, concurring in *Lamb's Chapel,* Scalia, J., joined by Thomas, J., noted that six "of the currently sitting Justices" have disagreed with *Lemon*—Rehnquist, C.J., and White, O'Connor, and Kennedy, JJ., in addition to themselves: "For my part, I agree with the long list of constitutional scholars who have criticized *Lemon* and bemoaned the strange Establishment Clause geometry of crooked lines and wavering shapes its intermittent use has produced. See, e.g., Jesse H. Choper, *The Establishment Clause and Aid to Parochial Schools—An Update,* 75 Cal.L.Rev. 5 (1987); William P. Marshall, *"We Know It When We See It": The Supreme Court and Establishment,* 59 S.Cal.L.Rev. 495 (1986); Michael W. McConnell, *Accommodation of Religion,* 1985 S.Ct.Rev. 1; Philip B. Kurland, *The*

test, when applied with proper sensitivity to our traditions and our caselaw, supports the conclusion that both the crèche and the menorah are permissible displays in the context of the holiday season. * * *

Rather than requiring government to avoid any action that acknowledges or aids religion, the Establishment Clause permits government some latitude in recognizing and accommodating the central role religion plays in our society. *Lynch; Walz.* Any approach less sensitive to our heritage would border on latent hostility toward religion, as it would require government in all its multifaceted roles to acknowledge only the secular, to the exclusion and so to the detriment of the religious. A categorical approach would install federal courts as jealous guardians of an absolute "wall of separation," sending a clear message of disapproval. In this century, as the modern administrative state expands to touch the lives of its citizens in such diverse ways and redirects their financial choices through programs of its own, it is difficult to maintain the fiction that requiring government to avoid all assistance to religion can in fairness be viewed as serving the goal of neutrality. * * *

The ability of the organized community to recognize and accommodate religion in a society with a pervasive public sector requires diligent observance of the border between accommodation and establishment. Our cases disclose two limiting principles: government may not coerce anyone to support or participate in any religion or its exercise; and it may not, in the guise of avoiding hostility or callous indifference, give direct benefits to religion in such a degree that it in fact "establishes a [state] religion or religious faith, or tends to do so." *Lynch.* These two principles, while distinct, are not unrelated, for it would be difficult indeed to establish a religion without some measure of more or less subtle coercion, be it in the form of taxation to supply the substantial benefits that would sustain a state-established faith, direct compulsion to observance, or governmental exhortation to religiosity that amounts in fact to proselytizing.

[The] freedom to worship as one pleases without government interference or oppression is the great object of both the Establishment and the Free Exercise Clauses. Barring all attempts to aid religion through government coercion goes far toward attainment of this object. [S]ome of our recent cases reject the view that coercion is the sole touchstone of an Establishment Clause violation. See *Engel* (dictum) (rejecting, without citation of authority, proposition that coercion is required to demonstrate an Establishment Clause violation); *Schempp; Nyquist.* That may be true if by "coercion" is meant *direct* coercion in the classic sense of an establishment of religion that the Framers knew. But coercion need not be a direct tax in aid of religion or a test oath. Symbolic recognition or accommodation of religious faith may violate the Clause in an extreme case.[1] I doubt not, for example, that the Clause forbids a city to permit the permanent erection of a large Latin cross on the roof of city hall. This is not because government speech about religion is per se suspect, as the majority would have it, but because such an obtrusive year-round religious display would place the government's weight behind an obvious effort to proselytize on behalf of a particular religion. Speech may

---

Religion Clauses and the Burger Court, 34 Cath.U.L.Rev. 1 (1984); Robert Cord, *Separation of Church and State* (1982); Jesse H Choper, *The Religion Clauses of the First Amendment: Reconciling the Conflict,* 41 U.Pitt.L.Rev. 673 (1980). I will decline to apply *Lemon*—whether it validates or invalidates the government action in question—and therefore cannot join the opinion of the Court today."

1. [The] prayer invalidated in *Engel* was unquestionably coercive in an indirect manner, as the *Engel* Court itself recognized * * *.

[*Marsh* noted that "here, the individual claiming injury by the practice is an adult, presumably not readily susceptible to 'religious indoctrination,' see *Tilton,* or peer pressure, compare *Schempp* (Brennan, J., concurring)."]

coerce in some circumstances, but this does not justify a ban on all government recognition of religion. As Chief Justice Burger wrote for the Court in *Walz:* "[W]e will not tolerate either governmentally established religion or governmental interference with religion. Short of those expressly proscribed governmental acts there is room for play in the joints productive of a benevolent neutrality which will permit religious exercise to exist without sponsorship and without interference." * * * Absent coercion, the risk of infringement of religious liberty by passive or symbolic accommodation is minimal. [In] determining whether there exists an establishment, or a tendency toward one, we refer to the other types of church-state contacts that have existed unchallenged throughout our history, or that have been found permissible in our caselaw [discussing *Lynch* and *Marsh*].

II. These principles are not difficult to apply to the facts of the case before us. [If] government is to participate in its citizens' celebration of a holiday that contains both a secular and a religious component, enforced recognition of only the secular aspect would signify the callous indifference toward religious faith that our cases and traditions do not require; [the] government would be refusing to acknowledge the plain fact, and the historical reality, that many of its citizens celebrate its religious aspects as well. [The] Religion Clauses do not require government to acknowledge these holidays or their religious component; but our strong tradition of government accommodation and acknowledgment permits government to do so.

There is no suggestion here that the government's power to coerce has been used to further the interests of Christianity or Judaism in any way. No one was compelled to observe or participate in any religious ceremony or activity. Neither the city nor the county contributed significant amounts of tax money to serve the cause of one religious faith. The crèche and the menorah are purely passive symbols of religious holidays. Passersby who disagree with the message conveyed by these displays are free to ignore them, or even to turn their backs, just as they are free to do when they disagree with any other form of government speech.

[Crucial] to the Court's conclusion [in *Lynch* was] the simple fact that, when displayed by government during the Christmas season, a crèche presents no realistic danger of moving government down the forbidden road toward an establishment of religion. Whether the crèche be surrounded by poinsettias, talking wishing wells, or carolers, the conclusion remains the same, for the relevant context is not the items in the display itself but the season as a whole. * * *

[III.] Even if *Lynch* did not control, I would not commit this Court to the test applied by the majority today. The notion that cases arising under the Establishment Clause should be decided by an inquiry into whether a " 'reasonable observer' " may " 'fairly understand' " government action to " 'sen[d] a message to nonadherents that they are outsiders, not full members of the political community,' " is a recent, and in my view most unwelcome, addition to our tangled Establishment Clause jurisprudence. * * *

[A.] *Marsh* stands for the proposition, not that specific practices common in 1791 are an exception to the otherwise broad sweep of the Establishment Clause, but rather that the meaning of the Clause is to be determined by reference to historical practices and understandings.[7] Whatever test we choose to apply must

---

7. [T]he relevant historical practices are those conducted by governmental units which were subject to the constraints of the Estab- lishment Clause. Acts of "official discrimina- tion against non-Christians" perpetrated in the eighteenth and nineteenth centuries by States

permit not only legitimate practices two centuries old but also any other practices with no greater potential for an establishment of religion. [Few] of our traditional practices recognizing the part religion plays in our society can withstand scrutiny under a faithful application [the endorsement test].

Some examples suffice to make plain my concerns. Since the Founding of our Republic, American Presidents have issued Thanksgiving Proclamations establishing a national day of celebration and prayer. The first such proclamation was issued by President Washington at the request of the First Congress [and] the forthrightly religious nature of these proclamations has not waned with the years. President Franklin D. Roosevelt went so far as to "suggest a nationwide reading of the Holy Scriptures during the period from Thanksgiving Day to Christmas" so that "we may bear more earnest witness to our gratitude to Almighty God." It requires little imagination to conclude that these proclamations would cause nonadherents to feel excluded, yet they have been a part of our national heritage from the beginning.[9]

The Executive has not been the only Branch of our Government to recognize the central role of religion in our society. [T]his Court opens its sessions with the request that "God save the United States and this honorable Court." [The] Legislature has gone much further, not only employing legislative chaplains, but also setting aside a special prayer room in the Capitol for use by Members of the House and Senate. The room is decorated with a large stained glass panel that depicts President Washington kneeling in prayer; around him is etched the first verse of the 16th Psalm: "Preserve me, O God, for in Thee do I put my trust." * * * Congress has directed the President to "set aside and proclaim a suitable day each year [as] a National Day of Prayer, on which the people of the United States may turn to God in prayer and meditation at churches, in groups, and as individuals." [Also] by statute, the Pledge of Allegiance to the Flag describes the United States as "one Nation under God." To be sure, no one is obligated to recite this phrase, see *West Virginia State Bd. of Educ. v. Barnette,* [Sec. 2, I infra] but it borders on sophistry to suggest that the " 'reasonable' " atheist would not feel less than a " 'full membe[r] of the political community' " every time his fellow Americans recited, as part of their expression of patriotism and love for country, a phrase he believed to be false. Likewise, our national motto, "In God we trust," which is prominently engraved in the wall above the Speaker's dias in the Chamber of the House of Representatives and is reproduced on every coin minted and every dollar printed by the Federal Government, must have the same effect.

If the intent of the Establishment Clause is to protect individuals from mere feelings of exclusion, then legislative prayer cannot escape invalidation. It has been argued that "[these] government acknowledgments of religion serve, in the only ways reasonably possible in our culture, the legitimate secular purposes of solemnizing public occasions, expressing confidence in the future, and encouraging the recognition of what is worthy of appreciation in society." *Lynch* (O'Connor, J., concurring). I fail to see why prayer is the only way to convey these messages; appeals to patriotism, moments of silence, and any number of other approaches would be as effective, were the only purposes at issue the ones described by the *Lynch* concurrence. [No] doubt prayer is "worthy of appreciation," but that is most assuredly not because it is secular. Even accepting the secular-solemnization explanation at face value, moreover, it seems incredible to suggest that the

and municipalities are of course irrelevant to this inquiry, but the practices of past Congresses and Presidents are highly informative.

9. Similarly, our presidential inaugurations have traditionally opened with a request for divine blessing. * * *

average observer of legislative prayer who either believes in no religion or whose faith rejects the concept of God would not receive the clear message that his faith is out of step with the political norm.[10]

[B.] If there be such a person as the "reasonable observer," I am quite certain that he or she will take away a salient message from our holding in this case: the Supreme Court of the United States has concluded that the First Amendment creates classes of religions based on the relative numbers of their adherents. Those religions enjoying the largest following must be consigned to the status of least-favored faiths so as to avoid any possible risk of offending members of minority religions. I would be the first to admit that many questions arising under the Establishment Clause do not admit of easy answers, but whatever the Clause requires, it is not the result reached by the Court today.

[IV.] The case before us is admittedly a troubling one. It must be conceded that, however neutral the purpose of the city and county, the eager proselytizer may seek to use these symbols for his own ends. The urge to use them to teach or to taunt is always present. It is also true that some devout adherents of Judaism or Christianity may be as offended by the holiday display as are nonbelievers, if not more so. To place these religious symbols in a common hallway or sidewalk, where they may be ignored or even insulted, must be distasteful to many who cherish their meaning.

For these reasons, I might have voted against installation of these particular displays were I a local legislative official. But [the] principles of the Establishment Clause and our Nation's historic traditions of diversity and pluralism allow communities to make reasonable judgments respecting the accommodation or acknowledgment of holidays with both cultural and religious aspects. No constitutional violation occurs when they do so by displaying a symbol of the holiday's religious origins. * * *

JUSTICE O'CONNOR with whom JUSTICE BRENNAN and JUSTICE STEVENS join as to Part II, concurring in part and concurring in the judgment. * * *

II.   In his separate opinion, Justice Kennedy asserts that the endorsement test "is flawed in its fundamentals and unworkable in practice." * * *

An Establishment Clause standard that prohibits only "coercive" practices or overt efforts at government proselytization, but fails to take account of the numerous more subtle ways that government can show favoritism to particular beliefs or convey a message of disapproval to others, would not, in my view, adequately protect the religious liberty or respect the religious diversity of the members of our pluralistic political community. Thus, this Court has never relied on coercion alone as the touchstone of Establishment Clause analysis. To require a showing of coercion, even indirect coercion, as an essential element of an Establishment Clause violation would make the Free Exercise Clause a redundancy. [Moreover,] as even Justice Kennedy recognizes, any Establishment Clause test limited to *"direct* coercion" clearly would fail to account for forms of "[s]ymbolic

---

10. If the majority's test were to be applied logically, it would lead to the elimination of all nonsecular Christmas caroling in public buildings or, presumably, anywhere on public property. It is difficult to argue that lyrics like "Good Christian men, rejoice," "Joy to the world! the Savior reigns," "This, this is Christ the King," "Christ, by highest heav'n adored," and "Come and behold Him, Born the King of angels," have acquired such a secular nature that nonadherents would not feel "left out" by a government-sponsored or approved program that included these carols. [Like] Thanksgiving Proclamations, the reference to God in the Pledge of Allegiance, and invocations to God in sessions of Congress and of this Court, they constitute practices that the Court will not proscribe, but that the Court's reasoning today does not explain.

recognition or accommodation of religious faith" that may violate the Establishment Clause.

[To] be sure, the endorsement test depends on a sensitivity to the unique circumstances and context of a particular challenged practice and, like any test that is sensitive to context, it may not always yield results with unanimous agreement at the margins. But that is true of many standards in constitutional law, and even the modified coercion test offered by Justice Kennedy involves judgment and hard choices at the margin. He admits as much by acknowledging that the permanent display of a Latin cross at city hall would violate the Establishment Clause, as would the display of symbols of Christian holidays alone. Would the display of a Latin cross for six months have such an unconstitutional effect, or the display of the symbols of most Christian holidays and one Jewish holiday? Would the Christmas-time display of a crèche inside a courtroom be "coercive" if subpoenaed witnesses had no opportunity to "turn their backs" and walk away? Would displaying a crèche in front of a public school violate the Establishment Clause under Justice Kennedy's test? * * *

Justice Kennedy submits that the endorsement test [would] invalidate many traditional practices recognizing the role of religion in our society. * * * Historical acceptance of a practice does not in itself validate that practice under the Establishment Clause if the practice violates the values protected by that Clause, just as historical acceptance of racial or gender based discrimination does not immunize such practices from scrutiny under the 14th Amendment.[f] [On] the contrary, the "history and ubiquity" of a practice is relevant because it provides part of the context in which a reasonable observer evaluates whether a challenged governmental practice conveys a message of endorsement of religion. [Thus,] the celebration of Thanksgiving as a public holiday, despite its religious origins, is now generally understood as a celebration of patriotic values rather than particular religious beliefs.[g] * * *

III.   For reasons which differ somewhat from those set forth in Part VI of Justice Blackmun's opinion, I also conclude that the city of Pittsburgh's combined holiday display [does] not have the effect of conveying an endorsement of religion. [In] my view, Justice Blackmun's new rule that an inference of endorsement arises every time government uses a symbol with religious meaning if a "more secular alternative" is available, is too blunt an instrument for Establishment Clause analysis, which depends on sensitivity to the context and circumstances presented by each case. * * *

f. In contending that "specific historical practice should [not] override [the] clear constitutional imperative," Brennan, J., joined by Marshall, J., dissenting in *Marsh*, noted that "the sort of historical argument made by the Court should be advanced with some hesitation in light of certain other skeletons in the congressional closet. See, e.g., An Act for the Punishment of certain Crimes against the United States (1790) (enacted by the First Congress and requiring that persons convicted of certain theft offenses 'be publicly whipped, not exceeding thirty-nine stripes'); Act of July 23, 1866 (reaffirming the racial segregation of the public schools in the District of Columbia; enacted exactly one week after Congress proposed Fourteenth Amendment to the States)."

Brennan, J., concurring in *Schempp*, further observed that "today the Nation is far more heterogeneous religiously, including as it does substantial minorities not only of Catholics and Jews but as well of those who worship according to no version of the Bible and those who worship no God at all. In the face of such profound changes, practices which may have been objectionable to no one in the time of Jefferson and Madison may today be highly offensive to many persons, the deeply devout and the non-believers alike. [Thus], our use of the history of their time must limit itself to broad purposes, not specific practices."

g. Brennan, J.'s dissent in *Lynch* expressed a similar view.

JUSTICE BRENNAN, with whom JUSTICE MARSHALL and JUSTICE STEVENS join, concurring in part and dissenting in part.

* * * I continue to believe that the display of an object that "retains a specifically Christian [or other] religious meaning," is incompatible with the separation of church and state demanded by our Constitution. I therefore agree with the Court that Allegheny County's display of a crèche at the county courthouse signals an endorsement of the Christian faith in violation of the Establishment Clause, and join Parts III–A, IV, and V of the Court's opinion. I cannot agree, however, [with] the decision as to the menorah [which] rests on three premises: the Christmas tree is a secular symbol; Chanukah is a holiday with secular dimensions, symbolized by the menorah; and the government may promote pluralism by sponsoring or condoning displays having strong religious associations on its property. None of these is sound.

[I.] Even though the tree alone may be deemed predominantly secular, it can hardly be so characterized when placed next to such a forthrightly religious symbol. Consider a poster featuring a star of David, a statue of Buddha, a Christmas tree, a mosque, and a drawing of Krishna. There can be no doubt that, when found in such company, the tree serves as an unabashedly religious symbol. * * *

[II.] The menorah is indisputably a religious symbol, used ritually in a celebration that has deep religious significance. That, in my view, is all that need be said. Whatever secular practices the holiday of Chanukah has taken on in its contemporary observance are beside the [point.] Pittsburgh's secularization of an inherently religious symbol [recalls] the effort in *Lynch* to render the crèche a secular symbol. As I said then: "To suggest, as the Court does, that such a symbol is merely 'traditional' and therefore no different from Santa's house or reindeer is not only offensive to those for whom the crèche has profound significance, but insulting to those who insist for religious or personal reasons that the story of Christ is in no sense a part of 'history' nor an unavoidable element of our national 'heritage.' " * * *

III. Justice Blackmun, in his acceptance of the city's message of "diversity," and, even more so, Justice O'Connor, in her approval of the "message of pluralism and freedom to choose one's own beliefs," appear to believe that, where seasonal displays are concerned, more is better. * * * I know of no principle under the Establishment Clause, however, that permits us to conclude that governmental promotion of religion is acceptable so long as one religion is not favored. We have, on the contrary, interpreted that Clause to require neutrality, not just among religions, but between religion and nonreligion. * * *

The uncritical acceptance of a message of religious pluralism also ignores the extent to which even that message may offend. Many religious faiths are hostile to each other, and indeed, refuse even to participate in ecumenical services designed to demonstrate the very pluralism Justices Blackmun and O'Connor extol. * * *

JUSTICE STEVENS, with whom JUSTICE BRENNAN and JUSTICE MARSHALL join, concurring in part and dissenting in part. * * *

In my opinion the Establishment Clause should be construed to create a strong presumption against the display of religious symbols on public property. There is always a risk that such symbols will offend nonmembers of the faith being advertised as well as adherents who consider the particular advertisement disrespectful. [Even] though "[p]assersby who disagree with the message conveyed by these displays are free to ignore them, or even turn their backs," displays of this kind inevitably have a greater tendency to emphasize sincere and deeply felt differences among individuals than to achieve an ecumenical goal. The Establishment Clause does not allow public bodies to foment such disagreement.

Application of a strong presumption against the public use of religious symbols scarcely will "require a relentless extirpation of all contact between government and religion," (Kennedy, J., concurring and dissenting), for it will prohibit a display only when its message, evaluated in the context in which it is presented, is nonsecular. For example, a carving of Moses holding the Ten Commandments, if that is the only adornment on a courtroom wall, conveys an equivocal message, perhaps of respect for Judaism, for religion in general, or for law. The addition of carvings depicting Confucius and Mohammed may honor religion, or particular religions, to an extent that the First Amendment does not tolerate any more than it does "the permanent erection of a large Latin cross on the roof of city hall." Placement of secular figures such as Caesar Augustus, William Blackstone, Napoleon Bonaparte, and John Marshall alongside these three religious leaders, however, signals respect not for great proselytizers but for great lawgivers. It would be absurd to exclude such a fitting message from a courtroom,[13] as it would to exclude religious paintings by Italian Renaissance masters from a public museum.[h] Far from "border[ing] on latent hostility toward religion," this careful consideration of context gives due regard to religious and nonreligious members of our society. * * *

Notes and Questions

1. *Secular purpose under the "Lemon" test. Lynch* found that "Pawtucket has *a* secular purpose for its display": "The City [has] principally taken note of a significant historical religious event long celebrated in the Western World. [Were] the test that the government must have 'exclusively secular' objectives, much of the conduct and legislation this Court has approved in the past would have been invalidated."

Brennan, J.'s dissent in *Lynch,* reasoned: "When government decides to recognize Christmas day as a public holiday, it does no more than accommodate the calendar of public activities to the plain fact that many Americans will expect on that day to spend time visiting with their families, attending religious services, and perhaps enjoying some respite from preholiday activities. [If] public officials go further and participate in the *secular* celebration of Christmas—by, for example, decorating public places with such secular images as wreaths, garlands or Santa Claus figures—they move closer to the limits of their constitutional power but nevertheless remain within the boundaries set by the Establishment Clause. But when those officials participate in or appear to endorse the distinctively religious elements of this otherwise secular event, they encroach upon First Amendment freedoms. [The] Court seems to assume that forbidding Pawtucket from displaying a crèche would be tantamount to forbidding a state college from including the Bible or Milton's *Paradise Lost* in a course on English literature. But in those cases the religiously-inspired materials are being considered solely as literature. [In] this case, by contrast, the crèche plays no comparable secular role.

---

13. All these leaders, of course, appear in friezes on the walls of our courtroom.

h. As an example of government "reference to our religious heritage," *Lynch* noted that "the National Gallery in Washington, maintained with Government support [has] long exhibited masterpieces with religious messages, notably the Last Supper, and paintings depicting the Birth of Christ, the Crucifixion, and the Resurrection, among many others with explicit Christian themes and messages."

[It] would be another matter if the crèche were displayed in a museum setting, in the company of other religiously-inspired artifacts, as an example, among many, of the symbolic representation of religious myths. In that setting, we would have objective guarantees that the crèche could not suggest that a particular faith had been singled out for public favor and recognition."

Does the dissent's approach require that government have "exclusively secular" objectives? If so, is this inconsistent with the Court's subsequent opinion in *Jaffree* (joined by all the *Lynch* dissenters) that "a statute that is motivated in part by a religious purpose may satisfy the first [*Lemon*] criterion."

2. *Differing interpretations of the "coercion" test.* LEE v. WEISMAN, 505 U.S. 577, 112 S.Ct. 2649, 120 L.Ed.2d 467 (1992), per KENNEDY, J., held violative of the establishment clause the practice of public school officials inviting members of the clergy to offer invocation and benediction prayers at graduation ceremonies: "We can decide the case without reconsidering the general constitutional framework [in *Lemon*. The] school district's supervision and control of a high school graduation ceremony places public pressure, as well as peer pressure, on attending students to stand as a group or, at least, maintain respectful silence during the Invocation and Benediction. This pressure, though subtle and indirect, can be as real as any overt compulsion. * * *

"Finding no violation under these circumstances would place objectors in the dilemma of participating, with all that implies, or protesting. * * * Research in psychology supports the common assumption that adolescents are often susceptible to pressure from their peers towards conformity, and that the influence is strongest in matters of social convention.[a] [That] the intrusion was in the course of promulgating religion that sought to be civic or nonsectarian rather than pertaining to one sect does not lessen the offense or isolation to the objectors. At best it narrows their number, at worst increases their sense of isolation and affront.

"[I]n our society and in our culture high school graduation is one of life's most significant occasions. A school rule which excuses attendance is beside the point. Attendance may not be required by official decree, yet it is apparent that a student is not free to absent herself from the graduation exercise in any real sense of the term 'voluntary,' for absence would require forfeiture of these intangible benefits which have motivated the student through youth and all her high school years.[b] [To] say that a student must remain apart from the ceremony at the opening invocation and closing benediction is to risk compelling conformity in an environment analogous to the classroom setting, where we have said the risk of compulsion is especially high. See *Engel* and *Schempp.* * * *

"Inherent differences between the public school system and a session of a State Legislature distinguish this case from *Marsh*. [The] atmosphere at the

a. For criticism of the psychological evidence relied on by the Court, see Donald N. Bersoff & David J. Glass, *The Not–So Weisman: The Supreme Court's Continuing Misuse of Social Science Research,* 2 U.Chi.L.S.Roundtable 279 (1995).

b. Consider Steven G. Gey, *Religious Coercion and the Establishment Clause,* 1994 U.Ill. L.Rev. 463, 503: "But a citizen of Allegheny County may also be compelled to transact business in the county courthouse, which would inevitably require that person to pass by the prominent display of the birth of the Christian savior. If the Allegheny County citizen is not coerced by being required to respectfully pass by the religious display, why is the Providence student coerced by respectfully remaining silent during a one-minute prayer? Conversely, if 'the act of standing or remaining silent' during a graduation prayer is 'an expression of participation' in the prayer, why is walking by an overtly Christian display in respectful silence not also 'an expression of participation' in the display?"

opening of a session of a state legislature where adults are free to enter and leave with little comment and for any number of reasons cannot compare with the constraining potential of the one school event most important for the student to attend. * * *

"We do not hold that every state action implicating religion is invalid if one or a few citizens find it offensive. People may take offense at all manner of religious as well as nonreligious messages, but offense alone does not in every case show a violation. We know too that sometimes to endure social isolation or even anger may be the price of conscience or nonconformity. But, by any reading of our cases, the conformity required of the student in this case was too high an exaction to withstand the test of the Establishment Clause."

BLACKMUN, J., joined by Stevens and O'Connor, JJ., who joined the Court's opinion, concurred: "[I]t is not enough that the government restrain from compelling religious practices: it must not engage in them either. [To] that end, our cases have prohibited government endorsement of religion, its sponsorship, and active involvement in religion, whether or not citizens were coerced to conform."

SOUTER, J., (who also joined the Court's opinion), joined by Stevens and O'Connor, JJ., concurred: "The Framers adopted the Religion Clauses in response to a long tradition of coercive state support for religion, particularly in the form of tax assessments, but their special antipathy to religious coercion did not exhaust their hostility to the features and incidents of establishment. Indeed, Jefferson and Madison opposed any political appropriation of religion, [and] saw that even without the tax collector's participation, an official endorsement of religion can impair religious liberty. [O]ne can call any act of endorsement a form of coercion, but only if one is willing to dilute the meaning of 'coercion' until there is no meaning left. * * *

"Religious students cannot complain that omitting prayers from their graduation ceremony would, in any realistic sense, 'burden' their spiritual callings. To be sure, many of them invest this rite of passage with spiritual significance, but they may express their religious feelings about it before and after the ceremony. They may even organize a privately sponsored baccalaureate if they desire the company of likeminded students. Because they accordingly have no need for the machinery of the State to affirm their beliefs, the government's sponsorship of prayer at the graduation ceremony is most reasonably understood as an official endorsement of religion and, in this instance, of theistic religion."

SCALIA, J., joined by Rehnquist, C.J., and White and Thomas, JJ., dissented: "Three terms ago, I joined an opinion recognizing that 'the meaning of the [Establishment] Clause is to be determined by reference to historical practices and understandings.' * * * *Allegheny County* (Kennedy, J., concurring in judgment in part and dissenting in part).

"These views of course prevent me from joining today's opinion, which is conspicuously bereft of any reference to history [and] lays waste a tradition that is as old as public-school graduation ceremonies themselves, and that is a component of an even more longstanding American tradition of nonsectarian prayer to God at public celebrations generally.

"[Since] the Court does not dispute that students exposed to prayer at graduation ceremonies retain (despite 'subtle coercive pressures,') the free will to sit, there is absolutely no basis for the Court's decision. It is fanciful enough to say that 'a reasonable dissenter,' standing head erect in a class of bowed heads, 'could believe that the group exercise signified her own participation or approval of it.' It is beyond the absurd to say that she could entertain such a belief while pointedly declining to rise.

"But let us assume the very worst, that the nonparticipating graduate is 'subtly coerced' * * * to stand! Even that half of the disjunctive does not remotely establish a 'participation' (or an 'appearance of participation') in a religious exercise. * * *

"The deeper flaw in the Court's opinion does not lie in its wrong answer to the question whether there was state-induced 'peer-pressure' coercion; it lies, rather, in the Court's making violation of the Establishment Clause hinge on such a precious question. The coercion that was a hallmark of historical establishments of religion was coercion of religious orthodoxy and of financial support by force of *law and threat of penalty.* [I] concede that our constitutional tradition [has,] ruled out of order government-sponsored endorsement of religion—even when no legal coercion is present, and indeed even when no ersatz, 'peer-pressure' psycho-coercion is present—where the endorsement is sectarian, in the sense of specifying details upon which men and women who believe in a benevolent, omnipotent Creator and Ruler of the world, are known to differ (for example, the divinity of Christ). But there is simply no support for the proposition that the officially sponsored nondenominational invocation and benediction read by Rabbi Gutterman—with no one legally coerced to recite them—violated the Constitution of the United States.[c] To the contrary, they are so characteristically American they could have come from the pen of George Washington or Abraham Lincoln himself.

"The Court relies on our 'school prayer' cases, *Engel* and *Schempp.* But whatever the merit of those cases, they do not support, much less compel, the Court's psycho-journey. In the first place, *Engel* and *Schempp* do not constitute an exception to the rule, distilled from historical practice, that public ceremonies may include prayer; rather, they simply do not fall within the scope of the rule (for the obvious reason that school instruction is not a public ceremony). Second, we have made clear our understanding that school prayer occurs within a framework in which legal coercion to attend school (i.e., coercion under threat of penalty) provides the ultimate backdrop. * * * Voluntary prayer at graduation—a one-time ceremony at which parents, friends and relatives are present—can hardly be thought to raise the same concerns."[d]

3. *Prayer at other school activities—issues of government purpose and involvement.* SANTA FE IND. SCHOOL DIST. v. DOE, 530 U.S. 290, 120 S.Ct. 2266, 147 L.Ed.2d 295 (2000), per STEVENS, J., relied on *Lee* to hold "invalid on its face" the school district's policy authorizing a student election (1) to determine whether to have a student "deliver a brief invocation and/or message [at] varsity football games to solemnize the event, to promote good sportsmanship and student safety, and to establish the appropriate environment for the competition," and (2) to select "a student volunteer who is [to] decide what statement or

c. Compare Gey, supra, at 507: "If dissenting audience members at a state-sponsored public event may walk away from the affair without subjecting themselves to legal penalties, it should not matter whether a prayer given at that function incorporates the tenets of a particular sect, or comments unfavorably on the tenets of another sect. It should not matter even if the government sponsors a prayer overtly hostile to one or more faiths, so long as the dissenters are allowed to ignore the government's advice and practice their own beliefs freely."

d. How would the *Lee* Court—with Souter, J. replacing Brennan, J. and Thomas, J. replacing Marshall, J.—have decided the crèche issue in *Allegheny County*? See Jesse H. Choper, *Separation of Church and State: "New" Directions by the "New" Supreme Court,* 34 J. Church & State 363 (1992); Suzanna Sherry, *Lee v. Weisman: Paradox Redux,* 1992 Sup.Ct. Rev. 123.

invocation to deliver, consistent with the goals and purposes of this policy. Any message and/or invocation delivered by a student must be nonsectarian and nonproselytizing." The Court found "the evolution of the current policy [to be] most striking," pointing to the earlier practice of having an elected "Student Chaplain [deliver] a prayer over the public address system before each varsity football game," and to the title—"Prayer at Football Games"—of the most recent preceding policy, which was similar to the school's policy for prayer at graduations. The Court also emphasized the parties' stipulation that "students voted to determine whether a student would deliver prayer at varsity football games," all of which led the Court "to infer that the specific purpose of the policy was to preserve a popular 'state-sponsored religious practice.' "[a]

"[T]he District first argues that [the] messages are private student speech, not public speech. [But] these invocations are authorized by a government policy and take place on government property at government-sponsored school-related events. [Unlike] the type of forum discussed in [*Rosenberger* and similar cases, here,] the school allows only one student, the same student for the entire season, to give the invocation. [T]he majoritarian process implemented by the District guarantees, by definition, that minority candidates will never prevail and that their views will be effectively silenced. [This] encourages divisiveness along religious lines in a public school setting, a result at odds with the Establishment Clause. [And, in the context of a] broadcast over the school's public address system [at all varsity football games,] the members of the listening audience must perceive the pregame message as a public expression of the views of the majority of the student body delivered with the approval of the school administration."

As for "coercion," "we may assume [that] the informal pressure to attend an athletic event is not as strong as a senior's desire to attend her own graduation ceremony. [But] to assert that [many] high school students do not feel immense social pressure, or have a truly genuine desire, to be involved in the extracurricular event that is American high school football is 'formalistic in the extreme.' "

REHNQUIST, C.J., joined by Scalia and Thomas, JJ., dissented: "Even if it were appropriate to apply the *Lemon* test here, the district's student-message policy should not be invalidated on its face. [I]t is possible that the students might vote not to have a pregame speaker, in which case there would be no threat of a constitutional violation. It is also possible that the election would not focus on prayer, but on public speaking ability or social popularity. And if student campaigning did begin to focus on prayer, the school might decide to implement reasonable campaign restrictions.[b]

"[A]ny speech that may occur as a result of the election process here would be private, not government, speech. [Unlike *Lee*, the] elected student, not the

---

a. "[Further], the policy, by its terms, invites and encourages religious messages. The policy itself states that the purpose of the message is 'to solemnize the event.' A religious message is the most obvious method of solemnizing an event. Moreover, the requirements that the message 'promote good citizenship' and 'establish the appropriate environment for competition' further narrow the types of message deemed appropriate, suggesting that a solemn, yet nonreligious, message, such as commentary on United States foreign policy, would be prohibited. Indeed, the only type of message that is expressly endorsed in the text is an 'invocation'—a term that primarily de-

scribes an appeal for divine assistance. In fact, as used in the past at Santa Fe High School, an 'invocation' has always entailed a focused religious message."

b. The Court responded: "Under the *Lemon* standard, a court must invalidate a statute if it lacks 'a secular legislative purpose.' [E]ven if no Santa Fe High School student were ever to offer a religious message, [the] attempt by the District to encourage prayer is also at issue. Government efforts to endorse religion cannot evade constitutional reproach based solely on the remote possibility that those attempts may fail."

government, would choose what to say. [A] newly elected prom king or queen, could use opportunities for public speaking to say prayers. Under the Court's view, the mere grant of power to the students to vote for such offices, in light of the fear that those elected might publicly pray, violates the Establishment Clause.[c]

"[T]he Court dismisses the [policy's "plausible secular purpose"] of solemnization.[d] [But] it is easy to think of solemn messages that are not religious in nature, for example urging that a game be fought fairly. And sporting events often begin with a solemn rendition of our national anthem, with its concluding verse 'And this be our motto: "In God is our trust." '" Under the Court's logic, a public school that sponsors the singing of the national anthem before football games violates the Establishment Clause."

4. *Differing interpretations of the "endorsement" test.* (a) CAPITOL SQUARE REVIEW & ADVISORY BOARD v. PINETTE, 515 U.S. 753, 115 S.Ct. 2440, 132 L.Ed.2d 650 (1995), per SCALIA, J., relying on *Widmar* and *Lamb's Chapel,* held that petitioner's permitting the Ku Klux Klan to place a Latin cross in Capitol Square—"A 10–acre, state-owned plaza surrounding the Statehouse in Columbus, Ohio"—when it had also permitted such other unattended displays as "a State-sponsored lighted tree during the Christmas season, a privately-sponsored menorah during Chanukah, a display showing the progress of a United Way fundraising campaign, and booths and exhibits during an arts festival," did not violate the establishment clause: "The State did not sponsor respondents' expression, the expression was made on government property that had been opened to the public for speech, and permission was requested through the same application process and on the same terms required of other private groups."

The seven-justice majority divided, however, on the scope of the "endorsement" test. SCALIA, J., joined by Rehnquist, C.J., and Kennedy and Thomas, JJ., rejected petitioners' claim based on "the forum's proximity to the seat of government, which, they contend, may produce the perception that the cross bears the State's approval": "[W]e have consistently held that it is no violation for government to enact neutral policies that happen to benefit religion. Where we have tested for endorsement of religion, the subject of the test was either expression by the government itself, *Lynch,* or else government action alleged to discriminate in favor of private religious expression or activity, *Allegheny County.* The test petitioners propose, which would attribute to a neutrally behaving government private religious expression, has no antecedent in our jurisprudence. [O]ne can conceive of a case in which a governmental entity manipulates its administration of a public forum close to the seat of government (or within a government building) in such a manner that only certain religious groups take advantage of it,

---

c. The Court responded: "If instead of a choice between an invocation and no pregame message, the first election determined whether a political speech should be made, and the second election determined whether the speaker should be a Democrat or a Republican, it would be rather clear that the public address system was being used to deliver a partisan message reflecting the viewpoint of the majority rather than a random statement by a private individual.

"The fact that the District's policy provides for the election of the speaker only after the majority has voted on her message identifies an obvious distinction between this case and the typical election of a 'student body president, or even a newly elected prom king or queen.' "

"After *Lee,* what result if the class valedictorian begins her speech with a prayer? See Alan E. Brownstein, *Prayer and Religious Expression at High School Graduation: Constitutional Etiquette in a Pluralistic Society,* 5 Nexus 61 (2000).

d. The Court responded: "When a governmental entity professes a secular purpose for an arguably religious policy, the government's characterization is, of course, entitled to some deference. But it is nonetheless the duty of the courts to 'distinguis[h] a sham secular purpose from a sincere one.' (O'Connor, J., concurring in judgment)."

creating an impression of endorsement that is in fact accurate. But those situations, which involve governmental favoritism, do not exist here. * * *

"The contrary view, most strongly espoused by Justice Stevens [infra], but endorsed by Justice Souter and Justice O'Connor [and Breyer, J.] as well, [infra], exiles private religious speech to a realm of less-protected expression. [It] is no answer to say that the Establishment Clause tempers religious speech. By its terms that Clause applies only to the words and acts of government. It was never meant, and has never been read by this Court, to serve as an impediment to purely private religious speech connected to the State only through its occurrence in a public forum."[a]

O'CONNOR, J., joined by Souter and Breyer, JJ., concurred in part: "Where the government's operation of a public forum has the effect of endorsing religion, even if the governmental actor neither intends nor actively encourages that result, the Establishment Clause is violated [because] the State's own actions (operating the forum in a particular manner and permitting the religious expression to take place therein), and their relationship to the private speech at issue, actually convey a message of endorsement."[b]

STEVENS, J., dissented: "[W]hile this unattended, freestanding wooden cross was unquestionably a religious symbol, observers may well have received completely different messages from that symbol. Some might have perceived it as a message of love, others as a message of hate, still others as a message of exclusion—a Statehouse sign calling powerfully to mind their outsider status. [It] is especially important to take account of the perspective of a reasonable observer who may not share the particular religious belief it expresses. A paramount purpose of the Establishment Clause is to protect such a person from being made to feel like an outsider in matters of faith, and a stranger in the political community. If a reasonable person could perceive a government endorsement of religion from a private display, then the State may not allow its property to be used as a forum for that display. No less stringent rule can adequately protect non-adherents from a well-grounded perception that their sovereign supports a faith to which they do not subscribe.[c],[5]

---

a. Thomas, J., filed a brief concurrence, emphasizing that "a cross erected by the Ku Klux Klan [is] a political act, not a Christian one."

b. Souter, J., joined by O'Connor and Breyer, JJ., concurred "in large part because of the possibility of affixing a sign to the cross adequately disclaiming any government sponsorship or endorsement of it.

"[As] long as the governmental entity does not 'manipulat[e]' the forum in such a way as to exclude all other speech, the plurality's opinion would seem to [invite] government encouragement [of religion], even when the result will be the domination of the forum by religious displays and religious speakers. * * *

"Something of the sort, in fact, may have happened here. Immediately after the District Court issued the injunction ordering petitioners to grant the Klan's permit, a local church council [invited] all local churches to erect crosses, and the Board granted 'blanket permission' for 'all churches friendly to or affiliated with' the council to do so. The end result was that a part of the square was strewn with crosses, and while the effect in this case may

have provided more embarrassment than suspicion of endorsement, the opportunity for the latter is clear."

c. O'Connor, J., responded: "Under such an approach, a religious display is necessarily precluded so long as some passersby would perceive a governmental endorsement thereof. In my view, however, [the] reasonable observer in the endorsement inquiry must be deemed aware of the history and context of the community and forum in which the religious display appears. [An] informed member of the community will know how the public space in question has been used in the past—and it is that fact, not that the space may meet the legal definition of a public forum, which is relevant to the endorsement inquiry. [The] reasonable observer would recognize the distinction between speech the government supports and speech that it merely allows in a place that traditionally has been open to a range of private speakers accompanied, if necessary, by an appropriate disclaimer."

5. [O'Connor, J.'s] 'reasonable person' comes off as a well-schooled jurist, a being

"[The] very fact that a sign is installed on public property implies official recognition and reinforcement of its message. That implication is especially strong when the sign stands in front of the seat of the government itself. The 'reasonable observer' of any symbol placed unattended in front of any capitol in the world will normally assume that the sovereign [has] sponsored and facilitated its message. [Even] if the disclaimer at the foot of the cross (which stated that the cross was placed there by a private organization) were legible, that inference would remain, because a property owner's decision to allow a third party to place a sign on her property conveys the same message of endorsement as if she had erected it herself. [This] clear image of endorsement was lacking in *Widmar* and *Lamb's Chapel,* in which the issue was access to government facilities. Moreover, there was no question in those cases of an unattended display; private speakers, who could be distinguished from the state, were present. * * *

"The battle over the Klan cross underscores the power of such symbolism. The menorah prompted the Klan to seek permission to erect an anti-semitic symbol, which in turn not only prompted vandalism but also motivated other sects to seek permission to place their own symbols in the Square. These facts illustrate the potential for insidious entanglement that flows from state-endorsed proselytizing."

GINSBURG, J., also dissented, reserving the question of whether an unequivocal disclaimer, "legible from a distance," "that Ohio did not endorse the display's message" would suffice: "Near the stationary cross were the government's flags and the government's statues. No human speaker was present to disassociate the religious symbol from the State. No other private display was in sight. No plainly visible sign informed the public that the cross belonged to the Klan and that Ohio's government did not endorse the display's message."

(b) *"Reasonable observer."* Consider William P. Marshall, *"We Know It When We See It," The Supreme Court and Establishment,* 59 So.Cal.L.Rev. 495, 537 (1986): "Is the objective observer (or average person) a religious person, an agnostic, a separationist, a person sharing the predominate religious sensibility of the community, or one holding a minority view? Is there any 'correct' perception?" Compare Note, *Religion and the State,* 100 Harv.L.Rev. 1606, 1648 (1987): "[If the test] is governed by the perspective of the majority, it will be inadequately sensitive. [If] the establishment clause is to prohibit government from sending the message to religious minorities or nonadherents that the state favors certain beliefs and that as nonadherents they are not fully members of the political community, its application must turn on the message received *by the minority or nonadherent.*"

(c) *Ambiguities.* (i) Consider Steven D. Smith, *Symbols, Perceptions, and Doctrinal Illusions: Establishment Neutrality and the "No Endorsement" Test,* 86 Mich.L.Rev. 266, 283, 301–03, 310–12 (1987): "[E]vidence of the test's indeterminate character appears in [Arnold H. Loewy, *Rethinking Government Neutrality Towards Religion Under the Establishment Clause: The Untapped Potential of Justice O'Connor's Insight,* 64 N.C.L.Rev. 1049 (1986).] Loewy likes the 'no

finer than the tort-law model. With respect, I think this enhanced tort-law standard is singularly out of place in the Establishment Clause context. It strips of constitutional protection every reasonable person whose knowledge happens to fall below some 'ideal' standard. * * * Justice O'Connor's argument that 'there is al-

ways someone' who will feel excluded by any particular governmental action, ignores the requirement that such an apprehension be objectively reasonable. A person who views an exotic cow at the zoo as a symbol of the Government's approval of the Hindu religion cannot survive this test.

endorsement' test. In applying that test to particular controversies, however, he concludes that Pawtucket's sponsorship of a nativity scene violated the establishment clause, that Alabama's 'moment of silence' law probably did *not* violate the clause, and that ceremonial invocations of deity, such as those occurring in the Pledge of Allegiance or the opening of a Supreme Court session, *do* violate the 'no endorsement' test. In each instance, Justice O'Connor would disagree. [From] the Continental Congress[139] through the framing of the Bill of Rights[140] and on down to the present day, government and government officials—including Presidents [not] to mention the Supreme Court itself[141]—have frequently expressed approval of religion and religious ideas. Such history [at] least demonstrates that many Americans, including some of our early eminent statesmen, have *believed* such approval was proper. That fact alone is sufficient to show that the 'no endorsement' principle is controversial, not easily self-evident. [If] public institutions employ religious symbols, persons who do not adhere to the predominant religion may feel like 'outsiders.'[d] But if religious symbols are banned from such contexts, some religious people will feel that their most central values and concerns—and thus, in an important sense, they themselves—have been excluded from a public culture devoted purely to secular concerns. [We] might conclude, however, that any alienation felt by [the latter] groups, although perfectly sincere, should be disregarded because their dissatisfaction actually results not from particular governmental actions but rather from the very meaning of the establishment clause." Contrast Jesse H. Choper, *Securing Religious Liberty: Principles for Judicial interpretation of the Religion Clauses* 28–29 (1995): "[T]his would grant something that I find too close to a self-interested veto for the minority. [An] effective solution here would be to entrust this 'perspective-dependent' inquiry to an independent judiciary * * *. Although justices of the Supreme Court 'cannot become someone else,' they should, with their own solicitude for the values of religious liberty, either assume the view of a reasonable member of the political community who is faithful to the Constitution's protection of individual rights or ask whether a *reasonable minority observer,* who would be 'acquainted with the text, legislative history, and implementation of the [challenged state action],' *should feel* less than a full member of the political community.[112]"

(ii) Do government accommodations for religion (such as exempting the sacramental use of wine during Prohibition) violate the endorsement test? Consider Mark Tushnet, "Of Church and State and the Supreme Court": Kurland Revisited, 1989 Sup.Ct.Rev. 373, 395 n. 73: "They use religion as a basis for government classification, and they do [so] precisely in order to confer a benefit on some religions that does not flow either to nonbelievers or to all religions. [It] is difficult to avoid the conclusion that permissible accommodations, with their necessarily disparate impact, indicate some degree of government approval of the

---

139. [The] Continental Congress "sprinkled its proceedings liberally with the mention of God, Jesus Christ, the Christian religion, and many other religious references."

140. Shortly after approving the Bill of Rights, which of course included the establishment clause, the first Congress resolved to observe a day of thanksgiving and prayer in appreciation of "the many signal favors of Almighty God."

141. See, e.g., *Zorach* ("We are a religious people whose institutions presuppose a Supreme Being."); *Church of the Holy Trinity v. United States,* 143 U.S. 457, 471, 12 S.Ct. 511, 516, 36 L.Ed. 226 (1892) (asserting that "this is a Christian nation").

d. For support of O'Connor, J.'s approach in this setting, see Steven G. Gey, *When Is Religious Speech Not "Free Speech"?* 2000 U.Ill.L.Rev. 379.

112. Although this process is basically normative rather than empirical, the Court's judgment should obviously be influenced by the perception (if fairly discernible) of 'average' members of minority religious faiths and should be more strongly affected if their response is very widely shared.

practices." Compare Michael W. McConnell, *Religious Freedom at a Crossroads,* 59 U.Chi.L.Rev. 115, 150 (1992): "Any action the government takes on issues of this sort inevitably sends out messages, and it is not surprising that reasonable observers from different legal and religious perspectives respond to these messages in different ways. These examples raise some of the most important and most often litigated issues under the Establishment Clause, and the concept of endorsement does not help to resolve them."

(d) *None* of the opinions in *Capitol Square* invoked the *Lemon* test, which was barely mentioned. How would the *Capitol Square* Court have decided the crèche issue in *Allegheny*?

SECTION 2. FREE EXERCISE CLAUSE AND RELATED PROBLEMS

I. CONFLICT WITH STATE REGULATION

The most common problem respecting free exercise of religion has involved a generally applicable government regulation, whose purpose is nonreligious, that either makes illegal (or otherwise burdens) conduct that is dictated by some religious belief, or requires (or otherwise encourages) conduct that is forbidden by some religious belief. REYNOLDS v. UNITED STATES, 98 U.S. 145, 25 L.Ed. 244 (1878), the first major decision on the free exercise clause, upheld a federal law making polygamy illegal as applied to a Mormon whose religious duty was to practice polygamy: "Congress was deprived of all legislative power over mere opinion, but was left free to reach actions which were in violation of social duties or subversive of good order." CANTWELL v. CONNECTICUT, 310 U.S. 296, 60 S.Ct. 900, 84 L.Ed. 1213 (1940), reemphasized this distinction between religious opinion or belief, on the one hand, and action taken because of religion, on the other, although the Court this time spoke more solicitously about the latter: "Freedom of conscience and freedom to adhere to such religious organization or form of worship as the individual may choose cannot be restricted by law. [Free exercise] embraces two concepts,—freedom to believe and freedom to act. The first is absolute but, in the nature of things, the second cannot be. [The] freedom to act must have appropriate definition to preserve the enforcement of that protection [although] the power to regulate must be so exercised as not, in attaining a permissible end, unduly to infringe the protected freedom."

Beginning with *Cantwell*—which first held that the fourteenth amendment made the free exercise guarantee applicable to the states—a number of cases invalidated application of state laws to conduct undertaken pursuant to religious beliefs. Like *Cantwell,* these decisions, a number of which are set forth in Ch. 8,[a] rested in whole or in part on the freedom of expression protections of the first and fourteenth amendments. Similarly, WEST VIRGINIA STATE BD. OF EDUC. v. BARNETTE, 319 U.S. 624, 63 S.Ct. 1178, 87 L.Ed. 1628 (1943),[b] held that compelling a flag salute by public school children whose religious scruples forbade it violated the first amendment: "[The] freedoms of speech and of press, of assembly, and of worship [are] susceptible of restriction only to prevent grave and immediate danger to interests which the state may lawfully protect. [The] freedom asserted by these appellees does not bring them into collision with rights asserted

a. E.g., *Schneider v. Irvington,* Ch.7, Sec.6, I, A; *Lovell v. Griffin,* Ch. 7, Sec. 4, I, A (involving distribution of religious literature). See also *Marsh v. Alabama,* Ch. 10, Sec. 2.

b. Overruling *Minersville School Dist. v. Gobitis,* 310 U.S. 586, 60 S.Ct. 1010, 84 L.Ed. 1375 (1940).

by any other individual. It is such conflicts which most frequently require intervention of the State to determine where the rights of one end and those of another begin. [T]he compulsory flag salute and pledge requires *affirmation of a belief* and an *attitude of mind.* [If] there is any fixed star in our constitutional constellation, it is that no official, high or petty, can prescribe what shall be orthodox in politics, nationalism or other matters of opinion or force citizens to confess by word or act their faith therein."

It was not until 1963, in *Sherbert v. Verner* (discussed below), that the Court held conduct protected by the free exercise clause alone.

HOBBIE v. UNEMPLOYMENT APPEALS COMM'N

480 U.S. 136, 107 S.Ct. 1046, 94 L.Ed.2d 190 (1987).

JUSTICE BRENNAN delivered the opinion of the Court.

Appellant's employer discharged her when she refused to work certain scheduled hours because of sincerely-held religious convictions adopted after beginning employment. [Under] our precedents, the [Florida] Appeals Commission's disqualification of appellant from receipt of [unemployment compensation] benefits violates the Free Exercise [Clause]. *Sherbert v. Verner,* 374 U.S. 398, 83 S.Ct. 1790, 10 L.Ed.2d 965 (1963); *Thomas v. Review Board,* 450 U.S. 707, 101 S.Ct. 1425, 67 L.Ed.2d 624 (1981). In *Sherbert* we considered South Carolina's denial of unemployment compensation benefits to a Sabbatarian who, like Hobbie, refused to work on Saturdays. The Court held that the State's disqualification of Sherbert "force[d] her to choose between following the precepts of her religion and forfeiting benefits, on the one hand, and abandoning one of the precepts of her religion in order to accept work, on the other hand. Governmental imposition of such a choice puts the same kind of burden upon the free exercise of religion as would a fine imposed against [her] for her Saturday worship." * * *

In *Thomas,* [a] Jehovah's Witness, held religious beliefs that forbade his participation in the production of armaments. He was forced to leave his job when the employer closed his department and transferred him to a division that fabricated turrets for tanks. Indiana then denied Thomas unemployment compensation benefits. * * *

We see no meaningful distinction among the situations of Sherbert, Thomas, and Hobbie. We again affirm, as stated in *Thomas:* "Where the state conditions receipt of an important benefit upon conduct proscribed by a religious faith, *or where it denies such a benefit because of conduct mandated by religious belief, thereby putting substantial pressure on an adherent to modify his behavior and to violate his beliefs,* a burden upon religion exists. While the compulsion may be indirect, the infringement upon free exercise is nonetheless substantial" (emphasis added).

Both *Sherbert* and *Thomas* held that such infringements must be subjected to strict scrutiny and could be justified only by proof by the State of a compelling interest. The Appeals Commission does not seriously contend that its denial of benefits can withstand strict scrutiny;[a] rather it urges that we hold that its

---

a. In *Sherbert,* the state "suggest[ed] no more than a possibility that the filing of fraudulent claims by unscrupulous claimants feigning religious objections to Saturday work [might] dilute the unemployment compensation fund [but] there is no proof whatever to warrant such fears of malingering or deceit [and] it is highly doubtful whether such evidence would be sufficient to warrant a substantial infringement of religious liberties. For [it] would plainly be incumbent upon the [state] to demonstrate that no alternative forms of regu-

justification should be determined under the less rigorous standard articulated in Chief Justice Burger's opinion in *Bowen v. Roy:* "the Government meets its burden when it demonstrates that a challenged requirement for governmental benefits, neutral and uniform in its application, is a reasonable means of promoting a legitimate public interest."[b] 476 U.S. 693, 707–08, 106 S.Ct. 2147, 2156, 90 L.Ed.2d 735 (1986). Five Justices expressly rejected this argument in *Roy*. We reject the argument again today. As Justice O'Connor pointed out in *Roy*, "[s]uch a test has no basis in precedent and relegates a serious First Amendment value to the barest level of minimal scrutiny that the Equal Protection Clause already provides." See also *Wisconsin v. Yoder*, 406 U.S. 205, 215, 92 S.Ct. 1526, 1533, 32 L.Ed.2d 15 (1972)[c] ("[O]nly those interests of the highest order and those not otherwise served can overbalance legitimate claims to the free exercise of religion"). * * *

The Appeals Commission also attempts to distinguish this case by arguing that [in] *Sherbert* and *Thomas,* the employees held their respective religious beliefs at the time of hire; subsequent changes in the conditions of employment made *by the employer* caused the conflict between work and belief. In this case, Hobbie's beliefs changed during the course of her employment, creating a conflict between job and faith that had not previously existed. * * *

In effect, the Appeals Commission asks us to single out the religious convert for different, less favorable treatment. * * * We decline to do so. * * *

Finally, we reject the Appeals Commission's argument that the awarding of benefits to Hobbie would violate the Establishment Clause. This Court has long recognized that the government may (and sometimes must) accommodate religious practices and that it may do so without violating the Establishment Clause.[10] See e.g., *Yoder* (judicial exemption of Amish children from compulsory attendance at high school); *Walz* (tax exemption for churches). * * *

---

lation would combat such abuses without infringing First Amendment rights."

b. Burger, C.J., joined by Powell and Rehnquist, JJ., prefaced this statement in *Roy* as follows: "[G]overnment regulation that indirectly and incidentally calls for a choice between securing a governmental benefit and adherence to religious beliefs is wholly different from government [action] that criminalizes religiously inspired activity or inescapably compels conduct that some find objectionable for religious reasons. Although the denial of governmental benefits over religious objection can raise serious Free Exercise problems, these two very different forms of government action are not governed by the same constitutional standard. * * * Absent proof of an intent to discriminate against particular religious beliefs or against religion in general, the Government meets its burden [etc.]"

c. *Yoder* invalidated a law compelling school attendance to age 16 as applied to Amish parents who refused on religious grounds to send their children to high school, noting no "showing that upon leaving the Amish community Amish children, with their practical agricultural training and habits of industry and self-reliance, would become burdens on society because of educational shortcomings. [The] independence and successful social functioning of the Amish community for a period approaching almost three centuries [is] strong evidence that there is at best a speculative gain, in terms of meeting the duties of citizenship, from an additional one or two years of compulsory formal education."

Only Douglas, J., dissented: If parents "are allowed a religious exemption, the inevitable effect is to impose the parents' notions of religious duty upon their children. Where the child is mature enough to express potentially conflicting desires, it would be an invasion of the child's rights to permit such an imposition without canvassing his views."

On the question of "whether children should be afforded rights of religious exercise independent of their parents," see Emily Buss, *What Does Frieda Yoder Believe?*, 2 U.Pa.J.Con.L. 53 (1999).

10. In the unemployment benefits context, the majorities *and* those dissenting have concluded that, were a state voluntarily to provide benefits to individuals in Hobbie's situation, such an accommodation would not violate the Establishment Clause. See *Thomas* (Rehnquist, J., dissenting); *Sherbert* (Harlan, J., dissenting). [The conflict between the establishment and free exercise clauses is considered in Sec. 4 infra.]

Reversed.[d]

CHIEF JUSTICE REHNQUIST, dissenting.

I adhere to the views I stated in dissent in *Thomas* [where Rehnquist, J., stated: "As to the proper interpretation of the Free Exercise Clause, I would accept the decision of *Braunfeld v. Brown*, 366 U.S. 599, 81 S.Ct. 1144, 6 L.Ed.2d 563 (1961), and the dissent in *Sherbert*. In *Braunfeld*, we held that Sunday closing laws do not violate the First Amendment rights of Sabbatarians. Chief Justice Warren explained that the statute did not make unlawful any religious practices of appellants; it simply made the practice of their religious beliefs more expensive. We concluded that '[t]o strike down, without the most critical scrutiny, legislation which imposes only an indirect burden on the exercise of religion, i.e., legislation which does not make unlawful the religious practice itself, would radically restrict the operating latitude of the legislature.'[e] Likewise in this case, it cannot be said that the State discriminated against Thomas on the basis of his religious beliefs or that he was denied benefits *because* he was a Jehovah's Witness.[1] Where, as here, a State has enacted a general statute, the purpose and effect of which is to advance the State's secular goals, the Free Exercise Clause does not in my view require the State to conform that statute to the dictates of religious conscience of any group."]

Notes and Questions

1. *Scope of decisions.* After *Sherbert*, *Thomas* and *Hobbie*, may a state deny unemployment benefits (a) to member of a pacifist religion who agreed to produce tanks as a condition of employment and who was fired for subsequently refusing to do so because of religious beliefs, see *Employment Division, Oregon Dep't of Human Resources v. Smith*, 485 U.S. 660, 108 S.Ct. 1444, 99 L.Ed.2d 753 (1988); (b) to a Sabbatarian who is dismissed from a job in the post office for refusal to work on Saturday because to grant an exemption would require paying overtime to another employee?[a] May (c) a state deny worker's compensation to the widow of an employee who, after being injured at work, died because of his refusal on religious grounds to accept a blood transfusion?

2. *Other forms of government largesse.* If a state fluoridates drinking water, must it supply nonfluoridated water to persons whose religion forbids such "medicinal aids"? Consider Tribe 2d ed., at 1274: "Presumably the government could provide subsidized loans to beef producers without facing a colorable free

---

d. The opinions of Powell and Stevens, JJ., concurring in the judgment, are omitted.

e. *Braunfeld* continued: "Statutes which tax income and limit the amount which may be deducted for religious contributions impose an indirect economic burden on the observance of the religion of the citizen whose religion requires him to donate a greater amount to his church; statutes which require the courts to be closed on Saturday and Sunday impose a similar indirect burden on the observance of the religion of the trial lawyer whose religion requires him to rest on a weekday. The list of legislation of this nature is nearly limitless."

Query: If a statute makes a religious practice unlawful but the maximum penalty is a fine, does this impose a "direct" or "indirect" burden?

1. [T]he Indiana Supreme Court *has* construed the State's unemployment statute to make every personal subjective reason for leaving a job a basis for disqualification. [Because] Thomas left his job for a personal reason, the State of Indiana should not be prohibited from disqualifying him from receiving benefits.

a. See also *TWA v. Hardison*, 432 U.S. 63, 97 S.Ct. 2264, 53 L.Ed.2d 113 (1977), interpreting the Civil Rights Act prohibition against religious discrimination in employment as permitting dismissal of a Sabbatarian if accommodating his work schedule would require "more than a de minimis cost" by the employer. Brennan and Marshall, JJ., dissented.

exercise claim brought by people whose religion requires them to raise and eat only vegetables; or provide tax benefits to medical or military professionals without facing a claim brought by people whose religious tenets forbid such work. But the principles underlying [the distinctions between these policies and that in *Sherbert, Thomas* and *Hobbie*] resist ready definition."

3. *Rejections of free exercise claims.* (a) *Taxation.* (i) JIMMY SWAGGART MINISTRIES v. BOARD OF EQUAL., 493 U.S. 378, 110 S.Ct. 688, 107 L.Ed.2d 796 (1990), per O'Connor, J., unanimously held that the free exercise clause does not prohibit imposing a sales and use tax on the sale of religious materials by a religious organization. The Court distinguished *Murdock v. Pennsylvania*, 319 U.S. 105, 63 S.Ct. 870, 87 L.Ed. 1292 (1943) and *Follett v. McCormick*, 321 U.S. 573, 64 S.Ct. 717, 88 L.Ed. 938 (1944), which had invalidated license taxes for sellers as applied to Jehovah's Witnesses who went from house to house selling religious pamphlets, because of the "particular nature of the challenged taxes— flat license taxes that operated as a prior restraint on the exercise of religious liberty": "[T]o the extent that imposition of a generally applicable tax merely decreases the amount of money appellant has to spend on its religious activities, any such burden is not constitutionally significant. * * *

"Finally, because appellant's religious beliefs do not forbid payment of the sales and use tax, appellant's reliance on *Sherbert* and its progeny is misplaced. [Although] it is of course possible to imagine that a more onerous tax, even if generally applicable, might effectively choke off an adherent's religious practices, cf. *Murdock* (the burden of a flat tax could render itinerant evangelism 'crushed and closed out by the sheer weight of the toll or tribute which is exacted town by town'), we face no such situation in this case."

(ii) UNITED STATES v. LEE, 455 U.S. 252, 102 S.Ct. 1051, 71 L.Ed.2d 127 (1982), per Burger, C.J., held that the free exercise clause does not require an exemption for members of the Old Order Amish from payment of social security taxes even though "both payment and receipt of social security benefits is forbidden by the Amish faith": "The state may justify a limitation on religious liberty by showing that it is essential to accomplish an overriding governmental interest [and] mandatory participation is indispensable to the fiscal vitality of the social security system. [To] maintain an organized society that guarantees religious freedom to a great variety of faiths requires that some religious practices yield to the common good. [The] tax system could not function if denominations were allowed to challenge the tax system because tax payments were spent in a manner that violates their religious belief."

Stevens, J., concurred in the judgment: "As a matter of fiscal policy, an enlarged exemption probably would benefit the social security system because the nonpayment of these taxes by the Amish would be more than offset by the elimination of their right to collect benefits.[b] * * * Nonetheless, I agree with the Court's conclusion that the difficulties associated with processing other claims to tax exemption on religious grounds justify a rejection of this claim.[2]"

---

b. Stevens, J., found the distinction between this case and *Yoder* "unconvincing because precisely the same religious interest is implicated in both cases and Wisconsin's interest in requiring its children to attend school until they reach the age of 16 is surely not inferior to the federal interest in collecting these social security taxes."

2. [T]he principal reason for adopting a strong presumption against such claims is not a matter of administrative convenience. It is the overriding interest in keeping the government—whether it be the legislature or the courts—out of the business of evaluating the relative merits of differing religious claims. The risk that governmental approval of some and disapproval of others will be perceived as

(b) *Conscription.* (i) GILLETTE v. UNITED STATES, 401 U.S. 437, 91 S.Ct. 828, 28 L.Ed.2d 168 (1971), per MARSHALL, J., held that the free exercise clause does not forbid Congress from "conscripting persons who oppose a particular war on grounds of conscience and religion. * * *[23]": "The conscription laws [are] not designed to interfere with any religious ritual or practice, and do not work a penalty against any theological position. The incidental burdens felt by persons in petitioners' position are strictly justified by substantial governmental interests that relate directly to the very impacts questioned. And more broadly, of course, there is the Government's interest in procuring the manpower necessary for military purposes * * *."

DOUGLAS, J., dissented: "[M]y choice is the dicta of Chief Justice Hughes who, dissenting in *Macintosh,* spoke for Holmes, Brandeis, and Stone: '[Among] the most eminent statesmen here and abroad have been those who condemned the action of their country in entering into wars they thought to be unjustified. [If] the mere holding of religious or conscientious scruples against all wars should not disqualify a citizen from holding office in this country, or an applicant otherwise qualified from being admitted to citizenship, there would seem to be no reason why a reservation of religious or conscientious objection to participation in wars believed to be unjust should constitute such a disqualification.' "[d]

(ii) In JOHNSON v. ROBISON, 415 U.S. 361, 94 S.Ct. 1160, 39 L.Ed.2d 389 (1974), a federal statute granted educational benefits for veterans who served on active duty but disqualified conscientious objectors who performed alternate civilian service. The Court, per BRENNAN, J., found a "rational basis" for the classification and thus no violation of equal protection, because the "disruption caused by military service is quantitatively greater" and "qualitatively different." Further, the statute "involves only an incidental burden upon appellee's free exercise of religion—if, indeed, any burden exists at all.[19] [T]he Government's substantial interest in raising and supporting armies is of 'a kind and weight' clearly sufficient to sustain the challenged legislation, for the burden upon appellee's free exercise [is] not nearly of the same order or magnitude as" in *Gillette.* Douglas, J., dissented.

(c) *Tax exemption.* BOB JONES UNIV. v. UNITED STATES, 461 U.S. 574, 103 S.Ct. 2017, 76 L.Ed.2d 157 (1983), per BURGER, C.J., held that IRS denial of tax exempt status to private schools that practice racial discrimination on the basis of sincerely held religious beliefs does not violate the free exercise clause: "[T]he

favoring one religion over another is an important risk the Establishment Clause was designed to preclude.

23. We are not faced with the question whether the Free Exercise Clause itself would require exemption of any class other than objectors to particular wars. * * * We note that the Court has previously suggested that relief for conscientious objectors is not mandated by the Constitution. See *Hamilton v. Regents,* 293 U.S. 245, 55 S.Ct. 197, 79 L.Ed. 343 (1934); *United States v. Macintosh,* 283 U.S. at 623–24, 51 S.Ct. at 574–75, 75 L.Ed. 1302 (1931).

d. Did *Gillette* discard the "alternative means" approach found in *Sherbert*? Consider Tribe 2d ed., at 1266: "In light of the relative ease with which the conscientious-objector exemption has been administered throughout our history without placing a noticeable burden on the country's military manpower needs, a

court might well require a concrete showing of threat to such needs in order to justify abolition of the exemption. The use of conscientious objectors—even selective conscientious objectors—in paramedical or other non-military roles could meet both the personnel argument and the morale argument well enough to constitute a required alternative under *Sherbert.*"

19. * * * Congress has bestowed relative benefits upon conscientious objectors by permitting them to perform their alternate service obligation as civilians. Thus, Congress' decision to grant educational benefits to military servicemen might arguably be viewed as an attempt to equalize the burdens of military service and civilian alternate service, rather than an effort [to] place a relative burden upon a conscientious objector's free exercise of religion.

Government has a fundamental, overriding interest in eradicating racial discrimination in education [which] substantially outweighs whatever burden denial of tax benefits places on petitioners' exercise of their religious beliefs. The interests asserted by petitioners cannot be accommodated with that compelling governmental interest, see *Lee;* and no 'less restrictive means' are available to achieve the governmental interest."[e] Rehnquist, J., agreeing with the Court's free exercise analysis, dissented on the ground that Congress had not authorized the IRS denial of tax exemption.[f]

(d) *Internal government affairs.* LYNG v. NORTHWEST INDIAN CEMETERY PROTECTIVE ASS'N, 485 U.S. 439, 108 S.Ct. 1319, 99 L.Ed.2d 534 (1988), per O'CONNOR, J., held the federal government's building a road and allowing timber harvesting in a national forest did not violate the free exercise rights of American Indian tribes even though this would "virtually destroy the Indians' ability to practice their religion" because it would irreparably damage "sacred areas which are an integral and necessary part of [their] belief systems": "In *Bowen v. Roy,* we considered a challenge to a federal statute that required the States to use Social Security numbers in administering certain welfare programs. Two applicants for benefits under these programs contended that their religious beliefs prevented them from acceding to the use of a Social Security number [that had been assigned to] their two-year-old daughter because the use of a numerical identifier would ' "rob the spirit" of [their] daughter and prevent her from attaining greater spiritual power.' [The] Court rejected this kind of challenge in *Roy:* 'The Free Exercise Clause simply cannot be understood to require the Government to conduct its own internal affairs in ways that comport with the religious beliefs of particular citizens. Just as the Government may not insist that [the Roys] engage in any set form of religious observance, so [they] may not demand that the Government join in their chosen religious practices by refraining from using a number to identify their daughter. [The] Free Exercise Clause affords an individual protection from certain forms of governmental compulsion; it does not afford an individual a right to dictate the conduct of the Government's internal procedures.'

"The building of a road or the harvesting of timber on publicly owned land cannot meaningfully be distinguished from the use of a Social Security number in *Roy*. In both cases, the challenged government action would interfere significantly with private persons' ability to pursue spiritual fulfillment according to their own religious beliefs. In neither case, however, would the affected individuals be coerced by the Government's action into violating their religious beliefs; nor would either governmental action penalize religious activity by denying any person an equal share of the rights, benefits, and privileges. [However] much we might wish that it were otherwise, government simply could not operate if it were required to satisfy every citizen's religious needs and desires. A broad range of government activities—from social welfare programs to foreign aid to conservation projects—will always be considered essential to the spiritual well-being of some citizens, often on the basis of sincerely held religious beliefs. Others will find the very same activities deeply offensive, and perhaps incompatible with their own

e. Contra, Douglas Laycock, *Tax Exemptions for Racially Discriminatory Religious Schools,* 60 Tex.L.Rev. 259 (1982); Mayer G. Freed & Daniel D. Polsby, *Race, Religion, and Public Policy: Bob Jones University v. United States,* 1983 Sup.Ct.Rev. 1, 20–30.

f. Four justices also rejected the claim that Nebraska's denial of a driver's license to a

person whose sincerely held religious beliefs—pursuant to the Second Commandment prohibition of "graven images"—forbade her to be photographed, violated the free exercise clause. *Quaring v. Peterson,* 728 F.2d 1121 (8th Cir. 1984) (free exercise violation), affirmed by an equally divided Court, 472 U.S. 478, 105 S.Ct. 3492, 86 L.Ed.2d 383 (1985).

search for spiritual fulfillment and with the tenets of their religion. The First Amendment must apply to all citizens alike, and it can give to none of them a veto over public programs that do not prohibit the free exercise of religion. * * *

"[The] dissent now offers to distinguish [*Roy*] by saying that the Government was acting there 'in a purely internal manner,' whereas land-use decisions 'are likely to have substantial external effects.' [But robbing] the spirit of a child, and preventing her from attaining greater spiritual power, is both a 'substantial external effect' and one that is remarkably similar to the injury claimed [today]."[g]

BRENNAN, J., joined by Marshall and Blackmun, JJ., dissented: "[R]espondents have claimed—and proved—that the desecration of the high country will prevent religious leaders from attaining the religious power or medicine indispensable to the success of virtually all their rituals and ceremonies. [T]oday's ruling sacrifices a religion at least as old as the Nation itself, along with the spiritual well-being of its approximately 5,000 adherents, so that the Forest Service can build a six-mile segment of road that two lower courts found had only the most marginal and speculative utility, both to the Government itself and to the private lumber interests that might conceivably use it." Kennedy, J., did not participate.

EMPLOYMENT DIVISION v. SMITH

494 U.S. 872, 110 S.Ct. 1595, 108 L.Ed.2d 876 (1990).

JUSTICE SCALIA delivered the opinion of the Court. * * *

Respondents Alfred Smith and Galen Black were fired from their jobs with a private drug rehabilitation organization because they ingested peyote for sacramental purposes at a ceremony of the Native American Church, of which both are members. When respondents applied to petitioner Employment Division for unemployment compensation, they were determined to be ineligible for benefits because they had been discharged for work-related "misconduct." [We believe] that "if a State has prohibited through its criminal laws certain kinds of religiously motivated conduct without violating the First Amendment, it certainly follows that it may impose the lesser burden of denying unemployment compensation benefits to persons who engage in that conduct." * * *

[The] free exercise of religion means, first and foremost, the right to believe and profess whatever religious doctrine one desires. Thus, the First Amendment obviously excludes all "governmental regulation of religious *beliefs* as such." The government may not compel affirmation of religious belief, see *Torcaso v. Watkins,* [Part II infra], punish the expression of religious doctrines it believes to be false, *United States v. Ballard,* [Part II infra], impose special disabilities on the basis of religious views or religious status, see *McDaniel v. Paty,* 435 U.S. 618, 98 S.Ct. 1322, 55 L.Ed. 2d 593 (1978) [state rule disqualifying clergy from being legislators]; cf. *Larson v. Valente,* [Sec. 3 infra] or lend its power to one or the other side in controversies over religious authority or dogma, see *Presbyterian Church v. Hull Church,* [Sec. 3 infra].

But the "exercise of religion" often involves not only belief and profession but the performance of (or abstention from) physical acts: assembling with others for a worship service, participating in sacramental use of bread and wine, proselytizing, abstaining from certain foods or certain modes of transportation. It would be true, we think (though no case of ours has involved the point), that a state would

g. *Nature of remedy.* Is there a difference between the remedy needed to satisfy the free exercise claim in *Roy* and that in *Lyng?* If so, what about the required remedy in the other instances in which the Court has sustained the free exercise claim?

be "prohibiting the free exercise [of religion]" if it sought to ban such acts or abstentions only when they are engaged in for religious reasons, or only because of the religious belief that they display. It would doubtless be unconstitutional, for example, to ban the casting of "statues that are to be used for worship purposes," or to prohibit bowing down before a golden calf.

Respondents in the present case, however, seek to carry the meaning of "prohibiting the free exercise [of religion]" one large step further. They contend that their religious motivation for using peyote places them beyond the reach of a criminal law that is not specifically directed at their religious practice, and that is concededly constitutional as applied to those who use the drug for other reasons. [As] a textual matter, we do not think the words must be given that meaning. It is no more necessary to regard the collection of a general tax, for example, as "prohibiting the free exercise [of religion]" by those citizens who believe support of organized government to be sinful, than it is to regard the same tax as "abridging the freedom [of] the press" of those publishing companies that must pay the tax as a condition of staying in business. It is a permissible reading of the text, in the one case as in the other, to say that if prohibiting the exercise of religion (or burdening the activity of printing) is not the object of the tax but merely the incidental effect of a generally applicable and otherwise valid provision, the First Amendment has not been offended. Compare *Citizen Publishing Co. v. United States,* 394 U.S. 131, 89 S.Ct. 927, 22 L.Ed.2d 148 (1969) (upholding application of antitrust laws to press), with *Grosjean v. American Press Co.,* [p. ___ supra] (striking down license tax applied only to newspapers with weekly circulation above a specified level); see generally *Minneapolis Star & Tribune Co. v. Minnesota Commissioner of Revenue* [p. ___ supra].

Our decisions reveal that the latter reading is the correct one. We have never held that an individual's religious beliefs excuse him from compliance with an otherwise valid law prohibiting conduct that the State is free to regulate. [In] *Prince v. Massachusetts,* 321 U.S. 158, 64 S.Ct. 438, 88 L.Ed. 645 (1944), we held that a mother could be prosecuted under the child labor laws for using her children to dispense literature in the streets, her religious motivation notwithstanding. [The opinion also discusses *Braunfeld, Gillette,* and *Lee.*]

The only decisions in which we have held that the First Amendment bars application of a neutral, generally applicable law to religiously motivated action have involved not the Free Exercise Clause alone, but the Free Exercise Clause in conjunction with other constitutional protections, such as freedom of speech and of the press, see *Cantwell* (invalidating a licensing system for religious and charitable solicitations under which the administrator had discretion to deny a license to any cause he deemed nonreligious); *Murdock*; *Follett*, or the right of parents, acknowledged in *Pierce v. Society of Sisters* [Sec. 2 supra] to direct the education of their children, see *Yoder.*[1] Some of our cases prohibiting compelled expression, decided exclusively upon free speech grounds, have also involved freedom of religion, cf. *Wooley v. Maynard* [Ch. 7, Sec. 9, I] (invalidating compelled display of a license plate slogan that offended individual religious beliefs); *Barnette.* And it is easy to envision a case in which a challenge on freedom of association grounds would likewise be reinforced by Free Exercise Clause con-

---

1. [*Yoder*] said that "the Court's holding in *Pierce* stands as a charter of the rights of parents to direct the religious upbringing of their children. And, when the interests of parenthood are combined with a free exercise claim of the nature revealed by this record, more than merely a 'reasonable relation to some purpose within the competency of the State' is required to sustain the validity of the State's requirement under the First Amendment."

cerns. Cf. *Roberts v. United States Jaycees* [Ch. 7, Sec. 9, III] ("An individual's freedom to speak, to worship, and to petition the government for the redress of grievances could not be vigorously protected from interference by the State [if] a correlative freedom to engage in group effort toward those ends were not also guaranteed."). * * *

Respondents argue that even though exemption from generally applicable criminal laws need not automatically be extended to religiously motivated actors, at least the claim for a religious exemption must be evaluated under the balancing test set forth in *Sherbert*. Under the *Sherbert* test, governmental actions that substantially burden a religious practice must be justified by a compelling governmental interest. [We] have never invalidated any governmental action on the basis of the *Sherbert* test except the denial of unemployment compensation. Although we have sometimes purported to apply the *Sherbert* test in contexts other than that, we have always found the test satisfied, see *Lee, Gillette*. In recent years we have abstained from applying the *Sherbert* test (outside the unemployment compensation field) at all [discussing *Roy* and *Lyng*]. In *Goldman v. Weinberger*, 475 U.S. 503, 106 S.Ct. 1310, 89 L.Ed.2d 478 (1986), we rejected application of the *Sherbert* test to military dress regulations that forbade the wearing of yarmulkes. In *O'Lone v. Shabazz*, 482 U.S. 342, 107 S.Ct. 2400, 96 L.Ed.2d 282 (1987), we sustained, without mentioning the *Sherbert* test, a prison's refusal to excuse inmates from work requirements to attend worship services.[a]

Even if we were inclined to breathe into *Sherbert* some life beyond the unemployment compensation field, we would not apply it to require exemptions from a generally applicable criminal law. The *Sherbert* test, it must be recalled, was developed in a context that lent itself to individualized governmental assessment of the reasons for the relevant conduct. [As] the plurality pointed out in *Roy*, our decisions in the unemployment cases stand for the proposition that where the State has in place a system of individual exemptions, it may not refuse to extend that system to cases of "religious hardship" without compelling reason.[b]

Whether or not the decisions are that limited, they at least have nothing to do with an across-the-board criminal prohibition on a particular form of conduct.

---

a. For a careful review of the cases, both in the Supreme Court and in the U.S. courts of appeals for ten years preceding *Smith*, concluding that "despite the apparent protection afforded claimants by the language of the compelling interest test, courts overwhelmingly sided with the government when applying that test," see James E. Ryan, *Smith and the Religious Freedom Restoration Act: An Iconoclastic Assessment*, 78 Va.L.Rev. 1407 (1992). See also Jesse H. Choper, *The Rise and Decline of the Constitutional Protection of Religious Liberty*, 70 Neb.L.Rev. 651, 659–70 (1991).

b. For the view that the system of discretionary hearings involved in the unemployment cases presents "a fertile ground for the undervaluation of minority religious interests" and is therefore "vulnerable to a distinct constitutional objection," see Christopher L. Eisgruber & Lawrence G. Sager, *The Vulnerability of Conscience: The Constitutional Basis for Protecting Religious Conduct*, 61 U.Chi.L.Rev. 1245 (1994). For an empirical study reaching an opposite conclusion, see Prabha S. Bhandari, *The Failure of Equal Regard to Explain the Sherbert Quartet*, 72 N.Y.U.L.Rev. 97 (1997).

See also Ira C. Lupu, *The Case Against Legislative Codification of Religious Liberty*, 21 Card.L.Rev. 565, 573 (1999): "Long prior to *Smith*, our civil liberties tradition had recognized the dangers of permitting local officials to exercise licensing authority over expressive activity without the benefit of determinate criteria. The absence of such criteria invites discriminatory treatment of groups disfavored by local decision makers. Identical concerns [favor] aggressive implementation of [the] antidiscrimination principle of free exercise with the individual assessment principle which *Smith* purports to preserve."

For review of lower court decisions that have attempted to "evade" *Smith* through the "individual exemptions" analysis and the "hybrid rights exemption," see Carol M. Kaplan, *The Devil is in the Details: Neutral, Generally Applicable Laws and Exceptions from Smith*, 75 N.Y.U.L.Rev. 1045 (2000).

[We] conclude today that the sounder approach, and the approach in accord with the vast majority of our precedents, is to hold the test inapplicable to such challenges. [To] make an individual's obligation to obey such a law contingent upon the law's coincidence with his religious beliefs, except where the State's interest is "compelling"—permitting him, by virtue of his beliefs, "to become a law unto himself," *Reynolds*—contradicts both constitutional tradition and common sense.[2]

The "compelling government interest" requirement seems benign, because it is familiar from other fields. But using it as the standard that must be met before the government may accord different treatment on the basis of race, see [Ch. 9, Sec. 2, I], or before the government may regulate the content of speech, is not remotely comparable to using it for the purpose asserted here. What it produces in those other fields—equality of treatment, and an unrestricted flow of contending speech—are constitutional norms; what it would produce here—a private right to ignore generally applicable laws—is a constitutional anomaly.[3]

Nor is it possible to limit the impact of respondents' proposal by requiring a "compelling state interest" only when the conduct prohibited is "central" to the individual's religion. It is no more appropriate for judges to determine the "centrality" of religious beliefs before applying a "compelling interest" test in the free exercise field, than it would be for them to determine the "importance" of ideas before applying the "compelling interest" test in the free speech field. What principle of law or logic can be brought to bear to contradict a believer's assertion that a particular act is "central" to his personal faith? [I]n many different contexts, we have warned that courts must not presume to determine the place of a particular belief in a religion or the plausibility of a religious claim. See, e.g., *Thomas* [Part II infra]; *Jones v. Wolf,* [Sec. 3 infra]; *Ballard*.[4]

If the "compelling interest" test is to be applied at all, then, it must be applied across the board, to all actions thought to be religiously commanded. Moreover, if "compelling interest" really means what it says (and watering it

---

2. Justice O'Connor seeks to distinguish *Lyng* and *Roy* on the ground that those cases involved the government's conduct of "its own internal affairs." [But] it is hard to see any reason in principle or practicality why the government should have to tailor its health and safety laws to conform to the diversity of religious belief, but should not have to tailor its management of public lands, *Lyng*, or its administration of welfare programs, *Roy*.

3. [Just] as we subject to the most exacting scrutiny laws that make classifications based on race or on the content of speech, so too we strictly scrutinize governmental classifications based on religion, see *McDaniel;* see also *Torcaso*. But we have held that race-neutral laws that have the *effect* of disproprotionately disadvantaging a particular racial group do not thereby become subject to compelling-interest analysis under the Equal Protection Clause, see *Washington v. Davis* [Ch. 9, Sec. 2, III] (police employment examination); and we have held that generally applicable laws unconcerned with regulating speech that have the *effect* of interfering with speech do not thereby become subject to compelling-interest analysis under the First Amendment, see *Citizen Publishing Co. v. United States* (antitrust laws).

Our conclusion that generally applicable, religion-neutral laws that have the effect of burdening a particular religious practice need not be justified by a compelling governmental interest is the only approach compatible with these precedents.

4. [In] any case, dispensing with a "centrality" inquiry is utterly unworkable. It would require, for example, the same degree of "compelling state interest" to impede the practice of throwing rice at church weddings as to impede the practice of getting married in church. There is no way out of the difficulty that, if general laws are to be subjected to a "religious practice" exception, *both* the importance of the law at issue *and* the centrality of the practice at issue must reasonably be considered. * * *

[For the conclusion that "the Court has never required that the claimant establish either centrality or compulsion in order to receive protection under the First Amendment," see Steven C. Seeger, *Restoring Rights to Rites: The Religious Motivation Test and the Religious Freedom Restoration Act*, 95 Mich.L.Rev. 1472 (1997).]

down here would subvert its rigor in the other fields where it is applied), many laws will not meet the test. Any society adopting such a system would be courting anarchy, but that danger increases in direct proportion to the society's diversity of religious beliefs, and its determination to coerce or suppress none of them.[c] Precisely because "we are a cosmopolitan nation made up of people of almost every conceivable religious preference," and precisely because we value and protect that religious divergence, we cannot afford the luxury of deeming *presumptively invalid,* as applied to the religious objector, every regulation of conduct that does not protect an interest of the highest order. The rule respondents favor would open the prospect of constitutionally required religious exemptions from civic obligations of almost every conceivable kind—ranging from compulsory military service, see, e.g., *Gillette,* to the payment of taxes, see, e.g., *Lee,* to health and safety regulation such as manslaughter and child neglect laws, compulsory vaccination laws, drug laws, and traffic laws, to social welfare legislation such as minimum wage laws, see *Tony and Susan Alamo Foundation v. Secretary of Labor,* 471 U.S. 290, 105 S.Ct. 1953, 85 L.Ed.2d 278 (1985), child labor laws, see *Prince;* animal cruelty laws, see, e.g., *Church of the Lukumi Babalu Aye Inc. v. Hialeah,* [note 1 infra], environmental protection laws, and laws providing for equality of opportunity for the races, see e.g., *Bob Jones University.* The First Amendment's protection of religious liberty does not require this.[5]

[A] number of States have made an exception to their drug laws for sacramental peyote use. But to say that a nondiscriminatory religious-practice exemption is permitted, or even that it is desirable, is not to say that it is constitutionally required, and that the appropriate occasions for its creation can be discerned by the courts. It may fairly be said that leaving accommodation to the political process will place at a relative disadvantage those religious practices that are not widely engaged in; but that unavoidable consequence of democratic government must be preferred to a system in which each conscience is a law unto itself or in which judges weigh the social importance of all laws against the centrality of all religious beliefs. * * *

JUSTICE O'CONNOR, with whom JUSTICE BRENNAN, JUSTICE MARSHALL, and JUSTICE BLACKMUN join as to [Part II], concurring in the judgment. * * *

II.   [A] law that prohibits certain conduct—conduct that happens to be an act of worship for someone—manifestly does prohibit that person's free exercise of his religion [regardless] of whether the law prohibits the conduct only when engaged in for religious reasons, only by members of that religion, or by all persons.

---

c.   Contra, Gary Simson, *Endangering Religious Liberty,* 84 Calif.L.Rev. 441, 461 (1996): "[I]t is far from clear that the government's ability to govern effectively would be seriously undermined as a result. After all, since the legislative process generally makes allowance for the needs of adherents of mainstream religions, court-ordered exemptions typically would be limited in scope to affected members of relatively small groups."

5.   Justice O'Connor contends that the "parade of horribles" in the text only "demonstrates [that] courts have been quite capable of strik[ing] sensible balances between religious liberty and competing state interests." But the cases we cite have struck "sensible balances" only because they have all applied the general laws, despite the claims for religious exemp-

tion. In any event, Justice O'Connor mistakes the purpose of our parade: it is not to suggest that courts would necessarily permit harmful exemptions from these laws (though they might), but to suggest that courts would constantly be in the business of determining whether the "severe impact" of various laws on religious practice (to use Justice Blackmun's terminology) or the "constitutiona[l] significan[ce]" of the "burden on the particular plaintiffs" (to use Justice O'Connor's terminology) suffices to permit us to confer an exemption. It is a parade of horribles because it is horrible to contemplate that federal judges will regularly balance against the importance of general laws the significance of religious practice.

[If] the First Amendment is to have any vitality, it ought not be construed to cover only the extreme and hypothetical situation in which a State directly targets a religious practice. [*Yoder*] expressly rejected the interpretation the Court now adopts: "[T]o agree that religiously grounded conduct must often be subject to the broad police power of the State is not to deny that there are areas of conduct protected by the Free Exercise Clause of the First Amendment and thus beyond the power of the State to control, *even under regulations of general applicability.* [A] regulation neutral on its face may, in its application, nonetheless offend the constitutional requirement for government neutrality if it unduly burdens the free exercise of religion."

The Court endeavors to escape from our decisions in *Cantwell* and *Yoder* by labeling them "hybrid" decisions but there is no denying that both cases expressly relied on the Free Exercise Clause and that we have consistently regarded those cases as part of the mainstream of our free exercise jurisprudence. Moreover, in each of the other cases cited by the Court to support its categorical rule, we rejected the particular constitutional claims before us only after carefully weighing the competing interests. [That] we rejected the free exercise claims in those cases hardly calls into question the applicability of First Amendment doctrine * * *. [I]t is surely unusual to judge the vitality of a constitutional doctrine by looking to the win-loss record of the plaintiffs who happen to come before us.

[W]e have never distinguished between cases in which a State conditions receipt of a benefit on conduct prohibited by religious beliefs and cases in which a State affirmatively prohibits such conduct. The *Sherbert* compelling interest test applies in both kinds of cases. [A] neutral criminal law prohibiting conduct that a State may legitimately regulate is, if anything, *more* burdensome than a neutral civil statute placing legitimate conditions on the award of a state benefit.

[Even] if, as an empirical matter, a government's criminal laws might usually serve a compelling interest in health, safety, or public order, the First Amendment at least requires a case-by-case determination of the question, sensitive to the facts of each particular claim. Given the range of conduct that a State might legitimately make criminal, we cannot assume, merely because a law carries criminal sanctions and is generally applicable, that the First Amendment *never* requires the State to grant a limited exemption for religiously motivated conduct.

Moreover, we have not "rejected" or "declined to apply" the compelling interest test in our recent cases. See, e.g., *Hobbie*. The cases cited by the Court signal no retreat from our consistent adherence to the compelling interest test. In both *Roy* and *Lyng,* for example, we expressly distinguished *Sherbert* on the ground that the First Amendment does not "require the Government *itself* to behave in ways that the individual believes will further his or her spiritual development. * * * " This distinction makes sense because "the Free Exercise Clause is written in terms of what the government cannot do to the individual, not in terms of what the individual can exact from the government." *Sherbert* (Douglas, J., concurring).[a] Because the case sub judice, like the other cases in which we have applied *Sherbert,* plainly falls into the former category, I would apply those established precedents to the facts of this case.

a. For the view that the *Lyng* approach, which "seems to involve neither social science nor theology," attracts the Court because it functions to "reduce the number of claims that must be afforded the searching inquiry demanded by the free exercise clause" and to permit the Court to avoid resolving the diffi- cult issues of "cognizability of the asserted burden, the sincerity of the claimant, and religiosity of the claim," see Ira C. Lupu, *Where Rights Begin: The Problem of Burdens on The Free Exercise of Religion,* 102 Harv.L.Rev. 933 (1989).

Similarly, the other cases cited by the Court for the proposition that we have rejected application of the *Sherbert* test outside the unemployment compensation field are distinguishable because they arose in the narrow, specialized contexts in which we have not traditionally required the government to justify a burden on religious conduct by articulating a compelling interest. See *Goldman v. Weinberger* ("Our review of military regulations challenged on First Amendment grounds is far more deferential than constitutional review of similar laws or regulations designed for civilian society"); *O'Lone v. Shabazz* ("[P]rison regulations alleged to infringe constitutional rights are judged under a 'reasonableness' test less restrictive than that ordinarily applied to alleged infringements of fundamental constitutional rights"). That we did not apply the compelling interest test in these cases says nothing about whether the test should continue to apply in paradigm free exercise cases such as the one presented here.[b]

[As] the language of the Clause itself makes clear, an individual's free exercise of religion is a preferred constitutional activity. A law that makes criminal such an activity therefore triggers constitutional concern—and heightened judicial scrutiny—even if it does not target the particular religious conduct at issue. Our free speech cases similarly recognize that neutral regulations that affect free speech values are subject to a balancing, rather than categorical, approach. See, e.g., *United States v. O'Brien,* [Ch. 7, Sec. 2]; *Renton v. Playtime Theatres, Inc.,* [Ch. 7, Sec. 3, I]; cf. *Anderson v. Celebrezze,* 460 U.S. 780, 103 S.Ct. 1564, 75 L.Ed.2d 547 (1983) (generally applicable laws may impinge on free association concerns). * * *

Finally, the Court today suggests that the disfavoring of minority religions is an "unavoidable consequence" under our system of government and that accommodation of such religions must be left to the political process. In my view, however, the First Amendment was enacted precisely to protect the rights of those whose religious practices are not shared by the majority and may be viewed with hostility. The history of our free exercise doctrine amply demonstrates the harsh impact majoritarian rule has had on unpopular or emerging religious groups such as the Jehovah's Witnesses and the Amish.[c] [The] compelling interest test reflects the First Amendment's mandate of preserving religious liberty to the fullest

---

b. See also Michael W. McConnell, *Free Exercise Revisionism and the Smith Decision,* 57 U.Chi.L.Rev. 1109, 1127 (1990): "The Court also failed to point out that in [*Roy*], five Justices expressed the view that adherents to a traditional Abenaki religion under which computer-generated numbers are deemed to rob the individual's spirit of its power were entitled to an exemption from the requirement that welfare recipients provide a social security number on their application. This did not become a holding of the Court because one of the five Justices supporting the result concluded that this aspect of the case had become moot."

c. See also Douglas Laycock, *Formal, Substantive, and Disaggregated Neutrality Toward Religion,* 39 De Paul L.Rev. 993, 1016 (1990): "Of course, inadvertence can interact with hostility, or with an insensitivity that borders on hostility. Consider what might happen when Frances Quaring [fn. f supra] writes her legislator. She may get a sympathetic response and a legislated exemption. But her legislator may find it so impossible to empathize with her belief that he never seriously considers whether an exemption would be workable. Even if he

empathizes, the legislative calendar is crowded, and the original statute having been enacted, all the burdens of legislative inertia now work against an exemption."

Compare Eisengruber & Sager, supra, at 1304: "[After *Lyng,*] the political process responded to interests the judiciary had not protected, and the Bureau of Land Management relocated the road. [After *Lee,*] Congress accommodated churches that had religious objections to participating in the social security system. [After *Goldman,*] Congress granted relief. And [after *Smith,*] Oregon legislated an exemption to its law," and Congress protected religious use of peyote in all states. But contrast Dhananjai Shivakumar, *Neutrality and the Religion Clauses,* 33 Harv. Civ. Rts.—Civ. Lib. L. Rev. 505, 512 n. 28 (1998): "The rejection of meaningful judicial review will deprive free exercise claimants of one historically effective way of eliciting attention and public support in cases where substantial burdens are borne, namely, litigation. Many well-known examples of political accommodation were preceded by lengthy, well-publicized free exercise litigation."

extent possible in a pluralistic society. For the Court to deem this command a "luxury," is to denigrate "[t]he very purpose of a Bill of Rights."

III. The Court's holding today not only misreads settled First Amendment precedent; it appears to be unnecessary to this case. I would reach the same result applying our established free exercise jurisprudence.

There is no dispute that Oregon's criminal prohibition of peyote places a severe burden on the ability of respondents to freely exercise their religion. Peyote is a sacrament of the Native American Church and is regarded as vital to respondents' ability to practice their religion. * * *

There is also no dispute that Oregon has a significant interest in enforcing laws that control the possession and use of controlled substances by its citizens. [Indeed,] under federal law (incorporated by Oregon law in relevant part), peyote is specifically regulated as a Schedule I controlled substance, which means that Congress has found that it has a high potential for abuse, that there is no currently accepted medical use, and that there is a lack of accepted safety for use of the drug under medical supervision. In light of our recent decisions holding that the governmental interests in the collection of income tax, *Hernandez,* a comprehensive social security system, see *Lee,* and military conscription, see *Gillette,* are compelling, respondents do not seriously dispute that Oregon has a compelling interest in prohibiting the possession of peyote by its citizens.

[Although] the question is close, I would conclude that uniform application of Oregon's criminal prohibition is "essential to accomplish," *Lee,* its overriding interest in preventing the physical harm caused by the use of a Schedule I controlled substance. [Because] the health effects caused by the use of controlled substances exist regardless of the motivation of the user, the use of such substances, even for religious purposes, violates the very purpose of the laws that prohibit them. Moreover, in view of the societal interest in preventing trafficking in controlled substances, uniform application of the criminal prohibition at issue is essential to the effectiveness of Oregon's stated interest in preventing any possession of peyote. * * *

Respondents contend that any incompatibility is belied by the fact that the Federal Government and several States provide exemptions for the religious use of peyote. But other governments may surely choose to grant an exemption without Oregon, with its specific asserted interest in uniform application of its drug laws, being *required* to do so by the First Amendment. Respondents also note that the sacramental use of peyote is central to the tenets of the Native American Church, but I agree with the Court [that] "[i]t is not within the judicial ken to question the centrality of particular beliefs or practices to a faith." [This] does not mean, of course, that courts may not make factual findings as to whether a claimant holds a sincerely held religious belief that conflicts with, and thus is burdened by, the challenged law. The distinction between questions of centrality and questions of sincerity and burden is admittedly fine, but it is one that is an established part of our free exercise doctrine * * *.[d]

d. In *Boerne v. Flores,* Ch. 11, Sec. 3, O'Connor, J., joined by Breyer, J., argued that "the historical evidence [bears] out the conclusion that, at the time the Bill of Rights was ratified, it was accepted that government should, when possible, accommodate religious practice." Scalia, J., joined by Stevens, J., disagreed: "The historical evidence put forward by the dissent does nothing to undermine the conclusion we reached in *Smith.*" For an extensive review, see Michael W. McConnell, *Freedom From Persecution or Protection of the Rights of Conscience?: A Critique of Justice Scalia's Historical Arguments,* 39 Wm. & M. L. Rev. 819 (1998). For support at the time of the fourteenth amendment for O'Connor, J.'s position, see Kurt T. Lash, *The Second Adoption of the Free Exercise Clause: Religious Exemptions*

JUSTICE BLACKMUN, with whom JUSTICE BRENNAN and JUSTICE MARSHALL join, dissenting.

This Court over the years painstakingly has developed a consistent and exacting standard to test the constitutionality of a state statute that burdens the free exercise of religion. Such a statute may stand only if the law in general, and the State's refusal to allow a religious exemption in particular, are justified by a compelling interest that cannot be served by less restrictive means.

[I]t is important to articulate in precise terms the state interest involved. It is not the State's broad interest in fighting the critical "war on drugs" that must be weighed against respondents' claim, but the State's narrow interest in refusing to make an exception for the religious, ceremonial use of peyote. [The] State cannot plausibly assert that unbending application of a criminal prohibition is essential to fulfill any compelling interest, if it does not, in fact, attempt to enforce that prohibition. * * * Oregon has never sought to prosecute respondents, and does not claim that it has made significant enforcement efforts against other religious users of peyote. The State's asserted interest thus amounts only to the symbolic preservation of an unenforced prohibition. * * *

Similarly, this Court's prior decisions have not allowed a government to rely on mere speculation about potential harms, but have demanded evidentiary support for a refusal to allow a religious exception. [In] this case, the State [offers] no evidence that the religious use of peyote has ever harmed anyone. The factual findings of other courts cast doubt on the State's assumption that religious use of peyote is harmful. See *State v. Whittingham,* 19 Ariz.App. 27, 30, 504 P.2d 950, 953 (1973) ("the State failed to prove that the quantities of peyote used in the sacraments of the Native American Church are sufficiently harmful to the health and welfare of the participants so as to permit a legitimate intrusion under the State's police power"); *People v. Woody,* 61 Cal.2d 716, 722–723, 40 Cal.Rptr. 69, 74, 394 P.2d 813, 818 (1964) ("as the Attorney General [admits,] the opinion of scientists and other experts is 'that peyote [works] no permanent deleterious injury to the Indian' ").

The fact that peyote is classified as a Schedule I controlled substance does not, by itself, show that any and all uses of peyote, in any circumstance, are inherently harmful and dangerous. The Federal Government [does] not find peyote so dangerous as to preclude an exemption for religious use.[5] Moreover, other Schedule I drugs have lawful uses. See *Olsen v. Drug Enforcement Administration,* 878 F.2d 1458 (D.C.Cir.1989) (medical and research uses of marijuana).

The carefully circumscribed ritual context in which respondents used peyote is far removed from the irresponsible and unrestricted recreational use of unlawful drugs.[6] * * * *[7]

Under the Fourteenth Amendment, *88 Nw. U.L.Rev. 1106, 1149–55 (1994).*

5. [Moreover,] 23 States, including many that have significant Native American populations, have statutory or judicially crafted exemptions in their drug laws for religious use of peyote.

6. In this respect, respondents' use of peyote seems closely analogous to the sacramental use of wine by the Roman Catholic Church. During Prohibition, the Federal Government

exempted such use of wine from its general ban on possession and use of alcohol. However compelling the Government's then general interest in prohibiting the use of alcohol may have been, it could not plausibly have asserted an interest sufficiently compelling to outweigh Catholics' right to take communion.

7. The use of peyote is, to some degree, self-limiting. The peyote plant is extremely bitter, and eating it is an unpleasant experience, which would tend to discourage casual or recreational use.

Moreover, just as in *Yoder,* the values and interests of those seeking a religious exemption in this case are congruent, to a great degree, with those the State seeks to promote through its drug laws. See *Yoder* (since the Amish accept formal schooling up to 8th grade, and then provide "ideal" vocational education, State's interest in enforcing its law against the Amish is "less substantial than [for] children generally"). Not only does the Church's doctrine forbid nonreligious use of peyote; it also generally advocates self-reliance, familial responsibility, and abstinence from alcohol. There is considerable evidence that the spiritual and social support provided by the Church has been effective in combatting the tragic effects of alcoholism on the Native American population. * * *

The State also seeks to support its refusal to make an exception [by] invoking its interest in abolishing drug trafficking. There is, however, practically no illegal traffic in peyote. Also, the availability of peyote for religious use, even if Oregon were to allow an exemption from its criminal laws, would still be strictly controlled by federal regulations, see 21 U.S.C. §§ 821–823 (registration requirements for distribution of controlled substances); and by the State of Texas, the only State in which peyote grows in significant quantities. Peyote simply is not a popular drug; its distribution for use in religious rituals has nothing to do with the vast and violent traffic in illegal narcotics that plagues this country.

Finally, the State argues that, [if] it grants an exemption for religious peyote use, a flood of other claims to religious exemptions will follow. It would then be placed in a dilemma, it says, between allowing a patchwork of exemptions that would hinder its law enforcement efforts, and risking a violation of the Establishment Clause by arbitrarily limiting its religious exemptions. [But almost] half the States, and the Federal Government, have maintained an exemption for religious peyote use for many years, and apparently have not found themselves overwhelmed by claims to other religious exemptions.[8] Allowing an exemption for religious peyote use would not necessarily oblige the State to grant a similar exemption to other religious groups. The unusual circumstances that make the religious use of peyote compatible with the State's interests in health and safety and in preventing drug trafficking would not apply to other religious claims. Some religions, for example, might not restrict drug use to a limited ceremonial context, as does the Native American Church. See, e.g., *Olsen* ("the Ethiopian Zion Coptic Church [teaches] that marijuana is properly smoked 'continually all day' "). Some religious claims involve drugs such as marijuana and heroin, in which there is significant illegal traffic, with its attendant greed and violence, so that it would be difficult to grant a religious exemption without seriously compromising law enforcement efforts.[9] [Though] the State must treat all religions equally, and not favor one over another, this obligation is fulfilled by the uniform application of the "compelling interest" *test* to all free exercise claims, not by reaching uniform *results* as to all claims. * * *

Respondents believe, and their sincerity has *never* been at issue, that the peyote plant embodies their deity, and eating it is an act of worship and communion. Without peyote, they could not enact the essential ritual of their religion. [This] potentially devastating impact must be viewed in light of the

8. Over the years, various sects have raised free exercise claims regarding drug use. In no reported case, except those involving claims of religious peyote use, has the claimant prevailed.

9. Thus, this case is distinguishable from *Lee,* in which the Court concluded that there was "no principled way" to distinguish other exemption claims, and the "tax system could not function if denominations were allowed to challenge the tax system because tax payments were spent in a manner that violates their religious belief."

federal policy—reached in reaction to many years of religious persecution and intolerance—of protecting the religious freedom of Native Americans. See American Indian Religious Freedom Act. * * *[a]

Notes and Questions

1. *Discrimination.* (a) CHURCH OF THE LUKUMI BABALU AYE, INC. v. HIALEAH, 508 U.S. 520, 113 S.Ct. 2217, 124 L.Ed.2d 472 (1993), per KENNEDY, J., held that city ordinances barring ritual animal sacrifice violated the free exercise clause: "[I]f the object of a law is to infringe upon or restrict practices because of their religious motivation, the law is not neutral, see *Smith;* and it is invalid unless it is justified by a compelling interest and is narrowly tailored to advance that interest. [The] ordinances had as their object the suppression of [the Santeria] religion. The [record] discloses animosity to Santeria adherents and their religious practices; the ordinances by their own terms target this religious exercise; the texts of the ordinances were gerrymandered with care to proscribe religious killings of animals but to exclude almost all secular killings; and the ordinances suppress much more religious conduct than is necessary in order to achieve the legitimate ends asserted in their defense. [A] law that targets religious conduct for distinctive treatment or advances legitimate governmental interests only against conduct with a religious motivation will survive strict scrutiny only in rare cases. It follows from what we have already said that these ordinances cannot withstand this scrutiny."

SOUTER, J., concurred specially "for I have doubts whether the *Smith* rule merits adherence": Because "*Smith* refrained from overruling prior free-exercise cases that [are] fundamentally at odds with the rule *Smith* declared, [in] a case presenting the issue, the Court should re-examine the rule *Smith* declared."

BLACKMUN, J., joined by O'Connor, J., concurred only in the judgment: "I continue to believe that *Smith* was wrongly decided, because It Ignored the value of religious freedom as an affirmative individual liberty and treated the Free Exercise Clause as no more than an antidiscrimination principle." Moreover, "when a law discriminates against religion as such, as do the ordinances in this case, it automatically will fail strict scrutiny [because] a law that targets religious practice for disfavored treatment both burdens the free exercise of religion and, by definition, is not precisely tailored to a compelling governmental interest.[a]

"[This] case does not present [the] question whether the Free Exercise Clause would require a religious exemption from a law that sincerely pursued the goal of protecting animals from cruel treatment. [That] is not a concern to be treated lightly."

a. In 1993, Congress passed the Religious Freedom Restoration Act which effectively re-instated the *Sherbert-Yoder* test for generally applicable laws that burden religious practices. RFRA was held unconstitutional in *Boerne v. Flores*, Ch. 11, Sec. 2.

For the view that the "core meaning of the Establishment Clause" prevents congressional efforts "to regulate matters of faith directly or to tell states what relation their laws must have to the fostering of one or all religions," which "means that Congress may not try to dictate church-state relations even to vindicate religious toleration or free exercise," see Jed Rubenfeld, *Antidisestablishmentarianism: Why RFRA Really Was Unconstitutional*, 95 Mich. L.Rev. 2347 (1997).

a. See also James D. Gordon III, *The New Free Exercise Clause*, 26 Cap.U.L.Rev. 65, 89, 92 (1997): "[I]f a law restricts only religious conduct, it exempts nonreligious conduct that produces the same harm. The government cannot have a compelling interest in denying a religious exemption, because it already has shown its willingness to exempt everyone else. [Therefore,] the compelling interest test adds nothing to the analysis."

(b) *Scope*. Does the *Smith-Lukumi* rule bar only those laws whose "object is suppression" of a religious practice, or that "target religious conduct"? After *Lukumi*, what result in *Smith* if Oregon had permitted the medicinal use of peyote (or marijuana) in designated circumstances to relieve pain? Would the law barring other uses of peyote (including sacramental use) be "generally applicable"? Would it "target religious conduct"? Of what relevance is *Smith's* reaffirmation of *Sherbert's* "individualized governmental assessment" context? Consider Frederick M. Gedicks, *The Normalized Free Exercise Clause: Three Abnormalities*, 75 Ind. L.J. 77, 117–120 (2000): "[T]he free exercise of religion is a fundamental right, the protection of which is specified by the constitutional text [but] the Court is not treating free exercise rights like privacy, speech, travel, and other fundamental rights. [What] fundamental rights/equal protection analysis [Ch. 9, Sec. 5] requires in the context of incidental burdens on religion is that religious conduct be exempted from a law whenever exemption of such conduct would not present a substantially greater threat to the purpose of the law than already-exempt secular conduct. Fundamental rights/equal protection analysis makes clear that any law or government action that excuses—by administrative exemption, legislative exemption, or otherwise—one or more secular activities but not *comparable* religious practices creates a classification that impermissibly burdens the fundamental right of free exercise of religion, and thus should normally be subject to strict scrutiny."

What result under the *Smith-Lukumi* rule if a state prohibits *all* polygamous marriages after a religious group that engages in the practice becomes active in the state? See Garrett Epps, *What We Talk About When We Talk About Free Exercise*, 30 Ariz.St.L.J. 563 (1998). Is this any different than Hialeah's ordinances? For the view that there should be no free exercise violation if a law serves "a substantial secular purpose" regardless of its motivation, see Lino A. Graglia, *Church of the Lukumi Babalu Aye: Of Animal Sacrifice and Religious Persecution*, 85 Geo.L.J. 1 (1996): "[Hialeah's] only complaint against the church was that it conducted animal slaughtering exhibitions, and there is no reason to doubt the district judge's finding [that] the ordinances were 'not targeted at the Church of the Lukumi Babalu Aye, [but] meant to prohibit all animal sacrifice, whether it be practiced by an individual, a religion, or a cult.' [I]t applied equally [to] all other exhibitionistic killings, like those that are sometimes performed by entertainers or as part of college fraternity or other initiation ceremonies."

If a state bars ingestion of all alcoholic beverages but exempts sacramental use, may it bar ingestion of all hallucinogenic substances without exempting sacramental use? See Michael J. Perry, *Freedom of Religion in the United States: Fin de Siècle Sketches*, 75 Ind.L.J. 295, 305 (2000).

2. *Aid to parochial schools*. Is the Court's statement, that denial of financial benefits to parochial schools does not infringe the free exercise rights of attending children,[b] consistent with *Sherbert, Thomas* and *Hobbie*? With *Smith* and *Lukumi*? Could a student bus transportation program include all nonprofit private schools except parochial schools? See *Luetkemeyer v. Kaufmann*, 419 U.S. 888, 95 S.Ct. 167, 42 L.Ed.2d 134 (1974). Would affording aid to *all* schools (public and nonpublic) *except* those that are church-related "target religious conduct" (*Lukumi*)? Consider Jesse H. Choper, *Federal Constitutional Issues*, in School Choice and Social Controversy 235, 249 (Sugarman & Kemerer eds. 1999): "First, such a

---

b. See the dictum in *Sloan v. Lemon*, 413 U.S. 825, 93 S.Ct. 2982, 37 L.Ed.2d 939 (1973): "[V]alid aid to nonpublic, nonsectarian schools would provide no lever for aid to their sectarian counterparts."

program would plainly discriminate on its face against 'some or all religious beliefs,' violating the basic protections of the Free Exercise Clause, unless justified after strict scrutiny. Second, since all schools teach values, the state could be fairly seen as discriminating against religious viewpoints, much as the University of Virginia had done in *Rosenberger*, and would also be subject to strict scrutiny under the Free Speech Clause [see Ch.7, Sec. 1]. Unless Establishment Clause concerns with providing support to parochial schools are found to present a compelling government interest, both *Lukumi* and *Rosenberger* would appear to compel the inclusion of religious schools in any voucher program or other plan of aid to education that included nonreligious private schools."

Indeed, might it be argued that *Sherbert* would require aid for parochial schools even though public support was given only to public schools? If some religions impose a duty on parents to send children to religious schools, may these parents argue that, since they must pay public school taxes, the state's failure to support parochial as well as public schools imposes a serious financial burden on their exercise of religion? That "conditioning the availability of benefits upon their willingness to violate a cardinal principle of their religious faith effectively penalizes the free exercise of their constitutional liberties" (*Sherbert*); that there is no "compelling state interest to justify the substantial infringement of their First Amendment rights"? May these parents further argue that their position is stronger than *Sherbert*, *Thomas* and *Hobbie* because the purpose of granting an exemption in that case was *solely* to aid religion whereas there is a wholly nonreligious purpose in giving aid to all nonpublic schools—improving the quality of the secular education? What result after *Smith*? See Choper, supra, at 246-48.

3. *Balancing process.* Of what significance is it that all the decisions sustaining free exercise claims against government regulations of conduct (*Sherbert—Thomas—Hobbie, Yoder* and *Roy*) involved religious refusal to engage in conduct required by government rather than religiously dictated action forbidden by the state? What results in respect to the religiously mandated *inaction* in the following: (a) Citing for contempt person who refuses to serve on jury. See *In re Jenison*, 265 Minn. 96, 120 N.W.2d 515 (1963), vacated, 375 U.S. 14, 84 S.Ct. 63, 11 L.Ed.2d 39 (1963), reversed, 267 Minn. 136, 125 N.W.2d 588 (1963); (b) Statute requiring smallpox vaccination applied to person whose religion forbids medicinal aids. See *Jacobson v. Massachusetts*, 197 U.S. 11, 25 S.Ct. 358, 49 L.Ed. 643 (1905); (c) Court order of blood transfusion, to save life of pregnant mother and child, for woman of Jehovah's Witness faith which obligates adherents to "abstain from blood." Suppose the woman were not pregnant but had infant children? See *Application of Georgetown College, Inc.*, 331 F.2d 1000 (D.C.Cir.1964), cert. denied, 377 U.S. 978, 84 S.Ct. 1883, 12 L.Ed.2d 746 (1964). Suppose the woman were neither pregnant nor had any children? Suppose there were only a slight chance that the transfusion would save the life? That the woman is a brilliant scientist whose work is vital to national security? Suppose the transfusion is thought necessary not to preserve life but to bring back to good health? (d) School board's refusal to exempt children of "born again Christian" parents from using textbooks with subjects—such as "secular humanism," "pacifism," "magic," and "women's achievements outside the home"—that were contrary to their religious beliefs. See *Mozert v. Hawkins County Bd. of Educ.*, 827 F.2d 1058 (6th Cir. 1987), cert. denied, 484 U.S. 1066 (1988), discussed in Stephen L. Carter, *Culture of Disbelief* 168–76, 191–92 (1993). If the subject matter in a textbook (or a course) is contrary to children's religious beliefs, does *exposure* to the material (in the textbook or the course) impose a "substantial" enough burden to trigger the free exercise clause? See Gary J. Simson & Erika A. Sussman, *Keeping the Sex in Sex*

Education: The First Amendment's Religion Clauses and the Sex Education Debate, 9 S.Cal. Rev. L. & Women's Studies 265 (2000).

4. *Willingness of others.* In the case of *action* due to religious beliefs, should a distinction be drawn between action that is requested by the people affected and action that is imposed on others? Should the conviction of a religious Spiritualist for fortune telling be sustained despite the fact that fortunes were told only upon request? If not, how do you distinguish the polygamy cases?[c]

II. UNUSUAL RELIGIOUS BELIEFS AND PRACTICES

1. *Validity and sincerity.* In UNITED STATES v. BALLARD, 322 U.S. 78, 64 S.Ct. 882, 88 L.Ed. 1148 (1944), defendant was indicted for mail fraud. He had solicited funds for the "I Am" movement, asserting, inter alia, that he had been selected as a divine messenger, had the divine power of healing incurable diseases, and had talked with Jesus and would transmit these conversations to mankind. The Court, per DOUGLAS, J., held that the first amendment barred submitting to the jury the question of whether these religious beliefs were true: "Men may believe what they cannot [prove.] Religious experiences which are as real as life to some may be incomprehensible to others. [The] miracles of the New Testament, the Divinity of Christ, life after death, the power of prayer are deep in the religious convictions of many. If one could be sent to jail because a jury in a hostile environment found those teachings false, little indeed would be left of religious freedom."

(a) *Ballard* permits the prosecution to prove that, irrespective of whether the incidents described by defendant happened, he did not honestly believe that they had? If so, may the prosecution introduce evidence that the incidents did not in fact happen and that therefore defendant could not honestly believe that they did? Should this line of proof be permitted in the prosecution of an official of the Catholic church for soliciting funds to construct a shrine commemorating the Miracle of Fatima in 1930?

(b) Is it relevant that in *Ballard* the alleged divine revelation was made to defendant himself? Would it be material if the experiences had allegedly occurred at a definite time and place? Many Biblical happenings are so identified. Could the prosecution introduce evidence that Ballard was not physically present at the alleged place at the alleged time? If Protestant, Catholic or Jewish clergy were prosecuted and there was overwhelming scientific evidence disputing the Biblical doctrine, what would the jury be likely to find as to the honesty of the beliefs? Should the first amendment permit people to obtain money in the name of religion by knowingly making false statements? See Tribe 2d ed., at 1243–47.

(c) Should the prosecution be able to prove that defendant had stated on many occasions that he believed none of his representations but that by saying that he did he was amassing great wealth? Suppose it can be shown that a priest or rabbi is *somewhat* skeptical as to the truth of certain Biblical occurrences? See John T. Noonan, Jr., *How Sincere Do You Have to Be to Be Religious*, 1988 U.Ill.L.Rev. 713. Could Ballard be convicted on the ground that fraudulent procurement of money, just like polygamy, is conduct which may be constitutionally prohibited even if done in the name of religion?

c. For several recent approaches that evaluate a wide range of factors in considering religious exemptions from generally applicable laws, see Eugene Volokh, *A Common–Law Model for Religious Exemptions*, 46 UCLA L.Rev. 1465 (1999); Eugene Volokh, *Intermediate Questions of Religious Exemptions—A Research Agenda with Test Suites*, 21 Card.L.Rev. 595 (1999); Jesse H. Choper, *Securing Religious Liberty* ch. 3 (1995).

2. *What is "religion"?* May the Court determine that asserted religious beliefs and practices do not constitute a valid religion? Consider Jonathan Weiss, *Privilege, Posture and Protection—"Religion" in the Law*, 73 Yale L.J. 593, 604 (1964): "[A]ny definition of religion would seem to violate religious freedom in that it would dictate to religions, present and future, what they must [be]. Furthermore, an attempt to define religion, even for purposes of increasing freedom for religions, would run afoul of the 'establishment' clause as excluding some religions, or even as establishing a notion respecting religion."

Is it relevant that the beliefs of a group do not include the existence of God? TORCASO v. WATKINS, per BLACK, J., 367 U.S. 488, 81 S.Ct. 1680, 6 L.Ed.2d 982 (1961), invalidating a Maryland provision requiring a declaration of belief in the existence of God as a test for public office, stated: "Neither [a state nor the federal government can] impose requirements which aid all religions as against nonbelievers, and neither can aid those religions based on a belief in the existence of God as against those religions founded on different beliefs." The Court noted that "among religions in this country which do not teach what would generally be considered a belief in the existence of God are Buddhism, Taoism, Ethical Culture, Secular Humanism and others."

What if the Communist Party claimed religious status? Consider Paul G. Kauper, *Religion and the Constitution* 31 (1964): "What makes secular humanism a religion? Is it because it is an ideology or system of belief that attempts to furnish a rationale of life? But if any ideology, creed, or philosophy respecting man and society is a religion, then must not democracy, fascism, and communism also qualify as religions? It is not uncommon to refer to these as secular or quasi religions, for some find in these systems an adequate explanation of the meaning and purpose of life and the source of values that command faith and devotion. Certainly in the case of communism, with its discipline, its cultus, its sense of community, and its obligation to duties owing to the system, the resemblance to religion in the conventional sense is [clear]."

May a single person establish his or her own religion? Consider Milton Konvitz, *Religious Liberty and Conscience* 84 (1968): "[Many religions] had their origin in a 'private and personal' religious experience. Mohammed did not take over an on-going, established religion; the history of Islam records the names of his first three converts. John Wesley is given credit as the founder of Methodism. Mrs. Mary Baker Eddy was the founder of the Christian Science church. Menno Simons organized a division of Anabaptists that in due course became the sect known as the Mennonites. Jacob Ammon broke away from the Mennonites and founded the sect known as the Amish."

How important is it that the group has regular weekly services? Designated leaders who conduct these services? Ceremonies for naming, marrying and burying members? Does the first amendment extend only to those groups that conform to the "conventional" concept of religion? Consider Harvey Cox (Harvard Divinity School), N.Y. Times 25 (Feb. 16, 1977): "[C]ourts [often] turn to some vague 'man-in-the-street' idea of what 'religion' should be. [But] a man-in-the-street approach would surely have ruled out early Christianity, which seemed both subversive and atheistic to the religious Romans of the day. The truth is that one man's 'bizarre cult' is another's true path to salvation, and the Bill of Rights was designed to safeguard minorities from the man-on-the-street's uncertain capacity for tolerance. The new challenge to our pluralism often comes from Oriental religious movements, because their views of religion differ so fundamentally from ours." To what extent should a group's "brainwashing," mental coercion techniques affect its constitutional status as a "religion"? Compare Richard Delgado, *Religious Totalism: Gentle and Ungentle Persuasion Under the First Amendment,* 51 So.Cal.L.Rev. 1 (1977) with Note, *Conservatorship and Religious Cults: Divining A Theory of Free Exercise,* 53 N.Y.U.L.Rev. 1247 (1978).

Suppose that a group has certain characteristics of "traditional" religions, such as a holy book, ministers, houses of worship, prescribed prayers, a strict moral code, a belief in the hereafter and an appeal to faith, but also has announced social and economic tenets? (Methodism developed originally out of social concerns.) Consider Note, *Toward a Constitutional Definition of Religion,* 91 Harv.L.Rev. 1056, 1069 (1978): "[A] spokesman for the new 'liberation theology' within Catholicism argues that true religion is to be found in liberation 'as the creation of a new social consciousness and as a social appropriation not only of the means of production, but also of the political processes.' The church, he says, seeks 'the abolition of the exploitation of man by man.' The views of these and other significant Christian theologians coalesce around one important theme: the Christian church will find itself only by discarding what until now has been perceived to be religious and by immersing itself in the secular world." Does the first amendment encompass any political, philosophical, moral or social doctrine that some group honestly espouses as its religion?

UNITED STATES v. SEEGER, 380 U.S. 163, 85 S.Ct. 850, 13 L.Ed.2d 733 (1965), interpreted § 6(j) of the Universal Military Training and Service Act, which exempted from combat any person "who, by reason of religious training and belief, is conscientiously opposed to participation in war in any form. Religious training and belief in this connection means an individual's belief in a relation to a Supreme Being involving duties superior to those arising from any human relation, but does not include essentially political, sociological or philosophical views or a merely personal moral code."[a] The Court, per CLARK, J., avoided constitutional questions and upheld claims for exemption of three conscientious objectors. One declared "that he preferred to leave the question as to his belief in a Supreme Being open, [and] that his was a 'belief in and devotion to goodness and virtue for their own sakes, and a religious faith in a purely ethical creed.' " another said "that he felt it a violation of his moral code to take human life and that he considered this belief superior to his obligation to the state. As to whether his conviction was religious, he quoted with approval Reverend John Haynes Holmes' definition of religion as 'the consciousness of some power manifest in nature which helps man in the ordering of his life in harmony with its demands * * *; it is man thinking his highest, feeling his deepest, and living his best.' The source of his conviction he attributed to reading and meditation 'in our democratic American culture, with its values derived from the western religious and philosophical tradition.' As to his belief in a supreme being, peter stated that he supposed 'you could call that a belief in the Supreme Being or God. These just do not happen to be the words I use.' "

The Court "concluded that Congress, in using the expression 'Supreme Being' rather than the designation 'God,' was merely clarifying the meaning of religious training and belief so as to embrace all religions and to exclude essentially political, sociological, or philosophical views [and that] the test of belief 'in a

---

a. The statute was subsequently amended to omit the "belief in a Supreme Being" element. For the view that "religion" under the first amendment "involves some conception of God," see Michael S. Paulsen, *God is Great, Garvey is Good: Making Sense of Religious* *Freedom,* 72 Not.D.L.Rev. 1597, 1623 (1997): "Text and historical evidence of original meaning should settle the matter. If this seems illiberal today, that is unfortunate, but irrelevant to the task of textual interpretation of the constitutional provision the framers wrote."

relation to a Supreme Being' is whether a given belief that is sincere and meaningful occupies a place in the life of its possessor parallel to that filled by the orthodox belief in God of one who clearly qualifies for the exemption. [No] party claims to be an atheist * * *. We do not deal with or intimate any decision on that situation in these cases. [The] use by Congress of the words 'merely personal' seems to us to restrict the exception to a moral code which [is] in no way related to a Supreme Being. [Congress did] not distinguish between externally and internally derived beliefs. Such a determination [would] prove impossible as a practical matter."

In WELSH v. UNITED STATES, 398 U.S. 333, 90 S.Ct. 1792, 26 L.Ed.2d 308 (1970), petitioner, in his application for exemption, "struck the word 'religious' entirely and later characterized his beliefs as having been formed 'by reading in the fields of history and sociology.'" BLACK, J., joined by Douglas, Brennan and Marshall, JJ., held that, under *Seeger*, "if an individual deeply and sincerely holds beliefs which are purely ethical or moral in source and content but that nevertheless impose upon him a duty of conscience to refrain from participating in any war at any time, those beliefs certainly occupy in the life of that individual 'a place parallel to that filled [by] God' in traditionally religious persons." "Although [Welsh] originally characterized his beliefs as nonreligious, he later upon reflection wrote a long and thoughtful letter to his Appeal Board in which he declared that his beliefs were 'certainly religious in the ethical sense of that word.' * * * § 6(j)'s exclusion of those persons with 'essentially political, sociological, or philosophical views or a merely personal moral code' should [not] be read to exclude those who hold strong beliefs about our domestic and foreign affairs or even those whose conscientious objection to participation in all wars is founded to a substantial extent upon considerations of public policy. The two groups of registrants which obviously do fall within these exclusions from the exemption are those whose beliefs are not deeply held and those whose objection to war does not rest at all upon moral, ethical, or religious principle but instead rests solely upon considerations of policy, pragmatism, or expediency."[b]

3. *What is "religious belief"?* (a) Of what significance is it that the practice is an "age-old form" of religious conduct (*Murdock*)? Is a "cardinal principle" of the asserted religious faith (*Sherbert*)? Consider Laycock, fn. d, p. 1040 supra, at 1390–91: "Many activities that obviously are exercises of religion are not required by conscience or doctrine. Singing in the church choir and saying the Roman Catholic rosary are two common examples. Any activity engaged in by a church as a body is an exercise of religion. [Indeed,] many would say that an emphasis on rules and obligations misconceives the essential nature of some religions." Compare Donald Giannella, *Religious Liberty, Nonestablishment, and Doctrinal Developments—Part I. The Religious Liberty Guarantee*, 80 Harv.L.Rev. 1381, 1427–28 (1967): "Personal alienation from one's Maker, frustration of one's ultimate mission in life, and violation of the religious person's integrity are all at stake when the right to worship is threatened. Although the seeker of new psychological worlds [through use of hallucinogens] may feel equally frustrated when deprived of his gropings for a higher reality, there is not the same sense of acute loss—the loss of the Be-all and End-all of life. [A] different problem presents itself when an individual who does not believe in a supernatural or personal God asserts

---

b. In separate opinions, Harlan, J., and White, J., (joined by Burger, C.J., and Stewart, J.) dissented on the issue of statutory construction. For their views on the constitutional issue, see Sec. 4 infra.

See generally Note, *The Sacred and the Profane: A First Amendment Definition of Religion*, 61 Tex.L.Rev. 139 (1982). For criticism of "sincerity," see Comment, *The Legal Relationship of Conscience to Religion: Refusals to Bear Arms*, 38 U.Chi.L.Rev. 583 (1971).

conscientious objection to certain conduct because of its injurious effects on his fellow man. [T]his ethical belief may be held with such a degree of intensity that its violation occasions the same interior revulsion and anguish as does violation of the law of God to the pious." Under this approach, on what evidence should these factual questions be determined? Suppose a drug-use defendant claims "that its use was essential to attain a unique level of spiritual consciousness [and] compared the effect of depriving him of marihuana with that of forbidding a Catholic to celebrate the Mass"? Joel J. Finer, *Psychedelics and Religious Freedom*, 19 Hast.L.J. 667, 692 (1968).

For the view that "belief [in] 'extratemporal consequences'—whether the effects of actions taken pursuant or contrary to the dictates of a person's beliefs extend in some meaningful way beyond his lifetime—is a sensible and desirable criterion (albeit plainly far short of ideal) for determining when the free exercise clause should trigger judicial consideration of whether an exemption from general government regulations of conduct is constitutionally required," see Jesse H. Choper, *Defining "Religion" in the First Amendment*, 1982 U.Ill.L.Rev. 579, 599, 603–04:[c] "It may be persuasively argued that *all* beliefs that invoke a transcendent reality—and especially those that provide their adherents with glimpses of meaning and truth that make them so important and so uncompromisable— should be encompassed by the special constitutional protection granted 'religion' by the free exercise clause. [In] many ways, however, transcendental explanations of worldly realities are essentially no different [than] conventional exegeses for temporal outcomes that are based on such 'rational' disciplines as economics, political science, sociology, or psychology, or even such 'hard' sciences [as] physics. When justifying competing government policies on such varied matters as social welfare, the economy, and military and foreign affairs, there is at bedrock only a gossamer line between 'rational' and 'supernatural' causation—the former really being little more capable of 'scientific proof' than the latter. [Therefore, government's] plenary authority to regulate the worldly affairs of society [should] not be restricted because of the nature of the causes, which are all basically unverifiable, that different groups believe will produce consequences that the state seeks to achieve."[d] Compare Kent Greenawalt, *Religion as a Concept in Constitutional Law*, 72 Calif.L.Rev. 753, 763, 815 (1984): "No specification of essential conditions will capture all and only the beliefs, practices, and organizations that are regarded as religious in modern culture and should be treated as such under the Constitution. [Rather, determining] whether questionable beliefs, practices, and organizations are religious by seeing how closely they resemble what is undeniably religious is a method that has been implicitly used by courts in difficult borderline cases [and] is consonant with Supreme Court decisions."[e]

(b) *Judicial role.* In THOMAS v. REVIEW BD., Part I supra, petitioner testified that, although his religious convictions forbade him to manufacture

---

c. For criticism of this view, see Stanley Ingber, *Religion or Ideology: A Needed Clarification of the Religion Clauses*, 41 Stan.L.Rev. 233, 274–77 (1989); Note, *Religion and Morality Legislation: A Reexamination of Establishment Clause Analysis*, 59 N.Y.U.L.Rev. 301, 346–52 (1984); Note, *Defining "Religion" in the First Amendment: A Functional Approach*, 74 Corn.L.Rev. 532 (1989).

d. For the view that religion should be defined as dealing only with "quintessentially religious questions," "addressing the profound questions of human existence," "such as God's existence or the proper definition of life and death," see Tom Stacy, *Death, Privacy, and the Free Exercise of Religion*, 77 Corn.L.Rev. 490 (1992).

e. Accord, George C. Freeman, III, *The Misguided Search for the Constitutional Definition of "Religion,"* 71 Geo.L.J. 1519 (1983). See also Eduardo Peñalver, *The Concept of Religion*, 107 Yale L.J. 791 (1997) (supporting "analogical" approach that "takes into account the evolutionary nature of language" and "tries to minimize the scope for [western] judicial bias").

weapons, "he could, in good conscience, engage indirectly in the production, [for] example, as an employee of a raw material supplier." The state court, viewing petitioner's positions as inconsistent, ruled that "Thomas had made a merely 'personal philosophical choice rather than a religious choice.'" The Court, per BURGER, C.J. reversed: "The determination of what is a 'religious' belief or practice is more often than not a difficult and delicate task, [but] resolution of that question is not to turn upon a judicial perception of the particular belief or practice in question; religious beliefs need not be acceptable, logical, consistent, or comprehensible to others in order to merit First Amendment protection. * * * Thomas drew a line and it is not for us to say that the line he drew was an unreasonable one. Courts should not undertake to dissect religious beliefs because the believer admits that he is 'struggling' with his position or because his beliefs are not articulated with the clarity and precision that a more sophisticated person might employ.

"The Indiana court also appears to have given significant weight to the fact that another Jehovah's Witness had no scruples about working on tank turrets; for that other Witness, at least, such work was 'scripturally' acceptable. Intra-faith differences of that kind are not uncommon [and] the judicial process is singularly ill equipped to resolve such differences in relation to the Religion Clauses. [The] narrow function of a reviewing court in this context is to determine whether there was an appropriate finding that petitioner terminated his work because of an honest conviction that such work was forbidden by his religion."

4. *Variable definition.* May "religion" be defined differently for purposes of the establishment clause than the free exercise clause? Consider Marc S. Galanter, *Religious Freedom in the United States: A Turning Point?* 1966 Wis.L.Rev. 217, 266–67: "[For purposes of the establishment clause, the] effect and purpose of government action are not to be assessed by the religious sensibilities of the person who is complaining of the alleged establishment. It must be essentially religious in some widely shared public understanding. [But, for the free exercise clause, the] claimants' view of religion controls the characterization of their objection as a religious one." Does this analysis solve the dilemma of Leonard F. Manning, *The Douglas Concept of God in Government,* 39 Wash.L.Rev. 47, 66 (1964): "If religion need not be predicated on a belief in God or even in a god and if it may not be tested by the common consensus of what reasonable men would reasonably call religion, if it is so private that—so long as it does not inflict injury on society—it is immured from governmental interference and from judicial inquiry, [might] not a group of gymnasts proclaiming on their trampolines that physical culture is their religion be engaged in a religious exercise? And if Congress, in a particular Olympic year, appropriated funds to subsidize their calisthenics would this not [be] an establishment of religion?" See generally Note, *Transcendental Meditation and the Meaning of Religion Under the Establishment Clause,* 62 Minn.L.Rev. 887 (1978).

SECTION 3. PREFERENCE AMONG RELIGIONS

In BOARD OF EDUC. OF KIRYAS JOEL v. GRUMET, 512 U.S. 687, 114 S.Ct. 2481, 129 L.Ed.2d 546 (1994), a New York statute constituted the Village of Kiryas Joel—"a religious enclave of Satmar Hasidim, practitioners of a strict form of Judaism"—as a separate school district. Most of the children attend pervasively religious private schools. The newly created district "currently runs only a special education program for handicapped [Satmar] children" who reside both inside and outside the village. The statute was passed "to enable the village's handicapped children to receive a secular, public-school education" because when they previously attended public schools in the larger school district outside the village, they suffered "panic, fear and trauma [in] leaving their own community and being with people whose ways were so different." The Court, per SOUTER, J., invoked "a principle at the heart of the Establishment Clause, that government should not prefer one religion to another, or religion to irreligion. Because the religious community of Kiryas Joel did not receive its new governmental authority simply as one of many communities eligible for equal treatment under a general law, we have no assurance that the next similarly situated group seeking a school district of its own will receive one; [and] a legislature's failure to enact a special law is itself unreviewable.[a] [Here] the benefit flows only to a single sect, [and] whatever the limits of permissible legislative accommodations may be, it is clear that neutrality as among religions must be honored.[b] [The statute] therefore crosses the line from permissible accommodation to impermissible establishment."[c]

KENNEDY, J., concurred in the judgment: "[G]overnment may not use religion as a criterion to draw political or electoral lines. Whether or not the purpose is accommodation and whether or not the government provides similar gerrymanders to people of all religious faiths, the Establishment Clause forbids the government to use religion as a line-drawing criterion."[d]

SCALIA, J., joined by Rehnquist, C.J., and Thomas, J., dissented: "[A]ll the residents of the Kiryas Joel Village School District are Satmars. But all its residents also wear unusual dress, have unusual civic customs, and have not much to do with people who are culturally different from them. [I]t was not theology but dress, language, and cultural alienation that posed the educational problem for the children [and caused the Legislature to] provide a public education for these

a. Kennedy, J., disagreed, arguing that if another religious community were denied special legislative help, it "could sue the State of New York, contending that New York's discriminatory treatment of the two religious communities violated the Establishment Clause. To resolve this claim, the court would have only to determine whether the community does indeed bear the same burden on its religious practice as did the Satmars in Kiryas Joel. See *Olsen v. Drug Enforcement Admin.*, [p. ___ infra] (R.B. Ginsburg, J.) (rejecting claim that the members of the Ethiopian Zion Coptic Church were entitled to an exemption from the marijuana laws on the same terms as the peyote exemption for the Native American Church). While a finding of discrimination would then raise a difficult question of relief, compare *Olsen* ('Faced with the choice between invalidation and extension of any controlled-substances religious exemption, which would the political branches choose? It would take a court bolder than this one to predict [that] extension, not invalidation, would be the probable choice'), with *Califano v. Westcott*, 443 U.S. 76, 99 S.Ct. 2655, 61 L.Ed.2d 382 (1979) (curing gender discrimination in the AFDC program by extending benefits to children of unemployed mothers instead of denying benefits to children of unemployed fathers), the discrimination itself would not be beyond judicial remedy."

b. Compare Thomas C. Berg, *Slouching Towards Secularism*, 44 Emory L.J. 433, 468–

69 (1995): "[T]he legislature specifically accommodated the Satmars [because] their plight was unique: no other group of children was being denied effective special education because they were traumatized by the atmosphere of the mainstream public schools. [Even] if the children of other groups had been harmed by the public school ethos, few if any such groups live together communally so as to permit the solution of a geographically based school district such as that drawn for the Satmars." But see Ira C. Lupu, *The Lingering Death of Separatism*, 62 Geo.Wash.L.Rev. 230, 269 (1994): "Is it imaginable that New York State would create a new public school district at the behest of an insular group of Branch Davidians or members of the Unification Church, whose children—like the Hasidim—may suffer panic, fear, and trauma at encountering those outside their own community?"

c. Within ten days of *Kiryas Joel*, the New York legislature passed a new law allowing "any municipality situated wholly within a single school district" to form its own district if it meets designated criteria regarding population, enrollment and property wealth. Constitutional when used by the Village of Kiryas Joel?

d. For discussion of similarities and differences between the use of religion and race [Ch. 9, Sec. 5, B] in drawing political districts, see Abner S. Greene, *Kiryas Joel and Two Mistakes About Equality*, 96 Colum.L.Rev. 1, 27–57 (1996).

students, in the same way it addressed, by a similar law, the unique needs of children institutionalized in a hospital. "[T]he creation of a special, one-culture school district for the benefit of [children whose] parents were nonreligious commune dwellers, or American Indians, or gypsies [would] pose no problem. The neutrality demanded by the Religion Clauses requires the same indulgence towards cultural characteristics that are accompanied by religious belief."[e]

Notes and Questions

1. *Delegation of government power:* In *Kiryas Joel,* SOUTER, J., joined by Blackmun, Stevens and Ginsburg, JJ., found an additional ground for invalidating the statute: "delegating the State's discretionary authority over public schools to a group defined by its character as a religious community, in a legal and historical context that gives no assurance that governmental power has been or will be exercised neutrally." They relied on LARKIN v. GRENDEL'S DEN, INC., 459 U.S. 116, 103 S.Ct. 505, 74 L.Ed.2d 297 (1982), per BURGER, C.J., which held that a Massachusetts law (§ 16C), giving churches and schools the power "to veto applications for liquor licenses within a five hundred foot radius of the church or school, violates the Establishment Clause": "§ 16C is not simply a legislative exercise of zoning power [because it] delegates * * * discretionary governmental powers [to] religious bodies.

"[The] valid secular objectives [of protecting] spiritual, cultural, and educational centers from the 'hurly-burly' associated with liquor outlets [can] be readily accomplished by [an] absolute legislative ban on liquor outlets within reasonable prescribed distances from churches, schools, hospitals and like institutions, or by ensuring a hearing for the views of affected institutions at licensing proceedings. [But the] churches' power under the statute is standardless [and] may therefore be used [for] explicitly religious goals, for example, favoring liquor licenses for members of that congregation or adherents of that faith. [In] addition, the mere appearance of a joint exercise of legislative authority by Church and State provides a significant symbolic benefit to religion in the minds of some by reason of the power conferred. It does not strain our prior holdings to say that the statute can be seen as having a 'primary' and 'principal' effect of advancing religion. [Finally, § 16C] enmeshes churches in the processes of government and creates the danger of 'political fragmentation and divisiveness along religious lines.' "

REHNQUIST, J., dissented in *Grendel's Den:* A "flat ban [on] the grant of an alcoholic beverages license to any establishment located within 500 feet of a church or a [school], which the majority concedes is valid, is more protective of churches and more restrictive of liquor sales than the present § 16C. * * * Nothing in the Court's opinion persuades me why the more rigid prohibition would be constitutional, but the more flexible not. [It] does not sponsor or subsidize any religious group or activity. It does not encourage, much less compel, anyone to participate in religious activities or to support religious institutions. [If] a church were to seek to advance the interests of its members [by favoring them for licenses], there would be an occasion to determine whether it had violated any right of an unsuccessful applicant for a liquor license. But our ability to discern a risk of such abuse does not render § 16C violative of the Establishment Clause."

e. Is this persuasive when there is total congruence between a religion and distinctive cultural needs *and* the cultural distinctiveness is defined by the religion?

Scalia, J., joined by Rehnquist, C.J., and Thomas, J., dissenting in *Kiryas Joel*, argued that *Grendel's Den* had ruled that "a state may not delegate its civil authority *to a church*," and did not involve delegation to "groups of people sharing a common religious and cultural heritage": "If the conferral of governmental power upon a religious institution *as such* (rather than upon American citizens who belong to the religious institution) is not the test of *Grendel's Den* invalidity, there is no reason why giving power to a body that is overwhelmingly dominated by the members of one sect would not suffice to invoke the Establishment Clause. That might have made the entire States of Utah and New Mexico unconstitutional at the time of their admission to the Union."

2. *"Excessive government entanglement" in ecclesiastical disputes.* (a) In JONES v. WOLF, 443 U.S. 595, 99 S.Ct. 3020, 61 L.Ed.2d 775 (1979), a majority of the Vineville Presbyterian Church of Macon, Ga. voted to separate from the Presbyterian Church in the United States (PCUS). A commission of PCUS, acting pursuant to the PCUS constitution (called the Book of Church Order), declared the Vineville minority to be "the true congregation." The minority sued to establish its right to the local church property. The state court applied "the 'neutral principles of law' method for resolving church property disputes. The court examined the deeds to the properties, the state statutes dealing with implied trusts, and the Book of Church Order, to determine whether there was any basis for a trust in favor of the general church. Finding nothing that would give rise to a trust in any of these documents, the court awarded the property on the basis of legal title, which was in the local church, or in the names of trustees for the local church. [Without] further analysis or elaboration, [it] further decreed that the local congregation was represented by the majority faction, respondents herein."

The Court, per BLACKMUN, J., stated the established principle that "the First Amendment prohibits civil courts from resolving church property disputes on the basis of religious doctrine and practice. *Presbyterian Church v. Hull Church,* 393 U.S. 440, 89 S.Ct. 601, 21 L.Ed.2d 658 (1969). As a corollary to this commandment, the Amendment requires that civil courts defer to the resolution of issues of religious doctrine or polity by the highest court of a hierarchical church organization. *Serbian Eastern Orthodox Diocese v. Milivojevich,* 426 U.S. 696, 96 S.Ct. 2372, 49 L.Ed.2d 151 (1976)[a] Subject to these limitations, [however,] 'a State may adopt *any* of various approaches for settling church property disputes so long as it involves no consideration of doctrinal matters, whether the ritual and liturgy of worship or the tenets of faith.' *Maryland & Virginia Eldership v. Sharpsburg Church,* 396 U.S. 367, 90 S.Ct. 499, 24 L.Ed.2d 582 (1970) (Brennan, J., concurring).

"[W]e think the 'neutral principles of law' approach is consistent with the foregoing constitutional principles. [It] relies extensively on objective, well-established concepts of trust and property law familiar to lawyers and judges. It

a. *Serbian,* per Brennan, J., reversed a state court decision that the Mother Church's removal of respondent as bishop of the American–Canadian diocese was "procedurally and substantively defective under the internal regulations of the Mother Church and were therefore arbitrary and invalid": "[W]hether or not there is room for 'marginal civil court review' under the narrow rubrics of 'fraud' or 'collusion' when church tribunals act in bad faith for secular purposes, no 'arbitrariness' exception—in the sense of an inquiry whether the decisions of the highest ecclesiastical tribunal of a hierarchical church complied with church laws and regulations—is consistent with the constitutional mandate that civil courts are bound to accept the decisions of the highest judicatories of a religious organization of hierarchical polity on matters of discipline, faith, internal organization, or ecclesiastical rule, custom or law. [I]t is the essence of religious faith that ecclesiastical decisions are reached and are to be accepted as matters of faith whether or not rational or measurable by objective criteria."

Rehnquist and Stevens, JJ., dissented.

thereby promises to free civil courts completely from entanglement in questions of religious doctrine, polity, and practice. Furthermore, the neutral principles analysis [affords] flexibility in ordering private rights and obligations to reflect the intentions of the parties. Through appropriate reversionary clauses and trust provisions, religious societies can specify what is to happen to church property in the event of a particular contingency, or what religious body will determine the ownership in the event of a schism or doctrinal controversy. In this manner, a religious organization can ensure that a dispute over the ownership of church property will be resolved in accord with the desires of the members.

"[The] neutral principles method [does require] a civil court to examine certain religious documents, such as a church constitution, for language of trust in favor of the general church. [A] civil court must take special care to scrutinize the document in purely secular terms, and not to rely on religious precepts in determining whether the document indicates that the parties have intended to create a trust. In addition, there may be cases where the deed, the corporate charter, or the constitution of the general church incorporates religious concepts in the provisions relating to the ownership of property. If in such a case the interpretation of the instruments of ownership would require the civil court to resolve a religious controversy, then the court must defer to the resolution of the doctrinal issue by the authoritative ecclesiastical body. *Serbian*."

The Court vacated the judgment, however, since "the grounds for the decision that respondents represent the Vineville church remain unarticulated": "If in fact Georgia has adopted a presumptive rule of majority representation, defeasible upon a showing that the identity of the local church is to be determined by some other means, we think this would be consistent with [the] First Amendment. Majority rule is generally employed in the governance of religious societies. Furthermore, the majority faction generally can be identified without resolving any question of religious doctrine or polity. [Most] importantly, any rule of majority representation can always be overcome, under the neutral principles approach, either by providing, in the corporate charter or the constitution of the general church, that the identity of the local church is to be established in some other way, or by providing that the church property is held in trust for the general church and those who remain loyal to it. Indeed, the State may adopt any method of overcoming the majoritarian presumption, so long as the use of that method does not impair free exercise rights or entangle the civil courts in matters of religious controversy.

"[But] there are at least some indications that under Georgia law the process of identifying the faction that represents the Vineville church [must] be determined according to terms of the Book of Church Order. [That] would appear to require a civil court to pass on questions of religious doctrine. [Therefore,] if Georgia law provides that the identity of the Vineville church is to be determined according to the 'laws and regulations' of the PCUS, then the First Amendment requires that the Georgia courts give deference to the presbyterial commission's determination of that church's identity."

POWELL, J., joined by Burger, C.J., and Stewart and White, JJ., dissented, finding that the neutral principles "approach inevitably will increase the involvement of civil courts in church controversies": "Until today, [the] first question presented in a case involving an intrachurch dispute over church property was where within the religious association the rules of polity, accepted by its members before the schism, had placed ultimate authority over the use of the church property. The courts, in answering this question have recognized two broad categories of church government. One is congregational, in which authority over questions of church doctrine, practice, and administration rests entirely in the local congregation or some body within it [and] the civil courts enforce the authoritative resolution of the controversy within the local church itself. *Watson v. Jones*, 80 U.S. (13 Wall.) 679, 20 L.Ed. 666 (1871). The second is hierarchical, in which the local church is but an integral and subordinate part of a larger church and is under the authority of the general church. [Here], this Court has held that the civil courts must give effect to the duly made decisions of the highest body within the hierarchy that has considered the dispute. [By] doing so, the [civil] court avoids two equally unacceptable departures from the genuine neutrality mandated by the First Amendment. First, it refrains from direct review and revision of decisions of the church on matters of religious doctrine and practice that underlie the church's determination of intrachurch controversies, including those that relate to control of church property.[b] Equally important, by recognizing the authoritative resolution reached within the religious association, the civil court avoids interfering indirectly with the religious governance of those who have formed the association and submitted themselves to its authority."[c]

(b) *Scope of the decision.* After *Jones v. Wolf,* what results in the following situations: (i) A donor who made a bequest "to the First Methodist Church" seeks return of the money because subsequently a majority of the church's members decided to affiliate with another denomination. Suppose the bequest had been "to the First Methodist Church so long as it does not substantially deviate from existing doctrine"? (ii) A state statute makes it a crime for sellers to falsely represent food to be "kosher." See Kent Greenawalt, *Religious Law and Civil Law: Using Secular Law to Assure Observance of Practices with Religious Significance,* 71 So.Cal.L.Rev. 781 (1998). (iii) An adult sues a member of the clergy for "malpractice" based on consensual sexual acts with the plaintiff. See Scott C. Idleman, *Tort Liability, Religious Entities, and the Decline of Constitutional Protection,* 75 Ind. L.J., 219 (2000).

(c) *Proposed approach.* "The solution most of the time is to honor internal church agreements, just as a court would honor the internal agreements of a secular organization. Only when doctrinal decisions[d] or the imposition of external policies are involved[e] need a court refrain from deciding a dispute. This approach

b. In response, the Court pointed out that, under the dissent's approach, "civil courts would always be required to examine the polity and administration of a church to determine which unit of government has ultimate control over church property. In some cases, [the] locus of control would be ambiguous, and 'a careful examination of the constitutions of the general and local church, as well as other relevant documents, [would] be necessary to ascertain the form of governance adopted by the members of the religious association.' In such cases, the suggested rule would appear to require 'a searching and therefore impermissible inquiry into church polity.' *Serbian.* The neutral principles approach, in contrast, obviates entirely the need for an analysis or examination of ecclesiastical polity or doctrine in settling church property disputes."

c. In response, the Court contended that "the neutral principles approach cannot be said to 'inhibit' the free exercise of religion, any more than do other neutral provisions of

state law governing the manner in which churches own property, hire employees, or purchase goods. Under the neutral principles approach, the outcome of a church property dispute is not foreordained. At any time before the dispute erupts, the parties can ensure, if they so desire, that the faction loyal to the hierarchical church will retain the church property" by using reversionary clauses, trust provisions, etc.

d. "Few [cases] present the problem of governmental determination of religious doctrine. [More] common are a second group of cases in which the court is asked to determine which religious doctrine the embattled parties agreed to follow. This kind of question is very different and need not present the first amendment difficulties inherent in the first group of cases." Id. at 1414.

e. "[T]he application of judge-made rules of procedural fairness in associational governance, and the use of charitable trust rules of

serves both organizational autonomy and the other interests of the church and its members, while preserving the religious neutrality demanded by the first amendment." Ira M. Ellman, *Driven from the Tribunal: Judicial Resolution of Internal Church Disputes,* 69 Calif.L.Rev. 1378, 1444 (1981).[f]

LARSON v. VALENTE, 456 U.S. 228, 102 S.Ct. 1673, 72 L.Ed.2d 33 (1982), involved a challenge by the Unification Church ("Moonies") to "a Minnesota statute, imposing certain registration and reporting requirements upon only those religious organizations that solicit more than fifty per cent of their funds from nonmembers." The Court, per BRENNAN, J., noting that "the clearest command of the establishment clause is that one religious denomination cannot be officially preferred over another, [*Everson*]," and that the "constitutional prohibition of denominational preferences is inextricably connected with the continuing vitality of the Free Exercise Clause," held that the statute violated the establishment clause because it did not survive "strict scrutiny."[a] Assuming that the state's "valid secular purpose [in] protecting its citizens from abusive practices in the solicitation of funds for charity" is "compelling," the state "failed to demonstrate that the fifty per cent rule [is] 'closely fitted'" to furthering that interest. Moreover, the statute failed the third *Lemon* "test": "The fifty per cent [rule] effects the *selective* legislative imposition of burdens and advantages upon particular denominations. The 'risk of politicizing religion' that inheres in such legislation is obvious, and indeed is confirmed by the provision's legislative history [which] demonstrates that the provision was drafted with the explicit intention of including particular religious denominations and excluding others."

charitable assets [are issues that] present the potential for courts to impose government-created policies on religious organizations [rather than rules seeking to fulfill the parties' intentions]." Id. at 1421.

f. For the view that "freedom of church groups" should be preferred to "freedom of individual members," and therefore the rule of "deference" to church decisions should prevail over the "neutral principles" approach, see John H. Garvey, *Churches and the Free Exercise of Religion,* 4 Notre D.J.L.Eth & Pub.Pol. 567 (1990).

For the view that the Court should adopt "a framework based on neutral principles"; that "national churches should specify the range of authority of their highest courts in documents clearly designed for recognition under civil law"; and that "civil courts should await the determinations of those religious courts and then accept their determinations, unless those determinations are undercut by some gross failure of the religious courts to comply with their own rules," see Kent Greenawalt, *Hands Off! Civil Court Involvement in Conflicts Over Religious Property,* 98 Colum.L.Rev. 1843 (1998).

a. The Court rejected the argument that the statute was merely "a law based upon secular criteria which may not identically affect all religious organizations." This "is not

simply a facially neutral statute, the provisions of which happen to have a 'disparate impact' upon different religious organizations. On the contrary [it] makes explicit and deliberate distinctions between different religious organizations [and] effectively distinguishes between 'well-established churches' that have 'achieved strong but not total financial support from their members,' on the one hand, and 'churches which are new and lacking in a constituency, or, which, as a matter of policy, may favor public solicitation over general reliance on financial support from members,' on the other hand."

The Court found *Gillette v. United States,* Sec. 2, I supra, "readily distinguishable": "In that case, we rejected an Establishment Clause attack upon § 6(j) of the Military Selective Service Act of 1967, which afforded 'conscientious objector' status to any person who, 'by reason of religious training and belief,' was 'conscientiously opposed to participation in war in any form * * *.' Section 6(j) 'focused on individual conscientious belief, not on sectarian affiliation.' Under § 6(j), conscientious objector status was available on an equal basis to both the Quaker and the Roman Catholic, despite the distinction drawn by the latter's church between 'just' and 'unjust' wars. [In] contrast, the statute challenged in the case before us focuses precisely and solely upon religious organizations."

WHITE, J., joined by Rehnquist, J., dissented,[b] disagreeing with the Court's view "that the rule on its face represents an explicit and deliberate preference for some religious beliefs over others": "The rule [names] no churches or denominations. [Some] religions will qualify and some will not, but this depends on the source of their contributions, not on their brand of religion. [The Court's assertion] that the limitation might burden the less well-organized denominations [is contrary to the state's claim] that both categories include not only well-established, but also not so well-established organizations." Further, "I cannot join the Court's easy rejection of the state's submission that a valid secular purpose justifies basing the exemption on the percentage of external funding."[c]

Notes and Questions

1. *The Gillette rationale.* (a) Should the existence of a "neutral, secular basis" justify government preference—de jure or de facto—among religions? Consider Kent Greenawalt, *All or Nothing at All: The Defeat of Selective Conscientious Objection,* 1971 Sup.Ct.Rev. 31, 71: "If a sociological survey indicated that Protestants generally work harder than Catholics, the government might simplify its hiring problems by interviewing only Protestants. If the doctors of Catholic hospitals were determined to be on the average more qualified than those at Lutheran hospitals, aid might be limited to the Catholic hospitals. It is, of course, inconceivable that such legislation would be passed and its unconstitutionality is [apparent]." How significant was the Court's observation that the *Gillette* law "attempts to accommodate free exercise values"?

(b) Was the Draft Act of 1917, which exempted only conscientious objectors affiliated with some "well-recognized religious sect" whose principles forbade participation in war, also valid under the *Gillette* rationale? Consider 48 Minn. L.Rev. 776–77 (1964): "Since pacifism often arises from religious beliefs, a workable method for ascertaining sincerity may have to be couched in terms of those beliefs. Such a test should be permissible, even though it may theoretically 'prefer' some sincere conscientious objectors over others, if it reasonably advances the [statute's] purpose by aiding local draft boards in administering the act. For example, since membership in an organized pacifist sect may be better evidence of sincerity than the mere assertion of pacificist beliefs, a requirement to that effect should be permissible."

2. *The Larson rationale.* (a) Consider Jesse H. Choper, *The Free Exercise Clause: A Structural Overview and An Appraisal of Recent Developments,* 27 Wm. & M.L.Rev. 943, 958–61 (1986): "*Larson* should be seen as a free exercise clause decision parading in an establishment clause disguise. [The] major thrust of the Court's opinion [used] classic free exercise clause analysis[:] strict scrutiny. [Even if] the Minnesota statute did not specifically give preference to some religions over others, it did expressly deal with the subject of religion, and it resulted in favoring some and disfavoring others. In my view, it should have been as vulnerable—that is, subject to the same level of scrutiny—as a general, neutral law that says nothing about religion but that happens to have an adverse impact on some faiths, [as] in *Yoder.* The problem is that when the [pre-*Smith*] Court has invoked the establishment clause, it has applied a much more lenient test to laws that expressly deal with religion and subject some faiths to discriminatory treatment

b. Rehnquist, J., joined by Burger, C.J. and White and O'Connor, JJ., also dissented on the ground that appellee Unification Church had no standing.

c. *Gillette* held that there was no religious "gerrymander" if there was "a neutral, secular basis for the lines government has drawn."

than it has applied under the free exercise clause to general, neutral laws that come into conflict with religious beliefs. [In] reality, I believe that the Selective Service Act survived strict scrutiny in *Gillette* [because of the] powerful government interest in raising an army and the difficulties in administering a draft exemption based on 'just war' beliefs. [In] sum, the doctrine in *Gillette,* that a valid secular basis for de facto religious discrimination is enough to sustain it under the establishment clause, plainly supports Justice White's dissent in *Larson.* The *Gillette* doctrine, however, effectively has been abandoned, and rightly so.''

(b) HERNANDEZ v. COMMISSIONER, 490 U.S. 680, 109 S.Ct. 2136, 104 L.Ed.2d 766 (1989), per MARSHALL, J., found no violation of the establishment clause in not permitting federal taxpayers to deduct as "charitable contributions" payments to the Church of Scientology for "auditing" and "training" sessions. A central tenet of the Church requires "fixed donations" for these sessions to study the faith's tenets and to increase spiritual awareness. The proceeds are the Church's primary source of income:

Larson was distinguished on the ground that IRS disallowance for payments made "with some expectation of a quid pro quo in terms of goods or services [makes] no 'explicit and deliberate distinctions between different religious organizations.' [It] may be that a consequence of the quid pro quo orientation of the 'contribution or gift' requirement is to impose a disparate burden on those charitable and religious groups that rely on sales of commodities or services as a means of fund-raising, relative to those groups that raise funds primarily by soliciting unilateral donations. But a statute primarily having a secular effect does not violate the Establishment Clause merely because it 'happens to coincide or harmonize with the tenets of some or all religions.' *McGowan.''*

Because of the absence of "a proper factual record," the Court did not consider the contention of O'CONNOR, J., joined by Scalia, J., dissenting, that "at least some of the fixed payments which the IRS has treated as charitable deductions [are as much a 'quid pro quo exchange'] as the payments [here]": "In exchange for their payment of pew rents, Christians receive particular seats during worship services. Similarly, in some synagogues attendance at the worship services for Jewish High Holy Days is often predicated upon the purchase of a general admission ticket or a reserved seat ticket. Religious honors such as publicly reading from Scripture are purchased or auctioned periodically in some synagogues of Jews from Morocco and Syria. Mormons must tithe ten percent of their income as a necessary but not sufficient condition to obtaining a 'temple recommend,' i.e., the right to be admitted into the temple. A Mass stipend—a fixed payment given to a Catholic priest, in consideration of which he is obliged to apply the fruits of the Mass for the intention of the donor—has similar overtones of exchange. [Thus, the case] involves the differential application of a standard based on constitutionally impermissible differences drawn by the Government among religions." Brennan and Kennedy, JJ., did not participate.

3. *Preference for "religious" objectors.* Is Congress' limitation of draft exemption to "religious" conscientious objectors valid? Consider John H. Mansfield, *Conscientious Objection—1964 Term,* 1965 Relig. & Pub.Or. 3, 76: "[T]here are really no convincing reasons why the religious objector should be exempt and not the non-religious conscientious objector. [T]he religious objector's opposition rests on somewhat more fundamental grounds [and] makes reference to realities that can more easily be described as spiritual. But the non-religious conscientious objector's opposition does rest on basic propositions about the nature of reality

and the significance of human existence; this is what distinguishes it from objection that is not even conscientious." Does the "religious" exemption result in more or less government "entanglement" with religion than an exemption for *all* conscientious objectors?

SECTION 4. CONFLICT BETWEEN THE CLAUSES

The decision in *Employment Division v. Smith* appeared to have relieved some of the tension that had existed between the doctrines that the Court had developed under the establishment and free exercise clauses. But substantial questions remained, e.g., do (a) the decisions in *Sherbert (Thomas, Hobbie), Yoder* and *Roy,* and (b) statutes granting religious exemptions from laws of general applicability violate the establishment clause because they impermissibly aid religion?

CORPORATION OF THE PRESIDING BISHOP OF THE CHURCH OF JESUS CHRIST OF LATTER–DAY SAINTS v. AMOS

483 U.S. 327, 107 S.Ct. 2862, 97 L.Ed.2d 273 (1987).

JUSTICE WHITE delivered the opinion of the Court.

Section 702 of the Civil Rights Act of 1964 exempts religious organizations from Title VII's prohibition against discrimination in employment on the basis of religion. [The] Deseret Gymnasium (Gymnasium) in Salt Lake City, Utah, is a nonprofit facility, open to the public, run by [an] unincorporated religious association sometimes called the Mormon or LDS Church. Appellee Mayson worked at the Gymnasium for some 16 years as an assistant building engineer and then building engineer. He was discharged in 1981 because he failed to qualify for a temple recommend, that is, a certificate that he is a member of the Church and eligible to attend its temples. Mayson [contended] that if construed to allow religious employers to discriminate on religious grounds in hiring for nonreligious jobs, § 702 violates the Establishment Clause. * * *

"This Court has long recognized that the government may (and sometimes must) accommodate religious practices and that it may do so without violating the Establishment Clause." It is well established, too, that "[t]he limits of permissible state accommodation to religion are by no means co-extensive with the noninterference mandated by the Free Exercise Clause." *Walz.*[a] [At] some point, accommodation may devolve into "an unlawful fostering of religion," but this is not such a case, in our view. * * *

Lemon requires [a] "secular legislative purpose." This does not mean that the law's purpose must be unrelated to religion. [Rather,] *Lemon*'s "purpose" requirement aims at preventing the relevant governmental decisionmaker—in this case, Congress—from abandoning neutrality and acting with the intent of promoting a particular point of view in religious matters.

a. Consider Michael W. McConnell, *Accommodation of Religion,* 1985 Sup.Ct.Rev. 1, 34: "[S]ome government employees may view attendance at religious services on a holy day a sacred duty; they could make out a plausible free exercise case if the government refused them leave. Others may view attendance at services as no more than a spiritually wholesome activity; their free exercise claim would be much weaker. It is not unreasonable for the government to disregard these distinctions—to implement a general policy permitting leave for employees on the holy days of their faith. * * * Religious liberty is not enhanced by a rule confining government accommodations to the minimum compelled under the Constitution."

Under the *Lemon* analysis, it is a permissible legislative purpose to alleviate significant governmental interference with the ability of religious organizations to define and carry out their religious missions.[b] Appellees argue that there is no such purpose here because § 702 provided adequate protection for religious employers prior to the 1972 amendment, when it exempted only the religious activities of such employers from the statutory ban on religious discrimination. We may assume for the sake of argument that the pre–1972 exemption was adequate in the sense that the Free Exercise Clause required no more. Nonetheless, it is a significant burden on a religious organization to require it, on pain of substantial liability, to predict which of its activities a secular court will consider religious. The line is hardly a bright one, and an organization might understandably be concerned that a judge would not understand its religious tenets and sense of mission. Fear of potential liability might affect the way an organization carried out what it understood to be its religious mission. * * *

The second requirement under *Lemon* is that the law in question have "a principal or primary effect [that] neither advances nor inhibits religion." Undoubtedly, religious organizations are better able now to advance their purposes than they were prior to the 1972 amendment to § 702. But religious groups have been better able to advance their purposes on account of many laws that have passed constitutional muster: for example, the property tax exemption at issue in *Walz,* or the loans of school books to school children, including parochial school students, upheld in *Allen.* A law is not unconstitutional simply because it *allows* churches to advance religion, which is their very purpose. For a law to have forbidden "effects" under *Lemon,* it must be fair to say that the *government itself* has advanced religion through its own activities and influence. [Moreover,] we find no persuasive evidence in the record before us that the Church's ability to propagate its religious doctrine through the Gymnasium is any greater now than it was prior to the passage of the Civil Rights Act in 1964. In such circumstances, we do not see how any advancement of religion achieved by the Gymnasium can be fairly attributed to the Government, as opposed to the Church.[15]

We find unpersuasive the District Court's reliance on the fact that § 702 singles out religious entities for a benefit. [The Court] has never indicated that statutes that give special consideration to religious groups are per se invalid. That would run contrary to the teaching of our cases that there is ample room for accommodation of religion under the Establishment Clause. Where, as here, government acts with the proper purpose of lifting a regulation that burdens the exercise of religion, we see no reason to require that the exemption come packaged with benefits to secular entities. * * * *Larson* indicates that laws discriminating *among* religions are subject to strict scrutiny, and that laws "affording a uniform benefit to *all* religions" should be analyzed under *Lemon.* In a case such as this, where a statute is neutral on its face and motivated by a permissible purpose of limiting governmental interference with the exercise of religion, we see no

---

b. See also Wilbur Katz, *Note on the Constitutionality of Shared Time,* 1964 Relig. & Pub.Or. 85, 88: "It is no violation of neutrality for the government to express its concern for religious freedom by measures which merely neutralize what would otherwise be restrictive effects of government action. Provision for voluntary worship in the armed forces is constitutional, not because government policy may properly favor religion, but because the government is not required to exercise its military powers in a manner restrictive of religious freedom. Affirmative government action to maintain religious freedom in these instances serves the secular purpose of promoting a constitutional right, the free exercise of religion."

15. Undoubtedly, Mayson's freedom of choice in religious matters was impinged upon, but it was the Church [and] not the Government, who put him to the choice of changing his religious practices or losing his [job.]

justification for applying strict scrutiny to a statute that passes the *Lemon* test. * * * § 702 is rationally related to the legitimate purpose of alleviating significant governmental interference with the ability of religious organizations to define and carry out their religious missions. * * *

JUSTICE BRENNAN, with whom JUSTICE MARSHALL joins, concurring in the judgment.

[Any] exemption from Title VII's proscription on religious discrimination [says] that a person may be put to the choice of either conforming to certain religious tenets or losing a job opportunity, a promotion, or, as in this case, employment itself. The potential for coercion created by such a provision is in serious tension with our commitment to individual freedom of conscience in matters of religious belief.

At the same time, religious organizations have an interest in autonomy in ordering their internal affairs * * *. Determining that certain activities are in furtherance of an organization's religious mission, and that only those committed to that mission should conduct them, is thus a means by which a religious community defines itself. Solicitude for a church's ability to do so reflects the idea that furtherance of the autonomy of religious organizations often furthers individual religious freedom as well.[a] * * *

This rationale suggests that, ideally, religious organizations should be able to discriminate on the basis of religion *only* with respect to religious activities [because] the infringement on religious liberty that results from conditioning performance of *secular* activity upon religious belief cannot be defended as necessary for the community's self-definition. Furthermore, the authorization of discrimination in such circumstances is not an accommodation that simply enables a church to gain members by the normal means of prescribing the terms of membership for those who seek to participate in furthering the mission of the community. Rather, it puts at the disposal of religion the added advantages of economic leverage in the secular realm. * * *

What makes the application of a religious-secular distinction difficult is that the character of an activity is not self-evident. As a result, determining whether an activity is religious or secular requires a searching case-by-case analysis. This results in considerable ongoing government entanglement in religious affairs. Furthermore, this prospect of government intrusion raises concern that a religious organization may be chilled in its Free Exercise activity. * * *

The risk [is] most likely to arise with respect to *nonprofit* activities. The fact that an operation is not organized as a profit-making commercial enterprise makes colorable a claim that it is not purely secular in orientation. * * *

Sensitivity to individual religious freedom dictates that religious discrimination be permitted only with respect to employment in religious activities. Concern for the autonomy of religious organizations demands that we avoid the entanglement and the chill on religious expression that a case-by-case determination would produce. We cannot escape the fact that these aims are in tension. Because of the nature of nonprofit activities, I believe that a categorical exemption for such enterprises appropriately balances these competing concerns. * * *

JUSTICE BLACKMUN, concurring in the judgment.

---

a. For the view that the establishment clause requires an exemption from a neutral, generally applicable law that "interferes with the relationship between clergy and church" or "intrudes on religious organizations' sphere of autonomy," see Carl H. Esbeck, *The Establishment Clause as a Structural Restraint on Governmental Power*, 84 Ia.L.Rev. 1 (1998).

Essentially for the reasons set forth in Justice O'Connor's opinion, * * * I too, concur in the judgment of the Court. * * *

JUSTICE O'CONNOR, concurring in the judgment. * * *

In *Jaffree,* I noted a tension in the Court's use of the *Lemon* test to evaluate an Establishment Clause challenge to government efforts to accommodate the free exercise of religion: "On the one hand, a rigid application of the *Lemon* test would invalidate legislation exempting religious observers from generally applicable government obligations. By definition, such legislation has a religious purpose and effect in promoting the free exercise of religion.[b] On the other hand, judicial deference to all legislation that purports to facilitate the free exercise of religion would completely vitiate the Establishment Clause. Any statute pertaining to religion can be viewed as an 'accommodation' of free exercise rights."[c]

In my view, the opinion for the Court leans toward the second of the two unacceptable options described [above.] Almost any government benefit to religion could be recharacterized as simply "allowing" a religion to better advance itself,

---

b. In her *Jaffree* concurrence, O'Connor, J., added: "Indeed, the statute at issue in *Lemon* [can] be viewed as an accommodation of the religious beliefs of parents who choose to send their children to religious schools."

In this connection, consider Phillip Kurland, *Religion and the Law* 112 (1962): "The [free exercise and establishment] clauses should be read as stating a single precept: that government cannot utilize religion as a standard for action or inaction because these clauses, read together as they should be, prohibit classification in terms of religion either to confer a benefit or to impose a burden." For thoughtful comment, see Paul Kauper, *Book Review,* 41 Texas L.Rev. 467 (1963); Leo Pfeffer, *Religion–Blind Government,* 15 Stan.L.Rev. 389 (1963); John Mansfield, *Book Review,* 52 Calif.L.Rev. 212 (1964). For consideration of "the extent to which equality, as a constitutional value, constrains our understanding of religious guarantees," see Laura S. Underkuffler–Freund, *Yoder and the Question of Equality,* 25 Cap. U.L.Rev. 789 (1996).

Similarly, for the view that the free exercise clause should generally only guarantee "equality of treatment for those who act out of sincere religious belief" and should afford special protection only for acts of "worship," as defined, see Fernandez, *The Free Exercise of Religion,* 36 So.Calif.L.Rev. 546 (1963). For the view that free exercise claims should be treated "no differently than free expression claims," see Marshall, *Solving the Free Exercise Dilemma: Free Exercise as Expression,* 67 Minn.L.Rev. 545 (1983).

c. In *Jaffree,* O'Connor, J. added: "It [is] difficult to square any notion of 'complete neutrality' with the mandate of the Free Exercise Clause that government must sometimes exempt a religious observer from an otherwise generally applicable obligation. [The] solution [lies] in identifying workable limits to the Government's license to promote the free exercise of religion. [O]ne can plausibly assert

that government pursues free exercise clause values when it lifts a government-imposed burden on the free exercise of religion. If a statute falls within this category, then the standard Establishment Clause test should be modified accordingly. [T]he Court should simply acknowledge that the religious purpose of such a statute is legitimated by the Free Exercise Clause."

See also Abner S. Greene, *The Political Balance of the Religion Clauses,* 102 Yale L.J. 1611, 1644 (1993): "[I]f we construe the Establishment Clause to prohibit legislation enacted for the express purpose of advancing religious values, then the predicate for universal obedience to law has been removed. A religious conscientious objector may legitimately claim that because she was thwarted from offering her values for majority acceptance as law, she should have at least a prima facie right of exemption from law that conflicts with her religion. The Free Exercise Clause works as a counterweight to the Establishment Clause; it gives back what the Establishment Clause takes away." Compare Sherry, fn. d, p. 1086 supra, at 145: "This formulation can also be reversed: protecting the values of the Establishment Clause should constitute a compelling government interest sufficient to justify the impact of neutral laws on religious exercise. Whichever clause serves as the compelling interest trumps the other. Which formulation one prefers depends solely on whether one places a higher priority on the values of the Establishment Clause or on those of the Free Exercise Clause."

For the view that "there is much to be said for allowing broad interpretations of both clauses to remain in a symbiotic relationship, in dynamic 'tension,' thereby maximizing the goal of religious liberty for all Americans," see Derek H. Davis, *Resolving Not to Resolve the Tension between the Establishment and Free Exercise Clauses,* 38 J.Ch. & St. 245 (1996).

unless perhaps it involved actual proselytization by government agents. In nearly every case of a government benefit to religion, the religious mission would not be advanced if the religion did not take advantage of the benefit; even a direct financial subsidy to a religious organization would not advance religion if for some reason the organization failed to make any use of the funds. * * *

The necessary first step in evaluating an Establishment Clause challenge to a government action lifting from religious organizations a generally applicable regulatory burden is to recognize that such government action *does* have the effect of advancing religion. The necessary second step is to separate those benefits to religion that constitutionally accommodate the free exercise of religion from those that provide unjustifiable awards of assistance to religious organizations. As I have suggested in earlier opinions, the inquiry framed by the *Lemon* test should be "whether government's purpose is to endorse religion and whether the statute actually conveys a message of endorsement." [T]he relevant issue is how it would be perceived by an objective observer, acquainted with the text, legislative history, and implementation of the statute.[d] [This] case involves a government decision to lift from a nonprofit activity of a religious organization the burden of demonstrating that the particular nonprofit activity is religious as well as the burden of refraining from discriminating on the basis of religion. Because there is a probability that a nonprofit activity of a religious organization will itself be involved in the organization's religious mission, in my view the objective observer should perceive the government action as an accommodation of the exercise of religion rather than as a government endorsement of religion.

[U]nder the holding of the Court, and under my view of the appropriate Establishment Clause analysis, the question of the constitutionality of the § 702 exemption as applied to for-profit activities of religious organizations remains open.

Notes and Questions

1. *Draft exemption.* Did the statute in *Gillette,* exempting only "religious" conscientious objectors, impermissibly prefer religion over nonreligion? In WELSH v. UNITED STATES, Sec. 2, II supra, four justices addressed the issue. WHITE, J., joined by Burger, C.J., and Stewart, J., found it valid: "First, § 6(j) may represent a purely practical judgment that religious objectors, however admirable, would be of no more use in combat than many others unqualified for military service. [On] this basis, the exemption has neither the primary purpose nor the effect of furthering religion. * * *

"Second, Congress may have [believed that] to deny the exemption would violate the Free Exercise Clause or at least raise grave problems in this respect.

---

d. In *Jaffree,* O'Connor, J., added: "[C]ourts should assume that the 'objective observer,' is acquainted with the Free Exercise Clause and the values it promotes. Thus individual perceptions, or resentment that a religious observer is exempted from a particular government requirement, would be entitled to little weight if the Free Exercise Clause strongly supported the exemption."

Compare William P. Marshall, *The Religious Freedom Restoration Act: Establishment, Equal Protection and Free Speech Concerns,* 56 Mont. L.Rev. 227, 236 (1995): "Prior to *Smith,* one could argue that the Constitution demanded some accommodation from general laws of neutral applicability for free exercise interests. Legislative exemptions from neutral laws, which provided this accommodation, could therefore be defended as in accord with this constitutional mandate. The denial of the free exercise right in *Smith,* however, suggests that exempting religion from neutral laws is no longer based upon a constitutional requirement. Accordingly, after *Smith,* the strength of the state interest supporting the legislative exemption is necessarily diminished."

[If] it is 'favoritism' and not 'neutrality' to exempt religious believers from the draft, is it 'neutrality' and not 'inhibition' of religion to compel religious believers to fight * * * ? It cannot be ignored that the First Amendment itself contains a religious classification [and the free exercise clause] protects conduct as well as religious belief and speech. [It] was not suggested [in *Braunfeld*] that the Sunday closing laws in 21 States exempting Sabbatarians and others violated the Establishment Clause because no provision was made for others who claimed nonreligious reasons for not working on some particular day of the week. Nor was it intimated in *Zorach* that the no-establishment holding might be infirm because only those pursuing religious studies for designated periods were released from the public school routine; neither was it hinted that a public school's refusal to institute a released time program would violate the Free Exercise Clause. The Court in *Sherbert* construed the Free Exercise Clause to require special treatment for Sabbatarians under the State's unemployment compensation law. But the State could deal specially with Sabbatarians whether the Free Exercise Clause required it or not * * *."

HARLAN, J., disagreed, believing that "having chosen to exempt, [Congress] cannot draw the line between theistic or nontheistic religious beliefs on the one hand and secular beliefs on the other. [I]t must encompass the class of individuals it purports to exclude, those whose beliefs emanate from a purely moral, ethical, or philosophical source.[9] The common denominator must be the intensity of moral conviction with which a belief is [held]. *Everson, McGowan* and *Allen,* all sustained legislation on the premise that it was neutral in its application and thus did not constitute an establishment, notwithstanding the fact that it may have assisted religious groups by giving them the same benefits accorded to nonreligious groups.[12] To the extent that *Zorach* and *Sherbert* stand for the proposition that the Government may (*Zorach*), or must (*Sherbert*), shape its secular programs to accommodate the beliefs and tenets of religious groups, I think these cases unsound.[13]"

2. *Unemployment compensation.* (a) Did the Court's decisions in *Sherbert, Thomas* and *Hobbie* impermissibly prefer religion? In THOMAS v. REVIEW BD., Sec. 2 supra, REHNQUIST, J., dissented, finding the result "inconsistent with many of our prior Establishment Clause cases"[2]: "If Indiana were to legislate what the

9. * * * I suggested [in *Sherbert*] that a State could constitutionally create exceptions to its program to accommodate religious scruples. [But] any such exception in order to satisfy the Establishment Clause [would] have to be sufficiently broad so as to be religiously neutral. This would require creating an exception for anyone who, as a matter of conscience, could not comply with the statute. * * *

12. [I] fail to see how [§ 6(j)] has "any substantial legislative purpose" apart from honoring the conscience of individuals who oppose war on only religious grounds. * * *

13. [At] the very least the Constitution requires that the State not excuse students early for the purpose of receiving religious instruction when it does not offer to nonreligious students the opportunity to use school hours for spiritual or ethical instruction of a nonreligious nature. Moreover, whether a released-time program cast in terms of improving "conscience" to the exclusion of artistic or cultural pursuits, would be "neutral" and consistent with the requirement of "voluntarism," is by no means an easy question. * * *

2. To the extent *Sherbert* was correctly decided, it might be argued that cases such as *McCollum, Engel, Schempp, Lemon,* and *Nyquist* were wrongly decided. The "aid" rendered to religion in these latter cases may not be significantly different, in kind or degree, than the "aid" afforded Mrs. Sherbert or Thomas. For example, if the State in *Sherbert* could not deny compensation to one refusing work for religious reasons, it might be argued that a State may not deny reimbursement to students who choose for religious reasons to attend parochial schools. The argument would be that although a State need not allocate any funds to education, once it has done so, it may not require any person to sacrifice his religious beliefs in order to obtain an equal education. There can be little doubt that to the extent secular education provides answers to important moral questions without reference to religion or teaches that there are no answers, a

Court today requires—an unemployment compensation law which permitted bene-fits to be granted to those persons who quit their jobs for religious reasons—the statute would 'plainly' violate the Establishment Clause as interpreted in such cases as [*Lemon*]. First, [the] proviso would clearly serve only a religious purpose. It would grant financial benefits for the sole purpose of accommodating religious beliefs. Second, there can be little doubt that the primary effect of the proviso would be to 'advance' religion by facilitating the exercise of religious belief. Third, any statute including such a proviso would surely 'entangle' the State in religion far more than the mere grant of tax exemptions, as in [*Walz*]. By granting financial benefits to persons solely on the basis of their religious beliefs, the State must necessarily inquire whether the claimant's belief is 'religious' and whether it is sincerely [held.] I believe that Justice Stewart, dissenting in *Schempp,* accurate-ly stated the reach of the Establishment Clause [as] limited to 'government support of proselytizing activities of religious sects by throwing the weight of secular authorities behind the dissemination of religious tenets.' See *McCollum* (Reed, J., dissenting) (impermissible aid is only 'purposeful assistance directly to the church itself or to some religious [group] performing ecclesiastical functions'). Conversely, governmental assistance which does not have the effect of 'inducing' religious belief, but instead merely 'accommodates' or implements an independent religious choice does not impermissibly involve the government in religious choices and therefore does not violate the Establishment [Clause]. I would think that in this case, as in *Sherbert,* had the state voluntarily chosen to pay unemployment compensation benefits to persons who left their jobs for religious reasons, such aid would be constitutionally permissible because it redounds directly to the benefit of the individual."

(b) *Accommodation vs. inducement vs. imposition vs. coercion.* Consider Alan Schwarz, *No Imposition of Religion: The Establishment Clause Value,* 77 Yale L.J. 692, 693, 723, 728 (1968): "[T]he establishment clause [should] be read to prohibit only aid which has as its motive or substantial effect the imposition of religious belief or practice * * *. Exemption of Mrs. Sherbert [represents] a judgment that the exercise of Seventh-day Adventism is more worthy than bowling on Saturdays, but the exemption has no significant effect and arguably no effect at all upon whether someone becomes a Seventh-day Adventist. Similarly, the Sabbatarian exemption from Sunday closing laws does not induce one to become a Jew; draft exemption to conscientious objectors does not normally induce one to become a Quaker; closing the public schools on all religious holidays or on every Wednesday at 2 P.M. does not induce the adoption of religion; and compulsory Sunday closing, while implementing an independent desire to attend church services, has no substantial effect upon the creation of such desire. The availability of preferential aid to religious exercise may, to be sure, induce false claims of religious belief, but the establishment clause is not concerned with false claims of belief, only with induced belief." Does this distinguish *McCollum, Engel* and *Schempp* from *Sher-bert?* Do you agree with all of the *factual* assumptions made? Under this analysis, what result in *Epperson?* What of a small governmental payment to all persons who would lose salary because they have to be absent from their jobs in order to attend religious services? Would the state's failure to provide Mrs. Sherbert with unemployment compensation be the same as its not having on-premises released

person in one sense sacrifices his religious be-lief by attending secular schools. And even if such "aid" were not constitutionally compelled by the Free Exercise Clause, Justice Harlan may well be right in *Sherbert* when he finds sufficient flexibility in the Establishment Clause to permit the States to voluntarily choose to grant such benefits to individuals.

time and school prayer in that all of these actions simply "make the practice of religious beliefs more expensive"?

Compare Jesse H. Choper, *The Religion Clauses of the First Amendment: Reconciling the Conflict,* 41 U.Pitt.L.Rev. 673, 691, 697–700 (1980): "My proposal for resolving the conflict between the two Religion Clauses seeks to implement their historically and contemporarily acknowledged common goal: to safeguard religious liberty. [I]t is only when an accommodation would jeopardize religious liberty—when it would coerce, compromise, or influence religious choice—that it would fail. [For example, in *Yoder,* unless] it could be shown that relieving the Amish [would] tend to coerce, compromise, or influence religious choice—and it is extremely doubtful that it could—the exemption was permissible under the Establishment Clause. In contrast, in *Sherbert,* [the] exemption results in impairment of religious liberty because compulsorily raised tax funds must be used to subsidize Mrs. Sherbert's exercise of religion.[b] [In the draft exemption cases], draftees seeking exemption would have to formulate a statement of personal doctrine that would pass muster. This endeavor would involve deep and careful thought, and perhaps reading in philosophy and religion. Some undoubtedly would be persuaded by what they read. Moreover, the theory of 'cognitive dissonance'— which posits that to avoid madness we tend to become what we hold ourselves to be and what others believe us to be—also suggests that some initially fraudulent claims of belief in a personal religion would develop into true belief. Thus, a draft exemption for religious objectors threatens values of religious freedom by encouraging the adoption of religious beliefs by those who seek to qualify for the benefit."

(c) *Breadth of exemption.* In TEXAS MONTHLY, INC. v. BULLOCK, Sec. 2, II supra, Scalia, J., joined by Rehnquist, C.J., and Kennedy, J., charged that according to Brennan, J.'s plurality opinion, "no law is constitutional whose 'benefits [are] confined to religious organizations,' except, of course, those laws that are unconstitutional *unless* they contain benefits confined to religious organizations. [But] 'the limits of permissible state accommodation to religion are by no means co-extensive with the noninterference mandated by the Free Exercise Clause.' Breadth of coverage is essential to constitutionality whenever a law's benefiting of religious activity is sought to be defended [as] merely the incidental consequence of seeking to benefit *all* activity that achieves a particular secular goal. But that is a different rationale—more commonly invoked than accommodation of religion but, as our cases show, not preclusive of it. Where accommodation of religion is the justification, by definition religion is being singled out." Finally, "the proper lesson to be drawn from" the fact that the free exercise clause may not require the Texas sales tax exemption and "that *Murdock* and *Follett* are narrowly distinguishable" is that "if the exemption comes so close to being a constitutionally required accommodation, there is no doubt that it is at least a permissible one."[c]

---

b. See also Jesse H. Choper, *The Free Exercise Clause,* 27 Wm. & M.L.Rev. 943, 951 n. 25 (1986): "Under Justice Rehnquist's [and Professor Schwarz's] rationale, if a municipally-owned bus company wanted to waive the fare to take people to churches, it could do so. According to Justice Rehnquist, the waiver would not 'induce' religion, but would simply 'accommodate' a religious choice that already had been made. That may be true, but the waiver also would result in what the religion clauses protect against—the use of tax funds for exclusively religious purposes."

c. Why didn't Texas' exemption violate the establishment clause test articulated by Kennedy, J. (joined by Rehnquist, C.J., and White and Scalia, JJ.) in *Allegheny County v. ACLU,* Sec. 1, IV supra, because it gave "direct benefits to religion" and involved "subtle coercion [in] the form of taxation"?

BRENNAN, J., joined by Marshall and Stevens, JJ., responded: "Contrary to the dissent's claims, we in no way suggest that *all* benefits conferred exclusively upon religious groups or upon individuals on account of their religious beliefs are forbidden by the Establishment Clause unless they are mandated by the Free Exercise Clause. Our decisions in *Zorach* and *Amos* offer two examples. Similarly, if the Air Force provided a sufficiently broad exemption from its dress requirements for servicemen whose religious faiths commanded them to wear certain headgear or other attire, see *Goldman v. Weinberger,* that exemption presumably would not be invalid under the Establishment Clause even though this Court has not found it to be required by the Free Exercise Clause.

"All of these cases, however, involve legislative exemptions that did not or would not impose substantial burdens on nonbeneficiaries while allowing others to act according to their religious beliefs, or that were designed to alleviate government intrusions that might significantly deter adherents of a particular faith from conduct protected by the Free Exercise Clause. New York City's decision to release students from public schools so that they might obtain religious instruction elsewhere, which we upheld in *Zorach,* was found not to coerce students who wished to remain behind to alter their religious beliefs, nor did it impose monetary costs on their parents or other taxpayers who opposed or were indifferent to the religious instruction given to students who were released. The hypothetical Air Force uniform exemption also would not place a monetary burden on those required to conform to the dress code or subject them to any appreciable privation. And the application of Title VII's exemption for religious organizations that we approved in *Amos* though it had some adverse effect on those holding or seeking employment with those organizations (if not on taxpayers generally), prevented potentially serious encroachments on protected religious freedoms.

"Texas' tax exemption, by contrast, does not remove a demonstrated and possible grave imposition on religious activity sheltered by the Free Exercise Clause. Moreover, it burdens nonbeneficiaries by increasing their tax bills by whatever amount is needed to offset the benefit bestowed on subscribers to religious publications."

3. *Sabbath observance.* THORNTON v. CALDOR, INC., 472 U.S. 703, 105 S.Ct. 2914, 86 L.Ed.2d 557 (1985), per BURGER, C.J., held that a Connecticut law—which provided "that those who observe a Sabbath any day of the week as a matter of religious conviction must be relieved of the duty to work on that day, no matter what burden or inconvenience this imposes on the employer or fellow workers"—"has a primary effect that impermissibly advances a particular religious practice" and thus violates the establishment clause: "The statute arms Sabbath observers with an absolute and unqualified right not to work on whatever day they designate as their Sabbath [and thus] goes beyond having an incidental or remote effect of advancing religion."[d]

---

d. Rehnquist, J., dissented without opinion.

Consider Richard A. Epstein, *Religious Liberty in the Welfare State*, 31 Wm. & M.L.Rev. 375, 406 (1990): "[It would plainly be unconstitutional] if the state offered to pay a small sum out of public funds to the employer to defray the additional costs it had to bear to keep the religious worker on its payroll. [If] a public subsidy of religious workers is not acceptable under the establishment clause, then a public mandate of a private subsidy is unacceptable as well."

For the view that since "securing individual constitutional rights often (or almost always) imposes impediments to the smooth functioning of our system, if accommodations for religion impose only imprecise social/economic costs, then these prices of religious tolerance are permitted to be paid," see Jesse H. Choper, *Securing Religious Liberty*, 123–126 (1995).

O'CONNOR, J., joined by Marshall, J., concurred, distinguishing "the religious accommodation provisions of Title VII of the Civil Rights Act [which] require private employers to reasonably accommodate the religious practices of employees unless to do so would cause undue hardship to the employer's business": "In my view, a statute outlawing employment discrimination based on race, color, religion, sex or national origin has the valid secular purpose of assuring employment opportunity to all groups in our pluralistic society. Since Title VII calls for reasonable rather than absolute accommodation and extends that requirement to all religious beliefs and practices rather than protecting only the Sabbath observance, I believe an objective observer would perceive it as an anti-discrimination law rather than an endorsement of religion or a particular religious practice."

Was the purpose or effect of the *Caldor* statute any different than that of the *Amos* statute or the Court's decisions in *Sherbert, Thomas, Hobbie, Roy* and *Yoder? Amos* distinguished *Caldor* on the ground that in *Amos,* "appellee was not legally obligated to take the steps necessary to qualify for a temple recommend, and his discharge was not required by statute." Should it make a difference that, unlike the other cases, the Caldor statute sought to alleviate burdens on religion posed by private parties rather than the state?

Does the *Caldor* statute "promote" and "endorse" a particular "religion" or "religious belief" or "religious practice" any moreso than the Court's decisions in *Sherbert, Thomas, Hobbie, Yoder* and *Roy,* or than the statutory exemptions from the draft or Sunday Closing Laws? *Hobbie* distinguished *Caldor* as follows: "Florida's provision of unemployment benefits to religious observers does not single out a particular class of such persons for favorable treatment and thereby have the effect of implicitly endorsing a particular religious belief. Rather, the provision of unemployment benefits generally available within the State to religious observers who must leave their employment due to an irreconcilable conflict between the demands of work and conscience neutrally accommodates religious beliefs and practices, without endorsement."

In *Kiryas Joel,* Sec. 3 supra, SCALIA, J., joined by Rehnquist, C.J., and Thomas, J., disagreed with the Court's conclusion that New York had impermissibly preferred one religion: "[M]ost efforts at accommodation seek to solve a problem that applies to members of only one or a few religions. Not every religion uses wine in its sacraments, but that does not make an exemption from Prohibition for sacramental wine-use impermissible, nor does it require the State granting such an exemption to explain in advance how it will treat every other claim for dispensation from its controlled-substances laws. Likewise, not every religion uses peyote in its services, but we have suggested that legislation which exempts the sacramental use of peyote from generally applicable drug laws is not only permissible, but desirable, see *Smith,* without any suggestion that some 'up front' legislative guarantee of equal treatment for sacramental substances used by other sects must be provided."

Kennedy, J., expressed a similar view: "It is normal for legislatures to respond to problems as they arise—no less so when the issue is religious accommodation. Most accommodations cover particular religious practices."

Is a *general* rule for free exercise exemptions—as under *Sherbert-Yoder,* or the Religious Freedom Restoration Act (fn. a after *Smith*)—preferable to a specific exemption for religion (as the statutes in *Texas Monthly* and *Caldor*)? Consider Thomas C. Berg, *The New Attacks on Religious Freedom Legislation, and Why They are Wrong,* 21 Card.L.Rev. 415, 435–36 (1999): "Requiring the same standard for all religious freedom claims, in the less political forum of the courts, serves the goal of religious equality by minimizing the chance that only politically powerful groups will get accommodations, while individuals or very small groups without a lobbyist will escape the legislature's attention altogether.[89]"

4. *School prayer.* In *Jaffree,* O'CONNOR, J., applied her "solution"[e] to Alabama's moment of silence law: "No law prevents a student who is so inclined from praying silently in public schools. [Of] course, the State might argue that § 16–1–20.1 protects not silent prayer, but rather group silent prayer under State sponsorship. Phrased in these terms, the burden lifted by the statute is not one imposed by the State of Alabama, but by the Establishment Clause as interpreted in *Engel* and *Schempp.* In my view, it is beyond the authority of the State of Alabama to remove burdens imposed by the Constitution itself."

5. *Reconciling the conflict.* Assuming the validity of the distinction between *McCollum, Engel, Schempp* and *Jaffree* on the one hand, and the programs such as that in *Amos* and exemption from the draft etc. on the other, are the above approaches nonetheless undesirable because they result not merely in protection of free exercise (or neutrality or accommodation) but in relieving persons with certain religious beliefs of significant burdens from which many other persons strongly desire to be exempted? That, in this sense, there is "preference" for minority religions and "discrimination" against the other persons because of their religion or lack of it?[f]

Might religious exemptions be seen as "restorative or equalizing" (Galanter, note 4, Sec. 2, II supra)? Consider Gordon, fn. a in *Lukumi,* at 91–92: "In a democracy, laws inevitably will reflect the majority's values, and consequently, laws will tend to burden minority religions but not majority ones. Therefore, majority religions generally have a kind of inherent exemption from the force of law. In addition, politically powerful minority religions often are able to obtain express exemptions from legislation. Therefore, powerless minority religions will be the only religions without exemptions. The accommodation principle provides powerless minority religions with some measure of the same protection that other religions already enjoy in the democratic process." What about exemptions (accommodations) for majority (mainstream) religions? Consider Greene, fn. d in *Kiryas Joel,* at 74: "When a majority pushes for governmentally organized prayer in public schools or for the placement of its favored religious symbols in the halls of government, it is wrong to call such actions 'accommodation.' [But] when the effect of the majority's actions is to make life easier for a minority, there is no concern about an 'Establishment' of religion. It also seems wrong to say that accommodation of minority religions constitutes a symbolic endorsement of those religions; rather, accommodation in this context suggests that the majority is coming to the aid of a burdened minority, not that the majority agrees with the minority on any matter of religious truth." Compare Ira C. Lupu, *Uncovering the Village of Kiryas Joel,* 96 Colum.L.Rev. 104, 117–18 (1996): "If Jews are a relatively small minority in New York State but a sizable minority or a majority in some New York City area suburbs, may the state close public schools on Yom Kippur while the suburb is forbidden from doing likewise? May Pennsylvania accommodate Mormon traditions, while Utah may not?"

---

89. See Ira C. Lulpu, *Reconstructing the Establishment Clause: The Case Against Discretionary Accommodation of Religion,* 140 U.Pa.L.Rev. 555 (1991) (claiming that statute-by-statute legislative accommodations are unconstitutional because they reflect the varying political power of different religious groups).

e. See fn. c in *Amos.*

f. Should the Court "either suggest or require that an alternative burden be imposed on individuals who would otherwise qualify for religious exemptions"? Choper, fn. d supra, at 92.

Chapter 9

EQUAL PROTECTION

[handwritten margin note: - basis for governmental distinctions between different groups of people. But all laws draw lines - Drivers license - Bar exam → practice law - welfare]

Virtually no legislation applies universally and treats all persons equally; all laws classify (or "discriminate") by imposing special burdens (or granting exemptions from such burdens) or by conferring benefits on some people and not others. Under what circumstances do legislative classifications violate the fourteenth amendment's command that no state shall "deny to any person within its jurisdiction the equal protection of the laws"?[a]

Although the language of the equal protection clause is not confined to racial discrimination, the *Slaughter-House Cases,* Ch. 5, Sec. 1, III (the first decision interpreting the Civil War amendments), "doubt[ed] very much whether any action of a state not directed by way of discrimination against the negroes as a class, or on account of their race, will ever be held to come within the purview of this provision." At least as early as 1897, however, the Court invoked the equal protection clause to invalidate a commonplace economic regulation that obligated railroad defendants (but not others) to pay the attorneys' fees of successful plaintiffs. The Court acknowledged that "as a general proposition, [it] is undeniably true [that] it is not within the scope of the Fourteenth Amendment to withhold from States the power of classification." But, the Court continued, "it must appear" that a classification is "based upon some reasonable ground—some difference which bears a just and proper relation to the attempted classification—and is not a mere arbitrary selection." *Gulf, C. & S. F. Ry. v. Ellis,* 165 U.S. 150, 17 S.Ct. 255, 41 L.Ed. 666 (1897).[b]

Sec. 1 of this Chapter considers this "traditional approach" under the equal protection clause to general economic and social welfare regulations. Sec. 2 then deals with the "strict scrutiny" given to explicit racial and ethnic classifications,

---

a. By its terms, the equal protection clause does not apply to the federal government. Nonetheless, at least since its 1954 decision in *Bolling v. Sharpe,* Sec. 2, II infra, the Court has held that the due process clause incorporates equal protection norms binding on the federal government. Although its pattern of decisions has not been perfectly consistent, the Court has generally insisted that the "approach to Fifth Amendment equal protection claims [is] precisely the same as to equal protection claims under the Fourteenth Amendment." *Weinberger v. Wiesenfeld,* Sec. 3 infra;

see also *Adarand Constructors, Inc. v. Pena,* Sec. 2, VI infra. The principal exception to this general rule of "congruence" involves the treatment of aliens. Current doctrine subjects state discriminations against aliens to more searching judicial scrutiny than federal discriminations against aliens—a disparity considered in Sec. 4, I infra.

b. For an even earlier invocation of the equal protection clause to invalidate a classification of transportation rates, see *Reagan v. Farmers' Loan & Trust Co.,* 154 U.S. 362, 14 S.Ct. 1047, 38 L.Ed. 1014 (1894).

which the Court has deemed "suspect," as well as with related issues involving race. Sec. 3 reviews the Court's treatment of gender-based classifications. Sec. 4 addresses the use of a nondeferential standard of review for governmental action that disadvantages several other groups. Finally, Sec. 5 examines standards for equal protection review of classifications affecting what the Court classifies as "fundamental" rights.

SECTION 1. TRADITIONAL APPROACH

As seen in Ch. 5, the due process clause was the usual provision invoked by the Court in the first third of the twentieth century to overturn a great many economic and social welfare regulations. But despite Holmes, J.'s reference to the equal protection clause as "the usual last resort of constitutional arguments,"[c] the Court held during this period that approximately twenty state and local laws violated equal protection. For the most part, the Court at least purported to take a deferential approach that granted the states "a broad discretion in classification in the exercise of [their] power of regulation" and interposed the "constitutional guaranty of equal protection" only "against discriminations that are entirely arbitrary."[d] But compare the formulation used in *F.S. Royster Guano Co. v. Virginia*, 253 U.S. 412, 40 S.Ct. 560, 64 L.Ed. 989 (1920): "[T]he classification must be reasonable, not arbitrary, and must rest upon some ground of difference having a fair and substantial relation to the object of the legislation, so that all persons similarly circumstanced shall be treated alike."

The materials that follow concern the Court's equal protection scrutiny of economic and social welfare regulations since the late 1930s, when it abandoned active substantive due process review of such legislation.

RAILWAY EXPRESS AGENCY v. NEW YORK
336 U.S. 106, 69 S.Ct. 463, 93 L.Ed. 533 (1949).

JUSTICE DOUGLAS delivered the opinion of the Court.

[T]he Traffic Regulations of the City of New York [provide]: "No person shall operate [on] any street an advertising vehicle; [except for] business notices upon business delivery vehicles, so long as such vehicles are engaged in the usual business [of] the owner and not used merely or mainly for advertising."

Appellant [operates] about 1,900 trucks in New York City and sells the space on the exterior sides of these trucks for advertising [for] the most part unconnected with its own business. It was convicted * * *.

The court [below] concluded that advertising on [vehicles] constitutes a distraction to vehicle drivers and to pedestrians alike and therefore affects the safety of the public in the use of the streets. We do not sit to weigh evidence on the due process issue in order to determine whether the regulation is sound or appropriate; nor is it our function to pass judgment on its wisdom. See *Olsen v. Nebraska* [Ch. 5, Sec. 3 supra]. We would be trespassing on one of the most intensely local and specialized of all municipal problems if we held that this regulation had no relation to the traffic problem of New York City. It is the judgment of the local authorities that it does have such a relation.

---

c. *Buck v. Bell*, 274 U.S. 200, 47 S.Ct. 584, 71 L.Ed. 1000 (1927).

d. *Smith v. Cahoon*, 283 U.S. 553, 51 S.Ct. 582, 75 L.Ed. 1264 (1931).

[The] question of equal protection of the laws is pressed more strenuously on us. [It] is said, for example, that one of appellant's trucks carrying the advertisement of a commercial house would not cause any greater distraction of pedestrians and vehicle drivers than if the commercial house carried the same advertisement on its own truck. Yet the regulation allows the latter to do what the former is forbidden from doing. It is therefore contended that the classification which the regulation makes has no relation to the traffic problem since a violation turns not on what kind of advertisements are carried on trucks but on whose trucks they are carried.

That, however, is a superficial way of analyzing the [problem]. The local authorities may well have concluded that those who advertised their own wares on their trucks do not present the same traffic problem in view of the nature or extent of the advertising which they use. * * *

We cannot say that that judgment is not an allowable one. Yet if it is, the classification has relation to the purpose for which it is made and does not contain the kind of discrimination against which the Equal Protection Clause affords protection. It is by such practical considerations based on experience rather than by theoretical inconsistencies that the question of equal protection is to be answered. And the fact that New York City sees fit to eliminate from traffic this kind of distraction but does not touch what may be even greater ones in a different category, such as the vivid displays on Times Square, is immaterial. It is no requirement of equal protection that all evils of the same genus be eradicated or none at all. * * *

Affirmed.

JUSTICE RUTLEDGE acquiesces in the Court's opinion and judgment, dubitante on the question of equal protection of the laws.

JUSTICE JACKSON, concurring. * * *

The burden should rest heavily upon one who would persuade us to use the due process clause to strike down a substantive [law]. Even its provident use against municipal regulations frequently disables all government—state, municipal and federal—from dealing with the conduct in question because the requirement of due process is also applicable to State and Federal Governments. * * *

Invocation of the equal protection clause, on the other hand, does not disable any governmental body from dealing with the subject at hand. It merely means that the prohibition or regulation must have a broader impact. I regard it as a salutary doctrine that cities, states and the Federal Government must exercise their powers so as not to discriminate between their inhabitants except upon some reasonable differentiation fairly related to the object of regulation. [T]here is no more effective practical guaranty against arbitrary and unreasonable government than to require that the principles of law which officials would impose upon a minority must be imposed generally. Conversely, nothing opens the door to arbitrary action so effectively as to allow those officials to pick and choose only a few to whom they will apply legislation and thus to escape the political retribution that might be visited upon them if larger numbers were affected. Courts can take no better measure to assure that laws will be just than to require that laws be equal in operation. * * *

In this case, if the City of New York should assume that display of any advertising on vehicles tends and intends to distract the attention of persons using the highways and to increase the dangers of its traffic, I should think it fully within its constitutional powers to forbid it all. [Instead], however, the City seeks to reduce the hazard only by saying that while some may, others may not exhibit such appeals. The same display, for example, advertising cigarettes, which this appellant is forbidden to carry on its trucks, may be carried on the trucks of a cigarette dealer. [The] courts of New York have declared that the sole nature and purpose of the regulation before us is to reduce traffic hazards. There is not even a pretense here that the traffic hazard created by the advertising which is forbidden is in any manner or degree more hazardous than that which is permitted. * * *

* * * I do not think differences of treatment under law should be approved on classification because of differences unrelated to the legislative purpose. The equal protection clause ceases to assure either equality or protection if it is avoided by any conceivable difference that can be pointed out between those bound and those left free. This Court has often announced the principle that the differentiation must have an appropriate relation to the object of the [legislation].

The question in my mind comes to this. Where individuals contribute to an evil or danger in the same way and to the same degree, may those who do so for hire be prohibited, while those who do so for their own commercial ends but not for hire be allowed to continue? I think the answer has to be that the hireling may be put in a class by himself and may be dealt with differently than those who act on their own. But this is not merely because such a discrimination will enable the lawmaker to diminish the evil. That might be done by many classifications, which I should think wholly unsustainable. It is rather because there is a real difference between doing in self-interest and doing for hire, so that it is one thing to tolerate action from those who act on their own and it is another thing to permit the same action to be promoted for a price. * * *

NEW ORLEANS v. DUKES

427 U.S. 297, 96 S.Ct. 2513, 49 L.Ed.2d 511 (1976).

PER CURIAM.

[A 1972 New Orleans ordinance banned all pushcart food vendors in the French Quarter ("Vieux Carre") except those who had continuously operated there for eight or more years. Two vendors had done so for twenty or more years and qualified under the "grandfather clause." Appellee, who had operated a pushcart for only two years, attacked the ordinance.]

When local economic regulation is challenged solely as violating the Equal Protection Clause, this Court consistently defers to legislative determinations as to the desirability of particular statutory discriminations. Unless a classification trammels fundamental personal rights or is drawn upon inherently suspect distinctions such as race, religion, or alienage, our decisions presume the constitutionality of the statutory discriminations and require only that the classification challenged be rationally related to a legitimate state interest. States are accorded wide latitude in the regulation of their local economies under their police powers, and rational distinctions may be made with substantially less than mathematical exactitude. Legislatures may implement their program step by step in such economic areas, adopting regulations that only partially ameliorate a perceived evil and deferring complete elimination of the evil to future regulations. See, e.g., *Williamson v. Lee Optical Co.*[a] In short, the judiciary may not sit as a superlegisla-

---

    a. In *Lee Optical*, Ch. 5, Sec. 3, a statute that otherwise prohibited the fitting of eye-glasses without a prescription exempted businesses that sold ready-to-wear glasses. The

ture to judge the wisdom or desirability of legislative policy determinations made in areas that neither affect fundamental rights nor proceed along suspect lines; in the local economic sphere, it is only the invidious discrimination, the wholly arbitrary act, which cannot stand consistently with the Fourteenth Amendment. See, e.g., *Ferguson v. Skrupa*.[5]

[New Orleans'] classification rationally furthers the purpose which [the] city had identified as its objective in enacting the provision, that is, as a means "to preserve the appearance and custom valued by the Quarter's residents and attractive to tourists." The legitimacy of that objective is obvious. The City Council plainly could further that objective by making the reasoned judgment that street peddlers and hawkers tend to interfere with the charm and beauty of an historic area [and] that to ensure the economic vitality of that area, such businesses should be substantially curtailed in the Vieux Carre, if not totally banned.

It is suggested that the "grandfather provision" [was] a totally arbitrary and irrational method of achieving the city's purpose. But rather than proceeding by the immediate and absolute abolition of all pushcart food vendors, the city could rationally [decide] that newer businesses were less likely to have built up substantial reliance interests in continued operation in the Vieux Carre and that the two vendors who qualified under the "grandfather clause" [had] themselves become part of the distinctive character and charm that distinguishes the Vieux Carre. We cannot say that these judgments so lack rationality that they constitute a constitutionally impermissible denial of equal protection. * * *

Reversed.

JUSTICE MARSHALL concurs in the judgment.

JUSTICE STEVENS took no part in [the] case.

Notes and Questions

1. *The theory of equal protection.* In what sense were the challengers in *Railway Express* and *Dukes* afforded the equal protection of the laws? Does the Court effectively read the "equal protection" guarantee as establishing a requirement of "reasonable classification," under which individuals cannot claim that they personally have been treated "unequally" so long as it is reasonable to treat the general class of which they are members differently from other classes? See Joseph Tussman & Jacobus tenBroek, *The Equal Protection of the Laws*, 37 Calif.L.Rev. 341, 344 (1949).

Is this the only way in which the equal protection clause could sensibly be interpreted? Does the equal protection clause embody a moral principle that "government must treat everyone as of equal status and with equal concern"?

Court found no violation of equal protection: "Evils in the same field may be of different dimensions and proportions, requiring different remedies. Or so the legislature may think. Or the reform may take one step at a time, addressing itself to the phase of the problem which seems most acute to the legislative mind. The legislature may select one phase of one field and apply a remedy there, neglecting the others. [For] all this record shows, the ready-to-wear branch of this business may not loom large in Oklahoma or may present problems of regulation distinct from the other branch."

5. *Ferguson* [Ch. 5, Sec. 3] presented an analogous situation. There, a Kansas statute excepted lawyers from the prohibition of a statute making it a misdemeanor for any person to engage in the business of debt adjusting. We held that the exception of lawyers was not a denial of [equal protection].

Ronald Dworkin, *Freedom's Law* 10 (1996). Is the Court's approach consistent with this principle?

The Court has seldom tried to link its "rational basis" review of non-suspect classifications with the original understanding of the equal protection clause. Should it? Consider the suggestion of Dworkin, supra, at 10, that the equal protection clause "has a moral principle as its content" and that the Court should focus on what this moral principle requires, not on the framers' specific expectations about how the principle would be applied.

2. *Underinclusive legislation.*[a] Does the "one step at a time" approach to legislation that the Court permits in *Railway Express* and *New Orleans v. Dukes* permit officials to give preferential treatment to favored groups and thereby promote unfairness? Consider Michael Klarman, *An Interpretive History of Modern Equal Protection,* 90 Mich.L.Rev. 213, 250 (1991): "[The] facially bizarre classification [in *Railway Express*] probably was attributable primarily to the powerful lobbying arm of the city's newspapers. Several Justices were troubled by a classification difficult to justify in terms other than raw interest group power. While *Railway Express* came down unanimous as to result, the Court initially was divided five to four, with Justice Reed arguing (correctly) in his draft dissent that to sustain a law based on such a 'whimsical' distinction was essentially to render the Equal Protection Clause 'useless in state regulation of business practices.'" Compare Note, *Equal Protection,* 82 Harv.L.Rev. 1076, 1085 (1969): "To require that the state remedy all aspects of a particular mischief or none at all might preclude a state from undertaking any program of correction until its resources were adequate to deal with the entire problem. Second, in some instances, the state may not be convinced that a particular policy is a wise one, or it may prove impossible to marshal a legislative majority in favor of extending the policy's coverage any further. Thus, to demand application of the policy to all whom it might logically encompass, would severely restrict the state's opportunities to experiment."

3. *Protecting disadvantaged minorities?* When "politically disadvantaged minorities are affected," should "the legislative judgment [be] more critically regarded"? Note, 82 Harv.L.Rev. at 1125. Were the excluded vendors in *Railway Express* and *Dukes* disadvantaged minorities? If so, in what sense?

Consider Jesse H. Choper, *Judicial Review and the National Political Process* 75–77 (1980): "[A]lmost all, if not all, groups [in] the American political process are 'minorities.' Thus, each time any group loses any political battle in which it has an interest—and some group always does—it may lay claim to the label of 'political weakness' or 'submerged and beaten minority.' [It] is true that some minorities, because of their sophistication and combined arithmetical and financial strength, are more influential than others on most political issues; and that some groups with modest numbers may win powerful surrogates who give them forceful representation. Similarly, there are some minorities who are less effective than others on most legislative matters because of their geographic isolation, the general inexcitability or unpopularity of their ideas, their relative inarticulateness, their lack of numbers and resources, or because they are viewed with such resentment, distaste, or hatred that they can neither join working coalitions nor prevent hostile action. But there are many disparate groups who may legitimately claim to meet some or all of these varied criteria for judicial solicitude." See also

---

a. For the classic description of various types of legislative classifications, see Tussman & tenBroek, supra.

Terrance Sandalow, *The Distrust of Politics,* 56 N.Y.U.L.Rev. 446, 466–67 (1981): "Corporations [do] not vote, but those who argue that aliens should be accorded [special protection] do not frequently complain that corporations should also receive that protection because they lack political influence. Any attempt to appraise the inner workings of the political process must, as the illustration of the corporation suggests, examine the entire process to ascertain the extent of a group's influence. [But] what measure have we, other than an evaluation of outcomes [i.e., the desirability of the substantive policies enacted by the legislature]?"

4. *Legislative purpose.* Of what relevance was it in *Railway Express* that the state courts "declared that the sole purpose" of the law "is to reduce traffic hazards"? Would it be more accurate (and realistic) to describe the purpose as being "to promote public safety slightly by reducing the number of distractions on the sides of moving vehicles to the extent this is feasible without jeopardizing the economic well-being of those merchants who advertise on their own trucks"—a purpose to which the classification unquestionably was "rationally related"? See Note, *Legislative Purpose, Rationality and Equal Protection,* 82 Yale L.J. 123, 144 (1972). Is it not true that many government programs "involve goals that reflect an accommodation of various purposes which are determined by subtle or blatant policy trade-offs"? Id. That often "the legislature is simply a 'market-like arena' in which individuals and special interest groups trade with each other through representatives to further their own private ends"? Scott H. Bice, *Rationality Analysis in Constitutional Law,* 65 Minn.L.Rev. 1, 19 (1980).

Are such legislative purposes (or goals) "rational"? "Legitimate"? "Constitutionally permissible"? Consider Tussman & tenBroek, supra, at 350: "[T]he requirement that laws be equal rests upon a theory of legislation quite distinct from that of pressure groups—a theory which puts forward some conception of a 'general good' as the 'legitimate public purpose' at which legislation must aim, and according to which the triumph of private or group pressure marks the corruption of the legislative process." Compare Richard Posner, *The DeFunis Case and the Constitutionality of Preferential Treatment of Racial Minorities,* 1974 Sup.Ct.Rev. 1, 27: "[A] vast part of the output of the governmental process would be seen to consist of discrimination, in the sense of an effort to redistribute wealth (in one form or another) from one group in the community to another, founded on the superior ability of one group to manipulate the political process rather than on any principle of justice or efficiency. Yet it would be odd, indeed, to condemn as unconstitutional the most characteristic product of a democratic (perhaps of any) political system."

5. *Deference and the "underenforcement" thesis.* Consider the possibility— first advanced in Lawrence G. Sager, *Fair Measure: The Legal Status of Underenforced Constitutional Norms,* 91 Harv.L.Rev. 1212 (1978)—that the deferential test applied in cases such as *Railway Express* and *Dukes* does not reflect the "meaning" of the equal protection clauses, but instead embodies a judgment about the limits of effective judicial enforcement. "According to Professor Sager, the Equal Protection Clause of the Fourteenth Amendment expresses the principle that '[a] state may treat persons differently only when it is fair to do so.' If this is the norm, then the most familiar equal protection test, under which courts uphold classifications that are rationally related to any actual or hypothesized state interest, is an instance of constitutional 'underenforcement.' The Court has determined that allowing judges to make independent, case-by-case assessments of the fairness of statutory classifications would invite excessive litigation and generate unpredictable and conflicting results. This judgment about undesirable

consequences, rather than a decision about constitutional 'meaning,' has led the Court to develop a doctrine that prescribes broad judicial deference to legislative decisions." Richard H. Fallon, Jr., *Implementing the Constitution*, 111 Harv.L.Rev. 54, 64–65 (1997). Would adoption of a deferential standard on this basis reflect judicial abdication? A defensible recognition that the Court must sometimes share the function of constitutional "implementation" with other governmental institutions? See id.

———

NEW YORK CITY TRANSIT AUTH. v. BEAZER, 440 U.S. 568, 99 S.Ct. 1355, 59 L.Ed.2d 587 (1979), per STEVENS, J., upheld the exclusion of all methadone users from any Transit Authority (TA) employment. It reversed the federal district court's conclusion that, because about 75% of "patients who have been on methadone maintenance for at least a year are free from illicit drug use" and because the exclusion applied to non-safety sensitive jobs, it had "no rational relation to the demands of the job to be performed": "[A]ny special rule short of total exclusion that TA might adopt is likely to be less precise—and will assuredly be more costly—than the one that it currently enforces. If eligibility is marked at any intermediate point—whether after one year of treatment or later—the classification will inevitably discriminate between employees or applicants equally or almost equally apt to achieve full recovery. [By] contrast, the 'no drugs' policy now enforced by TA is supported by the legitimate inference that as long as a treatment program (or other drug use) continues, a degree of uncertainty persists.* * *

"[T]he District Court's conclusion was that TA's rule is broader than necessary to exclude those methadone users who are not actually qualified to work for TA. We may assume [that] it is probably unwise for a large employer like TA to rely on a general rule instead of individualized consideration of every job applicant. But these assumptions concern matters of personnel policy that do not implicate the principle safeguarded by the Equal Protection Clause. As the District Court recognized, the special classification created by TA's rule serves the general objectives of safety and efficiency. Moreover, the exclusionary line challenged by respondents [does] not circumscribe a class of persons characterized by some unpopular trait or affiliation, it does not create or reflect any special likelihood of bias on the part of the ruling majority. Under these circumstances, it is of no constitutional significance that the degree of rationality is not as great with respect to certain ill-defined subparts of the classification as it is with respect to the classification as a whole."[a]

WHITE, J., joined by Marshall, J., dissented: Both courts below "found that those who have been maintained on methadone for at least a year and who are free from the use of illicit drugs and alcohol can easily be identified through normal personnel procedures and, for a great many jobs, are as employable as and present no more risk than applicants from the general population. [On] the facts as found [one] can reach the Court's result only if [equal protection] imposes no real constraint at all in this situation. * * *

a. See also *Vance v. Bradley*, 440 U.S. 93, 99 S.Ct. 939, 59 L.Ed.2d 171 (1979), per White, J., (sustaining mandatory retirement at age 60 for federal Foreign Service personnel), conceding that the classification was "to some extent both under- and over-inclusive" but holding that "perfection is by no means required. [In] an equal protection case of this type, [those] challenging the legislative judgment must convince the court that the legislative facts on which the classification is apparently based could not reasonably be conceived to be true by the governmental decisionmaker."

"Of course, the District Court's order permitting total exclusion of all methadone users maintained for less than one year, whether successfully or not, would still exclude some employables and would to this extent be overinclusive. [But although] many of those who have not been successfully maintained for a year are employable, as a class they, unlike the protected group, are not as employable as the general population. Thus, even assuming the bad risks could be identified, serving the end of employability would require unusual efforts to determine those more likely to revert. But that legitimate secondary goal is not fulfilled by excluding the protected [class]. Accordingly, the rule's classification of successfully maintained persons as dispositively different from the general population is left without any justification and, with its irrationality and invidiousness thus uncovered, must fall before the Equal Protection Clause."

White, J., added in a footnote: "I have difficulty also with the Court's easy conclusion that the challenged rule was '[q]uite plainly' not motivated 'by any special animus against a specific group of persons.' Heroin addiction is a special problem of the poor, and the addict population is composed largely of racial minorities that the Court has previously recognized as politically powerless and historical subjects of majoritarian neglect. Persons on methadone maintenance have few interests in common with members of the majority, and thus are unlikely to have their interests protected, or even considered, in governmental decisionmaking. Indeed, petitioners stipulated that '[o]ne of the reasons for [the] drug policy is the fact that [petitioners] feel[ ] an adverse public reaction would result if it were generally known that [petitioners] employed persons with a prior history of drug abuse, including persons participating in methadone maintenance programs.' It is hard for me to reconcile that stipulation of animus against former addicts with our past holdings that 'a bare [desire] to harm a politically unpopular group cannot constitute a *legitimate* governmental interest.' *U.S. Dept. of Agriculture v. Moreno*, [p. 1161 infra]. On the other hand, the afflictions to which petitioners are more sympathetic, such as alcoholism and mental illness, are shared by both white and black, rich and poor.

"Some weight should also be given to the history of the rule. Petitioners admit that it was not the result of a reasoned policy decision and stipulated that they had never studied the ability of those on methadone maintenance to perform petitioners' jobs. Petitioners are not directly accountable to the public, are not the type of official body that normally makes legislative judgments of fact such as those relied upon by the majority today, and are by nature more concerned with business efficiency than with other public policies for which they have no direct responsibility. Both the State and City of New York, which do exhibit those democratic characteristics, hire persons in methadone programs for similar jobs.

"These factors together strongly point to a conclusion of invidious discrimination. * * *"

Notes and Questions

1. *Overinclusive legislation.* Measured against the problems that they were designed to address, the legislative classifications involved in *Railway Express* and *Dukes* were "underinclusive"; they did not purport to solve the entire problem, but took only a partial step. But many laws are "overinclusive": They subject an entire class to regulation, even though not every person within the class may pose the problem that the legislature seeks to address. In *Beazer*, for example, the challenged regulation was overinclusive insofar as some methadone users would have presented none of the risks associated with illegal drug use.

2. *Applicable standard.* Should the Court be more deferential to overinclusiveness because it "poses less danger than underinclusiveness, at least from the viewpoint of political accountability, for overinclusiveness does not ordinarily exempt potentially powerful opponents from a law's reach"? Tribe 2d ed., at 1049. Or is overinclusion "less tolerable than underinclusion, for while the latter fails to impose the burden on some who should logically bear it, the former actually does impose the burden on some who do not belong in the class"? Note, 82 Harv.L.Rev. at 1086.

UNITED STATES R.R. RETIREMENT BD. v. FRITZ

449 U.S. 166, 101 S.Ct. 453, 66 L.Ed.2d 368 (1980).

JUSTICE REHNQUIST delivered the opinion of the Court.

The United States District Court [held violative of the "equal protection component of the Fifth Amendment" § 231b(h)] of the Railroad Retirement Act of 1974. [Under the] Act's predecessor statute, a person who worked for both railroad and nonrailroad employers and who qualified for railroad retirement benefits and social security benefits received retirement benefits under both systems and an accompanying "windfall" benefit. [Congress] determined to place the system on a "sound financial basis" by eliminating future accruals of those benefits. Congress also enacted various transitional provisions [which] expressly preserved windfall benefits for some classes of employees.

* * * First, those employees who lacked the requisite 10 years of railroad employment to qualify for railroad retirement benefits as of January 1, 1975, the changeover date, would have their retirement benefits computed under the new system and would not receive any windfall benefit. Second, those individuals already retired and already receiving dual benefits [would] continue to receive a windfall benefit. Third, those employees who had qualified for both railroad and social security benefits as of the changeover date, but who had not yet retired as of that date (and thus were not yet receiving dual benefits), were entitled to windfall benefits if they had (1) performed some railroad service in 1974 or (2) had a "current connection" with the railroad industry as of December 31, 1974,[6] or (3) completed 25 years of railroad service as of December 31, 1974. * * *

Thus, an individual who, as of the changeover date, was unretired and had 11 years of railroad employment and sufficient nonrailroad employment to qualify for social security benefits is eligible for the full windfall amount if he worked for the railroad in 1974 or had a current connection with the railroad as of December 31, 1974, or his later retirement date. But an unretired individual with 24 years of railroad service and sufficient nonrailroad service to qualify for social security benefits is not eligible for a full windfall amount unless he worked for the railroad in 1974, or had a current connection with the railroad as of December 31, 1974 or his later retirement date. * * *

The District Court agreed with appellees that a differentiation based solely on whether an employee was "active" in the railroad business as of 1974 was not "rationally related" to the congressional purposes of insuring the solvency of the railroad retirement system and protecting vested benefits. We disagree and reverse.

6. The term "current connection" is defined [to] mean, in general, employment in the railroad industry in 12 of the preceding 30 calendar months.

[The] plain language of § 231b(h) marks the beginning and end of our inquiry. There Congress determined that some of those who in the past received full windfall benefits would not continue to do so. Because Congress could have eliminated windfall benefits for all classes of employees, it is not constitutionally impermissible for Congress to have drawn lines between groups of employees for the purpose of phasing out those benefits. *Dukes*.

The only remaining question is whether Congress achieved its purpose in a patently arbitrary or irrational way. [Congress] could properly conclude that persons who had actually acquired statutory entitlement to windfall benefits while still employed in the railroad industry had a greater equitable claim to those benefits than the members of appellees' class who were no longer in railroad employment when they became eligible for dual benefits. [Furthermore,] Congress could assume that those who had a current connection with the railroad industry when the Act was passed in 1974, or who returned to the industry before their retirement, were more likely than those who had left the industry prior to 1974 and who never returned, to be among the class of persons who pursue careers in the railroad industry, the class for whom the Railroad Retirement Act was designed.

Where, as here, there are plausible reasons for Congress' action, our inquiry is at an end. It is, of course, "constitutionally irrelevant whether this reasoning in fact underlay the legislative decision," because this Court has never insisted that a legislative body articulate its reasons for enacting a statute. This is particularly true where the legislature must necessarily engage in a process of line drawing. The "task of classifying persons for [benefits] inevitably requires that some persons who have an almost equally strong claim to favorite treatment be placed on different sides of the line," *Mathews v. Diaz*, [Sec. 4, I infra], and the fact the line might have been drawn differently at some points is a matter for legislative, rather than judicial consideration.

Finally, we disagree with the District Court's conclusion that Congress was unaware of what it accomplished or that it was misled by the groups that appeared before it. If this test were applied literally to every member of any legislature that ever voted on a law, there would be very few laws which would survive it. The language of the statute is clear, and we have historically assumed that Congress intended what it enacted. To be sure, appellees lost a political battle in which they had a strong interest, but this is neither the first nor the last time that such a result will occur in the legislative forum. * * *[a]

JUSTICE BRENNAN, with whom JUSTICE MARSHALL joins, dissenting.

[When] faced with a challenge to a legislative classification under the rational basis test, the court should ask, first, what the purposes of the statute are, and second, whether the classification is rationally related to achievement of those purposes. The purposes of the Railroad Retirement Act of 1974 are clear, because Congress has commendably stated them in the House and Senate reports accompanying the Act. A section of the reports is entitled "Principal Purpose of the Bill." It notes generally that "[t]he bill provides for a complete restructuring of the Railroad Retirement Act of 1937, and will place it on a sound financial basis," and then states: "Persons who already have vested rights under both the Railroad Retirement and the Social Security systems will in the future be permitted to receive benefits computed under both systems just as is true under existing law."[3]

---

a. Stevens, J., concurred in the judgment.

3. Several pages later, the reports again make clear that persons with vested rights to earned dual benefits would retain [them].

Moreover, Congress explained that this purpose was based on considerations of fairness and the legitimate expectations of the retirees. [The] classification at issue here, which deprives some retirees of vested dual benefits that they had earned prior to 1974, directly conflicts with Congress' stated purpose. As such, the classification is not only rationally unrelated to the congressional purpose; it is inimical to it. * * *

A. The Court states that "the plain language of § 231b(h) marks the beginning and end of our inquiry." [Since] the Act deprives appellees of their vested earned dual benefits, the Court apparently assumes that Congress must have *intended* that result. But by presuming purpose from result, the Court reduces analysis to tautology. It may always be said that Congress intended to do what it in fact did. If that were the extent of our analysis, we would find every statute, no matter how arbitrary or irrational, perfectly tailored to achieve its purpose. But equal protection scrutiny under the rational basis test requires the courts first to deduce the independent objectives of the statute, usually from statements of purpose and other evidence in the statute and legislative history, and second to analyze whether the challenged classification rationally furthers achievement of those objectives. The Court's tautological approach will not suffice.

B. The Court analyzes the rationality of § 231b(h) in terms of a justification suggested by Government attorneys, but never adopted by Congress. [But] this Court has frequently recognized that the actual purposes of Congress, rather than the post hoc justifications offered by Government attorneys, must be the primary basis for analysis under the rational basis test. * * *

The Court argues that Congress chose to discriminate against appellees for reasons of equity, [but, as] I have shown, Congress expressed the view that it would be inequitable to deprive any retirees of any portion of the benefits they had been promised and that they had earned under prior law. The Court is unable to cite even one statement in the legislative history by a Representative or Senator that makes the equitable judgment it imputes to Congress. * * *

[L]abor representatives demanded that benefits be increased for their current members, the cost to be offset by divesting the appellee class of a portion of the benefits they had earned under prior law. [In] fact, the [management and labor representatives] and Railroad Retirement Board members who testified at congressional hearings perpetuated the inaccurate impression that all retirees with earned vested dual benefits under prior law would retain their benefits unchanged. * * *

Of course, a misstatement or several misstatements by witnesses before Congress would not ordinarily lead us to conclude that Congress misapprehended what it was doing. In this instance, however, where complex legislation was drafted by outside parties and Congress relied on them to explain it, where the misstatements are frequent and unrebutted, and where no Member of Congress can be found to have stated the effect of the classification correctly, we are entitled to suspect that Congress may have been misled. As the District Court found: "At no time during the hearings did Congress even give a hint that it understood that the bill by its language eliminated an earned benefit of plaintiff's class."

Therefore, I do not think that this classification was rationally related to an *actual* governmental purpose.

Only in technical discussions and in the section-by-section analyses do the reports reflect the actual consequences of the Act on the appellee class. * * *

[Because] the Court is willing to accept a tautological analysis of congressional purpose, an assertion of "equitable" considerations contrary to the expressed judgment of Congress, and a classification patently unrelated to achievement of the identified purpose, it succeeds in effectuating neither equity nor congressional intent. * * *

FCC v. BEACH COMMUNICATIONS, INC.

508 U.S. 307, 113 S.Ct. 2096, 124 L.Ed.2d 211 (1993).

JUSTICE THOMAS delivered the opinion of the Court.

In providing for the regulation of cable television facilities, Congress has drawn a distinction between facilities that serve separately owned and managed buildings and those that serve one or more buildings under common ownership or management. [Under Cable Act § 602(7)(B), cable] facilities in the latter category are exempt from regulation as long as they provide services without using public rights-of-way. * * *

This case arises out of an FCC proceeding clarifying the agency's interpretation of the term "cable system" as it is used in the Cable Act. In this proceeding, the Commission addressed the application of the exemption codified in § 602(7)(B) to satellite master antenna television (SMATV) facilities. Unlike a traditional cable television system, which delivers video programming to a large community of subscribers through coaxial cables laid under city streets or along utility lines, an SMATV system typically receives a signal from a satellite through a small satellite dish located on a rooftop and then retransmits the signal by wire to units within a building or complex of buildings. The Commission ruled that an SMATV system that serves multiple buildings via a network of interconnected physical transmission lines is a cable system, unless it falls within the § 602(7)(B) exemption. Consistent with the plain terms of the statutory exemption, the Commission concluded that such an SMATV system is [not exempt] if its transmission lines interconnect separately owned and managed buildings or if its lines use or cross any public right-of-way. * * *

[The court of appeals held that "the Cable Act violates the equal protection component of the Fifth Amendment."]

Whether embodied in the Fourteenth Amendment or inferred from the Fifth, equal protection is not a license for courts to judge the wisdom, fairness, or logic of legislative choices. In areas of social and economic policy, a statutory classification that neither proceeds along suspect lines [e.g., race, national origin, religion, or alienage] nor infringes fundamental constitutional rights must be upheld against equal protection challenge if there is any reasonably conceivable state of facts that could provide a rational basis for the classification. Where there are "plausible reasons" for Congress' action, "our inquiry is at an end." *Fritz.* This standard of review is a paradigm of judicial restraint.

On rational-basis review, a classification in a statute such as the Cable Act comes to us bearing a strong presumption of validity, and those attacking the rationality of the legislative classification have the burden "to negative every conceivable basis which might support it." Moreover, because we never require a legislature to articulate its reasons for enacting a statute, it is entirely irrelevant for constitutional purposes whether the conceived reason for the challenged distinction actually motivated the legislature. *Fritz.* * * *

These restraints on judicial review have added force "where the legislature must necessarily engage in a process of line-drawing." *Fritz.* Defining the class of persons subject to a regulatory requirement—much like classifying governmental beneficiaries—"inevitably requires that some persons who have an almost equally strong claim to favored treatment be placed on different sides of the line, and the fact [that] the line might have been drawn differently at some points is a matter for legislative, rather than judicial, consideration." Ibid. The distinction at issue here represents such a line: By excluding from the definition of "cable system" those facilities that serve commonly owned or managed buildings without using public rights-of-way, § 602(7)(B) delineates the bounds of the regulatory field. Such scope-of-coverage provisions are unavoidable components of most economic or social legislation. [This] necessity renders the precise coordinates of the resulting legislative judgment virtually unreviewable, since the legislature must be allowed leeway to approach a perceived problem incrementally.

Applying these principles, we conclude that the common-ownership distinction is constitutional. There are at least two possible bases for the distinction; either one suffices. First, Congress borrowed § 602(7)(B) from pre-Cable Act regulations, and although the existence of a prior administrative scheme is certainly not necessary to the rationality of the statute, it is plausible that Congress also adopted the FCC's earlier rationale. Under that rationale, common ownership was thought to be indicative of those systems for which the costs of regulation would outweigh the benefits to consumers. Because the number of subscribers was a similar indicator, the Commission also exempted cable facilities that served fewer than 50 subscribers. * * *

Respondents argue that Congress did not intend common ownership to be a surrogate for small size, since Congress simultaneously rejected the FCC's 50–subscriber exemption by omitting it from the Cable Act. Whether the posited reason for the challenged distinction actually motivated Congress is "constitutionally irrelevant," and, in any event, the FCC's explanation indicates that both common ownership and number of subscribers were considered indicia of "very small" cable systems. * * *

Furthermore, small size is only one plausible ownership-related factor contributing to consumer welfare. Subscriber influence is another. Where an SMATV system serves a complex of buildings under common ownership or management, individual subscribers could conceivably have greater bargaining power vis-a-vis the cable operator (even if the number of dwelling units were large), since all the subscribers could negotiate with one voice through the common owner or manager. * * *

There is a second conceivable basis for the statutory distinction. Suppose competing SMATV operators wish to sell video programming to subscribers in a group of contiguous buildings, such as a single city block, which can be interconnected by wire without crossing a public right-of-way. If all the buildings belong to one owner or are commonly managed, that owner or manager could freely negotiate a deal for all subscribers on a competitive basis. But if the buildings are separately owned and managed, the first SMATV operator who gains a foothold by signing a contract and installing a satellite dish and associated transmission equipment on one of the buildings would enjoy a powerful cost advantage in competing for the remaining subscribers: he could connect additional buildings for the cost of a few feet of cable, whereas any competitor would have to recover the cost of his own satellite headend facility. Thus, the first operator could charge rates well above his cost and still undercut the competition. This potential for effective monopoly power might theoretically justify regulating the latter class of SMATV systems and not the former. * * *

The judgment of the Court of Appeals is reversed * * *. ✗ H

JUSTICE STEVENS, concurring in the judgment. * * *

The Court states that a legislative classification must be upheld "if there is any reasonably conceivable state of facts that could provide a rational basis for the classification," and that "[w]here there are 'plausible reasons' for Congress' action, 'our inquiry is at an end.' 'In my view, this formulation sweeps too broadly, for it is difficult to imagine a legislative classification that could not be supported by a "reasonably conceivable state of facts." Judicial review under the "conceivable set of facts" test is tantamount to no review at all.

Notes and Questions

1. *Legislative purpose.* Do *Fritz* and *FCC v. Beach Communications* signal that *actual* legislative purpose is never relevant to equal protection analysis? Is this a sensible and workable position? For the view that if "rationality is to be a meaningful standard of review, the court must conceive of its task as identifying the legislature's *probable* goals based on the available evidence," see Scott H. Bice, *Rationality Analysis in Constitutional Law,* 65 Minn.L.Rev. 1, 30 (1980).

2. *Reality and reform.* Is the Court's approach justified or explained by the likelihood, discussed p. 1152–53 supra, that the legislative arena is frequently, possibly even typically, one in which interest groups compete for self-interested advantages? Is this view descriptively accurate? If so, would more aggressive judicial review possibly help to foster a more publicly spirited and deliberative legislative process?

Consider the suggestion of Cass R. Sunstein, *Interest Groups in American Public Law,* 38 Stan.L.Rev. 29, 49–50 (1985), that "[t]he rationality requirement may [be] understood precisely as a requirement that regulatory measures be something other than a response to political pressure." See also Gerald Gunther, *In Search of Evolving Doctrine on a Changing Court: A Model for a Newer Equal Protection,* 86 Harv.L.Rev. 1, 44–46 (1972): "If the Court were to require an articulation of purpose from an authoritative state source"—"a state court's or attorney general office's description of purpose should be acceptable"—"rather than hypothesizing one on its own, there would at least be indirect pressure on the legislature to state its own reasons for selecting particular means and classifications [and thus] improve the quality of the political process [by] encouraging a fuller airing in the political arena of the grounds for legislative action." Is improving the political process a proper function of the judiciary? See generally John H. Ely, *Democracy and Distrust* 125–31 (1980).

harming an un-popular group is not a legitimate Purpose.

—————

UNITED STATES DEPT. OF AGRICULTURE v. MORENO, 413 U.S. 528, 93 S.Ct. 2821, 37 L.Ed.2d 782 (1973), per BRENNAN, J., applying " 'traditional' equal protection analysis," held that a provision of the Food Stamp Act—excluding "any household containing an individual who is unrelated to any other member of the household"—was "wholly without any rational basis": The exclusion "is clearly irrelevant to the stated purposes of the Act [to] raise levels of nutrition among low-income households. [Thus], the challenged classification must rationally further some legitimate governmental interest other than those specifically stated in the Congressional 'Declaration of Policy.'

"[The] little legislative history [that] does exist" indicates that the provision "was intended to [prevent] 'hippie communes' from participating in the food stamp program. [But equal protection] at the very least mean[s] that a bare congressional desire to harm a politically unpopular group cannot constitute a *legitimate* governmental interest." Nor does the classification "operate so as rationally to further the prevention of fraud" because, under the Act, "two *unrelated* persons living together" may "avoid the 'unrelated person' exclusion simply by altering their living arrangements so as [to] create two separate 'households,' both of which are eligible for assistance. [Thus], in practical operation, the [provision] excludes from participation [not] those persons who are 'likely to abuse the program' but, rather, only those persons who are so desperately in need of aid that they cannot even afford to alter their living arrangements so as to retain their eligibility."

DOUGLAS, J., concurred: "I could not say that [this] provision has no 'rational' relation to control of fraud. We deal here, however, with the right of association, protected by the First Amendment." Thus, the classification "can be sustained only on a showing of a 'compelling' governmental interest."

REHNQUIST, J., joined by Burger, C.J., dissented: "Congress attacked the problem with a rather blunt instrument, [b]ut I do not think it is unreasonable for Congress to conclude that the basic unit which it was willing to support [with] food stamps is some variation on the family as we know it—a household consisting of related individuals. This unit provides a guarantee which is not provided by households containing unrelated individuals that the household exists for some purpose other than to collect federal food stamps.

"Admittedly, [the] limitation will make ineligible many households which have not been formed for the purpose of collecting federal food stamps, and will [not] wholly deny food stamps to those households which may have been formed in large part to take advantage of the program. But, as the Court concedes, 'traditional' equal protection analysis does not require that every classification be drawn with precise mathematical nicety."

Notes and Questions

1. *Additional "purpose" cases. Moreno* is one of a small number of cases in which the Court has identified equal protection violations, purportedly pursuant to a rational basis test, based on judicial findings that the state acted for impermissible purposes. See *Romer v. Evans*, Sec. 4, IV infra (involving "animus" against homosexuals); *Cleburne v. Cleburne Living Center, Inc.*, Sec. 4, III infra (invalidating action predicated on "irrational prejudice against the mentally retarded"). See also *Village of Willowbrook v. Olech*, 528 U.S. 562, 120 S.Ct. 1073, 145 L.Ed.2d 1060 (2000) (finding that a plaintiff constituting a "class of one" could bring an actionable equal protection complaint based on allegations that "she has been treated differently from others similarly situated" and declining to consider an alternative theory of "subjective ill will").[a]

a. Cases in which the Court has found that a state's articulated justifications for a statute are constitutionally impermissible under the equal protection clause include *Zobel v. Williams*, Sec. 5, II infra, and *Metropolitan Life* *Ins. Co. v. Ward*, 470 U.S. 869, 105 S.Ct. 1676, 84 L.Ed.2d 751 (1985) (state tax that discriminated against out-of-state insurance companies for the purpose of "promoting local industry" "constitutes the very sort of parochial discrimi-

[handwritten notes at bottom:] Would think Comm. Clause issue. power — But Congress has given State violation to regulate — no Constitutional: no legitimate because • equal protection violation: Purpose of Comm. Clause

Are these cases consistent with the Court's approach in *Fritz*, supra, and *FCC v. Beach Communications*, supra? Do they "reflect the possible use of rationality review as a kind of magical trump card, or perhaps joker, hidden in the pack and used on special occasions"? Cass R. Sunstein, *Leaving Things Undecided*, 110 Harv.L.Rev. 4, 61 (1996). If so, when will the joker come out?

2. *Purpose inquiries and the judicial role.* Consider the suggestion of Fallon, *Implementing the Constitution*, supra, at 99, that when the Court applies otherwise deferential tests such as the rational basis test, scrutiny of legislative purposes is especially important: "When political officials act for constitutionally illegitimate reasons, they forfeit any reasonable claim to judicial deference." Note that this analysis leaves open which motives or purposes should be deemed impermissible. With respect to this question, *Moreno* can be read narrowly as holding only that "a bare congressional desire to harm a politically unpopular group" is not a constitutionally permissible purpose.[b]

It is now well settled that courts must inquire into legislative purposes in equal protection cases involving classifications that do not facially differentiate on the basis of race, but that are nonetheless alleged to reflect racially discriminatory purposes. See Sec. 2, III infra. If the Court can inquire into whether race-based animus motivated a statute, why should it not examine whether statutes reflect other kinds of animus?

———

The Court was undoubtedly correct when it said in *FCC v. Beach Communications*, supra, that the "rational basis" review applied in equal protection challenges is, in the generality of cases, "a paradigm of judicial restraint." Nonetheless, there are at least a few modern cases in which the Court, although employing the traditional "rational basis" standard, has held laws violative of equal protection.[c]

In LOGAN v. ZIMMERMAN BRUSH CO. (1982), Ch. 6, Sec. 5, I, a majority of the justices, without questioning the legitimacy of the state's purpose, employed "the lowest level of permissible equal protection scrutiny" and found a violation of equal protection. Appellant filed an employment discrimination complaint before an Illinois Commission, but the Commission inadvertently scheduled the hearing at a date after the statutory time period expired. The state court held that the time lapse, though it was not the fault of the claimant, deprived the Commission of jurisdiction and terminated the appellant's claim. BLACKMUN, J., joined by Brennan, Marshall, and O'Connor, JJ., found the statutory discrimination against claimants who did not get a timely hearing through no fault of their own to be "patently irrational in light of [the law's] stated purpose": "I cannot agree that terminating a claim that the State itself has misscheduled is a rational way of expediting the resolution of disputes. [The] state's rationale must be something more than the exercise of a strained imagination; while the connection between means and ends need not be precise, it, at the least, must have some objective basis. That is not so here." POWELL, J., joined by Rehnquist, J., concurred as to

nation that the Equal Protection Clause was intended to prevent.").

b. For recent studies of the use of purpose tests in constitutional law, see Fallon, supra, at 90–102; Ashutosh Bhagwat, *Purpose Scrutiny in Constitutional Analysis*, 85 Cal.L.Rev. 297 (1997).

c. See, e.g., *Eisenstadt v. Baird* (1972), Ch. 6, Sec. 2; *Baxstrom v. Herold*, 383 U.S. 107, 86 S.Ct. 760, 15 L.Ed.2d 620 (1966) (extensive procedural rights prior to civil commitment except for persons who are ending a prison term).

"this unusual classification": "As appellants possessed no power to convene hearings, it is unfair and irrational to punish them for the Commission's failure to do so."[d]

ALLEGHENY PITTSBURGH COAL CO. v. COUNTY COMM'N, 488 U.S. 336, 109 S.Ct. 633, 102 L.Ed.2d 688 (1989), per REHNQUIST, C.J., unanimously found an equal protection violation when a West Virginia county tax assessor "valued petitioners' real property on the basis of its recent purchase price, but made only minor modifications in the assessments of land which had not been recently sold," producing the result that "petitioners' property has been assessed at roughly 8 to 35 times more than comparable neighboring property, and these discrepancies have continued for more than 10 years with little change." The Court held that the county assessor's practice was not "rationally related" to West Virginia's rule "that all property of the kind held by petitioners shall be taxed at a rate uniform throughout the state according to its estimated market value."[e]

But compare NORDLINGER v. HAHN, 505 U.S. 1, 112 S.Ct. 2326, 120 L.Ed.2d 1 (1992), per BLACKMUN, J., which held that California's "acquisition value" system for initially assessing property (Proposition 13) "rationally furthers the State's ['legitimate'] interests in neighborhood stability and the protection of property owners' reliance interests." As in *Allegheny*, Proposition 13 "resulted in dramatic disparities in taxation of properties of comparable value." But "the Equal Protection Clause is satisfied so long as there is a plausible policy reason for the classification, *Fritz*, [and] *Allegheny* was the rare case where the facts precluded any plausible inference that the reason for the unequal assessment practice was to achieve the benefits of an acquisition-value tax scheme. By contrast, Proposition 13 was enacted precisely to achieve the benefits."

THOMAS, J., concurred in upholding Proposition 13 but would have "confronted [*Allegheny*] directly": "Even if the assessor did violate West Virginia law, she would not have violated the Equal Protection Clause. A violation of state law does not by itself constitute a violation of the Federal Constitution."

Would it be fair to say that the dominant thread of the Court's "rational basis" jurisprudence is extremely deferential, but that there is a recessive strain of cases in which the Court conducts a more searching review of legislative classifications?[f] Should the dominant strain wholly replace the recessive one? Should the recessive replace the dominant?[g]

d. For an argument that the "rationality" requirement does and should function as a balance of costs, benefits, and alternatives as well as the legitimacy of legislative purpose and the closeness of fit between means and ends, see Robert W. Bennett, *"Mere" Rationality in Constitutional Law: Judicial Review and Democratic Theory*, 67 Calif.L.Rev. 1049 (1979). But see Edward L. Barrett, *The Rational Basis Standard for Equal Protection Review of Ordinary Legislative Classifications*, 68 Ky. L.J. 845 (1980).

e. For the view that *Allegheny* "revived a doctrine that had lain dormant for fifty years," see Robert J. Glennon, *Taxation and Equal Protection*, 58 Geo.Wash.L.Rev. 261, 290 (1990): "The systematic and intentional undervaluation test [is] at war both with rational

basis review and with the broad latitude given states in creating tax schemes. [In] every instance that [the] Court [has] found that a tax scheme violated rational basis equal protection, [the] opinion was either poorly reasoned or over the dissents of Justices of great stature." Accord, William Cohen, *State Law in Equality Clothing*, 38 U.C.L.A.L.Rev. 87 (1990).

f. According to Robert C. Farrell, *Successful Rational Basis Claims in the Supreme Court from the 1971 Term Through Romer v. Evans*, 32 Ind.L.Rev. 357, 357–58 (1999), in the twenty-five years 1971–96, the Court upheld rational basis claims in ten cases, while rejecting such claims in one hundred other decisions: "The Court never explains why it has selected

g. See note g on page 1155.

SECTION 2. RACE AND ETHNIC ANCESTRY

I. HISTORICAL BACKGROUND

Racism and practices of race discrimination are deeply embedded in American constitutional history. Six of the thirteen original colonies—Maryland, Delaware, Virginia, the Carolinas, and Georgia—gave express legal support to slavery. At the Constitutional Convention, the existence of slavery was accepted as a political fact; there was no serious discussion of the Constitution forbidding slavery. On the contrary, at least three provisions of the original Constitution recognized and arguably countenanced slavery: Art. I, § 2, which based a state's representation in the House of Representatives on its free population and three-fifths of "all other Persons" within its territory; Art. 1, § 9, which barred Congress from abolishing the slave trade before 1808; and Art. 4, § 2, which provided that "no Person held to Service or Labor" under the laws of one state could escape that status upon flight to another state but, on the contrary, "shall be delivered up on the Claim of the Party to whom such Service or Labour may be due." Even in many "free" states, at the time of the Constitutional Convention and thereafter African–Americans were denied the vote, excluded from jury service, and separated from whites in most public conveyances.

In the ante-bellum years, the Supreme Court decided major cases involving the African slave trade,[a] the return of fugitive slaves,[b] slavery in the federal territories, and the rights of slaves in transit through free states—virtually all in a manner accepting slavery's basic lawfulness. The most notorious of the ante-bellum decisions involving slavery came in the *Dred Scott* case.

––––––

The plaintiff/appellant in DRED SCOTT v. SANDFORD, 60 U.S. (19 How.) 393, 15 L.Ed. 691 (1857), was born in slavery in Virginia but, in the company of his master, later traveled in the free state of Illinois and the free territory of Wisconsin, where slavery was prohibited by the Missouri Compromise. Following his return to Missouri, a slave state, Dred Scott was sold as a slave to Sandford. Scott thereupon brought suit against Sandford in federal court, arguing that he had attained his freedom under the law of Illinois and the law of Wisconsin (the "free" status of which was established by the Missouri Compromise). Scott predicated his claim of federal jurisdiction on diversity of citizenship, alleging that he was a citizen of Missouri and Sandford a citizen of New York. The Court, per

a particular case for heightened rationality. [None] of these cases [upholding rational basis claims] has had a significant precedential impact on subsequent cases."

g. For an illuminating comparison of American with German doctrine, and discussion of how the German Federal Constitutional Court characterizes "equal treatment in taxation as an aspect of civic equality" and "frequently finds equality violations in tax legislation," see Gerald L. Neuman, *Constitutional Equality: Equal Protection, "General Equality" and Economic Discrimination from a U.S. Perspective*, 5 Colum.J.Eur.L. 281, 308–09 (1999).

a. See, e.g., *The Antelope*, 23 U.S. (10 Wheat.) 66, 6 L.Ed. 268 (1825) (recognizing the right of foreigners to engage in the slave trade, if the laws of their nation permitted them to do so, but upholding prosecutions against American slave traders).

b. See *Prigg v. Pennsylvania*, 41 U.S. (16 Pet.) 539 (1842) (upholding the federal Fugitive Slave Act of 1793, which established federal procedures for the capture and return of runaway slaves, and invalidating a Pennsylvania law creating impediments to recaption of slaves).

TANEY, C.J., dismissed the suit. It held that Scott was incapable of becoming a "citizen" of Missouri eligible to invoke federal diversity jurisdiction; that Congress's effort in the Missouri Compromise to abolish slavery in federal territories was unconstitutional; and that whatever Scott's status in Illinois, after he had returned voluntarily to Missouri, his status was governed by the law of Missouri, which treated him as a slave:

"The question before us is, whether the class of persons described in the plea in abatement [are 'citizens' capable of invoking federal jurisdiction based on diversity of citizenship]. We think they are not, and that they are not included, and were not intended to be included, under the word 'citizens' in the Constitution, and can therefore claim none of the rights and privileges which that instrument provides for and secures to citizens of the United States. On the contrary, they were at that time considered as a subordinate and inferior class of beings, who had been subjugated by the dominant race, and, whether emancipated or not, yet remained subject to their authority, and had no rights or privileges but such as those who held the power and the Government might choose to grant them. [It] is difficult at this day to realize the state of public opinion in relation to that unfortunate race, which prevailed in the civilized and enlightened portions of the world at the time of the Declaration of Independence, and when the Constitution of the United States was framed and adopted. But the public history of every European nation displays it in a manner too plain to be mistaken. [Negroes] had for more than a century before been regarded as beings of inferior order, and altogether unfit to associate with the white race, either in social or political relations; and so far inferior, that they had no rights which the white man was bound to respect; and that the negro might justly and lawfully be reduced to slavery for his benefit. He was bought and sold, and treated as an ordinary article of merchandise and traffic, whenever a profit could be made by it. This opinion was at that time fixed and universal in the civilized portion of the white race. It was regarded as an axiom in morals as well as in politics, which no one thought of disputing, or supposed to be open to dispute; and men in every grade and position in society daily and habitually acted upon it in their private pursuits, as well as in matters of public concern, without doubting for a moment the correctness of this opinion.

"But it is too clear for dispute, that the enslaved African race were not intended to be included, and formed no part of the people who framed and adopted this declaration; for if the language, as understood in that day, would embrace them, the conduct of the distinguished men who framed the Declaration of Independence would have been utterly and flagrantly inconsistent with the principles they asserted; and instead of the sympathy of mankind, to which they so confidently appealed, they would have deserved and received universal rebuke and reprobation.[c]

"Yet the men who framed this declaration were great men—high in literary acquirements—high in their sense of honor, and incapable of asserting principles inconsistent with those on which they were acting. They perfectly understood the meaning of the language they used, and how it would be understood by others; and they knew that it would not in any part of the civilized world be supposed to embrace the negro race, which, by common consent, had been excluded from civilized Governments and the family of nations, and doomed to slavery. They

---

c. Consider the argument of Edmund S. Morgan, *The Great American Crime*, 45 N.Y.Rev.Bks. 13 (Dec. 3, 1998), that white Americans who exalt slave-owning founding fathers may tend subconsciously to look for reasons to blame blacks for somehow inviting slavery and may thereby reinforce racism.

spoke and acted according to the then established doctrines and principles, and in the ordinary language of the day, no one misunderstood them. The unhappy black race were separated from the white by indelible marks, and laws long before established, and were never thought of or spoken of except as property, and when the claims of the owner or the profit of the trader were supposed to need protection. * * *

"No one, we presume, supposes that any change in public opinion or feeling, in relation to this unfortunate race, in the civilized nations of Europe or in this country, should induce the court to give to the words of the Constitution a more liberal construction in their favor than they were intended to bear when the instrument was framed and adopted. Such an argument would be altogether inadmissible in any tribunal called on to interpret it. If any of its provisions are deemed unjust, there is a mode prescribed in the instrument itself by which it may be amended; but while it remains unaltered, it must be construed now as it was understood at the time of its adoption. [Any] other rule of construction would abrogate the judicial character of this court, and make it the mere reflex of the popular opinion or passion of the day. This court was not created by the Constitution for such purposes. Higher and graver trusts have been confided to it, and it must not falter in the path of duty. * * *

"[The] powers of the Government, and the rights of the citizen under it, are positive and practical regulations plainly written down. [It] has no power over the person or property of a citizen but what the citizens of the United States have granted. And no laws or usages of other nations, or reasoning of statesmen or jurists upon the relations of master and slave, can enlarge the powers of the Government, or take from the citizens the rights they have reserved. And if the Constitution recognizes the right of property of the master in a slave, and makes no distinction between that description of property and other property owned by a citizen, no tribunal, acting under the authority of the United States, whether it be legislative, executive, or judicial, has a right to draw such a distinction, or deny to it the benefit of the provisions and guarantees which have been provided for the protection of private property against the encroachments of the Government.

"Now, as we have already said in an earlier part of this opinion, upon a different point, the right of property in a slave is distinctly and expressly affirmed in the Constitution. The right to traffic in it, like an ordinary article of merchandise and property, was guarantied to the citizens of the United States, in every State that might desire it, for twenty years. And the Government in express terms is pledged to protect it in all future time, if the slave escapes from his owner. This is done in plain words—too plain to be misunderstood. And no word can be found in the Constitution which gives Congress a greater power over slave property, or which entitles property of that kind to less protection than property of any other description. The only power conferred is the power coupled with the duty of guarding and protecting the owner in his rights.

"Upon these considerations, it is the opinion of the court that the act of Congress which prohibited a citizen from holding and owning property of this kind in the territory of the United States north of the line therein mentioned, is not warranted by the Constitution, and is therefore void; and that neither Dred Scott himself, nor any of his family, were made free by being carried into this territory; even if they had been carried there by the owner, with the intention of becoming a permanent resident."[d]

d. For critical commentary on the "originalist" methodology of the *Dred Scott* case—its

II. DISCRIMINATION AGAINST RACIAL AND ETHNIC MINORITIES

The "evil to be remedied" by the equal protection clause, declared the *Slaughter-House Cases,* was "the existence of laws in the States where the newly emancipated negroes resided, which discriminated with gross injustice and hardship against them as a class." STRAUDER v. WEST VIRGINIA, 100 U.S. (10 Otto) 303, 25 L.Ed. 664 (1880)—the first post-Civil War race discrimination case to reach the Court—per STRONG, J., invalidated the state murder conviction of an African–American on the ground that state law forbade blacks from serving on grand or petit juries. In the course of its opinion, the Court observed that "the true spirit and meaning" of the Civil War amendments was "securing to a race recently emancipated [the] enjoyment of all the civil rights that under the law are enjoyed by [whites]. What is [equal protection but] that all persons, whether colored or white, shall stand equal before the laws of the States, and, in regard to the colored race, for whose protection the amendment was primarily designed, that no discrimination shall be made against them by law because of their color? The words of the amendment [contain] a positive immunity or right, most valuable to the colored race,—the right to exemption from unfriendly legislation against them distinctively as colored,—exemption from legal discriminations, implying inferiority in civil society, lessening the security of their enjoyment of the rights which others enjoy, and discriminations which are steps towards reducing them to the condition of a subject race.

"That the West Virginia statute respecting juries [is] such a discrimination ought not to be doubted. [And if] in those States where the colored people constitute a majority of the entire population a law should be enacted excluding all white men from jury service, [we] apprehend no one would be heard to claim that it would not be a denial to white men of the equal protection of the laws. Nor if a law should be passed excluding all naturalized Celtic Irishmen, would there be any doubt of its inconsistency with the spirit of the amendment. * * *

"We do not say that within the limits from which it is not excluded by the amendment a State may not prescribe the qualifications of its jurors, and in so doing make discriminations. It may confine the selection to males, to freeholders, to citizens, to persons within certain ages, or to persons having educational qualifications. We do not believe the Fourteenth Amendment was ever intended to prohibit this. Looking at its history, it is clear it had no such purpose. Its aim was against discrimination because of race or color."

PLESSY v. FERGUSON

163 U.S. 537, 16 S.Ct. 1138, 41 L.Ed. 256 (1896).

JUSTICE BROWN delivered the opinion of the Court.

[An 1890 Louisiana law required that railway passenger cars have "equal but separate accommodations for the white, and colored races." Plessy, alleging that he "was seven-eights Caucasian and one-eighth African blood; that the mixture of colored blood was not discernible in him; and that he was entitled to every right [of] the white race," was arrested for refusing to vacate a seat in a coach for whites.]

reliance on the original intent or understanding of the Constitution's framers and ratifiers—see Christopher L. Eisgruber, *Dred*

Again: Originalism's Forgotten Past, 10 Const. Comm. 37 (1993).

That [the challenged statute] does not conflict with the thirteenth amendment [is] too clear for argument. Slavery implies involuntary servitude,—a state of bondage * * *. This amendment [was] regarded by the statesmen of that day as insufficient to protect the colored race from certain laws [imposing] onerous disabilities and burdens, and curtailing their rights in the pursuit of life, liberty, and property to such an extent that their freedom was of little value; [and] the fourteenth amendment was devised to meet this exigency. * * *

The object of the amendment was undoubtedly to enforce the absolute equality of the two races before the law, but, in the nature of things, it could not have been intended to abolish distinctions based upon color, or to enforce social, as distinguished from political, equality, or a commingling of the two races upon terms unsatisfactory to either. [Laws] requiring their separation, in places where they are liable to be brought into contact [have] been generally, if not universally, recognized as within the competency of the state legislatures in the exercise of their police power. The most common instance of this is connected with the establishment of separate schools for white and colored children, which have been [upheld] even by courts of states where the political rights of the colored race have been longest and most earnestly enforced [citing cases from Mass., Ohio, Mo., Cal., La., N.Y., Ind. and Ky.].

Laws forbidding the intermarriage of the two races may be said in a technical sense to interfere with the freedom of contract, and yet have been universally recognized as within the police power of the state. [S]tatutes for the separation of the two races upon public conveyances were held to be constitutional in [federal decisions and cases from Pa., Mich., Ill., Tenn. and N.Y. It is suggested] that the same argument that will justify the state legislature in requiring railways to provide separate accommodations for the two races will also authorize them to require separate cars to be provided for people whose hair is of a certain color, or who are aliens, or who belong to certain nationalities, or to enact laws requiring colored people to walk upon one side of the street, and white people upon the other, or requiring white men's houses to be painted white, and colored men's black, or their vehicles or business signs to be of different colors, upon the theory that one side of the street is as good as the other, or that a house or vehicle of one color is as good as one of another color. The reply to all this is that every exercise of the police power must be reasonable, and extend only to such laws as are enacted in good faith for the promotion of the public good, and not for the annoyance or oppression of a particular class. [In] determining the question of reasonableness, [the state] is at liberty to act with reference to the established usages, customs, and traditions of the people, and with a view to the promotion of their comfort, and the preservation of the public peace and good order. Gauged by this standard, we cannot say [this law] is unreasonable, or more obnoxious to the fourteenth amendment than the [acts] requiring separate schools for colored children in the District of Columbia, the constitutionality of which does not seem to have been questioned or the corresponding acts of state legislatures.

We consider the underlying fallacy of the plaintiff's argument to consist in the assumption that the enforced separation of the two races stamps the colored race with a badge of inferiority. If this be so, it is not by reason of anything found in the act, but solely because the colored race chooses to put that construction upon it. [The] argument also assumes that social prejudices may be overcome by legislation, and that equal rights cannot be secured to the negro except by an enforced commingling of the two races. We cannot accept this proposition. If the two races are to meet upon terms of social equality, it must be the result [of] voluntary consent of individuals. * * * Legislation is powerless to eradicate racial instincts, or to abolish distinctions based upon physical differences, and the attempt to do so can only result in accentuating the difficulties of the present situation. * * *

Affirmed.

JUSTICE BREWER did [not] participate in the decision of this case.

JUSTICE HARLAN dissenting.

[No] legislative body or judicial tribunal may have regard to the race of citizens when the civil rights of those citizens are involved. * * *

It was said in argument that the statute of Louisiana does not discriminate against either race, but prescribes a rule applicable alike to white and colored citizens. But [e]very one knows that [it] had its origin in the purpose, not so much to exclude white persons from railroad cars occupied by blacks, as to exclude colored people from coaches occupied by or assigned to white persons. [The] fundamental objection, therefore, to the statute, is that it interferes with the personal freedom of citizens. * * *

The white race deems itself to be the dominant race in this country. And so it is, in prestige, in achievements, in education, in wealth, and in power. So, I doubt not, it will continue to be for all time, if it remains true to its great heritage, and holds fast to the principles of constitutional liberty. But in view of the constitution, in the eye of the law, there is in this country no superior, dominant, ruling class of citizens. There is no caste here. Our constitution is color-blind * * *.

In my opinion, the judgment this day rendered will, in time, prove to be quite as pernicious as the decision made by this tribunal in the *Dred Scott Case*. [What] can more certainly arouse race hate, what more certainly create and perpetuate a feeling of distrust between these races, than state enactments which, in fact, proceed on the ground that colored citizens are so inferior and degraded that they cannot be allowed to sit in public coaches occupied by white citizens? [The] thin disguise of "equal" accommodations for passengers in railroad coaches will not mislead any one, nor atone for the wrong this day done. * * *

I do not deem it necessary to review the decisions of state courts to which reference was made in argument. Some [are] inapplicable, because rendered prior to the adoption of the last amendments of the [constitution]. Others were made at a time [when] race prejudice was, practically, the supreme law of the land. Those decisions cannot be guides in the era introduced by the recent amendments of the supreme law, which established universal civil freedom * * *.

Notes and Questions

1. *Consistency.* Is *Plessy* consistent with *Strauder*? Consider the suggestion of Alexander M. Bickel, *The Original Understanding and the Segregation Decision,* 69 Harv.L.Rev. 1 (1955), that the framers and ratifiers of the fourteenth amendment may have contemplated a distinction between "civil" rights—basic or fundamental rights of citizenship—that the fourteenth amendment protected, and social or other lesser categories of rights, which it did not protect. If this suggestion is correct, would it explain the decision in *Plessy*? Justify it?

Compare John P. Frank & Robert F. Munro, *The Original Understanding of "Equal Protection of the Laws,"* 1972 Wash.U.L.Q. 421, 455: "We believe that the equal protection clause, in the eyes of its contemporaries, froze into constitutional law the existing common law obligation of transportation companies to take all comers and to eliminate any possibility of their segregation. Congress decided so often in this period that color classifications were not permissible for purposes of transportation that it is difficult to understand how equal protection could possibly be given another meaning."

2. *Surrounding attitudes.* Could the Court in *Plessy* truly have believed that if the forced separation of the races "stamps the colored race with a badge of inferiority," it is "solely because the colored race chooses to put that construction upon it"?[a] C. Vann Woodward, *The Strange Career of Jim Crow* 64 (1955), argues that race relations in the United States, but especially in the south, had worsened dramatically during the last two decades of the nineteenth century: "Economic, political, and social frustrations had pyramided to a climax of social tensions. No real relief was in sight from the long cyclical depression of the 'nineties, an acute period of suffering that only intensified the distress of the much longer agricultural depression. Hopes for [a variety of political reforms] had likewise met with cruel disappointments and frustration. There had to be a scapegoat. And all along the line signals were going up to indicate that the Negro was an approved object of aggression. These 'permissions-to-hate' came from sources that had formerly denied such permission. They came from the federal courts in numerous opinions, from Northern liberals eager to conciliate the South, from Southern conservatives who had abandoned their race policy of moderation in their struggle against the Populists, from the Populists in their mood of disillusionment with their former Negro allies, and from a national temper suddenly expressed by imperialistic adventures and aggressions against colored peoples in distant lands."

Could the Court have resisted the mounting tide of racism in the late nineteenth century, even if it had wanted to do so? Consider Michael Klarman, *The Plessy Era*, 1998 Sup.Ct.Rev. 303, 304–05: "One cannot begin to understand the Court's racist decisions without first understanding the racist times in which they were rendered. [Given] the background of race relations at the turn of the century and the limited capacity of the Supreme Court generally to frustrate public opinion, it may be implausible to think that the Justices realistically could have reached different results [in cases such as *Plessy*]" since, among other things, political officials especially in southern states might simply have ignored a Court ruling that mandated equal treatment of the races. (Professor Klarman distinguishes *Strauder* as a case in which it was relatively easy for the Court to ensure compliance with its decisions by simply reversing convictions in cases where its ruling was ignored.)[b]

Compare *Planned Parenthood v. Casey*, Ch. 6, Sec. 2: "[W]e think *Plessy* was wrong the day it was decided." According to Lofgren, supra, at 5, "the nation's press met the [*Plessy*] decision mainly with apathy."

3. *"Separate but equal".* Where did the Court get the "separate but equal" standard? Consider Michael Klarman, *An Interpretive History of Modern Equal Protection*, 90 Mich.L.Rev. 213, 229–30 (1991): "*Plessy*, the case first introducing separate-but-equal to the Supreme Court, apparently contemplated that unequal segregated facilities would be subject to justification just like any other sort of inequality. [E]quality was required in *Plessy* [only] because the Court could conceive of no rational explanation for a state's refusal to provide equal railway

---

a. Consider Charles Black, *The Lawfulness of the Segregation Decisions*, 69 Yale L.J. 421, 422 n.8 (1960): At this point in the Court's opinion, "[t]he curves of callousness and stupidity intersect at their respective maxima."

b. For discussion of *Plessy* and its background, see Charles A. Lofgren, *The Plessy Case: A Legal Historical Interpretation* (1987); Paul Oberst, *The Strange Career of Plessy v. Ferguson*, 15 Ariz.L.Rev. 389 (1973).

facilities for blacks. Racial classifications, in other words, were subjected to the same general rationality test which had come to govern equal protection review of economic regulation."[c] *(Shameful chapter in American History)*

Executive order 9066 under Authority Gen. DeWitt enacted a curfew for Japanese, then detention structures...

Why not ban racial classifications altogether?

KOREMATSU v. UNITED STATES

323 U.S. 214, 65 S.Ct. 193, 89 L.Ed. 194 (1944).

JUSTICE BLACK delivered the opinion of the Court.

[Following the Japanese attack on Pearl Harbor, President Franklin Roosevelt signed Executive Order 9066, which gave military officials the legal authority to exclude any or all persons from designated areas on the west coast in order to insure against sabotage and espionage. Congress implicitly ratified the Executive Order by providing that the violation of an implementing order by a military commander constituted a misdemeanor punishable by fine or imprisonment. Under the authority of the Executive Order, the War Relocation Authority subjected all persons of Japanese ancestry on the west coast to a curfew, excluded them from their homes, detained them in assembly centers, and then evacuated them to "relocation centers" in California, Idaho, Utah, Arizona, Wyoming, Colorado, and Arkansas. By the end of 1942, roughly 112,000 persons—over 65,000 of whom were U.S. citizens—had been involuntarily removed to relocation centers.]

Standard of review for racial discrim. are immediately susp.

Strict Scrutiny
- *classification must be precisely tailored to a compelling interest*

The petitioner, an American citizen of Japanese descent, was convicted in a federal district court for remaining in San Leandro, California, a "Military Area," contrary to Civilian Exclusion Order No. 34 of the Commanding General of the Western Command, U.S. Army, which directed that after May 9, 1942, all persons of Japanese ancestry should be excluded from that area. No question was raised as to petitioner's loyalty to the United States. * * *

history of use of racial discrimination
- *Animosity/hatred*
- *Racial inferiority*
- *immutable characteristic*

[A]ll legal restrictions which curtail the civil rights of a single racial group are immediately suspect. That is not to say that all such restrictions are unconstitutional. It is to say that courts must subject them to the most rigid scrutiny. Pressing public necessity may sometimes justify the existence of such restrictions; racial antagonism never can. * * *

- Skeptical of classifications effectiveness for legislation

- Political Powerlessness

Exclusion Order No. 34 [was] one of a number of military orders. [In] *Hirabayashi v. United States,* 320 U.S. 81, 63 S.Ct. 1375, 87 L.Ed. 1774 (1943), we sustained a conviction [for] violation of [a] curfew order [applicable only to persons of Japanese ancestry as] an exercise of the power [to] take steps necessary to prevent espionage and sabotage in an area threatened by Japanese attack.

In the light of the principles we announced in the *Hirabayashi* case, we are unable to conclude that it was beyond the war power of Congress and the Executive to exclude those of Japanese ancestry from the West Coast war area at the time they [did]. Nothing short of apprehension by the proper military authorities of the gravest imminent danger to the public safety can constitutionally justify either. But exclusion from a threatened area, no less than curfew, has a definite and close relationship to the prevention of espionage and sabotage. * * *

Here, as in *Hirabayashi,* "we cannot reject as unfounded the judgment of the military authorities and of Congress that there were disloyal members of that population, whose number and strength could not be precisely and quickly

c. Compare Lofgren, supra (arguing that the separate-but-equal doctrine emerged from common law cases involving the obligations of common carriers, gained hold in a number of state statutes, and achieved constitutional status in *Plessy*).

Are they using Strict Scrutiny? • Not strictly!

★ Would want to know: is espionage + sabotage actually imminent?

ascertained. We cannot say that the war-making branches of the Government did not have ground for believing that in a critical hour such persons could not readily be isolated and separately dealt with, and constituted a menace to the national defense and safety, which demanded that prompt and adequate measures be taken to guard·against it."

[This] answers the contention that the exclusion was in the nature of group punishment based on antagonism to those of Japanese origin. That there were members of the group who retained loyalties to Japan has been confirmed by investigations made subsequent to the exclusion. Approximately five thousand American citizens of Japanese ancestry refused to swear unqualified allegiance to the United States [and] several thousand evacuees requested repatriation to Japan.

[H]ardships are part of war, and war is an aggregation of hardships. [E]xclusion of large groups of citizens from their homes, except under circumstances of direst emergency and peril, is inconsistent with our basic governmental institutions. But when under conditions of modern warfare our shores are threatened by hostile forces, the power to protect must be commensurate with the threatened danger. * * *

It is said that we are dealing here with the case of imprisonment of a citizen in a concentration camp solely because of his ancestry, without evidence or inquiry concerning his loyalty and good disposition towards the United States. [But] we are dealing specifically with nothing but an exclusion order. To cast this case into outlines of racial prejudice, without reference to the real military dangers which were presented, merely confuses the issue. Korematsu was not excluded from the Military Area because of hostility to him or his race. He was excluded because we are at war with the Japanese Empire, because the properly constituted military authorities feared an invasion of our West Coast and felt constrained to take proper security measures, because they decided that the military urgency of the situation demanded that all citizens of Japanese ancestry be segregated from the West Coast temporarily, and finally, because Congress, reposing its confidence in this time of war in our military leaders—as inevitably it must—determined that they should have the power to do just this. * * * We cannot—by availing ourselves of the calm perspective of hindsight—now say that at that time these actions were unjustified.

Affirmed.

JUSTICE FRANKFURTER [who joined the Court's opinion], concurring.

[To] find that the Constitution does not forbid the military measures now complained of does not carry with it approval of that which Congress and the Executive did. That is their business, not ours.

JUSTICE MURPHY, dissenting.

[T]he exclusion, either temporarily or permanently, of all persons with Japanese blood in their veins [must] rely for its reasonableness upon the assumption that *all* persons of Japanese ancestry may have a dangerous tendency to commit sabotage and espionage and [it] is difficult to believe that reason, logic or experience could be marshalled in support of such an assumption. [The] reasons appear, instead, to be largely an accumulation of much of the misinformation, half-truths and insinuations that for years have been directed against Japanese Americans by people with racial and economic prejudices—the same people who have been among the foremost advocates of the evacuation. A military judgment based upon such racial and sociological considerations is not entitled to the great weight ordinarily given the judgments based upon strictly military considerations. Especially is this so when every charge relative to race, religion, culture, geographical location, and legal and economic status has been substantially discredited by independent studies made by experts in these matters. * * *

Moreover, there was no adequate proof that the FBI and the military and naval intelligence services did not have the espionage and sabotage situation well in hand during this long period. Nor is there any denial of the fact that not one person of Japanese ancestry was accused or convicted of espionage or sabotage after Pearl Harbor while they were still free, a fact which is some evidence of the loyalty of the vast majority of these individuals and of the effectiveness of the established methods of combatting these evils. It seems incredible that under these circumstances it would have been impossible to hold loyalty hearings for the mere 112,000 persons involved—or at least for the 70,000 American citizens— especially when a large part of this number represented children and elderly men and women. Any inconvenience that may have accompanied an attempt to conform to procedural due process cannot be said to justify violations of constitutional [rights].

JUSTICE JACKSON, dissenting.

Korematsu was born on our soil, of parents born in Japan. [Had] Korematsu been one of four—the others being, say, a German alien enemy, an Italian alien enemy, and a citizen of American-born ancestors, convicted of treason but out on parole—only Korematsu's presence would have violated the order. The difference between their innocence and his crime would result, not from anything he did, said, or thought, different than they, but only in that he was born of different racial stock.

Now, if any fundamental assumption underlies our system, it is that guilt is personal and not inheritable. [If] Congress in peace-time legislation should enact such a criminal law, I should suppose this Court would refuse to enforce it.

But [it] would be impracticable and dangerous idealism to expect or insist that each specific military command in an area of probable operations will conform to conventional tests of constitutionality. When an area is so beset that it must be put under military control at all, the paramount consideration is that its measures be successful, rather than legal. * * * I cannot say, from any evidence before me, that the orders of General DeWitt were not reasonably expedient military precautions, nor could I say that they were. But even if they were permissible military procedures, I deny that it follows that they are constitutional. If, as the Court holds, it does follow, then we may as well say that any military order will be constitutional and have done with it.

The limitation under which courts always will labor in examining the necessity for a military order are illustrated by this case. How does the Court know that these orders have a reasonable basis in necessity? No evidence whatever on that subject has been taken by this or any other court. There is sharp controversy as to the credibility of the DeWitt report. So the Court, having no real evidence before it, has no choice but to accept General DeWitt's own unsworn, self-serving statement, untested by any cross-examination, that what he did was reasonable. And thus it will always be when courts try to look into the reasonableness of a military order. * * *

[A] judicial construction of the due process clause that will sustain this order is a far more subtle blow to liberty than the promulgation of the order itself. A military order, however unconstitutional, is not apt to last longer than the military emergency. [But] once a judicial opinion rationalizes [the] Constitution to show that the Constitution sanctions such an order, the Court for all time has validated the principle of racial discrimination in criminal procedure and of transplanting American citizens. The principle then lies about like a loaded weapon ready for the hand of any authority that can bring forward a plausible claim of an urgent need. * * *

My duties as a justice as I see them do not require me to make a military judgment as to whether General DeWitt's evacuation and detention program was a reasonable military necessity. I do not suggest that the courts should have attempted to interfere with the Army in carrying out its task. But I do not think they may be asked to execute a military expedient that has no place in law under the Constitution. I would reverse the judgment and discharge the prisoner.[a]

Notes and Questions

1. *Standard of review.* The Court's invocation of "the most rigid scrutiny" appears to have been a doctrinal innovation. According to Klarman, note 3 after *Plessy*, at 232–33, previous discriminations—including discriminations based on race—had never before brought a suggestion from the Court that race-based classifications were categorically "suspect." Was the Court justified in formulating such a standard to test the validity of federal action under the due process clause? (Recall that the equal protection clause refers only to states, not to the federal government.)

Despite the Court's "grandiose rhetoric," is it credible that the Justices actually applied "the most rigid scrutiny" in *Korematsu*?

2. *The scope of the threat.* (a) Relatively little effort at fact-finding appears to have supported the military exclusion orders. Consider David M. Kennedy, *Freedom From Fear: The American People in Depression and War, 1929–1945* (1999), at 750–51: "As war rumors took wing in the weeks following Pearl Harbor, sobriety gave way to anxiety, then to a rising cry for draconian action against the Japanese on the West Coast. Inflammatory and invariably false reports of Japanese attacks on the American mainland flashed through coastal communities. [The] release at the end of January [1942] of a governmental investigation of Pearl Harbor proved the decisive blow. The report, prepared by Supreme Court Justice Owen Roberts, alleged without documentation that Hawaii-based espionage agents, including Japanese–American citizens, had abetted [Japan's] strike force. [Within days, General John DeWitt—the official responsible for the assessment of military necessity—] reported 'a tremendous volume of public opinion developing against the Japanese of all classes' [and he] soon succumbed to Rumor's siren himself [in the absence of any hard evidence of traitorous activity].

"While Korematsu's case began its slow journey through the legal system, DeWitt's deputy [was] drafting [DeWitt's] official explanation for [the Japanese exclusion. To] buttress the argument that forced evacuation was a matter of military necessity, [the deputy] laced the *Final Report* with hundreds of examples of subversive activities on the West Coast in the winter and spring of 1942. [But] Justice Department lawyers quickly saw that he had cooked his facts [and, in fact, had little or no evidence of actual attempted subversion.] Armed with [findings as to the unreliability of the *Final Report*,] Justice Department attorneys determined to disavow [it] in their presentation of the *Korematsu* case [but were overruled by top officials in the War and Justice Departments]. Ignorant of this [background],

a. The dissenting opinion of Roberts, J., is omitted.

the Supreme Court justices proceeded to deliberate on the *Korematsu* case deprived of a basis on which to challenge the factual assertions of the *Final Report.*

"[When] the Court pronounced on the *Korematsu* case on December 18 1944, safely after the November presidential election, the camps had already begun to empty."[b]

(b) Consider William H. Rehnquist, *All the Laws But One* 205–06, 210–11 (1998): "[In response to the criticism that the Court's review was too deferential,] one can only echo Justice Jackson's observation [that] 'in the very nature of things, military decisions are not susceptible of intelligent judicial appraisal.' [It is also sometimes suggested] that [citizens of Japanese descent] were relocated simply because the Caucasian majority [disliked] them. [The] Court's answer to this broad attack seems satisfactory—those of Japanese descent were displaced because of fear that disloyal elements among them would aid Japan in the war. [But] a narrower criticism has more force to it: [The Court should have distinguished between American *citizens* of Japanese descent and non-citizens of Japanese descent.] Even in wartime, citizens may not be rounded up and required to prove their loyalty. They may be excluded from sensitive military areas in the absence of a security clearance and may otherwise be denied access to any classified information. But it pushes these propositions to an extreme to say that a sizable geographic area may be declared off-limits and the residents required to move.

"The most frequently made charge on behalf of [non-U.S. citizen Japanese affected by the relocation orders] is that the government treated Japanese enemy aliens differently from enemy aliens of German or Italian citizenship. [But] there do not appear to have been the same concentrations of German or Italian nationals along the west coast in areas near major defense plants. [While] there were areas of German or Italian concentration on the eastern seaboard, [there was no live fear of] attacks from German bombers or the invasion of German troops. [And] aircraft production was highly concentrated on the west coast. [These] distinctions seem insufficient to justify such a sharp difference of treatment between Japanese and German and Italian aliens in peacetime. But they do seem legally adequate to support the difference [in] time of war."

(c) Compare Earl Warren, *The Bill of Rights and the Military*, 37 N.Y.U.L.Rev. 181, 192–93 (1962): "[*Hirabayashi* and *Korematsu*] demonstrate dramatically that there are some circumstances in which the Court will, in effect, conclude that it is simply not in a position to reject descriptions by the Executive of the degree of military necessity. Thus, in a case like *Hirabayashi,* only the Executive is qualified to determine whether, for example, an invasion is imminent."

As the Attorney General of California, Warren—the Chief Justice of the United States at the time of the Court's decision in *Brown v. Board of Education,* infra—played a "leading role" in enforcing the Japanese exclusion from his state. Consider David Halberstam, *The Fifties* 417–18 (1993): "The one serious blot on [Warren's] record was [his role in the Japanese relocation]. He was playing to the growing fear of sabotage and the country's anger against the Japanese, particularly in California. Later he expressed considerable regret for his actions, although he was somewhat defensive in his memoirs: In 1972, when he was interviewed on the subject, he broke down in tears as he spoke of little children being taken from

b. For vehement, relatively contemporary criticism of *Korematsu*, see Eugene V. Rostow, *The Japanese American Cases—A Disaster*, 54 Yale L.J. 489 (1945).

their homes and schools. [That] a record otherwise so admirable had a blot so serious was a reminder [that] even in the very best politicians there is always some fatal imperfection."

3. *Subsequent developments.* A 1980 Act of Congress established a Commission on Wartime Relocation and Internment of Civilians to study the Japanese relocation during World War II. The Commission concluded that: "The promulgation of Executive Order 9066 was not justified by military necessity, and the decisions which followed from it [were] not driven by analysis of military conditions. The broad historical causes which shaped [the exclusion decisions] were race prejudice, war hysteria, and the failure of political leadership. [A] grave injustice was done."[c] In 1988, President Ronald Reagan signed legislation formally acknowledging injustices imposed by the internment and providing for the payment of reparations.[d] In 1984, a federal district court relied on the Commission's findings in granting the writ of coram nobis and vacating the conviction of Fred Korematsu, the original defendant in *Korematsu*. See *Korematsu v. United States*, 584 F.Supp. 1406 (N.D.Cal.1984)[e]

BROWN v. BOARD OF EDUCATION

347 U.S. 483, 74 S.Ct. 686, 98 L.Ed. 873 (1954).

CHIEF JUSTICE WARREN delivered the opinion of the Court.

These cases come to us from the States of Kansas, South Carolina, Virginia, and Delaware. * * *

In each of the cases, minors of the Negro race [seek] the aid of the courts in obtaining admission to the public schools of their community on a nonsegregated basis. [In] each of the cases other than the Delaware case, a three-judge federal district court denied relief to the plaintiffs on the so-called "separate but equal" doctrine announced by this Court in [*Plessy*]. In the Delaware case, the Supreme Court of Delaware adhered to that doctrine, but ordered that the plaintiffs be admitted to the white schools because of their superiority to the Negro schools.

* * * Argument was heard in the 1952 Term, and reargument was heard this Term on certain questions propounded by the Court.

Reargument was largely devoted to the circumstances surrounding the adoption of the Fourteenth Amendment in 1868. It covered exhaustively consideration of the Amendment in Congress, ratification by the states, then existing practices in racial segregation, and the views of proponents and opponents of the Amendment. This discussion and our own investigation convince us that, although these sources cast some light, it is not enough to resolve the problem with which we are faced. At best, they are inconclusive. The most avid proponents of the post-War Amendments undoubtedly intended them to remove all legal distinctions among "all persons born or naturalized in the United States." Their opponents, just as certainly, were antagonistic to both the letter and the spirit of the Amendments and wished them to have the most limited effect. What others in Congress and the state legislatures had in mind cannot be determined with any degree of certainty.

---

c. Report of the Commission on Wartime Relocation and Internment of Civilians, Personal Justice Denied 18 (1982).

d. Civil Liberties Act of 1988, Pub.L.No. 100–383, 102 Stat. 903 (codified at 50 U.S.C. app. § 1989).

e. For further historical discussion, see Peter Irons, *Justice at War: The Story of the Japanese American Internment* (1983).

An additional reason for the inconclusive nature of the Amendment's history, with respect to segregated schools, is the status of public education at that time. In the South, the movement toward free common schools, supported by general taxation, had not yet taken hold. Education of white children was largely in the hands of private groups. Education of Negroes was almost nonexistent, and practically all of the race were illiterate. In fact, any education of Negroes was forbidden by law in some states. Today, in contrast, many Negroes have achieved outstanding success in the arts and sciences as well as in the business and professional world. It is true that public school education at the time of the Amendment had advanced further in the North, but the effect of the Amendment on Northern States was generally ignored in the congressional debates. Even in the North, the conditions of public education did not approximate those existing today. The curriculum was usually rudimentary; ungraded schools were common in rural areas; the school term was but three months a year in many states; and compulsory school attendance was virtually unknown. As a consequence, it is not surprising that there should be so little in the history of the Fourteenth Amendment relating to its intended effect on public education.

In the first cases in this Court construing the Fourteenth Amendment, decided shortly after its adoption, the Court interpreted it as proscribing all state-imposed discriminations against the Negro race.[6] The doctrine of "separate but equal" did not make its appearance in this Court until 1896 in *Plessy*, involving not education but transportation. [In] this Court, there have been six cases involving the "separate but equal" doctrine in the field of public education. In *Cumming v. Board of Education,* 175 U.S. 528, 20 S.Ct. 197, 44 L.Ed. 262, and *Gong Lum v. Rice,* 275 U.S. 78, 48 S.Ct. 91, 72 L.Ed. 172, the validity of the doctrine itself was not challenged.[8] In more recent cases, all on the graduate school level, inequality was found in that specific benefits enjoyed by white students were denied to Negro students of the same educational qualifications. *Missouri ex rel. Gaines v. Canada,* 305 U.S. 337, 59 S.Ct. 232, 83 L.Ed. 208[a]; *Sipuel v. Oklahoma,* 332 U.S. 631, 68 S.Ct. 299, 92 L.Ed. 247; *Sweatt v. Painter,* 339 U.S. 629, 70 S.Ct. 848, 94 L.Ed. 1114[b]; *McLaurin v. Oklahoma State Regents,* 339 U.S. 637, 70 S.Ct. 851, 94 L.Ed. 1149.[c] In none of these cases was it necessary

---

6. *Slaughter-House Cases; Strauder* * * *. See also *Virginia v. Rives,* 1879, 100 U.S. 313, 318, 25 L.Ed. 667; *Ex parte Virginia,* 1879, 100 U.S. 339, 344–345, 25 L.Ed. 676. [See generally Brief for the Committee of Law Teachers Against Segregation in Legal Education, *Segregation and the Equal Protection Clause,* 34 Minn.L.Rev. 289 (1950).]

8. In *Cumming,* Negro taxpayers sought an injunction requiring the defendant school board to discontinue the operation of a high school for white children until the board resumed operation of a high school for Negro children. Similarly, in *Gong Lum,* the plaintiff, a child of Chinese descent, contended only that state authorities had misapplied the doctrine by classifying him with Negro children and requiring him to attend a Negro school.

a. *Gaines,* in 1938, invalidated the refusal to admit blacks to the University of Missouri School of Law, despite the state's offer to pay petitioner's tuition at an out-of-state law school pending establishment of a state law school for African–Americans.

b. *Sweatt,* in 1950, required admission of African–Americans to the University of Texas Law School despite the recent establishment of a state law school for blacks: "In terms of number of the faculty, variety of courses and opportunity for specialization, size of the student body, scope of the library, availability of law review and similar activities, the University of Texas Law School is superior. [Equally troubling is that the] law school to which Texas is willing to admit petitioner excludes from its student body members of the racial groups which number 85% of the population of the State and include most of the lawyers, witnesses, jurors, judges and other officials with whom petitioner will inevitably be dealing when he becomes a member of the Texas Bar."

c. *McLaurin,* in 1950, held violative of equal protection requirements that African–American graduate students at the University of Oklahoma sit at separate desks adjoining the classrooms and separate tables outside the library reading room, and eat at separate times in the school cafeteria.

to re-examine the doctrine to grant relief to the Negro plaintiff. And in *Sweatt*, the Court expressly reserved decision on the question whether *Plessy* should be held inapplicable to public education.

In the instant cases, that question is directly presented. [T]here are findings below that the Negro and white schools involved have been equalized, or are being equalized, with respect to buildings, curricula, qualifications and salaries of teachers, and other "tangible" factors. Our decision, therefore, cannot turn on merely a comparison of these tangible factors in the Negro and white schools involved in each of the cases. We must look instead to the effect of segregation itself on public education.

In approaching this problem, we cannot turn the clock back to 1868 when the Amendment was adopted, or even to 1896 when *Plessy* was written. We must consider public education in the light of its full development and its present place in American life throughout the Nation. Only in this way can it be determined if segregation in public schools deprives these plaintiffs of the equal protection of the laws.

Today, education is perhaps the most important function of state and local governments. Compulsory school attendance laws and the great expenditures for education both demonstrate our recognition of the importance of education to our democratic society. It is required in the performance of our most basic public responsibilities, even service in the armed forces. It is the very foundation of good citizenship. Today it is a principal instrument in awakening the child to cultural values, in preparing him for later professional training, and in helping him to adjust normally to his environment. In these days, it is doubtful that any child may reasonably be expected to succeed in life if he is denied the opportunity of an education. Such an opportunity, where the state has undertaken to provide it, is a right which must be made available to all on equal terms.

We come then to the question presented: Does segregation of children in public schools solely on the basis of race, even though the physical facilities and other "tangible" factors may be equal, deprive the children of the minority group of equal educational opportunities? We believe that it does.

In *Sweatt*, in finding that a segregated law school for Negroes could not provide them equal educational opportunities, this Court relied in large part on "those qualities which are incapable of objective measurement but which make for greatness in a law school." In *McLaurin*, the Court, in requiring that a Negro admitted to a white graduate school be treated like all other students, again resorted to intangible considerations: "[his] ability to study, to engage in discussions and exchange views with other students, and in general, to learn his profession." Such considerations apply with added force to children in grade and high schools. To separate them from others of similar age and qualifications solely because of their race generates a feeling of inferiority as to their status in the community that may affect their hearts and minds in a way unlikely ever to be undone. The effect of this separation on their educational opportunities was well stated by a finding in the Kansas case by a court which nevertheless felt compelled to rule against the Negro plaintiffs: "Segregation of white and colored children in public schools has a detrimental effect upon the colored children. The impact is greater when it has the sanction of the law; for the policy of separating the races is usually interpreted as denoting the inferiority of the Negro group. A sense of inferiority affects the motivation of a child to learn. Segregation with the sanction of law, therefore, has a tendency to [retard] the educational and mental development of Negro children and to deprive them of some of the benefits they would receive in a racial[ly] integrated school system."[10] Whatever may have been the extent of psychological knowledge at the time of *Plessy,* this finding is amply supported by modern authority.[11] Any language in *Plessy* contrary to this finding is rejected.

We conclude that in the field of public education the doctrine of "separate but equal" has no place. Separate educational facilities are inherently unequal. Therefore, we hold that the plaintiffs and others similarly situated for whom the actions have been brought are, by reason of the segregation complained of, deprived of [equal protection].

Because these are class actions, because of the wide applicability of this decision, and because of the great variety of local conditions, the formulation of decrees in these cases presents problems of considerable complexity. On reargument, the consideration of appropriate relief was necessarily subordinated to the primary question—the constitutionality of segregation in public education. We have now announced that such segregation is a denial of the equal protection of the laws. In order that we may have the full assistance of the parties in formulating decrees, the cases will be restored to the docket, and the parties are requested to present further argument on Questions 4 and 5 previously propounded by the Court for the reargument this Term.[13] * * *

Notes and Questions

1. *Historical context.* Consider Klarman, note 3 after *Plessy,* at 241–42: "[I]t is far too easy to regard *Brown v. Board of Education* as an inevitable decision. Yet quite plainly it was not. Justice Frankfurter probably spoke for a majority of the Justices when he [recounted] that had the school segregation challenge been forced upon him in the 1940s he would have felt compelled to reject it. Indeed, the

10. A similar finding was made in the Delaware case: "I conclude from the testimony that in our Delaware society, State-imposed segregation in education itself results in the Negro children, as a class, receiving educational opportunities which are substantially inferior to those available to white children otherwise similarly situated."

11. Kenneth B. Clark, *Effect of Prejudice and Discrimination on Personality Development* (Midcentury White House Conference on Children and Youth, 1950); Helen L. Witmer and Ruth Kotinsky, *Personality in the Making* (1952), c. VI; Max Deutscher and Isidor Chein, *The Psychological Effects of Enforced Segregation: A Survey of Social Science Opinion,* 26 J.Psychol. 259 (1948); Chein, *What are the Psychological Effects of Segregation Under Conditions of Equal Facilities?,* 3 Int.J. Opinion and Attitude Res. 229 (1949); Theodore Brameld, *Educational Costs in Discrimination and National Welfare* (MacIver, ed., 1949), 44–48; *Frazier,* The Negro in the United States *(1949),* 674–681. *And, see generally Gunnar Myrdal,* An American Dilemma *(1962).*

13. "4. Assuming it is decided that segregation in public schools violates the Fourteenth Amendment

"(a) would a decree necessarily follow providing that, within the limits set by normal geographic school districting, Negro children should forthwith be admitted to schools of their choice, or

"(b) may this Court, in the exercise of its equity powers, permit an effective gradual adjustment to be brought about from existing segregated systems to a system not based on color distinctions?

"5. On the assumption on which questions 4(a) and (b) are based, and assuming further that this Court will exercise its equity powers to the end described in question 4(b),

"(a) should this Court formulate detailed decrees in these cases;

"(b) if so, what specific issues should the decrees reach;

"(c) should this Court appoint a special master to hear evidence with a view to recommending specific terms for such decrees;

"(d) should this Court remand to the courts of first instance with directions to frame decrees in these cases, and if so what general directions should the decrees of this Court include and what procedures should the courts of first instance follow in arriving at the specific terms of more detailed decrees?"

NAACP's choice prior to 1950 to refrain from direct attacks on school segregation, instead pursuing an equalization strategy, was largely owing to the organization's perception that the sociopolitical environment was not yet conducive to a segregation challenge. Nor did *Brown* ineluctably follow from [the] 1950 decision in *Sweatt v. Painter*. Justice Clark, for example, [wrote] in a *Sweatt* memorandum that he was not then prepared to invalidate primary and secondary school segregation. Southern resistance to grade school desegregation, Clark warned, would be of a different order than to graduate school desegregation. [When] *Brown* was first argued in 1952, the Justices were closely divided; their own subsequent tabulations indicated a vote somewhere between five to four for sustaining school segregation and six to three for striking it down."

After the Supreme Court had heard the initial arguments in *Brown*, and had decided to set a re-argument, Chief Justice Fred M. Vinson—who was generally unsympathetic to the plaintiffs' case—died, to be replaced by Earl Warren. Upon learning of Vinson's death, Justice Frankfurter is said to have remarked, "This is the first indication I have ever had that there is a God."[a]

2. *"Original understanding."* In setting *Brown* for re-argument, the Court specifically asked the parties to brief whether the fourteenth amendment was originally understood to bar segregation in the public schools. In its final opinion, however, the Court largely evaded discussion of the history, which in the view of most historians did not support the Court's result. According to a memorandum by one of Justice Frankfurter's law clerks (the future Professor Alexander Bickel), which the Justice circulated to the Court, the principal aim of the fourteenth amendment was to guarantee equality with respect to a set of what were then understood to be fundamental rights of citizenship—such as rights to own property and sue and be sued—that did not encompass rights involving public education.[b] See Alexander M. Bickel, *The Original Understanding and the Segregation Decision*, 69 Harv.L.Rev. 1, 12–13, 16–17, 46–47, 56–58 (1955). Apart from that specific claim,[c] there is a virtual consensus among historians that the equal protection clause was not widely understood at the time of its adoption to mandate desegregation in education.[d] On the contrary, following the ratification of the fourteenth amendment, a number of northern states continued either to tolerate or require segregation in their public schools. See Kluger, supra, at 633–34. Indeed, the Congress that proposed the fourteenth amendment maintained segregated schools in the District of Columbia. If the framers and ratifiers of the fourteenth amendment did not specifically understand or intend it to abolish segregation in public education, does it follow that the *Brown* Court should not have reached its decision?

Consider Bickel, supra, at 59, 61: "If the fourteenth amendment were a statute, a court might very well hold [that] it was foreclosed from applying it to

a. Quoted in Richard Kluger, *Simple Justice* 656 (1975).

b. For fascinating descriptions and interpretations of the Court's internal decisionmaking process, see Dennis Hutchinson, *Unanimity and Desegregation: Decisionmaking in the Supreme Court, 1948–1958,* 68 Geo.L.J. 1 (1979); Mark Tushnet, *What Really Happened in Brown v. Board of Education*, 91 Colum.L.Rev. 1867 (1991).

c. See Klarman, supra, at 235 & n. 95 (reviewing the historiographical debate and embracing the view that most of the four-

teenth amendment's drafters viewed it as protecting only fundamental rights).

d. See Klarman, supra, at 252 & n. 180 (citing and discussing authorities). For a rare dissenting view, based largely on unsuccessful Republican efforts in a *subsequent* Congress to forbid school segregation under the 1875 Civil Rights Act, see Michael W. McConnell, *Originalism and the Desegregation Decisions*, 81 Va.L.Rev. 947 (1995). For a critical response, see Michael J. Klarman, *Brown, Originalism and Constitutional Theory*, 81 Va.L.Rev. 1881 (1995).

segregation in public schools. [But] we are dealing with a constitutional amendment, not a statute. The tradition of a broadly worded organic law not frequently or lightly amended was well-established by 1866, and [it] cannot be assumed that [anyone] expected or wished the future role of the Constitution in the scheme of American government to differ from the past. Should not the search for congressional purpose, therefore, properly be twofold? One inquiry should be directed at the congressional understanding of the immediate effect of the enactment on conditions then present. Another should aim to discover what if any thought was given to the long-range effect, under future circumstances, of provisions necessarily intended for permanence. [With respect to the latter inquiry, the fourteenth amendment may have reflected] a compromise permitting [moderates and radicals] to go to the country with language which they could, where necessary, defend against damaging alarms raised [by opponents of broad racial equality rights], but which at the same time was sufficiently elastic to permit reasonable future advances [toward racial equality]."[e]

Consider also Ronald Dworkin, *Freedom's Law* 7–11 (1996), arguing that courts should give a "moral reading" to provisions, such as the equal protection clause, that "are drafted in exceedingly abstract language [and embody] abstract moral principles." According to Dworkin, "the equal protection clause [has] a moral principle as its content," and the function of the courts is not to discover what the framers and ratifiers understood that "principle" to mean, but what it *really* means: "Most of [the framers and ratifiers] plainly did not expect [the equal protection clause] to outlaw official racial discrimination in school. [But] they did not *say* anything about [school] segregation[,] one way or the other. They said that 'equal protection of the laws' is required, which plainly describes a very general principle, not any concrete application of it." The job of judges, says Dworkin, is "to find the best conception of constitutional moral principles—the best understanding of what equal moral status for men and women really requires, for example—that fits the broad story of America's historical record," including evolving social and moral understandings and relevant judicial precedents.

Does this approach give too much power to judges? See Dworkin, supra, at 14: "Constitutional scholars often say that we must avoid the mistakes of both the moral reading, which gives too much power to judges, and of originalism, which makes the contemporary Constitution too much the dead hand of the past. The right method, they say, is something in between. [But] they do not indicate what the right balance is. [Though] the call for an intermediate constitutional strategy is often heard, it has not been answered."

3. *Social science and the Court's rationale.* Did the result in *Brown* turn on social scientific data of the kind cited in fn. 11? Consider Edmund Cahn, *Jurisprudence,* 30 N.Y.U.L.Rev. 150, 157–58, 167 (1955): "It is one thing to use the current scientific findings, however ephemeral they may be, in order to ascertain whether the legislature has acted reasonably in adopting some scheme of social or economic regulation; deference here is shown not so much to the findings as to the legislature. It would be quite another thing to have our fundamental

---

e. Agreeing with Bickel that "most of the Fourteenth Amendment's drafters [intended] racial discrimination [to be] impermissible with regard to certain fundamental rights, rather than across the board," Professor Klarman argues that "rather than stating a racial classification rule, *Brown* elevated education to the level of other fundamental rights with regard to which the Equal Protection Clause forbade racial discrimination." See Klarman, note 3 after *Plessy*, at 235, 247. If the premise about the drafters' understanding is granted, should it be permissible for the Court to recognize that education had become a "fundamental right" in the intervening years as a matter of fact or common perception?

rights rise, fall, or change along with the latest fashions of psychological literature."

Does *Brown* rest on a finding that "in terms of the most familiar and universally accepted standards of right and wrong [racial] segregation under government auspices inevitably inflicts humiliation, [and] official humiliation of innocent, law-abiding citizens is psychologically injurious and morally evil"? Id. at 159.

4. *Contemporary criticisms. Brown* was highly controversial at the time of its decision and for a number of years thereafter. Some of the criticisms rested on the decision's reliance on social science, but probably the most celebrated critique protested that the *Brown* Court had failed to ground its decision in "neutral principles." Consider Herbert Wechsler, *Toward Neutral Principles of Constitutional Law,* 73 Harv.L.Rev. 1, 34 (1959): "[A]ssuming equal facilities, the question posed by state-enforced segregation is not one of discrimination at all. Its human and its constitutional dimensions lie [in] the denial by the state of freedom to associate, a denial that impinges in the same way on any groups or races that may be involved. [But] if the freedom of association is denied by segregation, integration forces an association upon those for whom it is unpleasant or repugnant. [W]here the state must practically choose between denying the association to those individuals who wish it or imposing it on those who would avoid it, is there a basis in neutral principles for holding that the Constitution demands that the claims for association should prevail?"

In reply, consider the following from a "draft opinion" of *Brown* by Louis Pollak, *Racial Discrimination and Judicial Integrity: A Reply to Professor Wechsler,* 108 U.Pa.L.Rev. 1, 27, 29–30 (1959): "[W]e start from the base point that in the United States 'all legal restrictions which curtail the civil rights of a single racial group are immediately suspect.' *Korematsu.* [T]here is special need for 'a searching judicial inquiry into the legislative judgment in situations where prejudice against discrete and insular minorities may tend to curtail the operation of those political processes ordinarily to be relied on to protect minorities.' See *United States v. Carolene Products,* n. 4 [Ch. 5, Sec. 3 supra]. We could not, therefore, sustain the reasonableness of these racial distinctions and the absence of harm said to flow from them, unless we were prepared to say that no factual case can be made the other way. [To] the extent that implementation of this decision forces racial mingling on school children against their will, [this] consequence follows because the community through its political processes has [chosen] compulsory education. [The resulting] coerced association [cannot] be said to emanate from this Court or from the Constitution. In any event, parents sufficiently disturbed at the prospect of having their children educated in democratic fashion in company with their peers are presumably entitled to fulfill their educational responsibilities in other ways."

See also Charles Black, *The Lawfulness of the Segregation Decisions,* 69 Yale L.J. 421, 429 (1960): "The fourteenth amendment [forbids] disadvantaging the Negro race by law. It was surely anticipated that the following of this directive would entail some disagreeableness for some white southerners. [When] the directive of equality cannot be followed without displeasing the white, then something that can be called a 'freedom' of the white must be impaired. If the fourteenth amendment commands equality, and if segregation violates equality, then the status of the reciprocal 'freedom' is automatically settled."

5. *Extent of the decision.* (a) Did *Brown* bar all forms of state-imposed racial segregation? Or did it apply only to public schools? For comment immediately

after *Brown,* consider Paul G. Kauper, *Segregation in Public Education,* 52 Mich.L.Rev. 1137, 1154–55 (1954): "[*Brown*] placed emphasis upon the intangible factors that make the *Plessy* doctrine inapplicable to public schools. Education is an experience and not simply an enjoyment of physical facilities. But with respect to common carrier and public recreational facilities, the emphasis is upon the enjoyment of the physical facilities and services so that it is more nearly possible to speak of equality of enjoyment within the pattern of segregation." Compare Robert McKay, *Segregation and Public Recreation,* 40 Va.L.Rev. 697, 724 (1954): "[T]here appears to be no reason to believe that the sense of inferiority engendered by segregation in recreation is any less than in education."

(b) After *Brown,* the Court, in summary per curiam decisions citing *Brown,* consistently held invalid state imposed racial segregation in other public facilities—e.g., golf courses, parks, playgrounds.[f] The one notable exception is *Naim v. Naim,* 350 U.S. 891, 76 S.Ct. 151, 100 L.Ed. 784 (1955), a case that came to the Court by way of appeal and involved the constitutionality of a Virginia statute forbidding inter-racial marriage. Apparently persuaded by Justice Frankfurter that the miscegenation issue aroused such "deep feeling" that a Court pronouncement would "have the effect of 'thwarting or seriously handicapping the enforcement of [our] decision in the segregation cases[,]' the Court remanded *Naim* to the Virginia Supreme Court on the pretext that the parties' domicile stood in need of clarification. After the state court belligerently refused to cooperate, the Justices narrowly voted to deny review, apparently preferring to permit an insolent state court to flout its authority than to stir up another hornets' nest in the immediate wake of *Brown.*" Klarman, supra, at 243. As a result, the Court did not confront the miscegenation issue until 1967 in *Loving v. Virginia,* p. 1187 infra. Was the Court's course of action in *Naim* an exercise of wise, prudent, and legitimate judicial statesmanship? A supine abnegation of constitutional responsibility? Compare Alexander M. Bickel, *The Passive Virtues,* 75 Harv.L.Rev. 40 (1961) with Gerald Gunther, *The Subtle Vices of the "Passive Virtues"—A Comment on Principle and Expediency in Judicial Review,* 64 Colum.L.Rev. 1, 11–13 (1964).

6. *Segregation by the federal government.* BOLLING v. SHARPE, 347 U.S. 497, 74 S.Ct. 693, 98 L.Ed. 884 (1954), per WARREN, C.J., held—on the same day as *Brown*—that public school segregation in the District of Columbia "constitutes an arbitrary deprivation [of] liberty in violation of the Due Process Clause" of the fifth amendment: "The Fifth Amendment [does] not contain an equal protection clause as does the Fourteenth Amendment which applies only to the states. But the concepts of equal protection and due process, both stemming from our American ideal of fairness, are not mutually exclusive. The 'equal protection of the laws' is a more explicit safeguard of prohibited unfairness than 'due process of law,' and, therefore, we do not imply that the two are always interchangeable phrases. But, as this Court has recognized, discrimination may be so unjustifiable as to be violative of due process.

"Classifications based solely upon race must be scrutinized with particular care, since they are contrary to our traditions and hence constitutionally suspect. ['Liberty'] extends to the full range of conduct which the individual is free to pursue, and it cannot be restricted except for a proper governmental objective.

[handwritten margin note: Ct. looked to purpose of Segregation]

f. For a detailed listing of these and lower court decisions, see William B. Lockhart, Yale Kamisar & Jesse H. Choper, *Constitutional Law: Cases—Comments—Questions* 1206 (3d ed. 1970).

Segregation in public education is not reasonably related to any proper governmental objective * * *.

"In view of our decision that the Constitution prohibits the states from maintaining racially segregated public schools, it would be unthinkable that the same Constitution would impose a lesser duty on the Federal Government."

BROWN v. BOARD OF EDUCATION (II)

349 U.S. 294, 75 S.Ct. 753, 99 L.Ed. 1083 (1955).

CHIEF JUSTICE WARREN delivered the opinion of the Court.

These cases were decided on May 17, 1954. [There] remains for consideration the manner in which relief is to be accorded. * * *

Full implementation of these constitutional principles may require solution of varied local school problems. School authorities have the primary responsibility for elucidating, assessing, and solving [them]; courts will have to consider whether the action of school authorities constitutes good faith implementation of the governing constitutional principles. Because of their proximity to local conditions and the possible need for further hearings, the courts which originally heard these cases can best perform this judicial appraisal. Accordingly, we believe it appropriate to remand the cases to those courts.

In fashioning and effectuating the decrees, the courts will be guided by equitable principles. Traditionally, equity has been characterized by a practical flexibility in shaping its remedies and by a facility for adjusting and reconciling public and private needs. [A]t stake is the personal interest of the plaintiffs in admission to public schools as soon as practicable on a nondiscriminatory basis. To effectuate this interest may call for elimination of a variety of obstacles in making the transition to school systems operated in accordance with the constitutional principles set forth in our May 17, 1954, decision. Courts of equity may properly take into account the public interest in the elimination of such obstacles in a systematic and effective manner. But it should go without saying that the vitality of these constitutional principles cannot be allowed to yield simply because of disagreement with them.

While giving weight to these public and private considerations, the courts will require that the defendants make a prompt and reasonable start toward full compliance with our May 17, 1954, ruling. Once such a start has been made, the courts may find that additional time is necessary to carry out the ruling in an effective manner. The burden rests upon the defendants to establish that such time is necessary in the public interest and is consistent with good faith compliance at the earliest practicable date. To that end, the courts may consider problems related to administration, arising from the physical condition of the school plant, the school transportation system, personnel, revision of school districts and attendance areas into compact units to achieve a system of determining admission to the public schools on a nonracial basis, and revision of local laws and regulations which may be necessary in solving the foregoing problems. They will also consider the adequacy of any plans the defendants may propose to meet these problems and to effectuate a transition to a racially nondiscriminatory school system. During this period of transition, the courts will retain jurisdiction of these cases.

The [cases are remanded] to take such proceedings and enter such orders and decrees consistent with this opinion as are necessary and proper to admit to public schools on a racially nondiscriminatory basis with all deliberate speed the parties to these cases. * * *

Notes and Questions

1. *"Individual" vs. "race" rights.* Was the decree consistent with *Brown I?* Since plaintiffs had only a limited number of years of school remaining, did postponement of relief partially or totally destroy the very rights the decree was intended to enforce? Does the "deliberate speed" formula assume that "Negroes (unlike whites) possess rights as a race rather than as individuals, so that a particular Negro can rightly be delayed in the enjoyment of his established rights if progress is being made in improving the legal status of Negroes generally"? Louis Lusky, *The Stereotype: Hard Core of Racism,* 13 Buf.L.Rev. 450, 457 (1963).

Consider the complaint of Thurgood Marshall that "the argument [to postpone enforcement of a constitutional right] is never made until Negroes are involved."[a] Compare Richard H. Fallon, Jr., *Implementing the Constitution* (2001) (asserting that "Marshall's claim bears the sting of truth, but it is not the whole truth," as there sometimes are other gaps between constitutional rights and constitutional remedies).

2. *"Deliberate speed" and the slow pace of desegregation.* Consider Morton J. Horwitz, *The Warren Court and the Pursuit of Justice* 29–30 (1998): "The Supreme Court's decision in *Brown II* reflected the justices' understanding that they were initiating a social revolution. The Court feared that because deeply entrenched Southern attitudes and institutions were completely unprepared for immediate desegregation, anything more than a gradualist approach would inevitably lead to violence. As it turned out, [gradualism] probably encouraged violence by allowing enough time for opposition to desegregation to build while holding out hope that the decision could be reversed. [*Brown II*] also encouraged Southern public officials to claim that they were performing their legal duties whenever they refused to integrate facilities because there was a threat of violence."

Consider also Richard A. Wasserstrom, *Racism, Sexism, and Preferential Treatment: An Approach to the Topics,* 24 U.C.L.A.L.Rev. 581, 602 (1977): "The Supreme Court's solution assumed that [only black children should go to black schools] until the black schools were brought up to par or eliminated. That is a kind of conceptual racism [that] accepts the dominant racist ideology [that] the claims of black children are worth less than the claims of white children."

Compare Lino A. Graglia, *The Brown Cases Revisited: Where Are They Now?,* 1 Benchmark 23, 27 (Mar.–Apr. 1984): "There can be little doubt that if the Court had ordered the end of segregation in 1954 or 1955 the result would have been the closing of public schools in much of the South, about which the Court could have done nothing. The principal impact would have been on poor blacks, and *Brown* could have come to be seen as a blunder and symbol of judicial impotence."

The Court's subsequent efforts to implement *Brown* are considered in Part IV infra.

LOVING v. VIRGINIA
388 U.S. 1, 87 S.Ct. 1817, 18 L.Ed.2d 1010 (1967).

CHIEF JUSTICE WARREN delivered the opinion of the Court.

a. Quoted in Paul Gewirtz, *Remedies and Resistance,* 92 Yale L.J. 585, 613 (1983).

This case presents a constitutional question never addressed by this Court: whether a statutory scheme adopted by Virginia to prevent marriages between persons solely on the basis of racial classifications violates [the] Fourteenth Amendment. [Appellants, a black woman and white man, were married in the District of Columbia, returned to reside in Virginia, and were convicted under the state antimiscegenation statute.]

Virginia is now one of 16 States which prohibit and punish marriages on the basis of racial classifications.[5] [The] state court concluded that the State's legitimate purposes were "to preserve the racial integrity of its citizens," and to prevent "the corruption of blood," "a mongrel breed of citizens," and "the obliteration of racial pride," obviously an endorsement of the doctrine of White Supremacy. [T]he State [argues] that the meaning of the Equal Protection Clause, as illuminated by the statements of the Framers, is only that state penal laws containing an interracial element as part of the definition of the offense must apply equally to whites and Negroes in the sense that members of each race are punished to the same degree. * * *

Because we reject the notion that the mere "equal application" of a statute containing racial classifications is enough to remove the classifications from the Fourteenth Amendment's proscription of all invidious racial discriminations, we do not accept the State's contention that these statutes should be upheld if there is any possible basis for concluding that they serve a rational purpose. [Here], we deal with statutes containing racial classifications, and the fact of equal application does not immunize the statute from the very heavy burden of justification which the Fourteenth Amendment has traditionally required of state statutes drawn according to race.

The State argues that statements in the Thirty-ninth Congress about the time of the passage of the Fourteenth Amendment indicate that the Framers did not intend the Amendment to make unconstitutional state miscegenation laws. Many of the statements [have] some relevance to the intention of Congress in submitting the Fourteenth Amendment, [but] it must be understood that they pertained to the passage of specific statutes and not to the broader, organic purpose of a constitutional amendment. As for the various statements directly concerning the Fourteenth Amendment, we have said in connection with a related problem, that although these historical sources "cast some light" they are not sufficient to resolve the problem; "[a]t best, they are inconclusive." *Brown*. We have rejected the proposition that the debates in the Thirty-ninth Congress or in the state legislatures which ratified the Fourteenth Amendment supported the theory [that equal protection] is satisfied by penal laws defining offenses based on racial classifications so long as white and Negro participants in the offense were similarly punished. *McLaughlin v. Florida*, 379 U.S. 184, 85 S.Ct. 283, 13 L.Ed.2d 222 (1964).[a]

The State finds support for its "equal application" theory [in] *Pace v. Alabama*, 106 U.S. 583, 1 S.Ct. 637, 27 L.Ed. 207 (1883). In that case, the Court upheld a conviction under an Alabama statute forbidding adultery or fornication between a white person and a Negro which imposed a greater penalty than that of a statute proscribing similar conduct by members of the same race. The Court reasoned that the statute could not be said to discriminate against Negroes because the punishment for each participant in the offense was the same.

---

5. [Over] the past 15 years, 14 States have repealed laws outlawing interracial marriages * * *.

a. *McLaughlin* invalidated a statute making interracial cohabitation a crime.

However, as recently as the 1964 Term, in rejecting the reasoning of that case, we stated *"Pace* represents a limited view of the Equal Protection Clause which has not withstood analysis in the subsequent decisions of this Court." *McLaughlin.* [The] clear and central purpose of the Fourteenth Amendment was to eliminate all official state sources of invidious racial discrimination in the States. [At] the very least, the Equal Protection Clause demands that racial classifications, especially suspect in criminal statutes, be subjected to the "most rigid scrutiny," and, if they are ever to be upheld, they must be shown to be necessary to the accomplishment of some permissible state objective, independent of the racial discrimination which it was the object of the Fourteenth Amendment to eliminate.[b] Indeed, two [justices] have already stated that they "cannot conceive of a valid legislative purpose [which] makes the color of a person's skin the test of whether his conduct is a criminal offense." *McLaughlin* (Stewart, J., joined by Douglas, J., concurring).

There is patently no legitimate overriding purpose independent of invidious racial discrimination which justifies this classification. The fact that Virginia only prohibits interracial marriages involving white persons demonstrates that the racial classifications must stand on their own justification, as measures designed to maintain White Supremacy.[11] We have consistently denied the constitutionality of measures which restrict the rights of citizens on account of race. There can be no doubt that restricting the freedom to marry solely because of racial classifications violates the central meaning of the Equal Protection Clause.

These statutes also deprive the Lovings of liberty without [due process].

Marriage is one of the "basic civil rights of man," fundamental to our very existence and survival. *Skinner v. Oklahoma* [Ch. 6, Sec. 2]. To deny this fundamental freedom on so unsupportable a basis as the racial classifications embodied in these statutes [surely denies due process].

Reversed.

JUSTICE STEWART, concurring.

I have previously expressed the belief that "it is simply not possible for a state law to be valid under our Constitution which makes the criminality of an act depend upon the race of the actor." *McLaughlin* (concurring opinion). Because I adhere to that belief, I concur in the judgment of the Court.

Notes and Questions

1. *Standard of review.* Is the constitutional test for laws that *classify* by race or ethnicity different from the test for laws that *discriminate* against racial or ethnic minorities? How crucial was it to the Court's ruling that the challenged statute had no legitimate purpose whatsoever?[a]

---

b. *McLaughlin* also stated that racial classifications were " 'in most circumstances irrelevant' to any constitutionally acceptable legislative purpose." Harlan, J., concurring, added that "necessity, not mere reasonable relationship, is the proper test"; this "test which developed to protect free speech against state infringement should be equally applicable in a case involving state racial discrimination—prohibition of which lies at the very heart of the Fourteenth Amendment."

11. [While] Virginia prohibits whites from marrying any nonwhite (subject to the exception for the descendants of Pocahontas), Ne-

groes, Orientals and any other racial class may intermarry without statutory interference. Appellants contend that this distinction renders Virginia's miscegenation statutes arbitrary and unreasonable even assuming the constitutional validity of an official purpose to preserve "racial integrity." We need not reach this contention because we find the racial classifications in these statutes repugnant to the Fourteenth Amendment, even assuming an evenhanded state purpose to protect the "integrity" of all races.

a. Cf. Deborah Hellman, *Two Types of Discrimination: The Familiar and the Forgotten,*

2. *Racial information.* ANDERSON v. MARTIN, 375 U.S. 399, 84 S.Ct. 454, 11 L.Ed.2d 430 (1964), held violative of equal protection a statute requiring that the race of candidates for elective office be on the ballot: "The vice lies [in] the placing of the power of the State behind a racial classification that induces racial prejudice at the polls."

May a national census include racial information? May a state, for statistical purposes, require designation of the parties' race on every divorce decree? See *Tancil v. Woolls,* 379 U.S. 19, 85 S.Ct. 157, 13 L.Ed.2d 91 (1964).

3. *Family issues.* PALMORE v. SIDOTI, 466 U.S. 429, 104 S.Ct. 1879, 80 L.Ed.2d 421 (1984), per BURGER, C.J., held that Florida's denial of child custody to a white mother because her new husband was black violated equal protection: "There is a risk that a child living with a step-parent of a different race may be subject to a variety of pressures and stresses not present if the child were living with parents of the same racial or ethnic origin. [But the] effects of racial prejudice, however real, cannot justify a racial classification removing an infant child from the custody of its natural mother found to be an appropriate person to have such custody."

May a state take race into account in assigning children to foster homes and in choosing adoptive parents?[b]

4. *Law enforcement issues.* May a police department use race as part of a "profile" of those who are most likely to engage in certain kinds of criminal activities and, therefore, should be watched especially closely or pulled over for minor traffic infractions?[c] Cf. *United States v. Brignoni–Ponce,* 422 U.S. 873, 885–86, 95 S.Ct. 2574, 45 L.Ed.2d 607 (1975) (ruling that the use of a "single factor" of Mexican ancestry is impermissible in Border Patrol stops, but that immigration officers may base stops on the "characteristic appearance of persons who live in Mexico [including such] factors as the mode of dress and haircut"). In a situation involving inter-racial tensions, may prison officials segregate prisoners by race? Cf. *Lee v. Washington,* 390 U.S. 333, 88 S.Ct. 994, 19 L.Ed.2d 1212 (1968).

III.   DE JURE vs. DE FACTO DISCRIMINATION

Part II of this Section involved laws that explicitly discriminated against racial and ethnic minorities. But intentional (or "de jure") discrimination may exist even though the law in question is racially "neutral" on its face: the law may be deliberately administered in a discriminatory way; or the law, although neutral in its language and applied in accordance with its terms, may have been enacted

---

86 Calif.L.Rev. 315 (1998), arguing that equal protection doctrine has developed to assess the legitimacy of "proxy discrimination"—involving the use of classificatory schemes to promote an extrinsic end—and deals awkwardly with "non-proxy" discrimination, in which a law's actual purpose is to advance or harm a particular group.

b. For discussion, see, e.g., Richard Banks, *The Color of Desire: Fulfilling Adoptive Parents' Racial Preferences Through Discriminatory State Action,* 107 Yale L.J. 875 (1998); Amanda T. Perez, Note, *Transracial Adoption*

and the Federal Adoption Subsidy, 17 Yale L. & Pol'y Rev. 201 (1998).

c. See Randall Kennedy, *Race, Crime, and the Law* 137–38, 141–45 (1997); David A. Harris, *The Stories, the Statistics, and the Law: Why "Driving While Black" Matters,* 84 Minn. L.Rev. 265 (1999); K.G. Jan Pillai, *Neutrality of the Equal Protection Clause,* 27 Hastings Const.L.Q. 89 (1999). See also Neil Gotunda, *Comparative Racialization: Racial Profiling and the Case of Wen Ho Lee,* 47 UCLA L.Rev. 1689 (2000) (comparing the 19th and 20th century evolution of profiling for Asian-and African-Americans).

with a purpose (or motive) to disadvantage a "suspect" class. This section concerns these additional types of "de jure" discrimination as well as government action that is racially neutral in its terms, administration, and purpose but has a discriminatory effect or impact.

YICK WO v. HOPKINS

118 U.S. 356, 6 S.Ct. 1064, 30 L.Ed. 220 (1886).

JUSTICE MATTHEWS delivered the opinion of the Court.

[A San Francisco ordinance made it unlawful to operate a laundry without the consent of the board of supervisors except in a brick or stone building. Yick Wo, a Chinese alien who had operated a laundry for 22 years, had certificates from the health and fire authorities, but was refused consent by the board. It was admitted that "there were about 320 laundries in the city [and] about 240 were owned [by] subjects of China, and of the whole number, viz., 320, about 310 were constructed of wood"; that "petitioner, and more than 150 of his countrymen, have been arrested" for violating the ordinance "while those who are not subjects of China, and who are conducting 80 odd laundries under similar conditions, are left unmolested."]

[T]he facts shown establish an administration directed so exclusively against a particular class of persons as to warrant and require the conclusion that, whatever may have been the intent of the ordinances as adopted, they are applied [with] a mind so unequal and oppressive as to amount to a practical denial by the State of [equal protection]. Though the law itself be fair on its face and impartial in appearance, yet, if it is applied and administered by public authority with an evil eye and an unequal hand, so as practically to make unjust and illegal discriminations between persons in similar circumstances, material to their rights, the denial of equal justice is still within the prohibition of the Constitution. [The] fact of this discrimination is admitted. No reason for it is shown, and the conclusion cannot be resisted that no reason for it exists except hostility to [Yick Wo's] race and nationality * * *.

WASHINGTON v. DAVIS

426 U.S. 229, 96 S.Ct. 2040, 48 L.Ed.2d 597 (1976).

JUSTICE WHITE delivered the opinion of the Court.

This case involves the validity of a qualifying test administered to applicants for positions as police officers in the District of Columbia. [T]he police recruit was required to satisfy certain physical and character standards, to be a high school graduate or its equivalent and to receive a grade of at least 40 out of 80 on "Test 21," which is "an examination that is used generally throughout the federal service," which "was developed by the Civil Service Commission, not the Police Department," and which was "designed to test verbal ability, vocabulary, reading and comprehension."

[The] District Court rejected the assertion that Test 21 was culturally slanted to favor whites and was "satisfied that the undisputable facts prove the test to be reasonably and directly related to the requirements of the police recruit training program and that it is neither so designed nor operates to discriminate against otherwise qualified blacks." [The Court of Appeals held] that lack of discriminatory intent in designing and administering Test 21 was irrelevant; the critical fact was rather [that] four times as many [blacks] failed the test than did whites. This

disproportionate impact [was] held sufficient to establish a constitutional violation, absent proof by petitioners that the test was an adequate measure of job
performance in addition to being an indicator of probable success in the training
program, a burden which the court ruled petitioners had failed to discharge. * * *

The central purpose of the Equal Protection Clause [is] the prevention of
official conduct discriminating on the basis of race. [But] our cases have not
embraced the proposition that a law or other official act, without regard to
whether it reflects a racially discriminatory purpose, is unconstitutional *solely*
because it has a racially disproportionate impact.

Almost 100 years ago, *Strauder* established that the exclusion of Negroes
from grand and petit juries in criminal proceedings violated the Equal Protection
Clause, but the fact that a particular jury or a series of juries does not statistically
reflect the racial composition of the community does not in itself make out an
invidious discrimination forbidden by the Clause. "A purpose to discriminate must
be present which may be proven by systematic exclusion of eligible jurymen of the
prescribed race or by an unequal application of the law to such an extent as to
show intentional discrimination." * * *

The school desegregation cases have also adhered to the basic equal protection
principle that the invidious quality of a law claimed to be racially discriminatory
must ultimately be traced to a racially discriminatory purpose. That there are
both predominantly black and predominantly white schools in a community is not
alone violative of the Equal Protection Clause. The essential element ["differenti-
ating] between de jure segregation and so-called de facto segregation [is] *purpose*
or *intent* to segregate." *Keyes v. School Dist.*, [Sec. 2, IV infra].

This is not to say that the necessary discriminatory racial purpose must be
express or appear on the face of the statute, or that a law's disproportionate
impact is irrelevant. [A] statute, otherwise neutral on its face, must not be applied
so as invidiously to discriminate on the basis of race. *Yick Wo.* It is also clear from
the cases dealing with racial discrimination in the selection of juries that [a] prima
facie case of discriminatory purpose may be proved [by] the absence of Negroes on
a particular jury combined with the failure of the jury commissioners to be
informed of eligible Negro jurors in a community, or with racially non-neutral
selection procedures. With a prima facie case made out, "the burden of proof
shifts to the State to rebut the presumption of unconstitutional action by showing
that permissible racially neutral selection criteria and procedures have produced
the monochromatic result."

Necessarily, an invidious discriminatory purpose may often be inferred from
the totality of the relevant facts, including [that] the law bears more heavily on
one race than another. It is also not infrequently true that the discriminatory
impact—in the jury cases for example, the total or seriously disproportionate
exclusion of Negroes from jury venires—may for all practical purposes demonstrate unconstitutionality because in various circumstances the discrimination is
very difficult to explain on nonracial grounds. Nevertheless, we have not held that
a law, neutral on its face and serving ends otherwise within the power of
government to pursue, is invalid under the Equal Protection Clause simply
because it may affect a greater proportion of one race than of another. Disproportionate impact [s]tanding alone [does] not trigger the rule that racial classifications are to be subjected to the strictest scrutiny and are justifiable only by the
weightiest of considerations.

There are some indications to the contrary in our cases. In *Palmer v.
Thompson*, 403 U.S. 217, 91 S.Ct. 1940, 29 L.Ed.2d 438 (1971), the city of

Jackson, Miss., following a court decree to this effect, desegregated all of its public facilities save five swimming pools which [were] closed by ordinance pursuant to a determination by the city council that closure was necessary to preserve peace and order and that integrated pools could not be economically operated. [T]his Court rejected the argument that [the] otherwise seemingly permissible ends served by the ordinance could be impeached by demonstrating that racially invidious motivations had prompted the city council's action. [W]hatever dicta the opinion may contain, the decision did not involve, much less invalidate, a statute or ordinance having neutral purposes but disproportionate racial consequences.[11]

[Test 21] seeks to ascertain whether those who take it have acquired a particular level of verbal skill; and it is untenable that the Constitution prevents the government from seeking modestly to upgrade the communicative abilities of its employees rather than to be satisfied with some lower level of competence, particularly where the job requires special ability to communicate orally and in writing. Respondents, as Negroes, could no more successfully claim that the test denied them equal protection than could white applicants who also failed. The conclusion would not be different in the face of proof that more Negroes than whites had been disqualified by Test 21. * * *

Nor on the facts of the case before us would the disproportionate impact of Test 21 warrant the conclusion that it is a purposeful device to discriminate against Negroes * * *. [T]he test is neutral on its face and rationally may be said to serve a purpose the government is constitutionally empowered to pursue. Even agreeing with the District Court that the differential racial effect of Test 21 called for further inquiry, we think the District Court correctly held that the affirmative efforts of the Metropolitan Police Department to recruit black officers, the changing racial composition of the recruit classes and of the force in general, and the relationship of the test to the training program negated any inference that the Department discriminated on the basis of race * * *.

Under Title VII [of the Civil Rights Act of 1964], Congress provided that when hiring and promotion practices disqualifying substantially disproportionate numbers of blacks are challenged, discriminatory purpose need not be proved, and that it is an insufficient response to demonstrate some rational basis for the challenged practices. It is necessary, in addition, that they be "validated" in terms of job performance * * *. However this process proceeds, it involves a more probing judicial review of, and less deference to, the seemingly reasonable acts of administrators and executives than is appropriate under the Constitution where special racial impact, without discriminatory purpose, is claimed. We are not disposed to adopt this more rigorous standard for the purposes of applying the Fifth and the Fourteenth Amendments in cases such as this.

A rule that a statute designed to serve neutral ends is nevertheless invalid, absent compelling justification, if in practice it benefits or burdens one race more than another would be far-reaching and would raise serious questions about, and perhaps invalidate, a whole range of tax, welfare, public service, regulatory, and licensing statutes that may be more burdensome to the poor and to the average black than to the more affluent white.[14]

---

11. To the extent that *Palmer* suggests a generally applicable proposition that legislative purpose is irrelevant in constitutional adjudication, our prior cases—as indicated in the text—are to the contrary; and very shortly after *Palmer,* all Members of the Court majority in that case [joined] *Lemon v. Kurtzman,* [Ch. 8,

Sec. 1, II], [which held that determining] the validity of public aid to church-related schools includes close inquiry into the purpose of the challenged statute.

14. Frank I. Goodman, *De Facto School Segregation: A Constitutional and Empirical Analysis,* 60 Calif.L.Rev. 275, 300 (1972), sug-

Given that rule, such consequences would perhaps be likely to follow. However, in our view, extension of the rule beyond those areas where it is already applicable by reason of statute, such as in the field of public employment, should await legislative prescription. * * *a

JUSTICE STEVENS [who joined the Court's opinion] concurring. * * *

The requirement of purposeful discrimination is a common thread running through the cases summarized [by the Court. But] in each of these contexts, the burden of proving a prima facie case may well involve differing evidentiary considerations. The extent of deference that one pays to the trial court's determination of the factual issue, and indeed, the extent to which one characterizes the intent issue as a question of fact or a question of law, will vary in different contexts.

Frequently the most probative evidence of intent will be objective evidence of what actually happened rather than evidence describing the subjective state of mind of the actor. For normally the actor is presumed to have intended the natural consequences of his deeds. This is particularly true in the case of governmental action which is frequently the product of compromise, of collective decisionmaking, and of mixed motivation. It is unrealistic, on the one hand, to require the victim of alleged discrimination to uncover the actual subjective intent of the decisionmaker or conversely, to invalidate otherwise legitimate action simply because an improper motive affected the deliberation of a participant in the decisional process. A law conscripting clerics should not be invalidated because an atheist voted for it.

My point [is] to suggest that the line between discriminatory purpose and discriminatory impact is not nearly as bright, and perhaps not quite as critical, as the reader of the Court's opinion might assume. I agree [that] a constitutional issue does not arise every time some disproportionate impact is shown. On the other hand, when the disproportion is as dramatic as in *Gomillion v. Lightfoot,* 364 U.S. 339, 81 S.Ct. 125, 5 L.Ed.2d 110 (1960)[b] or *Yick Wo,* it really does not matter whether the standard is phrased in terms of purpose or effect. * * *

There are two reasons why I am convinced that the challenge to Test 21 is insufficient. First, the test serves the neutral and legitimate purpose of requiring all applicants to meet a uniform minimum standard of literacy. Reading ability is manifestly relevant to the police function, there is no evidence that the required

gests that disproportionate-impact analysis might invalidate "tests and qualifications for voting, draft deferment, public employment, jury service, and other government-conferred [benefits]; [s]ales taxes, bail schedules, utility rates, bridge tolls, license fees, and other state-imposed charges." It has also been argued that minimum wage and usury laws as well as professional licensing requirements would require major modifications in light of the un-equal-impact rule. William Silverman, *Equal Protection, Economic Legislation, and Racial Discrimination,* 25 Vand.L.Rev. 1183 (1972). * * *

a. The Court also found no violation of the relevant statutory provisions. Stewart, J., joined only the constitutional aspects of the Court's opinion. Brennan, J., joined by Marshall, J., did not address the constitutional questions but dissented on statutory grounds.

b. In *Gomillion,* an Alabama statute changed the Tuskegee city boundaries from a square to a 28 sided figure, allegedly removing "all save only four or five of its 400 Negro voters while not removing a single white voter or resident." The Court held that the complaint "amply alleges a claim of racial discrimination" in violation of the fifteenth amendment: "If these allegations upon a trial remained uncontradicted or unqualified, the conclusion would be irresistible, tantamount for all practical purposes to a mathematical demonstration, that the legislation is solely concerned with segregating white and colored voters by fencing Negro citizens out of town so as to deprive them of their pre-existing municipal vote."

passing grade was set at an arbitrarily high level, and there is sufficient disparity among high schools and high school graduates to justify the use of a separate uniform test. Second, the same test is used throughout the federal service. The applicants for employment in the District of Columbia Police Department represent such a small fraction of the total number of persons who have taken the test that their experience is of minimal probative value [to] overcome the presumption that a test which is this widely used by the Federal Government is in fact neutral in its effect as well as its "purpose" as that term is used in constitutional adjudication. * * *

Notes and Questions

1. *Background.* Consider Michael Klarman, *An Interpretive History of Modern Equal Protection*, 90 Mich.L.Rev. 213, 295–97 (1991): "Scattered dicta in Warren Court decisions [suggested] that facially neutral legislation producing disparate racial impacts possibly violated the Equal Protection Clause regardless of legislative motivation. [But the Warren Court never definitively resolved] the constitutionality of de facto racial classifications. [The] first case [squarely raising the question whether a facially neutral statute with an underlying discriminatory intent violated equal protection] was *Palmer v. Thompson*, [supra, involving a city's closure of its] public swimming pools to avoid court-ordered integration. The city's action unquestionably had a constitutionally objectionable purpose, but its impact seemed nondiscriminatory: neither blacks nor whites could any longer enjoy public swimming pools. [*Palmer*] produced chaos in the courts, [including the Supreme Court, which divided 5–4 in finding no constitutional violation]. [By] emphasizing the difficulty of discerning legislative purpose, [*Palmer*] seemed to [signal that legislative purpose was irrelevant to equal protection].

"Lower courts [plausibly inferred that the Court, by rejecting an intent-based inquiry in *Palmer*,] had opted instead for the [disparate] impact theory of equal protection. [They were bolstered in this conclusion] by the Court's contemporaneous interpretation of Title VII [of the 1964 Civil Rights Act in *Griggs v. Duke Power Co.*, 401 U.S. 424, 91 S.Ct. 849, 28 L.Ed.2d 158 (1971), as establishing] a disparate impact test" under which employment tests with discriminatory impacts were invalid unless the employer could make a showing of "business necessity."

2. *The discriminatory purpose requirement.* Should "racially disproportionate impact" alone trigger special judicial scrutiny? Consider Tribe 2d ed., at 1516–20: "The goal of the equal protection clause is not to stamp out impure thoughts, but to guarantee a full measure of human dignity for all. [Beyond] the purposeful, affirmative adoption or use of rules that disadvantage [them,] minorities can also be injured when the government is 'only' indifferent to their suffering or 'merely' blind to how prior official discrimination contributed to it and how current official acts will perpetuate it. [S]trict judicial scrutiny [should be used] for those government acts that, given their history, context, source, and effect, seem most likely not only to perpetuate subordination but also to reflect a tradition of hostility toward an historically subjugated group, or a pattern of blindness or indifference to the interests of that group."

Compare Michael J. Perry, *The Disproportionate Impact Theory of Racial Discrimination*, 125 U.Pa.L.Rev. 540, 559–60 (1977): "Laws employing a racial criterion of selection are inherently more dangerous than laws involving no racial criterion. The former, unlike the latter, directly encourage racism [and] are usually difficult if not impossible to justify on legitimate grounds. [Laws] having a disproportionate racial impact [should therefore not trigger strict scrutiny, but] the standard of review [should be] more rigorous than that required by the rational relationship test. [In] determining whether a disproportionate disadvantage is justified, a court would weigh several factors: (1) the degree of disproportion in the impact; (2) the private interest disadvantaged; (3) the efficiency of the challenged law in achieving its objective and the availability of alternative means having a less disproportionate impact; and (4) the government objective sought to be advanced."[a]

Consider Richard H. Fallon, Jr., *Implementing the Constitution*, 111 Harv. L.Rev. 54, 84–86 (1997): The Court disfavors "effects" tests that trigger elevated scrutiny based on a statute's disproportionate impact on minority groups because "the Justices believe that for courts [strictly to scrutinize] every governmental act that [disadvantages] minorities would infringe too far on [governmental decisionmaking]. And for courts to engage in open-ended balancing of all acts [with racially disproportionate impacts] would invite too many inquiries that are too little determined by legal rules. [The] Court believes [that] the judicial role must be cabined to protect reasonable choices by politically accountable decisionmakers against too many costly and unpredictable assessments by courts."

3. *Context and perspective.* Consider the suggestion of Perry, supra, at 557–58, that the racially disproportionate impact of tests such as that used in *Washington v. Davis* is likely to be the "consequence of prior governmental action that was constitutionally and ethically offensive" and should, for that reason, "trigger a heavier burden of justification than that required of a truly neutral disadvantage." Compare Owen M. Fiss, *Groups and the Equal Protection Clause*, 5 Phil. & Pub.Afrs. 107, 145 (1976): "A true inquiry into past discrimination [requires] the courts to construct causal connections that span significant periods of time, periods greater than those permitted under any general statute of limitations (a common device used to prevent the judiciary from undertaking inquiries where the evidence is likely to be stale, fragmentary, and generally unreliable). The difficulties of these backward-looking inquiries are compounded because the court must invariably deal with aggregate behavior, not just a single transaction; it must determine the causal explanation for the residential patterns of an entire community, or the skill levels of all the black applicants."[b]

Consider David Crump, *Evidence, Race, Intent, and Evil: The Paradox of Purposelessness in the Constitutional Racial Discrimination Cases*, 27 Hofstra L.Rev. 285, 315 (1998): "On the question of whether racial discrimination is tied to intent, [or] whether it can be unconscious and accidental, blacks and whites are sharply divided. African–Americans, in polls, tend to see racism as an ongoing and pervasive condition of American life, while whites tend to think of it as individual actions or attitudes of bigotry that are the exception rather than the rule. Thus, whites tend to use the word 'racism' to refer to explicit and conscious belief in racial superiority. African–Americans mean something different by racism: a set of

---

a. Compare the balancing approach that the Court prescribed in *Pike v. Bruce Church, Inc.*, quoted in the introduction to Ch. 4, for assessing facially neutral regulations that incidentally burden interstate commerce: "Where the statute regulates evenhandedly to effectuate a legitimate local public interest, and its effects on interstate commerce are only incidental, it will be upheld unless the burden imposed on commerce is clearly excessive in relation to the putative local benefits. If a legitimate local purpose is found, then the question becomes one of degree. And the ex-

tent of the burden that will be tolerated will of course depend on the nature of the local interest involved, and on whether it could be promoted as well with a lesser impact on interstate activities." Could a similar approach be applied to statutes that "incidentally" burden racial minorities?

b. See also Eric Schnapper, *Perpetuation of Past Discrimination*, 96 Harv.L.Rev. 828 (1983); Paul Brest, *In Defense of the Antidiscrimination Principle*, 90 Harv.L.Rev. 1, 42 (1976).

practices and institutions that result in the oppression of black people.''[c] If this assertion is correct, does *Washington v. Davis* adopt a characteristically white outlook—that there can be no discrimination in the absence of personally invidious intent—and reject the perspective of minorities who regard themselves as victims of pervasive discrimination?[d]

4. *Judicial role.* (a) Is the Court's approach in *Davis* consistent with the theory, often traced to the *Carolene Products* case, Ch. 5, Sec. 3, that the courts have a special role in protecting "discrete and insular" minorities? Consider Fallon, supra, at 104–05: "Traditional minorities may suffer at least two types of disadvantage in the political and legislative processes. One is hostility. The other is a relative dearth of sympathy, empathy, or concern.[e] [The Court's approach gives no protection against the latter disadvantage and, in its indifference,] reflect[s] at most a thin, minimalist conception of the democratic processes to which courts are [asked] to defer."[f]

Compare Robert W. Bennett, *"Mere" Rationality in Constitutional Law: Judicial Review and Democratic Theory,* 67 Calif.L.Rev. 1049, 1076 (1979): "If members of racial minorities statistically obtain benefits and suffer detriments as one or another piece of legislation is passed without attention to its racial impact, they are obtaining, not being deprived of, equal protection of the laws. To forbid all legislation that disadvantages them would give them the gains from political bargaining without the losses. This would be so regardless of the degree of the racially disproportionate impact or the importance of the interest affected."

(b) Is *Davis*'s mandate of judicial inquiries into legislative purposes a sensible and manageable one?[g] Consider Fallon, supra, at 99, 102: Within a doctrinal regime in which the Court frequently defers to legislative judgments, such as under the "rational basis" test, "purpose tests single out a class of cases in which" political officials "forfeit any reasonable claim to judicial deference. [In this sense, purpose tests are] a lowest common denominator. The [Court] can often agree that action [taken] for forbidden purposes should be invalidated, even when no majority believes that relevant constitutional norms merit the further protections that other constitutional tests [would] afford."

5. *Intent and impact under other amendments.* The Court strongly suggested that discriminatory impact alone (in the absence of a showing of discriminatory

---

c. For an ambitious effort to develop a "New Institutional" theory of racism, which explains how entrenched assumptions and routinized patters can produce outcomes that are unfairly skewed along racial lines even in the absence of conscious discriminatory intent, see Ian F. Haney–Lopez, *Institutional Racism: Judicial Conduct and a New Theory of Racial Discrimination,* 109 Yale L.J. 1717 (2000).

d. See also Alan D. Freeman, *Legitimizing Racial Discrimination Through Antidiscrimination Law: A Critical Review of Supreme Court Doctrine,* 62 Minn.L.Rev. 1049 (1978) (arguing that *Davis* adopts a "perpetrator" rather than a "victim" perspective on the relevance of past race discrimination).

e. See, e.g., Charles R. Lawrence, *The Id, the Ego, and Equal Protection: Reckoning with Unconscious Racism,* 39 Stan.L.Rev. 317, 341–44 (1987).

f. See Barbara J. Flagg, *Enduring Principles: On Race, Process, and Constitutional*

Law, 82 Calif.L.Rev. 935 (1994) (arguing that *Davis* resolved two "competing institutional concerns"—(1) making "meaningful inquiries into legislative motive in order to discern the presence of discriminatory intent" is "difficult and inappropriate," and (2) "applying strict scrutiny in all disparate impact cases would engage the courts too extensively in overseeing social policy"—"in a direction adverse to the interests of substantive racial justice").

g. For a range of views, see, e.g., Paul Brest, *Palmer v. Thompson: An Approach to The Problem of Unconstitutional Motive,* 1971 Sup.Ct. 95, 116–118; John H. Ely, *Legislative and Administrative Motivation in Constitutional Law,* 79 Yale L.J. 1205 (1970); Kenneth L. Karst, *The Costs of Motive–Centered Inquiry,* 15 San Diego L.Rev. 1163 (1978); Ashutosh Bhagwat, *Purpose Scrutiny in Constitutional Analysis,* 85 Cal.L.Rev. 297 (1997).

intent) will not establish a fifteenth amendment violation in *Mobile v. Bolden*, Sec. 5, I, A infra, and *Rogers v. Lodge*, Sec. 5, I, A infra.

The Court considered the requisites for establishing a thirteenth amendment violation in MEMPHIS v. GREENE, 451 U.S. 100, 101 S.Ct. 1584, 67 L.Ed.2d 769 (1981). At the behest of citizens of Hein Park, a white residential district, the city closed West Drive, a street that traversed Hein Park and was used mainly by African–Americans who lived in an adjacent area. The Court, per STEVENS, J., agreeing that "the adverse impact on blacks was greater than on whites," found no violation of 42 U.S.C.A. § 1982 [quoted in Ch. 11, Sec. 1 infra] or the thirteenth amendment: "[T]he critical facts established by the record are these: The city's decision to close West Drive was motivated by its interest in protecting the safety and tranquility of a residential neighborhood. The procedures followed in making the decision were fair and were not affected by any racial or other impermissible factors. The city has conferred a benefit on certain white property owners but there is no reason to believe that it would refuse to confer a comparable benefit on black property owners. The closing has not affected the value of property owned by black citizens, but it has caused some slight inconvenience to black motorists.

"[T]he record discloses no racially discriminatory motive on the part of the City Council [and] a review of the justification for the official action challenged in this case demonstrates that its disparate impact on black citizens could not [be] fairly characterized as a badge or incident of slavery.

"[To] decide the narrow constitutional question presented by this record we need not speculate about the sort of impact on a racial group that might be prohibited by the Amendment itself. We merely hold that the impact of the closing of West Drive on nonresidents of Hein Park [does] not reflect a violation of the Thirteenth Amendment."

MARSHALL, J., joined by Brennan and Blackmun, JJ., dissented: "I [do] not mean to imply that all municipal decisions that affect Negroes adversely and benefit whites are prohibited by the Thirteenth Amendment. I would, however, insist that the government carry a heavy burden of justification before I would sustain against Thirteenth Amendment challenge conduct as egregious as erection of a barrier to prevent predominantly-Negro traffic from entering a historically all-white neighborhood. [I] do not believe that the city has discharged that burden in this case, and for that reason I would hold that the erection of the barrier at the end of West Drive amounts to a badge or incident of slavery forbidden by the Thirteenth Amendment."

Although *Washington v. Davis* rejected the "disparate impact" theory and held that a facially neutral statute violates the equal protection clause only if motivated by a discriminatory purpose, the Court did not address in detail what counts as a discriminatory purpose. The leading case addressing that issue involved gender, not race, but the Court's approach to identifying forbidden intent or purposes appears to be the same. PERSONNEL ADMINISTRATOR v. FEENEY, 442 U.S. 256, 99 S.Ct. 2282, 60 L.Ed.2d 870 (1979), per STEWART, J., upheld Massachusetts' "absolute lifetime preference to veterans" for state civil service positions, even though "the preference operates overwhelmingly to the advantage of males": "When a statute gender-neutral on its face is challenged on the ground that its effects upon women are disproportionately adverse, a two-fold inquiry [is] appropriate. The first question is whether the statutory classification is indeed neutral * * *. If the classification itself, covert or overt, is not based upon gender, the second question is whether the adverse effect reflects invidious gender-based discrimination. In this second inquiry, impact provides an 'important starting point,' but purposeful discrimination is 'the condition that offends the Constitution.' "

As to the first question, "The District Court [found] first, that ch. 31 serves legitimate and worthy purposes; second, that the absolute preference was not established for the purpose of discriminating against women. [Thus,] the distinction between veterans and nonveterans drawn by ch. 31 is not a pretext for gender discrimination. * * *

"If the impact of this statute could not be plausibly explained on a neutral ground, impact itself would signal that the real classification made by the law was in fact not neutral. But there can be but one answer to the question whether this veteran preference excludes significant numbers of women from preferred state jobs because they are women or because they are nonveterans. [Although] few women benefit from the preference, * * * significant numbers of nonveterans are men, and [too] many men are affected by ch. 31 to permit the inference that the statute is but a pretext for preferring men over women. * * *

"The dispositive question, then, is whether the appellee has shown that a gender-based discriminatory purpose has, at least in some measure, shaped [ch. 31. Her] contention that this veterans' preference is 'inherently non-neutral' or 'gender-biased' presumes that the State, by favoring veterans, intentionally incorporated into its public employment policies the panoply of sex-based and assertedly discriminatory federal laws that have prevented all but a handful of women from becoming veterans. There are two serious difficulties with this argument. First, it is wholly at odds with the District Court's central finding that Massachusetts has not offered a preference to veterans for the purpose of discriminating against women. Second, [t]o the extent that the status of veteran is one that few women have been enabled to achieve, every hiring preference for veterans, however modest or extreme, is inherently gender-biased. If Massachusetts by offering such a preference can be said intentionally to have incorporated into its state employment policies the historical gender-based federal military personnel practices, the degree of the preference would or should make no constitutional difference. Invidious discrimination does not become less so because the discrimination accomplished is of a lesser magnitude.[23] Discriminatory intent is simply not amenable to calibration. It either is a factor that has influenced the legislative choice or it is not. The District Court's conclusion that the absolute veterans' preference was not originally enacted or subsequently reaffirmed for the purpose of giving an advantage to males as such necessarily compels the conclusion that the State intended nothing more than to prefer 'veterans.' * * *

"To be sure, this case is unusual in that it involves a law that by design is not neutral. [As] opposed to the written test at issue in *Davis*, it does not purport to define a job related characteristic. To the contrary, it confers upon a specifically described group—perceived to be particularly deserving—a competitive head start. But the District Court found, and the appellee has not disputed, that this legislative choice was legitimate. [Thus, it] must be analyzed as is any other neutral law that casts a greater burden upon women as a group than upon men as

23. This is not to say that the degree of impact is irrelevant to the question of intent. But it is to say that a more modest preference, while it might well lessen impact and, as the State argues, might lessen the effectiveness of the statute in helping veterans, would not be any more or less "neutral" in the constitutional sense.

a group. The enlistment policies of the armed services may well have discriminated on the basis of sex. But the history of discrimination against women in the military is not on trial in this case.

"The appellee's ultimate argument rests upon the presumption, common to the criminal and civil law, that a person intends the natural and foreseeable consequences of his voluntary actions. * * *

" 'Discriminatory purpose,' however, implies more than intent as volition or intent as awareness of consequences. It implies that the decisionmaker, in this case a state legislature, selected or reaffirmed a particular course of action at least in part 'because of,' not merely 'in spite of,' its adverse effects upon an identifiable group.[25] Yet nothing in the record demonstrates that this preference for veterans was originally devised or subsequently re-enacted because it would accomplish the collateral goal of keeping women in a stereotypic and predefined place in the Massachusetts Civil Service."

STEVENS, J., joined by White, J., concurred in the Court's opinion, adding: "[F]or me the answer is largely provided by the fact that the number of males disadvantaged by Massachusetts' Veterans Preference (1,867,000) is sufficiently large—and sufficiently close to the number of disadvantaged females (2,954,000)— to refute the claim that the rule was intended to benefit males as a class over females as a class."

MARSHALL, J., joined by Brennan, J., dissented: "In my judgment, [ch. 31] evinces purposeful gender-based discrimination. * * *

"That a legislature seeks to advantage one group does not, as a matter of logic or of common sense, exclude the possibility that it also intends to disadvantage another. Individuals in general and lawmakers in particular frequently act for a variety of reasons. [S]ince reliable evidence of subjective intentions is seldom obtainable, resort to inference based on objective factors is generally unavoidable. To discern the purposes underlying facially neutral policies, this Court has therefore considered the degree, inevitability, and foreseeability of any disproportionate impact as well as the alternatives reasonably available.

"[T]he impact of the Massachusetts statute on women is undisputed. Any veteran with a passing grade on the civil service exam must be placed ahead of a nonveteran, regardless of their respective scores. [Because] less than 2% of the women in Massachusetts are veterans, the absolute preference formula has rendered desirable state civil service employment an almost exclusively male prerogative. [Where] the foreseeable impact of a facially neutral policy is so disproportionate, the burden should rest on the State to establish that sex-based considerations played no part in the choice of the particular legislative scheme.

"Clearly, that burden was not sustained here. The legislative history of the statute reflects the Commonwealth's patent appreciation of the impact the preference system would have on women, and an equally evident desire to mitigate that impact only with respect to certain traditionally female occupations. Until 1971,

---

25. This is not to say that the inevitability or foreseeability of consequences of a neutral rule has no bearing upon the existence of discriminatory intent. Certainly, when the adverse consequences of a law upon an identifiable group are as inevitable as the gender-based consequences of ch. 31, a strong inference that the adverse effects were desired can reasonably be drawn. But in this inquiry— made as it is under the Constitution—an inference is a working tool, not a synonym for proof. When as here, the impact is essentially an unavoidable consequence of a legislative policy that has in itself always been deemed to be legitimate, and when, as here, the statutory history and all of the available evidence affirmatively demonstrate the opposite, the inference simply fails to ripen into proof.

the statute [and] regulations exempted from operation of the preference any job requisitions 'especially calling for women.' In practice, this exemption, coupled with the absolute preference for veterans, has created a gender-based civil service hierarchy, with women occupying low grade clerical and secretarial jobs and men holding more responsible and remunerative positions. [Particularly] when viewed against the range of less discriminatory alternatives available to assist veterans,[2] Massachusetts's choice of a formula that so severely restricts public employment opportunities for women cannot reasonably be thought gender-neutral. The Court's conclusion to the contrary—that 'nothing in the record' evinces a 'collateral goal of keeping women in a stereotypic and predefined place in the Massachusetts Civil Service'—displays a singularly myopic view of the facts established below.[3]"

Notes and Questions

1. *Reversed roles.* Should and would the Court find a "discriminatory purpose" if the challenged law would not have been passed "if its racial impact had been reversed—if the disparate impact had been on whites rather than on blacks"? Eric Schnapper, *Two Categories of Discriminatory Intent*, 17 Harv.Civ. Rts.Civ.Lib.L.Rev. 31, 51 (1982). Is this an inquiry that a court is competent to conduct? Consider id. at 55–56: "The central issue [in *Feeney*] is whether Massachusetts would have adopted in 1896 a veterans' preference [that would have excluded 98% of all male applicants] or would have amended its statutes successively in 1919, 1943, 1949, and 1968 to assure such preferential treatment for new generations of predominantly female veterans. The all too familiar history of discrimination on the basis of sex in this country renders implausible the suggestion * * *."[a]

2. *The Court's definition.* Consider the argument of Reva Siegel, *Why Equal Protection No Longer Protects: The Evolving Forms of Status–Enforcing State Action*, 49 Stan.L.Rev. 1111, 1138 (1997), that "discriminatory purpose, as discussed in [*Feeney* and other cases], is a juridical concept that does not reflect prevailing understandings of the ways in which racial or gender bias operates, but instead functions to protect the prerogatives of coordinate branches of government."

———

Since *Washington v. Davis* and in light of *Feeney*, the Court has struggled recurrently with problems of proof in cases alleging discriminatory motives or purposes. As you read the next case and the notes that follow, consider what general principles, if any, govern the requisite inquiry.

ARLINGTON HEIGHTS v. METROPOLITAN HOUSING DEV. CORP., 429 U.S. 252, 97 S.Ct. 555, 50 L.Ed.2d 450 (1977), per POWELL, J., held that

2. Only four States afford a preference comparable in [scope]. Other States and the Federal Government grant point or tie-breaking preferences that do not foreclose opportunities for women.

3. Although it is relevant that the preference statute also disadvantages a substantial group of men, it is equally pertinent that 47% of Massachusetts men over 18 are veterans, as compared to 0.8% of Massachusetts women.

Given this disparity, and the indicia of intent noted supra, the absolute number of men denied preference cannot be dispositive, especially since they have not faced the barriers to achieving veteran status confronted by women.

a. For detailed development of this approach, see also David A. Strauss, *Discriminatory Intent and the Taming of Brown*, 56 U.Chi.L.Rev. 935 (1989).

petitioner Village's refusal to rezone land from single-family (R–3) to multiple-family (R–5), so as to permit respondent's construction of racially integrated housing, did not violate equal protection:

"*Davis* does not require a plaintiff to prove that the challenged action rested solely on racially discriminatory purposes. Rarely can it be said that a legislature or administrative body operating under a broad mandate made a decision motivated solely by a single concern, or even that a particular purpose was the 'dominant' or 'primary' one. In fact, it is because legislators and administrators are properly concerned with balancing numerous competing considerations that courts refrain from reviewing the merits of their decisions, absent a showing of arbitrariness or irrationality. But racial discrimination is not just another competing consideration. When there is proof that a discriminatory purpose has been a motivating factor in the decision, this judicial deference is no longer justified.

"Determining whether invidious discriminatory purpose was a motivating factor demands a sensitive inquiry into such circumstantial and direct evidence of intent as may be available. The impact of the official action [may] provide an important starting point. Sometimes a clear pattern, unexplainable on grounds other than race, emerges from the effect of the state action even when the governing legislation appears neutral on its face. *Yick Wo; Guinn v. United States,* 238 U.S. 347, 35 S.Ct. 926, 59 L.Ed. 1340 (1915); *Lane v. Wilson,* 307 U.S. 268, 59 S.Ct. 872, 83 L.Ed. 1281 (1939);[a] *Gomillion.* The evidentiary inquiry is then relatively easy.[13] But such cases are rare. Absent a pattern as stark as that in *Gomillion* or *Yick Wo,* impact alone is not determinative,[14] and the Court must look to other evidence.[15]

"The historical background of the decision is one evidentiary source, particularly if it reveals a series of official actions taken for invidious purposes. See *Lane.* The specific sequence of events leading up to the challenged decision also may shed some light on the decision-maker's purposes. *Reitman v. Mulkey,* [Ch. 10, Sec. 3 infra]. For example, if the property involved here always had been zoned R–5 but suddenly was changed to R–3 when the town learned of MHDC's plans to erect integrated housing, we would have a far different case. Departures from the normal procedural sequence also might afford evidence that improper purposes are playing a role. Substantive departures too may be relevant, particularly if the factors usually considered important by the decisionmaker strongly favor a decision contrary to the one reached.

"The legislative or administrative history may be highly relevant, especially where there are contemporary statements by members of the decisionmaking body, minutes of its meetings, or reports. In some extraordinary instances the

a. *Guinn* held that Oklahoma's literacy test for voting violated the fifteenth amendment because its "grandfather clause" effectively exempted whites. Oklahoma then immediately enacted a new law providing that all persons who previously voted were qualified for life but that all others must register within a twelve day period or be permanently disenfranchised. *Lane* held that this new law violated the fifteenth amendment.

13. Several of our jury selection cases fall into this category. Because of the nature of the jury selection task, however, we have permitted a finding of constitutional violation even when the statistical pattern does not approach the extremes of *Yick Wo* or *Gomillion.*

14. This is not to say that a consistent pattern of official racial discrimination is a necessary predicate to a violation of [equal protection]. A single invidiously discriminatory governmental act—in the exercise of the zoning power as elsewhere—would not necessarily be immunized by the absence of such discrimination in the making of other comparable decisions.

15. In many instances, to recognize the limited probative value of disproportionate impact is merely to acknowledge the "heterogeneity" of the nation's population.

members might be called to the stand at trial to testify concerning the purpose of the official action, although even then such testimony frequently will be barred by privilege. See *Tenney v. Brandhove,* 341 U.S. 367, 71 S.Ct. 783, 95 L.Ed. 1019 (1951); *United States v. Nixon,* [Ch. 3, Sec. 4].[18]

"[This] summary identifies, without purporting to be exhaustive, subjects of proper inquiry in determining whether racially discriminatory intent existed."

Both courts below found that the rezoning denial was not racially motivated.

"We also have reviewed the evidence. The impact of the Village's decision does arguably bear more heavily on racial minorities. [But] there is little about the sequence of events leading up to the decision that would spark suspicion. The area [has] been zoned R–3 since 1959, the year when Arlington Heights first adopted a zoning map. Single-family homes surround the 80–acre site, and the Village is undeniably committed to single-family homes as its dominant residential land use. The rezoning request progressed according to the usual procedures. * * *

"The statements by the Plan Commission and Village Board members, as reflected in the official minutes, focused almost exclusively on the zoning aspects of the MHDC petition, and the zoning factors on which they relied are not novel criteria in the Village's rezoning decisions. * * * MHDC called one member of the Village Board to the stand at trial. Nothing in her testimony supports an inference of invidious purpose.

"In sum, [r]espondents simply failed to carry their burden of proving that discriminatory purpose was a motivating factor in the Village's decision.[21] This conclusion ends the constitutional inquiry."

Notes and Questions

1. *Consequences of "discriminatory purpose."* If it is found that a law "was motivated by a racially discriminatory purpose," should the state be permitted to prove "that the same decision would have resulted had the impermissible purpose not been considered"? *Arlington Heights,* fn. 21. Or should the Court invalidate a racially motivated law and "remand to the legislature for a reconsideration [on] the basis of purely legitimate factors"? Robert G. Schwemm, *From Washington to Arlington Heights and Beyond: Discriminatory Purpose in Equal Protection Litigation,* 1977 U.Ill.L.F. 961, 1020.

2. *Proving intentional discrimination in the administration of a law.* (a) *Jury selection.* In CASTANEDA v. PARTIDA, 430 U.S. 482, 97 S.Ct. 1272, 51 L.Ed.2d 498 (1977), respondent challenged the grand jury that indicted him in 1972. He showed that, although 79% of the county's population had Spanish surnames, the average percentage of Spanish-surnamed grand jurors between 1962–72 was 39%. In 1972, 52.5% of persons on the grand jury list had Spanish surnames as did 50% of those on respondent's grand jury list. The Court, per

---

18. This Court has recognized, ever since *Fletcher v. Peck* [Ch. 5, Sec. 1, I], that judicial inquiries into legislative or executive motivation represent a substantial intrusion into the workings of other branches of government. Placing a decisionmaker on the stand is therefore "usually to be avoided."

21. Proof that the decision by the Village was motivated in part by a racially discrimina-

tory purpose would not necessarily have required invalidation of the challenged decision. Such proof would, however, have shifted to the Village the burden of establishing that the same decision would have resulted even had the impermissible purpose not been considered. If this were established, the complaining party in a case of this kind no longer fairly could attribute the injury complained of to improper consideration of a discriminatory purpose.

BLACKMUN, J., held that respondent had established a prima facie case of discrimination against Mexican–Americans: "While the earlier cases involved absolute exclusion of an identifiable group, later cases established the principle that substantial underrepresentation of the group constitutes a constitutional violation as well, if it results from purposeful discrimination. [T]he degree of underrepresentation must be proved, by comparing the proportion of the group in the total population to the proportion called to serve as grand jurors, over a significant period of time. [If] a disparity is sufficiently large, then it is unlikely that it is due solely to chance or accident, and, in the absence of evidence to the contrary, one must conclude that racial or other class-related factors entered into the selection process. [A] selection procedure that is susceptible of abuse [such as the Texas procedure under which jury commissioners had broad discretion in compiling grand jury lists] or is not racially neutral [also] supports the presumption of discrimination raised by the statistical showing. Once the defendant has shown substantial underrepresentation of his group, he has made out a prima facie case of discriminatory purpose, and the burden then shifts to the State to rebut that case."

Should the state's proof that a majority of the jury commissioners were Mexican–American rebut the prima facie case? See *Castaneda* (answering in the negative).[a]

(b) *Selective prosecution.* UNITED STATES v. ARMSTRONG, 517 U.S. 456, 116 S.Ct. 1480, 134 L.Ed.2d 687 (1996), per REHNQUIST, C.J., held that the defendants had failed to make out a prima facie case of racially selective prosecution and thus were not entitled to discovery on the issue of prosecutorial intent to discriminate. All 24 defendants in "crack" cocaine cases closed by the Federal Public Defender in the previous year were black. In addition, the defendants submitted "an affidavit alleging that an intake coordinator at a drug treatment center had told her that there are 'an equal number of caucasian users and dealers to minority users and dealers,' [an] affidavit from a criminal defense attorney alleging that in his experience many nonblacks are prosecuted in state court for crack offenses, and a newspaper article reporting that Federal 'crack criminals [are] being punished far more severely than if they had been caught with powder cocaine, and almost every single one of them is black.' " But this was not enough: "the claimant must show that similarly situated individuals of a different race were not prosecuted."[b] STEVENS, J., dissented: "I am persuaded that the District Judge did not abuse her discretion when she concluded that the factual showing was sufficiently disturbing to require some response from the United States Attorney's Office."[c]

a. For a detailed study of the Los Angeles superior court's grand juror selection process, and the conclusion that although the judges "exhibit no purposeful embrace of racial discrimination, they nevertheless" act repeatedly in ways that reflect and enforce the significance of racial status, see Ian F. Haney–Lopez, *Institutional Racism: Judicial Conduct and a New Theory of Racial Discrimination*, 109 Yale L.J. 1717, 1844 (2000).

b. For the suggestion that the *Armstrong* standard is virtually impossible to meet, and indeed establishes a nearly insurmountable bar to "obtaining discovery of information that would help to prove discriminatory intent when it does exist," see Angela J. Davis, *Prosecution and Race: The Power and Privilege of Discretion*, 67 Fordham L.Rev. 13, 18 (1998). See also Andrew D. Leipold, *Objective Tests and Subjective Bias: Some Problems of Discriminatory Intent in the Criminal Law*, 73 Chi.-Kent L.Rev. 559 (1998).

c. The Court has held in other cases that the trial court's decision on the ultimate question of discriminatory intent represents a finding of fact of the sort accorded great deference on appeal, particularly on issues of credibility. See, e.g., *Hernandez v. New York*, 500 U.S. 352, 111 S.Ct. 1859, 114 L.Ed.2d 395 (1991).

If users of crack cocaine are disproportionately black, whereas users of powder cocaine are disproportionately white, is it prima facie evidence of race discrimination if legislatures enact higher penalties for possession of crack cocaine than for possession of powder cocaine? If police and prosecutors devote far more resources to crack cocaine than to powder cocaine cases? See Note, 19 Cardozo L.Rev. 1149, 1153 (1997); see also Reva Siegel, *Why Equal Protection No Longer Protects: The Evolving Forms of Status–Enforcing State Action*, 49 Stan.L.Rev. 1111, 1139–40 (1997). Compare Kate Stith, *The Government Interest in Criminal Law: Whose Interest Is It, Anyway?*, in *Public Values in Constitutional Law* 158 (1993): "While it appears true that the enhanced penalties for crack cocaine more often fall upon black defendants, the legislature's action might also have been a laudatory attempt to provide enhanced protection to those communities—largely black . . .—who are ravaged by abuse of this potent drug." See also Randall Kennedy, *Race, Crime, and the Law* 369–75 (1997).

(c) *Executive appointments.* In MAYOR OF PHILA. v. EDUCATIONAL EQUALITY LEAGUE, 415 U.S. 605, 94 S.Ct. 1323, 39 L.Ed.2d 630 (1974), respondents contended that in 1971 the mayor had racially discriminated in appointments to the city's Nominating Panel for school board members. Approximately "34% of the population of Philadelphia and approximately 60% of the students attending the city's various schools were Negroes" but "the 1971 Panel had 11 whites and two Negroes." The Court, per POWELL, J., held the proof "too fragmentary and speculative" to establish "a prima facie case of racial discrimination." The statistics were "simplistic percentage comparisons [in] the context of this case"; because of the designated qualifications for Panel members, it could not "be assumed that all citizens are fungible for purposes of determining whether members of a particular class have been unlawfully excluded."[d]

3. *Peremptory challenges.* BATSON v. KENTUCKY, 476 U.S. 79, 106 S.Ct. 1712, 90 L.Ed.2d 69 (1986), per POWELL, J.—declining to follow *Swain v. Alabama*, 380 U.S. 202, 85 S.Ct. 824, 13 L.Ed.2d 759 (1965)—held that, using the same "combination of factors" as in cases such as *Castaneda*, "a defendant may establish a prima facie case of purposeful discrimination in selection of the petit jury solely on evidence concerning the prosecutor's exercise of peremptory challenges at the defendant's trial. [Then], the burden shifts to the State to come forward with a neutral explanation for challenging black jurors. [T]he prosecution's explanation need not rise to the level justifying exercise of a challenge for cause. [B]ut the prosecutor may not rebut the defendant's prima facie case of discrimination by stating merely that he challenged jurors of the defendant's race on the assumption—or his intuitive judgment—that they would be partial to the defendant because of their shared race, [because the] core guarantee of equal protection, ensuring citizens that their State will not discriminate on account of race, would be meaningless" if this were permitted.

REHNQUIST, J., joined by Burger, C.J., dissented: "[T]here is simply nothing 'unequal' about the State using its peremptory challenges to strike blacks from the jury in cases involving black defendants, so long as such challenges are also used to exclude whites in cases involving white defendants, Hispanics in cases involving Hispanic defendants, Asians in cases involving Asian defendants, and so on."[e]

---

d. White, J., joined by Douglas, Brennan, and Marshall, JJ., dissented.

e. *Georgia v. McCollum*, 505 U.S. 42, 112 S.Ct. 2348, 120 L.Ed.2d 33 (1992), per Black-

mun, J., extended *Batson* and *Edmonson v. Leesville Concrete Co.*, 500 U.S. 614, 111 S.Ct. 2077, 114 L.Ed.2d 660 (1991) (holding *Batson* applicable to civil litigants), to peremptory

4. *Capital sentencing.* McCLESKEY v. KEMP, the facts of which are set forth in detail in Ch. 6, Sec. 4, III, per POWELL, J., rejected the claim of a black petitioner subject to a sentence of death "that the Baldus study compels an inference that his sentence rests on purposeful discrimination." Unlike the jury selection cases, where "the factors that may be considered are limited, usually by state [statute], each particular decision to impose the death penalty is made by a [jury] unique in its composition, and the Constitution requires that its decision rest on consideration of innumerable factors that vary according to the characteristics of the individual defendant and the facts of the particular capital offense." Further, unlike the jury selection context, "here, the State has no practical opportunity to rebut the Baldus study" because "policy considerations" (1) "dictate that jurors [not] be called [to] testify to the motives and influences that led to their verdict" and (2) "suggest the impropriety of our requiring prosecutors to defend their decisions to seek death penalties, often years after they were made." Furthermore, "[r]equiring a prosecutor to rebut a study that analyzes the past conduct of scores of prosecutors is quite different from requiring a prosecutor to rebut a contemporaneous challenge to his own acts. See *Batson.*" Finally, implementation of laws against murder, which are "at the heart of the State's criminal justice system, [requires] discretionary judgments. [W]e would demand exceptionally clear proof before we would infer that the discretion has been abused."

BLACKMUN, J., joined by Brennan, Marshall, and Stevens, JJ., dissented, reviewing parts of the Baldus study in detail: "I concentrate on the decisions within the prosecutor's office through which the State decided to seek the death penalty and, in particular, the point at which the State proceeded to the penalty phase after conviction. This is a step at which the evidence of the effect of the racial factors was especially strong" and not adequately rebutted by the state.

"I agree [as] to the difficulty of examining the jury's decisionmaking process [but not with the] Court's refusal to require that the prosecutor provide an explanation for his actions * * *. Prosecutors undoubtedly need adequate discretion to allocate the resources of their offices and to fulfill their responsibilities to the public in deciding how best to enforce the law, but this does not place them beyond the constraints imposed on state action under the Fourteenth Amendment."

Does *McCleskey* absolutely foreclose selective prosecution claims involving the death penalty, or only establish that the Baldus study is not enough by itself to make out a prima facie case?[f] If the latter, what kind of showing would a

---

challenges by a criminal defendant: "Just as public confidence in criminal justice is undermined by a conviction in a trial where racial discrimination has occurred in jury selection, so is public confidence undermined where a defendant, assisted by racially discriminatory peremptory strikes, obtains an acquittal."

O'Connor and Scalia, JJ., dissented on the ground that there was no "state action" (as discussed in her dissent in *Edmonson*). Rehnquist, C.J. and Thomas, J., agreed, but concurred in the judgment because "*Edmonson* governs this case." On the merits, Thomas, J., added: "In *Strauder,* we put the rights of defendants foremost. Today's decision, while protecting jurors, leaves defendants with less means of protecting themselves. [B]lack criminal defendants will rue the day that this court ventured down this road that inexorably will lead to the elimination of peremptory strikes."

f. The Baldus study's strongest evidence of race-based disparities did not involve the race of the criminal defendant, but rather the race of the victim. If a criminal defendant (whether black or white) is targeted for the death penalty for having killed a white (rather than a black), is the criminal defendant the victim of a racially discriminatory intent? Does this depend on what counts as a racially discriminatory intent? See Evan Tsen Lee & Ashutosh Bhagwat, *The McCleskey Puzzle: Remedying Prosecutorial Discrimination Against Black Victims in Capital Sentencing,* 1998 Sup.Ct. Rev. 145.

challenger need to make? See John H. Blume, Theodore Eisenberg & Sheri Lynn Johnson, *Post-McCleskey Racial Discrimination Claims in Capital Cases*, 83 Cornell L.Rev. 1771 (1998).

5. *The "myth of intent"?* Is it fair to say that the Court requires individualized showings of discriminatory intent by relevant officials in *Armstrong* and *McCleskey*, but that it accepts general statistical evidence as highly probative in *Castaneda* and *Batson*?[g] Consider the suggestion of Crump, supra, at 331, that the Court's willingness to find discriminatory intent may depend partly on whether a finding of discriminatory intent would have remedial implications that the Court would find difficult or unacceptable: "In *McCleskey*, if one were to find a violation, it would be difficult to conceive a complete judicial remedy unless the State were either to abolish jury determinations of death sentences or to abolish capital punishment. In the driving while black situation [involving accusations that police tend to stop disproportionately large numbers of minority motorists], systematic judicial responses [requiring a racially proportionate number of stops] might interfere unacceptably with the government's responsibility to enforce traffic laws that benefit members of all races."

See also Richard H. McAdams, *Race and Selective Prosecution: Discovering the Pitfalls of Armstrong*, 73 Chi.-Kent L.Rev. 605, 605–07 (1998): *Armstrong* creates a situation in which "the defendant 'cannot obtain discovery unless she first makes a threshold showing [of] selective prosecution. [Yet] making a sufficient preliminary showing of discriminatory intent may be impossible without some discovery.' [As a result,] many meritorious claims will never be proven. [The] tradeoff implicit in *Armstrong* [can] be justified only by great hostility to the selective prosecution doctrine itself. [The Court appears to believe] that there are no 'meritorious' selective prosecution claims, either because there is no selective prosecution or because selectively prosecuted defendants should not be entitled to the relief they seek—dismissal of the charge."

Do you agree with Daniel R. Ortiz, *The Myth of Intent in Equal Protection*, 41 Stan.L.Rev. 1105 (1989), that the Court has used the allocation of burdens of proof of discriminatory purpose to obscure its own "balancing of competing individual and public interests" and its making "many of the ultimate value choices implicit in equal protection"?[h]

IV. REMEDYING SEGREGATION

Although there was prompt compliance with *Brown* in the District of Columbia and some border states, the initial response in the deep south was "massive resistance." See generally Robert McKay, *"With All Deliberate Speed": Legislative Reaction and Judicial Development 1956–1957*, 43 Va.L.Rev. 1205 (1957). As late as the 1964–65 school year, only 2.14% of black students in the eleven "southern states" attended schools in which they were not the racial majority. In the late 1950s, some states sought to comply with *Brown* by simply permitting students to apply for transfer to another school. Procedures were complex and time-consum-

g. See generally Sheila Foster, *Intent and Incoherence*, 72 Tul.L.Rev. 1065 (1998) (reviewing leading cases and arguing that the Court effectively accepts different concepts of intent, and transparently applies different burdens of proof, in different contexts).

h. See also Michael Selmi, *Proving Discrimination: The Reality of Supreme Court*

Rhetoric, 86 Geo.L.J. 279, 286 (1997) (arguing that "the Court never fully embraced its own rhetoric" and that the Justices have "acted like the political branches by treating the issue of race as a subject for compromise and continually subjugating concerns of racial equality to other purported interests").

ing; standards were vague, making it difficult to show that denials were due to race. See Note, *The Federal Courts and Integration of Southern Schools: Troubled Status of the Pupil Placement Act*, 62 Colum.L.Rev. 1448 (1962). Under the "all deliberate speed" of *Brown II*, and its insistence that "[s]chool authorities have primary responsibility for" implementing *Brown I*, the Court largely played a hands-off role for nearly a decade. During this period, the burden of grappling with the "massive resistance" campaign fell largely to the lower federal courts.

The Court's single notable intervention in the immediate post-*Brown* decade came in COOPER v. AARON, 358 U.S. 1, 78 S.Ct. 1401, 3 L.Ed.2d 5 (1958), also discussed in Ch. 1, Sec. 1, involving the Little Rock School Board's request to stay an integration plan that had been in operation at Central High School during the 1957–58 school year, but only after federal troops had been sent by President Eisenhower to protect black students from "extreme public hostility" engendered largely by the governor's and legislature's opposition. The opinion, unprecedented in that it was signed by all nine Justices (including those appointed since *Brown*), "unanimously reaffirmed" *Brown*. The Court agreed that "the educational progress of all the students [will] continue to suffer if the conditions which prevailed last year are permitted to continue," but denied the request for delay: "The Constitutional rights of [black children] are not to be sacrificed or yielded to the violence and disorder which have followed upon the actions of the governor and legislature." The difficulties, created by state action, "can also be brought under control by state action." *Brown* "can neither be nullified openly and directly by state legislators or state executive or judicial officers, nor nullified indirectly by them through evasive schemes."

By the early 1960s, whether because of or in spite of *Brown*, the climate had changed in various ways.[i] The "civil rights" movement had galvanized attention, much of it sympathetic. Lower federal courts had grown increasingly impatient with "tokenism" plans. See Alexander M. Bickel, *The Decade of School Desegregation: Progress and Prospects*, 64 Colum.L.Rev. 193 (1964). In 1964, Congress passed a sweeping civil rights act, two titles of which specifically dealt with schools. Title IV authorized the attorney general to assist in the development and implementation of school desegregation plans and, where such plans were not adopted voluntarily, empowered the attorney general to initiate lawsuits to remedy racial discrimination. Title VI barred federal financial assistance for any program administered in a racially discriminatory manner. Under Title VI, eligibility for federal aid to local school districts was conditioned either on compliance with existing court desegregation orders or, in the absence of such an order, on submission of a desegregation plan consistent with federal "guidelines."

In this evolving context, the Court, in GRIFFIN v. COUNTY SCHOOL BD., 377 U.S. 218, 84 S.Ct. 1226, 12 L.Ed.2d 256 (1964), addressed the situation in

---

i. For a pessimistic view of *Brown's* impact, see Gerald N. Rosenberg, *The Hollow Hope: Can Courts Bring About Social Change?* (1991). Compare Jesse H. Choper, *Consequences of Supreme Court Decisions Upholding Individual Constitutional Rights*, 83 Mich. L.Rev. 1, 25–28 (1984) ("although a congeries of complex factors contributed to the civil rights upheaval in the 1960s, [*Brown*] was the catalyst"). For the view that "racial change in America was inevitable owing to a variety of deep-seated social, political, and economic forces," and that "*Brown's* contribution to the civil rights movement of the 1960s was in creating a "political climate conducive to the brutal suppression of civil rights demonstrations" in the south, which, in turn, aroused "indifferent northern whites from their apathy, leading to demands for national civil rights legislation which the Kennedy and Johnson administrations no longer deemed it politically expedient to resist," see Michael J. Klarman, *Brown, Racial Change, and the Civil Rights Movement*, 80 Va.L.Rev. 7, 10–11 (1994). For diverse commentaries on this general thesis by David J. Garrow, Gerald N. Rosenberg, and Mark Tushnet, see 80 Va. L.Rev. 151–199 (1994).

Prince Edward County, VA., which in 1959 closed its public schools rather than comply with a desegregation order. Private schools, supported by state and local tuition grants and tax credits, were operated for whites. The Court, per BLACK, J., held that the closing denied African–Americans equal protection: "[Whatever] nonracial grounds might support a state's allowing a county to abandon public schools, the object must be a constitutional one, and grounds of race and opposition to desegregation do not qualify as Constitutional."[j]

———

GREEN v. COUNTY SCHOOL BD., 391 U.S. 430, 88 S.Ct. 1689, 20 L.Ed.2d 716 (1968): The population of New Kent County in rural Virginia was about half black. Although there was no residential segregation, the county's two combined elementary and high schools, previously segregated by law, remained wholly segregated in fact until 1964. In 1965, the Board adopted a "freedom-of-choice" plan to remain eligible for federal financial aid. After three years, no white child chose to go to the black school that 85% of the black children continued to attend. School buses traveled "overlapping routes throughout the county to transport pupils to and from the two schools."

A unanimous Court, per BRENNAN, J., held "it is against this background that 13 years after *Brown II* commanded the abolition of dual systems we must measure the effectiveness of [respondent's plan]. School boards [then] operating state-compelled dual systems [were] clearly charged with the affirmative duty to take whatever steps might be necessary to convert to a unitary system in which racial discrimination would be eliminated root and branch. [It] is incumbent upon the school board to establish that its proposed plan promises meaningful and immediate progress toward disestablishing state-imposed segregation. [Where] more promising courses of action are open to the board, that may indicate a lack of good faith; and at the least it places a heavy burden upon the board to explain its preference for an apparently less effective method. [The instant] plan has operated simply to burden children and their parents with a responsibility which *Brown II* placed squarely on the School Board. The Board must be required [to] fashion steps which promise realistically to convert promptly to a system without a 'white' school and a 'Negro' school, but just schools."

SWANN v. CHARLOTTE–MECKLENBURG BD. OF EDUC.
402 U.S. 1, 91 S.Ct. 1267, 28 L.Ed.2d 554 (1971).

CHIEF JUSTICE BURGER delivered the opinion of the Court.

[This case concerned desegregation of the Charlotte, N.C. metropolitan area school district, which had had a statutorily mandated dual system. A companion case involved Mobile, Ala. The history included the district court's rejection in 1969 of three plans submitted by respondent board of education; its acceptance of a plan prepared at its request by "an expert in education administration"; modification of the district court decree by the court of appeals; and the district court's subsequent rejection of a plan prepared by federal officials and its conclusion that either the education expert's plan or a new plan submitted by a minority of the school board was "reasonable and acceptable."]

If school authorities fail in their affirmative obligations ["to eliminate from the public schools all vestiges of state-imposed segregation"] judicial authority

j. *Griffin* was subsequently distinguished in *Palmer v. Thompson* (1971), involving the clos- ing of swimming pools, which was discussed in Part III supra.

may be invoked. Once a right and a violation have been shown, the scope of a district court's equitable powers to remedy past wrongs is broad, for breadth and flexibility are inherent in equitable remedies. [The] task is to correct, by a balancing of the individual and collective interests, the condition that offends the Constitution. [But] it is important to remember that judicial powers may be exercised only on the basis of a constitutional violation. * * *

School authorities are traditionally charged with broad power to formulate and implement educational policy and might well conclude, for example, that in order to prepare students to live in a pluralistic society each school should have a prescribed ratio of Negro to white students reflecting the proportion for the district as a whole. To do this as an educational policy is within the broad discretionary powers of school authorities; absent a finding of a constitutional violation, however, that would not be within the authority of a federal court. * * *

The central issue in this case is that of student assignment, and there are essentially four problem areas: * * *

(1) *Racial Balances or Racial Quotas.* [I]t is urged that the District Court has imposed a racial balance requirement of 71%–29% on individual schools, [reflecting] the pupil constituency of the system. If we were to read the holding of the District Court to require, as a matter of substantive constitutional right, any particular degree of racial balance or mixing, that approach would be disapproved [for the] constitutional command to desegregate schools does not mean that every school in every community must always reflect the racial composition of the school system as a whole.

[But] the use made of mathematical ratios was no more than [a] useful starting point in shaping a remedy to correct past constitutional violations. In sum, the very limited use made of mathematical ratios was within the equitable remedial discretion of the District Court.

(2) *One-Race Schools.* The record in this case reveals the familiar phenomenon that in metropolitan areas minority groups are often found concentrated in one part of the city. [T]he existence of some small number of one-race, or virtually one-race schools within a district is not in and of itself the mark of a system which still practices segregation by law. [But] the burden upon the school authorities will be to satisfy the court that their racial composition is not the result of present or past discriminatory action on their part.

An optional majority-to-minority transfer provision [is] an indispensable remedy for those students willing to transfer to other schools in order to lessen the impact on them of the state-imposed stigma of segregation. [S]uch a transfer arrangement must grant the transferring student free transportation and space must be made available in the school to which he desires to move. * * *

(3) *Remedial Altering of Attendance Zones.* [O]ne of the principal tools employed by school planners and by courts to break up the dual school system has been a frank—and sometimes drastic—gerrymandering of school districts and attendance zones. [Absent] a constitutional violation there would be no basis for judicially ordering assignment of students on a racial basis. All things being equal, with no history of discrimination, it might well be desirable to assign pupils to schools nearest their homes. But all things are not equal in a system that has been deliberately constructed and maintained to enforce racial segregation. The remedy for such segregation may be administratively awkward, inconvenient and even bizarre in some situations and may impose burdens on some; but [this] cannot be

avoided in the interim period when remedial adjustments are being made to eliminate the dual school systems.

No fixed or even substantially fixed guidelines can be established as to how far a court can go, but it must be recognized that there are limits. The objective is to dismantle the dual school system. [When] school authorities present a district court with a "loaded game board," affirmative action in the form of remedial altering of attendance zones is proper to achieve truly non-discriminatory assignments. * * *

(4) *Transportation of Students*. [No] rigid guidelines as to student transportation can be given for application to the infinite variety of problems presented in thousands of situations. Bus transportation has been an integral part of the public education system for [years]. Eighteen million of the nation's public school children, approximately 39%, were transported to their schools by bus in 1969–1970 in all parts of the country.

The importance of bus transportation as a normal and accepted tool of educational policy is readily discernible in this and the companion case.[11] * * *

The decree provided that [trips] for elementary school pupils average about seven miles and the District Court found that they would take "not over 35 minutes at the most."[12] This system compares favorably with the transportation plan previously operated in Charlotte under which each day 23,600 students on all grade levels were transported an average of 15 miles one way for an average trip requiring over an hour. In these circumstances, we find no basis for holding that the local school authorities may not be required to employ bus transportation as one tool of school desegregation. Desegregation plans cannot be limited to the walk-in school.

[The] reconciliation of competing values in a desegregation case is, of course, a difficult task with many sensitive facets but fundamentally no more so than remedial measures courts of equity have traditionally employed. * * *

Notes and Questions

1. *A transformed obligation?* Consider John Jeffries, *The Right–Remedy Gap in Constitutional Law*, 109 Yale L.J. 87, 102 (1999): *Green* "transformed the constitutional obligation [recognized in *Brown*]. Most courts had thought it a sufficient response to *Brown* that the government stop requiring separation by race. So-called 'freedom of choice' plans, if fairly implemented, directly answered *Brown*'s finding that segregation violated the Constitution if, but only if, required by law. In *Green* [the] Court charged formerly de jure school districts with the 'affirmative duty' to undo the effects of prior practice and achieve a 'unitary' school system without racially identifiable schools."

2. *Scope of the duty.* Do *Green* and *Swann* require school boards that had de jure segregated systems to take "*whatever* steps might be necessary" for "mean-

---

11. During 1967–1968, for example, the Mobile board used 207 buses to transport 22,-094 students daily for an average round trip of 31 miles. During 1966–1967, 7,116 students in the metropolitan area were bused daily. In Charlotte–Mecklenburg [m]ore elementary school children than high school children were to be bused, and four-and five-year-olds travel the longest routes in the system.

12. The District Court found that the school system would have to employ 138 more buses than it had previously operated. But 105 of those buses were already available and the others could easily be obtained. Additionally, it should be noted that North Carolina requires provision of transportation for all students who are assigned to schools more than one and one-half miles from their homes.

ingful and immediate progress toward disestablishing state-imposed segregation" (*Green*)? Or need they only adopt plans that are "reasonable, *feasible* and workable" (*Swann*)? Who determines what is "feasible"? Consider Frank I. Goodman, *Racial Imbalance in the Oakland Public Schools: A Legal Analysis* 69 (1966): "Whether a particular course of action is 'feasible' depends largely upon which elements of the situation are assumed to be fixed and unalterable and which are regarded as freely variable. If, for example, one accepts as a 'given' the basic validity of the neighborhood school concept and the existing facilities and financial resources of the school district, the range of 'feasible' desegregation measures is apt to be rather limited. Drop these assumptions and the range of feasibilities becomes broader. Assume, finally, that money is no obstacle, and that proximity to schools can be dismissed as a mere matter of 'convenience,' and nearly *everything* becomes feasible." Consider also Owen M. Fiss, *The Charlotte–Mecklenburg Case—Its Significance for Northern School Desegregation,* 38 U.Chi. L.Rev. 697, 702 (1971): "[Under *Swann*,] if there is a conflict between integration and other values, integration will generally prevail."

Should the scope of the duty under *Green* and *Swann* depend on the level of public resistance or hostility to busing or other remedies? See Paul D. Gewirtz, *Remedies and Resistance,* 92 Yale L.J. 585 (1983).

Should the scope of the duty depend on the efficacy of busing and other remedies in producing an enhanced quality of education for minority children? On the effect of judicially prescribed remedies on the overall quality of schooling within a school district?

3. *Beyond primary and secondary education.* BAZEMORE v. FRIDAY, 478 U.S. 385, 106 S.Ct. 3000, 92 L.Ed.2d 315 (1986), per White, J., held that *Green's* "affirmative duty to desegregate" has "no application" to the 4–H and Homemaker Clubs (which had been deliberately segregated until 1965) operated by the North Carolina Agricultural Extension Service, even though a majority of the clubs remained uniracial in 1980: "While school children must go to school, there is no compulsion to join 4–H or Homemaker Clubs, and while School Boards customarily have the power to create school attendance areas and otherwise designate the school that particular students may attend, there is no statutory or regulatory authority to deny a young person the right to join any Club he or she wishes to join."

Brennan, J., joined by Marshall, Blackmun, and Stevens, JJ., dissented: "Nothing in our earlier cases suggests that the State's obligation to desegregate is confined only to those activities in which members of the public are compelled to participate."[a]

Compare UNITED STATES v. FORDICE, 505 U.S. 717, 112 S.Ct. 2727, 120 L.Ed.2d 575 (1992), per White, J., holding that Mississippi had the same obligation to dismantle what was once a de jure dual university system—and continued to include five almost completely white and three almost completely black schools— as would apply in the context of primary and secondary education: "That college attendance is by choice and not by assignment does not mean that a race-neutral admissions policy cures the constitutional violation. [If] the State perpetuates policies and practices traceable to its prior system that continue to have segre-

---

a. For the view that the core harm of de jure school segregation was "distorting the socializing process of public schools" by "inculcating a belief in the inferiority of African–Americans," and, therefore, that "racial imba- lance has less importance in an institution" like 4–H clubs, see Kevin Brown, *Has the Supreme Court Allowed the Cure for De Jure Segregation to Replicate the Disease,* 78 Corn. L.Rev. 1 (1992).

gative effects—whether by influencing student enrollment decisions or by fostering segregation in other facets of the university system—and such policies are without sound educational justification and can be practicably eliminated, the State has not satisfied its burden of proving that it has dismantled its prior system." The Court remanded the case for review "in light of the proper standard."

SCALIA, J., concurred on the ground that "the District Court should have required Mississippi to prove that its continued use of [particular admissions] requirements does not have a racially exclusionary purpose and effect," but dissented from "the Court's [applying] to universities the amorphous standard adopted for primary and secondary schools in *Green.* * * * *Bazemore's* standard for dismantling a dual system ought to control here: discontinuation of discriminatory practices and adoption of a neutral admissions policy. [Like] the club attendance in *Bazemore* (and unlike the school attendance in *Green*), attending college is voluntary, not a legal obligation, and which institution particular students attend is determined by their own choice."[b]

At the time of *Brown* and through the decade thereafter, school segregation was widely regarded as a southern problem, defined by de jure one-race schools. But if there was a *remedial* obligation of previously discriminatory systems to achieve a "unitary" status without racially identifiable schools, the issue arose whether it should take a history of formal, de jure segregation—and if so, how extensive a history—to trigger that obligation.

KEYES v. SCHOOL DIST., 413 U.S. 189, 93 S.Ct. 2686, 37 L.Ed.2d 548 (1973), was the Court's first case involving segregation that had never been statutorily mandated. The district court found that the Denver School Board—by school construction, gerrymandering attendance zones, and excessive use of mobile classroom units—"had engaged over almost a decade after 1960 in an unconstitutional policy of deliberate racial segregation with respect to the Park Hill Schools," and ordered desegregation. However, although the "core city schools" were also segregated in fact, the district court found that the school board had no segregative policy as to them and declined to order their desegregation.

The Court, per BRENNAN, J., reversed, first holding that since, in the southwest, Negroes and Hispanics "suffer identical discrimination in treatment when compared with the treatment afforded Anglo[s,] schools with a combined predominance of Negroes and Hispanics [should be] included in the category of 'segregated' schools." It then held that "where plaintiffs prove that the school authorities have carried out a systematic program of segregation affecting a substantial portion of the students, schools, teachers and facilities [it] is only common sense to conclude that there exists a predicate for a finding of the existence of a dual school system" because "racially inspired school board actions have an impact

---

b. O'Connor and Thomas, J.J., also filed separate concurring opinions.

Consider Note, *Mississippi Learning: Curriculum for the Post–Brown Era of Higher Education Desegregation,* 104 Yale L.J. 243, 259–60 (1994): "In choosing which schools to maintain, states like Mississippi will close weaker schools due to scarcity of resources. Because the dual system shortchanged historically black schools for years, the weaker schools undoubtedly will be the historically black ones. [Thus,] *Fordice* has made it more difficult to argue simultaneously for the preservation or quality schools and for the maintenance of colleges with almost exclusively African–American enrollments."

beyond the particular schools that are the subjects of those actions. This is not to say, of course, that there can never be a case in which the geographical structure of or the natural boundaries within a school district may have the effect of dividing the district into separate, identifiable and unrelated units. Such a determination is essentially a question of fact to be resolved by the trial court [but] such cases must be rare."

Finally, emphasizing "that the differentiating factor between de jure segregation and so-called de facto segregation [is] *purpose* or *intent* to segregate," the court held "that a finding of intentionally segregative school board actions in a meaningful portion of a school system [creates] a prima facie case of unlawful segregative design on the part of school authorities, and shifts to those authorities the burden of proving that other segregated schools within the system are not also the result of intentionally segregative actions. This is true even if it is determined that different areas of the school district should be viewed independently of each [other]. In discharging that burden, it is not enough, of course, that the school authorities rely upon some allegedly logical, racially neutral explanation [such as a "neighborhood school policy"] for their actions. Their burden is to adduce proof sufficient to support a finding that segregative intent was not among the factors that motivated their actions." Further, "if the actions of school authorities were to any degree motivated by segregative intent and the segregation resulting from those actions continues to exist, the fact of remoteness in time certainly does not make those actions any less 'intentional.'

"This is not to say, however, that the prima facie case may not be met by evidence supporting a finding that a lesser degree of segregated schooling in the core city area would not have resulted even if the Board had not acted as it [did]. Intentional school segregation in the past may have been a factor in creating a natural environment for the growth of further segregation. Thus, if respondent School Board cannot disprove segregative intent, it can rebut the prima facie case only by showing that its past segregative acts did not create or contribute to the current segregated condition of the core city schools."[a]

POWELL, J., filed a lengthy separate opinion, asserting that "the facts deemed necessary to establish de jure discrimination present problems of subjective intent which the courts cannot fairly resolve." "In my view, we should abandon [the de jure-de facto distinction] and formulate constitutional principles of national rather than merely regional application. [In] imposing on metropolitan southern school districts an affirmative duty, entailing large-scale transportation of pupils, to eliminate segregation in the schools, the Court required these districts to alleviate conditions which in large part did *not* result from historic, state-imposed de jure segregation. Rather, the familiar root cause of segregated schools in *all* the biracial metropolitan areas of our country is essentially the same: one of segregated residential and migratory patterns the impact of which on the racial composition of the schools was often perpetuated and rarely ameliorated by action of public school authorities. This is a national, not a southern phenomenon. And it is largely unrelated to whether a particular State had or did not have segregative school laws. * * *

"I would hold [that] where segregated public schools exist within a school district to a substantial degree, there is a prima facie case that the duly constituted public authorities [are] sufficiently responsible to impose upon them a national-

a. Burger, C.J., concurred in the result. Douglas, J., joined the Court's opinion but stated "that there [is] no difference between de facto and de jure segregation." White, J., did not participate.

ly applicable burden to demonstrate they nevertheless are operating a genuinely integrated school system. [A] system would be integrated in accord with constitutional standards if the responsible authorities had taken appropriate steps to (i) integrate faculties and administration; (ii) scrupulously assure equality of facilities, instruction and curricular opportunities throughout the district; (iii) utilize their authority to draw attendance zones to promote integration; and (iv) locate new schools, close old ones, and determine the size and grade categories with this objective in mind. [An] integrated school system does not mean—and indeed could not mean in view of the residential patterns of most of our major metropolitan areas—that *every school* must in fact be an integrated unit."

Powell, J., further argued for "special caution" concerning "any proposal as disruptive of family life and interests—and ultimately of education itself—as extensive transportation of elementary age children solely for desegregation purposes. As a minimum, this Court should not require school boards to engage in the unnecessary transportation away from their neighborhoods of elementary age children."

REHNQUIST, J., dissented: "[I]t would be a quite unprecedented application of principles of equitable relief to determine that if the gerrymandering of one attendance zone were proven, particular racial mixtures could be required by a federal district court for every school in the district. [U]nless the Equal Protection Clause [be] held to embody a principle of 'taint,' [such] a result can only be described as the product of judicial fiat. * * *

"The drastic extension of *Brown* which *Green* represented was barely, if at all, explicated in the latter opinion. To require that a genuinely 'dual' system be disestablished, in the sense that the assignment to a child of a particular school is not made to depend on his race, is one thing. To require that school boards affirmatively undertake to achieve racial mixing in schools where such mixing is not achieved in sufficient degree by neutrally drawn boundary lines is quite obviously something else."

COLUMBUS BOARD OF EDUC. v. PENICK

443 U.S. 449, 99 S.Ct. 2941, 61 L.Ed.2d 666 (1979).

JUSTICE WHITE delivered the opinion of the Court.

The public schools of Columbus, Ohio, are highly segregated by race. In 1976, over 32% of the 96,000 students in the system were black. About 70% of all students attended schools that were at least 80% black or 80% white. Half of the 172 schools were 90% black or 90% white. * * *

We have discovered no reason [to] disturb the judgment of the Court of Appeals, based on the findings and conclusions of the District Court, that the Board's conduct at the time of trial [in 1975] and before not only was animated by an unconstitutional, segregative purpose, but also had current, segregative impact that was sufficiently systemwide to warrant the [systemwide] remedy ordered by the District Court. * * *

First, [t]he Board insists that, since segregated schooling was not commanded by state law ["at least since 1888,"] and since not all schools were wholly black or wholly white in 1954, the District Court was not warranted in finding a dual system. But the District Court found that the "Columbus Public Schools were *officially* segregated by race in 1954"; and in any event, there is no reason to question the finding that as the "direct result of cognitive acts or omissions" the

Board maintained "an enclave of separate, black schools on the near east side of Columbus." Proof of purposeful and effective maintenance of a body of separate black schools in a substantial part of the system itself is prima facie proof of a dual school system and supports a finding to this effect absent sufficient contrary proof by the Board, which was not forthcoming in this case. *Keyes.*

Second, both courts below declared that since the decision in *Brown II*, the Columbus Board has been under a continuous constitutional obligation to disestablish its dual school system. [Each] failure or refusal to fulfill this affirmative duty continues the violation of the Fourteenth Amendment. [Whatever] the Board's current purpose with respect to racially separate education might be, it knowingly continued its failure to eliminate the consequences of its past intentionally segregative policies. * * *ª

Third, the District Court [also] found that in the intervening years there had been a series of Board actions and practices that could not "reasonably be explained without reference to racial concerns," and that "intentionally aggravated, rather than alleviated," racial separation in the schools. These matters included the general practice of assigning black teachers only to those schools with substantial black student populations, a practice that was terminated only in 1974[;] the intentionally segregative use of optional attendance zones, discontinuous attendance areas, and boundary changes; and the selection of sites for new school construction that had the foreseeable and anticipated effect of maintaining the racial separation of the schools. * * *

[It] is urged that the courts below failed to heed the requirements of *Keyes, Washington v. Davis,* and *Arlington Heights,* that a plaintiff seeking to make out an equal protection violation on the basis of racial discrimination must show purpose. [But] the District Court correctly noted that actions having foreseeable and anticipated disparate impact are relevant evidence to prove the ultimate fact, forbidden purpose. * * *

It is also urged that the District Court and the Court of Appeals failed to observe the requirements [of] *Dayton Bd. of Educ. v. Brinkman (Dayton I),* 433 U.S. 406, 97 S.Ct. 2766, 53 L.Ed.2d 851 (1977), which reiterated the accepted rule that the remedy imposed by a court of equity should be commensurate with the violation ascertained, and held that the remedy for the violations that had then been established in that case should be aimed at rectifying the "incremental segregative effect" of the discriminatory acts identified. In *Dayton I,* only a few apparently isolated discriminatory practices had been found; yet a systemwide remedy had been imposed without proof of a systemwide impact. Here, however, the District Court [and the Court of Appeals] repeatedly emphasized that it had found purposefully segregative practices with current, systemwide impact. * * *

Affirmed.ᵇ

JUSTICE REHNQUIST, with whom JUSTICE POWELL joins, dissenting.

The school desegregation remedy imposed [is] as complete and dramatic a displacement of local authority by the federal judiciary as is possible in our federal

---

a. In *Dayton Board of Education v. Brinkman (Dayton II)*, 443 U.S. 526, 99 S.Ct. 2971, 61 L.Ed.2d 720 (1979), a companion case to *Columbus,* the Court, per White, J., added: "[T]he measure of the post-*Brown* conduct of a school board under an unsatisfied duty to liquidate a dual system is the effectiveness, not the purpose, of the actions in decreasing or increasing the segregation caused by the dual system. [T]he Board has a 'heavy burden' of showing that actions that increased or continued the effects of the dual system serve important and legitimate ends."

b. The concurring opinions of Burger, C.J., and Stewart, J., and the dissenting opinion of Powell, J., are omitted.

system [—] 42,000 of the system's 96,000 students are reassigned to new schools. There are like reassignment of teachers, staff, and administrators, reorganization of the grade structure of virtually every elementary school in the system, the closing of 33 schools, and the additional transportation of 37,000 students. * * *

Today the Court affirms [in] opinions so Delphic that lower courts will be hard pressed to fathom their implications for school desegregation litigation. I can only offer two suggestions. The first is that the Court, possibly chastened by the complexity and emotion that accompanies school desegregation cases, wishes to relegate the determination of a violation of [equal protection] in any plan of pupil assignment, and the formulation of a remedy for its violation, to the judgment of a single District Judge. * * * "Discriminatory purpose" and "systemwide violation" are to be treated as talismanic phrases which once invoked, warrant only the most superficial scrutiny by appellate courts.

Such an [approach] holds out the disturbing prospect of very different remedies being imposed on similar school systems because of the predilections of individual judges and their good faith but incongruent efforts to make sense of this Court's confused pronouncements today.

[Alternatively, the] Court suggests a radical new approach to desegregation cases in systems without a history of statutorily mandated separation of the races: if a district court concludes—employing what in honesty must be characterized as an irrebuttable presumption—that there was a "dual" school system at the time of *Brown I,* it must find post-1954 constitutional violations in a school board's failure to take every affirmative step to integrate the system. Put differently, *racial imbalance* at the time the complaint is filed is sufficient to support a systemwide, racial balance school busing remedy if the district court can find *some* evidence of discriminatory purpose prior to 1954, without any inquiry into the causal relationship between those pre-1954 violations and current segregation in the school system.

[The] Court's use of the term "affirmative duty" implies that integration be the pre-eminent—indeed, the controlling—educational consideration in school board decisionmaking. It takes precedence over other legitimate educational objectives subject to some vague feasibility limitation.

[O]bjective evidence [of segregative intent] must be carefully analyzed for it may otherwise reduce the "discriminatory purpose" requirement to a "discriminatory impact" test by another name. [In] a school system with racially imbalanced schools, *every* school board action regarding construction, pupil assignment, transportation, annexation and temporary facilities will promote integration, aggravate segregation or maintain segregation. Foreseeability follows from the obviousness of that proposition. Such a tight noose on school board decisionmaking will invariably move government of a school system [to] the courthouse. * * *

Once a showing is made that the District Court believes satisfies the *Keyes* requirement of purposeful discrimination in a substantial part of the school system, the school board will almost invariably rely on its neighborhood school policy and residential segregation to show that it is not responsible for the existence of certain predominantly black and white schools in other parts of the school system. [But that argument is blocked by the District Court's reliance] on a general proposition that "there is often a substantial reciprocal effect between the color of the school and the color of the neighborhood it serves." [As a result, there is] no room for *Keyes* or *Swann* rebuttal either with respect to the school system today or that of 30 years ago. * * *

Notes and Questions

1. *Scope of the decisions.* Consider Daniel R. Ortiz, *The Myth of Intent in Equal Protection*, 41 Stan.L.Rev. 1105, 1132–33 (1989): In *Columbus*, the Court "held that plaintiffs could satisfy the intent requirement by showing that the district had acted purposefully to segregate the schools as far back as the time of [*Brown*]. In other words, plaintiffs could temporally transfer discriminatory motivation from any time between 1954 and the present in order to prove current de jure segregation. Thus, de facto segregation in any area where the state had purposefully discriminated at or after the time of *Brown I* became unconstitutional. In large parts of the country, then, despite the de jure/de facto distinction, current disparate effects, not motivation, became the operative liability standard."

2. *"De facto" school segregation.* (a) Would it have been politically and constitutionally tenable for southern school systems to be under an "affirmative duty" to desegregate while northern school systems with comparably large minority populations and with histories of public and private racism were not?

In his concurring opinion in *Keyes*, Powell, J., quoted from Frank I. Goodman, *De Facto School Segregation: A Constitutional and Empirical Analysis*, 60 Cal. L.Rev. 275, 297 (1972): "Ohio discarded [legally mandated segregation] in 1887, Indiana in 1949, [New York in 1938, New Mexico and Wyoming in 1954 (85 Harv.L.Rev. 85 n. 72 (1971))]. [T]here is no reason to suppose that 1954 is a universally appropriate dividing line between de jure segregation that may safely be assumed to have spent itself and that which may not. For many remedial purposes, adoption of an arbitrary but easily administrable cutoff point might not be objectionable. But in a situation such as school desegregation, where both the rights asserted and the remedial burdens imposed are of such magnitude, and where the resulting sectional discrimination is passionately resented, it is surely questionable whether such arbitrariness is either politically or morally acceptable."

(b) Would it have been preferable for the Court to adopt the suggestion of Powell, J., concerning the definition of the constitutional right? The scope of the requisite remedy?

Would finding a constitutional violation on the basis of racial disparity alone be inconsistent with *Washington v. Davis*? Consider Frank I. Goodman, supra, at 306: "If it is true that de facto segregation [generates] feelings of racial inferiority in black school children, the injury is one they incur distinctively as blacks, solely on account of their race. [In] that sense, the neighborhood school policy can be said to inflict a 'racially specific' harm [differing] in kind from that inflicted by examples of state action that hurt blacks more than whites, but hurt the individual black no more than his white counterpart."

3. *Interests of minority children and parents.* (a) Consider David J. Armor, *Forced Justice: School Desegregation and the Law* 8–9 (1995), which argues that the course of the Court's school segregation decisions has been deeply influenced by the "harm and benefit thesis" that "segregated schools harm the education and academic achievement of minority children" and, correlatively, that "[d]esegregation benefits [educational] and occupational outcomes for minority children while improving race relations for everyone." According to Armor, the actual

validity of this thesis is deeply contested among social scientists today,[c] but early and particularly influential articulations of the thesis came in 1966, in a report by a team of sociologists headed by James Coleman,[d] and in a 1967 report by the United States Commission on Civil Rights, *Racial Isolation in the Public Schools*, which concluded explicitly that: "Negro children who attend predominantly Negro schools do not achieve as well as other children, Negro and white. Their aspirations are much more restricted than those of other children and they do not have as much confidence that they can influence their own futures." Should the Court have been influenced by the "harm and benefit thesis"? Should it have consulted the sociological literature more broadly? Ignored the sociological literature?

Compare Mark G. Yudof, *Equal Educational Opportunity and the Courts*, 51 Tex.L.Rev. 411, 436 (1973): "One study of the psychological impact of segregation on black children has found that the black child's self-concept is inversely related to the proportion of white students in the school; the whiter his school the lower the black child rated himself. Other studies have reached the opposite conclusion. Studies of the relationship between personality development and segregation are similarly conflicting. [Moreover,] available studies are inconclusive as to whether integration in fact accelerates academic achievement. Further complicating the evidence are the many additional variables that may alter the effect of integration or segregation: the degree of interracial hostility, the percentage of black students in relation to the school population, the socio-economic makeup of the student body, the existence of ability grouping, and the attitudes of parents, teachers, and administrators."

(b) Although generally supportive, minority communities have not been unanimous in their welcoming of mandatory busing. See, e.g., Derrick Bell, *And We Are Not Saved: The Elusive Quest for Racial Justice* 112–13 (1987) (arguing, via a fictional character named Geneva Crenshaw, that "rather than beat our heads against the wall seeking pupil-desegregation orders the courts were unwilling to enter or enforce, we could have organized parents and communities to ensure effective implementation for the equal-funding and equal-representation mandates").

(c) Although the precise causal factors are much debated, efforts to achieve school desegregation frequently encountered an obstacle widely described as "white flight." A famous and influential study published in 1975 attributed white flight largely to desegregation orders and policies. See James S. Coleman et al., *Trends in School Segregation, 1968–73* (1975). Others see the phenomenon as having other more deeply rooted socio-economic causes. But "almost all participants in the debate agree that there are some forms of desegregation plans (particularly mandatory plans busing many white students in heavily minority central cities) that accelerate the decline of white enrollment." Gary Orfield, Susan E. Eaton and the Harvard Project on School Desegregation, *Dismantling Desegregation* 316 (1996). What weight should the Court give to a phenomenon of this kind in defining constitutional rights? In identifying the scope of constitutional remedies?[e]

4. *Judicial role.* The federal courts' involvement in the crafting of busing remedies—in north and south alike—gives rise to a variety of questions about the practical and constitutional limits of the judicial role. For criticisms of the breadth

---

c. For further discussion, see Part VI infra.

d. James S. Coleman et al., *Equality of Educational Opportunity* (1966).

e. See Paul D. Gewirtz, *Remedies and Resistance*, 92 Yale L.J. 585 (1983); Paul D. Gewirtz, *Choice in Transition: School Desegregation and the Corrective Ideal*, 86 Colum.L.Rev.728 (1986).

of discretion exercised by federal courts in entering and enforcing school desegregation plans, notably including intrusions on local political authorities, see, e.g., Lino A. Graglia, *Disaster By Decree* (1976). In a detailed review of the *Keyes* litigation, Graglia criticizes the district judge's findings of deliberate segregation and concludes that "perhaps nothing emerges more clearly [than] the fact of the almost totally unrestrained freedom of choice district judges possess in 'desegregation' litigation": "If this one judge had found—as he should [have]—that the racial imbalance in the schools was not the result of racial discrimination by school officials, the travail of Denver would have been at an end. Never in our history has the fate of so many people so importantly depended on the whim of a single, unelected, lifetime official."

Even at the high tide of the era of judicially enforced busing, the Court insisted that the scope of judicial remedies must be limited to the scope of judicially identified constitutional violations—even when the Court, as in *Columbus*, relied heavily on presumptions to identify the scope of the remediable violation. As a practical matter, a significant implication of this principle was a prohibition against so-called "interdistrict remedies."

In MILLIKEN v. BRADLEY, 418 U.S. 717, 94 S.Ct. 3112, 41 L.Ed.2d 1069 (1974), the district court found that various actions of the Detroit Board of Education, the State Board of Education, and the Michigan legislature (e.g., barring use of state funds for busing) produced de jure segregation in Detroit; that, because of the city's racial composition, desegregation plans limited to Detroit "would accentuate the racial identifiability of the district as a Black school system, and would not accomplish desegregation." Thus, the district judge ordered a plan encompassing 53 neighboring suburban school districts (in Oakland and Macomb counties). The Court, per BURGER, C.J.,—emphasizing that, apart from one "isolated instance affecting two of the school districts," the record "contains evidence of de jure segregated conditions only in" Detroit—reversed, stating the issue as "whether a federal court may impose a multidistrict [remedy] absent any finding that the other included school districts have failed to operate unitary school systems within their districts, [that] the boundary lines of any affected school district were established with the purpose of fostering racial segregation [, or that] the included districts committed acts which effected segregation within the other districts, and absent a meaningful opportunity for the included neighboring school districts to [be] heard on the propriety of a multidistrict remedy or on the question of constitutional violations by those neighboring districts":

"The controlling principle [is] that the scope of the remedy is determined by the nature and extent of the constitutional violation. *Swann.* [Before] imposing a cross-district remedy, it must first be shown that there has been a constitutional violation within one district that produces a significant segregative effect in [another].[a] The constitutional right of the Negro respondents residing in Detroit is to attend a unitary school system in that district."

WHITE, J., joined by Douglas, Brennan and Marshall, JJ., dissented: "The Court of Appeals [concluded] that an interdistrict remedy 'is supported by the status of school districts under Michigan law and by the historical control

a. Is this allocation of the burden of proof consistent with *Keyes*? Are there reasons for a presumption of segregative intent or effect in a *Keyes*-type situation but not in a *Milliken*-type one?

exercised over local school districts by the legislature of Michigan and by State agencies and officials.' Obviously, whatever difficulties there might be, they are surmountable; for the Court itself concedes that had there been sufficient evidence of an interdistrict violation, the District Court could have fashioned a single remedy for the districts implicated * * *.

"I am even more mystified how the Court can ignore the legal reality that the constitutional violations, even if occurring locally, were committed by governmental entities for which the State is responsible and that it is the State that must respond to the command of the Fourteenth Amendment."

MARSHALL, J., joined by Douglas, Brennan, and White, JJ., dissented: "Ironically purporting to base its result on the principle that the scope of the remedy [should] be determined by the nature and the extent of the constitutional violation, the Court's answer is to provide no remedy at all [thus] guaranteeing that Negro children in Detroit will receive the same separate and inherently unequal education in the future as they have been unconstitutionally afforded in the past. * * *

"The State's creation, through de jure acts of segregation, of a growing core of all-Negro schools inevitably acted as a magnet to attract Negroes to the areas served by such schools [and] helped drive whites to other areas of the city or to the suburbs. [Having] created a system where whites and Negroes were intentionally kept apart so that they could not become accustomed to learning together, the State is responsible for the fact that many whites will react to the dismantling of that segregated system by attempting to flee to the suburbs."

Compare HILLS v. GAUTREAUX, 425 U.S. 284, 96 S.Ct. 1538, 47 L.Ed.2d 792 (1976), upholding an order requiring the federal Dep't of Housing (HUD) and the Chicago Housing Authority (CHA)—both of which had authority to operate outside the city of Chicago—to undertake remedial efforts outside the city where the identified violation had occurred. Is *Gautreaux* faithful to the principle that "the scope of the remedy is determined by the nature and extent of the constitutional violation"?[b] Did *Milliken* adopt an unnecessarily limited view of the right in question?[c] Of the responsibility of the state of Michigan for the discriminatory practices of its subdivisions?

Consider Gary Orfield, *Metropolitan School Desegregation: Impacts on Metropolitan Society*, 80 Minn.L.Rev. 825 (1996): "[T]he more extensive the desegregation plan, the better. [Broad plans are less likely to produce 'white flight.'] Positive outcomes may reach well beyond educational benefits and desegregation levels to community race relations [by giving] an entire metropolitan community an interest in resolving racial tensions by maintaining the quality of schools in all parts of a metropolitan area, city and suburbs alike." Do concerns of federalism explain the Court's condemnation of interdistrict remedies in *Milliken*? If so, how and why?[d]

---

b. See Stephen B. Kanner, *From Denver to Dayton: The Development of a Theory of Equal Protection Remedies*, 72 Nw.U.L.Rev. 382 (1977).

c. See Norman C. Amaker, *Milliken v. Bradley: The Meaning of the Constitution in School Desegregation Cases*, 2 Hast.Con.L.Q. 349 (1975); Charles R. Lawrence, *Segregation*

"Misunderstood": The Milliken Decision Revisited, 12 U.S.F.L.Rev. 15 (1977).

d. For a listing of subsequent cases imposing interdistrict remedies, see Note, *Interdistrict Remedies for Segregated Schools*, 79 Colum.L.Rev. 1168 n. 5 (1979). See generally Robert A. Sedler, *The Profound Impact of Milliken v. Bradley*, 33 Wayne L.Rev. 1693 (1987).

After a plan to eliminate a dual system has been put in place, what additional obligations, if any, result from "re-segregation" that occurs as a result of "white flight" or other shifts in the student population of a public school system? And when can it be said that a defendant has satisfied its remedial obligations?

In PASADENA CITY BD. OF EDUC. v. SPANGLER, 427 U.S. 424, 96 S.Ct. 2697, 49 L.Ed.2d 599 (1976), a court ordered plan to remedy de jure segregation resulted in no racially imbalanced schools in 1970, but this situation lasted only one year; by 1974, five of the district's 32 schools were over half black. The Court, per REHNQUIST, J., reversed the district judge's order "to require annual readjustment of attendance zones so that there would not be a majority of any minority in any Pasadena public school": "[The] quite normal pattern of human migration resulted in some changes in the demographics of Pasadena's residential patterns, with resultant shifts in the racial makeup of some of the schools. [But] these shifts were not attributed to any segregative actions on the part of the defendants. [H]aving once implemented a racially neutral attendance pattern in order to remedy the perceived constitutional violations on the part of the defendants, the District Court had fully performed its function of providing the appropriate remedy for previous racially discriminatory attendance patterns."[a]

OKLAHOMA CITY BD. OF EDUC. v. DOWELL, 498 U.S. 237, 111 S.Ct. 630, 112 L.Ed.2d 715 (1991): Eight years after a federal court finding that "unitariness had been achieved," the school board adopted a new neighborhood assignment plan (SRP). Its asserted purpose was to alleviate greater busing burdens on young African–American children caused by demographic changes and to increase parental involvement. This resulted in about half the schools becoming primarily uniracial. The Court, per REHNQUIST, C.J., held that a desegregation decree should be dissolved if the board has "complied in good faith [since] it was entered" and "the vestiges of past discrimination have been eliminated to the extent practicable. [The] District Court should then evaluate the Board's decision to implement the SRP under appropriate equal protection principles. See *Washington v. Davis, Arlington Heights.*"

MARSHALL, J., joined by Blackmun and Stevens, JJ., dissented: "I believe a desegregation decree cannot be lifted so long as conditions likely to inflict the stigmatic injury condemned in *Brown I* persist and there remain feasible methods of eliminating such conditions." Souter, J., did not participate.

In FREEMAN v. PITTS, 503 U.S. 467, 112 S.Ct. 1430, 118 L.Ed.2d 108 (1992), the district court had found that the De Kalb County (GA) School System had "achieved unitary status [with] regard to student assignments, transportation, physical facilities, and extracurricular activities," but not in respect to "teacher and principal assignments, resource allocation, and quality of education." The Court, per KENNEDY, J.,—emphasizing that "returning schools to the control of local authorities at the earliest practicable date is essential to restore their true accountability in our government system"—remanded the case for more specific findings and held that "while retaining jurisdiction over the case, the

---

a. Marshall, J., joined by Brennan, J., dissented on the ground that a "unitary system"   had not been established. Stevens, J., did not participate.

court [may] withdraw judicial supervision with respect to discrete categories in which the school district has achieved compliance with a court-ordered desegregation plan [and] need not retain active control over every aspect of school administration until a school district has demonstrated unitary status in all facets of its system.

"[Among] the factors which must inform the sound discretion of the court in ordering partial withdrawal are the following: whether there has been full and satisfactory compliance with the decree in those aspects of the system where supervision is to be withdrawn; whether retention of judicial control is necessary or practicable to achieve compliance with the decree in other facets of the school system; and whether the school district has demonstrated, [its] good faith commitment to the whole of the court's decree * * *.

"As the de jure violation becomes more remote in time and these demographic changes intervene, it becomes less likely that a current racial imbalance in a school district is a vestige of the prior de jure system. The causal link between current conditions and the prior violation is even more attenuated if the school district has demonstrated its good faith. [It] was appropriate for the District Court to examine the reasons for the racial imbalance before ordering an impractical, and no doubt massive, expenditure of funds to achieve racial balance after 17 years of efforts to implement the comprehensive plan in a district where there were fundamental changes in demographics, changes not attributable to the former de jure regime or any later actions by school officials. The District Court's determination to order instead the expenditure of scarce resources in areas such as the quality of education, where full compliance had not yet been achieved, underscores the uses of discretion in framing equitable remedies. * * *

"There was no showing that racial balance [in student assignments] was an appropriate mechanism to cure other deficiencies in this case. It is true that the school district was not in compliance with respect to faculty assignments, but the record does not show that student reassignments would be a feasible or practicable way to remedy this defect."

SCALIA, J., concurred: "Racially imbalanced schools are [the] product of a blend of public and private actions, and any assessment that they would not be segregated, or would not be *as* segregated, in the absence of a particular one of those factors is guesswork. [Only] in rare cases such as this one and *Spangler*, where the racial imbalance had been temporarily corrected after the abandonment of de jure segregation, can it be asserted with any degree of confidence that the past discrimination is no longer playing a proximate role. Thus, allocation of the burden of proof foreordains the result in almost all of the 'vestige of past discrimination' cases. [Our] post-*Green* cases provide that, once state-enforced school segregation is shown to have existed in a jurisdiction in 1954, there arises a presumption, effectively irrebuttable (because the school district cannot prove the negative), that any current racial imbalance is the product of that violation, at least if the imbalance has continuously existed.

"In the context of elementary and secondary education, [the] extent and recency of the prior discrimination, and the improbability that young children (or their parents) would use 'freedom of choice' plans to disrupt existing patterns 'warrant[ed] a presumption [that] schools that are substantially disproportionate in their racial composition' were remnants of the de jure system. *Swann*.

"But granting the merits of this approach at the time of *Green*, it is now 25 years later. [Since] a multitude of private factors has shaped school systems in the years after abandonment of de jure segregation—normal migration, population growth (as in this case), 'white flight' from the inner cities, increases in the costs of new facilities—the percentage of the current makeup of school systems attributable to the prior, government-enforced discrimination has diminished with each passing year, to the point where it cannot realistically be assumed to be a significant factor.

"[While] we must continue to prohibit, without qualification, all racial discrimination in the operation of public schools, and to afford remedies that eliminate not only the discrimination but its identified consequences, we should consider laying aside the extraordinary, and increasingly counterfactual, presumption of *Green*. We must soon revert to the ordinary principles [that] plaintiffs alleging Equal Protection violations must prove intent and causation and not merely the existence of racial disparity, see *Washington v. Davis*."[b]

BLACKMUN, J., joined by Stevens and O'Connor, JJ., concurred only in the judgment of remand, stressing that "the District Court's jurisdiction should continue until the school board demonstrates full compliance with the Constitution." Thomas, J., did not participate.

———

MISSOURI v. JENKINS, 515 U.S. 70, 115 S.Ct. 2038, 132 L.Ed.2d 63 (1995), involved the 18–year school desegregation litigation for the Kansas City, Missouri School District (KCMSD). The Court, per REHNQUIST, C.J., found that "the District Court has set out on a program to create a school district that was equal to or superior to the surrounding [suburban ones]. This remedy has included an elaborate program of capital improvements, course enrichment, and extracurricular enhancement not simply in the formerly identifiable black schools, but in schools throughout the district. [The] District Court's remedial order has all but made the KCMSD itself into a magnet district [designed] to attract nonminority students from outside the KCMSD schools. But this inter district goal is beyond the scope of the intra district violation identified by the District Court." Consequently, "the District Court's order [of] across-the-board salary increases for instructional and noninstructional employees [and its] order requiring the State to continue to fund the quality education programs because student achievement levels were still 'at or below national norms at many grade levels' cannot be sustained."

THOMAS, J., added a concurrence: "Two threads in our jurisprudence have produced this unfortunate situation, in which a District Court has taken it upon itself to experiment with the education of the KCMSD's black youth. First, the court has read our cases to support the theory that black students suffer an unspecified psychological harm from segregation that retards their mental and educational development. This approach not only relies upon questionable social science research rather than constitutional principle, but it also rests on an assumption of black inferiority. Second, we have permitted the federal courts to exercise virtually unlimited equitable powers to remedy this alleged constitutional violation. [When] a district court holds the State liable for discrimination almost 30 years after the last official state action, it must do more than show that there are schools with high black populations or low test scores. [The] exercise of this authority has trampled upon principles of federalism and the separation of powers and has freed courts to pursue other agendas unrelated to the narrow purpose of precisely remedying a constitutional harm."

b. Souter, J., concurred.

SOUTER, J., joined by Stevens, Ginsburg, and Breyer, JJ., dissented: "We are not dealing here with an interdistrict remedy in the sense that *Milliken I* used that term. [*Milliken* involved the consolidation of 53 surrounding districts with the Detroit school district and an order for mandatory busing throughout the enlarged district. It] did not hold [that] any remedy that takes into account conditions outside of the district in which a constitutional violation has been committed is an 'interdistrict remedy,' and as such improper in the absence of an 'interdistrict violation.' To the contrary, by emphasizing that remedies in school desegregation cases are grounded in traditional equitable principles, we left open the possibility that a district court might subject a proven constitutional wrong-doer to a remedy with effects going beyond the district of the wrongdoer's violation, when such a remedy is necessary to redress the harms flowing from the constitutional violation."

Notes and Questions

1. *The end of school desegregation?* Consider Bradley W. Joondeph, *Missouri v. Jenkins and the De Facto Abandonment of Court–Enforced Desegregation*, 71 Wash.L.Rev. 597, 681 (1996): "No longer does the Court focus on the effectiveness of the desegregation remedies in eliminating the vestiges of de jure discrimination 'root and branch.' Instead, it emphasizes that court-enforced desegregation was intended to be a 'temporary measure,' and that local control of elementary and secondary education is 'a vital national tradition.' The Court's primary concern appears to be what it has termed the 'ultimate objective' in desegregation cases: 'to return school districts to the control of local authorities.' "

Compare Richard A. Epstein, *Recognizing the Limits of Judicial Remedies: The Remote Causes of Affirmative Action, or School Desegregation in Kansas City, Missouri*, 84 Calif.L.Rev. 1101, 1102 (1996): "[T]he Supreme Court [should] abandon now the hapless search for legal remedies for the remote causes of a present unpalatable state of affairs [in urban public education]. The process of mending—or ending—public education should be conducted by fashioning the best responses we can to the challenges the system now faces, without being deflected by a misguided search for [past] wrongs."

Consider also Mark V. Tushnet, *The "We've Done Enough" Theory of School Desegregation*, 39 How.L.J. 767, 767, 779 (1996): "After its periodic outbursts of support for African–American interests—provoked by a combination of idealism and self-interest—white America ordinarily decides it has done enough, and withdraws.[b] [For] the Court's majority *Jenkins* was a school desegregation case in which an overly aggressive federal judge pushed beyond the limits of his authority. It did not matter that the case did not involve forced busing, the issue that had propelled opposition to desegregation orders for twenty years. It did not matter that the case did involve a program that used incentives rather than coercion to produce schools likely to have substantial numbers of white and African–American students. It did not matter [that] *Jenkins* involved a desegregation plan that actually might work. [The] Court agreed with a majority of white Americans: 'We've done enough,' the Justices said."

What has been the empirical effect of the Court's decisions? According to Wendy Parker, *The Future of School Desegregation*, 94 Nw.U.L.Rev. 1157, 1159, 1189, 1221 (2000): "[T]wo empirical studies covering the court-ordered desegrega-

---

b. For an earlier iteration of similar themes, see Derrick Bell, *Brown v. Board of* *Education and the Interest–Convergence Dilemma*, 93 Harv.L.Rev. 518 (1980).

tion of 192 school [districts] disprove the perception that school desegregation litigation is coming to an end. Despite [a] number of high profile cases being dismissed, the vast majority of school desegregation [orders have not been terminated.] [F]ew school districts have sought unitary status, and *Dowell* has had little, if any, effect on the number of school districts seeking and acquiring unitary status. [The] true problem [is that] school desegregation litigation [orders are] largely characterized by disregard and neglect. Plaintiffs have suffered from courts' failure to pay attention to the efficacy of court-ordered remedies, while defendants may comply with senseless remedial orders."

2. *Desegregation today.* During the period 1968–1989, "the percentage of white students in larger school systems [that most blacks attend] has fallen markedly, from 73 to 52 percent of the total enrollment. There has been a modest increase in the percent of black students, from 19 to 25 percent, but the largest increase has occurred for Hispanic students, whose proportion has grown from 6 to 17 percent. Asian students increased from less than a percent to about 4.5 percent." David J. Armor, *Forced Justice: School Desegregation and the Law* 170 (1995).

Consider Gary Orfield & John T. Yun, *Resegregation in American Schools* (1999): "The percentage of black students in majority white schools in the South fell from a peak of 43.5% in 1988 to 34.7% in 1996"—roughly where it was in 1970. Nationwide, in 1996 the typical black student attended a school that was only 32.7% white, and the average Latino attended a school that was only 29.9% white. Whites, on average, attend schools in which their classmates are 81% white.

3. *Achievements and failures.* In the wake of the Court's recent cutback on the scope and duration of desegregation orders, experts are sharply divided on whether efforts to promote school desegregation should be counted a success, a failure, or a mixture of both. Compare Gary Orfield, Susan E. Eaton and the Harvard Project on School Desegregation, *Dismantling Desegregation* (1996) (reaching the relatively optimistic conclusion that desegregation has increased the welfare of African–American students and warning that resegregation threatens to take away educational and social benefits that minority students have achieved)[c] with Armor, supra, at 112–14 (concluding that court-mandated desegregation has largely failed to improve educational quality for minority students and also failed to achieve unattainable goals of social and economic equalization).[d] As Armor, supra, at 76, says, "there is still no definitive study of the relationship between school desegregation and educational achievement, and no group of studies has generated consensus among social scientists."

Consider Armor, supra, at 182: "Mandatory [busing] plans produced greater interracial exposure [than] voluntary [plans relying on 'magnet' schools] during the first several years of implementation, but the voluntary magnet plans produced greater exposure over the long run" because they are less prone to causing "white flight." Compare Orfield et al., supra, at 280, 286–87 (suggesting data on

c. See also James S. Liebman, *Implementing Brown in the Nineties: Political Reconstruction, Liberal Recollection, and Litigatively Enforced Legislative Reform*, 76 Va.L.Rev. 349, 356–57 (1990), reviewing studies in the 1980s finding that "northern desegregation has a substantial positive effect on black students' achievement," and that "more certain is desegregation's positive impact on dropout, teenage pregnancy, and delinquency rates; on the likelihood that blacks will attend and succeed at college (particularly four-year colleges), secure

employment in predominantly white job settings, and live in integrated neighborhoods as adults; and on the salary levels blacks attain in the labor market."

d. For a depiction and indictment of the current state of education of black children, see Pamela J. Smith, *Our Children's Burden: The Many–Headed Hydra of the Educational Disenfranchisement of Black Children*, 42 How.L.J. 133 (1999).

the success of magnet schools are inconclusive and that magnet schools may tend to decrease funds available for and educational quality at other schools).[e]

Does the trend toward resegregation suggest that there are underlying problems that judicially mandated desegregation could not or did not address? For the view that residential segregation presents a structural problem beyond the reach of judicial remedies, see Nancy A. Denton, *The Persistence of Segregation: Links Between Residential Segregation and School Segregation*, 80 Minn.L.Rev. 795 (1996).[f]

4. *Desegregation and affirmative action.* Suppose that a school system has used race-based assignment policies as a means of disestablishing a "dual" system and, as a result, has been released from any judicially enforceable obligation to desegregate under the equal protection clause. May such a school system continue on a voluntary basis to use race-based assignment schemes as a means of preserving racial integration? Does it matter if a state constitution imposes an affirmative obligation to combat de facto as well as de jure segregation?[g] Increasingly, the courts have treated questions such as these as involving the permissibility of race-based "affirmative action"—a topic discussed in Part VI infra.

V. REPEALS OF REMEDIES AND RESTRUCTURINGS OF THE POLITICAL PROCESS THAT BURDEN MINORITIES

In HUNTER v. ERICKSON, 393 U.S. 385, 89 S.Ct. 557, 21 L.Ed.2d 616 (1969), after the Akron, Ohio city council enacted a fair housing ordinance, the voters amended the city charter to prevent "any ordinance dealing with racial, religious, or ancestral discrimination in housing without the approval of the majority of the voters of Akron." The Court, per WHITE, J., held this "explicitly racial classification" violative of equal protection. Although the law "on its face" treated all races "in an identical manner, the reality [was] that the law's impact [fell] on the minority," since "[t]he majority [needed] no protection against discrimination." Placing "special burdens on racial minorities in the governmen-

---

e. Consider James E. Ryan, *The Influence of Race in School Finance Reform*, 98 Mich. L.Rev. 432, 435 (1999), asserting that "contrary to conventional wisdom, most minority districts are not relatively underfunded, but they are likely to become so when they lose funds that have been directed to them through court-ordered desegregation decrees." In another article, however, Ryan argues that money alone cannot solve race-based problems of educational inequality: "Although it is possible that school finance reform could have been a helpful supplement to desegregation, it is a poor substitute. [We] should not expect school finance reform to solve the problems created by the failure to desegregate many urban schools. [School] finance reform has done little to improve the academic performance of students in predominantly minority school districts." James E. Ryan, *Schools, Race and Money*, 109 Yale L.J. 249 (1999).

f. For discussion of the distinctive problems that arise in a multi-racial context, in which a remedial plan fashioned to achieve black-white integration may begin to function "as an affir-

mative action program for Whites and non-Chinese minority groups, while sharply restricting opportunities for equally and higher scoring Chinese–Americans," see Haeryung Shin, Note, *Safety in Numbers? Equal Protection, Desegregation, and Discrimination: School Desegregation in a Multi–Cultural Society*, 82 Corn.L.Rev. 182, 185 (1996).

g. See *Sheff v. O'Neill*, 238 Conn. 1, 678 A.2d 1267 (Conn.1996) (holding that Connecticut law imposes an obligation to dismantle racial and ethnic isolation in education, regardless of whether officials previously acted with discriminatory intent). For discussion, see Kevin Brown, *The Implications of the Equal Protection Clause for the Mandatory Integration of Public School Students*, 29 Conn.L.Rev. 999 (1997) (concluding that "despite initial appearances, the recent Supreme Court cases do not preclude the State of Connecticut from discharging its affirmative obligation to dismantle racial isolation," since the state has a compelling interest "in the proper socialization of public school students").

tal process [is] no more permissible than denying them the vote." Black, J., dissented.

In WASHINGTON v. SEATTLE SCHOOL DIST., 458 U.S. 457, 102 S.Ct. 3187, 73 L.Ed.2d 896 (1982), shortly after appellee implemented a mandatory busing plan to reduce de facto school segregation, the Washington electorate adopted Initiative 350, providing—with a number of broad exceptions—that "no school board [shall] directly or indirectly require any student to attend a school other than the school which is geographically nearest or next nearest the student's place of residence." The Court, per BLACKMUN, J., relied on *Hunter v. Erickson* in holding that Initiative 350 violated equal protection: "[T]he political majority may generally restructure the political process to place obstacles in the path of everyone seeking to secure the benefits of governmental action. But a different analysis is required when the State allocates governmental power non-neutrally, by explicitly using the *racial* nature of a decision to determine the decisionmaking process.

"[D]espite its facial neutrality there is little doubt that the initiative was effectively drawn for racial purposes. [T]he District Court found that the text [was] carefully tailored to interfere only with desegregative busing.[a] [It] in fact allows school districts to bus their students 'for most, if not all,' of the nonintegrative purposes required by their educational policies.[6] [It] is true [that] the proponents of mandatory integration cannot be classified by race: Negroes and whites may be counted among both the supporters and the opponents of Initiative 350. [But] desegregation of the public schools, like the Akron open housing ordinance, at bottom inures primarily to the benefit of the minority, and is designed for that purpose. [Given] the racial focus of Initiative 350, this suffices to trigger application of the *Hunter* doctrine.

"We are also satisfied that the practical effect of Initiative 350 is to work a reallocation of power of the kind condemned in *Hunter*. The initiative removes the authority to address a racial problem—and only a racial problem—from the existing decisionmaking body, in such a way as to burden minority interests. Those favoring the elimination of de facto school segregation now must seek relief from the state legislature, or from the statewide electorate. Yet authority over all other student assignment decisions, as well as over most other areas of educational policy, remains vested in the local school board. [As] in *Hunter,* then, the community's political mechanisms are modified to place effective decisionmaking authority over a racial issue at a different level of government.[17]"

POWELL, J., joined by Burger, C.J., and Rehnquist and O'Connor, JJ., dissented: "This is certainly not a case where a State [has] established a racially discriminatory requirement. Initiative 350 [is] neutral on its face, and racially neutral as public policy. Children of all races benefit from neighborhood [schools].

---

a. "The initiative envisioned busing for racial purposes in only one circumstance: it did not purport to 'prevent any court of competent jurisdiction from adjudicating constitutional issues relating to the public schools.'"

6. At the beginning of the 1978–1979 academic year, approximately 300,000 of the 769,040 students enrolled in Washington's public schools were bused to school. Ninety-five per-

cent of these students were transported for reasons unrelated to race.

17. [While] Justice Powell [finds] it crucial that the proponents of integrated schools remain free to use Washington's initiative system to further their ends, that was true in *Hunter* as well * * *.

"Nothing in *Hunter* supports the Court's extraordinary invasion into the State's distribution of authority. [Initiative 350] simply does not place unique political obstacles in the way of racial minorities. In this case, unlike in *Hunter,* the political system has *not* been redrawn or altered. The authority of the State over the public school system, acting through Initiative or the legislature, is plenary. Thus, the State's political system is not altered when it adopts for the first time a policy, concededly within the area of its authority, for the regulation of local school districts. And certainly racial minorities are not uniquely or comparatively burdened by the State's adoption of a policy that would be lawful if adopted by any School District in the State.[13] * * *[14]"

In CRAWFORD v. LOS ANGELES BD. OF EDUC., 458 U.S. 527, 102 S.Ct. 3211, 73 L.Ed.2d 948 (1982), after the state courts had ordered substantial busing to remedy de facto school segregation which the state courts had found violative of the state constitution, the California electorate amended the state constitution by adopting Proposition I, providing that "state courts shall not order mandatory pupil assignment or transportation unless a federal court would do so to remedy a violation of the Equal Protection Clause." The Court, per POWELL, J., found no violation of equal protection, "rejecting the contention that once a State chooses to do 'more' than the Fourteenth Amendment requires, it may never recede. [E]ven after Proposition I, the California Constitution still imposes a greater duty of desegregation than does the Federal Constitution. The state courts of California continue to have an obligation under state law to order segregated school districts to use voluntary desegregation techniques, whether or not there has been a finding of intentional segregation. The school districts themselves retain a state law obligation to take reasonably feasible steps to desegregate, and they remain free to adopt reassignment and busing plans to effectuate desegregation.[12]

"[Proposition I] does not embody a racial classification. It neither says nor implies that persons are to be treated differently on account of their race. * * *

"Were we to hold that the mere repeal of race related legislation is unconstitutional, we would limit seriously the authority of States to deal with the problems of our heterogeneous population. * * *

13. The Court repeatedly states that the effect of Initiative 350 is "to redraw decision-making authority over racial matters—*and only over racial matters*—in such a way as to place *comparative* burdens on minorities." But the decision by the State to exercise its authority over the schools and over racial matters in the schools does not place a comparative burden on racial minorities. In [*Hunter,*] "fair housing legislation *alone* was subject to an automatic referendum requirement." By contrast, Initiative 350 merely places mandatory busing among the much larger group of matters—covering race relations, administration of the schools, and a variety of other matters—addressed at the State level. Racial minorities, if indeed they are burdened by Initiative 350, are not *comparatively* burdened. In this respect, they are in the same position as any other group of persons who are disadvantaged by regulations drawn at the State level.

14. The Court's decision intrudes deeply into normal State decisionmaking. Under its

holding the people [apparently] are forever barred from developing a different policy on mandatory busing where a School District previously has adopted one of its own. This principle would not seem limited to the question of mandatory busing. Thus, if the admissions committee of a State law school developed an affirmative action plan that came under fire, the Court apparently would find it unconstitutional for any higher authority to intervene unless that authority traditionally dictated admissions policies. As a constitutional matter, the Dean of the Law School, the faculty of the University as a whole, the University President, the Chancellor of the University System, and the Board of Regents might be powerless to intervene despite their greater authority under State law. * * *

12. In this respect this case differs from the situation presented in *Seattle.*

"*Hunter* involved more than a 'mere repeal' of the fair housing ordinance: persons seeking anti-discrimination housing laws—presumptively racial minorities—were 'singled out for mandatory referendums while no other [group] face[d] that obstacle.' By contrast, [Proposition I] is less than a 'repeal' of the California Equal Protection Clause. As noted above, after Proposition I, the State Constitution still places upon school boards a greater duty to desegregate than does the Fourteenth Amendment.

"Nor can it be said that Proposition I distorts the political process for racial reasons or that it allocates governmental or judicial power on the basis of a discriminatory principle. [The] remedies available for violation of the antitrust laws, for example, are different than those available for violation of the Civil Rights Acts. Yet a 'dual court system'—one for the racial majority and one for the racial minority—is not established simply because civil rights remedies are different from those available in other areas."

BLACKMUN, J., joined by Brennan, J., although joining the Court's opinion, concurred "to address [the] critical distinctions between this case [and] *Seattle*": "State courts do not create the rights they enforce; those rights originate elsewhere—in the state legislature, in the State's political subdivisions, or in the state constitution itself. When one of those rights is repealed, and therefore is rendered unenforceable in the courts, that action hardly can be said to restructure the State's decisionmaking mechanism. While the California electorate may have made it more difficult to achieve desegregation when it enacted Proposition I, [it] did so not by working a structural change in the political *process* so much as by simply repealing the right to invoke a judicial busing remedy. Indeed, ruling for petitioners on a *Hunter* theory seemingly would mean that statutory affirmative action or antidiscrimination programs never could be repealed, for a repeal of the enactment would mean that enforcement authority previously lodged in the state courts was being removed by another political entity.

"In short, the people of California—the same 'entity' that put in place the state constitution, and created the enforceable obligation to desegregate—have made the desegregation obligation judicially unenforceable. The 'political process or the decisionmaking mechanism used to *address* racially conscious legislation' has not been 'singled out for peculiar and disadvantageous treatment,' *Seattle*, for those political mechanisms that create and repeal the rights ultimately enforced by the courts were left entirely unaffected by Proposition I."

MARSHALL, J., dissented: "I fail to see how a fundamental redefinition of the governmental decisionmaking structure with respect to the same racial issue can be unconstitutional when the state seeks to remove the authority from local school boards [as in *Seattle*], yet constitutional when the state attempts to achieve the same result by limiting the power of its [courts].

"Proposition I is not a 'mere repeal.' [B]y denying full access to the only branch of government that has been willing to address this issue meaningfully, [Proposition I] is far worse for those seeking to vindicate the plainly unpopular cause of racial integration in the public schools than a simple reallocation of an often unavailable and unresponsive legislative process."

Notes and Questions

1. *Facially neutral statutes, disparate impact, and the political process.* Is the result in *Seattle* consistent with *Washington v. Davis*, Part III supra? Why does a facially neutral statute trigger heightened judicial scrutiny?

(a) Did the proponents of Initiative 350 restructure the political process, or merely use it to achieve the outcome that they desired? Would it count as a "restructuring" of the political process if the voters adopted an initiative that, without generally withdrawing the power of local school districts to implement busing plans, simply forbade school busing in the Seattle district?

(b) What does the Court mean when it says in *Seattle* that "there is little doubt that the initiative was effectively drawn for racial purposes"? Does it mean that there was a racially invidious intent, such as underlay the antimiscegenation statute in *Loving v. Virginia*, Part II supra? If so, couldn't the initiative have been invalidated on that ground alone?

Consider Cass R. Sunstein, *Public Values, Private Interests, and the Equal Protection Clause,* 1982 Sup.Ct.Rev. 127, 149, 157–58: "A classification [that] singles out a racial problem for special and disadvantageous treatment [is] peculiarly likely to be supported by invidious justifications. Like the heightened scrutiny applied to facial racial classifications, heightened scrutiny in *Hunter* is justified by a suspicion that improper justifications are at work. [But] arguments against busing are less likely to be animated by racial bias than are arguments against legislation preventing discrimination in housing. *Seattle* might therefore have been treated differently from *Hunter* on the ground that invidious motives may well not have been at work."

2. *Crawford and the political process.* Is *Crawford* persuasively distinguishable from *Seattle*? Does the distinction depend on the proposition that a restructuring of the remedies available through the judicial process is not a restructuring of the political process? That the busing remedy was withdrawn by the same, statewide electorate that adopted the California constitutional provision under which it was granted in the first place?

A California constitutional amendment, adopted by the voters as Proposition 209, mandates an end to affirmative action by the state: "The state shall not [grant] preferential treatment to any individual or group on the basis of race, sex, color, ethnicity, or national origin in the operation of public employment, public education, or public contracting." Does Proposition 209 violate the constitutional principles underlying *Hunter* and *Seattle*?[a]

3. *Applicability to non-suspect classes.* ROMER v. EVANS, 517 U.S. 620, 116 S.Ct. 1620, 134 L.Ed.2d 855 (1996), Sec. 4, IV infra, invalidated an amendment to the Colorado constitution that forbade the state and its subdivisions to "enact, adopt or enforce any statute, regulation, ordinance or policy" protecting homosexuals against public or private discrimination. The amendment had the effect of nullifying several local ordinances and an executive order by the governor of Colorado, and the Colorado Supreme Court, whose judgement the Court affirmed, had relied on "precedents involving discriminatory restructuring of governmental decisionmaking" such as *Hunter* and *Seattle*. But the Court, per KENNEDY, J., without further discussion of the Colorado Supreme Court's ground for decision, rested on the different rationale that the challenged amendment, which "declar[ed] that in general it shall be more difficult for one group of citizens than for all others to seek aid from the government," was too broad and undifferentiated to be rationally related to any legitimate state purpose. The amendment's very breadth "raise[d] the inevitable inference that the disadvantage imposed is born of

a. See *Coalition for Economic Equity v. Wilson,* 122 F.3d 692 (9th Cir.1997) (holding that it does not, at least on its face). For the contrary view, see Vikram D. Amar & Evan H.

Caminker, *Equal Protection, Unequal Political Burdens, and the CCRI,* 23 Hast. Con.L.Q. 1019 (1996).

animosity toward the class of persons affected." SCALIA, J., joined by Rehnquist, C.J., and Thomas, J., dissented. In the absence of animus, would the rationale of cases such as *Hunter* and *Seattle* apply to legislation that made it more difficult for non-suspect classes to use the political process to achieve protective legislation?[b] What result if, for example, a state forbade its subdivisions to enact any legislation protecting cigarette smokers against private discrimination?

VI. AFFIRMATIVE ACTION AND "BENIGN" DISCRIMINATION

REGENTS OF UNIV. OF CALIFORNIA v. BAKKE

438 U.S. 265, 98 S.Ct. 2733, 57 L.Ed.2d 750 (1978).

JUSTICE POWELL announced the judgment of the Court.

This case presents a challenge to the special admissions program of the petitioner, the Medical School of the University of California at Davis * * *.

For the reasons stated in the following opinion, I believe that so much of the judgment of the California court as holds petitioner's special admissions program unlawful and directs that respondent be admitted to the Medical School must be affirmed. For the reasons expressed in a separate opinion, my Brothers The Chief Justice, Justice Stewart, Justice Rehnquist, and Justice Stevens concur in this judgment.

I also conclude [that] the portion of the court's judgment enjoining petitioner from according any consideration to race in its admissions process must be reversed. For reasons expressed in separate opinions, my Brothers Justice Brennan, Justice White, Justice Marshall, and Justice Blackmun concur in this judgment. * * *

I [†] [The medical school reserved 16 out of 100 places in its entering class for members of minority groups, apparently defined as "Blacks," "Chicanos," "Asians," and "American Indians."] Allan Bakke is a white male who applied [and was rejected, even though] applicants were admitted under the special program with grade point averages [and] Medical College Admissions Test scores significantly lower than Bakke's. * * *

II. [Powell, J., found that Title VI of the Civil Rights Act of 1964—which provides that "No person in the United States shall, on the ground of race, color, or national origin, be excluded from participation in, be denied the benefits of, or be subjected to, discrimination under any program or activity receiving Federal financial assistance"—proscribes "only those racial classifications that would violate the Equal Protection Clause or the Fifth Amendment."]

III. A. [P]etitioner argues that the court below erred in applying strict scrutiny to the special admissions programs because white males, such as respondent, are not a "discrete and insular minority" requiring extraordinary protection from the majoritarian political process. *Carolene Products Co.*, n. 4 [p. 298 supra.

---

b. Compare Stephen M. Rich, Note, *Ruling by Numbers: Political Restructuring and the Reconsideration of Democratic Commitments After Romer v. Evans*, 109 Yale L.J. 587 (1999) (seeing *Hunter* as directly relevant to *Romer* and cases involving intentional disadvantaging of identifiable minority groups, even if they are not suspect classes) with Jay S. Bybee, *The*

Equal Process Clause: A Note on the (Non)Relationship Between Romer v. Evans and Hunter v. Erickson, 6 Wm. & Mary Bill Rts. J. 201 (1997).

† Justice Brennan, Justice White, Justice Marshall, and Justice Blackmun join Parts I and V–C of this opinion. Justice White also joins Part III–A of this opinion.

These] characteristics may be relevant in deciding whether or not to add new types of classifications to the list of "suspect" categories or whether a particular classification survives close examination. Racial and ethnic classifications, however, are subject to stringent examination without regard to these additional characteristics. [*Hirabayashi; Korematsu.*]

B.   This perception of racial and ethnic distinctions is rooted in our Nation's constitutional and demographic history. The Court's initial view of the Fourteenth Amendment was that its "one pervading purpose" was "the freedom of the slave race * * *." *Slaughter-House Cases.* [Later, however, as] the Nation filled with the stock of many lands, the reach of the Clause was gradually extended to all ethnic groups seeking protection from official discrimination. * * *

Petitioner urges us to adopt for the first time a more restrictive view [and] hold that discrimination against members of the white "majority" cannot be suspect if its purpose can be characterized as "benign."[34] [But it] is far too late to argue that the guarantee of equal protection to *all* persons permits the recognition of special wards entitled to a degree of protection greater than that accorded others. * * *

Once the artificial line of a "two-class theory" of the Fourteenth Amendment is put aside, the difficulties entailed in varying the level of judicial review according to a perceived "preferred" status of a particular racial or ethnic minority are intractable. [T]he white "majority" itself is composed of various minority groups, most of which can lay claim to a history of prior discrimination at the hands of the state and private individuals. Not all of these groups can receive preferential treatment and corresponding judicial tolerance of distinctions drawn in terms of race and nationality, for then the only "majority" left would be a new minority of White Anglo–Saxon Protestants. There is no principled basis for deciding which groups would merit "heightened judicial solicitude" and which would not. * * *

Moreover, there are serious problems of justice connected with the idea of preference itself. [P]referential programs may [reinforce] common stereotypes holding that certain groups are unable to achieve success without special protection based on a factor having no relationship to individual worth. [In addition], there is a measure of inequity in forcing innocent persons in respondent's position to bear the burdens of redressing grievances not of their making. * * *

If it is the individual who is entitled to judicial protection against classifications based upon his racial or ethnic background. [When legal classifications] touch upon an individual's race or ethnic background, he is entitled to a judicial determination that the burden he is asked to bear on that basis is precisely tailored to serve a compelling governmental interest. * * *

---

34. In the view of Justice Brennan, Justice White, Justice Marshall, and Justice Blackmun, the pliable notion of "stigma" is the crucial element in analyzing racial classifications. The Equal Protection Clause is not framed in terms of "stigma." Certainly the word has no clearly defined constitutional meaning. It reflects a subjective judgment that is standardless. *All* state-imposed classifications that rearrange burdens and benefits on the basis of race are likely to be viewed with deep resentment by the individuals burdened. The denial to innocent persons of equal rights and opportunities may outrage those so deprived and therefore may be perceived as invidious. These individuals are likely to find little comfort in the notion that the deprivation they are asked to endure is merely the price of membership in the dominant majority and that its imposition is inspired by the supposedly benign purpose of aiding others. One should not lightly dismiss the inherent unfairness of, and the perception of mistreatment that accompanies, a system of allocating benefits and privileges on the basis of skin color and ethnic origin. * * *

C. Petitioner contends that on several occasions this Court has approved preferential classifications without applying the most exacting scrutiny. * * *

The school desegregation cases are inapposite. Each involved remedies for clearly determined constitutional violations. [Here,] there was no judicial determination of constitutional violation as a predicate for [a] remedial classification.

The employment discrimination cases also do not advance petitioner's cause. For example, in *Franks v. Bowman Transportation Co.,* 424 U.S. 747, 96 S.Ct. 1251, 47 L.Ed.2d 444 (1976), we approved a retroactive award of seniority to a class of Negro truck drivers who had been the victims of discrimination—not just by society at large, but by the respondent in that case. While this relief imposed some burdens on other employees, it was held necessary " 'to make [the victims] whole for injuries suffered on account of unlawful employment discrimination.' " [But] we have never approved preferential classifications in the absence of proven constitutional or statutory violations. * * *

IV. [The] special admissions program purports to serve the purposes of: (i) "reducing the historic deficit of traditionally disfavored minorities in medical schools and the medical profession," (ii) countering the effects of societal discrimination; (iii) increasing the number of physicians who will practice in communities currently undeserved; and (iv) obtaining the educational benefits that flow from an ethnically diverse student body. It is necessary to decide which, if any, of these purposes is substantial enough to support the use of a suspect classification.

A. If petitioner's purpose is to assure within its student body some specified percentage of a particular group merely because of its race or ethnic origin, such a preferential purpose must be rejected not as insubstantial but as facially invalid. Preferring members of any one group for no reason other than race or ethnic origin is discrimination for its own sake. This the Constitution forbids. E.g., *Loving.*

B. The State certainly has a legitimate and substantial interest in ameliorating, or eliminating where feasible, the disabling effects of identified discrimination. [That] goal [is] far more focused than the remedying of the effects of "societal discrimination," an amorphous concept of injury that may be ageless in its reach into the past.

We have never approved a classification that aids persons perceived as members of relatively victimized groups at the expense of other innocent individuals in the absence of judicial, legislative, or administrative findings of constitutional or statutory violations. [Without] such findings of constitutional or statutory violations,[44] it cannot be said that the government has any greater interest in helping one individual than in refraining from harming another. Thus, the government has no compelling justification for inflicting such harm.

---

44. Justice Brennan, Justice White, Justice Marshall, and Justice Blackmun misconceive the scope of this Court's holdings under Title VII when they suggest that "disparate impact" alone is sufficient to establish a violation of that statute and, by analogy, other civil rights measures. [This] was made quite clear in the seminal decision in this area, *Griggs v. Duke Power Co.,* 401 U.S. 424, 91 S.Ct. 849, 28 L.Ed.2d 158 (1971): "*Discriminatory preference* for any group, minority or majority, is precisely and only what Congress has proscribed. What is required by Congress is the removal of *artifi-* *cial, arbitrary, and unnecessary barriers* to employment when the barriers operate invidiously to discriminate on the basis of racial or other impermissible classification." Thus, disparate impact is a basis for relief under Title VII only if the practice in question is not founded on "business necessity," or lacks "a manifest relationship to the employment in question." Nothing *in this record*—as opposed to some of the general literature—even remotely suggests that the disparate impact of the general admissions program at Davis Medical School [is] without educational justification.

Petitioner does not purport to have made, and is in no position to make, such findings. Its broad mission is education, not the formulation of any legislative policy or the adjudication of particular claims of illegality. For reasons similar to those stated in Part III of this opinion, isolated segments of our vast governmental structures are not competent to make those decisions, at least in the absence of legislative mandates and legislatively determined criteria. Cf. *Hampton v. Mow Sun Wong* [Sec. 4, I infra]. Compare n. 41, supra. * * *

To hold otherwise would be to convert a remedy heretofore reserved for violations of legal rights into a privilege that all institutions throughout the Nation could grant at their pleasure to whatever groups are perceived as victims of societal discrimination. That is a step we have never approved.

C. Petitioner identifies, as another purpose of its program, improving the delivery of health care services to communities currently underserved. It may be assumed that in some situations a State's interest in facilitating the health care of its citizens is sufficiently compelling to support the use of a suspect classification. But there is virtually no evidence in the record indicating that petitioner's special admissions program is either needed or geared to promote that goal. The court below addressed this failure of proof: "The University concedes it cannot assure that minority doctors who entered under the program, all of whom express an 'interest' in participating in a disadvantaged community, will actually do so. It may be correct to assume that some of them will carry out this intention, and that it is more likely they will practice in minority communities than the average white doctor. Nevertheless, there are more precise and reliable [ways to achieve this end]."

D. The fourth goal asserted by petitioner is the attainment of a diverse student body. * * * Academic freedom, though not a specifically enumerated constitutional right, long has been viewed as a special concern of the First Amendment. [Thus,] in arguing that its universities must be accorded the right to select those students who will contribute the most to the "robust exchange of ideas," petitioner invokes a countervailing constitutional interest, [and] must be viewed as seeking to achieve a goal that is of paramount importance in the fulfillment of its mission. * * *

Ethnic diversity, however, is only one element in a range of factors a university properly may consider in attaining the goal of a heterogeneous student body. Although a university must have wide discretion in making the sensitive judgments as to who should be admitted, constitutional limitations protecting individual rights may not be disregarded. [As] the interest of diversity is compelling in the context of a university's admissions program, the question remains whether the program's racial classification is necessary to promote this interest.

V. A. [P]etitioner's argument that this is the only effective means of serving the interest of diversity is seriously flawed. [The] diversity that furthers a compelling state interest encompasses a far broader array of qualifications and characteristics of which racial or ethnic origin is but a single though important element. Petitioner's special admissions program, focused *solely* on ethnic diversity, would hinder rather than further attainment of genuine diversity. * * *

The experience of other university admissions programs, which take race into account in achieving the educational diversity valued by the First Amendment, demonstrates that the assignment of a fixed number of places to a minority group is not a necessary means toward that end. An illuminating example is found in the Harvard College program:

"In recent years Harvard College has expanded the concept of diversity to include students from disadvantaged economic, racial and ethnic groups. [When] the Committee on Admissions reviews the large middle group of applicants who are 'admissible' and deemed capable of doing good work in their courses, the race of an applicant may tip the balance in his favor just as geographic origin or a life spent on a farm may tip the balance in other candidates' cases. * * *

"In Harvard College admissions the Committee has not set target-quotas for the number of blacks, or of musicians, football players, physicists or Californians to be admitted in a given year[a] [but] in choosing among thousands of applicants who are not only 'admissible' academically but have other strong qualities, the Committee, with a number of criteria in mind, pays some attention to distribution among many types and categories of students."

In such an admissions program, race or ethnic background may be deemed a "plus" in a particular applicant's file, yet it does not insulate the individual from comparison with all [others]. The file of a particular black applicant may be examined for his potential contribution to diversity without the factor of race being decisive when compared, for example, with that of an applicant identified as an Italian–American if the latter is thought to exhibit qualities more likely to promote beneficial educational pluralism. Such qualities could include exceptional personal talents, unique work or service experience, leadership potential, maturity, demonstrated compassion, a history of overcoming disadvantage, ability to communicate with the poor, or other qualifications deemed important. * * *

This kind of program treats each applicant as an individual in the admissions process. The applicant who loses out [to] another candidate receiving a "plus" on the basis of ethnic background will not have been foreclosed from all consideration [simply] because he was not the right color or had the wrong surname. It would mean only that his combined qualifications, which may have included similar nonobjective factors, did not outweigh those of the other applicant. His qualifications would have been weighed fairly and competitively and he would have no basis to complain of unequal treatment under the Fourteenth Amendment.

It has been suggested that an admissions program which considers race only as one factor is simply a subtle and more sophisticated—but no less effective—means of according racial preference than the Davis program. A facial intent to discriminate, however, is evident [in] this case. No such facial infirmity exists in an admissions program where race or ethnic background is simply one element—to be weighed fairly against other elements—in the selection process. [And] a Court would not assume that a university, professing to employ a facially nondiscriminatory admissions policy, would operate it as a cover for the functional equivalent of a quota system. * * *[53]

a. The portion of this paragraph of the Harvard program—omitted by Powell, J., in his opinion but reprinted in full in an appendix to the opinion—is as follows: "At the same time the Committee is aware that if Harvard College is to provide a truly heterogeneous environment that reflects the rich diversity of the United States, it cannot be provided without some attention to numbers. It would not make sense, for example, to have 10 or 20 students out of 1,100 whose homes are west of the Mississippi. Comparably 10 or 20 black students could not begin to bring to their classmates and to each other the variety of points of view, backgrounds and experiences of blacks in the United States. Their small numbers might also create a sense of isolation [and] thus make it more difficult for them to develop and achieve their potential. Consequently, when making its decisions, the Committee on Admissions is aware that there is some relationship between numbers and achieving the benefits to be derived from a diverse student body, and between numbers and providing a reasonable environment for those students admitted."

53. [There] also are strong policy reasons that correspond to the constitutional distinction between petitioner's preference program

B. [W]hen a State's distribution of benefits or imposition of burdens hinges on the color of a person's skin or ancestry, that individual is entitled to a demonstration that the challenged classification is necessary to promote a substantial state interest. Petitioner has failed to carry this burden. For this reason, that portion of the California court's judgment holding petitioner's special admissions program invalid under the Fourteenth Amendment must be affirmed.

C. In enjoining petitioner from ever considering the race of any applicant, however, the courts below failed to recognize that the State has a substantial interest that legitimately may be served by a properly devised admissions program involving the competitive consideration of race and ethnic origin. For this reason, so much of the California court's judgment as enjoins petitioner from any consideration of the race of any applicant must be reversed.

VI. With respect to respondent's entitlement to an injunction directing his admission to the Medical School, petitioner has conceded that it could not carry its burden of proving that, but for the existence of its unlawful special admissions program, respondent still would not have been admitted. Hence, respondent is entitled to the injunction, and that portion of the judgment must be affirmed.

Opinion of JUSTICE BRENNAN, JUSTICE WHITE, JUSTICE MARSHALL, and JUSTICE BLACKMUN, concurring in the judgment in part and dissenting. * * *

I. [C]laims that law must be "color-blind" or that the datum of race is no longer relevant to public policy must be seen as aspiration rather than as description of reality. This is not to denigrate aspiration; for reality rebukes us that race has too often been used by those who would stigmatize and oppress minorities. Yet we cannot [let] color blindness become myopia which masks the reality that many "created equal" have been treated within our lifetimes as inferior both by the law and by their fellow citizens. * * *

III. [A] government practice or statute which [contains] "suspect classifications" is to be subjected to "strict scrutiny" * * *. [But] whites as a class [do not] have any of the "traditional indicia of suspectness: the class is not saddled with such disabilities, or subjected to such a history of purposeful unequal treatment, or relegated to such a position of political powerlessness as to commend extraordinary protection from the majoritarian political process."

Moreover, [this] is not a case where racial classifications are "irrelevant and therefore prohibited." *Hirabayashi*. Nor has anyone suggested that the University's purposes contravene the cardinal principle that racial classifications that stigmatize—because they are drawn on the presumption that one race is inferior to another or because they put the weight of government behind racial hatred and separatism—are invalid without more. See *Yick Wo*. * * *

On the other hand, the fact that this case does not fit neatly into our prior analytic framework for race cases does not mean that it should be analyzed by applying the very loose rational-basis [standard]. Instead, a number of considerations—developed in gender discrimination cases but which carry even more force when applied to racial classifications—lead us to conclude that racial classifications designed to further remedial purposes "must serve important governmental objectives and must be substantially related to achievement of those objectives." *Craig v. Boren*, [Sec. 3, I infra].

and one that assures a measure of competition among all applicants. Petitioner's program will be viewed as inherently unfair by the public generally as well as by [applicants]. Fairness in individual competition for opportunities, especially those provided by the State, is a widely cherished American ethic. * * *

First, race, like "gender-based classifications too often [has] been inexcusably utilized to stereotype and stigmatize politically powerless segments of society." While a carefully tailored statute designed to remedy past discrimination could avoid these vices, see *Califano v. Webster,* [Sec. 3, I infra] we nonetheless have recognized that the line between honest and thoughtful appraisal of the effects of past discrimination and paternalistic stereotyping is not so clear and that a statute based on the latter is patently capable of stigmatizing all women with a badge of inferiority. State programs designed ostensibly to ameliorate the effects of past racial discrimination obviously create the same hazard of stigma, since they may promote racial separatism and reinforce the views of those who believe that members of racial minorities are inherently incapable of succeeding on their own.

Second, race, like gender and illegitimacy, is an immutable characteristic which its possessors are powerless to escape or set aside. While a classification is not per se invalid because [of this], it is nevertheless true that such divisions are contrary to our deep belief that "legal burdens should bear some relationship to individual responsibility or wrongdoing," and that advancement sanctioned, sponsored, or approved by the State should ideally be based on individual merit or achievement, or at the least on factors within the control of an individual.

Because this principle is so deeply rooted it might be supposed that it would be considered in the legislative process and weighed against the benefits of programs preferring individuals because of their race. But [t]he "natural consequence of our governing processes [may well be] that the most 'discrete and insular' of whites [will] be called upon to bear the immediate, direct costs of benign discrimination." [Thus] our review under the Fourteenth Amendment should be strict—not " 'strict' in theory and fatal in fact," because it is stigma that causes fatality—but strict and searching nonetheless.

IV. Davis' articulated purpose of remedying the effects of past societal discrimination is, under our cases, sufficiently important to justify the use of race-conscious admissions programs where there is a sound basis for concluding that minority underrepresentation is substantial and chronic, and that the handicap of past discrimination is impeding access of minorities to the medical school.

A. At least since *Green v. County School Bd.,* [Part IV supra], [a] public body which has itself been adjudged to have engaged in racial discrimination cannot bring itself into compliance with the Equal Protection Clause simply by ending its unlawful acts and adopting a neutral stance. Three years later, *Swann* [Part IV supra] [held] that courts could enter desegregation orders which assigned students and faculty by reference to race, and that local school boards could *voluntarily* adopt desegregation plans which made express reference to race if this was necessary to remedy the effects of past discrimination. Moreover, we stated that school boards, even in the absence of a judicial finding of past discrimination, could voluntarily adopt plans which assigned students with the end of creating racial pluralism by establishing fixed ratios of black and white students in each school. *Swann.* * * *

[O]ur cases under Title VII [have also] held that, in order to achieve minority participation in previously segregated areas of public life, Congress may require or authorize preferential treatment for those likely disadvantaged by societal racial discrimination. Such legislation has been sustained even without a requirement of findings of intentional racial discrimination by those required or authorized to accord preferential treatment, or a case-by-case determination that those to be benefitted suffered from racial discrimination. These decisions compel the conclusion that States also may adopt race-conscious programs designed to overcome substantial, chronic minority underrepresentation where there is reason to believe that the evil addressed is a product of past racial discrimination.[42] * * *

B. [Davis] had a sound basis for believing that the problem of underrepresentation of minorities was substantial and chronic and that the problem was attributable to handicaps imposed on minority applicants by past and present racial discrimination. * * * For example, the entering classes in 1968 and 1969 [included] only one Chicano and two Negroes out of 100 admittees. Nor is there any relief from this pattern of underrepresentation in the statistics for the regular admissions program in later years.

Davis clearly could conclude that the serious and persistent underrepresentation [is] the result of handicaps under which minority applicants labor as a consequence of a background of deliberate, purposeful discrimination against minorities in education and in society generally, as well as in the medical profession. From the inception of our national life, Negroes have been subjected to unique legal [disabilities]. The generation of minority students applying to Davis Medical School since it opened in 1968—most of whom were born before or about the time *Brown I* was decided—clearly have been victims of this discrimination. [T]he conclusion is inescapable that applicants to medical school must be few indeed who endured the effects of de jure segregation, the resistance to *Brown I,* or the equally debilitating pervasive private discrimination fostered by our long history of official discrimination, and yet come to the starting line with an education equal to whites. * * *

C. The second prong of our test—whether the Davis program stigmatizes any discrete group or individual and whether race is reasonably used in light of the program's objectives—is clearly satisfied by the Davis program. * * *

Unlike discrimination against racial minorities, the use of racial preferences for remedial purposes does not inflict a pervasive injury upon individual whites in the sense that wherever they go or whatever they do there is a significant likelihood that they will be treated as second-class citizens because of their color. This distinction does not mean that the exclusion of a white resulting from the preferential use of race is not sufficiently serious to require justification; but it does mean that the injury inflicted by such a policy is not distinguishable from disadvantages caused by a wide range of government actions, none of which has ever been thought impermissible for that reason alone.

In addition, there is simply no evidence that the Davis program discriminates intentionally or unintentionally against any minority group which it purports to benefit. The program does not establish a quota in the invidious sense of a ceiling on the number of minority applicants to be admitted. Nor can the program reasonably be regarded as stigmatizing the program's beneficiaries or their race as inferior. The Davis program does not simply advance less qualified applicants; rather, it compensates applicants, whom it is uncontested are fully qualified to study medicine, for educational disadvantage which it was reasonable to conclude

---

42. [Justice Powell] would not allow [the university] to exercise such power in the absence of "judicial, legislative, or administrative findings of constitutional or statutory violations." [But] the manner in which a State chooses to delegate governmental functions is for it to decide. California, by constitutional provision, has chosen to place authority over the operation of the University of California in the Board of Regents [who] have been vested with full legislative (including policymaking), administrative, and adjudicative powers. [W]e, unlike our Brother Powell, find nothing in the Equal Protection Clause that requires us to depart from established principle by limiting the scope of power the Regents may exercise more narrowly than the powers that may constitutionally be wielded by the Assembly. * * *

was a product of state-fostered discrimination. Once admitted, these students must satisfy the same degree [requirements]; they are taught by the same faculty in the same classes; and their performance is evaluated by the same standards by which regularly admitted students are judged. Under these circumstances, their performance and degrees must be regarded equally with the regularly admitted students with whom they compete for standing.

D. We disagree with the lower courts' conclusion that the Davis program's use of race was unreasonable in light of its objectives. [A]s petitioner argues, there are no practical means by which it could achieve its ends in the foreseeable future without the use of race-conscious measures. With respect to any factor (such as poverty or family educational background) that may be used as a substitute for race as an indicator of past discrimination, whites greatly outnumber racial minorities simply because whites make up a far larger percentage of the total population and therefore far outnumber minorities in absolute terms at every socio-economic level. * * *

E. Finally, Davis' special admissions program cannot be said to violate the Constitution simply because it has set aside a predetermined number of places for qualified minority applicants rather than using minority status as a positive factor to be considered in evaluating the applications of disadvantaged minority applicants. For purposes of constitutional adjudication, there is no difference between the two approaches. In any admissions program which accords special consideration to disadvantaged racial minorities, a determination of the degree of preference to be given is unavoidable, and any given preference that results in the exclusion of a white candidate is no more or less constitutionally acceptable than a program such as that at Davis.

[That] the Harvard approach does not also make public the extent of the preference and the precise workings of the system while the Davis program employs a specific, openly stated number, does not condemn the [latter]. It may be that the Harvard plan is more acceptable to the public than is the Davis "quota." If it is, any State [is] free to adopt it in preference to a less acceptable alternative, just as it is generally free [to] abjure granting any racial preferences in its admissions program. But there is no basis for preferring a particular preference program simply because in achieving the same goals that [Davis] is pursuing, it proceeds in a manner that is not immediately apparent to the public.[b] * * *

JUSTICE MARSHALL.

[I]t must be remembered that, during most of the past 200 years, the Constitution as interpreted by this Court did not prohibit the most ingenious and pervasive forms of discrimination against the Negro. Now, when a State acts to remedy the effects of that legacy of discrimination, I cannot believe that this same Constitution stands as a barrier. * * *

The position of the Negro today in America is the tragic but inevitable consequence of centuries of unequal treatment. Measured by any benchmark of comfort or achievement, meaningful equality remains a distant dream for the Negro [—comparing Negro and white statistics on life expectancy, infant mortality, median income, poverty, unemployment, and percentages in professions].

In light of the sorry history of discrimination and its devastating impact on the lives of Negroes, bringing the Negro into the mainstream of American life

---

b. The separate opinion of White, J.—concluding that Title VI does not provide for a private cause of action—is omitted.

should be a state interest of the highest order. To fail to do so is to ensure that America will forever remain a divided society. * * *

Since the Congress that considered and rejected the objections to the 1866 Freedmen's Bureau Act concerning special relief to Negroes also proposed the Fourteenth Amendment, it is inconceivable that the Fourteenth Amendment was intended to prohibit all race-conscious relief measures. [T]o hold that it barred state action to remedy the effects [of] discrimination [would] pervert the intent of the framers by substituting abstract equality for the genuine equality the amendment was intended to achieve.

[H]ad the Court [held in *Plessy*] that the Equal Protection Clause forbids differences in treatment based on race, we would not be faced with this dilemma in 1978. We must remember, however, that the principle that the "Constitution is color-blind" appeared only in the opinion of the lone dissenter. [F]or the next 60 years, from *Plessy* to *Brown,* ours was a Nation where, *by law,* an individual could be given "special" treatment based on the color of his skin. * * *

I fear that we have come full circle. After the Civil War our government started several "affirmative action" programs. This Court in the *Civil Rights Cases,* [Ch. 10, Sec. 1 infra], and *Plessy* destroyed the movement toward complete equality. For almost a century no action was taken, and this nonaction was with the tacit approval of the courts. Then we had *Brown* and the Civil Rights Acts of Congress, followed by numerous affirmative action programs. *Now,* we have this Court again stepping in, this time to stop affirmative action programs of the type used by the University of California.

Justice Blackmun. * * *

I yield to no one in my earnest hope that the time will come when an "affirmative action" program is unnecessary and is, in truth, only a relic of the past. I would hope that we could reach this stage within a decade at the most. But the story of *Brown,* decided almost a quarter of a century ago, suggests that that hope is a slim one. At some time, however, beyond any period of what some would claim is only transitional inequality, the United States must and will reach a stage of maturity where action along this line is no longer necessary. Then persons will be regarded as persons, and discrimination of the type we address today will be an ugly feature of history that is instructive but that is behind us. * * *

It is somewhat ironic to have us so deeply disturbed over a program where race is an element of consciousness, and yet to be aware of the fact, as we are, that institutions of higher learning, albeit more on the undergraduate than the graduate level, have given conceded preferences up to a point to those possessed of athletic skills, to the children of alumni, to the affluent who may bestow their largess on the institutions, and to those having connections with celebrities, the famous, and the powerful. * * *

[In] order to get beyond racism, we must first take account of race. There is no other way. And in order to treat some persons equally, we must treat them differently. We cannot—we dare not—let the Equal Protection Clause perpetrate racial supremacy. * * *

Justice Stevens, with whom The Chief Justice, Justice Stewart, and Justice Rehnquist join, concurring in the judgment in part and dissenting in part.

[Bakke] challenged petitioner's special admissions program [and the] California Supreme Court upheld his challenge and ordered him admitted. If the state court was correct in its view that the University's special program was illegal, and that Bakke was therefore unlawfully excluded from the medical school because of his race, we should affirm its judgment, regardless of our views about the legality of admissions programs that are not now before the Court.

[Stevens, J., then construed the state court opinion as containing no "outstanding injunction forbidding any consideration of racial criteria in processing applications."] It is therefore perfectly clear that the question whether race can ever be used as a factor in an admissions decision is not an issue in this case, and that discussion of that issue is inappropriate.

[Stevens, J., then interpreted Title VI as prohibiting "the exclusion of *any* individual from a federally funded program 'on the ground of race.' "] It is therefore our duty to affirm the judgment ordering Bakke admitted * * *.

Notes and Questions

1. *"Benign" and "invidious" discrimination.* Should race-based classificatory schemes that aim to advantage previously disadvantaged minorities be evaluated under the same constitutional standard as schemes that are invidiously motivated and designed to stigmatize?

a. *History.* Consider Jed Rubenfeld, *Affirmative Action*, 107 Yale L.J. 427, 430–32 (1997): "In July 1866, the Thirty–Ninth Congress [that] had just framed the Fourteenth Amendment [passed] a statute appropriating money [for] 'the relief of destitute colored women and children.' In 1867, the Fortieth Congress— the same body that was driving the Fourteenth Amendment down the throat of the bloody South—passed a statute providing money for [the] destitute 'colored' persons in the [the District of Columbia]. Year after year in the Civil War period [Congress] made special appropriations for [the] 'colored' soldiers and sailors of the Union Army. [What] do [these statutes] prove? Only that those who profess fealty to the 'original understanding' [cannot] categorically condemn color-based distribution of governmental benefits."[a] Compare the view of Lino Graglia, *Racially Discriminatory Admission to Public Institutions of Higher Education,* in Constitutional Government in America 255, 263 (Collins ed. 1980), that arguments such as this risk proving "too much": "It is equally clear that the fourteenth amendment was not intended to prohibit school segregation either."

b. *Moral relevance and permissibility.* Is the relevant constitutional principle that government should not classify by race?[b] Or is it that government should not use race as a basis to demean, suppress, or stigmatize?[c]

c. *Political representation.* Consider John H. Ely, *The Constitutionality of Reverse Racial Discrimination*, 41 U.Chi.L.Rev. 723, 735–36 (1974): "When the group that controls the decision making process classifies so as to advantage a minority and disadvantage itself, the reasons for being unusually suspicious, and, consequently, employing a stringent brand of review, are lacking. A White majority is unlikely to disadvantage itself for reasons of racial prejudice; nor is it likely to be tempted either to underestimate the needs and deserts of Whites

a. See also Eric Schnapper, *Affirmative Action and the Legislative History of the Fourteenth Amendment*, 71 Va.L.Rev. 753, 784–89 (1985).

b. See Eugene Volokh, *Diversity, Race as Proxy, and Religion as Proxy*, 43 U.C.L.A.L.Rev. 2059, 2076 (1996).

c. See Rubenfeld, supra; cf. Jerome M. Culp, Jr., *Colorblind Remedies and the Inter-* *sectionality of Oppression: Policy Arguments Masquerading as Moral Claims*, 69 N.Y.U.L.Rev. 162, 171 (1994): "The genuine moral goal associated with race is to end race-based oppression. Colorblindness may sometimes accomplish this moral goal, but it is not the goal itself. Therefore, the color-blind principle [must] be seen as a policy argument and not a moral precept."

relative to those of others, or to overestimate the costs of devising an alternative classification that would extend to certain Whites the advantages generally extended to Blacks. [Whether] or not it is more blessed to give than to receive, it is surely less suspicious." Compare Terrance Sandalow, *Racial Preferences in Higher Education: Political Responsibility and the Judicial Role,* 42 U.Chi.L.Rev. 653, 694–99 (1975): "[This] analysis [is] troublesome on several grounds. First, in American politics majorities [typically] are coalitions of minorities which have varying [interests]. Resolution of the dispute depends upon which of the minorities is more successful in forging an alliance with those groups which are less immediately affected. The issue whether state schools ought to adopt preferential admissions policies is no exception. The immediate beneficiaries of these policies are the minorities which receive preferential treatment. But there is no reason to suppose that the costs of such policies are borne equally by sub-groups within the white population. To the extent that they are not, the discrimination—though nominally against a majority—is in reality against those sub-groups."

2. *Justifications for affirmative action.* Numerous justifications have been offered for affirmative action programs—that is, for programs that take race or group status into account for the purpose of increasing the participation of previously disadvantaged or excluded groups. Some of the asserted justifications are predominantly based on past injustices, while others emphasize anticipated future benefits. A third class of justifications views affirmative action as a safeguard against current, sometimes subconscious, bias.

(a) *Backward-looking justifications.* (i) Affirmative action is often defended as a *remedy* for past discrimination, but a remedy of a somewhat unusual kind. Undeniably there is a long national history of discrimination based on race. In many cases, however, the particular institution implementing an affirmative action program either has not engaged in or refuses to acknowledge that it has engaged in past discrimination. Moreover, even if the implementing institution has engaged in past discrimination, the beneficiaries of its affirmative action program are unlikely to be those particular individuals against whom it has discriminated. (The beneficiaries of the program may of course have been the victims of discrimination by other institutions and individuals—of "societal discrimination.") Finally, the costs of the remedy may be felt not by the institution itself, but by "innocent" whites.

(ii) A slightly different argument is that society itself, through acts of governmental commission (discriminatory acts) and omission (failure to forbid or remedy private discrimination), is substantially responsible for currently skewed patterns of distribution in which whites (on average) are much more materially and educationally advantaged than blacks (on average) and that affirmative action is therefore justified as a form of class-based reparations for society's wrongs. Are the premises of this argument, which depend on collective or group-based notions such as "societal" discrimination against a "class" defined by race, consistent with the proposition that the Constitution protects the rights of "individuals"?[d] Is the entire theory of the equal protection clause—in particular, its focus on the acceptability of legal *classifications*—inherently group-based? See Owen M. Fiss, *Groups and the Equal Protection Clause,* 5 Phil. & Pub.Aff. 107, 108 (1976) (so arguing).

d. For a negative answer, see Charles Fried, *Metro Broadcasting, Inc. v. FCC: Two* *Concepts of Equality,* 104 Harv.L.Rev. 107 (1990).

(b) *Forward-looking justifications.* Forward-looking justifications look less to past discrimination than to the anticipated benefits to be reaped from affirmative action programs.

(i) One view is that a more nearly proportionate distribution of opportunities and benefits to members of traditionally disadvantaged groups is a general good— either to break any association of race or ethnicity with subordinated social class or to demonstrate the society's equal openness to members of groups that are socially salient.[e]

As a practical matter, affirmative action in education "is confined to 'elite' colleges and universities, namely, the most academically selective fifth of four-year institutions, where scores on the Scholastic Aptitude Test averaged 1,100 or more."[f] But consider Sylvia A. Law, *White Privileges and Affirmative Action*, 32 Akron L.Rev. 603, 620 (1999): "A strictly race-neutral policy of admission to undergraduate schools would reduce the numbers of blacks admitted by 50 to 75 percent. Eliminating affirmative action would have a particularly stark impact on the legal and medical professions. Under race-blind policies, blacks would make up only 1.6 to 3.4 percent of the students accepted to the 173 law schools approved by the ABA. Eliminating affirmative action from medical education would reduce black enrollment by 90 percent."

Consider also Samuel Issacharoff, *Can Affirmative Action Be Defended?*, 59 Ohio St.L.J. 669, 684 (1998): "The academic goals of excellence in teaching and research require [elite] public universities to be highly selective in their admission of students. At the same time, they are public institutions that must serve, and be seen to serve, all the people of the state. Public education is part of the process by which skills and credentials are created and cannot be simply a reward for pre-existing skills and credentials, many of them created at earlier stages of the public education system. [Only] affirmative action permits a school to admit the very best white students and the very best black and Mexican–American students in more than token numbers. [A] modest preference in admissions can produce large gains in the public university's ability to serve its integrative mission, without significant cost to its pursuit of excellence. No other method achieves both missions."

(ii) Another, narrower view is that race, in some situations, may be a powerful indicator of a person's capacity to perform a socially valuable function. In *Bakke*, for example, Powell, J., recognized that people from minority backgrounds might introduce a distinctive perspective in academic institutions. It is sometimes also argued that black teachers provide needed role models to black students (and thus, because of their race, are more effective teachers in some contexts than otherwise similarly talented whites) and that black police officers, other factors being equal, may be able to function more effectively than white police officers in some situations. On this view, affirmative action is not, in some contexts, an exception to principles requiring merit-based distribution; on the contrary, race can sometimes be a component or indicator of "merit"—conceived as the capacity to perform socially valued functions effectively. See Richard H. Fallon, Jr., *To Each According to His Ability, From None According to His Race: The Concept of Merit in the Law of Antidiscrimination*, 60 B.U.L.Rev. 815 (1980); Kenneth L. Karst & Harold W. Horowitz, *Affirmative Action and Equal Protection*, 60 Va.L.Rev. 955 (1974).

---

e. Cf. Kathleen M. Sullivan, *Sins of Discrimination: Last Term's Affirmative Action Cases*, 100 Harv.L.Rev. 78, 96–97 (1986).

f. Thomas J. Kane, *Racial and Ethnic Preferences in College Admissions*, 59 Ohio St.L.J. 971, 971–72 (1998).

Is race likely to be an accurate indicator of the distinctive views and perspectives underlying the aim of "diversity"? Of the capacity to generate distinctive insights that are valuable in practical deliberations or the search for truth?[g] Is it morally objectionable to allow race to be treated as a measure of a person's capacity or merit? Is it dangerous to associate race with merit in a society that has often viewed whiteness as a sign of worth and membership in other races as an indicator of likely inability, vice, or treachery? See Randall L. Kennedy, *Racial Critiques of Legal Academia*, 102 Harv.L.Rev. 1745, 1807 (1989); Volokh, supra, at 2076.

(c) *Present and prophylactic justifications.* A final set of justifications for affirmative action maintains that existing, "meritocratic" distributive schemes are often skewed in several ways: (i) familiar merit measures often test for and reward traits that tend to be disproportionately possessed by whites, even when those traits are not relevant to performance; (ii) the same measures overlook *other* traits that are equally relevant to excellence in practical performance; (iii) merit testing frequently has a subjective component, and whites administering such tests may be culturally sensitized to recognize the merit of white more readily than of black candidates. On this view, affirmative action is a prophylactic needed to correct for predictable corruptions in meritocratic ideals and their implementation.[h]

Among its implications, this asserted justification rejects the assumption that "affirmative action means that unqualified, or lesser qualified, individuals will be selected over more qualified individuals."[i] Indeed, it assumes that "[r]acial discrimination"—which affirmative action aims to correct—"is powerful precisely because of its frequent invisibility, its felt neutrality"[j] as reflected in "meritocratic" standards.[k]

Would this rationale for affirmative action, if persuasive, support a "quota" system? If so, how should the size of the quotas be fixed? Consider Susan Sturm & Lani Guinier, *The Future of Affirmative Action*, 84 Cal.L.Rev. 953, 956, 1011–13, 1035 (1996), arguing that the current debate over affirmative action characteristically, but mistakenly, assumes the legitimacy of "existing selection and admissions conventions." "We are mired in a testocracy that, in the name of merit, abstracts data from individuals, quantifies those individuals based on numerical rankings, exaggerates its ability to predict those individuals' future performance, and then disguises under the rubric of 'qualifications' the selection of those who are more sociologically privileged [since scores on standardized tests tend to correlate strongly with family income]." In place of reliance on standardized tests, Professors Sturm and Guinier propose selection processes in which applicants get "a meaningful opportunity to learn and perform in the position as part of the application process." To select the applicants to be given learning opportunities, they urge consideration of "weighted" lotteries sensitive to "the needs, interests, and possibilities of the particular institutional setting."

g. For affirmative answers, see, e.g., Kimberle Crenshaw, *Race, Reform, and Retrenchment: Transformation and Legitimation in Antidiscrimination Law*, 101 Harv.L.Rev. 1331, 1336 (1988); Mari Matsuda, *Affirmative Action and Legal Knowledge: Planting Seeds in Plowed–Up Ground*, 11 Harv. Women's L.J. 1, 12–13 (1988).

h. See, e.g., Jody Davis Armour, *Hype and Reality in Affirmative Action*, 68 U.Colo.L.Rev. 1173 (1997) (citing evidence of current bias and discrimination).

i. Michael Selmi, *Testing for Equality: Merit, Efficiency, and the Affirmative Action Debate*, 42 UCLA L.Rev. 1251, 1251 (1995).

j. Patricia J. Williams, *Metro Broadcasting, Inc. v. FCC: Regrouping in Singular Times*, 104 Harv.L.Rev. 525, 544 (1990).

k. See Richard Delgado, *Rodrigo's Tenth Chronicle: Merit and Affirmative Action*, 83 Geo.L.J. 1711 (1995); Daria Roithmayr, *Deconstructing the Distinction Between Bias and Merit*, 85 Cal.L.Rev. 1449 (1997).

3. *The Bakke "standard."* A principal issue dividing the parties in *Bakke*, and to some extent the Court, was the question of the appropriate legal standard by which to judge the constitutionality of voluntarily adopted affirmative action programs. Four justices opted explicitly for an "intermediate" standard (between strict scrutiny and rational basis review). Powell, J., whose position was dispositive, instead purported to apply "strict scrutiny," under which even "benign" race-based classifications are impermissible unless necessary to serve a compelling government interest.

Do you agree with the way that Powell, J., applied the "strict scrutiny" standard to the various state interests asserted in *Bakke*? Does a public university, exercising its academic freedom, have a "compelling" interest in an ethnically "diverse student body" that would contribute to a "robust exchange of ideas". Consider Wayne McCormack, *Race and Politics in the Supreme Court: Bakke to Basics,* 1979 Utah L.Rev. 491, 530: "Most educators would agree that some element of diversity in a student body is healthy," but this "is simply not the most honest statement of the objective of [most affirmative action] programs. [Further,] it is hard to believe that racial classifications disfavoring racial or ethnic minorities could be justified by a school's claim of academic freedom. This justification would be considered ludicrous if advanced as a basis for preferring members of the white majority."[1]

4. *Affirmative action and stigma.* Do affirmative action programs unfairly stigmatize minorities in general, and their intended beneficiaries in particular, by creating the impression that minorities could not be expected to satisfy meritocratic norms without special preferences? Do they give rise to what Professor Carter calls "the best black syndrome"—the perception that highly able and successful minorities have risen to coveted positions only as a result of affirmative action. Consider Stephen L. Carter, *Reflections of an Affirmative Action Baby* 69 (1991): "Supporters of [racial] preferences cite a whole catalogue of explanations for the inability of people of color to get along without them: institutional racism, inferior education, overt prejudice, the lingering effects of slavery and oppression, cultural bias in the criteria for admission and unemployment. All of these arguments are most sincerely pressed, and some of them are true. [But] they all entail the assumption that people of color cannot at present compete on the same playing field with people who are white." Compare T. Alexander Aleinikoff, *A Case for Race Consciousness,* 91 Colum.L.Rev. 1060, 1091 (1991): "Despite assertions by whites that race-conscious programs 'stigmatize' beneficiaries, blacks remain overwhelmingly in favor of affirmative action. Would we not expect blacks to be the first to recognize such harms and therefore to oppose affirmative action if it produced serious stigmatic injury?"

5. *Individualized judgments and quotas.* Is there any practical distinction between (a) a separate, identified program for minority admissions and (b) a program in which racial background can be counted as a "plus," and those

---

1. Compare Arnold H. Loewy, *Taking Bakke Seriously: Distinguishing Diversity from Affirmative Action in the Law School Admissions Process,* 77 N.C.L.Rev. 1479 (1999) (defending the diversity rationale) with Jim Chen, *Diversity in a Different Dimension: Evolutionary Theory and Affirmative Action's Destiny,* 59 Ohio St.L.J. 811, 822–23 (1998) (arguing that the "diversity" sought by affirmative action, which exalts the significance of race and levels differences among racial minorities, "is in many ways the polar opposite of [genuine] diversity" and concluding that the diversity rationale for affirmative action should be abandoned). See also Mark R. Killenbeck, *Pushing Things Up to Their First Principles: Reflection on the Values of Affirmative Action,* 87 Calif.L.Rev. 1299 (1999) (arguing that affirmative action should be upheld only insofar as it promotes diversity that improves education in ways capable of social scientific demonstration).

administering the program—in order to get the desired "diversity"—monitor the number of admittees who fall within relevant categories? Consider Vincent Blasi, *Bakke as Precedent: Does Mr. Justice Powell Have a Theory?* 67 Calif.L.Rev. 21, 60 (1979): "[I]t is almost always a bad thing for constitutional standards to be based on the purported perceptions of the populace regarding what is fair or rational rather than on well-considered and explicitly defended arguments respecting fairness and rationality. [I]f admissions programs are to be evaluated not on the basis of what they really entail but instead in terms of how they are generally perceived, educational institutions can only regard the constitutional standard as a legitimation of subterfuge and hypocrisy."

6. *Which groups and individuals?* (a) If affirmative action is constitutionally justifiable for some minority groups, is it equally justifiable for all?[m] Consider Deborah Ramirez, *Multicultural Empowerment: It's Not Just Black and White Anymore,* 47 Stan.L.Rev. 957, 962–63 (1995): "In 1960, blacks constituted 96 percent of the minority population. Today, the phenomenal growth in the Asian and Latino communities has altered the mix [so] dramatically that blacks now make up only about 50 percent of the population of people of color [and people of color represent about 25 percent of the total population according to the 1990 census]. [As] a result, affirmative action remedies originally designed to address the legacy of suffering and discrimination experienced by African–Americans are increasingly benefiting *other* people of color. [If] blacks are indeed uniquely disadvantaged, does the 'lesser' history of discrimination against Latinos and Asians entitle them to a lesser remedy, or no remedy at all?"

Consider J. Harvie Wilkinson, III, *The Rehnquist Court and the Search for Equal Justice,* 34 Tulsa L.J. 41, 60 (1998): "[I]t is inconceivable that a multiracial society could be constructed on anything other than transracial legal standards. [According] to the 1990 census, roughly half of native-born 35–34 year old Asian Americans and two-fifths of Hispanics married spouses of a different racial or ethnic group. [To] devote prodigious efforts to devising the correct racial categorizations of American citizens is about as divisive an enterprise as it is possible to imagine. [The] more diverse America becomes, the more compelling the color-blind ideal remains."

(b) Consider Ian F. Haney Lopez, *The Social Construction of Race: Some Observations on Illusion, Fabrication, and Choice,* 29 Harv.C.R.C.L. L.Rev. 1, 10 (1994): "I write as a Latino. [My] older brother, Garth, and I are the only children of a fourth-generation Irish father [and] a Salvadoran immigrant mother. [We] both have light but not white skin. [Interestingly], Garth and I conceive of ourselves in different racial terms. For the most part, he considers his race transparent, [and] he relates most easily with the Anglo side of the family. I, on the other hand, consider myself Latino and am in greatest contact with my maternal family." How, generally, should race be defined for purposes of administering race-based classifications?[n] Is it constitutionally permissible under *Bakke* for a state university to grant an admissions "plus" to an African–American applicant whose views on political issues are deemed to reflect a characteristic "black" or "minority" perspective, but to deny a similar preference to an African–American candidate whose views are deemed too mainstream?

---

m. For diverse views, see, e.g., Paul Brest & Miranda Oshige, *Affirmative Action for Whom?,* 47 Stan.L.Rev. 855 (1995); Michael Gottesman, *Twelve Topics to Consider Before Opting for Racial Quotas,* 79 Geo.L.J. 1737 (1991); Richard H. Fallon, Jr. & Paul C. Weil-er, *Firefighters v. Stotts: Conflicting Models of Racial Justice,* 1984 Sup.Ct.Rev. 1, 44–50.

n. See Christopher A. Ford, *Administering Identity: The Determination of "Race" in Race-Conscious Law,* 82 Cal.L.Rev. 1231 (1994).

(c) In order to maintain a diverse student body, may a public educational institution with competitive entrance requirements place a cap on the maximum number of students that may be admitted from any racially defined group? Could it give race-based, individualized preferences (as in *Bakke*) to promote the same end, even if the effect was to exclude Asian–Americans with higher scores than whites? See Jerry Kang, *Negative Action Against Asian Americans: The Internal Instability of Dworkin's Defense of Affirmative Action*, 31 Harv.C.R.-C.L.L.Rev. 1 (1996) (arguing that a ceiling on Asian–American admissions as part of an affirmative action program would have a stigmatizing effect and should be held unconstitutional).

7. *Educational affirmative action in practice.* William G. Bowen & Derek Bok, *The Shape of the River: Long–Term Consequences of Considering Race in College and University Admissions* (1998), presents the results of the first comprehensive, long-term study of affirmative action in 28 academically selective colleges and universities (based on data involving more than 80,000 undergraduates who matriculated in 1951, 1976, and 1989). The authors' assessments are generally highly enthusiastic. Among their conclusions are these: (i) In 1989, blacks made up about 7% of the classes in the colleges that they sampled; without affirmative action, the number of black entrants would been between 2.1 and 3.6 percent. (ii) Although the black drop-out rate was 11% higher than that for whites, 75% of the blacks in the 1989 cohort graduated from their original institution, and 79% graduated from some college, within six years. (iii) Black graduates of the elite schools earned considerably more on average than black graduates of non-elite schools. (iv) Almost twice as many blacks as whites from the 1976 cohort participate in community service organizations.

For a sustained critique of the methodology and argumentation of *The Shape of the River*, see Abigail Thernstrom & Stephen Thernstrom, *Reflections on The Shape of the River*, 46 U.C.L.A.L.Rev. 1583 (1999). Among the Thernstroms' major arguments are that black students admitted under what they call "racial double standards" tend not to do as well academically as students admitted without regard to race; that admissions policies at elite institutions have little impact on the socio-economic fabric of African–American life; and that racial categorization perpetuates habits of mind antithetical to egalitarian ideals.

8. *Economically or class-based affirmative action.* Would affirmative action based on class or ethnic background be fairer or more constitutionally acceptable than affirmative action based on race?[o]

(a) It is sometimes asserted that there should be a preference in educational admissions for applicants from relatively less advantaged backgrounds, regardless of race. The underlying idea is that equal opportunities should be open to those born with equal natural talents. To many, the moral attractiveness of this ideal seems intuitively obvious. Others are more skeptical—wondering, for example, why the "natural" allocation of talents should define the baseline for measuring distributive justice.[p] But there is no doubt, is there, that a class or economically based affirmative action program would be constitutionally permissible if adopted solely to advance an ideal of justice defined without reference to race?

o. For a an introduction to the debate, see, e.g., Richard D. Kahlenberg, *The Remedy: Class, Race, and Affirmative Action* (1996); Richard H. Fallon, Jr., *Affirmative Action Based on Economic Disadvantage*, 43 U.C.L.A.L.Rev. 1913 (1996) (exploring the philosophical foundations of the fairness argument); Deborah C. Malamud, *Assessing Class–Based Affirmative Action*, 47 J.Leg.Educ. 452 (1997).

p. See Fallon, *Affirmative Action Based on Economic Disadvantage*, supra.

(b) Many proponents support class-based affirmative action on the ground that it would provide many of the benefits of race-based affirmative action— notably, much greater minority representation than would occur without any affirmative action at all—but without triggering the constitutional difficulties and social divisions caused by race-based affirmative action. But there are varying estimates of the extent to which class-based affirmative action would succeed in promoting racial diversity in higher education, for example, and many observers are quite pessimistic. See, e.g., Thomas J. Kane, *Racial and Ethnic Preferences in College Admissions*, 59 Ohio St.L.J. 971, 971–72 (1998): "Although blacks and Hispanics would benefit disproportionately from policies favoring low-income applicants, minorities constitute only a small fraction of all high-scoring disadvantaged youth. As a result, substituting class-based for race-based preferences would not suffice to maintain racial diversity at academically selective colleges." An additional consideration is that the African–American students currently attending elite institutions tend not to come from the poorest black families. See Bowen & Bok, supra, at 50.

(c) If class-based affirmative action program is racially neutral on its face, but is implemented for the *purpose* of achieving a racially defined effect (i.e., heightened minority representation), should it be subjected to rational basis review or to strict judicial scrutiny? Under *Washington v. Davis*, a facially neutral statute adopted for the purpose of advantaging whites and disadvantaging racial minorities would trigger strict scrutiny. Does the converse also hold? Kathleen M. Sullivan, *After Affirmative Action*, 59 Ohio St.L.J. 1039, 1050 (1998), argues that where the aim is diversity, "the government action is taken despite, rather than because of, the effect on white interests."[q] Do you agree?

9. *Bakke's authority. Bakke* was the last case involving affirmative action in higher education to be decided by the Supreme Court.[r] In *Hopwood v. Texas*, 78 F.3d 932 (5th Cir.1996), the court of appeals, in invalidating an affirmative action plan implemented by the University of Texas Law School, explicitly rejected Justice Powell's *Bakke* opinion and held that the use of race as a factor in law school admissions was "per se proscribed." According to the two-judge majority, "Justice Powell's view in *Bakke* is not binding precedent," because much of his opinion "was joined by no other justice," and his argument in *Bakke* never garnered a majority. Did the court of appeals fail to account for the significance of Part V–C of Powell, J.'s *Bakke* opinion, which a majority of the Court did join?[s] Compare *Wessmann v. Gittens*, 160 F.3d 790 (1st Cir.1998) (invalidating an affirmative action plan on the ground that its heavy focus on race did not promote true "diversity" and noting that the circuits are split on the question of whether the aim of educational diversity is a compelling governmental interest).

The Supreme Court denied certiorari in *Hopwood* on the last day of its 1995 Term. 518 U.S. 1033, 116 S.Ct. 2580, 135 L.Ed.2d 1094 (1996). In an accompanying statement, Ginsburg, J., joined by Souter, J., noted that the University of Texas Law School had announced its abandonment of the affirmative action

---

q. See also Kim Forde–Mazrui, *The Constitutional Implications of Race–Neutral Affirmative Action*, 88 Georgetown L.J. 2331 (2000).

r. For the argument that "[a] careful look at the arguments made and analyzed in *Bakke* demonstrates that nary a new argument has been advanced" since, see Michael Selmi, *The Life of Bakke: An Affirmative Action Retrospective*, 87 Geo.L.J. 981 (1999).

s. See Lackland H. Bloom, Jr., *Hopwood, Bakke, and the Future of the Diversity Justification*, 29 Tex.Tech.L.Rev. 1 (1998) (noting that a Court majority never specifically subscribed to Powell, J.'s, diversity rationale, but defending reliance on Powell, J.'s analysis based on other considerations).

program challenged in the lower courts, under which it evaluated minority applicants under separate processes and standards from those used to evaluate others, and thus said "we must await a final judgment on a program genuinely in controversy before addressing the important issue raised in this petition."

In response to the *Hopwood* decision, the state of Texas adopted a so-called "10–percent plan," under which all students in the top 10 percent of the graduating class in every Texas high school are eligible for admission to the University of Texas's flagship campus. This plan has apparently had some success in maintaining minority enrollment, but less than the affirmative action plan that it replaced. Some critics have protested that the 10–percent plan will have a serious adverse effect on the quality of the student body and ultimately on the quality of undergraduate education.[t] Compare David Orentlicher, *Affirmative Action and Texas' Ten Percent Solution: Improving Diversity and Quality*, 74 Notre Dame L.Rev. 181, 182 (1998): Largely "unnoticed is the fact that the [10–percent] approach may do much to improve the public primary and secondary schools by altering incentives for school quality. Current incentives encourage politically influential parents of school-aged children to prefer a two-tiered educational system in which their children attend the stronger schools and the children of the politically weak attend the poorer schools. Under the Texas approach, parents have less to gain from concentrating their children at stronger schools and more to gain from dispersing their children over a larger number of schools. Accordingly, Texas' ten percent policy may lead to a public school system with smaller disparities in quality from school to school."[u]

WYGANT v. JACKSON BD. OF EDUC., 476 U.S. 267, 106 S.Ct. 1842, 90 L.Ed.2d 260 (1986), involved a minority preference in teacher lay-offs. When a budget crisis required cutting teaching positions, the school board, pursuant to a contract with the local teachers union, laid off more senior white teachers in order to retain less senior minority teachers. The court of appeals upheld the school board's action as justified by its interest in "providing role models for its minority students, as an attempt to alleviate the effects of societal discrimination." Although there was no majority opinion, five Justices agreed that the school board had violated the Constitution.

Writing for a plurality,[a] POWELL, J., found that race-based preferences must be subjected to strict scrutiny. The plurality concluded that the school board had no compelling interest in remedying "societal discrimination," and suggested that "prior [institutional] discrimination" supplied the only permissible justification for "race-based remedies." But even if the school board had discriminated in the past, "the burden that a preferential-layoffs scheme imposes on innocent parties" would be too great to be constitutionally acceptable. "While hiring goals impose a diffuse burden, often foreclosing only one of several opportunities, layoffs impose the entire burden of achieving racial equality on particular individuals, often resulting in serious disruption of their lives. That burden is too intrusive" and

---

t. See, e.g., Ronald Dworkin, *Affirming Affirmative Action*, 45 N.Y.Rev.Bks. 91, 98 (October 22, 1998).

u. See also William E. Forbath & Gerald Torres, *Merit and Diversity After Hopwood*, 10 Stan.L. & Pol'y Rev. 185 (1999).

a. Burger, C.J., and Rehnquist, J., joined in all, and O'Connor, J., in parts, of the opinion.

therefore fails the requirement that a race-based remedy be "narrowly tailored" to achieve its ends.

O'CONNOR, J., concurring, subscribed to the view that "racial classifications of any sort must be subjected to 'strict scrutiny.'" Under this standard, she "agree[d] with the plurality that a governmental agency's interest in remedying 'societal' discrimination [cannot] be deemed sufficiently compelling to pass constitutional muster." Even if the school board had discriminated in the past, it had attempted to justify its layoff program by reference to discrimination with respect to student assignments, not faculty hiring, and the remedy was not closely tailored to the violation. With respect to other possible compelling government interests: "[A]lthough its precise contours are uncertain, a state interest in the promotion of racial diversity has been found sufficiently 'compelling,' at least in the context of higher education, to support the use of racial considerations in furthering that interest. And certainly nothing the Court has said today necessarily forecloses the possibility that the Court will find other governmental interests which have been relied upon in the lower courts but which have not been passed on here to be sufficiently 'important' or 'compelling' to sustain the use of affirmative action policies."

WHITE, J., wrote a brief opinion concurring in the judgment, but did not specifically endorse any standard of review.

Dissenting, MARSHALL, J., joined by Brennan and Blackmun, JJ., found the school board's actions adequately justified by its interest in "preserv[ing] the levels of faculty integration" achieved during the 1970s by an affirmative action program of unchallenged validity. It was a mistake to regard laid-off whites as singled out to bear a unique and disproportionate burden. The aim of the contract between the school board and the union was to apportion the burden of layoffs that were not deserved by anyone, and there was no basis for thinking that "the tradition of basing layoff decisions on seniority is so fundamental that its modification can never be permitted."

In a separate dissent, STEVENS, J., argued that the equal protection clause permits "inclusionary" but not "exclusionary" use of racial classifications to promote legitimate government purposes. He would not have asked whether the race-based preference was justified "as a remedy for sins that were committed in the past," but whether by maintaining "an integrated faculty" it provided educational benefits that "could not be provided by an all-white" faculty.

Notes and Questions

1. *Race and merit.* If the government, in *Bakke*, had a compelling interest in achieving a diverse student body, why did the school board, in *Wygant*, not have a compelling interest in retaining a diverse faculty?[b] If layoff decisions had been based on individualized assessments, rather than seniority, could a faculty member's contribution to faculty diversity have been treated as a "plus"?[c]

b. Compare Robert A. Sedler, *Racial Preference and the Constitution: The Societal Interest in the Equal Participation Objective*, 26 Wayne L.Rev. 1227, 1236, 1248, 1250, 1254 (1980) (arguing that, under the logic of Powell, J.'s opinion in *Bakke*, "there is strong societal interest in [the] equal participation of blacks * * * whenever a 'black [can] bring something that a white person cannot offer,'" and that

this extends to *all* "institutions of government, the 'power professions,' such as law and medicine, [and] the economic system").

c. In *Taxman v. Board of Education*, 91 F.3d 1547 (3d Cir.1996), the Third Circuit held that a policy similar to that in *Wygant*—but grounded in an explicit rationale of diversity, as opposed to remedying societal discrimination—violated federal antidiscrimination stat-

2. *Weight of burden.* Should it matter that *Wygant* involved a lay-off, not a hiring, decision and that the dislocations attending a job loss are likely to be significantly greater than the hardships of not getting a job in the first place? See Richard H. Fallon, Jr. & Paul C. Weiler, *Firefighters v. Stotts: Conflicting Models of Racial Justice*, 1984 Sup.Ct.Rev. 1, 28–31 (so arguing).

RICHMOND v. J.A. CROSON CO.

488 U.S. 469, 109 S.Ct. 706, 102 L.Ed.2d 854 (1989).

JUSTICE O'CONNOR announced the judgment of the Court and delivered the opinion of the Court with respect to Parts I, III–B, and IV, an opinion with respect to Part II, in which THE CHIEF JUSTICE and JUSTICE WHITE join, and an opinion with respect to Parts III–A and V, in which THE CHIEF JUSTICE, JUSTICE WHITE and JUSTICE KENNEDY join. * * *

I. On April 11, 1983, the Richmond City Council adopted the Minority Business Utilization Plan (the Plan). The Plan required prime contractors to whom the city awarded construction contracts to subcontract at least 30% of the dollar amount of the contract to one or more Minority Business Enterprises (MBEs) [defined] as "[a] business at least fifty-one (51) percent of which is owned and controlled [by] minority group members." "Minority group members" were defined as "[c]itizens of the United States who are Blacks, Spanish-speaking, Orientals, Indians, Eskimos, or Aleuts." [The] Plan declared that it was "remedial" in nature, and enacted "for the purpose of promoting wider participation by minority business enterprises in the construction of public projects." The Plan expired on June 30, 1988, and was in effect for approximately five years.

The Plan authorized the Director of the Department of General Services to promulgate rules which "shall allow waivers in those individual situations where a contractor can prove to the satisfaction of the director that the requirements herein cannot be achieved." * * *

The Plan was adopted by the Richmond City Council after a public hearing. Seven members of the public spoke to the merits of the ordinance: five were in opposition, two in favor. Proponents of the set-aside provision relied on a study which indicated that, while the general population of Richmond was 50% black, only .67% of the city's prime construction contracts had been awarded to minority businesses in the 5-year period from 1978 to 1983. It was also established that a variety of contractors' associations, whose representatives appeared in opposition to the ordinance, had virtually no minority businesses within their membership.

[There] was no direct evidence of race discrimination on the part of the city in letting contracts or any evidence that the city's prime contractors had discriminated against minority-owned subcontractors. [Representatives] of various contractors' associations questioned whether there were enough MBEs in the Richmond area to satisfy the 30% set-aside requirement. [One] noted that only 4.7% of all construction firms in the United States were minority owned and that 41% of these were located in California, New York, Illinois, Florida, and Hawaii. He predicted that the ordinance would thus lead to a windfall for the few minority

utes. The court did not reach the constitutional question, and the parties settled before the Supreme Court, which had granted certiorari, could review the question. Compare *Wittmer v. Peters*, 87 F.3d 916, 920 (7th Cir. 1996), cert. denied, 519 U.S. 1111 (1997), which upheld a hiring plan for a prison boot camp that used race as a hiring criterion for camp lieutenants. In an opinion by Judge Posner, the court explicitly rejected a role-model theory, "because of lack of substantiation and [its] well-nigh unlimited reach," but held that the argument for black lieutenants was "backed up by expert evidence the plaintiffs did not rebut."

firms in Richmond. Council person Gillespie indicated his concern that many local labor jobs, held by both blacks and whites, would be lost because the ordinance put no geographic limit on the MBEs eligible for the 30% set-aside.

[The case was brought by a contractor whose low bid on a city project was not accepted because of failure to comply with the Plan's requirements. A] divided panel of the Court of Appeals struck down the Richmond set-aside program as violating both prongs of strict scrutiny under the Equal Protection Clause * * *.

II. [In *Fullilove v. Klutznick,* 448 U.S. 448, 100 S.Ct. 2758, 65 L.Ed.2d 902 (1980)], we upheld the minority set-aside contained in § 103(f)(2) of the Public Works Employment Act of 1977 (the Act) against a challenge based on the equal protection component of the Due Process Clause. The Act authorized a four billion dollar appropriation for federal grants to state and local governments for use in public works projects [and] contained the following requirement: "Except to the extent the Secretary determines otherwise, no grant shall be made under this Act [unless] the applicant gives satisfactory assurance to the Secretary that at least 10 per centum of the amount of each grant shall be expended for minority business enterprises." MBEs were defined as businesses effectively controlled by "citizens of the United States who are Negroes, Spanish-speaking, Orientals, Indians, Eskimos, and Aleuts."

The principal opinion in *Fullilove,* written by Chief Justice Burger,[a] did not employ "strict scrutiny" or any other traditional standard of equal protection review. The Chief Justice noted at the outset that although racial classifications call for close examination, the Court was at the same time, "bound to approach [its] task with appropriate deference to the Congress" [and that] Congress could mandate state and local government compliance with the set-aside program under its § 5 power to enforce the Fourteenth Amendment (citing *Katzenbach v. Morgan,* [Ch. 11, Sec. 3]).

The Chief Justice next turned to the constraints on Congress' power to employ race-conscious remedial relief. His opinion stressed two factors in upholding the MBE set-aside. First was the unique remedial powers of Congress under § 5 of the Fourteenth Amendment: "[It] is fundamental that *in no organ of government, state or federal, does there repose a more comprehensive remedial power than in the Congress,* expressly charged by the Constitution with competence and authority to enforce equal protection guarantees." (Emphasis added).

[In] reviewing the legislative history behind the Act, the principal opinion focused on the evidence before Congress that a nationwide history of past discrimination had reduced minority participation in federal construction grants [and] concluded that "Congress had abundant historical basis from which it could conclude that traditional procurement practices, when applied to minority businesses, could perpetuate the effects of prior discrimination."

The second factor emphasized by the principal opinion in *Fullilove* was the flexible nature of the 10% set-aside. [A] waiver could be sought where minority businesses were not available to fill the 10% requirement or, more importantly, where an MBE attempted "to exploit the remedial aspects of the program by

a. Burger, C.J.'s opinion was joined by White and Powell, JJ. Powell, J., also concurred separately. Marshall, J., joined by Brennan and Blackmun, JJ., concurred. Stevens, J., dissented for reasons discussed below. Stewart, J., joined by Rehnquist, J., dissented on the ground that, generally, "under our Constitu- tion, the government may never act to the detriment of a person solely because of that person's race," and that "a judicial decree that imposes burdens on the basis of race can be upheld only where its sole purpose is to eradicate the actual effects of illegal race discrimination."

charging an unreasonable price, i.e., a price not attributable to the present effects of prior discrimination." The Chief Justice indicated that without this fine tuning to remedial purpose, the statute would not have "pass[ed] muster."

Appellant and its supporting amici rely heavily on *Fullilove* for the proposition that a city council, like Congress, need not make specific findings of discrimination to engage in race-conscious relief. Thus, appellant argues "[i]t would be a perversion of federalism to hold that the federal government has a compelling interest in remedying the effects of racial discrimination in its own public works program, but a city government does not."

What appellant ignores is that Congress, unlike any State or political subdivision, has a specific constitutional mandate to enforce the dictates of the Fourteenth Amendment. The power to "enforce" may at times also include the power to define situations which *Congress* determines threaten principles of equality and to adopt prophylactic rules to deal with those situations. See *Katzenbach v. Morgan.*

[It seems clear,] however, that a state or local subdivision (if delegated the authority from the State) has the authority to eradicate the effects of private discrimination within its own legislative jurisdiction. This authority must, of course, be exercised within the constraints of § 1 of the Fourteenth Amendment. [As] a matter of state law, the city of Richmond has legislative authority over its procurement policies, and can use its spending powers to remedy private discrimination, if it identifies that discrimination with the particularity required by the Fourteenth Amendment. * * *

Thus, if the city could show that it had essentially become a "passive participant" in a system of racial exclusion practiced by elements of the local construction industry, we think it clear that the city could take affirmative steps to dismantle such a system. It is beyond dispute that any public entity, state or federal, has a compelling interest in assuring that public dollars, drawn from the tax contributions of all citizens, do not serve to finance the evil of private prejudice. Cf. *Norwood v. Harrison* [Ch. 10, Sec. 3].

III. A. [The] Richmond Plan denies certain citizens the opportunity to compete for a fixed percentage of public contracts based solely upon their race. To whatever racial group these citizens belong, their "personal rights" to be treated with equal dignity and respect are implicated by a rigid rule erecting race as the sole criterion in an aspect of public decisionmaking.

Absent searching judicial inquiry into the justification for such race-based measures, there is simply no way of determining what classifications are "benign" or "remedial" and what classifications are in fact motivated by illegitimate notions of racial inferiority or simple racial politics. Indeed, the purpose of strict scrutiny is to "smoke out" illegitimate uses of race by assuring that the legislative body is pursuing a goal important enough to warrant use of a highly suspect tool. The test also ensures that the means chosen "fit" this compelling goal so closely that there is little or no possibility that the motive for the classification was illegitimate racial prejudice or stereotype.

Classifications based on race carry a danger of stigmatic harm. Unless they are strictly reserved for remedial settings, they may in fact promote notions of racial inferiority and lead to a politics of racial hostility. We thus reaffirm the view expressed by the plurality in *Wygant* that the standard of review under the Equal Protection Clause is not dependent on the race of those burdened or benefitted by a particular classification. * * *

Even were we to accept a reading of the guarantee of equal protection under which the level of scrutiny varies according to the ability of different groups to defend their interests in the representative process, heightened scrutiny would still be appropriate in the circumstances of this case. [B]lacks comprise approximately 50% of the population of the city of Richmond. Five of the nine seats on the City Council are held by blacks. The concern that a political majority will more easily act to the disadvantage of a minority based on unwarranted assumptions or incomplete facts would seem to militate for, not against, the application of heightened judicial scrutiny in this case. * * *

Justice Powell's opinion [in *Bakke*] applied heightened scrutiny under the Equal Protection Clause to the racial classification at issue. His opinion [contrasted] the "focused" goal of remedying "wrongs worked by specific instances of racial discrimination" with "the remedying of the effects of 'societal discrimination,' an amorphous concept of injury that may be ageless in its reach into the past." He indicated that for the governmental interest in remedying past discrimination to be triggered "judicial, legislative, or administrative findings of constitutional or statutory violations" must be made. Only then does the Government have a compelling interest in favoring one race over another.

In *Wygant,* * * * Justice Powell, writing for the plurality, again drew the distinction between "societal discrimination" which is an inadequate basis for race-conscious classifications, and the type of identified discrimination that can support and define the scope of race-based relief. * * *

B. [The] District Court found the city council's "findings sufficient to ensure that, in adopting the Plan, it was remedying the present effects of past discrimination in the *construction industry*." [A] generalized assertion that there has been past discrimination in an entire industry provides no guidance for a legislative body to determine the precise scope of the injury it seeks to remedy. It "has no logical stopping point." *Wygant.* "Relief" for such an ill-defined wrong could extend until the percentage of public contracts awarded to MBEs in Richmond mirrored the percentage of minorities in the population as a whole.

Appellant argues that it is attempting to remedy various forms of past discrimination that are alleged to be responsible for the small number of minority businesses in the local contracting industry. [While] there is no doubt that the sorry history of both private and public discrimination in this country has contributed to a lack of opportunities for black entrepreneurs, this observation, standing alone, cannot justify a rigid racial quota in the awarding of public contracts in Richmond, Virginia. * * *

It is sheer speculation how many minority firms there would be in Richmond absent past societal discrimination, just as it was sheer speculation how many minority medical students would have been admitted to the medical school at Davis absent past discrimination in educational opportunities. Defining these sorts of injuries as "identified discrimination" would give local governments license to create a patchwork of racial preferences based on statistical generalizations about any particular field of endeavor.

These defects are apparent in this case. The 30% quota cannot in any realistic sense be tied to any injury suffered by anyone. [None of the] "findings" [relied on by the district court,] singly or together, provide the city of Richmond with a "strong basis in evidence for its conclusion that remedial action was necessary." *Wygant.* There is nothing approaching a prima facie case of a constitutional or statutory violation by *anyone* in the Richmond construction industry.

The District Court accorded great weight to the fact that the city council designated the Plan as "remedial." But the mere recitation of a "benign" or legitimate purpose for a racial classification, is entitled to little or no weight. Racial classifications are suspect, and that means that simple legislative assurances of good intention cannot suffice. * * *

In the employment context, we have recognized that for certain entry level positions or positions requiring minimal training, statistical comparisons of the racial composition of an employer's workforce to the racial composition of the relevant population may be probative of a pattern of discrimination. See *Teamsters v. United States,* 431 U.S. 324, 337–338, 97 S.Ct. 1843, 1855–1856, 52 L.Ed.2d 396 (1977) (statistical comparison between minority truck drivers and relevant population probative of discriminatory exclusion). But where special qualifications are necessary, the relevant statistical pool for purposes of demonstrating discriminatory exclusion must be the number of minorities qualified to undertake the particular task. *Hazelwood School Dist. v. United States,* 433 U.S. 299, 308, 97 S.Ct. 2736, 2741, 53 L.Ed.2d 768 (1977), *Johnson v. Transportation Agency,* 480 U.S. 616, 651–652, 107 S.Ct. 1442, 1462, 94 L.Ed.2d 615 (1987) (O'Connor, J., concurring).

In this case, the city does not even know how many MBEs in the relevant market are qualified to undertake prime or subcontracting work in public construction projects. Nor does the city know what percentage of total city construction dollars minority firms now receive as subcontractors on prime contracts let by the city. * * *

Finally, the city and the District Court relied on Congress' finding in connection with the set-aside approved in *Fullilove* that there had been nationwide discrimination in the construction industry. The probative value of these findings for demonstrating the existence of discrimination in Richmond is extremely limited. By its inclusion of a waiver procedure in the national program addressed in *Fullilove,* Congress explicitly recognized that the scope of the problem would vary from market area to market area. * * *

In sum, none of the evidence presented by the city points to any identified discrimination in the Richmond construction industry. We, therefore, hold that the city has failed to demonstrate a compelling interest in apportioning public contracting opportunities on the basis of race.

[The] foregoing analysis applies only to the inclusion of blacks within the Richmond set-aside program. There is *absolutely no evidence* of past discrimination against Spanish-speaking, Oriental, Indian, Eskimo, or Aleut persons in any aspect of the Richmond construction industry. * * *

IV. As noted by the court below, it is almost impossible to assess whether the Richmond Plan is narrowly tailored to remedy prior discrimination since it is not linked to identified discrimination in any way. We limit ourselves to two observations in this regard.

First, there does not appear to have been any consideration of the use of race-neutral means to increase minority business participation in city contracting. [Second,] the 30% quota cannot be said to be narrowly tailored to any goal, except perhaps outright racial balancing. It rests upon the "completely unrealistic" assumption that minorities will choose a particular trade in lockstep proportion to their representation in the local population.

Since the city must already consider bids and waivers on a case-by-case basis, it is difficult to see the need for a rigid numerical quota. [But unlike] the program upheld in *Fullilove,* the Richmond Plan's waiver system focuses solely on the availability of MBEs; there is no inquiry into whether or not the particular MBE seeking a racial preference has suffered from the effects of past discrimination by the city or prime contractors. * * *

V. Nothing we say today precludes a state or local entity from taking action to rectify the effects of identified discrimination within its jurisdiction. If the city of Richmond had evidence before it that nonminority contractors were systematically excluding minority businesses from subcontracting opportunities it could take action to end the discriminatory exclusion. Where there is a significant statistical disparity between the number of qualified minority contractors willing and able to perform a particular service and the number of such contractors actually engaged by the locality or the locality's prime contractors, an inference of discriminatory exclusion could arise. Under such circumstances, the city could act to dismantle the closed business system by taking appropriate measures against those who discriminate on the basis of race or other illegitimate criteria. In the extreme case, some form of narrowly tailored racial preference might be necessary to break down patterns of deliberate exclusion. * * *

Proper findings in this regard are necessary to define both the scope of the injury and the extent of the remedy necessary to cure its effects. Such findings also serve to assure all citizens that the deviation from the norm of equal treatment of all racial and ethnic groups is a temporary matter, a measure taken in the service of the goal of equality itself. Absent such findings, there is a danger that a racial classification is merely the product of unthinking stereo-types or a form of racial politics. * * *

Affirmed.

JUSTICE STEVENS, concurring in part and concurring in the judgment.

[I] believe the Constitution requires us to evaluate our policy decisions—including those that govern the relationships among different racial and ethnic groups—primarily by studying their probable impact on the future. I therefore do not agree with the premise that seems to underlie today's decision, as well as the decision in *Wygant,* that a governmental decision that rests on a racial classification is never permissible except as a remedy for a past wrong.[1] I do, however, agree with the Court's explanation of why the Richmond ordinance cannot be justified as a remedy for past discrimination, and therefore join Parts I, III–B, and IV of its opinion.

[T]he city makes no claim that the public interest in the efficient performance of its construction contracts will be served by granting a preference to minority-business enterprises. This case is therefore completely unlike *Wygant,* in which I

---

1. In my view the Court's approach to this case gives unwarranted deference to race-based legislative action that purports to serve a purely remedial goal, and overlooks the potential value of race-based determinations that may serve other valid purposes. With regard to the former point—as I explained at some length in *Fullilove*—I am not prepared to assume that even a more narrowly tailored set-aside program supported by stronger findings would be constitutionally justified. Unless the legislature can identify both the particular victims and the particular perpetrators of past discrimination, which is precisely what a court does when it makes findings of fact and conclusions of law, a

remedial justification for race-based legislation will almost certainly sweep too broadly. With regard to the latter point: I think it unfortunate that the Court in neither *Wygant* nor this case seems prepared to acknowledge that some race-based policy decisions may serve a legitimate public purpose. I agree, of course, that race is so seldom relevant to legislative decisions on how best to foster the public good that legitimate justifications for race-based legislation will usually not be available. But unlike the Court, I would not totally discount the legitimacy of race-based decisions that may produce tangible and fully justified future benefits.

thought it quite obvious that the School Board had reasonably concluded that an integrated faculty could provide educational benefits to the entire student body that could not be provided by an all-white, or nearly all-white faculty.

[T]his litigation [also] involves an attempt by a legislative body, rather than a court, to fashion a remedy for a past wrong. Legislatures are primarily policy-making bodies that promulgate rules to govern future conduct. [It] is the judicial system, rather than the legislative process, that is best equipped to identify past wrongdoers and to fashion remedies that will create the conditions that presumably would have existed had no wrong been committed. * * *

The class of persons benefitted by the ordinance is not [limited] to victims of [identified] discrimination—it encompasses persons who have never been in business in Richmond as well as minority contractors who may have been guilty of discriminating against members of other minority [groups.]

The ordinance is equally vulnerable because of its failure to identify the characteristics of the disadvantaged class of white contractors that justify the disparate treatment. That [class] presumably includes some who have been guilty of unlawful discrimination, some who practiced discrimination before it was forbidden by law, and some who have never discriminated against anyone on the basis of race. Imposing a common burden on such a disparate class merely because each member of the class is of the same race stems from reliance on a stereotype rather than fact or reason.[9] * * *

JUSTICE KENNEDY, concurring in part and concurring in the judgment.

I join all but Part II of Justice O'Connor's opinion * * *.

[The] process by which a law that is an equal protection violation when enacted by a State becomes transformed to an equal protection guarantee when enacted by Congress poses a difficult proposition for me; but as it is not before us, any reconsideration of that issue must await some further case. * * *

The moral imperative of racial neutrality is the driving force of the Equal Protection Clause. Justice Scalia's opinion underscores that proposition, quite properly in my view. The rule suggested in his opinion, which would strike down all preferences which are not necessary remedies to victims of unlawful discrimination, would serve important structural goals, as it would eliminate the necessity for courts to pass upon each racial preference that is enacted.

Nevertheless, given that a rule of automatic invalidity for racial preferences in almost every case would be a significant break with our precedents that require a case-by-case test, I am not convinced we need adopt it at this point. [My] reasons [are] as follows. First, I am confident that, in application, the strict scrutiny standard will operate in a manner generally consistent with the imperative of race neutrality, because it forbids the use even of narrowly drawn racial classifications except as a last resort. Second, the rule against race-conscious remedies is already less than an absolute one, for that relief may be the only adequate remedy after a judicial determination that a State or its instrumentality has violated the Equal Protection Clause. I note, in this connection, that evidence which would support a judicial finding of intentional discrimination may suffice also to justify remedial

---

9. There is, of course, another possibility that should not be overlooked. The ordinance might be nothing more than a form of patronage. But racial patronage, like a racial gerrymander, is no more defensible than political patronage or a political gerrymander. But unlike the Court, I would not totally discount the legitimacy of race-based decisions that may produce tangible and fully justified future benefits.

legislative action, for it diminishes the constitutional responsibilities of the political branches to say they must wait to act until ordered to do so by a court. * * *

JUSTICE SCALIA, concurring in the judgment.

I agree with much of the Court's opinion, and, in particular, with its conclusion that strict scrutiny must be applied to all governmental classification by race, whether or not its asserted purpose is "remedial" or "benign." I do not agree, however, with the Court's dicta suggesting that, despite the Fourteenth Amendment, state and local governments may in some circumstances discriminate on the basis of race in order (in a broad sense) "to ameliorate the effects of past discrimination." The benign purpose of compensating for social disadvantages, whether they have been acquired by reason of prior discrimination or otherwise, can no more be pursued by the illegitimate means of racial discrimination than can other assertedly benign purposes we have repeatedly rejected. See, e.g., [Wygant]. At least where state or local action is at issue, only a social emergency rising to the level of imminent danger to life and limb—for example, a prison race riot, requiring temporary segregation of inmates, cf. Lee v. Washington, 390 U.S. 333, 88 S.Ct. 994, 19 L.Ed.2d 1212 (1968)—can justify an exception to the principle embodied in the Fourteenth Amendment that "[o]ur Constitution is color-blind, and neither knows nor tolerates classes among citizens," Plessy (Harlan, J., dissenting) * * *.

A sound distinction between federal and state (or local) action based on race rests not only upon the substance of the Civil War Amendments, but upon social reality and governmental theory. It is a simple fact that what Justice Stewart described in Fullilove as "the dispassionate objectivity [and] the flexibility that are needed to mold a race-conscious remedy around the single objective of eliminating the effects of past or present discrimination"—political qualities already to be doubted in a national legislature—are substantially less likely to exist at the state or local level. The struggle for racial justice has historically been a struggle by the national society against oppression in the individual States. [What] the record shows, in other words, is that racial discrimination against any group finds a more ready expression at the state and local than at the federal level. To the children of the Founding Fathers, this should come as no surprise. An acute awareness of the heightened danger of oppression from political factions in small, rather than large, political units dates to the very beginning of our national history.

In my view there is only one circumstance in which the States may act by race to "undo the effects of past discrimination": where that is necessary to eliminate their own maintenance of a system of unlawful racial classification. [This] distinction explains our school desegregation cases, in which we have made plain that States and localities sometimes have an obligation to adopt race-conscious remedies. While there is no doubt that those cases have taken into account the continuing "effects" of previously mandated racial school assignment, we have held those effects to justify a race-conscious remedy only because we have concluded, in that context, that they perpetuate a "dual school system." We have stressed each school district's constitutional "duty to dismantle its dual system," and have found that "[e]ach instance of a failure or refusal to fulfill this affirmative duty continues the violation of the Fourteenth Amendment." Columbus. * * *

I agree with the Court's dictum that a fundamental distinction must be drawn between the effects of "societal" discrimination and the effects of "identified" discrimination, and that the situation would be different if Richmond's plan were "tailored" to identify those particular bidders who "suffered from the effects of past discrimination by the city or prime contractors." In my view, however, the reason that would make a difference is not, as the Court states, that it would justify race-conscious action but rather that it would enable race-neutral remediation. Nothing prevents Richmond from according a contracting preference to identified victims of discrimination. While most of the beneficiaries might be black, neither the beneficiaries nor those disadvantaged by the preference would be identified *on the basis of their race.* In other words, far from justifying racial classification, identification of actual victims of discrimination makes it less supportable than ever, because more obviously unneeded. * * *

It is plainly true that in our society blacks have suffered discrimination immeasurably greater than any directed at other racial groups. But those who believe that racial preferences can help to "even the score" display, and reinforce, a manner of thinking by race that was the source of the injustice and that will, if it endures within our society, be the source of more injustice still. The relevant proposition is not that it was blacks, or Jews, or Irish who were discriminated against, but that it was individual men and women, "created equal," who were discriminated against. And the relevant resolve is that that should never happen again. Racial preferences appear to "even the score" (in some small degree) only if one embraces the proposition that our society is appropriately viewed as divided into races, making it right that an injustice rendered in the past to a black man should be compensated for by discriminating against a white. Nothing is worth that embrace. Since blacks have been disproportionately disadvantaged by racial discrimination, any race-neutral remedial program aimed at the disadvantaged *as such* will have a disproportionately beneficial impact on blacks. Only such a program, and not one that operates on the basis of race, is in accord with the letter and the spirit of our Constitution. * * *

JUSTICE MARSHALL, with whom JUSTICE BRENNAN and JUSTICE BLACKMUN join, dissenting. * * *

My view has long been that race-conscious classifications designed to further remedial goals "must serve important governmental objectives and must be substantially related to achievement of those objectives" in order to withstand constitutional scrutiny. Analyzed in terms of this two-prong standard, Richmond's set-aside, like the federal program on which it was modeled, is "plainly constitutional." *Fullilove* (Marshall, J., concurring in judgment).

Turning first to the governmental interest inquiry, Richmond has two powerful interests in setting aside a portion of public contracting funds for minority-owned enterprises. The first is the city's interest in eradicating the effects of past racial discrimination. * * *

Richmond has a second compelling interest in setting aside, where possible, a portion of its contracting dollars. [When] government channels all its contracting funds to a white-dominated community of established contractors whose racial homogeneity is the product of private discrimination, it does more than place its imprimatur on the practices which forged and which continue to define that community. It also provides a measurable boost to those economic entities that have thrived within it, while denying important economic benefits to those entities which, but for prior discrimination, might well be better qualified to receive valuable government contracts. In my view, the interest in ensuring that the government does not reflect and reinforce prior private discrimination in dispensing public contracts is every bit as strong as the interest in eliminating private discrimination—an interest which this Court has repeatedly deemed compelling. See, e.g., *Roberts v. United States Jaycees*, [Ch. 7, Sec. 9, III].

The remaining question with respect to the "governmental interest" prong of equal protection analysis is whether Richmond has proffered satisfactory proof of past racial discrimination to support its twin interests in remediation and in governmental nonperpetuation. [Richmond] acted against a backdrop of congressional and Executive Branch studies which demonstrated with such force the nationwide pervasiveness of prior discrimination that Congress presumed that " 'present economic inequities' " in construction contracting resulted from " 'past discriminatory systems.' " The city's local evidence confirmed that Richmond's construction industry did not deviate from this pernicious national pattern.

In my judgment, Richmond's set-aside plan also comports with the second prong of the equal protection inquiry, for it is substantially related to the interests it seeks to serve in remedying past discrimination and in ensuring that municipal contract procurement does not perpetuate that discrimination. [The] majority takes issue [with] two aspects of Richmond's tailoring: the city's refusal to explore the use of race-neutral measures to increase minority business participation in contracting, and the selection of a 30% set-aside figure. [But] the majority overlooks the fact that since 1975, Richmond has barred both discrimination by the city in awarding public contracts and discrimination by public contractors. The virtual absence of minority businesses from the city's contracting rolls, indicated by the fact that such businesses have received less than 1% of public contracting dollars, strongly suggests that this ban has not succeeded in redressing the impact of past discrimination or in preventing city contract procurement from reinforcing racial homogeneity. * * *

As for Richmond's 30% target, the majority states that this figure "cannot be said to be narrowly tailored to any goal, except perhaps outright racial balancing." The majority ignores two important facts. First, the set-aside measure affects only 3% of overall city contracting; thus, any imprecision in tailoring has far less impact than the majority suggests. But more important, the majority ignores the fact that Richmond's 30% figure was patterned directly on the *Fullilove* precedent. Congress' 10% figure fell "roughly halfway between the present percentage of minority contractors and the percentage of minority group members in the Nation." The Richmond City Council's 30% figure similarly falls roughly halfway between the present percentage of Richmond-based minority contractors (almost zero) and the percentage of minorities in Richmond (50%). * * *

I am also troubled by the majority's assertion that, even if it did not believe generally in strict scrutiny of race-based remedial measures, "the circumstances of this case" require this Court to look upon the Richmond City Council's measure with the strictest scrutiny. The sole such circumstance which the majority cites, however, is the fact [that] "blacks comprise approximately 50% of the population of the city of Richmond" and that "[f]ive of the nine seats on the City Council are held by blacks."

While I agree that the numerical and political supremacy of a given racial group is a factor bearing upon the level of scrutiny to be applied, this Court has never held that numerical inferiority, standing alone, makes a racial group "suspect" and thus entitled to strict scrutiny review. [T]he "circumstances of this case," underscore the importance of *not* subjecting to a strict scrutiny straitjacket the increasing number of cities which have recently come under minority leadership and are eager to rectify, or at least prevent the perpetuation of, past racial discrimination. In many cases, these cities will be the ones with the most in the way of prior discrimination to rectify. * * *

Nothing in the Constitution or in the prior decisions of this Court supports limiting state authority to confront the effects of past discrimination to those situations in which a prima facie case of a constitutional or statutory violation can be made out. [The] meaning of "equal protection of the laws" thus turns on the happenstance of whether a State or local body has previously defined illegal discrimination. Indeed, given that racially discriminatory cities may be the ones least likely to have tough, antidiscrimination laws on their books, the majority's constitutional incorporation of state and local statutes has the perverse effect of inhibiting those States or localities with the worst records of official racism from taking remedial action.

Notes and Questions

1. *Standard.* A clear majority in *Croson* agrees that affirmative action programs should be upheld only if closely tailored to serve a compelling government interest. But does a majority also agree on what this standard means in practice?

2. *Compelling interests.* (a) State and local governments have a compelling interest in remedying their own past discrimination, but how close must they (and should they have to) come to identifying specific violations with the attendant risk of liability—in order to act on this basis? Must they show a "strong basis in evidence" for conclusions that "approach[] a prima facie case of a constitutional or statutory violation"?

(b) Does *Croson* permit a state or local lawmaking body to implement affirmative action remedies in exercising its "authority to eradicate the effects of private discrimination within its own legislative jurisdiction"? If so, is its approach consistent with *Wygant*? How does *Croson*'s reference to eradicating the effects of private discrimination within its jurisdiction relate to its condemnation of remedies intended to "remedy[] the effects of societal discrimination"?[a]

3. *Close tailoring.* Suppose that the City of Richmond could have established past discrimination that it had a compelling interest in remedying. (a) Could it immediately have implemented race-based preferences, or would it need to have attempted other, race-neutral measures—or at least demonstrated their futility— first?[b] (b) Could it have established numerical targets for minority subcontractors? If so, how large could such targets be? (c) What waiver mechanisms would have been necessary?[c]

4. *"Individual" and "group" justice.* (a) Consider the position of Charles Fried, *Metro Broadcasting, Inc. v. FCC: Two Concepts of Equality*, 104 Harv. L.Rev. 107, 108–09, 111 (1990), that O'Connor, J., for the *Croson* plurality, reads

a. For discussion, see Ian Ayres & Fredrick E. Vars, *When Does Private Discrimination Justify Public Affirmative Action?*, 98 Colum.L.Rev. 1577 (1998).

b. Consider Ian Ayres, *Narrow Tailoring*, 43 UCLA L.Rev. 1781 (1996), arguing that the Court's preference for race-neutral remedies is inconsistent with its demand for narrow tailoring, since a remedy for discrimination against racial minorities can be more narrowly tailored if only minorities benefit.

c. For debate concerning the scope of *Croson*, compare Joint Statement, *Constitutional Scholars' Statement on Affirmative Action After City of Richmond v. J.A. Croson Co.*, 98 Yale L.J. 1711 (1989) with Charles Fried, *Affirmative Action After City of Richmond v. J.A. Croson Co.: A Response to the Scholars' Statement*, 99 Yale L.J. 155 (1989). See also *Scholars' Reply to Professor Fried*, 99 Yale L.J. 163 (1989).

the equal protection clause as embodying an "individualistic" conception of fairness, whereas the position of the dissenters rests on a conception of "group" justice. On the individualistic conception, Fried says, race-based remedies are permissible only to compensate for past wrongs by an individual wrongdoer; this is why remedies for "societal" discrimination are inappropriate. But how "individualistic" is a position that requires identified wrongdoing as a predicate for race-based remedies, but then allows the benefit of those remedies to flow to persons not proven to be the victims of the identified wrongdoing? In other words, the position identified (and defended) as individualistic requires individually identified wrongdoing, but then—once the wrongdoing is identified—allows group-based remedies in at least some circumstances. Does this asymmetry make sense?

(b) Compare the more consistently individualistic position taken by Scalia, J., concurring. Does the logic of individualism—including such notions as individual responsibility, merit, and desert—establish the correctness of his view?

(c) Does the dissenting position of Marshall, J., necessarily reflect the "collectivist" assumption that racial groups "hav[e] a status independent of and even superior to that of individual group members"? Fried, supra at 109.[d]

5. *Preferences for majorities.* Should it have mattered to the analysis in *Croson* that blacks held more than half the seats on the Richmond city council? That the set-aside program benefitted a range of groups with diverse histories and current economic statuses? Did the facts illustrate a serious risk of race-based division and resentment engendered by "a form of racial politics"?

ADARAND CONSTRUCTORS, INC. v. PENA
515 U.S. 200, 115 S.Ct. 2097, 132 L.Ed.2d 158 (1995).

JUSTICE O'CONNOR announced the judgment of the Court and delivered an opinion with respect to Parts I, II, III–A, III–B, III–D, and IV, which is for the Court except insofar as it might be inconsistent with the views expressed in JUSTICE SCALIA'S concurrence, and an opinion with respect to Part III–C in which JUSTICE KENNEDY joins. * * *

I. In 1989, the Central Federal Lands Highway Division (CFLHD), which is part of the United States Department of Transportation (DOT), awarded the prime contract for a highway construction project in Colorado to Mountain Gravel & Construction Company. Mountain Gravel then solicited bids from subcontractors for the guardrail portion of the contract. Adarand, a Colorado-based highway construction company specializing in guardrail work, submitted the low bid. Gonzales Construction Company also submitted a bid.

---

d. The Court has held that a voluntary affirmative action plan adopted by a private employer, not subject to constitutional constraints, need not be predicated on past discrimination by the employer itself to be permissible under Title VII of the Civil Rights Act of 1964—which, inter alia, makes it "unlawful [for] any employer, labor organization, or joint labor-management committee [to] discriminate against any individual because of his race, color, religion, sex, or national origin in admission [to] any program established to provide apprenticeship or other training."

United Steelworkers v. Weber, 443 U.S. 193, 99 S.Ct. 2721, 61 L.Ed.2d 480 (1979), per Brennan, J., held that "an affirmative action plan—

collectively bargained by an employer and a union—that reserve[d] for black employees 50% of the openings in an in-plant craft-training program until the percentage of black craftworkers in the plant is commensurate with the percentage of blacks in the local labor force," was justified by the interest in alleviating a racial imbalance in the employer's workplace. The Court found, 5–2, that "It would be ironic indeed if a law triggered by a Nation's concern over centuries of racial injustice [constituted] the first legislative prohibition of all voluntary, private, race-conscious efforts to abolish traditional patterns of racial segregation and hierarchy."

The prime contract's terms provide that Mountain Gravel would receive additional compensation if it hired subcontractors certified as small businesses controlled by "socially and economically disadvantaged individuals." Gonzales is certified as such a business; Adarand is not. Mountain Gravel awarded the subcontract to Gonzales, despite Adarand's low bid, and Mountain Gravel's Chief Estimator has submitted an affidavit stating that Mountain Gravel would have accepted Adarand's bid, had it not been for the additional payment it received by hiring Gonzales instead. Federal law requires that a subcontracting clause similar to the one used here must appear in most federal agency contracts, and it also requires the clause to state that "[t]he contractor shall presume that socially and economically disadvantaged individuals include Black Americans, Hispanic Americans, Native Americans, Asian Pacific Americans, and other minorities, or any other individual found to be disadvantaged by the [Small Business] Administration pursuant to section 8(a) of the Small Business Act." Adarand claims that the presumption set forth in that statute discriminates on the basis of race in violation of the Federal Government's Fifth Amendment obligation not to deny anyone equal protection of the laws. * * *

[Adarand's] claim arises under the Fifth Amendment to the Constitution, which provides that "No person shall [be] deprived of life, liberty, or property, without due process of law." Although this Court has always understood that Clause to provide some measure of protection against *arbitrary* treatment by the Federal Government, it is not as explicit a guarantee of *equal* treatment as the Fourteenth Amendment * * *. Our cases have accorded varying degrees of significance to the difference in the language of those two Clauses. We think it necessary to revisit the issue here.

A. Through the 1940s, this Court had routinely taken the view in non-race-related cases that, "[u]nlike the Fourteenth Amendment, the Fifth contains no equal protection clause and it provides no guaranty against discriminatory legislation by Congress." *Detroit Bank v. United States*, 317 U.S. 329, 337, 63 S.Ct. 297, 301, 87 L.Ed. 304 (1943). [But the Court departed from this view in *Korematsu*, which] began by noting that "all legal restrictions which curtail the civil rights of a single racial group are immediately suspect [and] courts must subject them to the most rigid scrutiny." * * *

In *Bolling v. Sharpe*, the Court for the first time explicitly questioned the existence of any difference between the obligations of the Federal Government and the States to avoid racial classifications [and] concluded that, "[i]n view of [the] decision [in *Brown*] that the Constitution prohibits the states from maintaining racially segregated public schools, it would be unthinkable that the same Constitution would impose a lesser duty on the Federal Government." [After intervening decisions,] in 1975, the Court stated explicitly that "[t]his Court's approach to Fifth Amendment equal protection claims has always been precisely the same as to equal protection claims under the Fourteenth Amendment." *Weinberger v. Wiesenfeld*, [Sec. 3, III infra].

B. [After some disagreement about the standard for assessing race-based governmental action designed to benefit historically disadvantaged groups, a majority, in *Croson*,] finally agreed that the Fourteenth Amendment requires strict scrutiny of all race-based action by state and local governments. But *Croson* of course had no occasion to declare what standard of review the Fifth Amendment requires for such action taken by the Federal Government. *Croson* observed simply that the Court's "treatment of an exercise of congressional power in

Fullilove cannot be dispositive here," because *Croson*'s facts did not implicate Congress' broad power under § 5 of the Fourteenth Amendment. * * *

Despite lingering uncertainty in the details, however, the Court's cases through *Croson* had established three general propositions with respect to governmental racial classifications. First, skepticism: " '[a]ny preference based on racial or ethnic criteria must necessarily receive a most searching examination.' " [*Wygant*.] Second, consistency: "the standard of review under the Equal Protection Clause is not dependent on the race of those burdened or benefitted by a particular classification." [*Croson*.] And third, congruence: "[e]qual protection analysis in the Fifth Amendment area is the same as that under the Fourteenth Amendment." [*Buckley v. Valeo*, Ch. 7, Sec. 10 supra.] Taken together, these three propositions lead to the conclusion that any person, of whatever race, has the right to demand that any governmental actor subject to the Constitution justify any racial classification subjecting that person to unequal treatment under the strictest judicial scrutiny. * * *

A year [after *Croson*], however, the Court took a surprising turn. In *Metro Broadcasting, Inc. v. FCC*, 497 U.S. 547, 110 S.Ct. 2997, 111 L.Ed.2d 445 (1990), the Court [held] that "benign" federal racial classifications need only satisfy intermediate scrutiny, [but] did not explain how to tell whether a racial classification should be deemed "benign," other than to express "confiden[ce] that an 'examination of the legislative scheme and its history' will separate benign measures from other types of racial classifications."[a] * * *

By adopting intermediate scrutiny as the standard of review for congressionally mandated "benign" racial classifications, *Metro Broadcasting* departed from prior cases in two significant respects. First, it turned its back on *Croson*'s explanation of why strict scrutiny of all governmental racial classifications is essential. "Absent searching judicial inquiry into the justification for such race-based measures, there is simply no way of determining what classifications are 'benign' or 'remedial' and what classifications are in fact motivated by illegitimate notions of racial inferiority or simple racial politics. * * * " We adhere to that view today. * * *

Second, *Metro Broadcasting* squarely rejected one of the three propositions established by the Court's earlier equal protection cases, namely, congruence between the standards applicable to federal and state racial classifications, and in so doing also undermined the other two—skepticism of all racial classifications, and consistency of treatment irrespective of the race of the burdened or benefitted group. * * *

The three propositions undermined by *Metro Broadcasting* all derive from the basic principle that the Fifth and Fourteenth Amendments to the Constitution protect *persons*, not *groups*. It follows from that principle that all governmental action based on race—a *group* classification long recognized as "in most circumstances irrelevant and therefore prohibited"—should be subjected to detailed judicial inquiry to ensure that the *personal* right to equal protection of the laws has not been infringed. These ideas have long been central to this Court's understanding of equal protection, and holding "benign" state and federal racial

---

a. *Metro Broadcasting*, per Brennan, J., upheld FCC policies granting preferences to minority ownerships in the acquisition and transfer of broadcast licenses on the basis of the governmental interest "in enhancing broadcast diversity." The opinion was joined by Justice White, who had joined the plurality opinion in *Croson*; it distinguished *Croson* as having established the level of scrutiny applicable to affirmative action programs initiated by state and local governments, not to federal affirmative action. O'Connor, J., joined by Rehnquist, C.J., and Scalia and Kennedy, JJ., dissented.

classifications to different standards does not square with them. "[A] free people whose institutions are founded upon the doctrine of equality" should tolerate no retreat from the principle that government may treat people differently because of their race only for the most compelling reasons. Accordingly, we hold today that all racial classifications, imposed by whatever federal, state, or local governmental actor, must be analyzed by a reviewing court under strict scrutiny. In other words, such classifications are constitutional only if they are narrowly tailored measures that further compelling governmental interests. To the extent that *Metro Broadcasting* is inconsistent with that holding, it is overruled.

[In his dissenting opinion,] Justice Stevens * * * claims that we have ignored any difference between federal and state legislatures. But requiring that Congress, like the States, enact racial classifications only when doing so is necessary to further a "compelling interest" does not contravene any principle of appropriate respect for a co-equal Branch of the Government. It is true that various Members of this Court have taken different views of the authority § 5 of the Fourteenth Amendment confers upon Congress to deal with the problem of racial discrimination, and the extent to which courts should defer to Congress' exercise of that authority. We need not, and do not, address these differences today. * * *

C. "Although adherence to precedent is not rigidly required in constitutional cases, any departure from the doctrine of stare decisis demands special justification." [But] "stare decisis is a principle of policy and not a mechanical formula of adherence to the latest decision, however recent and questionable, when such adherence involves collision with a prior doctrine more embracing in its scope, intrinsically sounder, and verified by experience." Remaining true to an "intrinsically sounder" doctrine established in prior cases better serves the values of stare decisis than would following a more recently decided case inconsistent with the decisions that came before it; the latter course would simply compound the recent error and would likely make the unjustified break from previously established doctrine complete. In such a situation, "special justification" exists to depart from the recently decided case.

D. [Finally,] we wish to dispel the notion that strict scrutiny is "strict in theory, but fatal in fact." The unhappy persistence of both the practice and the lingering effects of racial discrimination against minority groups in this country is an unfortunate reality, and government is not disqualified from acting in response to it. As recently as 1987, for example, every Justice of this Court agreed that the Alabama Department of Public Safety's "pervasive, systematic, and obstinate discriminatory conduct" justified a narrowly tailored race-based remedy. See *United States v. Paradise*, 480 U.S. 149, 107 S.Ct. 1053, 94 L.Ed.2d 203 (1987).[b] When race-based action is necessary to further a compelling interest, such action is within constitutional constraints if it satisfies the "narrow tailoring" test this Court has set out in previous cases.

IV. Because our decision today alters the playing field in some important respects, we think it best to remand the case to the lower courts for further consideration in light of the principles we have announced. The Court of Appeals, following *Metro Broadcasting* and *Fullilove*, analyzed the case in terms of intermediate scrutiny. [It] did not decide the question whether the interests served by the use of subcontractor compensation clauses are properly described as "compelling."

b. *Paradise* upheld a *judicially* ordered race-conscious remedy. The Court was unanimous that the federal government has a compelling interest in remedying proven race discrimination. Per Brennan, J., it found the particular order at issue to be "narrowly tailored," and thus upheld it, by a closely divided vote of 5–4.

It also did not address the question of narrow tailoring in terms of our strict scrutiny cases, by asking, for example, whether there was "any consideration of the use of race-neutral means to increase minority business participation" in government contracting, [*Croson*,] or whether the program was appropriately limited such that it "will not last longer than the discriminatory effects it is designed to eliminate," *Fullilove*, (Powell, J., concurring). * * *

JUSTICE SCALIA, concurring in part and concurring in the judgment.

I join the opinion of the Court, except Part III–C, and except insofar as it may be inconsistent with the following. In my view, government can never have a "compelling interest" in discriminating on the basis of race in order to "make up" for past racial discrimination in the opposite direction. Individuals who have been wronged by unlawful racial discrimination should be made whole; but under our Constitution there can be no such thing as either a creditor or a debtor race. That concept is alien to the Constitution's focus upon the individual. To pursue the concept of racial entitlement—even for the most admirable and benign of purposes—is to reinforce and preserve for future mischief the way of thinking that produced race slavery, race privilege and race hatred. In the eyes of government, we are just one race here. It is American.

It is unlikely, if not impossible, that the challenged program would survive under this understanding of strict scrutiny, but I am content to leave that to be decided on remand.

JUSTICE THOMAS, concurring in part and concurring in the judgment.

I agree with the majority's conclusion that strict scrutiny applies to *all* government classifications based on race. I write separately, however, to express my disagreement with the premise underlying Justice Stevens' and Justice Ginsburg's dissents: that there is a racial paternalism exception to the principle of equal protection. I believe that there is a "moral [and] constitutional equivalence," (Stevens, J., dissenting), between laws designed to subjugate a race and those that distribute benefits on the basis of race in order to foster some current notion of equality. Government cannot make us equal; it can only recognize, respect, and protect us as equal before the law.

That these programs may have been motivated, in part, by good intentions cannot provide refuge from the principle that under our Constitution, the government may not make distinctions on the basis of race. As far as the Constitution is concerned, it is irrelevant whether a government's racial classifications are drawn by those who wish to oppress a race or by those who have a sincere desire to help those thought to be disadvantaged. There can be no doubt that the paternalism that appears to lie at the heart of this program is at war with the principle of inherent equality that underlies and infuses our Constitution. See Declaration of Independence ("We hold these truths to be self-evident, that all men are created equal, that they are endowed by their Creator with certain inalienable Rights, that among these are Life, Liberty, and the pursuit of Happiness").

These programs not only raise grave constitutional questions, they also undermine the moral basis of the equal protection principle. Purchased at the price of immeasurable human suffering, the equal protection principle reflects our Nation's understanding that such classifications ultimately have a destructive impact on the individual and our society. Unquestionably, "[i]nvidious [racial] discrimination is an engine of oppression." It is also true that "[r]emedial" racial preferences may reflect "a desire to foster equality in society." But there can be no doubt that racial paternalism and its unintended consequences can be as poisonous and pernicious as any other form of discrimination. So-called "benign" discrimination teaches many that because of chronic and apparently immutable handicaps, minorities cannot compete with them without their patronizing indulgence. Inevitably, such programs engender attitudes of superiority or, alternatively, provoke resentment among those who believe that they have been wronged by the government's use of race. These programs stamp minorities with a badge of inferiority and may cause them to develop dependencies or to adopt an attitude that they are "entitled" to preferences. * * *

In my mind, government-sponsored racial discrimination based on benign prejudice is just as noxious as discrimination inspired by malicious prejudice. In each instance, it is racial discrimination, plain and simple.

JUSTICE STEVENS, with whom JUSTICE GINSBURG joins, dissenting.

[There] is no moral or constitutional equivalence between a policy that is designed to perpetuate a caste system and one that seeks to eradicate racial subordination. Invidious discrimination is an engine of oppression, subjugating a disfavored group to enhance or maintain the power of the majority. Remedial race-based preferences reflect the opposite impulse: a desire to foster equality in society. No sensible conception of the Government's constitutional obligation to "govern impartially" should ignore this distinction. * * *

The consistency that the Court espouses would disregard the difference between a "No Trespassing" sign and a welcome mat. It would treat a Dixiecrat Senator's decision to vote against Thurgood Marshall's confirmation in order to keep African Americans off the Supreme Court as on a par with President Johnson's evaluation of his nominee's race as a positive factor. It would equate a law that made black citizens ineligible for military service with a program aimed at recruiting black soldiers. An attempt by the majority to exclude members of a minority race from a regulated market is fundamentally different from a subsidy that enables a relatively small group of newcomers to enter that market. An interest in "consistency" does not justify treating differences as though they were similarities. * * *

III. [The] majority in *Metro Broadcasting* [was] not alone in relying upon a critical distinction between federal and state programs. In his separate opinion in [*Croson*], Justice Scalia discussed the basis for this distinction. He observed that "it is one thing to permit racially based conduct by the Federal Government— whose legislative powers concerning matters of race were explicitly enhanced by the Fourteenth Amendment—and quite another to permit it by the precise entities against whose conduct in matters of race that Amendment was specifically directed." [In] her plurality opinion in *Croson*, Justice O'Connor also emphasized the importance of this distinction when she responded to the City's argument that *Fullilove* was controlling. * * *

Presumably, the majority is now satisfied that its theory of "congruence" between the substantive rights provided by the Fifth and Fourteenth Amendments disposes of the objection based upon divided constitutional powers. But it is one thing to say (as no one seems to dispute) that the Fifth Amendment encompasses a general guarantee of equal protection as broad as that contained within the Fourteenth Amendment. It is another thing entirely to say that Congress' institutional competence and constitutional authority entitles it to no greater deference when it enacts a program designed to foster equality than the deference due a State legislature. * * *

JUSTICE SOUTER, with whom JUSTICE GINSBURG and JUSTICE BREYER join, dissenting.

[I] agree with Justice Stevens' conclusion that stare decisis compels the application of *Fullilove*. Although *Fullilove* did not reflect doctrinal consistency, its several opinions produced a result on shared grounds that petitioner does not attack: that discrimination in the construction industry had been subject to government acquiescence, with effects that remain and that may be addressed by some preferential treatment falling within the congressional power under § 5 of the Fourteenth Amendment. Once *Fullilove* is applied, [the] statutes in question here (which are substantially better tailored to the harm being remedied than the statute endorsed in *Fullilove*) pass muster under Fifth Amendment due process and Fourteenth Amendment equal protection.

The Court today, however, does not reach the application of *Fullilove* to the facts of this case, and on remand it will be incumbent on the Government and petitioner to address anew the facts upon which statutes like these must be judged on the Government's remedial theory of justification: facts about the current effects of past discrimination, the necessity for a preferential remedy, and the suitability of this particular preferential scheme. * * *

In assessing the degree to which today's holding portends a departure from past practice, it is also worth noting that nothing in today's opinion implies any view of Congress's § 5 power and the deference due its exercise that differs from the views expressed in the *Fullilove* plurality. The Court simply notes the observation in *Croson* "that the Court's 'treatment of an exercise of congressional power in *Fullilove* cannot be dispositive here,' because *Croson*'s facts did not implicate Congress' broad power under § 5 of the Fourteenth Amendment," and explains that there is disagreement among today's majority about the extent of the § 5 power. [Thus,] today's decision should leave § 5 exactly where it is as the source of an interest of the national government sufficiently important to satisfy the corresponding requirement of the strict scrutiny test.

[The] Court has long accepted the view that constitutional authority to remedy past discrimination is not limited to the power to forbid its continuation, but extends to eliminating those effects that would otherwise persist and skew the operation of public systems even in the absence of current intent to practice any discrimination. * * *

When the extirpation of lingering discriminatory effects is thought to require a catch-up mechanism, like the racially preferential inducement under the statutes considered here, the result may be that some members of the historically favored race are hurt by that remedial mechanism, however innocent they may be of any personal responsibility for any discriminatory conduct. When this price is considered reasonable, it is in part because it is a price to be paid only temporarily; if the justification for the preference is eliminating the effects of a past practice, the assumption is that the effects will themselves recede into the past, becoming attenuated and finally disappearing. Thus, Justice Powell wrote in his concurring opinion in *Fullilove* that the "temporary nature of this remedy ensures that a race-conscious program will not last longer than the discriminatory effects it is designed to eliminate."

Surely the transition from the *Fullilove* plurality view (in which Justice Powell joined) to today's strict scrutiny (which will presumably be applied as Justice Powell employed it) does not signal a change in the standard by which the burden of a remedial racial preference is to be judged as reasonable or not at any given time. If in the District Court Adarand had chosen to press a challenge to the reasonableness of the burden of these statutes, more than a decade after *Fullilove* had examined such a burden, I doubt that the claim would have fared any differently from the way it will now be treated on remand from this Court.

JUSTICE GINSBURG, with whom JUSTICE BREYER joins, dissenting.

[I] agree with Justice Stevens that, in this area, large deference in owed by the Judiciary to "Congress' institutional competence and constitutional authority to overcome historic racial subjugation." * * *

The statutes and regulations at issue, as the Court indicates, were adopted by the political branches in response to an "unfortunate reality": "[t]he unhappy persistence of both the practice and the lingering effects of racial discrimination against minority groups in this country." The United States suffers from those lingering effects because, for most of our Nation's history, the idea that "we are just one race," (Scalia, J., concurring), was not embraced. For generations, our lawmakers and judges were unprepared to say that there is in this land no superior race, no race inferior to any other. * * *

The divisions in this difficult case should not obscure the Court's recognition of the persistence of racial inequality and a majority's acknowledgment of Congress' authority to act affirmatively, not only to end discrimination, but also to counteract discrimination's lingering effects. Those effects, reflective of a system of racial caste only recently ended, are evident in our workplaces, markets, and neighborhoods. Job applicants with identical resumes, qualifications, and interview styles still experience different receptions, depending on their race. White and African–American consumers still encounter different deals. People of color looking for housing still face discriminatory treatment by landlords, real estate agents, and mortgage lenders. Minority entrepreneurs sometimes fail to gain contracts though they are the low bidders, and they are sometimes refused work even after winning contracts. Bias both conscious and unconscious, reflecting traditional and unexamined habits of thought, keeps up barriers that must come down if equal opportunity and nondiscrimination are ever genuinely to become this country's law and practice.

Given this history and its practical consequences, Congress surely can conclude that a carefully designed affirmative action program may help to realize, finally, the "equal protection of the laws" the Fourteenth Amendment has promised since 1868. * * *

For a classification made to hasten the day when "we are just one race," (Scalia, J., concurring), [the] lead opinion has dispelled the notion that "strict scrutiny" is " 'fatal in fact.' " Properly, a majority of the Court calls for review that is searching, in order to ferret out classifications in reality malign, but masquerading as benign. (lead opinion). The Court's once lax review of sex-based classifications demonstrates the need for such suspicion. * * *

Close review also is in order for this further reason. As Justice Souter points out, and as this very case shows, some members of the historically favored race can be hurt by catch-up mechanisms designed to cope with the lingering effects of entrenched racial subjugation. Court review can ensure that preferences are not so large as to trammel unduly upon the opportunities of others or interfere too harshly with legitimate expectations of persons in once-preferred groups. * * *

While I would not disturb the programs challenged in this case, and would leave their improvement to the political branches, I see today's decision as one that allows our precedent to evolve, still to be informed by and responsive to changing conditions.

Notes and Questions

1. *Congruence.* Should congressionally mandated affirmative action be subject to the same standard of review as affirmative action implemented by state and local governments? O'Connor, J.'s plurality opinion had defended a divergence of standards in *Croson*, as had the majority opinion in *Metro Broadcasting*. Why did O'Connor, J., change her mind—or did she?

2. *Original understanding.* Why did Scalia and Thomas, JJ., who frequently insist upon the central significance of the original understanding of the Constitution's language, pay no apparent heed to the original understanding in this case? Should the original understanding matter? If so, should it also be relevant that *Adarand* arose under the due process clause of the fifth amendment (which contains no explicit "equal protection" clause) rather than the fourteenth amendment?

3. *Applying strict scrutiny.* (a) Which congressional grounds for implementing race-based affirmative action programs would count as "compelling"? Remedying "societal" discrimination is not a "compelling" interest for the states, under *Croson*, but does Congress have a compelling interest in remedying discrimination occurring anywhere within the nation? If so, how specifically must Congress identify the area, or sector of the economy, within which identified discrimination occurs? Are there other compelling national interests—possibly forward-looking interests analogous to the diversity interest deemed compelling in *Bakke*? Would the diversity interest advanced in *Metro Broadcasting* count as "compelling"?

(b) Does the close tailoring requirement apply to federal affirmative action with the same stringency that it applies to affirmative action by state and local governments?

(c) What is the relevance, if any, of Section 5 of the Fourteenth Amendment—which provides that "[t]he Congress shall have the power to enforce, by appropriate legislation, the provisions of this article"—to the constitutional permissibility of congressionally mandated affirmative action? In *Adarand*, O'Connor, J., noted that "[m]embers of this Court have taken different views" about this question, but said that there was no need to address it. Since *Adarand*, the Court has held that the Section 5 power is exclusively a power to prevent or remedy *state action* that violates the Constitution and that federal statutes enacted under Section 5 must be "congruent" and "proportional" to the pattern of unconstitutional action to which they are addressed. See Ch. 11, Sec. 3.

4. *Varieties of affirmative action.* Consider Erwin Chemerinsky, *Making Sense of the Affirmative Action Debate*, 22 Ohio N.U.L.Rev. 1159, 1159–60 (1996): "The major problem with the debate over affirmative action is that it treats affirmative action as if it were one type of government action for a single purpose. [A] meaningful discussion of affirmative action cannot focus on affirmative action as if it is a monolithic concept, but rather must focus on what types of race-based actions are permissible under what circumstances." See also Akhil Reed Amar & Neal Kumar Katyal, *Bakke's Fate*, 43 UCLA L.Rev. 1745, 1779–80 (1996): "There is a proud American tradition of treating education differently from other spheres: Education is different—special—because it teaches Americans how to become full citizens in a heterogeneous, pluralistic scheme of democratic self-government. * * * *Adarand*-like set-asides set us apart, but *Bakke*-like affirmative action [in education] brings Americans together. [This] coming together of Americans to teach and to learn from each other is an inspiring event to behold." Do you agree?

For a comparative perspective on constitutional doctrines involving affirmative action, see Ruth Bader Ginsburg & Deborah Jones Merritt, *Affirmative Action: An International Human Rights Dialogue*, 21 Cardozo L.Rev. 253 (1999).

SECTION 3. DISCRIMINATIONS BASED ON GENDER

I. DEFINING THE LEVEL OF SCRUTINY

Prior to 1971, the Court used the deferential "traditional approach" (see Sec. 1 supra) to test the constitutionality of classifications based on gender. *Muller v. Oregon,* 208 U.S. 412, 28 S.Ct. 324, 52 L.Ed. 551 (1908), per Brewer, J., upheld a law barring factory work by women for more than ten hours a day, reasoning that "as healthy mothers are essential to vigorous offspring, the physical well-being of a woman becomes an object of public interest and care."[a] *Goesaert v. Cleary,* 335 U.S. 464, 69 S.Ct. 198, 93 L.Ed. 163 (1948), per Frankfurter, J., upheld a law denying bartender's licenses to most women, reasoning that "the fact that women may now have achieved the virtues that men have long claimed as their prerogatives and now indulge in vices that men have long practiced, does not preclude the States from drawing a sharp line between the sexes, certainly in such matters as the regulation of the liquor traffic."[b] Finally, *Hoyt v. Florida,* 368 U.S. 57, 82 S.Ct. 159, 7 L.Ed.2d 118 (1961), per Harlan, J., sustained a law placing women on the jury list only if they made special request, stating that "woman is still regarded as the center of home and family life."[c]

The first decision holding sex discrimination violative of equal protection, REED v. REED, 404 U.S. 71, 92 S.Ct. 251, 30 L.Ed.2d 225 (1971), per BURGER, C.J., involved a law preferring males to females when two persons were otherwise equally entitled to be the administrator of an estate: "A classification 'must be reasonable, not arbitrary, and must rest upon some ground of difference having a fair and substantial relation to the object of the [law].' The question" is whether the classification "bears a rational relationship to a state objective that is sought to be advanced by the [law]." It was contended that the law had the reasonable "objective of reducing the workload on probate courts by eliminating one class of contests" and that the legislature might reasonably have "concluded that in general men are better qualified to act as an administrator than are women." But "to give a mandatory preference to members of either sex over members of the other, merely to accomplish the elimination of hearings on the merits, is to make the very kind of arbitrary legislative choice forbidden by [equal protection]."

Invalidates sexual discrimination

a. But see *Adkins v. Children's Hospital,* 261 U.S. 525, 43 S.Ct. 394, 67 L.Ed. 785 (1923) (minimum wage for women violates due process), overruled, *West Coast Hotel Co. v. Parrish,* Ch. 5, Sec. 3.

b. See also the concurring opinion of Bradley, J., joined by Swayne and Field, JJ., in *Bradwell v. Illinois,* 83 U.S. (16 Wall.) 130, 21 L.Ed. 442 (1873), which upheld a statute denying women the right to practice law against challenge based on the privileges or immunities clause: "[T]he natural and proper timidity and delicacy which belongs to the female sex evidently unfits it for many of the occupations of civil life. [The] paramount destiny and mission of woman are to fulfill the noble and benign offices of wife and mother. This is the law of the Creator."

c. *Hoyt* was effectively overruled in *Taylor v. Louisiana,* 419 U.S. 522, 95 S.Ct. 692, 42 L.Ed.2d 690 (1975), holding that a similar statute, operating largely to exclude women from jury service, deprived a criminal defendant of the sixth and fourteenth amendment right to an impartial jury drawn from a fair cross section of the community.

Did *Reed* really involve "rational basis" review, or did the Court in fact apply elevated scrutiny? Consider Catharine A. MacKinnon, *Sexual Harassment of Working Women* 108 (1979): "It would have been considerably more rational, factually based, not arbitrary, and substantially related to the statutory purpose to presume that men would be the better administrators if most women were illiterate and wholly excluded from business affairs. Yet this reasoning would reveal a society in severe need of prohibitions on sex discrimination."

———

Reed was followed by FRONTIERO v. RICHARDSON, 411 U.S. 677, 93 S.Ct. 1764, 36 L.Ed.2d 583 (1973), which invalidated a federal statute permitting males in the armed services an automatic dependency allowance for their wives but requiring servicewomen to prove that their husbands were dependent. BRENNAN, J., joined by Douglas, White, and Marshall, JJ., argued that "classifications based upon sex [are] inherently suspect and must therefore be subjected to close judicial scrutiny." The plurality found "at least implicit support for such an approach in [*Reed's*] departure from 'traditional' rational basis analysis": "[O]ur Nation has had a long and unfortunate history of sex discrimination. Traditionally, such discrimination was rationalized by an attitude of 'romantic paternalism' which, in practical effect, put women not on a pedestal, but in a cage. * * *

"As a result of notions such as these, [statutes] became laden with gross, stereotypical distinctions between the sexes and, indeed, throughout much of the 19th century the position of women in our society was, in many respects, comparable to that of blacks under the pre-Civil War slave codes. Neither slaves nor women could hold office, serve on juries, or bring suit in their own names, and married women traditionally were denied the legal capacity to hold or convey property or to serve as legal guardians of their own children. And although blacks were guaranteed the right to vote in 1870, women were denied even [that] until adoption of the Nineteenth Amendment half a century later.

"It is true, of course, that the position of women in America has improved markedly in recent decades. [But] in part because of the high visibility of the sex characteristic, women still face pervasive, although at times more subtle, discrimination in our educational institutions, on the job market and, perhaps most conspicuously, in the political arena.[17]

"Moreover, since sex, like race and national origin, is an immutable characteristic [the] imposition of special disabilities [would] seem to violate 'the basic concept of our system that legal burdens should bear some relationship to individual responsibility.' And what differentiates sex from such non-suspect statuses as intelligence or physical disability [is] that the sex characteristic frequently bears no relation to ability to perform or contribute to society.

"[The] Government [maintains] that, as an empirical matter, wives in our society frequently are dependent upon their husbands, while husbands rarely are dependent upon their wives. Thus, the Government argues that Congress might reasonably have concluded that it would be both cheaper and easier simply conclusively to presume that wives of male members are financially dependent upon their husbands, while burdening female members with the task of establishing dependency in fact.

---

17. It is true [that] when viewed in the abstract, women do not constitute a small and powerless minority. Nevertheless, in part be- cause of past discrimination, women are vastly underrepresented in this Nation's decision-making councils. * * *

"The Government offers no concrete evidence, however, tending to support its view that such differential treatment in fact saves the Government any money. [And any] statutory scheme which draws a sharp line between the sexes, *solely* [for] administrative convenience [violates equal protection]."

POWELL, J., joined by Burger, C.J., and Blackmun, J., concurring, would rely "on the authority of *Reed* and reserve for the future any expansion of its rationale" because of the "Equal Rights Amendment, which if adopted will resolve [the] question." Stewart, J., concurred, "agreeing that the [statutes] work an invidious discrimination." Rehnquist, J., dissented.

Notes and Questions

1. *Basis for heightened scrutiny.* Should sex-based classifications be treated as "suspect"? If so, on what basis?

(a) *Economic disadvantage.* Women, on average, earn lower incomes than men;[a] own less property; and are more likely to be below the poverty line.[b]

(b) *Historical discrimination and prejudice.* How persuasive is the analogy of historical gender-based discrimination to discrimination based on race? In her brief in *Reed*, Ruth Bader Ginsburg—now a Justice, but then arguing as a lawyer—wrote that being a woman, like being of a minority race, is "an unalterable identifying trait which the dominant culture views as a badge of inferiority justifying disadvantaged treatment in social, legal, economic and political contexts." The brief also quoted Note, *Sex Discrimination and Equal Protection: Do We Need a Constitutional Amendment?*, 84 Harv.L.Rev. 1499, 1507 (1971): "The similarities between race and sex discrimination are indeed striking. Both classifications create large, natural classes, membership in which is beyond the individual's control; both are highly visible characteristics on which legislators have found it easy to draw gross, stereotypical distinctions. Historically, the legal position of black slaves was justified by analogy to the legal status of women. Both slaves and wives were once subject to the all-encompassing paternalistic power of the male head of the house. Arguments justifying different treatment for the sexes on the grounds of female inferiority, need for male protection, and happiness in their assigned roles bear a striking resemblance to the half-truths surrounding the myth of the 'happy slave.' The historical patterns of race and sex discrimination have, in many instances, produced similar present day results."[c]

a. "For full-time year round workers, on average, a woman earned 71.4% of what a male worker earned in 1995 (as opposed to 58.9% in 1977)." Mary Becker, *The Sixties Shift to Formal Equality and the Courts: An Argument for Pragmatism and Politics*, 40 Wm. & Mary L.Rev. 209, 253 (1998). Among other possible explanations, "statistical discrimination" against women may be economically rational if women are less likely than men to be willing to work long hours or to work uninterruptedly for the same firms for long periods of years. See Samuel Issacharoff & Elyse Rosenblum, *Women and the Workplace: Accommodating the Demands of Pregnancy*, 94 Colum.L.Rev. 2154, 2159–71 (1994). On the other hand, it may be economically rational for women to "invest" less in job training and expend less effort in their jobs if they are in professions that "discriminate against women and thus reward their investment less than that of men." Cass

R. Sunstein, *Why Markets Don't Stop Discrimination*, in *Reassessing Civil Rights* 22, 29 (Ellen Frankel Paul et al. eds. 1991). See also Edward J. McCaffrey, *Slouching Towards Equality: Gender Discrimination, Market Efficiency, and Social Change*, 103 Yale L.J. 595 (1993) (arguing for a corrective to achieve the enhanced "social efficiency" that would result if the labor market provided greater incentives for women).

b. In 1997, 20.4 million females, compared with 15.2 million males, were below the poverty line. Bureau of the Census, U.S. Dep't of Com., Ser. P–60, No. 201, *Poverty in the United States: 1997* at 2 (1997). See also Peter B. Edelman, *Toward a Comprehensive Antipoverty Strategy: Getting Beyond the Silver Bullet*, 81 Geo.L.J. 1697 (1993).

c. But cf. Ruth Bader Ginsburg, *Speaking in a Judicial Voice*, 67 N.Y.U.L.Rev. 1185,

Compare Richard A. Wasserstrom, *Racism, Sexism, and Preferential Treatment: An Approach to the Topics*, 24 U.C.L.A.L.Rev. 581, 589–90 (1977): "[T]o be female, as opposed to being black, is not to be conceived of as simply a creature of less worth. That is one important thing that differentiates sexism from racism: The ideology of sex, as opposed to the ideology of race, is a good deal more complex and confusing. Women are both put on a pedestal and deemed not fully developed persons. They are idealized; their approval and admiration is sought; and they are at the same time regarded as less competent than men and less able to live fully developed, fully human lives—for that is what men do." See also Catharine A. MacKinnon, *Reflections on Sex Equality Under Law*, 100 Yale L.J. 1281, 1289, 1298 (1991): "The African American struggle for social equality has been the crucible for equality law in America. [The] inequality of women to men deserves a theory of its own."

(c) *Lack of political power.* As of 1998, women held only 11.5% of the seats in the House of Representatives, 9% of the seats in the Senate, and 21.6% of the positions in state legislatures. See Becker, supra, 40 Wm. & Mary L.Rev. at 253–54. Moreover, historical discrimination against women might be taken to suggest that, within the terms of the *Carolene Products* footnote, p. 298, supra, gender-based prejudice and stereotypes of women constitute "a special condition, which tends seriously to curtail the operation of those political processes ordinarily to be relied upon to protect minorities, and which may call for a correspondingly more searching judicial inquiry." On the other hand, women are a not a minority, but a majority, of the national population.

Consider John H. Ely, *Democracy and Distrust* 166–69 (1980): "The very stereotypes that gave rise to laws 'protecting' women by barring them from various activities are under daily and publicized attack. [Given] such open discussion [the] claim that the numerical majority is being 'dominated' [is] one it has become impossible to maintain except at the most inflated rhetorical level. It also renders the broader argument self-contradictory, since to make such a claim in the context of the current debate one must at least implicitly grant the validity of the stereotype, that women are in effect mental infants who will believe anything men tell them to believe. [But] most laws classifying by sex [probably pre-date women's suffrage]: they should be invalidated. [To] put on the group affected the burden of using its recently unblocked access to get the offending laws repealed would be to place in their path an additional hurdle that the rest of us do not have to contend with in order to protect ourselves—hardly an appropriate response to the realization that they have been unfairly blocked in the past. [If, however] women don't protect themselves from sex discrimination in the future, [it] will be because for one reason or another—substantive disagreement or more likely the assignment of a low priority to the issue—they don't choose to."

Compare Tracy E. Higgins, *Democracy and Feminism*, 110 Harv.L.Rev. 1657, 1668 (1997): "By invoking women's political authority as a justification [for modern laws discriminating on the basis of gender, defenders of such laws] simply

1198–1209 (1992), noting "a reason that distances race discrimination from discrimination based on sex": "Most women are life partners of men; women bear and raise both sons and daughters. Once women's own consciousness was awakened to the unfairness of allocating opportunity and responsibility on the basis of sex, education of others—of fathers, husbands, sons as well as daughters—could begin, or be reinforced, at home. When blacks were confined by law to a separate sector, there was no similar prospect for educating the white majority."

assume[] that, given preexisting preferences, women (like any other interest group within the polity) are free to exercise their power unproblematically through the democratic process. Yet, the preferences of [women] are not independent of [existing distributions of power and opportunities]. The existing power structure contributes to the entrenchment of particular preferences, which in turn influence the democratic process."

(d) *Moral irrelevance.* Does it matter that, for many people, gender would be relevant for many purposes even in an ideal world? That separate men's and women's restrooms convey no inherent message of superiority or inferiority? For a subtle discussion, see Wasserstrom, supra.

2. *Original intent or understanding.* No one suggests that the fourteenth amendment was originally intended or understood to bar gender discrimination. Is this relevant? Dispositive? Was Powell, J., right in thinking that the Court should hesitate to move too quickly while it appeared that the proposed Equal Rights Amendment might resolve the question? This proposed amendment—that "equality of rights under the law shall not be denied or abridged by the United States or by a State on account of sex"—was approved by 35 states (three less than required for ratification) at its expiration in 1982.[d] What are the implications, if any, of the failure of a proposed Equal Rights Amendment to win adoption by the requisite number of states?

CRAIG v. BOREN

429 U.S. 190, 97 S.Ct. 451, 50 L.Ed.2d 397 (1976).

JUSTICE BRENNAN delivered the opinion of the Court.

The interaction of two sections of an Oklahoma statute prohibits the sale of "nonintoxicating" 3.2% beer to males under the age of 21 and to females under the age of 18. The question to be decided is whether such a gender-based differential constitutes a denial to males 18–20 years of age of the equal protection of the laws in violation of the Fourteenth Amendment.

[To] withstand constitutional challenge, previous cases establish that classifications by gender must serve important governmental objectives and must be substantially related to achievement of those objectives. * * * Decisions following *Reed* [have] rejected administrative ease and convenience as sufficiently important objectives to justify gender-based classifications. * * *[6]

Reed has also provided the underpinning for decisions that have invalidated statutes employing gender as an inaccurate proxy for other, more germane bases of classification. Hence, "archaic and overbroad" generalizations concerning the financial position of servicewomen, *Frontiero,* and working women, *Wiesenfeld* [Part III infra], could not justify use of a gender line in determining eligibility for certain governmental entitlements. Similarly increasingly outdated misconceptions concerning the role of females in the home rather than in the 'marketplace and world of ideas' were rejected as loose-fitting characterizations incapable of

---

d. See generally Barbara A. Brown, Thomas I. Emerson, Gail Falk, & Ann E. Freedman, *The Equal Rights Amendment: A Constitutional Basis for Equal Rights for Women,* 80 Yale L.J. 871 (1971).

6. *Kahn v. Shevin,* [Part III infra], and *Schlesinger v. Ballard,* [Part III infra], upholding the use of gender-based classifications, rested upon the Court's perception of the lau-

datory purposes of those laws as remedying disadvantageous conditions suffered by women in economic and military life. Needless to say, Oklahoma does not suggest that the age-sex differential was enacted to ensure the availability of 3.2% beer for women as compensation for previous deprivations.

supporting state statutory schemes that were premised upon their accuracy. *Stanton.* In light of the weak congruence between gender and the characteristic or trait that gender purported to represent, it was necessary that the legislatures choose either to realign their substantive laws in a gender-neutral fashion, or to adopt procedures for identifying those instances where the sex-centered generalization actually comported to fact.

[We] turn then to the question whether, under *Reed,* the difference between males and females with respect to the purchase of 3.2% beer warrants the differential in age drawn by the Oklahoma statute. * * *

We accept for purposes of discussion the District Court's identification of the objective underlying [the challenged statute] as the enhancement of traffic safety. [The] appellees introduced a variety of statistical surveys [to support the statute, but the] most focused and relevant of the statistical surveys, arrests of 18–20–year-olds for alcohol-related driving offenses, exemplifies the ultimate unpersuasiveness of this evidentiary record. Viewed in terms of the correlation between sex and the actual activity that Oklahoma seeks to regulate—driving while under the influence of alcohol—the statistics broadly establish that .18% of females and 2% of males in that age group were arrested for that offense. While such a disparity is not trivial in a statistical sense, it hardly can form the basis for employment of a gender line as a classifying device. Certainly if maleness is to serve as a proxy for drinking and driving, a correlation of 2% must be considered an unduly tenuous "fit." [Indeed,] prior cases have consistently rejected the use of sex as a decision-making factor even though the statutes in question certainly rested on far more predictive empirical relationships than this.

Moreover, the statistics exhibit a variety of other shortcomings that seriously impugn their value to equal protection analysis. * * *[14] None [of the surveys] purports to measure the use and dangerousness of 3.2% beer as opposed to alcohol generally, a detail that is of particular importance since, in light of its low alcohol level, Oklahoma apparently considers the 3.2% beverage to be "nonintoxicating."

[W]hen it is further recognized that Oklahoma's statute prohibits only the selling of 3.2% beer to young males and not their drinking the beverage once acquired (even after purchase by their 18–20–year-old female companions), the relationship between gender and traffic safety becomes far too tenuous to satisfy *Reed's* requirement that the gender-based difference be substantially related to achievement of the statutory objective. * * *

JUSTICE POWELL concurring.

I join the opinion of the Court as I am in general agreement with it. I do have reservations as to some of the discussion concerning the appropriate standard for equal protection analysis and the relevance of the statistical evidence. * * *

With respect to the equal protection standard, I agree that *Reed* is the most relevant precedent. But I find it unnecessary, in deciding this case, to read that decision as broadly as some of the Court's language may imply. *Reed* and subsequent cases involving gender-based classifications make clear that the Court subjects such classifications to a more critical examination than is normally applied when "fundamental" constitutional rights and "suspect classes" are not present.

---

14. The very social stereotypes that find reflection in age-differential laws are likely substantially to distort the accuracy of these comparative statistics. Hence, "reckless" young men who drink and drive are transformed into arrest statistics, whereas their female counterparts are chivalrously escorted home. * * *

I view this as a relatively easy case. [T]his gender-based classification does not bear a fair and substantial relation to the object of the legislation. * * *

JUSTICE STEVENS concurring.

I am inclined to believe that what has become known as the two-tiered analysis of equal protection claims [is] a method the Court has employed to explain decisions that actually apply a single standard in a reasonably consistent fashion. * * *

In this case, the classification [is] objectionable because it is based on an accident of birth, because it is a mere remnant of the now almost universally rejected tradition of discriminating against males in this age bracket, and because, to the extent it reflects any physical difference between males and females, it is actually perverse.[4] * * *

The classification is not totally irrational. For the evidence does indicate that there are more males than females in this age bracket who drive and also more who drink. Nevertheless, [i]t is difficult to believe that the statute was actually intended to cope with the problem of traffic safety, since it has only a minimal effect on access to a not-very-intoxicating beverage and does not prohibit its consumption. [But] even assuming some such slight benefit, it does not seem to me that an insult to all of the young men of the State can be justified by visiting the sins of the 2% on the 98%.

JUSTICE REHNQUIST, [with whom CHIEF JUSTICE BURGER was "in general agreement"] dissenting.

The Court's disposition of this case is objectionable on two grounds. First is its conclusion that *men* challenging a gender-based statute which treats them less favorably than women may invoke a more stringent standard of judicial review than pertains to most other types of classifications. Second is the Court's enunciation of this standard, without citation to any source, as being that "classifications by gender must serve *important* governmental objectives and must be *substantially* related to achievement of those objectives." The only redeeming feature of the Court's opinion, to my mind, is that it apparently signals a retreat by those who joined the plurality opinion in *Frontiero* from their view that sex is a "suspect" classification for purposes of equal protection analysis. I think the Oklahoma statute challenged here need pass only the "rational basis" equal protection analysis expounded in [prior cases].

[T]here being no plausible argument that this is a discrimination against females,[2] the Court's reliance on our previous sex-discrimination cases is ill-founded. It treats gender classification as a talisman which—without regard to the rights involved or the persons affected—calls into effect a heavier burden of judicial review.

The Court's [standard of review] apparently comes out of thin air. The Equal Protection Clause contains no such language, and none of our previous cases

---

4. Because males are generally heavier than females, they have a greater capacity to consume alcohol without impairing their driving ability than do females.

2. I am not unaware of the argument from time to time advanced, that all discriminations between the sexes ultimately redound to the detriment of females, because they tend to reinforce "old notions" restricting the roles and opportunities of women. As a general prop-

osition applying equally to all sex categorizations, I believe that this argument was implicitly found to carry little weight in [several decisions upholding classifications designed to compensate women for actual or presumed employment and economic disadvantages]. Seeing no assertion that it has special applicability to the situation at hand, I believe it can be dismissed as an insubstantial consideration.

adopt that standard. I would think we have had enough difficulty with the two standards of review which our cases have recognized—the norm of "rational basis," and the "compelling state interest" required where a "suspect classification" is involved—so as to counsel weightily against the insertion of still another "standard" between those two. How is this Court to divine what objectives are important? How is it to determine whether a particular law is "substantially" related to the achievement of such objective, rather than related in some other way to its achievement?

[Under the] applicable rational-basis test [the] evidence suggests clear differences between the drinking and driving habits of young men and women. Those differences are grounds enough for the State reasonably to conclude that young males pose by far the greater drunk-driving hazard, both in terms of sheer numbers and in terms of hazard on a per-driver basis. The gender-based difference in treatment in this case is therefore not irrational.

Notes and Questions

1. *Level of scrutiny.* Is the intermediate level of equal protection scrutiny applied in *Craig* soundly justified? If so, on what basis?

2. *Protection of men.* Is there any reason why statutes discriminating against *men* should be subject to heightened equal protection scrutiny? Is it plausible to think that both men and women are semi-suspect classes? Tribe 2d ed., at 1564–65: "It is no surprise that many of [the leading] sex discrimination cases were brought by male plaintiffs, since legislative assumptions about traditional sex roles often impinge on the rights of both men and women [by impliedly derogating the capacity of women to function effectively outside the home]. [In defending gender-based classifications,] the government's almost uniform argument [has] emphasized the [benefits achieved by reliance on] the accurate and therefore 'rational' assumption of traditional male and female inclinations and capacities. The Supreme Court's thoughtful response [has] recognized the argument's essence as self-fulfilling prophecy: The 'accuracy' of government's assumption is derived in some significant degree from the chill on sex-role experimentation and change generated by the classifications themselves."[a]

3. *Application in Craig.* Did *Craig* rest on the conclusion that the challenged law was unlikely to save any lives through a reduction in traffic accidents attributable to drinking by 18–21–year-old males? That it was unlikely to save enough lives to be constitutionally tolerable?

Or was the point that the state, in order to be able to restrict the sale of 3.2% beer to young men, must also prohibit sales to women of the same age? Should the state, in order to achieve important ends (such as saving lives by improving highway safety), be required to impose restrictions that it regards as unnecessary (as well as those it thinks vital)? What theory (or theories) of the equal protection clause would support such a view?

---

a. On gender roles, see also Dale Spender, *Man Made Language* (2d ed. 1985); Christine A. Littleton, *Reconstructing Sexual Equality,* 75 Calif.L.Rev. 1279 (1987); Frances E. Olsen, *The Family and the Market: A Study of Ideolo-* *gy and Legal Reform,* 96 Harv.L.Rev. 1497 (1983); Catharine MacKinnon, *Feminism, Marxism, Method, and the State: Toward Feminist Jurisprudence,* 8 Signs 635 (1983).

UNITED STATES v. VIRGINIA

518 U.S. 515, 116 S.Ct. 2264, 135 L.Ed.2d 735 (1996).

JUSTICE GINSBURG delivered the opinion of the Court.

Virginia's public institutions of higher learning include an incomparable military college, Virginia Military Institute (VMI). The United States maintains that the Constitution's equal protection guarantee precludes Virginia from reserving exclusively to men the unique educational opportunities VMI affords. We agree.

Founded in 1839, VMI is today the sole single-sex school among Virginia's 15 public institutions of higher learning. VMI's distinctive mission is to produce "citizen-soldiers." [Assigning] prime place to character development, VMI uses an "adversative method" modeled on English public schools and once characteristic of military instruction. [This model] features "physical rigor, mental stress, absolute equality of treatment, absence of privacy, minute regulation of behavior, and indoctrination in desirable values." [VMI] cadets live in spartan barracks where surveillance is constant and privacy nonexistent. [Entering] students are incessantly exposed to the rat line, "an extreme form of the adversative model," [which] bonds new cadets to their fellow sufferers and, when they have completed the 7–month experience, to their former tormentors.

In 1990, prompted by a complaint filed with the Attorney General by a female high-school student seeking admission to VMI, the United States sued the Commonwealth of Virginia and VMI, alleging that VMI's exclusively male admission policy violated the Equal Protection Clause of the Fourteenth Amendment. [The district court upheld the policy, but the court of appeals reversed, finding an equal protection violation. Following the remand, the state of Virginia proposed a remedial plan, under which the state would adopt] a parallel program for women: Virginia Women's Institute for Leadership (VWIL). The 4–year, state-sponsored undergraduate program would be located at Mary Baldwin College, a private liberal arts school for women, and would be open, initially, to about 25 to 30 students. Although VWIL would share VMI's mission—to produce "citizen-soldiers"—the VWIL program would differ, as does Mary Baldwin College, from VMI in academic offerings, methods of education, and financial resources.

The average combined SAT score of entrants at Mary Baldwin is about 100 points lower than the score for VMI freshmen. [While] VMI offers degrees in liberal arts, the sciences, and engineering, Mary Baldwin, at the time of trial, offered only bachelor of arts degrees. [Under the proposed remedial plan,] VWIL students would participate in ROTC programs [but in] lieu of VMI's adversative method, [VWIL would offer] "a cooperative method which reinforces self-esteem."

Virginia represented that it will provide equal financial support for in-state VWIL students and VMI cadets, and the VMI Foundation agreed to supply a $5.4625 million endowment for the VWIL program. Mary Baldwin's own endowment is about $19 million; VMI's is $131 million. Mary Baldwin will add $35 million to its endowment based on future commitments; VMI will add $220 million. [Both the district court and the court of appeals held that the proposed remedial plan satisfied the Equal Protection Clause.]

The cross-petitions in this case present two ultimate issues. First, does Virginia's exclusion of women from the educational opportunities provided by VMI—extraordinary opportunities for military training and civilian leadership development—deny to women "capable of all of the individual activities required of VMI cadets," the equal protection of the laws guaranteed by the Fourteenth Amendment? Second, if VMI's "unique" situation—as Virginia's sole single-sex public institution of higher education—offends the Constitution's equal protection principle, what is the remedial requirement?

We note, once again, the core instruction of this Court's pathmarking decisions in *J.E.B. v. Alabama ex rel. T.B.*, [Part II infra], and *Mississippi Univ. for Women*, [Part III infra]: Parties who seek to defend gender-based government action must demonstrate an "exceedingly persuasive justification" for that action. [The] burden of justification is demanding and it rests entirely on the State. The State must show "at least that the [challenged] classification serves 'important governmental objectives and that the discriminatory means employed' are 'substantially related to the achievement of those objectives.' " The justification must be genuine, not hypothesized or invented post hoc in response to litigation. And it must not rely on overbroad generalizations about the different talents, capacities, or preferences of males and females.

The heightened review standard our precedent establishes does not make sex a proscribed classification. Supposed "inherent differences" are no longer accepted as a ground for race or national origin classifications. See *Loving v. Virginia*. Physical differences between men and women, however, are enduring. [Sex] classifications may be used to compensate women "for particular economic disabilities [they have] suffered," *Califano v. Webster*, [Part III infra], to "promote equal employment opportunity," see *California Federal Sav. & Loan Assn. v. Guerra*, [Part III infra], [and] to advance full development of the talent and capacities of our Nation's people.[7] But such classifications may not be used, as they once were, to create or perpetuate the legal, social, and economic inferiority of women. [Measuring] the record in this case against the review standard just described, we conclude that Virginia has shown no "exceedingly persuasive justification" for excluding all women from the citizen-soldier training afforded by VMI.

[Single-sex] education affords pedagogical benefits to at least some students, Virginia emphasizes, and that reality is uncontested in this litigation. Similarly, it is not disputed that diversity among public educational institutions can serve the public good. But Virginia has not shown that VMI was established, or has been maintained, with a view to diversifying, by its categorical exclusion of women, educational opportunities within the State. In cases of this genre, our precedent instructs that "benign" justifications proffered in defense of categorical exclusions will not be accepted automatically; a tenable justification must describe actual state purposes, not rationalizations for actions in fact differently grounded.

[Neither] recent nor distant history bears out Virginia's alleged pursuit of diversity through single-sex educational options. In 1839, when the State established VMI, a range of educational opportunities for men and women was scarcely contemplated. [In] admitting no women, VMI followed the lead of [the] University of Virginia, founded in 1819. [Beginning in 1894,] Virginia eventually provided for several women's seminaries and colleges. [By] the mid–1970's, [however,] all [had]

---

7. Several amici have urged that diversity in educational opportunities is an altogether appropriate governmental pursuit and that single-sex schools can contribute importantly to such diversity. Indeed, it is the mission of some single-sex schools "to dissipate, rather than perpetuate, traditional gender classifications." We do not question the State's prerogative evenhandedly to support diverse educational opportunities. We address specifically and only an educational opportunity recognized by the District Court and the Court of Appeals as "unique," an opportunity available only at Virginia's premier military institute, the State's sole single-sex public university or college.

become coeducational. [The] University of Virginia introduced coeducation [in 1970] and, in 1972, began to admit women on an equal basis with men.

Virginia describes the current absence of public single-sex higher education for women as "an historical anomaly." But the historical record indicates action more deliberate than anomalous: First, protection of women against higher education; next, schools for women far from equal in resources and stature to schools for men; finally, conversion of the separate schools to coeducation. [In] sum, we find no persuasive evidence in this record that VMI's male-only admission policy "is in furtherance of a state policy of 'diversity.' "

[Virginia] next argues that VMI's adversative method of training provides educational benefits that cannot be made available, unmodified, to women. Alterations to accommodate women would necessarily be "radical," so "drastic," Virginia asserts, as to transform, indeed "destroy," VMI's program. [The] District Court [found] that coeducation would materially affect "at least these three aspects of VMI's program—physical training, the absence of privacy, and the adversative approach." And it is uncontested that women's admission would require accommodations, primarily in arranging housing assignments and physical training programs for female cadets. It is also undisputed, however, that "the VMI methodology could be used to educate women."

The notion that admission of women would downgrade VMI's stature, destroy the adversative system and, with it, even the school, is a judgment hardly proved, a prediction hardly different from other "self-fulfilling prophecies" once routinely used to deny rights or opportunities. [Women's] successful entry into the federal military academies, and their participation in the Nation's military forces, indicate that Virginia's fears for the future of VMI may not be solidly grounded. [Virginia], in sum, "has fallen far short of establishing the 'exceedingly persuasive justification' " that must be the solid base for any gender-defined classification.

In the second phase of the litigation, Virginia presented its remedial plan— maintain VMI as a male-only college and create VWIL as a separate program for women. [Having] violated the Constitution's equal protection requirement, Virginia was obliged to show that its remedial proposal "directly addressed and related to" the violation, i.e., the equal protection denied to women ready, willing, and able to benefit from educational opportunities of the kind VMI offers. Virginia described VWIL as a "parallel program," and asserted that VWIL shares VMI's mission of producing "citizen-soldiers" and VMI's goals of providing "education, military training, mental and physical discipline, character [and] leadership development." [But] VWIL affords women no opportunity to experience the rigorous military training for which VMI is famed. Instead, the VWIL program "deemphasizes" military education, and uses a "cooperative method" of education "which reinforces self-esteem."

[Virginia] maintains that these methodological differences are "justified pedagogically," based on "important differences between men and women in learning and developmental needs," "psychological and sociological differences" Virginia describes as "real" and "not stereotypes." [As] earlier stated, [however], generalizations about "the way women are," estimates of what is appropriate for most women, no longer justify denying opportunity to women whose talent and capacity place them outside the average description. "[S]ome women, at least, would want to attend [VMI] if they had the opportunity"; "some women are capable of all of the individual activities required of VMI cadets" and "can meet the physical standards [VMI] now imposes on men". It is [for] these women [that] a remedy must be crafted.[19]

[In] myriad respects other than military training, VWIL does not qualify as VMI's equal. VWIL's student body, faculty, course offerings, and facilities hardly match VMI's. Nor can the VWIL graduate anticipate the benefits associated with VMI's 157–year history, the school's prestige, and its influential alumni network.

[Virginia's] VWIL solution is reminiscent of the remedy Texas proposed 50 years ago, in response to a state trial court's 1946 ruling that, given the equal protection guarantee, African Americans could not be denied a legal education at a state facility. See *Sweatt v. Painter,* [Sec. 2, II supra]. Reluctant to admit African Americans to its flagship University of Texas Law School, the State set up a separate school for Herman Sweatt and other black law students. [This] Court contrasted resources at the new school with those at the school from which Sweatt had been excluded [and held that] the Equal Protection Clause required Texas to admit African Americans to the University of Texas Law School. In line with *Sweatt,* we rule here that Virginia has not shown substantial equality in the separate educational opportunities the State supports at VWIL and VMI. * * *

JUSTICE THOMAS took no part in the consideration or decision of this case.

CHIEF JUSTICE REHNQUIST, concurring in the judgement.

Two decades ago in *Craig v. Boren,* we announced that "to withstand constitutional challenge, * * * classifications by gender must serve important governmental objectives and must be substantially related to achievement of those objectives." [While] the majority adheres to this test today, it also says that the State must demonstrate an " 'exceedingly persuasive justification' " to support a gender-based classification. [To] avoid introducing potential confusion, I would have adhered more closely to our traditional [standard].

[I] agree with the Court that there is scant evidence in the record that [diversity] was the real reason that Virginia decided to maintain VMI as men only. [Even] if diversity in educational opportunity were the State's actual objective, [however,] the State's position would still be problematic. The difficulty [is] that the diversity benefited only one sex.

[Virginia] offers a second justification for the single-sex admissions policy: maintenance of the adversative method. [But a] State does not have substantial interest in the adversative methodology unless it is pedagogically beneficial. While considerable evidence shows that a single-sex education is pedagogically beneficial for some students, and hence a State may have a valid interest in promoting that methodology, there is no similar evidence in the record that an adversative method is pedagogically beneficial or is any more likely to produce character traits than other methodologies.

The Court defines the constitutional violation in this case as "the categorical exclusion of women from an extraordinary educational opportunity afforded to men." By defining the violation in this way, [the] Court necessarily implies that the only adequate remedy would be the admission of women to the all-male institution. [I] would not define the violation in this way; it is not the "exclusion of women" that violates the Equal Protection Clause, but the maintenance of an

---

19. Admitting women to VMI would undoubtedly require alterations necessary to afford members of each sex privacy from the other sex in living arrangements, and to adjust aspects of the physical training programs. Experience [at the United States military academies] shows such adjustments are manageable.

all-men school without providing any—much less a comparable—institution for women. * * *

Justice Scalia, dissenting.

* * * Much of the Court's opinion is devoted to deprecating the closed-mindedness of our forebears with regard to women's education, and even with regard to the treatment of women in areas that have nothing to do with education. Closed-minded they were—as every age is, including our own, with regard to matters it cannot guess, because it simply does not consider them debatable. The virtue of a democratic system with a First Amendment is that it readily enables the people, over time, to be persuaded that what they took for granted is not so, and to change their laws accordingly. That system is destroyed if the smug assurances of each age are removed from the democratic process and written into the Constitution. So to counterbalance the Court's criticism of our ancestors, let me say a word in their praise: they left us free to change. The same cannot be said of this most illiberal Court, which has embarked on a course of inscribing one after another of the current preferences of the society (and in some cases only the counter-majoritarian preferences of the society's law-trained elite) into our Basic Law. Today it enshrines the notion that no substantial educational value is to be served by an all-men's military academy—so that the decision by the people of Virginia to maintain such an institution denies equal protection to women who cannot attend that institution but can attend others.

[In] my view the function of this Court is to preserve our society's values regarding (among other things) equal protection, not to revise them. [Whatever] abstract tests we may choose to devise, they cannot supersede—and indeed ought to be crafted so as to reflect—those constant and unbroken national traditions that embody the people's understanding of ambiguous constitutional texts. More specifically, it is my view that "when a practice not expressly prohibited by the text of the Bill of Rights bears the endorsement of a long tradition of open, widespread, and unchallenged use that dates back to the beginning of the Republic, we have no proper basis for striking it down."

The all-male constitution of VMI comes squarely within such a governing tradition. For almost all of VMI's more than a century and a half of existence, its single-sex status reflected the uniform practice for government-supported military colleges.

[To] reject the Court's disposition today, however, it is [only] necessary to apply honestly the test the Court has been applying to sex-based classifications for the past two decades. [Only] the amorphous "exceedingly persuasive justification" phrase, and not the standard elaboration of intermediate scrutiny, can be made to yield [the] conclusion that VMI's single-sex composition is unconstitutional because there exist several women (or, one would have to conclude under the Court's reasoning, a single woman) willing and able to undertake VMI's program. Intermediate scrutiny has never required a least-restrictive-means analysis, but only a "substantial relation" between the classification and the state interests that it serves.

[It] is beyond question that Virginia has an important state interest in providing effective college education for its citizens. That single-sex instruction is an approach substantially related to that interest should be evident enough from the long and continuing history in this country of men's and women's colleges. But beyond that, [there was] "virtually uncontradicted" [expert evidence introduced in this case tending to show the benefits of single-sex education].

[Besides] its single-sex constitution, VMI [employs] a "distinctive educational method," sometimes referred to as the "adversative, or doubting, model of education." [It] was uncontested that "if the state were to establish a women's VMI-type [i.e., adversative] program, the program would attract an insufficient number of participants to make the program work"; and it was found by the District Court that if Virginia were to include women in VMI, the school "would eventually find it necessary to drop the adversative system altogether." Thus, Virginia's options were an adversative method that excludes women or no adversative method at all.

There can be no serious dispute that single-sex education and a distinctive educational method "represent legitimate contributions to diversity in the Virginia higher education system." As a theoretical matter, Virginia's educational interest would have been best served (insofar as the two factors we have mentioned are concerned) by six different types of public colleges—an all-men's, an all-women's, and a coeducational college run in the "adversative method," and an all-men's, an all-women's, and a coeducational college run in the "traditional method." But as a practical matter, of course, Virginia's financial resources, like any State's, are not limitless, and the Commonwealth must select among the available options. [In] these circumstances, Virginia's election to fund one public all-male institution and one on the adversative model—and to concentrate its resources in a single entity that serves both these interests in diversity—is substantially related to the State's important educational interests.

[The] Court argues that VMI would not have to change very much if it were to admit women. The principal response to that argument is that it is irrelevant: If VMI's single-sex status is substantially related to the government's important educational objectives, as I have demonstrated above and as the Court refuses to discuss, that concludes the inquiry. [But] if such a debate were relevant, the Court would certainly be on the losing side.

[Finally], the absence of a precise "all-women's analogue" to VMI is irrelevant. [VWIL] was carefully designed by professional educators who have long experience in educating young women. [None] of the United States' own experts in the remedial phase of this case was willing to testify that VMI's adversative method was an appropriate methodology for educating women.

[The] Court's decision today will have consequences that extend far beyond the parties to the case. [Under] the constitutional principles announced and applied today, single-sex public education is unconstitutional. [Although] the Court [purports] to have said nothing of relevance to other public schools [and to have considered] only an educational opportunity recognized [as] "unique," [footnote 7, supra], I suggest that the single-sex program that will not be capable of being characterized as "unique" is not only unique but nonexistent.

[A broader] potential of today's decision for widespread disruption of existing institutions lies in its application to private single-sex education. Government support is immensely important to private educational institutions. [When government funding is challenged, the] issue will be not whether government assistance turns private colleges into state actors, but whether the government itself would be violating the Constitution by providing state support to single-sex colleges. For example, in *Norwood v. Harrison*, [Ch. 10, Sec. 3 infra], we saw no room to distinguish between state operation of racially segregated schools and state support of privately run segregated schools. [The] only hope for state-assisted single-sex private schools is that the Court will not apply in the future the principles of law it has applied today. * * *

Notes and Questions

1. *Requirement of an "exceedingly persuasive justification."* Did Ginsburg, J.'s opinion alter the test applicable to gender-based classifications? Compare Cass R. Sunstein, *Leaving Things Undecided*, 110 Harv.L.Rev. 4, 75 (1996) ("[T]he Court did not merely restate the intermediate scrutiny test but pressed it closer to strict scrutiny."), with Denise C. Morgan, *Anti-Subordination Analysis After United States v. Virginia: Evaluating the Constitutionality of K–12 Single–Sex Public Schools*, 1999 U.Chi. Legal F. 381 (1999) ("[T]he 'exceedingly persuasive justification' language in *Virginia* does not indicate a shift from intermediate to strict scrutiny of sex-based classifications.").

2. *Means and ends.* Did the Court invalidate the scheme involved in *VMI* because the state's articulated ends were not "important" enough or because its means—gender classification—were not related closely enough to those ends? For both reasons? Deborah Hellman, *Two Types of Discrimination: The Familiar and the Forgotten*, 86 Calif.L.Rev. 315 (1998), distinguishes between "proxy" discrimination, in which a classifying trait is used as a means to achieve some other end, and "non-proxy" discrimination, in which the state views the advantaging (or disadvantaging) of one group as an end in itself. According to Professor Hellman, *VMI* involved "non-proxy" discrimination for which the Court's analytical framework is ill-suited. Compare Mary Anne Case, *Two Cheers for Cheerleading: The Noisy Integration of VMI and the Quiet Success of Virginia Women in Leadership*, 1999 U.Chi.L. Forum 347, 358–59: "What really mattered to VMI was [its] cult of masculinity. [This] makes *United States v. Virginia* [like] the many race cases from *Plessy v. Ferguson* through *Brown* and *Loving*." Do you agree?

II. DIFFERENCES—REAL AND IMAGINED

Whatever standard of scrutiny applies, the Court has consistently assumed that differences between men and women sometimes justify different treatment. But a recurrent problem has been to distinguish "real" differences and permissible distinctions based upon them from impermissible reliance on and reinforcement of gender-based stereotypes. As you read the cases in this section, consider how consistent and successful the Court's efforts have been, and how much the Court has been aided—if at all—by the doctrinal tests that it has purported to apply.

GEDULDIG v. AIELLO, 417 U.S. 484, 94 S.Ct. 2485, 41 L.Ed.2d 256 (1974), per STEWART, J., held that exclusion of "disability that accompanies normal pregnancy and childbirth" from California's disability insurance system "does not exclude [anyone] because of gender * * *. While it is true that only women can become pregnant, it does not follow that every legislative classification concerning pregnancy is [sex-based]. Absent a showing that distinctions involving pregnancy are mere pretexts designed to effect an invidious discrimination against the members of one sex or the other, lawmakers are constitutionally free to include or exclude pregnancy from the coverage of legislation such as this on any reasonable basis, just as with respect to any other physical condition. [The] program divides potential recipients into two groups—pregnant women and nonpregnant persons. While the first group is exclusively female, the second includes members of both sexes. The fiscal and actuarial benefits of the program thus accrue to members of both sexes. [There] is no risk from which men are protected and women are not. Likewise, there is no risk from which women are protected and men are not.[21]"

BRENNAN, J., joined by Douglas and Marshall, JJ., dissented, finding "sex discrimination" in the state's "singling out for less favorable treatment a gender-linked disability peculiar to women [while] men receive full compensation for all disabilities suffered, including those that affect only or primarily their sex, such as prostatectomies, circumcision, hemophilia and gout."[a]

DOTHARD v. RAWLINSON, 433 U.S. 321, 97 S.Ct. 2720, 53 L.Ed.2d 786 (1977), per STEWART, J., upheld the exclusion of women prison guards from duty in "contact positions" in all-male prisons: "In this environment of violence and disorganization, it would be an oversimplification to characterize [the exclusion of women] as an exercise in 'romantic paternalism.' [A] woman's relative ability to maintain order in a male, maximum-security, unclassified penitentiary could [be] directly reduced by her womanhood. There is a basis in fact for expecting that sex offenders who have criminally assaulted women in the past would be moved to do so again if access to women were established within the prison. There would also be a real risk that other inmates, deprived of a normal heterosexual environment, would assault women guards because they were women."[b]

MICHAEL M. v. SUPERIOR COURT, 450 U.S. 464, 101 S.Ct. 1200, 67 L.Ed.2d 437 (1981), upheld a "statutory rape" law that punished the male, but not the female, party to intercourse when the female was under 18 and not the male's wife. REHNQUIST, J., joined by Burger, C.J., and Stewart and Powell, JJ., observed that "the traditional minimum rationality test takes on a somewhat 'sharper focus' when gender-based classifications are challenged. See *Craig* (Powell, J., concurring). [But] this Court has consistently upheld statutes where the gender classification is not invidious, but rather realistically reflects the fact that the sexes are not similarly situated in certain circumstances. * * *

"We are satisfied not only that the prevention of illegitimate [teenage] pregnancy is at least one of the 'purposes' of the statute, but that the State has a strong interest in preventing such pregnancy.[7]

"Because virtually all of the significant harmful and inescapably identifiable consequences of teenage pregnancy fall on the young female, a legislature acts well within its authority when it elects to punish only the participant who, by

---

21. Indeed, the [data indicated] that both the annual claim rate and the annual claim cost are greater for women than for [men.]

a. Cf. *Cleveland Bd. of Educ. v. LaFleur,* 414 U.S. 632, 94 S.Ct. 791, 39 L.Ed.2d 52 (1974) (invalidating a requirement that pregnant teachers go on leave on the ground that an "irrebuttable presumption" of inability to teach during pregnancy violated due process).

b. For criticism, see Christine A. Littleton, *Equality and Feminist Legal Theory,* 48 U.Pitt.L.Rev. 1043, 1049–50 (1987).

7. Although petitioner concedes that the State has a "compelling" interest in prevent-

ing teenage pregnancy, he contends that the "true" purpose [is] to protect the virtue and chastity of young women. As such, the statute is unjustifiable because it rests on archaic stereotypes. [Even] if the preservation of female chastity were one of the motives of the statute, and even if that motive be impermissible, petitioner's argument must fail because "[this] court will not strike down an otherwise constitutional statute on the basis of an alleged illicit legislative motive." *United States v. O'Brien,* [Ch. 7, Sec. 2].

nature, suffers few of the consequences of his conduct. It is hardly unreasonable for a legislature acting to protect minor females to exclude them from punishment. Moreover, the risk of pregnancy itself constitutes a substantial deterrence to young females. [A] criminal sanction imposed solely on males thus serves to roughly 'equalize' the deterrents on the sexes.

"[The] State persuasively contends that a gender-neutral statute would frustrate its interest in effective enforcement. Its view is that a female is surely less likely to report violations of the statute if she herself would be subject to criminal prosecution. In an area already fraught with prosecutorial difficulties, we decline to hold that the Equal Protection Clause requires a legislature to enact a statute so broad that it may well be incapable of enforcement."

BLACKMUN, J., concurred: "I [cannot] vote to strike down the California statutory rape law, for I think it is a sufficiently reasoned and constitutional effort to control the problem at its inception. [I] am persuaded that, although a minor has substantial privacy rights in intimate affairs connected with procreation, California's [efforts] to prevent teenage pregnancy are to be viewed differently from efforts to inhibit a woman from dealing with pregnancy once it has become an inevitability. * * *

"I think [it] is only fair, with respect to this particular petitioner, to point out that his partner, Sharon, appears not to have been an unwilling participant in at least the initial stages of the intimacies that took place the night of June 3, 1978.* Petitioner's and Sharon's nonacquaintance with each other before the incident; their drinking; their withdrawal from the others of the group; their foreplay, in which she willingly participated and seems to have encouraged; and the closeness of their ages (a difference of only one year and 18 days) are factors that should make this case an unattractive one to prosecute at all, and especially to prosecute as a felony, rather than as a misdemeanor. But the State has chosen to prosecute in that manner, and the facts, I reluctantly conclude, may fit the crime."[a]

BRENNAN, J., joined by White and Marshall, JJ., dissented: "None of the three opinions upholding the California statute fairly applies the equal protection

---

* Sharon at the preliminary hearing testified as follows: * * *

"We were drinking at the railroad tracks and we walked over to this bush and he started kissing me and stuff, and I was kissing him back, too, at first. Then, I was telling him to stop * * *.

"[T]hen he asked me if I wanted to walk him over to the park; so we walked over to the park and we sat down on a bench and then he started kissing me again and we were laying on the bench. And he told me to take my pants off.

"I said, 'No,' and I was trying to get up and he hit me back down on the bench and then I just said to myself, 'Forget it,' and I let him do what he wanted to do. * * *

"Q. Did you have sexual intercourse with the defendant?

"A. Yeah. * * *

"Q. You said that he hit you?

"A. Yeah.

"Q. How did he hit you?

"A. He slugged me in the face.

"[The Court]: Did he hit you one time or did he hit you more than once?

"The Witness: He hit me about two or three times. * * *"

a. Stewart, J., also concurred, noting "that the statutory discrimination, when viewed as part of the wider scheme of California law, is not as clearcut as might at first appear. Females are not freed from criminal liability in California for engaging in sexual activity that may be harmful. It is unlawful, for example, for any person, of either sex, [to] contribute to the delinquency of anyone under 18 years of age. All persons are prohibited [from] consensual intercourse with a child under 14. [Finally,] females may be brought within the proscription of § 261.5 itself, since a female may be charged with aiding and abetting its violation. [A]pproximately 14% of the juveniles arrested for participation in acts made unlawful by § 261.5 between 1975 and 1979 were females. Moreover, an underage female who is as culpable as her male partner, or more culpable, may be prosecuted as a juvenile delinquent."

analysis this Court has so carefully developed since *Craig*. [The] plurality assumes that a gender-neutral statute would be less effective [in] deterring sexual activity because a gender-neutral statute would create significant enforcement problems. [But] a State's bare assertion [is] not enough to meet its burden of proof under *Craig*. Rather, the State must produce evidence that will persuade the Court that its assertion is true [and the] State has [not].

"The second flaw in the State's assertion is that even assuming that a gender-neutral statute would be more difficult to enforce, the State has still not shown that those enforcement problems would make such a statute less effective than a gender-based statute in deterring minor females from engaging in sexual intercourse. Common sense, however, suggests that a gender-neutral statutory rape law is potentially a *greater* deterrent of sexual activity than a gender-based law, for the simple reason that a gender-neutral law subjects both men and women to criminal sanctions and thus arguably has a deterrent effect on twice as many potential violators. Even if fewer persons were prosecuted under the gender-neutral law, as the State suggests, it would still be true that twice as many persons would be *subject* to arrest."

STEVENS, J., also dissented: "[T]hat a female confronts a greater risk of harm than a male is a reason for applying the prohibition to her—not a reason for granting her a license to use her own judgment on whether or not to assume the risk. Surely, if we examine the problem from the point of view of society's interest in preventing the risk-creating conduct from occurring at all, it is irrational to exempt 50% of the potential violators. * * *

"Finally, even if my logic is faulty and there actually is some speculative basis for treating equally guilty males and females differently, I still believe that any such speculative justification would be outweighed by the paramount interest in even-handed enforcement of the law. A rule that authorizes punishment of only one of two equally guilty wrongdoers violates the essence of the constitutional requirement that the sovereign must govern impartially."

Notes and Questions

1. *Difference and justification.* Consider Laurence H. Tribe, *Constitutional Choices* 241 (1985): "That 'the sexes are not similarly situated' in such cases as *Michael M.* and *Dothard* would not, to anyone less mesmerized [than the Court] by the ideal of law as a mirror of nature, be thought to *justify* a gender discrimination as noninvidious; it would instead raise the question whether such discrimination formed part of the law's systemic support for male supremacy." Viewing the problem through this different "lens," Professor Tribe concludes that "[t]he law must be prepared to act [by] affirmatively combating the inequities that result when we all too casually allow biological differences to justify the imposition of legal disabilities on women." Tribe, 2d ed. at 1577. Do you agree? How might this approach be applied to *Dothard*? To *Michael M.*? What would be the costs?

In "high-rape" areas, may female students be subjected to an earlier curfew than males? May women employees, because women live longer, be required to make larger contributions than men to a state pension fund? See *Los Angeles Dep't of Water & Power v. Manhart*, 435 U.S. 702, 98 S.Ct. 1370, 55 L.Ed.2d 657 (1978) (violation of Title VII). May only women be required to wear tops while swimming?

2. *Feminist criticisms of statutory rape laws.* Consider Frances Olsen, *Statutory Rape: A Feminist Critique of Rights Analysis*, 63 Tex.L.Rev. 387, 404–07

(1984): "Feminists charge that [statutory rape laws] are harmful to women on both a practical and an ideological level. First, as an effort to control the sexual activities of young women, statutory rape [laws] interfere[] with the sexual freedom of the underage female. [They] violate the female's right [to] be as free sexually as her male counterpart. [Second, g]ender-based statutory rape laws reinforce the sexual stereotype of men as aggressors and women as passive victims. The laws perpetuate the double standard of sexual morality [in which] sex is an accomplishment [for men but a debasing activity for women]. * * *

"Unfortunately, [however,] invalidating statutory rape laws altogether [might] undermine the right of young women to be free of unwanted sexual conduct. [Since the stereotypes that statutory rape laws reinforce may have a basis in current social reality, underage] females might discover that although the abolition of [such] laws would protect their rights against the state, it would remove some of their already-minimal protection against individual men. [Among other needed protections,] statutory rape laws may prohibit certain instances of sexual assault that should be considered illegal, but cannot be prosecuted as forcible rape.[94]"

3. *Discrimination and the dissenting opinions.* On what basis did the dissenting Justices object to the statute in *Michael M.*? Consider Olsen, supra, at 418–19: "[T]he statute discriminates in two different ways: it outlaws sexual intercourse by minor females, but not by minor males, and it protects minor females from exploitative intercourse with anyone, but does not protect minor males from exploitative intercourse with females who are above the age of consent. The dissenters ignored the first discrimination altogether and appeared confused about the second."

According to Professor Olsen, the dissenting Justices would have regarded the law as "gender-neutral" as long as it punished underage women and their sexual partners equally for engaging in the same sexual acts—even if it allowed minor males (but not minor females) to engage in intercourse with partners above the age of consent. Id. at 419. Should the latter discrimination be regarded as constitutionally objectionable? Why did none of the dissenting Justices allude to it?

Professor Olsen also argues that the "revision" that the dissenting Justices would have found acceptable "would be the worst alternative for women, because it would increase the coercive aspects of the California law and diminish any protective elements it now might have. A woman would find it more difficult to use statutory rape laws as a shield against male aggression [because] the woman would have to admit that she had violated the law in order to prosecute the male * * *." Id. at 419–20.

Do you agree? (Consider the testimony in the *Michael M.* case as reported in the footnote to Blackmun, J.'s opinion.) What are the implications, if any, for what the content of statutory rape laws should have to be in order to pass constitutional muster?

4. *The focus on "difference."* Should the constitutionality of gender-based classifications be based on an assessment of whether males and females are relevantly "different"?

---

94. [The] testimony [in *Michael M.*] provides one example. The man hit the female in the face two or three [times]. Presumably this could not be prosecuted as forcible rape because before intercourse took place the female gave what is considered legal consent.

(a) Consider Deborah Rhode, *Gender and Justice* 2–3 (1989): "The law's conventional approach to gender issues has focused on gender difference. [Within] this framework, sex-based discrimination remains justifiable if the sexes are different in some sense that is related to valid regulatory objectives. [But] this difference-oriented approach has proved inadequate in both theory and practice. As a theoretical matter, it tends toward tautology. It permits different treatment for those who differ with respect to legitimate purposes but provides no standards for determining what differences are relevant and what counts as legitimate. As a practical matter, this approach has both over-and undervalued gender differences. In some instances, biology has determined destiny, while in other contexts, women's particular needs have gone unacknowledged or unaddressed. [Reliance] on 'real difference' [has] often done more to reflect sex-based inequalities than to challenge them."

(b) Consider the suggestion of Martha Minow, *Introduction: Finding Our Paradoxes, Affirming Our Beyond*, 24 Harv.C.R.C.L.L.Rev. 1, 2–4 (1989), that feminist scholarship addressing issues of "difference" has included at least three stages: "[T]he first stage articulated women's claims to be granted the same rights and privileges as men [including] rights to vote and to hold the same jobs as men. The second stage advocated respect and accommodation for women's historical and contemporary differences. For those writing in this second stage, the problem needing redress was the undervaluation or disregard for women's historic and persistent interests, traits, and needs. Examples of second-stage goals include obtaining pregnancy and maternity leaves from paid employment, pursuing comparable worth to revalue traditional women's work, and elaborating special rights for women to respond to rape, battery of women by men, and self-determination about whether to conceive or bear a child.

"The third stage rejects the preoccupation with similarities and differences between men and women. As third-stage representatives see it, this preoccupation has itself helped perpetuate the degradation and subordination of women. Focusing on the similarities and differences between men and women threatens to preserve men as the starting point for analysis. For example, an unstated male norm makes pregnancy and maternity leaves 'special treatment,' contrasted to the 'normal treatment' given to employees. But these programs are special only in comparison with background rules that treat as the norm the person—a man—who never gets pregnant."[a]

(c) Would it be better to declare that a "rule or practice is discriminatory [if] it participates in the systemic social deprivation of one sex because of sex"? Should the "only question for litigation [be] whether the policy or practice in question integrally contributes to the maintenance of an underclass * * * because of gender"? For a discussion of this "anti-subordination" approach, see Catharine A. MacKinnon, *Sexual Harassment of Working Women* 117 (1979).

---

a. See also Martha Minow, *Making All the Difference* 230–39 (1990); Elizabeth V. Spellman, *Inessential Woman* (1988); Patricia A. Cain, *Feminist Jurisprudence: Grounding the Theories,* 4 Berk. Women's L.J. 191 (1989–90); Kimberle Crenshaw, *Demarginalizing the Intersection of Race and Sex: A Black Feminist Critique of Antidiscrimination Doctrine, Feminist Theory and Antiracist Politics,* 1989 U.Chi. Legal F. 139; Angela P. Harris, *Race and Essentialism in Feminist Legal Theory,* 42 Stan. L.Rev. 581 (1990); Carrie Menkel–Meadow, *Mainstreaming Feminist Legal Theory,* 23 Pac. L.J. 1493 (1992); Patricia Williams, *The Obliging Shell: An Informal Essay on Formal Equal Opportunity,* 87 Mich.L.Rev. 2128 (1989).

ROSTKER v. GOLDBERG, 453 U.S. 57, 101 S.Ct. 2646, 69 L.Ed.2d 478 (1981), per REHNQUIST, J., upheld a Military Selective Service Act (MSSA) provision "authorizing the President to require the registration of males and not females": "The case arises in the context of Congress' authority over national defense and military affairs, and perhaps in no other area has the Court accorded Congress greater deference. [This is not] to say that Congress is free to disregard the Constitution when it acts in the area of military affairs. [But in] deciding the question before us we must be particularly careful not to substitute our judgment of what is desirable for that of Congress, or our own evaluation of evidence for a reasonable evaluation by [Congress].

"No one could deny that under the test of *Craig,* the Government's interest in raising and supporting armies is an 'important governmental interest.' [Nor did Congress, in excluding women from draft registration,] act 'unthinkingly' or 'reflexively and not for any considered reason.' The question of registering women for the draft not only received considerable national attention and was the subject of wide-ranging public debate, but also was extensively considered by Congress in hearings, floor debate, and in committee. * * *

"Congress determined that any future draft, which would be facilitated by the registration scheme, would be characterized by a need for combat troops. [Since] women are [statutorily] excluded from combat, Congress concluded that they would not be needed in the event of a draft, and therefore decided not to register them. [The] exemption of women from registration is not only sufficiently but closely related to Congress' purpose in authorizing registration. See *Michael M.; Craig; Reed.* [It] realistically reflects the fact that the sexes are not 'similarly situated' in this case. *Michael M.*

"In holding the MSSA constitutionally invalid the District Court relied heavily on the President's decision to seek authority to register women and the testimony of members of the Executive Branch and the military in support of that decision. As stated by the Administration's witnesses before Congress, however, the President's 'decision to ask for authority to register women is based on equity.' * * * Congress was certainly entitled, in the exercise of its constitutional powers to raise and regulate armies and navies, to focus on the question of military need rather than 'equity.' * * *

"Although the military experts who testified in favor of registering women uniformly opposed the actual drafting of women, there was testimony that in the event of a draft of 650,000 the military could absorb some 80,000 female inductees [to] fill noncombat positions, freeing men to go to the front. In relying on this testimony, [the] District Court palpably exceeded its authority when it ignored Congress' considered response to this line of reasoning.

"In the first place, assuming that a small number of women could be drafted for noncombat roles, Congress simply did not consider it worth the added burdens of including women in draft and registration plans. * * * Congress also concluded that whatever the need for women for noncombat roles during mobilization, [it] could be met by volunteers.

"Most significantly, Congress determined that staffing noncombat positions with women during a mobilization would be positively detrimental to the important goal of military flexibility. [The] District Court was quite wrong in undertaking an independent evaluation of this evidence, rather than adopting an appropriately deferential examination of *Congress'* evaluation of that evidence."

MARSHALL, J., joined by Brennan, J., dissented:[a] "The Court today places its imprimatur on one of the most potent remaining public expressions of 'ancient canards about the proper role of women.' [W]e are not called upon to decide whether either men or women can be drafted at all, whether they must be drafted in equal numbers, in what order they should be drafted, or once inducted, how they are to be trained for their respective functions. In addition, this case does not involve a challenge to the statutes or policies that prohibit female members of the Armed Forces from serving in combat. It is with this understanding that I turn to the task at hand. [In] my judgment, there simply is no basis for concluding in this case that excluding women from registration is substantially related to the achievement of a concededly important governmental interest in maintaining an effective defense. * * *

"[The] Government makes no claim that preparing for a draft of combat troops cannot be accomplished just as effectively by *registering* both men and women but *drafting* only men if only men turn out to be needed.[11] Nor can the Government argue that this alternative entails the additional cost and administrative inconvenience of registering women. This Court has repeatedly stated that [administrative convenience] is not an adequate constitutional justification under the *Craig* test.

"The fact that registering women in no way obstructs the governmental interest in preparing for a draft of combat troops points up a second flaw in the Court's analysis. [The] majority simply assumes that registration prepares for a draft in which *every* draftee must be available for assignment to combat. But [this] finds no support in either the testimony before Congress, or more importantly, in the findings of the Senate Report, [which] concluded [that] drafting '*very large numbers* of women' would hinder military flexibility. [But the] testimony on this issue at the congressional hearings was that drafting a limited number of women is quite compatible with the military's need for flexibility. In concluding that the Armed Services could usefully employ at least 80,000 women conscripts out of a total of 650,000 draftees that would be needed in the event of a major European war, the Defense Department took into account both the need for rotation of combat personnel and the possibility that some support personnel might have to be sent into combat. [The] combat restrictions that would prevent a female draftee from serving in a combat or combat rotation position also apply to the 150,000–250,000 women volunteers in the Armed Services. If the presence of increasing but controlled numbers of female volunteers has not unacceptably 'divide[d] the military into two groups,' it is difficult to see how the induction of a similarly limited additional number of women could accomplish this result."

Notes and Questions

1. *Agreement and disagreement.* All justices in *Rostker* appear to agree that it is constitutionally permissible for the armed services (a) to exclude women from combat positions[a] and (b) in the event of a draft, to conscript males only. Why?

---

a. White, J., joined by Brennan, J., dissented separately.

11. Alternatively, the Government could employ a classification that is related to the statutory objective but is not based on gender, for example, combat eligibility. Under the current scheme, large subgroups of the male population who are ineligible for combat because of physical handicaps or conscientious objector status are nonetheless required to register.

a. For an attack on the combat exclusion, see Michael J. Frevola, *Damn the Torpedoes, Full Speed Ahead: The Argument for Total Sex Integration in the Armed Forces*, 28 Conn. L.Rev. 621 (1996).

Would it be fair to say that the majority and dissenting justices differ mostly if not exclusively about the implications of their shared assumptions?

2. *Male burdens and benefits.* Consider Catharine A. MacKinnon, *Feminism Unmodified: Discourses on Life and Law* 38 (1987): "Excluding women is always an option if equality feels in tension with the pursuit [of a desired end]. They never seem to think of excluding men. Take combat. Somehow it takes the glory out of the foxhole, the buddiness out of the trenches, to imagine us out there. You get the feeling they might rather end the draft, they might even rather not fight wars at all than have to do it with us."

Compare Leo Kanowitz, *"Benign" Sex Discrimination: Its Troubles and Their Cure,* 31 Hast.L.J. 1379, 1394 (1980): "[A] casual glance at the treatment males have received at the hands of the law solely because they are males suggests that they have paid an awesome price for other advantages they have presumably enjoyed over females in our society. Whether one talks of the male's unique obligation of compulsory military service, his primary duty for spousal and child support, his lack of the same kinds of protective labor legislation that have traditionally been enjoyed by women, or the statutory or judicial preference in child custody disputes that has long been accorded to mothers vis-à-vis fathers of minor children, sex discrimination against males in statutes and judicial decisions has been widespread and severe."

3. *Feminist divisions.* Consider Wendy W. Williams, *The Equality Crisis: Some Reflections on Culture, Courts, and Feminism,* 7 Women's Rts.L.Rep. 175, 189–90 (1982): "As for *Rostker,* the conflicts among feminists were overtly expressed. Some of us felt it essential that we support the notion that a single-sex draft was unconstitutional; others felt that feminists should not take such a position. These latter groups explicitly contrasted the female ethic of nurturance and life-giving with a male ethic of aggression and militarism and asserted that if we argued to the Court that single-sex registration is unconstitutional we would be betraying ourselves and supporting what we find least acceptable about the male world.[b]

"To me, this latter argument quite overtly taps qualities that the culture has ascribed to woman-as-childrearer and converts them to a normative value statement, one with which it is easy for us to sympathize. This is one of the circumstances in which the feeling that 'I want what he's got but I don't want to be what he's had to be in order to get it' comes quickly to the surface. But I also believe that the reflexive response based on these deeper cultural senses leads us to untenable positions. [To] me, *Rostker* never posed the question of whether women should be forced as men now are to fight wars, but whether we, like them, must take the responsibility for deciding whether or not to fight, whether or not to bear the cost of risking our lives, on the one hand, or resisting in the name of peace, on the other. And do we not, by insisting upon our differences at these

---

b. Compare Carol Gilligan, *In a Different Voice* (1982), suggesting that women tend to have a different moral framework—more concerned with issues of relationships and of caring—from the characteristically rights-based outlook of men. Questions raised about Gilligan's theory include (i) whether the characteristic difference that she identifies in fact exists; (ii) whether, even if it does, it is the result of social conditioning rather than reflective of a "natural" difference between men and women; and (iii) whether governmental action predicat-

ed on the notion that women have a distinctive moral perspective helps to perpetuate a stereotype that works to women's overall disadvantage. For a sustained effort to apply ideas derived from Gilligan to legal contexts, see Robin West, *Caring for Justice* (1997). For feminist commentary on and criticism of Gilligan's work, see Mary Joe Frug, *Progressive Feminist Legal Scholarship: Can We Claim "A Different Voice"?,* 15 Harv. Women's L.J. 37 (1992); MacKinnon, supra, at 32–45.

crucial junctures, promote and reinforce the us-them dichotomy that permits the Rehnquists and the Stewarts to resolve matters of great importance and complexity by the simplistic, reflexive assertion that men and women 'are simply not similarly situated?' "[c]

Alabama sued J.E.B. for paternity and child support on behalf of T.B., the mother of a minor child. The state used 9 of its 10 preemptory strikes to remove male jurors.[a] J.E.B. v. ALABAMA ex rel. T.B., 511 U.S. 127, 114 S.Ct. 1419, 128 L.Ed.2d 89 (1994), per BLACKMUN, J., held that the state's action violated equal protection: "[T]he only question is whether discrimination on the basis of gender in jury selection substantially furthers the State's legitimate interest in achieving a fair and impartial trial.[6] [R]espondent maintains that its decision to strike virtually all the males from the jury in this case 'may reasonably have been based upon the perception, supported by history, that men otherwise totally qualified to serve upon a jury might be more sympathetic and receptive to the arguments of a man alleged in a paternity action to be the father of an out-of-wedlock child, while women equally qualified to serve upon a jury might be more sympathetic and receptive to the arguments of the complaining witness who bore the child.'

"We shall not accept as a defense to gender-based peremptory challenges 'the very stereotype the law condemns.' [Respondent] urges this Court to condone the same stereotypes that justified the wholesale exclusion of women from juries and the ballot box.[11] Respondent seems to assume that gross generalizations that would be deemed impermissible if made on the basis of race are somehow permissible when made on the basis of gender. * * *

"When state actors exercise peremptory challenges in reliance on gender stereotypes, they ratify and reinforce prejudicial views of the relative abilities of men and women. Because these stereotypes have wreaked injustice in so many other spheres of our country's public life, active discrimination by litigants on the basis of gender during jury selection 'invites cynicism respecting the jury's neutrality and its obligation to adhere to the law.' [Our] conclusion that litigants may not strike potential jurors solely on the basis of gender does not imply the elimination of all peremptory challenges.[14] Neither does it conflict with a State's

---

c. For further commentary, see Diane H. Mazur, *A Call to Arms*, 22 Harv. Women's L.J. 39, 44 (1999) (arguing that a consistent application of most feminist approaches should "not only permit, but would demand, greater feminist support for military service by women").

a. J.E.B. used all but one of his preemptory strikes to remove female jurors, but any issue thus raised was not before the Court.

6. Because we conclude that gender-based peremptory challenges are not substantially related to an important government objective, we once again need not decide whether classifications based on gender are inherently suspect. See *Mississippi University for Women*, [Part III infra]; *Harris v. Forklift Systems*, 510 U.S. 17, 26, 114 S.Ct. 367, 373, 126 L.Ed.2d 295 (1993) (Ginsburg, J., concurring) ("[I]t remains an open question whether 'classifications based upon gender are inherently suspect.' ").

11. [The] Equal Protection Clause, as interpreted by decisions of this court, acknowledges that a shred of truth may be contained in some stereotypes, but requires that state actors look beyond the surface before making judgments about people that are likely to stigmatize as well as to perpetuate historical patterns of discrimination.

14. The popular refrain is that *all* peremptory challenges are based on stereotypes of some kind, expressing various intuitive and frequently erroneous biases. But where peremptory challenges are made on the basis of group characteristics other than race or gender (like occupation, for example), they do not reinforce the same stereotypes about the group's competence or predispositions that have been used to prevent them from voting, participating on juries, pursuing their chosen professions, or otherwise contributing to civic life. See Barbara Allen Babcock, *A Place in the*

legitimate interest in using such challenges in its effort to secure a fair and impartial jury. Parties still may remove jurors whom they feel might be less acceptable than others on the panel; gender simply may not serve as a proxy for bias. Parties may also exercise their peremptory challenges to remove from the venire any group or class of individuals normally subject to 'rational basis' review. Even strikes based on characteristics that are disproportionately associated with one gender could be appropriate, absent a showing of pretext.[16]"

O'CONNOR, J., concurred: "[T]oday's important blow against gender discrimination is not costless. [A] plethora of studies make clear that in rape cases, for example, female jurors are somewhat more likely to vote to convict than male jurors. Moreover, though there have been no similarly definitive studies regarding, for example, sexual harassment, child custody, or spousal or child abuse, one need not be a sexist to share the intuition that in certain cases a person's gender and resulting life experience will be relevant to his or her view of the [case.] Individuals are not expected to ignore as jurors what they know as men—or women. [These] concerns reinforce my conviction that today's decision should be limited to a prohibition on the government's use of gender-based peremptory challenges."[b]

SCALIA, J., joined by Rehnquist, C.J., and Thomas, J., dissented: "Today's opinion is an inspiring demonstration of how thoroughly up-to-date and right-thinking we Justices are in matters pertaining to the sexes (or as the Court would have it, the genders),[1] and how sternly we disapprove the male chauvinist attitudes of our predecessors. [The] hasty reader will be surprised to learn, for example, that this lawsuit involves a complaint about the use of peremptory challenges to exclude *men* from a petit jury. * * *

"The Court [spends] time establishing that the use of sex as a proxy for particular views or sympathies is unwise and perhaps irrational. The opinion stresses the lack of statistical evidence to support the widely held belief that, at least in certain types of cases, a juror's sex has some statistically significant predictive value as to how the juror will behave. This assertion seems to place the Court in opposition to its earlier Sixth Amendment 'fair cross-section' cases. See, e.g., *Taylor v. Louisiana* ('Controlled studies [have] concluded that women bring to juries their own perspectives and values that influence both jury deliberation and result'). But [the] Court's fervent defense of the proposition *il n'y a pas de différence entre les hommes et les femmes* (it stereotypes the opposite view as hateful 'stereotyping') turns out to be, like its recounting of the history of sex discrimination against women, utterly irrelevant. Even if sex was a remarkably good predictor in certain cases, the Court would find its use in peremptories unconstitutional. * * *

Palladium, Women's Rights and Jury Service, 61 U.Cinn.L.Rev. 1139, 1173 (1993).

16. For example, challenging all persons who have had military experience would disproportionately affect men at this time, while challenging all persons employed as nurses would disproportionately affect women. Without a showing of pretext, however, these challenges may well not be unconstitutional, since they are not gender-or race-based. See *Hernandez v. New York.*

b. Kennedy, J., concurred. Rehnquist, C.J., filed a dissenting opinion.

1. Throughout this opinion, I shall refer to the issue as sex discrimination rather than (as the Court does) gender discrimination. The word "gender" has acquired the new and useful connotation of cultural or attitudinal characteristics (as opposed to physical characteristics) distinctive to the sexes. That is to say, gender is to sex as feminine is to female and masculine to male. The present case does not involve peremptory strikes exercised on the basis of femininity or masculinity (as far as it appears, effeminate men did not survive the prosecution's peremptories). The case involves, therefore, sex discrimination plain and simple.

"The core of the Court's reasoning is that peremptory challenges on the basis of any group characteristic subject to heightened scrutiny are inconsistent with the guarantee of the Equal Protection Clause. That conclusion can be reached only by focusing unrealistically upon individual exercises of the peremptory challenge, and ignoring the totality of the practice. Since all groups are subject to the peremptory challenge (and will be made the object of it, depending upon the nature of the particular case) it is hard to see how any group is denied equal protection. That explains why peremptory challenges coexisted with the Equal Protection Clause for 120 years. This case is a perfect example of how the system as a whole is even-handed. [F]or every man struck by the government petitioner's own lawyer struck a woman. To say that men were singled out for discriminatory treatment in this process is preposterous. [That] is why the Court's characterization of respondent's argument as 'reminiscent of the arguments advanced to justify the total exclusion of women from juries,' is patently false. Women were categorically excluded from juries because of doubt that they were competent; women are stricken from juries by peremptory challenge because of doubt that they are well disposed to the striking party's case. There is discrimination and dishonor in the former, and not in the [latter]."

III. "BENIGN"–"COMPENSATORY"– "REMEDIAL" DISCRIMINATION

Probably the paradigmatic forms of historic gender discrimination, as of race discrimination, involve classifications predicated on the assumption that one sex is less competent, trustworthy, or deserving than the other. Some gender-based classifications explicitly reject this assumption; they may have as their aim compensating women for past discrimination, public or private, or expanding opportunities for women. In cases of purportedly "benign" discrimination, one question involves the standard of judicial review that ought to apply. The cases also reflect—albeit to varying degrees—a concern that gender-based classifications, even when their ostensible aim is to help women, may reflect and possibly reinforce stereotypes that redound to women's overall disadvantage. As you read the cases in this section, consider how consistent a theme that this has been, and ought to be, in the Court's decisions. Is concern about harmful stereotypes an aspect of the level of scrutiny that the Court applies or a factor independent of the standard of review?

CALIFANO v. WEBSTER

430 U.S. 313, 97 S.Ct. 1192, 51 L.Ed.2d 360 (1977).

Per Curiam.

[Social Security Act § 215(b)(3)'s formula—which has since been amended—afforded the chance of higher old-age benefits to female wage earners than to similarly situated males.]

To withstand scrutiny under [equal protection], "classifications by gender must serve important governmental objectives and must be substantially related to achievement of those objectives." *Craig.* Reduction of the disparity in economic condition between men and women caused by the long history of discrimination against women has been recognized as such an important governmental objective.

Schlesinger v. Ballard, 419 U.S. 498, 95 S.Ct. 572, 42 L.Ed.2d 610 (1975);[a] *Kahn v. Shevin,* 416 U.S. 351, 94 S.Ct. 1734, 40 L.Ed.2d 189 (1974).[b] But "the mere recitation of a benign, compensatory purpose is not an automatic shield which protects against any inquiry into the actual purposes underlying a statutory scheme." *Weinberger v. Wiesenfeld,* 420 U.S. 636, 95 S.Ct. 1225, 43 L.Ed.2d 514 (1975).[c] Accordingly, we have rejected attempts to justify gender classifications as compensation for past discrimination against women when the classifications in fact penalized women wage earners, *Califano v. Goldfarb,* 430 U.S. 199, 97 S.Ct. 1021, 51 L.Ed.2d 270 (1977);[d] *Wiesenfeld,* or when the statutory structure and its legislative history revealed that the classification was not enacted as compensation for past discrimination. *Goldfarb; Wiesenfeld.*

[The] more favorable treatment of the female wage earner enacted here was not a result of "archaic and overbroad generalizations" about women, or of "the role-typing society has long imposed" upon women such as casual assumptions that women are "the weaker sex" or are more likely to be child-rearers or dependents. Rather, "the only discernible purpose of [§ 215's more favorable treatment is] the permissible one of redressing our society's longstanding disparate treatment of women." *Goldfarb.*

The challenged statute operated directly to compensate women for past economic discrimination. Retirement benefits [are] based on past earnings. But as we have recognized, "[w]hether from overt discrimination or from the socialization process of a male-dominated culture, the job market is inhospitable to the woman seeking any but the lowest paid jobs." *Kahn.* Thus, allowing women, who as such have been unfairly hindered from earning as much as men, to eliminate additional low-earning years from the calculation of their retirement benefits works directly to remedy some part of the effect of past discrimination.[5]

[T]he legislative history is clear that the differing treatment of men and women in former § 215(b)(3) was not "the accidental byproduct of a traditional way of thinking about females," *Goldfarb* (Stevens, J., concurring in the result), but rather was deliberately enacted to compensate for particular economic disabilities suffered by women. * * *

a. *Schlesinger,* per Stewart, J., upheld a federal statute providing for the discharge of naval "line" officers who had not been promoted for nine years (males) or thirteen years (females): Because of Navy restrictions on combat and sea duty for women, "Congress [may] quite rationally have believed that women line officers had less opportunity for promotion than did their male counterparts, and that a longer period of tenure for women officers would, therefore, be consistent with the goal to provide women officers with 'fair and equitable career advancement programs.' "

b. *Kahn,* per Douglas, J., upheld a property tax exemption for widows (but not widowers) on the ground that the law was "reasonably designed to further the state policy of cushioning the financial impact of spousal loss upon the sex for whom that loss imposes a disproportionately heavy burden."

c. *Weinberger,* per Brennan, J., held that Social Security Act § 402(g)'s payment of benefits to the wife—but not to the husband—of a deceased wage earner with minor children violated equal protection because it "unjustifiably discriminated against women wage-earners": as in *Frontiero,* an " 'archaic and overbroad' generalization [underlies] the distinction drawn by § 402(g), namely, that male [but not female] workers' earnings are vital to the support of their families." Unlike in *Kahn,* "[i]t is apparent both from the statutory scheme itself and from the legislative history of § 402(g) that Congress' purpose [was] not to provide an income to women who were, because of economic discrimination, unable to provide for themselves."

d. *Goldfarb* held that Social Security Act § 402(f)'s payment of benefits to a widow of a covered employee, but not to a widower unless he proves dependency on his deceased wife-employee, violated equal protection.

5. Even with the advantage[,] women on the average received lower retirement benefits than men. "As of December 1972, the average monthly retirement insurance benefit for males was $179.60 and for females, $140.50."

Reversed.

CHIEF JUSTICE BURGER, with whom JUSTICE STEWART, JUSTICE BLACKMUN, and JUSTICE REHNQUIST join, concurring in the judgment.

* * * I question whether certainty in the law is promoted by hinging the validity of important statutory schemes on whether five Justices view them to be more akin to the "offensive" provisions struck down in *Wiesenfeld* and *Frontiero*, or more like the "benign" provisions upheld in *Ballard* and *Kahn*. I therefore concur in the judgment [for] reasons stated by Mr. Justice Rehnquist in his dissenting opinion in *Goldfarb*: ["Favoring aged widows is scarcely an invidious discrimination. [It] in no way perpetuates the economic discrimination which has been the basis for heightened scrutiny of gender-based classifications, and is, in fact, explainable as a measure to ameliorate the characteristically depressed condition of aged widows."]

ORR v. ORR, 440 U.S. 268, 99 S.Ct. 1102, 59 L.Ed.2d 306 (1979), considered "two legislative objectives" for an Alabama statute providing that only husbands may be required to pay alimony—(1) to "provide help for needy spouses, using sex as a proxy for need," and (2) to "compensat[e] women for past discrimination during marriage, which assertedly has left them unprepared to fend for themselves." The Court, per BRENNAN, J., held that the statute failed the *Craig* standard: "Under the statute, individualized hearings at which the parties' relative financial circumstances are considered *already* occur. There is no reason, therefore, to use sex as a proxy for need. Needy males could be helped along with needy females with little if any additional burden on the [state]. Similarly, since individualized hearings can determine which women were in fact discriminated against vis-à-vis their husbands, as well as which family units defied the stereotype and left the husband dependent on the wife, Alabama's alleged compensatory purpose may be effectuated without placing burdens solely on husbands."[a]

MISSISSIPPI UNIV. FOR WOMEN v. HOGAN

458 U.S. 718, 102 S.Ct. 3331, 73 L.Ed.2d 1090 (1982).

JUSTICE O'CONNOR delivered the opinion of the Court.

[Mississippi University for Women ("MUW"), "the oldest state-supported all-female college in the United States," denied Hogan admission to its School of Nursing solely because of his sex.[b]]

* * * Our decisions [establish] that the party seeking to uphold a statute that classifies individuals on the basis of their gender must carry the burden of showing an "exceedingly persuasive justification" for the classification. The burden is met only by showing at least that the classification serves "important governmental objectives and that the discriminatory means employed" are "substantially related to the achievement of those objectives."[9]

a. Blackmun, J., concurred. Burger, C.J., and Powell and Rehnquist, JJ., dissented on procedural grounds to which Stevens, J.'s concurrence responded.

b. The Court declined "to address the question of whether MUW's admissions policy, as applied to males seeking admission to schools other than the School of Nursing, violates the Fourteenth Amendment."

9. [Because] we conclude that the challenged statutory classification is not substantially related to an important objective, we need not decide whether classifications based upon gender are inherently suspect.

Although the test [is] straightforward, it must be applied free of fixed notions concerning the roles and abilities of males and females. [Thus,] if the statutory objective is to exclude or "protect" members of one gender because they are presumed to suffer from an inherent handicap or to be innately inferior, the objective itself is illegitimate. See *Frontiero*.

If the State's objective is legitimate and important, we next determine whether the requisite direct, substantial relationship between objective and means is present. The purpose of requiring that close relationship is to assure that the validity of a classification is determined through reasoned analysis rather than through the mechanical application of traditional, often inaccurate, assumptions about the proper roles of men and women. The need for the requirement is amply revealed by reference to the broad range of statutes already invalidated by this Court, statutes that relied upon the simplistic, outdated assumption that gender could be used as a "proxy for other, more germane bases of classification," *Craig*, to establish a link between objective and classification. * * *

The State's primary justification for maintaining the single-sex admissions policy of MUW's School of Nursing is that it compensates for discrimination against women and, therefore, constitutes educational affirmative action. [A] state can evoke a compensatory purpose to justify an otherwise discriminatory classification only if members of the gender benefitted by the classification actually suffer a disadvantage related to the classification. We considered such a situation in *Webster* [and *Ballard*].

In sharp contrast, Mississippi has made no showing that women lacked opportunities to obtain training in the field of nursing or to attain positions of leadership in that field when the MUW School of Nursing opened its door or that women currently are deprived of such opportunities. In fact, in 1970, the year before the School of Nursing's first class enrolled, women earned 94 percent of the nursing baccalaureate degrees conferred in Mississippi and 98.6 percent of the degrees earned nationwide.

Rather than compensate for discriminatory barriers faced by women, MUW's [policy] tends to perpetuate the stereotyped view of nursing as an exclusively woman's job.[14] By assuring that Mississippi allots more openings in its state-supported nursing schools to women than it does to men, MUW's admissions policy lends credibility to the old view that women, not men, should become nurses, and makes the assumption that nursing is a field for women a self-fulfilling prophecy. Thus, we conclude that, although the State recited a "benign, compensatory purpose," it failed to establish that the alleged objective is the actual purpose underlying the discriminatory classification.

The policy is invalid also because [the] State has made no showing that the gender-based classification is substantially and directly related to its proposed compensatory objective. To the contrary, MUW's policy of permitting men to attend classes as auditors fatally undermines its claim that women, at least those in the School of Nursing, are adversely affected by the presence of men.[17]

---

14. Officials of the American Nurses Association have suggested that excluding men from the field has depressed nurses' wages. To the extent the exclusion of men has that effect, MUW's admissions policy actually penalizes the very class the State purports to benefit. Cf. *Wiesenfeld*.

17. Justice Powell's dissent suggests that a second objective is served by the gender-based classification in that Mississippi has elected to provide women a choice of educational environments. Since any gender-based classification provides one class a benefit or choice not available to the other class, however, that argument begs the question. The issue is not whether the benefitted class profits from the classification, but whether the State's decision to confer a benefit only upon one class by means of a

Affirmed.

CHIEF JUSTICE BURGER, dissenting.

I agree generally with Justice Powell's dissenting opinion. I write separately, however, to emphasize that [s]ince the Court's opinion relies heavily on its finding that women have traditionally dominated the nursing profession, it suggests that a State might well be justified in maintaining, for example, the option of an all-women's business school or liberal arts program.

JUSTICE POWELL, with whom JUSTICE REHNQUIST joins, dissenting.[c]

[T]he Court errs seriously by assuming [that] the equal protection standard generally applicable to sex discrimination is appropriate here. That standard was designed to free women from "archaic and overbroad generalizations." *Ballard.* In no previous case have we applied it to invalidate state efforts to *expand* women's choices. * * *

By applying heightened equal protection analysis to this case, the Court frustrates the liberating spirit of the Equal Protection Clause. It forbids the States from providing women with an opportunity to choose the type of university they prefer. And yet it is these women whom the Court regards as the *victims* of an illegal, stereotyped perception of the role of women in our society. The Court reasons this way in a case in which no woman has complained, and the only complainant is a man who advances no claims on behalf of anyone else. His claim [is] not that he is being denied a substantive educational opportunity, or even the right to attend an all-male or a coeducational college. It is *only* that the colleges open to him are located at inconvenient distances.

* * * I would sustain Mississippi's right to continue MUW on a rational basis analysis. But I need not apply this "lowest tier" of scrutiny. [More] than 2,000 women presently evidence their preference for MUW by having enrolled [there.] Generations of our finest minds, both among educators and students, have believed that single-sex, college-level institutions afford distinctive benefits. There are many persons, of course, who have different views. But simply because there are these differences is no reason—certainly none of constitutional dimension—to conclude that no substantial state interest is served when such a choice is made available.[17]

Notes and Questions

1. *"Affirmative action" preferences for women.* Does *Webster* suggest that classifications enacted to remedy past discrimination against women will be tested under "intermediate" scrutiny? Does *Hogan* alter or supplement the framework for analysis? Does *United States v. Virginia*? Should gender-based affirmative action be subject to less stringent scrutiny than race-based affirmative action? The circuits are split on this issue in the wake of *Croson* and *United States v. Virginia.* See Jason M. Skaggs, *Justifying Gender–Based Affirmative Action Under United States v. Virginia's "Exceedingly Persuasive Justification" Standard*, 86 Calif.L.Rev. 1169, 1174–76 (1998).

discriminatory classification is substantially related to achieving a legitimate and substantial goal.

c. Blackmun, J.'s brief dissent—agreeing essentially with Powell, J.—is omitted.

17. [It] is understandable that MUW might believe that it could allow men to audit courses without materially affecting its environment. MUW charges tuition but gives no academic credit for auditing. The University evidently is correct in believing that few men will choose to audit under such circumstances. This deviation from a perfect relationship between means and ends is insubstantial.

What government interests, if any, should be sufficiently "substantial" to support gender-based affirmative action? Remedying past "societal" discrimination? "Diversity" in education? In employment?[a] In government contracting?

2. *Single-gender schools.* In *Hogan,* the Court stated that it was "not faced with the question of whether States can provide 'separate but equal' undergraduate institutions for males and females." Does *United States v. Virginia,* supra, establish that single-gender education is never permissible? Compare footnote 7 of the majority opinion in that case with the assertions of Scalia, J., dissenting. Consider Amy H. Nemko, *Single-Sex Public Education After VMI: The Case for Women's Schools,* 21 Harv. Women's L.J. 19, 76 (1998): "Public single-sex schools for women and girls can be justified, even if such schools for men and boys cannot. [The] existence of such schools is substantially related to important governmental objectives of preparing girls and women for success, engaging their abilities, and encouraging them to become leaders." Do you agree?[b]

3. *Single-sex athletic programs.* May public schools have separate athletic programs for boys and girls? May boys be excluded from "girls' teams"? Girls from "boys' teams"? According to Note, *Boys Muscling in on Girls' Sports,* 53 Ohio St.L.J. 891, 892–93 (1992), most lower courts have held that " 'separate but equal' teams remain a constitutionally permissible alternative to gender-integrated teams. [The] important governmental objective in denying boys access to girls' athletic teams has been articulated as: 'maintaining, fostering, and promoting athletic opportunities for girls' and 'redressing past discrimination against women in athletics and promoting equality of athletic opportunity between the sexes'; in short, 'redressing the disparate opportunities available to males and females.' Most courts addressing the issue have found a substantial relationship between excluding boys from girls' teams and providing equal opportunities for females. Hence, exclusion is considered a permissible means of achieving this objective."

Do you agree with this analysis? Is it consistent with the Court's frequent admonition in cases involving race-based affirmative action that equal protection rights attach to individuals, not groups?

4. *Pregnancy and maternity leaves. General Electric Co. v. Gilbert,* 429 U.S. 125, 97 S.Ct. 401, 50 L.Ed.2d 343 (1976), held that Title VII's prohibition of sex discrimination did not prevent companies from excluding pregnancy from their disability plans. In response, Congress enacted the Pregnancy Discrimination Act,

a. Does the validity of this interest depend on the controversial claim, often associated with Carol Gilligan's *In a Different Voice* (1982), discussed in note 3 after *Rostker,* that women's characteristic moral framework tends to differ from that of men? Cf. Suzanna Sherry, *Civic Virtue and the Feminine Voice in Constitutional Adjudication,* 72 Va.L.Rev. 543, 592–613 (1986) (suggesting that O'Connor, J.'s approach to constitutional interpretation is partly a valuable and distinctive reflection of her gender).

b. For a discussion of the effects of sex-segregated education, as well as analysis of the constitutional issue, see Nancy Levit, *Separating Equals: Educational Research and the Long–Term Consequences of Sex Segregation,* 67 Geo.Wash.L.Rev. 451, 454 (1999) (asserting that "social science research is absolutely clear that separation on the basis of identity characteristics creates feelings of individual inade-

quacy and instills beliefs about group hierarchy"); Denise C. Morgan, *Anti-Subordination Analysis after* United States v. Virginia: *Evaluating the Constitutionality of K–12 Single–Sex Public Schools,* 1999 U.Chi.Legal F. 381 (1999) (arguing that single-sex schools are constitutionally permissible when they "are voluntary, educationally beneficial, allow alternatives to traditional gender identities and roles, and do not harm women's economic or political status"); Lucinda M. Finley, *The Uneasy Legacy of Plessy v. Ferguson for Sex and Gender Discrimination,* 12 Ga.St.U.L.Rev. 1089, 1118 (1996) (asserting that "[c]urrent research demonstrates that the efficacy of single-sex education may be sex-specific—limited to young women—because it offers an environment free from female-specific forms of educational discrimination, such as silencing, discouragement, and male-peer harassment").

42 U.S.C.A. § 2000e(k) (1978), which defined sex discrimination to include pregnancy discrimination. Some states have given maternity leave rights that go beyond that afforded to non-pregnant employees who are unable to work. Is this sex discrimination? See *California Federal Savings & Loan Ass'n v. Guerra,* 479 U.S. 272, 107 S.Ct. 683, 93 L.Ed.2d 613 (1987) (protection for physical disabilities associated with pregnancy with no similar protection for disabilities unrelated to pregnancy is neither inconsistent with nor preempted by federal antidiscrimination statutes).

In order to pass muster under the equal protection clause, should a state statute providing post-natal maternity leaves also have to make identical provision for paternity leaves? Is an approach based upon "special treatment" for women a "double-edged sword"? See Wendy W. Williams, *The Equality Crisis: Some Reflections on Culture, Courts, and Feminism,* 7 Women's Rts.L.Rptr. 175, 196 (1982) ("[i]f we can't have it both ways, we need to think carefully about which way we want to have it"). Does the phrase "special treatment" presuppose a male perspective?[c]

Consider Katharine T. Bartlett, *Feminist Legal Methods,* 103 Harv.L.Rev. 829, 842 (1990): "Although feminists have split over whether women have more to lose than to gain from singling out pregnancy for different, some would say 'favored,' treatment, they agree on the critical question: what are the consequences for women of specific rules or practices?" Should this also be the critical question under the equal protection clause?

SECTION 4. SPECIAL SCRUTINY FOR OTHER CLASSIFICATIONS: DOCTRINE AND DEBATES

Are there are other classifications besides those based on race and gender that should be subject to special scrutiny? If so, by what criteria should those classifications be identified?

I. ALIENAGE

Up to the late 1940s, the Supreme Court found a "special public interest"[a] in rejecting almost all challenges to state discriminations against aliens involving such activities as land ownership, *Terrace v. Thompson,* 263 U.S. 197, 44 S.Ct. 15, 68 L.Ed. 255 (1923); killing wild game, *Patsone v. Pennsylvania,* 232 U.S. 138, 34 S.Ct. 281, 58 L.Ed. 539 (1914); operating poolhalls, *State of Ohio ex rel. Clarke v. Deckebach,* 274 U.S. 392, 47 S.Ct. 630, 71 L.Ed. 1115 (1927); and working on public construction projects, *Crane v. New York,* 239 U.S. 195, 36 S.Ct. 85, 60 L.Ed. 218 (1915).[b] But *Takahashi v. Fish & Game Com'n,* 334 U.S. 410, 68 S.Ct. 1138, 92 L.Ed. 1478 (1948), relying on both Congress' "broad constitutional

---

c. For further commentary, see, e.g., Lucinda M. Finley, *Transcending Equality Theory: A Way Out of the Maternity and the Workplace Debate,* 86 Colum.L.Rev. 1118 (1986); Christine A. Littleton, *Reconstructing Sexual Equality,* 75 Calif.L.Rev. 1279, 1297–1300 (1987); Herma Hill Kay, *Models of Equality,* 1985 U.Ill.L.Rev. 39; Herma Hill Kay, *Equality and Difference: The Case of Pregnancy,* 1 Berkeley Women's L.J. 1 (1985); Wendy W. Williams, *Equality's*

Riddle: Pregnancy and the Equal Treatment/Special Treatment Debate, 13 N.Y.U. Rev. L. & Soc. Change 325, 351–80 (1984–85).

a. *Truax v. Raich,* 239 U.S. 33, 36 S.Ct. 7, 60 L.Ed. 131 (1915).

b. *Truax,* however, invalidated Arizona's forbidding employers of five or more persons from hiring over 20% aliens.

powers in determining what aliens shall be admitted to the United States" and the fourteenth amendment's "general policy" of "equality," invalidated California's denial of licenses for commercial fishing in coastal waters to aliens lawfully residing in the state. *Graham v. Richardson,* 403 U.S. 365, 91 S.Ct. 1848, 29 L.Ed.2d 534 (1971), took a much further step. Reasoning that "aliens as a class are a prime example of a 'discrete and insular minority,' " the Court ruled that "classifications based on alienage [are] inherently suspect and subject to close judicial scrutiny" and held that state laws denying welfare benefits to aliens violate equal protection.

SUGARMAN v. DOUGALL, 413 U.S. 634, 93 S.Ct. 2842, 37 L.Ed.2d 853 (1973), applied the close scrutiny prescribed by *Graham* to Section 53 of New York's Civil Service Law, which required citizenship as a condition of public employment in positions subject to competitive examination. The Court, per BLACKMUN, J., held that Section 53 unconstitutionally discriminated against aliens: "It is established, of course, that an alien is entitled to the shelter of the Equal Protection Clause[,] that aliens as a class 'are a prime example of a "discrete and insular" minority (see *United States v. Carolene Products Co.* [fn. 4, p. 298 supra]),' and that classifications based on alienage are 'subject to close judicial scrutiny.'

"[We] recognize a State's interest in establishing its own form of government, and in limiting participation in that government to those who are within 'the basic conception of a political community.' We recognize, too, the State's broad power to define its political community. But in seeking to achieve this substantial purpose, with discrimination against aliens, the means the State employs must be precisely drawn in light of the acknowledged purpose.

"Section 53 is neither narrowly confined nor precise in its application. Its imposed ineligibility may apply to the 'sanitation man, class B,' to the typist, and to the office worker, as well as to the person who directly participates in the formulation and execution of important state policy. The citizenship restriction sweeps indiscriminately. [At the same time, other provisions] of the Civil Service Law, relating generally to persons holding elective and high appointive offices, contain no citizenship restrictions. Indeed, even § 53 permits an alien to hold a classified civil service position under certain circumstances. In view of the breadth and imprecision of § 53 in the context of the State's interest, we conclude that the statute does not withstand close judicial scrutiny. * * *

"While we rule that § 53 is unconstitutional, we do not hold that, on the basis of an individualized determination, an alien may not be refused, or discharged from, public employment, even on the basis of noncitizenship, if the refusal to hire, or the discharge, rests on legitimate state interests that relate to qualifications for a particular position or to the characteristics of the employee. [Neither] do we hold that a State may not, in an appropriately defined class of positions, require citizenship as a qualification for office. [Such] power inheres in the State by virtue of its obligation, already noted above, 'to preserve the basic conception of a political community.' [O]fficers who participate directly in the formulation, execution, or review of broad public policy perform functions that go to the heart of representative government."

IN RE GRIFFITHS, 413 U.S. 717, 93 S.Ct. 2851, 37 L.Ed.2d 910 (1973), which was decided the same day as *Sugarman*, per POWELL, J., invalidated Connecticut's attempt to exclude resident aliens from practicing law: "[T]he status of holding a license to practice law [does not] place one so close to the core of the political process as to make him a formulator of government policy." Burger, C.J., and Rehnquist, J., dissented in *Griffiths*.

REHNQUIST, J., dissenting in *Sugarman* and *Griffiths*, stated: "The Court, by holding in these cases and in *Graham*, that a citizen-alien classification is 'suspect' in the eyes of our Constitution, fails to mention, let alone rationalize, the fact that the Constitution itself recognizes a basic difference between citizens and aliens. That distinction is constitutionally important in no less than 11 instances in a political document noted for its brevity. [Indeed,] the very Amendment which the Court reads to prohibit classifications based on citizenship establishes the very distinction which the Court now condemns as 'suspect.' [The] language of that Amendment carefully distinguishes between 'persons' who, whether by birth or naturalization, had achieved a certain status, and 'persons' in general. That a 'citizen' was considered by Congress to be a rationally distinct subclass of all 'persons' is obvious from the language of the Amendment. * * *

"The mere recitation of the words 'insular and discrete minority' is hardly a *constitutional* reason for prohibiting state legislative classifications such as are involved here. Our society, consisting of over 200 million individuals of multitudinous origins, customs, tongues, beliefs, and cultures is, to say the least, diverse. It would hardly take extraordinary ingenuity for a lawyer to find 'insular and discrete' minorities at every turn in the road. Yet, unless the Court can precisely define and constitutionally justify both the terms and analysis it uses, these decisions today stand for the proposition that the Court can choose a 'minority' it 'feels' deserves 'solicitude' and thereafter prohibit the States from classifying that 'minority' differently from the 'majority.' I cannot find, and the Court does not cite, any constitutional authority for such a 'ward of the Court' approach to equal protection."

AMBACH v. NORWICK

441 U.S. 68, 99 S.Ct. 1589, 60 L.Ed.2d 49 (1979).

JUSTICE POWELL delivered the opinion of the Court.

This case presents the question whether a State, consistently with the Equal Protection Clause, may refuse to employ as elementary and secondary school teachers aliens who are eligible for United States citizenship but who refuse to seek naturalization. * * *

[*Graham* for] the first time treated classifications based on alienage as "inherently suspect and subject to close judicial scrutiny." Applying *Graham*, this Court has held invalid statutes that prevented aliens from entering a State's classified civil service, *Sugarman*, practicing law, *Griffiths*, working as an engineer, *Examining Bd. v. Flores de Otero*, 426 U.S. 572, 96 S.Ct. 2264, 49 L.Ed.2d 65 (1976), and receiving state educational benefits, *Nyquist v. Mauclet*, 432 U.S. 1, 97 S.Ct. 2120, 53 L.Ed.2d 63 (1977). * * *

In *Sugarman*, we recognized that a State could, "in an appropriately defined class of positions, require citizenship as a qualification for office." [*Sugarman* thus contemplated that the] exclusion of aliens from [influential] governmental positions would not invite as demanding scrutiny from this Court.

Applying the rational basis standard, we held last Term that New York could exclude aliens from the ranks of its police force. *Foley v. Connelie*, 435 U.S. 291, 98 S.Ct. 1067, 55 L.Ed.2d 287 (1978). Because the police function fulfilled "a most fundamental obligation of government to its constituency" and by necessity cloaked policemen with substantial discretionary powers, we viewed the police force as being one of those appropriately defined classes of positions for which a citizenship requirement could be imposed.[a] * * *

The rule for governmental functions, which is an exception to the general standard applicable to classifications based on alienage, rests on important principles inherent in the Constitution. The distinction between citizens and aliens, though ordinarily irrelevant to private activity, [denotes] an association with the polity which, in a democratic republic, exercises the powers of governance. The form of this association is important; an oath of allegiance or similar ceremony cannot substitute for the unequivocal legal bond citizenship represents. It is because of this special significance of citizenship that governmental entities, when exercising the functions of government, have wider latitude in limiting the participation of noncitizens.

In determining whether, for purposes of equal protection analysis, teaching in public schools constitutes a governmental function, we look to the role of public education and to the degree of responsibility and discretion teachers possess in fulfilling that role. Each of these considerations supports the conclusion that public school teachers may be regarded as performing a task "that go[es] to the heart of representative government."

Public education, like the police function, "fulfills a most fundamental obligation of government to its constituency." *Foley*. The importance of public schools in the preparation of individuals for participation as citizens, and in the preservation of the values on which our society rests, long has been recognized by our decisions [*Brown I*]. [In] shaping the students' experience to achieve educational goals, teachers by necessity have wide discretion over the way the course material is communicated to students. [Further], a teacher serves as a role model for his students, exerting a subtle but important influence over their perceptions and values. Thus, [a] teacher has an opportunity to influence the attitudes of students toward government, the political process, and a citizen's social responsibilities. This influence is crucial to the continued good health of a democracy. * * *

As the legitimacy of the State's interest in furthering the educational goals outlined above is undoubted, it remains only to consider whether [the statute] bears a rational relationship to this interest. The restriction is carefully framed to serve its purpose, as it bars from teaching only those aliens who have demonstrated their unwillingness to obtain United States citizenship. Appellees [in] effect have chosen to classify themselves. They prefer to retain citizenship in a foreign country with the obligations it entails of primary duty and loyalty.[14] [New York has] made a judgment that citizenship should be a qualification for teaching the young of the State in the public schools, and [the statute] furthers that judgment.

Reversed.

a. *Cabell v. Chavez–Salido*, 454 U.S. 432, 102 S.Ct. 735, 70 L.Ed.2d 677 (1982), extended *Folie* to probation officers. Marshall, J., joined by Brennan, Blackmun, and Stevens, JJ., dissented in *Folic*. Blackmun, J., joined by Brennan, Marshall, and Stevens, JJ., dissented in *Cabell*.

14. As our cases have emphasized, resident aliens pay taxes, serve in the armed forces, and have made significant contributions to our country in private and public endeavors. No doubt [many] would make excellent public school teachers. But the legislature, having in mind the importance of education to state and local governments, may determine eligibility for the key position in discharging that function on the assumption that *generally* persons [who] have not declined the opportunity to seek United States citizenship, are better qualified than are those who have elected to remain aliens. * * *

Justice Blackmun, with whom Justice Brennan, Justice Marshall, and Justice Stevens, join, dissenting.

[T]he New York classification is irrational. Is it better to employ a poor citizen-teacher than an excellent resident alien teacher? Is it preferable to have a citizen who has never seen Spain or a Latin American country teach Spanish to eighth graders and to deny that opportunity to a resident alien who may have lived for 20 years in the culture of Spain or Latin America? The State will know how to select its teachers responsibly, wholly apart from citizenship, and can do so selectively and intelligently. * * *

[Further], it is logically impossible to differentiate between this case [and *Griffiths*]. One may speak proudly of the role model of the teacher, of his ability to mold young minds, of his inculcating force as to national ideals, and of his profound influence in the impartation of our society's values. Are the attributes of an attorney any the less? [The attorney] is an influence in legislation, in the community, and in the role model figure that the professional person enjoys. * * *

Notes and Questions

1. *Aliens as a suspect class.* How persuasive is the argument that discriminations against aliens should be subject to strict scrutiny?

(a) Is it sufficient to justify strict scrutiny that aliens are a "discrete and insular" minority? Should it be relevant that the Constitution, as Rehnquist, J., pointed out in *Sugarman*, assumes the relevance of citizenship for at least some purposes—including the distribution of rights to vote and to hold some federal political offices?[a] Compare T. Alexander Aleinikoff, *Citizens, Aliens, Membership and the Constitution*, 7 Const. Commentary 9, 21 (1990): "[T]he textual references to citizenship can be read two ways. Either the framers thought that their Constitution was really about citizens and therefore constantly reminded us of that; or they thought their document was primarily about persons, and therefore mentioned citizens in particular situations as a special case. [M]uch can be said for the latter [approach]."

Consider Tribe 2d ed., at 1545: "Because aliens are ordinarily eligible to become citizens, alienage [is] not an unalterable trait. That aliens do not vote might be seen as demonstrating their lack of political power; but, at least if it is alien disenfranchisement that is being challenged, it would seem oddly circular to rely on the very practice challenged to establish the propriety of so strictly scrutinizing it as to make very probable its invalidation."[b]

(b) Does the history of prejudice against aliens justify strict scrutiny?

(c) Does the relevance of alien status to some legitimate government purposes suggest that alienage-based classifications, like gender-based classifications, should be subject to a form of intermediate scrutiny? See *Developments in the*

---

a. See also Earl M. Maltz, *Citizenship and the Constitution: A History and Critique of the Supreme Court's Alienage Jurisprudence*, 28 Ariz.St.L.J. 1137 (1996).

b. Compare Gerald M. Rosberg, *Aliens and Equal Protection: Why Not the Right to Vote?* 75 Mich.L.Rev. 1092, 1106 (1977): "[E]xcluding [aliens] from the political process clearly requires the strictest review of all, for it is the very fact of exclusion that made the classifica-

tion suspect and necessitated strict scrutiny in the first place." But cf. Jamin B. Raskin, *Legal Aliens, Local Citizens: The Historical, Constitutional and Theoretical Meanings of Alien Suffrage*, 141 U.Pa.L.Rev. 1391, 1395 (1993) (arguing that "state enfranchisement of non-citizens is neither forbidden by the Constitution, as is commonly assumed, nor compelled by it" and should be subject to local decision).

Law—Immigration Policy and the Rights of Aliens, 96 Harv.L.Rev. 1286, 1432–33 (1983).

2. *"Political function" exception.* (a) Is the Court's governing principle—that it is permissible for states to exclude aliens from functions related to "the process of self-government" but not to discriminate against aliens generally—a sound one? Consider Note, *A Dual Standard for State Discrimination Against Aliens*, 92 Harv.L.Rev. 1516, 1531–33 (1979): "Some dual standard [appears] fundamentally consistent with general equal protection doctrine interpreted in light of distinctions the Constitution makes on the basis of citizenship. [But despite *Foley's*] attempt to draw an analogy to exclusion of aliens from voting and holding high office, the existence of those exclusions only underscores the need for close review of other measures disadvantaging aliens. [Since] aliens are politically powerless because of their disenfranchisement and disqualification from high office, [the] political decision to bar aliens from the police should be stringently scrutinized."

(b) Are the Court's applications of the "political function exception" persuasively reasoned? With *Ambach* compare BERNAL v. FAINTER, 467 U.S. 216, 104 S.Ct. 2312, 81 L.Ed.2d 175 (1984), per MARSHALL, J., which held that Texas could not bar an alien from becoming a notary public: "We emphasize, as we have in the past, that the political-function exception must be narrowly construed; otherwise the exception will swallow the rule and depreciate the significance that should attach to the designation of the group as a 'discrete and insular' minority for whom heightened judicial solicitude is appropriate."[c] Was the political function exception narrowly construed in *Ambach? Foley? Cabell?*

3. *The role of the supremacy clause.* In addition to holding that classifications discriminating against aliens are constitutionally suspect, *Graham* found that "an additional reason why the state statutes [challenged in] these cases do not withstand constitutional scrutiny emerges from the area of federal-state relations. [State] laws that restrict the eligibility of aliens for [welfare] conflict [with] overriding national policies in an area constitutionally entrusted to the Federal Government. [In] *Takahashi* it was said that the States 'can neither add to nor take from the conditions lawfully imposed by Congress upon admission, naturalization and residence of aliens in the United States or the several states.'"

TOLL v. MORENO, 458 U.S. 1, 102 S.Ct. 2977, 73 L.Ed.2d 563 (1982), per BRENNAN, J., held that a University of Maryland rule—flatly denying "in-state" tuition to nonimmigrant aliens with G–4 visas (issued to employees of certain international organizations and their immediate families)—violated the Supremacy Clause. The Court observed that "Commentators have noted [that] many of the Court's decisions concerning alienage classifications, such as *Takahashi*, are better explained in preemption than equal protection terms. See, e.g., Michael J. Perry, *Modern Equal Protection; A Conceptualization and Appraisal*, 79 Colum.L.Rev. 1023, 1060–65 (1979). [Read] together, *Takahashi* and *Graham* stand for the broad principle that 'state regulation not congressionally sanctioned that discriminates against aliens lawfully admitted to the country is impermissible if it imposes additional burdens not contemplated by Congress.' To be sure, when Congress has done nothing more than permit a class of aliens to enter the country temporarily, the proper application of the principle is likely to be a matter of some dispute. But [in] light of Congress' explicit decision not to bar G–4 aliens from acquiring domicile, [the Maryland rule] surely amounts to an ancillary 'burden not contemplated by Congress.' [Further, as] a result of an array of treaties, international agreements, and federal statutes, G–4 visa holders employed by

c. Rehnquist, J., dissented.

[various international organizations] are relieved of federal, and in many instances, state and local taxes, on the salaries paid by the organizations. [The Maryland rule] frustrates these federal policies."[d]

REHNQUIST, J., joined by Burger, C.J., dissented: "[T]hat a state statute can be said to discriminate against aliens does not, standing alone, demonstrate that the statute is preempted. [A] state law is invalid only if there is 'such actual conflict between the two schemes of regulation that both cannot stand in the same area,' or if Congress has in some other way unambiguously declared its intention to foreclose the state law in question. [The] Court offers no evidence that Congress' intent in permitting respondents to establish 'domicile in the United States' has any bearing at all on the tuition available to them at state universities." As for tax relief, "First, the Federal Government has not barred the States from collecting taxes from many, if not most, G-4 visa holders. Second, as to those G-4 nonimmigrants who *are* immune from state income taxes by treaty, Maryland's tuition policy cannot fairly be said to conflict with those treaties in a manner requiring its preemption."[e]

4. *Discrimination against "illegal aliens."* PLYLER v. DOE, 457 U.S. 202, 102 S.Ct. 2382, 72 L.Ed.2d 786 (1982), Sec. 5, IV infra, "reject[ed] the claim that 'illegal aliens' are a 'suspect class.' [U]ndocumented status is not irrelevant to any proper legislative goal. Nor is [it] an absolutely immutable characteristic since it is the product of conscious, indeed unlawful, action." But the Court, per BRENNAN, J., invalidated a Texas statute denying free public education to illegal alien *children,* stressing both the special status of the children—who can " 'affect neither their parents' conduct nor their own status"—and "the importance of education," both to the children themselves and to the nation more generally, since so many undocumented residents were almost certain to remain in the United States.[f]

Under *Plyler,* may states permissibly deny welfare to illegal alien adults? To illegal alien children? May states permissibly refuse to furnish illegal aliens with emergency medical care? See Gerald L. Neuman, *Aliens as Outlaws: Government Services, Proposition 187, and the Structure of Equal Protection Doctrine,* 42 U.C.L.A.L.Rev. 1425 (1995) (arguing for "a limited extension of *Plyler* that forbids the states to exclude 'illegal' alien adults from a minimal level of government services"). Might the denial of some services to illegal aliens be impermissible under "rational basis" scrutiny?

5. *Federal discrimination.* (a) It has long been held that the national government has power "to exclude aliens altogether from the United States, or to prescribe the terms and conditions upon which they may come to this country."

d. Blackmun, J., who joined the Court's opinion, concurred, vehemently denying the suggestion in Rehnquist, J.'s dissent that "decisions holding resident aliens to be a 'suspect class' no longer are good law."

e. O'Connor, J., concurred in part and dissented in part: "I conclude that the Supremacy Clause does not prohibit the University from charging out-of-state tuition to those G-4 aliens who are exempted by federal law from federal taxes only." See Jesse H. Choper, *Discrimination Against Aliens,* in Jesse H. Choper, Yale Kamisar & Laurence H. Tribe, 4 *The Supreme Court: Trends and Developments 1981–82* 5, 14–21 (1983) for the view that (1) *Toll*'s use of the supremacy clause was a "salutary development," but that (2) "the Court's major difficulty resulted from its going beyond its premise and getting into the gory details of whether the University of Maryland regulation actually came into some direct conflict with congressional policy"; "Justice Rehnquist's argument was fairly strong once you accept *his* premise" of what is required for preemption. For further discussions of the relation between federal immigration policy and state obligations to aliens, see Stephen H. Legomsky, *Immigration, Federalism, and the Welfare State,* 42 UCLA L.Rev. 1453 (1995); Evangeline A. Abriel, *Rethinking Preemption for Purposes of Aliens and Public Benefits,* 42 UCLA L.Rev. 1597 (1995).

f. Burger, C.J., joined by White, Rehnquist, and O'Connor, JJ., dissented.

Lem Moon Sing v. United States, 158 U.S. 538, 15 S.Ct. 967, 39 L.Ed. 1082 (1895). Relying on this traditionally recognized authority, MATHEWS v. DIAZ, 426 U.S. 67, 96 S.Ct. 1883, 48 L.Ed.2d 478 (1976), per STEVENS, J., upheld a federal statute denying Medicare benefits to aliens unless they have (i) been admitted for permanent residence and (ii) resided for at least five years in the United States. Although "aliens and citizens alike, are protected by the Due Process Clause, [i]n the exercise of its broad power over naturalization and immigration, Congress regularly makes rules that would be unacceptable if applied to citizens.

"[T]he responsibility for regulating the relationship between the United States and [aliens] has been committed to the political branches of the Federal Government. Since decisions in these matters may implicate our relations with foreign powers, and since a wide variety of classifications must be defined in the light of changing political and economic circumstances, such decisions are frequently of a character more appropriate to either the Legislature or the Executive than to the Judiciary. [The] reasons that preclude judicial review of political questions also dictate a narrow standard of review of decisions made by the Congress or the President in the area of immigration and naturalization.

"Since it is obvious that Congress has no constitutional duty to provide *all aliens* with the welfare benefits provided to citizens, the party challenging the constitutionality of the particular line Congress has drawn" [—allowing benefits to some aliens but not to others—] "has the burden of advancing principled reasoning that will at once invalidate that line and yet tolerate a different line separating some aliens from others. [Since neither of the two requirements] is wholly irrational, this case essentially involves nothing more than a claim that it would have been more reasonable for Congress to select somewhat different requirements of the same kind. [But] it remains true that some line is essential, that any line must produce some harsh and apparently arbitrary consequences, and, of greatest importance, that those who qualify under the test Congress has chosen may reasonably be presumed to have a greater affinity with the United States than those who do not."

Why do the arguments for treating aliens as a suspect class, if valid with respect to state legislation, not apply equally to the federal government and federal legislation? Does the disparity of standards for scrutinizing state and federal legislation survive *Adarand Constructors, Inc. v. Pena,* Sec. 2, VI supra?

Congress' power to exclude aliens or impose conditions on their admission to the United States does not imply a power to deny them all constitutional rights while they are here. E.g., *Almeida-Sanchez v. United States,* 413 U.S. 266, 273, 93 S.Ct. 2535, 2539–2540, 37 L.Ed.2d 596, 602–603 (1973) (fourth amendment); *Wong Wing v. United States,* 163 U.S. 228, 237, 16 S.Ct. 977, 980–981, 41 L.Ed. 140, 143 (1896) (fifth and sixth amendments). Does the Constitution thus require that a line be drawn between Congress' relatively plenary power over immigration and its much more limited power to impose special disabilities on aliens once they are lawfully resident in the United States?[g] Consider the views that (i) "courts have wrongly assumed that every federal regulation based on *alienage* is necessarily sustainable as an exercise of the *immigration* power"[h] and (ii) the provision

g. See, e.g., Linda S. Bosniak, *Membership, Equality, and the Difference that Alienage Makes,* 69 N.Y.U.L.Rev. 1047 (1994). For the further-reaching argument that cases establishing the plenary power doctrine upheld discrimination against immigrants based on race, and therefore ought to be rejected as unsound in light of *Brown v. Board of Education* and subsequent doctrine, see Gabriel J. Chin, *Segregation's Last Stronghold: Race Discrimination and the Constitutional Law of Immigration,* 46 UCLA L.Rev. 1 (1998).

h. T. Alexander Aleinikoff, *Federal Regulation of Aliens and the Constitution,* 83 Am. J.Int'l L. 862, 869 (1989).

involved in *Mathews* "was not in any obvious way concerned with immigration."[i] Should a "substantive limit to the exercise of a federal power of national self-definition derive[] from the idea that alienage is a stage of transition from outsider to full member?"[j]

(b) HAMPTON v. MOW SUN WONG, 426 U.S. 88, 96 S.Ct. 1895, 48 L.Ed.2d 495 (1976), per STEVENS, J., held that a federal Civil Service Commission regulation, generally barring resident aliens from civil service employment, denied "liberty without due process of law": "[T]he federal power over aliens is [not] so plenary that any agent of the National Government may arbitrarily subject all resident aliens to different substantive rules than those applied to citizens. * * *

"When the Federal Government asserts an overriding national interest as justification for a discriminatory rule which would violate the Equal Protection Clause if adopted by a State, due process requires that there be a legitimate basis for presuming that the rule was actually intended to serve that interest. [We] may assume [that] if the Congress or the President had expressly imposed the citizenship requirement, it would be justified by the national interest in providing an incentive for aliens to become naturalized, or possibly even as providing the President with an expendable token for treaty negotiating purposes; but we are not willing to presume that the Chairman of [CSC] was deliberately fostering an interest so far removed from his normal responsibilities."

The Court reviewed the history of the regulation dating to 1884, concluding that it "cannot fairly be construed to evidence either congressional [or presidential] approval or disapproval of the [rule]. [Thus,] our inquiry is whether the national interests which the Government identifies as justifications for the Commission rule are interests on which that agency may properly rely in making a decision implicating the constitutional and social values at stake in this litigation. * * *

"The only concern of [the] Commission is the promotion of an efficient federal service. In general it is fair to assume that its goal would be best served by removing unnecessary restrictions on the eligibility of qualified applicants for employment. With only one exception, the interests [put] forth as supporting the Commission regulation at issue in this case are not matters which are properly the business of the Commission. That one exception is the administrative desirability of having one simple rule excluding all noncitizens when it is manifest that citizenship is an appropriate and legitimate requirement for some important and sensitive positions. Arguably, therefore, administrative convenience may provide a rational basis for the general rule.

"[But there] is nothing [to] indicate that the Commission actually made any considered evaluation of the relative desirability of a simple exclusionary rule on the one hand, or the value to the service of enlarging the pool of eligible employees on the other. [Of] greater significance, however, is the quality of the interest at stake. Any fair balancing of the public interest in avoiding the wholesale deprivation of employment opportunities caused by the Commission's indiscriminate policy, as opposed to what may be nothing more than a hypothetical justification, requires rejection of the argument of administrative convenience in this case."[k]

i. Gerald M. Rosberg, *The Protection of Aliens From Discriminatory Treatment by the National Government,* 1977 Sup.Ct.Rev. 275, 334.

j. Hiroshi Motomura, *Immigration and Alienage, Federalism and Proposition 187,* 35 Va.J.Int'l L. 201 (1994).

k. Brennan, J., joined by Marshall, J., joined the Court's opinion "understanding that there are reserved the equal protection ques-

REHNQUIST, J., joined by Burger, C.J., and White and Blackmun, JJ., dissented: "The Court's opinion enunciates a novel conception of the procedural due process guaranteed by the Fifth Amendment, and from this concept proceeds to evolve a doctrine of delegation of legislative authority which seems to me to be quite contrary to the doctrine established by a long [line of] decisions. * * *

"[Once] it is determined that [CSC] was properly delegated the power by Congress to make decisions regarding citizenship of prospective civil servants, then the reasons for which that power was exercised are as foreclosed from judicial scrutiny as if Congress had made the decision itself. The fact that Congress has delegated a power does not provide a back door through which to attack a policy which would otherwise have been immune from attack."

Did *Hampton* express a constitutional conclusion about powers that Congress may not permissibly delegate to the Civil Service Commission? A statutory conclusion about the powers that Congress actually had delegated? A judgment that the federal rule discriminating against aliens could be justified only by the considerations that actually motivated the decisionmaker?

II. ILLEGITIMACY AND RELATED CLASSIFICATIONS

MATHEWS v. LUCAS

427 U.S. 495, 96 S.Ct. 2755, 49 L.Ed.2d 651 (1976).

MR. JUSTICE BLACKMUN delivered the opinion of the Court.

[The Social Security Act provides survivor's benefits to children who are "dependent" on the deceased parent at time of death. Legitimate children and some classes of illegitimate children are statutorily presumed to be dependent; other illegitimate children must prove "that the deceased wage earner was the claimant child's parent and at the time of his death, was living with the child or was contributing to his support." Appellees, illegitimate children, proved that the deceased was their father but "failed to demonstrate their dependency by proof that [he] either lived with them or was contributing to their support at the time of his death, or by any of the statutory presumptions of dependency." Appellees "urged that denial of benefits in this case, where paternity was clear, violated the Fifth Amendment's Due Process Clause, as that provision comprehends the principle of equal protection of the laws, because other children, including all legitimate children, are statutorily entitled, as the Lucas children are not, to survivorship benefits regardless of actual dependency."]

[T]he District Court concluded [that] legislation treating legitimate and illegitimate offspring differently is constitutionally suspect * * *. We disagree.

It is true, of course, that the legal status of illegitimacy, however defined, is, like race or national origin, a characteristic determined by causes not within the control of the illegitimate individual, and it bears no relation to the individual's ability to participate in and contribute to society. The Court recognized in *Weber v. Aetna Casualty & Surety Co.*, 406 U.S. 164, 92 S.Ct. 1400, 31 L.Ed.2d 768 (1972), that visiting condemnation upon that child in order to express society's disapproval of the parents' liaisons "is illogical and unjust. Moreover, imposing disabilities on the illegitimate child is contrary to the basic concept of our system

tions that would be raised by congressional or Presidential enactment of a bar on employment of aliens by the Federal Government." President Ford subsequently issued such an executive order. Valid? See *Vergara v. Hampton*, 581 F.2d 1281 (7th Cir.1978), cert. denied, 441 U.S. 905 (1979); *Jalil v. Campbell*, 590 F.2d 1120 (D.C.Cir.1978).

that legal burdens should bear some relationship to individual responsibility or wrongdoing. Obviously, no child is responsible for his birth and penalizing the illegitimate child is an ineffectual—as well as an unjust—way of deterring the parent." But where the law is arbitrary in such a way, we have had no difficulty in finding the discrimination impermissible on less demanding standards than those advocated here. *Levy v. Louisiana*, 391 U.S. 68, 88 S.Ct. 1509, 20 L.Ed.2d 436 (1968).[a] And such irrationality in some classifications does not in itself demonstrate that other, possibly rational, distinctions made in part on the basis of legitimacy are inherently untenable. Moreover, while the law has long placed the illegitimate child in an inferior position relative to the legitimate in certain circumstances, particularly in regard to obligations of support or other aspects of family law, see generally, e.g., Krause, *Illegitimacy: Law and Social Policy* 21–42 (1971); Gray & Rudovsky, *The Court Acknowledges the Illegitimate,* 118 U.Pa. L.Rev. 1, 19–38 (1969), perhaps in part because the roots of the discrimination rest in the conduct of the parents rather than the child, and perhaps in part because illegitimacy does not carry an obvious badge, as race or sex do, this discrimination against illegitimates has never approached the severity or pervasiveness of the historic legal and political discrimination against women and Negroes.

We therefore adhere to our earlier view, see *Labine v. Vincent*, 401 U.S. 532, 91 S.Ct. 1017, 28 L.Ed.2d 288 (1971),[b] that the Act's discrimination between individuals on the basis of their legitimacy does not "command extraordinary protection from the majoritarian political process," which our most exacting scrutiny would entail.

Relying on *Weber*,[c] the Court, in *Gomez v. Perez*, 409 U.S. 535, 538, 93 S.Ct. 872, 875, 35 L.Ed.2d 56 (1973), held that "once a State posits a judicially enforceable right on behalf of children to needed support from their natural fathers there is no constitutionally sufficient justification for denying such an essential right to a child simply because its natural father has not married its mother." The same principle, which we adhere to now, applies when the judicially enforceable right to needed support lies against the Government rather than a natural father. See *New Jersey Welfare Rights Org. v. Cahill*, 411 U.S. 619, 93 S.Ct. 1700, 36 L.Ed.2d 543 (1973).[d] * * *

Congress' purpose in adopting [the] presumptions of dependency was obviously to serve administrative convenience. While Congress was unwilling to assume that every child of a deceased insured was dependent at the time of death, by presuming dependency on the basis of relatively readily documented facts, such as legitimate birth, or existence of a support order or paternity decree, which could be relied upon to indicate the likelihood of continued actual dependency, Congress was able to avoid the burden and expense of specific case-by-case determination in the large number of cases where dependency is objectively probable. Such pre-

---

a. *Levy,* per Douglas, J., involved a statute denying illegitimate children the right to recover for the wrongful death of their mother: "[The test] is whether the line drawn is a rational one [but] we have been extremely sensitive when it comes to basic civil rights and have not hesitated to strike down an invidious classification even though it had history and tradition on its side."

b. *Labine,* per Black, J., upheld a law denying an illegitimate child the same rights as a legitimate child in inheriting from its father who dies intestate even though the father had publicly acknowledged the illegitimate child.

c. *Weber,* per Powell, J., invalidated a law denying dependent, unacknowledged, illegitimate children recovery of workmen's compensation for the death of their father, finding the discrimination "justified by no legitimate state interest, compelling or otherwise."

d. *Cahill* invalidated a law denying welfare to households with illegitimate children.

sumptions in aid of administrative functions, though they may approximate, rather than precisely mirror, the results that case-by-case adjudication would show, are permissible under the Fifth Amendment, so long as that lack of precise equivalence does not exceed the bounds of substantiality tolerated by the applicable level of scrutiny.

In cases of strictest scrutiny, such approximations must be supported at least by a showing that the Government's dollar "lost" to overincluded benefit recipients is returned by a dollar "saved" in administrative expense avoided. Under the standard of review appropriate here, however, the materiality of the relation between the statutory classifications and the likelihood of dependency they assertedly reflect need not be "scientifically substantiated." Nor, in any case, do we believe that Congress is required in this realm of less than strictest scrutiny to weigh the burdens of administrative inquiry solely in terms of dollars ultimately "spent," ignoring the relative amounts devoted to administrative rather than welfare uses. Finally, while the scrutiny by which their showing is to be judged is not a toothless one, the burden remains upon the appellees to demonstrate the insubstantiality of that relation.

Applying these principles, we think that the statutory classifications challenged here are justified as reasonable empirical judgments that are consistent with a design to qualify entitlement to benefits upon a child's dependency at the time of the parent's death. [It] could not have been fairly argued, with respect to any of the statutes struck down in [*Cahill, Gomez, Weber, and Levy*], that the legitimacy of the child was simply taken as an indication of dependency, or of some other valid ground of qualification. Under all but one of the statutes, not only was the legitimate child automatically entitled to benefits, but an illegitimate child was denied benefits solely and finally on the basis of illegitimacy, and regardless of any demonstration of dependency or other legitimate factor. In *Weber*, the sole partial exception, the statutory scheme provided for a child's equal recovery under a workmen's compensation plan in the event of the death of the father, not only if the child was dependent, but *also* only if the dependent child was legitimate. [Here], the statute does not broadly discriminate between legitimates and illegitimates without more, but is carefully tuned to alternative considerations. The presumption of dependency is withheld only in the absence of any significant indication of the likelihood of actual dependency. * * *

Reversed.

MR. JUSTICE STEVENS, with whom MR. JUSTICE BRENNAN and MR. JUSTICE MARSHALL join, dissenting.

In this statute, one or another of the criteria giving rise to a "presumption of dependency" exists to make almost all children of deceased wage earners eligible, [including many] who are no more likely to be "dependent" than are the children in appellees' situation. Yet in the name of "administrative convenience" the Court allows these survivors' benefits to be allocated on grounds which have only the most tenuous connection to the supposedly controlling factor—the child's dependency on his father.

I am persuaded that the classification [is] more probably the product of a tradition of thinking of illegitimates as less deserving persons than legitimates. The sovereign should firmly reject that tradition. The fact that illegitimacy is not as apparent to the observer as sex or race does not make this governmental classification any less odious. It cannot be denied that it is a source of social opprobrium, even if wholly unmerited, or that it is a circumstance for which the individual has no responsibility whatsoever. * * *

Notes and Questions

1. *Origins of discrimination.* Consider Harry D. Krause, *Equal Protection for the Illegitimate,* 65 Mich.L.Rev. 477, 498–99 (1967): "There has been a long history of discrimination against the illegitimate. The medieval church, in both its concern for the family and its aversion to illicit sex, reinforced the basic self-interest of the father, which self-interest may ultimately have been most directly responsible for the situation of the illegitimate. It was natural that men, as legislators, would have limited their accidental offsprings' claims against them, both economically and in terms of a family relationship, especially since the social status of the illegitimate mother often did not equal their own. Moreover, their legitimate wives had an interest in denying the illegitimate's claim on their husbands, since any such claim could be allowed only at the expense of the legitimate family. Against these forces have stood only the illegitimate mother and the helpless child, and thus it is not surprising that our laws are inconsiderate of the child's interests."

2. *The level of scrutiny.* Although the Court's decisions reveal somewhat less than perfect consistency in stating the equal protection standard applicable to illegitimacy cases, CLARK v. JETER, 486 U.S. 456, 108 S.Ct. 1910, 100 L.Ed.2d 465 (1988), unanimously concluded that between the "extremes of rational basis review and strict scrutiny lies a level of intermediate scrutiny, which generally has been applied to discriminatory classifications based on sex or illegitimacy. To withstand intermediate scrutiny, a statutory classification must be substantially related to an important governmental objective." Applying that standard, *Clark* invalidated a statute providing that child-support actions for out-of-wedlock children must be brought before the child turns six. Although acknowledging an important state interest in avoiding litigation of stale or fraudulent claims, the Court found the six-year statute of limitations not substantially related to that interest. The six-year period was not necessarily a reasonable one, given the social pressures that might stop an unmarried mother from filing a claim, and "increasingly sophisticated tests for genetic markers permit the exclusion of over 99% of those who might be accused of paternity" regardless of when a claim is filed.

3. *Discrimination against parents of unmarried children.* (a) GLONA v. AMERICAN GUAR. & LIAB. INS. CO., 391 U.S. 73, 88 S.Ct. 1515, 20 L.Ed.2d 441 (1968), invalidated a Louisiana statutory provision barring a mother's suit to recover for the alleged wrongful death of her illegitimate child. Although acknowledging the state's legitimate interest in "dealing with 'sin,'" the Court, per Douglas, J., held that there was no "rational basis for assuming that if [a] mother is allowed recovery [in a wrongful death case that] the cause of illegitimacy will be served." It was "farfetched to assume that women have illegitimate children so they can be compensated in damages for their death."

Do the interests underlying heightened scrutiny for statutes that discriminate against illegitimate children support similarly elevated scrutiny for statutes that discriminate against the *mothers* of illegitimate children?[e]

(b) NEW JERSEY WELFARE RIGHTS ORG. v. CAHILL, fn.d supra, invalidated a provision that limited eligibility for a particular welfare program to otherwise qualified families "which consist of a household composed of two adults of the opposite sex ceremonially married to each other." Accepting the argument that "the challenged classification [in] practical effect [operates] almost invariably

---

e. See Note, *Equal Protection for Unmarried Parents,* 65 Ia.L.Rev. 679 (1980).

to deny benefits to illegitimate children while granting benefits to those children who are legitimate," the Court ruled the state unconstitutional, "for there can be no doubt that the benefits [are] as indispensable to the health and well-being of illegitimate children as to [others]." REHNQUIST, J., dissenting, protested that the challenged statute "distinguishes among types of families," not legitimate and illegitimate children. Is *Cahill*'s treatment of the challenged statute as involving a discrimination against illegitimate children (which was rendered in 1973) consistent with the 1976 holding of *Washington v. Davis*, Sec. 2, III supra? Should there be elevated scrutiny of statutes that discriminate against the unmarried parents of illegitimate children or against household units including illegitimate children and their unmarried parents?

See CALIFANO v. BOLES, 443 U.S. 282, 99 S.Ct. 2767, 61 L.Ed.2d 541 (1979), per REHNQUIST, J., upholding a provision of the Social Security Act that granted "mother's benefits" to a deceased's widow or divorced wife but not to the mother of his illegitimate child. The Court, noting that the illegitimate child received child's benefits, reasoned that the "mother's benefits" program "was not designed [for] child-care subsidies. Instead Congress sought to limit the category of beneficiaries to those who actually suffer economic dislocation upon the death of a wage earner and are likely to be confronted at that juncture with the choice between employment or the assumption of full-time child-care responsibilities. In this [light,] Congress could reasonably conclude that a woman who has never been married to the wage earner is far less likely to be dependent upon the wage earner at the time of his death."[f] Consider Amy L. Wax, *The Two–Parent Family in the Liberal State: The Case for Selective Subsidies*, 1 Mich.J. Race & L. 491 (1996), arguing that equal protection doctrine should permit welfare policies designed to encourage two-parent families, due to evidence that children raised in two-parent households have fewer behavioral problems and tend to do better academically than children from single-parent homes.

(c) MILLER v. ALBRIGHT, 523 U.S. 420, 118 S.Ct. 1428, 140 L.Ed.2d 575 (1998), upheld a provision of the Immigration and Naturalization Act that provides automatic naturalization for illegitimate children who are born abroad to mothers who are American citizens, but establishes various procedural barriers for the illegitimate children of citizen fathers and non-citizen mothers who wish to become American citizens. STEVENS, J., announcing the judgment of the Court in an opinion that was joined only by Rehnquist, C.J, framed the question as involving the permissibility of a classification based on gender; the statute distinguished unmarried fathers from unmarried mothers, but was justified by important governmental interests. Although Stevens, J., concluded that deference to the political branches' immigration powers dictated a narrow standard of review, he believed that the statute would also survive "the heightened scrutiny that normally governs gender discrimination claims."

SCALIA, J., joined by Thomas, J., concurred that the plaintiff's claim must fail, but did not reach the question whether the statute worked an unconstitutional discrimination: "The complaint must be dismissed because the Court has no power to provide the relief requested: conferral of citizenship on a basis other than that prescribed by Congress."

O'CONNOR, J., joined by Kennedy, J., also concurred in the judgment, on the ground that the statutory distinction between children of illegitimate mothers and

---

f. Marshall, J., joined by Brennan, White, and Blackmun, JJ., dissented, finding that the program, "both in purpose and effect, is a form of assistance to children," and that its discrimination against illegitimates violates equal protection.

children of illegitimate fathers was supported by a rational basis. According to O'Connor, J., rational basis review applied because the plaintiff—an illegitimate child claiming citizenship—lacked standing to assert the rights of fathers of illegitimate children to be free from gender-based discrimination in transferring citizenship to their offspring. Although upholding the provision under a rational basis standard, O'Connor and Kennedy, JJ., did "not share Justice Stevens' assessment that the [challenged] provision withstands heightened scrutiny."

BREYER, J., joined by Souter and Ginsburg, JJ., dissented. He reasoned that the statute discriminated on the basis of gender, that heightened scrutiny therefore applied, and that the discrimination was not adequately justified. Noting that O'Connor and Kennedy, JJ., had also opined that the statute could not withstand heightened scrutiny (if heightened scrutiny were properly brought to bear), Breyer, J., concluded that "a majority of the Court agrees [that] '[i]t is unlikely [that] any gender classifications based on stereotypes can survive heightened scrutiny.' "[g]

Apart from issues of gender-based discrimination, did the statutory scheme involved in *Miller* discriminate against illegitimate children? Should it have been subjected to heightened scrutiny on that basis?

III. MENTAL RETARDATION

CLEBURNE v. CLEBURNE LIVING CENTER, INC.

473 U.S. 432, 105 S.Ct. 3249, 87 L.Ed.2d 313 (1985).

JUSTICE WHITE delivered the opinion of the Court.

A Texas city denied a special permit for the operation of a group home for the mentally retarded. [Permits under the zoning ordinance must be renewed annually and applicants must "obtain the signatures of the property owners within 200 feet of the property to be used."] It was anticipated that the [Featherston] home would house 13 retarded men and women, who would be under the constant supervision of CLC staff members. * * *

[The] general rule [under the Equal Protection Clause] is that legislation is presumed to be valid and will be sustained if the classification drawn by the statute is rationally related to a legitimate state interest. *United States R.R. Retirement Bd. v. Fritz; Vance v. Bradley,* [Sec. 1 supra]. [White, J., then surveyed recognized exceptions to the general rule, involving discriminations based on race, alienage, national origin, gender, and illegitimacy.]

We have declined, however, to extend heightened review to differential treatment based on [age]. The lesson of *Murgia,* [Part V infra], is that where individuals in the group affected by a law have distinguishing characteristics relevant to interests the state has the authority to implement, the courts have been very reluctant [to] closely scrutinize legislative choices as to whether, how and to what extent those interests should be pursued. In such cases, the Equal Protection Clause requires only a rational means to serve a legitimate end.

g. The Court's previous cases involving discrimination against unmarried fathers, both decided by 5–4, are hard to reconcile. Compare *Caban v. Mohammed,* 441 U.S. 380, 99 S.Ct. 1760, 60 L.Ed.2d 297 (1979) (holding violative of equal protection a New York statute granting the mother—but not the father—of an illegitimate child the right to veto the child's adoption) with *Parham v. Hughes,* 441 U.S. 347, 99 S.Ct. 1742, 60 L.Ed.2d 269 (1979) (upholding a law denying the father—but not the mother—of an illegitimate child the right to sue for the child's wrongful death unless he had legitimated the child).

Against this background, we conclude [that] the Court of Appeals erred in holding mental retardation a quasi-suspect classification. [First, those] who are mentally retarded have a reduced ability to cope with and function in the everyday world. [T]hey range from those whose disability is not immediately evident to those who must be constantly cared for. They are thus different, immutably so, in relevant respects, and the states' interest in dealing with and providing for them is plainly a legitimate one. How this large and diversified group is to be treated under the law is a difficult and often a technical matter, very much a task for legislators guided by qualified professionals and not by the perhaps ill-informed opinions of the judiciary. Heightened scrutiny inevitably involves substantive judgments about legislative decisions, and we doubt that the predicate for such judicial oversight is present where the classification deals with mental retardation.

Second, [both national and state] lawmakers have been addressing the[] difficulties [of the retarded] in a manner that belies a continuing antipathy or prejudice and a corresponding need for more intrusive oversight by the judiciary. Thus, the federal government has not only outlawed discrimination against the mentally retarded in federally funded programs, but it has also provided the retarded with the right to receive "appropriate treatment, services, and habilitation" in a setting that is "least restrictive of [their] personal liberty." * * * Texas has similarly enacted legislation that acknowledges the special status of the mentally retarded by conferring certain rights upon them, such as "the right to live in the least restrictive setting appropriate to [their] individual needs and abilities" * * *. [It] may be, as CLC contends, that legislation designed to benefit, rather than disadvantage, the retarded would generally withstand examination under a test of heightened scrutiny. The relevant inquiry, however, is whether heightened scrutiny is constitutionally mandated in the first instance. * * *

Third, the legislative response, which could hardly have occurred and survived without public support, negates any claim that the mentally retarded are politically powerless in the sense that they have no ability to attract the attention of the lawmakers. * * *

Fourth, if the large and amorphous class of the mentally retarded were deemed quasi-suspect, [it] would be difficult to find a principled way to distinguish a variety of other groups who have perhaps immutable disabilities setting them off from others, who cannot themselves mandate the desired legislative responses, and who can claim some degree of prejudice from at least part of the public at large. One need mention in this respect only the aging, the disabled, the mentally ill, and the infirm. We are reluctant to set out on that course, and we decline to do so.

Doubtless, there have been and there will continue to be instances of discrimination against the retarded that are in fact invidious, and that are properly subject to judicial correction under constitutional norms. * * * Our refusal to recognize the retarded as a quasi-suspect class does not leave them entirely unprotected from invidious discrimination. To withstand equal protection review, legislation that distinguishes between the mentally retarded and others must be rationally related to a legitimate governmental purpose. [The] State may not rely on a classification whose relationship to an asserted goal is so attenuated as to render the distinction arbitrary or irrational. See *Zobel v. Williams*, [Sec. 5, II infra]; *U.S. Dep't of Agriculture v. Moreno*, [Sec. 1 supra]. Furthermore, some objectives—such as "a bare * * * desire to harm a politically unpopular group," *Moreno*—are not legitimate state interests. * * *

The constitutional issue is clearly posed. The City does not require a special use permit in an R–3 zone for apartment houses, multiple dwellings, boarding and lodging houses, fraternity or sorority houses, dormitories, apartment hotels, hospitals, sanitariums, nursing homes for convalescents or the aged (other than for the insane or feeble-minded or alcoholics or drug addicts), private clubs or fraternal orders, and other specified uses. [I]n our view the record does not reveal any rational basis for believing that the Featherston home would pose any special threat to the city's legitimate interests * * *.

The District Court found that the City Council's insistence on the permit rested on several factors. First, the Council was concerned with the negative attitude of the majority of property owners located within 200 feet of the Featherston facility, as well as with the fears of elderly residents of the neighborhood. But mere negative attitudes, or fear, unsubstantiated by factors which are properly cognizable in a zoning proceeding, are not permissible bases for treating a home for the mentally retarded differently from apartment houses, multiple dwellings, and the like. * * *

Second, the Council [was] concerned that the facility was across the street from a junior high school, and it feared that the students might harass the occupants of the Featherston home. But the school itself is attended by about 30 mentally retarded students, and denying a permit based on such vague, undifferentiated fears is again permitting some portion of the community to validate what would otherwise be an equal protection violation. The other objection to the home's location was that it was located on "a five hundred year flood plain." This concern with the possibility of a flood, however, can hardly be based on a distinction between the Featherston home and, for example, nursing homes, homes for convalescents or the aged, or sanitariums or hospitals, any of which could be located on the Featherston site without obtaining a special use permit. The same may be said of another concern of the Council—doubts about the legal responsibility for actions which the mentally retarded might take. If there is no concern about legal responsibility with respect to other uses that would be permitted in the area, such as boarding and fraternity houses, it is difficult to believe that the groups of mildly or moderately mentally retarded individuals who would live at 201 Featherston would present any different or special hazard.

Fourth, the Council was concerned with the size of the home and the number of people that would occupy it. [But] there would be no restrictions on the number of people who could occupy this home as a boarding house, nursing home, family dwelling, fraternity house, or dormitory. [At] least this record does not clarify how, in this connection, the characteristics of the intended occupants of the Featherston home rationally justify denying to those occupants what would be permitted to groups occupying the same site for different purposes. * * *

The short of it is that requiring the permit in this case appears to us to rest on an irrational prejudice against the mentally retarded. [Thus, the] judgment of the Court of Appeals is affirmed insofar as it invalidates the zoning ordinance as applied to the Featherston home. * * *

JUSTICE STEVENS, with whom THE CHIEF JUSTICE joins, concurring.

[O]ur cases reflect a continuum of judgmental responses to differing classifications which have been explained in opinions by terms ranging from "strict scrutiny" at one extreme to "rational basis" at the other. I have never been persuaded that these so called "standards" adequately explain the decisional process. Cases involving classifications based on alienage, illegal residency, illegitimacy, gender, age, or—as in this case—mental retardation, do not fit well into sharply defined classifications.

[I] have always asked myself whether I could find a "rational basis" for the classification at issue. The term "rational," of course, includes a requirement that an impartial lawmaker could logically believe that the classification would serve a legitimate public purpose that transcends the harm to the members of the disadvantaged class. Thus, the word "rational" * * * includes elements of legitimacy and neutrality that must always characterize the performance of the sovereign's duty to govern impartially. The rational basis test, properly understood, adequately explains why a law that deprives a person of the right to vote because his skin has a different pigmentation than that of other voters violates [equal protection]. We do not need to apply a special standard, or to apply "strict scrutiny," or even "heightened scrutiny," to decide such cases.

In every equal protection case, we have to ask certain basic questions. What class is harmed by the legislation, and has it been subjected to a "tradition of disfavor" by our laws? What is the public purpose that is being served by the law? What is the characteristic of the disadvantaged class that justifies the disparate treatment? In most cases the answer to these questions will tell us whether the statute has a "rational basis." The answers will result in the virtually automatic invalidation of racial classifications and in the validation of most economic classifications, but they will provide differing results in cases involving classifications based on alienage, gender, or illegitimacy. But that is not because we apply an "intermediate standard of review" in these cases; rather it is because the characteristics of these groups are sometimes relevant and sometimes irrelevant to a valid public purpose, or, more specifically, to the purpose that the challenged laws purportedly intended to serve.

Every law that places the mentally retarded in a special class is not presumptively irrational. The differences between mentally retarded persons and those with greater mental capacity are obviously relevant to certain legislative decisions. * * *

[The record in this case] convinces me that this permit was required because of the irrational fears of neighboring property owners, rather than for the protection of the mentally retarded persons who would reside in respondent's home. * * * I cannot believe that a rational member of this disadvantaged class could ever approve of the discriminatory application of the city's ordinance in this case. * * *

JUSTICE MARSHALL, with whom JUSTICE BRENNAN and JUSTICE BLACKMUN join, concurring in the judgment in part and dissenting in part.

The Court holds [the] ordinance invalid on rational basis grounds and disclaims that anything special, in the form of heightened scrutiny, is taking place. Yet Cleburne's ordinance surely would be valid under the traditional rational basis test applicable to economic and commercial regulation. [The] Court, for example, concludes that legitimate concerns for fire hazards or the serenity of the neighborhood do not justify singling out respondents to bear the burdens of these concerns, for analogous permitted uses appear to pose similar threats. Yet under the traditional and most minimal version of the rational basis test, "reform may take one step at a time, addressing itself to the phase of the problem which seems most acute to the legislative mind." * * *

The refusal to acknowledge that something more than minimum rationality review is at work here is, in my view, unfortunate in at least two respects.[4] The suggestion that the traditional rational basis test allows this sort of searching inquiry creates precedent for this Court and lower courts to subject economic and commercial classifications to similar and searching "ordinary" rational basis review—a small and regrettable step back toward the days of *Lochner v. New York*. Moreover, by failing to articulate the factors that justify today's "second order" rational basis review, the Court provides no principled foundation for determining when more searching inquiry is to be invoked. Lower courts are thus left in the dark on this important question, and this Court remains unaccountable for its decisions employing, or refusing to employ, particularly searching scrutiny. * * *

I have long believed the level of scrutiny employed in an equal protection case should vary with "the constitutional and societal importance of the interest adversely affected and the recognized invidiousness of the basis upon which the particular classification is drawn." *San Antonio Ind. Sch. Dist. v. Rodriguez* [Sec. 5, IV infra] (Marshall, J., dissenting). See also *Dandridge v. Williams* [Sec. 5, IV infra] (Marshall, J., dissenting). When a zoning ordinance works to exclude the retarded from all residential districts in a community, these two considerations require that the ordinance be convincingly justified as substantially furthering legitimate and important purposes.

First, the interest [in] establishing group homes is substantial, [for] as deinstitutionalization has progressed, group homes have become the primary means by which retarded adults can enter life in the community. * * *

Second, the mentally retarded have been subject to a "lengthy and tragic history" of segregation and discrimination that can only be called grotesque. [E]ven when judicial action *has* catalyzed legislative change, that change certainly does not eviscerate the underlying constitutional principle. The Court, for example, has never suggested that race-based classifications became any less suspect once extensive legislation had been enacted on the subject.

For the retarded, just as for Negroes and women, much has changed in recent years, but much remains the same; outdated statutes are still on the books, and irrational fears or ignorance, traceable to the prolonged social and cultural isolation of the retarded, continue to stymie recognition of the dignity and individuality of retarded people. * * *

The Court's [assumption] that the standard of review must be fixed with reference to the number of classifications to which a characteristic would validly be relevant [is] flawed. [Our] heightened scrutiny precedents belie the claim that a characteristic must virtually always be irrelevant to warrant heightened scrutiny. * * * Heightened but not strict scrutiny is considered appropriate in areas such as gender, illegitimacy, or alienage because the Court views the trait as relevant under some circumstances but not others. [An] inquiry into constitutional principle, not mathematics, determines whether heightened scrutiny is appropriate. Whenever evolving principles of equality, rooted in the Equal Protection Clause, require that certain classifications be viewed as *potentially* discriminatory, and

---

4. The two cases the Court cites in its rational basis discussion, *Zobel* and *Moreno*, expose the special nature of the rational basis test employed today. As two of only a handful of modern equal protection cases striking down legislation under what purports to be a rational basis standard, these cases must be and generally have been viewed as intermediate review decisions masquerading in rational basis language.

when history reveals systemic unequal treatment, more searching judicial inquiry than minimum rationality becomes relevant. * * *[24]

In light of the scrutiny that should be applied here, Cleburne's ordinance sweeps too broadly to dispel the suspicion that it rests on a bare desire to treat the retarded as outsiders, pariahs who do not belong in the community. The Court, while disclaiming that special scrutiny is necessary or warranted, reaches the same conclusion. Rather than striking the ordinance down, however, the Court invalidates it merely as applied to respondents. I must dissent from the novel proposition that "the preferred course of adjudication" is to leave standing a legislative act resting on "irrational prejudice," thereby forcing individuals in the group discriminated against to continue to run the act's gauntlet. * * *

Notes and Questions

1. *Tiers of scrutiny.* Are the Court's justifications for refusing to apply heightened scrutiny persuasive? Is the dissent persuasive that the Court *in fact* applies heightened scrutiny? That equal protection analysis both is and should be too complex to be captured in a short list of tiers or standards of review?

2. *"Rationality" and morality.* Do you agree with Stevens, J., that inquiry into the "rationality" of a law "includes elements of legitimacy and neutrality" and assessment of whether the sovereign has acted "impartially"? Is this approach consistent with the *Carolene Products* footnote, p. 298 supra, and suggested limitations of the judicial role in equal protection cases to the protection of discrete and insular minorities? Consider the suggestion of Bruce A. Ackerman, *Beyond Carolene Products*, 98 Harv.L.Rev. 713, 737, 741 (1985), that "*Carolene*'s emphasis on 'prejudice' " cannot mask the need for the courts to make substantive judgments of fairness, since "[o]ne person's 'prejudice' is, notoriously, another's 'principle.' " According to Professor Ackerman, the responsibility for substantive review of the fairness of legislative classifications cannot be limited to cases involving discrete and insular minorities. As Ackerman points out, women are not

---

24. No single talisman can define those groups likely to be the target of classifications offensive to the Fourteenth Amendment and therefore warranting heightened or strict scrutiny; experience, not abstract logic, must be the primary guide. The "political powerlessness" of a group may be relevant, but that factor is neither necessary, as the gender cases demonstrate, nor sufficient, as the example of minors illustrates. [W]e see few statutes reflecting prejudice or indifference to minors, and I am not aware of any suggestion that legislation affecting them be viewed with the suspicion of heightened scrutiny. Similarly, immutability of the trait at issue may be relevant, but many immutable characteristics, such as height or blindness, are valid bases of governmental action and classifications under a variety of circumstances.

The political powerlessness of a group and the immutability of its defining trait are relevant insofar as they point to a social and cultural isolation that gives the majority little reason to respect or be concerned with that group's interests and needs. Statutes discriminating against the young have not been common nor need be feared because those who do

vote and legislate were once themselves young, typically have children of their own, and certainly interact regularly with minors. Their social integration means that minors, unlike discrete and insular minorities, tend to be treated in legislative arenas with full concern and respect, despite their formal and complete exclusion from the electoral process.

The discreteness and insularity warranting a "more searching judicial inquiry" must therefore be viewed from a social and cultural perspective as well as a political one. To this task judges are well suited, for the lessons of history and experience are surely the best guide as to when, and with respect to what interests, society is likely to stigmatize individuals as members of an inferior caste or view them as not belonging to the community. Because prejudice spawns prejudice, and stereotypes produce limitations that confirm the stereotype on which they are based, a history of unequal treatment requires sensitivity to the prospect that its vestiges endure. In separating those groups that are discrete and insular from those that are not, as in many important legal distinctions, "a page of history is worth a volume of logic."

a minority at all, and illegitimates, in his terms, are neither discrete (readily identifiable) nor insular (geographically clustered).

Do you agree with Marshall, J., that equal protection analysis should depend on both the classification used by government and the nature of the burden or benefit being distributed?[a]

3. *Retreat from Cleburne?* The Court appears to have applied a much less stringent form of "rational basis" review in its one post-*Cleburne* case involving the equal protection rights of the mentally retarded. HELLER v. DOE, 509 U.S. 312, 113 S.Ct. 2637, 125 L.Ed.2d 257 (1993), per KENNEDY, J., upheld a Kentucky scheme that allows the involuntary commitment of the mentally retarded under less stringent standards than those employed for the involuntary commitment of the mentally ill. Treating as canonical the formulation that "a classification 'must be upheld against equal protection challenge if there is any reasonably conceivable state of facts that could provide a rational basis for the classification,' " the Court concluded that the lesser standard of proof was justified because it was "reasonably conceivable" that violent behavior by the mentally retarded was easier to predict than such behavior by the mentally ill, and because the treatment afforded to the mentally retarded is less invasive than that provided to the mentally ill.

SOUTER, J., joined by Blackmun and Stevens, JJ., dissented: "While the Court cites *Cleburne* once, and does not purport to overrule it, neither does the Court apply it, and at the end of the day *Cleburne*'s status is left uncertain. * * * While difficulty of proof, and of interpretation of evidence, could legitimately counsel against setting the standard so high that the State may be unable to satisfy it (thereby effectively thwarting efforts to satisfy legitimate interests in protection, care, and treatment), that would at most justify a lower standard in the allegedly more difficult cases of illness, not in the easier cases of retardation. We do not lower burdens of proof merely because it is easy to prove the proposition at issue, nor do we raise them merely because it is difficult. * * * Kentucky is being allowed to draw a distinction that is difficult to see as resting on anything other than the stereotypical assumption that the retarded are 'perpetual children.' "[b]

IV. SEXUAL ORIENTATION

ROMER v. EVANS

517 U.S. 620, 116 S.Ct. 1620, 134 L.Ed.2d 855 (1996).

JUSTICE KENNEDY delivered the opinion of the Court.

One century ago, the first Justice Harlan admonished this Court that the Constitution "neither knows nor tolerates classes among citizens." *Plessy v. Ferguson* (dissenting opinion). Unheeded then, those words are now understood to state a commitment to the law's neutrality where the rights of persons are at stake. The Equal Protection Clause enforces this principle and today requires us to hold invalid a provision of Colorado's Constitution.

[The] enactment challenged in this case is an amendment to the Constitution of the State of Colorado, adopted in a 1992 statewide referendum [and referred to]

---

a. See also Julie A. Nice, *The Emerging Third Strand in Equal Protection Jurisprudence: Recognizing the Co–Constitutive Nature of Rights and Classes*, 1999 U.Ill.L.Rev. 1209.

b. Blackmun, J., dissenting, observed that he would subject laws discriminating against

individuals with mental retardation to heightened review. O'Connor, J., concurring and dissenting in part, agreed with Souter, J.'s analysis of the differential burden of proof requirements.

as "Amendment 2," its designation when submitted to the voters. [The] amendment reads: "No Protected Status Based on Homosexual, Lesbian, or Bisexual Orientation. Neither the State of Colorado, through any of its branches or departments, nor any of its agencies, political subdivisions, municipalities or school districts, shall enact, adopt or enforce any statute, regulation, ordinance or policy whereby homosexual, lesbian or bisexual orientation, conduct, practices or relationships shall constitute or otherwise be the basis of or entitle any person or class of persons to have or claim any minority status, quota preferences, protected status or <u>claim of discrimination</u>. This Section of the Constitution shall be in all respects self-executing."

[The] State's principal argument in defense of Amendment 2 is that it puts gays and lesbians in the same position as all other persons. So, the State says, the measure does no more than deny homosexuals special rights.[a] This reading of the amendment's language is implausible. We rely not upon our own interpretation of the amendment but upon the authoritative construction of Colorado's Supreme Court, [which held that] "The immediate objective of Amendment 2 is, at a minimum, to repeal existing statutes, regulations, ordinances, and policies of state and local entities that barred discrimination based on sexual orientation." [Under Amendment 2 as thus construed, homosexuals], by state decree, are put in a solitary class with respect to transactions and relations in both the private and governmental spheres. The amendment withdraws from homosexuals, but no others, specific legal protection from the injuries caused by discrimination, and it forbids reinstatement of these laws and policies.

The change that Amendment 2 works in the legal status of gays and lesbians in the private sphere is far-reaching, both on its own terms and when considered in light of the structure and operation of modern antidiscrimination laws. That structure is well illustrated by contemporary statutes and ordinances prohibiting discrimination by providers of public accommodations. "At common law, innkeepers, smiths, and others who 'made profession of a public employment,' were prohibited from refusing, without good reason, to serve a customer." The duty was a general one and did not specify protection for particular groups. The common law rules, however, proved insufficient in many instances, and [most] States have chosen to counter discrimination by enacting detailed statutory schemes.

Colorado's state and municipal laws typify this emerging tradition of statutory protection and follow a consistent pattern. The laws first enumerate the persons or entities subject to a duty not to discriminate. The list goes well beyond the entities covered by the common law. The Boulder ordinance, for example, has a comprehensive definition of entities deemed places of "public accommodation." They include "any place of business engaged in any sales to the general public and any place that offers services, facilities, privileges, or advantages to the general public or that receives financial support through solicitation of the general public or through governmental subsidy of any kind."

These statutes and ordinances also depart from the common law by enumerating the groups or persons within their ambit of protection. [In] following this approach, Colorado's state and local governments have not limited anti-discrimination laws to groups that have so far been given the protection of heightened equal protection scrutiny under our cases. Rather, they set forth an extensive

---

a. For a discussion of "special rights" and their distinction from "equal" rights, see Peter J. Rubin, *Equal Rights, Special Rights, and the Nature of Antidiscrimination Law*, 97 Mich. L.Rev. 564 (1998).

catalogue of traits which cannot be the basis for discrimination, including age, military status, marital status, pregnancy, parenthood, custody of a minor child, political affiliation, physical or mental disability of an individual or of his or her associates—and, in recent times, sexual orientation.

Amendment 2 bars homosexuals from securing protection against the injuries that these public-accommodations laws address. That in itself is a severe consequence, but there is more. Amendment 2, in addition, nullifies specific legal protections for this targeted class in all transactions in housing, sale of real estate, insurance, health and welfare services, private education, and employment.

[Not] confined to the private sphere, Amendment 2 also operates to repeal and forbid all laws or policies providing specific protection for gays or lesbians from discrimination by every level of Colorado government. The State Supreme Court cited two examples of protections in the governmental sphere that are now rescinded and may not be reintroduced. The first is [an] Executive Order which forbids employment discrimination against " 'all state employees, classified and exempt' on the basis of sexual orientation." Also repealed, and now forbidden, are "various provisions prohibiting discrimination based on sexual orientation at state colleges."

Amendment 2's reach may not be limited to specific laws passed for the benefit of gays and lesbians. It is a fair, if not necessary, inference from the broad language of the amendment that it deprives gays and lesbians even of the protection of general laws and policies that prohibit arbitrary discrimination [such as statutes subjecting agency action to judicial review under the arbitrary and capricious standard and making it a criminal offense for a public servant knowingly, arbitrarily, or capriciously to refrain from performing a duty imposed by law]. At some point in the systematic administration of these laws, an official must determine whether homosexuality is an arbitrary and thus forbidden basis for decision. Yet a decision to that effect would itself amount to a policy prohibiting discrimination on the basis of homosexuality, and so would appear to be no more valid under Amendment 2 than the specific prohibitions against discrimination the state court held invalid.

[The] state court did not decide whether the amendment has this effect, however, and neither need we. [Even] if, as we doubt, homosexuals could find some safe harbor in laws of general application, we cannot accept the view that Amendment 2's prohibition on specific legal protections does no more than deprive homosexuals of special rights. To the contrary, the amendment imposes a special disability upon those persons alone. Homosexuals are forbidden the safeguards that others enjoy or may seek without constraint. They can obtain specific protection against discrimination only by enlisting the citizenry of Colorado to amend the state constitution or perhaps, on the State's view, by trying to pass helpful laws of general applicability. This is so no matter how local or discrete the harm, no matter how public and widespread the injury. We find nothing special in the protections Amendment 2 withholds. These are protections taken for granted by most people either because they already have them or do not need them; these are protections against exclusion from an almost limitless number of transactions and endeavors that constitute ordinary civic life in a free society.

[If] a law neither burdens a fundamental right nor targets a suspect class, we will uphold the legislative classification so long as it bears a rational relation to some legitimate end. Amendment 2 fails, indeed defies, even this conventional inquiry. [Even] in the ordinary equal protection case calling for the most deferential of standards, we insist on knowing the relation between the classification adopted and the object to be attained. [By] requiring that the classification bear a rational relationship to an independent and legitimate legislative end, we ensure that classifications are not drawn for the purpose of disadvantaging the group burdened by the law.

Amendment 2 confounds this normal process of judicial review. It is at once too narrow and too broad. It identifies persons by a single trait and then denies them protection across the board. [It] is not within our constitutional tradition to enact laws of this sort. Central both to the idea of the rule of law and to our own Constitution's guarantee of equal protection is the principle that government and each of its parts remain open on impartial terms to all who seek its assistance. [Respect] for this principle explains why laws singling out a certain class of citizens for disfavored legal status or general hardships are rare. A law declaring that in general it shall be more difficult for one group of citizens than for all others to seek aid from the government is itself a denial of equal protection of the laws in the most literal sense. * * *

Davis v. Beason, 133 U.S. 333, 10 S.Ct. 299, 33 L.Ed. 637 (1890), not cited by the parties but relied upon by the dissent, is not evidence that Amendment 2 is within our constitutional tradition, and any reliance upon it as authority for sustaining the amendment is misplaced. In *Davis*, the Court approved an Idaho territorial statute denying Mormons, polygamists, and advocates of polygamy the right to vote and to hold office. [To] the extent *Davis* held that persons advocating a certain practice may be denied the right to vote, it is no longer good law. *Brandenburg v. Ohio*, [Ch. 7, Sec. 1, I]. To the extent it held that the groups designated in the statute may be deprived of the right to vote because of their status, its ruling could not stand without surviving strict scrutiny, a most doubtful outcome. *Dunn v. Blumstein*, [Sec. 5, II infra].

[A] second and related point is that laws of the kind now before us raise the inevitable inference that the disadvantage imposed is born of animosity toward the class of persons affected. "[I]f the constitutional conception of 'equal protection of the laws' means anything, it must at the very least mean that a bare * * * desire to harm a politically unpopular group cannot constitute a *legitimate* governmental interest." *Moreno*, [Sec. 1 supra]. Even laws enacted for broad and ambitious purposes often can be explained by reference to legitimate public policies which justify the incidental disadvantages they impose on certain persons. Amendment 2, however, in making a general announcement that gays and lesbians shall not have any particular protections from the law, inflicts on them immediate, continuing, and real injuries that outrun and belie any legitimate justifications that may be claimed for it.

[The] primary rationale the State offers for Amendment 2 is respect for other citizens' freedom of association, and in particular the liberties of landlords or employers who have personal or religious objections to homosexuality. Colorado also cites its interest in conserving resources to fight discrimination against other groups. The breadth of the Amendment is so far removed from these particular justifications that we find it impossible to credit them. [It] is a status-based enactment divorced from any factual context from which we could discern a relationship to legitimate state interests; it is a classification of persons undertaken for its own sake, something the Equal Protection Clause does not permit. * * *

JUSTICE SCALIA, with whom THE CHIEF JUSTICE and JUSTICE THOMAS join, dissenting.

[In] rejecting the State's arguments that Amendment 2 "puts gays and lesbians in the same position as all other persons," and "does no more than deny homosexuals special rights," [the] Court considers it unnecessary to decide the validity of the State's argument that Amendment 2 does not deprive homosexuals of the "protection [afforded by] general laws and policies that prohibit arbitrary discrimination in governmental and private settings." I agree that we need not resolve that dispute, because the Supreme Court of Colorado has resolved it for us. [The] Colorado court stated: "[I]t is significant to note that Colorado law currently proscribes discrimination against persons who are not suspect classes, including discrimination based on age, marital or family status, veterans' status, and for any legal, off-duty conduct such as smoking tobacco. *Of course Amendment 2 is not intended to have any effect on this legislation, but seeks only to prevent the adoption of antidiscrimination laws intended to protect gays, lesbians, and bisexuals.*" (emphasis added). [This] analysis, which is fully in accord with (indeed, follows inescapably from) the text of the constitutional provision, lays to rest such horribles [as] the prospect that assaults upon homosexuals could not be prosecuted. The amendment prohibits *special treatment* of homosexuals, and nothing more. It would not affect, for example, a requirement of state law that pensions be paid to all retiring state employees with a certain length of service; homosexual employees, as well as others, would be entitled to that benefit. But it would prevent the State or any municipality from making death-benefit payments to the "life partner" of a homosexual when it does not make such payments to the long-time roommate of a nonhomosexual employee.

[Despite] all of its hand-wringing about the potential effect of Amendment 2 on general antidiscrimination laws, the Court's opinion ultimately does not dispute all this, but assumes it to be true. The only denial of equal treatment it contends homosexuals have suffered is this: They may not obtain *preferential* treatment without amending the state constitution. That is to say, the principle underlying the Court's opinion is that one who is accorded equal treatment under the laws, but cannot as readily as others obtain *preferential* treatment under the laws, has been denied equal protection of the laws. If merely stating this alleged "equal protection" violation does not suffice to refute it, our constitutional jurisprudence has achieved terminal silliness.

The central thesis of the Court's reasoning is that any group is denied equal protection when, to obtain advantage (or, presumably, to avoid disadvantage), it must have recourse to a more general and hence more difficult level of political decisionmaking than others. The world has never heard of such a principle, which is why the Court's opinion is so long on emotive utterance and so short on relevant legal citation. And it seems to me most unlikely that any multilevel democracy can function under such a principle. For *whenever* a disadvantage is imposed, or conferral of a benefit is prohibited, at one of the higher levels of democratic decisionmaking (*i.e.*, by the state legislature rather than local government, or by the people at large in the state constitution rather than the legislature), the affected group has (under this theory) been denied equal protection. To take the simplest of examples, consider a state law prohibiting the award of municipal contracts to relatives of mayors or city councilmen. Once such a law is passed, the group composed of such relatives must, in order to get the benefit of city contracts, persuade the state legislature—unlike all other citizens, who need only persuade the municipality. It is ridiculous to consider this a denial of equal protection, which is why the Court's theory is unheard of. * * *

I turn next to whether there was a legitimate rational basis for the substance of the constitutional amendment—for the prohibition of special protection for homosexuals.[1] It is unsurprising that the Court avoids discussion of this question, since the answer is so obviously yes. The case most relevant to the issue before us today is not even mentioned in the Court's opinion: In *Bowers v. Hardwick*, [Ch. 6, Sec. 2 supra], we held that the Constitution does not prohibit what virtually all States had done from the founding of the Republic until very recent years—making homosexual conduct a crime. [If] it is constitutionally permissible for a State to make homosexual conduct criminal, surely it is constitutionally permissible for a State to enact other laws merely *disfavoring* homosexual conduct. [And] a fortiori it is constitutionally permissible for a State to adopt a provision *not even* disfavoring homosexual conduct, but merely prohibiting all levels of state government from bestowing *special protections* upon homosexual conduct. Respondents (who, unlike the Court, cannot afford the luxury of ignoring inconvenient precedent) counter *Bowers* with the argument that a greater-includes-the-lesser rationale cannot justify Amendment 2's application to individuals who do not engage in homosexual acts, but are merely of homosexual "orientation."

[Assuming] that, in Amendment 2, a person of homosexual "orientation" is someone who does not engage in homosexual conduct but merely has a tendency or desire to do so, *Bowers* still suffices to establish a rational basis for the provision. If it is rational to criminalize the conduct, surely it is rational to deny special favor and protection to those with a self-avowed tendency or desire to engage in the conduct. Indeed, where criminal sanctions are not involved, homosexual "orientation" is an acceptable stand-in for homosexual conduct. A State "does not violate the Equal Protection Clause merely because the classifications made by its laws are imperfect." Just as a policy barring the hiring of methadone users as transit employees does not violate equal protection simply because *some* methadone users pose no threat to passenger safety, see *New York City Transit Authority v. Beazer,* [Sec. 1 supra], [Amendment] 2 is not constitutionally invalid simply because it could have been drawn more precisely so as to withdraw special antidiscrimination protections only from those of homosexual "orientation" who actually engage in homosexual conduct.

[The] Court's opinion contains grim, disapproving hints that Coloradans have been guilty of "animus" or "animosity" toward homosexuality, as though that has been established as Unamerican. Of course it is our moral heritage that one should not hate any human being or class of human beings. But I had thought that one could consider certain conduct reprehensible—murder, for example, or polygamy, or cruelty to animals—and could exhibit even "animus" toward such conduct. Surely that is the only sort of "animus" at issue here: moral disapproval of homosexual conduct, the same sort of moral disapproval that produced the centuries-old criminal laws that we held constitutional in *Bowers*.

[But] though Coloradans are, as I say, *entitled* to be hostile toward homosexual conduct, the fact is that the degree of hostility reflected by Amendment 2 is the smallest conceivable. The Court's portrayal of Coloradans as a society fallen victim to pointless, hate-filled "gay-bashing" is so false as to be comical. Colorado not only is one of the 25 States that have repealed their antisodomy laws, but was among the first to do so. But the society that eliminates criminal punishment for

---

1. The Court evidently agrees that "rational basis"—the normal test for compliance with the Equal Protection Clause—is the governing standard. The trial court rejected respondents' argument that homosexuals constitute a "suspect" or "quasi-suspect" class, and respondents elected not to appeal that ruling to the Supreme Court of Colorado. And the Court implicitly rejects the Supreme Court of Colorado's holding that Amendment 2 infringes upon a "fundamental right" of "independently identifiable class[es]" to "participate equally in the political process."

homosexual acts does not necessarily abandon the view that homosexuality is morally wrong and socially harmful; often, abolition simply reflects the view that enforcement of such criminal laws involves unseemly intrusion into the intimate lives of citizens.

There is a problem, however, which arises when criminal sanction of homosexuality is eliminated but moral and social disapprobation of homosexuality is meant to be retained. [Because] those who engage in homosexual conduct tend to reside in disproportionate numbers in certain communities, and of course care about homosexual-rights issues much more ardently than the public at large, they possess political power much greater than their numbers, both locally and statewide. Quite understandably, they devote this political power to achieving not merely a grudging social toleration, but full social acceptance, of homosexuality.

By the time Coloradans were asked to vote on Amendment 2, [three] Colorado cities—Aspen, Boulder, and Denver—had enacted ordinances that listed "sexual orientation" as an impermissible ground for discrimination, equating the moral disapproval of homosexual conduct with racial and religious bigotry[, and] the Governor of Colorado had signed an executive order [directing] state agency-heads to "ensure non-discrimination" in hiring and promotion based on, among other things, "sexual orientation." [I] do not mean to be critical of these legislative successes; homosexuals are as entitled to use the legal system for reinforcement of their moral sentiments as are the rest of society. But they are subject to being countered by lawful, democratic countermeasures as well.

That is where Amendment 2 came in. It sought to counter both the geographic concentration and the disproportionate political power of homosexuals by (1) resolving the controversy at the statewide level, and (2) making the election a single-issue contest for both sides. [The] Court today asserts that this most democratic of procedures is unconstitutional. Lacking any cases to establish that facially absurd proposition, it simply asserts that it *must* be unconstitutional, because it has never happened before. [But, as] I have noted above, this is proved false every time a state law prohibiting or disfavoring certain conduct is passed, because such a law prevents the adversely affected group—whether drug addicts, or smokers, or gun owners, or motorcyclists—from changing the policy thus established in "each of [the] parts" of the State.

[But] there is a much closer analogy, one that involves precisely the effort by the majority of citizens to preserve its view of sexual morality statewide, against the efforts of a geographically concentrated and politically powerful minority to undermine it. The constitutions of the States of Arizona, Idaho, New Mexico, Oklahoma, and Utah *to this day* contain provisions stating that polygamy is "forever prohibited." Polygamists, and those who have a polygamous "orientation," have been "singled out" by these provisions for much more severe treatment than merely denial of favored status; and that treatment can only be changed by achieving amendment of the state constitutions. The Court's disposition today suggests that these provisions are unconstitutional, and that polygamy must be permitted in these States on a state-legislated, or perhaps even local-option, basis-unless, of course, polygamists for some reason have fewer constitutional rights than homosexuals.

[Has] the Court concluded that the perceived social harm of polygamy is a "legitimate concern of government," and the perceived social harm of homosexuality is not? [I] strongly suspect that the answer [to the last question is] yes, which leads me to the last point I wish to make: [To] suggest [that] this constitutional amendment springs from nothing more than " 'a bare * * * desire to harm a politically unpopular group,' " is nothing short of insulting. (It is also nothing short of preposterous to call "politically unpopular" a group which enjoys enormous influence in American media and politics, and which, as the trial court here noted, though composing no more than 4% of the population had the support of 46% of the voters on Amendment 2.) [When] the Court takes sides in the culture wars, it tends to be with the knights rather than the villeins—and more specifically with the Templars, reflecting the views and values of the lawyer class from which the Court's Members are drawn. How that class feels about homosexuality will be evident to anyone who wishes to interview job applicants at virtually any of the Nation's law schools. The interviewer may refuse to offer a job because the applicant is a Republican; because he is an adulterer; [or] because he went to the wrong prep school or belongs to the wrong country club. But if the interviewer should wish not to be an associate or partner of an applicant because he disapproves of the applicant's homosexuality, *then* he will have violated the pledge which the Association of American Law Schools requires all its member-schools to exact from job interviewers: "assurance of the employer's willingness" to hire homosexuals. This law-school view of what "prejudices" must be stamped out may be contrasted with the more plebeian attitudes that apparently still prevail in the United States Congress, which has been unresponsive to repeated attempts to extend to homosexuals the protections of federal civil rights laws.

[Today's] opinion has no foundations in American constitutional law, and barely pretends to. The people of Colorado have adopted an entirely reasonable provision which does not even disfavor homosexuals in any substantive sense, but merely denies them preferential treatment. Amendment 2 is designed to prevent piecemeal deterioration of the sexual morality favored by a majority of Coloradans, and is not only an appropriate means to that legitimate end, but a means that Americans have employed before. Striking it down is an act, not of judicial judgment, but of political will. * * *

Notes and Questions

1. *Rationale of decision and standard of review.* What standard of review did the Court apply in *Romer*? Was it "ordinary" rational basis review?[a]

If so, the crucial move is to distinguish the expression of moral disapprobation, which is a legitimate governmental purpose, from the expression of animus, which is not. Does the Court provide a tenable basis for its distinction?

(a) Why did the majority make no reference to *Bowers v. Hardwick*? Is the result in *Romer* consistent with the result in *Bowers*? Is it an adequate answer to say that whereas due process methodology looks backward at "tradition" and traditional morality, equal protection analysis is appropriately critical of traditional, stereotyped, and prejudicial thinking? See Cass R. Sunstein, *One Case At a Time: Judicial Minimalism on the Supreme Court* 156–57 (1999); see also Barbara J. Flagg, *"Animus" and Moral Disapproval: A Comment on Romer v. Evans*, 82 Minn.L.Rev. 833 (1998).

After *Romer*, when, if ever, is it permissible for the state to discriminate against those who commit homosexual acts of the kind involved in *Bowers*? Against "homosexuals" as a class defined by their sexual orientation, proclivities, or state of mind, regardless of whether they have engaged in sexual acts of the kind held prohibitable in *Bowers*?

a. See Larry Alexander, *Sometimes Better Boring and Correct: Romer v. Evans as an* *Exercise of Ordinary Equal Protection Analysis*, 68 U.Colo.L.Rev. 335 (1997).

(b) A number of commentators have argued that "status-based" (even if not conduct-based) discriminations against homosexuals target a paradigmatic discrete and insular minority who have been the victims of historic "prejudice" and should, therefore, be subject to strict judicial scrutiny.[b] Did *Romer* implicitly reject this position?

(c) Is *Romer* best explained as involving a "pariah principle" that "forbids the government from designating any societal group as untouchable, regardless of whether the group in question is entitled to some special degree of judicial protection, like blacks, or to no special protection, like left-handers (or, under current doctrine, homosexuals)"? Daniel Farber & Suzanna Sherry, *The Pariah Principle*, 13 Const.Comm. 257, 258 (1996).

(d) Commentators have described *Romer* as "narrowly" written and shallowly theorized;[c] as opaque; and as notable for its "unwritten pages."[d] Do you agree?

2. *Culture wars?* Consider the observations of Richard F. Duncan, *Wigstock and Kulturkampf: Supreme Court Storytelling, the Culture War, and Romer v. Evans*, 72 Notre Dame L.Rev. 345, 372 (1997): "[The majority and dissenting opinions] tell clashing and fascinating stories about the culture war that is currently raging in our [society]. Justice Kennedy paints [Colorado] as the hate state. This is the narrative [that] is currently dominant among America's progressive elites. Justice [Scalia] understands [Amendment 2 as] an attempt by 'tolerant Coloradans' to prevent civil rights laws from being used to legitimize homosexual conduct and delegitimize traditional notions of sexual morality."[e]

Did the Court inevitably have to choose one of these narratives in *Romer*? Cf. *Boy Scouts of America v. Dale*, Ch. 7, Sec. 19, III, holding that a New Jersey statute barring discrimination on grounds of homosexuality violated the Boy Scouts' protected right to freedom of expression. Although the case presented no equal protection issue, Stevens, J., joined by Souter, Ginsburg, and Breyer, JJ., dissenting, described hostile attitudes toward homosexuals as "prejudices."

3. *Gender discrimination?* Is discrimination against homosexuals a form of sex discrimination appropriately subject to intermediate scrutiny? Consider Andrew Koppelman, *Why Discrimination Against Lesbians and Gay Men is Sex Discrimination*, 69 N.Y.U.L.Rev. 197, 208 (1994): "If a business fires Ricky, or if the state prosecutes him, because of his sexual activities with Fred, while these actions would not be taken against Lucy if she did exactly the same things with Fred, then Ricky is being discriminated against because of his sex."[f]

---

b. See John H. Ely, *Democracy and Distrust* 162–63 (1980); see also Eric A. Roberts, *Heightened Scrutiny Under the Equal Protection Clause: A Remedy to Discrimination Based on Sexual Orientation*, 42 Drake L.Rev. 485 (1993). Should it matter to this analysis whether homosexuality is an "immutable" characteristic? For a negative answer, see Janet E. Halley, *Sexual Orientation and the Politics of Biology: A Critique of the Argument from Immutability*, 46 Stan.L.Rev. 503 (1994). See also Kenji Yoshino, *Assimilationist Bias in Equal Protection: The Visibility Presumption and the Case of "Don't Ask, Don't Tell,"* 108 Yale L.J. 485 (1998) (arguing that equal protection doctrine wrongly treats visible and immutable characteristics (such as race or gender) as more suspect than invisible characteristics (such as sexual orientation)).

c. Sunstein, supra, at 138–62.

d. Lynn A. Baker, *The Missing Pages of the Majority Opinion in Romer v. Evans*, 68 U.Colo.L.Rev. 387 (1997); see also Janet E. Halley, *Romer v. Hardwick*, 68 U.Colo.L.Rev. 429 (1997) (emphasizing the importance or *Romer*'s silences).

e. See also J.M. Balkin, *The Constitution of Status*, 106 Yale L.J. 2313, 2316–21 (1997) (describing a culture war within the opinion and presenting a theory of status groups and unjust status hierarchies).

f. See also Sylvia A. Law, *Homosexuality and the Social Meaning of Gender*, 1988 Wisc. L.Rev. 187; Cass R. Sunstein, *Homosexuality and the Constitution*, 70 Ind.L.J. 1 (1994) (arguing that discrimination against homosexuals reinforces traditional assumptions concerning

If this argument is a good one, does it support a right to same-sex marriage under the equal protection clause?[g] Are prohibitions against gay marriage analogous to the antimiscegenation statute invalidated in *Loving v. Virginia*? See Koppelman, supra. Compare William N. Eskridge, *Multivocal Prejudices and Homo Equality*, 74 Indiana L.J. 1085, 1104–07 (1999), noting that whereas antimiscegenation statutes tried to support a race-based hierarchy, bans based on same-sex marriage do not attempt to inflict a harm or stigma based on sex, but one based on sexual orientation.

4. *"Don't ask, don't tell."* The United States military now observes a "don't ask, don't tell" policy, codified in 10 U.S.C.A. § 654(b), under which homosexuals remain subject to exclusion from the armed services, but the military will not seek to discover evidence of homosexual acts or orientation when it is not openly disclosed.[h] Although the constitutionality of this policy has not come before the Supreme Court, the courts of appeals are unanimous in upholding it in the aftermath of *Romer*.[i] In *Able v. United States*, 155 F.3d 628 (2d Cir.1998), the Second Circuit reasoned that it was constitutionally obliged to give deference to military judgments and credited as rational the government's stated rationales of maintaining unit cohesion, reducing sexual tension, and promoting "esprit de corps." The court also said that unlike Amendment 2 in *Romer*, the military policy is targeted at homosexual conduct, not homosexual status. Is this analysis persuasive?[j]

5. *The future of gay rights litigation.* (a) As is pointed out by Eskridge, *Multivocal Prejudices and Homo Equality*, supra, so-called gay rights litigation is likely to involve challenges to at least three analytically different kinds of statutes: (i) those involving explicit discrimination against homosexuals, (ii) laws that only apply to same-sex behavior (such as bans on gay marriage and same-sex sodomy), and (iii) statutes with a discriminatory effect, such as general sodomy laws. How much does the analysis change with the kind of statute in issue?

(b) Consider the argument of Chai R. Feldblum, *Sexual Orientation, Morality, and the Law: Devlin Revisited*, 57 U.Pitt.L.Rev. 237 (1996), that a persuasive constitutional argument that anti-gay discrimination violates the equal protection clause must ultimately confront the argument that homosexual conduct is wrong: The legitimacy of discriminatory legislation depends on the validity of the end that the state is seeking to promote.[k]

---

the general superiority of heterosexual males and devalues the sexual "passivity" traditionally associated with women). Compare Craig M. Bradley, *The Right Not to Endorse Gay Rights: A Reply to Sunstein*, 70 Ind.L.J. 29 (1994).

g. For a sustained argument in favor of a constitutional right to same-sex marriage, see William N. Eskridge, *The Case for Same-Sex Marriage: From Sexual Liberty to Civilized Commitment* (1996).

h. The prohibition extends (i) to those who have engaged in or solicited homosexual acts, unless "such conduct is a departure from a member's usual and customary behavior" and the member's continued service "is consistent [with] discipline, good order, and morale," and (ii) to anyone who "has stated that he or she is a homosexual or bisexual," unless there is evidence that the member does not engage in and

does not have "a propensity to engage in" homosexual acts. For detailed discussion and criticism, see Janet Halley, *Don't: A Reader's Guide to the Military's Anti–Gay Policy* (1999).

i. For criticism, see Yoshino, supra.

j. The courts of appeals have also rejected free speech challenges to the "don't ask, don't tell" policy. For discussion, see Tobias Barrington Wolff, *Compelled Affirmations, Free Speech, and the U.S. Military's Don't Ask, Don't Tell Policy*, 63 Brooklyn L.Rev. 1141 (1997).

k. See also Peter M. Cicchino, *Reason and the Rule of Law: Should Bare Assertions of "Public Morality" Qualify as Legitimate Interests for the Purposes of Equal Protection Review?*, 87 Geo.L.J. 139 (1998).

Compare Andrew Jacobs, *Romer Wasn't Built in a Day: The Subtle Transformation in Judicial Argument Over Gay Rights*, 1996 Wisc.L.Rev. 893, arguing that when judicial discourse is framed in moralistic terms, as in *Bowers*, gays tend to lose, whereas when cases are framed as involving hostile discrimination against a beleaguered group, as in *Romer*, gays tend to win.[l] Given that the data set is very small, does this seem a plausible and sustainable pattern?

(c) Consider the suggestion of Sunstein, *One Case at a Time*, supra, at 161–62, that even if the best understanding of the Constitution would forbid discrimination on the basis of sexual orientation, the Court should not move swiftly to enforce that understanding, certainly in the area of gay marriage and possibly in cases involving the military: "If the [Court] accepted the view that all states must authorize same-sex marriages in 2001, or even 2003, we might well expect a constitutional crisis, a weakening of the legitimacy of the Court, an intensifying of hatred of homosexuals, a constitutional amendment overturning the Court's decision, and much more. Any court should hesitate in the face of such prospects. It would be far better for the Court to [start] cautiously [as it did in *Romer*] and to proceed incrementally," stopping short of the steps most likely to trigger widespread opposition or outrage.

Should the Court accept Sunstein's premise that the equal protection principle forbids discriminations on the basis of sexual orientation? His conclusion that the Court should stop short of enforcing that principle to its ultimate limits?[m] What significance, if any, should attach to the fact that the Court's opinion in *Romer* begins by quoting Justice Harlan's dissent in *Plessy v. Ferguson*?[n]

6. *International developments*. (a) The Canadian Supreme Court has ruled that discrimination based on sexual orientation violates the equal protection provision of the Canadian Charter of Rights and Freedoms. See *Vriend v. Alberta*, 1998 WL 1044511 (Can.Sup.Ct. April 2, 1998). See also *M. v. H.*, No. 25838 (Can.Sup.Ct. May 20, 1999) (declaring invalid the opposite-sex definition of "spouse" in Ontario's Family Law Act and mandating civil equality for same-sex couples).

---

l. See also Toni Massaro, *Gay Rights, Thick and Thin*, 49 Stan.L.Rev. 45 (1996) (developing complementary themes).

m. See also Richard Posner, *Should There Be Homosexual Marriage? And If So, Who Should Decide?*, 95 Mich.L.Rev. 1578, 1585 (1997): "[P]ublic opinion is not irrelevant to the task of deciding whether a constitutional right exists. When judges are asked to recognize a new constitutional right, they have to do a lot more than simply consult the text of the Constitution and the cases dealing with analogous constitutional issues. If it is truly a new right, such as a right to same-sex marriage would be, [judges] will have to [consider] moral, political, empirical, prudential, and institutional issues, including the public acceptability of recognizing the new right." Compare *Baker v. State of Vermont*, 744 A.2d 864 (Vt.1999), which, although stopping short of declaring a right to gay marriage, holds that denying gay domestic partners the benefits available to married couples violates the Vermont state constitution.

n. For other notable contributions to the voluminous literature on *Romer*, see Symposium, *Gay Rights and the Courts: The Amendment 2 Controversy*, 68 U.Colo.L.Rev. 285 (1997); Akhil Reed Amar, *Attainder and Amendment 2: Romer's Rightness*, 95 Mich. L.Rev. 203 (1996); Roderick M. Hills, Jr., *Is Amendment 2 Really a Bill of Attainder? Some Questions About Professor Amar's Analysis Of Romer*, 95 Mich.L.Rev. 236 (1996); Joseph S. Jackson, *Persons of Equal Worth: Romer v. Evans and the Politics of Equal Protection*, 45 U.C.L.A.L.Rev. 453 (1997); John C. Jeffries & Daryl J. Levinson, *The Non–Retrogression Principle in Constitutional Law*, 86 Calif.L.Rev. 1211 (1998); Andrew Koppelman, *Romer v. Evans and Discriminatory Intent*, 6 Wm. & Mary Bill of Rts.J. 89 (1997); Robert F. Nagel, *Playing Defense*, 6 Wm. & Mary Bill of Rts.J. 167 (1997); H. Jefferson Powell, *The Lawfulness of Romer*, 77 N.C.L.Rev. 241 (1998); Louis Michael Seidman, *Romer's Radicalism: The Unexpected Revival of Warren Court Activism*, 1996 Sup.Ct.Rev. 67.

(b) The European Court of Human Rights has held that a British prohibition against homosexuals in the military violates the European Convention for the Protection of Human Rights and Fundamental Freedoms, but the Court rested its ruling on a provision guaranteeing "respect for * * * private and family life," not an anti-discrimination article that is at least partly analogous to the equal protection clause. See Rhonda K.M. Smith, *International Decisions: Lustig–Prean & Beckett v. United Kingdom, Smith & Grady v. United Kingdom*, 94 A.J.I.L. 382 (2000). A claim that discrimination against homosexuals is a forbidden form of sex discrimination has failed in the European Court of Justice. See Laurence R. Helfer, *International Decisions: Grant v. South–West Trains, Ltd.*, 93 A.J.I.L. 2000 (1999). Compare the respective decisions of the U.S. Supreme Court in *Bowers v. Hardwick* and *Romer v. Evans*.

(c) The South Africa Constitution of 1996 is the first national constitution expressly to list "sexual orientation" as a ground on the basis of which "[t]he state may not unfairly discriminate." *Id.*, § 9(3).

V. OTHER CHALLENGED BASES FOR DISCRIMINATION

1. *Age.* MASSACHUSETTS BD. OF RETIREMENT v. MURGIA, 427 U.S. 307, 96 S.Ct. 2562, 49 L.Ed.2d 520 (1976), per curiam, upheld—"under the rational basis standard"—a law requiring uniformed state police officers to retire at age 50. After first rejecting the contention "that a right of governmental employment per se is fundamental" and thus makes the legislative classification subject to "strict scrutiny" (see Sec. 5 infra), the Court continued: "While the treatment of the aged in this Nation has not been wholly free of discrimination, such persons, unlike, say, those who have been discriminated against on the basis of race or national origin, have not experienced a 'history of purposeful unequal treatment' or been subjected to unique disabilities on the basis of stereotyped characteristics not truly indicative of their abilities. The [Massachusetts statute] cannot be said to discriminate only against the elderly. Rather, it draws the line at a certain age in middle life. But even old age does not define a 'discrete and insular' group, *Carolene Products Co.*, n. 4, in need of 'extraordinary protection from the majoritarian political process.' Instead, it marks a stage that each of us will reach if we live out our normal span. Even if the statute could be said to impose a penalty upon a class defined as the aged, it would not impose a distinction sufficiently akin to those classifications that we have found suspect to call for strict judicial scrutiny."

MARSHALL, J., dissented from "the rigid two-tier model [that] still holds sway as the Court's articulated description of the equal protection test," urging a "flexible equal protection standard" of the kind discussed in his concurring opinion in *Cleburne*, supra: "[T]he Court is quite right in suggesting that distinctions exist between the elderly and traditional suspect classes such as [blacks]. The elderly are protected not only by certain antidiscrimination legislation, but by legislation that provides them with positive benefits not enjoyed by the public at large. Moreover, the elderly are not isolated in society, and discrimination against them is not pervasive but is centered primarily in employment. The advantage of a flexible equal protection standard, however, is that it can readily accommodate such variables. The elderly are undoubtedly discriminated against, and when legislation denies them an important benefit—employment—I conclude that to sustain the legislation the Commonwealth must show a reasonably substantial interest and a scheme reasonably closely tailored to achieving that interest."

See also *Vance v. Bradley*, 440 U.S. 93, 99 S.Ct. 939, 59 L.Ed.2d 171 (1979) (upholding mandatory retirement at age 60 for federal Foreign Service personnel); *Gregory v. Ashcroft*, 501 U.S. 452, 111 S.Ct. 2395, 115 L.Ed.2d 410 (1991) (upholding Missouri's mandatory retirement for judges at age 70). On discriminations against children, see generally Tribe, 2d ed. at 1588–93. An issue much litigated recently in the lower courts involves juvenile curfew ordinances adopted as crime prevention measures. Constitutionally permissible?[a]

2. *Wealth*. Laws that explicitly distinguish on the basis of wealth or poverty, and work directly to the disadvantage of the poor, are rare.[b] Today, laws seldom if ever prescribe that the poor cannot vote, attend public universities, utilize legal processes, or receive medical care in public hospitals. The disadvantage experienced by the poor more typically arises from the discriminatory impact of statutes that condition opportunities on the payment of money, or that draw lines—such as those separating relatively poor from relatively wealthy school districts—that strongly correlate with wealth. Equal protection issues involving discriminatory impact on the poor are discussed in Sec. 5, Parts II–V infra.

Rare though they may be, should explicit discriminations against poor people be held "suspect"? Although the Warren Court *stated* on several occasions that "lines drawn on the basis of wealth or property" "render a classification highly suspect,"[c] the Burger Court observed in 1973 that the Court had "never held that wealth discrimination alone provides an adequate basis for invoking strict scrutiny,"[d] and, in 1980, *Harris v. McRae*, Sec. 5, V infra, said that "this Court has held repeatedly that poverty, standing alone, is not a suspect classification. See, e.g. *James v. Valtierra*."

JAMES v. VALTIERRA, 402 U.S. 137, 91 S.Ct. 1331, 28 L.Ed.2d 678 (1971), per BLACK, J., upheld Art. 34 of the California Constitution, which provided that no "low-rent housing project"—defined as any development "for persons of low income"—could be constructed unless approved by local referendum: "Provisions for referendums demonstrate devotion to democracy, not to bias, discrimination, or prejudice." A "law making procedure that 'disadvantages' a particular group does not always deny equal protection." Nor were "persons advocating low-income [housing] singled out": Mandatory referendums were "required for approval of state constitutional amendments, for the issuance of general obligation long-term bonds by local governments, and for certain municipal territorial annexations."[e]

MARSHALL, J., joined by Brennan and Blackmun, JJ., dissented. Under California law, "publicly assisted housing developments designed to accommodate the aged, veterans, state employees, persons of moderate income, or any class of citizens other than the poor, need not be approved by prior referenda. [Art. 34 is] an explicit classification on the basis of poverty—a suspect classification which demands exacting judicial scrutiny."[f]

---

a. See Craig Hemmens & Katherine Bennett, *Out in the Street: Juvenile Crime, Juvenile Curfews, and the Constitution*, 34 Gonz. L.Rev. 267 (1998–99); Brian Privor, *Dusk 'Til Dawn: Children's Rights and the Effectiveness of Juvenile Curfew Ordinances*, 79 B.U.L.Rev. 415 (1999).

b. But cf. *Edwards v. California*, 314 U.S. 160, 62 S.Ct. 164, 86 L.Ed. 119 (1941), invalidating, under the commerce clause, a California statute making it a misdemeanor knowingly to transport a non-resident indigent into the state.

c. *Harper v. Virginia Bd. of Elections*, Sec. 5, I infra, and *McDonald v. Board of Elec. Comm'rs*, 394 U.S. 802, 89 S.Ct. 1404, 22 L.Ed.2d 739 (1969).

d. *San Antonio Ind. School Dist. v. Rodriguez*, Sec. 5, IV infra.

e. Cf. *Hunter v. Erickson*, Sec. 2, V supra.

f. Douglas, J., did not participate.

Do you agree that *James* involved "an explicit classification on the basis of poverty"? What result if the state were to make it a crime for a person without visible means of support to refuse employment? If it were to discriminate against the poor in offering admissions to prestigious state universities due to the risk that those without minimum resources would drop out for financial reasons (and thus squander some of the state's investment in their education)?

Consider Frank I. Michelman, *On Protecting the Poor Through the Fourteenth Amendment,* 83 Harv.L.Rev. 7, 21 (1969): "[I]f money is power, then a class deliberately defined so as to include everyone who has less wealth or income than any person outside it may certainly be deemed [to] be especially susceptible to abuse by majoritarian process; and classification of 'the poor' as such, may, like classification of racial minorities as such, be popularly understood as a badge of inferiority. Especially is this so in light of the extreme difficulty of imagining proper governmental objectives which require for their achievement the explicit carving out, for relatively disadvantageous treatment, of a class defined by relative paucity of wealth or income."[g] Compare Ralph K. Winter, Jr. *Poverty, Economic Equality, and the Equal Protection Clause,* 1972 Sup.Ct.Rev. 41, 97–98: "Race is [the] basis of a stereotype which served as a systematic vehicle of governmental discrimination. Moreover, it is not a stereotype with a pretense at being related to individual merit, even though it [is] unalterable by the individual. [But] poverty is not absolutely unalterable for all those afflicted by it. The history of this nation is a history of virtually all of its people bettering themselves [economically].[h] Beyond that, [t]here simply has not been any legislation invoking a poverty classification even remotely resembling the widespread, official, racial segregation of schools and other facilities. To the contrary, there is an enormous amount of legislation [to] help the poor. [Finally], to the extent low income is related to low productivity—and it is to a large extent—poverty is not entirely unrelated to individual merit. One need not adopt productivity as the sole criterion of merit to say that poverty resulting from low productivity is far different from legal exclusion from public facilities because of one's race." See also Robert H. Bork, *The Impossibility of Finding Welfare Rights in the Constitution,* 1979 Wash.U.L.Q. 695, 701: "In the past two decades we have witnessed an explosion of welfare legislation, massive income redistributions, and civil rights laws of all kinds. The poor and the minorities have had access to the political process and have done very well through it."

SECTION 5. "FUNDAMENTAL RIGHTS"

I. VOTING

A. DENIAL OR QUALIFICATION OF THE RIGHT

HARPER v. VIRGINIA STATE BD. OF ELEC., 383 U.S. 663, 86 S.Ct. 1079, 16 L.Ed.2d 169 (1966), per DOUGLAS, J., overruling *Breedlove v. Suttles,* 302 U.S. 277, 58 S.Ct. 205, 82 L.Ed. 252 (1937), held that Virginia's $1.50 poll tax as "a prerequisite of voting" was "an 'invidious' discrimination": "[T]he right to vote in state elections is nowhere expressly mentioned" in the Constitution, but "once the franchise is [granted] lines may not be drawn which [violate equal protection]."[3]

g. See also Stephen Loffredo, *Poverty Democracy, and Constitutional Law,* 141 U.Pa. L.Rev. 1277 (1993).

h. See also Comment, 85 Harv.L.Rev. 129 (1971): "The poor seem to be a less cohesive and less readily identifiable group than are racial minorities. Because the class of 'poor' is constantly in flux, the reinforced sense of stigma which characterizes de jure racial classifications is probably mitigated even where explicit wealth classifications are concerned."

3. [While] the "Virginia poll tax was born of a desire to disenfranchise the Negro," we do

Language of rational Basis review

But also
Strict
Scrutiny
- classification
• ability to
pay
- interest-
Vote

"Long ago in *Yick Wo*, [Sec. 2, III supra], the Court referred to 'the political franchise of voting' as a 'fundamental political right, because preservative of all rights.' * * * Wealth, like race, creed, or color, is not germane to one's ability to participate intelligently in the electoral process. Lines drawn on the basis of wealth or property, like those of race, are traditionally disfavored. See *Edwards v. California*, [Sec. 4, V supra] (Jackson, J., concurring); *Griffin v. Illinois; Douglas v. California*, [Part III infra]. To introduce wealth or payment of a fee as a measure of a voter's qualifications is to introduce a capricious or irrelevant factor. * * *

Poll tax was historically used for racial discrim

But: what about a Fee For drivers licence...

"In determining what lines are unconstitutionally discriminatory, we have never been confined to historic notions of equality" and "notions of what constitutes equal treatment for purposes of the Equal Protection Clause *do* change" [citing *Plessy* and *Brown*, Sec. 2, II supra]. "Our conclusion, like that in *Reynolds v. Sims*,[a] is founded not on what we think governmental policy should be, but on what the Equal Protection Clause requires.

"We have long been mindful that where fundamental rights and liberties are asserted under the Equal Protection Clause, classifications which might invade or restrain them must be closely scrutinized and carefully confined. See, e.g., *Reynolds; Carrington v. Rash*."[b]

Classification: • Ability to pay

BLACK, J., dissented: "[U]nder a proper interpretation of the Equal Protection Clause States are to have the broadest kind of leeway in areas where they have a general constitutional competence to act. [P]oll tax legislation can 'reasonably,' 'rationally' and without an 'invidious' or evil purpose to injure anyone be found to rest on a number of state policies including (1) the State's desire to collect its revenue, and (2) its belief that voters who pay a poll tax will be interested in furthering the State's welfare when they vote. [And] history is on the side of 'rationality' of the State's poll tax policy. Property qualifications existed in the Colonies and were continued by many States after the Constitution was adopted. [The Court] seems to be using the old 'natural-law-due-process formula' to justify striking down state laws as violations of [equal protection]."

HARLAN, J., joined by Stewart, J., dissented: "The [equal protection] test evolved by this Court [is whether] a classification can be deemed to be founded on some rational and otherwise constitutionally permissible state [policy].[3] *Reynolds* [also] marked a departure from these traditional and wise principles. [I]t was probably accepted as sound political theory by a large percentage of Americans through most of our history, that people with some property have a deeper stake in community affairs, and are consequently more responsible, more educated,

not stop to determine whether [the] Virginia tax in its modern setting serves the same end.

a. *Reynolds*, Part B infra, was among the first of the Court's "one person, one vote" decisions.

b. *Carrington*, 380 U.S. 89, 85 S.Ct. 775, 13 L.Ed.2d 675 (1965), held a Texas provision, barring members of the military who moved to Texas from voting in state elections so long as they remained in the military, "an invidious discrimination": "We deal here with matters close to the core of our constitutional system." Only "where military personnel are involved has Texas been unwilling to develop more pre-

cise tests to determine the bona fides on an individual claiming to have actually made his home in the state long enough to vote." " 'Fencing out' from the franchise a sector of the population because of the way they may vote is constitutionally impermissible."

3. I think the somewhat different application of the Equal Protection Clause to racial discrimination cases finds justification in the fact that insofar as that clause may embody a particular value in addition to rationality, the historical origins of the Civil War Amendments might attribute to racial equality this special status. * * *

more knowledgeable, more worthy of [confidence. It] is all wrong, in my view, for the Court to adopt the political doctrines popularly accepted at a particular moment of our history and to declare all others to be irrational and invidious * * *."

KRAMER v. UNION FREE SCHOOL DISTRICT

395 U.S. 621, 89 S.Ct. 1886, 23 L.Ed.2d 583 (1969).

CHIEF JUSTICE WARREN delivered the opinion of the Court.

[§ 2012 of the New York Education Law] provides that in certain New York school districts residents [may] vote in the school district election only if they [or their spouse] (1) own (or lease) taxable real property within the district, or (2) are parents (or have custody of) children enrolled in the local public schools. Appellant, a bachelor who neither owns nor leases taxable real property, [claimed] § 2012 denied him equal protection * * *.

[I]t is important to note what is *not* at issue in this case. The requirements of § 2012 that school district voters must (1) be citizens of the United States, (2) be bona fide residents of the school district, and (3) be at least 21 years of age are not challenged. * * *

[S]tatutes distributing the franchise constitute the foundation of our representative society. Any unjustified discrimination in determining who may participate in political affairs or in the selection of public officials undermines the legitimacy of representative government. [Therefore,] if a [statute] grants the right to vote to some bona fide residents of requisite age and citizenship and denies the franchise to others, the Court must determine whether the exclusions are necessary to promote a compelling state interest. See *Carrington*.

[The] presumption of constitutionality and the approval given "rational" classifications in other types of enactments are based on an assumption that the institutions of state government are structured so as to represent fairly all the people. However, when the challenge to the statute is in effect a challenge of this basic assumption, the assumption can no longer serve as the basis for presuming constitutionality. And, the assumption is no less under attack because the legislature which decides who may participate at the various levels of political choice is fairly elected. * * *

The need for exacting judicial scrutiny of statutes distributing the franchise is undiminished simply because, under a different statutory scheme, the offices subject to election might have been filled through appointment[10] [since] "once the franchise is granted to the electorate, lines may not be drawn which are inconsistent with [equal protection]." *Harper*.

Nor is the need for close judicial examination affected because the district [and] the school board do not have "general" legislative powers. Our exacting examination is necessitated not by the subject of the election [but] because some resident citizens are permitted to participate and some are not. * * *

Besides appellant and others who similarly live in their parents' homes, the statute also disenfranchises the following persons (unless they are parents or guardians of children enrolled in the district public school): senior citizens and others living with children or relatives; clergy, military personnel and others who

---

10. Similarly, no less a showing of a compelling justification for disenfranchising residents is required merely because the questions scheduled for the election need not have been submitted to the voters.

live on tax-exempt property; boarders and lodgers; parents who neither own nor lease qualifying property and whose children are too young to attend school [or] attend private schools.

[A]ppellees argue that the State has a legitimate interest in limiting the franchise in school district elections [to] those "primarily interested in such elections" [and] that the State may reasonably and permissibly conclude that "property taxpayers" (including lessees of taxable property who share the tax burden through rent payments) and parents of the children enrolled in the district's schools are those "primarily interested" in school affairs. * * *

[A]ssuming, arguendo, that New York legitimately might limit the franchise in these school district elections to those "primarily interested in school affairs," close scrutiny of the § 2012 classifications demonstrates that they do not accomplish this purpose with sufficient precision to justify denying appellant the franchise.

[T]he classifications must be tailored so that the exclusion of appellant and members of his class is necessary to achieve the articulated state goal.[14] Section 2012 does not meet the exacting standard of precision [because it permits] inclusion of many persons who have, at best, a remote and indirect interest in school affairs and on the other hand, exclude[s] others who have a distinct and direct interest in the school meeting decisions.[15] * * *

JUSTICE STEWART, with whom JUSTICE BLACK and JUSTICE HARLAN join, dissenting. * * *

Clearly a State may reasonably assume that its residents have a greater stake in the outcome of elections held within its boundaries than do other persons [and] that residents, being generally better informed regarding state affairs than are nonresidents, will be more likely [to] vote responsibly. And the same may be said of legislative assumptions regarding the electoral competence of adults and literate persons on the one hand, and of minors and illiterates on the other. It is clear, of course, that lines thus drawn cannot infallibly perform their intended legislative function. Just as "[i]lliterate people may be intelligent voters," nonresidents or minors might also in some instances be interested, informed, and intelligent participants in the electoral process. Persons who commute across a state line to work may well have a great stake in the affairs of the State in which they are employed; some college students under 21 may be both better informed and more passionately interested in political affairs than many adults. But such discrepancies are the inevitable concomitant of the line-drawing that is essential to lawmaking. So long as the classification is rationally related to a permissible legislative end, therefore—as are residence, literacy, and age requirements imposed with respect to voting—there is no denial of equal protection.

Thus judged, the statutory classification involved here seems to me clearly to be valid [and] the Court does not really argue the contrary. Instead, it [asserts] that the traditional equal protection standard is [inapt]. But the asserted justification for applying [a stricter] standard cannot withstand analysis. [The] voting

14. Of course, if the exclusions are necessary to promote the articulated state interest, we must then determine whether the interest promoted by limiting the franchise constitutes a compelling state interest. We do not reach that issue in this case.

15. For example, appellant resides with his parents in the school district, pays state and federal taxes and is interested in and affected by school board decisions [but cannot vote, whereas] an uninterested unemployed young man who pays no state or federal taxes, but who rents an apartment in the district, can [vote].

qualifications at issue have been promulgated not by Union Free School District, but by the New York State Legislature, and the appellant is of course fully able to participate in the election of representatives in that body. There is simply no claim whatever here that the state government is not "structured so as to represent fairly all the people," including the appellant.

[§ 2012] does not involve racial classifications [and] is not one that impinges upon a constitutionally protected right, and that consequently can be justified only by a "compelling" state interest. For "the Constitution of the United States does not confer the right of suffrage upon any one."

In any event, it seems to me that under *any* equal protection standard, short of a doctrinaire insistence that universal suffrage is somehow mandated by the Constitution, the appellant's claim must be rejected. * * *

Notes and Questions

1. *Classification as "fundamental."* What is the effect of classifying voting as a "fundamental" right under the equal protection clause (but not the due process clause)? Should (does?) the Constitution embrace a right to vote or simply a right of equality in voting?

Consider FORTSON v. MORRIS, 385 U.S. 231, 87 S.Ct. 446, 17 L.Ed.2d 330 (1966), upholding a Georgia election procedure under which, if no gubernatorial candidate received a majority of the popular vote, the state legislature elected the governor from the two candidates receiving the most votes: There is no federal constitutional provision "which either expressly or impliedly dictates the method a state must use to select its governor. A method which would be valid if initially employed is equally valid when employed as an alternative."

2. *Denial of voting to residents.* Should a state be able to deny the vote to those who cannot pass a literacy test? See *Lassiter v. Northampton County Board of Elections,* 360 U.S. 45, 79 S.Ct. 985, 3 L.Ed.2d 1072 (1959) (constitutional). Does *Lassiter* survive *Harper?* May a state deny the vote to smart seventeen-year-olds? Compare *Oregon v. Mitchell,* discussed in Ch. 11, Sec. 3 infra (upholding an age requirement for voting in state elections). To felons? *Richardson v. Ramirez,* 418 U.S. 24, 94 S.Ct. 2655, 41 L.Ed.2d 551 (1974) (constitutional). To members of the military? See *Carrington v. Rash,* supra (unconstitutional invidious discrimination).

3. *Denial of voting to non-residents.* Alabama extended a city's police and sanitary regulations and its business-licensing powers (at reduced fees) to residents of adjacent, unincorporated communities, but did not permit them to vote in city elections. Constitutional? See *Holt Civic Club v. Tuscaloosa,* 439 U.S. 60, 99 S.Ct. 383, 58 L.Ed.2d 292 (1978) (constitutional).

4. *The character of democracy.* Do voting exclusions necessarily make assumptions about the character and purpose of democratic politics? What assumptions?[b] Should the community be permitted to confine the franchise to those likely to focus on its long range interests? Would this mean that students of voting age could be excluded? If an appropriate test could be devised, should the community be permitted to confine the vote to those with substantial knowledge of its customs, habits, and traditions? Should the community be permitted to confine

---

b. See James A. Gardner, *Liberty, Community, and the Constitutional Structure of Politi-* *cal Influence: A Reconsideration of the Right to Vote,* 145 U.Pa.L.Rev. 893 (1997).

the vote to those with a commitment to its shared values? If not, why are resident aliens forced to take an oath on becoming citizens?

5. *Special purpose elections.* With *Kramer*, which restricted participation in school district elections only, compare SALYER LAND CO. v. TULARE LAKE BASIN WATER STORAGE DIST., 410 U.S. 719, 93 S.Ct. 1224, 35 L.Ed.2d 659 (1973), per REHNQUIST, J., which upheld California statutes permitting only land-owners to vote in "water storage district" elections and apportioning votes according to the assessed valuation of the land within the districts, even though in one of the districts a single corporation held a majority of the votes: "[Appellee], although vested with some typical governmental powers [including the power to condemn private property and issue bonds], has relatively limited authority." Apart from water acquisition, conservation, and distribution (including the fixing of charges), "it [does] not exercise what might be thought of as 'normal govern-mental' authority, [and] its actions disproportionately affect landowners" because of the method of allocating project costs and service charges. "In short, there is no way that the economic burdens of district operations can fall on residents qua residents, and the operations of the districts primarily affect the land within their boundaries." Thus, the franchise restriction is valid unless " 'wholly irrelevant to achievement of the regulation's objectives.' " And as to appellants' "reliance on the various decisions of this Court holding that wealth has no relation to resident-voter qualifications," because "the benefits and burdens to each landowner in the District are in proportion to the assessed value of the land," "we cannot say that the California legislative decision to permit voting in the same proportion is not rationally based." Douglas, J., joined by Brennan and Marshall, JJ., dissented.

The Court itself characterized *Salyer* as an "exception."[c] Is it a defensible exception? If so, what are its limits?

B. "DILUTION" OF THE RIGHT: APPORTIONMENT

REYNOLDS v. SIMS

377 U.S. 533, 84 S.Ct. 1362, 12 L.Ed.2d 506 (1964).

CHIEF JUSTICE WARREN delivered the opinion of the Court.

[Although the Alabama constitution required the legislature to reapportion decennially on the basis of population, none had taken place since 1901. The federal district court held the existing malapportionment violative of equal protec-tion. Under] 1960 census figures, only 25.1% of the State's total population resided in districts represented by a majority of the members of the Senate, and only 25.7% lived in counties which could elect a majority of the members of the House of Representatives. Population-variance ratios of up to about 41–to–1 existed in the Senate, and up to about 16–to–1 in the House. * * *

Gray v. Sanders, 372 U.S. 368, 83 S.Ct. 801, 9 L.Ed.2d 821 (1963),[a] and

---

c. Compare *Cipriano v. Houma,* 395 U.S. 701, 89 S.Ct. 1897, 23 L.Ed.2d 647 (1969) (invalidating statute confining vote to property taxpayers in elections for issuance of municipal bonds by a municipal utility); *Phoenix v. Ko-lodziejski,* 399 U.S. 204, 90 S.Ct. 1990, 26 L.Ed.2d 523 (1970) (invalidating statute con-fining vote to real property taxpayers in elec-

tions for issuance of general obligation bonds for financing various municipal improve-ments).

a. *Gray* invalidated the "county unit sys-tem" employed in Georgia primaries for state-wide offices, under which the candidate receiv-ing the highest number of votes in each county

Wesberry v. Sanders, 376 U.S. 1, 84 S.Ct. 526, 11 L.Ed.2d 481 (1964),[b] are of course [relevant to but] not dispositive [of] these cases involving state legislative [apportionment]. But neither are they wholly inapposite. [*Gray*] established the basic principle of equality among voters within a State, [and] *Wesberry* clearly established that the fundamental principle of representative government in this country is one of equal representation for equal numbers of people, without regard to race, sex, economic status, or place of residence within a State. Our problem, then, is to ascertain [whether] there are any constitutionally cognizable principles which would justify departures from the basic standard of equality among voters in the apportionment of seats in state legislatures.

A predominant consideration in determining whether a State's legislative apportionment scheme constitutes an invidious discrimination [is] that the rights allegedly impaired are individual and personal in nature. [Since] the right of suffrage is a fundamental matter in a free and democratic society [and] is preservative of other basic civil and political rights, any alleged infringement [must] be carefully and meticulously scrutinized. * * *

Legislators represent people, not trees or acres. Legislators are elected by voters, not farms or cities or economic interests. As long as ours is a representative form of government, [the] right to elect legislators in a free and unimpaired fashion is a bedrock of our political system. [It] is inconceivable that a state law to the effect that, in counting votes for legislators, the votes of citizens in one part of the State would be multiplied by two, five, or 10, while the votes of persons in another area would be counted only at face value, could be [constitutional]. Of course, the effect of state legislative districting schemes which give the same number of representatives to unequal numbers of constituents is identical. * * *

Logically, in a society ostensibly grounded on representative government, it would seem reasonable that a majority of the people of a State could elect a majority of that State's legislators. [T]o sanction minority control of state legislative bodies would appear to deny majority rights in a way that far surpasses any possible denial of minority rights that might otherwise be thought to result. [T]he concept of equal protection has been traditionally viewed as requiring the uniform treatment of persons standing in the same relation to the governmental action questioned or challenged. With respect to the allocation of legislative representation, all voters, as citizens of a State, stand in the same relation regardless of where they live. Any suggested criteria for the differentiation of citizens are insufficient to justify any discrimination, as to the weight of their votes, unless relevant to the permissible purposes of legislative apportionment. Since the achieving of fair and effective representation for all citizens is concededly the basic aim of legislative apportionment, we conclude that the Equal Protection Clause guarantees the opportunity for equal participation by all voters in the election of state legislators. Diluting the weight of votes because of place of residence impairs

---

obtained "two votes for each representative to which the county is entitled in the lower House of the General Assembly," and the winner was determined on the basis of the county unit vote. Because counties were not represented in the state legislature in accordance with their population, counties comprising only a third of the state's population had "a clear majority of county units." Emphasizing that the case did not involve legislative districting, the Court held that equal protection requires that "once the geographical unit for which a representa-

tive is to be chosen is designated, all who participate in the election are to have an equal vote."

b. *Wesberry* struck down Georgia's congressional districting statute, under which some districts had more than twice the population of others: "[T]he command of Art. I, § 2, that representatives be chosen 'by the people of the several states' means that as nearly as is practicable one man's vote in a congressional election is to be worth as much as another's."

basic constitutional rights under the Fourteenth Amendment just as much as invidious discriminations based upon factors such as race, or economic status. Our constitutional system amply provides for the protection of minorities by means other than giving them majority control of state legislatures. * * *

We are told that the matter of apportioning representation in a state legislature is a complex and many-faceted one. We are advised that States can rationally consider factors other than [population]. We are admonished not to restrict the power of the States to impose differing views as to political philosophy on their citizens. We are cautioned about the dangers of entering into political thickets and mathematical quagmires. Our answer is this: a denial of constitutionally protected rights demands judicial protection; our oath and our office require no less of us. [To] the extent that a citizen's right to vote is debased, he is that much less a citizen. [A] nation once primarily rural in character becomes predominantly urban. Representation schemes once fair and equitable become archaic and outdated. But the basic principle of representative government [remains]—the weight of a citizen's vote cannot be made to depend on where he lives. Population is, of necessity, [the] controlling criterion for judgment in legislative [apportionment]. This is the clear and strong command of our Constitution's Equal Protection Clause. This is an essential part of the concept of a government of laws and not men. This is at the heart of Lincoln's vision of "government of the people, by the people, [and] for the people." * * *

We hold that, as a basic constitutional standard, the Equal Protection Clause requires that the seats in both houses of a bicameral state legislature must be apportioned on a population basis. [We] find the federal analogy inapposite and irrelevant to state legislative districting schemes. [T]he Founding Fathers clearly had no intention of establishing a pattern or model for the apportionment of seats in state legislatures when the system of representation in the Federal Congress was adopted. Demonstrative of this is the fact that the Northwest Ordinance, adopted in the same year, 1787, as the Federal Constitution, provided for the apportionment of seats in territorial legislatures solely on the basis of population.

The system of representation in the two Houses of the Federal Congress [is] based on the consideration that in establishing our type of federalism a group of formerly independent States bound themselves together under one national government. [A] compromise between the larger and smaller States on this matter averted a deadlock in the constitutional convention * * *.

Political subdivisions of States [never] have been considered as sovereign entities. Rather, they have been traditionally regarded as subordinate governmental instrumentalities created by the State. * * *

[The] right of a citizen to equal representation and to have his vote weighted equally with those of all other citizens in the election of members of one house of a bicameral state legislature would amount to little if States could effectively submerge the equal-population principle in the apportionment of seats in the other house. * * * Deadlock between the two bodies might result in compromise and concession on some issues. But in all too many cases the more probable result would be frustration of the majority will through minority veto in the house not apportioned on a population [basis].

We do not believe that the concept of bicameralism is rendered anachronistic and meaningless when the predominant basis of representation in the two state legislative bodies is required to be the same—population. A prime reason for bicameralism, modernly considered, is to insure mature and deliberate consideration of, and to prevent precipitate action on, proposed legislative measures.

Simply because the controlling criterion for apportioning representation is required to be the same in both houses does not mean that there will be no differences in the composition and complexion of the two bodies. [The] numerical size of the two bodies could be made to differ, even significantly, and the geographical size of districts from which legislators are elected could also be made to differ. [T]he Equal Protection Clause requires that a State make an honest and good faith effort to construct districts, in both houses of its legislature, as nearly of equal population as is practicable. We realize that it is a practical impossibility to arrange legislative districts so that each one has an identical number of residents, or citizens, or voters. Mathematical exactness or precision is hardly a workable constitutional requirement.

[So] long as the divergences from a strict population standard are based on legitimate considerations incident to the effectuation of a rational state policy, some deviations from the equal-population principle are constitutionally permissible, [b]ut neither history alone, nor economic or other sorts of group interests, are permissible factors in attempting to justify disparities from population-based representation. Citizens, not history or economic interests, cast votes. Considerations of area alone provide an insufficient justification for deviations from the equal-population principle. Again, people, not land or trees or pastures, vote. Modern developments and improvements in transportation and communications make rather hollow, in the mid–1960's, most claims [for] allowing such deviations in order to insure effective representation for sparsely settled areas and to prevent legislative districts from becoming so large that the availability of access of citizens to their representatives is impaired. * * *

A consideration that appears to be of more substance [is] according political subdivisions some independent representation in at least one body of the state legislature, as long as the basic standard of equality of population among districts is maintained. [In] many States much of the legislature's activity involves the enactment of so-called local legislation, directed only to the concerns of particular political subdivisions. And a State may legitimately desire to construct districts along political subdivision lines to deter the possibilities of gerrymandering. However, permitting deviations from population-based representation does not mean that each local governmental unit or political subdivision can be given separate representation, regardless of [population].

* * * Decennial reapportionment appears to be a rational approach to readjustment of legislative representation in order to take into account population shifts and growth [and] if reapportionment were accomplished with less frequency, it would assuredly be constitutionally suspect. * * * [d]

[Clark and Stewart, JJ., concurred in the result in *Reynolds*, but JUSTICE STEWART, joined by JUSTICE CLARK, dissented in two of the companion cases in an opinion sharply at odds with the *Reynolds* rationale:]

First, says the Court, it is "established that the fundamental principle of representative government in this country is one of equal representation for equal numbers of [people]." [But] this "was not the colonial system, it was not the system chosen for the national government by the Constitution, it was not the

---

d. In addition to *Reynolds*, the Court invalidated apportionments in Colorado, *Lucas v. Forty–Fourth Gen. Assembly*, 377 U.S. 713, 84 S.Ct. 1459, 12 L.Ed.2d 632 (1964); Delaware, *Roman v. Sincock*, 377 U.S. 695, 84 S.Ct. 1449, 12 L.Ed.2d 620; Maryland, *Maryland Comm.* for *Fair Rep. v. Tawes*, 377 U.S. 656, 84 S.Ct. 1429, 12 L.Ed.2d 595; New York, *WMCA, Inc. v. Lomenzo*, 377 U.S. 633, 84 S.Ct. 1418, 12 L.Ed.2d 568 (1964); Virginia, *Davis v. Mann*, 377 U.S. 678, 84 S.Ct. 1441, 12 L.Ed.2d 609.

system exclusively or even predominantly practiced by the States at the time of adoption of the Fourteenth Amendment, it is not predominantly practiced by the States today." Secondly, says the Court, unless legislative districts are equal in population, voters in the more populous districts will suffer a 'debasement' amounting to a constitutional injury. [I] find it impossible to understand how or why a voter in California, for instance, either feels or is less a citizen than a voter in Nevada, simply because, despite their population disparities, each of those States is represented by two United States Senators.

[My] own understanding of the various theories of representative government is that no one theory has ever commanded unanimous [assent]. But even if it were thought that the rule announced today by the Court is, as a matter of political theory, the most desirable, [I] could not join in the fabrication of a constitutional mandate which imports and forever freezes one theory of political thought into our Constitution, and forever denies to every State any opportunity for enlightened and progressive innovation * * *.

Representative government is a process of accommodating group interests through democratic institutional arrangements. * * * Appropriate legislative apportionment, therefore, should ideally be designed to insure effective representation in the State's legislature, in cooperation with other organs of political power, of the various groups and interests making up the electorate. In practice, of course, this ideal is approximated in the particular apportionment system of any State by a realistic accommodation of the diverse and often conflicting political forces operating within the State.

[The] fact of geographic districting, the constitutional validity of which the Court does not question, carries with it an acceptance of the idea of legislative representation of regional needs and interests. Yet if geographical residence is irrelevant, as the Court suggests, and the goal is solely that of equally "weighted" votes, I do not understand why the Court's constitutional rule does not require the abolition of districts and the holding of all elections at large.

[Throughout] our history the apportionments of State Legislatures have reflected the strongly felt American tradition that the public interest is composed of many diverse interests, and that in the long run it can better be expressed by a medley of component voices than by the majority's monolithic command. [The] Equal Protection Clause demands but two basic attributes of any plan of state legislative apportionment. First, it demands that, in the light of the State's own characteristics and needs, the plan must be a rational one. Secondly, it demands that the plan must be such as not to permit the systematic frustration of the will of a majority of the electorate of the State. * * *

JUSTICE HARLAN, dissenting [in all the cases decided that day.]

The Court's constitutional discussion [is] remarkable [for] its failure to address itself at all to the Fourteenth Amendment as a whole or to the legislative history of the Amendment pertinent to the matter at hand. [I] am unable to understand the Court's utter disregard of [§ 2 of the fourteenth amendment], which expressly recognizes the States' power to deny "or in any way" abridge the right of their inhabitants to vote for "the members of the [State] Legislature," and its express provision of a remedy for such denial or abridgement. The comprehensive scope of the second section and its particular reference to the state legislatures precludes the suggestion that the first section was intended to have the result reached by the [Court].

The history of the adoption of the Fourteenth Amendment provides conclusive evidence that neither those who proposed nor those who ratified the Amendment believed that the Equal Protection Clause limited the power of the States to apportion their legislatures as they saw fit. Moreover, the history demonstrates that the intention to leave this power undisturbed was deliberate and was widely believed to be essential to the adoption of the Amendment.[e] [N]ote should [also] be taken of the Fifteenth and Nineteenth Amendments. [If] constitutional amendment was the only means by which all men and, later, women, could be guaranteed the right to vote at all, even for *federal* officers, how can it be that the far less obvious right to a particular kind of apportionment of *state* legislatures—a right to which is opposed a far more plausible conflicting interest of the State than the interest which opposes the general right to vote—can be conferred by judicial construction of the Fourteenth Amendment?

[The] consequence of today's decision is that in all but the handful of States which may already satisfy the new requirements the [courts] are given blanket authority and the constitutional duty to supervise apportionment of the State Legislatures. It is difficult to imagine a more intolerable and inappropriate interference by the judiciary with the independent legislatures of the States. [No] set of standards can guide a court which has to decide how many legislative districts a State shall have, or what the shape of the districts shall be, [or] whether a State should have single-member districts or multi-member districts or some combination of both. No such standard can control the balance between keeping up with population shifts and having stable districts. In all these respects, the courts will be called upon to make particular decisions with respect to which a principle of equally populated districts will be of no assistance whatsoever. * * *

Although the Court—necessarily, as I believe—provides only generalities in elaboration of its main thesis, its opinion nevertheless fully demonstrates how far removed these problems are from fields of judicial competence. Recognizing that "indiscriminate districting" is an invitation to "partisan gerrymandering," the Court nevertheless excludes virtually every basis for the formation of electoral districts other than "indiscriminate districting." In one or another of today's opinions, the Court declares it unconstitutional for a State to give effective consideration to any of the following in establishing legislative districts: (1) history; (2) "economic or other sorts of group interests"; (3) area; (4) geographical considerations; (5) a desire "to insure effective representation for sparsely settled areas"; (6) "availability of access of citizens to their representatives"; (7) theories of bicameralism (except those approved by the Court); (8) occupation; (9) "an attempt to balance urban and rural power"; (10) the preference of a majority of voters in the State. So far as presently appears, the *only* factor which a State may consider, apart from numbers, is political subdivisions. But even "a clearly rational state policy" recognizing this factor is unconstitutional if "population is submerged as the controlling consideration * * *."

I know of no principle of logic or practical or theoretical politics, still less any constitutional principle, which establishes all or any of these exclusions. [L]egislators can represent their electors only by speaking for their interests—economic, social, political—many of which do reflect the place where the electors live. The Court does not establish, or indeed even attempt to make a case for the proposi-

---

e. For refutation of Harlan, J.'s lengthy historical argument, see William Van Alstyne, *The Fourteenth Amendment, The "Right" to Vote, and the Understanding of the Thirty-* *Ninth Congress*, 1965 Sup.Ct.Rev. 33; Edward Goldberg, *Mr. Justice Harlan, The Uses of History, and the Congressional Globe*, 15 J.Pub.L. 181 (1966).

tion that conflicting interests within a State can only be adjusted by disregarding them when voters are grouped for purposes of [representation].

[The] Constitution is not a panacea for every blot upon the public welfare, nor [does] this Court [serve] its high purpose when it exceeds its authority, even to satisfy justified impatience with the slow workings of the political [process.]

Notes and Questions

1. *Results.* By mid–1968, "congressional district lines were redrawn in thirty-seven states"; "only nine states had any district with a population deviation in excess of ten per cent from the state average, while twenty-four states had no deviation as large as five per cent from the state norm"; every state legislature "had made some adjustment, and it seemed probable that more than thirty of the state legislatures satisfied any reasonable interpretation of the equal-population principle." Robert McKay, *Reapportionment: Success Story of the Warren Court,* 67 Mich.L.Rev. 223, 229 (1968).

According to John Hart Ely, *Democracy and Distrust* 120–21 (1980), the leading contemporary concerns about *Reynolds* quickly proved misguided: "Justice Frankfurter used to say that reapportionment was a 'political thicket' that courts should avoid. [Sometimes this charge] meant that there can be no administrable standard for determining the legality of apportionments. [But] that is nothing short of silly. [The] 'one person, one vote' standard [is] certainly administrable. In fact administrability is its long suit, and the more troublesome question is what else it has to recommend it. On other occasions the 'thicket' criticism has signaled a 'realist's' point, that a reapportionment order is one unusually calculated to get the Court in trouble, dangerously to decrease its prestige. [But] the critics were wrong on this one: the equal weighting of everyone's vote turned out to be a notion with which most people could sympathize."

But consider Pamela S. Karlan, *The Rights To Vote: Some Pessimism about Formalism,* 71 Tex.L.Rev. 1705, 1705 (1993): "Chief Justice Warren called *Reynolds v. Sims* his most important opinion 'because it insured that henceforth elections would reflect the collective public interest—embodied in the "one-man, one-vote" standard—rather than the machinations of special interests.' Measured against that ambition, *Reynolds* has been a spectacular failure. Advances in the technology of districting have stripped the substantive principles of one-person, one-vote of any real constraining force."

2. *Supermajority requirements.* GORDON v. LANCE, 403 U.S. 1, 91 S.Ct. 1889, 29 L.Ed.2d 273 (1971), per BURGER, C.J., upheld a West Virginia rule that forbade political subdivisions from incurring bonded indebtedness or increasing tax rates beyond designated limits without 60% approval in a referendum: "The defect [in previous cases] lay in the denial or dilution of voting power because of group characteristics—geographic location and property ownership—that bore no valid relation to the interest of those groups in the subject matter of the [election]. In contrast we can discern no independently identifiable group or category that favors bonded indebtedness over other forms of financing. Consequently no sector of the population may be said to be 'fenced out' from the franchise because of the way they will vote."

The Court added in a footnote that "[w]e intimate no view on the constitutionality of a provision requiring unanimity or giving a veto power to a very small group. Nor do we decide whether a State [may] require extraordinary majorities for the election of public officers."

3. *Permissible population deviation.* The Court has permitted considerably less deviation from the one person, one vote requirement for congressional districts than for state and local elections.[a] KARCHER v. DAGGETT, 462 U.S. 725, 103 S.Ct. 2653, 77 L.Ed.2d 133 (1983), per BRENNAN, J., invalidated a percentage deviation in New Jersey's congressional districts of 0.7%. But justifiable deviations were not ruled out: "Any number of consistently applied legislative policies might justify some ['minor population deviations'], including, for instance, making districts compact, respecting municipal boundaries, preserving the cores of prior districts, [preserving voting strength of racial minorities], and avoiding contests between incumbent Representatives. [The] state must, however, show with some specificity that a particular objective required the specific deviations in its plan rather than simply relying on general assertions [as here]." On the other hand, GAFFNEY v. CUMMINGS, 412 U.S. 735, 93 S.Ct. 2321, 37 L.Ed.2d 298 (1973), per WHITE, J., held that a Connecticut state legislative reapportionment with a maximum deviation of 7.83% was "insignificant" and "required no justification by the state."[b]

MAHAN v. HOWELL, 410 U.S. 315, 93 S.Ct. 979, 35 L.Ed.2d 320 (1973), per REHNQUIST, J., upheld Virginia's state legislative apportionment, which had a maximum percentage deviation from the ideal of "16.4%—[one] district being overrepresented by 6.8% and [another] being underrepresented by 9.6%. [T]he minimum population necessary to elect a majority of the house of delegates was 49.29%": "In *Kirkpatrick v. Preisler,* 394 U.S. 526, 89 S.Ct. 1225, 22 L.Ed.2d 519 (1969) and *Wells v. Rockefeller,* 394 U.S. 542, 89 S.Ct. 1234, 22 L.Ed.2d 535 (1969), this court invalidated state reapportionment statutes for federal congressional districts having maximum percentage deviations of 5.97% and 13.1% respectively. [I]t was concluded that [*Wesberry's*] command 'permits only the limited population variances which are unavoidable despite a good-faith effort to achieve absolute equality, or for which justification is shown.'

"[*Reynolds* suggested] more flexibility was constitutionally permissible with respect to state legislative reapportionment than in congressional redistricting. Consideration was given to the fact [that] there is a significantly larger number of seats in state legislative bodies to be distributed within a State than Congressional seats, and that therefore it may be feasible for a State to use political subdivision lines to a greater [extent].[l] * * *

a. *Avery v. Midland County,* 390 U.S. 474, 88 S.Ct. 1114, 20 L.Ed.2d 45 (1968), held that *Reynolds* applied to a county body with "general responsibility and power for local affairs" but left open the status of special purpose units of government "affecting definable groups of constituents more than other[s]." See also *Hadley v. Junior College Dist.,* 397 U.S. 50, 90 S.Ct. 791, 25 L.Ed.2d 45 (1970) (extending *Avery* to junior college district).

b. See also *Brown v. Thomson,* 462 U.S. 835, 103 S.Ct. 2690, 77 L.Ed.2d 214 (1983), per Powell, J., which upheld Wyoming's allocation of one seat in its House of Representatives to its least populous county, resulting in a maximum deviation of 89%. The Court emphasized that "appellants deliberately have limited their challenge to the alleged dilution of their voting power resulting from the one representative given to Niobrara County" rather than "the state apportionment plan as a whole."

O'Connor, J., joined by Stevens, J., expressed "the gravest doubts that a statewide legislative plan with an 85% maximum deviation would survive constitutional scrutiny despite the presence of the State's strong interest in preserving county boundaries. I join the Court's opinion on the understanding that nothing in it suggests that this Court would uphold such a scheme." Brennan, J., joined by White, Marshall, and Blackmun, JJ., dissented.

l. See also Douglas Hobbs, *Book Review,* 16 UCLA L.Rev. 659, 682 (1969): "[C]ongressmen are assumed to represent the state as a whole as well as their district; state legislators, on the other hand, are expected to be more parochial. Therefore, there is arguably a better case on the state [level] for allowing deviation based on local communities of interest. In addition, on the state level population variations in one house can be compensated for in the other.

"Neither courts nor legislatures are furnished any specialized calipers which enable them to extract from the general language of the Equal Protection Clause [the] mathematical formula which establishes what range of percentage deviations are permissible, and what are not. [While] this percentage may well approach tolerable limits, we do not believe it exceeds them."

5. *Calculating the population base.* BURNS v. RICHARDSON, 384 U.S. 73, 86 S.Ct. 1286, 16 L.Ed.2d 376 (1966), per BRENNAN, J., upheld a Hawaii plan that used *registered voters* as the population base, which, "probably because of uneven distribution of military residents—largely unregistered," produced results significantly different than if total population figures had been used: States are not "required to include aliens, transients, short-term or temporary residents, or persons denied the vote for conviction of crime in the apportionment [base]. The decision to include or exclude any such group involves choices about the nature of representation with which we have been shown no constitutionally founded reason to interfere. [But use] of a registered voter or actual voter basis [is] susceptible to improper influences by which those in political power might be able to perpetuate underrepresentation of groups constitutionally entitled to participate in the electoral [process]. [W]e hold that the present apportionment satisfies the Equal Protection Clause only because on this record it was found to have produced a distribution of legislators not substantially different from that which would have resulted from the use of [state citizen population, which is] a permissible population base."

MOBILE v. BOLDEN

446 U.S. 55, 100 S.Ct. 1490, 64 L.Ed.2d 47 (1980).

JUSTICE STEWART announced the judgment of the Court and delivered an opinion in which THE CHIEF JUSTICE, JUSTICE POWELL, and JUSTICE REHNQUIST join.

The City of Mobile, Ala., has since 1911 been governed by a City Commission consisting of three members elected by the voters of the city at-large. [This] is the same basic electoral system that is followed by literally thousands of municipalities and other local governmental units throughout the Nation.

[The] constitutional objection to multimember districts is not and cannot be that, as such, they depart from apportionment on a population basis in violation of *Reynolds* and its progeny. Rather the focus in such cases has been on the lack of representation multimember districts afford various elements of the voting population in a system of representative legislative democracy. "Criticism [of multimember districts] is rooted in their winner-take-all aspects, their tendency to submerge minorities, [a] general preference for legislatures reflecting community interests as closely as possible and disenchantment with political parties and elections as devices to settle policy differences between contending interests." *Whitcomb v. Chavis,* 403 U.S. 124, 91 S.Ct. 1858, 29 L.Ed.2d 363 (1971).

Despite repeated constitutional attacks upon multimember legislative districts, the Court has consistently held that they are not unconstitutional per se, e.g., *White v. Regester; Whitcomb; Burns v. Richardson; Fortson v. Dorsey,* 379 U.S. 433, 85 S.Ct. 498, 13 L.Ed.2d 401 (1965). We have recognized, however, that such legislative apportionments could violate the Fourteenth Amendment if their

This [is] impossible in congressional district-   ing."

purpose were invidiously to minimize or cancel out the voting potential of racial or ethnic minorities. To prove such a purpose it is not enough to show that the group allegedly discriminated against has not elected representatives in proportion to its numbers. A plaintiff must prove that the disputed plan was "conceived or operated as [a] purposeful device[] to further racial discrimination." *Whitcomb.*

This burden of proof is simply one aspect of the basic principle that only if there is purposeful discrimination can there be a violation of [equal protection]. See *Washington v. Davis; Arlington Heights; Personnel Adm'r v. Feeney*, [Sec. 2, III supra]. Although dicta may be drawn from a few of the Court's earlier opinions suggesting that disproportionate effects alone may establish a claim of unconstitutional racial vote dilution, the fact is that such a view is not supported by any decision of this Court.[13] More importantly, such a view is not consistent with the meaning of the Equal Protection Clause as it has been understood in a variety of other contexts involving alleged racial discrimination. *Davis* (employment); *Arlington Heights* (zoning); *Keyes*, [Sec. 2, IV supra] (public schools); *Akins v. Texas*, 325 U.S. 398, 65 S.Ct. 1276, 89 L.Ed. 1692 (1945) (jury selection).

In only one case has the Court sustained a claim that multimember legislative districts unconstitutionally diluted the voting strength of a discrete group. [*Regester*] upheld a constitutional challenge by Negroes and Mexican–Americans to parts of a legislative reapportionment plan adopted by the State of Texas. [T]he Court held that the plaintiffs had been able to "produce evidence to support the finding that the political processes leading to nomination and election were not equally open to participation by the group[s] in question." In so holding, the Court relied upon evidence in the record that included a long history of official discrimination against minorities as well as indifference to their needs and interests on the part of white elected officials. * * *

Regester is thus consistent with "the basic equal protection principle that the invidious quality of a law claimed to be racially discriminatory must ultimately be traced to a racially discriminatory purpose." [But] where the character of a law is readily explainable on grounds apart from race, as would nearly always be true where, as here, an entire system of local governance is brought into question, disproportionate impact alone cannot be decisive, and courts must look to other evidence to support a finding of discriminatory purpose. [I]t is clear that the evidence in the present case fell far short of showing that the appellants "conceived or operated [a] purposeful device[ ] to further racial discrimination." *Whitcomb.*

[T]he District Court [affirmed by the Court of Appeals] based its conclusion of unconstitutionality primarily on the fact that no Negro had ever been elected to the City Commission, apparently because of the pervasiveness of racially polarized voting in Mobile. The trial court also found that city officials had not been as responsive to the interests of Negroes as to those of white persons. On the basis of these findings, the court concluded that the political processes in Mobile were not equally open to Negroes, despite its seemingly inconsistent findings that there

---

13. The dissenting opinion of Justice Marshall reads the Court's opinion in *Dorsey* to say that a claim of vote dilution under the Equal Protection Clause could rest on either discriminatory purpose or effect. [Although] the Court recognized that "designedly or otherwise," multimember districting schemes might, under the circumstances of a particular case, minimize the voting strength of a racial group, an issue as to the constitutionality of such an arrangement "[w]as not [presented]."

The phrase "designedly or otherwise" [was] repeated, also in dictum, in *Burns*. But the constitutional challenge to the multimember constituencies failed in that case because the plaintiffs demonstrated neither discriminatory purpose nor effect.

were no inhibitions against Negroes becoming candidates, and that in fact Negroes had registered and voted without hindrance. * * *

First, [i]t may be that Negro candidates have been defeated, but that fact alone does not work a constitutional deprivation.

Second, [evidence] of discrimination by white officials in Mobile is relevant only as the most tenuous and circumstantial evidence of the constitutional invalidity of the electoral system under which they attained their offices.

Third, the District Court and the Court of Appeals supported their conclusion by drawing upon the substantial history of official racial discrimination in Alabama. But past discrimination cannot, in the manner of original sin, condemn governmental action that is not itself unlawful. The ultimate question remains whether a discriminatory intent has been proved in a given [case].

Finally, the District Court and the Court of Appeals pointed to the mechanics of the at-large electoral system itself as proof that the votes of Negroes were being invidiously canceled out. But those features of that electoral system, such as the majority vote requirement, tend naturally to disadvantage any voting minority [and] are far from proof that the at-large electoral scheme represents purposeful discrimination against Negro voters.

We turn finally [to] Justice Marshall's dissenting opinion. The theory [appears] to be that every "political group," or at least every such group that is in the minority, has a federal constitutional right to elect candidates in proportion to its numbers.[22] Moreover, a political group's "right" to have its candidates elected is said to be a "fundamental interest," the infringement of which may be established without proof that a State has acted with the purpose of impairing anybody's access to the political process. This dissenting opinion finds the "right" infringed [because] no Negro has been elected to the Mobile City Commission.

Whatever appeal the dissenting opinion's view may have as a matter of political theory, it is not the law. The Equal Protection Clause [does] not require proportional representation as an imperative of political organization. * * *

It is of course true that a law that impinges upon a fundamental right explicitly or implicitly secured by the Constitution is presumptively unconstitutional. See *Shapiro v. Thompson,* [Part II infra]. See also *San Antonio Ind. School Dist. v. Rodriguez,* [Part IV infra]. But plainly "[i]t is not the province of this Court to create substantive constitutional rights in the name of guaranteeing equal protection of the laws," id. [In] *Whitcomb,* the trial court had found that a multimember state legislative district had invidiously deprived Negroes and poor persons of rights guaranteed them by the Constitution, notwithstanding the absence of any evidence whatever of discrimination against them. Reversing the trial court, this Court said: "The District Court's holding, although on the facts of this case limited to guaranteeing one racial group representation, is not easily contained. It is expressive of the more general proposition that any group with distinctive interests must be represented in legislative halls if it is numerous

---

22. The dissenting opinion seeks to disclaim this description of its theory by suggesting that a claim of vote dilution may require, in addition to proof of electoral defeat, some evidence of "historical and social factors" indicating that the group in question is without political influence. Putting to the side the evident fact that these gauzy sociological considerations have no constitutional basis, it remains far from certain that they could, in any

principled manner, exclude the claims of any discrete political group that happens, for whatever reason, to elect fewer of its candidates than arithmetic indicates it might. Indeed, the putative limits are bound to prove illusory if the express purpose informing their application would be, as the dissent assumes, to redress the "inequitable distribution of political influence."

enough to command at least one seat and represents a majority living in an area sufficiently compact to constitute a single-member district. This approach would make it difficult to reject claims of Democrats, Republicans, or members of any political [organization]. There are also union oriented workers, the university community, religious or ethnic groups occupying identifiable areas of our hetero-geneous cities and urban areas. Indeed, it would be difficult for a great many, if not most, multi-member districts to survive analysis under the District Court's view unless combined with some voting arrangement such as proportional repre-sentation or cumulative voting aimed at providing representation for minority parties or interests. At the very least, affirmance [would] spawn endless litigation concerning the multi-member district systems now widely employed in this country." * * *

JUSTICE BLACKMUN, concurring in the result.

Assuming that proof of intent is a prerequisite to appellees' prevailing on their constitutional claim of vote dilution, I am inclined to agree with Justice White that, in this case, "the findings of the District Court amply support an inference of purposeful discrimination." I concur in the Court's judgment of reversal, however, because I believe that the relief afforded appellees by the District Court [ordering a new form of government "of a Mayor and a City Council with members elected from single-member districts"] was not commensu-rate with the sound exercise of judicial discretion. * * *

JUSTICE STEVENS, concurring in the judgment.

[While] I agree with Justice Stewart that no violation of respondents' consti-tutional rights has been demonstrated, my analysis of the issue proceeds along somewhat different lines.

[T]his case draws into question a political structure that treats all individuals as equals but adversely affects the political strength of a racially identifiable group. Although I am satisfied that such a structure may be challenged under the Fifteenth Amendment as well as under the Equal Protection Clause of the Fourteenth Amendment, I believe that under either provision it must be judged by a standard that allows the political process to function effectively. * * *

[No] case decided by this Court establishes a constitutional right to propor-tional representation for racial minorities. What *Gomillion* [Sec. 2, III supra] holds is that a sufficiently "uncouth" or irrational racial gerrymander violates the Fifteenth Amendment. [The] fact that the "gerrymander" condemned in *Gomil-lion* was equally vulnerable under both Amendments indicates that the essential holding of that case is applicable, not merely to gerrymanders directed against racial minorities, but to those aimed at religious, ethnic, economic and political groups as well.

My conclusion that the same standard should be applied to racial groups as is applied to other groups leads me also to conclude that the standard cannot condemn every adverse impact on one or more political groups without spawning more dilution litigation than the judiciary can manage. [N]othing comparable to the mathematical yardstick used in apportionment cases is available to identify the difference between permissible and impermissible adverse impacts on the voting strength of political groups. * * *

In my view, the proper standard is suggested by three characteristics of the gerrymander condemned in *Gomillion:* (1) the 28–sided configuration [was] mani-festly not the product of a routine or a traditional political decision; (2) it had a significant adverse impact on a minority group; and (3) it was unsupported by any neutral justification and thus was either totally irrational or entirely motivated by a desire to curtail the political strength of the minority. These characteristics suggest that a proper test should focus on the objective effects of the political decision rather than the subjective motivation of the decisionmaker.

[The] standard for testing the acceptability of such a decision must take into account the fact that the responsibility for drawing political boundaries is generally committed to the legislative process and that the process inevitably involves a series of compromises among different group interests. If the process is to work, it must reflect an awareness of group interests and it must tolerate some attempts to advantage or to disadvantage particular segments of the voting populace. [Accordingly], a political decision that is supported by valid and articulable justifications cannot be invalid simply because some participants in the decision-making process were motivated by a purpose to disadvantage a minority group. [A] contrary view "would spawn endless litigation concerning the multimember districts now widely employed in this Country," and would entangle the judiciary in a voracious political thicket.

JUSTICE BRENNAN, dissenting.

I dissent because I agree with Justice Marshall that proof of discriminatory impact is sufficient in these cases. I also dissent because, even accepting the plurality's premise that discriminatory purpose must be shown, I agree with [Marshall and White, JJ.,] that the appellees have clearly met that burden.

JUSTICE WHITE, dissenting.

[The] District Court and the Court of Appeals properly found that an invidious discriminatory purpose could be inferred from the totality of facts in this case. * * *

JUSTICE MARSHALL, dissenting. * * *

The Court does not dispute the proposition that multimember districting can have the effect of submerging electoral minorities. [Further], we decided a series of vote-dilution cases under the Fourteenth Amendment that were designed to protect electoral minorities from precisely the combination of electoral laws and historical and social factors found in the present cases.[4] [Although] we have held that multimember districts are not unconstitutional per se, there is simply no basis for the plurality's conclusion that under our prior cases proof of discriminatory intent is a necessary condition for the invalidation of multimember districting.

[Under] this line of cases, an electoral districting plan is invalid if it has the effect of affording an electoral minority "less opportunity [than] other residents in the district to participate in the political processes and to elect legislators of their choice," *Regester*. It is also apparent that the Court in *Regester* considered equal access to the political process as meaning more than merely allowing the minority the opportunity to vote. *Regester* stands for the proposition that an electoral

---

4. [T]hough municipalities must be accorded some discretion in arranging their affairs, see *Abate*, there is all the more reason to scrutinize assertions that municipal, rather than State, multi-member districting dilutes the vote of an electoral minority: "In statewide elections, it is possible that a large minority group in one multi-member district will be unable to elect any legislators, while in another multi-member district where the same group is a slight majority, they will elect the entire slate of legislators. [In] at-large elections, [t]here is no way to balance out the discrimination against a particular minority group because the entire city is one huge election district. The minority's loss is absolute." Barbara Berry & Thomas Dye, *The Discriminatory Effects of At-Large Elections*, 7 Fla.St.U.L.Rev. 85, 87 (1979). * * *

system may not relegate an electoral minority to political impotence by diminishing the importance of its [vote].

The plurality fails to apply the discriminatory effect standard of *Regester* because that approach conflicts with what the plurality takes to be an elementary principle of law. "[O]nly if there is purposeful discrimination," announces the plurality, "can there be a violation of [equal protection]." That proposition [fails] to distinguish between two distinct lines of equal protection decisions: those involving suspect classifications, and those involving fundamental rights. * * *

Under the Equal Protection Clause, if a classification "impinges upon a fundamental right explicitly or implicitly protected by the [Constitution], strict judicial scrutiny" is required, *Rodriguez,* regardless of whether the infringement was intentional. As I will explain, our cases recognize a fundamental right to equal electoral participation that encompasses protection against vote dilution. Proof of discriminatory purpose is, therefore, not required to support a claim of vote dilution.[10] The plurality's erroneous conclusion to the contrary is the result of a failure to recognize the central distinction between *Regester* and *Davis:* the former involved an infringement of a constitutionally protected right, while the latter dealt with a claim of racially discriminatory distribution of an interest to which no citizen has a constitutional entitlement. * * *

Reynolds and its progeny focused solely on the discriminatory *effects* of malapportionment. [In] the present cases, the alleged vote dilution, though caused by the combined effects of the electoral structure and social and historical factors rather than by unequal population distribution, is analytically the same concept: the unjustified abridgement of a fundamental right. It follows, then, that a showing of discriminatory intent is just as unnecessary under the vote-dilution approach adopted in *Dorsey* and applied in *Regester,* as it is under our reapportionment cases. * * *

The plurality's response is that my approach amounts to nothing less than a constitutional requirement of proportional representation for groups. That assertion amounts to nothing more than a red herring. [Appellees] proved that no Negro had ever been elected to the Mobile City Commission, despite the fact that Negroes constitute about one-third of the electorate, and that the persistence of severe racial bloc voting made it highly unlikely that any Negro could be elected at-large in the foreseeable future. Contrary to the plurality's contention, however, I do not find unconstitutional vote dilution in this case simply because of that showing. The plaintiffs convinced the District Court that Mobile Negroes were unable to use alternative avenues of political influence. They showed that Mobile Negroes still suffered pervasive present effects of massive historical official and private discrimination, and that the city commission had been quite unresponsive to the needs of the minority community. Mobile has been guilty of such pervasive racial discrimination in hiring employees that extensive intervention by the Federal District Court has been required. Negroes are grossly underrepresented on city boards and committees. The city's distribution of public services is racially

---

10. [Although] the right to vote is distinguishable for present purposes from the other fundamental rights our cases have recognized, surely the plurality would not require proof of discriminatory purpose in those cases. The plurality fails to articulate why the right to vote should receive such singular treatment. Furthermore, the plurality refuses to recognize the disutility of requiring proof of discriminatory purpose in fundamental rights cases. For example, it would make no sense to require such a showing when the question is whether a state statute regulating abortion violates the right of personal choice recognized in *Roe v. Wade.* The only logical inquiry is whether, regardless of the legislature's motive, the statute has the effect of infringing that right. See, e.g., *Planned Parenthood v. Danforth,* [Ch. 6, Sec. 2].

discriminatory. City officials and police were largely unmoved by Negro complaints about police brutality and "mock lynchings." The District Court concluded that "[t]his sluggish and timid response is another manifestation of the low priority given to the needs of the black citizens and of the [commissioners'] political fear of a white backlash vote when black citizens' needs are at stake."

[T]he protection against vote dilution recognized by our prior cases serves as a minimally intrusive guarantee of political survival for a discrete political minority that is effectively locked out of governmental decisionmaking processes. So understood, the doctrine hardly " 'create[s] substantive constitutional rights in the name of guaranteeing equal protection of the laws,' " [but] is a simple reflection of the basic principle that the Equal Protection Clause protects "[t]he right of a citizen to equal representation and to have his vote weighted equally with those of all other citizens." *Reynolds*.

[The] plurality's requirement of proof of *intentional discrimination* [may] represent an attempt to bury the legitimate concerns of the minority beneath the soil of a doctrine almost as impermeable as it is specious. If so, the superficial tranquility created by such measures can be but short-lived. If this Court refuses to honor our long-recognized principle that the Constitution "nullifies sophisticated as well as simple-minded modes of discrimination," it cannot expect the victims of discrimination to respect political channels of seeking redress. I dissent.

————

ROGERS v. LODGE, 458 U.S. 613, 102 S.Ct. 3272, 73 L.Ed.2d 1012 (1982), per WHITE, J., affirmed a decision that the at-large election system for a Georgia County Board of Commissioners violated equal protection: "The district court [demonstrated] its understanding of the controlling standard by observing that a determination of discriminatory intent is 'a requisite to a finding of unconstitutional vote dilution' [and] concluded that the [system] 'although racially neutral when adopted, is being *Maintained* for invidious purposes.' [For] the most part, the district court dealt with the evidence in terms of the factors [that had been used by the district court in *Mobile*], but as the court of appeals stated: 'Judge Alaimo [did] not treat [those factors] as absolute, but rather considered them only to the extent that they were relevant to the question of discriminatory intent.' Although a tenable argument can be made to the contrary, we are not inclined to disagree with the court of appeals' conclusion that the district court applied the proper legal standard. * * *

"The Court of Appeals [stated that the] District Court correctly anticipated *Mobile* and required appellees to prove that the at-large voting system was maintained[a] for a discriminatory purpose. The Court of Appeals also held that the District Court's findings not only were not clearly erroneous, but its conclusion that the at-large system was maintained for invidious purposes was 'virtually mandated by the overwhelming proof.' [This Court has] noted that issues of intent are commonly treated as factual matters [and] has frequently noted its reluctance to disturb findings of fact concurred in by two lower courts."

POWELL, J., joined by Rehnquist, J., dissented: "[T]he Court's opinion cannot be reconciled persuasively with [*Mobile*]. There are some variances in the largely

a. For commentary on the Court's handling of the intent issue, see C. Edwin Baker, *Outcome Equality or Equality of Respect: The Sub-* *stantive Content of Equal Protection,* 131 U.Pa. L.Rev. 933, 983–84 (1983).

sociological evidence presented in the two cases. But *Mobile* held that this *kind* of evidence was not enough. * * *

"The Court's decision today relies heavily on the capacity of the federal district courts—essentially free from any standards propounded by this Court—to determine whether at-large voting systems are 'being maintained for the invidious purpose of diluting the voting strength of the black population.' Federal courts thus are invited to engage in deeply subjective inquiries into the motivations of local officials in structuring local governments. Inquiries of this kind not only can be 'unseemly,' they intrude the federal courts—with only the vaguest constitutional direction—into an area of intensely local and political concern.

"Emphasizing these considerations, Justice Stevens argues forcefully [that] subjective intent is irrelevant to the establishment of a case of racial vote [dilution].[b] I agree with much of what he says [but] would not accept this view. 'The central purpose of the Equal Protection Clause [is] the prevention of official conduct discriminating on the basis of race.' *Davis*. Because I am unwilling to abandon this central principle in cases of this kind, I cannot join Justice Stevens's opinion. [But] in the absence of proof of discrimination by reliance on the kind of objective factors identified by Justice Stevens, I would hold that the factors cited by the Court of Appeals are too attenuated as a matter of law to support an inference of discriminatory intent."

Notes and Questions

1. *Multimember districts.* In *Mobile*, the Court considered a challenge to a "multimember" or "at-large" district. On the history of such districting arrangements, see Samuel Issacharoff, *Polarized Voting and the Political Process: The Transformation of Voting Rights Jurisprudence,* 90 Mich.L.Rev. 1833, 1839–40: "The widespread use of multimember electoral systems dates from the turn of the century, when an unusual alliance of northern Progressives and southern Redeemers endeavored to curtail the ability of community-based political machines, depicted pejoratively as ward heelers, to deliver the spoils of power to their local political bases. By eliminating the local bases of voting power of, respectively, urban working-class ethnics and freed slaves, the turn-of-the-century reformers hoped to centralize political power through the use of at-large and multimember election devices. These election schemes allow for serial voting that, in the context of a majority voting bloc, will reward a cohesive majority with superordinate representation."

In *Mobile*, the multi-member districting scheme made it difficult for a minority group to elect even a single representative. In the 1990s, however, some scholars began to urge the use of *modified* at-large systems, involving cumulative voting, in which "each voter is given the same number of votes as open seats, and the voter may plump or cumulate her votes to reflect the intensity of her preferences," as preferable to single-member districts as a means of enabling minority groups to form coalitions and elect representatives of their choice. Lani Guinier, *The Tyranny of the Majority* 149–53 (1994). For further discussion of such schemes, see Part D infra.

2. *Group rights?* Is the right at issue in *Mobile* inherently a "group" rather than an individual right—a right of (some) groups to be able to elect a representative of their choice?[a]

---

b. Stevens, J.'s long dissent expanded his views expressed in *Mobile*.

a. See generally Vikram Amar & Alan Brownstein, *The Hybrid Nature of Political*

Consider Larry Alexander, *Still Lost in the Political Thicket (or Why I Don't Understand the Concept of Vote Dilution)*, 50 Vand.L.Rev. 327, 336 (1997), arguing that beyond a requirement that each district have equal numbers, the concept of vote dilution makes no sense. Because literally any districting scheme will make it more difficult for members of some groups to elect a representative than would an alternative scheme, every plan "dilutes" some group's votes; and "[i]f every plan dilutes votes, we might as well say that no plan does." Do you agree?

3. *Proportional representation.* Stewart, J., asserts that the theory of Justice Marshall's dissenting opinion in *Mobile* would require "proportional representation" of groups, such that "every 'political group,' or at least every such group that is in the minority, has a federal constitutional right to elect candidates in proportion to its numbers." Is this a fair charge? Should there be a right to proportional representation?[b] Could such a right be limited to racial groups?

4. *Voting rights act.* After the *Mobile* decision, Congress amended the Voting Rights Act of 1965, p. 1359 infra, in a manner that has been interpreted to obviate the need for proof of discriminatory purpose in cases asserting statutory claims of vote dilution.

DAVIS v. BANDEMER

478 U.S. 109, 106 S.Ct. 2797, 92 L.Ed.2d 85 (1986).

[Democrats challenged Indiana's 1981 state apportionment—enacted by Republican majorities in both houses of the legislature and signed by a Republican governor—on the ground that it "constituted a political gerrymander intended to disadvantage Democrats on a statewide basis." A majority of the Court, per White, J.—relying on cases such as *Baker* and *Reynolds* (indicating "the justiciability of claims going to the adequacy of state representation in state legislatures"); *Mobile, Whitcomb, Regester* and *Rogers* ("racial gerrymandering presents a justiciable equal protection claim"); and, particularly, *Gaffney v. Cummings,* [note 3 after *Reynolds*],[a]—held that a "political gerrymandering claim [is] justiciable."]

JUSTICE WHITE announced the judgment of the Court and delivered [an] opinion in which JUSTICE BRENNAN, JUSTICE MARSHALL, and JUSTICE BLACKMUN joined * * *.

We [agree] with the District Court that in order to succeed the Bandemer plaintiffs were required to prove both intentional discrimination against an identifiable political group and an actual discriminatory effect on that group. [As long as redistricting is done by a legislature, it should not be very difficult to prove that the likely political consequences of the reapportionment were intended.[11]

We do not accept, however, the District Court's legal and factual bases for concluding that the 1981 Act visited a sufficiently adverse effect on the appellees' constitutionally protected rights to make out a violation of the Equal Protection

Rights, 50 Stan.L.Rev. 915 (1998) (arguing that political rights have an irreducibly hybrid nature, with a group as well as an individual dimension).

b. For an illuminating and spirited defense, see Note, *The Constitutional Imperative of Proportional Representation*, 94 Yale L.J. 163 (1984).

a. *Gaffney* ruled that the fact "that virtually every Senate and House district line [in Connecticut] was drawn with the conscious intent to create a districting plan that would achieve a rough approximation of the statewide political strengths of the Democratic and Republican Parties, the only two parties in the state large enough to elect legislators from discernible geographic areas" did not invalidate the plan.

11. That discriminatory intent may not be difficult to prove in this context does not, of course, mean that it need not be proved at all to succeed on such a claim.

Clause. The District Court held that because any apportionment scheme that *L
purposely prevents proportional representation is unconstitutional, Democratic
voters need only show that their proportionate voting influence has been adversely affected. Our cases, however, clearly foreclose any claim that the Constitution
requires proportional representation or that legislatures in reapportioning must
draw district lines to come as near as possible to allocating seats to the contending
parties in proportion to what their anticipated statewide vote will be. *Whitcomb;
Regester.*

The typical election for legislative seats in the United States is conducted in
described geographical districts, with the candidate receiving the most votes in
each district winning the seat allocated to that district. If all or most of the *L
districts are competitive, [even] a narrow statewide preference for either party
would produce an overwhelming majority for the winning party in the state
legislature. This consequence, however, is inherent in winner-take-all, district-
based elections, and we cannot hold that such a reapportionment law would
violate the Equal Protection Clause because the voters in the losing party do not
have representation in the legislature in proportion to the statewide vote received
by their party candidates. * * *

In cases involving individual multi-member districts, we have required a
substantially greater showing of adverse effects than a mere lack of proportional
representation to support a finding of unconstitutional vote dilution. Only where
there is evidence that excluded groups have "less opportunity to participate in the
political processes and to elect candidates of their choice" have we refused to
approve the use of multi-member districts. *Rogers.* See also *United Jewish Orgs. v.* ✓
Carey; Regester; Whitcomb. In these cases, we have also noted the lack of
responsiveness by those elected to the concerns of the relevant groups. *Rogers;
Regester.*[12]

These holdings rest on a conviction that the mere fact that a particular
apportionment scheme makes it more difficult for a particular group in a particular district to elect the representatives of its choice does not render that scheme
constitutionally infirm. This conviction, in turn, stems from a perception that the
power to influence the political process is not limited to winning elections. An
individual or a group of individuals who votes for a losing candidate is usually
deemed to be adequately represented by the winning candidate and to have as
much opportunity to influence that candidate as other voters in the district. We
cannot presume in such a situation, without actual proof to the contrary, that the
candidate elected will entirely ignore the interests of those voters. This is true
even in a safe district where the losing group loses election after election. Thus, a
group's electoral power is not unconstitutionally diminished by the simple fact of
an appointment scheme that makes winning elections more difficult, and a failure
of proportional representation alone does not constitute impermissible discrimination under the Equal Protection Clause.

As with individual districts, where unconstitutional vote dilution is alleged in
the form of statewide political gerrymandering, the mere lack of proportional
representation will not be sufficient to prove unconstitutional discrimination.

Not going to proportional representation

---

12. Although these cases involved racial
groups, we believe that the principles developed in these cases would apply equally to
claims by political groups in individual districts. We note, however, that the elements
necessary to a successful vote dilution claim
may be more difficult to prove in relation to a
claim by a political group. For example, historical patterns of exclusion from the political processes, evidence which would support a vote
dilution claim, are in general more likely to be
present for a racial group than for a political
group.

No judicially manageable standard:

But: Proportional representation
However: not System required
by the Constitution

Again, without specific supporting evidence, a court cannot presume in such a case that those who are elected will disregard the disproportionately under-represented group. Rather, unconstitutional discrimination occurs only when the electoral system is arranged in a manner that will consistently degrade a voter's or a group of voters' influence on the political process as a [whole].

In a challenge to an individual district, this inquiry focuses on the opportunity of members of the group to participate in party deliberations in the slating and nomination of candidates, their opportunity to register and vote, and hence their chance to directly influence the election returns and to secure the attention of the winning candidate. Statewide, however, the inquiry centers on the voters' direct or indirect influence on the elections of the state legislature as a whole. And, as in individual district cases, an equal protection violation may be found only where the electoral system substantially disadvantages certain voters in their opportunity to influence the political process effectively. In this context, such a finding of unconstitutionality must be supported by evidence of continued frustration of the will of a majority of the voters or effective denial to a minority of voters of a fair chance to influence the political process.

Based on these views, we would reject the District Court's apparent holding that *any* interference with an opportunity to elect a representative of one's choice would be sufficient to allege or make out an equal protection violation, unless justified by some acceptable state interest that the State would be required to demonstrate. [S]uch a low threshold for legal action would invite attack on all or almost all reapportionment statutes. District-based elections hardly ever produce a perfect fit between votes and representation. [Inviting] attack on minor departures from some supposed norm would too much embroil the judiciary in second-guessing what has consistently been referred to as a political task for the legislature * * *.

The view that a prima facie case of illegal discrimination in reapportionment requires a showing of more than a *de minimis* effect is not unprecedented. Reapportionment cases involving the one person, one vote principle [provide] support for such a requirement. In the present, considerably more complex context, it is also appropriate to require allegations and proof that the challenged legislative plan has had or will have effects that are sufficiently serious to require intervention by the federal courts in state reapportionment decisions.

The District Court's findings do not satisfy this threshold condition to stating and proving a cause of action. In reaching its conclusion, the District Court relied primarily on the results of the 1982 elections: Democratic candidates for the State House of Representatives had received 51.9% of the votes cast statewide and Republican candidates 48.1%; yet, out of the 100 seats to be filled, Republican candidates won 57 and Democrats 43. In the Senate, 53.1% of the votes were cast for Democratic candidates and 46.9% for Republicans; of the 25 Senate seats to be filled, Republicans won 12 and Democrats 13. The court also relied upon the use of multi-member districts in Marion and Allen counties, where Democrats or those inclined to vote Democratic in 1982 amounted to 46.6% of the population of those counties but Republicans won 86 percent—18 of 21—seats allocated to the districts in those counties. These disparities were enough to require a neutral justification by the State, which in the eyes of the District Court was not forthcoming.[15]

15. The District Court apparently thought that the political group suffering discrimination was all those voters who voted for Democratic Assembly candidates in 1982. Judge Pell, in dissent, argued that the allegedly disfavored group should be defined as those voters who

More than results of one election

*↙ (
↙F*

Relying on a single election to prove unconstitutional discrimination is unsatisfactory. The District Court observed, and the parties do not disagree, that Indiana is a swing State. Voters sometimes prefer Democratic candidates, and sometimes Republican. The District Court did not find that because of the 1981 Act the Democrats could not in one of the next few elections secure a sufficient vote to take control of the assembly. Indeed, the District Court declined to hold that the 1982 election results were the predictable consequences of the 1981 Act and expressly refused to hold that those results were a reliable prediction of future ones. The District Court did not ask by what percentage the statewide Democratic vote would have had to increase to control either the House or the Senate. The appellants argue here, without a persuasive response from appellees, that had the Democratic candidates received an additional few percentage points of the votes cast statewide, they would have obtained a majority of the seats in both houses. Nor was there any finding that the 1981 reapportionment would consign the Democrats to a minority status in the Assembly throughout the 1980's or that the Democrats would have no hope of doing any better in the reapportionment that would occur after the 1990 census. Without findings of this nature, the ⚡*PP* District Court erred in concluding that the 1981 Act violated the Equal Protection Clause.

The District Court's discussion of the multi-member districts created by the 1981 Act does not undermine this conclusion. For the purposes of the statewide political gerrymandering claim, these districts appear indistinguishable from safe Republican and safe Democratic single-member districts. Simply showing that ⚡*L* there are multi-member districts in the State and that those districts are constructed so as to be safely Republican or Democratic in no way bolsters the contention that there has been *statewide* discrimination against Democratic voters. It could be, were the necessary threshold effect to be shown, that multi-member districts could be demonstrated to be suspect on the ground that they are particularly useful in attaining impermissibly discriminatory ends; at this stage of the inquiry, however, the multi-member district evidence does not materially aid the appellees' case. * * *

In response to our approach, Justice Powell suggests an alternative method for evaluating equal protection claims of political gerrymandering. In his view, courts should look at a number of factors in considering these claims: the nature ⚡*L* of the legislative procedures by which the challenged redistricting was accomplished and the intent behind the redistricting; the shapes of the districts and their conformity with political subdivision boundaries; and "evidence concerning population disparities and statistics tending to show vote dilution." [T]he crux of Justice Powell's analysis seems to be that—at least in some cases—the intentional drawing of district boundaries for partisan ends and for no other reason violates the Equal Protection Clause in and of itself. We disagree, however, with this ⚡*PP* conception of a constitutional violation. Specifically, even if a state legislature ⚡*L* redistricts with the specific intention of disadvantaging one political party's election prospects, we do not believe that there has been an unconstitutional

Powell's Factors (rejected by ct.)

could be counted on to vote Democratic from election to election, thus excluding those who vote the Republican ticket from time to time. He would have counted the true believers by averaging the Democratic vote cast in two different elections for those statewide offices for which party-line voting is thought to be the rule and personality and issue-oriented factors are relatively unimportant. Although accepting

Judge Pell's definition of Democratic voters would have strongly suggested that the 1981 reapportionment had no discriminatory effect at all, there was no response to his position. The appellees take up the challenge in this Court, claiming that Judge Pell chose the wrong election years for the purpose of averaging the Democratic votes. The dispute need not now be resolved.

discrimination against members of that party unless the redistricting does in fact disadvantage it at the polls.

Moreover, as we discussed above, a mere lack of proportionate results in one election cannot suffice in this regard. [E]qual protection violations may be found only where a history (actual or projected) of disproportionate results appears in conjunction with ["strong indicia of lack of political power and the denial of fair representation."] The mere lack of control of the General Assembly after a single election does not rise to the requisite level. [But] Justice Powell's view would allow a constitutional violation to be found where the only proven effect on a political party's electoral power was disproportionate results in one (or possibly two) elections. * * *

In rejecting Justice Powell's approach, we do not mean to intimate that the factors he considers are entirely irrelevant. The election results obviously are relevant to a showing of the effects required to prove a political gerrymandering claim under our view. And the district configurations may be combined with vote projections to predict future election results, which are also relevant to the effects showing. The other factors, even if not relevant to the effects issue, might well be relevant to an equal protection claim. The equal protection argument would proceed along the following lines: If there were a discriminatory effect and a discriminatory intent, then the legislation would be examined for valid underpinnings. Thus, evidence of exclusive legislative process and deliberate drawing of district lines in accordance with accepted gerrymandering principles would be relevant to intent, and evidence of valid and invalid configuration would be relevant to whether the districting plan met legitimate state interests.

This course is consistent with our equal protection cases generally and is the course we follow here: We assumed that there was discriminatory intent, found that there was insufficient discriminatory effect to constitute an equal protection violation,[19] and therefore did not reach the question of the state interests (legitimate or otherwise) served by the particular districts as they were created by the legislature. Consequently, the valid or invalid configuration of the districts was an issue we did not need to consider.

* * * We recognize that our own view may be difficult of application. Determining when an electoral system has been "arranged in a manner that will consistently degrade a voter's or a group of voters' influence on the political process as a whole" is of necessity a difficult inquiry. Nevertheless, we believe that it recognizes the delicacy of intruding on this most political of legislative functions and is at the same time consistent with our prior cases regarding individual multi-member districts, which have formulated a parallel standard. * * *

JUSTICE POWELL, with whom JUSTICE STEVENS joins, concurring [on the issue of justiciability], and dissenting.

[T]he plurality expresses the view, with which I agree, that a partisan political gerrymander violates the Equal Protection Clause only on proof of "both intentional discrimination against an identifiable political group and an actual discriminatory effect on that group." The plurality acknowledges that the record in this case supports a finding that the challenged redistricting plan was adopted for the purpose of discriminating against Democratic voters. The plurality argues, however, that appellees failed to establish that their voting strength was diluted

19. In most equal protection cases, it is true, a discriminatory effect will be readily apparent, and no heightened effect will be required, but that is the only real difference between this type of equal protection claim and others.

statewide despite uncontradicted proof that certain key districts were grotesquely gerrymandered to enhance the election prospects of Republican candidates. * * *

The Equal Protection Clause guarantees citizens that their state will govern them impartially. In the context of redistricting, that guarantee is of critical importance because the franchise provides most citizens their only voice in the legislative process. Since the contours of a voting district powerfully may affect citizens' ability to exercise influence through their vote, district lines should be determined in accordance with neutral and legitimate criteria. When deciding where those lines will fall, the state should treat its voters as standing in the same position, regardless of their political beliefs or party affiliation. [*Reynolds*] contemplated that "one person, one vote" would be only one among several neutral factors that serve the constitutional mandate of fair and effective representation. * * *

The [most] basic flaw in the plurality's opinion is its failure to enunciate any standard that affords guidance to legislatures and courts.[10] [This] places the plurality in the curious position of inviting further litigation even as it appears to signal the "constitutional green light" to would-be gerrymanderers. * * *

A court should look first to the legislative process by which the challenged plan was adopted. Here, the District Court found that the procedures used in redistricting Indiana were carefully designed to exclude Democrats from participating in the legislative process [which] consisted of nothing more than the majority party's private application of computer technology to mapmaking. [T]he only data used in the computer program were precinct population, race of precinct citizens, precinct political complexion, and statewide party voting trends. * * *

Next, the District Court found [how] the mapmakers carved up counties, cities, and even townships in their effort to draw lines beneficial to the majority party. [The] redistricting dissects counties into strange shapes lacking in common interests, on one occasion even placing the seat of one county in a voting district composed of townships from other counties. Under these conditions, the District Court expressly found that "the potential for voter disillusion and nonparticipation is great," as voters are forced to focus their political activities in artificial electoral units. Intelligent voters, regardless of party affiliation, resent this sort of political manipulation of the electorate for no public purpose. * * *

[When] the plan was completed, Republican leaders announced that the House map was designed to yield 56 "safe" Republican seats and 30 Democratic seats, with the remainder being "tossups." Republicans expected that their Senate map would regularly produce 30 Republican seats and 8 to 10 Democratic seats so that Republicans would maintain their grip on the Senate even if Democrats won the remaining seats. In short, the record unequivocally demonstrates that in 1981 the Republican-dominated General Assembly deliberately sought to design a redistricting plan under which members of the Democratic party would be deprived of a fair opportunity to win control of the General Assembly at least until 1991, the date of the next redistricting. * * *

---

10. * * * I cannot agree, as the plurality suggests, that a standard requiring proof of "heightened effect," where invidious intent has been established directly, has support in any of our cases, or that an equal protection violation can be established "only where a history (actual or projected) of disproportionate results appears." If a racial minority established that the legislature adopted a redistricting law for no purpose other than to disadvantage that group, the plurality's new and erroneous standard would require plaintiffs to wait for the results of several elections, creating a history of discriminatory effect, before they can challenge the law in court.

Appellees further demonstrated through a statistical showing that the House Plan debased the effectiveness of their votes [reciting the 1982 election statistics in White, J.'s opinion. Moreover, since] half of the Senate membership is up for election every two years, the only election results under the challenged plan available at trial [showed] that, of the seats up for election in 1982, Democrats were elected to 13 seats and Republicans to 12. [It] was appellees' contention that most of the Senate seats won by Democrats in 1982 were "safe" Democratic seats so that their party's success at the polls in that year was fully consistent with the statewide Republican gerrymander. This contention is borne out by the results of the 1984 Senate election. In that election, Democratic candidates received 42.3 percent of the vote, and Republicans 57.7 percent. Yet, of the 25 Senate positions up for election, only 7 were captured by Democrats.

The District Court found, and I agree, that appellants failed to justify the discriminatory impact of the plan by showing that the plan had a rational basis in permissible neutral criteria. [As] the plurality opinion makes clear, [a] colorable claim of discriminatory gerrymandering presents a justiciable controversy under the Equal Protection Clause. Federal courts in exercising their duty to adjudicate such claims should impose a heavy burden of proof on those who allege that a redistricting plan violates the Constitution. [T]his case presents a paradigm example of unconstitutional discrimination against the members of a political party that happened to be out of power. The well-grounded findings of the District Court to this effect have not been, and I believe cannot be, held clearly erroneous. * * *[25]

JUSTICE O'CONNOR, with whom THE CHIEF JUSTICE and JUSTICE REHNQUIST join, concurring in the judgment.

[T]he legislative business of apportionment is fundamentally a political affair, and challenges to the manner in which an apportionment has been carried out— by the very parties that are responsible for this process—present a political question in the truest sense of the term.

To turn these matters over to the federal judiciary is to inject the courts into the most heated partisan issues. It is predictable that the courts will respond by moving away from the nebulous standard a plurality of the Court fashions today and toward some form of rough proportional representation for all political groups. The consequences of this shift will be as immense as they are unfortunate. I do not believe, and the Court offers not a shred of evidence to suggest, that the Framers of the Constitution intended the judicial power to encompass the making of such fundamental choices about how this Nation is to be governed. Nor do I believe that the proportional representation towards which the Court's expansion of equal protection doctrine will lead is consistent with our history, our traditions, or our political institutions. * * *

The step taken today is a momentous one, which if followed in the future can only lead to political instability and judicial malaise. [Federal] courts will have no alternative but to attempt to recreate the complex process of legislative apportionment in the context of adversary litigation in order to reconcile the competing claims of political, religious, ethnic, racial, occupational, and socioeconomic groups. Even if there were some way of limiting such claims to organized political

---

25. As is evident from the several opinions filed today, there is no "Court" for a standard that properly should be applied in determining whether a challenged redistricting plan is an unconstitutional partisan political gerrymander. The standard proposed by the plurality is explicitly rejected by two Justices, and three Justices also have expressed the view that the plurality's standard will "prove unmanageable and arbitrary." (O'Connor, J., joined by Burger, C.J., and Rehnquist, J., concurring in the judgment).

parties, the fact remains that the losing party or the losing group of legislators in every reapportionment will now be invited to fight the battle anew in federal court. [The] Equal Protection Clause does not supply judicially manageable standards for resolving purely political gerrymandering claims, and no group right to an equal share of political power was ever intended by the Framers. [Unlike racial minorities], members of the Democratic and Republican parties cannot claim that they are a discrete and insular group vulnerable to exclusion from the political process by some dominant group: these political parties *are* the dominant groups, and the Court has offered no reason to believe that they are incapable of fending for themselves through the political process. Indeed, there is good reason to think that political gerrymandering is a self-limiting enterprise. See Cain, *The Reapportionment Puzzle* 151–159 (1984). In order to gerrymander, the legislative majority must weaken some of its safe seats, thus exposing its own incumbents to greater risks of defeat—risks they may refuse to accept past a certain point. Similarly, an overambitious gerrymander can lead to disaster for the legislative majority: because it has created more seats in which it hopes to win relatively narrow victories, the same swing in overall voting strength will tend to cost the legislative majority more and more seats as the gerrymander becomes more ambitious. More generally, each major party presumably has ample weapons at its disposal to conduct the partisan struggle that often leads to a partisan apportionment, but also often leads to a bipartisan one. * * *

Furthermore, the Court fails to explain why a bipartisan gerrymander—which is what was approved in *Gaffney*—affects individuals any differently than a partisan gerrymander. [As] the plurality acknowledges, the scheme upheld in *Gaffney* tended to "deny safe district minorities any realistic chance to elect their own representatives." If this bipartisan arrangement between two groups of self-interested legislators is constitutionally permissible, as I believe and as the Court held in *Gaffney,* then—in terms of the rights of individuals—it should be equally permissible for a legislative majority to employ the same means to pursue its own interests over the opposition of the other party.

[The] Court has in effect decided that it is constitutionally acceptable for both parties to "waste" the votes of individuals through a bipartisan gerrymander, so long as the *parties* themselves are not deprived of their group voting strength to an extent that will exceed the plurality's threshold requirement. This choice confers greater rights on powerful political groups than on individuals; that cannot be the meaning of the Equal Protection Clause. * * *

Vote dilution analysis is far less manageable when extended to major political parties than if confined to racial minority groups. First, [d]esigning an apportionment plan that does not impair or degrade the voting strength of several groups is more difficult than designing a plan that does not have such an effect on one group for the simple reason that, as the number of criteria the plan must meet increases, the number of solutions that will satisfy those criteria will decrease.

[Second,] while membership in a racial group is an immutable characteristic, voters can—and often do—move from one party to the other or support candidates from both parties. Consequently, the difficulty of measuring voting strength is heightened in the case of a major political party. * * *

Moreover, any such intervention is likely to move in the direction of proportional representation for political parties. This is clear by analogy to the problem that arises in racial gerrymandering cases: "in order to decide whether an electoral system has made it harder for minority voters to elect the candidates they prefer, a court must have an idea in mind of how hard it 'should' be for minority voters to elect their preferred candidates under an acceptable system." Any such norm must make some reference, even if only a loose one, to the relation between the racial minority group's share of the electorate and its share of the elected representatives. In order to implement the plurality's standard, it will thus be necessary for courts to adopt an analogous norm, in order to assess whether the voting strength of a political party has been "degraded" by an apportionment, either on a state-wide basis or in particular districts. Absent any such norm, the inquiry the plurality proposes would be so standardless as to make the adjudication of political gerrymandering claims impossible.

[Because] the most easily measured indicia of political power relate solely to winning and losing elections, there is a grave risk that the plurality's various attempts to qualify and condition the group right the Court has created will gradually pale in importance. What is likely to remain is a loose form of proportionality, under which *some* deviations from proportionality are permissible, but any significant, persistent deviations from proportionality are suspect. Courts will be forced to look for some form of "undue" disproportionality with respect to electoral success if political gerrymandering claims are justiciable, because otherwise they will find their decisions turning on imponderables such as whether the legislators of one party have fairly represented the voters of the other.

Of course, in one sense a requirement of proportional representation, whether loose or absolute, is judicially manageable. If this Court were to declare that the Equal Protection Clause required proportional representation within certain fixed tolerances, I have no doubt that district courts would be able to apply this edict. The flaw in such a pronouncement, however, would be the use of the Equal Protection Clause as the vehicle for making a fundamental policy choice that is contrary to the intent of its Framers and to the traditions of this republic. The political question doctrine as articulated in *Baker* rightly requires that we refrain from making such policy choices in order to evade what would otherwise be a lack of judicially manageable standards.

[To] allow district courts to strike down apportionment plans on the basis of their prognostications as to the outcome of future elections or future apportionments invites "findings" on matters as to which neither judges nor anyone else can have any confidence. Once it is conceded that "a group's electoral power is not unconstitutionally diminished by the simple fact of an apportionment scheme that makes winning elections more difficult," the virtual impossibility of reliably predicting how difficult it will be to win an election in 2, or 4, or 10 years should, in my view, weigh in favor of holding such challenges nonjusticiable. Racial gerrymandering should remain justiciable, for the harms it engenders run counter to the central thrust of the Fourteenth Amendment. But no such justification can be given for judicial intervention on behalf of mainstream political parties, and the risks such intervention poses to our political institutions are unacceptable. * * *

Notes and Questions

1. *Judicial manageability.* Consider Tribe 2d ed., at 1083: "Justice White's opinion for the Court on the justiciability issue [equated] the Court's decision to intervene in the case with the Court's determination in *Baker v. Carr* to hear claims relating to the disparate size of election districts. Yet the two kinds of intervention are surely distinct. Although the *Baker* Court did not itself announce the one person, one vote rule, that rule was looming on the near horizon; the *Baker* Court had no reason to fear that no judicially manageable standard could be found. The Court in *Bandemer* had every reason to fear such an eventuality."

2. *A heightened effects requirement.* Consider Karlan, note 1 after *Reynolds*, at 1715–16: "In cases involving claims of racial vote dilution, the Court focused on the *racial* aspect of the cause of action, which allowed it to borrow the discriminatory purpose requirement from general equal protection doctrine. [This] stringent purpose requirement was extraordinarily difficult for plaintiffs to meet. By contrast, when the Court was faced with a claim of political gerrymandering, in [*Bandemer*,] it could hardly use the purpose requirement to pretermit the claim; given the overtly partisan nature of the redistricting process, nearly *every* districting scheme was intended to maximize the election of members of the redistricting party at the expense of other parties' candidates. So, in the area of political gerrymandering, the Court developed a heightened effects [requirement.] This test, like the purpose test in racial vote dilution cases, was virtually impossible to meet." For a discussion of how the *Bandemer* standard has proved "virtually impossible to meet" in practice, see Samuel Issacharoff, *Judging Politics: The Elusive Quest for Judicial Review of Political Fairness*, 71 Tex.L.Rev. 1643, 1670–75 (1993).

3. *Partisan interests.* (a) Is one person's gerrymander another person's good government? Consider Ronald H. Brown & Daniel Hays Lowenstein, *A Democratic Perspective on Legislative Districting*, 6 J.L. & Pol. 673, 679 (1990): "The most common 'neutral' criterion Republicans try to impose [is] compactness. The usual way of levying a political attack on a districting plan is to show diagrams of selected oddly-shaped districts. This is supposed to prove that the plan is an outrageous gerrymander. [The] real reason the Republicans promote the compactness requirement is that it tends to work systematically to their [benefit]. Inner-city areas tend to contain Democratic voters concentrated in extraordinarily high percentages. Many surrounding affluent areas are predominantly but not nearly so overwhelmingly Republican. Accordingly, it may be relatively easy to draw compact districts separating these areas and thereby to accomplish the objective of a Republican gerrymander—a small number of overwhelmingly Democratic districts surrounded by a larger number of much closer but still safely Republican districts."

But cf. Martin Shapiro, *Gerrymandering, Unfairness, and the Supreme Court*, 33 UCLA L.Rev. 227, 240 (1985): "If geography favors the Republicans in an ungerrymandered world, that is a purely fortuitous result, unforeseeable by either party when it chose its ideologies and clienteles. Such stacking ought to be considered extraneous to the goal of constraining the self-serving actions of the legislatures." For a comprehensive attempt to show that the removal of politics from redistricting is an illusory goal with the conclusion that judges should keep out, see Daniel Lowenstein & Jonathan Steinberg, *The Quest for Legislative Districting in the Public Interest: Elusive or Illusory*, 33 UCLA L.Rev. 1 (1985). But see Bernard Groffman, *Criteria for Districting: A Social Science Perspective*, 33 UCLA L.Rev. 77 (1985).

(b) It would be possible to program a computer to draw district lines without regard to voters' political affiliations. See Issacharoff, supra, at 1695–1702; Michelle H. Browdy, *Simulated Annealing: An Improved Computer Model for Political Redistricting*, 8 Yale L. & Pol'y Rev. 163 (1990). Would such an approach be desirable? Should it be judicially mandated? Compare Peter Schuck, *The Thickest Thicket: Partisan Gerrymandering and Judicial Regulation of Politics*, 87 Colum.L.Rev. 1325, 1337 (1987) (arguments against a structure permitting gerrymandering "overlook important complexities and values in our political life, project incomplete visions of democratic representation, and invite innovative political remedies that should not be mandated by our federal courts").

C. EQUALITY IN THE COUNTING AND RECOUNTING OF VOTES

BUSH v. GORE

531 U. S. 98, 121 S.Ct. 525, 148 L.Ed.2d 388 (2000).

PER CURIAM.

[After a machine count and recount of ballots in the 2000 Florida presidential election, Democrat Albert Gore trailed Republican George W. Bush by fewer than 1,000 votes. Returns from other states made it clear that the winner of Florida's electoral votes would have an electoral college majority. With the election thus in the balance, Gore sought further manual recounts in selected, heavily Democratic Florida counties, and a complex series of legal battles unfolded. Among the signal events was a United States Supreme Court decision, entered on December 4, vacating a decision of the Florida Supreme Court that effectively extended the deadline established by Florida's Secretary of State for the completion of recounts. When the deadline for "recounts" passed with a full manual recount having been completed in only one county, the legal battles entered a second phase in which Florida law permits legal "contests" of disputed elections. In an appeal from a lower court ruling, the Florida Supreme Court, by 4–3, ordered a manual recount of all so-called "undervotes"—ballots on which the earlier machine counts had failed to record any presidential choice—in one of the counties in which Gore had sought a recount and further directed a manual recount of "undervotes" in all counties. Many of the "undervote" ballots were punchcards on which voters using a stylus had apparently left hanging "chads" or produced "dimples" but made no full perforation. In determining when votes should be recorded, the Florida Supreme Court said only that election officials and lower court judges should follow the legislatively prescribed standard of attempting to discern "the will of the voter."

[Bush immediately sought a Supreme Court stay of the Florida Supreme Court's ruling, alleging that the state court's decision lacked any foundation in pre-existing Florida law and thus violated both a federal statute and the command of Art. II of the federal constitution that the choice of presidential electors should occur "in such Manner as the [state] Legislature"—as distinguished, Bush argued, from the state constitution or state courts—"may direct." Bush also contended that the unelaborated "will of the voter" standard for counting or not counting ballots with hanging chads and dimples would produce unjustified disparities and violate the due process and equal protection clauses. The Supreme Court stayed the Florida Supreme Court's order on Saturday December 9—just three days before what a majority of the Justices understood to be a Florida statutory deadline of December 12 for the completion of proceedings bearing on the final certification of the state's electors. The Court held oral argument in the case on Monday December 11 and handed down its decision shortly after 10 p.m. on December 12.]

* * * When the state legislature vests the right to vote for President in its people, the right to vote as the legislature has prescribed is fundamental; and one source of its fundamental nature lies in the equal weight accorded to each vote

Was Fl. Sup Ct.
mis-applying Fla. Law?
- Process for counting
undervotes, unconstitutional. (Sup ct.)

Sec. 5, I, C   VOTING: EQUALITY IN COUNTING   1357

and the equal dignity owed to each voter. See [*McPherson v. Blacker*, 146 U.S. 1, 35, 13 S.Ct. 3, 36 L.Ed. 869 (1892)].

The right to vote is protected in more than the initial allocation of the franchise. Equal protection applies as well to the manner of its exercise. Having once granted the right to vote on equal terms, the State may not, by later arbitrary and disparate treatment, value one person's vote over that of another. See, *e.g.*, *Harper v. Virginia Bd. of Elections*, [supra]. * * *

The question before us [is] whether the recount procedures the Florida Supreme Court has adopted are consistent with its obligation to avoid arbitrary and disparate treatment of the members of its electorate. * * *

For purposes of resolving the equal protection challenge, it is not necessary to decide whether the Florida Supreme Court had the authority under the legislative scheme for resolving election disputes to define what a legal vote is and to mandate a manual recount implementing that definition. The recount mechanisms implemented in response to the decisions of the Florida Supreme Court do not satisfy the minimum requirement for non-arbitrary treatment of voters necessary to secure the fundamental right. Florida's basic command for the count of legally cast votes is to consider the "intent of the voter." This is unobjectionable as an abstract proposition and a starting principle. The problem inheres in the absence of specific standards to ensure its equal application.

[T]he standards for accepting or rejecting contested ballots might vary not only from county to county but indeed within a single county from one recount team to another. The record provides some examples. A monitor in Miami–Dade County testified at trial that he observed that three members of the county canvassing board applied different standards in defining a legal vote. * * *

[The Court also expressed concern about the disparate treatment of so-called "overvotes," involving ballots on which a voter made a mark next to the name of more than one candidate. Under the recount scheme mandated by the Florida Supreme Court,] the citizen whose ballot was not read by a machine because he failed to vote for a candidate in a way readable by machine may still have his vote counted in a manual recount; on the other hand, the citizen who marks two candidates in a way discernable by the machine will not have the same opportunity to have his vote count, even if a manual examination of the ballot would reveal the requisite indicia of intent. * * *

In addition [the] Florida Supreme Court's [order] did not specify who would recount the ballots. The county canvassing boards were forced to pull together ad hoc teams comprised of judges from various Circuits who had no previous training in handling and interpreting ballots. Furthermore, while others were permitted to observe, they were prohibited from objecting during the recount.

The recount process, in its features here described, is inconsistent with the minimum procedures necessary to protect the fundamental right of each voter in the special instance of a statewide recount under the authority of a single state judicial officer. Our consideration is limited to the present circumstances, for the problem of equal protection in election processes generally presents many complexities.

The question before the Court is not whether local entities, in the exercise of their expertise, may develop different systems for implementing elections. Instead, we are presented with a situation where a state court with the power to assure uniformity has ordered a statewide recount with minimal procedural safeguards. When a court orders a statewide remedy, there must be at least some assurance

But: undervotes weren't counted because machine didn't
Punch out the Chad
• Other counties used optical scanners.
* Voters were not treated equally

that the rudimentary requirements of equal treatment and fundamental fairness are satisfied. * * *

Upon due consideration of the difficulties identified to this point, it is obvious that the recount cannot be conducted in compliance with the requirements of equal protection and due process without substantial additional work. * * *

The Supreme Court of Florida has said that the legislature intended the State's electors to [be chosen] by December 12. That date is upon us, and there is no recount procedure in place under the State Supreme Court's order that comports with minimal constitutional standards. Because it is evident that any recount seeking to meet the December 12 date will be unconstitutional for the reasons we have discussed, we reverse the judgment of the Supreme Court of Florida ordering a recount to proceed. * * *

[REHNQUIST, C.J., joined by Scalia and Thomas, J.J., joined the per curiam opinion, but wrote separately, concluding that the Florida Supreme Court violated Art. II by applying rules of decision at odds with those mandated by the Florida legislature.]

Justice STEVENS, with whom Justices GINSBURG and BREYER, join, dissenting.

* * * [Although we have previously found equal protection violations] when individual votes within the same State were weighted unequally, [we] have never before called into question the substantive standard by which a State determines that a vote has been legally cast. And there is no reason to think that the guidance provided to the factfinders, specifically the various canvassing boards, by the "intent of the voter" standard is any less sufficient—or will lead to results any less uniform—than, for example, the "beyond a reasonable doubt" standard employed everyday by ordinary citizens in courtrooms across this country.

Admittedly, the use of differing substandards for determining voter intent in different counties employing similar voting systems may raise serious concerns. Those concerns are alleviated—if not eliminated—by the fact that a single impartial magistrate will ultimately adjudicate all objections arising from the recount process. Of course, as a general matter, "[t]he interpretation of constitutional principles must not be too literal. We must remember that the machinery of government would not work if it were not allowed a little play in its joints." *Bain Peanut Co. of Tex. v. Pinson*, 282 U.S. 499, 501, 51 S.Ct. 228, 229, 75 L.Ed. 482 (1931) (Holmes, J.). If it were otherwise, Florida's decision to leave to each county the determination of what balloting system to employ—despite enormous differences in accuracy—might run afoul of equal protection. So, too, might the similar decisions of the vast majority of state legislatures to delegate to local authorities certain decisions with respect to voting systems and ballot design. * * *

If we assume—as I do—that the [Florida Supreme Court] and the judges who would have carried out its mandate are impartial, its decision does not even raise a colorable federal question. What must underlie petitioners' entire [case] is an unstated lack of confidence in the impartiality and capacity of the state judges who would make the critical decisions if the vote count were to proceed. [The] endorsement of that position by a majority of this Court can only lend credence to the most cynical appraisal of the work of judges throughout the land. [Although] we may never know with complete certainty the winner of this year's Presidential election, the identity of the loser is perfectly clear. It is the Nation's confidence in the judge as an impartial guardian of the rule of law.

Justice SOUTER, with whom Justice BREYER, joins, dissenting.

* * * I would [remand] the case to the courts of Florida with instructions to establish uniform standards for evaluating the several types of ballots that have prompted differing treatments, to be applied within and among counties when passing on such identical ballots in any further recounting (or successive recounting) that the courts might order. * * *

Justice GINSBURG, with whom Justice STEVENS, joins, dissenting:

* * * Ideally, perfection would be the appropriate standard for judging the recount. But we live in an imperfect world, one in which thousands of votes have not been counted. I cannot agree that the recount adopted by the Florida court, flawed as it may be, would yield a result any less fair or precise than the certification that preceded that recount. See, *e.g., McDonald v. Board of Election Comm'rs of Chicago*, 394 U.S. 802, 807, 89 S.Ct. 1404, 1408, 22 L.Ed.2d 739 (1969) (even in the context of the right to vote, the state is permitted to reform " 'one step at a time' "). * * *

Justice BREYER, with whom Justice STEVENS, Justice SOUTER, and Justice GINSBURG, join, dissenting.

* * * By halting the manual recount, and thus ensuring that the uncounted legal votes will not be counted under any standard, this Court crafts a remedy out of proportion to the asserted harm. [I]n a system that allows counties to use different types of voting systems, voters already arrive at the polls with an unequal chance that their votes will be counted. I do not see how the fact that this results from counties' selection of different voting machines rather than a court order makes the outcome any more fair. Nor do I understand why the Florida Supreme Court's recount order, which helps to redress this inequity, must be entirely prohibited based on a deficiency that could easily be remedied. * * *

Notes and Questions

1. *Breadth of principle.* Can the principle of fair treatment of votes and voters be limited to the context of judicially supervised recounts in statewide elections?

2. *Great cases.* According to Holmes, J., dissenting in *Northern Securities Co. v. United States*, 193 U.S. 197, 400, 24 S.Ct. 436, 468, 48 L.Ed. 679 (1904): "Great cases like hard cases make bad law. For great cases are called great, not by reason of their real importance in shaping the law of the future, but because of some accident of immediate overwhelming interest which appeals to the feelings and distorts the judgment." Did *Bush v. Gore* make bad law? Good law? Any law applicable beyond its peculiar facts?

D. RACIAL GERRYMANDERING REVISITED: "BENIGN" OR "REMEDIAL" RACE–CONSCIOUS DISTRICTING

Recent cases involving the constitutionality of state efforts to create so-called "majority-minority" voting districts—in which racial groups that are a minority of the overall population constitute a majority within a particular district—arise against the background of the Voting Rights Act of 1965 ("VRA"), 42 U.S.C. § 1973c. VRA § 2 provides a cause of action for claims of minority vote dilution, and Congress specifically amended the Act in 1982 to establish that discriminatory results may prove a violation of § 2, even in the absence of proof of discriminatory intent. To date, the Court's most important decision interpreting § 2 is *Thornburg v. Gingles*, 478 U.S. 30, 106 S.Ct. 2752, 92 L.Ed.2d 25 (1986), which held that plaintiffs may prove a § 2 violation by establishing that (i) a minority community is large and compact enough to constitute the majority in a voting district, (ii) the minority community is politically cohesive, and (iii) the majority has engaged in racially polarized voting practices.

Section 5 of the VRA imposes an additional requirement that any proposed districting changes in covered jurisdictions should not be "retrogressive" with respect to the representation of racial minorities. To enforce this requirement, § 5 provides that covered jurisdictions must "pre-clear" proposed districting changes with either a federal court or the Department of Justice. As commentators have noted, the VRA not only permits, but sometimes actually requires, policy-makers to be race-conscious in drawing electoral districts. See Daniel Hays Lowenstein, *You Don't Have to Be Liberal to Hate the Racial Gerrymandering Cases*, 50 Stan.L.Rev. 779, 780–83 (1998).

In UNITED JEWISH ORGANIZATIONS v. CAREY, 430 U.S. 144, 97 S.Ct. 996, 51 L.Ed.2d 229 (1977), the Court rejected an equal protection attack on a race-conscious districting plan implemented by the state of New York to comply with the VRA. In order to create a majority-minority district, the state deliberately divided a Hasidic Jewish community among several state legislative districts, thus splintering what previously had been a dominant voting majority. By a 7–1 vote, the Court rejected the challenge, but fractured badly concerning the rationale. The plurality opinion, written by White J.—but joined in relevant part only by Rehnquist and Stevens, JJ.—stated that the New York plan "represented no racial slur or stigma" and that there was no discrimination against white voters "as long as whites[,] as a group, were provided with fair representation."[a]

After largely disappearing for a decade or more, attacks such as that in *UJO* began to surface again in the aftermath of the 1990 Census, when the Department of Justice mounted aggressive efforts pursuant to its pre-clearance role to insist that states create as many majority-minority districts as possible.[b]

SHAW v. RENO

509 U.S. 630, 113 S.Ct. 2816, 125 L.Ed.2d 511 (1993).

JUSTICE O'CONNOR delivered the opinion of the Court.

[As] a result of the 1990 census, North Carolina became entitled to a twelfth seat in the United States House of Representatives. The General Assembly enacted a reapportionment plan that included one majority-black congressional district. After the Attorney General of the United States objected to the plan pursuant to § 5 of the Voting Rights Act of 1965, the General Assembly passed new legislation creating a second majority-black district. Appellants allege that the

---

a. Concurring opinions were filed by Brennan, J., and by Stewart, J., joined by Powell, J. Marshall, J., did not participate.

b. The surrounding political motivations were complex. See Samuel Issacharoff, Pamela S. Karlan, & Richard H. Pildes, *The Law of Democracy: Legal Structure of the Political Process* 582 (1998): "Republicans were delighted to pack pro-Democratic minority voters into new majority-minority districts, thereby drawing away from the electoral strength of Democratic incumbents. By the time the Clinton administration assumed office in 1993, the battles over redistricting were waged in terms of preserving the districts of newly elected Democratic minority representatives—not a group a Democratic administration was likely to abandon."

revised plan, which contains district boundary lines of dramatically irregular shape, constitutes an unconstitutional racial gerrymander. * * *

The voting age population of North Carolina is approximately 78% white, 20% black, and 1% Native American; the remaining 1% is predominantly Asian. The black population is relatively dispersed; blacks constitute a majority of the general population in only 5 of the State's 100 counties. [The] largest concentrations of black citizens live in the Coastal Plain, primarily in the northern part. The General Assembly's first redistricting plan contained one majority-black district centered in that area of the State. [I]t moves southward until it tapers to a narrow band; then, with finger-like extensions, it reaches far into the southern-most part of the State near the South Carolina border. District 1 has been compared to a "Rorschach ink-blot test," and a "bug splattered on a windshield."

The second majority-black district, District 12, is even more unusually shaped. It is approximately 160 miles long and, for much of its length, no wider than the I–85 corridor. It winds in snake-like fashion through tobacco country, financial centers, and manufacturing areas "until it gobbles in enough enclaves of black neighborhoods." Northbound and southbound drivers on I–85 sometimes find themselves in separate districts in one county, only to "trade" districts when they enter the next county. Of the 10 counties through which District 12 passes, five are cut into three different districts; even towns are divided. At one point the district remains contiguous only because it intersects at a single point with two other districts before crossing over them. One state legislator has remarked that "[i]f you drove down the interstate with both car doors open, you'd kill most of the people in the district." * * *

An understanding of the nature of appellants' claim is critical to our resolution of the case. In their complaint, appellants did not claim that the General Assembly's reapportionment plan unconstitutionally "diluted" white voting strength. They did not even claim to be white. Rather, appellants' complaint alleged that the deliberate segregation of voters into separate districts on the basis of race violated their constitutional right to participate in a "color-blind" electoral process. [This] Court never has held that race-conscious state decisionmaking is impermissible in all circumstances. What appellants object to is redistricting legislation that is so extremely irregular on its face that it rationally can be viewed only as an effort to segregate the races for purposes of voting, without regard for traditional districting principles and without sufficiently compelling justification. For the reasons that follow, we conclude that appellants have stated a claim upon which relief can be granted under the Equal Protection Clause.

[R]edistricting differs from other kinds of state decisionmaking in that the legislature always is aware of race when it draws district lines, just as it is aware of age, economic status, religious and political persuasion, and a variety of other demographic factors. That sort of race consciousness does not lead inevitably to impermissible race discrimination. [W]hen members of a racial group live together in one community, a reapportionment plan that concentrates members of the group in one district and excludes them from others may reflect wholly legitimate purposes. The district lines may be drawn, for example, to provide for compact districts of contiguous territory, or to maintain the integrity of political subdivisions.

The difficulty of proof, of course, does not mean that a racial gerrymander, once established, should receive less scrutiny under the Equal Protection Clause than other state legislation classifying citizens by race. Moreover, it seems clear to us that proof sometimes will not be difficult at all. In some exceptional cases, a reapportionment plan may be so highly irregular that, on its face, it rationally cannot be understood as anything other than an effort to "segregat[e] voters" on the basis of race. *Gomillion*, in which a tortured municipal boundary line was drawn to exclude black voters, was such a case. So, too, would be a case in which a State concentrated a dispersed minority population in a single district by disregarding traditional districting principles such as compactness, contiguity, and respect for political subdivisions. We emphasize that these criteria are important not because they are constitutionally required—they are not—but because they are objective factors that may serve to defeat a claim that a district has been gerrymandered on racial lines.

[A] reapportionment plan that includes in one district individuals who belong to the same race, but who are otherwise widely separated by geographical and political boundaries, and who may have little in common with one another but the color of their skin, bears an uncomfortable resemblance to political apartheid. It reinforces the perception that members of the same racial group—regardless of their age, education, economic status, or the community in which they live—think alike, share the same political interests, and will prefer the same candidates at the polls. We have rejected such perceptions elsewhere as impermissible racial stereotypes. By perpetuating such notions, a racial gerrymander may exacerbate the very patterns of racial bloc voting that majority-minority districting is sometimes said to counteract.

The message that such districting sends to elected representatives is equally pernicious. When a district obviously is created solely to effectuate the perceived common interests of one racial group, elected officials are more likely to believe that their primary obligation is to represent only the members of that group, rather than their constituency as a whole. This is altogether antithetical to our system of representative democracy. * * *

For these reasons, we conclude that a plaintiff challenging a reapportionment statute under the Equal Protection Clause may state a claim by alleging that the legislation, though race-neutral on its face, rationally cannot be understood as anything other than an effort to separate voters into different districts on the basis of race, and that the separation lacks sufficient justification. It is unnecessary for us to decide whether or how a reapportionment plan that, on its face, can be explained in nonracial terms successfully could be challenged. Thus, we express no view as to whether "the intentional creation of majority-minority districts, without more" always gives rise to an equal protection claim. * * *

Justice Souter apparently believes that racial gerrymandering is harmless unless it dilutes a racial group's voting strength. As we have explained, however, reapportionment legislation that cannot be understood as anything other than an effort to classify and separate voters by race injures voters in other ways. It reinforces racial stereotypes and threatens to undermine our system of representative democracy by signaling to elected officials that they represent a particular racial group rather than their constituency as a whole. * * *

The dissenters [also] suggest that a racial gerrymander of the sort alleged here is functionally equivalent to gerrymanders for nonracial purposes, such as political gerrymanders. This Court has held political gerrymanders to be justiciable under the Equal Protection Clause. See *Bandemer*. But nothing in our case law compels the conclusion that racial and political gerrymanders are subject to precisely the same constitutional scrutiny. In fact, our country's long and persistent history of racial discrimination in voting—as well as our Fourteenth Amendment jurisprudence, which always has reserved the strictest scrutiny for discrimination on the basis of race—would seem to compel the opposite conclusion.

[Finally,] nothing in the Court's highly fractured decision in *UJO*—[which] the dissenters evidently believe controls—forecloses the claim we recognize today. [The] plaintiffs in *UJO*—members of a Hasidic community split between two districts under New York's revised redistricting plan—did not allege that the plan, on its face, was so highly irregular that it rationally could be understood only as an effort to segregate voters by race. Indeed, the facts of the case would not have supported such a claim. Three Justices approved the New York statute, in part, precisely because it adhered to traditional districting principles. [Nothing] in the decision precludes white voters (or voters of any other race) from bringing the analytically distinct claim that a reapportionment plan rationally cannot be understood as anything other than an effort to segregate citizens into separate voting districts on the basis of race without sufficient justification. Because appellants here stated such a claim, the District Court erred in dismissing their complaint.

Justice Souter contends that exacting scrutiny of racial gerrymanders under the Fourteenth Amendment is inappropriate because reapportionment "nearly always require[s] some consideration of race for legitimate reasons." "As long as members of racial groups have [a] commonality of interest" and "racial block voting takes place," he argues, "legislators will have to take race into account" in order to comply with the Voting Rights Act. Justice Souter's reasoning is flawed.

[That] racial bloc voting or minority political cohesion may be found to exist in some cases, of course, is no reason to treat all racial gerrymanders differently from other kinds of racial classification. Justice Souter apparently views racial gerrymandering of the type presented here as a special category of "benign" racial discrimination that should be subject to relaxed judicial review. As we have said, however, the very reason that the Equal Protection Clause demands strict scrutiny of all racial classifications is because without it, a court cannot determine whether or not the discrimination truly is "benign." * * *

Racial classifications of any sort pose the risk of lasting harm to our society. They reinforce the belief, held by too many for too much of our history, that individuals should be judged by the color of their skin. Racial classifications with respect to voting carry particular dangers. Racial gerrymandering, even for remedial purposes, may balkanize us into competing racial factions; it threatens to carry us further from the goal of a political system in which race no longer matters—a goal that the Fourteenth and Fifteenth Amendments embody, and to which the Nation continues to aspire. It is for these reasons that race-based districting by our state legislatures demands close judicial scrutiny. * * *

JUSTICE WHITE, with whom JUSTICE BLACKMUN and JUSTICE STEVENS join, dissenting.

The facts of this case mirror those presented in *UJO,* [where] five of the Justices reasoned that members of the white majority could not plausibly argue that their influence over the political process had been unfairly canceled or that such had been the State's intent. Accordingly, they held that plaintiffs were not entitled to relief under the Constitution's Equal Protection Clause. On the same reasoning, I would affirm the district court's dismissal of appellants' claim in this instance.

The Court today chooses not to overrule, but rather to sidestep, *UJO.* It does so by glossing over the striking similarities, focusing on surface differences, most notably the (admittedly unusual) shape of the newly created district, and imagining an entirely new cause of action. Because the holding is limited to such anomalous circumstances, it perhaps will not substantially hamper a State's legitimate efforts to redistrict in favor of racial minorities. Nonetheless, the notion that North Carolina's plan, under which whites remain a voting majority in a disproportionate number of congressional districts, and pursuant to which the State has sent its first black representatives since Reconstruction to the United States Congress, might have violated appellants' constitutional rights is both a fiction and a departure from settled equal protection principles. * * *

I summed up my views on this matter in the plurality opinion in *Bandemer.* Because districting inevitably is the expression of interest group politics, and because "the power to influence the political process is not limited to winning elections," the question in gerrymandering cases is "whether a particular group has been unconstitutionally denied its chance to effectively influence the political process." [By] this, I meant that the group must exhibit "strong indicia of lack of political power and the denial of fair representation," so that it could be said that it has "essentially been shut out of the political process." In short, even assuming that racial (or political) factors were considered in the drawing of district boundaries, a showing of discriminatory effects is a "threshold requirement" in the absence of which there is no equal protection violation, and no need to "reach the question of the state interests [served] by the particular districts."

To distinguish a claim that alleges that the redistricting scheme has discriminatory intent and effect from one that does not has nothing to do with dividing racial classifications between the "benign" and the malicious—an enterprise which, as the majority notes, the Court has treated with skepticism. Rather, the issue is whether the classification based on race discriminates against anyone by denying equal access to the political process.

[I]t strains credulity to suggest that North Carolina's purpose in creating a second majority-minority district was to discriminate against members of the majority group by "impair[ing] or burden[ing their] opportunity [to] participate in the political process." The State has made no mystery of its intent, which was to respond to the Attorney General's objections by improving the minority group's prospects of electing a candidate of its choice. I doubt that this constitutes a discriminatory purpose as defined in the Court's equal protection cases—i.e., an intent to aggravate "the unequal distribution of electoral power." But even assuming that it does, there is no question that appellants have not alleged the requisite discriminatory effects. Whites constitute roughly 76 percent of the total population and 79 percent of the voting age population in North Carolina. Yet, under the State's plan, they still constitute a voting majority in 10 (or 83 percent) of the 12 congressional districts. * * *

Racial gerrymanders come in various shades: At-large voting schemes, see, e.g., *Regester,* the fragmentation of a minority group among various districts "so that it is a majority in none," otherwise known as "cracking;" the "stacking" of "a large minority population concentration [with] a larger white population;" and, finally, the "concentration of [minority voters] into districts where they constitute an excessive majority," also called "packing." In each instance, race is consciously utilized by the legislature for electoral purposes; in each instance, we have put the plaintiff challenging the district lines to the burden of demonstrating that the plan was meant to, and did in fact, exclude an identifiable racial group from participation in the political process.

Not so, apparently, when the districting "segregates" by drawing odd-shaped lines. In that case, we are told, such proof no longer is needed. Instead, it is the State that must rebut the allegation that race was taken into account, a fact that, together with the legislators' consideration of ethnic, religious, and other group characteristics, I had thought we practically took for granted. Part of the explanation for the majority's approach has to do, perhaps, with the emotions stirred by words such as "segregation" and "political apartheid." But their loose and imprecise use by today's majority has, I fear, led it astray. The consideration of race in "segregation" cases is no different than in other race-conscious districting; from the standpoint of the affected groups, moreover, the line-drawings all act in similar fashion. A plan that "segregates" being functionally indistinguishable from any of the other varieties of gerrymandering, we should be consistent in what we require from a claimant: Proof of discriminatory purpose and effect.

The other part of the majority's explanation of its holding is related to its simultaneous discomfort and fascination with irregularly shaped districts. Lack of compactness or contiguity, like uncouth district lines, certainly is a helpful indicator that some form of gerrymandering (racial or other) might have taken place. [But] they do no more than that. In particular, they have no bearing on whether the plan ultimately is found to violate the Constitution. Given two districts drawn on similar, race-based grounds, the one does not become more injurious than the other simply by virtue of being snake-like, at least so far as the Constitution is concerned and absent any evidence of differential racial impact. [A] regularly shaped district can just as effectively effectuate racially discriminatory gerrymandering as an odd-shaped one. By focusing on looks rather than impact, the majority "immediately casts attention in the wrong direction—toward superficialities of shape and size, rather than toward the political realities of district composition."

Limited by its own terms to cases involving unusually-shaped districts, the Court's approach nonetheless will unnecessarily hinder to some extent a State's voluntary effort to ensure a modicum of minority representation. This will be true in areas where the minority population is geographically dispersed. It also will be true where the minority population is not scattered but, for reasons unrelated to race—for example incumbency protection—the State would rather not create the majority-minority district in its most "obvious" location. * * *

Although I disagree with the holding that appellants' claim is cognizable, the Court's discussion of the level of scrutiny it requires warrants a few comments. I have no doubt that a State's compliance with the Voting Rights Act clearly constitutes a compelling interest. * * *

The Court, while seemingly agreeing with this position, warns that the State's redistricting effort must be "narrowly tailored" to further its interest in complying with the law. It is evident to me, however, that what North Carolina did was precisely tailored to meet the objection of the Attorney General to its prior plan. * * *

State efforts to remedy minority vote dilution are wholly unlike what typically has been labeled "affirmative action." To the extent that no other racial group is injured, remedying a Voting Rights Act violation does not involve preferential treatment. It involves, instead, an attempt to equalize treatment, and to provide minority voters with an effective voice in the political process. The Equal Protection Clause of the Constitution, surely, does not stand in the way. * * *

JUSTICE STEVENS, dissenting.

[I] believe that the Equal Protection Clause is violated when the State creates the kind of uncouth district boundaries seen in *Gomillion* and this case, for the sole purpose of making it more difficult for members of a minority group to win an election. The duty to govern impartially is abused when a group with power over the electoral process defines electoral boundaries solely to enhance its own political strength at the expense of any weaker group. That duty, however, is not violated when the majority acts to facilitate the election of a member of a group that lacks such power because it remains underrepresented in the state legislature—whether that group is defined by political affiliation, by common economic interests, or by religious, ethnic, or racial characteristics. [If] it is permissible to draw boundaries to provide adequate representation for rural voters, for union members, for Hasidic Jews, for Polish Americans, or for Republicans, it necessarily follows that it is permissible to do the same thing for members of the very minority group whose history in the United States gave birth to the Equal Protection Clause. A contrary conclusion could only be described as perverse.

JUSTICE SOUTER, dissenting.

[Unlike] other contexts in which we have addressed the State's conscious use of race, see, e.g., *Croson; Wygant,* electoral districting calls for decisions that nearly always require some consideration of race for legitimate reasons where there is a racially mixed population. As long as members of racial groups have the commonality of interest implicit in our ability to talk about concepts like "minority voting strength," and "dilution of minority votes," and as long as racial bloc voting takes place, legislators will have to take race into account in order to avoid dilution of minority voting strength in the districting plans they adopt. [A] second distinction between districting and most other governmental decisions in which race has figured is that those other decisions using racial criteria characteristically occur in circumstances in which the use of race to the advantage of one person is necessarily at the obvious expense of a member of a different race. * * *

In districting, by contrast, the mere placement of an individual in one district instead of another denies no one a right or benefit provided to others. [Under] our cases there is in general a requirement that in order to obtain relief under the Fourteenth Amendment, the purpose and effect of the districting must be to devalue the effectiveness of a voter compared to what, as a group member, he would otherwise be able to enjoy. * * *

There is thus no theoretical inconsistency in having two distinct approaches to equal protection analysis, one for cases of electoral districting and one for most other types of state governmental decisions. Nor, because of the distinctions between the two categories, is there any risk that Fourteenth Amendment districting law as such will be taken to imply anything for purposes of general Fourteenth Amendment scrutiny about "benign" racial discrimination, or about group entitlement as distinct from individual protection, or about the appropriateness of strict or other heightened scrutiny. * * *

Notes and Questions

1. *Constitutional injury.* What exactly is the constitutional injury or harm to the plaintiffs in *Shaw*? Is the shape of the district itself all, or part, of the problem? Consider Richard H. Pildes & Richard G. Niemi, *Expressive Harms, "Bizarre Districts," and Voting Rights: Evaluating Election–District Appearances After Shaw v. Reno,* 92 Mich.L.Rev. 483, 494, 506–07, 509 (1993): "[V]ote dilution is not involved in this case. [With] effective control of more than a proportionate

share of seats, white voters [could] not prove [that] the redistricting plan diluted their relative voting power. [One] can only understand *Shaw* [in] terms of a view [that the injury is an] expressive harm [that] results from the ideas or attitudes expressed through a governmental action, rather than from the more tangible [consequences] the action brings [about.] *Shaw* [rests] on the principle that, when government appears to use race in the redistricting context in a way that subordinates all other relevant values, the state has impermissibly endorsed too dominant a role for race. The constitutional harm must lie in this endorsement itself: the very expression of this value reductionism becomes the constitutional violation."

Do you agree? Compare John Hart Ely, *Standing to Challenge Pro–Minority Gerrymanders*, 111 Harv.L.Rev. 576, 587 (1997): "[G]iven racial block voting, the [white] filler people [who are typically included to make up roughly forty percent of a majority-minority district] are being denied the opportunity to elect one of 'their own.' [This] intentionally achieved inability on the part of filler people to elect someone of their own race can in turn be labeled harmless [by] asserting that there is no disadvantage whatsoever in being represented by someone not of one's own race. [But this] can't be true if the entire enterprise of pro-minority gerrymandering is to make any sense at all."[a]

2. *Minority representation.* Are efforts to create majority-minority districts a form of affirmative action that should be subjected to the same level of scrutiny as other affirmative action initiatives? Is the deliberate creation of majority-minority districts an especially objectionable effort to rig the political process? See John Hart Ely, *Gerrymanders: The Good, the Bad, and the Ugly*, 50 Stan.L.Rev. 607, 629–30 (1998). Or, given the frequent reliance on the political process to protect minority interests (as, for example, under the doctrine of *Washington v. Davis*), should efforts to ensure effective minority representation trigger less judicial skepticism than other forms of affirmative action?

How might the role of elected representatives be changed, improved, or compromised by majority-minority districting? Consider K. Anthony Appiah & Amy Gutmann, *Color Conscious: The Political Morality of Race* 154–55 (1996): "The prospect of greater descriptive and substantive representation of black voters provides good reason to recommend [majority-minority districting], not because blacks 'think alike, share the same political interests, and will prefer the same candidates at the polls' but because blacks [are] more likely [to] place the interest of overcoming racial injustice near the top of their political agenda. [The] electoral influence of black citizens would be most effectively expanded by reforms that encourage the formation of cross-racial coalitions. But there is ample evidence that majority-white districts in the South rarely form cross-racial coalitions. Quite the contrary; as the black voting population in Southern electoral districts increases from a small to a sizable minority (approaching and exceeding 40

---

a. The question of injury is of course closely linked to questions of standing, and issues of standing in vote-dilution cases have generated both recurring judicial controversies and a large literature of their own. In *United States v. Hays*, 515 U.S. 737, 115 S.Ct. 2431, 132 L.Ed.2d 635 (1995), the Court held unanimously that, regardless of race, "a voter who lives within a challenged district has standing, whereas a voter who lives outside the district normally does not." Samuel Issacharoff & Pamela S. Karlan, *Standing and Misunderstanding in Voting Rights Law*, 111 Harv. L.Rev. 2276, 2276 (1998). Is this holding consistent with the "expressive harms" theory of Pildes, supra? Consider Issacharoff & Karlan, supra, at 2279: "[T]here is no coherent theory of injury that justifies the standing rule the Court has established. [The] Court has made a hash of standing and injury in the *Shaw* context because of its deep ambivalence and confusion about race, the meaning of the right to vote, and the structure of the political system." Notable contributions to the standing literature include Ely, supra, and Issacharoff & Karlan, supra.

percent), the district tends to become more racially polarized, and white voters tend to form tighter, all-white coalitions, electing white representatives whose politics do not appeal to black voters."

See also T. Alexander Aleinikoff & Samuel Issacharoff, *Race and Redistricting: Drawing Constitutional Lines After Shaw v. Reno,* 92 Mich.L.Rev. 588, 612–13 (1993): "What is the evidence that race-conscious districting exacerbates racial bloc voting, or that it sends a message to an elected representative that she need only represent members of her group? There is only rudimentary evidence of the relative quality of representation and responsiveness in racially drawn districts, none of which is referred to by the Court, and none of which supports the categorical assertion that representation from such districts is fundamentally different from that afforded other constituent groups who form a majority in a congressional district. [Furthermore,] claiming that representatives should look primarily to interests beyond their district calls into question the entire edifice of geographically based districting."

3. *Beyond territorial districting?* Could problems of "vote dilution" and the representation of minorities be successfully alleviated through the use of voting schemes that do not rely on territorially based voting districts? Consider Lani Guinier, *The Tyranny of the Majority* 149 (1994): "[M]odified at-large systems used in corporate governance, such as cumulative voting, should be considered. Under a modified at-large system, each voter is given the same number of votes as open seats, and the voter may plump or cumulate her votes to reflect the intensity of her preferences. Depending on the exclusion threshold, politically cohesive minority groups are assured representation if they vote strategically. Similarly, *all* voters have the potential to form voluntary constituencies based on their own assessment of their interests. As a consequence, semiproportional systems such as cumulative voting give more voters, not just racial minorities, the opportunity to vote for a winning candidate."

Would such voting schemes be desirable? A federal statute, 2 U.S.C. § 2c, requires that the states establish "a number of districts equal to the number of Representatives" with "no district to elect more than one Representative." Apart from that restriction, would modified at-large systems that are designed to enhance minority representation be subject to any degree of heightened judicial scrutiny?[b] Are there any circumstances under which such systems should, or could, be imposed by courts?

———

MILLER v. JOHNSON, 515 U.S. 900, 115 S.Ct. 2475, 132 L.Ed.2d 762 (1995), involved Georgia's creation of three majority-minority congressional districts (out of a total of eleven) in response to the Justice Department's earlier refusals to grant preclearance under the Voting Rights Act to plans that created only two such districts. Georgia's population was about 27% black. One of the majority-minority districts created by the state—the Eleventh—cut through eight counties and five municipalities. The Court, per KENNEDY, J., held that this plan violated equal protection because "race was the predominant factor motivating the drawing of the eleventh district.":

"Our observation in *Shaw* of the consequences of racial stereotyping was not meant to suggest that a district must be bizarre on its face before there is a

b. See Steven J. Mulroy, *Alternative Ways Out: A Remedial Road Map for the Use of*   *Alternative Electoral Systems as Voting Rights Act Remedies,* 77 N.C.L.Rev. 1867 (1999).

constitutional violation. * * * Shape is relevant not because bizarreness is a necessary element of the constitutional wrong or a threshold requirement of proof, but because it may be persuasive circumstantial evidence that race for its own sake, and not other districting principles, was the legislature's dominant and controlling rationale in drawing its district lines. The logical implication, as courts applying *Shaw* have recognized, is that parties may rely on evidence other than bizarreness to establish race-based districting.

"[The] courts, in assessing the sufficiency of a challenge to a districting plan, must be sensitive to the complex interplay of forces that enter a legislature's redistricting calculus. Redistricting legislatures will, for example, almost always be aware of racial demographics; but it does not follow that race predominates in the redistricting process. [The] plaintiff's burden is to show, either through circumstantial evidence of a district's shape and demographics or more direct evidence going to legislative purpose, that [the] legislature subordinated traditional race-neutral districting principles, including but not limited to compactness, contiguity, respect for political subdivisions or communities defined by actual shared interests, to racial considerations. * * *

"[Whether] or not in some cases compliance with the Voting Rights Act, standing alone, can provide a compelling interest independent of any interest in remedying past discrimination, it cannot do so here. [When] a state governmental entity seeks to justify race-based remedies to cure the effects of past discrimination, we do not accept the government's mere assertion that the remedial action is required. Rather, we insist on a strong basis in evidence of the harm being remedied. [The] State does not argue, however, that it created the Eleventh District to remedy past discrimination, and with good reason: there is little doubt that the State's true interest in designing the Eleventh District was creating a third majority-black district to satisfy the Justice Department's preclearance demands. [It] does not follow, however, that the plan was required by the substantive provisions of the Voting Rights Act. * * *

"Georgia's drawing of the Eleventh District was not required under the Act because there was no reasonable basis to believe that Georgia's earlier enacted plans violated [§ 5]. Georgia's first and second proposed plans increased the number of majority-black districts from 1 out of 10 (10%) to 2 out of 11 (18.18%). These plans were 'ameliorative' and could not have violated § 5's non-retrogression principle.

"[T]he Justice Department's implicit command that States engage in presumptively unconstitutional race-based districting brings the Voting Rights Act, once upheld as a proper exercise of Congress' authority under § 2 of the Fifteenth Amendment, into tension with the Fourteenth Amendment. [We] need not, however, resolve these troubling and difficult constitutional questions today. There is no indication Congress intended such a far-reaching application of § 5, so we reject the Justice Department's interpretation of the statute and avoid the constitutional problems that interpretation raises."

O'CONNOR, J., concurring, added: "Application of the Court's standard does not throw into doubt the vast majority of the Nation's 435 congressional districts, where presumably the States have drawn the boundaries in accordance with their customary districting principles. That is so even though race may well have been considered in the redistricting process. But application of the Court's standard helps achieve *Shaw*'s basic objective of making extreme instances of gerrymandering subject to meaningful judicial review. I therefore join the Court's opinion."

GINSBURG, J., joined by Stevens, Souter and Breyer, JJ., dissented: "Although the Georgia General Assembly prominently considered race in shaping the Eleventh District, race did not crowd out all other factors, as the Court found it did in North Carolina's delineation of the *Shaw* district. Of the 22 counties in the District, 14 are intact and 8 are divided. That puts the Eleventh District at about the state average in divided counties. [And] notably, the Eleventh District's boundaries largely follow precinct lines. Evidence at trial similarly shows that [political considerations] went into determining the Eleventh District's boundaries. * * * Tellingly, the District that the Court's decision today unsettles is not among those on a statistically calculated list of the 28 most bizarre districts in the United States, a study prepared in the wake of our decision in *Shaw*. * * *

"To accommodate the reality of ethnic bonds, legislatures have long drawn voting districts along ethnic lines. Our Nation's cities are full of districts identified by their ethnic character—Chinese, Irish, Italian, Jewish, Polish, Russian, for example. The creation of ethnic districts reflecting felt identity is not ordinarily viewed as offensive or demeaning to those included in the delineation. [If] Chinese–Americans and Russian–Americans may seek and secure group recognition in the delineation of voting districts, then African–Americans should not be dissimilarly treated. Otherwise, in the name of equal protection, we would shut out 'the very minority group whose history in the United States gave birth to the Equal Protection Clause.' "

————

BUSH v. VERA, 517 U.S. 952, 116 S.Ct. 1941, 135 L.Ed.2d 248 (1996), struck down congressional districts crafted to meet what Texas argued was needed to meet the requirements of the Voting Rights Act. Although race was a factor in drawing the lines, Texas argued that the predominant factor was the protection of incumbents. O'CONNOR, J., joined by Rehnquist, C.J., and Kennedy, J., agreed that avoiding contests between incumbents was a legitimate districting consideration, and she emphasized that the "decision to create majority-minority districts was not objectionable in and of itself." O'Connor, J., noted that "[o]ur precedents have used a variety of formulations to describe the threshold for the application of strict scrutiny" and cited as possible triggering standards for strict scrutiny language from both *Shaw* ("so extremely irregular on its face that it rationally can be viewed only as an effort to segregate the races for purposes of voting, without regard for traditional districting principles") and *Miller* ("race for its own sake, and not other districting principles, was the legislature's dominant and controlling rationale"). Noting that strict scrutiny does not "apply to all cases of intentional creation of majority-minority districts," she nonetheless concluded on the facts that strict scrutiny was appropriate because race had predominated over legitimate districting considerations. Among the findings weighing in favor of the application of strict scrutiny were "that the State substantially neglected traditional districting criteria such as compactness, that it was committed from the outset to creating majority-minority districts, and that it manipulated district lines to exploit unprecedentedly detailed racial data."

"As we have done in each of our previous cases, in which [compliance with Section 2 of the Voting Rights Act] has been raised as a defense to charges of racial gerrymandering, we assume without deciding that compliance with [Section 2's] results test [can be] a compelling state interest." O'Connor, J., concluded, however, that the Texas districts were not narrowly tailored to meet the requirements of the Voting Rights Act because the act does not require a state to create districts that are not reasonably compact:[a] "If, because of the dispersion of the minority population, a reasonably compact majority-minority district cannot be created, the [Voting Rights Act] does not require a majority-minority district; if a reasonably compact district can be created, nothing in [the Voting Rights Act] requires the race-based creation of a district that is far from compact."

THOMAS, J., joined by Scalia, J., concurring, maintained that the intentional creation of majority-minority districts should be enough to invoke strict scrutiny: "In my view, application of strict scrutiny in this suit was never a close question," because "a majority-minority district is created 'because of,' and not merely 'in spite of,' racial demographics." Kennedy, J., concurring separately, strongly suggested he would join Thomas and Scalia, JJ., on that point if the issue were presented.

STEVENS, J., joined by Ginsburg and Breyer, JJ., dissenting, denied that race was a predominant consideration in the formation of the Texas districts and maintained that the creation of districts that were not reasonably compact was consistent with the Voting Rights Act (though he conceded that liability could be imposed only if the state could have created a reasonably compact majority-minority district). He also vehemently questioned the underlying premise of *Shaw*, in which the Court "struck out into a jurisprudential wilderness that lacks a definable constitutional core and threatens to create harms more significant than any suffered by the individual plaintiffs challenging these districts."

SOUTER, J., joined by Ginsburg and Breyer, JJ., dissenting, raised administrability, separation of powers, and federalism objections to the Court's *Shaw* jurisprudence: "The result of [the Court's] failure to provide a practical standard for distinguishing between lawful and unlawful use of race has not only been inevitable confusion in statehouses and courtrooms, but a consequent shift in responsibility for setting district boundaries from state legislatures, which are invested with front-line authority by Article I of the Constitution, to the courts, and truly to this Court, which is left to superintend the drawing of every legislative district in the land."

O'CONNOR, J., who wrote the plurality opinion in *Bush v. Vera*, also wrote a separate concurring opinion in which she attempted to summarize "the rules governing the States' consideration of race in the districting process[:] First, so long as they do not subordinate traditional districting criteria to the use of race for its own sake or as a proxy, States may intentionally create majority-minority districts, and may otherwise take race into consideration, without coming under strict scrutiny. See [the plurality opinion and the dissenting opinions of Stevens and Souter, JJ.]. Only if traditional districting criteria are neglected and that neglect is predominantly due to the misuse of race does strict scrutiny apply.

"Second, where voting is racially polarized, § 2 [of the Voting Rights Act] prohibits States from adopting districting schemes that would have the effect that minority voters 'have less opportunity than other members of the electorate [to] elect representatives of their choice.' § 2(b). That principle may require a State to create a majority-minority district where the three *Gingles* factors are present— viz., (i) the minority group 'is sufficiently large and geographically compact to constitute a majority in a single-member district,' (ii) 'it is politically cohesive,' and (iii) 'the white majority votes sufficiently as a bloc to enable it * * * usually to defeat the minority's preferred candidate.'

a. The Court reached the same conclusion, again over the vigorous dissents of Stevens, J., and Souter, J., both joined by Breyer and Gins- burg, J.J., in the companion case of *Shaw v. Hunt* ("*Shaw II*"), 517 U.S. 899, 116 S.Ct. 1894, 135 L.Ed.2d 207 (1996).

"Third, the state interest in avoiding liability under [§ 2] is compelling.[b] If a State has a strong basis in evidence for concluding that the *Gingles* factors are present, it may create a majority-minority district without awaiting judicial findings. Its 'strong basis in evidence' need not take any particular form, although it cannot simply rely on generalized assumptions about the prevalence of racial bloc voting.

"Fourth, if a State pursues that compelling interest by creating a district that 'substantially addresses' the potential liability, and does not deviate substantially from a hypothetical court-drawn § 2 district for predominantly racial reasons, its districting plan will be deemed narrowly tailored. Cf. (plurality opinion)(acknowledging this possibility); (Souter, J., dissenting)(same); (Stevens, J., dissenting)(contending that it is applicable here).

"Finally, however, districts that are bizarrely shaped and non-compact, and that otherwise neglect traditional districting principles and deviate substantially from the hypothetical court-drawn district, for predominantly racial reasons, are unconstitutional. (plurality opinion)."

Notes and Questions

1. *The applicable test.* Is the "dominant purpose" test applied in *Miller* and echoed in *Bush* a workable one? How does it relate to the test applied in *Shaw*? Consider John H. Ely, *Gerrymanders: The Good, the Bad, and the Ugly*, 50 Stan.L.Rev. 607, 611–12 (1998): "Dominant purpose tests aren't simply vague and manipulable: they are incoherent. Consider Desmond's decision where to go to law school. He chose Yale because it was small and good. But which of those was his dominant motivation? [Maybe] this question will tell us: Would he have chosen a good big school over a bad small school? Well, how big? How bad? Harvard versus Lilliput. Not fair: Harvard's quality clearly exceeds Lilliput's intimacy. Give me a more balanced choice. How about Harvard versus Stanford? Actually Stanford's about as good as either Harvard or Yale, but Desmond's afraid of earthquakes. He went to Yale because it is small and good and the ground stays put. Well, then, Chicago: Now there's a toddlin' town. Yeah, but it's also hog butcher to the nation, and Desmond's a vegetarian. He went to Yale because it's small and good and the ground stays put and they don't torture animals. Which was 'dominant'? [And] you choose only one law school. Drawing a voting district involves an infinity of choices. [How] could one suppose the whole monstrosity to have a 'dominant purpose,' unless it's to accommodate as many little purposes as possible?"[a]

2. *Racial and political gerrymanders.* If a state can draw voting district lines predominantly based on considerations of political affiliation, does it make sense that the state cannot equally make a decision based on racial identification? If racial minorities predominantly joined a third, race-based political party, could a state draw district lines with the predominant purpose of creating a district in which members of that party were a voting majority?[b]

---

b. The four dissenters in *Vera* (who also dissented in *Hunt*), together with O'Connor, J., supported this proposition.

a. Compare *Hunt v. Cromartie*, 526 U.S. 541, 119 S.Ct. 1545, 143 L.Ed.2d 731 (1999). Per Thomas, J., the Court stated that the intentional use of race to create districts with slightly less than a majority of minority citizens could be subject to equal protection challenge, but found that summary judgment was inappropriate, due to controversy whether the legislature's predominant purpose in creating the district involved race or party politics. Stevens, J. joined by Souter, Ginsburg, and Breyer, JJ., concurred.

Is it peculiar (or acceptable) for the Court to treat incumbent-protection as an acceptable purpose in the drawing of voting districts, as it did in *Bush v. Vera*, but to look askance at efforts to create majority-minority districts? Does current law invest whites with "an equal protection right not to be part of [majority-minority districts] that have an odd shape," but not invest racial minorities with any corresponding right "not to be part of majority white districts that have an odd shape"? Jamin B. Raskin, *The Supreme Court's Racial Double Standard in Redistricting: Unequal Protection in Politics and the Scholarship That Defends It*, 14 J.L. & Pol. 591, 606–07 (1998).

3. *The challenge to legislatures.* Consider Pamela Karlan, *The Fire Next Time: Reapportionment After the 2000 Census*, 50 Stan.L.Rev. 731, 733–34 (1998): "Federal law imposes essentially seven substantive constraints on the apportionment process. Under the [equal protection clause], a plan must (1) comply with one person, one vote; (2) avoid purposeful discrimination against racial minorities; (3) avoid excessive political gerrymandering; and (4) not 'subordinate [] traditional race-neutral districting principles' to racial considerations. Under the Voting Rights Act of 1965 [p. 1359 supra], as amended, a plan cannot (5) result in a dilution of minority voting strength (section 2) or (6) reduce minority voting strength relative to prior levels (section 5). Finally, federal law requires, at least regarding a state's congressional delegation, that a plan (7) use single-member districts." Is this a manageable set of requirements?[c] Is the existing legal equilibrium a stable one?[d] If not, what should replace it?

RICE v. CAYETANO, 528 U.S. 495, 120 S.Ct. 1044, 145, 145 L.Ed.2d 1007 (2000), per KENNEDY, J., invalidated Hawaii's granting only to "Hawaiians" (descendants of those inhabiting the Islands in 1778) the right to vote for trustees of a state agency that administers programs for "Hawaiians": "The ancestral inquiry mandated by the State implicates the same grave concerns as a classification specifying a particular race by name. One of the principal reasons race is treated as a forbidden classification is that it demeans the dignity and worth of a person to be judged by ancestry instead of by his or her own merit and essential qualities. An inquiry into ancestral lines is not consistent with respect based on

b. See Terry Smith, *A Black Party? Timmons, Black Backlash and the Endangered Two-Party Paradigm*, 48 Duke L.J. 1 (1998).

c. For a range of commentary, most of it critical, see (in addition to sources already cited): David M. Guinn, Christopher Chapman & Kathryn S. Knechtel, *Redistricting in 2001 and Beyond: Navigating the Narrow Channel Between the Equal Protection Clause and the Voting Rights Act*, 51 Baylor L.Rev. 225 (1999); Daniel Hays Lowenstein, *You Don't Have to Be Liberal to Hate the Racial Gerrymandering Cases*, 50 Stan.L.Rev. 779, 780–83 (1998).

d. Consider Samuel Issacharoff, Pamela S. Karlan, & Richard H. Pildes, *The Law of Democracy: Legal Structure of the Political Process* 608, 610 (1998): "[T]he Supreme Court [has] reached the merits and upheld two plans against *Shaw* claims: *Lawyer v. Department of Justice*, 521 U.S. 567, 117 S.Ct. 2186, 138 L.Ed.2d 669 (1997) [and] *DeWitt v. Wilson*, 515 U.S. 1170, 115 S.Ct. 2637, 132 L.Ed.2d 876 (1995), summarily aff'g (affirming) 856 F.Supp. 1409 (E.D.Cal.1994). Notably, neither plan involved district lines drawn by overtly political actors: the Florida State Senate district challenged in *Lawyer* was the product of a federal court settlement; the California state legislative reapportionments challenged in *DeWitt* were the product of three retired California judges appointed by the California Supreme Court as special masters. [Consider] the systemic incentives that the Court's decisions [might] create. If race-conscious districting is effectively permissible when done by courts but not by legislatures, does this turn the Court's original reluctance to enter the political thicket on its head?"

the unique personality each of us possesses, a respect the Constitution itself secures in its concern for persons and citizens.

"The ancestral inquiry mandated by the State is forbidden by the Fifteenth Amendment for the further reason that the use of racial classifications is corruptive of the whole legal order democratic elections seek to preserve."

STEVENS, J., joined by Ginsburg, J., relying on *Morton v. Mancari*, 417 U.S. 535, 94 S.Ct. 2474, 41 L.Ed.2d 290 (1974), dissented because of the "compelling similarity, fully supported by our precedent, between the once subjugated, indigenous peoples of the continental United States and the peoples of the Hawaiian Islands whose historical sufferings and status parallel those of the continental Native Americans."

II. TRAVEL

SHAPIRO v. THOMPSON

394 U.S. 618, 89 S.Ct. 1322, 22 L.Ed.2d 600 (1969).

JUSTICE BRENNAN delivered the opinion of the Court.

These three appeals [are from federal courts] holding unconstitutional [Connecticut, Pennsylvania, and D.C. statutes denying welfare] to residents [who] have not resided within their jurisdictions for at least one [year].

There is no dispute that the effect of the waiting-period requirement [is] to create two classes of needy resident families indistinguishable from each other except that one is composed of residents who have resided a year or more, and the second of residents who have resided less than a year, in the jurisdiction. [T]he second class is denied welfare aid upon which may depend the ability of the families to obtain the very means to subsist—food, shelter, and other necessities of life. [We] agree [that the statutes deny equal protection]. The interests which appellants assert are promoted by the classification either may not constitutionally be promoted by government or are not compelling governmental interests.

Primarily, appellants justify the waiting-period requirement as a protective device to preserve the fiscal integrity of state public assistance programs. It is asserted that people who require welfare assistance during their first year of residence in a State are likely to become continuing burdens on state welfare programs. Therefore, the argument runs, if such people can be deterred from entering the jurisdiction by denying them welfare benefits during the first year, state programs to assist long-time residents will not be impaired. [But] the purpose of inhibiting migration by needy persons into the State is constitutionally impermissible.

This Court long ago recognized that the nature of our Federal Union and our constitutional concepts of personal liberty unite to require that all citizens be free to travel throughout the length and breadth of our land uninhibited by statutes, rules, or regulations which unreasonably burden or restrict this movement.

Alternatively, appellants argue that even if it is impermissible for a State to attempt to deter the entry of all indigents, the challenged classification may be justified as a permissible state attempt to discourage those indigents who would enter the State solely to obtain larger benefits. [But] a State may no more try to fence out those indigents who seek higher welfare benefits than it may try to fence out indigents generally. [W]e do not perceive why a mother who is seeking to make a new life for herself and her children should be regarded as less deserving because she considers, among other factors, the level of a State's public assistance. Surely such a mother is no less deserving than a mother who moves into a particular State in order to take advantage of its better educational facilities.

Appellants argue further that the challenged classification may be sustained as an attempt to distinguish between new and old residents on the basis of the contribution they have made to the community through the payment of taxes. [But this] would logically permit the State to bar new residents from schools, parks, and libraries or deprive them of police and fire protection. Indeed it would permit the State to apportion all benefits and services according to the past tax contributions of its citizens. The Equal Protection Clause prohibits such an apportionment of state services.[10]

We recognize that a State [may] legitimately attempt to limit its expenditures, whether for public assistance, public education, or any other program. But a State may not accomplish such a purpose by invidious distinctions between classes of its citizens. It could not, for example, reduce expenditures for education by barring indigent children from its schools. [Thus], appellants must do more than show that denying welfare benefits to new residents saves [money.]

Appellants next advance as justification [four] administrative and related governmental objectives allegedly served by the waiting-period requirement. * * *

At the outset, we reject appellants' argument that a mere showing of a rational relationship between the waiting period and these four admittedly permissible state objectives will suffice, [for] in moving from State to State or to the District of Columbia appellees were exercising a constitutional right, and any classification which serves to penalize the exercise of that right, unless shown to be necessary to promote a *compelling* governmental interest, is unconstitutional. Cf. *Skinner v. Oklahoma*, [Ch. 6, Sec. 2]; *Korematsu; Sherbert v. Verner*, [discussed in Ch. 8, Sec. 2, I].

The argument that the waiting-period requirement facilitates budget predictability is wholly unfounded. The records in all three cases are utterly devoid of evidence [of use of] the one-year requirement as a means to predict the number of people who will require assistance in the budget year. * * *

The argument that the waiting period serves as an administratively efficient rule of thumb for determining residency similarly will not withstand scrutiny. [Before] granting an application, the welfare authorities investigate the applicant [and] in the course of the inquiry necessarily learn the facts upon which to determine whether the applicant is a resident.

Similarly, there is no need for a State to use the one-year waiting period as a safeguard against fraudulent receipt of benefits; for less drastic means are available, and are employed * * *.

Pennsylvania suggests that the one-year waiting period is justified as a means of encouraging new residents to join the labor force promptly. But this logic would also require a similar waiting period for long-term [residents.]

We conclude therefore that appellants [have] no need to use the one-year requirement for the governmental purposes suggested. Thus, even under traditional equal protection tests [the classification] would seem irrational and unconstitutional. But [s]ince the classification here touches on the fundamental right of interstate movement, its constitutionality must be judged by the stricter standard

---

10. We are not dealing here with state insurance programs which may legitimately tie the amount of benefits to the individual's contributions.

of whether it promotes a *compelling* state interest. Under this standard, the waiting period requirement clearly violates the Equal Protection Clause.[21]

[The Court rejected the contention that Social Security Act § 402(b) approved imposition of one-year residence requirements. But] even if it could be argued that the constitutionality of § 402(b) is [in issue,] Congress may not authorize the States to violate the Equal Protection Clause. * * *

Affirmed.

CHIEF JUSTICE WARREN with whom JUSTICE BLACK joins, dissenting.

[§ 402(b)] intended to authorize state residence requirements of up to one [year.] Congress, pursuant to its commerce power, has enacted a variety of restrictions upon interstate travel. It has taxed air and rail fares and [gasoline]. Many of the federal safety regulations of common carriers which cross state lines burden the right to travel. And Congress has prohibited by criminal statute interstate travel for certain purposes. * * *

The Court's right-to-travel cases lend little support to the view that congressional action is invalid merely because it burdens the right to travel. Most of our cases fall into two categories: those in which *state* imposed restrictions were involved, see e.g., *Edwards v. California,* [Sec. 4, V supra], and those concerning congressional decisions to remove impediments to interstate movement, see, e.g., [*United States v. Guest*, 383 U.S. 745, 86 S.Ct. 1170, 16 L.Ed.2d 239 (1966)]. *Aptheker v. Secretary of State,* [Ch. 6, Sec. 3] is the only case in which this Court invalidated on a constitutional basis a congressionally imposed restriction. *Aptheker* also involved [a] claim that the congressional restriction compelled a potential traveler to choose between his right to travel and his First Amendment right of freedom of association. [*Aptheker*] thus contains two characteristics distinguishing it from the [instant case]: a combined infringement of two constitutionally protected rights and a flat prohibition upon travel. [Here], travel itself is not prohibited. Any burden inheres solely in the fact that a potential welfare recipient might take into consideration the loss of welfare benefits for a limited period of time if he changes his residence. Not only is this burden of uncertain degree,[5] but appellees themselves assert there is evidence that few welfare recipients have in fact been deterred by residence requirements.

The insubstantiality of the restriction imposed by residence requirements must then be evaluated in light of the possible congressional reasons for such requirements. [Given] the apprehensions of many States that an increase in benefits without minimal residence requirements would result in an inability to provide an adequate welfare system, Congress deliberately adopted the intermediate course of a cooperative program. [Our] cases require only that Congress have a rational basis for finding that a chosen regulatory scheme is necessary to the furtherance of interstate commerce. See, e.g., *Katzenbach v. McClung*. I conclude that residence requirements can be imposed by Congress as an exercise of its power to control interstate commerce consistent with the constitutionally guaranteed right to travel. * * * *a

---

21. We imply no view of the validity of waiting period *or* residence requirements determining eligibility to vote, [for] tuition-free education, to obtain a license to practice a profession, to hunt or fish, [etc. These] may promote compelling state interests on the one hand, or, on the other, may not be penalties upon the exercise of the constitutional right of interstate travel.

5. [I]ndigents who are disqualified from categorical assistance by residence requirements are not left wholly without assistance. Each of the appellees in these cases found alternative sources of assistance * * *.

a. As to whether the "federalistic dimension" of the right to travel should limit Congress' power to affect it, see Kenneth Karst,

JUSTICE HARLAN, dissenting. * * *

In upholding the equal protection argument, the Court has applied an equal protection doctrine of relatively recent vintage [—the] "compelling interest" doctrine [which constitutes] an increasingly significant exception to the long-established rule that a statute does not deny equal protection if it is rationally related to a legitimate governmental objective. The "compelling interest" doctrine has two branches. [The] "suspect" criteria [branch today] apparently has been further enlarged to include classifications based upon recent interstate movement, and perhaps those based upon the exercise of *any* constitutional [right].

I think that this branch of the "compelling interest" doctrine is sound when applied to racial classifications, for historically the Equal Protection Clause was largely a product of the desire to eradicate legal distinctions founded upon race. However, I believe that the more recent extensions have been unwise. [When] a classification is based upon the exercise of rights guaranteed against state infringement by the federal Constitution, then there is no need for any resort to the Equal Protection Clause; in such instances, this Court may properly and straight-forwardly invalidate any undue burden upon those rights under the Fourteenth Amendment's Due Process Clause.

The second branch of the "compelling interest" principle is even more troublesome. For it has been held that a statutory classification is subject to the "compelling interest" test if the result of the classification may be to affect a "fundamental right," regardless of the basis of the classification. This rule was foreshadowed in *Skinner* [and] re-emerged in *Reynolds v. Sims.* It has reappeared today in the Court's cryptic suggestion that the "compelling interest" test is applicable merely because the result of the classification may be to deny the appellees "food, shelter, and other necessities of life," as well as in the Court's statement that "[s]ince the classification here touches on the fundamental right of interstate movement, its constitutionality must be judged by the stricter standard of whether it promotes a *compelling* state interest."

I think this branch [is] unfortunate because it creates an exception which threatens to swallow the standard equal protection rule. Virtually every state statute affects important rights. This Court has repeatedly held, for example, that the traditional equal protection standard is applicable to statutory classifications affecting such fundamental matters as the right to pursue a particular occupation, the right to receive greater or smaller wages or to work more or less hours, and the right to inherit property. Rights such as these are in principle indistinguishable from those involved here, and to extend the "compelling interest" rule to all cases in which such rights are affected would go far toward making this Court a "super-legislature." [W]hen a statute affects only matters not mentioned in the federal Constitution and is not arbitrary or irrational, I must reiterate that I know of nothing which entitles this Court to pick out particular human activities, characterize them as "fundamental," and give them added protection under an unusually stringent equal protection test. * * *

[Because] a legislature might rationally find that the imposition of a welfare residence requirement would aid in the accomplishment of at least four valid governmental objectives, [I] can find no objection to these residence requirements under [equal protection].

The next issue [is] whether a one-year welfare residence requirement amounts to an undue burden upon the right of interstate travel[, which I conclude] is a "fundamental" right [that] should be regarded as having its source in the Due Process Clause of the Fifth Amendment.

[In] my view, a number of considerations militate in favor of constitutionality. First, as just shown, four separate, legitimate governmental interests are furthered by residence requirements. Second, the impact of the requirements upon the freedom of individuals to travel interstate is indirect and, according to evidence put forward by the appellees themselves, insubstantial. Third, these are [cases] in which the States have acted within the terms of a limited authorization by the national government, and in which Congress itself has laid down a like rule for the District of Columbia. Fourth, the legislatures which enacted these statutes have been fully exposed to the arguments of the appellees as to why these residence requirements are unwise, and have rejected them.

[Fifth, the] field of welfare assistance is one in which there is a widely recognized need for fresh solutions and consequently for experimentation. [Sixth, the] statutes come to us clothed with the authority of Congress and attended by a correspondingly heavy presumption of constitutionality. * * *

Notes and Questions

1. *Theory of the decision.* (a) *Scope of the "right to travel."* If a state simply eliminated welfare, or granted lower payments than other states, would this "touch on the fundamental right of interstate movement" just as harshly as the programs in *Shapiro?* Would state policies of this kind be invalid under *Shapiro* "unless shown to be necessary to promote a *compelling* governmental interest"?

(b) *Equal protection or due process?* Does Harlan, J.'s contention—that "when the right affected is one assured by the Constitution, any infringement can be dealt with under the Due Process Clause"—make superfluous the *Shapiro* approach of finding a fundamental right to travel under equal protection?[a] Or does *Shapiro's* equal protection analysis add another dimension to the problem by distinguishing between the state interests needed to justify reducing expenditures generally and reducing expenditures by denying benefits to recent travellers?

(c) *Relation of right to travel and equal protection.* Is the central rationale of *Shapiro* that the state must not create "invidious distinctions between classes of citizens" based on whether those in one class have exercised their right to travel? If so, which discriminations should be classed as "invidious"?

2. *Bona fide residence requirements.* (a) After *Shapiro,* may a state deny welfare assistance to transients who have no intention of remaining permanently in the state? Consider the suggestion of Edward Barrett, *Judicial Supervision of Legislative Classifications—A More Modest Role for Equal Protection,* 1976 B.Y.U.L.Rev. 89, 117, that *Shapiro* did not really involve "the interest in freedom of travel" but rather "only the narrower interest in freedom of interstate migration"—i.e., to "resettle, find a new job, and start a new life."

(b) The Court has declined to invalidate bona fide residence requirements in a number of contexts. McCARTHY v. PHILADELPHIA CIVIL SERVICE COMM'N, 424 U.S. 645, 96 S.Ct. 1154, 47 L.Ed.2d 366 (1976), per curiam—involving a Philadelphia fireman who was terminated when he moved to New Jersey—held that "a municipal regulation requiring employees of the city [to] be

a. For support of this view, see Arnold Lo-ewy, *A Different and More Viable Theory of Equal Protection,* 57 N.C.L.Rev. 1 (1978); Mi- chael Perry, *Modern Equal Protection: A Conceptualization and Appraisal,* 79 Colum.L.Rev. 1023 (1979).

residents of the city" did not impair the "right to travel interstate as defined in *Shapiro*," which questioned neither "the validity of a condition placed upon municipal employment that a person be a resident *at the time* of his application," nor "the validity of appropriately defined and uniformly applied bona fide residence requirements."

Similarly, MARTINEZ v. BYNUM, 461 U.S. 321, 103 S.Ct. 1838, 75 L.Ed.2d 879 (1983), per POWELL, J., upheld Texas' denial of free public education to children who, apart from their parents or guardians, reside in the school district "for the sole purpose of attending" the public schools: "A bona fide residence requirement [with] respect to attendance in public free schools does not violate the Equal Protection Clause [nor does it] burden or penalize the constitutional right of interstate travel, for any person is free to move to a State and to establish residence there. [A]t the very least, a school district generally would be justified in requiring school-age children or their parents to satisfy the traditional, basic residence criteria—i.e., to live in the district with a bona fide intention of remaining there—before it treated them as residents." MARSHALL, J., dissented, mainly on the ground that an "intention of remaining" is not a proper criterion for a bona fide residence requirement.

Compare DOE v. BOLTON, Ch. 6, Sec. 2, which invalidated the residency requirement of the Georgia abortion law: "Just as the Privileges and Immunities Clause, Art. IV, § 2, protects persons who enter other States to ply their trade, so must it protect persons who enter Georgia seeking the medical services that are available there. A contrary holding would mean that a State could limit to its own residents the general medical care available within its borders." On Art. IV, § 2, see generally Ch. 4, Sec. 4. Is *Doe* consistent with *McCarthy* and *Martinez*?

3. *Waiting-period requirements in contexts other than welfare.* (a) *Voting.* DUNN v. BLUMSTEIN, 405 U.S. 330, 92 S.Ct. 995, 31 L.Ed.2d 274 (1972), per MARSHALL, J., held that Tennessee's voting registration requirements—of residence in the state for one year and in the county for three months—violate equal protection. Although "States have the power to require that voters be bona fide residents of the relevant political subdivision," it is the "additional *durational* residence requirement which appellee challenges. [Here], whether we look to the benefit withheld by the classification (the opportunity to vote) or the basis for the classification (recent interstate travel)," the classification must be "*necessary to* promote a *compelling* governmental interest."

First, as for the state's interest in "preventing fraud [by] keeping nonresidents from voting, [the] record is totally devoid of any evidence that durational residence requirements are in fact necessary to identify bona fide residents." Second, "the State cannot seriously maintain that it is 'necessary' to reside for a year in the State and three months in the county in order to be minimally knowledgeable about congressional, state or even purely local elections."

BURGER, C.J., dissented: "It is no more a denial of Equal Protection for a State to require newcomers to be exposed to state and local problems for a reasonable period such as one year before voting, than it is to require children to wait 18 years before [voting.] Some lines must be drawn. To challenge such lines by the 'compelling state interest' standard is to condemn them all."[b]

---

b. *Marston v. Lewis,* 410 U.S. 679, 93 S.Ct. 1211, 35 L.Ed.2d 627 (1973), per curiam, upheld Arizona's 50–day durational residency requirement for state and local elections as "nec-essary to permit preparation of accurate voter lists." *Burns v. Fortson,* 410 U.S. 686, 93 S.Ct. 1209, 35 L.Ed.2d 633 (1973), upheld a similar Georgia provision.

(b) *Medical care.* MEMORIAL HOSPITAL v. MARICOPA COUNTY, 415 U.S. 250, 94 S.Ct. 1076, 39 L.Ed.2d 306 (1974), per MARSHALL, J., held an Arizona statute—requiring one year's residence in the county for indigents to receive nonemergency hospitalization or medical care at county expense—violative of equal protection: "Although any durational residence requirement impinges to some extent on the right to travel," *Shapiro* "did not declare such requirements to be per se unconstitutional." It is only a state classification that "operates to *penalize* [indigents] for exercising their right to migrate to and settle in that state" that "must be justified by a compelling state interest. [*Dunn*] found that the denial of the franchise, 'a fundamental political right,' was a penalty [and *Shapiro*] found denial of the basic 'necessities of life' to be a penalty. Nonetheless, the Court has declined to strike down state statutes requiring one year of residence as a condition to lower tuition at state institutions of higher education.[12] Whatever the ultimate parameters of the *Shapiro* penalty analysis, it is at least clear that medical care is as much 'a basic necessity of life' to an indigent as welfare assistance." For reasons similar to those in *Shapiro,* the state has not met its "heavy burden of justification."

REHNQUIST, J., dissented: "[F]ees for use of transportation facilities such as taxes on airport users,[12] have been upheld [against] attacks based upon the right to travel. [T]he line to be derived from our prior cases is that some financial impositions on interstate travelers have such indirect or inconsequential impact on travel that they simply do not constitute the type of direct purposeful barriers struck down" in *Shapiro.* "The solicitude which the Court has shown in cases involving the right to vote, and the virtual denial of entry inherent in denial of welfare benefits—'the very means by which to live'—ought not be so casually extended to the alleged deprivation here. Rather the Court should examine, as it has done in the past, whether the challenged requirement erects a real and purposeful barrier to movement, [or] whether the effects on travel, viewed realistically, are merely incidental and remote."

(c) *Divorce.* SOSNA v. IOWA, 419 U.S. 393, 95 S.Ct. 553, 42 L.Ed.2d 532 (1975), per REHNQUIST, J., upheld a one-year residency requirement to file for divorce: The laws in *Shapiro* and *Maricopa* "were justified on the basis of budgetary or record-keeping considerations which were held insufficient to outweigh the constitutional claims of the individuals. But Iowa's divorce residency requirement is of a different stripe. [A] decree of divorce [will] affect [both spouses'] marital status and very likely their property rights. Where a married couple has minor children, a decree of divorce would usually include provisions for their custody and support. With consequences of such moment riding on a divorce decree issued by its courts, Iowa may insist that one seeking to initiate such a proceeding have the modicum of attachment to the State required here."

MARSHALL, J., joined by Brennan, J., dissented, relying on *Boddie v. Connecticut,* Part III infra: The right to divorce "is of such fundamental importance" that the law "penalizes interstate travel within the meaning of *Shapiro, Dunn,* and *Maricopa.*"

---

12. See *Vlandis v. Kline* [412 U.S. 441, 93 S.Ct. 2230, 37 L.Ed.2d 63 (1973), invalidating a conclusive statutory presumption that a student who applied from out of state was, therefore, a non-resident for tuition purposes for the entire period of attendance at a public university. *Starns v. Malkerson,* 401 U.S. 985, 91 S.Ct. 1231, 28 L.Ed.2d 527 (1971), summarily affirmed a Minnesota regulation denying a student the opportunity to show residency for tuition purposes until the student had lived in the state for one year.]

12. See *Evansville-Vanderburgh Airport Auth. Dist. v. Delta Airlines,* 405 U.S. 707, 92 S.Ct. 1349, 31 L.Ed.2d 620 (1972).

(d) *The decisions' rationales.* Do the cases explain how the Court determines whether a "waiting-period" requirement "operates to *penalize*" the right to travel? In both *Dunn* and *Maricopa* the Court conceded "that there is no evidence in the record before us that anyone was actually deterred from traveling by the challenged restriction" but observed that "*Shapiro* did not rest upon a finding that denial of welfare actually deterred travel." Could the cases be rationalized on the view that classifications based on duration of residency are invidious when they involve eligibility for some benefits or opportunities but not for others? Does the Court *presume* that withholding of certain benefits (but not others) deters travel? Would this explain the "basic necessity of life" emphasis in *Shapiro* and *Maricopa?* Does it account for the result in *Sosna?* In *Dunn?*[c] See Part IV infra. Is *Dunn* explicable on other grounds? See Part I supra.

Should the decisions turn on whether residency requirements reflect a "reasonable concern for proof of domiciliary intent"? See William Cohen, *Equal Treatment for Newcomers,* 1 Const.Comm. 9, 19 (1984).

———

ZOBEL v. WILLIAMS, 457 U.S. 55, 102 S.Ct. 2309, 72 L.Ed.2d 672 (1982), per BURGER, C.J., held that Alaska's scheme of distributing its revenue from state-owned oil reserves to its citizens "in varying amounts, retroactively based on the length of each citizen's residence, violates the equal protection rights of newer state citizens." The Court ruled that two stated objectives—"creating a financial incentive for individuals to establish and maintain Alaska residence, and assuring prudent management of the [oil revenues] and the State's natural and mineral resources"—were "not rationally related to the distinctions Alaska seeks to draw." And, under *Shapiro,* the objective of rewarding "contributions of various kinds, both tangible and intangible, which residents have made during their years of residence," was "not a legitimate state purpose. [Such] reasoning could open the door to state apportionment of other rights, benefits and services according to length of residency. It would permit the states to divide citizens into expanding numbers of permanent classes. Such a result would be clearly impermissible."

BRENNAN, J., joined by Marshall, Blackmun, and Powell, JJ., joined the Court's opinion, adding that "the Citizenship Clause of the Fourteenth Amendment [bars] degrees of citizenship based on length of residence. And the Equal Protection Clause would not tolerate such distinctions. In short, as much as the right to travel, equality of citizenship is of the essence in our republic. [Thus], discrimination on the basis of residence must be supported by a valid state interest independent of the discrimination itself. [L]ength of residence may, for example, be used to test the bona fides of citizenship—and allegiance and attachment may bear some rational relationship to a very limited number of legitimate state purposes. Cf. *Chimento v. Stark,* 353 F.Supp. 1211 (D.N.H.), affirmed, 414 U.S. 802 (1973) (seven year citizenship requirement to run for governor); U.S. Const., art. I, § 2, cl. 2, § 3, cl. 3; art. II, § 1, cl. 4. But those instances in which length of residence could provide a legitimate basis for distinguishing one citizen from another are rare."

O'CONNOR, J., concurred: "A desire to compensate citizens for their prior contributions is neither inherently invidious nor irrational. Under some circum-

c. For the view that *Sosna* may be distinguished from *Shapiro* and *Maricopa* because of the absence of impermissible state "motivation," see Loewy, fn. a after *Shapiro,* at 38–39;

J. Morris Clark, *Legislative Motivation and Fundamental Rights in Constitutional Law,* 15 San Diego L.Rev. 953, 984–90 (1978).

stances, the objective may be wholly reasonable.[1] Even a generalized desire to reward citizens for past endurance, particularly in a State where years of hardship only recently have produced prosperity, is not innately improper. The difficulty is that plans enacted to further this objective necessarily treat new residents of a State less favorably than the longer-term residents who have past contributions to 'reward.' [Stripped] to its essentials, the plan denies non-Alaskans settling in the State the same privileges afforded longer-term residents. The Privileges and Immunities Clause of Article IV [addresses] just this type of discrimination.

"[I] believe [that] application of the Privileges and Immunities Clause to controversies involving the 'right to travel' would at least begin the task of reuniting this elusive right with the constitutional principles it embodies. [I] conclude that Alaska's disbursement scheme violates [the] Privileges and Immunities Clause" because there is nothing "to indicate that noncitizens constitute a peculiar source of the evil at which the statute is aimed" and no " 'substantial relationship' between the evil and the discrimination practiced against the noncitizens. *Hicklin v. Orbeck,* [Ch. 4, Sec. 4]."[d]

REHNQUIST, J., dissented: "[T]he illegitimacy of a State's recognizing past contributions of its citizens has been established by the Court only in certain cases considering an infringement of the right to travel, and the majority itself rightly declines to apply the strict scrutiny analysis of those right-to-travel cases. The distribution scheme at issue in this case impedes no person's right to travel to and settle in Alaska; if anything, the prospect of receiving annual cash dividends would encourage immigration to Alaska."

SAENZ v. ROE

526 U.S. 489, 119 S.Ct. 1518, 143 L.Ed.2d 689 (1999).

JUSTICE STEVENS delivered the opinion of the Court.

In 1992, California enacted a statute limiting the maximum welfare benefits available to newly arrived residents. The scheme limits the amount payable to a family that has resided in the State for less than 12 months to the amount payable by the State of the family's prior residence. The questions presented by this case are whether the 1992 statute was constitutional when it was enacted and, if not, whether an amendment to the Social Security Act enacted by Congress in 1996 affects that determination.

The word "travel" is not found in the text of the Constitution. Yet the "constitutional right to travel from one State to another" is firmly embedded in our jurisprudence. [In] *Shapiro*, we reviewed the constitutionality of three statuto-

---

1. A State, for example, might choose to divide its largesse among all persons who previously have contributed their time to volunteer community organizations. If the State graded its dividends according to the number of years devoted to prior community service, it could be said that the State intended "to reward citizens for past contributions." Alternatively, a State might enact a tax credit for citizens who contribute to the State's ecology by building alternative fuel sources or establishing recycling plants. If the State made this credit retroactive, to benefit those citizens who launched these improvements before they became fashionable, the State once again would

be rewarding past contributions. The Court's opinion would dismiss these objectives as wholly illegitimate. I would recognize them as valid goals and inquire only whether their implementation infringed any constitutionally protected interest.

d. For views generally supportive of O'Connor, J.'s analysis, see David Bogen, *The Privileges and Immunities Clause of Article IV,* 37 Case W.L.Rev. 794 (1987); Note, *State Parochialism, the Right to Travel, and the Privileges and Immunities Clause of Article IV,* 41 Stan. L.Rev. 1557 (1989).

ry provisions that denied welfare to residents of [states] who had resided within those respective jurisdictions less than one year immediately preceding their applications for assistance. Without pausing to identify the specific source of the right, we [squarely] held that it was "constitutionally impermissible" for a State to enact durational residency requirements for the purpose of inhibiting the migration by needy persons into the State. We further held that a classification that had the effect of imposing a penalty on the exercise of the right to travel violated the Equal Protection Clause "unless shown to be necessary to promote a compelling governmental interest" and that no such showing had been made. In this case, California argues that [its statute], unlike the legislation reviewed in *Shapiro*, [does] not penalize the right to travel because new arrivals are not ineligible for benefits during their first year of residence. California submits that, instead of being subjected to the strictest scrutiny, the statute should be upheld if it is supported by a rational basis and that the State's legitimate interest in saving over $10 million a year satisfies that test.

[The] "right to travel" discussed in our cases embraces at least three different components. It protects the right of a citizen of one State to enter and to leave another State, the right to be treated as a welcome visitor rather than an unfriendly alien when temporarily present in the second State, and, for those travelers who elect to become permanent residents, the right to be treated like other citizens of that State.* * *

What is at issue in this case [is the] third aspect of the right to travel—the right of the newly arrived citizen to the same privileges and immunities enjoyed by other citizens of the same State. That right is protected not only by the new arrival's status as a state citizen, but also by her status as a citizen of the United States. That additional source of protection is plainly identified in the opening words of the Fourteenth Amendment: "All persons born or naturalized in the United States, and subject to the jurisdiction thereof, are citizens of the United States and of the State wherein they reside. No state shall make or enforce any law which shall abridge the privileges or immunities of citizens of the United States."

Despite fundamentally differing views concerning the coverage of the Privileges or Immunities Clause of the Fourteenth Amendment, most notably expressed in the majority and dissenting opinions in the *Slaughter-House Cases*, it has always been common ground that this Clause protects the third component of the right to travel. Writing for the majority in the *Slaughter-House Cases*, Justice Miller explained that one of the privileges conferred by this Clause "is that a citizen of the United States can, of his own volition, become a citizen of any State of the Union by a bona fide residence therein, with the same rights as other citizens of that State." * * *

Neither mere rationality nor some intermediate standard of review should be used to judge the constitutionality of a state rule that discriminates against some of its citizens because they have been domiciled in the State for less than a year. The appropriate standard may be more categorical than that articulated in *Shapiro*, but it is surely no less strict. * * *

Because this case involves discrimination against citizens who have completed their interstate travel, this State's argument that its welfare scheme affects the right to travel only "incidentally" is beside the point. Were we concerned solely with actual deterrence of migration, we might be persuaded that a partial withholding of benefits constitutes a lesser incursion on the right to travel than an outright denial of all benefits. But since the right to travel embraces the citizen's right to be treated equally in her new State of residence, the discriminatory classification is itself a penalty.

It is undisputed that respondents and the members of the class that they represent are citizens of California and that their need for welfare benefits is unrelated to the length of time that they have resided in California. We thus have no occasion to consider what weight might be given to a citizen's length of residence if the bona fides of her claim to state citizenship were questioned. Moreover, because whatever benefits they receive will be consumed while they remain in California, there is no danger that recognition of their claim will encourage citizens of other States to establish residency for just long enough to acquire some readily portable benefit, such as a divorce or a college education, that will be enjoyed after they return to their original domicile. See, e.g., *Sosna*; *Vlandis v. Kline*.

Disavowing any desire to fence out the indigent, California has instead advanced an entirely fiscal justification for its [scheme]. The enforcement of [the statute] will save the State approximately $10.9 million a year. The question is not whether such saving is a legitimate purpose but whether the State may accomplish that end by the discriminatory means it has chosen. An evenhanded, across-the-board reduction of about 72 cents per month for every beneficiary would produce the same result. But our negative answer to the question does not rest on the weakness of the State's purported fiscal justification. It rests on the fact that the Citizenship Clause of the Fourteenth Amendment expressly equates citizenship with residence: "That Clause does not provide for, and does not allow for, degrees of citizenship based on length of residence." *Zobel*. Neither the duration of respondents' California residence, nor the identity of their prior States of residence, has any relevance to their need for benefits. Nor do those factors bear any relationship to the States's interest in making an equitable allocation of the funds to be distributed among its needy citizens. As in *Shapiro*, we reject any contributory rationale for the denial of benefits to new residents. [S]ee also *Zobel*. [In] short, the State's legitimate interest in saving money provides no justification for its decision to discriminate among equally eligible citizens.

The question that remains is whether congressional approval of durational residency requirements in the 1996 amendment to the Social Security Act somehow resuscitates the constitutionality of § 11450.03. That question is readily answered, for we have consistently held that Congress may not authorize the States to violate the Fourteenth Amendment.

REHNQUIST, C.J., joined by Thomas, J., dissented: The Court today breathes new life into the previously dormant Privileges or Immunities Clause of the Fourteenth Amendment—a Clause relied upon by this Court in only one other decision, *Colgate v. Harvey*, 296 U.S. 404, 56 S.Ct. 252, 80 L.Ed. 299 (1935), overruled five years later by *Madden v. Kentucky*, 309 U.S. 83, 60 S.Ct. 406, 84 L.Ed. 590 (1940). It uses this Clause to strike down what I believe is a reasonable measure falling under the head of a "good-faith residency requirement." Because I do not think any provision of the Constitution—and surely not a provision relied upon for only the second time since its enactment 130 years ago—requires this result, I dissent. * * *

I agree with the proposition that a "citizen of the United States can, of his own volition, become a citizen of any State of the Union by a bona fide residence therein, with the same rights as other citizens of that State." *Slaughter-House Cases*. But I cannot see how the right to become a citizen of another State is a necessary "component" of the right to travel, or why the Court tries to marry these separate and distinct rights. A person is no longer "traveling" in any sense of the word when he finishes his journey to a State which he plans to make his home. Indeed, under the Court's logic, the protections of the Privileges or Immunities Clause recognized in this case come into play only when an individual *stops* traveling with the intent to remain and become a citizen of a new State. [At] most, restrictions on an individual's right to become a citizen indirectly affect his calculus in deciding whether to exercise his right to travel in the first place, but such an attenuated and uncertain relationship is no ground for folding one right into the other.

No doubt the Court has, in the past 30 years, essentially conflated the right to travel with the right to equal state citizenship in striking down durational residence requirements similar to the one challenged here.* * *

The Court today tries to clear much of the underbrush created by these prior right-to-travel cases, abandoning its effort to define what residence requirements deprive individuals of "important rights and benefits" or "penalize" the right to travel. Under its new analytical framework, a State, outside certain ill-defined circumstances, cannot classify its citizens by the length of their residence in the State without offending the Privileges or Immunities Clause of the Fourteenth Amendment. The Court thus departs from *Shapiro* and its progeny, and, while paying lipservice to the right to travel, the Court does little to explain how the right to travel is involved at all. Instead, as the Court's analysis clearly demonstrates, this case is only about respondents' right to immediately enjoy all the privileges of being a California citizen in relation to that State's ability to test the good-faith assertion of this right. * * *

In unearthing from its tomb the right to become a state citizen and to be treated equally in the new State of residence, however, the Court ignores a State's need to assure that only persons who establish a bona fide residence receive the benefits provided to current residents of the State. [T]he Court has consistently recognized that while new citizens must have the same opportunity to enjoy the privileges of being a citizen of a State, the States retain the ability to use bona fide residence requirements to ferret out those who intend to take the privileges and run.* * *

If States can require individuals to reside in-state for a year before exercising the right to educational benefits, the right to terminate a marriage, or the right to vote in primary elections that all other state citizens enjoy, then States may surely do the same for welfare benefits. Indeed, there is no material difference between a 1–year residence requirement applied to the level of welfare benefits given out by a State, and the same requirement applied to the level of tuition subsidies at a state university. The welfare payment here and in-state tuition rates are cash subsidies provided to a limited class of people, and California's standard of living and higher education system make both subsidies quite attractive. Durational residence requirements were upheld when used to regulate the provision of higher education subsidies, and the same deference should be given in the case of welfare payments.

The Court today recognizes that States retain the ability to determine the bona fides of an individual's claim to residence, but then tries to avoid the issue. It asserts that because respondents' need for welfare benefits is unrelated to the length of time they have resided in California, it has "no occasion to consider what weight might be given to a citizen's length of residence if the bona fides of her claim to state citizenship were questioned." But I do not understand how the absence of a link between need and length of residency bears on the State's ability to objectively test respondents' resolve to stay in California. There is no link between the need for an education or for a divorce and the length of residence, and yet States may use length of residence as an objective yardstick to channel their benefits to those whose intent to stay is legitimate. * * *

The Court tries to distinguish education and divorce benefits by contending that the welfare payment here will be consumed in California, while a college education or a divorce produces benefits that are "portable" and can be enjoyed after individuals return to their original domicile. But this "you can't take it with you" distinction is more apparent than real, and offers little guidance to lower courts who must apply this rationale in the future. Welfare payments are a form of insurance, giving impoverished individuals and their families the means to meet the demands of daily life while they receive the necessary training, education, and time to look for a job. The cash itself will no doubt be spent in California, but the benefits from receiving this income and having the opportunity to become employed or employable will stick with the welfare recipient if they stay in California or go back to their true domicile. Similarly, tuition subsidies are "consumed" in-state but the recipient takes the benefits of a college education with him wherever he goes. A welfare subsidy is thus as much an investment in human capital as is a tuition subsidy, and their attendant benefits are just as "portable." More importantly, this foray into social economics demonstrates that the line drawn by the Court borders on the metaphysical, and requires lower courts to plumb the policies animating certain benefits like welfare to define their "essence" and hence their "portability." * * *

I therefore believe that the durational residence requirement challenged here is a permissible exercise of the State's power to "assur[e] that services provided for its residents are enjoyed only by residents."

JUSTICE THOMAS, with whom THE CHIEF JUSTICE joins, dissenting.

Unlike the Equal Protection and Due Process Clauses, which have assumed near-talismanic status in modern constitutional law, the Court all but read the Privileges or Immunities Clause out of the Constitution in the *Slaughter-House Cases*. * * *

Unlike the majority, I would look to history to ascertain the original meaning of the Clause. At least in American law, the phrase (or its close approximation) appears to stem from the 1606 Charter of Virginia, which provided that "all and every the Persons being our Subjects, which shall dwell and inhabit within every or any of the said several Colonies [shall] HAVE and enjoy all Liberties, Franchises, and Immunities [as] if they had been abiding and born, within this our Realme of England." [The] colonists' repeated assertions that they maintained the rights, privileges and immunities of persons "born within the realm of England" and "natural born" persons suggests that, at the time of the founding, the terms "privileges" and "immunities" (and their counterparts) were understood to refer to those fundamental rights and liberties specifically enjoyed by English citizens, and more broadly, by all persons. [Justice] Bushrod Washington's landmark opinion in *Corfield v. Coryell* reflects this historical understanding. [Justice] Washington's opinion in *Corfield* indisputably influenced the Members of Congress who enacted the Fourteenth Amendment. When Congress gathered to debate the Fourteenth Amendment, members frequently, if not as a matter of course, appealed to *Corfield,* arguing that the Amendment was necessary to guarantee the fundamental rights that Justice Washington identified in his opinion. * * *

That Members of the 39th Congress appear to have endorsed the wisdom of Justice Washington's opinion does not, standing alone, provide dispositive insight into their understanding of the Fourteenth Amendment's Privileges or Immunities Clause. Nevertheless, their repeated references to the *Corfield* decision, combined with what appears to be the historical understanding of the Clause's operative terms, supports the inference that, at the time the Fourteenth Amendment was adopted, people understood that "privileges or immunities of citizens" were fundamental rights, rather than every public benefit established by positive law. Accordingly, the majority's conclusion—that a State violates the Privileges or Immunities Clause when it "discriminates" against citizens who have been domiciled in the State for less than a year in the distribution of welfare benefit—appears contrary to the original understanding and is dubious at best.

As The Chief Justice points out, it comes as quite a surprise that the majority relies on the Privileges or Immunities Clause at all in this case. [Although] the majority appears to breathe new life into the Clause today, it fails to address its historical underpinnings or its place in our constitutional jurisprudence. Because I believe that the demise of the Privileges or Immunities Clause has contributed in no small part to the current disarray of our Fourteenth Amendment jurisprudence, I would be open to reevaluating its meaning in an appropriate case. Before invoking the Clause, however, we should endeavor to understand what the framers of the Fourteenth Amendment thought that it meant. We should also consider whether the Clause should displace, rather than augment, portions of our equal protection and substantive due process jurisprudence. The majority's failure to consider these important questions raises the specter that the Privileges or Immunities Clause will become yet another convenient tool for inventing new rights, limited solely by the "predilections of those who happen at the time to be Members of this Court."

Notes and Questions

1. *Relationship to Shapiro.* Consider Laurence H. Tribe, *Saenz Sans Prophecy: Does the Privileges or Immunities Revival Portend the Future—Or Reveal the Structure of the Present?*, 113 Harv. L.Rev. 110, 125–26, 154, 198 (1999): "*Saenz* cannot be understood as a simple corollary of *Shapiro* and its progeny. Rather, it appears to represent a new generation of constitutional ideas altogether. [The] holding of *Saenz* reflected the Court's vision of governmental design in a federal union of equal states, and not primarily the Court's perception of a personal right ineluctably flowing from constitutional text or deeply rooted tradition. [The] component of the right to travel confirmed in *Saenz* involved the elaboration of a structural principle of equal citizenship more than the protection of an individual right. [*Saenz*] revealed a Court far more comfortable protecting rights that it can describe in architectural terms, especially in terms of federalism, than it is protecting rights that present themselves as spheres of personal autonomy or dimensions of constitutionally mandated equality."[a]

2. *Rule of decision.* Consider Roderick M. Hills, Jr., *Poverty, Residency, and Federalism: States' Duty of Impartiality Toward Newcomers*, 1999 Sup.Ct.Rev. 277, 279–80, 282, 331, arguing that *Saenz* reflects a nondiscrimination theory:

---

a. See also Mark Tushnet, *The New Constitutional Order and the Chastening of Constitutional Aspiration*, 113 Harv.L.Rev. 29, 106 (1999): "[T]he Court's reliance on the Privileges or Immunities Clause allowed the Court simultaneously to connect itself to the *outcome* reached by the Warren Court in *Shapiro* and distance itself from the Warren Court's *doctrine.*"

"[O]nce a new resident demonstrates that he or she is a bona fide resident, then states are categorically barred from drawing distinctions that burden the new resident based on length of residence." Professor Hills disagrees with this approach. According to him, states may be reluctant to expend their resources creating costly public goods such as public university systems if they must share those goods on an equal basis with temporary residents who may come just to enjoy those goods—as the Court appears to recognize in its discussion of "portability." Yet, writes Hills: "*Saenz* reaches the right result for the wrong reason. California's discrimination [is] suspect because it involves discrimination in a means-tested redistributive program—welfare benefits. This sort of discrimination against indigent newcomers is suspect because, unlike restrictions on divorce decrees or college education, it is likely to be rooted in cultural animosity rather than fiscal self-defense. Such cultural animosity is impermissible [because it is] so threatening to our sense of national citizenship. [The] argument against durational residence requirements for welfare is not an argument that classifications burdening the indigent are generally constitutionally suspect. Rather, [the] Fourteenth Amendment prohibits all durational residence requirements designed to maintain the current demographic character of the state against what the current population regards as socially undesirable migrants."

3. *Privileges or immunities rationale.* What is the significance of the Court's reliance on the long dormant privileges or immunities clause? Consider Kevin Newsom, *Setting Incorporationism Straight: A Re-interpretation of the Slaughter–House Cases*, 109 Yale L.J. 643, 744 (2000): "[*Saenz*] indicates that the Court might be poised to reevaluate the role of the Privileges or Immunities Clause in our constitutional system." Compare Tribe, supra, at 197–98: "Even as one who has long advocated overruling the *Slaughter-House Cases* and taking up the cudgels of privileges or immunities, [I] am hard-pressed to read nearly so much significance into *Saenz*. Ours is [an] era of largely unexamined preferences for [structure-based constitutional interpretation, as in a number of cases and doctrines protecting constitutional federalism]. I see *Saenz* more as a monument to that truth than as a herald of a new dawn in constitutional doctrine."

III. ACCESS TO THE COURTS

GRIFFIN v. ILLINOIS, 351 U.S. 12, 76 S.Ct. 585, 100 L.Ed. 891 (1956), held that a state must furnish an indigent criminal defendant with a free trial transcript (or its equivalent) if it were necessary for "adequate and effective appellate review" of the conviction. BLACK, J., joined by Warren, C.J.,and Douglas and Clark, JJ., found that "both equal protection and due process emphasize [that in] criminal trials a state can no more discriminate on account of poverty than on account of religion, race, or color. Plainly the ability to pay costs in advance bears no rational relationship to a defendant's guilt or innocence and could not be used as an excuse to deprive a defendant of a fair trial. [It] is true that a state is not required by the federal constitution to provide appellate [review]. See., e.g., *McKane v. Durston*, 153 U.S. 684, 687–88, 14 S.Ct. 913, 914–15, 38 L.Ed. 867 (1894). But that is not to say that a state that does grant appellate review can do so in a way that discriminates against some convicted defendants on account of their poverty. * * *

"All of the States now provide some method of appeal from criminal convictions, recognizing the importance of appellate review to a correct adjudication of guilt or innocence. [Thus] to deny adequate review to the poor means that many of them may lose their life, liberty or property because of unjust convictions which appellate courts would set aside. [There] can be no equal justice where the kind of trial a man gets depends on the amount of money he has."[a]

———

DOUGLAS v. CALIFORNIA, 372 U.S. 353, 83 S.Ct. 814, 9 L.Ed.2d 811 (1963), per DOUGLAS, J., relying on *Griffin*, held that a state must appoint counsel for an indigent for "the first appeal, granted as a matter of [statutory right] from a criminal conviction." It disapproved California's system of appointing counsel only when the appellate court made "an independent investigation of the record and determine[d] it would be of advantage to the defendant or helpful to [the] Court": [A] state can, consistently with the fourteenth amendment, provide for differences so long as the result does not amount to a denial of due process or an 'invidious discrimination.' Absolute equality is not [required]. But where the merits of the one and only appeal an indigent has as of right are decided without benefit of counsel, we think an unconstitutional line has been drawn between rich and poor.

"When an indigent is forced to run this gantlet of a preliminary showing of merit, the right to appeal does not comport with fair procedure. [There] is lacking that equality demanded by the Fourteenth Amendment where the rich man, who appeals as of right, enjoys the benefit of counsel's examination into the record, research of the law, and marshalling of arguments on his behalf, while the indigent, already burdened by a preliminary determination that his case is without merit, is forced to shift for himself. The indigent, where the record is unclear or the errors are hidden, has only the right to a meaningless ritual, while the rich man has a meaningful appeal."

HARLAN, J., joined by Stewart, J., dissented from the Court's reliance, as in *Griffin*, "on a blend of the Equal Protection and Due Process Clauses," believing that "this case should be judged solely under the Due Process Clause": "States, of course, are prohibited by the Equal Protection Clause from discriminating between 'rich' and 'poor' *as such* in the formulation and application of their laws. But it is a far different thing to suggest that this provision prevents the State from adopting a law of general applicability that may affect the poor more harshly than it does the rich, or, on the other hand, from making some effort to redress economic imbalances while not eliminating them entirely.

"Every financial exaction which the State imposes on a uniform basis is more easily satisfied by the well-to-do than by the indigent. Yet I take it that no one would dispute the constitutional power of the State to levy a uniform sales tax, to charge tuition at a state university, to fix rates for the purchase of water from a municipal corporation, to impose a standard fine for criminal violations, or to establish minimum bail for various categories of offenses. Nor could it be contended that the State may not classify as crimes acts which the poor are more likely to commit than are the rich. And surely, there would be no basis for attacking a state law which provided benefits for the needy simply because those benefits fell short of the goods or services that others could purchase for themselves.

"Laws such as these do not deny equal protection to the less fortunate for one essential reason: the Equal Protection Clause does not impose on the States 'an affirmative duty to lift the handicaps flowing from differences in economic

a. Frankfurter, J., concurred in the result. Burton, Minton, Reed and Harlan, JJ., dissented. For analysis of *Griffin*, see Michael Klarman, *An Interpretive History of Modern Equal Protection*, 90 Mich.L.Rev. 213, 265–67 (1991).

circumstances." To so construe it would be to read into the Constitution a philosophy of leveling that would be foreign to many of our basic concepts of the proper relations between government and society. [N]o matter how far the state rule might go in providing counsel for indigents, it could never be expected to satisfy an affirmative duty—if one existed—to place the poor on the same level as those who can afford the best legal talent available."

As for due process, "we have today held [that] there is an absolute right to the services of counsel at trial. *Gideon v. Wainwright,* 372 U.S. 335, 83 S.Ct. 792, 9 L.Ed.2d 799 (1963). But [a]ppellate review is in itself not required by the Fourteenth Amendment, [and] thus the question presented is the narrow one whether the State's rules with respect to the appointment of counsel are so arbitrary or unreasonable, *in the context of the particular appellate procedure that it has established,* as to require their invalidation." Clark, J., also dissented.

ROSS v. MOFFITT, 417 U.S. 600, 94 S.Ct. 2437, 41 L.Ed.2d 341 (1974), per REHNQUIST, J., held that *Douglas* does not require counsel for discretionary state appeals or for applications for review in the Supreme Court: "[The] duty of the State under our cases is not to duplicate the legal arsenal that may be privately retained by a criminal defendant, [but] only to assure the indigent defendant an adequate opportunity to present his claims fairly in the context of the State's appellate [process]."

DOUGLAS, J., joined by Brennan and Marshall, JJ., dissented: "The right to discretionary review is a substantial one, and one where a lawyer can be of significant assistance to an indigent defendant. It was correctly perceived below that the 'same concepts of fairness and equality, which require counsel in a first appeal of right, require counsel in other and subsequent discretionary appeals.'"

M.L.B. v. S.L.J.

519 U.S. 102, 117 S.Ct. 555, 136 L.Ed.2d 473 (1996).

JUSTICE GINSBURG delivered the opinion of the Court.

[A Mississippi chancery court terminated M.L.B.'s parental rights to her two young children. M.L.B. tried to appeal, but Mississippi required that she pay record preparation fees of $2,352.36 in advance. She could not afford to do so, and her appeal was dismissed.]

[Concerning] access to appeal in general, and transcripts needed to pursue appeals in particular, *Griffin* is the foundation case. [The] *Griffin* principle * * * "is a flat prohibition" against "making access to appellate processes from even [the State's] most inferior courts depend upon the [convicted] defendant's ability to pay."

[We] have also recognized a narrow category of civil cases in which the State must provide access to its judicial processes without regard to a party's ability to pay fees. In *Boddie v. Connecticut,* 401 U.S. 371, 91 S.Ct. 780, 28 L.Ed.2d 113 (1971), we held that the State could not deny a divorce to a married couple based on their inability to pay approximately $60 in court costs.[b] [Soon after *Boddie,*] in

---

b. In *Boddie,* the Court reasoned: "[M]arriage involves interests of basic importance in our society. [Without] a prior judicial imprima- tur, individuals may freely enter into and re- scind commercial contracts, for example, but we are unaware of any jurisdiction where pri-

United States v. Kras, 409 U.S. 434, 93 S.Ct. 631, 34 L.Ed.2d 626 (1973), the Court clarified that a constitutional requirement to waive court fees in civil cases is the exception, not the rule, [and approved] fees, totaling $50, required to secure a discharge in bankruptcy. *Ortwein v. Schwab*, 410 U.S. 656, 93 S.Ct. 1172, 35 L.Ed.2d 572 (1973) [adhered] to the line drawn in *Kras* [and rejected a challenge to] an Oregon statute requiring appellants in civil cases to pay a $25 fee. [A]s *Ortwein* underscored, this Court has not extended *Griffin* to the broad array of civil cases. But tellingly, the Court has consistently set apart from the mine run of cases those involving state controls or intrusions on family relationships. [The Court here cited and discussed what it described as the "two prior decisions most immediately in point": *Lassiter v. Department of Social Servs.*, 452 U.S. 18, 101 S.Ct. 2153, 68 L.Ed.2d 640 (1981), which held that indigents involved in proceedings aimed at the termination of parental rights were entitled to a case-by-case determination of their need for appointed counsel, and *Santosky v. Kramer*, 455 U.S. 745, 102 S.Ct. 1388, 71 L.Ed.2d 599 (1982), which held that an elevated standard of proof is constitutionally required in parental termination proceedings.]

[The] Court's decisions concerning access to judicial processes [reflect] both equal protection and due process concerns. [The] equal protection concern relates to the legitimacy of fencing out would-be appellants based solely on their inability to pay core costs. The due process concern hones in on the essential fairness of the state-ordered proceedings anterior to adverse state action. [Nevertheless], "[m]ost decisions in this area," we have recognized, "res[t] on an equal protection framework," [for due] process does not independently require that the State provide an appeal.

[Unlike *Washington v. Davis*,] the Mississippi prescription here at issue [is] not merely *disproportionate* in impact. Rather [it is] wholly contingent on one's ability to pay, and thus "visi[ts] different consequences on two categories of persons;" [it applies] to all indigents and do[es] not reach anyone outside that class. In sum, under [a broad] reading of *Washington v. Davis*, our overruling of the *Griffin* line of cases would be two decades overdue. It suffices to point out that this Court has not so conceived the meaning and effect of our 1976 "disproportionate impact precedent."

Respondents and the dissenters urge that we will open floodgates if we do not rigidly restrict *Griffin* to cases typed "criminal." But we have repeatedly noticed what sets parental status termination decrees apart from [the] mine run [of] civil actions, even from other domestic relations matters such as divorce, paternity, and child custody. To recapitulate, termination decrees "wor[k] a unique kind of deprivation." In contrast to matters modifiable at the parties' will or based on changed circumstances, termination adjudications involve the awesome authority of the State "to destroy permanently all legal recognition of the parental relationship." Our [decisions], recognizing that parental termination decrees are among

vate citizens may covenant for or dissolve marriages without state approval. [Due] process requires, at a minimum, that absent a countervailing state interest of overriding significance, persons forced to settle their claims of right and duty through the judicial process must be given a meaningful opportunity to be heard."

c. *Kras* noted the difference between proceedings involving bankruptcy and marriage: "[A] debtor, in theory, and often in actuality, may adjust his debts by negotiated agreement with his creditors. [Thus,] *Boddie*'s emphasis

on judicial exclusivity finds no counterpart in the bankrupt's situation." Moreover, unlike free speech or marriage, bankruptcy is not a "fundamental right." Stewart, J., dissented: "[In] the unique situation of the indigent bankrupt the government provides the only effective means of his ever being free of these government imposed obligations. [The] Court today holds that Congress may say that some of the poor are too poor even to go bankrupt."

the most severe forms of state action have not served as precedent in other areas. We are therefore satisfied that the label "civil" should not entice us to leave undisturbed the Mississippi courts' disposition of this case.

For the reasons stated, we hold that Mississippi may not withhold from M.L.B. "a 'record of sufficient completeness' to permit proper [appellate] consideration of [her] claims."[a]

THOMAS, J., joined by Scalia, J., and Rehnquist, C.J., in part, dissented: Today the majority holds that the Fourteenth Amendment requires Mississippi to afford petitioner a free transcript because her civil case involves a "fundamental" right. The majority seeks to limit the reach of its holding to the type of case we confront here, one involving the termination of parental rights. I do not think, however, that the new-found constitutional right to free transcripts in civil appeals can be effectively restricted to this case. The inevitable consequences will be greater demands on the States to provide free assistance to would-be appellants in all manner of civil cases involving interests that cannot, based on the test established by the majority, be distinguished from the admittedly important interest at issue here.

[I] do not think the equal protection theory underlying the *Griffin* line of cases remains viable. [The lesson of *Washington v. Davis*] is that the Equal Protection Clause shields only against purposeful discrimination: A disparate impact, even upon members of a racial minority, [does] not violate equal protection. The Clause is not a panacea for perceived social or economic inequality; it seeks to "guarante[e] equal laws, not equal results."

[M.L.B.] defended against the "destruction of her family bonds" in the Chancery Court hearing at which she was accorded all the process this Court has required of the States in parental termination cases. She now desires "state aid to subsidize [her] privately initiated" appeal—an appeal that neither petitioner nor the majority claims Mississippi is required to provide—to overturn the determination that resulted from that hearing. I see no principled difference between a facially neutral rule that serves in some cases to prevent persons from availing themselves of state employment, or a state-funded education, or a state-funded abortion—each of which the State may, but is not required to, provide—and a facially neutral rule that prevents a person from taking an appeal that is available only because the State chooses to provide it.[1]

The *Griffin* line of cases ascribed to—one might say announced—an equalizing notion of the Equal Protection Clause that would, I think, have startled the Fourteenth Amendment's Framers. In those cases, the Court did not find, nor did it seek, any purposeful discrimination on the part of the state defendants. That their statutes had disproportionate effect on poor persons was sufficient for us to find a constitutional violation. In *Davis,* among other cases, we began to recognize the potential mischief of a disparate impact theory writ large, and endeavored to contain it. In this case, I would continue that enterprise. Mississippi's requirement of prepaid transcripts in civil appeals seeking to contest the sufficiency of the evidence adduced at trial is facially neutral; it creates no classification. The

a. Kennedy, J., concurring, would have rested on the due process clause "given the existing appellate structure in Mississippi" though he also observed that "the authorities do not hold that an appeal is required even in a criminal case."

1. *Harper* struck down a poll tax that directly restricted the exercise of a right found in that case to be fundamental—the right to vote in state elections. The fee that M.L.B. is unable to pay does not prevent the exercise of a fundamental right directly: The fundamental interest identified by the majority is not the right to a civil appeal, it is rather the right to maintain the parental relationship.

transcript rule reasonably obliges would-be appellants to bear the costs of availing themselves of a service that the State chooses, but is not constitutionally required, to provide. Any adverse impact that the transcript requirement has on any person seeking to appeal arises not out of the State's action, but out of factors entirely unrelated to it.[b]

Notes and Questions

1. *Distinctions among access cases.* Has the Court successfully distinguished cases in which the Constitution mandates assistance to indigents seeking access to the courts from those in which it does not?

2. *Relation to Washington v. Davis.* Is Thomas, J., correct that *M.L.B.* is inconsistent with *Davis*? Consider Note, *Disparate Impact on Death Row: M.L.B. and the Indigent's Right to Counsel at Capital State Postconviction Proceedings*, 107 Yale L.J. 2211, 2229 (1998): "For the first time in twenty years, a majority of the Court has limited *Davis*'s discriminatory purpose requirement. [The] Court should [extend its rationale] to recognize a fundamental rights exception to *Davis*[]."

May a state require indigents to pay a marriage license fee? Require a "court access fee" of an indigent plaintiff who seeks to enjoin an ordinance allegedly violating first amendment rights? May a public hospital deny abortions to indigents who cannot pay the established service charge? Cf. *Maher v. Roe*, Part V infra.

3. *Due process or equal protection?* Consider Richard H. Fallon, Jr., *Implementing the Constitution*, 111 Harv.L.Rev. 54, 116, 117 (1997): "*M.L.B.* stands as a paradigmatic example of what Professor Sunstein calls judicial minimalism: the opinion is 'incompletely theorized' in at least one sense, and probably in two. First, the opinion offers no broad theory of either due process or equal protection. Second, it is quite likely that at least some of the Justices constituting the majority were themselves uncertain how to give a deep, principled account of why the judgment was correct. [The] Justices obviously believe that a shallow justification [of a Court decision] in terms of precedent at least sometimes satisfies their obligation of fidelity to the Constitution. [But] when the Court's majority declines a dissenting opinion's express challenge to justify its decision at a deeper level, it refuses to accept the full discipline of articulate justification that helps to support the legitimacy of judicial review."

1970's: Ct. began to draw back from creating Fund. rights.

IV. WELFARE AND EDUCATION

DANDRIDGE v. WILLIAMS, 397 U.S. 471, 90 S.Ct. 1153, 25 L.Ed.2d 491 (1970): Maryland's Aid to Families With Dependent Children Program gave most eligible families their computed "standard of need," but imposed a "maximum limitation" on the total amount any family could receive. The Court, per STEWART, J., held that the statutory ceiling did not violate equal protection: "[H]ere we deal with state regulation in the social and economic field, not affecting freedoms guaranteed by the Bill of Rights, and claimed to violate the fourteenth amendment only because the regulation results in some disparity in grants of welfare

Max. Amount on benefits to poor Families

#not Fund. upheld

b. In another section of his opinion, Thomas, J., argued that he would overrule *Griffin* in a proper case, but would, in any event, confine *Griffin* to criminal cases. Rehnquist, C.J., did not join that section of the opinion.

Legislative problem – LUS? const'l problem ⟹ not judices sice problem to Solve

Just because 2nd law does not mean UnConst.

payments to the largest AFDC families.[16] In [this area] a state does not violate [equal protection] merely because the classifications made by its laws are imperfect." "It is enough that the state's action be rationally based and free from invidious discrimination."

"To be sure, [many cases] enunciating this [standard] have in the main involved state regulation of business or industry. The administration of public welfare assistance, by contrast, involves the most basic economic needs of impoverished human beings, [but] we can find no basis for applying a different constitutional standard. [By] combining a limit on the recipient's grant with permission to retain money earned, without reduction in the amount of the grant, Maryland provides an incentive to seek gainful employment. And by keeping the maximum family AFDC grants to the minimum wage a steadily employed head of a household receives, the State maintains some semblance of an equitable balance between families on welfare and those supported by an employed breadwinner.

"It is true that in some AFDC families there may be no person who is employable. It is also true that with respect to AFDC families whose determined standard of need is below the regulatory maximum, [the] employment incentive is absent. But the Equal Protection Clause does not require that a State must choose between attacking every aspect of a problem or not attacking the problem at all. [T]he intractable economic, social, and even philosophical problems presented by public welfare assistance programs are not the business of this Court."[a]

MARSHALL, J., joined by Brennan, J., dissented:[b] "[T]he only distinction between those children with respect to whom assistance is granted and those [denied] is the size of the family into which the child permits himself to be born. [This] is grossly underinclusive in terms of the class which the AFDC program was designed to assist, namely *all* needy dependent children, [and requires] a persuasive justification * * *.

"The Court never undertakes to inquire for such a justification; rather it avoids the task by focusing upon the abstract dichotomy between two different approaches to equal protection problems which have been utilized by this Court.

"[The] cases relied on by the Court, in which a 'mere rationality' test was actually used, [involve] regulation of business interests. The extremes to which the Court has gone in dreaming up rational bases for state regulation in that area may in many instances be ascribed to a healthy revulsion from the Court's earlier excesses in using the Constitution to protect interests which have more than enough power to protect themselves in the legislative halls. This case, involving the literally vital interests of a powerless minority—poor families without breadwinners—is far removed from the area of business regulation, as the Court concedes. * * *

"In my view, equal protection analysis of this case is not appreciably advanced by the a priori definition of a 'right,' fundamental [and thus invoking the 'compelling' interest test] or otherwise.[14] Rather, concentration must be placed

16. Cf. *Shapiro*, where, by contrast, the Court found state interference with the constitutionally protected freedom of interstate travel.

a. See also *Lindsey v. Normet*, 405 U.S. 56, 92 S.Ct. 862, 31 L.Ed.2d 36 (1972) (the assurance of adequate housing is not a fundamental right).

b. Douglas, J., dissented on the ground (agreed to also by Marshall and Brennan, JJ.) that the Maryland law was inconsistent with the Social Security Act.

14. [T]he Court's insistence that equal protection analysis turns on the basis of a closed category of "fundamental rights" involves a curious value judgment. It is certainly difficult to believe that a person whose very survival is

Classification:
-Relative importance of interest to Individual
-State interest in denying

* Sliding Scale for E.P

Strict Scrutiny vs. Rational basis b/c: world is not clearly divided

upon the character of the classification in question, the relative importance to individuals in the class discriminated against of the governmental benefits which they do not receive, and the asserted state interests in support of the classification. * * *

"It is the individual interests here [that] most clearly distinguish this case from the 'business regulation' [cases]. AFDC support to needy dependent children provides the stuff which sustains those children's lives: food, clothing, shelter. And this Court has already recognized [that] when a benefit, even a 'gratuitous' benefit, is necessary to sustain life, stricter constitutional standards, both procedural[17] and substantive,[18] are applied to the deprivation of that benefit.

"Nor is the distinction upon which the deprivation is here based—the distinction between large and small families—one which readily commends [itself]. Indeed, governmental discrimination between children on the basis of a factor over which they have no control [bears] some resemblance to the classification between legitimate and illegitimate children which we condemned [in cases discussed in Sec. 4, II supra]."

On examination, the asserted state interests were either "arbitrary," impermissible, of "minimum rationality," "drastically overinclusive," or "grossly underinclusive." "The existence of [other] alternatives [to satisfy asserted state interests] does not, of course, conclusively establish the invalidity of the maximum grant regulation. It is certainly relevant, however, in appraising the overall interest of the State in the maintenance of the regulation [against] a fundamental constitutional challenge."

SAN ANTONIO IND. SCHOOL DIST. v. RODRIGUEZ

411 U.S. 1, 93 S.Ct. 1278, 36 L.Ed.2d 16 (1973).

JUSTICE POWELL delivered the opinion of the Court.

This suit attacking the Texas system of financing public education was initiated by Mexican–American parents [as] a class action on behalf of school children throughout the State who are members of minority groups or who are poor and reside in school districts having a low property tax base. * * *

Recognizing the need for increased state funding to help offset disparities in local spending [because of sizable differences in the value of assessable property between local school districts,] the state legislature [established the] Minimum Foundation School Program [which] accounts for approximately half of the total educational expenditures in Texas. [It] calls for state and local contributions to a fund earmarked specifically for teacher salaries, operating expenses, and transportation costs. The State [finances] approximately [80%]. The districts' share, known as the Local Fund Assignment, is apportioned among the school districts under a formula designed to reflect each district's relative taxpaying ability. * * *

The school district in which appellees reside, [Edgewood,] has been compared throughout this litigation with the Alamo Heights [District. Edgewood] is situated

at stake would be comforted by the knowledge that his "fundamental" rights are preserved intact. * * *

17. See *Goldberg v. Kelly*.

18. [See] *Kirk v. Board of Regents*, 273 Cal.App.2d 430, 440–441, 78 Cal.Rptr. 260, 266–267 (1969), appeal dismissed, 396 U.S. 554 (1970), upholding a one-year residency requirement for tuition-free graduate education at state university, and distinguishing *Shapiro* on the ground that it "involved the immediate and pressing need for preservation of life and health of persons unable to live without public assistance, and their dependent children."

in the core-city sector of San Antonio in a residential neighborhood that has little
commercial or industrial property. [A]pproximately 90% of the student population
is Mexican-American and over 6% is Negro. The average assessed property value
per pupil is $5,960—the lowest in the metropolitan area—and the median family
income ($4,686) is also the lowest. At an equalized tax rate of $1.05 per $100 of
assessed property—the highest in the metropolitan area—the district contributed
$26 to the education of each child for the 1967–1968 school year above its Local
Fund Assignment for the Minimum Foundation Program. The Foundation Program contributed $222 per pupil for a state-local total of $248. Federal funds
added another $108 for a total of $356 per pupil.

Alamo Heights is the most affluent school district in San Antonio. [Its] school
population [has] only 18% Mexican-Americans and less than 1% Negroes. The
assessed property value per pupil exceeds $49,000 and the median family income
is $8,001. In 1967–1968 the local tax rate of $.85 per $100 of valuation yielded
$333 per pupil over and above its contribution to the Foundation Program.
Coupled with the $225 provided from that Program, the district was able to supply
$558 per student. Supplemented by a $36 per pupil grant from federal sources,
Alamo Heights spent $594 per pupil.

[M]ore recent partial statistics indicate that [the] trend of increasing state aid
has been significant. For the 1970–1971 school year, the Foundation School
Program allotment for Edgewood was $356 per [pupil and] Alamo Heights
[received] $491 per [pupil].[35] These recent figures also reveal the extent to which
these two districts' allotments were funded from their own required contributions
to the Local Fund Assignment. Alamo Heights, because of its relative wealth, was
required to contribute out of its local property tax collections approximately $100
per pupil, or about 20% of its Foundation grant. Edgewood, on the other hand,
paid only $8.46 per pupil, which is about 2.4% of its grant. [Finding] that wealth is
a "suspect" classification and that education is a "fundamental" interest, the
District Court held that the Texas system could be sustained only if the State
could show that it was premised upon some compelling state interest. * * *

II. [The] wealth discrimination discovered [is] quite unlike any of the forms
of wealth discrimination heretofore reviewed by this Court. [The] individuals who
constituted the class discriminated against in our prior cases shared two distinguishing characteristics: because of their impecunity they were completely unable
to pay for some desired benefit, and as a consequence, they sustained an absolute
deprivation of a meaningful opportunity to enjoy that benefit. [For example,]
Douglas v. California [provides] no relief for those on whom the burdens of paying
for a criminal defense are, relatively speaking, great but not insurmountable. Nor
does it deal with relative differences in the quality of counsel acquired by the less
wealthy.

[Neither] of the two distinguishing characteristics of wealth classifications can
be found here. First, [there] is reason to believe that the poorest families are not

---

35. [I]t is apparent that Alamo Heights has
enjoyed a larger gain [due] to the emphasis in
the State's allocation formula on the guaranteed minimum salaries for teachers. Higher
salaries are guaranteed to teachers having
more years of experience and possessing more
advanced degrees. Therefore, Alamo Heights,
which has a greater percentage of experienced
personnel with advanced degrees, receives
more State support. * * * Because more dollars have been given to districts that already
spend more per pupil, such Foundation formulas have been described as "anti-equalizing."
The formula, however, is anti-equalizing only if
viewed in absolute terms. The percentage disparity between the two Texas districts is diminished substantially by State aid. Alamo
Heights derived in 1967–1968 almost 13 times
as much money from local taxes as Edgewood
did. The State aid grants to each district in
1970–1971 lowered the ratio to approximately
two to [one].

*[handwritten top margin: how do you determine meaningful? – Outcomes – employment – add'l education –Input = # – testing :teacher audits :class size :curriculum * very difficult to create a standard]*

[handwritten left margin: rejection?]

necessarily clustered in the poorest property districts. A [recent] Connecticut study found, not surprisingly, that the poor were clustered around commercial and industrial areas—those same areas that provide the most attractive sources of property tax income for school districts. * * *

Second, [lack] of personal resources has not occasioned an absolute deprivation of the desired benefit. The argument here is not that the children [are] receiving no public education; rather, it is that they are receiving a poorer quality education [than] children in districts having more assessable wealth. [A] sufficient answer to appellees' argument is that at least where wealth is involved the Equal Protection Clause does not require absolute equality or precisely equal advantages. [Texas] asserts that the Minimum Foundation Program provides an "adequate" education for all children in the State. [No] proof was offered at trial persuasively discrediting or refuting the State's assertion. * * *[60]

[Appellees] sought to prove that a direct correlation exists between the wealth of families within each district and the expenditures therein for education. [But] appellees' proof [fails].

This brings us [to] the third way in which the classification scheme might be defined—*district* wealth discrimination. Since the only correlation indicated by the evidence is between district property wealth and expenditures, it may be argued that discrimination might be found without regard to the individual income characteristics of district residents. * * *

However described, it is clear that appellees' suit asks this Court to extend its most exacting scrutiny to review a system that allegedly discriminates against a large, diverse, and amorphous class, unified only by the common factor of residence in districts that happen to have less taxable wealth than other districts. The system of alleged discrimination and the class it defines have none of the traditional indicia of suspectness: the class is not saddled with such disabilities, or subjected to such a history of purposeful unequal treatment, or relegated to such a position of political powerlessness as to command extraordinary protection from the majoritarian political process.

We thus conclude that the Texas system does not operate to the peculiar disadvantage of any suspect class. But [recognizing] that this Court has never heretofore held that wealth discrimination alone provides an adequate basis for invoking strict scrutiny, appellees [also] assert that the State's system impermissibly interferes with the exercise of a "fundamental" right [requiring] the strict standard of judicial review. * * *

Nothing this Court holds today in any way detracts from our historic dedication to public education. [But] the importance of a service performed by the State does not determine whether it must be regarded as fundamental for purposes of examination under the Equal Protection Clause. [In *Shapiro*, the] right to interstate travel had long been recognized as a right of constitutional significance, and the Court's decision therefore did not require an ad hoc determination as to the social or economic importance of that right. [*Dandridge*] firmly reiterates that social importance is not the critical determinant for subjecting state legislation to strict scrutiny. * * *

[handwritten right margin: • what is a fund. right for E.P. purposes • just because important not nece. fund. • Is right to educ. granted in Constn.]

60. [If] elementary and secondary education were made available by the State only to those able to pay a tuition assessed against each pupil, there would be a clearly defined class of "poor" people—definable in terms of their inability to pay the prescribed sum—who would be absolutely precluded from receiving an education. That case would present a far more compelling set of circumstances for judicial assistance than [this one].

*[handwritten bottom margin: What about college? or is this FN only limited to elementary educ * what is he talking about?]*

The lesson of these cases [is that it] is not the province of this Court to create substantive constitutional rights in the name of guaranteeing equal protection of the laws. Thus the key to discovering whether education is "fundamental" is not to be found in comparisons of the relative societal significance of education as opposed to subsistence or housing [or] by weighing whether education is as important as the right to travel. Rather, the answer lies in assessing whether there is a right to education explicitly or implicitly guaranteed by the Constitution. *Dunn;*[74] *Skinner.*[76]

Education, of course, is not among the rights afforded explicit protection under [the] Constitution. Nor do we find any basis for saying it is implicitly so protected. [But] appellees [contend] that education is distinguishable from other services and benefits provided by the State because it bears a peculiarly close relationship to other rights and liberties accorded protection under the Constitution [in that] it is essential to the effective exercise of First Amendment freedoms and to intelligent utilization of the right to vote. In asserting a nexus between speech and education, appellees urge that the right to speak is meaningless unless the speaker is capable of articulating his thoughts intelligently and persuasively. [A] similar line of reasoning is pursued with respect to the right to [vote]: a voter cannot cast his ballot intelligently unless his reading skills and thought processes have been adequately developed.

We need not dispute any of these propositions. [Yet] we have never presumed to possess either the ability or the authority to guarantee to the citizenry the most *effective* speech or the most *informed* electoral choice. That these may be desirable goals [is] not to be doubted. [But] they are not values to be implemented by judicial intrusion into otherwise legitimate state activities.

[The] logical limitations on appellees' nexus theory are [difficult to perceive]. Empirical examination might well buttress an assumption that the ill-fed, ill-clothed, and ill-housed are among the most ineffective participants in the political process and that they derive the least enjoyment from the benefits of the First Amendment. * * *

[The] present case, in another basic sense, is significantly different from any of the cases in which the Court has applied strict scrutiny [to] legislation touching upon constitutionally protected rights. [These] involved legislation which "deprived," "infringed," or "interfered" with the free exercise of some such fundamental personal right or liberty. [We] think it plain that, in substance, the thrust of the Texas system is affirmative and reformatory and, therefore, should be scrutinized under judicial principles sensitive to the nature of the State's efforts and to the rights reserved to the States under the Constitution.

[A] century of Supreme Court adjudication under the Equal Protection Clause affirmatively supports the application of the traditional standard of review, which requires only that the State's system be shown to bear some rational relationship to legitimate state purposes. This case represents [a] direct attack on the way in

74. *Dunn* fully canvasses this Court's voting rights cases and explains that "this Court has made clear that a citizen has a *constitutionally protected right* to participate in elections on an equal basis with other citizens in the jurisdiction." (emphasis supplied). The constitutional underpinnings of [this right] can no longer be doubted even though, as the Court noted in *Harper,* "the right to vote in state elections is nowhere expressly mentioned."

76. *Skinner* applied the standard of close scrutiny to a state law permitting forced sterilization of "habitual criminals." Implicit in the Court's opinion is the recognition that the right of procreation is among the rights of personal privacy protected under the Constitution. See *Roe v. Wade.*

unwilling to recognize education as a fund. as right. *Stoped recognizing fund. rights.

Sec. 5, IV   **WELFARE & EDUCATION**   **1399**

which Texas has chosen to raise and disburse state and local tax revenues. [This] Court has often admonished against such interferences with the State's fiscal policies under the Equal Protection Clause [and] we continue to acknowledge that *L the Justices of this Court lack both the expertise and the familiarity with local problems so necessary to the making of wise decisions with respect to the raising and disposition of public revenues. Yet we are urged to direct the States either to alter drastically the present system or to throw out the property tax altogether in favor of some other form of taxation. No scheme of taxation [has] yet been devised which is free of all discriminatory impact. In such a complex arena in which no *L perfect alternatives exist, the Court does well not to impose too rigorous a standard of scrutiny lest all local fiscal schemes become subjects of criticism under the Equal Protection Clause.

[T]his case also involves the most persistent and difficult questions of educational policy, another area in which this Court's lack of specialized knowledge *L and experience counsels against premature interference with the informed judgments made at the state and local levels. [I]t would be difficult to imagine a case having a greater potential impact on our federal system than the one now before us, in which we are urged to abrogate systems of financing public education presently in existence in virtually every State. * * *

III. [The] State's contribution, under the Minimum Foundation Program, *F was designed to provide an adequate minimum educational offering in every school in the State. [In] part, local control [means] freedom to devote more money to the education of one's children. [While] it is no doubt true that reliance on local property taxation for school revenues provides less freedom of choice with respect to expenditures for some districts than for others,[107] the existence of "some *L inequality" in the manner in which the State's rationale is achieved is not alone a sufficient basis for striking down the entire system. [Nor] must the financing system fail because, as appellees suggest, other methods of satisfying the State's interest, which occasion "less drastic" disparities in expenditures, might be conceived. Only where state action impinges on the exercise of fundamental *L constitutional rights or liberties must it be found to have chosen the least restrictive alternative.

[If] local taxation for local expenditure is an unconstitutional method of providing for education then it may be an equally impermissible means of providing other necessary services customarily financed largely from local property taxes, including local police and fire protection, public health and hospitals, and public utility facilities of various kinds. [It has] never been within the constitu- *L tional prerogative of this Court to nullify statewide measures for financing public services merely because the burdens or benefits thereof fall unevenly depending upon the relative wealth of the political subdivisions in which citizens live.

[In] its essential characteristics the Texas plan for financing public education reflects what many educators for a half century have thought was an enlightened approach to a problem for which there is no perfect solution. We are unwilling to *L

---

107. Justice White suggests in his dissent that the Texas system violates [equal protection] because the means it has selected to effectuate its interest in local autonomy fail to guarantee complete freedom of choice to every district. He places special emphasis on the statutory provision that establishes a maximum rate of $1.50 per $100 valuation at which a local school district may tax for school maintenance. The maintenance rate in Edgewood when this case was litigated [was] $.55 per $100, barely one-third of the allowable rate. (The tax rate of $1.05 per $100 is the equalized rate for maintenance and for the retirement of bonds.) Appellees do not claim that the ceiling presently bars desired tax increases in Edgewood or in any other Texas district. Therefore, the constitutionality of that statutory provision is not before [us].

assume for ourselves a level of wisdom superior to that of legislators, scholars, and educational authorities in 49 States, especially where the alternatives proposed are only recently conceived and nowhere yet tested. * * *

IV. [T]his Court's action today is not to be viewed as placing its judicial imprimatur on the status quo. The need is apparent for reform in tax systems which may well have relied too long and too heavily on the local property tax. [But] the ultimate solutions must come from the lawmakers and from the democratic pressures of those who elect them.

Reversed.

JUSTICE BRENNAN, dissenting.

Although I agree with my Brother White that the Texas statutory scheme is devoid of any rational basis, [I] also record my disagreement with the Court's rather distressing assertion that a right may be deemed "fundamental" for the purposes of equal protection analysis only if it is "explicitly or implicitly guaranteed by the Constitution." As my Brother Marshall convincingly demonstrates our prior cases stand for the proposition that "fundamentality" is, in large measure, a function of the right's importance in terms of the effectuation of those rights which are in fact constitutionally guaranteed. * * *

JUSTICE WHITE, with whom JUSTICE DOUGLAS and JUSTICE BRENNAN join, dissenting.

[T]his case would be quite different if it were true that the Texas system, while insuring minimum educational expenditures in every district through state funding, extends a meaningful option to all local districts to increase their per-pupil [expenditures. But for] districts with a low per-pupil real estate tax base [the] Texas system utterly fails to extend a realistic choice to parents, because the property tax, which is the only revenue-raising mechanism extended to school districts, is practically and legally unavailable. * * *

In order to equal the highest yield in any other Bexar County district, Alamo Heights would be required to tax at the rate of 68 cents per $100 of assessed valuation. Edgewood would be required to tax at the prohibitive rate of $5.76 per $100. But state law places a $1.50 per $100 ceiling on the maintenance tax [rate]. Requiring the State to establish only that unequal treatment is in furtherance of a permissible goal, without also requiring the State to show that the means chosen to effectuate that goal are rationally related to its achievement, makes equal protection analysis no more than an empty gesture. * * *

JUSTICE MARSHALL, with whom JUSTICE DOUGLAS, concurs, dissenting.

[T]he majority's holding can only be seen as a retreat from our historic commitment to equality of educational opportunity. [The issue] is not whether Texas is doing its best to ameliorate the worst features of a discriminatory scheme, but rather whether the scheme itself is in fact unconstitutionally discriminatory. [Authorities] concerned with educational quality no doubt disagree as to the significance of variations in per pupil spending. [But it] is an inescapable fact that if one district has more funds available per pupil than another district, the former will have greater choice in educational [planning].

At the very least, in view of the substantial interdistrict disparities in funding, [the] burden of proving that these disparities do not in fact affect the quality of children's education must fall upon the appellants. Yet [they] have argued no more than that the relationship is ambiguous. * * *

Nor can I accept the appellants' apparent suggestion [that equal protection] cannot be offended by substantially unequal state treatment of persons who are similarly situated so long as the State provides everyone with some unspecified amount of education which evidently is "enough." [The] Equal Protection Clause is not addressed to the minimal sufficiency but rather to the unjustifiable inequalities of state action. [In] light of the data introduced before the District Court, the conclusion that the school children of property poor districts constitute a sufficient class for our purposes seems indisputable to me. [Whether] this discrimination, against [them] is violative of the Equal Protection Clause is the question to which we must now turn.

[The] Court apparently seeks to establish [that] equal protection cases fall into one of two neat categories which dictate the appropriate standard of review—strict scrutiny or mere rationality. But [a] principled reading of what this Court has done reveals that it has applied a spectrum of standards [which] clearly comprehends variations in the degree of care with which the Court will scrutinize particular classifications, depending [on] the constitutional and societal importance of the interest adversely affected and the recognized invidiousness of the basis upon which the particular classification is drawn. * * *

I therefore cannot accept the majority's labored efforts to demonstrate that fundamental interests, which call for strict scrutiny of the challenged classification, encompass only established rights which we are somehow bound to recognize from the text of the Constitution itself. * * *[59]

I would like to know where the Constitution guarantees the right to procreate, *Skinner*, or the right to vote in state elections, e.g., *Reynolds v. Sims*,[60] or the right to an appeal from a criminal conviction, e.g., *Griffin*.[61] These are instances in which, due to the importance of the interests at stake, the Court has displayed a strong concern with the existence of discriminatory state treatment. But the Court has [never] indicated that these are interests which independently enjoy full-blown constitutional protection. * * *

The majority is, of course, correct when it suggests that the process of determining which interests are fundamental is a difficult one. But I do not think the problem is insurmountable. [The task] should be to determine the extent to which constitutionally guaranteed rights are dependent on interests not mentioned in the Constitution. As the nexus between the specific constitutional guarantee and the nonconstitutional interest draws closer, the nonconstitutional interest becomes more fundamental and the degree of judicial scrutiny applied when the interest is infringed on a discriminatory basis must be adjusted accordingly. * * * Procreation is now understood to be important because of its

---

59. Indeed, the Court's theory would render the established concept of fundamental interests in the context of equal protection analysis superfluous, for the substantive constitutional right itself requires that this Court strictly scrutinize any asserted state interest for restricting or denying access to any particular guaranteed right.

60. It is interesting that in its effort to reconcile the state voting rights cases with its theory of fundamentality the majority can muster nothing more than the contention that "[t]he constitutional underpinnings of the *right to equal treatment in the voting process* can no longer be doubted." If, by this, the Court intends to recognize a substantive constitutional "right to equal treatment in the voting process" independent of the Equal Protection Clause, the source of such a right is certainly a mystery to me.

61. It is true that *Griffin* and *Douglas* also involved discrimination against [indigents]. But, as the majority points out, the Court has never deemed wealth discrimination alone to be sufficient to require strict judicial scrutiny; rather, such review of wealth classifications has been applied only where the discrimination affects an important individual interest, see, e.g., *Harper*. Thus, I believe *Griffin* and *Douglas* can only be understood as premised on a recognition of the fundamental importance of the criminal appellate process.

interaction with the established constitutional right of privacy. The exercise of the state franchise is closely tied to basic civil and political rights inherent in the First Amendment. And access to criminal appellate processes enhances the integrity of the range of rights implicit in the Fourteenth Amendment guarantee of due process of law. Only if we closely protect the related interests from state discrimination do we ultimately ensure the integrity of the constitutional guarantee itself. This is the real lesson that must be taken from our previous decisions involving interests deemed to be fundamental.

[In] the context of economic interests, we find that discriminatory state action is almost always sustained for such interests are generally far removed from constitutional guarantees. [But] the situation differs markedly when discrimination against important individual interests with constitutional implications and against particularly disadvantaged or powerless classes is involved. The majority suggests, however, that a variable standard of review would give this Court the appearance of a "superlegislature." I cannot agree. Such an approach seems to me a part of the guarantees of our Constitution and of the historic experiences with oppression of and discrimination against discrete, powerless minorities which underlie that Document. In truth, the Court itself will be open to the criticism raised by the majority so long as it continues on its present course of effectively selecting in private which cases will be afforded special consideration without acknowledging the true basis of its action.

[It] is true that this Court has never deemed the provision of free public education to be required by the Constitution. [But] the fundamental importance of education is amply indicated by the prior decisions of this Court, by the unique status accorded public education by our society, and by the close relationship between education and some of our most basic constitutional [values].

Education directly affects the ability of a child to exercise his First Amendment interests both as a source and as a receiver of information and [ideas]. Indeed, it has frequently been suggested that education is the dominant factor affecting political consciousness and participation.[72] * * *[74]

[We] are told that in every prior case involving a wealth classification, the members of the disadvantaged class have "shared two distinguishing characteristics: because of their impecunity they were completely unable to pay for some desired benefit, and as a consequence, they sustained an absolute deprivation of a meaningful opportunity to enjoy that benefit." I cannot agree. * * *

In *Harper*, the Court struck down [a] poll tax in toto; it did not order merely that those too poor to pay the tax be exempted; complete impecunity clearly was not determinative. [In] *Griffin* and *Douglas* [t]he right of appeal itself was not absolutely denied to those too poor to pay; but because of the cost of a transcript and of counsel, the appeal was a substantially less meaningful right for the poor

---

72. [I]t should be obvious that the political process, like most other aspects of social intercourse, is to some degree competitive. It is thus of little benefit to an individual from a property poor district to have "enough" education if those around him have more than "enough."

74. [Whatever] the severity of the impact of insufficient food or inadequate housing on a person's life, they have never been considered to bear the same direct and immediate relationship to constitutional concerns for free speech and for our political processes as education has long been recognized to bear. Per-

haps, the best evidence of this fact is the unique status which has been accorded public education as the single public service nearly unanimously guaranteed in the constitutions of our States. Education, in terms of constitutional values, is much more analogous in my judgment, to the right to vote in state elections than to public welfare or public housing. [Indeed,] we have long recognized education as an essential step in providing the disadvantaged with the tools necessary to achieve economic self-sufficiency.

than for the rich. [This] clearly encompassed degrees of discrimination on the basis of wealth which do not amount to outright denial of the affected right or interest.[77]

[It] seems to me that discrimination on the basis of group wealth in this case likewise calls for careful judicial scrutiny. First, [it] bears no relationship whatsoever to the interest of Texas school children in the educational opportunity afforded them [by] Texas. Given the importance of that interest, we must be particularly sensitive to the invidious characteristics of any form of discrimination that is not clearly intended to serve it, as opposed to some other distinct state interest. Discrimination on the basis of group wealth may not, to be sure, reflect the social stigma frequently attached to personal poverty. Nevertheless, insofar as group wealth discrimination involves wealth over which the disadvantaged individual has no significant control,[83] it represents in fact a more serious basis of discrimination than does personal wealth. For such discrimination is no reflection of the individual's characteristics or his abilities. And thus—particularly in the context of a disadvantaged class composed of children—we have previously treated discrimination on a basis which the individual cannot control as constitutionally disfavored. Cf. [citing cases involving discrimination against illegitimates, Sec. 4, II supra].

The disability of the disadvantaged class in this case extends as well into the political processes upon which we ordinarily rely as adequate for the protection and promotion of all interests. Here legislative reallocation of the State's property wealth must be sought in the face of inevitable opposition from significantly advantaged districts that have a strong vested interest in the preservation of the status [quo].

[Here] both the nature of the interest and the classification dictate close judicial [scrutiny. I] do not question that local control of public education, as an abstract matter, constitutes a very substantial state interest. [But] on this record, it is apparent that the State's purported concern with local control is offered primarily as an excuse rather than as a justification for interdistrict inequality.

In Texas statewide laws regulate [the] most minute details of local public education. For example, the State prescribes required courses. All textbooks must be submitted for state [approval]. The State has established the qualifications necessary for teaching in Texas public schools and the procedures for obtaining certification. The State has even legislated on the length of the school [day.]

Moreover, even if we accept Texas' general dedication to local control in educational matters, [i]f Texas had a system truly dedicated to local fiscal control one would expect the quality of the educational opportunity provided in each district to vary with the decision of the voters in that district as to the level of sacrifice they wish to make for public education. [But local] districts cannot choose to have the best education [by] imposing the highest tax rate. Instead, the quality

---

77. Even putting aside its misreading of *Griffin* and *Douglas*, the Court fails to offer any reasoned constitutional basis for restricting cases involving wealth discrimination to instances in which there is an absolute deprivation of the interest affected. [Equal protection] guarantees equality of treatment of those persons who are similarly situated; it does not merely bar some form of excessive discrimination between such persons. Outside the context of wealth discrimination, the Court's reappor-

tionment decisions clearly indicate that relative discrimination is within the purview of the Equal Protection Clause. * * *

83. True, a family may move to escape a property poor school district, assuming it has the means to do so. But such a view would itself raise a serious constitutional question concerning an impermissible burdening of the right to travel, or, more precisely, the concomitant right to remain where one is.

of the educational opportunity offered by any particular district is largely determined by the amount of taxable property located in the district—a factor over which local voters can exercise no control.

The study introduced in the District Court showed a direct inverse relationship between equalized taxable district property wealth and district tax effort with the result that the property poor districts making the highest tax effort obtained the lowest per pupil yield. * * *

In my judgment, any substantial degree of scrutiny of the operation of the Texas financing scheme reveals that the State has selected means wholly inappropriate to secure its purported interest in assuring its school districts local fiscal control.[96] At the same time, appellees have pointed out a variety of alternative financing schemes which may serve the State's purported interest in local control as well as, if not better than, the present scheme without the current impairment of the educational opportunity of vast numbers of Texas schoolchildren.[98] * * *

Notes and Questions

1. *Positive and negative rights.* Consider Richard H. Fallon, Jr., *Individual Rights and the Powers of Government*, 27 Ga.L.Rev. 343, 377 (1993): "Perhaps the most pervasive strategy in constitutional law is for courts to distinguish between negative and positive freedoms: to insist that constitutional rights stand as barriers against government coercion and discrimination, but do not require the government affirmatively to come to anyone's aid." Is this strategy generally defensible?[a] Does it recognize exceptions—for example, in cases involving rights to appointed counsel or the waiver of litigation fees? If there are recognized exceptions, do they compromise the general rule?

2. *Wealth classifications.* If *Rodriguez* involved a wealth classification, what exactly was the group that suffered from discrimination? Did the issue involve discriminatory impact rather than de jure discrimination? If so, did *Rodriguez* anticipate the approach of *Washington v. Davis* that in the absence of proof of discriminatory intent, discriminatory impact alone does not generally establish an equal protection violation?

Does *Rodriguez* hold that de facto discriminations against poor people are subject to strict scrutiny only if they involve a right "explicitly or implicitly guaranteed by the Constitution"? May *all* the prior "wealth discrimination" cases be explained on this basis? Or does the Court's fn. 60 suggest that a state payment requirement resulting in "an absolute deprivation" of an important (albeit not "fundamental") right requires strict scrutiny?

96. [Although] my Brother White purports to reach this result by application of that lenient standard of mere rationality, [it] seems to be that the care with which he scrutinizes the practical effectiveness of the present local property tax as a device for affording local fiscal control reflects the application of a more stringent standard of [review].

98. * * * Central financing would leave in local hands the entire gamut of local educational policy-making—teachers, curriculum, school sites, the whole process of allocating resources among alternative educational objectives.

A second possibility is the much discussed theory of district power equalization put forth by Professors Coons, Clune, and Sugarman in their seminal work, *Private Wealth and Public Education* 201–242 (1970). Such a scheme would truly reflect a dedication to local fiscal control. Under their system, each school district would receive a fixed amount of revenue per pupil for any particular level of tax effort regardless of the level of local property tax base. * * *

a. For criticism, see, e.g., Susan Bandes, *The Negative Constitution: A Critique*, 88 Mich. L.Rev. 2271 (1990).

3. *Identifying "fundamental" rights.* The Court decided *Rodriguez* in the same term that it decided *Roe v. Wade*, which is cited in fn. 76 as supporting the conclusion that the Court cannot recognize fundamental rights that are not "explicitly or implicitly guaranteed by the Constitution." How does the Court determine which rights are implicitly guaranteed? Consider Richard H. Fallon, Jr., *Implementing the Constitution* 50 (2001): "Scholars have [advanced] forceful arguments for constitutional rights to education, health care, and other practical prerequisites to the enjoyment of explicit constitutional guarantees. The argument for such rights takes much the same form as the argument supporting other recognized but not precisely delineated rights, such as the right to freedom of association. Although neither a right to freedom of association nor a right to effective education is expressly enumerated in the Constitution, effective speech and political activity often require association and collaboration, and they often require education as well. If we want to know why the Court has recognized a fundamental right to free association but not to effective public education, the explanation surely involves the Court's belief that the federal judiciary can sensibly enforce the former but not the latter. Implementing a right to effective public education would require assessments of educational quality that courts are poorly equipped to make, [and] a right to effective public education could draw the courts into general oversight of the government's budget process."

4. *Fundamental rights and basic necessities. Should* the Court recognize fundamental rights to governmentally provided goods and opportunities—such as welfare and education—that are of fundamental practical importance?[b]

(a) Consider Frank I. Michelman, *On Protecting the Poor Through the Fourteenth Amendment,* 83 Harv.L.Rev. 7, 13 (1969), arguing that the harms alleged in cases such as *Dandridge* and *Rodriguez* involve claims of "minimum protection" more than "equal protection": "[T]he only inequality turns out to be that some persons, less than all, are suffering from inability to satisfy certain 'basic' wants which presumably are felt by all alike; [if] we define the inequality that way, [the] injury consists more essentially of deprivation than of discrimination, [and the] cure accordingly lies more in provision than in equalization."

(b) What are the strongest philosophical and constitutional arguments for recognizing positive rights to governmental provision of the basic necessities of decent human lives? Consider the following theories:

(i) Rights should be determined on the basis of what is important to human beings. Welfare rights are undeniably important.

(ii) The Constitution assumes that persons are entitled to equal concern and respect. To deny welfare rights is to deny the concern and respect owed to every person.

---

b. For a range of views, see, e.g., Susan Frelich Appleton, *Beyond The Limits of Reproductive Choice: The Contributions of the Abortion-Funding Cases to Fundamental-Rights Analysis and to the Welfare-Rights Thesis,* 81 Colum.L.Rev. 721 (1981); Susan Frelich Appleton, *Professor Michelman's Quest for a Constitutional Welfare Right,* 3 Washington University Law Quarterly 715 (1979); Robert Bork, *The Impossibility of Finding Welfare Rights in the Constitution,* 1979 Wash.U.L.Q. 695; Erwin Chemerinsky, *Making the Right Case for A Constitutional Right to Minimum Entitlements,* 44 Mercer L.Rev. 525 (1993); Peter Edelman, *The Next Century of Our Constitution: Rethinking Our Duty to the Poor,* 39 Hast.L.J. 1 (1987); Stephen Loffredo, *Poverty, Democracy and Constitutional Law,* 141 U.Pa.L.Rev. 1277 (1993); Frank I. Michelman, *Welfare Rights in a Constitutional Democracy,* 1979 Wash.U.L.Q. 659; Ralph K. Winter, Jr., *Changing Concepts of Equality: From Equality Before the Law to the Welfare State,* 1979 Wash.U.L.Q. 741; R. George Wright, *Persons with Disabilities and the Meaning of Constitutional Equal Protection,* 60 Ohio St.L.J. 145 (1999).

(iii) The Constitution assumes that persons are citizens who will participate meaningfully in the democratic process including political dialogue about the future direction of the country. Citizens deprived of welfare rights are unlikely to participate effectively in the democratic process.

(c) Suppose the argument were convincing that fundamental rights to education and welfare are "implicit" in the Constitution. Would it necessarily follow that rights to education and welfare should be judicially enforceable to their "full conceptual limits"? Consider Lawrence Gene Sager, *Fair Measure: The Legal Status of Underenforced Constitutional Norms*, 91 Harv.L.Rev. 1212, 1227 (1978), arguing that there are some constitutional norms—including the equal protection norm at issue in *Rodriguez*—that the Court, for practical or institutional reasons, believes it is not competent to enforce fully; it lacks relevant expertise (for example, in school finance and management) and does not wish to federalize a broad area of traditionally local decision-making. The bite of Professor Sager's view lies in the proposition that political officials other than judges have an obligation—albeit a judicially unenforceable one—to "regulate their behavior by standards more severe than those imposed by the federal judiciary" in creating statutory entitlements.

Are claims to "equal" enjoyment of education and welfare more judicially manageable than claims of absolute constitutional entitlement?[c]

5. *Standards of equal protection review.* Is Marshall, J., correct that the Court "has applied a spectrum of standards" to assess claims under the equal protection clause? Should it have pursued a balancing or totality-of-the-circumstances approach in *Rodriguez*? In *Dandridge*? Why didn't the Court do so? Or did it?

PLYLER v. DOE, 457 U.S. 202, 102 S.Ct. 2382, 72 L.Ed.2d 786 (1982), per Brennan, J., held that a Texas statute (§ 21.031) denying free public education to illegal alien children violated equal protection: "Persuasive arguments support the view that a State may withhold its beneficence from those whose very presence within the United States is the product of their own unlawful conduct. [But the children] in these cases 'can affect neither their parents' conduct nor their own status.' Even if the State found it expedient to control the conduct of adults by acting against their children, legislation directing the onus of a parent's misconduct against his children does not comport with fundamental conceptions of justice. [Citing cases involving discrimination against illegitimates, Sec. 4, II supra].

"We reject the claim that 'illegal aliens' are a 'suspect class.' [U]ndocumented status is not irrelevant to any proper legislative goal. Nor is [it] an absolutely immutable characteristic since it is the product of conscious, indeed unlawful,

c. In the years since *Rodriguez*, state courts have had to address a number of issues involving education funding lodged under their state constitutions, many of which include provisions specifically guaranteeing rights to public education. According to James E. Ryan, *Schools, Race, and Money*, 109 Yale L.J. 249, 266–72 (1999), plaintiffs have enjoyed significant but by no means unanimous success in state constitutional litigation seeking educational adequacy, as opposed to equality. For further reviews of relevant state constitutional decisions, see Paula J. Lundberg, *State Courts and School Funding: A Fifty–State Analysis*, 63 Alb. L.Rev. 1101 (2000); Karen Swenson, *School Finance Reform Litigation: Why Are Some State Supreme Courts Activist and Others Restrained?*, 63 Alb. L.Rev. 1147 (2000); Deborah A. Verstegen & Robert C. Knoeppel, *Equal Education Under the Law: School Finance Reform and the Courts*, 14 J.L. & Pol. 555 (1998).

action. But § 21.031 [imposes] its discriminatory burden on the basis of a legal characteristic over which children can have little control. It is thus difficult to conceive of a rational justification for penalizing these children for their presence within the United States. * * *

"Public education is not a 'right' granted to individuals by the Constitution.[a] *Rodriguez*. But neither is it merely some governmental 'benefit' indistinguishable from other forms of social welfare legislation. Both the importance of education in maintaining our basic institutions, and the lasting impact of its deprivation on the life of the child, mark the distinction. [We] cannot ignore the significant social costs borne by our Nation when select groups are denied the means to absorb the values and skills upon which our social order rests.[20] [Thus], the discrimination contained in § 21.031 can hardly be considered rational unless it furthers some substantial goal of the State.

" * * * Faced with an equal protection challenge respecting the treatment of aliens, we agree that the courts must be attentive to congressional policy; the exercise of congressional power might well affect the State's prerogatives to afford differential treatment to a particular class of aliens. [But] there is no indication that the disability imposed by § 21.031 corresponds to any identifiable congressional policy. [We] are reluctant to impute to Congress the intention to withhold from these children, for so long as they are present in this country through no fault of their own, access to a basic education. [We] therefore turn to the state objectives that are said to support § 21.031. * * *

"First, appellants appear to suggest that the State may seek to protect the State from an influx of illegal immigrants. While a State might have an interest in mitigating the potentially harsh economic effects of sudden shifts in population, [t]here is no evidence in the record suggesting that illegal entrants impose any significant burden on the State's economy. To the contrary, the available evidence suggests that illegal aliens underutilize public services, while contributing their labor to the local economy and tax money to the State fisc. The dominant incentive for illegal entry [into] Texas is the availability of employment; few if any illegal immigrants come to this country [to] avail themselves of a free education. * * *

"Second, [appellants] suggest that undocumented children are appropriately singled out for exclusion because of the special burdens they impose on the State's ability to provide high quality public education. [In] terms of educational cost and need, however, undocumented children are 'basically indistinguishable' from legally resident alien children.

"Finally, appellants suggest that undocumented children are appropriately singled out because their unlawful presence within the United States renders them less likely than other children to remain within the boundaries of the State, and to put their education to productive social or political use within the State. Even assuming that such an interest is legitimate, it is an interest that is most difficult to quantify. The State has no assurance that any child, citizen or not, will employ the education provided by the State within the confines of the State's

a. Consider Michael Klarman, *An Interpretive History of Modern Equal Protection*, 90 Mich.L.Rev. 213, 288 n.342 (1991): "Internal documents suggest that four of the five Justices in the *Plyler* majority were prepared forthrightly to hold education a fundamental interest for equal protection purposes. * * * Justice Powell, however, who supplied the fifth [vote], balked at the idea of 'creating another heretofore unidentified right.'"

20. * * * Whatever the current status of these children, the courts below concluded that many will remain here permanently and that some indeterminate number will eventually become citizens. * * *

borders. In any event, the record is clear that many of the undocumented children disabled by this classification will remain in this country indefinitely, and that some will become lawful residents or citizens of the United States. It is difficult to understand precisely what the State hopes to achieve by promoting the creation and perpetuation of a subclass of illiterates within our boundaries, surely adding to the problems and costs of unemployment, welfare, and crime. It is thus clear that whatever savings might be achieved [are] wholly insubstantial in light of the costs involved to these children, the State, and the Nation."

BLACKMUN, J., who joined the Court's opinion, concurred: "I joined [the] Court in *Rodriguez,* and I continue to believe that it provides the appropriate model for resolving most equal protection disputes. [Classifications] involving the complete denial of education are in a sense unique, for they strike at the heart of equal protection values by involving the State in the creation of permanent class distinctions.

POWELL, J., who joined the Court's opinion, concurred "to emphasize the unique character of the case": "Although the analogy is not perfect, our holding today does find support in decisions of this Court with respect to the status of illegitimates. [Thus,] review in a case such as this is properly heightened. [These children] have been singled out for a lifelong penalty and stigma. A legislative classification that threatens the creation of an underclass of future citizens and residents cannot be reconciled with one of the fundamental purposes of the Fourteenth Amendment. In these unique circumstances, the Court properly may require that the State's interests be substantial and that the means bear a 'fair and substantial relation' to these interests.[3]"

BURGER, C.J., joined by White, Rehnquist and O'Connor, JJ., dissented: "[B]y patching together bits and pieces of what might be termed quasi-suspect-class and quasi-fundamental-rights analysis, the Court spins out a theory custom-tailored to the facts [and its] opinion rests on such a unique confluence of theories and rationales that it will likely stand for little beyond the results in these particular [cases].[b]

"[Once] it is conceded—as the Court does—that illegal aliens are not a suspect class, and that education is not a fundamental right, our inquiry should focus on and be limited to whether the legislative classification at issue bears a rational relationship to a legitimate state purpose. [I]t simply is not 'irrational' for a State to conclude that it does not have the same responsibility to provide benefits for persons whose very presence in the State and this country is illegal as it does to provide for persons lawfully present. * * *

"[Denying] a free education to illegal alien children is not a choice I would make were I a legislator. [But the] fact that there are sound *policy* arguments against the Texas legislature's choice does not render that choice an unconstitutional one. [While] the 'specter of a permanent caste' of illegal Mexican residents of the United States is indeed a disturbing one, it is but one segment of a larger problem, which is for the political branches to solve."

3. [I]n *Rodriguez* no group of children was singled out by the State and then penalized because of their parents' status. [Nor] was any group of children totally deprived of all education as in this case. If the resident children of illegal aliens were denied welfare assistance, made available by government to all other chil-

dren who qualify, this also—in my opinion—would be an impermissible penalizing of children because of their parents' status.

b. See generally Dennis Hutchinson, *More Substantive Equal Protection? A Note on Plyler v. Doe,* 1982 Sup.Ct.Rev. 167.

V. MEDICAL CARE: ABORTIONS

MAHER v. ROE, 432 U.S. 464, 97 S.Ct. 2376, 53 L.Ed.2d 484 (1977), per POWELL, J., held that Connecticut's refusal to provide Medicaid funding for elective or nontherapeutic first trimester abortions, even though it gives Medicaid for the costs of childbirth and "medically necessary" first trimester abortions, does not violate equal protection: "The Constitution imposes no obligation on the states to pay the pregnancy-related medical expenses of indigent women, or indeed to pay any of the medical expenses of indigents.[5] But when a state decides to alleviate some of the hardships of poverty by providing medical care, the manner in which it dispenses benefits is subject to constitutional limitations. * * *

"This case involves no discrimination against a suspect class. An indigent woman desiring an abortion does not come within the limited category of disadvantaged classes so recognized by our cases. Nor does the fact that the impact of the regulation falls upon those who cannot pay lead to a different conclusion. In a sense, every denial of welfare to an indigent creates a wealth classification as compared to nonindigents who are able to pay for the desired goods or services. But this Court has never held that financial need alone identifies a suspect [class]. See *Rodriguez; Dandridge*.[6] Accordingly, the central question in this case is whether the regulation 'impinges upon a fundamental right explicitly or implicitly protected by the Constitution.' "

In reasoning that "the Connecticut regulation places no obstacles—absolute or otherwise—in the pregnant woman's path to an abortion" the Court also found that "appellees' reliance on the penalty analysis of *Shapiro* and *Maricopa* is misplaced.[8]"

"Our conclusion signals no retreat from *Roe* or the cases applying it. There is a basic difference between direct state interference with a protected activity and state encouragement of an alternative activity consonant with legislative policy. * * * We think it abundantly clear that a State is not required to show a compelling interest for its policy choice to favor normal childbirth any more than a State must so justify its election to fund public but not private education.

"[We must therefore ask] whether Connecticut's regulation can be sustained under the less demanding test of rationality that applies in the absence of a

---

5. [Because] Connecticut has made no attempt to monopolize the means for terminating pregnancies through abortion the present case is easily distinguished from *Boddie*.

6. [*Griffin* and *Douglas*] are grounded in the criminal justice system, a governmental monopoly in which participation is compelled. Cf. n. 5, supra. Our subsequent decisions have made it clear that the principles underlying *Griffin* and *Douglas* do not extend to legislative classifications generally.

8. * * * Penalties are most familiar to the criminal law, where criminal sanctions are imposed as a consequence of proscribed conduct. *Shapiro* and *Maricopa* recognized that denial of welfare to one who had recently exercised the right to travel across state lines was sufficiently analogous to a criminal fine to justify strict judicial scrutiny.

If Connecticut denied general welfare benefits to all women who had obtained abortions

and who were otherwise entitled to the benefits, we would have a close analogy to the facts in *Shapiro*, and strict scrutiny might be [appropriate]. But the claim here is that the State "penalizes" the woman's decision to have an abortion by refusing to pay for it. *Shapiro* and *Maricopa* did not hold that States would penalize the right to travel interstate by refusing to pay the bus fares of the indigent travelers. We find no support in the right to travel cases for the view that Connecticut must show a compelling interest for its decision not to fund elective abortions.

Sherbert v. Verner, [Ch. 8, Sec. 2], similarly is inapplicable here. In addition, that case was decided in the significantly different context of a constitutionally imposed "governmental obligation of neutrality" originating in [the] Religion Clauses of the First Amendment.

suspect classification or the impingement of a fundamental right. This test requires that the distinction drawn between childbirth and nontherapeutic abortion be 'rationally related' to a 'constitutionally permissible' purpose. [The] Connecticut funding scheme satisfies this standard. *Roe* itself explicitly acknowledged the State's strong interest in protecting the potential life of the fetus. [The] State unquestionably has a 'strong and legitimate interest in encouraging normal childbirth,' [and subsidizing the] costs incident to childbirth is a rational means of encouraging childbirth."[13]

BRENNAN, J., joined by Marshall and Blackmun, JJ., dissented: "[The] disparity in funding [clearly] operates to coerce indigent pregnant women to bear children they would not otherwise choose to have, and just as clearly, this coercion can only operate upon the poor, who are uniquely the victims of this form of financial pressure. [*Roe* and its progeny held] that an area of privacy invulnerable to the State's intrusion surrounds the decision of a pregnant woman whether or not to carry her pregnancy to term. The Connecticut scheme clearly infringes upon that area of privacy."

The dissenters rejected the Court's distinction in this context "between direct state interference with a protected activity and state encouragement of an alternative activity consonant with legislative policy": "First Amendment decisions have consistently held [that] the compelling state interest test is applicable not only to outright denials but also to restraints that make exercise of those rights more difficult. See, e.g., *Sherbert*. [The] compelling state interest test has been applied in voting cases, even where only relatively small infringements upon voting power, such as dilution of voting strength caused by malapportionment, have been involved. [The] Connecticut scheme cannot be distinguished from other grants and withholdings of financial benefits that we have held unconstitutionally burdened a fundamental right. [The] governing principle is the same [as in *Sherbert*], for Connecticut grants and withholds financial benefits in a manner that discourages significantly the exercise of a fundamental constitutional right. Indeed, the case for application of the principle actually is stronger than in *Sherbert* since appellees are all indigents and therefore even more vulnerable to the financial pressures imposed by the Connecticut regulations."

MARSHALL, J., dissented: "[It] is all too obvious that the governmental actions in these cases, ostensibly taken to 'encourage' women to carry pregnancies to term, are in reality intended to impose a moral viewpoint that no State may constitutionally enforce. [The] impact of the regulations here fall tragically upon those among us least able to help or defend themselves.

"[*Rodriguez*] stated a test for analyzing discrimination on the basis of wealth that would, if fairly applied here, strike down the regulations. The Court there held that a wealth discrimination claim is made out by persons ['who] because of their impecunity [are] completely unable to pay for some desired benefit, and as a consequence [sustain] an absolute deprivation of a meaningful opportunity to enjoy that benefit.' Medicaid recipients are, almost by definition, 'completely unable to pay for' abortions, and are thereby completely denied 'a meaningful opportunity' to obtain them."

---

13. Much of the rhetoric of the three dissenting opinions would be equally applicable if Connecticut had elected not to fund either abortions or childbirth. Yet none of the dissents goes so far as to argue that the Constitution *requires* such assistance for all indigent pregnant women.

HARRIS v. McRAE, 448 U.S. 297, 100 S.Ct. 2671, 65 L.Ed.2d 784 (1980), addressed the constitutionality of Title XIX of the Social Security Act, which established the Medicaid program to provide federal financial assistance to states choosing to reimburse certain costs of medical treatment for needy persons. Since 1976, various versions of the so-called Hyde Amendment have limited federal funding of abortions under the Medicaid program to those necessary to save the life of the mother and certain other exceptional circumstances. The version considered by the Court contained no "rape or incest" exception to the funding prohibition. The Court, per STEWART, J., found no constitutional violation:

"The present case does differ factually from *Maher* insofar as that case involved a failure to fund nontherapeutic abortions, whereas the Hyde Amendment withholds funding of certain medically necessary abortions. [But] regardless of [how] the freedom of a woman to choose to terminate her pregnancy for health reasons [is characterized], it simply does not follow that [this freedom] carries with it a constitutional entitlement to the financial resources to avail herself of the full range of protected choices. The reason why was explained in *Maher:* although government may not place obstacles in the path of a woman's exercise of her freedom of choice, it need not remove those not of its own creation. [T]he Hyde Amendment leaves an indigent woman with at least the same range of choice in deciding whether to obtain a medically necessary abortion as she would have had if Congress had chosen to subsidize no health costs at all.

"[Acceptance of appellees' argument] would mark a drastic change in our understanding of the Constitution. It cannot be that because government may not prohibit the use of contraceptives, *Griswold,* or prevent parents from sending their child to a private school, *Pierce,* government, therefore, has an affirmative constitutional obligation to assure that all persons have the financial resources to obtain contraceptives or send their children to private [schools.]

"Again draw[ing] guidance from" [*Maher,* the Court also rejected the argument that the Hyde Amendment] violates the equal protection component of the fifth amendment": It "is not predicated on a constitutionally suspect classification. [Here,] as in *Maher,* the principal impact of [the] Amendment falls on the indigent. But that fact alone does not itself render the funding restriction constitutionally invalid, for this Court has held repeatedly that poverty, standing alone, is not a suspect classification." Thus, the Hyde Amendment need only satisfy the rational-basis standard of review and it does—"by encouraging childbirth except in the most urgent circumstances, [it] is rationally related to the legitimate governmental objective of protecting potential life."

STEVENS, J., joined by Brennan and Marshall, JJ., dissented: "[The instant case presents a] fundamentally different question [from that in *Maher*]. This case involves the pool of benefits that Congress created by enacting [Title XIX]. Individuals who satisfy two neutral criteria—financial need and medical need—are entitled to equal access to that pool. The question is whether certain persons who satisfy those criteria may be denied access to benefits solely because they must exercise the constitutional right to have an abortion in order to obtain the medical care they need. Our prior cases plainly dictate [the answer].

"Unlike these plaintiffs, [those] in *Maher* did not satisfy the neutral criterion of medical need; they sought a subsidy for nontherapeutic abortions—medical procedures which by definition they did not need. [This case] involves a special exclusion of women who, by definition, are confronted with a choice between two serious harms: serious health damage to themselves on the one hand and abortion on the other. The competing interests are the interest in maternal health and the interest in protecting potential human life. It is now part of our law that the pregnant woman's decision as to which of these conflicting interests shall prevail is entitled to constitutional protection.

"[If] a woman has a constitutional right to place a higher value on avoiding either serious harm to her own health or perhaps an abnormal childbirth[6] than on protecting potential life, the exercise of that right cannot provide the basis for the denial of a benefit to which she would otherwise be entitled. The Court's sterile equal protection analysis evades this critical though simple point. The Court focuses exclusively on the 'legitimate interest in protecting the potential life of the fetus.' [Roe] squarely held that the States may not protect that interest when a conflict with the interest in a pregnant woman's health exists. [The] Court totally fails to explain why this reasoning is not dispositive here.

"[Nor] can it be argued that the exclusion of this type of medically necessary treatment of the indigent can be justified on fiscal grounds. [For] the cost of an abortion is only a small fraction of the costs associated with childbirth. Thus, the decision to tolerate harm to indigent persons who need an abortion in order to avoid 'serious and long lasting health damage' is one that is financed by draining money out of the pool that is used to fund all other necessary medical procedures. Unlike most invidious classifications, this discrimination harms not only its direct victims but also the remainder of the class of needy persons that the pool was designed to benefit. * * *

"Having decided to alleviate some of the hardships of poverty by providing necessary medical care, the Government must use neutral criteria in distributing benefits. [It] may not create exceptions for the sole purpose of furthering a governmental interest that is constitutionally subordinate to the individual interest that the entire program was designed to protect."

Brennan, J., joined by Marshall and Blackmun, JJ., dissented, expressing "continuing disagreement with the Court's mischaracterization of the nature of the fundamental right recognized in *Roe* and its misconception of the manner in which that right is infringed [by] legislation withdrawing all funding for medically necessary abortions": "[W]hat the Court fails to appreciate is that it is not simply the woman's indigency that interferes with her freedom of choice, but the combination of her own poverty and the government's unequal subsidization of abortion and childbirth."

Notes and Questions

1. *The logic of the abortion funding cases.* Consider Tribe 2d ed., at 1346–47: "There is a certain logic [to the abortion funding cases]: if the abortion choice is constitutionally private, why should the state be prevented from declining to make it a matter for public funding? [But] this logic is far from inexorable. The government obviously has the constitutional *authority* to make abortion, like childbirth, available at no charge to the woman, either in a public facility or by public subsidy. The government's *affirmative* choice *not* to do so can fairly be characterized as a decision to enforce alienation of the woman's right to end her

---

6. The Court relies heavily on the premise [that] the State's legitimate interest in preserving potential life provides a sufficient justification for funding medical services that are necessarily associated with normal childbirth without also funding abortions that are not medically necessary. The *Maher* opinion repeatedly referred to the policy of favoring "normal childbirth." But this case involves a refusal to fund abortions which are medically necessary to avoid abnormal childbirth.

pregnancy, whether that alienation—or 'waiver'—was brought about voluntarily (by the woman's failure to save money for an abortion), or involuntarily (by economic circumstances beyond her control). After all, the unavailability of abortion to such a woman follows from her lack of funds only by virtue of the government's quite conscious decision to treat that medical procedure in particular as a purely private commodity available only to those who can pay the market price. The constitutionality of that decision is rendered dubious by the government's simultaneous decision to take *childbirth* procedures for the same poor women *off* the private market: the result, as Justice Stevens put it, [dissenting in *McRae*,] is a government program that self-consciously 'require[s] the expenditure of millions and millions of dollars in order to thwart the exercise of a constitutional right.' The state's position with respect to reproductive rights—rights it is bound to respect—is therefore neither as neutral nor as passive as a majority of the Court supposed in *Maher* and *McRae*."

2. *Abortion funding and constitutional caste.* Where "rights [are] too important to be reserved for selected privileged groups," observes Kathleen M. Sullivan, *Unconstitutional Conditions,* 102 Harv.L.Rev. 1413, 1498–99 (1989), "conditions on benefits that affect their exercise can pose a similar danger of hierarchy. * * * Government cannot universally criminalize abortion, nor universally burden it with heavy restrictions, at least in the first trimester. The only difference between such general bans and the selective subsidization of childbirth but not abortion for indigent women is the class affected. Dependency on government defines the class here. But what the government cannot restrict for all, it may not restrict for those over whom it has special leverage because of their dependency—especially where the displacement of private alternatives creates special responsibility. To hold otherwise would sanction a two-tier system of constitutional rights—a system of constitutional caste."

3. *Governmental purpose and its relevance.* Michael Perry, *Why the Supreme Court Was Plainly Wrong in the Hyde Amendment Case,* 32 Stan.L.Rev. 1113, 1122 (1980), observes that, although *Roe* does not forbid all government actions that might have the effect of making a woman prefer childbirth to abortion (e.g., the government could decide to fund childbirth *solely* in order to increase the size of the labor force), "*Roe* does require that government take no action, including the selective withholding of Medicaid funds, predicated on the view that abortion is per se morally objectionable—just as government has an undisputed obligation (to borrow one of the Court's own examples) not to take action predicated on the view that sending one's children to a private school is morally objectionable. [This means] that the central question in *McRae* ought to have been whether the Hyde Amendment is predicated on the illicit view. [The *McRae* majority] never even addressed that crucial question." After pointing out, inter alia, that Congressman Hyde stated that the purpose of his Amendment was "not to fund abortion because it's the killing of an innocently inconvenient pre-born child," Professor Perry concludes, id. at 1126, that "[i]t strains credulity to the breaking point to suggest that those charged with defending the Hyde Amendment in court could possibly establish that the view that abortion is per se morally objectionable did not play a but-for role in passage of the Amendment."

4. *Comparing abortion funding and the funding of religious education.* Consider Michael W. McConnell, *The Selective Funding Problem: Abortions and Religious Schools,* 104 Harv.L.Rev. 989, 989–91, 994 (1991): "[A]bortion funding and religious education funding seem to pose the same question of constitutional law: when is the government's refusal to fund a constitutionally protected choice an impermissible 'burden' on the exercise of the right? In both cases, the

Constitution protects the right to decide for oneself—whether to have an abortion or to carry the child to term, and whether to obtain a religious or a secular education for one's children. And in both cases, the government funds one alternative and not the other. [More] interestingly, the arguments made by proponents of abortion funding and religious education funding are essentially the same. [But] virtually everyone who supports funding of abortions opposes funding of religious schools, and virtually everyone who supports funding of religious schools opposes funding of abortions. [A] general theory of selective funding is vital to an intermediate jurisprudence of constitutionalism in the context of an activist state, lest the expanded powers of government obliterate the boundaries of constitutionally defined liberties."

Chapter 10

THE CONCEPT OF STATE ACTION

SECTION 1. INTRODUCTION

The "state action" doctrine has long established that, because of their language or history, most provisions of the Constitution that protect individual liberty—including those set forth in Art. 1, §§ 9 and 10, the Bill of Rights, and the fourteenth and fifteenth amendments—impose restrictions or obligations only on government. The subject received its first extensive treatment in the CIVIL RIGHTS CASES, 109 U.S. 3, 3 S.Ct. 18, 27 L.Ed. 835 (1883), which held, per BRADLEY, J., that neither the thirteenth nor fourteenth amendments empowered Congress to pass the Civil Rights Act of 1875, making racial discrimination unlawful in public accommodations (inns, public conveyances, places of public amusement, etc.)—"and no other ground of authority for its passage being suggested, it must necessarily be declared void." Although the issue presented did not simply concern the authority granted the *Court* under § 1 of the thirteenth and fourteenth amendments, but rather involved the scope of *Congress'* power under the final sections of these amendments to enforce their substantive provisions "by appropriate legislation" (a topic to be considered in detail in Ch. 12), the Court's discussion of "state action" remains the classic exposition.

The Court held that, under the fourteenth amendment, "individual invasion of individual rights is not the subject-matter of the amendment. [It] nullifies and makes void all state legislation, and state action of every kind, which impairs the privileges and immunities of citizens of the United States, or which injures them in life, liberty, or property without due process of law, or which denies to any of them the equal protection of the laws. [T]he last section of the amendment [does] not authorize congress to create a code of municipal law for the regulation of private rights; but to provide modes of redress against the operation of state laws, and the action of state officers, executive or judicial, when these are subversive of the fundamental rights specified in the amendment. * * *

"An inspection of the [Civil Rights Act of 1875] shows that [it] proceeds ex directo to declare that certain acts committed by individuals shall be deemed offenses, and shall be prosecuted [by] the United States. It does not profess to be corrective of any constitutional wrong committed by the states; [it] applies equally to cases arising in states which have the justest laws respecting the personal rights of citizens, and whose authorities are ever ready to enforce such laws as to those which arise in states that may have violated the prohibition of the amendment. In other words, it steps into the domain of local jurisprudence, and lays down rules for the conduct of individuals in society towards each other * * *. [C]ivil rights, such as are guaranteed by the constitution against state aggression, cannot be impaired by the wrongful acts of individuals, unsupported by state authority in the shape of laws, customs, or judicial or executive proceedings. [An] individual cannot deprive a man of his right to vote, to hold property, to buy and to sell, to sue in the courts, or to be a witness or a juror; he may, by force or fraud, interfere with the enjoyment of the right in a particular case; [but] unless protected in these wrongful acts by some shield of state law or state authority, he cannot destroy or injure the right; he will only render himself amenable to satisfaction or punishment; and amenable therefor to the laws of the state where the wrongful acts are committed. [The] abrogation and denial of rights, for which the states alone were or could be responsible, was the great seminal and fundamental wrong which was intended to be remedied."

The Court recognized that the thirteenth amendment "is not a mere prohibition of state laws establishing or upholding slavery, but an absolute declaration that slavery or involuntary servitude shall not exist in any part of the United States [and] that the power vested in congress to enforce the article by appropriate legislation, clothes congress with power to pass all laws necessary and proper for abolishing all badges and incidents of slavery, in the United States * * *. [T]he civil rights bill of 1866, passed in view of the thirteenth amendment, before the fourteenth was adopted, undertook to wipe out these burdens and disabilities, * * * namely, the same right to make and enforce contracts, to sue, be parties, give evidence, and to inherit, purchase, lease, sell, and convey property, as is enjoyed by white citizens. [At] that time (in 1866) congress did not assume, under the authority given by the thirteenth amendment, to adjust what may be called the social rights of men and races in the community; but only to declare and vindicate those fundamental rights which appertain to the essence of citizenship, and the enjoyment or deprivation of which constitutes the essential distinction between freedom and slavery.

"[It] would be running the slavery argument into the ground to make it apply to every act of discrimination which a person may see fit to make as to the guests he will entertain, or as to the people he will take into his coach or cab or car, or admit to his concert or theater, or deal with in other matters of intercourse or business. Innkeepers and public carriers, by the laws of all the states, so far as we are aware, are bound, to the extent of their facilities, to furnish proper accommodation to all unobjectionable persons who in good faith apply for them. If the laws themselves make any unjust discrimination, amenable to the prohibitions of the fourteenth amendment, congress has full power to afford a remedy under that amendment and in accordance with it."[a]

a. In *Bell v. Maryland,* 378 U.S. 226, 84 S.Ct. 1814, 12 L.Ed.2d 822 (1964), Goldberg, J., joined by Warren, C.J., and Douglas, J., examining the "historical evidence" in detail, concluded that the *Civil Rights Cases* were based on the assumption of the framers of the fourteenth amendment that "under state law, when the Negro's disability as a citizen was removed, he would be assured the same public civil rights that the law had guaranteed white persons," and that "the duties of the proprietors of places of public accommodation would remain as they had long been and that the States would now be affirmatively obligated to insure that these rights ran to Negro as well as white citizens." Black, J., joined by Harlan and White, JJ., disagreed. Cf. Tribe 2d ed., at 1694 n. 14. See generally John P. Frank & Robert F. Munro, *The Original Understanding of "Equal Protection of the Laws,"* 1972 Wash.U.L.Q. 421, 468–72. For the view that the *Civil Rights Cases* interpreted the fourteenth amendment to reflect the intent of its framers that the "prohibited state action is the *failure* to protect fundamental interests," see Alan R. Madry, *Private Accountability and the Fourteenth Amendment; State Action; Federalism and Congress,* 59 Mo.L.Rev. 499 (1994).

HARLAN, J., dissented: "Was it the purpose of the nation [by the thirteenth amendment] simply to destroy the institution [of slavery], and remit the race, theretofore held in bondage, to the several states for such protection, in their civil rights, necessarily growing out of freedom, as those states, in their discretion, choose to provide? [S]ince slavery [rested] wholly upon the inferiority, as a race, of those held in bondage, their freedom necessarily involved immunity from, and protection against, all discrimination against them, because of their race, in respect of such civil rights as belong to freemen of other races. Congress, therefore, [may] enact laws of a direct and primary character, operating upon states, their officers and agents, and also upon, at least, such individuals and corporations as exercise public functions and wield power and authority under the state. * * *

"It remains now to inquire what are the legal rights of colored persons in respect of the accommodations * * *.

"1. As to public conveyances on land and water. [R]ailroads [are] none the less public highways because controlled and owned by private corporations; that it is a part of the function of government to make and maintain highways for the conveyance of the public; that no matter who is the agent, and what is the agency, the function performed is *that of the state* * * *.

"Such being the relations these corporations hold to the public, it would seem that the right of a colored person to use an improved public highway, upon the terms accorded to freemen of other races, is as fundamental in the state of freedom, established in this country, as are any of the rights which my brethren concede to be so far fundamental as to be deemed the essence of civil freedom.

"2. As to inns. [A] keeper of an inn is in the exercise of a quasi public employment. The law gives him special privileges, and he is charged with certain duties and responsibilities to the public [which] forbids him from discriminating against any person asking admission as a guest on account of [race].

"3. As to places of public amusement. [W]ithin the meaning of the act of 1875, [they] are such as are established and maintained under direct license of the law. [The] local government granting the license represents [the colored race] as well as all other races within its jurisdiction. A license from the public to establish a place of public amusement, imports, in law, equality of right, at such places, among all the members of that public."[b]

Turning to the fourteenth amendment, "the first clause of the first section— 'all persons born or naturalized in the United States, and subject to the jurisdiction thereof, are citizens of the United States, and of the state wherein they reside'—is of a distinctly affirmative character. In its application to the colored race, previously liberated, it created and granted, as well citizenship of the United States, as citizenship of the state in which they respectively resided. [Further],

b. For general support of Harlan, J.'s thirteenth amendment view, see Arthur Kinoy, *The Constitutional Right of Negro Freedom,* 21 Rutg.L.Rev. 387 (1967). Although the Court has since ruled that the thirteenth amendment grants broad enforcement power to *Congress* (see Ch. 11, Sec. 2, I), the Court has confined its use of the amendment, absent congressional legislation, to holding state peonage laws invalid. See *Memphis v. Greene,* Ch. 9, Sec. 2, III. For application of the thirteenth amendment to the areas of "employ- ment discrimination and affirmative action, jury selection and peremptory challenges, and capital crimes and the death penalty," and for a review of recent scholarship that applies the thirteenth amendment to "racial hate speech legislation, reproductive rights, and federal prosecution of racially motivated violence" and to "abused children, battered women, and women coerced into prostitution," see Douglas L. Colbert, *Liberating the Thirteenth Amendment,* 30 Harv.Civ.Rts.Civ.Lib.L.Rev. (1995).

they were brought, by this supreme act of the nation, within the direct operation of that provision of the constitution which declares that 'the citizens of each state shall be entitled to all privileges and immunities of citizens in the several states.' Article IV, § 2.

"The citizenship thus acquired [may be protected] by congressional legislation of a primary direct character; this, because the power of congress is not restricted to the enforcement of prohibitions upon state laws or state action. It is, in terms distinct and positive, to enforce 'the *provisions of this article*' of amendment * * * all of the provisions,—affirmative and prohibitive * * *.

"But what was secured to colored citizens of the United States—as between them and their respective states—by the grant to them of state citizenship? With what rights, privileges, or immunities did this grant from the nation invest them? There is one, if there be no others—exemption from race discrimination in respect of any civil right belonging to citizens of the white race in the same state [by] the state, or its officers, or by individuals, or corporations exercising public functions or authority * * *. It was perfectly well known that the great danger to the equal enjoyment by citizens of their rights, as citizens, was to be apprehended, not altogether from unfriendly state legislation, but from the hostile action of corporations and individuals in the states. * * *

"But if it were conceded that the power of congress could not be brought into activity until the rights specified in the act of 1875 had been abridged or denied by some state law or state action, I maintain that the decision of the court is erroneous. [In] every material sense applicable to the practical enforcement of the fourteenth amendment, railroad corporations, keepers of inns, and managers of places of public amusement are agents of the state, because amenable, in respect of their public duties and functions, to public regulation. * * * I agree that if one citizen chooses not to hold social intercourse with another, he is not and cannot be made amenable to the law for his conduct in that regard. [The] rights which congress, by the act of 1875, endeavored to secure and protect are legal, not social, rights. The right, for instance, of a colored citizen to use the accommodations of a public highway upon the same terms as are permitted to white citizens is no more a social right than his right, under the law, to use the public streets of a city, or a town, or a turnpike road, or a public market, or a post-office, or his right to sit in a public building with others, of whatever race, for the purpose of hearing the political questions of the day discussed."

————

The basic doctrine of the *Civil Rights Cases*—that it is "state action" that is prohibited by the fourteenth amendment—has remained undisturbed. But the question of what constitutes "state action" has generated significant controversy. It is settled that the term comprehends statutes enacted by national, state and local legislative bodies and the official actions of all government officers.[c] The more difficult problems arise when the conduct of private individuals or groups is challenged as being unconstitutional. Although—as will be pointed out in the materials that follow (see, e.g., note 7 after *Shelley v. Kraemer,* Sec. 3 infra)—it

c. On the question of what constitutes a "government" agency, *Lebron v. National R.R. Passenger Corp.,* 513 U.S. 374, 115 S.Ct. 961, 130 L.Ed.2d 902 (1995), per Scalia, J., held that Amtrak—created by a special federal statute as a corporation "for the furtherance of governmental objectives," with the President having "permanent authority to appoint a majority of the directors"—"is part of the government for purposes of the First Amendment," even though the authorizing statute disclaims this fact. O'Connor, J., dissented.

has often been argued that the inquiries are misperceived, the questions that the Court has asked are whether the private actor (a) is performing a "government function," or (b) is sufficiently "involved with" or "encouraged by" the state so as to be held to the state's constitutional obligations. These subjects will be developed in the next two sections of this chapter.

Until recent decades, most cases involved racial discrimination (or, occasionally, denial of free speech). But, as will be detailed in Ch. 11, the enactment and strengthening of federal (and state) civil rights statutes since the 1960s has largely mooted the problem of private racial discrimination. Further, with the growth under the equal protection clause of the number of "suspect" and "quasi-suspect" classifications (see Ch. 9, Secs. 3 and 4) and the expansion under the due process clause of the procedural rights that the state must afford persons before depriving them of liberty or property (see Ch. 6, Sec. 5), an increasing number of cases (as will be seen in the final section of this chapter) have involved attempts to require "private" adherence to these constitutional responsibilities.

SECTION 2. "GOVERNMENT FUNCTION"

SMITH v. ALLWRIGHT, 321 U.S. 649, 64 S.Ct. 757, 88 L.Ed. 987 (1944), held the fifteenth amendment forebade exclusion of African–Americans from primary elections conducted by the Democratic Party of Texas, pursuant to party resolution. The Court, per REED, J., relied heavily on a case from Louisiana, *United States v. Classic* (1941), fn. b, Ch. 11, Sec. 1, II, which held that Art. I § 4 "authorized Congress to regulate primary as well as general elections, 'where the primary is by law made an integral part of the election machinery.'" *Classic* "makes clear that state delegation to a party of the power to fix the qualifications of primary elections is delegation of a state function that may make the party's action the action of the state. [The] right to participate in the choice of elected officials without restriction by any state because of race [is] not to be nullified by a state through casting its electoral process in a form which permits a private organization to practice racial discrimination in the election." Frankfurter, J., concurred in the result. Roberts, J., dissented.

———

TERRY v. ADAMS, 345 U.S. 461, 73 S.Ct. 809, 97 L.Ed. 1152 (1953), involved the exclusion of African–Americans from the "pre-primary" elections of the Jaybird Democratic Association, an organization of all the white voters in a Texas county that was run like a regular political party and whose candidates since 1889 had nearly always run unopposed and won in the regular Democratic primary and the general election. The record showed "complete absence of any compliance with the state law or practice, or cooperation by or with the State." The Court held the election subject to the fifteenth amendment.

BLACK, J., joined by Douglas and Burton, JJ., found that "the admitted party purpose" was "to escape the Fifteenth Amendment's command." The "Amendment excludes social or business clubs" but "no election machinery could be sustained if its purpose or effect was to deny Negroes on account of their race an effective voice in the governmental affairs. [The] only election that has counted in this Texas county for more than fifty years has been that held by the Jaybirds. [For] a state to permit such a duplication of its election processes is to permit a flagrant abuse [of] the Fifteenth Amendment."

CLARK, J., joined by Vinson, C.J., and Reed and Jackson, JJ., described the Jaybirds as not merely a "private club" "organized to influence public candidacies or political action," but rather a "part and parcel of the Democratic Party, an organization existing under the auspices of Texas law. [W]hen a state structures its electoral apparatus in a form which devolves upon a political organization the uncontested choice of public officials, that organization itself, in whatever disguise, takes on those attributes of government which draw the Constitution's safeguards into play."ᵃ

Only MINTON, J., dissented: The Jaybird's activity "seems to differ very little from situations common in many other places [where] a candidate must obtain the approval of a religious group. [E]lections and other public business are influenced by all sorts of pressures from carefully organized groups. [Far] from the activities of these groups being properly labeled as state action, [they] are to be considered as attempts to influence or obtain state action."ᵇ

MARSH v. ALABAMA, 326 U.S. 501, 66 S.Ct. 276, 90 L.Ed. 265 (1946): A Jehovah's Witness sought "to distribute religious literature on the premises of a company-owned town contrary to the wishes of the town's management." The town, owned by a shipbuilding company, had "all the characteristics of any other American town." Appellant was warned that she could not distribute the literature and when she refused to leave the sidewalk of the town's "business block," a deputy sheriff, who was paid by the company to serve as the town's policeman, arrested her and she was convicted of trespass.

The Court, per BLACK, J., reversed: Under *Lovell v. Griffin*, Ch. 7, Sec. 4, I, A, an ordinary municipality could not have barred appellant's activities, and the fact that "a single company had legal title to all the town" may not result in impairing "channels of communication" of its inhabitants or those persons passing through. "Ownership does not always mean absolute dominion. The more an owner, for his advantage, opens up his property for use by the public in general, the more do his rights become circumscribed by the statutory and constitutional rights of those who use it. Thus, the owners of privately held bridges, ferries, turnpikes and railroads may not operate them as freely as a farmer does his farm. Since these facilities are built and operated primarily to benefit the public and since their operation is essentially a public function, it is subject to state regulation." In balancing property rights against freedom of press and religion, "the latter occupy a preferred position" and the former do not "justify the State's permitting a corporation to govern a community of citizens so as to restrict their fundamental

---

a. Frankfurter, J., stated that the "vital requirement is State responsibility" and found it as follows: "As a matter of practical politics," "we may assume" "those charged by State law with the duty of assuring all eligible voters an opportunity to participate in the selection of candidates at the primary—the county election officials who are normally leaders in their communities—participate by voting in the Jaybird primary" "and condone" "a wholly successful effort to withdraw significance from the State-prescribed primary, to subvert the operation of what is formally the law of the State for primaries in this county."

b. Are these examples distinguishable because "the only election that has counted in this Texas county for more than fifty years has been that held by the Jaybirds"? Because the fifteenth amendment outlawed discrimination *on the basis of race or color* with respect to the right to vote? Would it be "state action" if one of the major political parties imposed a registration fee in order to attend its convention to nominate candidates (assuming this would be barred by the 24th amendment if done by a state)? See *Morse v. Republican Party of Virginia*, fn. d, p. 1000 supra. Suppose the party excluded African–Americans?

liberties and the enforcement of such restraint by the application of a State statute." Frankfurter, J., concurred. Jackson, J., did not participate.[c]

AMALGAMATED FOOD EMPLOYEES UNION v. LOGAN VALLEY PLAZA, 391 U.S. 308, 88 S.Ct. 1601, 20 L.Ed.2d 603 (1968), per MARSHALL, J.,—reasoning that a large privately owned shopping center was the "functional equivalent of the business district [in] *Marsh*"—held that it could not enjoin peaceful union picketing on its property against a store located in the shopping center. Black and White, JJ., dissented. Harlan, J., did not reach the merits.

Four years later, LLOYD CORP. v. TANNER, 407 U.S. 551, 92 S.Ct. 2219, 33 L.Ed.2d 131 (1972), per POWELL, J., held that a shopping center's refusal to permit antiwar handbilling on its premises was not state action. *Logan Valley* was distinguished because the picketing there had been specifically directed to a store in the shopping center and the pickets had no other reasonable opportunity to reach their audience. In *Marsh*, "the company town was performing the full spectrum of municipal powers and stood in the shoes of the State. In the instant case there is no comparable assumption or exercise of municipal functions or power." Marshall, J., joined by Douglas, Brennan and Stewart, JJ., dissented, finding "no valid distinction" from *Logan Valley*.

Finally, HUDGENS v. NLRB, 424 U.S. 507, 96 S.Ct. 1029, 47 L.Ed.2d 196 (1976), per STEWART, J.,—involving picketing of a store in a shopping center by a union with a grievance against the store's warehouse (located elsewhere)—overruled *Logan Valley* on the ground that "*Lloyd* amounted to [its] total rejection."[a] MARSHALL, J., joined by Brennan, J., dissented: "*Logan Valley* [recognized] that the owner of the modern shopping center complex, by dedicating his property to public use as a business district, to some extent displaces the 'State' from control of historical First Amendment forums, and may acquire a virtual monopoly of places suitable for effective communication. The roadways, parking lots, and walkways of the modern shopping center may be as essential for effective speech as the streets and sidewalks in the municipal or company-owned town."[b]

EVANS v. NEWTON, 382 U.S. 296, 86 S.Ct. 486, 15 L.Ed.2d 373 (1966): In 1911, Senator A.O. Bacon devised land to Macon, Ga., to be used as a park for whites only. After *Pennsylvania v. Board of City Trusts*, 353 U.S. 230, 77 S.Ct. 806, 1 L.Ed.2d 792 (1957)—holding that there is "state action" when public

----

c. Reed, J., joined by Vinson, C.J., and Burton, J., dissented, noting that "there was [no] objection to appellant's use of the nearby public highway and under our decisions she could rightfully have continued her activities [thirty feet parallel] from the spot she insisted upon using."

a. White, J., concurred in the result, finding that *Logan Valley* "does not cover the facts of this case [which concern] a warehouse not located on the center's premises. The picketing was thus not 'directly related in its purpose to the use to which the shopping center property was being put.'" Stevens, J., did not participate.

b. For a decision that the free speech and petition provisions of the California constitution require that "shopping center owners permit expressive activity on their property," see *Robins v. Pruneyard Shopping Center*, 23 Cal.3d 899, 153 Cal.Rptr. 854, 592 P.2d 341 (1979). For consideration under the National Labor Relations Act of the right of unions to engage in communicative activity on the employer's premises, see *Eastex, Inc. v. NLRB*, 437 U.S. 556, 98 S.Ct. 2505, 57 L.Ed.2d 428 (1978); *Scott Hudgens*, 230 N.L.R.B. 414 (1977).

officials act as trustees under a private will requiring racial discrimination—the city permitted African–Americans to use the park. When Bacon's heirs sued to remove the city as trustee, the Georgia courts accepted the city's resignation and appointed private individuals as trustees so that the trust's purpose would not fail.

The Court, per DOUGLAS, J., reversed, arguing, inter alia, that "the service rendered even by a private park of this character is municipal in nature," "more like a fire department or police department" than like "golf clubs, social centers, luncheon clubs, schools such as Tuskegee was at least in origin, and other like organizations in the private sector." "Mass recreation through the use of parks is plainly in the public domain and state courts that aid private parties to perform that public function on a segregated basis implicate the State in conduct proscribed by the Fourteenth Amendment. Like the streets of the company town in *Marsh,* the elective process of *Terry,* and the transit system of *Pollak,*[c] the predominant character and purpose of this park are municipal." White, J., concurred on a separate ground.

HARLAN, J., joined by Stewart, J., dissented: In *Pollak,* "state action was explicitly premised on the close legal regulation of the company by the public utilities commission and the commission's approval of the particular action under attack. The conclusion might alternatively have rested on the near-exclusive legal monopoly enjoyed by the company, but in all events nothing was rested on any 'public function' theory." In *Terry,* "none of the three prevailing opinions garnered a majority, and some commentators have simply concluded that the state action requirement was read out of the Fifteenth Amendment on that occasion."[d] *Marsh* is the "only Fourteenth Amendment case finding state action in the 'public function' performed by a technically private institution."

The failing of the majority's theory "can be shown by comparing [the] 'public function' of privately established schools with that of privately owned parks.[e] Like parks, the purpose schools serve is important to the public. Like parks, private control exists, but there is also a very strong tradition of public control in this field.[f] Like parks, schools may be available to almost anyone of one race or religion but to no others. Like parks, there are normally alternatives for those shut out but there may also be inconveniences and disadvantages caused by the restriction. Like parks, the extent of school intimacy varies greatly depending on the size and character of the institution."[g]

c. In *Public Utilities Com'n v. Pollak,* 343 U.S. 451, 72 S.Ct. 813, 96 L.Ed. 1068 (1952), a city transit company subject to public regulation was considered in "sufficiently close relation" with the government as to cause the Court to determine whether the company's playing of radio programs on buses violated due process.

d. Harlan, J., cited Thomas P. Lewis, *The Meaning of State Action,* 60 Colum.L.Rev. 1083, 1094 (1960), who argues that "voting is a purely governmental function. No private organization can decree that a majority vote shall entitle a candidate to public office, while most of the functions involved in [other] cases are those traditionally performed by private organizations or at least within their performance capabilities." See also Note, *The Strange Career of State Action Under the Fifteenth Amendment,* 74 Yale L.J. 1448, 1456–59 (1965).

e. For further consideration of "private schools," see note 3 after *Moose Lodge v. Irvis,* Sec. 3 infra.

f. Is there a "strong tradition" of private as well as public operation of parks in cities? Is it likely that, if Senator Bacon had not provided the park in *Evans,* the city would have provided its own?

g. Black, J., believing that "the Georgia courts decided no federal constitutional question," agreed with the position also stated by Harlan, J.'s opinion that "the writ of certiorari should have been dismissed as improvidently granted."

For subsequent litigation in respect to this park, see *Evans v. Abney,* Sec. 3 infra.

Notes and Questions

1. *Scope of decisions.* (a) In *Marsh,* could the shipbuilding company discriminate against African–Americans in hiring production workers? In hiring peace officers or street cleaners for the town? In *Smith,* could the Democratic Party refuse to hire Jewish secretaries? In *Terry,* could the Jaybirds refuse to hire black secretaries? May "private organizations" that perform "government functions" be subject to some constitutional limitations but not others?

(b) *Migrant labor camps.* A company that has a large commercial farm owns a housing area adjacent to it that is several miles from the nearest municipality. It has duplex homes and apartments for about half of the 300 farmworkers (and their families) who work on the farm either seasonally or year-round. It also has a store that sells food, a cafeteria, and a recreation center. Does *Marsh* or *Hudgens* govern the question of whether the housing units may exclude union organizers? See Note, *First Amendment and the Problem of Access to Migrant Labor Camps,* 67 Corn.L.Rev. 560 (1976).

(c) *Residential communities.* Homeowners own in common a 150 acre facility with 12,000 houses for over 35,000 people. The association furnishes services to the homeowners, establishes rules for common property and individual units, and assesses fees for its operations. Does *Marsh* or *Hudgens* govern the question of whether the association may refuse to rent to African–Americans? May refuse to permit residents (or nonresidents) to distribute political pamphlets on the privately owned "sidewalks" within the community? Of what relevance is the fact that the complex contains a "business district"? See Steven Siegel, *The Constitution and Private Government: Toward the Recognition of Constitutional Rights in Private Residential Communities Fifty Years After Marsh v. Alabama,* 6 Wm. & Mary Bill of Rts. J. 461 (1998).[a]

2. *Statutory bargaining agents.* Suppose a labor union, the exclusive bargaining agent for all employees by authority of federal law, does not bargain as strenuously for black employees? Consider Murphy, J. concurring in *Steele v. Louisville & N.R.R.,* 323 U.S. 192, 208, 65 S.Ct. 226, 234, 89 L.Ed. 173, 186 (1944): "While such a union is essentially a private organization, its power to represent and bind all members of a class or craft is derived solely from Congress. [I]t cannot be assumed that Congress meant to authorize the representative to act so to ignore the rights guaranteed by the Constitution. Otherwise the Act would bear the stigma of unconstitutionality under the Fifth Amendment." May the union, although bargaining fairly for black employees, bar them from union membership?

3. *"Private" function.* (a) If the activities of private groups may become a "government function," may certain official activities of government ever be considered a "private function"? Such as acting as trustee under a private will? Is the nature of the trust property relevant? In any case, does the state's official "entwinement" end the matter?

(b) If a privately owned amusement park contracts with a state deputy sheriff, who is regularly employed by the park, to enforce its racial segregation policy, may the state convict African–Americans, whom the deputy arrests when they refuse to leave the premises, for trespass? See *Griffin v. Maryland,* 378 U.S. 130, 84 S.Ct. 1770, 12 L.Ed.2d 754 (1964).

---

a. The "government function" issue is con-   sidered further in Sec. 4 infra.

(c) *State scholarships.* May a state university constitutionally award scholarships that the donor has designated for whites only? For persons of a particular religion? If the donor personally selects the scholarship recipients each year and racially discriminates, may the university constitutionally admit those selected? Is there a "difference of substance" between these two situations? May a state university constitutionally solicit scholarships to be awarded on racial bases? See generally Note, *Constitutionality of Restricted Scholarships,* 33 N.Y.U.L.Rev. 604 (1958).

JACKSON v. METROPOLITAN EDISON CO.

419 U.S. 345, 95 S.Ct. 449, 42 L.Ed.2d 477 (1974).

JUSTICE REHNQUIST delivered the opinion of the Court.

Respondent [holds] a certificate of public convenience issued by the Pennsylvania Public Utility Commission empowering it to deliver electricity [and] is subject to extensive regulation by the Commission. Under a provision of its general tariff filed with the Commission, it has the right to discontinue service to any customer on reasonable notice of nonpayment of bills.

Petitioner [claimed that respondent's failure] to continue providing power to her residence until she had been afforded notice, a hearing, and an opportunity to pay any amounts found due [was] "state action" depriving her of property in violation of the Fourteenth Amendment's guarantee of due process of law.

[The] mere fact that a business is subject to state regulation does not by itself convert its action into that of the State for purposes of the Fourteenth Amendment. [It] may well be that acts of a heavily regulated utility with at least something of a governmentally protected monopoly will more readily be found to be "state" acts than will the acts of an entity lacking these characteristics. But the inquiry must be whether there is a sufficiently close nexus between the State and the challenged action of the regulated entity so that the action of the latter may be fairly treated as that of the State itself. * * *

Petitioner first argues that "state action" is present because of the monopoly status allegedly conferred upon Metropolitan by the State of Pennsylvania. As a factual matter, it may well be doubted that the State ever granted or guaranteed Metropolitan a monopoly.[8] But assuming that it had, this fact is not determinative * * *. In *Pollak,* [we] expressly disclaimed reliance on the monopoly status of the transit authority. * * *

Petitioner next urges that state action is present because respondent provides an essential public service [and] hence performs a "public function." We have, of course, found state action present in the exercise by a private entity of powers traditionally exclusively reserved to the State. See, e.g., *Terry* (election); *Marsh* (company town); *Evans* (municipal park). If we were dealing with the exercise by Metropolitan of some power delegated to it by the State which is traditionally associated with sovereignty, such as eminent domain, our case would be quite a different one. But while the Pennsylvania statute imposes an obligation to furnish service on regulated utilities, it imposes no such obligation on the State. * * *

---

8. [In] fact Metropolitan does face competition within portions of its service area from another private utility company and from municipal utility companies. [As] petitioner admits, such public utility companies are natural monopolies created by the economic forces of high threshold capital requirements and virtually unlimited economy of scale. Regulation was superimposed on such natural monopolies as a substitute for competition and not to eliminate it. * * *

Perhaps in recognition of the fact that the supplying of utility service is not traditionally the exclusive prerogative of the State, petitioner invites the expansion of the doctrine of this limited line of cases into a broad principle that all businesses "affected with the public interest" are state actors in all their actions.

We decline the invitation for reasons stated long ago in *Nebbia v. New York,* [Ch. 5, Sec. 3], in the course of rejecting a substantive due process attack on state legislation: "It is clear that there is no closed class or category of businesses affected with a public interest * * *. The phrase 'affected with a public interest' can, in the nature of things, mean no more than that an industry, for adequate reason is subject to control for the public good. * * * "

Doctors, optometrists, lawyers, Metropolitan, and Nebbia's upstate New York grocery selling a quart of milk are all in regulated businesses, providing arguably essential goods and services, "affected with a public interest." We do not believe that such a status converts their every action, absent more, into that of the State.

We also reject the notion that Metropolitan's termination is state action because the State "has specifically authorized and approved" the termination practice. In the instant case, Metropolitan filed with the Public Utility Commission a general tariff—a provision of which states Metropolitan's right to terminate service for nonpayment. This provision has appeared in Metropolitan's previously filed tariffs for many years and has never been the subject of a hearing or other scrutiny by the Commission.[11] Although the Commission did hold hearings on portions of Metropolitan's general tariff relating to a general rate increase, it never even considered the reinsertion of this provision in the newly filed general tariff. * * *

The case most heavily relied on by petitioner is *Pollak*. There the Court dealt with the contention that Capital Transit's installation of a piped music system on its buses violated the First Amendment rights of the bus riders. [The] District of Columbia Public Utilities Commission, on its own motion, commenced an investigation of the effects of the piped music, and after a full hearing concluded [that] the practice "in fact, through the creation of better will among passengers, [tends] to improve the conditions under which the public ride." Here, on the other hand, there was no such imprimatur placed on the practice of Metropolitan about which petitioner complains. The nature of governmental regulation of private utilities is such that a utility may frequently be required by the state regulatory scheme to obtain approval for practices a business regulated in less detail would be free to institute without any approval from a regulatory body. Approval by a state utility commission of such a request from a regulated utility, where the commission has not put its own weight on the side of the proposed practice by ordering it, does not transmute a practice initiated by the utility and approved by the commission into "state action." At most, the Commission's failure to overturn this practice amounted to no more than a determination that a Pennsylvania utility was authorized to employ such a practice if it so desired. * * *

Affirmed.

JUSTICE MARSHALL, dissenting. * * *

Our state-action cases have repeatedly relied on several factors clearly presented by this case: a state-sanctioned monopoly; an extensive pattern of cooperation between the "private" entity and the State; and a service uniquely public in

---

11. Petitioner does not contest the fact that Metropolitan had this right at common law   before the advent of regulation.

nature. [Even] when the Court has not found state action based solely on the State's conferral of a monopoly, it has suggested that the monopoly factor weighs heavily in determining whether constitutional obligations can be imposed on formally private entities. See *Steele v. Louisville & Nashville R. Co.* * * *

The majority distinguishes this line of cases with a cryptic assertion that public utility companies are "natural monopolies." * * * Initially, it is far from obvious that an electric company would not be subject to competition if the market were unimpeded by governmental restrictions. Certainly the "start-up" costs of initiating electric service are substantial, but the rewards available in a relatively inelastic market might well be sufficient under the right circumstances to attract competitive investment. Instead, the State has chosen to forbid the high profit margins that might invite private competition or increase pressure for state ownership and operation of electric power facilities [, thus] to ensure that the company's service will be the functional equivalent of service provided by the State.

* * * I question the wisdom [of] focusing solely on the extent of state support for the particular activity under challenge. In cases where the State's only significant involvement is through financial support or limited regulation of the private entity, it may be well to inquire whether the State's involvement suggests state approval of the objectionable conduct. But where the State has so thoroughly insinuated itself into the operations of the enterprise, it should not be fatal if the State has not affirmatively sanctioned the particular practice in question.

[I]t seems to me in any event that the State *has* given its approval to Metropolitan Edison's termination procedures. [That] it was not seriously questioned before approval [suggests] that the Commission was satisfied to permit the company to proceed in the termination area as it had done in the past. * * *

I agree with the majority that it requires more than a finding that a particular business is "affected with the public interest" before constitutional burdens can be imposed on that business. But when the activity in question is of such public importance that the State invariably either provides the service itself or permits private companies to act as state surrogates in providing it, much more is involved than just a matter of public interest. In those cases, the State has determined that if private companies wish to enter the field, they will have to surrender many of the prerogatives normally associated with private enterprise and behave in many ways like a governmental body. And when the State's regulatory scheme has gone that far, it seems entirely consistent to impose on the public utility the constitutional burdens normally reserved for the State.

[The] Court has not adopted the notion, accepted elsewhere, that different standards should apply to state action analysis when different constitutional claims are presented. Thus, the majority's analysis would seemingly apply as well to a company that refused to extend service to Negroes, welfare recipients, or any other group that the company preferred, for its own reasons, not to serve. I cannot believe that this Court would hold that the State's involvement with the utility company was not sufficient to impose upon the company an obligation to meet the constitutional mandate of nondiscrimination. Yet nothing in the analysis of the majority opinion suggests otherwise.[a]

a. Brennan, J., dissented on procedural grounds. Douglas, J.'s dissent is omitted.

For a decision finding state action under the California constitution when a privately owned utility discriminates in hiring, see *Gay Law Students Ass'n v. Pacific Telephone & Telegraph Co.*, 24 Cal.3d 458, 156 Cal.Rptr. 14, 595 P.2d 592 (1979).

Notes and Questions

1. *The "power" theory.* (a) Of what significance should it be that Metropolitan was "the only public utility furnishing electricity to the city"? Might it be argued that the "power" held by certain organizations today was conceived by the framers of the fourteenth amendment to be only within the possession of government? That, under a "living Constitution," such "power" creates such a threat to individual freedom that it should fall within the purview of state action? See Note, *State Action: Theories for Applying Constitutional Restrictions to Private Activity,* 74 Colum.L.Rev. 656 (1974).

Does (should) the "power theory" approach extend to holding the only ice skating rink in town to the state's constitutional responsibilities? Or is it limited to an activity that "is of such public importance that the State invariably either provides the service itself or permits private companies to act as state surrogates in providing it"? Does this invoke the "public function"—or "government function"—approach (to be considered further in note 2 after *Flagg Bros. v. Brooks,* infra)? In any event, does *Jackson* preclude this line of analysis?

(b) Does (should) the "power theory" depend on state participation in conferring the status?

(i) *Corporations.* Consider Adolf A. Berle, *Constitutional Limitations on Corporate Activity—Protection of Personal Rights From Invasion Through Economic Power,* 100 U.Pa.L.Rev. 933, 942–43 (1952): "[A corporation should be] as subject to constitutional limitations which limit action as is the state itself. [The] preconditions of application are two: the undeniable fact that the corporation was created by the state and the existence of sufficient economic power concentrated in this vehicle to invade the constitutional right of an individual to a material degree. [The] principle is logical because [the] modern state has set up, and come to rely on, the corporate system to carry out functions for which in modern life by community demand the government is held ultimately responsible." See also Theodore J. St. Antoine, *Color Blindness But Not Myopia: A New Look at State Action, Equal Protection, and "Private" Racial Discrimination,* 59 Mich.L.Rev. 993 (1961); Arthur S. Miller, *The Constitutional Law of the "Security State,"* 10 Stan.L.Rev. 620, 661–66 (1958). Does this rationale apply to *all* corporations? Should it be restricted to entities "created by the state"?

(ii) *Labor organizations.* Suppose a large powerful union, without statutory authority or assistance, becomes the exclusive bargaining agent in a particular industry. May it constitutionally discriminate against African–Americans? See generally Harry H. Wellington, *The Constitution, The Labor Union, and "Governmental Action,"* 70 Yale L.J. 345, 346–50 (1961). If not, must such a union afford a member "due process" before expelling him? May such a union refuse to hire black secretaries?

(c) Does the "power theory" aid in analyzing the last series of questions? Might it be argued, for example, that a particular labor union has sufficient "power" in respect to job opportunities in the industry as to be constitutionally forbidden from racially discriminating among its members, but insufficient power over general job opportunities as to be constitutionally barred from using a religious test for its office employees? That the "state's duty to take preventive action [or the "state action" issue] varies with the magnitude of the discrimination and the consequent problem it creates"? Henry Friendly, *The Dartmouth College Case and the Public–Private Penumbra* 22 (1969). See generally Jesse H.

Choper, *Thoughts on State Action: The "Government Function" and "Power Theory" Approaches,* 1979 Wash.U.L.Q. 757; compare Gary C. Leedes, *State Action Limitations on Courts and Congressional Power,* 60 N.C.L.Rev. 747, 757–61 (1981).[b]

2. *Constitutional rights of "power holders."* (a) In COLUMBIA BROADCASTING SYSTEM v. DEMOCRATIC NAT'L COMM., Ch. 7, Sec. 8, I—in which the FCC had ruled that a broadcaster is not required to accept editorial advertisements—some justices addressed the question of whether the action of the broadcast licensee was "governmental action" for purposes of the first amendment. BURGER, C.J., joined by Stewart and Rehnquist, JJ., concluded that it was not: "The historic aversion to censorship led Congress [to] explicitly [prohibit] the Commission from interfering with the exercise of free speech over the broadcast frequencies. [Moreover,] the Commission has not fostered the licensee policy challenged here; it has simply declined to command particular action because it fell within the area of journalistic discretion. * * *

"Were we to read the First Amendment to spell out governmental action in the circumstances presented here, few licensee decisions on the content of broadcasts or the processes of editorial evaluation would escape constitutional scrutiny. In this sensitive area so sweeping a concept of governmental action would go far in practical effect to undermine nearly a half century of unmistakable congressional purpose to maintain—no matter how difficult the task—essentially private broadcast journalism held only broadly accountable to public interest standards."

BRENNAN, J., joined by Marshall, J., disagreed: "[T]he public nature of the airwaves, the governmentally created preferred status of broadcast licensees, the pervasive federal regulation of broadcast programming, and the Commission's specific approval of the challenged broadcaster policy combine in this case to bring the promulgation and enforcement of that policy within the orbit of constitutional imperatives. [Indeed,] the argument for finding 'governmental action' here is even stronger than in *Pollak,* for this case concerns not an incidental activity of a bus company but, rather, the primary activity of the regulated entities—communication.* * *[12]"

(b) *Newspapers.* Is the conduct of the only newspaper in a metropolitan area "state action"? May it offer free "society news" space to whites only? May it refuse to hire black employees? After the *CBS* case, may a licensed broadcaster engage in such actions?

---

b. For the view that the state action doctrine may be justified by values of pluralism, see Maimon Schwarzschild, *Value Pluralism and the Constitution: In Defense of the State Action Doctrine,* 1988 Sup.Ct.Rev. 129, 146–47: "[T]he essence of the doctrine is that it distinguishes between exercises of choice by the monopoly institutions of the state—which must conform to the Constitution—and exercises of choice by private persons acting, as private persons always do, with the protection of the state. This is an essential distinction for a society that wants to safeguard the diversity of its own values by limiting the reach of the constitutional norms that govern its public institutions."

12. [W]here, as here, the Government has implicated itself in the actions of an otherwise private individual, that individual must exercise his own rights with due regard for the First Amendment rights of others. In other words, an accommodation of competing rights is required, and "balancing" [is] the result. * * *

I might also note that [a] finding of governmental involvement in this case does not in any sense command a similar conclusion with respect to newspapers. [The] decision as to who shall operate newspapers is made in the free market, not by Government fiat. The newspaper industry is not extensively regulated * * *.

SECTION 3. STATE "INVOLVEMENT" OR "ENCOURAGEMENT"

SHELLEY v. KRAEMER

334 U.S. 1, 68 S.Ct. 836, 92 L.Ed. 1161 (1948).

CHIEF JUSTICE VINSON delivered the opinion of the Court.

[In two cases from Missouri and Michigan, petitioners were African–Americans who had purchased houses from whites despite the fact that the properties were subject to restrictive covenants, signed by most property owners in the block, providing that for a specified time (in one case fifty years from 1911) the property would be sold only to Caucasians. Respondents, owners of other property subject to the covenants, sued to enjoin the buyers from taking possession and to divest them of title. The state courts granted the relief.]

Equality in the enjoyment of property rights was regarded by the framers of [the Fourteenth] Amendment as an essential pre-condition to the realization of other basic civil rights and liberties which the Amendment was intended to guarantee.[7] Thus, [42 U.S.C. § 1982] derived from § 1 of the Civil Rights Act of 1866 which was enacted by Congress while the Fourteenth Amendment was also under consideration, provides: "All citizens of the United States shall have the same right, in every State and Territory, as is enjoyed by white citizens thereof to inherit, purchase, lease, sell, hold, and convey real and personal property." * * *

It is likewise clear that restrictions on the right of occupancy of the sort sought to be created by the private agreements in these cases could not be squared with the requirements of the Fourteenth Amendment if imposed by state statute or local ordinance. * * *

But the present cases [do] not involve action by state legislatures or city councils. Here the particular patterns of discrimination and the areas in which the restrictions are to operate, are determined, in the first instance, by the terms of agreements among private individuals. Participation of the State consists in the enforcement of the restrictions so defined. * * *

Since the decision of this Court in the *Civil Rights Cases,* the principle has become firmly embedded in our constitutional law that the action inhibited by the first section of the Fourteenth Amendment is only such action as may fairly be said to be that of the States. That Amendment erects no shield against merely private conduct, however discriminatory or wrongful.

We conclude, therefore, that the restrictive agreements standing alone cannot be regarded as a violation of any rights guaranteed to petitioners by the Fourteenth Amendment. So long as the purposes of those agreements are effectuated by voluntary adherence to their terms, it would appear clear that there has been no action by the State and the provisions of the Amendment have not been violated.

But here there was more. These are cases in which the purposes of the agreements were secured only by judicial enforcement by state courts of the restrictive terms of the agreements. * * *

That the action of state courts and of judicial officers in their official capacities is to be regarded as action of the State within the meaning of the Fourteenth Amendment, is a proposition which has long been established. [In] the

---

7. *Slaughter-House Cases* [Ch. 5, Sec. 1, III]. See Horace E. Flack, *The Adoption of the Fourteenth Amendment.*

Civil Rights Cases, this Court pointed out that the Amendment makes void "state action of every kind" which is inconsistent with the guaranties therein contained, and extends to manifestations of "state authority in the shape of laws, customs, or judicial or executive proceedings." * * *

One of the earliest applications of the prohibitions contained in the Fourteenth Amendment to action of state judicial officials occurred in cases in which Negroes had been excluded from jury service. [These] cases demonstrate, also, the early recognition by this Court that state action in violation of the Amendment's provisions is equally repugnant to the constitutional commands whether directed by state statute or taken by a judicial official in the absence of statute. * * *

The action of state courts in imposing penalties or depriving parties of other substantive rights without providing adequate notice and opportunity to defend, has, of course, long been regarded as a denial of the due process of law guaranteed by the Fourteenth Amendment.

In numerous cases, this Court has reversed criminal convictions in state courts for failure of those courts to provide the essential ingredients of a fair hearing. Thus it has been held that convictions obtained in state courts under the domination of a mob are void. Convictions obtained by coerced confessions, by the use of perjured testimony known by the prosecution to be such, or without the effective assistance of counsel, have also been held to be exertions of state authority in conflict with the fundamental rights protected by the Fourteenth Amendment.

But the examples of state judicial action which have been held by this Court to violate the Amendment's commands are not restricted to situations in which the judicial proceedings were found in some manner to be procedurally unfair. It has been recognized that the action of state courts in enforcing a substantive common-law rule formulated by those courts, may result in the denial of rights guaranteed by the Fourteenth Amendment. [Thus,] in *AFL v. Swing,* 1941, 312 U.S. 321, 61 S.Ct. 568, 85 L.Ed. 855, enforcement by state courts of the common-law policy of the State, which resulted in the restraining of peaceful picketing, was held to be state action of the sort prohibited by the Amendment's guaranties of freedom of discussion. In *Cantwell v. Connecticut,* 1940, [Ch. 8, Sec. 2, I], a conviction in a state court of the common-law crime of breach of the peace was, under the circumstances of the case, found to be a violation of the Amendment's commands relating to freedom of religion. In *Bridges v. California,* 1941, 314 U.S. 252, 62 S.Ct. 190, 86 L.Ed. 192, enforcement of the state's common-law rule relating to contempts by publication was held to be state action inconsistent with the prohibitions of the Fourteenth Amendment. * * *

We have no doubt that there has been state action in these cases in the full and complete sense of the phrase. The undisputed facts disclose that petitioners were willing purchasers of properties upon which they desired to establish homes. The owners of the properties were willing sellers; and contracts of sale were accordingly consummated. It is clear that but for the active intervention of the state courts, supported by the full panoply of state power, petitioners would have been free to occupy the properties in question without restraint.

These are not cases, as has been suggested, in which the States have merely abstained from action, leaving private individuals free to impose such discriminations as they see fit. Rather, these are cases in which the States have made available to such individuals the full coercive power of government to deny to petitioners, on the grounds of race or color, the enjoyment of property rights in premises which petitioners are willing and financially able to acquire and which the grantors are willing to sell. * * *

The enforcement of the restrictive agreements by the state courts in these cases was directed pursuant to the common-law policy of the States as formulated by those courts in earlier decisions. [The] judicial action in each case bears the clear and unmistakable imprimatur of the State. We have noted that previous decisions of this Court have established the proposition that judicial action is not immunized from the operation of the Fourteenth Amendment simply because it is taken pursuant to the state's common-law policy. Nor is the Amendment ineffective simply because the particular pattern of discrimination, which the State has enforced, was defined initially by the terms of a private agreement. * * * We have noted that freedom from discrimination by the States in the enjoyment of property rights was among the basic objectives sought to be effectuated by the framers of the Fourteenth Amendment. That such discrimination has occurred in these cases is clear. * * *

Respondents urge, however, that since the state courts stand ready to enforce restrictive covenants excluding white persons[,] enforcement of covenants excluding colored persons may not be deemed a denial of equal protection of the laws to the colored persons who are thereby affected. [But the] rights created by the first section of the Fourteenth Amendment are, by its terms, guaranteed to the individual. The rights established are personal rights. It is, therefore, no answer to these petitioners to say that the courts may also be induced to deny white persons rights of ownership and occupancy on grounds of race or color. Equal protection of the laws is not achieved through indiscriminate imposition of inequalities. * * *

Reversed.

JUSTICE REED, JUSTICE JACKSON, and JUSTICE RUTLEDGE took no part in the consideration or decision of these cases.[a]

Notes and Questions

1. *Authority of prior decisions.* Do the cases holding that "judicial action is state action" call for the result in *Shelley?* Consider Comment, *The Impact of Shelley v. Kraemer on the State Action Concept*, 44 Calif.L.Rev. 718, 724 (1956): "In the cases exemplifying 'orthodox' judicial violation the prohibited activity [e.g., barring black jurors] was practiced by the judge himself. [But in *Shelley*] the discrimination originated with private persons." May this be said about "convictions obtained under the domination of a mob"?

As to those cases (*Swing, Cantwell, Bridges*) involving "the action of state courts in enforcing a substantive common-law rule," consider Comment, 45 Mich.L.Rev. 733, 742–43 (1947): "The difficulty of attributing the discrimination effected by the covenants to the enforcing tribunal is not to be escaped by pretending that it forms an element of the common law from which the right to enforcement is derived. The common law is simply the policy of the state in certain of its aspects, [and] that policy as seen in respect to these facts looks no further than to the protection of property and contract rights." Did the state policy in *Cantwell* look any further than to the protection of public tranquility? Did it, in *Bridges*, look any further than to the protection of the integrity of the court? For careful analysis, see William W. Van Alstyne, *Mr. Justice Black, Constitutional Review, and the Talisman of State Action*, 1965 Duke L.J. 219.

a. For a history of the battle against restrictive covenants, see Clement E. Vose, *NAACP Strategy in the Covenant Cases*, 6 W.Res.L.Rev. 101 (1955).

Are the considerations in *Shelley* different from all of these cases because it involves equal protection rather than due process? Because these other cases involve the right of free speech? Should there be a distinction between civil suits and criminal prosecutions? Consider Comment, 45 Mich.L.Rev. at 746: "The theory of civil remedies is that the interest of the state in the protection of property and contract rights is ordinarily secondary to that of the individual citizen, [while a] criminal statute is an expression of state policy of a much higher order."

2. *Zoning ordinances(?).* Is *Shelley* supportable because "so long as it is unconstitutional for a state to require racial segregation by zoning statutes [it] is equally unconstitutional for the state to bring it about by any other form of state action"? Dudley O. McGovney, *Racial Residential Segregation by State Court Enforcement of Restrictive Agreements, Covenants or Conditions in Deeds is Unconstitutional,* 33 Calif.L.Rev. 5, 30 (1945). Is the source of the discrimination the same in both instances? Or is this a variation of the "government function" approach? Consider Issac N. Groner & David M. Helfeld, *Race Discrimination in Housing,* 57 Yale L.J. 426, 454 (1948): "Where covenants do not presently cover entire areas, experience shows that, if encouraged by court enforcement, covenants do in time cover all of the area available for desirable residences." See also William R. Ming, *Racial Restrictions and the Fourteenth Amendment: The Restrictive Covenant Cases,* 16 U.Chi.L.Rev. 203 (1949).

3. BARROWS v. JACKSON, 346 U.S. 249, 73 S.Ct. 1031, 97 L.Ed. 1586 (1953), held that an action by a co-covenantor to recover damages from a property owner who sold to an African–American was barred by equal protection. Would this suit, like the one in *Shelley,* involve "the full coercive power of government to deny [on] grounds of race [the] enjoyment of property rights"? Would the suit in *Barrows* have the same effect as a suit to enjoin a white property owner from breaching the covenant? See *Hurd v. Hodge,* 334 U.S. 24, 68 S.Ct. 847, 92 L.Ed. 1187 (1948).

4. *Other devices.* After *Shelley* and *Barrows,* consider the validity of:

(a) A deed conveying property on condition that if sold to an African–American it automatically reverts to the original grantor.

(i) Suppose the grantor sues to evict the black purchaser? Suppose the grantor retakes possession and the black purchaser sues to evict? Might a court deny relief in the latter situation on the ground that it had "merely abstained from action, leaving private individuals free to impose such discrimination as they see fit"?

(ii) Suppose a suit for declaratory judgment as to the validity of the reverter? If the reverter were declared invalid, could it be said "that the restrictive agreements standing alone cannot be regarded as a violation of [the] Fourteenth Amendment"? If it were declared valid, could a court deny the original grantor's suit to enjoin the black purchaser's taking possession? See generally Arthur S. Miller, *Racial Discrimination and Private Schools,* 41 Minn.L.Rev. 245, 276–80 (1957).

(b) A will devising property on condition that if the beneficiary marry a person "not born in the Hebrew faith" the property be paid over to someone else. Suppose the beneficiary marries a Catholic and the remainderman sues for the property?

(c) A child custody decree directing the father to pay private school tuition. Suppose the father refuses to pay because the school racially discriminates and the mother sues to enforce the decree.

5. *The limits of Shelley.* (a) Consider Comment, 44 Calif.L.Rev. at 733: "If obtaining court aid to carry out 'private' activity 'converts' such private action into 'state' action, then there could never be any private action in any practical sense. So entwined are our lives with the law that the logical result would be that almost *all* action, to be effective, must result in state action. Thus all private activity would be required to 'conform' with the standards of conduct imposed on the states by the fourteenth amendment."

(b) Evaluate the following analyses of *Shelley:*

(i) "Professor Louis Pollak [*Racial Discrimination and Judicial Integrity,* 108 U.Pa.L.Rev. 1, 13 (1959)] would apply *Shelley* to prevent the state from enforcing a discrimination by one who does not wish to discriminate;[b] but he would allow the state to give its support to willing discrimination. [H]is proposal requires important limitation of *Shelley,* and raises a number of possible objections. [The equal protection] clause seems to be designed to protect the victim against discrimination, not to protect an unwilling 'actor' against being compelled to discriminate. It would seem also an eccentric constitutional provision which protected the aggrieved against involuntary discrimination by private persons but not against voluntary private discrimination. Moreover, the distinction is offered as a definition of 'state action.' But whether the judgment of a court enforces a voluntary discrimination or compels a no-longer-voluntary discrimination, the discrimination is private in origin; in both cases it requires a court judgment to make the discrimination effective. [Finally,] in *Shelley* itself, is it acceptable to think of the case as one in which the state was compelling discrimination by a grantor of property who no longer wished to discriminate? In essence, the state was enforcing discrimination by the other parties to the covenant." Louis Henkin, *Shelley v. Kraemer: Notes for a Revised Opinion,* 110 U.Pa.L.Rev. 473, 477–78 & n. 10 (1962).

Compare Harold W. Horowitz, *The Misleading Search for "State Action" Under the Fourteenth Amendment,* 30 So.Cal.L.Rev. 208, 213 (1957): "There is involved here a question of the degree of effect of different forms of state action on a prospective Negro buyer's opportunity to purchase and use [land]. The state does not substantially deny the Negro that opportunity by *permitting* a private person to refuse to deal with him because of his race. This would be the situation where there was 'voluntary adherence' to the restrictive covenant by the landowner. But the state does to a far greater degree deny the Negro the opportunity to acquire land, because of his race, if it *compels* a landowner not to deal with the Negro. This is the situation where the state enforces the restrictive covenant after a landowner has decided not to adhere to it."

(ii) Since restraints on alienation of property are presumptively void, being valid generally only if the court finds the restraint a reasonable one and consistent with public policy, Restatement, *Property* § 406 (1944), was there state action in *Shelley* because the court placed its imprimatur on a racially discriminatory restraint? Might it be argued that, due to this, the source of discrimination was public rather than private? See Jesse H. Choper, *Thoughts on State Action,* 1979 Wash.U.L.Q. 757, 769–71.

---

b. See *Moose Lodge v. Irvis,* infra, for this application of *Shelley*—in the only opinion of the Court (apart from *Barrows v. Jackson*) that has relied on *Shelley* to find state action. Cf. also fn. 10 in *Flagg Bros. v. Brooks,* Sec. 4 infra, and note 1 thereafter.

(iii) Consider Barbara R. Snyder, *Private Motivation, State Action and the Allocation of Responsibility for Fourteenth Amendment Violations,* 75 Corn.L.Rev. 1053, 1985 (1990): "In ordering the enforcement of the covenant, the state court determined that the plaintiffs were entitled to judgment only after taking notice of the race of the Shelleys. [Thus], the Missouri court's decision was racially discriminatory on its face."

(c) Consider Comment, 44 Calif.L.Rev. at 735: "It is submitted that the doctrine of judicial enforcement as interpreted by *Shelley* is applicable only when the court action abets private discrimination which in the absence of such judicial aid would be ineffective. [Where] the private activity, admitted in *Shelley* to be valid in itself, is already effective, it is not to be said that the court, recognizing or failing to abolish the activity, is itself an arm of the discrimination; the situation has remained the same, court action or no. It is only where the proponents of discrimination, unable to further their ends privately, seek court aid is the state itself causing discrimination under *Shelley.*"

(i) Suppose plaintiff is denied relief in a breach of contract suit against a cemetery for refusing to bury an African–American because the burial lot purchase contract was restricted to Caucasians? What result under *Shelley*? Under the above theory? Would denial of plaintiff's cause of action make the discrimination "effective"? If the body had already been interred, could the cemetery obtain the court's aid in removing it?

(ii) Suppose a collective bargaining agreement authorizes discharge of employees for "just cause" and an employee is so discharged because he is black. What result in the employee's suit for reinstatement? What result in the employer's suit to restrain the employee from continuing to appear on the job?

(iii) Suppose a landlord seeks the court's aid to evict a tenant whose defense is that the eviction is solely on the grounds of race (or religion, or speech)? Suppose the tenant seeks to restrain the landlord from recovering possession of the leased premises? If the tenant refuses to give up possession and is forcibly evicted by the landlord, what result in the tenant's suit for assault? Would a desirable rule produce different results in the above situations?

(iv) What result in a suit by the state real estate board to revoke a broker's license for having sold property to an African–American contrary to the owner's instructions? In a suit by a citizen to force the state real estate board to revoke a broker's license for having refused to show property to African–Americans pursuant to the owner's instructions?

6. *Reconsideration of prior problems in light of Shelley.* (a) *Evans v. Newton.* (i) When the state court accepted the city's resignation and appointed private trustees to carry out the testator's discriminatory intent, was this state action that abetted otherwise private discrimination? If the city had not resigned and the state court had granted the relief sought to remove the city as trustee, would this be enforcing discrimination by one who did not wish to discriminate in violation of the *Shelley* rule?

If Senator Bacon had designated a private trustee who was unwilling or unable to act, a new trustee would be appointed by the court. Would discrimination by such an appointee be state action? In most states, charitable trusts are enforced by the attorney general. If Bacon's will had designated a private trustee who refused to discriminate, would an action by the attorney general to force the trustee to comply with terms of the trust violate equal protection? If the private trustee, in compliance with the terms, discriminates from the outset, would the attorney general's failure to seek to end the discrimination violate equal protection? What would be the effect of a court approving the trustee's accounts?

(ii) On remand, after *Evans,* the Georgia courts interpreted Senator Bacon's will and held that "because the park's segregated, whites-only character was an essential and inseparable part of the testator's plan," the "cy pres doctrine to amend the terms of the will by striking the racial restrictions" was inapplicable; that, therefore, the trust failed and the trust property "by operation of law reverted to the heirs of Senator Bacon." EVANS v. ABNEY, 396 U.S. 435, 90 S.Ct. 628, 24 L.Ed.2d 634 (1970), per BLACK, J., affirmed, finding that "the Georgia court had no alternative under its relevant trust laws, which are long standing and neutral with regard to race, but to end the Baconsfield trust": "[T]he Constitution imposes no requirement upon the Georgia court to approach Bacon's will any differently than it would approach any will creating any charitable trust of any kind. [T]here is not the slightest indication that any of the Georgia judges involved were motivated by racial animus or discriminatory intent of any sort in construing and enforcing Senator Bacon's will. Nor is there any indication that Senator Bacon in drawing up his will was persuaded or induced to include racial restrictions by the fact that such restrictions were permitted by the Georgia trust statutes." *Shelley* was "easily distinguishable" because here "the termination of the park was a loss shared equally by the white and Negro citizens of Macon."

BRENNAN, J., dissented: "For almost half a century Baconsfield has been a public park." When "a public facility would remain open but for the constitutional command that it be operated on a nonsegregated basis, the closing of that facility conveys an unambiguous message of community involvement in racial discrimination": "First, there is state action whenever a State enters into an arrangement which creates a private right to compel or enforce the reversion of a public facility" and, here, "in accepting title to the park," city officials agreed to that "if the city should ever incur a constitutional obligation to desegregate the park." Second, "nothing in the record suggests that after our decision in *Evans v. Newton* the City of Macon retracted its previous willingness to manage Baconsfield on a nonsegregated basis, or that the white beneficiaries of Senator Bacon's generosity were unwilling to share it with Negroes, rather than have the park revert to his heirs." Thus, contrary to *Shelley,* "this is a case of a state court's enforcement of a racial restriction to prevent willing parties from dealing with one another." Douglas, J., also dissented. Marshall, J., did not participate.

(iii) Was the Georgia courts' action "a judicial choice between two incompatible terms of his will"—"(1) to keep Negroes out of the park; and (2) to keep Baconsfield a park forever"—thus, state action placing its imprimatur on racial discrimination (see note 5(b)(ii) supra)? Comment, 14 Kan.L.Rev. 613, 625 (1966).

(b) *De facto school segregation.* Consider Comment, 31 Mo.L.Rev. 391, 397 (1966): "[*Shelley*] stands for the proposition that the state may not give discriminatory acts of private persons the force of law. Does not the local school board violate that proposition when [it] assures private persons that if they are able to keep their neighborhoods segregated their schools will be segregated also." Does the school board thus also encourage private housing discrimination?

7. *The balancing approach.* Is the ultimate solution in *Shelley,* and other cases, a balancing of *all* of the particular interests involved? Consider William W. Van Alstyne & Kenneth L. Karst, *State Action,* 14 Stan.L.Rev. 3, 44–45 (1961): "[There has been] an attempt to discover or invent the *kind* of state connection which will satisfy the state action requirement. It is suggested, for example, that the state acts in the sense of the amendment when it coerces private discrimina-

tion, but not when it simply lends its aid to such racial discrimination as private individuals may choose to practice. [This analysis] perpetuates the untenable distinction between the state action requirement on the one hand and the balance of 'substantive' constitutional interests on the other. This way of looking at the problem [is] even more dangerous than the suggestion's other unfortunate aspect: its assumption that every private discrimination is invalid once the right formal state connection has been found." See also Jerre Williams, *Mulkey v. Reitman and State Action,* 14 U.C.L.A.L.Rev. 26 (1966).

Compare Henkin, note 5(b)(i) supra at 496: "Generally, the equal protection clause precludes state enforcement of private discrimination. There is, however, a small area of liberty favored by the Constitution even over claims to equality. Rights of liberty and property, of privacy and voluntary association, must be balanced, in close cases, against the right not to have the state enforce discrimination against the victim. In the few instances in which the right to discriminate is protected or preferred by the Constitution, the state may enforce it."[c] Is it the contention that the inquiry is not whether state action is present but whether the state policy preference, expressed through its laws, between conflicting claims of individuals, denies equal protection?

Contrast Martin G. Gilbert, *Theories of State Action as Applied to the "Sit–In" Cases,* 17 Ark.L.Rev. 147, 161 (1963): "The primary weakness in Henkin's approach would seem to be that the responsibility of the state arises from its *power* to act in a given situation. It would seem much sounder to impute responsibility where there is a *duty* on the part of the state to act. Thus, where traditional state functions, such as running elections or operating a town, are involved, the state would seem to have a duty to see that these activities are conducted in a constitutional manner. Beyond [this], the state might have a duty to insure nondiscrimination by enterprises which occupy important positions of public interest. For example, if all the milk producers in an area refused to sell to Negroes, it would seem that the state would have a duty to insure that Negroes could purchase milk on equal terms with whites. In the case of the small corner diner, especially in an area which offers other sources of similar meals to the Negro, it would seem that the state has no duty to insure the Negro a meal there, even though the state would clearly have the power to do so. Here again, an ad hoc approach would be required."

See Harold W. Horowitz, *Fourteenth Amendment Aspects of Racial Discrimination in "Private" Housing,* 52 Calif.L.Rev. 1, 12–20 (1964): "The determination of the constitutionality under the fourteenth amendment of state law permitting a private person to discriminate, on racial grounds, against another private person in a specific fact situation requires consideration of various interdependent factors: the nature and degree of injury to the person discriminated against, the interest of the discriminator in being permitted to discriminate, and the interest of the discriminatee in having opportunity of access equal to that of other persons to the benefits of governmental assistance to the discriminator * * *. If there is extensive state participation and involvement related to the activities of the discriminator, it is more likely that those activities will be public in nature, with consequent public indignity and humiliation suffered by the person discriminated against, and more likely that denial of access to those activities will be of some significance to the discriminatee. [When] there is governmental assistance to the discriminator in carrying on his activities, and the assistance is being provided to

---

c. See also Charles L. Black, *"State Action," Equal Protection, and California's Proposition 14,* 81 Harv.L.Rev. 69, 83–109 (1967); Frank S. Sengstock & Mary C. Sengstock, *Discrimination: A Constitutional Dilemma,* 9 Wm. & Mary L.Rev. 59 (1967).

further the purposes of a governmental program designed to provide benefits for the public or a permissible segment of the public, the effect of the discrimination is to deny to the discriminatee the opportunity to have equal opportunity of access to the benefits of the governmental program."[d]

Compare Jesse H. Choper, *Thoughts on State Action,* 1979 Wash.U.L.Q. 757, 762: "[The balancing approaches] contradict a central feature of the fourteenth amendment. Although its major purpose was to augment the authority of the national government to secure certain constitutional rights, its primary thrust was to accomplish this goal by outlawing deprivations of these rights by state governments and their legal structures rather than by the impact of private choice. By effectively obliterating the distinction between state action and private action, these theories eviscerate the fourteenth amendment's restriction on the authority of the national government vis-à-vis the states regarding the regulation of the myriad relationships that occur between one individual and another. [A]t the initiative of any litigant who is offended by another person's behavior, these theories would subject to the scrutiny of federal judges, under substantive constitutional standards customarily developed for measuring the actions of government, all sorts of private conduct that because of political constraints and collective good sense would probably never be mandated by law. Further, by permitting private actors to violate constitutional norms when they have a constitutionally protected liberty interest to do so, these theories would delegate to federal judges the power to implement the vague mandate of the due process clause in speaking the final word about the validity of virtually all transactions between individuals. In doing so, the national judiciary would be required to determine whether private conduct was constitutionally immune from government control even though, because of general political sensitivity to individual autonomy, such private conduct probably would never be regulated by the state." See also Thomas P. Lewis, *The Role of Law in Regulating Discrimination in Places of Public Accommodation,* 13 Buf.L.Rev. 402, 416–18 (1964).

8. *"Sit-in" cases.*[e] (a) In PETERSON v. GREENVILLE, 373 U.S. 244, 83 S.Ct. 1119, 10 L.Ed.2d 323 (1963), an ordinance forebade restaurants to seat whites and blacks together. The Court, per WARREN, C.J., reversed trespass convictions of black youths who, when denied service at a lunch counter, refused to leave: "[T]hese convictions cannot stand, even assuming [that] the manager would have acted as he did independently of the existence of the ordinance. [When] a state agency passes a law compelling persons to discriminate [such] a palpable violation of the Fourteenth Amendment cannot be saved by attempting

---

d. For other discussions of a balancing approach, see Robert J. Glennon & John E. Nowak, *A Functional Analysis of the Fourteenth Amendment "State Action" Requirement,* 1976 Sup.Ct.Rev. 221; Thomas G. Quinn, *State Action: A Pathology and a Proposed Cure,* 64 Calif.L.Rev. 146 (1976); Anthony Thompson, *Piercing the Veil of State Action: The Revisionist Theory and a Mythical Application to Self–Help Repossession.* 1977 Wis.L.Rev. 1; Arval A. Morris & L.A. Scot Powe, Jr., *Constitutional & Statutory Rights to Open Housing,* 44 Wash. L.Rev. 1–56 (1968); David Haber, *Notes on the Limits of Shelley v. Kraemer,* 18 Rutgers L.Rev. 811 (1964).

For recent consideration of "balancing," see Erwin Chemerinsky, *Rethinking State Action,*
80 Nw.U.L.Rev. 503 (1985); William P. Marshall, *Diluting Constitutional Rights: Rethinking "Rethinking State Action,"* 80 Nw.U.L.Rev. 558 (1985); Erwin Chemerinsky, *More Is Not Less: A Rejoinder to Professor Marshall,* 80 Nw.U.L.Rev. 571 (1985).

e. In the early 1960s, the Court—employing a variety of doctrines, but never relying on *Shelley*—reversed a long series of trespass convictions of "sit-in" demonstrators who were protesting racial discrimination by restaurants and other businesses. The Civil Rights Act of 1964 (Ch. 2, Sec. 2, III) largely mooted the constitutional problem of equal rights in public accommodations.

to separate the mental urges of the discriminators."[f] Douglas, J., concurred.[g] HARLAN, J., noting "a clash of competing constitutional claims of a high order: liberty and equality," would have "the issue of state action" turn on the "question of fact" whether the restaurant "might have preferred for reasons entirely of its own not to serve meals to Negroes along with whites, [or] whether the ordinance played some part in [the] decision to segregate."[h]

(b) In BELL v. MARYLAND, 378 U.S. 226, 84 S.Ct. 1814, 12 L.Ed.2d 822 (1964), GOLDBERG, J., joined by Warren, C.J., and Douglas, J., relying on the historical view in Sec. 1, fn. a, cited *Marsh, Shelley, Terry* and *Barrows* for the view that "a State, obligated under the Fourteenth Amendment to maintain a system of law in which Negroes are not denied protection in their claim to be treated as equal members of the community, may not use its criminal trespass laws to frustrate the constitutionally granted right. Nor [may] a State frustrate this right by legitimating a proprietor's attempt at self-help."[i]

BLACK, J., joined by Harlan and White, JJ., dissented: Reliance on *Shelley* was "misplaced" because it established only these propositions: "(1) When an owner of property is willing to sell and a would-be purchaser is willing to buy, then the Civil Rights Act of 1866, which gives all persons the same right to 'inherit, lease, sell, hold, and convey' property, prohibits a State, whether through its legislature, executive, or judiciary, from preventing the sale on the grounds of the race or color of one of the parties. * * * (2) Once a person has become a property owner, then he [may] sell his property to whom he pleases and admit to that property whom he will; so long as *both* parties are willing parties, then the principles stated in *Buchanan v. Warley*, 245 U.S. 60, 38 S.Ct. 16, 62 L.Ed. 149 (1917) and *Shelley*

---

f. See also *Lombard v. Louisiana*, 373 U.S. 267, 83 S.Ct. 1122, 10 L.Ed.2d 338 (1963) (statements by city officials that sit-ins "would not be permitted" had "as much coercive effect as an ordinance"); *Robinson v. Florida*, 378 U.S. 153, 84 S.Ct. 1693, 12 L.Ed.2d 771 (1964) (state health regulations, requiring racially separate toilets in restaurants, impose "burdens bound to discourage the serving of the two races together").

If a statute requires private colleges to enact regulations for maintenance of order on campus, must such a college's procedures for dismissal of students comport with procedural due process?

g. See also Douglas, J.'s view that "state policy may be as effectively expressed in *customs* as in formal legislative, executive, or judicial action," *Garner v. Louisiana*, 368 U.S. 157, 82 S.Ct. 248, 7 L.Ed.2d 207 (1961) (concurring opinion) (cf. Kenneth L. Karst & William W. Van Alstyne, *Sit-Ins and State Action—Mr. Justice Douglas Concurring*, 14 Stan.L.Rev. 762 (1962)); and Brennan, J.'s view that *Peterson, Lombard*, and *Robinson* "together hold that a state policy of discouraging privately chosen integration or encouraging privately chosen segregation, even though the policy is expressed in a form nondiscriminatory on its face, is unconstitutional and taints the privately chosen segregation it seeks to bring about," *Adickes v. S.H. Kress & Co.*, 398 U.S. 144, 90 S.Ct. 1598, 26 L.Ed.2d 142 (1970) (separate

opinion). See further, note 2 after *Reitman v. Mulkey*, infra.

h. Consider Thomas P. Lewis, *The Sit–In Cases: Great Expectations*, 1963 Sup.Ct.Rev. 101, 110: "The Court [was] concerned with persons unknown and unknowable who might be affected by the cumulative pressure of such laws on a variety of proprietors in a variety of environments. [When] only the proprietor can know what his 'mental urges' are, and when even he might find difficulty in separating them, judicial review will be more effective for the mass of cases [if] the Court by the announcement of its rule makes it as certain as it can that proprietors and officials alike appreciate the precise status of segregation laws."

If federal law requires airlines to search passengers for weapons, should the issue of whether such a search by an airline employee is "state action" under the fourth and fourteenth amendments turn on whether the airlines would have conducted the searches regardless of the federal legislation?

i. See also Souter, J., dissenting in *Bray v. Alexandria Women's Health Clinic*, 506 U.S. 263, 113 S.Ct. 753, 122 L.Ed.2d 34 (1993): "[G]overnment enforcement of private segregation by use of a state trespass law, rather than 'securing to all persons [the] equal protection of the laws,' itself amounted to an unconstitutional act in violation of the Equal Protection Clause of the Fourteenth Amendment. Cf. *Shelley*."

protect this right. But equally, when one party is unwilling, as when the property owner chooses *not* to sell to a particular person or *not* to admit that person, [then] he is entitled to rely on the guarantee of due process of law [to] protect his free use and enjoyment of property and to know that only by valid legislation, passed pursuant to some constitutional grant of power, can anyone disturb this free use."

REITMAN v. MULKEY

387 U.S. 369, 87 S.Ct. 1627, 18 L.Ed.2d 830 (1967).

JUSTICE WHITE delivered the opinion of the Court.

[Section 26 of the California constitution], an initiated measure submitted to the people [in] a statewide ballot in 1964, provides in part as follows: "Neither the State nor any subdivision or agency thereof shall deny, limit or abridge, directly or indirectly, the right of any person, who is willing or desires to sell, lease or rent any part or all of his real property, to decline to sell, lease or rent such property to such person or persons as he, in his absolute discretion, chooses." The real property covered by § 26 is limited to residential property and contains an exception for state-owned real estate.

[Respondents] sued under § 51 and § 52 of the California Civil Code [forbidding racial discrimination "in all business establishments"] alleging that petitioners had refused to rent them an apartment solely on account of their race. An injunction and damages were demanded. Petitioners moved for summary judgment on the ground that §§ 51 and 52 [had] been rendered null and void by the adoption of [§ 26] after the filing of the complaint. [The California Supreme Court held that § 26] was invalid as denying [equal protection].

We affirm the judgment [which] quite properly undertook to examine the constitutionality of § 26 in terms of its "immediate objective," its "ultimate impact" and its "historical context and the conditions existing prior to its enactment." Judgments such as these we have frequently undertaken ourselves. *Yick Wo v. Hopkins, Lombard v. Louisiana, Anderson v. Martin.* But here the California Supreme Court has addressed itself to these matters and we should give careful consideration to its views because they concern the purpose, scope, and operative effect of a provision of the California Constitution.

First, the court considered whether § 26 was concerned at all with private discriminations in residential housing. [§ 26's] immediate design and intent, the California court said, was "to overturn state laws that bore on the right of private sellers and lessors to discriminate," [and] "to forestall future state action that might circumscribe this right." * * *

Second, the court conceded that the State was permitted a neutral position with respect to private racial discriminations and that the State was not bound by the Federal Constitution to forbid them. But [the] court deemed it necessary to determine whether [§ 26] invalidly involved the State in racial discriminations in the housing market. Its conclusion was that it did.

To reach this result, the state court [reasoned] that a prohibited state involvement could be found "even where the state can be charged with only encouraging," rather than commanding discrimination. [To] the California court "[t]he instant case [was one]" wherein the State had taken affirmative action designed to make private discriminations legally possible. Section 26 was said to have changed the situation from one in which discriminatory practices were restricted "to one wherein it is encouraged, within the meaning of the cited decisions"; § 26 was legislative action "which authorized private discrimination" and made the State "at least a partner in the instant act of discrimination * * *." The court could "conceive of no other purpose for an application of section 26 aside from authorizing the perpetration of a purported private discrimination * * *." * * *

There is no sound reason for rejecting this judgment. [It] did not read either our cases or the Fourteenth Amendment as establishing an automatic constitutional barrier to the repeal of an existing law prohibiting racial discriminations in housing; nor did the court rule that a State may never put in statutory form an existing policy of neutrality with respect to private discriminations. [It] dealt with § 26 as though it expressly authorized and constitutionalized the private right to discriminate [and] the court assessed the ultimate impact of § 26 in the California environment and concluded that the section would encourage and significantly involve the State in private racial discrimination contrary to the Fourteenth Amendment.

The California court could very reasonably conclude that § 26 would and did have wider impact than a mere repeal of existing statutes. [The] right to discriminate, including the right to discriminate on racial grounds, was now embodied in the State's basic charter, immune from legislative, executive, or judicial regulation at any level of the state government. Those practicing racial discriminations need no longer rely solely on their personal choice. They could now invoke express constitutional authority, free from censure or interference of any kind from official sources. * * *

This Court has never attempted the "impossible task" of formulating an infallible test for determining whether the State "in any of its manifestations" has become significantly involved in private discriminations. [Here] the California court, armed as it was with the knowledge of the facts and circumstances concerning the passage and potential impact of § 26, and familiar with the milieu in which that provision would operate, has determined that the provision would involve the State in private racial discriminations to an unconstitutional degree. We accept this holding of the California court. * * *

Affirmed.[a]

JUSTICE HARLAN, whom JUSTICE BLACK, JUSTICE CLARK, and JUSTICE STEWART join, dissenting.

[A]ll that has happened is that California has effected a pro tanto repeal of its prior statutes forbidding private discrimination. This runs no more afoul of the Fourteenth Amendment than would have California's failure to pass any such antidiscrimination statutes in the first instance. The fact that such repeal was also accompanied by a constitutional prohibition against future enactment of such laws by the California Legislature cannot well be thought to affect, from a federal constitutional standpoint, the validity of what California has done. [§ 26] is neutral on its face, and it is only by in effect asserting that this requirement of passive official neutrality is camouflage that the Court is able to reach its conclusion. * * *

There is no disagreement whatever but that § 26 was meant to nullify California's fair-housing legislation and thus to remove from private residential

---

a. Douglas, J., joined the Court's opinion, adding that "we deal here with a problem in the realm of zoning, similar to the one we had in *Shelley.* [When] the state leaves [the zoning] function to private agencies or institutions [including real estate brokers who are state licensees], it suffers a governmental function to be performed under private auspices in a way the State itself may not act. The present case is therefore kin to *Terry.*"

property transactions the state-created impediment upon freedom of choice. [But there was no finding] that the defendants' actions were anything but the product of their own private choice. [There] were no findings as to the general effect of § 26. The Court declares that the California court "held the purpose and intent of § 26 was to authorize private racial discriminations in the housing market," but there is no supporting fact in the record for this characterization.

[The] denial of equal protection emerges only from the conclusion reached by the Court that the implementation of a new policy of governmental neutrality [has] the effect of lending encouragement to those who wish to discriminate. In the context of the actual facts of the case, this conclusion appears to me to state only a truism: people who want to discriminate but were previously forbidden to do so by state law are now left free because the State has chosen to have no law on the subject at all. Obviously whenever there is a change in the law it will have resulted from the concerted activity of those who desire the change, and its enactment will allow those supporting the legislation to pursue their private goals.

[Every] act of private discrimination is either forbidden by state law or permitted by it. There can be little doubt that such permissiveness—whether by express constitutional or statutory provision, or implicit in the common law—to some extent "encourages" those who wish to discriminate to do so. Under this theory "state action" in the form of laws that do nothing more than passively permit private discrimination could be said to tinge *all* private discrimination with the taint of unconstitutional state encouragement. * * *

Notes and Questions

1. *Court's rationale.* (a) What was the specific basis for § 26's invalidity? Was it that it "constitutionalized the private right to discriminate" in housing, making it "immune from legislative, executive, or judicial regulation at any level of state government"—thus making it much more difficult for minorities to get governmental antidiscrimination help? Would this call for the same result even if California had never enacted anti-discrimination laws? Suppose a state provides that *all* legislation requires approval by ⅔ of the voters? All legislation having *anything* to do with the sale and purchase of real and personal property? Was § 26 a less "neutral provision"? Sufficiently "nonneutral"? Was *this* the thrust of the opinion? If so, does *Reitman* hold that racial discrimination in housing by private individuals in California is "state action"?

(b) Or did the Court rest on the finding (whose finding?) that § 26, given "the milieu in which that provision would operate," "would involve the State in private racial discriminations to an unconstitutional degree"? If so, could "mere repeal of existing statutes" so operate? Failure to enact a proposed antidiscrimination law? The mere absence of an antidiscrimination law? Consider Archibald Cox, *The Warren Court* 45 (1968): "The truth would seem to be that the absence of legal restraints gives encouragement of a sort to anyone minded to engage in discrimination, and any defeat of proposed restraints after strong public debate will give moral support to some persons who might not otherwise have been ready to discriminate. The degree of support that is given seems likely to depend upon a congeries of factors far more diffuse and subtle than the differences between repeal of a statute and amendment of a constitution." See Charles L. Black, *"State Action," Equal Protection, and California's Proposition 14,* 81 Harv.L.Rev. 69 (1967); Philip B. Kurland, *Egalitarianism and the Warren Court,* 68 Mich. 629, 668–70 (1970); Kenneth L. Karst & Harold W. Horowitz, *Reitman v. Mulkey: A Telophase of Substantive Equal Protection,* 1967 Sup.Ct.Rev. 39.

2. *State "encouragement" or "authorization."* (a) To what extent does *Reitman* establish the principle that state law which *encourages* (or *authorizes*) private conduct results in "state action"? Is this the basis for Brennan, J.'s view in *Adickes*? What result if "a state passed a statute which provided that individuals shall have the legal right to engage in racial discrimination in their own homes"? Jerre Williams, *The Twilight of State Action,* 41 Texas L.Rev. 347, 384 (1963). Consider William M. Burke & David J. Reber, *State Action, Congressional Power and Creditors' Rights: An Essay on the Fourteenth Amendment,* 46 So.Cal.L.Rev. 1003, 1105–09 (1973): "[The] basic principle limiting the scope of the fourteenth amendment would be destroyed by equating state action with action authorized or encouraged by state law. [California] statutory law authorizes [the] use of force in self-defense; the disposition of real and personal property; [the] creation of a contractual relationship; [the] execution of a will; the formation of a corporation [etc.]. If state authority or encouragement is a valid state action test, then all of the above forms of private conduct would present fourteenth amendment equal protection and due process problems. [The] fallacy in the thesis [is] most readily apparent when one considers the impact of judicial law. It is almost impossible to consider any form of activity that is not somehow authorized by state decisional law. [As] long as the law is permissive in nature and leaves the initial decision to take the action entirely within the realm of private choice, neither the state nor the individual should be held constitutionally responsible under the fourteenth amendment. [Further], constitutional significance should not attach to such extraneous considerations as whether the law restates a long-standing law, clarifies an existing law, changes the law, creates entirely new law or repeals existing law. [First], the effect of a statute as a form of state law authorizing private conduct is precisely the same regardless of the statute's longevity. [Second,] a holding that the statute is unconstitutional because of its newness or because it repeals an existing law considered more socially desirable by the Court [would] constitutionally freeze into state law every form of social legislation or decisional or administrative law deemed constitutionally proper by the Court and would thereby discourage states from experimenting in this regard. It would also produce anomalous and illogical results since the identical private conduct authorized and encouraged by the identical statutory or judicial law would be valid in some states under the fourteenth amendment but invalid in others solely because of the age of the state law in each jurisdiction."

Compare Note, *State Action: Theories for Applying Constitutional Restrictions to Private Activity,* 74 Colum.L.Rev. 656, 665–66 (1974): "Statutes enlarging common law rights clearly amount to an increase of private powers, while mere statutory codification of common law rights does not amount to authorization [and the] argument that such 'authorizing' statutes involve government by increasing private powers implies that an increase in powers through expansion of common law rights effected by the courts will constitute a government grant of power. Since any particular decision expanding the previously existing common law would thus constitute 'authorization,' the question arises as against when present common law rights are to be measured. The most reasonable starting point for 'state action' cases arising under the fourteenth amendment would seem to be the common law as of adoption of that amendment." See also Harold W. Horowitz & Kenneth L. Karst, *The California Supreme Court and State Action Under the Fourteenth Amendment: The Leader Beclouds the Issue,* 21 U.C.L.A.L.Rev. 1421 (1974).

(b) The "state 'encouragement' or 'authorization' " issue is considered further in *Flagg Bros. v. Brooks,* Sec. 4 infra.

3. *Repeal of discriminatory legislation.* Recall *Lombard*, *Peterson* and *Robinson*. Suppose all official pronouncements *requiring* discrimination are repealed or retracted? Is subsequent "private" discrimination in respect to matters previously covered by official pronouncements "state action"? Is the state "significantly involved" because its repeals have now made "private discriminations legally possible"? Have they "authorized" and "encouraged" discrimination? Or is this "mere repeal of existing statutes"? Is discrimination more "authorized and encouraged" by repeal of laws requiring discrimination or by repeal of laws forbidding it?

MOOSE LODGE v. IRVIS

407 U.S. 163, 92 S.Ct. 1965, 32 L.Ed.2d 627 (1972).

JUSTICE REHNQUIST delivered the opinion of the Court.

Appellee Irvis, a Negro, [who] was refused service [as the guest of a member] by appellant Moose Lodge, [claimed] that because the Pennsylvania liquor board had issued appellant Moose Lodge a private club license that authorized the sale of alcoholic beverages on its premises, the refusal of service to him was "state action" * * *.

A three-judge district court [entered] a decree declaring invalid the liquor license issued to Moose Lodge "as long as it follows a policy of racial discrimination in its membership or operating policies or practices." * * *

Moose Lodge is a private club in the ordinary meaning of that term. [It] conducts all of its activities in a building that is owned by it. It is not publicly funded. Only members and guests are permitted in any lodge of the order; one may become a guest only by invitation * * *.

While the principle is easily stated, the question of whether particular discriminatory conduct is private, on the one hand, or amounts to "state action," on the other hand, frequently admits of no easy answer. "Only by sifting facts and weighing circumstances can the non-obvious involvement of the State in private conduct be attributed its true significance." *Burton v. Wilmington Parking Authority*, 365 U.S. 715, 81 S.Ct. 856, 6 L.Ed.2d 45 (1961).

[*Burton* held] that a private restaurant owner who refused service because of a customer's race violated the Fourteenth Amendment, where the restaurant was located in a building owned by a state-created parking authority and leased from the authority. The Court, after a comprehensive review of the relationship between the lessee and the parking authority concluded that the latter had "so far insinuated itself into a position of interdependence with Eagle [the restaurant owner] that it must be recognized as a joint participant in the challenged activity, which, on that account, cannot be considered to have been so 'purely private' as to fall without the scope of the Fourteenth Amendment."

The Court has never held, of course, that discrimination by an otherwise private entity would be violative of the Equal Protection Clause if the private entity receives any sort of benefit or service at all from the State, or if it is subject to state regulation in any degree whatever. Since state-furnished services include such necessities of life as electricity, water, and police and fire protection, such a holding would utterly emasculate the distinction between private as distinguished from State conduct set forth in *The Civil Rights Cases* and adhered to in subsequent decisions. Our holdings indicate that where the impetus for the discrimination is private, the State must have "significantly involved itself with invidious discriminations," *Reitman,* in order for the discriminatory action to fall within the ambit of the constitutional prohibition. * * *

In *Burton,* the Court's full discussion of the facts in its opinion indicates the significant differences between that case and this: "The land and building were publicly owned.[a] As an entity, the building was dedicated to 'public uses' in performance of the Authority's 'essential governmental functions.'[b] The costs of land acquisition, construction, and maintenance are defrayed entirely from donations by the City of Wilmington, from loans and revenue bonds and from the proceeds of rentals and parking services out of which the loans and bonds were payable. Assuming that the distinction would be significant, the commercially leased areas were not surplus state property, but constituted a physically and financially integral and, indeed, indispensable part of the State's plan to operate its project as a self-sustaining unit.[c] Upkeep and maintenance of the building, including necessary repairs, were responsibilities of the Authority and were payable out of public funds. It cannot be doubted that the peculiar relationship of the restaurant to the parking facility in which it is located confers on each an incidental variety of mutual benefits. Guests of the restaurant are afforded a convenient place to park their automobiles, even if they cannot enter the restaurant directly from the parking area. Similarly, its convenience for diners may well provide additional demand for the Authority's parking facilities.[d] Should any improvements effected in the leasehold by Eagle become part of the realty, there is no possibility of increased taxes being passed on to it since the fee is held by a tax-exempt government agency. Neither can it be ignored, especially in view of Eagle's affirmative allegation that for it to serve Negroes would injure its business, that profits earned by discrimination not only contribute to, but also are indispensable elements in, the financial success of a governmental agency."[e]

a. If the space has been leased to a law firm, could it constitutionally discriminate among its clients?

b. If the Authority had municipal immunity from tort liability, is Eagle liable for a customer's food poisoning?

c. "Other portions of the structure were leased to other tenants, including a bookstore, a retail jeweler, and a food store. Upon completion of the building, the Authority located at appropriate places thereon official signs indicating the public character of the building, and flew from mastheads on the roof both the state and national flags." *Burton.* Query: If Wilmington, instead of including rental space in the parking building, had relied on rental income from other of its properties located throughout the city to help finance the parking facility, could lessees of these properties refuse to do business with African–Americans?

d. Suppose Eagle were located in a private building immediately adjacent to the public parking building?

e. *Burton* added: "It is irony amounting to grave injustice that in one part of a single building, erected and maintained with public funds by an agency of the State to serve a public purpose, all persons have equal rights, while in another portion, also serving the public, a Negro is a second-class citizen [but] at the same time fully enjoys equal access to nearby restaurants in wholly privately owned buildings. [I]n its lease with Eagle the Authority could have affirmatively required Eagle to discharge the responsibilities under the Fourteenth Amendment imposed upon the private enterprise as a consequence of state participation. But no State may effectively abdicate its responsibilities by either ignoring them or by merely failing to discharge them whatever the motive may be." Query: If the state sells surplus property without requiring its nondiscriminatory use because such a requirement would bring the city a lower price, may the purchaser constitutionally discriminate? If such a requirement were financially irrelevant but the state neglected to include it, may the buyer discriminate?

Harlan, J., joined by Whittaker, J., dissented: "The Court's opinion, by a process of first undiscriminatingly throwing together various factual bits and pieces and then undermining the resulting structure by an equally vague disclaimer, seems to me to leave completely at sea just what it is in this record that satisfies the requirement of 'state action.'" See generally Thomas P. Lewis, *Burton v. Wilmington Parking Authority—A Case Without Precedent,* 61 Colum.L.Rev. 1458 (1961).

Here there is nothing approaching the symbiotic relationship between lessor and lessee that was present in [*Burton*]. Moose Lodge quite ostentatiously proclaims the fact that it is not open to the public at large. Nor is it located and operated in such surroundings that although private in name, it discharges a function or performs a service that would otherwise in all likelihood be performed by the State. In short, while Eagle was a public restaurant in a public building, Moose Lodge is a private social club in a private building.

With the exception hereafter noted, the Pennsylvania Liquor Control Board plays absolutely no part in establishing or enforcing the membership or guest policies of the club which it licenses to serve liquor.[3] [The] only effect that the state licensing of Moose Lodge to serve liquor can be said to have on the right of any other Pennsylvanian to buy or be served liquor on premises other than those of Moose Lodge is that for some purposes club licenses are counted in the maximum number of licenses which may be issued in a given municipality. Basically each municipality has a quota of one retail license for each 1,500 inhabitants. Licenses issued to hotels, municipal golf courses and airport restaurants are not counted in this quota, nor are club licenses until the maximum number of retail licenses is reached. Beyond that point, neither additional retail licenses nor additional club licenses may be issued so long as the number of issued and outstanding retail licenses remains above the statutory maximum.

The District Court was at pains to [note that] an applicant for a club license must make such physical alterations in its premises as the board may require, must file a list of the names and addresses of its members and employees, and must keep extensive financial records. The board is granted the right to inspect the licensed premises at any time * * *.

However detailed this type of regulation may be in some particulars, it cannot be said to in any way foster or encourage racial discrimination. Nor can it be said to make the State in any realistic sense a partner or even a joint venturer in the club's enterprise. The limited effect of the prohibition against obtaining additional club licenses when the maximum number of retail licenses allotted to a municipality has been issued, when considered together with the availability of liquor from hotel, restaurant, and retail licensees falls far short of conferring upon club licensees a monopoly in the dispensing of liquor * * *. We therefore hold that, with the exception hereafter noted, the operation of the regulatory scheme enforced by the Pennsylvania Liquor Control Board does not sufficiently implicate the State in the discriminatory guest policies of Moose Lodge * * *.

The District Court found that [Regulations § 113.09] of the Liquor Control Board adopted pursuant to statute affirmatively require that "every club licensee shall adhere to all the provisions of its constitution and by-laws." Appellant argues that the purpose of this provision "is purely and simply and plainly the prevention of subterfuge." [There] can be no doubt that the label "private club" can and has been used to evade both regulations of State and local liquor authorities, and statutes requiring places of public accommodation to serve all persons without regard to race, color, religion, or national origin. * * *

Even though the Liquor Control Board regulation in question is neutral in its terms, the result of its application in a case where the constitution and by-laws of a club required racial discrimination [as Moose Lodge did in respect to membership and guest privileges,] would be to invoke the sanctions of the State to enforce a concededly discriminatory private rule. * * * *Shelley v. Kraemer* makes it clear

---

3. Unlike the situation in *Pollak*, where the regulatory agency had affirmatively approved the practice of the regulated entity after full investigation * * *.

that the application of state sanctions to enforce such a rule would violate the Fourteenth Amendment. * * *

Appellee was entitled to a decree enjoining the enforcement of § 113.09 [but] no more. The judgment of the District Court is reversed * * *.

JUSTICE DOUGLAS, with whom JUSTICE MARSHALL joins, dissenting.

My view of the First Amendment and the related guarantees of the Bill of Rights is that they create a zone of privacy which precludes government from interfering with private clubs or groups.[1] The associational rights which our system honors permits all white, all black, all brown, and all yellow clubs to be formed. [And] the fact that a private club gets some kind of permit from the State or municipality does not make it ipso facto a public enterprise or undertaking, any more than the grant to a householder of a permit to operate an incinerator puts the householder in the public domain. We must therefore examine whether there are special circumstances involved in the Pennsylvania scheme which differentiate the liquor license possessed by Moose Lodge from the incinerator permit.

[The opinion then agrees with the Court's disposition of Regulations § 113.09]. But there is another flaw in the scheme not so easily cured. Liquor licenses in Pennsylvania [are] not freely available to those who meet racially neutral qualifications. There is a complex quota system, which the majority accurately describes. What the majority neglects to say is that the Harrisburg quota, where Moose Lodge No. 107 is located, has been full for many years. No more club licenses may be issued in that city.

This state-enforced scarcity of licenses restricts the ability of blacks to obtain liquor, for liquor is commercially available *only* at private clubs for a significant portion of each week.[3] [A] group desiring to form a nondiscriminatory club which would serve blacks must purchase a license held by an existing club, which can exact a monopoly price for the transfer. The availability of such a license is speculative at best, however, for, as Moose Lodge itself concedes, without a liquor license a fraternal organization would be hard-pressed to survive.

Thus, the State of Pennsylvania is putting the weight of its liquor license, concededly a valued and important adjunct to a private club, behind racial discrimination. * * *

JUSTICE BRENNAN, with whom JUSTICE MARSHALL joins, dissenting.

When Moose Lodge obtained its liquor license, the State of Pennsylvania became an active participant in the operation of the Lodge bar. Liquor licensing laws [are] primarily pervasive regulatory schemes under which the State dictates and continually supervises virtually every detail of the operation of the licensee's business. Very few, if any, other licensed businesses experience such complete state involvement. [The] opinion of the [court below] most persuasively demonstrates the "state action" present in this case: * * *

"[After describing the regulations, mentioned in the majority opinion, the court below continued:] It is only on compliance with these and numerous other

---

1. [There] was no occasion [below] to consider the question whether perhaps because of a role as a center of community activity, Moose Lodge No. 107 was in fact "private" for equal protection purposes. The decision today, therefore, leaves this question open.

3. Hotels and restaurants may serve liquor between 7:00 a.m. and 2:00 a.m. the next day,

Monday through Saturday. On Sunday, such licensees are restricted to sales between 12:00 a.m. and 2:00 a.m., and between 1:00 p.m. and 10:00 p.m. * * * Club licensees, however, are permitted to sell liquor to members and guests from 7:00 a.m. to 3:00 a.m. the next day, seven-days-a-week. * * *

requirements and if the Board is satisfied that the applicant is 'a person of good repute' and that the license will not be 'detrimental to the welfare, health, peace and morals of the inhabitants of the neighborhood,' that the license may issue.

"Once a license has been issued the licensee must comply with many detailed requirements or risk its suspension or revocation. He must in any event have it renewed periodically. Liquor licenses have been employed in Pennsylvania to regulate a wide variety of moral conduct, such as the presence and activities of homosexuals, performance by a topless dancer, lewd dancing, swearing, being noisy or disorderly. So broad is the state's power that the courts of Pennsylvania have upheld its restriction of freedom of expression of a licensee on the ground that in doing so it merely exercises its plenary power to attach conditions to the privilege of dispensing liquor which a licensee holds at the sufferance of the state. * * * '' * * *f

Notes and Questions

1. *Court's rationale.* Does *Moose Lodge* rest ultimately on a "balancing approach"? See Note, *State Action and the Burger Court,* 60 Va.L.Rev. 840 (1974). Consider Note, *Developing Legal Vistas for the Discouragement of Private Club Discrimination,* 58 Iowa L.Rev. 108, 139 (1972): "[There is evidence that] large, nationwide fraternal orders which are segregated pursuant to national constitutions, [serve] substantially economic interests. Furthermore, a glance at the membership requirement and size of these clubs indicates they are not closely knit clubs involving a high quotient of intimacy. They are certainly not primarily religious or political in nature. Hence, under the balancing approach, the associational rights asserted by these clubs would not seem strong."

2. *Burton vs. Moose Lodge.* Consider Christopher D. Stone, *Corporate Vices and Corporate Virtues: Do Public/Private Distinctions Matter?,* 130 U.Pa.L.Rev. 1441, 1449–1501 (1982): "There are several ways to interpret the contrasting results in *Burton* and *Moose Lodge.* One way is to contrast the symbolic elements of the situation: after all, the parking authority building flew, quite literally, the flags of government. [Second,] in *Burton,* the government stood to capture essentially all the economic benefits of the discrimination, assuming perfect competition among bidders for the lease. Hence, the Court's decision prohibiting the arrangement eliminated from public revenues essentially the full measure of the ill-gotten gains. [T]he preponderant costs of setting a morally correct example will be borne by the public, which is exactly where they ought to lie. Note that the same consequence, the apportionment of essentially all 'fairness' costs on general revenues, would not result from a plaintiff's victory when the government is insuring mortgages, or guaranteeing loans, or is a regulatory licensor, as in *Moose Lodge.* [In] those situations, extending state action would concentrate costs on a distinct sub-group, a result that courts have been reluctant to decree."

3. *Private schools.* (a) NORWOOD v. HARRISON, 413 U.S. 455, 93 S.Ct. 2804, 37 L.Ed.2d 723 (1973), per BURGER, C.J., enjoined Mississippi's lending of textbooks to all students in public and private schools as applied to racially segregated private schools: "[T]hat the Constitution may compel toleration of private discrimination in some circumstances does not mean that it requires state support for such discrimination."

---

f. Irvis also complained to the Pennsylvania Human Rights Commission. *Commonwealth v. Loyal Order of Moose,* 448 Pa. 451, 294 A.2d 594, appeal dismissed, 409 U.S. 1052 (1972), upheld the Commission's ruling that the Harrisburg Moose Lodge was a "public accommodation" under state law and could not bar guests on the basis of race.

The textbook program, "enacted first in 1940, long before [there] was any occasion to have a policy or reason to foster the development of racially segregated private academies," may have been "motivated by [a] sincere interest in the educational welfare of all Mississippi children. But good intentions as to one valid objective do not serve to negate the State's involvement in violation of a constitutional duty. 'The existence of a permissible purpose cannot sustain an action that has an impermissible effect.' [citing school desegregation cases]." The lower court had found "that the textbook loans did not interfere with or impede the State's acknowledged duty to establish a unitary school system" since "the State's public schools are now fully unitary." The Court, although casting doubt on the finding, held it "irrelevant": "A State's constitutional obligation requires it to steer clear, not only of operating the old dual system of racially segregated schools, but also of giving significant aid to institutions that practice racial or other invidious discrimination."

Plaintiffs had failed to show that "any child enrolled in private school, if deprived of free textbooks, would withdraw from private school and subsequently enroll in the public schools." But "the Constitution does not permit the State to aid discrimination even when there is no precise causal relationship between state financial aid to a private school and the continued well-being of that school. A State may not grant the type of tangible financial aid here involved if that aid has a significant tendency to facilitate, reinforce, and support private discrimination. * * * Textbooks are a basic educational tool and, like tuition grants, they are provided only in connection with schools; they are to be distinguished from generalized services government might provide to schools in common with others. Moreover, the textbooks provided to private school students by the State in this case are a form of assistance readily available from sources entirely independent of the State—unlike, for example, 'such necessities of life as electricity, water, and police and fire protection.'" Douglas and Brennan, JJ., concurred in the result.

(b) In GILMORE v. MONTGOMERY, 417 U.S. 556, 94 S.Ct. 2416, 41 L.Ed.2d 304 (1974), a federal court enjoined the city's "permitting the use of public park recreational facilities by private segregated school groups and by other non-school groups that racially discriminate in their membership." The Court, per BLACKMUN, J., modified the decree in part: It "was wholly proper for the city to be enjoined from permitting *exclusive* access to public recreational facilities by segregated private schools" (emphasis added), which had been "formed in reaction against" the federal court's school desegregation order. "[T]his assistance significantly tended to undermine the federal court order mandating [a] unitary school system in Montgomery." But, "upon this record, we are unable to draw a conclusion as to whether the use of zoos, museums, parks, and other recreational facilities by private school groups *in common with others,* and by private nonschool organizations, involves government so directly in the actions of those users as to warrant" intervention (emphasis added). "It is possible that certain uses of city facilities will be judged to be in contravention of the parks [or school] desegregation order, [or] in some way to constitute impermissible 'state action' ascribing to the city the discriminatory actions of the groups."

The latter issue concerns "whether there is significant state involvement in the private discrimination alleged. * * * Traditional state monopolies, such as electricity, water, and police and fire protection—all generalized governmental services—do not by their mere provision constitute a showing of state involvement in invidious discrimination. *Norwood.* The same is true of a broad spectrum of municipal recreational facilities * * *.

"If, however, the city or other governmental entity rations otherwise freely accessible recreational facilities, the case for state action will naturally be stronger than if the facilities are simply available to all comers without condition or reservation. Here, for example, petitioners allege that the city engages in scheduling softball games for an all-white church league and provides balls, equipment, fields, and lighting. The city's role in that situation would be dangerously close to what was found to exist in *Burton* * * *."[a]

WHITE, J., joined by Douglas, J., concurred: "[T]he question is not whether there is state action, but whether the conceded action by the city, and hence by the State, is such that the State must be deemed to have denied the equal protection of the laws. In other words, by permitting a segregated school or group to use city-owned facilities, has the State furnished such aid to the group's segregated policies or become so involved in them that the State itself may fairly be said to have denied equal protection? Under *Burton,* it is perfectly clear that to violate the Equal Protection Clause the State itself need not make, advise, or authorize the private decision to discriminate that involves the State in the practice of segregation or would appear to do so in the minds of ordinary citizens." Marshall, J. generally agreed with White, J.

(c) *Significance of remedy.* In contrast to *Burton* (where plaintiff sought an injunction against Eagle Coffee Shoppe), since the only remedy sought in *Norwood* and *Gilmore* was against the state or city itself, did these cases really present any "state action" issue at all? Was the issue in *Moose Lodge* whether the club's refusal to serve Irvis constituted "state action"? Or was it whether Pennsylvania could grant a liquor license to a club that practiced racial discrimination? Are these constitutional issues the same? What result in *Marsh* if the leafletter sued the shipbuilding company for violation of her constitutional rights? Consider Robert C. Brown, *State Action Analysis of Tax Expenditures,* 11 Harv.Civ.Rts.-Civ.Lib.L.Rev. 97, 115–19 (1976): "[T]wo kinds of 'state action' cases should [be] distinguished: only in suits in which relief is sought against a private actor should the private actor's interests be taken into account. [Thus,] it is quite possible that a plaintiff proceeding under a state action theory might prevail in enjoining the government's action but fail in his efforts to enjoin the private activity." Compare Thomas R. McCoy, *Current State Action Theories, the Jackson Nexus Requirement, and Employee Discharges by Semi–Public and State–Aided Institutions,* 31 Vand. L.Rev. 785, 802 (1978): "Although this theoretical distinction has considerable superficial appeal, primarily because it is formulated in terms of balancing competing constitutional interests, closer inspection reveals no significant difference between the cases. [E]ither kind of suit presents the private actor with precisely the same basic option—either modify the private action to conform to fourteenth amendment standards or do without the state aid." Contrast Brown, supra, at 119 n. 102: "In some cases the pressure to conform private behavior to constitutional standards generated by the loss of assistance will be as coercive as an injunction. In such a case, however, the fact that withdrawing the aid had a strong influence on private behavior would imply a high level of significance of government involvement with the private actor. In that case it would be appropriate to impose relief on the private actor as well as on the government, so the remedy distinction would not apply."

a. Brennan, J., concurred in part but would enjoin *any* "school-sponsored or directed uses of the city recreational facilities that enable private segregated schools to duplicate public school operations at public expense."

In any event, since the practices in *Norwood* and *Gilmore* were not shown to be "motivated" to perpetuate racial discrimination, can these decisions be squared with *Washington v. Davis,* Ch. 8, Sec. 2, III? Given the doctrines that (1) public financial aid to parochial schools violates the establishment clause if either the *purpose or effect* advances religion (Ch. 9, Sec. 1, II), whereas (2) a racially discriminatory *purpose* must exist for violation of the equal protection clause (Ch. 10, Sec. 2, III), can *Norwood* be squared with *Board of Educ. v. Allen* (fn. a, p. 1038 supra)? See Jesse H. Choper, *Thoughts on State Action,* 1979 Wash.U.L.Q. 757, 765–69.

(d) What results in *Norwood* and *Gilmore* if the remedy sought had been to compel the private schools to desegregate? Should some or all private schools be held to the requirements of the equal protection clause?[b]

(i) *Financial aid.* If private schools receive extensive financial aid from the state, does it result in state action only in respect to a specific activity being funded? Consider Comment, *Tax Incentives as State Action,* 122 U.Pa.L.Rev. 414, 436 (1973): "This [theory] incorrectly assumes that government involvement that bears directly upon a specific activity of an entity can be meaningfully distinguished from government involvement that serves more generally to perpetuate that entity as a whole. It is an inescapable fact that general government assistance which perpetuates an entity operates indirectly to perpetuate the specific activities of that entity." May a person whose sole source of income is public relief constitutionally refuse to sell his home to African–Americans?

(ii) *Public control.* Suppose the private schools' curriculum and admission policy are subject to state regulation? If a state statute regulates election procedures of all voluntary organizations, is a social club barred from racially discriminating? If the state provides private schools with extensive financial aid and strict regulation, are the schools "state functions"? If the state licenses all barber schools and requires that all barbers attend such schools, are the schools "state functions"?

(iii) *"Government function."* Even without state aid or regulation, does "the spirit of [the segregation decisions] support the argument that education is a matter of such vital public concern that any action taken in regard to it must be subject to the prohibitions of the fourteenth amendment"? 56 Colum.L.Rev. 285, 287 (1956). Consider Glenn Abernathy, *Expansion of the State Action Concept Under the Fourteenth Amendment,* 43 Corn.L.Q. 375, 407 (1958): "[T]he only purely privately operated functions which properly should be considered as governmental are those which are indispensable to the maintenance of democratic government. [S]uch a definition does not go so far as to cover operations which are merely useful or desirable as aids to a more efficient or intelligently controlled government. If these are to be included, then we are no better off than if we equate governmental action with operations affected with a public interest. Education is desirable and useful in a democratic system but it is not indispensable [in] the sense that access to the ballot and the processes of selecting public officials is." If the state closed all of its public schools, would that make private schools "indispensable to the maintenance of democratic government"? If so, would some (all) private schools be barred from racially (sexually, religiously) discriminating?[c]

---

b. See *Runyon v. McCrary,* Ch. 11, Sec. 2, I, holding that a federal statute prohibits private schools from refusing to accept black students.

c. See generally Note, *The Wall of Racial Separation: The Role of Private and Parochial*

Schools in Racial Integration, 43 N.Y.U.L.Rev. 514 (1968); Note, *Segregation Academies and*

4. *Tax exempt organizations.* May government give tax exemptions (or permit tax deductions for donations) to private schools, fraternal groups and charitable foundations that fail to adhere to fourteenth amendment requirements? See generally Boris I. Bittker & Kenneth M. Kaufman, *Taxes and Civil Rights: "Constitutionalizing" the Internal Revenue Code,* 82 Yale L.J. 51 (1972). Consider Note, *State Action and the United States Junior Chamber of Commerce,* 43 Geo.Wash.L.Rev. 1407, 1423–24 (1975): "[T]he Internal Revenue Code's tax exemptions for charitable organizations are based upon the theory that the Government is compensated for the loss of revenue by being relieved of the financial burden that would otherwise have to be met by appropriations of government funds. [Where] the private entity is thus acting as a surrogate for the government, any discrimination connected with the performance of public services, even if not affirmatively approved by the government, subjects the victims to discrimination that would not have occurred had the government performed the services directly. The government cannot avoid these constitutional limitations by delegating its functions to private entities, even if the delegation is well-intentioned." See also Frank R. Parker, *Evans v. Newton and the Racially Restricted Charitable Trust,* 13 How.L.J. 223 (1967). Reconsider note 3(c) supra.

5. *Redevelopment housing.* Are major urban redevelopment housing projects, undertaken pursuant to statutory authority with benefit of public condemnation power and tax exemption, constitutionally barred from racially discriminating? How about ordinary private housing projects that receive public "aid" in the form of water and sewage disposal, police and fire protection? See Comment, *Application of the Fourteenth Amendment to Builders of Private Housing,* 12 Kan.L.Rev. 426 (1964); Note, *Nondiscrimination Implications of Federal Involvement in Housing,* 19 Vand.L.Rev. 865 (1966); 17 J.Pub.L. 175 (1968). Is urban redevelopment distinguishable from a small private housing project because the former has the effect of racial zoning? Is this a restatement of the "government function" theory? Is "state action" affected if the claim is that the housing project evicted a tenant without affording procedural due process?

SECTION 4. DEVELOPMENTS IN THE 1980s AND 1990s

RENDELL–BAKER v. KOHN

457 U.S. 830, 102 S.Ct. 2764, 73 L.Ed.2d 418 (1982).

CHIEF JUSTICE BURGER delivered the opinion of the Court.

[New Perspectives is a private school that] specializes in dealing with students who have experienced difficulty completing public high [schools]. In recent years, nearly all of the students at the school have been referred to it by the Brookline or Boston school committees, or by the Drug Rehabilitation Division of the Massachusetts Department of Mental Health. [In] recent years, public funds have accounted for at least 90%, and in one year 99%, of respondent's operating budget. [T]he school must comply with a variety [of] detailed regulations concerning matters ranging from recordkeeping to student-teacher ratios. [T]he regulations require the school to [maintain] personnel standards and procedures, but they impose few specific requirements.

State Action, 82 Yale L.J. 1436 (1973); O'Neil, *Private Universities and Public Law,* 19 Buf. L.Rev. 155 (1970).

For further consideration of this issue, see note 2(b) after *Flagg Bros. v. Brooks,* Sec. 4 infra.

[Petitioners were teachers and a vocational counselor discharged by the school for, inter alia, supporting student criticisms against various school policies and sued under 42 U.S.C. § 1983. The] core issue presented [is] not whether petitioners were discharged because of their speech or without adequate procedural protections, but whether the school's action in discharging them can fairly be seen as state action. * * *

In *Blum v. Yaretsky*, 457 U.S. 991, 102 S.Ct. 2777, 73 L.Ed.2d 534 (1982), [t]he Court considered whether certain nursing homes were state actors for the purpose of determining whether decisions regarding transfers of patients could [be] subjected to Fourteenth Amendment due process requirements. [Like] the New Perspectives School, the nursing homes were privately owned and operated. [T]he Court held that, "[A] State normally can be held responsible for a private decision only when it has exercised coercive power or has provided such significant encouragement, either overt or covert, that the choice must in law be deemed to be that of the State." In determining that the transfer decisions were not actions of the state, the Court considered each of the factors alleged by petitioners [here].

First, [the] State subsidized the operating and capital costs of the nursing homes, and paid the medical expenses of more than 90% of the patients. * * *

The school, like the nursing homes, is not fundamentally different from many private corporations whose business depends primarily on contracts to build roads, bridges, dams, ships, or submarines for the government. Acts of such private contractors do not become acts of the government by reason of their significant or even total engagement in performing public contracts.

The school is also analogous to the public defender found not to be a state actor in *Polk County v. Dodson*, [p. _____ infra]. There we concluded that, although the State paid the public defender, her relationship with her client was "identical to that existing between any other lawyer and client." Here the relationship between the school and its teachers and counselors is not changed because the State pays the tuition of the students.

A second factor considered in *Blum* was the extensive regulation of the nursing homes by the State. There the State was indirectly involved in the transfer decisions challenged in that case because a primary goal of the State in regulating nursing homes was to keep costs down by transferring patients from intensive treatment centers to less expensive facilities when possible.[a] [The] nursing homes were extensively regulated in many other ways as well. The Court relied on *Jackson*, where we held that state regulation, even if "extensive and detailed," did not make a utility's actions state action.

Here the decisions to discharge the petitioners were not compelled or even influenced by any state regulation. Indeed, in contrast to the extensive regulation of the school generally, the various regulators showed relatively little interest in the school's personnel matters. The most intrusive personnel regulation promulgated by the various government agencies was the requirement that the Committee on Criminal Justice had the power to approve persons hired as vocational counselors.[6] Such a regulation is not sufficient to make a decision to discharge, made by private management, state action.

---

a. Brennan, J., joined by Marshall, J., dissented in *Blum*: "[Not] only has the State established the system of treatment levels and utilization review in order to further its own fiscal goals, [but] the State prescribes with as much precision as is possible the standards by which individual determinations are to be made. [The] Court thus fails to perceive the decisive involvement of the State in the private conduct challenged by the respondents."

6. [The] Committee did not take any part in discharging Rendell–Baker; on the contrary,

The third factor asserted to show that the school is a state actor is that it performs a "public function." However, our holdings have made clear that the relevant question [is] whether the function performed has been "traditionally the *exclusive* prerogative of the State." [U]ntil recently the State had not undertaken to provide education for students who could not be served by traditional public schools. That a private entity performs a function which serves the public does not make its acts state action.[7]

Fourth, petitioners argue that there is a "symbiotic relationship" [as] in *Burton.* Such a claim was rejected in *Blum,* and we reject it here. In *Burton,* [i]n response to the argument that the restaurant's profits, and hence the State's financial position, would suffer if it did not discriminate, the Court concluded that this showed that the State profited from the restaurant's discriminatory conduct. [Here] the school's fiscal relationship with the State is not different from that of many contractors performing services for the government.[b] * * *

Affirmed.[c]

JUSTICE MARSHALL, with whom JUSTICE BRENNAN joins, dissenting.

[I]t is difficult to imagine a closer relationship between a government and a private enterprise. [The] school's very survival depends on the State. If the State chooses, it may exercise complete control over the school's operations simply by threatening to withdraw financial support if the school takes action that it considers objectionable. [Almost] every decision the school makes is substantially affected in some way by the State's regulations.[1]

[Under state law], the State is *required* to provide a free education to all children, including those with special needs. Clearly, if the State had decided to provide the service itself, its conduct would be measured against constitutional standards. The State should not be permitted to avoid constitutional requirements simply by delegating its statutory duty to a private entity. * * *

The majority repeatedly compares the school to a private contractor * * *. Although shipbuilders and dambuilders, like the school, may be dependent on government funds, they are not so closely supervised by the government. And unlike most private contractors, the school is performing a statutory duty of the State. * * *

In SAN FRANCISCO ARTS & ATHLETICS, INC. v. UNITED STATES OLYMPIC COMM., 483 U.S. 522, 107 S.Ct. 2971, 97 L.Ed.2d 427 (1987), USOC, to which Congress granted the right to prohibit certain uses of the word "Olym-

it attempted to use leverage to aid her. [T]here is no evidence that the Committee had any authority to take even those steps.

7. There is no evidence that the State has attempted to avoid its constitutional duties by a sham arrangement which attempts to disguise provision of public services as acts of private parties. Cf. *Evans v. Newton.*

[Compare Brennan, J., joined by Marshall, J., dissenting in *Blum:* "For many, the totality of their social network is the nursing home community. Within that environment, the nursing home operator is the immediate authority, the provider of food, clothing, shelter, and health care, and, in every significant re-

spect, the functional equivalent of a State. Cf. *Marsh.*"]

b. Does this adopt the "moral exemplar model" in note 2 after *Moose Lodge?*

c. White, J., concurred in the judgment (and in *Blum*): "For me, the critical factor is the absence of any allegation that the employment decision was itself based upon some rule of conduct or policy put forth by the State."

1. [By] analyzing the various indicia of state action separately, without considering their cumulative impact, the majority commits a fundamental error.

pic," enjoined petitioner from calling its athletic competitions the "Gay Olympic Games." Petitioner claimed that USOC's enforcement violated equal protection. The Court, per POWELL, J.—relying mainly on *Rendell–Baker*, *Blum* and *Jackson*— held that USOC is not a "governmental actor."

BRENNAN, J., joined by Marshall, J.—and "largely" by O'Connor and Blackmun, JJ.—dissented on the basis of "a symbiotic relationship sufficient to provide a nexus between the USOC's challenged action and the Government": "The Act gave the USOC authority and responsibilities that no private organization in this country had ever held. The Act also [authorized USOC] to seek up to $16 million annually in grants from the Secretary of Commerce, and afford[ed] it unprecedented power to control the use of the word 'Olympic' and related emblems to raise additional funds. As a result of the Act, the United States obtained, for the first time in its history, an exclusive and effective organization to coordinate and administer all amateur athletics related to international competition* * *.

"Second, in the eye of the public, both national and international, the connection between the decisions of the United States Government and those of the United States Olympic Committee is profound. The President of the United States has served as the Honorary President of the USOC. The national flag flies both literally and figuratively over the central product of the USOC, the United States Olympic Team.[d] [While] in *Burton* the restaurant was able to pursue a policy of discrimination because the State had failed to impose upon it a policy of non-discrimination, the USOC could pursue its alleged policy of selective enforcement only because Congress *affirmatively* granted it power that it would not otherwise have to control the use of the word 'Olympic.' "[e]

FLAGG BROS., INC. v. BROOKS

436 U.S. 149, 98 S.Ct. 1729, 56 L.Ed.2d 185 (1978).

JUSTICE REHNQUIST delivered the opinion of the Court.

The question presented [is] whether a warehouseman's proposed sale of goods entrusted to him for storage, as permitted by New York Uniform Commercial Code § 7–210, is an action properly attributable to the State * * *.

[R]espondent Shirley Brooks and her family were evicted from their apartment in Mount Vernon, N.Y., on June 13, 1973. The city marshal arranged for Brooks' possessions to be stored by petitioner Flagg Brothers, Inc., in its warehouse. Brooks was informed of the cost of moving and storage, and she instructed the workmen to proceed, although she found the price too high. On August 25, 1973, after a series of disputes over the validity of the charges being claimed by petitioner Flagg Brothers, Brooks received a letter demanding that her account be brought up to date within 10 days "or your furniture will be sold." A series of subsequent letters from respondent and her attorneys produced no satisfaction.

---

d. The Court responded that "all sorts of private organizations send 'national representatives' to participate in world competitions. Although many are of interest only to a select group, others, like the Davis Cup Competition, the America's Cup, and the Miss Universe Pageant, are widely viewed as involving representation of our country. The organizations that sponsor United States participation in these events all perform 'national representational,' as well as 'administrative [and] adjudicative role[s],' in selecting and presenting the national representatives."

e. The Court responded that petitioner "has failed to demonstrate that the Federal Government can or does exert any influence over the exercise of the USOC's enforcement decisions. Absent proof of this type of 'close nexus between the [Government] and the challenged action of the [USOC],' the challenged action may not be 'fairly treated as that of the [Government] itself.' *Jackson*."

Brooks thereupon initiated this class action in the District Court under 42 U.S.C. § 1983, seeking damages, an injunction against the threatened sale of her belongings, and the declaration that such a sale pursuant to § 7–210 would violate [due process].

It must be noted that respondents have named no public officials as defendants in this action. The city marshal, who supervised their evictions, was dismissed from the case by the consent of all the parties. This total absence of overt official involvement plainly distinguishes this case from earlier decisions imposing procedural restrictions on creditors' remedies such as *North Georgia Finishing, Inc., v. Di–Chem, Inc.,* 419 U.S. 601, 95 S.Ct. 719, 42 L.Ed.2d 751 (1975); *Fuentes v. Shevin,* 407 U.S. 67, 92 S.Ct. 1983, 32 L.Ed.2d 556 (1972); *Sniadach v. Family Finance Corp.,* 395 U.S. 337, 89 S.Ct. 1820, 23 L.Ed.2d 349 (1969).[a] [While] any person with sufficient physical power may deprive a person of his property, only a State or a private person whose action "may be fairly treated as that of the State itself," *Jackson,* may deprive him of "an interest encompassed within the Fourteenth Amendment's protection," *Fuentes* * * *.

Respondents' primary contention is that New York has delegated to Flagg Brothers a power "traditionally exclusively reserved to the State." *Jackson.* They argue that the resolution of private disputes is a traditional function of civil government, and that the State in § 7–210 has delegated this function to Flagg Brothers. Respondents, however, have read too much into the language of our previous cases. While many functions have been traditionally performed by governments, very few have been "exclusively reserved to the State."

One such area has been elections. *[Terry v. Adams; Smith v. Allwright.]*

---

a. *Sniadach* held that a statute—authorizing a creditor to get a summons from a court clerk and thereby obtain prejudgment garnishment of a debtor's wages—violated due process because the statute did not provide the debtor with prior notice and opportunity for a hearing.

Fuentes held that a statute—authorizing a seller of goods under a conditional sales contract to get a writ from a court clerk and thereby obtain prejudgment repossession with the sheriff's help—violated due process because the statute did not provide the buyer with prior notice and opportunity for a hearing.

North Georgia Finishing held violative of due process a statute authorizing a creditor to obtain prejudgment garnishment of a debtor's assets by filing an affidavit with a court clerk stating reasons to fear that the property would otherwise be lost. The Court distinguished *Mitchell v. W.T. Grant Co.,* 416 U.S. 600, 94 S.Ct. 1895, 40 L.Ed.2d 406 (1974), which had upheld a statute that, without requiring prior notice to a buyer-debtor, permitted a seller-creditor holding a vendor's lien to secure a writ of sequestration and, having filed a bond, to cause the sheriff to take possession of the property at issue. *North Georgia Finishing* emphasized that under the sequestration statute in *Mitchell,* unlike the garnishment statute at bar, the writ "was issuable only by a judge upon the filing of an affidavit going beyond mere conclusory allegations and clearly setting out the facts entitling the creditor to sequestration" and that the *Mitchell* statute "ex-

pressly entitled the debtor to an immediate hearing after seizure and to dissolution of the writ absent proof by the creditor of the grounds on which the writ was issued."

For general discussion of these cases, see Robert E. Scott, *Constitutional Regulation of Provisional Creditor Remedies: The Cost of Procedural Due Process,* 61 Va.L.Rev. 807 (1975); Linda J. Silberman, *Shaffer v. Heitner: The End of an Era,* 53 N.Y.U.L.Rev. 33, 53–62 (1978).

More recently, *Connecticut v. Doehr,* 501 U.S. 1, 111 S.Ct. 2105, 115 L.Ed.2d 1 (1991), held that a state statute authorizing prejudgment attachment of real estate upon plaintiff's ex parte showing that there is probable cause to sustain the validity of his or her claim—without a showing of extraordinary circumstances, and without a requirement that the person seeking the attachment post a bond—violated due process. Petitioner sought an attachment on respondent's home in conjunction with a civil action for assault and battery that he was seeking to institute against respondent in the same court. On the strength of statements in petitioner's affidavit, the court ordered the attachment. Only after the sheriff attached his property did respondent receive notice, which informed him of his right to a postattachment hearing. Instead, respondent filed a federal action, successfully arguing that the state statute violated due process.

A second line of cases under the public-function doctrine originated with *Marsh*. Just as the Texas Democratic Party in *Smith* and the Jaybird Democratic Association in *Terry* effectively performed the entire public function of selecting public officials, so too the Gulf Shipbuilding Corp. performed all the necessary municipal functions in the town of Chickasaw, Ala., which it owned. * * *

These two branches of the public-function doctrine have in common the feature of exclusivity.[8] Although the elections held by the Democratic Party and its affiliates were the only meaningful elections in Texas, and the streets owned by the Gulf Shipbuilding Corp. were the only streets in Chickasaw, the proposed sale by Flagg Brothers under § 7–210 is not the only means of resolving this purely private dispute. Respondent Brooks has never alleged that state law barred her from seeking a waiver of Flagg Brothers' right to sell her goods at the time she authorized their storage. Presumably, [a person] who alleges that she never authorized the storage of her goods, could have sought to replevy her goods at any time under state law. The challenged statute itself provides a damages remedy against the warehouseman for violations of its provisions. This system of rights and remedies, recognizing the traditional place of private arrangements in ordering relationships in the commercial world,[9] can hardly be said to have delegated to Flagg Brothers an exclusive prerogative of the sovereign.[10]

Whatever the particular remedies available under New York law, we do not consider a more detailed description of them necessary to our conclusion that the settlement of disputes between debtors and creditors is not traditionally an exclusive public function.[11] Creditors and debtors have had available to them

8. Respondents also contend that *Evans v. Newton* establishes that the operation of a park for recreational purposes is an exclusively public function. We doubt that *Newton* intended to establish any such broad doctrine in the teeth of the experience of several American entrepreneurs who amassed great fortunes by operating parks for recreational purposes. We think *Newton* rests on a finding of ordinary state action under extraordinary circumstances. The Court's opinion emphasizes that the record showed "no change in the municipal maintenance and concern over this facility" after the transfer of title to private trustees. * * *

9. Unlike the parade of horribles suggested by our Brother Stevens in dissent, this case does not involve state authorization of private breach of the peace.

10. [It] would intolerably broaden, beyond the scope of any of our previous cases, the notion of state action [to] hold that the mere existence of a body of property law in a State, whether decisional or statutory, itself amounted to "state action" even though no state process or state officials were ever involved in enforcing that body of law.

This situation is clearly distinguishable from cases such as *North Georgia Finishing; Fuentes;* and *Sniadach.* In each of those cases a government official participated in the physical deprivation of what had concededly been the constitutional plaintiff's property under state law before the deprivation occurred. The constitutional protection attaches not because, as in *North Georgia Finishing,* a clerk issued a

ministerial writ out of the court, but because as a result of that writ the property of the debtor was seized and impounded by the affirmative command of the law of Georgia. The creditor in *North Georgia Finishing* had not simply sought to pursue the collection of his debt by private means permissible under Georgia law; he had invoked the authority of the Georgia court, which in turn had ordered the garnishee not to pay over money which previously had been the property of the debtor. See *Shelley v. Kraemer.* * * *

11. It may well be, as my Brother Stevens' dissent contends, that "[t]he power to order legally binding surrenders of property and the constitutional restrictions on that power are necessary correlatives in our system." But here New York, unlike Florida in *Fuentes,* Georgia in *North Georgia Finishing,* and Wisconsin in *Sniadach,* has not ordered respondents to surrender any property whatever. It has merely enacted a statute which provides that a warehouseman conforming to the provisions of the statute may convert his traditional lien into good title. There is no reason whatever to believe that either Flagg Brothers or respondents could not, if they wished, seek resort to the New York courts in order to either compel or prevent the "surrenders of property" to which that dissent refers, and that the compliance of Flagg Brothers with applicable New York property law would be reviewed after customary notice and hearing in such a proceeding.

The fact that such a judicial review of a self-help remedy is seldom encountered bears wit-

historically a far wider number of choices than has one who would be an elected public official, or a member of Jehovah's Witnesses who wished to distribute literature in Chickasaw, Ala. * * *[12] This is true whether these commercial rights and remedies are created by statute or decisional law. To rely upon the historical antecedents of a particular practice would result in the constitutional condemnation in one State of a remedy found perfectly permissible in another.

[T]here are a number of state and municipal functions not covered by our election cases or governed by the reasoning of *Marsh* which have been administered with a greater degree of exclusivity by States and municipalities than has the function of so-called "dispute resolution." Among these are such functions as education, fire and police protection, and tax collection. We express no view as to the extent, if any, to which a city or State might be free to delegate to private parties the performance of such functions and thereby avoid the strictures of the Fourteenth Amendment. * * *

Respondents further urge that Flagg Brothers' proposed action is properly attributable to the State because the State has authorized and encouraged it in enacting § 7–210. Our cases state "that a State is responsible for [the] act of a private party when the State, by its law, has compelled the act." This Court, however, has never held that a State's mere acquiescence in a private action converts that action into that of the State. * * *

It is quite immaterial that the State has embodied its decision not to act in statutory form. If New York had no commercial statutes at all, its courts would still be faced with the decision whether to prohibit or to permit the sort of sale threatened here the first time an aggrieved bailor came before them for relief. A judicial decision to deny relief would be no less an "authorization" or "encouragement" of that sale than the legislature's decision embodied in this statute. [If] the mere denial of judicial relief is considered sufficient encouragement to make the State responsible for those private acts, all private deprivations of property would be converted into public acts whenever the State, for whatever reason, denies relief sought by the putative property owner. * * *

Here, the State of New York has not compelled the sale of a bailor's goods, but has merely announced the circumstances under which its courts will not interfere with a private sale. Indeed, the crux of respondents' complaint is not that the State *has* acted, but that it has *refused* to act. This statutory refusal to act is no different in principle from an ordinary statute of limitations whereby the

ness to the important part that such remedies have played in our system of property rights. This is particularly true of the warehouseman's lien, which is the source of this provision in the Uniform Commercial Code which is the law in 49 States and the District of Columbia. The lien in this case, particularly because it is burdened by procedural constraints and provides for a compensatory remedy and judicial relief against abuse, is not atypical of creditors' liens historically, whether created by statute or legislatively enacted. The conduct of private actors in relying on the rights established under these liens to resort to self-help remedies does not permit their conduct to be ascribed to the State.

12. This is not to say that dispute resolution between creditors and debtors involves a category of human affairs that is never subject to constitutional constraints. We merely address the public-function doctrine as respondents would apply it to this case.

Self-help of the type involved in this case is not significantly different from creditor remedies generally, whether created by common law or enacted by legislatures. New York's statute has done nothing more than authorize (and indeed limit)—without participation by any public official—what Flagg Brothers would tend to do, even in the absence of such authorization, i.e., dispose of respondents' property in order to free up its valuable storage space. The proposed sale pursuant to the lien in this case is not a significant departure from traditional private arrangements.

State declines to provide a remedy for private deprivations of property after the passage of a given period of time. * * *

Reversed.

JUSTICE STEVENS, with whom JUSTICE WHITE and JUSTICE MARSHALL join, dissenting.

[Under the Court's] approach a State could enact laws authorizing private citizens to use self-help in countless situations without any possibility of federal challenge. A state statute could authorize the warehouseman to retain all proceeds of the lien sale, even if they far exceeded the amount of the alleged debt; it could authorize finance companies to enter private homes to repossess merchandise; or indeed, it could authorize "any person with sufficient physical power" to acquire and sell the property of his weaker neighbor. [The] Court's rationale would characterize action pursuant to such a statute as purely private action, which the State permits but does not compel, in an area not exclusively reserved to the State.

As these examples suggest, the distinctions between "permission" and "compulsion" on the one hand, and "exclusive" and "non-exclusive," on the other, cannot be determinative factors in state-action analysis. There is no great chasm between "permission" and "compulsion" requiring particular state action to fall within one or the other definitional camp. [In] this case, the State of New York, by enacting § 7–210 of the Uniform Commercial Code, has acted in the most effective and unambiguous way a State can act. This section specifically authorizes petitioner Flagg Brothers to sell respondents' possessions; it details the procedures that petitioner must follow; and it grants petitioner the power to convey good title to goods that are now owned by respondents to a third party.

[P]etitioners have attempted to argue that the nonconsensual transfer of property rights is not a traditional function of the sovereign. The overwhelming historical evidence is to the contrary, however, and the Court wisely does not adopt this position. Instead, the Court reasons that state action cannot be found because the State has not delegated to the warehouseman an *exclusive* sovereign function.[8] This distinction, [is] inconsistent with the line of cases beginning with *Sniadach*.

Since *Sniadach* this Court has scrutinized various state statutes regulating the debtor-creditor relationship for compliance with the Due Process Clause. In each of these cases a finding of state action was a prerequisite to the Court's decision. The Court today seeks to explain these findings on the ground that in each case there was some element of "overt official involvement." [But] until today, this Court had never held that purely ministerial acts of "minor governmental functionaries" were sufficient to establish state action. [The] number of private actions in which a governmental functionary plays some ministerial role is

---

8. As I understand the Court's notion of "exclusivity," the sovereign function here is not exclusive because there may be other state remedies, under different statutes or common-law theories, available to respondents. Even if I were to accept the notion that sovereign functions must be "exclusive," the Court's description of exclusivity is incomprehensible. The question is whether a particular action is a uniquely sovereign function, not whether state law forecloses any possibility of recovering for damages for such activity. For instance, it is clear that the maintenance of a police force is a unique sovereign function, and the delegation of police power to a private party will entail state action. Under the Court's analysis, however, there would be no state action if the State provided a remedy, such as an action for wrongful imprisonment, for the individual injured by the "private" policeman. [Of] course, the availability of other state remedies may be relevant in determining whether the statute provides sufficient procedural protections under the Due Process Clause, but it is not relevant to the state-action issue.

legion;[12] to base due process review on the fortuity of such governmental intervention would demean the majestic purposes of the Due Process Clause.

Instead, cases such as *North Georgia Finishing* must be viewed as reflecting this Court's recognition of the significance of the State's role in defining *and controlling* the debtor-creditor relationship. [In *Fuentes*, the] statutes placed the state power to repossess property in the hands of an interested private party, just as the state statute in this case places the state power to conduct judicially binding sales in satisfaction of a lien in the hands of the warehouseman. "Private parties, serving their own private advantage, may unilaterally invoke state power to replevy goods from another. No state official participates in the decision to seek a writ; no state official reviews the basis for the claim to repossession; and no state official evaluates the need for immediate seizure. There is not even a requirement that the plaintiff provide any information to the court on these matters." Ibid. [Yet] the very defect that made the statutes in *Fuentes* and *North Georgia Finishing* unconstitutional—lack of state control—is, under today's decision, the factor that precludes constitutional review of the state statute. The Due Process Clause cannot command such incongruous results. If it is unconstitutional for a State to allow a private party to exercise a traditional state power because the state supervision of that power is purely mechanical, the State surely cannot immunize its actions from constitutional *scrutiny* by removing even the mechanical supervision. * * *

It is important to emphasize that, contrary to the Court's apparent fears, this conclusion does not even remotely suggest that "all private deprivations of property [will] be converted into public acts whenever the State, for whatever reason, denies relief sought by the putative property owner." The focus is not on the private deprivation but on the state authorization. [The] State's conduct in this case takes the concrete form of a statutory enactment, and it is that statute that may be challenged. * * *

Finally, it is obviously true that the overwhelming majority of disputes in our society are resolved in the private sphere. But it is no longer possible, if it ever was, to believe that a sharp line can be drawn between private and public actions. The Court['s] description of what is state action does not even attempt to reflect the concerns of the Due Process Clause, for the state-action doctrine is, after all, merely one aspect of this broad constitutional protection.

In the broadest sense, we expect government "to provide a reasonable and fair framework of rules which facilitate commercial transactions." This "framework of rules" is premised on the assumption that the State will control nonconsensual deprivations of property and that the State's control will, in turn, be subject to the restrictions of the Due Process Clause. * * *[b]

Notes and Questions

1. *Authority of prior decisions.* (a) Does the Court's use of *Shelley v. Kraemer* (in fn. 10) refute the dissent's objection that the Court's handling of the prior debtor-creditor decisions establishes the principle that "purely ministerial acts of minor governmental functionaries" constitute state action? If so, then

---

12. For instance, state officials often perform ministerial acts in the transferring of ownership in motor vehicles or real estate. It is difficult to believe that the Court would hold that all car sales are invested with state action.

b. The separate dissent of Marshall, J., is omitted. Brennan, J., did not participate.

would the Court have found state action in *Flagg Bros.* if the state courts had to be used to enforce the warehouseman's lien? Would this read *Shelley* for all it is worth? Does fn. 10 so read *Shelley*? In any event, is the dissent correct in complaining that "the very defect that made the statutes in *Fuentes* and *North Georgia Finishing* unconstitutional—lack of state control—is, under *Flagg Bros.,* the factor that precludes constitutional review of the state statute"?

(b) LUGAR v. EDMONDSON OIL CO., 457 U.S. 922, 102 S.Ct. 2744, 73 L.Ed.2d 482 (1982), per WHITE, J.,—involving a statute that authorized a creditor to file a petition with a court clerk and thus obtain a prejudgment attachment of a debtor's property which was executed by the sheriff—relied on all the debtor-creditor decisions as establishing the doctrine "that a private party's joint participation with state officials in the seizure of disputed property is sufficient to characterize that party as a 'state actor' for purposes of the Fourteenth Amendment." POWELL, J., joined by Rehnquist and O'Connor, JJ., dissented: "It is unclear why a private party engages in state action when filing papers seeking an attachment of property, but not [when] summoning police to investigate a suspected crime." Burger, C.J., also dissented.

(c) NATIONAL COLLEGIATE ATHLETIC ASS'N v. TARKANIAN, 488 U.S. 179, 109 S.Ct. 454, 102 L.Ed.2d 469 (1988): The NCAA is an association of virtually all colleges with major athletic programs, and its rules governing these programs are binding on its members. After its investigation that found 38 recruitment violations by the staff of the University of Nevada, Las Vegas (including 10 by Tarkanian, who was UNLV's basketball coach), NCAA imposed sanctions on UNLV and requested it to show cause why additional penalties should not be imposed if it failed to suspend Tarkanian. The Court, per STEVENS, J., conceded that UNLV's suspension of Tarkanian, which was clearly state action, "was influenced by the rules and recommendations of the NCAA," but held that this did not turn the NCAA's conduct into "state action," and thus the NCAA did not violate Tarkanian's right to procedural due process: Although, as a member of the NCAA, UNLV played a role in formulating its rules, "UNLV delegated no power to the NCAA to take specific action against any University employee. The commitment by UNLV to adhere to NCAA enforcement procedures was enforceable only by sanctions that the NCAA might impose on UNLV," and which UNLV could choose to ignore by withdrawing from the NCAA. And even if "the power of the NCAA is so great that the UNLV had no practical alternative to compliance with its demands," "it does not follow that such a private party [is] acting under color of state law." Finally, "in the case before us the state and private parties' relevant interests do not coincide, as they did in *Burton;* rather, they have clashed throughout the investigation, the attempt to discipline Tarkanian, and this litigation. UNLV and the NCAA were antagonists, not joint participants, and the NCAA may not be deemed a state actor on this ground."

WHITE, J., joined by Brennan, Marshall and O'Connor, JJ., dissented: "[I]t was the NCAA's findings that Tarkanian had violated NCAA rules, made at NCAA-conducted hearings, all of which were agreed to by UNLV in its membership agreement with the NCAA, that resulted in Tarkanian's suspension by UNLV. On these facts, the NCAA was 'jointly engaged with [UNLV] officials in the challenged action,' and therefore was a state actor."

2. *"Governmental function."* (a) *Dispute resolution.* Do you agree that the authority exercised by the warehouseman under the New York statute was not a "governmental function"? Consider 92 Harv.L.Rev. 128 (1978): "The exclusivity of the function's exercise may shed some light on this inquiry, but it does not give

a final answer to the basic question. Regardless of the fact that there are many ways to go about resolving a private dispute, the ability to conclude unresolved disputes by making authoritative determinations of rights in property is central to our conception of government's role in society. If a state chose to assign part of its judicial function to private tribunals, giving them all the authority of trial courts, there would be little doubt that a vital attribute of sovereignty was involved." What about judicial enforcement of (i) a private arbitrator's decision made pursuant to an earlier contract between the parties, or (2) the agreement to arbitrate? Of what relevance is the fact that arbitrators "are statutorily vested with broad judicial powers to administer depositions and discovery, including subpoena and sanction powers," and "receive the same 'judicial' immunity from civil liability that is reserved exclusively for the states' own constitutionally authorized judiciary"? See Richard C. Reuben, *Public Justice: Toward a State Action Theory of ADR,*" 85 Calif.L.Rev. 577 (1997).

What result in *Flagg Bros.* if the warehouseman's lien had not been "burdened by procedural constraints" and had not provided "for a compensatory remedy and judicial relief against abuse"?

(b) *Jury selection.* EDMONSON v. LEESVILLE CONCRETE CO., 500 U.S. 614, 111 S.Ct. 2077, 114 L.Ed.2d 660 (1991), per KENNEDY, J., held that use by a private litigant in a civil trial of a peremptory challenge to exclude jurors on the basis of race violated "the excluded jurors' equal protection rights": "[I]n determining whether a particular action or course of conduct is governmental in character, it is relevant to examine the following: the extent to which the actor relies on governmental assistance and benefits, see *Burton;* whether the actor is performing a traditional governmental function, see *Terry; Marsh;* and whether the injury caused is aggravated in a unique way by the incidents of governmental authority, see *Shelley* * * *.

"Although private use of state-sanctioned private remedies or procedures does not rise, by itself, to the level of state action, our cases have found state action when private parties make extensive use of state procedures with 'the overt, significant assistance of state officials.' See *Lugar.* [The] government summons jurors, constrains their freedom of movement, and subjects them to public scrutiny and examination. The party who exercises a challenge invokes the formal authority of the court, which must discharge the prospective juror, thus effecting the 'final and practical denial' of the excluded individual's opportunity to serve on the petit jury. [By] enforcing a discriminatory peremptory challenge, the court 'has not only made itself a party to the [biased act], but has elected to place its power, property and prestige behind the [alleged] discrimination.' *Burton.*

"[Further, a] traditional function of government is evident here. The peremptory challenge is used in selecting an entity that is a quintessential governmental body, having no attributes of a private actor. The jury exercises the power of the court and of the government that confers the court's jurisdiction. [If] a government confers on a private body the power to choose the government's employees or officials, the private body will be bound by the constitutional mandate of race neutrality [*Terry*]. If peremptory challenges based on race were permitted, persons could be required by summons to be put at risk of open and public discrimination as a condition of their participation in the justice system. The injury to excluded jurors would be the direct result of governmental delegation and participation.

"Finally, we note that the injury caused by the discrimination is made more severe because the government permits it to occur within the courthouse itself.

Few places are a more real expression of the constitutional authority of the government than a courtroom, where the law itself unfolds."[a]

O'CONNOR, J., joined by Rehnquist, C.J., and Scalia, J., dissented: "It is the nature of a peremptory that its exercise is left wholly within the discretion of the litigant. [The] peremptory is, by design, an enclave of private action in a government-managed proceeding.

"The Court amasses much ostensible evidence of the Federal Government's 'overt, significant participation' in the peremptory process. [The] bulk of the practices the Court describes—the establishment of qualifications for jury service, the location and summoning of prospective jurors, the jury wheel, the voter lists, the jury qualification forms, the per diem for jury service—[is] in furtherance of the Government's distinct obligation to provide a qualified jury; the Government would do these things even if there were no peremptory challenges. [That] these actions may be necessary to a peremptory challenge—in the sense that there could be no such challenge without a venire from which to select—no more makes the challenge state action than the building of roads and provision of public transportation makes state action of riding on a bus.

"[The] government 'normally can be held responsible for a private decision only when it has exercised coercive power or has provided such significant encouragement, either overt or covert, that the choice must in law be deemed to be that of the State.' *Blum*. [A] judge does not 'significantly encourage' discrimination by the mere act of excusing a juror in response to an unexplained request. * * *

"A peremptory challenge by a private litigant [is] not a traditional government function. [In] order to constitute state action under this doctrine, private conduct must not only comprise something that the government traditionally does, but something that *only* the government traditionally does. Even if one could fairly characterize the use of a peremptory strike as the performance of the traditional government function of jury selection, it has never been exclusively the function of the government to select juries; peremptory strikes are older than the Republic."

(c) *Education*. Would (should) the Court hold that private schools perform a "government function"? If so, under what circumstances? Consider Jesse H. Choper, *Thoughts on State Action*, 1979 Wash.U.L.Q. 757, 778: "[I]t is clear that the operation of elementary and secondary schools is not an enterprise that is 'traditionally *exclusively* reserved to the State.' But a comprehensive survey of school districts in the United States would surely show that virtually all maintained at least one public elementary and secondary school unless, because of some peculiar development, the educational needs of the community's children were historically always met by a privately funded school. Such a school—or at least one of such schools if there are several in the hypothetical community (and which one is *the* one may present a nice question)—is, in effect, serving as a substitute for the conventional public school that the school district would otherwise provide. In this sense, it is performing a function 'traditionally *exclusively* reserved to the State.' "

3. *The limits (or lack of limits) of the state action concept*. Do you agree that "an ordinary statute of limitations whereby the State declines to provide a remedy

---

a. For the view that *Edmonson* (and *Tarkanian*) "heralded a halt to the Court's retreat from the *Burton* totality approach," see G. Sidney Buchanan, *A Conceptual History of the* *State Action Doctrine: The Search for Governmental Responsibility*, 34 Hous.L.Rev. 333, 665 (1997), undertaking an up-to-date, comprehensive review of the entire subject of state action.

for private deprivations of property after the passage of a given period of time" is *not* state action? If it *is* state action, then is New York's rule—that "its courts will not interfere with a private sale" pursuant to a warehouseman's lien—also state action? If so, is it not true that "all private deprivations of property would be converted into public acts whenever the State, for whatever reason, denies relief sought by the putative property owner"? Of what relevance is it that "the State's conduct in *Flagg Bros.* takes the concrete form of a statutory enactment"? May a "state procedure" providing a "framework of rules which facilitate commercial transactions" be promulgated by common law as well as by statute? See generally Paul Brest, *State Action and Liberal Theory: A Casenote on Flagg Brothers v. Brooks,* 130 U.Pa.L.Rev. 1296 (1982); Frank I. Goodman, *Professor Brest on State Action and Liberal Theory,* 130 U.Pa.L.Rev. 1331–45 (1982).

DeSHANEY v. WINNEBAGO COUNTY DEP'T OF SOCIAL SERV.

489 U.S. 189, 109 S.Ct. 998, 103 L.Ed.2d 249 (1989).

CHIEF JUSTICE REHNQUIST delivered the opinion of the Court.

[I]n January 1982, [t]he Winnebago County Department of Social Services (DSS) interviewed [Joshua DeShaney's father about alleged child abuse], but he denied the accusations, and DSS did not pursue them further. In January 1983, Joshua was admitted to a local hospital with multiple bruises and abrasions. The examining physician suspected child abuse and notified DSS. [T]he county convened an ad hoc "Child Protection Team" [which] decided that there was insufficient evidence of child abuse to retain Joshua in the custody of the court. The Team did, however, decide to recommend several measures to protect Joshua, including enrolling him in a preschool program, providing his father with certain counselling services, and encouraging his father's girlfriend to move out of the home. [A month later] emergency room personnel called the DSS caseworker handling Joshua's case to report that he had once again been treated for suspicious injuries. The caseworker concluded that there was no basis for action. For the next six months, the caseworker made monthly visits to the DeShaney home, during which she observed a number of suspicious injuries on Joshua's head; she also noticed that he had not been enrolled in school and that the girlfriend had not moved out. The caseworker dutifully recorded these incidents in her files, along with her continuing suspicions that someone in the DeShaney household was physically abusing Joshua, but she did nothing more. In November 1983, the emergency room notified DSS that Joshua had been treated once again for injuries that they believed to be caused by child abuse. On the caseworker's next two visits to the DeShaney home, she was told that Joshua was too ill to see her. Still DSS took no action.

In March 1984, Randy DeShaney beat 4–year-old Joshua so severely that he fell into a life-threatening coma [and] is expected to spend the rest of his life confined to an institution for the profoundly retarded. Randy DeShaney was subsequently tried and convicted of child abuse.

Joshua and his mother brought this action under 42 U.S.C. § 1983 [alleging] that the State had deprived Joshua of his liberty interest in "free[dom] from unjustified intrusions on personal security" by failing to provide him with adequate protection against his father's violence. * * *

But nothing in the language of the Due Process Clause itself requires the State to protect the life, liberty, and property of its citizens against invasion by private actors. The Clause is phrased as a limitation on the State's power to act, not as a guarantee of certain minimal levels of safety and security. [Nor] does history support such an expansive reading of the constitutional text. [The Clause's] purpose was to protect the people from the State, not to ensure that the State protected them from each other. The Framers were content to leave the extent of governmental obligation in the latter area to the democratic political processes. * * *

Petitioners contend, however, that even if the Due Process Clause imposes no affirmative obligation on the State to provide the general public with adequate protective services, such a duty may arise out of certain "special relationships" created or assumed by the State with respect to particular individuals [and] that such a "special relationship" existed here because the State knew that Joshua faced a special danger of abuse at his father's hands, and specifically proclaimed, by word and by deed, its intention to protect him against that danger. * * *

We reject this argument. It is true that in certain limited circumstances the Constitution imposes upon the State affirmative duties of care and protection with respect to particular individuals [discussing *Youngberg v. Romeo,* Ch. 6, Sec. 2; *Estelle v. Gamble,* 429 U.S. 97, 97 S.Ct. 285, 50 L.Ed.2d 251 (1976); and other cases.]

But these [cases] stand only for the proposition that when the State takes a person into its custody and holds him there against his will, the Constitution imposes upon it a corresponding duty to assume some responsibility for his safety and general well-being. [I]ncarceration, institutionalization, or other similar restraint of personal liberty [is] the "deprivation of liberty" triggering the protections of the Due Process Clause, not its failure to act to protect his liberty interests against harms inflicted by other means.

[While] the State may have been aware of the dangers that Joshua faced in the free world, it played no part in their creation, nor did it do anything to render him any more vulnerable to them. That the State once took temporary custody of Joshua does not alter the analysis, for when it returned him to his father's custody, it placed him in no worse position than that in which he would have been had it not acted at all; the State does not become the permanent guarantor of an individual's safety by having once offered him shelter. [The] most that can be said of the state functionaries in this case is that they stood by and did nothing when suspicious circumstances dictated a more active role for them. In defense of them it must also be said that had they moved too soon to take custody of the son away from the father, they would likely have been met with charges of improperly intruding into the parent-child relationship, charges based on the same Due Process Clause that forms the basis for the present charge of failure to provide adequate protection. * * *

JUSTICE BRENNAN, with whom JUSTICE MARSHALL and JUSTICE BLACKMUN join, dissenting.

[T]o the Court, the only fact that seems to count as an "affirmative act of restraining the individual's freedom to act on his own behalf" is direct physical control. I [would] recognize, as the Court apparently cannot, that "the State's knowledge of [an] individual's predicament [and] its expressions of intent to help him" can amount to a "limitation of his freedom to act on his own behalf" or to obtain help from others. Thus, I would read *Youngberg* and *Estelle* to stand for the much more generous proposition that, if a State cuts off private sources of aid and then refuses aid itself, it cannot wash its hands of the harm that results from its inaction. [While] other governmental bodies and private persons are largely responsible for the reporting of possible cases of child abuse, Wisconsin law channels all such reports to the local departments of social services for evaluation and, if necessary, further action. * * *

The specific facts before us bear out this view of Wisconsin's system of protecting children. Each time someone voiced a suspicion that Joshua was being abused, that information was relayed to the Department for investigation and possible action. [A] private citizen, or even a person working in a government agency other than DSS, would doubtless feel that her job was done as soon as she had reported her suspicions of child abuse to DSS. [If] DSS ignores or dismisses these suspicions, no one will step in to fill the gap. [Through] its child-protection program, the State actively intervened in Joshua's life and, by virtue of this intervention, acquired ever more certain knowledge that Joshua was in grave danger. * * * My disagreement with the Court arises from its failure to see that inaction can be every bit as abusive of power as action, that oppression can result when a State undertakes a vital duty and then ignores it. * * *

JUSTICE BLACKMUN, dissenting. * * *

Like the antebellum judges who denied relief to fugitive slaves, the Court today claims that its decision, however harsh, is compelled by existing legal doctrine. On the contrary, the question presented by this case is an open one, and our Fourteenth Amendment precedents may be read more broadly or narrowly depending upon how one chooses to read them. Faced with the choice, I would adopt a "sympathetic" reading, one which comports with dictates of fundamental justice and recognizes that compassion need not be exiled from the province of judging. * * *

Notes and Questions

1. *"State of mind" of government officials.* (a) Consider David A. Strauss, *Due Process, Government Inaction and Private Wrongs,* 1989 Sup.Ct.Rev. 53, 57–59: "Suppose that police officers learn that a murder is about to occur that they can prevent with minimal cost. [They] decide not to [intervene] because the targeted victim is someone whom they believe is guilty of another crime. The officers would rather see him killed by private persons than brought to trial where, they fear, he might escape with an acquittal or a light sentence.

"This must be a case of government inaction, assuming that there is such a thing. The police officers did not instigate or facilitate the murder in any way, except to refrain from intervening. They did not make the victim worse off than he would have been if the officers had never become aware of the predicament." Do you agree that "this hypothetical case is indistinguishable from *DeShaney*"? Would "child protective service employees [not] violate the Due Process Clause even if they deliberately refuse to intervened because they wanted to see a child harmed (because of a grudge against a family or out of a bizarre belief that child abuse constitutes proper discipline, for example)"? Id.

(b) Should there be a constitutional difference between government inaction that is careless or inadvertent rather than deliberate? Consider Richard S. Kay, *The State Action Doctrine, the Public–Private Distinction, and the Independence of Constitutional Law,* 10 Const.Comm. 329, 357 (1993): "The harms that follow on a state's failure to act are, in a sense, happenstance. In the usual case no official person will have planned for those results to follow. Affirmative acts, on the other hand, are more likely to have been deliberate and, therefore, they are more likely to have been undertaken with a dangerous state of mind. [This] need not be so in every case, but it is a reasonable enough assumption to explain why the state may be thought more threatening when it acts than when it fails to act.''

2. *Limited government resources and affirmative obligations.* Consider Barbara E. Armacost, *Affirmative Duties, Systemic Harms, and the Due Process Clause*, 94 Mich.L.Rev. 982, 1024–25 (1996): ''Because the social-work context [will] involve more cases of possible child abuse or neglect than plausibly can be addressed, the line between claims that raise resource-allocation concerns and those that do not is difficult to draw. That is exactly what makes *DeShaney* hard. It is, on the one hand, not an 'easy' case for *nonliability*, as if it had involved a single report of child abuse that went uninvestigated or a claim that more social workers should have been assigned to a particular neighborhood. [T]hese sorts of claims rarely result in liability [at common law] because they raise the most serious resource-allocation issues. But *DeShaney* is also not simply a case where social workers 'on the scene' stood by and failed to intervene. The picture is much more complicated. The social worker was 'on the scene,' so to speak, of many potentially abusive situations involving many at-risk children. In order to evaluate the reasonableness of her behavior toward one child, one would want to know more about her obligations and behavior in connection with these other cases as well.''

3. *The exception for "custodial" situations.* Consider Strauss, supra, at 63–66: ''Many state laws [are] designed to promote the establishment and maintenance of families. Through schools and many other media, the government promotes the family unit and reinforces the authority of the parents. [What] is wrongful under the Due Process Clause, according [to] *DeShaney,* is to establish [prisons, state hospitals and other institutions] without taking care to protect those who are 'confined' within them. Since the state plays a role in establishing the family, it owes a duty of care to persons in Joshua DeShaney's position as well.''

Chapter 11

CONGRESSIONAL ENFORCEMENT OF CIVIL RIGHTS

The exercise of congressional authority under the commerce power to protect civil rights was examined in detail in Ch. 2, Sec. 2, III. But the potentially most pervasive sources of federal legislative power to enforce personal liberty are found in the final sections of the thirteenth, fourteenth, and fifteenth amendments which grant Congress power to enforce the substantive provisions of these amendments "by appropriate legislation."

SECTION 1. HISTORICAL FRAMEWORK

I. LEGISLATION

The Civil Rights Act of 1866, enacted pursuant to the thirteenth amendment, was the first Reconstruction Act seeking "to protect all persons in the United States in their civil rights." (See Ch. 5, Sec. 1, III) Its current provisions are:

42 U.S.C. § 1981. *"Equal rights under the law.* All persons within the jurisdiction of the United States shall have the same right in every State and Territory to make and enforce contracts, to sue, be parties, give evidence, and to the full and equal benefit of all laws and proceedings for the security of persons and property as is enjoyed by white citizens, and shall be subject to like punishment, pains, penalties, taxes, licenses, and exactions of every kind, and to no other."

42 U.S.C. § 1982. *"Property rights of citizens.* All citizens of the United States shall have the same right, in every State and Territory, as is enjoyed by white citizens thereof to inherit, purchase, lease, sell, hold, and convey real and personal property."

The 1866 Act then provided criminal penalties against any person denying such rights under color of law. With certain changes (the most important being addition of the word "willfully" in 1909, and the substantial increase of penalties in 1968), this has survived as a significant federal criminal statute enforcing civil rights:

18 U.S.C. § 242. *"Deprivation of rights under color of law.* Whoever, under color of any law, statute, ordinance, regulation, or custom, willfully subjects any inhabitant of any State, Territory, or District to the deprivation of any rights, privileges, or immunities secured or protected by the Constitution or laws of the United States, or to different punishments, pains or penalties, on account of such inhabitant being an alien, or by reason of his color, or race, than are prescribed for the punishment of citizens, shall be fined not more than $1,000 or imprisoned not more than one year, or both; and if death results shall be subject to imprisonment for any term of years or for life."

Doubt as to the adequacy of the thirteenth amendment to support the 1866 Act was a significant force leading to adoption of the fourteenth amendment. After the fifteenth amendment, Congress passed the Act of May 31, 1870, principally to enforce the right to vote guaranteed by the amendment. One section, barring private conspiracies, evolved as an important existing protection:

18 U.S.C. § 241. *"Conspiracy against rights of citizens.* If two or more persons conspire to injure, oppress, threaten, or intimidate any citizen in the free exercise or enjoyment of any right or privilege secured to him by the Constitution or laws of the United States, or because of his having exercised the same; or

"If two or more persons go on the highway, or on the premises of another, with intent to prevent or hinder his free exercise or enjoyment of any right or privilege so secured—

"They shall be fined not more than $10,000 or imprisoned not more than ten years, or both; and if death results, they shall be subject to imprisonment for any term of years or for life."

Next came the Ku Klux Klan Act of 1871, which made criminal private conspiracies against the operations of government officials or courts, or to deprive persons of equal protection of the laws. The Act also established civil liabilities that have evolved to be important existing provisions. One is the civil counterpart of 18 U.S.C. § 242:

42 U.S.C. § 1983. *"Civil action for deprivation of rights.* Every person who, under color of any statute, ordinance, regulation, custom, or usage, of any State or Territory, subjects, or causes to be subjected, any citizen of the United States or other persons within the jurisdiction thereof to the deprivation of any rights, privileges or immunities secured by the Constitution and laws, shall be liable to the person injured in an action of law, suit in equity, or other proper proceedings for redress."

Another is roughly the civil counterpart of 18 U.S.C.A. § 241:

42 U.S.C. § 1985. *"Conspiracy to interfere with civil rights.* * * * (3) If two or more persons in any State or Territory conspire or go in disguise on the highway or on the premises of another, for the purpose of depriving, either directly or indirectly, any person or class of persons of the equal protection of the laws, or of equal privileges and immunities under the laws; or for the purpose of preventing or hindering the constituted authorities of any State or Territory from giving or securing to all persons within such State or Territory the equal protection of the laws; [the] party so injured or deprived may have an action for the recovery of damages, occasioned by such injury or deprivation, against any one or more of the conspirators."

The final Reconstruction enactment in this area was the Civil Rights Act of 1875, dealing with racial discrimination in public accommodations, held invalid in the *Civil Rights Cases*, Ch. 10, Sec. 1.[a] No significant congressional action to enforce civil rights took place until the Civil Rights Act of 1957. The principal thrust of the 1957 Act and of the Civil Rights Act of 1960 was against racial discrimination in voting. The Civil Rights Act of 1964, although principally concerned with matters already considered, also dealt with voting. But the most comprehensive federal legislation in aid of the franchise is the Voting Rights Act of 1965 and its later Amendments. Finally, the Civil Rights Act of 1968 provides protection against interference with designated "federally protected activities," and against discrimination in housing,—both considered at several points infra.

II. JUDICIAL DECISIONS

Necessity of "state action" for violation of constitutional rights. (a) *In general.* Shortly after enactment of the Reconstruction civil rights laws, a series of decisions culminating in the *Civil Rights Cases* significantly limited their impact by interpreting the fourteenth (and fifteenth) amendments as barring only "state action," thus precluding congressional legislation against "private individuals" for violating rights of persons created by these amendments.[a]

(b) *Sec. 241 exceptions.* But the Court has long recognized that there is a limited category of constitutional rights, protected by § 241, that, as stated in UNITED STATES v. WILLIAMS, 341 U.S. 70, 71 S.Ct. 581, 95 L.Ed. 758 (1951), "Congress can beyond doubt constitutionally secure against interference by private individuals. [T]his category includes rights which arise from the relationship of the individual and the Federal Government. The right of citizens to vote in congressional elections, for instance, may obviously be protected by Congress from individual as well as from State interference. *Ex parte Yarbrough,* 110 U.S. 651, 4 S.Ct. 152, 28 L.Ed. 274."[b] The Court has also included, as "attributes of national citizenship," "the right of the people peaceably to assemble for the purpose of petitioning Congress for a redress of grievances"[c] and the "constitutional right to travel from one State to another."[d]

(c) *"Custom or usage" under § 1983.* ADICKES v. S.H. KRESS & CO., 398 U.S. 144, 90 S.Ct. 1598, 26 L.Ed.2d 142 (1970), involved a damages action against a restaurant for having deprived plaintiff of equal protection—alleging that defendant acted "under color [of] custom, or usage, of any State." The Court (Douglas and Brennan, JJ., dissenting; Marshall, J., not participating) held "that

---

a. .For general discussion and evolution of the Reconstruction civil rights legislation, see Eugene Gressman, *The Unhappy History of Civil Rights Legislation,* 50 Mich.L.Rev. 1323 (1952); Will Maslow & Joseph B. Robison, *Civil Rights Legislation and the Fight for Equality, 1862–1952,* 20 U.Chi.L.Rev. 363 (1953); U.S. Comm'n on Civil Rights, *Enforcement* 103–40 (1965).

a. .See *United States v. Cruikshank,* 92 U.S. 542, 23 L.Ed. 588 (1876); *Virginia v. Rives,* 100 U.S. 313, 25 L.Ed. 667 (1879).

b. *United States v. Classic,* 313 U.S. 299, 61 S.Ct. 1031, 85 L.Ed. 1368 (1941), included within this category the right to vote in a state congressional primary.

c. *Cruikshank,* fn. a supra (dictum).

d. Ch. 6, Sec.3.

a 'custom or usage' for purposes of § 1983 requires state involvement and is not simply a practice which reflects long-standing social habits, generally observed by the people in a locality"; it "must have the force of law by virtue of the persistent practices of state officials."

SECTION 2. REGULATION OF PRIVATE PERSONS

I. THIRTEENTH AMENDMENT

JONES v. ALFRED H. MAYER CO.

392 U.S. 409, 88 S.Ct. 2186, 20 L.Ed.2d 1189 (1968).

JUSTICE STEWART delivered the opinion of the Court.

[P]etitioners filed a complaint [that] respondents had refused to sell them a home [for] the sole reason that petitioner [is] a Negro. Relying in part upon 42 U.S.C. § 1982 [Sec. 1, I supra], the petitioners sought injunctive and other relief.[1] The [courts below] sustained the respondents' motion to dismiss [concluding] that § 1982 applies only to state action * * *.

[I]t is important to make clear precisely what this case does *not* involve. Whatever else it may be, § 1982 is not a comprehensive open housing law. In sharp contrast to the Fair Housing Title (Title VIII) of the Civil Rights Act of 1968, the statute in this case deals only with racial discrimination and does not address itself to discrimination on grounds of religion or national origin. It does not deal specifically with discrimination in the provision of services or facilities in connection with the sale or rental of a dwelling. It does not prohibit advertising or other representations that indicate discriminatory preferences. It does not refer explicitly to discrimination in financing arrangements or in the provision of brokerage services.[10] It does not empower a federal administrative agency to assist aggrieved parties. It makes no provision for intervention by the Attorney General. And, although it can be enforced by injunction, it contains no provision expressly authorizing a federal court to order the payment of damages. * * *

[It] is true that a dictum in [*Hurd v. Hodge*, 334 U.S. 24, 68 S.Ct. 847, 92 L.Ed. 1187 (1948)] said that § 1982 was directed only toward "governmental action," but neither *Hurd* nor any other case before or since has presented that precise issue for adjudication in this Court. * * *

On its [face] § 1982 appears to prohibit *all* discrimination against Negroes in the sale or rental of property—discrimination by private owners as well as discrimination by public [authorities.] Stressing what they consider to be the revolutionary implications of so literal a reading of § 1982, the respondents argue that Congress cannot possibly have intended any such result. Our examination of the relevant history, however, persuades us that Congress meant exactly what it said.

In its original form, § 1982 was part [of] the Civil Rights Act of 1866. [The Court then extensively examined antecedent statutes and studies and debate in

---

1. To vindicate their rights under § 1982, the petitioners invoked the jurisdiction of the District Court to award "damages [or] equitable or other relief under any Act of Congress providing for the protection of civil rights * * *." 28 U.S.C. § 1343(4). * * *

10. In noting that § 1982 differs from the Civil Rights Act of 1968 [we] intimate no view upon the question whether ancillary services or facilities of this sort might in some situations constitute "property" as that term is employed in § 1982. * * *

the Congress, contemporaneous with the proposal and ratification of the thirteenth amendment, in support of its conclusion respecting § 1982.]

Nor was the scope of the 1866 Act altered when it was re-enacted in 1870, some two years after the ratification of the Fourteenth Amendment. It is quite true that some members of Congress supported the Fourteenth Amendment "in order to eliminate doubt as to the constitutional validity of the Civil Rights Act as applied to the States." *Hurd.* But it certainly does not follow that the adoption of the Fourteenth Amendment or the subsequent readoption of the Civil Rights Act were meant somehow to *limit* its application to state action. The legislative history furnishes not the slightest factual basis for any such speculation, and the conditions prevailing in 1870 make it highly implausible. * * *

The remaining question is whether Congress has power under the Constitution to do what § 1982 purports to [do]. Our starting point is the Thirteenth Amendment, for it was pursuant to that constitutional provision that Congress originally enacted what is now § 1982. [It] has never been [doubted] "that the power vested in Congress to enforce the article by appropriate legislation," [*Civil Rights Cases,*] includes the power to enact laws "direct and primary, operating upon the acts of individuals, whether sanctioned by State legislation or not." [Id.]

"By its own unaided force and effect," the Thirteenth Amendment "abolished slavery, and established universal freedom." *Civil Rights Cases.* Whether or not the Amendment *itself* did any more than that—a question not involved in this case—it is at least clear that the Enabling Clause of that Amendment empowered Congress to do much more.[a] For that clause clothed "Congress with power to pass *all laws necessary and proper for abolishing all badges and incidents of slavery in the United States.*" Ibid. (Emphasis added.)

Those who opposed passage of the Civil Rights Act of 1866 argued in effect that the Thirteenth Amendment merely authorized Congress to dissolve the legal bond by which the Negro slave was held to his master. Yet [the] majority leaders in Congress—who were, after all, the authors of the Thirteenth Amendment—had no doubt that its Enabling Clause contemplated the sort of positive legislation that was embodied in the 1866 Civil Rights Act. [Surely] Congress has the power under the Thirteenth Amendment rationally to determine what are the badges and the incidents of slavery, and the authority to translate that determination into effective legislation. Nor can we say that the determination Congress has made is an irrational one. For this Court recognized long ago that, whatever else they may have encompassed, the badges and incidents of slavery—its "burdens and disabilities"—included restraints upon "those fundamental rights which are the essence of civil freedom, namely the same right [to] inherit, purchase, lease, sell and convey property, as is enjoyed by white citizens." *Civil Rights Cases.* Just as the Black Codes, enacted after the Civil War to restrict the free exercise of those rights, were substitutes for the slave system, so the exclusion of Negroes from white communities became a substitute for the Black Codes. And when racial discrimination herds men into ghettos and makes their ability to buy property turn on the color of their skin, then it too is a relic of slavery.

[At] the very least, the freedom that Congress is empowered to secure under the Thirteenth Amendment includes the freedom to buy whatever a white man can buy, the right to live wherever a white man can live. If Congress cannot say

a. For discussion of the use of judicial pow-   10, Sec. 1.
er under § 1 of the amendment, see fn. b, Ch.

that being a free man means at least this much, then the Thirteenth Amendment made a promise the Nation cannot keep. * * *

Reversed.

JUSTICE HARLAN, whom JUSTICE WHITE joins, dissenting.

[The] issue of the constitutionality of § 1982, as construed by the Court, and of liability under the Fourteenth Amendment alone, [present] formidable difficulties. [In a lengthy opinion, Harlan, J., relied on statements in prior Supreme Court opinions, the use of the word "right" in § 1982, the legislative history and debates of the Civil Rights Act of 1866 and of companion legislation, and on the ethics of the times to demonstrate that the Court's construction of § 1982 was "open to the most serious doubt" if not "wholly untenable."][b]

———

RUNYON v. MCCRARY, 427 U.S. 160, 96 S.Ct. 2586, 49 L.Ed.2d 415 (1976), per STEWART, J., relying on *Mayer's* interpretation of § 1982, held that § 1981, Sec. 1, I supra, prohibits private schools—that were operated commercially and open to the public in that they engaged in general advertising to attract students—from refusing to accept black students. POWELL, J., joined the opinion, but added that "choices, including those involved in entering into a contract, that are 'private' in the sense that they are not part of a commercial relationship offered generally or widely, and that reflect the selectivity exercised by an individual entering into a personal relationship, certainly were never intended to be restricted by" § 1981. Stevens, J., joined the court's opinion, feeling bound by, but disagreeing with, the statutory interpretation in *Mayer*. White, J., joined by Rehnquist, J., dissented on grounds of statutory interpretation.

Notes and Questions

1. *Scope of §§ 1982 and 1981.* (a) What other discriminations against African–Americans are presently prohibited by these provisions? Consider Louis Henkin, *On Drawing Lines,* 82 Harv.L.Rev. 63, 85–86 (1968): "Will no bequest stand up which includes a racial discrimination since that would deprive Negroes of 'the same right [to] inherit'? Has there been an easier answer to [Senator Bacon's] will all this time while the Court struggled with theories of state action to find escape from his discrimination [see *Newton* and *Abney,* Ch. 10, Secs. 2 and 3]? Indeed, [Title II of the Civil Rights Act of 1964] provides that certain places of public accommodations may not discriminate on the basis of race in selling goods and services; the Court's construction of § 1982, when applied to personal property, renders the title (and its limitations) superfluous. Moreover, by the Court's technique of construction, the right 'to make and enforce contracts' guaranteed by [§ 1981] should prevent a restaurant or hotel management from refusing on grounds of race to 'make a contract' for service with a Negro. Indeed, that construction should prevent any employer from refusing 'to make a contract' of employment with a Negro; and the fair employment provisions of the 1964 Act likewise become superfluous, as does the entire struggle, since the days of the New

b. The concurring opinion of Douglas, J., is omitted. For conflicting views as to § 1982's history, compare Charles Fairman, *Reconstruction and Reunion: 1864–1888, Part One* (1971) with Sanford Levinson, *Book Review,* 26 Stan. L.Rev. 461 (1974); Robert L. Kohl, *The Civil Rights Act of 1866, Its Hour Come Round at Last,* 55 Va.L.Rev. 272 (1969) with Gerhard Casper, *Jones v. Mayer: Clio, Bemused and Confused Muse,* 1968 Sup.Ct.Rev. 89.

Deal, to enact adequate fair employment legislation."[c]

(b) *Constitutionality*. Are the above racial discriminations "badges and incidents of slavery"? What of the practice by sellers of certain goods or services of charging African–Americans higher prices? See Note, *Discriminatory Housing Markets, Racial Unconscionability, and Section 1988*, 80 Yale L.J. 516 (1971). Is the initial question inaccurately stated? Do these instances "run the slavery argument into the ground" (*Civil Rights Cases*)?

Does the thirteenth amendment empower Congress to prohibit action that has a racially disproportionate impact, regardless of its purpose? Do §§ 1981–82 do so? See Note, *Section 1981: Discriminatory Purpose or Disproportionate Impact?* 80 Colum.L.Rev. 137 (1980); *Memphis v. Greene*, Ch. 9, Sec. 2, III.

2. *Scope of § 1985*. GRIFFIN v. BRECKENRIDGE, 403 U.S. 88, 91 S.Ct. 1790, 29 L.Ed.2d 338 (1971), was a damage action under § 1985. Allegedly, respondents had wilfully conspired to assault and terrorize petitioners—who "were travelling upon the federal, state and local highways"—in order to prevent petitioners "and other Negro–Americans [from] seeking the equal protection of the laws and from enjoying the equal rights, privileges and immunities of citizens under the laws"—including rights to free speech, association, petition for redress of grievances, "their rights not to be enslaved nor deprived of life, liberty or property other than by due process of law, and their rights to travel the public highways without restraint in the same terms as white citizens." The Court, per STEWART, J., held "that all indicators—text, companion provisions, and legislative history—point unwaveringly to § 1985's coverage of private conspiracies." And the "constitutional shoals that would lie in the path of interpreting § 1985 as a general federal tort law can be avoided" because the "language requiring intent to deprive of *equal* protection, or *equal* privileges and immunities, means that there must be some racial, or perhaps otherwise class-based, invidiously discriminatory animus behind the conspirators' action.[9]"

The Court then found *at least* two sources of "congressional power to reach the private conspiracy alleged." First, under § 2 of the thirteenth amendment, Congress was "wholly within its powers [in] creating a statutory cause of action for Negro citizens who have been the victims of conspiratorial, racially discriminatory private action aimed at depriving them of the basic rights that the law secures to all free men." Second, "the right of interstate travel is constitutionally protected [against] private as well as governmental interference." Since "it is open to the petitioners to prove at trial that they had been engaging in interstate travel or intended to do so, that [the] conspirators intended to drive out-of-state civil rights workers from the State, or that they meant to deter the petitioners from associating with such persons," this "could make it clear that the petitioners had suffered from conduct which Congress may [reach]."[d]

c. .Does § 1981 make *Moose Lodge v. Irvis*, Ch. 10, Sec. 3, incorrect? Or do other constitutional provisions (values) justify the decision?

9. We need not decide, given the facts of this case, whether conspiracy motivated by invidiously discriminatory intent other than racial bias would be actionable under the portion of § 1985(3) before us. [See *Carpenters, Local 610 v. Scott*, infra, holding that § 1985 does not "reach conspiracies motivated by economic or commercial animus."]

[See also *Bray v. Alexandria Women's Health Clinic*, note 3 infra, leaving open the question

of whether "an invidiously discriminatory animus" against women comes within § 1985, but holding that opposition to abortion does not reflect such animus because it does not involve "a purpose that focuses upon women *by reason of their sex*." Blackmun, Stevens and O'Connor, JJ., disagreed.]

d. Harlan, J., joined the Court's opinion but found it unnecessary to rely on the "right of interstate travel."

3. *Beyond racial discrimination.* (a) CARPENTERS, LOCAL 610 v. SCOTT, 463 U.S. 825, 103 S.Ct. 3352, 77 L.Ed.2d 1049 (1983), per WHITE, J., held "that an alleged conspiracy to infringe First Amendment rights is not a violation of § 1985 unless it is proved that the state is involved in the conspiracy or that the aim of the conspiracy is to influence the activity of the state": "The complaint in *Griffin* alleged, among other things, a deprivation of First Amendment rights but we did not sustain the action on the basis of that allegation and paid it scant attention. Instead, we upheld the application of § 1985 to private conspiracies aimed at interfering with rights [such as the freedom from slavery and the right to travel] constitutionally protected against private, as well as official, encroachment." Blackmun, J., joined by Brennan, Marshall and O'Connor, JJ., dissented. Does § 1985 provide a cause of action to whites who suffer injury because of their espousal of the rights of African–Americans?

In BRAY v. ALEXANDRIA WOMEN'S HEALTH CLINIC, 506 U.S. 263, 113 S.Ct. 753, 122 L.Ed.2d 34 (1993), an injunction was sought against anti-abortion demonstrators' trespassing on, and obstructing access to, the premises of abortion clinics. The Court per SCALIA, J., held that § 1985 does not apply to private conspiracies aimed against abortion because that involves "a right only against state interference." STEVENS, J., joined by Blackmun, J., dissented on the ground that § 1985 covers "a large-scale conspiracy that violates the victims' constitutional rights by overwhelming the local authorities." O'Connor and Souter, JJ., agreed with Stevens, J., in separate opinions.

(b) To what extent does *Mayer* empower Congress to define the substantive terms of the Civil War amendments? For example, pursuant to § 2 of the thirteenth amendment, may Congress "rationally determine" that discriminations against groups other than African–Americans are "badges and incidents of slavery"? See *McDonald v. Santa Fe Trail Trans. Co.*, 427 U.S. 273, 96 S.Ct. 2574, 49 L.Ed.2d 493 (1976) ("Congress is authorized under [§ 2] to legislate in regard to 'every race and individual' "). Consider Note, *Jones v. Mayer: The Thirteenth Amendment and the Federal Anti–Discrimination Laws*, 69 Colum.L.Rev. 1019, 1025–26 (1969): "[T]he Court's conclusion that housing discrimination *today* is a badge or incident of slavery is itself a recognition that the 'slavery' referred to in the thirteenth amendment now encompasses the second class citizenship imposed on members of disparate minority groups. By doing so, the Court has implicitly interpreted 'slavery' as the word has come to mean. [A] victim's people need not have been enslaved in order to invoke its protection. He need only be suffering today under conditions that could reasonably be called symptoms of a slave society, inability to raise a family with dignity caused by unemployment, poor schools and housing, and lack of a place in the body politic. By removing the time element from badges and incidents of slavery, an aggrieved party need not show a continuous link between his plight and actual slavery in order to benefit from the guarantees of the thirteenth amendment."[e] Compare Note, *The "New" Thirteenth Amendment: A Preliminary Analysis*, 82 Harv.L.Rev. 1294 (1969). Consider Jesse H. Choper, *Congressional Power to Expand Judicial Definitions of the Substantive*

---

e. For the view that *McDonald* strongly supports this approach, see Emily Calhoun, *The Thirteenth and Fourteenth Amendments: Constitutional Authority for Federal Legislation Against Private Sex Discrimination,* 61 Minn.L.Rev. 313 (1977). For criticism of *McDonald,* see Note, *The Thirteenth Amendment and Private Affirmative Action,* 89 Yale L.J. 399 (1979).

The Court has interpreted § 1981 "to protect from discrimination identifiable classes of persons who are subjected to intentional discrimination solely because of their ancestry or ethnic characteristics." *Saint Francis College v. Al–Khazraji,* 481 U.S. 604, 107 S.Ct. 2022, 95 L.Ed.2d 582 (1987) (Arabs); *Shaare Tefila Congregation v. Cobb,* 481 U.S. 615, 107 S.Ct. 2019, 95 L.Ed.2d 594 (1987) (Jews).

Terms of the Civil War Amendments, 67 Minn.L.Rev. 299, 313–14 (1982): "*Mayer* need not be interpreted as conferring any *definitional* authority on Congress. Rather, it can be persuasively argued on either of two theories that the Court upheld the Civil Rights Act of 1866 as only a *remedial* exercise of Congress's enforcement power under the thirteenth amendment. First, 'slavery' may be regarded as a status to be defined by the Court, [and] the 'badges and incidents of slavery' may be regarded, not as elements of that definition, but as stigmas and disabilities related to slavery. [Thus,] to say that Congress may rationally determine the badges and incidents of slavery is nothing more than to say that Congress may prohibit certain practices, although those practices themselves do not constitute slavery, when Congress rationally finds that their prohibition will help to *prevent* slavery.[83] Alternatively, since Congress's [remedial power] encompasses eradicating the *effects* of constitutional violations as well as preventing future ones, the congressional prohibition in *Mayer* may be readily sustained as an effort to eliminate the persistent legacies of the past condition of slavery."

4. *Self-executing force of thirteenth amendment.* Apart from federal legislation pursuant to § 2, are any (all) of the discriminations referred to above made unconstitutional by § 1 of "the Amendment *itself*"? If so, by what means should (can) the Court enforce § 1?

II.   STATE "INVOLVEMENT"

UNITED STATES v. PRICE, 383 U.S. 787, 86 S.Ct. 1152, 16 L.Ed.2d 267 (1966), involved indictments for conspiracy and substantive violations under §§ 241 and 242, Sec. 1, I supra, against three Mississippi police officials and fifteen "nonofficial persons," for having willfully killed three civil rights workers—the police officials first jailing the victims, then releasing them and intercepting them and, then, all 18 defendants "punishing" the victims by shooting them—thus depriving "the victims due process of law."

The Court, treating the case as raising issues "of construction, not of constitutional power," held that, as to the conspiracy count against the "private persons" under § 242, " '[I]t is immaterial to the conspiracy that these private individuals were not acting under color of law' because the count charges that they were conspiring with persons who were so acting." As to the substantive counts against the "private persons" under § 242, the Court, stating that the statutory language "under color of law" has "consistently been treated as the same thing as the 'state action' required by the Fourteenth Amendment," held that "private persons, jointly engaged with state officials in the prohibited action, are acting 'under color' of law for purposes of the statute. To act 'under color' of law does not require that the accused be an officer of the State. It is enough that he is a wilful participant in joint activity with the State or its agents," citing *Burton v. Wilmington Parking Auth.,* Ch. 10, Sec. 3. "[A]ccording to the indictment, the brutal joint adventure was made possible by state detention and calculated release of the prisoners by an officer of the State."[a] "Those who took advantage of participation by state officers in accomplishment of the foul purpose alleged must suffer the consequences of that participation."[b]

---

83. David E. Engdahl, *Constitutional Power: Federal and State in a Nutshell* 247–48 (1974) (emphasis added).

a. See also *United States v. Guest,* 383 U.S. 745, 86 S.Ct. 1170, 16 L.Ed.2d 239 (1966).

b. See also *Screws v. United States,* 325 U.S. 91, 65 S.Ct. 1031, 89 L.Ed. 1495 (1945) holding that it was no defense under § 242 that defendant's actions were in violation of state law: "Misuse of power, possessed by virtue of state law and made possible only be-

Notes and Questions

1. *"Participation"* of private persons with state officers. In *Price,* the "official" and "nonofficial" defendants all appeared to be actively and equally participating in the venture. Could private persons be constitutionally convicted under § 242 if they were "passive" participants with state officers? Suppose the private person were the "active" participant while the state officers were merely "passive"? See Thomas J. Klitgaard, *The Civil Rights Act and Mr. Monroe,* 49 Calif.L.Rev. 145, 168–69 (1961). Could the private person be convicted if all the state officers are acquitted?

2. Consider the constitutionality of the following prosecutions under § 242:

(a) Defendant sheriff beats prisoner to death because prisoner cursed the sheriff. Suppose the sheriff encounters a personal enemy on the street and beats him to death? Suppose this personal enemy declined to resist because he feared the consequences of a victory over a police officer? Suppose the sheriff first tells the personal enemy that he is under arrest?

(b) Defendant private citizen secretly enters a jail and beats a prisoner to death, thus preventing a fair trial by the state. Suppose the citizen joined the sheriff in beating the prisoner to death in order to obtain a confession?

(c) Defendant sheriff stands by while a private citizen beats to death the sheriff's prisoner, who is the citizen's personal enemy.

(d) Defendant private citizen is part of a mob that so intimidates parents of school children as to cause them to keep the children away from the school with the result that the school is closed. Suppose the private citizen intimidates state officials in an attempt to thwart their racial integration of public schools? See Stevens, J., concurring in *Great American Fed. S. & L. Ass'n v. Novotny,* 442 U.S. 366, 99 S.Ct. 2345, 60 L.Ed.2d 957 (1979).

(e) Defendant private citizen makes a "citizen's arrest" without probable cause. Suppose the citizen masqueraded as a policeman and made an arrest without probable cause? Suppose this citizen, dressed as a policeman, killed a personal enemy? Suppose the citizen, making an arrest without probable cause, were a private detective who became a "special police officer" by local law? See *Williams v. United States,* 341 U.S. 97, 71 S.Ct. 576, 95 L.Ed. 774 (1951).

(f) Defendant attorney, an "officer of the court," makes false statements in a sanity proceeding which result in the commitment of another person. Suppose defendant is court-appointed? See *Polk County v. Dodson,* 454 U.S. 312, 102 S.Ct. 445, 70 L.Ed.2d 509 (1981) (public defender does not act under color of law when performing traditional adversarial functions as appointed counsel).

(g) Defendant private citizen denies another person the use of a state park because of the latter's race? See *Guest* (Brennan, J., joined by Warren, C.J., and Douglas, J., concurring). Suppose the denial involved a privately owned trailer camp?

3.(a) *Civil Rights Act of 1968.* 18 U.S.C.A. § 245(b): "Whoever, whether or not acting under color of law, by force or threat of force willfully injures,

cause the wrongdoer is clothed with the authority of state law, is action taken 'under color of' state law. [It] is clear that under 'color' of law means under 'pretense' of law. Thus acts of officers in the ambit of their personal pursuits are plainly excluded. Acts of officers who undertake to perform their official duties are included whether they hew to the line of their authority or overstep it."

intimidates or interferes with, or attempts to injure, intimidate or interfere with—
* * *

"(2) any person because of his race, color, religion or national origin and because he is or has been—

"(A) enrolling in or attending any public school or public college;

"(B) participating in or enjoying any benefit, service, privilege, program, facility or activity provided or administered by any State or subdivision thereof;

"(C) applying for or enjoying employment, or any perquisite thereof, by any private employer or any agency of any State or subdivision thereof, or joining or using the services or advantages of any labor organization, hiring hall, or employment agency;

"(D) serving, or attending upon any court of any State in connection with possible service, as a grand or petit juror; * * *

"(F) enjoying the goods, services, facilities, privileges, advantages, or accommodations of any inn, hotel, motel, or other establishment which provides lodging to transient guests, or of any restaurant, cafeteria, lunchroom, lunch counter, soda fountain, or other facility which serves the public and which is principally engaged in selling food or beverages for consumption on the premises, or of any gasoline station, or of any motion picture house, theater, concert hall, sports arena, stadium, or any other place of exhibition or entertainment which serves the public, or of any other establishment which serves the public and (i) which is located within the premises of any of the aforesaid establishments or within the premises of which is physically located any of the aforesaid establishments, and (ii) which holds itself out as serving patrons of such establishments; or * * *

"(5) any citizen because he is or has been, or in order to intimidate such citizen or any other citizen from lawfully aiding or encouraging other persons to participate, without discrimination on account of race, color, religion or national origin, in any of the benefits or activities described [or] participating lawfully in speech or peaceful assembly opposing any denial of the opportunity to so participate—

"shall be fined not more than $1,000, or imprisoned not more than one year, or both; and if bodily injury results shall be fined not more than $10,000, or imprisoned not more than ten years, or both; and if death results shall be subject to imprisonment for any term of years or for life. * * * Nothing in subparagraph (2)(F) * * * of this subsection shall apply to the proprietor of any establishment which provides lodging to transient guests, or to any employee acting on behalf of such proprietor, with respect to the enjoyment of [the] accommodations of such establishment if such establishment is located within a building which contains not more than five rooms for rent or hire and which is actually occupied by the proprietor as his residence."

(b) Suppose a private individual murders a black person. It is clear that the *effect* (irrespective of the murderer's *intent*) is to prevent the victim's equal use of state facilities; that it prevents his right to be a juror, etc. These facts would be equally true if the victim were white. May the murderer be punished under the above statute? Under a more narrowly drawn federal criminal statute? Consider Archibald Cox, *Constitutional Adjudication and the Promotion of Human Rights*, 80 Harv.L.Rev. 91, 116 (1966): "The differences between purpose, awareness that a consequence must follow, conscious indifference, and responsibility for the natural and probable consequences of an act are far too elusive to measure the scope of congressional power. Furthermore, if violence and intimidation are actually interfering with the [right], there is scant practical relevance in the wrongdoers' motivation. The suggestion was once made that the power of Congress to regulate local activities under the commerce clause depended upon the intent with which the activities were conducted, but the idea was shortly abandoned in favor of legislative or administrative determination of the practical effects on commerce."

Does congressional power fail in the above instance because "its authority is confined to instances in which there is a special relationship between the person injured and the state"? Because there is "an utter lack of proportion between the federal punishment [and] the federal interest in safeguarding enjoyment of the constitutional right"? Or is "the responsibility for the federal system" left to Congress: "possession of congressional power should not be confused with its exercise"? Id. at 116–17, 119.

SECTION 3. REGULATION OF STATE ACTORS

SOUTH CAROLINA v. KATZENBACH, 383 U.S. 301, 86 S.Ct. 803, 15 L.Ed.2d 769 (1966): South Carolina challenged the Voting Rights Act of 1965— "the heart of [which] is a complex scheme of stringent remedies aimed at areas where voting discrimination has been most flagrant." The Court, per WARREN, C.J., referred to "the voluminous legislative history" that showed, inter alia, "unremitting and ingenious defiance of the Constitution," the enactment of literacy tests in Alabama, Georgia, Louisiana, Mississippi, North Carolina, South Carolina, and Virginia, still in use, which, because of their various qualifications, "were specifically designed to prevent Negroes from voting." It pointed out that "discriminatory application of voting tests" "pursuant to a widespread 'pattern or practice'" "is now the principal method used to bar Negroes from the polls," and that "case-by-case litigation against voting discrimination" under federal statutes of 1957, 1960 and 1964 has "done little to cure the problem."

"As against the reserved powers of the States, Congress may use any rational means to effectuate the constitutional prohibition of racial discrimination in voting. [The] basic test to be applied in a case involving § 2 of the Fifteenth Amendment is the same as in all cases concerning the express powers of Congress with relation to the reserved powers of the [states.] 'Let the end be legitimate, let it be within the scope of the constitution, and all means which are appropriate, which are plainly adapted to that end, which are not prohibited, but consist with the letter and spirit of the constitution, are constitutional.' *McCulloch v. Maryland* [Ch. 2, Sec. 1]."

The "coverage formula" of the Act applied "to any State, or to any separate political subdivision [for] which two findings have been made: (1) [on] November 1, 1964, it maintained a 'test or device,' and (2) [that] less than 50% of its voting-age residents were registered on November 1, 1964, or voted in the presidential election of November 1964. * * * § 4(b). [T]he phrase 'test or device' means any requirement that a registrant or voter must '(1) demonstrate the ability to read, write, understand, or interpret any matter, (2) demonstrate any educational achievement or his knowledge of any particular subject, (3) possess good moral character, or (4) prove his qualifications by the voucher of registered voters or members of any other class.' § 4(c)." Statutory coverage was terminated by a so-called "bail out" provision—if the area obtained a judgment from a three-judge federal court in the District of Columbia "that tests and devices have not been used during the preceding five years to abridge the franchise on racial grounds."

"In acceptable legislative fashion, Congress chose to limit its attention to the geographic areas where immediate action seemed necessary."

The areas covered, "for which there was evidence of actual voting discrimination,"—Alabama, Louisiana, Mississippi, Georgia, South Carolina and much of North Carolina—shared the "two characteristics incorporated by Congress into the coverage formula." "It was therefore permissible to impose the new remedies on the few remaining States and political subdivisions covered by the formula, at least in the absence of proof that they have been free of substantial voting discrimination in recent years." That there are excluded areas "for which there is evidence of voting discrimination by other means" is irrelevant: "Legislation need not deal with all phases of a problem in the same way, so long as the distinctions drawn have some basis in political experience." "There are no States or political subdivisions exempted from coverage under § 4(b) in which the record reveals recent racial discrimination involving tests and devices. This fact confirms the rationality of the formula."

In areas covered, § 4(a) suspended "literacy tests and similar voting qualifications for a period of five years from the last occurrence of substantial voting discrimination," and § 5 suspended "all new voting regulations pending review by [the Attorney General or a three-judge court in the District of Columbia] to determine whether their use would perpetuate voting discrimination."[a] Both were upheld as a "legitimate response to the problem," the Court recounting the evidence Congress had before it of prior discriminatory administration of old tests and use of new tests to evade court decrees.[b]

KATZENBACH v. MORGAN

384 U.S. 641, 86 S.Ct. 1717, 16 L.Ed.2d 828 (1966).

JUSTICE BRENNAN delivered the opinion of the Court.

[Section] 4(e) of the Voting Rights Act of 1965 [provides] that no person who has successfully completed the sixth primary grade in a [school] accredited by the Commonwealth of Puerto Rico in which the language of instruction was other than English shall be denied the right to vote in any election because of his inability to read or write English. [Thus, it] prohibits the enforcement of the election laws of New York requiring an ability to read and write English * * *.

The Attorney General of New York argues that an exercise of congressional power under § 5 of the Fourteenth Amendment that prohibits the enforcement of a state [law] cannot be sustained as appropriate legislation to enforce the Equal Protection Clause unless the judiciary decides—even with the guidance of a congressional judgment—that the application of the English literacy requirement prohibited by § 4(e) is forbidden by the Equal Protection Clause itself. We disagree. Neither the language nor history of § 5 supports such a construction.[7]

---

a. For examples of the Court's subsequent broad interpretation of "voting regulations" that are subject to the suspension provision of section 5, see *United Jewish Orgs. v. Carey,* Ch. 9, Sec. 5, I, D (new or revised reapportionment plan); *Rome v. United States,* infra (election of officials "at large" rather than by district; annexation of adjacent area thus increasing number of eligible voters).

b. Black, J., agreed "with substantially all of the Court's opinion" but dissented in re-

spect to § 5 of the Act: "[I]f all the provisions of our Constitution which limit the power of the Federal Government and reserve other power to the States are to mean anything, they mean at least that the States have power to pass laws [without] first sending their officials hundreds of miles away to beg federal authorities to approve them."

7. For the historical evidence suggesting that the sponsors and supporters of the Amendment were primarily interested in aug-

[A] construction of § 5 that would require a judicial determination that the enforcement of the state law precluded by Congress violated the Amendment, as a condition of sustaining the congressional enactment [would] confine the legislative power in this context to the insignificant role of abrogating only those state laws that the judicial branch was prepared to adjudge unconstitutional, or of merely informing the judgment of the judiciary by particularizing the "majestic generalities" of [§ 1]. Accordingly, our decision in *Lassiter v. Northampton Cty. Bd. of Elec.*, 360 U.S. 45, 79 S.Ct. 985, 3 L.Ed.2d 1072 (1959), sustaining the North Carolina English literacy requirement as not in all circumstances prohibited by the first sections of the Fourteenth and Fifteenth Amendments, [did] not present the question before us here: Without regard to whether the judiciary would find that the Equal Protection Clause itself nullifies New York's English literacy requirement as so applied, could Congress prohibit the enforcement of the state law by legislating under § 5? In answering this question, our task is limited to determining whether such legislation is, as required by § 5, appropriate legislation to enforce the Equal Protection Clause.

By including § 5 the draftsmen sought to grant to Congress [the] same broad powers expressed in the Necessary and Proper Clause.[9] The classic formulation of the reach of those powers was established by Chief Justice Marshall in *McCulloch v. Maryland* * * *. *Ex parte Virginia*, 100 U.S. 339, 25 L.Ed. 676 (1879), decided 12 years after the adoption of the Fourteenth Amendment, held that congressional power under § 5 had this same broad scope * * *. Section 2 of the Fifteenth Amendment grants Congress a similar power [and] we recently held in *South Carolina v. Katzenbach* that [the test was] the one formulated in *McCulloch.* * * * Correctly viewed, § 5 is a positive grant of legislative power authorizing Congress to exercise its discretion in determining whether and what legislation is needed to secure the guarantees of the Fourteenth Amendment. * * *[10]

There can be no doubt that § 4(e) may be regarded as an enactment to enforce the Equal Protection Clause. [S]pecifically, § 4(e) may be viewed as a measure to secure for the Puerto Rican community residing in New York nondiscriminatory treatment by government—both in the imposition of voting qualifications and the provision or administration of governmental services, such as public schools, public housing and law enforcement.

Section 4(e) may be readily seen as "plainly adapted" to furthering these aims of the Equal Protection Clause. The practical effect of § 4(e) is to prohibit New York from denying the right to vote to large segments of its Puerto Rican

---

menting the power of Congress, rather than the judiciary, see generally Laurent B. Frantz, *Congressional Power to Enforce the Fourteenth Amendment Against Private Acts*, 73 Yale L.J. 1353, 1356–1357 (1964); Robert J. Harris, *The Quest for Equality*, 33–56 (1960); Jacobus tenBroek, *The Antislavery Origins of the Fourteenth Amendment* 187–217 (1951). [But see Robert A. Burt, *Miranda and Title II: A Morganatic Marriage*, 1969 Sup.Ct.Rev. 81–100.]

9. In fact, earlier drafts of the proposed Amendment employed the "necessary and proper" terminology to describe the scope of congressional power under the Amendment. The substitution of the "appropriate legislation" formula was never thought to have the effect of diminishing the scope of this congressional power. See, e.g., Cong. Globe, 42d Cong., 1st Sess., App. 83 * * *. [But see Note, *Theo-*

ries of Federalism and Civil Rights, 75 Yale L.J. 1007, 1046 n. 200 (1966). Compare discussion in *Argument: The Oral Argument Before the Supreme Court in Brown v. Board of Education of Topeka*, 1952–55, 93–94 (Friedman ed. 1969).]

10. Contrary to the suggestion of the [dissent,] § 5 is limited to adopting measures to enforce the guarantees of the Amendment; § 5 grants Congress no power to restrict, abrogate, or dilute these guarantees. Thus, for example, an enactment authorizing the States to establish racially segregated systems of education would not be—as required by § 5—a measure "to enforce" the Equal Protection Clause since that clause of its own force prohibits such state laws.

community [—the] right that is "preservative of all rights." This enhanced political power will be helpful in gaining nondiscriminatory treatment in public services for the entire Puerto Rican community.[11] Section 4(e) thereby enables the Puerto Rican minority better to obtain "perfect equality of civil rights and equal protection of the laws." [It] was for Congress, as the branch that made this judgment, to assess and weigh the various conflicting considerations—the risk or pervasiveness of the discrimination in governmental services, the effectiveness of eliminating the state restriction on the right to vote as a means of dealing with the evil, the adequacy or availability of alternative remedies, and the nature and significance of the state interests that would be affected by the nullification of the English literacy requirement. [It] is enough that we be able to perceive a basis upon which the Congress might resolve the conflict as it did. There plainly was such a [basis]. Any contrary conclusion would require us to be blind to the realities familiar to the legislators.

The result is no different if we confine our inquiry to the question whether § 4(e) was merely legislation aimed at the elimination of an invidious discrimination in establishing voter qualifications. We are told that New York's English literacy requirement originated in the desire to provide an incentive for non-English speaking immigrants to learn the English language and in order to assure the intelligent exercise of the franchise. Yet Congress might well have questioned, in light of the many exemptions provided,[13] and some evidence suggesting that prejudice played a prominent role in the enactment of the requirement,[14] whether these were actually the interests being served. Congress might have also questioned whether denial of a right deemed so precious and fundamental in our society was a necessary or appropriate means of encouraging persons to learn English, or of furthering the goal of an intelligent exercise of the franchise.[15] Finally, Congress might well have concluded that as a means of furthering the intelligent exercise of the franchise, an ability to read or understand Spanish is as effective as ability to read English for those to whom Spanish-language newspapers and Spanish-language radio and television programs are available to inform them of election issues and governmental affairs.[16] Since Congress undertook to legislate so as to preclude the enforcement of the state law, and did so in the context of a general appraisal of literacy requirements for voting, see *South Carolina,* to which it brought a specially informed legislative competence,[17] it was

---

11. Cf. * * * *United States v. Darby* [Ch. 2, Sec. 2, II, B], that the power of Congress to regulate interstate commerce "extends to those activities intrastate which so affect interstate commerce or the exercise of the power of Congress over it as to make regulation of them appropriate means to the attainment of a legitimate end * * *."

13. The principal exemption complained of is that for persons who had been eligible to vote before January 1, 1922.

14. This evidence consists in part of statements made in the Constitutional Convention first considering the English literacy requirement * * *. Congress was aware of this evidence. See, e.g., *Literacy Tests and Voter Requirements in Federal and State Elections,* Senate Hearings 507–513; *Voting Rights,* House Hearings 508–513.

15. [O]ur cases have held that the States can be required to tailor carefully the means of

satisfying a legitimate state interest when fundamental liberties and rights are threatened, see, e.g., *Carrington v. Rash; Harper v. Virginia Board of Elections* [Ch. 9, Sec. 5, I, A]; *United States v. Carolene Products Co.* [Ch. 5, Sec. 3]; and Congress is free to apply the same principle in the exercise of its powers.

16. See, e.g., 111 Cong.Rec. 10675 (May 20, 1965), 15102 (July 6, 1965), 15666 (July 9, 1965). The record in this case includes affidavits describing the nature of New York's two major Spanish-language newspapers [and] its three full-time Spanish-language radio stations and affidavits from those who have campaigned in Spanish speaking areas.

17. See, e.g., 111 Cong.Rec. 10676 (Senator Long of Louisiana and Senator Young), 10678 (Senator Holland) (May 20, 1965), drawing on their experience with voters literate in a language other than English. * * *

Congress' prerogative to weigh these competing considerations. Here again, it is enough that we perceive a basis upon which Congress might predicate a judgment that the application of New York's English literacy [requirement] constituted an invidious discrimination in violation of the Equal Protection Clause.

[The Court rejected the contention that the "American-flag schools" limitation itself violates "the letter and spirit of the Constitution"].

Reversed.

JUSTICE HARLAN, whom JUSTICE STEWART joins, dissenting.

[The dissent first argued that the New York law was not forbidden by the equal protection clause itself.] I believe the Court has confused the issue of how much enforcement power Congress possesses under § 5 with the distinct issue of what questions are appropriate for congressional determination and what questions are essentially judicial in nature.

When recognized state violations of federal constitutional standards have occurred, Congress is of course empowered by § 5 to take appropriate remedial measures. [But the] question here is not whether the statute is appropriate remedial legislation to cure an established violation of a constitutional command, but whether there has in fact been an infringement of that constitutional command, that is, whether a particular state practice or, as here, a statute is so arbitrary or irrational as to offend the command of [equal protection]. That question is one for the judicial branch ultimately to determine. [In] view of [*Lassiter*], I do not think it is open to Congress to limit the effect of that decision as it has undertaken to do by § 4(e). In effect the Court reads § 5 of the Fourteenth Amendment as giving Congress the power to define the *substantive* scope of the Amendment. If that indeed be the true reach of § 5, then I do not see why Congress should not be able as well to exercise its § 5 "discretion" by enacting statutes so as in effect to dilute equal protection and due process decisions of this Court. In all such cases there is room for reasonable men to differ as to whether or not a denial of equal protection or due process has occurred, and the final decision is one of judgment. Until today this judgment has always been one for the judiciary to resolve.

I do not mean to suggest in what has been said that a legislative judgment of the type incorporated in § 4(e) is without any force whatsoever. Decisions on questions of equal protection and due process are based not on abstract logic, but on empirical foundations. To the extent "legislative facts" are relevant to a judicial determination, Congress is well equipped to investigate them, and such determinations are of course entitled to due respect.[a] In *South Carolina,* such legislative findings were made to show that racial discrimination in voting was actually occurring. Similarly, in *Heart of Atlanta* and *Katzenbach v. McClung,* [Ch. 2, Sec. 2, III], the congressional determination that racial discrimination in a clearly defined group of public accommodations did effectively impede interstate commerce was based on "voluminous testimony" which had been put before the Congress and in the context of which it passed remedial legislation.

But no such factual data provide a legislative record supporting § 4(e)[9] by way of showing that Spanish-speaking citizens are fully as capable of making informed

---

a. For the view that "Congress cannot alter the *normative component* of a judicial decision" but that "the *empirical component* [is] the province of Congress," see Irving Gordon, *The Nature and Uses of Congressional Power Under Section Five of the Fourteenth Amendment*

to Overcome Decisions of the Supreme Court, 72 Nw.U.L.Rev. 656 (1977). See note 1 after *Boerne, infra.*

9. There were no committee hearings or reports referring to this section, which was

decisions in a New York election as are English-speaking citizens. Nor was there any showing whatever to support the Court's alternative argument that § 4(e) should be viewed as but a remedial measure designed to cure or assure against unconstitutional discrimination of other varieties, e.g., in "public schools, public housing and law enforcement" * * *.

Thus, we have [here] what can at most be called a legislative announcement that Congress believes a state law to entail an unconstitutional deprivation of equal protection. Although this kind of declaration is of course entitled to the most respectful consideration, coming as it does from a concurrent branch and one that is knowledgeable in matters of popular political participation, I do not believe it lessens our responsibility to decide the fundamental issue of whether in fact the state enactment violates federal constitutional rights.

In assessing the deference we should give to this kind of congressional expression of policy, it is relevant that the judiciary has always given to congressional enactments a presumption of validity. However, it is also a canon of judicial review that state statutes are given a similar presumption, [and] although it has been suggested that this Court should give somewhat more deference to Congress than to a State Legislature,[10] such a simple weighing of presumptions is hardly a satisfying way of resolving a matter that touches the distribution of state and federal power in an area so sensitive as that of the regulation of the franchise. Rather it should be recognized that while the Fourteenth Amendment is a "brooding omnipresence" over all state legislation, the substantive matters which it touches are all within the primary legislative competence of the States. Federal authority, legislative no less than judicial, does not intrude unless there has been a denial by state action of Fourteenth Amendment [limitations]. At least in the area of primary state concern a state statute that passes constitutional muster under the judicial standard of rationality should not be permitted to be set at naught by a mere contrary congressional pronouncement unsupported by a legislative record justifying that conclusion. * * *

Notes and Questions

1. *Morgan's "substantive" branch. (a) Equal protection.* After *Morgan,* could Congress enact legislation prohibiting *all* state discrimination on the basis of alienage, illegitimacy and gender? Cf. Ch. 9, Secs. 3–4. Forbidding state discrimination against master antenna cable TV systems, opticians, debt adjustors and methadone users? Cf. Ch. 9, Sec. 1. Requiring that, in all instances in which state action has a racially disproportionate impact, the courts should balance the strength of the government interest against the disadvantage imposed on the racial minority? Cf. Ch. 9, Sec. 2, III.

(b) *Procedural due process.* After *Morgan,* could Congress impose the federal rules of civil and criminal procedure on the states on the ground that the fourteenth amendment requires that due process be accorded all litigants and that in "its discretion" the federal rules are "needed to secure the guarantees of the Fourteenth Amendment"?

(c) *Substantive due process.* After *Morgan,* could Congress enact the proposed Freedom of Choice Act (FOCA), H.R. 25, 102d Cong., 1st Sess. (1991); S. 25, 102d Cong.2d Sess. (1992), which would respond to *Planned Parenthood v. Casey,* [Ch.

---

introduced from the floor during debate on the full Voting Rights Act.

10. See James B. Thayer, *The Origin and Scope of the American Doctrine of Constitutional Law,* 7 Harv.L.Rev. 129, 154–155 (1893).

6, Sec. 2], by codifying the holding of *Roe v. Wade?* May Congress grant a federal right to "abortion on demand"?

(d) *State action.* If *Morgan* gives Congress "the power to define the *substantive* scope" of equal protection (and due process), does it similarly permit Congress to determine the question of what constitutes "state action"? For example, might Congress, in "exercise of its discretion," determine that any judicial enforcement of racial discrimination shall be prohibited? That racial discrimination in the sale and rental of housing exists because of the failure of the states to make such discrimination illegal, and that this state "inaction" is state action under the fourteenth amendment that should "appropriately" be "remedied" by federal fair housing legislation? For the view that the fourteenth amendment's "Privileges or Immunities Clause (coupled with the § 5 Enforcement Clause)" was intended "as an authorization of Federal legislation to prohibit private racial discrimination if the states did not," see Louis Lusky, *By What Right?* 181–203 (1975). See also Frantz, fn. 7 supra.

2. *Dilution.* (a) Does *Morgan* give Congress power "to dilute equal protection and due process decisions" of the Court? Consider Cox, supra, at 106 n. 86: "According to the conventional theory [enunciated in fn. 10 of *Morgan*], the Court has invalidated state statutes under the due process and equal protection clauses only when no state of facts which can reasonably be conceived would sustain them. Where that is true, a congressional effort to withdraw the protection granted by the clause would lack the foundation of a reasonably conceivable set of facts and would therefore be just as invalid as the state legislation. But while that is true in the realm of economic regulation, the Court has often substituted its own evaluation of actual conditions in reviewing legislation dealing with 'preferred rights.' It is hard to see how the Court can consistently give weight to the congressional judgment in expanding the definition of equal protection in the area of human rights but refuse to give it weight in narrowing the definition where the definition depends upon appraisal of the facts." Does the "answer" lie in a theory that justifies judicial review principally on the need to afford protection to certain minority "rights" from the majority will? Consider William Cohen, *Congressional Power to Interpret Due Process and Equal Protection,* 27 Stan.L.Rev. 603, 614 (1975): "[A] theory that distinguishes between congressional competence to make 'liberty' and 'federalism' judgments resolves the dilemma. A congressional judgment rejecting a judicial interpretation of the due process or equal protection clauses—an interpretation that had given the individual procedural or substantive protection from state and federal government alike—is entitled to no more deference than the identical decision of a state legislature. Congress is no more immune to momentary passions of the majority than are the state legislatures. But a congressional judgment resolving at the national level an issue that could—without constitutional objection—be decided in the same way at the state level, ought normally to be binding on the courts, since Congress presumably reflects a balance between both national and state interests and hence is better able to adjust such conflicts." See also Jesse H. Choper, *Judicial Review and the National Political Process* 198–200 (1980). For the view that this reasoning is supported by both constitutional structure and original intent, see Douglas Laycock, *RFRA, Congress, and the Ratchet,* 56 Mont.L.Rev. 145, 157–165 (1995).

BOERNE v. FLORES

521 U.S. 507, 117 S.Ct. 2157, 138 L.Ed.2d 624 (1997).

JUSTICE KENNEDY delivered the opinion of the Court.

A decision by local zoning authorities to deny a church a building permit was challenged under the Religious Freedom Restoration Act of 1993 (RFRA). * * *

Congress enacted RFRA in direct response to the Court's decision in *Employment Div. v. Smith,* [Ch. 8, Sec. 2, I]. *Smith* held that neutral, generally applicable laws may be applied to religious practices even when not supported by a compelling governmental interest. [Many] criticized the Court's reasoning, and this disagreement resulted in the passage of RFRA. * * *

RFRA prohibits "[g]overnment" from "substantially burden[ing]" a person's exercise of religion even if the burden results from a rule of general applicability unless the government can demonstrate the burden "(1) is in furtherance of a compelling governmental interest; and (2) is the least restrictive means of furthering that compelling governmental interest." * * *

Congress relied on its Fourteenth Amendment enforcement power in enacting the most far reaching and substantial of RFRA's provisions, those which impose its requirements on the [States.] Legislation which deters or remedies constitutional violations can fall within the sweep of Congress' enforcement power even if in the process it prohibits conduct which is not itself unconstitutional and intrudes into "legislative spheres of autonomy previously reserved to the States." *Fitzpatrick v. Bitzer,* 427 U.S. 445, 455, 96 S.Ct. 2666, 2671, 49 L.Ed.2d 614 (1976). [As examples, the Court discussed the practices that Congress had made unlawful in *South Carolina, Morgan* and *Rome,* note 3(c) infra] We agree with respondent, of course, that Congress can enact legislation under § 5 enforcing the constitutional right to the free exercise of religion. * * *

Congress' power under § 5, however, extends only to "enforc[ing]" the provisions of the Fourteenth Amendment. The Court has described this power as "remedial," *South Carolina v. Katzenbach.* The design of the Amendment and the text of § 5 are inconsistent with the suggestion that Congress has the power to decree the substance of the Fourteenth Amendment's restrictions on the States. Legislation which alters the meaning of the Free Exercise Clause cannot be said to be enforcing the Clause. Congress does not enforce a constitutional right by changing what the right is. It has been given the power "to enforce," not the power to determine what constitutes a constitutional violation. Were it not so, what Congress would be enforcing would no longer be, in any meaningful sense, the "provisions of [the Fourteenth Amendment]."

While the line between measures that remedy or prevent unconstitutional actions and measures that make a substantive change in the governing law is not easy to discern, and Congress must have wide latitude in determining where it lies, the distinction exists and must be observed. There must be a congruence and proportionality between the injury to be prevented or remedied and the means adopted to that end. Lacking such a connection, legislation may become substantive in operation and effect. * * *

The Fourteenth Amendment's history confirms the remedial, rather than substantive, nature of the Enforcement Clause.[a] [The] objections to the [Joint]

---

a. Contra, Douglas Laycock, *Conceptual Gulfs in Boerne v. Flores,* 39 Wm. & M. L. Rev.

Committee's first draft of the Amendment ["The Congress shall have power to make all laws which shall be necessary and proper to secure to the citizens of each State all privileges and immunities of citizens in the several States, and to all persons in the several States equal protection in the rights of life, liberty, and property."] have a direct bearing on the central issue of defining Congress' enforcement power. * * * Members of Congress from across the political spectrum criticized the Amendment, and the criticisms had a common theme: The proposed Amendment gave Congress [a] power to intrude into traditional areas of state responsibility, a power inconsistent with the federal design central to the Constitution. [Under] the revised Amendment, Congress' power was no longer plenary but remedial [and] did not raise the concerns expressed earlier regarding broad congressional power to prescribe uniform national laws with respect to life, liberty, and property.[b] * * *

The design of the Fourteenth Amendment has proved significant also in maintaining the traditional separation of powers between Congress and the Judiciary. The first eight Amendments to the Constitution set forth self-executing prohibitions on governmental action, and this Court has had primary authority to interpret those prohibitions. The [Joint Committee's first] draft, some thought, departed from that tradition by vesting in Congress primary power to interpret and elaborate on the meaning of the new Amendment through legislation. Under it, "Congress, and not the courts, was to judge whether or not any of the privileges or immunities were not secured to citizens in the several States." Horace E. Flack, *The Adoption of the Fourteenth Amendment* 64 (1908). While this separation of powers aspect did not occasion the widespread resistance which was caused by the proposal's threat to the federal balance, it nonetheless attracted the attention of various Members. As enacted, the Fourteenth Amendment confers substantive rights against the States which, like the provisions of the Bill of Rights, are self-executing. The power to interpret the Constitution in a case or controversy remains in the Judiciary. * * *

Any suggestion that Congress has a substantive, non-remedial power under the Fourteenth Amendment is not supported by our case law. In *Oregon v. Mitchell*, [400 U.S. 112, 91 S.Ct. 260, 27 L.Ed.2d 272 (1970)], a majority of the Court concluded Congress had exceeded its enforcement powers by enacting legislation lowering the minimum age of voters from 21 to 18 in state and local elections.[c] The five Members of the Court who reached this conclusion explained that [the] legislation was unconstitutional because the Constitution "reserves to

743, 766 (1998): "Senators and representatives argued [that] the enforcement power would add nothing if it were confined to the judicially enforceable meaning of the Amendment"; Steven A. Engel, *The McCulloch Theory of the Fourteenth Amendment: Boerne v. Flores and the Original Understanding of Section 5*, 109 Yale L.J. 115 (1999).

b. For the view that "although the *Boerne* Court properly rejected the plenary 'substantive' interpretation of Section Five, the Court's conclusion that judicial interpretations of the provisions of the Amendment are the exclusive touchstone for congressional enforcement power finds no support in the history of the Fourteenth Amendment," see Michael W. McConnell, *Institutions and Interpretation: A Critique of Boerne v. Flores*, 111 Harv.L.Rev. 153, 174–83 (1997).

c. A different majority—Black, Douglas, Brennan, White and Marshall, JJ.—voted to uphold this provision as to federal elections. Black, J., who was in both majorities, distinguished the situations on the ground (with which no other justice joined) that Congress had power under Art. I, § 4 to set qualifications for voters in federal elections. For an alternative rationale, see David E. Engdahl, *Constitutionality of the Voting Age Statute*, 39 Geo.Wash.L.Rev. 1, 38–39 (1970): "Since no *state* [has] a legitimate interest in protecting the integrity of *national* elections, it is difficult to imagine any state interest sufficient to justify, under the equal protection clause, any *state* exclusion of a significant 'stake-holder' in *national* elections."

the States the power to set voter qualifications in state and local elections." Four of these five were explicit in rejecting the position that § 5 endowed Congress with the power to establish the meaning of constitutional provisions. See (opinion of Harlan, J.); (opinion of Stewart, J., joined by Burger, C. J., and Blackmun, J.). Justice Black's rejection of this position might be inferred from his disagreement with Congress' interpretation of the Equal Protection Clause.[d]

There is language in our opinion in *Morgan* which could be interpreted as acknowledging a power in Congress to enact legislation that expands the rights contained in § 1 of the Fourteenth Amendment. This is not a necessary interpretation, however, or even the best one. [As] Justice Stewart explained in *Mitchell,* interpreting *Morgan* to give Congress the power to interpret the Constitution "would require an enormous extension of that decision's rationale."[e]

If Congress could define its own powers by altering the Fourteenth Amendment's meaning, no longer would the Constitution be "superior paramount law, unchangeable by ordinary means." It would be "on a level with ordinary legislative acts, and, like other [acts,] alterable when the legislature shall please to alter it." *Marbury v. Madison.* Under this approach, it is difficult to conceive of a principle that would limit congressional power. Shifting legislative majorities could change the Constitution and effectively circumvent the difficult and detailed amendment process contained in Article V. * * *

Respondent contends that RFRA is a proper exercise of Congress' remedial or preventive power. The Act, it is [said,] prevents and remedies laws which are enacted with the unconstitutional object of targeting religious beliefs and practices. See *Church of the Lukumi Babalu Aye, Inc. v. Hialeah,* [Ch. 8, Sec. 2, I] To avoid the difficulty of proving such violations, it is said, Congress can simply invalidate any law which imposes a substantial burden on a religious practice unless it is justified by a compelling interest and is the least restrictive means of accomplishing that interest. If Congress can prohibit laws with discriminatory effects in order to prevent racial discrimination in violation of the Equal Protection Clause, then it can do the same, respondent argues, to promote religious liberty.

While preventive rules are sometimes appropriate remedial measures, there must be a congruence between the means used and the ends to be achieved. * * * Strong measures appropriate to address one harm may be an unwarranted response to another, lesser one.

A comparison between RFRA and the Voting Rights Act is instructive. In contrast to the record which confronted Congress and the judiciary in the voting rights cases, RFRA's legislative record lacks examples of modern instances of generally applicable laws passed because of religious bigotry. [Rather,] the emphasis of the hearings was on laws of general applicability which place incidental burdens on religion. * * *

---

d. Black, J., stated: "Congress made no legislative findings that 21–year-old vote requirements were used by the States to disenfranchise voters on account of race. I seriously doubt that such a finding, if made, could be supported by substantial evidence. Since Congress has attempted to invade an area preserved to the States by the Constitution without a foundation for enforcing the Civil War Amendments' ban on racial discrimination, I would hold that Congress has exceeded its powers in attempting to lower the voting age in state and local elections."

e. For the view that "the scope of the definitional power" granted Congress in *Morgan,* "although by no means insignificant, may nonetheless be quite limited," see Choper, note 3(b) after *Mayer.*

Regardless of the state of the legislative record, RFRA [is] so out of proportion to a supposed remedial or preventive object that it cannot be understood as responsive to, or designed to prevent, unconstitutional behavior. It appears, instead, to attempt a substantive change in constitutional protections. Preventive measures prohibiting certain types of laws may be appropriate when there is reason to believe that many of the laws affected by the congressional enactment have a significant likelihood of being unconstitutional. See *Rome.* * * *

RFRA is not so confined. Sweeping coverage ensures its intrusion at every level of government, displacing laws and prohibiting official actions of almost every description and regardless of subject matter. [Any] law is subject to challenge at any time by any individual who alleges a substantial burden on his or her free exercise of religion.

The reach and scope of RFRA distinguish it from other measures passed under Congress' enforcement power, even in the area of voting rights. In *South Carolina v. Katzenbach,* the challenged provisions were confined to those regions of the country where voting discrimination had been most flagrant, and affected a discrete class of state laws, i.e., state voting laws. Furthermore, to ensure that the reach of the Voting Rights Act was limited to those cases in which constitutional violations were most likely (in order to reduce the possibility of overbreadth), the coverage under the Act would terminate "at the behest of States and political subdivisions in which the danger of substantial voting discrimination has not materialized during the preceding five years." The provisions restricting and banning literacy tests, upheld in *Morgan* attacked a particular type of voting qualification, one with a long history as a "notorious means to deny and abridge voting rights on racial grounds." [This] is not to say, of course, that § 5 legislation requires termination dates, geographic restrictions or egregious predicates. Where, however, a congressional enactment pervasively prohibits constitutional state action in an effort to remedy or to prevent unconstitutional state action, limitations of this kind tend to ensure Congress' means are proportionate to ends legitimate under § 5. * * *

The substantial costs RFRA exacts, both in practical terms of imposing a heavy litigation burden on the States and in terms of curtailing their traditional general regulatory power, far exceed any pattern or practice of unconstitutional conduct under the Free Exercise Clause as interpreted in *Smith.* [In] addition, the Act imposes in every case a least restrictive means requirement—a requirement that was not used in the pre-*Smith* jurisprudence RFRA purported to codify— which also indicates that the legislation is broader than is appropriate if the goal is to prevent and remedy constitutional violations.

When [the] Court has interpreted the Constitution, it has acted within the province of the Judicial Branch, which embraces the duty to say what the law is. When the political branches of the Government act against the background of a judicial interpretation of the Constitution already issued, it must be understood that in later cases and controversies the Court will treat its precedents with the respect due them under settled principles, including stare decisis, and contrary expectations must be disappointed. RFRA was designed to control cases and controversies, such as the one before us; but as the provisions of the federal statute here invoked are beyond congressional authority, it is this Court's precedent, not RFRA, which must control. * * *[f]

f. Does *Boerne* also invalidate RFRA as applied to federal laws? Compare Thomas C. Berg, *The Constitutional Future of Religious Freedom Legislation*, 20 U.Ark. Little Rock L.J. 715, 727–47 (1998) with Marci A. Hamilton, *The Religious Freedom Restoration Act Is*

JUSTICE STEVENS, concurring.

In my opinion, RFRA is a "law respecting an establishment of religion" that violates the First Amendment * * *.[g]

JUSTICE O'CONNOR, with whom JUSTICE BREYER joins except as to [the first two sentences below].

* * * I agree with much of the reasoning set forth in [the] Court's opinion. Indeed, if I agreed with the Court's standard in *Smith*, I would join the opinion. [But] I remain of the view that *Smith* was wrongly decided, and I would use this case to reexamine the Court's holding there. Therefore, I would direct the parties to brief the question whether *Smith* represents the correct understanding of the Free Exercise Clause and set the case for reargument. If the Court were to correct the misinterpretation of the Free Exercise Clause set forth in *Smith,* it would simultaneously put our First Amendment jurisprudence back on course and allay the legitimate concerns of a majority in Congress who believed that *Smith* improperly restricted religious liberty. We would then be in a position to review RFRA in light of a proper interpretation of the Free Exercise Clause. * * *

JUSTICE SOUTER, dissenting.

* * * Justice O'Connor's opinion [raises] very substantial issues about the soundness of the *Smith* rule. [In] order to provide full adversarial consideration, this case should be set down for reargument. [Since] the Court declines to follow that course, our free-exercise law remains marked by an "intolerable tension" and the constitutionality of the Act of Congress to enforce the free-exercise right cannot now be soundly decided. I would therefore dismiss the writ of certiorari as improvidently granted * * *.

Notes and Questions

1. *Institutional limits and judicial "underenforcement."* (a) Apart from the "history" and "design" of the fourteenth amendment, are there good reasons for affording Congress some role in respect to "substantive scope"? Consider Lawrence G. Sager, *Fair Measure: The Legal Status of Underenforced Constitutional Norms,* 91 Harv.L.Rev. 1212, 1217 (1978): "There are reasons which explain and to some degree justify federal judicial restraint in [applying the provisions of § 1 of the fourteenth amendment]. In the most general of terms, the claims for restraint typically turn on the propriety of unelected federal judges' displacing the judgments of elected state officials, or upon the competence of federal courts to prescribe workable standards of state conduct and devise measures to enforce them."[a] See also Lawrence G. Sager, *Justice in Plain Clothes: Reflections on the Thinness of Constitutional Law,* 88 Nw.U.L.Rev. 410, 422 (1993): "The Supreme Court superintends a sprawling establishment of state and federal courts, courts that will be called upon to review a wide range of governmental behavior, [some] of which will have been carefully disguised precisely to avoid judicial invalidation. The Court, accordingly, has good reason to adopt rules that are blunter, less nuanced, but which overall better serve its objective of securing compliance with

Unconstitutional, Period, 1 U.Pa.J.Const.L. 1 (1998).

g. The concurring opinion of Scalia, J., joined by Stevens, J., both of whom joined the Court's opinion, is omitted.

a. For the view that "Congress may expand the judiciary's role by identifying additional

suspect classes and fundamental rights and by increasing the level of scrutiny in specified types of equal protection cases," see Stephen F. Ross, *Legislative Enforcement of Equal Protection,* 72 Minn.L.Rev. 311, 335 (1987).

its underlying norm." See also David Cole, *The Value of Seeing Things Differently: Boerne v. Flores and Congressional Enforcement of the Bill of Rights*, 1997 Sup.Ct.Rev. 31, 76–77: "When the Court interprets a constitutional provision, it creates rights that cannot be altered except by a judicial departure from stare decisis or a constitutional amendment. And when the Court interprets the Fourteenth Amendment to impose duties on the states, it does so without the benefit of state representation. When Congress interprets the Fourteenth Amendment for purposes of statutory enforcement, by contrast, its interpretations are subject to amendment at any time by majority vote, and its deliberations structurally reflect the interests of the states."

(b) Do these considerations apply to RFRA? Consider McConnell, fn. b in *Boerne*, at 195: "Judicial interpretations of the Constitution are often influenced by institutional considerations, such as the principle of judicial restraint, that create 'slippage' between the Constitution as enforced and the Constitution itself. [*Smith*] was predicated on just such an institutional concern: the fear that there are no judicially manageable standards for balancing the impact of a law on religious freedom against its importance to the public interest. This judicial restraint serves democratic values. But [t]he democratic values underlying the doctrine of judicial restraint do not apply to Congress. [Its] decision to adopt a more robust, freedom-protective interpretation of the Free Exercise Clause did not 'alter' the Constitution or create 'new' rights. Rather, RFRA merely liberated the enforcement of free exercise rights from constraints derived from judicial restraint."

(c) *"Factfinding."* In *Mitchell*, Brennan, J.'s dissent stressed that "when a state [law] comes before the courts [it is] cloaked by the presumption [of constitutionality]. But this limitation on judicial review [stems] not from the Fourteenth Amendment itself, but from the nature of [the] judicial process [which] makes it an inappropriate forum for the determination of complex factual questions of the kind so often involved in constitutional adjudication. [Should Congress, however, pursuant to § 5] undertake an investigation in order to determine whether the factual basis necessary to support a state legislative discrimination actually exists, it need not stop once it determines that some reasonable men could believe the factual basis exists. Section 5 empowers Congress to make its own determination on the matter." And note Harlan, J.'s view in *Morgan* that Congress' determinations as to "legislative facts" are "entitled to due respect."

(d) Did *Boerne* adhere to these approaches? Consider Tribe 3d ed., at 960: "[RFRA] provided perhaps the least suitable context imaginable for making the institutional argument: Unlike most § 5 legislation, RFRA [was] aimed directly at judicial procedures and rules of decision for every federal and state court in the nation, and, as if to dare the Court to defend its turf, RFRA was written less like an ordinary statute than like an opinion reversing or overruling the Supreme Court's decision in *Smith*."

2. *Deference to Congress.* Consider McConnell, supra, at 188: "Unlike enactments under the Commerce Clause or most other sources of congressional power, interpretations of the Bill of Rights under Section Five limit the powers of Congress and the federal government to precisely the same extent that they limit the powers of the states. When Congress decides that the freedom of religion warrants greater protection than has been provided by the courts, the federal government will bear no less cost and inconvenience than the states. [Rather] than aggrandizing federal power at the expense of the states, legislation like

RFRA constrains the power and discretion of federal and state governments alike. This makes it exceedingly unlikely that Congress will act from anything other than a genuine interest in enforcement of constitutional freedoms."

3. *Congress's "remedial" power.* (a) How much of *Morgan's* "remedial" branch survives *Boerne*? May Congress outlaw *all* age and residence requirements for voting? Consider Alexander M. Bickel, *The Voting Rights Cases,* 1966 Sup.Ct. Rev. 79, 100: "[S]uppose Congress decided that aliens or eighteen-year-olds or residents of New Jersey are being discriminated against in New York. The decision would be as plausible as the one concerning Spanish-speaking Puerto Ricans. Could Congress give these groups the vote? If Congress may freely bestow the vote as a means of curing other discriminations, which it fears may be practiced against groups deprived of the vote, essentially because of this deprivation and on the basis of no other evidence, then there is nothing left of state autonomy in setting qualifications for voting."

(b) May Congress forbid all racial discrimination in housing? Consider Archibald Cox, *Constitutional Adjudication and the Promotion of Human Rights,* 80 Harv.L.Rev. 91, 120 (1966): "So long as Negroes are confined to racial ghettos, there will be actual or dangerously potential state discrimination in the quantity or quality of public services. [T]he isolation of unpopular minorities in poverty-stricken, socially and economically isolated neighborhoods, lacking political influence, invites a lower quality of state services. [*Morgan* held that] Congress might legislate to remove an obstacle to the state's performance of its constitutional duty not to discriminate in providing public services, even though the immediate subject matter of the legislation—there the requirement of English literacy—was not itself a violation of the fourteenth amendment. It follows that Congress may likewise legislate to eliminate racial ghettos as obstacles to the states' performance of that same constitutional duty, even though the immediate subject matter of this legislation—the practices that result in ghettos—do not themselves involve violations of the fourteenth amendment. The only important difference is that in *Morgan* the obstacle was itself a state law whereas discrimination in housing has a private origin. [But] that difference in the source of the threat to performance of the state's obligation is irrelevant."

(c) *De facto discrimination.* (i) ROME v. UNITED STATES, 446 U.S. 156, 100 S.Ct. 1548, 64 L.Ed.2d 119 (1980), involved the Attorney General's refusal to approve, under § 5 of the Voting Rights Act, various changes in the Rome, Ga.'s electoral system and a number of city annexations. A federal court found that the city had not employed any discriminatory barriers to black voting or black candidacy in the past 17 years and that the city had proved that the electoral changes and annexations were not discriminatorily motivated, but that they were prohibited by the Act because they had a discriminatory effect. The Court, per MARSHALL, J., affirmed: "[T]he Act's ban on electoral changes that are discriminatory in effect is an appropriate method of promoting the purposes of the Fifteenth Amendment, even if it is assumed that § 1 of the Amendment prohibits only intentional discrimination in voting. [See *Mobile v. Bolden,* Ch. 9, Sec. 5, I, B.] Congress could rationally have concluded that, because electoral changes by jurisdictions with a demonstrable history of intentional racial discrimination in voting create the risk of purposeful discrimination, it was proper to prohibit changes that have a discriminatory impact. See *South Carolina v. Katzenbach.*"

REHNQUIST, J., joined by Stewart, J., dissented: "Congress had before it evidence that various governments were enacting electoral changes and annexing territory to prevent the participation of blacks in local government by measures other than outright denial of the franchise. [G]iven the difficulties of proving that an electoral change or annexation has been undertaken for the purpose of discriminating against blacks, Congress could properly conclude that as a remedial matter it was necessary to place the burden of proving lack of discriminatory purpose on the localities. But all of this does not support the conclusion that Congress is acting remedially when it continues the presumption of purposeful discrimination even after the locality has disproved that presumption. Absent other circumstances, it would be a topsy-turvy judicial system which held that electoral changes which have been affirmatively proven to be permissible under the Constitution nonetheless violate the Constitution. [Thus,] the result of the Court's holding is that Congress effectively has the power to determine for itself that this conduct violates the Constitution. This result violates previously well-established distinctions between the Judicial Branch and the Legislative or Executive Branches of the Federal Government." Powell, J., dissented on narrower grounds.

(ii) Do you agree that *Rome* empowers Congress "to determine for itself [what] conduct violates the Constitution" and therefore does not survive *Boerne*? Consider Choper, note 3(b) after *Mayer*, at 331–32: "[*Rome's*] rationale permits Congress to create a 'conclusive presumption' of racial motivation with respect to specified state or local practices that Congress finds have been widely or consistently employed for the purpose of disadvantaging racial minorities—and thus effectively authorizes a congressional conclusion that such practices violate the substance of the fourteenth amendment. But this is a much narrower license than empowering Congress to declare that all state or local rules with a racially disproportionate impact violate equal protection for that reason alone. [A] variety of factors make it extremely difficult for plaintiffs to prove that a state legislative or administrative body has acted with discriminatory intent and make it much more appropriate for Congress than for the judiciary to combat the problem of illicit motivation. Thus, there are powerful reasons for Congress to choose not to rely upon district judges for the highly sensitive task of ascertaining racially discriminatory intent on a case by case basis in respect to state of local schemes whose real purpose Congress has grounds to suspect. [*Rome*] did no more than recognize this reality when is [used] what is principally a remedial or prophylactic rationale." Does this rationale support the application of Title VII of the Civil Rights Act of 1964's regulation of state employment practices that disqualify a disproportionate number of African–Americans (see p. 1182 supra)?

4. *"Dilution."* To what extent do the approaches in notes 1, 2 and 3 supra relate to Congress' inability to "dilute" fourteenth amendment rights?

(a) *Competence as to "facts."* Does *Miranda v. Arizona,* 384 U.S. 436, 86 S.Ct. 1602, 16 L.Ed.2d 694 (1966), rest on the *factual* assumption that there is "compulsion inherent in custodial surroundings" and thus "no statement obtained from the defendant can truly be the product of his free choice"? See Yale Kamisar, *Can (Did) Congress "Overrule" Miranda,* 85 Corn.L.Rev. 883, 913–25 (2000). Does *Mapp v. Ohio,* p. 354 supra, rest on the *factual* assumption that the exclusionary rule is a "deterrent safeguard without insistence upon which the Fourth Amendment would have been reduced to 'a form of words' "? Does *Gideon v. Wainwright,* 372 U.S. 335, 83 S.Ct. 792, 9 L.Ed.2d 799 (1963), rest on the *factual* assumption that a person "who is too poor to hire a lawyer, cannot be assured a fair trial unless counsel is provided for him"? Does *Brown v. Board of Education,* Ch. 9, Sec. 2, II, rest on the *factual* assumption that racially "separate educational facilities are inherently unequal"? Does *Planned Parenthood v. Casey* rest on *factual* assumptions that "informed consent" requirements and 24–hour waiting periods do *not* "impose an undue burden on a woman's abortion right"? See generally Ira C. Lupu, *Statutes Revolving in Constitutional Law Orbits,* 79 Va.L.Rev. 1, 37–46 (1993). If so, may Congress, pursuant to § 5, find the *facts* to be otherwise and legislate a contrary rule? What result after *Boerne*?

(b) *Line-drawing.* After *Boerne,* what deference is owed congressional action, pursuant to § 5, that precisely defines (i) how long a delay constitutes denial of the "right to a speedy trial," see *Barker v. Wingo,* 407 U.S. 514, 92 S.Ct. 2182, 33 L.Ed.2d 101 (1972); (ii) how great a deviation from absolute population equality among legislative districts constitutes a violation of the "one person-one vote" requirement, see Ch. 9, Sec. 5, I, B.

(c) *Conflicting constitutional provisions.* If de facto racial segregation in the schools arguably violates equal protection, and if use of racial criteria to alleviate de facto segregation also arguably violates equal protection (see Ch. 9, Secs. 2, III and 2, VI), what deference is owed congressional action, pursuant to § 5, dealing with these matters? See opinion of White, J., in *Welsh v. United States,* Ch. 8, Sec. 2, II.

(d) *Rights vs. remedies.* May Congress, pursuant to its remedial power under § 5, withdraw the "exclusionary rule" of *Mapp v. Ohio* on the ground that this does not "dilute" any substantive constitutional right but merely modifies a remedy for its violation?[b] (How about *replacing* it?) On similar analysis, may Congress forbid busing (or substitute alternatives) to remedy school segregation? Consider Note, *The Nixon Busing Bills and Constitutional Power,* 81 Yale L.J. 1542, 1570–71 (1972): "Because busing is one remedy among many, Robert Bork [*Constitutionality of the President's Busing Proposals* 21–22 (1972)] argues [that the anti-busing bill] leaves intact the duty *Brown* imposed upon formerly segregated school districts. Such an argument creates an artificial distinction between rights and remedies; the right which cannot be vindicated is not a right at all, and the most that can be said for the distinction is that it may be useful where a right can be vindicated in several ways. [If] busing is in some cases—as it was in *Swann*—the only remedy that would produce desegregation in any real sense, then Bork's argument falls. The real question about the constitutionality of the busing bills is the question that Bork hesitates to answer directly: to what extent does the Equal Protection Clause require that once segregated schools achieve a racial balance? *Swann,* of course, had a simple and direct answer: to the greatest extent possible." See also Ronald D. Rotunda, *Congressional Power to Restrict the Jurisdiction of the Lower Federal Courts and the Problem of School Busing,* 64 Geo.L.J. 839 (1976).

For the view that many judicial decisions implementing constitutional rights are not "true constitutional interpretations" but rather only "constitutional common law" rules that may be modified by Congress, see Henry P. Monaghan, *Constitutional Common Law,* 89 Harv.L.Rev. 1 (1975). Compare Thomas S. Schrock & Robert C. Welsh, *Reconsidering the Constitutional Common Law,* 91 Harv.L.Rev. 1117 (1978).

(e) *Definition of "dilution."* If Congress believed that more wrongdoers would be convicted and crime deterred by changing the *Miranda* rule, would such legislation "dilute" the due process rights of the accused, or "secure" the rights of the public generally not to be denied life or property without due process of law?

---

b. *Dickerson v. United States,* 530 U.S. 428, 120 S.Ct. 2326, 147 L.Ed.2d 405 (2000), per Rehnquist, C.J., invalidated a federal statute which was "intended [to] overrule *Miranda,*" "a constitutional decision of this Court": "Congress [may] not supersede this Court's decisions interpreting and applying the Constitution, see, *Boerne.*" Scalia and Thomas, JJ., dissented, arguing that the *Miranda* warnings were "only 'prophylactic' rules that go beyond the [constitutional] right against compelled self-incrimination."

Who should *ultimately* determine these issues? See generally J. Edmond Nathanson, *Congressional Power to Contradict the Supreme Court's Constitutional Decisions. Accommodation of Rights in Conflict,* 27 Wm. & M.L.Rev. 331 (1986).

(f) *"Human Life Bill."* What of the constitutionality of the following proposed statute, S. 158 and H.R. 900, 97th Cong., 1st Sess. (1981):

"Sec. 1. The Congress finds that present day scientific evidence indicates a significant likelihood that actual human life exists from conception.

"The Congress further finds that the fourteenth amendment to the Constitution of the United States was intended to protect all human beings.

"Upon the basis of these findings, and in the exercise of the powers of the Congress, including its power under section 5 of the fourteenth amendment to the Constitution of the United States, the Congress hereby declares that for the purpose of enforcing the obligation of the States under the fourteenth amendment not to deprive persons of life without due process of law, human life shall be deemed to exist from conception, without regard to race, sex, age, health, defect, or condition of dependency; and for this purpose 'person' shall include all human life as defined herein."[c]

(i) *Questions of "fact."* Do the issues of when "human life" begins and what is a "person" involve questions of fact? Consider Laurence H. Tribe, *Prepared Statement,* Hearings on S. 158 at 251: "Such questions [call] at bottom for normative judgments no less profound than those involved in defining 'liberty' or 'equality.' [They] entail 'question[s] to which science can provide no answer,' as the National Academy of Sciences itself acknowledged * * *. Congress cannot transform an issue of religion, morality, and law into one of fact by waving the magic wand of Section 5 [which] no more authorizes Congress to transmute a matter of values into a matter of scientific observation than it authorizes Congress to announce a mathematical formula for human freedom." See also Archibald Cox, *Prepared Statement,* id. at 340–41.

(ii) *"Dilution"* vs. *"expansion."* Does the Bill dilute the right to an abortion? Consider John T. Noonan, Jr., *Prepared Statement,* id. at 266–67: "In recognizing the unborn as persons, [the] Act treats no one unequally but gives equal protection to one class of humanity now unequally treated. * * * Necessarily, the expression of the rights of one class of human beings has an impact on the rights of others. The elimination of literacy tests in this way 'diluted' the voting rights of the literate. It is inescapable that congressional expression of the right to life will have an impact on the abortion right; but in the eyes of Congress, [there] will be a net gain for Fourteenth Amendment rights by the expansion and the attendant diminution."

5. *"Last word."* Would a contrary analysis in *Boerne* give interpretive "control" to Congress rather than the Court? (a) Consider William G. Buss, *Federalism, Separation of Powers, and the Demise of the Religious Freedom Restoration Act,* 83 Ia.L.Rev. 391, 415 (1998): "The fact that the particular result in the *Smith* case would ordinarily be altered by the RFRA is not tantamount to

---

c. For argument in favor of its validity, see Stephen H. Galebach, *A Human Life Statute,* 7 Human Life Rev. 3 (1981), reprinted in Hearings on S. 158, before the Subcomm. on Separation of Powers of the Senate Comm. on the Judiciary, 97th Cong., 1st Sess. 205 (1981); Thomas Nagel, *Prepared Statement,* id. 321. For exhaustive consideration, see Samuel Estr-eicher, *Congressional Power and Constitutional Rights: Reflections on Proposed "Human Life" Legislation,* 68 Va.L.Rev. 333 (1982). For an "institutional" perspective, see Stephen L. Carter, *The Morgan "Power" and the Forced Reconsideration of Constitutional Decisions,* 53 U.Chi.L.Rev. 819 (1986).

recognition that Congress has a power to overrule the Supreme Court or to make authoritative decisions about constitutional rights. [It] would mean simply that Congress had *enacted a statute* within its enforcement power. [*Smith*] would continue to determine the constitutional meaning of the free exercise of religion, and would govern any situation with respect to which the RFRA did not apply— because of a statute of limitations, a pleading failure, an Eleventh Amendment bar, or any other reason. If the RFRA were repealed, the constitutional rule established by *Smith* would govern."

(b) Consider McConnell, supra, at 184: "Acceptance of the 'interpretive' reading of Congress's Section Five authority does not imply that Congress has the final word on the Amendment's meaning. [The] question in a Section Five case should be whether the congressional interpretation is within a reasonable range of plausible interpretations—not whether it is the same as the Supreme Court's. An analogy might be drawn to the *Chevron* doctrine [see Ch. 3, Sec.2, I], which holds that courts should not overturn agency interpretations of their governing statutes as long as they are within a reasonable range of interpretations of the statutory language."

(c) Might the *Boerne* majority be swayed by the arguments in notes (a) and (b)?

6. *Spending power.* To what extent may Congress use the spending power to achieve the ends sought in RFRA? Consider Jesse H. Choper, *On the Difference in Importance Between Supreme Court Doctrine and Actual Consequences*, 19 Card. L.Rev. 2259, 2306 (1998): "Even under the very generous power given to Congress regarding conditions on grants to the states, *Dole* requires these conditions to be reasonably related to the purpose of the expenditure. Consequently, RFRA would probably have to be written into individual federal laws concerning the use of funds. As examples, conditions on [existing] federal spending could likely reverse [*Smith*] and replicate the results in [all the other Supreme Court decisions requiring religious exemptions from neutral, generally applicable laws]." See also Daniel O. Conkle, *Congressional Alternatives in the Wake of City of Boerne v. Flores: The (Limited) Role of Congress in Protecting Religious Freedom from State and Local Infringement*, 20 U.Ark.Little Rock L.Rev. 633, 668–83 (1998); Sayers–Fay, note 1(b) after *Dole*, Ch. 2, Sec. 3, II: "[B]y attaching carefully crafted conditions to a host of federal spending programs, Congress could accomplish some, but not all, of RFRA's objectives."[d]

7. *Further restrictions on § 5.* (a) *Equal protection.* KIMEL v. FLORIDA BD. OF REGENTS, 528 U.S. 62 120 S.Ct. 631, 145 L.Ed.2d 522 (2000), per O'CONNOR, J., explored *Boerne's* scope in the context of Congress' exercising its § 5 power— which may be used to abrogate the states' immunity from suits in federal court guaranteed by the eleventh amendment—to make states subject to federal court actions for violating the Age Discrimination in Employment Act: "We have considered claims of unconstitutional age discrimination under the Equal Protection Clause three times [and held that] age is not a suspect classification [Ch. 9, Sec. 4, V]. Our Constitution permits States to draw lines on the basis of age when they have a rational basis for doing so at a class-based level, even if it 'is probably not true' that those reasons are valid in the majority of cases.

"Judged against the backdrop of our equal protection jurisprudence, it is clear that the ADEA is 'so out of proportion to a supposed remedial or preventive object that it cannot be understood as responsive to, or designed to prevent, unconstitu-

---

d. See the Religious Land Use and Institutionalized Persons Act of 2000, which creates a RFRA-like federal right applicable, inter alia, to land use regulations in connection with "a program or activity that receives federal financial assistance."

tional behavior.' *Boerne.* The Act, through its broad restriction on the use of age as a discriminating factor, prohibits substantially more state employment decisions and practices than would likely be held unconstitutional under the applicable equal protection, rational basis standard. [Petitioners] contend that the Act's prohibition, considered together with its exceptions, applies only to arbitrary age discrimination, which in the majority of cases corresponds to conduct that violates the Equal Protection Clause. We disagree.

"Petitioners stake their claim [on] the 'bona fide occupational qualification' (BFOQ) defense. [But to] succeed under the BFOQ defense, we held that an employer must demonstrate either 'a substantial basis for believing that all or nearly all employees above an age lack the qualifications required for the position,' or that reliance on the age classification is necessary because 'it is highly impractical for the employer to insure by individual testing that its employees will have the necessary qualifications for the job.' Measured against the rational basis standard of our equal protection jurisprudence, the ADEA plainly imposes substantially higher burdens on state employers [at] a level akin to our heightened scrutiny cases under the Equal Protection Clause. * * *

"That the ADEA prohibits very little conduct likely to be held unconstitutional, while significant, does not alone provide the answer to our § 5 inquiry. Difficult and intractable problems often require powerful remedies, and we have never held that § 5 precludes Congress from enacting reasonably prophylactic legislation. Our task is to determine whether the ADEA is in fact just such an appropriate remedy or, instead, merely an attempt to substantively redefine the States' legal obligations with respect to age discrimination.[e]

"Our examination of the ADEA's legislative record confirms [that] Congress never identified any pattern of age discrimination by the States, much less any discrimination whatsoever that rose to the level of constitutional violation. The evidence compiled by petitioners [consists] almost entirely of isolated sentences clipped from floor debates and legislative reports. * * *

"Our decision today does not signal the end of the line for employees who find themselves subject to age discrimination at the hands of their state employers. [State] employees are protected by state age discrimination statutes, and may recover money damages from their state employers, in almost every [State]."[f]

---

e. For the view that, at this point in the opinion, *Kimel* accounts for the differences of "institutional competence" between the Court and Congress (note 1 after *Boerne*), and "does not ask whether Section 5 legislation remedies or deters conduct that a court in adjudication would find unconstitutional, but instead asks whether Section 5 legislation remedies or deters conduct that *is* unconstitutional," see Robert C. Post & Reva B. Siegel, *Equal Protection by Law: Federal Antidiscrimination Legislation After Morrison and Kimel,* 110 Yale.L.J. 441, 456–66 (2000).

f. The scope of the eleventh amendment is considered in detail in Federal Courts courses. But several recent decisions,—by the same 5–4 split as in *Lopez, Morrison, Printz* [Ch. 2, Secs. 2, IV and 5, IV], and *Kimel*—have interpreted it to similarly enforce principles of federalism and state sovereignty. *Seminole Tribe v. Florida,* 517 U.S. 44, 116 S.Ct. 1114, 134 L.Ed.2d 252 (1996)—overruling *Pennsylvania v. Union*

Gas Co., 491 U.S. 1, 109 S.Ct. 2273, 105 L.Ed.2d 1 (1989)—per Rehnquist C.J., held that, unlike under its § 5 power, Congress has *no* authority under the commerce clause to abrogate state immunity under the eleventh amendment, and *Florida Prepaid Postsecondary Educ. Expense Bd. v. College Savings Bank,* below, extended this limitation to other Art. I powers (patent clause). *Alden v. Maine,* 527 U.S. 706, 119 S.Ct. 2240, 144 L.Ed.2d 636 (1999), per Kennedy, J., while agreeing that the Fair Labor Standards Act could constitutionally be applied to states (see *Garcia,* Ch. 2, Sec. 5, IV), held that, just as under *Seminole Tribe* private parties could not sue states under such federal statutes in federal court without their consent, so, too, states could not be sued in their own courts under such circumstances:

"[T]he sovereign immunity of the States neither derives from nor is limited by the terms of the Eleventh Amendment. Rather, as the Constitution's structure, and its history, and the

STEVENS, J., joined by Souter, Ginsburg and Breyer, JJ., dissented, relying on their dissenting view in *Seminole Tribe*, fn. f: "Congress' power to authorize federal remedies against state agencies that violate federal statutory obligations is coextensive with its power to impose those obligations on the States in the first place. Neither the Eleventh Amendment nor the doctrine of sovereign immunity places any limit on that power. * * *

"Federalism concerns do make it appropriate for Congress to speak clearly when it regulates state action. But when it does so, as it has in these cases, we can safely presume that the burdens the statute imposes on the sovereignty of the several States were taken into account during the deliberative process leading to the enactment of the measure."

(b) *Due process.* FLORIDA PREPAID POSTSECONDARY EDUCATION EXPENSE BOARD v. COLLEGE SAVINGS BANK, 527 U.S. 627, 119 S.Ct. 2199, 144 L.Ed.2d 575 (1999), per REHNQUIST, C.J., concerned Congress' § 5 power to expressly make states subject to federal court actions for patent infringement: Although patents "have long been considered a species [of] 'property' of which no person may be deprived by a State without due process of [law,] Congress identified no pattern of patent infringement by the States, let alone a pattern of constitutional violations. [At] most, Congress heard testimony that patent infringement by States might increase in the future. [Further,] only where the State provides no remedy, or only inadequate remedies, to injured patent owners for its infringement of their patent could a deprivation of property without due process result.

"Congress [did] hear a limited amount of testimony to the effect that the remedies available in some States were uncertain. The primary point made by these witnesses, however, was not that state remedies were constitutionally inadequate, but rather that they were less convenient than federal remedies, and might undermine the uniformity of patent law.[9] [The] need for uniformity in the construction of patent law is undoubtedly important, but that is a factor which belongs to the Article I patent-power calculus, rather than to any determination of whether a state plea of sovereign immunity deprives a patentee of property without due process of law.* * *

"The legislative record thus suggests that the Patent Remedy Act does not respond to a history of 'widespread and persisting deprivation of constitutional rights' of the sort Congress has faced in enacting proper prophylactic § 5 legislation. [*Boerne*.] Though the lack of support in the legislative record is not determinative, [h]ere, the record at best offers scant support for Congress'

authoritative interpretations by this Court make clear, the States' immunity from suit is a fundamental aspect of the sovereignty which the States enjoyed before the ratification of the Constitution, and which they [retain] except as altered by the plan of the Convention or certain constitutional Amendments."

Souter J., spoke for the dissenters: "[T]oday the Court has no qualms about saying frankly that the federal right to damages afforded by Congress under the FLSA cannot create a concomitant private remedy. [The] Court calls 'immunity from private suits central to sovereign dignity,' [but] this dignity is [not] a quality easily translated from the person of the King

to the participatory abstraction of a republican State. [It] would be hard to imagine anything more inimical to the republican conception, which rests on the understanding of its citizens precisely that the government is not above them, but of them, its actions being governed by law just like their own."

9. It is worth mentioning that the State of Florida provides remedies to patent owners for alleged infringement on the part of the State. Aggrieved parties may pursue a legislative remedy through a claims bill for payment in full, or a judicial remedy through a takings or conversion claim.

conclusion that States were depriving patent owners of property without due process of law by pleading sovereign immunity in federal-court patent actions.

"Because of this lack, the provisions of the Patent Remedy Act are 'so out of proportion to a supposed remedial or preventive object that [they] cannot be understood as responsive to, or designed to prevent, unconstitutional behavior.' *Boerne.* Congress did nothing to limit the coverage of the Act to cases involving arguable constitutional violations, such as where a State refuses to offer any state-court remedy for patent owners whose patents it had infringed. Nor did it make any attempt to confine the reach of the Act by limiting the remedy to certain types of infringement, such as nonnegligent infringement or infringement authorized pursuant to state policy; or providing for suits only against States with questionable remedies or a high incidence of infringement."[g]

STEVENS, J., joined by Souter, Ginsburg and Breyer, JJ., dissented: "Sound reasons support [Congress' decision] to vest exclusive jurisdiction over patent infringement litigation in the federal courts. [The] principle that undergirds all aspects of our patent system[,] national uniformity, [supports] the congressional decision [to] consolidate appellate jurisdiction of patent appeals in the Court of Appeals for the Federal Circuit [which] would be undermined by any exception that allowed patent infringement claims to be brought in state court.* * *

"It is true that, when considering the Patent Remedy Act, Congress did not review the remedies available in each State for patent infringements and surmise what kind of recovery a plaintiff might obtain in a tort suit in all 50 jurisdictions. But, [g]iven that Congress had long ago pre-empted state jurisdiction over patent infringement cases, it was surely reasonable for Congress to assume that such remedies simply did not exist. Furthermore, it is well known that not all States have waived their sovereign immunity from suit, and among those States that have, the contours of this waiver vary widely.

"Even if such remedies might be available in theory, it would have been 'appropriate' for Congress to conclude that they would not guarantee patentees due process in infringement actions against state defendants. State judges have never had the exposure to patent litigation that federal judges have experienced for decades, and, unlike infringement actions brought in federal district courts, their decisions would not be reviewable in the Court of Appeals for the Federal Circuit. * * *

"Even if state courts elected to hear patent infringement cases against state entities, the entire category of such cases would raise questions of impartiality. This concern underlies both the constitutional authorization of diversity jurisdiction and the statutory provisions for removal of certain cases from state to federal courts. * * *

"Finally, this Court has never mandated that Congress must find 'widespread and persisting deprivation of constitutional rights,' in order to employ its § 5 authority. [The] Court's opinion today threatens to read Congress' power to pass prophylactic legislation out of § 5 altogether; its holding is unsupported by *Boerne* and in fact conflicts with our reasoning in that case. * * *

"The difference between the harm targeted by RFRA and the harm that motivated the enactment of the Patent Remedy Act is striking. In RFRA Congress

---

g. Tribe 3d ed., at 958–59, describes the opinion as "breathtaking": "Thus have laws enacted by Congress pursuant to § 5 suddenly been saddled with something between interme- diate and strict scrutiny, effectuating what can only be understood as a substantial, albeit not conclusive, presumption of unconstitutionali- ty."

sought to overrule this Court's interpretation of the First Amendment. The Patent Remedy Act, however, was passed to prevent future violations of due process, based on the substantiated fear that States would be unable or unwilling to provide adequate remedies for their own violations of patent-holders' rights. Congress' 'wide latitude' in determining remedial or preventive measures, see *Boerne*, has suddenly become very narrow indeed.

"[In *Boerne*,] the sweeping coverage of the statute ensured 'its intrusion at every level of government, displacing laws and prohibiting official actions of almost every description and regardless of subject matter.' [Here, the Act] has no impact whatsoever on any substantive rule of state law, but merely effectuates settled federal policy to confine patent infringement litigation to federal judges. There is precise congruence between 'the means used' (abrogation of sovereign immunity in this narrow category of cases) and 'the ends to be achieved' (elimination of the risk that the defense of sovereign immunity will deprive some patentees of property without due process of law)."

(c) *State action*. (i) UNITED STATES v. MORRISON, Ch. 2, Sec. 2, IV, per REHNQUIST, C.J., held that Congress had no § 5 power to grant a civil remedy to victims of gender-motivated violence despite Congress' (1) receiving "evidence that many participants in state justice systems are perpetuating an array of erroneous stereotypes and assumptions," and (2) concluding "that these discriminatory stereotypes often result in insufficient investigation and prosecution of gender-motivated crime, inappropriate focus on the behavior and credibility of the victims of that crime, and unacceptably lenient punishments for those who are actually convicted of gender-motivated violence":

"[S]tate-sponsored gender discrimination violates equal protection unless it 'serves "important governmental objectives and [the] discriminatory means employed" are "substantially related to the achievement of those objectives." '*United States v. Virginia*, [Ch. 9, Sec. 3, I]. However, the language and purpose of the Fourteenth Amendment place certain limitations on the manner in which Congress may attack discriminatory conduct. [Foremost] is the time-honored principle that the Fourteenth Amendment, by its very terms, prohibits only state action. * * *

"Shortly after the Fourteenth Amendment was adopted, we decided two cases interpreting the Amendment's provisions, *United States v. Harris*, 106 U.S. 629, 1 S.Ct. 601, 27 L.Ed. 290 (1883), and the *Civil Rights Cases*. [*Harris*] considered a challenge to § 2 of the Civil Rights Act of 1871. That section sought to punish 'private persons' for 'conspiring to deprive any one of the equal protection of the laws enacted by the State.' We concluded that this law exceeded Congress' § 5 power because the law was 'directed exclusively against the action of private persons, without reference to the laws of the State, or their administration by her officers.' [We] reached a similar conclusion in the *Civil Rights Cases*. * * *

"Petitioners rely on *Guest* for the proposition that the rule laid down in the *Civil Rights Cases* is no longer good law. In *Guest*, [t]hree Members of the Court, in a separate opinion by Justice Brennan, expressed the view that the *Civil Rights Cases* were wrongly decided, and that Congress could under § 5 prohibit actions by private individuals. Three other Members of the Court, who joined the opinion of the Court, joined a separate opinion by Justice Clark which in two or three sentences stated the conclusion that Congress could 'punis[h] all conspiracies—with or without state action—that interfere with Fourteenth Amendment rights.' [We] have no hesitation in saying that it would take more than the naked dicta contained in Justice Clark's opinion, when added to Justice Brennan's opinion, to cast any doubt upon the enduring vitality of the *Civil Rights Cases* and *Harris*."

Sec. 13981 "is directed not at any State or state actor, but at individuals who have committed criminal acts motivated by gender bias. [It] visits no consequence whatever on any Virginia public official involved in investigating or prosecuting Brzonkala's assault. The section is, therefore, unlike any of the § 5 remedies that we have previously upheld"—as in *Morgan, South Carolina v. Katzenbach,* and *Ex parte Virginia,* which were directed at states or state officials. The "remedy is not 'corrective in its character, adapted to counteract and redress the operation of such prohibited state laws or proceedings of state officers.' *Civil Rights Cases.*[a] Or, as we have phrased it in more recent cases, prophylactic legislation under § 5 must have a 'congruence and proportionality between the injury to be prevented or remedied and the means adopted to that end.'

"Section 13981 is also different from these previously upheld remedies in that it applies uniformly throughout the Nation. Congress' findings indicate that the problem of discrimination against the victims of gender-motivated crimes does not exist in all States, or even most States. By contrast, the § 5 remedy upheld in *Morgan* was directed only to the State where the evil found by Congress existed, and in *South Carolina v. Katzenbach,* the remedy was directed only to those States in which Congress found that there had been discrimination."

BREYER, J., joined by Stevens, J., "doubt[ed] the Court's reasoning," but did not "answer the § 5 question"[b]: "The Federal Government's argument [is] that Congress used § 5 to remedy the actions of *state actors,* namely, those States which, through discriminatory design or the discriminatory conduct of their officials, failed to provide adequate (or any) state remedies for women injured by gender-motivated violence—a failure that the States, and Congress, documented in depth." Breyer, J., argued that the *Civil Rights Cases* did not consider "this kind of claim," observing in that case that the statute "did 'not profess to be corrective of any constitutional wrong committed by the States' and that it established 'rules for the conduct of individuals in society towards each other, [without] referring in any manner to any supposed action of the State or its authorities.'

"[W]hy can Congress not provide a remedy against private actors? Those private actors, of course, did not themselves violate the Constitution. But this Court has held that Congress at least sometimes can enact remedial 'legislation [that] prohibits conduct which is not itself unconstitutional.' *Boerne.* The statutory remedy [may] lead state actors to improve their own remedial systems, primarily through example. It restricts private actors only by imposing liability for private conduct that is, in the main, already forbidden by state law. Why is the remedy 'disproportionate'? And given the relation between remedy and violation—the creation of a federal remedy to substitute for constitutionally inadequate state remedies—where is the lack of 'congruence'?

" * * * Congress had before it the task force reports of at least 21 States documenting constitutional violations. And it made its own findings about pervasive gender-based stereotypes hampering many state legal systems, sometimes unconstitutionally so. The record nowhere reveals a congressional finding that the

a. "There is abundant evidence [t]o show that the Congresses that enacted the [laws in the *Civil Rights Cases*] had a purpose similar to that of Congress in enacting § 13981: There were state laws on the books bespeaking equality of treatment, but in the administration of these laws there was discrimination against newly freed slaves."

b. Souter and Ginsburg, JJ., having found the law valid under the commerce clause, felt no occasion to reach the § 5 issue.

problem 'does not exist' elsewhere. [This] Court has not previously held that Congress must document the existence of a problem in every State prior to proposing a national solution."[c]

(ii) *Thirteenth amendment*? Consider Ira C. Lupu, *The Failure of RFRA*, 20 U.Ark.Little Rock L. Rev. 575, 581 (1998): "[I]t is certainly a plausible argument that violent spouses attempt to keep their mates in a form of physical and emotional bondage, and that Congress would therefore have a rational basis for finding domestic violence to be an instrument of domination analogous to enslavement." See also Lawrence G. Sager, *A Letter to the Supreme Court Regarding the Missing Argument in Brzonkala v. Morrison*, 75 N.Y.U.L.Rev. 150 (2000).

c. *Mitchell* unanimously upheld the extension *nationwide* of Voting Rights Act of 1965 § 4a's prohibition of "any test or device" (including literacy tests) "as a prerequisite for voting or registration." Black, J., reasoned that "Congress had before it a long history of the discriminatory use of literacy tests to disfranchise voters on account of their race. [A]s to the Nation as a whole, Congress had before it statistics which demonstrate that voter registration and voter participation are consistently greater in States without literacy tests." Harlan, J., added: "Despite the lack of evidence of specific instances of discriminatory application or effect, Congress could have determined that racial prejudice is prevalent throughout the Nation, and that literacy tests unduly lend themselves to discriminatory application, either conscious or unconscious. This danger of violation of § 1 of the Fifteenth Amendment was sufficient to authorize the exercise of congressional power under § 2. [While] a less sweeping approach in this delicate area might well have been appropriate, the choice which Congress made was within the range of the reasonable." Stewart, J., joined by Burger, C.J., and Blackmun, J., held: "Because the justification for extending the ban on literacy tests to the entire Nation need not turn on whether literacy tests unfairly discriminate against Negroes in every State in the Union, Congress was not required to make state-by-state [findings]. In the interests of uniformity, Congress may paint with a much broader brush than may this Court, which must confine itself to the judicial function of deciding individual cases and controversies upon individual records. * * * Experience gained under the 1965 Act has now led Congress to conclude that it should go the whole distance. This approach to the problem is a rational one; consequently it is within [the] power of Congress under § 2 of the Fifteenth Amendment."

Chapter 12

LIMITATIONS ON JUDICIAL POWER AND REVIEW

Judicial power is limited under article III to the resolution of "cases or controversies." But what are cases or controversies? Both the historical understanding and contemporary significance of these terms are both much disputed.[a]

A frequent starting point for thinking about the case or controversy requirement and the resulting limitations on the judicial power is *Marbury v. Madison*, p. 1 supra. Consider the argument of Henry P. Monaghan, *Constitutional Adjudication: The Who and When*, 82 Yale L.J. 1363, 1365–67 (1973), that *Marbury* provides support for two quite different ways of thinking about the judicial role, and its inherent limitations, in the constitutional scheme: "In important part, *Marbury* found the power of constitutional exposition to be an incident of the Court's obligation to decide the particular 'case or controversy' before it. [In] *Marbury*, Justice Marshall repeatedly emphasized the necessity for the judicial protection of 'vested' or 'legal' rights; and he declared that 'the province of the Court is *solely* to decide on the rights of individuals * * *.' Moreover, *Marbury*'s analogy of constitutional litigation to 'ordinary' common law litigation strongly suggested that the occasions for judicial review were limited to the protection of identifiable and concrete personal rights, similar to those protected by the common law courts. This view of the judicial function took deep roots, particularly as the nineteenth century wore on. And the Court, while quick to protect private rights from 'arbitrary' social legislation, repeatedly disclaimed any general commission to expound on the meaning of the Constitution. Professor Wechsler reflected this tradition when, writing in 1966, he denied that the Court had any 'special function' of 'policing or advising Legislatures or Executives,' and yet reasoned that where individual rights were at issue, the Court had an inescapable duty 'to decide the litigated case and to decide it in accordance with the [Constitution].' "

It is an implication of this first line of thinking about judicial review—which might be termed a "private rights" model—that the function of the courts is exclusively to resolve the rights of the particular parties before them, in the context of traditionally structured lawsuits involving specifically injured plaintiffs seeking relief from defendant wrongdoers.

---

a. See, e.g., Robert J. Pushaw, Jr. *Article III's Case/Controversy Distinction and the Dual Functions of Federal Courts*, 69 Notre Dame L.Rev. 447 (1994); Susan Bandes, *The Idea of a Case*, 42 Stan.L.Rev. 227 (1990).

But, Professor Monaghan notes, there is a rival conception of constitutional adjudication—what he terms a "special function" or might equally well be called a "public rights" model—with quite different implications for the appropriate exercise of judicial review. According to Professor Monaghan, supra, at 1369–71, a public rights model, fully as much as its private rights rival, traces its roots to *Marbury v. Madison*:

"Today there is virtually unanimous agreement that the Court has a 'special function' with regard to the Constitution because it is the final authoritative interpreter of constitutional text. [It] is, accordingly, today simply unacceptable for the Court to dismiss as *beyond judicial competence* challenges by Congress to the practice of the pocket veto or to presidential attempts to impound funds solely because traditional 'private' interests are not at stake; it is unacceptable to dismiss state challenges to federal authority or a case of far-reaching national importance, simply because the particular litigants no longer have a 'personal interest' in the outcome.

"Once the Court's 'special function' and the 'unique' character of constitutional adjudications are stressed, 'the old notion that the power to decide constitutional questions is simply incident to the power to dispose of a concrete case loses much of its substance.' * * * *Marbury* welded judicial review to the political axiom of limited government. * * *

"Because the Court has the 'special function' in our frame of government to declare authoritatively the meaning of the Constitution, at least when Congress so authorizes, the Court may properly render such pronouncements whether or not recognizable private interests are involved. A 'special function' model of judicial competence would perceive constitutional litigation as 'public actions,' which may or may not involve private rights. To a significant extent, the 'special function' model, in fact, has already been adopted, although its contours are vague."[b]

As you read the remainder of this Chapter, consider how far a "special function" or "public rights" model of constitutional adjudication has displaced and should displace the kind of limitations on the judicial function called for by a more traditional, private rights conception.

SECTION 1. ADVISORY OPINIONS AND EXECUTIVE REVISION

CORRESPONDENCE OF THE JUSTICES (1793)[a]

Letter from Thomas Jefferson, Secretary of State, to Chief Justice Jay and Associate Justices:

Philadelphia, July 18, 1793.

Gentlemen:

The war which has taken place among the powers of Europe produces frequent transactions within our ports and limits, on which questions arise of

b. Among the most influential pieces exemplifying a "public rights" or "special function" approach are Abram Chayes, *The Role of the Judge in Public Law Litigation*, 89 Harv. L.Rev. 1281 (1976); Owen M. Fiss, *The Forms of Justice*, 93 Harv.L.Rev. 1 (1979); Louis L. Jaffe, *The Citizen as Litigant in Public Actions: The Non–Hohfeldian or Ideological Plaintiff*, 116 U.Pa.L.Rev. 1033 (1968); and Cass R. Sunstein, *Standing and the Privatization of Public Law*, 88 Colum.L.Rev. 1432 (1988).

a. The letters are taken from 3 *Correspondence and Public Papers of John Jay* 486–89 (Henry P. Johnston ed. 1891), and the questions from 10 Jared Sparks, *Writings of George Washington* 542–45 (1836).

considerable difficulty, and of greater importance to the peace of the United States. These questions depend for their solution on the construction of our treaties, on the laws of nature and nations, and on the laws of the land, and are often presented under circumstances *which do not give a cognizance of them to the tribunals of the country.* Yet their decision is so little analogous to the ordinary functions of the executive, as to occasion much embarrassment and difficulty to them. The President therefore would be much relieved if he found himself free to refer questions of this description to the opinions of the judges of the Supreme Court of the United States, whose knowledge of the subject would secure us against errors dangerous to the peace of the United States, and their authority insure the respect of all parties. He has therefore asked the attendance of such of the judges as could be collected in time for the occasion, to know, in the first place, their opinion, whether the public may, with propriety, be availed of their *advice on these questions?* And if they may, to present, for their advice, the abstract questions which have already occurred, or may soon occur, from which they will themselves strike out such as any circumstances might, in their opinion, forbid them to pronounce on. I have the honour to be with sentiments of the most perfect respect, gentlemen,

> Your most obedient and humble servant,
>
> Thos. Jefferson.

The following are some of the questions submitted by the President to the Justices:

1. Do the treaties between the United States and France give to France or her citizens a *right,* when at war with a power with whom the United States are at peace, to fit out originally in and from the ports of the United States vessels armed for war, with or without commission?

17. Do the laws of neutrality, considered as aforesaid, authorize the United States to permit France, her subjects, or citizens, the sale within their ports of prizes made of the subjects or property of a power at war with France, before they have been carried into some port of France and there condemned, refusing the like privilege to her enemy?

18. Do those laws authorize the United States to permit to France the erection of courts within their territory and jurisdiction for the trial and condemnation of prizes, refusing that privilege to a power at war with France?

20. To what distance, by the laws and usages of nations, may the United States exercise the right of prohibiting the hostilities of foreign powers at war with each other within rivers, bays, and arms of the sea, and upon the sea along the coasts of the United States?

22. What are the articles, by name, to be prohibited to both or either party?

25. May we, within our own ports, sell ships to both parties, prepared merely for merchandise? May they be pierced for guns?

29. May an armed vessel belonging to any of the belligerent powers follow *immediately* merchant vessels, enemies, departing from our ports, for the purpose of making prizes of them? If not, how long ought the former to remain, after the

latter have sailed? And what shall be considered as the place of departure from which the time is to be counted? And how are the facts to be ascertained?

On August 8, 1793, the Justices wrote to the President refusing to tender the requested advice and explaining their decision as follows:

Sir:

We have considered the previous question stated in a letter written to us by your direction by the Secretary of State on the 18th of last month. The lines of separation drawn by the Constitution between the three departments of the government—their being in certain respects checks upon each other—and our being judges of a court in the last resort—are considerations which afford strong arguments against the propriety of our extrajudicially deciding the questions alluded to; especially as the power given by the Constitution to the President of calling on the heads of departments for opinions, seems to have been *purposely* as well as expressly limited to the *executive* departments.

Notes and Questions

1. *Grounds for the prohibition.* According to Charles Alan Wright, *Law of Federal Courts* 65 (5th ed. 1994): "[T]he oldest and most consistent thread in the federal law of justiciability is that the federal courts will not give advisory opinions, though at least by 1770 the power of the English judges to give advisory opinions was well recognized. Thus, the refusal to give advisory opinions must be based on 'the implicit policies embodied in Article III, and not history alone.' "[b]

2. *Pro's and con's of advisory opinions.* (a) Consider Comment, *The Advisory Opinion and the United States Supreme Court,* 5 Ford.L.Rev. 94, 108 (1936): "The advisory opinion, it is said [by Felix Frankfurter, *A Note on Advisory Opinions,* 37 Harv.L.Rev. 1002 (1924)], would distort the entire focus of the judicial function in that it would require the Court to express its judgment on abortive issues without the benefit of all the relevant facts which, in crucial constitutional questions, are the very heart of the case. In addition, the operation of the device would debilitate the creative responsibility of the legislature in that it would tend to induce reliance upon the judiciary, depriving the former of submitting its convictions to the test of trial and error and of accumulating new facts for the vindication of its judgment which, *a priori*, may run counter to settled legal principles."

(b) Is the opposition to advisory opinions justified by the necessity for antagonistic assertion of rights by one individual against another? Consider Note, 69 Harv.L.Rev. 1302, 1309–10 (1956): "Argument in advisory proceedings might in some situations provide more assistance to the court than would argument in a normal adversary proceeding. Representation of diversified interests might provide the justices with a more realistic perspective on the statute than representation of only two parties; and, unlike ordinary litigation where the prosecutor or plaintiff [may] be able to select an opponent with little interest in the proceeding

---

b. See also Stewart Jay, *Most Humble Servants: The Advisory Role of Early Judges* 149–70 (1997) (arguing that the position taken in the Correspondence of the Justices traced to historically peculiar considerations, including the concern of Federalist Justices to maintain foreign policy as an exclusive executive prerogative and to avoid embroilment in political controversy at a time when the Justices were eager to escape "circuit-riding" responsibilities).

or one who is peculiarly culpable, the parties seeking to appear will generally be strong antagonists."

(c) Does refusal to render advisory opinions help to symbolize the status of the Article III judiciary as an independent and co-equal branch of the national government, which cannot be impressed into service as a mere legal advisor to Congress or the President? Compare Russell Wheeler, *Extrajudicial Activities of the Early Supreme Court,* 1973 Sup.Ct.Rev. 123, 158 asserting that the position taken in the Correspondence of the Justices was "part of a broader attempt by the early Supreme Court to deemphasize the obligatory extrajudicial service concept, so widely held in the early period." Is the Supreme Court's capacity to function as an organ of sober second thought enhanced by its refusal to render opinions except as an incident to the resolution of concrete cases?

(d) In considering the policy grounds for the prohibition against advisory opinions, of what significance is it that advisory opinions are available in numerous other legal systems? Many European countries authorize courts to rule on "abstract" questions, and the European Court of Justice and European Court of Human Rights have explicit grants of jurisdiction to issue advisory opinions.[c] A number of state courts also render advisory opinions.[d]

3. *Identifying advisory opinions.* What makes the judicial expression of an opinion "advisory" in the constitutional sense and thus prohibited?[e] Are all judicial dicta forbidden advisory opinions?[f] Is it unconstitutional for courts to advance alternative grounds for decision? According to Evan Tsen Lee, *Deconstitutionalizing Justiciability: The Example of Mootness,* 105 Harv.L.Rev. 603, 644–45 (1992), the Court has used the term "advisory opinion" to embrace "[a]ny judgment subject to review by a co-equal branch of government," "[a]dvice to a co-equal branch of government prior to the other branch's contemplated action (that is, pre-enactment review)," "Supreme Court review of any state judgment for which there is or may be an adequate and independent state ground of decision," "[a]ny opinion, or portion thereof, not truly necessary to the disposition of the case at bar (that is, dicta)," and "[a]ny decision on the merits of a case that is moot or unripe or in which one of the parties lacks standing." But, Lee concludes, "only the first two of these usages denote a constitutional bar. The other three usages are a function of judicial discretion." Are there principled grounds for drawing the lines where the case law, as reported by Lee, draws them?

4. *Executive and legislative revision.* (a) Closely related to the prohibition against advisory opinions is a doctrine, most often associated with HAYBURN'S CASE, 2 U.S. (2 Dall.) 408, 1 L.Ed. 436 (1792), barring judicial judgments that are subject to executive or legislative revision. The Invalid Pensions Act of 1792

---

c. See Richard Fallon, Daniel Meltzer, & David Shapiro, *Hart & Wechsler's The Federal Courts and the Federal System* 98 (4th ed. 1996).

d. See *id.*

e. Sec. 5 of the Voting Rights Act of 1965 provided that in "a State or political subdivision covered by § 4(b) of the Act, no person may be denied the right to vote in any election because of his failure to comply with a voting qualification or procedure different from those in force on November 1, 1964. This suspension of new rules is terminated, however, * * * (2) if the area has obtained a declaratory judgment from the District Court for the District of

Columbia, determining that the rules will not abridge the franchise on racial grounds." Does this provision direct the district court to issue advisory opinions? Compare the opinions in *South Carolina v. Katzenbach,* 383 U.S. 301, 86 S.Ct. 803, 15 L.Ed.2d 769 (1966).

f. Compare Neal Kumar Katyal, *Judges as Advicegivers,* 50 Stan.L.Rev. 1709 (1998) (defending judicial advice-giving as historically legitimated and functionally useful) with Abner Mikva, *Why Judges Should Not Be Advicegivers,* 50 Stan.L.Rev. 1825 (1998) (taking a contrary view).

charged the federal circuit courts with determining whether applicants for federal pensions were disabled. Upon a finding of disability, the courts were to certify the applicant's name and a recommended pension amount to the Secretary of War. The statute then directed the Secretary to put the applicant on the pension rolls unless there were grounds to suspect "fraud or imposition," in which case the Secretary was to withhold the pension and report to Congress. The circuit courts, which included Supreme Court justices "riding circuit," uniformly refused to entertain applications for federal pensions. The unanimous view was that the business was not properly judicial; the possibility of executive and legislative revision deprived the judicial determinations of the finality required by Article III.

What exactly is objectionable about a judicial judgment being subject to executive or legislative revision? The judgments of lower federal courts are routinely subject to revision by higher courts. Consider Hart & Wechsler, note c supra, at 103: "There is at least one connecting theme between the Correspondence of the Justices and the opinions expressed in the reporter's footnote in *Hayburn's Case*: judicial independence requires that the Article III courts not be subject to enlistment by Congress or the Executive to act as subordinates to those two branches in the performance of their characteristic functions."[g]

(b) *Plaut v. Spendthrift Farm, Inc.*, 514 U.S. 211, 115 S.Ct. 1447, 131 L.Ed.2d 328 (1995), invalidated a statute purporting to re-open final judicial judgments that had dismissed suits for damages as time-barred. Compare *Miller v. French*, 530 U.S. 327, 120 S.Ct. 2246, 147 L.Ed.2d 326 (2000), which sharply distinguished judgments in suits for damages from judgments providing ongoing injunctive relief and upheld a statutory provision that mandates termination of injunctive remedies involving prison conditions unless stringent standards are met: "The provision of prospective relief is subject to the continuing supervisory jurisdiction of the court, and therefore may be altered according to subsequent changes in the law."[h]

SECTION 2. STANDING

I. THE STRUCTURE OF STANDING DOCTRINE

ALLEN v. WRIGHT

468 U.S. 737, 104 S.Ct. 3315, 82 L.Ed.2d 556 (1984).

JUSTICE O'CONNOR delivered the opinion of the Court.

Parents of black public school children allege in this nation-wide class action that the Internal Revenue Service (IRS) has not adopted sufficient standards and procedures to fulfill its obligation to deny tax-exempt status to racially discriminatory private schools. They assert that the IRS thereby harms them directly and interferes with the ability of their children to receive an education in desegregated public schools. The issue before us is whether plaintiffs have standing to bring this suit. We hold that they do not.

[Respondents] allege in their complaint that many racially segregated private schools were created or expanded in their communities at the time the public

---

g. See generally *Federal Judicial Independence Symposium*, 46 Mercer L.Rev. 637 (1995).

h. Souter, J., joined by Ginsburg, J., dissenting in part, would have remanded the case to the district court to determine whether a statutory "automatic stay" provision—terminating any injunction that a district court had not found to satisfy the new statutory standard within a specified time period—effectively "assumed the judicial function." Breyer, J., joined by Stevens, J., dissented on statutory grounds.

schools were undergoing desegregation. According to the complaint, many such private schools, including 17 schools or school systems identified by name in the complaint (perhaps some 30 schools in all), receive tax exemptions either directly or through the tax-exempt status of "umbrella" organizations that operate or support the [schools.][11] Respondents allege that the IRS grant of tax exemptions to such racially discriminatory schools is unlawful [under federal statutes and the Constitution, and they seek declaratory and injunctive relief].

[R]espondents do not allege that their children have been the victims of discriminatory exclusion from the schools whose tax exemptions they challenge as unlawful. [Rather,] respondents claim a direct injury from the mere fact of the challenged Government conduct and, as indicated by the restriction of the plaintiff class to parents of children in desegregating school districts, injury to their children's opportunity to receive a desegregated education. * * *

II. Article III of the Constitution confines the federal courts to adjudicating actual "cases" and "controversies." As the Court explained in *Valley Forge Christian College v. Americans United for Separation of Church and State, Inc.,* [Part II infra,] the "case or controversy" requirement defines with respect to the Judicial Branch the idea of separation of powers on which the Federal Government is founded. The several doctrines that have grown up to elaborate that requirement are "founded in concern about the proper—and properly limited— role of the courts in a democratic society." *Warth v. Seldin,* [infra]. * * *

The Art. III doctrine that requires a litigant to have "standing" to invoke the power of a federal court is perhaps the most important of these doctrines. "In essence the question of standing is whether the litigant is entitled to have the court decide the merits of the dispute or of particular issues." *Warth.* Standing doctrine embraces several judicially self-imposed limits on the exercise of federal jurisdiction, such as the general prohibition on a litigant's raising another person's legal rights, the rule barring adjudication of generalized grievances more appropriately addressed in the representative branches, and the requirement that a plaintiff's complaint fall within the zone of interests protected by the law invoked. The requirement of standing, however, has a core component derived directly from the Constitution. A plaintiff must allege personal injury fairly traceable to the defendant's allegedly unlawful conduct and likely to be redressed by the requested relief.

Like the prudential component, the constitutional component of standing doctrine incorporates concepts concededly not susceptible of precise definition. The injury alleged must be, for example, "distinct and palpable," and not "abstract" or "conjectural" or "hypothetical," *Los Angeles v. Lyons,* [infra]. The injury must be "fairly" traceable to the challenged action, and relief from the injury must be "likely" to follow from a favorable decision. See *Simon v. Eastern Kentucky Welfare Rights Org.,* [infra]. (These terms cannot be defined so as to make application of the constitutional standing requirement a mechanical exercise.)

The absence of precise definitions, however, [hardly] leaves courts at sea in applying the law of standing. Like most legal notions, the standing concepts have gained considerable definition from developing case law. [More] important, the law of Art. III standing is built on a single basic idea—the idea of separation of

---

11. * * * Contrary to Justice Brennan's statement, the complaint does not allege that each desegregating district in which they re- side contains one or more racially discriminatory private schools unlawfully receiving a tax exemption.

powers. It is this fact which makes possible the gradual clarification of the law through judicial application. * * *

Respondents allege two injuries in their complaint to support their standing to bring this lawsuit. First, they say that they are harmed directly by the mere fact of Government financial aid to discriminatory private schools. Second, they say that the federal tax exemptions to racially discriminatory private schools in their communities impair their ability to have their public schools desegregated. [N]either suffices to support respondents' standing.

Respondents' first claim of injury [might] be a claim simply to have the Government avoid the violation of law alleged in respondents' complaint. Alternatively, it might be a claim of stigmatic injury, or denigration, suffered by all members of a racial group when the Government discriminates on the basis of race. Under neither interpretation is this claim of injury judicially cognizable.

This Court has repeatedly held that an asserted right to have the Government act in accordance with law is not sufficient, standing alone, to confer jurisdiction on a federal court. In *Schlesinger v. Reservists Committee to Stop the War*, 418 U.S. 208, 94 S.Ct. 2925, 41 L.Ed.2d 706 (1974), for example, the Court rejected a claim of citizen standing to challenge Armed Forces Reserve commissions held by Members of Congress as violating the Incompatibility Clause of Art. I, § 6, of the Constitution. As citizens, the Court held, plaintiffs alleged nothing but "the abstract injury in nonobservance of the Constitution...." More recently, in *Valley Forge*, we rejected a claim of standing to challenge a Government conveyance of property to a religious institution. Insofar as the plaintiffs relied simply on "their shared individuated right" to a Government that made no law respecting an establishment of religion, we held that plaintiffs had not alleged a judicially cognizable injury. * * *

Neither do they have standing to litigate their claims based on the stigmatizing injury often caused by racial discrimination. There can be no doubt that this sort of noneconomic injury is one of the most serious consequences of discriminatory government action and is sufficient in some circumstances to support standing. Our cases make clear, however, that such injury accords a basis for standing only to "those persons who are personally denied equal treatment" by the challenged discriminatory conduct. [If an] abstract stigmatic injury were cognizable, standing would extend nationwide to all members of the particular racial groups against which the Government was alleged to be discriminating by its grant of a tax exemption to a racially discriminatory school, regardless of the location of that school. [A] black person in Hawaii could challenge the grant of a tax exemption to a racially discriminatory school in Maine. Recognition of standing in such circumstances would transform the federal courts into "no more than a vehicle for the vindication of the value interests of concerned bystanders." *United States v. SCRAP*, [infra]. Constitutional limits on the role of the federal courts preclude such a transformation.

It is in their complaint's second claim of injury that respondents allege harm to a concrete, personal interest that can support standing in some circumstances. The injury they identify—their children's diminished ability to receive an education in a racially integrated school—is, beyond any doubt, not only judicially cognizable but, as shown by cases [since] *Brown v. Board of Education*, [Ch. 9, Sec. 2, II supra] one of the most serious injuries recognized in our legal system. Despite the constitutional importance of curing the injury alleged by respondents, however, the federal judiciary may not redress it unless standing requirements are met. In this case, respondents' second claim of injury cannot support standing because the injury alleged is not fairly traceable to the Government conduct respondents challenge as unlawful.[22]

The illegal conduct challenged by respondents is the IRS's grant of tax exemptions to some racially discriminatory schools. The line of causation between that conduct and desegregation of respondents' schools is attenuated at best. From the perspective of the IRS, the injury to respondents is highly indirect and "results from the independent action of some third party not before the court." *Simon.* * * *

The diminished ability of respondents' children to receive a desegregated education would be fairly traceable to unlawful IRS grants of tax exemptions only if there were enough racially discriminatory private schools receiving tax exemptions in respondents' communities for withdrawal of those exemptions to make an appreciable difference in public school integration. Respondents have made no such allegation. It [is] entirely speculative, as respondents themselves conceded in the Court of Appeals, whether withdrawal of a tax exemption from any particular school would lead the school to change its policies. It is just as speculative whether any given parent of a child attending such a private school would decide to transfer the child to public school as a result of any changes in educational or financial policy made by the private school once it was threatened with loss of tax-exempt status. It is also pure speculation whether, in a particular community, a large enough number of the numerous relevant school officials and parents would reach decisions that collectively would have a significant impact on the racial composition of the public schools. * * *

The Court of Appeals relied for its contrary conclusion on *Gilmore v. City of Montgomery* [and] *Norwood v. Harrison*, [both discussed in Ch. 10, Sec. 3 supra. Neither], however, requires that we find standing in this lawsuit.

In *Gilmore*, the plaintiffs [alleged] that the city was violating [their] equal protection right by permitting racially discriminatory private schools and other groups to use the public parks. The Court recognized plaintiffs' standing to challenge this city policy insofar as the policy permitted the exclusive use of the parks by racially discriminatory private [schools]. Standing in *Gilmore* thus rested on an allegation of direct deprivation of a right to equal use of the parks. * * *

In *Norwood v. Harrison*, parents of public school children in Tunica County, Miss., filed a statewide class action challenging the State's provision of textbooks to students attending racially discriminatory private schools in the State. The Court held the State's practice unconstitutional because it breached "the State's acknowledged duty to establish a unitary school system." The Court did not expressly address the basis for the plaintiffs' standing.

In *Gilmore*, however, the Court identified the basis for standing in *Norwood*: "The plaintiffs in Norwood were parties to a school desegregation order and the relief they sought was directly related to the concrete injury they suffered."

---

22. Respondents' stigmatic injury, though not sufficient for standing in the abstract form in which their complaint asserts it, is judicially cognizable to the extent that respondents are personally subject to discriminatory treatment. See *Heckler v. Mathews*, [infra] [involving the denial of monetary benefits on an allegedly discriminatory basis]. The stigmatic injury thus requires identification of some concrete interest with respect to which respondents are personally subject to discriminatory treatment.

That interest must independently satisfy the causation requirement of standing doctrine.

[Here,] respondents identify only one interest that they allege is being discriminatorily impaired—their interest in desegregated public school education. Respondents' asserted stigmatic injury, therefore, is sufficient to support their standing in this litigation only if their school-desegregation injury independently meets the causation requirement of standing doctrine.

Through the school-desegregation decree, the plaintiffs had acquired a right to have the State "steer clear" of any perpetuation of the racially dual school system that it had once sponsored. The interest acquired was judicially cognizable because it was a personal interest, created by law, in having the State refrain from taking specific actions. * * *

III. "The necessity that the plaintiff who seeks to invoke judicial power stand to profit in some personal interest remains an Art. III requirement." *Simon.* Respondents have not met this fundamental requirement. The judgment of the Court of Appeals is accordingly reversed, and the injunction issued by that court is vacated.

JUSTICE BRENNAN, dissenting.

[In] these cases, the respondents have alleged at least one type of injury that satisfies the constitutional requirement of "distinct and palpable injury."[3] In particular, they claim that the IRS's grant of tax-exempt status to racially discriminatory private schools directly injures their children's opportunity and ability to receive a desegregated education. * * *

The Court acknowledges that this alleged injury is sufficient to satisfy constitutional standards. [Moreover,] in light of the injuries they claim, the respondents have alleged a direct causal relationship between the Government action they challenge and the injury they suffer: [Common] sense alone would recognize that the elimination of tax-exempt status for racially discriminatory private schools would serve to lessen the impact that those institutions have in defeating efforts to desegregate the public schools.

The Court admits that "[t]he diminished ability of respondents' children to receive a desegregated education would be fairly traceable to unlawful IRS grants of tax exemptions [if] there were enough racially discriminatory private schools receiving tax exemptions in respondents' communities for withdrawal of those exemptions to make an appreciable difference in public school integration," but concludes that "[r]espondents have made no such allegation." With all due respect, the Court has either misread the complaint or is improperly requiring the respondents to prove their case on the merits in order to defeat a motion to dismiss. For example, the respondents specifically refer by name to at least 32 private schools that discriminate on the basis of race and yet continue to benefit illegally from tax-exempt status. Eighteen of those schools [are] located in the city of Memphis, Tenn., which has been the subject of several court orders to desegregate. * * *

More than one commentator has noted that the causation component of the Court's standing inquiry is no more than a poor disguise for the Court's view of the merits of the underlying claims. The Court today does nothing to avoid that criticism. * * *

JUSTICE STEVENS, with whom JUSTICE BLACKMUN joins, dissenting.

[In the] final analysis, the wrong respondents allege that the Government has committed is to subsidize the exodus of white children from schools that would otherwise be racially integrated. The critical question in these cases, therefore, is whether respondents have alleged that the Government has created that kind of subsidy.

---

3. Because I conclude that the second injury alleged by the respondents is sufficient to satisfy constitutional requirements, I do not need to reach what the Court labels the "stigmatic injury." * * *

[If] the granting of preferential tax treatment would "encourage" private segregated schools to conduct their "charitable" activities, it must follow that the withdrawal of the treatment would "discourage" them, and hence promote the process of desegregation. [This] causation analysis is nothing more than a restatement of elementary economics: when something becomes more expensive, less of it will be purchased. [W]ithout tax-exempt status, private schools will either not be competitive in terms of cost, or have to change their admissions policies, hence reducing their competitiveness for parents seeking "a racially segregated alternative" to public schools, which is what respondents have alleged many white parents in desegregating school districts seek.

[Because] [c]onsiderations of tax policy, economics, and pure logic all confirm the conclusion that respondents' injury in fact is fairly traceable to the Government's allegedly wrongful conduct[,] [t]he Court [is] forced to introduce the concept of "separation of powers" into its analysis. [In doing so,] the Court could be saying that it will require a more direct causal connection when it is troubled by the separation of powers implications of the case before it. That approach confuses the standing doctrine with the justiciability of the issues that respondents seek to raise. The purpose of the standing inquiry is to measure the plaintiff's stake in the outcome, not whether a court has the authority to provide it with the outcome it seeks.

[As the Court has previously recognized,] the " 'fundamental aspect of standing' is that it focuses primarily on the *party* seeking to get his complaint before the federal court rather than 'on the issues he wishes to have adjudicated,' " *United States v. Richardson*, 418 U.S. 166, 174, 94 S.Ct. 2940, 2945, 41 L.Ed.2d 678, 686 (1974). [If] a plaintiff presents a nonjusticiable issue, or seeks relief that a court may not award, then its complaint should be dismissed for those reasons, and not because the plaintiff lacks a stake in obtaining that relief and hence has no standing. Imposing an undefined but clearly more rigorous standard for redressability for reasons unrelated to the causal nexus between the injury and the challenged conduct can only encourage undisciplined, ad hoc litigation.

[Alternatively], the Court could be saying that it will not treat as legally cognizable injuries that stem from an administrative decision concerning how enforcement resources will be allocated. This surely is an important point. Respondents do seek to restructure the IRS's mechanisms for enforcing the legal requirement that discriminatory institutions not receive tax-exempt status. Such restructuring would dramatically affect the way in which the IRS exercises its prosecutorial discretion. The Executive requires latitude to decide how best to enforce the law, and in general the Court may well be correct that the exercise of that discretion, especially in the tax context, is unchallengeable.

However, as the Court also recognizes, this principle does not apply when suit is brought "to enforce specific legal obligations whose violation works a direct harm." [Here,] respondents contend that the IRS is violating a specific constitutional limitation on its enforcement discretion. There is a solid basis for that contention. In *Norwood*, we wrote: "A State's constitutional obligation requires it to steer clear, not only of operating the old dual system of racially segregated schools, but also of giving significant aid to institutions that practice racial or other invidious discrimination."

Deciding whether the Treasury has violated a specific legal limitation on its enforcement discretion does not intrude upon the prerogatives of the Executive, for in so deciding we are merely saying "what the law is." * * *

In short, I would deal with the question of the legal limitations on the IRS's enforcement discretion on its merits, rather than by making the untenable assumption that the granting of preferential tax treatment to segregated schools does not make those schools more attractive to white students and hence does not inhibit the process of desegregation.[a]

Notes and Questions

1. *Origins of the doctrine.* The Court appears to have referred to "standing" on only eight occasions prior to 1965, with the earliest reference coming in *Stark v. Wickard*, 321 U.S. 288, 64 S.Ct. 559, 88 L.Ed. 733 (1944).[b] Prior to the modern age, the *typical* plaintiff in federal court may have suffered injury-in-fact, but the Court seems not to have regarded injury-in-fact as an absolute requirement of a judicially cognizable case or controversy under Article III.[c] What should be the relevance, if any, of this historical practice?

2. *Nature and purposes.* As Stevens, J., noted in *Allen*, the Court has frequently stated that standing doctrine addresses issues of parties—and focuses, in particular, on the nature and sufficiency of the litigants' asserted injury or interest in the litigation—rather than the fitness of the issues for judicial resolution or even the question whether constitutionally protected rights have been invaded. See, e.g., *Flast v. Cohen*, 392 U.S. 83, 95, 88 S.Ct. 1942, 1950, 20 L.Ed.2d 947, 958–59 (1968), Part II infra. What purposes are served by this distinctive focus on appropriate parties? Consider the following views:

(a) Judicial review is an anomalous and potentially precarious function in a predominantly democratic government, which should be permitted only where strictly necessary to stop concrete harms to identified individuals. See, e.g., *Valley Forge*, Part III infra.

(b) Concretely adverse interests sharpen the issues for judicial resolution and enhance the likelihood of illuminating argument. See, e.g., *Baker v. Carr*, Ch. 1, Sec. 2.

Compare Louis L. Jaffe, *The Citizen as Litigant in Public Actions: The Non–Hohfeldian or Ideological Plaintiff*, 116 U.Pa.L.Rev. 1033, 1038 (1968): "[T]he very fact of [an 'ideological plaintiff'] investing money in a lawsuit from which the plaintiff is to acquire no further monetary profit argues, to my mind, a quite exceptional kind of interest, and one peculiarly indicative of a desire to say all that can be said in the support of one's contention. From this I would conclude that, insofar as the argument for a traditional plaintiff runs in terms of the need for effective advocacy, the argument is not persuasive."

a. Marshall, J., did not participate in the decision.

b. See Cass R. Sunstein, *What's Standing After Lujan? Of Citizen Suits, "Injuries," and Article III*, 91 Mich.L.Rev. 163, 169 (1992). On the history of standing as a concept, see Steven L. Winter, *The Metaphor of Standing and the Problem of Self–Governance*, 40 Stan.L.Rev. 1371, 1418–25 (1988).

c. See, e.g., Winter, supra (arguing that, prior to the twentieth century, courts granted relief whenever a plaintiff asserted a right for which one of the forms of action afforded a remedy and that some of these forms, particularly the prerogative writs, permitted suit by persons lacking a distinctive personal stake in the dispute); Raoul Berger, *Standing to Sue in Public Actions: Is It a Constitutional Requirement?*, 78 Yale L.J. 816, 827 (1969) (asserting that when the Constitution was adopted, "the English practice in prohibition, certiorari, quo warranto, and informers' and relators' actions encouraged strangers to attack *unauthorized action*"); but see Bradley S. Clanton, *Standing and the English Prerogative Writs: The Original Understanding*, 63 Brook.L.Rev. 1001 (1997) (disputing that prerogative writs were available to persons without a personal stake in the relief sought).

(c) Restricting judicial review to cases brought by concretely harmed individuals reflects "three interrelated policies of Article III: the smooth allocation of power among courts over time; the unfairness of holding later litigants to an adverse judgment in which they may not have been properly represented; and the importance of placing control over political processes in the hands of the people most closely involved." Lea Brilmayer, *The Jurisprudence of Article III: Perspectives on the "Case or Controversy" Requirement,* 93 Harv.L.Rev. 297, 302.[d]

3. *Standing and the separation of powers.* The concept of standing, and the concerns about the scope of judicial power that underlie it, have attained prominence as plaintiffs increasingly have sought to use the Constitution as a sword to establish affirmative rights against the government, rather than as a shield against invasion of traditionally recognized liberty and property interests.[e] As *Allen* emphasized, separation-of-powers considerations are obviously at stake when plaintiffs ask courts to grant judicial remedies against other branches of government. But is standing doctrine, as formulated in *Allen* and elsewhere to focus on the plaintiff's personal stake in the controversy, a sensible response to those considerations? Might doctrines that focus on the nature of the issue sought to be adjudicated or the character of the relief requested permit a more straightforward assessment of the extent to which separation-of-powers concerns are implicated in particular cases?

4. *The doctrinal requirement of injury-in-fact.* The Court's insistence that standing minimally requires injury-in-fact has occasioned sharp disputes about what constitutes an "injury" in the constitutional sense.[f]

(a) *Non-economic injuries.* Although unwilling to find an actionable stigmatic injury in *Allen,* the Court has regularly accepted the proposition that non-economic injuries can satisfy the constitutional requirement, provided that they are pleaded with sufficient specificity.

(i) UNITED STATES v. STUDENTS CHALLENGING REGULATORY AGENCY PROCEDURES (SCRAP), 412 U.S. 669, 93 S.Ct. 2405, 37 L.Ed.2d 254 (1973), upheld the standing of a group of law students to challenge the failure of the ICC to prepare an environmental impact statement before declining to suspend a surcharge on railroad freight rates. The theory of the suit was that the surcharge on rail rates would result in damage to the outdoor environment in the Washington, D.C., metropolitan area that the students used for recreational purposes: higher rail rates would increase the cost of recycled products and thus occasion "the need to use more natural resources to produce such goods, some of which resources might be taken from the Washington area, and resulting in more refuse that might be discarded in national parks in the Washington area." If so, the result would be an injury to the plaintiffs' recreational interests.[g]

---

d. For a contrary perspective, see Mark V. Tushnet, *The Sociology of Article III: A Response to Professor Brilmayer,* 93 Harv.L.Rev. 1698 (1980).

e. For an exploration of these issues by then-Judge Scalia, which foreshadows more recent doctrinal developments, see Antonin Scalia, *The Doctrine of Standing as an Essential Element of the Separation of Powers,* 17 Suffolk U.L.Rev. 881, 894 (1983).

f. On this question, see generally Gene R. Nichol, Jr., *Injury and the Disintegration of Article III,* 74 Calif.L.Rev. 1915 (1986).

g. Even if *SCRAP* remains good law on the issue of what constitutes a constitutionally cognizable injury, it seems doubtful that the pleading would any longer suffice to satisfy the causation and redressability requirements, discussed below. See *Lujan v. National Wildlife Federation,* Sec. 3, II infra (noting that *SCRAP*'s "expansive expression of what would suffice" for standing "has never since been emulated by this Court").

(ii) In FRIENDS OF THE EARTH, INC. v. LAIDLAW ENVIRONMENTAL SERVICES (TOC), INC., 528 U.S. 167, 120 S.Ct. 693, 145 L.Ed.2d 610 (2000), the Court upheld standing under the citizen suit provisions of the Clean Water Act. The defendant argued that standing was defeated because the District Court, in imposing a penalty, ruled that the defendant's illegal actions had not been proved to "result in any health risk or environmental harm." But the Court, per GINSBURG, J., held that the relevant injury "is not injury to the environment but injury to the plaintiff" and that the plaintiffs suffered injury from their "reasonable concerns" that pollution had damaged land that they otherwise would have used. Scalia, J., joined by Thomas, J., dissented.

(b) *Injury and the equal protection clause.* HECKLER v. MATHEWS, 465 U.S. 728, 104 S.Ct. 1387, 79 L.Ed.2d 646 (1984), per BRENNAN, J., held that appellee had standing to contend that a statute denied him social security benefits on the basis of gender, even though the statute provided that if it were declared invalid the class of beneficiaries would be narrowed rather than broadened (thus resulting in appellee's receiving no benefits in any event): "[T]he right to equal treatment guaranteed by the Constitution is not co-extensive with any substantive rights to the benefits denied the party discriminated against. [Rather,] discrimination itself [can] cause serious non-economic injuries to those persons who are personally denied equal treatment solely because of their membership in a disfavored group. Accordingly, [the] appropriate remedy is a *mandate* of equal treatment, a result that can be accomplished by withdrawal of benefits from the favored class as well as by extension of benefits to the excluded class."

Is *Mathews* consistent with the holding of *Allen* that the stigma suffered by the plaintiffs did not constitute cognizable injury?

5. *Standing and the merits.* Consider the argument of William A. Fletcher, *The Structure of Standing*, 98 Yale L.J. 221 (1988), that it is a systematic mistake to conceive the standing inquiry as focused on the concept of "injury in fact" and abstracted from the existence of underlying rights. According to Professor Fletcher, people should always have standing to sue for redress of violations of their rights, and the standing question should essentially be one of what rights, if any, people possess under particular constitutional and statutory provisions. Under this approach, *Heckler* was rightly decided because the plaintiffs clearly asserted a right under the equal protection clause. With respect to *Allen*, the central question would become whether the plaintiffs had an enforceable right under applicable law to an injunction against the challenged conduct of officials in the Treasury Department. The answer to this question might of course depend on whether the defendants had caused the plaintiffs harm and whether relief would redress it—questions that the Court emphasized in *Allen*. But what, if anything, is gained by severing the question of standing—conceived as involving issues of injury, causation, and redressability—from the question of what judicially enforceable rights the Constitution confers on whom?

6. *The causation requirement.* (a) In WARTH v. SELDIN, 422 U.S. 490, 95 S.Ct. 2197, 45 L.Ed.2d 343 (1975), a variety of plaintiffs alleged that the town zoning ordinance in Penfield, N.Y., violated the Constitution and federal civil rights statutes. The Court held that none of the groups had standing. Among those whose claims were dismissed were low-income individuals who wished to live in Penfield and claimed that the town's zoning laws prevented construction of low-income housing in which they could afford to live. The Court, per POWELL, J., deemed it too uncertain that, "absent the [defendants'] restrictive zoning practices, there is a substantial probability that [plaintiffs] would have been able to

purchase or lease in Penfield and that, if the court affords the relief requested, the asserted inability of [plaintiffs] will be removed."

(b) In SIMON v. EASTERN KENTUCKY WELFARE RIGHTS ORG., 426 U.S. 26, 96 S.Ct. 1917, 48 L.Ed.2d 450 (1976), a class action on behalf of all persons unable to afford hospital services, the Court, again per Powell, J., held that plaintiffs lacked standing to challenge an IRS Revenue Ruling eliminating a requirement that non-profit hospitals provide some care for indigents in order to qualify for favorable tax treatment. The Court termed it "purely speculative" that "the denial of access to hospital services [from which the plaintiffs suffered] in fact results from the petitioners' new Ruling, or that a court-ordered return by petitioners to their previous policy would result in these respondents' receiving the hospital services they desire."

(c) Compare REGENTS OF THE UNIVERSITY OF CALIFORNIA v. BAKKE, Ch. 9, Sec. 2, VI, in which the Court upheld the standing of a white plaintiff to challenge a special admissions program for minority applicants to medical school. Writing on this point for a majority of five, Powell, J., rejected arguments that Bakke lacked standing because he had not shown that he would have been admitted but for the affirmative action program or that invalidation of the program would result in his admission. Bakke's injury, the Court held, consisted in his deprivation, on grounds of race, of the chance to compete for every place in the entering class.[h]

Does *Bakke* suggest that satisfaction of the causation requirement will frequently turn on how the alleged injury is characterized? Could the plaintiffs in *Warth*, *Simon*, and possibly *Allen* have established standing if they had only alleged denial of a constitutionally guaranteed chance or opportunity, rather than denial of a specific benefit? Consider Sunstein, note 1 supra, at 1464–69: "The central problem [is] how to characterize the relevant injury. [In *Simon*,] for example, the plaintiffs might have characterized their injury as an impairment of the opportunity to obtain medical services under a regime undistorted by unlawful tax incentives. In *Allen*, the plaintiffs themselves argued that their injury should be characterized as the deprivation of an opportunity to undergo desegregation in school systems unaffected by unlawful tax deductions. Thus recharacterized, the injuries are not speculative at all. [If *Simon*] was rightly decided, it was because the tax statutes have been interpreted so as to deny standing, not because of a problem with causation; and if people now thought to be indirectly or incidentally harmed by regulatory action or inaction are to be denied standing, it is because the denial is a sensible reading of congressional purposes in enacting regulatory legislation."

7. *Redressability*. In perhaps the majority of cases, the requirement that an injury be redressable can be viewed as an aspect of the causation requirement: if a

---

h. *Northeastern Florida Chapter of the Associated General Contractors of America v. City of Jacksonville*, 508 U.S. 656, 113 S.Ct. 2297, 124 L.Ed.2d 586 (1993), per Thomas, J., pursued a similar analysis, holding that the challenger to an affirmative action set-aside program need not show that, but for the program, the challenger would have received a concrete benefit: "The 'injury in fact' in an equal protection case of this variety is the denial of equal treatment resulting from the imposition of [a barrier that makes it more difficult for members of a group to obtain a benefit], not

the ultimate inability to obtain the benefit." The Court distinguished *Warth* on the ground that the plaintiffs in that case based their claim to standing on the denial of concrete benefits, not exclusion from the opportunity to compete for a benefit (in *Warth*, the benefit of zoning approval) on an equal basis.

Are the Court's standing holdings in *Bakke* and *Associated General Contractors* "racially suspicious"? Girardeau Spann, *Color-Coded Standing*, 80 Corn.L.Rev. 1422, 1423 (1995) (so arguing).

defendant has caused injury, relief against the defendant will ordinarily remedy the injury. Occasionally, however, the redressability requirement exercises independent bite.

In LOS ANGELES v. LYONS, 461 U.S. 95, 103 S.Ct. 1660, 75 L.Ed.2d 675 (1983), for example, the plaintiff had been choked to unconsciousness by the Los Angeles police after being stopped for a traffic violation. Alleging that the department had a policy of applying life-threatening chokeholds unnecessarily, Lyons sued for injunctive relief. Standing could not be grounded on the threat of future injury, the Court held, because it was too speculative that Lyons himself would be subjected to a choke-hold again. And, although Lyons undoubtedly had suffered an injury in the past, that injury could not be redressed by an injunction against future police conduct.[i]

As *Lyons* explicitly recognized, the plaintiff undoubtedly had standing to seek *damages* relief for the injury caused him in the past. What purpose is served by treating eligibility for injunctive relief—which the redressability requirement precluded—as a component of standing or the Article III case or controversy requirement? Wouldn't Lyons's claim to an injunction have been better addressed as a question of entitlement to equitable remedies? See Richard H. Fallon, Jr., *Of Justiciability, Remedies, and Public Law Litigation: Notes on the Jurisprudence of Lyons*, 59 N.Y.U.L.Rev. 1 (1984).

8. *Standing, manipulation, and the merits.* As Brennan, J., noted in *Allen*, numerous commentators have complained that "the causation component of the Court's standing inquiry is no more than a poor disguise for the Court's view of the merits of the underlying claims." See, e.g., Richard Pierce, *Is Standing Law or Politics?*, 77 N.C.L.Rev. 1741, 1742–43 (1999) (arguing that standing doctrine is widely manipulated and that in order to predict when standing will be upheld, lawyers should "ignore doctrine" and proceed on the assumption that "judges provide access to the courts to individuals who seek to further and political and ideological agendas of judges"). Do you agree?

9. *The prohibition against asserting third parties' rights.* As recognized in *Allen*, the Court has established a number of "self-imposed [or 'prudential'] limits on the exercise of federal jurisdiction" that are not directly mandated by Article III. Among these is a "general prohibition on a litigant's raising another person's legal rights." A celebrated example of the traditional doctrine is *Tileston v. Ullman*, 318 U.S. 44, 63 S.Ct. 493, 87 L.Ed. 603 (1943), which denied standing to a doctor to assert his patients' rights in challenging a state law prohibiting the use of contraceptives. Compare *Craig v. Boren*, Ch. 9, Sec. 3, I supra, in which a store owner was permitted to assert the equal protection rights of would-be customers not to be discriminated against on the basis of gender.

As *Craig* suggests, the general prohibition against third-party standing is not without exceptions. According to *Powers v. Ohio*, 499 U.S. 400, 410–11, 111 S.Ct. 1364, 1370–71, 113 L.Ed.2d 411, 425 (1991): "We have recognized the right of litigants to bring actions on behalf of third parties, provided three important criteria are satisfied: The litigant must have suffered an 'injury in fact,' thus giving him or her a 'sufficiently concrete interest' in the outcome of the issue in dispute * * *; the litigant must have a close relation to the third party * * *; and there must exist some hindrance to the third party's ability to protect his or her own interests." Are these sound and stable criteria to govern the assertion of third-party rights?

---

i. Marshall, J., joined by Brennan, Blackmun, and Stevens, JJ., dissented.

Might many cases characterized by the Court as involving "discretionary" decisions to permit standing to assert third-party rights be better analyzed as involving assertions by litigants of their own derivative rights? Consider Richard H. Fallon, Jr., *As-Applied and Facial Challenges and Third–Party Standing*, 113 Harv.L.Rev. 1321, 1331–32, 1360 (2000): "[E]veryone has a personal constitutional right not to be subjected to governmental sanctions except pursuant to a constitutionally valid rule of law. [The] notion that an 'invalid law' is not law at all underlies *Marbury v. Madison* [Ch. 1, Sec. 1 supra]. [M]any, if not most, seeming departures from the prohibition against third-party standing can be understood as applications of the [valid] rule requirement. For example, [a] doctor challenging anti-abortion legislation need not rely directly on her patients' rights, but can instead invoke a personal right not to be sanctioned except pursuant to a constitutionally valid rule of law."[j] According to Henry P. Monaghan, *Third Party Standing*, 84 Colum.L.Rev. 277, 278–79, 299 (1984), the "first party" view is preferable because it eliminates "unanalyzed and ungrounded notions of judicial 'discretion.'"

II. TAXPAYER STANDING AND OTHER STATUS–BASED STANDING ISSUES

In FROTHINGHAM v. MELLON, 262 U.S. 447, 43 S.Ct. 597, 67 L.Ed. 1078 (1923), a federal taxpayer contended that a federal statute providing funds to states undertaking programs to reduce maternal and infant mortality exceeded Congress' power, and "that the effect of the appropriations complained of will be to increase the burden of future taxation and thereby take her property without due process of law." The Court, per SUTHERLAND, J., dismissed "for want of jurisdiction." A federal taxpayer's "interest in the moneys of the treasury [is] shared with millions of others, is comparatively minute and indeterminable, and the effect upon future taxation, of any payment out of the funds, so remote, fluctuating and uncertain, that no basis is afforded for an appeal to the preventive powers of a court of equity." To permit such suits might result in attacks on "every other appropriation act and statute whose administration requires the outlay of public money * * *. The bare suggestion of such a result, with its attendant inconveniences, goes far to sustain the conclusion which we have reached, that a suit of this character cannot be maintained." A person asking the Court to hold a federal act unconstitutional "must be able to show, not only that the statute is invalid, but that he has sustained or is immediately in danger of sustaining some direct injury as the result of its enforcement, and not merely that he suffers in some indefinite way in common with people generally." Here, the complaint "is merely that [federal officials] will execute an act of Congress asserted to be unconstitutional; and this we are asked to prevent. To do so would be, not to decide a judicial controversy, but to assume a position of authority over the governmental acts of another and coequal department, an authority which plainly we do not possess."

FLAST v. COHEN, 392 U.S. 83, 88 S.Ct. 1942, 20 L.Ed.2d 947 (1968), per WARREN, C.J., upheld the standing of federal taxpayers to challenge federal

j. See also Robert Allen Sedler, *The Assertion of Constitutional Jus Tertii: A Substantive Approach*, 70 Calif.L.Rev. 1308, 1329 (1982). But see Matthew D. Adler, *Rights, Rules, and the Structure of Constitutional Adjudication: A Response to Professor Fallon*, 113 Harv.L.Rev. 1371 (2000).

expenditures for parochial schools under the religion clauses of the first amendment. The Court noted, at the outset, that standing doctrine blends "constitutional requirements and policy considerations" and implied that *Frothingham* rested largely on policy grounds. It framed the essence of the standing inquiry as distinct from the fitness of the issues presented for resolution on the merits: "[The] fundamental aspect of standing is that it focuses on the party seeking to get his complaint before a federal court and not on the issues he wishes to have adjudicated." But the Court then acknowledged that "in ruling on standing, it is both appropriate and necessary to look to the substantive issues [to] determine whether there is a logical nexus between the status asserted and the claim sought to be adjudicated [to] assure that [the litigant] is a proper and appropriate party to invoke federal judicial power [so as] to satisfy Article III requirements": "The nexus demanded of federal taxpayers has two aspects to it. First, the taxpayer must establish a logical link between that status and the type of legislative enactment attacked. * * * Secondly, the taxpayer must establish a nexus between that status and the precise nature of the constitutional infringement alleged."

"The taxpayer-appellants in this case have satisfied both nexuses * * *." With respect to the first, it sufficed that the "constitutional challenge is made to an exercise by Congress of its power under Art. I, § 8, to spend for the general welfare, and the challenged program involves a substantial expenditure of federal tax funds." With respect to the second, "appellants have alleged that the challenged expenditures violate the Establishment and Free Exercise Clauses of the First Amendment." In light of its historic purposes, the Establishment Clause "operates as a specific constitutional limitation upon the exercise by Congress of the taxing and spending power conferred by Art. I, § 8."

Frothingham was distinguishable. Although the "taxpayer in *Frothingham* attacked a federal spending program [and therefore] established the first nexus required," her general allegation that "Congress [had] exceeded the general powers delegated to it" failed to identify any specific limitation on spending that Congress had breached. The Court reserved the question whether "the Constitution contains other specific limitations" that would support standing by taxpayers to challenge federal expenditures.

HARLAN, J., dissenting, protested that the Court's dual nexus standard for taxpayer standing was "entirely unrelated" to the purportedly controlling standard of whether the plaintiff had the requisite personal stake to justify standing. "It is surely clear that a plaintiff's interest in the outcome of a suit in which he challenges the constitutionality of a federal expenditure is not made greater or smaller" by the nature of the program being attacked or the constitutional provision under which the attack is mounted. "[H]ow can it be said that Mrs. Frothingham's interests in her suit were, as a consequence of her choice of a constitutional claim, necessarily less intense than those, for example, of the present appellants?"

The plaintiff's claim did not rest on any distinctive individual stake in the outcome, but involved an assertion of standing to represent the public interest— shared equally by all citizens—in the observance of the establishment clause. "[I]ndividual litigants have standing to represent the public interest, despite their lack of economic or other personal interests, if [but only if] Congress has appropriately authorized such suits. [Any] hazards to the proper allocation of authority among the three branches of the Government would be substantially diminished if public actions had been pertinently authorized by Congress and the President."

Notes and Questions

1. *The double nexus test.* Was Harlan, J., correct that *Flast*'s double nexus requirement provided a flimsy and artificial measure of the plaintiff's "personal stake" in the outcome of the litigation—at least insofar as the "personal stake" requirement is somehow linked to taxpayer status and the notion that the taxpayer has suffered a pocketbook injury?

2. *Flast and the public action.* Was Harlan, J., also correct that (a) the injury suffered by the plaintiffs in *Flast*, if any, was essentially indistinguishable from that suffered by all other citizens and, thus, (b) the Court had effectively authorized "public actions" to vindicate the public interest in enforcement of the establishment clause?

What, if anything, is constitutionally troublesome about all citizens being able to sue to ensure governmental compliance with constitutional mandates? Would the problems be cured, as Harlan, J., suggested, by congressional authorization of such suits?[a]

If *Flast* did authorize public actions to challenge the constitutionality of federal spending under the establishment clause, note that the double nexus test, coupled with other express reservations in the opinion, left the Court the option of limiting citizen or taxpayer actions to suits under that provision only. Would it be fair to describe *Flast* as an *experiment* with public action lawsuits to enforce the Constitution?

Or is the concept of a "public action" possibly not a helpful one in this context? Consider the argument of Professor Fletcher, note 5 after *Allen*, supra, at 271–72, that the question should not be whether citizens or taxpayers should generally have standing to sue to enforce the Constitution, but whether "the purposes of the particular clause at issue will be best served by permitting federal taxpayers to sue to enforce its obligations." On this analysis, could *Flast*, which was brought under the establishment clause, be persuasively distinguished from *Frothingham*, in which the plaintiff relied, *inter alia*, on the "general welfare" limitation on spending of article I, § 8, and on the due process clause?

VALLEY FORGE CHRISTIAN COLLEGE v. AMERICANS UNITED FOR SEPARATION OF CHURCH AND STATE, INC., 454 U.S. 464, 102 S.Ct. 752, 70 L.Ed.2d 700 (1982), per Rehnquist, J., held that respondents lacked standing as taxpayers or citizens to challenge, as violative of the establishment clause, the giving of surplus federal property to a church college that trained students "for Christian services as either ministers or laymen": "While the [power of judicial review] is a formidable means of vindicating individual rights, when employed unwisely or unnecessarily it is also the ultimate threat to the continued effectiveness of the federal courts in performing that role. * * * Proper regard for the complex nature of our constitutional structure requires neither that the judicial branch shrink from a confrontation with the other two coequal branches of the federal government, nor that it hospitably accept for adjudication claims of constitutional violation by other branches of government where the claimant has not suffered cognizable injury. * * * Article III, which is every bit as important in its circumscription of the judicial power of the United States as in its granting of

---

a. For further discussion of congressionally   authorized standing, see Sec. 2, III infra.

that power, is not merely a troublesome hurdle to be overcome if possible so as to reach the 'merits' of a lawsuit.

"[R]espondents fail the first prong of the [*Flast*] test for taxpayer standing [in] two respects. First, the source of their complaint is not a congressional action, but a decision by HEW to transfer a parcel of federal property. *Flast* limited taxpayer standing to challenges directed 'only [at] exercises of congressional power.' * * * Second, [the] property transfer [was] not an exercise of authority conferred by the Taxing and Spending Clause of Art. I, § 8. The authorizing legislation [was] an evident exercise of Congress' power under the Property Clause, Art. IV, § 3, cl. 2. * * *

"Any doubt that once might have existed concerning the rigor with which the *Flast* exception to the *Frothingham* principle ought to be applied should have been erased by this Court's recent decisions in *United States v. Richardson* and *Schlesinger v. Reservists Committee to Stop the War* [both cited in *Allen*, Part I supra]. In *Richardson*, the question was whether the plaintiff had standing as a federal taxpayer to argue that legislation which permitted the Central Intelligence Agency to withhold from the public detailed information about its expenditures violated the Accounts Clause of the Constitution.[18] We rejected plaintiff's claim of standing because 'his challenge [was] not addressed to the taxing or spending power, but to the statutes regulating the CIA.' The 'mere recital' of those claims 'demonstrate[d] how far he [fell] short of the standing criteria of *Flast* and how neatly he [fell] within the *Frothingham* holding left undisturbed.'

"The claim in *Schlesinger* was marred by the same deficiency. Plaintiffs in that case argued that the Incompatibility Clause of Art. I[19] prevented certain Members of Congress from holding commissions in the Armed Forces Reserve. We summarily rejected their assertion of standing as taxpayers because they 'did not challenge an enactment under Art. I, § 8, but rather the action of the Executive Branch in permitting Members of Congress to maintain their Reserve status.'

"[*Reservists* and *Richardson* cannot] be distinguished on the ground that the Incompatibility and Accounts Clauses are in some way less 'fundamental' than the Establishment Clause. Each establishes a norm of conduct which the Federal Government is bound to honor. [W]e know of no principled basis on which to create a hierarchy of constitutional values or a complementary 'sliding scale' of standing which might permit respondents to invoke the judicial power of the United States. 'The proposition that all constitutional provisions are enforceable by any citizen simply because citizens are the ultimate beneficiaries of those provisions has no boundaries.' *Reservists*.

"The complaint in this case shares a common deficiency with those in *Reservists* and *Richardson*. Although [they] claim that the Constitution has been violated, [they] fail to identify any personal injury suffered by the plaintiffs *as a consequence* of the alleged constitutional error, other than the psychological consequence presumably produced by observation of conduct with which one disagrees. That is not an injury sufficient to confer standing under Art. III, even though the disagreement is phrased in constitutional terms. It is evident that respondents are firmly committed to the constitutional principle of separation of church and State, but standing is not measured by the intensity of the litigant's interest or the fervor of his advocacy. * * *

18. U.S. Const., Art. I, § 9, cl.7 ("[A]nd a regular Statement and Account of the Receipts and Expenditures of all public Money shall be published from time to time").

19. U.S. Const., Art. I, § 6, cl.2 ("[N]o Person holding any Office under the United States, shall be a Member of either House during his Continuance in Office").

"In reaching this conclusion, we do not retreat from our earlier holdings that standing may be predicated on noneconomic injury. See, e.g., *SCRAP.* We simply cannot see that respondents have alleged an *injury* of *any* kind, economic or otherwise, sufficient to confer standing. [Their] claim of standing implicitly rests on the presumption that violations of the Establishment Clause typically will not cause injury sufficient to confer standing under the 'traditional' view of Art. III. But '[t]he assumption that if respondents have no standing to sue, no one would have standing, is not a reason to find standing.' *Reservists.* This view would convert standing into a requirement that must be observed only when satisfied. Moreover, we are unwilling to assume that injured parties are nonexistent simply because they have not joined respondents in their suit."

BRENNAN, J., joined by Marshall and Blackmun, JJ.,[a] dissented: "The Court makes a fundamental mistake when it determines that a plaintiff has failed to satisfy [the] 'injury-in-fact' test, or indeed any other test of 'standing,' without first determining whether the Constitution [defines] injury, and creates a cause of action for redress of that injury, in precisely the circumstance presented to the Court. * * *[5] [One] of the primary purposes of the Establishment Clause was to prevent the use of tax moneys for religious purposes. *The taxpayer was the direct and intended beneficiary of the prohibition on financial aid to religion.* [Each], and indeed every, federal taxpayer suffers precisely the injury that the Establishment Clause guards against when the Federal Government directs that funds be taken from the pocketbooks of the citizenry and placed into the coffers of the ministry.

"[Whether] undertaken pursuant to the Property Clause or the Spending Clause, the breach of the Establishment Clause, and the relationship of the taxpayer to that breach, is precisely the same."

Notes and Questions

1. *Significance of Valley Forge.* Is *Flast*'s significance now pretty much restricted to cases challenging congressional spending under the establishment clause?[a] Should it be?[b] Is it disturbing that there may be constitutional violations that no one has standing to challenge?

2. *Generalized grievances.* Although *Valley Forge* appears to deny that the plaintiffs had suffered any injury at all, several of the cases on which it relied placed weight on the notion that "generalized grievances" are not appropriate for judicial resolution, but should instead be remitted to the political process. How is the line to be drawn between "generalized grievances" that will not support standing and genuine "injuries" that, even if widely shared, will?

(a) Should the political process be trusted to deal fairly with grievances that are widely shared? Consider Scalia, note 3 after *Allen*, supra, at 894–95: "[T]he law of standing roughly restricts courts to their traditional undemocratic role of protecting individuals and minorities against impositions of the majority, and excludes them from the even more undemocratic role of prescribing how the other

---

a. Stevens, J., dissented separately.

5. When the Constitution makes it clear that a particular person is to be protected from a particular form of government action, then that person has a "right" to be free of that action; when that right is infringed, then there is injury, and a personal stake, within the meaning of Art. III.

a. Compare *Bowen v. Kendrick,* Ch. 8, Sec. 1, II supra, applying the *Flast* exception for taxpayer challenges under the establishment clause to an exercise of Congress' power under the taxing and spending clause.

b. For critical commentary, see Gene R. Nichol, Jr., *Standing on the Constitution: The Supreme Court and Valley Forge,* 61 N.C.L.Rev. 798 (1983).

two branches should function in order to serve the interest *of the majority itself*. [U]nless the plaintiff can show some respect in which he is harmed *more* than the rest of [us] he has not established any basis for concern that the majority is suppressing or ignoring the rights of a minority that wants protection, and thus has not established the prerequisite for judicial intervention."

How does this analytical approach apply to *Valley Forge*? Were the plaintiffs, in (then-Judge) Scalia's terms, members of a "minority" or a "majority"? Does it matter? Should it? Compare Cass R. Sunstein, *What's Standing After Lujan? Of Citizen Suits, Injuries, and Article III*, 91 Mich.L.Rev. 163, 219 (1992): "[S]ome majorities are so diffuse and ill-organized that they face systematic transaction costs barriers to the exercise of ongoing political influence [and their interests may] require judicial protection."

(b) Consider again the suggestion of Fletcher, note 5 after *Allen*, supra, that the crucial question is not whether a grievance is widely shared, but whether it stems from a violation of the plaintiff's constitutional rights. Within this framework, it should be no obstacle to standing that some constitutional rights—such as the rights to be free of race-and gender-based discrimination and governmental establishment of religion, for example—are widely shared. But might it also be the case that some constitutional provisions—such as possibly the "incompatibility clause" involved in *Reservists*—create no enforceable rights at all? On what basis might distinctions between constitutional provisions that do and do not create individual rights be drawn?

(c) In FEC v. AKINS, 524 U.S. 11, 118 S.Ct. 1777, 141 L.Ed.2d 10 (1998). The Court per Breyer, J., upheld the standing of a group of voters to challenge a determination by the Federal Election Commission ("FEC") that the American Israel Public Affairs Committee ("AIPAC") was not a "political committee" as defined by the Federal Election Campaign Act of 1971 and, accordingly, that AIPAC had not violated the Act and was not required to make disclosures concerning its membership, contributions, and expenditures: "The FEC's strongest argument [is] that this lawsuit involves only a 'generalized grievance'" inadequate to ground standing. But the "language [disclaiming the justiciability of generalized grievances] to which the FEC points * * * invariably appears in cases where the harm at issue is not only widely shared, but is also of an abstract and indefinite nature—for example, harm to the 'common concern for obedience to law.'" By contrast, the injury of which the plaintiffs complained, that of being denied information through AIPAC's failure to make disclosures allegedly mandated by the statute, though "widely shared," was nonetheless concrete and specific; the case was analogous to those "where large numbers of voters suffer interference with voting rights" but all affected persons have standing.

Scalia, J., joined by O'Connor and Thomas, JJ., dissented, arguing that *Richardson* was not distinguishable: "[T]he Court is wrong to think that generalized grievances have only concerned us when they are abstract. One need go no further than *Richardson* to prove that—unless the Court believes that deprivation of information is an abstract injury, in which event this case could be disposed of on that much broader ground. [If] the effect is 'undifferentiated and common to all members of the public,' the plaintiff has a 'generalized grievance' that must be pursued by political rather than judicial means." The harm of being deprived of information fit that description: "The harm caused to Mr. Richardson [and Mr. Akins was] precisely the same as the harm caused to everyone else."

Is it (and should it be) crucial to the result in *FEC v. Akins* that Congress had authorized standing?

3. *Local and state taxpayer standing.* In denying the standing of a federal taxpayer to challenge federal expenditures, *Frothingham* distinguished the case of municipal taxpayers: "The interest of a taxpayer of a municipality in the application of its moneys is direct and immediate and the remedy by injunction to prevent their misuse is not inappropriate."

(a) Compare DOREMUS v. BOARD OF EDUC., 342 U.S. 429, 72 S.Ct. 394, 96 L.Ed. 475 (1952), in which a state court had held that Bible-reading in public schools was not an establishment of religion. The Court, per JACKSON, J., dismissed the appeal: Although municipal taxpayers have standing to enjoin "a measurable appropriation or disbursement of [municipal] funds occasioned solely by the activities complained of," there "is no allegation that this activity is supported by any separate tax or paid for from any particular appropriation or that it adds any sum whatever to the cost of conducting the school." Although state courts may render advisory opinions on federal constitutional questions, "because our own jurisdiction is cast in terms of 'case or controversy,' we cannot * * *. The taxpayer's action can meet this test, but only when it is a good-faith pocketbook action."

DOUGLAS, J., joined by Reed and Burton, JJ., dissented: "There is no group more interested in [the] public schools than the taxpayers who support them and the parents whose children attend them. [W]here the clash of interests is as real and as strong as it is here, it is odd indeed to hold there is no case or controversy within the meaning of Art. III, § 2 of the Constitution."

(b) ASARCO INC. v. KADISH, 490 U.S. 605, 109 S.Ct. 2037, 104 L.Ed.2d 696 (1989), per KENNEDY, J., held that the exception from the *Frothingham* rule for municipal taxpayers does not apply to state taxpayers: "[W]e have refused to confer standing upon a state taxpayer absent a showing of 'direct injury,' pecuniary or otherwise." BRENNAN, J., joined by White, Marshall, and Blackmun, JJ., did not join this part of the Court's opinion.

(c) Although denying that state taxpayers possess standing to challenge state expenditures in federal court, *ASARCO* also adhered to the rule, pronounced in *Doremus*, that state courts are not bound by Article III standing requirements even when ruling on federal constitutional claims. What happens, however, when a plaintiff who would not have standing in federal court sues in state court and prevails on the merits? Does the defendant then have standing to seek review of the state judgment in the Supreme Court? By a vote of 6–2, the Justices in *ASARCO* answered in the affirmative.

REHNQUIST, C.J., joined by Scalia, J., filed a partial dissent objecting to the disparity that *ASARCO* creates: "[A]lthough the *Doremus* case is good law for plaintiffs who lack standing but lost in the state court on the merits of their federal claim, it is not good law for such plaintiffs who prevailed on the merits of their federal question in the state courts." Consider Paul Freund in *Supreme Court & Supreme Law* 35 (E. Cahn ed. 1954): "I think it is a needed change to make standing to raise a federal constitutional question, itself a federal question, so that it will be decided uniformly throughout the country."

Would acceptance of Professor Freund's proposal unjustifiably intrude on the autonomy of state courts by prohibiting them to render advisory opinions, for example? See William A. Fletcher, *The "Case or Controversy" Requirement in State Court Adjudication of Federal Questions*, 78 Calif.L.Rev. 263 (1990) (noting that no such problem would arise if state advisory opinions were denied precedential or res judicata effect).

5. *Standing of voters.* Numerous cases have upheld the standing of individual voters to claim deprivations of constitutional voting rights of various kinds. See, e.g., *Baker v. Carr*, Ch. 1, Sec. 2 (alleging malapportionment in violation of one-person, one-vote requirement); *Rogers v. Lodge*, Ch. 9, Sec. 5, I, B (involving race-based dilution of voting power); *Davis v. Bandemer*, Ch. 9, Sec. 5, I, B (challenging political gerrymander). Why don't cases such as these involve mere "generalized grievances"?

In recent years, controversy has surrounded the question of what injury—if any—either white or non-white voters suffer when the legislature deliberately takes race into account in creating a majority-minority voting district as in *Shaw v. Reno*, Ch. 9, Sec. 5, I, D.[c] Over the protests of Justice Stevens, who has denied the presence of any actionable injury at all, the Court has held that white voters living within a district have standing to challenge it as an unconstitutional racial gerrymander. But UNITED STATES v. HAYS, 515 U.S. 737, 115 S.Ct. 2431, 132 L.Ed.2d 635 (1995), per O'Connor, J., held that persons living outside a voting district lack standing to bring a challenge. The plaintiffs had not suffered the "representational harm" of having their representatives feel especially beholden to a racially defined constituency, nor been subjected personally to racially discriminatory treatment.[d] Concurring separately, Stevens, J., analyzed the standing question as largely inseparable from the merits and concluded that the plaintiffs lacked standing because they had failed to allege a constitutional violation.

6. *Standing of legislators.* (a) In COLEMAN v. MILLER, Ch. 1, Sec. 2, an action was brought by 21 members of the Kansas senate and three members of the house of representatives to nullify the Kansas legislature's ratification of an amendment to the Constitution. The plaintiffs complained (1) that the lieutenant governor had broken a 20–20 tie in the senate by voting in favor and that he had no right to cast the deciding vote, and (2) that the proposed amendment "had lost its vitality," having been rejected over a thirteen-year period by 26 states and having failed to win ratification "within a reasonable time." The Court upheld standing: "[P]laintiffs include twenty senators whose votes against ratification have been overridden and virtually held for naught although if they are right in their contentions their votes would have been sufficient to defeat ratification. We think [they] have a plain, direct and adequate interest in maintaining the effectiveness of their votes."

(b) Compare RAINES v. BYRD, 521 U.S. 811, 117 S.Ct. 2312, 138 L.Ed.2d 849 (1997), per Rehnquist, C.J., holding that members of Congress lacked standing to challenge the constitutionality of the Line Item Veto Act ("the Act"), which authorized the President to "cancel" certain spending and tax benefit measures after signing them into law: *Coleman* "stands (at most * * *) for the proposition that legislators whose votes would have been sufficient to defeat (or enact) a specific legislative Act have standing to sue if that legislative action goes into effect (or does not go into effect), on the ground that their votes have been completely nullified." Although plaintiffs alleged that the Line Item Veto Act diluted the significance of their votes for bills that are subject to presidential cancellation, there was a "vast difference" between the "level of vote nullifica-

c. For a range of views, see, e.g., Richard H. Pildes & Richard G. Niemi, *Expressive Harms, "Bizarre Districts," and Voting Rights: Evaluating Election–District Appearances After Shaw v. Reno,* 92 Mich.L.Rev. 483, 492–516 (1993); John Hart Ely, *Standing to Challenge Pro–Minority Gerrymanders,* 111 Harv.L.Rev. 576 (1997); Samuel Issacharoff & Pamela Karlan, *Standing and Misunderstanding in Voting Rights Law,* 111 Harv.L.Rev. 2276 (1998).

d. See also *Shaw v. Hunt,* 517 U.S. 899, 116 S.Ct. 1894, 135 L.Ed.2d 207 (1996).

tion" in this case and that in *Coleman*. "We attach some importance to the fact that appellees have not been authorized to represent their respective Houses of Congress, and indeed both Houses actively oppose their suit. [N]or [does the decision] foreclose[ ] the Act from constitutional challenge (by someone who suffers judicially cognizable injury as a result of the Act). Whether the case would be different if any of these circumstances were different we need not now decide."[e]

(c) Under what circumstances, if any, would there be congressional standing to challenge the constitutionality of the actual or imminent dispatch of troops to foreign hostilities on the ground that unilateral presidential action effectively deprives legislators of the right to vote on whether to declare war? Compare *Holtzman v. Schlesinger*, 484 F.2d 1307 (2d Cir.1973) (denying standing) with *Dellums v. Bush*, 752 F.Supp. 1141 (D.D.C.1990) (upholding standing of members of Congress to raise anticipatory challenge to executive initiation of the Persian Gulf War without a declaration of war, but finding the suit unripe). Would members of Congress have standing to raise the claims in *Richardson*—e.g., to complain that the executive has unlawfully (or unconstitutionally) withheld information from them, thus impairing their ability to perform their legislative duties?

Consider Jesse H. Choper, *Judicial Review and the National Political Process* ch. 5 (1980), arguing that, unless individual constitutional rights that could not be altered by Congress are at stake, courts should not intervene in separation-of-powers disputes. According to Professor Choper, the line separating legislative from executive authority is ambiguous and shifting, the political process affords Congress and the President ample means for protecting their institutional interests, and the Court should preserve its institutional capital for the protection of individual rights.

III. CONGRESSIONAL POWER TO CREATE STANDING

LUJAN v. DEFENDERS OF WILDLIFE

504 U.S. 555, 112 S.Ct. 2130, 119 L.Ed.2d 351 (1992).

JUSTICE SCALIA delivered the opinion of the Court with respect to Parts I, II, III-A, and IV, and an opinion with respect to Part III-B in which the CHIEF JUSTICE, JUSTICE WHITE, and JUSTICE THOMAS join.

[The Endangered Species Act of 1973 (ESA) § 7(a)(2) requires federal agencies to consult with the Secretary of the Interior to "insure" that projects that they fund do not threaten endangered species. Regulations promulgated in 1978 construed the consultation requirement as extending to actions taken in foreign nations. In 1986, however, the Department of the Interior reinterpreted the ESA to require consultation only for actions taken in the United States or on the high seas. Several organizations filed suits challenging the new regulation as contrary to law.]

IIIA. [The Court first held that the groups and their members had failed to present sufficient evidence of injury in fact. Although affidavits testified that at least two members had previously traveled abroad to observe endangered species and intended to do so again,] [t]hat the women "had visited" the areas of [identified] projects before the projects commenced proves nothing. [And] the affiants' profession of an "inten[t]" to return to the places they had visited

---

e. Souter, J., joined by Ginsburg, J., concurred that the plaintiffs lacked standing. Stevens, J., dissented, as did Breyer, J.

[before]—without any description of concrete plans, or indeed even any specification of *when* the some day will be—do not support a finding of the "actual or imminent" injury that our cases require.

[No more persuasive are] a series of novel standing theories, [including] the "animal nexus" approach, whereby anyone who has an interest in studying or seeing the endangered animals anywhere on the globe has standing; and the "vocational nexus" approach, under which anyone with a professional interest in such animals can sue. Under these theories, anyone who goes to see Asian elephants in the Bronx Zoo, and anyone who is a keeper of Asian elephants in the Bronx Zoo, has standing to sue because the Director of AID did not consult with the Secretary regarding the AID-funded project in Sri Lanka. This is beyond all reason. [It is] pure speculation and fantasy, to say that anyone who observes or works with an endangered species, anywhere in the world, is appreciably harmed by a single project affecting some portion of that species with which he has no more specific connection.

B. Besides failing to show injury, respondents failed to demonstrate redressability. [Since] the agencies funding the projects were not parties to the case, the District Court could accord relief only against the Secretary. [There was no assurance that other agencies would feel bound by the Secretary's regulation, or that the withdrawal of American funding would cause projects to be terminated and the threat to endangered species thereby eliminated.]

IV. The Court of Appeals found that respondents had standing for an additional reason: because they had suffered a "procedural injury." The so-called "citizen-suit" provision of the ESA provides, in pertinent part, that "any person may commence a civil suit on his own behalf (A) to enjoin any person, including the United States and any other governmental instrumentality or agency [who] is alleged to be in violation of any provision of this chapter." The court held that, because § 7(a)(2) requires inter-agency consultation, the citizen-suit provision creates a "procedural righ[t]" to consultation in all "persons"—so that *anyone* can file suit in federal court to challenge the Secretary's (or presumably any other official's) failure to follow the assertedly correct consultative procedure, notwithstanding their inability to allege any discrete injury flowing from that failure. To understand the remarkable nature of this holding one must be clear about what it does *not* rest upon: This is not a case where plaintiffs are seeking to enforce a procedural requirement the disregard of which could impair a separate concrete interest of theirs (*e.g.,* the procedural requirement for a hearing prior to denial of their license application, or the procedural requirement for an environmental impact statement before a federal facility is constructed next door to them).[6] Nor is it simply a case where concrete injury has been suffered by many persons, as in mass fraud or mass tort situations. Nor, finally, is it the unusual case in which Congress has created a concrete private interest in the outcome of a suit against a

---

6. There is this much truth to the assertion that "procedural rights" are special: The person who has been accorded a procedural right to protect his concrete interests can assert that right without meeting all the normal standards for redressability and immediacy. Thus, under our case-law, one living adjacent to the site for proposed construction of a federally licensed dam has standing to challenge the licensing agency's failure to prepare an Environmental Impact Statement, even though he cannot establish with any certainty that the Statement will cause the license to be withheld or altered, and even though the dam will not be completed for many years. (That is why we do not rely, in the present case, upon the Government's argument that, *even if* the other agencies were obliged to consult with the Secretary, they might not have followed his advice.) What respondents' "procedural rights" argument seeks, however, is quite different from this: standing for persons who have no concrete interests affected—persons who live (and propose to live) at the other end of the country from the dam.

private party for the government's benefit, by providing a cash bounty for the victorious plaintiff. Rather, the court held that the injury-in-fact requirement had been satisfied by congressional conferral upon *all* persons of an abstract, self-contained, non-instrumental "right" to have the Executive observe the procedures required by law.

[The] question presented here is whether the public interest in proper administration of the laws (specifically, in agencies' observance of a particular, statutorily prescribed procedure) can be converted into an individual right by a statute that denominates it as such, and that permits all citizens (or, for that matter, a subclass of citizens who suffer no distinctive concrete harm) to sue. If the concrete injury requirement has the separation-of-powers significance we have always said, the answer must be obvious: To permit Congress to convert the undifferentiated public interest in executive officers' compliance with the law into an "individual right" vindicable in the courts is to permit Congress to transfer from the President to the courts the Chief Executive's most important constitutional duty, to "take Care that the Laws be faithfully executed," Art. II, § 3. It would enable the courts, with the permission of Congress, "to assume a position of authority over the governmental acts of another and co-equal department," *Frothingham*, and to become "virtually continuing monitors of the wisdom and soundness of Executive action." *Allen*. We have always rejected that vision of our role * * *.

Nothing in this contradicts the principle that "[the] injury required by Art. III may exist solely by virtue of 'statutes creating legal rights, the invasion of which creates standing.' " *Warth*. [T]he cases [previously cited by the Court] as an illustration of that principle involved Congress's elevating to the status of legally cognizable injuries concrete, de facto injuries that were previously inadequate in law (namely, injury to an individual's personal interest in living in a racially integrated community, see *Trafficante v. Metropolitan Life Ins. Co.*, 409 U.S. 205, 208–12, 93 S.Ct. 364, 366–68, 34 L.Ed.2d 415, 418–20 (1972), and injury to a company's interest in marketing its product free from competition, see *Hardin v. Kentucky Utilities Co.*, 390 U.S. 1, 6, 88 S.Ct.651, 654, 19 L.Ed.2d 787, 792–93 (1968)). As we said in *Sierra Club*, "[Statutory] broadening [of] the categories of injury that may be alleged in support of standing is a different matter from abandoning the requirement that the party seeking review must himself have suffered an injury." Whether or not the principle set forth in *Warth* can be extended beyond that distinction, it is clear that in suits against the government, at least, the concrete injury requirement must remain.

Justice Kennedy, with whom Justice Souter joins, concurring in part and concurring in the judgment.

[I] join Part IV of the Court's opinion with the following observations. As government programs and policies become more complex and far-reaching, we must be sensitive to the articulation of new rights of action that do not have clear analogs in our common-law tradition. Modern litigation has progressed far from the paradigm of Marbury suing Madison to get his commission. [In] my view, Congress has the power to define injuries and articulate chains of causation that will give rise to a case or controversy where none existed before, and I do not read the Court's opinion to suggest a contrary view. [In] exercising this power, however, Congress must at the very least identify the injury it seeks to vindicate and relate the injury to the class of persons entitled to bring suit. The citizen-suit provision of the Endangered Species Act does not meet these minimal requirements, because [it] does not of its own force establish that there is an injury in "any person" by virtue of any "violation."

The Court's holding that there is an outer limit to the power of Congress to confer rights of action is a direct and necessary consequence of the case and controversy limitations found in Article III. I agree that it would exceed those limitations if, at the behest of Congress and in the absence of any showing of concrete injury, we were to entertain citizen-suits to vindicate the public's nonconcrete interest in the proper administration of the laws. While it does not matter how many persons have been injured by the challenged action, the party bringing suit must show that the action injures him in a concrete and personal way. This requirement is not just an empty formality. It preserves the vitality of the adversarial process by assuring both that the parties before the court have an actual, as opposed to professed, stake in the outcome, and that "the legal questions presented [will] be resolved, not in the rarefied atmosphere of a debating society, but in a concrete factual context conducive to a realistic appreciation of the consequences of judicial action." *Valley Forge.* In addition, the requirement of concrete injury confines the Judicial Branch to its proper, limited role in the constitutional framework of government. * * *

JUSTICE STEVENS, concurring in the judgment.

Because I am not persuaded that Congress intended the consultation requirement in § 7(a)(2) [to] apply to activities in foreign countries, I concur in the judgment of reversal. I do not, however, agree with the Court's conclusion that respondents lack standing because the threatened injury to their interest in protecting the environment and studying endangered species is not "imminent." Nor do I agree with the plurality's additional conclusion that respondents' injury is not "redressable" in this litigation. * * *

JUSTICE BLACKMUN, with whom JUSTICE O'CONNOR joins, dissenting.

I part company with the Court in this case in two respects. First, I believe that respondents have raised genuine issues of fact—sufficient to survive summary judgment—both as to injury and as to redressability. Second, I question the Court's breadth of language in rejecting standing for "procedural" injuries. * * *

The Court concludes that any "procedural injury" suffered by respondents is insufficient to confer standing. It rejects the view that the "injury-in-fact requirement [is] satisfied by congressional conferral upon *all* persons of an abstract, self-contained, noninstrumental 'right' to have the Executive observe the procedures required by law." Whatever the Court might mean with that very broad language, it cannot be saying that "procedural injuries" *as a class* are necessarily insufficient for purposes of Article III standing.

Most governmental conduct can be classified as "procedural." [When] the Government, for example, "procedurally" issues a pollution permit, those affected by the permittee's pollutants are not without standing to sue. Only later cases will tell just what the Court means by its intimation that "procedural" injuries are not constitutionally cognizable injuries. In the meantime, I have the greatest of sympathy for the courts across the country that will struggle to understand the Court's standardless exposition of this concept today.

The Court expresses concern that allowing judicial enforcement of "agencies' observance of a particular, statutorily prescribed procedure" would "transfer from the President to the courts the Chief Executive's most important constitutional duty, to 'take Care that the Laws be faithfully executed,' Art. II, sec. 3." In fact, the principal effect of foreclosing judicial enforcement of such procedures is to transfer power into the hands of the Executive at the expense—not of the courts—but of Congress, from which that power originates and emanates.

Under the Court's anachronistically formal view of the separation of powers, Congress legislates pure, substantive mandates and has no business structuring the procedural manner in which the Executive implements these mandates. To be sure, in the ordinary course, Congress does legislate in black-and-white terms of affirmative commands or negative prohibitions on the conduct of officers of the Executive Branch. In complex regulatory areas, however, Congress often legislates, as it were, in procedural shades of gray. That is, it sets forth substantive policy goals and provides for their attainment by requiring Executive Branch officials to follow certain procedures, for example, in the form of reporting, consultation, and certification requirements.

[There] may be factual circumstances in which a congressionally imposed procedural requirement is so insubstantially connected to the prevention of a substantive harm that it cannot be said to work any conceivable injury to an individual litigant. But, as a general matter, the courts owe substantial deference to Congress' substantive purpose in imposing a certain procedural requirement. In all events, [t]here is no room for a per se rule or presumption excluding injuries labeled "procedural" in nature. * * *

Notes and Questions

1. *Statutory rights to sue and constitutional standing.* *Lujan* clearly rejects the notion that Congress may confer standing wherever it chooses, but it distinguishes between two kinds of cases. (a) In cases involving "actual" injuries that have not previously been viewed as adequate to support standing—perhaps because they are too widely shared—Congress' power to confer standing remains. See, e.g., *Trafficante* (involving loss of benefits of living in a racially diverse community). (b) In cases in which there was, previously, no actual injury, Congress cannot confer standing.

Will the notion of a concrete or actual injury bear the weight that *Lujan* places on it? In what sense was denial of an equal opportunity to compete to enter the University of California an injury in *Bakke*, but denial of the opportunity to purchase housing in an undistorted market not an injury in *Warth*? How did the alleged governmental violation of the establishment clause injure the plaintiff in *Flast*, but not those in *Valley Forge*? Why was "stigma" sufficient to ground standing in *Heckler v. Mathews*, but not in *Allen v. Wright*?

Consider Cass R. Sunstein, *What's Standing After Lujan? Of Citizen Suits, Injuries, and Article III*, 91 Mich.L.Rev. 163, 190 (1992): "[T]he real question is what harms *that people perceive as such* ought to be judicially cognizable. [W]hether there is a so-called nonjusticiable ideological interest, or instead a legally cognizable 'actionable injury,' is a product of legal conventions and nothing else." Is this argument persuasive? If so, should Congress be able to alter the prevailing legal conventions by legislation?

How would (and should) the Court resolve a hypothetical formulated by Professor Sunstein, supra, at 234: "Suppose [that] Congress attempts to create a citizen suit" by first legislating that "all Americans have [a] property right—a tenancy in common—[in] clean air anywhere in the country, or pristine areas, or the continued existence of endangered species anywhere in the United States or abroad. If this seems odd, we might note that Congress could surely create property rights in unowned land within the United States. [And] surely Congress' capacity to create property rights is not limited to land. If Congress thus creates property rights," can it then further prescribe that violation of those rights constitutes injury to all right-holders, and thereby authorize standing to sue by all citizens? *Lujan* appears to signal that it could not, but compare the opinion of Kennedy, J., joined by Souter, J., concurring.[a]

2. *More recent developments.* FEC v. AKINS, 524 U.S. 11, 118 S.Ct. 1777, 141 L.Ed.2d 10 (1998), per BREYER, J., upheld the power of Congress to confer standing on any "aggrieved" person who suffers the harm of "inability to obtain information" as a result of a decision by the FEC that reporting and disclosure requirements are not applicable to a private party. Although the interest in acquiring information was not protected at common law, and although "prudential" considerations might have precluded recognition of standing to sue based on so widespread an injury in the absence of a statute, Congress had specifically authorized suit under the Federal Election Campaign Act. Judicially imposed "prudential" limitations on standing therefore had to give way; the "failure to obtain relevant information" is a "concrete" enough injury to satisfy the requirements of Art. III.

SCALIA, J., joined by O'Connor and Thomas, JJ., dissented on the ground that the asserted injury was too generalized and undifferentiated to support standing, and a statute could not cure the constitutional defect. "If today's decision is correct, it is within the power of Congress to authorize any interested person to manage (through the courts) the Executive's enforcement of any law that includes a requirement for the filing and public availability of a piece of paper. This is not the system we have had, and it is not the system we should desire."

Consider Cass R. Sunstein, *Informational Regulation and Informational Standing: Akins and Beyond*, 147 U.Pa.L.Rev. 613, 617 (1999): "If Congress creates a legal right to information and gives people the authority to vindicate that right in court, the standing question is essentially resolved."

3. *Standing and the separation of powers revisited.* (a) Recall the Court's statement in *Allen v. Wright* that "the law of Art. III standing is built on a single basic idea—the idea of separation of powers." What should be the relevance of separation-of-powers concerns to the standing determination in cases such as *Lujan* and *Akins*?[b] Recall Harlan, J.'s suggestion in *Flast v. Cohen* that "public actions" should be permitted if but only if they are authorized by Congress. Does this analysis ignore the independent stake of the President and the executive branch in being free to administer the laws? Is it an adequate response to concerns of intrusion on presidential authority that "the Take Care Clause confers a duty [on] the President [to] enforce the law as it has been enacted" and that this duty should be as enforceable by the intended beneficiaries of legislation as by the targets of regulation (who would have undoubted standing to challenge the President's enforcement actions as beyond the bounds of law)? Sunstein, *What's Standing After Lujan*, supra, at 212.[c]

---

a. For further critical discussion of *Lujan*, see Richard J. Pierce, Jr., *Lujan v. Defenders of Wildlife: Standing as a Judicially Imposed Limit on Legislative Power*, 42 Duke L.J. 1170, 1194–95 (1993); Gene R. Nichol, Jr., *Justice Scalia, Standing, and Public Law Litigation*, 42 Duke L.J. 1141 (1993). For more favorable commentary, see Marshall J. Breger, *Defending Defenders: Remarks on Nichol and Pierce*, 42 Duke L.J. 1202 (1993); John G. Roberts, Jr.,

Article III Limits on Statutory Standing, 42 Duke L.J. 1219 (1993).

b. Compare Scalia, J.'s majority opinion in *Lujan* with his solitary dissenting opinion in *Morrison v. Olson*, Ch. 3, Sec. 2, III supra.

c. For a direct reply to Professor Sunstein, see Harold J. Krent & Ethan G. Shenkman, *Of Citizens Suits and Citizen Sunstein*, 91 Mich. L.Rev. 1793 (1993).

(b) In In FRIENDS OF THE EARTH, INC. v. LAIDLAW ENVIRONMEN-TAL SERVICES (TOC), INC., note 4 after *Allen*, supra, the Court upheld the standing of private plaintiffs to bring an action under the citizen suit provisions of the Clean Water Act seeking civil money penalties payable to the government. Per GINSBURG, J., the Court found it "likely, as opposed to merely speculative, that the penalties," although payable to the government, "would redress [plaintiffs'] injuries by abating current violations and preventing future ones."

SCALIA, J., joined by Thomas, J., dissented, finding the Court's reasoning inconsistent with *Linda R.S. v. Richard D.*, 410 U.S. 614, 93 S.Ct. 1146, 35 L.Ed.2d 536 (1973): "The principle that 'in American jurisprudence [a] private citizen lacks a judicially cognizable interest in the prosecution or nonprosecution of another' applies no less to prosecution for civil penalties payable to the State than to prosecution for criminal penalties owing to the State." Scalia, J., also raised, but purported not to "address," the question whether citizen suits for penalties payable to the government violate Article II by depriving the Executive Branch of enforcement discretion.

(c) The False Claims Act authorizes private citizens—called "relators"—to bring "qui tam" actions for civil penalties and damages against "any person" who procured payment on a false claim against the United States. On this issue, the Court held without dissent in VERMONT AGENCY OF NATURAL RESOURCES v. UNITED STATES EX REL. STEVENS, 529 U.S. 765, 120 S.Ct. 1858, 146 L.Ed.2d 836 (2000), that a relator had Article III standing. The Court, per SCALIA, J., first held that standing could not be supported on the basis of the relator's interest in recovering a bounty; "an interest that is merely a 'byproduct' of the suit itself" did not satisfy the article III requirement of injury in fact. Standing was sustainable, however, on the alternative ground that the relator, as the assignee of the government's claim, "has standing to assert the injury in fact suffered by the assignor." The Court was "confirmed in this conclusion by the long tradition of qui tam actions in England and the American Colonies."

Having resolved the "standing" question, the Court dropped a footnote: "[W]e express no view on the question whether *qui tam* suits violate Article II, in particular the Appointments Clause of § 2 and the 'take Care' Clause of § 3. [See] *Steel Co. v. Citizens for a Better Environment*, 523 U.S. 83, 102 n. 4, 118 S.Ct. 1003, 1016 n. 4, 140 L.Ed.2d 210 (1998) ('[O]ur standing jurisprudence, [though] it may sometimes have an impact on Presidential powers, derives from Article III and not Article II.')."[d]

Is this position consistent with that adopted by the Court in *Allen v. Wright*? If not, which is better supported?

4. *Congressionally authorized standing under the Administrative Procedure Act.* Apparently unaffected by the *Lujan* decision was Congress' most sweeping grant of statutory standing, § 10(a) of the Administrative Procedure Act (APA), which authorizes suit by "any person adversely affected or aggrieved by agency action within the meaning of a relevant statute." As consistently construed, the test for standing under the APA incorporates the constitutional requirements of injury-in-fact,[e] causation, and redressability, but suits under the APA also introduce the further complication of determining when a plaintiff is adversely affected

---

d. Stevens, J., joined by Souter, J., dissented on other grounds. Ginsburg, J., concurred in the judgment only.

e. Indeed, the emergence of injury as a central concept in modern standing law may be

traced to the leading case on standing under the APA, *Association of Data Processing Serv. Orgs. v. Camp*, discussed in this paragraph.

or aggrieved within the meaning of a relevant statute. The leading case, *Association of Data Processing Serv. Orgs. v. Camp*, 397 U.S. 150, 90 S.Ct. 827, 25 L.Ed.2d 184 (1970), attempted to give meaning to this requirement by formulating a so-called "zone-of-interests" test, which turns on "whether the interest sought to be protected by the complainant is arguably within the zone of interests to be protected or regulated by the statutory * * * guarantee in question." On the meaning of this test, and on standing to challenge administrative action more generally, see 3 Kenneth Culp Davis & Richard J. Pierce, Jr., *Administrative Law Treatise* 1–96 (3d ed. 1994).

SECTION 3. TIMING OF ADJUDICATION

I. MOOTNESS

DeFUNIS v. ODEGAARD

416 U.S. 312, 94 S.Ct. 1704, 40 L.Ed.2d 164 (1974).

PER CURIAM.

[Petitioner was admitted to the University of Washington Law School after a state trial court had sustained his claim that the school's special admissions policy violated equal protection. The Washington Supreme Court reversed, but its judgment was stayed. By the time the case was argued in the Supreme Court, petitioner had registered for the final term of his third year. Although the school stated that if its admissions policy were upheld, petitioner would be subject to it if he had to register for any additional terms, his present registration "would not be canceled [regardless] of the outcome of this litigation."]

The starting point for analysis is the familiar proposition that "federal courts are without power to decide questions that cannot affect the rights of litigants in the case before them." *North Carolina v. Rice*, 404 U.S. 244, 246, 92 S.Ct. 402, 404, 30 L.Ed.2d 413, 415 (1971). The inability of the federal judiciary "to review moot cases derives from the requirement of Art. III of the Constitution under which the exercise of judicial power depends upon the existence of a case or controversy." *Liner v. Jafco, Inc.*, 375 U.S. 301, 306 n. 3, 84 S.Ct. 391, 394 n. 3, 11 L.Ed.2d 347, 351 n. 3 (1964).

[A]ll parties agree that DeFunis is now entitled to complete his legal studies at the University of Washington and to receive his degree from that institution. A determination by this Court of the legal issues tendered by the parties is no longer necessary to compel that result, and could not serve to prevent it. DeFunis did not cast his suit as a class action, and the only remedy he requested was an injunction commanding his admission to the Law School. He was not only accorded that remedy, but he now has also been irrevocably admitted to the final term of the final year of the Law School course. The controversy between the parties has thus clearly ceased to be "definite and concrete" and no longer "touch[es] the legal relations of parties having adverse legal interests." *Aetna Life Ins. Co. v. Haworth*, 300 U.S. 227, 240–241, 57 S.Ct. 461, 464, 81 L.Ed. 617, 621 (1937).

[There] is a line of decisions in this Court standing for the proposition that the "voluntary cessation of allegedly illegal conduct does not deprive the tribunal of power to hear and determine the case, i.e., does not make the case moot." [E.g.,] *United States v. W.T. Grant Co.*, 345 U.S. 629, 632, 73 S.Ct. 894, 897, 97 L.Ed. 1303, 1309 (1953). These decisions and the doctrine they reflect would be quite relevant if the question of mootness here had arisen by reason of a unilateral change in the *admissions procedures* of the Law School. For it was the admissions procedures that were the target of this litigation, and a voluntary cessation of the admissions practices complained of could make this case moot only if it could be said with assurance "that 'there is no reasonable expectation that the wrong will be repeated.'" *United States v. W.T. Grant Co.*, supra. Otherwise, "[t]he defendant is free to return to his old ways," id., and this fact would be enough to prevent mootness because of the "public interest in having the legality of the practices settled." Ibid. But mootness in the present case depends not at all upon a "voluntary cessation" of the admissions practices that were the subject of this litigation. It depends, instead, upon the simple fact that DeFunis is now in the final quarter of the final year of his course of study, and the settled and unchallenged policy of the Law School to permit him to complete the term for which he is now enrolled.

It might also be suggested that this case presents a question that is "capable of repetition, yet evading review," *Southern Pacific Terminal Co. v. ICC*, 219 U.S. 498, 515, 31 S.Ct. 279, 283, 55 L.Ed. 310, 316 (1911); *Roe v. Wade*, Ch. 6, Sec. 2 supra], and is thus amenable to federal adjudication even though it might otherwise be considered moot. But DeFunis will never again be required to run the gauntlet of the Law School's admission process, and so the question is certainly not "capable of repetition" so far as he is concerned. Moreover, just because this particular case did not reach the Court until the eve of the petitioner's graduation from law school, it hardly follows that the issue he raises will in the future evade review. If the admissions procedures of the Law School remain unchanged, there is no reason to suppose that a subsequent case attacking those procedures will not come with relative speed to this Court, now that the Supreme Court of Washington has spoken. This case, therefore, in no way presents the exceptional situation in which the *Southern Pacific Terminal* doctrine might permit a departure from "[t]he usual rule in federal cases [that] an actual controversy must exist at stages of appellate or certiorari review, and not simply at the date the action is initiated." *Roe v. Wade*.

[W]e conclude that the Court cannot, consistently with the limitations of Art. III of the Constitution, consider the substantive constitutional issues tendered by the parties.[5]

JUSTICE BRENNAN, with whom JUSTICE DOUGLAS, JUSTICE WHITE, and JUSTICE MARSHALL concur, dissenting.[a]

[Many] weeks of the school term remain, and [a]ny number of unexpected events—illness, economic necessity, even academic failure—might prevent [petitioner's] graduation at the end of the term. Were that misfortune to befall, and were petitioner required to register for yet another term, the prospect that he would again face the hurdle of the admissions policy is real, not fanciful * * *.

In these circumstances, and because the University's position implies no concession that its admissions policy is unlawful, this controversy falls squarely within the Court's long line of decisions holding that the "[m]ere voluntary cessation of allegedly illegal conduct does not moot a case." *United States v.*

---

5. It is suggested in dissent that "[a]ny number of unexpected events—illness, economic necessity, even academic failure—might prevent his graduation at the end of the term." "But such speculative contingencies afford no basis for our passing on the substantive issues [the petitioner] would have us decide," *Hall v. Beals*, 396 U.S. 45, 49, 90 S.Ct. 200, 202, 24 L.Ed.2d 214, 218 (1969), in the absence of "evidence that this is a prospect of 'immediacy and reality.'" *Golden v. Zwickler*, 394 U.S. 103, 109, 89 S.Ct. 956, 960, 22 L.Ed.2d 113, 118 (1969).

a. Douglas, J., also filed a separate dissent on the merits.

Concentrated Phosphate Export Assn., 393 U.S. 199, 203, 89 S.Ct. 361, 364, 21 L.Ed.2d 344, 349 (1968).

[T]he Court concedes that, if petitioner has lost his stake in this controversy, he did so only when he registered for the spring term. But petitioner took that action only after the case had been fully litigated in the state courts, briefs had been filed in this Court, and oral argument had been heard. The case is thus ripe for decision on a fully developed factual record with sharply defined and fully canvassed legal issues.

Moreover, in endeavoring to dispose of this case as moot, the Court clearly disserves the public interest. The constitutional issues which are avoided today concern vast numbers of people, organizations, and colleges and universities, as evidenced by the filing of twenty-six amicus curiae briefs. Few constitutional questions in recent history have stirred as much debate, and they will not disappear. [Because] avoidance of repetitious litigation serves the public interest, that inevitability counsels against mootness determinations, as here, not compelled by the record.

Notes and Questions

1. *Possible bases of mootness doctrine.* Is the principle that "moot cases [are] beyond the judicial power" simply an application of the bar against advisory opinions? A reflection of the fact that "[t]here is no case or controversy once the matter has been resolved"? Charles Alan Wright, *Law of Federal Courts* 62–63 (5th ed. 1994). Or is the doctrine merely a judicially created rule for judicial economy? According to Evan Tsen Lee, *Deconstitutionalizing Justiciability: The Example of Mootness*, 105 Harv.L.Rev. 603, 611 (1992): "The marriage of Article III to the mootness doctrine was remarkably casual. The Supreme Court's first mention of Article III in connection with mootness came in a 1964 case [*Liner v. Jafco, Inc.*, 375 U.S. 301, 84 S.Ct. 391, 11 L.Ed.2d 347 (1964)] found not to be moot at all." Should the point in litigation at which a case becomes moot matter to the justiciability of the dispute? See *Honig v. Doe*, 484 U.S. 305, 108 S.Ct. 592, 98 L.Ed.2d 686 (1988), in which Rehnquist, C.J., concurring, answered in the affirmative, while Scalia, J., dissenting, responded in the negative.[b]

2. *Capable of repetition, yet evading review.* If, in a suit by citizens alleging that a state law has denied them the right to vote, the case is not decided before the election has been held, is the case moot? The Court has held that, under certain circumstances, a case is not moot if the issue presented is "capable of repetition, yet evading review." See, e.g., *Moore v. Ogilvie*, 394 U.S. 814, 89 S.Ct. 1493, 23 L.Ed.2d 1 (1969). In such cases, to what extent should the Court be assured that the litigant before it will again be *personally* affected by the challenged government action? See *Weinstein v. Bradford*, 423 U.S. 147, 96 S.Ct. 347, 46 L.Ed.2d 350 (1975) (requiring a likelihood that the plaintiff personally will be affected).

Is acceptance of jurisdiction in cases capable of repetition, yet evading review incompatible with the view that moot cases are outside Article III? See *Honig v. Doe*, supra (Rehnquist, C.J., concurring).

3. *Mootness and standing.* Although the Court on several occasions had

---

b. See also Gene R. Nichol, Jr., *Moot Cases, Chief Justice Rehnquist, and the Supreme Court*, 22 U.Conn.L.Rev. 703 (1990).

characterized mootness as "the doctrine of standing set in a time frame,"[c] the Court reconsidered that description in FRIENDS OF THE EARTH v. LAIDLAW ENV. SERVS. (TOC), INC., Sec. 2, I supra. After Friends of the Earth sued to enjoin a violation of the environmental laws, the defendants ceased their illegal conduct, and the court of appeals ordered the case dismissed as moot. Reasoning that all elements of Article III standing must persist throughout federal litigation, the lower court found it too unlikely that a judicial remedy would effectively redress any current injury to the plaintiffs.[d] The Court, per GINSBURG, J., reversed, holding that "the Court of Appeals confused mootness with standing": "[T]here are circumstances in which the prospect that a defendant will engage in (or resume) harmful conduct may be too speculative to support standing, but not too speculative to overcome mootness. [Standing] doctrine functions to ensure, among other things, that the scarce resources of the federal courts are devoted to those disputes in which the parties have a concrete stake. In contrast, by the time mootness is an issue, the case has been brought and litigated, often (as here) for years. To abandon the case at an advanced stage may prove more wasteful than frugal. This argument from sunk costs does not license courts to retain jurisdiction over cases in which one or both of the parties plainly lacks a continuing interest [but it] surely highlights an important difference between the two doctrines."

SCALIA, J., joined by Thomas, J., dissented on the ground that the plaintiffs never possessed standing.

4. *Mootness and class actions.* Suppose the *DeFunis* case had been filed as a class action. Would the result have been the same?

(a) In UNITED STATES PAROLE COMM'N v. GERAGHTY, 445 U.S. 388, 100 S.Ct. 1202, 63 L.Ed.2d 479 (1980), a federal prisoner filed a class action challenging the guidelines governing release on parole. The district court denied class certification and rejected the claim on the merits, and Geraghty himself had been released from prison before the case reached the Supreme Court. The Court, per BLACKMUN, J., held the case not moot: "[A]n action brought on behalf of a class does not become moot upon expiration of the named plaintiff's substantive claim, even though class certification has been denied. The proposed representative retains a 'personal stake' in obtaining class certification sufficient to assure that Art. III values are not undermined. If the appeal results in a reversal of the class certification denial, and a class subsequently is properly certified, the merits of the class claim then may be adjudicated pursuant to the holding of *Sosna*."

POWELL, J., joined by Burger, C.J., and Stewart and Rehnquist, JJ., dissented: "The Court makes no effort to identify any injury to respondent that may be redressed by, or any benefit to respondent that may accrue from, a favorable ruling on the certification question. Instead, respondent's 'personal stake' is said to derive from two factors having nothing to do with concrete injury or stake in the outcome. First, the Court finds that the Federal Rules of Civil Procedure create a 'right,' 'analogous to the private attorney general concept,' to have a class certified. Second, the Court thinks that the case retains the 'imperatives of a dispute capable of judicial resolution,' which are identified as (i) a sharply

c. See *Arizonans for Official English v. Arizona*, 520 U.S. 43, 68 n.22, 117 S.Ct. 1055, 1069 n.22, 137 L.Ed.2d 170 (1997), quoting *United States Parole Comm'n v. Geraghty*, 445 U.S. 388, 397, 100 S.Ct. 1202, 1209, 63 L.Ed.2d 479 (1980), in turn quoting Henry Paul Mona-ghan, *Constitutional Adjudication: The Who and When*, 82 Yale L.J. 1363, 1384 (1973).

d. The clearly available remedy under the Clean Water Act on which the "redressability" debate focused was a civil money penalty payable to the government, not to the plaintiffs.

presented issue, (ii) a concrete factual setting, and (iii) a self-interested party actually contesting the case.

"The Court's reliance on some new 'right' inherent in Rule 23 is misplaced. We have held that even Congress may not confer federal court jurisdiction when Art. III does not. Far less so may a rule of procedure which 'shall not be construed to extend [the] jurisdiction of the United States district courts.' Fed.Rule Civ.Proc. 82. [Although] we have refused steadfastly to countenance the 'public action,' the Court's redefinition of the personal stake requirement leaves no principled basis for that practice."

Is Powell, J., correct that *Geraghty* stretches the concept of the plaintiff's having a "personal stake" to the breaking point if not beyond? Can, and should, the implications be limited to mootness determinations in class actions?

(b) Consider Monaghan, supra, at 1366, 1383: "*Marbury's* analogy of constitutional litigation to 'ordinary' common law litigation strongly suggested that the occasions for judicial review were limited to the protection of identifiable and concrete personal rights, similar to those protected by the common law courts. * * * Perhaps more than any other single development, the mushrooming of class actions has rendered the private rights model [of *Marbury*] largely unintelligible."

II. RIPENESS

UNITED PUBLIC WORKERS v. MITCHELL

330 U.S. 75, 67 S.Ct. 556, 91 L.Ed. 754 (1947).

JUSTICE REED delivered the opinion of the Court.

[Appellants, federal civil service employees, sought a federal declaratory judgment that the Hatch Act's prohibition against taking "any active part in political management or in political campaigns" violated their first amendment rights. They also requested injunctive relief. Only one appellant (Poole) had actually violated the Act. The others alleged that they desired to do so by, inter alia, serving as party officials, writing articles and circulating petitions to support candidates, acting as poll watchers, and transporting voters to the polls.[a]]

At the threshold of consideration, we are called upon to decide whether the complaint states a controversy cognizable in this Court. [Except with respect to Poole, the affidavits submitted by the plaintiffs] follow the generality of purpose expressed by the complaint. They declare a desire to act contrary to the rule against political activity but not that the rule has been violated. * * *

As is well known, the federal courts established pursuant to Article III of the Constitution do not render advisory opinions. For adjudication of constitutional issues, "concrete legal issues, presented in actual cases, not abstractions," are requisite. This is as true of declaratory judgments as any other field. These appellants seem clearly to seek advisory opinions upon broad claims of [constitutional rights]. As these appellants are classified employees, they have a right superior to the generality of citizens, [but] the facts of their personal interest in their civil rights, of the general threat of possible interference with those rights by the Civil Service Commission under its rules, if specified things are done by

---

a. One did allege that, at the last congressional election, he wanted to be a poll watcher but was informed by a Civil Service Commission official "that if I used my watcher's certificate, the Civil Service Commission would see that I was dismissed from my job." This matter, the Court found, "had long been moot when this complaint was filed."

appellants, does not make a justiciable case or controversy. Appellants want to engage in "political management and political campaigns," to persuade others to follow appellants' views by discussion, speeches, articles and other acts reasonably designed to secure the selection of appellants' political choices. Such generality of objection is really an attack on the political expediency of the Hatch Act, not the presentation of legal issues. It is beyond the competence of courts to render such a decision.

The power of courts, and ultimately of this Court, to pass upon the constitutionality of acts of Congress arises only when the interests of litigants require the use of this judicial authority for their protection against actual interference. A hypothetical threat is not enough. We can only speculate as to the kinds of political activity the appellants desire to engage in or as to the contents of their proposed public statements or the circumstances of their publication. It would not accord with judicial responsibility to adjudge, in a matter involving constitutionality, between the freedom of the individual and the requirements of public order except when definite rights appear upon the one side and definite prejudicial interferences upon the other.

The Constitution allots the nation's judicial power to the federal courts. Unless these courts respect the limits of that unique authority, they intrude upon powers vested in the legislative or executive branches. [Should] the courts seek to expand their power so as to bring under their jurisdiction ill-defined controversies over constitutional issues, they would become the organ of political theories. Such abuse of judicial power would properly meet rebuke and restriction from other branches. [No] threat of interference by the Commission with rights of these appellants appears beyond that implied by the existence of the law and the regulations.

[Poole, however] has been charged by the Commission with political activity and a proposed order for his removal from his position adopted subject to his right under Commission procedure to [reply]. Since Poole admits that he violated the rule against political activity and that removal from office is therefore mandatory under the [act,] we see no reason why a declaratory judgment action, even though constitutional issues are involved, does not lie. [The Court then rejected Poole's challenge on the merits.]

JUSTICE DOUGLAS, dissenting in part:

[What] these appellants propose to do is plain enough. If they do what they propose to do, it is clear that they will be discharged * * *.[2] The threat against them is real not fanciful, immediate not remote. The case is therefore an actual not a hypothetical one. [T]o require these employees first to suffer the hardship of a discharge is not only to make them incur a penalty; it makes inadequate, if not wholly illusory, any legal remedy which they may have. [At] least to the average person in the lower income groups the burden of taking that course is irreparable injury * * *.[b]

---

2. The case is, therefore, unlike those situations where the Court refused to entertain actions for declaratory judgments, the state of facts being hypothetical in the sense that the challenge was to statutes which had not as yet been construed or their specific application known.

b. Black, J., agreed with Douglas, J., "that all the petitioners' complaints state a case or controversy" and further that "the challenged provision is unconstitutional on its face." Rutledge, J., agreed with Black, J., as to Poole; as to the others, however, the controversy "is not yet appropriate for the discretionary exercise of declaratory judgment jurisdiction." Frankfurter, J., concurred in the Court's opinion. Murphy and Jackson, JJ., took no part.

Notes and Questions

1. *Ripeness and standing.* Consider Erwin Chemerinsky, *Federal Jurisdiction* § 2.4.1 at 114–16 (3d ed.1999): "Ripeness [is] a justiciability doctrine determining *when* review is appropriate. [Specifically], the ripeness doctrine seeks to separate matters that are premature for review because the injury is speculative and never may occur, from those cases that are appropriate for federal court action.

"Although the phrasing makes the questions of who may sue and when may they sue seem distinct, in practice there is an obvious overlap between the doctrines of standing and ripeness. If no injury has occurred, the plaintiff might be denied standing or the case might be dismissed as not ripe. * * *

"To the extent that the substantive requirements overlap and the result will be the same regardless of whether the issue is characterized as ripeness or standing, little turns on the choice of the label. However, for the sake of clarity, especially in those cases where the law of standing and ripeness is not identical, ripeness can be given a narrower definition that distinguishes it from standing and explains the existing case law. Ripeness properly should be understood as involving the question of *when may a party seek preenforcement review of a statute or regulation.* Customarily, a person can challenge the legality of a statute or regulation only when he or she is prosecuted for violating it. At that time, a defense can be that the law is invalid, for example, as being unconstitutional."

As thus defined, does "ripeness" doctrine fulfill a function independent of standing doctrine? Compare *Abbott Laboratories v. Gardner*, 387 U.S. 136, 148, 87 S.Ct. 1507, 1515, 18 L.Ed.2d 681, 691 (1967) (asserting that the "basic rationale" of ripeness doctrine is "to prevent the courts, through avoidance of premature adjudication, from entangling themselves in abstract disagreements").

Is it a further function of ripeness doctrine, at least in some cases, to narrow the scope of disputes? Compare LUJAN v. NATIONAL WILDLIFE FEDERATION, 497 U.S. 871, 110 S.Ct. 3177, 111 L.Ed.2d 695 (1990), per Scalia, J., which held that the Interior Department's promulgation of a "land withdrawal review program" with the goal of making more federally owned land available for commercial uses was not "agency action" or "final agency action" under the Administrative Procedure Act (APA), and was not "ripe" for review: A "wholesale" challenge to the announced program was not appropriate. "[A] regulation is not ordinarily considered the type of agency action 'ripe' for judicial review under the APA until the scope of the controversy has been reduced to more manageable proportions, and its factual components fleshed out, by some concrete action applying the regulation to the claimant's situation in a fashion that harms or threatens to harm him."[c]

2. *Ripeness criteria.* In a much quoted opinion in *Abbott Laboratories*, the Court characterized the ripeness inquiry as having two aspects: (i) "the hardship to the parties of withholding court consideration" and (ii) "the fitness of the issues for judicial decision." How would these criteria apply to *Mitchell*? Were the plaintiffs in that case subjected to a considerable hardship—a choice between foregoing possibly protected political activity and risking the loss of their jobs? If

c. The Court, citing *Abbott Laboratories*, noted that a "major exception" to this general principle "is a substantive rule which as a practical matter requires the plaintiff to adjust his conduct immediately. Such agency action is 'ripe' for review at once, whether or not explicit statutory review apart from the APA is provided."

the issues were unfit for judicial resolution, in what sense were they unfit? Does the majority accept the proposition that "what these appellants propose to do is plain enough [and] if they do what they propose to do, it is clear that they will be discharged"? If not, should appellants have written their proposed speeches and letters and submitted them to the Court? Or should they have first submitted them to the Commission? But what if the Commission took the position that it would not give "advisory opinions"?

Are the criteria articulated in *Abbott Labs* sound ones?[d] Is the ripeness requirement, as distinguished from standing, constitutionally mandated? See Gene R. Nichol, Jr., *Ripeness and the Constitution*, 54 U.Chi.L.Rev. 153 (1987) (arguing that it is not).

3. *Ripeness and the merits.* (a) ADLER v. BOARD OF EDUC., (1952), 342 U.S. 485, 72 S.Ct. 380, 96 L.Ed. 517 (1952), upheld a state law disqualifying from employment in public schools any persons who advocate overthrow of the government by force, or who belong to an organization that so advocates, or who utter any treasonable or seditious words, or do any treasonable or seditious acts. The appellants, who sought a declaratory judgment in state court, were taxpayers, parents of school children, and teachers. The Court discussed only the merits despite FRANKFURTER, J.'s dissent that the case should be dismissed for want of "standing of the parties and ripeness of the constitutional question." In addition to arguing that both the scope of the statutory provisions and the definition of key terms were unclear, he stated: "The allegations in the present action fall short of those found insufficient in [*Mitchell*]. These teachers do not allege that they have engaged in proscribed conduct or that they have any intention to do so. They do not suggest that they have been, or are, deterred from supporting causes or from joining organizations for fear of the [statute's] interdict, except to say generally that the system complained of will have this effect on teachers as a group. They do not assert that they are threatened with action under the law, or that steps are imminent whereby they would incur the hazard of punishment for conduct innocent at the time."

Was *Mitchell* "overruled"? Consider Fritz W. Scharpf, *Judicial Review and the Political Question: A Functional Analysis*, 75 Yale L.J. 517, 531–32 (1966): "[In *Mitchell*] the Court may well have regarded the constitutional balance between the political rights of civil servants and the legitimate public interest in a neutral civil service as an extremely close one, depending very much upon the actual scope of enforcement and upon the concrete nature of the activities against which sanctions were to be applied. In [*Adler*], the *Mitchell* rule should have applied a fortiori. [But, for the Court majority,] the statute was clearly constitutional * * *. Justices Black and Douglas, dissenting, also saw no reason to worry about standing or ripeness. For them the statute was clearly unconstitutional * * *. The conclusion seems inevitable that Justice Frankfurter alone advocated avoidance because he alone defined the substantive issues in terms of a close balance between the equally legitimate interests of society in its self-preservation and of the teachers in their freedom of thought, inquiry and expression. Thus, in order to strike this balance in the particular case, Frankfurter would have had to know much more about the actual practices of enforcement and the degree of surveillance to which the teachers would be subjected than the bare text of an unenforced statute permitted him to know."[e]

d. For an exploration of the economic costs and benefits of the "anticipatory adjudication" with which ripeness doctrine is principally concerned, see William M. Landes & Richard A. Posner, *The Economics of Anticipatory Adjudication*, 23 J. Legal Stud. 683 (1994).

e. The Court more recently took an approach similar to that of *Mitchell* in *Renne v.*

(b) According to Nichol, supra, at 165–67: "The ripeness requirement consistently has been molded to meet the dictates of the substantive claim on the merits. For several decades, the Court has allowed pre-enforcement challenges to laws regulating speech. Laws threatening sanctions for expression are said to 'chill' potential speech. Rather than force citizens to curtail the exercise of their asserted first amendment rights in order to avoid prosecution, courts have permitted facial challenges to regulations of expression even before the institution of other legal proceedings.[f] [As] the Supreme Court ruled in *Keyishian v. Board of Regents*, [Ch. 7, Sec. 9, II,] it is not permissible to inhibit first amendment expression by forcing a teacher to 'guess what conduct or utterance may lose him his position' by violating a 'complicated and intricate scheme' of regulation.

"The law of the takings clause of the fifth amendment, however, has followed a very different path. The Supreme Court has characterized the takings inquiry as turning on 'ad hoc factual' determinations directed to 'particular estimates of [the] economic impact' on the property in question. [P]art of the concrete factual setting necessary to the demonstration of a takings claim, apparently, is a showing that the regulatory authority would deny approval for all uses that would enable the plaintiff to obtain a 'reasonable return' on its investment [citing *Penn Central Transp. Co. v. New York City*, Ch. 5, Sec. 4, II]. [It] is obviously more difficult, therefore, to present a ripe takings claim than a ripe first amendment challenge. [The] common theme [is] the examination of what it takes to state a concrete cause of action under the substantive principles upon which the claim is based."

4. *Remote or hypothetical threat of injury.* (a) Suppose plaintiffs wish to challenge the constitutionality of a state statute that the state has not enforced for a number of years. Is a challenge ripe, or is the threat of enforcement too remote and conjectural? Compare *Poe v. Ullman*, 367 U.S. 497, 81 S.Ct. 1752, 6 L.Ed.2d 989 (1961), finding that a long pattern of non-enforcement rendered a challenge to a state statute prohibiting the use of contraceptive devices non-justiciable, with *Epperson v. Arkansas*, Ch. 8, Sec. 1, III, finding no ripeness difficulty with a challenge to a forty-year-old statute making the teaching of evolution unlawful, despite the absence of any record of enforcement. Is it relevant to ripeness analysis whether the issue presented on the merits is a hard one?

(b) In O'SHEA v. LITTLETON, 414 U.S. 488, 94 S.Ct. 669, 38 L.Ed.2d 674 (1974), black and white residents who had protested racial discrimination in Cairo, Illinois obtained a federal injunction against state judicial officers, alleging a deliberate pattern of illegal bail, sentencing, and law enforcement practices against them due to their race and exercise of first amendment rights. Although some respondents "had actually been defendants in proceedings before petitioners and had suffered from the alleged unconstitutional practices," the Court, per WHITE, J., reversed: "Of course, past wrongs are evidence bearing on whether there is a real and immediate threat of repeated injury. [But] respondents here have not pointed to any imminent prosecutions contemplated against any of their number and they naturally do not suggest that any one of them expects to violate valid criminal laws. [Thus], the threat of injury from the alleged course of conduct they attack is simply too remote to satisfy the case-or-controversy requirement and permit adjudication by a federal court."[g]

Geary, 501 U.S. 312, 111 S.Ct. 2331, 115 L.Ed.2d 288 (1991), in which it held unripe a challenge to a California constitutional provision prohibiting political parties from endorsing candidates for non-partisan offices.

f. For detailed consideration of the question of whether laws allegedly violative of the first amendment should be held facially invalid, see Ch. 7, Sec. 1, III, C.

g. For similar analysis, see *Rizzo v. Goode*, 423 U.S. 362, 96 S.Ct. 598, 46 L.Ed.2d 561 (1976).

Even if there were "an existing case or controversy," however, "a proper balance in the concurrent operation of federal and state courts" precludes federal equitable relief. The decision below "would contemplate interruption of state proceedings to adjudicate assertions of noncompliance by petitioners. This seems to us nothing less than an ongoing federal audit of state criminal proceedings [that] is antipathetic to established principles of comity.[h] * * * Respondents have failed, moreover, to establish the basic requisites of the issuance of equitable relief in these circumstances—the likelihood of substantial and immediate irreparable injury, and the inadequacy of remedies at law. [I]f any of the respondents are ever prosecuted and face trial, or if they are illegally sentenced, there are available state and federal procedures which could provide relief from the wrongful conduct alleged."[i]

Is *O'Shea* consistent with *Epperson*? Note that the plaintiffs in *Epperson* wished to quarrel with the statute book, whereas those in *O'Shea* challenged an alleged pattern of official conduct and sought a remedy broadly affecting the management and administration of law enforcement agencies. Should either or both of these factors bear on the determination of ripeness?

(c) Suppose there is serious doubt about the constitutionality of an important federal statute, enacted to encourage the development of nuclear power. Is it relevant to the determination of ripeness that delayed resolution of the constitutional question would frustrate a key purpose of the statute—"the elimination of doubts concerning the scope of private liability"? See *Duke Power Co. v. Carolina Environmental Study Group, Inc.*, 438 U.S. 59, 98 S.Ct. 2620, 57 L.Ed.2d 595 (1978), discussed in Jonathan D. Varat, *Variable Justiciability and the Duke Power Case*, 58 Tex.L.Rev. 273 (1980). Should the determination of ripeness be influenced by the fact that Congress wishes a determination of constitutionality as quickly as possible? See *Buckley v. Valeo*, 424 U.S. 1, 113–18, 96 S.Ct. 612, 680–82, 46 L.Ed.2d 659, 741–44 (1976), Ch. 7, Sec. 10.

---

h. Compare *Allee v. Medrano*, 416 U.S. 802, 94 S.Ct. 2191, 40 L.Ed.2d 566 (1974), upholding a federal injunction against state police disruption of unionization efforts. For further discussion of the delicacy of federal interference with state law enforcement proceedings, see Richard Fallon, Daniel Meltzer, & David Shapiro, *Hart and Wechsler's The Federal Courts and the Federal System*, Chap. 10 (4th Ed. 1996).

i. Blackmun, J., concurred in the first part of the Court's opinion. Douglas, J., joined by Brennan and Marshall, JJ., dissented.

Appendix A

THE JUSTICES OF THE SUPREME COURT

Originally prepared by JOHN J. COUND

Professor of Law, University of Minnesota

The following data summarize the prior public careers of the justices of the Supreme Court. The first dates in parentheses are those of birth and death; these are followed by the name of the appointing President and the dates of service on the Court. The states in which the justices were residing when appointed and their political affiliations at that time are then given. In detailing prior careers, I have followed chronological order, with two exceptions: I have listed first that a justice was a signer of the Declaration of Independence or the Federal Constitution, and I have indicated state legislative experience only once for each justice. I have not distinguished between different bodies in the state legislature, and I have omitted service in the Continental Congresses. Private practice, except where deemed especially significant, and law teaching have been omitted, except where a justice was primarily engaged therein upon appointment. (Blackmun, Breyer, Burger, Douglas, Fortas, Ginsburg, Holmes, Hughes, Kennedy, L.Q.C. Lamar, Lurton, McReynolds, Murphy, Roberts, W. Rutledge, Scalia, Stevens, Stone and Van Devanter, in addition to Taft and Frankfurter, had all taught before going on the Court; Story, Strong and Wilson taught while on the court or after leaving it). The activity in which a justice was engaged upon appointment has been italicized. Figures in parentheses indicate years of service in the position. In only a few cases, a justice's extra-Court or post-Court activity has been indicated or some other note made. An asterisk designates the Chief Justices.

The accompanying Table of Justices on pages [3] and [4] has been planned so that the composition of the Court at any time can be readily ascertained.

(This material has been compiled from a great number of sources, but special acknowledgment must be made to the *Dictionary of American Biography* (Charles Scribner's Sons), the A.N. Marquis Company works, and Ewing, *The Judges of the Supreme Court, 1789–1937* (University of Minnesota Press, 1938).)

BALDWIN, HENRY (1780–1844; Jackson, 1830–1844). Pa.Dem.—U.S., House of Representatives (5). *Private practice.*

BARBOUR, PHILIP P. (1783–1841; Jackson, 1836–1841). Va.Dem.—Va., Legislature (2). U.S., House of Representatives (14). Va., Judge, General Court (2);

President, State Constitutional Convention, 1829–30, *U.S., Judge, District Court (5).*

BLACK, HUGO L. (1886–1971; F.D. Roosevelt, 1937–1971). Ala.Dem.—Captain, Field Artillery, World War I. Ala., Judge, Police Court (1); County Solicitor (2). *U.S., Senate (10).*

BLACKMUN, HARRY A. (1908–1999; Nixon, 1970–1994). Minn.Rep.—Resident Counsel, Mayo Clinic, (10). *U.S., Judge, Court of Appeals (11).*

BLAIR, JOHN (1732–1800; Washington, 1789–1796). Va.Fed.—Signer, U.S. Constitution, 1787. Va., Legislature (9); Judge and Chief Justice, General Court (2), *Court of Appeals (9).* His opinion in *Commonwealth v. Caton,* 4 Call 5, 20 (Va.1782), is one of the earliest expressions of the doctrine of judicial review.

BLATCHFORD, SAMUEL (1820–1893; Arthur, 1882–1893). N.Y.Rep.—U.S., Judge, District Court (5); *Circuit Court (10).*

BRADLEY, JOSEPH P. (1803–1892; Grant, 1870–1892). N.J.Rep.—Actuary. *Private practice.*

BRANDEIS, LOUIS D. (1856–1941; Wilson, 1916–1939). Mass.Dem.—*Private practice.* Counsel, variously for the government, for industry, and "for the people," in numerous administrative and judicial proceedings, both state and federal.

BRENNAN, WILLIAM J. (1906–1997; Eisenhower, 1956–1990). N.J.Dem.—U.S. Army, World War II. N.J., Judge, Superior Court (1); Appellate Division (2); *Supreme Court (4).*

BREWER, DAVID J. (1837–1910; B. Harrison, 1889–1910). Kans.Rep.—Kans., Judge, County Criminal and Probate Court (1), District Court (4); County Attorney (1); Judge, Supreme Court (14), *U.S., Judge, Circuit Court (5).*

BREYER, STEPHEN GERALD (1937–____; Clinton, 1994–____). Mass. Dem.—U.S., Special Assistant to Assistant Attorney General for Antitrust (2); Assistant Special Prosecutor (during Watergate) (1); Special Counsel of the Senate Judiciary Committee (1); Chief Counsel, same (2); Judge, Court of Appeals (10); Member (while a judge) of the United States Sentencing Commission (4), and of the Judicial Conference of the United States (4); *Chief Judge, Court of Appeals (4).*

BROWN, HENRY, B. (1836–1913; B. Harrison, 1890–1906). Mich.Rep.—U.S., Assistant U.S. Attorney (5). Mich., Judge, Circuit Court (1). *U.S., Judge, District Court (15).*

1789 1790 1791 1793 1795 1796 1798 1799 1801 1804 1806 1807 1811 1823 1826 1829 1830 1835 1836 1837 1841 1845 1846 1851 1853 1858 1862 1863 1864 1865 1867 1870 1872 1874 1877 1880 1881 1882 1888 1889 1890 1892 1893 1894 1895 1898 1902 1903 1906

Jay	Rutledge, J.	Cushing	Wilson	Blair	Iredell		Catron	McKinley	Field
Rutledge, J.	Johnson, T.				Moore	Todd			
Ellsworth	Paterson		Washington	Chase, Samuel	Johnson, W.	Trimble		Campbell	
Marshall, J.	Livingston	Story		Duval		McLean		Davis	
Taney	Thompson		Baldwin	Barbour	Wayne				
	Nelson	Woodbury	Grier	Daniel		Swayne			
		Curtis							
		Clifford		Miller			Harlan		
Chase, Salmon			Strong		Bradley				
Waite	Hunt		Woods			Matthews			
Fuller	Blatchford	Gray	Lamar, L.	Brown	Shiras	Brewer		McKenna	
	White, E.		Jackson, H.						
			Peckham						
		Holmes		Moody	Day				

Catron died in 1865, Wayne in 1867; their positions were abolished by Congress to prevent their being filled by President Johnson; a new position was created in 1869, which traditionally has been regarded as a re-creation of Wayne's seat.

1909 1910 1912 1914 1916 1921 1922 1923 1925 1930 1932 1937 1938 1939 1940 1941 1943 1945 1946 1949 1953 1955 1956 1957 1958 1962 1965 1966 1967 1968 1969 1970 1972 1975 1981 1982 1983 1986 1987 1988 1989 1990 1991 1993 1994

Stone · · Jackson, R.   Harlan   Rehnquist · · Scalia

Pitney   Sanford Roberts   Burton   Stewart   O'Connor

Hughes Clarke Sutherland   Reed   Whittaker White, B.   Ginsburg

Butler   Murphy   Clark   Marshall, T.   Thomas, C.

Lamar, J Brandeis   Douglas   Stevens

Lurton McReynolds   Byrnes Rutledge   Minton   Brennan   Souter

Cardozo Frankfurter   Goldberg Fortas   Blackmun   Breyer

· · Van Devanter   Black   Powell   Kennedy

White, E.   Taft   Hughes   Stone Vinson Warren   Burger   Rehnquist

** Fuller died in 1910 and White was named Chief Justice. Hughes resigned in 1941, and Stone was named Chief Justice. Burger resigned in 1986 and Rehnquist was named Chief Justice.

1909 1910 1912 1914 1916 1921 1922 1923 1925 1930 1932 1937 1938 1939 1940 1941 1943 1945 1946 1949 1953 1955 1956 1957 1958 1962 1965 1966 1967 1968 1969 1970 1972 1975 1981 1982 1983 1986 1987 1988 1989 1990 1991 1993 1994

*BURGER, WARREN E. (1907–1995; Nixon, 1969–1986). Va.Rep.—U.S., Assistant Attorney General, Civil Division (3), *Judge, Court of Appeals (13)*.

BURTON, HAROLD H. (1888–1964; Truman, 1945–1958). Ohio Rep.—Capt., U.S.A., World War I. Ohio, Legislature (2). Mayor, Cleveland, O. (5). *U.S., Senate (4)*.

BUTLER, PIERCE (1866–1939; Harding, 1922–1939). Minn.Dem.—Minn., County Attorney (4). *Private practice.*

BYRNES, JAMES F. (1879–1972; F.D. Roosevelt, 1941–1942). S.C.Dem.— S.C., Solicitor, Circuit Court (2). U.S., House of Representatives (14); *Senate (12).* Resigned from the Court to become U.S. Director of Economic Stabilization.

CAMPBELL, JOHN A. (1811–1889; Pierce, 1853–1861). Ala.Dem.—*Private practice.* After his resignation, he became Assistant Secretary of War, C.S.A.

CARDOZO, BENJAMIN N. (1870–1938; Hoover, 1932–1938). N.Y.Dem.— N.Y., Judge, Supreme Court (6 weeks); Associate Judge and *Chief Judge, Court of Appeals (18).*

CATRON, JOHN (1778–1865; Van Buren, 1837–1865). Tenn.Dem.—Tenn., Judge and Chief Justice, Supreme Court of Errors and Appeals (10). *Private practice.*

*CHASE, SALMON P. (1808–1873; Lincoln 1864–1873). Ohio Rep.—U.S., Senate (6). Ohio, Governor (4). *U.S., Secretary of the Treasury (3).*

CHASE, SAMUEL (1741–1811; Washington, 1796–1811). Md.Fed.—Signer, U.S., Declaration of Independence, 1776. Md., Legislature (20); Chief Judge, Court of Oyer and Terminer (2), *General Court (5).* Impeached and acquitted, 1804–05.

CLARK, TOM C. (1899–1977; Truman, 1949–1967). Tex.Dem.—U.S. Army, World War I. Tex., Civil District Attorney (5). U.S., Assistant Attorney General (2), *Attorney General (4).*

CLARKE, JOHN H. (1857–1945; Wilson, 1916–1922). Ohio Dem.—*U.S. Judge, District Court (2).*

CLIFFORD, NATHAN (1803–1881; Buchanan, 1858–1881). Me.Dem.—Me., Legislature (4); Attorney General (4). U.S., House of Representatives (4); Attorney General (2); Minister Plenipotentiary to Mexico, 1848. *Private practice.*

CURTIS, BENJAMIN R. (1809–1874; Fillmore, 1851–1857). Mass.Whig.— Mass., Legislature (1). *Private practice.*

CUSHING, WILLIAM (1732–1810; Washington, 1789–1810). Mass.Fed.— Mass., Judge, Superior Court (3); Justice and *Chief Justice, Supreme Judicial Court (14).*

DANIEL, PETER V. (1784–1860; Van Buren, 1841–1860). Va.Dem.—Va., Legislature (3); Member, Privy Council (23). *U.S., Judge, District Court (5).*

DAVIS, DAVID (1815–1886; Lincoln, 1862–1877). Ill.Rep.—Ill., Legislature (2); *Judge, Circuit Court (14).* His resignation to become U.S. Senator upset the agreed-upon composition of the Hayes–Tilden Electoral Commission.

DAY, WILLIAM R. (1849–1923; T. Roosevelt, 1903–1922). Ohio Rep.—Ohio, Judge, Court of Common Pleas (4). U.S., Assistant Secretary of State (1), Secretary of State (½); Chairman, U.S. Peace Commissioners, 1898; *Judge, Circuit Court of Appeals (4).*

DOUGLAS, WILLIAM O. (1898–1980; F.D. Roosevelt, 1939–1975). Conn. Dem.—Pvt., U.S. Army, World War I. *U.S., Chairman, Securities and Exchange Commission (3).* His was the longest tenure in the history of the Court.

DUVAL(L), GABRIEL (1752–1844; Madison, 1811–1935). Md.Rep.—Declined to serve as delegate, U.S. Constitutional Convention, 1787. Md., State Council (3). U.S., House of Representatives (2). Md., Judge, General Court (6). *U.S., Comptroller of the Treasury (9).*

*ELLSWORTH, OLIVER (1745–1807; Washington, 1796–1800). Conn.Fed.— Delegate, U.S. Constitutional Convention, 1787. Conn., Legislature (2); Member, Governor's Council (4); Judge, Superior Court (5). *U.S., Senate (7).*

FIELD, STEPHEN J. (1816–1899; Lincoln, 1863–1897). Calif.Dem.—*Calif.,* Justice, and *Chief Justice, Supreme Court (6).*

FORTAS, ABE (1910–1982; L.B. Johnson, 1965–1969). Tenn.Dem.—U.S. Government attorney and consultant (A.A.A., S.E.C., P.W.A., Dep't of Interior (9); Undersecretary of Interior (4). *Private practice in Washington, D.C.* Nominated as Chief Justice; nomination withdrawn, 1968. Resigned.

FRANKFURTER, FELIX (1882–1965; F.D. Roosevelt, 1939–1962). Mass. Independent.—U.S., Assistant U.S. Attorney (4); Law Officer, War Department, Bureau of Insular Affairs (3); Assistant to Secretary of War (1). *Professor of Law (25).*

*FULLER, MELVILLE W. (1833–1910; Cleveland, 1888–1910). Ill.Dem.—Ill., Legislature (2). *Private practice.*

GINSBURG, RUTH BADER (1933–____; Clinton, 1993–____); N.Y.Dem.— *U.S., Judge, Court of Appeals (13).*

GOLDBERG, ARTHUR J. (1908–1990; Kennedy, 1962–1965). Ill.Dem.—Major, U.S.A., World War II. General Counsel, USW–AFL–CIO (13). *U.S., Secretary of Labor (1).* Resigned to become Ambassador to U.N.

GRAY, HORACE (1828–1902; Arthur, 1881–1902). Mass.Rep.—*Mass.,* Associate Justice and *Chief Justice, Supreme Judicial Court (18).*

GRIER, ROBERT O. (1794–1870; Polk, 1846–1870). Pa.Dem.—*Pa., Presiding Judge, District Court (13).*

HARLAN, JOHN M. (1833–1911; Hayes, 1877–1911). Ky.Rep.—Ky., Judge, County Court (1). Col., Union Army, 1861–63. Ky., Attorney General (4). U.S., Member, President's Louisiana Commission, 1877. *Private practice.* Grandfather of:

HARLAN, JOHN M. (1899–1971; Eisenhower, 1955–1971). N.Y.Rep.—Col., U.S.A.A.F., World War II. N.Y. Chief Counsel, State Crime Commission (2). *U.S., Judge, Court of Appeals (1).*

HOLMES, OLIVER W., JR. (1841–1935; T. Roosevelt, 1902–1932). Mass. Rep.—Lt. Col., Mass. Volunteers, Civil War. *Mass.,* Associate Justice, and *Chief Justice, Supreme Judicial Court (20).*

*HUGHES, CHARLES E. (1862–1948; Taft, 1910–1916, and Hoover, 1930– 1941). N.Y.Rep.—N.Y., Counsel, legislative committees investigating gas and insurance industries, 1905–06. U.S., Special Assistant to Attorney General for Coal Investigation, 1906. *N.Y., Governor (3).* [Between appointments to the Supreme Court: Presidential Nominee, Republican Party, 1916. U.S., Secretary of State (4). *Member, Permanent Court of Arbitration, The Hague (4). Judge, Permanent Court of International Justice (2).*] Chief Justice on second appointment.

HUNT, WARD (1810–1886; Grant, 1872–1882). N.Y.Rep.—N.Y., Legislature (2). Mayor of Utica, N.Y. (1). N.Y. Associate Judge, and Chief Judge, Court of Appeals (4); *Commissioner of Appeals (4).* He did not sit from 1879 to his retirement in 1882.

IREDELL, JAMES (1750–1799; Washington, 1790–1799). N.C.Fed.—Comptroller of Customs (6), Collector of Port (2), Edenton, N.C., N.C., Judge, Superior

Court (½); Attorney General (2); Member, Council of State, 1787; *Reviser of Statutes (3).*

JACKSON, HOWELL E. (1832–1895; B. Harrison, 1893–1895). Tenn.Dem.—Tenn., Judge, Court of Arbitration (4); Legislature (1). U.S. Senate (5); *Judge, Circuit Court of Appeals (7).*

JACKSON, ROBERT H. (1892–1954; F.D. Roosevelt, 1941–1954). N.Y.Dem.—U.S., General Counsel, Bureau of Internal Revenue (2); Assistant Attorney General (2); Solicitor General (2); *Attorney General (1).*

*JAY, JOHN (1745–1829; Washington, 1789–1795). N.Y.Fed.—N.Y., Chief Justice, Supreme Court (2). U.S., Envoy to Spain (2); Commissioner, Treaty of Paris, 1782–83; Secretary for Foreign Affairs (6). Co-author, The Federalist.

JOHNSON, THOMAS (1732–1819; Washington, 1791–1793). Md.Fed.—Md., Brigadier–General, Militia (1); Legislature (5); Governor (2); *Chief Judge, General Court (1).*

JOHNSON, WILLIAM (1771–1834; Jefferson, 1804–1834). S.C.Rep.—S.C., Legislature (4); *Judge, Court of Common Pleas (6).*

KENNEDY, ANTHONY M. (1936–____; Reagan, 1988–____). Calif.Rep.—Calif. Army National Guard (1). *U.S., Judge, Court of Appeals (11).*

LAMAR, JOSEPH R. (1857–1916; Taft, 1910–1916). Ga.Dem. Ga., Legislature (3); Commissioner to Codify Laws (3); Associate Justice, Supreme Court (4). *Private practice.*

LAMAR, LUCIUS Q.C. (1825–1893; Cleveland, 1888–1893). Miss.Dem.—Ga., Legislature (2). U.S., House of Representatives (4). Draftsman, Mississippi Ordinance of Secession, 1861. C.S.A., Lt. Col. (1); Commissioner to Russia (1); Judge–Advocate, III Corps. Army of No. Va. (1). U.S., House of Representatives (4); Senate (8); *Secretary of the Interior (3).*

LIVINGSTON, (HENRY) BROCKHOLST (1757–1823; Jefferson, 1806–1823). N.Y.Rep.—Lt. Col., Continental Army. *N.Y., Judge, Supreme Court (4).*

LURTON, HORACE H. (1844–1914; Taft, 1909–1914). Tenn.Dem.—Sgt. Major, C.S.A. Tenn., Chancellor (3); Associate Justice and Chief Justice, Supreme Court (7). *U.S., Judge, Circuit Court of Appeals (16).*

McKENNA, JOSEPH (1843–1926; McKinley, 1898–1925). Calif.Rep.—Calif., District Attorney (2); Legislature (2). U.S., House of Representatives (7); *Judge, Circuit Court of Appeals (5); Attorney General (1).*

McKINLEY, JOHN (1780–1852; Van Buren, 1837–1852). Ala.Dem.—Legislature (4). U.S., Senate (5); House of Representatives (2); *re-elected to Senate,* but appointed to Court before taking seat.

McLEAN, JOHN (1785–1861; Jackson, 1829–1861). Ohio Dem.—U.S., House of Representatives (4). Ohio, Judge, Supreme Court (6). U.S., Commissioner, General Land Office (1); *Postmaster-General (6).*

McREYNOLDS, JAMES C. (1862–1946; Wilson, 1914–1941). Tenn.Dem.—U.S., Assistant Attorney General (4); *Attorney General (1).*

*MARSHALL, JOHN (1755–1835; J. Adams, 1801–1835). Va.Fed.—Va., Legislature (7); U.S., Envoy to France (1); House of Representatives (1); *Secretary of State (1).*

MARSHALL, THURGOOD (1908–1993; L.B. Johnson, 1967–1991). N.Y.Dem.—Counsel, Legal Defense and Educational Fund, NAACP (21). U.S., Judge, Court of Appeals (4); *Solicitor General (2)*.

MATTHEWS, STANLEY (1824–1889; Garfield, 1881–1889). Ohio Rep.—Ohio, Judge, Court of Common Pleas (2); Legislature (3). U.S., District Attorney (3). Col., Ohio Volunteers. Ohio, Judge, Superior Court (2). Counsel before Hayes–Tilden Electoral Commission, 1877. U.S., Senate (2). *Private practice.* His first appointment to the Court by Hayes in 1881 was not acted upon by the Senate.

MILLER, SAMUEL F. (1816–1890; Lincoln, 1862–1890). Iowa Rep.—Physician. *Private practice.*

MINTON, SHERMAN (1890–1965; Truman, 1949–1956). Ind.Dem.—Capt., Inf., World War I. U.S., Senate (6); *Judge, Court of Appeals (8)*.

MOODY, WILLIAM H. (1853–1917; T. Roosevelt, 1906–1910). Mass.Rep.— U.S., District Attorney (5), House of Representatives (7); Secretary of the Navy (2); *Attorney General (2)*.

MOORE, ALFRED (1755–1810; J. Adams, 1799–1804). N.C.Fed.—N.C., Col. of Militia; Legislature (2); Attorney General (9). U.S. Commissioner, Treaty with Cherokee Nation (1); *N.C., Judge, Superior Court (1)*.

MURPHY, FRANK (1893–1949; F.D. Roosevelt, 1940–1949). Mich.Dem.— Capt., Inf., World War I. U.S., Assistant U.S. Attorney (1). Mich., Judge, Recorder's Court (7). Mayor, Detroit, Mich. (3). U.S., Governor–General, and High Commissioner, P.I. (3). Mich., Governor (2). *U.S., Attorney General (1)*.

NELSON, SAMUEL (1792–1873; Tyler, 1845–1872). N.Y.Dem.—N.Y., Judge, Circuit Court (8); Associate Justice, and *Chief Justice, Supreme Court (14)*.

O'CONNOR, SANDRA DAY (1930–____; Reagan, 1981–____). Ariz.Rep.— Calif., Deputy County Attorney (2); Ariz., Assistant Attorney General (4); Legislature (6); Judge, Superior Court (4); *Court of Appeals (2)*.

PATERSON, WILLIAM (1745–1806; Washington, 1793–1806). N.J.Fed.—Signer, U.S. Constitution, 1787. N.J., Legislature (2); Attorney General (7). U.S., Senate (1). *N.J., Governor (3)*. Reviser of English Pre–Revolutionary Statutes in Force in N.J.

PECKHAM, RUFUS W. (1838–1909; Cleveland, 1895–1909). N.Y.Dem.—N.Y., District Attorney (1); Justice, Supreme Court (3); *Associate Judge, Court of Appeals (9)*.

PITNEY, MAHLON (1858–1924; Taft, 1912–1922). N.J.Rep.—U.S., House of Representatives (4). N.J., Legislature (2); Associate Justice, Supreme Court (7); Chancellor (4).

POWELL, LEWIS F. (1907–1998; Nixon, 1972–1987). Va.Dem.—Col., U.S.A.A.F., World War II. U.S., Special Assistant to the Attorney General on Selective Service (4). Va., Member, State Board of Education (8). *Private practice.*

REED, STANLEY F. (1884–1980; F.D. Roosevelt, 1938–1957). Ky.Dem.—Ky., Legislature (4). 1st Lt., U.S.A., World War I. U.S., General Counsel, Federal Farm Board (3); General Counsel, Reconstruction Finance Corporation (3); *Solicitor General (3)*.

*REHNQUIST, WILLIAM H. (1924–____; Nixon, later Reagan, 1972–____). Ariz.Rep.—U.S.A.F., World War II. *U.S., Assistant Attorney General, Office of Legal Counsel (3)*.

ROBERTS, OWEN J. (1875–1955; Hoover, 1930–1945). Pa.Rep.—Pa., Assistant District Attorney (3). U.S., Special Deputy Attorney General in Espionage Act Cases, World War I; Special Prosecutor, Oil Cases, 1924. *Private practice.*

*RUTLEDGE, JOHN (1739–1800; Washington, 1789–1791, and Washington, 1795). S.C.Fed.—Signer, U.S. Constitution, 1787. S.C., Legislature (18); Attorney General (1); President and Governor (6); *Chancellor (7).* [Between appointments to the Supreme Court: *S.C., Chief Justice, Court of Common Pleas and Sessions (4).*] He did not sit under his first appointment; he sat with a recess appointment as Chief Justice, but his regular appointment was rejected by the Senate.

RUTLEDGE, WILEY B. (1894–1949; F.D. Roosevelt, 1943–1949). Iowa Dem.—Mo., then Iowa, Member, National Conference of Commissioners on Uniform State Laws (10). *U.S., Judge, Court of Appeals (4).*

SANFORD, EDWARD T. (1865–1930; Harding, 1923–1930). Tenn.Rep.—U.S., Assistant Attorney General (1); *Judge, District Court (15).*

SCALIA, ANTONIN (1936–____; Reagan, 1986–____). Va.Rep.—U.S., General Counsel, Office of Telecommunications Policy (1); Chairman, Administrative Conference of the United States (2); Assistant Attorney General, Office of Legal Counsel (3); *Judge, Court of Appeals (4).*

SHIRAS, GEORGE (1832–1924; B. Harrison, 1892–1903). Pa.Rep.—*Private practice.*

SOUTER, DAVID H. (1939–____; Bush, 1990–____). N.H.Rep.—N.H., Assistant Attorney General (3); Deputy Attorney General (5); Attorney General (2); Associate Justice, Superior Court (5); Associate Justice, Supreme Court (7). *U.S., Judge, Court of Appeals (½) .*

STEVENS, JOHN PAUL (1920–____; Ford, 1975–   ). Ill.Independent.—U.S.N.R., World War II. U.S., Associate Counsel, Subcommittee on the Study of Monopoly Power, Committee on the Judiciary, House of Representatives (1); Member, Attorney General's National Committee to Study the Antitrust Laws (2). Ill., Chief Counsel, Special Commission of the Supreme Court. *U.S., Judge, Court of Appeals (5).*

STEWART, POTTER (1915–1985; Eisenhower, 1958–1981). Ohio Rep.—Lt., U.S.N.R., World War II. *U.S., Judge, Court of Appeals (4).*

*STONE, HARLAN F. (1872–1946; Coolidge, later F.D. Roosevelt, 1925–1946). N.Y.Rep.—*U.S., Attorney General (1).* Chief Justice, 1941–1946.

STORY, JOSEPH (1779–1845; Madison, 1811–1845). Mass.Rep.—Mass., Legislature (5). U.S., House of Representatives (2). *Private practice.*

STRONG, WILLIAM (1808–1895; Grant, 1870–1880). Pa.Rep.—U.S., House of Representatives (4). Pa., Justice, Supreme Court (11). *Private practice.*

SUTHERLAND, GEORGE (1862–1942; Harding, 1922–1938). Utah Rep.—Utah, Legislature (4). U.S., House of Representatives (2); Senate (12). *Private practice.*

SWAYNE, NOAH H. (1804–1884; Lincoln, 1862–1881). Ohio Rep.—Ohio, County Attorney (4); Legislature (2). U.S., District Attorney (9). *Private practice.*

*TAFT, WILLIAM H. (1857–1930; Harding, 1921–1930). Conn.Rep.—U.S., Collector of Internal Revenue (1). Ohio, Judge, Superior Court (3). U.S., Solicitor General (2); Judge, Circuit Court of Appeals (8); Governor-General, P.I. (3); Secretary of War (4); President (4). *Professor of Law.*

*TANEY, ROGER B. (1777–1864; Jackson, 1836–1864). Md.Dem.—Md., Legislature (7); Attorney General (2). U.S., Attorney General (2), Secretary of the Treasury (¾; rejected by the Senate). *Private practice.*

THOMAS, CLARENCE (1948–____; Bush, 1991–____). Ga.Rep.—Mo., Assistant Attorney General (3). U.S., Legislative Assistant (2); Assistant Secretary for Civil Rights, Department of Education (1); Chairman, Equal Employment Opportunity Commission (8); *Judge, Court of Appeals (1).*

THOMPSON, SMITH (1768–1843; Monroe, 1823–1843). N.Y.Rep.—N.Y., Legislature (2); Associate Justice, and Chief Justice, Supreme Court (16). *U.S., Secretary of the Navy (4).*

TODD, THOMAS (1765–1826; Jefferson, 1807–1826). Ky.Rep.—*Ky., Judge, and Chief Justice, Court of Appeals (6).*

TRIMBLE, ROBERT (1777–1828; J.Q. Adams, 1826–1828). Ky.Rep.—Ky., Legislature (2). Judge, Court of Appeals (2). U.S., District Attorney (4); *Judge, District Court (9).*

VAN DEVANTER, WILLIS (1859–1941; Taft, 1910–1937). Wyo.Rep.—Wyo., Legislature (2); Chief Justice, Supreme Court (1). U.S., Assistant Attorney General (Interior Department) (6); *Judge, Circuit Court of Appeals (7).*

*VINSON, FRED M. (1890–1953; Truman, 1946–1953). Ky.Dem.—Ky., Commonwealth Attorney (3). U.S., House of Representatives (14); Judge, Court of Appeals (5); Director, Office of Economic Stabilization (2); Federal Loan Administrator (1 mo.); Director, Office of War Mobilization and Reconversion (3 mo.); *Secretary of the Treasury (1).*

*WAITE, MORRISON R. (1816–1888; Grant, 1874–1888). Ohio Rep.—Ohio, Legislature (2). Counsel for United States, U.S.—Gr. Brit. Arbitration ("Alabama" Claims), 1871–72. *Private practice.*

*WARREN, EARL (1891–1974; Eisenhower, 1953–1969). Calif.Rep.—1st Lt., Inf., World War I. Deputy City Attorney (1); Deputy District Attorney (5); District Attorney (14); Attorney General (4); *Governor (10).*

WASHINGTON, BUSHROD (1762–1829; J. Adams, 1798–1829). Pa.Fed.—Va., Legislature (1). *Private practice.*

WAYNE, JAMES M. (1790–1867; Jackson, 1835–1867). Ga.Dem.—Ga., Officer, Hussars, War of 1812; Legislature (2). Mayor of Savannah, Ga. (2). Ga., Judge, Superior Court (5). *U.S., House of Representatives (6).*

WHITE, BYRON R. (1917–____; Kennedy, 1962–1993). Colo.Dem.—U.S.N.R., World War II. *U.S., Deputy Attorney General (1).*

*WHITE, EDWARD D. (1845–1921; Cleveland, later Taft, 1894–1921). La. Dem.—La., Legislature (4); Justice, Supreme Court (2). *U.S., Senate (3).* Chief Justice, 1910–1921.

WHITTAKER, CHARLES E. (1901–1973; Eisenhower, 1957–1962). Mo.Rep.—U.S., Judge, District Court (2); *Court of Appeals (1).*

WILSON, JAMES (1724–1798; Washington, 1789–1798). Pa.Fed.—Signer, U.S. Declaration of Independence, 1776, and U.S. Constitution, 1787. Although he was strongly interested in western-land development companies for several years prior to his appointment, his primary activity in the period immediately preceding his appointment was in obtaining ratification of the Federal and Pennsylvania Constitutions.

WOODBURY, LEVI (1789–1851; Polk, 1845–1851). N.H. Dem.—N.H., Associate Justice, Superior Court (6); Governor (2); Legislature (1). U.S., Senate (6); Secretary of the Navy (3); Secretary of the Treasury (7); *Senate (4).*

WOODS, WILLIAM B. (1824–1887; Hayes, 1880–1887). Ga.Rep.—Mayor, Newark, O. (1). Ohio, Legislature (4). Brevet Major General, U.S. Vol., Civil War. Ala., Chancellor (1). *U.S., Judge, Circuit Court (11).*

Appendix B

THE CONSTITUTION OF THE UNITED STATES

PREAMBLE

We the People of the United States, in Order to form a more perfect Union, establish Justice, insure domestic Tranquility, provide for the common defence, promote the general Welfare, and secure the Blessings of Liberty to ourselves and our Posterity, do ordain and establish this Constitution for the United States of America.

ARTICLE I

Section 1. All legislative Powers herein granted shall be vested in a Congress of the United States, which shall consist of a Senate and House of Representatives.

Section 2. [1] The House of Representatives shall be composed of Members chosen every second Year by the People of the several States, and the Electors in each State shall have the Qualifications requisite for Electors of the most numerous Branch of the State Legislature.

[2] No Person shall be a Representative who shall not have attained to the Age of twenty five Years, and been seven Years a Citizen of the United States, and who shall not, when elected, be an Inhabitant of that State in which he shall be chosen.

[3] Representatives and direct Taxes shall be apportioned among the several States which may be included within this Union, according to their respective Numbers, which shall be determined by adding to the whole Number of free Persons, including those bound to Service for a Term of Years, and excluding Indians not taxed, three fifths of all other Persons. The actual Enumeration shall be made within three Years after the first Meeting of the Congress of the United States, and within every subsequent Term of ten Years, in such Manner as they shall by Law direct. The Number of Representatives shall not exceed one for every thirty Thousand, but each State shall have at Least one Representative; and until such enumeration shall be made, the State of New Hampshire shall be entitled to chuse three, Massachusetts eight, Rhode Island and Providence Plantations one, Connecticut five, New York six, New Jersey four, Pennsylvania eight, Delaware one, Maryland six, Virginia ten, North Carolina five, South Carolina five, and Georgia three.

1554

[4] When vacancies happen in the Representation from any State, the Executive Authority thereof shall issue Writs of Election to fill such Vacancies.

[5] The House of Representatives shall chuse their Speaker and other Officers; and shall have the sole Power of Impeachment.

Section 3. [1] The Senate of the United States shall be composed of two Senators from each State, chosen by the Legislature thereof, for six Years; and each Senator shall have one Vote.

[2] Immediately after they shall be assembled in Consequence of the first Election, they shall be divided as equally as may be into three Classes. The Seats of the Senators of the first Class shall be vacated at the Expiration of the Second Year, of the second Class at the Expiration of the fourth Year, and of the third Class at the Expiration of the sixth Year, so that one third may be chosen every second Year; and if Vacancies happen by Resignation, or otherwise, during the Recess of the Legislature of any State, the Executive thereof may make temporary Appointments until the next Meeting of the Legislature, which shall then fill such Vacancies.

[3] No Person shall be a Senator who shall not have attained to the Age of thirty Years, and been nine Years a Citizen of the United States, and who shall not, when elected, by an Inhabitant of that State for which he shall be chosen.

[4] The Vice President of the United States shall be President of the Senate, but shall have no Vote, unless they be equally divided.

[5] The Senate shall chuse their other Officers, and also a President pro tempore, in the Absence of the Vice President, or when he shall exercise the Office of President of the United States.

[6] The Senate shall have the sole Power to try all Impeachments. When sitting for that Purpose, they shall be on Oath or Affirmation. When the President of the United States is tried, the Chief Justice shall preside: And no Person shall be convicted without the Concurrence of two thirds of the Members present.

[7] Judgment in Cases of Impeachment shall not extend further than to removal from Office, and disqualification to hold and enjoy any Office of honor, Trust, or Profit under the United States: but the Party convicted shall nevertheless be liable and subject to Indictment, Trial, Judgment, and Punishment, according to Law.

Section 4. [1] The Times, Places and Manner of holding Elections for Senators and Representatives, shall be prescribed in each State by the Legislature thereof; but the Congress may at any time by Law make or alter such Regulations, except as to the Places of chusing Senators.

[2] The Congress shall assemble at least once in every Year, and such Meeting shall be on the first Monday in December, unless they shall by Law appoint a different Day.

Section 5. [1] Each House shall be the Judge of the Elections, Returns, and Qualifications of its own Members, and a Majority of each shall constitute a Quorum to do Business; but a smaller Number may adjourn from day to day, and may be authorized to compel the Attendance of absent Members, in such Manner, and under such Penalties as each House may provide.

[2] Each House may determine the Rules of its Proceedings, punish its Members for disorderly Behavior, and, with the Concurrence of two thirds, expel a Member.

[3] Each House shall keep a Journal of its Proceedings, and from time to time publish the same, excepting such Parts as may in their Judgment require Secrecy; and the Yeas and Nays of the Members of either House on any question shall, at the Desire of one fifth of those Present, be entered on the Journal.

[4] Neither House, during the Session of Congress, shall without the Consent of the other, adjourn for more than three days, nor to any other Place than that in which the two Houses shall be sitting.

Section 6. [1] The Senators and Representatives shall receive a Compensation for their Services, to be ascertained by Law, and paid out of the Treasury of the United States. They shall in all Cases, except Treason, Felony and Breach of the Peace, be privileged from Arrest during their Attendance at the Session of their respective Houses, and in going to and returning from the same; and for any Speech or Debate in either House, they shall not be questioned in any other Place.

[2] No Senator or Representative shall, during the Time for which he was elected, be appointed to any civil Office under the Authority of the United States, which shall have been created, or the Emoluments whereof shall have been increased during such time; and no Person holding any Office under the United States, shall be a Member of either House during his Continuance in Office.

Section 7. [1] All Bills for raising Revenue shall originate in the House of Representatives; but the Senate may propose or concur with Amendments as on other Bills.

[2] Every Bill which shall have passed the House of Representatives and the Senate, shall, before it become a Law, be presented to the President of the United States; If he approve he shall sign it, but if not he shall return it, with his Objections to the House in which it shall have originated, who shall enter the Objections at large on their Journal, and proceed to reconsider it. If after such Reconsideration two thirds of that House shall agree to pass the Bill, it shall be sent together with the Objections, to the other House, by which it shall likewise be reconsidered, and if approved by two thirds of that House, it shall become a Law. But in all such Cases the Votes of both Houses shall be determined by yeas and Nays, and the Names of the Persons voting for and against the Bill shall be entered on the Journal of each House respectively. If any Bill shall not be returned by the President within ten Days (Sundays excepted) after it shall have been presented to him, the Same shall be a Law, in like Manner as if he had signed it, unless the Congress by their Adjournment prevent its Return in which Case it shall not be a Law.

[3] Every Order, Resolution, or Vote, to Which the Concurrence of the Senate and House of Representatives may be necessary (except on a question of Adjournment) shall be presented to the President of the United States; and before the Same shall take Effect, shall be approved by him, or being disapproved by him, shall be repassed by two thirds of the Senate and House of Representatives, according to the Rules and Limitations prescribed in the Case of a Bill.

Section 8. [1] The Congress shall have Power To lay and collect Taxes, Duties, Imposts and Excises, to pay the Debts and provide for the common Defence and general Welfare of the United States; but all Duties, Imposts and Excises shall be uniform throughout the United States;

[2] To borrow money on the credit of the United States;

[3] To regulate Commerce with foreign Nations, and among the several States, and with the Indian Tribes;

[4]   To establish an uniform Rule of Naturalization, and uniform Laws on the subject of Bankruptcies throughout the United States;

[5]   To coin Money, regulate the Value thereof, and of foreign Coin, and fix the Standard of Weights and Measures;

[6]   To provide for the Punishment of counterfeiting the Securities and current Coin of the United States;

[7]   To Establish Post Offices and Post Roads;

[8]   To promote the Progress of Science and useful Arts, by securing for limited Times to Authors and Inventors the exclusive Right to their respective Writings and Discoveries;

[9]   To constitute Tribunals inferior to the supreme Court;

[10]   To define and punish Piracies and Felonies committed on the high Seas, and Offenses against the Law of Nations;

[11]   To declare War, grant Letters of Marque and Reprisal, and make Rules concerning Captures on Land and Water;

[12]   To raise and support Armies, but no Appropriation of Money to that Use shall be for a longer Term than two Years;

[13]   To provide and maintain a Navy;

[14]   To make Rules for the Government and Regulation of the land and naval Forces;

[15]   To provide for calling forth the Militia to execute the Laws of the Union, suppress Insurrections and repel Invasions;

[16]   To provide for organizing, arming, and disciplining, the Militia, and for governing such Part of them as may be employed in the Service of the United States, reserving to the States respectively, the Appointment of the Officers, and the Authority of training the Militia according to the discipline prescribed by Congress;

[17]   To exercise exclusive Legislation in all Cases whatsoever, over such District (not exceeding ten Miles square) as may, by Cession of particular States, and the Acceptance of Congress, become the Seat of the Government of the United States, and to exercise like Authority over all Places purchased by the Consent of the Legislature of the State in which the Same shall be, for the Erection of Forts, Magazines, Arsenals, dock-Yards, and other needful Buildings;—And

[18]   To make all Laws which shall be necessary and proper for carrying into Execution the foregoing Powers, and all other Powers vested by this Constitution in the Government of the United States, or in any Department or Officer thereof.

Section 9.   [1] The Migration or Importation of Such Persons as any of the States now existing shall think proper to admit, shall not be prohibited by the Congress prior to the Year one thousand eight hundred and eight, but a Tax or duty may be imposed on such Importation, not exceeding ten dollars for each Person.

[2]   The privilege of the Writ of Habeas Corpus shall not be suspended, unless when in Cases of Rebellion or Invasion the public Safety may require it.

[3]   No Bill of Attainder or ex post facto Law shall be passed.

[4]   No Capitation, or other direct, Tax shall be laid, unless in Proportion to the Census or Enumeration herein before directed to be taken.

[5]   No Tax or Duty shall be laid on Articles exported from any State.

[6]   No Preference shall be given by any Regulation of Commerce or Revenue to the Ports of one State over those of another: nor shall Vessels bound to, or from, one State be obliged to enter, clear, or pay Duties in another.

[7]   No money shall be drawn from the Treasury, but in Consequence of Appropriations made by Law; and a regular Statement and Account of the Receipts and Expenditures of all public Money shall be published from time to time.

[8]   No Title of Nobility shall be granted by the United States: And no Person holding any Office of Profit or Trust under them, shall, without the Consent of the Congress, accept of any present, Emolument, Office, or Title, of any kind whatever, from any King, Prince, or foreign State.

Section 10.   [1] No State shall enter into any Treaty, Alliance, or Confederation; grant Letters of Marque and Reprisal; coin Money; emit Bills of Credit; make any Thing but gold and silver Coin a Tender in Payment of Debts; pass any Bill of Attainder, ex post facto Law, or Law impairing the Obligation of Contracts, or grant any Title of Nobility.

[2]   No State shall, without the Consent of the Congress, lay any Imposts or Duties on Imports or Exports, except what may be absolutely necessary for executing it's inspection Laws: and the net Produce of all Duties and Imposts, laid by any State on Imports or Exports, shall be for the Use of the Treasury of the United States; and all such Laws shall be subject to the Revision and Controul of the Congress.

[3]   No State shall, without the Consent of Congress, lay any Duty of Tonnage, keep Troops, or Ships of War in time of Peace, enter into any Agreement or Compact with another State, or with a foreign Power, or engage in War, unless actually invaded, or in such imminent Danger as will not admit of delay.

ARTICLE II

Section 1.   [1] The executive Power shall be vested in a President of the United States of America. He shall hold his Office during the Term of four Years, and, together with the Vice President, chosen for the same Term, be elected, as follows:

[2]   Each State shall appoint, in such Manner as the Legislature thereof may direct, a Number of Electors, equal to the whole Number of Senators and Representatives to which the State may be entitled in the Congress; but no Senator or Representative, or Person holding an Office of Trust or Profit under the United States, shall be appointed an Elector.

[3]   The Electors shall meet in their respective States, and vote by Ballot for two Persons, of whom one at least shall not be an Inhabitant of the same State with themselves. And they shall make a List of all the Persons voted for, and of the Number of Votes for each; which List they shall sign and certify, and transmit sealed to the Seat of the Government of the United States, directed to the President of the Senate. The President of the Senate shall, in the Presence of the Senate and House of Representatives, open all the Certificates, and the Votes shall then be counted. The Person having the greatest Number of Votes shall be the President, if such Number be a Majority of the whole Number of Electors appointed; and if there be more than one who have such Majority, and have an equal Number of Votes, then the House of Representatives shall immediately chuse by Ballot one of them for President; and if no Person have a Majority, then

from the five highest on the List the said House shall in like Manner chuse the President. But in chusing the President, the Votes shall be taken by States the Representation from each State having one Vote; A quorum for this Purpose shall consist of a Member or Members from two thirds of the States, and a Majority of all the States shall be necessary to a Choice. In every Case, after the Choice of the President, the Person having the greater Number of Votes of the Electors shall be the Vice President. But if there should remain two or more who have equal Votes, the Senate shall chuse from them by Ballot the Vice President.

[4] The Congress may determine the Time of chusing the Electors, and the Day on which they shall give their Votes; which Day shall be the same throughout the United States.

[5] No person except a natural born Citizen, or a Citizen of the United States, at the time of the Adoption of this Constitution, shall be eligible to the Office of President; neither shall any Person be eligible to that Office who shall not have attained to the Age of thirty five Years, and been fourteen Years a Resident within the United States.

[6] In case of the removal of the President from Office, or of his Death, Resignation or Inability to discharge the Powers and Duties of the said Office, the Same shall devolve on the Vice President, and the Congress may by Law provide for the Case of Removal, Death, Resignation or Inability, both of the President and Vice President, declaring what Officer shall then act as President, and such Officer shall act accordingly, until the Disability be removed, or a President shall be elected.

[7] The President shall, at stated Times, receive for his Services, a Compensation, which shall neither be increased nor diminished during the Period for which he shall have been elected, and he shall not receive within that Period any other Emolument from the United States, or any of them.

[8] Before he enter on the Execution of his Office, he shall take the following Oath or Affirmation: "I do solemnly swear (or affirm) that I will faithfully execute the Office of President of the United States, and will to the best of my Ability, preserve, protect and defend the Constitution of the United States."

Section 2. [1] The President shall be Commander in Chief of the Army and Navy of the United States, and of the militia of the several States, when called into the actual Service of the United States; he may require the Opinion, in writing, of the principal Officer in each of the Executive Departments, upon any Subject relating to the Duties of their respective Offices, and he shall have Power to grant Reprieves and Pardons for Offenses against the United States, except in Cases of Impeachment.

[2] He shall have Power, by and with the Advice and Consent of the Senate to make Treaties, provided two thirds of the Senators present concur; and he shall nominate, and by and with the Advice and Consent of the Senate, shall appoint Ambassadors, other public Ministers and Consuls, Judges of the supreme Court, and all other Officers of the United States, whose Appointments are not herein otherwise provided for, and which shall be established by Law; but the Congress may by Law vest the Appointment of such inferior Officers, as they think proper, in the President alone, in the Courts of Law, or in the Heads of Departments.

[3] The President shall have Power to fill up all Vacancies that may happen during the Recess of the Senate, by granting Commissions which shall expire at the End of their next Session.

Section 3. He shall from time to time give to the Congress Information of the State of the Union, and recommend to their Consideration such Measures as he shall judge necessary and expedient; he may, on extraordinary Occasions, convene both Houses, or either of them, and in Case of Disagreement between them, with Respect to the Time of Adjournment, he may adjourn them to such Time as he shall think proper; he shall receive Ambassadors and other public Ministers; he shall take Care that the Laws be faithfully executed, and shall Commission all the Officers of the United States.

Section 4. The President, Vice President and all civil Officers of the United States, shall be removed from Office on Impeachment for, and Conviction of, Treason, Bribery, or other high Crimes and Misdemeanors.

ARTICLE III

Section 1. The judicial Power of the United States, shall be vested in one supreme Court, and in such inferior Courts as the Congress may from time to time ordain and establish. The Judges, both of the supreme and inferior Courts, shall hold their Offices during good Behaviour, and shall, at stated Times, receive for their Services a Compensation, which shall not be diminished during their Continuance in Office.

Section 2. [1] The judicial Power shall extend to all Cases, in Law and Equity, arising under this Constitution, the Laws of the United States, and Treaties made, or which shall be made, under their Authority;—to all Cases affecting Ambassadors, other public Ministers and Consuls;—to all Cases of admiralty and maritime Jurisdiction;—to Controversies to which the United States shall be a Party;—to Controversies between two or more States;—between a State and Citizens of another State;—between Citizens of different States;—between Citizens of the same State claiming Lands under the Grants of different States, and between a State, or the Citizens thereof, and foreign States, Citizens or Subjects.

[2] In all Cases affecting Ambassadors, other public Ministers and Consuls, and those in which a State shall be a Party, the supreme Court shall have original Jurisdiction. In all the other Cases before mentioned, the supreme Court shall have appellate Jurisdiction, both as to Law and Fact, with such Exceptions, and under such Regulations as the Congress shall make.

[3] The trial of all Crimes, except in Cases of Impeachment, shall be by Jury; and such Trial shall be held in the State where the said Crimes shall have been committed; but when not committed within any State, the Trial shall be at such Place or Places as the Congress may by Law have directed.

Section 3. [1] Treason against the United States, shall consist only in levying War against them, or, in adhering to their Enemies, giving them Aid and Comfort. No Person shall be convicted of Treason unless on the Testimony of two Witnesses to the same overt Act, or on Confession in open Court.

[2] The Congress shall have Power to declare the Punishment of Treason, but no Attainder of Treason shall work Corruption of Blood, or Forfeiture except during the Life of the Person attainted.

ARTICLE IV

Section 1. Full Faith and Credit shall be given in each State to the public Acts, Records, and judicial Proceedings of every other State. And the Congress may by general Laws prescribe the Manner in which such Acts, Records and Proceedings shall be proved, and the Effect thereof.

Section 2.   [1] The Citizens of each State shall be entitled to all Privileges and Immunities of Citizens in the several States.

[2]   A Person charged in any State with Treason, Felony, or other Crime, who shall flee from Justice, and be found in another State, shall on demand of the executive Authority of the State from which he fled, be delivered up, to be removed to the State having Jurisdiction of the Crime.

[3]   No Person held to Service or Labour in one State, under the Laws thereof, escaping into another, shall, in Consequence of any Law or Regulation therein, be discharged from such Service or Labour, but shall be delivered up on Claim of the Party to whom such Service or Labour may be due.

Section 3.   [1] New States may be admitted by the Congress into this Union; but no new State shall be formed or erected within the Jurisdiction of any other State; nor any State be formed by the Junction of two or more States, or Parts of States, without the Consent of the Legislatures of the States concerned as well as of the Congress.

[2]   The Congress shall have Power to dispose of and make all needful Rules and Regulations respecting the Territory or other Property belonging to the United States; and nothing in this Constitution shall be so construed as to Prejudice any Claims of the United States, or of any particular State.

Section 4.   The United States shall guarantee to every State in this Union a Republican Form of Government, and shall protect each of them against Invasion; and on Application of the Legislature, or of the Executive (when the Legislature cannot be convened) against domestic Violence.

ARTICLE V

The Congress, whenever two thirds of both Houses shall deem it necessary, shall propose Amendments to this Constitution, or, on the Application of the Legislatures of two thirds of the several States, shall call a Convention for proposing Amendments, which, in either Case, shall be valid to all Intents and Purposes, as part of this Constitution, when ratified by the Legislatures of three fourths of the several States, or by Conventions in three fourths thereof, as the one or the other Mode of Ratification may be proposed by the Congress; Provided that no Amendment which may be made prior to the Year One thousand eight hundred and eight shall in any Manner affect the first and fourth Clauses in the Ninth Section of the first Article; and that no State, without its Consent, shall be deprived of its equal Suffrage in the Senate.

ARTICLE VI

[1]   All Debts contracted and Engagements entered into, before the Adoption of this Constitution shall be as valid against the United States under this Constitution, as under the Confederation.

[2]   This Constitution, and the Laws of the United States which shall be made in Pursuance thereof; and all Treaties made, or which shall be made, under the Authority of the United States, shall be the supreme Law of the Land; and the Judges in every State shall be bound thereby, any Thing in the Constitution or Laws of any State to the Contrary notwithstanding.

[3]   The Senators and Representatives before mentioned, and the Members of the several State Legislatures, and all executive and judicial Officers, both of

the United States and of the several States, shall be bound by Oath or Affirmation, to support this Constitution; but no religious Test shall ever be required as a Qualification to any Office or public Trust under the United States.

ARTICLE VII

The Ratification of the Conventions of nine States shall be sufficient for the Establishment of this Constitution between the States so ratifying the Same.

AMENDMENTS OF THE CONSTITUTION OF THE UNITED STATES OF AMERICA, PROPOSED BY CONGRESS AND RATIFIED BY THE LEGISLATURES OF THE SEVERAL STATES PURSUANT TO THE FIFTH ARTICLE OF THE ORIGINAL CONSTITUTION.

AMENDMENT I [1791]

Congress shall make no law respecting an establishment of religion, or prohibiting the free exercise thereof; or abridging the freedom of speech, or of the press; or the right of the people peaceably to assemble, and to petition the Government for a redress of grievances.

AMENDMENT II [1791]

A well regulated Militia, being necessary to the security of a free State, the right of the people to keep and bear Arms, shall not be infringed.

AMENDMENT III [1791]

No Soldier shall, in time of peace be quartered in any house, without the consent of the Owner, nor in time of war, but in a manner to be prescribed by law.

AMENDMENT IV [1791]

The right of the people to be secure in their persons, houses, papers, and effects, against unreasonable searches and seizures, shall not be violated, and no Warrants shall issue, but upon probable cause, supported by Oath or affirmation and particularly describing the place to be searched, and the persons or things to be seized.

AMENDMENT V [1791]

No person shall be held to answer for a capital, or otherwise infamous crime, unless on a presentment or indictment of a Grand Jury, except in cases arising in the land or naval forces, or in the Militia, when in actual service in time of War or public danger; nor shall any person be subject for the same offence to be twice put in jeopardy of life or limb; nor shall be compelled in any criminal case to be a witness against himself, nor be deprived of life, liberty, or property, without due process of law; nor shall private property be taken for public use, without just compensation.

AMENDMENT VI [1791]

In all criminal prosecutions, the accused shall enjoy the right to a speedy and public trial, by an impartial jury of the State and district wherein the crime shall have been committed, which district shall have been previously ascertained by law, and to be informed of the nature and cause of the accusation; to be confronted with the witnesses against him; to have compulsory process for obtaining witnesses in his favor, and to have the Assistance of Counsel for his defence.

AMENDMENT VII [1791]

In Suits at common law, where the value in controversy shall exceed twenty dollars, the right of trial by jury shall be preserved, and no fact tried by jury, shall be otherwise re-examined in any Court of the United States, than according to the rules of the common law.

AMENDMENT VIII [1791]

Excessive bail shall not be required, nor excessive fines imposed, nor cruel and unusual punishments inflicted.

AMENDMENT IX [1791]

The enumeration in the Constitution, of certain rights, shall not be construed to deny or disparage others retained by the people.

AMENDMENT X [1791]

The powers not delegated to the United States by the Constitution, nor prohibited by it to the States, are reserved to the States respectively, or to the people.

AMENDMENT XI [1798]

The Judicial power of the United States shall not be construed to extend to any suit in law or equity, commenced or prosecuted against one of the United States by Citizens of another State, or by Citizens or Subjects of any Foreign State.

AMENDMENT XII [1804]

The Electors shall meet in their respective states and vote by ballot for President and Vice-President, one of whom, at least, shall not be an inhabitant of the same state with themselves; they shall name in their ballots the person voted for as President, and in distinct ballots the person voted for as Vice-President, and they shall make distinct lists of all persons voted for as President, and of all persons voted for as Vice-President, and of the number of votes for each, which lists they shall sign and certify, and transmit sealed to the seat of the government of the United States, directed to the President of the Senate;—The President of the Senate shall, in the presence of the Senate and House of Representatives, open all the certificates and the votes shall then be counted;—The person having the greatest number of votes for President, shall be the President, if such number be a majority of the whole number of Electors appointed; and if no person have such majority, then from the persons having the highest numbers not exceeding three on the list of those voted for as President, the House of Representatives shall choose immediately, by ballot, the President. But in choosing the President, the votes shall be taken by states, the representation from each state having one vote; a quorum for this purpose shall consist of a member or members from two-thirds of the states, and a majority of all the states shall be necessary to a choice. And if the House of Representatives shall not choose a President whenever the right of choice shall devolve upon them before the fourth day of March next following, then the Vice-President shall act as President, as in the case of the death or other constitutional disability of the President.—The person having the greatest number of votes as Vice-President, shall be the Vice-President, if such number be a majority of the whole number of Electors appointed, and if no person have a majority, then from the two highest numbers on the list, the Senate shall choose the Vice-President; a quorum for the purpose shall consist of two-thirds of the whole number of Senators, and a majority of the whole number shall be necessary to a choice. But no person constitutionally ineligible to the office of President shall be eligible to that of Vice-President of the United States.

AMENDMENT XIII [1865]

Section 1. Neither slavery nor involuntary servitude, except as a punishment for crime whereof the party shall have been duly convicted, shall exist within the United States, or any place subject to their jurisdiction.

Section 2. Congress shall have power to enforce this article by appropriate legislation.

AMENDMENT XIV [1868]

Section 1. All persons born or naturalized in the United States, and subject to the jurisdiction thereof, are citizens of the United States and of the State wherein they reside. No State shall make or enforce any law which shall abridge the privileges or immunities of citizens of the United States; nor shall any State deprive any person of life, liberty, or property, without due process of law; nor deny to any person within its jurisdiction the equal protection of the laws.

Section 2. Representatives shall be apportioned among the several States according to their respective numbers, counting the whole number of persons in each State, excluding Indians not taxed. But when the right to vote at any election for the choice of electors for President and Vice President of the United States, Representatives in Congress, the Executive and Judicial officers of a State, or the members of the Legislature thereof, is denied to any of the male inhabitants of such State, being twenty-one years of age, and citizens of the United States, or in any way abridged, except for participation in rebellion, or other crime, the basis of representation therein shall be reduced in the proportion which the number of such male citizens shall bear to the whole number of male citizens twenty-one years of age in such State.

Section 3. No person shall be a Senator or Representative in Congress, or elector of President and Vice President, or hold any office, civil or military, under the United States, or under any State, who having previously taken an oath, as a member of Congress, or as an officer of the United States, or as a member of any State legislature, or as an executive or judicial officer of any State, to support the Constitution of the United States, shall have engaged in insurrection or rebellion against the same, or given aid or comfort to the enemies thereof. But Congress may by a vote of two-thirds of each House, remove such disability.

Section 4. The validity of the public debt of the United States, authorized by law, including debts incurred for payment of pensions and bounties for services in suppressing insurrection or rebellion, shall not be questioned. But neither the United States nor any State shall assume or pay any debt or obligation incurred in aid of insurrection or rebellion against the United States, or any claim for the loss or emancipation of any slave; but all such debts, obligations and claims shall be held illegal and void.

Section 5. The Congress shall have power to enforce, by appropriate legislation, the provisions of this article.

AMENDMENT XV [1870]

Section 1. The right of citizens of the United States to vote shall not be denied or abridged by the United States or by any State on account of race, color, or previous condition of servitude.

Section 2. The Congress shall have power to enforce this article by appropriate legislation.

Amendment XVI [1913]

The Congress shall have power to lay and collect taxes on incomes, from whatever source derived, without apportionment among the several States, and without regard to any census or enumeration.

Amendment XVII [1913]

[1] The Senate of the United States shall be composed of two Senators from each State, elected by the people thereof, for six years; and each Senator shall have one vote. The electors in each State shall have the qualifications requisite for electors of the most numerous branch of the State legislatures.

[2] When vacancies happen in the representation of any State in the Senate, the executive authority of such State shall issue writs of election to fill such vacancies: *Provided,* That the legislature of any State may empower the executive thereof to make temporary appointments until the people fill the vacancies by election as the legislature may direct.

[3] This amendment shall not be so construed as to affect the election or term of any Senator chosen before it becomes valid as part of the Constitution.

Amendment XVIII [1919]

Section 1. After one year from the ratification of this article the manufacture, sale, or transportation of intoxicating liquors within, the importation thereof into, or the exportation thereof from the United States and all territory subject to the jurisdiction thereof for beverage purposes is hereby prohibited.

Section 2. The Congress and the several States shall have concurrent power to enforce this article by appropriate legislation.

Section 3. This article shall be inoperative unless it shall have been ratified as an amendment to the Constitution by the legislatures of the several States, as provided in the Constitution, within seven years from the date of the submission hereof to the States by the Congress.

Amendment XIX [1920]

[1] The right of citizens of the United States to vote shall not be denied or abridged by the United States or by any State on account of sex.

[2] Congress shall have power to enforce this article by appropriate legislation.

Amendment XX [1933]

Section 1. The terms of the President and Vice President shall end at noon on the 20th day of January, and the terms of Senators and Representatives at noon on the 3d day of January, of the years in which such terms would have ended if this article had not been ratified; and the terms of their successors shall then begin.

Section 2. The Congress shall assemble at least once in every year, and such meeting shall begin at noon on the 3d day of January, unless they shall by law appoint a different day.

Section 3. If, at the time fixed for the beginning of the term of the President, the President elect shall have died, the Vice President elect shall become President. If the President shall not have been chosen before the time fixed for the beginning of his term, or if the President elect shall have failed to qualify, then the Vice President elect shall act as President until a President shall have qualified; and the Congress may by law provide for the case wherein neither a President elect nor a Vice President elect shall have qualified, declaring who shall then act as President, or the manner in which one who is to act shall be selected, and such person shall act accordingly until a President or Vice President shall have qualified.

Section 4. The Congress may by law provide for the case of the death of any of the persons from whom the House of Representatives may choose a President whenever the right of choice shall have devolved upon them, and for the case of the death of any of the persons from whom the Senate may choose a Vice President whenever the right of choice shall have devolved upon them.

Section 5. Sections 1 and 2 shall take effect on the 15th day of October following the ratification of this article.

Section 6. This article shall be inoperative unless it shall have been ratified as an amendment to the Constitution by the legislatures of three-fourths of the several States within seven years from the date of its submission.

AMENDMENT XXI [1933]

Section 1. The eighteenth article of amendment to the Constitution of the United States is hereby repealed.

Section 2. The transportation or importation into any State, Territory, or possession of the United States for delivery or use therein of intoxicating liquors, in violation of the laws thereof, is hereby prohibited.

Section 3. This article shall be inoperative unless it shall have been ratified as an amendment to the Constitution by conventions in the several States, as provided in the Constitution, within seven years from the date of the submission hereof to the States by the Congress.

AMENDMENT XXII [1951]

Section 1. No person shall be elected to the office of the President more than twice, and no person who has held the office of President, or acted as President, for more than two years of a term to which some other person was elected President shall be elected to the office of President more than once. But this Article shall not apply to any person holding the office of President when this Article was proposed by the Congress, and shall not prevent any person who may be holding the office of President, or acting as President, during the term within which this Article becomes operative from holding the office of President or acting as President during the remainder of such term.

Section 2. This article shall be inoperative unless it shall have been ratified as an amendment to the Constitution by the legislatures of three-fourths of the several States within seven years from the date of its submission to the States by the Congress.

AMENDMENT XXIII [1961]

Section 1. The District constituting the seat of Government of the United States shall appoint in such manner as the Congress may direct:

A number of electors of President and Vice President equal to the whole number of Senators and Representatives in Congress to which the District would be entitled if it were a State, but in no event more than the least populous state; they shall be in addition to those appointed by the states, but they shall be considered, for the purposes of the election of President and Vice President, to be electors appointed by a state; and they shall meet in the District and perform such duties as provided by the twelfth article of amendment.

Section 2.   The Congress shall have power to enforce this article by appropriate legislation.

Amendment XXIV [1964]

Section 1.   The right of citizens of the United States to vote in any primary or other election for President or Vice President, for electors for President or Vice President, or for Senator or Representative in Congress, shall not be denied or abridged by the United States or any State by reason of failure to pay any poll tax or other tax.

Section 2.   The Congress shall have power to enforce this article by appropriate legislation.

Amendment XXV [1967]

Section 1.   In case of the removal of the President from office or of his death or resignation, the Vice President shall become President.

Section 2.   Whenever there is a vacancy in the office of the Vice President, the President shall nominate a Vice President who shall take office upon confirmation by a majority vote of both Houses of Congress.

Section 3.   Whenever the President transmits to the President pro tempore of the Senate and the Speaker of the House of Representatives his written declaration that he is unable to discharge the powers and duties of his office, and until he transmits to them a written declaration to the contrary, such powers and duties shall be discharged by the Vice President as Acting President.

Section 4.   Whenever the Vice President and a majority of either the principal officers of the executive departments or of such other body as Congress may by law provide, transmit to the President pro tempore of the Senate and the Speaker of the House of Representatives their written declaration that the President is unable to discharge the powers and duties of his office, the Vice President shall immediately assume the powers and duties of the office as Acting President.

Thereafter, when the President transmits to the President pro tempore of the Senate and the Speaker of the House of Representatives his written declaration that no inability exists, he shall resume the powers and duties of his office unless the Vice President and a majority of either the principal officers of the executive department or of such other body as Congress may by law provide, transmit within four days to the President pro tempore of the Senate and the Speaker of the House of Representatives their written declaration that the President is unable to discharge the powers and duties of his office.   Thereupon Congress shall decide the issue, assembling within forty-eight hours for that purpose if not in session.   If the Congress, within twenty-one days after receipt of the latter written declaration, or, if Congress is not in session, within twenty-one days after Congress is required to assemble, determines by two-thirds vote of both Houses that the President is unable to discharge the powers and duties of his office, the

Vice President shall continue to discharge the same as Acting President; otherwise, the President shall resume the powers and duties of his office.

Amendment XXVI [1971]

Section 1. The right of citizens of the United States, who are eighteen years of age or older, to vote shall not be denied or abridged by the United States or by any State on account of age.

Section 2. The Congress shall have power to enforce this article by appropriate legislation.

Amendment XXVII [1992] *

No law, varying compensation for the services of Senators and Representatives, shall take effect, until an election of Representatives shall have intervened.

* On May 7, 1992, more than 200 years after it was first proposed by James Madison, the Twenty–Seventh Amendment was ratified by a 38th State (Michigan). Although Congress set no time limit for ratification of this amendment, ten of the *other* amendments proposed at the same time (1789)—now known as the Bill of Rights—were ratified in a little more than two years. After all this time, is the ratification of the Twenty–Seventh Amendment valid? Does it matter that many of the states that ratified the amendment did not exist at the time it was first proposed?

*

Index

References are to Pages

†